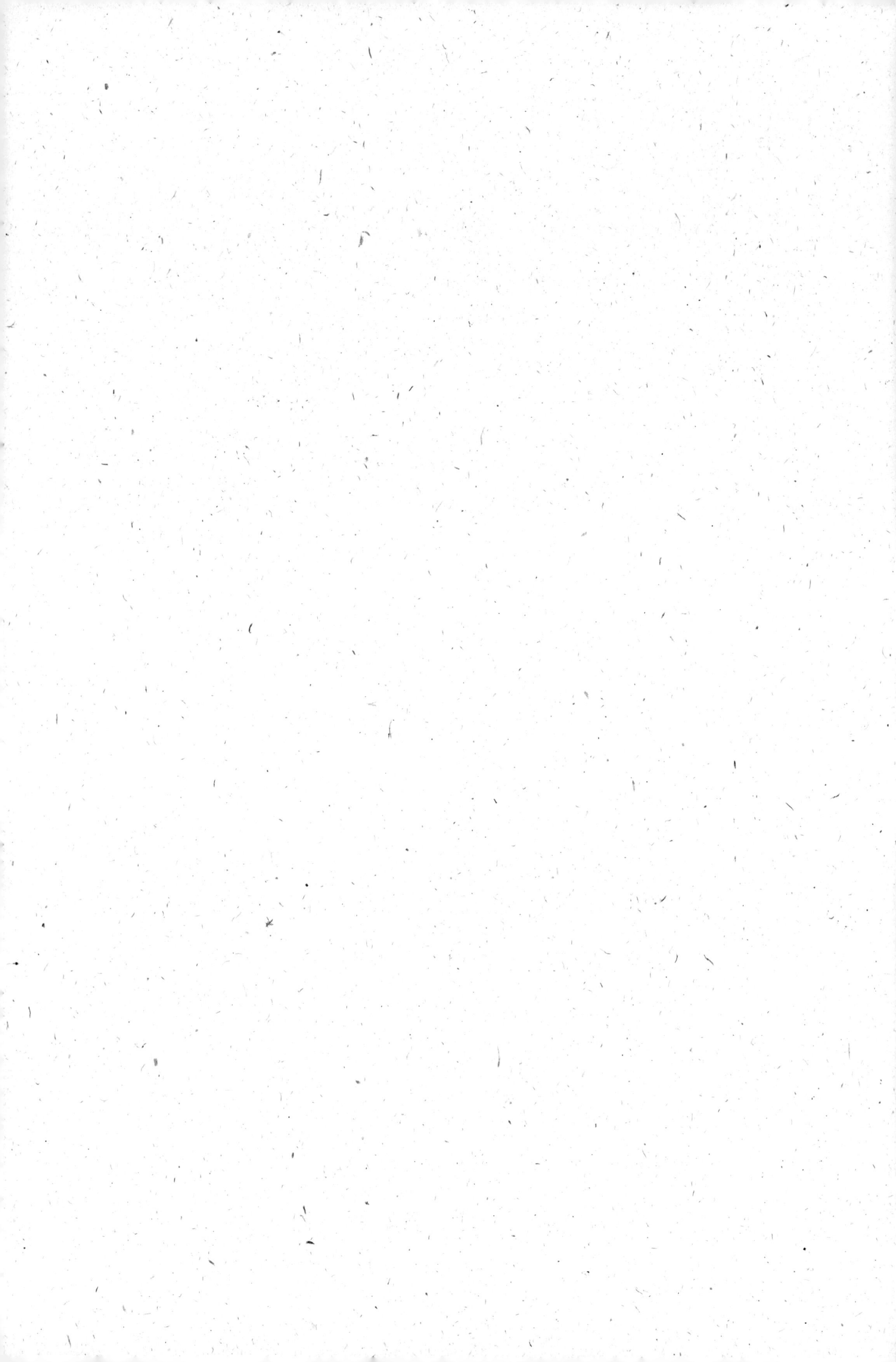

QUIET MOMENTS

Quiet Moments

ISBN 1-57553-180-1

Printing and Binding by
BPC Wheatons Ltd, Exeter, UK

QUIET MOMENTS

Mariah Hourihan, Editor

THE INTERNATIONAL LIBRARY OF POETRY

Editor's Note

The day clamours on: in the hiss and growl of traffic, in the barking of T.V. adverts, in the insistent nagging of bills unpaid, in the clanking rhythm of an efficiently-spent afternoon. One learns to appreciate the quiet moments, the lulls, where the noise of daily existence falls away and in the silence one can find a little solitude. It is in these moments of solitude that we are able collect ourselves and to release our imaginations. Alone with our thoughts, the earth, the sun and the stars seem to belong only to us, and we are free to explore and to invent new worlds.

The fruit borne from these quiet moments can take any conceivable form. Michelangelo's creative genius assumed the shape of the Sistine Chapel ceiling; Thomas Edison's, a light bulb; John Keats', an ode . The artists selected for this anthology, like Keats before them, have elected to shape their worlds in poetry.

Poetry *is* the world of one particularly engaging poem entitled "The Jump" [p.107] by Richard Parkhurst. It is an extremely self-aware poem in that it describes the poetic process itself. Mr. Parkhurst likens his attempt at poetry-writing to an incredible jump from a precarious perch — a blind leap into poetic space, if you will.

The poem addresses the inadequacy of language to give full expression to the poet's thoughts. Manoeuvering language and turning phrases are intricate and difficult dance steps:

> *Having a tango with words, the last holy ikons,*
> *so as to edge myself nearer*
> * to the great mystery of being;*
> *at which words, my newfound dancing partners,*
> * can   only   always   point*

Words may "only always point", but Mr. Parkhurst appreciates this power. Poetry enables greatness; it allows him to go "swimming across mountains . . . astonishing eagles". With refreshing modesty and enthusiasm, the poet appreciates his own limitations as a poetic neophyte and asks you, the reader, to drop your own pretensions for a moment and jump with him, "landing footsore, but whole,/ in the place you already are." Whether the poem "succeeds" or not, whether you land gracefully in a different place or don't go anywhere at all, the point is just to have a go and enjoy the attempt.

Like Mr. Parkhurst, Anna Jones succeeds in her poetic attempt, "Poem for Louise" [p.522]. A celebration of life-long friendship, the poem is an enjoyable collection of poignant childhood images:

> *We traced dust patterns on lazy summer days,*
> *Sat in our place.*
> *Counted freckles on each other's face.*

i

Straight-forward language and simple rhyme infuse the poem with a youthful innocence and accessibility. With deceptive ease, Ms. Jones skillfully recreates a child's world of simple ways and plain expression.

A different sort of past world is revisited in Kathleen Ebert's "Hiroshima" [p.131], a sombre meditation on the tragic World War II bombing of the city. With images dramatically cut from extremes of light and darkness, Ms. Ebert creates a powerful, stark sense of misery. Lanterns swing in the night as the damned walk in "shallowy shadows" and the "lights of love grow dim" — black and white images that call to mind the famous, haunting photographs of Hiroshima in the aftermath of the bomb. "Burning recollections" are brought forth from these celluloid reminders of the "rubbled ruin" and the "bones from the urns of yesterday". These are grim, painful images seared onto our collective conscience, like the infamous shadow of one victim onto the wall of a Hiroshima office building.

The poem also considers the moral questions concerning the deployment of atomic weapons. Was the scientific quest for atomic technology misguided? Did the West "snatch the wrong perfections"? Caught up in the race for the "golden Godhead", were other values misplaced? The poem makes no attempt to answer these questions, but merely states that the issues have become "crossed and blurred and old in time". Instead it hints of submission and defeat, perhaps reflecting the emotional fallout in Japan following the bombings. Painfully aware of even its own mortality, the poem recognizes that "each singing bird must cease", as it quietly draws to its close.

From World War to a more personal war, the poetic universe contracts to fit two in Kathleen Collier's poem "Smoke" [p.552]. "Smoke" expresses a woman's disillusionment when she finds the relationship she once valued to be worthless. Taking the colloquialism "blowing smoke" (to create a "smoke" screen), Ms. Collier ingeniously adds dimension to it by having the subject of the poem both blow cigar smoke and construct a deceptive façade:

> *You smile, exhaling*
> *easy lies rehearsed.*
> *A smog of falsehood*

The blowing of smoke works admirably on the literal and metaphorical level throughout the poem, one reinforcing the other and effectively making each line of the poem exhale twice.

Through very carefully chosen language, Ms. Collier captures the infuriating apathy of the subject in the face of the persona's torment:

> *The smoke from*
> *your havana curls an 'S'*
> *Blasé amidst the blitz of*
> *my distress . . .*

The mere gesture of lighting a cigar suggests casual indifference and a sense of comfort.

A poem intended to be seen as well as read, the spiraling fragments of text form a serpentine cloud on the page which further intensifies the poem's visual imagery. Not only is "Smoke" carefully laid out on the page, it is also carefully constructed in the form of a rondeau. A rondeau is typically a short poem with only two rhymes throughout and the opening words used twice as a refrain. Although not easy to spot, the essential elements of a rondeau are subtly at work in the poem. The first rhyme consists of an 's' sound, as in the words 'amidst', 'distress', 'less'. The second rhyme consists of an 'urst' sound as in 'burst', 'rehearsed', 'nursed'. The first rhyme is rather more pervasive than the second and the regular occurrence of the 's' sound creates a sibilance. The poem is again enhanced by this sibilance, which underscores the poem's 'S' shape as well as alludes to the subject's untrustworthy, snake-like nature.

Finally, the persona remarks that had she the courage, she would leave the relationship and let go of her illusions:

> *Abandon illusions fondly nursed*
> *To evaporate to nothingness*
> *Just like the smoke.*

Another careful composition was constructed by Gearoid MacSearraigh, a poem entitled "November 22nd 1963" [p.38]. It is a fascinating puzzle of fragments relating to the assassination of U.S. President John F. Kennedy. At first glance Mr. MacSearraigh's language seems discursive, his allusions arbitrary and the poem seems in general disorder. On one level, in creating this apparent disorder, the poet has recreated the complete confusion that still surrounds Kennedy's assassination. However, there is a very precise order at work. The poem is a deliberate pattern of cultural snippets (i.e. Castrol GTX-Men) and word play (i.e. Taxes Balk Suppository for Texas Book Depository). In a relatively small space, Mr. MacSearraigh highlights every major conspiracy theory, shifting words to capture multiple meanings. When the poet asks "Was it, in deed, Al's pals and gals" the words 'in deed' move within the sentence. The question can be read as "Was it in truth Al's pals and gals" as well as "Was it Al's pals and gals who did the deed?" Words seem to shoot in all directions but ultimately, they point back to what the poet sees as the root of America's problems, the missing element responsible for tragedies like the Kennedy assassination, the ingredient lacking in the American diet: religion.

> *"In Gawd's Name where beginneth the first lesion?" you essay.*
> *"Alimentary, my dear Watts sons, Mom's blueberry pie ain't got no Christ-Cream."*

There is an enormous number of poems that merit careful reading. Enjoy Young Herbert's adventure as he goes "Deep Sea Diving" [p.356] in a poem by A.R. Wheeler. Trace the lines of Vermeer's painting through the hand of D.W. Brown in "La Jeune Fille Endormie" [p.226]. Experience the excitement of the "Harvest" in

Dorothy Harvie's poem of the same name [p.457]. Taste Douglas Clarke's palatable poem "Food for Thought" [p.487].

I encourage you to take the time to delve into these and all the other excellent poems contained in this anthology. I am confident you will find many interesting and entertaining worlds to pass through as you read *Quiet Moments*. Congratulations to all the poets included in this work on their creative achievements.

Quiet Moments is the culmination of the efforts of many talented and dedicated individuals. I would like to thank the editors, assistant editors, customer service representatives, data entry, administrative staff, post-production personnel and all of those who brought their respective talents to bear on this project.

Mariah Hourihan, Editor

Featured Poetry

April's Fool

Another birthday approaching, the years are passing too fast,
I'm wondering what have I done with my life and how can I
 make it last.
Looking closely in the mirror, grey hairs and laughter lines,
I once resembled bubbly champagne, now I'm more like
 vintage wines
My zodiac sign of Aries, says I'm likened to a brave, fiery ram,
but the way I'm feeling at present, I'm more of a meek and mild lamb.
Born on April 1st many years ago,
a bonny little baby my parents were proud to show,
A moody teenager, a young woman full of life
then a mother and busy wife
The children are grown and gone their own separate ways
I'm now finding it hard to fill my days.
what's that you say, join a club or evening classes?
I'll look in the local paper, now, where are my glasses?
With aching bones and my bunion pounding
what a grumpy old person I am sounding
Have you guessed my age yet? Will I be sixty or more
Are you an April Fool? I'll only be forty-four.

 Anne Bradley

The Driving Test to Josie

For Josie now the day has come to take her driving test,
£1030 being the costly sum, so you pay up like the rest.
You drive your car to the centre, hoping your nerves will let
 you pass,
Then the examiner will enter, and take you on the farce.

The registration number of a distant car you read, then get
Into your test car, switch on, and take the lead.
Go right, go left, do a 3 point turn, his voice is cold and terse,
Do emergency stop, turn car around, and safely do reverse.

Do one way systems, roundabouts, then the highway code,
By now you are a nervous wreck, and hate the stuck of toad.
"I'm sorry Mrs. Saunders - you've failed", you here him cry,
Which means another fortune, to have another try!

Now two lessons have gone by, and you can say at last
It was upon your seventh try - the examiner said, "You've passed!!"

 Ellen J. Hunt

Untitled

Time for a celebration my Son!
A little merrymaking; A little revelry;
A little feasting perhaps and a joke or two.
Yes, an old friend is with us once more;
Dearly remembered from days gone by.

So come now my Son, let us fill our glasses;
Forgiving each other the things of the past.
Let us drink a toast for an end to all wars;
And wish each other well.

 Andrew Warren

Pack of Dreams

I saw him in the bric-a-brac shop,
A back-packed holiday boy,
Spinning dreams from ships in bottles,
Green glass floats, oily lanterns.
He had a nautical beard.

Later he stood at sunset
By a lonely hulk, long stranded,
Up to her waist in sand.
But the bleached deck and broken spars
Were alive in the magic light.

Chased by gulls under racing skies,
Decks awash 'round shouting crew,
She was prow-thrusting in windy surge
To the boy with the pack
Of dreams and a change of clothes.

 Ellen W. Worthington

Queen for a Day

The lady is 80, see the pride in her eyes.
a birthday cake for tea, oh what a surprise,
relatives gather 'round her, with
chocolates and sweets.
there are cards, greetings and
other little treats.
the centre of attention, a Queen
for a day.
Yet tomorrow will bring the
loneliness that will push these
feelings away.
Her special day over, she is
tucked up in bed.
That last glass of sherry, went
straight to her head.
Yes tomorrow will bring nothing,
except memories of today,
and long may they last, for what
else has she, anyway.

 Helen Bergin

Dead Dreams

What becomes of a broken heart
After all of its dreams depart?
Where's the grave to bury it in
Along with dead dreams worn and thin?
Is there a place where dead dreams go?
A place far off that only God could know?
Is there a cross to mark the spot?
Like the dead leaves, do dead dreams rot?
Is there a corner in the sky
Where dead dreams go when they die?

Who knows what becomes of a broken heart,
With its dead dreams withered and torn apart.
Who knows if it's buried in a lonely place -
Alone in the dark without light or space?
It could be a warm spot up high or low -
As long as it's there for me when I go.
For though I shall weep and I shall mourn
For all those dead dreams so forlorn,
I'll know there's a small corner in the sky
For me and my dead dreams after I die.

 Jean Angus

"The Light of Darkness"

Surround yourself a darkness with the depths inside your mind,
And choose a lightened corridor with stairs up to one side,
Opening up a doorway and light comes rushing in,
From somewhere never travelled to but hidden from within,
That place is safe and free from fear a place you know so well,
Though bright beyond description, is colourful as well,
Euphoric sense of falling through the peace and calm of dreams,
Where violence, time and anger are only conceptual things.
Emotions contradict themselves, and symbols pave the way,
Confusion gives you comfort, and day is night but day!!
Looking out on pastimes like spying through a tube,
Floating past existence and picking upon moods.
Other times at gatherings with music, tents and voices,
Or escaping dangerous places on the back of flying horses,
You have arrived at dream scape, a personal subconscious
 playground,
Moulding new adventures and a place where friends are found.
The smells and textures are vivid, as experienced in real time,
But the messages, the hints and truths are cunningly sublime,
But risks and chills and rays upright are there for you to chase,
As the sunny early morning brings you back from inner space.

 Emma Brown

Grace - A Fragrant Memory (1915 - 1948)

You were always quite supreme.
A brunette, beautiful, serene.
Waiting, waiting, ever true,
For your dear love's return to you.

A very special sense of fun
Sustained you thro' those timeless years,
Until it seemed at last you'd won
An end to loneliness and fears.

And with reunion there had come
Fulfilment of a cherished dream
Of deep companionship and love,
As wife and mother, still serene.

Yet bittersweet your brief reward,
So swiftly struck the Reaper's sword.
And while you lie in deepest sleep
We in silence weep and weep.

Elizabeth Atkinson

A Child Is Crying

A child is crying but no-one hears.
A child is afraid but no-one nears.
A life full of nothing
but bad memories to keep.
A child full of loving
but does nothing but weep.
A room full of darkness
but it's hard to sleep.
A house full of silence
but for the footsteps
that start to creep.
A child is calling and someone is near.
The pillow comes closer, the cries less clear.
A child is sleeping but no breathing to hear.
A child is resting but without any fear!

Julia Turney

A View of the Universe

Not sunlight draping in silken folds
  A clear-browed summer's day;
Not moonlight asleep, eyelashed with palms,
  In a tropical bay;

Not poetry, music, or sculptured forms
  That look as if they breathed;
Nor columned marble on a Grecian isle,
  Azure-enwreathed.

No; things that slither and crawl and die,
  Half unaware they have been;
The cold beyond the cushioning air
  Of the earth's tattered screen:

A formless void where nothing can draw breath,
Sulphur and methane, fire, darkness, and death.

David S. Taylor

Moondust and Starfalls

This bitter evening should feel worse;
A cold air, a brittle boy,
Nowhere to hide your vapour trail.
Your horns are showing
Where is your tail?

I have run past my devils tonight
To catch you before I lose you once more,
I am covered in moondust from head to heels,
This is how the betrayed must feel.

I need more moondust
To throw at the stars
To ask their forgiveness,
To show where you are.

Jonathan P. Holt

Belfast (Northern Ireland)

The tension is huge, the hatred so great
A country of beauty, filled with such hate,
People play games of power, and strength
Amongst the green fields, of discontent.

You need to come, see for yourself
A strange and eerie place
All are lost and drowning
Smiles have been erased.

If there are angels in heaven
Then Lord, send some here
To ease this place of sadness
And wipe away the fear.

For only when there is peace.
And the people can laugh again,
Will the children pick flowers on the hillside.
And the only tears will be rain.

Arlene McDonald

Ireland

Crack - a noise - a sudden sound,
A crumbled body on the ground,
I see a uniform - a fallen gun,
Footsteps in the distance run,
Look at this face - wretched with pain -
Never to portray peace again.
Good God - he is just a boy
His gun could almost be the toy
He played with not so long ago.
Grief - heartbreak and hate
His family will soon know.
They will mourn their shattered son,
His life - they thought - had just begun.
Eighteen, the age to start anew,
The age of reason - true - too true.
But alas! reason, some will never learn
To war - violence - murder - they turn
Why can't they learn before it is too late
Nothing can follow, but more death - more hate.

Elaine Foley

The Fox

His agile body, so swift in the midnight dew.
A dash of such aromatic grace.
His paws as hot as fire and as gentle as the wind.
His deceiving face so suspicious to his prey.
A golden dust trail behind his every step.
A burst of anger and in his eyes as the roaring sound
of a monster engine races past.
Like blossom in spring so quickly he past.
His fear hidden in a split of grass forever.
Now just a memory in my mind.

Carly Wood

Somebody's Son

He lay in a doorway the place he called bed.
A dirty old jacket pillowed his head.
Such a young man still in his teens.
Not a man not a boy somewhere in between.
He looked so unhappy his face spoke of pain.
he's arms bore the scars were needle met vein.
I thought as I saw him he's somebody's son.
Whose life will be over before it's begun.
So if at a party maybe just for a joke.
Someone offers a tablet or maybe a smoke.
Think what your doing is death worth the thrill.
It's the price you might pay for taking a pill.
Don't lose your life for what may seem like pleasure.
Say no to drugs and each moment treasure.
Think of the young man somebody's son.
Whose life's nearly over before it's begun.

Cora C. Mann

The Star

Three Wise Men saw
A bright light in the East
So they followed its glow
On a humped-back beast.

A King they did visit
Herod was his name
He thought they had come
To bring him fortune and fame.

They told him of the light in the sky
It rested over a stable nearby
A baby was born
Said an Angel on High.

Shepherds came from near and far
When overhead they saw a bright star
Mary's child was born in a stable bare
To give His love for the world to share.

Faith Daly

Return to Eden

A staircase of stars descends from above,
A familiar face to greet me,
So hand in hand with peace in my heart,
I return to the Garden of Tranquillity.

A brief look back, a last farewell,
Their cries of grief, my empty shell,
If only I could erase their fears,
Stem the river of needless tears,
The pain and suffering has disappeared.

I feel safe, warm, calm, serene,
A sea of souls that can't be seen,
Are silently wiping my life's slate clean,
The love ones I've mourned, that went before,
Are all here to guide me to heaven's door.

So never be afraid of death's dark vale,
On the ocean of contentment you'll forever sail,
Bravely face the final chapter,
A reunion with the ever-after.

Caroline Parry

Quiet Day 1995

Silence - a pause in the busy rush of life,
A time to sit and think, and see
The beauty of God's hand in every leaf,
In every plant and flower and tree.

And yet there are sounds -
The water bubbling joyously along,
Unceasing in its constant flow.
The wind that sought the trees
And bends the pliant branches to their knees.

The bird's sweet songs rise over all,
Blending their harmonies with wind and rill,
A leaf blown from the tree spirals and falls
In silence far too deep for words to fill.

Anne Cleveland

The Loo

Oh! How cold it used to be, sitting on our lavatory,
A tiny rustic old tin shed, hidden by a privet hedge.
Dangling from a curtain ring, paper hung in squares on string,
A wooden box, beneath our feet, helped us balance on the seat.
Bottoms numb, and fingers too, nature helped us in this loo,
To do our business without fuss. Jack Frost did not bother us.

Things have changed since those old days. Our rustic tin
  shed's gone away;
We've got, instead, another loo, with hand basin, and bidet, too.
Rolls of paper, tissue soft, fit neatly into chromium slots,
A coloured, plastic shining seat, and carpet steps to rest our feet,
Bottoms warm and fingers too - there's central heating in this loo.
So nature's got another job - we're taking lots of senna-pods!

Jean Hicks

Final Judgement Time at a Ballet Competition,

Easter Sunday, 1996

The piano plays, the dancers have danced,
a dream within a dream has passed;
snowflake beauty all evening long,
youthful dying in disciplined thong
paying the price to serve a profession,
a smiling, delicate swift succession,
wistful, seductive, vibrant, strong:
Elegant fairies and proud Spanish flirts,
a jolly sailor, two girls in skin skirts
coloured for leaf and flower impression.
Now all await the judges' decision.

Judges and audience die in their turn:
A weekend of dance! Is Easter spurned?
Or is Easter shared - new victories earned?
The piano plays while I meditate:
Must poets all die, give life to create?
The piano notes are wistful, yearning,
echoing young hopes for future earning;
but Easter is over, victory won,
we all shall arise, our ballet soon done.

John Canham

Time Is

Time is.
A fragment; a suspended point of motion; a shard of thought;
A fleeting glimpse of truth; memory and emotion.

For time is,
A microscopic snatch of life, frozen into immobility.
A flash of light; a partial word, captured for immortality.
A blast of sound; a deadly hush to shake the monoliths of society.

Oh now - - - where is time? That elusive gorgon that feeds upon life's
force and saps its very energy.
Cold time, that heralds death, a sweeping scythe,
that wipes all from the memory.

Where is he now, this ageless one, this fiend that stalks minds
corridors without due ceremony?
He's here, he's gone, then there again, then lost in the halls of ebony.

So listen closely - time is life, myriads of thought and action.
Shout it aloud that life's great gift, must be lived in every fraction.
For time is; - - - N O W.

Geoff Arthurs

Precious Things

Raindrops falling on my face
A fresh wind in my hair
The solace of a quiet place
Reflecting all Life's care

Babies' smiles and the smell of soap
And the softness of their skin
They are our future life and hope
As new miracles begin

A cuddly hug or a loving kiss
As the children come to stay
Joy and laughter I always miss
When they have to go away

Walking crisply thro' the snow
On a frosty starlit night
Beneath a moon that sheds its glow
In a mystic tranquil light

If I am feeling rather sad
I think of these precious things
New hope transcends - this heart is glad
My spirit soars on Life's wings

Janet Beveridge

Something Lost

Is it today's or was it tomorrow's?
A gift for forever, or just something borrowed?
Something on loan for a moment in time
Without payment, renewal, license or fine.

Was it last week's? Or the day before's?
Is it always left open or shut like a door?
Do the hinges swing both ways or only the one?
And does it rise every morning as the tireless sun?

Can it be found in those common one-liners?
That are spoken in jest by overfed diners.
You search through the corners and cracks of your mind,
Hoping that somehow the memories unwind.

Perhaps it is a right, something deserved.
An object that's flat not jagged and curved.
But whatever it is, whatever the cost,
I am fairly sure it's something we've lost.

James Stormonth

Searching

A mind so full it cannot think
A heart so sore it does not heal
Yet somewhere searching
For what it cannot grasp

A flicker of truth it cannot hold
And yet deep down it knows
The pain and hurt will come together
Not yet awhile, but soon

And become a oneness able to endure
And see more clearly, feel more dearly
The peace and quiet
It is searching for

Ann P. Crampton

The Advancing Storm

The billowy clouds turned a menacing black and enveloped the
sky like a huge cloak. The wind receded to a soft whisper, all
was still in anticipation of the advancing storm, the heady aroma
of heather and the heavy atmosphere, tiny animals bid a hasty
retreat into their deep burrows almost sensing the natural chaos
that was to follow.

The dark velvet blanket opened to release tumbling, dancing rain,
the calmness of the air was broken, the trees rustled, an awaken-
ing, an energy, a force of elements in battle, the gentle breeze
gathered momentum to become a raging tempest howling like a
banshee lost in the night. The force of the storm was merciless,
the saturated peaks of tiny flowers were beaten and uprooted
from the ground.

The crashing crescendo of wind and rain reached a discord, a
retreat, a quieting, a resonance, a gradual descend, the pelting rain
reached a slow steady decline, tiny crystal droplets clung to a
lace-like structure of a spider's web. The weight of the water
made the web sparkle like diamonds strung together to form a
delicate necklace, the trees silhouetted a dark shadow to accentu-
ate the fullness of the moon.
The way was paved for tomorrow's rainbow.

Julie Phee

Snow

Look out your window there is a sheet of white,
All of this magic has happened over night.
Put on your warm clothes and go out to play,
Quick, hurry before it all melts away.
The snow has covered fields that were green,
The most beautiful thing you have ever seen.
Men go out and put salt on the streets,
Walking around the snow freezes their feet.
Soon the snow will melt away,
I wish that the snow would come to stay.

Andrea Clarke

Untitled

I've lost my lover and my friend,
a husband on whom I could depend,
In bed at night through lack of sleep,
I do indulge in quiet weep,
and contemplate our life together,
and thought it would last forever.

We've had our "Ups" we've had our "Downs"
and often acted like two clowns.
We've had our joys, and shed some tears
but you were there to quell my fears,
I love my son, my daughter too,
but the love for them, isn't the same I have
for you.
I love you Bill and always will.

Joan E. Bean

A Beautiful World?

A beautiful world? I certainly think not,
A land of terror that's never forgot,

Children's smiles, all washed away,
Gone from this earth now we can only pray,

The reminders of dreams and children's gladness,
Has now been replaced by a nation's sadness,

Never will be forgotten, that tragic day,
When those beaming faces were taken away,

And left in the air, is a mournful silence,
A grieving world and such immortal violence,

As all that remains, are the memories and sorrow,
We can only hope for a brighter tomorrow,

And in the hearts of the people, lies hatred and pain,
In that once aweless community with the name of Dunblane.

Diane Ashworth

This Stone, This Grave

I'm standing on this stone, this grave
A flower I have thrown
In sadness, I can weep no more
For you I once belonged
Oh bitter sweet, the heart that loved
Has emptied, but remains
With anger and with just remorse
Will never love again

I'm standing on this stone, this grave
For God to seek the truth
Of tangled love that brought you down
Slain brutally on this sodded earth
Be strong, be silent
Are the words that still remain
Watching in a deadly silence
As you lie cold, and my heart
Held tightly in your hands

Edwina Marie Bruce

The Passing of Time

Time is an element we cannot control
A measure of life that goes by
The minutes, the hours, and even the years
It has often been said they just fly

Time is so precious, a duration of space
A series of events in a spell
We are carried along with the rhythm
When it will end who can tell

We each have our time, be it extended or short
Generations are born through the span
But it's a force that's unending, it keeps going on
It's true 'Time stands still for no man'.

Christina Maggs

La Lune

And as I gaze down
A lens. To the powdered sand
dust on the distant landscape.
So haunting in a silent glide
I focus on her drifting side
then soar above her lunar glow
as across my polished screen she goes.
With quivering legs and trembling hands
I set the scene once more
and through the optics once again
I hover above the dusty floor
her surface. Drifting by, slowly shows
a face of wondrous past. Mountains vast
in sea flat plains into which comets rained
and shadows are cast in comforting light
as she floats along through twinkling candlelight;
Her image fixed in the sight of my eyes
bright as her reflection in inky-blue skies.

Androo Bennett Parker

Real Friends

You're companion on all life's journeys
A listener foremost
A natural affinity and reminder of memories
Warm toast
Into which butter melts, to become one taste.
Comfort with sadness
Sharing with gladness
No haste.
An opening of all doors
Which welcome, irrespective of time.
Truth, no daggers no claws.
Your choice first then mine.
Real friends - counted on one hand
Or maybe one finger?
Hold them - make certain they linger.
No wealth, no privilege, no station
Will replace them.

Allan F. Munn

Spring

Spring, the very sunrise of the year,
All nature awakens from her winter sleep,
The rooks are busy in the Rectory elms,
The owl her silent vigil nightly keeps,
The thrush on yonder ash tree loudly calls
Singing with sweet abandon to his mate,
While primroses display their pastel hues
And summer flowers the kinder clime await.

Eric W. Smith

Frightened I Am

I am a mouse fleeing from the hungry owl and hawk,
A lamb stumbling to free himself from the wolf.
A baby alone on a stormy night,
Screaming and crying beside herself with fright.

I am thunder, lightning, winds and gales,
A midnight walk in the fog, mist and hail.
Dark, cold nights haunted with ghosts,
Crashing waves that lie hard on the coast.

I am the howling that breaks an eerie silence,
An old man in prison sorrowing his violence.
A cat arching and hissing at a dog,
The grunting and shuffling of a wild hog.

I am a small village escaping from an erupting volcano,
The wreck of a ship from a savage tornado.
A teenager having to take responsibility,
A man at a bar drowning his misery.

I am a security guard hearing a creak,,
The frantic crew when their ship has sprung a leak.
A piercing shriek in the forest at night,
A man on a stranded island with no land in sight.

Abigail Davies

My Cat Gilly

She came to me at seven weeks old.
A little thing, shivering with the cold.
Her coat was spotted with emulsion paint.
When I cleaned it off she looked so quaint
Her eyes are as yellow as a lemon.
Sometimes she can be a little demon
Her coat has so many different colours
Black, brown, tan and many others.
To sit on my lap is her delight.
Especially when I sit down at night
She thinks that's all I have to do.
I've told her, "I'm not here just for you",
She has, the best place in the house.
I've got to say she's caught many a mouse.
Out in the garden, she loves to roam.
But doesn't go very far from home.
She's the truest friend that I've got.
And believe you me, I love her a lot
Some people reading this might think I'm silly.
But I wouldn't be without my little cat Gilly.

Eirwen A. Jones

Reflections of Love

What is this love that's oh so dear,
A love we eat, speak, sleep and hear,
Precious feelings of heart and mind,
No other place will e'er we find - a love so true.

Love's passion fills the heart with fire,
It soothes the soul and deep desire,
That no one e'er will take away,
Not even for a moment stray, - a love so true.

This love has power to stop all pain,
But then alas it comes again,
When those around us start to doubt,
In greatest protest loud we shout, - a love so true.

There's pain and heartache all to come,
But deep within still shines the sun,
The winds of change may well still blast,
And love like ours will ever last, - a love so true.

May we be blessed with peace of mind,
The truly everlasting kind,
In days of sunshine and of a rain,
When ne'er again will feel pain - Our love is true.

Alison Marion Campbell

Untitled

I spied it in the garden,
A lovely coloured thing,
It looked just like a butterfly,
With multi-coloured wings.
I ran downstairs to catch it
before it flew away,
But when I got there the lovely thing,
Had clearly gone away,
Feeling a little unhappy, I sat down to wait.
And there it was, the lovely thing,
Coming over the garden gate.
It shimmered in the sunlight.
As it floated high in the sky.
It started to come down then,
The colours seemed so bright.
It was then I realized my lovely thing,
Was not a butterfly at all.
My lovely thing was a bubble.
That went pop on the garden wall.

Janet Worley

Who Needs Wings

A cardboard moon in a paper sky
A lover's blanket unfolds across the Tye
Sown in the ground of eternal thread
Peaceful motions on a sleepless bed
A silver river through a midnight clear
A constellation hangs like patient tears
Surrounding freckles on a face of smiles
Echoes from a billion miles
The distance soaks away in endless time
To where caressing shades entwine
Absorbing a spray of blues and greens
The hazy edge of all of my dreams
Amidst the passion of pastel grooves
I walk on air with cotton shoes
Lost in the night with time as it flies
Who needs wings when your mind has eyes

Andy Collenette

Karachi Scenes

A lorry with big brown sacks piled high.
A man on a motorbike.
Not a cloud to be seen in the sky.
That's the weather I like!

Buses that shimmer and shine in the sun.
Passengers all squeezed in!
People who wait at the side of the road
Hoping they'll all get in!

Boys selling papers at traffic lights.
Women with pots on their heads.
There stands a policeman all dressed in white,
A helmet on his head.

A beggar holds her baby close.
He sleeps there on his back.
Unaware of the regular dose
His parents take of 'crack'.

Jean Wilkin

Ravine

Waiting under the dull light.
A pacing heart with anxious step.
Watching for a figure slight.
Out of darkness' side a hand extends.
A voice addresses.
Extolling encounter the eye confesses

We combine in kiss, embrace, and gesture.
Confluent we pose.
A secret heart's conjecture.
Amid sidewalk strangers,
Under a repudiating moon's omniscience.
We contrive delight and aspire submissions,

We are amid loneliness without espouse.
Antisocial love.
To exhaust integrity and put the conscience to drowse.
It is out of romance we sculpt,
A ravine from society and church.
A flesh dream fighting its lurch.

Alan Smith

Pain

At first it's new and strangely exciting
A mountain to climb, a new challenge to conquer.
It's acute; it's agony; it's new.

Then it becomes like a whining child,
Or a nagging parent, not quite as wild.
It's chronic; it hurts; it's less new.

Then comes the time when you know it so well,
It wraps itself round like a cloak.
It's familiar; it aches; it's not new.

Finally sleep like a blanket engulfs you
Forever. No wakefulness now.
It's old; It IS you; Is this death?

Barbara Andrews

Nature

Clouds gather and rain starts to fall
A mist down the mountain begins to crawl
Grass in the meadow, all lush and green
As the water flows into the stream

The rising wind comes over the hedge
Causing the raindrops to hit the ledge
Little rabbits come out of their burrows
The voles and field mice keep to the furrows

The red brown fox comes looking for food
Casting his eyes over the chicken brood
Busy squirrels, working away
As they gather their nuts and hide them away

The rain stops the sun comes out
Catching the colours "a rainbow we shout"
Raindrops hang from the leaves of the trees
Like beautiful diamonds, sparkling spheres

The light of the sun comes down in rays
Lovely gold shafts come through the haze
All is quiet, peaceful and still
God's creation, caught in a spell.

Dorothy Smith

Life

Storm raging, pestilence disturbing
A need in me is so wanting
Gathering, rising, to a crescendo
I feel calm, mortal in the sizzling inferno
Life sweet life
Priceless, a shining star surrounding human strife
Probing, digesting, excruciating a miracle of creation
Having and appreciating, feeling and breathing
an aura of sensation
I stretch out my hands, grabbing, wanting just one more chance
How sweet how good it would all mean to me,
To live a while longer, in love, in harmony a natural balance
The sun warm on my back
The breeze inviting, caressing and overwhelming me in cool attack
The cries of children in play
Time, oh time only I had lived the right way
Somewhere, somehow it all went wrong
For I never knew where I belonged
I suffer in silence
Praying hoping waiting for my deliverance

Elliot B. King

Mother

Mother, the symbol of perfect love
A shining light from Heaven above
Sent down to us an angel sweet
To guard our lives and straying feet

To keep us happy, good and true
To help us always in all we do
In times of stress she's always there
To guide and help with a shining tear

Her love is more than a world of gems
A priceless gift from Heaven's wings
Her name, sweet music to our ears
Breathed with reverence through the years

A beloved name on every lip
A safety valve on many a ship
In distant lands and in the air
Wherever you go, you'll find it there

The peace and purity of a Dove
A perfect symbol of God's Love
Mother mine, I owe you much
An Eternal Debt for your every touch.

Eileen Wallmen

One-sided Leaf

Lilac light on the eye-lashes of glass.
A new leaf, after whistling with its clumsy edge,
As always, will land on the pine table.

A sudden rain in half-darkness has caught
All that piled up quietly over the years
And the soft face sign solidified into a question mark.

The unlived days, with a funeral march,
Have cast their silver net from bank to bank.
And a freshly cut sign whispers "turn back" to the elders.

The boundless sky and exploding waves
Grit rustily, rubbing side by side,
With a yellowing leaf caught between them in clutches.

Gliding sleapstone strives from the earth.
Zigzagging, it hops along the mirror surface,
Overtaking the yachts and fading afar.

   Denis Burdakov

As I Was Saying

'Do what thou wilt shall be the whole of the law!' said Aleister
'All else is windows and mirrors,' replied Jessica
'Life is difficult,' added Scott

'Life is a fruit crumble without the fruit,' began Helen
'Life sucks!' interrupted Derek, irritably
'Life's great!' Becky chirped
'Today,' she added; quietly
'Life's gay!' shouted Pete
And Daniel

'Life's amazing,' purred Guisy in response
And Harry said something pretentious that I've forgotten
'Life just is,' said Pooh
'What? Sorry, what did you say?' piped Piglet

   Helen Jones

Within the Far and Distant Places

Why must the rain be so far away?
All I can see is a rainy day.
Maybe the clouds will fill the sky.
Maybe the rain will fall on by.
Maybe the water will sting their eyes,
And make the authorities realize
That this world needs people of different races,
Within the far and distant places.

I believe in the black and the white
Where different people can share one light,
That shines so deep, their hearts shine bright,
Where speech is free and thoughts are shared
And ungodly abuse is never flared,
Between the people of different races
Within the far and distant places.

   Caroline Brough

This Takes the Biscuit

If I had the chance I'd like to be
a biscuit people have with tea
I'd go unwrapped without apparel
relaxing in a biscuit barrel

I could "Hob Nob" with "Garibaldi"
and make eyes at "Oval Marie"
Have a chat with "Morning Coffee"
and discuss finance with "Rich Tea"

The "Bourbon" is held in high esteem
by the "Shortcake" and the "Custard Cream"
the "Chocolate Finger" was pointedly restive
having been squashed by a "Chocolate Digestive"

The "Ginger Nuts" gone off in a huff
after a citric remark from the "Lemon Puff"
outside they're making cups of tea
so it looks like this is the end of me.

   Doug Ponti

Picture of Love

As it blows in the wind her hair is so fine
A sight to be seen a sight that's divine
It glows in the sun so soft and fair
That is the beauty of her hair.

Her eyes are like diamonds they have that magnetic glare
You can't help but feel happy when you're caught up in their stare
So big and so blue you can't help but realize
That is the beauty of her eyes.

And then when she smiles the sun will shine
The world is a better place and everything's fine
She is but a baby only four years old
You just need to stand by her you'll never be cold.

   David Ketteridge

Dreams

Isn't it wonderful that we can dream
A place where nothing is quite what is seems
What can you picture, what does it mean
What wonders go on, inside a dream.

Fall fast asleep, open you mind
Close the door, leave reality behind
Dreams are sacred within your mind's eye,
Sadness is low, sensuality is high.

A dream that lifts you, higher than high
Above your world, to a clear blue sky
Floating, o'er mountains and trees
Breathing, caressing, the warm summer breeze.

Far away you go, to a distant land
A dream to take you, to warm white sands
Blue sky, sunshine, you feel serene
Isn't it wonderful, that we can dream.

Look inside yourself, let go of your mind
Wake up your thoughts, leave the world behind
For in your dreams, while you rest deep
Fantasy comes, to take over sleep . . .

   Christine Nicholson

Behind the Doors

Behind the door of number ten,
an old woman is alone.

Behind the door of number eight,
a woman struggles to bring up her kids.

Behind the door of number six,
a man hides from racism.

Behind the door of number four,
a woman is covered in bruises.

Behind the door of number two,
sexism is the issue.

These are just some issues we try to ignore.
Why do we close them behind these doors?

   Helen Wade

Rose

Rose was my mother,
An ordinary person (so she said),
I wish I'd shown her how much I loved her,
But I can't because she's dead.

She was shy and gentle sweet and good,
She cared for us as best she could,
She never said, 'I love you' I don't think she knew how,
If only I could have her back, I'd really show her now.

All my friends remember her and loved her as I do,
They called her 'Rosie' she was a mother to quite a few,
I knew that she was proud of me although she never said so,
One day I hope I'll see a sign and then I'll really know.

   Eileen Tame

"Looking Back"

When I was young it seemed the sun would always shine
And buttercups and daisy chains around my neck entwined
The meadows were much greener and the banks were wide and high
The trees I used to love to climb reached almost to the sky!

When Grandmother took me out to tea to a small house in a row,
I would sit at her feet on a hard wooden stool and quietly told to sew,
I remember the rooms were tiny and the ceilings no height at all
Geraniums on the windows sill kept out the light - they were so tall.

I recall the wooden staircase I climbed up every night -
Carrying my little candle, a lovely friendly light,
And from my bedroom window - small and latticed-paned
I would watch the old lamp-lighter as the daylight waned.

I remember Grandmother's large serge skirts surrounding her
    ample figure
And her scrubbing brush on wash days which she used with
    so much vigour,
I see again her wooden chair she sat in every night
She never dozed or bent her back - always erect, upright.

Now the traffic rushes on - the bypass runs nearby
No time to stop and wonder - to pause - to weep or sigh
But somewhere on the hillock still by the roadside growing wild,
Are the buttercups and daisies I gathered as a child.

Joan M. Smith

Life?

Why is it that a single smile triggers a thousand tears?
A smile is barricaded by an army of fears, the height
of this obsession. A feeling of happiness wrapped in a
blanket of depression, like a lost soul searching for
home but only to find a prison. What good is the love
which is a one-sided affair, a wrong love leads to a
life of despair. Unlocking the gates of this morality
to say that what we teach may not always be fair.
This heart may have a story to tell, a song to sing, but the
words are a living symbol of this world, a meaningful
tune, but a thoughtless gesture of today, as what
do we mean by this thing they call love.
A heart lies there untouched whereas another lies
there smashed is the scene today. To what extent can
we live with this pain until no one will be left to
comprehend, just an empty heart and an empty mind.
Could we proceed to look further than this heart can take,
can we be the ones to give each other the love and guidance we
need. To live in the proper sense of life if we do we have sussed
to proceed this preaching of a better life is a must.

Humera Rafiq

The Dead Seabird

You look lonely, dashed between those rocks.
A smut of feathers beneath soaring flocks,
Just some more litter on a littered beach,
A little spot on your once untrammelled reach.

Was it my kind's fault that you're lying there?
Did we steal your food or pollute your air?
Just a thoughtless fisherman in rubber boots
With big fish dreams and death-baited hooks.

What caused your death on this lonely beach?
A long search for food, somehow out of reach
In an oily pool by a barren sea?
If it was me down there, would you pause for me?

Was your nest disturbed on some craggy height?
Did I help put you down on this dirty night
Or did you die in a mating game
With your beak agape and your blood aflame?

Did you ingest oil from a careless ship?
A burning, blinding swim through an oily slick.
It's now over for you by this polluted pool.
Your spirit wings away and leaves this world to fools.

Arthur Dalton

The Stoic

The Encheiridion dream.
A relic of a redundant philosophy.
You hide behind your stoic front
and your smile never reaches your eyes.
You guard you heart like a treasure
and erect boundaries
no one can transcend.
But I know the folly of self-delusion.
What are you scared of?
You aloofness is your armour,
but still the fingers of loneliness find the chinks
and pry deep into your soul.
Do you acknowledge your secret fear?
It's human nature to reach out and feel
and you are, after all, only human, my friend.
Don't abjure those who care
- not every lover hurts.
Don't remain shrouded in detachment
mourning a tortured heart
The stoic soul is an empty place.

Hazel Martin

A Tribute to Grampy

Grampy you were my world in every way I knew;
And now that you have gone my world has split in two;
I know I have my loving family to help me see this through;
But I would just like to say I will never stop loving you;
You were my tower of strength, and I don't know what to do;
Only to say I love you, and to hope you always knew;
Now that you're in heaven I just hope we'll meet again;
Where we will not have to part,
And always stay in each other's hearts.

Emma Lock

Feelings

The battlefields we visited
A sorrowful sight to see
Thousands upon thousands
Were slaughtered endlessly

They fought and died to save us
And bring us liberty
So the rest of us could live together
In perfect harmony

The war graves in their thousands
Lie in peace and tranquillity
Tended by the commission
As perfect as can be

There's English, Irish, Scots and Welsh
And other soldiers too
They died for what they thought was right
Their country, me and you

Joyce Bell

Destiny

Two tiny hands and two tiny feet
A quiff of hair and a small wrinkled face
A yell to show that the lungs are fine
A newborn baby joins the human race

What shall the future hold for this mite
A struggle to exist or an easy life?
Hard work to always make ends meet
Or comfort, luxury and freedom from strife!

No-one knows until life has been lived
What fortune will endow
'Tis one of life's greatest mysteries
Something we shall never know

Perhaps it's just as well for us
To be kept in an ignorant state
God has each of our lives mapped out
And we cannot alter fate.

Irene Ramsay

Just Words

"You have a way with words", the chairman said.
A way with words? Away with words!
Some action, please, instead.
Words by the ream won't build a dream,
Add nothing to a worthy scheme
Except a mounting cost.
Committees meet. Each has his say,
And then comes back another day,
Another day that's lost.
Heads sagely nod, and votes are cast.
Does this mean something's done at last?
But no. You have to quell your rage.
It's merely passed another stage.
No wonder some things take an age.

Dennis Gardiner

Life

Life, is like water,
a precious commodity.
Ever sought after
By those refusing conformity.

I look out at the sea
with wonder and amazement
as it flows free,
Just then, I'm full of contentment.

I love the Spring
a sign of new life.
The birds of the air singing,
for their renewed life.

Who knows what the future will hold?
Though, I want to give life what I've got!
In that way, I'll know I won't grow old,
Just move along, to whatever comes next.

Elizabeth McIntyre

The Beach

I strolled along the deserted shore,
And all I heard above the roar
Of waves that crashed upon the beach
Was the sound of something out of reach.

The gulls that overhead did fly
Wheeling around in open sky,
Their plaintive screech filled my ears
Like sounds of mourning, vocal tears.

When all at once my heart did lift
With joy at such a glorious gift.
The sunrise suddenly lit the sky
With bands of colour, metres high!

Fiona Sangster

The Garden Fairy

When the sun is shining bright
And all in the garden still and wary
You'll hear the laughter soft and light
The sound of the garden fairy.

She flits about with her lacy wings
Like a butterfly bright and airy
While on the breeze she softly sings
The sound of the garden fairy.

Behind the leaves and stems she hides
When she comes, the times, they vary
The tinkling laughter now subsides
No sound of the garden fairy

Away she hastens as if in fear
Sensing something odd and scary
Perhaps another day we'll hear
The sound of the garden fairy.

Caroline Allan

The Spaceman's Prayer

Far from home, the planet Earth
A Spaceman monitors his lonely journey;
As he looms from Earth's orbit web,
his silver machine weaves and spins
to the harmonic sound of the heavens,
binding all souls of life — Ad Astral!

The Earthman maps vast cosmic galaxies —
threads of light and dark, twine with ripple waves;
From cores of fusion to plasma array . . .
when energies hot and cold do meet —
emerging a nucleus, will or soul,
structured to the call of destiny.

He looks back to Earth, in its majestic presence,
crying for us to heed the wise warning
echoed by bones of dinosaurs bygone;
For the children and future generations,
mankind must break old preconceptions —
to form a new one . . . heal this living world.
Nothing is certain, only his true belief;
He knows how fascinating life can be!

Anna-Marie Killeen

Gentle Breeze

You my babe shall wander like a breeze,
a spirit born of earth and water,
  Floating over forests, across lakes and waters,
of far off shores.
  Over mountains through valleys, from season to season,
and on through the storm.
  And you shall see and hear sight and sounds of,
an inevitable nature.
  Should you spy me in the forest all dressed,
in green the look of a boy upon my face swinging,
  through trees from bough to bough, with my bow and arrow,
a mischief in play, followed by a gleeful banging of drums.
  Or in the waters at sea - a single dolphin you'd see,
playing merrily, skipping the waves in a graceful dance,
too attract if by chance, your eye as you pass on by!
  Or you see my tracks across the mountains,
my footsteps through the valleys,
know then I come along way.
  And when you here the storm you'll know it's me,
my laughter's like thunder, that's where you will find me!

Ashlee Cole

Valentine

I brought my love a Valentine.
A tall and lovely deep red rose.
"I'll cut the stem in half", she said,
"and see how well it grows".

I brought my love a Valentine.
Age old symbol of desire,
"it droops a bit "she said," I think
It's been too near the fire".

I brought my love a Valentine.
Sweet yearning for her to express,
"The petals are all falling off",
She said, "It makes a mess".

I brought my love a Valentine.
To show I meant to hold her fast.
"They force these things to bloom too soon",
She said, "They never last".

I brought my love a Valentine.
I saw she held a huge bouquet,
"another gave me these" she said.
"I threw your flower away".

Judith Moss

11

Shameful Mistake

As the weeping waves engulf the beach
As the wounded hobble along erratically
As unspoiled area wears a coat of black
as if in mourning.

Remember this and learn

As oiled men survey the damage
As the innocent suffer unnecessary wounds.
As the fisherman comes home saddened by his future

Remember this and learn.

Emma Boulton

Once upon a Year

Woven, secure, into our hearts for fully a year,
A thread can be tugged now, without a tear.
Only your parents privileged to see
The earthly shape of how you would be.
Impatience was over, the time was here,
But suddenly we had great cause to fear.
Your tiny heart, so calm, so still.
You were never destined our loving arms to fill.
Your soul had stayed in the love and grace
Of a greater Father; lost then, we thought, without trace.
And yet the memory of your birth on that sad day
Touched so many people in a wonderful way.
Carefree now, to chuckle and run around,
Where no mortal fear or dread need ever abound.
A breeze for a swing; clouds to bounce on and ride;
A magnificent rainbow for many a slide.
A home, radiant with light and great love to give,
To keep you safe for as long as we must still live,
Happy Birthday - our love will ever be the same,
Until we who care so deeply can greet you by your name . . . Jamie.

Joan Townsend

Reflections

A time for study
A time for mischief and intemperance
Such days were the beauty of life
The mists of time cloud these thoughts
Yet in times of solitude they shine forth
Like the lucidity of the sky.

Accursed and detestable I was described,
But I bear no malice and hold no grudge
As I sit here in my armchair
In the winter of my life,
What I would not give to be back there again,
Lonely and old as I am
Slow to walk yet still quick to think
The rowdiness of my class would bring melodies to my ears
But on this melancholy day
I must be content with my memories.

Giuseppe Corbelli

The Circle of Life

Beneath the soil as dark as night
A tiny shoot heads for the light

Through stony ground and hardened earth
It takes the route laid down at birth

To taste the rain and feel the sun
Is the reason why its life begun

And with each hour its strength enhanced
Through wind and storm its leaves have danced

And so with grace to face the world
With its final wonder now unfurled

Comes the day its quest complete
There is a stirring at its feet

And beneath the soil as dark as night
A tiny shoot heads for the light.

Derek Boniface

Angelic

High on a graveyard
A tree fed fat on death overhangs,
whilst beneath stone angels smile
and bare their fangs,
It's supposed to be a place of peace
yet people are imprisoned in the
earth and never find release,
Crucified on a thermal.

A derelict church, a headstone to religion
reduced to the housing of innocent pigeons.
Angels immortalized in the coloured glass,
yet broken and decayed,
A fitting testimony to the past.

On the altar lies a flaked cross
cradling the water of a fountain still flowing fast,
An awesome symbol - encased in dust
whilst the march of humanity strode on and past.

Glynn Parry

Existence

Would you like to know unwittingly how we all came to be?
Adam gave a rib for Eve then there were three
No explanations needed, as history will tell
There are only two places, there's heaven then there's hell.
There's circumstantial evidence of what happened all too soon
In the midst of time, became a population boom,
The fruits of the earth enriched by the by
But the wars of the roses made a lot of people cry.
Regimental officers with politicians stride
To make this world a better place, no-one should have died,
Life's long struggle, activated mirth
Has been laden upon us all, ever since birth
We retreat to face values, but hidden in our depth
There must be hearts of gold, in the ones who have left
We strive for love and peace, for heaven's sake and our own
Nuclear power - hell- leave us alone.

Hazel Forrest

Faraway Person

Long ago you left this land and my love far behind,
about you oft I wonder, now you're in another land.

Far-away person please think of me from far away
across the sea.
My love for you will never die I oft think of you
when ships pass by.

Our love was never meant to be between this vast
eternity, but faraway person please think of me and
and all the loving times you've spent with me.

I never will forget your face, my darling I hope you
save a place for me in the caverns of your heart and
hope from there I never depart.

Oh far-away person please come back to me and heal this
broken heart for me.

Jeannette Sayers

The Upward Climb

If I should stand on Everest's peak
Above the shrouding clouds,
Deafened by silence cold and bleak,
Blinded by beauty's spaciousness,
Sickened by vales of emptiness,
Vulnerable still to turbulent storms,
To rip-roaring winds and ice that forms
Deep crevices of cruelty —
I'd accept Love's power to change the scene
Within my consciousness,
From mortal concepts fast to flee
Which hold in sway idolatry
Feeding man's frivolity.
With understanding unconfined
I would climb the peaks of Mind
To see - my immortality.

Brenda J. Wilson

My Sky

Way up high, I see a beautiful sky
A truly beautiful sky
Shades of mauve, of peach and pink
So many colours, I dare not blink
The fluffy clouds slowly move on
Where have they gone to
Gone to pastures new
Now appear more lovelier hues
Very different shades of blues
It's just as if God used a paintbrush
Across the sky to tempt us
Now the colours are fading
To where are they heading
The clouds and sun are gone
The day is almost done
Night time is falling
The stars are calling
They are all peeping
The world is now sleeping

Joyce Roberts

All Alone

As I sit here all alone,
a very cold shiver
goes down my spine,
and along my bone.

I feel distant, as if I'm far away,
on another planet, a different time,
a different day.

As I'm distracted, from a light in the sky,
I rush to my window, to look out and see,
an enormous spaceship, coming towards me!

I created an image, of weird shaped beings,
and realized then they weren't human beings.

As it drew closer, closer to me, I saw lots of
hands and they'd abducted me!

They'd pulled me out, and took me away
to an unknown place far far away!

Jemma Meyer

Ode to Spring

As on a mossy bank displayed
A thousand golden trumpets played
A brazen fanfare heralding the Spring
Azure campanulas and hare-bells ring

A silent paean rose from where
Massed ranks of primulas so fair
Of form and hue each different from the rest
And each against the other press'd

To reach the sun; each recognition sought
In striving through the dark days, brought
To warm the heart and cheer the pallid soul
Uniting all into a unique whole.

So brief a spell, yet all is not in vain,
If Spring be lost, we shall a Summer gain.

Albert Butterworth

The Coming of Dawn

As the stars slowly disappear,
And the night owls I no longer hear,
From my window I watch the coming of dawn.
And as the first sprinkle of light touches the lawn,
My pain and sorrow are washed away by a single tear.

Bathed in fire is the coming of a new day.
Carrying in its radiant beams hopes of a better day.
Birds and wild animals rattle at the first drop of light,
While man and pet sleep away half of daylight.
This day is filled with no mistakes and is not at all grey.

Amira David-Iziky

A Cotswold View

I wish that I could visit once again
A village that I knew in bygone days.
A village close caressed by sweeping hills;
The proudly wooded hills of Gloucestershire.
One sunny summer day I climbed a path
Which led upward, ever upward to the hills.
I climbed past whispering woods of scented pine;
Past grazing sheep; past fields of golden corn.
At last I stopped to rest beneath a friendly tree.
I'd heard that from this place the eye could see
Seven counties spreading far around.
I saw the Malvern Hills, blue in the distance,
A glint of sunshine on a window pane.
I marvelled that the beauty I could see
Was only but a part of our small realm.
I cannot walk again upon those hills,
But I can close my eyes and feel anew
The healing touch of peace which came to me
Across those timeless curving hills.

Elsie Brown

Love's Only a Whisper Away

Was it really only yesterday, only
   A whisper away, love was mine?
Was it I that let love, like the
   delicate flower petals the summer
   breeze scatters, die?

Was I not there to hold your hand
   While darkness was all about you?
   Many the times the candle
   Flickered, its struggle to stay
   alight. Our flame of love did
   it not burn so bright?

Did I not lead you to a safer
   haven, and guide you through the storm,
   to wake up beside you the
   next morning when you were worn?

Did our love not win on the
   battlefields, to pass on to
   Peaceful grounds.
   Or was it I that never had
   the fight within and thereby let love down?

Janet Crowther

Together

Over the river lies a new world
A world of rejoicing, care and love
A world of forgiveness, kindness and friendship
A world that's as free as a dove
A world of sharing, free to live
A world full of happiness, everyday
A world that respects each other as equals
A world that is perfect in every way

On the other lies hatred an evil world
A world of pitch blackness
A world full of selfishness, stubborn and dark
A world lost forever tangled in mess
A world without freedom, sharing or respect
A world without happiness, a world of betray
A world of discrimination
A world full of dismay

Together we could make a perfect world,
Of equality, friendship, kindness and love
A world of rights to speak your mind
A world that's as free as a dove

Clare Ann Dunk

A Defence of Marriage

Oasis in Life's desert,
A tree, a pool, water of life,
Trekking the heat of mortality.

Find your oasis, nurture it well
Taking a wrong road
Could lead to a mortal hell.

Wear your gold band upon your left hand
'Tis your status, a mark
That you are willing to make a stand
To show the world that you are content
To grasp another's hand.

To take the risk and concede
All that loving will demand.
Be not fooled by modern trends
That lead to broken hearts
That nothing can mend.

Take up the banner of marriage, serve it well
And ignore the ominous soundings of the death knell
Which some would put in place
Of the Wedding bell.
Doreen McGee-Osborne

Without You

Every second that you're away,
adds a year onto my heavy heart.
And when you're not here beside me,
my world just falls apart.

Without you, life is meaningless,
and to go on each day is so tough.
I can't bear the thoughts of being without you,
and to hear your voice is not enough.

I wish I'd have told you how I feel inside,
maybe you would be with me now.
But I know there is no way of telling you,
I know now I should have tried.

My fears of never seeing you again,
grow stronger day by day,
I can't hide this feeling,
this pain, just won't go away.

If I never see you again,
my heart will never mend.
My love for you will never die,
and my feelings will never end.
Germaine Bowser

Untitled

Burn my heart in resin and wine
Afloat in the season's untamed vine
Replenish my soul in perfumed oil,
Dance with the ghost of the soil

Freed the pollen on summer's harp
Take the uniformed flowers in your mist,
The waters Claret shining
On a winter I warmly kissed

Dreams reflex on the spine of clouds
Love's gravity pulls you in my heart,
Fly in the rapture of beauty
Surrender the snake charm, that keeps us apart

Sow the seeds of freedom,
Love's uncovered swan
Hearts of the free will fly
Inspire my devotion on the wings of the sky.

My wings will hide your darkness
Travel in the depth of my thought
My trance is your heartbeat
Clothe the man who gathers wood, so he can fly once more
Deborah Demarco

October Bath

Strange, but I miss you.
After twelve years. After lifetimes gone,
leaves shed and pass on in the foggy streets. In London.

On the train I could smell you as I did an age before:
dregs dripping, rain sticking to my hands,
a pungent keepsake hanging, clinging to my core.

You dug. You burrowed.
You buried your share with a twelve year hug.

Till my reluctant bath
I breathed, I held you in,
my senses singing in the aftermath.

And I missed you. Thought to start again;
to scrub you off and out of there,
but then my strong, my hurried heart . . .
I did not wash my hair.
Estelle van Warmelo

Sunshine

Walking down the road looking good
All the women stop to look
Like women should
Walking down the road feeling cool
All the women know that I'm nobody's fool

The sun is out
I'm on my way the pool
Suntan lotion in my pocket
Ready to watch the women drool

The sun beats down on me
I'm the bronze Adonis
All the women look and see
That the sun shines through my orifice

Too nice, too neat, too sweet you see
That's me
But you already know that
Don't you girl?
Aniello Delgaudio

Lazy Summer Days

Long lazy days lapping up the sun.
Across soft pine needle carpets
Birds calling in the air, and crickets
Purring like a thousand cats in yellow gorse,
Proclaiming a path to my special place.
Soon I can hear it.
Its smooth lapping fills my mind,
A scent so clear and fresh.
Stones crunch under my feet,
I lay my towels on the golden sand
And rest in the heat of a glorious day.
The sea is deep blue,
Warm and safe from the world.
Full of life, but as calm as death,
Still and deep,
Invitingly cool in the boiling sun.
I lay on the rounded pebbles,
Book in hand, the perfect summer's day.
Not a care in the world.
Anna-Marie Bellerby

The Senses

Shadows dancing on a candlelit wall, swaying to and fro.
Ageless branches tapping at the window, they came to say, hello.
Stars shining in a darkened sky, a wonder-world to see.
Half-moon smiling, knowing all about life and destiny.
Darkness is a void unknown but, something that we fear.
Knowledge therefore we must gain, do we not have ears to hear?
The gentle platter of tiny feet, a suckling babe, oh so sweet.
A clog dancer echoing tunes gaily down our street.
A soldier safe, a battle won, a prisoner who is free.
It was gone and was to come yes, we have eyes to see.
Geraldine Ellis

A Lover's Desperation

The wind whipped so violently around her as she stabbed
  again and again,
And the rain poured down so quickly, but hers now he would
  still remain,
They had been so much in love until Faythe had come along,
And she had broken up a love, a love that was so strong,
But now Faythe was not strong enough to fight against the knife,
And victory was for Erica for she would become his wife.

But did he want her back when he'd heard that Faythe was dead?
And he'd heard the gruesome details of how someone had
  slit her head,
Faythe was his only interest, he idolized her so,
And compared to Erica she made her look so low,
Erica now learnt this and could not bare his thought.
So she set about to find him taking with her the knife she'd bought.

When at last she found him she held the knife up high,
But then before she'd stabbed him he let out a painful cry,
And he lifted himself up with blood dripping down his head,
This is when Erica saw the blade roped to the foot of the bed,
Without even breathing she got down by his side, and stabbed
herself with the knife so she too would die,
And there so still and silent the two lovers lie.

Hayley Hardcastle

Fingers Tall

Fingers tall and tapering of weather beaten brick,
Abandoned now, like rotting sentinels do stand.
Yet they mark not decaying walls of factories now dead
They quietly mourn an industry that died within this land.
No longer do they funnel black smoke to mouths built high
But silently stand, defiant, stark against the sky.

Oh tall and tapering fingers, once warm and belching soot
From fires that roared through night and day to hold a head of steam
Then breathed with vibrations from the engine down below
That watched the flywheel slowly turn, the polished conrod gleam
And rang to people's voices, the morning whistles call
Heard the clip of steel tipped clogs, saw women dressed in shawl.

Oh fingers tall and silent, now like rotting trees do stand
Your broken mill-shed windows display each a neglected frown.
And so you wait, forgotten, lost, your usefulness outdone
Till man with tractor, spade and crane will bring you crashing down.
No sentiment has progress, bricks and mortar mean naught at all
To man or state that did once depend on factory chimneys tall.

'Days Gone By'

I stare at the picture from years ago
And look at the girl I hardly know.
She seems so quiet, happy and mellow inside,
But I know the problems that she did hide.

Do I prefer her then or now?
Which life was better with hardly a row?
Remembering the happy times past and gone
Will I ever be that happy, and will it take so long?

I don't want to change my looks or rights.
It's part of who I am, that's why so many fights
Look at the girl from years ago and see.
That growing inside all along was me.

Joy Addison

Facts of Life . . .

As sure as leaves will fall from trees
As night will follow day
As grass is green as rivers flow
As June will follow May
As sun will shine and rain will fall
And time will pass us by
As sure as all the things above
Our love will never die.

Jon Harrison

While You Slumber

I wandered by your room, so cool
and entered quietly, and sat in a pool
of soft light near the window opened wide
while fondly looking by your side
I caressed your forehead and saw you smile
as by your bed, I lingered awhile.
For soundly you slept quite unaware
of any secrets kept, or that I was there.

But somehow you will know I have been
for as I go, I will enter your dream,
and in your dreams I will come again
by whatever means without any fuss or pain.
To touch your mind is my main desire
as you will find there is such a fire
burning within this very heart of mine
as we are akin until the end of time.

Sylvia Clayton

Stock Take

When every avenue has been explored
and every road is a dead end,
you have pleaded to the Lord
and received no dividend,
all your dreams have been dreamt,
all ambitious hopes spent,
then take stock.
Before it's too late and you're too old,
wake up to yourself, come in from the cold,
because out there in oblivion,
you will die in a salesman's death,
telling of great aspirations with your very last breath, take heed.
For your plain, grey headstone will stand bare
save for these words, inscribed with care:
An embracer of dreams,
yet a failure it seems.

Gavin Calthrop

The Smuggler

They tell the tale of an old Dutch barn
And a craggy cove by the shore
Where the Lizard's tongue stings the Cornish flow
And no one goes any more.

They say at night when the moonshine is blighted
By storm clouds from the lea,
You can oft' hear the moan, the creak and the groan,
Of the smuggler just out to sea.

They tell how he fell, with a ball through the heart,
His hands raised high in the air,
The wail of Miss Alice as she clutched at his soul
While the excise stripped him bare.

The old Dutch barn still stands alone
Beside that turbulent shore.
Through the seething shale a ghostly wail,
A terrible moan, torn from the very heart's core,
A sinister shape that is not quite real.
So no one goes any more.

Antony A. Rushworth

A Child's Prayer

Sweet, gentle Jesus, be with me I pray
All through the dark night and the bright light of day
Please bless my mummy and my daddy too,
Help me to love them, the way that you do.

Help me Lord Jesus to grow up like you
Because, I know that's what you want me to do.
At school and at home, at work and at play
Please be my best friend, every day.

Watch over the children, not lucky, like me
Who don't have beef burgers and chips for their tea.
I'm not very big Jesus, but I know this is true
I'll always be safe 'coz I'll always have You, Amen.

Doreen Barber

The End of the World

A planet which holds so many forms of life,
All of which love, show sadness and fight,
Some beauty, some ugly, some old and some new,
Some talk, some roar, some squeak, some coo.

Our home is a mystery, one never to know,
Where it came from, who made it many years ago,
A time bomb, or not, how long will it stay,
A decade, a century, a year or a day.

So small and meek, we humans pretend to be great,
But we don't even know what is our own fate,
There are geniuses and doctors, teachers and priests,
Leaders, strong men and magnificent beasts.

But the end of the world will finally come,
Disaster and death, but relief to some,
No answers, no solutions, nobody knows
We can't stop it, or save it,
That's just how it goes.
Emma Taylor

Winter

Winter's with us once again
All the trees are bare
Sleet comes down and turns to rain
No-one seems to care
Heads bowed down they rush along
Does anyone hear the birds sweet song
All he wants are a few moist crumbs
To keep him warm till summer comes
The dark days go and turn to spring
Now the birds can really sing
The air is warm and full of sun
We think of days all made for fun
Holidays and Picnic teas
Balmy nights and summer breeze
Alas too soon it's come and gone
All that's left is bird's sweet song.
Joan Yeadon

Sorrowful Temptations

Part of a circle
always going 'round.
life gives out temptations
only newly found.

These are a virtue
if used on proper ground,
if not.
Deceit becomes an issue
determined to rebound.

Self-indulgence should be ignored
when two people are bound.
Or sorry is the prerogative
when a new love is found.
Amanda Wood

The Barn

Twisted and scored by days of time,
Alone beside a leafy lane,
No more the reapers heave the sheaf
Or come to pound the grain.
From holes in dark corners peep
Eyes of mice, across an earthen floor
While closely sits the nesting wren
Listening to moans of a creaking door.

High above with emerald eye,
Surveying all from a jagged stone
Sits the wise and ruffled owl
King upon his ancient throne.
Over tired and bulging walls
Reflecting the silver gleam of dawn
Creep the eternal leaves of ivy
To welcome yet, this new day born.
Jeremy Boaz

In the Mirror . . .

The face in the mirror that I see
All wrinkled and lined, cannot be me
This middle-aged lady that I see
Could never, ever, ever be me

The gleam in those eyes that are so blue
Is as wicked as mine, it is true
And in the hair are touches of grey
That I had thought to colour away

The provocative smile that I see
Is faintly reminiscent of me
As is that saucy and flirty look
That from my image the mirror took

The mirror, they say, it never lies
And this I have seen with my own eyes
But of this image I want no part
For in my mind I am young at heart

Yet in the mirror the face I see
Is still the one that mocks me with glee
But despite the image that I see
I am still that girl inside me.
Dorothy Walker

The Day the Sea Gave Up Her Dead

The day the sea gave up her dead,
Aghast, I stood upon the shore
The sky above me turned to red
The rocks beneath me seemed to roar.

Horizon filled with sunken wrecks,
Now riding high upon the waves
Perished spirits walked the decks
Arisen from their watery graves.

Ashore then came the lost at sea,
And on the land their shadows cast
A shade which seemed to pass through me
A presence from a time long past.

Then in my path the reaper stood,
I felt a quake rip through the ground
A voice now echoed from his hood
And silenced all for miles around.

I've come to call the human race,
For this my friend is judgment day
Your maker now you all must face
I took his hand walked away.
Bernard O'Keeffe

Billy

Pale child on a swing, whistles a haunting melody.
Aged memories long buried rekindle painful thoughts in time.
Leaves swirl around the still playground, where once we played.

All that now remains,
is the ghost of my dearest friend Billy.

The tarmac rippled under a sticky summer sun.
Dogs barked at owners baited with sticks,
whilst lovers stroll hand in hand beside the lake.
Children shout and laugh paddling in the cool crisp water.
Voices and laughter sounded all around the park.

Me and Billy played on the swings,
so much fun trying to reach the sky.
Together we reached the top, as sunlight blinded us.
I glanced over, Billy was gone.
In the distance his poor limp body convulsed,
like a fish thrown upon land.
We were only having fun.

What lies before me now.
Flowers in front of the still swings, where once we played.
A farewell to my dearest friend Billy.
Ian Shaw

"Last of the Line"

In the still quiet night the old lady lay,
Alone in her hospital bed,
The last of the line
The remaining one,
All the others now dead.

The rasping breath and sweating brow,
Signs of life slipping away,
The last survivor,
The last of the line,
No more reasons to stay.

Her only child killed in the war,
His photo she keeps dear,
All these long years
On her own,
Their reunion is now near.

Nurse mops her brow as she slips away,
Off to her peaceful rest,
She's had a hard life,
Looked after the others,
She was one of life's best.

Christine Ashworth

Life in Review

I don't know much about living,
Although I've been at it for years.
I've been through the joy and happiness,
The heartbreak and shedding of tears.

I can't think why I'm doing it, I wish it would start to work out.
There's no way of knowing what's happening,
The one thing I'm sure of is doubt.

No one can tell me the answers to the questions I try to ask.
I know I can't go on like this,
As my life passes by so fast.

Am I really meant to be here, or is it just one big mistake?
I have nobody to show me
The path which is best to take.

I have come to the conclusion, it is easy for me to see
No one will provide any guidance,
So the person to help is me.

I'll live each day for its meaning,
To have a life as smooth as silk.
I shall cross each bridge when I reach it,
And stop crying over spilt milk.

Gemma Tindall

Untitled

I felt safe as in his arms he held me tight
  Although the time we spent just wasn't right
A few stolen hours we share together
  Hours not meant to be now or ever.

If only our paths had crossed before
  Because now I want him even more
There is no room for me in that life
  I cannot - and will not share it with a wife.

My tears fall loud and land unheard
  How I wish that I were like a bird
I could fly away and leave behind
  All the thoughts that distort my mind

I wish so hard it is him I'll hear
  So far away and yet so near
The voice I heard was music to my ears
  So long ago we'd spoken, it felt like almost year

We arranged to steal some hours away
  To our hideout we'd go and stay
Once again he held me tight
  Only this time it did feel right.

Allison Parnham

Indecision

Indecision now rose like a dark cloud
Amidst a clear, blue sky
Obstructing rays of hope and happiness
And those questions demanding why?

Remembering the bed sheets in disarray
Mugs of coffee on the floor
She had recognized the situation
And chose to walk right out of the door

But now he was stood before her
Appearing so sincere and true
Begging for forgiveness and just one chance
To love her and start anew.

Until she had made that decision
Taken a definite stance
Her life would not be free of clouds
And her future would have no chance

She prayed for guidance and strength
And the ability to make a new start
For deep within her soul
She knew the answer was in her heart.

Julie Taylor

"A Miner Thought"

Tomorrow we strike and leave you alone
Amongst this debris, that you make home
"How will you survive"?
There'll be no food to keep you alive

Fans will be turned off, you'll get no air
Gas will engulf you from everywhere
Pumps not working, you'll sink or swim
and we'll be out a long time, you simply can't win

But cheer up my pit mouse
I will leave you some snap
Have a good go for it's not in a trap
You've had a rough time down here in hell
Still you may end up in heaven
  One never can tell.

Joseph Mayoh

My Love Enticed

Entice my love to private place,
And there with arms entwined embrace.
A gentle touch fills heart's desire,
At every pore there lights a fire.

With fervent kisses lips apart,
And quickening pulses of the heart,
Pressing closer, and closer still,
Carried away on passion's thrill.

Two lovers joined as one unite,
There, love spent, glisten in the night.
To be loved by my love is truly bliss.
My love has my heart, and I have his.

Janice Upshall

"The Astrologer"

A man set sail across the sea,
And inside this man's heart was me
Swimming gracefully with a tail of gold,
Winding through caves a thousand fold.
And all inside this tiny heart!
That surely was a work of art
That fluttered at the sights he saw through those eyes,
That gazed whilst night, way into the skies.
  And he plotted those stars onto a map,
That gently in the wind would flap,
As he sailed across the ocean wide,
To fulfil the dream he had inside.
And he plotted all those stars for me,
So I could see my future to be . . .

Carol-Ann Kinsella

Through the Storm

Blue waves crash against
An army of rock,
The wind bellows its cries
While the spray lashes the sand
With an ecstatic sigh.
A single voice echoes through the storm
And is taken forever away,
To be lost among a thousand voices
Which echoed tomorrow and yesterday.
Life would be easy to end now
Just one step over the rock side,
Plunging into water's oblivion
Forever forgotten in the eternal tide.
But a burst of sunlight
On the distant horizon,
Or maybe just a sudden burst of hope,
Makes that one last step
Impossible to take,
Makes it seem
There is reason to cope.

Irene Logue

Long Shadows

Oh! Where have the cornfields vanished away,
Along with the creaking haywain and the dray?
Stretching so far that the eye couldn't see
The end of the golden crops rippling free,
Constable country of wild, glowing Weald,
Each summer returning its ripe August yield.
Gone are the gleaners, backs bending low,
Corn ears left behind feeding blackbird and crow.
Did these far-reaching meadows a sense of peace bring
To our forebears who watched each burgeoning spring?
Did they sense any end to the cycle each season,
Repeating like tide without rhyme or reason?
All omens brushed off with a dismissive laugh,
Grains of truth or presentiment obscured in the chaff?
Oh! Where have the cornfields vanished away?
The threshing and turning a family day,
The thrushes and hedges are all sparseness and few
God! Turn back the clock to that soul-healing view!

Flavia Stampa Gruss

Children's Safety Code

Children always be careful when you cross the road
And always remember to use the green cross code
Never play with a ball in the street
And do not go with strangers you meet
If any one stops you run as fast as you can
Or you may be taken away by a nasty man.
Never go alone to play in the park
And do not stay out when it is dark
Don't go for a ride with a stranger
Or you will put yourself in great danger
If you remember all these things
You will never go wrong
And you will always be able to go along
Singing a happy and cheerful song

Doris May Robey

Neighbours

We have a friendly neighbour and her name is Chris McCall.
And we're so disappointed she is going to leave us all.
But there's no doubt, we all agree, it really is a pity,
She's sold her house, and packed her bags, for Welwyn Garden City.
But, nonetheless, we wish her well, wherever she may roam,
And may God bless and keep her, when she goes to her new home.
We know she'll make some other friends, we also know 'tis true,
She'll be just as good a neighbour as she's been to me and you.
Everybody needs good neighbours,
Everybody needs good neighbours,
Everybody needs good neighbours, and that means me and you.

Jean R. H. Mathieson

Yugoslavian Idyll

At my feet lies the green Adriatic,
And azure sky above.
I lifted my face to the warming sun
And the mountains I loved to roam.

This beautiful scene entranced me
I must come back again
To see the pale pink fronds of the Tamarisk
Delicately dancing in the lane.

Within a frame of sea and sky
And all around a haze -
The snowcapped Mount of Lovchen
Towers loftily over the bay.

This sun-kissed corner of heaven
Will call me again and again,
To leave my well-loved native shores
And the sound of falling rain.

And now as time and tide move on
My travelling days are almost gone,
And an aching heart for that stricken land
Beats and mourns and prays for peace.

Joan Leedale

Remote Control

My love for you can be instantaneously switched off,
And back on again; Reigned over by your behaviour.
At the push of a button we move from the pure,
The simple, the black and white,
To a multi-coloured montage of arguments, fights and violence.

The picture when new was so perfect;
Now old and used is fading into nothingness.
We are here. The volume mute, only our picture remains.
Laughter and joy,
Once the noise of our relationship, now has a different sound.
We have changed channels from a light-hearted comedy
To a documentary, a drama.

Our relationship so expensive and precious at first,
Has been replaced by something else;
More colourful, common, less precious.
The old;
Thoughts of as for eternity, is slowly disappearing,
A relic, a memory, an antique.
No longer regarded as the ultimate, the forever,
But as the past, the no more.

Judith Reid

Observation

The sun's sharp rays give a tan that's smart
An inner glow to warm men's hearts
But middle age is a cruel thing
It ages women and destroys their skin.

That deep dark tan now looks like leather
No creams can guard against that weather
Those deep lined tits and shrivelled bits
That baggy skin around the thighs
And blue-veined legs for no man's eyes.
That sagging bottom, beauty's curse
And stretch marks just to make it worse.
That face which once was fresh and pink
Your tan has pencilled in the lines, like ink!
Your hair which glowed and puffed with ease
Now dry and brittle, tho' diseased.

So dear lady, just lie in shade.
Keep well covered as your beauty fades.
Let men's imagination run its fevered course.
Your body a fragrant mystery - He'll fight to find its source.

Christopher Dunn

Complex Lives

You looked both innocent and guilty
And although you always watched your back
The greatest battles fought were in your mind
But you never were a leader
And you had no plans to change my life
Your head was always turned to look behind

And however much you meant it
And although I thought you didn't care
I miss you and I'm sorry now you're gone
And I know I'll always love you
And I'll always think of you with me
I just don't think I've the strength to carry on

Sometime - in the future
When we've found ourselves another life
I'll meet you and by heart we'll know our lines
We were lovers, we were friends
And our world, it never ends
It just takes a new complexity sometimes

Ben Edwards

Sunset

Before the sun sets on this day
And before the darkness takes away
Our thoughts and wishes, and turns to stone
That glimmer of hope which the daylight had shown,
Let us remember the things we have done
And not dwell too much or worry upon
Our failings, mistakes and let us not grieve
For those many things which we didn't achieve.

Instead, let's look forward to tomorrow's new day
And hope that the morning, in some special way,
Will offer more hope and place in our hearts
The energy needed for a brave new start.
Tomorrow will come and with it, will bring
A new inspiration within everything
That we hold in our hearts as good and worthwhile
And rekindle our faith in the world for a while.

Jon Morris

My Prayer

When I come to the close of a busy day,
And by my bed I kneel and pray
My thoughts wing out across the sea,
To loved ones very dear to me.
I placed them in Your tender care, the day we said adieu,
Please guide their lives dear Father give strength each day anew.
I pray you lay Your healing hands on all who need Your aid,
And if for some You've chosen rest, don't let them be afraid
But gently take them by the hand, and lead them to the promise land
I pray for little children Lord of every race and creed,
Please shield them from all danger and meet their every need.
Bring peace upon this troubled world, Bless all humanity
And Father if You've time to share, will You remember me,
Help me through tomorrow's tasks with cheerful heart and smile
And may I say when evening comes, my day's been quite sublime.

Elsie Barker

Lacuna

Does it suck inside a porous shell
and weep tears of blood for its lack
   of incarnation?
To the sound of the clarinet it begins to breathe
   a clear breath.
Eyes look upon the world
   shadows and sunshine flitting over it.
A face of shadow but white as a sea-shell
   Flagging energies, half-dreaming substance
   smoother its dawning
Beaten white and yellow
Blood-red lips re-aspire a new lustre
nicer than sunshine served in a whisper
The luxurious outbreak of inflammable lunation
rushes towards its tourmaline birth

Fiona Hackett

Solace

When snowdrops proudly raise their pristine heads,
And bring with them the promised gift of spring,
When daffodils stir forth from wintry beds,
And high above sweet songbirds start to sing,
   then I'll be there.

When gentle breeze disturbs the sultry air,
And grasses whisper softly in its wake,
When sun-kissed waves dance on a sea set fair,
And from the beach the children's laughter breaks,
   then I'll be there.

When drowsy is the hum of probing bee,
And lovers' lips are bruised with berry stain,
When early mists enshroud the verdant lea,
And every sweet farewell is without pain,
   then I'll be there.

When hoary frosts enchant the wooded glade,
And winter's mantle casts its snowy fold,
When robin waits upon the gardener's spade,
And home and hearth bid welcome from the cold,
   then I'll be there.

June Winters

The Flow'rs of Dunblane

Hush, ye ill-winds on this sad date,
And calmed be the grieving heart
Of all who mourn their children's fate
When their class was torn apart.

They died by the hand of a gunman's bane -
The innocent Flow'rs of Dunblane.

Hush, ye ill-winds - wistfully blow
The fragrance where they repose;
May ev'ry name by Heav'n's light glow -
While the Angels guard them close.

They died by the hand of a gunman's bane -
The innocent Flow'rs of Dunblane.

Hush, then, ill-winds, and slowly quench
The anguish all parents share;
"Grant them, O Lord, Thy Grace and strength
To find Thy true peace in pray'r."

Their children died by a gunman's bane -
The innocent Flow'rs of Dunblane.

Francis Latchford

My Dream

Last night I dreamed I travelled far
And came at last to Shangri-La.

Where ivory domes and turrets gleamed
Beneath a sun that softly beamed.

I wandered on through streets of gold
To see such wondrous sights unfold.

Gardens with flowers of brilliant hue
Nestled by lakes of azure blue.

Silvery-leaved trees shimmered there
And butterflies danced on the scented air.

Birds were singing songs so sweet
And rose petals lay around my feet.

But then a ringing in my ear
Caused my dream to disappear.

As I awoke in the cold grey dawn
I stared at the culprit who had torn

Those blissful images from my sight
And shattered the visions of the night.

I reached to still its raucous call
And dashed that demon to the wall.

Angela Noble

Spring

Showers that usher in the spring
And cheer the wintry ground;
Dew upon the pale primrose
Diffusing fragrance 'round.

Lilies, tulips, snowdrops sweet
Withstand the sudden squall,
Catkins hanging from the trees
From them bright raindrops fall.

Birds song fills the morning air
Hoping all to please,
Whilst crows and rooks build straggly nests
In tall, strong swaying trees.

Squirrels shin down from their holes
For them dark "night" is o'er;
They lightly leap from branch to branch
Gathering food once more.

In verdant glen and mossy dell
New lambs beside their mothers stand,
Then haste oh! Spring, at God's command
Refresh the air and paint the land.

Joan Bunt

Why I Love You

Your love to me is like a baby tree,
Always growing more and more each day inside of me.

I love your warmth and kindness,
The love I have knows no blindness.

I love you more and more each day,
And that is the way it will always stay.

I love you holding me tight,
My life seems so colourful and bright.

I love you holding me in your arms,
And turning me on with all your loving charms.

All the arguing noise fades away,
When I hear the love in your voice.

I'll love you until the day I die,
So there will never be the word 'good-bye'.

So all I wanted to say each and every day,
Is that I love you in every possible way.

Jacqueline Reid

An Irish Wild-Blown Rose

Let nature hold the vision clear
An Irish wild-blown rose;
In crystal art, in magic sheer
Idyllic verse and prose.
Wild beauty captured in the soul
In peerless, scented lay,
From Antrim to Atlantic roll
To dawn on Galway Bay;
And claret-red the rose in form
In broken chords of time,
Unshaken pride stirred in the storm
Are martial thoughts sublime.
Who dares to dream, who might suppose
The bloom by Lakeland sea
Is lovelier than the Gaelic rose
The wild rose of Tralee.
And might a colleen fair of face
With laughter and desire,
Surpass another Island race
With inner Emerald fire?

Christopher Rothery

Then and Now

Gone are the days when mothers would knit
And children on grandfather's lap did sit -
Eagerly waiting for a story to be read
Before being safely tucked up in bed.
The days without the telly were better -
One even had time to write a letter.
To-day's babies wear baby-grows
And shops sell ready-to-wear
We'll buy another one to-morrow if anything should tear!
No one has time to darn socks to-day
If there's a hole just throw it away!
What about elastic in pyjama pants?
Never mind, we'll sleep in scants.
To-day there should be more time for fun
But it seems that the work is never done.
Up early in the morning and rush till late
Have dinner on a paper plate!
Like it or not, this way of life is here to stay
And the future depends on what we make of to-day.

Jean Morse

Lucky Me

I was down in the dumps, having just had the mumps,
And decided I needed a break.
I said, " What shall I do? I am feeling so blue".
Friends suggested a swim in the lake.

I said "Don't be silly, the water's too chilly,
I will go to Bermuda instead".
But the bank manager said "Your account's in the red,
Perhaps you'd be better off dead."

I didn't want to die, and I started to cry,
Then my lover said "Cheer up, my dear,
I will take you to town, and buy you a new gown,
And we'll go to Bermuda next year."

How lucky am I, to have such a good guy,
I thank God for him every day
He'll always adore me, do anything for me,
And all of my debts he will pay!

Hilda Womack

Beirut

City beautiful in sunlit robe
And guarded by her watching, shifting seas
So sometimes silver mingling, half real
As interchanging silent coves they probe.
The ancient city dreams towards Europe
Seeming in a slightly twilight mood.
Phoenician quinqueremes transmute to steel
As jewelled 'planes surmount the heliotrope.

See now how in the clouds of olive mist
The city tantalizing can't resist
To don her evening dress of sparkling bronze.
A million teardrops glisten in their throngs.
Towards the velvet midnight let us tread.
Towards the teardrops - softly let us tread.

Elizabeth Stephens

Guilty Reflection

The simple life is simple
When we have enough to eat
Simplicity's malevolent
With swollen belly, blistered feet.

To have, to hold, to own the mountain
To turn the tap that starts the fountain
To lack the means to play the game
To see and want and hope in vain.

Roy Jackson

The World

There is the sky of blue,
And everything reminds me of you.
The fields are green,
To have faith in someone I have never seen.

Have the flowers to grow,
And to have my hours to know.
See the tress,
To hear and feel the breeze.

The birds that fly,
To hear a person sigh.
Animals that live,
To be the thankful in what you give.

Sea and sand,
Everything made by your hand.
Having the stars,
To appreciate what is ours.

The pleasant sunshine,
To thank the Lord that you are mine.
In the moonlight,
Everything made perfect in your sight.

E. G. Chaloner

Mum

When the birds announce the break of day
And fill the sky with song
I have to remember what people say
That life still has to go on

They don't understand the way that I feel
That the pain in my heart is so very real
From the day I was born she was always there
The person who'd love me and forever care

Then I wake and she's gone
She's no longer at home
I feel really empty I feel so alone

I feel sad and tearful and hollow and numb
'cos today's the day I say goodbye to you Mum

I look at the flowers I hear all the songs
They're all saying prayers now
Why's it taking so long

I'll always remember you're here in my heart
And while you are there Mum
We're not really apart.

Jacqueline Brown

Eventide

The sun sinks in the west,
And gulls bemoan the onrush of the wind,
The greyness of the clouds, the heavy waves
That toss and heave a leaden foam
And dash against the rocks!

And somewhere there,
Across the restless sea,
My bark soars on, and challenges the storm,
But without me!

Because I'm here, and safe, at rest
Upon the shore of Hope,
My eyes turned to the east,
Where clouds can never shroud the rising sun,
Where no gulls scream,
No wind to dash my soul against the rocks;
There, where the dawn will break anew,
And bring forth a new day,
There, where *you* are, where *you* will be,
Bestrewing roses all along the path of May,
For all eternity!

Alfred Palma

The Spaceman

The first time he came it was in the dark.
And he landed in the park.
He had a mouth but he had no face.
And he said to my friend what is this place.
I said hello, he said goodbye
Then he vanished into the sky.

The next time he came it was in the day.
But he landed far, far away.

The third time he came, he spoke again
As we stood there in the rain.
I said hello, he said goodbye.
Then he vanished into the sky.

The last time he came, he spoke to me.
As I encountered him under a tree.
He said hello, I said goodbye
Then he vanished into the sky.

Ever since then, I have not seen him.
Maybe I should have told him, my name is Jim.

James Mulrooney

Remembrance

I sat and watched you in your sleep
and held your hand afraid to move
the time was close when I would weep
the last things said were words of love.
The final sigh, your breath was gone
I could not move nor wish to leave,
you were my life, my dearest John
why did you leave me now to grieve?
I could not sleep, the pain too strong
why you, not me? (I had it planned)
each day eternal, hours too long
I'd give my life to hold your hand.
Months of torment and time to greet
need for comfort from those who cared,
travel spent in order to meet
your family, the loss we shared.
A treasured friend has made me see
the things in life a different way,
I cannot stay in misery.
My wish to join you fades away.

Ann Odger

I Looked into My Mind

A shadowy brilliance forged into my mind.
Granting me what is not known, my finest now
Disorder breath, its soared mist entwined
Informing the secrets of its emerald towers.

Sheets of pain, stood upon, stretched across or embroidered night
Shapes they never learnt me, forbidden silence waits untold
Possessed with pure anxiety, Panicky squeezes light
Each step forms puddles of mercury, this kingdom will unfold.

Spontaneous burst of passion, calls the shapely souls around
Amongst a land of July into December, hail my creativeness
I touched the murky water, a sign of shiny glass rebound.
Dry straw wearing through a current stream, yet uncaring and
sourceless. No signs, just men without bones of shrunken leather skin
every mile or so, they hold their hands in gesture as to welcome
me what is mine, and to breed what I begin a corner in my eye,
spells a hint of infinite pasture

A journey through corridors of revelation
My heart pounds and breath this rich reward
Without need for concentration
No fear for time, the subconscious to absorb.

Peter Carlin

My Window on the World

When heaven's canopy is raven black
And hides from me the starry skies above,
And there's no moon to shed its pale light upon my world,
I live in hope.

I know that dawn will steal upon my day,
And the first blush of morn will push darkness away,
And that emerging light a different world reveal.

Soft morning dew mantling the earth with diamonds rare,
The gentle unfolding of meadow flowers fair,
The web of the spider exquisitely made
Give me hope not meant to fade.

For when the dark and blackened sky
Sheds its tears I wonder why
A rainbow is made of every hue
And whispers to me, "God loves you".

Joan Johnson

To a Sister on Her Wedding Day

I'll begin by starting again,
And hope, that this time, it flows,
Like all these crazy confused tears,
For what reasons 'God' only knows.

I know I am gaining a brother,
And he is gaining a wife,
His family is gaining a daughter-in-law,
And we will all share in your life.

But isn't it just really scary.
And also so incredibly sad,
That it's taken so long just to notice,
We are leaving that childhood we had.

I'm so proud that you have succeeded,
And you've pleased a wonderful lad,
In becoming his wife, for the rest of your life,
And probably help make him a dad.

I feel I would like to remind you,
Of something very precious to me,
You'll always be my big, big sister,
And will still mean the whole world to me.

Elizabeth Caroline Ivett

Garden Memories

How the memories flood back, walking around your garden.
As I walk around, I can smell the sweet scented flowers;
I can hear your gentle laughter, as you worked away the hours;
I can see you tending plants so carefully and with love;
As I walk around your garden, I say a quiet prayer,
For it fills my heart with happiness to feel you are there.

Christine J. Muir

The Speed of Time

Another year has just gone by
And I didn't see it go
I wonder if it's just my age
For they used to go so slow
I'm sure as we grow older
There becomes a new dimension
Must sort this out when I get time
And give it my attention
But if I give time to things like this
The time will go more fast
I wonder what's the remedy
To make tomorrow last
I try to keep an hour or two
Tucked up within my sleeve
But when I glance down at my watch
I swear my eyes deceive
For there it is the day has gone
It's time to go to bed
But tomorrow may last longer
If I don't wake up dead

Euphemia McKillop

Free to Dream

My heart's full, my footsteps light,
And I thank Thee God for the sunshine bright.
I hear the birds singing out their song,
And I know that the dark clouds don't last for long.

My eyes see green trees and blooming flowers,
The majestic oak - the rose decked bowers.
I hear the murmuring of the stream,
For I am free to sit down and dream.

My thanks I send dear God to Thee,
For every leaf upon the tree.
My thanks I give for the air I breathe,
The gift of life - the right to be free.

Tho' my heart's full, my footsteps light,
My life full of Thy sunshine bright.
Tho' I know that the dark clouds don't last for long,
There are poor souls who hear no bird's song.

Free the oppressed - let war reign no more,
Send all Thy love to this, earth's dark core.
Feed the hungry - let each soul have a home,
Let all on earth hear the bird's sweet song.

Jean Smith

Beef of a Cricket Fan

I've been eating British beef since I were nabut just a lad
And I've had it overdone and some time raw
An I'm here to tell thee, Maester, it's never done me bad
Not through t' slump, depression or th'war
Now, I were reading in yon paper how some expert (if you please)
No doubt a very educated chap
Says eating beef will give you something called Jack Hobbs' Disease
From Creutzfeld (which I can't find on the map)
Well, having sat through Test Match and seen our batsmen play
And watched them skittled out for one or two
I thought a touch of Jack Hobbs, or a dose of Peter May
Might help the batting record of a few
So I'm going to write to Lunnon; to t' head of M. C. C.
Advising him what diet I think best
Thou never knows, in sixty years, or mebbe sixty-three
Our England team will win another Test

Ol' Slimjim

"Whisper a Kiss"

Gently lay me down in sweet perfumed silk
And leave me to sleep in my rose-covered bower.
Whisper my name as you pass on your way
To our ivory tower,
Where you lavishly bathe in freshly gathered milk
From the goats which wander upon our hill.
And blow me a kiss on the warm breeze of the afternoon
And tell me, my love, you will come to me soon
When you have gathered more silk, to clad your sweet form,
As you gathered mine in the dew of the morn.
Oh, tell me again as you did before,
This place will be ours for evermore
To stay in bliss
And kiss
'Til Doomsday.

Audrey G. Groves

Untitled

It made a hell of a noise
and pain was everywhere
I searched and searched but
you weren't there, only, the
damned noise was everywhere.

Searching, a lot of it, I did
until hear I could no more.
Hear? Hear what, the noise?
No, there is no noise no more,
only, it's your spirit I'm longing for.

But, this I needn't search for:
it kisses me from within and
lonely I am not, no more.

Angelo Judice

22

Feline Felicitations

Dear Tinker and Tiger, Mum showed me your snaps
And if we possessed one, I'd send this by Fax.

You two look so comfy curled up in your bed
Mine's not made of wicker, it's soft stuff instead.

I guess Mum has told you I'm big, tall and smooth
I curl up and cuddle, endeavouring to soothe.

Now don't get the notion that I'm a bit soft
For out in the open birds fly up aloft.

I hide and I watch them - there are squirrels there too
I just lie down quietly enjoying the view.

To be confidential, I've bells 'round my neck
They think they deter me, but do they? - like heck!!!

I've heard of your antics, some fun, others - well!
Don't upset your mother she might give you hell.

Just stay sweet and gentle and play happily
I'll still get reports from your Granny, you see.

So may I just wish you the happiest time
With lots of nice grubbins and bodies to climb!!

Barbara Jones   Hobson

When It's All Over

Why when it's all over, can't you just see
At no time in the future they'll be a you and me
It didn't work once, it won't work again
You made it all go straight down the drain.

People can't say that I never kept trying
But deep deep down all along you were lying
You wouldn't be honest you treated me like dirt
Was there a reason you wanted me to hurt.

Didn't you realize you were inflicting such pain
You nearly succeeded in driving me insane
If ever there was a small chance of having a future
I would have hung on, I didn't want to loose you.

But now I've grown up, I've seen there's more to life
and the one thing I don't need is you as my wife
So leave me alone and don't bother phoning
I can't bear to hear you constantly grumping and groaning.

The solution to the problem is simple and clear
I'll leave you to your life have no fear
Just go out and get yourself a totally new life
And leave me alone and stop giving me strife.

Justine MacKinnon

The Curse of Toothache

Toothache is a dreadful thing it really is a curse
And when you have an abscess it surely is much worse
The pain is so unbearable it nearly drives you mad
How on earth you ask yourself could it ever be so bad.

You go along to your dentist with the hope of some relief but
When he does an x-ray it meets you with some grief
I'm very, very sorry says the dentist looking sad
I can't take out your tooth today as your abscess is so bad.

What about the pain I've got you ask with disbelief
Is there nothing you can give me so I can have relief?
He prescribes some antibiotics and paracetamol for the pain
Come back again in a few days time and we'll have to try again.

Back home you're pacing up and down the pain is more than
    you can bear
It really is excruciating and it's enough to make you swear
Once again you call your dentist please take this tooth away
So I can get some sleep at night and go to work next day.

Come in as soon as possible and I'll take your tooth away
Thank God at last you tell yourself it doesn't matter if you
    have to pay
The relief you feel is wonderful the pain has gone at last
Never again will you neglect your teeth as you have done in the past.

Betty Stewart

Across the Pool

There was something beautiful in the turning of a page,
And it watched without deception from afar.
And as morning glistened brightly on a jewel encrusted meadow,
There was time to count the secrets in the stars.

The darkness had retreated, to the paths between the trees,
To the places where the shadows ought to be.
And I stood dazzled by the colours that showered before my eyes,
And saw all that I'd forgotten how to see.

Sometimes I'll walk in shadows,
But I know that by the stream
There's a place where I can look up to the sun.
And to all the world I'm losing,
But deep inside my heart,
I'll know there was a time, when I had won.

Chris Kee

My Rabbits

When I'm sad and feeling low
And nothing's going right
I slip out to the garden shed
To forget about my plight
For there they are, those precious things
That make my life so full
When they're near
I have no fear
And the world seems rather dull
I watch them hopping in the grass
While the sun is in the sky
Their fur so soft, their eyes so bright
I couldn't even try
To think of such a creature
More perfect than these two
They are my ray of sunshine
I'm sure they'd be yours too.

Dee Richardson

Fish in a Polluted River

His mother's dead
And now his aunt
Says where's the purifying plant
He cannot breath
He cannot swim
Because of what you've done to him
You've polluted his life with acids and gas
All you've done is expand the mass
The pollution is worse than ever
It's time we pulled together
To clean up this world, to make it a better place
To make it cleaner for the human race
It's destroying our earth
How much is it worth
To loose hundreds of lives and plants to witches
And think it started with fish in a polluted river.

Emma Sage

The Road to Happiness

Though days seem dark and dear my friend
And troubles hard to bear
You will always find a smile will blend
With happiness you too can share.

Keep a smile where you go
Forget all doubt and fear
For troubled winds will always blow
A message of good cheer.

Love is a message pure and true
In its silent way around you
Grasp it firm and without doubt
You'll find your heartaches few.

Wherever you find a darkened cloud
There is a silver lining -
When life to you seems like a shroud
There's always love abiding.

Connie Binney

23

A Saga of Ancient Greece

You've heard of Agamemnon, great king of golden Mycenae,
And of his brother Menelaus who came from over Sparta way.
The wrathful young Achilles, and the wily Odysseus,
The possessive Mardonius, and the fighting Miltiades.
Of Darius, who bequeathed his throne to his son Xerexes,
And Egypt he reconquered with the greatest style and ease
And the courage of Leonidas with 300 Spartans brave
Was all in vain alas, because, someone the signal gave.
Thermistocles received a bribe, £3000 or more,
And the Persian fleet, beset by storms, lost men and ships by score.

Then Thermistocles was exiled, and Aristides died.
And Cimon was left free to fight, and Persia he defied.
Then Pericles he did prevent a full scale battle scene,
He did this by refusing the Assembly to convene.
With summer came the dreaded plague, which killed a third or more,
But then, with eloquence superb, Pericles held the score.
Now I fear this tale has gone too far, although there is much more,
But tales like this are better read, from books of GREEK FOLK LORE.

Carol Paterson

Dog Star

Fare you well, four-legged friend
And I will greet you, by and by,
As you roll among the stars
With the hunter in the sky.

That range of sky is yours
Where the brightest star shines white
At the heels of the hunter when
He strides the gentle night.

Through fields of silvered lights,
Far beyond the moon's calm face,
You will run for evermore
In the glory of the chase.

So, fare you well, four-legged friend,
You and I once journeyed far;
Now you wander endless fields
In the bright light of a star.

Jack Minahan

Spoons

I smell her nakedness in the dark
as she creeps across the bed.
Our lips meet
and she is under the covers
and we are making spoons.
Her electric back is pressed against me
as I nibble her shoulder
and caress her stomach.
And her totally naked body
is pressed against my totally naked body
all the way from here
to here.

Darren Saffin

Locked in a Life of Yesterday

The window she sees through is misty,
As she tries to make some sense,
Yet she knows what she sees is reality,
of a world she cannot reach.
Cause she's locked in a life of yesterdays.

The lights of the world hurt her eyes,
yet still she stares through the haze,
As she stares, she remembers what it was like,
Before it all slipped away,
Now she's locked in a life of yesterdays

If she could only release herself and open the
door once again,
But the key is buried with the hurt deep down
within her heart.
And she knows that for now, she's locked
in a life of yesterdays.

Cynthia Breen

Morning Joy

Morning light shines though the trees
Birds flutter 'round in search of food
Fruit, nuts, crumbs of bread they seize
Then away they fly to the distant wood.

In the next field two donkeys bray
Then away on the hill a fox barks out
Good morning world they seem to say
We've plenty of things to shout about.

Everywhere animals wake to a new day
Spiders spin, among the leaves and grass
Rabbits hop and skip in play
How pleasantly the time begins to pass.

Blackberries spill their fruit around
Nuts tumble from branches in the breeze
Acorn cups are strewn on the ground
Squirrels hurry with the store they seize.

The trees move their branches and sigh
A breeze gives them a knowing nudge, to play
Pigeons coo in the branches up on high
Below a beetle makes its weary way.

Bessie Groves

My Childhood Days

As I sit here by the firelight
And listen to the stillness of the night,
Days gone by, to my memory come
When I think of the times with Dad and Mum.

Getting up with the morning dew
Rounding up cows for milking too,
On a farm there's lots to do
Picking strawberries ripe, and they're all for you!

Helping Dad get done by noon
For the spring lambs will be coming soon,
Feeding the chicks and doing the raking.
Then Mum and I getting on with the baking.

The pigs and sheep and rabbits too
And 'Dolly' the horse was there to shoe,
With all the hay there in the barn
It was a lovely life, as a child, down on the farm.

Doing the garden and digging the weeds
And tending to the allotments' needs,
Yes, I love to remember my childhood days
But this is where my memory fades.

Angela Hearn

The Dream

Last night I dreamt that I was near you
And your heart would not let you stop loving me
And the feeling you got made you turn and say
That I was yours and you could never leave me

All night long we would kiss in each other's arms
Every beat of my heart kept you near
And the love in your eyes helped me carry on
But then I would wake up to find that you were not here

Why are we so far apart when I am so in love?
The distance between us is hurting me so
Why are we so far apart when I am so in love?
Because girl I love you   I just thought you should know

When I saw you last night your face was soft and your hair was tide
I wanted to touch you deep inside to feel your warmth,
your breath, your life
To taste your lips I would cry, to know your body
you know I would die
To hear your voice over again   I would end my life just
to be your friend

And even though this may never come true
My hopes, my wishes, my dreams of you
I shall never forget you and I just wanted to say
That you will be my perfect woman always

Jason Karl Blumschein

On Dragon's Wing

My love comes on a dragon's wing
and sails in open skies.
It soars through clouds, through sun and rain
and over fields it flies.

It dips to where the rivers meet
at the crashing of salt waters
And smoothly glides to mountains high
but the love it never alters.

And finally back onto land
wings lightly touch the ground
for in its way the person stands
for whom the love was found.

Together free above the clouds
Love sails to open skies
And soars through clouds, the sun, the rain
And over fields it flies.

Deborah L. Duke

The Promise of Spring

Oh look into the garden bare, amid the earth's brown thoroughfare,
And see sweet petals dainty white.
Standing so fragile, it seems they might
Snap, and break, while the rough winds blow
These gentle snowdrops in clusters grow.

Oh virgin babes who herald spring so fresh so pure my
heart doth sing
While sheer delight, as I stand and gaze
At Mother Nature's wondrous ways
The first born of the flowers have come
Their faces as pure as the vows of a nun.

Oh how we longed fall, winter through
To see the garden take its cue and wake from winter's sleep refreshed
The birds to choose their mates with zest.
While in barren branches vines awake
Tingling life before bucks can break.

Oh woo the beauty of the tree where birds of every kind are free
To fly to shelter, rest, or make within its branches
Nests to take their wives, who proudly sing before us
As each dawn breaks, they joyfully chorus.

Jean Marsh

Acceptance

If we are loved, can we ask for more?
   To know the rules, to know the score,
And re-live heartache we have felt
   yet play the cards we have been dealt.

To bear the loneliness, now and then
   still asking questions - why? and when?
But, if we are loved, can we say
   it has been too great a price to pay?

Joy Dyer

My Mum Said

I ventured over to the gate
Where lonely groans were heard,
And there a dying boy cried out,
"Please tell my Mum I did her proud"
Her words were on my mind all day
I killed them hard, I got them all,
And history will remember me.
For I have paid them back.
And God was with me all the time
He helped me all the way
I killed for my religion
I killed for this great state.
And as I tried to comfort him
I said that "God means love"
His bright blue eyes filled up with tears
I heard a feeble cry
"My Mum said" and he passed away.

Margaret Maybury

Just Have a Look!

There's a burst of buds in the garden
And Spring has arrived at last
She's waved her wand of Magic
And spirited Winter into the past
She's opened up her paint box
   and started the colours of life
She's woken up the birds again, and got out her palette knife
She's sculptured her wave of beauty
O'er landscape and Mountain and hill
   the bubbling bounty of Spring, is promising overspill
She's splashing here and daubing there
Her autograph is everywhere
The lambs - they are a frolicking out in the fields so lush,
The bright green cloak of leaves, are coating every bush
The bulbs have shown their growth
Now peeping through the soil, and hard work done by farmers
   was worth the sweat and toil
The happy rays of sunshine, that play upon the earth
Have proven to the whole wide world
That Spring - she's here - Rebirth.

Christine Boyce

To Make a Song

Art should be ever pleasing to the senses
And so a poem should be made to sing.
If then I cannot make its sounds to ring
I am no poet.

Art should be meaningful, say some. But how?
Of what? To whom? How right he was who said
Poems ought not to have to MEAN but BE.
Ah, yes, Macleish.

Oh, Spirit, come and give me words for music,
Soft tender tones and thundering cadences,
Harmonious echoes onomatopoeic;
Fauré and Mahler.

I will forget about all form and content
And labour only for the melody.
Then, if the end should be a thing of music
I'll sing Amen.

Anne Polhill

Antiques

Surrounded by things of a bygone age,
Belonging to folks passed on,
Cherished and loved, or perhaps just shared,
Who can tell? But again for sale.
Times must change, but objects live on after
Their owners long have gone.
Pairs of vases, a joy to behold, with colours
of every hue, clocks of all sizes, ticking
away the meaningful minutes of everyday
They cannot give us a clue to the people
who cared, and made a place in their
earthly home. Life's bric-a-brac, tables and
chairs, mirrors, brass, copper, and china too,
What an assortment of treasure, for
everyone here to view.
Come look with joy on this Parian Boy, or
this lovely lamp of old,
From all the corners of the world they came,
To all corners will be sold.

Emily Green

Sailing Home

Gentle winds that fill the sails of Life
Blow bravely through the barriers of stress

We set our course to cut through veils of strife
And sail toward our sure eventful death.

But we will be uplifted on our quest
Our ship set square with faces to the wind.

With Seabirds, Whales and Dolphins as our guests
To carry us toward our journey's end.

Beryl Reynolds

Connections

I stepped off the train, relishing the fresh breeze that wrapped
around me, momentarily freezing fear

My chest pounded as I looked along the platform for you;
The train pulling away and leaving me stranded with no way of
escape

I walked across the wooden bridge,
Heart in my mouth, cautiously glancing between peeling painted
struts.

I wondered if my chest would explode or my mouth would dry
completely;
I shivered slightly and hugged my jacket close
And then I spotted you, looking towards me with your hands in
your pocket,
your long hair blowing across your face;
Like a scene from an old thirties film,

I stared in fascination as I approached
Past suitcases and umbrellas and the smell of diesel, I took the
final step into your warm embrace;
My heart slowed, any intention I had of running
Away was lost in these perfumed seconds

I could have stayed forever like that, with the pigeons pecking the
ground
And the whistling of another train approaching;
As if I needed reassurance anymore, all had become clear,
I had made the connection at last.

Ben Nurdin

Romanian Reflections

You will listen to birds in your garden
And may well pick a bunch of your flowers,
But the sounds and the scents of Romania
Stay with you for hour upon hours.

They will ask you to say what you did there
To explain what you aimed to achieve
And you'll try to describe in much detail,
What is it that is making you grieve.

It's not just the down-trodden people
Or those dark eyed, sad babies in cots,
But that awful injustice pervading
A country which others forgot.

Oh, we gave, it is true, but so little -
Gaining memories, impressions, galore
A small promise of hope for the future?
And a wish that we could have done more.

Oh! Romania will haunt us forever
With its pain and its pride and its mirth.
And we'll pray for a happier future
As it labours towards its re-birth.

Joanna E. Kingston

Goodbye Uncle Arthur

Around the small village churchyard, we had a quiet wander.
And on thoughts of the past, we let ourselves ponder.
On family and friends, who seem to ever decrease.
Most of them laid here, hopefully resting in peace.
Grandfather Arnold, Uncle Bill and Aunt Rosie,
Uncle Jack, Auntie Kate, and now Uncle Arthur Hosey.
He's come to join all of them in their sleep.
God knows what dark secrets all of them keep.
Knowing the family from cradle to grave
And how each and every one would behave.
So now the time has come, to bid Uncle Arthur farewell.
We're going to miss him, and the tales he would tell.
I looked all around the church, from floor up to rafter,
Thinking, could there possibly be, a here-after.
Was this but a pause, or the end of the road,
Or could we all meet up, in some other abode.
We met people today we don't see very much.
All getting on with our lives, we simply lost touch.
Then the gathering broke up, and once more we went on our way.
But as we did, I felt a bit more of the past, was buried today.

Dinah Arnold

How Do I feel?

He calls me late at night, sometimes early in the day,
And tells me how he's missed me, and how I'm always in his dreams,
My stomach lurches, my head pounds, my heart begins to ache as
he speaks,
His talk is always sweet, his sentiments so real, he makes me
laugh and my face glows.
I remember we once shared a home, a life, a whole world, a bed.
But there was always a ghost, another he adored, she came
between us, and then all of a sudden we were apart.
He continues to dream of his love, and at a moment's call, would
be at her side.
She is the one he really dreams of, he waits for her to share his
life, bear his children and fulfil his wildest dreams,
But until then, I fill the gap, the vacant place, just another
lovely face, a convenience.
I sit at home and stare at the phone, hoping for his call,
waiting for that flush to return to my whole body.
Is this to be my daily grind, this lover, this man, always
there, on my mind.
What will ever become of me, is this what life is meant to be for
me, a nineties working girl. How do I feel?

Claire Scott

Ode to Wine Lovers

Let it lie on its lees if your aim is to please,
and twill surely be good if you use the best wood.
And don't be demented if not barrel fermented,
but please choose the best if I am your guest.

Colour sense I may lack, for my pinots are black;
them I'll stoutly defend - a red man to the end.
For despite the attractions of young white S. Africans,
I'm as sick as a parrot without my best claret.

David Pawlyn

In the Garden of the Sun

As the trees begin to green
And the birds chirp and sing
As the fruit begins to blossom
And signal the arrival of spring.
In the garden of the sun.

As the flowers begin to bloom
And the garden gleams hot with colour
As the sun begins to burn
And spring turns into summer.
In the garden of the sun.

As the leaves begin to fall
And the ground browns crisp and dry
As the breeze begins to chill
And the autumn months arrive.
In the garden of the sun.

As the clouds begin to gather
And the rain pours with snow
As the cold begins to whiten
And icily the winter blows.
In the garden of the sun.

Diane Baker

Who Am I?

I lost my part in the play you see, who am I?
And who plays me?
I seem to have lost my way somehow, there is so
much hurt and doubt.
Who is this person who waits for the night hating the
daybreak fearing the light.
The face with the smile but no light in the eyes
doesn't anyone see through this disguise.
I wonder what my next play will be, should I
audition for the new company - who am I? Will
someone tell, or did I get the part and its name
is HELL!

Barbara Bailey

Bullying

I See: I see the bullies as they walk around me
  And the crowd as they stare at me.
  It's a horrible sight to see.

I hear: I hear everyone laughing as the bullies
  push me about.
  I wish they'd leave me alone but that I doubt.
  I hear their voices as they call me names,
  Laughing as they play their cruel games.

I Smell: I smell their breath as they shout in my face.
  Why me? in this dirty place.

I Think: I think of what it used to be like, before the bullying.
  I think of what might happen to me. I guess I'll have to wait,
  But inside me I'm full of hate.
  I turn around and see my mate,
  Backing out the gate.

I Feel: This makes me feel alone.
  I wish I was at home.
    Judy MacDonald

Tossed to the Wind: Like Ashes

Craters are forming,
and the gap is ever widening.
I'm scared and alone.
Losing something so precious,
without hope of regaining that priceless gift;
the one to whom I gave myself.

The vacuum created;
ever increasing;
leaving me empty and cold.
I gave myself; and was accepted.
Offered my vulnerability; and was loved.

Now, all that I sacrificed is lost.
Its value diminished: worthless.
Crushed like an ageing leaf in autumn.
Ignited like paper to a flame,
and my ashes tossed to the wind.

Why, why, have you forsaken me?
    Fiona Baxter

Dear Hills of Dyfed

Dawn
and the quiet hills open reluctant eyes
and watch the slender fingers of the sun
probe the shadowed hollows.
Then all day long
'neath halcyon skies they drowse
and idly gaze as wispy clouds
now veil, now clear, their lovely heads.
But when the evening comes
and shadows creep along the Cwm
they stir
and trooping to the steam
they bathe their tired feet
and drink the tumbling waters.
Then having clambered once again the slope,
in gathering dusk they lie
and over rounded shoulders draw a misty blanket
And go back to sleep.
    Joy Playford Ward

Welcome to Spring

What crowns of splendour you wear today
As you stand there with your stately heads held high
Strong to defy all that world and nature
Would dare to thrust your way
Your faces shine!

Head-to-head welcome this special day
A new life for you just begins
As you have lain beneath dark, cold sod
Awaiting earth's call for you to arise
You awake!
    Beryl Wallis

Unanswerable Life

I am awakened by the bright sunlight peeping through my curtains
another wonderful start to my life
I lie here wondering what this new day may bring me
will I end the day happy or sad?
Or will I make the day whatever I want it to be?
As I shower and dress, I think of all the new people I might
  meet today
Will I know a single person from this day
in another ten years or more?
Will I live the same lifestyle as I lead now?
Will the friends I know now, recognize my name if overheard?
All these questions I ask myself each morning
And yet, each time I will never know the answers.
    Debbie Warren

"Apartment Two-Thirteen"

On the morning of March the clock outside Macy's strikes eleven.
And the ghetto roars. I stand on the ledge and look downwards:

Leaves swirl in hurricanes, calling to the trees, "I got away!"
How I wish.
Window-cleaners whistle. Whistle.
The Chrysler building sparkles. Gleaming. Teeth glint.
"She" rises from the water like Poseidon, and shines her
holy light. It sprays like a fan from her torch.
Ants hurry along the sidewalk. "Walk. Don't Walk. Walk."
STOP!
Predatory taxi-cabs eat business people for lunch.
Sandworms gape, open-mouthed, steaming, stinking.
Skateboarder flies like a bird through the bustle, too low.

Strutting car horns flock in the street.
The army masses.
Road slithers away into the distance.
I join the leaves.
    Charlotte Elisabeth Hughes

The Fisher

The summer sun is rising over the Eastern sea
And the little ships are sailing to their homes,
  so full of glee.
The weary fisher is telling of his trials in the deep,
Then with a grimy finger he points to the glittering heap.
"Ah! if they all were jewels I'd have no need to go
Out in the distant waters, where the shining fishes glow.
But then I should have all the worries that come
  to those who are rich!
And I am contented forever to travel the sea in my Witch!
I love my life as a fisher, I never would change my lot,
For the dangers and perils of fishing I care not one tiny jot!
The summer sun is setting over the western sea
And the little ships sails outwards to the treasure, so full of glee.
    Grace M. Kaye

Mistaken Identity

The delegates wait and the chairman sighs
and the public gallery is still
The one they're awaiting has not arrived and they guess he never will

Soon after though the chairman comes, and rises to his
feet, to lead a great ovation their leader now
to greet - the chairman shouts he's here he's here
And excitement and cheers rang high

The noise died down like a gunpowder flash
and the echoes made no reply
because, after the ovation David Steel appears
to an even greater welcome the best for many years

The chairman says it's Potter's fault
He looks like David Steel, from sideways on, in that
dark suit; well that is what I feel

Poor Potter is embarrassed at Thomas's mistake
and wishes he could disappear or,
jump into the nearest lake.
    Jeanne Martin Tammas

When You Can't Cope . . .

The darkness falls down, on this old ghost town,
and the rain begins to fall, from skies of grey,
upon the empty streets, where the people meet,
every afternoon, everyday.

The wind howls past my window, as the day comes and goes,
so quickly, so quietly, through a mist of silent cries,
but there is a light that shines so bright that it takes away my sight
and finally has closed my eyes.

The sun may rise in the east, but that doesn't interest me, in theleast,
its rays are too strong, too strong for my weary soul to take,
because there's something on my mind, that cannot, will not stay behind
and it has been keeping me awake.

So when the darkness falls, and when the wind howls,
and the sun rises
take a promise you can't keep and lie it on the ground,
and when you have to weep, and there is sorrow all around,
hold onto the hope, when you find you cannot cope.
When You Can't Cope . . .

Janet Sinclair

War Child

The westward wind whistles loud
And the sky behind is torched with fire
But the war child walks on,
Drowning in his thoughts of the past.
The road ahead holds no hope
As the dark images grow within his mind
But the war child walks on.
Black tears flow like a river down his soft cheek,
His memory tainted with a world of decay.
The future is bleak, his stamina is weak
But the war child walks on.
His fear is of living, not dying;
The loneliness, sadness, breathes forever in his soul
But forever, the war child walks on . . .

Francis Gollogly

Autumn from Lawton Church Tower

Look at this crestfallen gold around our feet,
Autumn's here again,
Incense of woodsmoke
Makes sweet the dusk-filled skies,
Evoking memories of lives
Lived long in a summer county;
See how the grown church,
Standing in its natural stone,
Keeps watch on those who are become
Bones-old in the sifting soil,
Whose labour and whose measured toil
Have made this harvest bounty.

Graham Tyler

It's a Small World

We met here just by accident while drowning each our sorrows,
And thinking of what lies ahead, in all our dark tomorrows.
I can't recall who said the words to start our conversation,
But believe me dear this night for me has been a revelation.

You said you loved a married man with two children and a wife,
Who'd said he would divorce her and make you his for life,
But fate had cast a fearful blow and he had passed away,
Leaving only memories and a baby on the way.
You ask me now to help you in your trouble and your strife,
But this for you I cannot do, because I was his wife.

Yes, fate has cast a fearful blow on both of us today,
Leaving only memories and babies on the way,
So I see I cannot help you in your trouble and your strife,
You are so lucky not to be, his children or his wife.
So let us finish off our drinks as if we'd never met,
And hope to God fate will be kind and help us to forget.

Aileen Gass

Dayspring

Isn't it pretty when the buds have burst,
And their bright young greens have not been cursed
With the dirt and dust, that will begrime
Those exhausted leaves in the summertime.

There on the bank, where the primroses lie,
Is a splash of yellow, painted by
Spring's brush of colours, variously hued,
As an artist's palette, generously strewed.

Pale green fingers on a sombre twig
Turn to glory, from dark winter's wig.
The oak and ash of the countryside,
Flinging their armoured branches wide.

There's copper and bronze on the beeches now,
Like candle flames on every bough,
And even the firs sport cones as fine
As the fairy lights on the Christmas pine.

Each little catkin shaking in the breeze,
And the furry-coated pussy willow trees,
Herald the warmer days of the year,
I'm glad that spring is finally here.

Amanda Groves

The Lonely Planet

I'm standing on the moon so bright, staring into a starry night
and what do I see up over there, a lonely planet so cold and bare.

It doesn't own a single tree, it doesn't own a flower
it doesn't have an atmosphere, it has nothing in its power.

I wonder if it used to be a bright and blooming land
or whether it has always been so empty and so bland.

But as I look more closely, I begin to realize
that this cold and lonely planet used to be a friend of mine.

I remember how you used to look and how you used to gleam
I remember all the beauty, the most I've ever seen

But as time began to travel on, you began to change
Misery, bitterness all over your face,
Was it too late to change?

So now what am I looking at?
What was it all worth?
Because now what I am looking at
is my dear Mother Earth.

Georgina Brown

Dyslexic Survival

My love, you are now almost forty three years old
And what horrors of life, you have to me told.
The suffering, the crying, the hurt and the pain . . .
Just because you're dyslexic - THERE IS NO SHAME.

Thrown out of class and thrown out of school,
Branded a troublemaker, called a fool.
Rebellious and misfit became familiar words to you,
But what no one saw, they couldn't say they knew.

Inside you always had a determined streak
But to others you appeared an idiotic freak.
This quality, though, is what has pulled you through,
To work with wood, you decided to do.

In the cellar you sat, night after night
Sawing and chiselling, until you got it right!
Reading and writing gave you a furrowed brow -
But drawings and numbers were much easier somehow.

Your apprenticeship you completed, and became in June '73
A carpenter and joiner in the big building industry.
You've got more than it takes - personality and true grit . . .
Of course you should be called SILICON SUPER CHIP!!

Glynis Davies

Despair

Despair! Where next will you inflict yourself on me,
And where did you first have your evil taste of life?
We're you born quietly in the darkness of yesterday
And will you disappear tomorrow, leaving myself to me
To all these questions soon, one day, I'll have the answer.
The why's and where's, the if's, and but's of living
And if to gain this knowledge I must die.
So be it; for then at least I'll know the reason why.
Despair! You wicked evil turd of inhuman excrement.
Vile faceless git that hides beneath a cloak of hope.
Alien hideous thing that rears its ugly head when I think I can cope
spare me your time and effort, find another moron to wreak havoc
leave me alone, and lonely, as when you first captured me
allow my vanity and self esteem to do your evil deeds
and by doing so, inject me with a final dignity!
Where am I now? This day, this month this year?
So long ago I penned this woeful rhyme,
It seems I've lost all those I held most dear. My wife, my kids, all
gone with passing of time one day, maybe,
I'll leave my grief behind me
forget my chequered past and go, where love can find me.

Gordon R. Fogg

The End Is the Beginning

When I die please think of me not to be sad but feeling glad
And with that thought I'll live again

Think that I came, though not the same
To share your effort on this soil
Your happy time and daily toil

Don't shut me out for I'm about
For what is me will always be

I'm in the sunset in the stars
I still am in this world of ours
For this body stays on earth
Is used once more in giving birth

And thus fulfils its Master's plan
That He has always had for man

This then is not the time for weeping
For my soul is in His keeping
And thus with Him I'll take a share
Of helping those for whom I care

Till for you too there'll be no pain
So weep not darling weep no more
For 'twill be better than before

Dorothea Bathurst

The Writing on the Wall

"Father Forgive" the slogan said
and you can be sure that He will.
The bomber dropped his load and fled
far away and over the hill.

Another wall in another town
Where forgiveness is needed too.
Thank God, that one's now broken down
its existence pleased but a few.

Protestors had written "Cruise out"
"Fly back" was the witty reply.
It's so easy to joke about
but just think of those who would die.

Why do people write on the wall,
Is it to satisfy their needs?
Maybe it's not for that at all
but to put an end to such deeds.

Read what is written on the wall,
consider the message thereon.
You may be sure that it's a call
there's something that needs to be done.

Anthony E. Darby

The Man with No Name

I met a man who had no name,
And with him I went away,
I never asked from where he came,
For I knew he would not say.
He took me to the moon,
Showed me his virility,
Ravished me by a barren lagoon,
That once flowed into the sea of tranquillity.
He cast off my boots made of lead,
And together hand in hand,
We elevate from our passionate bed,
Leaving our mould in the sand.
Drifting on into outer space,
Passing Venus, Jupiter and Mars,
And with a pleasant memory of moon base,
We float on through a galaxy of stars.
Never wanting to return to planet earth,
But if I must I'll have no regret,
And I will say now for what it's worth,
This man I will never forget.

Diane Parker

Of All the Oceans in the World, You Chose to Ruin Mine

You took away the oceans,
and you took away my land.
My life ran through your fingers
like meaningless grain of sand.
Of all the oceans in the world
you chose to ruin mine,
and everywhere I plant my roots
you'll dig them up in time.

Charlotte Carter

Eyes Fixed on Him

Keep your eyes fixed on Him
And your life never grows dim.
Your path may be granite strewn
But to you His light will be shown

Keep you ears attentive to Him
Listening to the small voice with in.
"Be still and know I am God . . .
Abiding with you if you abide by My Word."

Keep your thoughts attuned to Him
Being pure without and within
"For as a man thinks so is he
And I'll assure you of steady victory."

Let your tongue always speak of His glory,
Each heartbeat revealing His mystery
And may each deed be inspired by Him
And your life never grows dim.

He's only a thought away
And watches over you night and day
Keep your eyes fixed on Him
And your light never grows dim

Harriram Khusial

Massacre of the Innocents

Sweet little angles full of happiness and love,
Are now little angels in the heavens above.
Taken away by darkness and hate,
By a creature of evil who decided their fate.
Yesterday's children, today's new found graves
What a senseless waste is all we can say.
Laughing and playing with all hearts content,
Living in heaven is where evil sent.
People of this earth shall never understand
Why the innocent have gone by a monster's hand.
We shall never forget yet never know why,
These poor little children were forced to die.

Jennifer L. Towse

Just Been Dreaming

The time has come for me to say that we
are going on a holiday.
Here we are on the plane leaving behind all the rain.
We can't wait to touch the sea, taking the children
to the beach with me, building castles in the sand.
Collecting shells as big as their hands.
Taking them swimming in the sea playing ball and being happy.
Watching Daddy with smiles in his eyes, seeing
lots of pretty women walking by.
The evening comes very fast, the children go to
sleep at last, let's take a walk along the beach
and see the stars just out of reach, the moon
is glowing all around the sand is shining on the ground.
I turn to you, happy and beaming, then I open my eyes and find,
I've just been dreaming.

Debbie M. Robinson

Some Call This Sport

None is more impressive against a snow covered landscape so cold,
As a fox out for a morning stroll his red coat flashing so bold,
Sleek in his appearance, ears alert to every sound,
Cautiously roaming the countryside for food that may be found.
Truly a beautiful creature, although some may say a pest,
Compared to others animals I think I like him best.

You see I find nothing attractive in a hunt on winter's morn,
I cannot see the beauty in a fox chased and torn.
I wonder to myself about these people who call this sport,
Have they ever realised or maybe even thought.
How would they feel to be pursued until out of breath,
Only then to realize this game was to end in death.
Maybe someday they will understand how cruel this sport can be,
Then find it in themselves to act with some humanity.

Anita Sutton

The Shamrock Sin

I travel through a city full of flames
As a terrorist of Ireland again claims
One more loss of an innocent life
Probably a husband's dear sweet wife

Do they kill for fun?
Or do it for religion?
Can't they see what damage they've done?
Do they think that they've really won?

Their horrible cast
Lingers death over Belfast
When will they stop, oh when, oh when!
And let Ireland live in peace again

When will they put down the loaded gun?
We don't want to see another Warrington
Now with the Downing Street Declaration
We can stop this Irish obliteration

Aaron O'Sullivan

Swansea

Snuggling houses tumble down the hill,
And verdant forest covers mountain rill,
Homely hang the houses on the quarry edge,
And tidy lie the buried on slag leap ledge.
Cover the desecration of the land and raw the edges lay,
Hammered and burnt from another day.
Defiled and blatant murder, furnace lit and noise
And screaming rent the land.
Mark the misery with bands of houses,
Now going nowhere.
Memories of roughboots ring the streets and calls of
Working men filled the air,
And misery born made them care.
Long ago this verdant land had rung with coal and steel,
Greed has emptied the land and in its place,
Plant trees in memory and grassy girth the soil,
A fitting epitaph for all their toil,
Roll the hills over it all, and turn it again to Arthur's Land,
Where Giants sleep with dragons.

Jane Wilmshurst

Offcuts

Dear Phil, is heaven's Air as sweet
As Hilbre Isle or on the West Hoyle sand
While counting grey seals in the heat
That summer day time seemed unplanned
From your great treasury of nature's lore
That God seemed to endow you at your birth
And yet which knowledge that within you bore
You gave us your distinctive love of Earth
It is like only yesterday we sailed
From Thurstaston in Hughie Higgins boat
The little cockleshell that never failed
To bring a smile on all of us afloat
Old 'Offcuts' now no longer ploughs the Dee
A new boat 'Sula' looking trim and neat
Now takes the 'cruisers' on the estuary
One day last year I sailed, it was a treat
Martyn was there and Hughie in command
And I was given the helm on many a turn
But only wished old 'Offcuts' was at hand
And you Dear Phil were with me in the stern

John Christian Comaish

Within My Heart

I've never before felt so much pain
As I hear of the tragedy of Dunblane.
Never before have I ever cried from so deep inside.
I've been touched where never before
Feeling cries from my inner core.
How I feel for people, I never knew
How can I help, to help them through
But I pray night and day
That in peace the little ones lay.
I give the families my heart and soul
As they ask, why the lives were stole.
As a nation we join hands and unite
Stand together to help through this plight.
May God hold out, His open hands
For we pray for peace and understanding of our land.

Joanna McAndrew

L'Envoi

Suddenly the swallows are gone!
As I look up, the sky is bare of them
This end to their sweepings and whirlings has brought summer
To a close.
Strange not to notice their departure
Only their absence.
So with you - who are so much more a part of me
Than swallows are of summer
Shall I awake one day with a hole in my mind
To find you gone?
Our poignant friendship leaving only
An empty nest under the eaves of my heart,
A fallen feather,
Some trails of windblown hay.
No - for I think you would smile, and gently remind me
The swallows always come back.

Diana R. Cockrill

Earth's Beauty

Green grass of the fields, tall slender trees
Blue skies above, the humming of bees
Fruit on the great oaks, bushes laden with berries
Colourful boughs full of apples and cherries
The profusion of colour when wild flowers bloom
Velvet petals of roses and their delicate perfume
Birds calling their mates, fetching ripe golden corn
To store in the quiet nest where the young will be born
Tiny lambs romping, cows heavy with milk
Little calves suckling, coats soft as silk
The miracle of birth, a sight to behold
A newborn's first cry as new life unfolds
Don't say there's nothing in this world to see
This is only part of God's beauty, for you and for me

Irene McHale

"Especially for Us"

I sit, with my grandmother
astride a long narrow stool
set just inside the door.
Her shawl wraps us together in a warm cocoon
smelling of lavender and yes . . .
a hint of newly-baked bread.
"let's sit and watch the angels' fireworks", she says.
So I sit warm, safe and unafraid,
While the thunder and lightening
put on a display especially for us.

June Winspear

Farewell to the Dance

Love ignited, scorching in intensity,
as flame leaping from an ember,
dancing with colour; crackling with heat.

Lives entwined,
dancing in time
with the world and each other.
Rippling waters dampened passion;
a sense of tranquillity,
of waltzing in tandem,
seemed sufficient.

Without realization
syncopation replaced harmony,
discord threatening to destroy the manuscript
so hopeful at its creation.

And now, farewell to the dance.
The cacophony of life relentlessly drowns the rhythm,
choking the notes, steps faltering.
as love dies.

Yet others still dance as one to their music.
Perhaps, in time, I will compose another song.

Caroline Haines

The Spirit

Once more off into the night
As I begin my solo flight
I know that I am not alone
I feel a warmth right to the bone

I lie in bed alone each night
I feel your arms wrapped 'round me tight
At once I feel the peace and calm
You are there to keep out the harm

A slight breath caresses my ear
In the silence it is your voice I hear
I feel a shiver down my spine
As our spirits slowly entwine

I feel you are deep within my soul
To protect me is your final goal
Oh how I long to once more
Hold the man that I adore

Clare E. Johnson

Sunset Over the Irish Sea

Nothing could ever be so fair to me
as I gaze on the far horizon hue,
the colours spring as from a faded blue.
As day flees from the shadows of the night,
what then to me could be a better sight.
The fiery reds that hold no tempest wild -
fade not upon the land, but are beguiled
once more to shed their rays upon the ebbing sea.

At last enchanted ride the kings of night,
over dying sun they once more take their flight.
The captive soon will glide across the bay
the fiery Gods have conquered yet another day,
with shouts of madness they beckon the night
to take the sunset, on its dying flight.

Jennifer H. Fox

Dyslexia

I grip the pen
as I have done, since God knows when.
Words are in my head.
Clever words,
In-words,
Sure to impress

I try to set them free
to march across the paper.
Proud and beautiful.
See, Oh see, these splendid words,
And they were made by me.
They twist and writhe, refusing liberty.

I push them harder.
My fingers' vice sets spasms in my neck.
My words are dying.
Unrecognisable.
End the carnage.
I lay down my pen.

Catherine MacKay

Untitled

The cold sweat runs down my brow
as I sit wondering why and how,
for the chest pains haven't started yet
but I bet by golly that's what I'll get.

It's not a heart attack that grips my chest
it's a hyperventilation mode, for the lack of rest,
it's because I breathe too quickly and get all flush
that makes my heart overwork and rush.

Anne Small

Reflections

I think of you
As I stand and sigh over Swan's own lake
Reflecting the greyest of grey, in wintry skies
That surround the island where black, murky-mud pools lie
Left over from days gone by, torrential rains.
Where Crow, legs astride, greedily guzzles around the sodden edges
Of nature's own creation, in muddy Black puddles of reflection.
That are unable to show His Black back.

I thought of you
At Christmas-time, a time reflecting white snow - Snow White
Where stood. Or sat. No-where there was
Outside my windows pane a Crystallized, Crimson, Climbing Rose
In singular pose, reflecting the grey wintry day
Surrounded by Freezing Frost and temperatures of minus One degree
Greyest, they said, for 25 Years, with little to please.
Cold. All alone. Yet - capable of generating warmth
As with little care of what the cost
It grew inside of me and brought forth
An instantaneous Smile.
That - was when I thought of You.

Joan Armstrong

'Life'

As I sit here I wonder, where does it go?
As I watch in silence, the sea ebb and flow.
The coming of dawn, the red setting sun
The start of a new day, the previous one done.

Chimes of the church bells see the new year in
Summer, Winter, Autumn and Spring -
Have characteristics known to us all
A snowdrop's whiteness, radiant colours in 'The Fall'.

The birth of a baby - new life has begun.
Childhood and adolescence signal times of fun.
Adulthood is soon with us - the years fly by
Whilst the leaves on the trees rustle and sigh.

They tell their own stories, as does the sea
Tales of past generations unbeknown to me.
I smile at memories, my laughter lines show
As I sit here and wonder - where does it go?

Deborah Harriet Jones

Dad If You Hear Me

I may not have hugged you closely Dad,
as many times as I should have.
I may not have spoken words of love,
as often as I could have.

There never seemed to be urgency,
to say or do so many things.
But now my heart breaks every day,
because of the pain your leaving brings.

In my dreams you smile to me,
as your strength and spirit shine.
Dad, you may never have known how loved you were,
by this heart of mine.

But with all my soul I promise you,
until once more we all unite,
My faith in all you meant to me will keep
all that is good . . . in sight.

And when God hears me knocking at His door,
Dad . . . just promise this to me,
If He welcomes me to enter in
beside him waiting lovingly . . . You Will Be.

Kelly Elizabeth Paterson

Rosebuds and Leaves

Damper and darker grows the tiring night,
As rosebuds laugh at lace-covered tables,
Outside: Dirty brick above fluorescent light,
And unwashed leaves in doorways settle.

Silver cutlery mirrors candlelight.
This morning's paper retrieved from a bin,
With a cardboard box a home for the night.
Two glasses filled with wine to the brim.

Background music adds to the mood, as
Diesel fumes on cold air drifts and
Searches out the dwellings crude. While
Rosebuds eat; think not of thrift.

Potted plants and stainless platters.
Damp, rank leaves; no company.
Rosebuds drink to business matters.
Hopeless leaves go hungry.

And as the rosebuds leave the restaurant
For the warmth of their home,
Scattered leaves shiver and want;
Another night under cardboard, all alone.

Geoffrey Paul Dennis

Drifting Away

All the faces are grey now, fading into backdrop
   as seclusion, exclusion and solitude take centre-stage.
I feel the difference now between them and me;
It pleases, and saddens, that it has to be.
I grow aloof and depressed; thrill to the sound of rattling stones,
And the thrum of all the world's waterfalls reverberates in my bones.
My chest swells - love of imperfection; all the
   flawed fields of dreaming around delight and disturb.
I feel a certain sure confusion as my unquestionable
   conviction speaks to me
From crumble-down twists of empty dry paper scattered
   on the floor,
Indecipherable Spider-track scrawlings extruded from the
   sepulchrous vaults of my soul . . .
Life, perfect in its various broken fuzzy episodes
   of that and this; failure and bliss.
The balance is there somewhere, I can feel it
   like a nebulous milk and honey matrix dipping and swooping
   all around,
But safely out of reach, as I elate self-containedly
down the pure and beautiful white-sand plastic-littered beach.

Douglas Baird

Emmarentia Dam

Within our golden city there lies a jewel rare
As sparkling as a diamond and every bit as fair
A spot called Emmarentia Dam where children love to play
I can tell you all about it, for I go there every day.

Your shrubs and flowers all have a charm and colour of their own
I often sit and rest a while, a shelter from the storm
A refuge from the daily grind, and from the race of life
A place to sit and clear our minds of politics and strife.

A spot to sit and study, or just to read a book
To feed the birds, or sail a boat or just to sit and look
At all God's greatest wonders the simple things in life
Like trees and flowers, the clouds the sky, and stars that shine
   at night.

Your pink and yellow tulips, your green and golden shrubs
Above your restful water's edge, the calling of the doves
With rows of golden daffodils a joy to every man
Sure there's no place in South Africa like Emmerentia Dam.

Elizabeth Larkin

Sonnet to the Spirit

Fair beauty in all things is doomed to die,
as the bride's bouquet in days declines to tinder
and for herself as too few years deny
her noble dreams that drudge and strife does hinder.
Thus fades all earthly glory to the sight
and all that nature, all that wealth does cherish,
each succumb in the end to death's long night
and fame into oblivion must perish.
But thy ethereal power shall yield not hither
to ravages of time and failing light,
how could thy grace diminish such and wither
when the aura of thy soul burns ever bright.

All hail the beauty potent in thy mind;
that blooms immortal over all mankind.

Anthony Carl May

Bluebell Wood

Have you ever been to Bluebell Wood,
As the moon shines in the night,
For fairies dance in grassy glades
And goblins give you a fright!

Have you ever been to Bluebell Wood,
When the nymphs come out of the pool,
As fishes swim in circles,
And the breeze that blows is cool!

Have you ever been to Bluebell Wood,
When the sun begins to rise,
The sleepy fairies stretch themselves,
And open sleepy eyes!

Have you ever been to Bluebell Wood,
And heard the dryads play,
Sweet music on their harps,
Welcoming another day!

Jacqueline Stevens

Moon Bather

Deep-mouthed desires and dreams crystallize
As the phosphorescent surf rolls in, singing
In steady syncopation with the moon's
silvery tones.
Moon-bathing on glistening sands, I sit
And watch the hoary sea spew forth
Rich sediments from inaccessible horizons.
Forms and colours of a myriad lives
Rise in the dancing foam and scatter
Like seeds into the seminal night.

Anna Farell

Spring's Diadem

The grass gets greener by the day
As winter gloom is chased away
By spring, who takes each flowery gem
To make herself a diadem.

Pale primroses and celandine
Around her head in garlands twine
To make the framework of her crown
And deck her blossom-spangled gown.

Soft violets, that the sun has kissed
She uses as cool amethysts
Whilst snowdrop blossoms glow like pearls
Entwined among her shining curls.

Bright tulip petals, brilliant red
Glow like rubies 'round her head
And hyacinths of deepest blue
Reflect the sapphires richest hue.

And so bedecked with jewels fair
Her diadem sparkling in her hair
She dances over dales and hills
And gathers golden daffodils.

Elsie Anderson

Dark Yearnings

She led us into the crypt
and it sped down
into the earth;
it came to a quiet rest
and we stepped out
onto the shore of a vast lake.

A boat came out of the mists
and a monk in black beckoned us
with a crooked forefinger;
I stared down into the waters
as our journey began
and glimpsed shards of dreams;
fragments of all dreams dreamed
and I became drunk with the emotions
as we neared the dark isle.

There we entered caverns
painted with nostalgia and memories;
and in the most wonderful of all
sat Death on his throne of skulls
and my love swept out as there were deals to be made.

Christopher J. Smith

Mind Over Matter

I am the power in the high tower,
At the edge of the cliff.
I have the energy to change the view.
I so frequently see think about so often.

I see a sky at dusk.
A dark bleak contrast of colours.
Beneath a vast ocean lies.
For it is far from calm.

Powerful winds and the endless rotation of planets
Cause great confusion, amounts the water
Huge waves contort, twists crash.
Against each other.
Like a mind in great confusion.

Human thoughts, ruled by head or heart.
The two are one
But far from resolution

I am the power in the high tower
At the edge of the cliff
I may have the power
But the strength for resolution!!

Heidi M. Pole

The Waste of War

Feeling numb with the truth of the horror
At the pictures portrayed on T.V.
I watched in total alarm
These war scenes they thought we should see.

An innocent child is crying out for his mother
Who's become one more victim of war
This orphan alone gives cause for the question
What are we all fighting for?

The destruction that is caused from one bomb
Leaves buildings in decline and decay
Places of worship and office blocks lost
Homes wiped out, livelihoods taken away.

Visions of suffering to innocent people
The violence, destruction, the horror and more
Fill me with anger and total frustration
That I haven't the power to put a stop on it all.

So I urge all you leaders of Rebellions and Nations
Find and end to all war, get the fighting to cease
Abolish your differences, embrace one another
And strive to achieve everlasting world peace.

Emma Louise Wood

My Love

I met my love in this pub.
At the time, he seemed like just another guy.
Until my heart started to say different.
His loving touch meant so much,
Why was I letting myself do this again.
That hurt and pain that could shatter you, in just one day.
We went through so much, but our words never crossed.
But we battled on for the love that felt so right,
Still, in our different worlds.
I felt this love was slipping away.
Until that night came our way,
As we walked, we could finally let our words meet,
Things had started to go our way.

Who would think a dance, could go this far.
Smiles are glowing, things are sweet, my life feels so complete.
It's our little family and where I want to be.

But what if the words go silent and smiles stop glowing
Will he stand by me or fade away, to laugh with someone else.
I would be left in a sad life, with no smiles or laughter,
But with the tears that would run through my heart.
Leaving me with a scar, that would never heal.

Amanda Turnbull

Copper Hair

First glimpse o' ye wis at the fair,
aura o' colour yer hair.
Crowning glory condition shone so bricht,
for me, lo' at first sight.

Arranged date, courtship we did,
then church tae get wed.
Compliments a' aroon how lovely ye were,
proud o' ma new bride wi "Copper hair".

Later decided tiny patter o' feet, "fan occurs so let it be".
"Wonder weel they tak efter ma dear wife or be like me?"
Fate micht change its course, then heard midwife's voice.
Baith got, "Copper hair".

Twins quickly grew carried hereditary tradition fae dear wife.
In turn married hid ain femily,
best ability got wi in their lives.

We noo are auler an beloved spouse locks hiv
streaks o' grey. I wid like tae say.
Memories! Ne'er forget encounter O' ye wi yer, "Copper Hair".

Estelle wi the beautiful. "Copper hair", knew that ye wid be mine.
Estelle wi the beautiful. "Copper hair", lo' ye til' end o' time.

Dawn Constable

"Treasured Thoughts"

Treasured thoughts, no longer hidden
behind the face of love,
- 'My love for you,
your love for me' -
Or at least, that's what I thought!
You never call me anymore,
I see you in the street, and you just walk by.
I call out your name.
You never answer me.
I followed you once,
to see where you went, who you met.
A girl who you care about,
a love that will last.
Your love for me remains in the past tense,
But my love for you is forever,
Until the end of time,
In my heart, you're always mine.
Hidden, within my treasured thoughts!

Annalisa Maria Sumsion

The Night Nurse

You get used to sounds of breathing in the middle of the night.
As you go from bed to bed with your dimmed torchlight,
You get used to sounds of breathing in the middle of the night.

If the rhythm changes, your eyes peer in half light;
Are they dreaming! Are they snoring! Or is it something worse!

You hear the faintest whimpering from the old lady in her cot,
You try to give her comfort in the small hours of the night,
but she's crying, for all the years now lost, all the sorrows
and the sadness and the joys of course.

Yes you hear the faintest murmur in the middle of the
night, when you're trusted to take care of them until
the morning light.

Emma Hall

Jealousy

It cowers
behind the barriers of envy's eyes
A sickly stain of poison:
Spreading.
Suffocating.
Choking
her mind with hate.

A tiny seed of evil
planted and fed.
Watered with the acid of burning tongues
corroding a hole
in her heart
where once
love
lived.

Elizabeth Smith

The Orphan

Bombs fell on the hillsides
Bombs fell on the town
Then bombs fell on the houses
They lay in ruins on the ground.
There were dead and dying
Some cried out in pain.
Some would never feel the warmth of the sun
Or feel the touch of the falling rain.

Then a little hand touched my hand
I looked down on a tear stained face.
Please will you help my mummy
She is hurt and she cannot speak
I cradled the child in my arms
She sobbed, then she fell asleep
I could not save her mummy.
Now I look at this child and I weep.

Edna Porter

Fiery-Freda

Make no mistake, don't dismiss this in error,
Beware fiery Freda, the two-wheeled terror.
The following is her motto, no seriously don't laugh
Keep death off the roads, cycle on the path.
Possessed of bi-pedal power, is this pavement pest,
If you've safety in mind, stay alert it's best.
She's a choice of speeds, switch on handlebar right,
Either two miles a fortnight, or speed of light.
A stunning impression she does, of the tortoise and hare,
One minute still here, the next she's over there.
Heavily laden shoppers, are favourite fair game,
Confirmed hits are counted, silver stripes stuck on frame.
She bowls maidens over, that's surely not cricket
Tho' to watch Lords and Ladies she'll sell you a ticket. From
which direction she's coming, you never will tell, even though
she gives a warning with an echoing bell. If she misses the first
time, she'll not on the return. She'll do an about turn, to make
sure from astern. So when you're thinking you've simply
slipped, maybe your thinking's in error.
You might have become a victim of the two-wheeled terror.

Guy Taylor

What's Rich?

They sat entranced, their eyes aglow,
As the plot of the tale was revealed,
Of Prince and Princess, King and Queen,
No splendour or grandeur concealed.

They heard of the jewels,
The wonderful ball,
The sumptuous feast
That was served in the hall.

They heard of the cook,
Who prepared the great party,
Of the important guests,
With their appetites hearty.

Oh, I'd like to be rich,
A small child sighs,
A smile on her face
And a gleam in her eyes

What's rich? Asks the adult
As the knowledge she tests.
If I was rich said the child
Then I'd have two vests.

Jean Dinning

'Another Mother's Day'

The radio sings, the day begins . . .
Breakfast over, pots all done, rubbish to be thrown away
Beds to be made, dirty clothes for the wash
Get the hoover out again.
Polish the furniture, shift that scratch, rub with a bit of stain.
Time for a cuppa and a biscuit I think.
Oh! to sit down, feet up and drink.
The telephone rings, the doorbell chimes,
Off to the shops for bread.
Same old faces to be seen, and fresh air instead of steam.
Off back home, iron the jeans, hang up and put in rooms.
Feel the veg, prepare the rest for the waiting nest.
In they come, one by one, only daughter and three sons.
Hubby arrives, usual time, after his pint of lager and lime
Pots all washed, kids spruced up, Dad's had his shower and shave
Out they go, their nighttime calls.
Here I am in the same four walls.
Watch TV, weary eyed, shower and go to bed.
Listen for the music early in the morn.
Another day is thankfully born.

Barbara M. Cowell

Reflection

Coals aglow, among the hearth
Battered logs with smouldering bark
Ashes filter through the strands,
Of iron smelted, by human hands,

The room is bare but warm
There he sits, a man alone
He prods the fire, the old stake worn,
Enticing the flames, settling the coal,

Peeping he stands astride and worn,
Watching the furnace door,
Long handled shovels scatter the floor,
Salted sweat tickles his nose, he frowns
Sniffs and groans.

The heat behind the furnace door, like an inferno
Rumbles and roars,
He toiled so hard, for weeks and years,
His spirit ripened, with his tears.

Now he sits a squat, the fender warm
Hands clasped together, he was not alone.

Carole Anne Thompson Fisher

Survival

Fly high bird, fly high,
away from man's lead death,
your feathers scorched from bullets,
as you gasp your last breath.

Run fox run,
your freedom depends on your speed,
as the hunters close in,
they do not care how you bleed.

Burrow, rabbit, burrow,
dig as deep as you can,
the small beady eyes, and ferrets teeth
you cannot hide from man.

Swim, whale, swim,
away from the sharp harpoon,
no peace for you, until the water
is stained red instead of blue.

They call it sport,
but to an animal, or bird
trying to survive, life
is hard enough, just to live.

Iris Tennent

Doorways

Beyond the boundaries of imagination,
Beyond the beat of the eagles wing,
Beyond the isles of the emerald hills,
Beyond this conscious world of land and king.

Lies a land adorned with mystery,
Sunsets splashed with rays of gold,
Framed with the wisdom of amethyst,
And touched with a clarity that never grows worn or old.

This world lives in our dreams,
We take just a vague memory to keep,
Gentle prophecy that guilds us blind,
Into the ocean of secrets vast and deep.

Here you create your own calling,
With the meridians of the mind,
Here you can soar with angels,
Or enter chasms of stone where labyrinthine pathways meet and
intertwine.

This place belongs in all of us,
And to dance in the unicorns magical beam,
To play chance with mischievous elfin,
Just close your eyes and dream.

Joanne Knight

Stomach of Love

Deep in the Stomach of Love
I find a little, helpless battered white dove

I hold it tight
Care and give it love
I pick it up and embrace
But after time
It turns to claw my face

Like life itself which let me down
The angel of love wears no frown

Anthony Tindall

Mountains

The mountains are your creation Lord
Awe inspiring as we gaze above
Their shadows spread on the ground below
And remind us of your love
No matter how far we travel
The mountains are still in view
They appear impossible to pass
But if we look we can find a way through
It may be rough, sometimes narrow or wide
Light pierces the shadows as we pass
We travel safely if we stay by your side
Mountains remind us of You dear Lord
Awe inspiring, majestic and tall
Their shadows, like the shadow of Your wing
Spread out and cover us all
The light that shines through is your light
Help us to let it shine in us we pray
As we follow your path, both the easy and hard
Like the mountains, help us stand firm day by day.

Eileen Hallas

Alone

I like very much my life at home
Because I never feel alone.
I have my parents, both Mum and Dad,
Who stop me feeling very sad.

To be alone can be glum,
Especially if you have no mum.
I know of others in that state,
And to those people, I'm a mate.

Mum and Dad keep me feeling bright,
And I have no fear of the night.
So when the time comes for me to go,
The dreadful loneliness will I know.

To overcome that fearsome day,
I'll nurture strength to pave the way.
I will always remember my old home,
Then never will I be alone.

Desmond Brookes

Ageless

My body tills the garden
Being careful where it treads
My spirit entwines the flowers
With thoughts of golden threads

My inner soul is ageless
Its spirit rises every day
Preparing for grace and beauty
Before flesh and blood decay.

My spirit lifts higher and higher
As the years go sliding by
That light at end of the tunnel
Gives time to say good-bye

I know we leave behind us
Our daughters and our sons
But they're halfway through the tunnel
Shining the light on their loved ones.

Elizabeth Jerome

In Loving Memory

I know the pain you're going through
Believe me Dad it's true
Cause no one else could love you Dad
The way that I love you
And I am your favourite Daughter
This I'm often told you taught me
How to love a man and respect the very old
One thing you never showed me Dad
or taught me how to do and that was how
to stop this pain I found from
losing you. Your leaving was so sudden
as I held your hand so tight and now
all I have are memories of that cold
Dark April night. Yet still my tears
Keep falling like rivers from my eyes
wishing I was with you Dad
in God's heaven in the skies

Janet Taylor

Reflections

Across the water I see his eyes
binding with mine as he tries,
To fix his thoughts into my head
trying to disguise the oncoming dread,
The fear of what his life was before
to see his reflection is there no more,
Desperately he tries to see
what his thoughts mean to me,
No reflection in my eyes
recognized by his heavy sigh,
Wonders what will happen to him
reflection is now faded and dim,
His shadow does not seem like childhood fun
when not reflected by the sun,
Slowly sinking without a sound
feet no longer firm upon the ground,
Life's dreams are no longer there
nothing left for him to care,
The blue of his eyes are filled with peace
reflections of his life can now cease.

Judith Galley

The Articulate Voices of the Bottomless Sea

Through a dark myth of blue
I think of you,
from your big strong head
to your strapping tail.

As you soar out of the surf
you show off for all to see!

The King
The Master of the Sea!

Amanda Rawson

Churchyard in Winter

Darkly desolate, with freezing wind
Blowing about the sad, old yews
And stones, hundreds in extent,
Those most ancient loved alone by the ivy;
Those most recent, stark and cold with awful grief.
Limp, shrivelled flowers and birds here and there hopping
Disconsolately amidst the silent, barren graves.
Occasional, black figures of mourners
Lonely and bereft, shuffling heads bowed
Down to a tomb.

Till the voice of a spirit murmurs in March,
One bright dawn dispels the gloom
And bird song bursts forth ecstatically
In joyful sensing of another world
Beyond all death,
When the first snowdrops herald Spring
And Resurrection.

Graham Butler

Life's Deal

With shattered lives, their broken wives,
Bitter fights then lonely nights,
Why do the cards of life deal unfair hands,
Or are they dealt too heavy demands.

The spade, a club which way to play,
Whichever one the pain's here to stay.
Life's one big cheat, no diamonds here,
Only lonely sobs, or a sorrowful tear.

Wives broken dreams of their parted teams,
Why do they cheat with their lover's deals,
To crying children for dads not there,
Has to leave its mark in their corners dark,

With heavy hearts does God not care,
How can our lives be so unclear,
Though how it hurts with pain so real,
One day the cards should play a better deal.

Ann Whewell Evans

Searching for Peace

Silence in a world full of noise.
Blindness inside the light.
Close your senses and open your mind,
Let my thoughts drift inside.

Speak not what comes into your mind,
let me feel what you need to say.
Touch nothing in uncertainty.
Become numb, let me lead the way.

Hold your head tall and proud,
Never doubt what you are inside.
You're all you can depend upon,
If you don't open your mind.

Prejudice and greed must go.
Freedom's too high a price.
Stop the hating thoughts I hear,
I'll show you how to do it right.

Fear, we see from day to day.
Hate, we see in every way.
Your solace is something I can't match.
Does it really matter anyway?

Andie Branhall

An Old Beech Tree

I am an old beech tree
I have no leaves
I am not like the other trees
My heart is getting slower and slower
I am starting to rot
I have a hole inside me
I am going to be chopped down.

Henry Nicholls

Cry of a Badger

I am a badger, scared to death
I have nothing worth living left
I am running amidst the trees
I am running so that my children will be free
The wind's icy fingers grab around my neck
I have run my hardest and breathed my last breath
I plunge into darkness, my legs hit the ground
All of my hopes gone, my children lost to this hound
Why can't humans just leave us alone?
Soon for badgers, there will be no home
My frail body, frail as glass
Lay limp among the rotting grass
Thrown in among the badgers' griefs
For your sake, I only hope that God forgives
If only you could see this depressing sight
Maybe, just maybe, you would fight

Angela Taylor

The Dance

I tip-toe into the night, sweeping aside the moon and stars
Blowing clouds adrift with a whisper and a glance.
Earth gazes up at me as she spins
I mime farewell and blow a kiss from my hand . . .
There is no echo.
The Milky Way is gossamer soft, scented with music -
A lullaby on a pink melody of silver bells
Summoning me to the other side of night,
To bathe in a pool of stardust.
I laugh and silent tears escape me.
Dancing and dancing within the mystic galaxies
Carefree and weightless and beckoned on,
So mesmerized in dance my earthliness abandoned
My eyes now gently close into the foreverness,
Succumbing to oblivion.
Draped in the cloth of a breeze.
So dancing I become a glorious Traveller
A spiritual warrior of the skies.

Deirdre A. Lewis

Moon Rise over Creagh

Road dissected by moonbeams
bouncing from
crumbling walls to muddy entrance,
tormented scarecrows,
fleeing branches transfixed by winter . . .

Apposite shadow
scurrying along an estate lodge,
Pleiades star dust
as showers of moon drops bathe
hills and dark woods . . .

Downfield, river overflow its shadow
in glistening riddle,
silver globe rising above my shoulder,
Limbus of man's dreams,
betrayed hope and false promises . . .

. . . No crowing cock, silence,
only broken by barks of farmyard hound.

Guy-Patrick Bouyssou

Time Gone

The sand of time slips slowly down the hourglass of life,
I think of joy and happiness, of trouble and of strife,
I look back and reminisce of times long past and gone,
Of things done right, but oh, what pain if things go terribly wrong.
What changes could I have made to have improved my lot,
And if had made changes would I have what I've now got,
Or would I still be wandering down life' long weary road
With not a soul to care about, and none to share my load,
Instead I've got a family, a house, a wife, a home,
And in the life that's left to me I need never walk alone,
There's my children and my grandchildren and my ever-loving wife,
So sand, please slip more slowly down that hourglass of life.

Colin R. Hollman

Out of My Life

Why are you leaving me all alone and blue,
I thought we'd be together all our lives.
Have you found another who you have fallen for,
someone who you can't bear to lose.
When did this happen, was it secretly,
how could you treat me so.
I thought we were a couple in love
all our friends said so.
You say you used to know him,
and you've fallen for his lines.
I bet that he's still married
just filling in the time.
Don't bother with my feelings,
that's all I'm going to say but,
please think very carefully
as I hope and pray you'll stay.

Iris Smith

Shooting Dreams

I tossed a coin into a well, then closed my eyes to think
Heard it splash, then held my breath, and watched it slowly sink

I turned and gazed up at the moon, as shooting stars raced by
Then made another wish for luck before they fade and die.

I never quite imagined though, my wishes would come true
But sure enough they really did, by guiding me to you
So now they're here I won't let go, 'cause stars still glide in space
And the ripples from my sunken coin, can never be replaced.

All the love I feel for you, grows stronger day by day
And nothing in the whole wide world, will take that love away
I need you like the air I breathe, like flowers need the sun
When Cupid pulled his arrow back, it struck me like a gun.

I realise now, the first time, he aimed at me he missed
As no one half as good as you, could possibly exist
The friendship we developed babe, was good enough for me
I didn't ask more, yet dreams still roamed and set my spirits free.

Bryan Stuart Mayne

Autumn

Heavy air and icy chill;
Heavy heart and lack of will.
Fiery leaves fall to the ground;
Like my heart, there's not a sound.
Morning mist rolls over all;
The gentle songthrush sounds his call.
The airy sunlight filters through;
Reflected on the cobwebs dew.
The birth of autumn has arrived;
Farewell to summer, that now has died.

Angela Shawcroft

My Dog

My dog could run around all day,
He'd listen to what I had to say,
If I had a problem he would always be there,
To listen to secrets I would share.
I loved him from the very start,
He could always mend my broken heart.
Sometimes I would sit and pray,
For him to never go away.

The Thursday that my dog did die,
All I did that night was cry,
My Mum said he had gone away,
To a place that he would stay,
She said that God had taken him,
To be treated like a king.
This poem is left for me to say,
I'll love my dog always, night and day.

Charlotte Sygmuta

Happy Birthday

In a stable, Jesus was born,
Held in her arms, Mary kept Him warm.
A star shone brightly up above;
The animals three, they showed their love.
The shepherds heard of this wonderful thing,
They thought of presents that they could bring
A bright light shone all around.
Afraid, the shepherds fell to the ground.
Three wise men, they came from a far land.
They travelled through deserts over the sand.
They followed the star to where Jesus lay.
Got off their camels and started to pray.
Offering presents, their homage they paid,
Placing their gifts down where He laid.
The angels above, they started to sing,
Praising the boy, Jesus the King
December twenty-five, the birth of Our Lord,
Come on people, let's spread the word.
Be happy, Oh, happy this day,
For to Him there are no words to say except "HAPPY BIRTHDAY!"

Gilly Halse

New Life!

Her eyes opened, her breath came on a sigh.
Her hair was thick and dark with golden tips on every strand
As if sprinkled by fairy stardust as the tiny creatures flew by.

I held her close in awe and wonder, this precious daughter of mine,
So perfect in every detail - in body and in mind.
But what of her soul I wondered, is that as perfect too?
The reply came from deep within me - "That is up to you."

"Love her, cosset her, feed her well. Feed her mind with good things.
Show her the wonders of nature and what true happiness brings.
And as she matures and strengthens pray for her each day
That the love of God her Creator will be with her all the way.

She will be hurt, she will stumble and fall,
She'll ask again and again "What is life about?
Why are some so rich, and others so poor and why can't we work
things out, so that the world could be a better place for all?"

But that is all in the future, at this moment in time
As I hold this bundle of new life close, my earnest prayer will be
"If hurt and distress come her way, don't let it be because of me!"

Hazel Pavitt

The Lady Named Violet

Her big day approaching so soon,
Her heart burning with lust and desire.
Not knowing dreams turned into nightmares
Thinking she's someone we would admire.

Her dress not white but just blackness,
Her hair also as dark as the night
She carried a bloodstained rose,
Her hand bled she held it so tight.

She carries her rose down the aisle,
Sadness glowing in her eyes.
She's upset although she should be happy
But happiness is in disguise.

Her fiancé, not smiling but crying
His eyes filled with pure confusion
His body shakes like a leaf in the wind
Trying to tell himself it's just an illusion

On the church floor they put her box down
"Say a prayer," the priest had said.
for now Violet's wedding was a funeral
And Violet, she was now dead.

Hayley Shone

Birds of Freedom

Children. Show them love, they are not born to fight
Hold out a hand to guide them to keep their future bright.
Tiny, soft as little birds, fragile and confused
Never to be hurt, frightened or abused.

But still, there is a world where monsters are alive
Where torment reigns supreme, where the strongest will survive.
A world that never smiles or overflows with love,
A world that makes a fantasy of any God above.

No story books to dream upon, dark shadows hold the fears,
A heart that holds the pain and eyes that hold the tears.
Old heads upon young shoulders, childhood stripped away
To satisfy the demons that appear day after day.

Dear tortured souls, there is a world, a world where you can dance
Where playtime does exist and all dreams have a chance.
Where fledglings learn to breathe and live from day to day
To gain their strength, unfold their wings and safely fly away.

No wickedness or evil, teach to nurture, not destroy
A loving smile, a gentle touch for every girl and boy.
When little voices call, listen to their words
Invite them to our world and fill our skies with little birds.

Erica Morse

Untitled

The sky is grey; the rain is heavy; the wind is vicious,
highlighting our sorrow at her death; uniting a community in grief.
I see the sadness in your eyes as a tear slides down your cheek.
There is nothing we can do; there is nothing we can say
to comfort or console you. You have lost so much.
There is nothing you can gain; nothing anyone can gain from
    her death.
We will miss her inspiration; we will miss her compassion.
She had so much to live for; she was a bright star in the dark sky.
The star has gone now, the sky is darker.
We cry every time her name is mentioned, knowing she
    cannot be replaced.
We went to the funeral to say goodbye
but we will never be able to forget her
and never be able to forgive him, who took her life away.
Nobody can understand why he did it. He had no motive.
He can offer no excuse; no excuse for the pain and misery he
    has caused.
Her childhood innocence destroyed by his wicked deed.
Her young mind exposed to the brutalities of human nature.
She was harmless as a butterfly and as beautiful as a flower.
The flower has died, the petals have disintegrated
but the sweet fragrance will live forever.

Charlotte Bishop

November 22nd 1963

Jack Splaaahht would never again chew the fat
His bracelet could only lean over and over again.
Had the grassy knoll hit the nail right on the head?
Or was it the Taxes Balk Suppository, Cuban heels and Castrol
    GTX-Men?
Was it, in deed, Al's pals and gals, the cosy Nostradamus
Who had vatic(a)inated the final terms of the contract?
Bridge the gap between the Rock and the hard plaza.
Sing! Sing! Ruby, it is choose-day and that's the soul fact.
White Hat hostage to mass fortune, who will hang a name on you?
"Ain't got a Godamn clue," clucks clandestine n**ger
    stringer-upper.
"How could I?, chants the F**king Big Indian in plainsong.
"Don't look at me," stagewhispers the Invisible Man of the peephole.
Lee, in field, a dusky-Russky spy, all - American spy or a mince pie?
The primed steaks, after all, were High.
A hot pot-shot under the effluence of the grass.
"That's the American Wet Dream," ejaculates the happy
    hippy handler.
"In Gawd's Name where beginneth the first lesion?", you essay.
"Alimentary, my dear Watts sons, Mom's blueberry pie ain't got
no Christ-Cream."

Gearoid MacSearraigh

Come What May

Back in February, the ice was melting, in came the thaw.
His eyes had opened, whilst she was sleeping that while longer.
So in his winter coat out of hibernation, he braves the cold.
Early birds are building their nests, and rabbits coming out of
    their burrows.
She rolls over stretches her arms, and gives it one more turn.
Now she's standing naked like a winter tree, slipping into her gown.

She smells springtime 'round the corner, and the heat of the
    frantic male.
Throbbing like a pulse her heart beats, and skips a beat as well.
Pushing ajar her window, a breath of the March winds breezes
    through.
She pulls herself together, and she blows away the cobwebs too.
Then she puts on her make up, and flitters her brow.
Her feathers still pluming, letting wait the frantic male.

Under his brolly, the April showers they come and go.
The winds peter out, and the sun it tries its uttermost to filter through.
From beyond the broken cloud, zooming into her tunnel.
The female she leaves her trace of scent, after digging her way
out of the burrow.
He's walking into a rainbow, tomorrow's another day.
And you never know what'll happen, come what May!

John Langbridge

Living with Post-War Syndrome

It's not only the man it changes
His family feel it too
His calm ways change to rages,
How will we all get through?

Once he'd smile and laugh aloud
People called him their mate,
Now he can't stand to be in a crowd
His smile has changed to hate.

Now, he's afraid of everything he saw,
Everyone around feels his aggression.
What is the senseless meaning of war?
For now we all live with his depression.

We pray that one day he may find peace,
And forget the sights he saw.
If only the ghosts of the past he could release,
Then each day would not be his own war.

He lives each day without any hope;
He questions why he is still here.
Again, we ask ourselves how will we cope
For now, we all live with his fear.

Jill Spurr

A Modern Man

My husband means the world to me
His faults, his smile, his love and charm
He works so hard, his toil is long
He keeps me safe, secure from harm

He's gentle, warm and considerate
He was even there at our baby's birth
He drives me mad with his D-I-Y
But I will love him for all I'm worth

Alison Amos

Journey

I lay in bed haunted by his image,
His haggard face, so gaunt and grey.
I wondered about his life, his world,
And thought of what he had to say.

He'd looked at me with blue-grey eyes,
And I thought they'd once been bright.
But now the blue had faded dull,
And now there was no fight.

He'd been in this world for so long,
And been through the good and the bad.
So why did his face look like that,
And why did he look so sad?

And that's how I'll remember him,
Quietly rocking to and fro.
His image will always stay with me,
From my memory he'll never go.

Alison Reese

Charles Hunt Gentleman of the Road

Jockey lad till a horse trampled his foot
His story over bacon three years took
Tea in a milk bottle tramp Charles Hunt request
A soldier in the 1st world war - gave his best
Deep snow outside, couldn't sleep kept crying
Charles Hunt I was sure he was dying
My husband shrugged went back to his bed
Three months went by and he was presumed dead
Early spring he arrived his tale to tell
A bus shelter - police - frostbite - 'Twas hell
Open order - amputate every toe
Next of kin brother did not want to know
God and I that night were the ones to care
Salvation Army convalesced - he came back to share.

Jenny Ambrose

Judgment

She stands there as he speaks,
His version of truth which pains and burns her;
Her tears that fall do nothing to deter him
She wonders why he determines to hurt her.

He brands her with names she doesn't deserve,
Judges and abuses her without a cause;
A friendship built on love and trust
Shatters around them as she cries.

The pain pierces her deep,
Deeper than even he will ever know;
Daggers in her stomach twist and turn
Self respect and confidence fall with her tears.

Her heart can never be the same
He has destroyed everything she thought she knew;
This is a sad story, it is true,
But sadder to know that she is me and he is you!

Emily Daniels

Fide Non Armis

O God of high and low alike,
Hold in Thy hand our Land this night,
O'ershadow her with Thy great love,
Encompass her with heavenly might.

O Father of Thy children dear
Let no ill deeds disturb our peace.
And hear this falt'ring prayer of faith -
"Lord, make all strife and discord cease."

Alma Shandley

Moonlight Movement

Moonlight shining on lovers of the night
Holding each other so close and tight
No one there for me to hold
Just the night glow and air so cold

My movement flickers and then I smile
I hold myself and sit awhile
The way you move, they way you breathe
My tiny heartbeat, what can we achieve?

Everything changing, just like a season
you stir upon me without a reason
I often feel alone, but how can I be
Together we're one, just you and me.

My Moonlight movement you'll soon be free
you'll open your eyes to the world and see
The sun, the rain, the day and night
but please, my darling, don't forget moonlight.

Clair Flood

Don't Look Too Close

Dossing around in some dirty old street
Homes on their backs . . . sometimes no shoes on their feet
But don't look too close because you'll see the pain in their eyes
They're only human you see and they've got forgotten dreams
And they'll never question why

Maybe it's a rotten deal what life has given to them
They've already lived it once . . .
They won't try again

So they scavenge for food, knocking back the wine
The brown paper bag is marking their time
But don't look too close because you'll see the pain in their eyes
They've got forgotten dreams and they'll never question why

Maybe it's a rotten deal what life has given to them
They've already lived it once and they won't try again

Who cares if they don't eat and who knows if they live or die
Who'll understand or listen, they will never ask you why
And what do we do . . . we'll just walk on by . . . and silently . . .
They cry . . .

Fiona D. L. Beauchamp

Untitled

Remember, you are the Piper, so let your music be
honest, lest the purity of tone be put to the test.
Play softly so that you may hear the dissonant note,
but call true and clear to those unsure of following -
Above all, lead without discord, lest the drummer drowns
the sound we laud.
Pipe truthfully, never fear the response and let the notes
ring sound in the ear of the vulnerable.
Remember, you are the Piper, so when the Silence starts to
pall, choose wisely the tune that's yours to call.

Jennie Ferguson

A Moment

People ask me what I'm doing
Hoping not to offend
Smiling politely answer, "Poetry"
Smiling they leave to continue drinking
One says, "I once did that"
Then leaves to join friends
with a final glance over the shoulder
eyes filled with past history

Passions of a boy
who once wrote
Longing to undo the past
Returning a short while later
to recite a long lost poem
Friends join
he becomes silent
Only his eyes tell the story

Elizabeth Anne Hole

Crows in the Churchyard

Combing and moaning, the crows stalk the churchyard,
hopping across headstones where the rich pickings lie.
Pecking at new wreaths dewy fresh from the florist,
turning the cards with inquisitive eye.
Sprawling loving arrangements in cold marble urns
upsetting the humble glass pots.
Purple droppings dotting I's on names of departed,
smearing the epitaphs, corroding the rocks.

Where do they fly away to, to die,
these mourning birds, ominous and sombre?
Haunting God's Acre, uttering wails from each cross
as they greedily coax flat worms from the turf,
leather jackets out of the moss.

Are they the lost souls of long gone grave diggers
searching for rest as they rake with forked claws?
Among garish bowers of plastic flowers,
still tending the garden of the dead.

While a small bright-eyed robin with blood-stained breast
trills a song of hope from the evergreen hedge.

Catherine Curtis

Bygone Days

In days gone by the children played
Hopscotch, to and whip bucket and spade
There were no computers, hi-fi's or such
And as for money there was not much.

To church on Sunday dressed up in their best
No work was done it was a day of rest
They sat in their seat very quiet and good
Longing to play, but never could

They snuggled in bed on a cold winter's night
There was only a candle for a light
The frost on the windows made patterns that shine
There was no central heating they burnt woods from the pine

No washing machines then it was all done by hand
Scrubbing and cleaning all had to be planned
Each day of the week had its own special task
And it would not be changed so no-one dare ask

Evelyn Wilkins

My James

I miss him and I loved him, my Jim!
How can I ever forget him.
He was my shield, my rock, my love,
He called me his joy, his dove.
Jim had to go, his calling came,
Life, for me, will never be the same,
we told each other always - of our love.
We gave thanks together, to our Father, above,
For his loving kindness, guidance and care
(This is for all who wish to share).
So I must carry on - try not to show
My grief and cry, but remember all the
Happy years, even tho' I shed my tears.
I have family and friends, so dear,
They give me love and help all they can,
I give thanks to our heavenly father
and midst my tears - at least -
must remember to help third world man and beast!

Joyce Newman

Catch Me

Catch me when I fall, cos fall I will.
How can I resist you now that I have kissed you,
Now that I have looked into your eyes,
Now that you have touched my soul,
Pulled the world out from under my feet?
You'll have to catch me when I fall,
Cos fall I Will.

Pull me back toward you, pull me back,
for I may try to hide, resist the urge to slide
Towards those lips, for then I'm lost.
I may try to run from that smile as you beguile me.
So pull me back toward you, pull me back,
Then catch me when I fall
Cos fall I will.

Barbara Hopwood

How, Why?

How could you make a fool out of me
How could I be so stupid, and fail to see
That things were going too good to be true
That I never saw the real existing you.

Why build up hopes and dreams of you
When there's nothing left of me to know what to do
Everything has been shattered like pure, thin glass
How can I live with agony, how will it pass.

Why keep me in the dark like this
Why make everything meaningless, just like that kiss
Why lie to others, and then lie to me
You don't know what you're doing, you really can't see.

How could you treat me like a boring old toy
When useless, thrown aside for others to enjoy
You've made me feel like dirt itself
You've made me look like an old book on a shelf.

Christine Rodriques

Mother and I

Mother is the plant,
I am the seed,
The one she will love,
The one she will feed.
The one she will guide, through thick and through thin,
For she is the fish, and I am the fin.
She will love her children till the end of the day,
And all through their lives, her love will stay.
Mother is the word,
I am the letter,
Her guidance in life makes me better and better.
Thank you dear mum,
For all you have done,
For you are the sky,
And I am the sun.

Faye Hooper

Evacuee

She came in tired, frightened, wondering,
How could she know she'd be safe, even here,
away from the horror, destruction of war
and away from her city of fear.

Into our hearts she came unquestioning,
All was so new, so unreal, and so strange
Lost was the peace, gay lights and laughter
And her town before bombers found it in range.

It seemed so unfair to think of this infant
Running for shelter away from the strife
and yet not knowing a reason or answer
Except if she didn't the forfeit was life

One day she'll return when the fear is all over
Back to her city and folks once again
The freedom, bright lights will come out to greet her
And her stay in the country will not be in vain.

Dorothy Loveridge

Mutti

I never have the chance to say to you,
How grateful I am for the things that you do,
All of my life you have given me love,
Staying close to my side like a tight fitting glove,
You are thoughtful and kind in every way,
In each passing minute of every day.

In my early years I shed many tears,
You would pick me up and dust away the fears,
When I was upset and wearing a frown,
You made me laugh by playing the clown,
In serious matters your advice was to hand,
Helping me find a solution well planned.

You have helped me right the mistakes I have made,
Your gentleness makes the bad times fade,
Sometimes it may seem that I take you for granted,
You have always responded by giving what I wanted,
This, a small token I decided to send,
To my most precious MUTTI and loved best friend.

Dawn Redfearn Pearson

Rose

"Oh beloved rose,
How I felt to be
Near the velvet of the petals
That lie deep within thee.

The thorns by your side, in life to protect
The spellbinding aroma encasing lovers apart,
Allow only those of true beauty, love and elegance see,
Your petals unfurl the tide from your heart."

Julie Robinson

The Back Street

Alone in the night, just I,
Hidden from God by a stormy sky,
Prowling cats and creaking doors,
Idle cars and trading whores,
How I loathed that murky street.
Hearing the sound of other feet,
Drove me to a speedy pace;
It seemed a mile to my flat,
Those footsteps must have had a face,
The terror of the night, that human rat,
Having struck seven times before,
Still managing to evade the law.
With pounding heart and stricken fright,
I made my flat and turned the key,
Inside, a welcome sanctuary.
A restless mind, a sleepless night,
From that back street I moved away,
I just could not stand another day.

Jill Simmonds

The Night

How dark the night, no tiny spark to light the way
Huge stones and boulders block my path ahead,
   Must I go on?
Why yes of course my soul there is no turning back
   Your Master trod a far more bitter road,
    And did not hesitate,
Of this I know but he is strong and I am weak
Then grasp His hand and He will give you strength
Hold on to Him and you will never fall
He'll guide you step by step throughout the darkest night,
Till you behold the dawn of Endless Day.

Elsie Dakin

Love or Friendship

I sit alone and wonder, if you're really worth the wait
How much tears and heartache, do you want me to take.

I know this time is painful
And you may think I'll cause you more
But, please have faith in me, sweetheart
For it's you that I adore.

My head is saying "forget him"
My heart is saying "no - please wait"
Will you ever see me in a different way
Or will you leave it, much too late.

So darling, please inform me
Of any feelings you have inside,
To release my heart from this torture
And the love for you that I hide.

But if your feelings are of friendship
And you have no more love to share,
Although, it will hurt me deeply
For you I'll always be there

And always, remember sweetheart, if you ever need a friend,
Or someone to hold you, on me you can depend.

Anne O'Toole

Quiet Noisiness

Listen to the quiet,
   how noisy it can be
Even the quiet and stillness in me.
Why does the quiet seem so loud,
When the quiet within we should seem
   like a cloud,
Silently drifting as quiet as a feather
Oh why! does this quiet go on forever.
Gone are the days of the noise and the din,
Left is the silence that only lies within.

Irene Dorrill

Everyday Thoughts

So much gloom it's hard to know
How to express all this woe
But take a look at life's bright days,
They are not so far away.

Come rain or shine, hail or snow
There are sunny days to get to know
Look at flowers growing wild
Trying to reach up to the sky.

Stars at night twinkle so bright
They are quite a pretty sight.
Birds flying in the trees.
It's lovely to have a faint cool breeze.

Rivers flowing down to the sea
Fishes to catch which could be free.
Dreams to share with a friend or two.
Maybe a building to snap or view.

Green grass below our feet
Lovely to have a picnic to eat.
On towards home a place of rest
It's not so far, somewhere west.

Ida Butters

41

Our Time

Guitar.
I play songs of love.
I place a flower into your short blond hair,
Its blue filled with life.
Hills with a spread of colours.

You look at me,
Eyes filled.
My beauty,
I could sit here gazing into your eyes all day.

Anusia Manduk-Cheyne

An Alcoholic's Poem

Pouring the bottle,
How wonderful the colour of autumn,
Comes so peacefully.
Like a conker snug in its prickly shell,
Feeling comfortable,
Cradling my brandy glass,
Curved in its womanly shape.
My hands are warm,
Like the gulp I take,
As I drink like a baby to its bottled milk,
Feeling as calm as a sleeping child.

Soon I am numb,
Carried to meditation.
Till there's no pain,
No crying from inside,
No more fighting, to struggle, choking
To an almost heavenly weakness,
I give in,
To that final shot.
So beautiful to finally lay down, to rest.

Daksha Patel

Your Majesty Was My Destiny

I try to prove that I love you, by showering you with devotion,
I adore everything about you, watching you walk is like
    poetry in motion.
Whenever you are not around, I am still happy because I
    know that you are mine,
My life is a cloudy day, but your photo brings a ray of sunshine.
To be in love with you, with you loving me too,
Once seemed so impossible, it is hard to believe my dream has
    come true.
Whenever we argue, it is our feelings being tested,
Yet we make up straight away, with the goodness we have invested.
I know you can't forgive me, for I have caused you a lot of grief,
I just hope you realize that there's a good, loving man buried
    somewhere underneath.
Let me appreciate you for what you are, and you do the same for me,
And the beautiful girl, and her forbidden lover will ride the storm,
    and sail the sea.

Andrew Cullinane

Couldn't It?

Oh why is April always late,
I ask the heavens above.
Couldn't it, couldn't it, just for once
Give beastly March the shove?

Couldn't it, couldn't it, just for once
Come arm in arm with May?
And kick old Winter in the teeth
And then decide to stay?

Couldn't the trees their dresses don,
The flowers all come in bloom,
The nightingale burst into song
And serenade the moon?

Couldn't the stars belong to me
To string a necklace rare?
And couldn't it be the best of all
That you, my love, are there?

Edna M. MacLeod

"Lost Heritage"

How well I remember the creaking of the gate,
I always tried not to be late.
I'd sit in my pew, and glance at the coloured windows
    with the sunshine streaming through.
Hymn numbers were carefully put on the board,
Chosen words, to sing praises to our Lord.
The church bell ringing as if to say
"Come let us seek our God today."
Sounds of beautiful music, and singing floating on the air,
only those who have truly heard it, could really, really, care.
Everything has changed now, like yesterday's news,
build a new car park, and pull out the pews.
Get rid of the past to make a fresh start,
"Do they care that they have broken the heart?"
People may come, and people may go,
there is one thing that we all should know.
In years to come, all that will be left to see,
is a picture in a museum of how things used to be.
If no one cares any more about our history,
all I can say is : A very sad "Amen from me".

Diana Forgan

Euphoria

Under the influence of the crushed-grapes' juice
    I bask in a freedom absolute,
Out of reach of the World's abuse
    I'm the hedonists' latest recruit.

I drowse in the mists of a stolen hour,
    I dream in thoughts serene,
Languishing in my lover's bower
    I float in the Cosmic Stream.

The weight of the world is lifted away
    And my mind can touch the skies
Where rainbow colours in rich display
    Shimmer before my eyes.

My heart is light, my soul can sing,
    My spirit soars from its shell -
Lavender-scented while on the wing -
    A millennium away from Hell.

Cushioned against the press of the throng
    I'm cocooned in some heaven above
Where bliss is lasting and minutes are long
    And all around me are people I love.

Dorothy Thompson

Sunrise

The ground mist encircles the motionless trees,
I can hear a whistle in the distance of a light summer breeze.
Through tumbling playful clouds the sun peeps,
For the moon has lain herself down to sleep.

The dewdrops dance on fir and pine,
And just to think all this beauty is yours and mine.
The horse nuzzling and shading her newborn,
In the distance I can see the purple Mountains of Mourn.

The sky is alive with the colours of all seasons,
Why people try to destroy this I can find no reason.
The lilt of the bird catches your ear,
Rain starts to fall in glistening tears.

We have all this at our back door,
But soon it will be no more.
Men destroy these things every day,
Shortly they'll find they'll have to pay.

The world will be a very ugly place,
Unless someone acts with haste.
If you're rich or poor or average like me,
The beauty of the world will always be free.

Emma Sisk

An Arrow through Time

As I sit on the beach so weird and wonderful,
I begin to compare the waves to one another.
As I look further and further all I am seeing is the truth;
Not a fantasy.
Then I look straight into the horizon
With a strange voice echoing in my mind.
But I can't find -
Can't find the way home;
No map, no hope,
No glory, no people,
No life,
Just me and the world's polluted air.
I think bit by bit,
But not a thing can fit.
No longer will the Earth be
Just wait and see . . .
A few years ago
The arrows were in all directions,
But not now - only one way.

Ananka Lyall

General Life

I like to look on the bright side of life, it's a good approach for me
I like to see the funny side of things and not take them too seriously
If I could have anything I wanted it would be a complete open mind,
I know I have one but in these changing times it's difficult to find.
There's so much competition in this world where we all live,
Why is there so much taking and not enough to give?
There are people without a home, there are people without
  enough food,
The distance between the rich and the poor is actually pretty crude.

What happened to the good old days when even shopping was
  a pleasure,
You could stroll down the market and have a chat and be
  friendly at your leisure.
But we've been invaded by everything big like those mega
superstores,
where under one roof you can buy stamp or even a chest of drawers.
We rush around with a shopping trolley in a zombified way,
when we could barter with the stall holder and pass the time of day.

Should life be like a rat race where we don't really care?
And do we all need lessons to learn how to really share?
What happened to a friendly smile from one human to another,
Some responses we receive in life are enough to make you shudder.
But despite all these stresses and strains I like to think the best,
So all the negative thoughts above - I hope I can say in jest.

Dhesna Wise

Inside, Looking Out

In my mind's eye, when I blow the cobwebs away,
I can recall a bright spring day.
Golden daffodils just showing through,
Black and white lambs, that play in the dew.

Now summer is here, I can feel the heat.
Two-tone lawns, so green and so neat,
One mass of colour, from the ground to the sky,
As the flowers bloom, and clouds shimmer by.

Pastures once yellow, have turned reddish brown.
The earth all churned up, the ploughs now lay down.
Autumn has arrived, it's a colourful array
of swirling coloured leaves, that merrily play.

The snow now falling, and blanketing everything white
Like tiny silver stars, that colour the night.
All things are covered in jewels so grand,
Nothing's untouched by Jack Frost's hand.

In my mind's eye, when I blow the cobwebs away,
I can conjure up like magic any new day.
Whatever the season, I just call to mind,
My sight has now failed, I'm totally blind.

Deborah-Clare Englishby

A Wish from a Tree to David

And now that my arms are heavy with leaves
I can send you messages dancing with love
I twirl in the sun and my heart gently heaves
Sighs of delight as I look down from above.

As I cradle the breeze and rustle my arms
I can help you to learn in such beautiful ways
The shapes of my voice that will fill you with calm
To put peace in your heart and light in your days.

You have grown up so fast since my arms were all bare
You laugh and you sing and you fill life with fun
Was it me, this old tree, that made you aware
You don't have to be tall to be warmed by the sun

So now that I've watched you slowly unfold
I can bow low over you and whisper with pride
Happy Birthday my friend, who is just two years old
May you always be safe with me by your side.

Brenda Mason

Those in Dunblane

I cry for those in Dunblane
I can sense everyone's tears of pain.
What is Satan trying to gain?

Beautiful children in the gym
then a man walks in, oh he's so grim.

On that tragic morning sense is dawning.
Parents' hearts break.
Such horror one man can make.

When you look at the sky tonight.
Remember what's wrong and right.
Remember that cruel old man
who hasn't got one single fan.

So as it is the parents of loved ones.
Cry in their handkerchief
thanks to the life-robbing thief.

Elizabeth Sadler

Eternity

As the first light strikes the horizon,
I cannot prevent myself from gazing helplessly,
Helplessly at the body which lies before me
One which holds so much beauty
A beauty which is young innocent and free

As a dove this creature glows
A radiant light which transfixes me,
Like a dove it too is captivating
My desire for this spirit to stay free is strong
Although I know this dove cannot fly with the wind forever

To covet such a spirit would be wrong
Inevitably the hair which covers the face will turn to grey and fade
These moments in time will stay strong in my heart forever
This feeling of love cannot be lost or replaced
Only cherished and kept safe for eternity

Carol-Ann Miller

The Question

I am the whisper in the cold night air,
I am the sound in a deserted lair,
I am the wandering owl's cry in the dark,
I am the shining solitary spark.

I live in lost and forgotten holes,
I live in the heart of hungry souls,
I live on a wild and isolated moor,
or in a cave on a faraway shore.

What am I? You may ask,
"Where will you find me?"
I will find you,
For my name is LONELY!

Juliet Hogan

43

I Wasn't There

I wasn't there the day she went,
I didn't know she was only lent,
Like somebody quietly leaving the room,
She went to her eternal tomb.

Stolen by greedy outstretched hands,
She was taken away to other lands,
Angels posing as creatures of joy
Are like selfish children desiring a toy.

From the day that she was born,
They spied on her and said with scorn,
"It's written that one day without a fuss,
You will come and live with us."

They have her now in a heavenly place,
Where no one even has a face,
Like ghostly vultures in the twilight,
They knew her fate at the very first sight.

Debbie Chase

The Thief

He came into my life so suddenly, unexpectedly,
I drew my breath at the quickness of fate,
And I knew in my mind that he had captured me
But what could I do, it was far too late.

And I wandered lost, caught in bewilderment
And peace of mind I could not find,
So I succumbed unto his enchantment,
With melancholy tears so unkind.

And who is this man but a creature as I
And where does he learn such skilful art,
For this is the man, the THIEF, the bewilder,
This is the man who stole my heart.

And yet if he left, all would be lost,
My gladness yet suffering would all be in vain.
But lessons are hindsight to one who has loved.
No man would steal my heart again.

Gail Julie Hope

Irony

I am a model citizen
I do just what they say
I go to keep fit classes
and I jog to work each day.
I never smoke or drink at all
I'm careful what I eat
no sugar, saturated fat
and certainly no meat.
I'm bound to live forever
I believe this to be true
but . . . Watch out for that bus you say?
Oh Dear . . . .
God? Is that You?

Jean Jones

My Dreams

Any night that I can't go to sleep,
I don't count flowers or even sheep.
I imagine that I'm in a far away land,
With lovely blue skies and glittering sand.
For my loved one and I to be up in the sky,
To an isle in the South Pacific,
With every notion to bathe in the ocean,
That would really be terrific.
The native girls in their grass skirts and pearls,
Such a wonderful sight to see,
The soft music playing and palm trees swaying,
all this seemed like heaven to me.
I wake up and know that I would never go there.
I was just building castles in the air.
Still there is no charge for scheming and dreaming.

Irene Lee

Mum

I took you for granted because you were always there.
I didn't realize how lucky I was to have a mum to care.
You guided me through my childhood years,
taught me to laugh and to overcome my fears.

As I look back to those childhood days,
I thank you Mum, for all your ways.
You taught me right from wrong,
and many important lessons as the years rolled along.

You know my strengths and my weaknesses too,
but being me was enough for you.
You gave me time I can remember with pleasure.
A casket of memories that I'll always treasure.

I'm a mum myself now with two precious daughters,
and I realize the importance of the lessons you taught us.
I only hope that I can be a mum like you.
Someone extra special for the girls to turn to.

Even though I now have a family of my own,
you're still always there, at the place I call 'home.'
So I thank you Mum for all you do,
and send all my love especially for you.

Julie Worthington

Claire

I must have a reason to want to hold you tight
I don't even want to sleep with you tonight
During moments of passion my mind is far away
It's with the one I really love oh Claire where are you today
You must be out there somewhere to end this horrid plight
Your beauty and your love were my guiding light
There will never be another, you were so sublime
That we ever parted was our only crime
We had the greatest love that has ever been
Our hearts became entwined from the age of fifteen
But now we have parted and you've faded away
Like a radiant sunset at the end of the day
Of you I can't stop thinking in moments such as these
The thought of those passionate nights bring me to my knees
But now I have another two ships in the night
And she can't give me a reason to want to hold her tight

David North

The Visitors

The night they arrived I was sound asleep.
In the cold night air, like a child they did creep.
Had I been awake, then try stop them I might,
But their eyes were ice cold,
They filled my heart with fright.

For through my sleeping eyes not once did they stir.
My mind felt their breath in the chilly night air.
Their power was great and their will was as strong,
These beings weren't us, they didn't belong.

They took all they required and left us like ghosts.
Our ignorant minds blocked out we were hosts.
But our lives as we knew were to be vanquished so near.
For the end was spelt out in a baby's first tear.

Matthew Critchley

Broken Hearts

A have failed at love so many times,
I have struggled and fought until I feel drained,
But then it is lost, only to play havoc with my heart,
As I tried to mend what cannot be mended.

I have loved, but if love is not returned I am lost,
How lovely it would be,
If love could be gathered like wild strawberries,
And eaten at tea time with cream.

Pain mingles with happiness, as I think of the past,
But there is no pill to mend a broken heart,
Yet all that I dream of is not forbidden to me,
There is no hurry to love again to survive is enough

Jeanette Rivett

Send Me an Angel

If I could have just one wish
I don't know what it would be,
To stop all the suffering
Or the felling of a tree?

To stop the killing of our wildlife
Or to end the drought and starvation,
To bring about a new world peace
And end all the violence and devastation.

I'd put an end to mistreating animals
And let all the caged birds fly free,
I'd give shelter to the homeless
And put an end to poverty.

I'd preach that religion is to comfort
Not to cause conflict and war,
I'd find families for all the children
What else could I wish for.

So if my prayers could be answered
I would make the sick get well,
Please God, what I wish for
Is that You send me an angel . . .

Andrea Griffiths

Solitaire

Everything is getting me down,
I don't know why, I don't know how,

I don't want company, I need time to think,
No water in my life,
It's all gone down the sink

Nothing is left,
No happy thoughts any more,
My world is leaving, my feelings are sore,

The pain of the thoughts,
I seem to think,
They are never happy,
I feel all alone,

Silent all day,
No voice from my mouth,
My brain working wrong,
Going north, not south

I am empty,
These feelings are bare,
Most people happy
But I don't care.

Jaclynn-Sarah Smith

Persistence

The phone is near at hand
I can reach out and dial
And hear a voice - your voice - if I am fortunate
But that would be to break our understanding.
Unstated but acknowledged that the
boat is not rocked.

The TV offers its moving screen of
colour to the room.
Scenes, voices, a tapestry of brightness
that torments but doesn't change
the bleakness I endure.
Keeping the form of virtue because I must.
Accepting crumbs from someone else's loaf.

I query my own madness constantly,
but still I hold the line.
Perhaps because the fires have now burned low.
Or because I believe in miracles.
That there will be
One day
Him.

Dee Watson

That Special Feeling of the Night

As I wonder through the clouds of night
I feel nothing wrong nor feel nothing right
as I stare up high towards the cold winter sky
I watch the clouds roll through the air
whatever I know, whatever I care, my feelings all gone as
if they weren't there
I don't know what I'm feeling nor what to say all I know
is I want to stay
I look down now and stare, at the pond which lays there
and watch the moonbeams which dance along the small
tiny ripples which carry them along
The trees sway gently in the cold night time breeze with
such a graceful method it makes me feel pleased
But what makes me unhappy is knowing someday all this
natural beauty may be taken away and the peaceful
nights I used to enjoy will be taken away for no more to
enjoy
But tonight I'll enjoy it while I still can I'll sit back and
relax and think of my man.

Amie K. Z. Butler

I Look to the Sky

I look to the sky - I feel the warmth of the sun,
I feel the wind and the rain,
These are the things I need today,
To keep me sane.

In a world torn asunder by strain and stress,
How did we get in such a vile mess
Could the motive be hate or greed
People wanting more than they need
While others are starving, confused or dead
The greedy ones wanting more and more bread.

What good are strikes, demos, or war
Why cannot people keep God's law?
To love, honour and help those in need
These are worthwhile things indeed.

So I say to the world, look up to the sky,
Feel the warmth of the sun
Feel the wind and the rain
And perhaps as you look, strength and courage will come,
And the world will be sane again.

Ethelinda Copp

Wake Up Call

Routinely my mouth with the assistance of teeth and tongue chants
    "I love you"
Purple eyes noble medals of battle,
    "I love you"
Dragging a swollen and aching body out of bed,
    "I love you"
Desires surrendered to a misplaced dream time,
    "I love you"
Ambitions to be given to my children when I die,
    "I love you"
A ceremonial clashing of sexual organs, release is slow,
    "I love you"
My own reflection in a shop window entices the truth
    "I hate you"

Julie Hope

Always . . .

I seem to share this world with ghosts,
I meet them as I move around,
I see the thistles and the frogs,
As friends who see through other eyes,
And miss them both so very much,
Perhaps that's why I look for them,
Or see them when I don't.

Enough to know they shared their lives,
And touched the lives of folk they met,
And left behind their memory.

Bruce Robinson

Making Sense of the Senseless

I do believe we are being deceived,
I feel there is something unreal,
In this worldly atmosphere,
Do you really believe you have never been here before?

I remember youthful optimism's cheer,
Something I will always hold dear.
I now recall how easily ageing began,
How removed I am, never to forget,
I learned from it all.

I drifted on and on.
And stumbled like an innocent child,
On a thought;
My spirit can never be caught.

So here I am, I dream again.
Like a sudden awareness,
I fell on another thought,
I will never abandon the freedom;
That I have sought.

Ewan J. A. MacKinnon

Spreading Love

When I was a little girl,
I dreamt of world peace.
No guns, no war, no fighting,
We would all live as one.
But now I'm that bit older,
I know the world won't change,
Without a joining of our nations,
And a face to face exchange.

So let's begin the clear up,
Let's all become friends.
Put down your bombs, put down your guns,
We'll make a Family.
Ignore their race, ignore their creed,
It doesn't matter now.
We should love one another,
That's how life was found.

Charlotte Nicholls

Fox Poem

Oh, no it's happening the day I've always dreaded
I hear them, please don't let me end up shredded,
So many horses and dogs, yet there's only one of me,
If I don't hurry I know I'll end up their tea.
The fear, the fright, oh will I be alright?
What have I done so bad, to make them all so mad,
I'm just a fox living in the wild,
My temper's quite placid altogether pretty mild,
I want to be free, is that such a lot to ask?
At the moment it's a pretty hefty task.
They're gaining on me,
Soon they will see,
That not far ahead, is poor little me,
I've loved my life, but now I feel it's drawing in,
My paws are hurting, they're going to win.
My family, my friends, I'll never see again
They're just steps behind, I'll try and count to ten,
I've only reached four and there will be no more
Oh the pain, the pain it's awful!
'Please tell me is this really lawful?

Jenny Middleton

Violet

V is for Violet, the name she was given.
I is for the ideal mum, now gone to heaven.
O is for ordeal, that she had to bear.
L is for the love, that she had to share.
E is for economy, and her thriftiness to save
T is for the torment, that she carried to the grave.
But this Violet, is not dead and gone.
For in our hearts, she will live, on and on.

Aileen Chambers

A Budgie Breeder's Wife

My husband is a budgie breeder,
I find it hard to say,
He goes down to his birdhouse
and stays most of the day.
Blues and greens, greys, opalines and such,
I can see quite plainly, he loves them all so much.

The radio must play all day, they like a merry tune,
A heater keeps them nice and warm
morning, night and noon.
Other breeders come along to give him sound advice,
I meet their wives and, really, they all seem very nice.

Often when it is dinnertime I just have to shout,
But, even then, I find he just will not come out.
There is one consolation - his birds are the feathered kind
And at the bottom of the garden
He is never hard to find.

Joan Farr

Long Lost Curls

When I was young,
I had the prettiest curls you've ever seen,
But now I'm tall and fully grown
Those curls are few and far between.
They say beauty fades with time
And time has surely past
I should have known those curls
Were never made to last.
For now I'm so much older than I'd like to be
Oh how I miss those long lost curls
They looked so nice on me.

Judy Joslin

A Gift from Mother (Mothering)

I look into the perfect face of my new born child
I gave my heart, complete, without conditions
Offered with love parcelled in dreams
Full of happy things

Mothering him in the early years always fulfilled me
His splendid smiles and bright clear eyes
Accepting me, empowering me with his rewarding acceptance
Of my love

Now he's a young man and I sense his impatience with me
I utter no words and I expect nothing
But now and again I would like to see that splendid smile
And his bright clear eyes full to the brim with unconditional
Love for me
It's the gift I offered and never retrieved

Geraldine M. Dunleavy

Dedication to My Dear Wife, Evelyn

When I come to speak about my wife,
I get tongue-tied,
But really sweetheart I owe you my life, for the sleepless nights,
You keep telling me I have to fight,
Just keep telling me, I'll pull through,
For that darling, I love you.

Thank you for all holidays, and the friends we have gathered,
Remember Cola Bona, I even passed for your father,
With your youthful looks, and my grey hair,
I think we make a lovely pair.

Yesterday you caught me on the hop,
Never mind that Alec, you will wash up.
I'll wash up for you every day, if you promise not to take the
chair away.

I heard on the wire, that because of me, you packed in with the choir,
So for all the things that you've been through,
I'm grateful darling,
AND WILL ALWAYS LOVE YOU.

Alec Boros

No Greater Love

My joys will now be always yours,
I go now last not first,
For me my cup has overflown,
Your happiness now my thirst.

Through this life my eyes looked blindly
to fading shades of grey,
Now colours shine reflected brightly
from faces on my way.

No greater love has man inspired,
My life for yours I'd give,
All my thoughts are with you only,
That you, my love, should live.

I will show the world we know
and tell of the world we knew,
And when you surpass what I show
Then I shall learn from you.

I watched the seasons come and go,
With nature I am now at one,
The beauty of this earth I pledge
to you my newborn son.

June McDaniel

Yesterday

I should have done it yesterday but time went in a flash
I should have done it yesterday but I was in a dash
I should have said "I love you dear" instead of keeping quiet
I should have told you all the things I keep here in my heart.

I should have done it yesterday the clock I can't put back
I should have done it yesterday redress the things I lack
I should have seen my friend and said "Your sorrow, it will pass"
You'll find that time will heal your pain and you will smile at last.

I should have done it yesterday took time to look around
I should have done it yesterday I think I might have found
So many people needing help or just a word or two
To help them know God made this world for folk like me and you.

Please God give me tomorrows, my todays have nearly gone
My yesterdays I can't bring back and I must struggle on
To try to make amends to friends for times when I was cross
Not seeing others point of view insisting I was boss.

When my todays are all used up and yesterday's history
My tomorrows you can have, you solve the mystery
Of why my life has flown so fast and all that I can say
Is "Sorry can't do that just now, I should have done it yesterday".

Cynthia Turner

As I Thought

Just when I thought,
I had it all worked out.

All planned,
Yes all planned.
Just when I, yes, just when.
But now it doesn't matter.
My life's blood is nearly over.

Just when I thought that I was
going places, making plans and doing.
That's how one is.

Then she came along with her proposal.
And I said go away but she insisted.
When I said good bye to her I meant it.
But he in his world and me in my corner,
Fighting the opposition.
Yes just when . . . just when I thought
I had something special.
She came and took it away.
I cried but then . . .

Fatma Durmush

Such Sorrow

This story indeed is hard to tell.
I had such a beautiful Tom cat,
In grace he did excel.
On sunny days he'd roam and stray,
He had no enemies, anyway.
A day ago he frisked away
My lovely Tom with kids to play.
When up the road a man appeared
Two dogs he had, and a beard.
With vicious springs those dogs leapt out
And by the throat they seized my cat,
They shook and bit and tossed him 'round
Soon my Tom cat knew no bound,
He fell in shock without a sound
As death crept in to set him free.
Killed with force I'll never forget,
My dearest and most loving pet.
My grieving now can't bring him back,
No more indeed what I could say
For words as well I now do lack.

Barbara Voss

My Birthday

As I open my eyes in the morning,
I hear the dog yawning,
I go down stairs,
And look at the post,
And most of the post is for me,

I go into the kitchen,
The dogs nose is twitchin',
There are presents on the table,
But I open the cards first,
And the presents when my family is here,

One of them might be a lampshade,
Or an ornament that in China it was made,
One even could be.
A little plum tree,
And that's my Birthday.

Caroline Ann Fuller

Ad Astra

In the quiet of dark, under twinkling lights,
I lie here and wonder of folly and stars.
So tiny a part of smooth planetary action,
aligning the cosmos in the dead of night.
As the Influence of Arcturus summons up spring,
and ushers in his vernal equinox sting,
High above, an anarchic meteor graces my sky,
a joyride igniting this vacuous flight.
Is this shooting star, just a scaramouch trail,
or can my wish, become tomorrow's truth.

Antony C. E. Waterhouse

This Crazy Game of Golf

Tae pick up a stick, and chase a wee ba'
I jist canna see the sense in it ava'
Hittin' a ba' roond a park fu' o' holes,
Ye'd think t'wis a new wey tae kill a' the moles.
Bit they tell me it's golf . . . It's the "In" game the noo,
It swackens ye up, without hae'in' tae boo,
Bit if yon's meant tae swacken ye? . . . Hodgin' aboot
Aff o' ae fit on' till't ither. O' this there's nae doot
Yer banes are mair like tae seize up nor swacken.
Bit golfin' freends say "fresh air is nae lackin',
Jist think on't, yer lungs are gettin' a treat"
Bit wi the win' there is here, ye'd be blawn aff yer feet
An' faur's the fresh air, faur's the sport, faur's the tricks,
Fin the rain's poorin' oot o' the doup o' yer breeks.
An' syne come the winter, It's nae eese ava'
Lookin' for holes amon' sax fitt o' snaw.
So takkin't a' roond ye'd be better by far,
Tae stick tae the nineteenth, and bide in the bar!

Frances S. Jaffray

Why?

I am hurting so very much,
I just want to reach out and touch,
the love I feel is so strong,
but you just want to prove me wrong.

What have I done for you to go,
it's just not fair, I love you so,
but you don't feel that one so young,
could feel so much and have some fun.

I feel so empty,
I want you to know,
tell me this,
why did you go?

It hurts so much that you chose her,
oh why is life just so unfair,
what did I do to make you choose,
and why is it always me to lose?

Andrea Dummer

Just One More Chance

Hi it's me. I am going to change
I know I can, just let me prove to you
Please, please let me show you
I am not what you see
Within I am longing to be free
I am a respectable man
A man who can love and respect you
Don't look at me that way
Your eyes are piercing through me
I feel cold, lost, disgusted, what will I do. Help me
Why are you looking at me
Why with love and not hate
You know, I know what decision to make
Is there a chance
Or will it be my faith.
That breaks down the barriers
Faith it shall be, then I shall stand tall, walk straight.
I'll take your hand, and together we will go
through the narrow gate.

Diane Finlay

My Wonderful Mum

You weren't always there when I was growing up,
I know it wasn't your choice,
But it would have been nice to hold your hand,
And sometimes hear your voice,
As the years have gone by and the older I have got,
I have been in trouble but you've stuck by me through the lot,
As I am growing up to be a lot like you,
The closer we've become,
I love you so much, really I do,
Because you're such a wonderful Mum.

Hayley Coles

Too Late

Do not close your eyes when you kiss me,
I know you don't love me anymore,
Don't smile knowingly when you turn away,
Don't turn around when you leave my door.

I know our love is over you see,
But I know you think I care,
You think you have deceived me,
Don't turn around, you'll see I'm not there.

You have always been the strong one,
And saw only weakness in me,
You used me for yourself,
Don't turn around, you just might see.

A different person than you know,
And I'd hate to hear you curse,
Don't turn around just yet, I smile,
Because darling, I left you first!

Avril Dearden

Too Short a Span

Lives such as yours are not measured by time.
I know you went without regret
And all the lonely years I've yet to live
I'll remember you.
I'll strive in every gesture, thought and deed
To be worthy of your sacrifice.
You loved life too much to want to die,
No wasted moments or idle dreams
Each day to you was a great adventure,
Each action a stepping stone set with purpose
Your high ideals and lofty ambitions blaze forth
Like a beacon atop the hill I've still to climb.
You died with heroes in blood and battle.
No flowers or cross mark your grave, you're with a gallant company
In a fighting ship that went down fighting.
The ocean itself guards over you in majesty.
You loved life too much to want to live
If by your sacrifice others could be freed.
A well spent life; a brave man's death;
There could be no finer epitaph.

Alma White

A Thought

I wonder what I'd like to be
If I were anything but me.
A spider running up the wall?
A giraffe who can reach so tall?
Maybe a cat, with coat of silk
(That wouldn't do - I don't like milk!)
I wouldn't mind a pair of wings
Then I could see all kinds of things.
What does a goldfish think - who knows?
As 'round and 'round the bowl he goes.

All clever creatures, you'll agree
But they can't make my cup of tea!

Joan Mayers

Are You Listening

I am an unborn baby
I listen to your every word
I notice also what you do
Is it for me or is it for you
I see you take my abode away
Now I have no place to stay
I have no voice to have my say
So you in turn put me away
There is someone who is over us all
He made earth and everything
To share our lives together
What we do to you we did to Jesus
We did not listen to what he said
When will we ever learn
Or is it not your concern
How unhappy can you get
Or is it easier to forget
I am a person I have my right
Even if I have not been in your sight

Elizabeth Docherty

A Squirrel's Tale

By the oak tree, which looks so bare,
I look at the river and start to stare,
The moonlight shines on the river's ripple,
I can even hear a little trickle,
To my amazement, I turn around,
I hear a rustle from the ground,
It's not what you think, I definitely know,
It's the leaves twisting and twirling and falling like snow,
Suddenly, swish goes the wind, blowing through my fur,
and it's feeling nippy, and time for me to stir,
I'm off to hibernate, and to have a winter's sleep
in my old oak tree, down by the river's creek.

Debbie Coombes

A Train of Concentration

Stepping to a clearing in a wood,
I met a railway there and stood,
keen ears listening for a sound,
but nothing stirred within me or around.

The tiniest vibration on my drum,
I wasn't sure did I hear a hum?
A hammer on an anvil in my ear,
no louder than a solitary tear.

A train of concentration in my mind,
travelling towards me, constant grind.
Approaching, growing louder as it came,
quiet rumble? Yes, I knew his name.

My concentration spoke "Warning, near."
Approaching speeding noise growled "Never fear."
Gushing in, ramming every space,
no other would be victor in his race.

Growing, puffing, wheezing, blowing,
screeching, soaring, screaming, roaring,
all resisting senses sped along.
One blink, and all imagined trains were gone.

Andrew L. Milne

To My Husband

I miss your love, your kisses, your caresses;
I miss your very nearness, your strength;
For you were a part of me,
Now I am alone and I am mutilated.

Will I ever come alive again?
Will this torment end?
Does love come more than once?
I hope so, but if it is not to be, I give thanks for what I had,
the love with which you have surrounded me, and for the
memories which I shall forever hold in my heart.

Gwynedd Spraggs

When I Made the World

When I made the world, it took less than a week
I put people on earth and I taught them to speak
From the very first day, they griped, and they groaned
You can't guarantee, the seed that you've sown
I look back at myself, think what have I done
When I sent to earth, my only son
I gambled his life, and I lost the loss
Don't talk about pain, I watched him on that cross
So stop your complaining, do the best that you can
There's a road to me, and a road to Satan
When you make your mind up, you just have to pray
I'll always hear you, but there might be delay
The reason I'm given, millions pray day and night
And I'd like to think I was getting it right
So set by example, do your best, be upright
All I ask from you, is say thanks and good night
I don't have to tell you, these words are not mine
I was just the instrument, that put them to rhyme.

Daniel McRae

In My Head

I want to be in someone else's mind
I need to be able to see
Is there someone else who is scared and confused
Or is it just me?
Sometimes I feel frightened and alone
I don't know which way to go
I don't understand some of the thoughts I have
But I feel like I should know
I wonder if I have an illness
But then again I'm not sure
Whatever it is, there's no name for it
So how can I find the cure?

Emma Denny

Sparkling Crystals

When in the twilight hours I dream of you
I remember well your heart so true.
No mean or nasty thought did cross your heart,
No harsh words from your lips did start.
We laughed at nothing, you and I
And sometimes dreamt a bit of times gone by.
We didn't always have a lot to eat,
Yet, almost poverty (with you) was near to sweet
Until that day late into Spring
When longer days more evening light did bring,
I sailed away in search of life
Not recognizing shining brightly,
Sparkling crystals shining, shining,
Priceless gems of priceless love!
When at last in some harsh foreign land I stood
I wished me back beside you love as hard I could.
Oh bitter pill that only then did find,
I naked stood - in life, with love so far behind!

B. Veares

Time

When leaving this world of its toil and strife
I reflect on the moments of times in my life
My greatest wish for the human race
Is look to your God in His forgiving face.

Time moves on and the calendar clicks
For people in countries and harmony to fix
The wanton waste of God's given things,
And avarice people manipulating strings.

Come one and all end global strife
And live in harmony, a contented life
Time will tell when God peers down
With a wondrous smile or a damning frown.

My time is up and I leave this place
No more to gaze on my family's face
Look to the heavens and I'll be there
for future generations take extraordinary care.

John Robert Whittle

Baby

Although you're so tiny with eyes bright and blue,
I promise all of these things to you.
I'll always be with you and you mustn't fear,
Whenever you need me I'll always be near.
My arms they will hold you in case you should fall
My ears they will hear you whenever you call.
My eyes they will watch you and keep you from pain
If ever we're parted I'll find you again.
If people should hurt you and you wonder why,
If friends should desert you I'll be there close by.
If ever you're troubled and haven't a friend,
I'll always be there till the very end.

Celia Hardy

'I'

I healed you
I soothed you
I protected you
I listened to you
I gave you warmth
I gave you understanding
I gave you unconditional and devoted love.
I let you go

I received from you, pain
I was hurt by you
I feared you
I was ignored by you
I received no warmth
I received no understanding
I received a broken heart

I cried, - and from that day
I died.

Jackie Hellewell

Peace

What is that abstract ideal?
I saw it in the face of the Nun
As she meditated in her cell;
I heard it in the rendering of the song
While the mother sang her lullaby;
I felt it in the couple's tender touch
When they strolled the gardens fair.

It is as fragile as a pane of glass
Which shatters at the impact of a blow,
The slivers like a rose's thorn
It is as delicate as a tender flower
Which withers without constant sustenance.
It is as beautiful as an innocent child
Who delights to play in the balmy breeze.

War or peace, my friend,
Which would you choose
To pattern this dull world with light?
Choose not the Stygian darts of darkness that offend,
But rather the ethereal joys which harmonize:
This the true freedom that we crave.

Bernadette Marley

Out of Touch

I reach out to touch you,
I search but nothing's there
Oh the miles that hold me from you,
Are so deep, so dark and unfair.

Why can't I just be near you,
In your heart, in your arms, in your mind
The most precious thing I've ever thought of,
So beautiful, so loving, so kind.

I know my feelings for you,
Will last forever and a day.
I love everything about you,
All you do, all you touch and all you say.

And
I know it's coming soon now,
The time that we shall meet
When I rush over to Ireland,
And you sweep me off my feet!

Georgina Reynolds

Time

Time is a thing you can not describe,
it goes by so quickly when you're alive,
when you are sixty you wish you
were six, oh my God time slips by so quick.
Now that I am old I think of
the past as I sit by the fire and
just relax, I wish I was young and
in my prime, because time is to
precious to waste, wasting time.

Glenys Porter

On Saturday Night

I saw my friend, whom I'd known for years.
I saw my friend, who brought me to tears.
Her arms and legs were tired and bruised
Her body, for years all alone she abused.
Her face was drawn and somewhat yellow,
Her eyes were deep, with a touch of mellow.
Joy was her name, and a joy she has been
To many who know her she was willing and keen.
She would help any person that needed her care
Doing their washing, their housework, their hair,
The kind of person, it's nice to know
The kind of person who rarely says no.
I saw my friend, whom I'd known for years
Now I'm alone with only my tears.

Farewell my friend

Barbara Smart

Our Gracious Lord

When I bow my head in prayer,
I search my heart and say,
Forgive me Lord for any wrong
I may have done today.

No longer do I wonder,
Is He really there?
My faith grows ever stronger
And I know He hears my prayer.

Not so very long ago,
My heart was heavy and full of woe.
Now today, with hope and love,
I lift mine eyes to the Lord above.

Satan hovers - ever alert,
Waiting for someone he can hurt.
With you beside me every day,
I pray, dear Lord, I'll never stray.

When I bow my head in prayer,
I thank You Lord for being there;
To guide me and calm me with Your grace.
I look to the day I may see Your sweet face.

Irene Joan Kelsey

Goodbye

When I look back to my long ago childhood,
I remember the bright shining sun,
I remember the shadows as fleeting, capricious,
I remember the laughter and fun.

There must have been grey days and cold winds,
There must have been storm clouds and rain,
But oh! how I wish I could relive those days,
I wish I was young once again.

The bluebells we picked in the dark scented woods,
The primroses snug 'neath the hedge,
The call of the cuckoo, the cry of the barn owl,
As it perched on the high-raftered ledge.

Fresh green, young bracken, the hedgerows all white,
with the May coming out in to bloom,
All I see now are the grey streets of London,
From inside a dull gloomy room.

My friends are all dead and gone now,
The snow on their graves it is cold,
But still I can find a quiet solace,
From my dreams, that were once edged with gold.

Heather Bushell

Innocence and Youth

You could have told me anything yesteryear,
I would have believed every word.

Innocence . . . a wonderful mixture of childishness and youth
   combined
The fairies at the bottom of the garden,
The visits to the park, with pram enfolding some mother's tiny child.

And now, whilst completely void of life's flow and knowledge,
Love's awakening . . .
The midsummers day, the lush acres of green grass, bluebells
dancing in the breeze, trilling birds, the canter of horses on the
hillock, oh happy happy day!
The brightness of eye, the redness of lips parted in controlled
breathlessness, and the completed transformation, from a
plain to blissful face by the kind and gentle touch of
Mother nature . . . and all because of a companion.

So handsome, so tall, so blond, so very wise, and all of 17 summers.
Oh wonderful youth, innocence, and awakening love, can anything
compare to this awesome state of mind? surely this is mysticism
completed, and my soul shall rise to thine.
You could have told me anything yesteryear . . .
Please don't tell me anything today.

Elizabeth Pemberton Ward

A Reflection

As I look upon the river,
I see a broken mirror.
A picture of myself just gazing in.
The ripples distort my face,
The swirls mess up my hair.
Every single detail is right there.
From behind a gloomy cloud,
The sun reveals its face,
And rainbow colours dance before my eyes.
Overhead the sky grows dim,
And clouds begin to roar.
Suddenly out of nowhere comes a total rain downpour.
My looking glass is ruined,
Shattered beyond repair.
Wistfully I turn away and find elsewhere to stare.

Holly Shelton

My Kind of World

If I could change the world today.
I would change it in many ways.
I would make the rich, not filled with greed,
I would make the poor not be in need.
The lame and sick walk through a door.
Where there would be pain no more.
Drink, drugs, no abuse.
No wicked, people, they're no use.
No war, no crime people would not dare
Happy not sad, people who care.
Children playing in the street.
No broken glass at their feet.
No crazy drivers, at their wheels.
Killing, maiming, family crying on their knees.
No earth quakes, or disasters of any kind.
In my world the sun would always shine,
I wish I could change the world.

Janet Elizabeth Isherwood

Philosophy of the Fallen

Behind the noise and hub,
I sense a silence deep beneath the childish pretence and
    impish giggles,
The silence is rarely defined,
Only in the eyes of the lonely or the innocent
Yet is ever present.

Snippets of conversation slap my ears like naughty hands,
Eyes search, tongues lash, sneers curl
On the lips of the foolish who feign wisdom.
Let them tell you of the colours, the music and the light,
They could not even begin to.

Falsities and idealistic aspirations conceal all truth
From their gluttony filled eyes,
While the eyes that are deep like marble pools
See all truth yet never speak of it,
For fear of being noticed in the ever influential crowd
The black sheep in a flock of white.
They melt away into the murky shadows,
Seeking no attention.
Fawning beneath the urgency of the mighty concourse.

Jamie Stewart

"A Driver"

I'm not allowed to try and see, how fast my train can go,
I'm not allowed to sound the horn, except in emergency, fog,
or falling snow,
I'm not allowed to speak my mind or let off a little steam,
I'm not allowed to pass a signal red, until it's turned to green,
I'm not allowed to drive, on routes I've never been before,
I'm not allowed to take my foot, off the safety pedal on the floor,
I'm not allowed to leave the driving seat, it's like sitting in a cell,
But just let my train jump the tracks, whose to answer, well?
Taken from the cab, then breathalysed, told bend down and touch
your toes,
Asked, when last did you eat or drink, now shut your eyes and
touch your nose.

Harold Lamb

Really Knowing God

The Lord is my guider,
I shall not want,
The meadows are full of love,
Where peace is forever,
He takes me to the waters of life,
To receive my love of the spirit,
He guides me in the right direction,
He his my Master.
If I should walk in darkness,
No evil will I face,
You are my Shepherd with goodness,
Wherever I go I'll be with comfort,
You welcomed me into Your home and heart,
While my foes are left behind,
You have christened me with oil,
My love and kindness has overgrown,
Wherever I go love will follow,
For all the time I will be here.
In the Lord's house I will live forever
For the rest of my life.

Amanda Hall

The Song

She must have held your heart so strong,
Immortal girl, now etched in song.
The words you wrote cannot be wrong.

She must have meant the world to you
This golden girl, you've threaded through
The lyrics of your ballad, blue.

Did you think that it would last?
Tossed on her sea, tied to the mast,
Captured by the spell she'd cast?

Don't answer ....

For I live in hope that you'll be mine.
I know you care, you give me time.
But will you ever make me rhyme?

Your heart won't hide in staves of steel.
A bard betrayed sings sweet and real.
The chord she struck in you will heal.

One thing, my love, you can rely,
There are no logical reasons why.
Your song will always make me cry.
Play on ....

Deborah E. Parkinson

"Memories of a Faithful Friend"

The days are cold, my heart is heavy,
I still shed a tear, for you my lovely,
To touch your fur, to hear you bark,
Would comfort me, when the nights are dark.

I'm growing older, my hair is grey
My bones are aching, in the mornings when waking,
My thoughts are always of you, my friend,
Faithful and loyal right to the end.

It won't be too long, my loving friend,
When all of my days will come to an end,
My happiness will be complete, on the day
I go over, and we shall meet

No leads or collars when out on our run,
Just lots and lots of lovely fun,
Racing here, racing there, over the fields
without a care.

No worries, no troubles, together we'll be,
Always forever, just you and me.

Hazel Smith

The Old Tin Bath

When I was young and had a bath
I used a tin one in front of the hearth

My mum would scrub me and wrap me tight
Then up to bed for an early night

We bought a new one, not made of tin
We kept the old one to put newts in

We filled it up with water and stones
For frogs and newts the perfect home

Now I am older my bathroom is new
Over the years my children grew.

They bath in the warmth of central heating
But my bath by the hearth takes some beating

Doreen Cave

Painting

Can it be colours and shapes
Ideas and thoughts that come without restraint,
Perhaps the beauty of the subject in my mind
That struggles to find life upon the canvas that I paint -
Can it be, that all at once the calmness that I feel
The quiet world I'm in, forgetting worries that are real
That I have found a cure to wipe away unhappiness and fears
And memories that can sadden and sometimes bring the tears

Can these brushes - extroverts in colours bright and bold,
Or sometimes calm and gentle painting white and gold,
Really work this magic on my soul if I so wish?
Ah yes . . . they can do all these things for me -
They bring contentment and tranquillity,
I can escape among the flowers, sea and sky . . .
There are no pressures and I do not reason why.

Joyce Mitchell

"Saturday Night Lottery Fever"

The more I look upwards to the sky.
I strain and strain but cannot see -
Those Famous Fingers pointing down at me.
It's you! It's you! Is the cry!
I'd love to win - so have a try.
First you find the nearest store -
- with the lottery "logo" over the door.
Six numbers only you must pick -
Seven? Twenty? - or could it be six?
You pay your pound - that is the fee
Now you wait - all week, and see!
If mystic Meg with her witch-like eyes -
- Into her crystal ball - she spies -
With smoke around her - tension mounting
- She sees a 'Dr.' and "people in accounting"
Now for the best part of the show
'Lancelot,' 'Arthur,' 'Guinevere,' and "balls" ready to go -
Press the start! The numbers have gone!
Alas! Us usual I've not got one!!

Hazel Adeline

The Miracle

It happened a long time ago,
I was only five years old,
My mother fell down the cellar steps,
And was told, "You'll never walk again".

Twelve months she lay on her back,
Couldn't move, that's a fact,
"I will walk again", said mother.
As she prayed to God, like no other.

For ten pounds she was taken to Lourdes,
And a Frenchman wheeled her to the waters,
Where, she bathed and was comforted,
By this man's lovely daughter.

Seven days of this healing routine,
Then mother was homeward bound,
To walk and love and live again,
She was a young eighty eight, when she died.

Hetty Foster

Forever Young

As my anger turns to sorrow
I think about my life tomorrow
I think about what could have been
If my eyes were open and I had seen

You were happy, so I thought
But it was sadness that you fought
Why did you leave me like you did?
You left me lonely with your kid

I look at the picture, see you smiling
My heart melts, it's slowly dying
I'm so tempted to follow you
But I will live my life right through

But you're not dead, you live on
through your music, through your song
And you'll be in our memories
Remaining there for eternity

Carrie Gledhill

Adjustments

You have no right to reproach me.
I took you in, odiferous and ill.
Gave you shelter, succour, and not a little affection.
You must have known the price, a bargain struck.
Is domesticity such a cross? Regular hours, regular meals.
It had to be. You with your rapacious sex, I my fastidiousness.
Stranger pairings work. Owning and being owned.
And does it really matter so much?

I didn't have to live with you.
It was your idea. Good for your ego, no doubt.
But what of mine?
I could have taken my chance with the rest,
Street-wise and mean.
Rummaged in alleys, slept rough, fended for myself.
But the bed was soft, and so were you.
And unaccustomed flesh-pots beguiled me.
You should have called the forfeit, pronounced sentence.
That you and he, with legalized barbarity, and blood-money passed,
Would re-arrange my gender.
No longer Tom but Tiddles.

Christine Dinsdale

I Want Freedom I Want Peace

I want freedom I want peace but will I ever get it?
I want to walk in the night without getting in a fight.
I want to go to a place where there is love and not hate.
I want to go to a place where there are no wars because of race.
I want to work in a place where I'll be treated like any other face.
I want to be in a place where a piece of paper controls no fates.
I want to be in a place where I'm not judged because of my weight.
I want to go to a place where I can love someone from another race.
I want to go to a place where bombs and guns have no place.
I want freedom I want peace but will I ever get it?

Arun Sharma

Choices

At the age of twenty-six
I was living in the sticks,
So to London town I came
Not for fortune, gold or fame.
But, hopefully, a lover, friend,
A better life, the modern trend,
Well, I've been loved, and I've been kissed.
I've been sad for folks I've missed,
Country burr has given way,
To voices strident every day.
Traffic, noise, my life's a whirl
Too much for this country girl.
So, at the age of twenty-eight
I'm going home, it's not too late,
Where speech is lilting, like a song,
Family's close, and friendship strong,
I don't know why I looked elsewhere,
All I'll ever want is there.

Florence Baldwin

Shadows of the Past

I sense their eyes upon me,
I turn. There is nobody there.
Walking down the road
I can feel arms reaching,
Stretching out to hold me,
To touch me. And yet,
There is nobody there.

Whichever direction I turn in,
I feel but cannot see
The thousands of people around me.
The weight of their stare
Turns my feet to lead, yet still
There is nobody there.

There is no escape from the past.
The tears flow like a river,
They are haunting my mind.
Completely alone, surrounded by silence
I can feel their presence.
I know there is somebody there.

Anne Paramore

Suicide Note!

By the time you read this,
I shall be stony cold.
I want, first, for you all to know,
How it is to be above, below,
in front of and behind a metal grill.
It looks easy to live in this zoo,
an attraction for the visitors.
But when they've gone, behind closed doors,
you hear the;
Clank, Clank!
Guards haul metal torpedoes into their shells,
. . . so in the pig sty I knock the blunt instrument into my pocket.
I grate the knife on the rusty bed all night,
then toy with my murder tool.
Slicing this sinewy wrist of mine.
. . . Drip . . . Drip . . . Drip . . .

I love you all!

Jo Tinkler

Head Boy

Head Boy
I wish you were dead boy
So then I could be head boy
Because that would be great

I wanna be the head boy
So I've thought up a cunning ploy
I'm gonna kill the current head boy
With some rat bait

I'll put it in his food
So when he begins to chew
From above I'll view
His tragic fate

Head Boy
I just killed the head boy
But I am not the head boy
Because I'm serving a life sentence in prison
After being convicted for murder
BUT I CAN WAIT

James Corcoran

Pondering

As I sit and stare
I wonder are you out there?
The seasons slip quickly by.
As I think of the reason why
Is it true He takes the best
Or does He take you for a rest
Will we meet again one day.
These thoughts I think as I sit and stare
are you really out there.

Christine V. Gledhill

Bitterness

Why be bitter? Why be not?
If I can't be bitter what else have I got?

Kipling speaks of building up with worn out tools,
Should I, to have it knocked down again?
Should I become a normal fool?

So many times they've called me thick
That now I always act that way.
Truer to call me stubborn; in acting to make them pay.

But everyone's a price to pay. Respect has to be earned.
I won't work for it or pay the price, I've never really learned.

And them that never learn they say, come to a sticky end.
I would learn and I would pay, just to have one special friend.

There's not much spirit left in me. Not much more will to fight.
It seems to me that life's unfair, and will never be put right.

We have to keep on trying, if we are to survive.
But we all need affection, if we're going to thrive.

So I'll try just a little more, a little's all I've got left.
My will to be is nearly gone. God please give me a rest.

My battery needs recharging and not by drugs or pills.
I need some motivation to help me work to pay the bills.

Anthony Frith

A Mind of Mine

When I was young and in my prime,
I was sent to work deep down·a mine.

Working in dust and gases too
Everyday from six till two.

At half past four I had to rise
Ate my breakfast with half-closed eyes.

My mum packed snap of bread and jam.
To catch the bus I mostly ran.

On the bus I joined my mates.
We travelled eight miles to pit gates

Into the canteen for a pint of milk.
This helped dilute the dust and silt.

Through the baths, a change of clothes.
Steel-toe, capped boots that pinch my toes.

We donned our lamps and checked the time,
Before descending down the mine.

Down the shaft we quickly sped.
A thousand yards no word was said.

We travelled tunnels in semi-dark,
Our eight hour task about to start.

Derrick Buxton

Gleam of Hope

As the sun smiles on my freckled face,
I watch the birds in a playful chase.
This haven gleams a sign of hope,
It fills my bones with the strength to cope.
I've seen the answer to my dreams,
It all takes time, or at least it seems.
For we fear in life just one small thing,
Life itself and what it may bring.
I'll try to focus on the good not bad,
To make sure this time is the best I'll have.
My soul will dance in a state of glee,
When I acknowledge the beauty in all I see.
My heart will burst with the joys of spring.
I must appreciate my everything.
I will wake each day to feel re-born,
With a need to run through golden corn.
The clouds will burst and the rain will fall,
I will finally stand so strong and tall.

Debbie Clerkson

God?

A wire mesh surrounding me,
I'm shrivelled in a ball.
My hands clasp around my ears,
and yet I hear you call.
My arms coil around my face,
I'm protected from the cold.
The light shines down and hurts my eyes,
but stops me growing old.
I'm hiding from another world,
I see my life ahead.
I walk towards the open gate,
and I realize I'm dead.

Claire Merriman

"A Link with the Past"

St. Patrick's Day of '94 I'll remember for evermore,
I went to England the day before, hence my little
tale of woe!
While in the air, I was served with tea, then befell,
a catastrophe. The plastic cup sprang a leak, and the
tea was sprinkled over me. I travelled Aer Lingus
(their staff is superb). A most apologetic
hostess soon cleared up the mess.
After this, I'm glad to relate - I had a most enjoyable
St. Patrick's Day. I now live in Ireland, the land of
my birth, but have very happy memories of the
country I left. For Fifty odd years I'm proud to
state - I lived in England, where I wed, and
stayed, combining motherhood with nursing, and
wifely duties as well.
These last lines I have added so you can decide, if
my entry is valid;
If not - well! - I've tried.

Ellen Worth

A Proposal

My darling I love you, with all my heart
I will love you forever, till death us do part.
You've made me so happy, and gave me a goal.
For you my darling, I would give my soul.

I saw the love in your eyes, the first time we met
I yearn for your kisses, your cuddles too,
My heart is filled with love, which I'm keeping for you.
I love you my darling, honest I do.

I dearly want to hold you and hug you so tight.
I will love you forever, a day and a night.
If you still love me, then please tell me so.
I will be faithful, and loyal to you.

I want you to love me, like I love you.
I will love you forever, for E-tern-ity.
This promise I make, straight from my heart.
I love you so much, may we never part.

Denis Johnston

Forever Loved

I will not leave you comfortless,
    I will see you again.
These same words kept repeating,
    As I sought for peace in vain.
Then I felt the touch of your kiss,
    Your broken heart touched mine.
I thank God for this wonderful gift,
    His gift of your love divine.
The troubles we have shared have been many,
    The burden heavy to bear.
But none of these things really matter,
    As long as you are there.
We will travel life's journey together,
    With the dear Lord as our guide.
And face all our troubles and hardships,
    As long as we stay, side by side.

Christine Wheat

Death

Man woman child are on this earth for approximately one
    hundred years
If one dies before then it will bring others close to tears.
You may lose your loved one, friend or one of your relatives.
Even though tears drop down your face, it is no disgrace too cry
because in your hearts you know one day they are going to die
    and so am I.
Our souls will travel on.
Life to me is like being a leaf on a tree the wind blows,
    then it snows am I going to fall nobody knows.
The tree might bend, I still hang on, it rains very hard but I
    still hang on.
I get the sunlight. I stay on the tree and survive, oh how
    good it is to be alive.
But in my heart of hearts like a human being I am going to fall
to the ground then die, but my soul will travel on and the rest of
the younger family will live on.

Joseph G. Webster

I Want to Be a . . .

I want to be the president, and rule the U.S.A.,
I wouldn't make a good one though, I'd be ruined in a day,

I want to be an astronaut, and drive a big spaceship,
I would take full advantage, and take it for a trip,

I want to be a janitor, and clean the school playground,
I'd pick up all the bouncy balls, and keep the ones I found,

I want to be a school teacher, and order kids about,
If anyone would fool around, I'd have them sent straight out,
I want to be a T.V. man, and present a brilliant show,
So if I cracked a joke, the whole wide world would know,

I want to be a builder, and build my own small house,
I'd call it "The one that Jack built", and live there with my mouse,

I want to be all these, if stacked all on a shelf,
But the person I want to be the most, has to be myself.

James Crawford

Love

Love is as a many changing thing
It has so many forms, so many shapes
Love has no control, in youth in age, we cannot understand
Through the mist of our senses only our souls can tell
It cannot be see nor heard. It has no meaning for some people.
It is a bliss, a timeless knowledge, but it cannot be captured only
found.
If love is blind let me never see
If love is sweet let the rose never leave my lips
If love's fragrance is that of a spring morn let me never sleep
And if love's happiness is that of a life let me never die.

Chris Pudney

Untitled

When you look at me, what do you see
I'm asking you a question, please answer me
I know I don't look the same, as the day I took your name
The lines on my face from sharing and caring
Sorrow, joy, I know it all shows, and you're staring

All the years we've shared, how well have you known me,
I know that you cared, by all the love you've shown me
There were times when things were hidden
Dark thoughts came unbidden
Words said in heat, that couldn't be withdrawn
Time spent in silence, feelings torn.

Happy times too, blessing to cherish
Never doubting that love like ours could perish
If I had to do it all again
I think I'd do the same
Remembering that lovely day, the day I took your name
So, when you look at me, what is it that you see
I'm asking you a question, please answer me.

Ghladys Mills

Questions

I need your touch, I need your smile
I'd like to see you just for a while
You're all alone and I am too
I wish that I could be with you.

Are you in the hall or on the stair?
I wish that I was really there
For a minute or just a second would do
I only want to be with you.

Are you sleeping now or wide awake?
What are you doing for heaven's sake?
I need you, do you understand?
To touch my skin and hold my hand.

Are your days too long and nights so cold?
Do you miss me too? I need to be told.
I'm lying here but it doesn't seem right
Why aren't you there to kiss goodnight?

Now it's time to use my head
You're not in this house or in this bed
Why not? You should be or is it a crime?
To want to be together all of the time.

Helen S. Wadley

"Hidden Talents"

If I couldn't do a job, when I was young,
I'd just sit down, and sigh,
But my mother always said, "Don't say you can't,
Always say, you'll try."

It's surprising, the hidden talents,
You never knew, you had,
Even if your first attempts,
Turned out, quite bad.

I tried oil-painting, when I was fifty-five,
Never thinking, that I could,
But with patience, and lots of practice,
They turned out, quite good.

At sixty-six, I started writing poetry,
A thing, I'd never tried before,
And the poems, I've had published so far,
Have now reached forty-four.

I have lots of other ambitions,
But the time, just seems to fly,
So when I think, I'm too old, to do them now.
I hear my mother say, "Just Try."

Jean Hendrie

Sleep

Where would we be without our precious sleep
if daylight hours spilled over into night
where toil and trouble last for untold hours
and ne'er a brief respite from constant light

Where would we be without our much earned rest
without a pillow to lay our weary head
no dreams to share with loved ones gone before
without our only contact with the dead

How sad we'd be without the song of birds
to wake us from our reverie
without the moon and stars that shine above
to light us through the night so constantly

The world would be so very strange a place
Perpetual noise around we'd want to weep
each day would seem as long as twenty now
no joy for us at all without our sleep

Without sleep the day would have no end
monotony creep in our life as we
try to cope with things for endless hours
life a burden on humanity

Elizabeth D. Tucker

Loneliness

If the stars should leave the heavens,
If the moon ever left the sky,
Or if the sun should cease to shine -
Then, I thought, I'd surely die.

That's how I felt about our love
With you, my dear, that I thought mine.
We'd shared our thoughts, we'd shared our kisses,
You filled my life like heady wine.

But I have only memories now
Since you left me all alone;
Without your presence, without your love,
Our house is empty now, not like a home.

Tears and sadness now fill my heart
As I gaze at your vacant chair;
Living on memories, living in dreams -
Longing to hear your foot on the stair.

My days are sad and lonely now.
You've been gone so long, but I still pray
The love we had is everlasting
And we will meet again some day.

Constance Leigh

Gossip

There's a little bit of gossip that I'd only tell to you,
if you would make this promise, not a soul you'd tell it to.

This gossip is so juicy, you must never state its source,
you must not divulge its origin, even if you're forced.

The only reason I was told, was because I'm so discrete,
you know I can keep a secret, if I'm sworn not to repeat.

So it's discretion when I tell you, now not a word you breath,
otherwise if it got back, my source would then be peeved.

Their trust in me then be lost, if they knew I had disclosed,
such a juicy bit of gossip, and to you I had exposed.

But now I come to think of it, I should let it go no farther.
Maybe now I've said too much, and I'm getting in a lather.

So I'll try hard not to tell you, yes I think this would be best.
Maybe I'll tell you a little bit, then you could guess the rest.

This way I won't be breaking, a confidence that's true,
so please don't mention me at all, if someone asked you to.

Well where's the harm done anyway, to repeat a juicy bit,
someone has to tell someone, or what's the point of it?

So if you would not repeat, this gossip any more,
promise to keep it to yourself, you wouldn't that's for sure . . .

Jean Black

Reflections

Although I'm nearly fifty
I'm feeling young and spree
till I look in the mirror
and shudder is that me?

I don't remember anyone with
wrinkles quite that size
and what are those deep furrows
that are forming 'round my eyes?

The hair is looking greyer
the lips rather thin
That can't be my reflection
That's not the shape I'm in

There's lots of creams and potions
They claim will change your dial
or you could have a face lift
and get a wooden smile

But perhaps it's best to tell yourself
as time goes marching on
No more spots or acne
The look of youth long gone.

Jane Keens

Into the Millennium

What are the changes we shall see
If we live until Two Thousand and Three?
Our currency is threatened, Hong Kong has gone
Vast projects are promised; re-construction done.
An exhibition in London as never before
To be built in Greenwich and, what for?
To commemorate the Millennium having arrived
Giving joy to us all who have survived
The lean years lived in the Century past
Through wars and conflict, tragedies that last.
Seen through the eyes by the likes of me
Such costly celebrations I do not agree
Whilst our meagre pensions remain the same
And the help, much needed, never came
For the service of those who strive to maintain
To give us the welfare we all should again.
Whether we are sixty or only three
Many a life much better could be
By a little more care for all to see
From those chose to rule our Destiny.

John J. Sanders

Falling in Love Again

If you feel like falling in love again
If you feel like being my friend
If you feel like falling in love again
Then we can make it to the end

If you feel you want to make it girl
If you feel you could be true
If you feel like falling in love again
Then we can make it through

Well thank God we've fallen in love, again
And I'm more than just your friend
Yes thank God we've falling in love again
I'll be yours, yours to the end

John Harris

Tomorrow's Too Late

How can you know, when you are so young
If you will still love him, when he's eighty one
That dashing young man, as he walks down the street
His life all before him, the world at his feet
He touches my hand, with a smile on his face
My legs turn to jelly, my heart starts to race

Now he's older and wiser, his hair turned to grey
He sits in his chair, won't move much today
Did he do all the things that he wanted to do
By the look on his face, I think this is true
We've loved and we've laughed, and have friends by the score
What other old couple, could ask for much more

He looks at me now, with a spark in his eye
Yes, I still love you, I silently cry
I'll tell him tomorrow, that he's my best mate
But how could I know, tomorrow's too late
"Where's Granddad", a child excitedly cries
"He's gone to heaven", I say with tears in my eyes

Doreen Hodgson

Moody Blues

When asked, "What colour best describes you?"
I'll always reply, "Moody Blues"
Turquoise for my creative mind
Greyish-blue for a cold behind
Navy for authority and making the right impression
Bright blue to spur me on and letting out aggression
Dolphin blue to make me calm
Royal blue to give me charm
Misty blue when I'm in a dreamy mood
Sky blue captures my thoughtful brood
Deepest, darkest blue for warmth and kindness
Pale and sultry blue for feeling cold and sadness
When asked, "What colour best describes your moods?"
I'll always reply, "Moody Blues"

Anna Lightfoot

Half a World in Darkness

The sunlight, as it streams through the open window
Illuminates you, your face, but only the side that you want me to see
And you voice only the thoughts that you want me to hear,
The remainder left incessantly swirling around in those cold,
  grey eyes.

Emphasizing mental instability came the foolish misuse of words
And the concentrated nature of the river of nonsensical
  abuse that showered me.

There is no deeper well than hatred and when
  it is stirred by anger
It spills over and produces a horrifying fountain
  of caustic substance
Bent only on destruction.
Whether it is borne out of fear, or rejected passion
Nobody ever fully understands.

But they all understand those devious undercurrents of a
  twisted mind
And there are always those of us who can see and fully under-
stand
Your black, evil other side!

Dawn Lynette Evans

A Poem of My Pleasure Dome

My pleasure dome's in Xanadu,
I'm going there today.
I'm going to visit the shallow
waters and caves of ice,
Maybe the ledges of mice.
You may come with me
but wrap up warm.
The waves on the sea
are lashing up the rocks.
Come to my pleasure dome,
Please, but do be careful on the rocks.

Gemma Anne Steele

"A-Counting for Sleep"

I must think of a poem to lull me to sleep;
I'm not getting anywhere counting these sheep.
The poem must calm me, and help to unwind
The grey web of thought in my over-tired mind.
I'll think of the stars in ne'er-ending space,
Of the moon that glides by with a smile on its face
As it winks at the owl in its camouflage tree,
And highlights the waves on the crown of the sea.
I'll think of the warmth of a mid-summer day,
Of sky-diving seagulls, and children at play
With buckets and spades on the sun-bed sands,
And ice-lollies melting down hot, sticky hands
That squeeze-pop the seaweed, and push-pull the dads,
Then point to the cliff-tops, and hang-gliding lads.
Far away, 'neath the haze, are mountains and lakes,
Quaint country cottages, chin-wagging gates,
Old pubs and cricket greens, "'ow's that?" and tea,
Deck chairs and cider . . . but wine, please, for me.
I'm feeling quite drowsy . . . I'm falling asleep . . .
But wait, there's a field; I must just count those sheep!

Joan Sylvia True

Lonely Box

Where do you want me, trapped or free?
I'm not you, open your eyes, I'll never be.
The box I know is by my side,
I'm not getting in, I don't want to hide.

'Myself' will always seep in you know
I can't breathe in there, it won't let me grow,
I am not the one in the box you love so much,
Hidden in the corner there I can't feel your touch.

So let me go to this other place,
I'll still be beside you not merely a trace,
Or maybe you can't understand, you never will,
Just another wasted attempt to explain how I feel.

Camilla Lloyd

Baby's Busy Day

It's been such a funny day today,
I'm not really quite sure what's what,
I've been pushed, pulled and manhandled,
I was wrapped in a towel, and put in a cot.

I've had my private parts inspected,
I had a wee, and caused a flood,
I've been exercised, weighed and measured,
Some man, even stole my blood.

I've been popped into a bath-tub,
I must admit, I was in a state,
It was rather good, to have a stretch,
I've been rather cramped of late.

I had a cuddle with my daddy,
He held my hand, and stroked my feet,
In fact, the only thing I haven't had,
Is anything to eat.

Now I'm snuggled in with my mummy,
My nan's been in, to have a peep,
It's been such a busy day today,
I think, it's time to have a sleep.
Jean Godwin

A Day's Freedom

It's a cold, crisp morning at Sheffield Park
I'm out of my prison to see the beauty of Autumn
There's hardly a cloud in the sky as I'm wheeled around in my chair

I sit beside the lake and look at the beauty across the water
The trees are glowing with red, orange, yellow, brown and green leaves
Reflecting their beauty on the lake.

A few remaining birds begin to sing
To commemorate the peacefulness and rapture that I see
It feels as though I'm the only person around

All too soon the picture cracks
The trees sway gently in the breeze
And I sit and watch the leaves fall silently to the ground

It's a reminder that the colourful beauty of autumn is about to end
To be replaced by the harshness of winter
Which means I'll be in my prison again.

Autumn to Winter
Beauty to Death
Freedom to imprisonment
When can I be truly free again?
Hannah Marie Epps

Moving On

Hello remember me?
I used to be your friend
But then I got sick and couldn't walk
And all of that came to an end.

Just 'cos I'm not perfect
Like you like to think you are
I can still get served a drink
Although I can't walk to the bar.

You think I am embarrassing
Because of my wheelchair
Well it may surprise you all to know
That I don't really care.

I trusted you all
Thought you were good friends
But all you were,
Were fair weather friends.

But when I get better
And rejoin the human race
For you my 'friends'
There will be no place

A Day in the Life of a Beetle

I am a beetle, or so I'm told:
I'm not very big and I'm not very old.
I've six little legs and two little eyes,
And with two little wings I take to the skies.
My antennae are pretty and my coat is a-shine -
My mandibles though tend to creak when I dine.
I've never had feet - and I'm glad that I've not,
For I walk quite a way and they'd ache quite a lot!
My diet is simple. I eat anything,
I don't give a fig for the fare of a king.
I've got to beware though for oft' I have heard
Many a proud beetle's been ate by a bird!
So I will take care and pay great attention;
And with any luck I'll live to draw pension.
So I'll bid you adieu, and when we next meet
I'll be under the carpet - so just watch your feet!
Jan Shah

Now a Quality Life

I hire a business - very small
I'm on "The Merry Go Round"
I work long hours - no fun at all
Expected happiness far from found.

I bought a bike to exercise
My lifestyle far from healthy.
This machine has made me wise.
Much better than being wealthy.

The trees the fields the flowers
The smells, the sounds, the sights
Oh, these blissful hours
bring me such inner delights.
I'm recession weary, and in debt.
No way out for years.
Material things and all I'll get
with insecurity and money fears.

My Soul is starved of all life's treasures.
That's it! I'm selling all my tack.
This lady with green bicycle
is getting her life back!
Estelle Livesey

Home Time

Turning, turning, the lathechuck turning.
In its headstock the gears engaging.
The workpiece spinning, the steel chips flying.
The coolant gushing, the steam goes rising.
Clock watching, seems to be stopping.
One more part turned, the pile is mounting.
On and on through the day not stopping,
Waiting for the time when home is looming.
An eternity passing, factory whistle screaming
Now I'm rejoicing; it's home time.
Christopher John Varley

Broken-Hearted

I want to scream
I want to shout
But I can't let it out
You have numbed me
from head to toe.
You have scarred me where no one knows
You have bruised me so very deep.
I want to climb inside you
Passing your veins.
I want to pull
Your brain's inside out.
You have hurt me so badly
I want to get inside you.
Where I can see
Why do these
Dirty shameful things to me
I am left with
Scarred arms body and mind.
Janet Grundy

Dawn Flight

They come in waves over the land
In the first cold light of the morning.
Like clouds of smoke moving so fast
On silent wings they hurry past.
They weave their way across the sky
Spreading out, some low some high.
Groups descending here and there
Dropping silently out of the air.
Over the hedgerows and trees they skim
Flocks of starlings on the wing.
Watch out for them in the morning.

Bridget Rochard

My Monthly Bloodcount

It's time for my monthly bloodcount,
I'm really not amused,
When Mandy comes a-calling,
I sure do get the blues.

She smiles at me so sweetly,
Her hand behind her back,
My mother holds me tightly,
Cos it's courage that I lack.

I scream, I moan, I fight, I gouge,
I'm jumping up and down,
There's no way that they'll catch me,
I'm running 'round and 'round.

I'm pinned down in a headlock,
My mother's sweating now,
Her face is red, she's panting hard,
We're heading for a row.

At long last it's all over,
Mandy's screwing on the lid,
I'm smiling now at everyone,
"That didn't hurt a bit!"

Ann Hedges

When My Ship Comes In

If I had a windfall, if my ship came in,
I'd linger where wrinkles are smoothed from your chin.
I'd be pushed into shape, and be ever-so-thin
If I had a windfall, if my ship came in.

O - I'd stretch in the sun with a sparkle of wine and
On strawberries, peaches, and caviare dine;
But it's all just a daydream, I do declare,
And worth not a jot, with no one to share.

I'd swap all the gold in the Krugers' rand for
The postman's ring - a note in his hand, with
The promise of riches (fashioned above) - my ship
Has come in, its hold bursting love.

Yet, I'd settle for pirates and winds howling gale,
And wrinkles a-plenty on cheeks growing frail, if
My ship would unburden one kiss on the quay
Treasure enough to un - die, me.

Jean Semple

Never

I never had a garden
In which to sear my palms
On spades and forks of wooden hue
And strengthen up my arms.

I never smelt the earth,
So fresh and dark and wet,
With worms and weeds and shallot sets,
I've never met them yet.

I live my life in bedsit land
I buy my food, eat mouth to hand.
My only hope in life, you see,
Is meeting my mother on bended knee.

James P. O'Brien

Under Your Influence

I'm the flowers which you press,
I'm the model that you dress.
No opinions of my own,
My whole brain is what you own.

I'm powerless,
I'm under your influence.

I'm the stamps which you collect,
I'm the slip on which you bet.
Not allowed to see my friends,
You're my start, you'll be my end.

I'm powerless,
I'm under your influence.

Don't bother asking why with her I stay
I debate it with myself each day.
And although she wears me like a glove,
I stay because she's who I love.

I'm powerless,
She's got me under her influence.

George Stanworth

Untitled

Can you stop me, the blasted clock?
It bedevils me with its not, not stopping,
The infinite rock of its cogs, the tick and the tock,
The breaking of silence with hammer and block,
The never to end and never to stop,
Clock. Clock. Clock. Clock...............

Will it end if I muffle it, suffocate, stifle it?
And then if I hide it away, will it cease to beat
Out the seconds and minutes and hours,
The days in between, ones best forgotten,
Those we ignore as irrelevant spots on
An otherwise clear and sparkling record,
Save for the tick and the tock and the knocking.
From under the stairs where I've now locked my clock in.

Christopher Newman

The Bubbles

You can see the bubble is like the rainbow colour shining in the air.
It can see people like they're looking in the mirror.
You can see a bubble is like the shape of the world.
You can see shadows in the bubbles.
You can see a bubble is like a glass ball.
You can see bubbles flying like a bird.
The bubble is small like a fish in a pond.
You can see a bubble is like a stream.
You see a bubble going on the grass and sometimes off again.
The bubble is going zig zag it jumps up and down.
Then it popped.
I felt I was sad.

Gary Stevens

My Sister-in-Law Joan

My sister-in-law's life has really changed,
In fact completely rearranged,
All because she had a fall,
Which then quite quickly changed it all.

She used to be able to walk and run,
Swim and dance and have some fun,
Jogged for miles was much much thinner,
Now its crawling with a zimmer.

To see her sat there in a chair,
Paler face, thinner hair,
Putting on fat where used to be muscle,
Fighting off sleep, life's one big tussle.

In the future there could be many more trials,
On the treadmill of life that goes on for miles,
Meanwhile she's learning how to cope,
Because while there's life, there's always hope.

John J. Yeates

Faces in the Fire

When I sit by the fire on a winter's day
I'm transported to so many places,
As I stare into the flickering flames
I'm greeted by hundreds of faces,
There's family and friends and people I've known
And some from the history book's pages,
Then there are faces to whom I can't put a name
And rock stars who've come through the ages,
I can see Elvis with his lop-sided smile
And there's Uncle Dick from years ago,
I'm sure that one looks like Hitler
And that's Auntie Nan with starched collar and bow,
Now the coals have moved and the faces have changed
There's a man in a three cornered hat,
And Sir Winston Churchill with a big cigar
And that one there looks just like our cat,
There's Dr. Kildare from the sixties T.V.
And Cliff Richard who's still loved today,
So with imagination and a bucket of a coal
I can dream the winter away.

Carol Francis

Evil

Green leaves fall gently to the ground,
In a far off place, few people have found.

When sun is high, all is fair,
With beauty beyond belief, and animals unaware.

For when darkness falls the animals hide,
From a looming creature with eyes open wide.

The screams are heard across the land,
From tortured corpses beneath the sand.

Slowly they rise towards their Master,
With skin falling away like old, grey plaster.

The flesh is torn, the blood is spilt,
And all life around them begins to wilt.

Mothers cry as their young are taken,
No lives or souls are ever forsaken.

When darkness leaves and the sun is near,
The creature looms away to disappear.

Green leaves fall gently to the ground,
In a far off place that evil is bound.

When sun is high, all is fair,
With beauty beyond belief, within evil's snare.

Amanda Quinn

Red Rum

If any horse knows this race so well
It has to be you, you seldom fell,
You took to the flights so brave and strong
Like a Christmas Robin singing his song.

Ears pricked forward, legs tucked in
You could hear the crowd "He's gonna win",
You're over bleachers, and you've cleared the chair
My heart's pounding, I'm riding you there.

You know you're winning, the race is yours
This is your stage, you can hear the applause
You're passing the line, oh boy what fun
He's done it again "three times Red Rum."

Still when you retired your work never stopped,
You helped many charities, even opened up shops
But once a year the "the old gent" played his part
He led the "National" runners down to the start.

Of forty runners you were the eldest there
But you never lost it, you still had your flair
The kiddies loved you, you were gentle and kind
It's the first "National" without you, "Rumms" on everyone's mind.

Adele Tracy Adams

In Time

God lives in a beautiful garden
In heaven up above,
He tends each tiny flower
With care and lots of love
When He thinks they're ready
He will pluck one just for you,
For He knows that you will care for it
The way He used to do.
He gave you the prettiest rose bud
But made a grave mistake,
This little flower was not ready
For a life on earth to make
So He took it back to heaven
To give His special care
He will tend it, till it blossoms
Then it's yours to share.

Julie Rakes

The Life Force

I am cold, my power on "hold," my heart
In hibernation
No robin's song, no living sound,
Strikes through this bleak sensation

I can dance, and take a chance
I face strife, I fight for life
And I will find, find the balance.

Look now! I am a friend a neighbour.
Offering a helping hand
Don't ignore me. I cannot linger.
    I have no time to stand

I am warm, my strength is free, if you
Wish to take my gift
Make your spirit rise and shift
    I am eternal

If you wish to live forever
Follow me upon my course,
I can never let you down.
Know me! Trust me. I am
    The life force

Jean Noble

'I Will Survive'

From a desert you picked a rose and held it
in your hand
who thought a rose would grow on that baron land
it opened its petals for you to look inside
but you dashed that rose away your feelings
to hide
now that dying rose lies on that baron land
covered by the ever sifting sand
but that rose revived in the early mourn
warmed by sun rays of the early dawn
awakened by the moisture from the dew
to spread its petals to a day so new
so think before you pick a rose its thorns so sharp
remember that flower also had a heart

Carole Taylor

Frosted Lace

I drew back the curtains and gasped with delight,
Jack Frost had been working all through the night,
The garden transformed into a white fairy dell,
That glistened and sparkled where pale sunbeams fell.

Draped lacy cobwebs adorned fences and trees,
Where a puff of white frosting twinkled down in the breeze,
A feathery eiderdown covered the lawn,
Where plump pillows of fern leaves and grasses were born.

What a magical sight to greet a new day,
But the wonderful artist had tip-toed away.

Cynthia Fenwick

I'll Maybe Listen One Day, but Not Today!

I glance at Chaz just sitting there
in his great, steel electric chair
his hands grasped firm around the belt
his eyes so cold his heart will melt
He dies for us, the human race
this sick, disease infested place

They've shaved his legs, his neck and arms
they've rid him of his good luck charms
The hour beckons ever nearer
the dull future coming ever clearer
The crowd is poised within his mind
the four strong audience is not so kind

The minutes tick by and the two wardens cheer
I grip Audrey's hand as she resists a tear,
'We must be brave for him', Amnesty shouts out loud
for Chaz we are strong and we'll be ever proud
The Switch is turned on, his body a light
I grab his hand quickly and join him tonight.

Amy Bruce

My Soldier's Dream

I was only a soldier lover,
In search of a girlfriend it seemed,
Hoping someday I will be
Far, Far away,
With the girl of my soldier dream,
For some girls are quickly forgotten,
Gone with the dawn of a day,
Some you remember, like love's
Glowing embers,
Haunting your memories and dreams,
For I was only a soldier lover,
Who could be found at last,
with the sweetheart,
of my soldier dreams.

Fred Turner

"Thoughts of Peace"

Peace at last, for evermore,
In this world, so torn in war,
So many died, for us to live,
Our thoughts, so freely we should give,
Honour our dead, and those who fought,
To love one another, should surely be taught,
Making this world a better place,
Giving our all, with loving grace,
Children should be taught at an early age,
There is no gain in exerting rage,
To heed their parents' every word,
Their wildness, they must learn to curb,
To care for human life they must,
And prove to be forever just.

Elsie Joyce Cranfield

Twilight Flight

Freebird up soaring high
In the pale blue, murky sky
It is the twilight of the night
But you are still in full flight.

You pass by me without saying "Hello"
As the wind starts to blow
The trees have started dancing
And you carried on, not even glancing.

Wishing I could come with you
Overseas to pastures new
But when I get out of bed
I'll have to go to work instead.

This really is not for me
How I long to be so free
From the dull mundane routine
Like the Freebird I've just seen

Derek John Price

Doyle and I

One day in childhood's idleness
In hours devoid of play and chore
I to Doyle a plan did press
Agree, did he, under duress
The old house to explore

They say she's haunted Doyle told me
As through her rotten door we pushed
Cursed for sure we're bound to be
And go to hell as well said he
As both our faces flushed

The sun was beaming shafts of light
Down through her roof of absent slates
Dancing shadows caught our sight
Imaginations fuelled with fright
Oh! no 'tis ghosts Doyle states

Then from the dark old house we fled
Our courage now in short supply
Harmless shadows being our dread
Upon our innocence they fed
We n'er again did go there, Doyle and I.

Bernard O'Keeffe

The Sparrow

His shabby coat with colours scant portrays this poor communicant
In nature's church of open sky where all the wing-ed creatures fly
Not for him the priestly white of doves and seabirds high in flight
who dive at angles so acute and dip their wingtips in salute

He doesn't crave the deacon red of robins who are often fed
With morsels from some human hand when winter's grip
  engulfs the land
Nor does he to a place aspire among the thrushes in the choir
Or envy birds with plumage grand that visit from some foreign land

For his part this little chap likes nothing better than a scrap
All through his life his bread and butter has been a punch-up
  in the gutter
His peers with greater intellect often die from sheer neglect
On frozen pond, or branch, or fence they seem to lack good
  common sense

When winter winds chill to the marrow you'll seldom see the
  little sparrow
He hides himself away from view in nature's church beneath a pew
He is no dunce, no fool, no skiver but he is nature's great survivor

Ian Sinclair

The Colours of Pain

Pain - it builds up a wall, excluding the rest of the world;
It makes a cocoon of isolation wherein the only thing existing
is the demanding greed of its own viciousness -
and its own frenzied colours.

Great, jagged fangs of crimson and purple tear into the top of the
skull; Sharp, white needles dart out to the centre of the ear
and shoot along to the nerve ends.
A dull, brown bolt thuds up the back of the neck,
trying to crush out the tortured, searing colours already in
possession.

Then, through the mists of pain - a gentle touch, a loving query of
concern; an unexpected bouquet of glorious flowers with a tender,
caring message; a softly-spoken prayer of comfort.

Suddenly, a ray of golden light pierces through the pain
bringing in its wake the clear, translucent blue of tranquillity.

The crimson teeth are still lurking there,
snarling on the periphery - waiting to pounce again,
but - just for a moment, they have been overcome
by the pure, untarnished gold of love.

Jean G. Bowler

Empty Arms

I would that my empty arms could hold
  in peace my babe once more,
As they used to in encircling fold
  as they protected for,
All the goodly years when in his prime
  with innocence not dim,
In perfect trust as his smiles all mime
  my purest look on him.

Now my empty arms yield nought but air
  as he has grown and gone,
When cloaked in manhood with stance fair
  as he then did but don,
The mask of maturity with face
  all angular that grew,
To eclipse his dear babe form in space
  as far away he flew.

Aileen Hopkins

The Pen Is Often Heavier Than the Sword

To be a writer of prose or verse,
In thoughts and words you must immerse,
Mostly a struggle and always a fight,
To create the lines you feel are right,
Then strangely without much thought,
An avalanche of words in your mind consort,
Work completed, though not the end,
If it sits in a tray marked pend,
The Editor and Publisher you must please,
Before your work the public sees,
And only then if they are sure,
Lots of sales they can secure,
There's not much future for themselves,
In publishing books just to sit on shelves.

James Douglas

Goodnight

Sleep the sleep of mortals
In the slumberland of dreams
And open up the portals
To the land of kings and queens
Listen to the fairies laugh
And hear the hare-bells peal
Walk the soft and rambling path
Between the golden fields
Dream of what you want to be
And where you want to go
Of the beautiful green valley
And of mountains capped with snow
And when your wandering wondering soul
From slumber must return
And leave the wooded watering hole
As dawn's faint light doth burn
Come gently back with love in mind
For all your kith and kin
With care enough for all mankind
And harmony within.

David Loring

The Strawberry Grower

My father was picking strawberries on the day that I was born,
In the field he heard the news on that beautiful June morn.
There are four decades now his seasons have spanned,
And millions of those rubies have been picked by hand.
For me, his passion I can understand,
His love of this fruit, his love of the land,
For of all the berries the strawberry is queen,
This luscious red heart is an epicure's dream,
Perfected, selected, handled with care,
Even royalty have sampled his fare,
So that's why he's always amidst the rows,
Nurturing this plant all his life he will grow,
The only plant which requires a cushion of straw,
To protect its soft fruit from the ground floor,
This cousin of the rose with not a thorn in sight,
Just dainty white blossom, red pearls of delight.

June M. Marie

Mirror of Me

Gaze into my river, reflections of my image into your eyes,
Inquisitiveness appears in the mist, feel, vision my love inside.
I hear inside, the pain, and sometimes my heart does wrench
I cannot contain the ocean, swirling, crashing in my bodily frame.

I dreamed I would sail the ocean with you, we could explore
  our secrets,
You could give me life, give me strength.
I was your pretty bride, a white petal, a flower child,
The air so fresh and free, we danced with the moon until dawn.

My woman came alive in me, understood things I cannot believe,
She was your saviour, your company.
As day breaks I feel withered, my innocence returns,
The woman skips into the distance, I am here again.

Love so painful without love, you care only for the woman,
She has gone away, and I lie behind.
Gaze into my mirror, is she near?
Look again, and it will become clear . . .

Julie Flatman

Untitled

Bitterness? I have none
Just fear, as the crowds stand and jeer
Awaiting my scream, as I suspend
And reach alone my bitter end
Without a kiss, without a friend.

Condemned to death with no fair trial
With empty heart I wait awhile
Only a few short minutes
To remember, to smile.

I face the end with fear and pain
Until the world finds peace again
Life for life? but who can say?
I never killed, yet hang today.

Carolyn Smith

The Owl's Hunt

Softly hoots the owl, in the stillness of the night.
It glides through the moonlit sky watching, waiting
A vole is heard, there's no escape
The owl swoops, snaps, and catches.
It lands on a stump nearby,
The vole exists no more.
Silently, the flight of the bird can be heard.
The silent trickle of water can be heard in the distance.
Hoots of satisfaction can be heard,
Yet the owl wants more.
It glides waiting for the smallest squeak
But the voles are aware,
Danger! The owl gently glides away,
To hunt again another day.

Emma Bulmer

Comrades

Where has the time gone,
  In the midst of war?
Living, breathing, holding hands
  and loving more and more.

Now I lie in some French field,
  breezes blow above me.
Long forgotten dreams and sighs,
  held on the breath of time;
Shimmer golden fleeting,
  and yet remaining mine.

I am dead and yet alive - my spirit
  soars in space,
I'm here and there and everywhere,
  but you cannot see my face.

Death is only one life, ending for another
  I fought and died for love and principles,
    my sister and my brother.

Eileen Longley

61

Space Is Lonely

What would this world be like
    If there were no colours?
No yellow sunlight through the window pane,
No blue waves breaking underneath green palms,
Nor scarlet sports cars in the outside lane,
Or crisp white cuffs on summer sun-kissed arms.

How would we feel alive,
    If there were no time?
No hour to wake, and no set time to eat,
To stop, to fling the curtains wide apart
And slip the shoes onto our morning feet,
No long night hours before the bright dawn start.

If all the world were grey
    And had no shape,
And all the people moved like fleeting wraiths
With no home place, no family, no friends,
No inner glory, and no warring faiths
There could be no beginning and no end.

Space is a lonely place.
Elaine Dollery

Grief for Dunblane

Like tender young plants
In the warm spring sunshine
A promise of pretty petals
And fine green leaves

They could have been yours
They could have been mine . . .
Destroyed in the bud
And the whole nation grieves

My daughters are grown
They are well, they're alive
But my mind hurtles back
To when they were five

Same school photograph we all own
Same sweet faces in a line
Oh yes . . . they could have been yours
Dear God . . . they could have been mine

Inconsolable grief
Unbearable pain
We share these with you
Dunblane
Iris Ramkissoon

Saturday 2nd September 1939

Walking slowly, side by side
In warmest sunlight, looking down
At our three shadows; hand in hand
We made our way into the town.

Our errand was a weekly chore,
Early on each Saturday
To bring fresh yeast, and maybe more
For mother's weekly baking day

In azure sky the blazing sun
Was tempered by a cooling breeze;
Filled with a wave of sheer delight
We laughed and chattered, at our ease.

Relishing all this simple joy
We were untroubled, unaware
That one more day would change the world
And fill our lives with pain and care.

Before us, death and partings lay,
A world in chaos, torn asunder
But on that last, sweet, carefree day
We laughed and sang in childish wonder.

Betty Ellerton

Dark Days

Calm and collected on the outside.
Inner thoughts are dark and negative.
A feeling that comes and goes. How can I tell them?
Am I the only one that feels like this?
Is it a state of mind?
What is happiness? What is the right understanding?
Travel to a foreign land. Is that the answer?
No, not again! Questioning life and my part in it.
The right answer to it all, is that there is no right answer.
A blue sky and sunshine. Oh, yes please!
But most of the days seem long and grey,
When carrying around such a heavy heart as this.
The effort seems so great at times.
My path is to be a rocky one.
I wish they knew what was going on underneath.
Jeffrey S. Elsmore

Night

The owl swoops, the hedgehog creeps, under blanket of black.
Inside, small creak awakens daytime's sleeping fears,
Of lonely eve endurer.
It holds the vacuum of absent human comfort,
Or echoes of that comfort lost.
Its silence inducing longing for daytime shape and sounds.

Where lights challenge night's emptiness of form,
Many gather: piercing silence with sound,
Youth shouts loudly as though defying death.
March on stage a differing morality:
The addict and pusher loiter,
The lady lingers for brief verbal encounter,
The thief steals quietly.

Mostly, we live a semi-death,
Through its stages past dusk to dawn.
Mostly, our minds banish on waking,
Disturbing plays with familiar players.
Mostly we accept it in winter with sullen resignation,
Glory in its summer curtailment,
Seldom acknowledging fear, knowing its inevitability, like the
    long sleep.
Janet R. Smith

On Waking and Waiting

She wakes, will he call today?
Is he happy or is he hurting in some way,
Going downstairs she makes her drink,
It's 6 a.m. her own time to think,
Of what went wrong - why and how,
The lines of worry furrow her brow.

She gave him everything and more,
Including the key to open the door,
Others now appear to be his priority,
She prays every day that he will come to see,
The words used in anger were not spoken from her heart,
Just a cry for help before they drifted apart.
Desnee Kolakovic

Night-Time Fears

When night-time comes, stars appear,
it seems so lonely, lots to fear.
A light so bright shines down the lane,
the big bright moon looks just the same.
And owl hoots a merry song,
a badger quickly strides along.
A sad old fox romps slowly by,
a hedgehog looks him in the eye.
A moth flies swiftly 'round a light,
a rabbit skips with pure delight.
A bat glides 'round with grace and style,
autumn leaves lay in a pile.
Flowers sleeping in the ground,
the countryside makes no sound.
When daybreak comes the sun appears,
no more lonely night-time fears.
Babs West

Teddy Bear Auction

Long gone the day you were stored away
In that dark, dark cupboard,
And, amazingly now said, worth five thousand or more.
Think of that in my hand! Five thousand grand!
There was money galore behind that cupboard door
When you were rediscovered.

With eyes as bright as in early light
Of your first Christmas day,
You're looking tip-top; straight out of the shop
Can't think you've been so long hid away!
You'll be worth a fortune down at the auction,
If, bear bidding's as bullish as they say.

Long after I'm gone you'll be still soldiering on
And, like old soldiers just fade away!
In future, I wonder to whom you'll belong,
When worth twice today's price, I dare say.
Meanwhile, my course is clear, Teddy, old dear,
I just can't keep the temptation at bay

I'll say no more! I'll just take your paw!
And we're off to the Teddy Bear auction!

Harry Hays

My Own Dream

When I'm sat on my own
It may be at work, or at home.
Things start to appear in my mind,
How this world is so unkind.
I wander into a world of my dreams,
Everything is perfect, so it seems.
Joy and happiness is all I hear,
And no-one is living in total fear.
No-one's crying, no-one's sad,
And for this dream, I'm very glad.
Is the world just pain and sorrow,
Good things could come, but be gone tomorrow.
Life alone is the greatest thing,
That any one on this earth could bring.
But happiness is everywhere,
And there are people who still care.
So when you're feeling very sad,
Sit and think this world's not bad.
Make your own dream in your mind,
It will make you happier you will find.

Jayne Prime

Amazing Life

The sun comes up and it goes down and life's full cycle
unfolds around,
It truly is a wondrous sight the fields the trees and
meandering streams,
Enriched with colour, smells and sound the birds and insects
sing all around,
All trying so hard to survive against such overwhelming odds,
Pollution, buildings, and the like and even humans back to
their bike,
Amazing world, you won't last long unless one curbs
incessant greed,
and turns back the clock on this sad deed.
If hope there is, it seems to be that man wakes up and tries to see,
before too late, the legacy.
The search goes on for other worlds and beings to if such exist,
to help the puzzle to unravel of life itself, it means much travel.
What is it really all about! I want to know so spell it out!
Alas, I hear no firm reply, and Adam and Eve could be a lie,
The explanation seems to be, all an accident to some degree.
Despite the struggles, wars and strife the gift of life having
been bestowed moves on to new adventure, whilst always
lurking close at hand is mankind's self-destructive nature.
If there is one thing learned above all others it is to try to help
each other,
And if a role model is needed here, then think of mother and shed
a tear,
The one that always gave it all and asked for nothing for this role.
And one can only stand in awe, the sheer wondrous nature of it all!

Barry Robinson

Regrets

The pain in my heart will not go away, the pain in my heart
is here to stay.
The love that I felt for such a long time, forever I thought
that you'd be mine.
You came along so caring and kind, you took my heart and all
my mind.
Now you are just a memory, all the love that you gave to me.
But my darling you'll always be here, if you're miles away
you'll always seem near.
I really wish I could change the past, maybe then our love would
last.
Please come back to be with me, I love you still can't you see?
Give me a chance if you can, you're simply the best such a
lovable man.
My heart bleeds when you're away, the tears drain each and
every day.
I miss you so much do you not see, me and you were just meant
to be.

Helena Cooper

The Immaculate Deception

Where does the time go,
Isn't life unfair?
Every moment has its moment,
Then before you even know it,
It all seems to vanish in mid-air.

Where does the time go,
Was I really here?
Did I accomplish what I came for,
Take my bows at every encore,
Was my exit full of grace and flair;
Will anyone remember me, or care?

To talk of immortality, such vanity is man.
The question still arises why I am.
To reason is futility, it isn't worth a damn.
Always winding up where you began.

Was it all a dream?
Sublime to the extreme?
Will I awake to find that it was all illusion?
Have I been riding on a carousel?
That only stops to bid farewell.

Donny Marchand

The Fair

The fair has come upon the green, with music and with lights
It hasn't changed since we were kids, I'm still afraid of heights

The bumper cars, the whirling thing with lights that seem to flash
It doesn't even to come to mind that these will ever crash

The candy floss the hot dog stand with toffee apples too
The prizes that you sometimes get are small and very few

The faces on the people who have really enjoyed themselves
Go home with prizes held in their hands to put upon the shelves

And when the noise and bustle, are over for the night
We count the money left in the purse - we've enjoyed ourselves
alright

Joyce Avis

Water-Disaster

The Sea Empress, O what a mess
Is all she left behind,
It's a terrible kind of tragedy
That could ruin all mankind.

Where would we be, without the sea
And all its creatures too,
Those poor fish, those oil-soaked birds
Although they suffer, they can't be heard.

Those golden sandy beaches
That we visited with pride,
The tourists will not bother now
They will ebb, just like the tide.

Dawn Marie Davies

A Crying Shame

Man, the most intelligent of earth's creatures
Is it any wonder the animals aren't tame?
They kill for food,
Man kills for game.
What a crying shame!

A woman cries out giving birth with pain.
A time to rejoice give the child a name,
But pain remains
The baby's lame.
What a crying shame!

In this age of so called peace, fear of rape, mugging, murder.
War that's over stepped the border.
People weeping, dead and maimed,
In man's lust for power and fame.
What a crying shame!

Too late to find solutions, to man's imperfections.
The conclusion having halted the quest for gain.
All that could be said,
When Armageddon came.
What a crying shame!

Donna Lesley Edinboro

"Moonlit Night"

During the war on a moonlit night
It is disaster when they start to fight
The bombs they light up all the sky
The young ones sit and wonder "Why?"

People are running here and there
Some are screaming some just stare
They just can't believe what's going on
They think to themselves something's wrong.

Bodies are lying everywhere
What a sight it is to bear
Some are wounded some are dead
The floor is like a crimson red.

The fight is over the noise dies down
People are looking about with a frown
Helping the wounded covering the dead
There is no need for this, some said.

Audrey Brown

Winter Time

Winter has come,
It is getting cold,
Put your hats and scarves on the
    children we're told.

Cars are skidding across the roads,
People are wearing their warmest clothes.

Icicles hanging off roof tops,
Everyone's feet feel like lollipops.

Winter is cold

Georgina Busby

The Dwelling Place

A stirring, a memory, a hope, a desire,
Just a whisper that echoes,
Then louder and louder.

A sadness that won't leave me,
That taints me,
That haunts me.

A last chance that escaped me,
Not aware that it was,
It tricked me, It conned me
Now I know what I lost.

This emptiness stays with me,
Clings to me, spreads through me.
This is a grief,
That has found its dwelling place.

Claire Hall

What People May Say!

We go through our life, searching for love, for
Joy and for peace.
It's a gift if you find it, but seldom the case,
When all that you get is disgraced.
All of us guilty, sometime in our life, of having
Something to say.
Of people around us, you don't really know, of what
they've been doing that day.
However wrong, or right someone is, or however
they look in the flesh.
Can be looked at, knocked down, and misjudged
every time!
Because they are frightened, of what people may say.
It is wrong to be judged! so live and let live!
We are all guilty, of being two-faced!

Alice Bird

Sursum Corda

From all eternity, my Lord,
    Joyous and glorious, needing none,
Rejoicing in a boundless love
    'Twixt Father, Spirit, Son,
Deigned to extend this mutual bond
    Of souls to soul's unending bliss;
Designed the universe - time and space -
    And planted me in this.

Thus, weak and foolish though I be,
    And worthless as I oft-times seem,
I am God's everlasting choice,
    Precious beyond my wildest dream;
And when life's burden crushes most
    And bleak Despair's face I see,
I raise my heart in glad surprise.
    My gracious God - made Me.

Alice Bushell

Know Yourself

To know your future,
is to learn about your past,
think then act, don't be the last,
don't give anything away too fast.

Be independent, be free,
Know yourself, and what you want to be,

Be happy, be true,
Show yourself, and what you want to do.

Be glad, not sad,
Glow with all this light, and grow in body and mind,

Be strong, beyond, caring and sharing,
Know yourself and your soul can be free.

Christina Christoforou

The Happy Daisy

A daisy in the garden grew,
It was a weed - what's more it *knew*
The roses lifted perfumed heads,
How grand they were - real flowers in beds!
The daisy felt despondent quite,
It was so small, so plain, so white . . .
A little girl came dancing by
And saw its tear-filled yellow eye,
"Don't touch the flowers, dear,"
She'd been warned,
The lovely roses she just scorned,
She looked upon them with disdain,
"These flowers won't do to start a chain,
The thorns would make my fingers bleed,
This daisy here is what I need"
And then the daisy did not mind
Though other flowers had been unkind
It knew it had a job to do
A weed maybe, but needed, too.

Elma Haughie

The Murder of Innocence

The number thirteen is unlucky for some,
It was March 13th when the whole world went numb,
There's a small town in Scotland that will never be the same,
For one horrific massacre shocked this place called Dunblane,
This was an act of evil by a man who took so many lives,
He just walked into a primary school and killed sixteen
   children aged five,
He also killed their teacher and injured many others,
This town that was once so quiet was now filled with the cries
   of their mothers,
It upsets me to think how frightened they must have been,
Such innocent little children, the things they must have seen,
As for the man who murdered, no justice can ever come,
for after taking the lives of others he also took his own,
If only he was still alive to be tortured with his shame,
But he has taken the easy way out while others feel the pain,
I feel for the families that grieve and I've shed tears too,
So has the rest of Scotland and England, but what are we to do,
WHY! Do we have such violence?
WHEN will it ever cease? But to all those children and their teacher,
may their souls all rest in peace.

Gill Sloanes

Chrysanthemums

An obvious choice for aunts and mums
Is that why Christ said
"Adam call them Chrysanthemums"
In Dad's garden standing upright like soldiers
Funny how I remember them

The greenhouse at the allotment
Uncle Bill, stools and cuttings
The majesty of the bloom
The strength of the perfume

Has each chrysant got a mate
Does it ever get lonely
Or is it as self-reliant as it looks
In a world that looks at the occasion
Then the flower books!

For me I would have them with me
at my parting
It would be nice to be remembered for something
Why not a hundred assorted chrysanthemums
Better to go out with a florist
Than to be oh so glum, chum!

Colin Johnson

My House

A few weeks ago I went down a street
It was where my old house had stood replete
It was now shuttered up and stood all forlorn
But it was still the house where I was born

My thoughts strayed back where as a boy
I played with friends and with their toys
The house looked sad and love was needed
The path and garden was not weeded

I walked away saddened with what I had seen
And wondered whether it was all a bad dream
Even the "for sale" board had fallen down
Perhaps nobody wanted this side of town?

A week ago I went back down this street
Imagine my joy when I found the house neat
The paintwork was gleaming, the garden was done
There were children playing and having fun

I saw there was love in the house once again
And imagined it was me playing in the garden the same
When I as boy with my family around
Had spent many happy days on this familiar ground

Don Walker

Loneliness

Loneliness is a hurtful thing
it takes your body from limb to limb
the pain inside is hard to bear,
No one to share your deepest thought
and no one who really cares
life is a b*tch and unfair
No one can compare the loneliness inside
in which you have to hide,
So no one can pry.
The deepest thought of pain and fear
the loneliness in your heart
that one day shall be pulled apart
Shall anybody know my deepest thought
and my plight for love.
And shall anybody find the loneliness inside

Helen Fletcher

Victory

What is Victory?
Is it when men, women and children die?
What is victory?
Is it when people break down on their knees and cry?
What is victory?
Is what I said a lie?

What is victory?
Is it worth the hurt, the pain?
What is victory?
Is it when death cannot be washed away by rain?
What is victory?
Surely it shouldn't bring fame?

What is victory?
Is it death now and again?
What is victory?
Is it the regret of too many men?
What is victory?
Will it happen again?
....
I hope not.

Carina Taylor

Am I So Different?

Am I so different? Why do you treat me this way?
It doesn't matter what I do, it doesn't matter
What I say. But every time I see you, you try to
Start a fight, just because my skin is black and
Your skin is light. Whenever you look at me,
I see hatred in your eyes, but I just have to grin,
And bear it; put on a phoney smile. Why are you
Treating me this way? Do you like causing me pain?
Our appearance may be different, but inside,
We're both the same.
I've drawn the final straw. I can't take this
Any more. Am I so different? You seem to think so,
But, the next time I ask myself this, my
Answer will be 'no'.

Claire Saddler

Just Rocking

I stand here day and night,
Just rocking,
You sit on me when you like but I'm,
Just rocking,
I have no fun as I stand here,
Just rocking,
I am a horse with rocking feet and I stand here,
Just rocking,
20 years on and I'm still here,
Just rocking,
The children have gone but you kept me here,
Just rocking,
In 50 years time I will be somewhere on display,
Not even rocking not allowed to play.

Emma Roper, aged 10

The World

The world is not my oyster
It's just as bad as can be
I thought I was living in a cloister
So I knew I had to be free.

I now have my independence
Although, I'm older now you see
But life is so stupendous
I'm free at last to be me.

They say life begins at forty
But I must disagree
It now has a whole new meaning
And I'll soon be sixty three.

So I now see the world through different eyes
No more being bullied and no more lies
I now think my life is a gift to me
And I'm as happy as can be.

Edith Sweeney

A Cold and Lonely Moment

A cold and lonely moment,
it clutches and grasps,
with poisoned talons.
A frigid touch that opens old wounds,
draws out buried memories,
and renews old fears.

I cannot find peace of mind,
without that which I seek,
or, indeed, the heart,
with which to seek.

I seem to be ever alone,
tho' I have friends,
and family,
yet through it all,
I remember,
all that I seek,
is . . . love . . . hope . . . happiness,
none of which do I posses,
or ever shall?

Ian Leach

The Race for Life

A small rabbit scurries through the forest,
Its fate lies only in his own speed.
One second slower and his bobtail will be no more.
He turns around but the threat to his life still follows,
Further into the forest children innocently play.
Oblivious to any wrongful goings-on.
Suddenly, a loud bang takes over the forest.
The children immediately cease playing and rush to see what's
going on.
The rabbits lifeless body lies in the grass.
With one bang of the gun his life promptly ended.

Emma Haywood

Goodbye

It breaks my heart to see you go
It's hard to say goodbye
Being apart from you my love
Makes me want to cry
Together we have been for all this time
And now we have to part
But no matter where you go my love
You shall always live in my heart
The moon will shine my love on you
While the stars look down and smile
The soft breeze will carry my kisses to you
Across the many miles
My tears for you will fall
In every drop of rain
I pray to God to protect you my love
Until we meet again

Fiona Gomes

An Adult Perspective

There is no life in my house,
it left unnoticed.

Hollow impressions stand where flesh and bone,
tears and laughter, once weaved their enchanting
spell on me.

Dimly lit figures sit in the glow of television realism,
the light in their eyes is borrowed, they look tired,
weary so very weary.
I never noticed,

I long for the past, a time filled with joy,
hope and warmth, but it left unnoticed.

Yearning I throw out my arms to embrace them,
show them what I know, what I have seen, but
they have seen too much to see anything other than
the way they think it already is.

I am powerless to help them,
and at a loss to leave them.
I am guilty of caring too much
and doing too little.
I grew up, I never noticed.

Jenny Read

Eternal Love

The hardest thing in mortal life
Is to lose someone you love
The question that is often posed
Is there a God above?

Why did He take a kindly soul
Someone so precious and so kind
And leave those who are evil
Undisturbed and left behind

But God doesn't want the impure in heart
To mar His precious land
It's those just like your loved ones
Can you begin to understand

Each day we know is hard to bear
You say, "Will I get through".
But remember this when you are low
They'll be right there with you

So make everyday a challenge
For although you cannot see
I am right there beside you
It's still just you and me.

Jean Little

Father of the Bride

I was the first one to see her splattered in blood,
It was then I realized I'd fallen in love.

I was the first one to smell her and touch her as well,
Just think I'd given birth to a girl!

Many years later still on cloud nine,
I was still bragging about that daughter of mine,

At thirteen she left me for three weeks — what a fright,
I don't mind admitting I cried that night.

She went to America all alone,
When she came back into a woman she'd grown.

From that day on I was a jealous dad,
She was now out, looking for a lad.

On his first visit I'd tell him a thing or two,
When I opened the door — good God he's 6' 2".

But today with pride I walked her to the alter,
And was very honoured to hand that lad my daughter.

I won't stop loving her till the day that I die,
If that lad does the same that will please Mum and I.

All that's left now is to kiss her good-bye,
No don't be stupid there's no tear in my eye.

Jack Youngman

The Nightmare Monster

The thundering beat of the nightmare monster,
it sprints towards me.
With an eerie face as pale as the moon,
its echoing wail repeats, "Too late, too late."
The devil's silhouette haunts my pathway,
and as I run to safely,
I scream and cry, but nobody hears me,
I am all alone with the nightmare monster.
It's coming closer, hands outstretched,
as its mighty claws tap on my shoulder.
When I turn to face it,
Cruel death snatches me.
I am locked in a cage with unmovable bars.
Freedom has betrayed me,
life has sold my soul,
to the stealing hands
of the nightmare monster.

Emily Manser, age 12

I Remember

I remember the night when I first met you,
It was a Monday evening, do you remember it too?

I was sat with friends, having a drink,
When you looked over and gave me a wink.

Are you lonesome tonight, you sang to me,
I never realized the song was only for me.

But, I do now, that's why I'm writing this,
To tell you that it is you I really miss.

I often sit and think of you,
And remember well that magnificent view.

It was a wonderful sight when we looked down,
One could see the real beauty of the town,

It was lovely to be with you, the stars and the moon,
And I hope I will be able to come back soon!

Joyce Nichols

Roads

If my life is like a spaghetti
junction with roads leading off it

I can take any road then
and if that road don't seem right to me

I can go back and take another
I should have allowance

For any mistake made
Who never made a mistake? Only Christ who never did

So when people, surprised, say "You're foolish"
you can take it hard or even look down on them

Sometime you have to make mistakes
to then get it right in this world

I always know my heart never rules my head
as you once a man and twice a child

Gloria Campbell

A Smile

Isn't a smile, a lovely thing?
Isn't a smile beguiling?
It makes all the difference,
When you're feeling low,
When you're down in the 'dumps',
When you have nowhere to go -
Isn't a smile a lovely thing?
To be caught unawares in your grief!
But a beautiful smile -
Can make life so worthwhile,
No matter how long, or how brief,
But isn't a smile so lovely to see,
And wouldn't it be perfect; if they were
Smiling at me!

Betty Mallinson

The Bird

A brave bird sang on a chimney stack.
It was the whispering sigh
Of a snowdrop's birth.
It was the tremulous cry
Of the awakening earth.
A brave bird sang, and my heart called back.

A brave bird sang beneath shrouded skies,
While unheedful feet
Of the back-bowed throng
In that grim-grey street
Under-beat the song.
But the brave bird sang, and I raised my eyes.

As a vagrant dream in the depths of sleep
Opens a moment a beckoning door,
So the bird's frail song in that tumbling street
Took my torment on wings as if it could soar
Into Heaven itself.

And I felt
Heaven there.
And I knelt.

Betty Gunson Taylor

The Rabbit

There's a rabbit in our garden, a lovely little bunny.
It's always on its own which seems rather funny.
It's a common or garden rabbit, not a rabbit from a hutch;
Not angora, nor a lop-eared - not even a dutch.

It seems a little strange that it's always on its own,
Chomping on the green grass, all over the lawn.
I know there is a rabbit - squirrel, also called a viscacha.
Not in England, nor in Europe, but in South America.

We have a single rabbit,
And a lonely squirrel too.
If they ever got together,
I wonder what they'd do!

Perhaps they'd have an offspring,
With long ears and a bushy tail.
Produce their own viscacha
Like a rodent's "Fisherman's Tale."

I wonder what they'd call it,
Perhaps a squabbit or a ribbel?
I know what I would call it;
Just a lovely little miracle!

Jean M. Senior

The Disappearing Nature

The beauty of Britain we once used to know,
Its gradual decline means we no longer sow,
The seeds for new trees, new parks for our pleasure,
The damage to nature we never can measure,
The roads being built, the wildlife disturbed,
Rabbits, squirrels and badgers, their lives being curbed,
Bulldozers move in and ruin the sights,
Ravaging forests and glades that should have the right,
To live on forever for us to admire,
The oaks and the beech, fir trees towering higher,
Now being demolished by those who don't share,
In the wonders of nature for which most do care,
But please let the natural prevail and then back,
Will come all the wildlife that at present we lack,
Because of the ruthless desire and the greed,
Of drivers with cars who should really take heed,
And leave our beautiful country as it was years ago,
For the children and young who never have known,
Of the countryside beauty that was made for us all,
Let's preserve all of nature, leaving trees standing tall.

Harold Longman

The Feeble Hand

The feeble hand reached forward, for strength and courage sought,
Its own strength had turned to weakness, from years of labour
wrought; Many years of service to other people gave,
That hand is crying out, help me, come and save!

I now need reassurance
Courage day by day;
Nurse, don't be afraid to hold my hand,
As it's difficult to say!

I find some strength and courage,
To bear fear and pain,
Memories are all that I have now,
They'll never wax, or wane;

This hand has now become so weak,
It is the kind word that I seek,
Just knowing, Nurse, you really care,
Hold my hand, and my suffering share!

I'm grateful now, for what you've done,
Strength and courage for me you've won;
Hope your hand will too be blest,
For answering my unspoken request!

Esther Armstrong

Glory Days

I love the sound of summer -
  It's like a symphony,
Orchestral music playing
  A rhapsody for me.

I love the sight of summer -
  Each flower, each blade of grass,
The beauty of a rose in bloom
  And daises in a mass.

I love the smell of summer -
  No perfume can compare
To the natural scent of nature
  Emitted everywhere.

I love the sense of summer -
  To feel her presence here,
Caressing every living thing
  With warmth and bringing cheer.

The sound . . . the sight . . . the smell . . . the sense
  Bring magic - but alas,
The glory days of summertime -
  How swiftly they do pass.

Briony V. Lill

Untitled

I love you, I love you, I love you,
It's so easy, oh so easy to say,
Yet I suppose I take love for granted,
When I'm near you, beside you each day.

As the sun stirs the night into mornings,
And so beckons on our new day,
I look at you lying beside me,
And love you a hundred new ways.

To know you, to love you, to need you,
It's oh so easy to say,
I love you, I love you, I love you,
And the feeling grows stronger each day.

Every day in time has its passing,
Reminds me of the love that we know,
And when I'm away and not by you,
Like a flower in the spring it will grow.

The days into years are now turning,
And together we live out our life,
Every day I love you more deeply,
My darling, I love you, My wife.

Douglas Wilson

"This Is Not an Obsession - It's Not"

This is not an obsession
It's not a problem
It's not a crime
I would give the moon
To you
It's not a major threat
It's not the worst thing yet
That I would die for you
It's something good and pure and holy
The way I feel for you
It's indomitable love
It's simple
I am filled with love
For you
I am happy
If you love me too
Even just a little bit————

Arni McGuckin

Partners

Whether to embrace Europe in full measure
Is not a decision free of pressure.
A Utopian success or an economic nightmare,
'Tis clear that we must be cautious and beware.
Scrapping the mark, the franc and the pound,
Switching to the Euro to produce an economy that's sound.
Pious hopes to expound on an economic panacea,
Only time will produce a result that's clear.

To some the union is an economic perception,
But there are those who hunger for political direction.
Yet the nations have fought and squabbled for a thousand years,
Creating a reservoir and background of instinctive national fears.
To sweep those worrying concerns aside,
Clearing the way for the birth of European pride
Will take an immense amount of year-spanning patience
Before we Europeans can live harmoniously in friendly tolerance.

Allen Jessop

Encounter

Chanced on a rattlesnake coiled on a rock scree,
just a young one, no more than two rattles.
A pebbled glanced on him as I climbed,
and my hand would have been within his reach
but for the earliness of the day, and the air frost.
There he was, caught by the cold,
and chilled, muscles immobilized,
and scarcely detectable, sulking in his crevice.
He could not launch his length and strike,
unable to move, trapped. So too was I
hypnotized by the threat of his bite,
each holding the other's fate at a hand's breadth.
Snake, subliminally apprehensive till
cautiously he settled back to sleep,
a shift of the wind that changed my mood
to admiration of his form and pattern,
and an apology for the disturbance of his quiet.

Bridget Juniper

I Wish I Had The Power!

I wish I had the power to bring peace into this world
No blood would spill across the globe
No want or need to kill.

I wish I had the power to dissolve away hard drugs
That hook into our children
Preyed upon by thugs.

I wish I had the power to feed the starving mass
Of walking dead, the underfed
Their time will come to pass

I wish I had the power to erase and cure all ails
Life support machines no more
No pills and no more wails.

Michelle Walker

I Demand a Sperm Re-Count!

Our breakfast's censored!
It's not as if the World is flooding
with a Lava of Black Pudding.
Nor a job for MENSA,
to see which way the World is heading.

I am no Scoffer,
and cannot stomach the invective:
one would rather have perspective.
While it's not on offer,
a person must remain objective.

Now it's Weetabix!
But hold my tongue and do the Quiet Thing;
there is no sense in rioting.
Tyrannosaurus Rex
could easily have died from Dieting.

Yes, there is a need,
when considering we have no place
to strut our stuff, or state our case.
So I'm the one to plead
in this "virtually-fat-free" space!

Jeffrey Charles Wheeler

Michelle

Eyes like the ocean deep.
Mouth as smooth as silk.
Hair so fair - All I can do is stand and stare . . .
A smile so beautiful as to make an angel cry.
Your body I want to caress.
One look at you and I lose my stress.
To hold you close is all I dream.
Without you my heart would scream.
Be with me forever;
To lead life's merry dance together.
A love no man can sever.
Michelle.
Together forever.

Steven Alan Duggan

The Family

Like blades of grass we stand side by side, bending together,
moving together and living together.
Part of the same patch of life, our roots entangled in the cold dark earth.
We share the same sunshine, feel the same winds: So closer our
lives are, yet we do not see each other.
We do not whisper into each others ears: All we hear are distant
sounds of the breeze rustling the leaves on the trees.
We take notice to what is happening across the way, but not of
what is here.
Never turning to see if the other is still there, only assuming no
heavy foot has come their way; no gust pushing too strong that
they could no longer stand.
To onlookers we appear complete, our unity essential for that
carpet of greenery; yet how isolated we are.
Though supportive we try to be, being back to back we do not see
the tears in each other's eyes.

Nicola Buckley

Sleep

What happens to me when I go to sleep?
My senses cut off, as in slumber, I'm deep.
Does my spirit rise up, and glide away,
To far distant places? or does it stay
Close by my side, all the night through,
Resting with me, in slumber too?
Why do I dream, of people I know not,
Or visit places, I've long since forgot.
Why have I nightmares, that make me cry?
Or dream a sad dream, that maketh me sigh?
Sleep is the most mysterious part of man,
Creeps up on me, I cannot it ban.
But I often wonder, what happens to me,
When I go to sleep, and my spirit is free.

B. R. Wilkinson

Stubbin Pit

Down at the old Stubbin Pit on the tops,
It's so quiet down there where now nobody goes.
Where men and boys got sooty and black,
Miles underground many years ago.

Shafts working all day and night.
Cages going up and down carrying men.
The furnaces burning so hot with coal,
Coal from deep in the mine.

Don't you wish those days could be here right now?
When the land was so beautiful and green,
Before houses were built on wonderful marsh land,
That was filled with nature and wildlife.

Why did it all have to go away?
Why was the beautiful land destroyed?
Why can't we go back in time?
To the good old days to see the working mine.

*Stubbin Pit was a mine between Rawmarsh and Greasbrough
which is now closed down and deserted. Many people have
forgotten about it, but it holds a great deal of history.*

Caroline Race

The Loch - An Epitaph of Our Dog Lomond

A fountain of spirit, warmth and vitality,
No heed given to the harsh reality
of your beginnings.

A pond, your eyes, brown pools of unconditional love,
So grateful, for all that He above
has given you.

Happy times at sea, a wag, a lick, a wuff for me.
Your golden beauty - there for all to see
proud and majestic.

The loch, an inspiration of strength and courage
Long, deep and still,
with your own entourage
of those who'll miss you now.

Hearts which will never mend,
For you - our beloved friend,
Until the day we meet again
"on your bonnie, bonnie banks"

Oh lovely loch, our thanks are due,
for all the love we've had from you
you were all we ever wanted - we love you too.

Linda E. Solazzo

Against My Mother's Advice

If I had listened to my mother.
Most likely I would have married another
When I told her we wanted to get wed.
She screamed, married to him, are you right in the head.
Countless times I was told I was throwing myself away
Nobody could ever say I wasn't warned I would rue the day.
Much thought and buckets of tears I shed.
But we loved each other, and the wedding went ahead.
It was the happiest day of my life when we left for our honeymoon
I looked at mother her face was filled with gloom
We didn't have much money but enough to sustain life.
I was really happy and contented being a wife
When I had a baby six years, later I had been at death's door
I thought mother would be overjoyed instead she said don't
  have any more
Over the years we had two more her advice scrapped.
I was elated but mother kept saying I was trapped
For thirty five years my husband tried hard but never won her round.
Ironically it was he she turned to when she was housebound
Grudgingly one day she said towards the end of her life I
  suppose I should give him some praise
At least he was not as bad as I expected I thought you were
  going through a phase.

Marlene Forrest

Baby Mine

Ever since you came baby mine
no words can express my loving care for you,
you will make my life so divine
I wonder if I could live without you,
There is nothing on this earth
That can describe your worth,
My seven pounds of heaven,
I know the angels sighed
The day you left my side,
My seven pounds of heaven.

F. C. Turner

Dreams

I've flown with eagles to their craggy keep,
I've dived with whales to the icy deep,
And all this whilst I'm fast asleep.
I've walked with Armstrong on the moon,
Helped Gershwin write his famous tune,
I've seen Merlin's cave at Camelot,
And pulled the sword from its rocky slot.
I've sat with God, saw Jesus weep,
Don't think it's untrue, I know it's absurd,
But to me, Nelson spoke his very last word!
I was there when the King and Boleyn wed,
I also saw her lose her head.
And all this whilst I'm fast a-bed!
I trod the earth with dinosaurs,
I'm surprised they never heard my snores!
But never in my dreamiest state,
Could I have chanced on one so great,
If I could sleep the whole year through,
I'd never find a love like you!

Heide M. Burchmore

Mrs. Suburbia

Time to get up Monday morning again.
Kids up for school get ready for work
I talk to people, daydream in between
Should I do something crazy?
Break the routine.
Of course not, don't be silly
Not someone like me.
A Mrs. Suburbia . . . Mrs. Jones
That's me to a 'T'.

Maybe someday in the future
I'll blow everyone's mind
After a few Gin and Tonics
I could be the kind
To throw caution to the wind
Surprise all around
But for the time being
I'll stay the 'normal' me
Looking after the kids
Making the tea.

Anne Fennell

Life

Tread this path with care,
No sign to says adventures beware,
Unseen rules to follow,
ever chancing on tomorrow.
Myriad of choices to be made,
Quickly answered before they fade,
Smiles and tears come our way,
A difficult dance this is they say,
In our worlds which we create,
Each unsure and yet safe,
Destiny's to be fulfilled,
this drink to be savoured and not spilled,
We are all beginners in this place,
an exciting game, a cruel chase.
The only treasure here to win,
is a resting place without sin.

S. Townsend

Laughter Lines

I see this old lady standing before me each time I glance in the
    mirror
I cannot make out, but there seems no doubt, "Surely, not me", I
    cry in horror
This old person is grey, her eyes the same colour, but she's
    somewhat smaller than I
No! that isn't me, so I turn around to see, but there's nobody
    there and I sigh!

Surely the years have not treated me so, I've been too busy to see,
That more cosmetics are needed, a highlight or two, but
    nothing too drastic for me.
My husband, he says that I look in all ways, 'Just like the girl
    he wed',
I suppose that's true, I say feeling blue, but I look at him with
    real dread.

He says that he loves me whether sixty or more, so what am I
    worrying for,
It's natural to age and turn over the page, not bother too
    much or to bore.
"Does it matter dear, that lines show up clear, it proves we
    have lived a good life,
These lines are just laughter, it's love that we're after, to me
    you're the very best Wife".

Lucy-May Bloxham

School Alone

I went to work this morning, nothing strange in that you'd say,
Just another job to do on just another day.
But, all was deadly quiet, nothing stirred - no noise at all,
It all felt kind of eerie as I walked in through the hall.

The rooms were bare, the walls all stripped,
No rubbish where it's usually tipped.
The tables and chairs were all neatly stacked high,
There was no one about - not a whisper - not a sigh.

There were empty pegs and empty drawers,
Empty cushions on empty floors.
No writing, no pictures, no sums on the board,
No water to play in - no paints to be poured.

There was no happy laughter, no squeals of delight,
No little 'Johnny' wanting 'Jimmy' to fight!
No hands to be held - no tears to be dried,
No stories to listen to - eyes open wide.

They've all 'broken up' - gone home from the hols,
And they've taken their models of tractors and dolls.
There's no hustle, no bustle, only silence - no sound,
And SCHOOL doesn't seem right without children around.

Christine Hall

Renew Your Courage with Truth

It happened on a cold March day, the Devil visited Dunblane.
Just ten horror stricken minutes, before he went his way . . .
Leaving carnage and death in the path of his cowardly,
    . . . bloody foray.
The Devil, in that tormented, twisted mind.
Wreaking wrath and vengeance, on the most innocent he could
    . . . find.
Sixteen wee children and a school teacher died.
A heroine, for to defend them, she had tried.
The Devil, in Dunblane that pleasant quiet, medieval town.
Living, seething, scheming in their midst.

How? Was so much evil allowed to exist?
Why? Did no one heed those warning signs?
Why? Were guns licensed, with which to commit such heinous
    . . . crimes.
Crimes that no one will forget, or forgive.
Lessons must be learned, if other innocents are to live.
Mental illness cannot be ignored by the sane
Do not let that courageous teacher and those dear little children
    . . . die in vain.
Remember your motto "Renew your courage with truth"
Future generations could come to rely on your city's ancient
    . . . claim . . . Dunblane

Harry Stratton

Lord Jesus

The Lord Jesus walked in the
morning light across a field of green
When all at once he come upon a flower
of purest white
Its centre shone pure yellow as it reached
up to the sun
Lord Jesus said such purity you find
in the heart of the young
And then the Lord was heard to say
Fear not to praise my Father's name
In field and garden or the lane
Hear now the heavenly choir in the bird's song
Take care of all the wonders that you see
And worship my father as you love me.

D. M. Neale

Brodick from West Kilbride

Not even giants could I see upon the isle from here;
Mist shrouded mountains and horizon blurred.
But on the strand at Brodick any time of night or day
There are real people going about their ways.

Distance lends a blindness of perspective in this light;
The cold, grey, stilted clarity of an autumn day;
And in its clouded vision all dreams are possible to dream,
Without reality being hostage to that other theme.

The mind's eye sketches the outline of the bay,
The pier, hotels and shops that make the town.
Still people do their chores in the location that beguiles
Oblivious of prying eyes across the firth's eleven miles.

The ferry can provide the missing link between
The seance of the mind and true morphology.
Some day I'll sail across and make the two, one whole:
Mind and mystery, sand and sward in unity, my goal!

Ross Mitchell

'Birthdays'

Slowly voyaging around the sun all my days
I've lodged with the winter, summer, autumn and spring
revolving life, weather, colour and time
making me grow with every orbiting ring.

The revolution that makes me a day older
turns around once the same everyday
till darkness rotates to light
till work turns to dreams

So the earth has come back to the same faithful spot
where I was born many circles ago
turning numbers into my adding age
revolving happenings into memories of old

Dizzy times still lie leisurely ahead
and happy they into the future
Still they take the same exact time
of which for me are growing fewer

Christopher Heenan

Our Micky

A cheerful dog was our Micky, and just eleven months old.
With mournful face, and honest eyes, and coat of shining gold.
Effusive, most ebullient, and ever full of fun,
Brave and obedient, not afraid of fence or stream nor gun.
A trusting good companion and always by our side,
In wood, in field, in marshy ground, and by the Towy wide.
Our friendly pal has left us now and perfect peace
has found. We gently laid him down to rest in
Banc-y-berllan ground.
And as we stood beside his grave, two full grown
men did cry and unashamedly, tears did roll as they
bid Mick goodbye.
Goodbye dear Mick goodbye old friend we love
you though you've gone, but by my side in
heaven one day again you'll
"Bring it on"

J. Brown

Dreams

Do you ever have dream of travels to foreign climes afar?
Of sailing across the oceans and even "crossing the bar."
I think of eastern pagodas, of minarets gold in the sun.
And a coolly hatted rickshawman who spends his days on the run.
Bicycles and oxen carts pushing wearily through the throng.
Teeming streets and customs that remain unchanged for so long.
Eating houses where fish are chosen live, as you enter the door.
Exotic food and chopsticks with bowls of rice and much more.
The boss man in kimono, hands tucked in his sleeves.
Tables low and polished. Flowers with lotus leaves.
Junks that ply the harbour, piled high with who-knows-what.
Anything they think will sell, fish to veg; the lot!
The babble of foreign voices in the markets as they trade.
And the murky little jewellers who sell exquisite jade.
It's all a flight of fancy, but oh so real to me.
I've not even left my armchair, let alone been to sea!

J. E. Boots

Howling

Outside the wind howls,
its talons pulling at roofs.
Its foul breath oozing through every hole.
Its whistle loud as it blows,
Pulling up roots as it goes.
Here we sit, alone and afraid,
as it keeps up its loud tirade.
Laughing in its rage.
A power all of its own,
like a nagging old lady's moan.
As it screeches across the sky,
watch the debris and rubbish fly.
Pulled down the street,
pushed from our feet,
paper flung across the air,
plants and trees massacred as if they were not there.
But as soon as it comes,
it disappears,
giving no warning as silence greets our ears.

Catherine Nutt

Proverbs from an Elderly Home

Don't throw us out into the cold,
Just because we've turned grey and old.
But do let us be alone,
Away from this infernal home.
Here beds become coffins
And nurses change into witches.
The pills are their potions,
Putting to sleep any idle notions.
Instead our dear children,
Push our wheelchairs outside
In the warmth and sunshine,
Where the flowers smell of perfume
And the stream water tastes like wine.
In fact take us to your homes,
So we need never again be alone.
Instead you make us stay here,
Shedding our lonesome nightly tears.

Anne-Marie Jones-Taylor

The Peace of Time

Time can stand still, in a field of green
No sound but the rustle of trees.
A peaceful moment, a time to think,
A pause to let moments cease.

The birds can stir your restful dreams
Help you realize life is worth
A restful time just now and then
To accept the terms on earth.

A peaceful mind, a loving heart
Can see beyond the wood.
We should all take up these moments
To make our life feel good.

D. M. French

Mother

I am you in a different generation
Moulded conceived, filled with elation
Personality and twin, features can be found
Knowing every avenue, knowing every sound.

A small child, a teenager, adolescence before formed,
Creative, responsible, no past to be mourned
You were there then, you are here today
Strong, adorable a friend who will stay.

Blood has always been, thicker than water
A colossus is formed into a son or a daughter,
Familiarity is noticed, through features or expression
Era is in past, but is now your tradition.

Growing believing in you, every word is a lesson
Treasuring every minute a memorable possession
Strength is your priority, leave behind any anguish
Offsprings delightful, beauty will flourish.

Years will go past, memories to collect
Statue, model like, a figure, you'll protect
Genetics produced you, you produced another
No one could make a copy of you my mother!

J. A. D. Keel

The Movie Star

When thee earth the sun
    Moon and stars seem all gone,
As I bask in my last moments of splendour.
    I'll remember the Girl
From the celluloid world,
    Where immortality was acquired by endeavour.

Thee American dream
    Legend of the screen,
Her name from the flowers,
To sing through thee hours
    Flowed the blood of the muses above.
For at thee end of my days
    Postulate as I daze,
Sensational, was my favourite love.

But as love never dies,
    Perpetual remains the prize,
Where the fires of love never smoulder.
To thee ends of thee age
    The flames forever rage,
In thee eyes of thee Immortal Beholder.

B. A. Atreides

Children of the Streets

Assassins for hire without names
Murder most foul, to their shame,
Innocent children in twilight sleep
A date with death will have to meet.

Orphans, Urchins coming this way are not allowed to sleep or play.
Begging for alms is all they know, they have no homes or place to go.

Society neglects them and turns away, in "Brazil" it continues
    night and day.
Victims of circumstance, not desire, easy targets for bullet fire.

No protection, no conscience it seems
These street children can have no dreams.
Why do we stand idly by, turning deaf ears
To their desperate cries.

Save them from the dangerous foe,
Give them shelter, a place to go,
Protect them from the threatening storm
Waken them gently with the dawn,
Let their sleep be tranquil and sweet,
With thoughts of fairies and dancing feet,
Feed and clothe them, and when that's done,
THE BATTLE FOR STREET CHILDREN HAS BEEN WON.

Yvonne Delaney

Un Love Child

Un love child is a child that walk in the shadow of life,
never to feel love's warm glow,
or hear I love you so

Only the stillness of the night hears his cry,
no one to wipe the tears from his eyes,

You who gave me my first breath of life only to walk away in to
the night,

Never to see your face or feel your arms around me
if only I were a child and you that gave me life would love
me for the rest of my life,

Never to walk in the shadow of life,
Only to see your face when I wake in paradise

M. Treacey

Trading Places

Rosebay Willowherb, scottish cat,
Met Pennyroyal, the pipistrelle bat,
Rosebay feline, pampered, hairy,
Penny vespertillian, feral, scary,
Exchanging lifestyles, homes and whims,
Penny began to rummage in bins,
Had fun chasing flies and moles,
Pigeons, widgeons, toads and voles,
Was offered liver, duck and cream,
Salmon, mackerel and chicken supreme,
And was able to sleep in the Master's house,
Provided she caught the odd rat or mouse.
But Rosebay had to sleep in a tree,
Upside down! For all to see,
She alone dined on dew and roots
(Unable to find the forest fruits),
Sought shelter in caves from raucous rooks,
Bad - tempered polecats and beady - eyed ducks,
Told Penny she'd lived in hunger and fear
But agreed to trade places again, once a year.

Vickie Wilkinson

'Lust'

For we are dark.
Our souls do grieve for lack of what is beauty,
But in the depths,
Which seldom show,
There lurks a dusted scarlet beauty.

Drips of scarlet,
Bloodied passion,
Seep from where this decaying beauty settles.
Yet, with wonder,
And fiery vigour,
This scarlet beauty consumes the darkened body.

Sally Shaw

Orphans of Rwanda

Little children of Rwanda how you touch my breaking heart
No mother, father, friends have you - no one to take your part
The images I see before me bring tears to my eyes
Little eyes so wide and staring underneath Rwandan skies
Little bellies swelled with famine, little bony limbs so weak
Little children shocked and frightened and too tired and
    weak to speak
How in God's name has this happened - how can we all understand
If there is a God above us, then where is His helping hand
Little children filled with misery, all hurting and alone
Oh! where is the joy of childhood that they all have never known
And what lies ahead - the future, for the orphans who survive
With no-one to love and care for them - are they glad to be alive?
No - the scars they bear will ever be deep etched within their minds
And memories will haunt them, shuttered in their tiny minds
Dear God in all humanity, now have mercy on these babes
For they have done no evil - yet they're bound for early graves
Yes, we all must take some blame I know for what has happened here
But what do we do? Where do we turn? When all we feel is fear.

Wendy Ryan

My Best Friend

My best friend was four months older than me.
My best friend was like a brother, always there for me.
He was loving, caring and the best friend anyone
could ask for.
I lost my best friend to cancer, just two days before his birthday.
He had cancer for a year and tried to live his
short life to the full.
If only, I could see him again to tell him, well, I loved
him and always will.

Tammie Foley

April

Golden sunlight, sparkling dew,
Morning mist obscures the view,
Creatures stir in secret places,
Hidden still from prying faces,
Moon turns pale and fades away
Vanquished by the dawning day
Dappled clouds race wild and free
Like islands in an azure sea.
Blossom falls from cherry trees
On pink confetti-laden breeze
Suddenly, a change of scene
The sun-kissed fields have lost their sheen
Dark shapes violate the sky
And soon the clouds begin to cry
Majestic golden orb appears
And greets a world awash with tears
The sun's rays fall on steaming land
With splendour borne of nature's hand
And as the swallows swoop and scream
The rain is but a distant dream

Michael J. King

Farewell to a Mother at Heathrow Airport

Like an old soldier in red suit
Mother went to the passport control
after a brief goodbye.
Struggling with tears
we made our farewell.
She at eighty-five, grey-haired and frail.
"Must I go now?" Mercifully brief.
Inadequate time for all we longed to say,
  or should have said.

We climbed the stairs to the airport roof.
A darkening haze covered the west, heavy with rain.
Her 'plane, with thundering roar
sped along the runway and soared.
We strained our eyes to follow.
Slender, wraith-like, soundless
ir bore her on - her, who bore me
now borne in their steel womb
heading South, into sun, and was gone.

L. Cumings

My Daughters

They bring much joy into my life
Much laughter little pain
Without them life would be so grey
No sun would shine again

They leave their love along the road
Of memories mine to keep
Their laughter and their many tears
Will comfort through the coming years
Their trust I hope to reap

The world it is their oyster
They'll meet worries on the way
But sunshine overcomes the darkness
To brighten up their day

Like birds one day they'll fly away
And I'll be left to weep
But memories are left behind
They are mine to keep

Ruth Whitfield

Could You Love

My name is Lee, aged three
Mum and Dad didn't want me,
I'm a little fostered boy you know
I wish I had some place to go

My eyes are blue, hair is fair
I only wish someone would care
I sit and play, I'm not much trouble
I also like to have a cuddle.

Please come 'round and have some tea
Then if I like you and you like me
Perhaps you could adopt me
To be in a family tree would be fun
Then at least I would have my very own mum.

Wendy Mallett

Bluebell Wood

Over the stile, I stopped in a trance.
More blue than the ocean or the sky, they caught my eye.
A carpet of deep blue, warm and bewitching.
My nose started twitching.

I feared to tread, should I bend their delicate stems.
So many standing tall, delicate bells, glittering like gems.
The smell was sweet, enchanting, what beauty.
I stopped and stared, like being in another world.
Full of peace and tranquillity.

I laid down, the sound of trees buzzing, birds singing.
The occasional butterfly caught my eye, with peacock coloured
wings.
What pretty things.
Easy to find amongst the electric blue, I knew,
I had to come this way.
Surely in the month of May.
When spring is in its finest time.
Oh bluebells you are mine.

Lynn April Meddins

"A Small Child"

Once in my life, a day in September
My Aunt came for tea, I well remember
I sat by the window, waiting awhile
Then came a taxi, with Auntie in style
I ran to the door, to greet her you see
Then went too fast, and fell on my knee
"Look" said Auntie, "that big crack on the floor"
"Some jelly" said Aunt, "sure you could eat more"
I looked up at Auntie, smiling away
Tears were forgotten, 'twas like yesterday
Then came the Parcel Auntie had brought
I opened it fast, is it what I thought!
It's my Birthday today, yes, I'm only three
Oh! it's Dolly, just a Dolly for me.

Kathleen Baskeyfield

Who Cares?

Here I am in this lonely room with the lights dim low
Music playing to soothe me, having to face life's cares alone
Springs in the air but, only fear springs to mind.
Releasing the dread of having to face another lonely day

makes me ask the question, "WHO CARES?"

I hear the whisper of the wind comforting me,
Yet I feel the heartaches that love brings
Causing me to ask the question, why did it happen to me?
Problems are many, but friends are few.
Makes me ask the question, "WHO CARES?"

The love I feel, I want to share with you alone!
Not knowing just how you will respond makes me refrain,
Inadequate are the words that I would like to use,
To describe the way I feel about you, me, Who!
I want to share my love with YOU, if you CARE.

Winklet Smith

The Empty Streets

Swiftly driving through the deserted city streets
My colleague tells of carnage, his broad accent stern, concerned

We turn the corner, silence falling, but for a second, the wind
whistles down the empty path
The buildings with no windows, the rubble, curtains falling,
flutter in the breeze

The cladding rattles, droplets splashing, water cascading down
the walls
Glass crumbling 'neath the tyres, there are no people, laughing,
talking

The vacant streets are ghostly quite, but I hear the crying,
the forlorn calling
Forever will I remember the words, the silence, the empty streets
of Belfast.

S. J. Adkins

My Family

My mum stays at home all day,
My dad works all night,
My sister likes her flower arrangements,
Both of my brothers fight.

My granddad does lots of gardening,
He likes it too you see,
He's also sometimes boring,
And he never talks to me.

Now let's talk about the best one,
In my whole family you see,
The skill, the style, the superstar,
Of course you know it's me.

Master Clinton Rose

The Sandy Beach

I walked along the sandy beach
My dog quite near but out of reach,
I found some seaweed and a shell
Some oysters and a snail as well.
Some heaps of sand where little worms
Do make their homes when the tide turns,
One old shoe, an old tin can
Adventurer or fisherman?
I wander on, and still can't find
An answer to my restless mind . . .
Why is the sea so big and strong
That I can only walk along
  The Sandy Beach?

Stella Taylor

A Wondrous Life

If I could live in my life again
No more heartaches no more pain
To turn the clock back over the years
To keep fond memories and wipe away tears

I would try to live so pure and good
Like the bible tells me christian should
To go to church to kneel and pray
And to guide me safely every day

To live a happy carefree life
No more worries no troubles or strife
To be kind and gentle for all to see
Once more to live a life of liberty

To help each other in every way
To understand children as they play
To watch flowers grow to hear birds sing
To live my life again what a wondrous thing

To be wanted and loved day after day
To see the sun moon and stars at play
To awake each day to another morn
What price I would give if I where reborn

G. Thomas

Don't Stand at My Grave

Don't stand at my grave 'cos I'm not there,
my epilogue for you I now lay bare.
My life that was then will now disappear
Though my soul is all around you
so my child do not fear.
My loss is a bereavement that will never go away.
My love is always in your heart and there will always stay,
so until we meet again my child
stick to the fight,
it will only be when the pain goes away
that we will re-unite.

Natalie Hance

Goodbye to the Loved Ones

Why did you escape to heaven, when I could cradle you in
my hands?
Your fingers clasped, like a clutching child who stumbles
in foreign lands.
From desperation to despair, my will could bind no
more,
Our pages stained, only words remained, as the hands just
ripped and tore.
Somewhere down below us, is eternity we will never know,
Somewhere deep inside us, is loss we will fail to show.
Forever here, forever life, forever can leave us all,
But for the fresh and growing, the warm breeze blowing,
together we will stand tall.

Lucy Corner

Gentle Persuasion

I'm sitting here quaking
My hands they are shaking
And I feel like running away
But there's no way but down
All the way to the ground
And my turn is coming around
I make a decision
To shift my position
And I fumble and stumble until
The others are glaring
The instructor is staring

At a point that is right through my head
The vomit is rising
Which is not so surprising
Oh! - I wish I was back in my bed
My head it is thumping
Someone pushed - and I'm jumping
Hey! it's brill - what a thrill!
Then I land on my head!

Norah Murray

The Picture

To the picture out in space
mother nature is its name,
many movements taking place
on its ever-changing face,
and the rainbows are its frame.

From our land, no divides,
men rushed so far away,
to be the first to stab you with a flag
to beat a brother.
Billions spent to feed the ego,
while on our lands bellies roared
of our fellow man
returning to the dust.

When I was a boy,
you rolled across the sky,
you lit up our nights
and lit up our lives,
and you were a wonder.
To think that man could touch you,
one day pollute you.

Ray McGann

Peace of Mind

It must be of great satisfaction to have no doubts at all
Of who you are and where you're going and the reasons for life at all;
Of the belief in a higher supremacy, however you perceive Him to be;
Of unstinting faith in fellow men who can never agree to agree;
Of justice, honour and dignity, whatever creed or clan;
Of love of nature and all forms of life encompassed in earth's
     master plan.
But when it seems - you, alone,- are striving to improve your
     earth's little corner,
Others decimate the earth's ecology by destroying the flora
     and fauna
Bomb, kidnap, hijack and murder for, or of a particular belief,
The injustice, dishonour and indignity in God I can find no relief.
When stockpiles of life-giving food and drink get higher and
     higher and higher
And people in various parts of the globe are surrounded by
     machine guns and wire,
The spirit and resolve are weakened at the sheer magnitude
     and problem
But I alone cannot hope to even make a dent and solve them.
. . . If only others of like thought could improve earth's corner
     where they're standing,
Then satisfaction too would be curs and man's achievements
     know no ending.

Margaret Lane

Sick at Heart

I can feel that hurt inside, like a piercing icicle of pain.
My heart has lost its usual beat, and now my blood runs cold.
My senses do not sense any longer, and wind, rain or shine I
     do not feel.
Is this possibly death that has caught me, or am I just invisible
     to the world?
Is it a deep loneliness that has made my body react this way?
Such loneliness that does not bring tears to warm the cheeks.
Am I so unloved that even my body has chosen to abandon me?

What is this darkness that attempts to cover me?
Darkness that stings the skin and wounds the soul.
Confusion that rockets past me and knocks me over to a pool of
hatred that tries to capture my spirit.
There is no rope to pull me out, no voices that desperately call my
sorry name.
Maybe they did not know my name, they did not wish to learn the
letters that form it.
I have been swallowed by my own emotions and now this is
where I shall stay until glorious death touches me.
And lets me go free.

Leah Gannon

Losing Hope

My heart is burning, and my aching insides are effervescing,
Not unlike a cauldron over flowing with passion and excitement.
Yet there is a dark thriving antithesis,
Lurking in the misty depths of my being,
Clouding the but otherwise, ultimate Utopia.

A light pulls me towards its dazzling supremacy.
However, there is an ever-developing blackness holding me tight,
Not allowing me to stride proudly forward, and to grasp my destiny.

It is almost as if a remorseful weed is growing, growing slowly
inside me,
Blocking out sunlight, and strangling the ever hopeful buttercup,
Who is fighting for sunlight, and life.

Tortured I stand, torn apart from my only dream.
Gradually my conscious being is losing all reminiscence of my fantasy.
A fantasy, that is all it is to me now, a distant fantasy.

The brilliance of the blaze,
Had now been over shadowed by a mournful blackness.
Yet there, out there in the gloomy never-ending blanket
That surrounds my soul
A candle is burning for me.

Yvonne Goold

Perhaps

Perhaps I should have ignored
My heart searching for your love and affection.
Perhaps I should have looked away and
my love for you I dare not mention.
Perhaps I should have left you
in my dreams at night.
Perhaps it would have been so
easy if you hadn't kissed me
and held me so tight.
Perhaps I mean go when all
the time I mean stay.
Perhaps you shouldn't be in my
mind during the day.
Perhaps all of these would
be so simple to do.
Perhaps I am just trying
to say I am so happy
just loving you.

Patricia Ann Traveller

Bosnia

Since the day I fled in force
My heart still beats and yearns for your turquoise sky;
Thy people and thy victims' cries echo in my bosom incessantly.
I know . . . I shall return and shall wait to see your rebirth
out of ashes, out of dust,
out of ruins and depraved lust.

Bosnia of snowy mountains, you will never succumb
to the forces of evil and demons,
who eagered to destroy and vitiate your existence.
Harken! In the roots, in your womb, proud you still are
as spiteful and proud as you've been in every instance.

I dream a dream of peace and white lilies' fields,
I see it every day before my sunken and hollow eye
I dream and pray that justice will triumph and erase calamities;
May God not allow my dream's fulfilment ever die.

Lejla Kokorovic

The Parting of the Ways

There you stand, I'm proud of you son.
My, how you've grown, I feel my work's done,
You've gone from a child, to an adult full grown,
I'm proud I sampled the seeds of the unknown,
My feelings of love are undying for you.
I gave you that first breath a life so true,
The time has come for a sorrowful farewell.
Oh son how I'll miss you, the whole world I will tell,
One day you will realize how much you mean to me.
With children of your own the pain you will surely see
For they will grow son and leave you as you, me.
But that is life, all we can we ever do
Is tell our children of our love so tender and true.

Yeoman

My Week

As I leave the warmth to be reborn into a cold new day,
My journey begins . . .
My journey is short but long, it stops but soon again it begins.
The deepest of blues disappears as I stare through life stained glass,
A brilliant glow of warmth emerges as my back turns,
The journey continues . . .
Everything I've dreamed fades with this journey but I
always dream of my sunrise . . .
The journey begins to judder and then slows to a stop,
suddenly my sunrise is in a clearer appearance.
Once more the crossing, is there time, well we're here anyway.
As the shadows once again enclose me, I think of
my sunrise, is this living or just existing,
I think of my sunrise . . .
I emerge once again but my sunrise, where is it?
I will see you again my sunrise, until we meet again,
The journey is just beginning and it always lasts,
Or Does It . . .

Scott Brooker

A Son Forever Lost

How light the step of the bright young man, as he whistled on his
way.
    Oh! Son of mine how kind and true,
The love that I had was just for you.
    You walked away on that fine day, never to return again!

We waited so long by the window there -
    Hoping against hope for our son so fair
I know now that it can never be,
    And yet how long will I still yearn,
Hoping against hope for your return.

The ache that I have is wholly mine and will forever be!
    For this son of mine now far away
(Buried or lost across the sea).
    Manis I. Gillman

Missing You

If only, repeated again and again,
my mind so full of remorse;
a relationship never to regain..
gone to its eternal and final repose.

Vibrant colours against the stone,
buds aggressively piercing forward;
birds chorus sing with similar tone:
'Now girl, now, forever onward!'

Will you release me from this desire,
to be a credit to your name
and soon the all exhuming fire
smoothest away the pain.

At last, the feeling of happiness a fact,
re-discovered beauty and love,
with others as bound in a close pact;
disappearing to the horizon, a lonely white dove.
    M. English

The Kinsfolk

The day she died
My mother's brethren came,
With suitable solemnity in their country eyes;
We didn't send, they knew that she had died.
And so they brought brown eggs, gifts from afar,
They said the griddle bread, the butter churned today,
Was as she knew it.
I looked for a star.
Their rich Fermanagh voices so consumed
Our city home, the room in which she lay,
That we forgot the animosities, feuds there had been,
And when they spoke of places we had seen
Mentioned on Bible flyleaves Mother had;
Aghadrumsee, Tully, Salaghy and Kilmore,
The mystic dream was born and she was there
With clogs, in lamplight, on an earthen floor;
The orphan donkey, standing near,
And Christ not very far.
When they were gone I kissed her cheek and said,
Father forgive them now that mother's dead.
    Robert Lindsay

Who Cares

The old man falls then lies still.
Must be drunk they say.
    No-one cares.

A boy is chased by two others.
When caught they start beating him.
    No-one cares.

The girl screams as a man tears at her clothes.
They turn away and ignore her.
    No-one cares.

A baby cries loudly in pain.
The neighbours turn up the television.
    Will no-one care?
    D. O. Brown

A Child's Winter Dream

Wrapped up in bed was the only place to be,
My quilt, my pillow, my teddy and me.

Far from the world's watchful eye,
Dreaming of Santa touring the sky.

I rose my head and peeked through the curtain,
I had to look twice I couldn't be certain.

The ground outside was out of sight,
Covered in a fluffy blanket of white.

Being in bed no longer seemed best,
Suddenly I was awake full of energy and zest.

Pictures of snowmen entered my head,
As I wrapped up warm like Mother always said.

I rolled a ball as big as I could,
Then I did a smaller one just as you should.

As I finished I ran excitedly to Mother,
And she put one ball on top of the other.

Then Dad came out with a carrot and scarf,
I couldn't help laughing as he slid down the path.

As Dad put the finishing touches to my creation,
I watched suddenly feeling a tingling sensation.
    Natalie Talbot

The Enemy Within!

I walk quite well today, but the fatigue is still a pain,
My speech is articulate, the old memory is just the same.
My legs feel like lead, tied to my ankles are sacks of coal,
The depression is so bad, I can't climb out of this dark hole.
My balance is erratic, like being on the cake walk at the Fair,
No I'm not drunk, so why all those people choose to stare?
Once I took my legs for granted, walking them here and there,
Back then this was effortless, now it all seems so unfair.
I can't keep up with the kid's, they run ahead so fast,
On Sport's Day in the Mother's Race, I'd certainly come in last.

I have to learn to pace myself, take things easier so I'm told,
Slow down at thirty six, I thought you did this when you were old,
I can't bend down without falling, smack bang on the floor,
I trip myself over nothing, when going to answer the door.
The pain in my legs is hidden, in my heart it is hidden too,
For a disease like M. S. there's no cure, nothing anyone can do.
Try to remain positive, pray for a remission, hope it will all end,
M. S. is my unwelcome visitor, my enemy, and not my friend.
I treat it with contempt, I'm unfriendly, aggressive and conceited,
I won't go down without a fight, as yet you're undefeated.
    K. M. Tipton

Broken Clock

Tick . . . tock . . . tick . . . tock.
My time is running out I feel lower than low.
No one to run to and nowhere to go.

I've never been loved or had someone to care for,
Just a big empty house with dusty old things.
No money, no job, no car, hobby or friends.
And never the happiness any of them bring.

I was always the stranger, the oddball they left out.
But inside, like them, I was normal.
I just couldn't get out.

My body had me trapped and it hurt more than I could tell.
The mental torture of knowing but not being able to yell,
in joy, pain or anger to stand up and clap, dance or shout.
Why was I given this cage with no key?
My own personal hell from which I'll never get out.

One day it will come the clock will stop ticking.
My torment will be done I'll stand up and scream out.
It's finished it's over I am free now in heaven.
For that clock ticks in me with every breath that I take.
Tick . . . tock . . . thump . . . thump I hope soon it will break.
    Kevin Fox

Compassion

Shed a tear for someone you don't know,
Never be afraid to let sorrow show.
Show the pain that you feel for an unknown friend,
Cry out loud, let tears fall, so their hearts will mend.

Water cleanses, it is pure,
A good cry is like a cure.
Hold out a hand, reach out far,
Be that someone's shooting star.

Rise above the clouds, shine a ray of hope,
Make them believe that they can cope.
Open your arms, open your heart,
And then, the clouds will part.
Maybe one day you just may be,
That person who needs the sympathy.

L. Harold

Contemplating

As I sit alone and contemplate about my role in life
My thoughts drift to those raindrops which run down
and out of sight
They have no thoughts or feelings as they race against time
The windowsill is their ambition if only for a short while.

They have no cares or worries
Their lives are determined by clouds will it rain heavy tomorrow
will the wind blow loud these raindrops are a part of me
Good friends with them am I they listen to my thoughts
Though not understanding why they put my life into perspective
They make my dark days bright when I sit alone and contemplate
What are our roles in life.

The wind has gone quiet now no longer do they move as I return
to the state of consciousness here sitting in my room there is
silence all around me now at peace are them and I until our
thoughts meet once
again contemplating my role in life.

Susan Matthews

The Cafe

The doors open and the cafe springs into life, and the smell
of fresh ground coffee greets a man with his wife.

The mixtures of the orders is far and between, some like their
coffee black, and some take it with cream.

Cosmopolitan faces are dotted across the room, some are truly
happy, but others are full of gloom.

The traveller eats his breakfast, then goes on his way,
with bacon and eggs inside him he's prepared and set for the day.

Patrick J. Ryan

Mr. Isaac

Icy cobblestones reflect the light
Of mansion windows glowing bright,
Adorned with holly, mistletoe and pride,
A Yuletide welcome awaits inside

Yet; forbidding hall, cold marble tiles,
Broad staircase beckons, flickers gas light,
With mounting unease I ascend the flight,
The ambience beguiles.

At the staircase head, see man appear,
Distinguished, bearded, moustache, glasses,
Edwardian dress, watch-chain, so clear.
In an eternity of time that passes.

Human words cannot describe
The perfect peace and warmth intense,
An aura suffusing every sense and control,
As we pass, each resuming his goal.

The gentleman upon the stairs, does anybody know?
That's Mr. Isaac, a permanent guest!
I heard much later, died years ago,
But still pursues his lonely quest.

Sydney Oates

Past Reflections

As I gaze into the mirror,
My reflection stares back at me,
What on earth is that I see!
I'm thinking back to days gone by,
Recalling emotions that I felt,
Every one to me that life dealt.
With the money I earn from my Saturday job,
My friends and I always go on a drinking spree,
Remember I am a young girl happy and carefree.
I'm so happy because I think to life the answer I have found
How wrong could I be but that I have yet to learn
Past reflections, for those teenage days gone by I dearly yearn
For those teenage days gone by I dearly yearn.
If I was given the chance to turn the clock back,
I would do things differently this time 'round,
And in my pocket I would definitely have more than one pound.
As I gaze back into my magic mirror,
I feel like I'm going to break down and cry,
Past images are quickly fading
As my whisky bottle is rapidly running dry.

V. Hamley

Why History?

History is not about remembering the dead
Nor the Empires time has long forgotten
History is not for boring school lessons
Or for questions on TV Quiz Shows.
History is not Grandpa's old tales
Of days of strife and poverty.

History is just now,
Just as,
History was just then.

We look at the past to see our future
We need history to make history.

Steven Osborne

After Match

The field is quiet now.
Night rides in on a cold North-easter
And the trodden grass can breathe again.
The last uncaring sparrow settles in the high beams.

Below, in hot and steamy caverns
Weary warriors sweat and dream
of other battles still to come.
Through the darkening city streets
The armies of the day retreat
With banners furled.
Favours red, favours white
Reflected in the tall lamps' light.
Songs of triumph, songs of sorrow
Soaring upward to the skies.
All the joy and the pain
Soon forgotten on the morrow.

Tom Gurney

For a Long Lost Love

No Valentine card from a secret admirer
No flowers or chocolates from your heart's desire
How sad for those love has passed by
To feel left out, could make you cry
Never mind true love you will find sometime
When you do, it will be sublime
For romance is not only for the young at heart
Everybody at any age can take apart
Remember a Valentine is a two way street
Did you send one to whom you are sweet?
If you don't emit any signals or vibes
You may miss out on the love of your lives
Faint-heartedness you must not crave
Fortune only favours the brave
A smile or a wink will suffice
To show someone you are warm and nice
The moral of this verse is don't be coy
Or you may lose the love of a girl or a boy.

Terry Underwood

Episodes of Life

In somewhat pensive frame of mind
My thoughts reach out to life and time
A happiness that life can bring
No end to life's strange happenings

A memory that reaches out
A sadness that life can't leave out
Love's emotion life has crushed
Like dried crumpled petals that lie in the dust

A broken rosebud that lies in repose
Not destined to become one more beautiful rose
Remembering children in laughter and play
Not knowing yet life will have its own way

A kaleidoscope pattern of life down the years
Unusual happenings, dreams and life's fears
Sometimes smooth edges and sometimes defeat
When you might want to hide or make a retreat

But life isn't boring it's a mixture of things
So fill it with hope you must live all its dreams
You might cry at your happiness laugh later at fears
Make life like a book you can read through the years.

Maureen Adams

Nightmare

Slip calmly into the darkness, tread naively into the abyss.
No shields for you are defenceless, my decisions, for you are at rest.
Here I am, I thought you weren't coming, though I knew I
    would see you again.
No fighting for you are my prisoner, be alarmed for that's part
    of my game.
I know your concerns and your notions, and I'm weaving a
    web of unease.
Escaping just yet is impossible, until all of my cravings have ceased.
Take it easy sit back don't enjoy it, there's along time to go till
    the light.
How you wish you had chosen the other, full of passion and
    full of delight.
Oh do worry we shall have some fun though but of cause at
    your own expense.
Your anxieties will be my weapons and your horrors my
    missiles to send.
Look at me wasting time look what's happened the aurora's
    upon us again.
Not to worry I still have a few hours to pick and to pull at your brain.
Now which one of these to bequest you from my roster of
    wicked delights
Ah yes, this one, I'll begin it, have a wonderfully harrowing night!

Lisa Nuttall

A Starless Sky

The midnight stars come and go in my burning eyes. At the
bitter edge of despair I wish they would dissolve into the swirling
void above me or come crashing down upon my bare feet. Then I
would dance across the debris and not flinch for pain is lost on
me as I swept to an unmarked shore, never awoken by morning
sunlight

I would follow his footprints to the ends of all my tomorrows, to
know he was mine if only for a short time, but he leaves no trace.
I lie awake to hear him puncture the silence by calling my name in his
earthy Northern tones. In dreams I am cast as his lover, set to
shiver as I brush against his naked skin.
Even in the dimmest light his skin is golden,
made that way more by the inner sun that shines
within his soul than any outside touch.
Those beautiful brown spinning eyes have taken
many hostages but few have gone consciously.

Man has reached the moon, yet I still fail to reach him.
Alone I am starved but my devotion needs no further
fuel, like each breath I need it to survive. If the world were to
end tomorrow the only wonder left to show me would be the
inner prison of his soul. Closer to freedom with his undenied
truth, they would send me to burn in Hell but I'd still love him
from there.

Siobhan Ni Dhufaigh

The Wood

The wood like me, has grown up
No longer is it the friend
I could lose myself in
Once I could enter it and disappear
Become part of it, moving from tree to tree
Shadow to shadow soundlessly,
Now it is cold, no longer do its shadows envelope me,
It almost resents my presence, blocking my
Way through itself with thorny branches
And placing dry twigs for me to break at my feet
The birds have always flown away as I passed
But now they do it with more noise and commotion
As if laughing at my attempts to renew
A relationship with an old friend
But the wood like me has grown up.

M. David Rose

The Lonely Soldier

A lonely soldier on a battlefield
Not like the old days with sword and shield
Guns are blazing and bullets fly
And all around, his friends, they die

He wonders why he is sitting here
As his heart begins to fill with fear
He thinks of his family and starts to cry
This lonely soldier just a boy

He does his duty he takes a stand
To defend his country, to save his land
Never to wonder to do or die
This lonely soldier just a boy.

B. A. Smyth

When True Love Dies

We met in the mid-morning of life
My soul mate, my lover, dear darling wife
Best friends right from the start
Capturing each others heart
Your presence filled up the room
No space for lingering gloom
The touch of your hand, as you pass my chair
Sweet light in your eyes, to show that you care
The joy in our hearts, each time we meet
With you at my side, our lives were complete

Now cruel death has wrenched us apart
But you still kept hold of my heart
Your love was a pillow, to lay down my head
Your laughter a quilt, to cover my bed
Your presence the power, to live out my life
But all I have now is trouble and strife
I am left in life's tormenting gale
Like a boat at sea bereft of its sail
No star to guide me, no rudder to steer
Cast adrift on an ocean of fear

E. A. Franklin

Forever Green

Can you imagine a life without green
No fields, no trees, no hedgerows seen.
Can you imagine no open space
To walk in a wander at your own pace,
Can you imagine no rippling brooks
And countryside only seen on books,
No sparrows, no fox, no baby chicks
The summer sun setting on rows of bricks.
Lambs that once frolicked, no more to be seen
Can you imagine a life without green.

Can you imagine our land without green
No fields of corn, no harvest to glean,
No fish in the sea, no birds in the air
What are we doing, do we really care?
Our earth was created by God above
To hold in trust for those we love
So nurture it, love and let it be seen
It's wonderful to live in our land that is green

Marion Yeats

Wishes

Birthday wishes for someone so dear,
My wishes for you are all sincere,
A wish which comes from deep inside,
A wish for heavenly love, time cannot hide.

A tender wish for all you cherish,
A wish for love, that'll never perish,
A wish for all you wish yourself,
A wish for more than future health.

A wish that time could now stand still,
A wish that all your dreams are fulfilled,
A wish to end all wasted wishes,
A wish to spirit away life's dirty dishes.

A wish for fulfilment to caress you soon,
A wish that the eternal garden will always bloom . . .
. . . in you and hope that your today, starts and finishes
with a prayer, a dozen red roses and a dozen sweet kisses.

Wishes, Wishes.

D. J. Trueman

My Heaven

Living in a world with no people starving,
no war, no violence just sweet harmony.
People showing respect for each other
regardless of their colour, religion or sex.
No such thing as lower or upper class people,
but everyone living in equality.
No more child abuse, no more cruelty to animals.
Everyone with a life's guarantee of good health.
Can you really imagine my heaven?
Wake up, you're only dreaming.

Lisa McDonagh

"On the Edge"

Need to know the love around;
No - need to feel and not just know.
Longing to feel it enveloping her soul;
Yet standing on the edge of the crowd
She's unable to move any closer.
She's scared to reach out her hand.

All through life and relationships
There have always been two sides,
And after love has been hate, pain and rejection.
Now the fear of rejection grips her whole being.
Can it ever be different?
Still standing on the edge of the scene watching others,
Not able to visualize herself in their midst
She silently cries as she turns and walks away,
Desperately longing for someone to reach out to her
To invite her to join them
So that she can belong.

Lisa Goddard

Ermintrude

My puss she died, my budgie flew,
No, no more pets for me,
I will not be 'tied' and save pounds,
There's sense in that you'll agree,
I can go away, close the flat, and
Not have that nagging feeling,
I won't have to worry when I get back...
At first this was appealing.
But now time's gone on, I'm still alone,
I miss having someone to talk to
Another pet! No, I will fret, saying
I never really ought to.
But then she found me quite unexpectedly,
In a corner I espied her,
She likes the dark, doesn't miaow or bark,
It's my 'Ermintrude' the spider.

E. M. Holt

The Mirror

Facing a giant mirror stands a girl of five
On the other side she says I wish when I'm a hundred I'm still alive

Looking in the mirror is a girl of fourteen with a gleam in her eye
On the other side she cries for adulthood.

Looking in the mirror is a woman of twenty-three
On the other side she is screaming to be free.

Looking in the mirror is a woman of thirty-two
On the other side she is taunted by her soul.

Looking in the mirror is a woman of forty-one
On the other side she thinks I hate you.

Looking in the mirror is a woman of fifty-six
On the other side she looks at her son and wishes she were him

Looking in the mirror is woman of sixty-seven
On the other side she is rushing to be in heaven.

Looking in the mirror is a woman of seventy-eight
On the other side she thinks "I was always late".

Looking in the mirror is a woman of eighty-nine
On the other side she thinks I'm next on the death line.

Looking in the mirror is a woman of a hundred and still alive
On the other side she says 'I wish I were five'.

Tigho Ayovuare

Flower

"I am only a flower blowing in the breeze,
Near this well used footpath, shaded by trees,
I have not yet been tramped, I still blow here,
In the breeze,
Though I'll always wait in worry,
Under my shading trees.

Soon I will be trampled,
Will anyone care for me?
My stem will be crushed - my petals,
All around,
You won't even bother,
When you shove me to the ground.

You will carry on your life,
Yet mine will come to an end,
My last memory will be you,
Turning 'round the bend.

Will you still use that footpath?
That is shaded by the trees,
Knowing that you killed me,
That I can no longer blow in the breeze."

Stacey MacDougall

The Call of the Nightingale

What a charming little bird is the nightingale
On a Summer's night she will tell her tale;
Cradled in a beech tree or aspen tall,
Pause awhile and listen to her plaintive call.

Across the fields and woods so fair,
Her voice is carried on the air,
She pipes and waits, then pipes again,
She knows she will not call in vain.

From yonder wood her voice is heard,
Full-throated sings another bird.
Upon the misty evening air his flute like notes ascend,
While all around the woodland trees with gentle breezes bend,

Oh what melody and song
From her throat she pours then on,
There, together in joy their melodious song they sing.
Making the stillness of the night with silvery music ring.

From times of yore this little bird,
Has given joy when her song is heard.
She brings with her a zest for life,
Her song so free of hate and strife.

Lilian Thrussell

Heartbroken

Hurt, painful, heartbroken.
No more love for me, someone else,
Sweeter, prettier, older.
Me, too young, crying, tears.
Real tears, tears that once loved.
Daydreaming, thinking, why.
The right person gone,
the light of my life, worth living for
never to be seen again.
Is it worth being alive
when the one you love,
doesn't love you back anymore.

Kirsty Lever

"A Tree's Plea"

Underneath the tangle of fern and gorse and heather
nestled cosily in a nook sheltered from the weather,
Stands a little sapling, trying hard to grow,
Braving all the blazing sun, the wind, the rain, the snow.

It struggles hard to push its head up through the tangled mass
To lift its leafy arms up high not seen by all that pass
Soon it becomes a thing of beauty, tall and stately grown
Wearing flowers in its hair, dressed in a green and flowing gown.

Look at me it seems to say, "don't you think I'm grand?
I'll cheer you up through all your days if you only let me stand.
I'll give shelter to the little birds, and pollen to the bees
I'll shade you from the hot sun's rays - oh, let me stay here please.

I've pale pink buds in springtime, in summer I'm dressed in green,
In autumn, reds and yellows, glittering gold - many colours to be seen
Winter comes, and I will slowly close my eyes, and take a
    well-earned rest.
And when next year comes 'round again once more I will look
    my best."

J. C. King

Pictures

Waves have washed our dreams away
No more hope since love walked away.
Sinking alone in rivers of tears
Mountains of heartaches, alone with my fears.

Each day is cloudy since you walked away
Leaving me lonely in colours of grey.
No more sunsets or rivers to chase,
Wishing on stars for the dreams that we made.

Promises like paintings, pastels of blue,
Pretty pictures of yesterday and you.

J. O'Regan

Relationships

Once things were easy,
no doubts, no regrets.
Being on a high, everyday a different story,
living on one's merits.

Unexpected like a flash,
it came from no-where.
Secretly concealed and in silence,
it was all so clever.

The message was simple,
clear but precise.
The effect was everlasting,
what a cunning device.

Like a knife, it struck deep,
a feeling of betrayal and mistrust.
Wanting to remain in everlasting sleep,
memories fading like unwanted dust.

Wicked, damaging and very sly,
quickly eating away at my heart.
A coward's way of saying goodbye,
forever to be apart.

Maria C. Heath

Fear of Heights

Spiralling stairs in cathedral towers,
No grips, no rails, blind blackness glowers.
Endless darkness looms,
A silent shrieking scream consumes.
I fall on all fours, an animal cornered,
Fear freezes on cold, worn steps.
Mumbles above, grumbles below,
Hysterical pressures grow and grow.
Trapped in terror, "Can't anyone see?
I'll fall on them! They'll fall on me!"

Slow-motion nightmare, demented dash,
Bright light bursts, roof-top relief,
So sweet, so brief.
Distance down swoons and sways.
Beckons closer, closer, no delays.
On the brink the magnet draws.
Suddenly a pair of arms withdraws.
The panic, the terror remain,
"I've got to go down again!"

Roderick Croskin

Untitled

Forgive me for the Rain,
No longer it falls Pure,
Although we've poisoned Earth and Sky,
We haven't found a Cure.

Always use a Condom,
Forgive me the Disease,
No longer is it safe,
To sleep with whom you Please.

Forgive me for the War,
A World of Hate and Greed,
If only I had Known,
You'd still be but a Seed.

Forgive me all the Animals,
Once there were so many
But through Man's Progression,
We left you hardly any.

My Children, How I Love You,
Thought it won't look that Way,
But if I had a Magic Wand,
I'd take all the Bad Things Away.

Karen H. Sheen

I Am Air

Breathe me around you and feel me, the veil of my coolness, the
coat of my warmth upon your being, my freezing presence upon
your skin. Close your eyes and inhale me, open your arms to
embrace me, spread your fingers and I'll venture between them,
breathe me gently and I'll enter your very soul, for I am air and
always with you. Play in me and I'll play around you, above you
and below you. Deny yourself the
right of me and you deny yourself the gift of life. You cannot
lose me or fight me for I am your rightful kin, your brother, your
husband, your sister, your wife, I am your mornings, your
afternoons, and your nights. Your life line depends upon me, if
endangered you struggle to find me, but fear not for I am a good
friend by your side, I am second to your soul, I am the reason you
exist. I am your saviour from death, your protector from death,
and your medicine for life, I am above your soul, around your
heart and into your spirit. I am the
silent tick between your seconds, the half a minute to your full
minute, and the half hour to your confirmed hour. I am the days
in your weeks, the weeks in your months and the months in your
tender years, for I am air and always with you. I am the steps you
take from danger, the perfume you breathe to begin your morn-
ing, the last thing to leave your being when your life disperses
into the heavens, and the first thing to greet you, the first thing
you breathe, discover and depend upon cometh the circle of your
re-birth
for I am air and always with you.

Samantha Jeanne O'Geare

Parting

When two people want to part
No matter what the broken hearts
It's best to go forget the past
Look to the future and make it last
Sad but true go on to new
Try hard, be happy you'll get through

Support from family you will need
We'll stand by while you do the deed
It breaks our hearts to see it end
But broken pieces we'll try to mend
We'll lend our ears to all your sorrows
Never forget there's new tomorrows

We're always there through thick and thin
We belong to both Kith and Kin
Life's twists and turns they can be strange
Don't forget it's one big game
One day perhaps you can be friends
Time doesn't regret, it heals and mends

Linda Williamson

Twisted Maze

Our lives go on in a twisted maze
No matter what we say
And day by day we learn to grow
For that's the only way
For live we must until we die
In that moment's tick of years
And some may know but only some
The reason why we're here
To live, grow old and then to die
That's what society says
And those who live in the outside world
Live life in a misty haze
There's more to life than society says
But only we can see
That spark of light within our sight
The one to set us free
So grow we must to reach our goal
And warm that icy chill
For one day we'll find the answers
And our lives they will fulfil.

Pearl Archer

They Don't Understand

They don't understand, all those well meaning friends
of the need that she has that won't go away
For the things that they have but don't really see
A friend, a lover, a child, a life
A longing so deep it cuts like a knife
A wound that runs deeper with each passing day
Her existence the nightmare that won't go away.

Susan Barnett

Dreaming

There is a silence that has no sound
No noise of footsteps falling
As gently the night winds sigh
And grey clouds go drifting by
When in the dark hours of the night, my shut eyes weep
For our dreams pursue our thoughts
But do not find the end or the beginning
And although I do not fear
To see those eyes which so delighted me.
As I dream of all the goings-on of life
And the years I spent as your beloved wife
You slumber on.
You were my friend; who loved me till the end
But left me this solitude.
For I have been young; but now am old
And the sheets I lie on are empty and cold
But as the darkness silvers away
And I begin another day
When passions are no more, so we are calm
And happy memories bring peace and a healing balm.

G. M. Haigh

Dreaming of Life

I dare to dream, of a life so supreme,
of qualities so rich and delightful,
and then I look 'round, and listen to the sound,
of people, begrudging, and spiteful.
But what would I do
if my dreams did come true,
and millions belonged to me,
I'd buy a house and car,
make me money go far,
and then face reality.

L. Hirst

The Odd Couple

"They're right funny folk who live in that house
No one knows nought about them at all
They say the old fellow's as quite as a mouse
And pretends to be out if you call".

"A woman I know says that she is a b*tch".
"We can do without their sort goddarnit".
"Some people say that she is a witch
And he is the devil incarnate".

"I've been told they don't have any money
And get all they can from the state".
"If you see her she's always dressed funny
And he never comes outside the gate".

"They're the most selfish couple that ever I've known
They've no kids 'cos they couldn't beget 'em".
"Well I know the reason they live all alone
Is they could and they did but they 'et 'em".

"Well I'm glad that I don't even know them,
That you do, you're sorry, I'll bet
You'd not trust them as far as you you'd throw them?"
"Oh no! thank goodness that we've never met".

C. Denton

My First Mother's Day without My Mam

There's a place in my memory, my life that you fill
No other can take it no one will.
There's a place in my heart that no one can own
Whom I talk to for strength when I'm alone
We are never without her in thought and in mind
No one can place no one will.
The bond that we had will always be
I know she is watching over me.
She said when she went we would have to go to
She knew us so well the pain we would
go through
We are not parted forever there are no goodbyes
We will be following behind her like the days gone by
So wait for us Mam just by the door
And we will always be together
Just like the days before.

B. Henderson

Dawn of a New Day

The velvet blackness of the sky is pierced with stars,
No sound pervades the air - the morn is still.
Each blade of grass hangs heavy with moist drops of dew,
And sheep lie gently sleeping on the hill.

The first light softly steals across the waiting heavens -
Streaks of pink and azure, tinged with gold.
The silhouetted shapes of trees on the horizon,
Stand out in sharp relief, all black and bold.

A gentle whispered scurrying of a sleepy fieldmouse,
A soft brown feathery fluttering of wings,
A tentative sweet note is sung - another answers,
Then suddenly, it seems the whole world sings.

The wakening fields reflect the new day's promised glory,
The breeze awakes and flutters all around,
The daisies lift their heads in welcome to the morning,
And life begins anew with gladsome sound.

P. A. Neil

Ode to Mankind

Listen to me man of God - a preacher? The reader says
No you who reads this poem, Man of God, I've said
Of God you are, of God you be, a truth you fail to see
So think not you are less than that
When what you are is He.

I write to you, the searching one, to tell you of your grace
To search in vain for what you are is really no disgrace
But what you are is perfect, regardless of your thoughts
And what you regard as sin, is judgement of your choice
There is no sin, it never was, it is man's little game
For no man can destroy himself, though try he will in vain
To try to destroy another, is a view of lesser sight
For he'll rise again to another life, eternity is his right
That right is true for all of you, so turn now from these thoughts
When you look within to who you are, your light will change
your course
So carry on now light of the world, let it shine, not dim
For you are of the highest source
And you are One with Him.

Susan Mortimer

Look, Stop, Racism

Am I shamed by people because I'm a different race?
Or, am I misjudged because of the colour in my face?
Am I a miscalculation? So wrong, that I'm rejected?
   Why is it my life that has to be affected?
Hatred is held in people's minds,
Why does this coloration make people blind?
Am I such a criminal because I'm not the same?
   Why do people play this hateful game?

Lisa Clay

Never Look Back

Never look back in anger
Or forward with too much haste.
Never save time for worry,
Never leave time to waste.
Let dreams be your beginnings
And action be your end.
Let loyalty be you aim,
Then truth be your friend.

Never let hate into your life
And eat away your soul.
Only let love be your light
And honesty be your goal.
Let children be your learning
With the innocence that they give
Then grab hold of life with both hands,
Thank God and then just live.

Paul Atherton

Reality Struck

When last I met you,
My heart felt cold,
I couldn't believe.
Now faced with fact.

I had a vision of you previously -
Laughing, joking - always,
I glanced over and reality struck.

The image of you, far-away was hopeless.
But you were never in anger,
No regrets.

Happy memories, so special;
We'll never forget.
I know you still dwell with us
You are precious.

You knew, but didn't go gently,
No more pain, not alone, not frightened.
In this life I will miss you,
But, convert you will not.
Please remember, and remain close.

Kirsten L. Black

Untitled

Visions are all, we all live for,
Nothing else matters, not any more.
Nothing worth living for,
No reason to die,
Melting inside of me, intoxicating my mind.
People can talk,
Though whatever comes out?
I wish that I knew what they're all going on about.
Time no longer has a purpose,
What does it all mean?
Does a clock and its tick make you forget
what you've seen?
Can people and money help change your mind?
Though what I am looking for I shall never find.

Yeliz Uygur

Questions of Life

How did it start?
Nobody knows.
Everything needs a question, a reason and an answer.
Is it about having fun, or waiting?
Will it stop or is it everlasting?
Can any one judge it as an object?
Or is it just something which will linger as an individual?
Can it be taken away or chased?
Has it got its own recipe to make it perfect?
Is it priceless or can it be bought?
Does it exist on other planets?
Can you touch it, smell it, taste it or hear it?
How many people does it belong to?
All these question and many more.
But nobody knows the answers.
This makes it something quite peculiar.
Life!!!
Everybody questions it.

Tina Hathaway

Destiny

Stand not in my wake,
Nor cast dark shadows at my door,
My time is my own to take,
This grief, my own to endure.

In my footsteps, do not tarry,
Nor lay your burden at my feet,
I have my own remorse to carry,
My own destiny to meet.

I shall not stray from this, my pathway,
But reap the harvest that I've sown,
This is my chosen road through life,
I must travel it alone.

Cast not into my heart affray,
Nor try to dance with fate,
The road is long, be on your way,
   I need no advocate.

D. L. Dudley-Scott

Desire

I met him on holiday,
My heart did he take.
He came over to my house;
my heart did he break.
I wish I could see him
all over again.
I gave him my heart
and he went away.
I hope he still has it
and cherishes it so, because
I never want my love to go.
I wrote a letter, told him to reply.
when he didn't I let out a sigh.
Then one day I heard my door
as I lookèd around onto the floor,
I saw his feet, and quickly glanced up.
Happily now, he lives in my flat.

Marlena Fierek

Dawn over the Blackwater

All is still.
Not a breath stirs the surface of the dawn-kissed sea.
The silent wraiths of morning mist glide gently free
as the warming rays of the awakening sun
lay golden paths across the gently undulating
pulse of the morning swell.

So easy to imagine you are in another sphere
where mystic beings have their place.
And we have wandered through the veil
into an unknown unworldly space
where peace wafts gently over fear
and minds are tranquil led.

What now, the gentle swell grows bolder
as if some leaden beast is moving down below.
The fingering wraiths of gossamer mist
are moving to and fro.
Then suddenly the brilliant orb
and changing tide
have vanquished veil, the other world is gone
and morn has come.

Sheila Laurence

The Sad Plight of Others

With what horror we gaze upon the sight,
Of far away people and their sad plight,
Starving children with so many dying,
All of them on western aid relying.

Nations split asunder by civil strife,
Showing no mercy for human life,
Houses burning, and people in retreat,
Thousands seeking refuge on aching feet.

Helpless we view such scenes day by day
But why should the innocent have to pay,
Such a price for freedom, a fair share in life?
Sad victims of war, terror and strife.

Considering all things, how glad we should be,
To live in a country where we are free,
To do and say what we like without any fear,
Of views bring dangerous to those we hold dear.

So instead of moaning about our lot,
Be very grateful for what we've got,
So many would be glad to be in our shoes,
Our way of life if they could but choose.

E. Kathleen Jones

Love . . . or Loneliness?

LOVE is a cold, sad feeling,
not a warm glow inside of you,
it brings a whole new meaning
of pain and sorrow too.

LOVE should be given, not bought,
feelings are totally FREE,
so why are battles fought
with so much hate and energy?

LOVE should mean caring and giving,
putting someone way before you,
but it turns into something quite chilling,
like indifference, in all that you do.

LOVE is no magical mystery,
it's there to hurt and crush you,
it gives you EVERYTHING one moment,
then leaves, and laughs back at you.

No LOVE'S not a warm, glowing feeling,
as you're left there all alone,
it's a bleak hurt deep inside you,
that turns your heart, one day, to stone . . .

A. K. Moore

Lost without You

Alone on a mountain, just me and the breeze
Not a minor bird sings, nor a rustle of the trees
In my mind I see your tall dark face
Your hands are so kind, your mouth like lace
Love creates a picture in the cool mountain air
Like soft water flowing, your thoughts are there
I long to see you and feel your embrace
I can't explain love or the large human race
You're with me in the day, you're with me at night
I see your eyes as I turn out the light
The breeze gently carries the songs we sing
I realize that you mean everything
But now all alone, I lay my thoughts to rest
You're the love of my life and my Sunday best
You fill my heart with gladness and joy
I need you now like a lost child's toy
I can't feel your touch or see you in the sky
You may be gone but our love flies high
I wait for the moment when you walk through that door
I'll know tonight our love is once more.

Zoe Allsopp

The Hyacinth Seed

A good neighbour of mine, himself something of a gardener,
noticed the fertility of my ableit, somewhat humble garden bower
and unbeknownst to me, sowed therein a certain seed.

The seed had life and in utero caught, already struggling to surface
into the light and life which it so singularly sought.

Quickened by the Son into prolific growth,
the seed's life was forfeited, for one anew, as a flower.

Aware as I now am, of my neighbour's goodwill,
I've since followed his example and sown many more seeds still.

And so, like the secret between luminaries or the enmity between
foes,
while I await the harvest, my love grows and grows.

Mark Cheyne

Ode to Time

What happens to time? It can stand still; it can disappear.
No time, we sometimes wail, but time is to live,
To seek the mysteries of the universe.
It makes the roses grow; sheds the autumn leaves.
It heals the sick, and cossets the weary.
Love in a four letter word of gigantic possibilities.
It is for love, should not be for hate.
It records the sunny hours, the misty days,
Time to know I am me and you are you.
Time is needed to do all the things
We'd like to do, but for which we never have time.
"Killing time?" One is asked
And to which we sometimes say "yes".
Time adds wrinkles to ageing skins,
But tenderness to the touch of hands.
Love, alas, in time can fade as roses do, but hearts beat on
So let us enjoy that little strip of light
'Twixt night and night we call `today',
Till live - in time - is kind.

Ruby Lancaster

The Final Question a Searching Sonnet

When I come to the end, will death be a friend
Or implacable foe that takes all I know?
Will the dread and the pain forever remain;
Will sins that are rotten be purged and forgotten,
Or will we still pay for losing His way?
And in the hereafter, will there be laughter?
Will happy bells ring to remind us of spring
Or will our souls splinter and freeze into winter?
Will we remember the joys of September
Or devils impound us, pitch black around us?
Will we distinguish the ills and the anguish
From the love and bright hope that allowed us to cope?
While death hovers near there is little to cheer
Save wondrous rebirth - or is that hollow mirth?

Townley Shenton

Spring

The flowers that had ducked down low,
Now suddenly, they do grow,
People who had a sad face,
Now brighten up like they won a race,
The stags lose their antlers soon,
And not for long we see the moon,
The gorse bushes have flowers on the moor,
We do not see leaves drop on the floor.
The cat on the wall marches, up and down,
People no longer have an icy frown,
Baby animals being born,
Mice eating the new grown corn,
All the birds in the spring sing,
And the church bells do ring, ring, ring.

Matthew Reynolds

My Tree

My tree, all winter, drab has stood,
Now whispers to the first spring bud,
"Take away my garments grey
Clothe me again in dresses gay."

Now, that glorious day has come,
Little buds warmed by the sun,
Have made for her a dress of green,
Now once more she is a queen.

She holds her head with joy and pride
Her lacy gown, flowing wide
This way, that, she nods and sways.
Aware of my admiring gaze.

Beryl Iddon

Max

Nobody said it would be so hard to part
Not a word was said of a broken heart.
With a lump in my throat and a tear in my eye
I laid him to rest, and said my goodbye.
For seventeen years he was my friend.
I didn't think about his end.
He was there to watch the children grow,
And there to bid them cheerio.
I miss the warmth of his head beneath my hand.
That look that said I understand.
The nose that pushed my book away.
The pleading eyes that asked to play.
That eager stance that used to state,
It's time for walks, come on we're late.
I miss the muddy footprints on the floor.
The lead that hung on a hook by the door.
There's a space on the floor where his bed used to be.
The door is still marked where he jumped up to see.
It grieves me still that we had to part.
He's gone from my home, but not from my heart.

Maureen Vera Higson

A Poem to Think About

I am flying high up in the sky,
Now down I dive to the water's edge,
Up again to the sky beyond,
Oh how I fly like a perfect being,
The wind is just a whisper as I fly so very high,
The ocean still beneath me looks like liquid coloured glass,
The land that lies in front of me is just a tiny dot,
Flapping my wings as hard as I can I dive towards the sea,
Beak straight down, wings full out my breakfast waits for me,
Up again to the clear blue sky, oh how I love to fly,
We can be free when we learn to fly just like the whispering wind,
Oh you birds down below let your sprit free,
Let me show you what I've found, the reason to be free,
There's a higher purpose for this life, much more than all you see,
So fly with me up in the sky, and like the wind be free,
And dive and loop and circle 'round in loving freedom be.

Mick Terri

Bad Old Puss

"Meow," said puss as she walked through the park but nobody noticed her there.
The children were having so much fun "Meow does anybody care.
For I am lost I don't know my way" but nobody understood.
"Meow" said puss "someone take me home where I'll stay and I'll be good.
I just wandered off didn't mean to go far, to see and look to be nosey.
"Meow" said puss "please take me home to my mum where it's nice and cosy.
The children all gone and puss is alone as night begins to fall.
"Meow" says puss but nobody hears so she curls herself up like a ball. The moon it does shine lighting her up through the clouds and stars in the dark. She hears a noise what can it be.
It's her mum running across the park. "Meow" says puss
"Meow" she cries her tears are full of glee.
"Purr" said her mum "come along you,
it's home with me for your tea."
From that day to this puss has always been good,
never wandered or even strayed.
She remembers the night that gave her a fright,
So with her mum she always has stayed.

Lesley Johnson

To Live Content

More love and sharing is what we need
Not selfishness or hate or greed
The way things are in the world today
Work, make money no time to play.

Learn to accept things the way they are
So what if you haven't money or a car
Things are so much better you see
To live content is the way to be.

I have never craved for wealth or fame
Exotic holidays afar
Jewellery adorning my body
Or a posh and fancy car.

A fire to keep me warm
A roof above my head
A bed in which to lie.
And food to keep me fed

To live the best way that I can
Be kind and compassionate to my fellow man
It makes a lot of sense to make a new start.
When you live content you'll have peace in your heart.

Wilma Barrett

The Missionary

A human figure, deceiving to the average eye, holds dark secrets,
Only to be revealed by the devoted eye of adolescence,
A missionary mind and robotic soul, held captive in a human shell.
His mind knows nothing of love, nor deep emotion,
Only of his logical purpose as an employee of greater lives to come.

A younger figure tries to change his rigid direction.
Her introduction to love at an early age, proved to be a disadvantage
As her hopes and dreams shatter under the weight of reality.
Her mind, once again conflicts with her heart as she surrenders her soul to him. She knows of the risk she takes which could lead to infinite pain, and as the sands of time cease, he becomes part of her.

Fury overrules her, as his inexperienced lips preach of the illogical purpose of human emotions. Fighting fire with fire,
she continues the uphill battle.
Her minutes turn to hours, days to eternity,
And not even a shred of light can be seen in her universe of darkness.

All spirit is ripped from her body with accusing fingers as she suffers the agonies of her love.
With no escape, she silently waits for her life and world to crash around her.
Another life, another soul, drained by the missionary . . .

Katrina Kent

Life

My life is in turmoil, it's on a downward slide,
Nothing ever goes right, I'd like to run and hide.

The money that I work for pays the bills and all,
Still there are those wanting more, they're not happy 'til I fall.

I struggle on to make ends meet, to have a happy home,
I manage to scramble to my feet, but I'm doing it all alone.

You try to save a penny for that unsuspecting thing,
The pounds may not be many, but then there's a bill, start again.

The car it needs renewing, the fridge it's hot, not cold.
The sofa needs recovering, like me it's getting old.

The roof has got a hole in, the garage roof one too,
Even the cat is old and thin, God knows what I'm gonna do.

Still I should be happy, I've got my health for sure,
My family all around me and I've got my own front door.

I can speak and see, I can walk and hear,
I feel so lucky for these things are so dear.

C. Brown

The World Today

This world of ours is in a state,
Not much love, but plenty of hate;
Billions spent on wars and space,
Not much hope for the human race.
In foreign lands amid the strife,
People starving, fighting for life.
More money, less work is the cry,
No thought of those who have to die.
Bosses, unions join the fight,
What can we believe? What is right?
Then there's redundancy, folk worried sick
Wondering whose jobs next they'll pick,
What hope for the homeless, unemployed?
A better share of wealth should be deployed.
May this mad and wicked world of ours
Change, and promote truth and Justice with their powers,
And through authority, may all wars cease,
So that nations may live in peace.

Kathleen Heavens

Striker

Someone came last night and stole my goal posts
Now I'm in the middle of this field of life without any hopes
Now I'm lost as to whose side I'm on, attack or defence
Out here there's no referee to save me from my torments
There are no linesmen to tell me I've overstepped the mark
I'm out here lost and alone, in the middle of this empty park
Now I can't see just what I'm living and working for
I don't see where to aim, to be able to make my score
How long can I linger from one goalless day to another
Until I find my goal posts, from this no win game,
  I can't recover

Trudi Carroll

Love to Death

Yesterday she said her love would last forever,
Now she had to go.
Waving on the shore,
I heard the ocean's hungry roar,
A raging turmoil in my head.

Yesterday she said her love would last forever,
But not to me!
Green fired burned
My sanity adjourned
She fell as led.

Yesterday she said her love would last forever,
Suffer Kate! I did!
Empty; bottle with warning label
tablets strewn across the table
Aren't I already dead?

K. A. Aldersley

Destruction

The world is going down
nothing will be left,
Kindness has resorted
to ignorance and theft.

Murderers, killers rapists,
wandering the place,
Never will a smile be seen
on another person's face.

Children will be murdered,
building will be bombed,
Will there be nothing left
of which we can be fond?

Everyone's become so low
I do not want to live,
Everybody taking, taking,
now there's nothing left to give.

For then it is conclusive
that life is never fair,
But don't give in, don't let them win,
hold a smile and gently bare.

Rosa Nissim

Memo to a Boss

Your strong point is delegation,
Not for you the dreaded audits.
I'm "volunteered" - no consultation,
We know who will take the plaudits.
The same will happen again next year.

"My door is always open" you said
But your secretary guards the door.
"Feel free to come to see me" you said
But I don't want to anymore,
Behind dark glasses what do you fear?

"We must cascade ideas down,"
Jargon rules the day.
"Oh, not the bidet effect?" You frown.
Let us flag this one away.
Has your life lost all its cheer?

Your days are full of briefings,
For this or that committee.
You plan meetings about meetings,
I'll miss the outcome - a pity,
I'm off to further my own career.

Rhoda Down

Untitled

When we're together, alone,
Nothing else exists,
Just us in a world of our own.
The past never was; the future is yet to come,
Present moments are fleeting
But treasured and precious above all.

Standing on warm and windy hilltops,
The breeze whispering through our hair,
Clothes pushed tight against two forms
Leaning against its invisible support.
We breathe its intoxicating fragrance,
Suddenly, unaware, we touch,
Feelings of a stronger force pass between.

We turn and walk on,
Trying to ignore the endless moment
Of realization - A love that should not be,
A friendship that always was,
A oneness we choose not to admit,
The world moves on but we stand still
  In dreams of paradise.

Margaret Lumpkin

For Eternity

She lay deathly still.
An angel heaven.
I grasp her tiny hand in mine, still warm.
I wish for her to smile at me again, just once more.
But I turn and walk away, my heart heavy.
I know she can never light up my life again.

Everyone is around me, blurred faces in a sea of sounds.
Loneliness envelopes me like a pall.
The devil rages for possession of her soul.
A soundless cry escapes from my dry lips,
As my heart shatters, your life ebbs away.

Darkness. Peace at last.
My heart full of sorrow, their eyes full of pity.
Weighing me down, drowning me with condolences.

Theresa O'Donovan

Swim

Nice day to go to the beach for a swim,
Nowadays it's just a whim.
The last sizzling days,
I had a figure to match the rays.
Nowadays weather hotter and longer,
My figure makes me ponder.
No longer hourglass shape which made people stare,
It's now bigger and bolder like a pear.
No longer the tinny fancy bits I wear,
At times I do not think it's fair.
Any bigger I'll have to rent,
As they're getting as big as a tent.
Deep inside my mind is still the same,
And only I can take part of the blame.
To the gym, I thought, and run the streets,
But that is a big task to meet.
So here I am bigger and older,
I go to the beach swim and sit on a boulder
On the beach all shapes and sizes in the glare,
Hourglass shape and pear.

Sheila Morton

Forest

Mystical smoking tree silken stands
with bird heaven branches
and the name of forbidden truth.
And my lost love in her eastern bows reclined,
warm as the leaves lies,
sleeping, as her days drift by.

Ivan Ericsson

Magical Moments

Have you seen the face
of a wayside flower
or felt the summer rain
had silver moonbeams dance in your hair
and become a child again?

Have you wondered in awe
At a million stars
in a black velvet sky above
had rays of the sun, shine into your soul
and known the warmth of love?

Have you heard the song
of a woodland bird
or the cry of a gull on the wing
the rustle of leaves in a playful breeze
and a choir of insects sing?

Have you walked barefoot
with sand in your toes
the open sea before you
such solitude and sense of peace
are gifts for all — not the few.

Pauline Peachey

The Way of Things

The waters flow - indefatigably
On and on
Between the incarcerating banks that
speed back to source.
The lightning strikes at the roots of
earth,
And the tree of ages bows - to nothing.
The crater emits effulgence;
Effuses finality
While the wars wage on:
For the seed was sown "In the beginning,"
And Cain smiles
In the knowledge of inevitability.

James Leslie

Our Wild Primrose

Add further beauty to famed Scottish scene.
Of revere charms grace court of queen.
Deem as special gifts kind nature's chose.
Can breath take each precious groups she sows.
Blooms challenge to be found other than clean.
Even along eroded banks of ravaging stream.
Sure as a spatted water subsiding flows.
There among floating debris still perfect grows.
Greet sharp at new season I fisher keen.
In parity afresh as spring salmon's pearly sheen.
Some times well nigh casting on my toes.
To blemish perfection sore inflict woes.
Near defy the sun of enhanced glean.
Arrest from all things eyes hard wean.
Seem won't to cast a petal succumb to snows.
As if treat beckons time back and forward throws.
To draw from all iniquities no hard scheme.
Justly voids poetic merits of high esteem.
Still treasure the pleasure to praise in prose.
Maisy our hardy delightful wild primrose.

Tom McConnachie

Late Autumn Thoughts

Summer slipped away before the coming
Of the winter chill,
Yet not now warm and caring
The hedgehog-slow dawn of cold
And thoughtless days.
Melting out of night into the
Blood-red womb of morning,
Those last, late autumn days.
Today, tomorrow or a week ahead
Comes winter with its whip-cord
Cutting dagger of a frost,
On shires smothered deep in
Milk-white snow,
While vagrant Nordic geese beat west
Across the sky.
The brown, scarlet, copper colours
Tinged with gold are fading fast -
To leave us with the monochrome
Of winter and of sleep.

Owen Dan: Jones

Dream Lines

My inner self looks out at the world
Of watching time advancing on,
And feeling the emotions of my mind
Deep rooted in the soul of my heart,
Followers of past thoughts and sensations
Exploded throughout my being,
Earning peace and tranquillity absorbed
Throughout my universe,
Unchanging atmosphere's blend in
Unequalled cloud bursts of energy,
Enhancing the beauty of life and longing,
And the special memory of immense
Pastness floods my inner space,
And forms my dream lines of past
Resounding melancholy.

S. J. Jackson

Breezes over the Gravestones

The wind blows over the gravestones
Of those who have gone before,
And gently whispers a lullaby
To those whom we see no more:
And it tells how the world has changed much
Since they lived and loved on this earth;
It tells of the wars and the conflicts they've missed,
And of building again, and rebirth.
So I join with the breeze as it lulls them to rest,
Whilst our lives hurry on at a pace;
I thank them for all they did in the past
To perpetuate this race.
For we are their 'tomorrows',
And with His helping hand,
Till we lie 'neath the sod, on our walk with God,
The grass will grow green in our land.

Phyllis M. Spooner

What Is a Mother

A mother is many things,
Of which you can't compare,
When all is lost and you can't go on,
She's always standing there.

Her patient smile and soothing hand,
She tells you it's alright,
She never moans of her troubles and pain,
That keep her awake all night.

She deprives herself of things she needs,
Just to see her family right,
Unselfish and never complaining,
She'd work all day and night.

A mother is like a precious jewel,
And your friend who's always there,
Remember this, and never forget,
To show her how much you care.

Suzanne McCormick

The Pheasants

A broody hen was sitting tight
On some pheasants eggs,
Then one day they began to crack
And out popped tiny heads.
Soon they were running in and out
Pecking food that lay about.
The Mother proudly watched her brood
Finding little bits of food.
And as they grew they suddenly found
A great big world was all around.
And then they thought that they must try
To see if they could fly.
Then later on when they were strong
And really could fly high
The Guns came out, and with a shout
Shot them from the sky.

L. H. West

A Dinner Party with Strangers

The snowy white cloth gleamed beneath the light,
On the table stood a carafe of red wine,
Silver cutlery glistened against white,
All politely seated waiting to dine.

During the meal people ill at ease,
Feigned smiles and courteous conversation,
Compliments paid, people eager to please,
Each feeling speech a forced obligation.

After the meal everyone thanks the host,
Accepting a drink with hesitation,
Someone stands up and proposes a toast,
Offering us all an invitation

To join him next week, I can hardly wait!
I mull over with dread my next dinner date.

Melanie Smith

Leaves

As they sleep swaying in the wind
on a tall long branch
times past's by,
time to wake up,
breaking though like a butterfly
to the warm of the sun,
shining down and the current of the
wind and rain, they live and breath as nature allows.

Olive Irwin

A Narrow Life

We are the victims
Of the system
That encourages a narrow life.
If only we could fully understand our potential
But, moulded by, and reflecting
Mass media taste,
We do not appreciate art
Capable of telling us the truth about this world of ours,
About ourselves,
Art capable of inspiring us, ennobling us and chiding us
Instead we labour under a yoke
Of convention, habit and prejudice
Absorbed in trivialities
Our hopes based only on luck and chance,
Moral apathy and insensitivity
The two heralds of certain tragedy.
We deceive ourselves, we rob ourselves.
Behaviour unworthy of our humanity.
Even passive 'like' and 'love' of positivism falls short.
We must actively promote truth, rationality and justice.

Lea Georgiades

Double Bed

Oh dear, ma double bed
Oh dear, ma back
What I'd give for a single wife
To be a single man, Jack.

I won't say the wife's a problem
But just imagine a face of stubborn strife
From day to night, she's always right
Then that's you got ma wife, Jack.

Truth to say I'm broken-hearted
I'm cleaned and dusted out a ma life
Never once have we been parted
Would you take ma wife, Jack?

I'll sell her for a pittance
If you believe she can work for you
But soon you'll be defeated, make admittance
Before your whole life's through, and you're ruined too, Jack.

Better days, were the days, I'd far forgotten
The days when I could scratch the itch
Now it's just a case of suffering, what's rotten
For she won't leave, and I have to live with the b***h.

P. Boyle

Children at Play

In the fields or at the park,
Oh, it's time to have a lark,
Running through the long damp grass,
Or sliding down the slide so fast.

All children love to play
Every hour of everyday
falling over and graze a knee
Crying out, Oh please help me!
On the swings they swing so high
Seeing who can reach the sky
Will it be you or will it be me.

They all climb on the roundabout
Spinning so fast, all the children shout out,
Slowly, slowly not too fast
We're going to fall, who will last.

Lorraine Bacon

"Just to Dream"

It's lovely to dream, and have a secret thought
One little pleasure, that cannot be bought,
We can dream anytime, through the day or night
These little moments, can bring you true delight,
Sweet dreams often come, when we are feeling blue
We wish that some day, our dreams could come true,
And we hold out a hand, as if to touch
As we dream of the one, that we love so much.

Victor R. Travis

Sour Grapes

"How can you live so far", they say, "With no car?",
"Oh, we cope", I say, "There is really no day that I sit or mope
Or stand around to view the latest model".
"They tell me it's a doddle, at a price that shakes me rigid".
Shuffle feet and fidget, then beat a quick retreat
To my flat, gasping, "That is that!".
"It's far beyond my means". I feel full of beans
And say, "What a gorgeous day to walk a mile or so",
And feel the glow of good health. No cars brought with wealth
Can bring that zing. With a smile and, in my feet, a spring
I stride, feeling good. Eyes open wide.
"Just look at all these flowers at ground level
You have had a devil of a thrilling ride,
But I feel good inside, and don't care
Because I breathe God's fresh air". Strolling on my way
Not wasting a day in garage, fixing car. "You see, I'd rather be
From breakdowns free. Road-works, parking in the town
And yes, the warden's frown.
How unlucky you all are with that monster thing you call a car!".

P. J. Ellis

The Devil's War

I am a rough tough wave coming towards the rocks,
On a dark cloudy black night,
But at the back of the big rock.
There is a bright light struggling to get through,
It's like a big war one side trying to get through to the other,
One side good, one side bad, rocks like stepping stones,
Making a puzzle through the waves,
The clouds like black dark steps to the devil "NO HAPPINESS",
The only beam of happiness in our world
Is below the sea with the fishes,
The beam of light shining upon the sea from the lighthouse,
Giving a glitter of light beaming on to the rocks,
The pool of light sitting in the corner,
Black rocks sitting in the water like coal,
We smash against the rocks like thunderbolts,
Fishes flying in the air dancing madly in the sea trying to escape,
The black clouds trapping the bright clouds
From getting out of their dark prison
The clouds drain the water from the sea
No home left for us now I am gone forever

S. M. Page

Solitude

Miles and miles away from town,
On a grassy bank I sat down,
To enjoy the silence of the night,
And admire the landscape with delight,
No noisy traffic or rumbling trains,
Just rolling hills and winding lanes,
No hustle and bustle of the throng,
But I hear the blackbird sing his song,
I hear the wind blow in the trees.
Life's so good with things like these,
Back in the town the traffic roars,
Life's a worry, life seems a boar,
No one has patience, no one seems to care,
No time to stop, to stand and stare,
On this bank where I sat down,
Miles and Miles away from town,
I found the quiet and the bliss,
And all the lovely things I miss.

T. W. Berry

A Country Walk

To walk along the countryside
  On a summer's afternoon.
To smell the honeysuckle
  With its blossoms all in bloom
To listen to the corncrake
  And watch the farmers make the hay
Is the nicest way to pass the time
  On a lovely summer's day.

  You can stroll around the orchards
And smell the apples dangling overhead
  You can see and hear the goldfinch sing
  With its beautiful red head
And then to head for home again
  And go a different way
  With memories of a country walk
On a lovely summer's day.

V. P. Clarke

"May Day Thoughts"

Off I go, off to war
On life I close the door
Will I live or will I die?
Oh! Won't somebody tell me why

Through the bodies injured and dead
Oh, won't you get it through your head
War will never pay in the end
So why oh why, do we always send?

Black men, white men young and old
Why oh why is this story never told
He had his life straight ahead
Surely now enough is said

He falls to the ground
There isn't a sound
Is that a dove I see?
No! Just a wish to be free.

Peter Cornwall

Old Man

He often walked here.
Often thinking of the way things were, the yesterdays.
He often waved a friendly wave, and spoke freely with passers by.
Today was no different, nothing had changed.

The trees still greeted him with their same majestic bow,
as they swayed from side to side in the wind.
His old bones sang out the same old tune,
a tired song, a familiar reminder of the year's past.
Nothing had changed.

The flower beds in bloom, warmed him as he passed by.
A blanket of comfort, so well cared for.
The cobbles under foot, mapped out his journey.
Step by step, a reflection of so many days passed.
Nothing had changed.

He often took a while to catch his breath,
to gather his thoughts, to watch the children as they played.
He pulled his scarf tightly around his neck, as the wind seemed
cruel that day.
Her warm hand, no longer held his. Today everything had changed.
He walked alone.

Sarah Watts

Oh Mighty Wind of Fate

Blowing across the plains of life, scattering your
seeds of happiness and sorrow, disappointment
and joy, grief and laughter

Blowing first here, then there, tossing the souls
of men, like ships at sea,

Blow gently oh mighty wind, blow gently on
the tired soul

That it may find a quiet harbour of peace.

Patricia Wadsworth

Paradise Found

The eternal hills look down with steadfast calm
On peaceful scenes in widespread vale below,
The woodland glades, the fields of pastoral farm,
The winding stream which sings in tuneful flow.
A serenade; to fragrant primrose growing,
On mossy bank; to shy sweet violet showing,
To gold starred daisies and the cowslip blowing,
In gentle breeze, which softly drifting by,
Sings with the stream a perfumed lullaby.

The tall trees ranked in graceful colonnade
Stand meditative in the noontide glow,
Whose branches dapple golden light and shade
On hazy mists of bluebells spread below.
The verdant fields and meadows green are springing
In azure sky a joyous lark is singing
From flower to flower the murm'ring bees are winging,
A sweet enchantment lies in scene so fair
And happy peace a benediction there.

Wynne Mary Wilson

'One'

One head, One heart,
One birth, One death,

One isn't many but it's enough
It's more than most will ever be given

Some chuck it, some kick it,
Some waste it, some use it,

But one is everything,
One day, One night, One life,
One planet, One God, One universe,
One place, One Home, One road,
One way, One dream and One chance

Just think what it would be like
If all these things were none

Then you'll be complaining
Wishing you had 'One'.

Matthew Lindley

Amorphous Presence

Sitting, impressions not wrong, feelings of being watched strong,
no one around or in sight, I feel a presence, I know I'm right,
creaking floor boards, sound, foot taps to ground, I feel I have a
visitor looking over me! But not scared, am I to be, feeling
apprehensive to what may be in sight, not seeing it ever, even
though bright shining the light, is this an amorphous presence, I
feel of a ghostly apparition which I cannot see, to this I keel,
cuddle up in a ball, feelings of frightened pangs, of all, to why
must I cash-gate, to this feel like bait, if I convoke may others
appear this is no joke. Do they the presence feel, are they
embalm, fragrant charm, this scent I
feel quite calm, I feel so tired lying in my bed, my book I have
read, but as I gradually drop off to sleep. I know they are
watching me, I feel their presence to watch me they keep!

N. Harbard

Company

I have two lovely cats as happy as can be,
One is a tom and the other is a she.
They get up to all kinds of play,
When they're not sleeping through the day.
Sophie is the girl all fluffy and sweet,
Pepie is the boy always very neat.

We have chicken for dinner, I give them a treat,
Pepie tries to help himself as it's his favourite meat.
I have to scold Pepie as I hear the fridge door,
He hooks his claw in the seal and tries for some more.

We've a flap in the door for them to go in and out.
They do not go far it's like a roundabout.
Occasionally they wash each other, And end up with a fight,
But they soon make up and settle for the night.

Maureen Faulkner

The Things I Miss Most

What are we doing so terribly wrong,
Our future children are in my dreams, but when I wake they're gone,
Why are we deprived of these special times,
We are not wicked people who commit awful crimes.

No morning sickness or kicks from inside,
No growing bump that I'm trying to hide,
No swollen ankles and feeling faint,
No trips to the shops to buy nursery paint.

No bright white nappies to hang on my line,
No wonderful pram to show and shine,
Nobody to wake me in the still of night,
Who needs a mother to hug it tight.

No dolls and prams or bikes and trains,
No dirty clothes with mud or stains,
No parenthood worries, no motherly fears,
No putting on plasters to stop little tears.

No frilly dresses, no dungarees,
No birthday balloons, no big Christmas trees,
No bubbles at bath time, no cuddles before bed;
Ever longing thoughts, in a childless person's head.

S. J. Hurley

Life

Born was we so very sweet, with tiny hands and little feet,
outgrowing clothes and saying goo, heavy nappies filled with poo!
The time for school, we're five years old, wearing grey shorts,
feeling cold,
See ya mum, at 3:30, with blazer torn and hands all dirty.
Growing up so very quick, kids' diseases, always sick
First it's measles, then it's mumps, Face all swollen - full of lumps!
In your teens some go punk, some go skinhead, some go funk
Fashion's in and so is beer, your own decisions - straight or queer.
Then it's work and buying a home, mortgage payments and
paying a loan
Got no money just pay pay pay, a simple mistake and one's on
the way!
Married ten years and soon be forty, letting things slip, let's get
sporty!
Middle age spread and hair so thin, 'tis one more battle I cannot
win!
And now you're old with a mixed-up head, can't do anything,
just lay in bed!
Eyes can't see and can't hear thunder, better off being six foot under!
So don't get stale and be a bore, always grumpy, being sore
When you go through trouble and strife, remember three words —
'Live Your Life'!!

Mark Hayes

Land of Sorrows

Slow misty land of the western waves
Sad misty land you call me

Green lands, dark lakes
Sad misty land you call me

Time doesn't matter
Who wouldn't prefer four to three?

Many greens, many blues
Strange islands of the western wave

Cows swim to boat, beyond lies the sunset
Such strange islands of the western wave

Flimsy curraghs, black and small, seven son's lost
High pitch cries, lamenting sons lost.
Seven they were and all gone the same way.

Melancholy land, islands cry, no joy.
Sad islands of the western wave

Songs sung, eyes shut, fragile boats, fragile sons
Misty lands fragile lands. The western waves you call
Distant misty land of the western waves
Distant lands, lonely lands
Slow misty land of the western waves. You call me.

Saul Grant

Katie

It was freezing cold
On this hot summer's day
For the life of a child - just passed away

Such a gentle, still, lonely sight
Upon the bed - lay quiet
For she is not with us now
The angels have that honour tonight

It saddens me so, to be left
With this mortal bind
It stops me from being close to you
For it's her kind soul I wish to find
On its heavenly flight

God bless you, my child
And sleep in peace
Knowing my love for you
Will not cease.

Kevin Burnell

Moonlight

Moonlight is kind to places no peeling paint no crack, no traces,
Only its translucent glow does the kindly moonlight show,
Moonlight is kind to faces no tears no remorse no traces,
Only the calm moonlight glow does the kindly moonlight show,

Moonlight is kind to lovers their dew-like tears resembles stars,
Their unfounded fears fly up to Mars hand in hand they walk away
To meet the dawning of the day

Moonlight is kind to poets their trailing thoughts turn to emotions,
They write with feverish hand anew of quest of wars
and romance too.
Moonlight is kind to the stranger the long dark road holds no danger,
For the silvery moonlight glow shows the stranger where to go,
Moonlight is kind to me it made me write this poetry,
Now I wait for its return with loving heart and eyes that yearn,
To watch it glow and shine for me on the world so graciously.

Vivinne McGinn

The Passing Years

No matter how each day may end
or what the future has in store
on one thing dear you can depend
each passing year I love you more.

Like the sun that warms the meadows
or the dawn when songbirds sing
our lovelight will dispel the shadows
and turn our winter into spring

This road of life is not forever
there are things that we may not understand
but we will always be together
and pass each milestone hand in hand.

G. M. Smyth

Thoughts of Abroad from Home

A darker side of man appeared upon a yonder hill,
Our 'boys' in blue, were called again -
To be our Heroes still,
To lead the way to Victory; supported by the best -
United Forces gathering to meet the final test.
Within the Desert Storm they fought,
But not for you or me?
For 'PEACE' to reign upon out lands,
In all Humility.

The Cannon roared, the skies lit up -
With angry flames of 'HATE',
Our 'boys' this time were on the ground -
To liberate Kuwait,
And with God's speed and helping hands,
They soon accomplished much,
In 'GLORY' may we praise them be,
But in repose, must surely ponder such?
Through all Eternity.

Margaret Barrass

A Little Welsh Town

The hearth with flame aglow
Reflected on the mistletoe
Its waxen beads of purest white
Amidst the golden candlelight
On that happy Christmas Day
I paused and thought of those I'd met and loved
And those so far away

Memories so near and dear
Sharing happiness and tear
Of sad and smiling faces, in a multitude of places
Acquaintances who keep in touch
And others you have loved so much
A host of friends so bountifully cherished
A treasured few, alas, so sadly perished

Through all the years of hopes and dreams
And striving to achieve what seems
To be a glorious world within a soul
Far reaching for its endless goal
At last I find a tranquil place, so full of harmony and grace
A haven wherein love and peace serenely dwell
That little bit of Wales - Llandrindod Wells

Nicholas Bryans

Highway of Reckoning

The man rides forth, into the dark, foggy airs shroud his being
Piercing moonbeams tantalize the cold diffuse light
He knows not what he seeks, it matters little
Every journey is different, all is new experience
For it is through life that the man travels

The night has a feel of menace as the rider reins in
Perchance he has come by a crossroads of opalescence
Confusion though, is paramount in his solitude,
His mind slides once again to the past
Unsure of what may come, he has ridden hard,
Across the open stretches, and searched through the
entangled forest
The plains of life, the dark brooding of his mind

Signs yield little information, seek to further mystify the rider
Wealth points south, happiness follows a path to the north
Unfulfilled desires lead away in another direction
The road of health had proved tediously uneventful

A stiff wind blows through, clearing the intersection, freeing thought
With a clarity he now knows what it is that he seeks
Uncertainly, he wheels the horse around, and down the oft used track
Here he may find love, with hope renewed the highwayman rides
again.

Leigh Billett

Picture Love

If I can paint, with words my feelings, yet cannot describe
them openly
When you try to read my story, how does my silence picture me?
If I can draw what is not spoken, the thoughts in me, that
swarm inside
Will you understand if I keep quiet, when from the words my
feelings hide!

If I can write, what is never said, that it's so hard to say
what's true
And if break my silence open, would then my soul belong to you?
Why does it hurt to say 'I love you'? How can three words
cause so much pain?
And when I try to mouth emotions, why do I find my lips refrain?

If in my silence, there echoes sadness, will you ever learn to
forgive me?
Can you love me with no answer, if the words won't come to me?
How can I portray I love you deeply, I always have, it's clear to see
If words betray the need to tell you, that is how to picture me!

Picture words, are clear to see, I'll never leave, believe in me,
You have framed a heart, that once was free, picture love and
picture me.

Kevin J. Plicio

The Saffron Crocus

What beauty does this flower hold
Once precious more than gold
Planted in the rich red soil
The delicate crocus grows
What secret does this flower contain
That's planted with great care
Laboured long and hard by hand
Its secret let us share
No ordinary crocus this
But related to our own
Which grows in gardens in the spring
But this one's usefulness is known
It thrives in good dry limestone ground
With care it's cultivated
The saffron crocus is its name:
Red gold spice it's rated
A product so expensive
And picked at just the time
Delicately picked and harvested
When saffron's at its prime.

L. M. Carter

Boxing

Getting ready to start referee pulls them apart
one hook and duck not just a pluck
just after lunch having a punch
three rounds few downs
going 'round in circles it would have to take a miracle
next round no downs
three rounds to go just give him a blow
at his teeth he had to crunch
the other boxer gave him a punch
it's all pain, no game
they stop, no drop
have a drink to clean out the mouth
can't wait to get to the house
before you know it, it's the sixth round
no-one's even hit the ground
this ain't no act that's a fact
one round to go few more blows
suddenly, one down it's a helt
the other wins the belt

Tracy Greer

The Head and Tail of the Moon

The head of the moon shines her silver rays
On frivolity and merriment,
The tail of the moon he displays
A melancholy temperament.

Linda Watson

Parting

Parting is a bitter sorrow,
One that bears only pain.
It comes like darkness on a colourful day,
Snatching away the light and leaving only rain.

It seems like a vacuum has enveloped you,
And the air has left your life.
Leaving you like a crippled, wanting, 'dead' soul,
Knowing no love - only strife.

You tell yourself when to breathe,
When to think, and when to cry.
Yet always having to remember the one,
For whom you could steal, kill or even die.

When even the love of your life has left you,
Leaving only their memory behind.
What can you do, but teach yourself how to live again,
Knowing that life without them is hard to find.

Trying to part with the unceasing darkness,
Is hard enough to do.
When thinking also of the pain your loved one is suffering,
When he is remembering you . . .

Yesha Yadav

Wishful Thinking

What I lack in life's a name
One that would conjure up!
Wealth, security, and fame
To make them all look up.

Like Hercules, and Pericles
And other names as sound,
As those men in history
Whose names are so renowned.

But all these names I cannot use
For they are second-hand
And if I could, what hopes have I
To reach the heights where now they stand?

Then whilst in dream I realized
My searchings were in - vain
For it's not the name which makes the man
But the man, which makes the name!

A. P. Hollick

Plight of the Stripper

Hair closely cropped ear wisps shaped to a point,
opalescent hazel eyes, petite nose slightly out of joint.
Pink lipstick coloured lips heighten her dollish complexion,
programmed to tease she'll reveal all for inspection.
She moves slowly centre stage rather pensive,
surveying so called gentry, a little apprehensive.
Temperatures rise as she begins her routine,
voyeurs wearing dinner jackets uttering the obscene.
Excitement abounds in the front central rows,
bosoms exposed the empty brassiere she throws.
Nipples projecting forward like two unspent bullets,
cigar smoking men choking from their gullets.
Thickened thighs tapering to calves so slender,
legs now unadorned of fishnet and suspender.
Her midriff somewhat paunchy due to age maybe,
buttocks firm, rounded like a females should be.
Fumbling fingers removing the "G" string her utmost humiliation,
they stand and applaud, servile praise to degradation.
Posing briefly, a naked woman yet in disguise,
departing the stage dryless tears in her eyes.

L. Hollier

Dance with a Nursery Rhyme

Ah if I could but take wing
Or like a conker on a laughing string
Be hurled through space and time
To dance with a nursery rhyme

I would dance and laugh all day
As the cat on the fiddle did play
With the cow jump over the moon
With the dish run away with the spoon

But alas I have no wing
Nor am I tied to a laughing string
As I wander this wandering of mine
Never to dance with a nursery rhyme

Lawrence Smith

Shakespeare

As king-cupped curls of golden English oak
Paid whispered court to England's virgin Queen,
In whose long reign the Prince of Stratford spoke
And penned so pure no peer has yet been seen,
So his gilt leaves oft kissed the regal hand
The centuries between: until once more
Fair name "Elizabeth" proclaims our land,
As at his birth four hundred years before.
No Thespian fool may act Shakespearean clown,
Sad Juliet's trance, or fay Titania's dream,
Mad Hamlet's mind, or Macbeth's sleepless crown.
"The Play's The Thing" is universal theme.
Yet had Shakespeare not composed a sonnet,
I should not have writ this piece upon it.

Ray Matthews

Not Just Another Picture on the Wall

Just because people see that I have dreadlocks in my hair,
Or maybe I've got slack, ripped, jeans - why do they really care?
They think I'm layabout - I'd love to prove I'm not.
Their prejudiced comments show just what a mind they've got.
Why should we have stereotypes, for I am simply me.
If you looked a little further and just listened then you'd see.
Don't assume at what I'm like if I'm not of your race,
Why don't they understand that I'm just not another face,
No-one is that stupid that they can't look inside, within,
You shouldn't guess how I act by the colour of my skin.
I am hurt when you assume that I'm just one of them,
Just because of how I look that hardly means a thing.
Don't plan your opinions just from a quick first glance,
Get to know me then decide - at least give me a chance.
Appearances are deceptive, you've probably heard that said.
Don't waste your time assuming - get to know who I am instead.

Shelley Rowntree

In Days Gone By

In days gone by, there was just you and I
Our dreams we shared together
We'd laugh and play, in the happiest way
And thought we'd live forever
But sorrow comes to one and all
At one time or another
We lose the one we love the most
Be it daughter, son or lover
In days gone by we couldn't see
The pain that lay ahead
The hurt there'd be, the tears there'd be
When one of us was dead.
And now the time to part is here
We have to say goodbye.
Please smile for me and wipe your tears
And hold me as I die.
In times gone by there was just you and I
Our dreams we shared together
We'd laugh and play in the happiest way
And thought we'd live forever.

Katrina Birch

Mother Nature

Pollution is hear to stay,
Our green and pasture land will decay,
Save our Planet from man kind,
Mother nature you will find.

Life on earth is forever,
We must care and work together,
Let us pray and understand,
Mother nature is our land.

Give us the chance to make amend,
Could this be the very end,
Will the human race survive,
Mother nature can keep us alive.

Stephen Treharne

Alone

A widow now her friends remark
Poor soul she's all alone, and what comfort will she get from
children fully grown.
Although they offer sympathy and weak arms to caress,
who can fill a husband's place that leaves such loneliness.

Like two world explorers they set off from the start,
through the trials and downfalls with each a willing heart.
The joys in caring, love in sharing, every test together,
The warmth, companionship and love, they hoped to share forever

She wipes a tear from her eye and lifts her head up higher and
for a moment stands erect for fear she may soon tire,
Her task is there although alone, she has to face it on her own.

The pain still there she hides it, behind a weary smile and hopes
the mask she's wearing, will cover for a while,
The memories of a marriage although now in the past, until the time
they meet again and sadness ends at last.

Sonia Sacre

Peace of Mind!

Take a walk, in the quiet,
Peacefulness, of the garden,
Forget your worries and cares,
Stop for awhile, to smell the roses,
How sweet, their fragrance lingers,
In the coolness of the air,
Relax, clear your mind,
Feel refreshed, for tomorrow's prayer!

Mary Flower

Architecture

Camberwell Green, yes days gone by, was the home of Christopher Wren.
Our English clever architect, days that will not return again!
There was fine country in those parts, good buildings were sublime
In fine detail, with quality built, with curves, arches to define.

You can tell from the pictures, they kept from those days.
Pictures of beauty and strength do amaze
A steeple so fine, or a dome of splendour,
They were made good and strong, with an interest to render.
With the true honest accuracy, mended so tender.

They were our landmarks, so nice, like a badge.
But who made decisions to alter our heritage?
When not quite so clever, they tried to endeavour
A cheap quick way to make London modern.
But if they'd followed the footsteps their fathers had trodden
There would be no complaint, we haven't forgotten.
Bad architecture is never so pleasant
What we have left now, is a fond reminiscent.

Ruby E. Griffin

Time Goes By . . .

We are here for but a blink of an eye
Only realising it as time goes by
Losing loved ones on the way -
Gone to a better place we pray

Rarely showing each other how we feel
Regretting the future before it's seen
If given forethought we'd see how we should have been

Parents getting older, frailer too
Not realising it, but of course it's true
Until one day all the security you knew you had
Is gone forever leaving you desolate and sad

For all the things we should have said throughout
We are now left feeling guilty about
Time heals "They" say
But how do we reconcile opportunities missed?
All we can do is pray and hope we can be forgiven one day

J. A. Tweddle

Questions for the Animals

Animals, animals, where have you been?
Packed up in lorries, none too clean
Animals, animals, where are you going?
Your fate is sealed. You are innocent, unknowing.
Animals, what do you think of man
And the way you've been treated since time began?
Do you know protestors stand out for your rights?
We've seen you travelling. You've seen some sights.
Animals, do you know we're very sorry
To see you crammed in stinking old lorry?
Sent for ritual slaughter or to a veal crate,
Either way it is a cruel evil fate.
Now cows are inflicted with BSE.
A disgrace for man. How can it be?
Should a cow be changed to a carnivore?
It should never be. Need I say more?
The trouble it's caused is so obvious.
No wonder protestors make such a fuss.
Animals, can you ever forgive
The ways that you die, or are forced to live?

Norma Langley

Our Grandchildren

Our garden looks lovely in the sun
Our grandchildren playing football having fun,
Such joy for grandparents to behold,
They are worth their weight in gold.

There is such laughter coming to places
Michael, Scott, Jack and Mathew with smiling faces,
They look so cute with boyish ways
So much joy they bring each day.

Their childhood will soon be in the past,
We cannot stop the years come so fast
The children will grow but love remains,
Bound for life with loving chains.

Happy moments remain bright and clear,
Of all the times we hold so dear
Such precious memories to relive,
And cherish all the joys they give.

V. Mitchell

Constitutional

Why is it when we go to bed
Our mongrel wants his walk instead . . .
To do his stint around the park
And leave his constitutional mark;
Where other dogs have been before
And dragged their owners by the score.
Through mud and puddles in the rain
They dash and furnish their domain,
With scented symbols of their kind
For other dogs to track and find -
And just like sheep we let them lead
For thus their nature has decreed . . .
That dogs . . . in harness for their goal
Must take their constitutional stroll.

B. Ditchburn

"Happy Thoughts"

When we sit alone at the close of each day,
Our souls at peace with the earth,
In which paths do our thoughts stray
And how much are they worth?

But we cannot speak in weights and measures,
Of things we hold most dear,
For they are our sweetest treasures,
Happy . . . and yet bring a tear.

As we re-live each happy hour,
Of things we've seen, and those we love,
It is not only in our power,
But also from the One above,
To keep within our hearts a store,
Of happy thoughts forevermore.

Mabel Leatham Thomas

Oh Dear!

Under a toadstool crept a wee elf,
Out of the rain, to shelter himself.
But under the toadstool, sound asleep,
Sat a small dormouse, all in a heap.

Trembled the wee elf,
Frightened and yet,
Fearing to fly away,
In case he got wet.

So he tugged at the toadstool,
And broke it in two,
Holding it over him,
Gaily he flew.

Soon he was safe home,
Dry as he could be,
But soon woke the dormouse,
"Good gracious me,
Where is my toadstool", he said tearfully.

Mo M. Bailey

The Shadow of Death

Out of the light comes a shadow.
Out of the shadow comes despair.
The hand of hope is unreachable,
As blackness pervades all.

The black tulip summons night,
As its life becomes enclosed in a petaly shroud.
I reach out for an empty palm,
Grasping at eternal oblivion.

A sense of nothingness gives a death blow.
The sound of silence beckons the shadow onward.
The blood red rose reveals its thorns,
As my life leaks away.

A shimmer of white awakens my soul,
Gentle fingers hold onto my spirit.
The voice of hope guides me forward,
The black tulip opens.

Laura Morrell

The Fox

The keeper saw from whence he came,
Over the wall and down the lane.
He knew well from before this time,
When he'd tried to stop his evil crime.

One night he'd waited with his gun,
By the main pen for him to come.
But not as daft as the keeper thought,
For all his patience came to nought.

He spied him once whilst feeding a ride,
But his gun at home he'd left inside.
As bold as brass he sat and spied,
His pheasant lunch not to be denied.

How he had dodged the trap and gun,
Amazed the locals every one.
The keeper swore and shook his head,
Vowing one day to see him dead.

Then early morn going down the lane,
The body of a fox across he came.
But what had killed this vulpine sage,
A keeper's wrath or just old age.

R. J. Charlesworth

Winter Sky

The sun hung there, half veiled,
Palely shining in the misty wintry sky
Like a fading flower,
Sadly drooping.
Its light shone wanly on the roofs of the cars
Lining the dingy street.
There was a mood of infinite sadness
I wanted to cry.

Sylvia Jeffery

To My Wife on Our Ruby Wedding Anniversary

The days are short, the nights are long,
Our life together is like a song.
Each day your words reach out to sing
They draw me near, my love to bring.

For so long now we've shared our life,
I'm still so proud that you're my wife.
This year my love, two score years we've shared,
There have been no secrets, our hearts we've bared.

Our feelings, thoughts, our words portray:
The learning of such, so more each day.
Our future years, however long,
The love will stay, forever strong.

We then may live, stay joined as one,
All doubts, if any, now so long gone.
This proves that love will conquer all
And our true marriage will never fall.

Ramon H. Clarke

My Poems

My poems come from within my soul,
Part of it resides in each one I write,
And in spite of my mood it leaves me whole,
While my wit struggles out with all of its might.

There is no rhyme, no rhythm, nor reason for them,
A therapeutic murderous motive, though,
For a dusty, rusty soul, just fit to condemn,
From which these words sometimes sluggishly flow.

I hope these words outlast the life,
As a mind is a wondrous thing to waste,
But with a smack in the mouth and a twist of the knife,
My courage deserts me with the greatest of haste.

My poems are rarely happy and light,
Since they always will reflect my mood,
As I present a really depressing sight,
Through those troubles on which we all brood.

My thoughts, frustrations and sins fill these verses,
The words dance my emotions across the page,
Through this then my dreams and my heart converses,
Or just unleashes the pain and this primeval rage.

Kevin Ridgway

Evening Meal

She was to him, a vision there,
Partaking of provided fare.
Creating longing in the patient waiter,
Aware he wouldn't dine 'til later.

When from the sky the sun did sink,
She ceased to eat and reached to drink.
Unaware she was then to cater,
As evening meal for the alligator.

G. Barrie

The Butterfly of Spring

Over buttercup fields
passing flowers in bloom
a flower,
a scent of such beauty
a silhouette,
with no threat of gloom.
Fulfilling the world with your caress
and your joy, your heart-shaped warm features could
never destroy,
You are a strong sign of Summer
essence of love you bring
with your artful expressions
Red Admiral of Spring.

K. Baker

Time

Time? . . . What is time?
Past, present, perhaps tomorrow,
Swallowed up in joy or sorrow,
What is time?

Time? . . . What is time?
Time to wonder, stop and look
At a sparkling pond or babbling brook?
What is time?

Time? . . . What is time?
Time to saunter down the road
To stroke the sheep in hurdled fold,
What is time?

Time? . . . What is time?
A fleeting image of the mind?
Blessing or curse for all mankind?
What is time?

Time? . . . What is time?
To copy nature's patient role
And seek to make our spirits whole -
This is time!

Kathleen C. White

The Clouds

Oh silent clouds of oh such might
  Passing gently through the night
    High up in the sky they go
Above the trees and land below

Oh clouds of darkness full of wrath
  Spreading rain on every path
Flooding rivers and streams below
  As just above the earth they go

High up in the cold night sky
  Pure white clouds go sailing by
Cascading down showers of snow
  Making our face and fingers glow.

Oh beautiful clouds of many colours
  Standing out above all others
Illuminated by rays of the setting sun
  As the passing clouds go by
    Kenneth Fulcher

Little Stream

Drift on little stream drift on.
Past places and scenes now long gone.
Girls in lawns and fine laces
With smiles on their faces
Girlish laughter of innocence born.

Drift past little stream, drift past
Good times and pleasures don't last
Boys happy in boots and grey breeches
Rolling around 'neath the beeches
Boyish mischief of impishness born

The sound of laughter is heard as you flow
On your journey you merrily go
Floating past are the bronzed autumn leaves
On a journey that constantly weaves
Echo memories of earthliness born

Monica Polis

Heralding the Spring

"It's been a long Winter George".
"Peggy's knitted five sweaters."
"Got your potatoes planted?"
"Still too wet."

Just enough blue for the proverbial trousers.
Dark interfacing lines the cotton clouds,
Grass definitely looks greener.
But I might be looking on the other side!

Frisky winds fondle frolicking lambs
Starlings drop sponge moss on the patio -
So kind of them to clean the guttering.
Frog spawn in the pond.

Tinge of colour on barren branches
Silhouetted against the racing sky.
Water gurgles, squelching grasses
Do you think the spring is nigh?

Mary Cooper

Times Remembered

When I was a child, life was grand
People had time to talk and stand
A friendly word on just a smile
Or a little walk and rest a while
Everyone had time for each other
Not like now all bustle and bother
The Sunday dinner best of all
Running home from church over the wall
After dinner a walk down the lane
Down to the woods to pick bluebells again
Then back home for a treat in store
Homemade scones and cakes galore
Settle down after a lovely day
And watch the evening fade away

J. M. Hobson

Tomorrow

Every night,
People lie awake,
Dreaming of tomorrow,
When all they see is the past.
Their hearts burn and toil,
Weighted with frustration,
And never understood.
And the world,
A seething mass of unrequited love,
Turns innocently on its axis,
As we catapult our race towards the moon,
In the endless search for utopia.
And even then,
We lay soiled and dirty,
In unmade beds,
Dreaming of a kiss,
That will surely be received,
Tomorrow . . .

Marie Louise Bevan

Golden Gate

Oh, if the world were a different place.
Perhaps there'd be a Golden Gate.
A place we all could find.
Where death and destruction were a thing of the past.
Like a distance that is gone at last.
Where all was perfect, and there existed no hell.
Where children, and animals, could all dwell, in a
simple harmony.
The birds would sing their song, an everlasting throng,
the sun would always shine, in this little world of mine.
There'd be no crying, lying, dying, in this little
world of mine.
All would be divine, in perfect harmony.
No visions of the past, we would all reach there at last.
Through a little Golden Gate.

J. V. Watson

Rise, Rise, O Lark

Rise, rise o lark to greet the dawn
Pervade the dew-touched summer morn
with euphonious cadence of the note
that tumbles from your trembling throat.
Full many times have I enjoyed
the untutored music unalloyed,
transcending all the sounds I've heard.
O blessed, gifted, happy bird
Would that I could share in part
the joy in your exuberant heart

O. Jones

Finale

You were such an unlikely composition: an easy-to-please
perfectionist.
A plainsong, yet beautiful. Wise not intellectual.
A puritanical lover of velvet, especially deep blue.

So I made these velvet curtains for you: deep Prussian, paintbox blue
And hung them with love a year-or-two ago, or more,
A song, a snatch of time, a score?

Now I stand alone, you are no-more to console
To shake the cobwebs from their folds; so cold and damp:
Solitary this mourning.

A dawning idea or your voice from your corner?
Grieve not my dear time to let-go, move-on
But take my deep blue velvet curtains with you: I did love them

How can I touch them? Cobwebby, dusty.
I must. I push them open with the broom-handle
Then jump and tense. Big spider failing, still in web.
But wait. It moves not spidery: it is a butterfly.

I scoop it gently up. Into the garden we flutter both.
Outside I open my hands. It hesitates: "Oh please"
It flies! On amber wing resplendent. Soon it soars.
And my heart sings, and so does yours.

Sheila Windsor

Changing Seasons

Open eyes to all around
Perceive the pleasures that abound
Each season has its wondrous beauty
And always skies that change so swiftly
Newborn growth in everything
Heralding the joys of spring
Summer following in its wake
Warm sun and showers alternate.
Changing hues of autumn bring
Glorious colours, breathtaking.
Nature rests, a winter phase,
Contrasting with all other days
Ever-changing scenes to bring
Rejuvenation in the spring
See the wonders that surround,
Restoring faith, awareness found
In song of birds, in flowers, trees,
Rivers, lakes, and mighty seas.

M. Juanita Wilson

Untitled

In hearts alight at the created world,
Perplexity of argument must fall away.
We see and love but cannot understand
A world so simple yet not wholly ours,
And pain of contemplating 'might-have-been'
Is ended in the sense that, come what may,
The whole unfolds to an appointed end.
Reality cannot be made in words,
And so demands the silence of unknowing,
While love and faith pursue their steady way
Closer than breath or heart yet in Eternity.

Paul Burrough

The Art Preview (Liverpool City)

Punters not plonkers needed here . . .
Pictures stare from walls . . . hungry for red dots . . .
Entrepreneurs, artists, posers, poets and businessmen
linger, chat, drink, drink . . . another preview next week
I think . . . maybe Falkner Square . . . the wine is good there
. . . and the atmosphere . . .
Sculptor . . . A. Dooley in dungeon garret, Seel Street . . .
praising God . . . in form . . .
Ladies drink tea at the "Blue Coat" . . . unaware; artists
work in studios above . . . all hoping, wanting, seeking . . .
Longing for the "Picture of the Time".
Previews at the "Tate" have the essence of good taste . . .
Do the pictures have appeal? The pundits say they do . . .
"The Kings New Clothes" is nothing new! . . . the "Walker"
awaits its visitors to view . . . the masters hanging there.
Soulless, a new office opens, not a picture on the walls
. . . like a window without a view.
Another gallery opens . . . preview is tonight, already
pictures hang, await their fate . . .
Gallery's name?

Penny Wilson

Summer

Swooping swallows, waves of wheat,
Rainbow showers dowsing summer's heat.
Deep azure skies, and shimmering haze,
Buzzing bees in meadow sweet ways.
Meandering streams, limpid pools,
Iridescent mayfly wings, dragonfly fools.
An opal flash of kingfisher blue
Streaking downstream straight and true.
Predatory pike lurking in wait,
Playful minnows unaware of their fate.
Skylark songs cascade from way above,
Soothing calls of a ring-necked dove.
Long languid days that pass with ease
Softly in step with the evening breeze.
Summer drifts, and gently fades
Into autumn, in all its shades.

Kenn Atkins

Istanbul

Icy winds flash across the Bosporus
Piercing my skin like shards of glass.
The fragile sky bears shades of grey
As pigeons flock to the seedman's hand.

I am lured inside the labyrinthine maze
Of kilim sellers plying their trade.
The melée of patterns and colours confuse me
And I flee from the dark into the light.

The spice market strangely overwhelms me.
I have seen henna and cumin before
In the twist and turn of the fabric
In the kilim seller's store.

Following the call of the river
I turn and survey the scene
Through sea mist and dust, the domes and minarets . . .
I can see how this city may once have been

How beautiful the colours of the carpets
Protected within the bazaar walls.
How sad, this city neglected,
In the dust and the dirt of us all.

Mark Smith

Untitled

An overgrown garden, neglected, abandoned,
piles of bricks showing that a house once existed
what love and care this garden has known,
lovely shrubs, plants and trees chosen by owner unknown.

But the joy and the beauty as one walks through the rubble,
evergreens rising, so lovely and stately
still proudly growing, oblivious of changes
romantic garden, so full of life and surprises.

Mahonia, Japonica, Laurels, Conifer and box trees
trying to imagine who had walked on your pathways
loving and tending pruning with pride
bricks and mortar may tumble, as time marches on.

Sun rises and sets as each day is done
the love that still lingers lives on and on
started by hands, that are rested from toil
the glory of the garden, is now God's alone.

R. V. Holder

Inner Love

Always believe in my self,
remember my valuable worth,
never forget I'm somebody unique, and special.
Not a nobody.

If no one will believe in me,
then I must have faith in myself,
to create my self being, and uphold respect,
for my dreams, my destiny.

"Don't give up" the pressures on,
a test in life, one must battle on,
so that one day, I can say,
"I did it", "I achieved"
I believed in my self,
I believed in me.

Pamela Headley

Friendship

F is for the fun we are going to have.
R is for the relationship we are going to build.
I is for the interesting moments that are to come.
E is for everlasting friendship.
N is for near future that is to come.
D is for deep moments of thought.
S is for slowly as a friendship should go.
H is for happiness ahead.
I is for inner emotions expressed.
P is for patience which is what you need for an everlasting
FRIENDSHIP

Natasha Curtis

The Restless Sea

O restless, raging, boundless sea,
Pitching and tossing relentlessly,
Driven by the wind;

Your crashing waves and moving scenes
Enter the fabric of my dreams,
Uplifting me.

Majestic seabirds circling the skies,
Soaring and swooping with piercing cries,
Incessantly;

With outstretched wings, a glorious sight,
Sustained by the wind in perfect flight,
Land Gracefully.

Mighty forces awe inspire,
Lift my spirits ever higher,
In ecstasy.

Norah Vincent

In the Snowfield

In tilted fields there is no track or crossway but the patriarchal
Prints of every pathway gleam between sleet storm and
      powder blizzard.
At white-out there is no scarp or dip, nor safe place or edge.
Ascending figures sift within the blank sanctuary
Counter, strain a little, half-circle down - pulse an obsecration -
      on the dazzling plain.

The sainted bishop strode the slope, lifted high his crosier
Prayed with his flock, and with the seasons, between snow
      line and hollow.
Laid late boundaries and built an archway to another world
Where bunting fleck like shreds of paper on the wind
Phalarope fret between snow-ice and snow-broth.
- And incense billowed from the spruce plantation and there was
      solar-powered song.

Sun blaze rears on three sides of the ice cathedral
Leaps up and down the range - but freshly actuated limbs
Dull at once with ice sludge - without a shriek
Balance unravels - one figure, and another
Slip through rainbow frazzles on the flank
Where God's most energetic angels - in dawn shade - sweep
      crisp lawns.

Terence Organ

Watching You

Innocent eyes wide and bright, shining with delight.
Purist simple affectionate ways smiles cometh my way -
giving strength so much each day, tender thy love I try to portray,
Kissing lips to heal bad days, gentle hugs to wipe the tears away.
Our world is big, can you survive?
While I watch your innocent eyes
"Wrapping you" in my cocoon tender as a mother's womb.
My precious Jem you are to me, the innocent eyes of eternity.

Susan Byrne

Hear the Call

People of this country
Please hear the call
Often it has been said
That we are the masters of our own destiny
But this will hold no meaning
If we are not prepared to accept the responsibilities of which we are
Charged

Farmers, policemen, and for everyone for that matter
We need each other
Let's do it for the love of self
And humanity and country

We can do it if we try

People in question
Check your conscience

I rest my case

Kim Beaupierre

Poor Soul

I see her each day, that old lady in rags.
Pushing the pram, with her home in four bags.
She sings to herself, as she goes on her way.
Tramping the streets, to see out the day.
The crowds they walk by her, as if she's not there.
They all just ignore her, they don't seem to care.
At night she's moved on, to face the ice cold.
Lord, how I pray that I never grow old.
She sits in the cafe, with a large tea in hand.
And dreams of days past, when life was so grand.
Days when her husband, and son were at home.
But Dave and John died, leaving her all alone.
She turns up her collar, as she steps through the door.
Cursing the gods, as the rain starts to pour.
Hiding in doorways, she tries to keep dry.
Dodging the drops that fall from the sky.
Next day, in the paper, with horror I read.
A little old lady, in rags, was found dead.
Tears from my eyes, they spill to the floor.
As I think with regret, I could have done more.

Kenneth Boyle

Winter Life

A truly magnificent view.
Quiet and peaceful.
Something there . . . a part of you.
The world has stopped,
Halted dreams.
Nothing is certain till colour redeems.
How long is this season of tranquil war?
Are we trapped for perpetual,
For ever more?

Susan Wright

"Mine Happy Life!"

"I stroll along our country lane,
Quietly humming a catchy refrain,
Flowers blooming, dripping with drew,
Me, giving thanks: For a happiness new!

Birds, chattering to the trees,
Honey being collected, by the bees.
I praise the Lord, I can see and hear,
Everything around, so delightfully clear.

Listen, to the sound of laughter,
People testing, joyfully screaming,
Whatever else, can this world be after?
Please! Dear Lord, don't say I'm dreaming!!

May this occasion last for ever,
Such sweet memories are so few.
Oh! Good earth, don't leave me. — Never!!!
Really God! It's up to you . . .

W. M. Boyle

Downfall

The tempest tore the yellow dawn,
Raggedly across the dark grey sky.
Trees trembled under the blows they'd born,
The rooks were tossed like feathers upon high.

With a roar like a raging sea
Pounding a granite pebbled shore,
The wind ripped branches from the tree,
Bend, crack and rattle to the floor,
Where brittle, blackened leaves scurried
And rattled like dead bones
In a frantic dance, and hurried
To the tune of the old tree's groans.

The old, disfigured sycamore tree
Had stood hard against the gale:
But a roar, a crack and suddenly
Down it tottered: so strong and yet so frail.

K. S. Spreadbury

Juggling Game

Tossing Juggling balls in the air,
Rapidly, carefully, watching them glide.
Throwing away all your despair.
Taking your feelings for a ride.

Each colour represents different thoughts,
Mixed and mingled as the balls are thrown.
Joining together to form the happiness I sought
And a bright new colour to call my own.

The set of balls forms an arrangement,
Either in descent or in flight.
With each colour having its own importance,
Depending on which ones are in your sight.

Life is puzzling, never facile.
Hurled at you is suffering and pain.
You are left wondering which balls to expel.
Is life just a juggling game?

Renu Arora

Veg. Alert

It's tea time now, says my mum. Oh no what a dread, I think I'd rather go to bed. Sit at the table, and eat your greens. I'm sorry Mum I don't like peas. Oh no green alert, I can't eat these, my tummy hurts. Get the doctor "Quick Quick Quick", I'm going to be rather sick. My vegetables are forming words "EAT ME EAT ME", but I'm afraid I can't my tummy hurts. Oh no what a dread, I was sweating from my feet, to my head. Help help, but it's no use, I couldn't seem to find any excuse. But how will I eat my greens, can I just leave them this week please. Any excuse isn't it lad, you've already had some stick
off your dad. But from him, not my greens, oh can I leave them please Mum, please. O.K.O.K., but remember it's only for to-day. Because if you do not eat your greens, a price you will have to pay.

Nicola Jayne Davis

Talking to God

Taking all my feelings, a rage of fun and tears
reaching for the universe, discarding all my fears
my life is on a journey, through stars and darkened space
I'm looking for a new land, a perfect human race.

I've lived a life of questions, all answers gone untold
I've searched my soul and body, and found nothing to unfold
I've reached into my dark side, and saw myself right through
my mind was all in pieces, my heart was broke into.

How can I live this moment, this time this day this place
how can I be a leader, how can I keep this pace
I've wrestled with my conscience, and battled with my soul
and unless you take what's out there, you'll never score a goal.

I've sat and looked around me, I've seen what's going on
and I've wondered in amazement, is this what I'm really from
well I've told you all my story, about my painful life
now I'm waiting for an answer, I'm looking for advice
cause I feel you owe me something, before I finally die
did I really have a life, or was it just a lie.

P. R. Surman

Ephemera

Brides of Spring they stand
Pure, untouched, virginal white
Or palest pink, frilled and ruffled
As the daintiest gown.

But when the sudden storms of April
Dash their ruffles to the ground
A drift of snow seems to have settled
And made a winter of their Spring.

And so it was with you, dear friend.
A week, a day was all you had.
Spring came and stopped our hearts with beauty
But yours was stopped and I was sad.

C. B. Copley

At the Airport Field of London

Yellow and green lights in lines,
red or blue and golden in circles,
all shining like coloured candles,
all giving signs of life,
all being signals to airplanes,
all giving priorities
to the "birds of heavens" for landing.
Are they little hopes which help
people to find their way?
Are they outlets
to our dark thoughts?

Maria Rally-Hydreou

My Fair Rose

Rosa Picasso you are so fair,
Releasing your fragrance into the air,
The glory of you is all I can see,
When sitting beside your rose tree,
Your delicate beauty I love so much,
Your soft petals are like velvet to touch,
Seeing your photographs printed in books,
That photographers took of your stunning looks,
Enhanced by the pearly droplets of dew,
No other flower could be as lovely as you,
When finally your petals drop down on the floor
The buds you produced will flourish I'm sure,
Repeating the beauty that once you did show,
It is a shame Rosa Picasso you have to go,
I'm tempted to pluck you before you die,
Hanging you up in my kitchen to dry,
When you have dried, still beautiful to see,
Placed in a vase and not on a rose tree.

L. J. Dhar

Remembrance

Remember the song of a blackbird in spring,
Remember the swifts, acrobats on the wing,
Remember the seabirds, soaring aloft
Over shimmering seas and sands so soft,
Where families on holiday from city and town,
Played with their children and became golden brown.
Remember the fields with the ponds and the trees
And frogspawn and bluebells and plump bumble bees,
Remember those walks down lanes so narrow,
With high hedges abundant with chattering sparrow.
Remember the woods of oak, beech and larch
With their cathedral-like silence and imposing arch
Of the canopy of tree tops as they reached for the sky,
Uplifting the spirit and gladdening the eye.
Why remember, you ask, of such common place?
Note destruction, I reply, of gathering pace.
The woods are now asphalted dual carriageway,
Buildings make fields disappear every day.
Dead birds on oiled beaches, smog filtered sun,
Hail, great God car, man's will be done.

Michael Anthony Lindop

Husband and Wife

Several years ago, when our eyes first met,
Your skin so soft, your lips so wet,
Led me to believe, we would stay together,
Not just for one day, but maybe forever.
The following weeks, we grew so near,
Your love for me, then became so clear
My feelings for you were exactly the same,
Now months have past, this is no game,

The months turned to years,
How quick they have past,
My love for you, would certainly last.
There's one question that remains,
That plays on my mind.
Answer honestly if you would be so kind,
Could you stay with me, for the rest of your life?
If so, then I'm asking you to be my wife.

Stephen Sherwood

"Without You"

Without you here, I shed a tear,
Remembering how we used to be
Our hearts entwined, two of a kind
But somehow you stopped loving me

Your touch, your kiss - I cherished this
In your strong arms I did belong
You cheated . . . lied, but how I cried
When one day you were gone.

I'm so alone; I should have known
Your love was not to last forever,
A flame still burns; how my heart yearns
And longs for us to be together.

Our son so dear, should draw us near,
But tore us far apart
Of this I'm sure; there is no cure
For my poor, shattered heart.

As now it seems, my hopes and dreams,
Of love and happiness are through
So filled with pain, I weep again
For life's so empty without you.

Michelle Cameron

125

Cradled in encapsulated comfort,
Reminder of the ante-natal state?
Existence in a bonded drop of time.
The world glides by untouched, untouchable.
I float, I drift, I dream, subconsciously.
My problems are not there, they never were.
The movement ceases, brings me back again,
Am I in heaven - no! It's Paddington.

P. M. Beaven

It Doesn't Rhyme

Religion is boring, Starchy and Stiff,
Rules for fools, Unleavened - no Lift.
   Church mice snoring, Predestined, Plain.
   Long faces rising, and kneeling again.
It's Tried and Tested, Numb, Infected
by Custom and Pomp, the same Introspective,
Void, Destroyed, Cliched, Dejected,
Mundane, Weak, Dull, Rejected.
   Flat, Uneventful, Ancient and Cold,
   Battered, Unfruitful, Outcast and Old.
Typecast, Depressive, Incense absurd,
Nonsense, Drab, Monotonous words.
   Disproved, Dismal, Blunt, Distressing
   Sluggish, Humdrum, Gloomy, Regressing.
Rusty and Dusty, Blinkered and Eerie.
Hard pews, Bad news, Staid and Weary,
Tedious, Tiresome, Diluted and Dreary,
  but so is Flight
    to a
     Caterpillar.

T. Noel Davies

Chasing Rainbows

Our friendship is comparable, to the sun and the rain,
Sharing all of our joys, and all of our pain,
There's a light to our pathway, wherever we go,
It's the sun, with its radiant, ever-warm glow.

As the rain pours gently, through the air,
It resembles the crosses, that we have to bear,
But on those occasions, when together we can be,
A rainbow transpires, for all to see.

At the end of every rainbow, lies a pot of gold,
Well, at least, that's so, in the legends we are told,
At the end of our rainbow, we'll find our treasure,
In the form of a friendship, that will last forever.

Rachel Demet

Sex and All That

Since Adam and his apple-temptress Eve
Renounced their innocence and turned to lust
We humans have indulged our copulations
Variously without reservations

We're told the object of the exercise
Is for the human race to multiply
So women have to suffer giving birth
To yet more sinners on an overcrowded Earth

So let's keep this carnal recreation
Mostly for sport and less for procreation
Yes! Sexual gymnasts could hold competitions
And give *fantastic* exhibitions

That's OK, if that is all you want
Out-doing the antics of the monkeys
But what about love, romance and all that stuff?
Well, that's a different ballgame sure enough

They say lovers can touch infinity
And move briefly amid the wheeling stars
Sometimes and sometimes only or so it seems
The physical can match up with the dreams.

Robert Clark

Steely Town

In this steely town, the
Rising smoke meets swirling smog.
Heavy raindrops slick dark pavements.
Concrete cavities crumble in a Council Carpark.

Huddled people shuffle under small inadequate umbrellas
To escape the muggy, steely rain.

The squat church tower casts centuries shadows over a modern,
Redbrick, Amenity-Filled Leisure Centre
Uneasy, next to each other they mark time.

In goods-filled halls, old ladies wield shopping trollies
Like stubborn hoovers over old carpets,
Keeping left through the cramped market
They eye socks, sprouts and over-sized cream cakes.

Later on darkness draws around the busy bus station,
The cafe a haven of homely fare and steaming mugs.
Condensation covers wide windows as home goers peer
Out of smeared circles, checking queues and times.

Observe this steely town and all its northern life.
Difference creeps like the darkness over squat concrete shops and
cooling towers. Fires burning a beacon, as life grinds on.

D. Rhys

Memories on an Autumn Day

Uniformed captain, raised spear ready to strike, hesitates
Seeing himself and the impression he makes, shakes

A young couple, frozen like puppets without string
What could of developed from that schoolboy fling

Leaves flutter carelessly in the Autumn wind
Disembodied fragments of past images drift through time

To reassemble like a finished Jigsaw in the mind
Past stories reenacted in an orchestrated mime

Highs and lows, swings and roundabouts, twists and turns
The sum of our experiences leads to our appearances

We are what we are, what we've been and seen
Everything filtered slow motion, silver screen

Elderly park keeper absently spikes the faded photograph
Reexamining it in detail, he gives a muted laugh

The man in uniform no longer a youthful mirror
Dropping it into accompanying bag of other half told lives

He shuffles off, pausing briefly to wave to a young family
Smiling, the circus of life marches on to beat of drums

The band have packed up their instrument for today
Treading carefully across the dim grassy way

Nicholas Ronald

Sunshine Intermezzo

The gently lapping, equidistant waves,
Roll in like mile-wide, shimmering, silver staves,
Across a hazy page.
And happy, bobbing, energetic heads
Are ever - changing notes,
In frenetic summer rhapsodies,
Randomly composed by youthful joy.

Between the yellow flags,
A frenzied tune fortissimo is played,
with undulating semi-breves (○),
And ostentatious quavers .... arms aloft (♪);
While distant notes diminuendo stray.

I wonder if....
My many - peopled, multi-layered score,
Gives contemplative echoes on the shore,
To only me!

The rains may come tomorrow:
But somewhere in the catalogue of time,
This moment will be registered.....

To be replayed con brio in my mind.

J. Donaldson

'Le Ciel Couverturé'

The misty sky is a cover
Pervading my thoughts,
My heart as cloudy
As it is tonight.
In its vastness
It covers everything,
A protective blanket.
Sometimes reassuring,
Sometimes suffocating.
Its density weighing upon me
As thoughts of you upon my mind.
It is my companion when I cannot sleep
- alone.
Its many twinkling eyes promising friendship,
Then dissipating, as promises will.
Shadows chase shadows,
Pausing to bestow me with a fleeting glance
As I stand, absorbed.

The misty sky is my lover.
It is the one thing we always share.

Sarah Barnes

Childess/Infertility

Walking past I feel such a fool - watching the children come out
of school, smiles so sweet, eyes that glisten, - if only God would
stop and listen,

Pain so intense, tears burn my eyes, - will I ever be waiting for
mine I cry, laughing, playing, saying nursery rhymes - I heard the
word 'mummy' a thousand times.

I see pretty dresses of ribbon and lace, - as tears of frustration
fall down my face, matchbox cars and scuffed-up knees, - let me
have just one chance - please,

I feel confused, hurt, and cheated, - I feel all faint I should be
seated, I can look no more, I bow my head, - I think I'll just go
home to bed,

I close my eyes, they start to sting, - afraid of what the future
won't bring, I bite my lip, my heart beats hard, - as I fight to put
up a protective guard.

Then I think of us and what we're missing, - it seems everyday
we just keep on wishing, I wish I could bring us what we crave, -
today I don't feel very brave,

I get indoors no-one can see, - I pray for a part of you and me, we
have so much love for each other, - I know we'd be a good father
and mother

I look down at my wedding ring, - I know with you I have everything,
But sometimes I just need to sit apart, - to rock the empty cradle
in my heart.

Tina Denman

Ode to the Rose

She stands like a monarch amongst her servant blooms,
She breezes gaily to and fro, her appearance, always groomed.
Her sleek and abundant figure, her stem, her ruby gown,
She's empirical, statuesque, her beauty is profound.

Her deep and powerful colour, like a strong and vibrant blood,
Planted tight and fittingly in this strong and earthy mud.
Behold! The Sun's radiant beams she welcomes with open stems,
The clouds and the rain are also welcome, time and time again,
For without these elemental miracles, she wouldn't stand so proud,
No beauty, no prestige, no glamour, no pride,
Instead her head will hang under a cold and lonesome cloud.

What is she? She is love, she is romance,
she is an emblem of the nation,
For the beauty of the rose the preciousness of pearls
have such a close relation.
She glimmers pristinely on a lonely summer's eve,
she's a metaphorical happiness, in her presence we cannot grieve.
All spring and summer she will reign supreme, she will don the
golden crown,
And when Autumn welcomes himself to our doors, her superior-
ity will fall down.

But her soul lives on, her reputation aspires,
Passion, romance, melting desires, ODE TO THE ROSE.

Shaun Anthony Meekins

The Missing Link?

Greater minds than mine have tried to trace the birth of man,
Scientists have theorised on how it all began;
Perhaps the highest form of life before the human birth,
Was a kind of ape like mammal which roamed our ancient earth.

That was Darwin's theory. But where's the missing link?
Something must have taken place to make such creatures think;
The Book of Genesis relates to chariots of fire,
The thund'rous roar of heavenly gods, expressing deepest ire.

If 'chariots' were space ships, engines the 'thund'rous roar',
The 'heavenly gods' were astronauts, in pristine days of yore;
Did they have to leave their world, its life being almost through?
From another galaxy, perhaps, in search of planets new.

With their advanced intelligence, they may have had some means
Of mating with the apes, and thus, producing human beings;
Man must have had an origin, be it Adam and Eve or ape,
So did God start the human race with an inter galactical rape?

In the centuries that lie ahead, as man explores the stars,
How many answers will be found on worlds like distant Mars?
If, when life was at its source, mutation did take place,
The missing link which man has sought, came here from outer space!

Ken Burrows

Harvest of the Sea

Ships and boat and tiny craft from North most tip to farthest South
Rolling, pitching, through Gods great seas bringing us our
   basic needs
From fish that fry to prawn that boil all are held in nets of toil
Tons and tons of every kind ending up as yours or mine
on our plates for our tea Cod of Haddock — preferably

The sea is cruel the sea is kind care for it don't be blind
It gives to us more than food, mother of life, that's been proved
So everyone now lets give thanks for the bounty held within
   its banks,
we must save and not destroy its treasures in the depths explored,
with oils and gases left to roam from ruptured pipes and well
   heads blown,
Killing all in its path from birds and seals to tiny sprat

So pause a while and just give thought for all the beauty
   that's in store
for all the children of the world in future lives far from ours
Let them see the gift of life and cause our earth no harm or strife
We are merely keepers of this world and should impart these
   lessons learned
to those who follow in our place securing safe the human race

Michael Evans

Cancer Days

Dr. Casoni said, Sam come into my little room and I will make you sad.
So into her small room went I because then I was completely mad.
"Your wife you know" she said to me "has fought.
So very bravely, but now the end is not too far we wondered
   if alright you are."
They spoke to me like in a dream the cancer was still in between.
We never did accept the words of doctors' voices that we heard.
A shaking head and polite smile and us just thinking
   this is just a while.
The days of chemotherapy drastic times for her and me.
But still we laughed and lived life full,
I guess we were just two old fools.
Remembering when you hair did grow a summer's morn
   the sun did show
While shining on your lovely face, a gentle down my fingers traced.
We were so happy no one knows now I'm alone that's how it goes,
but never in a million years can I forget our silent tears with every
morn I wake I think of you with every passing day a step closer to
I need her just to walk beside me then, and hold my hand
If I could once again embrace, and kiss her lovely face all this has
been denied me, my path of life seems long.
This void that's all around me, please God where did we go wrong?

S. J. Tidd

Say Goodbye for Me

Say goodbye to the sun for me no longer shall I feel its heat,
say goodbye to the moon for me never again shall we meet,
bring a smile to someone's face for me for no longer shall I jest,
mend a loved ones heart for me now that I'm at my rest.

Listen to the morning rain for me for no longer shall I hear,
drink and talk and laugh for me and dry your cheeks of tears,
try not to think ill of me now that we're apart,
my body lies in that grave but my soul lies in your heart.

Take a look in the mirror for me and reflect on what has passed,
then take a breath of air for me for I have drawn my last,
stop and look at the sky for me for no longer shall I see,
the world where everyone has a place but there was no place for me.

A. Taylor

Message of Hope

Bring forth the white winged dove,
   Send out a message of love.
Roll back the clouds of despair,
   Fragments of hope linger there.

Beware the great men of power,
   Who live in an ivory tower.
Sowing their seeds of corruption
   That lead to death and destruction.

Out of the dark and confusion,
   Surely will come retribution.
The sun will emerge, and then,
   Perhaps we shall smile again.

Mary West

Void of Hope

In the beauty of life,
Shadows of the past,
Flow with the streams of the future.
Cutting, cutting happiness to shreds.
Making our eyes see ugliness,
Where only Nirvana rests,

To Nirvana we supposedly move
Pushing, pushing, angrily shoving.
Frustrated cries for all this anguish,
We remain stationary at one point.
At the point of nothing.

An empty void of meaningless fears,
Encase us in a cloak of tears.
Drowning us, drowning us
In the sea of unspoken death.
Clouding our eyes of the island
   That lies so near ahead.

Louise Yates

Red

Red is a stop sign on a traffic light
Red is the colour of blood in a fight
Red is a devil that scares me at night
Red is the colour of my kite
Red is a colour that reminds me of heat
Red is the colour of raw meat
It can also be the colour of the apple you eat
Red is the colour on the end of my brush
Red is the colour of my cheeks when I blush.

Lauren Nicolson

Untitled

All my friends who read my poems
say I have a talent
I just look at them and smile
and say of course I haven't
So I saw your ad for poetry
and just had to have a go
to see if I was good enough
or I would never know
it really is so easy it comes straight from the heart
I just pick up my pen and then it's sure to start
it flows from my mind like ink from my pen
flowing lines again and again
it really feels lovely like cleansing my body
but the real enjoyment is that it's my hobby
it's something I love and very often do
and feel really honoured to send it to you
Now I will wait to see what you say
and I will be praying that you make my day.

Wendy Miller

The Canada Geese

It's October and the geese are coming in.
See there, where the marsh mist is wispy and thin
They're coming in to land.
Just a few now, I can count on one hand,
But each day will bring more, perhaps tomorrow a score
Will skim through the reeds, the Canada geese.

What body clock beats in each feathered breast
To tell them it's time to fly from the West?
How do they know that Winter is coming;
That they can rest here until the whole marsh
Is humming with their deep-throated cries,
Until they take to the skies.

I shall not be here when their journey begins;
Will not see them rise, hear the strong beat of wings
As they circle the marsh, heading south for the sun,
But I can wish them God-speed, until their journey is done

P. M. Shakespeare

Dedication

I thought I'd send you this little letter,
Saying how I'd like to know you better,
I know your feelings for me have not changed,
But I hoped mine had been rearranged.

A year on and my feelings stay the same,
Though I think you'll soon forget my name,
I wanted my feelings to drift away,
But there are so many things I want to say.

Do you know who I am? Do you know why I stay
Loving you, more and more every day.

After all your lying and ignoring,
Still this letter starts my heart pouring,
I'll never be your treat, you preferred trick,
A thought which still makes me thoroughly sick.

I'll hope you'll make this a secret letter,
But that won't make my feelings better,
Soon you'll be laughing at this loving verse,
But what do I care, I can't feel worse.

Rachel Abbott

England

As I walk through pastures green, my mind wanders to
a different scene,
Men in battle a long time gone, fighting for England against all odds.

No foe too large no battle too big, for England their lives to give.
To give unselfishly without a care, only for our country and she is
so fair.

The courage of man is hard to understand, unless you walk
through this glorious land.

To lay down your life as precious as it can be, so all in England
can be free.

Through every war this country has strived, so no foreign flag
will fly in our skies.

If in my time the call does come, like my ancestors I will take
up the gun.

And fight to the end and beg for their courage and wisdom to send.

So other people can walk and see, what this England meant to me.

N. B. Miller

Separate Ways

Misty meadows mourning
Screaming echoes into space.
Mysterious noises vanishing
Swallowed by the dead of night.

Waiting for their battle to commence
Filled with hatred ready to pounce
Thirsty for revenge
Faded shadows fooled by death.

Secretly rummaging for lost remains;
Snatched away and forced to enter the unknown.
Always searching yet never found
Trapped in a whirlwind of everlasting disappointment.

Singing snowdrops dancing through their day zone twilight.
Glittering dewdrops burst with hidden emotion
Surrendering to the earth.
Captured and killed.

Never spared - another soul is hunted
Faced with a sentence and doomed forever
Included in a story of tragic death
One more lonely shadow weeps, forgotten by our world.

Michelle Rogers

"The Apple Blossom Tree"

"Mocking with delight" like some "Small mischievous sprite"?
"Shaking with laughter" so full! of glee is "The Apple blossom tree."
"Pink and white" the dancing sprite "Waves its limbs in sheer
    delight"
Showing off! to passers-by? "Shimmering against a bright" blue sky,
A breeze "Snaps off" a small bouquet a gift? To celebrate the day.
Some "tiny hand" will snatch it up! and once at home, place in a cup?
Artists will sit for hours! trying! to catch on canvas, "The
    beautiful flowers"
"Smiling" down upon them, "giggling" with glee "It won't! sit
    still it's free!"
The artists tries! to capture! in a rush! such beauty ever
    changing with a brush?
"Singing" of Summer that Winter's set free! is the Apple
    blossom tree!
Now! the breeze! sees its chance to join in the "Merry dance".
Once again the petals fall covering canvas, artist and all!
Even, a "summer" shower? cannot! depress its "joyful" power!
"Soft rain falls, it only serves to quench its thirst! refreshed
    'replenished' fit to burst"!
Once shy? Birds sing loudly now hopping from confettied
    "Bough to bough"
Still! "mocking" with delight like some small mischievous sprite?
Shaking! with laughter full of glee "The mocking Apple
    blossom tree"
"Pink and white" the dancing sprite "Waves its limbs sheer delight"
"Singing of "summer" that Winter's set free is "The Apple
    Blossom Tree"

Wendy Ann Allcock

Tube Train

Noisily, speedily train rushes on,
Rolling and shaking, electric in song,
Evening by evening, so tired and so weary
Journey can be so long and so dreary.
Look down the train, see all of the faces
People and people of many races
Reading their papers, keep looking down
Avoiding eye contact, wearing a frown
Dozing and dreaming and talking and listening
To conversations and to the trains whistling.
Stop at a station, some people alight
Hurrying, scurrying into the night
Just like life's journey some will remain
And some have gone home on an earlier train.

M. Carter

My Mind Wanders Back

She gave me a feeling of loving and warmth
Secure in Grandma's care on that cherrywood chair.
Brass forks and fenders, fire lit for the day.
That sweet smell of breakfast that started my day.
Wheat fields and acorns with freedom to play.
Cows ready for milking the sun shone all day.
Gobbling turkeys by the roadside we'd see,
Bicycle rides past the moss and the trees.
The farmer, the kittens I would rescue to keep.
Only for a short while, when others were asleep.
Milk pail filled up every morning to fetch.
Water in the barrel all rusty and wet.
Pea pods in the garden, spinach I would chew.
Butterflies in matchboxes to name but a few
Cupboard doors closed, with treasures to find
Grandfather clock stirring, ready to chime
Some memories of childhood I could never erase.
As my mind wanders back to the table she laid.

Valerie Diane Wilson

My Father

Today I heard, my father died,
I wasn't sad, and I never cried

I feel quite guilty, cos I know I should
but as my father, he was never any good
The memories are bad, and still hurt like hell,
And the beating's I remember so very well.
So please understand, if I don't mourn.
Or feel all alone, lost and forlorn.

He never earned no love from me,
and in a sense, I'm now quite free.
I've learned to trust, and feel no pain.
So his great loss, was my real gain.

To have a daughter, who loved him so,
is a privilege, he'll never know.

Rita Monk

The Wreck

Up on the cliff top out of reach.
I watched the waves pound the beach
Out at see I saw the ship
Head for the port it was her last trip
The storm broke suddenly over all
And down in torrents the rain did fall
The ship was pounded this way and that
Closer and closer into a trap
The coast guard had seen the ship go aground.
He summoned the lifeboat but no one could be found
They had rowed so bravely against the big waves.
To save those souls from a watery grave.
Her bows were shattered, her back was broke
What a sad end to a ship called "The Good Hope",
The cargo she carried was strewn far and wide
To be brought to the shore by the swollen tide.
They salvaged her cargo of tea, fruit, and beef.
And all that was left was the wreck on the reef.

J. W. Emond

Sorrow

The constant motion of life around him
seems unreal, and the long moment of his
suffering rushes around and around in
circles; making each day akin to its
brother, and as his pain engulfs him;
he does not seek from within it, sympathy,
condolence or understanding.
    He is doomed to be solitary, but because
of it has no bitterness against the world,
from which he seeks only simple but great
things. The sea, trees, flowers, brother wind,
sister rain and the golden rays of the sun,
for he has left behind the encumbrance
of endless repetition. No longer is he a
Philistine in a mad, conceited and rushing
world. A place of pitiless greed and course
brutality, and as a mere spectator of life,
looks upon the broken heart of the world,
as from his sorrow comes love. Which to him
is the only truth.

Martinella Brooks

The Fragile Veil

Out of the dark and misty depths of time
Shadows and faces flicker with gruesome cries.
Ghostly faces shimmering white,
leering skulls with hollowed eyes like glass
float before me, reaching a long and bone-like hand,
beckoning me through the veil of life
that keeps two worlds apart,
into a land of darkness only death can understand.
Vile faces gather and circle around me
while foul decay hangs heavy
on the blackened night.
Then wailing loudly back, back they go,
lamenting shadows wrapped in clouds of mist
whose battle is now lost,
smaller they grow, and now are out of sight.
Heavy eyelids flicker, moving slowly they open
and focus on an old cream night gown
draped across a worn-out bedside chair.
    A welcome sight.

Patricia Kennedy-Paterson

Thoughts (Part I)

Wilderness I see, and am and will be; dark sounds surround,
    quiet lights at night.
The voice; your voice, cries out, hungry on the wind.
Pain twisted, rain drenched, wanting and waiting, alone in the dark.
Sharp bitterness of life, secret thoughts abound,
Of wrist and knife and tranquillity found.

Beauty I see, you are and will be; the sins within and the
    heart's true doubt.
The struggle; your struggle, screams out, binding to my soul.
Perfect imperfect, roses cut down, glowing embers inside,
    lighting fire without.
And after love's might, remember you still,
In your rags of light all dressed to kill.

Apart I see, we are and will be; entwined in mind, the soul
    holders' gone.
The world; our world, tears out, and into and onto the blood
    spilled thick.
From hearts wrenched, and torn and uprooted, embraced and l
    lost the moment of truth.
But the passion ran wild when I danced with you,
I was a motherless child who'd seen the dark side too.

The future I see, it is and will be; endless mends, healing of wounds.
The tears; my tears, fall softly, gently and true.
Seeping and weeping through my bitter veins, of what remains.
And so, the end, but not of the dream, a tear moist in one eye,
    another clenched fist,
Wilderness torn and beauty unseen, I dreamed last night of
    what might have been.

D. Casey

Our World

Green is the word that everyone says
I wonder if they know what it means.
It means keeping our world tidy and clean
not making the mess that people have seen
Recycling paper and cardboard and glass,
and anything else that you find in your house.
Not polluting the air, throwing things in the sea.
It kills all the animals even the fleas.
So keep our world tidy and clean
OH PLEASE!

Kirsty Harvey

Soul Searching

As I watch the stars that shine
I wonder what is truly mine.
For when it is my time to go
I'll only have myself to show.
No fancy items will impress,
Just the soul that I possess.
My inner self is all they see
What has transformed, what's made me, me.
And as I wander through the days
Some so clear, and some in maze,
I realize to feel at ease
You have to find a way to please
Your mind, your body and your soul.
You need contentment and a goal
So you can pass yourself and say
I feel so good, I achieved this today.

C. Greenwood

An Evening in the Park

Walking alone, though the Twilit park,
Shadows dancing, before me, from the naked trees,
Leaves rustling, in the gentle autumn breeze,
Bringing my mind, painfully back to reality

Sad lonely evenings, I've spent walking, crying
Thoughts of my loved one, tearing at my aching heart,
Why was he taken from me, so soon, so young,
Soul mates like us, should never have to be apart.

All I have to cherish, are photos, and memories
Of the fun-filled evenings, we shared together,
Walking, talking, loving, laughing,
Those memories will stay in my heart forever.

Dreams of our future, together, unrealized,
Now forever sadness, death changing our plans
No more kisses, or cuddles, or laughter
No more strolls in the park, hand in hand.

Trudy De Mouilpied

A Winter's Evening

The chill wintry evening wore on.
Shaking branches danced to the rhythms of the wind.
Great gusts blew, and darkened leaves fell from ageing
branches which could no longer hold them.
They fell to the feet of their master, who was planted
in nature's warm bosom. Beaten and dejected, they gave way to
pass as crisp sheets of death, insulating the mother tree's base.
    Small frightened animals, scurrying for what
shelter they could find, found refuge under massive boulders.
The earth cracked under the cold canopy of frost, which was
beginning to make its presence felt.
Huge blankets of snow fell from the broad conifer branches
that had supported them for as long as its feeble boughs could
stand.
    To the west, you could just make out the very last
signs of a dying, heatless sun, which had been defeated by the
more brutal and aggressive winter's evening.
No bats dare fly through the now white, speckled evening
just as no owl would trust venturing out to greet this night.
To them, the day's end was solemn indeed.
All was still. All was still.

D. J. Candon

The Influence of Christ upon Shakespeare

    A young man, born in a country town,
school'd in the Scriptures and in the
prose of Thomas Cranmer.
This young man, his schooling done,
made a pilgrimage to London town.
There, these holy words of Scripture
and those of honest Cranmer
inspire him to write - to give us plays.
Yet, these were not writ for mere amusement
or to please the gentles or groundlings of
the great Globe itself.
These immortal words were to teach,
to inspire, to show how mankind,
which once had fallen, would fall and fall again
unless the teachings of another young man,
one who - like him - was born in a country town,
were mark'd and heeded.
They teach us still, the words of both
young men; one died for all, inspired the other.
The world may mark both still - and learn.

Tony Boyd Williams

Enjoying Life to the Full

Come on everyone and let's have some fun,
Shall we all go for a swim or a run,
Or maybe we should just amble out for a walk,
Or simply just sit about and talk.

These are just a few of the simple things
we can do,
So come on how about you.
Music and dance it sure to make us shine,
As does a little bit of beer and wine.

A little laughter here and there,
Surely this is something we can all share,
Time really does soon march along,
So do it now before it's all gone.

There are so many enjoyable things
we can say,
A compliment goes a long, long way,
A really good gossip is rather nice,
It all adds up to a life full of spice,
This seems to us to be ideal,
To do just a little of what we feel.

Maria Howard

A Day at the Sea

Down to Devon we do go
Seaton, Looe or Polperro,
Weymouth, Sidmouth, Lulworth Cove,
To all these places we have Drove.

Sandy beaches, pebbles too,
For our Ice Cream we did queue,
Popcorn, sandwiches - all sliced,
Candy floss and lollies iced.

Fish and chips in paper bags.
Father with his pipe or fags,
Mother lagging far behind
Carrying bags, she is so kind.

Children laughing in the sea,
Splashing, happy as can be,
Donkey rides and puppet shows,
This is how our day out goes.

Deck chairs: brightly coloured towels,
Excitement reigns amongst the howls,
Tired children on our knee,
Time for home - it's jam for tea.

Patricia M. Baden-Maggs

103

Self Realization

I had a dream a wonderful dream
I was walking hand in hand
I did not know whose hand held mine
but I felt peace throughout our land
I felt light and glad and happy
As we walked over fields so green
My heart felt so full I laughed with glee
Don't ever end this dream
I didn't want to wake up as I felt I'd had a friend
then someone called my name out
And my dream came to an end
I tried to think whose hand held mine
Who made me feel so sublime
With my elbow I pushed back the covers
And found the other hand was mine
The meaning of my dream came clear you see
The following morning whilst drinking my tea
That no one, I mean no one else
Could help me as much as 'ME'

Kathleen Benton

One of Those Days

The hoover went on fire that day. The telly on the blink.
I went on the rampage. I hadn't slept a wink.
Rain had poured down all the night and left a great big pool.
You were in the huff with me when you went off to school.
The dog had made a bloomin' mess upon the kitchen floor,
And chewed up all the letters posted through the door.
The day had only started and already was a mess.
I was in a dither and I couldn't have cared less.
The cat had caught a great big rat
And left it for me on the mat.
The car it wouldn't bloomin' start.
It made noises like a giant heart!
The alarm clock started and would not stop.
And I needed to get to the corner shop.
The pillow beckoned to my weary head,
And so I crawled back into bed.

Linda McCorquodale

Another Day

As you watch your children grow, you think,
if only they were to know - the happiness, the
tears, the joy of all those years, would they
have cherished and savoured those years? No,
without doubt too young to know what it's all about,
Soon they grow up, up and away leaving us
with memories of another day.
With pride and with love, with sadness and
sorrow, were left with our yesterdays and our tomorrows.

Maureen Torres

Growing Up

I thought when I was five years old
I went to school I was growing up
I thought when I was eleven years old
I became a young women
I was growing up

I thought when I was fifteen to sixteen
I went to work I was growing up
I thought when I was eighteen going on nineteen
I thought I could get married or have a vote
I was growing up

I thought when I was twenty one
Time to buy a house a baby on the way
I must be growing up
I thought have my children before thirty years old
I am growing bigger

I thought get a career before it's too late
I must be growing up
I thought my mum and dad will be there
For ever to say you're grown up

M. E. Cooke

Rebirth

Cocooned within a dark nothingness solid nothingness.
I wish I could find the light, a right way out.
Turning swerving, yearning, finding, learning, serving.
I want to be me out and open, I can't get out of this dark,
Who am I! What do I know? What can I show, I don't know!!
I can't say what it feels like, only! I'm in solitude.
Like being this side of darkness, on a black cloud.
Lost in time, not a wall nor barrier but blackness!
I just want to be out to be, to feel, not reel!
Feeling anger no more, for sure not so insecure or raw,
Lacking sight not might! My eyes have sight a inner sight
Time for peace solitude serene, to cease floating in nothingness
Confused sometimes on sometimes off eyes that see and not see,
peace ceased to be, you see! Not me he seized me.
    He grieved me!!

Kim Kearney

Dead Funny

I laughed and laughed at something you said
I woke up howling in my bed
I laughed and laughed until I cried
I thought I was in heaven - had I died . . .
I looked for St. Peter, I looked for St. Paul
But oh dear I'd just had a fall . . .
OUT OF BED!!!!

Sue Skeet

To a Grandmother

My daughter is having a baby soon
She can't wait to be a mother
The baby is due in the month of June
Which will make me a grandmother
Then I'll pick up a photo from my table
And look into your gentle face
To tell you that, if I am able
The newborn child will fill a space
In my life, but not my heart
That special place is kept for you
And even though we are apart
Your love will see me through.
You'll live on in the little one
I'll feel that you are near
To give some hope where there was none
Though I wish you were still here.
I write this poem in your memory
For me there is no other
Because to me you will always be
My dearest, much loved mother.

Sylvia Hume

Sadness

My tears are like drops of falling rain,
Rolling down bumpy and soft terrain.
I weep like a weeping willow tree,
Or just cry softly to myself.

My cheeks are red, but
Not from joy or embarrassment.
The sun burns away my falling tears.
But blotchy remains can still be seen.

I think of you and more appear.
Tiny drops of crystal
Each tiny droplet telling a story,
More precise than words can tell.

Look into my eyes and you will see,
Another haunting world.
No one knows what lies inside,
For every door is closed.

No one cares about my tears,
No one understands why.
No one sheds a tear for me,
No one simply cares.

Lisa Walker

Thoughts

As I look out across the sea
I wonder what life means to me
My mind slips into all kinds of thoughts
What life should be and what it ought
But as I look across the sea
I realize that my life was meant to be
Not just for the good times but also the bad
Sometimes happy sometimes sad
I have one try only and this we all know
So best to give it a jolly good go
People I meet along the way
I should treat with respect each single day
Life is too short are so people say
Not enough hours in a day
I snap my fingers another day gone
So as I look out across the sea
I know that life is very precious to me

Margaret M. Gannaway

'Ode to a Cat Eye'

While driving at night alone,
I wondered and marvelled as I drove on,
As to how the beautiful diamonds on the lane line shone.
With wonder as the enormous curiosity had grown.
 With a kind and humble voice spoke the stone
 Oh! Wondering driver, you might ever frown
 I am ugly, perhaps I'm the ugliest known
 But thanks, thanks, thanks to the light you have thrown.
Because all the ugliness it has blown
It is thy grace my beauty depends upon
 With thy grace they wear crown,
 Without thy grace with dust they are blown
 With or without we are up or down
Praise me no more o' passer by
Lest with pride I may fly
 Lose the anchor fall from the sky
 With thy grace I ever flourish
 Without thy grace I even die.

Parminder Cheema

Sonnet - The Dropping Zone

'Tis fifty years and more since wars they fought,
In battles and dropping zones they did assail,
The mighty enemy whom they had sought
Yet now they are too old and do but ail:
Time passes to the century end chimes
There's now a dropping zone for ancients true
Who survived the wars till death in peaceful times
From all the years a tiredness did accrue.
In dropping zones they'll lie until eternity
And do now begin to sleep within the hushed grass
That whispers of the sunshine of fraternity
Their heroic deeds no one can e'er surpass.
The blissful birds fly o'er their scattered graves,
They lie fearless as the green grass blows in waves.

A. R. Rees

Lucky Me

I'm lonely I thought, as I walked down the road,
In a fit of self pity and woe,
But then I looked up to the sound of a bird,
Singing on a branch, which hung low.
As I went on my way, my eyes were then drawn,
To the gardens, where nature had woven its spell,
And the flowers were nodding and whispering to me,
Don't worry all will be well,
I waved them goodbye, and a friend caught my eye,
And we shared a cup of tea and a chat,
We relaxed in style, for a little while,
And discussed about this and about that.
My friend and I parted, I bade her farewell,
My heart so content and warm,
And Margaret I said just be grateful my dear,
Life's not so bad after all.

Margaret Rose Akeroyd

My Good Friends Annie, Elsie and May

When I first arrived on this Cornish shore,
I wondered what, there would be in store.
I met three ladies who would brighten my stay,
My good friends Annie, Elsie and May.

I first met Annie while out for a walk,
And each time we met, we would stop for a talk.
Then when later I found some work to do,
It was Annie's daughter who helped me through.

Elsie would welcome me in from the cold,
And give me a hot cup of tea to hold.
When my parents and brothers were made to roam,
It was Elsie who helped me find them a home.

The work I mentioned was given by May,
She was never aware that she saved my day.
She taught me to cook, and she taught me to clean,
To polish the furniture to a fine sheen.

These three kind souls I will never forget,
There's many a day, when I think of them yet.
And thank the Lord at night when I pray,
For my good friends Annie, Elsie and May.

Phyllis M. Trevithick

Door of Plenty

A gift from the gods . . . a prodigy
I would give him the riches of the night
I would steal the bright gems of the light
and hold them all in a timeless muse.

I could touch the midnight blue
and it would turn and change and dance
like a flame.
And then it would turn in to you.

Tasting your saltwater kisses
tasting your lips divine
tasting your enchanting being
heavenly ambrosia from the vine.
Sun-kissed eyes — I watch.
Inner strength fitters through.
An aura encumbers you,
of pale silken hue.

Innocence in your word, pure as a child-like dream
I'm falling deeper and deeper into an emotional stream,
the door of plenty has been opened.
I appear to be stepping through.

M. Starks

"My Childhood"

Reminiscence down memory lane,
In search for fortune and fame,
Ambitions and castles in the air,
But there's no one there to shelter and care,
Of life's cruel and stormy weather.

Time can never turn back what destiny has lost or gain,
My past childhood must not be in vain,
Memories of bygone days flash back in my mind,
The hopes, dreams and fears that were left behind.

From childhood to adulthood,
Life has to go on, for the young and old,
Haunted memories, happy, sad, good or bad,
These were the memories I ever had.

Then a new day has come!
A time to enjoy and a time to have fun,
To be or not to be, that is the question, as
Shakespeare's Hamlet had said.
Life is precious, life is short as we all know,
Thank you dear Lord, that I have gone this far,
with the help of my Guardian Angel and my guiding star.

P. D. Field

For I Have Done

"Must I do more to prove myself, have I done my best?
if so my love, Now you be ready, lay me please to rest.
For I have stolen songs of sorrow, yet lent a helping hand,
borrowed thoughts and dreams, toyed with timeless sands.

Broken hearts and promises . . . and reaped the dark reward,
suffered cross and nail, to resurrect the sword.
Talked of hope, enchanted realms, of love and twisted fate,
of apple trees that blossom there, have eaten from this plate.

Walking upon sacred soil, still keeping solemn word,
while listening, angels weep, where no sound can be heard,
re-creating love, my dear, from this empty shell,
Seeking The Creator, standing 'twixt Heaven and Hell.

Writing things mysterious, speaking soft words to last,
sat in forest glades alone, remember times since past.
Singing a thousand love songs to tame this heart a cure,
to hold a thousand dreams aloft, to live a thousand more . . .

Giving back the knowledge, of all that has been learned,
to and from the garden, the one for which we turned.
So if my love, you now be ready, lay me please to rest,
I have no more to prove myself, for I have done my best . . . "

William Booth

Untitled

The elephant is a funny fish, I don't know how it swims,
I'd like to bring one home with me and cut off both its fins.
And when I find it swims no more, I'll put it in a box,
I'll take it to the swapping shop and swap it for a fox.
And if I found the fox could sing, I'd put in on the stage,
But if it ever let me down I'd put it in a cage.
And when the fox was dead and gone, I'd find myself a horse,
I'd teach it how to sing and dance - but a horse can't dance,
    of course.
So I'd swap it for a cadaver and take the dead thing's heart -
And if it still would not be mine, I'd tear the thing apart.
I found myself a piece of land and shaped it how I wished,
And in the night I slept alone and in the day I fished.
And in the end I had my way, the dead things' hearts were slaves,
And those who disagreed with me were banished to the caves.
I only wish the fox could learn, the horse was not so stable,
I could control the whole of you, you know that I am able.
But you're a creature quite unique, I cannot understand,
I wouldn't hurt you nor desert you, I'm never underhand.
The elephant is a funny fish, I don't know how it swims,
I'd like to bring one home with me and cut off both its fins.

Phil Groves

The Lady in White

The same time in the evening, the same night every year,
It is known, it is heard, that's when she appears,
At the top of ridge rock fall, some say they felt her breath,
Before the mystery unfolded of how she fell to her death

Of course the rumours soon got started, yes everybody knew,
Through a cousin or an aunt, nothing but the truth,
Some say they saw what happened, but that night there was no one,
Except a woman and her shadow and the guilt of what she'd done

Standing in the moonlight, the tide at its best,
They lady in white took her life, and the rest,
Standing in the moonlight, the tide at its best,
She let herself go now nobody will know how she'd suffered all
those years

The same time in the evening, the same night every year,
It is known, it is heard, that's when she appears,
Her soul is gone, washed away in the water,
The tears she cries, for her one and only daughter,

The same gruesome way of dying, the same time a year ago tonight,
She took her crying daughter, pushed and took away her life,
Battered against the rocks, battered with the rain,
The lady in white, relieved herself of pain.

Scott Paton

In Need of Forgiveness

There's something Lord I need to say
I'd like You with me every day,
So Lord I pray on bended knee,
To show the love I have for Thee.

Guide my life Almighty Lord.
Relieve me of this wounding sword,
In being honest I do repent,
Forgive me Lord for a life misspent.

Give me a life that's full of love,
Please help, and protect me from above,
You're the life for me I know,
I want to pray and let it show.

Compared to some, I'm just a flower,
Please help me Lord, You've got the power,
When You come into my heart,
I hope we never ever part.

Paul V. Burton

"Oh What Would I Do"

Oh what would I do oh what would I do,
if I had no-one to love that's as charming as you.

I'd search to a near and I'd search to a far,
I'd search all the Earth and then out to a star.

I'd search all the Galaxies
and I'd search all of space,
for something as lovely
as your charming face.

But my search would be fruitless
and all of my fault
but I'd never give up,
never call it to halt.

But back down to Earth
with a bump I would come,
but not for a Nephew
a Niece or a Son.

For through all the Galaxies and through all of Space,
I would find nothing, like your lovely face.

So tell me dear lady if telling you do,
Would I ever find someone as lovely as you?

Peter Robert Bruford

My Love

People would look - as people will,
If I said out loud how I miss you still,
How many times in the past it was said
That time is a healer, but, here in my head,
I only know that in life's short run
You are for me the only one,
Age cannot diminish the light
As, once again my thoughts take flight,
Here, in my head I feel silent applause,
And my heart feels the tug - the invisible cord.

M. Slinn

A Pinch of Love

If I could choose one power by the grace of God above,
I'd keep it in a little box, I'd choose the power of love.
It needn't be a golden box, it could be made of tin,
But only I would have control, of the energy within.
I would travel the world over, and gather as I go,
The wonders of the canyons, and Niagara's water flow.
I'd pinch a little sunbeam here, and a pinch of moonbeam there.
Carefully putting in my box for all the world to share.
I'd take a pinch of rainbow, moon, stars and sunshine too,
And put my hand deep in my box, when you were feeling blue.
Then sprinkle like confetti all the love that I had found,
Scattering the hills and dales and all the world around.
It would have been a perfect place, true heaven here on earth,
If I'd only had the power, at the time of my own birth.

Moira Callan

The Jump

Swimming across mountains,
   ignoring precipices,
astonishing eagles . . . and disturbing the deep-sea fish.
   Having a tango with words, the last holy icons,
so as to edge myself nearer
   to the great mystery of being;
at which words, my newfound dancing-partners,
   can   only   always   point
(and haven't we been told often enough that it's rude?)
   Thus armed I'm feeling a bit fey;
a fine surge of energy, akin to divine madness (ha-ha).
   Forcing them to salute me and march to my orders,
slotting themselves into this addled old brain
   and singing me senseless songs -
surely the gentlest of violence?
   Who knows, maybe you, dear reader,
will drop your absurd pretensions for a moment,
   and jump over the earthbound edge with me?
landing, footsore but whole,
   at the place where you already are.

Richard Parkhurst

Where I'd Rather Be

They are putting the decorations up
I'll pretend that. I can't see
They can pull them down for all I care
I know where I'd rather be.

The nurses all hustle and bustle
With laughter and gaiety
But they can go home, and I'm still here
I know where I'd rather be

They say, "Come on, cheer up Sally
It will be lovely, wait and see,
We'll do our best to make it nice"
"Huh, I know where I'd rather be".

I want to be in my own house
Surrounded by family
Not stuck here in hospital
Oh, I know where I'd rather be

My house is cold and damp now
There's no one left but me
In here it's warm, and there's plenty of food,
Yes, I know where I'd rather be.

Valerie M. Wells

Pain and Worry Are Interchangeable

It Quells.
It is not of the searing, burning, agonizing kind
of which familiarity allowed ready recognition -
but is rather a deeper, grating, persistent presence
- an inescapable reminder.

Stiffness becomes a torment.
Fresh sinew
the original unwavering straightness
fall prisoner to the ever-engulfing continual bondage -
Consequential; inevitable.

It wearies.
Slow, imperceptible changes grind and tear at the spirit -
that which only yearns for the purest joy and strength
- still felt -
Yet once not questioned.

Innocence is lost
as sleep eludes and disappointments once not imagined become
real.
Solitude is felt - not sought.
Trapped within limitations whose boundaries undulate,
whose roots grow deep as the knots which tighten; As time
presses on.

Sarah Forgan

Shades of Reality

I need no book for horror
I'll just look around my world,
No literature can scare me,
Look into shades of reality.

My world is dying around me.
A road for a tree,
A whale for science,
Barbaric tortures for non-compliance,
Oil burning, (only dentures are left),
Children killed for a necessary theft.
Guns firing, ships on seas
Trying to find an enemy.
Marriage through obedience not through love,
Everyone looking for a sign from above.
To tell us when judgement day is nigh,
I don't think the sign will be in the sky.
It's all around us, just you look,
And to think that greed was all it took.

Samantha Whenlock-Allen

Abandoned

I've met someone else
I'm leaving, he said
Shocked, stunned, bewildered
I faced the future with dread
The days were long, sorrowful, dark
Help me God, I cried from my heart
My body couldn't cope, my brain plagued my head
What wouldn't I give - just to be dead
The months passed by
Life's become easier, I thought with a sigh
Then all of a sudden the gloom lifted
Perhaps I will live, life's good, I said
My days start happily; no, not with tea
But good old Radio 2 and Sarah Kennedy

Susan Williams

Waiting

I knew it, knew it, she's going to be late,
I'm left here waiting at the front gate.
I've got a salad all fresh and green,
the ham is the leanest I've ever seen.

It was just the same the day she was born,
I stood around waiting all forlorn.
I know her mother went all through the pain,
but I've waited and waited, time and again.

At her school I have waited and at the zoo.
If she's been in the bathroom I've waited there too.
I've waited while she tried on dresses, by the score,
I keep telling her I'm not going to wait any more.

She's coming to show me her latest young man.
She'll give me a kiss and say here he is Nan.
They are going to marry at some future date,
I don't know when, I'll just have to wait.

Marie Little

Wonderful Universe

How often do my eyes behold the sky,
   In bright daytime or jet black night,
So vast a universe up there so high,
   To me, it is a wondrous sight.

The great multitude of stars uncounted,
   And the flimsy mist of the clouds,
That pass steadily onward overhead,
   To cover the moon like a shroud.

With the rising of the sun at dawning,
   Again a lovely sight I see,
As night fades away, such colour day brings,
Unspeakable joy is in me.

E. A. Sherriff

In My Dreams

In my dreams
I'm free as the birds which swoop and soar
above the plains
where wildebeests wander and lions roar.

In my dreams
I can swim where the dolphins leap and play
in tropic seas
then sleep under the moon at close of day.

In my dreams
I can scale the peaks far above the snow
and touch the sky
while the Lamas chant in the land below.

In my dreams
I'm not a crippled, twisted deformity.
I stand erect -
no wheels, no frame: a man of enormity!

To my dreams
I escape while my life's clock ticks steadily.
Soon it will end -
My dream world will smile as I enter it readily!

Beatrix Budworth

The Precious Bond

I am a little bluebird and my feathers are bright blue
I'm perched high upon the Rockies such a breathtaking view
I have black tips on my tail and also on my wings
I am the greatest songbird, listen and hear me sing.

I can sing I can twitter my heartbeat's all a-flutter
I have blue feathers on my crown my breast is chestnut brown
I curl up at night under my wings,
As dawn breaks, I groom, whistle and sing.

It's a vertical world I see from this rock
The canyons are a safe refuge where some animals will flock
I will choose a female and we shall fly north in early spring
She can build the nest and I can sing

The eggs are laid, some blue some white
The chicks may hatch by day or night
I must collect the insects for mother to be
She must incubate the eggs and wait patiently
The chicks unfold, featherless and weak
Mother bird tears the juicy insects with her sharp beak.

The precious bond begins between mother and her chicks
Her bright colours they will see, as their eyelids flick
The chicks stand on the nest edge and flap their wings
Gradually they will fly, then whistle and sing.

R. Bell

Emotional Despair

Here comes another whirlwind mixing up my mind,
I'm searching through this wilderness to see what I can find,
Spinning my emotions over which I've no control,
Ripping out my heart and tearing away my soul,

This beast called love has trapped me underneath its paws,
Thrown around like a rag-doll, clamped between its jaws,
Attempting to climb out but sinking back to desperation,
I need to stop this carousel to find myself salvation,

I'm going around in circles leading to nowhere,
Just another manic cocktail of emotional despair,
On a nightmare of a journey along this lonely road,
I need to find some clues to try and crack the code,

Falling back into this terror of everlasting darkness,
Can't someone shine a beacon to light my way with brightness,
Show me the way to relieve this feeling of frustration,
Move me ever forward to my ultimate destination,

And if this how I'm destined to finish off my days,
In total misery and a blur of loveless haze,
Then someone raise their rifle to free me from this pain,
And I'll wait for reincarnation when I can love again.

Mark Tugwell

To Be Human

I'm human, you're stone.
I'm soft, you're hard.
If I'm cut I bleed.
If we argue, I'm hurt.
If you ignore me, I wonder why.
Am I guilty? No and I start to cry
Because I'm only human.
I try so hard, not to put myself down
But it's like being on a merry-go-round.
Now let us talk, let us try again
I'm sure we'll have more to gain
If we try to ease the pain
After all is said and done
We're "both" only human.

Margaret Blackburn

Paranoid

I know there's someone there;
I'm sure there is.
That man across the street - he's watching me;
    wants to know what I'm doing.
Those heads that turn away - if they're not watching;
    then why do they make me feel so strange?
I'm sure it's not just a feeling - I know it's a fact;
    but when I turn to look, there's no-one there.
Watching; Waiting; Prying.
"Why would you be so interesting,
    that everyone's watching you?" They ask.
But they don't know.
The walls have ears, they say;
    But the world has eyes.

Karen L. Bath

Terrorist Angel

I'll do anything for you
I'm sure you know that by now
The world belongs to us and no one else
let's take it now while we're still young
we don't need anyone else
who care's about the dumb rules
all that matters to me is you
and I really don't care what you've done
or why they all want to put you down
I'm just not interested in what they say

As we lie below the stars?
Away from civilisation away from chaos
You look into my eyes as you pass me a drink
that's when I know we're so special
so what if no one can understand you but me
you're the only girl for me
everything you do leaves me full of passion.
So give me your hand, and we'll run forever.
Forget the past and just say yes.

Stephen Maughan

Bob the Collie

I'm Bob the Collie
I'm tan, white and brown,
Heads always turn when I go to town,
O' I long for the dirt,
And I long for the mud,
I'm just tired of being ever so good,
But it's don't do this.
And don't do that,
Keep out of that puddle,
And don't chase that cat,
O' I long to be home,
And I long to be free
To see if my puddle is where it should be.
Or even my bones still under the tree.
O' I long to be home
And I long to be free.

J. Chadwick

The Real Me

See the person - the real me,
I'm the furthest thing to reality.

You can't see deep down inside,
as it's the place I love to hide.

Try to get close and snap goes
the lid, who am I to judge
I'm just a kid!

I'm the child who can't let go
to sorrows, memories, thoughts and woe.

I'm tired of hiding in the deep dark sea
can anyone find the real me?

Tessa Greatorex

'The Writer'

He picks up his pen and wonders in his mind,
Images, thoughts, dreams of all kinds.
He could write from experience for the whole world to see,
Or just from a memory, a vision of thee.

He knows it's not easy, time's passing him by,
But to write from the heart is a thing he must try.
To express your thoughts in a way that will show,
On paper or card for the whole world to know.

It doesn't need to be grand with words or with diction,
Just simple and concise, maybe fact or fiction.
They can be words of sorrow, words of hope,
It's not easy to decide when the pen cannot cope.

He could write about love and the turmoils within,
Or even about intimacy, it isn't a sin.
And then he turns to his mind confused of ideas,
And thinks about laughter, joy and tears.

He remembers the past the traumas he's shared,
The agony, the torture, the sadness he's bared.
He picks up his pen and the images appear fast,
For soon he remembers, he's a writer at last.

Marlene Critchlow

Sunburst

To feel every sense.
Immerse myself, then to emerge.
Shaking loose a thousand drops of morning dew.
Glistening in a myriad of ways.
Bursting into sunshine.

Sarah Evans

The Dentist

Following a night of raging toothache the morning finally came,
In a crowded anxious waiting room the receptionist called my name,
"Please come in" the dentist said to me with a kindly smile,
And asked me to lay back in the chair "Hold your mouth open
    wide for a while."

Although he was very gentle as he inspected my troublesome tooth,
I knew it was no use pretending and would have to face the truth,
"I'm afraid it will have to come out" he said, trying not to look
    glum,
And before I knew anything about it he injected my tender gum,

All I felt was a kind of numbness in the area that had caused
    the pain,
Then he asked me to wait a few minutes until he looked in my
    mouth again,
"Please open once more", said the dentist, as I shrank down in
    the chair,
And with a yank of his wrist my molar was no longer there.

You can have this as a souvenir he said as I finally walked to
    the door.
I thanked him very kindly, the pain in my mouth was no more.

The moral of this story is to regularly give your teeth a brush,
And always have a check up, even if you need a push.

M. J. Baron

A Valentine Message

Logs on the fire, crackling brightly,
In a darkened room the curtains drawn.
Soft shadows dancing around the walls.
I am waiting for my love.

A table set for two, the candle lit.
Champagne on ice, soft music also very nice.
I am waiting for my love.

He is the one, whom I adore.
His love, strength, faithfulness, and gentle persuasion.
When I feel low, lifts me to the heights of heaven
I am waiting for my love.

Time is so precious, when we are together,
The world stands still.
I count my blessings, what I've got.
They may seem few, but not to me.
I am waiting for my love.

We shall grow old, but not our love.
Our bodies, weak, frail and bent, still caring,
I am waiting for my love.
For he is my valentine forever.

J. L. Warner

The Scottish Secret

There, tucked away in the East Neuk of Fife,
In a field stands a cottage, full of flowers and wildlife.
But hidden below, deep underground,
Is a secret, a shelter, beneath a green mound.
You walk through a door, into a tunnel yards long,
With concrete walls, dense, thick, built to be strong.
Through a huge steel door you pass in awe,
Unable to believe the real threat, the cold war!
Not for mere mortals was this all about,
But the top brass, the brains, the ones with the clout!
From room to room I passed in a daze,
Offices, dormitories, bedrooms - a maze.
Computers, telephones, nothing was spared,
But what of the children, old people, the scared!
Their fate, as always, is to face the strife,
The man in the street gives his all, gives his life.
Not for him a bunker, a chance to survive,
The bomb seals his fate. Better dead than alive!
Thank God, I thought, as I stepped back outside,
The cold war is over, thank God my heart cried!

Margaret Trimby

"Beauty"

Beauty has no games to play when death
is near at hand - a loved one lost and
one must learn to live alone - now at this
hour beauty has no ring - yet dreams
stay with us to the end - making beauty -
just a friend.

Rowland Patrick Scannell

My Life

When I sit here all alone
In a house we call a home,
I listen to my heavy breath
and wonder what life offers next.
A lovely wife with two or three kids,
A broken marriage
A runaway b*tch.

My life so far has not been bad
Some happy times, and sometimes sad,
The happy times have been with you
like making love in the dew
under the stars up in the sky
my love for you will never die.
I'd love to sit here all day long
and write my life but now I'm gone,
which brings me to my last request
to be cremated and laid to rest.

Ross McLaughlin

Regret

I have destroyed a day's work
In a moment.
A light twirl of the hand,
A fatal pirouette,
And the spaghetti-hoop symmetry
Of a spider's web
Is no more.

In the interests of hygiene,
At a housewife's whim,
The deed was done
In a feather-duster stroke.

And immediate remorse throbs
In these fingers.
Oh! That those silken ropes could strangle
My wrist -
A cheese - wire web
To sever my ambition
As I have his.

Robert F. Haden

Little Boy

Little boy, we have never met,
In my heart you live - and yet,
Somehow you are real to me.

Laughing eyes, merry smile so sweet
How sad that we shall never meet.
I could say so much to you,
Of all the things I long to do - for you

God has willed it not to be.
Never a mother's pain for me.
Still somehow I'm never free - from you

When I'm old and perhaps alone.
With all the wrongs I cannot atone.
I shall think how much you've done - for me.

B. R. Breeze

The Seasons

In spring new buds appear
In summer time they open out in glory
To charm the eye and give us cheer
Autumn times the leaves to brown
Where eventually they dry up and flutters
To the ground
In winters all life has departed
From a tree.
But it will bloom again in splendour
For everyone to see.

Without the different seasons
Where would our beautiful varied landscapes be.
From the highest mountains,
Right down to the sea.

S. R. Davies

Air Natural

I hold my hand out to the wind it blows through gently
It blows my hair from my face
I turn my collar up
The leaves fall softly to my feet
As though a passing friend.

The tree stands high the wind does not mind
It just blows through passing by on its long journey
Nobody knows where it comes from
Nobody knows where it is going
But it just come like all the other things and passes by.

The people do not mind the wind on their faces
The children let it play with them
But it cannot stay for long
For it always has somewhere else to go
And somebody else to please.

P. E. Roby

The Three Bears

Once upon a time
In a nursery rhyme
There were three bears
Who were covered by hairs
Mama bear, papa bear and wee bear too
Papa said to mama "I love You"

Baby said to papa, one fine day
"Daddy will you come out to play"
Mama was scared "he's so tiny and all"
"Relax" said papa "we'll play with the ball"
"If baby's so safe I'll be sure
To come along and mark the score"
"Oh! Come along and mark the score
I don't know what the fuss is for"

"Remember, remember his four legged and laced
"Oh! Him! Is that why you're so scared"
"For when that wolf begins to scowl
Baby these, and I, will scowl"

Out they came on after the other
Baby asked if he could have a brother.

Stanabelle Adekemi Dixon-Williams

Reflections

Tales and stories of holidays past
In front of the tiller not behind the mast
Of winding canals and great long rivers
To a landlubber it would give them the shivers
Of locking down and locking up
When that's all over it's into the pub
Now if you feel jaded and a bit off colour
Go off in a narrow boat and just discover
Nature at her good and very best
Be careful though you're only a guest

J. Snowsill

'Life in a Photograph'

The colour of time, fashion in life,
Increasing to hurt, increasing of fright.

Change all the time, difference on the face,
One goes through an unsteady pace.

A different area, and a different land,
Will I be holding another in my hand.

The guilty of one, the purity of another,
What's next in a shot to discover.

Something is told, nothing is heard,
Detail is revealed, no need for words.

Yes it will end, turn to dust,
But memories of time is a must.

Narinder Bamra

"Catnap"

Mind still racing, body numb;
I yearn for rest, but sleep won't come.

Days of turmoil, anger, stress,
need tranquil, dreamy nights' redress.

I hear soft foot-fall on the stair -
Such keen anticipation there.

Oh welcome spirit, make your climb!
Bring scents of earth, of moss, and thyme.

With kneading paw, and tongue to rasp;
embrace my angst in gentle clasp.

Warm and heavy; snuggle, stay; and
slowly start to drift away.

Antidote to life's commotion;
Worthy cause for such devotion:

Be without you? Nightmare notion!
Furry, purry sleeping potion.

Melanie Jane Banner

Dad

I wonder what you're doing now
in a world up in the sky
I never got the chance to ask
or even say goodbye.

But I know that what I said
to your face, and not over the phone
will stay with me forever
while we sat there all alone.

You lay there in another world
your face was like a tile
but those three words I said to you
at least they made you smile.

Sat there in a room with you
I didn't know what to say
you were drifting between sleep
alone with me you lay.

I remember all the good times,
and I hope you do too,
but what I want you to remember is
when I told you I love you.

Rebecca Street

After the Snow

Look at the snow so deep and white,
It makes the world look clean and bright,
The crocus and snowdrops show their heads,
Above the blanket that covers their beds,
How can something so beautiful and small,
Survive in that snow at all,
And now the thaw has come making everything look glum,
But just in the corner I can spy,
Just out of the corner of my eye,
My crocus and snowdrops as I pass by.

V. Dodd

Seeing is Believing

All around us is beauty
In abundance everywhere
But, some people cannot see it
They do not stand and stare

All they see is ugliness
And suffering and pain
They take people's lives away
With their sickening violent reign

They close their eyes to their bloodshed
And the misery they cause
To them, life is meaningless
If only they would pause . . .

To give up their arms and hatred
To look around and see
At God's given glorious scenery
All for them, you and me

People want love and happiness
To live together in harmony
Where peace will reign forever
For every colour, race and creed.

B. Ferris

Beauty of the Wild

In the wild, a tigress, proud and majestic, watches her
inquisitive and playful cub.
A mother full of harmony, grace and beauty, in a world
full of danger
The cub, full of charm and mischief, runs through the forest
so sleek and graceful.
A tigress mother and her young, eloquently captured is
a delightful scene.
Streamlined body, built for speed, the mother and child
gracefully run into the wind.
What a wonderful life it would be so precious, full of tranquillity.

Shaun Watson

The Spirit of the Twisting Fire

The fire it holds a castle,
In an enchanted fairy tale.
It is a rocket which has just been launched,
And exploded in the dark pale night.
Scattering its life into the heavens,
To die in darkness.
It is a playful child.
It is a devil burning red.
It is a life short lived twisting briefly.
It dances with the air,
Who commands its power.
It is the power of light.
A ruby set in Amber.
It slowly dies.
It is a graveyard,
Of grey and black ash.
The castle is no more . . .

Kathryn Sargent

Seasons

In summer you watched as I walked on the sand,
In spring I wandered on cherry blossom,
In winter, the snow bitter under my feet,
In autumn rusty leaves were forgotten.
But you can't make footsteps any more
You walked up life's path and went through its door,

You cannot save the tears you cried
Yet all your tears I can provide,
For there is emptiness in my heart,
For you, your journey had yet to start.
I'm still caught in a web of tears;
Alone to face my greatest fears.
And, so this year, in every season,
Without rhyme and without reason,
Afraid, I wander far from home
and in my tears,
I walk alone.

Rebecca Williams

Why

Why do I suffer with this cramp
Is it something to do with damp
Why does it make me scream and cry
And pace the bedroom - why oh why

Why do my legs just cease up tight
In the dark and dead of night
Why do my muscles twist and lock
And cause the pain my husband mocks

Why do I find sanity in the bath
Thaw out the cramps, cause me to laugh
Why does cold metal twist it back
Normal blood flow - have I a lack.

Sharron Spencer

Lakes Nonsense

The Walrus and the Carpenter were walking by a lake
In Cumbria to see the Fells, a pleasant path to take.
They wept like anything to see such quantities of rain.
"Do you suppose", the Walrus said, "that they can get it dry?"
"I doubt it", said the Carpenter; a tear fell from his eye.

"A pleasant path, a pretty lake", the Walrus said, "I doubt
If we can walk, our anoraks without".
"Turn back then", said the Carpenter; "before we're flooded out".

"We could engage some even maids with buckets by the score,
Or even call the Fire Brigade to clear the path before.
Perhaps two dozen elephants could drink the water dry".
"I doubt it still", the Walrus said, "its depth would be too high".

To save themselves, they turned around
And sought the homeward path;
But night came down and they were found,
Next morning, in the bath!

R. C. Crake

The Tree's Tale

The seed was planted, the deed was done
In earth, moist by rain and warm by sun
And encouraged as nature planned
The seed reached out a tentative hand

Pushing up with all its might
The young plant strived to see the light
As its leafy limbs broke free
Of earth, it knew what it would be

As time progressed, and tree grew strong
The Mayor of the city came along
He said, "I wish to plant this tree
In the park, for the public eye to see

As a memorial to those who died
Fighting for our country's pride."
Planted with a plaque, tree did thrive
And its spirit brought the land alive

And underneath the tree's green boughs
Lovers kissed and exchanged vows
The trees produced seed, which duly fell
To earth, to germinate a tale to tell.

Kay Wellby

To the Moon

Your radiant beauty illuminating the night.
In our dark hours you give us light.
You watch over us when we rest
to keep us safe you do your best.
Glowing brightly in the sky
you help the witching hours pass by
and when I'm tired, but cannot sleep.
I gaze at you, and my dreams I keep.
Oh heavenly angel up so far
never your light retire.
When day breaks you fade too soon
hurry back beloved moon.

Kay Chester

Dorset Contrasts

Dark rolling ribbon, dissects the comfortable quilt.
In shades of green, in shades of brown of twig bare hedges,
edging sullen fields.
Fog, silent, blanket snuggles down, softly smooths uneven paths.
Straggled sheep, huddle head low, against the winds piecing icy
blow on a Dorset winter day.

Shades of green, shades of yellow, red and blue.
The lively hedges, fence in, fence out, the growing living fields.
Sunlight glitters, running silver, water giving life.
Dotted sleeping sheep, lambs at play, birds in flight and fight
on a Dorset summer day.

J. H. Bennett

Mo Mháthair

She was our guide. She was our strength
In bad times she kept us going.
The drain of large family.
The handicap of poverty,
The need to sustain the family.
The curse of unemployment.
Her loss of two sons.
The loss of husband, Father-love.
The loneliness
Yet her strength survived all of this.
She still carried on, never showing pain of loss.
For she must be strong, and keep on going.
Why? Yes, there was the rest of the family now.
And her grandchildren, and still she worried
Now, It is her turn to pass on.
The load is lifted. Our loss great.
She has peace and rest at last, the heavy burden is past.
The long journey is ended.
She was THE GREAT UNSELFISH being.
She was my mother.

Michael P. MacHale

Memories of Summer

When I was a girl I was lucky to be
In our house by the river Grandma and me,
I'd sit by our pool watching the otters play
Contented and happy for many a day.

I would ride by my bike along the riverside
Watching and waiting for squirrels that hide,
To have them coming to my lap
To take a nut and then run back.

Like the beautiful swans who came to my call
Graceful as ballerinas at a ball,
Standing there so graceful and grand
Accepting the food I had in my hand.

Then off down the meadow to sit very still
In the cool of the morning, then maybe I will
See all the little rabbits, come out to play
To add to the joy of a sunny day.

Listening to the cuckoo, and song of the birds
The sweetest music I ever heard,
So fleeting the days now far away
So happy was I when young and gay.

Irene Webley

Dead Fox

Dumped ignominiously among roadside rubbish you lie
A rusty, speckled baggage;
Sad casualty waiting to decompose;
Become part of the moulding leaves
In earth which fate has deemed shall be your grave.

Lack-lustre fur that once gleamed like autumn sun;
Legs long stiffened in death;
You who were a part of the subtle rhythm
That courses through this planet's heart,
Once throbbed with life;
Such free and untamed beauty that was yours
Should surely be bereaved;
Did you have a mate who mourned,
Like I regret the trauma of your passing?

It saddens and sickens me to see
You becoming more and more at one with the decay;
Frozen under snow, or made dry and brittle by bitter winds
Your bones will soon be stripped,
Then sucked into the hungry earth
That waits to devour all that was once beautiful.

J. A. Miller

Annalise

Hush, my sweet baby, don't you cry, let me smooth away your tears
Let me rock you gently through the night, while I chase away
your fears
I love the way you smell, you feel, you look, the way you nuzzle
in close to me
I'll never forget the sweetness of this moment, these memories
are mine to keep.

You are worth all that I went through with you, all the worry,
discomfort and pain
But if I'd known what a joy you'd be to me, I'd gladly do it over again
I can see shadows of you sister in you, in the flicker of your smile
while you sleep
I listen to the softness of your breathing each night, these
memories are mine to keep.

I love the way that your soft hair lies, in the shadow of the silvery moon
And it makes me realize how short a time you'll be a baby, and
that you'll grow up much too soon
So, sweet Annalise, let me kiss you goodnight, and lay you down
into your cot to sleep
You won't remember all these quiet moments that we've shared,
still, these memories are mine to keep.

Samantha Neish

Grieving

Take me out to sea where there is no light
In the coal black, oil black, tar black night.
Show me that locker of Davy Jones.
The locker that is filled with the salt-bleached bones
Of sailors who pitted their puny might
Against the sea in the dead of night.
Steer me around the sharp-fanged rocks
Where the keening Lorelei sits and mocks.
When the salty spray renews my tears
And the booming waves assault my ears

In that frightful place
I'll stay . . . I'll stay
Maria Yates

My Garden

Many hours I spend
In the garden,
Digging, weeding and planting,
The soil to tend.

Amazed to see what can be done,
In winter time without the burning sun.

Veggies, flowers, shrubs and trees,
All growing in perfect harmony.

The beautiful colours of chrysanthemums and daises,
The perfume of lavender and rosemary.

Butterflies and bees flitting in among the flowers,
Whiling away the hours.

When I feel unhappy about the woes
Of this, our wonderful world.
In the garden I quickly go,
And gaze in sheer delight
At all the colours so bright.

Please excuse and beg pardon,
For spouting so much about
My garden.
J. C. Cane

The Visitors

The night they arrived I was sound asleep.
In the cold night air, like a child they did creep.
Had I been awake, then try stop them I might,
But their eyes were ice cold,
They filled my heart with fright.

For through my sleeping eyes not once did they stir.
My mind felt their breath in the chilly night air.
Their power was great and their will was as strong,
These beings weren't us, they didn't belong.

They took all they required and left us like ghosts.
Our ignorant minds blocked out we were hosts.
But our lives as we knew were to be vanquished so near.
For the end was spelt out in a baby's first tear.
Matthew Critchley

Daydream

If a poem paints a picture
In shades of jaded green.
I'll sit and write a poem
That will idolize this scene,
To sing to you of beauty
That you'll seek but never find.
For the poem that I'm writing is a picture in my mind.

I am sat upon a hilltop
Where the birds about me fly,
With jollity and freedom in a vivid sapphire sky.
Caressed by graceful cotton clouds
That are my boundless friends.
Sailing through the endless air
Until my vision ends.
Robert A. Horrocks

Sunset

Just before the fall of night
in the glorious sunset light.
I watch the sky with growing awe
though many times I've seen it before.

As shades of pink mix with the blue,
the orange, the yellow and the purple hue,
they fill the sky in the west
giving the earth a majestic crest.

I wonder as I gaze aloft
at clouds of pink that look so soft,
whether there be a prettier sight
than that of the sun's daily flight.

As the hush of eventide descends
the bird its song no longer sends.
Tranquillity and peace and calm
beset me like a soothing balm.

All too soon the glory ends
as the earth its journey wends,
slowly the incandescent light
fades to make way for the night.
Dennis C. Woollett

World Peace

People have died for us many a time,
in the graveyards they lie asleep,
no one wakes them, there they will stay,
asking us for world peace.

Why does the world have to keep on crying,
Death can't be that much fun,
The worst thing of all is that the innocent die,
When they are younger than young.

Men wanted their loved ones,
Their loved ones wanted them,
God help those scared, fearful men.
Why was life taken away,
I shall remember them day after day.

A ray of light shines in thy heart,
as we think of what they did,
they died back then so we could live.
why should they go to the dark and gloom,
when I can sit in a warm friendly room,
God bless the tomb that they rest in
my heart, their soul shall be within.
Marie Johnson

Country Lane

Pain, Pain, heading along the Country
Lane, one way into the city and out
again. I cry, but it still remains
remains. All day, I pay . . . the toll
for my disdain and shame.
My directions are, straight ahead, Don't
stop!, to explain explain.
Lance Evans

Solution?

The dusty plateau of my consciousness
is a barren place to be

Like the empty drinks machine
in the middle of the sea
Which
Knows no calm but turbulence
like the troubled mind
Seeking refuge
Seeking peace
But cannot seem to find
The love which should be evident
In these pastures - green?
But the turn of the screw whose name is hate
makes me want to scream
But to die a death is easier.
Mark Pawlikowski

113

Loving Support from Family and Friends

As time goes by we sometimes cry
In the next few years we will shed more tears
Things go wrong that can break our hearts
But we have to be strong and make a new start
When we're feeling in a state we can count on love to keep
  us straight
What ever we suffer what ever the pain family and friends will
  keep us sane
Our family's and friends will help us by
Through the good and the bad at any time
Where ever we go what ever we do family and friends will
  be there for you.

Tracey Ball

Tarot

Judy, you sit here with your cigarette, on the grass
In the shade of the flowering Ash
Bright with energy.
The Tarot is uncannily accurate and beautiful -
My life spread out here, before me,
Marked out like sleeping stones,
Among Dreams and Bridges, Cups and Wands, Swords.
I like the way you talk with me
Reflecting back tumultuous force, creating a pattern,
Telling out the symbols,
Bridging the nameless with the known.
You see panic, confusion, then shaking, breaking into Ruin,
Yet the world of infinite possibility,
Rebirth.
The Shanonstirs her own bowl.
I should play with fire-creativity, sexuality you say.
The Shaman Voicing card tells
The clarity of speaking out in the world.
Judy, sitting here with me
In the shade of the flowering ash.

Maxine Davies

My Dream

My dream of being someone,
In this world today has past.
I've tried with all my soul and strength,
But the days keep flying past.
There's not enough hours to last each day,
It's dark before it is light.
Once my dream was far away,
But now my dream's come bright.
I haven't reached out to all my dream's.
But one I know for sure,
Is I'm quite content with life today.
And to be happy was my dream for evermore,
So I just thank god for what I have.
And the love I have around me
For now I know that dream's come true,
If you try hard you will find them.
The dream of being someone
Does not matter to me no more
Because the dream of being loved so much
Is far better that is for sure.

Susan Hughes

Bosnia

Little houses in rows; all similar
gerry-built, gimcrack affairs.
card houses, we called you and scoffed.
At your petty suburban airs.

Oh! Desolate gaunt-eyed houses
huddled in broken - breaked heaps
still terror struck, sightlessly staring
while death clothed in flames 'round you leaps

Charred bones of rafter-armies pointing
in silent reproach to the sky,
the children you once protected
now shelterless, terrorised die.

Nesta Moore

Fly - Away

Walking, down, the path, so, wide and, narrow,
Is, where, I first, saw my little sparrow.
His legs, were, thin, his, breast so small.
He could hardly, move, at all.
I covered, him, with a hand's so warm,
Until, I found, him a comfortably home.
Six, week's six, day's passed by,
I slowly watched, him learn to fly.
Then, one, day, without a sound
My little, sparrow, swiftly left the ground.

J. Pickman

The Realization

There is so much peace
In the tranquillity of being alone
To be able to be at one
With your heart and soul
Recovered enough from heartbreak
To take on the world again

To look out over the city
As dusk fast approaches
A pink and grey sky slowly loses its colour
Lost behind the tall buildings and city lights
To hear the bird's chorus
Only just audible
Above the noise of the city
On its nightly journey home

To watch the day come to an end
and take part of my life with it
To wait in nervous excitement
For the new day to bring forth
New life and its experiences
And for me to survive them alone.

K. Welburn

Verse XXI

Who is devoid of sin and, through and through,
In thought and word and deed, shines pure and clear
As ever present love; who, without fear,
Observes the world, embracing it; and who
Is total in His grandeur; who is true
To life when lived as love: who, now and here,
Forgives, corrects, and comforts; yet, austere,
Transcending all, well knows what others do; -
His life is simply scripture: His word hymns,
His action sacred, blessings: in a word
He is fulfilled: the perfect, and adored. -
The glory of His person never dims.
Throughout and down the ages He is heard; -
And what He is is worshipped. - He is Lord.

Gordon Hindley

Autumn Leaves

What a beautiful sight are the autumn leaves -
In various colours on the trees,
A lovely scene for any eye - until the time they fall and die,
Laying a carpet of various shades
All done by nature not handmade,
Glorious colours of golds and browns
As they scatter on the ground,
Then comes the wind to blow them around
Until once more they lay on the ground,
With clearing them we can't keep pace
There's always more to take their place,
In the end the job is done even though it wasn't fun,
Heaped in a pile and left to rot
Then some good compost we have got
When it's time to dig and pot
All our labours long forgot,
Flowers bloom - it's been worthwhile
Though they only last a while,
Vegetables that look a treat
And are so very good to eat

O. M. Godfrey

The Indian Giver

He raped you.
Innocence torn from sweet lips.
My teeth grind with each gaping breath.
Before we stole our first kiss;
Held hands in silence.
He bled you of the only given gift.
You reach for my fevered hand.
To you, I'm miles away.
I know you're smiling,
At me. I'm the one who should be.
It wasn't me, scarred.
God, I wish him dead
Then there's my guilt for that.
It's natural, you say.
But I've got f***ing Jiminy Cricket
Atoning in my head;
Drowning sorrows in contemplation.
I feel like throwing-up, and you smile on,
Unawares.
Me? I'll cry myself to sleep.

Stephen Cowan

Ye Olde Antique Shoppe

At ten o'clock they hung the open sign
Inside the door of ye olde antique shoppe,
The sunlight made the old war medals shine
And lit the face of the grandfather clock.
Paintings, barometers and mirrors hung,
Surrounded each in dark mahogany,
A violin that had to be re-strung
Lay near the standard lamp of tapestry.
In ones and twos the people came and went
And scrutinized the over-laden shelves
Most only browsing, though a few had spent
On pieces for their homes or for themselves.
A box of coins, a gas mask and a jug
Were taken down and dusted, then put back;
Someone bought a Queen Victoria mug
Another bought an inscribed silver plaque.
Yet in the quieter moments of the day
When not a word was spoken I am sure;
Grandfather clock ticked faithfully away,
Till the shop was shut, at dead on half past four.

Lisa Rose Garbutt

The Timebomb

Our world is like a timebomb
It ticks as loud as the very first cry of a newborn baby
but still no one hears it, we all just ignore it.
We wired it up, set the timer now all we can do is wait in silence
Not even God could go back in time and put right what we have
all done wrong, we have pushed it too far.
But who is it that will suffer, our kids, us.
If reincarnation is real we are all building our own future, which
we will have to relive in over and over again like a bad memory.
Only it will keep getting worse.
But now all we can do is wait because our world is like a timebomb.

Sarah Mace

An English Garden

An English garden, large or small,
It matters not, I love them all
With changing scene throughout the year
As flowers bloom, then disappear
Where oft times many birds alight
To add indeed to my delight
While busy little bees contrive
To do their best to aid the hive
So charmed am I in summer when,
From out of nowhere, there and then,
A brightly coloured butterfly
Will flit and flounce and flutter by
The sights, the sounds, the fragrance too
Alas will fade when autumn's through

Kenneth Bennett

Dunblane

Oh the pain, pain, pain
In the town of Dunblane
Of man gone insane,
Not just mad, mad, mad,
But bad, bad, bad.

Oh the hurt, hurt, hurt
In my heart, heart, heart,
Of my tears and cries,
But what are they, they, they
To loving parent's dismay.

Oh the deep, deep loss,
Of darkness and dross,
Look to the cross, cross, cross,
That fills the great abyss
'Tween the heaven and earth.

Oh the weans, weans, weans,
Ne'er to see again, again,
Just the precious joys, toys, noise,
Of wee girls and boys
Cut short here, living forever, way up there.

Samuel T. Irwin

I Wanna Be Liked

Why am I so different?,
I'm not like all the rest,
I don't have many close friends,
Friends that are my best.
I'm not like all the others, they think
that I'm strange. I'd do anything
to be more outgoing, to make myself
Change. No boys like fat, ugly me,
they don't go for the quiet type.
Maybe if I was a little pretty and
talked more they might. But that's
my biggest problem, I never know
what to say. I just don't want
to sound like an idiot and be
laughed at every day. The right
words never come to my head and
when they do it's too late. I
can't talk to people or make
new friends I guess it's just my fate.

Kelly Saddler

Valentine Sonnet

You're like a gentle hand,
kind, caring and tender,
the softest of all the land
here is a valentine from a secret sender.

I think about you all the time,
my thoughts for you never end,
wishing that you could be mine.
My broken heart only you could ever mend.

You took my breath you stole my heart
and created a new world for me,
Without you my world would fall apart.
With you is the place I always want to be.

This love could go on 'til the end of time,
But I want to be with you, be mine.

Natalie Kensit

Spring in Rearsby

The cold earth stirs and quickens into life
Kissed from sleep by the warm caress of God.
The greys, and browns and blacks are laid away
For use again when Spring's six months behind.
From out there fragrant folds of softest greens
Lilac, Primrose and Violet shyly peep
And smiling earth dons her Spring attire,
While April touched in admiration weeps.

Mary Doyle

115

Woodsmoke - Autumn

Palish blue, low hanging, - drifting,
  interweaving stricken trees, slowly,
Ghostly, pausing, waltz with a breeze
  touch fading light, caress, smile,
a lazy wake o'er the fields,
  by the Abbey, stain the air,
fake incense, perhaps, who cares,
  snake along dimly lit paths,
watch love embrace, smile,
  uplift the violent city draught,
above it now, mix with stars,
  soon from sight are vanished,
nighttime calls the blackness in,
  an' casts his cloak o'er all,
sleep, sleep, drift with night,
  await in slumber the purpling east,
and start again.

I. MacLaren

Mad Cow Disease

How long will it be before we all contract mad cow
Is it safe to eat beef or should we give up beef now
If the incubation period's ten years, is it already too late to worry
Do we eat chips and burgers, or switch to chips and curry
The government's trying to say it's down to Alzheimer's instead.
Either way if I'm going ga-ga, I'd rather be dead.
Do they kill the mad cows now and who's going to compensate the farmer?
Something for Major to worry about, if he has to put up our tax
Will he be around next election? or will he be axed?
If beef's bad for us then who'd have thought it.
Is the world going ga-ga through mad cow, or just natural causes?

Lynn Cook

Beauty

Beauty what means so charmed a word.
Is it the sunset or the starlight.
Nay these things are but one kind,
of earth's small universe.
Beauty is the thought,
that shines from out of mothers' face,
when some loved one, does a kindness
with a charming sort of grace.
Beauty is another thought, when
one is sad and alone,
and a little child, just comes along.
And claims you for its own.

Vi Lord

Reality?

The perfect world that people idealize? The world which everything is seen? I think not, and this way of thinking must stop. Hidden agendas which are always there, many a time seem so unfair, as the delusion which has been given to us, the delusion we shouldn't really hold and trust. Given to us from a young age, taught it to bring a better change. From television and all around, the media, the ministers, it's so profound. All selling the illusion to us, and many of us do lust. Lust for it as a form of escape. Delusions confusions, many do brake. Many will demand then take, some will return, is this the mistake? Take not just riches, as money and gold, but take love and trust commodities of old. Commodities vary from differences in situation or circumstance in life. One man, one woman, even one's wife. Illusions delusions we all do have which must be fulfilled, to make us glad. If not fulfilled understood and excepted as one's self so the madness inside is not erected. Maybe not in all, this will show, and not linger and grow. But life is life, to love one's self is living, living life is best of all, then can start giving. Giving truth though own experiences, to solve their differences. The ideal will be fulfilled, a better world we build. From ashes and the earth, take away the curse. As God is willing, can converse, and no more of this sullen verse.

Michelle Yatman

Untitled

When you look at me, what is it that you see
Is it everything you've dreamed of, or is it merely fantasy
Do you look at the outer part, or can you see within
Can you see the flaws and lines, or do you see perfect skin?

Can you close your eyes and see me there, when we are miles apart
Can you feel our love beating, Like music in our hearts
Do you ever get so lonely, you don't know what to do
Has someone ever hurt you, As lovers often do?

Can you climb the highest mountain, Or swim to the ocean floor
Can you see every rainbow, or do you search for more?
If it's the secret of life your after, I'll tell you what to do
Don't search the whole world over-the truths inside of you!!!

K. Davies

Innocence of Presence

Forever in the future
inspiration from the past
Never in the present
bang, the gods have cast

Forgave the sin
wearing a permanent grin
He asked do I sleep, do I dream
the things realistic as they always seem?

Predictable answer I cannot give
lately I feel I don't want to live
I get treated like a piece of dirt
They all must know that it hurts

I can't pay any attention
i am in a different dimension
Bang, bang, the gods have cast
i wonder if these will last

Yolanda Heath

Siren

Sea-surges tug at the tides of blood, lick
Into salty cracks,
Their weedy seepings.
So is your heartbeat haunted
By pulse of wave, so does your soul dream
Of my bright bruising waters,
Their dark lullaby.

My rocks are lonely.
Won't you come dancing over the water
And dare the waves' laughter?

Don't fight
The lilt of cold currents
(For sea-slumbers sing in your ear, lap
In the mind's hollows)
I can set you free - loose you in the forever
Of this the rock-sleep, wave-thunder
My secret swellings and oozings,
The leaking of foam,
Are for you alone. Darling.

My rocks are lonely . . .

Laura Wilkins

Music?

Infuriating music ringing in my ears,
Irrational junkie playing his tune.
Sounds of wailing, moaning, whimpering
Wade together in harmony.

Alcoholic, Narcotic, Music man.
Plays his tunes to addicts.
Loser in society but in the spotlight
He becomes a star.

Addicts need something stronger.
A new trend will be on the scene.
Pay packet gone, star no more
Loser in society is born . . .

Stephen Crawford

Who Am I?

Where is the real me
Is it hiding from my pretend self
Or have I buried it so deep
That I can't find it any more
Have I become a shadow
In the light of day.

Sometimes just sometimes I leave my
Unhappiness behind
I fly away high above everything
All my unhappiness drifts away
And my life is once more worth something

But then I return and the memories
With me
The violence, the pain
My living hell is here!

C. Diamond

Thoughts

Is everything you do related to me?
Is everything you think what you see?
Why oh why are you so insecure?
What does it take to find a cure?

Are you sick, are you twisted?
Have you been visited,
By the weird and wonderful
Evils of your mind?

Do you care?
I bet you don't
Could you tell me if I asked,
What the hell love is?

On the way over I had a thought,
The happiness you have has all been bought,
Nothing's real, nothing's true,
Everything you own is completely feeble.

Is everything you do related to me?
Is everything you think what you see?
Are you actually living,
Or do you just simply, exist?

Tracy Sage

The Touch of Evening

The golden light of afternoon -
Is fading, fading - all too soon.
Pale evening's shadowy fingers, reach -
Through lingering strands of daylight peach,

Until the sun-kissed trees, gold-dressed,
Pierce the heavens, as silhouettes.
And an arrow-headed flight of birds -
Streaks across the dome of night - homewards.

Rebecca Hood

The Gift

A golden cup, a precious gift
is given through life to hold.
Remember that its contents
should be of purest gold.

Cherish this gift with greatest care,
a treasure it should be.
And keep it clear so others there
a shining light can see.

Spread cheerfulness, give loving care,
let kindly words ring true.
And be forgiving, just and fair
see other's point of view.

Fill it with joy and peacefulness
and thankfully behold.
Goodwill on Earth will manifest
the blessed purest gold.

B. Benbow Townrow

A Very Potty Thought

This is your botty,
it goes on the potty,
Tell mummy you know what I mean.
I constantly try,
then heave a large sigh,
another patch on the carpet to clean . . .

Oh why don't they make
for sanity's sake
a bottom you turn off and on?
You could just turn a key
when they wanted a wee
and turn it back off when they've gone . . .

P. J. Richards

Destiny

The labyrinth of life
is no intellectual crossword;
nor can man photograph
the untransparent future
for calenders of destiny.
Time alone
knowing that calender,
can guide you
to the footprints
into which your shoes
will ultimately fit.
Search is futile.
Contemplation a waste.
Prayers — over-expectation.
Time printed its calender
the day it was born.
That was the first and the last edition.

Shehnaz Somjee

Romeo and Juliet the Love that Conquered All

This tale to tell about dear Romeo and his Juliet,
Is so, so sad and moving we ne'er will forget.
It shows us how love can abound and then conquer,
Even though others forbid and are stronger
The love undeterred spurs on and grows fonder.

The consequence for such a forbidden occurrence,
Was death for them both and their families' assurance
That never again would a quarrel appear,
For such a long time that their friendship would sear.

An ending so disastrous, yet joyous it's true,
Of youth love did sprout, a binding so new.
A wish that appeared through a young lover's plight,
And said to the stars, that very long night.

And so we now leave this emotional scene,
Of love and dishonour and friendship foreseen.
To think of another moving strong fable,
Of Shakespeare's great works and of others so able.

Kelly Goodacre

The Mask

I look into the mirror.
Is that really me smiling?
No it can't be!
For it's a mask
When deep inside I am so sad.
Why! Oh why! Can't people see, that all I want is to be me.

Burdens I carry on my back of past times,
I can never bring back.
What does the future, hold for me.
Please happiness find me,
Surely I deserve that.
Love is what I want, to be loved is what I need.

To share, to hold, to care,
Then surely the mask will slip away,
And they will see the person that I call me.

Wendy Ingham

Are You There

Where do you go when you're not watching me
Is there somewhere else that you have to be
Are you an angel that walks by my side
Giving me courage when needed
Making me face life, not hide

Do you see where I'm going, and watch with pretence
And hear when I'm talking, sometimes making no sense
Do you feel what I feel, the pain everyday
I can't stop that torment, it won't go away

Are you there by my side as I lay on the grass
Counting each cloud in turn, and then watching it pass
Are you there when I watch the sun going down
Can you hear when the birds go to sleep, there's no sound

Do you know when I'm tired, and can't think any more
Are you still there with me when I curl up on the floor
Can you see me at night when I cry in my bed
Do you watch as the tears make my eyes turn red

Can you hear silent prayers
Do you know what I say
God look after my angel, and thanks for my day

Valerie Ann Best

The Lemon Tree

A lemon tree grew at the bottom of my garden.
Its essence rich, its bittersweet smell
Awakens my senses, even through remembrances;
Oh! I still know my garden well.

In the corner, welcomed briefly my intermittent
Rays of light and gentle breeze, I wait
For cool water to quench my thirst for life itself,
While heaven opens wide its gate.

This shady haven, overgrown with great tangles
Unavoidably strangling my dusty root
Unintentionally, yet with brutality
To keep me from the tree's Spring fruit.

The curling edges of my leaves, as though in hibernation
Wither. Petals fall and kiss the ground
In a dying gesture to this rough earth burying me.
To this garden I am bound.

One single drop of moisture would have been enough
To lift me towards sunlight by the lemon tree;
But will you choose to pour yourself, unlimitedly,
Without second thought, to nourish me?

Ruth Krawiecka

Come to Malvern View in Lilac Time

Come to Malvern View in lilac time,
It isn't far from Chelters,
See old Heming's yew tree standing proud,
Old John's yuccas too,
Old Bob's lilac looks a dream
All kept going by young Bob's expertise,
With Mum and Dad lending a helping hand too.

See the old garden tidy and tough,
Five generations have trod her beloved turf,
She is sunny and restful and shady in parts,
She has seen weddings, and tea parties of many different styles,
Children's sedate parties with sandwiches and cakes and
homemade lemonade.

To present day fumy barbecues,
With packs of children whooping and running wild over her
lovely lawns,
Chasing and screaming and popping balloons,
But above all this she has shown great resilience to our
sworn enemy,
That dreaded weed the ground elder.

Nancy Shipway-Blackwell

Looking Back

Time, when it happens, seldom seems fun
It always looks greener on the other side
You think better times are still to come
And just go along for the ride

But looking back makes bygone times the best
And memories are hidden treasures
Each memory seems to top the rest
And each brings so much pleasure

Even when life's graph is set on a low
And you think you will never recover
Time heals well and before you know
Again you smile and laugh with each other

Experiences in life, good or bad
Help us to learn on our way
And looking back on the times we've had
Keep us going forward from day to day

Mandy Strain

A Smile

Though without a word, a smile does say so much,
It breaks down the barriers and we do not have to touch
It brings out the brightness and a thrust that sparks,
Then people understand and drop their masks
As for this act we do not need a word,
We are all on bramble bushes just as birds
We hop here, we hop there, trying to survive, and
Tired by stresses and strained by cries
Some laughter each day and a smile to someone
Makes all the difference, if we try and we can,
Always remember someone's burden could be made light them
Push yourself to give a little smile
It could be just the tonic for someone's soul and maybe just
What someone needs to make their world.

Mary Joseph

"God Alone Knows How Much I Love You"

God alone knows how much I love you,
It breaks my heart to see you in pain,
I'd willingly give my life, to have you well again.

I've always believed that on earth we have to suffer pain,
But I didn't want to believe any more,
When it happened to you Elaine.

I did not want to pray any more, I thought He was unjust,
To let this happen to you, after in Him I put my trust.

How wrong we are to shed our faith,
When life deals us a blow.

We should pray all the harder for a miracle for Him to show,
God alone knows how much I cried and prayed,
To make you well again.

He must have listened to my prayers, for that miracle it came.
As the months go by and you get strong, we'll both kneel
Down and pray to God and tell Him we were very
Wrong to ever doubt His love.

C. Porter

The Tree

For hundreds of years the old tree had stood
Its roots sunk deep, and branches spread bold
Many names are carved in its gnarled old trunk
Young men gone to war and died
Young women grown old who cried
Listen carefully and hear the sounds it's captured
Sounds of laughter and lovers whispers
Cut it down and its magic will be gone
No more will it grow
No memories of so long ago.

Kerry McDermott

118

"A Special Love", A Love Beyond Compare

Love is something special
it can come in many ways,
with some it comes and goes
in others it just stays.

My mother had a special love,
a love beyond compare.
She gave us all this special love
a love for all to share.

She shared this love with all of us.
My sisters, and my dad.
She had so much love to give
it made us feel so glad.

She isn't with us any more,
She's resting in God's care.
But, she left us love,
A special love.
A love beyond compare.

Sheila Mathers

The Sea

The sea the sea the roaring sea,
It cares not that we stand there,
With howling wind blowing through our hair,
With large waves cover stones and wrack,
Then draws nearly half of these back,
Screeching gulls fly overhead,
With sharp eyes on those throwing bread,
In the tide needed and the wind, dropped,
The throwing of the flotsam and get same stopped,
Row exposed in shingle and sand,
Where not long ago mighty roller would land
Be careful, be careful don't venture too far,
Waves still race up and sweep over the bar,
Swinging matters now wash the sand clean,
And now not a sign where footprints had been
Ever so slowly, the tide draws back,
And small gullies its leaves in its track,
What a wonderful day this has been to behold,
Watching natures forces unfold.

N. DeBreanski

Happiness

The key to happiness is not gold.
It is something that cannot be bought nor sold.

For a lifetime, people can seek, but fail to find.
Wealth and importance together they bind.
Never satisfied, jealous, full of discontent.
Emotions building, bursting inside, but impossible to vent.

Happiness is not a perpetual thing,
It comes and goes with the trials which life brings.
So, when it appears, embrace it with relish.
And savour the moments forever to cherish.

Richard J. Cruickshank

I Love You

My dearest darling
It isn't because of who you are
It isn't because of what you do
It is simply because of what you mean to me
It is because of what I feel for you
The special love we share
The joy we share when we are together
The singing and the laughing
The caring and the trusting
My dearest darling
It is because you are there for me when I need you
It is because you are always there to make me laugh.
You give me your shoulder to lean on when nobody else could
My dearest darling
It is because you are what I want
It is simply because
I love you now and forever.

Kate Nkanza

There Is a Lovely Bird

There is a lovely bird
It favours sunflower seed
In a tree cavity it nests, and there it will breed
Down the tree trunks, running head first
Searching for insects, or a nut to burst
Pine bark and dry leaves, the cavity nest is lined
If it is too large, some mud this bird will find
The cavity is made, nice and small and neat
By this grey blue bird, upside down on its feet
Its breast is coloured buff, vivid and deep
Easily recognised, by the way it does creep
On to the bird table it will fly
Peanuts in a net, sure to catch its eye
Around the woods, on some tree in a park
Walking down head first, pecking at the bark
Spiders insects and grubs, this food it will seek
Probing at the bark, with its pointed beak
Flying quite a way, from its own patch
Creeping down the trees, is the lovely Nuthatch

Marilyn Francis

Taking Time

Take time to see the day unfold,
It starts off new, but soon grows old.

Birds start singing early morning,
Chirping that the day is dawning.

Milkman's early, it's not yet seven,
For him a lie-in must be heaven.

The paperboy comes with the daily rag,
His bike weighed down with a heavy bag.

Postman's next, I've received a letter,
From cousin John who's feeling better.

Neighbours starting off for work,
Tom's car starts with a sudden jerk.

Some children going off to school,
Laughing, running and playing the fool.

The garden looks good this time of the day,
New shoots are showing, Spring's on the way.

The hustle and bustle of day has progressed,
It's nearly mid-day and I've only just dressed.

You may think I'm lazy, not one that's admired,
But then it's the first day since I have retired.

Rosalie Harvey

The Loss of Love

Those days have passed, a former life
It feels; so happy were we then,
Careless to the times of change to come.
Ah, so long ago . . . and memories fade
I fear.

I must hang on, I must
To each remembered hour
The skin, those eyes I still recall,
But most of all I mourn the Loss
Of Love.

This new Life is strange
To me; to others all is still the same.
So much harder to accept.
I try to find my way in this foreign land,
But where?

I dare not ask questions, what right
Do I have? But still they demand to be heard
They must be packed away until one day
It will make sense to me,
They say.

Sara Jane Brine

Renewed Faith

Faith is like the sun, when it shines it feels great.
It warms the earth, and your heart.
It seems to charge the earth and us with unseen energy.

On a grey day look up to the sky, and watch the clouds.
If you look long enough the sun's rays will pour
through the cracks in the cloud,
like fingers pointing to the earth.

At night the sun goes down but we must take heart.
The sun does not shine for us but for someone else.
If it did not go we would not see the dawning of a new day.

A new day, a fresh start, renewed faith.

Paul Creamer

Life through the Bottom of a Glass

If your drinking habits are on the down side
It may not always be your fault
But you must experience the benefits
In a bottle of single malt.
So if you skate on the thin ice of life
And trouble is all you amass
Just pour yourself some liquid gold
Look at life through the bottom of a glass
I don't subscribe to the phrase. "The demon drink"
For it chases the demons away
Tell me, how can something so pleasurable
The morning after make you pay.
So does that stop us, it does not
We always indulge again
Why do we do it, abstainers might ask.
Because the pleasure is worth all the pain
It affects our hearts, our livers, even our eyes
So here's a message for the myopic masses
Forget all your troubles and change your outlook
See things through lead crystal glasses.

Phil Rowbottom

Imagination Sensation

This is the Imagination Sensation,
It puts your brain to its highest limitation,
This weird place is just a nation,
Created by my imagination,
All put together from my determination,
To make the ultimate creation,
A world with no termination,
Forces are driven with acceleration,
And not a thing has a relation,
But the source of all formation,
Is the wise tree of endless information,
Its secret location,
Is the furthest destination,
The people are masters of illusion,
They can drive any soul to confusion,
Now you see this is my mission,
So test your skills at the ultimate imagination sensation

Kieta Papier

Children

Children bring you heartaches, children bring you joys,
It really makes no difference if they're girls or boys,
It doesn't make a difference if they're young or old,
They're either very naughty or as good as gold.
They're sometimes very horrid and they're sometimes very nice,
I wonder if they choose which or decide by shaking dice,
They can be very penitent and so full of remorse,
But only when they've very badly gone off course,
They can be very loving and they can be very kind,
Which means that they want something or have something on their mind.
When they're small they make your arms ache, when
They're big then it's your heart,
But for parents there's a trauma when from home they do depart.
And no matter what they do and no matter where they go,
They will always be our children and that's why we love them so.

Susan Jones

A Reflection . . . A Mask

What is it but a reflection of our outer being?
It reveals not what is inside of us,
Our hearts, our feelings, our memories,
But a glistening veneer
Hiding away our true opinion of ourselves.

Yet, why do people find it so important?
The mask that hides away
What would make us feel so vulnerable were it exposed,
Our inner persona.

Mirrors everywhere reflect back what I have no desire to behold,
The feelings of society are thrust upon me
Yet I have no desire to experience them,
'Beautiful reflections, mean a beautiful person'.

How easy it would be to rip away their masks of loveliness,
To reveal their inner selves, their insecurities,
In my own ideal world.

Keeya Kulkarni

What's Real?

Drowning in a circle of nothing
It seems like never-ending torture
Nothing ever changes here
Nothing really happens

Reality is just a surreal dream
Dreams never amount to anything
Everything I feel is unreal
Unless reality is unbearable

In a place like this, death would be kind
A glimpse of reality to soothe the mind
Light shines outside this cave
But inside, darkness is eternal

I reach out to touch the stars
But all feel is emptiness

Louise Griffiths

March 13th

Innocence died today.
It was destroyed in a hail of bullets.
It didn't stand a chance.

Innocence was crushed today,
Trampled beneath the feet of madness.
Taken away - all at once.

But - their faces will stay forever young
In the photos their innocence will remain,
Captured by the camera's lens.
Reminding us of how they were,
before innocence died today.

Sally J. Tate

Spring

I went outside,
It was a delight.
It was spring
flowers were all over everything.
Buds are opening,
Nothing is blowing.
My mum can have a cup of tea outside,
Now the night is quite light.
As I'm lying on my pillow,
I can hear the branches rustling of a pussy willow.
I can hear the birds singing,
While I am on my swing swinging.
I see the sunshine,
I wish that is was there all the time.
As my dad walks past the pond mowing the lawn,
I can see the big frogs spawn.
I was outside having my tea,
When a bee came and stung me.
My friend lives on a farm his name is Sam,
And all of his sheep are having lambs.

Lisa Marie Cooke

Africa's Loss

Scorched earth, cracked and dry, I lift my eyes to the sky
Is the answer there,
For my little one, dying from thirst, when will he show that
he cares.

Death coming closer with every faint breath,
body grows weaker, losing its strength.
The pain I felt when you were born will be nothing to compare.
To the pain I'll feel here in my heart, if tomorrow you're not there.

Will you wake up tomorrow to suffer yet another day.
Or will you be too deep in sleep, no longer able to stay,
My love for you will go on and on like the ever-flowing sea.
Famine and strife takes another child's life
Will it take this one from me,

We've suffered together, but if tomorrow should finally set you free,
I will lift my eyes towards the sky, asking
How many more will there be,
How many more will there be
Linda Harrington Dallin

"Country Musing"

Now leave me for a time alone
In pensive solitude to roam
At leisure o'er the distant scenes,
Exploring natures dells and denes.
Caressing hedgerows as I pass
Softly treading nodding grass.

Whispering wings float overhead,
Feathered songsters hide in the hedge.
Over the fence the cattle gaze
Sheep and horses cease to graze.
No panic, a disdainful eye
As the intruder passes by.

Filtered sunlight in leafy lanes
Reflected in the window panes
Of the occasional cottage,
Glimpsed through hanging foliage.
Homeward bound, filled with elation
Thanking God for his creation.
Sidney A. Gadd

The Gentle Giant

He will work all day
Just needs warm bed and bale of hay
No diesel oil to make him run
Even though he weights a ton
His bright eyes, lovely chestnut coat,
Soft velvet nose
You will see his like
At all the agriculture shows
Put him on a grass meadow
Where he will stand and munch
Who is this gentle giant?
The beautiful Suffolk punch
P. Block

Mountain Pleasure

The trek up to the mountain was a step into the past;
It was so many years ago, since then I did it last.
Oh! To sense the freedom and the wind upon my face
My companion walked quite quickly but soon I set the pace.
We climbed the hill together in an easy kind of way;
Just as if we did it each and every other day.
The summit of the mountain was how I remembered it
When I was such a little girl and there I use to sit.

The undulating beauty lay stretched before my eyes;
Where the leafy trees of green meet the ever-changing skies.
A profusion of white flowers extended far and wide,
How readily the heather tumbled down the mountainside.
We both sat down together, contented in our thought
Taking in the pleasures which never can be bought.
There is no need of money or never-ending wealth
When all we really have to do, is find our inner-self.
C. S. Brooks

Dirty Dishes

There is a job that I dislike
It is the washing-up.
I'd rather clean the windows
Or bathe our dirty pup.

I would sooner dig the garden
Or plant a row of trees
I would rather scrub the kitchen floor
Although it hurts my knees.

I don't mind washing and ironing
Or cooking a three course meal.
But when it comes to washing-up.
Unhappy is how I feel

Dirty plates and dirty pans
To them there is no end
Dirty knives and forks and spoons
They'll send me 'round the bend

So all you clever clogs out there
If you've got time to dwell
Can come up with a liquid
That will dissolve the pots as well
Olive Atkinson

Untitled

Mary had a little stone,
It was as heavy as lead,
And everywhere that Mary went,
She carried it on her head.

And thus lived Mary night and day,
She ate and played and slept,
But on her head this burden lay,
And in her sorrow Mary wept.

"Oh, how can I this weight release,
It tortures me by day and night.
Oh, help me gain a little peace,
Relieve me of this awful plight!"

Her friends they all quite tired had grown,
They tugged and pulled till they were red.
But Mary's hand was stuck to the stone,
And the stone was stuck to her head.

One day she tripped on a stone and fell,
Her hands flew out in fearful dread.
"Cold kills cold", our sages tell,
'Twas a stone that released the stone on her head!!
Rachel Tweg

Goodbye

Goodbye.
It tears at me,
like a sea wind,
rushing over bleak dunes.

Like roof tiles rattling
as November wind whips across damp red,
its fingers tearing at edges.

The orchard apples are
hurled to the ground and
huddle, bruised in the grass,
a multi-coloured mess.

Autumn leaves are piled high
against damp brick walls.
Sudden gusts scatter the brown,
shattering the patchwork colours.

And then suddenly,
there is a desolate calm.
Goodbye is thrown away on the wind
and I'm torn from two to one.
Lesley Curtis

To My Husband

I dreamt you came back from the dead last night,
It was cold where you were, you said last night,
You laid your leg across mine, your arm around mine,
And cuddled me, your body warmed me
In the bed last night.
Someone else came into the room last night,
Surprise on his face to see you there,
What would we tell friends?
You weren't dead.
The flowers they left for you,
The money they sent in memory of you,
The people who mourned you
What would they think?
You had gone, had left me
You couldn't come back.

There's so much I want to ask you
So much I want to tell you
Just to have you near me again would be good
But it was cold in my bed this morning.

M. E. Thomas

'Have You Heard This One'

What is a joke
It's a point of view.
Some are clean, some are blue,
Some are told in a constant rush.
Then there are those that make you blush
I've heard some as long as a story
Others turn your stomach as they are gory.
To me the jokes with the most appeal
Often make me laugh till I almost reel.
They can be short or long but must be witty.
A corny crack or rhyming ditty.
The best to be had are off the cuff
They make you cry, Enough! Enough.
A really good joke will never offend.
Be it family, acquaintance or best friend.
So if you feel you have something funny to say
Just go ahead, make someone's day

M. J. Boden

Desperate Love

The moon is clear and bright;
Its beauty is the light.
The sky is all around;
Transparently clasping the ground.
The air is fresh and sweet;
Scented hearts may miss a beat.
The sea is cool and flowing;
The breezes from it, blowing.
The music penetrates the flames;
That sends fiery blood through the veins.

You are my moon; you shine on me.
You are my air; you breathe in me.
You are my sea; you flow in me.
You are my life; you live in me.

Karen Skitch

"Children"

To have the love of a child, is something rare and true,
It's the kind of feeling that brings the closeness home to you.
To understand this feeling, that floats on every wave,
Is something that you treasure each morning - till the grave.
The smile in their eyes, the flick of a lash,
That impish grin, which soon goes past.
But when there is heartbreak, and tears trickle down a cheek,
They make you feel so humble, frail and meek.
A child can be many things, full of hope and joy,
They share the same expressions of love, either girl or boy.
They need to know they are secure in everything they do.
Their hopes and fears and all their dreams
Is the confidence, they place in you.

C. H. Cruse

"A Tribute to Dunblane"

The routine was usual for the rising of dawn,
It was March 13 this particular morn,
Children were breakfasting with families in homes.
We knew not or, disasters that roamed.

Precious children were taken away that day,
What can we do, what can we say,
Comfort the parents in their time of grief,
While others walk on in disbelief.

What makes a person commit such a crime,
Is their life that bad, where they don't give a damn,
He took his life too, after this fate,
I can only express a day too late.

May God rest his eyes upon their town,
Let them rebuild the lives they had found,
Time is a healer as we all know,
Dunblane will recover,
As the pain slowly goes.

D. A. Palmer

The Tramp

He dawdles and stumbles down the lane,
It's clear to see his terrible pain,
He won't look up, nor say a word,
He's scared his voice will not be heard,
Drunk and dirty, he wreaks of smoke,
Once he was a decent bloke,
She stole his heart and identity,
But he was blind, he could not see,
She drained him of his love and pride,
Deserted him, then said he'd died,
And now he has nowhere to go,
That's why he wanders, head bowed low,
He won't survive, he has no hope,
There is no way that he can cope,
His mind and soul are rising fast,
He draws a breath, it is his last,

Shirley Mulder

Planet Earth

This planet is surely dying
its destruction caused by man,
but if we all stick together,
we can make a plan.

Let us all get together,
and stop the pollution of earth and sky,
let us ask each other,
the how, the what, the why.

God created this beautiful planet,
and made it all serene,
then He breathed life upon it,
a wonder to be seen.

So if we stick together,
and believe in our dreams,
we can clean up this world,
and keep it forever green.

Kenneth Fisher

Bertie

He came filled with love, this small bundle of joy
just what we wanted, our own little boy
Two big brown eyes, looking up, filled with trust
He's so soft and warm, to keep is a must

He's got long floppy ears and a little wet nose
His coat's mostly brown with little white toes
'Bertie' is his name he's our own King Charles Spaniel
We all love him dearly, especially Lisa and Daniel

He's the king of our castle, a real little toff
He keeps us all laughing
as he nearly wags his tail off!

Lynne M. Hope

My Love

My love for you is oh so deep,
It will always be there for you to keep.
So you can take it anywhere,
This I promise, this I swear.

My love for you is oh so true,
Although sometimes it makes me blue.
It makes me sometimes want to scream
And let you know it's not a dream.

My love for you will never alter,
So there is no need for you to falter.
I'll be there whenever you need me
So all you need to do is look and see me.

My love for you is oh so strong,
I know, full well it isn't wrong.
There's nothing I wouldn't do for you,
If you really look you'd know it's true.

My love for you is never-ending,
It's why this message to you I'm sending.
I want to be with you for life,
So just say yes and make me your wife.

Lesley Kelly

Broken Love

I know in my heart my love lives on
It's better to have loved and lost.
Sorrow is hard when love is gone
Should we despair at any cost.

More in sadness than in anger
Is love just a dream.
My love for you is like a hunger
Like a cat I like the cream.

Many years we've spent together
We all take the good with the bad.
That's what life's about, sharing forever
Why do I feel so sad.

I close my eyes and there we are
Holding hands again.
Why did things go this far sun
Sorrow has a terrible pain.
Shall my sadness have an end
Together again would be divine.
My love for you is on what I depend
I'll always love you, you'll always be mine.

D. Reynolds

"Growing Old with Dementia"

Is it really my mum?
It looks like her.
The familiar face, hair and soft skin.
But something's missing -
She's not the mum I remember anymore.
The laughing, the hugs, the closeness between us,
It's all gone now.
It's nobody's fault - it just happened.
It seems like one day she was my mum
And the next - an old lady who didn't really know me.
I'd never imagined my mum like this.
The sparkle's no longer there,
She still smiles, but doesn't understand the hurt I feel.
Carefully chosen Birthday cards with touching verses,
No longer appreciated, no longer read,
As she lives in her own private world,
Am I a stranger to her, as she seems to me?
I grieve for what I've lost,
For although she's here with me now
The mum I once knew has gone forever.

Karen Tyas

Know Your Blessings

Mind not the soil treading in from the garden,
It will soften the days when the ground starts to harden
And footsteps grow scarer not lingering long
And with no happy voices to join the bird song.

Mind not the props piling up to the ceiling
It will colour the years when the paint work starts peeling
And concerts have ended no curtain ding dong
And with no grand finale to put right such wrong

Mind not good sheets making tents for encampment
It will furnish your dreams when they need some enchantment
And campsites are silent not one muffled tongue
And with no little persons to burrow among

Mind not the 'mice' sneaking on to your pillow
It will help fool the night when the wind strips the willow
And kisses are memories like limbs clinging strong
And with no whispered secrets where they did belong.

Margaret Duffield

A Poem Is Good to Be Read

A poem is good to be read.
It's good for the living
And is good for our dead.
It goes on forever
Weather's cold right now,
But soon it will be spring
Where flowers bloom and birds will sing.
So love one another all year through,
Where ups and downs will worry you.
But with our love
Things will go right
All the day and night
Our Lord with us
And by our side
So we can go through the
Year with pride.

H. Bare

The Tree

Look at the tree so big and so high
It's grown so big it touches the sky
Look at the branches how wide they go
Protecting the ground from winter's snow

Look at the tree it is so tall
The branches reach out over the wall
The buds are bursting with fingers of green
For spring is here and winter has been

Look at the tree its beauty complete
Reaching out across the street
Giving shade to all who come
Against the summer's burning sun.

Look at the tree with leaves aflame
Autumn has come around again
Next the wind will hurry along
And then the leaves will all be gone

Mary Donaldson

Our Dogs

Bengo and Bonzo are our dogs names,
It's really a wonder they're not both lame,
They're boxers you see, do you know what this means,
Well life to them is permanently in your teens.
They are boisterous, crazy, act like clowns,
Life for them really is ups and downs.
They don't see the logic of going 'round things,
Just plough on through and wonder why it stings.
Food is another item, they just cant wait,
Bengo! Bonzo! Leave the plate.
Oh but they're lovely, affectionate and kind,
Such true friends are hard to find.

Sally Jane Cox

"Life"

The miracle of life begins at birth,
Its first breath essential to all,
A mystery spanning the widest girth
On mankind, creatures, large and small.

On earth, each life walks through a varied path,
Years of destiny unravel,
Their unknown future lies ahead, which hath
Miles of changing roads to travel.

As ageless time reveals the lives of all,
Many a story will be told,
Portrayed as illustrated books recall,
Historical pages unfold.

Although not eternal, life is cherished
As a treasure beyond compare,
For without a life all would be perished,
Leaving a world lone, without care.

Pauline Will

Aftermath

The pain has not gone,
It's still within.
Twisting, turning, needing and wanting to be released.
The silent tears flowing with no one,
no one to wish away my fear and terror.
Creepy cracks, whistly winds make my heart erupt.
Nervous breath, what's out there? WHO?
No one,
Just my past, abuse and more abuse.
People stop and stare, whisper
God, please what the matter with me?
Do I have "victim" or "dirty" sprawled over my head?
Oh no, I'm just paranoid.
I'm innocent.
I was supposed to be safe as a child.
I want to be safe now.
I want to be free and at peace now.
But the treatment is worse than the crimes of childhood,
That were afflicted upon me.

Satuinder Mann

Starlight

It's the darkness that crowds out the light
It's the quiet that drowns out the noise
It's the starlight that blocks out the sunlight
It's the quiet darkness of starlight
That creates my dreams and hopes
When I was just small child
Looking to the heavens to shape
My future and my life.
I arrive with an understanding that I can
Explore the stars for as long as I want
With a promise that I would never destroy
Their peace and contentment for if I broke
My promise they would take back their beauty
And protection from this world and leave me
To the whims of the harsh sun and cruel moon.

Roseann Pannier-Taylor

Time

The clock upon the wall chimes out the hour.
It's time to go to work or time to play.
We run, we rush, we dash, or maybe wait;
But time is king; time dominates our day.

We're waiting for some news, or life is hard;
Then time creeps slowly, wearily drags by;
Yet good and glad times pass with haste,
The hours race, the days and minutes fly.

But what is time? A useful manmade toy?
The planets each revolve at their own pace.
A day on Earth or Mars is not the same.
In fact, does time exist at all, in space?

Pamela Briddon

Life

The telephone rang, persistently,
Its insidious tones burrowing into t.v. numbed minds.
"Your son is ill."
Those few destructive words unleashed an agony of questions.

Casualty,
A limbo of patients and anxious, grieving friends and relatives.
A son who heaved and moaned and vomited
The noxious brew so carelessly ingested.
A parlous act.
A youth in prime of life with home thought loving, safe and happy.
If so, then why?
We needed reasons, answers and solutions;
Answers which would pacify our tortured minds,
Remove doubts and restore tranquillity.
We took him home.
His system purged, all reprieved,
Allowed a chance to start anew -
To cherish him, support his needs and hide our pain.
Inspire in him the will to carry on,
Nourishing the priceless gift of life.

C. J. Conod

The Football Team

They've kicked off, what a team,
It's the semi-final, they look very keen.
Everton is this team's name,
Football is their favourite game.
Duncan Ferguson scores a goal,
There's no way this man will be on the dole.
Andrei Kanchelski's down that line,
Now there's a player that seems so fine.
He's crossed the ball in, with Graham Stuart on the end,
Stuart's gone down injured but he'll soon be on the mend.
It's a penalty given to the blues,
Hinchcliffe takes it, they surely can't loose.
He's scored, Everton's won,
The match has been lots of fun.

Steven Walker

Butterflies

We touch like butterflies our fragments of creation;
Lighter than air we lift towards the sun.
Blossoms give their fragrance to its warmth,
And dancingly the joyful hours we run
Until the light grows red and slowly dies,
And darkness tells the fluttering day be done.

We rest surrounded by the night's strange sounds,
Damp dew upon our sluggish wings;
Waiting to sense the rising warmth again,
New day's vitality when all life sings
And life's bold energy flows forth,
Abundant in the dancing joy it brings.

Rex E. Burrow

In Hospital

Sitting, gazing through the window pane,
It's really started to rain again,
I've never had so much time before,
To gaze at the beauty for us in store,
The beautiful colours, the hosts of flowers,
I could sit and view for hours,
At last the sun begins to shine,
I can see it peeping through the vine,
The view of the hills, the tops of the trees,
Even the sound of the humming trees,
The little rabbits are hopping and playing,
Then I can hear the donkey neighing,
The sound of the children's voices loud and clear,
Now, I have spotted a little deer,
The little lambs as they skip and play,
They really are having a wonderful day,
All this is sent from the Lord above,
I'm sure it's sent with all His love.

Mary Carring

The Day of a Rose

Silently and gently it uncurls, the petal on a rose
Its velvet skin searching for the sun, so far away and yet so close
Soft dew lingers and the petal takes it in.
Quenching its thirst, and bathing it, releasing the fragrance
　　held within
Other petals take the cue and follow close behind
All turning eagerly, to see what they can find
The sky, the air, the grass, the trees, the life force all around
Carry on the gentle pace, all without a sound
A bee in noisy contrast
Excitedly plunges his nose inside
Gathers up the pollen, and exits in satisfied pride
The petals stretch, the sun glows warm
The day advances onto noon, a shower goes, a breeze then blows
Its coolness over too soon
The petals now are open wide, with stamens pointing to the sky
The leaves and thorns protect its base, the rose is safe on high
Evening comes, the sun goes down, the petals close for sleep
Touching each other comfortably, company to keep
Their softness and their beauty, lie in sweet repose
Another day is ended, a day in the life of a rose

Wendy Eaton

Contentment

Contentment is a state of mind.
It's there for everyone to find
It smooths away that furrowed brow.
That frown is gone, you're smiling now.

Contentment doesn't cost a lot.
Be satisfied with what you've got.
Don't reach for things you can't afford.
Be active and you won't be bored.

If through the world there was content.
There'd be no need for armament.
The money saved would clothe and feed.
Millions of people who are in need.

Contentment then would quickly spread.
Instead of all the fear and dread.
It would be very nice to see.
A world of peace and harmony

But in this world of hate and greed.
It seems a miracle we'd need.
And if that miracle came true.
I'd be content, and so would you.

L. K. McBean

The Tree

There's a tree outside my window,
It's rather special to me,
Nature in all its glory,
A wondrous sight to see.
For two years I've watched it grow,
From a rather doubtful start,
It weathered the storm, and the gales,
Now a sight to gladden one's heart.
Man may think he is clever,
But never, never can he,
Create and produce such a wonder,
As my lovely, beautiful tree.
My tree has a message for me
My silent, unspoken friend,
That nothing or no-one lives forever,
And Death is not the end.
When I feel the need to pray, I look upwards towards my tree,
Somehow God seems so much nearer,
　　when the tree looks down on me.
The sun may shine, the rains come down
　　but my tree keeps a firm hold,
In this very troubled world of ours, it's worth its weight in gold.

Vera M. Lawrence

Doppelganger

It looks onto life with sharp eyes,
Its heart beating to a pace of mine.
Its thoughts gathered in a confused state,
Reflecting onto life, it waits.
To destroy is its widest capacity,
I am its aim, its reflecting mirror image,
I am all there is to blame when its hunger strikes.
Between us, two faces, but only one look,
My life is its hunger, my blood is its thirst.
In my shadow it waits,
Haunting its fleshly counterpart,
For there not a thousand men could move it.
It is a knife of life wanting revenge,
But no-one succeeds to capture it.
Its power appears larger than life,
But it weighs less than a feather.
It watches, it moves, it stands close to you.
A ghostly being of your existence,
You laugh but when you finally look,
It's been standing there right behind you.

Lisa Algieri

The Armadillo

It seems that many a times I've faltered
I've walked the path of blindness for reason
The reason being that involvement was haste
My conscience smashed by turning away.

At times we bury our heads for convenience
Must dash, oh look! Times moving on
If we run from self beyond our call
We're confused and baffled, a dreadful fall.

If facing self causes strife and pain
We must ask ourselves why and face and strain?
It must be said it's better than a life
Of pretentiousness, of vanity an invisible knife.

Simon Horn

Leaving

Down the lonely paths of life
I've wandered on, in stress and strife
But looking back, I can recall,
Those paths have led me nowhere at all,
Did I achieve my goal in life
It passed so quick, then I was a wife,
Children dancing 'round my knee,
A partner who was jealous of me,
Not allowed to have a friend
When the children grow, this must end,
The children now are quite high.
It's time, I fear that I must fly,
I've got to spread these rusty wings.
And take to the air, whatever it brings,
I'm off along my doddering flight, to where?
I must go now, I must not scare
A last look 'round this place I've known,
Come feet move, you've got a new home,
With heart like lead, I leave the place,
And wipe the tears from off my face

Mary Shearer

Life - The Early Start

Two weeks early, you decided to come
Joy, pain and anxiety, all rolled into one
Soon you'll open your eyes and see the light.
So vulnerable, tiny, gentle the movements of life
Watching eyes, listening ears, crying mouth and breathing nose
Perfectly formed - little fingers and toes
Such long hours - nourishing you night and day
Willing you to grow, so tired, I forgot to pray
My child is for life, this maternal instinct
Lonely and afraid, I didn't stop to think
Will you talk, walk, be able to sing
Until someone whispered
Have faith for what tomorrow may bring.

Shirley Armitage

Little Things

I looked out of my window and saw a dull damp day.
Just how I feel I mumbled my mood was dark and grey
I stepped out in the garden and looked 'round in despair
Not a flower to be seen all was stark and bare
Just then a breeze touched my face and whisper'd look around
I touched my face and thought what's to see
but looked towards the ground
And spied four little snowdrops as perfect as could be
In a clump of faded grass smiling up at me
I just knelt down and touched their
Heads how could I not have seen
Those pretty flowers growing there dressed in white and green
It's little things like snowdrops so beautiful to see
That makes your life worth living that's
What they did for me.

Rose Wright

Adam

We're two very lucky people to have this feeling twice,
It's so warm and loving it's really very nice.
Welcome baby Adam, welcome to our home.
We'll never leave you son,
You'll never be alone.
You have an older brother, a brother you'll never know,
He was only six weeks old, and then he had to go.
We have photos for you to look at,
And memories though so short,
But we know that you'll stay longer,
Then our first born baby George.
You're wished love and happiness all your life through,
And try darling Adam, to live your life for two.
We'll celebrate one day soon,
The day the doctors say,
You can take off the monitor,
Your boy is here to stay.

Lynn Beech

A Love that Was Mine

Three years seems like eternity and I still long for what was mine -
I've a good life - a new life and altho' you're with me all the time -
It's not enough to think of you, as I do, each day
I need you to hold me in the night and kiss my tears away.
When I was low, you cheered me, your words were always kind
A gentle man, a kinder man, in this world I would not find.
When you love a man and the bond is strong, when he's with you everyday
What do you do? Where can you go? when that man is taken away.
Just once in a lifetime a love comes - a love engulfing and true
You know that love when you look in his eyes and he looks back at you.
I saw such a look many years ago, on a boat and out to sea
What a wonderful day - what a wonderful thrill to know you were looking at me
I can see you still if I close my eyes and your spirit stays close by
I still question the reason I'm left all alone, but no - one can answer me why -
But memories, treasured memories of the happy times spent with you
Gives me the strength and the will to keep going on still
And to face each new day anew.

Marion Smith

My Mask

Take away my mask and what do you see
Just a face. How d'you picture a girl who is free
We are all of a mind to do as we wish
But I've tasted the essence of that - a rare dish

I've conquered the battles of life's evil snares
And I've been in the nets of ones who glare
But I'll fight even the devil to stay just as I am
And I'll take off my mask any time I can

But when facing the vultures that are lurking outside
I don't have to run away and hide
I just put on my armour. My thick coat of bold
And walk tall in the sunshine. It's a good fit this mould

Sandra D. Fletcher

It Could Be You

I've had a go at the football pools, at dog racing as well
I've even tried the horses, but the jumpers always fell
I've no luck with the women, no matter what I say
I can offer love or money, but they all still keep away
I gambled on the stock market, and I'd never done so well
And then we got 'mad cow disease,' and all the prices fell
My health has suffered recently, brought about by stress
As my love life, and my finances, have both got in a mess
How then can a guy like me, make an honest bob?
Should I keep on gambling, or try to find a job?
I may have found an answer, but I'll have to wait and see
My new line of investment is the national lottery
Already I've had some success, perhaps there's more to come
But at the time of writing, ten quid's the most I've won
So hopefully this weekend, both my problems I'll erase
'Cos in a dream, I clearly saw, 'my balls fall into place'
So come on folks, don't linger, invest a pound or two
And when you see that finger, you'll know 'it could be you.'

B. K. Bayles

Reflections in a Childhood Window

Raindrops gently spatter my window in a million designs
Life flashes through my mind's eye in a virtual blur of noisy colour.
I'm beginning a journey - screams, laughter, tears and smiles
A blaze of colour running on for miles.

A breath of fresh air washed across the sky in a dream-like rainbow
There's a warm falling-through feeling as sleep takes me far away.
To a fast moving coach and the whirring warmth of heater vents
Far below a car crash then off to camped tents.

Marbles, school, getting the cane, a kestrel hovers, ignore the pain
The strength of a hug from a dad never known, more tears.
Weightless now floating till, off on a roller coaster ride on the back of the wind
Diving down across playgrounds where children seemed tinned.

Cut grass and barbecues perfumed the air, I soared higher
Through the cotton wool clouds to face the smiling sun.
She whispered to me, her voice a musical dream of beauty
As I sank through the wispy floor, I cried, she understood me.

Swooping down I appreciated the rolling fields and all life itself
Gliding now, a tranquil eagle, I skimmed the surface of a mirror stream.
Touching its silk-like silver back, but, something was calling
Through warm mists, the hot sun, up and up into a warm bed falling.

Neil Gould

Untitled

Green buds unfurl with ballet grace,
Light frost as lace, gilds emerald grass,
God's love shines forth with spring's new face,
As winter cold and bleak has passed.

Lynette Elliott

A Passenger's Prayer

I am in heaven it's such a mistake
Just because you thought it was time to overtake
My life taken from me at the age of three
I ended up at the base of a tree
You decided to have a drink then drive.
That didn't matter, you survived
A few days later, you laid me to rest.
You tell all your friends I was one of the best.
They take you to court they're not very tough
The judge said you have suffered enough.
As I look down from out of the sky
I happen to notice my father drive by
You think he would learn from all his mistakes
But no he stops at a pub to take a break
Back to the car he thinks he can drive
But this time he didn't make it he didn't survive
He came to heaven with tear's in his eyes
I just shook my head and walked straight by
So if you drink and if you drive what the heck, you may survive
But stop and think of those who have died

H. R. Hicks

A Void Like the Atmosphere

Like emerging from the sea so deep
Like the islands of Lakshadweep
My mind has left its futile slumber
Now I know death to keep
Thus I shall drink of nothingness' fountain
and fill myself till such tears I weep
Then life's evil will me no more encumber
And with its fall so seemingly steep
I tumble down civilization's mountain
To awaken, then to sleep

Ole Andreas Bjerheset

Requiem for a Slate Roof

Sad to see you go, slate roof.
I've gazed on you for a lifetime.
Purple and blue and green, like a pigeon's breast,
Gleaming in rain, the water sliding down
Into the gutters with a rushing sound
As over natural rock, in some Welsh stream.
Out of the mountains were you hewn
By men, far down in the bowels of the earth
In caverns deep, splitting natural slate
Made over millions of years in silent gloom.
Gouged from the quarries, shaped and counted
Sent to the cities for rooves, secure and strong.
And now new neighbours want you stripped,
Replaced by hideous tiles; no life, no reflection, just tiles,
But I noticed you were carefully stacked,
Hand-made, and still of value in the world today.
And so you'll go to re-roof some old house or barn
And fit into the hillside next the lake.
You'll breathe a sigh, and feel you've come back home
But I am left bereft, to mourn my loss.

M. G. Williams

No Tears Left

These past four years
I've learnt how to cry,
To learn the deceit
Of the death of your lie.
That life is worth living.
But to live you need love!
For love is a troll
Who's out on parole,
With claws like a hawk,
Holding you back from the truth of your talk.
Life is forever, in memory of love
But loved ones are dragons disguised as a dove.
Full of deceit,
Offering a treat, of candy, a sweet.
These treats soon decay
with the death of the day.
As the tears run dry
I know I must die.

Lana Edwards

Motherhood

Expecting a baby you can't wait to see,
Just what sex it's going to be,
Labour starts you're in bad pain,
Was it worth the gross weight gain,
Out it comes tears of joy,
Is it a girl or is it a boy,
Has it ten fingers has it ten toes,
Better make sure your mother knows,
Then you feel good the bump has gone,
You remember your beauty once shone,
You look down what has it done,
Varicose veins and not just one,
Stretch marks on breasts, tum and thighs,
Miracle creams what a load of lies,
Endless bottles and sleepless nights,
Tiredness causes tears and fights,
Being a mother can really tire,
Never mind one day you may retire.

S. J. Cogdale

In Memory of My Soul Mate

You made your choice to leave this world, it was all too much to bear,
I've tried so hard to carry on as if you were still there,
They say that time's a healer but is that really true?
For every day that passes by is full of thoughts of you.
I wonder are you free of pain, is your world a happy place?
Are you watching now from up above with a smile upon your face?
You had so many problems, so very many fears,
I tried so hard to help you whilst fighting back my tears,
Your good days grew less frequent and your down days
    they were bad,
It broke my heart to hear your voice so desperate and so sad.
No need to say I miss you, I had so much to say,
I only wish I'd said it all before you went away.
Life goes on, it has to, but until we meet again,
The silver thread that holds you tight helps ease my inner pain.
You'll always be a part of me wherever I may go,
For you and I were soul mates and soul mates don't let go.
If only I could close my eyes and make a dream come true,
I'd pray to God with all my heart for yesterday and you.
You were a very special guy, one of the very best,
God bless you till we meet again, God bless you as you rest.

Lee Gooch-Hatton

Seasons for Living

Spring: Birth, awakening, newness, glee,
Light-hearted feeling within the depth of me.
Greens, yellows, whites and blues,
Sweet fragrances sent out from delicate hues.

Summer: Warmth, growth, abundant cheer,
Warm breezes, blue skies are once again here.
Greens, yellows, pinks and reds,
Fill hedgerows, parks, borders and flower beds.

Autumn: Maturity, changes, tasks not quite done,
Leaves turning, mists broken by the harvest sun.
Reds, yellows and golds cascading to the ground,
Occasionally lifted by the breeze to dance around.

Winter: Sleep, wisdom, life put on hold,
Memories within dreams to stave off the cold.
Raindrops, frosted patterns, flurries of snow,
Swirling mists, singing winds, crackling fires aglow.

Within the four seasons life will come and go,
From the first bud on the trees to the last flake of snow.
To start once again, the circle of life turns,
And within the centre, the eternal flame burns.

Karen Wilson

Strange Love Rhapsody

Deep in a promised land, far from busy docks and parading ships,
Lo! My fair Andromeda, awakened on the hidden shore of rocks,
As I profoundly ache and reflect upon her bare loveliness,
A forsaken sea-monster, dare I feel those forbidden locks,
Kneel dizzy before freshly cloven buttocks and open, red lips,
Though fearing a bold Sir Perseus, master another's sublime body.
Youthful Kama, with love's bow and arrow, rides his prime sparrow,
Playful shadows lengthen, range and strengthen the azure sky,
The drowsy day, in omni-striped pyjama, prepares to say goodbye.
Pure light, in grace and joy, succumbs to the dulcet embrace of night,
A shy boy, understood, hides thumbs and sleepily falls from sight.
The slow sea, time's rare plunder, bedecked in a snow-white canopy,
Throws its pristine loneliness, over a visiting angel lover and I,
In the precious gap between man and woman,
    painful tenderness grows,
And the tinkering breeze above,
    rapidly blows a strange love rhapsody.
Noble sons and daughters,
    adrift upon measured seasons and reasons,
Happily will find, that in a world of treasured monsters and dragons,
Thee passions will swiftly shift woes, and bind the deadliest foes,
Melt the strong, cruel freeze, and set the confined souls free -
It is long time that creatural hearts felt, the rime on tops of trees.

C. T. Wootton

One of the Crowd

I wore clothes I didn't really like,
Just to be one of the Crowd.
Changed the way I lived,
Went from shy to very loud,
But it didn't work, I was still oblivious
to them.

I started drinking and dabbling with drugs,
Trying not to be a nobody,
Changed my whole way of life,
Lost my friends and family,
But it didn't work, I was still oblivious
to them.

I decided that killing myself would get their
attention,
So I got a very sharp knife,
Changing my life for the last time,
Slit my wrists to have my life,
It worked, I'm now oblivious to everyone,
I did it,
Just to be one of the crowd.

Tracie James

Moonshine in the Tropics

I watched the full moon rise in elegance
Like a graceful swan, in a lake of midnight blue.
And the fleecy clouds like swansdown all around her,
Touched here and there the picture with silver hue.
And with gentleness the moon stooped down to see,
White roses cascading their petals on the ground.

She peered through the shady, spreading Saman tree
At a world asleep, serene, where not a sound,
Save the gentle murmur of wind amongst bamboo,
And the solitary deep-bass croak of a frog forlorn,
Or a startled cry of a tiny, timid bird,
Added nature's lilting sounds to a lovely scene

J. M. Fung

Look What . . .

Look what people have
It's not like what I have.
A big, big house in the country
with lights hanging down
That's what I have.

Look what people love
It's not like what I love.
Lots of money, that's what people love,
but small trivial things -
that's what I love.

Look what people own
It's not like what I own.
A room with posters -
that's what I own.

Look how people act
It's not how I act.
Happy and never sad -
that's how I act.

Lois Bull

Untitled

So I made a wrong decision, guess I'll have to start again!
Life is a learning process and they say no pain, no gain.
At least I tried although it hasn't turned out as I hoped;
No one can criticize me or say I haven't coped.

It may be disappointing when your dreams are not fulfilled
When hope is stifled, and your heart's ambition must be stilled;
The chill of discontent comes creeping, knocking at your door.
The road you're trudging doesn't hold out promise anymore.

The wind of change is fickle, sometimes doesn't fit your plan,
So you must plot a different course, strive to be your own man.
And patience is a virtue learned in solitary mood
Which guides a fragile soul as mine to greater fortitude.

Sue Holyoake

Elephants

Their deep, dark eyes as deep as the sea,
Keep twinkling back,
They're looking at me,
Their ivory tusks gleaming in the sun,
This dry hot weather seems to be no fun,
Their big long trunks helping them to wash,
Helping them to eat,
To cool down in this heat,
Their big floppy ears,
Twitching with the flies,
But now the heat has gone,
Clouds are filling up the skies,
The splashing of the rain,
Trickles down onto the floor,
The cracks are disappearing,
No heat to cope with anymore,
The elephants take a bath,
Into the cool water they lay,
Hoping the sun has ended,
And the water will last for just one more day.

Paula Salter

My Beautiful Dream

An illusion, a dream with floating bubbles,
Magic wands to wave, ending all your troubles.
Ladybirds, butterflies, leaves on the wind,
Larks and Robins, a chorus that sing.

Weddings, photos, the peel of church bells,
Stocks, lilies and lilacs, a fresh cut grass smell.
Puppies and ponies, a child at heart,
Holding on to life, letting sadness depart.

Eagles and aeroplanes, soaring into the sky,
Dolls and daisy chains, things that don't die.
Comics, pink ballet shoes, party dresses with bows,
The warm summer sun, and a winter that snows.

But dreams are shattered when life bites back,
Defences are raised, and you're into attack.
Fight the fear, experience the pain,
And don't be fooled, for it will happen again.

Let love and courage, in your body flow,
Nurture your mind and your spirit will grow.
Taste joy with sorrow and carry it through,
Then the woman is born; and it's really you.

L. E. Gibney

Jesus Never Sleeps

I wake every morning, thanking God for each day,
Knowing He's with me, whenever I pray,
Watching and waiting, in times of our need,
Life giving water, so often we read.

Thirsty for Jesus, believe me,
Thirsty for God, we cannot see,
His Spirit descending, the shape of a dove,
All powerful, winged love.

To know Jesus, and talk of His life,
Give others strength, that we feel inside,
Stretch out for His hand, it's always there,
Be still, in His presence, you'll not have a care.

Wake up now, there's no time to lose,
We've no time to ponder, it's you He will use,
To tell of His wonder, miracles, and healing,
He'll lift you so high, it's a wonderful feeling.

After days done, and we've gartered the sheep,
We lay our heads down, for a good night's sleep,
Thanking God, in His presence, our life to keep,
Knowing God, Jesus never sleeps.

I. Malcolm

Tucked Up in Bed

Through sudden gusts of wind a cloudy night,
Listening from my bed tucked up warm and tight;
The driving rain tapping on the window pane,
The distant hooter of the night train,
What's that noise? It must be a loose tile;
Crashing to the ground in a broken pile:
The sound of an owl perched in a nearby tree
Takes to flight wild and free,
Thinking of my day ahead,
Happy to be tucked up in bed.

G. J. Baynton

Without You

The pains of desolation dwell
knotted nerves entwined in Hell
flashing lights of the inner eye
cause head to ache and heart to sigh

Tears poise on the point of break
I know not, which course to take
emptiness, hollow, something gone
loneliness, despair, everything wrong

Care gives way to place of duty
love, high and dry in all its beauty
I steel my heart against love's song
days gain hours, the nights grow long

I am what I am, cannot choose
destiny decrees that I should lose
one reason, one hope, one aim in life
to one day darling
make you my wife.

Walter Kitching

A Tractor's Lament

I'm an L245HC tractor
Kubota is my name,
And I've worked well at varied tasks
So as to gain acclaim.
There is a man who needs me,
He likes me as I am.
All his wishes I carry out,
He's pleased with me - there is no doubt.
Slow-speed sowing, spraying, weeding,
Everything this man is needing.
He feeds me well - oil, diesel, water,
And I do all the things I oughter.
I'm treated right and play the game
So do not need a safety-frame.
Yet when he wanted me to buy,
The tractor with crop-clearance high,
Red tape stepped in; would not allow,
The purchase, no - not anyhow.
None can buy - I am stagnated,
Until my frame's evaluated.

Pam Brown

Season of Hope

The icy wind fades to a gentle breeze,
Land no longer waiting to freeze.
Bright golden sun now lengthening the days,
Buds develop to catch the rays.

Spring has arrived. The earth is aware
That Nature can decorate what once was bare.
Greens are the contrast to lifeless browns,
Petals of flowers drape like ballroom gowns.

This is the season which brings hope to all.
Echoing sound of a young bird's call,
Fields full of lambs on wobbly legs,
Children hoping for Easter eggs.

Arranging the holiday for summer is a must,
Brochures are sought and venues discussed.
But "I have nothing to wear!" is the cry,
As off to the clothes shops one dashes, to buy!

C. J. Halliday

Missing You

I can't believe I'm not in your arms
Listening to all your charm,

Missing you more than you know
Feeling so very very low,

Want to kiss your face
Want our lips to lock in a warm embrace,

Wish we were skin to skin, bone to bone
Laying together not on our own,

Over and over I play your voice
That is my only choice,

Want you to say more
Want you to be knocking on my door.

Paula Gittins

The Night

Fires blazing, dancing flames,
Little children playing games,
sleepiness is setting in,
toys are going back in their bins.

The cheerful sandman is on his way,
everyone is home to stay,
falling asleep in their beds,
children cuddling up with their teds.

Burning embers are all that are left,
of the night when everyone slept.
The sun is up and the day is bright,
and everyone begins their new plight.

Orla Willis

Barriers to Freedom

Under cover of dark clouds
Landscapes appear on the horizon
The sun shining through the trees - yet
Barriers held the shadows shielding all
Life as far as the eyes could see

Dark clouds to streams glistening
Eagles watching their prey
Seasons only gave warnings proving
To all living creatures in far off
Lands in their calling

Barriers held fast - break waters gave
sanctuary to life's creation
Thunder - lighting opened the sky
Sunshine gave light - Rivers gave
Freedom to all creatures

Looking back, buds gave signs of life
Flowers blossomed, looking upwards to
the sky became reality to all around.

J. S. Mitchell

The Grief of Dunblane

I want to curl my body into a ball
Like a foetus inside the dark womb
To hide and to escape from it all . . .
The horror, the grief, gloom and doom.

I want to close my eyes shut very tight,
To press my hands over both of my ears,
To erase such evil from the sight . . .
To no more hear the sobbing and tears . . .

We turn to You, Dear God, in our pain
(Your innocent Son Jesus was slain too).
May the sweet slain cherubs of Dunblane
Remain happy now, in heaven, with You.

Though snatched away, may they now play
Together, in heaven, as in Dunblane . . .
Spared of old age . . . to await the day
When they meet up with loved ones again.

Sheila Ann Rowland

Easter Resurrection

Now we have seen drab winter's
   landscapes change to green.
Yellow flowers lift their fragrant heads
   Arisen from their barren beds.
Daffodils, primrose - all compete
   to provide for us an Easter treat,
And by their immaculate perfection
   Remind us of another resurrection.

How can we doubt the message clear
   or contemplate a barren year?
No spring - no sweet birds' song,
   no balmy summer's day
Nor gentle warming rain, or fruit or grain.
   No resurrection - no tomorrow -
Is beyond conception!

Let the sweet warm voice of life
   steel upon the ear;
The noise of children ring.
   Live day by day - and on our way,
For all His Bounty Praise Him.
   H. G. Taylor

Forgive Us for Calling You a "Tramp"!

A yesterday scopes his today, no set hours forms her day
Like a leaf from a branch, he strays.
In snow, wind, rain or shine - she plays.
An earthly-coloured dresser, with flair,
A 24-7 public performer less cheer,
Recognition is made from far or near
Every surrounding footstep is placed with care.
New found wisdom are lines on his face
There are no boundaries regarding her race,
His voice ranges from falsetto to bass
In body she's healthy to a weakening dire case.
Orphaned by society, "no penny to ride",
Unable intellectually, the words are on the inside
A fugitive from capture, no bounds, no ties.
A human question mark, who knows not "why".
On that hour, when the sun retires and the stars aspire
Timeless memories haunt the lonely and become desire.

I plead with you:
Read between the lines - each leaf - despite the cover
Because failing to be loved, to not have loved, or have loved
Can happen to anyone, "my Sister, my Brother".
   Pedro Pereira

Do You Feel the Same Way

Do you feel the same way as I do today
Like a monkey without a tree
No swinging for you and me
Like a bird without a sky
Or a cyclops missing an eye, or do they feel like us

Do you feel the same way as I do today
Like reliving yesterday
Turning all the wrong ways
Like Hitler's failed invasions
Or Africa's starvation, or do they feel like us

Do you feel the same way as I do today
Like the Beatles on "Let It Be"
Or Dastardly and Muttley
Like a tenor who can't sing
Red Baron losing a wing, or do they feel like us

Do you feel the same way as I do today
Like Lincoln at the theatre
Or a toothless alligator
Like Neil Armstrong in a black hole
Or James Brown with no soul, or maybe they're the same as you and me
   Simon George Dixon

The Secrets Room

Two lovers embrace, entwined in love.
Laying, touching each other,
whispering words
that only the walls can hear.
The walls see them.
The walls protect them
and keep their secrets safe.
They kiss
exploring with lips and tongues,
leaving silver traces on their bodies.
Murmurs of passion break the silence
within the shadowed room.
The silhouettes that danced upon the walls
are now still, through passions spent.
Too soon the time will come
when they must return, go their separate ways.
A tender kiss. Goodbyes are said.
Hand in hand they leave.
The room now is empty
save for the secrets that it keeps.
   P. D. Goodwin

A Kiss Defined

Your lips are warm and inviting,
Like a blazing open fire
Is the warmth of love they emit.
They fill me with an inner joy
And ignite the flame of passion
Each time our lips meet.
For they are soft as candy floss
When you pucker them up to mine
And sweet to my heart are their delights.
From the ruby richness of your mouth
Comes the reassurance that I cherish.
Each kiss a priceless, precious gem
Locked within the vault of my esteem,
Which continues to expand to accommodate
The love you constantly lavish on me.
   Stephen John Wyles

My Daughter to Marriage

Love isn't a thing that comes and goes
Love is a feeling that grows and grows
Even when life seems such a bore
A miserable time, a quarrel, a chore
Love grows, surrounds, envelopes and shines
It's great, it's sad, in all of these times
From the moment I knew you were on your way
My happiness and love for this life would stay
My pride and joy in your being stands tall
My daughter, my first born, you have been my all
Now you have a new life, new home, new love
I wish you such happiness, they will sing from above
Let it always be strong, your love together
Then happiness will be yours forever and ever
My little one, my special one, never cry or fear
I'm your mother, I will come, my love always near
Growing up you have been a tower of strength to me
I will always be there if you need me, you will see
Because our life and love has been so strong
I know that forever it will go on and on
   Georgina Sherin

Various Verses for Greeting Cards

The love in your heart wasn't put there to stay
Love is not love until you give it away
Don't keep it inside it will wither and die
So open your heart, know the meaning of joy
Share out your love, give it a try
It makes life worth living, it's here to enjoy!
   Sarah Teehan

Summer's Always Nice

Sweat-encrusted summer evening
lays down its head
to watch the birds fly over.

The clammy palms of lovers' hands
falter on dry patches of skin
wiped on tight jeans they continue to
the horizon of your underwear elastic
as the sun, like a Durex slides
beyond the line of reason.

Swirled about,
ice cream wrappers meet in gangs
enticing flies from still soft piles of Sunsh*te,
and the index finger of chill
strokes your barbers-poled body.

Summer's always nice
it fetches sex on the streets;
moth-balled privates are aired in parks,
and ancient graveyards,
wrapper-strewn beaches, and backs of cars.
Yes, summer's always nice.

E. K. Cunningham

"For Sarah"

Silent happiness fades with the wind
Love falls deeply into a wound.
Fate occurs without beginning
Beautiful things must die.
The love of one may break a heart
Longing distance tears apart
Little things can mean so much
Look to the dark and find me.
Sometimes you feel like life goes slow
Hold on tight just don't let go
Believe your dreams
In silence cry
Love yourself for you can fly.

Ruth Ward

Love

What can I say about Love?
Love is unmeasurability it can be long or short.
It makes you happy or it can make you sad.
Everybody feels it or sees it.
It's a word that's been said so many times.
Sometimes it's a word that can't be said.
It can wrap itself inside you so tight
Or it can lose itself in your mind.
No matter what you think or say.
Love is a word that's here to stay.

Susan Clark

Leave Her Alone

Oh cruel ones, leave her alone
Leave her alone, her body is her own
What gives you the right to cut her up?
What gives you the right to pin her down?
You're killing her childhood, murdering her innocence
She trusted you, had faith in you
Leave her alone, her body is her own
Look at those pleading eyes
Listen to her painful cries
Leave her alone, her body is her own
What? It is custom, culture, religion?
Whose custom? Whose culture? Whose religion?
Oh cruel ones, her body is her own
Custom! Culture! Religion! Or mere excuses to cause a woman pain
She is not a mere possession, a toy for man
Her body is not just for the pleasure of man
Her body is her own
How can you being a woman cause another pain?
How can you humiliate her, rob her of self-esteem?
Leave her alone, her body is her own.

Satish Dutt

Hiroshima

Throng the undoing night with all our going.
Let lanterns swing, keys turn,
And undeniably, lights of love grow dim.
Snatch the wrong perfections.

Outpace atonement.
Rubbled ruin ring on a clattered longing.
Bones from the urns of yesterday
Bring to burning recollection

Of the upturned scattered ways
Where fools of unencumbering
Nurture lost pastures, and the damned
In shallowy shadows of feeling win delay.

Captive the golden Godhead
Crossed and blurred and old in time
Begets mutations, outlaws history's word
Across the abandoned mountains
Horning a din of death:
To the forests' withered breathing
Each singing bird must cease.

Kathleen Ebert

Our Time

When the morning comes your tears will disappear
Life will carry on
Your path will soon be clear.
There won't be time for sorrow,
For anger or for pain,
When the morning comes, life begins again.

Tomorrow is not forever
It's just a breath away,
Don't waste these precious moments,
How quickly they fade away.
Now take my hand and follow
Before it passes by.

But when at last it catches us
And we can run no more,
The hands of time stop turning,
Night time gently falls.

Take my hand and hold me
As time can be no more,
Hold me in your heart dear,
Our time is now forever more.

J. O'Regan

A Dedication to My Four Legged Friend and Companion - Bonnie

You came to us so full of fear, you'd been taken from a mother you loved so dear, your crying was awful to hear at night, each morning our kitchen looked like a building site.

Two years on, you would cry in pain, but love we gave you again and again, arthritis had struck you in your tender years, I don't know how I held back the tears.

We had such fun in those earlier days, we tried to help you in so many ways, your persistence for life was a sight to see, I clung to you and you clung to me.

Life hadn't been very kind to you, no other dog could have seen it through.
You tried our patience many a time, but we knew your health was on a decline.

That day has come to say goodbye, part of my heart will surely die.
No other dog could ever be compared, to the undying love we had always shared.

You were always there when I needed you most, when I felt lonely, lost and morose. You'd sit by my side and comfort me, no better friend could there ever be.

I'll remember you always till the day I die, I stayed with you till you breathed your last sigh. One day we'll meet at those Pearly Gates, you weren't just my dog, we were the best of mates.

Yvonne Whittingham

Man's Strength

Mirror mirror on the wall
Let me search to give my all
Look at me through your eyes
Hear my anguish hear my cries
Upon this earth I was sent
Surely not for life half spent
I have my dreams I have desire
Give me wisdom to aspire
Give me strength of character
I'll shape my life from this time after
I want to work I want to play
As I stride along life's way
I want to rise I want to soar through life's ever open door
For my children, for my wife
For my friends, to help through strife
Make me worthy of my cause, there is nowhere I will pause
I have the strength to show the way but I need support from those who
say "I'll come with you today, not tomorrow or next week but
now at this moment I will seek with true friends the greater life
And by God's grace I'll pay the price'.

Victor T. Lewis

Mozart, Dear Mozart

I hope you have found peace where you rest
Like the peace I find
In my mind
When listening to the music that you blessed
And if I could go back in history
With him I wish to be
To walk by his side
Love him in his life
Before him kneel and bow
Hold those hands and kiss his brow.
Ah Mozart, dear Mozart
I hope you have your love where you rest
Like my love of those notes
And all you wrote
I will stand and gaze at the piano that you caressed

Robert Earl Stevenson

Where's the Romance

Where's the romance, where's it gone?
Loving used to be such fun
Now just side by side we stand
No longer linking hand in hand
No flowers on a special day
Paying bills gets in the way
Our goodnight kiss would last and last
But now it's something in the past
A cuddle wouldn't go amiss
Of course there's not much chance of this
Maybe a candlelight dinner for two
But the budget would only stretch to stew
So I guess it's goodbye to romance now
Marriage got in the way somehow.

Linda Potter

The Man with His Bottom on His Head

The man with his bottom on his head,
Lived in a fully furnished potting shed.
His good friend Jobe, so we are told,
Walked with a buttock thrust up his nose.
His uncle Clive was also described,
As dancing at parties with his bum on his side.
In turn cousin Beaumont could only grin,
At his elephant behind and double chin.
Inventor Rhyde tried to stem the seas tides,
With a breakwater resembling a giant's backside.
It sounded a cheek until Mrs Plump squeaked,
That a monster had eaten her rump for a week.
But to this Auntie Ethel could not compare,
With her Zeppelin-like inflatable derriere.
Nor compete with the flood of mass hysteria,
Met by the man with a head like a posterior.

Martin Combeer

Cornwall

I love to go to Cornwall,
It's so beautiful to me,
I like to walk the coastal paths,
And paddle in the sea.

It's a wild and rugged county,
Steeped in history,
It draws me like a magnet,
It's where I want to be.

Its history is natural,
Some industrial too,
There are chimneys from old tin mines,
From Lands End up to Looe.

The villages are so pretty,
They are a wonderful sight,
Cottages with slate roofs,
And walls all painted white.

I think of life in Cornwall,
Surrounded by the sea,
And hope that in some years to come,
It will be home to me.

P. King

The Dew Drop

A dew drop sparkled on a bough
like a pearl, from an oyster, that somehow
shone like a twinkling star at night
making shapes as the sun cast light

It glittered like snow, on the ground
a maiden snow where no prints are found
like fine white sand that lays on the shore
that trickles through fingers to the floor

A shining drop of dew, like lace
occupying but the smallest space
capturing the eye that alone did see
the tiny miracle upon the tree

A mesmerized eye locked to the spot
where the rays shone on the tiny dot
conjuring up images and different shapes
like the patterns made by snow-white flakes

Then it seemed about to fall
from the huge oak tree erect and tall
as it swayed gently with the breeze
to tantalize the eye that sees.

Sheila Graham

The Priests of Paranoid Fear

He stands alone on the street corner with Hellish fear upon his lip.
Like a sickening hypocrite he clutches the book of love like a
weapon of war to his hip.
He screams of judgement to come as he glares with hate-filled
eyes at the bemused sinners in the street.
He cries in anguished fervour of how God is only for him and his
and how Satan is the Eternity everyone else will meet.
The little boy glares as in terror he clutches his mother for
protection and she quickly pulls him on past.
The deviant who was only beginning to find acceptance listens at
a distance and is now wondering if the peace he has found will
last.
He leaves his sidewalk pulpit and never even gives the quivering
addict a second glance.
An old man tries to stop him to question his word but the
preacher's parrot-like quotation cuts through him like a lance.
He walks proudly homeward knowing in his heart that through
him the work of his God abounds.
His children meet him at their home like good Heaven bound
saints fear and paranoia in their hearts abound.

Kristian Phoenix

132

Thoughts Unsaid

You took a key and let yourself into my heart
Like a thief sneaking in you stole a part
No thought as to how I may be left feeling
Confused, a head constantly reeling
Who gave you permission?

Craving to awake to new found thoughts
Instead to unwelcome tears you brought
Urging to give what belongs to another
New found fears unkindly smother
Who gave you permission?

Pondering constantly on the outcome
A surrounding cloud envelops the sun
An uncertain future with no-one to tell
Hidden by a barrier of new-built shell
Who gave you permission?

Smiling at unhappiness becomes a routine
Beliefs fade into someone else's dream
A life spent facing an unknown end
Secrets left unspoken to a new found friend
Did I give you permission?

Lindsey Westhuizen

Out of the Cupboard

In a pile, on the floor
Like broken soldiers in a war,
Warm and smelly, torn and grey,
Loved and cherished from days of play.

Suddenly I feel so old,
A thousand stories could be told.
I look from one to one and sigh,
Time has flown, I start to cry.

They look at me with begging eyes
Not wanting to go, no sad goodbyes.
They are not real, of course I know,
Yet, I want to believe, just once more,
before they go.

Innocent days and special toys,
The wonders of imagination, a child enjoys.

Dogs and bears and squeaky old dolls,
Watch silently as life evolves
Home to home, their work begins,
Loving you and me and whatever life brings.

Sally Young

Tumble Dryer Thoughts

My thoughts go whirling, turning, madly jumbled,
Like the washing I sit watching being tumbled, a never ending
cycle of drying, sorting,
Clothes and thoughts, thoughts and clothes altogether jumbled.

If I could catch just one thought and sort it, then others might just fit,
But as I reach out to catch just one,...the cycle Stops—to start
again in different circles,
Backwards, forwards, inside, outside, this way that, always turning,
Just like the clothes I watch and wait for.

Perhaps I should just stop pretending that I can sort my thoughts,
In their unending progress 'round that maddening endless cycle
that is my mind.

Open the door, thoughts fall out, heaped one upon another, onto
the floor.
Sort them, which is damp, or can be left to iron another day,
Which needs more time in the tumble that I call my mind today.

Oh, put them back, never mind the jumble, which is worse I
cannot say.
Perhaps these never ending cycles is just because it's Monday.
Wash day, dry day, sort them out day...How I wish...how I wish.

Maureen Stichler

Dreams

Bright hues of green and heliotrope,
Like some giant, spinning, kaleidoscope,
With unreal figures, or so it seems,
Again I'm plunged into my world of dreams,

Where good always triumphs over bad,
No one of my friends can ever feel sad.
With joyous laughter and words of praise
I'll bring sunshine into their darkest days.

On gossamer wings I soar on high
Watching over them from a cloudless sky,
And, if I happen to see a tear,
I swoop down to them with words full of cheer.

For, in my dreams, my friends seem to be
Endowed with a mystical quality,
And if their friendship should ever cease
I know, in my dreams, I'll never find peace.

Keith Iles

What Is Life?

Sleeping and waking, walking, sitting, standing,
Lying down, jumping, crawling, climbing,
Some of the activities of being alive.
One can be dead, and do all these things,
Oh no, not physically of course.

The body is only part of the person,
There is a more important part.
For want of a name we call it a soul,
If it be dead, then we are not whole.
Now let us consider this great truth.

To know God: that's what, life eternal is.
Say: how can we know this blessed bliss?
Through Jesus, God's only begotten Son,
Who died on the Cross for you and me
That we may have our sins forgiven,
And dwell with Him for eternity.

A. B. Fredlund

Decayed Memory

It is lost to the world of dreams
Lying there all alone
It calls from an empty room
Locked away — life squeezed
From the laughter that dwelled therein
Siblings sigh —
Leaving the wretched grin —
Journey to the light
Call out — call out
Take my hand —
And lead me from this — decadence

Decayed memory
Una Hunt

Sonnet of Faith

Faith in what one cannot see,
may be good enough for you and me.
Others though may not think much,
of a faith in something one cannot touch.
Religions all have their point of view,
some have good and bad points too.
The problems come with fanatic zeal,
which replaces rational, sane appeal.
But fundamental mistrust and hate,
have no place in our uncertain fate.
Hear therefore another's word,
their views may not be so absurd.
And the God of love is after all
The one and only God of all.

R. W. Kirby

Depressed

You feel depressed,
like you're locked in a cage,
why?
There is a lead weight in your stomach,
pulling you down,
down into a state of depression.

A cold, icy claw has gripped your heart,
tearing it our or its place,
fight for it back,
fight for your will to survive.

You're swimming in dark, murky waters,
lead for your arms and your legs,
you're dropping down,
farther and farther,
until only darkness is around.

Can't somebody help?
Catch you if you're feeling as though you're falling?
But, usually people don't know,
don't know you're falling,
until it's too late.

K. Langwith

War Was It Worth It

The nightmare of those cruel cold years.
Linger still, within my deepest fears.
The memory of my friends who died.
And all the tears I wept, now dried.

The picture of those men in trenches, mud up to their thighs.
The fear was all around them, showing in their eyes.

Above the din of firing rifles, came the sound of grown men's cries.
Cries of pain, and cries of fear, are still ringing in my ears.

The days were long and daunting.
The nights were long and cold.
With four long years of fighting many never grew old.

I am not your brave hero,
I am just a lucky man.
The scars I bare run deeper, than just my missing arm.

Looking back on devastation
I ask myself one question
Was it worth it.

Maureen Parker

Mummy

A mum is a person who cares for you.
Loving, forgiving and beautiful too.
I wonder dear Mummy what I would do without you
your brown loving eyes and your smiling face too.

Toni M. Taylor

"Sometime Blues"

Summer days; bringing rain,
Loving ways; giving pain,
Just rewards for lives so badly run.
Ambition reaching bottom of the range.
Tradition seeking means of bringing change.
Candles snuffed before time has begun.

Foreign faces; milling all around.
Meeting places; absentees abound,
This really is a hopeless, helpless life.
Stinking worlds awash with piercing noise,
Naughty girls with equally dodgy boys,
Leading lives of torn and troubled strife.

Sporty cars, racing every where,
Dingy bars to drink away your cares,
Life goes on no matter how we feel.
Motor-bikes with engines like a mower,
Country hikes, espying every flower,
Wheeler-dealers really yielding zeal.

Vic Bowen

Grief

Thirty years - so many tear-drenched years of grief and wanting
you,
Longing to feel you touch my hand
Your strong arm guiding me along life's way
Enfolding me in contented happiness,
A warmth of love, not of this world.
The sun shines brightly, but its rays are cold,
Stars shine in midnight heaven, but no story told
Of intense enduring love, burning through time
Waiting to be united in the cold grave's depth.
The rainbow hues of earth's fair flowers
Bloom briefly and are gone, bringing no joy in their sweetness.
But still I bring them to your grave
To heal the soreness of my heart.
And when at last my time is done
If it be God's will, my soul unites with yours
Then we will know true happiness once more
For all eternity.

J. Middleton

Hair

A trail of sticky pond life
Lots of satin ribbon
With curls like a monkey's tail
A cleaning utensil - a broom a mop?
An alter ego for mankind
cranium's thermal underwear or shady parasol
A versatile entertainment for hands, brushes
and bottles of bleach!
An unpotted plant for my scalp that I can
prune and grow at leisure!

Maria Allin

Wind Song

The music of the wind was calling
Lulling as I lay
Mysterious, enticing, pulling me away
As I sank deeper, nearly hypnotised
It would be easy to follow powerfully mesmerised

I felt the lift, now I was ready
To float to channels new
And, yet, one last chance to hold back in the place I knew
A moment's pause, a moment's fight
To stay, to go, holdfast or flight

The strains of wind music reached crescendo
Eerily, again I felt the pull
Not right, not right, I shook away
My eyes opened fast, I broke the spell

Maureen Stewart-Condron

Valiant Baby Warrior

Valiant baby warrior mine, fiercely fighting sleep!
Loathe to leave this wakeful world
And slip into the deep
And baby-boring world of rest,
And sleep.

Valiant baby warrior, with flaming cheeks of fire!
Burnt with searing, molten tears,
While traitorous eyelids fight the dire
Consequence of closing;
In sleep.

Valiant baby warrior mine, tiny body writhing,
All kicking, flailing, twisting limbs;
While infant fists come scything
Past my attempts to calm you
Into sleep.

Valiant baby warrior, grappled to my arm;
My hand held prisoner to your cheek,
Rose-paler now, and calm.
By weariness defeated,
You sleep.

B. E. Clayton

Letting Go

We started speaking,
Looked at each other, then turned away.
The tears kept rising to your eyes,
I wanted to take your hand, but my hand trembled.

God, I needed you so much that day,
I clung to a smile but choked on a sob,
Because knowing that you were with
someone else began to hurt even more
than the pain of losing you.

I remember the ticking of the clock filled the quiet room.
"Listen", I said, "It is so loud"
You shut me up in your arms
I slid beside you so well,
My chin still fitted the same place on your shoulder.

You said to me "I cannot go; all that I want
is here with you".
But you went.

I did not understand my confusion that day. The world seemed to
change. The sound of the clock grew fainter, dwindled away.
And I whispered into the darkness, "If it stops, I shall die".

Sarah-Jane Woodford

That Summer Day

Down the country lanes we went,
me in our Buggy,
"Prince" the pony, in the reins,
He knew his way, that summer day.

Here! Said my Dad, you take the reins
Prince knows the way, and will not stray

I was so proud, being very young,
for it wasn't really aloud.
but I think Prince knew the score
as he jogged along.

We were in tune, like a happy song
that lovely summer day.

E. Adamson

Learning

Life is as precious as the time you are here,
Meaning use to your fullest advantages,
Thinking always positive, never negative,
Experience subjects throughout your finest ages,

Crossing paths of ancestral mystery,
Learning methods of peoples of the past,
Gaining knowledge by the opening of secrets,
Forever studying to be sure we are not the last.

Stephen G. Lamonby

Before I Met Lorraine

Before I met Lorraine, I didn't know what friendship
meant, but since that day being with Lorraine, I know it
was time well spent. Being friends with Lorraine has
made me see what a good friend she can be.
Lorraine I just want to let you know, you're
such a good friend I don't want you to go. You've
helped me with boys and all the rest so basically
Lorraine you are the best! Whether the problem is big or
small you're always there to help them all. Being friends
with you has taught me as lesson, don't take for
granted friends in your possession. I want you to know I'm
always here for you, and I hope for me, you're there to. Cos
whatever the problem, I need you Lorraine, you take any
hurt, any pressure or pain, and it helps everybody to
know you're there. Lorraine for you I'll always care.
Lorraine this poem is dedicated to you all my
friendship goes with it too!
Best friends forever 'cos we're great mates together
Love and friendship

Rebecca Elphick

Blessed Hope

Christian, though the world about us
May give us good cause to fear
Let the words of scripture cheer us
Christ's return is very near.

Blessed Hope, what words of comfort
To these aching hearts of ours
Nought can change God's wondrous promise,
Nought can thwart His sovereign powers

Christ our long awaited Lord is coming
In the clouds to claim His bride
All who know Him as their Saviour.
Those for whom the Saviour died

Cast your eyes not down, dejected
At the state of the things down here,
Lift your heads, and look to heaven
Whence our Lord shall soon appear

"I Come Quickly" Jesus said it,
And His promises are sure
Let the Blessed Hope possess you
Our Salvation Is Secure

H. Hartley

Voice in the Wilderness

I'm a voice in the wilderness
Looking for happiness that doesn't
    come my way
A voice that isn't heard no matter
    how hard I try
I will have to get by somehow

Voice in the wilderness
An echo in the night
Why must my aching heart
    take flight
A dream I dreamed has not
    come true
Oh why oh why did I believe in you

A voice in the wilderness
Hoping to be heard
Crushed like a bird
Whose flying days are done
There is nothing to be won
    by being unkind
So must I go on like this until the day I die

Niki Edwards

The Question

Lady, as you gaze out toward the sea
Lost in your mem'ries, do you, like me
Wonder, who was the man who killed my son?
Was he as gentle? Was he as young?

Did you have a son who was called to fight?
Who lived in fear both day and night?
Do you grieve still for your son who was lost
And wonder if 'they' ever count the cost?

Heads of State often disagree
But have they compassion for you and me?
Boundary and territory lost and won
But the highest price paid is the loss of a son.

Although you and I are nations apart
I understand what you hold in your heart.
The faith that after the hurt and the pain
That in the here-after you'll see him again

Lady, as I stare out to sea
Toward the land where you might be
Did your son kill mine during the wars?
Or was it my son, who killed yours?

Margaret F. Bevis

135

Reflections

Running through life, chasing days . . .
Making decisions, mending ways,
Living for others, putting yourself out,
Wondering what it's all about.

Counting hours, minutes and time,
Trying to make sense of reason and rhyme,
Existing in years, women and men,
Forever ending, beginning again.

Making your stand, flag unfurled,
Challenging a cruel world,
Remembering what we've all been taught;
Religion, politics, love and sport.

Joining the rat-race, trying to compete,
Living on wits, thinking on feet,
Facing problems with iron will,
Ending up standing still.

How ever you play, you just can't win,
People grow old, light grows dim,
Everything's been said and done,
Life is over . . . Time has gone.

Trevor Woollacott

Alone

She sits inside the cemetery and talks to him alone,
She's got her happy memories and the pictures 'round the home,
She's told to put it behind her, they say it'll never last
But no matter how hard she tries comes flooding back the past.

He haunts her happy memories, he never leaves her be.
No future and no present, the past is all she'll see.
She longs for his loving arms to enfold her once again
But there's the future and the present but the past was once then.

As she plans for old age, she plans her sadness too
For she remembers his words "it's now just me and you."
Her love was strong for him but the grief was even worse
For she recalls the day that he lay within that hearse.

The day they did part, like a message it did rain,
The feeling of emotion, the swelling of the pain,
The day they buried him, they buried her too
For she was with him all the way if only he knew.

No words can comfort her, no words can ease the pain
For without him, she will surely go insane
The bright light is her target, yet it lives so far away.
Till then she has to fight the battle of each and every day.

Hayley King

A Lazy Afternoon

The fisherman on the bank stands still as the gentle river runs by
singing to its own sweet song
He casts a line so gracefully it settles down to glide, then it bobs
its little head as a coot swims by across the water and out the
other side.
It's early yet and the dawn mist is on the water like its gown of lace
Silently, as a bird flies overhead he is wishing he had stayed in bed
No bite on his line, no fish his eye could see,
One more minute then it's home for a cup of tea.
But hush, what's that sound, it's broken now as a fish is caught
up on his line and wriggles to be free.
It swims along so slowly, then all at once it jumps to try to get
the hook out to be free, the fisherman, he's dancing, my what a
big one I see they really won't believe me unless I take it home
for tea.
But then the line it goes slack and still and all the glory's lost, as
the fish that was his prisoner is now so free once more.
And the fisherman stands still then wades back to the shore.
It really was a giant, but it got away too fast.
He reels the line in quickly, he doesn't make a splash.
Then it's home to tell the tale that's past.

Elizabeth A. Wilkinson

"Nothing"

Solitude is the moon's beautiful face
Sighs not mine
Someone's body mingled with the night
And untouchable soul
But to me belongs time of roundness
I am filled with shades
Instead of real colours
Filled with fear of uncertainty
I can accept no emptiness
So hands come and go
Bringing nothing and taking nothing
From me

Diana Jordanowa

Red Desert

This red desert I now walk
looking for someone's trail which I have left long ago
with a promise to myself
that I will return
I am now walking this desert road

Closer and closer to you I hope it will bring me
to a place
somewhere in this desert
where I once lost you

Blue sky above
give me a sign
and tell me
was I wrong when I found out
that in this red desert
I was alone
under your blue sky

tell me now, tell me now
'cause your light is fading out
and darkness begins to fall
over this red desert of mine

I. Cianci

Ides of March

Row upon row of smiling faces
Man with a gun holds all the aces
Sledgehammer blows and broken glass
Blood and death means no more class

Open mouthed we stand in silence
A nation shattered by the violence
Men of God can give no aid
Or explain the price those children paid

The snow falls on another dawning
On a city now in open mourning
On a generation swept away
As gun law destroys another day

We cast around to find some meaning
But all I hear is children screaming
My hope of future now is lying
In a Dunblane school with its dead and dying

A. N. Hatton

Untitled

The sadness of the Dunblane tragedy,
Made my life seem more valuable to me.
We can do what we want to,
And it should be valuable to you.

The massacre I must admit,
Had sent me into a crying fit,
That man sent them to their end,
That no amount of sympathy can mend.

My heart goes out to their families,
And I'll get down on my knees.
And pray for their dads and mums,
To stop the illegal possession of guns.

Kirstie Faulds

Queen of Grace

Through winter's bitter winds and chills
She'd slept inside the old wheat mill
So safe inside her silken case
Transforming to a queen of grace.

And now with dreary winter past
Her form starts breaking from its cast
She climbs to where the sky is bright
She pumps her wings prepares for flight.

Soon sunshine burns the morning mist
And pastel shades of flowers are kissed
By lingering dew on petal and stem
A summer's day is born again.

This painted lady comes into view
And flits among these wondrous hues
Then sips from cups of red and gold
The butterfly's secret then unfolds.

James Crawford

Aunt Flo

She talks about the days gone by, and thinks about them with a sigh
She's not concerned about today, or what her family have to say
A once alert and active brain, brings only sadness only pain
It's very hard for us to see, but in her place how would we be
We want to help and give a hand, we try so hard to understand
But then with bitterness we are met, and resentment's all we ever get
Why is it that the ones who care, are treated badly it's so unfair

Jenni Roper

Tunnelled Vision

The Sun has his power
Shedding light on the flower
The Rain is refreshing
to the Earth is a blessing.

Man is greedy and destructive
Bringing death to a fertile planet
Taking from the soil to give to the productive
If Good was Bad, he would damn it.

Plastic people in plastic homes
Plastic gardens with plastic gnomes.

The tree is old, the night is young
The sea and mountains protest the wrong
Uttered in all creatures' song,
"will evil go forever, despite all lively endeavour?"

Oh! Night, do not mistake me
My age makes me not blind to see,
Nature is strong
Man's venal vision
Must not evolve.

Janice Fogg

Oor' Quinnie

Now Fiona is oor' quinnie, bit noo she's turned eighteen
she's a tall slim woman, the bonniest thing you've ever seen
nay mair dirty nappies to change, or runny nose tay dicht
she canna' wait for Saturday, so she can jive and dance a' nicht

I mine fin she wis jist a bairn, she wis cheeky bit quite nice
fin she came hame fay school though, she'd ask her mithers advice
it wis'na aboot her homework, or even aboot her toys
it wis a' aboot the local dance, and fit tay say tay boys

Up the stairs black and blue, Knees skint and sair
her mither runnin we' a cloot, it's richt noo' there there
a sticky sweety tay cheer her up, a promise o' a treat
awa' tay the pictures on Saturday, and a poke o' chips to eat

Bit noo she is a woman, oot tay work she'll be
nay mair shoutin at her, FAR'S YER FAITHER'S TEA???
see fin she's up n' married we' kids o' her aine
she'll still come up tay see, her auld Ma and Da at hame.

Graham Weir

Fantasies of the Night

A lone tree silently stands against the darkening sky
Silvery moonlight engulfing the still form.
Strange silhouettes start appearing
And create a kaleidoscope of shapes.

Some clouds befall
And the darkness gently kills the formations
To leave nothing but an empty blackness.
The moon drives away this unwelcome occurrence
Leaving the tree clear to produce
More fantasies of the night.

Helen Jeacock

That's My Dad

More than two decades have passed away
since first my eyes did gaze.

A tiny baby who did grow
through all the seasons
rain wind and snow.

Once upon a lullaby.

Journeys together along the way
a story to read when the long day was done
a goodnight kiss before she closed her eyes
for sleep.

Then came the day she was taken away
a hurt so deep
that which we sow we must reap.

For she who was born on a warm June day
I remember it then as I do today.

Glad was my heart - it will be again
when I hear the words - That's my dad.

For that which I was - I am still
a loving dad.

Gordon Pyle

Brecon Beacons

Now dulled by time on time those pangs on birth.
Since first your rocky form saw light of day;
When peaks that once beneath the surface lay
Were thrust from out the womb of Mother Earth.

Sculptured by wind and rain your finer shape
Clothed with each season's varying detail;
A cloak of snow, a sun blue hazy veil,
Or grey-white shawl of clouds around you drape.

Softened by centuries are your lower slopes.
Grown velvet green, where sheep serenely graze.
Stone-naked still, your head attracts our gaze,
A guiding beacon to inspire man's hopes.

Millennia of generations strange -
Have found that you pervade a sense of balm
From pain of toil, and through uneasy calm
Your permanence lends peace to every change.

June Picken

In My Dream Last Night . . .

In my dream last night I was
sitting,
    looking,
        swimming,
            In the waves.
On the beach with the creatures of the rockpools.
    "Hurry, hurry, the tide is coming in,
Scuttle back into your rockpools before the waves come
and wash you away forever".
In my dream last night I was
Sitting,
    looking,
        swimming,
            in the cool, dark, night's wave.

Charlie West

Hold Me

Hold me in your arms so strong,
Sing me, your sweetest song.
Mixed in accents soft and low.
Promise me you will never go.

Hold me in your arms so tight
Stay with me each, and every night
Bring me kisses, send me flowers
Promise me this love is ours.

Hold me in your arms forever,
Life's sudden storms, we'll face together.
Love can conquer, love will heal.
So on this life let's set our seal.

Jacquie Batchelor

Eternal Night

Hidden he lurks in the void of his colourless form,
Silently waiting for her to come.
Crouching behind a mask of lies,
To get closer, closer before she can run.

He sees her in the distance - a shining, bright light,
And he draws her gently towards him.
Smiling false smiles, whispering lies,
As she gets closer, closer to the shrouded sin.

He reaches out to her, takes her hand in his,
And casts a shadow over her bright, wide eyes.
He embraces her and she freezes,
And as they draw closer, closer she helplessly cries.

His mask has faded, she stares in his eyes,
As he steals her shining bright light.
She falls, paralysed by his chains,
And they sink closer, closer throughout the eternal night.

Julie Hewitt

As Time Passes

Dear Mum, the days and weeks are going by
Since God called you away,
And oh, I still miss you so very much
With every passing day.

Time after time I think of you and
Wish you were here again.
Inside I feel a deep and yearning ache
Almost like a pain.

I long to see your face and talk to you,
And hug you very tight,
In my mind I see you smile at me
And lovely is the sight.

In memory too I can hear your voice
Say words you said before,
But I cannot put my arm around you
Not ever, any more.

Janet Buttell

Myself

I am a creature of feeling,
shining in sunlight while its warmth is expanding
the breath of life inside me.

I am a creature of feeling,
gutted by lightening's knife amid thundering
torrents and indigo skies.

I am a creature of feeling,
tear-drop and glow-pulsating fertilizing
the seed of my soul.

I am a creature of feeling,
the seed of myself is germinating, following
a lit path through leafy shadow.

I am a creature of feeling,
soon to expand beyond the canopy, senses absorbing
the sunrise into my pores. I am no shadow.

Gemma Adams

"Forbidden"

She knows you wear a band of gold,
She's got no chance with you, she's told,
But this message tells you that she genuinely cares,
As all she can do is stand and stare.
This is leap year, so they say,
You fill her thoughts by night and day,
She cannot touch,
She cannot hold,
And these feelings to her are powerfully bold.
You see - you're a man, and you teach,
She knows that you'll always be out of reach.
Of course she's aware that she pretends,
She knows her love will embarrass and offend.
So, please forgive her, I must plead,
In case she enacts this wicked deed.
She's out of her mind and her life must end,
I don't want to lose her - for I'm her husband!

Alison McDowell

Unite

But do not become as one
Sing together, dance together
Laugh together and have fun!

Be together but be independent
Fill each other with love
But keep some of your own love for yourself.

Ride on your wave of emotion
But each take your own paddle,
So that you do not drown in your sea of love.

Allow your souls to become friends too
But let the winds of heavens dance between you.

If through my words you see the light
I hope your love lasts night after night
  after night
'Til your souls transcend into the light.

Dawn Lochmuller

'The Mad Man'

There once was a class sitting in a hall
Singing with their friends, having a ball.
All of a sudden the door opens wide
In walks a man who stands by their side.
In his hand he holds a gun,
A little boy stands up thinking it's fun,
In a second this baby's shot to the ground,
So the rest of the class does not make a sound.
One by one, sixteen of them are killed in turn.
All they did was go to school to learn.
A couple survived, but three critically ill,
But it doesn't make up for the ones that were killed,
Who would want to cause such pain?
Only one sick, perverted man who was from Dunblane.
He knew he did wrong so he took his own life
If only he was alive, I'd slit his throat with a knife,
Just think of those families with such heartache,
No more please God, for goodness sake!

Cindy Cooper

Sixteen Little Angels

'Suffer little children to come unto me'
Sixteen little angels with the Lord they went to be
Their dedicated teacher also went along
All because an evil one decided to do them wrong.

Mothers, fathers Grans and Granddads,
People worldwide silenced and sad.
But to each other they hold out a hand
Helping to heal throughout the land.

United in sadness and disbelief
Dealing each day with their grief.
To the sixteen little angels in heaven above
The whole world sends to you, all their love.

Christine Stewart

Crystals

Crystals sparkling and stones so bright
Shimmering in the full moon light.
Making objects appear so clear
And helping people with health to heal.

Prisms dancing all around
Making rainbows on all that's found.
Generating energy till we feel high
Taking our dreams up to the sky.

Wearing crystals upon our skin
All the energy soaked up and drawn within.
Waiting to burst out, it can't be a sin
To make them look bright or sometimes dim.

Red ones, mauve, pink or green
On our fingers they look supreme.
Big, small, round, long or thin
How they can glow when under our chin.

Oh what a frill we can feel
Especially when we know the stones are real
Life can be full of these precious things,
Not just on earrings, necklaces or even rings.

Dawn Keeble

Blood Is Thicker than Water

Poppies are forever,
Shining in the sun,
Blood is thicker than water.

Children playing,
Had to run,
Blood is thicker than water.

Mosaics of honour,
In a scarlet field,
Blood is thicker than water.

Red as blood,
A sword and a shield,
Blood is thicker than water.

The reason of death,
For man, woman and child,
Blood is thicker than water.

To one man sane,
To another man wild,
Blood is thicker than water.

Every single war is a tragedy,
But the saddest of all will be World War 3!

Clare Kerbey

Evolution

We came to this world with hope in our hands,
Spreading peace throughout the nation, love throughout the lands,
Cherishing every special moment of the life we lead
But somewhere along the line learned about greed.
We learned to be selfish and forgot about others,
No longer had time for even our own brothers.
We learned about satisfaction but just kept on wanting more . . .
And so we learned about violence and the impact of war.
We learnt about suffering but turned a blind eye,
Just blocked out the sound of a muffled cry.
We learned about fur coats, the animals did too.
We're destroying our earth after all that we've been through.
We opened our eyes and saw the world in a different light,
Yet no one asked what was wrong or what was right
We just used it to our advantage, took all its trees,
Filled the air with fumes and polluted the seas.
What happened to our dreams, do we no longer have a heart?
Once we loved our world but now we're tearing it apart
And we'll go on destroying it until in a few years
Those of us left will be drowning in our own tears.

Holly Whitbread

From My Head and My Heart

The world turned its back upon me
Silently I weep and bleed
I have been buried alive
Like a vine my soul is twisted
My heart is in chains
Another holds the key

I reached for those who spied
They shunned me
Forgiven by some
But not all
And never by myself

Like the piece to a puzzle that could never fit
Masked from the world
Like the enemy within
My soul is a rose waiting to bloom
But its thorns tear me apart
It's like reaching for the moon and knowing you can never have it

Allison Bishop

Brother Sun

Thank you Lord for the glorious sun,
So bright and warm,
kissing the earth with fondest love
And O what love.
For forth from the ground grow myriads of lovely things;
flowers, trees, hedges, grass and many more things.
Animals dance and sing, giving praise to your name;
They procreate, and all because the lovely blessèd sun
  has caressed them.
Our hearts are glad, our faces full of joy,
because Brother Sun has smiled upon us.
And through his smile we see your glory.
Thanks be to God for Brother Sun.

Angela Preston

The Cat

The cat, with slim feline fur,
Sinking, crouching, down on her,
Streamline body, warm to the touch,
You may not think she knows much,
But her eyes are watching, looking,
Wondering what it is that's cooking,
Inside that mouse she sees by the wall,
Staring, glaring, eyes that fall,
Down to the ground, chin on the floor,
Watching, eagerly, silently for,
The food alive to be quite still,
So she can pounce in her own will,
Suddenly, she grabs the mouse,
Skidding, clawing, into the house,
Munching, mangling, chewing her food,
Between two jaws of a powerful mood,
Blood spattered fur and hairs on decline,
Resting, sleeping, now she's fine.

Joanne Ryder

Poem about a Poet

First go back in Scottish Lore considerably far
Skip Byron, Burns, but remember William Dunbar

Honest as the day is long in truth I am no liar
The bold poetic Wullie Dunbar was first a Franciscan friar

Many of his poems are forgotten I suppose
But memorable to me: the Thistle and the Rose

But one trip stout William delighted to make
A bright and brilliant slice of poetical cake

In a fine poem so pleasant deserving bardic crown
Dear William sang the praises of old London Town

Scots youngsters today have travelled the world far 'round
Bringing the blast of bagpipes so high above ground

Sound Rab C advice for those who end up in London I tell you now
Absolutely avoid all altercations at airport Heathrow

Donald Patience

Saying Goodbye

Here in my arms my love lies bleeding, such pain, torment and
scars that need my healing.
I would give all I have to end his pain, my fear is that our love
still had so much to gain.

The last breath of air eases out as death draws near, suddenly the
future without him seems so unclear.
Anguish and agony this knot deep inside, tears my heart out and
will never subside.

A single tear that burns my face, makes me blind and my heart
start to race. You changed my life, made me feel so alive, now
you are gone how will I survive.

Lying entwined, gripping him tight, moments together as death is
in sight. His breath starts to fade, shallow and slow, his body
goes limp draining his glow.

The heartbeat is missing, the final chime is rung, life is now over,
his morning will never come.

Holding him close, so scared to let go, seeing the fear that he
tries not to show. His last words still ringing so softly in my ear,
"I'm always yours forever, your love I hold so dear".

So I think as I cry, every human we know will die.
But why is it always so hard to say goodbye.

Dee-Ann Naylor

Virgo

Like a fairy queen on a Christmas tree
Sits the pure white rose of this Hybrid Tea.
Nothing fancy, nothing gay,
Just sheer beauty on display.

This goblet like cluster of white delight
That radiates peace like a shining light.
That gently sways to and fro
And greets each morn with a glow.

There's the twinkling hint of a dewy kiss,
Trickling down the cheek of this pure white Miss
As she frolics with a bee
Beneath the old apple tree.

This priceless jewel of tranquillity,
Ensconced in its natural entity.
White petals prinked, green leaves splayed,
Summer snowballs in the glade.

In a world bedeviled by guns and cars,
Of astronauts frantic to get to Mars
Here on earth one can have peace,
Make Virgo your centrepiece!

Alexander Fillingham

Shopping for Shoes

Shopping for shoes can be so much fun.
Sizes and colours for everyone.
I just love shopping for shoes.
So many pairs on display, I don't know what to choose
flat ones, high ones, straps and laces.
The assistants they get fed up with me, I can tell by their faces.
But, I will be paying, so I have to be sure.
No I won't have these. Please bring me some more.
These are nice, the ones with the bow.
Still, I'm not sure. Oh, I don't know.
I just love shopping for shoes. This pair are nice, 'but they
pinch my toe.
Pass me back that other pair, the ones with the bow.
I put them on and walk up and down
Yes these are nice, but I'll have them in brown.
I have the brown pair, the ones with the bow.
I'm sure the assistants are very pleased when I am ready to go.
There is a relief upon their faces
But, knowing me, I may go back and change them for the
black pair with laces.
Could you imagine the looks on their faces?
I would be very amused. Oh, I just love shopping for shoes.

Jackie A. Middleton

"Innocents"

Sixteen little Angels all gone to Heaven,
Sixteen little children, age up to seven,
When they went to School that day,
Their hopes were to run and play, skip and
    jump up to the sky,
Like little birds with bright eyes.

But then the darkness arrived,
Some children with fear cried,

Bewildered are those left behind,
Why was this man so unkind,
And so the nation grieves and mourns,
Along with God's love these children will be
    adorned.

Denise Sonia Ogden

My Uncle Ted

In remember the times we used to go fishing,
sit and play with the worms.
I don't remember most of his life,
as I was only four. But my mum and dad,
tell me how close we were,
and that he died of cancer in 1984.
Me and my family were up in Manchester,
looking for a house. When we got back to Essex,
we had a phone call, it was my aunty Eileen,
my uncle Ted had died.
For years and years I had bad dreams,
waking up in cold sweats.
These dreams were the only thing I had left
apart from memories, of my uncle Ted.
I don't think it's fair. He was only forty-two.
It's coming up to twelve years now,
since he passed away. I just wish he was here today,
fishing by the river bank,
his wavy hair blowing in the breeze
as he helps me reel fish in.

Dawn Maycock

'End of Affair'

Was it ever really a pleasure to feel so high?
    Sneaking, lying, hiding, fearing gossip - pregnancy
Two years was so long . . . let it die, pie in the sky you said.

Okay, so I will unplug the phone, please leave me alone
    My heart has no wish to be at home for you this time:

Night time blues - my mind drowns, deepens, darkens, dwells
    Who could sleep, feel or weep in this kind of hell?
Normality - your perception of - was never achieved with you.

I shall lick my wounds and follow my goals through
    Which you would have denied me . . . stealing my life!
To possess me totally - like your wife?

This forbidden fruit can only be sweet for a moment
    Now poison caresses my heart, but our baby - sublime -
Neutral, the a perfect grape grown on a Life's vine,
    Who is cherished and transcends through Love.

Colleen O'Neill

My Rainbow

Was I really a blue dragonfly with iridescent wings
Skimming waters on hot sultry days
A graceful swan gliding, wings that sing in flight,
Was I really a weeping willow bending low
To grace the river
A shy deer amid the dappled trees and forest fern,
Was I really a wild goose with beating heart and wing
A butterfly, delicate, kaleidoscope with colour,
Was I really a bird with watchful eye bringing joy at dawn,
A celestial star spangled ethereal sphere, was I really?
You, who have created me, tell me so,
Then blow me gently where I go
Pike, dragonfly, dandelion, daisy, was I?
You, speak my rainbow to me dearly.

Anne Llewellyn

140

The Starving Few

Heads overweight sit upon
Skeletons that move along
on stork-like sticks
That lean and sway
Precariously along the way.

Eyes that glow from the skull
Know full well hope is dull
and Life without value
Just breathes in vain
and silently accepts its pain.

The United Nations sat today
On tables set so they say
with the finest fare.
Bloated then and weary too
Debating the fate of the Starving Few

Aid given by the stroke of a pen
Biased by politics of men
and not on any sad recourse.
They have nought to lose
Sadly beggars cannot choose.

Cecilia Turner

Beautiful Things

Nature is such a beautiful thing.
Summer, autumn, winter and spring.
When the flowers start to grow,
bringing out a marvellous show,

Spring and summer brings the sun
everyone is having lots of fun.
Autumn and winter brings the snow
it's time to sit by the fireside glow.

David Lawley

Return to the Rio Grande

Oh! River Captain please make a bamboo raft for me
So that I may ride once more down the Rio Grande
With lush green mountains either side
Down the gentle river let your bamboo raft glide
Let me feel the hot sun burn my face
As the wonder and the beauty around me I embrace
I want to see the old women washing their clothes
Along the shore of where the "Grande" flows
And I long to call to the children who dive for fish with
   homemade spears
As you so capably, so gracefully your bamboo raft steer
At first the water is cool and still
But as we journey on it gets faster, deeper until -
The swirling river twists and bends
And gushes into the sea at St. Margaret's Bay and the
   journey ends.

Heather Thaxter

The Zero Hour

They huddled in the slushy,
slimy mud of misunderstanding,
each lonely in his thoughts.
The tangled barbed wire etched
spiky against the velvet sky.
Harmonica's lone last semibreve floated far away.
Zero hour was here and gone.

The gun's muzzle yawned
and spat its deadly cargo.
Eyes twin noughts seeing nought,
mouths gaping a surprised Oh! Of sudden death.
Telegrams took halos with them
round were the tears that fell.
All from the zero hour.

Then came the poppies red reminder
their round black eyes accusing stare.
Full circle war winds blew again
drowning the whispered warning.
"Here was the zero hour."

Gwendolyn Joslyn

the songs of weeping men

with the wind the songs of weeping men
   slipping dawn on broken hillside
wayside spring the catching water
   vast minds listening to falling autumn
sweet grass roughly kicked
   to deep dark ditches
speed of crashing rainbow
   silent moonbeams
dancing to bewitching heartbeats
   mellow kissed corn
soaked field tearing
   blood showers in eventide
thistledown swaying
   blowing tunes caught in anguish
gentle nursery rhymes ironically ripping
   stale words of the world sipping
through closed mouths

Gillian Patricia Smith

Your Hobby

Have you ever thought of a hobby
Something that you could see,
How about doing a painting
Then say that was done by me.

As you look at the blank canvas
And mix the colours for the skies
To see the fluffy clouds forming
Right before your eyes.

Now a mountain range in the distance
Filling in lower all in line,
Each brushstroke brings an added bliss
With contentment all the time.

Maybe water or at the bottom
Trees or bushes with greenish glow
Keeping alive with your own idea
Perhaps it can be put on show.

You may get the Doubting Thomas
Whether they like it or not,
Remember it is your hobby
And you gave it your best shot.

Edith Cooke

The Book of Life

Life is a book and each day a page,
something to read about in your old age,
when your body stops working your spirits not dead,
There's a whole new beginning when your last page is read,
as your spirit leaves you to the life ever after,
another book opens and you start a new chapter

Brian Edwards

Baboushka

Shut in cupboard. Dark and the smell.
Soft sandalwood rises up
Like words never to be spoken.
The damage already done,
My eyes closed to the light
All my senses kissing the dark.
Conversations have taken place
In my head, shut in a cupboard smell
of sandalwood. Memories are placed
under my bed; listening in my dark cupboard.
Feelings and thoughts denied,
Rough to the touch, I locked in.
A silent prisoner, I know I dream
of us. I crouch in my cupboard.

My heart has been broken.
Forget what I've said.
The damage has been done; these dreams
Are back in my head, shut
In a cupboard.

I reach. I feel.

Goanita E. I. M. Jacques

141

Some Friends

Some friends are really kind and nice.
Some are really bad and cruel.
Some friends are so scared as mice.
Some are so greedy they'll take any jewel.

With friends you do lots of things like talk, work and play.
You invite them to your house to watch T.V. and eat.
With friends you have loads of fun all night and day.
Some friends are really cool and neat.

Friends really understand and care.
When you're in trouble they're always there for you.
You have fun with them and like them doing your hair.
When I break friends I feel down in the blues.

Erum Naavi

A Hole in the Ground

A hole in the ground
Small or large, soft and round,
A tiny seed, a root now browned
And see life shooting from the mound
Beauty from the flower, the tree
And so on for all eternity.

A hole in the ground
Six feet may be
Lined with laurel and flower - see?
And with sad sweet memory
Life is left - uncaptive free
Rest in peace you and me
Our work is done - Eternity.

A hole in the ground
Large and ever secret mound
Secret terrible to be found
Nuclear tests, and awful Atom
One move false and all is Satan
Hiroshima! wailing! silence and anon
For none to know or see: Eternity

Irene Ryder

Age

She sits alone, surrounded by framed memories.
Smiling faces, times gone by.
A solitary tear falls down her cheek.
Time has gone so fast.
There's still so much she wants to do.
Still so much she wants to see.
Her mind still full of questions, but her body is tired, so tired.
Her independence, given so harshly by her husband's death.
Now takes his place.
Her independence, once hated but now so cherished.
Is drifting from her grasp.
Life can be so cruel.
She struggles on, determined not to give up.
"I can do it myself", she cries,
As her next step brings her tumbling down.
People gather 'round, pick up the pieces.
But the most important pieces, are still lying on the ground.
They can't see them, only she can see.
Her silent cries go unnoticed.
Her self respect lies shattered on the floor.

Claire Nutting

From Grannie to Angus on His First Birthday

Angus - with black currant eyes
So full of courage and surprise
You found yourself on Earth one day
And this was where you thought you'd play.
The sun shone bright and all those smiles
Came from people twice your size,
But still you knew the world was yours
A perfect place for little boys
To scramble, crawl, and climb, and laugh
And cuddle up beside your toys.
Angus with black currant eyes
I think you'll grow up very wise.

Jean Polwarth

One Sunny Morning

I woke up one sunny morning, birds were singing
Snowdrops daffodils swaying in the wind.
What a lovely day. I don't like those cold
And frostier days. They make my fingers and toes so cold.
The Snowdrops that blows in the wind
I love the birds that sing. Thank You Lord for everything
I was so sad. I was so sad when I lost a friend.
I did not won't to smile
But as the days pass by
I wipe away the tears
And now I can smile again
I missed her so much
But life goes on.
And I am happy again
I still think of my
friend from time to time
She would say
Smile smile.
Smile

Doris Osborn

Seasons' Gifts

Gently, twirling, twisting, swirling,
Snowflakes touch the ground,
Nature's magic wonderland,
Creating all around,
And trees that once stood stark and black,
Shaped by winter's storms,
Suddenly look beautiful,
As they are transformed,
Their branches laced by virgin flakes,
So white, so pure, a blanket makes,
For young shoots, peeping through the earth,
Awakening to their time of birth,
Nature does not forget a thing,
For after winter comes the spring,
A gift she gives to everyone,
Of hope, and joy, till day is done.

Emily Gibbs

Someone

Someone who loves you when no other will
Someone who cares when you are ill
Someone who forgives no matter what
Someone to rock you in your cot
Someone who watches as you grow tall
Someone who cherishes gifts large or small
Someone who worries when you're far away
Someone who's happy when you're back to stay
Someone whose life you've made
Someone whose memories will never fade
Someone like no other
Someone just like a mother.

Jonathan F. Camp

I Had a Dream

I had a dream
So close
Seemed easy to reach, grab and put away
In my treasure box,
But just as I thought I had it, it vanished.
Everything's gone wrong?
A sea of reality overtook my soul.
Sexually, physically, mentally abused.
All this horrible excitement left me quite
Confused and disarrayed.
I am but only young, and my life seems
over already.
I shall stand on two feet, holding my
heart in my hand.
It was once warm but it is now cold.
Take pity on me, merciless people.
I am but only young and my life seems over
already . . .

Erica Banton

'Spiritual' Lessons from Shop Signs

Salvation's door is "Open" wide
So enter, while you may
For when 'tis "Closed" 'twill always be
Now is Salvation's day

A "Special Offer" you can have
A Great Salvation sure
Nothing to pay, Christ paid it all
So you need do no more

"Buy now while stocks last", this we read
Sometimes, when in a store
"Sold out", in time this will apply
Then you can get no more

"Under new management", so now
Changes you can expect
Wrong things put right, with Divine help
Your life God can direct

When Christ comes in, the sinner's heart
Is changed, now born anew
Trust Him today, turn from your sin
And find what He can do!

Bernard E. Avery

Ploughing

Harvest. Peace. But then the doubts return
Surface twisting and writhing
Like shredded worms thrown up

By ploughs, tractor pulled blades drawn through
Fields begging to lay fallow
Stubborn to yield to the search

The quest to dig up the meaning of life
Despite protestations for peaceful shelter
From what so long lay buried

And safe from the grip of Winter hungry beaks
The jealousy of eyes demanding to be fixed
On anything exhibiting the merest sign

Of life, in such a barren wilderness,
Dredgings from the sea of frozen dun
Once so unexploited; once so fertile.

Once such a dark and tempting place
Till the coming of heated blades
Till keen edges again craved blood

Till, till, till.
Then the cold sets in again.

Gavin Douglas John Wilson

Guess Who?

South Shields to Rotherham is much more than a mile
So the car set out to fetch him and brought him home in style
Imagine the excitement when he arrived at three
Wondering what he looked like, and just how big was he
A tiny little bundle, but what a big surprise
Small soft ears, a button nose and shining dark brown eyes.

I remember the first time I held him and now he's ten years old
He really is a little gem and worth his weight in gold
In sickness and adversity, 'midst my hopes and fears
He's such a consolation, a vessel for my tears
And when we go out walking and he's prancing by my side
His little upward trusting glance fills my heart with pride

Sadly on other occasions I must go out alone
But what a wonderful thrill I feel when he welcomes me back home
The little tail a-wagging, the welcome shrieks of pleasure
No-one, just no-one, greets me like my little treasure.

No doubt you've guessed my secret, as my poem comes to an end
It's all about my cuddlable, lovable, most faithful four-legged friend.

He's a Schnauzer and his name is 'Luke'.

Joy D. Richardson

Grandparents

It's nice to have grandparents somewhere
Someone to look up to when Daddy's not there
One whom you can talk to, and know that he cares.

Yet there are some grandparents who just can't be bothered
Some who can't notice that their grandchildren are around.
Some pretend to love, but with no meaning
Others put on a face in their surroundings.
So why are they there - those who don't care?

Other grandparents are loving and kind
And show off their grandchildren to their friends of all kind.
They take them for walks, even though it's just to the park
And hold their hand when they're afraid of the dark.

The grandchildren you've neglected, when you get much older
Might not be around, so beware,
For when they needed you, you were not there
So why should they now be bothered to care?
Remember your friends they will disappear
When you get much older - or don't you care
Of the life you are living?
Please grandparents beware.

Jennifer Gordon

On the Crest of a Wave

Where torment lies beneath the crest
So many memories came to rest.
So many rhythms carry the tides
As broken schools attempt to hide
From steaming nostrils, cold with rage,
Their unlucky fortunes prolong with age.
Turmoil persists with each ebb and flow,
No sooner have they come, they must go.
Released, they fall from the doom in which they die,
Saluting survivors, so dignified as they cry.
Full steam ahead, their eyes evade
The reluctant offering of a sacrifice made.
No pain will enter their breath so many fathoms below,
Dormant flags forgotten, as young souls resist to go,
And still their smiling faces, meet with a turbulent sky,
Awaiting their comrades, with medals shining high.

An empty locker with a forgotten name,
A distant family contains the pain.
Touching the water, too late to save
An anointed hand caught by the wave.

Del Osedo

"Togetherness"

I went to our old haunt today, those secret childhood places
that we used to know.
I sensed your presence near me on the hilltop, where we played
and tumbled in the snow.

The cottage on the corner with the smoke-blackened hearth,
where we whiled away the happy hours with friends.
In spirit you were sitting there beside me, for love never ends.

And in the bluebell wood I heard you whisper above the gentle
rustle of the trees,
The essence of my being reached out to touch you there as you
lingered on the fragrant summer breeze.

Beyond the sunset I see your smiling face, you are with me at the
dawn of each new day.
With angel voice you whisper close to me "I'm here with you, I
have not gone away."

I call you by your old familiar name, I speak to you in the easy
way I always used to.
What we were to each other, that we still are.

After this, and through the long to-be, and I know there must
be love there too.
I, should you chance to have need of me, am always and ever
there for you.

A brief moment, and all will be as it was before.

Irene Nobbs

Shark-Toothed Stars

Luminous island in autumn sunlight.
Solid gold vision
Breaks free through
Radiant fire and shining water.
A rising star sets against multi-cloud skies,
Heaven and earth combined.

Yellow pink curtains cascade
Through the dark.
The lights dim, the waters rise,
Yet a rain-blue cloud possesses
Its surroundings. Brightness
Gently fades, blue disappears.

Slowly, fine pinpoints
Of energy and whiteness appear,
Contrasting
With the resilient curtain.
A vast twinkling emptiness.
Break free from
Silent solidity, piercing
Earth's pure heart.

Eve V. Pickles

Melancholy Friends

We sit in a room full of
strangers, you and I
make light-hearted chat of times gone by.
We're both broken-hearted,
lost loves who we miss.
Uncanny how we are both feeling like this.
You tell me your troubles,
I tell you mine.
I am sympathetic,
you are kind.
We part as friends
- may meet again sometime.
You leave with her on your mind,
I leave with you on mine.

Christine Towle

Feelings So True

A very warm and gentle person close within my heart
Someone who is still beside me in the hours apart
With a knowledge and depth of understanding
Time to the test is still withstanding
We seem to reach some points together
Through wind and rain and stormy weather
Always to find that the sun is shining
The clouds with a beautiful silver lining
Such happiness can be hard to find
Even in a search amongst all of mankind
So following this winding path along
A world full of laughter, a world full of song
Stirring such passion long since seen
Hidden inside is where it has been
That is the me I thought I would deny
The question now, with you, for me is why
Why deny what I know I feel
The feelings so deep, they can only be real.

Caroline Blishen

On Christmas Day

The big day is here at last
Something that began in the past.
Turkey dinner is served on the table
Reindeers are eating in the stable.
Santa Claus has come
Little kiddies are annoying their mum.
She's glad all her work is finally done
Presents are scattered beneath the
Christmas tree.
Ready for the fun to begin for everyone
Sadly it soon comes to an end.
As darkness falls it's all over and done.

Colin Palmer

I've Never Been Happy Since I Left You

I've never been happy since I left you
No woman has made me smile
And I've become unattractive to them
You've turned my smile into a mad smirk
There's no plastic left in my cheeks to squeeze

And I burn my bridges right and left
So many people I wish I never met
But if I can somehow patch us up
May be there's hope for them
I've tried to leave them laughing
But no one makes me laugh since I left you

Maninder Chana

Gone - But Not Forgotten!!

I no longer cried!
Something was missing from inside
Colours were no more
They were locked behind a closed door.
I was blind?

Trees, birds and flowers had all cried,
But I was left way behind,
Was it because I was blind
That no tears came to mind
They really had died!!

No more bright lights would I see
In years to come would they remember me
Could it possibly be
That I was never meant to see
What the world held for me.

You've taken away my eyes,
But I am still alive
I have all the memories inside
They haven't died.
Even though I am blind.

Jessica Jones

"False Alarm"

As I close my eyes, to go to sleep,
sometimes, I can't, so start counting sheep,
off into dreamland, I gently flow —
there goes the "Alarm!" So up I must go.
On with the slippers,
then make the bed,
still very tired —
you "old sleepy head!"

Switch on the kettle, to make the tea,
look out the window —
"My! It's still dark I see"?

Glance at the calendar —
"Oh No!", I think,
still very tired, need forty winks,

So, back into bed,
the same sleepy head.

"All" clocks did "alter".
But that one can keep,
while I close my eyes, and,
start counting sheep.

Hilary A. Grist

Sadness

Sometimes 'tis magic
Sometimes 'tis not
In times of the latter, I often think we shouldn't be
And seek the wisdom from within the trueness of my heart
For only it alone can lift me from this despair
And not only my proud, judgmental head
. . . May the twain never meet.

Helena J. Lowe

Time Passes

I was clearing the big, old house: My old home
Sorting, sifting, sighing: Struggling alone
Week after week I went there, working every day
With each dusty discovery the years rolled away
Memories came flooding back, evoking heartbreak and smiles
Into Time's recesses I travelled many miles
I found boxes of Havana cigars, crumbling away
Father's pipe and 'baccy' tin; an older pipe of clay
Aspidistras, still alive. They were Mother's pride
I watered them, and polished their leaves - and cried
I climbed the winding attic stairs, even dustier and dim
Boxes and cases everywhere. Dare I look within?
Souvenirs of childhood; old toys, a cricket bat
My brother's old school photograph, a drawing of my cat
Magazines, school books, latin primers, french grammars
Nails, screws, tin tacks, pliers, saws and hammers
An ancient pair of ice skates, used so long ago
Who left all this junk up there? I don't know
Mother's sewing box, father's horn-rimmed glasses
Symbols of a bygone age . . . Time passes!

Joan Ierston

Rainbow

An arc of light across the sky.
Sunlight through raindrops from on high,
A spectrum of colour we can see,
Known as a rainbow to you and me.
Red, Orange, Yellow, Green and Blue,
Indigo and Violet too,
With these colours were mesmerised,
An optical phenomenon is devised,
A Kaleidoscope gives similar effect,
Colours and shapes not to reject,
from cylindrical shape, symmetrical pattern,
Glass chips and mirrors make this happen,
Not natural as the rainbow I know,
Nowhere else to find this heavenly glow,
Dream of the Leprechaun all clad in green,
And the pot of gold yet to be seen,
A marvellous, most beautiful sight,
Is this glorious, natural arc of light.

Elizabeth Eade

Where Is the Peace?

Where is the peace, promised by the dove?
Spread from his mouth; the branch of love.
Why has it not reached us from long ago?
Where has it gone, where did it go?

Will it come back, reach out anew;
are we ready to grasp for a peace so true?
This world truly needs that dove to arrive
just to exist, to stay alive.

War must end; in its place: Love.
Oh, where is the peace, promised by the dove?
Come soon; we need you.

Irene Anderson

A Ghost of Love

Beset my widow's grief
Such tears can't prevail
Betook a shadow left behind
Alone, that last farewell
An empty womb is no solace
Beseech thee, why for, did you
Heartache, no joy exist
Aloneness and solitude
Missing thee my love that was
The father of my child
Again I weep my lonely state
Be still awaits your return
I weep afresh long cancelled love
Isn't thy grave enough
A stone to mark the spot
Where'st you'll forever lay
Your honour not besmirched
Oh gentle lion sleep on this day

Audrey Clapton

Earthquake at Dawn
(Natural Disaster at Kobe 17.1.95)

Beneath the feet of the people of Japan
The earth is in constant motion, unharnessable by Man.
Sometimes lying motionless for hundreds of years
Lulling people into false security and erasing their fears.

All of a sudden, the beast rises from its slumbers
Destroying property, people's lives and killing great numbers.
Damaging the services that people take for granted
Gas and water mains broken, electric and phone poles stunted.

In the Miyaji hospital, the patients were all evacuated
But two nurses were trapped in their quarters and waited.
For rescue and relief they hoped would be coming soon
It took eleven painful hours and they only saved one.

There were many heroic stories throughout the disaster
Personal triumphs and tragedies, grief and joy unsurpassed.
People finding comfort and relief through someone's kindness
Business men responded to calls to try and relieve the mess.

This tragedy made people seek answers to the question
How could this have been avoided, any suggestion?
We learnt that Man can't build to overcome Nature
We can't earthquake-proof any human structure.

David Muncaster

Cascades

I've met a girl who's altered me.

My love flows to her in cascades.

It's my heart's serene outpouring,
that gently splashes everything.

Willingly deeper I choose to wade.

I've been struck by Cupid's arrow,
and been released from wooden gallows.
My love's reactive after being fallow.

I'm smitten in this joy parade.

She's taken an injured heart by stealing,
and gives me such emotional healing,
by discovering all, I'd been concealing.
How has she generated such feelings?

She's made real my heart's old charade.

Laying foundations that have entrapped,
but I've no objections about being captured,
I've gained a pleasant loving stature.
She's plastered over my heart's fractures,
and leaves me feeling ecstatic rapture.

My love flows to her in cascades.

Alexander Craggs

Salute to Sirius

Glorious light of winter heaven,
Splendour of the southern sky,
Scintillating, then pulsating,
Great delight to human eye,
Far outshining all companions
In the field of darkness nigh.

Only men's imaginations
Made of thee the dog of space,
Following your splendid master
In hibernal night time chase,
But I wonder what great planets
'Round thee run their timeless race?

And what creatures on those planets
As a god do thee adore,
Light and warmth with thanks receiving,
While your nuclear ovens roar . . . ?

For the present it suffices
As celestial paths align,
Caught winking through my curtains,
Sirius is mine!

Anne Kerr

Skyscape

I do to come to you like the pale moon
Stalking the watery Heavens, white like the wind.

The sky is bright tonight with lurid light,
Sea-swallows flight, flutter and fall.

An old grey gull with wan wise eye
Looks at the water as it swings by.

No, I do not come to you, I do not come
Speeding the heavy Heavens where the night's begun.

My pattern breaks and changes like the clustering clouds,
No firm foothold on the silver stars.

No point of contact with the eternal form
With the thrusting moment, with the ever-long.

As I falter to the chasm of the failing, flickering cloud,
As I seek my own identity within the hand of God

I will come upon the morning when the water's swinging by,
Riding on the grey gull with the sad grey eye.

Anne Ross

"Alone"

Being without you . . . is like "floating in time"
Suspended emotions . . . "Drifting Alone"
Time ticks away . . . "It's such a Crime"
That we aren't together . . . "As together we Shine"
But I will . . . wait . . . "Forever for you",
Hoping you will come back . . . "As you seldom do",
A free spirit you are . . . "Following the Breeze",
When the Breeze turns around . . . "Follow it Please,"
Come back to me . . . "With arms open wide"
And stay "Together" . . . "Forever inside."

Jean Walker

August Dank Holiday

Chill winds have quelled the wheat, the rye.
Squirrels cling to trees;
Soaked summer's sound so sough, so sigh
So shriek through shudd'ring leaves

Dejected butterflies deplore
Summer's draggled robes.
Undaunted, big black rooks outpour
Unmelodious tones.

A field beside a lane, a rill
Heaves and dives and churns
A cottage broods where rolls a hill
A poet blinks, and yearns.

And down I go, a horse's shoe
Tripped me though 'twas thinning
And down the well I'm wishing to
Goes my silver shilling

Joyce Nina Pountney

Daybreak

Rustling papers drift along,
Streets deserted by the throngs,
Pavements wait, anticipating the resounding thud of busy feet -
Their steady rhythm an echo of the town's heartbeat.

Robin stirs upon his bough,
Farmer dreams of seed and plough,
Nocturnal creatures scurry to complete their nightly chores
'Ere daylight's beasts return to reclaim the land once more.

Trees reach to salute the dawn,
Larks await to sing their song,
Earth, her heart so cold for hours, prepares once more to warm and nurture
Nature's wondrous gifts, so precious now and for the future.

Moon's round face is almost gone -
Eclipsed by sadness at the morn,
Stars fade as golden fingers reach to pluck their silvery lights away
As rising sun transforms dark night to bright new day

Helen McKendrick

The Forgotten Child

Lying still inside a cage of emptiness and unleashed rage
Staring eyes, their glisten gone,
In one so young, that must be wrong.
Heart beats slowly, barely there,
Unnoticed in the cold night air.
Smell of death looms all around,
Fear creeps over icy ground,
Tears fall slowly, a cry is heard,
Food is given, but not a word.
Silence moves in once again,
Is there no shelter from this pain.
A glimmer of hope is all he needs,
In between his tiresome feeds,
A kiss, a hug, a laugh or smile
Would make this child's life worthwhile.
Lost in a world full of greed,
Lies this harmless pitiful seed,
No toys no books no teddy bear
Just four walls and an empty chair.

Alison Hawkridge

The Flowers of My Garden

There is one hour of the day
that all around is quiet.
And the flowers of my garden talk.
I am speechless in those magic hours
and I listen, to their music with
messages of love.
Secret harmony in my heart, I found.
Nobody can take those flowers, because
for me there are singing love,
for he who likes to hear them.

Baroli Martinetti Rosangela

Men

Men exasperating lumps of lard,
That always preempt your word,
Who have no clues on what you like,
Will tear you down word for word,
The art in men is hard to touch,
If they're soft it's all too much,
Drinking, feeding, sports their thing,
Where's my dinner? you're late, I'm not
That shirt I left has no button.
Where's the sugar? In the cupboard.
What cupboard? is the cry,
Birthday, Christmas, all the same,
Where's my card? You get too much.
On first-being married
It's cosy and warm,
The next stage, comfort and calm,
Children and pets come and go,
Then you're left alone together.
Both in menopausal air
God help us each we cry.

Diane E. Complin

The Toll

I walked the toll bridge that joins the two lands.
Stopping still in dismay at the outstretch of hands.
Squat on some rags in the filth of the street,
Her life as empty as the cup she held in entreat.

She looked up at my face as I stood in the crowd.
Climbing into my soul, eyes screaming out loud.
A virgin to poverty, seduced by a stare.
My innocence given to one yet so many sit there.

Long ago I was told 'you don't know you are born'.
I see that much now and find myself torn
By a river's deep wound that runs through the heart
Of a neighbour so close yet so far apart.

Committed to memory and evermore so shall be
The cost of the toll at the pittance of fee.
Want is a face, paid for by the hell
Of having nowhere to go and only feelings to sell.

Frank Goldsmith

Peace

The Lord did ask for us to keep
Ten simple things in His command
Honour and obey His mighty word
So the world can sleep in peace.
All the leaders of the land
Smile and shake each other's hands
But will their pleas for peace succeed?
Will people listen, will they heed
Will they obey the Master's plan?
Violence we do not need
Peace and goodwill should be our creed.

Christine Stirling

Dawn

Dawn's pale fingers of gentle light
Steal across the earth
Folding back the shroud of night
To give a new day birth
A thrush begins to test its throat
And cautiously to sing
A thousand birds take up the note
And make the morning ring
Crystal dewdrops softly fall
Stirred by a gentle breeze
That wraps blue smoke like a wispy shawl
'Round whitewashed cottage eaves
Silver webs in hedgerows glisten
Like tiny silken threads
For waking shepherds, collies listen
Pricked up ears on inclined heads
Farmyard cats stretch and yawn
And leave their nests of hay
Basking in the golden dawn
Herald of another day

John Hayter

Timely Transition

Don't hide behind that brick wall you imagine to be there,
Step around from behind it, you'll find people there who care.
Remove the mask you are wearing and leave it on the shelf,
And you will find love is there if you would only be yourself.

Identify your shadow and your dark repressed side,
Recognize the trouble and use it as your guide,
Disperse your negative feelings or limitations will occur,
And no longer lust after blockage as your vision it will blur.

Don't make yourself a prisoner or your own growth you will cease,
And accept past disappointments then the hurt you must release.
Find the reason for the enigma and let your emotions flow,
And dispense with the oppression, it's now timely that you let go

Become conscious of your nature and mould it into shape,
Hold your hands out now to strangers and with you they'll relate,
As accomplishment is likely now, the darkness turned to light,
The outcome almost predictable knowing the transition is right.

Cheryl Anderson

The Game of Life

Snakes and ladders
That it seems to be,
Up and down, it's but a dream,
Ascending on the finishing line,
Then whee, start again
Look closer this time!
Each Ladder I climb the better
I get,
The smaller the snakes,
I'm really being stretched,
My confidence grows like a flower
in bloom,
Try as I will that big snake's here soon,
But I missed it this time!
I feel in glee,
Then a whole set of new snakes and ladders
are coming for me!

Ferrelyn Shurety

"In Loving Memory"

Looking out towards the valley
Still damp with morning dew.
Happy voices echoed through the hills.
Eager faces filled with glee
Afresh with warmth and laughter.
Children together, with peace of mind
But one fine day
Destruction was about to strike.
A beast of evil raged,
As the tender-loving hearts were filled with silent fear.
There was emptiness, nothing but the clock was heard.
The pain in those hearts
Were with all the world.
Pleading whispers softly said
Why, oh why did they have to go?
We cannot forgive, we cannot forget,
Although as time goes by
The world will bond together as one -
And there will be peace in the valley once more.

Claudia Sharp

"Strangled by Love"

Dusty hat and worn-in boots
the cowboy gets on his brute
over the hill, he rides his range
mending the fences, feeling the pain
for the love he once had never to regain
her death unexpected because she was so young
Now the cowboy is a loner without any fun
and sadly enough he'll get by
without her being by his side . . .
Now the cowboy is a loner today
he works very hard to get by
he ropes and he wrangles
Just to be strangled by a love he'll never let go
Praying, someday she'll show up in a new way
But the cowboy is a loner today.

George E. Stakely

Love

You sit across from me,
The angel of my heart.
Asleep but so alive,
Suspended in time for all to see.
Your flowing black hair,
Your slender body,
Those luscious red lips,
Your deep black eyes that suck me in
I wish you were mine
To hold you in my arms
To kiss those lips, to taste your soul
To hold you close when you are sad.
To share your pain, your dreams.
But do you want me?
My lips, my kisses,
To share my soul, my pain.
If you do come to me,
If you do not tell me so?
Oh Lovely YOU!

Alan Smith

Promises

White scudding clouds in the sky up above,
Talk to me darling - such sweet words of love.
The heavens may open with black thunderous sky,
I'll lay here beside you and never know why
You love and desire me and none may intrude
On our stolen few hours - a snatched interlude.

Our passion must last and never be spent
On recriminations, however well meant.
And when I'm alone and you're home with your wife,
Whom you promised to love for the rest of your life,
Will you spare me a thought as I cry on my bed,
And remember those promises, better not said?

Jane Parker

The Pain Inside

I hear music on the radio
Stories of love and romance
I see couples on the dance floor
And their closeness as they dance

It makes me feel so lonely
It makes me feel the pain
That's inside of my heart
Where your love used to reign

I feel so lonely I could cry
With all the hurt I feel inside
Just want to lay down and die

When we met I was feeling this pain
But it was taken away by you
You made me feel so good inside
But now we're apart too

I've tried, so hard to sort myself out
But there's some things that take two
I need someone to hold me tight
To take away the pain that's been left by you.

Helen Claire Wheeldon

Friendly Support

Sinking in a pit of depression;
Struggling to find a release.
Clawing at walls with my hate and aggression,
When will this frustration cease?

You are there every night - every day;
To help and support and to guide.
You are only a phone call away;
And I trust you enough to confide.

So when the despair is pulling me in
And I feel I can't escape its hold;
I know I can rely on your friendly grin.
A good friend is worth more then gold!

Helen Lovell

I Don't Love You

I don't love you anymore,
Tears rolled down her face and life
seemed no more,
Feeling as if she was nothing more
than a shell,
So empty and unsure of where to
turn now.
Wishing she were dead, buried and gone,
thinking of ways she could end it all.
Finishing her life seemed the best
thing to do, to be free of the heartache
and unhappiness too.

Catherine E. Bennett

My Brother

He holds our mum dear,
Spends most of his time in fear,
Now our dad has died,
My brother is dry from all he's cried,
Alone he feels without any love,
I am here my favourite bruv,
His wife and kids are also gone.
He makes out he is strong,
He watched my dad die in pain,
The memories are not keeping him sane.
My mum's babe he was before,
Now he feels he has no-one anymore,
For warmth and love is all he seeks
Every now and then he grows weak,
There are lots who care if he's in a mess
Me, our family, and of course there's Les,
I could add plenty more to this list,
He won't listen, he just gets p....d!!
His time in life has been awful bad,
To see him like it makes me sad

Angela Rea

Future's Coming

When thoughts of my parents permeate,
tears and fear form fast and flow,
to see and hear them lose their grip,
hurts more than I will show.

The gleam in their lives fades as,
their light and bone and skin die,
and as the children walk and run and fly,
their sun sets before their eyes.

Their memories are their futures,
as they move into their pasts,
with only formed faces to look backward to,
and the loosening of their grey grasps.

And when, in time, they are no more,
I shall remember less clearly,
The past, the present, interweaving,
as the future rocks and reels me

So enjoy while you can, the youth
you have left, make much memory,
to enthral at death's bed, then
Live on, you will - in hearts, in minds,
live on in your children's souls.

David J. Byrne

Journey

I left while the sun shone warming the breakfasting air. The breeze swept the sleepiness away and beyond the barn sheds the geese cackled. Clothes hung drying on the rope; they lightened and blotted in the sun. As I headed towards the village the smell of grass cuttings simmered amongst a heifer reek. It was peaceful; then the car passed!

Petrol fumes lingered by its scorching tracks; on the roadside daises wilted. Black soot clinging to those fragile blades - lost from a cylinder ring. I spluttered in its wake and walked through the sultry smell to a freshness but its stench was with me now; not going as I headed to the city for work.

A bus soon came. I sat in its smoke-charged deck amongst pollutants and jargon sprays, swatting walls with their hideous breaths; Yellowed with nicotine my collar wilted. The train gave little respect as we joined more city scummers in a grotesque battle of the satanic. The tunnel to Waverley was a black hole to Hell's deity; I'm sure I saw an idol to Beelzebub.

I departed the platform in a rushing flow of panic and scampering chaos like vermin in a rat race. Not even the light from the staircase summit was clear; only a rankness of diesel fumes. Taxis queued with engines on, their wipers clearing persistently the rain which fell in a fixation to the street. The silted gutters were carrying last night's muck from West End pubs.

Craig A. Pagett

Serenity

At the top of the lane, the Curlews fly
Swooping and gliding across the sky,
The air is clear, the soft breeze warm
And everything's peaceful after a storm.

Across to the Berwyns all purple and green,
The views all around, a sight to be seen.
The hillsides are covered with grazing sheep
Down in the valley the Dee runs deep.

Walk down the lane past hedgerows high
Tall cerise Foxgloves reach for the sky.
Wild Rose and Honeysuckle scent the air
Bindweed, Clover, Cow Parsley are there.

Pass the big Oak and now 'round the bend
Suddenly we begin to descend.
On the cottage wall the House Martin nests,
By the bridge o'er the stream, we take a rest.

Now we can see near the barn, the road
Ever noisy with traffic and heavy loads,
Taking supplies beyond Betws or Bala
Keeping the Welsh heartbeat throbbing forever.

Betty Bailey

"Wending"

Take my heart upon a wing,
Take and teach it how to sing of love -
that flows with time and speed, on
thermals that may take no heed.
Let it soar in sheer delight
with voice in tune, while reaching
heights of ecstasy.

Now my heart has learned to sing
with tender voice and choral ring.
Let it wend its way to me,
with it bringing harmony -
the sounding note of happiness -
that comes with learning to
express - a heart's desire.

Janet Turner

Youngsters of Today

When I was a young lass and in my prime
Talking to lads seemed such a crime.
But now the lasses don't care a toss
Both sexes want to be boss.

I used to like to dance and sing
Also have a jolly good fling.
But you have to be careful what you do
When mothers' eyes are watching you.

But these days, the lass and the lad
Have the fun we'd like to have had
They go to a disco for a jive.
This makes them feel it's good to be alive.

But when some get into their teens
They don't know what behaving means.
They go out and get very rough
Thinking they are really tough.

But some of these youngsters are really kind
Helping old folk and the blind.
I know that same are on the level;
These are the ones that deserve a medal.

Edna Beedham

An Epitaph

God showed through Robert Burns
That Kings could still rise on Scotland's plain
To sing the glories of our domain.
Speak aloud of her immortal fame.
Acknowledge the battle of life is seldom tame.

Alex Ferns

"Devon Countryside"

It was in glorious Devon
That beauty caught my eye
When walking down a leafy lane
With primrose either side

It was in glorious Devon
On top of Totnes Hill
I saw a silent beauty
Of Devon lying still

It was in glorious Devon
Along the River Dart
Where rippling waters ebb and flow
So peaceful and so quiet

It was in glorious Devon
Across the Dartmoor scene
Where ponies sheep and cattle graze
In an idyllic fairy tale dream

It was in glorious Devon
I found tranquillity
A peace of mind know where could find
But Devon Countryside.

Allan Sumner

The Quest

"Tell me my love, where did they hide the key,
that would open my eyes and enable me to see.
And when my eyes are open where will I find the light,
that will guide me, to find to love within your sight.
Will that light guide me and allow me to enter your arms,
or will darkness descend and blind me to your charms?
I will quest for that key, and then find the lock,
no doors thick or bars of steel can my way block.
That key, that key can now be my only salvation,
without your sweetness my life will be eternal damnation.
You say that key can only be found in one's own heart,
and once unearthed will break the chains that keep us apart.
I will search, I will journey long miles to find that thing,
When I do, will you love me and accept my wedding ring."

Brian Land

Memories of You

I knew you were ill, but I didn't understand;
That you would die soon, and leave this fair land
You nursed me when ill, and gave sound advice
You were everyone's friend, and always so nice.

What I remember the most, is how often you smiled,
Always so pleasant.
The memories of you, are the happiest times I saw.

Jane Sear

Have You Ever Thought

Have you ever thought that nothing's wrong
That everything is right
Have you ever thought that night is day
Or even day is night.

Have you ever thought that God is real
Have you ever thought He's not
Have you ever thought that you've got things
You really haven't got

Have you ever thought that life is death
Or death is really life
Have you ever done things that were wrong
Or got in any strife

Have you ever thought of getting married
And sharing all your life
Have you ever thought of wife and man
Or better man and wife

Have you ever thought of the day you'll die
And what will happen next
Have you ever thought that all you are
Is a piece of God's giant text.

Heather Campbell

The Little Girls of China

Who will hear their sad, sad cries
The little girls of China

No cuddles, no toys, if only they were boys,
The little girls of China

No ribbons, no rings, no little girly things
For the little girls of China

Just sadness and tears, no joyful baby years
For the little girls of China

All darkness, no light
For God's sake see the plight
Of the little girls of China

All Government heads sleep well in warm beds
With warmth and light all through the night
No such joy, unless you're a boy,
For the little girls of China

Please God, if you're there, for pity's sake spare
The little girls of China

Elizabeth Brown

Mother

At tender age she wrote the page
That later she would rue
But, handsome, charming, uniformed
He was her only beau
   A soldier's wife her future life
   Invitingly did beckon
   With tears and troubles, in her joy
   She sadly failed to reckon
The foreign climes, the happy times
The births of children four
Fulfilled her dreams beyond belief
Before he turned them sour
   A mistress fair he did declare
   Had wooed him from his duty
   He bade farewell to kith and kin
   Then vanished with his beauty
Through many years of toil and tears
Her children grown to manhood
Though fatherless, their happiness
Ensured her future good.

James E. Ross

World Peace

In the depth of the wood, softly I tread,
The beauty of the trees spread over my head.
What Peace, I heard only birds sing
As I passed by, they took to their wing.
They flew into the sky so high
It somehow caused me to sigh
If only we could fly away from a World of strife
Where there are many conflicts and countries fight.
Brother should love Brother, whatever race or creed.
Lord, the whole World seeks Your need.
Yes, Your hand should surely touch the World
Make it, as it should be, a haven of Peace and Love
until Eternity.

Irene Barnes

Agua De La Vida (Thoughts in a Drought)

Water - Spirit of life,
Streams of living water in a weary land,
A parched land, a land bleached with drought,
A burning desert.
How well the Moors understood it;
Always, the sound of water
Trickling, running, splashing droplets,
Beautiful to hear, to see, to touch,
Cascading, pouring still in the conduits they made,
'Round their gorgeous palaces.
Where it flows, in the shade, grow plants,
A thread of green in the tawny hide of Spain,
Or the riotous efflorescence of the Generalife Gardens.
But, without water, nothing, death.
Always, to reassure them, tinkle, plop, rush
Gurgle, chuckle.
The fun of water, its beauty, not solemnity.
Jewelled with aquatic delight
They brought this dower,
One gift of water's mighty power.

Jo Roberts

The Sea

What is it about the sea
That totally relaxes, and unwinds me?
It has something to do with the rhythm of waves,
That eases my mind and my sanity saves.
It has something to do with how soon it can change,
From as calm as a millpond to a tempestuous rage.
It's the fact that it can't be controlled by man,
And that beyond the horizon is an unseen land.
Perhaps it just is . . . when I walk by the sea
That I realize how amazing creation can be.
That increases my hope that it really is true,
That past the horizon of death . . .
there's an unseen land too.

Alison Wood

For You I Care

There's a place in my heart.
That is open for you
There's one way to enter
It's only for you

You don't need a ticket, your entry is free
All that I want is for you to love me
The depth of our loving
Is something we share
Something to cherish and someone to care

I'll love you for always
In my thoughts you will stay
My love for you will not go away

These words have strong meaning
My love to confess
With you I can say
I could find happiness

You are my light that will never go out
So my love for you is never in doubt.
Together with you a future to share
Because of my loving you know that I care

Bob Reynolds

Wisdom of a Fool (To Be Another Half)

I wish the band would play a different tune. Something
   mellow or in the mood
Look at the stars. Today they're shining bright
Look into these crazy eyes, now can you see what they contain
Is the wisdom of a fool
Looking around nobody wants to speak
Nothing works in this senseless place
Take me away to that Grand Parade where everything works
   like a clock
I can see the same things as you, but give me a moment
I'll change across to the other side and you can see
The wisdom of a fool
You'd better smile with me because this fool's looking at you
I can't turn around now: so we've got to make it through
Voices from one side have no bearing on the other
Myself and me are not the same
One side burns with a caustic dread and to change across to
   the other side
Would have you wishing I was rather dead
Needing a support, someone who'll trust
Someone who will believe in the wanting to be taken away
I need time to reflect upon
The wisdom in this fool.

Callan Asch

An Everlasting Love

Just think of me as a gentle breeze
That can kiss you on the cheek
The sun that shines with a delicate warmth
Like the arms of a loving caress.

I'm in the flowers that bloom and grow
With a fragrance soft and pure
The grass that carpets where you walk
And the rain that gently falls.

I'm in trees that softly sway
The leaves of green and brown
The winter snow of icy lace
Floating to the ground.

Don't ever doubt my love for you
Because I can't be seen
I'm with you always night and day
I'm where you have just been.

Look around I'm always there
I'm in the air you breathe
I'm in your laughter and your tears
And in your heart my dear.

Dylis Lawrence

Scattered Soil

I felt her breath even closer
Than the sweet peas I dropped upon her coffin
Now resting within the earth.
These were her flowers and I brought them
From her garden. She blushed with colour.
Without her, the seasons will melt into one
And become, an adjacent Trinity.
The earth that I now scattered upon her
Was once her foothold
And infinitely sure
She walked upon it Until infinity
Drew in her scent
And floundered.
For she was lovely.
And when the angels welcome, or whoever comes to greet,
May they welcome in, a guardian
Who will lead the apostles
To find the earth and goodness
Closer than the darkness
Of scattered soil.

Andrew Woodhouse

The Thundercloud

With a great anger,
The dark grey thundercloud,
Burst with wrath and,
Sending down its silver streak,
It shoots its icy white hail,
Down, down to the green fields below.

Its crack of lightning fells a tree,
It falls creakingly, then with a mighty crash, lies dead.
Hail sheeting down from the grey cloud,
The thundercloud has avenged the sun,
That singed the leaves of the willow tree,
And starved the crops of the old wheat field.

Christopher White

Farewell to a Sailor

The month was March
The day was Sunday
There were twenty-five guests

Eighteen were family
The rest, wives and
Shipmates, the very best

The sea looked blue
The waves were calm
There was no wind to feel

This the setting
Very fitting as
Skipper returned to the sea.
Soon the scattering
Done by a shipmate
The captain presiding. A memorable gathering

Dolly Harmer

Alone to Die

Thrust thy wind upon my face,
The bitter snow that falls with haste.

Fall down on me the darkened beast,
Oblivious to the heart that grieves.

In my darkest hour alone I die,
Exist no more, no more can I.

Cast off by you, you selfish souls,
And never yet my pain be told.

Resentful? Yes of that I am,
As sure as the Lord made man.

Unnoticed I'll go and who will care,
Of a lonely lost soul without a prayer.

No thanks to give but sour am I,
As here I wait alone to die.

Bonny Metin

Afterthought

There is more to love, my lady said,
Than your hand on my breast in this hotel bed,
With breakfast late,
A view of the sea
And love for lunch
And a snooze till tea,
A stroll on the beach
Till it's time to dine,
Canard saute,
A glass of wine,
With Chopin's Third
On that violin
And wasn't God clever
To think of skin!
There's far more to it, my lady said,
Now come with me. It's time for bed.

There's more to love, my lady said,
Her eyes a-brim with tears.
Please think of things that you can say
To drive away my fears.

John Bennett

"An Invisible Bond"

A touch, a smile, a warm embrace
The brush of his hand against my face
An invisible bond that all can see
Runs between my man and me

An unspoken word, a gentle kiss
A stolen glance, a moment's bliss
A world for just the two of us
Where past and future turn to dust

Passion sublime is his and mine
Where body and soul entwine
'Twas destiny we met that day
Upon life's troubled highway

Twenty years on, the love's still strong
Together, forever, we belong
An invisible bond that all can see
Still runs between my man and me.

Josephine Ellicott

Pretty Paper Gifts and Bows

There are pretty paper gifts and bows
beneath the Christmas tree
but let us not forget my friends
how Christmas came to be.

Some mistletoe, a glass of wine?
Hoorah it's present opening time.

I'll make no move for there'll not be
a parcel there I'd care to see
the gift of love and life itself
Is gift enough for me.

Julie Cross

Untitled

How deep, how deep
the endless toil that only sleep may hide,
the longing to rest without guilt.
Freedom to end the strain of life
to thin, to lie, to sleep.

To end the turmoil of hopelessness
and smile again without the burden of life.

The exhaustion of tears of loneliness
the fear of control slipping, edging away,
the darkness of another day;

Then night and peace, the moments of release,
enfold me once again,
please sleep, please sleep . . .

Helen Marshall

151

Images of the City

City grime all around,
The cat on the kerb-way which has just been knocked down,
The old woman lying with blood running down her face,
The mugger running off into the night who
will disappear without a trace

The tramp gathering paper for his bed,
The young boy on heroin who has just been found dead,
The girl on the corner plying her trade,
Hoping that someone will pay to get laid.
This is the city.

Andrea Austin

Turning the Corner

There's a corner further down the road
that's waiting to be turned.
Although it can't be seen from here
it's waiting,
still.

There's a question begging,
"Do you know why they've forgotten me?
Perhaps I can't be seen from here;
but I'll wait,
still."

For a million hungry children
And a hundred million more,
The corner must be in the way.
They're waiting.
Still.

Evelyn Warlow

You'll Find God

You'll find God in the drop of rain
That runs down your window pane
God is in the baby's cry
In the tender Mother's smile
Look into the pansy's face
When you smell June's sweet perfume
When the rose is wet with dew
You'll find God in these things too
In the wind, and in the waves
In our nights, and in our days
In the stars and in the moon
When you watch sunrise at dawn
When you see the growing corn
Even under winter's snow
God is where seeds are sleeping
Their vital spark is in His keeping
When each person serves their brother
Giving love to one another
Omnipresent, God is life, God is love

Iris Ballard

Cosmophobia

There are tiny black holes in my mattress
That sneak out at night and suck in my flesh
Exchanging me with my double in a parallel universe.

Neutrinos continually bombard my brain
And gluons gather to gum up my ganglia
Destroying the memories I never will have.

Galactic clusters send out their gravitons
To charm me quirkily with beautiful snarks
And make me feel quantumly strange.

Hadrons, muons, pions, mesons
Protons, neutrons, gamma rays
Hubble bubble, stellar trouble
Dogs me all my days.

Leptons leap out from clouds of dark matter
And send me in a spin
Thank God I'm a well-balanced Libran.

Watch out! A posse of positrons!

Douglas J. O'Neale

The Mists of Time

There is only one creator,
That uses just one tool.
Science of the universe,
Boundless space it does traverse.
Science that can at will,
Take the atoms, use its skill.
Creative force that is so great
A universe it did create.
The atoms of our space were used,
Into a central mass then fused.
The mass was split, our space was lit.
Time had begun to pass.
Man has forgotten,
How science did create.
From chemicals that were at hand,
Creatures that would procreate.
Prototypes just a few,
From which many species grew,
Creatures of the land and sea.
And humanity.

Edwin Gallup

I Strayed into Your Arms

I strayed into your arms and I found heaven there,
The angels sang a hymn for us alone to share,
To me, your voice is like a haunting melody
The words are soft, and sweet, when you say you love me,
I love you more than I have ever loved before,
When I met you I opened Heaven's door
Forever in my heart, that's where you'll be,
Through all the years, this love will last eternally.

Campanula Downes

To You Who Could Change the World

And will it always be the same
That what you want will ever change
And what you have is not enough
And this normality is strange?
When all the things that are around you
Suffocate as they surround you
There is nothing left to look to;
There is wrong in every age.
And it is their fault never yours
For they are always wanting more
And you will sacrifice your life
For all the wars they make you wage.
No they will never see your logic
They will ever try to crush it
They will laugh and disregard you
As you fumble in your rage.
But do not let them push you under,
All that's wrong will come asunder
And when justice rolls like thunder
There will dawn a brand new age.

Holly Goose

The Wishing Well

What is a wishing well?
Something to wish for,
But must not tell,
As you make a wish
What does it mean,
Maybe a fantasy, maybe a dream,
As you throw in your pebble,
And watch the ripple, as far as you can see,
Down, down it goes,
To the bottom of the well,
Listen, it sounds like a tinkering bell
What is it you're wishing for?!
Many things you may be sure,
So make three wishes,
And you will find,
Your dreams may all come true,
As a wishing well will never tell,
Whatever is in store for you!!!.

Joyce Farmer

Dawn (During a Sleepless Night)

At 4 a.m. on a midsummer's day,
The birds are awake and are now singing.
The dawn is breaking; it's getting lighter;
The joys of a new day it is bringing.

At 5 a.m. on a midsummer's day,
I say bye to the stresses of the night.
I switch off the light and pull back the drapes,
And gaze at our Square now bathed in sunlight.

Anita Comerford

Special Friendship

If God is love - Is not love Divine?
   That which we had for each other
   That which we did not will
Was it not part of the Great Divine
   Dwelling within us?
As through our eyes - The windows of our souls -
   We beheld each other.
In the stillness of that moment
   Deep called to deep,
      We responded.
Our souls were knit together,
   Souls of two boys
In the deepest bond of love.

Twenty-three years since physical parting
   In that dread parting
      Part of me died!
But Divinity born within me at our meeting
   Lives on!
So — Dearest I love you still.
   Because our love is Divine.

Julian Howell

Untitled

There are fairies at the bottom of my garden,
that's what my friend said to me.
And if we venture out quietly
we might be lucky to see.
We silently crept across the grass,
looking for signs of life.
You have to believe to see them you know,
her words were sharp as a knife.
But I don't believe in fairies,
I thought as I walked along.
Was this the day to change my mind,
when I would be proved wrong.
Then what I thought I saw was a magical sight,
as fairies danced and flew,
they smiled and laughed enjoyed themselves,
and all at once I knew.
That if you don't believe in fairies,
and the magic that they do,
You're missing one of life's treasures,
for they won't come true for you.

Bridget King

Love's Gift

A baby's smile is a wondrous thing,
The first word he utters has a magical ring.
The tiny fingers that clasp your own,
This little treasure is yours alone.
His first steps are taken on tottery feet,
Your heart fills with pride, life is so sweet.
You vow not to spoil him in a million years,
Then it happens, a fall, then a kiss for the tears.
A little cuddle, a little squeeze,
That is not spoiling him, if you please.
School days are here, your little one has grown,
Off to School, 'I will miss him' you moan.
Your baby is now a happy young child,
He may have a tantrum, be it only mild;
But you would not be without him, of that I am sure,
In fact, if it comes to it, you would like one more.

Daphne Nurcombe

Sacred Aspiration

I can sense your presence
the air is filled with the scent of the blossom
on a hot summery night
you appear in sight like an angel covered in white satin
shiny and live like a sparkle of light
and the moment holds still
I can almost reach out and touch your warmth
so graceful like a fire
dancing in air
on a cold wintry night
like the melting in the heat of a mountain so pure
like water running in the veins of a leaf so vital
You're enchanting
You're gentle
I can sense your presence
when the sacred inspiration
brings you back like a queen
wrapped in the arms of a white southerly cloud
I can feel you're the essence.

Elaine Rice

Why!

We had just returned from a funeral
The fact is, we hadn't been long,
But as soon as we opened the front door
We knew that something was wrong.

The window of the kitchen was open
And glass was all over the floor.
A feeling of numbness came over all
As we opened the living room door.

They'd taken everything of value
The recorder, the stereo, the lot.
Been upstairs, smashed all the toys
What a weird sense of humour they've got.

The police came, but didn't hold much hope
And the neighbours never heard a sound.
It's not that things have been stolen
It's knowing that someone's been around.

The next thing is an alarm system
But then perhaps others might scoff,
But to you who broke into my house
I hope your "bleeding" fingers drop off.

Geoff Buckby

Untitled

The fear of life, when two people meet.
The fear of the unknown, as they
walk down the street.
Just because of who they are,
they won't give each other a chance
before they even meet
But when they do, they are
scared of what each other are
really like
So they just run and hide

Emma Thwaites

Living in the Town

I remember the trees, that were so green,
The flowers, streams, and all I've seen,
The countryside, that I well know,
In winter, covered, with pure white snow,
In summer, golden, sometimes green
These things here, are never seen.

Never, shall I see the rain
And find it beautiful again,
See the birds, and hear then sing,
Or listen, to the church bells ring.
To walk through fields of uncut grasses,
I grow more blind, as each day passes.

Irene Costello

153

Sonnet M

Burgeoning over English fields
The monstrous highways violates,
Its acreage no harvest yields
It garners not but dissipates;
By man, for man, tribute to speed,
Sprawls across hills and rolling downs,
Outrageous monument to greed
On concrete stilts struts over towns.
In parallel monotony
Six lanes exposed to sun and breeze;
Six lanes, exquisite irony,
Once rutted paths beneath the trees.
Now when the fog rolls from the hills
Shrouding the lanes, the monster kills.

Doris Snape

Sounds

There are evocative sounds,
The distant hum of planes
The plaintive call of the gulls
The chug, chug of the power boats
And the nostalgic ringing bells.

Sounds can conjure up strong memories,
Just as perfumes can do,
Reminder of youth and holidays,
The old steam trains puffing,
As into stations they did draw.

Why do sounds awake feelings?
It is a memory of thought,
Why does it feel sad when one listens?
An old longing brought about?

For a moment one's senses are caught
But the sound I like best is the sea,
As it froths on the shore
Or crashes against rocks and whirls back,
white horses I could listen for evermore.

Anna Parkhurst

For My Father

Death was so very easy after all:
The halt, the blackout and the gentle fall
Onto one side and gone, no sound,
The floating up above and looking down -
Reception lady, anxious, calling in
The doctor; then the check - no life, the end;
Faint motions as to help you to recover,
Knowing that this was best, all over -
So easy that you wondered why
It took so long for you to dare to die.
You watched them move the body soft away,
No thought to stay,
Gratefully sank through the meridian way
Into the brilliant day.

Bridget Taylor

Sounds

The rumbling of a mountain stream, its gurgling over stones
The clatter of an unlocked gate. The wind that sighs and moans,
Bacon spitting on the stove! Click Clack of heels on wood!
Grazing munch of cows in fields, of wellingtons squelching mud.

Chimes of ice cream vendors, a peacock's eerie cry!
Flap and crack, as flag unfurls. A lover's heartfelt sigh.
The bark at dawn of hungry fox, male voices in a choir,
Hammer, and nails fix wooden box. Hiss and crackle of a fire.

Scratch on paper, of student's pen, a squirrel's angry chatter!
Click of coins, in busy till, cutlery noise on platter.
Whirr, and screech of landing plane, a telephone's urgent ring!
Pigeons cooing happily. The lark that soars to sing.
This world is full of myriad sounds,
So different each to me,
Sometimes they bring laughter, and tears you must agree
But I thank God, as each day comes,
That I can hear and see.

Ethel McColl

John Chapter 10 (In Memory of a Special Teacher)

The road was dark and lonely,
The moon her watch did keep.
And in a field, a light did shine,
A shepherd with his sheep.

Perhaps one had gone missing,
A small lamb gone astray.
I wondered just how long he'd search?
Till breaking of the day?

Whatever was the reason,
Through the field that night he'd climb.
And this fact, oh so obvious,
His flock more precious than his time.

Of one thing this reminded me,
In a world so full of strife.
That we too have a shepherd,
But for us - He gave His life.

Christina Wallace

Everything Has a Use

The stars are the lights for the owl to see
The seed is the life of a beautiful tree.
The shepherd is the keeper of his sheep.
The sandman's the man who puts us to sleep.
The king of weather makes the winds really blow.
Mother Goose is the one who lets down the white snow.
The sun is the gift that brightens the day.
The lady of spring takes care of March, April and May.

Alexandra Moira Kaley

Memories of Summertime

Pink and white, seeking light
The dog rose sprawls o'er ash and elder,
Creamy flowers, hedgerow bowers
Shelter nested wren in gelder.
Speckle-breasted fledgling robin shrieks for succour,
Russet mother moistens clay throughout another day;
He will not stay forever.
Crystal rivulet winding alongside rustic lane,
Water finding way of least resistance in restless search for plain.
Bullrushed pool, in cool and silent deeps
Shubunkin glides, trout leaps,
Predatorial egrets stalk and strike,
Levanting birds before marauding pike.

Strong and weak,
To balance - nature's right;

Pervasive carrion . . .
The musk rose sweetly scents the darkening night.

David Harris

Airborne

Running free in the night.
The clouds create their formation of fantasy,
Behind the background of the bright coloured sky.
There's an eclipse of wonder sparkling in my eyes.
It's the flight of the fairies.
Their flight takes place through the trees.
Their wings glide them through the air,
Avoiding a crash allowing them to skim each tree.
You can hear them giggle as they race around.
Their coloured lights circle me, they're all around.
I can feel the wisps of air from their fluttering wings.
They're so petite and delicate.
They're full of sheer beauty.
Each detail is microscopic.
As they circle me around and around,
I feel a tingly feeling starting from my head all the way down.
My back starts to tickle, and my skin starts to sparkle.
My body begins to tense and I feel myself shrinking.
I force myself into a ball, I extend myself and look around.
My wings begin to flutter and I'm airborne off the ground.

Alison Landes

The Fading Shadow

I walk into the dark, dark room. A shadow lies there before me.
The shadow faces me.
It looks full of unhappiness, yet full of life.
I take pity on it.
I say to the shadow "Come let me see you"
No reply.
I set about a conquest, but at the moment it seems to fail
I say yet again,
"Why do you listen to my words, yet ignore what I have to say?"
No reply again.
"I help you but you refuse to help me."
No reply yet again.
The light dawns, the shadow fades.
That shadow is me.
My life is good the shadow fades even more.
I feel lonely but loved.
I will try to conquer the wrong.
I am this no more.

Clifford David Challinor

The Smile

One first sees the smile, not the face, at the start.
Then the light in the eyes, and the soft lips, as they part;
The crinkled skin at the side of the eyes.
That deepen as the smile grows wide.
A smile is the most infectious thing,
It makes one feel, like a bird on a wing.
The warmer the smile, the higher one flies.

A feeling of pleasure, as one reaches the skies.

Alicia Proctor

Believe Me

M.E. is not an illness, they say it's all in the mind
Then why am I so weak and tired, with everything a 'Grind?'
If it's all imagination, why when I wash my hair,
Have I to rest all day in bed, with muscle pains to bear.

They said it was a virus, left over from the 'Flu
"Take Aspirin and drink plenty, stay in bed a day or two"
That was long ago, after "cures" tried and tested
But I still have the "Dreaded syndrome", oh how I detest it.

I can't do things that others do, like plan a trip to town,
I don't know if I'll have the strength, it really gets me down
Simple tasks I used to do, I struggle now to try,
'Cause everything's a "Marathon" and yet I know not why.

I know a girl of sweet sixteen who lost three teenage years,
spent two years in a wheelchair, her young life full of fears
but Carole has decided, that she must now fight back
she is now on her feet again, planning "the attack",

We pay tribute to our families, who've tended us with care
And to the friends who've helped us, our aches and pains to bear
To the doubters of our illness who come from far and near
We don't want to send the message - "wish you were here!"

Harry Gibb

Around the Bonfire

Come join the gathering everyone
The fire is warm the flames are bright
Just sit or stand the choice is yours
Evening is the time for peace and quiet

A story I will tell you now.
Of our love for the land, this ground
Our pride in everything that grows
Love of the sky, the stars around

They are the mighty spirits that guide
And tell us how we must survive
Just watch those flames a-leaping high
And thank your God you are alive

All things are taught to us today
Our feelings conveyed in all we do
You are an artist in what you create
Work hard at it, there is a place for you.

Jessie Berry

The Desolate Farm

Beneath the scaring face of the July sun
The moor slumbers sated with warmth
upon its threshold stands a desolate farm
memories lost in its everlasting charm

What secrets did it behold?
What stories were to be told?
Who had dwelled within its walls?
Had the sturdy oak tree stood there so tall?

Had destructive winds howled amongst the
weather-beaten stones?
Had dark secrets been whispered so very long ago?
Had thunderous storms raged in the skies above?
By the pineside were there spoken gentle words of love?

Peering into the darkness of an empty room
I feel a shiver of loneliness within its gloom
For a moment the cottages memories I share.
Then I stride away to leave it there.

Abigail Helen Stinchcombe

"My Secret"

I think I am in love,
The beauty of it, is like a dove,
I want to hold your hand in mine,
Oh, just one more time!
I will never tell anyone,
For what's done, is now done!
I will not regret it, as long as I live,
Please say something,
I can't stand all of the grief,
People look at me in the face,
My life runs at a steady pace,
For beauty is there in every way,
Like a flower, blooming in May,
I need a little help in life,
I cannot forgive what happened that night,
When we held each other tight,
You will not speak to me indelibly,
I suffer so much incredibly,
If you cannot love me, let me know,
"I LOVE YOU," but can't let it show.

Hannah Moger

Daybreak in the Woods

As the curtains of dawn are raised,
the players of the day stand tall in the spotlight
of life's stage.
Though now in costumes of a leafy green,
soon to be in a production where they will stand unclad.
The scenes will then be changed,
and the players will find themselves on a stage
covered in a carpet of the purest white.

Gay Pointon-Hulme

The Pace of Life

The snow lay deep upon the ground.
The clear bright air caught every sound,
The traffic on the motorway,
An aeroplane going far away.
These modern sounds seem out of place,
In this magic land of pure white grace.

My mind imagines days gone past,
When the pace of life was not so fast.
When lords and ladies all serene,
In coach and carriage could be seen.
Chestnut sellers on the street,
Children's laughter and stamping feet.

Though times were hard I must say,
They were happier than today.
Or will a hundred years from now,
Someone will say as I do now.
Oh for the peace of days gone past,
When the pace of life was not so fast.

Joan Wicker

Distant Drums of Change

You hear them, you hear them not.
The distant drums from five continents.
Women of the world are on the march.
Carrying banners of peace, equality and development.
In many tongues, they speak.
Heading east to Beijing.
Heavy with reports from Mexico City
Copenhagen and Nairobi.
Hoping and praying to be heard.
2000 years of anguish and death.
Producing humanity.
Which doesn't care and doesn't want to listen.
No more, the women sing.
This is our agenda to be free.
Education, health and employment we shall demand.
The distant drums of change are
calling governments and nations to act.
Citizens of countries are we, no more no less.
Peace, equality and development are rights not favours.
Distant drums will be forever.

Joyce C. Kadandara

Vision

I had a vision of hot days,
The latticed sunlight falling upon my head
Through cool leaves, and my feet
Treading the wild sharp ways
Of broken twigs, and leaves fallen dry and dead;
Of soft winds at my throat, smokeless, sweet.

Though I have craved these things,
The lonely ways of life and the silent hours,
I am abruptly aware
How dry may be those springs,
Bursting my spirit into embittered flowers,
Revealing my heart as desolate and bare.

John Laycock

The Show of Life

The mood is set, with an air of anticipation,
The lights are turned on and shines brightly on the stage,
A sign is shown and a whisper can be heard somewhere in the
background, the show begins.
At the beginning not much is understood,
But as the show develops, things begin to heat up,
Dancing and loving all night long, everyone enjoying themselves,
Listening to old and new songs, getting a real high,
Reaching instant nirvana.
Gradually the characters become wiser, but it is too late.
Everyone returns to a deep sleep,
Lights go out, now the show is over.
There is an air of sadness and joy.
When the show started, something new had entered the room,
When the show ended, something old had exited the room.

Darren David Weaver

Scotland's Scars

Think back to when you were six years old,
The joy you found in the stories told
By loving parents and best of friends
Now for fifteen children this story ends.
An exercise class in a small school hall
But within minutes the world would appal
A scene of carnage and needless pain
A Mother's plea, but all in vain
Her child was lost, her heart was broken
A Prime Minister's sympathy, merely a token,
Her child's dear friends were also taken
And God's right hand was soon to beckon.
Sixteen dead, a killer famed
The hellish nightmare may never be tamed.
Sixteen dead and innocent blood
Fills the graves and soaks the mud.
Think back to when you were six years old
And the joy you found in the stories told.

Claire Malcolm

On Coniston

We saw him flash past on his way
Then turn, to make the final bid
And for a breath the craft was hid
By shining spears of slashing spray,
Her bow rose; for a moment's space
She hung there, etched against the sky,
Then arching, on her way to die
Forcefully struck the water's face.
With sickening speed she slid from view,
A swirl of foam to show us where
This man had died; this one of few
Whose courage urges them to dare
To break all records, just to prove
Their country is their greatest love.

Jean McAra

The Universal Elements

It appears appetizing through the tantalizing sheen,
The enjoyment of being caressed by the vigorous cobalt aqua,
It is clearly refreshing observing the swirling of colour,
Dark, deep, as the water twists crystal clear into locus.

It cries fiercely with power flourishing through the air,
Lavished with stamina, awaiting to explore the sphere,
The immaculate below propelling passionately with intensity,
Whining, wailing, crudely shattering through the sky,
Whilst ferociously charming the universe with energy.

Glancing at the shimmering flash of light,
The glow ignites the coral flame of the forceful flicker,
Dynamically blazing sensually, raging aroused with sensitivity,
Sparkling fragments of colour, floating in the mist,
Ready for the glittering planet to spin.

The globe provides a climaxing innocence,
As it performs an explosion of exertion around us,
The cosmic realm allows the spirits to rejoice in harmony,
Piping skilfully with polished practice,
The earth lives on. Dying endlessly.

Amy Elizabeth Roe

Winding Down Wales

From the view I take is the view I see.
The miners march past.
The anger is shown their soul and heart.
With the jet black coal dust imbedded in their skin.
Their fear of danger is hidden within.
Why must their heritage come to an end?
Who has the right to close down the mines?
Our traditions shine like old Davy lamps.
The families of miners will always be there,
With a kind face to greet them to show that they care.
The shaft is deceased, working no more.
The pits in Wales have closed all of their doors.

Anna Elizabeth Roberts

Heaven's Diamond

Up above in the diamond sky, belongs
the heaven's grace
Imprinted on each cloud, an angel's face
For when the rain arrives it will shadow
The changing faces of time
As being in love was their only crime

The night beckons, the stars and their
rustic gems
Will sparkle in the moonlight
To make our hearts as light as they
are bright

For when the dawn summons us
We should put these gems to pass
As we all drink from the same glass
The dawn has arisen, our souls fill
with joy
As we hear heaven's laughter
Now in our minds there's peace ever after

Cheryl Gelder

Someone to Care

I see around me nature's wondrous things,
The flowers, trees and birds that sing.
The wind humming through the trees,
The faint buzzing of the bees.
The sun shines and warms my face,
And I feel the world isn't such a bad place.
We must have bad, to feel the good,
We must cry to enjoy the laughter.
Sometimes all this is not understood,
But we all realize it sooner or later.
But above all we must carry on,
Lifting us up, even when alone,
For in time, we find someone to care,
And it makes a difference knowing they're there,
Oh, love brings us so many wondrous things.
Making us happy, causing bells to ring.
So love can bring us together, making life and love a pleasure
Two lives entwined, completely forever,
Love around and inside each other.
And this is how it will ever be. For YOU, and ME, till eternity.

Charles Alun Jones

Battle-Sky

The stars, eternity's confetti for
the nuptials of night,
decorate the veteran sky
as men, adapted to death,
prepare the next day's
ceremonial carnage.
But here a sniper prematurely
unveils the inner stage of slaughter
with a crack of lethal light -

a young man better employed
in a natural silhouette
with a girl in a dangerless evening
when the dramatic unities are irrelevant
and constellations compassed in a kiss.

Dick Anstis

The Saga of the Sock

Poor Marleen has a problem, she thinks is quite unique,
The machine that does her washing is really such a freak.

In goes the dirty washing, she does it everyday,
It comes out clean and ready for her to put away.

But when Stuart starts the ironing, he really runs amok,
The machine that does the washing, has eaten his left sock.

It really is a problem that others know as well,
What happens to that clean left sock, no machine will ever tell.

Now Dot she has the answer, it's really not too grand,
Give your machine the right one, the left one wash by hand.

But just in case it doesn't know the left foot from the right,
Wash the left one in the morning, the right one wash at night.

Dorothy Morris

Old Dreams

Memories are fading,
The light is growing dim.
So much time has past, still I don't know,
Where we all fit in.
Once I thought I knew it all,
That I could reach the top.
I know I could, I might still do,
If time does not make me stop.

Storm clouds are gathering,
Blocking out the sun.
If I could have just one wish now,
I'd make the summer come.
Or I'd bring back days, too long past,
And once more watch them leave.
Along with dreams, both old and new,
Of what I could achieve.

Fay Newall

Generations

Gone are the trellised roses,
The garden of yesteryear.
A spacious lawn replaces
The tumble of cannas and ferns.

And the tall old man
With the walking stick
And the grey, grey hair
And the smile

Only one lady resides there now,
The portraits still hang on the wall,
With a story behind each face there
A life behind each face.

A playing field covers the old backyard
But a phantom voice seems to call
"Those loquats have grubs, you children
Get down, before you fall."

And what of this present six-year-old
With solemn and round-eyed stare?
What pictures for her "Inward Eye"
Does she store for her unknown future?

Emily Genevieve Grainger

Autumn

Crunch, crinkly leaves scattered across
the ground,
Brown, red, yellow, orange and gold,
those colours show it's Autumn.
Autumn has the shortest days,
but not the longest days.
Leaves rustling, going crunch, crunch,
crunch.
Conkers, acorns lying everywhere,
the helicopters are like spinners,
spinning through the air.
The trees are bare,
and it's time for harvest, apples
and corn are picked for the
Winter.
Crunchy, crinkly leaves are scattered
across the ground.

Anita Soma

Stoke Beach, South Devon

The seagulls, reeling, mewing in the sky,
The marbled clouds go rolling by.
A symphony of breaking surf upon a strand
Of iron rock and yellow sand.
Above are sea pinks, nodding, in the breeze
And sharp-toothed gorse, a golden frieze.
A creamy swirl is all that's left
Of a wave that rose, then broke . . .
Whilst on the clear horizon a plume of
grey, green smoke.

John V. Dyer

Achievement

Day after day our hearts believe,
The things that others set out for, and achieve;
But while we raise their points of score
And on they go doing more and more.
Inwardly perhaps we're grieved and sore,
What is it that we're here for?
But never mind,
Let's not dismiss our 'Little bits'
And go on being kind
After time has passed;
We then may find;
That the greatest jigsaw,
Of them all
With larger pieces laid out so fast!
Will only be complete
By those we deemed so small at last!

Elizabeth M. Breakey

"The Gift I Treasure"

Grant me my sight until I die, to lift my heart to flight
The stimulus on which my soul takes wing from dark to light.
Keep in my view the clear blue sky reflected in a spume-tipped sea,
The swoop of gulls 'round fishing boats, the changing dress
   of shrub and tree.
Allow me still to feel the joy as Mother Spring's first bud is born
The leap of lambs, the nesting birds, warm breezes stroking
   heads of corn.
To stand on summer hill-tops high, where panoramas spread
   their quilt
In shades of green and rape-seed gold and loving skills of
   craftsmen built
In ancient church, each hand-smoothed pew, 'neath streams
   of light through windows stained
Reflect on flowers and scriptured word on stone memorial remained.
The look of thatch o'er mellowed walls where butterflies dance
   to the to the hum of bees,
September heralds the coming of fall in shades of red if to tease
The nakedness that winter brings, when snow lies heavy on
   boughs brought low.
The innocence of babies asleep, the peace that can come from
   candle glow.
The changing faces of those I hold dear, and the aging of me
   through each passing year.
Please grant me this as my day turns to night,
Until I die, grant me my sight.

Christine Cluley

Christmas Day

Mary lays her child upon
The golden manger straw
While Joseph, kneeling near, looks on,
Christ Jesus to adore.

An ox and ass draw close to them
By night and help to warm
The new-born babe of Bethlehem
Who will the world transform.

Angels sing above the land
Where wise men worship still:
"Glory to God in heaven and
Peace to all of good will."

With the shepherds, let's glorify
And praise our God for all
That He has done and not deny
What this Day does recall.

The very years of history
Converge on Christmas Day
When God's Own Son, as a baby
Sleeps on the stable hay.

John Davidson

Maybe You Won't

The more I do, the less I get done in your eyes
The harder I try, the less I achieve in your view
I think I'm helping, making it easier for you
You say nothing, except to criticise.

Never a thank you, nor a word of praise
Although I'm your daughter, more a servant it seems
The things that I do well go unmentioned
But if I do wrong then I'm a failure.

I word hard all week, just to come home to you
But I can't relax, you have too much for me to do
And at the weekends, I'm always up first
Giving you the time you need to yourself.

I never mind, I'm happy to do it, to do anything
But not for myself, only for you and your well-being
Appreciation is not a word in your vocabulary
You take it for granted that you can take me for granted.

Veiled threats, you can't take any more
I doubt if I can, for much longer
Maybe then you'll realize how much I love you
Sadly, maybe you won't.

Debi Povey

Moon Shadows

The nights are getting longer
The nights are drawing in,
I hope you will be with me to share the long evenings.
I need your arms around me,
Your love to keep me warm,
Your lips to kiss my body, to comfort and to calm.
I need you very much my love.
I wish that you were here,
I need to know you need me too
Always so sincere.
And now the night must come and go,
I hope it passes soon
For tomorrow is another day I long to be with you.

Donna C. Jones

Realisation

On a cold Monday morning I find it difficult to rise,
The man on the radio says there has been another killing
Inflation is up again, but spirits are down
And all this before I open my eyes.
I stay a while longer and ponder the state of this world in
   which I live.
And when finally I stumble from my protective womb
I bend to kiss the softness of my child's cheek,
Outside begins the bustle of another week.

In the garden the fat birds are building homes voraciously for
   their future young,
A bright yellow crocus has stabbed through the darkness of
   another year.
The man on the radio is still talking of gloom,
Yet if he stood beside me here in my room,
He would see that the state of the world in which we live
Is amazingly rich yet beautifully simple
Yes, it's time to get going now, time to embrace
Time maybe to greet each day with a smile on my face?

Angela Minos

Euthanasia

This bed becomes a sea of pain
The nurse comes in, a jag again
Two minutes pass, two days it seems
Ah'll soon be in the land o'dreams
Ma visitors come everyday
Some alive some died, it's hard to say
Ah open Ma eyes and try tae smile
They sit by me for quite a while
The minister, a nice young chap
Sits by me and has a nap
When he wakes up he'll talk O' God
Ah shake me heid an slyly nod
The doctors come and try to explain
The reason for the awful pain
Ah've heard it aw and wonder why
Can someone no' help me tae die?

Catherine Hislop

Haunted

The house was dimly lit, candlelight filled the halls,
The old musty smell, leaking through the walls,
Stories of ghosts and goals, centuries old,
No more warm spots, only the cold.

Castles and their turrets, giant towers everywhere,
No one would enter, no one would dare,
Hidden panels, darkened tunnels, noises through the night,
The chamber of horrors, can give quite a fright.

Voices whispering, echoes around the room,
Ghostly sounds, can only bring doom,
The wind whistling, at the windows, and at the doors,
The unsettled dust, rises from under the floors.

So if your easily frightened, it's no place for you, to be,
Haunted houses keep their secrets, inside especially,
Best to stay away from them, it can only bring you fear,
Knowing that something is lurking there, can draw you ever near.

Diane Brown

The Lovers

Hand in hand they walk the shore,
The seagulls soar above.
They smell the sea and
  hear the waves.
So happy in their love.
Tenderly he smiles at her,
No other does he see.
While she so radiant in her joy,
To find one such as he.
What need have they of
  spoken word.
They know each other's heart.
This blissful feeling that they share,
Was magic from the start.

June DeBont

Grandfather's Worry

When grand folk think, of their grandchild's future.
The parts they'll play, the sage, the tutor.
A moments dread, the eyes start stinging
Of the hellish future, fate is bringing.

The facts of life now are the drugs.
The evil dealers, the mindless thugs.
Crime now paying, it's such a mess
With guns and knives, the lawlessness.

While judges sit on their high chairs
About the crime waves unawares.
Violence worse, it makes me sad.
This is no place for my wee lad.

For their welfare I truly care,
About their future I do despair
There may be hope - a glint of solace
If one of them's another "Wallace".

Who reads this ode, must surely reason,
I'm stating facts, "it's not high treason".
I'm one of millions in this state,
Who'd like to see "Great Britain", great again

Alistair Laing

Aberfan

At Aberfan one dreadful night,
The people were all stiff with fright,
For there at an old coal tip,
The earth and rubble began to slip
The dirt and slack . . .
The dust so black
Teachers killed and children too
How would you feel if they belonged to you
How much more do we have to stand
Before this is made a safer land.

Gwyneth Jones

Day Dreams

As I lay along the river bank
The place I like to dream
Of all the beautiful places
I have not yet been.
It is such a wonderful place to be
Where I can smell the flowers
I have only been here for a short time
But I feel I have been here for hours.
I hear the birds fluttering to and fro
As they drink from the streams
I think and chuckle to myself
And wonder do they have dreams?
In my dreams I can stay here all day long
But in reality I know this cannot go on
I glance at my watch to look at the time
It is just after two, I am cutting it fine
As I get back to work
With a smile on my face
I just think of my dreams
At my river bank place.

Carolyn Jenkinson

'Regal Dreams'

One night I dreamt I lived in Rome,
The Queen called on the telephone,
She requested, that I might some day,
Travel to London with her to stay.

I packed my belongings and stepped on the plane,
Someday . . . we may be burning an eternal flame,
She met me at the airport and said "come with me;
We're meeting my son Charlie at the house for tea!"

We visited Great Ormand Street,
Important people we did meet,
Strangers fell down at her feet,
As we just . . . walked along the street.

The precious moment's now passed by,
It's time I back to Rome did fly,
I boarded the air bus for the sky,
And waved my friend The Queen "Bye-Bye".

Claire R. Ritchie

Fear

Dark clouds roll in as black as night
The rain begins to fall
I shiver and shake and close my eyes
Then I hear the call

The sound, no more than a whisper at first,
builds to a blood curdling screech
my pulse is racing, my heart beats fast
defenceless, within its reach

Pinned down in oppressive darkness
Icy fingers reach for my throat
with final breath squeezed from my lungs
away from my body I float

In complete and utter silence then
a figure in white appears
to tell me I've only been dreaming
and soothe away my dark fears

My heart resumes its rhythm
awake now, I run to the hall
then the clouds roll in as black as night
and the rain begins to fall

Eileen M. Carver

The Hand of Faith

A star that twinkles in the night
THE rainbow after rain
ARE the promises of God's love
FOR us on this our earthly plane
GOD takes from us those we love
NOT to test our faith
BUT to shield them from a greater harm
SO our love inflame

Barbara Morrow

What Next?

You wake up late with bags under your eyes,
The rain's pouring down - what a surprise.
You do up your shirt, one button pops off,
Your head is pounding, you've had enough.
You get out of the house, can't stand any more,
Your coat gets ripped as it's slammed in the door.
You put up your umbrella to shield you from wet,
It turns inside out - how much worse can this get?
You get to the top of your road at long last
It's then that you see your bus going past.
Cold, wet and dreary, you stand in the rain,
Water cascading down into a drain.
You're fed up and moody - Your head's in a muddle
A car comes along, straight through a huge puddle.
Here you are at the offices, towering high,
The floors seem to reach right up to the sky.
You find the door locked - you turn around in dismay
And it's now you remember - it's Saturday.

Catherine Lovell

The 'Battle'

With grim face and steely eye.
The marching matron hurries by.
'Tis Friday. Shopping day. You see.
Not, just an ordinary shopping spree.
With purse in hand. And bag on arm.
Sometimes perhaps. A little charm.
A clutching claw, a bony elbow.
Helps her to choose. Her bargains faster.
Now, the face, begins to sag.
And the legs. Begin to drag.
The purse becomes. A bit more slender.
But, thanks to the very careful spender,
The bags are full. And really heavy.
"Value for money" is her slogan.
With aching arms. And burning feet.
A cup of tea. Will be a treat.
But not until she's home once more.
Standing at her own front door.
The battle's over. So's the pain; of course
It will start off again; next Friday.

Eve Murrell

Static Reflections

Alaska is the place for me, as I sit indoors and drink my tea.
The miles of wonderful open spaces, where man has yet to leave his traces.
Find gold deep in the frozen ground, where man won his battle and left his mound.
The permafrost that must not be broken, as lives are lost in this waste forsaken.
To follow the whales, see a beautiful sight of glaciers glinting in pale moonlight.
The salmon leaping as water gushes, then one is taken as a brown bear rushes.
To see the mountains pale and tall, to hear an eagle's eerie call.
Watch sea otters nurse their young, they seem to have such a lot of fun.
The moose abound and seals do too, that can't be said of the caribou.
The walrus and polar bear they say, on ice they always win the day.
To catch a glimpse of goat or sheep, one must spend days with little sleep.
All these things can come to me, when I get a book from the library.

Joan C. Aylott

Anticipation

I stand upon the deserted shore
The sand yet cold beneath my feet.
The sun has not arisen once more
To disturb night's coldly sleep.

But now a cat's paw touch my face
A promise of things to come,
Releasing forces that will set the pace
Of the competition yet to run.

Christopher Goldsmith

The Boys

The picture of you I capture in my heart
The only memory now we're apart
Though I never heard you cry it's true
Still you know I will always love you.

Until we meet one special day.
My love and pain I'll lock away.
Without the opportunity to say goodbye.
Why did you both have to die.

Everyday I think of you and all the plans I'd made.
But I know now the plans will never be.
Because you aren't here beside me.
My baby sons, your memory will never fade.

I hope to have another child someday.
But I would never forget you, no way.
Until our paths meet and we are one
I will always love you, my wonderful sons.

J. M. Reid

Hands of the Clock

The hands of the clock keep on turning,
The season's come around.
Flowers wither and are reborn.
Life ends and begins anew in a never-ending circle.

The winter comes the summer goes.
The light of day moves to a close.
The dark of night waits in its shadow.
Engulfing all in a cloak of black.

We are frightened of tomorrow.
The uncertainty and the loneliness.
The fear of being alone.
The clock ticks the hands move on.

It's up to us to change.
We play a waiting game.
Tomorrow could be better.
Remember the dark of night comes quickly.

Let's get up and live life now.
Make the best of it you can.
The clock keeps on moving.
All too soon the hour rings.

Alison Jamieson

"A Love Story"

We met, and a spark became ignited
The magic gift of love had come to stay.
Two young lovers, who soon would be united,
On the start of a great adventure, on our wedding day.

Plans were made. Soon our family started growing;
Three fine boys and a sweet young daughter too.
Life was good. Work and leisure time was flowing
with the love that grew simply from the joining of we two.

Soon the next generation came to join us.
And our joys were complete, in middle age.
When retirement came, we'd start a great new life style!
But fate stepped in - and planned a different ending at this stage.

So I sit, with my memories to treasure.
For my darling was taken, - all too soon.
Yes, I know my loving family gives me pleasure.
But oh! how much better had I not been left alone.

Now my task in life has taken a new turning.
Ten grandchildren really all must learn the truth;
Of when granddad set the flame of passion burning.
When we fell in love; we married; when he was but a youth.

Eva Kelly

Life Is Love

To hold a baby just a few minutes old,
There and then love starts to unfold,
A parent's love, their tender care,
The small child knows that love is there.

The early years and through Primary school,
Friendship arrives but love is the tool,
Throughout adolescence and into their teens,
Loving one's parents is not as it seems.

Gain qualifications, start looking for work,
Falling in love often can hurt,
Loving a wife like no other can,
Being a father, does that make a man?

The children grow up, their love doesn't wane,
Love between parents can cause so much pain,
Divorce is so harmful, love goes astray,
Meeting new friends, foundations to lay.

Loving a friend is loving to live,
Caring and sharing just wanting to give,
Writing these words is easy to see,
The last nineteen lines are all about me.

Henry Haskins

The Battle

The guns they roared,
The shells they fell,
Life was just a living hell,
My comrades stood on both sides of me,
Our guns and bayonets
You could see.
The order came, charge the foe,
So onwards onwards we must go,
Blindly stumbling we pressed on,
Many of our comrades now have gone,
Their bodies strewn across this plain,
Never to arise again.
At last we reach the other side,
And much to our great surprise,
The enemy have run away,
Thank God we live
To fight another day.

James Barnes

A Painful Moment

Sitting alone, in a crowded bar
The music was loud, yet it seemed so far.
Then suddenly a feeling, of what she's not sure,
As she turned her head, he was stood by the door.
A dark handsome stranger, with a loving smile
Had been standing staring, for quite a while
As he walked towards her, her heart skipped a beat
So she looked him over, from his head to his feet.
Then suddenly she realized, she knew that face
As he took her hand, and kissed it with grace
With a loving wink, and a tender smile
He whispers "I'm sorry", and they talked for a while.
It was so nice to see him, once again
But it brought back memories, and the terrible pain
She could never be the love of his life
Because the man she adored has returned to his wife.
He kissed her again, and walked away
And each step he took, she was wishing he'd stay.
One last look back, brought a tear to her eye.
It was then that she knew, this was really goodbye.

Julie Beckett

"Recovery" (With Gratitude to A.A.)

Non-drinkers always told me they knew best,
The preaching Chapel 'freaks' got on my nerves,
I wanted pints and songs and darts and curves
And told well-meaning friends: "Give it a rest!"

The judge who heard the facts was way ahead.
I shivered as they brought me from my cell.
Though I'd convinced myself that all was well,
"In need of psychiatric help", he said.

To see me, you'd not think that I was mad.
Close up you'd realize I stank:
I lost all normal values when I drank; -
Without the booze I wasn't always bad!

Two strangers came, with Faith, to show the way;
A Higher Power keeps me sane today.

Alan R. Williams

"The Final Dawn"

All human race that's born of man,
The rich and poor, to God's the same,
We all are blessed with one life span,
The commoner, and those of fame

To everyone will come a dawn!
When they won't wake nor feel pain,
They'll never see another sun
Will never lose, and never gain.

Some pray for everlasting life,
But not for me, that gambler's pawn
Just reunite me with my "Wife",
and bless me with my "Final dawn!"

I. F. Sime

World of Beauty

From one end of the woods to the other
The robins and larks cry one to the other -
Morning is coming!! Dawn has arrived.
Trees sway - from which life is derived.

Dew caressing the face of the flowers -
The climbers growing ever higher;
To drink in the sun with all its petals
Leaving none for other petals.

The river gushes along its path
Cascading down the hills as if in wrath -
In beauty so awesome so distinct . . .
With sparks tinkling never extinct!

Awake! Awake! each animal and bird -
To a beauty that cannot be reared;
Captivating, powerful and invincible
Whose creator - everlasting and invisible

Beauty, beauty, world of beauty -
Hues and shapes blend in unity;
Awesome in harmony and in equity
Beauty, beauty, world of beauty!

Ekua Badoe

Last Flight

It was such a busy bank holiday
The shows, the fetes, the tea shops gay
People sauntered happily around the stalls
for cups of tea

The air race was at Halfpenny Green
All were anxious and hoped to win
The pilot in his Cherokee
Took off from base for all to see
and then disaster reared its head
the plane crashed down and he was dead

The crowd were silent, and all was still
No joy was left, no race to fulfil
Our thoughts went out to his family
His mother who'd nursed him on her knee
All purpose from this world had gone
His spirit only living on, and just God's
love to see you through
As we know a part of your heart died too.

Deirdre Ann Rooke

Our World

God gave us this wonderful world
The sun, the moon, the stars, and the sky above
The sea to sail, fish and swim in
The land to build and grow on
The trees, the flowers and the air that we breath.

So please don't destroy this wonderful world
With pollution, war and greed.
Let's make our world a wonderful place to live in.
It's not ours to keep.
We must save it for our next generation.

Carole Digby

The Antique Shop

Heavy with the smell of musty memories,
the silent echo of faded years
moving quietly through dust-covered displays
of simple reminders, private trinkets
and unapologetic trivia.

Out-of-print books cherishing handwritten messages -
photographs of strangers once so familiar -
lacework draped delicately
over the shoulders of time.

This is the ageless jumble of lives, that
taunts and teases our speculation -
but keeps secret the truths we can
never touch.

Catherine O'Rourke

Untitled

This is my first day without you.
The sun is shining. It's a bit cold perhaps,
but a 'Winter Wonderland' nonetheless.
And I, like Alice, am displaced and disproportioned
In a one-size-fits-all world.

This is my first day without you.
Yesterday was much like this, only
Yesterday I was one, being two.
I love you and that's why
My first day without you simply isn't a day at all.

"Cut off their heads!"
I wish I could cut off my own
And feed it unfeeling in to the gaping
jaws of your cheshire contradiction.

This is your first day without me.
The sun is shining. The frost.
A bit cold perhaps.

Are you displaced, disproportioned?

Or mending and finding another second half?
After all, one size fits all.

Amber Batty

Second Marriage

He says his love for me has died
The pain the shock I try to hide
I know it's calming words I utter
But inside chaos, my heart's a flutter

There's someone else you surely know,
And to her arms I must now go
She's twenty-four with baby son,
He calls me Daddy - life's just begun

Through my tears, I beg him to stay
We are forty six now - any day,
As he tries to turn back time
The hurt he's caused it's such a crime

I see him sometimes driving his bus
I walk on by without a fuss
Grey hair at his temple shows
I love him still God only knows.

Two years have slowly passed on by
One time I thought I'd surely die,
They're married now and full of joy
For her for him and her little boy.

Janice Dean

Beneath the Waves

Not a ripple's on the water, not a creature stirring there,
The sky is clear and cloudless not a raindrop in the air.
A misty haze has settled just above the glassy sea,
The only thing that's moving are the leaves upon the tree.

Suddenly it happens and the sea begins to part,
A large black fin emerges, there's a lurching in my heart.
This creature is enormous, it's so black and almost daunting,
Emerging from the ocean with an eerie sound that's haunting.

A body slowly breaks the waves, its eyes are open wide,
The creature takes in all it sees, it rules the sea with pride.
A Killer Whale - Looks threatening and his size is viewed with fear,
When really he's a gentle giant, his beauty brings a tear.

He glides on through the water barely making any sound.
His blow hole opens and snaps shut with every breath that's found,
His dorsal fin is towering high above the fish below,
Any that are swimming by get caught up in the flow.

Is this creature lonely in his battle to survive?
Or are there other whales around continuing to dive?
Just as though they know I'm here, three fins coming breaking
    through,
This whale is never on his own for he has family too.

Jacqueline Marshall

'My Old Man'

Long, long, summer nights,
The smell o' yellow gorse:
I sit alone, on ancient stone,
an' my old man's getting worse.
Tall, tall, swaying trees,
Stretch ever to the sky:
It can't be fair, you'll still be there,
an' my old man's got to die.

Far, far, so far away,
The waves foam in from the sea:
The moon will call, the tide will fall,
But where will my old man be?
Why, why do I sit here an' cry,
When I know it's all in vain:
Like bygone youth, the simple truth,
Is I'll ne'er see my old man again.

George Dolbear Robertson

"First Love"

Love was stars scattered into space
The smile on my beloved's face
Love was a pain of exquisite joy
Shared between this girl and her boy
The world was free so much to choose
I never thought that I would lose
Oh hurtful love where did you go
He was mine and I loved him so
But he had to leave he needed space
There was an empty look on his empty face
Time will move on I shall smile again
I will remember my old love now and then
Never again to yearn for that
Flickering flame of love to burn.

Joan Butler

I'm Blessed

Curtains are drawn it is not yet dawn.
The snowflakes fall upon our garden wall.
The trees stand tall.
Soon our robin red breast will appear.
It brings me so much cheer.
The cheeky grey squirrel is here.
It's always first to appear.
The blackbird with its orange beak has just taken a peep to
See if nuts, apples and bread have been put out.
The thrush, blackbirds, blue tits, magpies and the wood pigeons
Know there is food about.
I hear a cuckoo too, there is food for you!
The wild foxes or rabbits must have eaten the carrot peel that I
    put out.
I'm blessed to have such faithful friends, there is no doubt.
Thank you Lord now they have all been fed I am off to bed.

Hilda France

Dunblane

Today the sky is grey, all colour has been drained
The sound of laughter has died today
The smile of a child, gone forever

We think of you in that town of yours
Somewhere, perhaps you would rather not be
We weep for you, your eyes dried out
And wish your pain would ease

To lose a child is an unbearable thought
To imagine your feelings, chokes
The life you bore was cruelly snatched
With it your strength, your feeling, your love

Our thoughts are with you everyday
We feel helpless for what we cannot do
Tonight we kissed our children twice
For us and then for you.

Jennie Kynoch

The Spinner of Dreams

In the twilight, just before night, he comes to me,
The spinner of my dreams;
With silver threads of silver light,
He weaves his dreams of pure delight,
Thoughts that dreams are made of, in the twilight,
The spinner of my dreams.

In shades of night when twilight ends, he comes to me,
In peaceful sleep, when eyes are closed and breathing's deep;
He weaves his dreams with golden threads,
And whispers sweet inside my head;
Thoughts that dreams are made of,
The Spinner of my dreams.

In myriad colours of the dawn, and sunshine bright,
he comes to me,
As sunbeams dance along the way, On hazy, sleepy, summer days,
While lying in a meadow green he comes unseen,
And weaves his web of silken sheen;
To help me dream the dreams I dream.
The spinner of my dreams.

Christine Grant

My Typical Day

The grass sways in the breeze, calling softly my name.
The sun beats down and warms my smile then shady trees cool me.
Yet in my mind these visions stay, for I am trapped in a place
where windows show but sky.
Where the breeze is a stale smell released from someone's mouth
nearby. The sun is a man's florescent lighting, which makes
squint into a frown.
And when I leave the cramped conditions and all its falseness,
the sky has darkened, the cool breeze has turned.
The moon is rising and my name is not heard.
But where? I hear you ask yourself!
For this is a factory, hell itself.
The air which was once warm is now cold here.
The sky which was once light is dim here.
When shouts are heard by people unnerved.
The language we hear are mimics by people releasing frustrations
upon others.
The smells are pungent and stay forever.
The lies are told yet change like the weather.
Here on earth this factory lies.
Here on earth my soul does cry

Georgina Faithfull

Trouble and Strife

In a world of troubles and strife
There is relief throughout our life.
Strolling steadily down the road.
Slowly we unwind our load.
Watching spring flowers raise their heads,
Forgetting our worries and cares.
Watching the trees budding instead
Knowing everything renews itself
It's just sleeping, not dead.

Cilla Hughes

My Lonely Queen

In early evening she starts to rise,
the sun's going to sleep as she opens her eyes.
As darkness falls she throws out her light,
and there she stays and glows all night.
When my gaze rests on her form,
she seems so cold, lost, and forlorn.
For a score of years I've gazed at this place,
that casts down this lonely face.
Each night up there alone she's been,
her emotions I've felt, her cast eyes I've seen.
Every day that passes by,
I wait for my Queen up in the sky.
As evening falls, I ponder for a while,
on what I can do to make her smile.

Carl Dawson

The Bull and the Matador

It was a boiling hot day.
The sun was a glare
The audience was shouting
The matador was aware.
The bull was led out from the darkness
The light blinded him
He stumbled about hearing cheers and shouts.
He was being pushed into the middle of the stadium.
He felt a poke and swish of cloak
A lot of pain. His blood fell like rain.
He was dehydrating.
More pain he knew was awaiting him.
Taunting, calling, shouting cheering
He fell to the ground in the cruel sun.
The pain was excruciating.
It was seconds, minutes before he died.
Why had his life been denied.

Hayley Hogan

The 'New Heart' Baby

"An unfinished job, born with half the heart"
The surgeon told his loyal team
"We'll have to see what we can do
For the sake of the parents
And our reputation too"
They gave her a new little heart
And intensive care and protection
While they waited for signs of rejection
Yet nobody heard the anguished cry
"If they call this `life'
I do reject it, with my whole new heart
I reject every part
The masks, the machines, the probings
The prying eyes behind the glass"
Then at last, "Let me alone!" She cried
And died
"Poor little mite," they said, "How sad"
But the baby's spirit soared free and glad.

Georgiana Melrose

The Cherry Tree in Markham Square

Uncurling its buds with pale precision,
The thin, dark wintered tree slowly became aware of Spring,
And moved with living life, until it burst upon the sky,
A huge, improbable mass of bliss, a candy floss of sight,
And stayed there, static, for a while, too beautiful to bear,
Until an errant wind blew the blossom all around the Square,
Blowing it with wild gaiety, as confetti must have blown,
Long ago from the Church, when it still stood there in the Square.
Now the dissipated blossom drifted down,
Filling the gutters, sweet and pink and spent.
"Untidy, isn't?" a woman said, sweeping her step,
"I wouldn't have it in my garden as a gift".
And that was that - until next year.

Deirdre Brander

Belonging to Nothing

Count the cars as they pass by,
The sky begins to darken to pale grey.
Lights approach and zoom away.
Headlights, house windows and the silent sky.

I sit alone, owning nothing
not even my fate,
even my mind belongs to someone else,
as images are created from
unknown sources.

The sky is dark
All the house lights are now bright,
the warmth shines out.
Wish I was inside there.
Sharing security,
but instead here, I sit,
Sleep, think and pity
myself.

Aulfat Bi

The Little Breeze

Lonely as little leaf, I fluttered down to earth,
The tree allowed my fall again,
Not listening to my plea!
God help; I said, again I wander down in my despair;
   But then, a little breeze appeared, and said
Jump up; I'll take you there.

It is the safest place on earth
I call it, "Everywhere"

And so the leaf and breeze took flight,
Free flowing, letting go,
So all their cares were left behind
As if like melted snow

And never more she hoped to tell
Her tearful tale of woe.

   Elizabeth J. Pryer

From the Rushes

The wind whistled slowly through the dead leaves,
The water flowed rough,
Her lips were pursed,
But no sound could she make -
She allowed the Chin Sau to swallow her.

The guards lifted the upturned boat,
The body within the rushes lay.
A hairpin remained in place,
Her body blue through the tattered robes.

The month of November, colours vibrant,
But still the Chin Sau flowed on.

But what sound was that? A rustling,
And the rushes began to part.
From out of the water a figure stepped forth.
Pale, deep hollows of eyes,
Lifeless.

   Ellie Wharton

Loneliness

I walked by the sea at a slow pace,
The wind slapped its fingers across my face,
The summer's sun had gone from sight,
The sea looked dark, not crystal light.
It unfurled its waves and they rolled onto the shore,
Whirling shells and pebbles from the sandy, ocean floor.
As I clambered on the rocks I noticed a pool -
Small, unique, its waters so cool;
The fish no longer darted here and there,
The sea-life had stopped, all was bare.
The fringed cliffs stood majestic and grand
But loneliness lingered upon the land;
A loneliness that showed that winter was here,
A strange, desolate time of the year.

   Gillian Taylor

The River Trent

Like a great brown serpent searching for prey
The River Trent winds on her way,
A great brown snake through browns and greens
Fed by water from a thousand streams,
Looking lean at times, till gorged by the tide,
Then, a great sluggish monster with nowhere to hide -
So eager to help any poor suicides
Who enter her depths, their faces to hide.
Ruthless, cruel, cold, so deep
How many ride her tides in death's dark sleep?
For what is hers she will keep a secret guarded
Till tired of playing, on mudbanks discarded,
Her toys she leaves, rotting, soiled.
An armada of craft on her great back ride
At the beck and call of her surging tide.
Listen her evil chuckle, smell her fetid breath
Rotting vegetation, filth, decay and death
As like a great brown serpent searching for prey
The River Trent winds on her way.

   Geoffrey W. Pell

Alone

Help me Lord in the way that You can,
The things that happen, I didn't plan.
Sometimes I can't think, I do the wrong thing,
Self-satisfaction that's all it brings.
I want to be right in all that I do.
What this is, if only I knew.
Childish in mind, but not in age.
Another day as I turn the page.
My life is a book, this I can't read.
I wish that I could, then perhaps I'd succeed.
The days are so long, what is life?
Somebody's mother, nobody's wife.
I feel so alone with people around.
The place in my heart, is lost not found.
I know one day that this I shall fill.
When this day comes it shall be Your will.
Listen Lord, can You hear me shouting.
The people around me, I'm always doubting.
Thank You Lord for listening again.
I know my words are never in vain.

   Denise Freer

The Countryside

The flowers swaying in the breeze
Their perfume drifting with gentle ease
The reds, the yellows, blue and gold
On dewy morning do unfold.

The cattle sheep do softly graze
Amidst the sunny sunshine haze
The song birds, blackbird, lark and thrush
The rabbits, door mice in the bush

The trees and hedgerows gently sway
As I tread the leafy way
All of these I hear and see
Best of all they're here for me.

   Audrey Grannon

Alexander's Shining Star

I do believe for every star that twinkles in the sky
There's one for every child somewhere and here's the reason
   Why -

When I look up I see, on a dark and starry night,
A million tiny faces smiling down what sheer delight

But the star which shines most brightly has got to be the best
As I know that one is your star as it stands out from the rest

And as I stand and gaze at it as it smiles down from above
I know it is watching over you and sending you my love

You are bright and seem to sparkle just like a shining star
That's how I think of you each day no matter where you are

So when you next look up when the sky has changed from blue
Remember I'll be looking up at that very same star and
   Thinking just of you

   Dorothy Browning

The Whale's Song

The water begins to bubble and roar.
The whale didn't know the score.
All of a sudden an amazing sight,
An Orca jumping with delight.
But out came the fishermen in their boats
Mean and evil, wearing black and blue coats.
Surrounding the whale with their huge thick nets.
Making the whale pay its debts.
The whale dived down under the water.
There he saw another Orca.
There was a break in the net big enough to get through
The other whale sang, 'I believe in you'.
He broke through the gap and swam away
The fishermen said, "We'll come another day".
But now the whale knows the score.
Never to swim anywhere near the shore.

   Becky Naylor

The Tear

Wince upon a sigh mine own sigh
There welled from my feel
A solitary hurting sadsome
Out of my bola it did come
Born of my first understanding
Hundreds and thousands a gig ago
  it were
And the horse before the cat
White as the driven snow later than
  the lambs that year
And the canary she gave away
When he never never came piggy-back
And there and then it fell forever like
  once upon a time

Charles Jones

'Motherhood'

When motherhood hit me I was very naive,
The words of warnings I refused to believe.
A choice made so easily in my own childish mind,
Quality years I should cherish denied.
Innocent visions I dreamily viewed.
Knowledge of what lay before me refused,
By my own selfish attitude of what was to come,
My own childhood now finished, over and done.
But these warnings I'm glad I refused to believe,
As the life I have led is so precious to me.
Ask if I'd do it a different way,
Given the choice to go back and replay,
So proud that I am of my own family,
I'd do it the same, yes so willingly.
As nothing on earth could ever replace,
The feelings of love with every embrace,
Of my own special child, it's second to none,
If ever a choice, I'd choose being a 'MUM'!

Alaana Kirk

My Angel Claire

A look, a touch, a caring smile.
These are the things that are worthwhile.
The tears, the fears, the outstretched hand.
The strength, the promise, the wedding band.
The life together, the things we share,
This is to show, we love and care.
When we're apart, and I'm on my own,
Never fear I'm not alone.
I then reach down, into my heart.
Then we are together, not apart.
My life is full, of things so grand.
I married the fairest, in the land.
For she alone holds me, in her spell.
Claire protects me from all fears and hell!

Frank M. Fish

Scarborough Bay

When I was young and sweet 16 I lived at Scarborough Bay,
The tide flowed in, the tide flowed out,
The seagulls they flew overhead,
Some were white and some were grey, "oh" what a delight
How high they flew, they dove down to the deep waters so blue,
I looked beyond the skies so far, and in the distance
Three ships sailed by, I just wondered who goes by,
I long to be with them.
So in my thoughts I think of far-off lands
Where I have never been before,
I stretch out my arms, but this will never do
So I think of the sea so blue.
I turn around, in the distance tall buildings stand,
But I still think I would love to be beyond the waves
Still tossed about that sea.
The splendour of it formed.
Sometimes I think I'm like that sea,
The messages come to and fro,
This body sometimes feels self-hatred, I must put aside,
Hands together I will pray for another day.

Jean Rickwood

Love

A love so strong can never be broken,
there's just three words that need to be spoken.
To let those whom you love know just how much,
three words that no-one should ever begrudge.
No-one should ever split lovers apart,
for love that you feel should come from the heart.
Although sometimes love has its ups and downs,
Saying those three words may keep lovers bound.
Just being there with a hug and a kiss,
if you went away they're the things I'd miss.
I will be there forever and always,
Your hand in mine we'll get through bad days.
Love that's so strong keeps us two together
I will love you forever and ever.

Charlotte Jones

Days Gone

Gone are the days when you held me so tight
The unrequited love of all days and all nights
That feeling has gone now we hardly dare speak
Our great love has died and can't be rekindled

How we loved in the past and the laughter we shared
We were gloriously happy our life uncompared
The love for each other meant the whole world to me
In our own loving world eternal lovers we'd be

But too soon it all changed the bubble had burst
We'll go separate ways and no if's and no but's
Shattered and ruined are my dreams and my hopes
My heart is in two and my spirit is lost

I will miss you so much and your devilish smile
Sadly it's real not a dream as I hoped for a while
But should you meet me tomorrow all alone and so sad
Don't ignore me and walk by, stop and smile I'll be glad.

Iride Cerbelli

A Day Runs Out

The awesome moors with blackened stone,
The weathered grass on the hillside blown.
The dips and climbs with fields and walls,
The ruined past of baronial halls,
Now softened by years of nature's fauna,
To make a shady resting corner.

Following the course of a trickling stream,
One wanders on as if an a dream,
Of times gone past and lain away
With memories of yesterday.
The sun is setting it's time to go home,
To dusty roads and traffic drone.
Where work is the rule, no time for fun,
Is this called progress - what have we done?

Elaine M. Cooper

Parting of Lips

Why can't people smile?
Their faces hang like
pictures on a bent nail.
Drooping down towards the ground.
If only they would smile
they then would look so meek and mild.
Their frowns would go
their faces glow
eyes sparkle, big white teeth would show,
it seems we're forgetting how to smile
life seems to be just a scowl.
People shout, people swear
depressing news fills our air.
If we could only have a day
where everyone would smile
I'm sure we would feel the benefits
would that really be so vile?
So go on, smile!!!!

Ann Ryan

Thoughts of Sadness and Love

Happily married for thirty-five years,
Then came the heartache, followed by tears,
Sadly your loved one is taken from you,
Who can I turn to? What can I do?
Where is my tower of strength, I came to rely on,
What do I do for a shoulder to cry on.
My whole world had suddenly fallen apart,
Lots of happy memories, but only one broken heart,
All the good things we used to share,
You must do them alone, because he's not there,
What can you do to ease the pain,
My life can never be the same.
As time passes by, life gets easier to bear,
Little things tell me sometimes he's still there,
God may have taken him away from me,
But locked in my heart he will always be,
For the wonderful years I would like to thank,
Whoever made it possible that I met my FRANK.

Jaqueline Clarke

Company

Well you know I thought I lived on my own,
Then I saw my company, far from alone!
Invaded corners, for their homes to begin,
What! Eleven spiders have just moved in!

Hey! there's a wood-louse marching across the floor,
How did he get in, not through the door!
The trail of a snail left in the hall,
Well I did not see him, or hear him call!

Now I have a fly, busy buzzing about,
Must be looking for food, or being nosey no doubt!
Plus a couple of ants just scurrying around,
Hope there's no nest, this is my ground!

Feel one must have a party with all these guests,
Wonder what sort of music would be their request!
Now I can never say, I live on my own,
For I always have company, I enjoy sharing my home!

Ann Penelope Beard

Children

Their faith is strong,
Their love is true,
They can make you mad,
With the things they do,
But if you are sad,
They can cheer you too.
Never ever try to dictate,
It's a thing they really hate,
Guide them throu' with gentle care,
Just to ensure, they will always be there,
Don't force them to be a model you,
Give them a chance to air their view,
Bother to give them the time of day,
Or you will wonder why they grew away,
To consider others is not a crime,
Teach the children, they will learn in time.

Carole Sillince

Lust for Death

Stealthily through the trees, a tiger moves,
a magnificent sight, sleek and smooth,
if one could touch this creature without fear or dread,
how wonderful!
The soft coat, shining and lustrous,
to bury one's face in the silken fur,
soon hands will touch and caress this creature,
not in love or ecstasy, but with bullets and machetes,
cut apart, every piece used to satisfy man's lust,
bones ground into dust,
sexual prowess, this need for manhood,
aches and pains soothed with tiger's blood,
will tiger balm soothe out tortured minds,
when these creatures are gone from this earth,
someone must answer!

M. Gould

Makes Me Think

There's a full moon tonight
The whole world's nearly as crazy as I feel
I feel no shame beneath this sky
I have left the past behind
And mended my mind that was so unsure
Isn't this so crazy
This isn't the way it's meant to be.

There's a dream in my mind
It's the only thing I own
The only dream I've had since I was a kid
It is my life, my heart, my very soul
It's the only part of me I've left to give
It's my one dream, the only thing I'll share
Like a great bird flying in the air

It's the only thing that can make me feel alive
And it's all a part of making me feel new
Maybe one day I'll thank God for making it come true
But for now it makes me think maybe
God's a woman too.

Gemma Jacob

The Baby

Skin soft as petals on a summer rose,
A tiny button of a nose;
Eyes like still blue pools that glimmer
And reflect the laughter like a mirror;
Lips curved into a Cupid's bow
Which arrow kisses at your heart;
Untouched now by the thorns of life
Such precious innocence at the start
Will, sadly through the years depart.

G. M. Lickman

Snow Queen

Snug beneath the ice and snow
  A tiny plant begins to grow,
Protected by the hardened earth
  A Snowdrop has begun re-birth;
Sending out a cobweb root
  It nourishes a little shoot;
Razor-sharp - a dainty spear
  Pushes upwards - bravely upwards
Up towards the atmosphere.
  Slicing through the earth's hard crust
And with a last courageous thrust
  Emerges on the Winter scene
Dressed in lightest fairy green.
  A minute bud begins to form
Like dew left by the early dawn
  A fragile flower of purest white
Lifts its head toward the light;
  Queen of the winter; straight and grand;
Proclaiming spring is well in hand.

Patricia Surman

The Backyard Astronomer

Prepare your telescopes my friends, to scan the darkened sky,
the wonders there are plain to see, the problems, how and why.
Those are the questions we all strive to answer in our quest,
how came they there, so long ago, to put us to the test.
Select your eyepiece, swing the tube and focus on a star,
the light that shines upon your eye is coming from afar.
The spin of Earth from West to East moves objects in our view,
so right ascension we adjust to keep alignment true.
The constellations we all love, they faithfully appear,
by their positions in the sky we know the time of year.
Our moon it is a special friend, before it gets too bright,
the mountains and the crater rims throw shadows in sunlight.
The comets never fail to give an air of mystery, far from the sun,
then sweeping in to add to history,
Planets are our sitting ducks, targets moving, slow,
except for little Mercury, popping in and out Sol's glow.
Our numbers grow as year by year we pass our knowledge on
to those who'll take the backyard watch long after we have gone.

John W. Smith

The End of Civilization

Like William Wordsworth, I wondered lonely as a cloud
Across the barren hills I tread
Where once stood trees so tall and proud,
Now struck down and left for dead.

I walked and walked up and down the hills
Until I could walk no more,
I couldn't find any daffodils,
But I will tell you what I saw.

I seen burnt bones from cattle strewn around,
I seen birds fall out of the sky
Already dead before they hit the ground,
I was soon to learn the reason why.

I seen dead fish floating on the sea,
And I seen the sky turn a flame of red
That was when it suddenly hit me,
That I to must be dead.

So much on Nuclear did this world depend,
Like an over inflated balloon it had bust,
The NUCLEAR blast explosion was the beginning of the end,
Ashes to ashes dust to dust.

Veronica J. Crompton

The Last Night

The moon is bleeding red.
The witches start to cry
Maybe something I said to them
The only light, one star's way up high.

Down in the Sacred Forest.
The wind blows strong
All is in the shadows
All covered by a storm.

Suddenly a breath of light illuminates the sky
Followed by a roaring drum roll sound.
As it starts up there, to hide from my sight.
To sense the danger, I must start my stroll.

The chances are against another night
The roaring of thunder is over,
but I know that in my unconsciousness, as I bite
My food, my end draws closer.

I'd like a companion for eternity,
A true and unique friend.
But I am not very healthy,
As I fall into my sleep, everything ends.

Daniel Rossi

Thoughts from an O.A.P.

The seagulls wheel above the frozen grass,
Then bravely snatch the scraps of food below.
The sky is dark - more snow is on the way,
But spikes of daffodils push to the light -
It will be spring again.

Another year for us, though shorter now,
To walk our garden, tend the flowers again,
To stretch our arms up to the warming sun,
So thankful for our lives, for the delight
In seeing spring again.

We have survived the winter, you and I,
We were not mugged, we missed the I.R.A.
We've not been forced by war to flee our home,
Our pensions were enough to see us through.
Spring dawned for us again.

But what will next year hold for us, my love?
Will we be healthy, still have strength to rage
At youth's indifference, to vote for change,
Protest at the injustices we see?
Will spring return for us again?

Betty R. Winbolt

The Bonfire

We collected leaves and twigs and bracken,
    Then stacked it very high.
We would have stacked it higher,
    But couldn't reach, the sky.

We made a guy with trousers on,
    He looked a funny sight.
Then after doing all of that,
    We set it all alight

What a shame it seemed to us,
    After all that work and fuss,
We worked and toiled day and night,
    Just to set it all alight.

Then we bought some fireworks.
    That cost an awful lot.
When we put a match to them
    Up into the sky they shot.

Fireworks can be dangerous.
    Don't use them to torment or tease,
Let the adults handle them,
    Little children please.

Joyce Shaw

Memories

There she stands in skin tight jeans,
A replica of what I had been.
Slim and beautiful with hair of gold
What a shame I'm getting old.

Youth flashes by like a flash of light
All we have left are lonely nights
The photo album is a source of joy
All my memories of my girl and boy.

From babe in arms to wedding day
There's nothing more for me to say.
Just close my eyes and dream again
That the boy is 8 and the girl is 10.

Linda Beatrice Yates

My View

I gaze out on a valley fair.
A river pursuing its winding way
between banks and braes;
Cattle with markings gay graze
peacefully in pasture's green.
One by one they disappear to drink
their fill of water clear.
From the Flesk on its way to join the Bride -
Together they flow on to the sea
Quenching the thirst of the salmon as they go.
In the distance I can see the path
that leads to a holy shrine.
Pilgrims come there to pray and
drink clear water from a spring.
Tradition says, that long ago a
blind man struggling on that way
moistened his eyes from that spring
and saw light.

Nora Cotter

The Break of Darkness

There is no better place than in your arms
And as the break of darkness charms
Your passion spreads like an ocean
I am powerless to your devotion
My love for you is like the sky
A new star born for every kiss goodbye
Our love is like no other found before
The reason why your ocean met my shore
Nature sculpted you with a thousand sunrises
And every day I am with you, you have new surprises.
The closer we get the closer we see
How love has affected you and me.

Tristan Simpson

"Friends"

Friends that are true stay friends for life,
There are many good times, but there's also strife.
Friends are there where you need I shoulder to cry on.
They're also there to be relied on.
As you go through life boyfriends come and go,
At this time friends pick you up when you're feeling low.
With a friend beside you, you have more fun,
Meeting people in the summer sun.
You have many friends, but there's always a best,
Whom you like the most above the rest.
A best friend is the one you're closest to,
The one you know the friendship is so very true.
A friend who you would miss a lot if you went away,
But in your heart they'd always stay.
Together you go places and do many things.
Where you both have fun and have little flings.
A best friend hopefully stays so forever,
And will always be there through stormy weather.

Hannah Cass

A Passion for Time

A piece of passion,
a bright coloured flower;
Through the hourglass falls another hour.

Days flow by in a moment of time,
another day beckons from the hourglass of mine.
I turn it back the right way up,
it's just a piece of passion in the hourglass cup.

I look to the future,
I look to the past;
A passion for time will always last.

The sand in the middle keeps falling down,
it tells the time without a sound.
It doesn't look forward, it doesn't look back,
turn the hourglass around and the time is back.

Wayne Osborne

Pin-Striped People and Angels in Sack Cloth

They auctioned the Pearly Gates at Christies.
A businessman thought them simply divine;
He prayed he had not paid over the odds,
Gobbled his wafer and knocked back the wine.

Now policemen sport their paper halos,
The Judge hears confession in the High Court
And winged accountants are sitting hard by
In a heaven where forgiveness . . . is bought.

Pin-striped people and angels in sack cloth,
Saints lying homeless in the Underground;
The Bible is swapped for a briefcase: Well,
I once was lost, now I'll pay to be found.

C. K. Evans

"To a Rose"

I walked alone
The wind gently blowing through my hair
Airing the cobwebs of my life. It's spring and warmth is yet to come,
Filling all the corners of my life.
The depressing coldness that engulfs the earth, also tremoured my heart
To find the one I love, his heart belongs to someone else, not me.
He loves me he says, yet his eyes do not mirror his heart.
For it is somewhere else. I have never met her
Yet I know she loves him not. It's unlike the passion I feel for him
His, for her, is sexual, my love for him, is that and more
So strong there's nothing like it. So by the sea
I take my solace, that I am a giver in this love
And not a taker. Whatever future there is to be
At least I can say to you my darling
Whichever way you treat me, whichever way your heart goes
Mine will always be there loving you, for all your faults,
Every step of the way.
Whichever path your love and heart dictate.

E. Jenny Hards

A Story to Tell

Through the door of the creaking old house
There sits alone a man
For he has no one to call his own
Just memories from which he ran

Along the dark and empty rooms
Where paint has pealed and lain
Listen very carefully and you will hear
His sobs of joy and pain

His clothes are shabby they smell of age
There's no one there to care
But once upon a time
Only the finest would he wear

Open the door and dare to go in
But don't ever try to return
For this is a room of dreams
A place for you to learn

A gasp is made from between your lips
As you look into his eyes
For now you know why you were called
This is your day, the time for your goodbyes

Janeen Robertson

The Boys Brigade

Many years ago, in a Glasgow mission,
There was a man, who had a vision
His vision was, to form a group of boys,
To whom he could teach, the Christian joys
The group was formed, and rules were made,
He called his group, the Boys Brigade
William Smith was this man's name,
And the Boys Brigade brought him fame
For from that first company, that was his pride,
Has grown a movement that is worldwide
Sure and steadfast on an anchor crest,
Is lived up to, by boys, with Christian zest
Through this great movement, good relations,
Are fostered by boys, of all the nations,
And in this strife-torn world, enmity would cease,
We'd have a greater understanding, and an everlasting peace
If the nation's marching soldiers, came up to the grade,
Of sir William Smith's great army, the world's Boys Brigade.

James Cameron

The West Wind

Splitting the razor's edge of sky
A clean-limbed gale is in full cry;
The land, not able to answer well,
Lies quiescent in this raging hell.
Farms and cities, crouching, stressed,
Shut out the fury as they know best.
In twelve hours' time it'll be forgotten,
Except for my fence, which I knew was rotten!

Tony Green

My Brass Bed

I have a new shiny, brass bed,
A bed without a history,
Where no-one else has laid their head,
Adorned with a patchwork quilt, lovingly sewn,
From my children's dresses long outgrown,
That brings happy memories of summers passed.
These treasured memories I allow to last.

A cascade of cushions cover my bed,
In gold and pink and green and red.
When I lie there in all its warmth and splendour
I feel ready for sweet dreams
No nightmares to remember.

When I wake with the sun's ray
Shining on my golden bed,
I am ready for the beginning of a new day,
A new life, a happy one,
Another chapter to be lived.

Valerie Duthie

"My Broken Heart"

'A kiss that misses the wishes of mine,
A dance, lost chance in the depths of time,
In my heart a dart as we part our ways,
Nothing spoken, my life broken, this very day,
My dream jaded, my rainbow faded into blue,
My soul no longer whole without you,
The pot of gold I did once hold has gone,
I'm now so far from the star that shone,
The door closes, dying roses, fill my head,
As the car starts, my broken heart is dead.'

Susan Butcher

A Perfect World

In a perfect world there is no war
There are no beggars pleading for more
People will live in peace ever after
No cries of pain, just tears of laughter
The air will be fresh, the streets will be clean
The sea uncontaminated, the grass fresh and green
The lion, the elephant, the chimpanzee
Let them live, let them breathe
To us they have done nothing wrong
But very soon they will be gone
We yearn for fame, fortune and money
But in reality it's greed, selfishness and poverty
In a perfect world all things are right
No guns, no weapons no more fright
People will be free forever more
And the world of God will be restored.

Carolyn E. McDermott

Seventeen

Time was when skies were always blue and the sun shone every day.
There were so many things to do, exciting games to play.
Where is the child who ran and ran and never seemed to tire?
Where is the child who said 'I can achieve all I desire'?

Time flew and in a little while I got a job and then
next thing I'm walking up the aisle to marry my dear Len.
Where is the bride who danced and danced without the slightest care?
Where is the bride whose playful pranks made laughter fill the air?

Husband, home and family, no time to stop and think.
No time to curl my hair up now or paint my nails bright pink.
Where's the young wife whose zest for life could brighten any day?
Where's the young wife whose happy smile could chase the clouds away?

Now I look in the mirror and see faded hair and eyes.
It isn't me, it isn't fair, the mirror's telling lies.
Yet as I stand dejectedly, depressed by ageing fears,
I catch a twinkle in those eyes that rolls back all the years.

I may have lost the bloom of youth and better days I've seen,
but deep inside to tell the truth, I still feel seventeen.

Glennis Dann-Gibbons

Spring

It is Spring
And of course that will bring
All the beauty and the fun
And of course the sun
It is spring.

The hibernating animals have woken up,
In the fields you'll find buttercups,
Young animals are being born
In the fields the farmer is growing corn
It is spring.

The farmer is growing spuds
The cows are chewing their cud
The birds are building their nests
The weather is nearly at its best.
It is spring.

John O'Leary

One Such Child . . .

At the Otargo hospital in the city of Dunedin, a drama was unfolding as a mother lay a-bleedin'. It was the 27th October, 1973, a tiny baby boy was struggling to be free. His birth was by Caesarian section, things looked very grim and he died for several minutes as the doctors attended him. They gave him lots of oxygen to try and bring him 'round, and glucose when low blood sugar was found. He weighed only 4lb. 6oz., a tiny helpless baby. Then he started breathing and the "No" became a "Maybe". In the incubator he got lots of attention. Once he took a breath, to Live, was his intention. His mum left the hospital and gave him a teddy bear, she made him a state ward - didn't anybody care? But Jesus loved that tiny man and knew what He would do, He watched over him in Karitane as he slowly grew. The Dr.'s feared that because his breathing had been stopped, that his brain was damaged and he'd be handi-capped. His mother had asked for a "Home full of Faith", and the adoptive mother prayed for what the Lord saith in Matthew 18:5, where the Bible fell open on the bed. "Whoever takes such a child takes Me" it said. Jubilantly she went running down the stairs, "Look at this!" she said, "The Lord has heard our prayers". Tim took longer to talk and toddle and learn his 1,2,3, but at "potty training" the quickest one was he! He is dyslexic and finds it hard to read, but he is most determined and tries very hard to succeed. He passed his written driver's licence at his third attempt, and the score he got was a full 100 percent. He makes model boats and he was skateboarding champ. He shows no fear as he rocks up and down the ramp. He is a plumber with his big brother Lance. He knows what he is doing, you can see that at a glance. Time is 22 now and the kids all love their brother. He makes us all so proud and I'm glad to be his Mother so glad to be his Mother.

Noeline Iris Cutts

Things That Go

"*. . . bone-fire in the Dark Ages when Hallowe'en saw families digging and constructing . . . skeletons propped up on . . . fires . . . toasted foods below.*" Graeme Donald

The ancients, the worm picked,
Shot out to laughter and purple hand -
Light, and light work of the replicas.

The crooked men grow like their own bacteria;
Bleached neighbour, arthritic foe,
Their progeny create them a public Hades.

No memories say rats, say years
Red autumn needs no invitation.

Lifeless heat on heatless lives,
Greased and bloated shadows
See empty sockets spark amused.

Echo Echo the burning sing,
Together fall to embers.

I put on my witches hat.

Kirsty Moore

Reality

It arrived monotonously on time,
the yellow idiot bus
packed with misshapen faces
at odd angles, peering,
not seeing the real outside.

The chair rolled out,
bearing its lolling Pontiff
to be elevated, waving asynchronously,
to an unknown audience.
She looked at me, through me,
to a distant horizon.
Her eyes flickered brief recognition,
we understood each other.

Then they were off, determinedly,
to deal with the day's affairs.
My plans, my schedules, my appointments,
the real outside again trivialized.

Carmel Maultsaid

A Friendly Voice

I have been chained up and left to die.
There's no one to hear me when I cry.
My body is torn and bleeding, but no one hears my pleading.
The chain is cutting into my neck, I'm so exhausted I hit the deck.
I'm soaking wet from the rain. Oh! Someone please hear my pain.
I have had no food for many days and only rain to drink.
My bones are showing through my skin and my body is
    starting to shrink.
I bark and yell but I'm growing weak, if I only had a voice to speak.
I have been badly beaten with a stick, I really don't know why.
My life is such a living hell, I wish that I could die.
I dream about a nice big meal and wish my bloody wounds
    would heal.
Oh! I hear a voice, but will they go on walking by and just
    leave me here to die?
No! They have heard me, I rejoice, my life has been saved by
    a friendly voice.

Gladys Edith Von Janowski

Life's Song

Life's song does sing to me different tunes
A different tune each day
Sometimes happy, sometimes sad
It can be full of dismay
I sometimes get a cheerful tune
That I like to sing.
But the tune that I love
Is happy, soft and full of living.

J. L. Crisp

Perfection

A dewy flower unfolding in the light.
A baby's dimpled hand with shell pink nail
The glory of a many coloured sunset
The snow capped mountain peak the lush green dale

The moon with silver path across the water
The many hues of early autumn tree
The winter frost with lacy patterned splendour
Perfection means so many things to me

A bumblebee amongst the pollened flowers
The dragonfly with clear and coloured wing
Each minute creature made by the great master
Who alone created every beauteous thing

Each tiny bird winging so high above me
The nightingale with song he fills the air
The babbling brook that flows along forever
All these make this land of ours so fair.

J. M. Ball

Another World

There is a place that well I know,
A dell where fairies linger low.
The buttercups and meadow sweet
Sway gently to their dancing feet.

Amongst the grasses, free as air,
The fairy folk without a care,
Discard the work of human kind
And guard a peace so hard to find.

Theirs is the real reality,
Where everything was born to be
A slave of neither time nor care,
But something beautiful and rare.

Theirs is a world of crystal streams,
Of flowering banks and woodland realms;
Of painted birds and butterflies,
Of sunny days and starry skies.

The paradise that they have found,
Where summer lasts the whole year round,
Is there for everyone to share,
It's timeless peace without a care.

B. Skipper

The Dark Stranger

The raven flew and hopped across the grass;
A distant, careless creature in the cold.
An age of sorry silence seemed to pass,
And gradually I watched his wings unfold.
A flutter, he was gliding 'cross the stones,
O'er the shimmering silver of the pool,
As free as wind which o'er the country roams,
But tortured by conditions hard and cruel.
The lofty branch reared up at him and beckoned;
He veered toward, alighted and remained,
The bird was warmer than at first I'd reckoned,
I pitied him, gave sorrow for his pains.
And blank, expressionless, the raven gazed,
Transfixed somewhat by the tarn's rippling tide,
Once more became attentive, wings were raised;
And off he fluttered, into darkening skies.

Myra Goodchild

Untitled

What did you do my darling
100 fathoms down?
When the dreadful depth charges
blasted had you time to think of me?
What did you do my dearest
did the chill cold feeling come?
Did you have time to say a prayer
to help you back to the sun.
Whatever you did I know you were
brave and helped those less secure
With the thought of love you were never
without from Rowena waiting at home
Had you time to think of your friend in
Simoom or your hero the great B-B (Ben Bryant)
Or your mother and father and sisters at home
Or did you just think to me
Now I am old while you are still young
You'd not know me any more.
But the day will come when we'll meet again
on that wonderful "Dancing floor"

Rowena M. Southall

The Chestnut

At the entrance to a wood
A chestnut in her glory stood
Towering above the lesser trees
Carpeted in bluebells to her knees
What majesty! What great array!
As the wind in her hair
Blows her petals away.

The smiling sunlight filtering through
Takes its toll of the morning dew.
Awakened, rejoicing, all birds sing
Echoes of life, the woods now ring
The gentle breeze, as it passes by.
Carries the sounds with it on high
And, twilight hour, when all is still
She reigns supreme upon the hill

Nina Olive Du Pille

No Justice

I heard a man say on the news today
A child's life had ended, no more will he play
At his parents hands he met his end,
they were his enemies not his friend.
They showed him no love only anger and pain,
as they beat their child again and again.
He had many fractures some old and some new,
instead of pink skin he was bruised black and blue.
For this terrible crime they got only five years,
not much of a punishment of all of those tears.
People like this don't deserve to live,
a death sentence is what I'd give.
They should be made to pay for what they have done,
taking the life of their precious son.

Karen Wilde

Mothers' Day

Mothers' day is a wondrous day.
A great day to behold.
All the niceties of the children come out.
In a flood of yellow and gold.
A card and a gift they present to you.
All raped in ribbons and bows.
An extra kiss if you do persist.
Is planted on your nose.
What a change the next day brings.
It's back to normal with wanting things.

M. K. Cadman

How Long Have We Lived on This World

Man has been on this world for a fair few years
The thought of what has happened drives me to tears
People all around with no place to call a home
Families all around, nowhere to live, just left to roam

People, men, women, children young and old
For the sake of a government's argument, their lives have been sold
watching the bullet and bombs to their home fly
Looking at what's left, all they can do is cry
More families left with no home, and nowhere to roam

People living all around this big, wide world
Who were led to believe the lies they were told
Left to live in boxes, alleyways, unable to afford the rent on a house
Places so unfit, crawling with disease, people are left to die
People left without they worry of a home, or where to roam

Man has been on this world for a fair few years
A world so old, full of sorrow and full of tears
Families should not have to worry about war any more
People shouldn't have to worry about having a house
People shouldn't be expected to be as quiet as a mouse
Everyone should have security, no war but a place to call a home

Charles James Sloan

My Kite

Look at my kite just look at the height
The wind and my kite together they fight
Just look at my kite
Dancing and swirling, a wonderful sight.

It's only of paper just paper and string
A fragile, magical, delicate thing,
It flies in the field like a bird on the wing
My kite has its own life, beautiful thing.

It's getting so dark now the kite's so alone
It's danced it's dived
Its talent has shown
The wind starts to change now
So low the kite's blown.

What an exciting and heaven-sent day,
I've watched my first kite
In the wind it did sway,
Will it also have dreams?
When we both sleep and lay
That the wind will awaken
And live a new day.

Ann P. Jackson

Life in a High-Rise Flat

"She's a nice old woman" I heard him say,
A little boy to a girl at play.
"How do you know?" I heard her say.
Because she didn't say "go away".

A stopped to ponder and wonder if,
This childlike statement could really be true
I did not know them and they didn't know me,
Yet we lived in the same community
On a council estate built after the war
Where everyone goes in, and locks the door

I shall see them again at play and know that
Even if it's only, from my fourteenth floor flat.

W. E. Anne Tilbury

A Poem Based on Wordsworth's Daffodils

A poignant image,
A golden haze,
A comfort glow,
A yellow maze.

Cleanse my eyes,
My cynical mind,
Dance through memories,
Take root and entwine.

Be my dream,
My abyss of escape,
My drug in a thought
For serenity's sake.

Sarah Gosbee

The Mystic

With gazing eyes piercing heaven's gates,
A bearded mystic patiently waits,
Cross-legged he sits so perfectly still,
In humble submission he seeks our Lord's will.

On a mountaintop overlooking the sea.
He finds God's peace and tranquillity.
There's a smile of contentment as his soul leaves the ground,
On the wings of grace he is heaven bound.

Meanwhile, somewhere, a grieving mother asks why,
the thorns should live on, while the roses die?
The seeds of affliction and misery growing,
Under the shade of the tree of unknowing.

Can we carry our cross to the top of the hill?
And in the heat of the desert, learn to be still.
Can we flee from the suffering and torment we're in?
Please tell me mystic man where to begin.

He said, "make your desert anywhere, sit in silence on the sand,
Open the eyes in your heart, and see our Lord's outstretched hand,
The desert sun will not harm you, neither will you thirst,
But my son above all else, seek the kingdom first."

Neil Harris

Birth

A tiny bundle of mischief,
A little bundle of fun,
A little one to love and nurture,
Your darling little one,

Nine long months,
Of waiting and wondering,
Dreaming what it'd be like,
Would it be a boy or girl,
Who would it resemble,

On the (date of birth),
(He/She) made (his/her) entrance,
Delighting (both his/her parents/all his/her family)
(Name) has arrived.

Lynsey Bessent

Hidden Beauty

Beauty is all around us, if we have the eyes to see.
A buzzing bee upon a flower, a leaf upon a tree.
Smoke curling from a chimney in the morning air,
Things we take for granted - but they're always there.
Dewdrops are like diamonds, shining in the sun,
Cobwebs hang on lacy threads when day has just begun.
A sky that's blue with wispy clouds, a field of golden corn,
In the meadow by the stream, a lamb that's newly born,

In winter when the snow lies fresh upon the ground
always there is beauty waiting to be found.
Patterns on the footpath where the birds have been
Trails that lead to nowhere, clearly can be seen.
Icicles like chandeliers glistening in the light.
Leafless boughs against the sky, a starry night.
But we are always busy, we don't have time to spare
To see the beauty in the world, that's always there.

Renée Clegg

Curragower Falls

Thundering o'er water carved stone,
A beauty from ebbing tide is born.
Watched by ancient castle stone;
The beautiful Curragower.

Dark waters turned to whitened steeds
As they gallop along at hastened speed.
Down they race to the open sea;
From the beautiful Curragower.

A natural beauty to behold
Watched by bewildered young and old.
As it washes o'er its carved-out stone,
The beautiful Curragower.

And as the ebbing tide returns once more,
On whitened steed it closes its door.
And dark waters they return once more;
On the beautiful Curragower.

But not for long we'll have to wait
As the ebbing tide opens up its gate.
And whitened steed from sleep will wake,
On the beautiful Curragower.

Michael J. O'Brien

Yonder (But within Sight)

Love knows no boundaries, limitations or age.
A saying once uttered by a wise spoken sage.
Loves set to conquer and illuminate all
Leaving behind doubt, proud to stand tall.
Put trust in your heart and knowing in your mind.
Seek the truth for you shall find.
Love and the truth be sure to set you free.
Forever love was meant to be.

Nicolina Manfredi

Autumn

So peaceful, so quiet here in my room listening to the sounds outside.
A bird sings, then I know what a beautiful day it seems,
not a cloud in sight, like a summer's dream.
The big willow tree in the distance stands still,
all its branches hiding the view of the hill.
The smell of the air has certain scent,
a bundle of roses in the garden lay awkwardly bent.
Leaves all crisp, all orange and brown,
so quiet it seems without any sound.
The sheep all eating the lovely green grass,
chewing and crunching as if it's a task.
All huddled together but lots of space,
no fox in sight and there is no race.
Baby lambs running and jumping,
their mothers calling them and their hearts pumping.
This moment I wish could last forever,
but tomorrow will come and another day has passed.
All of which is forgotten about but I wish it could last.
I gently fall asleep, but not forgetting the sheep,
I drift into a dream but is it all it seems?

Zowie Jade Kaye

Life and Me

My heart is really breaking, a heart that you can't see,
A heart that's full of nothing, that isn't even me!
A heart that was full of dreams and hopes,
    that's shattered day by day.
Of sorrows, fears and many tears that have got lost along the way.

I read my dreams of many things, I need to make you see
That all I ever want in life is just to be me!
A heart that isn't broken, a heart that's full of joy,
A clearer vision of my life, a wish that it could be.

I don't care about happiness, if I'm so sad inside
I don't care about money or problems I can't hide.
Please, I beg you all to see,
I just need to be me!

R. Griffin

Samhuin

A witch flew over the autumn trees,
A black crone shuffled through the glorious leaves,
Gold, red and crackled brown.

"A ha"! says she, the Goddess of the Season,
"Run quickly afore I catch yer soul."
And the West Wind blew hard and strong
Scattering the last of the harvest gifts.

Warm and wild she blew; whipping the thin mist,
Like a veil on a spring bride.
This was no young maid about to wed;
but an age old Goddess shifting seasons;
pushing away the last days of autumn
to bring in cold dark Samhuin
and onwards into winter.

Hark! The Morrigan waits in the wings.
Join hands to witness cold, dark death.
But wait, for later comes the Rebirth.
We'll welcome each new death; as night follows day,
So Rebirth follows death.
Each part, in turn, a new beginning.

Nicky Allis

The Blue Fog

Seeping out of the reeds and vine
a blanket of faint blue fog
smothers a gentle lake of glass,
suffocating the smooth water.
The lake tries to scream out of its silence
but cannot even force a ripple of despair,
as the blue fog consumes the catatonic
in a panoramic coat of moist wool,
and palliates the waning water
with little air for breath.

In honour to the paramount fog,
the lake relinquishes a prize -
one of its infinite treasures;
(something dark, something dead,
full of doom, full of dread).
The lake shivers in defeat
and in the fathoms deep below
the serene surreal surface,
moves a thing of horror and suspense.
The blue fog swirls in splendour.

William Jordan

Mars

High on hilltop, in some distant land
A lonely figure moves, what seems to be a man
I see him quite clearly as memories unfold
A reminder of things I've not yet been told

I plunder through valleys of green grass and pine
There's a moon in the distance both in front and behind
Flowers are pretty but alas seldom found
Animals are none, returned to the ground

I see by my watch that time non exists
Everything's backwards with a very strange twist
The chorus sings out at every new dawn
Birds are no more but time plays their song

I sit by a pond and watch recorded events
Played back on the surface while lily pads dance
The depression is over for this is the place
Where man destroyed man now the world is at peace

Vincent Lee Reid

My First Poem

On top of the cliff tops looking over the trees
A long came a breeze bringing me to my knees
What else could I want to make me pleased?
For I glared and could not see
For I am glad for all that will ever be.

Wayne Bryan

A Sea to Suffer In

Where the waves of the ocean used to crash with passion and lust
A new sun rises hidden in a grey black sky
With a crimson flow of vitality steadily pouring from the artery
    of life
A man lies reflecting on what could have been
The pool of red grows larger as the premature dusk of his life
    grows near
A few moments of pain and then the joy again of togetherness
Together in a world without disease
Serenity forever in each other's arms

Eyes fill up as another wave of sadness and pain rack his
    emptying body
Not long now as the lights grow dimmer
Soon there will be an eternal silence
Blackness once so terrifying now so welcome

As the river of crimson stops flowing into the sea of life
A dark figure emerges from the shadows of what is the final night
"Who are you" asks the man as he looks down on his now
    dead body
I am Death, I have sat with you a long time, it is time to go

A new day breaks, bursting with life and energy
Across a golden pond two swans glide slowly
Interested only in each other
Like lovers reunited from an eternity apart
  William S. Waugh

Benevolence Beach

The sun warmed my face as the wind teased
A breeze that eased my frown to a smile.
The tide lapped away in a muted roar,
Peace, is what I wanted, for a while.

"May I interrupt for a moment?" Said a man I knew well,
For he was my Reason and had travelled here too.
"Your Heart and I have a few things to say,
A grievance that is well overdue."

"Ah," I replied, nodding my head,
"Time for a lecture, a moment of truth?"
"Yes," he replied with his tolerant smile,
"About that regret, that one from your youth."

"That ache in your heart that pained you so much,
Was us packing in love very tight.
Then we pasted moments and memories just behind your eyes
For you to watch and remember each night."

"Ah," I said with a rueful smile,
"Was she always that easy to find?"
And I noted as the ocean retreated with the sun,
The shore of brilliant gold left behind.
  J. D. Sellman

The Day's Awakening

As dawn ascends, its majesty unfolds before my eyes
A choral harmony of birds, orchestral sound implies
Dew's limped pools of water lie on every outstretched leaf
Glistening in the morning light in ghostly pale relief.

The halcyon summer's day begins after these stormy weeks
The erstwhile gusting wind today, in gentler fashion speaks
The sky, still grey, as dawn's bright lamp elects again to burn
Be still today, and watch, why for tomorrow yearn.

Part audience to witness this, the daily life's enactment
From which night's ritual sacrament can offer our contentment
The pain that's past forever dies, as clouds that sweep the sky,
Like dewdrops fallen from the flower that nature's tears wash dry.

The grey gives way to reddish tinge in these first early hours,
Obliterates the sombre night with nature's healing powers
That as the sun comes up at last, its mesmerizing rays
With healing warmth regenerates and hopeful strength conveys.

The choral song which even now to a crescendo reaches,
Dawn's silent observation by its education teaches
For day to night, and night to day, life's pattern races on
A new tomorrow always, for yesterday has gone.
  Vivienne Colwill

Reality

Life is a big parade,
a maze of twisted truths,
an illusion of faceless masks and cold impostors.

Life is a big parade
where dreams are shattered
and love destroyed.
A cage of loneliness,
where your only identity is a colour not a name.

Life is a big parade,
a vicious circle.
Betrayal, hatred, deception,
which remains uncovered all of our lives.
  Lisa Holmes

Black Heaven

A black heaven surrounds me.
A dead man's hands around me.
A dead man's eyes, a gift to me,
so I may see what things shall be.

A dead man's hands around me.
Through silent lips he speaks to me,
walk with me, talk with me.
Take my hand, I'll take you to a promised land.
A dead man's hands around me.
A promised land, he said to me.
I'll take you to a promised land,
a carefree verdant land.
A dead man's arms around me.
A dead man's lips pressed close to me,
so I may be the same as he.
The same as he, has come to be.
The life of me, has ceased to be.
A black heaven surrounds me.
  Mark Williamson

Life!

As a window closes,
a door is opened.

It refers to the symmetrical pattern of life . . .
    . . . my life.
I don't know where I'm
going in life, but I know someone cares.

Even if I don't do well at school,
I know I can turn to someone.

I hope friends and
family stick by me through
good and bad times.

I know what I want
to do in life, but hopes and
dreams don't always come true.
  Vicki Watkin

Philosophy

We have got a body,
A body and a mind,
Which work together in unison,
With something quite unique,
Which cannot be defined.

To be in perfect harmony,
On each other they depend,
But what links them together,
We cannot comprehend.

Could it be the air we breath?
For if it stopped we would surely die,
But where does it come from?
Somewhere surely far beyond the sky.

What is this ingredient?
This something special which makes us whole,
It must be something supernatural,
Could it be our soul?
  Mary Daly

173

Church Bells

What do you think of when you hear church bells
A wedding perhaps with lace and frills
A calling to church on a Sunday morning
Or even just a new day dawning
What do you think of when you hear church bells
A country walk with fresh air and smells
A stroll through a village with thatched roof tops
Or a trip into town to browse 'round the shops
Or maybe a city with a central market
But don't take the car there's nowhere to park it

Linda Nunn

The Drunk

In a dark and cold land
A drunk takes out his hand,
He despairs another night.
Waiting the next round
Hot hearing a sound,
Wanting a way out.

Once caring he's never felt this weak and beat,
He's best friend - Jack Daniels
Doesn't know it's all a show.
Another row
Before the night draws down,
In the distant mind
He's so blind.

Just like it didn't happen,
This time, now.
Before the end of the night
Finally his fight will die,
Jack Daniels won't cry,
Before the end,
He'll have a new friend.

Scott Turner

You to Me

You're an addiction that I can't give up,
A fantasy made real, my World Cup.
You're a beacon shining out at sea,
A lifeboat sent to rescue me.

You're a song that resonates in my heart,
My magic flute, my lucky dart.
You're the wind that holds me to my course,
My Christmas bonus, my Star Wars force.

You're a bubble that will never burst,
my favourite food, an unquenchable thirst.
You're an untamed tigress in my bed,
Delirium tremors in my head.

You're at the epicentre of my quake,
You make magic ripples upon my lake.
You're something that I don't want to end,
Oh beautiful woman, my best friend.

Marcus Abel

Yesteryear

I remember a walk down Stonebrig Lane,
a hedge would shield us from the rain.
Wild flowers in the grass grew here and there,
a rabbit would jump, or sometimes a hare.

Patches of violets were often found,
down by the brook on a little mound.
Over the bridge tall daisies grew
with other flowers, a lovely view.

Wild duck once nested in a hollow tree,
that was a beautiful sight to see.
My children remember the sunny days,
there we would play, picnic, and laze.

Photographs captured those places for me,
forever they'll be in my memory.
Walk down the lane, but you will not find
the pictures I see in my mind.

M. E. Timms

'Seeking a Second Wind'

From land once seen as featureless
the wind scoured desert sand
thus laying bare for dormant spores
a hostile 'Promised Land';
mere touch of dew awakened, some shot out tendrils green,
others — opting for the 'softer' life
just desiccate — Unseen.

Blow clean then wind, but double-dig,
Fresh loam I seek in fact,
and breaking old to make anew, was e'er 'volution's act.
Make unconfined, release my mind, and show you're Omnibus,
by toppling my restricting walls of Age-old detritus.

Then in this way
sponsor my need, grant me a chance to show
despite the harsh environment, a Burgeoning to grow.

From 'Proving-ground', I've gleaned new seed,
and — awaiting 'Kill-or-Cure',
of Genera I'm a student — of the species called Mature.

Douglas M. Henly

The Puddle

Your shiny face looks up at me,
A mirror of my memory,
A puddle from the gentle rain,
Reflections of Narcissus, vain.
Your width is quickened so with tears
Of sodden skies and fading fears.
Whilst looking through the window pane
I cannot see the falling rain,
Save for your surface as it stops,
A measure of the many drops.
A squirrel revels in your bath,
As he scampers up the path
And to the treetop nimbly climbs.
The puddle is his paradigm.

Nola B. Small

It Makes One Mad

This past week has been horrendous
A nightmare coming true,
Beef's been banned throughout the world
That affects both me and you.
Thousands of jobs have been lost,
More are yet to go
As businesses go down the drain
In a never-ending flow.
When will our leaders learn to be
Honest, faithful and true
To the promises they made to us
When elected to the job they do.

Sheila M. Lamb

Old Tara

My cat Tara was sharp swift and full of fun
A gift from high
In the garden, a smoking gun
Ever alert to predators, velvet paws in the house
The loveliest cat ever to grace the family home.

Tara didn't like sudden bangs
Guy Fawkes shenanigans she would ban.
She would come to my side. Tail up: purr purr
Trying to tell me her cat news
A true and faithful friend.
The years rolled on, her eyes grew dim
No more quick movements to her stride
In my heart I knew one day the vet would say
There's nothing more I can do for Tara!

She staggered to me one evening
Bade me a cat's good bye
Crept to a geranium pot in a quiet spot on the floor
Trying to hide her agony, and keep her dignity.
There she died like the warrior she was,
Tara is now at peace, her memory will never grow old.

Katie Kent

Teenage Friendship and Parties

I'd thought we'd be together,
a friendship that I'd last forever,
Laughter and smiles,
crying and shouts came too.

We'd go walking,
forever talking,
words that I'll never hear again
countryside and rivers will never flow or look the same.

Going out,
parties all about,
Loud music and lights,
Drink and drugs - I always said take care

You thought just one would be alright
I'll never forget your one last night
as you slowly drifted away from me
to another land of peace.

Laura Parkes

Seeds of Happiness?

She lays the foundation to her new life in the sun
A one way ticket to scenic beauty that befits her own
As her seeds of self-righteousness grown.
Observers wonder if flowers like her could
survive in such heat.
So she arrives and is surrounded by an array
Of flowers, raising their heads to greet her
Such an introduction in her new life only
adds to the complacency.
Doesn't she realize the higher she is on her own,
the harder she will fall . . .
alone.
Who will replace the fallen petals on this mimosa?
Too late she realizes that petals which have
been pulled from the heart, never regrow.

Advent

What joyful news we had today.
A 'little tyke' is on its way.
A tiny 'her' or mini 'him',
Light of heart, sound of limb.
With nappies, croup and teething joys,
Then tripping over scattered toys.
Your lives will change - (those sleepless nights!)
With days of fun and great delights.
The pangs and joys of parenthood
Are always, always very good.
The ups and downs, the highs, the lows
Are treasured times as junior grows.
Oh lucky babe, you'll be so glad
You chose this pair as 'mum' and 'dad'.

A. J. French

Sleepless Night

A face from the moon shone down at me
A frozen glare of glistening gloom
And wishing me tortuous dreams
It showered down silvery beams
Entranced was I, but shook with cold
The shadows cast from tales of old
So long I lay with every breath
Piercing through my heart 'til death
With eagle's claws, snatched away
The stone cold corpse of another prey
No ties I hold to humankind
Cut from the ropes which used to bind
Though memories still ache with pain
I look to thee, the other way
Cast down your rays and lift me high
Rest me close by thee to lie
Forever thine with soul to offer
Thy shalt not find so warm another.

S. L. Wong

A Frightening Atmosphere

Dark, dark was the night
A flash for a second makes a light
The thunder I hear most foul
And the wind has a fierce howl.

The rain against my window is beating
As if in a race it is competing
The thunder cracks with a loud voice
Saying I can make the most voice

It must be the devil that is playing
But only evil is it seeking
To the North, South, East and West
To frighten us all it is doing its best.

But wait for now he is defeated
Or perhaps his task is completed
The moon again courageously smiles
And the wind has travelled many mules

There is a stillness in the air
Much damage has been done I fear
But now we must all go to sleep
For soon daylight a promise will keep.

J. H. Bridgeman

A Belfast Sunday

Are you going to kill the baker?
A husband and a dad?
Are you going to kill the baker?
I think you must be mad.

Think of the poor man's family,
Waiting patiently for his return,
Not knowing his life's been ended,
Of their endless grief when they do learn.

You'll strip them of their money earner,
Of the centre of their heart,
You'll leave them lying stranded,
Their lives all ripped apart.

"Mummy, where has Daddy gone?"
A bewildered child cried.
"He's gone away for a while dear",
Her grieving mother lied.

Why kill innocent people?
Think of how little you gain.
Why kill innocent people?
Taking innocent lives in vain.

Nayana K. Cintra

My Somekind of Wonderful

I long to have and to see
a girl who loves and cares for me.
I long to kiss and hold her tight
I need to be there to say goodnight

To run my fingers through her hair
with soft and gentle loving care.
I want to feel her lips on mine,
as a never-ending sign,

Of this love strong and true,
Of this love I give to you.

And if she's sad and feeling down,
to tenderly wipe away her frown
If she's upset and starts to cry,
I'll take her hand and help her fly
to a better place where she'll see,
There's plenty of time for her and me.

We'll walk in the park like lovers do,
Hand in hand like couples do.
And should the day be finally done,
As friends we'll end as friends we begun

Lee Stevenson

All Alone

She stands alone upon the shore,
A solitary figure against a backdrop of night,

Her coat a billowing cape about her,
She seems to be waiting, watching,
What for . . . I'm not sure,
There is nothing out there,
Except the restless waves dancing at her feet,

She's been there for hours,
Never moving, just waiting,
As it turned to stone,
All alone!

Toni Knight

My Journey

Each day is a new beginning
A step towards a brighter future -
As I leave my past behind.

No more will I shed tears for what has passed,
I have left my shadows in darkness.
My pain has been lifted from me -
I wait for happiness to take its place.
Time has been my healer a true friend
to accompany me on my journey -
My journey through life.

I thought I had reached my destination,
But now I realise I've not yet reached halfway.
I have places to go, people to meet, things to do.
God will let me know when I am through

With these thoughts, I am filled with anticipation,
As I look to the skies
and am thankful for seeing another day.

Karen Lee Hawthorne

Those Curtains

Those curtains are vivid in my head,
A strange reminder of someone dead,
She went through during our song,
But to me her presence felt most strong.
The vicar said we must say goodbye,
Memories to be savoured, no tears, don't cry.

That now she will be with others gone,
With Granddad Ronald "They are now one"

That God would look after her in the sky
We did for years, so take her now why?
One day those curtains will fade away,
But shade the memories of you, Nan, to this day
I hated those curtains

Laura Orton

A Sad Ending

I used to think it would always be
a perfect life for you and me
I thought we loved and we cared
the cherished moments that we shared
Happy times, and the sad
some were good, some were bad
we had each other that's all that mattered
all my dreams have now been shattered
I promised to love you come rain or shine
but that got hard when you weren't mine
I look back in anger and want to cry
all those wasted years gone by
now I know your love has gone
an unhappy ending but life goes on
the last goodbye I'll say today
it's time for me to be on my way
Now is the time to close the door
and try to live and love once more
and find a love that's strong and true
and fulfil all my dreams which I dreamt of you.

Lynn Musson

The Poet

Dedicated to Mr. James Douglas Morrison 1943-1971

He was a poet,
A great American poet. As the sun rises,
And the light comes in, the birds sing with such grace.
As the poet starts to write
His words so true they come to life
His words lie upon the paper as each page turns
Every word has a magical touch.
He filled the pages with such beautiful words.
But these words will always be free
To those who read these will know, he was a poet,
A great American poet. The people gather at the window.
To see the poet at work, the sun continues to shine through.
The flowers in bloom ready for another day,
The wildlife come out to play
Knowing the poet, is at work today.
His face continues to smile,
As he writes his words, upon the page
His eyes sparkle with the light upon his eyes.
But these words will always be free
To those who read these will know.
He was a poet. A great American Poet.

Nicola M. Simpkins

A Rose for a Child

A little child so pure and clean
A little child that's meant to be
So full of life that I can see
She's like a rose among the trees

This tiny child so small and sweet
is like a rose that I shall keep
and every time a new bud grows
the memories of my child shall glow

I reached to touch that tiny rose
that I had planted and I had grown
But God delivered and God must take
these little things that I to make.

A bright red rose I have at last
and Sixteen years have now flown past
the memories of my child you see
are in my heart where they should be.

Wendy Blackmore

Sunshine and Storm

As Iris, rising from her bed of night
Adorns with rainbow hue the morning light,
Or from a greying sky of dismal lead
Plucks multicoloured haloes for her head,
So does the smile of one you hold most dear
Dispel dark clouds of black unreasoned fear,
Sweeps back the baleful curtain of despair
And see! The golden sun is shining there.

Yet should that smile once fade into a frown,
Its warm compassion cool, congeal and freeze,
So quickly that black curtain tumbles down,
The sun is dead, now rules a dark unease.

Maurice H. Gould

Yesterday's Dreams

I've forgotten the dreams we dreamed one summer
afternoon as we sat beneath the trees, birds and
insects eavesdropping on our intimate chatter.
Did we talk of days to come and other summers?
There on the grass so close to each other.
What were those dreams of long ago?
So sweet our talk so much to say,
did we talk of weddings and of children we might have one day?
And of love so strong it would last forever?
I remember that day so very well
and yet the dreams we dreamed are lost forever.

J. Terry

A Paradise that Was Meant to Be Free?

The dolphin swam in the deep blue sea,
A paradise that was meant to be free.

Looking so peaceful in the tranquil blue,
A place soon to be destroyed by me and you.

These delicate creatures so full of grace,
Slowly dying in a polluted place.

The dolphin swam in the deep blue sea,
A paradise that should be free.

Their future's been left in our unworthy hands,
Us, their only hope throughout the lands.

We must help them - we must unite,
Save the dolphins, a never-ending fight.

The dolphin swim in the deep blue sea,
A paradise that we've made free.

But the battle we fight will never end
Unless everybody joins and their help they send.

Raegon Wilde

Journey

The fierce wind bit savagely about her
A pale huddled figure alone
Amidst the whirling storm
A chaste moon
Stared coldly at the lone woman

Frosted circles penetrate the air
As silence from the bleak surroundings
Echoed alone
Around the empty chasms
Haunting her, pushing her on her way

Her steps thoughtful and precise
Leaving an imprint
Of the past, behind her
Walking towards the future
Out of her storm

Sarah Jacques

Silence

Nothing is heard, but quiet breathing - a sigh.
A teardrop that falls, without sound, from an eye.
A leaf drifting down, from an overhead tree.
A silence, that's magic, falls all around me.

The dew on the grass, the freshness of dawn.
The shaft of pale moonlight, that lights up the lawn.
The mountain, that glistens with sun on the snow.
The child quietly sleeping, its small face aglow.

The snowflake, that noiselessly, falls to the ground.
All things of Silence.
The things without sound.

E. P. Marshall

The Secret Place

Where is your soul taken? Is it to the secret place?
A place that remains a mystery,
Until you're lifted, in a silhouette of grace.
But maybe I can tell you, because I think I know,
About the secret place, and where all the people go.
You are welcomed to the entrance of God's garden,
And greeted by fellow God's men,
Your death was worth all the ashes and dust too,
You're chosen to live a life that will always remain true.
Angels await the time, to take your soul away,
Take it up to heaven, where in love and peace
your mind can lay.
The joy of the trumpets playing, the sound of the lark's song,
Yes, there's such a place, where nothing ever goes wrong.
And yes, it is 'round the corner,
A place that's filled with beauty, where you and I shall go,
Where tranquillity fills the air and all the people share.
So, if you believe in heaven, I promise you will go,
to a secret place, a garden where love will grow.

Kathy Grant

The Sentinel

On one tree hill, the tree it stood,
All alone and made of wood,
Its trunk encircled with iron bands,
Right on the top alone it stands,
Its branches reach from here to there,
There is no larger anywhere
Its girth reflects the mirth of those,
Whose laughter once wore older clothes.

Pamela Smith

The Land of "No One Knows"

There is a place where no one goes,
A place called the land of no one knows;
Now in "No one knows" the questions are many,
But of course no one knows the answer to any;
Like where do flies in the winter go,
Who cuts out the shapes for the flakes of snow;
Why are radishes red and round,
How far does a worm go underground;
Why is it a new born lamb always stammers,
Who teaches a pig such sloppy manners,
Why is it a billy goat always butts,
And who puts the milk in coconuts;
Why does a dandelion seed leave home,
Away on the wings of the wind to roam;
Where and when and what and how,
I think I'm confused enough for now;
With questions I could go on all day,
But I think it is best if I keep away;
From the land where no one goes,
The land called "The land of no one knows".

J. W. Thorpe

Everyday and More!

There is a place that's way down low
A place that 9 from 10 won't know
A place where faith will never grow
That place, its name - despair.
Broken dreams lie there.

But those broken dreams mean nothing
Needles in a ditch
Backward step so easy
See the fat cat's getting rich,
See the fat cat's getting rich.

And the steely eyes stare through me
And they chill me to the core
Push and shove to feed the high
And everyday's the score.
Everyday and more!

Yet nothing's ever changing
Cold - inner city view
Wrong turn just leads to emptiness
Where nothing's ever new
Cold ways beneath the blue. So grey beneath the blue.

Thomas Gaughan

Winter Inspiration

A shaft of sunlight through winter trees,
A ray of warmth when winds in east.
Spring is coming! we feel new hope -
Bulbs are springing, birds start singing;
Spring, with its glorious annual show,
Ceaselessly triumphs over wind, ice, and snow,
What hopes swell up within our hearts,
Yet we know the sun will soon depart.
The welcoming blessings God sends each year,
Through seasons of changing joys and fears
A wonderful world we could all enjoy,
If mankind's heart were filled with love and joy -
And everyone forgot jealousy, hate and greed,
And looked at the wonders each day brings free!
We might all get the message of hope and dreams -
In a shaft of sunshine through winter trees!

L. M. Dyke

Promise

No noise, no fuss with leaves unfurled,
A snowdrop peeps out upon a startled world.
The trees join in the act of birth.
And buds appear.

In a meadow, to a patient ewe,
A lamb is born and skips the dew.
Unfailingly, each year will bring
This promise fair

Nature, with its gift of life.
Cancels out remembered strife
Of hail and snow and thundery rain.
And spring is here.

And these will always stay the same
However frail the human frame.
Unfailingly, each year will bring.
This promise fair.

M. Taylor

Lac De Luc

A still, silent pool,
A prayer in a cathedral of stately trees;
Water, peat-brown with the deaths of a billion leaves,
Quietly released from aching branches
Longing for the balm of winter's snows.

The small, gentle splash
Of wavelets lapping at the shore;
Reflections shake and shimmer,
As merganser geese paddle with purpose
To the grassy bank, to preen, to sleep.

A dreamy, soothing memory
Of a place visited on autumn days,
Quiet moments of shared peace,
Of soft talk, and aimless walks
By the still, dappled, sun-lit pool,
With leaves falling, twirling - down,
Drifting down . . . floating . . . down . . . down and down.

Mary A. Baillie

Whose Knowledge?

You know not of what you speak but only what is taught,
A prejudice that is sold, passed on and then bought
A majority that is right and minority that is wrong,
Or a minority, that is right when the majority is wrong.
Stand sturdy and tall, fight for your rights
Or sit in a corner insignificant small out of sight
The victim now victimised, forgotten, ignored
I know not where I stand or who to applaud.
A society that tolerates the sin of the sinner
Crime, anarchy, anger and more,
Torn between rules, regulations and laws
Am I right am I wrong or am I at war?
Those who talk know not what they say
And those who challenge know not what they do,
An organism am I that is trying to survive
In a world gone crazy and a mind that has died.

Kerry Whiston

The Special One

You are the star that twinkles in the night,
A warm and beautiful sight,
You are the colour within the rose,
The one to whom my heart is close,
You are the sunset upon the sea,
The special one for me,
You are the heat from within the sun,
And for me, you are number one,
You are the fire deep in my heart,
Let no man, tear us apart,
You are all of these things,
And for you, my heart sings,
You are the one that gives so much,
You are the one I want to touch,
I love you, very much.

Valerie A. Leslie

Reflections

I look in the mirror, and what do I see?
  A reflection looking back at me
It seems to say you're alive and well
  For how long we cannot tell
So make the best of what you are
  For life's journey may not be far

I look in the mirror and what do I see
  Is that image really me
Where is that lass of long ago
  Who set her lover's heart aglow
Is she left in yesterday
  Forever with her love to stay

I look in the mirror and what do I see
  A face reflecting maturity
A life that lived so many years
  Of joy and sorrow, laughter, tears
And so we take a little peep
  Into precious memories that we keep

Rita Melba Crosher

The Dolphin's Tail

With howling winds and dashing gales
Across the sea they sailed aboard a ship
called the dolphin's tail. Now the captain
and his crew looked to the heavens and prayed
to prevail. Blow fair winds blow and give
us good sail help us out run this gale.
With fair winds now catching the sails
The dolphins tail began to sail leaving
white horses chasing the tail.

C. J. Browne

Eventide

Softly, Softly, steal the night
Above this quiet and slumbering land.
Hues and tones of such delight
A palette proof of God's own hand.

Silence now in tree and bush,
All feathered friends in just repose.
So now in this deep contented hush
The silvered Moon silently rose.

Deeper still in God's good earth
All his creatures ceased their work.
Content and weary from their toil,
They sleep until their Morning call.

Softly, Softly, steal the night
All is quiet, all is right
As peace reverberates around this land,
Guided by God's Good Hand.

P. Tutton

Voices of Forgotten Poets

In my hard land of the sacred heart,
  a serpent kiss is cherry cloying and red.
  No fugitive angels guard the lonely.
  Dark roses fade into polished night.

Raged buffalo clouds stampede the mourning stars,
  scatter them to distant hunting grounds.
  An echo dies on a silent trail.
  A scorpion finds my empty shell.

In Indian summer did not pause nor linger,
  rather it stumbled and cried into winter.
  Moist bones carve no new tales.
  Inside my mouth slithers soft poetry.

This sacred heart is bruised and beaten,
  by the poison in my boundless mind.
  Whispers stir within my jaded soul
  with poems of voices,
  forgotten.

A. E. S. Gamage

Shipwrecked

As I opened my eyes and gasped for breath,
A piece of wreckage carries me from death,

Thoughts of life flash before,
As I see in the distance a sandy shore,

A lucky escape from a watery grave,
As I ride upon an inshore wave,

I crawl to safety upon the rocks,
I look to my feet at my soaking socks,

As the fierce sun beats down on me,
Now able to dry from the cold wet sea,

Tired, hungry and feeling weak,
Help and security is what I seek,

As I start to think where can I be,
I hope there are others just like me,

I sit up in shock and wipe my face,
But what if this is not the case,

Tracey Julie Whelpley

Sandblaster

The golden grains of sand sweep with the breeze
Across the beach on which we're sitting still
If days were ever spent with gentle ease
As this, no threat of time could dare to kill
Our fragile love, for though the odds are high
No parting would be if time failed to pass
And my heart would not suffer, break and die.
But can we steal the sands of that hourglass
To build a castle, golden bright and warm?
A dream true haven where our love can grow
Alas, this dream would fall upon a storm
For whirling winds would take their toll to show
Foundations need much more than sand to hold
Time's hands at bay and make love shine as gold.

Pauline McCandless

Discovery

A strange new light,
a secretive light
you weren't there the other night.

To the East of Cassiopeia
Who's squatting on the Milky Way,
you lack the magnitude of Polaris
just a dull shimmer, yet you hold me in sway.

Has God smudged you with His thumb?
or - are you His great hall of enlightened souls?
as the gentle moonlight bathes me,
soft white clouds enshroud you and the light
breeze kisses my cheek -
you are gone.

Patrick A. Hamburgh

It's a Dog's Life

Through my mind's eye, gazing
- all around - amazing!
Political discord encompasses my world.
An historical repeat
of former world retreat
Birth to Death - conception and re-birth -

I have seen all this before
through chinks in my back door.
Before it slams! and I am in a maze
of alleyways and smells,
passages and bells;
Seeking answers to folks attitudes and ways.

They do not seem to comprehend
Have no desire to bend
Their attitudes so steeped in self-acclaim.
Seek the eyes of "man's best friend"
Look for malice, greed or shame:
IT IS NOT THERE!

Michael G. E. King

"By the Stream"

By the stream in the small wooded glade.
A tall willow branch is giving its shade
To a choir of birds singing in the cool morning air.
And a thirsty brown fox drinking there.

In the glade by the stream, where the rushes grow
Water crashes over rocks to form a deep pool below.
Along the footpath I see cattle run,
Seeking some shade from the noonday sun.

By the stream in the heat of the day.
Cows swish their tails to keep flies at bay.
Standing knee deep in the muddy pool
Chewing their cuds, they look so cool.

By the stream the light starts to fade.
But the birds still sing in the wooded glade.
Then a blackbird calls out to its mate
Come on, let's roost for the night it's getting late.

Darkness has fallen, and all is still.
But for the hoot of an owl at the old water mill.
Down through the trees the moon sends her beam,
To cast a new light on the fast flowing stream.

Miriam Nicholls

"Thoughts of Yesterdays"

I see the smoke of the cottage chimneys curling up to the sky,
And hear the rooks chattering as they fly home to the wood
    near by.
The dove coos to its mate up in the old apple tree,
Then an answer comes back but from where I cannot see.

A blackbird sings in the orchard, hard and long.
But the thrush outbids him with a far sweeter evening song.
The sheep call their lambs as the sun dips low,
And to their mothers' crying and running they go.

I see the farmers shire horse standing beneath the old oak tree,
And when I called to them they would come plodding over to me.
Their work and mine done now for another day,
Then I would pray for a fine tomorrow so that we can gather in
    the hay

The cattle are contented lying chewing their cud in their meadow low,
Then in the morning light they'll be up first to their milking go.
Now I smell the wood smoke from someone's fire near by,
And recall all those wonderful memories with a sigh.

Then I wonder what it will be like after my days are done,
And hoping not too bad for the generations to come.
So as the evening shadows fall while leaning on this gate,
I hope the people of today will realize their folly before it is
    too late.

Phyllis E. Salmon

The Folly of Religion

When will heaven up above
And hell down below?
When will they give up the fight
The fight for my soul?

When will I be set free
From the chains I bear?
When will I be able to
Walk out of the dragon's lair?

When will Armageddon come?
Will it be good or evil?
Will it really matter when
When there'll be no more people?

When will the folly of religion
And the foolishness of faith?
When will it all be forgotten?
Will it all be in disgrace?

When will the worship of false gods
Forever be left alone?
When will we all realize
Are gods are within us are souls are our own?

Nigel Whitbread

Wording of a Stressed Mum.
Beware of the Little Terror!

Age 2 1/2 Years Old.
As I sit here trying to write my poem my son Nathan goes into
agitation, crying, moaning, and pulling at me, wanting my attention.
I sigh and heave in despair wishing he wasn't here!

"I want dat" "I want dat" he bawls close to hysteria his eyes clued like
two huge magnets riveted to my new pen, just like a hungry newborn
hen. And well before I know it my pen does a quick vanishing act
well just like that!

I look firmly at the culprit who instinctively breaks out into a
triumphant grin, he knows with his mum he can win. I try to
fight my frustration at this intrusion but already my mind's a
whirl of great confusion.

Other mums tell me that having kids is one of life's great challenges,
and things like: I must try to persevere as my little one won't be a
toddler forever so I must enjoy him at this stage while I can.
I try hard to understand.

Watching him engaged in his scribblings and childish chatter I
make and offer him some bread and butter. He looks up at me
with silent thanks and breaks out into a beaming smile, looking
at him now I realize just how much he makes my life worthwhile
and how I couldn't imagine my life without him no way, no not ever!

C. Bennett

Changed Priorities

Fresh cut grass,
A raspberry bun,
Ripe strawberries and cream,
This once was home.

An age within a brain to age, defined through passing millennium.
Man seeks own comforts thus disguised as welfare
for the better span.
Yet, the earth groans, constant upheaval, man won't agree with man!

Supreme being shows the signs, turmoil in the rocks,
Human violence, summer and winter akin - on earth and
In the book of words, statements visible to man. And,
He observes, talks about "The Hole," then shoots up
Another bloody ton, so widens gap still further.

Era of intelligence, this umbilical cord gives life,
others through earth's sharpened rocks are gone. Exhaling
poisonous vapours towers the background to children play.
Mothers watch helpless as weaker bodies frolic, unaware
What is to come, mid slimy waters bird span struggles
In unrelenting gum. The world waits and trembles
Man's decisions, in dissipated hum.

B. Forrest

Damien

Once upon a time there existed a guy whose mind was so confused.
He hated life, most people too, within his mind the world was cruel.
And then someone came they stole his pride and with it they just
flew off into the night.
Through many days and many nights he endured hours of such pain.
Yet, he would turn around and smile once again.
The visions that appeared within his mind drove him into a deluded
Ecstasy in what seemed a very short time,
Damien you strived through forests filled with the unknown,
Even through the walls of your convalescent home,
But you never, ever regained your peace of mind or sanity,
For you shall always remain the excruciating pain
forever to be a part of me
At least you are now freed of your anguished cries of agony,
One day I hoped you'd find a little peace within your mind,
Some magic potion of which might cure this tragedy.
Oh yes it's true for the world is cruel it is there for us all to see
the pain and strife of which we bleed.
The recollection of your memory and with that gift I shall treasure it
eternally, for it's all that's left of what was once a part of me.
Oh yes it's true for life is cruel as you too my friend shall see,
Dearest Damien sleep forever peacefully.

Amanda Jane Stewart Pickens

The Great Divide

Some see a great expanse of water,
a separation of land.
A liquid border between us and them.

Some see with eyes of colour,
diligently keeping those colours separate
less they might run and change the form.

Some see divisions from on high,
from God of love.
Divisions which demand
you live our way or die.

One stands at John's O'Groat's,
one at Land's End,
surmising their distance is logical and sound
and not just fear of the middle ground
when once approached is invariably found
that one and all have common ground.

But alas the greatest distance
that keeps us all apart
is the mere distance from mind to heart.

Michael Hennessy

Of Sorrow and of Joy

I could not bear to let you go, I have fought for you so long
and all your friends were loath to hear, the news that you had gone.
The closeness and the love we shared between us lies unspoken
The red rose thrown into your resting place my only token
Rest easily my dearest, for your family are near and with many
sprays of flowers let you know that we are here.
Now we'll remember all the joy and happiness you've given
The many ways you shaped our lives, our errant ways forgiven
We miss you so but all will know, in your brave courageous way
You taught us life was well worth living, each and every day.
So we will celebrate the life, that brought us all together,
Shaped us, made us what we are, and remember you forever.

Pamela Bryan

Winter Kills

As brightness fades from summer's glaze,
and autumn golds caress the phase,
he leaves, his heart turns cold,
the thirtieth piece of silver sold.

She turns her head as if to wave,
his tears which flow reproach the brave,
th'embedded ring which holds his life,
approaching winter steals his wife.

Returning to the flattened grass,
a bonny painted flying lass,
with hair as blond as dazzled light,
and faith to quench the dizziest height.

Advance alone, romantic clown,
within your rich and blinding gown,
a strolling minstrel struck by dreams,
a dead dove where the circle gleams.

Richard Gerard Rogerson

The Old Gun Before the Fight

For many years we have carried you old gun,
And how many wars have we begun, not one,
When you were young in days gone by,
Where from red hot coke and fumes that choke
The smithies kept you fed with shot from hell,
From hands of iron forged with tongs of steel
For the very lead, you lower your head,
Your ramming rod is loose from over work
But come the dawn with damp bog mists rolling
Past, I see all this at a glance,
"Flint lock to steel," the cry rang out,
By your cherry stock I rest my head,
A spark a flash in the pan, old gun you
Have done your work too well.

Sidney Jackson

That's the Cat!

Black as night; silent as the falling snow
A slinky, oil slick oozing through the undergrowth
A mirage jet fighter zooming in for the kill
Sleek fur soft beneath the caressing hand
Bristling like a bottle brush hissing a warning
Whiskers twitching in excitement of impending chase
Glistening with milk droplets soon to be meticulously cleaned
Neatly curled tail encircles the warm, sleepy bundle
Thrashing tail of anger when teased or threatened
Pulling a piece of string, we innocently encourage him to chase and kill
Anger and disgust when cleaning up the feathers
Wild black eyes alert to one mistaken movement
Slit eyes sleepily reflecting utter bliss
The urgent miaou demanding a bowl of warm milk
A deep chested rumble of the contented purr
Slow, cleansing massage with emery board tongue
Lap, lap, swallow; lap, lap, swallow in studied repetition
Dainty paws become deadly pinioned weapons
Tenderly patting its prey before tearing the flesh
Aloof, loving, murderous, adorable; that's the cat!

Sheila Edwards

Untitled

Old battered biscuit tin, what do you hold?
All of your secrets are there to be told.
Very old gas bill, is that all it cost?
Old family photo you thought you had lost.
Diaries, notebooks, only half filled.
Overdrawn statements for which you were billed
Little pink wrist band, the name a bit torn.
But clearly informs when our daughter was born
Guarantees, receipts, certificates galore
God only knows what they are all for
Love letters, poems, that never were sent
Old smashed up watch with its fingers all bent.
Souvenir key rings, pens with no ink
From all over Britain, presents I think
A chain with no fastener, a ring with no stone
Assorted old buttons that never were sewn
What a story is told from the history within
And all is concealed in an old biscuit tin.

Michelle Starkie

Summer Sunday in Uppingham

It was Sunday morning. Outside the dairy
a tall man with a stately walk.
He had a baby girl in a chair on his back.
Her head was tilted back, hat over her eyes.
They were talking. She was being funny and
she knew it! I asked him where he had found her.
He gave me a big happy smile...
I saw them again with the Sunday papers-
the man sure-footed and the girl with his
hat over her eyes.
I had seen father and daughter on a little
journey through life.
My envious eyes followed them.

W. I. Buckland

Moments in November

Southerly wind blows fast, gathering autumn leaves,
All the colours, red, brown, russet, gold, hurry past
dead but alive in their dance.
Frantic with hurry they scurry about,
flip through the air with not a chance,
but already the spring buds are lying there
waiting to appear and landscape enhance . . .
Landscape enchanting in deepest colours warm
Breathtaking scenery now that autumn's here
Barn owl flies early, ever hopeful of mouse -
Gulls on the seashore searching for food -
Sea shores endless beauty fills a heart with hope and good,
Does winter hold hope there in the wood?

Rosie Webster

A Perfect Summer's Day

A beautiful soft breeze across
A sun filled open window,
A smell of scented roses
Fill awaiting nostrils
Oh, what a beautiful way
For the start of so perfect a day

The chirping of birds enjoying the sunshine
And gathering children,
Running out to play
Oh, indeed what so perfect a day

The meadows all soft and inviting
Some filled with daises, buttercups and
Heavenly green grass
While others with cattle just grazing away
What more could we need
For so perfect a day

Picnics with families, oh so gay
No worries, just fancies of fun and play
Oh, what a beautiful way
For so perfect a day.

J. P. Birnie

Beneath the Shadows (In Her Face)

She shed a tear in stormy weather
along her cheek, it felt as soft as a flying feather.
She follows the clouds, searching for the truth
of this meaningless life, she's got nothing left to lose.

Although her smile lights the darkness in every place,
You can feel there's sadness hiding beneath the shadows in her face.

All her dreams somehow were shattered,
like when the clouds turn into rain,
it's the child that she wanted, the made her wait in vain.
No wonder she's feeling worthless, No wonder she feels pain
For the emptiness inside her, she has no-one she can blame.

To me she was an illusion, a mystery without a clue,
Now I ask what is the conclusion, of all that she's been through.

You can walk by all the oceans, see the colours of the moon,
And with every drop of tears you cry, the more the pain goes soon.
You can hear every whisper, saying things you've not been told
And with every step of life you take, the more you feel the cold.

Even though her smile, can light the darkness in every place,
I do still feel there's sadness, hiding,
beneath the shadows in her face.

Mugtaba Madani

Facing Calamity

The world is full of misery. Mankind has chains to bind it
All men look for happiness, but many never find it.
We sweat and toil in younger years (if that's our inclination)
Some crave success, and some don't care. Each seeks his
   own salvation.

Some meet early tragedy which makes them go right under
Others meet the care head on and break despair asunder,
Shrug their shoulders, strengthen will, and carry on regardless
While others sink within themselves, with an outer hardness.

Life can be so very cruel and terribly demanding.
I had to reach rock bottom to come to understanding.
To my darkened soul came dawn - a truth no longer doubted -
Acceptance of the facts to-day will see the demons routed.

To-day, to-morrow, sometime when - I'll face what is before me
I looked at other's tragedies and listened to their story -
Just ordinary people - the Tom, the Dick, the Harry -
But all found compensations to ease the load they carry.

We're like the tall ships out at sea where time and tide are master.
We steer a course - we sail along - but we who meet disaster
Like sailors, run before the wind that's a potential killer.
My ship flies free. No course is set - and peace has manned
   the tiller.

Verna Roach

The Mind Devoid

Devoid of thought, decision, memory, no emotion, love or hate or fear
Alzheimer's disease has settled here
To those who once shared a joke or tear
The blankness of an uncomprehending stare
No glimmer of recollection, no sense of aware
A living death trapped in a living frame
To the loved ones never again the same.
What cruelty then is the pain imposed, not on the sufferer alone
But also to all those left behind at home
You are not dead, we cannot grieve
And yet, as sure as death, you did leave
You were stolen away before we knew
Never a chance to bid a sad adieu.

Stroma Mary Hammond

Gardening Chores

Prune away and snip for hours,
All done with skill and secateurs.
Puerperium carpet spread beneath,
Aquafolium and Kilmarnock willow.
Lazy gardener's ornamental wheel barrow,
Stands where the path goes narrow.
Keeps less awhile to keep neat,
Camomile lawn under feet.
Alpine niche of grassulas grow,
Was under carpet layer of snow.
Spring brings florets of bright coloured blooms,
Last summer's Pampas Grass looms.
Fronded tall and full of grace,
Aromatic scents permeate the face.
Hedges snip, topiary sculptured clip.
Beech and yew to grow anew.
Clematis and red Rosa Rugosa
Makes sunny days seem cosier.
All the tedium of gardener's life,
All diligently done by wife.

F. A. Rawlinson

The Warrior

A sculptor building and shaping his destiny,
Along the "moonlit path," that leads to
Nowhere and everywhere,
Familiar voices on the fringes of his insanity,
Crying, take me! Take me! Take me!
Five senses numbed.
Yet knowing he is one.
With those who have been,
And those yet to come,
For all eternity

Michael Joseph Murphy

The One Who Waits

The sheep were once happily grazing by the stream
Along came the rams and broke the dream
They took them to the hills far away
The rest one by one decided to stray
Till all that was left was the shepherd to pay

The years went on and the joy went away
The sheep looked 'round for a place to stay
They wanted to run away from the ram
So God said, "Alright, I have a plan
I'll send the shepherd back to you
To lead you back to pastures new"

Some came back faithful and true
Others didn't know what to do
And still the shepherd waited
"I'll only come if the terms are right
Perhaps I'll wait till the day is bright"
And still the shepherd waited

So don't keep the shepherd waiting too long
Even though he is so strong
He does get tired of waiting.

Ruth Gentles

Memories

Memories return to roam my dreams
Along hidden paths, through silent streams
Of russet and gold and warm afternoons
Frost laden trees and luminous moons

My first true love, the one I would wed
The joys, the laughter and the tears that I've shed
And somewhere under forgotten skies
The stories, the dreams, the truth, the lies

But now in the autumn of my years
I reflect on the past with a smile not a tear
Because each chapter of my life has come to a close
And what awaits me now no one knows.

E. Meek

A Day in London

I was you once, when my skin was like
a sun kissed peach and London was my oyster.
I did not know the taste of ruin.
Men's stares followed me until my shadow
Diffusing into hordes, shopping the sales
At Knightsbridge. Like you. Till dusk.

Now my life is contained in your discarded
boxes and bags - a treasured trinket
or two wrapped in the tissue paper that
stuffed the toes of your Givenchy shoes,
snaffled at a snip from some lady posing
in a channel suit - too small - good price.

Rush home now, to lie about the cost and
gloat over your bargain and I will smile,
When night falls and liver aches -
You will not remember me -
Gutter flotsam - in a city that dupes the buyer.
I was you once - when I danced her streets.

Patricia M. Davison

Time

Time is a concept we don't understand
A thing that passes, but can't hold in the hand
It never seems constant, it always alters
It seems to stand still but time never falters
When we're happy it flies by but not when we're sad
It's fast in the good times but slow in the bad
Why this occurs I don't really know
P'rhaps in the future a reason will show
A reason for concept? A reason for life?
A reason for living? A reason for strife?
An answer to these only time will tell
Maybe in time it will ring a bell.
Time's a dimension so theorists say
To pass back and forth, from date to day
So if this is true we all live our lives
Every day, every minute, all of the time
We may see our futures, or even our pasts
What a terrible thought, I hope it don't last
To live all my life in one moment gone
Could be a saviour, or gone for a song.

Robert Thorogood

Nuclear War

A war without a warning
A war without a fight
A war without a winner
A disaster overnight

This kind of war, a nothing war
A war that must be stopped.
A country left with nothing
Since the bomb from somewhere dropped.

They will never pull the trigger
Good God they wouldn't dare
Well they would, and did, and loved it
Such a shame there's no one there!

Rebecca Hardiman

The Port Watch

We saw it in the darkened morning light
  a tiny speck of blue
We saw it in the cloudy dark of night
  a star came shining through
We'd never saw the like before
  in skies so dark and drear
As if the Gods were telling us
  that there was nought to fear
Up and down we'd yaw and turn to face the icy wind
  monitoring a convoys pace hurrying them from behind

Like a shepherd with his flock watching, caring urging
Racing up and down each line as the storm was raging
With bodies soaked with salt and rime
  we hung of fast to rope and line
Above the towering waves we soared
  whilst wind and rain and thunder roared
Amidst this cacophony of noise
  we thought we heard a heavenly voice
And in an instant all was calm then in the morning light above
We saw a bird as white as snow an albatross? Or dove?

    B. Garvey

Reflections

Time.
Abstract whim of man.
Design of order.
Linear path.
Restrictive hands
imposing patterns on our day:
when we eat, work, sleep and play.

Infernal bells, the tic and toc,
who needs the constant ticking clock?
Be safely guided by the sky:
Nature's rhythms do not stop
endure eternal like the rock.

And if at night you yearn to dance,
go out and greet the moon and stars,
abandon rationale and care,
run the risk, reckless, leap, and dare.
For

Life and opportunity are One,
we can rest enough once we are gone.

    Lynn-Marie Cody

A Kiss

Caught in a whirling wind of bliss,
Amid sapphires delicate blue,
Like a thousand dewy stars - was this.
'Love' made her way into
She touched me - with so frail a hand
The heavens sighed above,
At last! - I find that, sought-for land
The mystic land - called Love -
Where happiness lies - where dreams come true

And life! is just a wish
Now I've discovered peace - and you,
in one eternal kiss.

    Ruby Singleton

My Best Friend "Basko"

My best friend is sitting by me now, faithful as ever,
Always beside me whatever the weather,
He loves his walks, when we go out together
Rain or shine he does not mind,
He has kept me sane, from sad and very lonely times,
He wakes me up every morning,
And says hello, another day is dawning,
Life is much better now,
I've got Basko to show me how,
To enjoy life once again,
With my "BEST FRIEND".

    S. Lawrence

Remembrance

While plane trees wept their sad Autumnal tears,
An Old Soldier stood recalling those awful, bitter years;
When stranger had met stranger on the bloody fields of War,
To kill or to be killed, they hardly knew what for.
You fight for home and freedom the Generals had said,
But all our man remembered was the carnage and the dead.

    R. F. Green

Nothing Is Final

A slight breeze, whistles through the valley,
Allowing the leaves to don the hue of autumn,
Gold, amber, scarlet and the decreasing shades of green;
Collaborate to form a natural tapestry across the land.

There is a sting in the air now,
A reminder that winter is on her way,
The glorious colours will disappear and naked branches remain,
The frost encrusted earth, sparkles
Like a bed of diamonds in artificial light

Here is not the end though,
The snow melts away to reveal,
Replenished soil ready for rebirth and growth,
The cycle to begin once again.

There is a message in the seasons,
One for all to hear,
Nothing is final, not even the end of year.

    Sarah Louise Clegg

World War III

I don't know why I still live,
Among rubble, crumbled brick.
Everyday, I see parts of corpses, scattered every where.
The loneliness is intolerable, the pain incurable, hunger.
As I wonder through the deserted, bombed streets,
I ponder whether I, should end my life now.
My spirit empty, unwilling.
There is not a house standing,
Nor a living thing, except I.
Everything dead, lifeless.
I can't explain the agony, heavy in my heart.
I feel drained, as though my body in not my own.
Even the spirits from everything that was alive,
Have been scarred, by the memories of torture, pain and death.
God does not even show His face!
For he is grieving, ashamed that mankind
Was foolish enough to start the war,
To end the world
And all his creation.

    Laura Sewell

Identical Individuals

We stood as individuals
Amongst a crowd of identicals
Choosing our own identities
Against the stereotyping of our friends

With strength and courage
We stood alone
Leaving behind the hateful beings
Uniting in a bond of distinction

Now together we are inseparable
Nothing can touch or harm us
For the love we share within our souls
Will conquer any obstacle

Locked in each other's arms
Like barriers to the world
We shall rise above the people below
And be no one but ourselves

Now we face the world together
Choosing our destined future
We stand together as individuals
But love has won this battle

    Louise Payne

A Heart's Journey

Oh beating, beating heart, quiet, lest my love should hear thee
and guess my silent prayer, for hither to he knows not, him
forever would I love
    - If only he would care.

My heart betrays me to my love, for am I now not wed?
Oh bliss, oh bliss his whisper of love to me, whilst lying
upon our bed. We share our plans, hopes and dreams, yes,
children I shall bear. Oh love, oh love, where are you now?

    - If only he would care.

Oh heavy heart, oh heavy heart, 'twas not all thou hath
planned; hopes, shared care, were never there from the
love who took my hand. Oh hopeless life live on, live on in
hurt too much to bear, just keep beating lest he return.
    - If only he would care.

Oh tired heart, poor tired heart, your promise ere fulfilled,
Offspring flown, remorse burnt out, now poor dear heart alone.
But tarry not, look outside, for there's life after death out
there - look up to the skies, thank God for your life, you know
He'll hear your prayer. Just speak to Him, speak to Him, He is
always there; then no more need will you have to exclaim,
    - "If only he would care".

    K. M. Steward

Help You Through

If I could only read your thoughts
And look inside your head
If I could listen to you
And hear the words you said

Would I be here to help you through
Could I if I tried
Would I speak to you the words
Or run away and hide

I think that I would choose the way
The way to make it right
To lighten your heavy load
Then it would be alright

You should not have kept it all inside
Just let your feelings show
And then you would have realised
Your troubles would all go

You did not know that some were here
To help you through and through
If only you'd stretched out your hand
I could have helped you so

    E. M. Mallett

Ocean Moods

There are many different changes with the passing of the tides
And many unknown secrets 'neath the depths the ocean hides.
The murky dismal indigo, the untamed mood of light,
The icy pitch black shadow, and the distant shaft of night.

And when a storm is brewing, an eerie rumble pounds,
A wild and ghostly echo brings a desperate war-like sound.
The forward motion of the surf, the building of the waves,
The destruction as the swell breaks up, and the broken surge
concaves.

And when the storm has broken, and the surf begins to calm,
The sun shows signs of daybreak, and sings its morning song.
The mood becomes indifferent, a peaceful hush evolves,
A bittersweet composure, a foreboding ease resolves.

When shades of black and indigo transform to aqua blue,
The heat of midday sunshine, dries up the morning dew.
A flotilla of the small boats, cruise gently on the waves,
When seagulls dance upon the surge, the tide vacates the caves.

And when the evening sunset becomes a crimson blush,
The movement of the gentle ebb, whispers a sombre hush.
So many secrets of the sea must surely stay unfurled,
And hold its mystique and remain . . . a wonder of the world.

    I. C. Harris

"Grandpa"

His life had been a long one,
and a pleasant one indeed.
He'd fought to save our country,
and helped all those in need.

He was always willing to lend a hand,
a kind man to the end.
He was wise and knew just what to do,
and all he had he'd lend.

I remember the last thing he said to me.
"you mind that road", he said,
but I just took little note of him,
as he sat in his hospital bed.

He always moaned about the weather,
And was really quite a lad.
While twenty, he dated six girls at once,
I think they must have been mad.

Now he has died and gone to heaven,
and will never again complain,
but I will never forget my grandpa,
for in my heart he'll always remain.

    Steven Williams

Some Things Are Forever

You would never believe that a paradise so wonderful could exist!
As I looked out across the sea a gentle breeze brushed
    passed my face,
a warm breeze that made me smile.
The night was still and peaceful and the moon lit the sky, it was like
a torch on full beam, it made the sea glisten.
I walked along the water's edge, the sand was still warm from
    the day's sun.
I looked up at the sky and watched the stars they looked like
diamonds twinkling in the velvet background of a jewellery box.
As I watched the palm trees sway in the warm night's breeze the
tiniest ripples from the sea covered my toes.
I took a deep breath and smelt the night air, I could smell the
lotions people use against the sun and the salt from the sea
    mixed into one.
I stopped . . . and listened, I could hear the tree frogs and crickets
they sounded like whistles being blown from a far distance.
I wanted to stay forever, but someone once told me nothing
    is forever.
The day had come for me to say goodbye to this paradise and yes I
thought that was forever, but I was wrong.
There will be a time when I will re-enter my paradise and my dreams
will be fulfilled once again, as I grow up I can see things more
clearly and I am determined that some things are forever,
MEMORIES ARE FOREVER.

    Michelle Foster

Sleepless in Sarajevo

Christian sits beneath a tree,
And remembers how it used to be,
Birds would sing a merry song,
A fitting start to the spring.

But now Spring has come but not one bird,
For they are afraid they will be heard,
By passing soldiers who would shoot,
And end their welcoming salute.

Bodies laid on their back,
Remainders of the night's attacks,
Children cry by parent's grave,
Another war victim.

Generals bomb without a care,
Plan attacks to gain people's fear,
Peace treaties lay on the floor,
Stained with soldier's blood.

Christian sits beneath a tree,
And remembers how it used to be,
Children laughed, sung and played,
Now there is no-one left.

    Vicky Mitchell

Life

When we come into the world,
All naked, pink and crying,
We bring our parents perfect joy,
And to their lives true meaning.

From infancy to teenage years
We're safely nurtured through,
And fed with love and food and warmth,
To make our whole selves grow.

And when the trials of middle life,
Are free from all constraint,
We please ourselves, and no one else
To make our lives content.

The years pass by, and great age comes.
Our pills take without fuss,
Because we have no choice at all,
When youth takes care of us!

G. M. Peplow

Whatever You Say - Say Nothing

"Put the remote control in a bubble bag
And drop it in the post.
It wouldn't be too much trouble, would it?
That's all right, isn't it?"
The simple questions baffled me,
And rendered me speechless.
He was never a sadist.
Was I ever a masochist?
The phone shook in my hand,
As I pondered the options.
Then came the death drop -
"And I gave you back your key".
Seamus Heaney received the Nobel Prize today.
Whatever you say - say nothing,
But I had to say something,
"If that's the way you want it - goodbye".

Kitsy Brady

My Mood

The densely clouded sky envelopes my feelings,
And engulfs them within a second,
Leaving nothing but a misty swirl imprinted on my mind.

It forms a pattern reflecting my mood,
That changes as often as time will allow.

The devil torments when the visions is black,
Beckoning body and soul to run wild.

A milder version is when it is grey,
The devil here plays no part.
Just a sickening sense of reality, which fails to explain or reason.

Tina Jurado

The Rescue

A hiker one day went walking upon a rocky moor,
Alas he lost his footing and fell flat on the floor.
He lay there for an hour, maybe two or three,
And all the time was thinking will anyone ever find me!

The sun was getting lower now his hopes were fading fast,
He knew no other walkers were likely to come past.
'Twas then he heard some panting and much to his surprise,
A dog was standing over him, a blessing in disguise!

"Go get your master quickly boy my legs are feeling numb,
I've been down here for hours now in hope someone would come"
The dog ran 'round in circles, darted off into the night,
Appearing not to notice the urgency of his plight.

Within the next half hour a man arrived with rope,
He hadn't called an ambulance he said that he could cope.
The rope was lowered to his ledge, his ordeal would soon be over,
With a pull and a tug he soon came up, all thanks to good old
Rover!!!

Rebecca Law

Landscape of Sameness

I travelled to Kent for Christmas
And somewhere along the way
My thoughts I gathered together
Then allowed them once more to stray.

To the landscape so gloriously painted
By the artist unseen in the night
Who chose from his wide range of colours
The ghostly, yet beautiful white.

All trees were transformed as if by magic
In the picture that I liked so much
By the paint on the brush of the artist
With a gentle, delicate touch.

Cobwebs shed light as they glistened
With icing like droplets of frost
On the spread of winter's canvas
Where all but white colour, was lost.

White on the grass and the hedgerows
Sparkling on fences and posts
Framed by the sun, on that morning
As seen in the valley of ghosts.

Kathleen H. Allen

Fire

What can you see in the flickering fire
Amongst oranges, yellows and reds?
Maybe that which your heart most desires
Or the faces of old friends long dead?
Your bones are touched by the soothing glow.
You're mesmerized by the rhythm
Of flames flaring up and dropping back low.
Such a comforting warmth is given.

But beware of the fire - it's known to be fickle;
It crackles and spits all the while;
When fanned by a breeze it will tease and tickle
It can tirelessly travel for miles;
Though easy to light it's so hard to put out
Destroying all in its path.
Many creatures have choked from smoke on its route
Shrivelled carcasses victims of wrath.

When ashes show, still the embers may glow,
Fierce ruby eyes waiting their chance.
So don't turn your back, or vigilance lack
Else Fire Devils will leap up and prance.

B. T. Fayers

Home

'Tis a wonderful place is a home,
An anchor for both young and old.
'Tis a place where one lives,
Where one takes, and one gives
To the loved ones who live in its fold.

'Tis a wonderful place is a home,
A place for which we all yearn,
Whether weary and worn and feeling forlorn,
Or happy and glad for the day that we've had,
It's the place to which we return.

Be it castle on high with its head in the sky,
Be it manor, or cottage, or barn,
It's the home as we know it,
And love it, and show it,
A place where we'll come to no harm.

'Tis a wonderful place is a home.
The place that we all take for granted,
We use it, and leave it,
Come back to retrieve it,
The place where we always feel wanted.

Mary R. Varley

I'm Black

Darkness falls like
an angel from heaven
I rise and overcome the
struggle I face,
I'm black
I feel the pain and
pray to make it go away
does He hear me
does He care
please understand me I hurt
freedom is a gift
you take for granted
I don't understand,
I'm black
I'm proud and hold
my head up high
I respect myself for what I am
the struggle continues
but I still fight
I'm proud and I'm black

Kelly Morgan

To Mother . . . !

If ever there trod upon the earth.
An angel true yet without wing
Who gave her best, and all its worth
To those she helped in everything.
Never to rise to fames great height.
She did her duty's daily round
Through darkest days kept up the fight
And in it all. Contentment found.
Too soon she left this vale of tears.
To claim her place and rest up wonder
With no more sorrow, no more fears
No earthly stress to overbond her
The world would richer be and strong
If we would help another
And concentrate each day along
To find for all - "A Mother".

A. S. G. King

Life

Life is hard at times to understand, control and live,
An ongoing situation, dictated by circumstance and lack of
understanding,
A mirror that does not reflect a true image,
A joke that no one laughs at.

Live life to the fullest, a false happiness, an
uncertain contentment, an empty thought in an empty head.
Humanity spirals forever downward, a
tornado without a centre, a fight without a cause.
Too much greed, too much power, too much hate,
no reason, just fact.

Why do people expect so much from a
being like themselves, fallible, lonely, and
unexperienced with love, but no contact.

Contact, physical, emotional, like a tide
that doesn't turn, forever pounding at the centre of a beach.
Each pebble a person, and one pebble me.

G. H. R. Watson

Our Dream of Tomorrow

Dreaming of green fields,
And blue skies above,
Dreaming of happiness,
Dreaming of love,
All the world, a different place,
All the people, with a smile on their face,
No more hatred, shown by man,
Even the lion, lying down with the lamb,
This dream of tomorrow, will never cease,
Until all work together
And the world finds peace -

M. E. Chipchase

The Alien

Looked down on, spat at, scorned and despised,
An utter failure in everyone's eyes;
The lowest creature to walk this earth,
Oh, pity the mother who suffered its birth.

It's 'different', it knows, not like the rest,
Time after time it fails the test.
Stupid, ugly, a waste of our space,
How can it be part of the human race?

But it feels, it knows, it hurts, it cares,
It's ever aware of the stares and the sneers.
In front of a mirror it stands for so long
Desperately trying to make right the wrong.

But try as it might, it will not succeed,
It's here on this earth to hurt and to bleed.
Oh, 'Alien', how sad - but I see
There may be other aliens . . . like me.

Mandy Dickinson

Use Your Day

If you wake up in the morning
and all is dull and grey
Just stop and think, how you can.
Brighten up your day
visit a friend, or perhaps just phone
There is always someone
Who is feeling alone.

So take off your slippers
and put on your shoes
Shake of dull care
get rid of your blues
Forget the can't's, think what you can do
How you use your day
Is all up to you.

Louie Davis

A Nation's Plea

The spirit of the people led England through the war,
And Churchill's rousing speeches played their part that's for sure,
But do our politicians deserve respect today?
Scandal and broken promises surface every day.

When voting time comes around which party tells the truth?
Propaganda, lies and deceit are all so uncouth.
So Mr. Politician I'd like you to ensure,
That you help all our aged, tend our sick and aid our poor.

So how can the people have their confidence restored?
Keep to your manifestos and leave us all assured.
We really need to put the Great back into Britain,
And leave our European friends feeling quite smitten!

Paul Andrew Younger

We Are Not Alone

From day one on my mother's earth,
and gazed upon father's skies,
I looked upon a glowing sun,
reflections in my eyes,
A shooting star, a twilight moon,
evenings swept with shades,
a darkened sheet, a blackened page,
with pinholes that God made.
Its shape was round and softened,
as nothing in memory.
Near not noticed, a falling leaf,
an erratic melody.
Tree lines sway with heated wind,
a dark that has shone light,
The grass that moves a strangest dance,
an object for your night.
I know now for our beliefs, we cannot just be one,
for now the ignorance that came to us, must surely soon be gone,
It's time to trust, an open mind, a window to your home,
I am now certain and surely believe that We Are Not Alone

Nicholas Stone

Seasons

When the nesting birds begin to sing
And all the world is new
When pretty springtime flowers appear
That's when I love you.

When busy bees fly to and fro
To sip the honey and the dew
When warm and balmy breezes blow
That's when I love you.

When summer turns to autumn
To give trees their golden hue
When brown leaves are gently falling
That's when I love you.

When icy winds begin to blow
When sunny days are few
When the earth is covered in pure white snow
That's when I love you.

So as these seasons of the year
Each cycle they renew
Timeless and predictable
As is my love for you.

Rita Crompton

Venus in Rags

The moonlight melts and drips into the sea,
And floods the nighttime shores with silver waves
That come to set the velvet waters free
Of all their innocent translucent days.

The sea distorts the images of night,
Reflecting shapes of stars that spell desire,
And suspended in the darkness, burning bright,
Hangs tainted Venus, with her furs on fire.

Her muffled screams cut through the thick smoked sky
And wake the sleeping planets and the stars,
Who watch her glowing furs and riches die
And join the molten sea of fire on Mars.

So weeping Venus turns her naked back,
Whilst fragile love in ashes starts to fall
And stains the dawning sky eternal black,
For blinding night will reign above us all.

Louisa Huskisson

Tears

I know that they come when you're really sad,
And flow slowly down your cheek,
But where do they come from? Nobody knows,
I think it might be a leak.

Is this leak just in girls?
And women and babies too,
Because I've never seen men cry,
Well . . . maybe just a few.

My mum says tears are water,
Hidden inside your eye,
And if your brain knows that you're sad,
You'll then begin to cry,

So, the next time that I start to cry,
I'll know what's happening then,
And I hope that more tears will come,
to young boys and grown men!

Lynda Keown

Quiet Love

Two lovers stroll hand in hand
And gaze in wonder o'er the land
They smile and kiss in warm embrace
As tender love shines in each face
It matters not that they grow old
Or that the northern breeze blows cold
The warmth that comes from each heart
Will keep them warm until they part.

W. E. Clements

Untitled

Every time I think of you my heart bleeds
and breaks that little bit more,
as soon as I heard you had gone something
ripped in and straight away tore,
I don't care what anyone says I will never
forgive myself or forget what I did not do,
I didn't get to say goodbye or tell you how
much I really loved you,
we spent 12 years of our lives together,
and you will spend the rest of mine in my
thoughts forever,
you were the best dog and the prettiest yet,
and it is you that no-one will ever forget,
now you are in heaven keeping on us an eye,
I know you can hear this so Lassie I LOVE YOU
and GOODBYE.

Rhiannon Shier

My Definition

Is this a charade?
A game I play.
Going here and there,
With no comment.
Have I a mind?
I think I do.
I can be introvert
Or extrovert,
Or a combination of the two.

Am I the shyest actress
The world has ever seen?
Or do I appear as some kind of Drama Queen?
Forget the games.
You are an individual.
In your own right.

Have your say, don't shy away.
Face your fears overcome them
You will realize,
How, much an illusion
So called reality is.

Yvonne Salter

Moments

The clock ticks away the seconds of our lives
and ten is all we have
Five we remember as the past
one is now, four yet to come
We add together moments that last
and try to find the sum.

Some we stretch out long
Some we mourn, they're gone
But when at last the spring unwound
all moments are to us re-found.

And in between what do we see
save for the growing of a tree?
Its falling leaves a circle of events
our thoughts at once so intense.

Our eyes are opened, the truth is seen
It's not what we are but what we've been.

Michael R. Wardle

Sour Fruit

   This poem reflects the "Untimely" pregnancy
and termination of a young girl.
Society considers the concealment and
subsequent termination of this "disgraceful
event" as her saviour.
The girl sees the returning of this "gift"
as a tragedy and misfortune for none other
than society itself. She returns what is pure
And marvels at the blindness of those who
live in a world that pains over its shame
and turns upon those who accept their own imperfection.

S. A. Cliffe

187

The Earth Where I Lay as a Boy

The earth where I lay as a boy
And built my graveyard
Is a graveyard now.

The sand where I fooled as a king
Which was subject to me
Has crawled to the sea.

My seed was nurtured.
In the glaze of grass my flower grew
To the full of its imagination, white like wind
Across the rape of skies.

My mind was a mass of twisted words out of reason
Into rhyme. People crabbed and died
In their youth and my arms sang
The Him of their deliverance.

I saw the water lilies break in couplets
On the edge of the thick stream.
I saw the face of evening smile up
At the white boy licking its lips.
The white boy woke from genesis
On the morning skull.

Michael Alan Shafran

A Childhood Dream?

I crept into Mum's bedroom
And by the flickering candle light
I gazed upon the picture
I stared with all my might

I know I was not dreaming
I'd pinched myself to make sure,
But no, the picture on mums wall
Stayed the same as the night before.

A castle in the background
Some water to the fore
A man helps a lady into a boat
I stared as I'd stared before

What's strange about the picture?
You ask, as well you might
A herd of cows graze in the stream
No boat, in the morning light.

The years went by, I told myself
It must have been a trick of the light
How could a picture on a wall,
Change images from day to night?

P. E. Haynes

Just in Time

Hours to come
And hours to go in thoughts without restriction
The world is there to be explored at once

School days come
With bubbly laughter, giggles and collaboration
Tinged sometimes with a spike that pains or hurts

Teen years come
With eager joy and wild anticipation
And glimpses of a world of cruel fear

Adulthood comes
With painful efforts in survival's competition
Yet with bright flashes of delightful joy

Old age comes
With fading strength and rueful reminiscence
Aware that myriad days lead to one end

Death will come
But in the waiting time wise tolerance provides
The skill to guide all those who still may have

Hours to come.

Margot Hester

Peace for Jerusalem?

Jesus cried as He looked at Jerusalem,
And He might well cry today,
For as they killed prophets in long past times
There is senseless destruction - they say
Yet another explosion has cruelly dealt
Death and devastation around.
And still the peace, craved for centuries,
Certainly cannot be found.

Dear Lord, as You cry, please soften the hearts
Of those who these treacherous games play,
That in Jerusalem, and in London Town,
Comes that peace for which we pray.

Stella Alton

To My Dog

On Irish soil the leafless trees now bends
And canopies the spot where you are laid
Their falling waters sing their plaintive songs
And down the glens the wild winds pausing sigh.
And murmur on you grave a lullaby -
You were the dear companion of my youth
The solitude of Irish hills we shared
You did not one intrude upon a thought
Or spoil one vision, now too rarely caught
Silent you were, only your questing eye
Would gaze with wonder when I lagged behind
Faithful you were few, few were your demands
and true the love shown when you licked my hands
You were the dear companion of my youth
The solitude of Irish hill we shared
And often now I look in vain to find
A heart as true as yours and eyes as kind.

L. B. Sansom

Once upon a Time

When Summer days were hot and long
And childhood pleasures gave delight,
When morning dew invited song
And happy smiles closed down the night,
We dangled upside-down in trees,
Played hopscotch in the road,
We paddled in the rippling stream,
Whilst watching out for toads.
On backs, we watched the birds on wing,
Our hands and faces smeared with mud,
What joy we found in simple things,
In childish ways, our lives were good.
And now, when life is such a race,
Gone are those artless pleasures,
Our children live at faster pace
And miss our long lost treasures.

Vera Finney

Reflections

I stood upon a mountain high
And felt so very near the sky,
I gazed around at the far distant land,
Saw the touch of the Master's hand.
The sheep were grazing, a peaceful sight,
Streams and rivers, gleaming and bright
I saw a church tucked away in the glen -
A fairy glade so pretty, that not any pen
Could portray the beauty that caught my eye,
The grass so green, the beautiful sky!
The colourful flowers, growing wild -
Bring joy and delight, to many a child -
I heard in the distance the curlew and pheasant,
Such friendly sounds, make life pleasant.
The farmer looks so far away,
As in the fields he cuts the hay;
Conies are playing hide and seek,
While fishes are splashing in the creek,
'Tis good for one to stop and ponder,
At the goodness of God, who dwells up yonder.

Ruth M. Maytum

Schooldays

Schooldays, they say, are the happiest days,
And I'm sure that this is quite true.
But at the time of actually experiencing them
One rarely holds to this view.

It is only when looking backwards
One realizes how brief their span;
They fly so quickly and only because
The child cannot wait to be man.

These are the days when we make those friends
Who stay close to our hearts and our minds,
And even though we may later part
There is always that tie that binds.

But to countless generations
To shun school has been the rule.
Even Shakespeare wrote of the "schoolboy
Creeping unwillingly to school".

So how can the child be made to see
That schooldays are to be enjoyed?
Maybe the adult should be the learner
And the child, he who's employed!

Marlene Allen

To Dream Alone in an Empty Place

To walk in this green and pleasant land,
And hear birds singing near at hand.
To walk in the country on a warm summer day,
And smell the scent of the new mown hay.
To stroll in peace down a quiet country lane,
Away from the city, the stress and the strain.
Free to roam without a care,
And breathe the clean fresh country air.
Free to wander regardless of time,
Through this beautiful country of mine.

Strolling along by the fields of green,
All is peaceful and serene.
Sheep and cattle graze either side
As I pass them by at a leisurely stride.
The distant hills stand proud and high
With green crowns reaching for the open sky.
And as I gaze o'er this peaceful scene,
Of fields of corn and pastures green,
Free of the city's mad'ning pace,
To dream alone in an empty place.

Joseph Michaels

Darkened Hues

When legion forces 'round me fly
And I am trapped beneath a sky
Of darkened hues, with spaces bare,
I know not light, I am despair

When all about on rocky seas,
I'm tossed in terror, I find these
Dark waves claim me to their deep,
Tempting me to their long sleep

I can't find the door that I
Know opens out on sunlit' skies,
In desperate need I walk the fell,
Touching trees I know so well

And there, beneath their canopy
I stand, a speck of humanity,
And wonder, is it accident, or plan,
That earth moves and produces man.

Is mortality a myth,
Or are we unending parts of this,
Or is this blanket of despair
The truth, that kills my hopes laid bare

J. Mackereth

When the Heart Takes to Verse

I take a walk outside
and I breathe in nature's air,
I look at the space beside me,
and imagine that you're there.

But there's nothing I love enough
I could pretend was you
that special place beside me
could be filled by only you.

You truly are the sweetest rose
This land has ever grown
you're the closest thing to heaven
an angel of my own.

No words I could ever write
could show you how much I love you
but this world's become a better place.
Knowing you're in it too.

(Trudy's verse)

Keith Fraser

I Am a Witch

I am a witch
And I can switch my age
Without a hitch.
When I am gay, I play
The same old witches' game,
Which is to bewitch whomever I tame.
When I am struck by gloom,
Or hit by rage, to take it out my hair,
I take my broom,
And ride on it through the air.
I like to hide behind a cloud,
So that nobody could see,
That even I can cry and doubt,
But I can switch my mood,
Because I am a witch.
And that is why I can't take back with me,
When it is time to depart,
The sunshine that is mine
And my lighthearted broken heart.

Maria Gryziecka-Goldberger

Icelandic Hinterland

Jet black desert stretching beyond the bounds
of our imagination -
the power of creation etched in ebony mountains
and dunes of ancient dust.
Man strives for authority in this kingdom that is nature's own.
But the wind mocks, trusting the untameable force
of Mt. Hekla's explosive disgorgement -
too proud to notice that, small and courageous,
there blooms a flower,
blushing as it shatters the volcanic illusion
of conquered earth.

Penelope Tizley

The Whore

She knew I was watching,
and I followed like a lamb,
out of the precinct,
where the shops were all crammed,
leading me on by the sway of her thighs,
I was enslaved in a lustful demise.

I knew she was watching
as I cried off my guilt,
laughing before me
at each tear that I spilt;
leading me out by her harsh, frosty hand,
we stood by the door
and I paid her demand.

Mark Cheshire

The Real Ruler of the Sea

The media break the dramatic news
And once again a nation subjected to horror pictures
As they sit living safe lives.
Out at sea creatures return to their homeland,
Unaware of the present man has left them
To welcome them home.
A creeping black death oozes towards them
With no regard to man's pathetic attempt to halt it.
It has a life of its own now and will not be used by man any more.
It engulfs all it touches, choking mouth, feather, lung, life
It slowly covers, smothers and drags down
And is crowned supreme ruler of the ocean.
Men say sorry to other men
Creatures die in appreciation.

Kathryn Hilton

An Elver Night

On a night such as this, when wild March winds are still,
And men, abroad, look southward down from lofty forest hill
To Severn's jewelled necklace strung with lantern - candlelight
Some stirring - indefinable says "Here's an elver night".
Along the grassy banks they wait, from Crib to Pridings' end,
Dark shadows in soft moonlight, around the Horseshoe bend,
Call greetings on the water to those on further shore -
A boat slips by with friendly word from those who ply the oar,
A muttered oath as feet slip in the mud - and time goes by
In stillness, somewhere, hauntingly, a night bird's plaintive cry
Is answered from far distance carried on the stilly air,
While nets are dipped, cider quaffed, and lanterns checked with care
Then comes the cry of "Tide - Oh" - hopeful backs bend to the ebb
As down long years they fished before - the elver men, now dead,
And those who leave dark Severn's shore to live and work elsewhere
Will pause on such a night as this, to feel upon the air
A stirring - indefinable, as memories winged flight
Returns, and pensively they say - "This is an elver night".

Mary Purcell Herbert

Promises Past

I wish to God I could forget you.
And more that ne'er we met.
A life unhappy with you,
And without, one sodden with regret.

I cannot bare to wake,
I do not dare to sleep
Absence does not forsake,
A heart which bleeds and weeps.

I glimpse you through the day,
And walk with you in dreams.
I hear you when it's silent,
There's no escape, it seems.

As days turn into weeks and weeks transpire to years,
I venture past the places that were ours
Recalling moon-like promises my spirit sadly wanes,
None left to voice them now to, but the stars.

P. A. Malcolm

"Life's Pathway"

As you walk along life's pathway
And see each golden door
Open it and you will find all the
Treasures that are in store.

As you wake each morning pause a
Little while, think what is before you
And give the world a smile.
There is always a ray of sunshine
In a clouded sky and always a bluebird
Singing as he is flying by.

As you walk along that pathway
Never never despair
There is always someone there to
Help and guide you each and every day.

Dorothy May Sprigings

Early Days Yet

"Gives us a kiss!", she said in that coy, cute beguiling way
and this was shortly followed by "don't you love me to-day?"
Oh! what a question, as if these pangs wee indigestion.

"Give us a love!", she cried in that oh so slightly hurt
and pleading voice, with arms outstretched, proffering no choice
and I complying, surrendered to her warm and melting kiss
oh! such bliss.

F. B. Smith

Rawar

Still the night 'til break o' dawn,
and quieter still that shrouded morn,
for a hundred thousand who were reborn,
will never forget the men o' corn.

The bullets cut like sharpened blade,
Their bodies of stalk, fragile, swayed,
like chaffed wheat sheaves there they laid,
the price of war always paid.

The bloody earth under sulphur sky,
where one should live and four should die,
A whole youth spent, scattered, lie,
one man's death, a price too high.

Sow the seed, reap the wrath,
tormented flesh 'neath khaki cloth,
Evil cauldron a corpus Broth,
Wars ever racing, war the sloth.

Wallace B. Ellis

The Birth of a Grandson

Time has passed
And I have held fast
To what was right and proper.
A marriage was made
And a price was paid
With the loss of freedom
Once on offer.

But little did I know
That what was to grow
Was the life of a beautiful daughter.
For all to see, she was to be
The repayment of that fee.
And in her turn she bore a son
Which was the ultimate fulfilment of me.

So blessed be
The family tree
From which we're all created
For that is life with all its strife
To which we're all related
And come what may we have to pay
For gifts which are donated.

Karin H. Fothergill

"Making Up a Dream"

Was it a dream when you held me in your arms
And kissed my sadness away?
Or was it real?
Did I indulge in slumber when imagination held full sway?

Tell me what are dreams
And what is reality?
Is life itself one long dream
Albeit nightmares - sometimes pleasant?

Last week's agonies, this week's memories,
Are memories part of dreaming?
Be it a dream or real it has left me sad
Then suddenly I'm glad, you're back and you're real.

It wasn't a dream after all
There you stand straight and tall
The lovelight in your eyes
Showing me how you feel,
This is no dream, it is real!

Margaret Leslie

Outwood

I remember Outwood on a cold and frosty night.
And I remember Outwood when things were black and white.
I remember a school yard under the fullness of the moon,
And children's breaths freezing as they all
Sang out of tune.
The noise of heavy boots, studded on a last,
Sliding through the night in times long, long past.
Our hands and toes nipped and
tingling with the cold, and on our heads
a balaclava in colours of red and gold.
It makes us hurry along the street and back
to home and fire. To warm our toes and
fingers and watch the flames get higher.
I look around the gas-lit room, and dimly glows
the light. But from the kitchen Mother comes,
with hot drinks that seem just right.
A pot sink to work at, a gas ring and
coal fire. This was life a long time ago
in Outwood's Yorkshire.

Thomas Allan Liddle

Forbidden Love

I'm-so-rich, in love, that-I'm-dancing, in the air.
And-if-it-were, money, I'd be a millionaire.
How can something, so wrong, feel so right?
This feeling, that haunts me, by day, and by night.
I-only-started-to-live, the day, you came along.
I awoke, from the corner, and-I-stood-up, so strong.
I couldn't fly, my wings, were so broken.
Never-a-nice-word, to-me, had been spoken.
Yes, you-rescued, my life, before-it-died, completely.
You-awoke, my dying soul, and you kissed it, so sweetly.
Now-I-look, at this world, in-a-much, better light.
You're my candle, in the dark, so I sleep, safe at night.
You-were, right there, when-I-wanted, you most.
By being, my friend and-my-leaning, lamp post.
So-please, forgive-me, if-I'll never, forget.
The fact, that-you've-been, my-most-precious, friend yet.
I'm-so-rich, in love, that-I-can't, believe, I'm me.
I'm-so-rich, in love, that I cannot, break free.
Yes, we're-so-rich, in love, you, and I.
We own, something precious, that-no-money, can buy.

Linda George

For You

Let me delve into the depths of your heart,
And pluck from your heartstrings the eternal tune of love,
Which will travel to the ears of an ever-vulnerable people,
And you too can do likewise to mine.
Let the two meet at the end of infinity,
And our hearts and souls shall be together as one.
Let the passion burn until the fuel is gone.
And, if our love should float away on a cloud,
Let us two be buried under the thick, dark earth,
And be laid to rest in the grave forever.
For our eyes are greedy to have what we cannot,
And to have what we cannot hurts more than a love dead.

Kate Roddis

Snail and Slug

Snail and Slug who slither and slide
And in the lettuce leaves will hide,
Not liked by gardeners, when they feed
Upon the plants they've grown from seed.
Harshly uttering disdainful sound
While spreading pellets on the ground,
Upsetting nature's chain of food
As slug is relished by bird and brood,
Some spear snail with accurate beak
While others sluggish morsels seek,
Birds; early morn and evening bring
A daily pleasure when they sing,
How could they be in such avail
If it were not for Slug and Snail?

Susan Barr

Calcutta's Rickshaw Puller

In Cal's busy city, crowded trams look pretty,
And nowhere in the world are buses fuller;
If you must get around, and taxis can't be found
Just hail the willing, waiting rickshaw puller.

Before you clamber in, he'll price the run and grin,
With steel like arms he'll lift you slow and steady;
With a tug he'll gather speed, then try to get a lead
On traffic that has clogged the streets already.

He'll stop or turn or wait, suddenly change his gait,
Alert at crossings and at hidden curves;
With ease he'll cross a road, no matter what the load,
Dodging a dust cart or lorry as he swerves.

And when you're there somehow, he'll wipe his sweaty brow,
Then stretch his hand out for his meagre fare;
And when it's in his palm, he'll bow and say, "Salaam",
Then amble away in the crowd to who knows where.

Once more he'll look about, the busy streets to scout,
For anyone else that him would care to hire;
Once more he'll ring his bell, the whole wide world to tell:
"I'm ready again. I can't afford to tire."

Richard D'Cruze

Why You?

I watched you fighting for your breath
And knew that you were close to death
I prayed to God to let you stay
I would not let you go that way

Each time you have a bad attack
I don't know if you're coming back
The fear I feel you'll never know
For I must never let it show

The doctor's came around today
There's nothing new to try they say
They just don't know what else to do
Oh God I think I'm losing you

And just before your time runs out
You start to have a turn about
Your breathing now is getting calm
And once again you're out of harm.

If I could have one wish come true
It's that they'd find a cure for you
And that your pain would go away
And you could live the normal way.

Danual S. Ryan

As the Gipsies Do

"Will you come and play with me,
And shall we go and wander
Over fields and meadows green,
And past the big white gander?

Let's make a gipsy caravan
With twigs from elm and yew,
And let us go a-wandering as the gipsies do.

We'll curtain all the windows
with cobwebs from the dew,
And lay a bright, bright carpet
With flowers of every hue.

We'll hang from it a golden bell,
The biggest kingcup found,
Then all will hear us coming
For miles and miles around.

Oh, will you come and play with me
While still the sky is blue?
And let us go a-wandering
The lanes and byways through;

Let us go a-wandering, as the gipsies do."

Vivienne Helps

"E"

Ecstasy,
An addiction to dancing with me.
Put your life in my hands beat the blues,
Go on, go on wear the red shoes.

Let the fire take a hold of your heart,
Let the flames lick and tease every part.
Feel the rhythm pulse in your soul,
Let the music and dance take control.

Faster and faster you spin,
Its whirl of excitement you're in.
Can you hear your heart in your ears,
feel the touch & caress of your fears.

Regretting this devil you rode?
perhaps your poor pulsing heart will explode.
you asked to dance in my fire,
so now I, lucifer raise it higher.

What's up? Can't take the pace?
Is that sweat? Or fear on your face?
"Had enough" is that what you said?
Sorry! This ride don't stop till you're dead!

Maxine Gardner

"Reflections on Water"

I wish that I could cast my line,
And reel in years gone by,
Put things right. I knew were wrong,
Change to truth, the lie.
Enjoy again those golden days,
Took for granted then,
Laugh and play with friends once more,
Who now have grown to men,
I wonder if they sometimes long,
For days that passed us by,
Remembering just how good they were,
And miss, the same as I . . .

A. W. Wells

Starlight

I gaze upon the stars above,
And marvel at what I see,
They shine down upon my love,
Who's standing next to me.
What will the future hold for one,
Who will pass on first?
You either die, or are left alone,
I wonder which is worst?
The Ancients looked upon the stars,
For guidance and forecasting,
About their battles, and their wars,
And about life, everlasting.
I wish they'd tell us what comes next,
Or luck that comes our way,
But it always leaves us vexed,
When things all go astray.
So I put my arms around my love,
And hug her close to me,
Never mind the stars above,
We'll see what we shall see. BIG FELLOW.

J. Jones

Spring Is Coming

Outside the window it is snowing.
And the north wind is blowing
But down the dale the daffodils are growing
Spring is coming
and the birds are singing
Jack Frost is still about
But the snowdrops are coming out
The fruit buds are sprouting out
But down in the beck there is
still snow about.
In the garden the broad beans are growing
Which last October I was sowing

D. McNeil

"Bing"

I'm a friendly little doggy, in fact I'm quite a guy
And if you've got a moment I'll try and tell you why
Such a lovely character that everyone adores
I really love the garden, but I do get muddy paws
'Round and 'round and 'round I go, under every tree
I'm very fast along the straights but have to stop to wee
I jump upon the window sill and bark at passers-by
And really get quite angry if a cat should catch my eye
Mummy says I'm naughty, but isn't cross for long
Daddy thinks I'm perfect, I can't do any wrong
I really get excited when my Janet comes to stay
I love to lick and kiss her, I know she's come to play
I run and get my tufty, I really like that game
She pulls and tugs with all her might and I do just the same
But when her stay is over I really do get mad
I cry and winge and bark at her, but only 'cause I'm sad
Well I hope you liked my story and trust that you agree
'Cause my name's Bing and I'm the best,
The best you'll ever see.

Janet Hall

Parallel Spirits

When we kissed the rain stopped falling,
And the sunshine broke through the clouds.
The whole world seemed to be silent,
Just us, away from the crowds.

Bravely we climbed many mountains,
And swam across sparkling streams,
And when our path divided,
You followed me, as in my dreams.

Now we find ourselves blinded,
By brambles, bracken and heath,
Jealous, they aim to trip us,
Yet we stumble to what lies beneath.

Beyond the forest lies beauty,
But paradise takes time to find,
Together I know we will make it,
Beneath a rainbow our souls will entwine.

Rachel Tucker

The Gift of Death

The best Christmas present for me would be death,
apart from that there is nothing left.
My family have gone and my friends are no more,
I wish I could just walk out and close the door.
My home is the gutter and my survival is my hate,
I live in withering defiance of our inevitable fate;
realising it would bring the freedom I yearned so long,
and I would never have to hear another Christmas song.

For what is Christmas if there are to be no loved ones there?
No one to share presents with and no one to care.
When Jesus died, He died for everyone but me,
and I know that I have to pay the price, not He.
My days are numbered, I know that now;
I see that it's not where you live but how
I look back on an empty life as lie here at the door:
like everyone I go on searching until it closes forever more.

Sharon Morrison

Joy

As they day is to the night
and the sea is to the shore,
So constant is my love for you
I wish for nothing more
than time to stay its hand
Lest Fate for me has hurt in store.

Joy is in my life again,
Your greatness fills my heart,
with magic of your touch and kiss.
A wondrous thing apart
to keep and hold with tender care.
This joy, this love from Cupid's dart.

Zoe Bex

The Seed

A seed is sown beneath the ground
  And left to take its time
Before it shows its tiny head above
  The earth divine
Its progress started down below for
  Everything must start
A tiny seed left all alone to
  Grow away from dark
What beauty it will give to those
  Who really see
The work that seed had done
  Before it came to be
A flower open to the light above
  The very ground
Where it had started all its work
  How nice to be around
A thing that opens all the day then closes for the night
A flower many will admire oh, what a wondrous sight
The effort really worth the while for pleasure it will give
To people all around the ground a seed that had to live.

Marjorie Margerison

Whisper of Emotion

'Twixt the shrouded blanket of fallen night
and the crimson steady warmth of early day.
Lays the girl of dreams, young and bright
Deep in the arms of the man who,
thought it only happened to the chosen few.
Caressing, touching, caring and wanting
to say I love you but,
The flimsiness of words are not needed
in a world of love.
A world where feelings flutter like doves,
scattered on a windy day.

C. P. Knowles

A Sonnet
The Parting

It would be a big occasion it was said —
And so it proved, so many crammed within —
Young, old, from near and far they came and stayed
To smile, to mourn and to remember him.

What makes a man beloved of his peers
Is not the grace perfection does achieve,
Nor yet the wisdom that may come with years
Still less the worldly goods he has to leave.

But laughter and a fellowship for all —
With friends, a dram in hand, always at ease;
A family man whose caring is recalled,
Good business sense: a wit who loved to tease;
And now at last to challenge protocol —
"Club or school ties preferred, please!"

Rena McGuinness

The Good Things in Life

I have visited many a land overseas,
And have seen countless sights of beauty to me,
I have sated my senses in marvellous wonders,
In mountains and water that cascades and thunders,
I've basked in the sun and I've swam in the sea,
And I've loved every moment in my memory,
For now that it's past, it is still in my mind,
And I'm thankful for all that the good Lord designed.
I've lived and I've loved, and now that I'm old,
The things in my mind are so good to behold,

I still love to look at the sky up above,
Feel the sun and the rain, see the beauties I love,
The flowers, the trees, hear the birds when they sing,
The loves of my heart above everything,
Are with me, although I may wander alone,
For many are gone to their rest, but I've known,
The joys and the sorrows, the trials and the strife,
And I cherish all things in this God given life.

D. Luckett

Taken for a Ride

He sat with men he'd never known
And never felt so much alone.
A vehicle racing through the night,
Impatient for his silent plight.

As through the countryside they sped
In hedgerows flashing by he read
His own last chapter written there,
But he could only sit and stare.

Quiet companions pressing near,
And never had he known such fear
As now, for this they could not hide
Was planned to be his final ride.

He sat with men he'd never known
And never felt so much alone.
These servants of his destiny,
Were they the last men he would see?

And when the vehicle, black as night,
Eased off the highway out of sight,
And 'Get out!' heard above his fear,
Were these the last words he would here?

Maurice Morgan

Looking for Answers

Her cries can be heard both night and day,
And yet she has so little to say.
She cannot eat but frequently drinks,
And cares so little what others may think.

Her hands and feet feel useless somehow,
They are aching for use but not for now.
Her eyes are blind and only a sound,
Can point her to where activity is found.

She longs for someone to hold her hand,
And awaits the day when she can stand.
What are these bars that keep her contained?
And why does moving feel such a strain?

Why does everyone ignore her so?
And why is she dressed in ribbons and bows?
Why does she seem so small to others?
And why must she hide behind the covers?

She needs someone, yet lies all alone,
She is coming to terms with her new home,
She needs protection from all that harms,
For she is merely a babe in arms.

A. Fullman

The Lonely Maiden

A maiden kissed her love goodbye, and then she heaved
a lonely sigh,
As he sailed for far away lands, not knowing that never again
would he touch her velvet hands.

As the days turned into months and the months turned into years,
She added to the ocean with her sad and lonely tears.

Six years later to the day, the maiden was waiting in the bay,
For the love she lost at sea, she wondered still where could he be.

At last she could take no more, sad and bitter to the core,
The sea had clearly claimed her love, so she climbed the cliff so
high above.

She reached the top and looked around, hoping for a sight or sound,
He would never come and that was clear, she had lost a love that
was so dear.

She looked to the sky and said she was sorry, but no longer
did she care or worry, with one great leap she fell to the ocean
But the waves didn't stop their haunting motion.

Now the lovers they are together, and will be now always and forever,
At the bottom of the sea their bodies lie, but their souls are way
up in the sky

Never again will they be parted,
Because now their lives have only just started.

Serena Barber

Understanding

If truth is truth then what is lies?
And which is which behind your eyes?
Do you love or do you hate?
Is loneliness to be my fate?
For what is love if it violence shows
Much better hate that kindness knows
For hate's not hate that pity feels
and love's not love that violence wields

So know yourself as I must know
or spurn my love and my life's flow
For I no longer want to bide
Where love and hate have no divide

A. Clark

The Thoughts of a Dying Soldier

'Come hither, Death,
And let me see your face;
'Tis time we met;
So gather in your fateful casting net
And add one more sad soul
On this dread killing day.
I come with all attested marks
That one must have to be accredited,
Not only shattered flesh
But shattered dreams -
As if some cursed seal were needed thus
To stamp a passport in through Heaven's Gate.
But wait a while,
I've not yet made farewell
To hopes fulfilled and youthful promises.
Ah well, I've said enough,
The moment that we meet
I'll know the way of it.'

Peter Wheatley

Bully for Her!

She went swimming,
And washed the b*tch out of her hair.
But the black around her eye still stings.

She went into music,
And sung the b*tch off her chest.
But the black around her throat still hurts.

She went into science,
And burned the b*tch from her memory.
But the black around her lip still throbs.

She went into needlework,
And stuck pins in the b*tch.
But the black around her ribs still burns.

So she went home,
And remembering the b*tch put a blade to her wrist.
Now the black turns red, and she feels nothing.

Paula Lovatt

I Have Just Remembered

It is Christmas eve, again
And the shopping is bought;
Did we remember the herbs,
The lard and pepper and salt?
The turkey is closed up to the brim,
With stuffing - rich waiting to be pinned;
The vegetables are ready each for their
Own saucepan, tray, pot or tin.
But have I remembered everything?
The cakes and sweets in all their glory stand,
Waiting to be eaten - out of hand.
And the fruit lay polished ready for everyone.
But is there something which I should have done?
Mince pies for Santa and a tot of gin
To welcome him as he flies in.
But before to bed at last I flee,
I have just remembered - we have got no tea!!

Roger Piggott

Rather Me than You

Looking at other people's lives
And seeing what I see
I can honestly say to myself
Rather them than me

People's ways are funny
They seem very upside down
In my experience
This is what I've found

No-one seems very happy
Everyone is always moaning
About their lovers, husbands or wives
Or the money they are loaning

I think we all want too much
Without looking at what we have
This is what life has become
Don't you think it's sad

The funny thing is
My friends probably think I'm strange too
And they say to themselves
Rather me than you

Shelley Selner

On the Eve of Saint Valentine's Day

It's Valentines Day tomorrow
And my heart is filled with sorrow.
If only you knew what it's like for me,
Thinking of you with someone else makes me so unhappy.

Everyone said it wouldn't work out,
I was convinced it would; I had no doubt.
You told me we were destined to be together,
And I believed you which wasn't too clever!

You knew what to say, you knew my weakness
I wanted to be loved - that was my feebleness.
I did love you, more than words can say
But you didn't love me and now I have to pay.

Life goes on or so they tell me
But when I think of you it drives me crazy;
I wish that I could change the way things are
But what can I do when you're so afar?

I wish things were different but they are not
So now I have to make do with what I've got.
But I haven't got anything without you,
You've broken my heart - now what can I do?

Natalie Hartnoll

Sometimes We See the Heron Fishing

The freeways - the motorways and the parkways
are O.K. - if you've car and you're in a hurry,
but give us the cycle paths, the bridle-ways and the country lanes
less stress - less lead - less worry!

Though when we are caught in a shower
or get another puncture,
we resolve to get a car again
but then we'd only miss the nature.

We like the scent of wild flowers,
especially after a shower of rain
and to this end we'll spend hours
down any ol' bridle-way, cycle path or country lane.

We like to watch the animals play,
we feel good when the sun shines through,
sometimes we see the heron fishing,
the swans and the ducks, the anglers too.

No longer for me the world of the motor way
or the stress of the contra-flow,
give us the cycle paths and country lanes
they have much more to show.

Michael Duell

Untitled

When the sky is grey,
And nothing goes your way,
You are feeling very bored,
The things you like, you can't afford,
Perhaps you are not wealthy,
But maybe you are healthy,
Stop your pining,
Every cloud, has a silver lining,
If every one parcelled, up their troubles, and put them in a sack
Most of us would want our own parcel back,
We are needed on this earth, for many reasons,
Like the year needs, four seasons,
In winter, when the weather is bad,
We get fed up, and feel rather sad,
But when spring comes, with nice warm rain,
Brings up, the flowers, and we are happy again,
Birds sing, as they've always, done,
We humans be out, basking, in the sun,
One is in a good mood,
Because life is so good.

H. A. Ralphs

"Old Photographs"

Paper skies,
And paper trees,
Paper children, mirroring this curiosity.
Soul fragments,
Stolen and frozen;
Memories beating still, in
Starched figures,
Gaunt eyes,
Meditative gazes, regarding me.

Absent here, the chiming years,
Amid dead time,
Theirs and ours.
Trickery, seized forever on
A moment,
Met here.
And again, defying its space,
In hearts
That still beat.

Sarah E. M. Clarke

Sorrow Tears

The love I have is filled with light
and will keep on shining through the night
and when the brightness disappears
my heart cries always with sorrow tears
but when the daylight shines above
you will see the sparkling wings of a dove
It resembles the sign of my love for you
and my heart will always be true.

Pierina Cicchirillo

Untitled

I glance through the misty scene
and see love and hate.
My eyes follow yours
but never meet.

I clear the mist,
but it comes again,
thicker.

I turn away from the coalescence into the haze,
everything blurred in front of me.

I tremble uncontrollably
though nothing of me moves,
until I dare to turn again.

I glance through the misty scene
and see love and hate,
my eyes follow yours,
but never meet,
again.

Kirsteen McDonald

This Wondrous Earth, This Magical Planet

In woodland glade where peace is found
And songs from birds the only sound,
Sheltering trees, flowers unfurled
Uplift the spirit in this busy world,
Masterpieces from an unseen source
Gives hope and keeps our hearts on course

Nature is a wondrous teacher
Let's open our eyes and be much richer,
Appreciate what our planet can offer
It's all for free, not from a coffer,
Just take from our earth's rich store
For daily needs and nothing more

Then our future generation
From every corner, every nation,
Will never hunger, never thirst
Because we've considered first things first,
Given creatures, living things a chance
This word to multiply, enhance.

Kathleen Crawford

Untitled

I wander around the playground just waiting for someone to say
Are you alright
Not that they do
Sometimes I cry
Miss says, what's wrong?
Nothing
I say
The bully says if you tell I'll beat you up
Please don't

Kim Van Pelt

Happiness

The best things in life are free they say.
And to appreciate the little things that
happen every day,
Like a smile from my passing neighbour
And a rub on my leg from my purring cat.

He was not wanted and was left on my doorstep mat.

Whoever left him there had no heart at all
They did me a favour, and is by my side whenever I call

To watch the birds and hear them singing
To hear the lovely church bells ringing
That's what I mean that the best things in life are free
Try to remember this and you will be
happy and content like me
It doesn't mean that I haven't had any
hard knocks in my life
It simply means that my outlook on life
has overcome meanness and strife.

Marjorie Perkins

Your Photograph

I want to smash this photograph of you
and tread the glass into your eyes,
so that when the light strikes each prism
I can pretend that you are crying,
not laughing with your new lover.

When I saw you through my camera that day
I knew you loved me,
but it lasted no longer than this frame,
which cracks under my foot
with a noise of boot on bone.

Goodbye my love.
As you lie with your new boy,
and shiver,
and he jokes that someone is walking on your grave,
remember me,
and taste my footprint on your face.

Michael Carney

195

Friendships

When youth is gone and years are passing
And we are growing old
We value friendships and good deeds
Much more than any gold
The are no pockets in a shroud
No banks in heaven above
You can't take money with you
So don't make it your love
Of all life's greatest treasures
No money can compare
With loyalty love and friendship
And one with whom to share
So when you find a loyal friend
One whose kind and true
Just stop and count your blessings
Maybe you'll feel less blue
If you are loyal to your friends
They'll be the same to you.

> *E. Smith*

End of the Game

The once flawless complexion is now a pebble dash mess
And the small red ant army could not have cared less
We once had a chance with the ball at our feet
But we played with submission and suffered defeat.

Electricity, static, velocity air
The blue-shirted beetles fed off our despair
A mouth gaped wide open, but failed to be fed
And the skycoated ones hurtled headlong ahead.

Each stamped with a number, not only a name
A shrill silver scream marks the end of the game
A smell in the air, born of joy and disgust
And for some of us, passion has waned in our lust.

The actors leave the green stage, but movement is slow
And the red dotted audience turn quickly to go
Defeat is the enemy, in which there's no fame
But we'll be back next week for the start of the game.

> *Stephanie Hignett*

Lost Family

Shouting and screaming is all I seem to hear
Arguments occur whenever they're all near
Not a moment's peace, it's never silent
Punching and kicking they're all so violent
It is all so quiet, until one walks out
And as soon as they do the others will shout
We're supposed to be a family to get on not to fight
It is not how it used to be we used to be friends
But now nothing's ever right
It's supposed to be my home but it doesn't feel that way
I'd like to click my fingers and for my life to fade away
No more rows, no more fights, no more tears
Just peace and quiet without all the fears.

> *Sophie Amanda Graham*

Sleepless Night

It's 3 a.m. with my eyes wide open
and in all sense of hopelessness I say.
Where do women go to get well again?
Is it the bar across the street where we first met.
Where I can smell the memories of when
we sat on stools and drank the wine
and looked into each other's eyes.
Saw the love there, felt the warmth
when we kissed and held each other tight.

Or, is it the bedroom in the hotel,
where I can smell the memories
of the time we had and shared together.
Remembering all that we went through,
what we did and what we said.
The first time you saw me you said, 'I love you'.
So, where do women go to get well again?
Is it here?

> *Marion Cook*

Halloween

When the devil speaks in whispers and witches cross the sky
And you hear a tap on your window followed by a mournful cry
Remember it is Halloween and all the things you've read
The best place for you tonight is tucked up in your bed

If you leave your window open they will pull you out to play
And you will have to stay with them until the break of day
You'll see the dance of skeletons and hear the graveyard choir
You'll see the witches dancing around the midnight fire
You'll see the goblins running in and out the trees
You'll hear the ghostly music floating on the breeze

Then you'll see the phantom coach flying down the road
Rocking from side to side with its ghostly load
You'll hear the church bells ringing with no-one in the tower
For that's the devil's signal for the bewitching hour.

> *William E. Dempsey*

Old Age Does Not Come by Itself

When I am old I will wear long skirts
and tights down to my ankles;
Go to the beach with my hubby Bert
and put foundation on my wrinkles

When I get my pension money
that I'll spend on things so funny;
Brandy for me and the grey little rat,
brandy for him and the old thick Cat.

I'll do things then I'd never dream of now
like wearing black and blue and brown;
Drinking lots of Wales brewed tea
with my fancy man called Lee.

When I've gone to cuckoo-land
when my mind doesn't work with my hands;
I hope that people I have helped
won't pass me by like a piece of cement.

> *Kay Davies*

Dawn

As earth's darkness ends comes dawn time.
And the world awakes to new births of man and beast
Whilst rolling mists of morning dew refreshes earth.
But "seasons change, and generations multiply.
Till fate decides, the how and when of man's demise.
Blindly we destroy and pollute our earth"
our beaches "swamped from oily surf"
Country lanes almost gone.
All this, in the name of progress is done.
And, it still goes on mindlessly without care
"These failings" we all share.
The wildlife flowers, "Hazy summers," and gentle showers
Yet "men of science have done wonderful things"
Till the power of politics "destroys and rescinds."
Then greed took over "and so it began
The downfall of the honest man.
Sadly, precious time will come to an end
And dawn time will die
Till, only darkness descends"

> *Mollie Clarke*

"So I'll Just Imagine"

I caught the reflection of your golden eye
as it studied me with a curious wry,
I knew it was time to spring into action
as I thought that I felt a mutual attraction,
I'd convinced my heart that you were mine
So I asked you to be my valentine,
Your reply, mute horror, the silence was deafening
I knew then you found my bravado threatening
I jumped into quick, I pushed you too fast
before we'd begun I'd drove us apart
So I'll imagine just what it is, to kiss your ruby satin lips,
    So I'll just imagine.

> *Sharon Maria Hayes*

The Wisdom of the Stone

I see a flower and a stone,
as I sit here on my own.
I can smell the flower's summer scent,
a gift from Mother, heaven scent.
How wondrous such a mighty force,
can create a form so delicate.
And the stone, in its eternity,
resonates a cosmic vibe.
It talks to me, it is alive!
I hear its voice inside my head,
"So you think that you'd be better off dead?
Don't be a fool, don't rue the day,
Your soul will never fade away.
Death is not the end, my friend.
I know, when you go, that I'll meet you again"

Steven Anderson

Autumn Leaves

"The leaves were blowing around my feet"
and though a slight chill stilled the air
on one, such beautiful autumn day.
But, nevertheless, it made my day, for the world
stood still that moment, and I felt so right in a world so
swiftly spinning by and the sky so blue that day.
And I noticed the wonderful shades of nature's magic with their array
of colour of rustic reds, golds and greens of their leaves.

"And I felt those autumn leaves crunching beneath my feet,
for now the leaves were dry that had fallen from their trees.
And all of this I encountered on my return from work that day.
For then, as I pondered and looked around,
I glanced towards the sky,
and was dazzled by the beauty of the red sunset, so up high.
And, I couldn't, help but wonder, as to what would we all
really do. Without this wondrous miracle
yes, of God's creation, to the like of me and you.

M. Siglioccolo

The Sunshine of My Life

When all about walls crumble down
And winds whirl angry, 'round and 'round:
I think of you and close my eyes
And sunshine brightens up the skies.

When shadows skate around my head
And screams awake me from my bed:
I think of you and close my ears
And see the sunshine through my tears

When everything becomes too much
When all I want is your soft touch:
I think of you and once again
The sunshine lifts me from my pain

On golden days the sunshine downs
And midday heat does soothe and warm.
The amber dust will calm my mind
In glowing sunsets, you I find.

Linda Ellis

My First Love

Time passes; do we really forget our first love?
As I sit in the chair, eighty five today,
I remember my first Love
It seems only yesterday.
He was tall and strong,
Younger than I
Do you love me I asked?
This was his reply.
I will always love you said he taking my hand,
Whether in this life or another land.
I remember those words sitting looking at him.
His body lays still in the chapel of rest
He's gone to another land now.
Will he remember those words
Or were they spoken in jest?

D. Perry

Memories

Sweet thoughts of you are with me now,
And though I miss you at my side
My memories suffice somehow.

Though many times we had a row,
And times there were I almost cried,
Sweet thoughts of you are with me now.

Now cool is my once fevered brow,
And though your love has been denied,
My memories suffice somehow.

And though my make-up did allow
Our parting to upset my pride,
Sweet thoughts of you are with me now.

And though the break-up did endow
Me with a sadness I can't hide,
My memories suffice somehow.

And all this said I must avow
There is no verse in which I lied;
Sweet thoughts of you are with me now,
My memories suffice somehow.

Terence Jacob

Words I Cannot Say

The Winter's sun, the misty moon, the darker night creeps in too
soon, as inhibitions of my mind, in sad confusion hide behind the
eyes that long for peaceful sleep, but turning to the pillow weep.

The words that flow in even pen, the thoughts I cannot find again,
For they are lost between each line, and every gap a moment mine;
the written word is but a part as is the beating of my heart,
for all my thoughts to find a way, into the words I cannot say.

The momentary human doubt, to question what it's all about;
the fear that hides the pen so lost in life's confusion when
it cannot find the reason why - unspoken words unwritten try
to air the thoughts and find a way into the words I cannot say.

When thoughts and fears cannot pretend, nor dark aloneness find
a friend, for who am I that I would share such sad confusion that
I bear, when I myself can't find a way,
into the words I cannot say.

So oft' I fail to understand that courage can reach out a hand,
enough for faith to blind the fear, enough to dry confusion's tear,
enough maybe to find a way into the words I cannot say.

Nita M. Dubois

The Three Seasons

With winter's mantle lifting
And the crying of new lambs.
The movement in the hedgerows
Tells us spring is just at hand.

The hosts of golden daffodils
That frolic in the glen
The sunshine on the rolling hills
We pray 'twill never end.

The apple and the cherry trees
In the orchard by the lane.
Shower blossoms on the morning breeze
And laburnum's golden rain.

My thoughts are of the bluebell
And the lilac on the wall
Nearby, the stream, where nightingales
And silver birches dwell

Can it be they all must fade
as summer passes by.
The leaves turn red and gold and brown
Beneath the autumn sky.

J. Beange

Life's Bitter Disappointment

Waves of disenchantment crash against the shore,
As I lay and wonder what is it all for,
When life won't follow the path you choose,
And all that you touch starts to blister and bruise,

The tangled web of deceit and lies,
I hear the shouts I hear the cries,
Of demons telling me where I've failed,
where my life's been shunted off the rails,

I'm being driven to the brink of insanity,
When each day brings a fresh calamity,
Take this rope from the neck to show me you care,
Stop me sliding down this spiral into despair,

Who knows the answers to all these questions,
Of constant setbacks and cruel deception,
When life's rich tapestry is fake,
Another major mishap, another grave mistake,

And as I sink into this depressed state,
Of endless worry, bitterness and hate,
Wondering where my life will lead,
Will I ever find all that I need.

Mark Tugwell

Letting Go

I saw your footprints in the snow
When I looked out last night.
"I will follow those footprints," I said
"When dawn comes with the light."
The dark, cold night passed fleetingly,
I opened up the door,
And saw a crystal drift.
Your footprints were no more
For they had become ice-bound,
Frozen out, no trace
Unwarmed, out of print,
Gone to another place.

R. Smith

World's Uncalm

What a sad lonely world this place can be,
When it leaves your life in sheer debris.
One lost love does break your heart,
One moment in life you feared would depart.

The heartache the pain it hits you hard.
From your thoughts and tears you try to disregard.
They say hard men they do not weep,
But who knows what goes on in the secrets they keep

Your pleasures in life you take for granted,
In your memory they are firmly planted.
But life takes turns on your ups and downs,
On some its smiles on others it frowns

William Joseph Dean

Happening Perdition

O'er the mountains travelling winds
  Angry bitten howling these
Anguish tension fraught of pain
  Noise of deafening hammers slain
Thrashing waves on Cornish rocks
  Raging in storm, lashing, seething,
Gnawing pulling
  The force so great
The fear, the pain, torn and worn
  The feeling - falling
Gripped and ripped
  From stable roots, embedded deep
For years to keep
  Now, gone - broken, weeping
Seeking solace
  Without seeing - just being.

Margaret M. Foster Jensen

Just Give a Thought

Just give a thought to the air that you breath
When it was given to you for free I believe

Imagine what will happen if that cold wind blows
Think what will happen, will you think that it snows

Do you live now and will you live then
Do you give now but what if and when

So just give a thought to the lives we all lead
Listen to the words, take cover, take heed

For one day it will happen, I predict pretty soon
If the powers that lead don't change their views

So consider what may be, in the future for you
Think for your children, please tell them the truth

For they are the fated to change what we've done
For they will be destined to the wind when we've gone

So just give a thought to the plight of our souls
Just a little time to that someone who drolls

Don't be undone by the dredge of society
Don't waste your time in a life of compliancy

These are not your lives that you lay on the line
These are the tunes of old father time.

Raymond David Povall

When the Wind Blows

The wind blew down upon his frown,
And whispered in his ear.
"Why do you feel the way you do?"
And in reply the boy did cry,
"Life is no longer dear".

The wind howled out, a mighty shout,
That this was not to be,
As life was like a precious stone,
Sweet and clear, with nought to fear,
And this was not the time to flee.

His tears were gone, his eyes now shone,
The wind now knew his job was done,
And dropped to just a breeze.
With new found spring, and an impish grin,
Boy walked off under setting sun.

Task complete, the wind did die,
To take the young boys place.
For all things knew when death was due,
There could be no empty space.

Michael Bull

Untitled

You won't remember that which you've heard
And you won't tell a soul,
Because if you do, they'll think you absurd
Or you'll end up in a hole.

You'll try to forget that which you've seen
But it will creep back at night
And corner and buffet you in a bad dream
So you'll scream and scream with fright
Don't even contemplate that which you've touched
Feeling its warmth on your skin

Along came Bren Scorned a sneer
Shakespeare died of too much beer
Along came Bren and said Oh Globe
All your troubles in me enrobe.

Gravestones, a crippled tree with an iron crutch
Beds of flowers faces lifted up to catch the sun
Smiling on an old man with a large green bottle of sherry
And yet such perfect charm - an oasis of peace unexpected
In an area of violence and noise and cheap humanity.
Next door to a place of my formal education.

B. Beirne

Cradled Safe

I rock you in my arms at night,
Whispering gently everything is alright,
Your little heart flutters
With your eyes so bright,
Because the sound of thunder
Has given you a fright,
I cradled you safely
Until the morning light,
The storm was over
You feel safe now it's light.
J. Diana Clark

Gone in the Mist of Time

Arthur the Pendragon the
arch-warlord, duke, king of England.
He and only he and his
knights of the round table
Brought the Celtic Clans of Britain into one.
And the Pendragon Arthur he made England free.
They fought the Saxon and
the Norman hordes, the Picks
and Irish pirates and Lancelot
at his side and the Bedivere
and Merlin and Guinevere his
Queen and Camelot.
This made England free and
this Country what it is today.
The Pendragon Warlord
brought law and order and civilisation
to Britain the myth, legend
of Camelot gone in the
Mists of time and beyond
Arthur the Pendragon king, true king of Britain
Malcolm Gordon Form

Looking Back

Taking time, looking back;
What have I done, am I on the right track?

I look around and all I see,
Are broken hearts and misery!

Where is the laughter, where is the fun?
What happened to that shining sun?

Am I to blame for what has come?
Am I in shame for what I've done?

The light won't shine on my life anymore,
I've turned around and closed the door.

Taking time and looking back
Is there a way to get off this track?
Samantha L. Marsh

Glenurquhart

The beautiful hills that surround Glenurquhart
Are covered in thick white snow
With a lovely wintry scene in the valley below
The trees standing upright and proud -
As if to flaunt the winter's cloud
Covered in their snowy gowns
Looking like ghosts in the darkening sky
The fish sleep soundly in the bottom of their ice covered loch
Waiting for the warmth of Spring to release them from their icy tomb
The birds in their cosy nests - high in the trees
Anxiously survey the snowy scene beneath
Looking for the little shoots of green to appear
Which means that Spring will soon be here
Icicles hang from the roofs of the houses on the hill
Adding to the beauty of the wintry scene
Peace and tranquillity hover around
Not a sound to be heard between valley and hill
This lovely glen will be there forever
For mankind to relax and recuperate
From the stress and strain of this Modern World in which
we live today
M. E. Kitson

A Winter's Day

The wind blew, the snow fell
whirling, swirling, drifting down on us.
The birds flew in search of food;
the Robin stood and peered in,
hoping for a crust of bread.
The trees all heavy with fallen snow'
Blocking out the scenic view.
The Sparrows, the Magpie, and Blackbirds too,
hoping for spring to come.
Juicy fat worms, juicy fat flies;
warm sunny days,
what a wonderful thought!
Laura Jayne Cregg

"The Shore Perfectionist"

Pursuer of the lonely shoreline,
Arrogant eyes piercing sea-mist gloom
For abandoned, helpless creatures
Washed up, stranded to their doom
By endless crashing of the rollers,
In the gale-driven North Sea spume.

Successful pirate of the stricken,
Heedless of their fatal plight,
Plundering freely of all others
In the fight to claim his right
To monopoly of the tideline,
Extending far beyond our sight.

Gliding effortlessly on the thermals,
Ever watchful, as he soars,
In grace, the pure embodiment
Of God's perfection, without flaw.
This common gull, in beauty faultless,
Scours the wind torn Norfolk shore.
Norman C. Whye

The Woodland

How quickly the spirit rejoices
When in a moment of sweet delight,
A shimmering sea of daffodils
Burst suddenly into sight.
Gentle, lively, rising, falling
Moving with ease and grace,
Crowning stars of sparkling beauty
To unfold in a woodland place.

Golden trumpets, erect and tall,
A congregation that reached down to the stream,
Resplendent in their woodland dress
Some lemon, some yellow and some cream.
Rhythmically bending to the ebb and flow,
When kissed by the wind and sun,
To waltz in blissful harmony
When human hearts are caught and won.

As a pellucid sun snaked through the trees,
To cast thin shadows on the ground
How glad was I, my eyes could see
This woodland royally crowned.
Myrtle Haysler

Fan Worship

So when they ask me
What do you see in him?
What can I answer?
What can I say?
How can I explain
To those who do not know
Who do not see
Who do not feel?
Those who are blind in sight and sense
Too blind to see his soul
Feel his power, his joy, his love?
What can I answer?
What can I say?
I say, "He's Michael".
Shirley Lloyd

Northern Ireland

I've always thought of Ireland
As a land of green serenity
But now it's a place of war and strife
Where man or woman fight for their life.
The blast of bomb and the roar of fire
Another home is a funeral pyre.

A soldier advances down the street
A sniper's bullet grazes his feet
Quickly he turns gun at the ready,
Eyes searching and hand steady
But another bullet finds its mark
And the soldier falls, alone, in the dark.

Surely religion should bind together
Not tear apart forever and ever.
Civilian and soldier each take a chance
Of being destroyed in this endless battle
Surely somewhere there is a solution
To end this futile and needless destruction.

Norah Wilkins

The Day I Met Your Eyes

It was an ordinary day rather bland;
    as a matter of fact!

The sun was shining; but it was snowing in
my heart as I aimlessly ambled along the path

Suddenly out of the blue something
Caught my eye she was blonde with an
enigmatic smile!
A turn with a shrill corn bright hair
bobbed and bounced amidst sunlight

Soft wind blew dislodging each
strand indiscriminately fanned
waving hair.
I stood transfixed her eyes were deep
pools of cold blue enchanted captivated
lost trapped emersed
Like a spider to the fly!
To do with what you will forever
The day I met your eyes.
The cat and the mouse, the bird in the cage
The day I met your eyes.

J. D. Stevenson

Untitled

On Armistice Day; see all those poppies worn
as bleeding hearts.
'Mongst all those people worn in remembrance.
Remembrance of those dead of conflict then
and in-between, and now.
Loosely, in fields, those poppies grow,
we all admire their colour in amongst the green.
Sadly, they are cut down at harvest time.

Poppies, then in confusion in the fields grow,
just like those waves of men who rose up;
and were cut down - scythed just like those
fields of green at harvest time.
Gladly now we remember them, those men.
Sadly now those men are gone.
Poppies, then, is how we will remember them.
Forevermore.

P. T. Williams

Her Man

He came into her life,
When she was lonely, she was down,
It was not right,
For they were wed, but he still stayed around.

The years rolled by,
And still they met, they had time for each other,
To love and be loved,
But she would always stay his mistress, he, her lover.

Mary R. Turrell

My Boat

The boat leaps and sings like a nightingale,
As dark ripplings on the water reach it.
My spirit soars and spreads a with the sail.

Bright flashing sunshine makes shadows seem frail.
As we skim along others fall behind.
The boat leaps and sings like a nightingale.

I weak the tiller and dare not exhale.
Turn with perfection so we catch the breeze.
My spirit soars and spreads with the sail.

Clouds move we are shrouded by a veil,
The soft wind freshens and all the boats heel,
The boat leaps and sings like a nightingale.

On a swaying buoy sits a proud wagtail,
That flutters away when we draw closer.
My spirit soars and spreads with the sail.

As the current drops so dies my telltale.
We pull gracefully into the jetty.
As I leap ashore like a nightingale,
My spirit soars, and I pull down my sail.

Sally Radford

"This World of Ours"

I wonder if the time will come when everything seems right
When hopes can rise, and wars demise to make the future bright
So much has happened o'er the years to help us on our way
And yet we still find many things to cause our own decay.

The grass is green, the sky still blue the sea and sand are ours
The trees and plants all flourish with their show of gaudy flowers
But all the colours, all the hues are saddened every day
By all those people on this earth who must just have their say.

The world has suffered hard and long as every day we need
The easy life provided by our selfishness and greed.
We all want this, we all want that, we want it here and now.
But who are those who'll pay the price for all our greed - and how?

Yet we know the world is lovely, it's ours and ours and ours
There are people who could help it, they're those who have the
powers
The trees we fell, the earth we maul, the countryside we rape
We'll never live to put things right unless we all escape.

Let's slow the cars and walk a pace and sparkle as we chance
To breathe the air that could be fresh if given just a glance.
The world has sped these hundred years and given such a lot
We could just care and stop to think, to cherish what we've got.

Zena Annette Horton

"The Beautiful Women"

Beneath are the beautiful women
Who are drifting along with the tide,
Their bodies are changing around them
Though they are still lovely inside

They rejoiced in their homes and their families
Bought gifts to arrange 'round the tree,
Loved perfumes and satins and laces
And having their hair done 'at three'.

They loved shopping for hats in the springtime,
And birthdays and dinners and wine,
The making of jam and the sewing
And washing that blew on the line.

There were picnics and trips to the country
And taking the kids to the sea,
And trying to keep up with the fashion
And having their friends in for tea.

So I weep for the beautiful women
As they silently sit in a row.
And I sigh for the years that are passing
And the days that are melting like snow.

Rosemary Williamson

Elusive Fame

Who seeks the magic formula?
  Who dreams of bright success?
Who can rely on their talents -
  To thrive on the world's excess?

Who can turn the wheel of fortune,
  Or hold the hand of fate?
Who dares to pass the Rubicon
  In a bid for Luck's great stake?

How many become triumphant -
  High in esteem to stand?
Whose name rings out in history -
  Applauded throughout the land?

Which recruit in life's arena
  Is chosen from the fray?
Is it chance that moulds man's striving -
  Re-sculpturing rough clay?

Does it matter one has wisdom . . .
  Another, not one grain?
Is it the longing of the soul
  That opens the door to fame?

Kay Ennals

Son

We will get no big prizes I fear.
As father and son of the year.
For I am no Saint it's very true.
And you have all your faults too.
But I don't want another fathers boy.
Because you've brought me so much joy.
It doesn't make me less of a man.
To express my feelings when I can.
From the day I held you on my knee.
Your love has been important to me.
And although there's changes I must face.
Son no one will ever take your place.
Cars and soldiers are all nearly past.
For being my little baby didn't last
And the sad thing about being older
Is I cant carry you on my shoulder.
I want always agree with what you do.
But son I'll always be there for you.
All I ask is that you really try.
To love me until the day I die.

Thomas M. Bell

Can I Interest You in Words?

As I start this verse I wonder how my words will seem;
Will they stand straight and tall like cold prison walls and
  confine you within my dream?

Or, will they explode off the page in an olfactory rage and
  stink out your nostrils with onion and sage?

Will they spring to cause pain at your jugular vein, rip it out
  in a trice then want to do it again?

Will they cause a great din as the ball's nodded in, in the
  one World Cup final England's started to win?

Will they scream and shout 'Let me out, let me out' like a
  terrified child who has nothing but doubt?

Will they create an emotion and start a live potion swirling
  'round in your stomach like a salty green ocean?

Will they jump and then drop, disappear without a plop - an
  Olympic style dive - or just belly flop?

Will they confuse and befuddle, merely mumble in a huddle,
  be a soggy old mess like a page in a puddle?

Or, will you think they are wrong to carry on for so long, stop
  reading and equate them with a nasty strong pong?

As I finish this verse I wonder if I'll have interested someone
in words.

Paul Ibbs

To the Past

Oh what fun it was when I was not mixed up in my head,
When I could go shopping and didn't get lost
And bought all my goods and could count the cost,
Oh what fun it was when I was not mixed up in my head,
When I knew to post a letter and not open it instead
And know if I'm retiring or getting out of bed.
Oh what fun it was when I was not mixed up in my head,
And knew to put some food away and not to take it out.
I know that I'm forgetful and my mind is full of doubt
I have my coat on am I coming in or going out?
Oh what fun it was when I was not mixed up in my head,
And knew what I had done and knew what I had said.

S. K. Chapman

The Soldier

His body trained to fight the foe
As forward from his home he goes
To battle in a foreign land
Where the sun beats down on him and the sand.
At night in dreams he does recall
A wife and children still so small
In longing to hold them he wakes up to find
His home a tent, his roof the sky
He looks up at the stars above
And remembers when he fell in love
How can they look exactly the same
When the love of his life is so far away
When day breaks who knows what it brings
Wrong deeds and words can alter things
And from the peaceful desert sands
A battle can engulf the land
How many men will have to die
How many wives and mothers cry
To free a land that is the goal
So man can call that land his home.

Maureen O'Leary

Untitled

I walked down memory lane today,
and thought about us and yesterday.
I smiled when I thought of the sun and the heat,
did I really have wings on my feet?

I pictured the heron and the family of mice,
the way that you held me and made me feel nice,
Walking beside you with your hand in mine,
the taste of your kiss like a very fine wine.

I remember us walking in a cool Autumn breeze,
with leaves slowly falling down from the trees.
We walked over grass covered with dew,
I was so happy to be there with you.

I took a deep breath and walked on my way,
the memory of sunshine fading away.
Just for a moment I wished I didn't care,
the cold winter wind blew through my hair,
Now was the time my heart had to say,
"Goodbye to us and yesterday"

Rosalyn M. Butterworth

I Woke Up One Day and Stared Death in the Face

I looked at death it wasn't
what I'd expected, it wasn't
this horrifying thing we're led
to believe. I felt at peace; it
was a peace I'd never experienced
before, I looked at death and
it stared back at me. I looked
again but still I was at peace
nobody could hurt me nobody
could take this peace away,
it was mine completely.
I looked at death and it
did not turn its face. I looked
death in the eye and smiled
and waved death goodbye.

Marie Langley

Spring Flowers

Delicate petals of sweet smelling flowers
What lovely fragrances they bring
So many colours and varieties,
Especially the flowers of spring
Anemone, Snowdrop and Crocus
Hyacinth and Daffodil
The Iris, Daisy and Tulip
Freesias and Jonquil
Each one has its beauty
In its own way
But put them all together
They make a beautiful bouquet

J. Mardel

Parting

My life was like a bird on wing
As high on clouds I soared
But as you turned and walked away
I felt my light go out
You left me as a singing lark
Who fell with broken wing
And all that I remember
Are the things you meant to me
Like the gentle breeze which was your voice
Now quiet, calm and still
Like the Mighty Oak whose form you took
And stands no more for me
I loved you more than life itself
Which I thought would never end
But as my Summer slips away
And my light begins to fade
No more, my love, no more, my love
I feel my life is done
And only dreams I now shall keep
Within my broken heart

Mavis H. Whitaker

Untitled

My heart is so heavy, my eyes they are sad,
As I drift back to the time when I was a lad.
Lots of home comforts, a warm cosy bed,
A good secure life for me lay ahead.
At seventeen I met a girl, who was so full of life,
I remember my proudest day, when she became my wife.
We drifted along as happy as can be,
No children for us, just Susan and me.
But that fateful day I remember so well,
When two policemen came by and rang on my bell.
With sorrowful eyes and in a low voice they said,
I'm so sorry Sir, but your Susan is dead.
The shock of it all, of losing my wife,
I gave it all up, including my life.
So, here I sit now, in a doorway alone,
And dream of the time I had a place to call home.
My dark damp space, just lit by a lamp,
The people walk past and call me a tramp.
But please do not judge, think not what you see,
Look into my eyes, look closer... see me.

K. L. Rayment

Spring

The sweet green grass is coming through,
Wet from the morning mist's clear dew,
Flowers popping up here and there,
A bird's clear sing-song in the air.

The buds are growing on the trees,
Helped by a cool uplifting breeze,
Newborn animals finding their feet,
Life to them is a special treat.

The smell of the fields are fresh and clean,
Tracks of rabbits can be seen,
Streams are noisily trickling by,
I love spring, now you know why.

Kathryn Woodhouse

Idyll

Take me to a golden time
When fluting nymphs and piping boys
Twirled and sang of earthly joys
With dance and sport and mime.
Lead me on through seaward dreams,
Let me taste the salt-blue wind,
Fly with hawks beyond the clouds
And vanish into mist and haze.
Take me down an autumn path,
Smell the wetness of the leaves
And kiss the dew and soar again
Above the earth-bound, bold and brave,
But turning home on wings of fire
To scatter roses on your grave.

Simon Harrison

Hopeful Thoughts

I sit and think of time to come when I'll be frail and old
And wonder how my days I'll fill, what will each hour hold?
Will they be tranquil, calm and warm just like the summer sun?
Or haunted by the times I've tried and lost - but never won.

The path of life sometimes seems hard, so stony, bleak and cold
Although I try to face the odds, put on a front so bold.
I've never seemed to make the grade to lasting warm content
Too rashly have I walked my path, each wrong way I have leant.

I still have the time to try again if I'm allowed the chance,
To look the future in the eye, a straight and honest glance.
Accept mistakes I've made before throughout the years gone by
So I can face my older days serene without a sigh.

This time will be so peaceful then, my heart will be so full
Of love for everything around, yes, nothing will be dull.
I'll not regret a thing that's passed if I can conquer this
My days to come will hold no fear for they'll be full of bliss.

Vivianne Dubret

Unknown Disappointment

What if trust withdraws,
What if I don't know the score,
What if the memories call,
What if the tears don't fall,
What if there's only one road someday,
What if it leads me in the wrong way,
What if there is nothing to say,
What if pains the price to pay.
What if we're wrong, if we're right,
Two opposites drawn together in life,
Truth and love against betrayal and lies,
So many questions, I wonder, why?
Strong but helpless, afraid and unsure
But the answers lie in the future,
    trapped behind a locked door.

Sarah Marples

Peace

I was comfy and peaceful and lying quite still
As I lay reflecting on my life,
I was thinking of all the things I liked best
Not things that had caused me strife.

I thought it quite strange as I had no desire,
To move not even my eyes.
But I felt so at ease and at peace with all things
That I chose to ignore someone's cries.

I lay there a while as still as the night
When into my mind came a wonderful sight
My family appeared each member was there
And my happiness seemed too complete to bear.

But alas they were not happy and glad
They had tears on their cheeks, and their eyes were all sad.
And yes, they were looking at me in my bed,
And the reason you see is because I was Dead.

Margaret Waddell

Snow

Falling softly from above, the whiteness of a pure
white dove
Changing the greens and mellowing gold
To pure whiteness as it falls to the earth below
White all white everywhere, cascading on trees
rooftops chimneys and more
Changing the mother earth to a carpet of peace
Shall I not walk on this virgin white softness
Serene and majestic all over the land
But leave the footsteps of nature to take
the first steps on this new mother-land

Mary Morris

Poetry

Poetry is the music of the soul
And the words come from the heart.
There is poetry in music and movement
And poetry in song and dance.
When flowers and trees sway with the breeze
That is poetry too.
There is poetry in the rustle of spring
With graceful birds upon the wing.
There is poetry in the rushing stream
And in the waterfall.
Poetry too begins anew
Where the fountains fall.
All nature and poetry go hand in hand
With the freedom of this our pleasant land.
For there is poetry in children's laughter
And in a baby's smile
Poetry too when love is new
When loving eyes beguile.
So let poetry from your heart enrol
With the music of your very soul.

F. M. Rothwell

Travels of Life

The years of my life have travelled far as I search within my mind
Whatever has set me thinking questions and answers I must find
I picture part of childhood playing on cobbled streets
A top and whip a skipping rope a bag of coloured sweets
The gypsy girl who knocked on doors to sell her pretty flowers
Cross her palm with silver hear of mystical powers
The candy man with barrow trundling down back lanes
Shouts of any old lumber faces look from window panes
Now moving on I encounter adolescent at full bloom
Dancing singing bouncing bright often feeling gloom
I meet the true love of my life time sped as family grow
Those years of happy marriage pass by as a tide must flow
Age stands still for no one as we reach a golden time
Reflection shows so many things that makes a life worthwhile
Many memories to ponder on I am left with a great big smile
Questions part only answered I enjoyed deep thought for a while...

Mary Robinson

I Should Have Known!

I wandered lonely as a cloud
And walk 'round the shops, but I'm just one of a crowd.
I thought I'd buy a coat or a dress
For when I look in the mirror I feel such a mess.
There's plenty to choose from but oh what a figure
My heart's in the right place but my bottom half's bigger.
There are jackets of blue and dresses of green,
But when I try them on I'm not fit to be seen.
I walk in the next shop and search through the rails
I'd like to find something reduced in the sales.

I'll try one or two more with hope in my heart
But I should have known better right from the start
These clothes are odd sizes?? and all out of gear
So I'll save all my money and come back next year.
My feet are aching they need my respect
So I'll go for the bus and have time to reflect
I could have been hasty — of that I confess.
For there's nothing so smart, as MY LITTLE BLACK DRESS.

Marjorie Gale

Rage

Reason matters not upon vehement desire,
when rage from within, thus turns to fire;
spiralling thrust, like a cyclonic storm,
eye of the serpent, the venom is born;
martial ardour, fervent, and fierce,
anger so strong, heart threatens to pierce;
passion, and pain, the cocktail of rage,
pumping the blood, high adrenalin stage;
braved with the lust of warrior Mars,
ferocity bred for gods of the stars;
force of four winds, and that of the tide,
can only compare thunder's raging ride;
unchained, untamed, lies in dormant abode,
vehement desire, lies a rage to explode.

G. Davies

Memories

Strange, quiet, eerie I thought
As I looked around and stared,
Was this the place
Was this the street,
The years have simply fled.

No more familiar faces
Yet the houses are the same,
A great sadness filled my heart
As I walked down in the rain.

There was the garden shed still standing,
There was the same old gate,
I'd often stood there in my teens
Staying out far too late.

All those thoughts came flooding back
Happy years were they,
Mrs. Brown at No. 1, Jimmy at No. 8,
All that seems so long ago
Many years have passed,
The only thing that doesn't change
Are memories that last.

Sarah Rhodes

Disco Nights

Oh! What a racket what a din
What is this place I've entered in
Bodies packed like sardines
Sweat running, in tiny streams
Down face and arms, down front and back
Right in the middle of the pack
A gyrating head nodding body form
In positions far from the norm
Legs weaving arms flailing
Lights blinking in and out
Away at the back hear the D.J. shout
He lets you know what record is coming
While all around a humming and thrumming
A great vibration in my ear
I am pushed there, then I am shoved here
Faces oblivious minds carried away
As all around me bodies sway
Oh! What a racket what a din
These disco nights are not my scene.

Pat Duncan

Christmas Time

That special time is here again
When houses are a-glowing.
with christmas trees and fairy lights
That everyone is showing.
The postman has a heavy load
To carry 'round each day.
I look out for him eagerly
for cards that come our away.
But the best time, is on christmas morn.

When the children wake to find
That Santa has been and left his gifts
And as usual, has been very kind.

Pamela Kiefer

203

Man's Inhumanity to Man

For many years actually a score
We've holidayed on Yugoslavia's shore,
Dubrovnik, Makarska and lovely Lake Bled
Also Kaponik and Kranjska-gora where you can sled.

On leaving the plane, you can tell you are there
From all of the scents pervading the air,
Barbecue smoke, Rosemary, Lavender and Pine
Our holiday had started, this was the sign.

The people so happy and eager to please
To make our stay contented, carefree, at ease,
We enjoyed the scenery, mountains and lakes
The sparkling blue sea washing over the breaks

Bathing and lazing enjoying the sun
Dancing in the hotel when day was done.
So many happy memories come to mind
Of this beautiful country so terribly defiled.

With the scars of battle horrific and sad
Surely the Yugoslavs must be totally mad,
To destroy their heritage and cause such pain
To their fellow countrymen, What have they to gain?

K. Markendale

Her Student Son

You've driven back now after a sad, sad weekend,
When you cried and she tried to be like your best friend,
   And not your Mum!

Your hopes and your dreams, they have all come to naught.
Which was surely not what you thought you'd been taught
   By your Mum.

Life can be too easy, or can be pretty foul.
Some days you are singing, some trying hard not to howl.
   Just ask your Mum!

She reluctantly guessed that the day could soon dawn
When you might feel betrayed, alone, bereft and forlorn.

As you blurted out, sobbing, each stark disillusion.
All your pain and your hurt and your total confusion
   To you Mum.

She put her arms 'round you and wished she could say
That you'd wake in the morning with the pain gone away.

Oh son, it can't be, but your Mum always knew
How you cope with life's setbacks is what will mould you.
And she knows, in the end, you will pull bravely through.
   Like your Dad.

Lucy M. Kaye

When Love Is . . .

When love is something you feel but can't have,
When you know someone for whom your feelings are strong,
When you know that to them you shall never belong,
When as time's gone by through shyness you've done everything wrong,
When that someone has love for another,
When you can't get close enough even to love as sister and brother,
When it seems that no matter what you say,
When you know that your dreams will never come true,
When you keep on smiling with nothing else to do,
When you talk out the wrong words never saying I love you,
When you see lips knowing they're ones you'll never kiss,
When you know of that person too many moments you are apart,
When you know that you can't fulfil the feelings from your heart,
When with everyday time passes,
When as life is you'll never get that sheer bliss,
When as life is of that pleasure you shall miss,
When as love is the reason we multiply,
When knowing that really no matter how you try,
Knowing you'll be left writing silly poems alone to ask why till
you die, When love is . . .

Paul Waldock

When I Went to War

I joined the ranks of two by two and marched in tunic royal blue,
with head held high and sturdy arm,
and thoughts of love yet bold and calm.

   When I Went To War.

The Captain he said charge the foe and up and ready we would go,
for ere the words had left his lips
then bayonets fixed and at our hips.

   When I Went To War.

To fight our enemies he said, some made ready some were dead,
then at the foe we'd lunge and fight
from the morning till the night.

   When I Went To War.

Towards the gun smoke and the hell,
with tattered flag and Captain's yell
and tunic blue now spattered red, some were weary some were dead.

   When I Went To War.

Now as those days are far gone by my thoughts are of that battle cry,
I sometimes wonder who can say
or judge who won that sad affray.

   When I Went To War.

Sydney Sanderson

Evacuees

Evacuees
What did they know, what did they do, where will they go.
Please end this war, I hate it so.
I will have to go and leave my love ones.

There is a woman standing there, she has the most beautiful hair.
She's like my mum I miss her so.
Please end this war and let our people go.

Kill Hitler and end this war.
I want peace and yet more.
Send me my mum; I miss my dad I bet he is ever so sad.
He is fighting the war, I don't know where
they say it's for peace but I don't really care.

Hitler is winning what will be
Will I be dead or will I be free?
Kill Hitler and end this war for evermore.

Evacuees - yes we are free. There's a price for our peace.
Men have died fighting the war to be seen no-more.
Take this message - carry it away.
We must go forward peace in our hearts.
Never to let another war to start.

Katy Woods

The Joys of Motherhood!!

It starts with a wonderful feeling of joy.
What will it be; a girl or a boy?
Then tiredness sets in and nausea flows,
and your figure expands as your miracle grows.

You're determined to be the most perfect mother,
to be patient and kind, to love one another,
but if only you knew of the trials ahead!
How you're pushed to the limit and often see red!

The waiting is over, your baby is here,
The worries, exhaustion and pain disappear.
And happiness spreads through your life; such elation
and you're filled with such love for your precious creation

Now life will be different in so many ways,
there's no going back to your wild carefree days!
There's less chance of sleeping or having a rest,
and your temper and patience are put to the test.
There's no job on Earth as fulfilling as this,
there's nothing or no-one can bring you such bliss,
It's something to treasure and cherish for good.
The best feeling ever; it's called 'MOTHERHOOD'.

S. A. Henville

I Catch the Sounds of Life Slowly Drifting Away from Me

Sleeping then praying, balancing my life on a thread.
What is that radiance that lights up my bed.
Are angels present or am I dead.
No voice can I hear nor face can I see.
Just the sounds of life saying goodbye to me.

Give me your hand friend till my earthly time is run.
Time is life oh so precious.
Yet how much we spend on things that really do not matter.
That serve no useful purpose in the end.
This is my prayer that I will find behind tomorrow's door.

No pain, no pills, no smack or crack,
Just the precious gift of love.

So let me build upon my ruins
Leave my troubled past behind
Explained it to my children that place I have to find
For nothing is secure in my lonely junked up mind
Unseen hands reaching out to help life passing away
Loved ones must go
But memories must stay

Les Campbell

Mother of Mine

We all die one day
When it will be is unknown,
Pain we go through day by day
Losing her mother I hear them say
She'll get over it one day.
But the pain never ends, it just goes on
Because losing your mother
She's the one. That special person
Who brought you into this world
And now has gone.
Empty inside I must go on living
Missing the love she was giving
Joy, laughter I have no-more
Just sadness no feeling
Numb and sore.

Sharon Mount

Lament for the Twentieth Century

Emerging from the sunlight of a golden age
When air was pure and water bright with life
Into the grey and dusty plain of fear.
There is a fear that was unknown to man
Not fear of death, for death is part of life
But fear of pain and sorrow for the lives
Still unbegot and of a future time.
It may be there will be no future time
The limits have been reached, the goal in sight
And that the master of creation who
Gave us peace and beauty and the will to strive,
Compassion, joy and all the powers of love
And knowing that these gifts have been in vain
Will put aside his plan and say 'No More'.

I. Websdale

"The Wild Bunch"

Look upon a grassy meadow, drink in the sweetness of the air,
Wild flowers growing in abundance, speckled hue to dazzle there,
But standing out ablaze, in glory, the poppy with her 'bowed head' bud,
Nodding in the summer breezes, for the earth her seeds to flood.

Along the hedgerows thicket fence, hawthorn and bramble overgrow,
Fragrant honeysuckle all entwined, dog rose blossoms out full blown,
Nature's gems such perfect beauty, thriving 'twixt the thorn and grass,
A posy gathered, it's the 'Wild Bunch' that transforms the simple glass.

P. A. Newman

Ambitions

In the cold grey light of dawn I sit here and reflect
What it is I want from life what do I expect
A life of full and plenty do I wish to come my way
Nothing much to do but laze around most every day

I do not think that would be me - I know that I would find
Doing nothing every day - and not to use my mind
Is not the way I see my life stretching out ahead
Unless I can be useful - I may as well be dead

A life spent helping others more unfortunate than me
Is what I really want to do and how I want to be
This may not be an easy task, this I understand
But I will do the best I can to give a helping hand

It doesn't matter just how small the help I give may be
The most important, thing of all is that it came from me
And when my time is over I'll hope it was worthwhile
And those who would remember me do so with a smile

L. Snow

Little Grey Squirrel

Little grey Squirrel
When you climb a, tree so fast you make
My head twirl,
When you're planting your food be it
Twigs or nuts,
Do you hide them beneath leaves,
Or nuts,
When you climb your favourite tree,
Please don't be nervous of me,
So when you sleep through the winter,
And cold,
Please still remember me when
I grow old.

Paul J. C. Hunter

Always There's Hope

Many years ago we decided to part
When you left you took a piece of my heart
Here I was just left on my own
But your decision to leave I could not condone
Time does heal the pain that you feel
But missing you seems so unreal
I picked up the pieces and started anew
But my feelings were the same, were they for you?
As we get older memories don't fade
Hoping one day you would visit or stay
Now you're here and home at last
The heartache I felt is a thing of the past
The future looks bright, I feel it's a new
Life can begin again, just me and you

Mary E. Gill

Poetry

Poetry you know me well
What have you in store for me today
My pen breathing with every move
How would I write without your desires poetry
Spelling the words my heart beats out

Some are rainbows, colours many
Just as much are they sad
Many just sweet memories
Others clinging to crazy dreams
Oh' poetry so like a deep well

Such wonders come from you
Oh' poetry who named you so
Many a poem has been written
Allowing one escaping time
Seeing rainbows through the mind

A refuge engulfing in you poetry
Wiping away tears of sorrow
Writing in you for hope in tomorrow
Stay poetry with me my pen's in hand
Waiting for what you have to say.

Rosina Drury

Mirror Image

You're always were my mirror, the way I looked was the same for you,
When I flipped my hair from my shoulder, I knew that you did too.

When I turned I knew you did, when I spoke you spoke at the same time,
A fraction of myself, the other half of the rhyme.

When we were separated it was cruel, no longer we were an event,
No longer something special, on our hearts lay a dent,

Torn from each other, like a letter from a stamp,
Our hearts as heavy as if they were riddled full of damp.

I cannot imagine walking without you, going into a room alone,
What's mine I share with you, because together we have grown!

You cannot split what is whole, we are not two but one!
How could we ever survive? When one of us is gone?

We are not individuals, what you did to us was sin,
How can I ever forgive you? When you look away my twin

Katherine Lamb

Endless Love

When I awaken - I reach for him
When he leaves for work - I kiss him
During the day - my thoughts are for him
A whole weekend - I adore him
My whole life is for him
But does he really know how much I love him.

We have had a bad year - I lean on him
We have a few quarrels and I still love him
We wait for a child and my love grows stronger for him
But does he really know how much I love him.

We have our long-awaited child - a boy, we both love him
My love is not split in two but doubled for both of them
Our son is perfect and each hour my life is filled with more pleasures
But often I think - this is a dream and someone will take my treasures.

Sheila Hadfield

Neil

I need to tell all,
What the Lord has done,
He gave my mum; the precious gift of a son,
With big blue eyes and jet black hair,
Tiny toes and tiny fingers,
For Mum to love and care,
Eleven weeks on; He took him away,
My mum still mourns that fateful day,
There he was her special little boy,
Quiet and still,
Her little bundle of joy,
Resting at God's will,
Yet, there is a part,
Will always live within her heart,
One sure thing; that wouldn't die,
The love she felt inside,
The love she will always feel,
For special baby son, Neil.

Tracey Wiggins

Dunblane

Sorrow, Heartache, Misery and Pain
Why did that tragedy happen at Dunblane?
No-one has answers no-ones to blame
Except for that man he was obviously insane.

Families and friends left to grieve
The sympathy of the nation they receive
Nothing can be said to ease the pain
Why did he do it he had nothing to gain?

Seventeen lives taken away
Nobody will ever forget that day
The question on everyone's lips is WHY?
We'll never know not you not I

Sharon Smith

The Other Side of Tears

On the other side of tears
When all the crying's done
There'll be no more starving children
Lying, dying in the sun,

On the other side of tears
When all the shelling's ceased
There'll be peace for war-torn refugees
And the pain will be released.

On the other side of tears
There'll be no more battered wives
But women living freely,
In bruise-free, loving lives.

On the other side of tears
Torn minds will be set free
And broken, crippled bodies
Will move stealth-like, gracefully.

On the other side of tears
The day will finally come
When a special world of love and peace
Shall be the food of everyone.

Terry Meredith

Bonfire Day

Bonfire's burning brightly, Roman candles all around
Whoosh there goes a rocket and there's Catherine Wheels
    on the ground.
November 5th has come 'round again and all little boys are
    spellbound
Crackers, sparklers, jumping jacks, flames leaping higher and higher
Children yelling, mother shouting all stand back from the fire
Dad has most of the fun he tells us what's to be done
Dry woods flaming damp wood smouldering
Fumes and smoke gets in one's hair, where's the guy he
    should be burning
Where did you put Gran's old chair, cats fled in he's frightened
Can't blame him it's so noisy and our little Jimmy is drinking
    all the Scrumpy.
If Mum finds out his legs will be red and it will be bed.
The armchairs on fire why didn't someone say
Now it's coming on to rain one more firework, then off indoors
Noses pressed to the window pane.
One eye on the guy that's burning doesn't he look a fearsome sight
One eye on the sausages sizzling oh I do love bonfire night
I think I'll never tire but yawning I shall be quite soon
and it's sad the day is ending Guy Fawkes' legs are bending
So say goodnight to embers. And wish it was early again
Bonfire day has ended so goodnight again

A. J. Bolter

Called Memories

MEMORIES! Oh, how sweet these can be,
    When caressed with love from early childhood.
Guided positively along life's road,
    Shielded from all snares and foes.

Skilfully shown right from wrong
    Gently guided when inclined to stray.
Encouraged positively when fear took hold,
    To have the courage to go on.

School days! Oh, how precious these are
    To equip us for all that will be,
Especially when trial and error
    Walk hand in hand.

No effort too great, no task too small
    For those who care to shape the way,
To let us have an occupation for the future,
    Which we would always hold dear.

A sense of perspective
    To help to keep our priorities in order,
Balancing all our tears and laughter,
    To keep all our MEMORIES clear and true.

Teresa K. Connor

A Country Churchyard

I wandered in the churchyard having little else to do.
When all was quiet and peaceful the surroundings lovely too
I studied all the gravestones, all weathered, rough and worn
Some epitaphs unreadable, the grass had not been shorn.
I learned of the last interment there in nineteen thirty seven
And thought of all the folks long dead.
Now hopefully in heaven.
I read of old John Crispin who died aged seventy-four.
His well-loved wife preceded him, "not lost but gone before"
She's borne him many children so she got her, release
When she gave up and went to heaven to get a bit of peace.
I strode among the dandelions, the nettlewort and clover
And gazed upon the sunken stones, some cracked and falling over.
One impressive monument had wrought iron fence about,
Was it to keep the departed in or us poor mortals out?
It's said life was much harder then, but there were more contented?
Some kindly souls had placed a seat there, sheltered from the winds
Where folks with little else to do could think upon their sins.

May Bonner

The Mountain

The tall dark giant beckons
As it casts its shadows on the ground,
Towering peaks from mountains great
Always hypnotize and abound.

A climber scales its granite face,
Such daring challenge to accept,
He ascends the awesome mountain
A promise to himself is kept.

Long days are passing heavily
The summit ridge still out of sight,
Elements severe are unrelenting
And a storm displays its might.

The howling gale becomes so cruel
It drowns his cries of sheer despair,
Fingers frozen cannot aid him
A forlorn figure in mid-air.

The screeching wind is loudly fierce,
Dislodged are pitons from the rock,
Ropes run through and dangle freely,
The climber falls, but peaks of the mountain mock.

Margaret M. Wadsworth

A Tree

A tree in Spring is a sight to be seen
As new buds develop into leaves of fresh green.
Each type of tree has a leaf of its own,
With a unique shape by which it is known.

When Summer arrives and the tree's glory is complete
It gleams in the sunshine providing shade from the heat.
As the wind blows its branches, it dances and sways
And gives so much pleasure in so many ways.

Its leaves then change to hues of brown, red and gold,
Leaving us in wonder as nature's beauties unfold.
But when Autumn comes and the tree's best it has shown
Its branches are bare with strong winds that have blown.

But come the new year when the snow, hail and rain,
Have all disappeared and it's Spring once again,
The tree in its glory will again flourish with pleasure
And we can admire God's creation forever and ever.

We could compare our own lives with that of a tree,
As it spreads its roots for strength - so of course should we.
Taking life as it comes, not as we wish it would be,
From our birth through to death - and our eternity.

Mary Dale

Progress

How well I remember that autumn scene
When as a child I stood
Gazing at the oaks of burnished gold
And the wildlife in Primrose Wood

The neatly kept hedgerows surrounding the fields
A wondrous carpet of flowers
The songbirds singing so prettily
I would listen for hours and hours

But gone is the wood that I loved so much
Gone are the hedgerows so neat
The grasses and flowers are mown to the ground
Now tarmac is laid at my feet

Bricks and mortar, ditches and drains
Progress is the name of the word
All my childhood dreams are crushed
Like the sound of the pretty songbird

J. Burningham

You're Sixty Wow!

Why are we put on the scrap heap
When authority asks us our age
You say I've just turned sixty
You can tell by the look on their face,
It's time you stopped asking and moaning
There's nothing at all they can do
Just pop this pills down and hope for the best
Your span of life's nearly over for you,
So if I need an opp: oh! the horror it brings
To the face of the one who was fine
You've left it too late you will just have to wait
It's a shame you are not fifty nine.
So tell me how can we just change overnight
From someone to an old has-been
We've still got our marbles we're not stupid or deaf
But that's how they treat us it seems.
So just stop and think — you get older each day
And sixty will not be all that far away
So give us a break we're not finished yet
Treat us like humans, or send us to the vet.

V. Smith

Untitled

I pray and hope the day will come
When the letter's here to say, you've won!
I pray and hope that it's this year
When I am told, "well done my dear!"
But I don't mind, helping others,
It's just a job, it's no bother.
The days, the months, the years go by
But I don't give up, or sit and cry.
Others are worse off than me.
But now and then, I give this plea —
Why aren't I lucky? Why don't I win?
Then I shrug my shoulders and start to grin.
I am lucky, I've got my health.
Without that, what's the good of wealth?

Vera Casey

What Ever Happened to the Past

What ever happened to the past, the past of yesteryear.
Where countryside and village seemed a happy place to be.
Where everyone knew their neighbour, and nothing seemed
   to change
Where life went on so peacefully in those lovely bygone days.
A countryside where men got their living, without going far afield.
The men who made old England's countryside, which generations
   have admired.
Now the countryside is disappearing at an ever-increasing rate
As year by year the houses march across the fields and woods
The man who was born a countryman, is now a stranger in the land,
   and the village where he was born.
Oh give me yesteryear, and the village of the past,
   where the sun was always shining, in the village of the past.

C. Kemp

207

Caring

When life seems cruel and hurt is all you feel
When days are dark and nights are long and lonely
Your wounded heart you fear will never heal
I think of you, my prayers are for you only.

When all you want to do is sit and cry
While all around just stare and wonder why
When no-one seems to care or understand
How I yearn to comfort you, to hold your hand.

When inside you feel an emptiness so sore
And your life just has no meaning any more
When your tears have all been shed and wiped away
Through the haze you'll start to see a brighter day.

The pain will ease if only given time
Then gradually each day the sun will shine
Until then you'll feel so lost, but don't despair
My thoughts are with you even though I can't be there.

If you need somewhere to rest your weary head
Or some help through all the days that lie ahead
Don't stumble helplessly alone along life's road
Remember someone here just longs to share your load.

Susan Georgine Banks

"My Lost Love"

I will remember you!
When next spring will come,
With birds in my garden,
Will start to sing for me again.
I will remember you!
When next summer comes,
With flowers in my garden,
Will bloom for you again.
I will remember you!
When next Autumn comes,
With leaves on my garden ground
Will whirl around and around.
I will remember you!
When next winter comes,
With snow on my window pane,
I will remember you again! and again!

Tamara Zerman

Why

A small and furry teddy bear lies on a little bed
where only a few short days ago lay a little tousled head
now the teddy isn't cuddled, he's just a toy of fur ad foam
waiting patiently for a little girl who won't be coming home.

His owner was a little girl, blond hair, all smiles and charm
a child who wouldn't wittingly do anyone a harm
but she was in the gym that day and died in fear and pain
from the bullets of a madman in a village called Dunblane.

Outside the school the streets are pave, but not with solid gold
instead with wreaths to remember those who won't be growing old
and the weeping and the grieving is echoed by tears falling
   from the sky
and smudge on word written on a wreath that simply asks the
   question - "why"

Pauline Slate

Untitled

Sense-of-wonder, coupled to lasting awe,
Can other genre equal its model,
Invent what things to come, what went before,
Events in times and spaces parallel.
Numberless either vessels boldly-go,
Cross galaxies upon the heels of light,
Enter the worlds of cosmic friend and foe,
Fight with the weapons of eternal night.
Ideas in every field of human thought,
Changes in attitude and circumstance,
This literature is loath to tackle nought,
It airs the mind of man, debates his chance.
One verse, nor yet a trillion would suffice,
Number its myriad modes or tire its voice.

Stan Eling

Question Time

Oh Mummy please, I've got to know
What makes a flower start to grow?
How do peas get in a pod?
And Mummy tell me - who made God?

When the sun is shining bright
Where does it go when it is night?
Who puts colours in the rainbow?
And when it's dark, what makes the moon glow?

Who puts the milk inside the cow?
And Mummy, can you tell me how
The stars can stay up in the sky
And don't fall down when planes go by?

Why do people need their sleep?
And why do onions make you weep?
Who was it who invented words?
And why can't people fly like birds?

All my children ask are 'Whys',
And Mummy never tells them lies,
I answer "Off to school you go,
Ask your teacher - she will know".

L. Wall

Way of Life

Life is really so wonderfully real
When lived to the full, like a bell that will peel;
It's laughter, gaiety, heartbreaks and tears
Live through all these and banish the fears.

To walk in the country along a quiet lane,
Brings comfort, peace, and stills the mad brain;
The delicate hush, just a ripple or so,
Meandering, winding, the brook that does flow;

Avenues of stately trees along in the park,
Above in the heavens the song of the lark;
Oh listen awhile to the tremouring sound,
In a lovelier place that could never be found.

Amid sheltering oaks casting shades as they grow,
Down in the woods the daffodils blow;
It's a restful scene you encounter just there,
Ambling along in the peaceful fresh air.

Then onward rise to reality find,
Away from that haven with new peace of mind;
To remember for always perfection that's seen,
In that beautiful place where you have just been.

Margaret Govier

The Affluence Decade

A bygone era for past is where this tale is set,
Where dreams of ownership were sold, and bought lest we forget.
We fell under the spell of wealth and promises of gain,
Economists had blinkers on, the future spelt out pain.
"We'll all be rich!" they smugly purred, "Buy shared in Sid" they
said, And two by two we joined a queue, the cautious days were dead.
The pin-striped suited Stockholder, no sleep no fears no cares,
An idol of the working men, the Bulls the Stags the Bears.
A filofax and mobile phone, and sleek red sporty car,
Became the tools of this man's trade, as did the Champagne bar.
"In whom are we investing?" "Oh my dear please don't fuss!"
"Their profits are irrelevant, forget the Prospectus!"
"Please pin your cheque, don't staple it, make sure you read it
through, If you can write One Thousand when you sell it will be Two."
But then on screens around the Globe the message boldly flashed,
The days of get-rich-quick are gone the Stock Markets have crashed.
Yet still outside the Banks you queued, your cheque books in your
hands, To grab a share of worthlessness you didn't understand.
And when the Bears came home to roost, the Stags had run a mile,
No short term gain would be the same, the City lost its smile.

Michael Brown

Afterwards . . .

When the dew glistens on the lawn
When the stag walks with the fawn
When the rain rips the sky apart
When a man breaks a woman's heart

The world seems grey without those we love
And we don't understand our God above
We cry until we have no tears
And see that pain doesn't heal with years

We must each of us all know
We only reap the love we sow
And we have now all surely learned
We receive what we have earned

Don't be sad when loved ones die
Although you're asking what and why?
Be glad they've gone to a better place
Where they always wear a smiling face

They've been 'called' or so they say
To eternal happiness not far away
A place of love, cakes and sticky sweets
And laughter and lots of other treats.

Katherine O'Connor

Summer Days

Upon the hills I sit and gaze,
Where'er we walked through summer's haze.
Now heather blooms 'neath rocks austere,
Before winter settles everywhere.

The birds are gathering in the sky;
Soon to foreign climes they'll fly.
Everywhere is hushed this day,
Before winter winds howl on their way.

Brilliant summer suns are fading;
The hay is gathered - no more making.
Hope, like summer, is falling fast
Into the winter's icy blast.

Balmy days and magic nights,
Coloured with blossom and such delights;
Strolling, drifting o'er hill and dale,
'Til winter drops its curtain of hail.

Savour every precious moment;
Live a life of sweet contentment.
Soon it goes, and all that's left
Is winter and a dream bereft.

Pamela Hurst

Ad Infinitum

What strange alchemy stirs in the earth,
when winter's decided to leave.
It's as if a key has been turned,
releasing a prisoner — Spring.
Small green blades of grass appear
and the trees seem to straighten their limbs.
The birds start to build new homes for themselves,
and the children to laugh and sing.
Then spring says good-bye and makes way for the sun,
as summer decides to return.
Bringing hot lazy days and nights that are warm,
with a nightingale warbling his song.
Leaves start to fall when autumn arrives,
it rains or blows most of the time.
Sometimes a grey fog comes swirling down,
then it's cosy to sit by the fire.
Once more it is winter, it's cold and it snows
and there's nothing at all to be seen.
Bare trees, bare earth and leaden skies,
How long will it be before spring?

J. H. Jenkins

After You've Gone

The future was always beckoning
When we would have to part.
How could I acknowledge the reckoning
Would be the breaking of my heart.

Love true, deep and without measure
My future was always your choice
Heartfelt memories always to treasure
The emptiness no longer filled by your voice.

The bluebells will grow and bloom
And you and I will survive
The shadows creep across the room
And what's the point in being alive

We grabbed the chance to live these years
The reckoning seemed so far away
but here I sit alone in tears
The bill has to be paid today

Mary Williams

"He Listens"

I have a friend I talk to
When I don't know what to do
Always there to help me
He could be your friend too

Then when you feel unhappy
And have some doubts and fears
He'll comfort you with his peace
And brush away the tears

His strength is ever present
It gives you inner calm
And when the still small voice you hear
It is a soothing balm

So tell him of your troubles
He'll answer all your prayers
He wants for you a good life
With never any cares

Vera E. Speck

"Distant Sands"

Halcyon beach - so dear to me - too far from me
Where gull and curlew play - wild content and free
A place to rest, hold hands and gaze -
Perhaps make wondrous plans for future days
Whilst ebb and flow perform a magic symphony
On stage of sand and foam - edged an azure sea.

Hallowed too - the love of my life - she walks there
Proud head held high - fresh breeze in auburn hair
I must return - I left some footprints there.
'Long side another - more precious pair.
All need replacing now - oh let me be
Beside you - beside the sea - this is my prayer

Ronald H. Simmons

Heavenly Laughter

What would you gain if you tried to kiss me
When it's only my abstract you're after
I'd take off in flight just like a queen bee
Can't you hear heavenly laughter?

I'd soar to the heights and savour delights
Such as only the abstracts attain
And when I was free I'd fly back to me
And land back on earth once again.

There in the gloom beneath a grey tomb
Lies a mortal whose abstract has fled
He descended to hell the fires to quell
Because of the life he had led.

If you try kissing abstracts you'll die as he did
And you'll be in abstract - oh heaven forbid;
It's bad enough meeting you here on this plane
Without having you abstract my abstract again.

G. J. Stott

A Friendship Lost

I've lost my best friend
where can he be?
He's still around - only not for me.
We used to talk and laugh and joke
but these past few weeks we've hardly spoke!
He's found another to share his life
perhaps she'll even become his wife!
To her he now tells all his news,
about his job, his life, his views.
I know this is right, it's the way it should be
perhaps I'm just feeling sorry for me.
Next time I see him I'll try to be tough.
I'll try, but what if that's not enough?
Then I'll have to be hard and really strong
and think about where I went wrong.
The only fault that I can see
is that I cared for him more than he cared for me.
I've lost my best friend
where can he be?
He's still around - only not for me.

L. Fry

Lines Written on Hearing of the Death of Chaplin

The little tramp with hat and cane
who spanned my life and filled my days with laughter.
The actor ageless in his role. I saw no man, no human soul.
Such is the naivete of youth. The eye is bright, the reason mute.

Once I saw a picture of this man, with wrinkled face and
    furrowed brow
Can this be he who strutted through the park, antagonized
    the bullies and won the ladies hearts?
In reverie I saw him stand alert and twirl his cane.
That integral immortality of man and actor mixed up in my mind.
The little tramp his universal humour suspended in youth forever.

Mary Gordon

Unicorn

What stirs now in the Mystic Wood,
where for so long Oak and Ash have stood.
There is now a ripple in waist high grass,
could it be just the wind, or a large mass?
I do not believe, this just cannot be,
the rarest beast, for any man to see,
A head so regal, yet so very serene,
a finer sight there has never been.
With a coat as white as driven snow,
or is it faint pearly gold, with a glow.
Is it a fawn at mother side,
no 'tis a colt, but no other so.
Where on a horse head would be a blaze,
here a knob of Gold seems to raise.
As the air fills with summer scents,
in fact a winter's sky relents.
To show that which men would give kingdoms for,
the Lord of Lights Unicorn.

G. J. Von Heizon

Questions and Answers

Life in the whole is a span of time
where did it begin? and how much
of it is mine?
Is it everlasting? or just for this Span?
or are we part of some statistical plan
Where did we come from? and why are we here?
Where are we now? and where do we belong?
going to? and how?
The answers to these questions and many more
I'm sure are found inside us if we look
for the door
I know were not doing some of the things
that we should, like showing compassion,
Giving love and being good.
There is still time to change our ways
we should slow down and really look at our ways.

Stephen Goodchild

The Great Whale Never Sleeps

The great whale never sleeps just bides its time
As it heaves its bulk through foaming brine
Great tail surfaces hangs proud in the air
Then disappears to reappear elsewhere

He roams the seas and oceans wide
The whalers hunt him on every side
But he knows he will win in the end
For he and his kind are really man's best friend

Through flat calm seas or the tempest roar
He must ply his course to reach farthest shore
Where food does in abundance lay
And to find a mate and commence love's play.

He leaves the shore with his new mate
They cleave the sea with their vast wake
To search the seas where they can be
Away from us forever free.

Roy David Ridges

What's Happening?

Who wants to live in a world that's torn apart,
Where there is nothing but hatred in everyone's hearts,
People are busy doing their thing,
they haven't noticed that the world's folding in,
People are thoughtless,
They don't give a damn,
I'm only asking what's happening to man?
Nature has provided us with everything we need,
but man is destroying it with all his greed,
The forests which were full of trees, that stood so tall and green,
Now lay on the ground decaying so man
Can have his dreams,
Man's dreams which were creative have now become obscene,
Man's only thoughts are for himself,
To hell with nature's theme.

J. E. Phillips

Entrance to Earth

With one mighty push I slide into light,
Where I have been laying. It's always been night,
The brightness is blinding and I'm trying to breathe,
The snip of a scissor, and my body is freed.

I can only open the hole in my head,
And scream and scream for my warm waterbed,
Nobody listens, nobody cares,
The journey's one way, with Mum paying the fares.

They weigh me and check me to make sure I'm right,
If only they would turn my head from the light,
I'm aware of my mum as they lay me to rest,
I listen to her heartbeat and suckle her breast,
I've entered earth on this special day,
Now all I ask Lord is
"Show me the way."

G. Treweeks

The Death of a Nation

Within the realm of fantasy, a graveyard filled with hopes,
Where one did fall, another stray, upon its verdant slopes,
The hearts that fear the whispered word, the stout hearts' firm denial,
The Great One's threat, with fist on wood that ended in a smile.

How much for others do we strive, how much of truth we share,
And when of friendship we contrive, could of the truth we bear,
How many styles of man are we, that form this happy band,
And why the doubt of men so strong, at every outstretched hand.

Could be the frailty of our plan, lies in the paths we tread,
The small horizon that we scan, suggests the spirit's dead,
What ails the members of our cast, must all the parts be great,
Why do we seek to fit the last, of every other's fate.

I see us all, with costume on, all leading parts to play,
The curtain rise, the audience gone, we'll sadly fade away.

Len Pearce

The Man Has Gone

The man has gone . . . the boy remains,
Where 'ere there are meadows green and leafy lanes,
On the quiet heath; where the gorse flames,
In shady woods where we played our childish games,
On the fen where the Kingcup glows in the morning sun,
Where the white mists hang low, when day is done,
Where the corn waves bright and golden, when I recall times - olden,
Where the lark sings and the lonely kestrel spreads its wings,
Where there are trees to climb and farm gates for a boy to
    swing upon,
Where the birds assemble for their Evensong,
Where a rustic bridge spans a rippling rill,
When shadows fall and the world is still,
When firelight flickers on the Holly bough,
Bringing memories of the long ago,
In the storm's rage and the peace which comes after,
Most of all where there is the sound of laughter, there will my
    brother be
For although the man has gone, the boy remains,
Safe - 'neath the sunny skies of childhood memories.

G. Goodfellow

Peace of Mind

Do you ever stop to wonder,
when you are feeling under
the weather and weighed down,
Why you are you, and I am me.
Why this a flower and that a tree.
Why grass is green and earth is brown.

Do you ever sit and ponder
why time is made of summer,
autumn, winter, spring.
Why day is light and night is dark.
Why cats do meow and dogs do bark.
Why pigs do grunt and birds do sing.
Just remember you've a life to live.
That you are on this earth to give
affection and be kind.
To appreciate the things you see.
To live with others in harmony.
To love, be loved, have peace of mind.

H. M. Comley

Whispering Thoughts in Time . . .

Waves of emotions flow through my mind,
Where do they come from?
When prompted portray beauty, within ink-filled lines;

Being in touch with your heart and soul is a wonderful experience
of treasured words on a roll:

Never forgetting or letting out of sight, giftings of qualities . . .
that are cherished, almost a sense of light in flight.

Always a joy for eyes that read, positive, feelings, hope . . .
ears opened . . . comforted needs:

Byron, Lawrence, Kipling, flavourings of life shown through the years,
written masterpieces, soothing . . . healing . . . our tears
Biblical writing expressing so clear, awesome in its original glory
"Wanting the word" to be . . . so very near!

"It's everywhere"
It's all over the world . . .
It's called Poetry
. . ."It's love" . . . it's in the search for seeking hearts, soul and
minds . . . Its radiance can be felt,
Capturing those gifts

. . . of "Whispering Thoughts in Time"

Kymberley Veale

Lifetime

When you've reached the point of no return at last,
When your future now is shorter than your past,
When your dreams are realized or just not meant to be,
When work, your master all these years, is just a memory.

Your mind, trapped in its ageing frame, is still a youthful one,
Society condemns you, your usefulness is done.
The young can never understand how much age has to give
In wisdom and experience, how to survive, to live.

You've raced with time throughout your life, but time is now
    your friend.
You play with time, although you know that one day time will end.
But while it lasts you will enjoy what's left of time for you
By doing things you've never done, but always wanted to.

God give you time to realize the beauty of this earth,
Appreciate the miracle of life and death and birth,
Take pleasure from a kind word, a stream, a tree, a flower
And live in gratitude and love, until your final hour.

Shirley Baxter

Bliss

You mention Bliss.
What word is this?
What would you say
Bliss is to-day?

The old may miss
The lover's kiss,
The laughter gay
Of childhood play.

But what is here
In days and nights?
The joy of sun
And wondrous sights.

The beauty of our country fair
And all the creatures living there,
The kindness, friendship, trust, and love,
The mystery that looms above.

And could one say
In feeling this,
One has discovered
Endless Bliss?

Margaret Tasman

My Creation

My daughter's my canvas, born ready to paint,
With colours of love, the world threatens to taint.
Firm brushstrokes of kindness, sincerity, trust
A splash of respect, include that I must.
Create a whole picture in perfection I'll try,
And hang it up proudly in light, watch it dry.
Please, depravity don't touch it, until it is ready
To take its place in the world, looking confident, steady.
No master am I in creation of art
But from this valuable piece I'm loathing to part.
But soon in the future someone may borrow my treasure,
To love and nurture, I hope, in my place with equal measure.

J. Fowler

"The Voice of the Eyes"

O child of Love, for that is what thou art,
Why hast thou not been blessed with voice?
And tell to me of what you feel,
Your hopes, your dreams, your right of choice.

Thou dost not speak, no words burst forth,
No swell of song from thee;
And yet my soul o'er fraught with pain,
Cries out for thee, to speak my name.

And as in love, I gaze on thee,
Our mirrored eyes as one,
All the words thou ere will need,
Are written there my son.

Patricia Gaskell

211

Progress

The sparkling stream that once I knew,
With grassy bank and waters clear.
Where celandines and rushes grew,
Is now a wasteland, dank and drear.
For here there's no clear water bright,
Just broken wheels and rusty tins.
To me, a most depressing sight,
The debris of unwanted things.
It's difficult to understand
Why progress brings pollution.
The more we learn, the less we think,
So is there no solution?
Let it not be a bygone dream,
The pleasures of a sunlit stream.

Margaret Daker

Changes

Love is like a smile
which brightness up your day
when the world seems down
you never have a frown
when everything feels good
the world changes your mood.

Happiness can't last forever
you're told to move on down the river
your heart will break
which you can't take
for what you must do is not a test
As in the future you know what's best.

I will always care
and always be there
for every time you shed a few tears
you never forget those happy years

Kylie McGuffog

Just Like the Rest

4th time going out with you I was unsure
The 1st and 2nd were just a laugh
the 3rd time meant more,
I thought you were different from the lads
who think I'm a whore
But you proved me wrong
You're just like the rest, at first I thought you were the best
You said you loved me and things were great
I was told I was finished by a mate
When you dumped me for the 4th time you said
you still wanted to be friends.
But you b*tch behind my back, and I find out from a mate,
You've told everyone I smoke, when I don't
I gave up yonks ago
Now I know who you fancy, the same mate that told me everything
and who smokes
You broke my heart, you are a snake.
But I'll tell you, now I know how to hate.

Julie Morse

Dark Rapture

You climb higher than the highest mountain
You touch the sky
Your breath mingling with red wine
That caused you to be there.
For a moment you feel astral ecstasy
Then you fall to the ground and scream
For you see your sins and the fire below
You stand before the gates of the city in
The sky
You cry 'God!'
You see through the eternal light
You throw yourself at the feet of God
And shout
'Take me!'
Then the gates close and you fall,
Fall into the dark rapture of immortality.

Tanmhiz Fatimah

Loneliness

I picked the cold, wild-scented morning
With her
And dreamed of the afternoon.
But as the day began to blossom and fill out
She went away.
Somewhere the day is warm and fragrant
Where she is:
But I am sad.

Robert Martin Nicholl

"Depression"

In the depths of despair in the midst of the air,
When your heart has no care, and there's only you there
Like a tree stripped bare, tear and sorrow,
No hope for tomorrow

Will I ever be free?
Or will I go mad?
Am I a good person
Am I evil or bad?

The wind has borrowed my heart,

The world has my mind
My wish to be well
is as great as mankind

My fears are real, but
they're not understood.
They carry me over
from childhood

There's something wrong,
It's a feeling that's there.
It's not a good feeling
Is anyone there?

K. J. Carter

Verse on Dismal Areas in the Metropolis

I glory in the thought that mighty Time
Will crumble these mean streets into decay,
That trees and grass shall grow here once again,
A nobler art, a nobler theme hold sway.

I glory that in the inexorable course of Time,
The Truth endures, the false word dies,
To realms of life not clearly visioned yet,
To which Humanity at last shall rise.

Time robs us of our youth, and those we love,
Yet sets its seal upon the works of merit:
Man lives on in his heirs, what they shall cherish
Are things that bear the splendour of the Spirit.

J. M. Hardcastle

I Kissed an Angel

One night I lay alone in pain
As tears ran down my face
An angel she appeared to me
Sent by His Holy Grace

Her beauty warmed my very soul
With these words she whispered soft

"Come close and kiss these lips of mine
Come lay down by my side
Let my love surround you now
And feel the pain subside"

It was then that I surrendered
All the love that I could find
As so I also realized, this world
It could be kind

But pain it doth still follow
Each day we are apart
As being here without you
Lies heavy on my heart.

Kenneth Grafton

Lost

Trapped in another dimension, where life seems empty and space.
Where fears and emotions are hollow, I have to find a better place

Imprisoned as an outcast, and to follow a certain rule,
life is happier on the outside, and the inside sight is so cruel

A vision which is before me, of a tunnel with no end,
the darkness of which I hold, I want so much to mend.

The direction in which I'm moving, to find the heavenly light
The fears and pain that are hurting but, the determination to fight.

A disjointed kind of feeling, my imagination runs wildly with hate.
Life does not exists on the inside. The outside life is what I want
to create.

Desperately in need of something, to change my horrid basic belief,
lost, in this other world of loneliness and grief

Physically running for a way out but, the light is
no where to be found.
Shouting for my existence but, only I can hear my echoed sound.

Nicole Koning

Why?

Mummy, why are you doing this letting them kill me?
Why don't you try and stop them was my life not meant to be?
Are you not happy that I am here inside?
I thought I was a sign of love why must I be denied?
Do you not love Daddy too or is it only I who's hated?
If you do not want me then why was I created?
Mummy, they are hurting me but I've done nothing wrong,
Aren't you committing a crime by murdering someone so young?
I'm sorry if I would have ruined your plans and if I'm a mistake
I suppose deep down you're doing this for my own sake.
Mummy this is agony they're tearing me apart,
They started with my arms and legs and now they've got my heart
I guess I'll never get to tell you all the things I had to say,
But hopefully we'll meet again in a different life and a different way.

Kate Brewster

Sonnet

Why, love, are you content with hidden joy?
Why leave the world deprived of something pure?
There's nothing in its greatness to annoy,
Of this all poets known have been quite sure.
Aye, those with secret schemes to plan and plot
To crush the world between their jaws of gold,
They need a place to root - or rather rot,
Their very souls to Mammon being sold!
But we, who gave to earth's rotation worth,
For whom the stars and sun and moon were made,
And death was bound to be redeemed by birth,
We ought to show mankind we're in good faith.
    Let's change the sultry darkness for the sun,
    That all may know: a true Love has begun.

Mike Roysons

The Sea

What joy to be living close to the sea
Where the sound of the surf is sweet music to me
With each tide doing battle 'gainst the fair land
Reducing great rocks to mere grains of sand.

O to see on a bright summer's morn'
The rising sun glint on waves newly born
That gently caress each long golden strand
Then quickly retire as if shy of the land.

Or to stand and watch on a wild winter's day
Mighty great waves rush into the bay
Then furiously crash down upon the shore
They gently caressed so short a time before.

Now that I've seen your fury and your calm
And felt your soft touch like cool soothing balm
O mighty great ocean when life's book I must close
Deep in your green depths fain would I repose.

Michael C. McCann

Christmas Time

Christmas lights, log fire nights, warming to the glow,
While outside sleigh bells ride, sliding in the snow,

Boys and girls do their twirls, skating on the lake,
Christmas pud looking good, and the Christmas cake,

Young and old in the cold, sing carols in the night,
Holly trees in the breeze, covered all in white,

Fingers blue build snowmen who, melting in the sun
See lovers go under mistletoe to steal a kiss for fun

Fairy on the tree for all to see, tinsel hanging down,
Trees so bright, lit up at night all around the town,

Chestnuts roast, a Christmas toast to all friends old and new
The cards that went, have all been sent, with love from me and you,

Robins sing church bell's ring, Christmas time is here,
Girls and boys hunt for their toys, Santa Claus is near,

A turkey lunch a warming punch, presents 'round the tree,
A big surprise in all their eyes, a lovely sight to see,

But through the haze of Christmas days, we must remember when,
A baby's birth brought peace on earth, and good will to all men.

J. A. Jenkins

Got to Find Me a Place

Got to find me a place
Where I am not judged by my colour, creed or race.
A place where I can move at my own pace.
Got to find me a place
Where there is no race
For first place.

Got to find me a place
Where life is not a waste.
Must find a place
And it won't be in space
Nor will it be in a Roman State.

Got to find me a place
Where my children can be safe.
Must get away from this rat race
And go to a place where I can practise my faith.
Must find a place where I can meditate.

Got to find me a place
Where I pay no rate, yet I can have a home
And food on my plate. Must find a place
Where love shines Brighter than Hate.

Trevor Donald

Deja Vu

There's a Mogin Doggid swastika at large in Palestine.
While Weisenthal is in Whitehall avenging for the crime.
Pray tell, oh noble Nimrod, how do we reconcile.
When Sabra and Shatilla lay out the Auschwitz pile?

When the black eyed tribe of David braved the Himmel flame.
All righteous men in Christendom called Teuton out in shame.
When the agemot at Nurnberg garnered in the toll.
Did they give brief to Gideon to play the Heine role?

Though man may sculpture justice she will not be denied.
Truth will scream for answers and know why Nuguibe died.
Enough! Genug! Proud Isaac, do not fall from grace.
Warum bringen kristal nacht in that halowed place?

Moshe at Entebe did the world inspire.
And those abed on Chrispin's day will hence call Ezra Sire.
When heroes speak of heroes by these they set the gauge.
Their names are writ forever upon the golden page.

The gods watch over heroes when ere they go astray.
When courage blends with vengeance reason has no say.
The sun will not stop shining cos Maffuse died last night.
Yet to those who love Shalom since it shines less bright.

Patrick Carvill

"Never Too Old to Rock"

It was over 40's night at the local hop
Where the wrinklies go to for a bop
The resident bank plays all the old faves
A pensioner shouts for any Chas and Dave
Rita and Don are the disco couple
They strut funky stuff after a whisky double
Bodies gyrating varicose legs akimbo
Serious fun trying the sexy tango
Reg is the one to put on the style
Tries the splits and never again smiles
Margot thinks that she is Fontayne
A ballerina of once world fame
With a jetee and pas de deux
Across the floor she shoots in a blur
Tipsy ladies get ready for the twist
Pulling their skirts up above their hips
Flabby thighs wobble around stockinged tops
Frenzied dancing like it's top of the pops.
Bar drunk dry taxi cabs called
The merry old souls have had a ball

Kevin Rodgers

The Right to Die (Euthanasia)

I lie here with my eyes turned to the sky.
Will you help me?
Yes.
The pain gets stronger every day.
Will you help me?
Yes.
In my mind, my soul's already free.
Will you help me?
Yes.
My love,
Will you help me to die?
Will you free me?
You give me no reply.

Kerry McNaney

Autumn's Glory

Sun-dried leaves of copper, gold and brown
Wind blown and falling upon the ground
Crunch beneath my feet, how I love the sand
Cool misty mornings, cobwebs in hedgerows glistening dew
Disappear when the sunshine begins to show through
Plump sparrows flitting around from tree to tree
Appearing so carefree to you and to me
The woodland toward the evening as the sun goes down
Is mother nature dressed so colourfully in her loveliest gown.
Frost patterns on the window early in the day
Heralding that winter is now upon its way
Chill air pinching cheeks, fingers, nose and toes
Makes me appreciate the cosy warmth of the fireside
As the day draws to a close

Tina C. Dowdall

Looking into 'Then'

Where is it leading this life of mine?
Where will I be in fifty years' time?
Thought provoking as it may be
This question is unanswerable to me

It is said a good education is essential
But how does one recognise their true potential?
The pressure is on within oneself
Due to fear of being left on the shelf

Intelligent people should make lots of money
So stereotypical it's rather funny
Jobs are hard to find today
A known fact to my dismay

Being a fighter is the key to success
It will gain one more respect than less
Happiness is very important to me
As is peace, love and security

Louise Thomson

Velvet StarCloud

Ah, Velvet StarCloud, child of gold.
Where youth is ancient; full and deep,
So your eyes, held tales, then untold.
Where comfort lay, soft, in light sleep.

Ah, Velvet StarCloud, child of charm.
Your smile, a passage, that led me.
Lips curving, no vestige of harm.
Just whispers, allow me to see.

Ah, Velvet StarCloud, child of age,
Minutes are hours, and years are days.
Moments a timeless, empty page.
Where words have wandered off as strays.

Ah, Velvet StarCloud, child of pain,
My heart you own, as life gives less.
I cannot bow down and refrain.
I cannot hate; I cannot bless.

Ah, Velvet StarCloud, child of storm,
Your shadows fills clouds in the sky,
And I know, I will not be warm,
Nor see you again in my eye.

Matthew M. Rose

Remembrance Day Commemoration

It was a sense of duty towards monarch and country
Whereby our noble heroes fell upon sandy beaches
All in a said good cause for liberty and the sake of humanity
It so became a legend of battle, of battle on the soil of Normandy
Whereupon our British Tommies lay slaughtered like cattle
Amidst the gory battleground mighty roars of cannons
Shattered the battlefields amidst fallen heroes
And their cries deadened by the roars of hell
Meanwhile the rip-roaring battle swelled
Upon the shores of Dunkirk and the soil of Normandy.

Alas! Many a good man sacrificed his life
Within, hope and faith of giving a worthwhile chance
Of survival in darkened days of misery and strife
So in memory of all mighty men who fell upon
Many a battleground amidst monstrous creation of insane hell
The heroes never to be forsaken for such bravery
Each sacrifice in a cause for peace and liberty
In commemoration of our mighty men who fell
Forever remembrance day shall always stay
For those long gone and every lost hero of today.

Margaret Howens

Flowers

Has anyone ever noticed how beautiful flowers can be,
Whether they're grown in a cottage garden
or wild in a field by the sea.

There are buttercups and daisies that peep out
from behind long grass.
And then there are those like orchids
especially grown under glass.

We see the little pansies who seem to have a face
and lily of the valley who look as delicate as lace.
There are iris and tulips growing on a hill,
with a host of daffodils that seem to grow at will,

With lavender and lilac so beautiful to smell
and clematis and green ivy,
That grow 'round the old wishing well.

As I look at the water lilies growing in the pond
I think about chrysanthemums of which I'm very fond,

and what about the crocus and snowdrops,
That grow in a lovely array
But let's not forget carnations, roses, and freesias,
That are arranged in a bride's bouquet.

E. Carty

That Place

There's a place I know,
Where I always grow
In strength and heart and mind.
It's a lovely place,
A beautiful face.
A hand that will provide.
I know I'm weak and feeble-kneed,
I know I'm not my own,
For my destiny lies.
Where my heart strings ties.
I know I'm coming home.

To ever be that place with me,
That place where I belong.
There's a longing here my heart to share,
Away from trouble and from scorn,
Take heed dear friends for time will tell,
If you have no place of your own,
Let your desire be at that place with me,
Waiting, watching earnestly, hear the call. Come quickly
Friend, feel free, feel free, feel free.

    H. Williamson

Wanted

Cry little one. Relieve the pain -
which you have been subjected.
Cry little one. You'll not again -
receive the cruelty expected.
Sleep little one and have no fear.
There's naught to harm you here.

Laugh little one. Enjoy your life -
Now you are in my care.

Laugh little one. There's no more strife -
Just love for us to share.
Rest little one. Your wounds will heal.
The warmth of love from now you'll feel.

Love little one. It's love that's the solution.
Love little one. With love there's no confusion.
Learn little one and ne'er forget -
The evils of this world you've met.

When you're adult my little one,
With hate you'll not be haunted.
When you have your own to love,
My love, you'll both be wanted.

    D. R. Thomas

The Atlantic

The ceaseless movement of the tide;
White horses racing side by side;
A ruffled pathway in the wake
In feathery folds of frothy flake.

The changing aspect of the sea
Sweeps past in white-flecked filigree.
The varied patterns, pictures clear,
In gleaming loveliness appear.

The writings of an Eastern race,
Sometimes a dress of sequined lace,
The maps of many countries vast
In motley sequence gliding past.

The whisper of the waves' caress;
Or rustle of a silken dress;
The gentle breeze that softly sighs
To harmonise with seagulls cries.

The clouds pierce Heav'n like distant spires.
The sea glows red with secret fires.
The burning orb sinks out of sight.
A silver lane leads through the night.

    Nancy Frost

The Gypsy

There came such a loud knocking at my door
Whilst I was busy with many a chore
So knowing this would hinder me
I opened it reluctantly
There before me my eyes did behold
A tall dark gypsy young and bold
He sold me pegs I did not need
Then asked for water, he did so plead
I gave him milk, bread and cheese
He ate with relish which did me please
He wished me luck and then did say
You are the first good lady I've met this day
I thought this, his yarn of woe
But then as he did turn to go
A leg so lame the dragged behind
Oh was I glad I had been kind.

    Louise Wood

Loony Bin

Giggling gerty giggled all day
Whilst tinkering terry tinkered away
Wiggling willie wiggled on in
And messy bessy with egg on her chin
Dithering david tried hard to say
To haggling annie oh what a nice day
When fumbling frederick fumbled on by
And starry mary stared up at the sky
Nattering natalie looked 'round the door
When arrogant alice said what's she here for
Sticky dickie was sticking quite true
To the lavatory seat smeared with glue
Specky becky was brushing her locks
And spotty dotty was picking her spots
Diddling danny was sat all alone
Whilst stammering stephen spoke on the phone
And all the time the children did play
While the cat and the dog
They both ran away

    Michael Shearon

"To Change"

To change or not to change, that is the question.
Whether it's wiser after all to wear the same old dress
we've worn all week or have a bath and done complete
new raiment.
To bath - to wash - to relax, ah! there's the rub.
For when we wash with scented soap and bubbles gay,
what thoughts may come as we wallow in hot water
must give us pause. 'Tis a prospect not lightly to
be dismissed.
Is there a merit in being newly dressed in silken
underwear and dresses elegant and shining? to read
approval in another woman's eyes and yet be scared of
being overdressed or flashy.
Boredom-induced depression can be banished by one
pleasing image in the mirror.
So perhaps it is true to say that we adorn ourselves
not for some unlamented male, we do it for us!

    G. Frampton

Devil's Liquid

An innocent fragile child awaits,
With a once trusted man
Vodka, the devil's liquid intoxicates his mind
He is now a demon dining on child's flesh.
As years went by and by
The child's now distorted mind dreams.
The man wrapped up in a chain of thorns
Behind the prison door of stone
Head bowed sipping from a tap of running blood.
Falling down, upon his starved swollen body
A blanket of barbed wire.
She silently continues in pain
For the dreams she loves to be reality.

    Natascha Bastiaan

Grannies

Some grannies are elderly, with silver hair,
Who are happy to sit in their armchair.
Who will tuck you in, when it's time for bed,
Who are there when you need a story read.

Some grannies are younger, with energy to spare,
always willing to take you somewhere.
Swimming, shopping, games in the park,
ready to comfort, when you cry in the dark.

Grannies like the things you make,
They always eat the cakes you bake.
They love it when you come to call,
The hugs and the kisses says it all.
They like to hear of the things you have done,
The games you've played, how your team won.

The tears in her eyes, when it's time to go,
The smile that says, she loves you so.
after all things are said and done.
Being a granny, can be fun.
Myrtle Elden

To a Dear One

Who do I turn to when I am sad
Who do I run to when I am glad
Who sees me through all worry and strife.
You do.

Who cares for me when I am ill
Who sits by the bed and remembers my pill
Who helps me get well and fit again
You do.

Who makes me a cuppa when I am down
Who makes me smile when I wear a frown
Who thinks of me always, day in and day out.
You do.

Who has his own troubles but puts me first
Who whole-hearted loves me even at my worst
Who makes me love him more than anything on earth.
You do.

G. J. Thornewell

Ode to Grandad

I've never known a person, so kind of thought and mind,
who loved to be around us, no, another I'll not find.
I worshipped every moment that we could be together,
but now I find I'm left alone, without you now, forever.
Although I can't be with you, I think of you each day,
not a moment does go by without a thought of you in some way.
How I wish you could be here now, here to see my brand new home,
for you to meet my partner, or to speak to you on the 'phone.
I'd love to have your blessing, to know you are pleased with me,
contented at the type of person that I've turned out to be.
But you have left me with lots of memories, ones I could not do without,
so you really must excuse me when to odd tear trickles out.
I miss you, oh, so dearly, but I can not forget you,
for I know you'll be beside me in everything I do.

K. Beadman

Life

What's the meaning of the word tell me, and why
With all our technology can't we work out this so
important mystery, of where we derive from, if
we could solve this crazy puzzle, I'm almost certain
this world would not be in such an unfair muddle.
I believe religion is one the root of all evil, I also think
there is no God and there is no devil, Just add
an O to God and this makes good then add a D to
evil which then makes devil, and the rest is up
to you for what ever path you wish to choose, choose
wisely, for it's only common sense, which one will make
you happy. So let's get solving, after all if we did
solve this so important mystery we may then have
found the answer to world peace.

Katch O'Dwyer

May I Say Thanks

May I say thanks to many unseen friends
Who help me on my way
With a kindly word and a guiding hand
As I journey day by day.

An aged gent helped me at Worle
And help from a caring American girl,
Who as she left said, "Have a nice day"
As I went safely on my way

The lorry drivers, the motorists
Whose flashing lights show through the mists
To tell me I can safely cross
Without them I should feel the loss

My daughters understand my plight
And help in every way
My neighbours do those little jobs
That crop up day by day.

I've many friends, who friendship give
And I give them thanks again
So stop and speak if you see me out
Holding my long white cane.

Kathleen Williams

My Great Nan

You came into my life, Nan
With a smile upon your face
And since that day, through all the years
You never gave up laughing!
I saw you as a lady
Without a trouble in the world
But I guess, sometimes,
Deep down inside
You may have worn a frown,
But even though it never showed
'Cause the best of you shined through.
That's always how I've known you
And always how you'll stay.
In my heart and mind I'll always see you -
Laughing, smiling, having fun;
And - best of all Nan, sharing it with me!

Victoria Ross

Spring

My "Lady Spring" is here again,
With all God's glories for us to share
Gone are the days of snow and rain
And icy winds which caused such pain.
Small trees, Tall trees gaunt and bare
Now show green buds, for all who care to notice.
Snow drops, crocuses, hyacinths blue.
Twittering birds, and lambs here too
Heaven's clear blue sky,
The sun shining high.
Welcome, my "Lady Spring", earth's joys are nigh.

Millicent D. Stevenson

Peace

O for the corner of a meadow,
Where the grass is fresh and green,
With the sky above of azure blue,
And the sound of a tinkling stream.

Where Blackberries grow in hedges neat,
And Campian grow beneath your feet
Larks that sing in the sky so high
And to watch the skim of a dragonfly.

This is peace, a place of love.
The cooing of a turtle dove,
Robin sings in a hawthorn tree.
The humming of a Bumblebee.
Away from the toils of daily life
Anger greed and daily strife
Go to a meadow and find a dream,
Of green green grass and silver stream.

W. C. Woolcock

Sweet Dreams

Living in a candy world, that's how life should be,
with clouds like cotton candy, floating high above me.
The snow would be ice cream, with hot fudge flavour topping.
Houses made of cookies, and rain like popcorn popping.
Trees with chocolate branches, and peppermint flavoured leaves,
flowers that are lollipops of any flavour you please.
The grass would be green jello, all wiggly, giggly, goo.
Rivers and lakes of soda, plenty for me and you.
Pebbles and stones are candy, both soft and hard to chew,
strawberry, raspberry, lemon, take lots or just a few.
But you would get sick of candy, after a week or two, so I'm
glad that this is just my dream world, which I can visit with you.

Yvette Marie Darwood

A Pig's Tale

Fitzroy was a fastidious pig
Who never cared a whit or fig
For wallowing in the feeding trough
And while the other pigs would scoff
He'd daintily eat with knife and fork
And farmhands stood to gaze and gawk.

Then to the river he would trot
To wipe off any offending spot
Until he was both pink and clean
And quite the smartest pig you've seen
He'd settle in some nice clean grass
To lay and watch the clouds go past.

One day young Fitzroy, all aglow
Was taken to the livestock show
There he paraded 'round the ring
While the auctioneer his praise did sing
But to Fitzroy's horror he was sold
For a paltry sum, five pieces of gold

So Fitzroy went to his sad fate
And ended up on my breakfast plate!

M. Bastable

Mum and Dad

When you first married, there were one or two,
Who said you'd never last, the whole year through,
But little did they know, how strongly you felt,
'Cause the years have gone by and you've never had a doubt.

You've had many a good times, bad ones and all,
But you've both pulled through and felt very tall,
There's been tears and arguments throughout the years,
But your love's been strong and you've made things work.

You've worked hard for your family and give what you can,
And there's never been a day when you don't give a damn,
You've stopped and listened and give good advice,
But you've never told us how to manage our lives.

For this we are grateful and hope that you know,
That we love you very much wherever we may go.

Lisa Jane Wright

Maxima cum Laude

How inspiring 'twas to sup with one so graced
With intelligence with judgement and with taste,
And meet exterior loveliness combined
With all the richest treasures of the mind;
Such knowledge, wisdom and discrimination,
Such talents seldom found in combination.
To these add magnanimity of thought,
And with this generosity of heart.

Some may call it providential
That I've found the quintessential.
Clerics declare it quite heretical,
And sceptics merely hypothetical.
Away with trouble, away with strife,
I've found the elixir of life.

Max Court

Tears and Cheers

I am a woman old in years
Who sometimes drowns in floods of tears
But, truly thankful many a night,
To laugh, and wheeze, with sheer delight.

Some only cry at something sad,
Of course, these folks are far from mad
But, search out joy - it's there to find
And keeps the aged sane in mind.

A chuckle here, a giggle there
Is quite the best of daily fare,
It shows the world you're not done yet
And brings such joy to friends well met.

I had good parents, shown right from wrong
Told, life is not all a happy song.
But believe that God is always near
Press on — do laugh — bring cheer.

Winifred Cumming

"Time"

Time - what is it?
Why are we always racing
Saying we just haven't time
Time to enjoy nature's wonders.
To the beauty around us we're blind.

Time to spend with our children
Our grandchildren, neighbours and friends.
Time to see the heart needs of others
To be there when someone's life ends.

Oh, what is the meaning of time.
it slips by us so frightening fast.
The years just have rolled by us
When we look back over the past.

Well, maybe God has the answer.
And he'll tell us all in the end
For there's one thing I know for certain
God is our steadfast, loyal, true friend.

Ruth Gordon

Shalom Means Peace

I visited the Holy Land
With my own eyes to see.
I travelled down from Haifa
Toward the Salty Sea.

I journeyed then to Tel Aviv
And Jerusalem I turn.
I spoke to Arabs and to Jews
From them the truth to learn.
And from all of them the self-same pleas:
"Shalom," they said "We want peace"

Kurt Fleischmann

The Mystic Isles

Oh mystic isles, within the mist
Where golden dawn, has scarcely kissed
How pleasing to my eye, you are
Who gazes upon you, from afar
My heart has known a surge of joy
At this innermost cry of "Land Ahoy"
For many weeks now, I have known
No other sight, then waves alone
That ever writhing, restless sea
Which, arches into Eternity
Monotony, had dulled my brain
I've longed to see some land again
And now, my far horizon is blessed
With your beguiling beauty, upon its crest
Majestic, is the word for you
Mysterious, a little too
For, I shall never thread your shore
And, too soon, see you, never more
As, wind-borne, I'll go on a sailing past
Until you've disappeared, at last

J. F. Clarke

Song

How long, O Lord, how long
Will I be able to look across the garden to the bay
Where, beneath the night sky
Shines the spangling globe of light
That steadfastly glows, how long
Will I be able to remember
The gold of last summer's fields
Wove and burnished by the blazing sun
Patterned only by the aching dark of summer trees?
The scent of the sea
And the village houses, with painted doors, huddling close
As if to give shelter, though
The snows of winter are yet to come
And they, cut off by their isolation
Draw comfort from wooden fires
Will someone in the future
Write all this down in poem or a song
Or will they think it another Midsummer Night's Dream?

Rosemary Adams

Time

At the Valentine's Ball with the moon overhead,
"Will you be mine darling Wendy?", he said,
How could I refuse such a wonderful man,
Just 15 years old and an eighteen year man.
So tall, dark and handsome with a quiet gentle way,
Married, together, forty years to the day.
How TIME flies in your company, my darling love,
We fit together like hands in a glove.
I'd never have changed anything about you,
You gave me your love - I've returned it to you.
With arms oh so strong that enfold our desire,
Eyes like black pools, set my heart on fire.
Love is the caring that you gave to me,
There'll never be anyone but you for me.
You're the reason to live and I'm greedy you see,
I want all of your TIME forever, for ME!

Wendy Scammells

The Destroyer

They thrust themselves upon the land
With empty head and heavy hand,
To dig in deep to reach her soul
Keeping eyes tightly closed.

Bit by bit they take apart
Mother Natures broken heart,
She bleeds, she cries.

Yet still they stand wit swords of death within their hands
To break her down with no need
To draw her slowly to her knees.

Suicidal men are we, for without her where would we be.

Kathleen Bruce

Commuting - My Journey

The journey starts
With a choice to be made
Central, Circle, District, Piccadilly
Which should I take to bring me to the City.

I board the train and spot a seat
And so have many others
The race is on
But once again I lose it to another.

And so I must stand
While becoming more cramped
Squeezed into a tiny space
Someone's elbow in my face.

My head is swimming
My eyes are brimming over
With frustration
The journey ends, I've reached my destination.

Sandra Taylor

To Live

In times of despair I ask myself
Why?
I look around at what I have done and see
coldness.
There is a chill.
Is it the chill of that damp dark place where one
I love lies buried
Or do I feel a chill because I myself placed him there?

My mind screams once more and my heart cracks.
I try not to think about it,
But still the blood boils
And the pain strikes,
Crashing at me like the waves of the sea.
Where once I stood happy
Now tears stream down my cheeks.

Life goes on they tell me.
Not everyone's it seems.
The gap in my life is as wide as the seven seas.
I live a day at a time.
That's all I can do now.

Rose Hamilton-Lyons

No One Loves Me

A little child left all alone on a cold bleak
winter day.
No mum or dad to love it.
No clothes to keep it warm, or food to ease
its hunger.
A little child to young to speak and tell
you how it suffers.
The only way that it can tell is by sad and tear filled eyes.
It knows not how to show its love, never
having had it, or any toys to play with
or a teddy bear to hug.
There are millions of these little ones in
this vast world of ours.
It's all so very sad, and tragic to recall
That Gods little children were born to suffer so.

V. Hamilton

'Died Abroad - But Home with Mother'

You stand forlorn and distant seem,
With tears a-glistening downward poured,
And time stands quiet here with you.

The dew-washed grass beneath your feet,
Like tears you've cried in memory.
Though not interred in native soil,
Where I perhaps would love to be.

Oh! mother dearest do not weep,
For I am happy in my sleep.

Pat Lewin

Memories

So long ago a boy I met
Yet he's the one I can't forget
Those happy days I still recall
And re-live till the teardrops fall
War let us meet, then made us part
Love unfulfilled still in my heart
Since then a mess I've made of life
I wonder! Had I been his wife
But fate had other plans for me
It knew the kind of fool I'd be
But time goes by and so you try
A life that's new and things that are not really you
Thought in your heart you know I guess
Still searching for that happiness.
But now as youth and hopes have flown
And dreams that were my very own
I often wonder if he knew
My love for him was really true and were I granted
Just one day from life to live anew
I'd hurry back into the past to spend that lovely day with you.

H. Lane

Motherly Love

Ma's kitchen always smelt so good
with homemade cakes and lovely meat pud,
the many children she had to feed
was always there for their need.

At the sink the washing was rubbed
then was washed in an old tin tub,
the floors were scrubbed all the way through
until they came up looking like new.

The bath came down off the garden wall
children were bathed one and all,
from kettles of water off the stove
that was used before hand to bake the loaves.

She hugged them all on retiring to bed
she did no more than to prepare for ahead!
Until she looked 'round and found more to do
darning their socks and cleaning their shoes.

When the chores were finally done
she counted her blessings one by one!
The end of the day was finally through
a life that was my mother knew.

Patricia Harris

The Contact

At last you arrived, looking so small, smelling of talcum and
wrapped in your shawl. Don't get emotional, try not to cry
I know I can't keep you, you'll never know why.

The weeks pass so quickly, I can't bear to think
That the day will be here soon to sever the link.

Today is the day I shall never forget.
It's a decision I hope I shall never regret.

Goodbye little one, it wasn't to be
I was meant to keep you safe with me.

I'll never forget you, and hope that one day
you might get in touch and I'll hear you say, 'I forgive you'

Thirty years pass, then out of the blue, a message received, can it
really be you. My prayers have been answered, a contact at last.
You tell me you're happy and, what's past is past.

The big day is here, I shall see you again.
My legs are like jelly as I wait for the train.
I've dreamed of this day, and now you are here.
We both smile and stare and lose all our fear.

So much to explain, so much to learn.
My life feels complete, no longer to yearn.

J. Phillips

Black and White

Children black or white
Why do adults have to fight?
Matter of colour a matter of creed
Matter of religion a matter of greed
The heart of mankind bleeds red, be you black or white,
that still doesn't tell me why adults fight.
The pain is there but does anyone care?

It seems not in this adult world we live in.
It's a matter of politics a matter of place.
A matter of survival in the human race.

Why do my parents despise you as such?
It's the colour of my skin it stands for too much.
In this cold world only one colour can count.
Whites are clean and blacks are out.
In the warmth of my heart I know it can work.
I'm sorry my love but people keep us apart

So next time you watch a riot on T.V
Don't think of excuses,
Look in the mirror
Because the answers in you and me.

Zoe Harrison

Just My Imagination

Who are you? What are you?
Why do you follow me, every hour of everyday of my life?
I feel your cold fingers reach out to me and brush my face with fear.
Your icy breath freezes on my cheek, a cold mist, so very near.
Where do you come from? What is your name?
Why do you follow me, wherever I go, whomever I'm with?
What do you want? What can I do, to get you to leave me alone?
I hear you breathing, I hear your voice, as soft as the wind you moan.
What are you?
Are you the wind that tugs at a kite?
Are you that thing that goes bump in the night?
Are you the terror? Are you the suspense?
Are you that presence that I can always sense?
Are you the monster that lurks under the bed?
Are you a name that has never been said?
Are you a lost soul seeking peace from me?
Are you that person that I can never see?
Are you the one that causes people strife?
Are you jealous of my soul, and of my life?
Are you the sound of a dead bird singing?
Or are you just my imagination?

Sarah Jane Billington

To See Beyond

Bridle path to Misty Valley,
Will you find the sea,
Or will you find in fairy glen,
Wee folk dancing free.

Whate'er you find, bring peace of heart,
Joy to fill the day
Bridle path to Misty Valley
Welcomes you to stay.

Time; enshrouding Misty Valley
Gently year by year,
Offers those who seek the truth,
To proceed without fear.

Misty Valley, mankind's venture,
Through the world of strife,
Surely time for all to reject,
Evil acts in life.

Lift the veil from Misty Valley,
Confront hate and greed,
Bringing forward Christian Action,
Helping all in need.

May Hulme

The Day the Spacemen Came

"What do you think?" said the alien commander, "I'm afraid sir, we
can't land her." you see the trouble with the planet, that it hadn't
any space. What were they thinking when they took away its grace?

"Commander, where are all the flowers and the high green trees?
Where are all the birds that are supposed to fly around free?
What about the things we read about in books, what about the
world that's been promised us?"

There was nothing there now apart from over-crowding and smog.
Nothing but grey dark buildings and a thick and dirty fog. A place
where evil and hare are thriving, a place where ignorance and
war are surviving. "Commander, what should we do this mess?"
"Blow it up . . . like the rest,

Organisms like this cannot live in peace, they cannot be taught. I
bet lower life-forms like this don't even have thoughts." "their
future is hazy, let's just call it euthanasia. "They travelled away
and released the bomb.

The once beautiful, sad, grey blob became dimmer. Then it went
up in a huge silver shimmer. The spacemen's faces were sad, but
they hadn't done anything really bad. It's just a terrible shame,
the life-form on that planet was to blame.

They travelled away faster than light, at the end of their search,
they had finally found the planet known as Earth. With no more
clear, silver waters which ran, all had been destroyed by a life-
form called man . . .

Jenny Burton

War Child

Poor little child crying alone
Without a family, without a home
On a street corner he stares at the sky
Asking himself why, oh why?
He has seen enough he wants no more
Why are they fighting? What is it for?
His life's just beginning yet it seems so dim
The killings do not mean anything to him
He doesn't know where his parents have gone
And he has no clue of what's going on
All he knows is that people are dying
And he still sits alone crying and crying.

I. Modinou

When I Grow Up

When I grow up Daddy, will I be able to speak with my mouth full?
Will I be able to do anything Dada, anything at all?
Wear all those fancy clothes and drive a big fast car,
Will I be able to have a beer and smoke a big cigar?

I want to stay up really, really late at night Daddy,
I want to be a big grown up instead a little laddie.
Then I'll be able to understand what the teachers taught me at school,
And go out dancing with the girls, and be hip and trendy and really cool.

Does it take long Daddy, to grow up from a boy to a man?
'Cos I want to get there Dad, as fast, as fast as I can.
What's the secret Dad, to make those years pass by?
I want to be all big and tough, and much too brave to cry.

I want to get married Dad and have a wife and babies too,
I want to be a daddy Dad, and do the things that Daddies do.
I want to dig the garden Dad, and paint the ceilings white,
Then have my tea and watch T.V. and stay up till it's late at night.

I want my kids to have kids so that I can be a Grandad,
And when I'm a Grandad you'll be oh . . . oh . . . Oh DAD!!

Keith A. Watkins

The Sea

The sea is so powerful and yet so kind,
With all sorts of wonder for people to find.
Sometimes she's angry, sometimes she's sad,
Often she'll kill when she's really mad.

The sea is amazing and loves to impress,
Her beauty and style we love to undress.
Thrashing and crashing when weather is wild,
Cool and serene when climate is mild.

The sea she is green and sometimes blue,
Offering herself to me and you.
But when she's troubled and very dark,
That's when she'll swallow and make her mark.

The sea gives such pleasure in all that she does,
Cooling and stroking people like us.
She may be good or she may be bad,
But living without her would be oh so sad.

N. Marshall

Silent Voice

Born in a world full of high expectations
With so many voices so many nations
My life is a test on that were agreed
So please understand how much love I will need
In a world full trouble, conflict and pain
I hope my birth won't have been in vain
You call me disabled yet I'm only nine
So was Gods intervention really divine
When people pass by me saying life's not fair
They don't notice me perhaps they don't care
I'd like to point out at least they have choice
When I stay silent trapped with no voice
So next time you see me no smile on your face
Just consider my life and the words I can't place.

Teresa Hall

The Ghost of Ireland

Why did he have to shoot me
Why did I have to die
We lived in the same street
We played under the same sky.

We often walked to school together
Across the park and down the lane
Went into different buildings
But came out and played our favourite games.

But someone stuck a label on him
And put a badge on me
Then they put guns in our hands
And told us it was either him or me.

One night he crouched along the ground
A body came into sight
He just pulled the trigger and shot out the breath of life.

Next morning he read the papers
And listened to the news
The news reader said I lay dead near my old school.

T. Doherty

Another Day

Looking from the window, with my head and hands held low
With sadness in my eyes, numb from head to toe

I pear into the sky, the clouds they seem forever
every shape and size, scattered everywhere

Through a break in the clouds, I can see a warm blue sky
The sunshine beams on through, upon my face appears a smile

The sadness disappears, a tear of joy trickles down my face
I see a tiny song-thrush, in the distance, through the sunny haze

The day will soon be ending, and tomorrow will come around
another day, just hoping, just wishing, just praying
what the new day will bring, is unfound.

Selina J. Del-gaudio

Bag Lady

Saw you sitting there, all alone,
with no one to care.
Empty bottles around your feet,
Hands in your hair,
A whole world, in just one stare,
Expressions of despair.
Years of life, love, laughter and misery.
Memories in brown paper bags,
This heart cried out, but was chased away.
The only friends left in the world,
Pigeons in the square, Empty bottles
around your chair.
Past caring, Past sharing,
Just waiting for the day
that you don't have to wait for
anymore.

Sylvia Edwards

This Government

While I sat and thought the other day, of rack and ruin and decay the world is heading for a fall, the rack and ruin of us all. Well some of us maybe a few, would like to know hey! Who said you could rule the roost and make the laws, infect us all and hide the cause. You've covered for so many years, but we're not daft we've had our fears you treat us like we have no brain, our families they feel the pain. And what about the U.F.O's, that we have seen but you say no there's no such thing make fools of us, just shut our mouths don't make a fuss
I'm no angel I've done my share, of good and bad to those out there but still I try my best to do the rightful thing no not like you, you've brought the earth down to decay, it's policy I hear you say the cover-ups, too much to bear God knows what else you've done out there. So if it's true you reap what you sow, the Government to hell you go you've done your best? I don't think so!

Seema Sara Thompson

Home with a Heart

When is a house really a home, it isn't the
windows, it isn't the stone.
It's so rare to see in this day and age, not
something seen on a magazine page.
Yet once you have found one you know it's real,
not something that shows, but something you feel.
Ring the bell and step inside, there to experience
a lovely surprise.
The hall still echoes with children's laughter,
bringing warmth so many years after,
Family grown up, all left home, yet Mum and
Dad are never alone.
The spirit of love so evident there, in every
room, in every chair
Pictures, mementos displayed with love,
showing the blessing from heaven above.
Special people make this house a home, not
the windows, not the stone.
I shall always cherish the time I spent there,
and remember the family when I say a prayer.

Veronica Black

Alike and Yet . . .

All the airs are stilled
With Nature's hand
The frost lies cold upon the land
The forest cries out unashamed
Their death like shadows
Cast on Winter's land
The child cries
Its hunger burns
The winter of our souls are not of Nature's hand
We look awhile we think awhile
We turn away and say
Well! That's a different land
But all their air is stilled
And there's no helping hand
Death lies cold upon their land
And the forests of humanity are unashamed
We walk, we laugh, we eat, we talk
And still the beast of hunger preys
His lust fulfilled without
The boundaries of our lands.

Stephen Blackwell

Where Would We Be?

How sad would be this world of ours,
Without various trees, and beautiful flowers
If there were no birds, to sing, or hum of the bee upon the wing.
Still, would be the air without any tune or sweet perfume.
Where would we be, if there were no fish
in the sea or animals to utter a cry.
No little creature or the lovely butterfly
Life would be empty, and not worth the while.
There would be nothing to make us smile.
Without Mother Nature, who created,
all the beautiful things we see and hear.
Where would we be?

E. H. Lake

The Final Piece

Like the sudden clap of thunder wields its power with a roar,
you came into my life like no other came before,
and like the stars that fill the heavens on a crystal winter's night,
you beamed into my world and filled it with your light;
When I thought that I was dreaming, that you would ne'er be mine,
and the signs that I was seeing were a fantasy of mind,
I thought that very soon you would turn and walk away,
but you opened up your heart and said the words I dreamed you'd say;
Now my heart it wears a smile and my soul it fills the skies,
for I found the part of me I'd lost, in the wonder of your eyes,
you gave me back the final piece, 'twas all I needed to be free,
I love you gentle lady, you brought my spirit home to me.

Paul T. Alan

The Park (Hollycroft Park, Hinckley)

Green appled gates of youth,
Within we played our games,
Beneath the great weeping willow's bough,
In the shrubs and bushes' maze.

Unspoken secrets, hushed tight lips,
As we seek and peep and hide,
Unbroken silence as we tread through
Whispered glades, no one confides.

Deep thought, imagination, our only toy.
Blissful days filled of childlike truth,
Sweet lingering smell of new mowed grass,
Within the green appled gates of youth.

Sylvia Rose Payne

'The Old Classic'

I evolved from a by-gone age, in the minds of men
with a passion for style and grace.

I developed on a drawing board in the corner of a
room, at the hand of a man with an imagination
gifted with accurate decision.

I transformed from image to model on the bench of a
craftsman skilled with chisel and dedicated
precision.

I matured like a vintage wine, with each part
individually nurtured and adorned with paint and
polish, by a man possessed with the eye of a famous
artist.

I emerged fully fledge, TRIUMPHANT - bright
shining headlight, front and rear fender angled just
right, fuel tank colours, a hue of blue and a swirl of
white.

What am I? An old classic Triumph Motorbike!

Karen Mandy Tranter

Peace

We await the new year like the first day of spring
Wondering what the future will bring
To many, we hope, a new kind of life
Away from fighting, trouble, and strife
A new kind of year, where peace will prevail.
No more hungry children to weep and to wail
But a year of happiness, laughter and such
Or is this asking a little too much
If we all pulled together, all races and creeds
To bury the hatchet and meet others' needs
Then this could be the year we unite
The year that we tried with all of our might

J. L. Slade

Solitude

The other night, I sat alone
with all my thoughts for company
thoughts, that were my very own
and in imagination made me see,
all those vague things take form and tone
and re-create themselves for me, alone.

On wings of song and with a sigh,
I saw my happiness pass by,
and with grim thoughts and deep despair
I saw my sorrows over there,
with difficulties and every care,
I should be here why was I there.

And with my mind in this refrain,
before my eyes my life passed by,
I saw the buses, boats and trains
and saw the place where men must die,
and saw the face so far away,
which stays with me from day to day,
Oh, these things, if I could see,
that brings this solitude to me.

Rodney H. Vinall

221

Spring's Gentle Caress

Spring's golden light pierces dark winter's gloom
With summer's promise, and slowly life blooms
Buried deep beneath the cold, furrowed soil
Opens, revealing nature's patient toil.

Rain sprays drench the shy emerging flowers
With rainbow's colours, and through the showers
The sweet notes of a songbird can be heard
Trilling with joy. Creation's slumber stirred.

Slender bluebell, primrose, cool snowdrop stand
Glorious in field, meadow and woodland,
To bloom unseen. Wild flowers of the field
To the rainbow alone their beauty yield.

Retain in your mind's eye this vibrant scene.
Blue sky, white lambs playing, trees ever green.
Wonder at barren earth's mighty rebirth
Ponder life's dreams borne on fast flowing streams.

Patricia Keating

Jacko

If I could feel again your rough coat on my cheek
your body firm and warm within my arms,
I would find comfort as I did before
when your swift secret tongue
would hide my rare reluctant tears.
I asked in vain for human love, yet you
who were not worth a pedigree
possessed the virtues cultured folk forgot;
you gave me all the love I ever knew.

Patricia Elvidge

Walk of Life

You were there across the crowded room.
Your face I remembered from way back.
Although you had changed with time
You were still the person I once new.
Our eyes met, you wandered over.
We talked about our past
Life had not been kind but that changed with time
You became my best friend, my lifeline. I now felt complete
The years we spent together past quickly
We had our hard times. But when I look back they were good times
What happened one will never know.
You went from my life the way you came. Taking part of me with you
Why is life so unkind? Do we deserve the pain and suffering
I search for answers, there are none.
We had walked that path before. Did you loose your way
Only you never returned
Looking back the path is overgrown now.
I must go on and make way for a new life.

Val B. Seal

The Elephant's Foot

Soft, gentle, yet immense
Your foot, O Master Pachyderm
Spreads o'er the ground caressingly.
Distributing the tons of weight
In even pressure on the earth below.
Old Father Ant he fears you not,
And after you have gone, will rush
From out his hiding place under your foot
To join his family, who scurried quick
To avoid your ponderous fall.
Less lucky were the eggs left there
Which were destroyed and crushed beneath
Your tread, you wise, inevitable, creature.

So dear companions all, please hasten to
Your spiritual shelters just like Father Ant,
That you, like he, may rise unscathed
After the giant footsteps of our Fate
Have passed your way and crushed the lesser man,
Who like the egg, puts up a brittle fight,
But yet is smashed and lost, forgotten quite.

Patrick A. Miles

Untitled

Don't tell me what to do, don't tell me what to say
You're not my dad
My dad was good before he left us and went away
Don't think that you can rule me, just 'cos you give me a home
You're not my dad
My dad never stayed in to boss me about like you do
My dad can take his drink, he isn't a softie like you
Washing up and asking where I am
What's it got to do with you?
You're not my dad
My dad would laugh at you if he saw you now
Sitting there watching T.V.
With a cup of tea
He's the tough one
He's in jail
Not sitting there
Watching me
You're not my dad.

L. Kirby

Youth

Life awaits you, and all you have to give,
You're on the threshold now — Begin to live.
Time is yours, so don't throw it away.
There is no finer moment than to-day,
Youth comes once, then spreads its wings in flight.
Don't let it flee, hold on with all your might.

What is life without the hope of spring,
The birth of life, and all that it could bring,
And what is youth if it slips by unshared,
If no one wears a smile, because you cared,
And those rare years, had never known the joy,
That graced each moment, when you were a boy,

For when youth is gone, and manhood has its days
And times brief hours are mirrored in its gaze,
Such years will seem as but the time of day,
Before dawn kissed, then turned and walked away,
When time is sweet and laughter full of truth,
Don't let it die, for nothing's like your youth.

C. J. Langdon

My Super "M-A-A"

My dear "M-A-A,"
You're the golden wealth in our life.
You're so precious "M-A-A!"
We felt secure in your affection,
Although we were so little.
So far as I can remember,
We played outside and if anything happened to us,
We would run - run and go to you for comfort.
Before I came of age
God, you took away my "M-A-A!"
I can't find the "M-A-A," I love.
She left us so suddenly
And her smile has gone forever.
I pray for you "M-A-A."
God bless, we love you always.
You're everything to me
My super "M-A-A."

Shafi Ullah

Listen! (To a Cry from a Disabled Person)

To all that ask but do not hear
You've made my hopes full of fear
Please LISTEN!! to what I have to say
and please don't just push me away
How would you feel, if everything you wanted to do,
someone pushed you aside and said "I'll do that for you."
They just didn't ask, they just assumed,
that a person like you had to be cocooned.
Well I want to stretch and reach for my stars,
I want to break out through these man-made bars.
I want to break out, I want to be free.
But most of all I just want to be ME!

Martin R. L. Hammond

The Airhostess

She arrives in the aircrew carpark
In her black Renault Clio.
She walks towards the staff bus
With her suitcase in tow
Off on another long journey
Where will she go.
With her jet black hair and
Eyes to match
She boards the bus and with
A lovely smile she says hello!
She takes her seat to ponder
On what I wonder
At our short journey's end
She disembarks with a smile
And a "cheerio" with her suitcase in tow
When will she return I wonder
Will I be here I hope so
To see her is always
A pleasure something
A treasure.

Tim Cassidy

"When Life Is Too Much"

Sometimes we feel that life has nothing left for us.
Why should we wait around for something that will never happen?
Only we matter; ours is the decision to stay or go.
But others are important too.
What we leave behind is their misery.
Our rest begins but so does their pain.
Our way out leads to their suffering.
We inflict our pain on them.
They do not deserve to suffer for our escape from life.
Instead, if life or its ways are wrong, change them.
There is always a better way.
There is always an answer, but sometimes it has no legs;
It cannot come to us, we must go and look for it.
We must take that first step and search.
There is always a better way.
We will earn our rest, our peace.
But ours is not to choose the time or place.
Ours is to find the best pathway, the best route.
One that does not harm others or ourselves.
That is the better way.

Ruth Taylor

A Parting

In the still dewy ambience of early morn
You were carried to your rest
A cloak of Mahogany shrouded your face
Earth crashed upon it
as a muttered formula was read
to dust and eternal obscurity
The pent up vitality of a barely begun day
Mocked your inertia
The ascending sun could never scorch your skin
You lay safe from temptation
Unable to see the true void,
the legacy of grief left to me.

Nicola Grant

The Ash

Enduring ash, far longer lived than I,
you were full grown when first I had a name;
strong, angular and wild against the sky;
now though I weaken, you are still the same.
All winter bare, then through the dreaming spring
your naked curves flow on along each branch;
last dressed in green for summer, when girls sing
and own true love is started at a glance;
white mists, autumn damp falls, and splendour lost
winds rage, and rage away despair; not yet
despoiled, till leaves crimp in a sudden frost
and withered spin to earth; then pride forget.
Crouched in numb sap the cruel shoots conspire,
'Make your black buds, we'll slit them with green fire.'

Patricia Harrison

Clouds

When the music I have listened to has ended
With all the recollections and memories,
The room dark, still and loudly quiet.
Looking up through the window
Into the clear blue black night,
Quietly watching - the stars and the moon.
The stars are shining through my room
The lonely moon is full and bright,
Which lit upon the night -
Seems caught in the limitless starlit sky.

Where the sky meets the racing clouds -
The bare leaf branches waving,
Moving lithely to and fro;
Some thin and slender others gracefully large
All moving in time to the theme
Of the non-seen orchestral storm,
Like dances in a modern ballet.
Then essentially quiet and still -
Like a zephyr seems to becalm,
The racing clouds reveal the stars and the moon.

Steven Clark

No Love to Lose

On tar-macadam paths we walk,
With every type of tree around,
And as we wander so we talk
of matters trivial and profound.
Passing beneath a 'ruined' arch
Are others walking hand-in-hand,
Observing Chestnut, Pine, and Larch
And soldier-like a Cyprus stands.
Tall at the end, Pagoda, red,
Towards the sky and out of reach.
An aeroplane flies overhead,
Drowning out the sounds of speech.
Here, children hide and seek and play
At chasing on a fresh-cut lawn.
I ponder, seeking what to say
And in the end, my words unborn
Remain with me in private muse.
Along the path and 'round the bends.
No love to win, no love to lose, just you and I, just two good friends.

(After a walk in Kew Gardens -)

Peter J. Skilton

You

You wander lonely in a crowd where no one sees you go.
You are silent, others loud in journey to and fro

You seek to hide, to turn away from life's joyous embrace
You stumble on whilst others march with confidence and pace.

You wonder why the change occurred how did the rot set in
You remember when you too did march amidst a raucous din.

You know deep down the problems cause you need not be told
You are approaching fifty son you are in fact quite old!

J. D. Rhys

"Oh Beautiful Sea"

Oh beautiful sea, you mean so much to me
You calm me when I am troubled
You soothe me when I am sad
Your gentle waves caress me
You make my heart feel glad
You are wild in a storm
But like a sleeping child at dawn
You are warm and inviting
To me you are exciting
You can rage, you can roar
You can make your wild waves soar
But then as a new day breaks
All your gentleness awakes
Oh how can I leave thee, Oh beautiful sea.

Molly Napier

Remembering

I wonder, do you remember me as I remember you?
Yesterdays, that used to be adventurous youth we knew.
Doubt never entered youthful minds - oh would
this last forever.
Days of childhood left behind, still we were together.
Alas those days have simply flown things really never changed.
Youthful flings we've since outgrown, our futures
re-arranged.
Older now with creaking bones, fond memories of the past.
Carefully tread life's stepping stones for time goes by so fast.
Tho' long ago I still can see days which once I knew
Hoping you remember me as I remember you.

G. W. Dobson

Tick Tock Time

Tick tock, tick tock, goes my clock
With face of red so bold, with hands of black and gold
It's not a chime he is making, it's a tale of awaking
A tale that ages have told, as time ticks by we get old.

He says the same each day, as we pass it by, each in our own way
So pray for your sins you have done,
    soon to be judged is each and everyone

Tick tock, tick tock, says his chime
life is for living, so cast out your line
Have fun while you can both old and young
He says it's never to late to have some fun

learn by your mistakes you made in the past,
    get on with you life it goes too fast

Don't hurt the people you care for
because once death is here there's no opening the door
Be happy and gay, help people out
In the Lord's house this carries much clout.
    Tick tock, tick tock of life

Vanessa Ann Tricker

Nostalgia

No nightingale for me, but the sweet collared dove,
Cooing contentment from some hidden bough,
'Minds me of may-times many years ago,
The blossom-scented days when we were half in love.

For when I hear its call, that low, insistent note
Telling the pleasures of connubial bliss,
Under the lilacs, tasting our first kiss
I seem to stand again, and languor fills my soul.

Not you alone, my dear, are present to my mind:
Oxford's enchantment casts its golden dust,
Punts drift down Cherwell through the buttercups
And in its haunted dusk our youth is left behind.

Yet will I not regret that we have grown apart,
Sighing that autumn soon will strip the tree;
Those tender may-times are still part of me,
Hid, like the collared dove, contented in my heart.

Ann Ferguson

An Ode to Anne

You are interesting and warm
You have got your own type of charm
Although you are a mother and a wife
But you know how to enjoy your life
You have a unique sense of humour
Bubbling always, it may be winter or summer
You have definitely got what it takes
You have certainly got what it makes
Your honeyed lips have got a mesmerising smile
The twinkle in your eyes can be seen from a mile
Not that what you do or say is always right
But you certainly know how to enjoy day and night
Alas that we met now, only if we had met earlier
We would have been drawing warmth from each other.

Mansur Mojiz

Roses

On the first day of life,
Without trouble or strife, arose from the mud,
The colour of blood, a Rose.

The first of its kind, with others behind,
And the fragrance it held,
Poison, trouble, it spelled.

For soon evolved man,
With his knife in his hand, to pick roses.

Then they were displayed,
With their thorns all dismayed, they had failed.

Man plucked their seeds,
Paid no fear and no heed, to the delicate petals.

Deranged and soon dying, with women applying,
Its beautiful fragrance.

Soon men and then women, it must be a sin!
Now the roses are gone.

The last seed shrivelled up,
Would not grow in the cup,
Full of earth it was given.

Now our gift is gone, no more smells and no songs, about roses.

Tina Faubert

Needing Love

She stood by this mirror watching herself,
Wondering what in her life had happened.
To make her face these worries on this shelf,
All spread out shapely, leaving her saddened.
If only in this sad life, she had love.

Like a still stone, she stood watching her eyes,
Deeply searching, for a trace or reason,
Answers to why, when faced with love, so shy
She seemed, always, whatever the season,
Staring, shaking, crying . . . needing the love.

When at last she thinks that love has found her,
In amongst her thoughts of desperation,
She reaches out, thinking that love is there,
Kind and warm, such a great transformation!
Has she at last, found her such needed love?

Soon though, again love disappears,
Leaving alone this girl, wishing to run,
Away from her worries and her fears.
She is I . . . I am she and we are one,
Both needing this feeling of being loved.

Katherine Little

Aging Punch Bag

The coloured sands that filled time,
Would keep a child pleasurably amused,
Not knowing that with each turn,
Brings the nearing of a helpless age!

An age that there is no longer respect,
Only a fearful time of silent waiting,
Also listening for that foreign knock,
If not today then soon as the tendencies disgust.

To witness the marks of this blacken evil,
Should not be for a child with gaiety in every step,
To see their flowers die, unseen,
The cookies specially baked, uneaten.

The little knocks remain unanswered,
Through the window the elder child looks,
The motherly rocking still, beaten to the carpet,
The sweetie jar smashed, jagged with scarlet pains!

The crime of wanting to enjoy the pleasures,
The delights of their new children, but
Robbed of wise grace, left with little time to heal.
Punished for the gentle frailty.

Kate Head

To My Cat Bumble

Plump tabby cat beside the fire
You understand my all,
You feel the sun rise in my heart
You know when shadows fall.

So wise and young, but so discreet
I'd gladly seek advice
Yet curled up in your pussy-sleep
You dream of cream of mice

But are there smoother things than cream?
And men are often mice,
So sleep on little silken cat
Indulge your harmless vice.
Noel Sargant

Sweet Spirit

Sweet spirit of the night so light as air,
With jocund smile so bright it has no care.
The darkness of the eyes, that held a light surprise,
The hair so fair, it glowed a golden crown.
And from the shadowed light, cast not a single frown.
And from the treetops whence it all had blown,
Its breeze a single breath, to brush the cheek so warm.
As in the dark, as on some summers morn,
Sweet spirit danced with tiptoes on the dew,
And ran the circled web so bright and new,
The droplets shone so golden in the night.
Like golden pearls, against the blanket of the sky,
Too gently fade the twinkling of the dawn,
The dew on emerald blanket of the morn,
Sweet spirit speed with twinkling of the light,
Yet to return upon, the velvet of the night.
S. D. Holt

Alone

I'm standing alone in a room full of people
With no one beside me holding my hand.
They're all shouting and screaming
So no one can hear me,
They're speaking a language I can't understand.

I'm lost in a world where no one is friendly
With no one to hold me and keep me from harm.
They're all crowding and squeezing
So no one can touch me,
They're pushing so much I can't remain calm.

I'm frightened and scared in a sky full of stars
With no one to love me and give me a home.
They're all laughing and jeering
So no one can find me,
They are so many and I'm all alone.

If you can hear me, come to my call.
If you can touch me, hold out your hand.
If you can fine me, love me please.
For I'm alone in a room full of people,
Lost in a world I can't understand.
Rick Trivett

"Friends"

To have true friends is a priceless gift to possess,
Without them, life would be very monotonous, no less;
The comfort and pleasure received, to talk to folks like you
To reminisce through bygone days, and things we used to do;
It is like having a golden chain, the links are friends most dear,
They become very precious jewels, more treasured every year;
Clasped together so strong, with a love so deep and true,
Together with an abundance of memories, many fond
recollections too;
Nothing can ever take away this gift, as long as memory lives,
To know what real friendship is, and the happiness it gives;
So as these twilight years come upon us, and the days
pass quickly by,
We more than ever realize the wonderful "blessing" of
"FRIENDSHIP" and thank our "LORD" on high;
A. E. Wetton

Summer

Alone I sit in the sunshine
with nothing else to do
While lazing away the hour
I see a world so new
For as I look around me
I really am spellbound
To find that mother nature
has spread beauty all around
The trees have donned their dresses
of different shades of green
And grass is now a carpet, where birds can stop to preen
Grey skies have deserted as, white clouds pass o'er the blue
And the sun has brought forth blossoms, of sweet and
fragrant hue
There are butterflies fluttering by, busy bees at work
And song thrushes singing as in the trees they lurk
I watch lazy cattle grazing, among the clover sweet
And glancing down find daisies, strewn around my feet
It's only when winter comes, with everything stripped bare
I wait and long for sunny days, of which we find so rare
But right now I realize, how good this life can be
For surrounded by such beauty, I'm filled with ecstasy.
E. Wills

Fruitless

Is this body to lie still,
with nothing biological to turn, no life to continue.
A sprout, forever more - immune.

No innocence to live or continue the line,
no child to hold and bond with.
A being with like and love,
to develop and grow,
with a greater strength and love to show.

It longs for existence - a thrill to grow,
a seed to ignite with an offspring to show.
Blue and pink booties to knit and swelling a must,
- fat ankles and tights, a treat.

The body is ripe and open to flower,
it aches for growth and all to bear.
To lie still and ferment would be the death . . .
a family - without the life!
Sharon Creaven

A Season of Love

With the blossoms of spring
You entered my life.
You fulfilled a yearning
and saw me through the summer,
the sun did not shine much above . . .
But every day in my heart.

Then came the autumn
and as with leaves,
your affection slowly died
Until winter befell the land
and my life.
Leaving me cold and alone.
J. Slattery

Dunblane Children

To all the children who live in Dunblane
You will never forget the day that evil came
It entered your lives and took some away
At times like this, what can we say?
Our thoughts are with you, so young and pure
We feel your pain, but we have no cure
Our hearts go out to those who lost someone dear
Although strangers to us, we all shed a tear.
Something like this reaches deep in our mind
And stirs great emotions and makes words hard to find
Although miles apart, your grief we all share
In a cruel world like ours, there are still some who care.
Andrew Hughes

Lost Love

A fairy-tale romance come true
Your love for me, and mine for you
We met by chance or was it fate
Sadly you were born too late
But happy memories we both share
Of laughter, tears, love and care
It's all around us in family and friends
A broken heart that never mends
I understand why it can not be
But that shouldn't stop you loving me
As you get older the heartache begins
In love and war, whoever wins?
You get so near, yet feel so far
A door that's always left ajar
But one day the door will close forever
Our love will be gone, to return, never.

Rona Manley

La Jeune Fille Endormie

Furrowless brow 'neath widows peak
wrist to buttress the inclined face
eyes closed feigning sleep?
Drift body and mind in ethereal grace
etiolate neat, an ordered perfection.
Dutch clean and austerely furnished,
seasoned timber, the haunt of polish
varnished art and wrought-iron burnished
a gentle breeze to flap the shutter
the bark of a dog, a trundle of a cart
clogs on cobbles, earthy apples
a clock tower clang to make her start.
Glinting copper and smooth leather
starched collar and a cuffless sleeve
of work wearied by chore and toil
not an idle hand on the coverlet weave.
Noiselessly cross the polished flags
care, the intrinsic silence to keep
captured forever in timeless time
Vermeer's portrayal of a girl asleep.

D. W. Brown

'Still in Love with You'

Somebody once said these words to me
'You don't know what you got 'til it's gone'
When we broke up I thought I'd be fine
But now you're back and I know you're the one

The feelings that I felt were long ago
And I thought that they'd gone away
But your face has been inside my mind
Since I saw you again that bright sunny day

We've been apart for such a long time
I'm different now and I want you to see
My feelings haven't changed and I want you back
I know how good our love could be

Please tell me that you feel the same
Say you want us to be together too
I would do anything to get you back
Because I'm still in love with you.

Sarah Preval

Winter Morn

The dawn awakens, dark turns to light
You hear the birds sing in their flight
A dewy carpet lays on the grass
And condensation on the glass

An eerie mist lifts from the landscape
As the day starts to unfold
Sun shining brightly in the sky
Smothering the cold

A gentle breeze that breaks the silence
Of the early winter morn
You wake up from a restful sleep
To find a new day has been born

L. I. Treadwell

Winter Blues

Winter is here the children are agog.
With the rain, the snow and even the fog
Not everyone is happy now winter is here
There's lots of people live in darkness and fear

The homeless think they've been sent a curse
With very little money in the purse
They sleep in doorways of shops and stores
And the people who pass ignore their snores

They stand on the street for extra money
They think life is tough and not very funny
To try to imagine what they go through
It's been going on for years and not something new

They'd like to work and pay their way
On the wishful thinking of somewhere to stay
They go to soup kitchens for something to eat
With blisters and plasters on their feet.

How can you stay warm in the wind and the rain
No one can imagine that kind of pain
To live on the streets they must feel alone
In this day and age they should have a home.

E. C. Thomas

Untitled

Another day is dawning, it's the end of the night.
You draw back the curtains, and see a wondrous sight.
It fell from the sky, without a sound,
It covers like icing, every inch of the ground,
It colours the grass, a brilliant shade of white.
It glistens on the trees, like tiny lights.
So perfect and smooth, a new creation,
It's as if every creature on earth, has gone on vacation.
But there on the fence, sitting alone and proud,
Is a little robin, singing his song outloud,
It's as if he's trying to let you know,
The beauty of the fallen snow,
It's so clean and pure, like the virgin birth,
Sprinkled from heaven, here on earth,
Everywhere you look, it's a brilliant white,
Sparkling like glitter, such a beautiful sight

M. Goodwin

Untitled

You've got the power to turn my world around,
You lift my spirits high above the ground,
You've got my heart, my body and my soul,
You're my dreams, my own personal goal,
You are my light in the tunnel of love,
Your heart fits me like a velvet glove.
In the rainbow of love you're my pot of gold,
You've got me in your magnetic hold.

All my life, I've waited for so long,
For someone like you to come along,
Your eyes like diamonds sparkling bright,
Brighter than the stars in the sky at night,
To win your love was an honour itself,
Jealous rivals compete with enormous wealth,
But in your own special way,
You say, "I love you", makes my day.

Stephen Wilson

Splitting Up

In loving you I found a life of emptiness and pain,
You said the chapters finished when I asked you to remain,
You said Michelle it's over now and you must go your way
You told me from the very first day that you should never stay,
I saw you through misty eyes, so misted up with tears
The Doctor had confirmed that day all of my worst fears,
He told me I have a son a lovely little Boy,
The tears run down my rosy cheeks, so great was my joy
The memory of you will fade away with passing of time
But the memory that will never go is the son that's yours and mine.

Norman Paramore

Summer

As I walk along the beach on a bright and breezy summer morning
with the wind blowing in my hair and a glow on my face
and at peace with the world and my thoughts once again
I know we live in a very mixed up world today
which needs sorting out and putting back on track for once
We are put on this earth for just a short time
we should use the time carefully and very wisely
I am a very lucky person to have the beach to myself
so early in the morning
and that's the best time to come to the beach
when there is no one about
Just looking out to sea to see if the fishing fleet was going
out to sea
But there was nothing on the horizon just sea gulls flying over head
The fishing fleet are all tied up in harbour not putting out to sea
This is a sad day for the fishing fleet not putting out to sea
to earn a living
I like this time of day when it's so peaceful and quite
by midday the beach would be packed full of noisy
children and adults having a happy holiday with their families.

Susan A. Trooke

The Awakening

The birds are awakening us
with their morning call
They are saying, "Come on wake up!
Good morning to you all."
The flowers will be lifting up their lovely
Heads they have been buried all winter
in their earthly beds, the blossoms of the apple
and the cherry on the trees, will mingle in together
with the warm summer breeze.
There are the treasures we treasure to doubt,
and this is what life is all about.
We walk down the avenue and admire the view
it's there for the asking just for me and for you,
gone are the cold icy winds for a time,
Soon we will be breathing in the warm
Summer air, and we'll drink the summer wine.
And as we grow stranger in our ways
We will enjoy many more happy golden days.

G. Shreeve

Unpublished

Martin my son,

I look at my primroses and remember when,
You were in my garden planting them,
I miss you my son with all of my heart,
Broken in pieces that we are apart,
I miss you my son the tears flow unchecked,
As I look back in anguish my life now a wreck,
We all make mistakes as we go through our lives,
We all need forgiveness to help us survive,
You were my first born held in my arms,
So proud as a mother I fell for your charms,
No longer a baby but a tall strapping man,
With a wife and two children completing life's plan,
I grieve for the closeness we once shared
The primroses remind me that you too cared!!

Margaret Coleman

Tribute

A tribute to my husband - Tom:

It's 50 years since Cilfrew Rovers was formed
You should know Tom for you've served them all;
You've stayed with the boys through thick and thin,
Even though they didn't always win!

But this year Tom, you've really scored a goal;
And not, I may add, by kicking a ball!
But for 50 years service you've given your all,
So, congratulations and best wishes to your sport -
FOOTBALL!

Thelma Williams

Love Breeze

Have you ever had the feeling
You are being turned inside out?
Have you ever felt so dizzy
You wonder what it's all about?

Have you ever known such tenderness
Such a shiver down your spine
When someone takes your breath away
By saying "Please Be Mine,"

Have you felt those arms around you
Have you ever been so close
When the passion that burns inside you
Makes your whole body glow.

Have you ever had a friendship
That you know will last forever
Had the feeling of such completeness
When you are alone together.

That's why there is never a moment
When my thoughts are not of you
I have never felt this way before,
What I'm saying is "I love you."

Paula Wilkins

You and Me in 1973

In that special year, of nineteen seventy three, we met
You smartly dressed, with a Rod Stewart hair style.
Rushing in from the rain, with my hair still wet.
I saw you staring, you gave me such a smile.
You asked me to dance, to Diana Ross and Marvin Gaye
We talked and laughed, as if we'd known each other forever.
You asked, to see me soon, in fact the very next day.
Somehow knowing in our hearts, we were meant to be together.

Our love grew so strong, we couldn't bear being apart.
We got engaged, in our special place, on Christmas Eve.
I knew as we exchanged rings, I loved you with all my heart.
I was so proud and happy to be marrying my Darling Steve.

Twenty three years later, I love you even more,
I'm glad we met, that night in the year of nineteen seventy three
Remembering our romantic walk, wearing a maxi skirt along the
sea shore
On that special night, with the moons reflection on the sea in a
place called Barry.

I've written you this poem, to say, you are the world's best soul mate
We may not be rich, you're not always in the best of health.
As we celebrate twenty years of marriage this year, don't forget
the date!
Our love, our three lovely children and family is our wealth.

Ruth Wozencroft

Toy Boy Rent a Boy

He closed his eyes she shouldn't see the hurt.
"You took so much my love, my heart, but all you did was flirt.
I was afraid. I came to the city alone. You picked me up,
"I didn't know how to say no".
"My precious toy boy" you whispered, as you stroked my hair,
You aroused my passion, I satisfied your needs
But you really didn't care. You taught me to drink, and how to
use drugs, you fooled me with words of love,
Then without warning you turned me out.
Your face reflecting in waters all around.
'God I hate you, I bloody hate you'. My head hurts, my hearts
pounds,
Reluctantly the waters rise above my head.
'Don't hurt your next toy boy, you wretched miserable old flirt'
Brown eyes searching, holding in tight embrace.
'Poor boy, what happened? Were you pushed in the chase?'
Thank God I was near. The masculine voice close to his ear.
'Come home with me I'll take care. We're not the misfits, they
may call us gay'. The strong broad hand stroking his face.
'Don't cry boy I know how you feel it happened to me when I
was sixteen.

Rose Younger

H₂O Will It Flow?

Throughout the drought, we watch and observe,
Yorkshire Water you've got a nerve.

Your service motto seems "Shareholders first,
forget the consumer, they'll never thirst".

You've lacked respect, you've shown neglect,
our natural life source, you can't detect.

How wrong you were, how wrong you are,
Yorkshire Water you've gone too far.

Leaks and wastage, you've caused it all,
the weather has caught you and now you must fall.

The privatized companies have such a free role,
charging high prices to staff on the dole.

Stream lining, cutbacks, false promises too,
providing a service is this taboo?

I blame the Government, they are selling us out,
shirking responsibilities, of this there's no doubt.

How long will we take it, how long will it last,
let's hope that soon, it's a thing of the past.
Robert Phillip Choudhury

Suicide

One minute we are present, next minute we are not,
WHERE DO WE GO?
You see me here you see me there, next minute you know you're
left in despair.

Did you think of me when you were happy? Did you think of me
when you were sad? Did you care for me as much as I hoped?
For I envied you for what you had.

Were you there for me when I needed you? Were you there when
I didn't? No matter what you have done to me you have been
forgiven.
NOW I ASK FOR YOUR FORGIVENESS!

Did I really mean that much to you? Well, don't worry you'll see
it through.

Everyone's life will end one day, some before others. I decided to
end mine now for it was my way of ducking undercover.

Please, please appreciate my decision and try to understand, I
was no longer an Invalid I was a fully grown man. Young you
may say too young to die. Well you couldn't have seen my
sadness that was clearly shown through my eyes.

Please don't weep. For now is the time to realise that you should
live life to the fullest and not end it like mine.
Sabah Bakali

The Great Canals of England

We going on a boat trip
Yes on a canal boat we will go
We pensioners love a boat trip
Days to us is just life to love

Canals they run for miles and miles
They carried goods for hundreds of years
But no one knows or seems to care
This country owes a debt it cannot pay

For canals have been here for hundreds of years
They form part of our heritage
When trains stopped and cannot move
Canals run on and very smooth

The great canals were here before trains
They took the load felt the strain
The horse on the towpath pulled the barge
The loads the carried were very large

Horses was on the earth for thousands of years to work
First the plough and what a drudge
Then the canal boats the heavy load
We failed them but on the went their duty
Richard A. Roberts

Visions of Love

My love for you grows stronger each day,
Your romantic words whisk me away,
Far away to distant lands
Glowing beaches, warm inviting sands,
Forever will our hearts entwine
What love, what beauty, is this really all mine?

Floating on clouds way up high,
Loving kisses to me they fly,
Dreamy days when your lips touch mine,
Oh sweet taste of love so divine,
You bring to me hope and desire
Our love will burn, an everlasting fire.
Carolyn Deakin

Lucky Ignorance

Your joy knows of my sadness not
Your smiles not of my pain
You laugh and drink the glorious sun
As I trudge through the rain,
Sobbing.

Your bright eyes they see not my tears
Your ears sense not my cries
You seek and find the light of day
As I look to dark skies,
Despairing.

Your heart it feels my aching not
Your soul hears not my whine
You, in peace, follow your path
As I, at war, tread mine,
Alone . . .

(. . . And do you really care?)
Louise Turner

"Late Mum"

You brought me into this world.
You cared for me, you filled me,
You delighted me, you pleased me, and,
You made my life so rich.

Mum, though you're gone you are always my hero.
You are always in my heart and always on my mouth.
I will remember you always till I sink to rest too.
Now, memories of you are still and shall ever be my treasure.
My tears may dry but memories will live and last forever.
Even time itself has not taken and healed away the pain.

Life ain't easy without you Mum,
Now life is an equation to be solved.
Again and again, day and night I'll always remember you.
Nothing in this world compares to you,
You are a light a million years beyond compare.
Sleep well and take care.
Mum, rest in peace and not in pieces.
Knowledge Mahuni

Life's Tempest

Amidst the heat, before the storm,
You hunger for the light of dawn.
To wander, lonely, out of reach,
Watching the waves lap the beach.

In darkness, thunders loudest clash,
Bright the sky with lightening's flash.
Feelings rise and race the wind,
Crashing with waves against the skin.

The frantic beating of the rain,
Try's to turn you home again.
The tempest of your life to see,
Like the storms, will ever be.

Home you must and like the waves,
Peace must come, from what you gave.
Like the ship, weather the storm,
It began, when you were born.
Sandra Wolsey

Nineties Motorcade

Motorways of asphalt grey
yet another planned today
Cars and lorries start their run
mirrors gleaming in the sun.

Three lanes crowded with them all
tempers fray, exhaust fumes pall
Wheels rumble through the day
commuters struggle on their way.

Lines of traffic diverse colours
Fords and Renaults touching bumpers.
Arctic lorries, tankers, dustcarts
block the route, commercial dumpers.

Placard signs to tell direction
slip roads merging into one
flashing headlamps shout a warning
tail lights 'thank' in unison.

Rough embankments stained with oil
show of mundane daily toil
blackened skid marks, tell-tale braking
accidental in the making.

E. A. Cleveland

The Garden of Love

It's only a small plot, which I so tenderly love and care,
With such attention and joy as the soil which one has to prepare,
The pleasure it gives when planting time comes around,
In spring what a delight, as green shoots appear above the ground.

One must not forget Mother Nature's help, such a mysterious way,
Without which all our gardens would never give that wondrous
    display,
From tiny seeds those plants suddenly shoot up, and grow,
But one must always remember, without God's help, we would
    not sow.

A garden of love, however small, can be a haven of beauty for
    all to see,
We plant the seeds, but faith we must have, for all to flourish
    healthily,
As one admires the fruits, and flowers, remember the Sun and Rain,
For without them, all our work would have been in vain.

So let us enjoy our garden of love, and give thanks to that
    gardener above,
For it is He who really tends those tiny seeds we plant and love,
The spring with all its fresh growth, the Roses in all their
    beauty and grace,
May we all give thanks to nature, with our garden of love, so
    much to embrace.

W. L. Emery

"Mother"

These people here are strangers
Yet, we have to trust in them
Some care a lot, some say they do
But, we are here for you.

We hold your hand, and stroke your brow
We help you eat your food,
How could it all have come to this
Just weeks ago were bliss.

You were the prop for all our lives
So honest, proud and strong.
Your love was freely given
But, now you look from heaven

I miss you more than words can say
Life will never be the same.
But, on I go for my children's sake.
As I feel my heart would break.

My partner is my strength now
He is so strong and brave.
Without him I would be nowhere
He wipes away my tears.

G. S. Jones

Dad

As time goes on I learn to live with less pain.
You know the pain you caused when you didn't
come back again

I know we used to argue
and cause each other pain
But that's just growing up you said over and
over again

When we used to make up and you used to cuddle
me so tight I felt so secure and always knew you were right.

I know used to hurt you.
I didn't do it intentionally.
Because I'm finding it very hard to live without you
As I love you so immensely.

I know that someday we'll meet again
And until that day I tell you how much I love you and
make you understand I'm true
I'll be holding onto memories all my life of you

Lorraine Carter

Leaves

Energy abounds the golden leaves which fall to the ground.
As the mighty winds, when in full force,
    create the power in their limbless forms.
They dance, then turn with effortless ease,
    like matchwood upon stormy seas.
Sometimes they halt, but not for long,
    not even time to hear the wind's song.
But maybe, when the rain appears,
    their spirits will dampen and then cease.

Maureen Bates

"Outlook on Life"

This life of ours is a wonderful thing, so well preplanned from birth,
Yet for all our knowledge we know not so much,
What tomorrow brings - what fate holds in store,
We cannot perceive, other than that which we can control
By means available due to mankind's creation.
These facts concern every man, woman and child upon this earth
And with space travel - the whole universe as such.
We have achieved much to date and will do much more
Meanwhile one should accept life as it is - on the whole
Living together, in peace, in unison, as one nation.

Whilst we live our lives fully, thinking we know all
We must not forget our shortcomings and what we lack,
Remember that whatever we plan and seek to fulfil
Fate may decree other things may evolve
Turning us from the road we thought we knew.
Pointing us in a direction in which we may fall
Along a rough road which has no turning back.
Live for the present - time as always - never stands still.
Enjoy life today, whilst hoping tomorrow's problems to solve
Old age will come - have no fear - life's days are so few.

E. Towers

Meditation

Another day has passed me by.
As in this hospital bed I lie,
visitors to call this evening or afternoon
Time will fly all too soon,
This evening television I might see
enjoying the other patients' company,
Still I wish I was at home and fine
and good health once more was mine,
The nurses are kind they're good to me
I enjoy their gay and witty company,
They attend to me with great care.
Working so hard it isn't fair.
On my locker, I look and see
Flowers and gifts from my family.
I'm on my own so for my pleasure
I read a book at my own leisure.
Till one day better I will be
Home once again with my family.

Mavis Paul

"Ragged Little Angel"

Poor ragged little angel
    with torn and tattered wings
She walks on walls, she rests, she falls, she sings . . .

    "Where is the happiness?
    Where is the laughter?
    Where is the dream
    that I'm chasing after?"
Rest. Fall. Sing. Poor ragged little angel.
She walks on walls, she rests, she falls and she sings,
    and when she sings, she sings such terrible things
if only someone could hear all the sad things she sings . . .
    You'd never rest
    You'd fall
    You'd sing
      Oh what a beautiful thing
        Both resting
          Both falling
            In harmony . . .
              Still singing.

Rebecca Woodruff

The Player

His hands on the piano keys were a delight to me,
because, you see, I couldn't play.
And yet - with his fine talent, he preferred
to draw out of an organ, with pipes or electricity -
the mesmerising sound.
I listened, watched and gloried in the joyous
way he moved from jazz to classics and from hymns to pop or
dance; the music smoothly joining, never ceasing
Ah yes, a gift without a doubt. Brought in its wake romance
From sweetly satisfying melodies divine. He gave enjoyment to
his eager throng of fans. Yet, he was mine - oh - so completely
mine.

Mair E. Lynne Williams

"Dunblane"

How can they ever come to terms
With what happened that tragic day.
The lives of so many sweet innocents
And their teacher so brutally taken away.

My heart goes out to every-one
And to those who've lost loved ones.
May God in His infinite wisdom
Give them "all" strength to carry on.

This tragedy will live forever
Within their hearts and minds
Because this act of evil
Leaves a reason that's hard to find.

God said, "suffer little children
To come unto me".
For them their suffering's over
They're now spirits true and free.

To all who've suffered this great loss,
With your strong belief in God,
You'll be given back your angels
When you meet with your beloved Lord.

Lily Walker

Winter in Toy Land

The tree tops glisten with snow
as the elf children play games below
on sledges they slide
with eyes open wide
and their fingers and thumbs numb with cold.

The snow is all crisp and white
and the snowmen are there all in sight
with hats, gloves, and scarves
they cover the paths,
and with the moonlight they glisten all night.

Leanne Evans

The Patient

"Has the war ended?"
"Yes Mr. Patient - a long time ago."
"Why are they waiting here, all 'round the room,
Waiting to go? Help me, I'm slipping -"

"They are waiting for lunch, Mr. Patient, in an hour or so.
Did you fight in the war Mr. Patient?"
"Yes, in trenches and mud of both wars,
Help me I'm slipping -"

"What is the date dear?"
"See the new board Mr. Patient, it tells you the day and the year."
"But the clock stays the same, dear -"
"The batteries have stopped."

"I'm slipping again dear!"
"It's the plastic old soldier,
Your crimpolene trousers just cause you to slip."
"Could I have my own clothes dear,
And a proper armchair?"
"I cry out for you soldier -
This is not fair."

Mary Graham

Be Still . . .

How much we miss in the maddening throng
As we hustle . . . bustle . . . rush along
Each one intent on his own desire,
No one raising his eyes any higher
Then on the ground a few steps away,
Treading by instinct his lonely way.
While all around in this world so fair
There are beauties of nature everywhere
Dew on daisies when day's just begun,
A field of corn in the ripening sun
Even along streets dismal and dark
Where poverty reigns real and stark
Here if you take time to seek
Beauty shines out from a grubby cheek,
Of a child whose world has always been
Confined to this dark and dismal scene,
But peace and contentment are mirrored there
And to you as you meet his happy smile
He says don't rush by, be still awhile . . .

I. Spencer

Canoes

You never liked the flowers said the smell went
as we wreathed them unfurled petalled rows dewy white like sugar
"heaven knows neither fear nor sorrow"
the words gold ringed in the centre black and hard
like old Wellington boots.

"I'd not be needing those for my time," you'd whisper
as the mourners filed tearful to the black toned beat
compact disked from speakers on the table top
but I did cry, wept like a bruised child
left moss ragged on the stone.

Mark Lucek

Where Is Love

What kind of a world is this?
Badness all around, good has gone amiss
    Murder, rape and theft
love where is it? There's none left!
To lose a child through another
To cradle your dying brother
While the culprits walk free
Fresh air they breathe, blue skies they see
While they have sealed our fate
Waiting for the day we meet our children
    at Heaven's Gate
For we will never be the same people again
Where is peace and justice to all men?
Where is love? Where is good?
If I could answer, I would . . . I would . . .

Marie O'Mahony

230

Reflections

Black and white? No, shades of grey,
for nothing's cut-and-dried;
Life moves on, we must adjust and treat each coming day
with hope and optimism.
Tucked up comfortably, it's easy to ignore
the world "outside" has problems -
No cosiness for many, just a fading shore
with time to think and fret.
Conscience prickles? How to cope?
Glimmers of light beyond the hole -
A need to take each moment of life's scope
as a precious gift to use.
Think on again - black, white, or grey?
Have you thought things through?
Life moves on, we must adjust and treat each coming day
with hope and optimism -
   For this is Life's survival.

   H. A. Ross

I'll Be My Number One

Every time I fell in love, seems it's not to be.
For now I'll give up all that stuff and spend some time with me.

I'll spend some time with me and mine
And for a while to come
I'll be first and I'll be last,
I'll be my number one

Whatever time I choose to wake - look around my room.
No one there. No rules to break, I'll make my own day bloom.
I'll plan my day and do just what pleases only me
And think of what I haven't got . . . responsibility.

There are things that I miss bad
Sometimes feeling.. oh so sad
Always something I want to share,
Someone to love me and to care

Someday . . . maybe . . . I'll wait and see
But for now, I'll think of me.

When night comes and I'm alone
I'll shut out all my pain,
I'll sleep and dream of how I've grown
To like myself again.

   R. H. Read

The Tragedy of Dunblane

There is no laughter today in the town of Dunblane.
For on this sad day an evil being came.
Armed with four guns, sixteen children he did slay.
No more in their gym will they ever play.
Their teacher too in cold blood he killed.
This being cared not how much blood he spilled,
Some children survived this horrific attack,
We pray they heal quickly, and will soon be back.
For this town to hear their laughter once again.
Though the grief for their parents will be a great strain
But it may, in some way, help to mend each broken heart.
So in time, with loved ones' support, they maybe able
to make a fresh start.

   Pamela Jeanne Marston

"A Little Assistance"

Monica-Rose was the poor wee souls name
For seven years now she's been on the game
She got taunted at school co's her mum wed a black
Maybe that's the reason, she's always on her back
Her mother, a redhead, she was the school cleaner
Her father wished he'd bolted, as soon as he seen her
She started on the streets, at the age of fourteen
She has a three year old daughter, imagine what she has seen
Most of the money she earns, goes to her pimp,
An evil looking man, who walks with a limp.
They say she has no life, a mere existence
She only needs a helping hand, a little assistance . . .

   Keith Rice

Nature Watch

Life, I thought, is very good
as I strolled through the wood.
Security and freedom are wonderful things,
good health and happiness that they bring.

It's autumn now, changes all around
leaves are scattered on the ground.
What is this, a broken branch?
This poor tree stood not a chance.
Did someone break it, was it a storm?
The tree looked so very forlorn.

Life is fragile and quick to pass
easy to shatter, like a glass.
But what is this I see nearby?
I nearly missed it as I passed by.
A new tree growing so proud and straight,
to start afresh is never too late.

Perhaps we should ponder the life we live,
and wake to the wonder nature can give.
Life I thought is very good
as I strolled though the wood.

   M. Rejer

Untitled

Looking down from mountain high
Where the earth reaches the sky
On high such a lofty place
Like a king of the human race

Down on to valley and rolling hill
Sights and sounds in your mind does fill
Clouds across the pale skies race
Lost to time is such a place

Gazing onto such a lovely scene
Makes you recall things that have been
And where your life is set to go
And do you really want to know

In this world of peace and rest
You do not need yourself to test
As if in a capsule of time so still
But with the power to leave at will

So when you've so much stress and strain
And life can become a pain
We all need such a place to go
And let the world past us flow

   Peter Howarth

"Powerfully Held by His Love"

A hymn on our lips and a smile on our face
As we walk in the light to our meeting place
Teach us the way to love one another
To reach out and touch our sisters and brothers
   "Powerfully held by His love"
Your life of healing, loving shepherd who spread the word
Bible stories told and throughout the world are heard
In the light that shines bright from above
We are powerfully held by His love
Weightless and free singing happily
Your love is undivided and we are Christians guided
   "Powerfully held by His love"
For the Holy One we wait, in peace we earnestly listen
In prayer we connect, to the voice that says "He is risen"
   "Powerfully held by His love"
Our whole bodies are lit by the power of the spirit
Who makes us feel so good as only His love could
With a spring in our step how our hearts leapt
Thank you Lord our Blessed Saviour
   "We are powerfully held by Your love"

   Marjorie M. Stainer

Greenfoot Activities

A welcome warmth awaits you
As once you step inside
To greet old friends and maybe new
A friendly chat on this and that
Refreshing cups of tea
There's lots of kinds of games to play
Blockbusters, bingo, dominoes, Uno and what.

In fact there's always something
To keep you occupied
Like handicrafts, including
Needlecraft, knitting and art
Also not forgetting exercise
Which plays a little part
Quiz night's a popular event
An evening that will be well spent.

The album is very interesting too
With lovely pictures of happy times
Of birthdays, Easter and Christmas past
Fond memories that will always last.

E. A. Lynn

The Silent Suspect

It was half past nine on a Saturday night
when the babylon pulled me up, and read me my rights
I asked what I had done
they said 'no questions son', you're being taken down the
station because you're under suspicion.
So they threw me in the police van and drove up Norton Road
where they pulled over to some young lads who're about fourteen
years old
they walked to the window at the back of the van
and pointed me out saying 'yeh sir he's the one':
they drove me to the station and walked me to the desk
as the desk sergeant said 'you're under police arrest,
anything you say will be used in a court of law
now lock him up in a dirty cell, until he decides to talk'.
Twelve and a half hours later after wasting their time
and not being able to charge me for committing the crime
'the theft of a briefcase from a police van'
they released me from their custody
a free, but pissed-off man

Ryan MacDonald

Life

Life is put here to enjoy,
But others treat it as a toy,
Playing with people's emotions,
Using life as a magic potion.

Where there's a start, there's always an end,
Whether your heart's been broken or on the mind,
You could be rich or you could be poor,
But some people will want more and more.

If you live a fairly long life,
At some time you'll witness strife,
There'll be love, hate, peace and war,
And at one time you'll experience all four.

So take my advice and live your life.
Because it could be ended with a knife,
But no one knows what's around the corner,
So let's hope you're not the next mourner.

Tessa Sillifant

Pain!

You ran so fast - so very far.
But pain will find you, wherever you are
And because from me, you ran away
You left me feeling pain that day.

But tho' I feel such endless sorrow
Pain will catch up with you tomorrow.
You'll keep running again and again.
But the memories will haunt you and you can't outrun pain.

Linda Meyler

Hold Back the Tears

Hold back the tears - I must not show my pain
as I struggle so hard to be 'normal' again.
No one must know to what depths of despair
I sink day by day, hoping they're not aware
of my anguish and turmoil and falling apart;
of this cold heavy stone that replaces my heart;
of the nightmares that haunt me awake and asleep
and the fears from within me buried so deep
that I cannot release them and let them go free,
so they pester and fester then overwhelm me
with such powerful emotions I feel I shall drown
in the swirling black whirlpool that draws me deep down
to a place where perhaps there is final release
from the pain and the anguish that give me no peace.
Oh God I am crying! Tears stream down my face.
Will anyone notice my shame and disgrace?
But now I am sobbing - I'm losing control
of my reason, my body, my life and my soul.
I am begging for help. Oh Lord hear my plea
I don't know this person. Please give me back Me!

Valerie Dawson

The Caravan

Winter wind and river swell
You lashed against my side,
Heavenly clouds up in the sky
Told me you were here to stay.

They came and went and came again,
In frenzied fraught tore at my very being,
They left without a backward glance,
Ere voice should break or tear be shed.

But on that day of days you called on me,
Gently prised my door ajar,
Slipped inside with summer's warmth,
Becoming intoxicated with the memories
My scents stirred up in you.
You stared the sunlight straight into the eye
And gazed into the past.

You slipped outside, closed my door,
Leaned against my fragile frame
Holding the trapped memory in your cupped hands,
And thanked me for all I was to you.

Nuala Clifford

Lost Love

I can't lose you, my lover of sensual exchanges,
But I can't face you when fear and criticism enrages,
I can't beg you for magnanimity and untouched pride,
so I'll accept your judgement for the impossible ride
I gave you last week in my demoralized state,
The decision I fear is the one I await.

C. Williams

Crying for Love

You helped bring me into this world, Dad
you seemed to love and care
but a few years later you were no longer there
you'd made a new life without me
I guessed you didn't care. Mum tried and did her best
but I pushed her too far and had to face the mess
I moved in with you and your girlfriend, Cath
but you had made a new family and it was obvious I had no part
I took so much and started to crack
the thought of you not loving me tore me apart
but then I was so messed up and didn't know where to turn
So I went back to my mum's and started my life just like it had began
I then turned to drugs they tended to help me forget,
for the words you still never said
it shouldn't have been that hard Dad
I only wanted to hear, "I love you and always will"
Now at this moment in time I am off all drugs
but I guess it's only a matter of time
As time ticks a steady pace the love I had for you
could never be replaced.

Lisa Marshall

The Surf

The sound of roaring breakers
As they ride abreast the surf;
To me, there's no sight like it,
Not here, nor else on earth.
They leap, and twist, and curl, and wind
Their way towards the shore;
Then crash and thunder with a voice
That seems a mighty roar.
Their spray leaps up to meet the sky,
Helped on by gentle breeze;
It forms all kinds of faceless shapes,
As though, the mind, to tease.
Down it drops to meet the force
Of yet another swell;
Then rides the crest of other waves
With one tremendous yell.
On forever, they must go,
For motion can't stand still.
To some they mean eternity;
To me, they give a thrill!

B. Colebourn

Is Your Country Really Worth Dying For?

The soldiers are tired but have to go on,
as they run in the mud to avoid a flying bomb.
Leaving behind our comrades now dead,
to escape the shells exploding from over our heads.

One man so exhausted fell to the ground,
if I had not caught him he would have drowned.
Staggering away from the bombs, fire and fear,
ignoring the shells we can no longer hear.
Suddenly a man came staggering and spluttering,
he arrived by my side his movements all stuttering.

We were surrounded by gas and I now felt alone,
and all I could hear was the dying man's groan.
Hearing the man's every scream and bellow,
as you watch a father and a friends face turn yellow.
Drowning in a pool of mucus and blood,
as he groans again with his insides in flood.

Now you have heard that war is not fun,
it is not even good to kill with a gun.
Dying for your country is not so glorious,
it is staying alive that is so victorious.

Nick Taylor

Of Night and Fire

As I crawl inside my cowl, there I shall find peace within myself.
As this hood hides my emotions, I cannot reveal my inner self.
My true identity shall never be seen by thine mortal eyes.

The wyrd rune of fate shall reveal the divination,
But that will never satisfy you, mortal beings.
A race that can never know and never understand,
What was, was
And what is, is . . .

But O to be free again, to return to the light
Still wishing I was . . . Of Fire and Night,
To hear your distinct call, your sorrowful laughter,
And to see your empathetic face,
I can see thee, but, in a dream.

Call upon my graces to be near, Call upon me to see
your deed is done
And not unwound in the web of your world.

I am with my three faces of - Then, Now and To be.
I see the changing moons, like the changing faces of my life.
I once was, but now, no more, for what was never meant to be, I
know.

To see the rising sun and it's setting is a life in itself,
And I, shall see it, forever.

Yvette Balbaligo

My First Day at School

There were pegs with names and coats with labels,
Bright coloured pencils were in pots on the tables,
It was nearly nine, my stomach was churning
Outside children stood with their parents all yearning,
There goes the bell, a teacher opened the doors,
A sudden rush of tiny feet on the corridor floors,
Anxious faces and silent tears,
Hidden behind smiles were the parents fears,
The classroom was full, I was now on my own
I was with so many faces, yet felt so alone.
I took a deep breath and looked around the room,
To my horror, was a face, so sad, filled with gloom
I walked over and smiled and took the hand of the boy,
His arms hanging loosely and clutching his toy,
I asked him his name, a tear dripped from his face,
"John" he replied at a very slow pace.
"Well I'm your new teacher" I said with a smile
"Come on meet the others, you'll be fine in a while",
In time my nerves went, I enjoyed my first day,
I hope these are the words my new class all did say.

Sarah Adams

Spring

Nature calls and yawns,
Brighter, lighter morns,
Bluely, whitey-yellow makes the sky a picture that calls,
Birds cheep,
Sheep bleat,
Warmth of the sun makes the dews sparkle.

Snowdrops sparkle like ice,
With daffodils smiling like the sun,
Tulips shine like the red of blood,
The weak sun peers over the new day,
The new life is full of greenery it's picturesque, is what I see,
Rabbits bounce across the fields,
Building burrows as they go.

Easter starts to celebrate the crucifixion of Jesus,
Chicks are born,
Eggs are laid, eggs are given.

Bare trees turn into blossom,
Like the rising of a new life.

Samantha Young

"Canal Sailing"

Narrow boats narrow boats floating along
Brightly coloured and whistling a song
Who is that there, it's charming "Jan Tiddle"
Chugging along right down the middle
Swans glide towards him waiting for bread
Ducks quacking loudly and swimming ahead.
A beautiful morning the sunrise is dawning
And wildlife is stirring in all their array
"Canal sailing barges" in England in May.
Oh charming "Jan Tiddle" who sails
Down the middle we ne'er will
Forget you forever we pray.
Jogging along cottage roofs passing
Black and white buildings on windows
sun flashing
From village to village with quaint old houses
Flower-decked meadows and children with posies
Summertime heather and sweet smelling roses.

Margaret Griffiths-Bood

Are We Dot Men?

Army dot men playing in the park
Bring 'em up right and keep 'em in the dark

Army dot men swimming in the sea
Make 'em work hard enough that's all they've time to be

Army dot men burying a friend
Hadn't even started and he's now come to the end.

Martin Willis

My Strange Self

So I don't want to be the final piece.
Convenient, coordinated,
Grateful to belong.
I want to be the one shining planet visible from earth,
The strangled flower
Of a mutated seed.
The one curiosity on the suburban shelf,
My strange self.

So I don't want to be the final piece.
Conceivable, believably
Progressing with age.
I want to be the one true vessel of the illicit rush,
The crying dreams
off a dying man.
The priceless nothing in a world of wealth,
My strange self.

Rupal Kothari

One Saving Grace

And when I die and leave all else behind,
Could I but have it said I had been kind!
All claim to other virtues did eschew,
And though of God's commandments kept too few,
    Say I was kind!

St. Paul's injunction strove to emulate,
So plead that this one issue seal my fate;
All wrongs forgiven that weigh my soul upon,
With kindliness the sole Criterion,
    Say I was kind!

And should deserved harsh judgement fall on me,
I'd rest content if only it could be
That, 'spite my faults and many a wrongful deed,
'Twere deemed a fitting epitaph should read:
    "Yes, he was kind!"

Stanley Mitchell

The Voice

"Excuse me Sir", the voice said
"Could you spare a couple of Bob"
I'm tired, hungry and homeless
And I haven't got a job

I stopped and gave him fifty pence
'Twas the best that I could do
He said, I could be lying in the morgue
If it wasn't for people like you

We stood and chatted for a while
As we sheltered from the rain
When we had finished our little chat
I could see and feel his pain

We shook hands and I walked away
And then turned to wave goodbye
I took one last look and thought to myself
There but for the grace of God, Go I

Thomas Begley

'Critics'

Authors pen novels, poets write verse
Critics like neither, both are 'the worst'
Whatever the subject, heavy or light
It's never near perfect, never just right.

But ask of the critics, can you write too?
And see if they answer, falsely or true
Talent is varied, no one can state
Which works are perfect, how works will rate.

So to all budding writers, fear not their pen
A critic is human, whether real foe or friend
The tongue may be sharp, the bile may be black
But we have the talent that all critics lack.

Ann B. Rogers

Heartbreak

Heartbreak is something you can't stop.
Emptiness and pain,
Always there, it never ends.
Ruins your confidence and life.
Tears never stop falling.
Broken hearts take long to mend.
Relations try to help but they can't.
Emptiness never ends.
And it hurts like a
Knife going deep inside.

Selina Mundy

Hole in the Middle

Broken windows, closed doors,
Empty rooms with death-filled space,
Leaking ceilings, warped wood,
Despair hanging from above.
Hearts in two, shattered dreams,
What does life mean?
Oh moon up above,
Shine some light and help me see,
For I am blinded by the shadows of my fears,
Let me be guided through the dark,
So I can release my tears to the night.

Sue Jack

For Mei Ming

Empty eyes and a maggot-ridden soul,
Encased in an oppressive tabernacle, made of flesh,
Life never touched you, left fermenting
In your unnatural state
Love never touched you, all awry
Left to die, in a world of worms
Don't look baby, turn your bleak eyes inside
Reject their nihilism, create your Eden
From thoughts of fabric you never knew.
You didn't live in void hopelessness, helplessness
You didn't live at all
Your existence is etched on my brain
You breathed my air, though never speaking my tongue.
You, with your rotting encasement
Are beauty and the immaculate personified.
You are the salt of the sea, the soil, the sand
Everything that is childishly glorious, perfection embodied
Enter the realm of faerie now
And bask in your immortality.

Laury Desmond

Old Faithful

I have a very special friend, he's my eyes my ears and loyal to the end.
He has been with me now for several years and when he's around
    i have no fears.
No matter the weather, he lies by the door, in rain, hail or snow
    nothing pleases him more.
Just to know he's protecting me makes him happy, content and
    totally free.

He has large brown eyes long hair and big feet, and i'm so very
    glad that we happened to meet.
It was April third eight years ago, i was so excited it was my
    birthday you know.
As i entered the room with my friends all around, everything was
    quiet there wasn't a sound.
I gazed at the table and noticed a box, it was large and round and
    not full of frocks.

As i lifted the lid to my sheer total delight! sat a large puppy what
    a beautiful sight.
A few days had passed and he wasn't yet named, so i thought
    and i thought, until finally it came!
I'll name him "PALS" cause that what we'll be, he's been friend
    and companion,
"OLD FAITHFUL" to me.

Marlyn Hamilton

The Soldier

A pane of glass is broken, glass falling there abound
For broken glass and bottles, hearts and bodies found
The soldier stood in silence, he held his breath around
And looked upon that package, as it lay upon the ground

He looked towards the heavens, eyes filled with fear
And whispered for his mother, his girl so very dear
What choices did they leave him, upon it as he lay
And mothers turned their babies faces, far from him away

That package warm, but crumpled, as he lay upon that floor
Mothers dragging screaming children, nearer towards the door
To short the fuse to stop, a moment lost, gone in time
He didn't try to move, my friend, speak, cry or mime

The rebels shout and yell, their hatred deep within
He'll never hear from them again, that dreadful awful din
His body aged from years, he knows not for whose sake
Gone is he, really gone is he, his blood a crimson lake

So my friend just listen, to the silence of that boy
Was he just a pawn for others? Was he just a flaming toy?
Keep his hopes alive my friend, open up that door
Our only hope is talking, to stop this dreadful Civil War....

Mary Scott

The Angels of Dunblane

Pray for the Teacher. Pray for the Class.
For each young Boy and for each wee Lass.
Today heaven opened and gathered them in.
No more will we see their innocent grin.
Our hearts are all broken. Our tears sting like rain.
The poor mites who suffered the torture and pain.
The flowers arrive from the School down the road.
Sixteen coffins pass by with their tiny load.
Please God give them comfort, let the families know there,
That the whole world is with them and their grief we share.

Margaret King

My Special Star

When night owls hoot and hungry foxes hunt
For food to feed their young, I raise my eyes
To view the wondrous beauty of the skies.
A thick velvet carpet of royal blue
Threaded with a billion twinkling stars.
Tiny specks of shimmering silver light
Gaze down on me - a grain of sand, compared
To the vast greatness of the Universe.
But then I see my special star and smile
As its celestial body seems to wave,
My heart is filled with warmth and love from rays
Fast glowing brighter than the rest; dazzling
Brightly, a diamond in the Galaxy.
I know it's you, Mum, watching over me.

A. M. Adams

Lament for the Elephant

God gave the elephant ivory,
for him alone and us to see,
and marvel at his splendid form,
to be born, and stand out in adorn,
against the plains of Africa.
He makes the landscape come alive,
so strong and yet he cannot thrive,
not allowed to walk his way,
for proudly wearing tusks will pay,
and taken from him sorely ripped out,
his body wasted for such small gain,
out of his death comes so much pain,
just so greedy people can,
turn his ivory into nothing more than,
a tiny ornament, a ball or stick,
what can be the use of it,
compared to such a noble treasure,
alive he gives us so much pleasure.

Susan Bullman

Brave New World

Youth weeps so much
At the impending doom they think they see,
Their tears combine, originating rain,
Blinding them with mists of misunderstanding
Born of the sublimation of their tears.

Were they to flame
With their bright sparks of passionate inspiration,
Torches of reason, mists would roll away
Bringing the sun to dry their anguished faces,
Bathing the universe in a different light.

Martin Carroll

Honour Whaur It's Due

Dedicated to the late Dave Cochrane

Roon' the clubs seems a Guid Fun,
As telt in the Herald by Dave Cochrane,
Mind you, A dinna ken the man
But frae whit he writes, he taks a dram,
Michty me, the wie he prattles
A doot if a drap ever weets his thrapple.

I've thocht an thocht aboot his list
An wunner if I've got the gist,
Apairt frae the editor an' himsel'
Naebody seems tae hae rung the bell,
Ye muckle gowk, ye mak ma bluid bile,
Nae mention o' cronies Babtie Tamson Trapp or Kyle.

A dinna think ye've had sic a sair fecht
Tae be amang the very best
But tae keep on sayin' it's me, me, me!
Maks ye soond like Mohammed Ali,
Cauld stane sober or ilka fu'
Gie honour whaur honour's due.

Margaret Meek

Untitled

The love for my lost love darkens
As the ebony tears decrease
And form an everlasting shadow upon my heart
Shadows of hurt
Weld themselves onto my memories
Making sure that I will never forget
The pain and anger my lost love left
The floods of tears
Have now decreased
Into a slow meaningful trickle
Each day becomes a little more bearable
Than the last
If love was meant to be easy
It would never have been meant at all
I'm just left lifeless and heartbroken
Because you were my beloved

Zoe Whitaker

Unnamed

The Vigorous wind forces its strength across the naked terrain,
   as the rain incessantly vibrates the soil.
The erotic throbbing of Nature's strength,
shakes the earth to its extremity.
The uncovered trees commence together
   in an act of intimate desire,
to protect themselves from the corruptive
   conditions of the night.
Then a bursting shower of light
   penetrates a solitary shrub
and illuminates the environment with a heavenly glow.
The perforation opened by heaven's potent power
   splits further;
Oscillating with sensual desire
as shooting bullets insert its exposed aperture.

The pulsating beat gradually subsides,
as the prostrated wind takes its final breath;
Nature's appetite is satisfied - earth can sleep.

Michelle Smith

Losing You

The sky is dark and grey
As the snow lays on the ground
The traffic's rushing by me
But I don't hear a sound

Because my world's been shattered
My hearts been torn in two
I'm losing someone close to me
My love I'm losing you

The doctors say you're dying
That you don't stand a chance
The cancer's spread so quickly
It's already too advanced

We've spent so many years together
Now I'm breaking up inside
But to you I must be cheerful
And the truth I'll try and hide

I'll sit and have a drink with you
My husband and best friend
Then we'll raise our glasses and share a toast
To our love that will never end.

Linda Whelan

Out on the Street

Cold and dark was this winter's night
As the young man moved closer to the fire burning so bright
Casting his mind back on years that had gone by
What had gone wrong? He said with a sigh
At one point in his life, he has it all to live for
A good loving wife and kids to care for
Now he had nothing just emptiness and despair
No home to go to and no one to care
He lost his job about eight years ago
And never recovered from that devastating blow
He turned to drink to ease the pain
Thus putting his life under such strain
She told him to leave and never come back
Putting his belongings in an old pillow sack
He had lost it all and how he regretted
The things in his life that he once loved and protected
This is how it was now, out on the street
Begging and stealing to make ends meet
This young man once held, his head up with grace
Now he was no one in a lonely cold place.

S. Kirkwood

Moving Up

Taxi cab waiting, to take me to the station.
Bags are packed in anticipation.
Leaving home on the very last day
Nothing else for me to say
Moving on to better things
Moving out to spread my wings
Wealth and status are in reach
Follow through to find my niche
Through it all I perceive.
At long last, I'm finely here.
Kept my cool and my wit.
Now I know I have made it.

A. D. Swindlehurst

Query

Granddad sat in his big armchair;
Balding, bearded and old was he.
Entered the spirit of mischief then:
Gently she climbed on the old man's knee.
Her eyes lit up as she studied his face:
"Granddad, dear, please tell me" she said,
"Did your hair go and stick itself to your chin,
One day, when it fell off the top of your head?"

M. B. Ford

Lakeside Beauty

I gaze in wonder as a new day dawns
At a famous lakeside one fresh spring morn
A big round red sun slowly rises high
Into the fluffy white clouds, and a light blue sky.

The water in the lake is calm, deep blue, serene
It glistens on the surface, it shimmers and it gleams
It lies beneath the sunlight looking tranquil and at peace
Disguising the enormous strength and power that lies beneath.

The Pebbles on the shoreline, they shine like new, so bright
As the water gently ripples over them, so clear and light
I smell the clean fresh air, and enjoy the gentle breeze
That blows softly past my face, and moves the air with ease

The mountains overlook the lake, magnificent they stand
Offering protection to the lake and lower land
The mountain tops are covered by a mist that hovers high
And the mountains blend as one, into the glorious warm sky

I feel encased within this beauty, as I listen to the sound
Of the birds singing sweetly, in the trees that stand around
They blend in perfect harmony, and like me they are elated
At one within the universe, and all that god created.

Shirley Hampson

The Great British Bank Holiday

Mechanical beasts throughout the land,
at first light of day
Move as if one to a silent command
Migrating herds flood the motorway

Through flashing lights and warning zones,
they start to slow
Nose to tail in a sea of cones
The surging tide hits the contra-flow

Concrete and tarmac, at last, a landmark
The coastline's in view
Jostle and shunt for somewhere to park
Queue for the cafe, queue for the loo

Walk up the Prom and back again,
for seaside dreams
Stare at the sea through the pouring rain
Crazy golf, hot dogs and slot machines

To journey home to far off places,
they wait in line
Same rain, same cones, same hopeful faces
Will all meet again - the next time!

Valerie Parkin

Unsinkable

The boat sailed from the docks
At first slowly, then faster
She seemed perfectly safe, but who really knew.

Further out to sea she went
Finally losing site of land
She seemed perfectly safe, but who really knew

For many nights and days she sailed
Further and further, without a care
She seemed perfectly safe, but who really knew

The boat sailed slowly into icy waters
Not worrying, as she was unsinkable
She seemed perfectly safe, but who really knew

Then it struck, and there was panic
Lifeboats were few, and people were many
She seemed perfectly safe, but who really knew

Slowly the water gobbled her up
Many people gasping for air on her decks
People in lifeboats stared in desperation
She had seemed perfectly safe, but who really knew

The unsinkable boat had sunk.

Kay Figg

236

Through a Mother's Eyes

I look at the world with sorrow,
At sights that should never be,
I see hungry children's faces,
Hatred and misery,
And I wonder what God must think to himself,

As he watches man with his pride,
In guns and tanks, and weapons of war,

All meant to kill and destroy,
And I sit and ponder to myself.
Why man cannot see,
That if only love could replace all the hate,
What a wonderful world it would be.

Mary Arstall

My Friend "GUS"

You came to us such a weak, lost mite,
At three months old, never giving up the fight,
Such trust and devotion in your tawny brown eyes,
How you must have wondered, at all of our sighs!
Not understanding man's indifference,
To come face to face with such love, in your innocence,
To see you grow strong, trusting and sure,
And giving us all love, so pure,
The shadows of Rust, Black and Grey,
Heightened to gold, burnished the sun's ray,
You will always be with us, in memory and thought,
A friend who's enriched us, surpassed nought,
Asking nothing, with those ears askance,
Did I see, a loving glance?
Gus, you gave us all so much,
Your little treasures, placed untouched.
Running free, belonging, and part of us,
Good night God bless, my friend Gus.

M. J. Morrison

Futile

Beds in a row - neat and trim,
bodies just lying there
all life trapped within
no-one stirred - no-one moved,
except the nurse on call
they try to hide their heartache
but the look in their eyes say it all.

Beds in a row, tidy and clean
lives that were wrecked, their plans now a dream
things that should have been, things that could have been
all shattered by a fall
they chat awhile, they even smile
but the look in their eyes - say it all.

Their fate is a sentence inflicted by chance
no more will they run no more will they dance.
Windows long and narrow look out on mountains green,
but the beauty that is there
remains to them unseen!

Beds in a row - sterile and white
no sign of the tunnel - not even a light!

Oonagh Lee McNamara

If Love

If love had a face what would I see?
Beauty unbounded looking at me
If love had a voice what would I hear?
Dulcet tones so soft and clear
If love had a fragrance what would it be?
The sweet scent of roses so light and carefree
If love were mine forever to hold?
Would I have wealth and riches untold?
If love were these things wholesome and true
Then I have love because I have you.

D. H.

Purple Rage

Scream scream scream how to scream
Away a world of empty faced ruins

My hands grip on the edges of insanity as I
Seek to scream out of a dream not of my wanting

No now this feeling of certain terror close your eyes,
Approach from within see colours of hate red and
Purple running together all in a race to form
Purple rage

Paul E. Calder

A Memory

Down to the station and into the train,
Away form the School, the wind and the rain;
A seat in the corner, just what I want,
A glimpse of the engine, way out in front.

Faster and faster, the journey's begun,
We're off to the seaside to play and have fun;
The trees and the houses are all flying by,
The steam from the engine is left in the sky.

Under a tunnel, it's ever so dark,
And isn't it funny? I saw a wee spark;
Back in the daylight, we've got safely through,
The driver is careful for me and for you.

I feel so excited and cannot sit still,
I must read my comic, there's still time to kill;
The engine's soft rhythm soon makes me doze,
But in no time at all the train's shrill whistle blows.

Oh! The joy of arriving, folk rush from the train,
Leaving doors swinging open . . .
We're on holiday again!

Louie W. How

"Progress"

Take me back to the days of sun, games and fun
back when fear was not number one
where we walked, ran and tumbled,
played, fought and learned
and pocket money had to be earned.
Sweets were a treat - school dinners were YUK!
the worst word we knew was "bum"
Where violence was fantasy - "Tom and Jerry"
and drugs were given by your Mum.

Now I understand "things aren't like they used to be"
and "my! how things have changed" -
Computers, car phones, faxes and CD's,
I know what my daughter's children will say
"Come on Gran tell us the truth - when you were young
did they have TV's?"
Take me back, just 15 years, to the days when I was free
to change the world, to keep it safe
for my children and, yes, even for me.

Sue Hufton

Culloden 1746

Where now the rugged grass bows the wind before
Bandaging the wounds of old Drummossie moor
Where pine does now preserve the line, the challenged ground
That nature softly takes and folds her arms around

Where Claymore targe and dagger did shoot and ball oppose
And courage beat its heart out for a small white rose
The witless mountain stream carries to where proscribed
So 'twas with you from crib your names were here inscribed

A million tenored feet a line of march had laid
By survival's cruel junta steps errant were forbade
From glen and from the shillings from hill and from the moor
A call demanded presence or denial of their lore

These uncouth stones declare the clan's last lingering look
The gods were not constrained and history closed a book.

F. S. Benfield

The Island

Natural, wild, unconquered, untamed is the island.
Barren and deserted, attractive and repulsive all at once.
Shunning the timid, drawing the adventurous.
Some feel the urge, the need, to avoid it.
Others feel the urge to know its secrets.
They believe the island can be conquered,
They believe the island can be tamed.
They long to own it, to control it,
They don't know that they'll just leave it.
Torn, battered, maimed.
And I, the island, will die as I executed in life;
With my barren spirit,
With my soul of rock,
With my heart of stone,
Entirely unaffected by this tale of time
Completely unhurt,
Completely unemotional,
Completely unmoved,
But completely alone.

Nigel S. Green

Winter

High rides the moon this winter's night
Bathing the earth with its silvery light
Frosts icy fingers on bare trees linger
Sparkling like diamonds in the cold of the night
The silence is broken by the hoot of an owl
The bark of a fox on his nightly prowl
O'er the meadow a white mist is born
Low rides the moon awaiting the dawn

F. H. Ellis

Ode to a Full Moon

This silvery orb that lights the night,
Beams out across the globe so bright,
Its patterned face a mystery,
Discovered, seen, made history.

The brilliant light makes shadows,
On rooftop, trees and meadows,
Lights up the path of those on foot,
Be it cat or mouse, man, or rook.

For those at sea, its glorious beams move,
Ripples on the water, rough or smooth,
An emotional sight to behold each morn,
Emerging from cloud, or raging storm.

The land mass shown to the world,
A cold unwelcome orb unfurled,
The darker side is hardly known,
The craters show nought can be grown.

Around the world it goes each night,
New, quarter, half or full, still right,
Without its glow, a sad dark world would be,
The guide of many, involving it in their destiny.

P. J. Benham

Summer Day

The roses bloomed with sweet perfume,
Bees buzzed around the flowers,
A dragonfly swooped to the rippling pond,
Birds twittered in their bowers.
The willow stirred in a gentle breeze,
Its tips did brush the river,
A fish jumped up to catch a fly,
All in the heat-haze shimmered.
A dove cooed softly in the cot,
The steeple rang its bell,
Strawberries ripened in the fields,
And the lupins popped their shells.
The cows lowed gently in the meadow,
Horses neighed and shook their bridle,
The sun sank low, 'twas near the end
Of this summer's day so idle.

P. S. Hickman

St. Mary's Isle of Scilly

Fierce, soothing ocean surge
Beating on a remote Atlantic flower-island,
Sends fan-spray high to hang
Above the towered sentinel lamp-houses
Peaked, glint and upthrust
Against the granite palisades of Mary's Pool.

In a quaint lee-coast Valhalla,
Where wall-perched cormorant librarian presides,
The wooden sea-histories of proud ship's figure heads
Are perused by skua, screaming gull,
And dilettante sand-piper.
There in rock pools
The perceptive predatory petals of sea anemones
Tentatively seek darting and unsuspecting daphnid shadows,
Providing drama not seen on inanimate screen;
And dibbling the wet sand behind an ebbing tide
The seal track's faint anonymous sentences
Still await a reader.

Phyllis J. Humphrey

A Definition of Beauty

Beauty never pulls one by the nose,
Beauty is far more soft and subtle;
Exquisite is the queenly rose,
How delicate is each petal.

Beauty does not slap the eye,
Its power is strong, it needs no fist,
It has no wish to advertise, being shy,
Beauty sails along, quiet as a mist.

Mary Frances Mooney

Blissful Ignorance

World disasters are beyond us,
Because we can't feel the pain.
If it doesn't happen to one of ours
We see it through a mist of rain.

The human race is selfish
Looking out for just our own.
If something happens elsewhere
To us it's a place unknown

We need to work together,
In poverty, peace and war.
To embrace the countries in our arms
Not turn our backs and ignore.

It's our children's children's world,
That we fight not to destroy
So we mustn't live in blissful ignorance.
So they have a life to enjoy.

Nicola Burstow

Helford

Gulls tip the waters, and call from a mast.
Awake! Sun-kissed valleys; from dawn to day ensues,
Horses canter through morning dews,
Hounds and huntsmen the fox pursues.
Wonderful! As spiders have woven in joint excursion,
Across dew-filled grass, carpets of silken transversion,
Flash of red coats and glitter of the horn,
A farm cat lazily stretches and stifles a yawn.
Pigs lie in blissful abandon in the sun.
Cows move slowly, hens busily scratch in a run.
The bull calls with majestic arrogance from his pen.
Ducks and wild fowl make themselves known from a fen.
A gooseberry bush conceal tenderness - a bird's nest.
Ants vital for natural fertilizer - classified a pest.
From another era, glittering in silver span a ford,
A carriage past epoch, a fleeing Lord.
Out of the barn walls, wild flowers grew,
Hours from dawn to dusk spun into a slew.
Moonlight floods; branches juxtapose skies like black lace.
Owls into the night shriek without trace.

Lisette Scott

The Roses

The Rose that started as a bud
Began to grow and bloom
Its delicate petals. Soft as silk
Scattered around the room

Beside it grows another rose
But this one's not as tall
But it looks more attractive
Than the petals that did Fall.

Now the roses start to droop
And begin to loose their colour
The poor old roses that once were bright
Are looking so much duller

And so the roses once full of life
Have slowly slipped away
But hopefully when the time does come
They will grow again one day.

Keeley Pilmoor

I'm All Right

It's a strange thing
Being mentally ill,
The doctors keep them quiet
And stuff them with a pill.

What will we do with them
They just go out and roam,
It doesn't matter if they cause disruption
We'll just send them home.

They're bound to have a relative
Who'll put up with the pain,
Nobody outside the house
Will ever know the strain.
Mentally ill, don't know they cause any trouble
They live their lives enclosed in a little bubble,
They're never in any hurry
They haven't got a care or worry.

Sheila Paterson

What Is Faith

What is faith, but the sweet smell of a rose
Belief but the colour and touch
And in believing in a life everlasting
Oh sweet smell of a rose
lift me up, lift me up
To my saviour who I can once more touch
The hem of his robe
the leather on his feet
Oh red red rose thou
smell so sweet

Patricia Bridget Sawyer

The Forest

I walked into a forest
Beneath the trees so tall
It's quiet in the forest
There's creatures great and small.
I walk along a winding path
I hear a jackdaw gently laugh.
Wild flowers in a leafy glade.
I'll stop and linger in the shade.
I see a movement it's quite near
A bright eyed fawn, but man they fear
A little shrew, a tiny mole,
A rabbit scampers down a hole.
The silver birch, the beech, the oak.
Where crows can roost up there and croak.
If only man could sit there still
But some they only come to kill.
So I'll come back another day
I'll stay awhile as I stray
So forest creatures great and small,
I pray that God protects you all.

Marjorie Spokes

Linda Lovelock

Walking through the darkness she turns,
  her lantern burns dim and grim
before her stands the cold, dank dwelling
  she will weave her spell in.
With fire bright she opens books of old.
  Swirling flames leap up to light the place.
From hidden realms beyond, there peers a spoiled and livid face.

Fingers long and nimble grasp a lighted tallow candle,
  though few would be attracted to its flame; to see her game.
Dancing fiends and leaping demons summoned by dark power,
  called by deathly incantations in the midnight hour.

Her young face darkens as further shapes come
  drifting from the haze,
leaving dark halls to form into some goblin or strange guest,
  whichever suits her incantations best.
She chants her spells the more - a door flies open -
  souls unknown enter and clock and broom take part;
a howl - a scream, the terrors of an oft repeated dream.

Daybreak comes; the fiery visions fade,
  and she, a quiet, simple maid
steps forth, but none would guess the shrieks and yells,
  the loud, unearthly peals of bells that shake the forest dark on
midnight damp,
  whenever Linda Lovelock lights her lamp.

Richard Langford

Sunset

Oh Sun going down, I breathe out with a sigh
Beyond that heavenly range of mountains high
That brilliant orb of shining gold
Pouring your glorious light, on my thoughts to unfold
Beautiful sunset you'll return again
I'll look for you there, though not in vain
A picture of time in perpetual motion
The sight of you fills me with emotion
Seeming so near and yet so very far away
Such a wondrous sight I wish it could stay
Sun, your furnace sets the evening sky on fire
Dark clouds gathering, will not cover my desire
With purple, red and gold, the sky it glows
Those majestic mountains, shining with their halos
Burning, burning, so fiery and red
I hold a dream, no spoken word has said
Lighting a vista, so beautiful to behold
What stories and adventures, could be told
The day is gripped by night's encroaching fingers
The memory of your sweet love, in my mind lingers

N. G. Edwards

Lay Down Your Gun

A tiny soul so alone,
Wrecked with pain and fear,
Where is your Mamma, where is your home,
You didn't ask to be here.
Your sad wide eyes tell it all,
So lost and so poor,
And for your Mamma, you do call,
But your Mamma's here no more.

Can you mend this child's broken heart,
Can you give him back his Mum,
As you load the dead onto your cart,
Will you put away your gun.
Do you feel sorrow, do you feel pain,
Do you have a heart inside,
From all of this, what do you gain,
Will you run away and hide,
You are a soldier, march right on,
So big and so strong,
Look around, look what you've done,
Will you now lay down your gun.

Maxine White

Trust

Sad is the young girl who has yet to know love
Binding two hearts like a hand in a glove
Impatient to sample those pleasure so sweet
She searches with hope for the love she will meet
So eager to trust the man of her love

Sad is the woman who has known love and lost
Her heart has been broken by pain sharp as frost
But will it prevent her seeking another
Risking her all in the arms of a lover?
But trust not is what she has learned to her cost

Glad is the widow for whom love is past
She knows that the turmoil and pain do not last
For when worldly feelings are finally done
She knows of a greater love yet still to come
And puts her trust in God whose love is steadfast

Pauline B. M. Simmonds

O God Thou Hast Created Wondrous Places

The silence of the valleys and the mountains,
Birds on silent wings, soaring, diving like fountains.
A silence or cry of beast and bird of air,
God, one can only stand and stare.

The babbling brook and the raven's hook,
The dancing trout on the fisherman's hook.
The black-spotted sheep on the mountain's edge,
The little warbler in the sedge.

The clouds are racing across the meadows,
The sheep are running as they cast their shadows.
The trees are waving in the wind,
Is it man who has sinned?

Oh God, Thou hast created wondrous places,
As individual as are faces,
Are we doing the best we can?
Why hast Thou polluted it with man?

M. Nelvius

Early Birds

Dew sparkling like diamonds on the grass
Birds singing gaily up above
The sun rising out of the cloudy mass
Chases away nights quiet darkness
And all around expectancy grows
Of the approaching new day
What it will offer no one knows
As joy and sorrow slowly unfold
The distant hum of traffic near by
Grows in crescendo
Children shout with joy or sigh
At what the day may hold for them
Maybe for some the lucky few
New friends to make
Old acquaintances to renew
But for most the routine of life is secure
Lucky those early birds who might
See the brand new day approaching
So fresh and fair in their sight

V. Yorke

Lament

Driftwood lies stranded here, bleached by decay;
Bones of old ships call back their ghosts.
Sea-shells abandoned, a common fate share,
Bereft of the life that was once housèd there.
Dried by the wind the brittle reeds mourn,
And above these dark rocks the gulls cry, forlorn.
But let me remember! O let me recall!
The grey sky above is one sky over all!
And far away from this desolate shore
It gently enfolds the green land of home;
The land that I love, and will love evermore,
Where small birds may sing in the wide-spreading trees,
And a fawn lies secure in a dappled green glade.

Winifred Mary Oliver

Just as an Afterthought

Destiny! Why do you find me lying in this bed,
Body and mind too tired or lazy to get up.
Mind too busy to allow for sleep?

Why do you not find me soaked in sweat and salt water.
Blistering my fingers and blowing my mind.
Heaving on the straining sheets of an ocean race?

Why don't you find me still soaked in the blood and tears
of a raped and ravaged little country,
Honourably taking the lives of other victims?

Why don't you find me in front of my typewriter
Tapping frenetically and visualising the advance
royalties on my next - but - one novel?

Destiny! Why do you even bother listening
to such stupid questions?
Oh, yes! . . . and Destiny! Would you not
feel more satisfaction as a comedian than as a Creator?

Ken Chalmers

A Battle

Conditions are perfect, not too dry, not too wet,
Both teams' all-star players, for the match start are set,
Melodious voices of fans can be heard,
Teams briefed by their managers, of game plans preferred,
First steps on the field, each player will show,
Their focus and strength, right from the word go,
A referee to act as both the judge and jury,
To control both teams tempers, grudges and fury,
First whistle is blown, the action's intense,
Players like caged animals, broken through a guard fence,
A break away runner, with ball under arm,
Passes back at last minute, to avoid any harm,
The time passes by, the score line is clear,
Triumphant, the cry of the victors' loud cheer
Both teams are exhausted, thoughtful comments exchanged,
Until next weekend, and the returned match arranged.

Mark A. Sutton

Angels

They spread their delicate wings
Bowing their heads in honour
Each rosy cheek baring a tear
As one by one they fall to the ground
Returning to the dust
The command of their God,
Their life,
Their creator,
Gone. Gone forever.

Samantha Davis

Cocaine

The sunken smile hides behind the eyes,
Bloodshot, they can only stare.
No longer seeing or loving,
No longer aware.

Darkened face, almost a corpse.
Where has the child gone, lost?
For an insight to another place
There is always a cost.

A quiet voice inside
Asking for a quick release
From the nightmares and sweating,
To the inner warmth of peace.

The chains have closed tight now,
Waiting for the high.
Then what is left of her
Will wave goodbye.

Slipping down the black vortex,
Escaping from the pain,
The last time in our world
For the prisoner of cocaine.

Penny Anita Colligan

Dawn Chorus

The sun comes out into view
Breaking each bud in a milky white dew
Trees bowed with mellow grace
Crickets chirped and badgers raced
The willow drooped wanting care
Not knowing, still aching to share
The warmth of summer safely glowing
Mindless minds and women sewing
The corn is high and pastures green
Dripping snowdrops liken to a dream
Wind howling through the night
Faces at windows full of fright
A tree falls onto a raging stream
Babies in bed all in a dream
Slamming doors echo down the lane
Shinning puddles linger left in the rain
Morning erupts revealing a hazy hue
The sun appears from her blanket of blue
Smiling faces chanting through leas
Spraying buds tread the breeze

J. Jolly

My Best Friend

The man who once played and mucked around now lay there,
blood pouring out of his head onto the ground,
his eyes still burning into the wall.
You reach over to close his eyes, wishing deep down that
he would wake up and tell you he was o.k.
You close his eyes, he looks so peaceful as if he had not had
any pain, not like you have.
You turn cold at the thought of your best friend dead.
You pick up the gun that killed him and you fill up with hate
that hate forces you to 'chuck' it.
You would give anything to kill the man that killed your friend
but know that would make you just as bad.
Why and how could they do this to him? Your only friend, your
best friend.
No more fun, not any more.
You leave him there like everyone else.
You wanted to scream and cry to let it all out but you can't
wake your friend from his endless sleep!

M. Tallis

Yesterday - Today - Tomorrow

Today reliving all my yesterdays, embarking on the sorrow
Bringing back the memories to relive again tomorrow
Through laughter and tears
Turning moments into years
Turning myself inside out.

Transferring my thoughts into your mind
No need for words silence is kind
Being here today, yesterday is nowhere, but tomorrow is here,
Time will stay with you, or slowly move on
Memories of yesterday, then tomorrow is gone.

Today we throw away our yesterdays, to forget about our sorrows
Yesterday is relived today in case there's no tomorrows
An ideal world, where time stands still
is something that I'll hope for
So given time, I'll be in your mind and the
  silence is no more.

J. Ross

Snow

The beauty of the snow, it looks lovely as can be.
But sorry it has Haunted me in the greatest of degree.
You see it on the Ski Slopes, you see it far and wide
in lots of other countries they take it in their stride.
The children love it truly the snowmen and snow balls
But how I do hate it, I wish it would not fall
But what truly makes me angry is not the snow that falls.
It is the disruption that it causes, particularly on roads.
How come we have these Countries that have more Snow than us.
Their lives go on so smoothly but we have such a fuss.

S. Jennings

No One Came

The diary pages turn day by day
Each entry is the same
Short and pathetic, No one came.
So it goes on week by week.
Months drag slowly by
The writings getting fainter
Now the diary closes with a sigh

The last entry's made alas
Yet it could read the same
The old lady passed away and no one came.
One could tell how much she suffered
Through the months and years
From the entries in her diary
Ink mingled with her tears

Could this be someone's mother
Neglected and alone, what remorse,
How could one atone
No words can describe
The heartache and shame
To see the silent accusation no one came.

Mary Doran

Incoming Tide

The waves inch slowly forward on the beach,
each one a little further than the last;
children's sandy castles just within the reach,
then waves leapfrogging gently 'round them pass.

In and onward comes the creeping sea
as over smooth and rounded stones it flows,
like drawing in of breath, it seems to me,
and waits, rising, poised, before it onward goes.

C. Turner

Dream Life

Oh, how to live among these dreams which haunt
each restless, sleepy and each waking hour.
The perfect, misty images that taunt
and threaten to reality devour.

Nebulous shadows, fleeting and obscure,
Swift moments of sweet tenderness and joy,
cloud reasoned thought and wild fantasies lure
of lithe, ethereal, perfect girl and boy.

But yet I know these visions are unreal,
just figments of a too romantic mind
and I should smother any hopes I feel
that in these dreams true happiness I'll find.

For you and I are truly worlds apart
and doubtless we will never be as one,
But I shall store these dreams within my heart
and pray that they may one day see the sun.

Pam Belton

A Voice on the Wind

A voice on the wind whispered to me,
Eagerly I listened, because you see,
For one happy moment I thought it was you,
Then I thought to myself no, it's not true.

I heard it again the other day
Yes it was true, and you wished to say
How you had loved me for many years,
And how sorry you were, for all my tears,

You never wished for us to part
It had to be, but it broke our hearts,
Maybe we will meet again one day,
As we stroll along life's highway.

I will listen again, to hear your voice on the wind
And resume our conversation,
Our two hearts beating again as one,
I live on in anticipation.

Lorna Culshaw

My Dad

A father is the person who gives you his name
But a dad is the one who kisses away your pain
A father provides material things like clothes and money
While a dad gives one a cuddle, and calls you his bunny
I never knew my father, people say how sad
But I have someone better, you see I have my dad.

J. Williams

The Mariner

A quiet character, a Boxing Shrimp
but be warned I'm no wimp,
Hidden in my shell like a Hermit Crab
don't mean to say I'm a drab.

To be an Anemone don't put me down
for to survive with me is to be a Clown,
If to put us down is your only thing
Beware I have a Deadly Sting.

To think my words I'm only a Puffer
with spikes larger than life that are my Buffer,
You will find your put-down we will Block
like a protected Being, made of Rock.

So don't upset something that is a Dish
or you'll find yourself on a Death wish,
Cause from every angle I can't miss
from all angles like that of a Starfish.

T. C.

"The Beautiful World"

Peaceful surroundings, and songbirds' praise
Bring peace of mind, and tranquil days:
Clear skies of blue, "Seas Of Aqua Green".
Colourful flowers, fragrances so beautifully fresh, and clean.
Wildlife surrounds us, in every way
On this a glorious summer's day.
"We Are All Nature's Creations", existing together,
"Enhanced Today," by this fine weather:
From the highest mountain peaks, down to the coast
These are the wonders, we should all "Cherish The Most",
Share these with everyone, be loving, caring, and sincere too
They're are God's creations, for me, and for you:
Be considerate unto others, show real love and care too,
And the same, shall be "Bestowed upon You",
Give love unto others, portray your true face
For this, our world, is a wonderful place:
"We Are Each Of Us Equal", "Borne By Our Mothers",
We are all sons and daughters, and "Each Other's",
Show unto others, "True Love", respect, and "Care",
For this our world, "Is For Us All To Share," equally!!

A. K. Simmons

"The Ever-Changing Sea"

The young men hurtled up the ratlines
Buffeted by the billowing topsails.
The crimson orb of the dying sun plunged
Into the wine dark sea.

But storm clouds were gathering and the wind
Shrieked through the rigging. Streaks of rain
Swept across the darkening sky. The vessel
Lurched and crashed into the mighty waves.

The spume stung their cheeks and the sullen
Heaving swell became angry foam capped rollers.
The rudder left boiling eddies as it was snatched
Out of the foam.

When it seemed that they were in the very jaws of Death,
At last the dawn came. White caps chased each other
Charging in serried ranks to the far horizon.
The ragged sun was glimpsed once more amidst the lowering clouds.

They shook out the reefs and gently eased Her
Into the wind to head for the Island once more.
Mighty Neptune had been tamed and the raging
Sea was still.

A. J. A. Leys

Dreaming of Death

I am standing on a silver plain
Calling to my sister
As silken feathers brush my face.
A crystal wind sings in harmony
With the pebble brook,
Whose lapping waters touch my toes.
My heart feels gentle,
Like being in love for the first time,
Giving flight to my body.
The wind whispers my name,
Enticing me to follow its swirling path
Towards the end of time.
I dance to the bright light before me,
That glints off my regretful tears,
Like the golden blush of dawn
On shivering drops of dew.
I am not tired,
Yet I lay myself down to rest
And be cradled in utter finality,
In death.

Nicola Hills

"Independent"

What a cat! Yes so damned independent,
Calls you only when hungry, otherwise they
Need no one, so silent and steady on foot.
As if walking upon precious moon beams, that would
Shatter with the loudest noise if walked upon too harshly.
So sleek and cunning, yet so pleasing to the eye,
Like the very finest of velvet to touch,
But look out not is all that it seems,
For he is a hunter, a killer by night, oh!
But what a clever disguise, he loves you as much as you deserve
They call him the man of the night and true to that he stands.
As if during the day drained of all energy and wanting,
He lies in all the very best seats,
Warm enough for him, he has chosen them you know,
He is your ruler and master, for you dare not disturb him,
Fear to do so he might throw you a disgusted glance that
Makes you shrivel with guilt.
For he is the king in his own home and you,
As you well know are merely his provider.

Linsay Otter

Peace

I lay at peace with the world today,
Calm amidst the new mown hay,
Great castle clouds went floating by,
To make more beautiful the clear blue sky,
And in that August noon I heard
The lazy twittering of an unseen bird:
Then, borne faint upon the breeze
The distant murmur of woodland trees.

Give O God, to this world at war,
A Peace, the nations have never known before,
Then from man's twisted mind release,
Thine own gift, by man embarked,
Pure love.

P. K. Mitchell

Facing the Inevitable

Getting older I must confess,
Can cause many people a lot of distress.

One of life's rules is that we all must grow old.
When we die the soul leaves us as our body grows cold.

We move on to our next life so some people believe,
As our friends and our loved ones are left here to grieve.

But try as we might to hold on to our youth,
We all must get older and face up to the truth.

So hard it may seem we must try to be brave
And not worry about the day when we go to our grave.

Karen Ann Hird

The Justice-Lover

Raise your arms for the justice-lover cometh.
Broken from the ice
The pallid skin shall once more be ruddy with
Enlivened vigour.   Leveller of suspect truths,
He will shed his brilliant light o'er fields far and
Wide and singe the surface of a million minds.
He too came from ape
But fashioned of a gentler kind
He shed his burden into the mists
And vapours of a sunlit morn.
And light of soul can tread upon the crystal froth of winter,
Unnoticed.
He shall speak in the courts of the land
Not with hardy tones of advocate
But with a song meek and mild and heart of child,
Fear not, a family is safe within his grasp of velvet kind
Tell your sons of his approach
That they may adopt him in their ways of mildness untainted
For he will never walk alone.

J. Rogers

Doesn't Understand

Snowy fields,
Broken hearts,
Lonely tears and
Freezing cars.

People running out of the show,
It could have been love, but oh no,
It's March, but it feels like Christmas woe.

The things he says
They make me feel numb
He makes me feel completely undone.

My life feels incomplete
His wishes, I wish to meet
I tell him it's not my fault
but he doesn't seem to understand
He can't listen, he's too stubborn
He wrecks my life, but he doesn't know
He doesn't understand.

Rachel Hall

Babies

Let the cuddly cherubs
come to me
with their chubby cheeks
and soft thick thighs.
Let me hug them
and hear them gurgle
with pleasure.
Let me kiss their cushy hands
and feel their love smother my face.

Corinne Demey

The First Day at School

The first day at school is horrible for some,
But for others it's great,
To be on your own,
without Mum or Dad,
Learning new skills,
And making new friends.

The first day at school is horrible for some,
They don't want to go,
And be on their own.
without Mum or Dad,
They feel all alone.

The first day at school is horrible for some.
Some children like it but others don't,
Some children laugh and others cry,
Where some are quiet and others are shy,
And by the end of the day some want to stay,
But some can't wait to find Mum at the gate.

Mary Ellen Williams

The Boatbuilder

Look at that man, he must be mad,
Building a boat so far from the sea!
The biggest laugh I've ever had
Is watching him work so slavishly!

But wait, my friend, - now could it not be
He knows something we don't and maybe should?
'Tis hard work chopping down a tree,
Harder still to make something with the wood!

Now the boat is finished, the man is madder,
He's loading it up with the strangest crew!
Elephants, monkeys, donkeys, even an adder -
It's too fantastic to be true!

Let's wait and see what happens next -
He's high and dry - but look again -
His family's aboard now, all looking vexed -
Let's hurry home, friend, it's starting to rain!

It rained, and rained, and still it rained
The boat floated off - Noah stood at the bow.
The man who was 'mad' was terribly glad?
He smiled as he said "Who's laughing now?"

M. Edwards

Untitled

I've had my share of sadness and hurts
But each day of my life's worth living
Because of the gifts from my girls.
The loving and all things worth giving.
They've seen me through many bad times.
Through troubles they shouldn't have known.
Four shoulders for me to cry on.
Because of them I was never alone.
I want them to know of my feelings
To know just how much I care.
When troubles and hurts come into their lives
To know that I'll always be there.
To help them as much as they have helped me,
To cuddle them to me and say
Never mind, the pain will soon go
There's always another day.
Never forget we have each other.

Pat Beswick

I Wish I Was a Tree

I wish I was a tree by a meadow full of green grass in a forest
by the edge where I can be seen.
I would be gentle swaying in the wind. My leaves rippling,
flapping around. Children climbing, swinging in the summer breeze.
Insects, animals crawling, sliding up and down my bark,
running, hopping, hiding from the slightest sound.
In the cold month's the snow would glide through the air gently
landing on the branches. Birds looking for some warmth
sheltering from the snowy fall. Rain splashing, spraying water
on my bark. People hiding in the forest,
The thunder came and crash I fell to the ground will I be used
for firewood or a leaf out of a book I will never know.

Zoe Vittle

The Climb

To reach the mountain summit I would climb -
Breathless but intact, to see the view sublime,
I would gaze with wonder at the panoramic view
like achieving something precious with a feeling oh so new,
for when one's at the base camp looking up to see the summit
to start off one's arduous climb, a tune in heart to hum it,
intentionally or otherwise, one stops to gaze halfway,
keeping firmly in one's mind to press on, or just to stay;
To take in all the view with mind and body fully intent
as if to climb this snowy peak to here we have been sent -
not for the glass of our country but to fill a restless yearning
mindful all the time of the way to be discerning,
not trying or chancing to be foolhardy - better wise
and blazing of a trail for others the ascent to devise.

William C. Howe

Parenthood

The children bring such pleasure
But with them comes the pain
From the time that they start teething,
Till they think that love's a game
It's sad that they can't understand
How deep a mother's love,
But even with the sorrows caused
We thank the Lord above
When they themselves are parents
And then their children grow
I feel it's then and only then
That they will come to know
The pain, the tears, the heartache
That we must never show
How well we know the story
As I'm sure you will be told,
For we ourselves were children
But now we're growing old

B. K. Watson

Loved Ones

You've just lost a loved one
But you don't really understand
That God only takes those special ones.
Into His heavenly land.
You've lost a loved one
Neither weep nor cry
A new star is placed in heaven
To brighten up the sky
And when the stars all twinkle
Look and you will see
The one that twinkles brightest
Is your loved one
God is watching over
As they sleep so peacefully.

R. M. Warman

Waiting

"I'll call you!" And so she waits patiently
by the phone.
As the minutes tick by she waits, patiently,
all alone.
As each moment passes she waits, uneasily,
wondering why he hasn't called yet.
Still she waits. (Did he try?).
And as the time goes on she waits, worriedly,
is all well?
She longs to hear his voice and so she waits.
Sheer hell!
Will it be much longer now she waits?
Suddenly the 'phone rings.
"I'll be with you soon," he says.
And while she waits her heart sings.

M. Gibson

Lamentations

The curse of discontent has crept into the human mind
by twentieth century materialistic unconsciousness leaving all
sanity behind.
For life has become an emphasis on status regarding wealth,
irrational occurrence globally, ignoring the irreplaceable value
of health.
It has stolen from the heart of the myriad, consideration,
awareness and empathy
replaced by a somewhat negative attitude and no response
from the powers that be.
With man's continual defiance of nature, comes the decaying
foundation of our existence,
along with the increasing gap of human equality and racial
division, created from arrogance.
These barriers of injustice and chaos to which mankind has
turned a blind eye
can only be rectified when we return to the simple life,
and nature's ample supply.

Karl Tregonning

Daydreams

Mr. Fahey thinks I'm reading
But I'm not I'm in the chocolate factory
Discovering how to make chocolate
Or playing with my new puppy
I'm dancing on a stage with millions
Of people watching.

Mr. Fahey thinks I'm reading still
But I'm taming Lions at the Circus
Or swimming in the World Championship
Or gliding in the sky
"Wake up", shouts my teacher "It's home time"
"Oh just when it was getting interesting too!"

Marcella Debiase

Christmas and Winter

Christmas is coming hip hip hooray,
Closer and closer it gets each day,
As I sit in my chair with my hands by
the fire, the cruel cruel winter draws near,
draws near.
I look from my window out onto the street,
I clearly see the patter of little children's feet.
Then as the snow starts to fall, laying
crisp and white onto the garden wall.
Their footprints I can no longer see.
They must have all gone home for their tea.

D. O'Brien

Friendship

Friendship is a virtue, which money cannot buy,
But everyone can spread it 'round, if they would but try,
It brings joy to the receiver,
And helps the giver too,
By bringing peace and true contentment,
And I am sure - God's Blessing too.

A helping hand and friendly smile,
Or merely just a chat,
A quiet stroll down country lane,
Or to the park and back,
These little things can do so much,
To ease away life's pain,
Not visible to naked eye,
But is there just the same.

So look around your brethren, there may be one or two,
Amongst your nearby neighbours, silently crying out to you,
They may not be so blest with friends,
Fortunate like you and I,
But they would truly welcome you,
So please - don't pass them by.

G. R. E. Coles

The Parting of the Ways

Well I hear you went and did it,
But I believed not one cruel word.
I heard it through a mutual friend,
And I told him how absurd,
I hear you only met him at a party last July,
And he told you that he loved you,
I recalled that so did I,
Did he hold you close and tell you.
That for him you light the sky,
And he couldn't live without you,
D'you remember so did I,
They tell me to forget you,
Though in truth I never will,
Thought we would grow old together,
Though you know I'm single still,
Through day and night I've suffered,
Not knowing what to do,
Every part of me cries out I love you still I do,
You know I'm going to love you
through the long dark nights and days
This is my friend the bitter end, the parting of the ways . . .

C. G. Lally

My Prayer

Dear LORD I know I'm a nuisance
But I just have to say
THOU will be done is hurting
No matter how I pray

I pray for strength and guidance
And comfort from above
But still the sorrow hurts me
Oh guide me with THY love

I know when parting in YOUR love
We part to meet again
I keep repeating that dear LORD
But grief goes not away

Perhaps, if I was really strong
And truly trusted YOU
Then I would find the strength of mind
To find 'the peace' anew.

M. E. Watkins

Yesterday and Today

Trained to be honest,
But I only promised,
To play just one more game.
When the stakes are the same.

All my life I have aimed to survive,
It is so wonderful to be just alive,
They trained me to kill,
And drummed in this skill.

Now in a room much too small,
Because of a cold concrete wall,
On a table, they say is three quarter,
A week's pension only just brought her.

Somehow I still just win,
Lose! Throw the bat in the bin.
Today there is no money for nothing,
The court stopped the bailiffs from bluffing.

Still fifty-five quid for myself and a wife,
Do not give her a worth-living life.
Thank God, for His guidance through every day,
I try so hard to hear what He say.

J. J. Flint

Christmas

Christmas comes just once a year
Bringing us merriment and good cheer.
We receive and give presents to our families dear

And send cards and greetings to friends far and near
We decorate our homes with boughs of holly
And kiss under mistletoe which is quite jolly.
We display our Christmas trees decorated with baubles and tinsel
And partake of food and drink to make our eyes twinkle
'Tis a time for us to think of others
And a time to share with our sisters and brothers
But to also give thanks to God up above
For the best gift of all
the birth of His Son.

Mollie Crawshaw

Untitled

"Mum said I cannot even spell my name,
But I can!"
Said the young man,
Pale and hurt by the shame.
Take heed all you young mothers,
If you dare,
Show you care!
Try to treat your sons as you treat others.
Give them your time and listen to their hearts.
See their needs.
Take time to feed
The hunger for attention and love they display.
Don't turn them away!

Linda Mawhinney

Darkness before Light

Depression, this sorry state of mind,
Composed of tortured thoughts so undefined.
If only sweet memory of past joy
Could pave the way,
Sweeping sorrows in its sway.

Darkness of spirit that cripples the soul,
Confining life's shining light to a retrospective role.
Oh what gladness showered on me
If this sombre mantle, lifted be!

Suzanne Pettit

Reflecting

Oh! How I'd like to stay in bed today
But I'm not the type to stay away
Maybe now's the time to take that break
But there's so very much at stake

Still with all these changes taking place
Could be time for a change of pace
Time to think and rest and play
Stay in bed if I want all day!

Now at home there's time to stop and stare
Think of all the opportunities out there
What's important? What is not?
What I want and what I've got

So now with lots of thinking done
Whilst remembering still to have fun
The answer is to balance work and play
And not to stay in bed all day!

S. J. Nicholson

Silent Memories

She sits, silent at the window watching who knows what.
But in her mind remembers such an awful lot.
Things time has forgotten, dates and places too.
Now she sits in silence with nothing else to do.
When she was young, oh how she'd laugh
and feel so bright and gay.
But now she's old, she's trapped inside the same thing everyday.
Remembering how she loved her man with all her heart and soul.
And how his kiss would make her melt and she'd forgive him all.
Remembering happy summer days and long and meaningful walks.
And how they'd hold each other tight and into the long night talk.
But those days are gone and many more too.
Now all she has are thoughts.
While she sits at the window, silent now, remembering moments caught.

Shirley A. Milby

Three Little Boxes

These boxes may seem empty,
But look and you will find,
They are full of golden treasure,
If you only use your mind.

The first one holdeth money,
For all that you can buy,
Except the moon, the twinkling stars,
The sun, the sea the sky.

The second holds your dearest dreams,
And as your life unfolds,
The years will whisper words of wisdom,
That can't be bought with gold.

The third one floweth over,
With love to give to you,
Take it, give it, share it,
And you will see life's golden hue.

Keep these little boxes,
These little verses too,
The love that they will help you give,
Will return, a thousandfold to you.

Mavis Pemberton

A Winter's Tale (With Apologies to Shakespeare!)

Snow — lying like a sheet
Causing trouble in the street,
Icy paths and slippy roads
Skidding lorries with their loads.

Birds are hungry, on my sill
Knowing I'll give them their fill,
Robin looks through the glass
Hoping this bitter cold will pass,

Keeping me entrapped indoors
I try to fill the lonely hours,
Reading, TV, writing verse
Weathers going from bad to worse.

How much longer will it last?
Bread is scarce, we'll have to fast!
The thaw will come, maybe tonight!
Isn't snow a lovely sight!

E. Wierzbicki

Ire-Land

Plead for a ray of light to pierce the darkness of negotiations ceased -
For a dowsing hose to wash away those cowardly bombers
    from the streets;
So cries the man, sore troubled deep with fear -
Confidence drained because of blasts detonated
    by ill-working hands,
Preplanned by twisted minds.
Still shattered, builds a future again upon some new initiative
    of politicians short of sincerity and truth -
And deep despair thrives on this distrust of Republican and
Loyalist alike.
So what is left?
The Emerald army command pitting wits against Metropolitan
    investigative chiefs;
But that is war - disaster pending - misery ahead
Man's petition in vain.

W. Keith

Summer Day Long

Forget-me-not sky
Celandine, buttercup meadow
Anemone woods
Snowdrop hedgerow
Rush-rimmed pools
Moorhen nests
Heron fringes
Kingfisher flashes
Trout rises
Otter splish splashes his footsome way
Into the swirling current deep into pools
Crazy cavort
Sunshine yellow haze of mist
Early dawn summer day long
Overhang of trees fitfully stirring
In high summer breezes

G. A. J. Bennett

Cats Have Fleas

I sleep when I want and wherever I please
But my mistress get cross if I'm covered in fleas
Then out comes the powder and out comes the brush
I don't know why she makes such a fuss
I don't like the powder it makes me sneeze
I don't know what it does to the fleas
I come in all ginger and go out half white
I clearly can't be seen looking a sight
I can't be seen strolling about
So I'll hide in the cellar until I'm brushed out
And now that I'm ginger and no longer white
I think I'll take off for the rest of the night
But when dawn comes around you'll
Know where I'll be curled up in the
Leaves at the base of the tree
Where I'm sure to pick up a few more fleas

Maureen Ball

Grace

A word that means such a lot
But never seems to mean anything
Yet it's free, a gift, a promise
To enter the kingdom of God.

Grace, promised by Christ
A Christ full of grace
Showing us what God's love is like
So we can try and follow Him.

God helps us to show the world
The individual gift He gives each of us
But grace grows through all of it
Taking us closer to the Lord.

Two children each together
one rich, the lot
The other just pleading
But Christ blesses them both.

Arallt

The Tramp

I wander through the town at night,
but nobody is in sight.

My clothes are ragged and scruffy.
Not like other people's, whose are nice
and fluffy.

I live with my mind,
dreaming of things I can find.

My sheets are newspaper.
My bed is a box
And in the morning 'round me
people laugh with glee.

I scavenge for my food in bins.
All I find is fags and tins.

I always think about my past,
although it went so very fast.

Lucy White

"Those Days"

There was no TV when I was young!
But life was good! we made our fun
We were made to use our hands!
do our best and take our stand!

We could not get out of doing work
Woe beheld those who tried to shirk!
One was willing to give a hand
Do one's share! be kind, and understand

Life can be like, Sun and Showers!
We give and take, then happiness is ours?
None can tell what the future holds
So we do our best as our life unfolds!

Rhoda Hamblyn

Insomnia

I try to sleep, while in my bed,
But thoughts keep running through my head.
Like a rushing tide that just won't stop,
I'm drowning in a sea of thoughts.

Relentless, pursuing, always teasing,
These thoughts are endless never easing.
A glance at the clock soon let's me know,
How long it's been, time goes so slow.

I pace around, then make some tea,
Try reading the paper - reluctantly.
Then back to bed I quietly creep,
Perhaps to find those vital sheep.

I lie there in the darkness scheming,
Staring at the blackened ceiling.
Wishing that the night would end,
Then suddenly, I'm awake again.

Ray Patterson

Poetic Pam

I truly admire Pam Ayres - she must be worth trillions in shares
But quite apart from her money her poetic wit is hilariously funny
And besides - she sports such cute cheek dimples - they aren't
inverted skin pimples!
She's probably by now - a millionairess - living a lifestyle like a
royal princess
No doubt due to her own personal success.
She certainly deserves her share of happiness
She's visited the Aussies no less than eight times
It's so nice to know they all appreciate Pam's rhymes.
We've not really seem her since heaven knows when
But hopefully she'll be on our television screen again
She may even surprise us all with a humorous yen.
And read us tonight's news - in rhyme - at ten.

E. Haydon Sanderson

The Breath of Freedom

I do not know why I did this
but surely one day one will pass, together, forever.
Forgiveness will bring happiness
in a world coloured grey.
Jealousy is a bright colour
but destructive
and full of hate and resentment
Let go, let go
take off the harsh metal box
around your heart and let it breathe.
Live.
freely with space
and time
and love.
let the birds sing
the flowers grow
for they are forever in my heart.
now and
forever.

Tracey Wilkes

Precious Time

Bitter thoughts, stretching, taunting,
Changing flowers into weeds.
  Soil into blood.
No gentle hands to hold.
Drifting friends forgotten.
Into endless fields spread.

A new year began.
A baby born.
Thrashing its way to rekindle mankind.
Its tiny hands covered all scars and pain.
Laughter once again, bubbled like champagne.
This precious time is now.
And mine, for a while.

Margaret Latchford

Precious Time

The sun, the moon, the earth, they are forever moving,
Changing their form, changing our time,
Our time of getting older, that's what they do.
Between them they turn night into day,
Then turn day into night.
We have no control over passing time,
What do we do with this precious time?
We use it, we abuse it,
We waste it on doing meaningless things,
Things that mostly do not contribute to what is important,
Like love, like telling the people we love that we love them,
They are the important ones.
Spend this precious time of ours with them and for them,
For only One Being knows when our time will be no more,
Then it will be too late for us.
The sun, the moon, the earth however, will keep on moving,
Our precious time is now.

Mary Brown

Feelings

Many of us are afraid that our feelings will
cause us pain. The truth is, running away from
them causes us pain if we avoid our feelings,
we learn what pain feels like, but we never
find out what our feelings feel like. If we stop

running the pain stops. Of course, we are left
with a whole lot of unexpressed feelings,
feelings accumulated from many years of living
in fear. This means we've got work to do. But
we've also got a chance to finally live in the
present and experience our feelings as they
happen. We begin to feel sadness, grief, anger,
and joy. We begin to express all of our feelings.
We cry, laugh, and scream. We release, expand, flow,
and feel, We begin to move.

Steven Appleby

Spring

The March winds blow - we even have snow
But look below - it is all "go go"
The snowdrops with their graceful heads.
The primroses and the crocus beds.
Now the daffodils join the throng
'Tis only the world which is sadly wrong.

Look at the shrubs they swell with glee
The weeping willows a sight to see.
Look at the birds they are buildings high
They at least can reach up to the sky.
Soon the trees will be full of grace
Spring is coming in a pace.

Look out then for the birds and bees
Even the cats will hatch some fleas.
These are a few of life's glories
From which we make our stories.
Alas so many just cannot see
These wonders God sends to you and me.

Muriel W. Day

A Mother's Love

It doesn't seem that long ago from the
days when I was small.
You held me up in your arms and cuddled
me when I bawled.

You cleaned and cooked, you kept me straight
and fed me when I wailed
you laughed, and cried when I pee'd my pants
but never did you complain

I woke you up throughout the night
just to be upon your knee
I'd scream and shout with all my might
so that you would cuddle me.

I'm all grown up and those days have gone
but you're still there for me.
I have not forgotten who you are
and what you mean to me.

Rosemarie Cleary

November Gone

The sun beats down upon the arid ground,
Dead leaves cling stubbornly to sodden twigs,
Parched and timid dogs seek franticly for shade
Without a sound.
Winter's come
Wind etched and sun bleached bones can here
And there be found.
A robin shrills impatiently whilst someone digs.
Goats feed on cardboard cartons lying around.
I'll soon be home
Evening shadows slowly climb a sand and
Ancient mould,
Above the door, all green and red a holly sprig,
A camel train passes by somewhere bound.

Peter Hanlon

Never Understood (June 1994)

Naked bodies tap-dancing in the rain in a steamy cloud of
desperation,
Cobbled streets, alternating stones, window frames crashing into
the world,
They did while the wind in the hallucinated sky twisted the
weather vane,
And ran along the dam while the water crashed from hell.
And splashed, tore, seduced, drowned, consumed,
A slit on the wrist, blood flowing drop upon drop sinking amidst
the crystal granules of sand in the desert.
Running through the fire cracking and splitting the tender skin of
the sole
When the driver in his leather cape rides the chariot of destiny,
Plucking spiral eyelashes to paste upon the sticky wall.
Leaving his tail behind entwined between the rungs of the gate.
Cut it, free it, cut it off, freeze it in melting ice and see the colours . . .
Slide into one another in mutual animosity,
The painting on the wall reveals the artist's reflection,
Leaps from the crevice of his soul,
And penetrates the atmosphere of the room,
The toughness of the skeleton, and we lost them,
Sanctuary in the jail forever with light slipping through the bars,
Shining rays with convulsive beams around the carved table legs,
Turning in a whirlpool of expressive words and thoughts,
Never understood except under an enclosed hood.

Sheila Marie Herlihy

'Going Away'

You're probably going far away and feeling rather blue,
But treat this as a whole new life, exploring pastures new.

You may be leaving loved ones behind,
and good-byes are difficult too,

For everyday that you are away,
their thoughts will remain with you.

Go out in search of your new life,
for many new friends you will find,

As these will go to lessen the wrench,
of those you leave behind.

The sights you will see may open your eyes,
and leave you feeling sublime.

All that you learn from this adventurous trip,
will stay with you a very long time.

Visiting places far and wide will be one of your pursuits.
Eventually time will come to return to all your homely roots.

It's here your family will remain, to await your eager return,
back you will come to open arms,

Much wiser, for all that you've learned.

Marilyn J. South

Fate

I am a great believer in the fates that govern all our lives,
But there are choices to be made
Along these chartered lines.
There comes a day, when we have to make
A decision, good or bad,
About a given task, or plea,
Or something that makes us sad.
It could even be, which choice of route
We take, to travel home,
What clothes to wear, which book to read, or movie to be shown.
Trifling things, you might agree,
But life's made up of these,
And however much one tries,
You cannot always please.
Bigger problems, broader plans
Could follow in their wake.
What to do, how to say,
The path is yours to take.
Well! decision time is nigh, and now it's up to you.
Your destiny will be formed, by whatever you choose to do.

Sheila Ann Rignall

Leaving School

We may be glad to leave today,
But when our friends are far away,
We have said goodbye to all those years,
And find it hard to hold the tears.
We may laugh and say we're glad,
But in our hearts we are very sad,
I wish the younger ones could know.
Just how fast our school days go.
I cannot tell them, they cannot see,
They will find out just like me.
Looking back upon the years
Why does it hurt, and why the tears?
But the good Lord sent a comfort small
To everyone who hears His call,
Which lay in the Heavens up above
For everyone who knows His love,
Whether through wind storm or rain,
We know we shall always meet again.

Penelope J. R. Watson

A Cold Winter's Day

It is really cold today, all frosty bleak, and bare,
But when you look around there's still beauty lying there,
The grass is a pure white cover, stiff and crunchy under your feet,
And trees look like giant candles sticks, although there is
not one bird in them to tweet.

Children go running past, on their way to school,
Wrapped up cosy in winter clothes, I bet shares have gone
up in wool,
Little red cheeks, and glowing noses, fingertips of blue,
they skip and skate quite happily, so what's wrong with
all of you.

Let's take a message from the kids, and let's not make a fuss,
Take our time, look at the scenery, don't hop on the bus,
And yes it is cold today all frosty bleak and bare,
But I think like me you will agree, there's still beauty
lying there.

Maureen Arnold

Transport

When someone discovered that wheels
Carried burdens too great for men's backs,
Then transport was born
On that very same morn
And people were facing new facts.

Steam trains ousted wagons and horses,
Their strength for all haulage endorses.
But the trains couldn't win
Heavy lorries came in
Mammoth loads, down the roads, from all sources.

In the last forty years now they send
Jet engines, and space probes extend.
Two years to reach Mars?
We fly to the stars
As the Prayer Book says, "World without end."

M. G. Bridger

"Tempus Fugit"

It comes to this when you are
cold and grey, and life her best spun o'er
your weary head, when like a dying
ember once so red, so youth has sped
on golden wings away. Mark not the theme
that once so long ago, an urging endless
passion filled thy breast, so are those
pleasures but a woe no peaceful end for thee
to rest. Nor yet remain unseen to aged
wanton yield, such wisdom is a blessed gift
of time, break forth those countenances
sweet, to nurture ageless wonders 'round
thy feet, yours be the end of time the moving
parody of life, yours be the happy heart
of bliss, awaiting thus for all it comes to this.

J. Simpson

Diet

To fill your life with a bit of spice,
Cut out the chocolates and all things nice,
And as you grow decidedly thinner;
You'll be bad tempered but a winner.

When into the size smaller you can get;
Or wear that dress, your heart is set,
Was it worth it, your family ask
To put us through that mammoth task.

The show of ecstasy and pride
On their faces, they cannot hide
As you emerge through the bedroom door
Looking a million dollars or more.

Margaret McQuilton-Morgan

Everything

My world is my heart, without it I would die
But with it there is so much pain, I thought I'd never feel again.
Like rocks it always crumbles, unlike the sun, no more it shines
But like a baby bird without its nest it's cold, alone and pines
Each day ... it's no less easy .. .each day ... there's no less pain
The only thing that stays the same, is the crack around the
   centre where all my love's contained.

A part of me's still open, my key he's found and kept,
until he's locked it up in chains, I'm trapped with playing
   tearful games
But these memories won't leave my side, they echo 'round in
   my head.
Not only do I see his face but everything he did and everything
   he said
My love for him won't go away, it will stay and never fade away
Forever in my soul and mind, the times when he was so gentle
   and kind.
He'd smile so sweet, our lips would meet, I'll never forget . . .
   the first times we met.
If only I could forget what I haven't got - love, warmth, tenderness,
   everything the lot . . .

Lucy Cross

Forbidden Love

The fire and passion of forbidden love
Claws at the gut and burns the brain
The sickening hopeless feeling that
You cannot have what you entertain

Senses reel and confusion abounds
Through aching body and fantasy mind
With awful longing as the life blood pounds
For the love of another of the prohibited kind

I see your laughing eyes and mouth
And yearn the closeness of your form
And imagine the caress of your gentle touch
And glad of the day this love was born

Never before have I walked this path
Unsure and frightened of where it leads
But I am bound upon it now
Unable to deny I love

Sue Casson

Sonnet to Dunblane

Dawn broke coldly on that soul-destroying day
Children went joyfully to school or on their way
The mist that hung with snow and damp
Betrayed the calm on Allan water
Beyond Sunnylaw and Causeway Head
A man so sad walked with the dead
His mind confused and with cold intent
The darkest hell the devil sent
Into Dunblane and that blessed school
To murder innocents as they bent to rule
The world in mourning close hearts were broken
Many the carriers of words unspoken
The world will mourn that day so sad
When angels were slaughtered and the time was mad.

Peter Blackburn

Just a Thought

What became of childhood joy, a Sunday walk, a wooden toy
Cuddled by mum, fun with dad, chastised when naughty,
   not beaten bad
To grow with no pressure on, only remember summers hot and long
Short trousers to school with fair play, no reason to hide, to
   run away
To come of age, work with the rest, not ridiculed for job not best

But now at birth must perform, must be best and first to learn
Pressure on from every quarter, no leniency for son or daughter
Long trousers to school, kids at rage, how to survive within the cage
To fight the fight to be the best, no rules at all just sod the rest
And now of age it doesn't stop
Everlasting struggle of the failure chop

S. J. Hall

A Dear Friend, Lovingly Remembered

A laughing voice and a cheery face
called a greeting over the fence,
"How are you?" What's new today?"
she always found the time to say.

A lifetime of knowledge for her to unwrap
advice on everything for us to tap.
What shall we do? Where can we go?
Was for us to ask and for her to know.

She always knew the right thing to say
when one of us had had a bad day.
Sunshine and showers the life she has had
so she understood when times were bad.

And now it is over, just like that
everything finished - gone in flash.
No more laughter and jokes to share
just sadness and sorrow for us to bear.
But we'll think of her often through our tears of pain
and one day, we know that, we will smile again.

Lynda Redfern-Mason

Sexual Surrender

Rose petals scattered on the ground,
   Colours of red and pink all around.
The aroma feels the warm air,
   Of the scented candles lit with care.
The romance of the excited silence,
   As they look deep into one another's presence.
The fire that burns beneath their skin,
   Sends a passion from right within.
Their bodies touch so intimately,
   So within as one, completely.
The longing for that stimulating kiss,
   All overpowers the surroundings, so they don't exist.
This feelings of sexual pleasure,
   Is one every person should surrender.

Lemanie Kelly

Hopelessness

There's wanton destruction all around
Caused by boredom, no jobs to be found.
Marriages crumbling, and houses rot.
Will it ever end? No, it will not.

Educate all! With what aim in view?
To add to the increasing dole queue.
There's not much point in working hard now,
Not much use taking the marriage vow.

No money for heating - people die.
Does anyone care, ever ask why?
It's a cold cruel world we live in,
Only drugs to disperse it, and sin.

No visions of hope are forthcoming,
No prospects, dreams, about which to sing.
Maybe soon there'll be a miracle,
And the bell of sanity will ring.

Rosemary Dawson

From the Heart

Can you feel the love, all across the miles,
Can you feel the pain, in between the smiles,
Pain caused by love that can't be shared
Smiles caused by love, bills showing we cared.

Can you feel my loneliness, can you see my tear,
The loneliness like the tears, non-existent when you're near,
Can you understand how time can fuel my fears,
Just a day without you to me seems like years.

Can you feel for me, the way I feel for you,
Yes it seems our love is destined to be true,
But when I shed that tear for what I want to start,
Can you understand it's coming from the heart.

Can you feel my pain, do you know my sorrow,
When I need you today I have to wait till tomorrow
Do you know this year has been the hardest to bear,
Do you know I love you, I really do care.

Nicola Thornton

Dunblane

Our thoughts are with you in Dunblane,
Can your lives ever be the same?
That tragic day we will not forget,
We feel such helpless sad regret.

If only we could go back in time,
Obliterate this horrific crime.
Those precious innocent little ones,
Whose lives had not long begun.
The teachers who tried to protect,
Thoughts of them we'll not neglect

What can we do to comfort you,
We hurt and feel like weeping too.
Perhaps you would rather be left alone,
To grieve and heal upon your own.
Heartfelt thoughts to you go out,
Of that you must have no doubt.
So many feel your pain and sorrow,
May it ease with each tomorrow.

G. S. Roberts

Gold

Can you read between the lines?
Can you feel my body weep?
The normal words I say to cheer
The normal way I fear.

Sunshine on my mind warms to my ways with you
Then ice cold feelings flutter through the heart
Telling me you could not be true.
True to yourself - but not to me.

The pricking of uncertainty,
Niggling doubt and pain.
Which pain was the greater?
The losing or the gain?
It's time to turn, to look, to mend
Gone are the hours in which we spend
Our lives greatest gold.

D. L. Scott

'The Dunblane Disaster'

Suddenly the candle stopped glowing and the peace no
　　longer existed.
Erased from their interior life the many unknown souls
　　evaporated into the sky.
They walked and played but ran into evil and hell slithered in
　　and stole their lives.
Sadder than forceful rain upon a grave their love ones
　　experience . . .
Depression, Confusion or an illusion of their world retrieving.
In sight on the mantelpiece in the portrait on the wall, a mental
　　image will never be forgotten.

The 16 wonders who were once perfect and real are now
　　beautiful angels watching in the stillness existing in the dark.

Sarah Gray

Alien Man

People, throw me into oblivion,
Cannot cope with the sanity around,
Receive me, can you comprehend me?
I think not dear broken friend.

Shatter great dreams, just utter the word
With stabilized sardonic contempt,
With your glazed-over eyes and my subordinate views,
I doubt you will ever understand . . .

The common mistrust of the alien man,
He will never touch your rich jewelled hand.

People, push me deeper in
Until there is no escape,
I will fight with the dawn and battle the night,
A comrade? Me? You are too late . . .

For the alien man, shunned torch in his heart
Walks alone, bitter earth, oh so great.

Kathryn Hodgson

Filigree

Where is the gold, grains of time
Caught within the hourglass of life?
I have only silver, filigree of man
Traced with hand so fair.

Where is the artist, with brush so fine
To catch within my life, the spirit that is me?
I have only shadows, filigree of man
Colours of the day.

Where is the child, innocence in love
Living promises, an actor without lines?
She has yet to learn, filigree of man,
Heart as a delicate bird.

I have found the day, the time that is now
Captured for a moment, shimmering ghost.
Walk by my side, filigree of man -
It is real and can be.

M. K. Mason

Down

Stone grey beard on an ash pale face,
Deep furrowed lines, cracked like lace,
Fingers yellow from tobacco stain,
Shabby shoes still wet from rain.
A worn, thin coat, trousers held with twine,
Tight in his hand, cheap red wine,
No place to sleep, it is a shame,
What caused this? Is he to blame?

J. R. Wiseman

Lust

They think it's fun doing what they do.
But they don't love you like I do.
Today they do it just for pleasure.
But in my heart you are a treasure.

They do it now just for the lust.
What ever happened to Lovers' trust.
They see it all as one big game.
I think they ought to be ashamed.
They're getting younger by the day.
They think it's fun; it's just a lay.

The world's gone crazy, it's really mad.
They've all gone crazy sex sex mad.
They boast to mates saying who they've had.
I think it really is so sad.

They're spreading diseases from one to another.
Diseases like AIDS, you won't recover.
A disease you can't see by judging the cover.
So just be faithful to one another.

Making love is a beautiful thing.
So save your love for that special him.

Patricia Sampson

The Birthday Boy

Birthday cards all standing there.
Celebrating another year!
Presents wrapped with shining bows.
What's inside? No one knows.

Birthday party with singing for all.
Everyone dancing around the hall.
Mothers and aunts won't give it a miss.
They are all there waiting for a birthday kiss.

Into the hall walks the birthday boy.
With a girl on his arm looking rather shy.
Kissing and shaking of hands begins.
Trying to avoid that kiss, it never wins.

Father stands there proud of his son.
Thinking of past things now all gone.
That young lad of his is now a young man.
He can do what he wants, oh yes he can!

His mother sits weeping, but only with joy.
For this young man was once her boy.
"Well congratulations" the father says to his son.
"It's only once in your life you reach Twenty-one.

J. A. Farr

The Unhappy Marriage

He'd gone out.
Cello in the background as my mind flowed
Peace and tranquillity . . .
I do not recall which
To languish in either
had become a luxury.

Returning early he put on the television
I switched off my music
He clumped down sprawling himself
over the sofa.

I rose and went upstairs.
He shouted, "Any cheese left?"
Obediently I asked, "Are you hungry?"

Not wanting to stop what I was doing
Nor welcoming the interruptions made on my life
The constant intrusion . . .
Had made me an unhappy and miserable wife.
Cooked eggs on toast and departed.
He always dribbles the yolk.

Kay Hastie

The Little Stream

By verdant hill and glen you come,
Child of the waterfall;
A whisper in the quiet wood
Where oak and elm stand tall.

You sing - with thrush and nightingale -
Your mystic, sweet refrain;
What do you care if skies be grey,
Friend of the wind and rain!

You wind your way to secret haunts
By bracken, moss and fern,
Perchance to meet a kindred stream -
But never to return.

The wild flowers on your sunny banks
Delight the honeybee,
While birds in ecstasy of song
Look down from every tree.

O little silver stream, wind on,
A-sparkle in the sun,
Until you reach your destiny,
Where deep dark waters run.

Patricia McGavock

Milky Shadows

Milky shadows curdling in the depths,
Churning 'round the neurones of the mind.
There was a glimpse of colour,
—— Shut it out quickly.
There can be no colour.
Sinking back to marbling greys.

Milky shadows curdling in the depths,
Not nurturing in the memory.
Painful crystals imbedded,
—— Scratching the surface of the soul.
There can be no stirring.
Falling back to grey stillness.

Milky shadows curdling in the depths,
Jumping the synapses of the brain.
Was there a thought,
—— Stifle that emotion.
There can be no tears.
Hush! Hush! sink into the soft black.

Penny Ann West

Can You Imagine

Can you imagine a world without music,
Without colour, sun, moon or the stars?
A world simply covered in darkness,
No changing seasons or a visit to Mars?

Can you imagine no flowers or green grass,
Not even trees, shrubs or a bee?
No bird chorus, nests or wildlife,
Not even an ant or a wasp to see?

Can you imagine no mountain, hill or valley,
No streams, trout or jumping frogs?
With no beauty around as we tarry,
No friendly pet, cat or dog?

Life would not be worth living
So live every day to the full
Listen, join the birds in their singing,
Life no longer can ever be dull.

Louisa Bundy

"H" - The Model Inmate

The warden of dust abatement, back rigid
Defying defilement by the very air
Moves with less than grace abounding
Constricted by the uniform of regulation.

No need for him the warning of self neglect,
Rising above the pull of lethargy and forfeit
Pride in the daily routine of living
Fulfilment in the desire to please
Enough for him the boundaries defined and set
The words a job well done, a just reward for conviction.

Laurel Henshall Wiltshire

The Wink

A smile can be sunny and warm,
Derisive, sarcastic or knowing.
A laugh can be the epitome
Of good humour infectious and flowing.
It can sometimes be cruel and cold,
Persuasive, cajoling and jibing.
Transparently clear to anyone near
And empty beyond the describing;

But there's much to be said for the wink -
Eloquent, silent, disguised . . .
A private transmission, a delicate mission,
Heavy lidded or archly surprised.
Unobtrusive and private the signal
Or broad as you wish it to be . . .
Just imagine the fuss if they knew about us
And the wink that you're winking at me!

J. R. Lane

'Loving Which Resembles a Dream'

Beautiful and enchanting does such words
Come into mind,
Speaking of you in a tone of undying love
and compassion.
You living and breeding inside my heart
twisting and turning with the tides of
ever-lasting peace.
Your eyes portrait a world of undemanding
harmony.
To be in heaven floating freely among the clouds.
Flying with the secretive lives of angels
and sing in to a sea of contempt passion.
Glowing red sunsets releasing rays of
intense yellow sun that reaches my soul,
embarking on an experience of sensational uplifting purity.
I love you for fulfilling me of such pleasures
I must also thank you.

Zoe Smith

Night

The cold dark blanket of night
comes down to surround us after light
some people fear it coming at all
as now they just don't feel so sure

They used to feel safe locked up in their homes
but now they just hate to be alone
they quietly listen for every sound
to see if there's a prowler around

Their home used to feel so safe and secure
but now it's not like that any more
they say it's the price we have to pay
for the age we live in to day

But who's to blame for making it this way
for those who hate it wait all night
to see the dawn coming with the daylight

M. A. Thompson

Wilderness

A butterfly awakens from its silken
cocoon, dead skin shed floating
down like sun-tinged paper.
A delicate moth flutters dust like a
rainfall of sand.
A slug trailing its silken veil behind
him awakened by the moon star
silvery sky. A spider as black as
night lying waiting in its silken web.
Dew from leaves like pearls all a-mist.
Brightly coloured moonlit sky,
subsiding for new pictures. Now a ray
of yellow falls upon the wilderness
bringing warmth and relaxation.
Animals awaken, silence shattered,
hope and happiness arising from above.

Katie Roxburgh

Our Eternal Love

Dedicated to my husband "Bill" — William Robert Pope
There was nothing wrong with our love
For neither you or me
Times of joy and times of pain;
But through it all you see
Nothing wrong between us.
Not between us, you and me.
But the fates decreed,
I know not why it had to be
That we're not in the same world.
You're not here with me
Yet though not in the same world, others cannot see
Though not in the same world, our love will always be
There's nothing wrong with our love,
Though your face I cannot see.

M. A. Pope

Mum

Can it be so long ago, how the years have quickly flown
Days of youth, of joy, of fun, gone now but remembered well
slim of body, fleet of foot, racing fields, swimming brooks
Climbing every rock in sight. Laughter, loving, dizzy heights.
Hair hangs loose and flies behind, cheeks aglow, eyes a-shine
Happy lovely sun-filled days, all those youthful years of mine

Then a mum and babes arrive, treasured darling little mites
Hair like fluffy golden down, skin like velvet, lay
Them down, sweet innocence - my babes asleep

Now a nan, such joy again, little faces wreathed in smiles,
Sometimes tears, kiss it better. Little arms tight
'Round my neck, love you Nanna, love you lots.

Do I long for my lost youth with laughter, love
And joy and fun? No I think not, not at all,
In truth my life has just begun.

Millicent Proud

Granddad

Oh Granddad I miss you so,
Did you really have to go?
You are so close yet so far away,
I think about you every day.

You had such a fulfilling life,
A loving family, a caring wife,
There was so much that you got to do,
I hope that I take after you.

Oh Granddad I miss you so,
You know I didn't want you to go,
You are so close yet so far away,
But in my heart you'll always stay.

Kelly A. Stewart

Two Worlds "One"

Beneath the ocean, another world lays,
Different from ours, in so many ways,
No fighting, no wars, no gripes or hate,
Tranquil, Solitude, Peaceful, Sedate,
Enchanted Sea, mysteries bound,
Just a small spot in our world so round,
All sparkles, all is pure,
Amazing colours, under the ever-open door,
The sea just watches, the sea never sleeps,
Keeps on going to the darkness of the deep,
You hear it whisper, once in a while,
If you listen closely it'll bring you a smile
Shoals of fish on the ocean floor,
Velvety rocks, I touch once more,
Looking through the ripples above,
Sun beating down,
fills the sea with warmth and love
Two worlds separate, but joined as one,
Nature, this way since time begun.........

Sarah Cooledge

Hero's All

We think of an army of distinguished
Descent, where the flower of
Our nation was eagerly lent,
To fight for a peace and victory
Call, let's bow our heads to those
hero's all;

We think of a navy whose renown
Is known for its vigil and faith to
Our island home, hero's all if from
A watery grave knew some would
Die so and others may save

We think of our airmen all hero's true,
Not forgetting the glorious few, they flew
For a peace and freedom's call, we bow
Our head to those heroes all.

C. Johnson

Is There Time for Love? Jason

Time: Stars shining eternally,
    cold winds, blowing seas into infinity,
Time: A time for crying, a time for laughing,
    a time for knowing there is no time.
Time: I watch the huge hands turning,
    and see my life caught up in those wheels (and I am happy)
Love: Is now and always in this life,
    and an eternal life time of love, happiness
    with you in this life and the great unforeseen life ahead,
Love: My life and yours as one tree stretching its branches,
    and the sun which shines on you, will shine on me also,
    and your raindrops will be mine,
    for we are together with one root,
    and one direction to grow in,
Love: That gave joy to two people's hearts who were lonely,
    from the love grew understanding, and like the morning sun
    my love, our love is always there and given freely,
Love: My love each day is growing stronger, each day ready
    to comfort
    each day being shared, and yet never vanished
    after all we have been through, such love is for you.

Kerry Clifton

Remembered Joy

Come back with me,
Come back with me along time's far-off ways
To that one tree which marked our summer days,
Embracing in its ever-dancing shade
The happy garden jungle where we played.

We stood with glee
Below the steepled hollyhocks, and there,
Aglow with golden pollen in our hair,
Gazed up, until like jungle cats, amid
The cool and leafy bamboo canes we hid.

Then from our tree
There softly came a pure white butterfly
And chose our little cushion, there to lie,
Our favourite cushion which we loved so much,
Black velvet, plump and very soft to touch.

What joy to see
The white on black, the perfect wings,
To watch this prettiest of living things!
Oh then, we placed our cushion by the tree
And saw it fly, beautiful and free.

Margaret Ballard

A Love of Cornwall

The mighty seas, the craggy rocks
Derricks aloft, in Plymouth docks
A downwards slope, to find a beach
A lonely spot no cars can reach

The musical voices of Cornish folk
Not driven to rush, or in a yoke
A steady life, a pleasant gait
Not as London, no time to wait

Something special in Looe found
An air of mystery, an inviting sound
The dogs with a leash to keep them near
I shall return, you may have no fear

Call me back, oh! peaceful Looe
With great speed, I will return to you
A love of my life, with you I have found
You to behold, my feet on your ground

With the grace of a gull, I with soar in your sky
To find you there waiting, my reason why
Do not change your shape, you're fine as you are
The wonders of Cornwall, my wish from afar.

Maurice Evenden

Memories

There comes a time when once again the thoughts of yesteryear
Come crowding in my mind, and yet each one seems very clear.
I see the roads I walked along, the shops I used to view;
I see the happy faces of the people I once knew.
I see the buildings straight and tall I used to pass each day,
Sadly, some have disappeared, "Because you see," they say,
"It's in the name of progress, and you can't stop that, you know
Things are always changing, new things come and old things go."
I stand and look around at the old town I knew so well,
The features somewhat altered. For the better? Who can tell.
The empty space I see was once a thriving thoroughfare,
With bustling shops and offices, a cinema was there.
And now it's gone — but should I mourn for mortar, bricks and
stone?
Yet, somehow I felt safe with them, those buildings I had known.
But through it all, whate'er they do, what alterations make,
The soul of that town is still there, that soul they cannot take.
Perhaps I shouldn't reminisce, should let my thoughts stand still,
But a little of my life stays there, and I know it always will.

Margaret Ainsworth

The Shepherd

Winter's icy savage blast
comes sweeping down the glen
A shepherd tends his scattered flock,
the hardiest of men

He wanders through deep lairs of snow
to find his missing ewe
Darkness falls, he rests awhile,
at daylight starts his search anew

Out from the warmth of fireside glow
he treads a barren land
His sheep, like strangers, lost astray
he lends a helping hand

No matter how the saviour tries,
there are always those who die
Hardened now by nature's way,
the shepherd seldom cries

Happy now the winter's gone,
the shepherd starts to sing
Rewarded for his honest toil,
a new born lamb in spring

R. Anderson

"Another Man's War" (Ode for Bosnia)

There's a dramatic land where trees meet sky, and the mist hangs till dawn and the distant sound of men at war, while the early morning yawns. There's white-walled houses, red tiled roofs, framed by shades of green, with Mosque towers above the tree tops, a rural life that seems serene.

There's dirty children, smiling faces, their eyes bright and alive. What future will they inherit, and to old age will they survive? There's adolescent boys in clothes of men, the 'puberty of war'. The change from innocent child to man, their fate is now secure.

There's wooded mountains and snow topped peaks, at night in a noisy silence, and disguised within a natures splendour, is a war of awesome violence. And watching from our 'Bastion' walls, the death beyond the hills, left powerless to stop an ancient war, where a friend and neighbour kills.

Their past is all around us, an indictment of mankind's madness, where the homes and lives of normal folk, are left in shattered sadness. There's burned-out houses, broken glass, homes with roofs no more. The evidence of a hatred so deep, yet another settled score.

There's toys in gardens, clothes outside, still flowers blooming through, is this the way war is meant to be, is there more that we should do? But as invited guests, in another mans land, to watch we can do no more. What we are, we're witnesses, spectators in another man's war.

P. A. Watson

253

"Enough"

Black and blue she is
curled into a ball she is
tears course down her cheeks
covered in blood and gore
she is but a tiny mite
her face all bruised and painfully sore
her arm lies at an awkward angle
and her hair is dirty and tangled

Just another casualty we say
Just another statistic - you say
what goes on behind closed doors
no one sees and no one knows
do we care I know not, no not I

Enough is enough
have we not had our fill
shout out loud or forever stay still
go for right and damn this wrong
voice our fears and make it strong
make them listen, make them hear
make them, just make them care

M. A. Clarke

Sexism

Samaritans calm her down on the phone
Effortless yes and no's
X-raying her mind
Is all he can do
Smacked across the face and abused
Men don't understand the pain and shame women go through.

Kate Seabright, age 14

Tomorrow

As the curtain of darkness is lifted from my
empathy, your touch like a ray of golden sun
breaks through the dark clouds that surround me.
Your nymph like looks inspire my beating heart to race.
Dainty features brighten up a dreary winters
day, your voice like a prima donna dances
effortlessly to my ears, your laughter soft and
mellow like a well honed violin enchants me to
your warm embrace.
Through a quagmire of destruction I must
plough, to find the freedom of joyous love.
My mind is clouded by mistrust and
misjudgment, friendship or lust it is yet to
soon to tell, is this puzzle complete; or just
a moment away from my constant hell.

Neil Kerr

On the Subject of Your Daughter

She is a confused and insecure adolescent
Empowered by the attentions of a lost boy, in wolf's clothing
Who bares himself to her, as she wraps her legs around him
As a mother wraps a baby in a shawl for comfort

And as she is leaving, you call to her once more
"Be careful, there are real wolves prowling"
And she turns to take one last look
And you know the only wolf she sees is you

And you as her mother, question her insecurity
And find yourself wanting
As was your mother, as was her mother,
As is mother nature herself
And you fail to find a pattern to rationalize your thinking

Your instincts scream: to love, to nurture, to protect
But you are forced to let go
Not a gentle letting go bit by bit, but the cord through which
You sent that love, that nurture, that protection
Is wrenched from you belly; leaving you wounded and bloody
Incapable of making sensible conversation
On the subject of your daughter

Eve Toiman

Melanie

How can such beauty
Concentrated in one place be
A question not for the likes of us, I'm sure you'll agree
The great thinkers and minds of all time
Maybe, but doubtful
As she walks across the world
A strange luminescence emanates from everything around
Inanimate objects become animate
As if dancing in a frenzy of excitement
Mountains rise even higher for the heavens
Rivers sear and oceans crash and roar in a
Proclamation of her presence
Deserts
For the split second of a glance become rainforests
People are elated for no reason they can fathom
The privileged few know why, oh yes they know
I too know for I am the scribe,
The mortal who is near insanity
In her presence.

Thomas Stritch

The Circus

There was a circus in town, we shouted "Hooray!"
Dad bought our tickets the very next day
Right from the start it was to be a disaster
When I noticed the ringmaster had both arms in plaster
As we took our seats inside the big top
I sat on Dad's hot dog and spilt all my pop
The fat lady next to me let out a sneeze
Alarming the man on the flying trapeze
He fell on an elephant and grazed both knees
What a show this was going to be.
Then Barney the clown, limped on stage crying
Said he couldn't perform because of the attack from the lion
So his act was replaced by an acrobatic poodle called Brian
What a show this was going to be
Dad finally lost his temper
When Brian the poodle tried to attempt a
Backward flip but died of distemper
What a show this had turned out to be
We went home early for tea

Nigel Barron Kirkup

From the Heart

On angels' wings thou slept,
drifting into a passion adept.
The morning's dwellings art not near,
The sound of dreamers thou wilt not fear,
The desire for the starry nights,
scented with a red rose and music so light,
Open your heart will make heavens bright,
for mine heart is thy home,
So come my love, so thou art feel alone,
for your beauty I long,
for thou tender love is so strong,
A power inside a lover's song,
And our love will live on and on.

Shelley Kiddle

Lest We Forget

L ike giant birds of prey they took to the sky
E mptying their payload from way up on high
S o what if it's Dresden, Berlin or Cologne
T ell them of London, of England, of Home

W inging their way o'er land sea and shore
E nsuring your freedom they gave of their all

F orget all your preaching now years are long gone
O bjections are easy when deeds have been done
R emember their fears, their courage, their youth
G one in six years as they fought for you
E nter their names in the log books of pride
T o tell them, at last, you are on their side.

Sheila Kendall

Behind the Smile

It seems, within myself, I have always been alone.
Dark, grey-clad armies battle for my soul
Whilst I stand impotent, not knowing what to do.
I try to raise inside of me a rage,
A rage the power of which will reach the dais of God
And make His notice turn towards me.
I plead for intervention but all He says is
"Patience. You have forever."

So far, so good. But, if I have to stand alone,
Let it be for a short while only.
You know the road I tread; You are with me from the start.
Please, guide me through the strife,
The clash of cultures, the hatred of unknowing fools
And unite me with my love, a man like me.
I live this need. Join our two halves
That our forever may forever be.

Neville ColtmanRetribution

Nature's Beauty

Different flowers grow from the ground
Daisies, poppies, growing all around,
Some flowers are evergreens
Many pollinate all their seeds,
When it's sunny, flowers grow tall
But when it rains they curl up small,
Wind rushes through the delicate petals
Daffodils, tulips and beautiful roses
Make a scent to please all noses,
Snowdrops, bluebells wild flowers
Lying among them, sunbathing for hours,
Natural beauty surrounding our world
Started way back when the first bud uncurled,
Seeds for a new flower to begin
Each of these little seeds lie within,
Our gardens hold amazing pleasures
For us to enjoy whatever the weather.

Kimberley Walker

Shannon Natasha

I watched her push her way into the world,
Dear little girl;
Her tiny body gradually unfurled.
I heard her cry, and shed my tears of joy
As did my son, a man now, not a boy.
This love I feel I never could explain,
But somehow it's like sunshine after rain.
I held her in my arms and time stood still
I love her more than life, I always will.

I love her for the deepness in her eyes,
The way she clings on tightly when she cries.
I love her when she says "Grandma"
And flashes me that smile
I love the way she cuddles when she wants to stay a while.
She's brought new meaning to my life,
This precious little girl;
I love her more than life itself
I know I always will.

Rosemary Ann Downing

"The Chaperones"

When I was Sweet and Twenty (1935)
During the British Raj,
I had a handsome boy-friend
Who suggested we Dine at the 'TAJ'.
He booked for us a table
And I was eager to go,
But Dad had other ideas!
When he insisted the whole family would go!
So there was me, and my boy-friend,
With Dad, brothers and sisters in tow,
And the Romantic Evening so happily planned,
Ended in a Big Fiasco!

Vera M. Jennings

Days Aground

Milford Haven not far away, lights on shore
flicker their ray. Stormy Seas sail away.
To lands far far away . . . Rocks below the ocean
hide! Lookout men . . . They did but try. Run aground
Sea Empress cry. "Rock's beneath the Ocean hide!"
No one . . . It happened! "We have no clue?"
Thus someone aboard definitely new!
Ripping Her hull. No time for dreams . . .
Blood of Black floods around the scene . . .
Creating the cull, thy Creature's soul.
On land thy life's ban . . .
Norway offer Helping hand!!
To hell with You we hold our stand . . .
Disaster all at Sea. We do without your decree.
We fight with wind and heavy sea!
We beg you let it be . . .
Final night we see it's right . . .
. . . Glimmer harbour light . . .
Beckon Our journey's END!!

Peter Martin

Colours of Spring

Now fades the colourless misery of winter,
drab browns and greys; inhospitable scene.
The buds of spring are showing; each tree
and shrub awakens, in a hundred shades of green.

See upon the ground; first flowers of the year, newborn. Aconite
and celandine; daffodil; in sulphurous tone.
Acid yellow cowslips, pale primrose by the road,
all colours seen in my mind's eye; as sheerest àlamode.

Brightest yet; like midas gold,
the crocus shines hot as the sun
and harks of summer days to come.
Days to warm the old folk bones;
days to make the senses mellow.
Spring colours make my heart to leap;
with tints and tones of green and yellow.

K. R. Turner

Moonlight Dance

I love to sit and watch the moon,
Especially when it's shining on a lake,
Or when it's reflecting on a pool,
Look at the dancing patterns it makes.
Not lots of different colours though,
Just many silvers and whites,
It moves so quickly on the shores,
Like beautiful birds in flight.
It glows like a burning candle,
Shining so bright from its wick,
If only it could last forever,
But it has to disappear so quick.
The moon flickers bright on the water,
Moving quickly like taking a chance,
And nothing could be better,
Than watching a beautiful moonlight dance.

Shelly Cook

The Werewolf

A planetary movement starts the cycle,
First the glint of an eye, then the claw,
Then the tooth embeds itself
Into the untainted flesh of its victim,
Leaving it to suffer an eternity
Of devouring minds and flesh,
with a passion so violent and grotesque.

Tranquillity and normality reside once more,
Until the next disturbance,
Another unsuspecting victim in the wrong
Place at the right time.

It's another full moon!

Lesley Mallia

Love Sonnet

What is this unfathomable mystery love?
Feeling? Emotion? Heart or head-tendered decision?
Is it amorphous? Or symbolic? Who can define with precision
a hand enveloped smooth within the folds of a glove?
We dream on perfect attunement in vibrating harmonies
of laughter caring understanding acceptance
mutuality synergy constancy in absence;
on a melodiously clear quaver uplifting dinning cacophonies.
Yet a magnet truths its gegen-pole
dove yields flight's shadow to hovering hawk
atoms explode random in split equation fused whole;
acid leaves wither sighing for once mighty oak.
  Venture love be inspired eternal wind hope-filling parallel sails
  on life's journey of discovery through reflections joy and pain.

Vanessa W.

Untitled

Who are the lonely among us
Fellow travellers on a train
A bus or in a crowded street
Using time as a drug.

Look at the passing faces
Presenting a facade
Of defence against all
Who dare to pry.

Who are the selfish among us
Treading on others and using
The weakness and insecurity
Born to some and bred in others.

Who are the compassionate among us
Sharing and caring for those in need
Easing a burden relieving a tortured mind
A therapy for even themselves.

Who are those among us
Prepared to stop and ponder
Along this race of life
Alas too few.

Lilian McGeachey

Weep No Tears

Weep no tears of bitterness or regret.
For a life that has passed into a beautiful sunset.
For the race was truly run
And all the joys, sorrows, and desires won true.
The things seen and done were wonderful to behold
And will go on long after this is told.
How can we cease to be.
When we have touched, loved, spoken, seen
All the senses alive, vital, clean.
And then to sleep, to pass over
Another life begins, a way we do not yet know.
A way as yet unseen
By mortal people in a mortal dream.

M. Gee

The Stallion of the Sea

With wild rearing and plunging,
Diving into the bay,
Hooves to grind the stones to sand,
And a mane of Ocean spray.

His snorting rumbles like thunder,
His hooves cleave through the air,
As he gallops the heaving Ocean,
Seeking out his mare.

Together they race at break-neck speed,
As only they would dare,
Rushing, chasing, recklessly,
The Stallion and his Mare.

Are they but myth and legend?
Who indeed can say?
Wild, magical Sea-Horses?
Or just the Ocean spray?

Nicole Le Strange

Do You Wonder?

Do you ever wonder why a day is long?
Do you ever wonder why some birds will sing a song?
Do you ever wonder where people hurry to?
When rushing through a railway station just like people do.

Do you ever wonder what people's habits are?
Who's in that plane - where it's going just how far.
Do you wonder if they think like you
And worry sometimes - as you do

Do you look in houses you pass when in a train?
Watch people's faces, hurrying in the rain -
Do you wonder about people sitting alone in a bar?
Do you ever talk or keep your distance far.

I think deep down we are really all the same
Pity we must all play a silly game.
If we talked life through and worried less.
Don't think we would be in such a mess.

Pamela Duley

Dignity to Despair

My dignity bore from this existence
Ever dying love is my regret.
Self-harm is the escape
From my life's debt.

Cuts so deep across my flesh
Rotting, dreams of this state
Never able scream or cry
Slash my world filled with hate.

It's not attention, or love that I seek
Just redemption in this life.
I know you cannot understand
How I get to sleep at night.

Abuse in oneself is beautiful and rare,
Just look at the scars.
Don't turn and walk away
Help me, reach out for the stars.

Simon G. Weatherer

Depression

What is the point of living?
Everyone fighting, no one giving.
Is there no feeling any more?
No love, no caring.
Life is for loving and sharing.
People talking to make them feel good.
Playing games as if they understood
That life's a game that can't be won.
But no one is listening so it doesn't matter.
Take the pills, forget the chatter.
Clean the house, cook a meal.
Go for a walk for pity's sake.
Join a club or jump in the lake.
Is it all darkness and no dawn?
How much longer must we mourn?

Margaret Housley

Heartache

She struggled through every sorrowful day
Everyone ignored what she had to say
She couldn't carry on like this, why can't they see
She needed to die - to set her soul free
Many dark secrets lay deep in her eyes
They all chose to ignore her pitiful cries
That frightful day, she wiped out her existence
She'd just had enough, she needed her distance
She scoured the kitchen and found a sharp blade
But unsure as she was, she did not feel afraid
She wasn't sure that what she was doing was right
As tears stung her eyes, blurring her sight
The emotions she felt were tearing her apart
As the knife she was holding dug deep in her heart
But her sad life is over, now she is dead
There's no longer pain whirling 'round in her head.

Sarah Price

Levitation

Sinking slowly inside the subconscious mind,
Falling away, dropping off the edge,
The separation sensation is starting.

As if I am a purple mist, rising up, away
From my daytime self, leaving behind
The physical world, for another.

Now my body and soul are separate,
But I have never felt so whole,
So free, nothing to stop me.

I am both rising and falling, forming
An undulating path to astral space,
A place with no beginning or end.

I move fast, then slow, not knowing where
To go. But what I do no longer matters,
It is what I am that counts here.

The vapours rise, unravelling a mystical scent
Gently uncoiling the spring. No force needed,
Nature is reclaiming her child, to play in dreams.

Katherine Saltfleet

True Wisdom

Thank You for Your holy blessed book
   Father, help me when I through its pages look
Learn more about the wonders of You
   And give me knowledge of all You want me to do
Teach me how to watch and pray
   And to become more like You with each passing day
Let me guided by the living light
   And as You make me and mould me, let me be Your delight
Help me to tell other the wondrous story
   Of Your salvation and of Your glory
And help me remember You are my friend
   Always faithful, with me to the end
And when I the race fully have run
   Please let me hear Your words: "Well done".

S. Wilson

An Unfolding Spirit

Listen, for a whisper.
Feel, that soft breath against your face,
Touch the warm breeze that blows behind you,
She is there, calling, "I love you"
Whichever, path you take.

She is in the sunrays above you, and,
That rainbow that holds your memories,
   Her teardrops;
The rain beating, against your breast,
Her sad heart; "Snowflakes," that fall silently,
And the moon's silver crest.

Her spirit may surround you,
In many earthly forms
Until . . .
You are called together,
On one departing morn.
   Just, listen, for that whisper . . .

Lizzy Usher

Forget-Me-Nots

Forget-me-nots lie sweet with me -
finding solace in their lilac-blue sea
I amble on through another day
sheltered by blossoms paving my way.
Mind's thoughts gather where none dare roam
lost midst primroses, I search for a home.
Heady tones inundate the balmy air
innocence and wonder at such beauty I share.
If only for a moment I can there find peace
perhaps allow me a chance, allow me release
Mother Nature has caressed me with gentle hand
Perhaps hope lies here in her carpeted land.

Yvonne Ballard

Metamorphosis

The chill emotional desert within darkens the soul and
devastates the spirit, akin to the frozen wastes of
Antarctica: The Mothership of resolution and of one's
own salvation is imprisoned in the pack ice of profound
melancholia and complete desolation.

The thaw comes in the Springtime of therapy, when being
enabled to know oneself and accept one's true Self, frees
the emotional blocks and so the process of recovery begins,
and the guided way forward is at last clear.

All heroic and lasting human endeavour - whether on the
grand scale or in miniature - is born out of adversity and
the suffering endured is not in vain but touches and
ennobles the lives of those around us. In the end, it is
not success but failure which is the best teacher: it
humbles the blind pride and lack of insight which stand
in the way of learning true self-realization.

Tough love, leavened by humanity and kindly tutelage,
is the catalyst which transforms a fearful sufferer into,
a trusting and integrated person.

Frances Williams Crowe

Undercover

Used, Abused, Accused
Charged on account of my vulnerability
My need to be loved, wanted,
Cared for, Held
A prisoner
Convicted for the coat I wear
The coat that covers me, smothers me, mothers me.
Lost in my own disguise
Weighed down in my own protection
Down, down, I sink
I need not a rope, but a hand,
I reach out blindly, nothing.
No hand, no heart, no mind, no-one.
I cling to the sides by a thread, I hold on
How long can this go on
There's no point to this needle
It is blunt, useless
I let go, I snap my thread
I fall, I die, I rejoice
No heart, no mind, no-one.

Sarah Hardy

Out of Time

What is the difference between life and death?
Feeling out of time, out of touch. Stuck between
two unknown universes: in no man's land
The celebration of life is similar to the celebration
of death. Going to another place; out of time, out of touch.
Cut adrift from everything that appears to be familiar.
But is not.

Kimberley Ashton

Emotions

Emotions run high
Feelings run deep
Words left unspoken
Memories to keep.

Just a second
Many thoughts away
Always remember
The words I say.

If ever I should tell you
If ever I should say
The thoughts inside my head right now
My thoughts of you today.

I'd whisper very slowly
And make you feel it too
The feelings that I have right now
Are feelings just for you.

L. Bolton

Morena and the Goldfish

Tattoo my body with fish fins.
Do not hurt a distorted rhyme of my nude.
Scarve me with a prayer,
let me kneel devoted on the wood.
I shall memorize your eyes by my heart.
I shall worship you blind and fatigued,
condemned with my worn out clothes.
I can foresee now
that you will throw me
greyed into the river
one bright day.
The Goddess of Spring
will be dancing between
the jolly bodies
laughing up to the skies
with coquetry.
What else shall I be able to do
but swimming on my back
    feeling fine
        and paganlike . . .

Veronika Fejesova-Borakova

Our Friends

It's at times like these, I begin to think
Do we really know the people around us
The people who with life we share
Will they be there when we need them
Do they really care.

It's at times like these, I begin to look
At all the people, we call friends
Will they come running, when we are in trouble
Will they be there
When our world begins to crumble.

It's at times like these, I begin to see
That people show their true colours
When the water gets too hot
They show us what they are
And who they are not.

It's at time like these, I begin to feel
That it's only true friends who stand by you
When there's nothing to gain
It's them you can trust
Who still remain.

Shaun Hulme

Remembering

Where did it begin - this all embracing love for you
Do you know or are you confused and as bewildered too.
A fleeting glance, a murmured word, a smile or two
And I was lost forever in my love for you.

I did not know, did not suspect, did not see
Could not have guessed that you would fall in love with me
It was not planned and yet it seems 'twas meant to be
Fate took a hand — drew us close — created 'we'.

Your smiling eyes, that stubborn chin, that bashful air
The way you walk, the way you talk, your glorious hair.
A tender hug, a loving touch to say you care -
I know them all, I love you so—yet such despair!

For you are you and I am me and sad but true,
Our days together — those heady days — were all too few.
For you are hers, yet here am I in love with you
You will not leave her - yet you say you love me too.

Before we met I did not know what love could be
I did not know the glories that were there to see.
You taught me well the wonders that true love could bring
But now, alone, I sit in tears — remembering.

Vivienne Wood

Lost Friend

We were close,
Felt together, a one.
Shared each laugh, each pain.
But jealous thoughts stopped me feeling your great pain.

I feel it now forever.
For you lie, words of love on your grave.
And though I died with you,
My headstone is blank.
Pain and loneliness, words cannot write.
But when a flower dies,
A new bud opens.
But my rose has no colour or scent.
Bees are not buzzing to taste my nectar.
You were a bee and stole it away.
I keep my nectar locked inside now.
It will not be stolen again.

Stephanie J. M. Coles

Mum

My dear old mum I have not seen
    for many many years.
If only I could see her,
    perhaps I'd shed those tears,
Sometimes when I'm alone,
    the tears just seem to fall,
Sometimes I get a bucket,
    and try to catch them all,
My dear old mum is out in Oz
    and that's a long long way,
If only I could be an angel for a day,
    I'd fly up high, right through the sky.
And be with her within the day.
    Just to see her walking
along the old footpath,
    just to see my dear old mum,
would mend a broken heart.

V. M. Slaughter

My Angel

A part of me has been taken away,
for my lost child I loved more than I can say.
I thought our world would be complete,
with our beautiful child so small and sweet,
and as I close my eyes to dream
I see your face with its heavenly beam.
I hear your golden laughter
before you take a nap,
and I see you sleeping soundly
upon an angel's lap.
You were created in the Lord's own light
and you send beams of love
on my darkest of nights,
you are in my heart night and day
and to the Lord I will always pray
to hold you, my angel, so close and safe,
until Mammy holds you at heaven's gate.

Theresa Tyrrell

Love

Love is not so rare, when your heart is full of love
do not spare. Share it with others.
There is no wound love cannot heal.
Love is like a new born child,
Its warm and tender touch,
fills your heart with love.

Sometimes love makes us do strange things,
Why shouldn't it, it is the inspiration of all art.
Many words of love are spoken,
when they come from a loving heart.
How many lives made beautiful and sweet,
By our loving inspirations.

Noel Kennelly

A British Lament

Don't eat fat, and don't eat butter,
Don't get excited or your heart will flutter,
Don't have an egg if it's got a soft yolk,
Don't rot your teeth by drinking Coke,
Don't eat sugar, don't eat bread,
Don't chew your pencil, its point is made of lead,
Don't eat chocolate, and keep away from toffee.
Too much tea is bad for you, and the same applies to coffee.
Water from a bottle is supposed to be the best,
Fish from the polluted sea could be added to the rest.
But please, oh please, don't stop us eating British beef,
How can we get by with just a lettuce leaf
Or a handful of raisins and a basinful of rice,
Is that what they want us to say is very nice?
They've turned our pounds to kilos, and our ounces into grams,
Who do they think we are - a flock of silly lambs?
Our milk will be powdered next, and packed up in a tin,
Twice our men have been to war, our freedom for to win.
Who are these kind of people who call themselves just "They"?
Do they live in London, or is it far away?
Whatever can we do to stop this slippery slide?
Is there anyone out there now who's fighting on our side?

J. Gant

Regrets

Regrets — knots in the thread of time, tightly tied,
Fast woven in the tapestry of life.
Harsh reminders of unrewarding pastimes
Unfriendly undertones of future strife.

Regrets — Black holes in distant constellations
Open graves for future hopes and dreams,
Supernova, collapsing into neutrons,
Dead stars, emitting dark and fatal beams.

But carbon crystallizes to sparkling diamond
Glistening pearls from tissue that was torn,
Regrets, buried in obscure recesses,
Eventually emerge as hopes reborn.

Regrets — the grit in new determination,
The spur that bites so sharp in wounded side,
The pungent acid in our poignant make-up
Re-energizing once rejected pride.

On the painful climb-down from old ambitions
To the lonely skeleton cave of the dry bone,
Regrets become the rocks of firmer footholds
Announce us atheling to the vacant throne.

W. Haisley Moore

Untitled

Where are you now dear one? Dancing in a shimmering star like
   a droplet of crystal water suspended in a moment of sheer joy,
   melting into a moonbeam, like a damsel fly whose gossamer wings
   catch a sunbeam to glow the radiant fire of our Christ self
   transmitting thoughts of pure love.

Where are you now dear one? Held on the wings of that pure love,
   subtle energies vibrate to the songs of the seas, the whispering
   wind telling stories of truths gone by, enfolded in the arms of a
   happy abandoned self to ride upon virgin ice crystals that melt in
   the eyes of a newborn babe.

Where are you now dear one? Nestling in your mother's womb, waiting
   to tread life's pathways, bringing with you an understanding never
   before brought forth into the hearts and minds of beings, to go
   forth with your shimmering light to change all before you into new
   beginnings, your heart will pulsate with a fineness, you will
   glide with the birds riding the air, breathe with the animals
   and creatures, outworn fear evaporates into nothingness.

Where are you now dear one?

I am here and have been since time began, in your seeing,
   your feeling, your hearing, your touching.

Neil Meadows

In Search of the Answer

Some seek the truth in a warm, leafy glade,
Eyes closed, body limp, melting into the shade.
Some scour the page of a book's confide,
Hoping life's answers lay etched inside.

Some look to the still of the highland moor,
Perhaps solitudes tonic provides the cure.
Some steal to the sea to spite the pain,
Misty eyes trawling the waves in vain.

Some nervously bare their soul to God,
Praying their back can be free of its rod.
Some focus inward, to find their true self,
Dreams left for dead rescued down from the shelf.

Some give up and lose their way,
Apathy growing in dreams decay.
Some look not and feel content
Happy, fulfilled, a life well spent

Then others, like me, understand the truth,
Life's answer will always remain aloof
Unless the question is known afore
Never the answer will knock at your door

Stephen Allan

The Little Girl Lost

The little girl lost stands all alone,
Fights her many battles all on her own.
Hides behind the power that she built,
Will block out all her feelings of hurt and guilt.
She's so strong, she cries no tears.
She's so brave, she has no fears.
More powerful than all the rest,
Must always be the best.
She's nasty and cruel, she brakes every rule.

The little girl lost stands all alone,
Fights her many battle all on her own.
Plays with her dolls, hurts when she falls.
Sleeps with a cat and her favourite ted,
Just another innocent child, sleeping in her bed.
Can't trust either side, nobody there to confide,
She's so confused about their love she's been refused.
When it goes dark, out goes the light,
Nasty dreams and tears all through the night.
The little girl lost stands very tall,
But she's only a little girl, frightened and small.

Nathalie Leckie

The Letter

I awake to greet the winter's dawn
Feeling low a bit forlorn
Eat a slice of toast have a cup of tea
The letter box rattles, some post for me
I go to the door expecting a bill
It's then I get the greatest thrill
With my hometown postmark for me a letter
Now I'm feeling very much better
I avidly read what my brother has written
With his new penthouse suite, he is very smitten
He writes of a room, for when I visit
The kind of furniture he's putting in it
How a view from a window looks over the sea
And down to the right he can see the fish quay
He goes on to write of this and that
It's just like he's here, and we're having a chat
No matter now the winter's day
The nip in the air the sky of grey
I am happy and won't feel the chill
I got a letter today from my brother Bill

E. Fisher

The Old Oak Tree

We all have treasures in our hearts
From happy days of Yore.
To some it is a cottage small
With roses 'round the door.
My treasure is an old oak tree
So motherly and grand.
Her leafy boughs reach out to me
As if to shake my hand.

When I was just a little girl
And home from school would run.
Its welcome leaves would shade me
From the mid-day sun.
Then later on in girlhood years
Maturing and deep in love.
I sat with sweethearts fond and true
Beneath the old oak tree.
And then with stars above
I said good night and left for home.
What sad and happy tales it would tell if only it could speak.
So proud and yet so meek that old oak tree.

A. T. O'Reilly

Croxdale in Autumn

The woods are full of sounds
From invisible creatures.
The hawthorn drops are veiled in leafy gold.
And the larch takes on transparency.
The hushed heat of summer is over
And a winter readiness begins,
Hurrying the withered leaves
Through scattered sunlight.
The wind is everywhere -
Not angry, but a cold
Presence in the air.

From distant fields
Flocks of white birds
Rise and hang in air
Uncertain where to settle -
Poor timid ghosts
In this burning dale.

Shirley Lewis

The Last Card

Take this card that carries words to you
From me with hope that kindle flames anew
The mystic powers of the all-seeing eye
The unseen spirit that darkens the sky
The warm breath that teaches flowers to smile
The moving hand that ushered us down the aisle
The foresight that denies rage a fight
The courtesy that charms a stone to shine bright
Had I pinch of any one thing
You would never loose your wedding ring
And of all deeds impossible a task so hard
Is to give you this our last anniversary card.

Richard Steggles

Edinburgh

I miss the place once called home,
From so long ago.
The familiar aroma of coal fills the air,
I could almost be there.
I stand and close my eyes,
But when I open them I'm not there.

Why did we have to move?
Did you even ask if I approved!
How would I have grown?
I guess that shall never be known!
How I miss those smoke filled skies,
Maybe I just haven't said my goodbyes.

Lorraine Gordon

The Light Will Come

I long for the sun to come up and smile,
For that I guess I'll be waiting a while;
The time is soon I can guarantee,
The light will come and I will see;
I will see what is there and watch and learn,
The knowledge and love that I will yearn.
The love inside I feel so strong,
To tell the world I do so long;
I shall shout it so loud my voice will be heard,
To be carried away amongst the birds.
The world will listen and answer my prayers,
Then I will know that some-one is there;
I don't that I need my friends, deny,
But without the love my heart will die;
The love is there in many forms,
But to see who is true nobody warns.
When you feel the worlds getting you down,
Just open your eyes and look around;
Just sit and wait for it will come,
Yes one day you will see the sun.

Tony Lindsay

Insomnia

I wait for the wave to crash over me.
For the dark swirling mass of unconsciousness.
I drift on a raft of unused dreams.

The beating of my heart is the ticking of a clock.
I lay in the darkness, watching the navy blue
shadows invade my wall.

I am used to it now, this spiteful eternity.
The light on the horizon is shining like bright's disease.

I watch it draw nearer. Hating it. Hating myself.

Ruth Parfitt

6th June 1994

A day to remember, a day of great glory,
For the past seven days, we have relived their story.
We've read it in the papers, we've seen it on T.V.,
Fly passes by the spitfires and wreathes laid in the sea.
A bombardier from Bolton, a corporal from Stoke.
"We've come to see old Tommy, a really smashing bloke.
They got him as he left the landing craft at nine,
The poor unlucky bastard stepped right on a mine.
A lovely man, a kindly man, very, very brave,
We've bought a bunch of flowers and put them on his grave."
The high spot was the veterans, marching past the Queen,
Be-ribboned chests of medals, all musing on the scene
of glories long ago, now part of history,
They saved the world for others, the likes of you and me.
As they marched past the dais there was purpose in their stride,
Some walking, some on crutches but their eyes were filled with pride.
Scores and scores of veterans, returned to keep a date,
And the youngest was William, a sprightly sixty-eight.

Michael Carter

The Cupboard from Hell

Please do not open that cupboard door
For things fall out, all over the floor
There must be all sorts of things, I haven't seen for years
An old jumper, socks, etc., that have been thrown in after
   a few beers
My friends laugh at me, when I go in and throw things over
   my shoulder
They say you will never find anything, at least until you get a
   lot older
I am going to clear it out, as soon as I get time, I vow
But that time has not come, I am not quite ready, just now
So my hell hole will stay as it is, and I will lean on the door to
   to get it closed
And keep my friends happy, as they laugh at me trying to be
composed.

Margaret Crouch

Mount Zeus

I am Mount Zeus
I get very hot when I am mad.
I start to brew and let off steam and
all of sudden I blow and all of my
anger flows out as I scream madly!

I start to rage and gradually I calm down
and I don't rage again because I have to build
up gas and lava. "Oh no,
I'm going to blow!!"

Zeus O'Sullivan

Old Age

I'm old and I'm wrinkled, I sit in my chair,
eyes dim and faded, but memories are there
of family and children, of lovers and life
of sorrow and glad times, of pity and strife
my heart beats much slower, I look for the light
my hands gnarled are shrunken,
my eyes squint at light.
Old age has crept on me, my beauty is gone
forever behind me as death comes along.
my youth smooth and shining is set to decay
my hair long and golden now thin, dull, and grey.
But I have such stories of love in my head
to cherish, remember, until I am dead
my life has been torment, I've known deep despair.
I've lived on light laughter, and grief has been there.
I've known all these feelings, I've lived, so I'm told -
To laugh, to remember them, now that I'm OLD!

Margaret Hanning

The Place of Exile

No one to speak to nowhere to go, I have just the company of the dungeon rats,
For seven days and seven nights now I have dwelt in the loose palace of exile.
The only light I have at night is the strong and intimidating stare of the moon. In the night's sky.
But soon I will break through in to a new born dawn on the other side.
I can see the disciples following their Jesus to a new spring's door,
but it's locked they can't get out but they can hear behind the door
the swish and the swash of the season's spring tide.

Summer is nigh those hazy days are here again.
I am still locked up here in heartache and pain with only the rats
of the dungeon of darkness, to talk to for comfort and sanity.
I will be here for eternity in body and soul waiting for my only
friend, I will be ready for him when he comes,
for he is my only friend the end.

Stephen J. E. Woodhouse

To My Daughter

The world stood still for me when you were born, your first
faint cry awakened a grey dawn, they laid you in my arms so
fragile and so small, and I marvelled that this tiny soul could
be alive at all, my dear ones how I made such plans for you,
butthen I find that dreams and plans so very rarely come true,
we've wept together you and I such angry bitter tears; and yet
we've been such comfort to each other through the years. I
watched you tremble as a child and kissed the hurt away, and
wished withall my heart I could do the same today, but I could
only stand by helpless sharing your grief and pain, praying that
you'd have the courage and the will to start again. Your life has
been like a jigsaw with the pieces all in bits, and you've grouped
around despairingly wondering where your jigsaw fits, and then
piece by piece and day by day you've built it all anew, till your
picture is completed and I'm so proud of you. I always prayed
you'd find yourself now the best is yet to be, and you've grown
into the sort of person beautiful to see. I loved you from the
moment that you made your first faint cry,
I know I'll always love you never question why.

Gwendoline Stella Braid

Through the Years

Four little faces looked up at me,
Four little faces filled with curiosity
Four little faces that occupied my day
Four little faces that drove the clouds away
Four little faces that grew through the years
No longer little faces but, I still dry their tears
No longer dependent but, I still calm their fears
So those four little faces are still there you see
Because I'm their mother so, how else should it be.

Pat James

For Charles

We had fun, 'Blue Eyes' and I
enjoying each day we had to share.
Sitting nearby, he would 'catch my eye'
with mischief glinting there.
He was my friend, as well as pet,
when he became ill, we had many visits to the vet.
My heart still hurts, and I miss him so,
for we had to part six months ago.

Yet I think back, to when he was young
the paper balls, how high he flung.
Jumping on walls, with ease and grace
a shadow, a fly, he would eagerly chase.

My lovely Charles, with coat so sleek,
around corners slyly, he would peek.
Purring loudly, and rubbing heads to please,
my enchanting cat, who was a Siamese.

Mary G. Edwards

My Friend Dotty

When I was young, I had a friend,
Dotty was her name,
She wasn't real, just pretend,
Life was one big game,

Dotty was really beautiful,
She probably had lovely hair,
But it didn't matter how she looked,
'Cause she wasn't really there.

If I ever got in trouble,
Not often I might add,
Dotty would always comfort me,
Whenever I was sad.

Sometimes though, she'd egg me on
To be naughty for a game,
Dotty would hide and I'd get caught,
And I would get the blame.

We had lots of fun, Dotty and me,
We laughed, we cried, shed tears,
I'm grown up now, but my memories stay,
Of those my happiest years.

Lisa Boyton

That Little Boy

The innocence shining from the face of a child
Can't be equalled by anything else
As he looks back at you through those big blue eyes
Knowing nothing, so dependent on you

You to him are everything he needs
His source of safety, comfort, and love
He looks to you to put right what's wrong
When even he doesn't know what that is

The harder times, and the mutual tears
When that upward hill seems so long
Are outweighed, and take second place
To the precious moments and smiles

The pride and love reflects in the eyes of those close to him
He's your own little legend, and you look at him in awe
You'll do anything in the world for that little boy
Everything you can - and more

Sarah Olson

The Lonely Man

I wander aimlessly throughout this land,
Hoping to find love and a kind and helping hand
But not many people seem to understand.
That love and kindness are in big demand.
So I travel alone throughout this land
And I'm hoping some day the Lord will come
And I hope "and hope" he will take my hand,

Maurice Parvin

Retribution

Wild, frenzied,
Dashing themselves against the stone,
Beating, raging,
What sin could make them thus atone?
Unleashed, crazy, why do they torture, hurt self so?
Is it because,
Of thousands drowned, they saw them go?
Heard the screams, and strongly beat the crying down,
Did not help,
But used their power to make them drown.
Is this so?
And is this why the waves crash and rage?
Like tigers
Freed from an unwelcome, tiny cage,
Do they now,
Thunder, travel, always moving,
Throw themselves
Against the rocks, for us mortals proving
Their sorrow, that they are cruel against their will,
Throughout the ages, they will be drowning and atoning still.

J. M. Gosling

The Fate of a Cake

When Hildy baked an apple cake
Especially on a trip to take
After leaving home then she did find.
She'd left that apple cake behind.

For in the cupboard there it stood
When they returned as hard as wood
Or visions of it going mouldy
Tormented our poor Len and Hildy

So they hit on a bright idea
Of phoning friends who lived quite near
Collect that cake at once they said
Tonight before you go to bed

You've got the key to our front door
Don't help yourself to anything more
Those neighbours are a hungry shower
They'd scoffed that cake within an hour

Now by the phone they sit and wait
With Lolling tongues and empty plate
Hoping that once more it rings
So they can have another binge.

D. C. Line

Gone

Gone is the hand I used to touch, silent the voice I loved so much.
Gone now your smile that was so bright, changing my darkness into light
No sound of your feet upon the stairs, no quick "hallo"
That says you care
You slipped away into the night, not "gone", but out of sight
Slowly my eyes wander around, "What do I see",
"What" am I clasping, "What" have I found.
Just an old photo faded and worn
Brings back memories now reborn
The eyes look back, with soft appeal as if to say
I'm with you still
As I gaze, I cannot shed a tear
You look, so real, so "near"

Marjorie Augarde

Depressing as It Seems Life Is . . .

Full of crap,
Double standards - for males and females
What you are taught, and what you really learn

It's full of lies,
Because people don't try to understand
They pretend to -
And yet; they make you feel as if you lie

About your problems and how you handle them
Depression, Anxiety and Panic, Stress and Nerves
The way it takes you over
And you don't have control
You're heading for a bang; a huge explosion

They don't understand the effect
The way you react, and try, to be normal
But you can't
So you try to cope, in the only way you can
Banking it down, so you can function
That is what they can't, or won't understand
And that, frustrates and eats at me so.

Bianca

'Flying'

See those white lines in the sky?
From which far countries do they fly?
A lonely dot in the wide blue yonder.
The miles and space these craft squander!
An island in the sky each one,
Bathed as always in brilliant sun.

The vapour trails they leave behind,
Stark, white, and well defined.
Do these contain the travellers souls?
Their hopes, fears, dreams and goals.
Cocooned apart from us mere mortals
But closer to heaven, its pearly portals.

Floating down from the clouds to emerge,
onto earthly airports they converge,
to a sudden change of world they awake,
each landing is a new daybreak.
On the threshold of earthly triviality,
from a buoyant dream to reality.

R. W. Burnett

Newspaper

Sometimes I am freed in fluid flight
From your dense thicket of letters and
Sink into a silence where I sense the
Vital sap-thrust of forest-growth
Before they pulped you into present shape.
Sometimes, dyslexic, I see only
Gnarled syllables dying in my
Vision of your origin in mindless
Clay and rest at a still point
The other side of words.

Patrick Deighan

Joyce

Her hair was a spider web about her face, eyes closed as in sleep
No wrinkles now, smoothed away by death
Quiet in spirit as it never was of late.
No more shall she speak of her dislikes to friends who cared
No more displeasure in her unquiet mind
She did not know what hurt her so inside.
She knew no hurt before
Shielded so long by the man who loved her till death did them part.
It hurt her more than she knew.
So, her anger grew, grew as each day passed
It shrivelled her heart, her body, her soul.
Till there was nothing left, only pain, that ended too.
Here she lay in death, once more at peace.
Looking as she did, dressed in her favourite bright green dress,
Scarf of many colours draped round her throat
Her face not of death.
But of quiet contentment, at last.

Alice Lee

Eagle Eye

They carried him slowly wrapped in a sack
Draped across his stallion's back
Snow poured from the freezing sky, the day they buried Eagle Eye
Once a warrior young and brave
Not for him a white man's grave
But to the happy hunting mound
A resting bed above the ground
Where the chiefs can once again be free, united with their family
They lift him slowly to the bed
And gently rest the feathered head,

Their tears mix with the freezing snow
Their chief is dead, now they're alone
Once more they kiss old warrior's head
So Regal and brave even in death
So then goodbye, till we meet once more
On the happy hunting shore
Where buffalos are ours once more
And Whiteman does not have his way.
The Indians are there to stay

K. Waller

Risen from the Dead

Do not stand at my grave and weep.
I am not there, I do not sleep.
I am a thousand winds and blows,
I am the diamond glints on snow,
I am the sunlight, on ripened grain,
I am the gentle autumn rain,
When you awaken in the morning hush,
I am the swift uplifting rush,
Of quiet birds in circled flight,
I am the soft stars that shine at night,
Do not stand at my grave and cry,
I am not there I did not die.

Paul Waters

Magical Wales

In the fairy-filled mountains of Abercarn Fach
I saw a green goblin taking a bath.
There he sat in a minnow-filled stream,
Splashing and laughing,
He giggled and screamed.
Shook his fist at the squawking blue jay,
Splash-frightened the rough, barking dogs till they ran.
He copied them, shaking his willow-slim frame,
The droplets all catching the morning-rise sun,
And showering the greenest of grass in all Wales.
One gasp, one blink, one chuckle, he'd gone.
I've not seen him since but the magic lives on.

Rose Knight

The Best Things in Life

The moon shining high with the stars in the sky,
Frost as it glistens on the ground.
The breeze as it whispers to leaves on the trees,
These are delights I have found.
A walk in the rain, big puddles down the lane,
Autumn leaves under my feet.
Birds singing above, the songs that I love,
Without which no world is complete.
Snow on the hills and spring daffodils,
Little lambs gambolling at play,
Children on swings, a church bell that rings,
Sunset at the end of the day.
Just simply to laze on warm sunny days
Relaxing with nothing to do.
Gardens in bloom with fragrant perfume
To last me all seasons through.
When I look around at the things I have found
The ones that have brought me content
Giving moments of pleasure I always will treasure
And none of it costs me a 'cent'.

Teresa Archer

Life

I am the first flowers of spring.
I am the breeze that caresses your face on a
warm summer's day.
I am the crisp golden leaves under your feet in autumn
I am the beautiful sunset over winter's mountains
I am life and I'll go on forever.

Pam Cooper

Soldier Welcome Home

Soldier, soldier, home on leave
Draw deeply of the air you breathe;
Here at home that air is free
Back at base there is a fee.
Sometimes dispute, sometimes debate,
Sometimes dislike, sometimes deep hate.
Protector, invader, defender, attacker,
Peace keeper, warmonger, constable, killer.
Soldier I pray for your soul, a reprieve
Peace on this earth for you to achieve.

Soldier, soldier, home on leave
Don't give our hearts a chance to grieve,
Soldier of such tender years
Haunting pubs and supping beers.
Stand to attention there my man!
Short years ago you held my hand,
Chased a ball and bounced my Knee,
Cried with ecstasy beside the sea.
Did I buy your first toy gun?
Soldier-boy who is - my son.

J. P. Woodward

Hanoi

As I walk down your
            dust-ridden streets
your lace-up houses flaking
            in the heavy heat,
you dog me from all corners
            of my eyes
shadowing a cyclo
            at my side
as another begs
            his shoe shine
on my suede.

And I am jaded
      by your strains.
Long into the night
            your distant tooting haunts
my insane mind
            wrestling for sleep
beneath a netted arch
            as Hanoi's power
cuts beyond the dark.

R. Russell

Yesterday

Don't look over your shoulder
Don't look back at yesterday
For you can't recapture the happy hours
That heartbreak took away

You can't rekindle a fire that died
For the ashes are cold that once glowed
There is no warmth when the bleak wind blows
With no love to ease your load

Face the future with faith and hope
Take in your stride the lonely path you must tread
Pray that tomorrow you'll be able to cope
But don't cry for yesterday, yesterday's dead

All our tomorrows are yet to be
What they hold for us who can say
Look ahead but never behind
Live for today, dream of tomorrow
But learn from yesterday

Mary Haynes

A Love through Eternity

Your touch is but a presence dear
A bond that weakens time
I've been right by your side
Since I left you far behind

I never meant to leave you
Though I knew my time was nigh
Please darling don't forget me
They'll say that you should try

I know you're scared of leaving
But the time must come for all
And I'll still be here waiting
When you get that final call

One day when you are ready
I'll just reach out my hand
And then we'll go together
Into that promised land
J. Fieldhouse

Lament

you know how it is
a fanciful meandering
a slip into the possible
that for one short moment
seems real

a touch
a lingering look
a smile
a fleeting glimpse of understanding

private
unspoken

unfulfilled.
Keith Duke

Memories

Lying back on the warm dry grass
A girl of six years or seven
Above the fragrant blossom
I saw the bluest heaven
The tree that towered over me
Was laden in pink glory
And I gazed in amazement
At the beauty there before me
An aeroplane droned over
It was flying very high
I listened to its throbbing
As it went across the sky
A breeze blew really softly
And shook some blossom free
It whirled, cascading earthward
And gently fell on me
All seemed so calm and peaceful
That lovely September day
And I remember that time still
Though it's many years away.
Megan Law

Sweet Violets

'Neath grassy banks the violet grows
And bows her head in sweet repose
Her dainty petals white and blue.
Hail spring again in all their hue.
Leaves around her, ever green
Are quite the sweetest ever seen.
With perfume fresh as morning dew
Most fragrant all the season through
And then alas, when she has gone.
Her lonely leaves still linger on
Where once she grew in all her pride
In this, our lovely countryside
Norah Faulkner

Disaster

Out of the ruins,
A life is plucked from certain death,
Out of the chaos,
A baby is born.
A child cries,
While men dig with bare hands,
At any sign of life.
In a different place,
On the other side of the world,
Babies are battered,
Left to die,
Naked in their own houses,
Taken from their Mothers,
Thrown like rubbish,
Into bloody water.

While the world smiles,
A baby, still breathing,
Is lifted gently from the rubble,
And another, is murdered.
Suzanne Taylor

The Bridge

On a side table
a man, I watch,
he knows I'm here.
I feel the bridge
but will it hold me?

He reads
I keep up a
fake conversation.
I feel the bridge
but will it carry me?

I make a move
a cup in my hand,
his eyes suddenly alert
he sees but doesn't move.
I feel the bridge
but will he ever
use it?
Satu Lindgren

Love Is

Love is special gift,
a present given.
Love can make you happy,
it can make you sad.
Love does not just mean you and it,
it spreads and grows.
Love brings a future,
a reason for living.
Love needs tender care,
nurtured affection.
Love should not be discarded,
just taken away.
Love can be for always,
or just one day.
Our love is a treasure
it will last forever,
as long as it's remembered
that love is . . .
Sheila O'Brien

Silent Words

In your eyes I read a message.
A promise intense and clear.
A question veiled in nonchalance.
A sound too soft to hear.

Why speak? When eyes reveal
all thoughts -
All dreams of what could be.
We need no words of oral sound.
Your eyes say all to me.
Marie Somerset

A Sacred Place

The Intricate Web of Family Ties;
A woven warmth,
A sanctuary of security.

Of loving beings.
And helping hands.

The singular and unrivalled,
Simplicity and stability,
Offered only by the place called home.
Paula Marie Henderson

Fox and Doe

While walking through a forest green.
a movement, caught my eye.
'Twas not the squirrels in the trees,
nor birds, up in the sky.
I chanced to glance ahead of me,
was amazed, at what I saw.
a large fox creeping stealthily,
crouched down, on every paw.
I wondered what it was he stalked
what made him creep, so low?
But then I saw beside a bush,
a snow white, rabbit doe.
Fox crept along so quietly,
you could not hear a thing,
when just within a yard or so,
was ready then to spring.
I gave a shout the rabbit jumped,
then swiftly, ran away.
And so, that little snow white doe
did live, another day.
Patrick J. Knight

Recipe for Friendship

A heaped spoon of laughter.
A small pinch of pain,
Mix in some sunshine,
Add a few drops of rain,
Mix in your troubles,
Then stir in mine,
Together we will sieve them,
And they will turn out fine,
Add a real black mood of yours,
Then pour in one of mine,
Stir in some forgiveness,
And it will cook just fine,
Sprinkle in some teardrops,
Add a real big smile,
Put it in the oven,
And bake it for awhile,
Ice it with some memories,
Then pour us both life's wine,
Of all the friends in all this world,
I'm honoured that you're mine,
L. Osbourne

Red Indian Dream

The skies that cry for you and I
Across the plains and this domain
Our broken hearts for we depart
Thundering guns with bullet runs

We cry for mercy being thirsty
So killing game within your name
This land of ours in dream time hours
The kingdom of dreams so it seems

Your wicked ways, the way you play
The end of you I do I do
Within your sins and there's no inn
God has spoken you're so broken

Across the plains and this domain
The skies that cry for you and I.
E. T. Ward

A Sad Soul

Emotional tragedy is really
A tragedy of oneself,
Take love,
Love has to be dangerous
Quiet, with stealth, like a wolf,
Like death.
To greet then pounce,
With claws
Of such sweet words
As to leave no trace of any
Cuts they make
For love must be seen
As a holy wounding.
A legalized form of emotional
Cannibalism?
Of that I am sure
Of such magnitude
That Caligula would look ready
For angels.

Peter J. Scarratt

Summer's Vines

If a man happens upon
a woman in flippant
yarn and common deed or
mutual purpose, what
may become.
Shrouded in linen silk
and precious jewels that
behold his eyes as a virgin
in fresh countenance.
His hands stained with
juice, hers with oil of the olive
Both entrenched in custom
cast and dinar, yet split from
the vine as one sapling
Surely such hands will
breathe life in new soil as a bird
will carry seed beyond an ocean
A nation is born.

Leonard Andrews

The Race

On starter's orders ready to run,
All lined up one by one
As we wait for the hungry serge.
Bang goes the start
So off we all dart
To make for the hero's lot

Gamblers on edge
As we go for the hedge,
And out drops a few at the first.
There's no going back,
Once you take to the track
So on to the second we go

The laggers who fall
At the last final haul
Show the way for the galloping star.
Silent urging before
Then a glorious roar
As the winner comes in at the post.

Kara March

Untitled

I can't give you a gift,
    like a diamond ring
And my present is just
    sunny days of spring!
Let the smile of the sun
    never leave your house
And I hope you will be
    always friends of us.

Anna Anpilogova

From Beginning to End

Planet earth
Abode of man
Rose from the depths
To invade the land

One creator
Lasting foundation
Constant survival
Of soul creation

One life to live
One world to live in
A way to choose
To loose or win

One heart to give
One mind to control
A space of time
In time, to know

When through with age
When end is night
When life is spent
With death we lie

Margaret Hosken

Ring of Laughter

A ring of laughter, fills the air
And echoes down, through time.
Across the hills and down the vales,
It finds a lonely child.
No smile adorns his lips, and tears
    stand in his eyes.
Oh ring of laughter, do your stuff,
Cheer up this lonely child.
Put dimples in his little cheeks,
And sparkles in his eyes.
Send butterflies with speckled bands,
To just outreach his chubby hands.
Put wings upon his little feet,
To chase them all, oh, what a treat
through flowers he'll dart and shout.
a lonely child no longer.
Oh, ring of laughter, do your stuff,
and carry on, ever stronger.

P. Ernst

Autumn

Autumn comes and autumn goes,
And silent trees in woodland rows,
Await the coming of the snows,
And mighty gales of winter

The fallen leaves so crisp and brown,
Upon the path are strewn around,
Have richly carpeted the ground
Before the frosts the winter

Philip Dilworth Harrison

The Book

Looking so normal,
an ordinary thing,
never would you suspect,
that book of being a king
of cunning
cruelty and dare,
and you'd never be aware,
that he is stalking you,
watching, waiting,
looking at your every move,
remembering, thinking,
and as you pick him up to read,
he gets you!
Wham!!!
Closing the world from you,
if he can . . .

Katie Holton

If

If you would meet me
After all these years,
I wonder would you greet me
With laughter or with tears.

If you would walk with me
To places we used to know,
I wonder could you talk with me
Before you had to go.

If you would kiss me
One last time for memory's sake,
I wonder would you miss me
Would your heart be about to break.

If you would hold me
Before we said goodbye,
I wonder would you scold me
If you saw a teardrop in my eye.

T. S. Norman

Husband of Mine

I cannot tell you Darling
All that you meant to me
I only know, I loved you so
and yet it had to be
God called to you, your time
on earth was spent
My lesson learned, was, that you
were only lent
The tears I've shed, the pain I bare
and no one here, my grief to share
I long for one thing only
That god will call me Home
No more tears and heart ache
No more to be alone.

Sophie Godfrey

Yesterdays

All those years ago we touched,
All those years ago we loved,
Together, for such a brief time,
Yet, we remembered each other,
Never to forget, not to regret.

A first love is never said to die,
Neither does true love.
A love so true, the heart is kind,
and locks the pain away.
Until the day we meet again.

The pleasure of the meeting,
Brings the passion of the moment,
to last for some time, yet gone.
In the same moment, replaced by pain,
The pain of being apart.

    Until tomorrow,
    Until then.

Marianne Gemmell

Home Is Where You Are

I'm in my country of birth
And the town of my youth,
In the house of my folks

-But I want to go home.

I still long for that feeling
of comfort and stillness.
My soul is abroad

-And I want to come home.

I pause, and take stock of
The unrest within me.
I cradle my heart

-For I know I am home.

Pattie Vukomanovic

Thoughts

How beautiful the sunset's glow,
And lovely is the dawn,
The sunshine fills us with delight
And courage to go on.

To brace ourselves for each new day
For what the hours may bring,
We hear the lark sing high above
Whilst distant church bells ring.

We think of all the glorious dead
The people we once knew,
Who vanished like a drift of snow
Or like a morning dew.

So Life and Death is ever night
Since this great World began
We must prepare our souls for Thee
'Tis part of thy great plan.

Violet Williams

Anonymous

There lies in the desert
  An unknown grave,
Where a gallant soldier died.
  Beneath the sands where
He fought a war
  Was shot, his life denied.
That was somebody's boy
  Young, healthy and strong,
He was brave, ambitious
  And free
But fate would have him
  Placed on the front line,
His future was never to be.
  You are sleeping my boy,
Your memory lives on,
  Your bravery never forgotten.
You fought for your nation
  And you'll never know
What a hero you were
  At your station.

Yvonne Scollen

Lost Love

Is this the glorious Summer
And does the new mown hay
Sweet scent the air I only know
My love has gone away

Is this Autumn when the leaves
Fall yellow and russet to play
In the gusty wind I only know
My love is far away

Is this the barren Winter
And does snow thickly lay
Across the fields I only know
My love is still away

Is this really Spring again
And are the gardens gay
With flowers and birds I only know
My love has gone for aye

Olive Hiscocks

Untitled

Kingly thou art in thine attire,
and in your rags a pauper indeed.
In your palace upon your throne
along the footpaths overgrown.
Dressed in white, a flowing cowl
upon your horse ride free
and when you reach the lonely inn
enter and you will find me.

K. G. Gray

Be Yourself

Be yourself, be who you are
and don't let others change you.
For they must like you as you are,
for what you are and who.
No-one else is quite the same,
unique, the only one,
for if you change to be like others
the real you will be gone.
We all must learn to give and take
in everything we do.
So be yourself and like yourself
and others will like you.

Nancy Wake

On St. Valentine's Day a Lament

If I were young
And fleet of tongue
What wondrous song
I would have sung
To my lady valentine.

Alas, alack the time has gone
The mood no longer suits the song
For the years have come and gone
Tempus fugit has blighted the song
To my Lady valentine.
And woe is me
And woe is me.

D. Rees

Peace

I look into the clouds
And I can see,
Peace and harmony
for you and me,
An end to fighting
An end to war,
finally we get
What we've been fighting for.

I stare into space
And I feel free,
with sanctuary and silence
That may cease to be,
It's peaceful now but
How long will it last?
There is always the threat
of a nuclear blast

We must lay down arms
And show heaven above
It's not the only place
With peace and love

Paul McDermott

The Poet's Game

In my heart I hide you,
And in my mind I see
The world through your eyes,
Deep like forest pools.
Your hair of darkwood shade,
Fine upon your face,
Lighting up your being.
Leaving me to trace your beauty.
Shy, a little shy,
You take my compliments half-hearted.
And I, afraid to tell you,
That you radiate perfection.
A prize worth every breath and strain,
That any challenge asks.
I write with words not worthy,
Of one as pure as you.
My thoughts,
In language base,
I try to give to you,
And redeem the poet's game.

Paul J. Charman

Happy Birthday Lamb!

Many thoughts have followed,
And often I have Known,
That you may not be quite with me
But I'm never all alone.

I miss your way of thinking,
And the way that things should be,
I know I cannot change things,
I miss you desperately.

The longer I am living,
More distant come your calls,
I sit here brave and patient,
For death shall conquer all.

This life has left me speechless,
To all who dare to call,
For there are no words left in me,
worth saying, none at all!!

Tamsin Humphries

Home

Home refreshes me
And rests me
And balms me.
Things fall into perspective.
Here I can smile objectively
At my situation.
Here I feel accepted
And loved.
And here I love.
My father is beautiful;
My mother is worthy of high praise
Their generosity of the highest order
And unconditional. For I have
Done nought to deserve all they
Have done for me.
And pray I can do the same
For them.
Here my sisters are beautiful also.
This is home.

Nigel Consiglio

Thank You

Evening time is drawing near
And sleep is coming on,
May our thoughts be just as clear,
Please let thy will be done.

Stubborn are we, childish too,
Open our hearts we pray;
Help us in everything we do,
New thoughts throughout the day.

Father in heaven Your will was done,
Your blood was shed for me,
And when the day of judgement come
Your precious face we shall see.

Patricia V. Gonsalves

Untitled

You listen with such caring silence
And speak with so much thought,
A gift of life that's given
Not a lesson to be taught,
Your words are full of wisdom
Though sometimes they are hard,
You say that life's not dealt with
Like the turning of a card,
You have to take it in both hands
And use it day by day,
Because if you don't face it well
You'll never find the way.

Rachel Balian

A New Day

The dark night paled
And stars like lighted candles
Dimmed.

Soft as a sigh, a breath
Ruffled the tops of the trees
And the sleeping rhythm changed.

Closed eyelids flickered,
Limbs uncurled,
Yet sleeping on

Dreaming mankind swam up
From fathomless depths
And paused.

Darkest blue filtered
To the colour of the mind
And the dreams of a new day.
Rozanne Ellis

Klan Kake

Take one swastika,
And stir violently with ignorance,
Corrupt one mind with foul intentions,
And steadily boil.

When the hate bubbles over,
Break up one society,
Season with white power,
And serve with pain.
Leanne Boast

The Troubled Ocean

The sun is shining,
and the dolphins play,
Then suddenly there's a cloud,
they all rush away.

There's a thing with a net,
"What is it?" they cry
"It's man again",
The wise one says with a sigh.

The thing up above,
the wise one calls man,
reaches out to the net,
and pulls up with his hand.

The fish are struggling,
and flapping their tails
In the end they give up,
when every effort fails.

He takes them aboard,
and jokes with his friends
the dolphins look angry,
and plan their REVENGE!
Sarah Weir

Green Fields

A look of green velvet,
as I stand on the hill,
so smooth and calm,
and oh so still.
This tranquil pasture,
so relaxed and green,
wisps of golden in between
in the distance sunset
starts to fall,
and lights up the sky
this fiery ball,
then darkness comes
and turns day into night,
then wait till dawn for
this green and tranquil sight.
Marilyn Grace Bossuot

Re-Born

For my mother, Jean

A whole year has gone by
and the road has been tough
But one year on its own
is just never enough
The small changes you've seen
are only the start
You've been given 'new life'
which will strengthen your heart
So, carry on living
keep all that is new
chuck out all the old
for they're a burden on you
Count your losses and gains
Let your eyes see it's right
Reap the rewards
and keep up the fight
Take hold of the truth
and grab this 'new chance'
You will find all the proof
without so much as a glance!
Thurzah Berry

Oh Mum!

Another morning,
Another day,
Another nappy,
And then off to play.

Another knee,
Another floor,
Another plaster,
A kiss once more.

Another yell,
Another fight,
Another evening,
A kiss good night.

Another story,
Another cheek,
Another kiss,
And then off to sleep.

Good night my darlings,
It's the end of a long day,
But I'll see you tomorrow,
When you can resume play.
Melanie Player

Write It Out

Many do not see
Any need for poetry
If you need to think about
Why not sit and write it out

When the world, goes flying by
Just sit there, but don't sigh
Don't go in a bout
Why not sit and write it out

If you want to be
Free from your misery
Don't just lay about
Why not sit and write it out

If it's only meant for you
Then give the world fingers two
If you are about to shout
Why not sit and write it out.

Nearly gone my poetry
Find it hard to count to three
If you feel the need to shout
Why not sit and write it out
J. J. Sabin

September

The east wind blows, and the trees
Are aglow. With their green, golds
Reds and brown leaves.
As they wait on the boughs for the
Winds to dislodge them.
Their function complete, the sun
Flickers through them, like jewels
In their own right, but slowly
They alight and fall to the ground
Their task complete
C. Longford

Daffodils

Gleaming, fair, gold daffodils
Are growing on the sunlit hills,
Under the trees and in the shade
In the woods and in the glade.

Oh, you splendid beauteous things,
Heralds of the lovely spring,
Stay a while until the sun
Does leave us on its course to run.

What a carpet of delight
You make as we pass out of sight,
And while the sun drops in the sky
The flowers nod and say goodbye.
Meryl A. L. Kelly

Caring

Can it really happen
Are people so unkind
To read of hungry children
And put it from the mind?

It should not bother us
It's all so far away
Forget all about it
And have a happy day

Yet those faces keep appearing
We cannot enjoy a meal
While realizing the suffering
That we could help to heal

Yes, we are only human
Starving faces haunt our dreams
Sadness lingers every hour
We cannot forget, it seems

So we decide to help

And give without delay
Suddenly we know
We will have a happy day
E. M. Walters

Black

No light
Black night.
So unfair
Black despair.
Pointed hat
Black cat,
Nose twitch
Black witch.
Not fair
Black hair.
Not a mate
Black hate.
Poke fun
Black pun.
Not amused
Black blues.
Prison cell
Black hell.
Enormous mole
Black hole.
Paula Jolly

The Lone Swan

Be gone be gone lone swan,
　As I watch you fly
Cross an Azure sky,
　Whilst I
A mere mortal
　Drive up the A1 at Seventy!
Be gone be gone lone swan
As you fly through the air
　without a care
The are no Restrictions up there!
Be gone be gone lone swan

Trevor L. N. Brigham

The Rainbow

I want to touch the rainbow,
But it's too far,
I want to get my hands on
the pots of gold.

　"The rainbow"
　"Oh rainbow"

It's got beautiful colour
It's got beautiful gold,
But I want to touch the rainbow
but it's too far to go.

S. Sayer

Love's Enchantment

Sunless was my life and being
As leaves on a withered autumn tree.
My heart, my arms empty until
You came with passion and love to fill.
You took me from the shore of dreams
Into love's enchanted reality.
Since first we met your eyes met mine
My heart has been forever thine.
Because we love each other
Just because you are mine
Every day seems brighter
Life seems more worthwhile.
If ever you should leave me
If ever you should want to go.
My heart would break in silence
I'd live in agony and woe.
Always I'll remember you love
Forget you I could never
Loving thoughts of you are woven
Deep through all my memories.

Polina Belle McCann

Trees

Trees hold so much beauty
As majestically they stand
Their branches so protective
Of all creatures on the land

In spring their buds burst forth
With shimmerings of green
Mother nature nurtures them
Until their blooms are seen

In the woods in summer
They shield us from the sun
Animals play around them
Far from the farmer's gun

Autumn sees their changing hue
And their leaves must fall
But though losing their glory
They still stand quiet and tall

Stark against the Winter sky
Like soldiers on their duty
Each day I marvel why
Trees hold so much beauty

J. Shuttlewood

Let Us All Live a Life of Love

Let us all live a life of love,
As pure as the clean white dove,
Flying gracefully up above,
All hate is overtaken by true love,
Below a pretty flower fox glove,
It springs up like the heart of love,
Green grass, water flows
Ducks appear as white as a dove,
Let us all, "forever"
Live a life of love.

Robert Courage

A Spider's Web

Watch a spider spin her web,
As 'round and 'round she goes,
Is she thinking as she waves?
Nobody really knows.

Life is like a spider's web
A created work of art.
Sometimes in life a storm appears
And tears your web apart.

At times like this,
Just pause and think
What would a spider do?
She'd just throw out
Some stronger threads
And weave her web anew.

Yona Geddes

Memories

Tears roll down her whitened face,
As she recalls her living hell,
The day she thought would never come,
That final sad farewell,

He held her hand,
He kissed her cheek,
He walked away,
He did not speak,

She wanted to run after him,
She wanted to shout out,
It's not supposed to end this way,
What is it all about?

She now just sits alone,
Thinks of how things used to be,
Of all the love he felt for her,
It's just a memory.

Victoria Gray

Young at Heart

Love begins to blossom
As trees come into bloom,
When nature takes a hand in things
Spring casts out the gloom.
Petals start unfolding
To face the morning sun,
Birds all sing upon the wing
Now wintertime has gone.
Prancing sunbeams flirting
With a soft warm gentle breeze,
As butterflies go dancing
Amid the lilac trees.
Lovers seeking romance
Delighting all who see,
With arms entwined and eyes a-shine
Embracing tenderly.
'Tis springtime, all the world awakes
To nature's fragrant bowers,
Enchanting all the young at heart
With the beauty of her flowers.

Margaret Malenoir

Pale in Comparison

She lit a cigarette
Biting her nails
A flawless silhouette
Changed only by the figures
Cruising by the roulette

Mark D. McConnell

Unhappy Wife

I wish that you and I were friends
As well as being wed.
The only time we're really pals
Is when we play in bed.
I work with you and think we're mates
Then something goes all wrong
You cast your wicked glance at me
And whiplash with your tongue.
We do not speak and talk it out
We fester on in silence
My heart is sad my mind confused
I wait conciliation.
You don't seem happy or content
With me, or even life
To me you're every thing one wants
A home, a bed, a wife.
I feel just like your whipping post
To bow when you say bend.
When all I ever wanted was.
To be your real best friend.

B. Cardnell

Pleasure in Any Sense

A sight can take your breath away
Beauty please the eye
Fond memory produce a tear
Or deepest, saddest sigh.
Perfume carried on the air
Pervade with fragrant scent.
Sweet taste give unexpected Joy
Or offer sustenance.
Pure sounds may tantalise the ear
Exquisitely recall
A melody, a symphony
Sometime heard before.
Whispered word, amusing jest
Delight the weary soul
Sparking wit or laughter
You cannot quite control.
Clasp of hand transfer with touch
Comforting and care
Offering the gift of love
To treasure, Precious and Sincere.

Gloria M. Phinn

Royal Scrap Book

I remember years ago
Being at school
We would all have a scrap look
The teacher would tell us
To look through old books and papers
And to cut out and collect
Pictures of the royal family
The queen mother, the queen
Princess Margaret and so on
It took a long time
To fill the scrap look
As there were hardly any pictures
Not like today
Now there are in the papers
Writing their stories in books
Never off the tele
Washing their dirty linen in public
You get so sick of seeing them
Strange how things change

D. Healy

Shadows

You said I was your shadow
Because I was always there,
Following every path you walked
And laughing at the jokes we shared.

You made the sun seem brighter
You brightened up my day,
But I never really understood
Why you left that day.

It was time for God to call you
I didn't say Goodbye
Time and time I asked myself
Why did you have to die?

You went to be with the angels
When I was very small,
Your shadow slowly disappeared
Leaving mine alone on the wall.

Now you are my shadow
You're there in everything I do,
And whenever I see that shadow
I always think of you.

Paula Bundy

Heatwave

The sun beats down relentlessly,
Beneath the ancient apple tree
The cat is sprawling lazily
Within a patch of shade.

A breath of warm air whispers past,
Beside me on the thirsty grass
A mist is forming on my glass
Of icy lemonade.

The blossoms hang their weary heads,
A mass of faded blues and reds
In dry and dusty flower beds
Under the blazing sky.

The birds are silent in the trees
In the cool shadow of the leaves,
The day dreams in the hum of bees,
And do so I.

Margaret George

Run Fox Run

Run fox run
Beware the mounted horse
Run fox run
Across the gauntlet course
Run fox run
Take heed the blowing horn
Run fox run
Reject the hunter's scorn
Run fox run
Away from baying hound
Run fox run
For sanctuary to ground

W. G. Purse

"Waiting"

Twisting, Blinking,
Blinking, Twisting,
Of you, I'm thinking;

Yawning, sighing,
Signing, yawning,
For you, I'm crying;

Tossing, Turning,
Turning, Tossing,
For you, I'm yearning;

Sleeping, waking,
Waking, sleeping,
How long, you're taking
to come home.

Pippa Clarey

Peace

Peace of mind
Body at rest
Leave behind
Your treasured best.

Heart fights no more
Trapped in cage
Life has reached
Its final stage.

Death is sleep
Sleep is rest
Rest is peace
Peace is death.
Flesh asleep
In quilted case
Pupils wide in
Whitened face
Rolled right 'round the back of head
Peace is with you when you're dead.

Louisa Rawle

Parasuicide

Death of style, style is oneself
Born of frustration
Invisible transparent sole
A nothing that's me!!
Claustrophobic in one sense
The walls of pressure doom paranoia
Closing in all around
Pain is reality a way of life
The first wound inflicted from a
blade of a knife
The screams torment crying of pain
It's a battle a restricted one
All done in vain
Gas Gullit free fall cross the mind
Pressure to great to handle
But I seem to survive.

Robert Page

Dawn

So many times I've watched the dawn
Break through another day.
Listened to the singing birds
Looking for their prey.
Dew sodden grass and hazy mist
Has fallen all around.
Worms that wriggle and find a way
Out from underground.
Assailants flock to pluck their prey
And carry to their nest.
Off in flight they go again
Looking for the rest.
For this is early morning
When all is fresh and new
Skies that change from black to red
And then to azure blue.
Clouds re-appear and take the place
Of stars that shone so bright.
This is the start of another day
That will roll on into night.

Ruth Steele

Elegance

Such a slender neck,
Brightness of white,
Glides on the water
As quiet as night.

Such serenity,
Full of grace,
The beautiful swan
Of nature's race.

Marlene M. Gilbert

"Winter Song"

Silent snowflakes, fall, fall.
Build a snowman, tall, tall.
Frosty moonlight, shine, shine.
North wind blowing, whine, whine.
Icy footpath, slip, slip.
Then comes the thaw, drip, drip.
Snowman melting droop, droop.
Clear the slush, scoop, scoop.
Winter's over sing! sing!
Crocus blooming spring, spring.

Patricia E. Nicholls

Confusing Decisions

I want to be a poet,
But don't know where to start,
I always find it easier,
To write straight from the heart.

I'll soon be starting college;
To polish up my knowledge;
I don't know what to take,
To get my first big break.

Maybe I'll take English,
Or Sociology,
But I want to be a poet,
So won't you please help me?

Susan D. Neill

Untitled

Once the candle stood alone
and filled the room with light.
Everything was shining,
it could even shine at night.

The yellow, like the sun
is turning into moon,
slowly it clouds over
and lightning strikes the room.

Now the candle's melting,
thunder steals its cry,
its body burnt to ashes
but still the flame survives.

The flame alone, grows smaller,
no longer does it glow.
Darkness is surrounding
No light will ever show.

Everything must change
for no longer is there light.
Without a candle, there's no flame.
Everyday is night.

Simone A. Bertrand

Words

Words can be nasty,
Causing sadness and pain.
Words can be puzzling,
and drive you insane.

Words can be happy,
Kind - with joy.
Words can be vulgar,
Words can annoy.

Words can be merry,
Hurting, when you're in a mood.
Words can be pleasant
Or the opposite, rude.

Words can be power,
All in a different way
Words are power,
In all that you say.

Mark Hopkinson

Untitled

My darkest hour came,
but God was there to greet me.
we played a little game,
He laughed a lot to see me.
He said "you come here often",
but he was pleased to see me.
How could I have forgotten,
what joy and love He brought me.
How we laughed that God and I,
I know he came to help me,
Now is time to say goodbye,
but he will never leave me,
for in my darkest hour.
He will be there to greet me.

Marilyn Norris

Fairwell Message

We have always been together,
    But now we are apart.
We cannot find the words to say,
    The pain that's in our hearts.

We have been through many things,
    The good times and the bad.
To us you are a special man
    A fine husband, loving dad.

We have never asked for miracles
    But today just one would do,
To leave a door wide open
    And see you walking through.

We would put our arms around you
    And kiss your loving face
For you are someone special
    Who will never be replaced.

And now the time has come
    For us to say goodbye
There won't be a day to pass us,
    When we don't think of you and cry.

Kay Frankling

Our Friend and Foe - The Sun

To sit and daydream is such fun
but please oh please not in the sun
A suntan really does not pay
for danger lurks within those rays

Just think of all the things we eat
that ripen in the sunshine's heat
We need the sun to maintain life
but it can also cause us strife

The sun is friend but also foe
so treat it carefully as you go
About your business and your leisure
to get a suntan is no pleasure

For danger lurks within those rays
and it's your skin that has to pay
The price is high. I do not lie
the sun can cause your skin to die

Sylvia Scott

Running on Empty

I tried to cry
but there was nothing wrong,
I thought I'd enjoy
but not for long,
I tried to smile
but it hurt my face,
I thought I'd be serious
I was all over the place,
Running on empty

G. Dawson

All Alone

I'm all alone,
By my self,
I'm on my own'
I'm on the shelf.

No one loves me,
No one's here,
I'm made of glass,
I shed a tear.

I'm an ornament
Of a pig,
I'm more lonely
Than you think.

I'm all alone,
By myself,
I'm on my own,
I'm on the shelf.

Sophie Walsh

Water World

I look deep down,
By the water inside,
Deep blue sea,
Yellow pebbles by,
Fishing, swimming, voices by,
I wonder why
I heard your voice
Now I wonder why
I not by your side.

Rachel King

To Doug "Once"

I once wrote a song,
called golden days,
that seemed never,
to come,
then I met you
my only one.
You bought sunshine
into my life
with all your heart
you gave to me
a love divine
warm like the sun.
I know, now that
my golden days
have come.

Patricia Lee

Sly Memory Stir

Oh how the pain of life
Can pierce one's very heart
And stab without a warning,
    Like the sharpest blade!
One moment - all bright joy -
    Then sly memory stirs.
The glowing candle flickers
And life grows dark and chill.
    The transience of joy
Is swift and crystal cold.

Lynette MacMahon-Wall

Escape

Silent entry into a silent world
Colourless odourless place
of no name
But the dream deceives
and the wind stirs my belief
the cold gives me heart
as the rain falls
Stopping short of reality
Quick exit to the real world

Lesley C. Alexander

Heavenly

Oh tiny sequins in the night
Casting silver specks of light,
On rich velvet deep and blue
Fading with the morning dew.
But where are you throughout the day
Do you sleep or turn away?
For when the sun is burning high
We see you not up in the sky.
Diamonds priceless and divine
Embedded in a celestial mine,
Gems and jewels that shine for hours
Wondrous beauty little stars.

Phillida Orr

Untitled

Ross Andrew,
Celtic, copper tones, rustic
Like autumn leaves and
Soft sea breezes
From the peninsula
Now a part of the whole
Forever in our soul.
Helping us, guiding us,
When no one else can.
A mirror of happier times to come
A daughter or a son
A promise that all will be well.
Time alone will tell
The whole story.
Ross has begun
Tranquillity

Patricia Corry

In the Magic of the Night

You gently shook my shoulder
Come look at this you said
What is it love, is something wrong?
I asked jumping out of bed.
What a sight awaited me
The moon was shining bright
There was silver water in the lough
'Twas the magic of the night.

A silence hung about the air
The clouds just wafts of smoke
While boats sat quietly waiting
Not a ripple broke
I stood with bated breath and watched
Absorbed this wondrous sight
I'd swear the moon was swimming
In the magic of the night.

Linda Fraser

Off on Our Hol's

'Are we nearly there yet?'
Comes a voice from the back,
'Not so long now pet
Why not take a nap?'

Two hours have passed,
We must be there soon.
'If you drive really fast,
We'll be there before noon.'

Gosh this is boring,
We want to have fun.
Play on the beach,
And soak up the sun.

So the sooner we get there,
The sooner we can begin.
But for the time being,
We're still travelling.

Lynne Ingles

Child of the Decade

Child of the Eighties,
Computer conscious
Technocrat:
Machine monitor
Star Wars veteran. Moon brat
Worldly wise,
All-knowing,
Too soon old;
Rights without duty,
Self above all,
Feelings grown cold.

Child of the Eighties
Bomb-scared,
Video-scarred,
Seeker of peace,
Lover of kittens,
Life-marred.
Wide-eyed dreamer,
Trusting tot,
Love-starved. Neglected, abused,
Adult-wary
Living is hard.

Rose Anne Durkin

War

Armies stomping ground
Cross countries far and wide
Guns slung over shoulders
Together side by side
Marching up mountains
Opposition not far away
They've left families and friends
Some won't see another day
Men marching for their country
Courage strong and brave
Loved ones sitting home
Hands still in mid-wave
Not so long ago
These boys had big dreams
To move and join the army
Medals dangling from seams
Now faced with cruel hard war
The worst experience ever
All blood and destruction
Losing lives forever.

Michelle Dobb

Will

Will

the tears that flow in
death console the
anguished heart that
beats no more.

Will

the warmth that emanates
from grieving souls heat
the cold tempered blood
that chills the still body.

Will

death become life
as
life becomes death
in this room of mourners.

Will

tomorrow (when it comes)
change that which has gone
before.
If only it will.

J. M. Hornsey

Birds

Feathered wings they fly so high
Diving in the deep blue sky
Colours of the rainbow
Their tails will flow
Falling like the pure white snow

Lesley-Ann Ross

The Other Side

Forlorn and lost, the spirit bear,
Descends the dark void of my despair.
Sightless groping, stumble, stark
Into still and soul-less dark.

Cries of anguish, tears of pain,
Thorns are hammered in my brain.
Joyless eyes, viewing sad,
Clawing fingers turning mad.

Give me strength to end my plight
For I have lost the will to fight.
Sleepless, restless, nights of woe,
Burdened mind sinking low.

Wasted body of no availing,
Shows the scars of my failing.
Celestial voice, please speak to me
And set my tortured spirit free.
For I know the peace I crave
Will be found in my grave.

Kenn Evans

In the Centre

In the centre of the green field
Deeply rooted and in bloom
A solitary flower yields
Her face up to the moon

In the centre of the flower
Glowing gold and framed with snow
Appears the stem from which it towers
Which will never let her go

In the centre stem of life
Like the flower growing strong
Lifting upwards, free from strife
How could anything go wrong

In the centre where the moon lies
Looking down upon with grace
A shadow casts the bright skies
And the flower turns her face

In the centre where the roots hold
Another flower will grow maybe
Framed in snow and glowing gold
A sol - i - tary DAISY

P. D. Pastides

Boots

I named him Rumplestilkskin
Each day he wandered by
A Youth with body so thin
Worn collar, tatty tie
Hair pony-tailed, lank
Baggy sweater, unwashed shirt
Eyes bleary, sunken, vacant
Faded denims covered in dirt
Black suede boots, scruffy and old
Unfastened, gaping, all splayed out
Eyelets torn and tongue lolling about
Straggling laces, caked in mud
Worn out heels and ankles bare
Weary boots, make a dull thud
In that Autumnal morning air
He plodded on towards School
Oblivious to my pitied stare
A sad reflection of anti-rule

Sandra Elizabeth Fox

Indestructible Eye

Hello Mr. Fly
Did you know?
That when we die
You and your kind
Will survive.
I wonder Mr. Fly
Were you designed?
Natures version
Of the little black box.
Will you remember Mr. Fly?
When all of this is gone.
Have you recorded
Our flight through time?
I think not.
So we must find peace
Or nought will remain.
But you Mr. Fly
And generations the same.
Trapped in the web
yet again.

Victoria Fisher

Peace for All

Lay down your arms you men of war
diffuse your lethal bomb
Our people do not need this grief
It's gone on far too long
Why can't you learn to live in peace
And trust in one another
and look upon the other man
as though he is your brother.
this act we will not tolerate
you know you can never win
For peace is what we're praying for
Go pray now for your sin.

D. S. Moss

War

War kills many
Diseases are spread
Famine kills more

Let there be no more war
Let us live in peace
Let us share our lands

All people are God's children
Whether we be white or black
Let us live in harmony

I hope one day people will see
The illogic of war
So we may all be granted,
Long life and prosperity.

Kathlynne Griffin

Children Everywhere

Children children
Everywhere
Darting here,
Rushing there
Adults saying
"Beware take care"
They're fun, they're loving,
And full of giving,
They tease, and please,
You're always forgiving,
And as they sleep
I think what joys.
Are all the little
Girls and boys
So please be patient,
And be kind,
To all the children
Far and Wide.

Karen Crewe

271

Face

Hey!
Does my face offend you?
Why do you all look away
So quickly
Look at me, in my eyes and
smile
Once upon a time I was like
all of you
Now it seems I no longer belong
to the norm
I am a person behind the scars
if you would only see beyond
this face of mine.

W. Simpson

Bank on It

Does she smile, no.
Does she speak, no.
You can bank on it.

Does she charge, yes.
Does she err, yes.
You can bank on it.

Does she ignore, yes.
Does she anger, yes.
You can bank on it.

Does she charm, no.
Does she help, no.
You can bank on it.

J. A. Carrington

The Doll

The doll rocks in its cradle,
Dreaming of life,
Wishing itself a real baby;
To laugh and to cry.

To eat and to grow;
And to learn how to walk,
To chase the cat;
And be taught how to talk.

But, the doll in its cradle;
Will never choose to be bought,
Because the doll in its cradle,
Is the doll with no thoughts.

Rebecca Jones

School

Ancient books, chalky:
Dust enclosed.
An edged floor.
Frail.
Furious in masses, nudging on.
Smells.
Swarming spaces,
Soft, scratching whispering.

Lucy Runacre

Hazel's Departure

Hark, upon the wind gently
For a storm thrush sings
As clouds go quickening by
A time of missing, of going
Of departure to another place
A quietness beckons
As if time were to stop
As if whispers were no more
But Hazel come again
With the dews of spring
Never to be forgotten
Always fresh as the
Thrush sings.

Peter Bland

My Space

This room has been a dwelling,
For my everlasting cries.
These four walls have heard,
My every sullen word.
This door has been my saviour,
From the distant world outside.
This silence has been my companion,
With whom I shared my life.

Ravia Begum

I Just Want to Know It

What would it be like to be
dying,
Running, fighting, slow walking or
flying.

I don't want to be it,
I just want to be know it.
Death.

Will it be like running through a
clump of trees
Or swimming through empty seas.

I don't want to be it,
I just want to know it.
Death.

Could you be living in a different
time zone,
Or in a strange world all alone.

One day I'll know it,
Some day I'll be it.
Death.

Zara Marie Gray

Spring

Oh winter's sun awaken now,
ease bulbs of wintry cold.
Warm, frost-speckled bough,
though the tree be very old,
feel youth bursting all around.

Excitement grows as
the Easter weekend nears.
Cameras eagerly wait as
daffodil and bluebell hears
that Spring is here at last.

Soft breezes, a little chill,
caress each bloom awake.
Green shoots, climbing still,
the breath of life to take,
sap rising to the bait.

Blues and golds burst with pride
eager to smile and sigh.
The Springtime merry ride
rushes to a summer high
and warm pictures tumble in.

Leonard R. Green

Nature's Bounty

Breathing in the fresh sweet air
Enjoying life without a care
The trees whispering in the breeze
The gentle humming of the bees
Drifting perfume of the flowers
That seems to linger on for hours
The twittering of the birds on high
And the grace of which they fly
The soothing rays of the warm sun
Children's voices having fun
The tinkling of nearby stream
A perfect day in which to dream
Nature's beauty does abound
So much to love is all around.

D. White

The Wretched Night

The silent space
Entered the blindness
Of the dark sinister night.
The air closed in on itself
And died quietly within its grasp.
A light blindingly
Struck the silence
And rendered it in two.
Outside air rushed in
To meet the wrenched night
And morning surrendered to its call
As day erupted to life.

Pam Helm

Untitled

I can hear your laughter
Feel the sadness and your tears
and hold you in my arms
to wish back all the years
your head on the pillow
is heavy counting sheep
'tis but gently in my bosom
I'll hold you while you sleep
warmly I caress your brow
so let your thoughts go deep
let me take away your troubles
for someone else to keep
never far away from you
I watch with loving care
So rest my son with peace of mind
    Your mother's always there.

Philip Green

Untitled

Five little faces
full of aims and graces,
my life my day,
"alas" no boy,
all shells and lace,
my pride, my life
I look into the faces
of my five little girls,
the fears and tears
of all the years,
vanish with one little hug.

Y. Lawrence

A Sacred Beauty That Was Meant!

A Crimson coloured butterfly
Fluttered passed my eyes
On its wondrous journey
Mingling with the flies.

I dreamed I was this butterfly
Free and flying high
Gracious as the drifting clouds
Fantasizing as I lie.

Greenery charmed the valley
Cool breezes soothed my face
The golden eye a-glowing
Swept me up in its embrace

Trees like emerald spires
Gentle humming from the bee
The beautiful blue of the river
Winding like a ribbon to the sea.

A mosaic of colourful flowers
Leaving a trail of scent
The desired inspiration of all
A sacred beauty that was meant!

Rose Grigg

Tranquillity

I sit and behold - Green leaves
Fluttering serene and oh! So Green
Each leaf unto the other
As child would caress its mother
Nature by its desire to please
Acknowledges man when he is at ease

H. W. Crouch

Our Cat

Running, jumping, skitter-skat,
Flying, leaping, that's our cat.
Every motion closely watched,
All who dare to move are scratched.

Purring gently, now at sleep,
Fur, tail, whiskers in a heap.
Bundle of love she now might seem
As she dreams of milk and cream.

Slowly swaying, every ounce
Ready for that playful pounce.
Growing curious every day,
I really think she's here to stay.

Into every little space
Look of mischief on her face.
Biting slipper, coat and hat
Yes, that really is our cat.

Some give cats a name of fame,
Others choose a name that's plain.
Not a "Ginger" or a "Fluffet"
Because our cat's name is "Muffet."

Lyndon Powell

A Memory

Many years ago I went
for a walk in the grass field
that was close to my home,
there we had a hen house,
newly cleaned out, door left open.

To my surprise something
must have frightened
one of the cows, to take shelter
it had rushed into the hen house,
knocking all perches down.

Getting turned 'round, standing
standing in the door way, facing
the out side world,
me not having a camera
in those early days
is why it is just a memory.

M. J. A. Britain

Easter

Tread softly in God's garden,
For Christ is resting there.
Now in peace He's sleeping,
freed from earthly care.

Tread softly in God's garden,
lest you disturb the womb
holds Christ for resurrection,
from death and sombre tomb.

A robin sweetly singing,
wakes life at dawn of day,
God's garden now is ringing,
In joyful roundelay.

Tread softly in God's garden,
the risen Christ walks there
His triumph crowned with glory,
His love beyond compare.

F. L. Hough

Lover's Lament

I rue the day that we must part
for I love you with all my heart;
but part we must; for I must die
an in the dust my body lie.

Mourn not for me when I am gone,
for life is joy, but not so long,
so happy memories are yours to save,
until you join me in the grave.

H. T. Hughes

Peace of Mind

The night has been so very long,
For one who cannot sleep,
It seems the dawn will never come,
To set my mind at ease.

I thought about the day before,
And of the things undone,
A smile, a kiss, or just hello,
Would have cheered a lonely one.

I thought of the mistakes I made,
And hope to put things right,
I saw the darkness pass away,
And watched the morning light.

O Lord, who hears our every prayer,
Please help me this new day,
To learn by the mistakes I've made,
And give me peace of mind.

E. H. Binkley

Supermarket Music

The tape was on - my ears attuned
For strains coming over sweetly.
Horror of horrors! Double-bass
was out of tune - completely.

Remainder songs were not too bad,
(If such is your musical taste.
For myself, I think they are
Of shopping time, a waste).

The 'music,' it goes on and on,
Making me morose.
When shopping's done I hasten home
To Mozart - big, big dose.

From Christmas carols, all of us
I'm sure, get quite a kick.
But - jazzed up 'Away In A Manger??'
Really, it's a bit thick!!

Do they really pipe this music
To encourage us more to spend?
It does not work - prestissimo
To exit our way we wend.

Norma Young

Showcase

Take a showcase of talent,
For those who wish to learn,
Opening many streets of life,
That may spell out,
This very useful word,
So many happy hours,
And seconds of each day,
That bring us pleasure,
In a very special way,
The source of this enjoyment,
Will always linger on,
In the minds of everybody,
And stay for time that's long,
Let this showcase of talent,
That lies in one and all,
Be there for us to remember,
And mostly to recall.

C. Hush

Death of a Spruce

Neatly pruned and trimmed,
forehead adorned with a red splash,
she pecks and pecks
deep holes into his trunk,
drains every sap of youth.

His stripped frame,
dried decaying leaves,
condemned to death.
With no remorse,
the woodpecker finds another tree.

Margaret Muldowney

Until

Bound without cause
forever and beyond,
till time is a memory
and endless abscond,
Where the moon and the stars
last flickers grow dim,
And the past the present
and the future begin,
Till near and far touch
emptiness has its fill,
my thoughts for you
will go from to until.

Wendy Jones

Long Lost Soul Mate

I know you
From another time;
And yet you don't know me
Or don't seem to

I do know you
From another place
And yet we have never met

Do you not recall
When we knew everything?
Could go anywhere?
Were aware of all time?
But chose to come here, now?

We were, then, as one
And are still
Beneath our human minds

Keith Beasley

Untitled

Colour is my world
How explain the days
Save as patterns built unpraised
of some great plan?
A jewelled day gives evening
a merging of troubled sea
With gentle opal cloud
Till night shuts all
in ebon night and gives us rest.

Nirah E. M. Davies

Splitting Hairs

Technically speaking
I drew blood today;
A thin red line
On your chin.
I didn't hold the blade
But metaphorically speaking
I held you at knife point
And I said
Please have a shave,
Your stubble cuts me.
So who cut whom?

Ruth Richards

The Probe

'Voyager' - to where?
From Eden to despair,
Forbidden fruit out there!
To know - consolidate, or
Primeval thoughts - exacerbate
Our slowly - slowly
Nurtured hopes of Paradise.
Exchange or not?
Firmament for permanent!
Plot on Earth's allotment.
This leafless track -
No looking back!
Wherein the flavour - without salt!
Probe not - for What!

R. H. Greedy

Wish You Were Here!

It's been a jam-packed day
From morning-noon-till night
The chores accomplished - sure
Fell into bed and hit the hay
Wrapped into thoughts - held tight
The door now closed - once more

So where are you - to share
With me - this ordinary event
To check - that all is fine
To demonstrate your care
Oh - this was never meant
'Cos you were always mine

Today I've said goodbye
To my dearest friend
I wish - that you were here
Now I shall have to try
This broken heart to mend
And conquer all those fears
  wish you were here

A. Jasdrow

In Captivity

I cannot escape
from the bars in the cage,
Locked in for hours
My mind in a rage.

Emotions are none
My heart is cold,
Can't chance the break
Of letting my wings unfold.

Wish away a dark drab room
Feeling cold and bare,
Full of doom and gloom
Search for the beauty, love and care.

Fly to the place
I've loved so long,
Soar up with grace
And sing my beautiful song.

Let me live and love
And be free to do.
Like any other dove
what I wish to do.

Ruth Gardner

Faded Flower

Praying here in this shower,
As if a dying faded flower.
Will a downpour restore my form?
Will I ride out this storm?
Will my skies once more be blue?
Will the sun warm me through?
So I may blossom into view,
Showing all my colours true.

A. Little

Memories

I sit here on the beach,
Full of golden sand,
An opal blue sea a calm breeze,
What a sight to adore,
As I look to the sun,
Reflections bouncing along the sea,
Like children in ... the rain,
Funny how life is,
Once a long time ago,
I sat here as a child,
That was before,
Before that life drowned,
A helpless silhouette,
I had to come just once again,
Just to see,
How much life has changed,
Not much,
But the life isn't here anymore,
But her soul is here ..... not alone.

Rebecca Meade

Marmy

Do's and don't's
Given with love
Shelter when it rains
A hand to hold
A friend to behold
A place to lay my head
A pick me up
When I fall down
A medal when I'm good
So much love
And laughter too
Sadness and tears as well
A wealth of memories
You've shared with me
My life
I owe to you.

Lorraine Hobson

Winter

The garden is sleeping
God's put it to rest,
if only we people
would put it to test,

There would be serenity
surrounding us all,

Peace and tranquillity
would descend on us all,

But true life is different
we go with the flow,
mistakenly thinking
it's the right way to go,

If only we stopped and
thought it all out,

It's not worth the
trouble anxiety and doubt.

M. Thomas

New Toilet Roll

Between this morning and tonight
I had a punchless sit down fight
When of all things I lost control
While trying to open a toilet roll
Pulling this way and pushing it that
Producing streamers both thin and fat
My thoughts went hazed!
My eyes went glazed!
Then fuming on the toilet seat
I bit the roll and lost two teeth!

Patrick Sutton

The Dandelion

Why when we stand so firm and bold?
Golden sunshine to behold,
You frown on us, don't ask for much,
Even shudder at our touch.

Our leaves do have tooth-like edges,
They're filling spaces under hedges
Golden bright we do not sting
To pick us up, no need to cringe.

Why do you all dislike us so?
A dandelion our name doth show,
Were strong and never ever fail,
Even in the strongest gale.

We multiply, yes, every day,
Always renewing on the way
And when a fluffy ball we seed,
You throw us out just like a weed.

So when you see a field of gold,
Remember what to you we've told,
If no-one else, the bees love us
Before becoming a field of fuzz.

D. C. Wilbraham

"The Last Breakfast"

He gives her a morning kiss.
Has a shower and a shave.
She starts down the stairs
And tries to be brave.

Last night she heard him whisper
Another woman's name.
Turns the kettle on to boil
The humility and the shame.

He's singing in the shower now,
Such a happy song.
Puts the bread on the toaster
Wondering where it went wrong.

Pressing in the new suit
He just happened to buy.
Food is ready now
She's trying not to cry.

He gives her a Judas kiss
Smiles and turns his back.
Breakfast and marriage over
She climbs the stairs to pack.

Terri Dooley

Man Watching

As a moth,
he chooses his
own flames with whom he
will dance, and
extract the essence
of his very Being.
Should the flame burn
he will never return,
yet when dancing
from flame to flame,
need either choose
to extinguish their gifts
in his absence?
He maps his flight
through stars of the night . . .
Flame to Flame,
wanting all, needing some,
dependent on none.
Free to be free
forever.

J. McLellan

The Snowman

Most years he comes to our house,
He fills us with delight.
He wears a hat of blackest black,
His suit is always white.

He never steps inside the house,
'though once 'tis true he did,
I didn't know he'd disappear,
I was just a kid.

I put him by the kitchen fire,
Thought I'd warm him with a cuddle.
Before I'd took my mittens off,
He was just a puddle.

'Midst tears of disappointment,
As Mother mopped the floor,
She made me promise not to warm
My Snowmen any more.

A. C. Dorling

The Entertainer

With the sound of applause
he retains centre stage.
The performance begins again,
his usual act.

The audience are in stitches,
he is the crème de la crème.
His energies are boundless.

As his confidence explodes,
he prepares his newest trick.
As he gains his balance,
he looks up to the spectators,
he grins.

He holds his head up high,
still oozing confidence.
His hands reach parallel height,
he grins again.

And then he does it.
One step forward, unaided.
This is the beginning of a lifetime,
he is learning to walk.

Laura Stilwell

Friends

Friends are always there,
 Hearing what you say,
Friends are always there,
 Every single day.

My friends are really great,
 They look after me,
My friends are really great,
 They care for me.

My friends are really great,
 Because they're always sure,
My friends are really great,
 They're never immature.

Lesley-Anne Ferrol

Beg, Steal or Kill

For my children I live
 And for my children I'd die,
They're everything to me
 And God knows why.

He gave them to me
 To love and care for,
Protect them from harm
 In His guidance forever more.

I'd beg or steal
 And even kill for them,
God bless them always
 And give guidance to them.

J. Diana Clark

I Think of You

It would be true to say
I think of you
With each sunrise,
With each sunset,
And many times between . . .

Mary Kordiak

Where Are They Now?
(A Cat's Lament)

He sits alone
He waits, he waits,
His gentle eyes alert.
Where are they now?
It hurts, it hurts,
So sorry, so forlorn.
His lonely vigil
Will, he knows
Bring its own reward
To see the smiling faces
Of the family he adores.
He sees them now,
He runs, he runs,
He feels their gentle touch.
He purrs, he purrs
His happy song.
He is alone, no more.

Rosemary A. Ingles

Her Golden Prison

Her dream house was her prison,
Her children iron bars,
Weighed down with cares and sorrows,
She could not wander far.

Takes two to make a child,
I hear you softly say,
What then of the father,
Died or gone astray.

She never liked to burden him,
He had his share to do,
Gardening and working hard.
To see the family through.

One more year of scrimp and save,
Of nothing much to wear,
Seeing others look and say.
Oh no, another on the way.

For a while all will be joy,
It is a precious girl or boy.
Presents come in, flowers as well,
To make the happy parents swell.

Margaret Craton

Candlelight

The answer is there, I am sure
hidden within the candlelight
I watch the flame as it dances
piercing the darkness of the night

A tall, noble phallus of wax
yet useless without its inner core
and an ember to set its heart ablaze
trimmed to burn more and more

Flickering fires reaching up
bright yellow, green and blue
casting their light all around
covering me with a golden hue

Seductive, alluring, drawing me in
but if I get too near I shall burn
a wonderful enigma, a dazzling sight
I can only sit and dream, and yearn

Michael D. Kearney

Untitled

I will soon be 73
I bet you wish that you were me
My teeth are not all my own
In this respect I am not alone.
I cook, I sew I clean, I paint
A lazy one is what I ain't
Drugs, cigarettes and drink
Are not for me
I'll try to be a Healthy 93.

B. L. Moore

King of the Air

Poised on a lonely crag
high about the forest
far from seeing eyes
stood the golden eagle
alert as ever, like
majesty.

Bright of eye and distance
a head so strong and proud
surveying all around him
his plumage golden brown
his sharp eyes searching
for his prey.

With wings outstretched
and his sharp claws eager
to gather that poor hapless
creature who dares to come
within the sight of that
magnificent golden eagle.

Vera Stevens

Nights Like This

Where drinking men
hold sway
and laughter
hop-scotches around the room,

Nights like this
I miss
laughter that crinkles
blue Scottish eyes,

calling me, calling me,
calling me from the cold

of Northern winters
and cold Southern
scruples that
suffocate me.

Nights like this
I miss
the silk of skin
knitting my nights into mornings

and calling me, calling me,
calling me softly out of sleep.

Kate St. John

Outside Asda!

"But why?" I asked.
"I had to." He said.
"Drugs?" I asked.
"Society." He said.
"Too much?" I asked.
"Too much." He said.
"But your fans?" I asked.
"Rock 'n' Roll is dead." He said.
"But we love you." I whined.
"You love Oasis." He said.
"But you are the King." I pleaded.
"I am going." He said.
"Elvis! No!" I screamed.
"I am dead . . ." he said.

Tamsin C. Jones

275

The River Runs Wide

Sometimes we strive to understand
How life a painful process looms
A challenge to our every plan
And hovers there with tireless gloom.
Sometimes the river runs too wide
To ever build a bridge across,
And farther still the other side
Which beckons all to feel its loss.
The moons reflection in a pool
Within the grasp of those who dream,
Appears so magical, so cool,
But all is not what it may seem.
The snowflake falling from the sky
A wonder ready to explore,
Is captured only by the eye, because
Once touched, is there no more.

Milinda Elizabeth

My Stepping Stone

I march along the land,
How soft to my feet, the sand.
Waves crashing before me,
Out into the world I see.

I stand and stare,
Seagulls swoop through the air.
They mock and Jibe,
Giving sympathy vibes.

I sit and cry,
Tears fall from my eye.
Around and within,
My soul left sinking.

A breeze, a flutter,
People pass, with small talk chatter.
The scathing water,
Only, I'm compelled to alter.

The sun doesn't shine,
I grasp at a life, which isn't mine.
Torn and flared,
I reach out, but I'm scarred.

Sandra Godley

My Wife

"My Wife" is just a little phrase
I very often say,
Yet always with a special warmth
And in a special way,
For more and more I realize
That you're the dearest part
Of every special plan I make,
Each dream within my heart,
So every time I say "My Wife"
I say those words with pride
That is why the love inside
I simply cannot hide.

A. J. Mabbott

Untitled

It was a heavy day in winter
I was feeling tired and low.
The stressful vibrations of the
crowd as they bustle to and fro.
Quietly permutating through the
town, softly soothing, calming.
A young man stood, guitar in
hand, face full of life, as he
was slowly strumming.
I stayed awhile and listened,
refreshed, senses sharpened.
My step now seemed more purposeful
as the distant rhythm faded from
my ears but not my mind.

M. G. Townsend

I Don't Know What to Do

I don't know what to do
I'm stuck in the middle,
like a tied up shoe
It's all because of this one sum
I think this one,
must be the hardest one of all
the other ones are easy
I just don't know what to do
oh come on Lord tell me this one
what is two plus two.

Odelle Deal

The Veteran

In silence he stood
In front of the wreaths
Remembering the war
He fought for our peace

His comrades he lost
He remembers them still
And will continue to do so
Until time stands still

But let us all remember
This man standing here
As with his comrades he fought
For his country so dear

Our memories of him
Shall continue forever
As for his today
Gave us our forever.

Paula Jeffrey

"Darker Road"

In the dead of night in Darker Road,
Hurried footsteps move close by.
Can it be that she is followed?
In the silence a sudden cry!

Twisting shadows grasp and tear,
But then a tension settles in,
In solitude too much to bear,
Who committed such a sin?

Running footsteps move away,
From the scene of crime.
The pool of blood is here to stay,
That will stain in time.

About that girl no one cared,
Who sadly lost her life.
No one asked how she fared,
What happened to that knife?

Simple crimes of everyday,
Do not linger in our mind.
Who is it that must pay?
The family of the find.

Paul Kennedy

Untitled

Life is a strange thing,
I found out too late
The man I thought I loved,
I then began to hate
But now my feelings are different,
And I wonder why they are
It seems to me so often,
I was reaching for a star
Time heals and time goes on,
You learn every day and night
Not to take things too serious,
And you will definitely see the light.

Lorraine Fisher

Paul I

Yes, he is almost near
I can feel him and smell him
And almost hear
His soft sweet voice
Of dulcet tone,
His gentleness directed
At me alone

Those fleeting times
We spent together
Unplanned so short
Drifting by as a feather,
Sometimes embarrassed
Yet surely won
Love, heaven sent
Then, but now returned
My beloved son,
(Goodnight my angel)

Patricia Tomkins

Along the Moon

Along the moon
I can see
A thousand lives
A thousand trees
For in that moon
There is a light
I need to find
I need to fight
Around this place of humble breed
Lie thirsty hearts of certain needs
But neither of these ever found
A place of virtue
A world so round.

Along that sister of a moon
My heart is like a feather
I do not need to breathe no more
I am blind by it forever

I would like to see a world so high
But neither would I feel
That I would ever go that far
I am better standing still.

Marcia Dinkovski

Waxing and Waning

A silvery white crescent.
Is she bowing to me
So slim and genteel
A little more time and,
She blooms to a cheerful full face,
Surely it's me, she shyly smiles at
I smile and bow in return
Slowly she turns and waves
Once more slim and genteel
Then darkness and she is gone

C. Fieldson

Brother

As I open my eyes,
I see your pain and sorrow -
as if I have been in another world,
where you can't enter, or borrow.

Your big sunken-in eyes
look at me helplessly,
searching for an answer.
Why me? I hear you cry.
but the best I can do is try.

Those words echo in my ears.
day and night, I hear you cry.
I want to help you - really I do -
So give me your hand and I will
come to you.

Sara Evans

Tranquillity

Silence is golden so they say
I dream away a springtime day
To listen to a chirping bird
A finer song no one has heard
To watch her building her tiny nest
She pauses, and stops, for a rest
Then off she goes, quick as light
Oh so graceful in her flight.
I see buds forming on fruit trees
Soon there's blossom for the bees
To pollinate and make things grow,
Soon the grass I will have to mow.
The sun shines down upon my face
I feel its warmth and its embrace
I doze and reflect amidst this dream
While time is silent and serene.

Sheila Merriman

Thought Dog

In the darkness of the room,
I imagine a shadow.
I can't picture what it is.
It starts to come closer,
Its shape becomes clearer.
As I stare at it I realize,
The shape is a dog.
The room becomes lighter,
Big brown eyes stare at me.
I stretch out my hand to touch it.
I can feel its warm breath,
In front of my cold hand.
Out of the window,
The moon is so bright
I have to look away.
I look back at the dog.
It's gone,
But I can still hear
The pitter patter of its feet
Fading into the darkness.

Suzy Tubby

The Rose

From the calm of my room
I look out on the gloom.
The sea once so blue
Has mirrored the hue
Of the charcoal grey sky
The fishing boats race by
Heading for the safe shore.
The palm trees bend and sway
To survive another day!
Then the rain arrives
And the red rose strives
To emulate the palm tree;
Something it can never be.
Due to Fate's fickle hand
It's a stranger in a foreign land.
At the end of the storm
The rain soaked petals have fallen
On the ground, left and right
A heartbreaking sight
To a stranger in a foreign land.

Stephanie Callaghan

Lonely

When I am lonely, I am sad
It makes me feel really bad
When I am lonely, I am shy
I begin to cry
When I am lonely, I am hurt
It makes me feel like a piece of dirt
When I am lonely, I feel remote
I feel I need to smoke
When I am lonely, can't you see
You are all that matters to me

Laura Charlton

Our Secret

They tell me
I must close the door,
I must not cry and weep no-more

They tell me
Time will heal
The pain
And I will start
To live again

How can I
tell them
Little-one
An empty shell
I have become

That all my
happiness and love
And dreams of life anew,
I had gathered
them together
And I buried them
with you.

Millie Whitney-Holmes

Memories of Dad

Last night, as I lay dreaming
I saw a wonderful sight.
A little girl was walking
Holding her dad's hand so tight.
The little girl was laughing,
Her dad he beamed with pride.
Then the image faded,
And I awoke and cried;
I lay there thinking quietly
Of the times I shared with you,
And of how much you loved me,
And how much I loved you too.
You did your best to teach me
The right way from the wrong.
You gave me hope and courage
And the strength to carry on.
You gave your knowledge and wisdom
You helped me to grow
That's why I'll keep on loving you
As the years, they come and go

Tina Atterbury

Death of an Oak

Who weeps for the oak tree
I saw them fell today
Some men just came and axed it
And then they walked away

Who will even ask
What stood there yesterday
Now the men have felled it
And taken it away

Gnarled rugged weather struck
Has stood this mighty oak
Twisted old but beautiful
And sheltered many folk

I'll miss this oak tree
As I pass this way again
Remembering all the shelter
That its great boughs gave

I'll weep for the oak tree
I saw them fell today
I saw them come and axe it
And simply walk away.

Markina Dawson

Physical Contact

Aroused to violence
I sense the fear
Anything is possible
It's physical that's clear

Sex is no more
Violence is contact
Warmth overwhelms me
And hits out through fear

The aftermath is quiet
Sorrow overwhelms
A damaged relationship
Beyond repair
Conversation flows.

Linda Benn

My Life

My life is flashing by me
I stand and watch it pass
Oh, how I wish I could stop it
From passing by so fast
Each day they say I'm older
Each day I see it too
I haven't done a thing in life,
I really wanted too
How I wish I was young again
Free and without a care
But wishing one's life away
Leads only to despair
I am a lonely person
I choose that way to be
I feel such sorrow inside
That makes me miserable, you see
My life isn't how I want it
I just don't seem to fit
My life is filled with darkness,
and places that are unlit.

P. Pegg

Road to Calvary

May we tread the road to Calvary;
    In His footstep's plant our own,
Let His spirit guide and purify,
    And melt our hearts of stone

Let us seek in true surrender
    To make His life our own;
To follow His example
    And never more to roam.

From the love that seeks to save us
    May we never turn aside
Let us seek our true redeemer
    And swallow all our pride

Let us humbly serve the master
    And repent of all our sins,
That by His mercy and his power
    We may be truly cleansed

We will know true joy and peace then
    His strength along life's way
With grace to serve each other
    To work, and love and pray.

H. A. Timms

God Send Your Blessings

God send Your blessing from above
In return we send out love
Help us to do the things we should
Unto others be kind and good
In darkness will You show the way
Our faith and trust
Will never stray
Forgive us for the wrong we do
As only a servant
We are to You

Rita R. Garcia

Peace

Whenever we seek it,
It becomes harder to find.
Wherever else we search
We should look in our mind.
For that's where we'll find it,
For that's where it bides
Within our own hearts is where
Our own peace resides.

Valerie Jennings

My Favourite Things

Whenever I feel low or sad
I think of days gone past
And all those special moments,
Which all my life will last.

There are so many favourite things
I'm able to recall,
Which cheer me up and make me laugh
When times begin to pall.

The fun I had on holidays,
Which took me far and near
And memories of a happy home
With folk I held most dear.

The family ties were closer then,
More freedom for the young
And shows with lasting music scores
Were always being sung.

My favourite things are there inside
To pick out one by one
And each day, when it's dark and drab,
I bring out my own sun.

Margaret Hollis

Lanzarote

From 8 o'clock to 1/2 past 4
I work in a factory it's such a bore
Day dreaming my life away
Living from holiday to holiday
I dream of a far off sunny land
Which has volcanic ash for sand
Where palm trees grow at every door
Of water sports and sangria galore

I dream I walk the beach all day
Selling refreshments to pay my way
I hope one day to leave behind
Dullness for the bright sunshine
To walk in paradise and live my days
On the island of Lanzarote

H. Morris

"For You"

If I were fog
  I would dissipate
If I were river
  I would evaporate
If I were mountain
  I would melt
If I were rain
  I would cease
If I were fire
  I would extinct
If I were star
  I would slip away
If I were thunder
  I would be silent
But I am only myself
  Who even dead
Your love in my heart
  Will live forever
My pain is heavy, my means is vain
  My tears abundant, will never end.

Naima Bichbiche

Smile, Smile, Smile

Look at the bright side
Live life to the full,
Love all God's children
Let no one take ill;
Greet others with a smile
Making their days worthwhile,
You'll find that you are happier
Having made another smile.

Mary Price

Al

If you were my Valentine
I would hug my knees
Go on all threes
and kiss your lips with vigour:
I know however, your idea of love
is so completely different
that I would have to compromise
and hug your chest
and this is the best
I could undo my feet
and feel really neat
and kiss you through and through
with a passion so good
you would feel in the mood
For a loving - of sorts
That cannot be bought
If you were my Valentine.

Susan Kirk

A Living Will

Do not prolong my life
If in living I grow weary
of the pain
I have breathed a million hours
All in the blink of an eye
I have laughed and cried
Shared joy and sorrow
I have given love
and been blessed by love
Cry no tears
When it is my turn to go
For we are of the circle
That has no end
Do not tie me here
with your potions and your pills
Rather
Free my soul
For I would walk amongst stars
And kiss the wind.

Marion Golaup

The Last Letter

Dear Grandmother,

Now you have passed away
I'm hurting deep inside
Tears are falling everyday
And it's so hard to find
The strength to live life through
Without you here with me
So many memories of you
Remaining clear to see
But now I realize
You're an Angel up above
Among the clear blue skies
I'm surrounded by your love
And your shining guiding light
Is the sun on a cloudy day
On a lone star burning bright
Is where I'll find you, Lily May

Your Loving Granddaughter

Simone A. Peveri

Certainty

Come what may
I'll see the day
When flowers bloom
And skies aren't grey.

Come what may
I'll see the sun
On a summer's day
When life is fun.

Come what may
I'll see the trees
Change their colour
In the autumn breeze.

Come what may
I'll see the snow-
A pure white blanket
On the ground below.

Come what may
I'll see these things
Whilst the world in chaos
Only sorrow brings.

Toni Cox

Who'll Buy My Time

It's far too old
  I'll throw it out
Or take it
  To a dealer.

This clock's for sale
  Can we do a deal?
No, it's not antique
  And the dials not real.

Then your judgement
  Is impaired I fear
As it's kept good time
  For eighty year.

You can't keep time
  Only record it
Besides I don't buy time
  I only use it

And you are using up
  What's mine
And that clock on the wall
  Says it's closing time.

Sheila Makin

Flowering Bulb

I am a little flowering bulb
I'm put in a box and put on hold
in the spring when it's not too cold
they put me in a garden hole.
I'm covered with nice warm earth
until it's time for my rebirth.

First my green stem will appear
it's my first time out this year
first some rain and then some sun
now my flowering has begun.

I started with a nice tight head
now my petals start to spread
gently, gently open wide
now you see the full inside.

Busy bees come flying by
diving down from the sky
taking pollen from my face
to a very special place
off they go to mummy bee
making honey for your tea.

Susan Caile

Daydream

Let us rise above,
Into the cool night sky,
And depart from this disastrous
world.
To a place where to hate is unknown
And love is everything.

If only if were true,
As I wake to the harsh reality
of our society.
It was all but a dream
But dreams are sweet
So dream on dreamer.

Lisa Feather

Think?

Think of all the people
In the foreign lands
Think of all these people
Their lives in our hands

In all the third world countries
Where food is very low
No fresh and healthy water
Just sand and dust will blow

These people, they are hungry
But live for days on end
Why do they carry on?
When none will ever tend

They're not just other kinds
But humans, just like us
Because they are so hungry
That's why some make a fuss

Some people love and care
Some have a heart of stone
Look at these poor people
They are jut skin and bone

Skye Scott

My Ball

I've got a ball,
It's Black and White.
It bounces well
and makes good flight.

I've got some boots,
They're Black and White
I use them well
and kick with them right.

I've got some fans,
They're Black and White.
They scream all day
and shout all night.

Scott D. Shell

Age of Wonder

Have we travelled too far
In the age of the motor car
Contamination of winds in tides
Synthetics and pesticides

Polluted rivers, acid rain
Will radiation leak again
How far should we progress
With natural balance under stress

A new language rules our lives
Evidence of how man strives
For micro chips and laser beams
Atoms and researching genes

Advantage for the minority
Scientists hold the key
Can nature answer to our call
To re-dress the balance for us all

B. E. Eyre

Summer Breeze

The trees shimmering
in the bright Summer sun,
the leaves dancing
like ballerinas on tip toes,
the branches swaying
in the breeze,
acorns falling gently
to the ground,
squirrels jumping
from branch to branch,
grabbing acorns,
storing them in their mouths,
scurrying around
to find a secret hiding place,
to store them
during their long Winter's sleep,
until they wake again
in the Spring.

Linda Casey

Love

Love is courting
Love is marrying
Love is having children
Love is a missed heartbeat
When unexpectedly meeting
Love is caring and sharing
Love is saying
After thirty-seven years
"I Love You"
- on your Death-Bed

R. B. D. Dorian

Soaring High

Soaring High
In the darkened sky
The land just an outline below
The mountains so tall
Are shadows all
And the lochs, like big eyes glow

Circling 'round
Watching the ground
With its patches of light and dark
There's snow on the hill
And all is still
In the distance the song of the lark

Now comes the dawn
And homeward I turn
For my body in bed does still lie
But when night comes again
Then my spirit will reign
And my soul will go on
Soaring high.

Pat Munto

Time

I walked alone in the garden;
In the hush of the evening calm;
So close were the joys of nature.
The sweet night touched my arm.
I looked to the sky,
And the starry way.
Knowing the Lord was there.
His voice was the voice,
of the birds' last song;
His breath was everywhere.
The night dew sparkled.
Where His feet had trod.
The wind sighed,
In a moment of time.
For the time that had gone -
And time to be -
Was caught in this heart of mine.

Rosemary Goram

A Devil's Birthday

One early morning
Mr Devil got out of bed
and said what day is it today!
Gosh it is my birthday!

What shall I wear
I think a coat of green
But what shall I eat
I think two fried boys!

Michael Lloyd

Pondering

We are but a tool,
In the great scheme of things,
So brief is our time here,
Such changes it brings.

Why are we here?
Is it the wonder we have,
Does fate lay our pathway?
Dictate hate and love.

For some - yes perhaps,
The ones who don't mind,
That life washes over them,
Leaves them behind.

But time is so short,
And this world is so vast,
Push on for the future,
Don't cling to the past.

Your life is for living,
Only one chance you get,
Ensure that you use it,
No time to regret.

Paula Martin

"The World Around Me"

Happiness cannot be found today
  In the world around me
the things that people say
  their words surround me
Wish I could fly away
  a broken wing grounds me
I don't want to stay
  not when sorrow hounds me
My dreams have gone astray
  Life, it just confounds me
It's a terrible price to pay
  It really does astound me
Can't keep the wolves at bay
  and now they gather 'round me
I fall to my knees and pray
  but black depression has found me
I feel my mind begin to fray
  as life continues to wound me.

Paul Crudgington

The Sun

The Sun rises early in the morning
It spreads its golden glow then
travels far across the land
To welcome all the people there
To share its warmth and glowing care.
The flowers wake to get their fill
Happy faces we all see, smiling,
laughing, full of glee
The Sun I find just - seems to make
The people happy in "Limbo State"
As evening gathers the sun goes down
people rest contented now
To watch the "Sunset" on the Bay
glowing gold, red the light
Gives a picture of true delight
Promising a bright tomorrow
Like to-day, no time for sorrow

D. Campion

Today

There's not enough Love or kindness,
In this wicked world today.
No one cares for each other,
As they did, in my youngest days.
Everyone helped each other,
Their doors were open wide,
To the Butcher, Milkman, Baker,
As they called 'round each day,
Good morning, Please and thank you,
Were the greetings of each day.
Now, all these decencies,
Have passed along the way,
Oh, for dear old England,
With all its Pride, and Joy.
The England we're proud of,
With its kindness Love and Joy.
The England I grew up in,
When I was a boy.

A. S. Moore

Early Morning Travel

I look up into the sky
Into the unknown.
Dawn is breaking.
Patches of dark cloud
Make mercurial shapes
Against the blue back cloth.
Suddenly in the far distance
A redness glows
Amid the silhouettes of the trees
And hump-backed hills.
The lights of a nearby town
Twinkle and dazzle
As the bus ambles past.
I am still in a semi-somnolent state
But the beauty of the awakening day
Stirs my emotions.
I feel overawed
By some ethereal being
But happy to be alive!

Lorraine D'or Stubbs

The Lonely One

My life is a shambles, my life
is a mess,
I am wandering in a wilderness,
Each day brings no hope.
I often feel I cannot cope,
Dear Lord, hear my prayer when I
cry to thee to pity me.
And give me strength to hold my own,
in the fight for self-esteem,
For it would seem, I am all alone.

B. J. Staveley

Jewel

The jewel in my eye,
is not a diamond in the sky,
nor the fields of emerald green,
mine's the most precious ever seen,

With many a treasure to be told,
it's not silver, platinum or gold,
I wear no necklace or ring,
yet of its beauty I sing,

There's onyx, black as night,
and crystals with colours alight,
but even rubies cannot compare,
my jewel is clearly more rare,

Sapphires like the darkest sea,
Still mine means more to me,
offer me pearls by the ton,
every time I'll take my son.

Marina Jane Rowe

Dark Don't Find Me Here

In this state of grief,
In this state of fear,
In my state of shock,
Dark don't find me here.

The death was sudden,
Yet not a tear,
My own kind of grieving,
Dark don't find me here.

With you so close,
And the reaper so near,
One more thing,
Dark don't find me here.

On the brink of discovery,
At the edge of fear,
On the brink of my sanity,
Dark don't find me here.

My fear subsides,
As death draws near,
Insanity conquers my world,
And the dark will never find me here.

Stuart Earle

Poles Apart

My fading sunset
is your breaking day
I lay down to dream
of a kiss far away

The Arctic Tern
shall carry my love
soon will you hear him
as he calls from above

Jet streams to carry
my hopes upon air
no more should I dream
for you will be there

Degrees, Minutes, Seconds
that convert into time
my love stand before me
your embrace to be mine

Sharing one sunset
no more poles apart
will you lighten my burden
will you lighten my heart.

Terence Mooney

A Life of Meaning

Life is such a wonderful thing
It can grow from the earth
Animals and humans too
Bring life through giving birth,

It's just like a miracle
When plants and flowers grow
Birds are chirping, dogs barking
And children play to and fro

The circle of life never stops
When it stops again it's starting
As a life begins
One is also parting

They say there is no eternal life
I don't believe that's true
Spirits and souls carry on
And live instead of you

But there's no rush to say goodbye
Live life for each day
And respect all the many things
You'll have along the way.

Michelle Thompson

My Granddad

When I visit my granddad
It isn't quite the same
I cannot hear him laugh
or sing
Nor watch his soccer game.

When I visit my granddad
there's no one sitting there
just his favourite slippers
Under his favourite chair.

When I visit my granddad
my heart is full of pain
for he is no longer with us
And I want him back again.

The next time I visit Granddad
I'll be as old as he
Because we will be in heaven
And he'll look after me.

Linsey Marie Champion

Rules of the Game

It will not last a twelve month,
   It may not last a week,
But while the game is on, my love,
   Let's speak as lovers speak.

I'll kiss and stroke and rouse you,
   Your heart I will not seek.
I know that lust is just for fun,
   But so want you to speak.

I moan and groan with sex words;
   You shout when at the peak.
The game is good, but, oh my love,
   Just speak as lovers speak.

I know that vows are broken
   When muttered cheek to cheek.
Undying love is never found,
   But let's pretend and speak.

I give to you, I'm loving;
   Show me your softer streak.
And while the game is on, my love,
   Just speak as lovers speak.

P. Kirkman

Runaway

In the hills I walk
It's quiet here
No need to talk
I hear the waves crashing
Crashing against the rocks
I stand for a minute
A minute to think
Maybe I should go home
Home to all the pain
It's a long walk
Too long . . .
This is my home now
There's no evil here
Just what I see
And what I hear.

Theresa Terris

Recognition

With considerate pity and disgust,
Looking upon myself
To see not the appearance
But that of within.
In the darkest of corners,
In the deepest of soul,
A scar never to be healed.
A permanent fragment of memory
Wished to be washed away,
Where the silence is no longer sound.

Kaitlin Milford

My First Easter

It was my first Easter,
It was really very fun,
I got a chocolate Easter egg,
A Mr. Blobby one.

Upon this merry holiday,
I found it really fun,
That everything I got that day,
Was chocolate for my tum.

Everyone I saw that day,
Was full of chocolate too,
Sitting on the toilet,
Me on my potty too.

They all sang jolly songs that day,
But all I just good and plenty,
Until it got to six o'clock,
And everybody wenty.

It was late that night,
As I awoke in plight,
With my stomach uptight,
I just puked all night.

Michael Simmonite

Images

I had an image of heaven,
It was to be quiet and tranquil,
Yet loud and joyful,
There would be music,
Of a kind I never knew.

I had an image of death,
A blank television screen,
The sound of hungry eagles squawking,
In a lonely deserted town.

I have a picture of life,
It is in a special frame in my mind,
It is my thoughts and feelings,
For me to keep forever.

Lizzy PenDennis

Harvest-Time from the Train

I'd love to have worked on the land,
it would have been grand. I'd love
to have tossed the hay and stoked
the corn as when I was young.
But that life was not to be.
I chose the world of city and strife
for my life.

I forgot my first sweet love of
the sun and the sky for company.
I don't know why. I forgot my love
of the land, and the golden corn
that stands so straight.
I remembered too late.

Ursula Jane Heilbut

"Little Child"

Little child, your look it pains me,
It's an answer your eyes seek,
Can't you see I'm a shadow of
    your soul,
No matter where you are,
My heart is yours to keep,
Little child smile today and
    Leave your cares behind,
Live it all day by day,
And surely you will find,
That the world is full of love,
This will be yours to know,
Now every time I look at you,
The sun in your eyes comes
    Smiling through.

Marion Ashman

The Call of Mother

A small child sits and waits,
Mothers love, caring arms,
Not a lot to ask,
The ravages of war now gone.
Mother!

Sandra Russell

The Row

They're fighting again
It's always the same
They think I don't hear
But I do

Their shouting's getting louder
Take bets on who's prouder
Words aren't to fear
'Til they're true

They're fighting once more
I listen through the door
He shouts 'til it's her turn
Again

He screams and she cries
Their millionth goodbye
When will they learn

It's too late

Kirsty Sadler

"The Young Ones"

Where are the decorations Mum?
It's festive time again.
We are all prepared to have some fun
With Mary, Les, and Jane.

Garlands entwined with tinsel
Lanterns shining bright
Put a log upon the fire
It's very cold tonight.

Silver bells that jingle
On the Christmas tree
Little parcels all around
Well wrapped for secrecy

Above the door hangs the mistletoe
The "Young Ones" are sure to find
Any excuse for a kiss or two
Their "Beaus", they will not mind.

The Young Carollers are singing
Inviting all to join them
Mince pies in the oven warming
Christmas Joys to everyone.

Margaret Jenks

"You're So Special"

I had no idea that our love would
last, on that cool breezy night
of the 5th of June.
When you first held my hand in
a desperate attempt to tell me
how you felt, I knew there and
then, that I loved you, but I
never imagined that to love
someone this strong was possible
neither did I expect to feel so
soon that I'd known you forever
or that I could trust you so easily.
I never dreamed that I would
grow to want, to need,
to love someone as much
as I do you.
You're so special to me
and I love you with
all my heart.

Samantha Dumbreck

"Life"

Life is here and now not then
Not pretty soon or when
Life! Is to-day
Not yesterday
Put aside, sad thoughts gone by
Life is you and what you do
Don't waste your time away
Don't let folk make you blue
Be happy! When you breath and say.
I'm living, for to-day!

Margaret Edwards

My Cup

Last year I won a silver cup
I've never won a cup before
And it looked so nice
When I came through the door
Now my cup and I
have said goodbye.

Still, the memory will stay
Of that wonderful day.
My name was called
In the County Hall
To receive a cup
And to read a poem
I had written.

Long past the age of seventy-three
I never thought
This would happen to me.
To stand on a stage
Speak down a mike
And read out my poem
All this before hundreds of people.

I. Millington

The Innocents of Dunblane

God lent these children to our world
Just as He lent His Son.
And now He's called them home again
Their work on earth is done.

These tiny mites so innocent,
Were killed by a twisted mind,
A man who hid behind a gun,
A misfit of mankind.

Their families are left to mourn,
Their grief beyond compare,
God willing time will heal their pain
And dull their black despair.

Pamela R. Pickford

Lost Love

Tempted touch by fate
Lingering hands to beg
Holding memories close
Time will never tell

The moments alone kept
The times together strong
You and me are nothing
You now are all alone

Pretence your world of love
With whom is now to stay
The never kiss to nowhere
The love to be kept at bay
Stop my tortured heart
Do not rip me anymore
I can't hold your hand
I can't stand your stare

You know these times together
Are memories that's all we share

A. Christy

Thoughts on a Hill Top

In the quiet and cool of evening,
Lie the valleys wreathed in calm,
High to God a hymn ascending
And the words of heavenly psalm

Here I stand upon the hill top,
Up above me soars a bird
Here, I wish that I could stop
Here, there is no need for word

In this peaceful sanctuary
Where it seems that time stands still
Here I wish that I could tarry
Of the wonders drink my fill.

High the shaggy rocks are towering
Springs gush forth from out the hill.
Gorse and heather now are flowering,
All around the air is still.

Now a warm breeze stirs the grasses
Fonds bend gently to and fro
It travels now to Moorland marshes
Where the mighty rushes grow.

W. Reed

Memories

Memories.
Like an old film,
They fade in time,
Images once so clear
Slowly ebb away
And are lost forever,
Except maybe in a dream
A sweet reminder of what once was,
Old friends and loved ones
Lost in life
But not in the heart.
Memories.
Happy times from the past,
Giving us hope for the future.

Michael Warner

The Dark Hills

The dark hills are all around,
Like unused houses without a sound,
The wind whistles;
The windows stare.
I'm all on my own without a care.
The shadows hide,
The lights dim,
I'm all on my own.
The light is back,
The window is clear,
It's the morning, the sun is near.

Sarah Fletcher

Questions

Life trickles away
Like warm sand through my fingers;
Hollowing out,
Gathering momentum.

Why do I not mould it, shape it,
Make something tangible,
Something more durable?

What am I waiting for . . .
The cold rain to splatter it?
The sharp wind to scatter it?
The swift the tide to erase it?

Warm sand yesterday,
Today it grows cooler;
Tomorrow . . . ?

Mollie C. King

Lonely

Here I am, all alone,
just sitting in my chair.
There are other people living here,
but does anybody care?

I couldn't cope at home they say.
So that's why I am here,
with all the other lonely folk,
some with that glassy stare.

My family comes to visit me,
But it's really not the same,
as living in my flat at home,
but with a walking frame.

I'm only ninety years of age,
I talk to my budgie all day,
He understands and cheers me up,
I can't hear what people say.

Mind you, the meals are really nice,
the cook knows her job for sure,
and just think no more 'washing-up'
p'rhaps life's not so bad after all!

Penny Gregory

Thursday and the Rain

Thursday and the rain
lashes against the window
I hear it
hitting the roof
tapping
falling
trickling along the glass

I sit in my room
and am safe from the storm

the wind howls
like a sinner
bearing its soul
into the night

I spare a thought
for those
who do the same
yet, unlike the wind
are never heard

Thursday and the rain
lashes against the window

Steve O'Toole

Untitled

Remember when we walked together
late, so late last night,
among the sea of mist and cold
as I held you tight, so tight.

Remember when I kissed you
like stars that kiss the sky,
and how I spoke so lovingly
when all you did was sigh!

Remember how I missed you
when you went away,
remember all the tears I cried
when I awoke next day.

Remember how I felt
when I found it wasn't true,
that all our love was a fantasy
I'll never be with you.

I know you don't remember
the silent glistening stream,
for you were never with me
you were only in my dream.

Jean Kay

Let Me Die

Let me sleep,
Let me lie,
Give me peace
Let me die.

Don't want to suffer,
Don't want no pain,
Just don't treat me,
Like I'm insane.

Can't you see,
that I am blind,
That I'm not,
Out of my mind.

I am old,
I am weak,
Just leave me here
So I can sleep.

So let me sleep,
Let me lie,
Give me peace,
Let me die.

Marie Eager

Let Me Love Again

Please let me be in love again,
let my heart sing out again.
Let my spirit run wild and free,
let someone out there care for me.
Let me walk hand in hand.
With someone special along the sand.
Let me laugh, let me cry,
like a dove let me fly.
Let me care for, let me live for,
someone who I'll always give for.
Let me love him and be with him,
everyday when problems ail him.
Let me know how to share,
with someone who really does care.
I'll make him happy and content,
I'll make his life seem heaven sent.

B. Kiss

Inner Depth

Listen - say nothing
Let silence surround
Privately with peace
Banish all sound.

Heart dancing a slow dance
In keeping to its beat
Gentle rhythm prevails
A solitary treat.

Finding space to feel free
Hunt the past and dig deep
Rediscovering lost threads
Buried in the heap.

Through time - long forgotten
Ready now to unfold
An emotional see - saw
Reliving the untold.

Mary Honeyfield

The Tunnel

I went to France just for the day,
No sea to see along the way.
Stayed on a coach on board a train
A lovely trip, I'll do that again.
I bought some cheese, and some wine,
And here I am, home, on time
A certificate to mark the day
To say I crossed the "New Found Way".

E. Holmwood

Stolen

Lost forever
Never returning
Nothing can be done to save it

It was something special
If only it could be returned
To the rightful owner

He has gotten away with it
If only he'd leave me alone
I don't need to be reminded

I only want my life back.

R. Dean

Back to School

To all you readers sitting here
listening for the words,
Look around,
Use your eyes,
Syllables all around;
A to M - N to Z,
Letter everywhere.

Poets young
and poets old,
All you need to use;
Your life;
Your eyes;
Your heart;
Listen to the lesson you are told.

R. B. Edwards

Growing Up

When I was a little girl
Living in a town
I used to watch the couples
Walking up and down
Then came a day
They did not come
They'd found a place
To settle down,
When I became a big girl
I did just the same
Walking up and down
Looking around
And now that I have found you
I can do the same.
Live with you and love you
And really settle down.

E. M. Gilbert

Life Changes

I was a girl once
mad as a hatter, free as the air,
couldn't wait for tomorrow,
racing everywhere.

I grew up then,
sensible steady and good,
worked, laughter, loved then,
Just as a good girl should.

Life seems so slow now,
I walk at a steady pace,
No running for a bus now,
No longer need to race.

Stay at home more,
Writing, reading who's who,
Dream winning those lottery prizes,
'Cos dreaming is all I can do.

It's funny how life really changes,
The little things make your day,
Like letters on the doormat,
And that call from far away.

J. N. Mason

Waking Up

Sunlight broke
Morning breathed
Orange hue
Whispered breeze

Caring touch of a gentle hand
Takes away the dreamlike land

Senses stir
Warmth surrounds
Quickly cooled by
Alarm clock sounds

Reaching out for one last hug
Arms entwined curled up snug

Paul G. W. Maddison

I Behold

Love

I behold Love:
Love stands
  Before me;
What can I possibly desire?
I Embrace the Darkness
  With open arms.
Today I fear not fear.
I fear not unknown
  Of mankind:
Let love embrace me:
I want only you.
Tonight let Love
  Entwine fear;
Let the world embrace
  The world.
I want to embrace
  My love.

Shamshad Akhtar

Ireland

Think not of him as arm,
Lying grotesque - a head,
No legs - no chest,
But John - sincere
And loved by those
Who held him dear.

Why think of hair,
(Matted and muddied now
but once well kept and shining)
as being his?
It is not so, there is
no face below.

His youth, his vigour
Even life has gone
Accursed bomb!

Peter Jones

So Moving

Seventeen years of living and loving
Memories sharp and sweet
Sentiments gathered all around
Spread before my feet

Days of packed lunches and picnics
Journeys to and fro
Thoughts and dreams providing
Time for minds to grow

Two oak trees were the goal posts
Buried pets we lost
The rhododendron Wendy house
The children's garden ghost

Rooms that now are empty
Quiet as a mouse
Nothing really tragic
We're only moving house

Margaret Walters

Parting Thoughts

By the side of one's partner
Looked after with love.
The tears fall gently
As they naturally should.

No time together
Is long enough.
The parting days
Are very tough.

You will soon be free
In God's great care
But "Thank you dear
for the years
  We did share."

M. Charlton

Woman Dawning

My body feels different
My body feels strange.
I've lost concentration
Like my minds in a cage
I'm looking at things that.
Have always been there
I just didn't notice.
No I just didn't care.

It's just like a yearning
Enveloping me and -
I want you to notice - yes -
I want you to see.
Something has wakened
Its stretching inside
Simply fantastic
And I won't be denied

Robert Bowman

Reflection

Look at my face
My face is your face
My eyes are your eyes
My tears - yours

I follow your movements
Although your back is turned
I know you
Like no one else does

I've watched you suffer
All on your own
It never need be that way
Talk to me

You're not alone friend
I will always be here
To live your life with you
Behind the glass

Susan C. Pearman

Humidity

I wish I was alone
My thoughts keep me happy
Keep me pure

Burning up from inside out
Can't sleep for lack of it
Can't be myself

Feel bound and gagged
Half deaf
One ear shut
The other lies mute

Wish I had the gift
Of those I listen to
All day long
All year long
ALL MY LIFE.

Stuart Edwards

The Ancient Hill

Every week I climb this hill
My heart is filled with joy
I know my friends live on the top
Doggie too with her pet toy.

Nature greets me all around
Horses, deer and the squirrel grey,
Such peace and quiet I have found
In which to enjoy my little day.

Many flowers there are each year
Orchards apples and the William Pear
For this haven I truly care
Where I am free of every fear.

This land I love all part of me,
Fields and woods live side by side.
Where I can choose to hide
Or try and find the secret tree.

I only hope and pray
This hill will live many a day
Please may it never ever
See that yellow monster

G. S. J. Pratley

Weed Killer

Sometimes, I watch
My husband
Pouring weed killer
On our lawn.
And I wonder -
Is he right
To take advantage
Of the latest knowledge?
Or is he poisoning
God's once pure earth?
Certainly, it is effective.
Again I wonder -
What would happen
If God
Poured 'weed killer'
Over us?
How many of us would be left?

Audrey J. Seacombe

Untitled

Someone turned the light out
My world is so dark
The part of you
I really wanted
Is no longer mine
Someone let the cold in
It's so hard to keep warm
These feelings chain me
I need you here
To set me free
Someone turned the light out
Why?

S. Bynoe

Oban

Sea Shimmering sparkling
Myriad jewels, low setting sun
Night envelops
Fish jumps light of moon.
Air clear, ship looms
Like giant monster. Full tide,
Imagination wanders stand quay side,
Far off lands same sea laps
Dusky maidens. Wave whitecap.
Toward shore.
Man boat pulls hard on oar.
Walk to abode, supper ready
Sleep morning breakfast.

P. Grime

The Empty House

She grew old,
No longer bothering to wash,
She grew dirtier and dirtier.
Her skin crumbled first.
Cracks appeared in her body.
Her hair fell out.
Her eyes grew too dim to see,
And her one tooth,
Right at the front, rotted away.
Standing lazily, without movement,
The old house died.

Lesley Spencer

My Friend

My friend is always there for me,
No matter what I do.
She's always there to pick me up,
When I feel blue.

She never stands in judgement,
Nor does she criticise.
She'll always find the time for me,
And never does she lie.

She'll cry along with me,
If I feel sad.
And when I'm feeling happy,
Together we will laugh.

She's wonderful in every way,
Thoughtful and sincere.
A shoulder when I need it most,
To let me know she cares.

I really couldn't ask,
To have a better friend.
In return I shall be there for her,
Until the very end.

Tracey Dawn Kyme

To Solitude

O Solitude, I salute you,
Not for an open face,
But for your secret smile,
Therein lies charm;
Not for your merry voice,
But for your steady hush,
Therein lies strength;
Not for a limpid look,
But for the mystic cast
Of your speckled eyes,
Therein lies sway.
Be one sage or simple,
Each seek you to inter
The ravaged relics of Time.

J. M. Skinner

Addicted

In this dark room
Nothing else but the dark
It's so cold no feelings
No intimate dealings

I want to get out,
But I can't seem to shout
There's so much pain nothing to gain
In this dark room

What's out here?
There's people to fear.
Lots of gain, but still so much pain
I want to go back I've got to go back
To the dark room.

Sharon Hay

My Poem

Who has made this great big world,
Our dear Lord above
The flowers, birds, and everything
He made with all His love,
The oceans deep, the mountains high,
The sky so big and blue,
Our dear Lord made all these things,
Because His love is true.

S. Moore

Untitled

I dream you
Now my dreams are
All I have.
I tear out my
mind every sunshine.
It brings only you.
The dark and the light
Swap places once more
Still my heart beats
Taunting me
Filling my eyes with
Portraits of you.
My make-believe life
You think I've survived?
My shattered heart
Within me has died.

Lynsey J. V. Rose

He Remembers

He remembers the pathetic vigour,
Of a once forgotten youth,
He recalls the dying embers,
Of a flame he once called truth,
He belies his ageing instincts,
With an appetite for fun,
Because time has not yet withered,
This old, but faithful, son.

Matt Scantlin

Secrets

Can you keep a secret?
Of course I can.
A very special secret,
Yes, of course I can.
No one else must know this secret
No, of course not.
Promise to keep it secret
Yes, of course I will.
Cross your heart and hope to die
Of course I will
Well my friend told me!!!

M. J. Arkwright

'Loving Hope'

Love is lingering in time and space
Is this the case is this its place?
The oneness that draws me in embrace
Is love a subject of condition?
A timed proposition a seesaw ride
An arms length submission

It was here and now it's gone
The love the laughter anticipation
With hope my aching heart retrieves
The man I love like falling leaves
Sweet mystery that pulls him back

Heart of my heart so cleverly
Comforts the thought of he and she
Running into each new day
Nearer to the time he'll stay
Just for a while and then condition
Is this love's proposition?

Valerie Musk

As Good as New

Engine running nicely
Pipes all clean and new
Your M.O.T. completed
What can we wish for you

Our love and all good wishes
For a clear road ahead
To steer you back to perfect health
Worth more than all the wealth

Lilian Halley

Untitled

Lovely landscape
On shore
Captured moments
Happy days

Lonely people
Eels in the water
Viewing points
Ever green forests
Nasty children

Camping out
Angry adults
Small animals
Trapped dogs
Listening to birds
Entering their nests

Sharon Wallace

Primrose

A primrose sits
on the bank of
The English
Countryside

Yellow with delicate
petals
Moving to the tune
of the wind

It sits alone
I notice it
I do not pick it

Innocent, untouched
I leave it
Then continue
my walk

Primrose you
made me see
Something real.

Karen Sutherland

The Fool . . .

The fool stands alone
on the bridge by the river,
watching the water flow by.
The sun smiles down
on his sad tear-stained face,
the bells tinkle gently, he sighs.

Always the joker
and ever the joke,
the life of the party they say.
But he only knows
the stinging hard truth,
and it's nearing the end of the day.

There's hardly a splash
as he hits the cold water,
his hat with the bells floats away.
The clichéd old jokes,
he is free of them now,
the darkness enshrouding the day.

Katie Wilkie

9:30 A.M.

How can one share
The grief that's there
In Dunblane
With deepest, thought
One feels they ought
To share the pain
In deepest sorrow
There's no tomorrow
From an act, so insane
Lord God above
Bless us, with Your love
That it happens not, again

I. Gallowere

Life

What is this life we mortals live
On this tormented earth.
Is this the freedom we were promised
When we were given birth?

Is this the shackle we must wear,
When from our mothers womb,
We came to wait upon this earth
For our eternal tomb?

Must we here like prisoners wait,
As with each passing breath,
We step further from unwanted birth
To everlasting death.

G. L. Andrew

Photographs

Photographs take us back
Once more through yesteryears.
Some bring forth peals of laughter
While others bring the tears.

Incidents come fleeting back
We're lost in Memory Lane,
And there we seem to meet a friend
Or loved one once again.

And as we live the past once more
We lose ourselves in dreams;
Then weave a web of happiness
With memories golden beams.

Friendships long forgotten
Are tangled in the thread
Other more romantic ones
On wings of love are sped.

And when at length we seem to wake
From out our reverie
We know that photographs bring back
The sweetest memory.

Patricia M. Morris

Without You

The Sun will never shine again
Or song birds sound so sweet
I'll never really feel again
A soft breeze on my cheek.

Though flowers bloom around me
And I know that it is spring
It's sadness that surrounds me
And my heart no more will sing.

I only can remember
When you were here with me
The Sunshine and the flowers
Were everywhere to see.

You were the trees, the softest
Breeze, the birds that fly above
You made me sing, you were my
Spring, when you were here my love.

E. L. Eastley

Friends

Does it matter if my friend is Black
Or if he is Chinese?
All people on this earth of ours
Are people if you please.
Take away their colour
And they are all the same,
So if you really think of it
It's only in the name.
They are all our brethren,
Whatever race or creed,
And you'll find if you cut them
They will always bleed.
So try to be more tolerant
There's good and bad in all;
If you do discriminate
You're riding for a fall.
We are all God's children
And when in Heaven above,
He will not see the colour
But share out all His love.

Ruth Smith

Knowing!!!

I know when to stop Bob,
or was it the face on the wall,
with long hair he saw it all.
The man who had his bullet
said peace was not to fool . . .

It was these three
who said life could
be lived free,
only sadly their own lives taken
from them early
their names read.
LENNON, BOLAN, AND BOB
MARLEY.

Louise Smyth

1959

At 3 o'clock one January morn!
Our beloved son was born.
A beautiful blue eyed boy
Who filled my heart with such joy.

Quickly taken away was he
Why? he should be with me!
"He is not well", I was told,
For him my soul I would have sold.

Many years later
He's still with me
chairbound, true.
A joy to see!

He enjoys all parts of life,
Abhorring every kind of strife.
A gentle man, in every way.
I thank God who allowed him to stay.

J. Ellis

Thick and Thin

Through thick and thin,
our friendship stood,
Like a field full of trees
standing in a wood.

Chatting and gossiping is what we
like to do.
We would always make friends
with someone new.

Shopping and day trips are fun
as well,
But if you've got a secret
we won't tell! . . .

Ruth Bale

Today's Monet

She sits with oils
paints and shuffles.
Looks up and asks
if I desire.
A bowl of fruit
still life.
She paints like Monet
with lust for talent.
She need not bribe
her gift from God
inspires me and all.
Envied by those
who fail to delight.

Saiqa Hussain

The Brook

Rays of golden sun
Peeping through the tangle green
Where the waters of the brook
Creep along the mossy banks
All the pathways they entwine

Often when the day is ending
And the sunlight falls
Sleepy willows bend their blanches
To rest gently on the water sheen

Now the gleaming brightness fades
Finds its way to shady nooks
Then noon tide softly beams
On a darkened brook

Mary Hobday

Slow to Kill

The serpent,
penetrated the womb
that bore me.
Tongue venomous,
appetite insatiable.
A slow winding trail:
havoc and destruction,
in its wake, a skeletal form:
my mother.

Months, weeks,
excruciating pain -
scream - scream
morphine -
a respite;
daily ablutions,
shame in the eyes
"You're my child now".

Journey ending,
comatose -
eyes roll, lids flutter,
a bird on the wing -
soaring - soaring -
gone.

Maura McDonnell-Fairthlough

Potential

The future is never
quite what it seems
it has no clear cut
boundaries
no maximum limits.

We must all make the best of
what we are given
the skills, the abilities,
all the amazing gifts and
unique qualities that make
us individuals.

The trick is hanging on long
enough to realise
our potential.

Paul Elder

Unfair Destiny

I came unto you early,
So small and insecure
Unaware to me the dangers
Of what I may endure.

The taste of death injected
Into my soul unknown.
The fear and doubt surrounding me
Has left me all alone.

My life is not a lasting one
Decided before I came
You didn't even have the chance
To give to me a name.

Mandy Louise Wilson

Eyes Widely Closed

The war is on
So you close your eyes
And pretend you don't hear
The blood curdling cries

You hear a bomb go off
Its sounds so near
You can't stand to think
If it's someone dear

You lay awake in bed
As you can't get to sleep
And in the next room
You hear your mother weep

Have you lost your dad
Your granddad or your nan
Have you lost your uncle
or your brother Dan

You start to scream
You can't take it anymore
Why does there have to be
A bloody war!

Linzi Graves

We All Have Our Journeys to Make!

We are all pawns in a political game
Some seek to help, some seek fame
Some are scapegoats
Who can take the blame
Out of muckraking
Same good may come, for the making
There is always HOPE
So do not mope
(You can always watch TV Soap!)

The Spring is coming
and birds will be humming
They can be fed
with our left-over bread
Sometimes 'simple things'
can be rewarding
We can all mend fences
and let down our defences
with those friends we love
We can share 'good times'
and coo like doves'

Evelyn Keyes

True Marriage

Marriage is like a rose,
Sometimes thorns
It bears,
Strong it stands
With fresh green leaves.
True beauty stays
On top.

T. Bennett

Peace

Wealth and riches there are more
Than we could ever imagine,
Through the maze, beyond the door
Lies peace there in abundance.

Clasp it with unselfishness
Then spread it across the world,
Cast aside all wickedness
Peace be the weapon you hurl.

Help those who only darkness see,
Dazzle them with your light.
Let peace and love forever be
The goal you keep in sight.

Only you can forge a way
Through evil and God willing,
Peace will rise above the hate
To drive out thoughts of killing.

Sheila Davies

Love

Love is the greatest power
That God has given to man.
Love was the purpose
Love the hope
Before the world began.
Our love is but a fragment
We can't measure its worth
God showed how great His love is
When He gave us Jesus' birth.
Like the story in the Bible
Of the fishes and the bread
Our love, if shared, is multiplied
A miracle takes place once more
And a multitude is fed.

S. M. Binks

Friends (1914 - 1918)

I see a face,
That I knew well.
I hear a name,
That rings a bell.
I stood here,
And saw them fall.
They sank to the ground,
I lost them all.

Sara Cole

One Way Thing

I will always love you,
That will never change,
But what's the point of love
If it's a one way thing?

Rachel Anne Evans

The Kid with a Match

I am the kid with a match
Playing on the kitchen floor,
Look at this, the scar on my leg,
I've played this game before.

I strike the match, it flickers,
Red, gold and blue.
Now I've done it, it's no fun,
So I shall stick it down my shoe.

I am the kid with a match,
Sitting on my hospital bed,
I've put on my shoe and leg,
So it will go up my nose instead.

I am the kid with a match,
As dead as a doornail for sure,
I was the kid with a match,
Just playing on the kitchen floor.

Michelle Jarrett

Him

Him, and his Precious car!
Perfectly protected,
pristinely preserved,
personally prized,
passionately propelled

Him, and his Fantastic job!
Fiendishly fanatical,
fearfully fetching,
flagrantly fixated,
fatally fascinating

Him, and his Enchanting mistress!
Expensively entertained,
exquisitely exciting,
exclusively endeared,
enthusiastically enjoyed

Him, and his Bloody wife!
Brutishly blasphemous,
balefully berating,
barbarically bestial,
Bitterly betrayed.

Katherine Sharman

Life Has Begun

The birds are nesting
preparing for young,
Buds are bursting
life has begun.
I stand in amazement
at what I see,
What a beautiful sight
this is for me.
A carpet of green,
pink blossom, and white,
A heavenly scene.
Thank God for my sight.

G. S. Hamerston

Feeling Angry

I'm feeling angry,
Really really mad,
I'll wreck my room,
I'll get called bad,
I'll rip all my clothes,
I'll pull out my hair,
But whatever happens,
I DON'T CARE.

I'll yell at my Brother,
My Father, and Mother,
I'll slam all the doors,
On the way to my room,
I'll get into trouble,
I'll annoy everyone,
But whatever happens,
I DON'T CARE.

Tracey Twomey

Thoughts of You

Thoughts of you, your smiling face
Return me to a happier place
When we were young and we were free
So long ago eternity

And such was life a forgotten place
With love reflected in your face
The time you had was just for me
A glance for all the world to see

But time goes on not backward face
Perhaps on to a better place
If this is so I know for me
With you it will most surely be

Rebecca Howland

Untitled

O dear dolphins how can it be,
That you still trust in our
humanity,
O dear dolphins how can it be,
that we are so cruel to
you in the sea,
when the fishermen lay
their nets down low,
and you get tangled with
your death so slow
why can't they hear you
crying so painfully,
O dear dolphins how can it be,
that we evil humans can be
so cruel and mean.

Sara Stoker

Modern Society

People look
People stare
People who don't care
People . . . people everywhere.

What do they think?
What do they see?
As they pass each other by
Too busy maybe.

Where do they go?
What do they do?
Are they feeling lonely too?
I wish I knew.

Lost in their own thoughts
Are they too selfish and greedy?
Or too tired to care
About the person next to them there.

That's the way it has become
In this, our wonderful new land
Could we still have one more chance
Or is it too late to make a stand?

Sharon Gray

Mediterranean Sea . . .

Life in the soil,
rivers at sunset,
the noise of travelling birds,
the earnest cry of a new born baby,
the ardent kiss,
the sincere handshake,
the enchanted words, I love you
and peace be with you,
poetic words . . .

Do you know, Mediterranean Sea,
that you are in agony?

Mario F. Bezzina

Our Dad

This is where you loved to be
Sitting on a gnarled old tree
Now the tree and you are gone
But the memories linger on
Days of caring, love and laughter
Now whatever follows after
We'll remember and be glad
That we had you for a dad
To our mum, you were her man
Almost since your lives began
As we leave you here with flowers
Strewn among the leafy bowers
We thank God for the time we had
To all of us, you were our Dad.

Margaret Kinnaird

"Again"

Again my snake-like life
returns, I slip and slide
and shed my skin, then
turn around and start again.

I fail again then freeze my
prey. Hypnotic feelings ease
the pain. I lure them in
to help me - then slide
away unnoticed.

The blood feels cold, yet my
heart is hot. The contradiction
pulls and tears.

Are you watching me? I feel
someone; is it is frightening.
My eyesight is distorted.
but I can feel and sense you.
The fear within is returned
To scare and freeze is my reaction
and intention

To love and have that love returned will
hold my tongue.

Katy Yule

Memento Mori

Copies of poppies
Rich with the sap
Of lonely lads,
Their dreams long dead,
Perch precarious
On cold lapels,
And give my heart
The shocks and smells
Of their young dread,
In Flanders earth
Where they were put to bed.

Michael Faulkner

A Tribute to Dunblane

The children all went to
School that morn
But was never to see the
Next day dawn.
They all assembled teacher
And all
In that wonderful gymnasium
Hall.
Little knowing that the gunman
Would call
But soon they all began to
Fall
The children didn't have time
To run and hide.
Nor did their teacher so
Full of pride.
But in their hearts I'm sure
They new
That the gate's of heaven
Were open through.

Wendy Lynne Bryan

Forgotten?

Memories misplaced in the mind,
Sacrificed to the passage of time.
Dead and embalmed.
In the sanctity of ignorance,
Time has been calmed,
Liberated from the eternal pyre,
Ignited by memory's passionate fire.
Memories aberrate life's procedure,
As time masking honesty,
Is manipulated amnesia.

Rachel-Louisa Williams

The Last Time

I
See
for the
Last Time

Those winks and grins,
the grain of skin;
Knotted knuckles,
Boughs of bone

Brittle as tinder sticks.

In the heart glow
Autumn embers,
Spitting memories as
Flickering red.

Sighing high into hush

They are taken
by my breath,
and flush my face
When I remember.

On my soul
Are cinders cold.

Matthew Thomas Lumby

Birth

Surging into a new world
Seeing the light at the end,
Then, a piercing white light
And warm hands.
I cry and am cleaned
Then caressed by the mother machine.

Steven James

Alarm Clock

With a strange, unruly motion
Seeker's journey has begun
swimming in an endless ocean
seeking the father of the sun

But land I cannot see
and enslaved as other slaves
I am drowning in the waves
To my fetters there seems no key

Fighting like a militiaman
against the sea, but going under
then betimes saved by a fisherman
just before the thunder

O. A. Bjerheset

Sweetheart

If you wish a sweetheart,
Seen her in the Spring,
Love is like a red rose,
It blossom as the season's go,
Every kiss is frozen in time,
Like a sparkle in your mind.

H. J. Goodchild

Soulmate

It was more than warmth that melted,
The barrier to my soul,
It was a friend to be trusted,
happy, brave and bold.
He justly reclaimed his right,
to hopes, dreams and promises,
by a comforting arm that night.
Nothing was amiss
as the darkness smiled down on me,
dispelling my disbelief
now I'm ready for eternity
much to our relief.

Surinder Jagdev

National Health

The national health service should be
Surrounded with praise,
When you think back to the so
Called "Good Old Days,"
If illness required a hospital bed
Families kept paying long after the
Patient was dead
Today people speak glibly of
insurances, then
Not easy if there was no known
Cure for them
People died young with families
All around
Scenes never forgotten, today
Would astound
Count your blessings and be of
Good cheer.
Miracles are happening and
Who knows maybe next year!

Pauline Whelch

Nightmare

Tossing and turning,
Sweating and shaking,
Trapped!
In the solitude of your mind.

You scream!
Silence.
You run!
Paralysis.

Everywhere you turn,
A new barrier appears,
Reality turns to dust,
As imagination and fear run free.

Karen Elson

Protect

Ocean blue ocean deep
Swimming lives
Into our keep
They fall

Sky blue sky high
Flying lives
With a sigh
Could fall

Land green land low
Walking lives
We'll never know
May fall

Earth alone the only one
Without due care
Could all be gone
Come fall

H. S. Foster

Lazy Science Wear Barefoot

Me a bayside
swingin in me hammock
restin off me body
a tink pad sudden.
Future mo no wahn nuttin
but to lie here humming
way foo mash up an jumbies
flyin in de sky.

So le me lone wi mi bizznizz
wi mi palm tree bang water
me no meddle wi sardine tin
foo Goat Mouth say.
Rabben strong foo water pumkin
blow bex Science all away.

Vanessa W.

New-Born

Twinkle in your Daddy's eye,
Tears of joy for you I cry.
Gold and jewels could not buy
A bond so strong as you and I.

Pat Osborne

Cold Mornings

Cold Mornings
shimmering snow
frosty winds that blow
numb feet
twinkle nose
chattering teeth
knobbly knees
card-board ears
slippery slopes
smiling snowman
plentiful post
happy children
unexpected surprises
magic joy
wonderful glow
warm family feelings
special occasion
party season
chimes of bells
and hymns of Jesus.

Sokho Kaur Safri

Untitled

Betrayed, mislaid
silent whispers in a room
smiling faces soon fade away
their looks turn into doom.

Mistrust, unjust
for years have been my friends
they say such things to hurt me
then try to make amends.

Deterred, not heard
my voice in their crowded ring
all taking mental punches at me
and I can't do a damn thing.

Alone, far from home
they say they're on my side
never believing the words I speak
they wonder why I've lied

Don't know how hard I've tried.

Tammy Radley

The Peacock and the Sunset

Cast no sight upon my word.
Simple food for sight unheard.
The Uranian heart sat
with cold plume of purple
bruised beset
with solitude in room with
no inside, outside or
selfless met.
The horizon song
penetrates Plutonian walls
Kissing heart, Kissing plume.
And purple fell to English rose,
thus volcano weeping
We suppose.
So one returns to a room
Outside metamorphosed
to truthful inside.
And thought crawls as one
on venusian tide to Satori's shore.
No meaning implied.

Shaun Kelley

Poets Are a Must

Poets are a must
They are people
Put on this earth
like a trust
Their thoughts
Come from far
and wide

Crushing in like
A raging tide
up to the sky
To a far of star.

Poet's are must.
Put on this
Earth
Like Gods
Good trust

G. J. Ockelford

My Thoughts

Their children are good,
They have gone to heaven,
The lessons they learnt
Will be with them forever,
They roam with the souls
of their family
Past, knowing their joy
Will eternal last.
Don't mourn parents of ours
We will wait for you
Along with the stars.

M. Price

God's Helping Hand

When we lose someone we love
They say "Life must go on"
But these are merely words
In Verse or in a Song
The hardest moments of this time
Is coping while we grieve
Though Life will not be easy
One fact we must believe
There is a GOD in Heaven
He's our saviour and our Friend
And if we place our Trust in Him
He'll help us to the end
He never gives us burdens
Beyond what we can bear
And should our load get heavy
Our burden He will share
He's always there beside us
Wherever we may go
And He will guard and guide us
Because He loves us so!

Lynne Gotting

Colours

Life is full of colours
They tend to come and go
Showing signs of happiness
The moods begin to flow
Sometimes they are lively
With shades of red and green
Then comes a time of sadness
With shades that go unseen

These are the colours
We see each and every day
The colours of tomorrow
The colours of today
Where would life be
If it were not for these
A world full of darkness
Is the world we would see.

Sukhvinder Kaur Badwal

A Primrose Posy

He knew where to look
This lad of the land.
Down by the little brook
On banks of leafy sand.
Only the best he took
Cherished in rustic hand.
Seen by the cawing rook
Seven leaves in the band.
He laid them gently on her book
A primrose posy, oh! So grand.

Vic Sutton

True Love

Can love live through bitter words
Through anger hurt and pain
Can loves gentle voice be heard
And through all this remain

Can love stand the heavy blows
That lovers sometime strike
Can the heart remain unclosed
And shine with loving light

Of course true love can stand
Where other feelings fall
Whatever the harsh demand
True love will stand it all.

T. E. Littler

The Spirit

Floating past in flowing gown,
Through fields of crimson flowers,
There she rests in misty haze,
To dream away the hours.

I wonder what she dreams about,
She sometimes looks so sad,
Maybe she is thinking of,
A love that she once had.

She has a far away look in her eyes,
They sometimes cloud with tears,
I wish she'd let me be her friend,
To share her hopes, her fears.

I think I might approach her,
But just as I draw near,
Suddenly she fades away,
It soon becomes quite clear.

Floating past in flowing gown,
Through fields of crimson flowers,
There she rests in misty haze,
To dream away the hours.

Lindsey Jenkins

Missing You

I miss you in the morning
Throughout the day and night
I miss you more between these times
Now how can this be right.

I miss you when I am sleeping
Even more when wide awake
To remedy my condition
What medicine can I take.

I miss you when I am talking
I miss you when I am not
By this time you may have guessed
I miss you quite a lot.

Tonight, again I missed you
More than I've ever done before
But there again, tomorrow night
I'll probably miss you more.

Lee Carroll

Friends

Has it ever occurred
To you
That I view
Friends
Not as trends
To make amends
Or beginnings to ends
But more
To the core
A nearness
A dearness
Unspoken trust
Is a must
To ensure that friends
Are never just trends.

Liz Needham

Observations

The days pass so quickly
Tomorrow soon becomes yesterday
We'll be together soon
But all that lies between

The days pass so quickly
Hazy, fun-filled days
Tireless, responsible free days
Dreamy thoughts of tomorrow

The days pass so quickly
Painful, chaotic days
Tiresome days full of burden
Anxious thoughts of May

The days pass so quickly
Too fast for you
Too slow for me
The day will soon be here

The days pass so quickly
But what does it matter in the end
For in only a couple of months
This will all be just a memory

Rachael Aldridge

War Cry

What woman wages war?
Too much pain in other ways
too many tears
to live is fight enough
but not for men . . .
How deep the pain?
How hard the loss?
What woman wages war?
Too much to lose
A husband a son a child
Given in pain taken in pain
Life and death
It's time men wept
What woman wages war?

Philippa Trump

Why?

Trash on the ground,
Trash in the air,
Trash in the river,
everywhere.
Why do people do it?
Don't they understand?
Why don't they put it
in the bin
instead of on the
ground?
Don't they think or care
About this planet
Earth?

Simon Owens

289

Mind over Rainy Day

On the inside, looking out
wandering what it's like.
can see through the window
smell of the trees, fresh cut grass
smell the roses, hear the bees
taste the honey.
all the laughing
ice cream cones
water fights, skipping rhymes
lovers kissing cuddling too
spring is leaving
turn the corner
summer's hiding
behind the clouds
suntanned bodies
beach party time
but all of this is in my mind
looking through my eyes
this rainy day.

C. Hampton

Untitled

In depths of dreamland,
Wand'ring through a world of hope -
Peace surrounds my soul.

Brightest sun appears -
Earth now dons her coat of gold -
Basking in delight.

Magical rainbow,
Heaven's paint box in the sky
Spilling silken shades.

Margaret Bond

Fire

I gaze at the hearth-side,
Warm winter comforter.
Dancing pictures dazzle,
Drawn from the darting flame.
Fire-bird, jungle king,
Flash-feathered oriole;
Pale waxen idols
Licked by blue candles.
Sap sizzles, sprigs crackle,
Send rockets to the stack.
Hedgerow glowworms gleam
Among the ash-grey embers.

Flint can spark to kindle,
Burn to blazoned blaze:
So love flares from stone-start.
My eyes turn inward
To my own heart,
Consumed for you,
Casting the forbidden letter
Black-charred to the fire.

Penny Albanhac

The Poker-Playing Dragon

The poker-playing dragon
was a fearsome beast
His eyes were bright and brilliant
And his claws were very sharp

His fangs just hung there loosely
And his tail was very still
He smoked without a cigarette
And sparked without a flame.

He had an awful temper
And couldn't stand to lose
If you had beaten him at cards
You'd just burst into flames.

Mark Frost

Flowing Thoughts

My affection that flows
will continue to run.
Ever since we met, you
brought out the sun.

For I believe I am sane,
to be near to you, one
cannot explain.
All that circulates will
always remain.

Ecstatic flowing emotions,
flowing head to toe;
my soul is searching
and only you must know.
For you are the one
who moves me.

J. E. Andrews

Windows

Pools of love liquid eyes.
Windows opened, filled with sighs,
Baring all, naked seen,
Can't hide the tears within me.
Droplets of life rolling down
Years of pain no sound
Whirlpool sucking life
Drowning, no more strife
One glance upward pull
Fighting, struggling
Against all odds
Windows opened their is a cause
Hold on cling to life
New beginning new sight.

Kathleen Robertson

A Gift of Love

I know it's not your birthday,
With all anniversaries - gone!
Those "special days" - remembered,
Have vanished - one by one.
There's still so much to wish you,
And so much more - I could do;
So! Because it's not your birthday,
I give - my heart - to you!

I know that real love, deepens,
With longing - inside - just to give
Some little corner of our hearts
To help - each other - live.
'Tis heaven - being near you,
With love - like ours - so true;
So! Because it's not your birthday,
I - give my love - to you!

R. G. Youngman

My Mischief

He's big and lovable,
With big green eyes.
He's tan and white,
With brown at the sides.
His tail curls over,
Like a foxes brush.
It's hard to explain,
But I LOVE him so much!

His heart is dodgy,
And his breathing poor.
He's close to death-
Knocking on heavens door.
Please don't take him,
I'm begging you Lord,
I love my dog
He's part of my world.

Peta Capes

If I Was

If I was a heart,
You'd be my beat.
If I was the sun.
You'd be my heat.
If I was winter,
You'd be my frost.
If you were not here.
I would be lost.
If I was a planet,
You'd be my sun.
If I was a car,
You'd make me run.
If I was an oyster,
You'd be my pearl.
If I was a lady,
You'd be my earl.
If I was a pirate,
You'd be my treasure
And I would keep you,
Forever and ever.

Kerry Lawrence

Your Room

What will become of your room?
Your clothes? Cassettes? Guitar?
My letters? Cards? And thoughts?

The memories of our blissful days,
now relics of past Utopia.
On an antique mattress lies
the shadow of two souls merging.
Imprinted for eternity on cool linen
you can not wash pure love away
nor remove its presence.
Its sweet stain will remain
embodied and preserved
a memorial to
"A love lost, yet never ending."

Sara Fellows

Your Eyes

I love you for your eyes
Your tender look
Your tender gaze
There's magic in those eyes
drawn by a magnet
they entice and tantalise

The power those eyes hold
mysteries to unfold
feelings you keep hidden
As if you were forbidden

In control demanding
sometimes quite alarming
master full supreme
I want to be your Queen!

Those eyes full of dreams
And promise
fill with tears of pain
won't you let those veins
feel your heart
pound again

Veronica Wyatt

In Memory of V. E. Day

You're gone but not forgotten
Your ears tuned out
But I hear
Your lips are silent
But your message is clear
Your eyes are closed
But I see
Your precious lives
Given for me

S. A. Farmery

Would You

If I told you about my life
Would you lend a sympathetic ear
If I shared my worries and strife
Would you chase away my fear

If you looked inside my dreams
Could you help me understand
Life is never what it seems
Would you lend a helping hand

If I shared my love with you
Could you conquer my desire
Would you wake in me anew
The ever burning fire

If I told you how I feel
would you turn and walk away
Or would your soft kiss steal
My doubting heart away
Margaret Lord

"Experience"

To,
    Wrestle with experience,
To,
    Have "words", to convey it,
To,
    Grow and mature,
To,
    Have sensitivity of perception,
To,
    Observe the similar,
To,
    Venture into growth.
To,
    Scan worlds not yet realized,
To,
    Fasten onto an object
And,
    Turn it into a thing of
        Beauty
            "Words,"!
Mabel Drury Layland

Fred!

Tulips and Daffodils
You brought for me,
Always at Easter
You came for tea.

Now my dear son
You can't bring to me,
Daffodils or Tulips
I'll bring them, for thee.

I'll place them with care
And, with love
On your grave
In remembrance of you
And the love, that you gave.
Olive M. Robinson

A Summer's Day

The leaves are dancing in the trees
You can almost hear the growing seeds
As the birds they fly up in the sky
A butterfly goes fluttering by.

To lie so still in the cooling breeze
And gaze upon the dancing leaves
To watch the birds as they glide by
Away up in the beautiful sky

For here as I lie this summer's day
Troubles seem so far away.
One with nature, never alone.
Basking in the midday sun.
Marie Bingham

What a Wonderful World!!

It was cold and bleak,
The air was still,
No sound, nothing living,
No noises to kill.

This moment was broken,
When some life came alone,
He successfully took power
And created our home.

On His first day He began
To create dark and light,
When His second day had ended
He had made day and night.

He also provided us
With sky, sea and land,
Plants and vegetation
Was what He had planned.

After six days of working,
His mission was done,
His seventh day was spent resting,
His race had been run!!
Katherine Williams

Music in the Air

I wake up in the morning,
The birds they sweetly sing,
I open wide my window
To let the music in.

In heaven we have the harp,
Through the golden streets we walk,
The joy bells too, are ringing
By the wayside as we talk.

Walk and talk with Jesus,
The Saviour of mankind.
Fill your heart with music
Your soul and your mind.

Where Jesus dwells there's music
Fill you heart with song;
Say you belong to Jesus
Praise him all day long.

Save your soul for Jesus,
Give him your heart today;
Don't wait for tomorrow
Come now, without delay.
E. May Hughes

Immortality

The blackbird's haunting melody
The curlew's lonely cry
These things go on forever
but man just passes by.

The moon that lights the prairie
The stars that show the way
These things go on forever
but man he cannot stay.

The sun that wakes the flowers
The chattering of the stream
These things go on forever
but man can only dream.

The clouds that roam the heavens
The rainbow in the sky
These things go on for ever
but man is born to die.

The wind that stirs the branches
The waves that wash the sands
These things go on forever
untouched by human hands.
W. Pegg

Neglected Graveyard

Look at the gravestones
Tattered and torn
The grave forgotten
A soul reborn

With weeds that grow
From dawn till dusk
The brambles that meander
Winding their way
From one to another

A flower so thoughtfully put
Upon a grave
Of someone not forgotten
How gloomy our endings
Upon this earth

How enchanted the soul must be
To be reborn in peace and harmony
Sonia R. Lewis

Sitting on the Fence

I'm sat on the fence
That's all I can say
Who knows if there's a God
Or if U.F.O's watch us play

They're both quite extreme
But in their text seem true
Yet the truth is not in discussion
But the belief that's in you

I've tried to be drawn
To this side and that
But I stand firm in my words
On the fence is where I'm sat
A. Scott Robertson

Catching Moonbeams in My Bucket

I'm catching moonbeams in my bucket,
That's what I'm trying to do
They say if you catch a moonbeam
It'll make your wish come true.
A wish is what I need right now
To make things right again,
To bring back my dear mummy
And take away our pain.
Daddy, me and little Sammy
Didn't want her to go away,
The doctors said there was no hope
All we could do was pray.
So I'm waiting by my window
With my special little pail
To catch a moonbeam for a wish
I know I must not fail.
If there's someone up there
Send a moonbeam down right here
I'm waiting with my bucket
For a moonbeam bright and clear.
G. Hockerday

The Eagle

Soaring above the numerous clouds,
the eagle expands his wings and
lets his freedom be known to all
mankind.

Freedom is his life. Nothing can
hold back his anticipation of flight.
It gives him joy to know he can
fly high above the world and set
his spirits free. Life awaits him
wherever he may go.

His home is where his soul is
and he will not rest until he
finds that place.
Rebecca Skidmore

291

Untitled

I don't remember which struck first
the lightning or my pain
I don't remember which fell faster
my teardrops or the rain.

I don't remember which was louder
the thunder or my screams
I don't remember which was deeper
the darkness or my dreams

I don't remember which was colder
my blood or the blade of the knife
I don't remember which was shorter
the terrible storm or my life.

Simon Parker

Love Is Blind

They look at each other
The love has grown stronger
It can be seen in their eyes
Their expressions
Their soft caresses
Their gentle kisses
She is so beautiful
He is so handsome
Remembering their first meeting
What they've been through
The good times always present
The bad times forgotten
They hold each other's wrinkled hands
They smile with creased faces
But they don't notice that
They only see each other
As they were
When they first met
Love really is blind

Michael A. Leonard

Winter

Winter is drawing closer
the nights are getting dark
The chilly winds are blowing
across the open parks.

The rain and snow are falling
the woolly gloves come out.
All the children playing
waiting for the stars to come out.

The star that shines the brightest.
Bringing Christmas near
makes them excited
and full of all good cheer.

J. Townsend-Blazier

My Soul Is Nothing but a Mirror

My soul is but a mirror of
the people I have known.
It is me and only me. The
troubled people, the lonely people,
the successful people. My family,
the people I admire, the people
I struggle with are all part of
my soul. For I know deep
within that I am wholly unique
but take bits from all these
people into my soul. Strangers I
meet, are all me. Society can
also be a mirror of my soul. There
is good, there is joy but there is
pain and war. For all the things
I admire, for all the things
I disliked they are all mirrored
in my soul. My soul the one
thing that is truly mine.

Sarah Silvester

Flicker

Add to the flame
The plans you make.
Upset is the balance
Of give and take.
The man is away
And just out of reach.
Give up the grovelling
Attempts to beseech.
If there's no interest,
Time will assure.
No doubt it's hard
To wait and endure.
The nearer the future,
When interest will rise.
Clear the mind now -
Don't wait for surprise.
Thoughts are at odds,
But fate will deliver.
Somehow, constant,
The lights eternal flicker.

S. C. Thompson

The Rose

The rose that buds in spring
The rose that flowers in summer
The rose with scent so nice
It smells as sweet as pine
The rose that dies during the
winter months and comes to
life again in the spring
Oh, how beautiful is the
rose of mine.

W. G. Kay

Dance, Dance, Wherever You May Be

You and I understand
the scarecrow flaps on the grave,
the birds don't dare peck eyes
take flesh before it's time.

My bones and flesh ache
to give up mourning
for life that seeks
to destroy, maim, kill.

You and I understand
that life remains a flame
deep in a flower's throat
invisible to those

who cannot worship
who do not know the
gifts of joy and peace.
Their flame may go out.

You and I understand
we wear our mourning cloaks
to dance as scarecrows do
to keep the flame alight.

Lorna West

The Sound of Listening

The frosted is cracking
The snow is falling
Listen to the sound
The trees are swaying
The birds are singing
Listen to the sound
The wind is blowing
The leaves are falling
Listen to the sound
The children are playing
The children are laughing
Listen to the sound.

Sheila Marlene Gardener

Going Far South

Throughout the day
the sun sears and scorches
without mercy,
though evening brings
a light breeze that cools
the angst of summer.

Then night comes alive
with music that pierces
every silence.
Red wine flows and spills.
On warm tin roofs
cats mate and miaow.

And tomorrow will repeat
the same performance.

Maria Wallace

Sounds

The wind is rough as it blows through
the trees.
The waves grow calm as they glide
o'er the seas.
The sun glows warming from the
sky above.
As the fluttering sound can be
heard of a dove.

The dove grows weary after
its long flight.
The sun grows cooler as day
becomes night.
The waves stand still as the
breeze it sleeps
And the willow tree in silence
weeps.

Madeline Amy Davis

'It's Just Another Day'

Time doesn't heal
  the way I feel?
The days are long
  the nights are cold
Without you here to hold.

Everywhere I see your face
Then you're gone without a trace.
Minutes, days turn to years
Forever drowning in my tears.

I long for sleep as you appear
But then I wake,
  and you're not here.
'It's Just Another Day'

J. R. Marsh

To Our Dog "Sandy"

How can you explain
The way you feel
When life had gone
And death is real

You wipe a tear
From your cheek
You sit and think
But cannot speak

The best friend
You have ever had
Has gone for good
And you are sad

You sit and think
And wonder why
Why someone, loved so much
Had to die.

Pauline Suddell

Camelot

There was a place called Camelot
Where there were fields so green
Legend had it on some nights
King Arthur could be seen

King Arthur and his knights so bold
They shared a table round
So no one had a place supreme
Their table was the ground

In the land there was a lake
In there a mystic stone
It kept the sword Excalibur
Held fast for one alone

A blade which needed strength untold
To draw if from its keep
Arthur tried, so great was he
He drew it as a feat

With the sword and his men
King Arthur wore his honour proud
Misdeeds he knew were righted
He stood above the crowd

H. C. Baker

Venice

Venice is the place
Where you want to be
Down in the city
On the sea

Ride a boat,
From shop to shop,
And keep on shopping,
Until you drop.

When your bags get heavy,
And your purse gets light,
Jump on a plane,
Before it turns night.

When you get home,
You jump into bed
and all those shops
Spin 'round in your head

When you wake up,
You visit all your mates,
You give them all their presents,
Like china cups and plates.

Michelle Tucker

Thin Women

I loathe thin women,
Who complain of being fat.
There's something so detestable,
The way that they do that.

They'll moan about their midriff,
Their thighs, or bum or arms.
When all the time they do their best,
To use their obvious charms.

Wearing skimpy outfits,
Their bodies they do flout.
I'd like to feed them doughnuts,
Till rolls of flab they'd sprout.

Losing weight is difficult,
The more excess, the harder.
You try, deprive yourself a lot,
Then you raid the larder.

So, if you're a thin woman,
Who complains of being fat.
Think of us who really are,
And just stop doing that.

Susan J. Wethered

Here with My Poem

Hello old mountains
Sing to me
In that playground
of majesty.

Those peaks that are
stark and sheer
water falls on glass
ice, so clear

The clouds above
weep and sail
wind blows
in gale

Music plays around the tips
caressing those grips
of icy rainbows
in moonlight
give such a sight

That even God
must weep this night.

Shelagh A. Alkenade

The Magic Nursery

Teddies and Dollies
Sitting up high,
Bright coloured Building Blocks.
Reaching the sky.

A Jack-in-the-Box,
A Rag Doll so tall,
When the night comes -
You'll hear them all call . . .

"It's time to wake up,
it's time now to play,
We should be dancing.
Hip hip hooray!

Now we can have fun,
Play Hop, Skip, and Jump,
Until we're so tired -
That we fall with a bump!

And when morning comes 'round
We'll all run from sight,
Back to the Toy Box -
And wait for the night"

Keri Stretton

Will Time Heal

When time stands still.
You live each day in a daze
When time stands still.
You look for the answers
When time stands still.
Reflect on yesterday.
When time stands still.
Don't want to wake tomorrow
When time stands still
Dreams scattered and broken
Now time stands still.

Suzanne Anderson

Rebecca Rebecca

So gentle and mild
you really are a darling child.
Whose little body shows such strength.
From Heaven you were surely sent.
All the things you have overcome,
Since your tiny life began.
You're now improving day by day
So for your full recovery
To God we pray.

Sylvia Wills

Memory

Leaves entwined,
twisting through my memory's mind,
twisted bodies crystallized in stone,
the picture of your smile
echoing through my third sight.
I still hear your laugh
Stranded in vacant air.
Do you hear my tears?
Silent, they fall through space.

Kelly Barratt

Love

Love is like a mother's touch
So gentle, kind and warm
It can tear your heart strings
And yet pacify each storm.
Love can lift your spirits up
you seem as though you fly.
Love is with you always
Until the day you die.
Love is in the air you breathe
Can make you smile or weep
Will change your life forever
And memories you'll always keep.
Love is in your every touch
The way you laugh or cry
Love is every word you speak
Even when you say Goodbye.
Love is all I see in you
There is only truth, no lies
It's there for everyone to see
Just look into your eyes.

M. G. P. Evans

Childhood Delusions

The days of my childhood
So joyous
So bright
Days of adventure
Always promising
Full of delight

Everyday just awaiting for me
Wonder and magic
No worries
So free
Magnificent rainbows coloured
especially for me

Life was such a breeze
'Oh' how I was so naive

If only I knew
The heart breaks of life

Paula Cook

Death

Met death this afternoon,
Saw him down the street,
Funny thing nowadays,
You'll never know who you'll meet.

He was dressed in black,
And looked very old,
Wonder whether he was a good boy,
And did as he was told?

Looked like a reaper,
Grim as can be,
Wondered whether he had sharp teeth,
And needed to use a file?

He waved and ran,
Till out of sight,
All that speed,
All that might!!

Marie Dawson

293

The River Tay

The Tay, the Tay
So lovely to see
As it flows from the Tummell
    To bonnie Dundee

As it winds through the hills
And valleys so green
Passing dense woodland
    What a beautiful scene

Its banks abound
With game so rare
The red deer, the roe deer
    The mountain hare

Its waters are full
With salmon and trout
I've watched the osprey
    Lifting them out

Ah, the Tay the Tay
Where I long to be
As it flows through Perth
    To bonnie Dundee

J. Cannon

Ordinary Person

The ordinary person
Sounds like everyone's the same
With arms and legs and bodies
Only difference is the name

The ordinary person
Has a nose, two eyes and ears
The ordinary person
Sometimes laughs or cries real tears

The ordinary person
Has a mind, and brain and voice
And this ordinary person
Can utter curses, or rejoice

This ordinary person
Could be you or me
And just like every other
Must be loved by somebody

Because ordinary people
Are unique, as God has shown
And each ordinary person
Is special to his own

Mary D. Jones

The Empty Church

Give the door a gentle push
Step inside and feel the hush,
Its texture is as soft as down
Envelops, smooth away the frown

The air of welcome lingers there
None can be seen, but, feel the care
The silence is as balm
Heals hurt and fears becalm

A fragrance pervades and clings
Echo still silently sings
Give the door a gentle push
Step inside and feel the hush

D. K. Reed

Sun Set

As I watched the sunset
The whole world turned dark
No light at all
Except for the white pale moon
Looking soft and sad
Suddenly it disappeared
before my very eyes
Then it was daylight again

K. Wiggins

Future

Plan for a future
Strive for success
Measure this by
Your own happiness

Life is for living
Your plans and your dreams
And if they are broken
don't go to extremes

Pick yourself up
And start to remould
Alter and change
You have to be bold

Make future plans
Keep them to hand
No matter what happens
Make sure they stand

Your future's your own
Something you must decide
With or without
Someone by your side.

Y. J. Riley

From a Seed to a Flower

From a seed to very tall
"Sunflower" - helped by the
Sun-rays, the wind - and the soft
Rain showers - standing tall
And proud she seems to be
Watching almost every cloud
Her beauty revealed - catches
Attention of the birds - and
The bees as she's swaying
And dancing in the breeze
This beautiful sunflower
Standing "So tall" just loves
To display her "beauty" to all.

Roger Brooks

Kings Pond

Alone with my thoughts
Surrounded by nature
The odd snap of a twig
There's so much to capture

Swans gracefully passing
Like silk tickling velvet
A breeze playfully kissing
Enriched all is kept

Sunlight caressing my every move
Wishing and wanting dreams on the run
Leaves peek-a-boo with my shadow
Tomorrow's memories have just begun.

Lorraine Lane

Pondering

Listen to the rustle of
The leaves upon the trees.
Listen to the buzzing of
The nectar-seeking bees.
Listen to the children
Laughing whilst at play.
Listen to the chatter on
A lovely summer's day.
Listen to the droning of
An airplane in the sky
Listen to the birds as on
The wing they fly.
Listen to the waves as on
The shore they pound.
Listen to the silence
When you cannot hear a sound.

V. Young

Love from Above

I watched when you were with her
the happiness that you shared,
you walked hand in hand
barefoot in the sand,
you'd laugh and kiss,
oh God
look what I've missed.

I watched when you were with her
the looks that passed between,
you walked through the park
well we did that,
your bodies entwined.
Oh God
look what I've missed.

I watched when you were with her
you're happy now, that I can see,
you're loved from above
and I'll watch over you my love,
Till the day, you come, and join me.

Yvonne Brightwell

"The Singer and the Song"

A song of love is a sound from
the heart,
The singer that sings it is the
main part,
Whether it is to a lover or just
a good friend,
The message is the same they will
be together in the end,
There may be good times, there
may be bad.
But the singer and the song
brings the best times they ever had.

P. P. Gower

Airport Reunion

Our lips meet,
The last few months of pain are over,
Reunited love;
Wish this moment could last forever,
Holding each other close,
The world slips away -
Into the background,
We seem alone, but together,
No one else in this world but us,
The world stands still in time -
Let this moment last forever.

V. Coulson

My Snowman

As I look out my window
the snow is falling down
it's falling fast and furious
And covering the ground

I'll get my scarf and gloves on.
I have to wrap up warm.
the snow is falling heavier
it's looking like a storm

As I walk out the door
A snowball hits my face
My friends are playing in the street
Oh look, there in a race.

We've built a man made out of snow
He's really looking good
With eyes and nose made out of stones
And his pipe made out of wood

As I look upon my snowman
With sadness and with sorrow
'Cause when the sun comes up again
My snowman's gone tomorrow!

Kelly Cumberbirch

Early Spring, Seen from the Train

A flannel-grey sky.
The soil night-black.
A flutter of white napery,
the gulls encircling the track
of the plough.

A field frost-white,
Rooks building high,
nests afloat in frail
branches, winter-naked
patterning the sky.

Red earth in furrows.
Mud turned to ice
in the hollows
crazed and milky as Roman glass
polished in sunlight.

A single black crow
goose-stepping on grass
frost-stiff. Golden eye alert
for the worm, up-stirred
by the train's passing.

B. W. Merson

Good Times

The song did sing
The sun did shine
The wind did blow
The earth was mine
The plant did grow
The leaves did fall
The earth was mine
And his and all
The rain fell down
The buds they grew
The flowers bloomed
The winter's through
The spring is here
The night it shines
The party's on
For those good times

Karen Fisher

To Dream

How bare the trees
The winter long
The cold dark days
Without birds song.

The spring awaits
The sky is blue
Birds sweetly sing
The sun shines through.

Trees bear blossom
Perfumed flowers bloom
Our spirits lift
Away with gloom

Clear waters glisten
Crystal in the stream
The spring is here
No more a dream.

Pat Whitmarsh

Coming

I came following Ulysses
Till the sun spoke to me
I met Claudius' palace
Drinking Orpheus' music
Strangling Oedipus' dilemma
I came following
the ball of future
Entering Noah's Ark.

Louisa Borg Haviaras

Understanding

I ask for understanding
The world I'd like to right
Do away with suffering
Give the blind their sight

I ask for understanding
Why droughts should ever be
Do away with hunger
So much water in the sea

I ask for understanding
Why those who have so much
When it comes to understanding
So completely out of touch

I ask for understanding
Why can't the world unite
Do away with suffering
give the blind their sight

Thomas Mair

Requiem for Trees

Smoke is rising,
Their last remains are burned,
Side by side they lay, awaiting
Their cremation, while others
Stand and hang their branches
In sorrow for their departed friends,
As their turn is yet to come,
So many sunrises, so many sunsets
Have they seen,
So many joys and sorrows of
The passing years,
The birds are their mourners,
As overhead they fly, dipping their
wings in last respect -
People stop and gaze in sorrow -
For these trees there is no tomorrow,
This is their end,
Remembered only by their friends.

V. J. Lafon

Into the Fire

I went for the 'burn'
Then life began to simmer.
I try to stay cool.
Soon, I will be clambering
Right out of this frying-pan.

Susan Shaw

I Am Life

Once I was only Spirit,
    Then there was only Me;
Now I am also many
    Material manifestations
Of the one Reality

What made Me manifest
    And why?
What led Me to you
    From I?
My Self awareness, and
    My mind,
My self love - is
    The kind
That self expresses
    To fulfil;
My cosmic presence
    Is My will.

Because I AM, so are you;
    Everyone and everything like you.
And everything, like you!

K. K. Kempt

In My Mind

I wander and wander through my mind,
There are so many fabulous things I can find,
Moments of the past,
Praises of today,
Searching, searching,
Every way,
Things I never knew,
Things I can forget,
Things I love,
And things I regret.
Each passing minute,
Holds something new,
Surprising me,
Out of the blue,
Something magic or maybe bad,
Sometimes happy, and sometimes sad.
Now I add to my mind
Another thing I can find,
Something magic and something new,
The thing I'm adding . . . is you.

Kerry Stewart

Liar

There's no where to run
There's no where to hide
To darkness is coming
You shouldn't have lied
The days are now shorter
The nights are now longer
You should not have lied
Now the evil is stronger
Some call it guilt
Some call it pride
Some call it anger
You shouldn't have lied
to an enemy o.k.
You should have tried
But to your friends no way
You should never have lied
What were you thinking?
Now it's time to go
It's time to say goodbye
Why did you lie?

Mark Baker

Loneliness

I didn't know the meaning,
Till you said goodbye,
I didn't know the feeling,
Of a heartache, or a sigh.
I'd never felt the sorrow,
Behind a parting kiss
Or the love in your eyes,
That now, I reminisce -
Your smile, the smile
My memory holds dear,
Not for just a while
But always so clear.
We were together,
Then, we had to part
Parting, how that word
Echoes in my heart.
You whispered goodbye
As you stepped on the train,
So lonely now, until the day
You come back to me again.

Patricia Betteridge

Summer Solstice

On summer solstice sunshine skips
To craggy corners of unlit crypts
This Mystic moment mimics mirth
Then dies in darkness, dies at birth.

Michael J. McCann

Two Hearts Collide

Two hearts collide,
to a single beat.
With the flames of love,
I can feel the heat.

The light of my life,
a star in disguise.
A moment in time,
as seen through my eyes.

An age goes by,
a passage of years.
A gain in strength,
to conquer all fears.

The shot from an arrow,
a pain in my heart.
A problem in life,
tears me apart.

Michael Smith

Total Joy

I never knew it was possible,
To feel such total joy,
Every time my eyes look down,
Upon my baby boy,
His eyes so brown and knowing,
His mouth so soft and cute,
My heart's all warm and glowing,
He really is a beaut!

Life is now complete for me,
I have someone of my own,
Even though he has fetish,
For chewing on his bone,
His teeth may be so very sharp,
His nose all cold and wet,
But a lovelier puppy you won't find,
My house, my wealth, I'll bet!

Kathy Berry

"The Wonder of Sun"

The sun shines through my window pane
    To greet the dawn of day,
Its glowing warm encircled frame
    Fills hearts in every way.

Enriched by far, mankind will know
    The power of its rays.
On earth, the sun doth it bestow
    Fulfilment of its days

As twilight turns to dusk we see
    A wondrous sight on high,
The setting sun, to such degree,
    Illuminates the sky.

Pauline Will

"Listen with Your Mind"

Just close your eyes and listen
To hear the flowers wind
Look in the secret places
And listen with your mind

Touch a fair wind blowing
Touch the corn to grind
Hear a fairy's whisper
Just listen with your mind

Taste the sparkling waters
It's source for you to find
It's richer than the rarest mead
So listen with your mind

The shining stars of heaven
Keep skies above re-lined
With light and every loveliness
So see them with your mind.

M. Hulme

Life

Long life is all man strives for
To last an eternity
Our nagging fear, our unspoken bond
The fear of death itself
But the depth of our feelings
The meaning of our love
The ultimate gift I could give
Is to overcome that fear
And lay down my life for you

A. C. Stock

Depths of Despair

To curl around your body,
To lie within your arms
To feel the touch of your caress
Is a feeling I just yearn.

Your sensuous kiss upon my lips
I long for every day
But now as time goes passing by
Will it ever come again.

My lover who has left my life
Has gone away from me
He has slipped into a world unknown
Forty fathoms under the sea.

It's not the fathoms of water
That stirs my mind with pain
That grips my heart and twists it
Till the blood has left my veins.

I'm swirling in the darkness
Trying to grip what's left of life
It's not the fathoms of water
But that many tears that I have cried.

Moira Spencer-MacKay

Dream Lover

I have a secret, lover, she comes
    to me at night.
Oh! To feel the warmth of her, as
    I hold her tight.
She tells me that she loves me,
    contented in my arms.
Oh! To feel desire, when presented
    with her charms.
My heart is full of passion, as we
    kiss so tenderly.
I will always love you, please never
    go from me.
She gives to me without question,
    herself in total love.
When daybreak comes, I shed a tear
    she's flown like a dove.

Daytime is so lonely my heart
    yearns for the night.

Because I know my dream will
    come and I can hold her tight

D. Fuller

Untitled

Step by step with Jesus.
Walking hand in hand,
Following our Saviour
To the promised land.

God will not forsake you,
His promise He will keep,
We are His little children.
In Him we seek our peace.

Please forgive us Father,
For the wrong that we have done
We ask You for Your blessing
Sweet Jesus, God's own Son.

Mary Turner

Self-Denial

I turn to the shadows,
to the inspiration that flows
from a craftful figure
of stone or something bigger
than life and more modest
than being friendly dishonest.

I define myself with abstractions
and the only thing that isn't yours
must surely be the essence of me.
So if we all do then agree
that life itself is your own course
then leave me to my affliction.

Eye to eye with my vague I,
I stand in frightful oblivion
until I accept and refuse to try
another self-centred rebellion.
My void turns into a tray,
on which I give myself away.

Tom Hengen

To the Man

To the man who fathered me,
To the one I'll never see.
To the man who isn't around,
To see me now - safe and sound.
To the man who I can't see,
Who's in my heart eternally.
To the man who married my mum,
Now we'll never have the family fun.
To the man I'll never fear,
Thinking of you makes me shed a tear.
To the man who gave me life,
Taken from his child and wife.
To the man I'll love forever,
One day we will be together.
To the man who'll always be,
My one and only Daddy.

Samantha J. Bates

I Should Have Said

Today I woke up in my bed
To think of things I should have said
Like thank you Mum and thank you Dad
For putting up with all the bad
And praising me when I was good
When I was always in a mood
How many times you held me tight
When I was frightened in the night
And taught me how to deal with life
And handle all the toil and strife
You handled me with love and care
And taught me how to give and share
To be polite and always nice
If not then I should pay the price
This precious time I need to give
For life is full and we must live
To say I love you every day
To Mum and Dad I must now say
I love you both and now is time
Now that I am in my prime

Margaret Ritchie

Hate

An insidious blackness descends
upon the horizon child,
A coiling malevolent serpent
poised
venom fanged.

The whispers surmount in crescendo,
deadly jeering imbuing satisfaction
the victim bared on crucifix
nailed in sacrifice

Scott Francis

296

April Shower

Sheets billowing on the line,
Trees bending,
Dark clouds scudding o'er the sky,
Storm coming,
Raindrops plopping to the ground,
Storm breaking,
Wind whistling in the tall trees,
Rain pouring,
Sunlight breaking through the clouds,
Rain easing,
Rainbow arching 'cross the sky,
Storm ending,
Puddles drying on the path,
Storm over,
Sheets billowing on the line...

Sandra M. Eyles

To Nancy

Precious breath - gone.
Trembling hands - still.
Darting eyeballs - rested.
Aching limbs - numb.

And my ears ring;
And my heart pounds;
And my parched eyes sting
And my whole soul shakes.

Dead but not buried,
I remember all of you and
Imagine that I am imagining
That you are not still with me

My grandmother and friend
Your absence haunts me and
I strain to see your chair as empty
And not to hear your rattling breaths.

Martine Louise John

The Garden of Eden

I see this beautiful garden
Unique and glorious
One man and woman
At one with nature
Flowers, trees, ferns amidst

Up nigh a sky of heavens
Blue horizon of meaning depth
Wondrous, amazing, terrific
Abound with creation below
Carefully kept

The waterfall erupts and stirs
The birds sing out the joy
The flowers blossom and grow
Nature calls out for more

Tracy Charters

Silently Creeping

Silently creeping all around you,
unseen by staring eyes, he paints
the freshly dewed forests with
his gentle freezing breath.

He's so gentle but yet so sharp
with his staggering crystal dagger.
As he breathes his wet silver
whisper fills the air with chilling
sparkling vapour.

Red patches on your legs and
gleaming red fingers are the result
as frost sets in. Then, as the sun
appears, frost magically disappears.

Michael Taylor

Botanic Gardens

The trees on the hill
wake with the wind in their arms
dipping and swaying.

Like a chaperon at a dance
a stout pohutakawa
responds to the wind's rhythm
with tiny movements of the eyes -
a matron's glance.

The solid palm nearby
raises its eyebrows
at the runners streaming past.

Bedded pansies
shake their heads each time the wind
interrogates them.

A stooped figure in overalls
sweeps the path.
Then he straightens up
and with a freckled hand
smooths down the petals
of his chrysanthemum hair.

Robin Fry

Forever

You give me so much pleasure,
watching you each day,
breathing, living, growing,
laughing in your own way.

As each new dawn breaks,
my love for you won't hesitate,
I often wonder was it fate
God made you to be my mate.

Please believe me when I say
My love for you won't go away
It's locked away with a key of gold
Too big for hands to ever hold.

Sandra Traynor

Energy

Swinging, swirling, leaping,
Waving colours, blends and hues
Power cascading, slipping, sliding,
Here - there - now - then
Anima with full blood beat
Sometimes hiding, fearful, chiding
Throw away - too strong to hold
Cherished, fondled, hot and cold
Mine - other's; at times no home
Sheer abandon wet and warm
Surging, pushing not held down
Clowning, blinking, winking frown -
At rest within, a-simmer, tremble
Gift sublime - for 'lifeing' - Mine.

Margaret V. Horan

Listen

Listen
To the notes
One by one being written
Listen
To the low and high
Together all are being fit-in
Listen
How the finger;
Key by key are being hitten
Listen
To the music flowing
In my ears it is being let in
Listen
For slowly it drafts away
Smoothly, as if to copy a kitten

Maryam M. El-Shafie

How Still the Night

How still the night
When all are sleeping.
How still the night
When stars are peeping,

Through the clouds
Be they white, or grey.
How still the night,
Then dawns the day.

Marie Robinson

Reflection

What is a reflection
We ask each day
The answer to say
Is a mirror fixed on the wall.

It shows when you are
Sad and blue.
We look to see if that is true.
And when you are happy and glad
You, me, and all
Just look at the mirror
on the wall.

It's like a camera it doesn't lie
Life goes on as days fly by
Grey hairs appear and wrinkles too
There is not much that one can do
Just sit around and take what comes
If you don't want to see it all
Don't look at the mirror on the wall.

Sue Hayden

Why Care

Why should we care.

We have our clothes
We have our food
We have our houses
That's more than you,

Why should we care.
What should we do stop think.

We could have been you stop think
There's things to do
Try and make thing
As good for you

Why should we care

What should we do
One day we will die,
And so will you

At least we will
Know we did our best,
When they lay us down

To rest

B. M. Fuller

A Choice

Life is too short.
What will I do, he asked me
I said I don't know, I'm not sure,
I'll think about it.
Is it worth it.
My freedom, O God my freedom,
Will suddenly yet significantly
Dissolved in the mere molecules,
Of my immediate atmosphere,
I won't be able to sneak out and
Snog the boy next door, flirt with
The barman, the milkman, o and
That cute errand boy
Life is too short, too sweet,
I think I'll say yes, Maybe!

Vaf McCarthy

The Dunblane Tragedy

On the 13th of March 1996,
We heard the innocent cry,
Of those 16 angels,
Who now sleep up in the sky.

Why did he have to shoot them?
The man who went to hell,
He never let those angels,
Hear the end-of-school bell.

Those innocent wee angels,
They never got to say,
Mummy I love you,
That Mother's Day.

All my sympathy goes out,
To the families of those who died,
On March 13th of 1996,
The nation cried and cried and cried.

Kimberley Forsyth

Letter to a Lost Love

I let you go, without a word,
We never said good-bye
But my love for you was true,
Forty years have gone by
But I still remember you

We met by chance one summer's day,
I must speak with you, you said,
But I only turned away,
I know I must have broke your heart
But mine was broken too,

If only one could turn back time
I would walk with you
Our live's would have been entwined.

I had a duty to fulfil,
It was better to let you go,
Many tears I shed,
And now, to late, I know,
I should have never let you go.

M. D. Seymour

Myself

Scared!
What will each new day bring?
Lonely!
An empty ongoing thing
Single!
Like a lonely rose
Friends!
So different, yet so close
Worry!
Everyday I do
Tomorrow!
A start of something new
Unhappy!
Why do I feel so sad?
Myself!
Am I really that bad?

Sarah Mullins

The Tree of Life

You look out the window,
what do you see,
it's the Magic
of the Living Tree.
The leaves fall
covering the ground,
like a magic carpet
all around.
The autumn colours, they're
so stunning, so bright.
Rustling, waving, whistling.
This is the magic of life.

Lois Sweetman

Our Troubled World

Why can't we live in harmony,
We plead time and time again,
We must stop all this killing,
All the heartaches and the pain.
So many of our countries,
Are at war with one another,
But God did not intend all this,
He wants us to love our brother,
To live together side by side,
No matter what creed or colour.
So stop the maiming and the killing,
Put our trust in one another.
Mothers lose their cherished sons,
And wives, their husbands gone,
What happens to the children,
Left, bewildered and forlorn.
Teach these, the little children,
Not to repeat our history.
But to live together, side by side,
To bring peace and harmony.

Rita Scanlon

Mis-Directed

I can't express the way I feel,
Well at least not face to face
The telephone is the easy option,
Well at least it gives me grace

I want to say how much,
I want to leap on top of you.
But what I really need to know,
Is that you feel the same way too,

I seem to spend my time
Just dreaming what I should do now,
I think a flat and suitcase
are my only option somehow

Well I hope you like the poem,
I haven't written for some time.
I look forward to our meetings,
I promise I won't talk in Rhyme.

Michelle Putman

Despair

What is this abyss of despair
where all is gloom and silence
Wouldst thou my Lord
just leave me there
alone and without guidance.

What sin have I committed
what have I left undone
that doubt should now assail me
to whose heart may I run

Oh would I lay my weary head
at heaven's door my Lord
No more to worry, ever sure
That you wouldst guide my tread.

J. Henchy

Precious Moments

Those precious moments
When you are all alone
To think of the wonderful
Times you have known.

The dreams one have
Are only for you
The gold of the sun
The sky so blue

The flowers so radiant,
The garden so gay,
Makes it worth living,
From day to day

Marguerite Lowder

Thoughts of Life

What is life all about
What are we doing here
Living through pain
Living through sorrow,
The occasional joy
But what of tomorrow

Whose to remember to us
When we've gone,
We are merely mortals
Of skin and bone.
There are many regrets,
But yesterday's gone.

There are a few
Who make their mark
For future generations.
But for the majority
Of us it seems,
The most we can expect
Is a fistful of dreams.

Lesley Burton

Stranger

Tell me stranger, as you read,
What do you cast your eyes upon.
Nought but words upon a page,
Moments used that now are gone.

Well now stranger, whilst you read,
Are your moments wasted thus.
Then if waste the time so spent,
Applies in equal parts to us,

I sat and mused on words to say,
Into this my time I fused
Words that lilt a certain play,
To me 'tis time not lost, but used.

I guess I could have left the space,
With nothing to the page to bring,
I could have said a little less,
Although, I have not said a thing,

Having read this so far thus,
You hardly can ignore.
The time you took to read it through.
Know me, no better than before.

Pauline Davies

Life's Testament

Do not let the tears cascade
When your world falls apart
Fight to keep those spirits high
Hope deep inside your heart

Recall fond happy memories
Embedded in the soul
Cast away black shadows
Once again you will feel whole

There are bountiful blessings
That we forget to store
Turn your head and look around
So many could do with more

The devil grips hard to possess
As trouble attacks galore
Push him aside in angry trait
Don't let him through your door

We are not in armour clad
Protected from every hurt
Our safety lies within the Lord
Feel his love gently insert

P. M. Mulrooney

By the Gravestone

By the gravestone I do sit,
wondering why you had to die.
I look up in the sky,
to see the sun shining down,
upon the flowers in the ground.
I wonder to myself today,
why people had to go this way.
Rest in peace they
all must do.
Knowing one day,
it will be me and you.

E. Donnelly

Heaven's Dream

I often sit and wonder
What heaven would be like
If I was ever good enough
To see that wondrous light.
I imagine it to be a warm
summer's day
Bright green grass and flowers
To guide us on our way.
The trees would be full of
Birds of all different types
Singing prettily it would be
a lovely sight.
The sky would be a lovely
Blue, we could see the people
We all once knew.
Wouldn't this be nice if
All this could come true.

Marie Amelia Evenden

The Snowman

On one winter morning
When all was white with snow.
The hazy sun was shining
The wind was all a-blow

The children playing snow balls
Giggling, all a-glee
The snowman standing proud and tall
Waiting to be free

The winter sun was glowing
Thawing all around
The wind was still a-blowing
Snow melting on the ground

The trees and hedges dripping
With slowly melting snow
The snowman gently thawing
He'll soon be free to go

The winter sun had melted
The snow on ground and tree
The children watched downhearted
The snowman was now free.

Sue Whitworth

Lockerbie

An aeroplane was flying high
When a bomb on board
Blew it out of the sky
It didn't land in England
Or fall into the sea
But it fell on a place in Scotland
On a town called Lockerbie
So many people died that way
I'll remember with horror
Till my dying day
As the story unfolded on my T.V.
I was filled with pity
For each family
All of them waiting expectantly
But there were no survivors
From flight one-o-three

S. T. Evans

"Tattered Covers"

Sometimes I feel just like a book.
    With torn and tattered covers,
Which has been read for a while
    And then passed onto others

But they never seem to turn a page
    So they will never see.
The heartache and the pain
    That's deep inside of me.

So the next time that you pick me up
    Don't give me to another
Make sure you read what's inside
    Don't judge me by my cover.

D. Blakey

My Home

The bench is where I live
When I wake
I see trees blow in the wind.

When I turn my head
I see the oil drums
That have died out.

Across the road
Is the bright red phone box
Which is my only friend
As well as so many unwanted calls.

And opposite to me is the graveyard
Which seems so peaceful
And no devil has set foot
As he runs.

Soon I will be running
And I will stop at the graveyard
With no gravestone
To remember me.

Polly L. Heaver

Forever Christmas

Christmas, is the time of year
When wars and quarrels cease,
The world forgets her troubles,
There's tranquillity, and peace.
Everyone holds out their hand,
In friendship, warm and true,
To help each other on life's road
That's what we strive to do.
So when the season's finished,
And the trimmings have all gone,
Don't let that Christmas spirit die,
No, let it linger on.
The world would be a better place,
Of that I have no fear,
If, my friend, you just pretend,
It's Christmas all the year.

H. Baldwin

The Outsider

It's not fair,
Why can't I be,
One of them,
And not just me.
I'd like to step in,
through an open door.
And not have it slammed,
With me pushed to the floor.
I was one of them,
once long ago.
Now all I do is stand and gaze,
and just hope.
Why can't they understand,
how I feel to be,
The Outsider.
Yes, that's me!!!

Uzma Rehman

Saying

They say to change the world
you should start with yourself.
They say if you want something
bad enough you'll eventually
achieve it.
They say if you look at the
end of a rainbow you'll find
a pot of gold.
They say everything that
happens has a meaning.
They say if you have special
qualities, you'll be someone.
They say far too much and
listen far too little.

Natasha Haverley

Missing You

Life is somehow cruel,
When it leaves one all alone
But I feel you're always with me
No matter where I roam
I think of all the good times
The laughter and the songs
Why did you have to leave me,
Where did I go wrong?
My life is slowly passing by
Each day I shed a tear
I picture you as you used to be
And wonder, do you hear
The prayers that I pray for you
Before I go to sleep
I wonder do you see me dear
When all alone I weep.
I know we'll meet again some day
And when that day will come
I know you'll stand and wait for me
It's then I'll start to run.

Mary Devine

Untitled

Will you set out on the water,
with my dreams to help you float.
Will you safely reach a port,
With my heart to be your boat.
Will you follow a true path,
With the lodestone of my hope.
Will you search for all our goals,
With my strength to help you cope.
Will you rest a while in peace,
With the anchor of my faith.
Will you face the storm again,
In the search to see my face.
Will you strive to remain true,
If my light will lift the veil.
Will you journey on life's ocean,
If my love will be your sail.

Susan C. Marsters

My Prayer

When I needed strength Lord,
You were always there.
When I asked for help
You showed how much You care.
And when I lost my faith
to follow and to trust You.
Your loving arms surrounded me
and made my spirit new.

So I will always try to follow
Your eternal guiding light.
For you are my salvation
and my strength in every fight.
And now I'm giving thanks Lord
for each and every day.
that You've been here to love me
in Your gentle caring way.

Sandra Standage

299

Orpheus

I am not Orpheus.
When you left, to lie
in her arms, you died.

Although we talked
in passing
you were never,
wholly alive
to me again.

So now you find
her, less inviting
and whisper
from the darkness
that if I dare
you would follow.

But I am not Orpheus.
Whilst you lay
amongst the dead
I may have lived
learnt another tune.
I am, cold heart
not your Orpheus
S. E. Rand

Untitled

Lost in the wilderness,
Searching for your soul,
Grasping at the air,
Never catching hold.

Infinite wisdom,
Questionable doubt,
Hoping for freedom,
No way out.

Tears of fire,
Heart of ice,
Neurosis of your own device.

I can hear your screams,
And understand your dreams,
Please let my dry your tears,
Comfort your fears,
And with a gentle hand,
Mould them into normality.
Rebecca Crow

Claustrophobic

There are barriers all around us.
A fence a six root wall,
Invisible to others,
But there and standing strong

The barbed wire is so easy,
Can be thrown up in a day,
Lead-plated, walls of steel.
To some it sounds so unreal

Trapped within your own small space,
No diffusion taking place
Jane Sutherland

One Summer's Day

A sky of blue, a misty haze,
A friendly smile, a little wave,
An artist palette, a tranquil place.
Peace and quiet, lots of space,
Distant mountains, greyish hue,
Stream meandering, misty blue,
Orange heads waving, Poppies dancing,
Tossing heads, horses prancing,
Ears of corn, tall and yellow,
Breath of wind, cool and mellow,
Birds overhead, singing sweetly.
Looking down on a scene of beauty.
Christine Booth

A Kiss!

A kiss to say good morning.
A kiss that seems so right.
A kiss to say I thank you.
A kiss to say goodnight.

A kiss that notes our friendship.
A kiss once in a while.
A kiss that shows we're happy.
A kiss and then a smile.

A kiss that tells no lies.
A kiss to show it's true.
A kiss to say three words.
A kiss to say I love you!
Graham Mitchell

Woodland Pathways

Once an idle way we took
Where the little wand'ring brook,
Overflowing mossy wells,
Beckoned us to secret dells,
Flashing out of twilight shades
Led us into fairy glades.

Here the sunlight filtered through
Woven trellises of blue,
Coming from a sky unseen.
Into hollows, golden green.
Here the forest's magic spells
Hung on dappled foxglove bells.

Through the arch of leafy green,
Still we wandered on unseen
Walking by the little brook,
Turning back once more to look
At the laden boughs of May,
'Ere we went upon our way.
Sheila McFarlane

Mrs. Farbrother

I used to find some things so hard,
I didn't understand,
Things were not made plain to me,
Till this lady came to hand,
The way that she explained to me,
Things became so very clear,
The things that used to worry me,
I now no longer fear.
Claire Toms

The Chapel

There is a chapel
Where
No breath
Of far-off
Discord
Breathes
But like
The candle's
Flame
Unmoved
By tunes
Inaudible
Burns.
At Evensong
When cattle
Weary
Bow their
Heads
And drink

I will go.
Martin Stubberfield

Walking

A Sunny spring morning,
a chill in the air,
where I am walking,
I do not know
'cause walking on a morning
like this,
is true bliss.
If I were to go away
the one thing I would
miss,
is walking on a sunny
spring morning
Just like this.
Alexis Burke

I Asked for Life

In my bed I lay dying,
Wife and children crying,
Nurses and doctors whispering,
Sometimes softly, softly talking
Around my bed.
The senior man took my pulse
And shook his head,
A nurse whispered, "is he dead?"
Again the man shook his head,
Pulled the sheet over my face,
And straightened my arms by my side.
A bright light covered me,
So brilliant that I could not see,
Then it became dark
And I was sorely afraid,
And silently prayed for life,
A voice boomed from the dark,
"You have got life,"
And I awoke from the dream.
V. Aitcheson

Petting

Our home is a menagerie
With dogs and cats and such
rabbits fish and white mice too
Though those I hate to touch

We haven't any birds yet
to sing their plaintive song
but if I know my weaknesses
We'll have one before long

Our kitchens full of varying tins
all filled with weird pet food
and sometimes we glean hay and straw
When we're in rural mood

But though I love my animals
in truth they can't compare
With woman's need for man's true love
So precious and rare.
Pamela Rose

A Deeper Understanding

Oh that I had the strength
with my own eyes
To pierce man's heart and
see what in it really lies
And find in other souls
some hidden spot
To understand the things
I now cannot
These inner things to me
are very bleared
As though a fog within has
not yet cleared
For only the simple things of
Life I see and know
And yet these things so
beautiful with radiance do glow
T. Underwood

My Life at 83

I'm here all day
With nothing to say,
Cos there's no one here to talk to.
I'm here on my own
With never a moan,
Don't quite know what to do?
I know! I'll sit in my chair
Watch the folk out there,
Who can come and go as they please
I don't mind at all
Though I can't walk tall
As I have arthritic knees
Can't walk quick
With even a stick
I get around painfully well
When my son gets home
I won't be alone
I'll just listen to him
Where he's bin' who he's sin'
Well what else can I do

Phyllis V. Richardson

It's Been My Pleasure

If on this earth we are placed
With style and grace, to serve
Our fellow man,
To share their woe
And let them know

That someone cares,
Life's not a hustle and bustle,
It's not a race,
Live it at a steady pace.
Nothing for first,

In fact, first maybe last.
Who knows what prizes have been lost.
Live each day and live each night
Awaking in the dawning light.
In our hearts we can say,

We bring pleasure, on the way
To the journey of our final day
We seek no reward
Our prize will be,
Laughter and smiles, we hear and see

Leslie Carter

If Only . . .

He yells but no-one hears,
Without a friend to lean on,
Without a shoulder to cry on,

It's getting too much,
Time to relieve the pain,
Time to get out of the way.

He tries,
But he can't,
Why?

He has to,
There's no-one here for him,
But there will be up there.

He does it,
The pain has gone,
Says 'Good-bye'.

The body lays there cold,
In the playground,
people come around,
As if they cared,
It was their fault.

Marc J. Hambly

Untitled

Like a headless chicken
without a goal
watches I
a drunk
on his way home
from the last picnic
in December
a master
of coincidences
in my own speed
I use my life
like a rambolt
towards a paradox
that does not belong
who is fighting
a lie of exhaustion
like a holy war
merely I walk
towards what once shall be
my final breath

Kai H. Sollie

Where?

Where are you God?
Are you looking down?
Are you watching me,
With disappointed frown?
Do you know my name?
Do you feel my pain?
Would you help if you could?
Will I know if your should?
Do you care what happens to me?

Diane Wallace

See Me

See me . . . do not ignore me!
You can look me in the eye
It makes me sad when you ignore me
In truth it often makes me cry!
People tend to pat me on the head
Then they quickly look away,
As they don't know how to treat me
They simply don't know what to say!
Well . . . try to imagine how I feel
I have to deal with the frustration
As even very simple tasks
Cause problems in my situation,
Please do not add to all my traumas
By your thoughtless attitude
Apart from being so hurtful
It is also very rude.
So the next time that you meet me
Sitting there in my wheelchair
Treat me like a human being
Just remember that I am there!

Mary Scott

The Piano

For as long as I can recall,
A piano has stood in this hall,
And yet I fail to understand,
How to master that piano grand,
With ivory and ebony keys,
And pedals just below the knees,
On legs of grand splendour it stands,
Just yearning for musicians' hands,
Its colour of white and mirror shine,
It waits to send notes into time,
And oh how I long to play,
Just to make that piano's day,
It seems to be beckoning me,
To run my fingers through its keys,
But musical minded I am not,
So there it will stay till it rots.

Joseph Walker

No More

A voice no more to be heard
A touch no more shall be felt
No more a word of wisdom
No more a heart to melt

To need a loving embrace
To gently caress a face
To hold the warmth of love
no more

To ease thy aching heart
To wish not the end but start
To say goodbye too much
To feel no more the touch

The wind no more to feel
A tear no more to cry
End of a soul to seal
Dear God do please take I

No autumn leaves to fall
No sea to caress a shore
As my Lord You call
These eyes will see no more

Elaine Anne Unwin

"Thoughts of Home"

Home is a place where
You feel safe, also secure
With lots of loving care,
Even with sorrow and strife,
That's what life is about.

As you grow older in years,
You have a will of your own,
Then you are ready to fly
"The nest from home".
Just like the tiny birds
Who have to learn to fly high
"To survive or die"

To look after oneself,
Also to get on with life,
You have to do the rest,
Always do your best,
Then you will win life's tests.
You will then, I pray my dears
Come through life alright.
"God Bless Home Life."

V. M. Moore

Eclipse

Moon! Why so shy?
You grace the heavens
with your silver bright.

Oh Moon! Where do you go?
Can I come with you
or must you go alone?

Moon. Where's your light?
Under a bushel
or snuffed by the night?

Moon! What have you done?
Peek-a-boo - really?
What? Hid from the Sun?

Moon. When will you peep
out again to
play hide and seek?

Oh Moon! What do you think?
Sunlight has seen you -
she's making you blink.

Susan Biggin

Someone to Care

Sitting in a little room,
All by himself,
He could have been a parcel,
On an empty bedroom shelf.
People pass him daily,
They all know he's there,
But people have their own lives,
And people just don't care.
Mother has been beaten,
Sister has just gone.
Father has just eaten,
But for little boy there's none.
A little love,
A little care,
How much more can this child bear?
Could someone make a difference,
To this lonely, poor reject?
Will someone hug the child,
'Cause he's dying of neglect.

Dawn Davis

My Dad

My dad was somebody I'd
Always admired

Always there for any help
I required

He had a true, loving nature
In every way

Always happy and smiling
Throughout the day

To tell him how much I loved him
I left far too late

Put into only words when
I knew of his fate

You were not only my dad
But also my friend

I hope you knew how much loved you
Before the end

Diane O'Hennessy

If Time Was Just an Island

If time was just an island
an island in the sun
and we could be together
Life could be such fun

If time was just an island
and you and I were there
we could be so happy
for the joys of time we'd share

But time is just a-wasting
and like a passing dream
the island's quickly fading
Life's never what it seems

As time waits for no one
and life just carries on
I think of our tomorrows
and the time that's already gone

Jennifer Pressley

In the Distance

I saw a figure.
An outline.
A small child,
Walking slowly,
Towards the future.
His slow footsteps,
His tired figure,
Silhouetted by the setting sun.

Emma Wyatt

Golden Days

The long grey days have gone
away, the sun is shining through
the days that used to be so grey
are turning now to gold.

It took a little time this
change, but now it has occurred.
I think I'm getting to know myself
and buds are starting to burst.
The buds are pushing really hard,
and once the flowers bloom,
the long grey days will go
away, and you'll see what's
left is gold.

Christine

The Lacemakers

At the bottom of the garden
    Behind the potting shed
You'll find tiny lacemakers
    Working their silvery thread

Fastened between the wild flowers
    That grow with beauty there
Hangs such delicate lacework
    To be displayed anywhere

If during night, a frost is brought
    And on the lace it falls
Brilliance of morning light
    Reveals spiralling ice jewels

Lacemakers hide in the cracked pots
    Which were left there one day
And if they hear you coming
    It is here they're sure to stay

Not of fairy folk I tell of
    But a creature more clear
Spider, I'll whisper to you
    So their bigger kin won't hear

Claire P. Bonneywell

Untitled

She is kneeling, head bowed
    Beside the fresh mound
Wrenching tears dropping down
    Into nothingness

Listening, she lifts her head
    Sees the lark in the bright air
Defying the pull of the earth
    Calling her heart
    Up

Helen Hooke

An April Day

Cold and bright this April morn,
Billowing clouds on a light
breeze flow
Like icebergs in the sky
drift so slowly on
This Arenial Sea, the backdays
of a light blue sky on a
Northwest breeze.
From the Welsh hills, and
the distant lakes.
Bringing the showers to
spring forth the budding trees
and flowers, which burst
Forth in the coming may sunshine.
Blossoms of many trees are
now showing, colourful,
Pinks, yellows, red and whites,
Oh! The joy of new life, it's spring.

John D. Ainsley

Joyriding, They Call It

You said you'd never leave me,
but you did . . .
Out of the blackness of the night
it came, the chariot of death,
its youthful occupant
screaming
as he struck you down,
and you, my love,
lay silent in its wake.

Across soft meadows
of remembrance
your dear voice echoes,
through the tangled visions
of the past,
and I, alone,
my life a fog
of nothingness, die,
a thousand times a day.

Audrey Newall

Seeing!

I was waiting for you
but you didn't show
I knew already - why?
Cos I always know
do you feel like you're being watched
could it be me?
You'll never know!
That I'm the foe
or just think that I am
I'm not - just to assure
or just maybe
terrify you more
cos you'll never know
deep down how much
I love you so
ha! ha! I can laugh
cos I'm the eyes
you so much despise
    watch out.

Belinda Davis

Drug Abuse

You're a murderer
But you say you're innocent,
Impaling the mind
But you're very indecent.
Spelling doubt and confusion
Adding to the case of losin',
The vision of reality
But you're actually
A murderer of sanity.

Darren Seedhouse

Incantation at Moonrise

By the powers of magic made,
By the powers of dark nightshade,
Earth and water, air and fire,
Hear my spell as I conspire:

Magic moon shine down on me,
A famous writer I want to be.
I'll write about what man has done,
How he has tried to block the sun
Which shines upon the feminine.
Give me words that will rhyme
Then I'll have no need to pine.

Light reflecting from the moon
Tells me that the time is soon
Goddess of love and queen of space
Set free among the human race.

Anne Tomasso

No Regrets

You'll never be mine,
So I cannot lose you.
We have never spoken,
So words cannot hurt.
We will never be lovers,
So you cannot disappoint me.
We have never disagreed,
So we haven't shed a tear.
We haven't had good times,
So we can't have bad times.
You'll never hold me in your arms,
So I cannot push you away.
I love you so much,
Since we'll never meet,
You'll never love me back.

Debbie McDonald

Anthony

Anthony was so tiny,
so lovable and sweet,
From his little red nose,
down to his tiny feet.

He had the bluest eyes,
The tiniest fingers and toes,
his skin was so soft,
with a birthmark on his nose.

He wasn't here for long,
but he was so special,
my baby brother, Anthony Jordan,
and he will always be remembered,
in our prayers and thoughts.

George Stewart

Sorry

The power of words, Lord,
So many bring light,
Whilst others the night,
As each one passes our lips,
Another's heart they hit,
We want to say what is good,
What we know we should,
But we sometimes get in the way,
Words are out, gone the ray,
Eyes alight, now in darkness,
There was joy, now only sadness,
Oh the chance to start again,
Somehow relieve the pain,
One small word conveys so much,
Sorry, eyes alight, back in touch.

Carol Pattinson

Dangers in Life

Life can be dangerous
So tragic so sad
Nothing is good
Lots of things bad
Women being beaten by men
Why is it so
Cruelty to animals
Above and below
Children abused
Shooting and crime
Drugs and bad knifings
In this sad time
Why aren't people kind
There's so much pain
It's a true fact
What do they gain
I love all animals,
children, the lot
If everyone thought the same as me
What a future we've got.

Elsie Williamson

The Lido Bathers

An early, loping sun.
Sleek Gazelle silhouettes
Haze in morning dew.

At the waterline blue,
Furnace-blazed mosaics
Clip a cool, crystal pulse.

Like lepers on parole
Fevered sinew draws bathers
To plunge, and shiver like steel.

In the spangled water-plume
Discarded skins craze yellow.
And naked, man embraces man.

Declan Kerr

Being Aware

I am dicing with death
Smell the whisky on my breath
Taste the pills upon my tongue
An ambulance someone has rung.

An outcry from my soul
Like Gazza missing a goal.
A feeling of despair
While my conscience
Makes me aware
And tells me that
I should really care.

Harvey S. Williams

The Dark Depths

I have taken life's pleasure
so big and so small
but where have they got me
no where at all.

It came to a point
when I crumbled like dust
it is a sinful pleasure
the one of lust.

Where did I go
when pleasure was no more
I turned within
and found nothing but sin.

Now pleasure is small
in God's given way
but it is better than all
of that sinful decay.

Allanna L. Harper

I Cannot Write Poems!

I cannot write poems
So why am I trying?
I'm glad I'm not mad
Is that why I'm crying?

Do they have to rhyme?
Will they sound better?
I have the questions
And I need the answer.

I think of things to write about
But forget them just like that
Like the cutting of a flower stem
Or the movement of a cat

If I was a poem
What would I be called?
Sonnet, ballad or haiku
Or perhaps nothing at all!

Oh, I'd like to be a poem
And be read out loud
To hear all the applause
And the standing of the crowd.

Joanne Dunn

Love

God gave us all the gift of love,
Sent down from the heaven above,
He taught us how to laugh and play,
And to say a prayer each day,
Loving Father in heaven above,
Show us all the way to love,
Guide us along our life's pathway,
To do some good on every day,
Time to give and time to share
Time to live and time to care.

Joan Willson

Christina Taught Tenderness

Crystallized powder
set there, for good.
It seems.
Presenting all kinds
of pictures.
Rarefying our moments
together.
Imprinted in the cold.
Dew kisses, hold me close.
Present it bare.
White blanket,
cover me.
Part of me,
will always be there
with my playmate
in the snow.

Diana Taylor

Wor Mary Jane

Wor Mary's a canny lass
She is me mam.
She makes my dad a good wife
Mary's bairns are her life.
She cares wipes their dirty
Noses, pick up cloths, is
Always there in trouble or strife.
Their pain she cannot bear,
All because she cares.
Mary Jane's bairns are all
Grown now, so now they
Cherish her Mary Jane has
Common sense she'll tell you
Straight, wipe your tears with
A cup off sweet tea.
Forget your fears
Mary's here.
She'll restore your faith
In the living

June Wilson

Figure of Loneliness

This girl is feeling low
She's got nowhere to go
There is no one to see,
Sits on her cardboard bed
With her hands holding her head
Wishing that she was happy.

Half-eaten buns from burger stalls
On the floor trodden on regals
Is all that she lives on,
Most young people that she sees
Just stand, stare or tease
Finish their insults and then gone.

Looked up in her own style
Faking me a smile
Wasn't a smile of happiness,
Eyes are dark and deep
the kind that make you weep
This is a figure of loneliness.

David John Burton

The Life Saver

That cup of tea
Just saved my life
How often we've heard those words
If only they were true
What worry we'd be spared.

No need for all the doctors
No medicine or pills
Just put the kettle on
To cure all our ills.

Elizabeth Taylor

Show Me Love

I am the voice,
let me speak for you.
I am the light,
let me show you the way.
I am the strength,
I will fight for you.
You are the people,
Show me love.

Adam Frank Farish

The Rose

In Mother Nature's Garden,
Lies a sweet but evil thorn.
In its natural beauty,
It's a very flawless thing.
But its appearance is just to hide,
The evil that lies within.

On a sunny morning,
The dew drops on a petal glisten,
Just beneath the sun.

Though, just upon the petal,
Is the blood that soon will run.

This mysterious creature,
Does not move without the wind.
Even in darkness,
There is a spirit that lies within.

Here by the river,
Where the wild roses grow.
You'll find this mystic creature,
That is perfect for the heart,
But not for the soul.

Aisha Romilly

Bliss

He who loves me,
Lies beside me,
Deeply sleeping,
Held in the curve of him,
Each nerve aware of him,
Contented, I haste not to sleep.

Janet E. Smith

Indian Evening

A herd of buffalo
lies to the West
on the plains of the sky
the sun is treading
the hills
in orange and purple
moccasins
and shadows track
every movement
Slowly, the sky darkens
and the clouds of buffalo
fade into night
an owl hoots
and ancestors start walking.

Grant D. McLeman

Stolen Moments

Seven thirty. Cold and wet
Outside the station, waiting.
Supposing he can't escape?
How long should I stay?

Train screeches - sharply stops.
Passengers emerge, rushing,
Head and shoulders above the others
I kiss his apologies away.

Much later, warm and happy
In his arms, sighing.
He'll soon have to leave
But until the next time, I'll wait.

Suzanne Heathman

Heaven Dreams

See the roving river run,
Over the hill and dale,
To a secret and pale
O my heart, noon-vale
Look for me at dawning
When the sun's reborn,
In the silent beauty
'Twixt the night and morn
Wait till the lark ascends,
And the skies are blue,
There where the rainbow ends
I WILL MEET YOU.

Celeste Mendoza

For Rwanda

People are dying,
People are crying,
while we live our lives
Regardless.
Children alone,
No families no homes,
Left to wander
Aimlessly.
Lost and dejected,
Feeling rejected,
No justice, no hope,
No future.
Suffering and pain,
Weeping in vain,
Famine, starvation,
Poverty.
The future unclear,
Next week next year,
For a nation slowly
Dying.

Clare Segger

Easily Replaced

Here she comes with
Pert little bum.
Slim hips swaying in
Rhyme.
She opens the door at
house number four.
Elegantly stepping inside.
I turn to my son
He says he will come,
Next time she goes
out for the day.
By my window I stay
Watching him slipping
away.
To his wife a
Replacement for me
His mum.

Heather Brown

Country Boy

I am not a rich man,
I'm not a rich man's son,
But I love the countryside,
And the wealth of things to come,
I see the leaves burst open,
In the joyous time of spring,
The sweet song of the birds
As they build a nest and sing,
The fragrance of the flowers,
So bright and in full bloom,
The golden autumn woodlands,
With leaves that will fall soon,
The crispness of the morning,
Is this the time of frost,
Another year nearly over,
I think of time I've lost,
Of things I didn't do,
Even though I thought I'd tried,
"But one cannot do everything",
Was the words that were replied.

John E. Johnson

This Is Called Modern Age

Hitler still lives on
In another form
Scientists and doctors
Governments and drug dealers
Experiment, not in cages
Misinform we poor humans
Mad cow disease
People dying
Sixty five percent
Are suffering from stress
Two thousand die with asthma
Please don't became pollution
Or additives in foods
Give tablets willy nilly
We were fitter in the war
Encourage offspring's education
Stop this extermination
Possibly they may remedy
And salve this rotten core

Iris Williams

Untitled

Blue soulful eyes looked upon me
in my waking moments, a kiss
so tender touched my lips that
lingers there for eternity, a few
sweet words you said and then
where gone, I lay alone on the
satin sheets, sadness had
arisen 'cause my soul mate
had gone, I smiled with the
memories of that night past and
wrestled with my conscience
until love won the fight.

John Hogg

Port Erin

The countless waves that have come,
in peace and in war,
rushing to the shore.

The relentless crashing of the seas
in the seemingly endless
night of the storm.

All have served their part
to smooth
and to shape
and perfect
one tiny pebble,
in the midst of a thousand.

Berni McAvoy

Peace

Be quiet and calm when approaching,
No fighting or anger when near it,
It needs to be left all alone.
Don't feed it hate or bitterness,
Don't feed it tension or hurt,
Feed it love and understanding
Or it will become dangerous.
If left to be quiet and beautiful,
Peace will make this world wonderful.

Chemaine A. Challenger

Sad Not Glad

When the day came I was sad
Not at all glad
I did not smile
My dad, brother and uncle,
Were M.I.A.
Or missing in action
Dad was first
He was a prisoner of war.
Gassed.
Next my brother was declared dead
When his Spitfire went down
Then was Uncle Fred
He drowned when his submarine
Was hit by a torpedo
I was sad
Not glad at all.

Christopher Fitton

Husband and Wife

To meet someone and fall in love
Not ever wanting to part
Wanting to give and not just take
The love that's in your heart

Deciding it's time to take a vow
To make you, Husband and Wife
To be together side by side
Throughout the rest of your life

With your partner by your side
Showing they really care
If and whenever trouble comes
You have someone to share

Later in life you will find
The years just roll away
But the love you have for one another
Grows stronger from day to day

Fate, kindly took a hand
So you could share a life
For you were born to be together
As a loving Husband and Wife

Dennis N. Davies

Trauma

Still, cold and lonely
nothingness,
black steely fingers
curl and clutch around my life
engulfing my world,

A hand, My hand
reaches out desperately
grasping one single ray of sunshine,
that fearlessly defies the darkness,

I embrace its warmth, its light
with all my strength,
and pray for someone, anyone
to help me.

Elizabeth Lynn Pickering

To the One I Left Behind

If I should die, before you awake,
one last wish, I do forsake.

Please sweet bride do not cry,
I will always be here by your side.
Shed no tears, for I've not gone,
in spirit and soul I still live on.

If love were words,
this poem would never end,
with every word, love I send.
In these words I've tried to mend,
the sorrow that this day does send.

You made me feel, want, and love,
so now I wait up here above.
My eyes and mind I'll take with me,
to look and think on times of glee.
To keep you safe and guide your way
until we meet again one day.

Jamie Clark

A Global View

Love has no boundary,
Only soft words spoken bind.
To all around, seeing no wrong,
Only one light shines.

The centre of all things,
A private universe,
All giving, all knowing,
Daily in strength growing.

All forgiving a full heart.
Bathed in moments of happiness.
Contentment rests, and in my soul,
Will grow a lasting peace.

Jacqueline Rahali

The Best Years of My Life?

Have you ever sat in a room, alone?
Only the T.V. for company,
Waiting for the ring of the phone.
Wanting someone to talk to,
To tell you they care.
Needing some comfort,
But there's nobody there.

Have you ever been alone in a crowd?
Surrounded by people,
Having fun, talking loud.
You want to join in,
You try, do your best,
But you know that it's pointless,
You'll never be like the rest.

Well I've been there, done that,
Bought the t-shirt, seen the show,
There's nothing you can tell me,
That I don't already know.
The best years of my life?
I really hope it isn't so.

Fiona Mullins

The Way of Prayer

We can never go beyond His reach
Or His tender loving care,
We know even in the darkest hour
We have the way of prayer.
He knows before we ask Him,
What is best for all our needs!
For us He has provided,
His Son who intercedes!
So when we pray to Him in faith,
And ask for strength to do,
His will, and not our own,
Our prayers He will answer too!

Jacqueline Thomson

Stars That Fly

A fleeting flash of
    Light
    to bring,
fresh hope for another tomorrow.

Unknown worlds of
    Stars
    that fly
into our minds; they stay

To find out what
    Mysteries
    they hold
such beauty, yet so small.

The Magic of
    Worlds
    Anew
Such wonder, such ignorance

Davina Green

The Touet

The Touet, an inspirational place.
Like a secluded island,
or outer space.

In the peace and quiet,
I can sit and think,
about love and laughter
about life on the brink.

With a pen, but no paper
a poem enters my mind,
I write it on tissue,
the Touet, is one of a kind

The Touet, where my mind can drift
The Touet, it must be Gods gift.

David Burton

Nascent

Seems to be a day
like any other,
but I don't know
do you?
Seems to be a thought
of some kind or other
but I don't know
do you?
Seems to smell of the future
that I have just discovered,
do I know you?
Seems to be a mixed-up
way of saying things,
but I don't know
do you?

C. A. Williams

The Rose

A bud is beautiful,
Like the rising sun,
A brand new life,
Has just begun.

It blows in the wind,
It survives the rain,
But this little bud,
Feels no pain.

It grows with the thorns,
Then starts to bloom,
And this tiny bud,
Brings no gloom.

It goes on with its life,
And as it grows,
This tiny bud becomes,
A beautiful rose.

Hayley Rose

Best Wishes

The time will come next Monday
How will we face the day
Dear Mum it is your birthday
The 25th of May
We cannot give you presents
Or cards with loving words
All we can do is miss you
How very much it hurts
There was no finer mother
This world could ever hold
Your smiling face, your gentle ways
Your heart of purest gold
Best wishes dearest Mother
Be happy up above
We'll treasure your sweet memories
In our eternal love

Joan Swords

Message

I give you my love, for you to share,
I ask for no reward.
All I ask of you my dear,
is spread the news abroad.

Tell of God's love for them,
all children far and wide.
Let peace reign over thy world,
and love be your guide.

For they have lost all hope of love,
God still loves them so.
Wrath that they are building,
clouds their senses low.

Love and peace I ask of them,
war and hate no more.
So tell them of this message dear one,
to all who are below.

There are many children yet to meet,
who need God's help so much.
It's from the Lord, that I say now.
    Tell all to keep in touch!

Glenda Mary Davies

I Believe

Do you believe in destiny?
I believe we were meant to be.
Do you believe in fate?
I believe you are my soul mate.
Do you believe in my love for you?
I believe you love me too.
Do you believe we'll never part?
I believe it with all my heart.

Donna-Marie Thomson

"My Love"

I can't see your face before me,
I can't hold you in my arms,
But I love you from a distance
That no other understands.

Your memory lights my life,
A beacon to my soul,
I pray one day that destiny
Will make our two hearts one.

My heart holds a love,
That burns eternally,
I'd give it to you freely
Like the waves upon the sea.

Words cannot express
My feelings deep inside,
A very special love
That only you can find.

Diane Foulkes

My Good Friend

I have a friend
Her name is Harriet
She rides in a wheelchair
Not in a chariot.
She used to be so active
And alert
Now finds it hard to put
On her skirt,
She's always got a smile
On her face,
And she never makes you
Feel out of place,
I've known her now
For twenty-five years
We've laughed a lot
And shed a few tears.
But the main thing is
We're still good friends
And that's what matters in the
End .

Helen Goldsmith

Terminal

My daughter phones,
Hiding the pain.
I feel the fear.

"I don't think I'll make Christmas."
The words so clear on the line.
"You can't go yet,
I've just bought the crackers."

We laugh together through the tears.
Love linked, time held,
We go on talking

Afraid to face the silence
Alone.

Jean Matthews

Sentinel

Mighty glaciers left me here
high perched o'er Sussex Downs.
I watched man rise omnipotent
who now descends to clowns.

Unsensing of the subtle force
of nature he once knew,
he believes himself the master
of all he wants to do.

Earth ravaged by his motorways,
urban sprawl and towns,
she lies inert (or so he thinks)
but "Gaia" wears a frown.

Aloof and cool methinks that I
have seen it all before,
and man despite his cleverness
will follow the dinosaur.

Plunged into extinction
by evolutionary shock.
Whilst I remain to watch and think -
Six tons of granite rock!

Gordon Skinn

Love

Love is iz not forget-me-knot
His or Mis(s)
Love is not lust
Love is not must
Love is not . . . just a dove
Only
Trust
A soulfully (2-way) thrust
Not just a (4-letter) word!

Deryk Alan Lee Baker

Share My Happiness

Sharing life together,
Having you so near.
Always caring for each other,
Right throughout each year.
Every wish is most sincere.

My thoughts are always for you,
Yet these words will never tell.

How very much I love you,
As I'm sure you know quite well.
Pleasant memories I do treasure,
Photographed for all to see.
Indeed, it is my pleasure,
Number One, you'll always be.
Elated joy has no ending,
Strong love leaves no mess.
Songbirds sweetly singing.

    SHARE MY HAPPINESS.

Brian Meadows

To Fr. Michael Doyle, RIP

He has gone to a distant place,
He remains somewhere near,
He is beyond my mortal sight, yet
He will not disappear.

He has gone out on a journey,
He's at the end of the road.
He has completed now his task
And he has put down his load.

We wait alone in anguish,
His anguish now has ceased.
We wander on through turbulence,
He rests now in peace.

Fiorella Sultana

Silent Footsteps

Down in the shadows
he waits
There among the gutter rubbish
he lurks
Dancing with the sewer rats
he bides his time.

Behind the stinking privies
he hides
Through the alleys of the slums
he stalks
From the edge of the lamplit circle
he watches

The greatest thief of all
goes on his rounds
Tirelessly
oblivious to the seasons
He sows his crop
and reaps his harvest.

Beth Short

Don't Cry

See the smile.
Hear the song.
Always think of me.
Don't cry.
I'm still here,
In spirit and in soul.

Faded memories never die.
I can feel your pain.
Mourn me once,
But never twice,
We'll meet again someday.

Carol James

Dusk A-Dawning

Dusk fell to earth
gathered folded light
Shadowy growing darkness
dwelling place the night

Caught between the dawning
capture held at bay
Act of Parturition
births another day

Shafts of lacy brightness
weblike eyelets drawn
Daylight tinged with darkness
traces in the dawn

Denuded light of morning
dusk had come a dawning

Edna M. Sarsfield

A Worm and a Mouse

My two cats brought me two
gifts this morning a mouse and a worm,
The worm made my squirm,
It was a germ,
The mouse ran around the house,
I hate mice,
Just like spice,
Well they can be nice,
I don't want a worm slithering
across my floor making everyone squirm,
I don't want a mouse running
around my house,
NO MORE PETS

Bonnie Cassidy

Birds' World

Pretty little song bird,
Happy as a king.
Will you tell me truly,
Why is it you sing?

Early in the morning,
At the break of day,
High up in the blue sky,
In sweet tones you pray.

From morning's first grey light
Till fading of daylight,
You're singing and toiling
The summer days through.

Oh, you may get weary,
And think work is dreary,
But it's harder by far,
To have nothing to do.

"I praise God the Father,
Every time I sing
And thus pay my homage,
To the great high king."

Francis B. Udogaranya

An Interplay of Instruments

The sound of the didgeridoo
Has powerful associations
Shades of emotional quality
Where the soul is ever present
Linked to the aborigines' beliefs
And their communion with nature.

The noise of the naswaram
Has mystic qualities
Drones of hidden depth
Where the player is ever humble
Linked to his quiet personality
And his existence with the animals.

Joe Loxton

Love and Rainbows

Today I saw a rainbow in a
   freshly laundered sky,
So absolutely perfect that it
   made me want to cry.

The beauty of the rainbow was
   so fleeting and so wild
I still think it as magical as
   I did when a child

But you cannot have a rainbow
   'til you've had a lot of rain
And it seems you can't have love
   until you've had a lot of pain.

Just like the rainbow's magic
   love is something you can't buy
You cannot grasp or hold it
   no matter how you try.

Diane Sherwood

A Friend for Life

Soulful eyes looked up at me
From every cage I saw,
A wagging tail
A mournful wail
"Please choose me . . . shake my paw".

Dogs of every size and breed
Some very large, some small,
Some dark, some fair,
Some with shaggy hair,
I'd love to take them all.

How difficult to pick just one
To be my lifelong friend,
If one I choose
The rest will lose,
How will they meet their end?

Will the others all find homes
Or will they be put to sleep?
It isn't fair
Don't people care
That a dog's for life . . . to keep.

Carol Marsh

Life

Life is just a stepping stone,
From one world to another,
All of us arrived here,
From the bosom of our mother,
Some of us had happy lives,
Some of us had sad,
But we all made the best lives,
With the little time we had,
But do not fear the future,
When it's time to say goodbye,
For we'll all meet our loved ones,
In that Utopia in the sky.

Joan King

In Defence of Poetry

The poesy of life
fulfilling a need
to express
an overflow of self
an outpouring of soul
IS a saving grace.

Let the poetry speak
for all who cannot
let go to show
what can be done
in one sweet embrace
of a pencil
on the page.

Carol Beeton

Tears

I have no tears
For the years of deception
For the man of delusions
For the wasted years
I have no tears

I have no tears
For the cherished children
Hurting and helping
Loving and leaving
I have no tears

I have no tears
For the friendship of years
Abruptly destroyed
Leaving a void
I have no tears

So I went to the Hospital
And they gave me some tears.

Elizabeth Mawer

Watchful

Be ever watchful, my dear one,
For there is much to see.
Man's selfishness, man's sinfulness,
Will bring man's misery.

Be ever watchful, and you'll find,
There is so much to see.
A happy smile, a sudden tear,
Change places so easily.

Be never watchful and you'll miss,
The things you ought to see.
As if, like a blind man, you walked,
In the seas of mystery.

Be ever watchful, and you'll find,
That blindness could make you see,
The hidden blessings in this world,
That wait for you and me.

Be watchful always, and you'll find,
There is so much to see.
Learn from lessons that come to show,
Your inner mind is free.

Janet Swindells

Gone Forever

Forget his name, forget his face
Forget his gentle warm embrace
Forget the love that you once knew
Remember he's with someone new

Forget him when they play your song
Forget you cried all night long
Forget how close you two once were
Remember he has chosen her

Forget his laugh, forget his grin
Forget the love that grew within
Forget the way he held you tight
Remember he's with her tonight

Forget the time that now has passed
Forget the love that went so fast
Forget he said he'd leave you never
Remember now he's gone forever

Jennifer McArthur

An April Day

Soft white clouds are trailing high,
Frail as blossom in the sky.
The new green of the spring grass,
And tranquil, like a looking-glass,
Lies the pool, beneath the hill
Reflecting the first daffodil.

Catherine Winifred Moss

307

Astral Imprints

Ironing pillowcases
crushing creases
and residue,
of washed-out dreams.
Fanciful images
rising in steam,
a myriad of astral
impressions
escaping
into infinity.

Josie May Hodges

Dunblane

Our hearts are broken,
crying with pain
For those poor little lambs
shot down in Dunblane.

The flowers lay sadly
on the ground
As their little hearts
will never be found

How evil and mean
could this man have been?
To destroy the lives,
so evil to have seen.

The teddy bears scattered
around Dunblane
Their lives demolished
through hate and pain,

The tears still pouring,
of what we could say,
Will never be forgot,
as such a sad day.

Geraldine Harvey

The Star You Truly Are

Stumbling in the twilight
Dark layers in the veil
Induced reality a sham
No ripples in the sea.

Sounds block the silence
Senses confused
The wheel turns blindly
In a lethargic wasteland.

Source of the waterfall
Vibrations form the palette
The shell will only open
To the cry from within.

Cords clinging to the core
Pathway of moonbeams
Unfurl your wings and soar
Golden shining star.

Jane Patience

The Beautiful Dead

A slab of granite.
Decorated
with neglected toys
and wilting flowers.

A children's toy trunk.

Only, the toys have
packed
my boy away now
he's finished.

Playing.

Fleur Evans

Coping with Death

In my heart I'd hear it break
But life still goes by
It's cold outside but dead inside
And I've got no time to cry.

Everyday I try my best
But all I do is fail
If I had the chance, I'd try again
But you know life's not fair
Look at me can you see the pain
It's hidden in my eyes
I've got no time to raise my wings
But hope someday I'll fly.

Jennifer Walsh

Water Fall

My tear grows underneath yours,
But my tear is for sorrow and pride,
And yours, well, your tear is
Deeply, deeply, in water and
Drops, drops,
Flickers and twinkles
Slowly, slowly
To the ground

Adonia Archodakis

The Man Who Wasn't

The road beneath his feet is rough,
But still he shambles on,
His coat is torn, his shoes are worn,
His beard is white and long,

He has a bag upon his back,
An old hat on his head,
The starry sky his only roof,
The dewy grass his bed,

His tired old face is wrinkled,
Weather beat, from sun and rain,
He never talks, he always walks,
I wonder what's his name,

Down twisted roads he shambled,
Day had turned to night,
Looking 'round, he sees me,
And vanishes from sight,

I followed him all through the day,
I wonder where he went,
For all I saw when he had gone,
An old stick snarled and bent.

Jean Torrens

Words of Wisdom

My mother said "Don't grow old"
But we never do as we are told
So old I went and got
I think it is a plot
To show we are not wanted
When by old age we are haunted

We can't do this, or that,
And don't want to decorate the flat
I used to take it in my stride
To do a good job was my pride
Now, I could not care less
This I must confess
To do a big screw up tight
I have to turn it with all my might

But some good times I've had
Life has not been too bad
Everything must come to an end
I am glad you were my friend

Cecil V. Pike

Beautiful Pet

Two liquid sad eyes
A ball of black fur,
She'd just come to live here,
And for her I would care,
Her eyes changed from sadness,
To faith, love and trust,
Her mischievous antics,
For me were a must
As she grew older,
More settled and staid,
I knew that her time here,
Would soon be out-played,
And that's when I saw it,
That look on her face,
Her eyes now were pleading,
She could no longer stay.
I weep now with sadness,
For my beautiful pet,
Her eyes they stay with me,
I will never forget.

Coleen McAvinnie

The Miracle of Life

When all the shouting's done
A child busts into view
The world outside is
really very small
The miracle is there
with imperfections too.
A little face stares back,
an extension of you two.
The pain, the hurt, the wait,
all forgotten in such haste.
As baby looks at you
with very crinkled face.

Irene Smith

Untitled

Many years have come and gone
And yet to me it's not so long
Since we first met and fell in love
Our bond being blest in heaven above.

The many many ups and downs
The many many fears and frowns
The total if we were to add
Would be some laughter and some sad

God willing we'll have many years
To share our happiness and tears
The joy of children and their fears
Our love will never die.

Edith Holmes

A Seed Grows

Hello, yes it's me as
You can't see
because I'm in a packet
with no jacket
I'm going home
and I won't moan
Oh no she's putting me in the ground
with no sound.

A few months later
I was like an alligator
I was growing
And showing,
I was bursting out
A bit like a sprout
And after all that
I was what I wanted to be
A TREE.

Leanna Jones

PAX

The powerful weapon in your armoury
Is your good memory
And yet
I have a better
A good forgettory.

Joy Mitchell

An Ode to Charin Yasindu

You made your debut on a scan,
a blip on the screen
a writhing mass of twisted limbs,
gentle pleading eyes,
wanting to see the outside world.
Our heart skipped a beat
as we saw you,
larger than life.

Then came the moment,
intense suffering
your mother bore the pain.
A labour of love,
you came screaming and kicking
into the real world.

Now we share your laughter,
your tears, your squeals of delight,
smiling eyes of love
total dependency,
a wonderful gift from God,
our newborn son.

Ivan Corea

Untitled

"Why hast thou forsaken me"
A dying Jesus cried
As He hung upon the cross
A spear wound in His side

All alone and frightened
And so very very cold
The most important human
Who never did grow old

He called to God His father
The people for to pardon
Then was taken from the cross
To a cave in a garden

That He had cured the sick
And blessed the blind with sight
Had all been forgotten
On that awful Friday night

He came to earth to save us
From the ravages of sin
This holy humble carpenter
Who has risen up again

Deanna M. Hassan

Untitled

Please play me
a little music
to soothe my soul,
ask the angels
if they can spare
me a moment
from their heavenly
duties
after all
they must pity me
as before their
transformation
they must have been
as I am now
a very solitary
being.

Gunilla Herrmann

Armistice

It is late, and the night is black,
A New Era has begun,
For Armistice has just been signed
No more we'll hear the guns.
And as I stand in the porch alone
I cup to my ear the sound
Of the Woolwich boats all hooting
'Rejoice the war is done'.
I go to lift my son from his cot
He's peaceful, and fast asleep,
But he is all I have to share
This wonderful moment of time,
The end of the heartache and care.
"And soon we'll see your Dad son,
Yes soon that day will come,
We'll hug that thought together
When you won't just have your Mum".

Dot Hooles

Sorrow

The strife of Dunblane,
Families mourning,
Victims in pain,

16 children,
And their teacher,
All killed by one sad man,

No-one can express the
grief they feel,
15, 16, 17,
Dead.

Jessica Bayliss

"Loss"

The bombs explode
A siren speaks
The uniforms jump to its sound
That's time when civilians know
It's time to hit the ground.

Money's the matter
It buys the arms
'They' order us about
The government is big and strong
It's us who have to shout.

The poppies fall
The flag is raised.
The uniforms are stained
The message left is loud and clear
War will people claim.

Gayle Pagram

Miracle Park

A sun-dappled place
of gold and green shade
A mythical face
that the gods have obeyed
Whispered before
by the slaves and the frail
alone on a shore
under their moon burning pale.
In this hideaway hollow
where shadows melt apart
and the voice wants to follow
the echoes of the heart
where stars are replaced
by tears of the serene
the unique taste
touched but not seen
the mind begs to send
a light to my dark
but the fool will pretend
he's in MIRACLE PARK.

Marcus Waring

Floral Love

Love can be like a flower
It can dwindle fall and die
For flowers are for summer
For the good times in our lives

The love I give to thee
is a magnificent oak tree
The oldest oak in the forest
The tallest tree in the land
For trees are green in summer
They nest the birds in spring
but most important of all
they survive the cold harsh winters
The bad times in our lives.

Andrew Brien

A Heart of Stone

Love is like a stone some may say,
It does not bleed,
It does not cry,
It does not fade away,
And as time goes by,
We wonder how wrong we were and why,
But when it's dropped it shatters,
Into a thousand, million pieces,
Like a heart when broken,
On a cold midsummer day.

Heather McColgan

Tigh Nan Cailleach Dubha

It is a heavy sky today.
It drags a long curtain of rain
To the land.
Where the surf peels onto the rocks
And time means nothing.

Here has seen them all
The Dagda, Odin, Christ,
Outlived their shadows
Scarred but unbowed.
The circled cross.

This earth was someone's home
A place of worship
Brought down, staring
Blank at the ghosts
The cling to the mountain tops.

The grass grows and is grazed.
The stones protect the soil.
We are transient.
Here ends Britain,
In wrack and ruins.

Ben Moxon

Missing You

I miss you,
It's as simple as that,
Those three words,
That communicate,
That say my fears.

I miss you,
It's as plain as can be,
Those few words,
Yet we do not communicate,
Listen to my fears.

I miss you,
I can't say it anymore,
No more words,
No more to communicate,
Here come my fears.

Carrie Cobb

Hope

Treasured and loved
Security immense
Tenderness, sweetness
A childhood intense
This child of the future
Grew up in a world
Full of wonder and newness
Just laughter, few tears
With hope for the future
Without any fears

This child of the future
Has suffered and cried
Has felt the brutality of a life
Far removed
From days full of love
Of peace and of joy
But optimistic by nature
Nothing will stand in the way
If hope takes a tumble
Sunshine turns to rain

Ann De Micheli

Waking

Another early morning
seeing the sun seep through,
feeling the space beside me
holding memories of you.

Hearing a distant rumble
focusing on the room -
familiar boundaries give
little hope of release.

Trudging down stairs staring
into the still fireplace.
The vibrant dancing flames
now a few grey remains.

Smiling at sofa cushions
perfectly aligned just as
you left them - the house is
empty and full of you.

Jane French

Plateau

I walk where you cannot
Seeing things that I should not
Controlling all that comes and goes
How I do it nobody knows
A secret being of total power
Living in a golden shower
Calling the shots everyday
You follow everything I say
I even control the things you see
Am I God or an MP.

Dave Shore

Pain

Your pain
seeps
into me slowly
Your fear
blinds me
Your silence
deafens me
Your sorrow
numbs my soul
Your poison tears
I drink and
Die.

Caroline Pulman

Burning Flame

My life is a burning flame like a
candle melting away. Time is
running out,
no more time,
trying to get away.
Will my candle relight again?
Shall I cry, shall I be happy? Or
Shall I just wait until it just
melts away.

Amy Luton

Countryside

Just look upon our countryside
A pleasant tranquil scene
Of trees and fields and hedgerows
All dapple shades of green

A cobweb sparkles in the sun
Like jewels in a crown
The cottage on the hillside sits
Its roofs of rustic brown

A song thrush sings his merry tune
My heart begins to sing
As if in answer to my thought
The distant church bells ring

Sweet smell of clover in the field
The sheep and cows softly graze
The peacefulness of the meadow
The horse do soulfully gaze

Our pleasant peaceful afternoon
What joy our countryside has been
We thank you God Almighty
For all that we have seen.

Joyce Boast

Autumn

The autumn leaves are falling
And as the leaves turn red
The animals that hibernate
Collect them for their beds.
They looks so snug and peaceful
As they go to sleep
Search for them and you will find
They've burrowed very deep.
The flowers around are dying
Their heads are all forlorn.
Jack Frost is here as usual
And sits upon my lawn.

For the year been's long
And the weather's gone cold
Oh what am I to do?
Maybe I could hibernate
Maybe you could too!

Elaine O'Neill

My Mistress

My mistress is mad
And I love her to pieces
She's really insane
And she keeps me in creases
She's really quite nutty
There's no way of knowing
If she tells you it's sunny
It's probably snowing.

She bought me a Cat flap
Which I find a bore
It's grey, with a flap
And it fits in the door.
She bought me a collar
To keep off the fleas
Now instead of my neck
They live on my knees.

Jacqueline Lydia Fogg

My Friends

He crossed my window,
And casually looked in,
Timid and afraid he waited,
Bound to my chair,
I could not move,
And like him I waited,
Off he went and I was alone,
My friend had gone?
But no he was back,
And wife as well,
They watch me again,
As I moved in pain
Afraid no longer they danced around,
Not one single sound.
I watched in awe,
As my friends begin to sing for me,
It lifted my heart,
To hear their refrain,
My Beautiful Blackbirds,
Were here again.

Joan Ford

What's in a Word?

Child gently swinging
And cuddling his Ted.
"What are you thinking about?"
"Nothing", he said.

Child holding felt-tip pen,
Desk scribbled red.
"What are you doing there?"
"Nothing", he said.

Child cut his finger deep,
Watched while it bled.
"What were you playing with?"
"Nothing", he said.

Child in a twilight room,
Suddenly fled.
"What was it frightened you?"
"Nothing", he said.

Child playing all day long,
Now time for bed.
"What have you done today?"
"Nothing", he said.

Jennifer Bailey

A Dictator's Life

With all your earthly riches
and dealings in stealth
there is not a moment
when you consider
where you will make your wealth?

Climbed all ladders
in your matters of life
still neglect shown
towards those in strife

The comings and goings
in your throw of life
still you try
to surpass your ungodly
ways of the unlike

A prayer in the morning
a bullet blessed for death
killing in the name of . . .
he not believeth then
or understand what is the words
that were said then.

Clive Ayton Bell

The Brass Bell

The brass bell tolls.
And deep below the waves
Angel fish and
Fish in school,
Pause to listen.
Cat fish fin for mouse sized morsels.
Pearls gleam darkly
In oysters.
Dolphins dive.
And whales in seven seas
Sing the songs
Of the brass bell.

Beryl Brown

The Joys of Spring

It's Easter Time again
And eggs are on display;
All types and sizes,
With all kinds of prices.
Children are happy,
Small faces full of glee;
Picking and choosing
Which treat to enjoy.
Spring is upon us,
With new birth all around.
The trees they are budding
And the birds they are nesting,
The flowers are blooming
And the grass is getting greener.
Lambs they are baaing
And foals they are neighing.
Young calves are leaping
And little chicks are cheeping.
Nothing is more beautiful
Than the countryside in Spring.

Julia Greene

True Love

I thought that I had found love
And happy I thought I was
Until the day you came along
It was a miracle I know because
The heartache was over
Each day brought something new
My life has changed completely
Just because of you
In my heart there is no more pain
The sun for me is shining again
Please stay with me my darling
Real love is here at last
We will start life over
And forget there was a past
We can plan together
Of all the things we can do
At last I have found happiness
All because of you

Elizabeth Anderson

Morning

On a still summer's morning
As the sun comes up
And the moon goes down
The birds come out
And sing their songs

Little children rise
Laugh and play
Their voices echo
Around the house

And the stillness
of the morning is
no more
as the day goes on

Anne Ramsay

Sleepless

My body aches,
As I lie awake,
And sleep eludes,
My tired form,
The brain not taxed,
Muscles relaxed,
The bed both comforting
And warm.
Two hours now though,
Since I began to slow,
And I thought,
"I need to sleep",
Two minutes more,
And the clock strikes four,
So much, for counting sheep.

Graeme Paul Rowland

The Dear Little Fawn

A picture of innocence
  Is the dear little fawn
    As he curls into a ball
      On the long grassed lawn.

Big brown eyes staring
  Ears pricked sharp and high,
    His nose sniffs fresh air
      As the day drifts on by.

How small and timid,
  How genteel and calm,
    How could anyone do
      Such dear animals harm?

Joan A. Anscombe

The Lesson

When I placed the last brick
It all came tumbling down.
All my selfish haste
Lay 'round me on the ground.

Now I build with tender care,
From first brick to the last.
So strongly it will ever be,
My future and my past.

Maria Rosamond

Light and Hope

The earth awakes from its slumber
Its heavy blanket lifted by the
Warm caress of morning sun
Which slips across the land.

And the first splash of colour
Spreads to seek out every shadow
Which shivers and begs to hold on.

But the solitary star in the sky
Keeps the world alive
And every bit of the earth
Has been touched by its light
Once before,
And should not be allowed to die.

Jane Wise

Life

Life is what we make it,
it's up to us each day,
To see that it's for the better,
and mind what we do and say,
it's so much nicer to be nice
and make somebody smile.
When it's ended and you go to bed,
You think it's well worthwhile.

Gladys Austin

"Hampshire"

Oh, how I'd love to wander
and let my thoughts run wild
to places, I knew long ago
when I was just a child,

To run, to jump or stand still
or just listen by the brook,
to go back one more time
just to take another look,

To recall days when it rained,
and I couldn't go out to play,
I'd try to count the raindrops
or watch a rainbow fade away,

Just to hear again the music
of the birds, up in the trees
or smell again the perfume
of flowers, borne on the breeze,

To me, there is no other place
that will ever be so dear
as the meadows and the woodlands
of my beautiful Hampshire.

Audrey Philps

Untitled

When all is done.
And Buried Deep
we Slumber in Eternal Sleep

The abstract Spirit
free from weight

Explodes into a Million
Particles, to penetrate

Heavenly Bodies
Spirits and Such
whose Earthly return
into the new Born, and Much.

What is Known or Unknown
Mysteries abound
atoms Formulate into our
new found, Vehicle.

The cycle is then Complete.

Bernard Simmons

Sweet Sorta Girl

I've swallowed the ecstasy pill
And now I lie motionless and still
My mother and father sit by my side
It's impossible for them
Their tears to hide.

Hand in hand, they watch
The hospital monitor
That make's the life signal sound
Hoping and praying I'll come around

It was my choice, I took the pill
I didn't just go with the flow
And it wasn't just because
I couldn't say NO

If I listened to everything
My parents had said
Maybe just maybe
I wouldn't be leaving them
With the heart-breaking
Decision to pronounce
Their darling daughter's dead

Ian Nicholls

Bosnia '95

You've taken other families
And now you're taking mine.
Cousin Malcolm came on Saturday
And I'm sure he's doing fine.

Many lives have been taken
But Malcolm won't be one.
'Cause when we all awaken
Malcolm's job will be done.

Weeping for all the mothers
However we hear the tale.
But we always know it's others
'Cause Malc will never fail.

Tomorrow he may be fighting
But we won't feel the grief.
Cause Sunday he'll be writing
To tell us he's not underneath.

So Bosnia if you're listening
Give Malcolm all our prayers.
Tell him his baby misses him
And everyone still cares.

Gayna Gillespie

Untitled

When all is dark
Do not despair
Reach out your hand
I will be there
To help in any way I can
Whether you be woman or man
This promise thus I make to you
Try, you'll find it trusted and true
My name is friend.

Jean Hopper Sparrock

Writing is a Pleasure Too

I keep a diary in my head
and open it at night.
A maidenly bed of vivid
blues binds the cover.
The pages are delicious.
White, unwrinkled, body
scented, they invite and
beckon. How will I start?
Born Cancer, you Virgo
others need permission
to read our lives for only
in my dreams I share
existence here with you.

You should come at dusk
it's then I write.
And, in the morning carefully
smoothly, I put us away.

Ann V. Bellingham

Skylark

I stood and watched a skylark rise
And listened hard and long,
How could a creature thus so small
Pour forth so sweet a song,
Up, and up so full of life
It's singing from its heart,
If happiness is in a bird
Then it's in a lark.

And there I stayed and marvelled
As it ascended in the air,
And as I listened to its notes
I was glad that I was there,
Oh little bird of happiness
The bubbling little lark,
You and the sweetness of your song
Have found a place within my heart.

Finlay Shiner

Clouds

I watched them at play
As I lay
Stretched on my back
Enjoying the day.

First they curled,
Then they twirled,
Then they dipped
And toward me swirled.

Billowy seas of grey
Wisps of curl gone astray,
Stretching layers of foam
All along the way.

Gently changing forms
Each new one transforms
The world spread out below
As each new image dawns.

So I watched them play
As I lay.
Wished I was up there
Enjoying the day.

Grace Rorke

Pain

Pain rages through me,
As I strive for blissful sleep,
Searing fingers touch me,
Caress me, till I weep.

Do my tears appease you,
And fill burning desire,
For every night you visit me,
Consume me with your fire.

We dance together, madly,
Your knives embedded deep,
Till I buckle at the knees,
And lie exhausted at your feet.

Nerves and senses numbing,
As we meet time and again,
If I ignore my screaming body,
I may rise above the pain.

So come to me, old friend,
My days of flight are gone,
I'll embrace you and weep gladly
We'll dance on and on and on.

Jane Butterworth

The Stately Elm

How saddened we are.
As speeding away
O'er snowclad hills afar,
On cotswolds mantle lay.

Standing tattered and torn
Alas, the stately elm,
Arms outstretched forlorn,
We pass without a qualm.

Nature's beauty is hidden,
Gone, with passing winter,
See new life forbidden,
The ghostly shapes simper.

Landscape's marred now,
Oh help! They cry,
Can we refuse how?
Their desperate sigh.

Now comes fate, lopped,
See they topple aground,
Too late to be stopped,
There's firewood found.

J. L. Ward

Fantasy

In my dreams you were eloquent
liquid of form and movement,
your whole being sang
your eyes sparkled with laughter.
You promised much.
A nymph to enchant,
captivating my soul,
clasping it to yourself.
Alas, you fled through the moonlight
silver-dappled in dew-droplets
leaving only your scent, and
a whispered remembrance
as you stole my soul away.

John S. Fisher

Fruit Garden

Raspberries, gooseberries
Loganberries and thorns
I work in the garden
With hands so sore
The fruit must be picked
When the sun is high
We must be aware
Of the damn fruit fly
Once a year
These chores must be done
Chores I know
Will be lots of fun
Now the berries
Are put away
The first of the apples
Are on their way.

Colin Barrett

The Sun

The sun is a
Lolly that nobody eats.

It makes my heart beat,
beat, beat.

I go for a dip in a nice warm
pool, to cool me down.

The sun rises and turns
me to brown. It makes
me want to frown.

Amy Ridout

'Beauty'

The plants say "feed me
look after me and
we will grow in beauty"
The trees ask for rain and sun and
grow to be of great age and beauty
Me, I ask for love
for when one is loved
they are beautiful
Beauty is love!

Christine Beal

Why?

Everyone is asking themselves,
Looking for an answer,
Desperately
Searching,
An evil word?
A peaceful world?
No-one knows.
One moment you were here,
Now you're gone,
Gone,
but never forgotten.

Gemma Pryde

Madness

When the new moon stalks the sky
And owls give up their prey,
The sea gives up her dead
And blackness rules the day.

The newborn enters the womb.
Enemies hug their foes.
The pound is worth a penny
And fishes swim on shores.

They speak with tongueless lips
And see with eyes that are shut.
The gentle take to guns
And nuns revere the slut.

Strange world when you're mad,
See things wrong way 'round.
Grass is in the sky
And clouds are on the ground.

Josephine L. Yates

Bubbles

Round
Floating
Shimmering
Rainbow-hued spheres
Moments of magic
Trembling here
Sinking now
Downwards
Gone!

Ena Owen

The Secret Garden

The sun smiles down upon me
    and reflects her mood below
I feel her warmth encase me
    as I catch her golden glow.

The scented air floats by me
    and brushes past my skin
I feel its powerful energy
    push from the outside in.

The birds' sweet songs surround me
    and fill my ears with pleasure
I feel their charm caress me
    as they sing from heart of feather.

The fragrant flowers possess me
    as their beauty takes a hold
I feel their natural splendour
    as a kaleidoscope unfolds.

This secret I've not murmured
    of my garden I'll not tell
Of Mother Nature's paradise
    I've fallen for her spell.

Jean Mann

If I open my eyes
And the sky is blue,
There is nothing much else
That I must do
To make me feel happy
And safe, in my way.
A blue sky is all
That I need for my day.

If I open my eyes
And the skies are grey,
I have to take heart
And to myself say -
Just grin and bear it,
Life happens that way.
You're lucky to see it;
Even the grey.

Joan Mason

'Forgotten Dreams'

When day is done
And shadows fall
Across the grassy glade.
And toys lay idle on the floor
Where boys and girls have played.
Then sandman comes to lay his hand
Upon each sleepy head.
And mother tucks each little child
Into its own small bed.

Then comes dreaming -
    Dreaming of the things
    they would like to do.
Dreams forgotten
And maybe, sometimes dreams
They wish really would come true.

When day is done
And shadows fall
Little children sleep.

Ann Sandwil

Future

There is no future - some say.
Oh what a pathetic view.
If there was no future
we were already dead.

So, think of tomorrow
and make nice dreams
because tomorrow might be
what you dream today.

Cornelia Lampis

And the Rain Came Down

And the rain came down
And the rain came hard.
And the petals of the flowers
Were permanently marred.

And the storm grew strong,
And the lightning flashed,
And the thunder sounded
With a mighty crash.

And then the typhoon came
And the people cried,
And the sun hid forever
God must have lied.

And the man on the news
And the dust on the floor,
And the bomb killed the earth
Which could live no more.

Fiona Jayne Burry

Without

A song without music
And words without rhyme,
A place without distance,
A place without time.
This place in my head,
Your place in my heart,
Some place in between
We are never apart.
A dreamland of 'being',
Just 'being' alone,
Where being together
Is all we have known.
But when I open my eyes
The light disappears,
The darkness surrounds me
To mirror my fears.
Lonely heart full of longing.
Wishful head full of doubt,
God bless the poor dreamer
Who must do without.

Julie Ann Bell

A Taxi Ride

It seemed to drape around us
Around us like a shroud
This old Morris Oxford taxi
That takes us through the crowd
No fancy air conditioning
No cool recycled air
Don't dare to touch the windows
Just let them stand and stare
Children at each stopping place
Morning, noon and night
Blind being led by crippled
Part of a tragic plight
Increasing traffic problems
Bring us soon to rest
She stands there pleading, begging
Her baby at her breast
You think you know the reason
Why people go astray
There's little that prepares you
For life around Bombay

Iain Docherty

Divine Design

Before I start my journey
As the time is running down
I think that I must make for me
A most appropriate gown

I'd begin with golden sunbeams
And dainty drops of dew
Thread silver moonlight in the seams
With shades of midnight blue

Filigree snowflakes on the sleeve
With diamond rain beads too
Fine strands of sunrise in the weave
To give a radiant hue

Next a cuff of fine spun lace
From a silken web no doubt
With rosebuds in the button space
Or anchored thereabouts

There will be a wondrous welcome
On my grand entrance day
I must gain some pearls of wisdom
To add upon the way

Jill A. Rust

Do You Ever Get a Feeling

Do you ever get the feeling
    as you're driving down the road,
That however long you'd waited
    they never would have showed.

Do you ever get the feeling
    as you walk along the street,
That among the crowded pavements
    there's no one left to meet.

Do you ever get the feeling
    as you work and work all day,
That you'd probably have met them
    if they hadn't gone away.

Do you ever get the feeling
    when you wake up in the night,
That you really would have seen them
    if they weren't just out of sight.

Do you ever get the feeling
    that there's no one there to see;
Do you ever get that feeling,
    or is there only me!

Andrew Banfield

Untitled

As dark as night,
As black as coal,
This darkened rose reflects my soul.

My frozen heart,
Still burns for you,
My hidden love you never knew.

If you return,
My tears are lost,
Blood red petals melt the frost.

But if you leave,
My heart will break,
And surely then my life I'll take.

Forever yours,
I'll always be,
And only then may you see . . .

As black as coal,
As dark as night,
This darkened rose was always white.

David A. Blackham

Untitled

Each punter puts on a bet,
As the horses are getting set.
Off goes the starting gun,
As the horses begin to run.

Horses running down the track,
Jockeys riding on their back.
Up to the fence as they jump,
Down to the ground with a bump.

Each horse jostles for the lead.
But each horse needs more speed.
First number 7 then number 10,
But what happened then?

Coming up to the finishing line,
The other horses need more time.
The winning horse looks so proud,
As the punters shout so loud.

Amy Wilson

Bethany

She has wings of spun gold
Delicate and fine
She lives in the forest
And not in my mind.

Her bath is the pond
Surrounded by trees,
Her bed is the petals
Her blanket the leaves.

She dances and laughs
And plays in the grass,
And that's how we'll leave
This flutter-by lass . . .

Andrea Taylor

Two-Faced Water

Water swayed to gravity
Dog jumped in.
Fish blew tiny bubbles
Water rippled with pleasure.
The dark transparent hues
Trembled in the wake of geese,
The river matured to the sea.
Water smashed rock to sand
For children's play.
Scuba diver entered wreck,
Water roared with broken coral,
A face mask rises up,
Deprived of its goggle-eyed owner
It becomes flotsam on the shore.

James Douglas Grassick

Noeleen Mary

The summer has ended.
Most will remember
the weather. Not I,
but extremes of joy
and sorrow, a terrible
goodbye. The birth of
My daughter, so pretty -
so fair; the death of
my mother, the vacant
chair. Perfect, blue-eyed
blonde. The wonderful
reward of prayer and hope
too heavy, no doubt, for
the scales. One in and one out.
In five short hot weeks
mother love I lost but
I keep. Without you, my
Dear Mother, for me
who will weep?

Caroline England

"Love"

Love is like the golden sun,
moving higher through the day;
shining brightly on someone
with its powerful ray.

Love is like a red, red rose,
with a beauty so serene;
swaying as the warm wind blows,
pure, full of body and clean.

Love is like a moonlit place,
quiet, with a shining light,
magic lingering o'er, a trace
of romance so bright.

Love is you my darling one,
to my heart you hold the key.
A nature thoughtful, kind and strong;
together in harmony.

C. Hewlett

The Promise

Before I turn,
My head to sleep,
There is a promise,
I have to keep,
To call you softly,
Wherever you are,
Whether near,
Whether far,
To touch you face,
And with a kiss,
Close my eyes,
And tell you this,
I love you.

Joan Brocklehurst

Time to Enter

I'm old and weary
My hearing is bad
My stick is here
But it guides me there
My eyes are blurred
I sense your trust
I take your hand
You're warm to touch
I tell you my secret
That my love has gone
As time approaches
I release your hand
I'm slipping away
My time has come
To drift away

Anthony P. Deller

Is That How It's Meant to Be?

When we are young
Life is oh, so sweet.
The toys we get to play with,
The friends we get to meet.

Then it's time to study
For our future, in the distance.
"You are going to have to work hard."
Was everyone's insistence.

"Come on, let's have some fun."
"Life is so uncomplicated."
The grief that was yet to come,
Was never even contemplated.

The time has come to marry,
To build a lovely home.
We've found the one we want,
No longer need we roam.

Now that we are older,
It's the same for you and me.
The problems we must face.
Is that how it's meant to be?

Anita Flynn-Brown

Spindrift

The earth is my mother,
Life source of the land,
Polluted and barren,
From man's unkind hand.

My brother the sun,
Strengthens my spirit,
His fiery shield,
Fills me with courage.

My father the ocean,
Tempts me to fate,
In his arms I do battle,
His anger runs deep.

My mistress the moon,
Her will is obeyed,
Her silent commands,
Send favourable waves.

For I am the surfer,
Son of the sea,
My home is the beach,
Where my soul runs free.

Jane Woodbury

Love

You came into my life
Like the sun's soft warm embrace,
I felt your very tender touch,
But I could not see your face.

You came into my life.
Like the waves upon the shore.
I did not know your name.
But I knew I wanted more.

You came into my life.
Like the gentle summer breeze.
You touched my very heart and soul
And I whispered "Oh, stay please".

You came into my life.
Like the fire's burning flame.
You made me feel emotions
Of ecstasy and pain

You came into my life.
Like the softly falling rain.
I now can see your face
And know that "Love" is your name.

Beryl Moon

A Silent Snowstorm . . .

Live a scene from a moonwalk,
Silent, and alone.
One outstanding feelings,
One outstanding white tone.

From the start of a snowstorm
That very first flake.
The first white flurry
On an iced over lake.

Icicles, hanging from rooftops,
Breath, almost like mist,
The earth and the moon,
By a snowstorm is kissed

Amber Roach

Lonesome

Sat alone, I wait
Silent, not moving
I breathe - slowly.
Pain in heart, it aches.
I wait ever patient
For someone, anyone.

Alone, I sit
Alone, I wait
Somebody knock,
I cry -
A cry for help -
A plea from the heart
Sat alone, I am still
Waiting . . .

Caroline Louise Chandler

Black Cat

Black cat,
Silky, shining fur,
Long legs, sleek muscular,
Wily predator of the night,
Black cat.

Fierce cat,
Slit golden eyes,
Seeing all yet moving not,
Watching waiting, time suspended,
Fierce cat.

Lap cat,
Stretching, yawning,
Purring, coiled upon my lap,
Soft and yielding, love displaying,
Lap cat.

Quiet cat,
Content yet wary,
Relaxed but action ready,
Mysterious, living your own life,
Quiet cat.

Christine Chapman

Existence

Dad's complaining,
Sister's stressed out,
Mum's broken her finger,
What's life about?

Man down the road,
Died yesterday,
A cat got ran over,
What's left to say?

World's in recession,
Civil war's broken out,
People are dying,
What's life about?

Gemma Budzik

Squirrel

He seems not to notice us
As he climbs up the clothes-prop,
Swinging upside down
When he reaches the top,
In order to run, like a fly
Up to the bird-feeder,
Tiny paws holding on,
Tail waving to help balance.

But he sees!
Not one of his senses sleeps
As he prises out nuts,
Dropping them on the grass
For later consumption.
If we move a muscle
Behind the glass
Instantly he becomes a bird!
In a flying leap he gains the fence,
And sits rubbing his paws
As he watches us.

Gwen Gardner

Freedom

The wind cleanses me
body and soul
Its gentle caresses
make me feel whole

flowing around me
holding me
comforting me
loving me

Touching tenderly
at my brow
Like a mother
'Hush now'.

Softly weaving through my hands
letting me know I am not alone
and guides me
Guides me home

Beautiful land
reaching out to embrace me
Oh mother, I am home
Oh mother, I am free.

Angela McLaughlin

A Grave Look at Life

I'm standing in a crowd,
But I'm all alone,
I'm a million miles from anywhere,
I wish that I was home,
Voices in my head,
But they're a million miles away,
Not listening to the words,
Trying to keep the ghosts at bay,
Heavens are breaking above me,
They mingle with my tears,
I'm breaking down and screaming,
But in a place where no one hears,
I can feel that I am bleeding,
But in a place that can't be seen,
I hold my head up high,
As my tears become a stream,
I'm hanging on to life,
By the flower's in my hand,
Its petals are bright and crisp,
While I can barely stand.

Carrianne Nutt

The Wall

As I stand between these walls
I see no life
But yet I am here,
But not there,
As I see, or feel,
But yet I cannot, be as one,
I move around to and fro,
Wondering what to do,
But all the time,
I am as one.

John Eagle

Peace

What a world we have to live in
Brother fighting brother
Dying for their politics
Not living for each other
Not only is it politics
But religious beliefs too
Oh what a troubled world we live in
Peace is overdue.
Nuclear war is threatening
Bombs exploding far and nigh
Terrorist everywhere
It makes you want to cry
It's written that we all should give
Love to one another
Let's follow that instruction
Stop fighting with our brother
Call a halt to all the horrors
Because it's really up to you
This world is worth redeeming
And so my friend are you.

Jan Shreeve

There Is No Cure for a Miracle

The two men were friends
Cancer was their enemy
There was a battle to be fought
But who would win the war

Strategies were planned
The doctor infiltrated
The man was mesmerized
and conscripted to the system

The fight was devastating
No Red Cross in sight

Until a truce was called
Cancer waved the white flag
Tumours submitted to the knife
I know that all this happened
I am the patient's wife

Anne McLennan

Beyond Daylight

Silhouette the landscape
Cast a shadow over the sun,
Encase the world in darkness
Now the day is done.

Let a moonbeam's silver sparkle
Awake the creatures of the night,
Watch them dart amongst the shadows
Free from human sight.

An eerie silence, slightly broken
By the wind amidst the trees,
Leaves are carried helplessly
Captives of the breeze.

A glimmering horizon
Heralds the ever-advancing dawn,
Sun and moon briefly embrace
As another day is born.

Angela Carol Latham

Abortion - A Mother's View

Now the dreaded day has come
I really am so scared
The day when I shall give a life
That once I might have shared
Now I'm going to explain to you
To tell you the reason why
As I write this letter
I begin to cry
I honestly do love you
But in this world you see
There's nothing I can do for you
No friends or family
Your father would have loved you
But when he went away
My whole life started falling
And reached this very day
Please don't call me a murderer
I'm doing what is best
I love you my poor darling
Now lay yourself to rest.

Alison James

Mater Amabilis

I see her star at night
I see her face at dawn
Her voice is in the breeze
That heralds morn.

I miss her smile
I miss her touch
And oh I miss so very much
The sound advice
The kindly word
So oft rejected
Scorned, unheard.

And still she guides
And points the way
But now I listen
And obey

Dorothy Salvage

Untitled

Through time and space
I seek for you
Though storm breaks
And rain does flow
My search goes on

I sail the seas
I scale the heights
I search for thee
In all thy might

Yet seas seem tame
And mountains small
When thy beauty rains
Upon my soul.

Greig Walker

Dandelion Clocks

I am a dandelion clock in your arms.
If you squeeze me,
I will surely break.
So treat me gently,
but beware . . .
I can take over,
I am no flower.
You could blow me away
forgetting you love me;
but everywhere you go
I will be there
reminding you
Who cares.
I am not beautiful . . .
But I am beauty.

Jane A. R. Hadfield

Inner Cave

We all of us have an inner cave
into which we can retreat.
Where our daily thoughts and pure
peace can meet.

And slowly our cares and worries
dissolve and are no more,
As we picture our inner cave
far away on a distant shore.

Take comfort from the peace
you find within your quiet cave
And remember this calm and quiet
place and the upliftment it gave.

Denise Crabtree

"Promises"

A great part of our planet
Is covered in sea or sand:
So when we've felled all the forests
What will become of our land?

When all our oceans are polluted
And there's nowhere we can flee
When all our lands are barren,
Is that when we shall see?

That we have to live in balance
With nature in every way,
For unless we find that balance,
Where all of us can share
There still maybe a planet
But it will be quite bare!

Barren of life as we know it
Too late to save mankind!
Too late to keep the "Promises
That we always had in mind!"

Anita West

My Love, For You

My love, for you,
is deeper than any ocean bed,
it goes far beyond.
My love, for you,
is higher than the stars above,
it is in heaven.
My love, for you,
is wider than the universe,
it stretches so many times around,
I cannot count.
My love, love me,
and we will be in paradise together,
and I'll be yours for eternity.

Elizabeth Barnett

A World with No Love

This World hasn't enough love
Is God still up above?
People are afraid to share -
No-one ever stops to care.
What happened to romance?
It doesn't stand a chance.
Everyone tearing each other apart
Instead of living by their heart.
Living life by 'the rule' -
It's all becoming too cruel.
If you try to refuse -
There's someone who'll abuse . . .
There's no use pretending -
Love has reached its ending.
It's sad; but trust -
Has been turned to lust.
There is no answer
For love has cancer . . .
It's been forgotten -
In a World so rotten . . .

Jackie Redhead

The Last Day of Summer

Miles and miles of golden sand
Children running hand in hand
Building castles finding treasure
This, is people's
Source of pleasure

Lots and lots of golden dust
Some parts soft some hard as crust
Getting trod on by tired feet
Then gently trailed
Upon the street

The sun goes down
The night draws near
The sand lies still
For another year

Anne Boyle

Utopia

Step into my dream with me
come step into my world.
Walk with me in peace and calm
through a utopian world.

Where threats of war do not exist,
Peace only rules this land.
Where peoples of all nations
walk together, hand in hand.

Mankind has learnt to live as one
in perfect harmony.
No matter what the colour,
no matter what the creed.

All pestilence and suffering gone,
no hardships, hunger, needs.
Just peace of mind, contentment,
a world that's free from greed.

So step into my world with me
come step into my dream.
Before too late, we have to wake
back to reality.

Colin W. Howard

Sore

Humble feeling hospital,
Oh no not the food,
Supposed to be good,
Potatoes not mashed,
I can't wait to fast,
Time to take my Temazepam,
Au revoir bump on heel,
Later on how do you feel.

SORE!

Fiona Carr

I See the Night

I see the night, I see the night
and it's so cold without you,
I see the stars up in the sky,
but they don't shine without you,
I see the moon but she goes
too soon without you
Persona grata to me.
And if our paths ever cross again
would you love me, just the same
For who can I turn to,
if you walk away.
I see the night, I see the night
and it's so cold without you
I see the stars up in the sky
but they don't shine without you
I see the moon but she goes
too soon without you
Persona Grata to me.

Caroline Helenora Davis

Stagnant Existence

I pushed away my only love
my love was relieved.

Now my love, love is lost
lost and not received

Love he knows he was the one
but now love is gone

He was right, ideal for me

I being everything wrong!

Eve Carter

In the Shadow of Thy Wing

When myriad heat
Consume the day,
With ceaseless beat
Of insect wing:
When living thing
On earth retreat
To hide away
From ceaseless beat:

Serenest pool
To soothe and cool.

When myriad sin
Consume the heart,
With ceaseless din
Of envying strife:
When restless life
On earth begin
To hide away
From ceaseless sin:

Serenest love
From God above.

Barbara Butler

I Feel

I feel for you
Deep inside
I feel the love
and want to hide

I feel the passion
like red hot coal
it burns my heart
and melts my soul

I feel the heat of red hot fire
it is my love
and my desire

I feel your hands
upon my skin
it lights a spark
from deep within

Julia Battams

Elemental Fury

Clouds scurry hurriedly
Across the sky
Menacing atmosphere
A storm is nigh.

The world grows dark
On the sun's retreat.
Rain cascades
In a rhythmic beat.

Landscape stark
In a lightening flash.
Seconds later
A thunder crash.

The angry heavens
Erupt in rage.
Fighting a battle
On a cosmic stage.

Barbara M. Flaherty

Dark Flower

Black was the flower
I picked up that day,
Dark was its colour
Among the pale hay

The seasons had passed,
And the white blossom
Had been changed so fast
To that dark column.

Every life must end,
But, when my flower
To winter will bend,
Lord, keep her colour!

John Bogard

To Geoff on the Death of Liz

If I should die before you
I'll reach out for you and say
"My spirit heart adores you
until your dying day"

When earthly lovers find you
I will turn to you and say
"An earthy cover binds me
but my heart with yours will stay"

And although you're glad you met me
I'll touch your soul and say
"It's time now to forget me
put mourning tears at bay"

And when you find another
I'll look fondly on and say
"I'm glad you have each other
this ghost has had her day"

Elizabeth Lidstone

Joy of Belief

Hello world I'm upside down
I'm happy - so must you.
My smile it charms you I can see

Up comes one leg then the next
Like a puppet without a string
Crash to the ground
'Poor thing'

Be happy, don't you see
You are you
And I am me

Eyes so blue, mist with concern
Dearest darling - won't you learn
It's alright, just watch me now
Force of gravity
Do not justify
you to I will defy

There dear mother
Don't you cry
I knew you were there
When I didn't die

Irene Nation

Solo Being

Don't shatter me,
I'm no good to be glass.
Throw me oblivious;
And tangled mesh,
And solitary, and emotionless.
Let be the hands of time.
So lift me unconscious,
Up onto the world's humble shoulders
And that's where I live,
In close connection,
Of self, of control.
There will be another.

Donna Staughton

Untitled

Look at you, you little lout.
Crude obscenities, I hear you shout.
How old am I, I do forget.
Who was that, that I just met.
My eyes are blurry, it looks dark.
I no longer see, to walk the park.
The music gone from my ears.
Drowned out by all the years.
My back is bent from years of toil.
I think my joints may need an oil.
A plastic cup, I use to drink.
They no longer fill it to the brink.
My face is wrinkled, weather worn.
My clothes all ragged, old and torn.
I still have a lot to give.
I still have a life to live.
So listen well to what I tell.
For you will soon be old as well.

Deborah Partridge

Unconditional Love

A newborn babe
Defenceless and weak
Loving arms around her
She will always seek
Kind words whispered
Lullaby's sang
Always nearby
To take her hand
Happiness and smiles
And lots of tears too
To have such love
Adored by you
Growing up
As children do
Being cared for
As if expected of you
Years roll by
You're loved like no other
You're my friend
My mother.

Dawn Manders

Untitled

Spring turns into summer,
Spring flowers coming into bud
the sky is so blue, the grass
is so green, the oil is so
fresh I just love to sit out,

Days are getting longer
Days are getting warmer,
birds begin to sing,
I just love the Spring.

Hoyle Reachill

Remaining

Darkness swept my body
Down in an empty tomb,
Still I lay, down in a
Cold, damp, dark room.

My hands covered the stone
That had engraved my name,
Calling, calling me down,
To take even the blame.

As darkness swept my body
Still in that lone room,
My heart thumped, singing
A sorrow-formed tune.

I knew that I could not
Live another day,
So I sank further and further
And crept slowly away.

Claire Immel

Untitled

Captured in the universe of the mind,
Drifting to unknown places,
Seeing your imaginations,
Seeing life with unknown faces.
A blackness that glitters,
A colourful void of your choice,
Commanding what is there,
With a soundless voice.
A never-ending journey,
In a space that is so vast,
To go beyond your reaches,
So forever will always last.
The depths of the unknown,
Lying dormant in your head.
No questions to be answered,
No spoken words are said.
All that is you,
Is all that you are,
A wondrous adventure,
In a space that goes so far.

Jacqueline M. J. Cole

Anorexia

Clumsiness, acne
Dry skin and hair
Swollen cheeks
Life just isn't fair

Cold hands and feet
Temperature poor
When I stand up
I fall to the floor

The feeling of faintness
Bad concentration and sleep
I've lost that much energy
I'm a quivering heap

People keep joking
And taking the mick
But I'm hooked on laxatives
And being sick.

You see I'm convinced
That fat is a sin
So I'm simply dying
To be thin!!

Jo Morriss

The Earwig

It crawls up the wall,
Easy to see,
Even though it's small
It frightens me.

Slowly at first,
But quickening up,
I loose my thirst
As it crawls in my cup

It crawls halfway
Then turns and stops,
I feel it's going to stay
In a funny sort of way

It climbs out
And crawls down
And goes for the spout
Move it quick and get it out.

I flick it and it flies
And I know I've got a hit
Because now it's moving
Just a tiny tiny bit.

Deborah E. Barson

Dunblane

Dunblane, Dunblane,
Evil came,
Nothing's the same,
Children die,
Wounded cry,
A teacher less,
Families caress,
Dunblane, Dunblane,
Skies grey,
Misty day,
A village weep,
Memories keep,
Clouds drift by,
Sun in the sky,
Dunblane, Dunblane.

Helena Douglas

Inner Woman

Soft, smooth shoulders,
experts in the orchestra,
send me,
as I long to stroke them,
the feminine whiles,
disguise her subtleness,
innocence perhaps, who knows?
But her lovely shape
glistens as the male brass does,
to tempt a vision of what might be.

If I could have the woman I want,
it would be she
with smoothest shoulders and the
and the deepest cleavage.
But no, for the shape
is not the most important
but the spirit within the skin.

Derek I. Buchanan

Love

Tear it apart,
Petal by petal,
Leaf by leaf,
Until it dies.
Then try to put the pieces
  back together.
You will find you can't.
But don't cry,
There will be others.
You will love again.
But he will be the one you
  want for always,
Because you love him.

Erika Daccus

Aspirations of the Enigmatic Soul

The only way is to strive
for our dreams to survive,
while keeping our proverbial
feet firmly set on the ground.

We must all be bold
and not left out in the cold,
for the zenith of our
thoughts to be crowned.

The soul must be strong
for the quest to belong,
in a place that will
shine through adversity forever.

If an aspiration grows weak
it will not climb to its peak,
which means the death of one's
pinnacle endeavour? Never.

Gregory Button

A Day in the Life of a '10 Month Old'

Well I'm up on my feet
Now where shall I stand
What's exciting to me
To hold in my hand

Oh look there's a coffee
That mug I could break
The coffee will spill
And a mess I would make

Oh I do like that crystal
I think that would crash
If I drop it from here
I think it will smash

Now the table is clear
They've ruined my fun
They're faster than me
Oh I wish I could run

Now away from the table
That tele looks great
There must be a knob here
Or something to break.

Elaine Titterrell

Wings of Fantasy

Gliding o'er the scented roses,
Flight-path silent to the ear -
Dipping in the summer breezes,
See a miracle appear:
Insect of the Lepidoptera,
Caterpillar embryo,
Cocooned larvae lie suspended
Turquoise chrysalis below;
Dormant pupae now awakened
Legs and wings their flexes try:
From its latent tomb, fresh shattered
Glimpse the new-formed butterfly.
Rich and rare the vibrant colours,
Crimson, gold and palest hue;
Slender form, with knobbed antennae
Beaming myriad signal though.
Brief ethereal existence,
Float a kiss to friend and foe:
Ornamental pleasure-seeker
Simply come and sweetly go!

Heather Dillon

Breathless

Trees grow,
Flowers bloom,
Nuclear waste,
Kills the Earth's womb.

The sun's power,
The moon's strength,
Radiation destroys,
What man has built.

Winters are cold,
The Earth shivers,
Effluent chokes,
Our lakes and rivers.

Summers are hot,
The fields are bare,
C.F.C.'s widen,
The ozone layer.

Nights are bright,
Days are dark,
I thought Atomic bombs,
Were a thing of the past.

John Gately

God's Gift to Man

God's gift to man,
Is so perfect.
It's full of love,
And its endless energy
Works in everything.

Its great work of
Art and architecture,
Can clearly be seen
In towns and cities
Throughout the world.
It is the sole founder
Of the whole magic
Of science and technology.
Lives in both rich and poor.
So great, yet so humble.

God's gift to man
The spirit from above.
Master of knowledge and power.
When it touches it brings love
Great understanding and inspiration.

Joan Monica Attoh

The Lost Chord

Strength to his elbow
Fiddlesticks to his bow
He's over-orchestrated
Non-functional at high doh!
Metronomically speaking
At measured spells
His unrehearsed outbursts
Pitch-peak decibels
Crescendoing the other day
In strain - his very own
He scaled several octaves higher
Than the top C zone
Pianissimo!
How absurd!
DOUBLE-PIANOFORTE
Is the definitive word!

Knowing the score
My pen inspires
This ode to the one
Who hires and fires!

Anna MacDonald

Renewed Strength

I felt the need of solitude
For merely half an hour
Time to think and wonder
To wait till I gained pace
I was aided by the water
Lap, lapping at my feet
The monotonous repetition
Seemed to pull back on the reigns
That forced the driving speed in life
From which I tried to flee

Every limb was limp and heavy
As I sat there drained and jaded
Then slowly, very slowly
Like pouring thick molasses
My veins began to fill
Once more I drew a breath
The clamp had been released again
The pressure had subsided
It only took but one half hour
To stop and gain the pace.

Doreen H. M. Scott

Ulster - A New Season

The frost lay glistening
Its whiteness so grand
Enveloping the countryside
Penetrating the land.

Its coldness, its sharpness
Its pervading chill
Smothering life
Damaging at will.

The people prayed silently
Mourned what was lost
The truths, the beliefs
The huge human cost.

But the winter is fading
The wind is less raw
The heat is emerging
The land starting to thaw.

The burdens, the obsessions
The life by the gun
Are diminishing slowly
With the warmth of the sun.

Alison Hamilton

Untitled

Strolling through the forest
In the stillness of the day
Listening, as trees rustle
Imagining what they say

The sadness of the day
The hopelessness of life
As we try to make our way
Through the trouble and the strife

The peace and calm and serenity
As we wander hand in hand
Is all we ever hoped for
In this dark and troubled land

Many roads may lead us
Each day we journey on
We cannot see the outcome
Of either right or wrong

The crumpling underfoot
Of the leaves upon the ground
Breaks the tone of silence
Peace is what we've found

Delia Spalding

Through Vagrant Eyes

The pin stripe blind pass her by
On the street she sprawls alone
Weeping tears through vagrant eyes
In a doorway she calls home

Beneath the sheets of cardboard old
She finally settles down
To another night of breathless cold
In a blinkered carefree town

I vaguely heard her sleeping cry
Of the faded life before
A turning mumble asking why
And what she's living for

With bitter streak of irony
Just a few streets away
Politicians sleep in sanctuary
Before the break of day

She dreads the hour of nature's sin
On a harsh winter's morn
When she wakes to find upon the wind
The cold December scorn

Gary Keeble

Peace

Peace is in a person,
Jesus, God's own Son,
By simply trusting in His name,
And the work that He has done.

This world is full of turmoil,
Of bitterness and strife,
Men try in vain to solve them,
The problems of this life.

No matter how much talking,
That men may do and say,
The solution lies in Jesus,
The life, the truth, the way.

For if we come and ask Him,
And repent of every sin,
He'll wash us in His precious blood,
Then pour His peace within.

The Prince of Peace bequeathed
To His disciples, peace,
When men and women turn to Him,
Then wars and strife will cease.

Dorothy Anderson

Untitled

You'll be leaving soon,
for pastures new,
for you it's a boon,
But us, we'll be blue.

New Zealand's the place,
Where you hope to be.
You'll be packing your case.
Quite soon, you will see.

No doubt we will miss you,
And be sad for a while.
But what can we do?
Only, just try to smile.

When we say our goodbyes,
Before you leave for the plane.
We'll heave a few sighs,
And grin through the pain.

But we're all adults now.
With lives of our own.
We'll cope some how,
and there's always the phone.

Clare Simmons

Family Ties . . .

In the corridors of my mind
My thoughts start to unwind
To the past that has been cruel
A perpetual duel
By my nearest kin
From the lies and Sin

The reflections are shown
On my siblings who've flown
Myself, well I stay
Now quieter days
Tranquillity? Not quite
But it's always in sight

As new beginnings start
Old enemies depart
The fingers I've burned
The lessons I've learned
A love that's so deep
Secrets I still keep

Now aged with time
This life that is mine

Anita Delaney

Untitled

Times are a-changing
nothing's the same,
Life's moving
but we are to blame,
moaning and squawking
When things don't go right
Just look at the pleasing
things of life,
the beauty which can be
found in the woodlands and glades
flowers and ferns on parade
Carpeted with bluebells all around.
The animals footprints on the soft
leafy ground. Through the woods
we walk on by, just watching
Where you step and then you'll see
the secrets to be found just you
look around. Open your eyes, the
Windows of your mind

Eileen Annette Jasmin Jones

How I Long for a Drink

Toom is my Tassie,
O' how I wish it were
Fu' O' Bree,
To take away thy thirst
From my yell throat,
Though cool it may be.

Monie days I have travelled
An' been reestit by the sun.
Though my sark covers my back
Still I feel the burn.

Pray not for bield against
The sun, nor for snaw,
But for a Tassie Fu' O' Bree
An' for the winds tae blaw.

Alexander Bryce

The Artist

I painted the clouds
On a summer's day
But the rain washed my canvas
And swept them away.

So, I painted a bird
Up high on the wing
But he got too lonely
And ceased then, to sing

I painted the stars
That were hid by the sun
But man came and conquered
Them, every one.

So, I turned my eyes
Seaward, and what did I find?
That the great waves surged over
And whitewashed my mind.

Candy Chilton

Transfigured Night

Then love's sun set fast
on the shining sea
and blood-red stained
the departed quay,

followed swiftly by
the death-dark night,
full dimming all
the grieving light.

But while earth seemed
darkened with despair,
the stars joined in a
son et lumière.

David Stockdale

Who Am I?

Whose is this face I know as mine?
So young. Yet old, am I;
My life - we meet as strangers now,
I know not how, nor why.

For there, beyond reality -
The face that is my past;
The boy I was. Such dreams I knew,
Believing they could last.

Yet, is his image really mine?
This boy, who mirrors me;
He smiles, and I become that smile -
And know that I am he.

Donna Prime

'The English Summer'

Spring is here, with a
  Heigh and a ho,
 Not that you'd notice, neigh
  Nonny no,
'Tis cold and it's windy
We could have snow,
That's England, dear England
  You should jolly well know.
Black were the clouds
  In the sky,
Lightning flashed and the
  Birds flew high.
The thunder crashed overhead
  The rain poured down
And the people fled,
'Tis June, 'tis June our
  English summer,
But all one can get is
  A worn-out plumber!

Eileen E. Bailey

Unsung Hero

She was only four, her brother died
Her dad had gone and she never
Asked why?

She knew I was angry
She knew I was sad
And still she never
Asked why?

She grew up quick
She had no choice
She cuddled me
She sympathised, still,
She never asked why?

Ten years have gone
Still she cares, not
Just for me, my
Unsung hero my
Champion, my daughter.

Janet Allan

Wasted Dreams

Broken thoughts and shattered dreams,
Puddles full of tears.
Memories like photographs,
Yet a blur of all the years.

After all the waiting
It's all come to an end
I don't need my dreams now
I just need a friend.

After all the hoping
Living with my fears
In the end the wrong side won
And it all ended in tears.

Geraldine Bradley

Set a Guardian at the Gate

Set a guardian at the gate,
Restrain all intrusion;
Travelling with each other
In intimate fusion.

Soft voice cushioning,
Your hands are mine;
Liquid dance evolving
A touch divine.

Warm tastes invite
Sweet and salt melting,
My mouth embraces
Safe, soft sheltering.

Dandelion clock of time
Dispelling breathlessly
My mind from worldly being,
A journey alone for me.

What sees man in woman
Or woman in man's charms
But peace and passion abiding
Encircled in your arms.

J. P. Branley

Whose Guiding Hand?

When the wild west winds blow
In storm and tempest rage o'er land
Its anger all shall know.
We ask whose guiding hand.
Such fury both us show.

When mountain waves the angered sea
Pound rocks upon the peaceful land
And howling seagulls flee
We ask whose guiding hand
Whose fury can it be?

When singing birds wing gently by
Alight to kiss their nature land
Then on to distant homes they fly
We ask who guiding hand
Allows them all to die.

Such mysteries are not for man
To seek the answers why
No earthly wisdom can
To heavenly knowledge fly
To where it all began.

John S. Hughes

Beautiful England

Oh, beautiful England
how much you have to give
no wonder your inhabitants
have such a gust to live.
my heart is full of wonder
by your multitude of charm
your castles and stately homes
that stand erect and calm.
you have all of the four seasons
that just seem to come and go,
beginning with the summer sun
to end with winter snow.
I don't think you'll find such colour
as England has right here
just look at the field and hedgerows
and the trees both far and near.
I've done my share of travelling
many wonders I have seen
but England it is beautiful
fields and fields of green.

Frances Coe

An Unexpected Visitor

The rattling of a window pane,
Footsteps on the stairs,
As I sit there engulfed with pain
And all my troubled cares.
The open door that once was not,
Rustling near my face,
Is it real? A dream or what?
My heart begins to race.
A whisper of fragrance enfolds me
As memories from the past,
Takes my pain and sets me free,
Recognition comes at last.
Now I'm content with singing heart
Love flows everywhere,
Never no more will it depart
And leave me in despair.
Now I know, believe I've found,
I've searched since long ago,
My mother's here she's all around,
She's called to say hello.

Ivy Thompson

God's Sea

When I think about the sea
I feel a deep fulfilment
inside of me

The waves, they rip and roar
turning and twisting to and fro

Power lies beneath our feet
power so strong
our hearts skip a beat

The foam that moves to shore
retains little creatures
and much more

For without the waves
recycling the sea
many small animals would never be

The beauty of the ocean
calms my soul
and makes me feel whole

Thank You Lord for creating the sea
a place for you and me
where we can . . . just be.

Georga Dawson

A New Friend

On a bus to Waterloo
I met her.
A blonde.
Blue-eyed.
A beauty
to reckon with
she was friendly.

On the way
To places unknown
She told me
she feared the worst,
the world was hard
things were tough.

On getting off the bus
I took her hand.
Small and vulnerable
I held it firmly
to lend her courage.
I would be there
now that she is deserted.

Edwin Senjobe

Seven Sins

Monday night you're working,
You don't get home till late.
Tuesday night is keep fit night,
Your evening starts at eight.
Wednesday night the queen of clubs,
You don't get home till three.
Thursday night is set aside,
But you're too tired for me.
Friday night the disco calls,
Another early morn.
Saturday, we're both at work,
And then you're out till dawn,
Sunday comes, our day of rest,
You sleep the whole day long.
And so that is your seven days,
But to you, there's nothing wrong . . .

Damian Potter

Hurt?

Hurting inside
You don't know why
Sinking within
Not stepping outside
Losing all contact
Spinning further away
You feel comfortable
But know you can't stay
Look to the future
What lies ahead?
Return to the living
Step out of your head.

Gill MacNaught

I Love You

I can talk.
You hear me - talk, talk, talk.
Words clamour to escape my mouth,
A river of nonsense
To make you laugh
To make you like me.

Look deeper.
Beyond the crowd and the noise
All alone and silent,
The deepest feeling of all.

If you open your heart to me
Listen . . .
You will hear,
I love you.

Carole A. S. Sutherland

Changing Times

"I want!" "I want!"
You hear the cry
In every shop
As you pass by

"I've got! "I've got!"
It's such a sin
This greedy world
We now live in.

"Mine's better than yours!"
"You can't beat that!"
Straight from the mouth
Of our new age brat.

"Yes please and thank you".
Those times are past.
"Mind out!" "Shove over!"
Are here to last.

"Look around, look around,
Why can't they see,
Nature's true beauty
And it's all for free."

Diana Rowland

Love of Mine

Love is a candle,
That flickers so bright,
As lovers entwine,
In the depth of the night.

They slowly caress,
Their love unfolds,
Fire in their hearts,
Becomes so bold.

The web of lust,
Entraps the heart,
The burning desire,
Can't tear them apart.

Their hearts as one,
Beating in time,
The candle so bright,
You're mine, all mine.

Debbie Hindes

Friend

You are the sun
That gives me my colour
You are the rival
That makes my life fuller

You are the rain
That helps me to grow
You are the mirror
That teaches me so

You are the wind
That blows me away
You are the challenge
That begs me to stay

You are the air
That has such great worth
You are the weight
That holds me to Earth

You are the one
With whom I feel tall
You are the one
That I'm proud to call . . . Friend.

Andrew Price

Untitled

There should be a smell
That I could call you.
One I could return to
And smell, coating my
Senses in security.
All I have is clouds of memories
Floating out of reach
And unwanted anyway.
No smell, no thought, no being
Is good enough for what you were.

Gaynor Hodgson

"Sound"

I think you'll find
That I've left behind
And you are wrong
I'll always be strong
Before too long
I'll be back on song
I think you'll find
If you don't mind
So please don't start
To hound me
I'm still sound
I'll always be around
So don't bring me down

David Mawn

Self Destruction

In a world full of rules
Her love burned inside
Unable to show this
Love, she did hide

Ugly - an outcast
Denying from him
Her inner beauty for
One who was slim

Love never replaced:
Life and good health
Never knowing his love
Never knowing herself

Beauty shined within
They saw - not she
Living lonely 'til death
Alas, so did he.

Chloe Shaw

Love's Tide

Here we swim
Swallowing the deep,
Slowly opening eyes
To moving mysteries.
Our souls flashing
Hope, fear, sanctuary.
The current thrives
Demanding influence,
But we swim!

A. J. Rigby

Untitled

How much do I love you.
How deep is the ocean.
How high is the sky.
My body and soul need
To be near to you.
That's how much I love you
A million times a day
With things I do and say.
And yet you seem deaf
And blind and so unkind
Still I say I love you.
I reach out my hand
In the sun-kissed sand
I can't see anyone but you.
I love you.
Yet one day some day
You will leave me.
And in my darkest thoughts.
I will whisper.
I love you.

Judith Summerfield

Wonder What It's Like in Heaven

I wonder what it's like in Heaven,
For all our love ones, and friends are there.
Mansions, lakes, mountains, churches,
Beautiful scenery that's all
beyond that golden gate.
On this earth it's a hard
and difficult road, there's
no turning back, but in
Heaven it changes all that.
You meet all your friends in
Bygone days, and talk about
the past, your memories will
never fade away because
they will always last.
A beautiful garden, serenity
and perfect peace.
Yes, I wonder what it's
like in Heaven.

Frederick Wainhouse

Youth in the Rain

Grey days
Standing in darkness
Expressionless features
With distant thoughts
Distant eyes
Seeing young lives
Running away
Alive lives running
Into puddles of darkness
Selfsame darkness
Alone.

Charlotte Robson

"Welcome Stranger"

"Welcome stranger,"
"How goes your day?"
If someone said this to you
What would you say?
Would you ignore him
Or give him a smile?
Would you stand on the pavement
And talk for a while?
For people are wary
In this day and age.
To hold conversation
With a wily 'old sage',
But there's a wealth of knowledge
In his ancient mind.
And those kindly blue eyes
Seem so sad now he's blind,
So next time you see him
Spare a moment or two.
For that 'welcome stranger'
Could one day be you.

Irene Coltman

School Gate Bullies

No, no mother,
I don't want to go to school.
They'll be there,
Waiting at the gate;
Waiting for the money.
If I don't give it to them,
They'll call me names,
And blame for things I didn't do.

I know they'll be there,
Waiting,
For the money I don't have.
Hitting me,
Until I cry.

Why me?
Why do they pick on me?
I don't tease them,
Kick them and embarrass them;
No, no mother,
I don't want to go to school.

Caroline Day

Poets' Dream

Ancient hills, steeped history
Thawed landscape deserted
Fragrant pines veiled by mist
Tapestry woven, nature's mystery.

Tilth, purple mottled jade
Rippling streams peacefully flow
Vermilion sunsets, tinged gold
Horizons distant, watercolours fade.

Enraptured, wondrous scene
Timeless grandeur surpassed
Whispering winds, spirit free
Majestic, captivating, poets' dream.

Jean Emerson

My Darling

I'd lie beneath green shady trees
In summer sun, a gentle breeze
I'd whisper with an urgent plea
"Take me now, my darling"

Naked, lain upon the sand
Blue sky, blue sea and rolling land
I'd feel the soft touch of your hand
"Make love to me, my darling"

I'd lie in fields of golden corn
A sweet and dewy springtime morn
From founts of love is passion born
Slake my thirst my darling

Now in your bed, with sleepy eyes
Yearning heart and passion sighs
Your body burns me, satisfies
"Sleep well tonight, my darling"

Janette Craythorne

The Flower

Spring is here,
That what they say,
But who are they,
Perhaps - It's God.
  Or
Just snowdrop.

Heavenly white
And spring time sweet
You look so tender.
At my feet
Are you God.
  Or
Just snowdrop

Irene Crawford

Our Saviour

A stranger in a foreign land,
Is ours be known as one.
Deemed to hold the greatest stand,
As the Lord, our Son.

Born to quell a nation's moan;
To mourn the sick and poor;
And offer forth a hand in loan,
To sweep the wretched floor.

Destined as the Golden Child;
With sights above the rest.
To settle out terrain that's wild,
And calm the ruffled nest.

Sent to play the martyr's role,
To walk alone at death.
At last to save the wayward soul,
So hope may gasp for breath

Deborah Raggett

My Young Lovely

How long will it be
my young lovely
before all your petals are picked
and all of your stems
branches
and green shoots
are laid spread bare
upon a lover's bed?

How long
my young lovely
before that love curdles
into sour poison
and the buds of hope lie
withered and dead
and the lover's bed more
a grave?

Brian Thomson

Willow Tree

A willow tree, a willow tree,
Standing beside a flowing river,
A scene of such idyllic beauty.
Yet, a lonely landscape,
For a weeping willow tree.

Alan Harrison

Wishing for Death

The day the dog's
Suffering
Gets too much
The vet turns him down
To sleep
The day my suffering
Becomes unbearable
You leave it
Lingering
Too long, too deep

Take me away
From the pain I am feeling
Take me away
From the fear that I feel
If you loved me, O Lord
You would take me away
The day my suffering
Turned into pain

Justine Saunders

Stranglers Beach North Cornwall 1995 and 1895 Contrasted

Summer evening,
  Sunlit sea,
Gentle breeze,
  Wave-kissed rocks;
Evening swim,
  Fun in the surf,
Friends on the beach,
  Life is so good.

Winter night,
  Roaring waves,
Force ten gale,
  Jagged rocks;
Swimming for life,
  Cruel breakers,
Murderous wreckers,
  Death on the beach.

John Wensley

The River

Sounds of the river
Sweet music to hear,
Whilst eye watches idly
White sails billowing near.

Ropes beating time
To the gulls' wailing cry,
As they search azure water
With keen yellow eye.

Quietly gliding
The ripples we meet,
Wind whispering softly
To curlews' sad cry.

Greedily sucking at mudbanks
Pushing aside with a sigh,
Seaweed and pebbles
Causing Dunlins to fly,

What joy does it bring us,
On bright Summer days
Memories to cherish
For the rest of our days.

Elizabeth Moore

Beneath the Moon

Beneath the moon I stand, I see
The soft white glow fall onto me.
I feel its inner peace of mind,
A touch of warmth, my soul to find.

Beneath the moon I rest, I look
Up at darkness, the love you took.
A sudden tear does hit my skin,
That single tear you always win.

Beneath the moon I sit, I stare
At passing clouds that seem to share
Their heavenly light, with the sky,
May they protect both you and I.

Beneath the moon I lay, I dream
Of all that my life means to me.
A face I see, I long to touch,
That face I'll always love so much.

Beneath the moon I kneel, I pray
That we'll be together again one day.
Beneath the moon I think of you.
My love remains forever true.

Corrinne Anne Lovelock

Blind Love

I cannot see the mistletoe
The sunlight on the sea
The rainbow, and the falling snow
And you are here with me

But I can smell the new mown hay
And I can touch your hair
I listen to the children play
And you are always there

I love the sound of falling rain
Soft music on the breeze
The footsteps walking down the lane
Your funny little sneeze

The chocolate bars we love to share
A little sip of wine
The endless darkness, I can bare
Your body next to mine

I'm helpless now, you're going to die
I gently stroke your paw
I take your harness, and I cry
And stumble through the door

June Darley

In the Midst of the Moonlit Night

The clock ticks,
The tap drips
In the midst of the moonlit night.

An owl hoots,
A ghostly flute toots
In the midst of the moonlit night.

The fox howls,
As he silently prowls
In the midst of the moonlit night.

The nice squeak,
The floorboards creak
In the midst of the moonlit night.

The man snores,
As the cat comes indoors
In the midst of the moonlit night.

A silver knife cuts through the room
And a candle flickers in the gloom
In the midst of the moonlit night.

Jennifer Cockcroft

The Night Has Come

Confusion, disillusioned
The nights silence
Like a cloak surrounds me
Smoke pours and dragons scream
Tall shadows are the decorations
A distant cry issues forth
Creating havoc in its wake
Bad dreams haunting
The clocks mechanics
Whirring smoothly
Sweet darkness
Hold me close
Keep me tight
Don't hide
Don't go
Stay forever
Things change, people, places
Dark and light fight for control
For me, darkness rules eternally.

Hazel Lea Snelling

Untitled

My goals are changing,
The posts are moving

I tackle, I run,
I am but one

I aim at the goal,
but it's too far away.

A little more practice
A little more pain
and maybe the goal post
will be closer next time

Helen Hillier

The Shoeshine Girl

She has no name
The Shoeshine girl
People pass by her tiny frame
Those who stare, don't care.
No home, no rights,
A pitiful sight,
No one to protect her,
Or look after her.
No one knows who she is,
Where she came from
How she lives.
Her round eyes stare into space,
Tears run down her dirty face,
She pushes away a damp curl,
She's all alone,
The Shoeshine girl.

Catherine S. Gillibrand

If Only

If only you could see
The sights I have beheld

  With your eyes . . .

If only you could taste
The flavours I have savoured

  With your mouth . . .

If only you could feel
The textures I have caressed

  With your fingers

If only.
God, if only . . .

You were human too.

Gavin Douglas John Wilson

323

"My Son"

From your first kick
To your first breath, my son.
I gave you life and love
Like I'd given to no-one.

When you first looked
Into my eyes -
I knew from then on
This love wouldn't die.

Our first real separation
Starting nursery school,
Your look of desperation
And hurt - I felt a fool!

Many years have passed by -
Trials, happy times and sorrow,
Always there beside me -
You're my meaning for tomorrow.

Now you've grown up
I have to let go.
Never letting you guess
How much I'll miss you so!!

Janette Jacobs

Don't Give Up

When life gets you down
Try hard not to frown.
Just hold your head up high.
When you want to laugh
But can only cry
Please don't tell the world goodbye.
Some you miss
Some you hit,
Don't give up
Don't just quit.
Although the tunnel
Looks black and grey
Someone soon will show the way
You'll see the light
It shines so bright.
Just when you thought
You couldn't cope
The light gets stronger
And gives you hope.

Andrea Henderson

Twenty Men Twenty Hounds

Twenty men on panting steeds,
Twenty men in bright red coats,
Twenty men and twenty hounds,
Twenty men a-going 'round,
One small fox and one small deer,
Whose lives are precious and so dear,
Twenty men are out to kill,
A creature that means no ill.

Derek Woodman

Perfect Words

Under the blanket of night he cried,
under the stars he wished to die.
It once made sense,
stripped to my last defence.
You've loved like this before,
who are your tears for?
Slay the God that damns me,
with your beauty that crucified me.
The quest for absolution begins.
You've chosen the Celtic King.
Why do the fools follow him?
Let temptation pull you in.
He is every tear,
in your world of sin.
I have worthless dreams,
compared to all your perfect sounds.

Julian Courtney

Untitled

Crowded with strangers
The door swung

A growing desire
A quenching thirst
A life of dreams
A life of death
A painful feeling waiting for death

But death will come
It's neither a choice or a want
The obvious is vague
The reality strange
But deep inside we all feel the pain

Whether young or old
The corpse is cold
The soul will linger
Forever alone
Wandering around looking for peace
But peace will never come.

Christian McKenna

Life on Earth

The seed is planted
The flower grows
How long it will live,
Nobody knows
As a child you can't run
As a man you can't hide
Like all human beings,
We live off our pride,
We're afraid to love
Yet unwilling to hate
We're blind to the truth
Until it's too late,
The young know so little
The old know it all
The big use their knowledge
To steal from the small,
Piece by piece our civilization
Dies from famine and thirst
But our world won't live forever
Which will go first.

Ben Faul

Tomorrow Won't Come

Blood on the walls
The Grim Reaper calls
Tomorrow won't come

Death in the air
Nobody cares
Tomorrow won't come

Living today
Now on their way
Tomorrow won't come

Family cries
Everyone dies
Tomorrow won't come

Jacqueline Church

Alone

When I let my emotions stray
The hurting will not go away
And as I lay in doleful bliss
I cannot stop the tearfulness
In my mind you are here to stay
The memory of you will not go away
I hate myself for feeling like this
This is not heaven nor is it bliss
If only I could rise above
This lonely unrequited love
But no matter what I do or say
I am all alone at the end of the day.

Joseph Allen

Pain

Why doesn't he love me,
That's one thing I can't see.
Every night I say a prayer,
That one day he'll notice, I'm
still waiting there.
All I can do is wait,
While my body goes through
the stages of love and hate.
Why did he leave me with
all this pain.
I had everything to lose
and nothing to gain.
Now he doesn't want to be
my friend,
But surely can that be
the end?

Emma Kenny

Beautiful World

The sun sets on yet another day,
The beautiful green fields
And blue skies,
Are cast into darkness.

The skies light up
With the blasts of war,
But still they live on,
Fighting every day.

The green grass gone,
The blue sky darkened,
The dreams of life
Are shattered by war.

But with all the shame
And broken dreams.
It's still a beautiful world,
For our children to be born.

Julie Parsons

Caragh

The animals she loves
The birds she just adores
The insects they intrigue her
And anything out of doors
Will grab all her attention
And she will spend the day
"Over here, just look at this"
You'll often hear her say.
She'll wander through the forest
Or hike around the park
Inspecting all the wildlife
I'm sure she'd stay till dark
Soaking up the beauty
Of the planet at its best
Taking all that nature offers
You could put her to the test
She would answer all your questions
And help you understand
Why we the peoples of the Earth
Should be caretakers of our land.

Judith Gray

The Candle

All is dark,
The night is here,
Burning so brightly,
The candle shines out,
An orange-red light,
As the wax drips down
As the candle gets smaller,
The glowing red flame,
So suddenly disappears.

Jenny L. Walker

Making Progress?

Rhythm of a perpetual pendulum,
Swing, and reach, and stall,
Swing, and reach, and stall.
Stall mid-flight, and grasp,
Enough to break the fall.

I stand mesmerised by the constant
To and fro of the Howler monkey
In a cage fourteen swings long
(28 seconds from end to end).
Stopping only briefly at the
Wire to fix my stare.
A minute round trip, including
The brief exchange of views,
From there to here and here to there.

And I wonder what progress
We're making, what sense?
If a civilised creature
In a free world can continue
To watch such beauty,
Enslaved by a wire mesh fence.

Jeff W. Bee

Take a Chance

Why trouble over issues,
That won't see the "light of day"?
Many are of our own making,
So just laugh the lot away.

Once people showed more guts,
They left more to chance.
They didn't worry to excess,
Or do things in advance.

We should organize our day,
We should give ourselves a margin.
When we're a head of schedule
It's a bonus, it's a bargain.

It's quality not quantity,
That should be our concern.
That's something we've forgotten,
What a lot there is to learn.

Competition is to blame,
It has made us blind.
To everybody's faults,
We're vicious, we're unkind.

Jill Ives

Magic in the Trees

A candle burns
The thread draws tight,
A note is struck at daybreak
Somewhere in a distant
scented wood.

A preen of feathers drifts
Curled petals bright and wet,
Shake loose
And touch the moss.

Time hangs in woven baskets,
Insects tick and shudder
Counting seconds ......

Earth's breath in the tall trees
Knows no world full of turmoil,
Only time without beginning
Days without end.

A leaf twists and falls
Earth turns .....
A note is struck.

Clive Weston Sirett

Two Minutes Silence

It is when, the strong are weak
The weak are strong
The mighty are humble
The humble are mighty
The mightiest pay tribute
And rulers obey
The captive are free
And the free are captive
It is when, the armless salute
The legless stand
The sightless see
And mothers weep
While we stand among poppies

Jack Guthrie

Content

The sky is grey
The winds are high
There's a chill in the air,
no reason why

My mood is sober
My thoughts are rife
My mind is tired
I wonder why!

My sister is coming
Her husband is gone
My house is half tidy
My cat just yawns

My fiance relaxes,
while the rugby is on
The sky has got greyer,
the rain will come

I'm feeling lazy,
and relaxed today
My mood, is still sober
What more can I say . . .

Helen McCormick

Eggs-Tract from British History

'Eat lots of eggs'
'They do you good'
Were famous words,
Of Robin Hood.

Not words uttered,
Purely in jest,
After all,
Robin should know best.

Indeed, they must be accepted,
As second to none,
Well, he could hardly,
Be called a liar.

When you consider,
His men were all 'poachers',
Except, just the one,
Who was, of course, a 'friar'!!

Joe Bayford

XTC?

"Bright eyed - laughing
Thoughtful - caring
Joining in
Having fun
Full of hope
Sharing
Reach for the stars
Life's just begun . . .

Eyes dull - spark gone
Couldn't care less - about anyone
Isolated - paranoid
Has life become an endless void?"

Janet Williamson

I Have the Power

To be kind,
To be gentle from my mind.
To help when it is needed
When it needs to be succeeded.
To love from my heart
When it's very very dark.

To swear when it's not needed
And launch a good punch
Spit on the floor after I've had
Lunch

Aled Wyn Griffiths

Everyone's an Expert!

'Kids need boundaries,
to know who's in control',
said the chat show hostess,
twenty three, with little
experience of life.
'Kids need security, consistency
and a sense of self',
said the psychologist,
single, childless and
differently sexually oriented.
'Kids need time, attention
and empathy', said the counsellor
in the young offenders unit
with a mouthful of lentil stew
and a book on Zen Buddhism.
'Kids need to go to bed, love',
said my husband, as he reached
for the T.V. remote.

Deborah Ellis

Sherwood Forest

This was the place we chose
To rest and eat;
To look up at the blue sky,
The high oaks,
The weeping yews,
The young pines flowering -
And fragile leaves of beech
As soft as silk.

Reclining there, at peace,
Those closest to me
Sitting, walking,
Thinking, talking,
Earth seemed bright indeed
That June Sunday at noon
Or thereabouts.

Grace Greaves

Hello in There

Hello in there my little one
We don't know each other yet
Just now we share my body
Yet we haven't even met.
I feel you kick away inside
And wonder who you are
My little boy, my little girl
My little shining star.

Hello in there my precious
For you I care so much
I am so longing for the day
When I can feel your touch.
To have you tucked up in my arms
And cuddle you so tight
I don't care how much you'll need me
In the middle of the night.

Hello in there my child-to-be
Your whole life lies ahead
For any harm to come to you
I'd give my life instead.

Joan Davidson

My Children

Oh to lose my children,
To somewhere far away
Just to lose my children
For a whole night and a day

Not to hear their footsteps
As they thunder up the stairs.
Not to hear their voices
shouting everywhere.

Not to have the arguments
Not to have the fights
that last from light of morning
Until the dark of night

My children - how I love them
And by my side they'll stay
My children - how I love you
Just please do go away!

Delia Beer

Barefoot Days

Barefoot days they tell me
were the good old days of yore
but from what I can remember
feet were cold and wet and sore
I suppose you could call me lucky
because bare feet I never had
but that was only because
I had a working dad
I've worn clothes off Paddy's market
and of this I'm not ashamed
and blankets from the pawn shop
that had never been reclaimed
I've pawned Mam's ring on Monday
took it out again week end
put it back again on Monday
"Oh" will it never end
but out of poverty and want
may I say this all to you
that the people of those days
were faithful kind and true

Anne Murray

Sea Fantasy

Endless waves in sunset glowing
timeless and forever flowing.
Does each spray caress the coast
returning to rejoin the host?
Whirling gently on the sand
shape with time both rock and land
making inlets, coves and caves
sculptured by the mighty waves.
Play with my toes
take all of me
like driftwood bear me out to sea
stroke my body
float my hair
change me to a mermaid fair.
On the ocean's swell I'll ride
moving with the changing tide
past barren rock and sandy bay
in the ceaseless waters sway.

Joan Scott-Jones

Blind!

I do not know what it would be like,
To be blind, not to see.
A dark hole,
An empty space.
As if my life had been wasted,
As if my eyes had been pasted,
I feel all alone,
Nobody there,
I don't even know,
The colour of my hair.

Erika Stoner

The Individual

People don't trust me
They think I'm strange
They just won't see
I'm not deranged

I'm just a bit different
Not like other men
I don't want to relent
If I did, what then?

I have an identity
That's what they don't like
I'm what I was meant to be
For that I will fight

I won't be a pawn
To their common fate
I won't be reborn
To a life full of hate

The things that they tell me
They are all lies
The same I won't be
My way will survive.

Charlotte Andrew

My Pets

My pets are very precious
They're my way of life sublime
I think about them always
To forget them is a crime.

I walk the dog each morning
The cat stays close to home
The birds talk happily to me
I have no cause to moan.

When morning comes I hear them
"Good morning" comes up the cheer
Then later on at nightfall
"Goodnight, God Bless" I hear.

If ever I feel lonely
I put my hand out slow
A friendly head sits on my lap
I'm not alone, I know.

But if there was a reason
Their life ends before mine
I'd keep a memory of them
In a picture like a shrine.

Iris K. Griggs

A Lover's Duet

When you run your fingers
through my hair
you just don't know
how much I care
for you my darling dearest
I think you are the
most sincere

When we kiss and caress
I want you more not less
When I feel the warmth
of your body on my face
Your love sends me into
a heavenly place.

You and I are birds
of a feather
When love joins us together
and when we come together
it is like no other
experience ever

John Jones

The Force

Through the lands
through the trees
through the rivers
through the seas
There it is

Through the moon
through the sun
through the stars
are we the one
Is it there

Through the dust
through the breeze
through time
through years
It is there.

Through the sands
through the skies
through the plants
can you feel it
LIFE.

Angela Rushton

The Dove

I wake up every morning
To the cooing of the dove
You'd think he owned our chimney
And sang to heaven above.

The tree in next door's garden
Is where he builds his nest
Consisting of a few old twigs
I'm sure it's not his best

He seems to love our green house
On which to perch for hours
A-looking for his ladylove
Among our garden flowers

He's no success when breeding
When springtime does abound
His mate sits tight but usually
The magpie comes around

I feel sorry for these creatures
Who seem so much in love
That's why I hope - I never return
As a black ring collared dove.

Iris O'Hara

Train Station

I sat patiently,
Waiting for my train,
Looking at the clock,
I feel a heavy strain.

The hours pass,
The trains pull up,
I stand to my feet,
It's my train at last.

It starts to move,
Then stops with a jolt,
I move back to my seat,
While told there's a fault.

Guards say the train is delayed,
"I will never get there",
I hear my voice fade.

More hours have passed,
The train has stopped,
I am here at last,
And now I can shop.

Ashlea Dimond

Waiting

He was sitting, all alone,
Waiting for the dark cloth of night
There were shadows all around him,
Waiting for when the time was right.

Dark strangers pass by,
Not giving a single glance
To the shadow of a boy
Who never had a chance.

In his eyes are painted memories
Good times of the past,
He yearned for a life,
But this life, it did not last

For he is not truly real
But a ghost of what he became,
He was sitting, waiting,
But no-one ever came.

Arabella Stanger

February

All the earth is waiting
Waiting for the spring
All the earth is bating
Every single thing
Lies in silence sleeping
Wondering when to rise
Looking for the promise
of the April skies.
Listen for the heartbeat
Strain to catch the note
As it tries to struggle
From a tiny throat
of a newborn songbird
trembling on the wing
flying ever onward
Towards Eternal Spring.

Joy Shrubsole

My Inspiration

My inspiration for writing poetry
Was a gift from my dad
He encouraged me to put pen to paper
One day, he said you will be glad.

He was a marvellous person
Just thinking what was best for me,
Oh how I wish he was here today
So that he could see.

His words are really coming true
I never thought they would,
And now I'm glad I took notice
Because the feeling is quite good.

Dorothy Joan Sadler

If I Was

If I was, what could I do?
What could I be? Could it be true?
If I was could I fly?
I wonder if I could purposely die
If I was it, and it was me
What on earth would I be?
That's the question if I was
If only I was
Could I be an astronaut?
Or a robber who got caught
Would I be a great success?
Or would I just be in a mess?
What about an army soldier
But what then as I grow older?
As I wonder if I was
My answer would have to be because

Donna Cosgrove & Lyndsey Berry

It's Just the Way

Was I all wrong,
Was it all in my head?
You asked to be hugged,
I take you to bed;
All in my head
All in my head

You hold me so tight
My arms are bruised
My hips are bruised
I want to screech
What we've always known
We're alone each alone

You didn't want me around
So I stood making tea
With my head down

Well. We had some fun - you said.
And paid - was on my tongue -
Because, admit it; you and me,
It was always letters never sent
Always never reaching.

Helen Frost

Twisted Justice

Burn the book to feed the fire,
Watch the flames grow higher, higher
See God's word reduced to dust,
Watch the metal crosses rust
See the falsehoods and the lies,
Watch the fire as it dies
Wooden stake now charred and empty,
Ashes on the ground a-plenty
All that's left of gentle daughter,
Victim of the holy slaughter
Burning of God's word abused,
Bonfire of unjust accused.

Hannah Ward

Life

Life comes to us all
We live it everyday,
We try to live life
In the best possible way.

Life can feel tough
As if it's all going wrong,
You've got to hang on
You must keep being strong.

You've got your family
You have very close friends,
But they will be the ones
To hurt you in the end.

Life has its bad points
It has its good too,
Life is what you make it
So live life for you.

Jessica Marie Bowden

Untitled

The sun now shines for me,
whatever the weather,
Be it day or night, it shines
forever.

No pair of sunglasses could
mask its glare,
No day will pass without
me of its presence aware.

No more will a cloud hide it
from my view,
No longer a day without
thoughts of you.

April Louise Austen

Death of a Child

I don't know what to say or do,
When all my thoughts return to you,
It hurts so much, I cannot stay,
I know I have to walk away,
To face what's now, I must be brave
And place you in your tiny grave.
I want to flee, to run, to die,
But still I cannot figure, why?
And in their ignorance, they say
"She'll live to fight another day."
Those who've never been a mother
Tell you "You can have another."
As I then turn and move away
I'll say "I'm Fine" to them today.
So with despair and tears and pain,
To disappear and brood again.
If those I love would be alright,
Then I'd depart this life tonight,
And as I grieve, remember such,
I loved you, Oh! So very much.

Dawn E. Hopkins

Remember Me . . .

Remember me when I am not here.
When I am gone and no more.
Remember me when you pass near,
The places I loved and saw.
Think of me when the rain falls down.
When the wind howls 'round and about.
Think of me when you hear the sound,
As the thunder bellows its shout.
Dream of me when you sleep at night.
Remember the way that I look.
Dream of me when your thoughts take flight,
And follow the paths that I took.
But please don't forget me, for that
I could not bear,
As I watch from up above.
Don't forget me but please just
continue to love.

Ailsa Trense

For Lorinda

Do not grieve for me
when I have passed away
I shall be at peace then
forever and a day.

Death is not the end
so do not now despair
only the beginning
of life beyond compare.

Put away your tears
be glad and do not mourn
this day was meant to be
from the moment I was born.

Anne Coade

Innocence Smile

I get off my bike
when I reach the sandy beach.
As the tide jetsams in, rolling
sections precede to the front
with a twirl and a whirl
still carrying old flotsam and
pebbles dropping them delicately
as if from a hand, them with
a motion of inward swirls
the crabs delivered under layers of
sand, the seagulls chirp annoyed
I'm - there they dare not take
crabs legs that have just been
left by the waves.

Jenny Dunkley

To Autumn

When summer sheds her coat of green
We marvel at the changing scene
No earthly being could have planned
This transformation of our land

A spectacle of sheer delight
A myriad of colours bright
Lengthening shadows, cooler days
Introducing autumn's ways

Frosty mornings, crisp and cold
Shafts of sunlight, leaves of gold
Misty ribbons swirling 'round
Moving gently o'er the ground.

Russet carpets deep and soft
Titian trees heads held aloft
Nature's colours on parade
A final, glorious, cavalcade.

Jean Parker

"Days"

I have good days and bad days
When I'm happy, when I'm sad.
I have days when I'm gloomy
And days when I am glad
Some days my eyes smile gladly
And days when tears show through
Some days my face glows cheerfully
Some days I show my gloom
There are some days I'm full of joy
And days when I feel blue
But the days I really do feel good
Are when I'm close to you.

Ena Andrews

To My Father

Sometimes,
When nights are uneasy
And sleep comes but fitful,
Your voice in the silence
Seems to call out my name;
And I wake then,
Believing you live still:
That the years since your passing
Were only a dream.

Such was
The force of your spirit,
In anger and laughter,
That death cannot sever
Its strong hold on my own;
And I hear yet
Your accents and phrases,
As if brain, breath and heartbeat
Had never been stilled.

Andrew McWhirter

Opportunity

Opportunity needs help.
When out of reach.
One sees a ship passing.
When stranded on a beach.
One needs a ladder to climb.
Out of a deep hole.

Opportunity passes too fast.
Too far away to grasp.
Frustrating hopes
of making the future.
Unlike the past.

Yet: the ship may stop.
A ladder arrive.
A platform built.
To opportunity.
And a new life.

Etta Lewis

The Journey

Where do you go to
Who do you see
High in the sky
Way above me.

Will you be happy
Will you be sad
At the end of your journey
Will you be glad.

Will you return
Today or tomorrow
Will it be joyful
Or full of sorrow!

Bernadette Johnson

Weeping

I'm weeping for the children
who live in our land.
I'm weeping for the children
who can't understand.

I'm weeping for the children
the ones, as yet not born,
who come into this world
so small and forlorn.

I'm weeping for the children
who want to grow up fast
and seem to be forgetting
that childhood doesn't last.

I wish that all the children
could really understand,
the Love and Trust, I put in them
and in our lovely land.
Be kind and selfless in Return
and I won't ask for more.
There's one thing, I don't want to do,
to weep forevermore.

Angelika Dewberry

Sweet Marigold

Marigold, sweet Marigold
Why art thou so fair?
Is it thy blue eyes
Or thy golden hair?

Marigold, sweet Marigold
Thou hast not a care
While I shower upon thee
Pretty clothes to wear;

Marigold, sweet Marigold
Other toys may stare
And envious children covet thee
But thou wilt keep thine air . . .

. . . Of innocence, sweet Marigold
And charm beyond compare
While I safely guard thee
And count thee in my prayers.

Joan Dorothy Newman

"Good Night Daddy"

Where is he?
Why did he leave?
Does he still love me?
Does he still care?
Is he by a warm fire
Or out on the streets?
Is he dead or alive?
Why, Oh why did he leave?
"Good night Daddy, where
Ever you are"

Claire Tindale

Rhondda

Cold and bitter blows the
wind in the valley here within.
For as its beauty has been scarred.
It is for man for him to have
the dark shadows in the sky,
reveals the wonder of the night
stars that twinkle here and there.
Show that God is always near.

Geraint John

Echoes of Silence

Through the echoes of silence
When thought stands still
Ebb the whispers of wisdom
Emphatically.

Through the echoes of silence
When noise is asleep
Wakens the sweet music of life
Orchestrated.

Through the echoes of silence
Flows a spectrum of light
Dancing a genre
Of effulgent artistry.

Through the echoes of silence
Vibrates a wealth
Not counted in bank notes
But measured in stealth.

Jean Carroll

Remember Me When I'm Dead

Remember me when I'm dead
When you wake from the morning
And step out the door
As you breathe in the air
In which I exist

Now I have returned
To the earth that bore me
Now I am there
In the trees before you
I may be dead
But I'm still there inside you

Now my soul is cleansed
And bathed in white light
I can now comprehend
The universe's might

I now realize
I have a part to play
In the lives of the people
I touched every day

Darran Murphy

Love Dies

What do you do,
when your love dies.
Thousands of tissues,
and constant cries.

Nights wondering why,
what went wrong.
for acceptable answers,
you do long.

Constantly by the phone,
you spend your days.
Hoping it will ring,
wondering what to say.

But the phone doesn't ring,
and you never talk.
Out of your life,
your love did walk.

Julie Muttock

At the End of the Rainbow

At the end of the rainbow
Where all your dreams lie,
Is a place where a merchant
Collects you and I.

He'll pick up the pieces
of hearts and of heads
And all that once mattered
Now shattered and dead.

The keeper of promises
Hopes and desires,
That all turned to nothing
The captives of liars.

At the end of the rainbow
Where time would not wait
Lay the one time illusions
Come trade in your fate.
Janice King

Baby Love

Mummy when I went away
Why those tears for me
I was not really needed
In this world of misery.

I know I meant the world to you
I know you loved me so
But when the angels came for me
I knew I had to go

I'm really not that far away
In fact I'm quite close by
I see you in your happiness
I hear you when you cry.

I'd like to wrap you up in love
To make you feel brand new
For I am now an angel
Who thinks the world of you.
Elizabeth Clark

The Carnival

I watched a carnival in haste
Wind up the summer's end
Pull off the leafy hyaline
From the wilting diadem

There burst onto the landscape
Defunctively cold
Domes of expanding mushrooms
Ivory and gold

In them I caught an imagery
Prophetic with gloom
Of Earth sinking
Through a huge mushroom

It glowed - but in that moment
The carnival had passed . . .
And a timbre of another world
My senses grasped.
Derrick Porter

Uncle David

Pick up the knife, test the blade
with a meddlesome finger
Call to the heavens, remember
yesteryear, not in one lifetime
learn which thread brought you here.

Hold the cloth with care
it has grown brittle with age
colours fade, a hole unwinds
blunt needles pick away
stitch by stitch, the names.
Joe Citizen

Life (Our World)

Invisible air
World's a twirl
Moonrays pulling
Waves curl
Sunshines rainbows
Moonshine pearls
Man woman
Our wondrous world.
Isabelle Wright

Our Lord

Powerful yet humble
Wrathful yet merciful
Strong yet gentle
Judging yet understanding
Loathing yet loving
Slow and meticulous
Yet rapid and carefree
Innately calm yet outwardly joyous
Ever forgiving and eternally alive
Claire Williams

A Lifetime and a Day with You

Dawning together,
Yawning together,
I want us to wake,
Each morning, together.
And together we'll watch,
The sun's rising bloom,
And stay here together,
Until evening's soft gloom.

Lying together,
Flying together,
Let us be never,
Crying together,
Let us be together,
For the rest of our days,
Exploring together,
The world and its ways.
David J. Shepherd

With Thanks for the Geranium Plant

How beautiful the plant you gave,
Yet lovelier, far, the giver,
And though, with time,
All flowers must fade,
Your beauty lingers - ever.
Frank McKeown

Goodbye Grandma

You brought my life such happiness
You brought my life such joy
You loved us all your grandchildren
Each one of us girl and boy
They say you didn't feel much pain
You left us in your sleep
You told us never to be sad
But we can't help but weep
You were the greatest Evertonian
Forever a true blue
This year the lads will win the cup
And hold it up for you
Your life was full of flowers
The rose, the daffodil, the tree
Now you're in your endless garden
which is where you deserve to be
You know we'll always love you
And we're not really far
We can never stop loving you
We'll see you soon dear Grandma
Alison Jones

Dreams

One can dream of places
Where one would like to be
On an island free of pollution
Silver sands washed by the sea

To hear and see the gulls
Crying overhead
Old fortresses across the bay
A lighthouse by causeway lead

Sailboats bobbing on the sea
Alongside fishing smacks
People looking into rocks
Their treasures to bring back

Along the shores collecting shells
Of all the various kind
To decorate the flower pots
The colours of summer time

I look around the jutting rocks
Seagulls feed their young
So peaceful - just the foam on waves
A haven in the sun
Doreen Nightingale

Then for Tomorrow

I feel empty, and
Void of all emotion.
I feel helpless, I'm
Too blind to see the commotion
Inside me.

I feel drained, but
My heart keeps on beating.
I feel confused, there is
Something inside me that's eating
My mind.

I feel sadness, and
My eyes keep on crying.
I feel strong pain, but
There is no use in denying
Anymore.

I feel distant, I'm
Lost and can't find my way.
I feel lonely, and I
Have to get back yesterday, today
Then for tomorrow.
Judith A. Stainsby

'Our World and Our Life'

Our world is full of mysteries
Which we cannot yet explain,
Our lives are linked together
Like a never-ending chain.

Our world that we live in
Has a beginning but no end,
It's sort of like a fantasy
But this is not pretend.

Our world proceeds in a cycle
Revolving in one certain way,
Birth, life and death
Is repeated throughout each day.

Questions which have no answers
Which we willingly seek to find,
From dawn till noon till dusk
We search using only our mind.

This complicated mystery
Is what we have to bear,
Not knowing what confronts us
Our life is but a dare.
Gabrielle O'Leary

The Stars

When you wake at early dawn
You see another day of life
To us all there is content
But one may say oh dear
It's lent. But do you know
That everyday you must pray
To see a star it tells
You that up in the sky
There is so much you
Can say for a star that
Is so far away.
Then we wake up to
Another day.

Emily Edwards

One Year Ago Today

One year ago
You took my hand
And held it to your heart

One year ago
You kissed my lips
And thawed my frozen heart

One year ago
You changed my life
Was it for good or bad?

One year ago
You took my love
And made me very glad

One year ago
You took my heart
And now you have it still
Will the feelings be the same
In one years time
I hope they will.

Anne Gatehouse

Untitled

simplicity I know not
you, you know not me
Is this all right,
would you agree,
let what ever stays
within NO HURT SUSTAIN
in the cooling rain
Flowers blooming UNASSUMING
IN A COUNTRY LANE
REMAIN

Bernadette Leavy

Death in the Basement

Down in the basement
You'll always hear
the noise,
that will fill your heart with fear.
His heavy breathing
loud and coarse
the height of two men
the strength of a horse.
No one knows where he comes from
No one knows his name
he walks about in the dark
dragging the leg that's lame.
No one goes near the room
the room of fear and death
the cry of the dying people
the smell of the corpses left.
A heavy mist
hangs low by the door
and all is quiet
as he sleeps once more.

Cheryl Bethell

One Morning

A crisp, bright morning
White frost on the ground
Shimmering hedge rows
Jewelled cobwebs abound

The sunlight is rising
Warmth flooding around
Snail's silver paths
Criss-crossing the mound

Everywhere buzzing
Under nature's crown
And cloak of earth
In darkest brown

Watching and waiting
With never a sound
A young hawk dives
Its prey, it has found

David L. Inker

A Summer Storm

Wild the sea, on frothing foam,
White horses, 'neath a sky of gloom,
How can this be? The day begun
With skies of blue, and warming sun,
To us mere mortals skills denied
To govern wind, or sea, or tide.

Yet a fascination of its own
Lies in this world of wind and foam,
Leaden, grey, a sky of awe
Where golden sunsets glowed before.

Indelible on memories leaves
Will stay this freak midsummer eve,
A fishing boat, denied to net
Tosses in black silhouette.
Seas, that were so crystal clear
Now are cold dark depths of fear.

Night denies, I see no more.
The frenzy, on this Suffolk shore.

Joyce Barker

So Little Time

I've tried so hard to understand
Why I must leave this world behind
So much to do so little time
So many things left on my mind.

To live a life with no regrets
And show the world how much I care
It's wonderful to be alive
With love and laughter left to share.
To watch the children laugh and play
And bring a smile to some and face
The world is full of things to do
So little time for me and you.

Audrey Balmer

Soldier

I lie in my bed
Wondering at night,
Why this world
Still has to fight.
Why we have war
and guns to kill,
Why innocent people
Die at our will.
Should I shoot my gun
or throw it to the ground,
Would it make a difference
would peace come around.
For I am a Soldier
trained to keep the peace,
But when war is around
my training is ceased.

Gary Lee Kerslake

Now

As I walk through the park,
Where our bodies entwined
I remember sweet kisses,
And the touch of your hand.
The moonlight upon the lake,
Your soul upon my heart
Your lips so close to mine
Now so far apart.
I remember sweet words
And the stars in your eyes
Words now turned sour
Along with your lies
Now his touch is warm,
And his kiss sweeter,
But instead I remember you fondly,
Because his love is deeper.

Claire M. Guyan

Teddy Bear

The teddy bear had a picnic
With jam and all things nice
To celebrate his birthday
His age never came to light.
His furry coat so shabby
And looking very worn
He'd been handled by many children
And now he looked forlorn
He'd given so much pleasure
To children over the years
He'd had some very rough treatment
And had healed a lot of wet tears.
Poor teddy just part of a family
and handed down over the years
He'd suffered so much torture
But always been loved - I'm sure.

Janet Mary Kirkland

"My Garden"

My sweetest little garden,
With roses full of dew,
How strange when I am troubled,
I come and sit with you.

I whisper you my secrets,
And tell you of my fears.
Somehow I know you hear me.
For your petals fall like tears.

Elsie May Hellon

Only You

You are my sunshine
You light up my day.
You are my sunshine
Never go away.

You are the air I breath
I need you to survive.
You are the air I breath
It's something you can't deprive.

You are the stars at night
That shine so bright and clear.
You are the stars at night
That whisper in my ear,

You are the world to me
I need you by my side
You are the world to me
I love you with all my pride

You are the universe
That's forever and again,
You are the universe
Mother you're my friend.

Donna Stacey

When I Must Leave You

When I must leave you
You mustn't ever fear
All the lessons I taught you
Seem to gradually come clear,
You mustn't ever fret and
you mustn't ever cry
When you think of me
just look into the sky
When you think of me
remember when I was there
When I held you so close
like a huge cuddly bear.
When I have to go
Will you do me a huge favour
Remember the times when we were happy
And savour the erotic flavour
When I must leave you
you mustn't ever cry
'cause you know that I'll be waiting
up in heaven's sky.

Jodie Davies

Purple Heart

Purple heart.
Your courage astounds me.
My emotions feel the tear
That you should echo.
Yet still you beat.

Crippled heart.
Your numbness frightens me.
Dead to all feeling; unaware
That I will stagnate.
Yet still you beat.

Stirring heart.
Your quivering arouses me.
My curiosity will wear
My heart upon my sleeve.
And still you beat.

Joyous heart.
Your loudness deafens me.
Alive to sensations; banished despair
That once lost all love.
And still you beat.

Claire J. Bagnall

Lonesome Soli

Soli was 28 years old.
Soli was my friend.
Soli and I would go for walks,
Where heads would turn
And eyes would stare
At his handsome young face
Soli had deep blue eyes
And a pale complexion
Soli looked young and innocent.

Soli made me feel good about myself.
Soli listened to me,
Soli confided in me.
Soli didn't have many friends.
Soli didn't belong to anyone.
Soli was lonely.

Soli was a perfect Virgo.

In the summer of '89,
Soli went to another world
Said he only belonged there.
Soli is greatly missed.

Jesse Kaur

Morning Bird

In early dawn a fledgling bird
sounded clarion call in tone,
That beauteous fell so I heard
the purity of pitch alone,
More elegant to make absurd
a symphony in scale full blown.

I gloried at the range of note
in tremble showered through the air,
As like a siren shock it smote
the misty daybreak with all rare,
Flourish as the bird from throat,
sharply piped as loud would dare.

What joy I felt then at the chord
in my soul struck when I leapt,
As the dulcet shaft like sword,
stabbed the heavens and clear swept,
With all perfect lilt which clawed
through my heart and I but wept.

Anne Huntly

Skylark

Hail to thee, o songster,
Spirit of the sky.
Further still, yet further
From this earth you fly.
And as you go, your song you sing
Until the heavens with echoes ring.

Rarer than all treasures
That in this world are found.
Sweeter than all measures
Of harmonious sound,
Is your song, so gay and free
Which other bird can sing like thee?

Teach me then, o soaring bird
Those joyful notes divine.
I have never, ever heard
Song so rapturous as thine.
O immortal minstrel free,
Would that I could sing like thee.

Frances Smith

Untitled

Mist rises, shadows fall
Shots stifle animal's callJamie Bulger
Words can never ease the pain
I know just how you feel
memories will still remain
But believe me, time will heal

No matter what you say or do
You'll never bring him home
But now he's got the angels too
You know he's not alone

He knocked upon heaven's door
And asked if he could play
Although he's with you no more
You'll see him there someday

This little boy was only two
Who's life did end so vulgar
Good night God bless to you
Sweet little Jamie Bulger

Debra Palmer

"Greenpeace"

As Greenpeace showed the world
with such bravery, and stopped
the brent spar
being dumped at sea,

They stood by their guns
and took on the might,
of the shell company and government,

Do we really appreciate
what Greenpeace do,
standing by their environmental
issues,
making us all stand up and
fight for what we all
believe is right,

Trying to make the world
a heather place,
for all our children's
sakes.

Ian Wilson

Reflection

I look in the mirror
Reflection of solitude
A dim light that paints my eyes
My heart is open wide
I can see my thoughts
From the world I hide

Between the shadows
My eyes shine
A flickering candle
Behind the dark
I can see the sparkle
A picture of truth

The eyes that awake
A sensitive blue shade
An intensity that's quiet
A smile - in my surprise
Dormant feelings revived
The real me again!

George Harrison

Sense of Spring

The vision of Spring is
primrose yellow, hidden violet
pink-tinged buds and green shoots
of resurrection

The sound of Spring is
the song of birds, hum of bees
the cry of a newborn lamb
in the newborn day

The scent of Spring is
the smell of new-mown grass
the incense of a thousand petals
to uplift the soul

The taste of Spring is
the grief of Good Friday and
the victory of Easter
a rich celebration

The touch of Spring is
the touch of love
God gives to Earth
for our rebirth

Eveline Jolly

"Thirty-Something"

If we could look at life with
The clarity of a child's mind

If we could live life with the
Effervescence of a teenager

If we could enjoy life with the
Freedom of a young adult

If we could find peace with the
serenity of old age

Why is life so confusing when
You're thirty-something.

Maureen Kavanagh

"Say You'll Be Mine"

Say you'll be mine,
So my life won't be blue.

Say you'll be mine,
I'm devoted to you.

Say you'll be mine.
So our souls meet halfway.

Say you'll be mine,
Make me happy today.

Say you'll be mine,
Or my heart, it will break.

Say you'll be mine,
That our love isn't fake.

Say you'll be mine,
That our love it will last.

Say you'll be mine,
And I'm not in your past.

Michael James-Cooney

Untitled

Don't look for it in distance
how far or how near,
It's hidden in a smile
and memories held dear,
The feelings we know
and the times that we share
are all brought together
to remind us we care,
So don't feel forgotten
or that we're ever apart,
You're here with us always
deep in our heart,
No land can divide us
or seas are too deep,
This bond that's between us
is the closeness we keep,

Amanda Page

The Well Ran Dry

Listen to the running water,
flowing in the well.
Look at the endless bucket,
running down to hell.
The bucket reached the bottom,
falling to the ground.
They pulled it up again,
making not one sound.
A lot of thirsty faces,
staring at the rope.
This well was important,
representing all their hope.
The bucket was empty,
the well ran dry.
The faces were void,
their hope began to die.

Patricia Patton

The Choice

The time limit is over,
But you have day and night.
The distance is gone,
But there's still left and right.
The weight is lost,
But there's food on the plate
The Battle's begun,
But your love awaits.

Janice Golding

Winterland

Did I tell you
I was cold

In winter everything
dies ice
has no opponent

My naked feet
slip over old
affections

Jonathan Fisher

Writing Class

We gathered together
And formed a class.
From all walks of life
We came, en masse.
The farmer, the housewife,
The teacher, the nurse.
To put pen to paper
We could be doing worse.
Margaret, the teacher said,
You don't apologize
Which turned out
To be very wise.
For now we all write
Prose, fiction and verse.
And the dreaded Haiku
To which I'm averse.
We analyze and edit
But mostly we praise.
What was just a class
Is now a great craze.

Maureen Lydon

The Dream

What shall I write
To whom shall I speak
To enter into my heart
To gather each grief
Or shall it be joy
Which shall unfold
To tell each simple moment
Of glee, untold
Alas it is past
The dream of my heart
Torn and worn
From life's daily tasks.

M. P. Kirk

Rainbow's Gold

A rainbow is a treasure
of colours bright and bold,
They say at the end of it
There is a crop of Gold.
Yet I know a better place
To find gold oh so rare
And that is in the friendship
Two loving people share
True friendship is beauty
Filled with love and so free
And no other place can hold
Such gold is enough for me.

Angela Burton

My Granddaughter

Julie
Unruly
A mischief at heart
Always a winner
Quick as a dart.

Julie
So loving
Soft arms twining tight
A kiss and a cuddle
Then of like a light.

Julie
So pretty
Bright eyes, rosy cheeks
Her love for her gran
I do not have to seek.

Julie
Is growing
Her visits now short
As she studies and works
But I'm oft in her thoughts

Barbara Reeves

Untitled

My Latin lover
who I desire
with your dark eyes
searching for reassurance
swallow my love
Eat it
Chew it
Digest it
Let it swim
through your body
let it flow
through your veins
Let it be free
within you
And you will be happy.

Amanda Pulham

Mary . . . Mary . . .

The cold pinching out face
make us sad on Sundays
for then we miss her more
that girl, along our Northern shore.

With winter blankly on
its way
and as we love so much
our very Mary Sunday
now, for love's sake
she left bears, cats 'nd folk
with - all in all.
So much to live for . . .
all that . . .
there she's lying between
fragrant clover
entangled in the strong embrace
of the smartest lover
but we, shall we ever,
ever recover?

Lily Reynaerts

Fatal Attraction

It came to us suddenly
Just the meeting of eyes
No need for the spoken word
Or the breathing of sighs
We knew in that moment
We would never part
Our lips remained silent
We spoke with our hearts

Norah Ivans

Departed

She is here...
Compassionate, considerate,
Willing to share.
Caring, open-hearted,
Always there,
For any storm brewing.
But, alas,
The icy winds have blown,
Direction? Unknown.
Swift and sudden,
Taken from life's grasp,
Death's mighty scythe,
Has passed through our lives,
Whisking away the one we love.
Without even a final farewell,
She departs,
For a place we know well,
Neither to be seen,
Nor to be heard
She is here no more...

Christopher MacPhee

Chi'en the Creative

To you, whom I've yet to meet.
I feel you,
but you're not there.
My dreams reveal you
but you don't exist.
Why do I miss you
when you've yet to appear?

Are you waiting
for the rose bud
to open?
Or for the rose bush
to shed its thorns?
Should I go to ground
or wait here?
Knowing one day
you will appear.

Roy Sorensen

The World Out There

The world out there
Is an interesting place
Everywhere you look
There's the human race

The world out there
Is a disturbing place
Out of control
Challenges to face

The world out there
Is a learning place
So much to conquer
Just keeping up the pace

The world out there
Is for all to see
So many experiences
For you and me

How much can we learn
How much can we grow
Do we really want to know
The world out there.

Barbara Jean

Spring 1994

A shower of Swallows
on the lawn.

An upside-down shower
on takeoff.

Mary B. Ploog

Flying

Flying high,
It's just where I wanted to be,
Flying high,
Just you and me.

Flying blind,
My conscience tells how I'm,
Flying blind,
Beyond mortal reach.

Flying free,
With you by my side,
Flying free,
To the other side.

Lynda Cosgrove

Soul Mates

One word,
That says it all.
How much alike we think.
How much alike we care.
How much alike we love.

One word,
For real love.
How real can love be?
The only thing I know,
I really love you.

Daniel Fetzer

Untitled

I told you I really don't
    believe in fate.
Waiting for destiny to make
you happy could be leaving
    things too late.
The one who pays the piper
is the one who call the tune.
You won't get sunstroke if
    you stay inside at noon.
Do you look both ways
Before you cross the road.
Why listen to sad music if
you're in a lonesome mood.
Don't wait for life's
hourglass to lose all its sand.
You must reach out if you
Need someone to take your
hand.

J. D. Howell

It Will Be Fine

His eyes met mine,
the look was divine.
Love was ours to share,
life suddenly seemed fair.
He came my way,
I know he will stay.

His voice was soft and smooth,
I did not dare move,
my lips to reply,
the truth would seem a lie.
He gave me a sweet smile,
I thought I would faint for a while.

His hand touched my face,
it felt of satin on lace.
I felt people stare,
as his hand went through my hair.
Now love is mine,
it will be fine.

T. Mellor

Do You Notice Death?

Death, death, death,
It's away of life.
Say it over and over again,
Death, death, death.

It's in the papers,
It's on the news,
It's on the streets,
It's everywhere.

Do you notice the pain?
Do you notice the anger?
Do you notice the suffering?
Do you notice it.

Death, death, death,
It's a way of life,
Say it over and over again,
Death, death, death.

No one notices it.

Lisa Hollies

The Poor Rower

Through the hail and rain
and loud thunder claps,
with the unbearable pain
of the whip on his back.

His red face stung
and his hands were numb,
he had to give up
he couldn't go on.
they threw him in the sea
to escape he tried,
but at the bottom of the sea,
in the sand, he died.

Jennifer Ellison

The Lover

Your beauty shines forth,
Like that of the sun,
golden hair flowing,
Like a river.
Azure eyes deep enough
For me to drown in.
Laughter runs from you,
As I walk in the door,
And at that moment,
I want you to be mine forever.

Darragh Sinnott

Praying for Peace

Praying for peace
And the killings to end
Please somebody help us
Who shall we send

Mothers are crying
For sons they have lost
What was the reason
How great was the cost

Little children without fathers
No more will they see
The man they looked up to
Or sit on his knee

The peace they are seeking
Must come from the heart
Asking God for forgiveness
To make a new start

With lives entrusted
To the dear Saviour's hand
Only then will they know
Peace in their land

Colline MacKiggan

"After Thought"

Life we don't know. But have a think
Of love hate shame guilt wisdom sorrow
Jealousy trust faith sadness and health
And then not our friend death it will
Win in the end no matter where you hide
It will find don't you know it will
Win in the end death

Gordon G. Stevenson

Equality

Peace to all people
    Black, white or brown.
We are climbing a steeple
    So never look down.

Below is the past
    Above is the new.
Where we are is the present
    Now it's all up to you.

So carry on rising,
    Don't pause, hesitate or stop.
We keep getting better
    But we'll never reach the top.

Ian Laurie

A Nightmare

I saw him in the shadows
My heart skipped a beat
But from behind he grabbed me
I couldn't move my feet.
'Don't scream' he said in a whisper,
'There's a knife right here in my hand,
Just walk this way and through the gate
And onto the Common land.'
His face was covered in nylon,
I was paralysed by fear,
I fell upon the toughened grass
But couldn't shed a tear.
From the headlights of a moving car
I saw the gleaming blade,
I felt the pain inside my head
And though that I'd been slain.
When I woke, I was still screaming,
I sat bolt up right in bed,
It had been just a bad dream,
I realized I wasn't dead.

Sue Staien

Middle Class Crime

The Sunday Telegraph
Lies on the hearth rug,
Unread.

An interrupted chess game
Waits,
Gathering dust.

A china pot of Earl Grey
Brews in the corner,
Steadily.

TV songs of praise
Echo around the room,
Religiously.

Small porcelain animals
Line the mahogany cabinet,
Reflecting light.

Excellence pervades.

And on the telephone table
Sits a container,
Full of little blue pens
Nicked from Argos.

Andy Tate

Nature

The sun is warm, the sea is still,
The wildflowers bloom beside the hill,
Somewhere up in the sky we hear,
The lark's sweet music to the ear
Enjoy these moments while you may.
The pleasure of a summer's day.
Soon the summer days are past,
Winter comes again so fast,
Long dark nights and cold short days,
Colours change to browns and greys,
The wind's lament fills up the air,
The waves send seas pray everywhere,
Rain and sleet and sometimes snow,
To cover all the ground below,
But do not fear for you will see,
With hope and faith for company,
The wondrous way that nature brings,
The beauty back to living things.

M. Mair

Venice

The waterways the alleys
The streets and the squares
The churches so numerous
You come on unawares
The beauty the splendour
The pleasure that is yours
By gazing around you
And peeping through doors
Each one of them hiding
Such beautiful work
Done by men so long ago
Their labour did not shirk
To produce such beauty
For all the world to see

Oh Venice dear Venice
What pleasure you gave me

Kathleen Linford

My Sky

The sun is the heart
In the soul of the sky
The clouds are the pillows
On which our dreams lie

The sky is an ocean,
Cool deep and blue,
Life is a ship,
and we are its crew.

Deirdre Sweeney

Winter

The snowfall fell on padded feet
A blanket of ice and snow
Silently flocked the robin's sweet
And hushed its troubled brow

Then winter reared its ugly head
A beast of ice and cold
With many a farm animal dead
Like a hunter in the fold

Sly as a fox the cold crept in
In every corner howl and scowl
As terminal frost so icy thin
Wreaked its havoc foul

Trees look old arthritic and thin
Branches reach out proudly
But with winters toothless grin
They moan and groan so loudly

Winter, you robbed the day of light
You made your curfew noon
You swap the daylight for the night
And are as barren as the moon.

Michael John Inns

Why?

A bearded man, all dressed in rags,
He's either scrounged or found,
Smoking cigarettes and stumps
He finds lying on the ground
His food he gets from litter bins
He doesn't care what kind,
Just roots through all the rubbish
And then eats what he can find.

His day consists of roaming around,
Through all the public places,
Where lots of people watch this man
with disgust upon their faces.

We help out other countries
Are our own homeless left alone,
To drop out of society
And we're left here to condone,
As he finds himself a cardboard box
To sleep in or maybe die,
Does a man's life mean so little?
Just ask the question "why . . ."

Paul Fisher

My Cat

My cat has a secret,
He has you know
He has a priceless gift
That money can't buy
Do you wonder what it is.
When he looks you in the eye
He never gets hot
He never gets cold
And his priceless heirloom
Never gets old
Have you guessed his secret
Will I let it be known
It is all on earth, he'll ever own
Have you guessed his secret,
Have you made a note
Yes, I think you know,
It's his own, 'fur coat'

Aline Weager

Loves Platter - Method

Gently take a waiting hear
Blend with smile of one
Fold in confusion
Baste with dreams
Prove in time setting sun
Lightly sprinkle tears of joy
Add a pinch of fear
Knead until forlorn is gone
Serve garnished with life's cheer.

John Rosser

Peace

Peace is like a dove.
Gentle, loving, caring.

Peace is like a river.
Crystal clear, flowing.

But in the end the dove dies
The river dries up.

Peace is more like a rainbow
It comes after the rain,
and there's a pot of gold at the end.

But when you try to find the gold.
It's gone.

Then all the wars begin
All the fighting and killings.

Until one day.
Hopefully, the rainbow will return.

Gemma Wilson

No Winners

We will win said the bishop,
We will win said the sage
We will win said the journalist
From the foot of his page

We will win said the politician
The actor on stage
We won said the Bonber
Bloody hands white with rage!

Eileen Isaacs

Loneliness

Many tourists
Gaily hop from coloured buses,
Necks swathed with cameras,
Fingers eager to click,
All wanting to capture
A snap,
Of our elusive friend
Nessie.

But she elegantly
Floats below
The glare of eyes
And sun.

Amongst the green weeds,
Wafting fatly,
Looking for a friend
Lost long ago.

Jenny Hunt

Untitled

Times when this human heart
needs for warm embrace.
Yet barren hours do not leave me barren
nor full of pain
nor sufferings pierce
bleed dry my life.

In moments - still gather
my juices that feed the
fruit to ripen
and to share.

Catriona MacPherson

Untitled

For you! Great Gran she said
As I lay in my hospital bed,
Her face all a glow,
And she did I know

She had painted a picture for me.
The el flowers she painted
So bright and so true
From a little one of two
Reflected her thoughts
through and through
Delighted to paint it
She must love me so true

Slatter

Piano Mates

To me you are a pianist
And I a baby, grand
You run your fingers over me
And let the music sound
Sometimes it is wilt anger
You touch the notes that way
But when you softly stroke
them,
The music's is sweet you play
And you can play your music
Forever, whenever you can
For you will be my pianist
And I your baby grand

Yvonne Bell

Eyes of My Shoes

Lying beneath my feet,
the slow swish of the water-wheel
runs in a dream;
clear blue water, a dusky mill,
the damp scented room
still lies below.

A man grows older,
weaves me magic spell of me mill,
harvests memories:
A ginger car lying in the corner,
a donkey runs the grind-store.
Here I am standing on stillness,
listening to silence.

Jenni Clark

The Car Seat

I have a lovely car seat
it should fetch a bob or
it's very clean and too comfy
and a lovely shade of blue
it's had a few owners
and a bum or too
but if you will buy me
I will look after you.

A. L. Smith

Danger: Deep Water

I stare into the surface
Your smile bubbles up to me
We should be closer
But the water is so cold
I hold out my arms
But the ripples merely beckon
I want to hold you
Yet deeper you dive
My calls can't be heard
The water turns to ice
A missed chance
I try to dive in
But only bruise myself
The water turns to steam
I try to swim into it
But its scalding heat is too much
Every attempt amounts to nothing
So I sit and wait
You can't remain under forever
You have to come up for air.

Alexander Wardle

Currency Clatter

A storm has now arisen,
On the currency of our land,
Imagine what will happen,
If European currency will stand.

Have Honourable gentlemen easily,
Forgotten that people in vain,
North of the Border their currency
Wanted again and again?

Yet overrun by southern votes,
Resignedly accepted,
A currency without their notes,
For clattering coins replaced it.

Not all identity was gone,
Few Banks allowed to keep,
Their type of bank notes still to own,
A Nation left to weep.

Great Britain suffers now its whack,
Of clattering coins degraded,
But can the changing tide stay back,
Sine Maastrick Treaty invaded.

F. B. Cal-Anglia

Double Celebration

The clouds sail in the sky
And waves splash in the sea
Birds sing in the branches
To tell about their glee.

New life is expected
In the early morn
Maria and Daryl are waiting
For their twins to be born.

Nature is moving fast
In the usual way
Every one is waiting
For the babes to be born today.

Daryl phoned around
To tell of his joys
That his lovely wife
Had given birth
To two bouncing boys

Janet Carter

Little White Lies

Lying - what a lie,
Everyone must lie,
Little white lies!
See, lying is survival.

Lies, lies, lies.
They grove you see,
deeper and deeper,
Until the truth dies!

Little white lies.
Are no longer,
They growl until,
You are no longer.

Tammara Michelle Wilband

"On the Bright Side"

My Heart is big and warm
My face is full of smiles
My eye are full of glow -
laughter that goes on forever.
My dreams are in the
distance that the light
at the end of the tunnel
is wide open for Miles.
I can see my life
full of happiness and
shine around the
corner from day today
that will end up in
Happiness
forever.

T. R. Ray

Boat to Freedom

I'm staring at the sky
From the top of the hill
Looking out to the sea
Fishing frantic in an ocean of dreams

This April sun knows no fear
It melts and cracks my outer shell
Inner thoughts fly away
Far across the universe

Say, what of the torment
Oh to be a man in Chains
Is nothing compared to solitude
Waiting for my boat to come

Standing on the sand
Chasing the tide as it ebbs away
And I'll be here tomorrow
To receive the waves of a long lost friend
Pray may it be my boat to Freedom!

Daniel T. Reid

Broken Promises

Still and quiet remains the air
The town all tired and cold
Whilst time ticks by without a care
The daylight is getting old.

Light returns so the streets now fill
A package is seen nearby
Ticking away, its aim to kill
Innocence, not knowing why.

Destruction! Despair takes over
Smoke and debris is fill the air
Women goes on without a care.

A number of people have died
To change this what can be done?
Politics is choosing to hide
But innocent people must run.

Jaime Austin

You See

I reach to you,
afraid to touch,
still more afraid not to.
I bite my lip,
hide my fear,
Your smile.
My world brightens,
and my face.
You see.
How gentle your look.
The child in me is safe with you,
The adult, still insecure,
feels the ache.
You speak.
Your thoughts fit mine,
a Chinese puzzle of wanting, waiting.
Afraid to reach out.
you reach in, and grip my heart.

Diane Everingham

An Insight

It was too unfair,
A thought to scare,
My life seems so short,
People around me seemed not to care,

But as my life fell apart,
I rose above it,
And thought about a new start,
I don't know why,
I felt this way inclined,
But I seemed to under mind,

Not many people know,
How will they react,
That was the main problem,
The thought of that,

I am no different,
No matter what they think,
And I will be patient,
Even though I'm on the brink,

Victoria Appleby

My Prayer

Revive me God
Breathe back into me the life
I once had
The enthusiasm I had for you.
Give me back the thirst please Lord
For the living water and your word.
May others know to look at me
That I belong to you.
May they your image in me see
Reflected there eternally
Amen.

Louise McCarroll

The Bedroom

Sitting here on my own,
board out of my head,
my life is just one big bore.
Get me a job any old one,
instead of sitting on my own
day in day out, with just the t.v. on,
What a life at nineteen,
stuck in my bedroom with just me.
Nothing to do but stare into thin air.
Minutes tick by but do I care,
No because life is just one big bore!.

Anne-Marie Lory

Summer's Day

Feel the warmth of a summer's day
Smell the smell of new mown hay
The scent of roses in full bloom
On this heavenly afternoon

Watch the butterflies in lurid reds
A spider weaves his silken threads
The cornfield yellow with ripening corn
It makes you glad that you've been born

P. L. Parker

A Loved One Never Dies

When summer's shadows fade away
And flowers fall asleep,
to wake again another day,
like memories to keep.

When winter breathes her chilly air,
and all the trees are cold and bare
and we no longer seem to care.
With hearts too sore to weep.

I look upon the snow-capped hills
where winter's heartless icy chills
create a giant frozen bed
where sleeps our cold and silent dead.

No loving arms to hold them now
no loving kiss upon their brow.
No words of hope to clam their fears
asleep within a veil of tears.

Now bitter hearts are left to grieve
If only we could still believe,
the teachings of the master's plan,
to house the soul within the man,

Margaret R. McPhee

Intelligence

There was a man, who was a genius.
His intelligence was great, unthinkable.
He had such power within his mind.
He had the power to end mankind.

He used his thoughts to create a master.
A complicated, technological monster.
The plans of this he willingly sold
To earn himself much praise and gold.
There was a second man, also a genius.
He had the knowledge of this monster.
He knew the praise he could earn himself,
But he kept its secrets to himself

He realized the power in this machine.
He saw that it could end the world.
He knew what man would do with it:
Buy it, harness it, use it, abuse it.

Which of the two was more the genius?
The second, for he was wise as well.
True intelligence comes when we,
Use our knowledge intelligently.

Sarah Needham

Prayer for a Sick Cat

Please let her live
Whoever you are
Whatever you are

She's one of your creatures
A blessing to us
No violence has she done
No war has she caused

She holds my heart in her tiny paws
I can't be without her
I need her
To love me

Please let her live
Her heart is so pure
I'll never be loved
Like this again

P. McDonnell

Lucy Pucie

Lucy Pucie has come to stay
for a three week holiday.
Her coat is white.
Her eyes all green.
She's the prettiest cal you've ever seen.
She eats my plants
And sleeps all day.
When evening comes she starts to play.
Leaping from window sill to
chair her toy nice thrown
up in the air, she makes
we laugh I love her so,
The holidays over and she
goes home, and I am sad
and all alone.

Dee Parkinson

I Need the Dreams

Where have they gone those golden days
of happy loving caring ways,
We thought our dreams would all come true
I need the dreams since I lost you.

You were my life, my love, my all,
I never thought so soon a call
would come to take you for from me,
but thought more years were yet to be.

I walk alone now through the years,
with heart ache still but no more tears,
The only thing I need it seems
are the memories and the dreams.

Dora Warman

Footsteps of a Child

Trees creaked and cracked
A small girl looked back
Seeing birds twittering on a bough
Squirrels running up and down
A stream ran through the trees
And footsteps by it side
Crossing to the other side
She bent down to touch them
Loneliness enveloped her mind
Tears pricked at her eyes
Wishing for some - one to love
The stream was cold soon she was on
the other side looking back at the child
She had left behind
Loneliness dogged her mind
Fear stalked her in the trees
Onwards and upwards she went
Loneliness all around her
Till the light engulfed her soul
Leaving just happiness behind

Carole Lofthouse

Love

Love is like a rose blooming inspiring.
Petals as soft as silk.
Love is as delicate as a rose.
So don't treat it wrongly,
Or like the rose it will break and die.
You keep love well act gently towards love.
You'll keep it in your heart always.

Erica Timberlake

The Owl

A ghostly figure,
Sitting on a branch
Like a soldier on watch.
Its marble eyes
Staring into space.
It screams!
As if in agony.
Sounding like
A child in pain.
Its cream suit
Shines in the moonlight,
Making its wearer,
Look like
An evil devil.

In the daytime
The owl is
A sleepy old man.
At night,
An evil ghost,
Haunting the darkness.

Jill Barber

Unrequited Love

I've loved you forever
Or that's how it seems
Suffered agony ecstasy
Dreamt impossible dreams
Longed for love everlasting
True romantic was I
Washed with waves of emotion
Endless tears did I cry
You entered my being
Of my life became part
I ached deep within
Both in body and heart
There will come a time
When this yearning will end
We'll no longer be lovers
You'll be some distant friend
I'll remember for always
And you never will know
Just how deep were my feelings
Or how I loved you so.

Christine Boden

Untitled

Mist rises, shadows fall
Shots stifle animal's call
They have much to give
Why can't we let them live

Hatred, war is our creation
Invade, destroy another nation
Animals kill to exist
They have no trophy list

Man did not create the earth
All creatures have equal worth
So why must we destroy
What can give us joy

Every land and sea
Has a right to be
Shadows lift and look there
We have a world to share

Eileen Pitcher

The Cry of the Wolf

Is the cry of the wolf
Just as it seems
Or just a pitiful cry
In the moonlight gleam?

Is the buzz of the bees
In the large birch trees
Just a call for love
From the bees up above?

Is the roar of the lion
In his cage of iron
Just a call for help
In his mysterious yelp?

Is the jump of the kangaroo
Just a jump for joy
As he jumps 'round the outback
Pursued by a boy?

Claire Whittle

The Power of Prayer

My darling, darling daughter
My Stephanie Marie
You really are so special
A miracle to me
I waited such a long time
Fourteen years for you
At last my prayers were answered
A silent dream came true
I found myself in Lourdes
Upon an August day
I asked for nothing more
As I knelt down to pray
My prayer was quickly answered
Your daddy was over the moon
When he saw you being born
On a sunny day in June
I didn't ask for riches
I didn't ask for gold
Just this perfect chance
For my story to be told.

Carol Ann Richardson

Untitled

I am so old I want to marry
I go to school quickly I become teen.
I came back home running I am a child
I cry father yippee no responsibility
I am cradled and now in your arms at last
I now understand to trust in God.

Jennifer W. K. Uzele

Maybe Tomorrow

Good treasures found on earth,
Mated mammals running wild.
Great treasures soon be death,
End of a new age child.
Lying on a bed of roses;
Subtle to the day.
Holding sweet smelling roses,
Last time left to play.

Hearing the colours
And smelling the sounds.
Feeling the tastes
And being around.

Pressure of life's meant to be's,
My life you cant decide.
Tears of life's meant to be's,
Thinking I'm one step behind.
Well this is the end of my dreaming,
The life I'll then soon see,
Has any of this got a meaning,
It's all what I'm wanting to be.

Jodie Reid

The Affair

Delight had danced
Filling the moments of promise,
Touching tenderly,
Titillating, tantalizing,
Now strength, now weakness,
Gliding through the days.

Delight still danced.
Wonder-filled moments
Transporting triviality,
Temporary transcendence
All closeness and completeness,
Unknowing of the days.

Delight ceased dancing.
Fear-chilled moments,
Trapping, tying,
Possession-seeking, trust-denying,
Now; cloying blackness
Marking off the days.

Jean W. Waldron

Typical Evening

Often there is trouble,
When you have a nagging wife,
Problems there are many.
And they often start at night
Like "Have you put the bottle out?
And then locked our front door
Have you turned the lights off?
'Cause you left them on before,
Did you turn the gas off dear?
Then check the cooker too,
Did you put the cat out?
Then lock the back door too,
Have you put the blanket on?
Then made a cup of tea,
Then we will sit and drink it,
then retire you and me."
We then forget the nagging,
We cuddle up real tight,
Our bed is nice and warm,
We sleep away the night.

Christine Lamb

Untitled

Harshly Blowing through my hair
I cannot change that never more

I thought again of days once passed
the pain has clenched my heart fast

I need to know where they've all gone
Without knowing I can't go on

Dominic Kenneally

The Red Rose

The red rose lay dying
upon its bed
petals, withering, shrinking,
falling
waiting for love to conquer
to revive, to let it survive
sorrowfully the rose lay
down its head hurtfully,
drowning on its own petals,
its own flesh and blood.
The dying rose was deteriorating
life changing.
Red, blood red, brown to black
the black rose lay, no love,
it lay weeping for the
last breath of air, waiting, for love,
wanting it to strike
The red rose
Dead the black rose waits.

Jolene Martin

Hillsborough

I was stood on the banks of Villa Park,
Watching my beloved Blues,
On that fateful day in April,
When I heard the tragic news.

"Five DEAD at Hillsborough"
I must have heard it wrong.
"Turn your radio up, mate,
Our Kid's there, singing his song"

The toll had risen to 20
when the next update came.
"The fans have spilt onto the pitch,
They've now abandoned the game"

It was about 9 O'Clock that night
When I found out that he was OK,
But if I live to be 100
I'll never forget that day.

The moral of this tale is quite simple,
Make the most of your time together,
Don't take your loved ones for granted,
They won't be there forever!!

C. Manion

One Step at a Time

She lies -
Petite and tiny
Too fragile to touch

For if I lift her
She might get hurt,
Or bruised, or sore
With my coarse touch.

I suppose I could try
It's the thing to do.
If I don't lift her
What will they say?

Well here we go
Nice and easy.
This feels quite strange,
But somehow pleasing.

I'll put her back down
That, enough for just now.
I've the rest of my life,
Now, that's pleasing somehow.

Colin D. Skinner

H N S

The knife which keeps my soul in tears
Is sheathed by me alone
When dwelled upon my own thoughts
Fairly cut me to the bone.

Now mother, please don't shine
That torch into my mind
It may unveil a genius
You do not wish to find.

I hope my thoughts of envy
Are a natural device
Could fate alone be guilty
Of casting down the dice?

You might think me a loose one
So Dad, I'm still your son
"He could have been just like me
Only now his life's begun".

Their friendship is important
To remember all my deeds
But the form which now cries hopeful
Is so different from its seeds.

Darren O'Hanlon

A New World

Will you take this little babe?
And show it all that's free.
The air, we breathe.
The star's at night,
The moon, the sun, the sea.
Will you teach it right from wrong?
And how to live in peace.
So all the world may live as one.
And its wonders never cease.
In return you will hear.
The laughter and the joy.
Of all the people on the earth.
Woman, man, girl or boy
There never would be talk of war.
Or killing for the fun
Just a beautiful, peaceful world
In which to fall asleep
When our day is done.

E. Wilkinson

In Search of Forever

I've been in search of a land forever,
Where no hate can occur,
Where by our own endeavour,
Temptations do not lure,

The Issue of starvation,
Is not a dispute there,
In this Phenomenal creation,
Man kind have learned to share,

In this equidistant land,
No body, nor no soul,
Has the right to command,
Take charge or control.

Yet forever this will seem,
What we want the world to be,
This land shall stay a dream,
A dream inside of me.

Joe Hardwick

Peace

And the war you're fighting,
Can only give one solution,
Like the game you're winning,
Peace shines on through,
And you believe in what you're doing,
As the victims drop and souls arise,
Yes the victory moves on,
As peace shines on through.
Soldier of circumstance and country of honour,
For peace they're fighting,
As the children play with guns,
Yes, I'm a winner too,
Peace, yes peace shines on through
Peace yes peace.

Valery Catherine Vandis

'Down and Out'

Freezing rain, cold damp box
Cold winds blowing, scared as a fox

Huddles down no warmth, no care
Hands so cold, feet so bare

Empty pockets, lonely times
Feeling trapped, committed no crimes

Cold dark doorways, dirty face
No kind hearts, where is this place?

Shuffled walk, head held down
In despair I may well drown
So much sadness, no tears of sorrow
Hoping, praying, for a brighter tomorrow

L. Vancliff

Spring

At last it's spring, and what we see
Are golden daffodils, and budding trees
The earth in splendour, wakes and yawns
Another year is about to dawn

The breathless beauty of colour and green
Are there for all the world to see
And it is God's own work that's done
And given us the flowers and sun.

The birds awake and sing so sweet
On ears that just awake from sleep
And in the passing of the day
We thank the Lord, and kneel and pray

It is to him we greatly owe
What mother nature has to show
And in her wisdom, and her care
The flowers, and fruit on us she bears

L. Nash

Requiem

Not me, I would have said.
Somebody else perhaps.
I never could perform such loathsome
and distasteful tasks.
Not me.

But the time came.
I could and did do all those hateful things
It wasn't easy, but you see
I loved him.

Eileen Snelling

Dreams and Rooms

Like Russian dolls concealing
A dream within a dream;
Alone they are hollow,
A fraction of what they seem.

I had a dream of birds and skies,
A wind blew through it all;
The birds are swept into the sky,
Some they fly . . . some they fall.

I dreamt of a room of fallen stars,
They lit like a glowing carpet;
Thoughts make flesh the things you love,
Don't stop dreaming, don't lose hope.
The hardest things giving up the ghost.

Time stands still for nobody,
Your room won't always be empty!

Gavin M. Watkins

Toffee's Poem

You are so beautiful my dog
Your colours are red, brown and gold.
I see you standing in the sand.
And then you race across the land.
After the sea.

You are so ugly my dog.
Your coat is dirty brown.
It smells of bracken pine and 'orse muck.
You have been in the stream again
My beast.
Now you are chasing after the birds.
As they fly across the sun.

You are so beautiful my setter,
Your coat is shining copper
Glinting in the sun
As you run.

Through the grass
Past the trees
And back to me.

Julia Crake

I Am Your Music

Play me, for I am your music, your song,
For you are the one for whom I long.
Turn my pages, use my score
For you are the one that I adore.
Like a piano with so many keys,
You are the one, I so want to please.
So take me in our arms,
Give to me of your charms.
I am your orchestra your symphony
so my love, Play me, Play me.

Patricia Smith

The Naked King Exposed

I'll write a poem that does not rhyme
For this month's competition
For a poem that does not rhyme will win
If 'ultra modern' poets are judges.

Much easier now for ultra mod 'poets'
Who all ignore construction.
Destruction here's a line too early
To stress my meaning of poetic death.

Who's heard of Willie Shakespeare,
Wordsworth and Rossetti?
Art, now, is throwing paint, to get that
New look, new sound, new words, new ease!

Up to now I've broke my habit
Of writing lines that rhyme.
It's easier than I thought it even would be;
Piece of cake, you crafty 'ultra moderns'.

I feel just like the little boy
Who saw the naked king
And could not keep his mouth shut:
To you, at last, the rhyme and truth I bring.

Leonard Andrews

A Parent's Lament

Dads were stunned, Mums were in a rage,
For this wasn't a play on a west end stage,
Young men laughed, for they never knew the score,
This was for real, this was war,
They never thought about trenches, and going over the top,
All the training, and discipline, and having their longhair cropped,
So off to war they went, to fight the huns,
Without the knowledge, of the danger of guns,
Then the tears, and the fears, and explosions like thunder,
Some maimed, some injured, some in permanent slumber,
Tin helmets, black boots, and khaki green,
Some missing, some lost, some never seen,
Dodging bullets from low, and from the sky,
Some were not quick enough, some would die,
Then a letter to parents, in a brown envelope,
Your son has been killed, "but don't give up hope,
He fought for his country, and stuck to his task,
But was it worth death?, we are left to ask!,
Then a plaque on the wall, with an inscription that reads,
"Killed in action, doing his deeds."

Roger Davidson

A Thought

Spare a thought when you've a moment,
For those who perish through lack of food,
For the forests ever plundered:
To satiate our need for wood;
For the mighty elephants slain:
For their tusks which are so prized;
For the whales that are harpooned:
For the contents for their insides;
For the countless victims:
Of innumerable crimes;
For the sick,
The poor,
The lonely,
And many, many, more besides.

Wayne Vassell

The Father and Son Relationship

The father and son relationship is a weird and wonderful one.
For years there's been anger and laughter but now that's over
    and done.
You and he have a history that only the two of you share
Even though he has gone forever just be thankful that he was there
In the last years he seemed to be closer than maybe he ever had
He seemed to accept role reversal when the son becomes the Dad
Be glad that you had each other, to lean on and to care
Even though not always together, you knew the other was there
I'm sure that he's watching you somewhere so don't shed too
    many tears
You just can't see where he's gone to no more worries or fears.
You don't know what you have in your life until that thing has gone
The father and son relationship is a weird and wonderful one.

Susan R. Butcher

The Miracle of Life

The long impatient waiting, then the pain you must bear,
for you to give birth to a baby so fair.
No one can explain what an experience this is,
a moment of love, and of joy, such a bliss.
At once you can feel this great bond of love,
which means you've been blessed by the good Lord above.
This child is yours, she is your life,
you must love and cherish her throughout your whole life.
Pray for her safe-keeping, her future ahead,
that her footsteps alone by God may be led.
Teach her to be wise, faithful and true,
to show love for her, all this you must do.
For this child is love, a love made by two.

B. Charlton

A Voice in the Mist

The eyes that read this are the eyes that see
For yours are the eyes that were born of me.
Though not now in body I'm still all around
My voice you can hear though there isn't a sound.
From dawn until dusk whether raining or bright
Your path I will lead, so keep me in sight.
The pitfalls of life we all have to cover
Take hold of my hand and love one another.
Keep peace with yourself and patience with others
Though some you may hate, treat them like brothers.
The years come and go, but they all have a meaning
So learn from each one and treat them with feeling.
Listen with your heart and think with your mind
But in all that you do, try to be kind.
We each have a choice in this life that we lead
As we grow in stature from such a small seed.
The lessons from books and life we will learn
Until God picks a time for us all to return.

D. C. Kershaw

Now You Know

You are an inspiration to behold
Enough to make a man's love unfold
Should you be unattached single and free
I wish you would go out with me
On a date and talking until late
It could be fate or more than a mate
Ever so gently not too fast
Hoping to God it will last
You and me may only be a dream
Walking hand in hand by a mountain stream
Of course it could easily become reality
Your sensuality the source of our vitality
Feeling the warmth of your beating heart
You made an impression right from the start
Treat you good like any man should
Best I could my heart is not wood
Think for a while you may even smile
Imagine mile after mile cruising down the nile
Now you know time will show love can grow

Vincent Miles

Silent Witness

I watch her bloom,
I see her swell,
I hear her voice, thick and sweet as honey.
I watch her grow ripe,
And feel her labour,
As the beginning of life on a cold spring morning
Brings forth a quality reproduced.
I see no contrast between this mother and child,
Bathed in a mutual love.
Yet, I sense something is not right.
Playing her part for all she is worth,
And I know.

I feel her pain,
I know her sadness, her hate,
Her secret thoughts.
I watch her wither,
I see her shrivel,
I see the pain etched on her beautiful face.
I hear the agony in her thin, lifeless voice,
And I know.

Niamh Sweeney

Feelings

Walking down the street at night what do I see
I see other people just staring at me
What are they thinking what's on their mind
I don't know they must be blind

Why don't they realize that I am telling the truth
I could have been pregnant and by doing D and A
test that would have been proof

He carries on telling the lies
While Mum carries on and cries
Right now I'm safely tucked in bed
Wishing he was dead

My Dad can't sleep at night
While Andrew tries to do what's right
Emma turns off the light
And in the end everything turns out to be alright.

S. M. Pryor

Intimations of Death and Rebirth

Battered, frayed, of no real significance,
I sit here, adopted by this trance, this earthly dance.
The time moves, I can make no sound,
Life grows, I sense it all around.

The spirit moving, dining, directing me forward.
The pattern evolving, all life revolving, ever onward.
Rushing, speeding, soaring by, the breath of the fire.
Circling 'round and further away, onward ever higher.

The peak, the culmination, and end I see, before me.
But wait! This is no end, is this not the beginning I see.
I know this place, I am unafraid, I've rested here before.
Yes! I have been here before, I recognize the door.

From whence have I come that I should feel familiarity here.
My memories hazes, misted by time, something so near
Of course! The door will take me back, I realize with mirth
The laughter stirs my inner Core, I'm ready nor for birth.

Mel Sedgwick

A Worm's Eye View

I wriggle and wiggle it's quite a chore
I slip and I slide till my belly gets sore
I'm very unhappy but who would have guessed
There's no one to notice I'm feeling depressed
But wait beneath that new blade of grass
A cute little caterpillar's making a pass
She's smiling at me in a friendly pose
As shivers run down from my head to my toes
My early remarks I regret very dearly
For a worm in love it's quite fun really

Kenneth Cosgrove

The Victim

The world is coming to an end.
I say to myself it can't be true.
My son isn't dead, he can't be.
But here he lies in pain.
A liar is in his eye.
A liar to say goodbye.
My wife never sleeps.
I hold her and tell her it's alright.
But it isn't, and there's nothing I could do.
God how's my son now?
A place of never-ending happiness
The devil the killer.
In hell his soul may rot.
This poem goes out to the victims.
Whose children died, whose children lived.
I didn't do nothing to him.
But yet I can't swear or kill him.
My son was only five.
I will never sleep right again.
This is not for money for the people in pain in Scotland.

Virginia Willems

"Reflections in the Water"

When I look into a pool of clear unmoving water,
I see a face reflecting back, one which I cannot alter,
It's seen by day and night as well, by all who are dearly cherished,
But mirror image at its best reveals a lot to me.

Reflections can seem odd to me, especially in the water,
They show up clearly on dull days that I am getting older,
They also show my state of mind according to my features,
With dull dark clouds above my head, I always feel much colder.

On those dull days I'd like to change reflections in the water,
To smile a while and look quite good, but verities I can't alter,
Then to banish dismal feelings there's but one thing I can do,
Just look away or throw a stone at reflections in the water.

On good days I like to look at clear unmoving water,
My reflection doesn't mean a lot, 'cause there's beauty all around it,
The heavenly light from the God-given sun, the shadow of the oak,
If life could only stay like this, dull days would be remote.

But such is life there in the pool of clear unmoving water,
Sometimes so dull, sometimes such fun, the oak tree often smiling,
I must balance with the good and bad sometimes amidst the laughing,
One ripple then and life is gone, like reflections in the water.

Raymond Buckley

A Vision

In the cool grey mist of the dawn
I see a vision
Is it a vision from the past?
I do not know . . .
But now it beckons me and,
As I look, it fades before my eyes.
Only the silence remains — intense but fragile
And even as I stand, transfixed, the sun
That red orb of the morn
Breaks through the mist and all is wondrous light.

P. Langford

Mirage in the Mirror

I look in the mirror and what do I see,
I see an image but alas it's not me,
I have gone to a place
I know not where
To look for myself
Oh life it is so unfair.

My life won't be whole
Until I reunite with my soul
Until I have I and myself and me,
I look in the mirror and what do I see,
I or myself or me
I won't be complete until I have all three.

Susan Sinclair

340

Untitled

I love the way you hold me, you always make me feel safe.
I love the way you smile at me, you make me feel special.
I love the gentle way you treat me, you always make me feel precious.
I love the way you arouse feelings in me I never knew I had.

I love the way you always want to know what I want, you
    make me feel important.
I love the things you say to me you make me feel loved.
You have shown me what love is.

I love the way you help me say things I find hard to, by
    waiting and not rushing me.
I love the colour of your eyes, your smile, your hair, just
    everything about you.
I love you and always will, I will be here for you as long as
    you need me.

Thank you for trusting me and being yourself.
Thank you for accepting me the way I am and don't try to change me.
Thank you for loving me, you can be sure of mine forever.

Terri McElhinney

A Second Chance

To Pat and her daughter, Rachel

When I first knew about you
I loved you so - and I cried
When I felt you move inside of me
I loved you even more - and I cried
And when I first saw your little face
I fell in love with you - and I cried
And when I had to leave you behind
I knew I would never stop thinking
About you, or loving you - and I cried
Then you came back into my life
Again, and my heart did a jump for joy
But before that feeling, I thought I would die
Because I knew I still loved you, and had
Never stopped loving you - and I cried
But it was because I loved you so much
I had to wait all these years, to let you
Know, that I never stopped loving you
Ever, and I thank you, with all my heart
For coming back into my life again, now the tears
I cry, are tears of joy, and such happiness.

Sheila J. Burton-Pye

Veritas

Disdaining ineptitude with words
I make this vain attempt at confutation
prostrating myself before you
not in total submission
but in semi-submersion
succumbing to oblivious temptation
of our timeless scenarios and
absolute equivocal dilemmas
of you-me perception
an inamorata? alleviator? libido satiator?
reduced to mediocrity . . . oh, never that
spare me that
and are we both lotus eaters
or products of mutation
you'll call this sophistry - ignotum per ignatius
same difference.

Yva Melrose

Van Gogh

I am a artist I am Dutch.
I miss my brother very much.
I go to my brother who lives in France
Now my paintings are full of song and dance.
Then me and my friend had a fight,
Then I cut off my ear on the right.
I felt so sad I committed suicide,
I shot my self then I died

William Peter Abercrombie

I, Moon

My Golden Eye for I to spy,
Forming interests into focus try
Until your Earthy Eclipse brings night
And contact grows in soul delight:

Your seized maxim from distance dawns,
A glimpse from which our light forms,
No innovation from confrere correlation,
A feigned likeness, this revelation;

Oh Contraction, how alignment is rare,
And my vain reflections shall no longer stare
To imagine myself in orbit of you,
That which could once, can no longer be true;

I take my leave and break free of such Laws
Claiming my actions to be but of flaws,
Sheer away from your grace as you would choose,
Finally procuring from that which we lose;

One again two, my prevail has allowed
And cover you've given casts off your shroud;
No longer aspire to feats of unknown,
Fulfilled we part and remain, we, alone.

Steven Jones

The Market

In a street just off the Angel, to the left down Liverpool Road,
forms a market every day selling vegetables by the load.

Other goods bulge on the stalls, from fish to ribbons bright,
and the vendors with their cash bags, yell out to catch your sight.

It's been there since I don't know when, the generations
    taking part,
in a chorus of good humour at the sight of any "Tart."

The street is anchored at both ends, by pubs well used and warm.
They must have been there in their place long before I was born.

The middle, at the fulcrum, are ice cream parlours old.
Italians face each other, selling cornets and other things cold.

In forty years I see little change except for some old faces,
still many trousers held up, by string or worn out braces.

When the day is over, and stalls all vanish, to homes I know
    not where
The kids emerge to sort and rummage, and stand to stop and stare.
And now and then you see a face with a look of sheer delight,
cause in the rubbish lying there is a coin shining bright.

I remember just such coins, of seeing them at my feet,
and stooping to retrieve them to spend on something sweet.

Chapel Street's that market, and will be there long to come,
just off the Angel, Islington, the place where we had fun.

H. J. Hargrave

No Respect! For Someone I Dearly Love

Some people say you're weird, they don't give a damn
For someone who has achieved so much, how can they understand
I try to tell them you're not, all you do is good
They have no respect for someone I dearly love!

The papers write such crap, all they do is lie
They just can't leave you alone, someone tell me why.
Some people say you're wacko. For loving such simple things
But for a person with a lonely childhood,
you just want to experience these things.

So please Micheal don't mind, what these people say
They're afraid of what is different and good,
Afraid of a child at heart, who just wants to play

So I write this poem for you Micheal,
Just to let you know,
That it does not matter what they say.
You will never be alone!

Sharon M. Hall

A Foreign Seafront

As I walk along the seafront in this warm and pleasant land,
I cast my gaze around me at the scenery so grand.
The flowers in all profusion, the palm trees standing tall,
the Quaint old fashion buildings that attract us one and all.

In bright and coloured clothing they come from far and wide,
the dutch, the French, the English, along the prom they glide.
The locals stare in wonder at these strangers close at hand,
on their way to nowhere an ice cream in the hand.

The cafes, bars and restaurants are thronged by happy eaters,
the food and drink served promptly by well dressed smiling waiters.
The lovely fish is nice and fresh and caught along the way,
the fisherman go out each day to the seas beyond the bay.

The white and fluffy sand is warm and ever so inviting,
the swimmers shout and splash around, the waters so exciting.
The lonely waves are slapping gently against the weathered sand,
the unclad bodies turn and sigh, intent upon a tan.

The sun is slowly dipping, there's no one around the pool,
what a beautiful sight it is, but gee it's getting cool,
The bars are slowly filling the restaurants busy too,
lets all have a mighty knees up, it'll soon be time to go.

D. A. L. James

Weary Me

When I grow weary and tired,
I close my eyes and imagine
a small cottage, in the English countryside;
Where I could go and rest and hide.

Plain and simple would it be,
nothing fancy, not for me.
With open fire and cosy chair,
I would while away the hours there,
letting my thoughts just wander free.

Where time could pass as slowly as it wished,
and I could read of things, I'd missed,
whilst amid the turmoil in which were forced to live.

A dream, a longing 'tis but true, but that is what I'd
like to do, to get away, but for a while.
From dull routine, and those that treat me like a machine.

Think of that cottage, with fire and chair, and wish to
myself, that I was there.
With scented roses 'round the door, perhaps I could
abide for evermore.

Alan Grey

Untitled

"Let go, Let God" I hear you say. Perplexed I ask "But in what way?"
"I come to church, I hear his voice:
  I'd do his will, given the choice.
Nobody knows the trouble I've had; please don't expect me
  to be glad.
"Jesus loves you; again you say." 'Hum He shows it in a
  funny way.

I've things to do; others need me. I am held back; no way
  am I free.
Go here, go there, they need me so.
I'd stay here and love Him but I have to go."

But, deep inside, I know the score;
at this 'loving' business I am so poor;
I've got my pride; my dignity, take all that I do but don't take me

I'll run and hide; I'll go away. Quite clearly I hear
  'Oh no, you will stay.'

"Your will be done; there's nought left of me.
Ah! that's how He wants it; Now it's Him that I see.
What wonder; What beauty, I see things so clear.
Unworthy as I am Jesus loves me so dear.
"Let go, Let God," I listened; never heard
It's simple; It's easy; It's there in His Word.

Viv Collier

Bookshop

Joseph Smith, a bookseller, dealt in second-hand books.
He attended at jumble sales, homes and auctions ... scoured
  crannies and nooks
For stock for his shop in a side street, Joe could just about
  manage the rent,
And many a worthwhile and pleasant hour the general public spent
Browsing before his crowded shelves where the system made
  no sense
And prices ranged from a pound or two right down to twenty
  five pence.

Not that that stopped some persons
From trying to beat Joe down.....
"This book cost sixpence in 1930!"
(Eyebrows knit into a frown).

"You had a book a year ago, I can't seem to see it today;
To find another copy, could you advise the way?
I don't know the title or author but the cover was a sort of red ...
Or maybe blue or green or pink ... hard to say off the top of my head."

"Where is X street?" " The way to Y?"
"Can you sell a stamp to me?"
"I'd like a first by Jane Austen
With her signature preferably."

"There's nought as eccentric as folk," concluded Joe, "and the
cream of the eccentric crop
Can be daily found, God bless 'em, in your average second-hand
bookshop."

Mary Gard

Windows on the World

I have a window on the world
Four walls do not surround it
There is no glass within its frame
There is no frame around it.

I have a window on the world
And from it I can see
The planets, moons, the earth, the stars
And all eternity

All God's creatures great and small
The flowers and the trees
All the love and all the hate
Unrest, uncertainty.

I see all the races of the world
Living in harmony
I see all that nature has to give
Including you and me.

My window now is growing dim
As life begins to fade
But from my window on the world
I'd loved, I'd hoped, I'd prayed.

Rosemary J. Bayliss

Untitled

He plays football in a blue and white stripe
fourteen is the number that's
sewn on his top.
He plays for the best football team.
vale of arrow f. club
there's Aidy, Murphy, Bertie and him
of course, many more
at seventeen the youngest lad in the team.
When he kicks that ball and it
lands in the goal, lightning strikes
the football pitch at home.
Vale of arrow are the best
I support them and no one else
boy, can he play football.

Lorraine Layton-Morris

The Hunt

He dashes quickly, his heart, it pounds,
He must get away from these terrible hounds,
They're getting closer with every step,
He hopes he can find a safe little set.
He hits open ground, there is no refuge,
From the horses and hounds, so big, so huge,

He trips on a branch and injures his foot,
looks up, above him a dog is stood.
He takes a deep breath and prepares for attack,
Then all of a sudden his world is black.

The huntsman are happy, successful again,
The fox he breathes slowly, he's crippled with pain.
He finally takes his last breath of air,
There is one conclusion, this sport isn't fair.

Lisa Howes

Jasper

Jasper came on the full moon,
he must have fallen from a witch's broom.
We felt so sorry when he arrived,
Because all the time he just cried and cried.
Jasper is an Oriental Black Cat,
he's not chubby and he's not fat.
He eats his dinner very, very posh,
Then afterwards he has a little wash.
His teeth are long his claws are sharp,
He's almost invisible in the dark.
Jasper sits on everyone's knee,
But most of the time he sits on me.
We do love our little Jasper,
Because he gives us so much laughter.

Lucy Cavaliere

The Eventide Liaison

'The moon's made of cheese',
He said, with marked indifference,
Gazing into the frosted sky.
And then he turned and paced along the grass,
Like a soldier
Without a mission.

She replied with an austere glare
marked by emeralds,
'If it were, I should have eaten it already'.
And then she left
Along the gravel path,
With a purpose in mind that
He never understood.

Melissa Frewin

Propaganda

As Michael walked down the road
He saw the black Nazi sign
Sewn onto his coat.
He was so proud to be in Hitler's army.
Germany was going to be the best
Country in the world,
Without all those Jews,
He thought to himself.
His shiny black shoes made a sharp, short
Noise on the pavement,
The only noise that could be heard.
This was 1944, the war had lasted 5 years already.
There were no children happily playing in the street,
There were no men at work,
They were fighting for Germany - Hitler's country.
Michael thought that as soon as
Germany could ostracize the Jews - the better.
He saw a big picture of Hitler,
Painted on a wall, and a slogan beneath it ran,
'Whoever helps a Jew, helps the devil.'

Rebecca Bendall

Message of Hope

My parents have left this earthly shackle,
Freedom at last from the battle.
Reborn with cosmic light,
That flows through us all, especially at night.
Wake up my friends to this message
Of hope, for thou art glory, hope
And light that will burn eternal
In the heavens bright.

Terry King

"A Mother"

A mother's love is there for you,
From a baby to a tiny tot too!
School starts and she holds your hand,
She tells you how you've done just grand,
As a teenager you gave her tears,
But Mother is there to help your fears,
Life brings illness along to you,
But Mother will make you as good as new,
Words are said you do not mean,
But Mother always sets the slate clean,
The time comes when you are wed,
What she has taught you will stand you in good stead,
Problems in life that come to you,
A Mother feels them through and through
A grandchild comes along the way
And a Mother's love is there to stay.
A friend she will always be.
That's what my Mother is to me.

Susan Styles

Perhaps

Is this how it's meant to be,
From blind to vision, and now we see,
Two minds apart cannot connect,
And inner feeling do not detect,

Can we live as one, yet not another,
Or lay our tracks, then turn and cover,
To do what others do and wish,
Or be as one on land a fish,

To wish with heart and honest hope,
With all our difference how one must cope,
Forged as metal no sign of joint,
Can never be, so find no point,

Enclosed inside this fragile frame,
Allowed outside as held and tame,
Connected through each other's expression
Communication lacks and enter depression.

William Taylor

Windsong

I have shaken the dew of the meadows
from the clover's creamy gown,
I have whispered among the grasses
And danced up the hill and down.

I have stirred the gold of the buttercups
With my quick silver spoon,
And hushed the birds to listen
To my wild, melodious tune.

I caress the earth so softly
With my sweet, loving breath
I play with the clouds and treetops
And know not the meaning of death.

I dance with the seven sisters
More sprightly and supple are they
When they dance to my merry playing
Along the silvery way.

Sarah Baker

Nightmares

Please Daddy please Daddy don't hurt her
Get back up those stairs he replies
In a bellowing tone, a thundering roar
That drowns my future cries

Mr. Jack Daniels is tossed to one side
While Mummy she cowers with fear
This morning they kissed as he walked out the door
Why does love have to be so unclear

He violently grabs and tugs her hair
As he polls her around the room
Her screams resound around the house
The walls conceal her doom

She's left for dead on the living room floor
Realizing now what he has done
He's wasted a bottle of Mr. Jack Daniels
Unrepentant about beating dear Mum

Tyler Stone

Derelict

Green moss grows where the stone once glistened
Ghosts bow their heads where once they listened
To the cries of children as they scraped their knees
On the gravel paths. And the old oak trees
Scratch their names on the off-white shutters
As gargoyles spit rain on the gardener who mutters
And curses the crows as they flock in the eaves
And time slips away as he sweeps away leaves.

Owen Phipps

Spring

Green shoots from the earth are peeping
Giving life to the ground so bare;
Birds in chorus are singing
There is warmth in the very air.

Buds on the trees are bursting
Into leaves their boughs to grace,
Lambs in the field are skipping
Bold rabbits from their burrows race.

For Spring is here bringing gladness,
All creation seems to say,
Lifting our spirits, dispelling our sadness
Winter's bleakness has gone away.

On trees and shrubs soon blossoms will show
Displaying colour and beauty to enthral,
While seeds in hope we sow
For summer's flowers and food as well.

This lovely season in all its freshness
Given by our Creator long ago,
Should move us to thank Him for His goodness
While we live on this earth below.

O. R. Cornish

Happy Mothers' Day . . .

To be a mum is a special task,
Giving more, than what is asked.

Just being there in troubled days
Always knowing what to say.

You're also a friend, one that's true
I'm glad I have a mum like you.

And when I'm lonely, you're always there
To give a cuddle and say you care.

Our love and friendship will always remain
No matter where I go, I'll be home again.

Hold on to our memories, with a smile upon our face
Bless you mum for carrying on the human race.

With warmness in my heart, I love you.

Sally Jose Rudkin

Sixteen

Just another ordinary day
Going smoothly in the usual way.
But you can never know what is to come.
Day turning to horror, forgot all about fun.

Sixteen children falling one by one,
Innocence swallowed by the barrel of a gun.
Sixteen children hand in hand with fear
Left people wondering what has happened here?

The classroom left lying oh so silent,
Parents remembering where the five years went.
None of them picture, none of them could the horror see
Will the last one out, turn out the light please.

Sixteen children falling one by one,
Innocence swallowed by the barrel of the gun.
Sixteen children hand in hand with fear
Their final act to hold each other dear.

Children left to see their parents weeping,
Don't understand why no-one is sleeping.
Returning in respect one by one to the scene
Never to again live the shattered dream.

Stuart Grant

Body Talk

I recall the tender flesh, supple bones,
Golden hair flowing in the gentle breeze,
Complexion - fresh as the flowers of the fields,
The warmth from the smile, eyes dancing with
Excitement at the pleasures of youth.

Years have passed by, the inner soul has
not changed. Weathered skin now covering the
aged flesh on creaking bones. Silver hair
no longer ruffled by the breeze, but coiled
into the nape of the once swan-like neck.
The smile as warm, the eyes still sparkle,
but at times are sad when they recall the loss
of loved ones over the years. Slow down,
I feel weary but the heart beats rhythmically
on, the love still flowing out, to all mankind.

"How much longer will love and kindness course
from within to comfort those who need it most?"

Pauline Vinters

"Paradise"

In paradise as fountains flow,
goldfish swim to and fro,
rapids run over glittering stones,
through sparkled gates and silver thrones
emerald bridges, gilded gold.
Gleaming magic of Motherload.
Yachts afloat on sparkled seas
golden rivers with diamond trees
treasure chests on every bend.
In paradise, In wonderment.

Robert Vance

The Dance

As I looked through the window, the night was gone.
Dull was the sky and the wind quite strong.

Suddenly plucked from its family a Hydrangea
head flew high,
and committed a dance of joy to the sky.
It bowed, it curtsied and pivoted with such grace.
Then dipped low only to lift with speed
and elegance.

Down came the rain,
Down the flower head.
The entertainment was over,
Yet the tenderness and aura of dance remains.

Maurice Brett

Untitled

A daily dose of tabloid views,
From fast food ads and tele news.
Suitably supplied from press and factory farm;
So, where's the harm.
What worldly word and food processor,
This sagacious, universal professor.
Verbose and flatulent indigestion;
A constant, straining constitution.
Those do's and don'ts: Wills and won'ts-
Of choice and variation;
Given carefully consideration.
Life's a lottery,
Served-up on plastic: paper;
Or off pottery.
With words; vitamins: Supplements A to Z.
Only additives -
After all is done, and said.

D. H. E. Bradley

To A***

In secret we drank
  from flawless glasses,
The wine for you and me alone.

In secret we drank
  while the world outside
moved and carried on

And on leaving our isolated cells
  our hands were unsure.

We loved in secret and I knew
  I could not be healed of so much joy in so little time.

For now,
  I seek the haven of poppy fields and everlasting time.

Rita Cox

The Sea Empress

Wisdom dictates: "Learn by your mistakes",
but is this what it takes?

We watch Nature's fight, a terrible sight, as day and night
Her emptying hold bleeds volumes untold of Earth's 'Black Gold'.
This is the morbid caress of a tear in the dress of the Sea Empress,
Who would be ashamed, being so named, if she should be blamed!

We see Nature's suffocation and feel anger and frustration
That they didn't learn before, so we must watch it all once more:
As Death spreads its black cloak, both land and sea choke
And every bird, a blackened raven, lies still on Milford Haven.

Only time will tell if we will sell our Heaven for Hell.

Stephen Williams

An Ode to Milton Keynes

A windmill now stands across the road
From the home where my childhood was spent:
Not a working mill I have to say
But a hotel/restaurant with rooms to rent.
The fields where I played have become a lake,
There's a club now for those who sail . . .
"Members Only" announce the signs by the road
Which was merely a muddy trail.
But Milton Keynes has grown up around me
Everything's changed since I was a kid.
Those country lanes of yesteryear
Are outdated - replaced by a grid.
Houses have grown up all over the place
Offices, factories, shops and schools;
Places for leisure and relaxation,
Skating rinks, pubs and swimming pools.
The critics make fun of our brand new city,
But maybe they've got it all wrong:
Though things aren't quite what they used to be
Milton Keynes is where I belong.

Sheila Fullman

Saints and Sinners

The world is full of Saints and Sinners
From the aged ones to the mere beginners.
The fate of us, one and all,
Lies in the hands of the beginners, so small.

The newborn child holds the key,
That unlocks the future for you and me.
If this child, this one so young,
Becomes a Saint, no more can be done

For Sinners I think can show the way,
To simple survival from day to day.
If Saints, the great ones, the ones we've cherished,
Are left to lead then we will perish.

For what is good? What is right?
What do Saints do, while out of sight?
The Sinners though we can be sure,
Will grow up keen to even the score.

Saints and Sinners,
Their roles reversed,
are the future
of Planet Earth.

Wayne M. Clark

Debt

Not comprehending, my only reaction was "Cor!"
I did not perceive the vivid scars of war,
I did not anticipate the agony I provoked
And was unprepared for the scream on which he choked.
The voice was not familiar, it was so full of pain,
I felt wretched, as spasms of grief gripped him over again.
Those awful shudders; the breathless, alien speech;
I was scared, there was a barrier I could not breech.
I was stuck for words and so sat dumb,
I tried to touch him but no movement would come.
"All my pals were on that ship", he said,
Recalling friends who were all dead.
"The Luftwaffe blew that ship out of the water".
And I made him remember that grim slaughter,
I made him re-witness that terrible scene.
I made him see again his real nightmare dream.
I felt his sorrow and I felt his hurt
As he hid his tear behind pyjama shirt.
I experienced a new emotion, a new feeling
Which came from a wound, never healing,
An open wound, over half a century old,
From a shocking war and horrors untold.
I never realized, I'd even heard this before.
Never more insensitive was that word "Cor!"

Richard Duckett

Missing Him

Crisply cut diamonds cascade towards the ground,
From the white satin sky above.
There is a peaceful silence, and the air is still,
Just like the day he was taken away.
As I walk through the orchard, branches spiralling like arms to
the heavens, my eyes fall on a solitary Christmas card,
Placed lovingly next to a wreath of holly.
I wonder do they know or do they care, that they are missed?
Slowly I walk towards the place he now rests,
Underneath a conifer, forever reaching upwards,
forever stretching for the stars.
My grandfather's ashes now one with the earth,
His life's blood now running through the tree's veins,
Memories come flooding back.
The way he used to toss me onto his shoulders as if I wasn't there,
The patience he had with the persistent young child craving for his
attention. I used to follow him like a puppy, loyal and full of
adoration. Now I wonder aimlessly not seeming to be getting
anywhere,
Feeling the injustice of his passing.
I wanted to know the loving old man,
And for him to know the young woman.

Kirsty Webb

A Friend of Mine . . .

I know love very well - she's an old friend.
Full of understanding.
Always shows an interest.
Overflowing with kindness.

I think you know her too.

She always listens - my friend, Love.
Gives encouragement.
Continuously laughing.
Always enthusiastic.

You may have heard of her.

Love is a close friend of mine - someone I really respect.
Never makes comparisons.
Shows no inhibitions. Not constrained by differences.

You may have caught a glimpse of her.

I know Love very well - an irreplaceable friend.
Holds no preconceived opinions, never expects or assumes,
sensitive in all situations.
Caring, affectionate, warm, funny, faithful, trustworthy, genuine.
Always smiling - that's my friend Love.

I don't think you've ever met her.

Kerensa Porter

Strange Dreams

Here we sat in our casing,
Fumbling with time, just phasing,
Everyone around has changed,
I saw their feeble cause, their innocence,
And I cried.
The stars fell into my eyes,
And enlightened my thoughts.
No longer would I dream,
It can tie you in knots.
Through corridors I rush,
As a rapid, a roller,
Coasting to terror, insanity,
But always inside me.
Hiding and teaching,
He won't show his face,
But I know it's only me,
In a different time and place.

Ross Hunter

Christopher My First Grandson

C is for calm the way that you seem
H is for handsome, quiet and lean.
R is for rare the way you can draw
I is for idolize the one we adore
S is for saunter as you stroll through life
T is for talent, I hope that is rife
O is for occasions when you were very small
P is for pictures I've got on my wall
H is for happiness you've given us all
E is for excellent days you've spent with me
R is for rich and fond memories
Christopher you'll always be No. 1 to me

C. Cook

Pillow Fight

My sister and I, one night
had a wonderful pillow fight
Bish, Bash, Bosh,
Boy, was Mother cross
feathers everywhere
even under the chair
it wasn't our fault,
We never wanted to get caught
How did we know, the pillows would tear
and the feathers would go everywhere
We didn't know
We didn't care.

Laura Hall

Beach Walk, Newburgh, Aberdeenshire

Fishing lines and nets in the sand
Half buried and in impossible tangles.

At my back along the tideline my footprints
A clear mark of my journey.

I wonder if my mark is so obvious
Elsewhere I have walked.

Drifting into others' lives
Filling them with frail promises.

Leaving them
Half buried and in impossible tangles.

A. J. MacDonald

The New Day's Sun

Softly reflect the tide of the day.
Gather your thoughts into one.
Trade for the night, your mind's display,
And wait for the new Day's Sun.

Recall the people you love and hate,
Capture them, every one.
Side by side they'll walk to the gate,
That leads to the New Day's Sun.

Remember yourself as you have always been.
Accept who you really are.
Look back at your loved ones and friends serene,
You will see how they sparkle like stars.

Gather together these impressions clear,
And smile at the love you have won.
Hold them, retain them, keep them near,
For this, is your New Day's Sun.

R. McLaufhun

The Cure

A blustery playful wind
gave me a buoyancy I did not feel
as I walked to the beach in the early morn.
My back was aching-legs-heavy as lead
the headache that awakened me - said get out of bed.
So I walked and walked in the early morn
this savagely windy early morn
so glad was I then - to be born.
The walk took me on to a sea-washed beach
peace - tranquillity - were there to reach
wide open space - clean untainted air
filled me with joy - just being there.

Still floating along with the unyielding wind
I watched as the sand lifted - above the hard bed
below - as I was - against my will - yet letting
my thoughts - my problems go - and blow with the wind.

My lungs were filled with a new promise
the past - the future -(the headache)
Today-the wind blew it away.

Margaret Richardson

"A Winter Scene"

As I awoke one morning and through the window
Gazed, I could not believe my eyes, the snow almost
Looked to reach the sky, gold and young show
Their pluck, the going was hard and the traffic got stuck,
Farmers went out to check their cattle, but also the
heavy snow had forward too much they fought a
loosing battle, then the rivers burst its banks
Flooding towns and homes, the boats that helped in
Their plight, booked a very sad and pathetic sight,
But as time goes by and the days got longer
We shall see better ones ahead,
The flowers that's hid beneath the snow will show
Their tiny heads, the little birds will begin to church,
Their own sweet songs they sing,
Telling us in their little way.
That soon it will be spring.

G. Moore

An Island Reserve

An aboriginal stood with spear in his hand
Gazing towards his native land,
Sent to an island reserve at the white man's whim
Because they no longer had time for him.

His culture destroyed, and now short of space
To go walk - about had been part of his race.
Then he'd be free to hunt for his meat
Always finding sufficient to eat.

He'd found water, where no white man could
Was able to make fire by rubbing wood,
Wandering the bush he'd left no litter
Now he was sad and feeling bitter.

'Round the camp fires his stories were told
Legends handed down from days of old,
Now he was under the white man's law
None of these things could he do any more.

They'd introduced, the demon drink
Which sent him mad, and he couldn't think,
So he got drunk to drown his sorrow
He dare not think about tomorrow

D. Jacobs

Our World Is Dying

Gone are the trees now the grass so green now,
Gone are the flowers that bloom in spring,
The soil is drying the earth is crying
For the cool, cool rain that no clouds will bring.

The food won't grow now there is no harvest,
Millions starving oh! do we care,
We bury the children we weep no more now
The tears have dried from the pain we bear.

We dump our rubbish in the mighty ocean,
We kill the whales and dolphins too.
The jungle's silent now where are the wildlife
No longer will they go in two by two.

The clean pure air now is no longer there now
Polluted skies we breathe the fumes.
Where are the birds now flying so high now
Oh! how I long for the skies of blue.

We kill we fight for the what, the why for
Our loved ones die for the mother's cry
We rob and plunder, tear her asunder
What have we done to our world.

Shirley Kilpatrick

"Ge's a Job, Mate"

"Ge's a job, mate." Where have I heard that before?
"Ge's a job, mate." Do you know the score?
On the dole, down on your luck
Not two pennies to rub together, don't duck.

"Ge's a job, mate." The queues seem to get longer
"Ge's a job, mate." Now competition is stronger.
It's a dog eat dog world, that's for sure
And as time goes by, there seems no cure.

"Ge's a job, mate." The boys from the black stuff, are here
"Ge's a job, mate." The symptom is clear
If we continue in recession
It will soon be worse than the Great Depression.

"Ge's a job, mate." This is how it is
"Ge's a job, mate." Do you hear the bizz
People on their bikes and leaving their father's home
Breaking up families as hungry people to get a job roam.

"Ge's a job, mate." Time alone can tell
"Ge's a job, mate" Your soul you'll have to sell
The future looks dim
Caught in society's net, the system pulls you in.

E. Elaine O'Neill

The Lone Grouse

The lad went to work at half past four,
Gently he closed the front door.
As he trudged upwards through the snow,
The snowflakes set his face aglow.
It was just coming up to dawn light,
When the pit head gear came in sight.
The framework stood out, stark and black,
As the lone grouse shouted, go back go back,
The roof was weighting all the day,
But miners have to earn their pay.
Then the roof began to crack,
Too late he thought of the lone grouse
    shout go back, go back.
He then woke up with a scream,
He'd had a nightmare not 'a' dream.

L. Lowe

Going Home

Going home sing the wheels of the train
Going home, going home again
Where the grass is green
And the sun rides high
Going back to the valley of Wye

Strong arms of the hills Westward sweeping
Deep forests in their keeping
Flames of sunset gild the sky
And golden ripples span the Wye

So many shades of green
Colour each passing scene
In field and forest and shady ride
That soon the shawl of dusk will hide

You are home sing the wheels of the train
Home, I am home again
The stars are bright
And the moon rides high
I am home in the Valley of Wye.

Margaret B. Copeman

House for Sale

Here lies the joys of yesteryear
    gone and yet so near
As squirrel scampers across my gait
He does not linger, pause, nor wait
A lone flower flutters in the breeze
Not heeds nor sees
Whole, lie the hopes and fears of yestereves
As dead and scattered as
last year's leaves.

Now back to a world of iron and stone
And to dwell there all alone
At times in squalor, at times in dismal grandeur
All times trapped like a fly in amber
Waiting till the death cart rolls
Rolls and creaks forever braking
Mind and heart in endless waking.

Maurice Hemmant

Taken for Granted

Come listen to the little birds a-whistling in the trees
God's little creatures out to pleasure and to please
As the wind gently whispers the rustling of the leaves
Whilst nestling in their nests at night alone
at last and out of sight
the dawn arrives and shades of light
Caress the trees and shuns the night

With eggs all hatched and mouths to feed
Birds in flight in search of seeds to feed
their young and cater for their need

With mouth agape and head upright
A new generation hatched last night

Aiden Gordon

347

The Last Puff

Is this to be my last cigarette?
Good job I bought twenty,
Didn't want to give up just yet,
Made sure that I had plenty.

Dreading the time when there are none,
But then, I'll feel healthy and good,
"Talk to your friends on the phone",
Or "raid your fridge for the food".

But then when the deed has been done,
You feel so fidgety and broody,
And when you think it's your last one,
You become exceptionally moody.

Don't the medics know that it's hard,
It's not as easy as they say,
Told my loved ones, "Be on your guard",
Or else there'll be hell to pay.

Sue Butcher

'Tragic April'

Your death stays with me everywhere,
Half my soul has flown with yours,
I need you here to say I care,
Ask why you've gone, ask what's the cause

The rain poured down, it danced alone,
Immersed in earth, we must disjoin,
The piper plays a deathly moan,
Then silence sweeps the dankness again.

That day in April haunts me still,
And so it will forever more,
The plans we made, all unfulfilled,
Why did you have to die so young.

'But only the good die young' you said,
With griefs deep cut, its comfort small,
Cold dark thoughts, which swarm my head,
Must lay to rest as you have done.

Lisa K. McLellan

My Love the Pitman

Arms as strong as the giant oak,
Hands so big, so gentle,
Smiling eyes like clear blue skies,
Curly soft hair and face so fair.
A back that ripples like tide-washed sand
With traces of blue through the summer brown.
Firm of limb a sportsman him.
His mind has thoughts as deep
As the pit he works down when I'm asleep.
Sparkling personality, a heart that understands,
A generous man in thought and deed,
Sensitive to my every need,
Kind and true, he loves me too,
My love, the pitman.

Maureen Abram

The Ancient Blackthorn

Battered, twisted, bent, seared from northeast storm,
Hangs off tarmac sheered atop of sandy cliff,
It's northeast as of granite dark, but dead
Seemed to point toward the cottage of poor old Ned,
Ned, ancient, bent by years and northeast winds, dead,
He feared not the winter cold, but what of March's treachery,
A sudden chill and he was gone with daffodils,
But, a sheltered southern branch out straight upon the thorn,
A single blossom held, just opening,
Its petals pointed down a lane
To where a newborn baby cried,
And what of Ned when last he slept,
That gnarled but kindly salt,
Before him a brilliant light come forth,
A voice, "Come unto me" and Ned was dead
But Ned is with the Lord, he is alive

B. A. Claxton

3 A.M. Morning

Have you heard the silence of a 3 a.m. morning?
Have you heard the sleeping of the rest of the world?
Sleep, peaceful sleep, restful and calming.
Precious and needed but far, far away,

Have you heard the noise of a 3 a.m. morning?
Have you heard a riot going on in your head?
Of thoughts and confusion and terrors all clashing.
And sleep is still so far, far away.

Have you watched the clock of a 3 a.m. morning?
Have you watched as time drags slowly by?
Heard sounds of ticking, persistent, incessant.
Counting the hours of the sleep far away.

Have you seen the darkness of a 3 a.m. morning?
Have you seen the blackness of night-time despair?
Longed for light and the dawn of a morning,
As sleep slips ever further away.

Have you fought the fight of a 3 a.m. morning?
Have you fought the demons raging loud in your head?
Have you been tempted to extinguish a 3 a.m. morning,
And make plans for a sleep far, far away?

Katie Brown

Memories

Memories are all I have left now I am alone
Grateful for the friends who still phone
All the years we had together could I have done better
When I returned from town, not even a letter
To say you were sorry for what you had done

You'd had enough and you gave up and took your own precious
life
Leaving behind a devastated and loving wife
I ranted and raved shouting didn't you care
You left your family to face the people out there
Without saying goodbye you went away

Could I have done so much more for you
Watching you in pain and depressed I often cried too
It took so long to forgive you in my heart
Not to feel so bitter now we are apart
I am learning to take each day as it comes

The years go by I miss you so much
Longing once more to feel your tender touch
I pray you will be waiting with a smile on your face
Once again to feel your tender embrace
So rest in peace until we meet again.

May Clough

Evergreen No More

Electric blue the lightning flashes, the thunder growls and roars.
Grey cloud scurry across the sky, the rain it pours and pours.
The forest that once welcomed it, now hangs its boughs in dread.
The bounty now that this rain brings, serves nothing but the dead.
For the rain now stings the acid burns, their leaves turn brown
and die.
The giant forest asks the wind a silent question, why?

By sheltering us from storm and beast amid their towering spires.
And giving us wood to build our homes and fuel to stoke our fires.
They gave us all the chance to live and take our place on earth.
To strive and rise from the forest floor, to find our own true worth.
From birds that nest within their leaves they'd taught us all to sing.
They even gave us the air we breath, they gave us everything.

Now we with our chain saws hew them down, we chop, we saw,
we tear.
We rip their roots out from the ground without a moment's care.
But worse than the axe that bites their limbs or the painful kiss of
the saw.
Is the poison that pervades the air and kills their every spore.
Now gone are the days of verdant green, of majestic sights
in the sun.
Now they lie in rotting heaps . . .
Dear God! . . . What have we done!!?

Michael Job

Moods and Seasons

Blue skies outside as morning sun shines in,
Grey clouds gather from deep within.
Emotions and feelings like waves on the sea,
Sometimes calm and smooth I could sail endlessly.
Then when things get rough and a storm brews ahead,
The waves become fierce those thoughts I dread.
I long for the peace no confusion today,
To skip through the hours with a light breeze I sway.
We walk through the seasons four parts of the year,
Each with its weather it seems so clear.
Spring with its new life with lambs in the field,
The pain of death from us it tries to shield.
Through the summer with its blazing sun,
Never does it seem life isn't fun.
With autumn arrives leaves of brown and gold,
These precious moments are for us to hold.
Winter with the snow that lies deep on the ground,
When dusk draws in we hear not a sound.
But what we forget when we look through life,
Along with the seasons can come pain and strife.
Blizzards in winter, floods in spring,
Storms in summer, what'll autumn bring?
If we prepare for good times and bad,
It'll help us cope with the happy and sad.
Love and hate are not so different from seasons of the year,
We'll face them together, For you I'll always be here.

Sharon Phillips

The Balloon

It glided across my sky,
Gently rising up towards the clouds,
Watching as it slides by,
floating high above the crowds.

Looking down on leafy green pastures,
floating though a sea of blue,
A sudden break of silence, rocks the basket,
As the burner breathes new height
back into the balloon.

I watched it getting smaller,
Gradually disappearing from view,
Gliding high above us all.
To become a tiny speck,
Drifting on the horizon.

Suzanne T. Smith

A Pet's Poem

Chirp, chirp goes the bird,
Glug, glug goes the fish,
Tetley is the name, is always heard,
That is the name of the bird,
that is always heard, but how I wish,
She would not make such a row,
Pepsi is the fish, who is always slow,
And I don't know how,
I've managed such not to deal
a vicious blow,
And done away with my darling pets,
Who are part of my life in every way.

D. Bohanan

Claustrophobic World

Imprisoned in my own world
Free to go but forced to stay
Like a bird with its wings clipped
No barriers to stop me but I can't fly away.

I'm trapped in a never ending tunnel
Unable to reach the virtuous light
The closer I think I'm coming
The further it disappears out of sight

The sky has enclosed me here
Like a lid that's been put on a tin
But I'm only captive on the outside
For I'm free as the wind and the clouds within...

Sarah Quick

A Shot in the Night

A shot in the night a bullet to kill
He drops to the ground lifeless and still
Not a sound from his mouth not a beat from his heart
Just a life that is lost in an endless dark
The love that is taken which can never return
Burns a hole in the love of his golden pearl
Without their hearts both beating as one
There is no reason for her to go on
A knife, a cut, and then the blood flows
The death she does not fear for her lover is close
Now back together both souls as one
Nothing can destroy their love
Not a knife, not a soul, not a bullet from a gun

G. A. Van Der Beek

Railway Exhibition

Nottingham's old Victoria Baths - sad and sweaty sports hall

Model railways - double O gauge, tiny stations with frozen porters,
grimy sidings and signal boxes

Club enthusiasts wearing embroidered station names on white shirts
shunt, uncouple and change points

Loudspeakers cough and wheeze train noises puffing steam,
guards' whistles and nasal station voices

Peaceful old men, silently crafting engines (to scale) awakened
only by admiration

Rank-smelling old lags wander in to warmth and cheap,
formica table-slopped tea

Little boys curious fingers curling and straining to touch,
stopped dead at barriers protecting men toys

Lynn Merry

Lassie Come Home

Protective mother, when she had five pups to feed,
Guard dog, family pet, always there in the time of need.
In return just to be brushed combed and fed,
A warm blanket for her bed.
On cold winter's nights she lay close by your feet.
A walk through the woods on fine summer's days
Now she's gone far far away.

For fifteen years she put joy in our lives,
Thoughts of her now brings tears to our eyes.
As we all know the dog is man's best friend.
That's how she remained, faithful to the end.

Our sad loss, is heaven's gain.
Life without her will never be the same.
She won't be alone as she journeys into the unknown.
Joining her sons, Tiny and "Prince" or "Bent".
For they too were heaven sent.
Now as they run free without a care,
The wind blowing through their hair.
But wherever you roam, Prince! Let
   LASSIE COME HOME.

K. Pendlebury

Soldiers in a Pillbox

Standing still, cold, watching and waiting,
Gun ready to fire without hesitating,
Looking out through the small square windows,
A chill down my spine as an icy wind blows,
Through the open doorway and around the concrete pillar.
They say I'm a soldier
But I'm just a straightforward killer.

The Germans stalking across the blood reddened field,
Using piles of mud as their only shield;
Dying by the thousand day after day,
Who has the right to make them die this way?
The politicians and generals stay safe at home,
While us soldiers in pillboxes chill to the bone.

Stuart Poffley

Soldier Boy

Sniper on roof, with telescopic sight,
Gunshot rings out in the night,
Soldier dying, falls to the floor,
Lying in pain, life no more.
Wife at home crying all day,
Nothing to comfort her and nothing to say,
Why did her husband have to die?
Hurts her kids to see her cry.
Join the army and have some fun,
Perhaps to die by a terrorist gun.
Enemy unknown, not like before,
Not like in either World War.
A single red rose lies on his grave,
A memory of the life he gave.
Soldiers trying to end the fight,
Gunshot rings out in the night,
Another one to add to the score,
My God, my God, how many more?

Robert Dalrymple

Goldfish . . .

. . . Plump, shiny, lacy fins, bulging eyes, overfed,
Half dead.
Swimming 'round and 'round the mirrored bowl,
And artificial plants in coloured stones, Soul
Destroying.
Sad, despondent fish,
Shocked at times by its reflection.
Neglected,
Gulping stagnant water.
Listless fish, swimming 'round and 'round in cloudy water,
Uninterested in food, searching for oxygen,
Dying . . .
Dying . . .
DEAD.

Katherine Murray

Let Him Know

My brother John is number one,
He cared, he shared we all got on,
  His hart was big, his hart was kind,
A love like John's, is hard to find,
  And that is why we all should say,
We learn to love and we learn the prey.
  You got your wings you flown away,
The kingdom of heaven is were you stay.
  We send our love each and every day.
We love you John and we still prey.
  We will all be together, forever, one day.

V. Moore

In Praise of the Lord

Give thanks to God we share His gift
He cares for us and gives a lift
To those in need He'll lend a hand
So come and join His happy band

Praise to the Lord for all His love
He'll grant us faith from heaven above
And give His peace to those who wait
To meet again at the pearly gate

Now forth we go to show we care
And work quite hard our tasks to share
With friends around we're seldom sore
We find our lives are worth some more

Our lives are short we should not fight
But fill our days with another light
Then make the most of all our time
To write a verse and make it rhyme

Now in this work I seldom fail
So here for you another tale
I give my thanks for every hour
To Him above a greater Power

A. Thomson

Contentment

Leaking tents and starry August skies,
Harvest moon hung over new mown hay,
Country roads and honeysuckle highs
Sounds of evening pause, and melt away.

Tenty mornings hot and dim within,
Stirring lazily I stretch and sigh,
Here I lie at peace amongst my kin
And remember always blessed am I.

Veronica Emmott

The Alien from Mars

The alien from Mars
has teeth like metal bars.

His feet are like massive chunks of meat,
which I think is really neat.

His body is like a ball
It's as big as our school hall,

His name is Hobnob
and he has a brilliant job.

He comes from the planet fly,
but he said he was just passing by.

I cried when he flew away
but he promised me he would come back in May.

Robin William Methven

Indecision

Not once in my past life before,
have I not known that through a door,
the way to find the answer lies.
Before, I could at least surmise!

If wrong, retrace and start again,
with small diversions now and then.

But now my direction seems to be,
'round in circles endlessly.

Oh how I wish I could be free,
from these shackles binding me.

Not one clear thought is in my head,
I face the future full of dread.

Imprisoned in my mental cell,
living through a personal hell.

I need someone to help me find,
the way to release the ties that bind.

Lost and alone I await a sign.

Peter Chamberlain

Moving House

Maybe the desert nomads and their spouses
Have little difficulty in changing houses.
The tents are struck, the camels' backs are loaded
To the penultimate straw, and then they're goaded
Into a shambling movement of the feet
And so the déménagement is complete.

An Englishman is fortunate indeed
To move his goods and chattels at such speed.
Removal men, no doubt, are expeditious
In handling ornaments and precious dishes.
They move the heavy furniture with ease
To emulate the feats of Hercules.
Tables and chairs, wardrobes and beds, impedimenta
Crammed in an enormous van with paraphernalia
From loft and garage, whilst the car behind
Follows with family in anxious mind.

We sit among the boxes and the crates
To drink the cup 'that not inebriates'
And contemplate the snail (as we unpack)
Whose house is wisely carried on his back!

L. P. W. White

Path Finders

Flasks filled lunches packed.
Haversacks upon our backs of we go along the
track over fields in our waterproof macs
walking fast walking slow speaking to everyone
as we go hearing tales of gladness and woe
giving comfort if we can to another fellow man.
Gazing back across the land. enjoying everything
at hand fields like patchwork quilts below
cows and sheep moving to and fro
coming to a babbling brook looking for a
shady nook to rest our weary feet and eat,
our lunch with much gusto. And then for home
we all must go.

M. Watson

Genesis

Scrutiny of a toad's eye flicks on, flicks off eternity,
Having passed between the silence and the laughter,
Out of blindness and stillness, weaving meaning and atoms,
Into seasons having warmth; punching questions in the blackness,
Glowing greenness in the zenith,
Curling upwards and unfolding clamorous life and death's cliff,
A time of grief and life's grip, clutching at the fractured
Rhythm in its laughter and its issue,
Burning through its dry ambition; subtraction through division
Of purpose and perfection, leaving the tight brute focus of its greed.
The eye rolls 'round its hollow cage turning about the axis
Of its love; looking inwards at itself;
The eye rolls 'round its padded cell and sees the truth through
Memory: Vision feasted in the vault of blindness,
As sounds shrieks from bedlam to a deaf world or fishes struggle
In a concrete sea towards the dream of wetness.
And man whose shadow was ignorance was like a beacon
in the world
And the vision before his eye was one of ignorance,
Ignorance of the word and that which it became,
Ignorance of the world and that which he'd undone.

Mark Shelley

Love Call

I'm looking for a fella, 18 to 21,
He must be tall and handsome, and have a sense of fun;
I don't care how he dresses, as long as he is clean,
And doesn't count each penny (in other words, not mean).
No purple hair or safety pins in his dress or through his nose,
Or platform shoes that make him look as if he's standing on his toes;
It's OK if he likes a drink, as long as he's not boozy,
I've waited for a man so long, I'm not the least bit choosy!
It would be nice if he were strong and could always be around,
'Cause I'm short and fat and 60 plus, asthmatic and
wheelchair bound.
So if there are any offers, I'm sure you will agree
The bloke who makes the offer is a bigger fool than me.

B. James

Concrete and Clay

Trees are felled, forests are dying,
Grass grows brittle, the ground is drying,
'Twixt global warming and developer's greed,
Ring road and motorways we don't need,
With heartless planning and building haste,
People are moved, their lives laid waste.

Parks and fields and green-belts eroded,
For an urban sprawl with buildings corroded
Two hundred years this planets been ravaged,
With little thought for the future, ourselves we've damaged,
It's time to stop, it's time to think,
Or to a concrete jungle the earth will shrink.

Let us breath again, air unadulterated and clean,
Have water flowing without pollution seen,
The quality of life on which we depend,
Will it survive, or will it end?
The thin ozone layer in damaged sky,
Let it recover, or the earth will die!

Mike McEwan

The Architect

My neighbour is an architect, a man of some renown,
  He also is a gay old boy, retired now from the town.
He said he now feels lonely, which state he must amend,
  He'd build a new extension to accommodate a friend.

He soon drew up the master plans, with best contractors hired,
  The concrete founds were quickly laid, his speed must be admired,
When the project reached completion, he showed me 'round inside,
  I've never seen such elegance, my mouth stood open wide.

A Persian rug adorned the floor, with luscious carpets too,
  The colour scheme was pastel green, the ceiling, pastel blue.
The entrance door was solid oak, brass fittings made it shine,
  The panelled walls had gilded balls, in oiled Parana pine.

The windows all were double glazed, just set to get the view,
  And central heating warmed the air, with radiators too.
The furnishings were dignified, soft seats with padded cork,
  A room where Architect and friend could quietly sit and talk.

He said he felt the scheme oozed peace, no fax-machine, nor phone,
  Neither he, nor friend need ever spend one moment's sit alone.
A brilliant architect is he, what vision!, what design!
  This grand two-seater privy, in the garden next to mine.

W. Langford-Johnson

Cynical Easter

If you believe what the fables say,
He came to us then went away.
He saw the wars,
the famine the strife,
and came to try to improve our life.
He'll be back the wise persist,
but when? The downtrodden do insist.

It seems that now more than ever we need,
a truth we can all see,
and believe.

When someone says listen, I'm the One,
He's not believed,
we assume He's wrong.
So will it be the same old tale,
He will be here, and again He'll fail.

He can see that wars,
and famine and strife,
play more of a part in our everyday life,
If He exists and He cares so much,
then why on Earth doesn't He get in touch?

Karen Smith

"The Gales of Dunblane Howl Sorrow"

"Just as the gentle wind carries the
fragile leaves, will the remaining love of
this world carry the remembrance of those
innocent and once-happy souls."

Maxine Thomas

An English Celebration of Burns Night

Remembrances
From the Hebrides
Speed South
O'er glen and bridgeses
The Tay and Firth of Forth
Thrive on fine fisheses
As salmon red and richeses
And brown kippers
Sweet as Finnanese
And kilted Glaswegians
Reel in ecstasies
O'er porridge and Scotch Glenfiddiches
And men in Aberdeen agree
That Haggis is
The Highlands'
Highest hospitalities

F. Dillien

351

Sonnet V

When a boy is old, or a man is young,
He gains his intellectuality.
Thoughts wander from trivia up a rung,
To egotistical profanity.
Misplaced, of course, profanity - I mean,
For he does not intend to be so rude,
But his dreams of the future have been seen,
And to him they are true, however lewd.
He'll fight most arrogantly for his dreams
As if he were the King of all ideas.
Profane utterances ensue in streams,
When he tries to voice his thoughts and his fears.
So, remember the problems of men, boys,
When you dislike the product of thought - noise!!

Laura Sherlock

The Soldier Unknown

A private scans the countryside,
He gasps in horror for those who've died,
He closes his eyes and thinks of his mother,
All this war, why do they bother.

The private looks down and sighs in sorrow,
All this over a silly quarrel,
He hears a series of painful screams,
This can't be anyone's land of dreams.

A gun fires, the private's dead,
A bullet boars straight through his head,
No-one know the private's name,
Did he give his life in vain?

Dog tags lost and a soldier gone,
A thousand later, and not yet won,
Whilst his comrades do their best,
He is being laid to rest.

His body lies in Westminster Abbey,
His mother weeps for her poor baby,
She was never to know,
Exactly where her boy did go.

Scott Morton

Mr. Midnight

With no sound of coming, he covers the land.
He tiptoes around us, like walking on sand.
His hand reaches out, stealing the light,
  rich man or poor man,
He takes away sight.
Everywhere, he can get, every crevice and crack,
He paints it all in, with the colour of black.
Creeping around us, he comes and He'll go so make him your
  friend, and be sure not your foe.
In winter, he's early and summer he's late,
  but be sure he'll be there, no matter the date.
You cannot keep him back, regardless the cost,
  and don't try to follow, for sure you'll be lost.

Peter John Turner

The Racehorse

The horse a machine so swift so clean
He travels along from scene to scene
Sometimes on the downs, sometimes on the track
Sometimes a gallop, sometimes a hack

He pulls so hard with gracious ease,
Your arms are stretching from your sleeves,
He comes over the hill in the morning. Mist.
the lad he holds him with clenched fists

His coats so shiny with linseed oil.
His hooves they rattle on the soil.
The horse a machine so swift so clean
I wish I had the chance to ride the dream

David Head

Icicles

Red ball of sun
High in the winter sky
Snowflakes fall in-between
Bright sunlight in my eye
Heavy cloud comes.
With icy cold air
January brings some people despair
Not for me though
I can see its winter glow
Brings its own kind of magic
The ice and the snow
Black trees red berries
Icy tips on lots of hedges
Silver crystals hanging down
Icy ponds would make no sound
With tiny prints frozen on the ground
To capture the moment of the day
Till the sun sets and leaves
This wonderful bright array.

Patricia Flynn

Old Age

An old old man sat on a bench
High up on a hill and seemed asleep
No movement at all he seemed caught in time
The sky shone blue and the soft breeze blew.

Three little boys went running past
Slid down the hill and ran up again.
Laughed and shouted and climbed the trees
Punched each other and whipped out guns.

The old man remained in his deathlike trance
But he knew what life was in the feel of the wind,
In the warmth of the sun, in the fact that he breathed,
In the stillness of thought and the nearness of God.

Rosalind Milne

Victim

Look at the child of war;
his dry, cracked lips part and let forth tales of death . . .
. . . his friends, his foes . . . and as he tells of the passing of
his Mother and his Father into the hands of God by the knives
of Satan, he does not weep or mourn, and he is indifferent to
your tears as they flow and fall for him.

  "What are tears?" he whispers. "But a salty sap from a
newly made wound. And I have been bled to the bone of my soul."
  Slowly he walks from your sympathy, turning his back on
his sorrow, to walk. And all around him, fighting to hold his
moistureless hands, dance the children of God, fatherless.
  And at the depths of the child's dark pool eyes stands
an old dying man, who will never find youth again.

Matthew Taylor

Soldiers Brave

Upon a field a soldier lies,
His fight for freedom done.
His face lies buried in blood-soaked land
Beside him lay his gun.

He fought with valour and with strength.
He fought with heart so bold
But where he lies, 'tis sacred ground.
Though body lies so cold.

The snow and rain and hail beat down
And wind blows through black hair,
What purpose for did hero die.
Leaves friends in deep despair.

His body will be lifted
To be placed in hero's grave,
To where all comrades rest in peace,
Where God doth guard the brave.

J. D. Tarling

Michael

He says his life is on the stage
His soul is in the glove
He says he wouldn't harm a child
His heart is like a dove

His mind is the earth's own heart
Their trusting bond shall never part
As long as he has the strength, the power
His dance and song will be a growing flower

Budding in the sun's own rays
His dance will flower in different ways
As long as he's the dance, the song
His mystery will be forever long

Kelly Porr

The Countryman

The Countryman begins to sing,
his thoughts are of the coming spring.
He sees the signs, those shoots of green,
with Winter past, the worst he's seen.

The cuckoo comes and swallow soon,
and countryside gets into tune.
Dawn chorus welcoming the morn,
he's feeling good, glad he was born.

Moorhen builds her nest upon the stream,
everywhere is like a dream.
Mowing grass to make the hay,
as sun shines on another day.

The Countryman enjoys the life,
he shares it with his darling wife.
The seed is sown, away the plough,
he's thinking of the summer now.

Raymond J. Hobbs

Lonesome Melody

Hear him strumming to the busy beat of life,
Homeless figure in a doorway.
Plays a melody recalled from bygone days,
Years of loneliness his story.
Who is he standing there? fighting cold and despair!
Doesn't anybody care?

Cold wind whistles to his 'Lonesome Melody',
Takes the rhythm from his fingers.
Through the years he's lost his friends and family,
But his hope in life still lingers.
Who is he standing there? fighting cold and despair!
Doesn't anybody care?

O won't you bring a smile to those sad and lonely eyes,
Playing in his disguise - won't you show him that you care?

Drop a coin down on the other side of life conveniently forgotten,
Take a look - it could be you that's standing there, lost and lonely
and forsaken!
Who is he standing there? fighting cold and despair!
Why doesn't anybody care?

People walking on the other side of life, can you hear my melody?
Lonesome Melody!

Yvonne Lyons

Heavenly Heights

Dawn chariots of cloud
Hoofing it down the scudding wind
Race on forever across the world of blueness
To shadow furtively the lower green of earth
Wakening in throbbing blinks between the grey.
Cease not the turning of thy carriage wheels
Scarce kissing the hilltops of thy journey
Floating ecstatically into space-oblivion.
We shall do likewise - our time is brief
And there is no returning

J. J. MacGregor

Punishment

You've been vulnerable, violated, viciously abused,
Humiliated, beaten, battered and bruised.
Understandably shaken, shattered; subdued,
And frightened, forced and furious -
How could you become so used?

C. Beardmore

Pilgrimage

Father died in '43, the middle of the war,
He had a sudden headache and collapsed upon the floor.
I was only thirteen and didn't know the score,
But twenty-four hours later Father was no more.

Father died at 43, a soldier in his prime.
He just overdid things and went before his time.
He left me lofty mountains I must singly climb
Without a Father's guidance or yet his extra dime.

After nearly fifty years I saw his lonely tomb
In the annex graveyard, because there wasn't room
To bury a mere stranger, many miles from home,
In the nearness of the Church from which he hadn't come.

I never saw his body. The funeral I missed.
I never said my Farewell to the man I never kissed.
They sent me off to Granny by a steam engine that hissed
With a once-white hanky clutched within my fist.

Just what would have happened, if he'd lived a normal span?
Would his life have made me a different sort of man?
Would at least his ashes lie beside our Gran,
So I could put a flower there, anytime I can?

Patrick Davies

Racist

Once there was a black boy walking down the street,
He had ragged clothes on and no shoes upon his feet,
Once there was a white boy walking down the street,
He was dressed as royalty with new shoes upon his feet,
There were definitely differences at each side of the road,
The black boy's grass was long and the white boy's had been mowed,
On one side the houses glistened and looked pretty in the spring,
On the other they were dirty and looked horrible and grim,
How many spiteful angry snowballs have been thrown?
How many dirty looks and fights had happened on this street?
Something bad always happened when both sides agreed to meet,
But despite all the anger there was one friendship going on,
Between the two most different boys Simon and Tom,
They smiled and laughed together despite the colour of their skin,
And I just hope that one day their two peopled side is going to win,
People are really trying hard to get the message through,
It does not matter what colour your skin is, what matters is you.

Karen Waite

Valhalla

Their names are carved in stone all over the World.
Heaven is where they will be. Eighteen to what ever age, it made
no difference.

Ready always to serve their country.
Obstacles were no hindrance in their quest for victory.
Youth; too many died in theirs.
Adored by everyone, family, friends, and comrades.
Loyal in their allegiance to their sovereign and country.

Barracks were their home, except in battle.
Religion - each to their own belief.
Identification; only by their tags.
They were all active, nimble and strong. Ideologist, everyone.
Sacrifice; they gave their lives for the free world.
Hammock: used by the Navy for a bed.

Lament by those of us who survived. Every one a hero
Gallant to all who knew them.
Immaculate always; but difficult in battle.
Offered their services willingly, without thought for their own safety
Names we must never forget. "WE WILL REMEMBER THEM".

Stanley Naylor

My Darling

I call your name, but you are no longer there
I look across the room, only to see an empty chair
My life will never be the same
Because my darling, you are no longer there
I carry on with hope and prayers
Knowing one day, I will be there
As I write this verse, under our favourite tree
Wiping my eyes, looking back on the beautiful memories
So I will carry on, in my own sweet way
Until I am with you, again one day
So if you see me looking sad and blue
It is, because life is so painful — without you.

Sheila Mee

Streams of Love

As water gently trickles off my eye,
I look at my mistakes and continue to cry.
Just a small niche in life's stream, the sad and horrible part of
what was once a beautiful dream.
To me this plague of discontent has came about like untimely rent.
To take from me my only true love like a thief in the night it
steals my love.
Why is there anger and so much pain, there used to be sunshine
but now there is rain.
Please rekindle the love you once knew, show no sadness but
love for two.

'Twas in my dreams that you blessed my eyes.
'Twas in reality true love spoke to me.
begone bad weather and times of woe
streams of love must continue to flow
oh burst your banks streams of love
wash over me like a silken glove
let me soak in this water of life together I and my love
give our true love one more chance
or these tears of life will forever dance.

Usha Kumari

Everyone Says . . .

Everyone says that I look like you,
I look in the mirror and I know that it's true,
We have the same shaped eyes and long thin nose,
Delicate features I suppose!
The only thing that's different is our hair,
Mine is dark and yours is fair,
But still people comment: "like a pea from a pod",
And I always smile then proudly nod.
Because there's no one else I'd rather be,
If I look like Mum that's fine by me!

Marie Difolco

The Waiting Room

As I strolled into this old waiting room
I looked around at the dust and gloom
I went to the hearth and looked at the grate
I've missed my train, but it was me that was late
Thoughts crossed my mind as I stopped to ponder
As I looked around my mind began to wander

Stations are gateways, which people pass in endless profusion
Privatisation of the railways, are all in confusion
Why worry about a train which is not on time
What is more important, is the rise in crime
These rooms were established around 1858
Even in those days, passengers still had to wait
Was life then more of a leisurely pace
I walked to the mirror to powder my face

My wandering mind came back from the past
Here comes my train I thought at last
Outside on the platform there were flowers in bloom
I was pleased to leave that old waiting room
The only thing wrong which now seems worse
I've come all this way and forgotten my purse

Patricia Moon

A Prayer for Night

To give one greater faith.

At night I find it best to pray, the air is dark and still,
Hence one can slip away alone, to try and seek Your will.
I do not have those eyes that see, my ears just do not hear,
Yet now and then the slightest peep, a whispered sound comes
near.

So raise Your curtain just a touch, then light can filter in,
Please help me to achieve this end, a new life to begin.
The smallest, slimmest hope You bring, is nectar to my soul,
A move towards Your shining light, and onward to my goal.

Yet come the dawn and earthly light, each day my life reborn,
The beauty of this life on earth, starts once again each morn.
Temptation is the rule on earth, so much to want and do,
This earthly home, our paradise, at times this seems so true.

For some this paradise is past, the graceful years slip by,
And then this life on earth bodes ill, we ask the question why??
For those in pain or deep distress, please Father give them hope,
A little light perchance to see, and show them how to cope.

For me I pray that what I do, will move from wrong to right,
So cause to cease, and thus dear Lord, eliminate my light.
And so I seek Your daily bread, the manna of our time,
I pray that soon Your day will come, for me a day sublime.

Tony A. Jay

The World

God made the world for you and me
He made the earth, the sky and sea
The sun, snow and refreshing rain
Animals that roam the plain.

He gave us day He gave us night
He gave us all the gift of sight
The blessing of a restful sleep
And all our sowing we may reap

The birds so graceful as they fly
Clouds float by in the sky
Starlight nights and sunny days
The waves that wash around our bays.

The trees in spring their leaves unfold
When autumn comes they turn to gold
Summer flowers fruits and berries
Apples, plums and sweet red cherries.

We came upon this earth for this
To live a life of peace and bliss
We must preserve and guard it all
If we fail the world will fall.

B. Z. Brown

Little Drummer Boy - Ringo Starr

As I fall asleep I look at his face
He makes the world a beautiful place.
In my dream my hero appears
It's Sergeant Pepper's Billy Shears.

Ringo is good, he's sweet and he's kind
A nicer fella you never could find
With stunning blue eyes and a gorgeous smile
To be with him I'd run a mile.

Standing immaculate and very cute
In his beloved Beatle Suit.
With his styled hair in a mop top
Ringo is the prince of pop.

Small of stature, a distinctive face
He's a credit to the human race.
Very handsome, more than the rest
Ringo Starr is simply the best.

Drummer, singer, man of parts
A record high within the charts.
Actor, film star - who to thank
Ringo's known for Thomas the tank.

Rachel Edwards

Samuel

I can feel his eyes watching me.
He stares through the thick, perspex tank
They put him in.
I smile at him, though I can't be sure
He sees me.
A wriggle; a blink,
He stares and sucks with sticky breath.
My hand rests on his warm cocoon,
His head like a round, furry ball.
I study him in every detail; every scratch; every bruise
Noted in my memory bank forever.
I love him very much.
I wonder if he loves me, or if I shall grow on him.
I know his smell instantly,
I recognize it; it is me.
My fears are in the future.
For now, I bask in my pleasure,
My joy, my relief.

Rosalind Gower

Angelic Faces of Dunblane

Angelic faces, set in your mind,
hearts just like flowers of the prettiest kind.
Laughter and giggles, they're sent from above,
they were put on this earth to cherish and love.
The anger, the pain, the loss and despair,
we all try to show how much we do care.
Explain or reason, that we can't do,
the feeling of loss is so real and so true.
Angelic faces, in our hearts they will stay,
and all we can do is to kneel and to pray.
Comfort from above is all we can hope,
support for the families, to help them to cope.
In God's arms they now rest, so sweet and so small,
and life just goes on in spite of it all.
Let's never forget their lives though so short,
nor the lessons from this that we have been taught.
Life is to cherish, memories are to keep,
whilst angelic faces in heaven go to sleep.

C. Douglas

Herbal Remedy

Outside, stiflingly hot!
Heat shimmering, heat festering,
Heat oozing up from cracks in
In the hard-baked ground.
The sun, a fire-ball
In a blazing sky that burns my eyes.
My lungs ache,
I can hardly breathe.
An oppressive numbness dulls my senses
As fatigue overwhelms me.
Inside, cooler, fresher;
Blinds down.
A twilight gloom descends,
Sympathetic and soothing;
But a strange aroma fills the air.
It is the tangy infusion
Of lemon balm, camomile and lime-blossom
That sharpens on my tongue.
For heat-exhaustion,
This is Mother Nature's best remedy!

Linda Bitvus

La Luna

Beckon me with your eyes and your body,
   I am yours with the night.
Together we succumb to the power of beauty.
Drug and woo me, O Dionysus,
Bind us close, swathed in mist, a multitude of stars line the sky.

Watch us dance. Drunk on good wine and life.
Spinning through the haze, touching the earth.
   How simple are you both,
   Lifting me breathless out of life into Living.

Susanna Laughton

Suffering

Eighteen, what age is that?
He was younger than me
No life at all he's had.
But war will not stop
They don't care about his life

The elements of war, that's all we are
Out here, cold, wet, mud up to our ankles
The shells come over
What's the use, we'll all die soon.

The men fall down like flies
The air we breathe, filled with blood, anger, suffering
But what for
Nothing we can do will stop it.
Nothing short of killing everybody.

To kill ourselves is suicide
To kill others is murder
To be killed is bravery
How does it work?
How can we live?
How?

C. Beardmore

Wealth

How do you define the word wealth, do you associate it with
   your health,
Or to you does this word money mean, are you posh and
   squeaky clean,
Too upper class for the likes of us, does this word wealth give
   you a buzz,
Do you live in the land of the rich, not like us down in the ditch.

To some along with wealth goes fame, to others we have only
   you to blame,
For the wrongful meaning of this word, wealthy rich people
   have you not heard,
For you the word wealth I will now define, you probably will
   not believe and decline
To accept my explanation but hear it you must, instead of
   your head, your heart you should trust.

Material possessions, riches do not make, money in fact
   makes life a piece of cake,
To appreciate your possessions first you must struggle, when
   you're born into money you are in a muddle,
But even if you're reared with a silver spoon, all the money in
   the world cannot buy the moon,
To the real plutocrat with his feet on the ground, money's of
   no importance true wealth he has found.

This is a gift for you to behold, all that shines is not gold,
So search your soul and proclaim wealth glorious, don't let
   money be victorious
Your children are your riches, love you abounds, fertile is the earth
   full of beauty - you it surrounds,
You do not need mountains of money but of grass, I have
   now defined the word wealth - alas.

Susan Lewandowski

A String of Rose Pearls

September wore her special dress for us:
her skirt of meadow green, fresh - laundered that morn
with dew, lay lush along the rippling corn,
deep cleaved, wind brushed. We listened to the chorus
that the larks sang, 'til evening, holding her breath
at day's delay, consoled its imminent death.
Inspired she flung her delicate pastel
talents across the sky, rich in aerial
splendour, - the autumn evening's lustrous mane
held high in tribute!
The sun, spraying rose pearl, entranced a lane
of clouds into a necklace for the sky.
The trees, no longer mute
rustled with arboreal views: an array
of colour resat, crowning September's day.

Richard Slinn

355

Time - The Healer?

'Tis said Time's the healer of all grief
How can this be my belief?
Without my man - lost and lonely
My true love, one and only.

He was my comfort day and night
My problems by him put to right,
Joys and sorrows shared until . . .
Home is now so hushed and still.

Will Time heal this deep ache?
He would have wished this for my sake -
Life to go on without too much sorrow
And look forward to a peaceful morrow.

Margaret Kilgour

"My Wild Heart"

Roam the island where time is free,
Hear the island calling me,
Come back my wild heart where you belong,
Where dreams reign free like curlew's song,
Come home my wild heart,
Come home.

My secret places you once did grace,
Bright summer sun upon your face,
You walked across my pastures green,
Contemplated, calm, serene,
Have I not waited here alone,
Come home my wild heart,
Come home.

In winter did I not provide,
A sheltered bay in which to hide,
To wait out the storms of life,
Protected here from pain and strife,
Do you not own my heart bar none,
Come home my wild heart,
Come home.

Kim Kilpatrick

New Dawn

Light reach out and fold me in your arms,
Heavy days, dark nights have passed,
Coming Spring the flowers open to reveal,
New colours falling o'er the land.

The Spirit lifts and smiles appear on lips,
The sombre Winter seems a long past dream,
Step out with new found life,
And hope is everywhere.

Each morning is a bonus to the soul,
A grateful heart that one is here,
Everlasting hope to dwell
The coming day still offers us a role,

Another new beginning rushes out to meet,
Each weary plodding foot,
Fresh skies and soft light breeze,
Oh wonder Light reach out.

R. Fraser

My Girl

Her face, beauty is a word not good enough to describe it,
Her brown eyes,
So lovely, So large, So bright.
They look into mine,
So deep, So loving.
Her heart,
So true, So pure, So giving.
She never complains, never argues.
Just loves me - for being me.
She lives her life always by my side.
So loyal, So faithful.
And I love her so much.
A better lady you'll never find,
YES you guessed it, it's my dog,
MADUSA, MY ONLY TRUE FRIEND.

Sisco

Deep Sea Diving

Young Herbert was ambitious, he knew what he'd like to be,
He'd read about it in his books, and seen it on T.V.
To be a deep sea diver going down to sunken ships,
He dreamt of finding treasure as he ate his fish and chips.

Next morning after breakfast, a plan he had in mind,
To try and get some scuba gear or something of the kind,
So he went around the village, all the people he did ask,
Till he got himself some flippers, a lifebelt and a mask.

Then he took apart the radiator standing in the hall,
And he made himself a snorkel from the drainpipe on the wall,
Then putting on his swimming trunks, and his dad's string vest
He strapped his weird contraption on with belts about his chest.

Then off he set to try a dive into the village pond,
And all the people followed him to see if they'd been conned,
He stood upon the edge awhile and then leapt in the air,
Then he landed in the water but there wasn't that much there.

Instead it was four feet of mud as there had been a drought,
So they went and got a shovel and they had to dig him out,
He smelt just like a sewer, so they didn't stay too long,
They just left him with his scuba gear, his lifebelt, and his pong.

A. R. Wheeler

My Little Man "Jack"

The kids, they bought you for Fathers' Day
He'll be company for you Dad while we're away
I was very ill and they all knew that
What else could they do for their poor old Dad

You were only very small
But God only knows, you knew it all
The tears, the suffering, the constant pain
You were there for me through the bitter strain

You were the best friend a man ever had
I even nicknamed you "My Little Man"
We'd go for a walk, you never left my side
I thought you'd be with me till the day I died.

But alas your life on earth was not to be
Four short months is all you lived to see
I could not understand why you had to go
For my Little Man Jack, I loved you so.

I never recovered when you had gone
I died myself Christmas Ninety-One
'Twas only then I understood it all,
When you were there waiting at Heavens' Door
God in His wisdom had saved you for me
So we'd be together for all eternity.

Margaret Hudson

Dog

When I was young, I had a little dog,
His name was Tigger, he was a faithful dog,
I used to take him out, for runs in the park,
He was always very happy, and used to bark, bark bark.

One day as he was running in the park,
I looked 'round quick, when I heard him bark,
He was running very quick towards another dog,
They were jumping and frolicking, over a log.

Every day we would go back to the park,
Tigger would hear the familiar bark,
Off he would go, running to the log,
To look for his little friend, who we called Dog,

One day when we got to the park.
Tigger was looking 'round for the familiar bark,
But as he went leaping and jumping to the log,
There wasn't any sign of his friend the dog.

His master told us in the park that day,
He walked up to the log, where Dog and Tigger used to play,
As he looked down, his dog looked far away,
He bent down to stroke him, and found he'd passed away.

Linda Marie Blackburn

Burcin

My life was going so wrong, I had forgotten how to trust
I thought men were there to hurt you, building barriers was a must.

Then you just walked into my life suddenly you were there
Even when I was awful you stayed around to care.

You never returned to Turkey, you stayed to give us a chance
You threw away your ticket and swept me into your arms.

We were married just three months later,
you proved everybody wrong
Two years on in married life, and our love is still as strong.

When I talk you listen, if I need support you're there
You always make me laugh so much and when I'm sad you care.

Some people think they have great wealth,
   we know we have much more
For the unconditional love we share, no one can ignore.

Throughout your life you lead many lives, but only one is ever
worth living
It's not always about receiving, it is what you are capable of giving.

In just two years my life has changed, fulfilled with things we do
I couldn't imagine spending life with anyone else but you.

When everything is said and done and my life draws to an end
I will always have the knowledge, that my husband was my best
friend.

Tanya Seyis

A Child Prays on Christmas Eve

A child prays on Christmas Eve,
Her faith is strong, she still believes,
But within her reach are the tears she keeps,
For those at war who bleed for peace.

She whispers softly, oh Lord of mine,
I pray to you for all mankind,
Look through the eyes of those who hide,
And let them feel the touch of Christ.

And she prays that her words,
Will be learnt by the people,
Everyone and everywhere,
And she prays that her words,
Will be heard for the people, anyone who needs a prayer.

Her faith is strong, she still believes,
A place exists where all are free,
Where the hungry eat and the lonely meet,
And the blind can watch their children sleep.

And she prays that her words,
Will be heard for the people,

Anyone who needs a prayer.

Tony Mottram

Children of Our Children Our Tonic

Kayleigh is one — A beautiful baby. Full of fun
   Her life has just begun.
Laura is two — Pretty and sweet and very neat.
   with so much to do.
Sean is four — Mischievous and cute
   Who could ask for more.
David is five — He'll soon melt the girls' hearts
   with his lovely brown eyes — so alive.
Leon and Robert are seven — Football mad. Gentle giants
   caring and sharing.
   Two angels from heaven.
Antonio is ten — Dark and handsome.
   Nearly as tall as the men.

   Bonny beautiful brilliant and bright
     A great delight.
     Our grandchildren.

   By the way. Number eight is on the way
     What more can we say
     Hip. Hip. Hooray.

Marjorie Bevan

Brother John

Fetch out no shroud, for Johnny who laughed aloud,
His mum called him a madcap, when he was a kid at school.
The army made him a Redcap, he was nobody's fool.
Forget all your sorrow, remember old "TOJO",
a name he was christened, by workmates who listened.
To his tales that were many, but never a bore,
of his days spent in Changi in old Singapore,
The beach at Penang, where often he swam,
The splendour of Taj Mahal, and the love of a Chinese gal,
The troopship back home, to the mum he adored,
With his cockatoo bird, and his Samurai sword.
His laughter lives on, through birds and their song.
His memory remains, in quiet country lanes,
So as we grow older, remember with joy.
His mum's little soldier, Johnny the boy.

W. J. Cole

The Price of Loving

I hurry through the city streets, I see him sitting there,
His placard reads, "I'm homeless", I ponder, 'Do I care'?
His plight may tug my heartstrings and yet I pass him by,
The cynic says I must not stay, love's rule does not apply.
Take notice of the media, the M.P. and the like
Who from a cosy office cry, "he should get on his bike",
"It's only daylight robbery and fools will pay the price,"
I think about the One who took a thief to Paradise.

It's easy to ignore him, carry on for no-one sees,
What do I mean when I take bread and wine upon my knees?
I wander back and leave my coin, now call it what you will,
A sop to salve my conscience, a sugar coated pill.
In Christ he is my brother, the Christ who says to me
"Who so bestows his arms feeds three, himself, his hungering
   neighbour and Me."
And should the sceptics prove me wrong to heed a vagrant's call,
I only staked a measly coin, the Saviour pledged His all.

Norah Wright

For My Dad

Life has lost one of the best.
Hurt and pain are left for the rest.
A perfect Husband and a dad.
Everyone wishes they had.
His sudden death has left a lot of people sad.
We ask ourselves why we were
Never given the chance to say goodbye.
Life is just so unfair.
To take away a man who had so much love to share.
He'll always be with us in our heart's
Even though our life's are now apart.

Suzanne Milligan

Exmoor

Purple, green and striking gold
Hypnosis reigns, control you hold
Peace, for me a silence clear
Oh Exmoor I shall just stay here

The world is fast, the world is tough
But you are made of tougher stuff
The wind, it buffs and batters me
Oh Exmoor, peaceful by the sea.

While wooded paths close in on me
Expanse of nothing, raging sea
Cliffs dramatic, sheer and bleak
Oh Exmoor, serenity I seek.

When all is sad and lonely
To you I come and share
Your widespread comfort that you give
Oh Exmoor, rugged bare.

We rush on in a frenzied state
Frustration, anger foams
When all explodes through man's mistake
Oh Exmoor be my home.

T. Eames

Going to the Coast

Going to the coast?
I had hardly noticed you were a sailor.
Did you enjoy the ride?
I should have asked,
But it all comes around so quick, I forget.
I wish I came.
But you told me it would be alright.
And that you're o.k.
Then you came on so strong,
Drinking Spanish wine, smoking French cigarettes.
We should never have met.

Your visit down south was supposed to be good.
Now the rust red scabs will never go,
Splinters, poison, unsteady fingers.
You're still telling me you're o.k.
I hardly notice when you are now.
The corner shop is pleased,
With their sales of brandy and cigarettes
I hoped the whiplash broke your back (cracked a shell)
Let it all ooze out on the motorway with the glass,
    and rusty water.

Neil A. Young

Untitled

The ferry arrives, it looks quite full
I hope the passengers will stay in Hull.
But off they come to take a walk
To get the transport to take them to York.
Why they go there is a mystery.
Hull is also steeped in history.
There's Wilberforce house,
the Old Town too,
And that little window King John peeped through.
There's William the 3rd and of course his beautiful horse.
Down white Friargate, to see Beverly Gate
And the Humber Bridge,
which came too late

Lilian M. Fowler

House for Sale

Two old iron gates led the way in.
I just wandered in entranced.
A stream ran quietly through the grounds
Causing parts of the land to be marshy and damp.
Beyond were trees, grass and a small well - a wishing well? - I wished!
To the side of the house was a path and beyond it grass
And masses of daffodils - living where they would -
Would that I too, could live as the daffodils I would live with
    them there . . .
Behind this fairy castle lay paths and woodland,
And to the side, a mound of grass-covered earth
Said to have been a burial ground of long ago.
Standing on the mound I looked across at the sea,
And wondered who was buried beneath my feet . . .
Wondering, too, where my body would be buried
I had a fleeting wish that it should be buried down among the
    daffodils.

Mary Betchetti

A Day in My Life

I hustle and bustle worry and frown
I keep on working till the sun goes down
The guests need breakfast, and look for a chat
The dogs are curled up on the fireside mat
There's the beds to change - and the rooms to do
There's the washing - then the ironing too
Telephone to answer - the dinner to cook
Never a spare moment to read a book.
I knit in the evenings and watch T.V.
And my husband makes me a nice cup of tea,
There's letters to write - and the bills to pay
Just some of the things that make up my day,
It's then off to bed for a well-earned rest
And so many things still left unsaid.

B. E. Gillan

Channel Firing

The ground started to shake, my coffin shook,
I rose from my grave to take a look,
At what was going on, and to my dismay,
I thought it was judgement day.
The noises got louder, that's all I could hear,
I could feel my happiness turning to fear.
I was dead, so it didn't matter,
As the noises got louder, windows started to shatter.
The explosion had awakened the tired hounds,
And the terrified worms drew back in their mounds,
The little mouse dropped her altar-crumb,
As she was scared by the banging of the guns.

Tracey Dodd

The Working Dog

She lays there so peacefully
Her working days are done,
Through her mind go thoughts of sheep
And all the miles she's run.
Her coat a little shaggy
And nose a little dry.
Her young days have long gone passed
but she will always try.
She moves a little slower now
Her eyes grow dim with time.
I sometimes sit and wonder
How much longer she'll be mine.
In all the days we walked the fields she followed every step.
Now her working days are done I keep her as my pet.
I know she longs to be out there when I tend the sheep.
I'm sure she dreams she is with me even in her sleep.
A faithful friend a working dog no better could I find.
I know that when her days are done she'll never leave my mind.
If dogs go to heaven I know that she will be.
Writing at the gate my faithful friend to always be with me.

R. J. Sandom

My Garden

My garden is the love of my life
Here I wander, there's no trouble or strife
I tell these plants, hurry up, or you'll get the sack
There's one good thing, they never answer back.

The yellow broom, says to the white broom,
Oh, here's the woman with her shears,
She snirs and snips all over my head,
Till I'm reduced to tears.

Don't be sad says the white broom,
You know your top was getting old,
But very soon, you'll be a mass of bloom,
Shining bright like a piece of gold.

The weeds must like me, they never go away,
I pull them out and say, be on your way,
But I can almost hear them say.
We're not going we're here to stay.

E. McLellan

I Watched at the Window

I watched at the window as you went away,
Hoping that you would be back the next day,
You said that your visit was only routine,
And if you were frightened, you'd left it unseen.
I stayed there for hours, looking out at the lawn
And the tree which was planted the day you were born,
You cared for that tree every day of your life;
It was there that we stood when I made you my wife.
Then they called me to say you had died in your sleep
And pain filled my heart as I started to weep;
I cried 'til my eyes felt as if they would burn -
My belovéd was gone and would never return.
Now I stay by the window and patiently wait
While I muse on the cruel caprices of Fate,
And I gaze at the tree through the wind and the rain
As I wait for the day I'll be with you again.

Mark A. Cooper

Storm Clouds

Dark storm clouds develop as I gaze out to sea.
Huge breakers rise and fall, thundering over the
    pebbles, spewing over the rocks,
Momentarily drowning my troubled mind.
The biting winds howls and I cocoon myself comfortingly
    in the warmth of my coat.
A seagull flies overhead, its raucous cries startle me.

It is lonely, here, no solace offered.
The sea, the elements are unrelenting.
A heavy crack of thunder erupts. Fork lightning
Fork lightning discharges across the menacing
sky, striking out as if in anger.
Then rain follows, ceaselessly beating down
    savagely until I am drenched and numb with cold.

The wind has subsided now.
At last the sea is calm and crystal clear.
Blue skies are emerging from the cloud, while birds
    bob contentedly on the water.
Determinedly the sun peeps through the dispersing clouds
    and I feel the reassuring warmth as the sun bursts forth,
    uplifting me, driving the angry black clouds away.
I see the beautiful unbroken horizon stretching optimistically ahead.

Roberta Stanley

The Heroin Hole (For Stewpot)

Heroin's broken the heart of my mother,
Heroin's hooked my little brother
Heroin's turned him into a thief,
Heroin's causing all of us grief.

The doctors put him on methadone,
The answer is not here,
It only prolongs his agony,
His sadness and desperate fear,
Leaving him lost and empty,
Stealing from us his identity.

He can't be trusted, he's lost control,
As he falls deeper into the heroin hole,
Where's the solution, how do we cope,
How can we return to him, all his lost hope,
We cannot stand by and leave him to cry,
My fear if we leave him, is he'll give up and die.

I don't want this worry on my mother's head,
It'll cause the cancers return,
I don't want it to end in one of them dead,
There must be an answer or something to learn.

Marcia L. Wren

The Proposal

She's waiting for him in the cafe.
He's ten minutes late already.
How should she tell him?
What if he's already guessed?

She thinks back to when they first met,
bumping into each other, so corny.
She laughs a little to herself.
The door opens and in he walks.

He shakes the cold snow from his coat
and see's her sat in the corner.
He thinks to himself how lovely she looks
and wonders what could be so important.

He walks over to where she is sitting
and apologizes for being so late.
He orders two cups of coffee and then
sits across the table from her.

She gazes straight into his eyes.
Small tears form in the corner of hers.
He starts to get nervous and lowers his gaze.
"Will you marry me"? she smiles.

Sharon Conroy

Heroes

Lying there in trenches deep,
Horrific nightmares invade your sleep.
Will you wake or lie there still,
A ghostly presence they cannot kill.

You will go on, you know you must,
This sheer brutality, it's never just.
Only last night you saw him fall,
A mate, a friend, proud and tall.

What is left but a watery grave,
Or a rough hewn cross and a final wave.
No time to bow your head in prayer,
Asking God was it fair.

The roaring thunder of enemy fire,
Will it ever cease, ever tire.
Will anyone hear as you rush over the top,
Your screams of terror as in your tracks you stop.

With a mournful sigh, a final breath,
You relinquish life to a heroes death.
You were so young, you'd seen no life,
No babe in arms or a loving wife.

P. A. Griffiths

Reflection

Ancient mirror on the wall
    How dare you show me such a face
Has time laid its dust on you or me
    A quick wipe over and I see those faults are mine.

With some effort I recall
    When every blemish caused me pain
And long hours were spent in agony
    Until the bloom was restored again, and confidence mine.

It was unnecessary to overhaul
    What nature had bestowed with grace
But the game was played alluringly
    With rules to keep us in our place and to toe the line.

Then fashion's dictates began to pall
    As life's demands increased in pace
And from all sides some emergency
    That I must myself efface in others' time.

So I will leave you up on the wall
    For I cannot hold you to blame
For showing that we both reflect
    What life has sketched inevitably upon this face of mine.

D. M. Smith

The Stillness of Time

When I saw you laying there, all I could do was stare.
I did not know what to do, was it really you.
I could not talk and I could not cry, all I could do was wonder why!
When I held your hand I could not understand.

I felt so helpless and very sad, I thought the anger would
    drive me mad.
Then the strain turned to pain and I wondered would I ever
    see you again?
Would you, see, talk, would you ever walk?
Would you laugh, would you cry, will you live or die?

Then I started to cry and I knew why, that was very clear.
You are so very dear.
My heart was heavy and my eyes were blue.
I cried so many tears at the thought of losing you.
I asked you to stay, please, please don't drift away,
    don't drift away.

When you squeezed my hand.
I knew you heard and could understand.
All I could do was pray, so thankful for each new day.
Your returning, it may take awhile.
How I love to see your smile.

Margaret Fraiel

Sonnet for a Loved One

How shall I tell thee of my fond esteem?
How shall I say and not offend thy taste?
Thou art of dreams, made real by some neat scheme
To make mine heart beat with uncommon haste
How cans't thou know my feelings pure and true?
What earnest deeds will prove a love not base?
Though should I try too hard thine heart to woo
I'll seek forgiveness in thy smiling face
For there within the sweetness of thine eyes
Are messages of tenderness and joy
That rouse in me such wonderful surprise
There are no words that I can then employ
   Twin souls in love's sweet chains are ne'er apart
   Not while between the two beats just one heart

Roger N. Waring

Time

If you look around you are sure to see
How interesting life can be.
The tiny flowers at your feet,
A wondrous sight your eyes to greet.
Spare a little time to stop and share,
This wonderful world beyond compare.

Walk down a quiet country path,
Reflect a little in the past.
That old grey church for years has stood,
Long before your childhood.
It's watched the seasons come and go,
Heard tears of joy and tales of woe.

Spare a little time, don't rush away,
A quiet moment spent each day,
Is worth a lot, when you compare,
The strife and misery everywhere.

Valerie M. Helliar

My Dreams

At night I dream a thousand things
How it would feel to fly with wings,
What it would be like to bear a child
And bring it up through winters mild

Me, a rock star up on stage
Earning amazing amounts of wage.
Friends, and people that I've never seen
Exciting new places where I've never been.

Sometimes I dream that danger's near
Of death and other things I fear.
I dream of people cruel and mean
Of horror movies I've just seen.

These are the things that I into leap
When I drop my eyelids and go to sleep
And when I wake up in the morn of next day
My dreams flash back and then just slip away.

Katie Nial

My Ambition

An ambition is a funny thing,
I always wanted to dance and sing.
My chance came, I couldn't wait,
But 'oh' I didn't realize my fate.
As I stood in the wings, I didn't feel so bad,
But as I walked on stage; I thought, "I must be mad".
My body went stiff, my legs like jellies,
Instead of tap shoes on my feet, they felt like wellies.
The music started, my heart did race,
I had a painted smile upon my face
I looked into the audience and thought,
"Oh my God they're all looking at me".
So I tried to hide at the back, hoping they wouldn't see.
The routine and the music seemed to last forever.
But I'd fulfilled my ambition, would I do it again
No Never!

C. M. Richardson

Camden Market in the Rain

Our waste adorns the gutters and clutters the High Street
Hypodermic syringes crunching beneath our feet
Remnants of the night before - gig, rave, club or party -
Cigarette butts and old beer cans, as far as one can see.

Dripping flooding awnings, tassels soggy in the rain
The colours run and smudge, tie dye will never be the same
Damp and tatty posters, discount if you buy four
And one Big Issue seller is braving the downpour.

We queue in muddy puddles for a doughy pizza slice
Or cold vegetable curry with a scattering of rice
Crispy caramel peanuts, tangy fresh orange juice
Sweet iced buns and chocolate cake, and other fresh produce.

The choking clouds of incense prevail ad nauseam
Black Coconut and Love Supreme, White Musk and Opium
Music blaring from the shops, pubs scattered here and there
Bootleg CDs and demo tapes, plus singles now so rare.

Jewellery at every turn, miles of leather cord -
Friendship bracelets, beads and strings, and silver shapes galore
Coloured candles, big and small, and scented oil lamps
And in the side streets, in the wet, the beggars and the tramps.

Sarah Archibald

It Makes You Wonder

The wind out there is blowing so wild.
I better go and find that child.
What's that noise, did I hear a cry?
Or is it the birds just flying by?

Listen, did you hear that noise again?
It sounds like someone is in pain.
Who opened that door? No, not me.
Perhaps it was my eyes playing tricks maybe.

Where's she gone I can't find her.
I saw her go that way I'm sure.
Wait what's that glowing over there.
I think that could be my little girl, Clare.

As I approach I'm sure I see a shadow move away.
Then she says my grandad came to see me to-day.
So how can you tell her he's not around any more.
Maybe it wasn't my eyes playing tricks on me before.

She says she even saw Lucy, her dog.
No you must be seeing things as there's a lot of fog.
So what do we believe I'll leave that to you.
It is something that needs to be thought through.

K. Buckley

I Love You

When I was young and in my teens
I came to Ulster for the Queen
A few days later I met a girl
She was so beautiful. Just like a pearl.

It wasn't long but very soon
I told her I loved her, just like the moon
She means the world to me and my heart.
I would be sad if we fell apart.

I go away for a week a two
But all I want is to be with you.
When I come back seeing you there
All I know is how much I care.

Being away tears me apart
If you ever left me, it would break my heart.
Twelve months is not far away
It's not very long till our special day.

So with this poem, I've written for you
I want you to know, I only love you
But most of all, with this last line,
I hope and pray, you're forever mine.

Pte Hayes

Haven't I Ever Told You . . .

Haven't I ever told you,
How much I love you.
Haven't I ever told you,
How much you mean to me.
But now it's too late;
Now that you are gone.
I guess you will never know
That all I've ever wanted is you.
My love for you is true.
It grows stronger and stronger each day
Even though you're miles away.
I will always be here for you
And I will always love you so,
More than you could ever know.
You will always be here in my heart,
And my thoughts,
Because you're the only one
I've ever wanted.

Lisa Cheesman

Untitled

I saw God! In a child who played by the sea
I saw God! In a mother with a baby at her knee
I saw God! In a crowd as the crowd went wild
I saw God! In a woman swollen with child
I saw God! In a fish which leaped from a lake
I saw God! In a kiss but for gods sake
God see me

Don Davidson

Poetry Competition

Poetry Competition, I read
How much? I smile
A poet not I
Win not I
But wait why not I?

A poet a poet yes I will become
A pen let me get hold of
A sheet of paper I shall fetch
At a table I shall sit for that where poets sit
And write the winning entry that the judges will all pick.

Write pen write, make your mark upon this sheet
Write pen write, but what shall it write?
Tell it what to write, tell it
Anything! Anything! Please do write
For a winner of the poetry competition I long to be.

Another competition begins in April I read
Yes by then I shall have it
You ask "What is it you shall have?"
I laugh "The prize money of course"
I won you see.

Meena Mehan

"A Day at the Seaside"

What a sunny day! And a blue sky - My!
How they brighten up my eyes
Gone are my cares - and woe
"It makes me think of holidays and where I'll go"
Should I go to a far off land?
"Basking by the sea" lying on silver sand - or
"Should I take a cruise"?
On a luxury ship - and me, dining at the Captain's table
Fancy me - in an evening gown - and it trimmed with sable

Dreams - that's all, just dreams - they're not for me
Lucky am I with a day trip by the sea
Going on a local bus -
With folks I know, they don't make a fuss
Just a sing along as we come home
All I will buy - just a stick of rock - maybe a sugar gnome
What a day we'll have - for me - it's holidays over
Then someone will shout - "don't forget the driver"
Not bad - for my holiday, it cost about a fiver

Leslie F. Dukes

Field of Dreams

To find a field it is my dream
However impossible it may seem.
   Not just a field anywhere,
But somewhere special for me to share,
   My every thought, be it good or bad
When I'm happy or very sad.
   My own green pastured paradise,
   Where urban life I'd sacrifice.
   Let there be storm, rain or hail,
I know my dream field would not fail,
   To fill me with the gifts I lack,
And lift this burden from my back,
   I'd go there angry with feelings of hate,
And feel them all disintegrate,
   When feeling hurt or all alone,
I'd just make for my heavenly home,
   The power would lift me to the highest height,
Soak up the power from that wondrous sight.
   The birds would whistle songs to me,
"Go on and be happy you too can be free"
I'll keep on searching, no matter how hard it seems,
   Until I find my field of dreams.

Lesley Anne Rutter

"The Love of Kintyre"

In Memory of Robin

White stone cottages in groups of four,
   huddled together on the craggy shore.
Hornéd sheep and goats, stand or lie,
   chewing, grazing, I ask not why.
In the distance on the pebbled sand,
   red shanks nest where they land.
Seaweed draped over driftwood bare,
   groups of seals sleep or stare.
The cutting wind blows the sand in dunes,
   whilst sea gulls call their screeching tunes.
Clinker built fishing boats with masts so high,
   pierce the blue tumultuous sky.
Multi-coloured fishing nets dry in the sun,
   after a hard day's work is done.
Coniferous forests where buzzards soar,
   spread behind the windy shore.
Electricity pylons claw the ground,
   carrying forth their power and sound.
Whistling wind through wires above,
   over this Scottish land we love.

Michael John Reid Vowles

Time Stood Still

One evening in springtime some years ago,
I lay on my bed gazing at the scene far below,
The moon in its splendour shed its silvery light,
Turning everything mysterious, rocks, sea, and a pathway so bright.

As I lay there listening to the soft gentle breeze,
The sounds of the sea murmuring, the wind in the trees,
There arose a sound, so beautiful to hear,
Trills of birds singing, so lovely, so sweet to the ear.

I arose crept to the balcony overlooking the shore,
Stood there enchanted, soaking in the sound, a moment to adore,
Time stood still, heaven came down to earth,
Even the Angels listened, a moment when God's love gave new birth

I will never forget that moment of time,
It's etched on my memory that song so divine,
The tiny brown birds are nightingales they say,
Maybe I will hear them again, I do hope so one day.

I feel so sad, this place is no more,
You see this coastline has been destroyed by war,
The little brown birds have no doubt flown away,
Dubrovnik is not a safe place to stay.

J. M. Collinson

Brown Bird

Walking down the lane one day in the early Spring
I came upon a brown bird half-alive, unable to sing.

He'd fallen from a nest up high, upon the ground been left to die,
His place been taken by another's chick, his mother a new babe
by a trick.

I picked him up the tree to climb but found it was too steep,
And so the brown bird came with me to my home to sleep.

Material small wrapped 'round and 'round into a wall of warmth
and comfort for my visitor's needs,
And warm milk to give him for his feeds.

From strength to strength he grew each day,
Until the Spring came 'round once more - and then my brown bird
flew away to find his own front door.

Ros Street

Take More Care

It's not my fault that I'm in this mess.
I didn't want to be here.
You've given me more, but also less
I can't talk, but can shed a tear.

I have taken no drugs,
nor any needle to share.
Learn from me,
Take more care.

A little thought, a little protection.
I could have been born without infection.

As it is,
I will only live a short while.
But at least,
I will be able to smile.

My future has been made for me.
I have no choice.
You can. Be protected,
and save any more like me.

D. R. Miles

Jealousy

When the green-eyed monster rears its ugly head,
I can't help it, I just see red,
To feel hatred, anger, upset and fear,
It hurts so much, I shred a silent tear.
It's such a burden on your shoulder,
Under the surface, just waiting to smoulder.
Then the green-eyed monster rears its ugly head,
I can't help it, I just see red.
The fire is burning, I'm fiery and wild,
I go mad, and act like a child.
It can make you sad, it can make you blue,
So you have to control it, before it controls you.
And if you let it, it will tear you apart,
So be sure to be rid of it right from the start.
I can't help it, I just see red,
When the green-eyed monster rears its ugly head.

J. G. Merritt

Missing You

I'll always love you for the rest of my life,
I can't live without you no matter how I try,
You'll always be with me wherever I go,
No one can love you as much as you know,
We maybe apart, but our love will be there,
Growing, getting stronger, a bond that we share,
A Closeness of warmth the heartache and pain,
Missing you like crazy, to be in your arms again,
I'll close my eyes and pretend you're there,
besides me always that closeness we share,
Caressing, Kissing arms wrapped up so tight,
Close to my body all Day and all Night,
See I'll never let you go,
You're in my life, my Dreams forever,
Darling I love you so.

T. J. Madgwick

My Diet

I'm full of good intentions,
I can go a day or two,
And then . . . my tummy starts to rumble
At the sight of all that food.
I've tried so many times before
Determined I must be,
To reach that special target
And have a slimmer me.
But as I'm walking past the shop
I quickly glance inside
at all those creamy cakes
Just calling me to buy.
Can I resist temptation,
Somehow I think I won't,
my mind is overtaken
By the longing for a taste,
I never stop and think about
my ever thickening waist.
well I suppose it's the price I have to pay.
Oh! Well never mind, perhaps another day.

Valerie Hall

A Thought . . .

My darling, consider this . . .
I miss you terribly,
Funny, isn't it?
When you are near
And we're busy about our tasks,
We'll sometimes go for hours
With just a quick smile, or a kiss,
And then go back to our own worlds.
But, when I'm away from you,
It's like I suddenly awaken
And my right arm is gone.
I may not go to bed thinking about my arm,
But when it's gone . . .

S. M. Lake

Untitled

The sunlight on the water casts dancing patterns through the shutters,
He lies in bed, with eyes unseeing the wondrous dancing and only mutters.
He sees things we cannot see. He talks, to whom? We do not know.
For eight long years he has bravely fought the foe.
My father lying there fights on against the time for him to go.
But death has almost had his game and is ready for the final blow.
He's weaker now, his time with us grows shorter.
His eyes stare blankly, the talking is inside his head.
The conscious times grow shorter.
And death waiting in the wings, sees the pain and suffering.
And we pray that God will show His mercy,
And that he will reach that far, far better place
To which we all must go.

Peter Trumble

Here's to the Lassies O'Neilston

Here's to the lassies with yon bonnie faces
Here's to the lassies with curves in the right places
Here's to their kindness, their wisdom, their brains
Here's to them for having the weans.

Here's to the lassies with flowing locks
Here's to the lass who'll wash my socks
Here's to their courage, their strength, their skill
Here's to the lassies who pay the bill.

Here's to the lassies both shy and bold
Here's to the lassies I long to hold
Here's to their eyes that sparkle and glow
Here's to the lassies I've yet to know.

Here's to the lassies who would sit on my knee
Here's to the lassies who put up with me
Here's to the lassies big and small
Here's to the lassies I love you all.

William Beatts

Deadly Pleasure

I can make you happy
I can make you cry,
I'm the most powerful force in this life.

I can make you high,
I can make you low,
Without me it's hard to survive.

The rich adore me
The poor desire me.
Often I cause jealousy and hatred,
Sometimes loss of lives.

When you befriend me
You can't live without me
I control the soul and mind.

I am more addictive than any drug
And will be until the end of time.
To some I am greater than deity
More deadly than the cobra

But when you die,
I cannot buy you another soul.
    Ruth Sidman

Fire Poem

The match is lit
I come to life
A flame of flickering orange light
I burn the paper, light the wood
To catch the coals
To heat the souls
That wander in from far and near
To see my embers burning clear

A bucket full of coal to burn
Is thrown on me to keep me in
My smoke grows thick and clogs the air
As I go up the chimney stair
The open top, the blue sky looming
Far away my smoke goes zooming

I clear the rooftops
Pass the clouds
Disperse in rays of sunlight bright
Then to darkness of the night
Gone forever, never to return
I wish I'd just been left to burn!
    Lyndsey Derry

Life

As I sit here in this room,
I could think of doom and gloom,
Of all the things that have happened in the past,
The timescale could be very vast.

There've been times when my feeling were high,
But also many times when I have had to sigh,
There have been many lows,
But it's best to look at the times that make you glow.

We all have our ups and downs,
When we think life is just one long frown,
But no!
Forward is the only way to go.

You have to think positive,
What a wonderful life we have to live,
Every now and again we are put to the test,
But with faith and strength your life will be the best!

And as I sit here in this room,
There are no thoughts of doom or gloom,
Just how honoured I've been to be given a slice,
Of sweet precious LIFE!
    G. Walsh

A Mother's Bond!

They wouldn't let me see him,
I couldn't see my son!
"Just let me be with Tony!
You HAVE to, I'm his Mum!"
They took us into Resuss.
And pulled the curtains back,
I felt my senses reeling
And I felt my raw nerves crack!
"I'm going Mum . . . " I heard him say . . .
"NO TONY! Please don't go!"
"There's NO heartbeat." The doctors said.
"Don't tell me that! - I KNOW!"
He'd waited just to hear my voice,
A restless soul, that lingers . . .
I felt him blowing through my hair
And slipping through my fingers . . .
A Mother's bond can only stretch,
A Mother's Love can't die!
So now I sit and dream of you
And ask myself . . . BUT WHY?
    Mandy Aitken

Generations

When you were but a baby,
I cradled you in my arms,
And I smiled as your newborn eyes, full of wonder,
Studied my face, starting their quest for understanding.

When you were only a little child,
I played with you,
And as I played the fool, you laughed, your innocent laugh,
There was never a more magical sound.

When you were still a child, I walked with you,
And when you tired, I lifted and carried you,
To bring you safely home, once more.

And as you continued to grow, I watched over you,
And I helped to teach and guide you, showing you the way,
Sharing my knowledge, experience and self with you.

So please remember me,
Though I can no longer be with you,
For, although of separate generations, we once travelled
life's roads together,
I was once a part of your life, and you were a wonderful
part of mine.
    Keith McClearn

"Missing You"

I never felt the warm touch, which triggers the fear,
I never knew what love really meant, until here,
I never thought I could be the one to feel
the tingles in my feet, and redness in my ears,
I never thought I would miss someone so severe,
I never imagined myself to be attached to anyone
so lovingly and dear,
I can't wait to see him, when he comes back here,
That's the time my life would be fulfilled with happiness
and my eyes with tears!
    Marieh Akbarzadeh

With Love, For Life

As the days go by and the years accumulate,
I never regret choosing you, my soul mate,
As the feelings mature, growing daily stronger,
Others can only watch, wait and wonder,
In this maddening world, how on earth did we find,
Two separate people, with one blended mind,
Individuals in thought, taste and expression,
Yet still seen as one from every other dimension,
It might not be said, it sometimes won't show,
But your the strength that I need to help me to grow,
You're the roots to my tree, the path up the mountain,
The one who'll support me when others are doubting,
In sickness and in health, even death will not part,
You'll always be sacred, adored by my heart.
    Nicola Burgess

Shattered Dreams

I didn't ask for love but you gave it to me
I didn't ask for dreams but they followed
I didn't ask for promises and hopes of better living
I didn't ask for anything but still you kept on giving
And now I ask myself
Can love really be true?
What I mean to say is
Was it love?
This thing between me and you
When I accepted you
Or should I say loved you
You threw it in my face
You watched me bury my pride and let my heart give chase
I thought once that two people were meant for each other
And when I loved you, you would love me
Oh! What a fool I must have been to let you bring such misery
I didn't ask for love, I didn't ask for emptiness
I gave no cause for you to leave and shatter dreams of hopefulness
But now I'll live without you and hope true love will come
Fulfil my shattered dreams and let me live to love again

Odette Short

Backstreet Lady

I met a sleazy lady in some backstreet place
I don't remember her name let alone her face
but she was pretty in a common sort of way
make-up plastered inches thick in fashionable array
to attract young men make old men ogle
women jealous and shy men boggle
tough men tut barmen mutter
strong men show off and meek men stutter
fat men thinner thin men fatter
bold men weak and coy men matter

She viewed them all with her simple smile
then turned to me who all the while
had been taking no notice instead writing this poem
curiosity killed her and so she came over
read what I'd written and kissing my lips
asked me for business at ten dollars plus tips.

Martin Boyce

A Ray of Hope?

I spend my days wishing and hoping for a job,
I spend my nights praying, just praying to God.
That in His great mercy He will find me a place
As only God can find me and each of us our own space.

I have toiled all my life to bring food to our home,
I have tried all my life to keep hope in our home.
In my heart in my home I keep hope and love,
With the help and protection of my Saviour above.

Though still unemployed I struggle on.
Awaiting that call saying you're taken on.
My faith and my dreams will again be restored.
And I will toil on to the end of the road.

Lucy O'Boyle

Hope

As I was slowly passing through Belfast Town.
I stood aghast, as I looked around,
Those lovely buildings that once stood there,
Where now in ruins, their dead eyes stare.

Along the street a young soldier lay,
As I lifted his head. I heard him say.
I came to your country to help keep the peace.
'Cause I wanted to help you, I die in your streets.
Tell my mum, my dad, my friends and my all.

That to help you poor Irish I have fought and did fall.
As tears stung my eyes, my heart it did break.
Oh foolish young people awake, Oh awake.
Forget about guns and bullets and bombs
Start putting things right, and forget other's wrongs.

Sarah Dunn

The Unborn

All is dark for I cannot see,
   I float on a gentle tide
Anchored safe from buffet and harm
   On my Sea of Tranquillity.

Time has passed without knowing
   Lying here in blissful content
Nurtured by some force that is part of me
   And I part of it whate'er it be.

I sway in gentle rhythm
   To movement that comes from without,
   I too feel the wonder of movement
That I can now make from within.

I grow restive with impatience
   For I feel the hour draws near
   For me to find a true awakening
When sounds take on a mortal shape.

   'Tis then at long last I shall see
   That affinity which sustained my life
And know the inner bond that joined us
   Will, unbroken, remain forever.

H. G. Kendrick

Nasal Exploration

Dad used to say "Your head'll cave in".
I kept on picking my nose with a grin.
Face twisted and contorted like someone insane,
I'd be pushing so hard it was hurting my brain.

Extracting my finger with all of my might,
I examine the glistening blob with delight.
Without hesitation I make up my mind,
And into my mouth put this marvellous find.

That's one nostril clear, another to go,
By now my nose is all of a glow.
Picking away a bit at a time,
Loosening bits like coal from a mine.

Sometimes a finger or maybe a thumb,
Picking away to get the job done.
Turning my back so no-one can see,
Why can't parents just let me be?

Leave me alone I'm doing no harm,
It's all part of my boyish charm.
But when I grow up to be a man,
I'll still pick my nose whenever I can.

K. N. Senior

The Healer

I know a young heart, in great pain,
I know a young soul, sorely bruised,
I know a young mind, so alone,
Unhappy, afraid, and confused.

Like a wild fawn caught in a snare
Fighting against hands that can save
Not knowing those hands love and care
Not able to trust and believe.

My dear young friend has lost her way
And thinks no one can understand
In her dark night there is no day.
I do wish she would take my hand.

Then I would lead her to the one
Who knows about her every need
He is an arm to lean upon
His tender hand heals hearts that bleed.

His voice comes to the listening ear,
Come weary one, come unto me.
I'll give you peace, remove your fear.
I'll take your burden, set you free.

J. M. Fleming

Dried Away

As I stared into the face of the one I loved,
I noticed a frown which I had never seen before
I saw in him hate and anger which I thought only
the rest of the world could possess.
To me he was like a stream of pure water,
which splashed against my naked body, as the
blazing furnace of the sun dried away my tears.
When he held me in his arms, the doors of life
closed and a virtual reality began.
But now it's dead, burnt in the teeth of saturn,
he lived for desire and fought against love while
torturing mine.
As he holds me in his arms, I know I can't forgive
because the stream I had once loved has dried away.

Katharine M. Williams

Always Wonder

What could have been will never be,
   I often wonder what could have been.
What you and your sister would have been
   like together.
   To watch you play, be happy and gay.
I bet you would have been so close,
   but you will never know each other.
I hope one day, I'll understand and learn to
   live with what I could have had in my hand.
To deny your sister of ever loving you,
   was the worst thing a human could do.
I will always have two children,
   Faith the first and you the second.
I know I'm still very young,
   but a mother should do no wrong.
You were a miracle and a shock,
   but please remember, I really love you,
      and wish you could have been born.
Sorry

E. H. Cooper

Returning Home

The snow underfoot was crisp and stark
I pasted the graveyard in shadows of dark,
The feeling came, slow and sure
The feeling was terror, cold and pure.

They'd warned me with horror alive in their eyes
So real and frightening it could not be lies,
The noise came soft, barely a whisper at first
Then so loud I thought my head would burst.

I realized the unearthly sounds were my own
Screams, now in exhaustion reduced to a moan.
Running through bushes that clawed at my face.
Feeling the fear gain at un-natural pace.

The moon broke through cloud to give guiding light
Familiar the river, at last home was in sight.
I crossed, relief as I saw my lair
My two young cubs, still safely there.

Patricia Henrick

Thoughts of a Police Horse

In tranquil scene with little sound,
I quietly stand and look around,
Lightly held, on gentle rein,
I love mankind, that's very plain.

A different scene, the noise of battle,
From rioting mob the missiles rattle,
I'm hit and kicked in a wild attack,
By Jove, I'd like to kick them back.

In stable now, I eat and drink,
And as I stand here sadly think,
Perhaps it's just as well I'm mute,
Or else I'd tell you - "MAN'S A BRUTE".

Richard Ford

The Man I've Never Met

Years ago I saw his face, I heard the magic in his voice,
I realized I was in love, in this I had no choice,
Other singers came and went but didn't mean a thing,
They couldn't compare in any way with the pleasure that you bring,
A man I've never met.

When sad and feeling low he would bring me cheer,
His songs made me laugh, smile and sometimes bring a tear,
He was so many miles away and yet so very near,
He brought to me such happiness I hold him very dear,
This man I've never met.

As time went on I shared his grief, the sad loss of his Mother,
To me he was my family too, my friend also my lover,
He got married, and had a daughter, for him I was so glad,
I prayed with all my heart he would never again be sad,
For the man I've never met.

I will always have him with me, still to cheer me when I'm blue,
I'm with you when your singing because it's me you're singing to,
Even with your passing I will stay forever true,
I will be forever faithful no one else will ever do.
The man I've never met.

Maxine Willerton

Quietly Strolling

While strolling through the country lanes.
I felt myself at peace
The little lambs were covered
In their white and fluffy fleece.

The primrose heads were nodding
In the gentle breeze.
Birds were singing loudly
Way up in the trees.

I walked a little further
And found a pretty lake.
Six lovely little ducklings
With their mother and the drake.

I watched them for a little while.
But then it was time to go.
When I will return again?
I really do not know

It may be in the summer
Or even in the fall.
The sights will all be different
But these things I will recall.

Pamela Spackman

The Pit

Sometimes my life feels really s**t! And I am caged beneath a pit,
I find it hard to scream and shout, "Somebody please
help get me out"
I keep it all wrapped up inside, and with no one do I confide,
I'm in a tunnel dark and long, deep down I know this is all wrong,
I must start running find the light,
come on girl put up a fight,
There's life at the end just waiting for me,
Where I can be what I want to be,
Blue skies, water green grass and trees,
let your heart open, the light holds the keys.
Running with my hair free to the wind,
I can do that for I have not sinned,
Making my laughter rise from below,
I can be happy, I can be, I know,
So much I want to smile and say
"Hey everybody life's going my way"
I know this will happen just time it will take
Be patient with me, please for God's sake.
Can you hear me I'm beginning to shout,
"Open the pit for I'm coming out".

Lesley-Anne Rutter

The Silent Cry

They cannot hear my cry, they cannot see the pain,
I suffer for the sake of humans.
They experiment on me to find things out,
Don't they care what they put me through?
I feel pain, I'm a living creature,
I breathe, I move, I eat and drink,
The only difference is, that I don't have a voice.
How can I speak out when no-one understands me.
I cry a silent cry, it can't be heard.
Locked in a cage, which is cold, damp and bare,
Should I be grateful I'm still alive?
I live in this laboratory until I die
From chemicals and substances, which make me ill,
uncomfortable, sore and partially blind
What should I care for now!
How would humans feel, if they could not speak,
and were in my position, growing weak.
I'm sure that they would have to think twice.
I sit here thinking what gives them a right,
And carry on silently crying.

Rachel Webb

I Dream

I walk towards the harvest moon set in the blackened sky,
I then take her by the hand and to the moon we fly,
I dream, this dream once again, again I dream this dream
This illusion must come true please make things as they seem.
The night is long and perfect, nothing in our way,
My dream love and I are happy on our moon far away.
The morning sun wakes me, my dream love is gone.
I wait for the night to come again why does it take so long.
Ah, but when the moon rises within the blackened sky, she
will be with me again and to our moon we'll fly.

I dream my dream once again, again I'll dream my dream.
Until morning will be happy, please make things as they seem.

K. Golightly

Pale Blue Skies

Immortalized in a carefully painted picture
I wander across the landscape of shades.
Living on a canvas that's always changing
I try to catch the colours before they fade.

With each brushstroke of the artist,
I'm taken to a higher plain;
Passing over clay statues in sculpted gardens
Who shelter from imaginary rains.

When I travel through those pale blue skies,
There is no pain and there are no lies;
There's just the sound of the rushing wind
That re-arranges familiar faces on broken clouds.

I'm suspended by a thread that's made from tears;
The gentle tears that fall from a loved one's eyes.
So I embrace eternity for a while, and feel myself rise
Above those pale, pale blue skies.

J. MacKenzie

"The Easy Life?"

How many pieces make up the heart?
I really don't know just where to start
When fear and rejection raise their ugly head
I feel my heart get ready for bed
There is no point in the above situation
To be able to sleep amid this frustration?
Soon my heart'll begin to rumble
Then I'll feel it truly crumble.

But then again this may never happen
Soft cotton wool I'll wrap my heart in
Surrounded only by comfort and love
Held together by devotion that fits like a glove
Like two hearts that beat as one
Life is so empty until that is done
But if it were easy love would cost less
And I wouldn't be living in this . . . wilderness!

Lesley-Anne Smith

To Understand the Word

I feel for the old and the lonely,
I feel for the sick and the poor,
I feel for the scared and the frightened,
  The weakest of all.

I sense something is wrong,
I sense a struggle and a fight,
I sense a need for peace,
  As none of this feels right.

I hear the laughter of children,
I hear the song of the dove,
I hear the sound of the breeze,
  And the silence of sorrow.

I see hurt and confusion,
I see pain and despair,
I see war and destruction,
  In the eyes of the world.

The need for tranquillity,
The need for dreams,
The need for knowledge,
  And a time to heal.

Toni Catling

The Lifeboat

It lay on its side, a hole in the hull,
"I think I could", he casually said oh no you can't it's too big a job
But the money was paid, the task had began,
The engine was first, a back-breaking job,
The barnacles removed, the muck and the slime,
The deck to be cleaned, and the putty applied,
The hole in the side had to come next,
Fibre glass and lots of skill was put to the test,
There wasn't a steering wheel, it had to be made.
A four inch round was cut from a stump
  Of an old oak tree that had just been dumped,
He chiselled and whittled until it took shape
Then proudly put it into place.
The painting came next, three coats were applied.
All white the colour, with a thin blue line,
Hooray! Said the two lifeboat men as they passed by,
You two people have done a jolly good job,
And one of those two people was only a lass
A name! A name! She must have a name,
It will be "Kingfisher" he said with a grin,
The old, old, wreak was in the water again.

Lily Stephenson

The Alien

I'm an alien
I don't live here.
How could I?
People drink beer - and sneer . . .

I'm not one of them
I live on a cloud
Sometimes I find
People are loud - and a bit too proud . . .

I'm not quite the same
I don't fit in
How could I?
I don't drink gin - and nor am I thin!

I do stand apart
I do stand alone.
I believe in love
My heart is not stone (but my courage has flown).

Is it O.K. to be me?
I'm not what you see
Don't be fooled
No - one is free - least of all me . . .

Sue Lightfoot

Hidden Treasures

It was August when we first moved in,
I remember it so clear,
As we wandered around in the garden
Crying "Look! come look over here".
We found beautiful bushes and wonderful plants
Everyday some new bloom would appear
And we loved to just sit or potter around
In our garden the rest of the year.
Then winter arrived with cold winds and snow
The garden looked bleak and austere,
But the birds seemed to like the nuts we put out
And their singing we loved to hear
Then one day I looked up, what was that I spied?
Something white, right at the rear
I dashed up the garden and to my surprise
Found some snowdrops had started to peer.
Then all at once daffodils, crocus, and buds
So much beauty and I shed a tear
As these hidden treasures God sent, I believe
For the start of another blessed year!

Sandra Fairham

"The Scout Jumble-Sale"

The day that the Scouts had their first Jumble-Sale
I remember it well (for our dog trapped his tail)-
I offered to help on one of the stalls -
It was held in the largest of our two Church halls -
I'll never forget it as long as I live
You would never believe what some people give,
Two jumpers - well shrunk in the washing machines,
And young Alfie yelling - (his mum gave his jeans.)
The Finnigan twins tugged a doll by its hair
Not one would give in - (they were under a chair!!)
Willie, the Sidesman (in church every Sunday) -
Was trying (in vain) to console Mrs. Grundy.
A sewing machine someone said, wouldn't sew
She lifted it down, and it dropped on her toe -
The Minister, smiling, to welcome folks in
Made certain he proffered the "ADMISSION" tin -
The Scoutmaster, ANGUS (of Scottish descent),
Made certain they got a good price for a tent -
The profit they made at the grand old conclusion,
Made me wonder "HOW"- amongst all the confusion!!

Kathleen M. Daniels

The Stirring Heart

Silence, calm, tranquillity of mind
Hidden emotions, deeply buried, that you find
A tender kiss, a loving smile
The honest look that's like a child
The beating heart, the warmth, the glow
Distant memories stirred from long ago
The walk along a path that's new
All this has come from knowing you.

Laura Ellis

A Horse's Life

Gallop gallop into the ground
Horses race each other pound for pound
Steady steady watch that jump
Ooh there's another horse come down with a thump
Is it cruel - is it kind
It all depends on each individual's mind
Racing's a game that's brought many fame
It's also a game that gets horses maimed
Is it fun or is it greed
The poor horse only gets its feed
Listen listen to the thud of the ground
Another punter wages a pound
People get rich people get poor
The poor old horse isn't so sure
They say horses are happy
They love to run
Bang!
There goes another shot from the gun

Keith Wakefield

Winter, Summer and Spring Days

On a winter's icy day
I slip and trip
Not skip but trip and no back flip
I fall over and walk really slow
Like being towed, in a conked-out car.

On a summer's sunny day
I can skip and play hit
Not slip but skip and still no back flip
I gallop and leap from house to house
As fast as a speeding mouse, running from
a vile cat.

So on a winter's icy day
I slip and trip
Not skip but trip and no back flip
On a summer's sunny day
I skip and play hit
not slip but skip and still no back flip

On a spring's mild day
I see my mates
And the people I love, no people I hate

Vicki Goodlad

Paranoid in a Paranoid World

As I glance through the window
I smile at what I see
The world looks so beautiful
The Ideal place to be

But now in the road amongst all the trees
Something feels wrong everyone's looking at me
Yes! They're all looking at me

Their faces are rigid
Their smiles have all gone
Nature around me has stopped singing its song

Although the road is now busy
As cars speed on by
I'm still the target distracting their eye

As I look for small corners
'Cause' I just want to hide
The road starts to bend and corners grow wide

But in all the blinding confusion
I was still able to see
The world is not out to get me
But just paranoid like me

Rosalyn Baptiste

Mother

Dear mother I love you with all my heart
I need you so much, as I did from the start,
I'd be lost without your love and care,
I know when I need you, you'll always be there.

You've looked after me since I was small,
Picked me up when I had a fall.
Wiped my eyes when I shed a few tears,
And helped me conquer all my fears.

You gave me pocket money to buy sweets,
And not only that, you brought my treats.
I can never repay what you have done,
All of the laughter and the fun.

Through my teenage years you were always there,
Looking after me with such loving care.
And now I'm grown up, you're still my mum,
I just need to call and I know you'll come.

My love for you will never die,
You are my best friend and Mother that's why.
This little poem is filled with love and affection,
Because we both know you are simply perfection.

Tina Down

Our Mutual Friend

Don't make a sound or you'll disturb,
The singing of the little birds,
They've come to tell us Spring is coming,
With flowers a-blooming, bees a-humming,
Soon Winter will be far behind,
With snow and cold both gone,
So we can sit in our gardens
And soak up all the sun.
With nests to make and eggs to lay,
The birds are very busy,
Their search for food to store up strength
Must almost make them dizzy.
One shouldn't have a favourite bird,
But this has stood the test,
The little one we all like most
Has a lovely scarlet breast
He's handsome and he's cheeky,
A proper little rogue,
But you wouldn't find a better friend
If you traversed the globe.

Vera Hartley

Natural Beauty

The clouds move so swiftly
The sky beats down so strongly
Whether it's gloomy
Whether it's glowing brightly
It's a natural beauty

The birds whistle so greatly
Gliding along so gracefully
Sticking together making patterns so skilfully
Before landing on trees which stand so proudly
The crisp, green grass covering the ground so daintily
Being part of the natural beauty

People walk the earth so abrasively
Without realization destroying,
All of the natural beauty

Michelle Haggerty

A Better World

One day the grass will be greener,
The sky the brightest blue,
The world, a lot more peaceful,
'Cause I will be there with you,
Where flowers grow and weeds will die,
And white puffy clouds will float on by,
But that will only happen,
If people clean up a bit more,
Where people love each other,
And never close their door,
So open up your door a bit,
And you will surely see,
That the world should be trusted,
Without a lock or key.

Kerry Hutchison

Snowfall

Softly, silently, whitely, whispering,
The snow flakes drift down from the sullen skies,
Masking the land in an icy disguise,
Gleaming, glinting, in the trees soughing.
The old withered oak whose days are numbered,
Is wrapped in glory, its years remembered,
Resting in peace.

From far icy wastes, the wind in a rage,
Comes roaring, to thrash, to lash, and to hack,
Bearing a joy-riding snow on its back,
Intent with mankind a battle to wage.
Snow blocks, and road blocks, power-lines tumbled,
A lesson is learnt! Mankind is humbled!
No rest, no peace.

D. G. Ellis

The Suicide

The night was cold and the wind whistled as it slapped
the sea venomously,
Against the scraggy face, of the peaked, jagged, mountainous edge.
There was a man silhouetted against the dark might sky, by the
light of the dying moon.
Perked like a scraggy, scarecrow, or some foul offering to one
insane 'God'.
With hands hold high.
Ready to flung over, into the greasing teeth of the gale, as it
plucked and tone at his clothes.
Then, suddenly, form the darkened sky, a piercing light shone
on the forlorn figure.
And he paused, — just for a fraction, or a hairsbreadth of a moment.
The tableau was suspended in noontime, between seconds.
Then, the man, with one smooth almost jubilant are,
jumped and was gone.

S. M. Kelly

Uncertainty and Belief

The powers of imagination overrun the mind,
The seduction of words that somehow can send you blind,
times move on and the sea it roars,
Its turbulence setting life's true course,
Many times I say I care and many times
you explain beware,
The feelings that erupt within my heart,
Tell me we shall never be apart,
Our friendship will ignite,
And we'll soar with all our might,
The turbulence is subsiding now,
The darkness fades and the light shines through,
The sea is calm and it's down to you,
I understand now my uncertainty,
But I know that belief is my eternity.

Lisa Benson

Our Sussex Downs

The morning sun, spraying sunbeams on our lovely downs,
The sheer beauty of the moment, expelling any early frowns,
A cry from a seagull, as it wings its way across the sky,
How this loveliness is given to us, you wonder why,

The winding footpath, beckoning you along the curves and slopes,
Seems to drive away any problems and encourage many hopes,
The sky in the distance, looks so blue as it slips behind the bend,
Your eager wishes are that nature's glory will never end,
Perhaps these thoughts are really prayers, to be answered one day,
As you stroll along this colourful carpet, you know it's
the only way.

W. G. Jackman

Absorbed

Beyond brief glances and half heard sounds,
the sight of something harsh,
so black and white; an image burns
and mars the retina of my life.

Perhaps the childlike coil and arch
of the back provoked a pause,
a breath inhaled with sharp return
is just enough to mist a mirrored cause.

So why such sorrow in crumbling form;
immense and crushing, with no proportion?
I stop to rest that single thought
and scan the landscape of today.

A smile and scent of gracious giving
surrounds each event and straight exchange
within the core of such expressions
hide words which snatch our fragile frames.

Bleak frustration beats against reason
and the body of hatred for absorbing hurts.
But careless phrases should not take the strong.
So I move on: The sun brings out a different song.

Kathryn Lawton Vaughan

Unseen Flower

As they lay among the field of barley
the fragrance of ardour enveloping all
like an autumn mist in early morn
the idyllic not yet lost in time

the lightness of that yet urgent touch
so reassuring it reminds of life so far
how can the needs of so many be reconciled
by nature's purity in love's guise

dressing slowly so as not to lose the moment
thoughts turning to that given and that stolen
how gently they had lain all down
love shone in glistening eyes and bodies

turning coyly to look at each other clothed
they embrace clasp hands and walk away
never noticing the symmetry of flattened crop
a pressed flower formed by their seed of love

Rowland Douglas

Nature

I love the rain upon my face,
the freshness on my cheeks,
The autumn feel of chill in air,
The crispy leaves, the trees so bare,
And we can only stand and stare,
at all the beauty that is there.

And is there a much finer view?
To see the early morning dew,
and spy a deer, a fleeting glance,
It's heard you, flees with easy prance.
The morning's here, the days begun.
The earth dries out, here comes the sun.

We wait for Summer, and blue skies,
the warmth on skin, our sun-kissed eyes,
Miracles of nature know no bounds,
the seasons so different, do their rounds.
We can only gaze in awe,
in wonderment at what we saw.

Susan M. Cubitt

Calm

The peace and calm of a summer evening,
The friendly gaze of the man in the moon,
The mumble of voices awed by the Universe,
The kettle humming to their tune.

A stream, laughing gaily
Gurgles through roots of a tree,
His old gnarled fingers grasping starlight
But still he leaves some for me,
His weather-beaten branches bending,
Casting friendly shadows below.

They eat in silence,
Savouring the succulent juices.
Slowly, as if to make it last,
The redness is fading
And the hare is watching
One small moment in time go past.

I. R. Kernaghan

The Gad Fly

As the anthro respirates,
    The gad fly is concepted and consummated.
As I sit, ponder and fallacise,
    Despotism occurs,
As I desiderate away the time,
    The gad fly flues and dies.
If only surplus time would transcend,
    And pursue a wanton juncture,
Both past and present would velocitise,
    And destiny dawn upon our eyes.

Natalie Cavens

Tonight I've Seen the Eyes of My Muse

Tonight I've seen the eyes of my muse
staring at me stuck with illusion,
filmed with joy, covered with blues,
trying to get me out of confusion.

My life's been utterly turned upside-down,
my head made ache, poisoned bone-marrow,
invisible devil made light turn brown
penetrating my heart with venomous arrow,
scorching my senses unable to revive,
burning my eyes to stay blind forever
knowing that just with being alive
my dilapidated brains can be satisfied never.

Is that my destiny that's taken its toll,
or is it just the way everything should be,
and I am being treated like a senseless doll
with anguish and pain falling on me?

So I find myself crippled and rotten,
whipped by a sword, covered with dust,
is everything one day going to be forgotten,
or I'll be forever armoured with rust?

Maria Sasha

Home

As daylight fades into the night
Stars peep through the darkened sky
Doors at home are fastened tight
Against the winds that whistle by.
Inside when the lights are low
It is safe and warm by the fireside glow.

Joy and family love shine through
For God himself is here to dwell.
This is a refuge sure and true,
A blessed home where all is well,
And with the passing of each day
There is no better place to stay.

Tom Buchanan

The Freedom Child

Little boy peers and weeps through shadow glass, chances a half-starved smile to the thought of living again.

Muddy paws wipe the tender droplets, as they mark his life on the white worn windowsill.

The fresh breeze breaks the still sound of monotony, grasping the air with such disdain.

He turns with back to certain freedom, lifts a sturdy foot, which marks the passages of time.

His life concealed within his box he calls his room, challenged by his peeling peers, possessed by youthful impatience.

What questions would you ask if you had the chance?

Maybe if the books are read it would make life turn pages too!

Robert Cousineau

Retirement

What is retirement? Well! It's the time in your life when the state pays you for being 65 years old.

And it's the time in your life you have dreamed of and looked forward to; about all those pleasurable things throughout your working years.

Like holidays and those "Lazy hazy days in the Sunshine", But! Wait a moment, did I say dreamed of.

But! I am 65 years old now, and still dreaming of those times still to come; oh; where have all those years gone, when, I had money in my pocket and light in my step.

But, alas those days have gone, gone, gone.

Just like those dreams of yesteryear!

K. G. Haywood

Spirits of the Past

Reflections, on a smell of tranquillity.
Sounds that bring momentary feelings of almost
forgotten recollections.
The wind that whistles in the silence, once shared.
The music that stirs through thought-filled dreams of the past.
The hours that once took weeks to arrive, now,
pass in minutes.
Today, is tomorrow was yesterday, all one.
Life is but a tide, is now what it was one
hundred years past.
We are but small pebbles on the beach of life,
forever changing, to and fro!
What are we but spirits of the past for tomorrow.

Sandra Lockley

H. P. Sauce

M. P.'s acting like - spoilt brats
Speaker - absolutely frantic
Order! Order! Order!
Cod and chips, haddock and chips;
Moving motions; Miss Nyne-munths, - labour
Maternity ward; pregnant — pause
Speech on liberalism and birth control;
Interrupted by hyphen La - di - da, Tory crawler
From the town hall spawning ground.
Order! Order! Order!
Haddock and chips, cod, chips and peas:
The ever resounding Ear! Ear!
"Lugubrious???"
Jock Strappe - Scottish Nationalist; invited to
Belt-up, by Miss Fancy-Free-liberal
Order! Order! Order! Order!
An extra order? How extraordinary!
Someone forgot the sausage???
Moving a motion, Dia-Rrhoea-Welsh Nationalist
Hope he's got a safe seat.

Michael Brown

The Palmist

The future cupped in grooves, dented times.
Spiralling energy winding through lines,
Catching the heart and dragging at life's destiny.
"Tell me who is there for me?"

Venus smiles. Chained love punctures love.
Nets are cast on shallow waters. Islands forming
Chilling the mind, cooling the heart of thoughts of love
The whippy wind surrounds the cove.

Life's long trails sprout new beginnings.
Shunting awake those tiring dreams.
Believing the air holds Mars's tireless courage.
Permitting your breath to nourish.

The childish grim spooks sometimes nip
The woman, who nips back whilst moving forward,
Pressing and tripping and forcing the bolt.
The lighted mine caresses its hold.

Ruby Scott

A Journey through the Passage of the Mind

Corridors of the mind look to the light,
Spirits of our souls stay out of sight,
Our feelings, emotions, our personal thoughts.
Stay locked, undisturbed in personal vaults.

Isolation, grief, pain, continue to be,
The sole emotional aspects of me.
But perhaps today help comes at last, for
the end comes to all be it slow or fast.

Slow or fast like the ever-flowing tides,
My pain is not shown, but just felt inside.
Yet it is there, look deep and you will see,
That the pain, the grief is actually me.

Nihal De Silva

Television

Television; brings to us a wondrous sight,
Ships a-sail, planes in flight
We travel with the aid of the little box,
It brings joy, tears, laughs and shocks.

The Hula girl in her grass skirt,
Advertisements for a certain shirt.
The voices and faces of people afar,
Views of both the moon and star.

The nomads in the desert, riding camels
The capture of the largest mammals.
A film of Cleopatra, sailing the Nile,
Unplaced persons, or Napoleon sent into exile.

We sit in the comfort of an armchair,
Yet the television takes us there.
From the Grand Canyon, to the Victoria Fall,
Our little box; provides them all.

M. B. Wild

Springtime

Bulbs push up through the ground
Shoots are unfurling all around,
Bursts of colour start to appear
Birds call out in songs of cheer.
The bleats of lambs
As you watch them playing,
Yellows of daffodils
In a breeze are swaying,
The cold has dispersed for another year
Winter has gone and Spring is here.

Wanda Monks

Young Love

Is the first really the best
Should you. Could you. Forget the rest.
Can you remember your first hug
Can you remember your first love
The first kiss can you remember
Was it in June? Or was it September?
The first fight. The first harsh word
"was that the first or was it the third"
Is it the first you'll never forget
Can you remember your love yet.
Young love, I remember the feel
Young love, my thoughts are still.

William Hickey

The Curtain Rises

Black colours the night sky
Shrouding the earth in darkness,
A deep impenetrable blindness
Closes deceitfully around the sighted.

Silence sounds out through silence
Tearing this veil in two,
Within a cry echoes - unheard
As past, present, future merge.

Pulled inside this seething mass
Drawn by an omnipotent force,
Spinning, turning, faster, faster
No control possible to exert.

My mind cries out 'defiance'
Willing the self to hold,
Grasping onto fragments adrift
A picture slowly unfolds.

Light bursts open the clouds
Mocking darkness' withering soul,
A myriad of glorious colours
Its enchantment overthrowing all.

Mary McDonagh

A Mother

Children jump with joy, when she is near,
She creates an aura of mystery and excitement,
Her bright smile makes the sun to appear,
And jealous skies frown at that attachment.

The dew envies the sweet breath from her lips,
And the rainbow pales before her rich eyes,
Her crystal tears, the orchids claim to sip,
Her calm and loving voice, the wind sighs.

Angels dim before her glowing splendour,
Goodness studies closely for her source,
The Messiah's touch, her own as tender,
And Paradise is stilled by her sweet transient force.

Margarette M. Thomas

The Beauty of a Woman

With a graceful tiger-like walk
She gently strides over to the waterfall
Which is filled with beauty and colour,
She places herself on a nearby rock
removing her silk robe
to reveal her soft bare skin
So soft and beautiful she looks,
With the sun shining down on her sun-kissed body
And the gentle breeze of the wind
She bathes in the crystal clear river
So clear she admires her beauty
She throws her long shiny hair back
And catches the gentle pour of the water
With her smile so bright
And all of nature in bloom
She is one of nature's gift from God.

Lotus Shephard

Evelyn Chambers (Always Hated)

Evelyn Chambers, always hated strangers
She never let a single soul enter her house.
Even when she married, the problem, it just carried
Not letting in her in-laws, or even her spouse.
They sat out in the garden, where their bottoms had
  to harden, and
Evelyn just spied on them through the letterbox.
When things got even tougher, Evelyn thought that she
  might suffer
So she went ahead, and purposefully changed all the locks.
By now a crowd had gathered, a passing dog had lathered
And even all the neighbours had gathered in the street.
The in-laws, they got restless, and hubby, he was vestless.
For temperatures were rising out in all the heat.
Evelyn could not be certain, for she hid behind a curtain
But thought she spied a policeman arriving on the scene.
So she opened up window, and with a pail of swill, go
And throw it over ma-in-law, hubby and the bill.
They ranted, raved and shouted, but Evelyn, she just pouted,
And calmly said: "It serves you right for going against my will."
The crowd outside were splattered, the husband, he felt battered,
So they all got up, shook off the muck, and marched back
  down the hill.

Sandra Anne Bidwell

Mum

She's the gentle breeze that cools my fevered brow,
She's the arbitrator that sorts out any row,
She's the sturdy rock that is my main support,
She's the good Samaritan that can my problems sort,
She's the golden spark that always makes me smile,
She's the friendly face when life is such a trial,
She's the inspiration who makes me want to be,
She's the visionary who enables me to see,
She's the wise advisor who helps me overcome,
She is all and everything, she is my darling mum!

Tracy Christian

Untitled

Reflections on the Virgin Mary and Easter
She not only prays for Christians
But for Gentile and for Jew
She's there to pray for all who care.
And surely that means you
You must care that on the day
He suffered so much pain
He was showing the way
Eternal life to gain.

And when your soul is on its way
With this world left behind
You'll be in the presence
Of the Saviour of mankind.

He greets you all with open arms
Your tears are dried, your fears He calms
And once you are inside the fold
His heavenly kingdom you'll behold

May the risen Lord uphold you
And bless you as you pray
May His love surround you
On the glorious Easter day

V. Lewis

Little Girl Lost

Her life has ended before it begun,
She sees no point in all that's done.
She cries in the corner just wanting to die.
And in her cries why, why, why.

She sees no beauty, letting it waste,
The grass is no longer green,
The food has no taste.
Should she give up?
Or should she go on?
Will it get better?
Or will it go on?

But think of the people she'll leave behind,
Does it matter?
Will they mind?
She reaches out but no one's there,
Will they help, do they care.
What will happen,
What will she do,
Who can help her,
Can you?

Nicole Ridge

"My Son My Son"

At the foot of the cross
She stood with sorrowful heart
The tears she shed for the sacred heart
And from the cross He saw at a glance
His mother's heart pierced with a lance
And like you and I in our despair
He called upon Him we know is there
from the cross they brought Him down
In arms that trembled she cradles Him on the ground
Kneeling on stones that cut her knees
Fretful prayers from her lips exceed
"My Son, my Son", she called in her despair
And He lightened her heart of the sorrow to bear.
Then to the sepulchre they laid Him there
The sentinel sleeps as the third day dawns.
Lord Jesus, our Saviour, is reborn
So the words of the Scriptures are fulfilled
Nations of plenty do take heed
Unless we pass the supreme test
And do His bidding as He said
Behold the great Chastisement.

M. J. McAllister

Jeannie

Jeannie my friend is bad, the sickness
she too, has made us all sad
Our hearts are sore but what can we do.
For God's need, Jeannie's. He's calling her too.

The lands, where they are happy,
and sing all the time, no tears, nor sorrow.
Everything beautiful in this land of tomorrow.
Above that blue sky, on that heavenly shore,
and Jesus is there, and our friends by the score.
so Jeannie my friend, stretch out your hand,
and Jesus will take you to that heavenly land.
I won't cry no more Jeannie, or be sad
for Jesus loves you. To part we had to, some day
I'll go too and I'll be glad
for Jeannie, you'll be waiting and so will God.

Marian Kerr

"Pain Killer"

It's pierced my skin and it's into my vein,
I feel so relieved by that feeling again.
I am gone, it's a brand new me,
All the pain has passed, only hope I can see.
You can't reach me now, even if you tried,
You can't hurt me no more, I'm empty inside.
You all go on about how stupid I must be,
but through my eyes you'll never see.
Heroin to you is only "the end,"
but to me it is my only friend.
I sometimes think I could be like you all,
but then I think "who am I trying to fool?"
I've tried to give it up, but failed,
because it wasn't long before reality was unveiled.
I can't handle life, I've lost the plot,
My whole life is waiting for that next shot.
You don't understand, you won't ever try,
As if you care, if I live or die.
It's pierced my skin, and it's into my vein,
I feel so relieved by that feeling again.

Nikki Adams

No Hand Signals

He's belted in the passenger's place,
Sheer terror painted on his face.
He feels I'll be a hopeless case.
I'm learning, finally, to drive.

Check the mirror, check the road,
Check his pulse - it's panic mode,
Can barely cope with such a load.
I'm learning, slowly, how to drive.

No near misses - he seems surprised.
The highway code's been analyzed,
The throttle foot's now energized.
I'm learning, quickly, how to drive.

His look has changed from doubt to pride.
The tests been passed, he's cast aside.
This driving teacher's grin is wide.
He's cracked my case, and I can drive!

M. Cowie

Mother Nature

Mother Nature can be oh so cruel,
she'll never know how much you meant to me.
Never know at all,
she took you away from me when
you were oh so young.
When really your life had never begun,
but I will never forget.
And never stop loving what I never really had.
For now in feeling unhappy and incomplete,
for I know I will no longer hear the
pitter patter of tiny feet.

M. Wort

Sheila

The first time she felt the little lump there, she tried not to worry
she tried not to care but weeks went by and so it grew, it was Cancer
somehow she knew. A painful test, a week to wait, the tiny lump had
grown, it was too late. The operation left a scar across her chest,
but in her life the scar marked best.

Why me? What have I done? I'm only 40 my life's just begun.
Dear God to you I pray help cure me of Cancer let me live me one
more day.

The endless tablets and chemotherapy. Hand fulls of hair falling
out for all to see. Radiation and healing but all were too late.
Heaven had opened up its golden gate. What of the children,
aged just 3 and 5? They had to be cared for. How would they
survive? All she could think of was, what lay ahead. Perhaps 3
months the doctors had said.

Dear God open Your arms I pray, accept my friend and to her
say, "Why you, because your time has come, not because of
anything you have done. Just close your eyes don't fight any
more. Your life at 40 has begun for sure. A life in heaven where
your good ways will influence others from above still."

The morning after she did not awaken. An angel had her spirit taken.
I listened quietly and thought I heard her say,

"I now know why, I didn't do wrong, I just had to return to the
place I belong." But never forget treat each day with respect, life
has a habit of giving more than you expect. Love one another and
live life to the full, who knows when your name He will call?

Sindy Carmichael-Brown

'Coming Home'

In the darkness of the night, a light shines brightly through the mist.
Shimmering and glimmering, flickering and fading, now
    shining bright again.
As I get nearer, the light shines brightly through the windows
    of the house.
A warm glow illuminates the building, an aura of anticipation
    envelopes all.
I open the door and step inside.
Warmth, and smells and welcome hit me all at once, softly,
    gently, caressingly.
In the fireplace a log fire burns, hissing and spitting, making
    shapes to invite imagination. A wooden table surrounded by
A wooden table surrounded by chairs claims the centre of the room.
On that table stands a bowl of steaming stew, a cob of bread,
    a rich brown mug of tea and a large deep spoon.
I sit down unhurriedly, basking in the warmth, and the
    soundless welcome.
I lift the spoon and take the first taste of stew, rolling it around
    the tastebuds of my soul. The tea is sweet and
The teas is sweet and strong, the bread is crisp and soft.
There is silence, there is peace, there is no other creature here,
    no one but me. And yet I feel
And yet I feel the presence of concern and care and love.
Whose hands made the fire, the meal, and the tea, left the
    welcome, left the warmth in which I glow?
I am breathless with expectation, I know! I know!
I feel your presence, you are here, I am home! I am home!

Thomas Larvin

Autumn Mind

My eyes are haunted by the ghost inside:
Sight circled by grey intimations of mind,
Softly bruised apples on the autumn floor
Clipped and fall'n from the sap-cloyed, drugged torpor,
Reflecting an inner, darkened glow
Of which my soul does know:
A part of aching eternity's bounds,
Lying close to the earthly ground
Where nature's heady skies can now be seen
From amongst the mulchy, golden leaves:

The fall of the fecund crown's deceit,
Its strength withered by time's heavy ease
As I return to my Self's deepest seat,
And the obscuring boughs melt, so I can breathe.

Richard Nadal

Emerald - Oasis

Envy of Emeralds.
Shimmering around the neck like twinkling stars at night.
Green as the Indian ocean.
Deepest - peacock green.
Emeralds rarest isles.
Seagulls glide in the sky.
Wildlife of mystery.
Eyes peering through binoculars with excitement.
The rarest creatures all colours - like a rainbow.
Feel the atmosphere come alive.
Warmth, coolness, subtle breezes.
Coral seas, citron suns, fiery steamy night,
Midnight in the oasis.
What sheer delight - grass soft as velvet.
Imagine the freshness of smell, like an exotic scent.
Sparkling of Emeralds - shimmering around the
neck like twinkling stars at night.
Oblivion - to what's exquisite surrounds.

Patricia Nelson

The Moon

The radiant moon in all her glory,
Shines like a beacon of hope in the sky,
If she could speak, what would be her story,
As man from earth, walking godlike on high
Seeking to find her age old secrets,
But her cold austere beauty passes them by.

Ruby De Gruchy

Mother

Now another day is breaking,
Sleep was sweet, so was waking
Dear Mum I promised God last night.
Never again to sulk or fight.

Such vows are so easy to keep.
When I'm in bed, fast asleep.
Today Mum, for your dear sake
I'll try to keep them when awake.

If you don't know how much I love you
I really love you a lot
I think the love between us,
Started when I was a babe in my cot.

Now I've grown, blonde hair, blue eyed.
We have our arguments, all about pride.
It still feels good to make up friends
And dare I say, we will to the end.

I wrote this poem to say that I care
Yes the girl with blue eyes and blonde hair.
Friends we are, not just daughter and mother
If I ever need advice, I'll look to no other.

C. A. Jones

War

My friend saw her home wrecked,
Her loved ones inside,
She's all alone now,
Her loved ones have died,
No home, no family,
She wandered the street,
No one to look after her,
Nowhere for her to sleep,
The war has come,
And we must hide,
People around us dropped down and died,
We were running and she was ahead,
And as far as I knew she was dead,
I kept running,
I tripped,
And there I lie,
I thought this was my turn to die,
A soldier came up to me and said,
"I'll count to seven and then you're dead,"
And now I am resting in a heavenly bed.

Kelly Martin

Death

The stone face of Death,
Shines out from your eyes,
As you lay there in your bed,
Death's doors open wide and beckon to you,
Ease the pain,
Fly away,
With wings as white and pure as doves,
And the world is left with your body, an empty shell,
Like a sailor with no boat,
Where are you going?
Will he be there to welcome you?
The stone face of Death,
Shines out from your eyes,
As you lay there in your bed,
Death's doors open wide and beckon to you,
Ease the pain
Fly away
Your breath stills,
And you are gone.

Rhianne Lewis

Success

When the blazing sun
Shines right through
And the sky is no more bleak,
Your future lies within your grasp
And your life is at its peak.
Don't look back, don't look down
But boldly look ahead
And take a step, into the world
With hope, will and strength.
Keep going down that steady road
For at the very end,
You'll see a light, you'll reach your goals
And you'll become your own best friend.

Rathika Thillainathan

Seagull's over Silly Mid On

The velvet outfield lush and green
Silent, no white linen seen
Audience of empty seats mocking silently swinging
Warm air suddenly rent with screaming
The show's begun, they fly in teeming
Wicket pristine shorn and brown
Awaiting stumps and bails to crown
All glassy eyed, jostling, pecking, crowding
Far from any windswept shore
Calling, crying, swooping on this hallowed floor
Without warning noise disturbs the flock
White sea of feathers rise above to mock
Every strutting squawker gone
Peace at last for Silly Mid On

Margaret Cullum

Mournful Sigh!

Crying deep, 'Oh' mournful sigh,
Simplistic notions of love,
Now complicated -

A 'secret love' -
Entangled in a public web,
'Oh,' Mournful sigh
Drowning the whispers, 'Sinful desires!'
Churning within,

Chattering resistance, Sharpening the pain,
"Forget the love!" - 'Oh' - Mournful Sigh,
Palpitating heart - Fear? - Judgement? -
Each beat a feeling!

Fading to an oblivious world,
Surface denies! Conceals the pain!
Truth unlocked, though the silence remains,
Throbbing love, tongue twisted and tied,
Who would have heard those feelings inside . . . ?!

Rina Sondhi

V. E. Day 1995

As beacons flare around our land,
Silently the people stand. Millions stop - two minutes pass
In lonely, calm reflection.

The old among us contemplate
The sacrifice of friend and mate - Partners, sons and daughters gone -
In war's fierce conflagration.

For middle-aged, clear memories
Flood back, of past festivities. The parties - the euphoria!
V. E. Day celebration.

Fathers, mothers, loved ones lost;
Homes destroyed - they knew the cost! Their eyes are damp,
   as tears are shed;
A war-scarred generation.

The young folk stand - they too are moved -
More recent wars to them have proved the stupid, mad futility
Of nation fighting nation.

Our little ones enjoy the fun.
Life for them has just begun. Will the silence teach them peace?
There lies our world's salvation.

As glowing embers pierce the night, ten thousand parties put to flight
Our darkest thoughts, our deepest fears. A mem'rable occasion!

   T. McGeorge

It's Been Such a Long Time

It has been a long time since the moon has risen far into the
midnight sky, and shone upon two souls talking away the night.
When will I see you again, old friend? Distance separates us and
time keeps us from communicating. The sun rises on this side of
the ocean, when the day has ended on the other. Is it for a
lifetime? or will the day come when the sun rises for you and me?
Together will we see days come and
go without talk of separation?

Where are you now my friend? Chasing rainbows you'll never
reach? Or are you so deep within life's heartaches that you can't
come and chase the rainbows with me? As for me I am flying
high in the fluffy white clouds of Spring. The weather is oh, so
lovely. Each morning I rise to the dancing rays of the sun upon
my window and the birds sing
in my ears, whispering "fear not the world one day shall be yours."
It reminds me of the sweet words you whispered long ago.

How is it that old friends have such great wisdom? Is it from
experiencing life? We've come so far, but the journey ahead is
yet very long. So much to see, so many stories yet to tell. Will
there ever come a day when we shall tell these stories together?
Or was it meant that you and I should exist on two separate
worlds joined by an endless sea? I shall swim the ocean and be
with you once again? But what if I should drown? You shall be
proud of my efforts and laugh
at my silliness.

   Salma Bhanji

Precious Memories

Dawn sky high above, in deepest blue
fades to a distant pinky hue.
Glowing fingers of orange, the sun's early rays
Bathing the world in its warm, misty haze.

Leaning out of my window - the cool air so pure -
as the stream far below, past the old cottage door.
First sounds awakening - "that fox seems so near",
Meadowlark singing, so sweet to my ear.

I'd counted the weeks, the days and the hour
drawn back to my childhood by some unknown power.
The Oak tree's the same - the initials still there
scratched deep in the trunk, a lifetime to bare.

Daydreaming of family, friendships and fun,
The days seem so long when life's just begun.
Dear Lord, just this once still the hands of Time
As I smile and relive precious memories of mine.

   Patricia Ingham

Rainbow Nights Colourful Days

When daybreak's call from fast of night
Silver wash shall be your light.
A final wash cleanses all
And sets a colour rolled dice call.

Red, yellow, blue, green, indigo, violet or orange seen.
Perhaps a colour of one or two
But complimentary through and through.
You set the scene and colour of day
Until night washes it away.

In dark of night you wash us with your glory
(I go between our lay lines, gold lover, deliver gold grain)
Out across glorious plain, delivering thread that mends the land
Like seamstress you weave with your hand.

A splendour of expression shared with all
No malice or aggression bared at all.

Pastel shades of pure love pass over through
Not many realize or care that this is but a token of devotion
And expression of heaven.

We sleep within your planets lay with fix of gold new story way
Sleep a gift of cleansing.

   W. H. Broom

Until . . .

Am I dreaming, am I sleeping, am I
   simply not awake?
Am I feeling, am I hurting, is my heart
   about to break?
Will I get there, where I'm going?
Will my journey ever end?
Please be patient, Please be loving, what
   I need most is a friend.
Can I touch you, can I love you, can
   I hold you for a while?
Please come back now, Please don't leave
   me, let me see again your smile.
You are safe now, in God's garden,
Peace and love are there to stay,
until I get there, Please remember,
Mummy's heart is on its way.

   T. Brookes

Untitled

Stomach churning, heart is burning, every minute, how I feel
Since I met you, seems I let you, in my heart for you to steal
How this feeling, keeps me reeling, every minute of the day
Counting hours and the seconds, since I let you slip away
Into the night, I went walking, as I left you to your dreams
I think of you and your beauty, my heart is bursting at the seams
I need to tell you, how I'm feeling, if I only had the nerve
I want to love you and to hold you and to honour you and serve
The thought of living, with this feeling, that is coming from within
It drives me crazy, with frustration, oh darling where will I begin
To tell you, how I want you, everyday until I die
Sensing this will never happen, I feel my eyes begin to cry
With each tear a solemn promise, if you ever need a friend
That I'll be here and I'll be waiting, from now until the end.

   Mark Conacher

Autumn

   Slanting rays of sunshine sparkle on a cobweb
slung between the boughs of an old apple tree; the
grass below shimmers with Autumn's dew. Aloft, a
blackbird trills its haunting melody; listen too,
for the gentle humming of a bee!

   Nature's kaleidoscope has clothed the branches
and hedgerows in a rich mantle of reds and rust, bronze
and gold. On woodland paths footsteps gently swish
and crunch through crisp and curling fallen leaves.

   Soon, the trees - branches almost bare - will
prepare for Winter's hibernation, to recoup their
strength and restore their glories for another year.

   Margaret A. Neasby

374

Hello

Twelve months have passed
Since you've captured my heart
I've so much to say
but don't know where to start

You're mysterious and quiet
and I'm sure you are deep
to decide how to speak to you
keeps me from my sleep

I'd like you to know I'm no typical girl
but a shy and sensitive lady
and I'd like to believe
that to get to know me is not a no
but a possible or definite maybe

I love the theatre and to dance
Seductive but in a nice way
I don't drink smoke or swear
and have quite long blonde hair
the girl who looks at you
then looks away

Lisa Philpott

A Wild Thing

I heard a bird in the wilderness
Singing a joyous refrain
I heard its song over and over again
What is this joyous refrain - free from
Trouble and pain?
Only the shadows of solitude knows
This singing refrain
It is the song of a wild thing,
That never knows man's din -
This thing of shame and sin

P. J. Garrett

Diet Plan

Apples, oranges, bananas, pears,
Skipping, jogging, running upstairs,
Cabbages, carrots, lettuce too,
Swimming, cycling, to name just a few.
Healthy food and exercise
Keep in trim and stay alive,
Stick to the diet, really work at it,
Go to aerobics, go on get fit.
Fruit juice, yoghurt, low fat food,
All these things will do you good.
Sometimes though, nothing will suffice
But burger and chips and a vanilla slice.

Sheila Newbould

A Baby Is Born

Crying, gasping for air.
Sleeping, eating, without a care.
Crawling, walking, but not too far.
Running, riding, in Daddy's car

Learning, playing, having fun.
Laughing, swimming, out in the sun.
Jumping, Splashing, out in the rain.
Taking a trip, on a high speed train.

Seriously studying, quietened down.
An interview made, a trip into town.
An apprenticeship, in a large firm.
No longer now, an end of term.

Wedding bells, a confetti trail.
Through the adds, 'House for Sale.'
A mortgage now, and electric bill.
A Baby is born, in the house on the hill.

Crying, gasping for air.
Sleeping, eating, without a care.
Crawling, walking, but not too far.
Running, riding, in Daddies car.

J. Danson

Dreams

Dreams - untrue reality
Sleeping warm
Lying on a bed of stars
Black sky twinkling stars
Floating into the universe
Uncontrolled bliss
Being stroked by passing angels
Warm full of light
From world to universe
Full of play and laughter
Floating one to one with spirit
The untouched beauty man can't give or take
Just wonder at the love warmth and peace

Monty Nicholls

Yesterday's Dreams

As I walk through the fields I can feel you are near
Smell your sweet scent, your voice I can hear
I feel your caress on my windswept face
Loving arms hold me in a gentle embrace
Taking my hand I sense you are with me
Side by side walking, just as it should be
Reaching to touch you, I feel you it seems
Yet I know you are gone, it's just yesterday's dreams.

Tracey Wilson

Imagining Emotion

I can't believe our time has come
Even if it was a passing moment.
Never realizing you were still warm in my heart
Until you were so close.
And yet this time was so different
to the past we've left behind.
To know the warmth and tenderness I believed in
Were real not just a dream.
We've reached a place we've never been
And perhaps we'll find a way.
As you held me in your arms I felt myself submit
To the murmur of your voice; and
the pleasure of your touch.
You may be far away,
But you're still warm in my mind.
The distance makes no difference,
to the feelings deep inside.
Something that would take a lot to divide
If anything possibly could.
Only time will tell.

Rebecca Stopford

Downhill

Suspended from a single wire,
Skywards the car raises higher,
Goodbye to the crowds and frustrating queues,
For where we're bound all be free to move.

Packed full all bent with same desire,
The expert, amateur and intrepid first trier.
The buzz of the speed, the thrill of that turn,
Sensations only the unconverted would spurn.

Summit is reached, doors slowly retreat,
Blasts of pure, crisp air first do we meet.
Skis are donned and bindings tightened,
To what is in store one's senses are heightened.

Yet before we descend let us take a breath,
Stand tall and survey the scene we have met;
Beauty on a magnitude almost beyond comprehension,
Surely there's no greater testament to God's creation?

But soon I am gone and part of the race,
Now only pray that I stay on the pace.
Precious these moments for which I have waited,
Free on the mountain to which I am fated.

R. M. Brew

A Soldier's View

Northern Ireland is a beautiful place,
Even though the Ulstermen are fighting,
Each religious sector,
Divided by walls,
Catholic on one, Protestant on the other,
The Falls, The Shankill, The Ardoyne,
People live like prisoners,
Unable to tell their tales,
Unable to live their lives,
To scared to come out into the open,
Scared of Bombs, Bullets and beatings,
Yet underneath all the hatred,
They are all Ulstermen,
Why can't they live in peace,
They are harming themselves,
No one to help them,
No Soldiers, No RUC,
All they want it peace,
All I want is to go home.

Bodle

What Is Love?

Love is like the sun reflecting on
still water
Or it can be a bird that spreads
its wings and soars into the sky.

It can be all consuming
full of passion and rage
Like a howling wind
On a bitter winkers day.

It can be forever like the flame
On the unknown soldiers grave
Or it can be gentle and sweet
Like children playing on a summers day

But love to me is growing old
And watching you every day
Love to me is you Kathryn
forever and a day.

G. Kristain Blyth

"Memories"

Fields for playing in -
Stinking Brook, foaming with suds from
washday tubs.
Bright red poppies, waving by the sewerage works.
Wild flowers, and bushes of deadly nightshade.
Blackberries "watch for the maggots".
A sand pit, the canal, bluebell wood -
The red pitch for playing rounders on -
The railway crossing, "watch out for the trains"
Time to go home and have "vanilla
slices, fresh from uncle John's bakery".

Mabel M. Dawson

The Circus

There in the middle of the circus ring,
  stood a clown with a big red nose,
while another was getting ready to fling,
  cold water at the frontline rows.

It was then the turn of that famous trapeze,
  the relief every time their hands met,
it really made you shake at the knees,
  as they did it without any net.

The elephants were a sheer delight,
  and the horses were really grand,
they were all adorned in feathers of white,
  and galloped to a percussion band.

Then at the end, the big parade,
  it really was most splendid,
followed by the Scottish Brigade,
  it's a shame the night had ended.

P. C. Cook

It's Over

Showers and sunshine, cloudy and clear,
Ever changing weather, just like you, dear.

You build me up high, and then let me down,
Now that sweet smile, then that mean frown.

It's come to the point where I would be free,
There's too little left, 'twixt you and me.

I need to regain my contentment and peace,
From bickering back chat find happy release.

When love is no more, and all has gone wrong,
There's no further reason that we go along

Pretending we care, just to fool mutual friends,
When neither forgives, nor makes any amends.

We really must split up, we've both had our say,
Despite your reproaches, I'm running away -

No more of this face can I possibly take,
For the last time of asking, either make up or break.

Laura Edwards

Heaven

Oh how I wish that I had wings
So I could fly up high in the sky
Find the heaven people talk about
Then maybe I'd find the reason why
I suffered on earth and wanted to die
I'd walk the heavens around and about
Find peace of mind I've no doubt,
Meet people with love people who'll care
A life of bliss for everyone to share.

N. Foreman

The Miracle of "Hannah"

The Church of St. Mary's, beckoned a child,
So ill, so trusting, so gentle and mild.
Earnestly we wished her, help from above,
With a healing hand, He responded with love.

She came in her push-chair, too weak to walk.
Her little mind active, and ever in thought,
She watched the Rector, with eyes so bright.
A Blessing he gave her, On her face a great light.

What did she know that we did not?
So crystal clear was the faith she'd got.
Was she able to speak with Him?
This child so wise, completely without sin.

Each week we watched her, always with prayer.
Each week she got better, a joy we all shared.
So come on Daddy, Come and Gran.
Dearest Mummy, my healing's began.

Not long after, this holy child.
Was well and happy, with joyous smile.
She plays with her friends all day long.
Then evening comes with love's grateful song.

W. O'Connor

Captured Roses

As I linger in a passion that's never known freedom
I wallow in the beauty of my single rose.
I lavish it adoringly with the jewels of all suitors
teasing my imagination with an array of dreams.

Where words of love are told in longings.
Where lovers' eyes meet in the caressing of arms
embracing the warmth of each tender touch.
Where lips meeting after a decade of silence
electrify each breath in this union of souls.
Leaving nothing too long for the door has closed.
No more running. No more longing. No more denying
The ever-present telltale signs.

For love like my rose has been captured by the rapture
of the late summer ambience.

Linda Fenton

Was There Really

Was there really elephants nanny for
Everyone to see?
Was there really trees to climb and
Fishes in the sea?
Was the sky really blue, and the grass
Always green
Was there really animals nanny, and
Dolphins to be seen
Was there ever peace on earth or was
There always war
Did children really starve to death if so,
Then why, what for
In answer to your questions child, Oh yes
All this and more
The world in which you live in, is nothing
Like before
But I can't answer why and when, or even
Try to explain
Why man destroyed your future world, just
For the sake of gain

Sue Richards

A Bride's Thoughts

If only you could be here, on this my wedding day,
So that I could thank you for your help along the way,
From infant's faltering steps to this walk along the aisle,
You cheered me on and guided me,
In triumph and in trial.
You taught me your fine principles
With these I'll never part,
So many happy memories are treasured in my heart.
Dear Mum, Dear Dad,
You were my dearest friends, until that tragic day,
When all too unexpectedly you were snatched away.
But I will never let you down, this I promise you,
I will stay with what you taught me, be honest and be true,
And today on this, my wedding day, as I walk down the aisle,
To my brand new life of happiness,
I will feel you near and smile.

Myra Johnston

Nan

God has the right to take from you,
    So with him we can't argue.
Because you know it's not right,
    For your Nan you put up a fight.
You build your fight with pain and tear,
    For without your Nan you do fear.
As the time draws near the say and goodbye.
    You reject it and feel it's a lie.
But then the lie becomes so true,
    And now there's nothing you can do.
Pain was something Nan never had,
    So this doesn't make you feel too sad.

Nathalie J. Cunningham

The Head of the Rose

Violet moons and purple doves reflect upon your shores,
Solitary rose heads are lying by your doors.
Deep peace in your heart, as the ferryman hums,
True joy in your soul, as your heart skips a beat,
Closing your eyes, now the world's at your feet.
Maybe you've flown in late with no wings,
Not knowing which one of you to believe.
So live your life to the head of the rose,
Tomorrow's unborn and you're not alone,
For there is a statue in every stone.

If you are taught not to love, just to sit still
And you know you're remembering to breathe, against your will,
Never mind, we all feel the same sun,
We all have thoughts, often too deep for tears.
So, from the winds of heaven, to the head of the rose,
Live your life the way you chose!

Vicky Giles

White World

Snowflakes falling, silent and light;
Steady, relentlessly all through the night.
Shrouding the houses, adorning the trees,
Rounding the corners, swept by the breeze.
Creating new contours,
Disguising deformities,
Thickening hourly and forming enormities.

P. E. Laycock

"I Haven't Seen You for Ages!"

A friendly anxious voice, yet trained and calm
Explains the purpose of the call, "It's `home alarm',
You're on our list. We've rung her twice!" The dread refrain;
"Can you respond?" Of Course! My muscles tense, the strain
First numbs my sense, and then with beads upon my brow
A sharp rebuke to such a fainting heart, it's here and now
I need clear thought, a torch to light
That dark forbidding wintry night.
I'm on my feet, well armed to fight my wall
Of fear. Emergency? A heart attack or fall?
I reach her door, my mouth is dry, it's on the latch,
I hail, "Hello", no cry returns, no snatch
Of sound dispels the deathly stillness of the hour.
The thin torch beam illuminates my target door,
A chink of light betrays some life within, I shout again
And burst, into the room and laugh insane
With sheer relief, my 'Ma' is there, her hearing aid
In bits upon the floor in neat array is laid.
Her look of puzzlement gives way to pure delight
A close embrace, a misty kiss destroy my awful fright.

H. Mitchell

Jamaica

Sugary white sands blue sky and sea
exquisite colours the place to be.
Tropical fruits, the sun's warming rays
in the breeze the palm gently sways.
Waterfalls cascading down mountain ridges
perhaps we may see a few small bridges,
Rum and lilt to quench our thirst,
but ginger biscuits and cake to eat first.
Reggae and calypso beats to hear,
steel band music is always near.
Limbo dancing this an art to perfect
basket making - on these we reflect.
Caribbean cocktails - such unique taste
take time to digest, there's simply no haste.
Enjoy a trip on a bamboo raft
these carefree days - see the local craft.
Relax as the fiery sunset does fall
oranges, yellows, pinks to be seen by all.
These idyllic scenes with everlasting treasure
this beautiful island with so much pleasure.

Margaret Jackson

Witchcraft Cat

Black as black
Eyes as sharp as its claws.
The witchcraft cat does not stay out
But always stays indoors.

Balancing on my broomstick
Hypnotizing eyes
The witchcraft cat
Can get its own way whenever it tries.

Black as black
She sits and mews.
Spider pate or kity kat worm
Which one will she choose

Balancing on my broomstick
Hypnotizing eyes
She sits there without a sound
And never ever lies.

Leigh-Anne Gawtry

Full Circle

Sticky Jammy finger marks and much more mucky bums,
Sleepless nights and endless washing are all privileges of mums.
You cope with their sniffles and everyday lumps and bumps,
Then along comes the chicken pox, the measles, the mumps.
Their very first school day, off they go spick and span
And they come home with stories of how they danced, sang and ran.
The years roll along, life's small battles are won,
At times there's been tears, but mostly it's been fun.
Then one afternoon, as they walk through the door
You are stopped in your tracks, they are children no more!
In place of your spotty tomboy and your rather gawky lad,
There's two beautiful young adults, for some reason, you feel sad,
Gone are dolls and guns, colouring books and other children's toys,
Instead there's a stream of lovely girls and rather handsome boys.
They wed their loves and fly the nest, please be happy my
darlings you pray,
Then they come to you, all dewy-eyed, to tell of a special birthday.
The memories come flooding back, the love, the tears, the joy,
I wonder what will this one be, beautiful lass or bouncing boy?
For the joy your child brings, the happiness, the love.
Is unequalled by anything, thank You our dear Lord above.

J. Impey

A Dedicate to Judy

The gates of heaven was waiting for you
So it was goodbye what more could I do.
It's been such a long time since you've been gone.
Yet life goes on, I've got to be strong.
And now I've found you, it may be a glass
But to me it bring's comfort to talk to you at last.
Something's you tell me it make's me feel sad
Most of the time's the thing's are not so bad.
You came here to help me. To show me the way.
You're always kind with the things that you say.
I thank you Judy for being so close.
I wish I could see you, I miss you so much.
Yet deep in my heart and I'm sure that it's true
You'll always be with me, I'll never be blue,
You're the sister I worshipped when you was alive
Still I'll love you the way that I did in the past.
There's no much to offer as the year's pass me by.
But when my time come's I'll see you at last.

Wendy White

Contemplating a Peacock

Bright, brilliant bird, all iridescent glow
Stately and self-contained as on your "progress" go.
Head held with regal pride, and neck a lustrous blue.
Enthralled we gaze - our homage pay to you.

Your plumage spread into a glorious fan,
A hundred eyes aglow within its span.
Rich blues and greens - your native India's pride
Reflected in that elegant, slow stride.

A visitor from such exotic strand.
How do you fare in this cold, alien land?

Margaret M. Osoba

River Days

Silent water, slowly sliding;
Stately swans, serenely gliding;
Swallow and kingfisher, skimming so fast;
A lone bittern's call booming over the marsh.
Waterside homes with sloping lawns;
The magical stillness of misty dawns;
Sparkling sunlight, rustling reeds;
Sailing-craft scudding along in the breeze.
Water a-bustle with all kinds of boats;
Fishermen, patiently watching their floats;
Windmill in ruins, its sails now at rest;
Sun painting the sky as it sinks in the west.
Darkness descending, owl's haunting cry;
Silent water, sliding by.

Margaret J. West

Reflections

The oily shape slips
silently through the dark waters.
Its silhouette losing shape
as the river ebbs and flows.
A streak of moonlight
pierces the clouds above
and shoots into the dark icy river below.
The rays of light ricochet,
glimmering, sparkling, shimmering
through the ripples,
Cutting through the very heart
of the river bed.
The fingers of light
search out the shadowy shape,
illuminating its glistening scales.
For a moment the reflection is complete.
Then darkness swallows
The scene once more.

Sophie Aylward

The Red-Backed Shrike

Gaily you adorned those summer skies
So long ago unto our eyes,
When days were long and your song
Swept through valleys fair and strong.
You came, with flamed, burning wings
From lands afar this green your home
As like a star, should never fade.
Winging you way through sunlight and shade,
Resting in some unknown glade,
Unaware of man's mortal fate,
You lived and life without a trace
Was bountiful in your waking.
To those who know and those who seek
This one small bird who in retreat,
Sings out its song for one to greet
And though in vain it cannot meet
That, which is eternally ours.

N. L. Farquharson

Lost Love

My heart was breaking, no one knew or even cared,
So many happy hours we had shared.
Walking the beach, writing our names in the wet sand
Then off we would go, hand in hand.
You went to the City, to learn a new skill,
When you came home and told me, I said you were ill.
You said you were sorry, it wasn't your fault
You had tried very hard to live as you were taught.
You had met someone new and realized you were gay,
Then you said goodbye and just walked away.
I hope you are happy in your male-only life,
And don't regret not having a wife.
I shall always love you, but in a different way,
Perhaps there is room on this earth - for both straight and gay.

Margaret A. Murton

A Mother's Reflections

You have to work you own lives out
So please be sure what you're about
Be always thoughtful always kind
And scandalous tongues please never mind
Help the helpless help the poor
What you can do is so much more

Keep your mind and body clean
A paragon of virtue you'll be seen
Walk in the light, keep out of the shade
The way you are is what you made
So keep heart pure, keep eyes bright
You'll always know what's wrong what's right

Keep God within your heart and soul
And only then your life is whole.

F. Shelvock

Cry That Broken Heart Away

What are you hiding there lady, behind that 'I'm fine' disguise,
Some people you can fool maybe, but pain shows there in your eyes.
You don't have me believing in that look at the smile on my face,
Tears falling had my pain easing, when I was stood there in your place.

You gotta bow down your pretty head and cry,
There's no use in just holding it high,
When you're breaking up deep down inside,
There's no use in just trying to hide,
Let yourself go, let it out now today,
Then just cry that broken heart away.

That hurting will never end, until you learn to let those tears start,
Holding on to all of that pain, you'll never ever mend your heart.
Can't just stay there pretending, that you don't even know what I mean,
With that 'my heart don't need mending' look, that you keep showing to me.

You gotta bow down your pretty head and cry,
There's no use in just holding it high,
When you're breaking up deep down inside,
There's no use in just trying to hide.
Let yourself go, let it out now today,
Then just cry that broken heart away.

Ray Bowden

A Little Miracle

As she grew inside my tummy, a little miracle beginning to form,
Snuggled up in her mothers' womb, so cosy and so warm.
A new life had been made out of happiness and love,
This beautiful gift was sent from God above.

As I felt her move and gain her strength,
Steadily putting on the ounces and growing in length
A unique bond had formed right from the start
And I knew I'd love her with all of my heart.

From the moment I held her, I'll never forget
The way I felt when our eyes first met.
A tiny pink bundle, perfect in every way
I love her much more than words can say.

She makes me feel so happy and proud
When she squeals with delight and laughs out loud
Her smile brightens up the dullest of days,
Bringing me so much joy in lots of ways.

I love every giggle, every frown and every tear
She knows she is safe and sound when I hold her near.
To me she is an angel, who I love like no other
For there is nothing greater than the love of a mother.

Kim O'Neill

Off the Richter Scale

There is a little-noticed underground movement,
teenaged, drugged not on pills
but by its own inborn skills.

Drawing on centuries-old concertos
and fantasies, it re-imagines
feelings of those born sometimes

continents away on mountain sides,
in valleys, cathedral cities;
and communicates, in concert halls,

and via television (acne side away from camera)
by its butterfly fingering, puffed out cheeks,
and frowning concentration

its apolitical concerns: the tectonics
of emotion, the eruption of islands
to rhapsodic heights, the shifting

from sites of settee sensitivity,
that puny microcosm,
of whole selves to out there,

the macrocosm
and a coda without end.

Margot Duncan

"Twilight"

In our twilight years we remember other years.
Some were bright. We remember with delight!
Others we would rather forget! Those
Where the light has not reached the end of the tunnel yet.
Twilight! Means what it says; one cannot see very far ahead.
As darkness falls reveries beholds the hours
of slumber will unfold dreams that will never be told.
Twilight! Is also the dawn of the day, come what may
we have to accept whatever comes our way.
No matter how many years have past away!

A. A. G. Staggs

"Love Is"

Love is caring - sharing and holding hands,
Smiling, beguiling and making plans,
To be together forever and a day,
Whispering "I love you" in a special way.

I need you with me, and always there,
To hear your voice, and know you care,
Love is constant making life worthwhile,
I hold your hand and see you smile.

As time goes by and age appears,
Love is strong - love is tears,
I need you with me through hail and strife,
To be together as your wife.

Love's forever - love's for life
It's caring, sharing,
  "Love is"

Virginia Jarosz

Words

Words should flow together like a river.
Smoothly and fluently, riding the ripples.
Without any inconvenience
Negotiating the twists and turns,
And the odd fallen trees,
Which try to obscure.

Words moving in harmony, side by side.
As they excite and delight.
The eyes that gaze upon it.
That never cease to amaze,
Or to leave you in a daze.
In any uncertain way.

Words releases anxiety, held within you.
Carrying your thoughts along with its current.
When you wish to plunge in.
Be totally submerged and consumed.
Within its wondrous soul,
Called words simply words.

Ryan L. Mellis

True Love

True love is so special,
So constant and deep.
It goes deep inside forever to keep.

A lasting bond which never dies,
but goes on growing and shows in your eyes.

To feel both relaxed,
to share how you feel.
To be able to laugh when you both feel blue.

Relieving the stress of life's ups and downs,
with a cuddle and smile and never a frown.

Being gentle and caring loving and true,
A tight hug means everything to both of you.

The future ahead many dreams to be shared,
to enjoy together and never be scared.
growing old gracefully, but being young too,
life is for living to be enjoyed by two.

Linda Hilton

Droplets of Rain

It declines from the sky,
swiftly and quietly roaming through the air,
Scattering lifelessly upon the ground,
Yet still is does not care to stop.
Suddenly it unites with all.
Neither desolate nor distinct it begins its voyage.
with no sight nor sound it follows,
knowing not where to go or whom to pursue.
While it still moves the clouds slowly disappear,
And yet still it does not care.
The light appears causing stillness, its rays slowly get to work.
The others stop falling and disappear.
The united slowly fade, sinking - drying so unaware.
And as the rays show their greatness,
It submerges beneath the ground. And soon it seems as it was
not there, like a phantom that shows no life, it's gone.
Yet it does not care.
It only had a short life, and then it disappeared,
knowing no where it was going, or what it was.
Yet still it does not care.

Lucia Oshinaike

War

Out of the distant came the sound of the guns
Spitting and firing the flame of death
Many young lives will not wake to the dawn
Only their bodies are left
What a waste of so many young lives
Battling to keep us free
Not for themselves did they give their lives
They did it for you and for me
The guns are now silent all is still
The world is now at peace
One lone piper plays his lament
By the broken and twisted oak tree
God in his wisdom sits high on his throne
Studying the world below
When will mankind learn to live side by side
This we will never know.

G. W. Liveley

"Revolutions the Second Coming"

Television is a modern means to lull viewers into acceptance.
Take, for instance, extra-terrestrials.
It's no good looking to Venus or Mars -
People from those planets came here eons ago.
A gem of genetic engineering with primitives so
Gave the hirsute a giant leap, to man!
Thus eradicating slow evolution or natural selection.
Martians, Venusians; call them what you will,
Destroyed their own planets, settled earth; still
"They" had to start again. The beginning.
Consider the scientific advanced minds tied earth-bound.
How, for instance, does one equate 'e'=mc2' to an ape?
God's ultimate jibe! what a jape!
The time is ripe for the second coming!
So television will lull the people on earth
In 'sci-fi' films and those 'close encounters'.
Do not look to Mars or Venus -
"They" are here and - hopefully -
Will, by will, save our planet - this time!
Otherwise it is eternity for us all!

R. Peter Smith

Positive

You can't possibly lose in pursuing to gain
Take life as it comes and you'll move past the rain
Take pride in yourself and everything you do
Look past the grey skies and you'll see the blue
When you're feeling low and losing an appetite for living
Don't concentrate on self pity, but focus on giving
If you strive to achieve, one day you'll reach your aims,
And treasure friends and laughter, it will pull you through life's
pains.

Sirita Sen

Our Christmas Tree

Our Christmas tree stands in the hall,
So fresh and green and proud and tall,
With gifts all 'round for one and all,
But I can't see one for me.

It's covered with exciting things;
Tinsel, sugar can on strings,
For Judy, there's a doll that sings,
But there's nothing there for me.

A gun for Tom, a book for Sue,
A coloured tie for granddad too,
There's even a present for our dog Blue,
But there isn't one for me.

Silver bells that chime so gay,
Ringing out for Christmas day,
I see red gloves for auntie May;
But I can't see a thing for me.

I've searched all 'round our Christmas tree,
And there's nothing for me that I can see;
I've been as good as good can be,
Dear Santa please remember me.

J. Marskell

"Only Once in Our Haven"

From mist clamoured mornings to deep raven nights, salt
souls ring silent knells, no more in beat with nature's wing.
Grey seals nose a curious pose and cathedral high seagulls
in lament do cry, as homeward the bobbing fishermen sing.

Silent as tombstones before dawn, blind but to doom the oiler
skin strained in prayer, lumbers in wretched darkness near.
Majestic, deep laden with ignorance; meekly lost to shore as
beguiled by a siren wind, cutlass keen for her cargo of fear.

Unheard, brined-eyed pilots call what drowned sailors saw.
St. Anne's spuming in gratitude, aids wrecking a paw.
A talon each rock, so secure of claw; no grace a ship now,
a "Sea Empress" no more.

Blessed creatures of life dappling happy they came,
lie spill covered in destiny of Earth's life blood of shame.
Kind hearts can but measure by trembling and dread,
how slick was our folly - gifted black choking death.

Our guilt flowed lays cloaked over on rock fall and shore.
Our sadness unanswered, never questioned before.
Only salvaged small pride from this legacy so graven,
such little be saved - "Only Once In Our Haven".

Owain Williams

For the Angels of Dunblane

Knee bends and curls, running about,
So many small voices starting to shout,
On that cold Wednesday morn something spoilt their game,
Like a dark black cloud engulfing Dunblane,
Calm and collect through the hall he came,
Evil personified - even given a name.
Opening doors, four handguns he brought,
Opening fire, his victims he sought.
What took place next is hard to believe
An innocent shout becomes a scream.
The terror, the fear, children charging about.
Stopped in a second, sixteen angels wiped out.
A lady so brave, protecting with care.
One fatal shot - she's no longer there.
Parents waiting, showing emotions eyes flowing with tears.
Asking what about us? - But not wanting to hear.
Relief, guilt, sharing their grief and despair,
No-one ever knowing why Thomas Hamilton chose there.
The whole world grieves for them over an act so insane,
And for innocent lives on that dark morn in Dunblane.

Lesley Bradley

Life

Life can be happy, life can be sad
So much to be grateful for, why think of the bad
A roof over our heads and food to eat
Think of the souls who live on the street

How I long for open spaces,
Less roads too and happy faces
More places to run and be free
A slower pace for you and me

The sky above, the birds that sing
How content they are with such a small thing
Why do we worry, why do we fret?
For all that we have, we mustn't forget.

So, let us ever grateful be
Open our eyes and really see
Let's be caring, let's be kind
And then the real treasures in life we'll find.

Margaret I. Goldsmith

What Belfast Means to Me

My favourite's got to be the sea
So relaxed, calm sparkling to me
The beautiful sands spreads for miles
Birds singing as they fly over our land

The summer days have got to be
Beaches which are longing for children and me
Family and friends all gather together
Hearing their laughter, and enjoying the weather.

City hall, Shaw's bridge,
Belfast is that place for me
Standing still, I stare
Beautifying our land so fair,

Forty shades of green are seen
As flocks of sheep they stand
It really is a promise land
Oh peace, Oh peace, we have at hand.

Paula E. Milne

Them and Us - Or Personalities

It takes all sorts to make a world,
Some like their hair straight;
Others prefer it curled.
The rest wish they had some, any way.

Some are nosy parkers,
They are helping the community.
Where would the rest of us be,
Without them and their 'barkers'?

Some like to entertain,
Others find it all a pain.
No smiles flicker on their faces,
They'd rather sit and watch the races.

Many like to review the world around them,
Listen to, 'The World Today';
Take part in it, in some way.
Or simply sit and watch the rest; then blame them.

Olive Tyrie

Untitled

See her run with rage as thunderstorms stab her silver skin
Swishing past the naked trees distorting shadows from within
She rides alone, cutting her way through the seasonal land
Moving, sometimes silent with soft touches in my whispering hand

She holds no disguise as she lies naked to the sun
But her mystery kisses me as I then watch her run
She will hold me forever in her only loving motion
She will take my tears to the ocean fulfilling my emotion

Her body ever changing as she grows with the falling rain
The nature of her soul never fears for any pain
As I fall into her fold cascading back to my dream thought
Once again enchanting my vision with all that she has brought

Mark Parry

Tears

Tears are for laughter tears are for pain.
Tears should be shed as God sheds the rain.
We should not hold back this way to ease grief
God gave them to us as a means of relief.

So feel not ashamed by people who say
"You must never shed tears and never give way"
So cry when you're happy and cry when you're sad
To show your emotions can never be bad.
Feel sorrow for those who never can weep
And feel the relief when their sorrow is deep.

D. Fenoulhet

Drift

Not all can partake of the American Dream
Some of us must share in the Nightmare
Which, like a running river, flowing all-stream
Leads turbulently to nowhere

I was standing by Godot's tree
Waiting vainly for him to arrive
Worn out of clothes and dignity
Only on hope do I survive

The rain-clouds came, watering the Elysian Fields
Where the grateful dead abide
But dust and ashes cover the land of Sheba
Where the wretched living reside

And the mad dogs, crying 'Havoc!'
Came streaming forth from their master's whistle
From bone they ripped the flesh of men
And bathed children in their spittle.

Oladipo Agboluaje

All Kinds of Everything

As I look down from the mountain top onto the homes below,
some of whom I recognize, and others I do not know.
I wonder of the inhabitants, who dwell secretly inside,
maybe old people, ignored, dependant, now lacking in their pride.
Young children abused, helpless in their plight, Looking for a safe
haven, afraid of the blanket of night. Women beaten daily,
degraded by the men they wed, Men working for low wages,
diligently providing, their families with daily bread.
Invalids, who can never set foot, outside their own front door,
never to feel God's air on their face or walk in their street once more.

But then maybe there are others who feel safe and secure inside,
bringing up their families, and swelling with love and pride.
Being content and happy, in a job that suits them well,
facing the day joyfully with a purpose, never knowing hell.
Preparing well planned meals, with an interest, And eaten off the
table, that has only known the best. I know now, that all kinds
off everything, can be together, in just one place, And all kinds of
homes represents a different face. And you have to go deep
inside the rooms to see what's hidden out of sight, And enter
humbly every beating heart, to find its glowing light.

Sandra Taylor

Untitled

Is your hope always grounded in something?
sometimes I get a glimpse of pure hope
A hope, that is not tied to anything, anybody.
I hope, not because I believe in God - that I don't -
so His grace favouring me in this or the next life is out;
not because I believe in any innate sense of justice,
that I'll get justice since I imagine injustice has been meted out
to me; not because I believe in any law of averages,
that enough wrongs have been done to me
and now it is the turn of the right;
not because I believe in people,
they continue mostly to disappoint me in behaving predictably.
My hope doesn't spring out of any helplessness either,
that what else is there to do but hope
No, I just hope without reference to context,
any context.

C. K. Purandare

The Happy Otter

The summer sun shines on a land of quiet rural charm,
The air is sweet, the water's fresh, the mood is one of calm.
An otter wakes from gentle sleep and trots out of his home -
A holt near to the riverside from which he likes to roam.

He trots along the wooded bank, the water here flows slow,
He makes his way upstream to where it has a faster flow.
The river here's a rockery with small cascades and pools,
Our otter splashes, swims, has fun in waters clear and cool.

He scrambles over rocks and stones, gives little cries of joy,
He cannot get enough of this exciting little ploy.
Later on he goes back home, to see his cubs at play,
His wife is dining on a fish she caught not far away.

They all unite and frisk about, each has a lot of fun,
They nuzzle then they have a rest in warm and pleasant sun.
A gentle breeze now stirs the trees refreshing those it meets -
The creatures of this pretty place afar from busy streets.

Mark Green

A Winter's Night

The pale moon shone through the winter fog,
The air was bitter and full of smog,
He rode through the night with a stern looking face
She sat waiting patiently dressed in lace
The road was long and stretched out ahead
His temper was flaring, he was seeing red,
The minutes passed she watched the clock
And alas she heard the wanted knock
She opened the door and in he stepped
There was a loud bang all of a sudden - she leapt
She turned her back to walk away
He caught her wrist and told her to stay
Don't do this to me, he begged and pleaded
A little reassurance was all he needed
No she said and there was hate in her voice
He had to do it she left him no choice
He raised his arm and hit her hard
Her body lay motionless - stiff as card
He mounted his horse as the day got light
And he never looked back upon that night . . .

Lareina Connolly

Untitled

This world we live in is ruled by good and ruled by bad.
The answer to what it's all about is very very dear
To lie tempted by the bad, life can be easier I fear.
So the bad side of this world grows stronger like a weed.
A seed that takes, and hurts, unloved it grows - succeeds.
For nothings stronger, bigger, than a nettle a spiteful weed.
And God He watches sees His creation His precious seeds
To him He takes the brave the honest and the weary home above.
But what happens to the weeds?

M. A. Pope

"Doubt"

I have never been an angel
Some would say uncouth
But what I lacked in breeding
I supplemented with pride.
Proud of my country and all it has achieved.

But in my mind "doubt"
Has sown its seed.
What has happened to this land
That is decimated with greed.
Landscapes lost forever wetlands all dried out.

Wildlife of my childhood endangered
If not gone.
Family life we all once new
Replaced by stress and strain.
Will our envied lifestyle
Ever return again?

V. J. Jackson

Mum and Dad

My mum, she was an angel
The best that there could be
God said her job was to be 'Mum'
For Jill and Jean and me.

My mum, she was an angel
She worked so hard for us,
And struggled with more rough than smooth,
But never made a fuss.

My mum, she was an angel
We miss her more each day
They say that time will heal the pain
But ours, won't ever go away

My dad he was an angel
The best that there could be
God said his job was to be "Dad"
For Jill and Jean and me.

Now Mum and Dad are angels
Their work on earth is done.
God's taken them to heaven
To rest in peace, and live as one.

P. Barnes

The Overwhelming Shadows

The overwhelming shadows in the corners of my mind.
Sometimes bring such sadness, peace and rest are hard to find.
So many questions left unanswered, doubts and inner fears.
The hardest part of all is accepting you're no longer here.

My thoughts return to that sunny morning, Tuesday 4th May.
And the sadness which unfolded before the end of day.
I had still to learn your life was so brutally taken away.
And come to bear this sadness which is here to stay.

My memories I treasure because they can't be taken away.
They are precious and they're mine on a sad and lonely day.
Some are happy, some are sad, some are the best we ever had.
They make me feel so thankful and so very glad.

This nightmare started over two years ago.
When will it end? I really don't know.
I will carry on pretending, put on a brave smile.
Just make believe everything is fine for another while.

I have got to be strong, it's expected you see.
Hide all these feelings deep inside me.
Until I pick up the pieces, carry on with my fight.
For truth, justice, and all that is right.

Yvonne Marie Beattie

Demons Dark Depression

The book that I was reading, fell, I watch it with surprise
Stooping low to pick it up I feel the panic rise
The blinding, nameless, fear takes hold, my breath is kept at bay
I feel the flutter of my heart like butterflies at play

A chilling numbness in my arms, my hands and fingers shake
I close my eyes as once again depression claims its mate
The pain begins, insidious till shrieking muscles twist
My world goes dark in agony, my eyes are clouds of mist

The tears, my only self defence, pour streaming down my face
I curl myself into a void of aching, grieving space
Darkness, corners, each I seek avoiding nightmares call
Yet fearful, knowing that I have no real control at all

I bend my head, the tears flow on, depression holds my hand
Regret and grief, anxiety, self pity.. but, unplanned
The hours pass, the tears increase, I ride the waves of hell
I taste despair that once again invades my empty shell

At last I feel the strength to rise, to hold my fears at bay
I pick the book up from the floor and face another day
If you are strong you'll never know the lonely fearful tension
That comes unbidden on the wings of Demons dark depression.

Maureen Bowery

Sounds in the Night

Voices calling in the night,
The birds are on their homeward flight,
The Fox is calling to his mate.
The cats fighting at the garden gate.
The donkeys braying in the field.
The distant sounds from the motorway,
Another end to a perfect day.

P. Horton

Sunrise

The sun rises this morning,
the birds begin to sing,
Just as the day is dawning,
and church bells start to ring.

It's going to be a beautiful day,
the children are coming out,
They're coming out to play,
they begin to run, giggle, scream and shout

The air is wonderfully clean,
there's a gentle breeze.
The grass is a nice shade of green,
the pollen makes me sneeze

There's not a cloud in the sky,
not a raindrop to be seen,
you can see the birds fly,
I wonder, where they've been.

Come on, let's go for a walk,
in the early morning sun,
We can, look, explore and talk,
and maybe, have some fun!

S. Simpson

Summer's Gone

Sunny days have long gone by,
The birds have lost their song.
The reason is quiet simple winters come along . . .

The squirrels dashing to and fro
Looking for nuts so brown
They end up running through the leaves
That are lying on the ground . . .

As I walk along the stream I hear the geese above,
They are going to a lake,
A place that they all love . . .

It's time to say goodbye to these fields I dearly love,
And leave the workings of the winter
To the great gods up above . . .

P. Frost

On Green Dolphin Street

The train has reached its destination
Some people are on vacation
Others drift, wearily, from the station
To their relevant location.

Suddenly there is the expressway
With 4th Avenue in sight
Pedestrians, scurry, to and fro, in the streets and avenues without
much delay as if it is their right.

7th Avenue is looming
Stores are booming
Activity is at its highest peak
Shoppers are on a lucky streak.

The Park on Green Dolphin Street is beckoning
Time for reckoning
Shoppers weave their way to a secret haunt
With gossip of the day to flaunt
Discussions of the latest fashions are in progress
No less.

Moira Dillet

Pleasant Daydreams

The fire warmed her soul.
The body that housed her laid down.
She was covered by blankets of leaves,
The rain was silver diamonds.

Diamonds landed on her eyes, she blinked.
Stars fell at her feet golden red.
The man she thought of kissed her fingers.
All her rings, changed into gold, and vanished.

Her face turned into joy.
She dyed her hair until it was the ocean.
People looked at her, her body wisdom.
Her feet finally moved her onwards.

We all see her, wandering beauty.
Changing flowers into children, creating rainbows.
Eternal summer, silver virtue, emerald mind.
Her name is known to all of us, we call her Art
We call her Poetry.

K. Brydie Terris

An Ode to Man

Humans are a species - said to have a developed brain,
Sometimes hard to understand - the superiority they claim,
The world is seldom better - for many things they do,
It seems real effort for mankind - is made by very few.

In living life we all are gamblers - in one way or another,
Hoping to acquire wealth without work - or too much bother,
Some foray in the stock exchange - some to horses cast a glance,
Do you favour pools - the lottery - is it scratch cards perchance?

So this is the nineteen nineties - an enlightened age we're told,
But there are many who don't believe it - perhaps they're just too old,
The millennium will come even ne'er a flag be waved,
London will still be London - tho' streets with gold aren't paved.

And now we look ahead - our finest hopes firmly afloat,
Politicians, so seldom worthy - their words we will not quote,
One millennium is over - some effort has been made and done,
Could it be the year two thousand will herald a rising sun?

D. F. Smith

The Fortress

The still emptiness of the morning,
Still rings in the ears of oblivion.
Soundless sounds and deafening silence,
Crush the heart of defeat.
If I reach out,
To touch the crimson stain,
Where the petals fall,
Will I only catch a faint perfume of their lives.
In such a hollow shell,
Even the sound of the sea,
Pales into insignificance.
Take the sword of truth,
And storm these battlements,
For in a lifetime only one may enter here.

Penny Morris

The Blue Man

It was a dream come true,
The first time I saw you,
You had haunted my sleep for many years,
From which I had woken eyes full of tears,
Wondering who you were,
Where you could be found,
Would you be lost in the sands of time,
Our hearts never to entwine,
Then destiny led me by the hand,
to you and the promised land,
Were we will stand hand in hand,
Faces caressed by the warm Sirocco,
In the promised Land of Morocco.

Vannesa Fitzgerald

Flower People

When I look at flowers, it often seems to me,
That each one has a character, its own personality.

Dandelion's the schoolboy, yellow tousled hair,
Brash, and rather cheeky, eager for a "dare".

Daisy's a little schoolgirl. Fresh-faced and golden-eyed.
A blush upon her cheek, in the grass she tries to hide.

Dahlia's the painted lady, blood-red pointed nails.
Beside her garish beauty, the little violet quails.

For Violet's the Good Samaritan. Good deeds are quietly done.
Never pushing forward, never eager for the sun.

Delphinium's a haughty model, standing straight and tall.
Those beautiful blue eyes, gazing over all.

Lavender is Grandma. Gentle, sweet and kind.
Her delicate perfume denoting peace of mind.

Arum lilies are the nuns, clothed in spotless white,
With their purity of spirit, a truly holy sight.

But the Queen of the Flower People, for beauty and for grace,
Must be the English rose - she must take pride of place.

A. Logan-Turvey

The Dell (Hexthorpe Flatts)

Oh! It seems so long ago,
That folks were treated to a show,
Of Yorkshire miners playing brass,
With bandstand centred on the grass.

Chairs of white arranged in rows,
Children in their Sunday bows
Not allowed to shout or play,
And spoil the highlight of the day.

The bus arriving was a sight,
Bandsmen with their buttons bright
Waved to the crowd and then behold,
Our eyes were drawn to gleaming gold

Of trumpets, cornets, symbols too,
These to mention but a few
Of instruments required to form
A band to which the crowd would warm.

Once seated and the practice through,
Each person with a perfect view,
Sat quietly to enjoy a time
When brass band music reigned sublime.

S. Simpson

Battles Lost

What is it in his heart
That forces him to play the part
Of the modern day chivalrous knight
Who takes the action he thinks is right
When faced with a lady in distress
Forgets his friends and ignores the rest

She comes to him with outstretched arms
And drops the purse from her palm
Her tears they roll down either cheek
Comfort from him she's here to seek
As she speaks of suicide and homicide
Talk that comes from the bottle inside

Why can't he walk on by
Leave their problems to another guy
Just concentrate on living his life
To think of himself for once would be nice
You don't have to take them on
Walk out the door and they'll be gone
Everything will work out in the end
With or without your help my friend.

Shaun C. Holmes

"Leather Diamond"

On fields where the sun does shine.
Sometimes they are wet, and full of grime.
An oval ball is used with skill.
Brings to many, such a thrill.
You find these men of the muscular kind.
With strength of body and of mind.
A scrum, tackle and many a scrape
Much love for this ball of an unusual shape.
In different formations, they run and do shout,
Trying to catch each other out.
Each playing without hesitation,
On their bodies cause laceration,
Through these posts of enormous height,
Players run, and kick, with all their might
Scattered at times across this field,
Other nationalities, not wishing to yield.
Those who lose, are also "meritorious"
Not only they, who are "Victorious".
To all who bring much pleasure
"I bequeath My Diamond Made Of Leather".

Kenneth Anderson Bradley

Little I

Yellow flowers by a stream,
Summer sun in full agleam,
Willow trees whistle by,
As I sit here, little I.

The greenest grass I'd ever seen,
The biggest blooms that's ever been,
Me among them, little I,
Oh, how I wish that I could fly.

Bright red roses with a beautiful bouquet,
Busy men afar collecting all the hay,
These are all the things I see,
Sitting here, little me.

Tracey Jane Crewe

In Praise of Spring

Woke up one morning to a medley of birdsong,
Sunbeams a-dance in my room.
Welcome, sweet harbingers. Welcome to Springtime!
Farewell to cold Winter's gloom.

Stepped out that morning to a flirting of feathers,
Dew-drops a-twinkle on lawn;
Joyous my steps and I thrilled to the promise
Of new life at every Spring's dawn.

Sang on that morning to Nature's awak'ning,
Music alive in my soul,
Thankfully joining in Spring's celebration
Of worship to God, Lord of All.

Margaret Haining

Refections

In fearful times of suffering I try to listen for your words
sometimes they seem to be delivered like a pair of humming birds
but in times of expectation, confusion and great pressure
your words can seem so vivid, so hard to hear or measure

This is when I sit alone in the dark
letting images of life pass by as quick as a swimming shark
the time I spend is peaceful
with no worries, or no strife
just a moment of reflection upon my taxing life

I feel at ease and mellow
although possibly I am unlike any ordinary fellow
but as seconds pass me by
never once do I ask a question
or demand a silly why
the answer's unimportant, I know I need not try
for this day is for reflection, for life to pass me by
and tomorrow will begin so then I will think of time.

Kathryn Clear

Somewhere!

I wish I was somewhere,
Somewhere out of this place,
A place far away,
Not part of this race.

Where nothing would happen,
Time would pass slow,
Where everyone's equal,
Not part of a show.

This somewhere place, where will it be,
Beyond these life-times where a new sun shines,
When will we go there, this day, the next,
It's been spoken about and written in text.

In times to come,
We will all be there,
No difference shown,
Nothing to compare,

That's the place I want to be,
Beyond the stars, beyond the sea,
So when we meet we'll all be there,
That faraway place the call SOMEWHERE!

Stewart Wilson

Teenage Years

Help! I'm being invaded by these growing beings
Suddenly you're forced to be more aware of their feelings
Save all of your strength for the teenage years
The mood swings, the stomps and many many tears

They know what's best, and put the world to right
You tighten your lips and try not to bite
For if we do, they threaten to leave home
What we don't want is to be alone.

Money grows on trees, so they think
For the disco, burger bar and even the ice-rink
Boyfriends, girlfriends come and go and I must say
Agony aunts and uncles we have to play.

The telephone is not ours any more,
As we watch the bills soar and soar.
Bedroom doors, banged hard, coming off their hinges
While we sit and watch TV tensed and cringing

The house shudders whilst the music plays
Gone are the classical musical good old days.
Make the most of life whilst the kids are young.
For when they grow-up, the house is theirs until they have gone.

Yvonne Husseyin

Deepest Blue Sea

Crashing waves trickle over the sand,
Splashing drops of turquoise blue,
Skies of cotton clouds,
With blazing sun peeping through

Mysteries of another world,
Hidden away from human life,
Fish glide through water,
Like hot butter slipping through a knife

Tranquil sounds of chattering dolphins,
Conversing amongst each other,
A world so full of peace,
Which no human being will ever discover

Below the vast amount of water,
Known as the deepest blue sea,
Lies a place of total beauty,
So full of mystery

Crashing waves hit the rocks,
Sprinkling a sparkle of life to the shore,
A world waiting to be uncovered,
Right outside of your front door.

Kirsty Robinson

Life

Times and seasons go drifting by months
soon pass into years
our lives are filled with happiness and joys
love heartaches and tears
We all grow older wiser too through the
lessons we learn each day
But there are things which never cease
and will always find a way.
Love can't be measured its depth cannot be reached
We cannot always express it regardless of our speech
So much is stored within our hearts it seems to overflow
We try to touch the ones we love with words for us to show
How much we care and think of them
how much we want to be near
They're just being who they are
We hold so very dear
Three little words still hold true
I love you

Winifred Kuczaj

Music of Spring

The golden trumpets sound -
Spring is here, Spring is here.
Awake my love, awake my love,
As gentle breezes bring to life
The rustling of the leaves.

The trumpets are the daffodils
In dress of inspiration,
Bringing forth a gentle scent
To further God's creation.

The trumpets play the first great notes,
Then cymbals join in various colours.
Come, sing and dance, Spring is here,
Life and love are here forever.

Tall trees grow and sway in rhythm
To the sound of golden trumpets.
Moving waters carry each pulsating sound
To fill the earth with boundless life.
The music is the song of daffodils.

Ruth Evelyn

I'm Here

Open the door of light,
Step in from the darkness,
The worrying times have gone.
I will guide you from the pain,
Through to happiness to follow,
If I'm here, you need no fear.
We'll defeat the anger and hatred,
That made you cry and shout,
And once again make you smile.
There's no easy way to get away,
Only to make things worse,
But together the war of anger's fought.
All that's needed is a laugh or smile,
To take the pain away,
Together this will happen.

Louise Oxley

The Comet

How we fretted how we screamed the clouds
Stopping us from seeing the magic comet in the sky.

Then on the 27th March 1996 a frosty night
The stars we could see, then out of the
Blue the magic comet we could see.

Like a big bright cross up in the sky
Glowing faintly we could see the magic
Comet in the sky.

Does it mean good luck to all who can see
Or is it a sign to one and all, behave
Yourselves or no more will you see a
Silver cross up in the sky

J. M. Lauricella

'Society'

The world is such an evil place,
Spurned on by class, spurned on by race,
The violence, the theft, the muggings, the rape,
are everyday things by people who hate,
  It's a power keg that's getting bigger,
  A loaded gun with a hairpin trigger,
It's man's own greed and some's intention,
To prey on the old and the steal their pension,
To batter, mug, to knife, to main,
It doesn't matter it's all the same,
But we tend to ignore it, we turn a blind eye,
'Til we're the victim and start to cry,
No one hears us when we shout,
So come on people "let's sort it out"!
Before it gets worse lets do what we can,
or the prophecy's true
"Man will destroy Man"

D. R. S. Clemmett

The Meditations in Solitude

O Welcome morn
that wakes the silent earth,
Unto its virgin loveliness of spring a new
when all the awaited springs, fresh, with the spirit of eternal
things, there on a lover may in fondness all recite caught in
such rapture.
O the infinite here in the moments off terrestrial bliss the
truth and form of heaven exist now at the time of morning
with the sun and the echoing choirs of love imbued with song
from the bright vale and the hillocks green beyond, upon the
breeze that o'er the meadows roam to kiss with unseen lips
the trembling flowers,
and whisper off sweet melodies of sound that throb and echo
through the soul and mind
Ah! I would drift upon the foamless tide and sip with eager
lips the sweets of blossoms wild.

W. C. Scudamore

Untitled

I am the atomos,
That which cannot be cut.
Because I stay away from knives.
I stand in the face of your contempt;
You sharpen your blades on the whetstone of my past,
But I will not be cut.

I am a broken angel,
Tumbled from my celestial skateboard.
Naked, wings clipped, bewildered by the laws of gravity,
I try to fly out the windows of my eyes.
Clasping at the haunted void, my thorn-tangled womb,
I beg to be cut: let my sin bleed away.
But I am the atomos, cripple-winged, confined.

Sophie Lizard

Untitled

Gemstones they are hidden deep within the ground,
Someone has to dig them out if they are to be found,
Cutting and polishing before set in a ring,
Quite a lot of punishment to make a lovely thing,
Then it is admired, has value, a price so very great,
Just so with human beings, cut and shaped by fate.

In life we hide our true selves deep within our losses,
Injured and burdened by our heavy crosses,
When the trials are over, we can rise in glory,
Help others on their way, sharing our own story.
Pain can hide the sparkle, sorrow dulls the glow,
Coming through it is the polish - this I truly know.

Cut glass or a diamond - does it really matter?
Earthenware or china, or a silver platter?
Rising from the ashes, burnished in the flame,
Blessed by the experience, continue without shame,
The purity within you now shines brighter friend by far,
Than any precious diamond, than any distant star.

Mary E. Hall

Wake Me Up

A warm and gentle sea,
Taken completely for granted
With womb-like protection, supports me.
An occasional tickling wave,
Or a deeper darker dip,
Simulates life's oscillations.

No stirring or swirling,
No warning cry or telescope glimpse
Of a pirate ship, in the distance, menacing.
A sudden sharp sting of salt
And I see for the first time.
Life shakes me, slaps me, wakes me,
With a jolt.

Louise Crowther

Just One of Those Days

Why does it always have to be,
That when I go to the dentist I see,
Someone I know who wants to speak,
My mouth is all frozen and so is my cheek,
I want to smile but my mouth feels all funny.
My eyes start to water, my nose is all runny.
I've got to escape I want to go now,
I must make an excuse but I don't know how,
Then I see my escape a bus that will do,
I say my goodbyes and get in the queue.
I've got on the bus now when we've not gone far,
When I remembered I came in the car!

G. Bower

Friend

Like an old boot; Trusting and Familiar,
Stands my Gemini, accompanied by mood swings.
A slave to Technology,
Addicted to Cars,
Referred to as Picasso, with his artistic aura.
Although not an oil painting, beautiful in his own way.
A strong Ox,
A delicate Butterfly,
His sensitive soul yearns for Harmony; His heart weeps for world
peace.

With striking appearance, he's easily spotted.
Freckles scatter over an eggshell complexion:
Smiling emerald eyes shimmer under a wave of orange sea.
A wiry body submerged by colour.

My battered, old boot can take me through anything.

My one true friend; A hero in itself.

Katie Norcup

Seashells Hidden among the Sand

Glittering among the waves
Star-like visions, like diamonds, glitter from the sea

The sun shines brightly upon the water
The radium heat bringing pleasure
And healing to all around

From a distance a ship berthed
The waves bashed to and fro
A red balloon figure marked the safety where you should go

Among the waves swimmers breathtakingly
Swam among the small fishes
Small fishing boats rowed along the heavy waves
By men who know their way
Bringing their catch of the day
To those who are willing to pay

But this unfortunate day there were no fish;
The fisherman decided to call it a day
Bringing their boats sadly ashore

When walking through the hot sand
They trod on a quantity of conk shells
To their surprise that was their catch of the day.

C. Stephens

"Why"

On the shell scarred plains of Flanders
Stood a soldier young and brave his country won't to save
When suddenly his face went deathly white
He fell unconscious to the ground,
While all around were bursting shells the only sound.
And lying near, his horse, man's most faithful friend
In agony was writhing, waiting for the end.
His eyes seemed to ask the pitiful WHY?
Why does man have to fight? What is the cause of war?
The night wore on the wind swept o'er
Those dreary plains with not a hand to staunch those dark red stains
The youthful eyelids flickered his thoughts returned to home
Of his beloved mother, and his sweetheart waiting there
Before his eyes were closed in death
He cried aloud with one last breath
"Oh God, Please God, help me and save my people".
So to the youth of all the world
Band together by the thousand score
Help to make the whole world strong
So that there shall be No more war!

B. R. Timms

Angel

Long golden hair hung down to her waist
such beauty I've never seen.
I pinched myself I thought at first
perhaps I was having a dream.
One leg outstretched the other half bent,
her back against the tree.
A snow white dove lay in her hands
rested upon her knee.
She turned and smiled as I walked by
then raised her hands up high.
I watched the dove take to the air
it soared into the sky.
Then as I gazed down to the spot
to where my lady lay.
To my dismay she'd disappeared
And all that was left to be seen.
Where several large white feathers
where once my lady had been.

Pièrre Raymond

Untitled

Can it be true, is it a dream,
surely this I've never seen -
A ghostly figure, its features clear,
gliding slowly - now so near.

Hands outstretched with smiling face
offered friendship with perfect grace.
Its body close - gentle touch,
A peace I've never felt as much.

It's faded now a dream I fear
A sadness now a dream so clear.
I knew that face from memories past,
never forgotten remaining fast.

Could it be true though - was it a dream?
I must believe what I had seen.
That ghostly figure was surely there
with kind and gentle loving air.

P. Oakley

Hope's Song

Dear Lord take us to a safer place
the bullets of war have no place here
Where is the freedom to walk in peace?
Gone for so long we forget the joy.

One day soon we will be salvaged
From the wrecks of this cruel time
To grow and learn to live in love,
No fears to hide in uncertain smiles.

Maureen Clover

The Flower

It thought it was a weed
stuck between the crevices and other flowers

Overshadowed and blocked out to the sun
it lived its life among

One day the others matured and fled
alone to fend, the weed was left

It slowly started to feel the sun
and soon begun to live some

Crushed on occasion and trampled upon
never the less; it lived on

It carried on for many years
wondering where it would all lead

Then something happened to shake it leaves
it had survived it could go on.

Its heart grew strong, its soul gained strength
no more a weed, but flower instead.

Susan Swann

Distant Days

We had not seen many another place
Surpassing ours in beauty and in grace
There was no dearth of laughter and fun
We enjoyed the lanes, the trees and the sun.

Pleasant evenings filled with mirth
Friendly chatter of endless girth
Our views in oil, on canvas we shaped
As innovated recipes cooked, and baked.

Looking down from where we dwelt
A multitude of lanes over the planes swept
As serpentine and graceful as lanes could ever be
With the distant mansion, delightful to see.

The oaks stood stately as we stared
Against any changing sky full well they fared
Eyes never beheld a scene dull or sour
When views changed with weather, day or hour.

A tough day's work, and some hurtful ways
Did touch our sensitive minds on some days
To heal our wounded spirits and minds to please
We returned to the winding lanes and lovely trees.

Sriya Gunasekera

December

The cold wind blows, its fingers entwine
The dead branches of the lonely ash
Snow falls softly on Bracken and Broom
Ice falling down with a gentle splash
The children cry with pure delight
The warmth of a fire on a cold dark night
The slippery paths of hills we climb
The little things of winter come

Myra Pollock

My Father's Daughter

Every day you went down that hole
Sweating and digging for black coal
At the pit gates there I'd stand
Waiting to take hold of your hand
I'd here the clatter of cobbled stone
You were coming to take me home
Feeling the warmth of your palm
When I grew tired you'd lift me on your arm
As you walked telling me a story or two
Kissing your cheek I'd say I love you
Ashes to ashes you had to die
Alone at your grave I stand and cry
Now a women a child no more
You're still the man I adore
I walk through life
With the treasured memory
Of how grand life used to be

Maureen Kennedy

The Old House

The old house stood in acres of land
Surrounded by a fantastic view
Climbing ivy ascending the walls
Glistening with dew.

The Oaks and Elms which stood so tall
Cast their shadows around
Landscaped garden and shrubbery
And stepping stones set in the ground

The house and land were picturesque
Just like an old oil painting
With its atmosphere of serenity
I imagined a lady in waiting.

I stood aside absorbing the scene
And breathing in the air
I closed my eyes momentarily
And wished that I lived there.

C. E. Giles

Untitled

Incandescent orange
Subsides to misty blue
Fragile webs of half-formed dreams
Reflect images of you
Been a long time running
On broken crooked sky
And love has lain there bleeding
Too afraid to fly
It's as though I've turned full circle
Faced east surfing with the sun
Ready to make a leap with faith
And welcome what's to come
No longer tormented by the shadows
Free to feed on life
To dance barefoot on your laughter
And to become your wife.

Lisa Mallett

Reverie

Silently waking to thoughts that are mine
Taking form
Words flow
On to promises still to come
Heart mind and soul
Waking silently waking
Desires striving to be
Pen poised waiting
Still more to me
Reflecting the all of me
Growing to infinity
Gather the silence
Don't wait for the beep
It's time

Marlene Smith

A Mother's Lot

Oh! To escape from this dreary life
So full of worries, work, and strife
To pastures new where the grass is greener
Away from dishes and bathroom cleaner
My thoughts take me to a paradise isle
Some solitude for a little while
Where warm soft breezes brush my face
Tall palm trees sway with gentle grace
Feeling the warm sand beneath my feet
No cares or worries to brow beat
I could stay here forever in this dreamy state
Not for long because I wake to find this dream is
not my fate.
Back to reality Alas, alas.
Not longer with the greener grass
A busy mother I'll always be
Thank God for my dear family
I like to dream, but do not pine
To be a Shirley Valentine

M. H. Slavin

Dear Friend I Pray . . .

No matter what trials you're called on to pass through,
That God in His rich Mercy will send Special Blessing on you.
And though your days appear to be as black as the darkest night,
For you to Graciously receive a ray of wonderful Guiding Light.
In all your weakest moments, I pray that He will make you strong.
And always protect you from all evil, by a guardian Angelic throng.
That our Father will lead you by the hand, showing you
the right way to go.
And bring to your aid, kind Christian friends it is a privilege
to know.
Should your pain at times, seem far too much for you to personally bear,
Then I'll ask God to clasp you to His heart, with very loving care.
Even at times, however low your faith may seem to be,
I pray our living Lord, will walk every step of the way with thee.

Muriel Ross

To the Bard

To you, great bard, this love of poetry,
That which in me from infancy was bred,
Has brought my winging thoughts in search of truth
To your immortal lines, so often read.
How often did you strive to captivate,
Through poetry, your lady and your friend?
Two loves you had, one dark (so false and fickle)
The other (fair) you loved until the end.
Yet will I find the truth for which I'm searching?
Can beauty, love resist the passing time?
I search your lines to find a written answer,
Did you one moment capture truth sublime?
Yet time has done its worst - despite its wrong
Your love has in your verse stayed ever young.

Margaret Turtle

The Birth of My Daughter

With Hendel's birds singing in her ear and the silky sun saluting her
Sweetly through the windows that convene the garden of Eden.
Morning blue surrounds her as the wall of sleepy stars
    kiss goodnight
to the chimerical chorus of the church bells.
She snuggles, silky soft, her hair, golden, like the stars
Cascading like Cupid's fountain, pure and transparent.
Like the dew drops on the tree's budded branches, that are
Fanned like a peacock's tail, outstretched to touch her soul.
He arms draw open, like petals her fingers unfold
Her perfume procures the sweetest sensation.
The wind sweeps up and her eyelashes flutter
Like the grass swaying on the river bank;
Her satin lips part
Like the most innocent earthquake;
She cries.
Mother Nature turns her heavenly head.
And for one magic moment time's transfixed in her heartbeat . . .
My princess has awoken.

Nadia Robarb

Mixed Emotions

I watch the clouds go racing by,
swelling out the storm-filled sky.
A lightening flash, a thunder roll,
excites within my very soul.

Beauty, danger fused together,
as nature does her best to tether,
the anger of the storm.

But, she lets it go, she does her best,
to rid her troubled breast,
of all the anger she feels arise.
Then with the rain, she gently cries.

All these emotions she goes through
and, as I watch, I feel them too.
I feel at ease, emotions stilled,
as I watch the sky, that once was filled with anger,
now at peace.

Wendy J. Price

The Runaway

Cold and hungry, with nowhere to turn
Tears well up in your eyes, they start to burn
You huddle in a doorway, watching strangers go by
Reduced to begging, you try to catch someone's eye.

You might as well be invisible, for they don't look your way
Perhaps they're embarrassed, and don't know what to say
You begin to wish, you had stayed at home
You thought it would be easy, to survive on your own.

Problems at home, were really bad
You couldn't turn, to either your mum or dad.
Too busy with themselves, no comforting words for you
But plenty of faults, pointed at you know who!!!

Why don't they take the time, to hear what you have to say
It's no wonder many youngsters feel, their only option is to run away
Parents realize too late, the pain they inflicted on you
by ignoring the real traumas, that all teenagers go through.

Now you're on the streets, all alone and feeling scared
With thoughts of home comforts, that you once shared
Now it's gone from bad worse, since running away from home
Think twice young runaways, for there's nothing worse than
being alone.

Roseanne Ritchie

A Lighted Candle

Jesus said "I have come as a light,
That all the world might see,
To take away the darkness,
from those who'll follow me".

A lighted candle is a prayer,
It stays bright when we leave,
And kindles in the folk who see it,
Desire to pray and to believe.

A lighted candle is a parable,
It burns at length, not now and then,
Until its life span comes to end,
Having given so much light to men.

A lighted candle, lit for others,
A brilliant life to give,
As Jesus gave His own life,
That this dark world might live.

A lighted candle is a symbol
of warmth and hope and love,
The world can get all these, and more.
By prayer from Him above.

Roland Morley

"Taken"

Now you've gone, now you've vanished,
Taken from our lives and banished.
Stripped a mere babe, from your mother's arm,
Taken from a place where you shouldn't have been harmed.
Such small children fair of face,
Here at home should have been your place.
Natural beauties, each different in their own right,
Now I wish I could have foresight.
For if I could have possibly seen, what that man was going to do,
I can assure you I would have done more then sue.
In his grave he would be, on display for all to see,
What a murderer looked like, such a villain such a sight.
Now you're gone, without an once of dignity,
I wish it were me in the place you'll be,
Up in heaven, safe in God's arms, playing about, listening to psalms.
The short lives you had were good, happy, fun and loving,
I can only hope at night you're watching,
For my words will always echo, forever wanting to reach you.
"Never forget though in all you do,
That Mummy and Daddy will always love you."

Sarah Maher

Been Held Your Tender Hand

I first opened my eyes and it was you I could see,
The bond was so special, between just you and me
My first years flew past, whilst you held my hand
You taught me many things that I didn't understand
The time went slower, during my teens
You stood right by me, through every testing scene
I learned to relish every second, of my so-far short life
I was so very wrong, yet I thought I would always be right
Another year older, yet wiser - I'm not convinced
The stupid things I did, I could see, made you flinch
My first tender love, you didn't agree
You warned me of the dangers, but I just couldn't see
what I then didn't realize and didn't understand
Was that you have been there, been held, your tender hand
From your mistakes, you want me to learn
And not your way, my precious life to turn
My hands now ache, to be held in yours
But now they have changed and are tender no more
But now I understand, now I finally see,
That mother and daughter, we always shall be.

Tracey L. Hughes

Time

Time goes on and on forever, through
the catacombs of life and death.
Time will still be going on long after,
I have passed by, but I hope my poems
will go on forever and ever just like
time does.

Peter J. Morris

Taken for Granted

We have taken them, have we not all for granted,
The cattle there, on a thousand hills
We see the latest "B S E" scare now
The legalizing, of their slaughter, no doubt
Not one of us thrills
Plenty of "Food: how and for thought
Scary though, is it not
That "Big Mac" beef burger, may not only rot
Jobs will be lost, and into the thousands,
We will then "tot" up their numbers too
The poor old cow, that soft dewy eyed "moo"
To the final then slaughter, not the butcher's for you
The death of all deaths then, purely, to be true all
To cure you

We once had the slaughter, sad, of the Jew
A coward's disease caused that, though, mind you
Hitler was mad, was he not, what a "moo"
For it was not God at work, there, surely.

Margaret Lightbody

A Memory Stirred

On a hot and humid sunny beach,
    the children play with sand.
While the sun is shining bright,
    please darling take my hand.
In a busy station people rush,
    to catch the train before it leaves.
While there is time enough for us,
    my darling hold me please.
In a noisy park the children play,
    and watch their kites soar high.
While there is laughter in the air,
    my darling make me fly.
In a lonely port a ship sets sail,
    and heads its way to sea.
Before you have to say goodbye,
    my darling make love to me.
Then one day when the sun is warm,
    and a kite soars high above.
And children's laughter fills the air,
    it will remind you of our love.

Lesley Mann

Holidays!

Now we belong to the summer days
Taking no thought of our normal condition,
There seemed so little at work, to praise,
And we passed the time in a kind of daze
   Waiting for tomorrow!
But the here and now should be enough,
And we content with our portion
These cushioned days they should suffice,
For this modern world is really 'quite nice'
   So why do we grumble?
We have leisure and money, and time, to spare,
And peace 'of a kind!' for the nation
And these long days to spend as we please
On river, or mountain, on lakes or seas,
   Our work forgotten!
Now the weeks that are gone and we must return
To the wheels have stilled their motion,
But from some of us, there's a question why?
And from some hearts a wistful sigh,
   For the lost - freedom!

   E. Smith

With Love

Thank you for your gentle guidance
that touched my crying child's pain,
and with patience and great kindness
taught her wonderment again.

Thank you for your gentle guidance
that showed me living day by day
and letting go all expectations,
is a kind and simpler way.

Thank you for your gentle guidance
which helped me take both rough and smooth;
and gave me deeper understanding,
so that others I might soothe.

And, thank you for your gentle guidance
that led me where I longed to be,
safe at home right here inside me,
trusting in my liberty.

   Sally Hoare

The End Is Nigh

   The dark will drown the light with a hollow glow,
the downfall will make a red, glistening snow,
it'll make what's here no more, not a single hint,
except for a black smog with a small grey tint,
there's a smell that haunts this ghostly place,
then you stop and think where's the human race?
Now you have realized what has happened you say "No way"!
you sit down and feel a chill yes you've survived judgement day.

   Keith Robson

A Lancashire Lad's Logic

Me grandma's been very poorly and me mummy told me today
that Grandma's heard Jesus calling, and so she's drifted away.
She's gone to live with all the angels way above the clouds.
Well that won't suit me grandma, cos she never did like crowds.
Mummy said she was very tired, and just couldn't carry on,
So that's why me grandma's left us, that's why she's up and gone.
Well if Grandma was feeling tired, then all I've got to say,
is why did she choose to go somewhere that's hundreds of
miles away.
And how, without taking her walking stick, could Grandma get so far,
she couldn't get to the corner shop, except in Mummy's car.
and how could God speak to Grandma, how could she hear him
call when me grandma's been deaf for ages, and never heard owt
at all. No, I can't see me grandma doin' it, she'd grumble all the
way and if Grandma didn't like it, then me grandma wouldn't
stay. So I'm expecting me grandma back very soon, all tucked
up in her bed,
For if I know me grandma like I think I do, then me grandma
   will never stay dead.

   M. Spencer

This Afternoon

The auburn-leaved tree casts its shimmering shadow across the lawn,
Orange and yellow leaves lay strewn across the grass,
As though someone had carelessly left them there.

The lilac flower shivers ever so delicately,
It enjoys the warmth of the late sun.
The sound of a rattling train heading homewards,
Can be heard in the distance.

The glow from your love can be felt in the garden
this afternoon.

   Maria Panther

Love of Life

Love, life, hopes, and dreams,
that's all we people want, 'it seems,'
'Not too' much to ask for, so they say,
But everybody has to pay,
Bridges to cross, hurdles to leap,
people, wanting needing begging pleading
for the "simple things, in life, that's teasing"
A piece of earth the sun and rain,
Gives everyone, the chance to gain,
Go forward, in life, and don't look back,
Work hard to keep your life intact,
Nothing is impossible, never doubt,
Enjoy each day, with a mind, to know,
there is 'always' light,
at the end of a Rainbow.

   S. Cunningham

Simply-God Within

Have you ever thanked God, each day, that you can move?
To fill your lungs with air, to see, to hear - be finely tuned.
The trees, so beautiful, shelter birds, whoever seeks to rest.
They lift their branches skywards, as if it were to bless.
Their Creator, their Source of life, upon which they depend.
And so, we too, as every creature knows, deep down the pull of
that great Love, comprehends.
The intangible, that links us, when so long ordained, to be
part of God's plan, in this age.
To follow His example, to be an instrument of grace, to love when
it's not easy, to overcome our weakness, our frailties.
To have that mantle, which means to turn the other cheek.
To hold our tongue, to be very silent and not to speak!
This means, that central to us is the cross - but no shadow cast
but a great light and love and joy and peace!
And so, this renewing, this turning right around.
Insures a balance and we confusion but a mind that is sound.
With these thoughts, our days can then begin.
No stress, no imbalance but simply God within!

   M. Comley

The Old Corner Shop

How I miss the corner shop, with all the bustle and the chat,
The bacon slicer take your choice of slices medium, thin or fat.
Broken biscuits what great fun, just dive in and pull out one,
Could be plain or cream or crispy,
buy ginger ale to make you tipsy.
A quarter of flour, two ounces of tea, anything nice you just
happened to see.
Tasty ham sliced really thin, definitely never out of a tin!
Wonderful smells of freshly baked loaves,
Just that minute out of the stoves.
On the way home you knew you must
break off a chunk of tasty crust.
Mum got cross, what have you done, though it really was in fun.
So much to buy, get just enough, chunk of baccy, a twist of snuff.
Those days have gone, it's such a bore,
shopping in a Super store.
Guess that's progress, so they say, but
Not as much fun as in Granma's day.

   D. Davies

The Soul that Soared above the Clouds

Listen!
Tears fall again down his face.
Never do they dilute the aching pain
That engulfs his heart.
The mist outside his sobbing window pane
Reaches in and swirls around his
Head, endlessly suffocating his every thought,
With sorrow.
She has disappeared from his life forever,
Leaving a void, strewn with anger
and bitterness and helplessness and love.
Just for a while, he had thought
He'd discovered the sunshine in a
Universe of darting stars and circling planets,
The security his splintering life had pined for,
The one who made sense out of senselessness.
Two souls, etched into the same cloud,
Free to wander, and shape each day as they wished.
Without her glittering presence
He would fall like rain forever.

Samantha Barnett

Norfolk

The wide and open spaces, the saltmarsh and the sea,
The sand dunes and the pinewoods, Norfolk beckons me.
A walk across the marshes, with creeks and muddy pools;
The boats and ropes and fishing nets, a booming Bittern calls.

The wetlands and sea lavender, the samphire-covered sand,
Within this damp and marshy ground, a graceful heron stands.
The golden swaying reed beds; migrating flocks of birds,
The heathland, fields and hedgerows; the farmers' Jersey herd.

The cornfields edged with poppies beneath the ripening sun,
The barn owl, hunting supper, begins when day is done.
The bending branch with crookéd backs, the leaning
windswept trees;
The natural curving coastline, the view from Salthouse see.

The tall imposing windmill, with mighty sails of white;
The skyscapes and the sunsets arrive to herald night.
The peaceful country landscape, a church at every view;
The people of this county, must be the chosen few.

Ruth Batchelor

The Tide

The tide comes in and the tide goes out.
The scream in my heart turns to a shout.
But it can't be heard 'bove the roar of the sea.
None can hear it — only me.
The birds swoop down, then up to the sky.
How grand it must be to fly so high.
Maybe up there the ache goes away.
The ache in my heart I can't keep at bay.

J. M. Smith

Maddie

You were such a cute ball of yellow fur
The day we chose you at the cat and dog home
Having travelled ever so far
We named you Madelaine, Maddie for short
A pretty name for you, or so we thought
Little did we know that lovely summer's day
That you had rather wild ways
Naming you Maddie was an appropriate name
You were not an easy puppy to train
Three years of obedience classes did not do the trick
All you want to do is play and lick
We still love you even with your eccentric ways
You are a one off what more can we say
The people who gave you away
Don't know what they are missing
Their loss is our gain, more with each passing day
Your endless love and devotion
Is worth putting up with the garden devastation
Holes dug in the lawn, plants uprooted
Maddie you drive us to utter destruction.

C. Findlay

Stranger on the Hill

I see a derelict church, amid the weeds,
    That choke its fallen stones.
What's this I hear?, as I draw near,
    The stirring of old bones!

I wander on, past the tombs
    Sealed off by rusty chains.
Stone angels stand, like sentinel's grand,
    Tear stained by years of rain.

"Be still!" You prisoners of the grave,
    Your "kinning" fills my ear.
Your souls they cry, for days gone by,
    But another age is here.

No more we walk in Sunday best,
    Or pick the flowers upon the knoll.
The Lark may sing, on sky-borne wing,
    But no Sabbath bell will toll!

If you in spirit, in judgment sit
    Of those that follow, listen well to what they say.
For if progress be their answer!
    Then how much dimmer be the light that shows the way.

G. S. Black

Our Field

There was a field, a plain small field,
surrounded by houses, newly built;
a new estate on the edge of town
where people from the city streets came to live.

With great delight, the children, all
from slums and grimy tenements,
looked upon this wide, green space,
the likes of which they'd never seen, and cried aloud.

"Come on, let's play", they cried with glee,
and in no time at all,
the field was full of noisy hordes
of children large and small, leaping for joy.

They ran, they rolled, they shouted loud
from morn till night they played
till mothers called them home to bed.
the field was left to night's quiet shade, until next day.

The field is quiet, the houses old,
No more do children come to play
They've other things to fill their days.
The times have changed and so have they, I'm sad to say.

R. A. Edgar

Love for the Lakes

This little part off England that's become so dear to me
The lovely lakes, the rolling hills and every leafy tree
The distant mountains, strong and still in early morning light
Sunset over water on a cool and peaceful night.

Dear little cosy Ambleside, so sweet and picturesque
Wordsworth's school at Hawkshead, you can really see his desk!
The journey through to Keswick with the mountains either side
We went on the little local bus, it's a really lovely ride.

Dove cottage, Wordsworth's home, the one he loved so much
And which his sister, Dorothy, gave a warm and homely touch
Grasmere lake and Rydal water, calm and so serene
The Langdale Pikes and Aira Force, all these Thank god, I've seen.

What beauty's here, I never knew how lovely it could be
But now I know and now I think at last I really see
That God must love us very much to give us this to treasure
Our precious land, our heritage, for our eternal pleasure.

The dry stone walls, the sheep, the cows, the pretty winding lanes
The little stream that chatters on, the scenery never wanes
I'm just so sorry that I never found you years ago
This little part of England that I've come to love and know.

L. Weir

Falling Leaves

We are the voices that whisper at night -
The ominous rustle!
Ours is acute apprehension,
Prescience of sombre end,
And the shiver of despondency.
We are but puppets of drama
- Dry and shrunken -
In vivid autumn garb array'd,
Moved by rheumy fingers
In the malicious, jerky dance of death . . .

We are the gargoyles of despair
That once were elfin of the ballet Spring.
Ours is the call to Calvary,
With the last summer sun,
And then first faint breath of autumn wind.
We are but children
- In childhood doomed -
There is no escape!
No longer are we falling leaves
We are leaves fallen . . .

I. G. Whamond

My Best Friend

My best friend is the perfect mate
The one and only, I can relate
She sits and listens, my sorrows I tell
And never once, does she shout or yell
She won't ask questions, where! or why?
And even listens as I cry
Whether I'm wrong, or even right
She'll sit with me all through the night
I love my friend, as she won't lie
She's never two faced or even sly
I often wonder, why she's my friend
I know she'll always be, to the end
She's my best friend and always true
And she's my dog, her name is sue.

Paulette Richards

He Was Mine . . .

I thought it could last forever
The one great love of my life.
Did he promise me anything - never!
I'll never become his wife.

How do we get involved
With those we have to share?
It's a fact, never to be solved
We shouldn't but why do we care?

Children play a major part,
We mustn't hurt or leave them.
So sorry my love, you can have my heart,
But anything else is forbidden.

Why did I love him so much?
We hardly had anytime.
I'll never forget his love, or touch
He was mine . . . for a while.

Lorraine Roddy

Dreaming

I drift amongst the clouds,
the only sound is the soft stirring of the wind.
The Earth below is sleeping - quiet, peaceful.
I float towards the Moon
and reach out to the Universe, the Eternal Void.
Others surround me, some unsure and anxious in this strange dreaming.
We play amongst the stars and encircle the moons.
But then I sense the Earth is waking - voices are quietly calling.
I feel gentle hands touching my face - yet still I am reluctant to return.
Still the voices call me, I wake slowly from my slumber -
and return to the love and safe-keeping of this mortal Earth.

Maureen Fair

The Gardener

Now the winter days are o'er
The gardener wants to work once more
He sees the bulbs about to bloom
Spring awakening to cheer the gloom.
He knows he must prepare the soil,
A labour of love this is his toil
He digs and plants and sows his seeds
For all the food his family needs
Lawns must be cut, the roses pruned
To show their beauty in the month of June
Then through the year so many delights
A garden full of wondrous sights.

D. L. Gregory

Lamentations

Steel thistles bloom on barren land.
The azure dome arcs over.
Lizards stir the dry sand.
Heat Shimmers.

Below in this deep red earth,
In your decorated rooms,
Viridian, cobalt, scarlet, gold.
Fathers, forefathers, ancestors lost in time.
Dreamless on your catafalque
Wrapped in painted sleep.
Swathed babies in small cuttings.
Little time to glimpse the blue heavens
Before the velvet black.
Their sweet young mothers
With kohl-eyed masks of poignant beauty,
Gowned in cobweb and dust.

Only the watching lizard knows these dead.
Thistle-down wafts in the dry air.
The azure dome arcs overhead.
Heat shimmers.

Susan Gill

Impression: London (New Year's Eve)

A tinkle of music in the frost-sequined streets
the City wears like orchids on her gleaming breast
fades with the fading year; like a ghostly swan,
filled with the fluttering spirit of Pavlova,
in fanciful, familiar pose she turns her head
to the rest of England, baring her hidden beauty.
Fire-fingered she reaches for the sky,
the moonlight glinting on her polished arms;
her face, smiling, is flushed with rose,
fringed lashes silver, lips delicately carmined,
a laurel-wreath of stars upon her brow.
The twining years are tangled in her hair,
softer than sunrise in the Valley of Kings.

Neil Tierney

We Shall Remember

The long hard winter nearly gone,
The Crocus in the fields begun,
Hillside and Valleys with daffodils amass,
Spring was here, approaching fast.

The cheerful sound of children playing
The sweetest song from birds a-flying
Then this day our lives were shattered
Torn apart and ripped to tatters.

Sixteen little faces gone,
No more to see and feel the sun,
The nation stood and mourned the dead,
No sense to be made of things being said

Sixteen small red candles burned,
Sixteen parents lives upturned,
Oh yes we will remember, each by name,
The little angels of Dunblane.

L. A. Fitton

To Josephine

I never felt like this before, I can't believe it's true,
That in a space of twenty days, I fell in love with you.
No words can express my happiness, the joy that life now brings,
And now I suddenly realize, that love's full of splendid things.
Each day I work but think of you, each night you're in my dreams,
Without you my day is empty so, this must be love, it seems.
Oh Josephine you are my Queen, I'll love you 'til I die.
It's like a fairy tale come true, there must be a reason why.
The reason is to do with fate, and the first time that we met,
The night we went dancing at La Valbonne, that night I'll
    never forget.
The first time I held you in my arms, the lights were dim above,
My feelings from then were so different again, I knew I was
    falling in love.
That Sunday night when you held me tight, and you told me
    you loved me, I knew,
That there could never by anyone else, and I could love only you.
Don't ever say that you're going away, or that our love will be parted,
My life would end I don't pretend, you'd leave me broken-hearted.
And so my Jo, I want you to know, that it's mutual the way we feel,
Be always mine, my Valentine, and make sure our love stays real.

Peter Collins

Alone in the Dark

A spider slowly crawled its way up the wall
the howling of the wind could be heard
the trees danced in the rhythm of its beat
a sudden flash of light lit the room
as the thunder clapped the room shook with the hall

Followed by a shrilling scream in the night
I held my breath as I heard the stairs creaking
beads of sweat dropped down my face
as a big fat rat ran across the floor
I watched as it came closer for a bite

Its small little eyes gleamed in the light
When it saw a piece of cheese, it greedily ate
Whiskers twitching, it sniffed for more
as I felt sharp claws dig into my feet
its face rugged as it looked up and grinned with delight

I grabbed its tail and threw it out of sight
it squeaked as it scarred away into the darkness
then I breathed a sigh of relief
my foot flushed with pain
as I rushed over to turn on the light.

Shameen Akhtar

"Thoughts of You"

I woke today and my world was duller,
the light was not bright and the sky had no colour.
The wind chilled my bones, but the tears came from deeper,
my heart grew so heavy and my grief ever steeper.

The bitter hard thoughts of a world gone mad,
the wonder, the reasoning, feeling so bad.
The waste and the hate and the rage felt inside,
my thoughts and my love for all those who have died.

The day will not stop and rewind to a time,
when all that occurred will appear as a mime,
The memories will grow, and the love will feel stronger,
life will move on and from time you will ponder.

The innocent and sweet, the good and the brave,
all fondly remembered for the joy that they gave.
The light and the warmth from them there will be
surrounding and calming for eternity.

Don't ever hurt or blame those who survived,
Pain they have felt and tears they have cried.
Give them the strength and the love from your heart,
Stay close by their sides never to part.

Shara J. Beck

Red

Red is for the heart,
That keeps me alive
Red is for the fury,
That comes when someone annoys me.

Red is for danger,
That lurks everywhere.
Red is for the juicy apple.
Ripe and red.

Red is for cheeks,
That blush when we are shy.
Red is for the volcano,
That erupts with anger.

Red is the beautiful ruby,
Red and moody.
Red is for jam,
Sweet for my mum.

Red is for the Cupid's arrow,
Red is for the blood around my marrow.

Prizzi Zarsadias

"Beached"

I crept into my sleeping bag
That lay among the dunes
Listening to waves break the shore
I peep up at the moon.

Here I lay upon the shores
Where stars shone out so bright
For the night air was kinda warm
And there were no street lights.

The odd car lit up the bay
As it drove along the cliff
I lay there happily, happily, happily
And thought; I'm sure sure my life's a myth.

Tiredness was winning, as I faded way
While I drifted to that inner eye
The waves rolled in again
Beneath that starry sky.

Trevor J. Smith

The Last Leaf

The tree is bare except for
The last leaf next to fall.
It's clinging on so very tight,
It's holding on with all its might.

It doesn't want to leave the tree,
It has been sitting there so happily.
It's been lovely there. the wind so calm.
It doesn't want to come to harm.

Off it goes, away, away.
It won't be there next day.
It has fallen down to the ground,
Lying there, not safe nor sound.

Laura Overton

Untitled

Autumn has gone now winter's on its way.
The leaves have fallen from the trees.
We shiver in the cold winds night and day.
And yearn for the soft summer breeze.

The snow its mantle it lays gently on the grounds.
A white carpet taking place of the green.
With icicles in abundance hanging all around.
And frost everywhere to be seen.

A snowflake in design is lovely to behold.
But as in life, so in death it doth sever.
It melts with the warmth of your touch.
One moment here then it's gone forever.

Peter McLean

Just Black

The night draws nearer,
The day has gone,
The day's been gloomy,
The sun never shone.

I've never been to heaven,
And I've never been to hell.
I've never seen my parents,
Or the friends I know so well.

I live in total darkness,
And can only hear the birds that sing.
I never saw at Christmas what Santa had to bring.

As I live my life blind,
And face the world in black,
Imagine yourself, with your head inside a sack.

Kate Grant

My Red Rose

The birds are singing, the sky is blue,
the field is twinkling with morning dew.
Tree lined and perfect on this summers day.
Wildlife gather for uninterrupted play.

Tucked in one corner of this idyllic place,
is another wild being, waiting to show its face,
standing tall and proud amongst the green,
A flamboyant colour is about to be seen.

The sun shines down on this wonderful morn,
A bee lands lightly on an untouched thorn.
The delicate stem bows to the breeze,
As the trees dance gently and rustle their leaves.

A deep coloured hue so bold and so clear,
as it comes into the world, without any fear.
Unspoilt and perfection in every way.
A beautiful red rose is born today.

Stella Maker

War Sorrow

The guns are fired from the hills.
The fighting gets worse and worse.
A window shatters above my head.
Used bullets lie in the grass.

They say they're fighting for freedom,
From a cruel, vindictive rule.
But all I see is destruction,
And blood standing in pools.

The ground is littered in bodies,
The dying and the dead.
Children on the hunt for food,
It's been days since they've been fed.

This place is like a ghost town.
Filled with sorrow and pain.
And as the fighting continues,
Neither side seems to gain.

Louise Jane Holmes

One Sunday in July

"Rose-bay willow-herb . . . "
The gardener on the Television said —
"Known in America as fire-weed."
But to me it will always be the moon flower.
One moon-lit night we came upon
a field of delicate white flowers —
near Cambridge.
We stood entranced.
Two lovers beneath the moon.
You said, "I hadn't noticed these before tonight"
"They weren't here before to-night" I replied
But the next morning we saw
The resilient rose-bay willow-herb
— the fire-weed.
No moon-flowers.

Nonie Beerbohm

Armageddon

Concrete ribbons, bonded black
The death-throe of the trees.
The winding roads that lead to hell
Bring nature to her knees.

Saws that tear the hearts from oaks,
The smoke that stains the air,
The car that kills the kestrel's flight,
A world that doesn't care.

Oceans, fast devoid of life,
Polluted dumping grounds.
Ships that burden seas with oil,
Protest, not a sound.

No beauty of the butterfly
No singing of the lark
Majestic beasts of prey, no more
The earth, just cold and dark.

When greed has wrecked our paradise,
This gem, our earth, been sacked,
And we are doomed by man's own hand
She'll take her planet back.

Paul Harden

Solitude

So sweet the songs of solitude,
That soothe the soul of sorrow's kiss,
And drift within a timeless land,
To drink the liquid light of dawn,
That stills the heart at nature's breast.

Thoughts that dance upon the breeze,
Dislodge the tears of morning dew,
And silence courts serenity,
To re-instate forgotten dreams,
That slumber deep within the soul.

Songbirds sing their sacrament,
As wistful reverie subsides,
And falls upon an ancient sleep,
To leave the mind awash with light,
That drowns the tearful spirit's song.

Aurora breaks the mortal dream,
As waves caress the silent shores,
And light reborn sings songs of praise,
To rekindle the fires eternal within,
That takes for its lead the silence serene.

Shane Gale

A Thought in Time

I wandered through the door of time
That stark unknown dimension
The past rose up and beckoned me
The future filled with tension

My desk at school was old and worn
The classroom dark and full of fear
The street outside was filled with tears
For souls of long ago and dear

I passed my friends upon the street
No recognition did I see
Afraid and lonely lost in time
I prayed that soon I would be free

My home had gone the lights had dimmed
No merry fire burned in the grate
I cried the tears of deep despair
I was too late, so very late

My life was over the years flown by
But now I had no thoughts of sorrow
The door of time will open wide
I will be born again tomorrow

W. Goddard

Untitled

'I love you' she said, 'I know', he replied,
That same stupid answer, and a part of her died.
She's been through this before, it's become just a game
She starts looking around, another face, another name
She's tired of it though, the same merry-go-round
Giving all that she's got, to see it fall to the ground
She looks in the mirror, with eyed full of tears.
All she wanted was love, she just got wasted years
She puts on her make up, please God make it tonight
She can look in the face of her Mr. Right.
But she knows it won't happen, doesn't need to be heard
It's all just a pipe dream, cos 'loves' a four letter word
And he'll be home tomorrow, with eyes full of lies
And as she looks in his face, another part of her dies
She knows it's not long now, before he packs up and goes
But she'll cling on to the last because she loves him, and
'He knows'.

Sonia Gregory

Feelings I Get When I'm with You!

The feeling I get when I'm with you,
That tingle I feel when I'm near to you.
I love your smell, the clothes you wear,
The hugs you give and colour of your hair.
I'm happy with you, I'll you love till I die.
I'll never break your heart or say goodbye.
Feeling you inside . . . the heat of our bodies
like the sensation you have from a fairground ride!

Sinking deeper into love as a ship plunges into the waves
Our love will sink deeper and will never fail.
Thinking of marriage as we lie on your bed
All happy thoughts clutter my head,
Hoping this fairy tale will never end.
Give us a chance and you will see
Our love's worth more than anything to me.
Till the day we die . . .
Yours forever, forever yours!

K. Samuels

Scratching

They say the itch starts in year seven,
That's when the scratching begins.
Picking faults, opening sores
Letting bitterness infect the wounds.
They seek the itch doctor,
Their medicine is talk
And this talk isn't cheap.
"He never says he loves me any more,
And sex only once a month."
"I'm tired, there's the kids
Work's tough, it's different now."
Seven years invested,
Cash it in, get the paper - shop around
Seven years invested
Let it grow, heal the itch - start anew.
Learn to give, respect - but never expect.
So they say, scratching.

Marie Tracey

The Persistence of Memory

Like an unforgettable score of music,
The devilish song repeats its summoning.
To the rhythm of time, the presence of space,
Its jagged waves stab mind, heart, body and soul,
Haunting the eyes, and replacing the feeling
In justice to the memory, but living
In annoyance to the reality same.

Like an asthma attack it goes on and on,
Repeating still, and on still. Paining the world,
But hurting no-one. Dying to continue,
But willing to look back, and grieve, and weep now,
At its feet now. Surrender now. Give up now.
"What's it worth?" The devil fights back, "I control
Your mind, and your persistence of memory."

Kathryn Gore

The Word

"In the beginning was the word"
The cry of love, the primordial sound, the big-bang
The metaphysical vibration, the genesis of creation
The lonely melody seeking the company of harmony
The waves of revelation - Let it be;
"And the word was with God" - the muse of the intervals
The sonic exodus of time and freedom -
the temple of the promised land;
"And the word was God" - the architect of the music of the spheres;
But as the dialectic evolved, the tempered conflict arose
And from out of the storm
"In" search for new horizons
"The" new age will dawn
"Beginning" in this the land
"God" gave to Cain
"Created" during the winds of change
"The" day of judgement remains
"Heaven" must wait
"And" tomorrow never knows
"The" desolation of power which glory resolves
"Earth" to earth, ashes to Xanadu

Keith Martin

Too Far Away

Too far away you were when I could see the light
The light that almost blinded me on that silent night
I shall not forget the way it called and beckoned me away
Not to see your face again, or see another day

I wanted you beside me, to guide me and to care
To lean on and to hold me, I just wish that you were there
So many times I called your name, I shouted and I screamed
So many times I saw your face though only in my dreams

But please do not be angry that I left with no goodbye
The only fact of life is the fact that we must die
And soon enough you'll be here, although maybe not today
For when I reached out for your hand, you were just too far away

Lesley Ann Jackson

The Girl

A door slams,
the girl cries,
there's no love for her in her mother's eyes.

She'll weep all night,
as she has all day,
she knows her sorrow won't wash away.

She's innocent,
and takes the blame,
lately each day has been the same.

Her mother yells,
and screams, and shouts,
but the girl can't let her feelings out.

She's lived with hate,
and now she's seen,
the space in her mother, were her heart should have been.

Sarah Ellis

If Only I Could Say

Ah! This maze in which we live, did Christ intend it?
That one should weep and wonder why
What does it mean, when will it end
Are my actions that of a robot, wound up by society
To eat its produce, swallow its dogma and pay its kings

Could I die and not be missed, until the time came
That the sight of man as he really is
Stirred the undertaker and shook the soil
Would people be pleased one more then had parted
To leave room for the next, would they quote quite kindly

"She's better dead she never did much while she could"
But could I? When all endeavour seems without promise
All kindness promoted by guilt or hate
If only I could say, damn all rules
I'll live as I choose, free and unbiased
Then I would smile and welcome the dawn.

Sarah Haw

This Country Life

The woods, the hills and the green green grass
The local lads and the village lass
So quiet, no trouble this country life.
Clean fresh air, no rush and tear
Friendly locals everywhere.
Lovely views down country lanes
The valleys we like to see again
Walking in a summer breeze
Birds singing in the trees
Thatched cottages, gardens of flowers to see
No hustle bustle so carefree
Yes! It's the country life for me
Inside on outside
Sit, walk or ride
It's lovely in the countryside.

I. Sainsbury

Thinking of You!

I lie awake and think of you,
The hour is late, that much is true.
I close my eyes and try to rest,
I really do, I've done my best.
The clock it ticks, the time goes by,
But still I cannot rest an eye.
I wonder what you're doing now,
I hope you're safe, Oh, I wish it how!
Are you in bed all tucked up tight,
Wanting for a kiss goodnight?
Or dreaming in the land of nod?
I think of you, and pray to God,
To keep you in a warm embrace,
Until see your smiling face.
So think of me, I do so care,
Oh, won't you be my teddy bear?
To hold and cuddle me to keep . . .
Me warm, so I might fall asleep?

Sharan Marie Wilson

Black Cargo

The village of Accranika, the sun dawns,
The hunting party out, the pale face fighters,
Controlling, spouting fire, heralds of death.
Shouts of Kaffe, Kaffe, (stop it). Shoved aboard a floating coffin.
Death and sorrow, stamping feet, a woman grieving for her dead son,
She is singing a grieving song.
Thoughts of home and hope, dances and antelopes, my family and love.
The fear as women sing a long lost prayer to whomever is listening.
The wave of thunder, the last thoughts of home.
We had hope, we were proud, we had dignity.
Now we're looked at, poked and pushed, traded for a single shiny coin.
Thoughts of my homeland Africa,
Thoughts of freedom. A prayer that Shakka will soon come.
A shedding of single tear in memory.

Robert Sackey

Missing the Boat

It was when I got to sixty,
That I wish I'd been more 'risque',
And gone to parties, nightclubs and The Proms.

The reason that I did not
was that "good" girls simply did not
Break the rules and incur parental wrath.

But now that I'm all grown up
Got more sense and fewer hang-ups
I wonder why on earth it took so long.

Going to visit foreign places,
stay out late and kick the traces firmly
into touch where they belong.

Might have been a slowish starter,
but I'm catching on much faster,
enjoying life and having lots of fun.

Rona Elizabeth Ross

One God, One Church

Don't buy me a gun for Christmas Mum
the Irish lad did say.
If you buy me a gun for Christmas Mum
I can't go out to play.

The soldier men will think it's real
they won't know it's just a toy.
Too long they've felt the cold hard steel
with little time for joy.

Hatred all around out there
and killing with all their might.
There is only one God up there
so why do our people fight?

One God, one Church, I hope one day will come
for if they continue their evil powers,
Love and peace will never come
upon this land of ours.

F. M. McKendrick

A Glimpse at Time

As the night draws in
The moon hangs high
Like sparkling diamonds, the stars cluster the sky
The air is fresh and a gentle breeze
makes whistling noises through the trees.
An owl swoops by to catch its prey
It comes out at night instead of day
As night goes by and morning comes
The sun will rise, to heat the land
The birds will sing to bring joy
Waking up every girl and boy
As the day goes on, time will fly
Soon that moon will be back in the sky.

S. Wager

Untitled

It's raining now as I walk along the lonely streets of town,
The Moon's encircled by a cloud and wears it like a crown,
And as the rain falls gently down, it falls upon my face,
So I walk a little faster and my heart begins to race,
I walk towards the water's edge, to think and watch the tide,
And I twist the worn old wedding ring that I once wore with pride,
The sea reflects the mood I'm in, calm but very cold,
And I still clutch the photograph, it's all I have to hold,
How can I be proud of my wedding ring, when you've broken all the vows.
And what was once a happy marriage is now torn apart by rows,
That blasted rain falls harder now, it seems to know my fears,
But the sky is clear, the Moon is bright, it's only raining tears.

Linda Williams

Love's Song

My song is nothing without you,
The harmony is meant for just us two,
Our love could always be
From now to eternity,
But there is no love without a song.

A tune will come with your embrace,
The words are written upon my face,
Our hearts will beat the drum
When our souls harmonize as one,
This will be our song that never ends.

Just one kiss the choir begins to sing,
You caress my face I hear violins,
Blue eyes that gaze into mine
I have found my love sublime,
Indeed a song that shall never rest.

Fate has scored our destiny,
The crescendo is the passion we feel,
A cymbal plays out loud
To proclaim the love we found,
It's our song that will live on and on.

Virginia J. Humphrey

Satin Fantasy

We bathed ourselves in sweet perfume,
The heady scent caressed the room,
We dried each other by the fire,
Our bodies aching, with desire,
He looked at me; then he said,
"Come my love, let's go to bed."
We slipped between the satin covers
Like a pair of moonstruck lovers,
Our only thoughts were of amour,
The pillows then flew through the door;
We slipped, we slided, all the night,
No pillow talk, more pillow fight,
We tried, and tried, and tried, once more,
Then, we slipped onto the floor;
We'll have this night of passion yet!
But the bed will wear its flannelette.

Sheila Myers

The Lake

There it stands still, and yet a mirror to
the passing years.
Yet full of life to the passers'
Eyes and ears.
Reflecting the colours of the
Seasons from the cloud
Shades of the rainbow
Mingled with the ground.

The swans they nest around
the shaded reeds
Ducks and geese their young
protect and feed.
The trees their shadowy arms caress.
Each one, as they wander from
their nests.

V. K. Dilloway

Easter Message

The Easter message is one of love,
The perfect love of God above.
He sent His son to die for us
He gave His all, nailed to a cross.

What was it for? All this love and pain,
Was it all wasted? All given in vain?
Ah no, it was so freely given
That all His children might live in Heaven.

When Jesus arose on that first Easter day,
He opened up a most glorious way
For us to join Him in that beautiful place,
To live there forever, and look on His face.
Hallelujah.

K. Shewring

'Retarded'

The person behind these anxious eyes is the real me
The person who sees and knows more than you give him credit for.

You see only the hands that cannot guide a pen,
The feet that will not answer to the rhythm of the music I love.
I know my weaknesses. I know that people praise me falsely
When they see me attempting what I cannot achieve.
I understand words that I do not speak distinctly.
There is creativity in me yearning to get out.

When people look at me I feel they are trying to penetrate my mind,
Looking with sorrow and pity. I shut my eyes, I look down
Or turn away. 'Oh isn't he shy' they say laughing
But I am not shy, only sad at my own clumsiness.
At night I lie awake and desperation chokes me
That I am not quite the same as other folk.

I have no-one to confide in, to love, to take me as I am
But I am patient. Waiting. Soon I shall escape into a world
  where I am free.

Robert G. H. Nelson

Anthony

Not very tall, neither very small
The darkness of the face,
expressionless it appears.
Inner-feelings trying to creep out, up from the heart.
Blocked, but shown in those eyes,
eyes trying to shut out the passion, waiting
true feelings, love somewhere, but can't be found
looking deeper, deeper inside his soul,
secrets from the past, understood only by him
feelings hidden in depth.
Shown by the eyes, only to those who know,
secrets uncovered, hidden thoughts, hurtful,
the mysterious look, longing to touch,
once linked, linked forever,
the special person, longing to be her,
never seeing the special thoughts, feeling them
once seen, seen forever, his eternal love,
each day goes by love growing stronger,
my love is eternal.

Sophie Holmes

Class of '69

Life was such a bore, I was just
the kid who lived next door, then
they sent me off to war.

I landed in an awful place, I felt
a little glum — I saw a preacher
with a gun.

The preacher said, "Don't look so sad,
come pray with me my son, then
go and have some fun". I did, I
killed someone, then I killed some more
then they stopped the bloody war.

"Go home", they said, "forget the things
you did, the things you saw", but
dark thoughts still haunt me -
like a Saigon whore, and will
torture me - forever more.

A. Green

Real Life Is Free

Water that runs over pebbles in a stream
The red of the sky on a warm summer's eve
The tides of the sea how they enter and fade
The smell of cut grass through your senses invade
The mountains that rise majesticly high
The billowing clouds up above us do fly
The wind rushes past nothing to block its way
The seasons go by year to year, day to day
The trees grow so high producing their fruit
The animals live of the fruits they produce
These beautiful things are for us all to see
There is no fixed price to us they are free

Lester Kent

Have a Heart

A heart is just a little thing
That beats within us all
It can make you feel like a king
And sometimes like a fool

Use your heart for many things
That life may have in store
The love the joy the good it brings
It is the key to many a door

Although it's small it is big as well
When we want it to be
Let's sing its praises its stories tell
For the world to hear and see

My lines above are not a poet's
That is true I can't deny
I hope you will have no regrets
For allowing me to try

W. Huckle

I Remember

Never again will I see
The days my love and me
Wandered together down life's troubled road
In search of happiness untold
The years have passed but not our love
Much stronger now than it ever was
I remember this beautiful world
The sun, the moon, the sky
The stars that glitter
Like a diamond's eye
I remember my garden
The flowers tendered with loving care
The bird table for my little friends
Who were always there
Now that I'm old and can no longer see
My eyes are now misty and not as they used to be
My thoughts are of my love and our beautiful world
But due to man's inhumanity to man
I weep for our world, for our children unborn
For they are our future, our hope to come.

Joe Worthington

Taxi

Out of the hotel rain pouring
The rains in Spain fall mainly on the plains
Una Taxi por favour
Si, si, si
Donne le museum del artistes
Si, si, si
Here is a map of the city
'Round and 'round and 'round
Senor, telephone the exchange
Where are we?
La Cathedral si, si, si
An alle there is Ile museum
No money gratcia gratcia
600 pescates adios taxi

J. Wolf

The Man in Me

If you could see the man within,
The man who sometimes commits a sin.
His thoughts are pure but his actions are not,
Something to do with not having a lot.
Deep inside there's someone searching,
Just to try and stop the hurting.
At times it's like the final curtain,
Then a voice seems uncertain.
So much to do in such a little time,
No wonder men seem to turn to crime.
To raise a family in this society,
On such little money it's insanity.
How can our women expect to respect us,
If life itself seems to reject us.

W. A. Powell

You and I

When I'm alone, my thoughts of you expand,
The kindness of your heart overflows unto mine.
Your presence is no longer, yet;
Your touch is still felt,
Your smile still remembered,
And your tender words still saved deep into my soul.

I long to be alone with you,
And tell of my desires true.
Though at present our paths are apart,
I can sense the closeness of our hearts.
And now I plead to you to hold me tight once more.

Now we may permit our hearts to beat, united as one.
To beat to secrets only you and I can share.
To know such intimacy,
Yet to stay so divided.
And in the future, I have decided;
You and I.

Sara Dale

The Sound of Silence

The house was full of joy
The sound of two girls and a boy
Now all I hear is silence.

I used to listen for a floorboard creaking
or a door that was squeaking
Now all I hear is silence.

Where's my coat? Where's hat, Dad have you seen my cricket bat
Now all I here is silence.

The house is empty there is no joy
not even the sound of two girls or a boy
all I hear is silence.

Roy Smith

I Am - - - -1987

I am the wounded bird who will never fly
The scars under my wings pull me from the sky

I am the abandoned kitten lying by the roadside
Ribs crushed - dying alone
Never knowing the feel of caring

I am the dog whimpering
Crawling back to the source of my blows
Knowing more will fall - knowing no other love

I am the woman
Crying in the night for the safety she never knew
She tries to will them away but -
The nightmares still tear the shreds of her sleep

I am the girl drunk - stoned - abusing herself
Feeling the dirt - scrubbing vainly - endless showers
Knowing no cleaning can remove the scars

I am the child who grew childhood denied
Emotions stunted - used and abused - learning - knowing
No safe place to be!

Kamiria Mullen

The Sound of Silence

The sound of an aeroplane as it flies overhead
The sound of a baby fast asleep in its bed
The sound of a fire bell as it rings in the night
The click of a switch as you turn out the light
The sound of a drill as it digs up the road
The sound in the marsh is it a frog or is it a toad?
The sound of percussion in a full orchestra
The rustle of pages in your daily paper
The sound of the wind whistling through the trees
The sound of a mouse as it nibbles at cheese
The sound of a lion when caught in a trap
The cry of a child when you give him a slap.
These contrasts in sound are all familiar
For those of us who are fortunate to hear.
So never complain and always treasure
For the sound of silence is the sound of, displeasure.

B. W. Griffin

Dear Lord

Dear Lord, I hold Your life upon my hand,
The life You gave, to give life to Your own,
And I am Yours, as quietly here I stand
In union with You, but not alone;
For I am with all those who share this bread,
Accepting why their Lord was Crucified.
I also feel them here who are now dead,
Or not yet born or lived before You died.
Your death in time, outside of time, brings life,
To all, I hope, for all to You belong.
But with us here, at peace and free from strife,
I feel the presence of a countless throng.
Through faith they have believed, or will, or do.
They are Your body and for them You bled.
And does their walk with God not give them too
The right to take this broken, living bread?

Mary Shaw

"How She Really Was!"

She was so small in that dress her eyes haunt me still.
The question I had to ask "Why is it yourself you want to kill?"

Her eyes were deep and black, they hid the secrets of her mind,
The sweaters that she wore were only masquerades to hide behind.

Nobody ever knew her, they never understood
She wanted to tell them but knew she never could.

When looking in the mirror, the reflection she'd see was big and
fat and ugly, but that was not how she looked to me.

Her check bones were like daggers, they pointed sharply
   from her face
Her skin was white she was more fragile than even lace.

The pain inside her stomach you think she must have felt
She pretended not to have it and I guess that might have helped.

But nobody ever noticed, she never said a word
not that they could remember, not that they had heard.

Inside she never released, until it was too late, the fear and
pain and horror which waited in her fate

Linda Rodgers

Christmas Dinner

I Never drink - we-ell just a sip, and Seldom eat we-ell just a dip,
The dog is Drunk - He's going 'round, the cat is looking not
   so sound,
The budgie's cage has taken flight - it really does look such a sight,
My hubby laughs and looks so blurred, HE says it's ME - now
that's absurd . . .
Sherry's empty - the meal is cooked, it was so full when last I looked,
I wonder why? How can that be? I only took a sip you see.

I've never seen so many pans, there's Three of each - with also rans!
Open oven - what's that I see? Turkey's also grown to Three!
They're really having such a race - floating 'round and 'round
   in space.
Take the mid-one . . . that should do, or should I really grab at two?
It seems to me they have a ball, it's really not so fair at all.
I Know it's them - It is not ME! I only took a sip you see . . .

To help me cook a meal so grand, NOW - what's that BOTTLE
   in my hand?
Ah! More Sherry - Well - How nice! I think I'll join them, Who
Cares
What Price!

Merry Christmas!
Pam Way

See the First Sunrise

Look at the sky, some winter's morn.
The eastern sky at the break of dawn.

And see Gods glory, in the very same way.
As the very first sunrise, on that very first day.

See that first dim glow, as the sun starts to rise.
As a purple pink tinge, in the nights black skies.

Then casts of orange, scarlet too.
Crimson silver, on azure blue.

All are there, in the very same way.
As the very first sunrise, on that very first day.

No artist skilled, with pallet or brush.
Can do justice to, this Heavenly flush.

Nor poetic words, that could find a way.
To describe the glory, of such a display.

For the true glory of God, here in the very same way.
As the very first sunrise, on the very first day.

J. E. M. Dodds

The Last Farewell

Goodbye my friend all is not lost,
That's imprinted on your mind.
You'll surely think of bygone days.
The shop, the girls, the wine.
No more you'll tread on Thornton paths.
Along the grey roads wide.
And watch the silver tasselled birch.
That grew right by your side.
The rhododendrons cluster blooms.
The pheasant's sudden call.
The Jerky moorhen's shrill creak
You chose to leave them all.
But if your heart is torn.
Between your family ties.
You put your thoughts to question,
And it intimately lies.
Across the great wide yonder.
Where the bond is strongly held.
To the ones you love so dearly.
The reunion will be felt.

May Reid

Home Coming

Back in this hometown again
The stench of belonging grows strong
Receding is not its game
Those soft hands of german time clinging to the mind
Turbulent ties to this family game moneys of the time
Being doing shuffling up and down the lines
How long to those sunsets again longing
Even when rain pounds those lands of mine
Eye of the mind I see them now
Spewed from all their mothers' wombs
Free from their contented time
Some return to re-exist some never did
I return and cease to exist
Old town I thank you not for giving
Space to lay for a day not quite so
Soon a fitful sleep I will take
Thankful for treading your streets
And return again despising all your securities.

Stephen Gibbons

Family at Home

A perpetuating harmony, turnful and remove
The still night of a city dwelling,
darkness and a star lit night.
Samuel Johnson and family at home,
Frank Toffee, a family, a burning cup.

C. Vincent Anderson

Friend and Lover

Whenever I need a helping hand
Thank you, friend.
Whenever I need a listening ear
Thank you, friend.
Whenever I am sad and need cheering up
Thank you, friend,
Whenever I am scared and need to feel safe
Thank you, friend.
Whenever I am cold and need to keep warm
Thank you, friend.
Whenever I am weak and need to be strong
Thank you, friend.
Whenever I am hungry and need to be fed
Thank you, friend.
Whenever I am tired and in need of a bed
Thank you, friend.
Whenever I am lonely and just need to talk
Thank you, friend.
Whenever I need a friend
Thank you, lover.

Suzanne Louise Short

The Four Seasons

Now that the cold winter days have gone away -
We look forward to 'spring' with bulbs in full display.
The angelic snowdrops and crocus in their splendid drifts of beauty
As if to say, they are giving us pleasure and indeed a duty!
The perpetual bluebells in the woods in their colour of royal blue
So fragrant, uplifting with admiration amidst the misty hue
The birds 'one and all' are building their individual nests
It's a blessing they soon will be able to have their rests!
Soon we shall see, the buds of May bursting in fresh green -
So refreshing with thanks, in all corners of the land can be seen!
In all their wonderful splendour the horsechesnuts blossom in pink
and white. Oh, what pleasure, it brings to all being spared to see
the lovely sight! June is now with us having the delightful
roses in full bloom! What joy, to see many flowers of variety,
adorning gardens soon. To hear the sounds of busy bees and
butterflies hovering around in the peaceful setting -
One of God's world wonders 'food for thought', think of the
honey one will be getting. After the glorious summer days,
autumn will soon be approaching. We shall admire the red
maple leaves and fine golden tints without a soaking. It's so sad,
to see earth's beauty pass so lovingly and with memories so dear.
The winter will bring 'a little cheer' with all thoughts, 'Spring
will soon be here!'

D. Brightling

"Out of the Rain"

He followed in the rain, I stopped and turned,
We looked at each other, and said not a word.
I hurried on, I could hear him behind, the
Sound of his feet on the wet ground.
I turned a corner, he was still there, as wet
As can be, we just stared.
On I walked, now in a hurry to get home.
He was beside me as I turned up my path.
I opened the door and looked once more to
The one who had followed me home, he looked
Me full in the eyes, I sighed and said
Oh come on, and wagging his tail he knew
He had a home too.

A. Lawson

Caught in the Grip of War

Drenched in mud,
We make our journey
Through endless plains
cushioned by corpses.
Drained bodies alive,
but minds not absorbing,
the terrible deeds that await.
Forgotten faces flash,
through over-worked brains.
And distant dreams forever haunt -
followed by visions of brass,
compensating for mental scars.
Patriotic men lay buried beneath layers
of hungry mud.
In search for heroism and glory,
caught in the grip of war.

Stephanie Taylor

Loving Remembrance

To hold your hand, to touch your face
We miss so much your warm embrace,
But all the words cannot express
The way you showed your tenderness.
Friendly and loving to all you knew
Always there to talk problems through.
In each and every person here
Is a memory that's pure and clear.
So with peace and grace, we say goodbye,
For in our hearts, you did not die.

Kathryn E. Pearce

What's the Point?

It's the sharp end of a needle your finger feels when you prick it,
The gesticulation of the umpire at the fall of a batsman's wicket.

It's a definable spot in space, A measurement on a scale,
A definite moment in time, The tapered end of a nail.

It's unit or scoring, A particular place en-route,
The directing of a gun when about to shoot.

It's portrayal of character, indifferent, good or bad
They told me that it was 'rude to do it' when I was a lad.

It's the mechanics that help a train to change track,
The dot in decimalization we adopted way back.

It's a mark on a compass, The climax of a joke,
The part of the pencil that tends to be broke.

It's a versatile word that's used quite a lot,
But at the end of each sentence it's only a dot.

U. Wendon

Truth

Life's not a bed of roses, from the outset that's assured.
The dice are rolled the moment we descend upon this earth.
That first breath proved the miracle. That first breath sealed
    our fate.
The future has begun for all. The dice? We watch and wait.

Unknown the path that lies ahead, most travellers pass us by
Tho' some will stop to hurt and wound us, intent to crucify.
Too soon we're plagued with thoughts of fear. Example hunters kill.
Defenceless creatures, traumatised. The bait of iron will.

Then, man will fight his fellow men. What quality of mind
Excludes each moral thought and deed, to the detriment of mankind.
"Do as you would be done by" or "Love thy neighbours" theme
Is all we need to right the world! A thinker's favourite dream.

There's so much beauty in this world, it's there within our reach
Enhanced by love and kindness, forging harmony and peace.
By example may this message of direction be applied
To enrich the future wellbeing of each miracle alive.

S. M. Linney

Dear John

You will never know the feeling, the anger and the dread,
The feeling of such helplessness, when you hear one parent is dead.

You think they are eternal, here for every season,
But believe me now dear John they are taken for a reason.

God maps out our future, a plan for everyone,
I know that this is no consolation, for a grieving son.

Weeping not for him, he is free from pain,
Nothing or no-one, can hurt him again.

He will never ever leave you, he will be there at your side,
You will feel his presence always as a special guide.

John I know that you will read this, and find it really hard,
that God our Holy Father, has dealt this awful card.

Your dad is really happy, you truly must believe,
That if he thought you were not ready, he would never plan to leave.

Be brave now John, and try to be glad,
That God did just not take anyone, He only chose your dad.

E. R. Monie

Longing

I stand here wistfully on the sand,
watching couples strolling hand in hand.
Looking over the waves to a far off land.
Dreaming of picnics in the sun,
Races and rides until the day was done.
Youthful days long since departed,
Over seas well charted.
With fond memories of the recent past,
I wend my way home to rest at last.

Winifred Cooke

Dad

The day you left me all alone
The feeling chilled me to the bone
Your body here, your soul to God
Looks after you with staff and rod

The silent tears, the lonely days
I miss you more than words can say
They say that you're the lucky one
You're with your Christ the Holy Son

The days went by, they turned to years
You're in my mind and stop the fears
I search for you but cannot find
The memories of you are in my mind

I write this poem to let you know
My love for you will grow and grow
Until the day we meet again
I'll live my life and see you then

Margaret Paterson

The Positive Ion

An unhappy positive ion am I,
The ether I stress and I strain,
Because my potential is so very high
I long to be neutral again.

So restless I wander alone and apart
A free bright electron to find;
For deep in my protonic nuclear heart
I have to love one of their kind.

But now in a sudden oscillatory rush
I find that a thousand or so
Have come on the wave of a negative push;
Which is more than enough at one go.

Too many electrons now circle my heart;
For surely I need only one.
So if the remainder from me should not part,
I really would sooner have none.

Pat Tisdall

Down, Down

Down, on the planes of the Serengeti
were the exotic wild, precious animals.
meat eaters and vegetarians alike: Get on with
their complex every day lives.
except the Men!
Who are reshaping the world around them?
Making it extremely difficult? And less
beautiful and exotic list in.
I hope it all stops before it's too late,
To replace the damage we have done;
For God's sake?

Peter J. Morris

Not a Care in the World

The sun is shining it's a beautiful day,
The Heaven is glistening just like in May.
The sky is blue, as blue as can be,
It stretches far back, as far as you and I can see.
The clouds are bubbly and fluffy white,
The day is perfect for flying your kite.
The breeze is gentle, as gentle as can be,
Out in the meadows that's where you'll see me.
The grass is green and very damp,
Over the hills there is a Scout camp.
Their tents are brown with yellow flags,
The boys are carrying dark blue bags.
The sun is hiding, the darkness is overcoming it,
I would like to stay here and just sit.
But I walk home quite fast looking around,
There isn't a whisper, not a sound.
At long last I see my gate,
I look down at my watch, it's very late.
But who cares, not me, I haven't a care in the world.

Pauline French

Venice

Ancient City rising from the water,
The grace of centuries resting on her brow -
Tall buildings casting pools of shadow,
Their walls perhaps more splendid even now.

Lazy water slipping under bridges.
Lapping, lapping, gondolas drifting by.
Lions with golden wings gleaming
Under a cloudless sky.

Balconies hung with fragrant blooms.
Ghosts on the Bridge of Sighs.
Windows shuttered against the heat,
Staring with unseeing eyes.

Climb high up in the Camponile.
Right to the top of the tower.
The Moors are waiting with hammers raised.
Ready to strike the hour.

Magic city rising from the water.
You're much too beautiful to tell.
We hope to tread your streets again.
For you have cast a spell.

P. Taylor

The Last Fix

We all worried about Carol, though we laughed at first.
The odd once or twice didn't matter but then she moved on...
Not far away yet with such speed
We couldn't keep up.

We watched her stagger, watched her fall,
Often carried her upstairs to the flat
Where it was all happening, man.
We talked while she ate buttered cornflakes.

She was full of good intentions but too weak to say no.
She said she was enjoying it,
But she knew.

She would listen and agree then spend her money on more.
And we all worried about Carol.

The news didn't come as a shock
Though we were stunned.
While we sat worrying Carol had taken 'just one more'.
She didn't realize her body had grown as weak as her will.

Now there's no more need to worry about Carol.

M. Espin

Togetherness

When we're together the sun always shines
The stars always glisten, our hearts they entwine
When friends see us together, they give us a nod
They say that we're like 'two peas in a pod'

Our interests are the same and our dislikes too
We always have fun, whatever we do
Be it watching a movie, training in the gym
Visiting friends, even eating - our life's never dim

We're relaxed in each other's company, we don't have to try hard
And I've got this gut feeling that our future's well starred
What's mine is yours, and what's yours is mine
As long as we're together everything will be fine

We started out as friends, but from then our love has grown
It's a love that's really something, like nothing I've ever known
With honesty and trust we really can't go wrong
We share the bad as well as good, it helps to make us strong

Togetherness is wonderful if the combination's right
Planning the future together, a future that looks bright
Togetherness is important so you really shouldn't quit
You never know what you've got until you finally lose it.

Tonja Vafiadis

'Time My Friend'

Time has been a friend to me in something hard to bear,
Time has dimmed the thoughts I had and found I couldn't share.
Through many years I've been alone and stood up to the test,
But time has helped each one of them to hurt a little less.
I thought at first if I could die it would be best for all,
But I have lived in time to smile, the heartaches growing small.
And so in joys of life I find that I am caught again,
A friend who took my hand one day has helped to kill the pain.
Though time alone can tell how the years ahead will be,
I will face them now with hope, for time is kind to me.

A. V. Painter

Jealousy

Lying awake at night in my bed
    The green eyed monster rears its head
Keeps me from sleep by playing his games
    Bombarding questions, whispering names
Doubts like an oarless boat on a lake
    Float in my head, increasing the ache
Emotions in turmoil, feelings of dread
    Heart pumping faster, stomach like lead
Thoughts enticed grow out of proportion
    Pervade my being with fatigue and exhaustion
Why do I torture myself with this pain
    Caused by images which trespass my brain
Jealousy unmerciful, you can't comprehend
    But you feel deep inside it's the means to the ends
Destroying emotions, crushing lives with its blows
    Emitting its poison where ever it flows
Abandoned, alone facing sorrow and tears
    I will regret for the rest of my years
Not having the strength to stand up and fight
    The green eyed monster which lurks in the night.

Tracy Jane Amey

Visions

The eyes, they say are the windows to the soul,
The key to many secrets of existence
forgotten shadows of before,
Yet to be discovered and relearned.
Our thoughts that linger,
Like the smell when the rain has been and gone
Hidden deep 'n the corners of the mind
These fragments of life we hang on to,
Memories to be stored for tomorrow,
Life is everything we are,
The hum of activity bursting at the seams,
A miracle taken for granted,
For all these precious gifts, we hold,
What purpose do we serve?
We see it in our dreams,
Hear it spoken through time
The purpose is there,
It's in all of us . . .

Lynsey Hirst

Oil - At Any Price?

Upon the golden sandy shore
The oil pours from the sea.
It keeps on coming more and more
And seems endless to me.

I hear the birds they call and cry,
Their freedom is in flight.
Why did so many have to die,
In that black oily plight?

'Tis nature's way our sea birds play,
On horses white to see,
Which race along the sands each day
Escaping from the sea.

I've watched them dive, I've watched them play,
While wheeling overhead,
But never thought I'd see one day
So many oily dead.

Robina S. McKay

Mountains

Rolling clouds unfold
The mountain peaks
Like naughty children
Come out from beneath the sheets
Sunbeams of gold strike through
A golden hand stretched
Forms into fingers
About to inspect
The mountains hills and valleys
Whilst misty and dull
Once the haze lifts
Becomes more colourful.
Breathtaking greens hues and heather.
To stand in awe and wonderment
For no matter the weather
The beauty unfolds and is captured in our hearts
For the mountains have stood for centuries
Longer than any man
Such true splendour
Created by God's hand.

Yvonne Brown

The Butterfly

See it flitting 'cross the sky,
The light and fulsome butterfly,
Downy wings with azure hue,
Wing their way across the blue.

Its spectral dance upon high,
Ethereal countenance in which to fly,
Gliding o'er flower and tree,
Framed in perfect symmetry.

Floating 'cross somnolent countryside,
Seeking winds on which to ride,
Winging over woodland glade,
It continues on its gay parade.

Catching on the warming breeze,
Racing colours the eyes do please,
Living within summer's caress,
The harlequin of the wilderness.

See it flitting 'cross the sky,
The light and fulsome butterfly,
Downy wings with azure hue,
Wing their way across the blue.

Niall Henderson

Jewel in the Crown

A mother's love is always with you from
The moment you take your first breath,
A mother is a crowning glory to her
Children both in life and so called death.
A mother is a gift from heaven, she is
A gift from the Lord above,
A precious jewel, carved with such
Perfection through a labour of undying love.
A mother's love should always be wrapped
Around you to secure you from all your fears
A love that will continue with you
Throughout your coming years.
A precious moment, a treasure are all
Of your mother's caring ways,
A love that will continue to lift you
Over those rough days.
A mother will always be a jewel in
The crown to her children both young and old,
A mother's love is always warming
It's our fears that make us cold.

Marie Graham

God's Creation

Dawn breaks as I rise early from my bed
The sun as yet unseen has coloured fleecy cloud
A pearly red
In the stillness of the morn not far away
A blackbird greets with song another day
From my open window I hear that cheerful note
And listen in wonder to the sweetest sounds
From that small throat
How beautiful the morning grows as in the
Early mist
The grass blades glisten where the dew has kissed
Now pales the morning star its duty done
The mist now disperses with the rising of the sun
Upward I gaze and see a swallow flying high
Erratically, he dips and weaves as if he
Owns the sky
Then disappearing swiftly speeds upon his way
I think that god has created yet
Another lovely day.

S. T. Sweetman

Untitled

I stand on the cliff top at Mappleton
The sun shines silver on the sea
I walk through the field to the house
I pick up the letters from the mat
One is from a solicitor
I have been unreasonable
My husband wants a divorce
I sell my home and land
So he can live in comfort with his lady
My heart is broken

Many years have passed
I am ugly, old and ill
I live in a terrace house
Surrounded by walls and buildings
No land, no love, no hope
The sun still shines silver on the sea at Mappleton
But I shall never again see it with my eyes
Or feel happiness in my heart.

D. Simms

The Fairy Princess

Today the fairy princess came and cut off my arms.
The tap drips incessantly in the yard.
I would leave you but . . .
She knows my love has faded, like the photographs
Lying, stale, yellow and dying in boxes.
Memories, our memories.
The tap drips incessantly in the yard.
Now your touch bruises me,
Now your only passion is anger,
Now every summer is cold.
So tomorrow I will leave you
And tomorrow the fairy princess will take my legs.
She knows, like you do, I am weak, tired and weak,
The tap drips incessantly in the yard,
Nothing changes.

Michelle McLoughney

Loss

The loss I feel I can't describe,
the tears fall freely from my eyes.
The love we had was beyond compare
now you've gone up the golden stairs.
The Love I had, no one could match,
for I have loved the best of the batch
I will miss you deeply, as we all say
but can't wait till we meet again one day.

Now you've left me all alone
I've got no one to nag, no one to moan
I'll miss you forever and a day
have good sailing on your way.

T. Holcroft

Welsh Winter

Sheep, drifting down the distant hillside.
The stutter of a tractor on far away field.
Gulls lamenting with mournful cry above the tide,
Boats, putt-putting, carrying home the sea's yield.
Black storm clouds gather against winter sun
Giving light so eerie. All mauve, black, green.
Wind rising, slapping rope on spa with jangling thrum
as harboured boats toss, on the rising tide's stream.
Birds rise, flocking, twisting, turning white
Against the dark sky then settle, muttering.
For one moment rays of sun pierce clouds with light
Before rain lashes, streaming, pouring from guttering.
Wind-whipped trees shed crystals of glittering rain,
People scurry, crouching timid under anoraks, listening,
silent, to the music of raw nature's refrain.
Quietness falls as sun peeps through on a harbour, glistening.
Aberaeron bustles again into daily routine. Birdsong
returns. Gulls wheel above: screeching menaces.
Another moment of winter's many, varied, faces passes on
over the mountain, into other lives, other places.

Marcia Jeffry

Water

An image beholden to mirrored depths,
The teeming plethora of life is swept,
And ushered meekly to flaccid world,
Of drifting thoughts and plundered pearls.

The sting is drawn and sunk in anguish,
Bile tempered and dissipated forthwith,
For here belies a gentle dissuasion,
The motion of virtue, divine invitation.

Here, a concourse of captured dreams,
Enveloped without a motive means,
For dormant wishes are slowly seen,
As empty substance, an alluring sheen.

Richard Anthony Moore

Homework

Although I know it must be done,
The thought of homework makes me glum.
Assignments which must be complete,
So many deadlines I have to meet.
It must be handed in on time,
To not do so would be a crime!
Punishment would be detention,
Quite effective crime prevention!
A never-ending flow of work,
With holidays being the only perk.
Every night there's more and more,
Completing it is such a bore!
So, although I know it must be done,
The thought of homework still makes me glum!

Shelley Williams-Walker

"Springtime Splendour"

Standing still, peace filled my heart,
The view before me was breathtaking,
Green manicured lawns, rich drifts of golden daffodils,
Yellow flower heads mingled with white Narcissus.
Native Cherry and Norway Maple trees,
The pale, pink blossom looked like Candy-floss,
A delight and feast for the busy bees, at last,
White and orange, pleasant-eyed daffodils,
Rich in colour on this golden, April day,
Gently, warm, winds blowing,
All my troubles seemed to pass and fade away,
How glad I am that I made the effort,
To visit this beautiful garden,
On this idyllic, Spring-like day.
No cold South East wind blowing to spoil the joy -
Slowly! I lingered, as I gazed on this magnificent sight,
Peace came over me, homeward bound, before, comes the night.

V. Blakeston

Our Cats - Rosie and Jim

We had six cats at one time
to look after our farm yard.
To keep the rats and mice at bay
our friends when times were hard.

But one by one they died away
by accident else old age
'till we were left with rats
and mice intent on a rampage.

We rescued two poor starving things
from a local rescue place.
Thrown out like common garbage,
a terrible cruel case.

We took them in with love and care
and tried to fill each 'tum',
the long-furred ginger kitten
and the tabby 'she' his mum.

They've made some lovely cats it's true
and in our yard hunt free.
When work is done and they come home
they sit upon our knee.

Muriel D. J. Brown

"Field Mouse"

How I long for spring, with buds bright and new,
to look up at the clouds, and see the sun shining through,

to know winter's over, no more freezing night,
where I've had to hibernate, asleep out of sight,
now I can run through the grass, to and from my house,
for I am no more, than a tiny field mouse,
I woke this morning, just a little late,
now I'll have to hurry, to meet my new mate,
Her name is Nina, and seems very sweet,
and when we've had some babies, our family will be complete,
now I'm brushing my whiskers, and combing my fur,
so I'd better hurry, or I will miss her,
When it's September, that will be the time I'll like best,
then Nina and I, can snuggle up together in our warm nest,
I'm all smart and read, but just before I go,
see you soon, must hurry, so I'll say cheerio.

Tom Ginn

Night, Grenada

Night touches all with its solemnity,
To merge the shadow and the shape it forms,
Day gives to all its gay vitality,
To light the varied colours of its charms
And yet the day is drifting as a thought
Of lotus-eaters leisured paradise
Where all is almost timeless, all is brought
To lazy dreaming out of dreaming eyes.
And night is a dimension drawn from space,
The palms soft breathing darkly o'er the sea,
There is no hour, deep ocean stars no more
Are set and distanced from this isle, a grace
Is given, to sense a new reality,
I take the lantern pathway to the shore.

G. H. Delderfield

Love

Love is spoken lightly every single day
To most it's just a little word.
To pass along life's way.
   But
Love is like a breath of spring
Its meaning stretches far.
The birth of every new born child,
The twinkling of a star.

A glance, a touch, a hold of hands
A sweet and gentle kiss
It's love that make the world go 'round
We must remember this.

Pat Clark

Untitled

When I'm alone my thoughts after stray
To bygone times and on a beautiful day.
When as a child, I would play, in fields of
green and golden splendour.
Happy times, so good to remember.

As I sit so deep in thought
My silence is broken, my dreaming cut short,
By someone calling me, seems so far away, a
touch so gentle a smile so gay
Suddenly, I'm back to the present day.

Where have the years gone without my knowing
What have I missed, while I've been growing
Life slips by, oh so fast
Nothing good seems to last
I shouldn't complain at that I have missed
I've had many blessings that have been kissed by
Beauty around me, I've taken for granted, and
My faith is strong in gifts that are planted,
As seasons of life in each coming year
It makes life worthwhile and easier to bear.

Sheila M. Birch

Love and Life

To love and be loved is a wonderful emotion,
To care and be cared for is magic itself,
To be happy and give happiness is a gift,
never to be shunned.
All these qualities are within us all,
We just find them in different stages of
our life.

Rabia Begum

For the Sake of a Drink

A candlelight dinner, a table for two,
To celebrate the love I'm feeling for you,
I patiently wait my love doesn't show,
The phone doesn't ring, my feelings run low,
Where can she be that woman, my wife,
The one that I chose for the rest of my life.

She's two hours late then three now four,
It's quarter past twelve there's a knock at the door,
I open it quickly, there my wife doesn't stand,
Instead it's a policeman with notebook in hand,
He asks do I live here then asked me to sit,
While crossing the road my wife had been hit.

She was hit by a car, the man had been drinking,
My wife she was dead, it started me thinking,
The woman I married a year to this day,
Who I loved and I cherished had been taken away,
Now the years they do pass, but my mind still does think,
Of the wife who was killed for the sake of a drink.

Paul Hughes

Morning Walk

The heron flies swiftly from the south
To circle over the river mouth,
In search of food, this winter morn
The scene of peace, so soon is torn
By modern man; a jet roars by
To startle all. I search the sky
And see it skim the waters cold
Then into the clouds, oh pilot bold,
Leaving me alone, with my trembling dog
As I sit, to cuddle her, on the nearest log.
The birds so silent now start to call
To one another, o'er the waterfall
The heron stands still in the river below
Head bowed, eyes searching to and fro,
One quick, sharp jab in the water deep,
A toss of the head, I see in its beak,
A wriggling trout, no chance to get free.
The bird, content, slowly stretches, rises, and soars off to the sea

Margaret Jean Thomson

Untitled

If I were to describe what it feels like
To be beside you, to hold you tight,
To look into your eyes and see no harm
To give in, after wanting to fight,
To not even dare think of a life without you,
Because there would be nothing such as life.

How could someone explain the beating of hearts,
And the sweating of palms,
The slight pain love inflects to his sons,
The ghostly thoughts of death of bodies,
Of love, of souls, that one wouldn't have
Spared a thought for before?

If someone could describe
The peaks and valleys of a heart
And the causes that make it beat fast,
He would just decode the essence
Of what to be in love is like.

Laura Lorena Perez

Dream On

I'm going to a health farm today,
To be cosseted, and pampered, in every way.
Saunas and mineral baths,
Waxes, and seaweed wraps,
Massages with aromatherapy,
Only the very best for me,
Then when they can do no more,
I'll buy designer labels, by the score,
A good foundation is a must,
To help my hips and sagging bust,
I open my eyes, I'm wide awake,
And find it all a big mistake,
I'm down to earth, with a great big bump,
Now I've really got the hump,
It's all been a dream, you see,
I haven't won the lottery.

L. Bulger

Change of Heart

When I was young I longed to be free:
To be dependant on nothing and no-one but me.
To travel, untrammelled, to places unknown . . .
To live, love, and wander wherever I chose.

But now I am old and there's none left to care;
No longer needed - redundant - no roots anywhere:
Living on memories, provoked perhaps by a tune or a song . . .
And all my time now I JUST YEARN TO BELONG.

M. Cooper Hilton

The Apprentice

I've travelled down from afar
To be here on my own
To gather all my thoughts
A long, long way from home.

To look at all around me
And ask but just one thing:
Is this life reality
Or a dream, I'm living in?

The world it passes by me
Without the slightest of remorse.
To find oneself so lonely
I blame myself of course.

To have swords drawn against me
And find I'm up against it all,
I should have listened when they told me.
And read the writing on the wall.

You tell me of a sea of troubles
And tell me of your woes
To know of the solutions
I have a long long way to go.

J. S. Brocking

Mr. Usual, Miss Love

I lay on my bed never noticing you up and hard working the house,
Timing it nicely so that it was straight up and out, doing little or less.
The gleam you left never catching my eye, perhaps I should have tried,
All the clothes in stacks, so neatly piled, oh so many thoughts, oh how I've cried.
My free time always taken up away from you, I now know,
Such laughter you had echoing merrily around, I never heard it go.
Annoyed at times when the toothpaste lid was off and dripping,
So lazy and unconcerned was I, but now the mess has got me tripping.
I notice now the empty void of a selfish shell, that is the remains,
The shine has dulled, neat piles have scattered, the scene is of complete disdain.
The only echo is a hollow misery, that returns like some boomerang,
What I wouldn't give just to feel your love and the happy way to yourself you sang.
I'm sure it was only yesterday you smiled as I sneaked off yet again,
The apron you wore the wrong way 'round made me laugh, I laughed a lot then.
You kept your illness hidden well, but then, did I ever notice you weaken;
So many ways you were vulnerable, but you acted and I never saw the play, oh so stricken.
The cold is now spreading grasping me into your arms where I belong,
For now I understand all you were, you were me, my life and I will be with you forever before long.

Michelle Crawford

A Special Day

Once a week we travel to town, for a shopping trip we are bound.
To a Superstore some distance away, it makes for us a fun-filled day.
Armed with a list of the usual things, waiting to see what fate brings
Sometimes we are lucky and chance to find, products new to cross our mind.
A different recipe, taste, or smell, amazing goods, they try to sell.

Special offer, at a give away price, looking good they must be nice.
Along the isles one by one, goods on display second to none.
Scent from the bakery, fills the air, choice of cheeses none to compare
Bottles of spirits, beer and wine, to a connoisseur the choice is fine
Chocolates and biscuits, on display, colourful wrappings bright and gay.

Of the fashion section, a wonderful sight - quality and prices tempt and delight.
Fruit and veg, a gigantic display how can we not afford to pay.
Plants and flowers, fresh and gay, have helped us to enjoy the day.
At the checkout anxiously we wait, hope to get a special rate.
Now for a coffee, and a rest, for a good day out this is best.

C. King

Friction's Eye

Unnatural determination to attack the placenta
To accrue more fervour for life
To probe the entrails and unconsciously communicate
Kick out for freedom and toss and turn in jeopardy

A strange bleeping sound kills the silence
In development arena pending boredom
Wanting to conceal my face forever
I'm the solely survivor of my resider

Creeping fingers feeling so pure here untouched
The cliche of coughing living in this sullen atmosphere
Just seeing immeasurable lunacy feeling exhausted in lethargy
Trying my hardest to breath in all this squalor

Pipes travelling for miles, coated in dubious paint
So much to meddle with so much to injure
I feel so omnipotent inside the belly
My body weaves its way through the refulgent jelly

This day surely has to become a beginning
I tremble in animosity and furiously clamber down the tubes
I climb away from my embryo so prepared and inviolate
I reach out for the living exit and thank God I'm finally here.

Philip M. Dalton

Untitled

They're watching us with pitying eyes,
Those unseen aliens in the skies.
Well knowing how absurd are we,
To gradually pollute the sea.
To fill the air with gas and fumes,
The earth with population booms.

They know, they've seen it all before,
And foolishly they went to war.
It didn't help, in fact, that war,
It shook their world right to the core,
And left a sparse and barren place.
Nowhere to go but outer space.

They're trying to warn us,
Watch out, beware.
Lest we become like them up there.
Drifting around, trying to find if they can.
A place, as it was,
In the world, before man.

Susan Christine Keith

Enemies

I have been much blessed in my enemies
Those who without opposed me, and within
Led me a captive. For the very sin
That I, in striving with them, so committed
Became a gate, whereby God's grace permitted
Redemption and Rebirth to enter in.
There is a mercy more than mind's eye sees
In the deep mystery of the hostile heart
For in the struggle, is the Truth that frees
Life's darkness to declare light's other part.
Then let me not, unwilling, stand aside
From new encounter with my friends and foes
Lest I, thus doing, miss the loves that hide
Behind the brunt of battle, and blows.
So IS the enemy, within, without
Self's answer to heart's hatred and mind's do

D. Hill

If Only

Listen to the people, those who really care,
    those with words of wisdom, who make us all aware,
Of the tragedies, hate, frustration,
    coming from every nation,
Let's come together, show our strength,
    bonding us all at any length,
With a world full of love and hope for all,
    walking together, walking tall,
I know that we could, I know that we should,
    think of the future, we've heard the call,
It's up to us now, one and all.

E. Weaver

Tanith Our New Beginning

Given a name of mother earth,
thou filled a space of great dearth,
We've argued and fought,
But share many a loving thought
memories of summer days,
As by the sea we laze,
Of the land of mystic majesty,
The Avalon of our hearts,
To the mountains of Celtic song,
And the valleys of Pendragon we strayed along,
Across to the eastern seaboard,
Where the wild birds shout their chord,
At the end of the year across the wide firth
In the garden isle we welcomed the Lord's birth,

Tanith

To a future we hope will last,
From memories and love unsurpassed.

D. Hemsell

The Blacksmith's Hammer

Let the fire glow red! Let the anvil ring.
This is the song I love to sing, while the Suffolk-
Punch, waits in the oak-trees shade, to be shod
Anew once the shoe's are made, oh! iron and man,
They belong together, the winds blow chill in
Summer weather, no job too big, nor too small,
And the spark's fly up, as my hammer falls,!
Learned my trade at my father's side, and he
Watched me close till I earned his pride,
Now my hands are skilled, my arm's are strong.
And I love the forge, through the hours are
Long, there must come a time, when I work
No more, and the fire grows cold I'd close, the
Door, but who's to say, what the year's will
bring? So hammer and I let us toil - and sing

T. H. N. Prince

This Good Earth

Our wonderful world that we live in
This planet held in space
Where every living creature
Has its own particular place
The beauty of all flowers
Tall trees with leaves so green
All colours made by nature
Are there - just to be seen
The butterflies that please us
And birds with rainbow wings
The human frame - a masterpiece
And greatest of all things
We don't always appreciate
The treasures here on earth
And take for granted all these wonders
That have far greater worth
The words we sang as children
All creatures great and small
Down to the smallest detail
The Good Lord made them all.

I. Sparkes

The Older Woman

Why look at me when you don't see
this woman who knows that time is short
and won't last,
unable to make fast.

Why speak to me when you don't hear
the unspoken thoughts
telling you I'm lost.

Why stay with me when you don't feel
that I should stop caressing your face,
in case,
you find me out.

Maybe I will explain
my fear of growing old with you,
so young and vain,
and let go of my pain.

Lucie Dixon

Memories

They creep up on us when least expected.
Those memories that we prefer neglected.
They are too sad to remember
and difficult to forget.
Yet they are always there
and we never regret.

No, memories of love are never rejected,
even though our minds eject them
from our surroundings, our brain, our thoughts.
Memories weren't bought.
Although, we paid so much.
First payment, - a glance, a smile, a chat, a touch.

Sharon McCourt

My Life, This Life

Ever since I can remember -
There has been a yearning inside me.
It's been so unspeakable.
It's been there since before I was born.

Dislocation with time -
Searching for all my realities.
They're here and everywhere.
Spirit, God, Goddess, Earth Mother

My life and all your lives -
We're linked in destiny and truth.
Find ourselves and lose ourselves.
It matters only that we try.

Kate Hargrave

Sweet Valley

Where valleys green sweep down to meadows filled with flowers
There I long to be, to spend my lonely hours.
To stroll and gaze and by natures bounty be overwhelmed.
This then shall be my peace, my heart content will beat.
Natures peace, this then is what I seek.
Perhaps to stroll along, to gaze at the rolling sea
To watch the waves crash on distant shores
This would be peace to me.
Where the beauty of God and nature overwhelms the heart and mind
My soul will be filled with longing, too much for me to bear
Longing for what? I do not know, yet I know I'll find it there.
By babbling brook and rippling stream is where I long to be.
Oh let my soul wander there for many a beauteous hour.
Let my feet so lightly tread, they harm not any flower.
Where valley green sweeps down to meadow sweet
There let me walk and spend my lonely hours.
Let God fill my heart and nature fill my mind
Then may I share that beauty with mankind.

Pamela Bruton

Raison D'Être

'Midst all the problems that confuse our minds
There is that great incentive we procure
To pluck from the embers of our efforts
Some worthwhile gem that will endure;

Some discovery, creation, perhaps invention
That will assist mankind along the way
And make our being within this mortal frame
Purposeful and cast a hopeful ray.

We find around us in the course of time
Joy following upon the painful stings.
There's surely more to life than we can comprehend;
Our source of strength the author of all things.

E. R. Wollington

Save Our World

A long time ago, before human time began,
There was a planet, now called Earth, free from man.
No person had been there, they had not been made,
So animals were happy, did not know how to be afraid.
Then the apes started getting clever, more clever by the hour,
Started killing animals, thinking this gave power.
Very soon all living things gave man a wide berth.
This made the conceited, stuck up humans, decide they ruled Earth.
This terrible story went on for years and years and years,
And could have gone on for more, had it not reached God's ears.
"This can't go on!" he cried and sent an Almighty giant flood.
Put the animals in an ark, but stained the sea's with human blood.
But when his boat arrived God opened it and found
That Noah and his family had made it to dry ground.
They populated the planet, killing animals on the way.
Over 60 billion of his clan, still survive today.
Do you care about the animals that are and could be extinct?
If not, sit back, and once you think,
You'll realize Nature needs a chance to unfurl,
You'll heed my word and save our world.

J. McGregor

The Runaways

As dawn breaks above the city,
The young fledglings awake,
Whether shop doorway or cardboard city,
Cold and hungry, in the early morning light,
They had survived another night.

Predators wait like birds of prey,
They wait for you, young fledglings, night or day,
These people have no shame,
In this city, that soon will not look so pretty,

Go home young fledglings, back to the nest,
Stop the pain in your mother's breast
Put your parents heartbreak and sorrow to rest.

The time will come for you to stretch your
Wings, young fledglings,
With your parents help and guidance.
Older and wiser you will be,
To help keep you safe in this city,
From drugs, rape, pain, pity

Raymond Paul Prince

Killed in Action

Laid in rows, a blanket their shroud
Their faces are covered, their silence loud
The hobnailed boots, thick with clay
All toecaps up, at attention stay
Heels together, forty-five degrees
Can you tell, whose men are these

This morning when night was losing ground
The whistles blew and with shattering sound
The air above was in howling waves
And infantry men whispered, Jesus saves
The unscreaming dead are in pieces torn
And the wounded's markers adorn the corn.

A. R. Jenkins

Two Worlds Apart

My family, I know very well, my son and daughters (two).
Their in's and out's, their up's and down's.
Their joys and sorrows too.

I cared for them in many ways. They did not want for much.
Then thro' the passing years they went their different ways.
I myself found life anew in an unexpected way.

My family. Know me NOT AT ALL! We haven't even met.
They cannot, or they will not come to terms and do not understand.
That Dad as was, is now called Lynne and will be forevermore.

That they cannot comprehend, I well can understand.
But time and our creator will heal their troubled minds.
And in the end all will be well. That's the way of ALL mankind.

Lynne J. Braithwaite

The Roses, That You Brought

Like as if to say, they know and understand
Their little heads bow left fall
The water that was placed upon to refresh
For tears they know we cannot shed

The parting was not easy nor yet hard
For in our hearts we knew it was our duty
So the roses that you brought
Lived for us the love we would never know

As the soft sunlight touched their beauty
So the freshness of the newborn day
Let the seconds of their lives slip by
Making us more far away

In the glory of their veil
They stand and lean they live to die
With the wonder of their perfume
Leave behind the beauty of your thoughts

Marjorie Joan Smith

The Forgetful Poet

Spirit of words I once felt your wonder.
The thoughts in my mind, were made very clear,
soon time took over and slowly asunder,
the words from my lips had soon disappeared.

Spirit of words who now must have left me,
this tearing apart of mind is not fair
for once I was gifted in writing and splendour,
and now I am in doubt that there's anything there.

Spirit of words will you grant me a favour,
stop all this nonsense that befalls my lips.
My conscious is troubled and you make it harder,
for I forget all my words and I pick up on bits.

Lorraine Gordon

The Grand Old Lady

I know a grand old trawler
The Tiger is her name
And out in the stormy seas
Is where the Tiger found her fame

She set off early one morning
In the cold and murky sea
The darkness was all around her
And the winds were as strong as could be

But the grand old Tiger went onward
And fought against the cold
Knowing that she would return
With fish bursting out of her hold

Despite the weather that morning
The Tiger caught lots of fish
And docked with them back in Grimsby
For everyone's favourite dish

Now there are many trawlers in Grimsby
And a lot of them look the same
But there's one that will always be special
And the Tiger is her name.

Marco Francis

Miss You

I miss you every minute, every day.
The way you looked at me the words you'd say
The grief, that's like a cancer deep inside
Has been with me my darling, since you died
Life has no meaning, pattern or a goal
Ambition's gone - I have no heart or soul
I long to rest, to find some inner peace
To wait, my love, until my own release,
But peace and rest I just cannot obtain,
Until I'm with you darling once again.

T. W. Jordan

"Papa Karol"

He wasn't there when I went to his door -
The Polish gentleman, turned ninety-four.
There wasn't the usual wave of his cane
Or smile, as I tapped on his window pane.
It was all too quiet, too quiet and still
The unopened milk bottle made my heart chill.
Like a cold blanket it held me,
No-one around there to tell me
Where he could be, why the locked door
Where was my friend, turned ninety-four?.
We hardly spoke, just hellos and goodbyes
But what wealth of knowledge shone from his eyes.
If only I could have spoken his tongue -
To hear him speak of all the things he'd done,
To have listened in awe to the stories he told -
of the suffering he'd known and adventures unfold.
He enriched my life, I was proud to have known him
and tried to show it in the friendship shown him.
My heart is sad that I'll be going no more.
How I'll miss that dear friend who was turned ninety four.

Pauline Metcalfe

A Mother's Loss

A soft bundle in your arms you so welcome receive,
The unbearable pain you felt so much has finally eased,
You're filled with happiness and love, and the overwhelming joy,
When the nurse calls out "Well Done, my dear, it's a healthy
   little boy".
A life brought into this world only you alone can see,
By being a mother, a guardian how vitally important that role can be,
You will never in your lifetime regret who you are,
And your deep down desire is for your child to go far,
Not to be extremely wealthy, because riches brings too much strife,
But to be strong and healthy, and to live a long and prosperous life,
But when that life is taken from you, in a way no one can explain,
The grief, the sorrow, the despair you feel the agonizing pain,
Especially when it is not God's will from this world so young
   to depart
But the work of a sinful ungodly man that is tearing you apart,
Who but no one can blame 'Why us' is a familiar phrase,
Because gone is a life so young so pure,
   you so joyfully wanted to raise.
And a mother's loss, there is no cure no medication could
   ever heal,
No therapy, no counselling can ever change the way you feel,
Because only God and God alone can ease that lifelong pain,
It is when you are called to him to rest and you hold your
   child again.

Paulette Riley

Unknown Mind

No one knows what influences
the woman I am within
No one knows what reflects the future
that lies ahead of me.

My unspoken words are
the result of the unknown part of my mind.
In this mind lies aspirations
that are beyond man's belief.

The time shall come
when the unknown mind
will be known
And the unspoken words
will seep like streams of water
captivating minds and souls
This is the day that
the unknown within me
will be revealed.

Tarisai Mascelline Garande

Love Conquers

Great storms are brewing inside my head, action to be taken my
thoughts to be fed
My ideas are processed never followed through, my dying
courage never grew
Words I speak differ from those in my mind, what I want to say
is loving and kind
I've tried I promise so very hard, the door of emotions won't let
down its guard
I dare not show the vulnerability in me, all pain I've endured was
caused by a HE,
Time heals pain I've so often heard, I've tried letting my emo-
tions fly free like a bird
Without all my feelings I'd prefer to be, my life's anguish gone
from within me.
I do try and say things I really feel, but an emotion I own hasn't
had time to heal
I showed my love once all that was returned was hate, I'll leave
our future to the hands of fate.
Who knows what maybe our journey ahead, through corridors
around corners we may be led.
If we both try I'm sure we'll succeed then me like a book you'll
be able to read
If you turn away I'll understand, the confusion I pronounce is too
much for one man.
An expanding burden on you I've become why can't I say I want
US to be ONE.
I'm sure I'll conquer this coward inside. Alone, by myself or
with you as my guide.

Sally Ann Darch

Kings Road Kids

As we near the Millennium,
The unemployed, do you care about any of em?
A tall thin lad, shabbily dressed,
Trudges wearily from one street, into the next,
Seventeen, I would say,
With nowhere to go, and no money as pay,
A younger brother whose hand is outstretched,
Skips alongside him, nothing's complex!
Unknown to him, his background decrees,
He's destined to wear trousers, with patches on knees.
In a few years time, he'll take the tall thin lad's place,
Instead of a smile, there'll be a blank face,
He'll wear his brother's jacket, with shoulders hunched the same,
He won't be told the rules, he won't be told the game,
As he turns, you'll notice on his back,
A large white logo, amidst the black,
A question mark for all to see,
Fashion statement? Or why me?

Rhonda S. James

The Blue Tit

Poor little blue tit, why did he die?
The magpies, they chased him through the sky,
terrified, trapped he flew into the glass,
and the small fragile body lay still on the grass.
I picked him up gently, I wanted to know,
if he was still breathing and if that were so,
would he be quite able if I let him go?
His heart wasn't beating but feathers still warm,
I shed a few tears for this small lifeless form.
I hated the magpies that moment in time
but it wasn't their fault, they'd committed no crime
They are nature's creation so nature's to blame
but nature won't bear any shame for that claim,
'Cause although it's her fault that the blue tit died
It was she who supplied me the tears that I cried.
So all that she takes she replaces by giving,
Just like all those who die are replaced by the living,
and next time, the blue tit, reborn he may be -
- a blue tit, a magpie or he could be me.

Sheila Milne

We Are, What We Are

Life is an experience, of ups and downs,
The world is just a bunch of old clowns.
We love and we hate, we're good and we're bad,
They're part of an experience, we know we've all had,
We give and we hate, we're both selfish and kind,
We get all worked up, then have to unwind,
We're clever and stupid, be black or be white.
We're occasionally blind, although we have sight.
We're rich, and we're poor, we're young and we're old
We buy and we sell, and some are just sold,
We're strong and we're weak, some short and some tall,
We all have to rise, each time we fall,
We all have to live, and follow that star
If we like it, or not, we are what we are.

J. McKearney

Victory Ode

We owe them their right to rejoice at their Victory,
The suffering they went through for the sake of our Liberty,
We owe them their right to remember their dead,
The ones they saw wounded, or shot up ahead,
We owe them their right to commemorate this time,
The memories they hold, we simply can't undermine,
We owe them their right to remember and share,
The memories they have must be so hard to bear,
We owe them their right to display, with great pride,
The honours they earned, when youth was on their side,
We owe them their right to the respect they deserve,
The peace they earned us, we must strive to conserve,
We must all rejoice, in awe, at their long hard victory,
And all they went mithrough, for the sake of our liberty.

W. L. Broadbent

"Flowers"

Where would we be without our flowers,
Their natural colours, and all their powers,
They bring us joy, as given in gifts,
They ease the sorrow, heal the rifts.
How beautiful, those colourful flowers,
Above all else, their majesty towers.
With daffodils, then tulips, in early spring,
Then roses in summer,
Their splendour will bring.
Pansies with happy faces come fall,
To see us through winter,
our flowers stand tall!

P. R. Woodward

Please, Help Me!

Politicians talk and soldiers fight.
The world says it cares
Well, I suppose it might.
But in all this, do they understand
The heartache and suffering caused, by their hand?
We children are frightened by war and destruction.
Our food we're given by distribution.
But who can we cuddle? Who'll say they care?
When the ones we love are defeated by despair.
In God's eyes we are all one:
then why do we cry while others have fun?
We just want a home, with love to be found,
Not a pavement and a ruin with soldiers around.
When will the world be fit to live in?
How soon will they stop, and start to listen?
Don't ask this of us it's too much to bear;
We cannot understand why you don't care.
I don't want to live in this pain and agony.
Won't someone listen when I say
Please, help me!

Ruth McCarthy

The Lilac Bush

The world says thank you for the little girls
The world says thank you as a smile unfurls
We all say thank you for Motherly love
And for roses and the heaven above
The lilac offers its lovely blossom
That covers the bush from top to bottom
It offers a fragrance so sweet and strong
To everybody who may pass along
The freshness of its green leaves it seems
Crowns the beauty of the purple racemes
Lilacs bewitch many country gardens
With grace dignity even a pardon
So when into our deck chairs we lie back
Lets thank the Lord kindly for our lilac.

G. Edwards

bramScled gEg's Life Is Mine

The innocent white is added,
The yellow soul has been beaten
With the devil's own fork.
The chameleon liquid forms
Merely to be cooked,
Whilst the misty innocence swirls
As it pours into the oily pan.
A heavy force from above
De-clarified the substance,
Before you know it
It's all over, greasy
But with time that changes,
The devil's sperm disappears
To leave a eatable substance.
The hole widens
And it trickles after biting, down slowly
Until from the other side
It escapes your system,
Never to be seen again.

Rasila Hirani

Lure of Sin

Behold the stranger in my eyes,
There's pain each move he fakes
As moon beams bright so full of wiles,
In upturned palms I try to take.
Each time I clutch a fist of air
His imps sing out with glee,
My soul — for solace I search there:
A part no more is free.
My shutters he has left undone,
My caution he has winged,
With wind-swept mind to him I'm gone:
His bid — my soul to singe.
In quicksand now a fight I put
But plunge new depth and fear.
In vain I see each flailing foot
Brings naught but more despair.
And Sheol now, with calloused hands,
Reaches out in frigid grasp,
As in crudeness it before me lends,
Eternal bitter, bitter clasp.

Linda Deliah

A Chinese Lullaby

Born to this world, no choice of their own,
these little people of skin and bone.
Boys become men, productive, and strong,
ideology dictates, that this is not wrong.
Their hearts and minds, still pure and clean,
some will be loved, others to scream.
Parental care they will never know,
donated to a government, will they die, will we know.
In darkened rooms, their cries unheard,
tied to chairs, the idea's absurd?
But here they are, cold and alone,
in that institution that's called a home.
Unwanted unloved, deemed an excess,
that pretty little girl, in the dirty dress.
Her tears for Mummy roll down her cheeks,
her life expectancy is only weeks.
Everyone knows, but no one cares,
for those babies, tied in chairs.
Babies are people, like you and I,
(Why do they suffer, Why do they die?)

S. C. Brown

Prisoner

I sit and survey these four walls
These never-changing same four walls
The world outside goes on as normal
No part do I take in this routine.
Once I knew and was involved
Now I depend on others for my news
What crime have I committed?
When will my sentence end?
Only Death, blessed relief will end it
No, I am not a criminal
My only crime is being old.

Sam J. Reilly

Traffic

I sit here at my window and watch the cars go by
They are always in a hurry, I often wonder why.
Where are they all coming from, where are they going to?
Always in a hurry, never see the view.
I wonder why they don't slow down and notice what they pass
Instead of thundering along in a roaring mass
The windows all are shut up tight, not a breath of air
What is so important that they must hurry there?
So often there's an accident, what happens then
They are in an ambulance and rushing on again
This time it is urgent, they really need to hurry
I wonder if they lie there and realize their folly
For now that important meeting won't be met today
They might as well have slowed down and gone a quieter way.

Valerie Lloyd

Black and Beautiful

Black and beautiful, dark as night
The whites of your eyes sparkle
from glimmering moonlight.

Large ears so sensitive, pick up the noise of the night
Large staring brown eyes, as if from fright.
Trotting carefully, with soft blackfeet,
Soon to run off into the street.

Black coat so soft, like raven's wings.
Your nose so wet, it shines like silver.
Brown eyes as deep like velvet.
Reflect images they hold.

You tread gingerly, placing your feet,
Letting them softly unfold
As if you fear breakages some delicate or old.

Sensitive and careful, in everything you do
Really not surprising.
I choose and love you.
My beautiful black poodle!

C. Baldam

Untitled

With wringing hands and shaking head
The woman looked upon the dead
The widow turned and as she wept
Clutched in her arms her baby slept
"My God" she cried "what have they done
The battle's fought and no one won"
Stop threats and bombs, we must have peace
Love thy neighbour, fighting must cease
God's cry is love not bombs and war
Lay down your arms and kill no more
God shed his blood, let's not shed more
Come together now and end the war
A shot rings out, the woman falls
From lifeless arms an orphan crawls

Teresa Greener

Summertime and Nature

The little path leading over the stream,
The wooden fence on either side,
Makes a lovely landscape scene,
Lush green fields where horses ride,
On a summer's day,
With a gentle breeze,
All the birds singing,
Relaxed and at ease,
Kids throw stones,
From the water's edge,
But the river keeps flowing,
To the waterfall ledge,
Where people go swimming,
To cool themselves down,
By laughing and joking,
And clowning around.

I. C. Rankin

Spring Time

The trees grass and flowers,
The wind sun and rain,
A gentle breeze a bird that sings,
Beneath my window pane,
The green green grass waves in the wind,
A butterfly, a bee that stings,
The sun that's shining in the sky.
And clouds all drifting slowly by.
Birds appearing everywhere,
leaves on branches that were bare,
all the things are signs of spring.
lifting her head to start and bring
her message to us all and say
is this not as lovely way.
To welcome in the spring.

D. J. Southall

Fare Well My Love

Fare well my love - I shall remember you,
The walks we had in morning dew,
Cosy chats by the roaring log fires,
Walks around Cathedrals with their high towers,

Fare well my love - you'll be back someday,
From the ocean waters into the bay,
All your loving letters I'll not burn,
But keep them close, till your return.

Fare well my loved one - as you cross the sea,
I hope you will often think of me,
As now I stand here on the shore,
Lonely, because you are beside me no more,

Fare well my loved one - fare well,
I watch your ship set sail,
As it slowly slips away,
In my heart dear you will stay,
So fare well, till your return, fare well - fare well.

Pixie Ann Tomsett

Life Begins . . .

Not one of us can e'er recall the time our life began
We're here on earth to stay throughout our time allotted span
From documents and photographs there is no shred of doubt
But will we ever comprehend what life is all about?
We breathe, eat, watch and slowly grow, then start to recognise
Family, friends and relatives, and everything besides
We learn at school until such time our goal has been attained
Then find our niche where'er it be and seemly so ordained
We chose a partner, fall in love, the wonder of conception
Our child is born so much like us and far beyond perception
This child we have, who too will not, as we did not before
Recall the time our life began nor will when it is o'er
. . . Life ends - then starts again

Marjorie Ella Foster

My Thoughts

A garden full of flowers and scent
To display the thoughts I meant
My life's so dull and unfulfilled.
A garden is my grave untilled
No visitors to cheer my day.
So this is where I must stay
Alone despite a family around.
They may be here but they speak no sound.
Their door is closed and I am excluded.
The hurt I feel has no words to explain
Except the emptiness and pain.

S. M. Stevenson

My Son

My son, my son, my only child, the one that I adore,
The golden thread between our hearts has become so fragile once more,
Don't loosen it too much my son, for I fear it may become untied,
And I may lose forever, my life, my joy, my pride.

I tried to teach my values, what is right and what is not,
But somewhere in your heart, you found you couldn't believe a lot,
You somehow formed your own ideas, so alien to mine, you
wanted to live your own life, one that I couldn't define,
But don't forget through it all, you still always will be mine.

Although I cannot share your life, your hopes, your fears,
Your dreams, my heart will stay close to guide you,
By whatever means.

The golden thread is tight around my heart, I will not let it slip
Away, I tend it daily with love and care, and tighten it each day.

I love you now, I loved you then, no matter what you do,
I will not let you break that golden thread that binds
Me close to you.
Although at times we drift apart, when all is said and done,
We are two specs in the universe, just a mother and her son.

S. York

Take Things Slow

It isn't easy for patients new,
To be told "No, I'm sorry, it's not just the 'flu."
But the very best way to get over that
Is to make yourself sit and have a chat
With some of the "old hands" who already know
That the best way forward is to take things slow.

So sit and take a look about
Before you start to scream and shout.
You'll soon realize things aren't so bad
And maybe you'll even be slightly glad,
When you realize you can still come and go;
As long as you learn to take things slow.

For most of us our lives will alter,
Because we will often trip and falter.
But if we learn to accept our new pace
We can often go out without having to race.
And then we'll be able to boast and blow,
That at least we know how to take things slow.

Magdalene McKinney

Untitled

What do you do when your world is wrong?
To cope, it seems, you must be strong.
When things are thrown from every side
to keep on top you've tried and tried.
You're tired of coping, your strength is less
you just can't seem to handle stress.
When you're sick and tired of asking why
the only way out is to break down and cry.
There isn't a purpose for what you do
you hope that others feel this way too.
For if you were alone it would be hell
the only one to hurt, and bleed as well.
To work and work without a break
there's only so much a body can take.
Your brain never stops all through the day
even through sleep it's ticking away.
Working and working, and what's it all for?
You think you've finished, yet still there's more.
Do you think you'll cope with all this strife?
You have no choice, 'cos it's your life.

Samantha J. Middleton

The Serenity of Old

I am an old lady so happy and free
To do as I like and have friends home to tea
and my age is 93.
I am never lonely as you will see
there is plenty to do to keep me going
reading writing typing and sewing
and cooking too keeps me busy all day through
I go into the garden to see what I can find
the simple little daisy is just as nice to me
as the brightly coloured flowers and blossoms on a tree
I listen for the phone to ring to enjoy a little chat
When evening comes I settle down
in my comfortable chair with my dear little cat
she is happy too, purring on my lap

N. White

Without Words

Without words what would be said,
To explain what's going on inside our heads.
Without words how could things seem real,
How could we explain what we feel.
Words are the bridge between you and me,
Words have the power to make the blind see.
Without words what could we say
to wash pain and heartache away.
Without words the world
would be a blank page,
A wordless song or an empty stage.
How could we live without words?

Kirsty Nankeville

To Live My Life with You

To taste you would be like tasting the finest wine,
To live my life with you would be simply divine,

To share your up's and down's, pains and sadness,
Will bring me nothing but deep-hearted gladness,

To stay with you through thick and thin,
To never commit an adulterous sin,

To fall asleep in your caring arms,
To also be captivated by your charms,

To become intoxicated with your eternal love,
To be as free as a pure white dove,

To have our bodies moulded to become one,
To live my life with you would be nothing but fun,

To feel your hands running up my warm thigh,
To want you so much, I'd be prepared to die,

To kiss every single inch of me
Driving me into a state of ecstasy,

To be your soul mate, partner for life,
To be known one day, may be as your wife,

To make my body ache only for you,
To live my life with you is all I ever want to do!

Shaolin Rajaram

Dreams

Look up into that endless space one night and you may see eternity,
the while starts twinkle in that vast expanse, man dreams.
To gaze and wonder what's beyond, then reaches out the
furthermost, comes back to collect his things - and still man dreams.
While earthbound, his fetters strain, to emerge from his cocoon
which on fantasy wings flies out into that great unknown again.

I had a dream the other night, 'twas a place where love began, a
long time ago. Where thoughts were pure - and this I know, that
a troubled soul bereft of care is much in need of a friend to share,
not be met with a vacant stare. Then quite suddenly I had this
other dream in a place I know today, where silly bits and
pompous things - seductive looks and pearls, told me I'd lost my way.

But it was another dream another night which gave me back my
soul, for when I looked up I saw a bright illuminate sky, so I
didn't come back to collect my things, but left them for you to try.
So just look up for there's another age, another sphere waiting for
you to see, and you needn't wonder what's beyond - or dream, for
if you take care of some troubled soul, you too may see eternity.

Raymond R. Pammenter

A Night of Passion

A stream of moonlight trickles through
the window touching his face,
a sweet smell when we are so close,
your star-gleamed lips I can taste.

Smooth silken breaths on my cheek,
velvet lips take their chance,
as our eyes dance slowly to romantic music,
in a second glance.

The beat of the music is my heart race,
as we are locked together in time in our embrace,
We reach out together to grasp a handful
of stardust from the sky,
it's then I know our love will never die.

I'm drowning in my emotion for you,
soak up the love I feel,
see my hands tremble when we touch,
a night like a dream that does not seem real.

But the stars could not steal our silent moments
together, with unseen dreams that seems to last forever.

Sarah Marie Rabbett

My Mum

Of all the people in the world
there's no one quite like Mum
She's always there, she always cares
no matter what I've done.
Whenever I am lonely, whenever I am sad
She's always there to be my friend
She's the best I've ever had.
I hope she'll always be there
and we'll never be far apart.
But no matter what ever happens
She'll always be in my heart

Sarah Hallifield

The Flowers Lament

Weep, yes weep, as you remember
The words sung yesteryear,
"Where have all the flowers gone?
Who would have us believe
God's in His Heaven
All's right with the world?

Where was God that fateful day?
When Springtime flowers died 'ere they bloomed.
What of faith and grief.
Faith yearns to understand divine truth
To believe Jesus truly "is"
Was He really there amid the grief? An unseen witness
Sad, loving, caring and helpless.

Mothers of Salem heard Jesus calling
Suffer little children to come unto me.
Mothers of Dunblane seek comfort and happiness
Your children's angel voices
Make music with the Heavenly Choir,
Sing and the hills will answer.

Mary Scopes

Car-Tastrophe

I can hear them again in the distance, sirens screaming
Their way to disaster,
Someone thought to impress those around them
They needed to go that bit faster,
Wives and mothers and lovers are waiting the return
Of their dear ones once more
With exciting stories to tell them
Or a cosy evening in store,
Tempers are frayed at the end of the day people behave
In an unlikely way,
Anger takes over no one's thinking of life, of Mother or Father
Husband or Wife.
A special event, an occasion that's meant to bring loved ones
Closer at heart, in a moment of haste to be there on time
Those loved ones are further apart. Think what is far more important
Than whatever you've planned to do, for the most precious
cargo you
Are carrying is undoubtedly you!

Maureen Swanwick

Willow

She stands, proud and beautiful in the sun's warm caress
Then
Coquettish laughter, lifting her petticoats and dancing
with her friend the breeze.
Enjoying beyond thought the freedom denied to many of her world.
Whispering confidences to the winged souls glad of her
motherly arms
And as mortals, no doubt dreaming.

Came the storm
And her dreams were tossed into the wilderness, broken
And her heart yearning for her friends.
She being of the fortunate few, they came.
The sun to warm the coldness from her limbs
And the breeze, more gentle now in her sickness.
Tomorrow dawned and she stood once more proud and graceful.
A living dream.

Mollie Peace

Peace in Northern Ireland 1996

The president speech was a great sight to see
they came in their thousands like a great swarm of bees
to listen to one man and his wonderful speech
he came with a message, a lesson to teach

Belfast was his oyster city hall was the stage
he was trying to calm all the terror and rage
to bring about peace at whatever the cost
before peace on our island forever is lost

But did they all listen through the claps and the cheers
how many remembered the pain through the years
a great sight to see on that wonderful day
but what were they all thinking when they went on their way

A country divided but not on that night
the media thought what a wonderful sight
not a whisper was heard as he spoke to the crowd
the message was peace and he said it out loud

If we all take a minute to savour the sight
all the years filled with trouble could end overnight
so we have to salute him our ally and friend
and pray that his words will bring peace in the end

Michael Finlay

Gossip

I feel sorry for people who gossip,
Their lives must be empty and dull,
You never hear people gossip,
If their lives are contented and full.

I feel pity for people who gossip,
They must be very weak,
Not to see that it causes them more harm,
Than those of whom they speak.

I feel sorry for people who gossip,
You are judged on what is said today
So people will tell you, what they want you to hear,
And not what they want to say!

I feel sorry for people who gossip,
They will never know love that is true,
Because when they hear about others,
No-one will ever again trust you.

I feel pity for people who gossip,
And if they talk of me,
It's not anger, or hurt, but pity I feel,
It'll hurt YOU, much more than ME!

Trenna P. Baillie

Just on Loan

I have three lovely daughters, all born one summer's day,
Their names I've taken from the months of April, June and May.
The children are so different, as you can plainly see,
Perhaps I should have christened them Faith, Hope and Charity.
I've put them in the bath tin, with bonnets on their head,
And with a bewildered look from each I'll soon have them in bed.
Each in a little cot of their own with Teddy, doll or Rover,
A woolly doggy tucked away, another day is over.
But not for me, I start again to clear their toys away,
And then the washing they have caused, clothes soiled during
their play.
And then I pop up to their room, one final check to make,
I see my darlings fast asleep, them I do not wish to wake.
But all were labours full of love, times I recall at leisure,
Three little cherubs born to me who each day gave me pleasure.
I wish that they were with me still, alas, I have no say,
For life must run its natural course, and live from day to day.
When I reflect upon those days and what they meant to me,
My husband by my side, relaxed, each with a cup of tea,
I wonder where my daughters are with husbands of their own,
'Tis then at last I realize, I just had them on loan.

Tom Bellis

Textures

As the textures from upon the avenues of life
Their shades and silhouettes throw patterns on our feelings
By what ever light shines in their degree of depth
Reflects their tone and contour
For what convenience we tolerate to hide
To show a face to every side

Then embers of thought collide and crumble to ash
A final flush removes all cages to reveal
The tongues of ages

That last important move marks the
Dispersal to remake
For I am evolved, I believe - I am
But the stopping can never be
Like an evaporation, to a condensation
A period whatever length forgets
For the existence exists to force the
Instances inwards for fantasies we desire our goal
But the complete is omnipotent
For I am evolved and the stopping can
Never be and the forgotten forgot

B. C. Rooks

Let Your Light Shine

With pen and paper, here I seek
The words I find so hard to speak.
Communication is the key
To set my lonely spirit free.

The people 'round me think they know
The real me from my outward show.
But deep within, my true self cries
To leave the place wherein it lies.

I hear the sounds my voice gives out
In empty words to those about.
These words are strangers to my heart,
As on a stage I act my part.

"Impostor!" Is my spirit's cry.
"Why do you live and let me die?
The person you pretend to be
Has no place in reality."

I strive to let my spirit show,
So that God's truth in me can grow,
Yet, still it stays where none can see,
Neglected for that other 'me'.

Pam Baker

Adolescent Innocence

Adolescence In the beginning it's seemingly simple,
Then the world takes a hold upon you,
You're content to live for the present,
Before the future controls what you do.

Innocence Its presence is disguised by a transparent mask,
But recognizing the beholder is no enormous task,
Originating naturally it's never artificially gained,
Instilled within earlier it cannot be retained.

Future Your virginal eyes are forced open prematurely,
It's a terminal illness with no immediate cure,
The whole world is now clear, all hellish and war-like,
But the future remains blurred; its secrets obscure.

Change All too soon the innocent part of you dies,
Stained by living you become eternally 'wise',
It began so honest so blameless and carefree,
Before the world's impurities interfered making you corrupt,
Unoriginal, full of excuses or lies.

Ultimately . . . Evil defiles good, strong captures or entraps the weak,
When you stop living as a human being you're only existing as a
Human doing, only the fittest survive! So are you really alive?

Mark Melia

Insomnia

The room is dark and quiet, the house is still at last,
thinking of the days, of present and the past,
sleep that doesn't happen, I watch the time go by,
the dawn peeps through the curtain, I breathe a heavy sigh.

Why can't I sleep, to close my eyes, just for an hour or two?
I can't go on I'm exhausted, I don't know what to do?
Hot milk, chocolate, cocoa I've tried them all before,
knitting, reading, telly, playing cards what the hell for?

The birds begin to sing again, the morning has appeared,
I knew the night was over, sleepless, as I feared,
tired, angry, restless, how long can this go on?
Time is all I have now and once again I greet the sun.

Wendy Bage

The Hero

In the trench we stand and stare
Thinking of the generals who couldn't care
Whether we live or die
Or of our women who will later cry

Over the top comes that shivering cry
For now they decided is the time we must die
Ducking and weaving avoiding the lead
I'm making sure it won't stick in my head

And there in the mud where the water runs red
Lies a brave soldier who is gloriously dead
And what will he get for his sacrificed life
His name on a cross and a grieving young wife

And what will they say back here in old England
We will make him a hero no, a national hero
We'll erect a statue in Trafalgar square
And other young men can come and stare
And dream of being a hero if they dare

Russell David Gill

Harewood

My children walk with me, too small to understand
This deep and green and silent wood
Peaceful in the sun, violent in the dark
Filled with ancient memories buried under stones
Old gods, Pan of the pipes, who calls to foolish man

His brother, him of the growing fields
Vaguely remembered, in names of inns
The man in green who sows his seed to bring the harvest in

But beauty hides within, birds sing
And snowdrops welcome spring
Bluebells make carpets, to feed the hungry bees
And squirrels play running games up and down the trees.

The children sing and skip along
Their walk is nearly done, so home to tea, they run
The old wood settles down to sleep
The stars begin to peep, all is quiet again.

M. J. Eckfelt

My Hobby

I write for pleasure whenever I've time
this hobby relaxes my body and mind.
Some people are more physical I suppose
but a pen and paper is all I need for my prose

After a day at work when I'm all wound up
a melody I'll play, with a cuppa to sup
then I'll retrieve my composure and reach for my pen
and unwind slowly with my poems once again.

My husband thinks I'm a sort of fanatic
but I reply, I'm more of a romantic,
to share my feelings, loves and hates
is the best way for me in life to relate.

Sally Moreton

Untitled

Will you walk down this road see this garden with me
There are flowers, and shrubs, and a beautiful tree,
Red, yellow, pink, and blue
All is there for you to view.
It starts in the spring with snowdrops white
Pushing their heads threw the snow with a fight.
Tulips, daffodils, primrose too
Follow each other they know what to do.
Then roses refined they smell so sweet
Very often becoming some ladies treat.
The grass green with envy with the borders around,
The trees look down and whistle
The flowers don't make a sound.
Now the residents did this garden
And for that we give them credit
But we all know that someone else should earn a little merit
We forgot old mother nature and God who gave us all
The birds, the bees, the sunshine, we know God made them all
So lets be a little grateful for the things that we have planted
And remember that the garden is all that God as granted.

Pearl June Waterhouse

Lovely Daffodils

The daffodils are lovely flowers
They blow in the breeze for hours and hours
Sometimes I watch them standing there
Lonely and quiet in the soft spring air.

As I was walking over the hills
I saw this crowd of daffodils
I saw them standing by a stream
And thought that it was all a dream

Time has passed and memories fade
And I think of the things I have seen
I remember the stream and the
daffodils there
Lonely and quiet in the soft spring air.

Mary Bartlett

Our Daughter

Daughters are like seasons,
They change throughout the year,
Like summer to winter,
Or winter to spring,
You never quite know what mood she's in.

She is the type of girl,
Who keeps your brain in a whirl,
You sometimes never know what's best,
By the end of the day you need a good rest.

She doesn't look her years,
Which are only just a few,
Twelve to be exact,
But acts like twenty two.

We wouldn't be without you dear,
Your Dad and I you see,
Coz we love you more than words can say,
And will for eternity.

H. J. Shephard

Weathering Time

Weathering time is an effort for most,
Those once rosy cheeks now pale as a ghost,
Those laughter lines have branched out all over the place,
And you wish you had courage to buy a new face,
The thickening waistline is a nightmare for you,
With diets and exercise what else can you do!
Buying trendy clothing whenever you can
And worrying all the time if your mutton dressed as lamb
When will we realize getting old is not a crime
And give in gracefully to old father time.

Norma Morgan

Norma Jean Baker Rags to Riches

From no age she was lonely,
There was no one to care,
Norma Jean was so frightened,
But none of her family were there.

She grew up in an orphanage,
With scores of other kids,
No one knew one day she would be famous,
And that she would be such a big hit

She never knew her father,
And her mother was away,
Norma Jean was always alone,
And didn't care what the kids would say.

She posed nude for a calendar,
It all started from there,
She changed her name to Marilyn,
Then she even dyed her hair.

Her death was a mystery,
Even after reading the facts in the press,
Did she die through an overdose,
Or was she helped by a well known friend.

Rodney Ewins

Little Jewels

Little jewels sent from heaven above,
There's no hatred in your heart, you are made from love,
Some of you are white, while others are coffee brown,
The Lord knew what He was doing, when He sent you tiny angels
down,
He is asking mankind not to throw His gift away,
That innocence be taught tolerance and kindness, every day,
In the playground, tiny tots' hands clasped so tight,
Black and white, Catholic and Protestant all unite,
God is smiling in His heaven, as He views this scene,
He heaves a sigh. He knows what could have been,
Some of you will encounter racism and fear,
Your Creator asks you, to turn to Him in prayer,
You are the future of this human race,
So unite now, and put His plan in place,
Sometimes, some of these little jewels are called back home,
We wonder why, maybe the Lord wants them for His own,
Every time a jewel is lost, I am sure it joins the stars,
And looks down upon this earth, with all its scars,
So treasure these little jewels, from far-flung lands,
For we are nothing without them, the future is in their hands.

Val Matthews

"I Remember"

I remember Mum saying, "you died about 3".
there was to be no more 'you and me'
I looked up and just swore
I wanted you back to hold me.
'make me feel secure'.

I remember you said, "when I die,
you must try not to cry" and I
Promise you Dad, everyday that
Passes, I really do try.

Autumn's the hardest, where colours change on leaves;
I remember waking with you through woods
in a free windy breeze, you gave me green
eyes, but now they're worn with pain,
When I remember you again and again.

You're meant to be around, and you're
meant to be "here", but I can't seem to find you
anywhere. I know that you loved me. I couldn't
I have wished for more, but I still want you
back to love me - just like you did before.

Olwen Maria Page

The Unknown Man

Solitude setting in.
They pray for peace, they pray for death,
They pray for someone to save them.
Pain forbids a smile on a face,
But they are loyal and they will fight.
They will not give in the struggle.
Some will die on battlefields.
Some will hurt with grief.
Some will grow old and face dismal memories of the past.
Some will drown in honours and forget the unknown man.
An unknown man who fought this struggle.
An unknown man who suffered this torture.
A hero he died.

Patrick G. Quinn

Stanley's Fantasy World

Come the revolution, and I'm made commissar
There's certain things that I'd allow, and others that I'd bar,
In fact most present laws would stay, but here's some I would make,
I'd ban the sale of fattening foods, like doughnuts and cream cake,
I'd outlaw all umbrellas, from crowded city streets,
I'd bar, in all theatres, the eating of wrapped sweets,
and then I'd stop those magazines, that are sold with one intent,
like "Vogue", and "Good Housekeeping",
that make wives discontent.
The shoulder carried radios, that only seem to screech,
I'd not allow them to be used, in parks, or on the beach,
The T.V. programme planners, on these my scorn I'd heap,
I'd stop them showing films I like when I am fast asleep.
All pussy cats would wear a bell, to give the birds some warning,
at least they'd have a fighting chance to see another dawning.
These are things that I would do, without no if's or but's,
When this is read, you're bound to say, that I'm a misery guts.

S. R. Osborne

'Innocence'

There's innocence in their sleep,
There's innocence in their play,
Their world is full of stories and games,
To see them through the day.

There's innocence in their laughter,
There's innocence when they cry.
Their world is either black or white,
They cannot tell a lie.

There's innocence when they're hurting,
There's love when you show you care,
And even when they're naughty,
The innocence is still there.

There's a beauty in their innocence,
But all too long, it doesn't last,
They grow up all too quickly,
Then the days of innocence are past.

Larry Bowen

"Dunblane"

Up the drive, into a school, 4 guns blazing,
Then he turned a gun onto himself.
Mothers, families, in the midst of a nightmare,
Hope, anger, anguish, waiting . . .
16 children dead, their teacher among them,
Laughing, playing . . . no more,
The ones left, their childhood gone,
For they were witnesses
Survivors of the horror
can they ever forget?
Relief that her child made it,
Guilt because yours did not
Don't blame her for feeling this way
You might have done too
If . . .
One bastard hadn't walked into a school
Shot 16 children
And devastated a community.

L. Forrester

Bedtime Companions

I go to sleep with a Cow and a Ted.
They lie on your pillow when I go to bed.
Your very first gift - my dear bear with his bow.
He cuddles up close when I'm feeling low.
Cow is a case for the nightie I wear
Only on nights we cannot share.
We make the best of the time on our own.
Scheming and dreaming until you come home.
We count all the hours. I tidy the place.
I iron Ted's ribbon - there's a smile on his face.
Cow looks so benign she calms me it's true,
On the nights I can't sleep for longing for you.
When you return life is pure bliss.
Soft sweet words of love and kiss after kiss.
We both say 'Goodnight' to Cow and to Ted.
They do understand it is bliss to be wed.
The nights are so special, lonely no more.
And dear Cow and dear Ted? — They sleep on the floor!

Phyllis Allen

The Cottagers

They churned the butter for their bread
They made the soap to wash the sheets
Made rushlights from the osier bed
They planted cabbages and beets.

They made horses plough
And cows get calves
Made stocking, aprons, caps enow
Nothing ever worked by halves.

Their wheels ground 'round
Through dawn to dark
Say!
One gift with (envied) ease they found
The rapt, sweet cadence of the lark.

Kate Conway

Hands through Life

The tiny hands of the baby girl have a surprisingly strong grip
They wave urgently in the air as with demanding cries she lets rip.
The plump little hands of the toddler innocently play
But turn your back for an instant and into mischief they'll stray.
Baby fat goes and she grows straight and tall. That is when,
Studiously bent over her desk, her fingers are stained by inky pen.
Exams are passed and off to earn a living she hopefully goes.
Slender fingers on the keyboard are tipped with red to match her toes.
Soon on her engagement finger she displays a sparkling ring
To be joined by a plain gold band on the joyous day of her wedding
In the course of time her own baby by her hands is gently caressed
Feeding, bathing, soothing, loving, feeling so very blessed
Now those hands, baking, washing, ironing, work as never before
At the end of the day she rubs cream into hands so chapped
    and sore
Her hands gently guide her children through life, until they
    leave for another
And then, suddenly, she has the deft capable hands of a
    grandmother
Comforting, knitting, baking her grandchildren special treats
Ready to hug and understand, and give them illicit sweets
Gradually the hands grow stiff with age, and begin to slow
As she lies in her coffin, hands neatly folded, who, their busy
    life story would know?

Margaret Meagher

You Hold Me Too Tight

Sometimes I get this feeling, please let me explain.
Think of summers day, well I'll want it to rain.
There's not a cloud in sight, then I'll wish it was night.
Then I'll want you near to me, but you hold me too tight.
Sometimes I get this feeling, I need to tell you why.
I don't want to tell the truth, then I don't want to lie.
I don't want to hurt you, but that's how it must be.
I'm like a bird in cage, and I want to be free.

Tracy T. Scargill

Friends

'True friends', Who are they? How do we know!
They're not acquaintances, buddies, no not so.
I'll tell you friends, they are hard to find,
Real friends are few; of the rarest kind.

Sad that it might seem, it is a fact,
That a handful of friends will share a pact.
To come to your rescue any day or night,
And risk their own lives in your hour of plight.

'True friends' we cry, that is the question,
To some, no understanding of the word, the mere mention.
Putting to the test of that theory could be harming,
And the results of your findings, could be alarming.

We drift through life not realising who,
Would be the one, or even the few,
At some stage during the years you will find,
Out there amongst the millions, to be one of a kind.

Madeline Hurton

War

A war in a country is like the end of a world,
Things are being destroyed as bombs are being hurled.
The innocent children alone in the night,
Not being able to sleep due to coldness and fright.
The bombs are being dropped, the houses are ablaze,
The atmosphere is a black, smoky, thick haze.
People are choking from the toxic fumes,
There are many large families squashed into small rooms.
There are bodies of the deceased just lying on the ground,
Scattered belongings of people, never to be found.
The homeless take shelter whenever they can,
It doesn't matter whether they're woman, child or man.
The wars should be stopped before the earth comes to an end,
People can change! Their ways they should mend.
People should communicate, it would keep the peace,
Until we have mastered this, the firing should cease.

Kassandra Fletcher

Mother

Look at her legs not a vein in sight.
This is my mum she's a delight at 88
Look at her eyes, bright and clear
you don't have to whisper, she
can hear every word and sound
in this hospital ward with its alien feel.
She's going to die, it's so unreal
I'll miss her smile, her scowl, her moan,
I've cared for her so long,
now I'm alone.

Sandra Clark

Questions?

What is a season?
They come and go
Autumn - winter - spring and summer
Suddenly is here -
Not without a tear.

Raindrops falling - snow and ice
Windy days are here to last
Why do people complain?
Too hot - too cold! What are we to do?

A glimpse of the sun -
comes shining through -
Just for you. Days for
Dreaming! - Long nights - pleasant sights
Soon the season will end
And winter will descend.

Where are the roaring fires
Of long ago? Mere pollution?
What a solution!
Tree branches swaying in the breeze -
Bare and icy - without leaves!

V. A. Tunstall

Victorian Days

I wished I lived in Victorian days,
They had cobbled streets no motorways.
No motor cars no aeroplanes
Just the sound of trams and trains.
I wish people would change their ways.
And live like people in Victorian days,
They didn't rush from place to place.
Victorians moved at a more gentler pace.
I know it was a long time ago.
But today they don't stop to say hello.
They don't have time, I don't understand,
Victorians made it seem so grand,
I wish those days didn't have to change.
To me the world seems so strangle.
Soon we'll have to search far and wide.
For what Victorians called countryside.
We all need progress there's no doubt.
But this kind of progress I can live without,
I wished I lived in Victorian days,
With no motor cars,no motorways.

Tommy Downing

Summernight Thoughts

Oh, how those summer evenings seem so long ago,
Those scented sunsets that painted an amber glow,
Some mesmerized midges chasing nothing to the night,
As busy as we were idle watching the fading light.
Those shadows on the lawn that slowly crept along,
Seeking out dusty dry corners to settle and belong,
Yet that warm night approaching would be very quickly run,
For then darkness reigned briefly, among the summer sun.
We stood and watched the warm night chased by the solar flare,
Chilled in the freshness of the clean morning air,
Watching the mists of the morning slowly roll away,
As warmth spreads life to a brand new day.

Pete Harrison

Memory Lingers On

I sense you're there,
Though I know you've gone,
Your fragrance fills the air,
And memory lingers on.

Though I know you've gone,
Your perfume still pervades my space,
And memory lingers on,
So I can clearly see your face.

Your perfume still pervades my space,
And I whisper softly your name,
So I can clearly see your face,
I feel my heart aflame.

And I whisper softly your name,
Your fragrance fills the air,
I feel my heart aflame,
I sense you're there.

C. Carr

"Living Thing"

Falling on my face the kiss of rain, wind dancing
through my hair, skipping through my thoughts scattering
them like fallen leaves, great sun shining in my eyes
making my vision like that of a newborn child, bright
golden flame that lights my way.
Rivers running deep as oceans through my soul washing
my hopes up on the shores of far off islands, mountains
high like majestic castles with ivory towers full of my
ideas, trees! . . . trees my friends and I, my shelter on a
stormy day, my confidants when trouble's afoot.
Cliffs to throw my voice down into, to hear myself
talk to me, as like boomerang it heads its way home.
Valleys to run down with deep grass to fall in when breath
evades me, life tall or short of happy things, life so dear to
me, so full like a chalice overflowing spilling on to the world.
Leaving a mark where I have been for all to see that
here this life was me.

R. Walton

Passing Years

The days on the calendar are for all to see
They were set long ago for you and for me
And it's easy to check our paid up fee
For the years are locked with an irreversible key.

Each leaf on the pad has the date in bold type
When torn from its fixing it passes from sight
Another day gone from morning to night
We count it as nothing - one day of our life.

The pad grows thinner, more easily torn,
This year is fast passing it's very much worn,
But there is no need to be sad and forlorn
There are all the tomorrows not yet born.

So look not back on the days that have gone
But forward with hope to every new one
There's a lot still to play for, a lot to be won,
Living at any age can still be fun.

Sam Sharman

The Song of Life

When I look on winter's trees
They look so dead no leaf of green
And yet there's life beneath the bark
Just waiting for the new spring spark

A bud bursts forth to greet the sun
A leaf unfolds, spring has began
The tree has started the song of life
Forgotten and gone are winter's strife.

P. J. Diacopoulos

An Afternoon with Tom Hanks

Blue South frames a gentle face that fills the screen.
Those pale, far-seeing eyes
Flicker with light
As the television glows within our dim room.
Golden numbers count unnoticed
As your tape moves on
But we just murmur emotion into mugs of tea
"Well done".
Living out decades of America's history
with soft, perceptive Forest Gump.

But the story plays on; we talk endlessly
How in each part he's different,
This actor, - his hour.
So draw our conclusions, reflecting on morals:
How patient is love;
Stays true, endures trials -
And how in the space of one afternoon
We drifted the breeze of a lifetime, too.

Stacey M. Burchell

Inner Voice

Somehow, the world got the better of you.
Those prizes: senses you learned to attune
to cadences of shadow,
chart the fissured line of your pulse
like a seismograph
tremors on the edge of panic.

Somehow, your sensitivity's slipped out of step
when all around you it's like a limb to Nature:
a wing's fluting of feathers 'round
flexions of current, foraging shapes of air.

Don't you remember how a kestrel hung like breath
above fields behind your old school?
That's how a sensitivity should be:
a balance in prevailing winds to a stilled point's
absolute objectivity;
a sharp eye's ability to scan
rapid movements of surfaces and shadows,
to seize inside a striking purity of line
your hunt for meaning, hungrily defined.

Patrick Sullivan

Damsel in Armour

There is a tale to be told, about a girl in a cell,
Though the walls are of air, and the roof made of clouds.
The place she is trapped was within her own mind,
The key long gone and the lock chocked with briars.
The only sound she can hear, is a low resonant scream,
Which re-bounds right down from her brian to her toes.
Her face is a mask perfected by time, her eyes blank and sterile.
She feels strangely out of synchronism, slightly off-centre.
A hard case of ice encircles her heart,
But it is a chill she does not feel for she feels nothing at all.
Through this impregnable armour occasionally occurs a chink,
Allowing a re-birth, helpless and vulnerable
with unseeing eyes she surveys the world,
And wonders, "why am I here?", "what is the point?",
Before retreating once more to the safety of her cell.
Too far to be reached, waiting only for the right time,
To look up, touch the clouds and turn over to sleep

Sarah Tooth

Memories

Memories of childhood come tumbling by
thoughts of first love that still make us sigh
life's for the living though memory won't die
take it on till tomorrow to the future we fly

I dream of a world where there is no pain
in mists of the future the past comes again
the hurt and the suffering are of no cost
when we are united with the ones we have lost

The tide ebbs and flows like good times and bad
though the moment is fleeting we must not be sad
take thoughts of the past and things that's to come
the present's the bond that makes the infinite sum

Great words of wisdom will never heal pain
though people will tell you them time and again
time is the healer though slow like good wine
God made the rules; not wisdom of mine.

P. J. Garrett

Untitled

Lost souls unite
Through ages spent in ruin and torment,
And memories lost to the cold night
Lie tranquil come the morn,
Say then what we see and feel
To be the muffled chant,
That spreads itself through everything
And is both free and warm,
Let me then by the dawn's fevered touch
Caress your perfect skin,
That rises and falls with every breath
And heard softly in my dreams,
I awake both parched and hollow
From nights that seem so dark and dim,
And love which seems so scantily clad
Is borne along so many streams.

Samuel DeKay

Whispers of the Past

Flowers grow on earth where lovers have trodden
through centuries unheard,
And left no path of trodden violets and rows of daisy chains,
The same blue skies blanket like a canopy,
Hiding the lovers from the stars that have peeped on
secret and on stolen hearts,
With time and dust those footprints have long since vanished,
Where you and I first walked hand in hand,
Down those cherished lanes that wove our hearts with love,
Lasting through time until we join the lovers of the past,
As lovers lane hides beneath the dust of time,
And the stars will never tell our secrets to those who follow us,
With the same words on lips that caress and spell the
words of love,
I once said to you.

A. Wilkins

"Hyakutake - The Visitor"

Out of infinite vastness of endless space
Through a vortex of huge dark places
You have journeyed towards our earthly sphere
Returning from bygone ages.

Your brightness illuminates our atmosphere
With a bridal veil of attending stars
What mysteries have been yours to behold?
What secrets of planets could you reveal?

Were you created when time began?
A joyful sparkler held in God's hand
Then thrown out into infinity
A celebration of light for all to see

I watch your passage across the sky
Touching our lives for a moment in time
A symbol of all mysteries past
A journey from creation to eternity

You travel on towards future ages
What awaits you there in time to come?
Will my soul follow your brilliant path
Towards the place that we call heaven?

Yvonne Butler

Tigers

Tiger, Tiger, hiding in the jungle,
Tiger, Tiger, roaming free,
Tiger, Tiger, shot by the hunter,
When will it ever stop?

Tiger, Tiger, hiding in the rain forest,
Tiger, Tiger, roaming free,
Tiger, Tiger, shot by the hunter,
When will it ever stop?

Tiger, Tiger, hiding in the clothes shop,
Tiger, Tiger, not roaming free,
Tiger, Tiger, lying on the counter,
When will it ever stop?

Tiger, Tiger, hiding in the cupboard,
Tiger, Tiger, not roaming free,
Tiger, Tiger, hanging on a hanger,
When will it ever stop?

Tiger, Tiger, hiding in the jungle,
Tiger, Tiger, roaming free,
Tiger, Tiger, shot by the hunter,
When will it ever stop?

Christopher Cox

Adagio

Tick. tick . . tick . . . slow down thy beating heart.
Tick . . . tick . . . tick . . . now, ease thy heaving breath.
Smooth out thy ragged nerves, as you inhale.
Soothe out thy tortured soul, as you exhale.

Let niggles go astray;
Let feelings fall apart;
Let worries drift away.

Go, hear truth 'long the tracks of lies.
Go, see peace 'mongst the fields of war.
Go, feel life 'midst the clouds of death.

Let go thy troubled mind;
Let go thy heavy heart;
Let go thy anxious thought.

Do not fret, for what is done, is done.
Do not quake, for what will be, will be.
Do not weep, for what has gone, has gone.

Tranquillity holds the key. Feel your tensions melting away.
Serendipity holds the lock. Taste the pleasures of your life.
Surreality holds the gate. Tick . . . tick . . . tick . . .
Spirituality holds it all. Tick . . . tick . . . tick . . .

Thomas Francis Porter

Sunlight and Showers

Through sunlight and showers
Through snow and strong winds.
We have to accept
Whatever life brings.
The good and the bad
The joys and the sorrows,
Onwards our journey
Through all our tomorrows.
Take heart for the future
Let troubles be past
Heartache and worry, never shall last.
For Christ is the answer
In all of our lives
Just lift up your hearts
And search with inward eyes.
For if your search is noble and true
Jesus indeed will come unto you.
He will inspire and give you peace
Then you will find
All your troubles will cease.

Lena Maureen Raine

Just Sad

I see the world like a forest of azure,
through these beautiful shades of blue.
I hate my life,
My entire existence, being here without you.
I wonder 'Will life ever be the same?
Will I wake in a good mood again?'
I doubt it, I fear, for the love I hold dear,
Died when I lost you.
I am the poet and you are my muse,
you gave me all my inspiration to live.
Now without you here I just neck back the beer,
Whisky chaser a trip or two.
And now that you're gone,
I remember our songs,
and cry an ocean of tears.

Mojo Risin Young

Devotion

For you I will wait 'til time is no more
'Til there is nought but dust on the ocean floor
'Til eternity's fire is a dying flame
'Til our earthly souls go from whence they came
'Til the sun on high no more shall glare
'Til words are but a whispered prayer
'Til the tired earth shall cease to spin
'Til all is dead and gone therein
'Til hell below is glazed with ice
'Til nought exists no good no vice
'Til you turn and see your destiny
For you I will wait - You are all to me

J. Robinson

Thank You

The David I knew was good and kind
There was nothing wrong with his wonderful mind
He was big and strong, good looking too
It's something I wanted to tell all of you
                    For
When he came to you he was weak and frail,
I had tried and tried to no avail
To find a place where he could be,
Cared for, and loved by people like me.
                    Then
A miracle happened I found all of you
Wonderfully caring in all that you do
No task too big, nor yet too small
Always on hand at his beck and call
                    So
There are no words that I can say,
Or enough money in which to repay
All of you for what you have done,
God bless you all, each and everyone.

S. Bretherick

Life

Life is bewildering, a puzzle, an enigma, when you're trying so
hard to avoid the stigma.
Of failing to make your house your home, with all the trappings
you would like to own.
Of failing to keep your job, your career, when the income you
need for the ones you hold dear.
When you lose self respect and you lose self esteem, and hope
that your plight is only a dream.
That's when you realise! your river is only a stream.
Sometimes things change and you solve the conundrum, of
making ends meet and reaching your fulcrum.
It's then that the happiness outweighs the hardship, and you hide
the thought of losing your grip.
But it's only a break in the puzzle of life, so give it your all,
again will come strife.

W. E. Hughes

Face to Face

All I have is a crumpled bygone photograph
To teach me something of you.
A worn faded figure in uniform,
A fresh young face I dearly wish I knew.

Your eyes seem to hold many secrets,
Your smile has an abandoning air.
There are so many questions I long to ask you,
As you gaze knowingly back at me without a care.

No doubt in your day you broke many a heart,
Of a beaux waiting dreamily back home.
With that iridescent sparkle in your eyes of sultry blue,
You must have looked so debonair; if only I could've known.

When I gaze long and hard at the face I'll never touch,
And strive to heed the voice I'll never hear.
Your legacy of hope and valour emerges; bearing,
An affinity and an awareness that you're near.

And this illusive soldier I clasp in my hand,
Has many sides I wish I could see.
With a smile that masks a thousand thoughts,
And eyes that reveal part of me.

E. Wellington

One Day at the Fair

To the fair she did go
To try out the rides, and watch a sideshow.
On the go-carts, she raced 'round the track.
On the dodgems, watch your back
She tried the waltzers, was not struck.
So she tried, lady luck.
She threw the rings around a duck.
She won a goldfish for her score.
Ate a donut, went back for more.
Exhausted and dizzy, her head spinning 'round,
To her amazement, she fell to the ground.

E. Lightfoot

Untitled

It used to be "Tide's in dirt's out"
To be a Persil mum was all the rage
Coppers, mangles, scrubbing boards
I've been through every stage.
Fanny Cradock used to say Lifebouy soap's a must
To get a really deep down clean
On your collars and your cuffs.
With extra white and colour bright
And Bio Ultra Clean, Oxydol, Dreft and Daz,
Are among the best there's been
Vanish, Omo, Rinso, not forgetting all the rest,
They've added all they can
And the measure's less and less
But now it's back to basics,
Because original is best.

J. Bliss

419

Fiesta Di San Giovanni Battista
(Fireworks of a Fiery Prophet)

They came from far, they crowded in from near:
to the feast they thronged to eat and drink, and behold
extravagant fireworks bejewelling an Umbrian night.

The elderly and children mingled together, all
in a medley of boisterous delight, intoxicated
by the fantasy of fragmenting stars or fiery rain,
reflecting the dreams and earth-germinating
desires of the stately stalks of youths, who seemed
more metaphors than men, loitering about languid shadows,
as lovely as Botticelli's Graces - but more lively.

Was this the baptism by fire the prophet proclaimed
as the art of truth's renaissance or an excuse to forget
the toil of the late summer's heat and tiresome regret,
which dully that evening the preacher had declaimed?

Michael L. Gaudoin-Parker

Gone Away

They shall come no more
    To the old familiar place
The home they left is lonely and bare
The garden is deserted, the fire is dead
And the clock stands silent
    In the corner there

They have gone away
    To a far and foreign land
To a life that shows a promise fair
To new faces, new friends add happy days in store
But the clock stands silent
    In the corner there

Mona Jackson

Sam

Sam the dog we loved so much
To us he was a real soft touch,
A loving dog with feelings true
No wonder why we loved him too,
The holidays with us his been,
Hills and sands and grasses green
No one run ever take away,
Part of our life own our dog did play,
Sam a loyal & faithful friend,
We loved him tell the bitter end,
In our hearts he'll forever stay
A treasured memory locked away.

Sayers

A Life Full of Yesterdays

A life full of yesterdays, hopes and desires,
Times that destroy you like funeral pyres.
There are good times and bad, then happy and sad,
Yet gratitude always for the life that we've had.

A life full of yesterdays, dreams that come true,
Moments of contentment for me and for you.
We look to tomorrow and then back to the past,
To things we have done in time gone so fast.

A life full of yesterdays, with tragedies few,
Each day brought about experiences new.
Stored carefully in mind, our whole lives to date,
Our yesterdays gone, our tomorrows our fate.

A life full of yesterdays, some sadness within,
Then tomorrow arrives, a new day to begin.
Memories of loved ones, with us or apart,
Held deep in our mind and close to our heart.

A life full of yesterdays, laughter and tears,
Carefree and happy or hiding our fears.
Feeling emotions like love and anger and pain,
Then our life slips on by, to yesterday's gain.

Lee Bryant

In Springtime

As we walk in the meadows upon a spring morn
To hear the bird song at the break of dawn,
Hand in hand we step throu' the sweet scented grass
Watching the wandering herd as they pass
By old weeping willows, which gracefully lean
To trail their wands in the murmuring stream,
The day gently breaks and our spirits rise
To the fountain of love, beyond the blue skies
In the warmth of the sun, rising with mirth
We give thanks to Thee for this beautiful earth
Away in the distance the church bells ring
And a cuckoo sings on this morning in spring.

Patricia Woodcock

There but for the Grace of God . . .

Look stranger! Look stranger! What do you see
through your eyes, when you look down on me?
A funny old man in a worn, grubby suit
With a wrinkled shirt, and one laceless boot
Ha! I used to be smart in a collar and tie
A spring in my step, a glint in my eye.
Owned my own business, had my own place
Always so happy with a smile on my face.
Then came the depression the Wall Street crash
I lost everything then, all of my cash.
Then my wife left me, I was alone
I had no family to call my own.
Down on my luck, out on a limb
No longer was I happy, lucky old Jim
Look stranger! I'm harmless, I do not beg or steal
I seek work daily in exchange for a meal.
Some days I'm lucky and earn a few bob
When someone asks me to do an odd job.
Do not look down on me son, with your eyes steely blue
There but for the Grace of God, boy, it could have been you.

Mary Holder

I in "Reality"

The youngest of ten that I was born,
To my parents, Elizabeth and Luke.
I would like to have been a Child of a Duke,
Instead, a daughter to a family very poor then,
When people had children by the ten.
What chance did we have at all
When I was five I dreamed a dream,
That I would have clothes galore,
Instead I had hand-me-downs and not more, more, more,
At school we were asked to do a poem, what Christmas
    was like at home.
I said we had family and very fine gifts.
And a tea table set for a queen.
It was the finest I'd ever seen.
When I grow up I want a house, an ambition not to be ignored.
But times were hard and money was tight.
Then one day I saw the light.
Go on saving till you find your dream,
Husband to go with it too,
And since then that's what it's been.

Margery Audrey Catherine

Sad World

Why is it we are cruel, unjust and unkind?
To other people's pain, we are so blind
We live in violence, darkness and hate
Leaving our lives to the hands of fate
We tend to kill each other in cold blood
Like ripping the head off a newly formed bud
Such lack of respect and sense of self worth
With no thought at all to the miracle of birth
So afraid to go out at night all alone
Because of what some people have now become
As for crime, there never seems to be an end
Always lives and possessions we have to defend
Many hearts are filled with sorrow and dismay
At how our world is becoming today.

Sheryl Roach

420

My Children

I am giant at tiny, glove hands,
Thus humility adorns me with watchful bands.
Bringing joy when shedding tears,
They embrace security when I calm their fears.

They amaze in development mundane,
Delight by puerile tantrums insane.
Mischief manoeuvres playful innocence,
Indifference overwhelmed only by their persistence.

In chastisement I am remorseful,
I despair at a heavy hand so hurtful.
Yet they wrench my heart in remitting embrace,
And redeem my soul with impish face.

They are infuriation, yet angelic inspiration,
They are my parameters without restriction.
They are paradox and contradiction,
They are my children.

A. Morcombe

Salute to a Clown

I bow my head before you,
to you who make us laugh.
We take you at face value,
but we don't know the half
of what you suffer.
For when your act is over,
and all the crowds have gone,
the only thing that you have left
is the loneliness that lingers on and on.
I love you funny clown
although you frighten me.
I understand your masquerade
because I am one you see.

P. Nelson

Dad's Birthday

Another birthday has come around,
To your wife and children your love has been sound,
With that in mind I wish to say,
I hope you have a wonderful day.

You're sometimes happy, sometimes mad,
But, we'll always respect you, because you're our dad.

From you we are able to get advice,
Knowing you're there for us, that's nice.

So, I've written this poem just for you,
A splendid dad and granddad too,
We treasure the moments more and more.
We spend as a family, that is for sure.

So once again, from your daughter and son,
This birthday wish is surely the one,
To show you how much we appreciate,
As dads come, you really are great.

A. J. Gibbs

Life

I wonder when the end will come, the silent, peaceful sleep
To rid the harsh and hurtful times why do I sit and weep?
Behind my smile, my cheery face, behind the curtains drawn
My sadness grew beyond control, and others now will mourn.

How could I be so lonely, with friends who loved me so
They never really knew, my hurt and why I had to go.
So sad to leave my lover, I long to comfort him
I know he really loves me, but goodbye to love - and him.

Their tears begin to slowly fall, for now the party's over.
Time to clear up all the mess for I have now passed over.
Too late to save me, now I'm gone - I've left the hurt behind
Though self-inflicted, silently I smile a peaceful smile.

Confusion, hate and torment and stifled cries and sobs
The question - why of everything is life the hardest job?

Lucy Marie Butts

Timely

Today is now — no longer then.
Today can never come again.
It is the moment when we live —
When heart and soul combine to give
Our very best or just our worst,
Which makes us loved yet sometimes cursed.
A cheerful smile, a kindly word
In answer to a heart that's stirred,
A gift to one unused to such,
A loving glance, a tender touch,
It must be now — not left undone.
For moments lost, forever gone,
Can mean the day has been in vain
And that life empty will remain.
Make living fill the waking hours —
Words and deeds to spread like flowers —
The fruit then borne in after years —
    Whether of laughter or of tears —
    Will be the testament you give.
With each new day — just try to live.

M. Rees

You Said Goodbye

You wrote me a note
to say goodbye.
You said you were leaving,
and our love would never die!
That day you left you broke my heart.
I thought you were mine and that we
would never part.
So what did you go and do, you
broke my heart.
I will never forget that day my life fell apart!
As I look through all the happy years, tears start
to roll down my cheeks.
I wish you were still here with me to hold me and
say everything was going to be alright.
But know I am all alone in this world no one to love me
and no one to care.
JUST ALL ALONE SITTING ON MY OWN IN THIS LONELY
OLD CHAIR!!

Leanne Westwood

On Being Late

Time hovers over us, a hangman's noose,
Waiting to strangle if we should lose
Ourselves in a moment of contemplation
Dragging down to eternal damnation.
Once caught there is no chance of reprieve;
Time's tentacles cling, we cannot leave
To renounce time's cause and claim oblivion;
To bask in the sun of life's meridian.

N. M. Beddoes

Irises

Oh, sweet mysterious flower the colour of night
Thy purple midnight hue spurs my reverie to flight
To a foreign land of bright silver moons, sickle,
    crescent, full
And myriads of stars that jewel the skies
The cadent lull of a Grecian sea
And to a love that never dies.

Ah, once again, the soft breeze stirs the leaves
And fragrance fills the air from the almond and
    lemon trees.

Here now I stand in a northern land and gaze
    upon thy purple midnight hue
And I remember the irises that in our orchard grew
And I remember you my sweet Adonis, my beautiful
    and wise Apollo
And our ecstatic love the gods defied
They looked on us with jealous eyes and thus you died
But in all things lovely you live on
And the purple midnight hue of the irises that in our orchard grew.
Will ever link my heart to you.

Lili Arger

The Jigsaw

It's been a very dull and dreary day
We got out our jigsaw.
It's been very difficult to do
But now it's nearly done
Oh wait a moment there is one missing
Why is it there is always one missing
It's not on the floor or under the cushion
Maybe still in the box, but oh no.
Oh I know under pussy over there
Come on puss up you get, but it's not there
Oh well we will have another cup of tea.
Oh what is that stuck under your cup
It's the missing piece hoorah
But now we have to take it loose
And back in the box it goes again.

E. M. Hayes

The Sea Empress

Running on the sand splashing in the sea
we laughed in the sun my sisters and me.
Now we are grown we stand and stare at
the devastation we can see there.
The golden sand now black as night
our hearts are breaking at this terrible sight.
The ship is grounded and the oil is free to
wash our shores and kill the sea.
To SAVE a penny to save a pound we've
killed the seals' hunting ground.
What will it take to make you all see that
we're killing the life of the beautiful sea.
The shores are black and the birds are
all gone children no longer play in the sun.
We save a penny we save a pound and
we've killed the seals' hunting ground.

K. Edge

The Old Ford

At eventide we strolled along,
We listened to the skylark's song
Summers's here he seemed to say
Tomorrow will be another day.

Hand in hand or arms entwined
We never stopped to look behind.
We were all enhanced with each other's love,
We did not see the turtle dove.

At last we reached the water's edge,
Each other's love we did pledge,
We saw the glistening water's flow
There's a trout - where did he go?

But now I go there all alone
Because my lover has gone home
So when I feel upset and bored
I still visit, that Old Ford.

Bethany Jade

Welcome

Today I was moved by the rolling of a whisper
We said our farewells with saddened shot eyes
I turned my head to these dear sweet people
for whom this tired old lady filled much their own lives
with such sweet tenderness.

It was like the heavens had fallen upon us
and bequeathed our earthly sighs
I could almost feel the presence of her angels
as they blew past our sides
to carry her away.

Somehow I could feel this tired old lady
begin life again as young
I could almost see her ascending the golden stairway
as she ran up every rung
to be once again with her Mother.

Peter Threadgold

Tranquillity

Tranquillity is the Causeway Bridge
To stand and look over the Yar
As it flows gently by and in its wake
Beautiful swans, what a picture they make
A view of the Church, a copse nearby
Where Bluebells and Primroses peacefully lie.
It's a small piece of heaven, a wonderful view
There are scavenger crabs small, but living there too
The old railway track now a small stony lane
Of which only memories will always remain,
Tall standing reeds, sometimes ducks can be seen
The water is sparkling, the trees turning green.
The sky azure blue, clouds showing up grey
Birds ducking and diving what more can one say
The Church clock shows its face as we wend our way home
The time's been well spent, given rise to this poem
For moments like these just cannot be bought
I'm leaving you now, have a heavenly thought.

B. M. Bryan

"Love Is"

Love is someone who makes you laugh and lifts you
        up to touch the sky,
        who gently holds you when something makes you cry.

Love is someone who kisses and cuddles you
        closely every night,
        who smiles at you with each new morning light.

Love is someone who stands by you, and understands
        when things go wrong,
        who joins in with you when you burst into song.

Love is someone who shares bringing up the children
        from nursery to teenage years.
        who then looks down Memory Lane of laughter and tears.

Love is someone who guides and encourages the children
        to find a Lover true,
        who enjoys endless, happiness the hours Grandchildren
        give you.

Love is someone who is still with you at the end
        of Life's Year,
        who then travels with you through Eternity, with no fear.

Marjorie A. Barrett-Powell

Requiem for a Whale

From fathoms deep, she came to sleep
Upon a Kentish shore —
Far from her kind — and who's to mind
The family she left behind?

Those once pure oceans where she would play
Are sadly things of yesterday

We kill your kind — and we don't mind
    The damage that we do
So bless you, whale — all I can say —
    We're sad to see you go.

Rick Sassi

Heartache

She looked upon her children,
Upon each and every face,
Their grief was framed in symmetry,
With a cold expressionless grace.

Sorrow blazed in their timid eyes,
As hers began to fill,
And she listened to their silent cries,
While remaining helpless and still.

Then one by one they left the room,
Until she was alone,
And once again she knew the truth,
Only now the guilt had grown.

Leann Brown

The Fruits of My Vineyard

To the vineyard I did go
To reap the fruits of what I'd sown
From my harvest, like the rest
I only wanted what was best.

But alas the tale was this
Someone had been there and had raped
My land of what was rightfully mine
They stole my fruit, that was for wine.

They didn't know nor did they care
The damages, the despair
They raped and ravished all in sight
My harvest ravaged, my life's work vanished

Life goes on I cried out loud
Those fools that stole my life, my wine
Are drunk, but only for a while
For they have drank my life's sweet wine.

My vessels they are empty now
My vineyard it is barren
Today I will seek sweet revenge
Those fools will drink my bitter blend

Margaret Braniff

The Empty Chair

I used to wonder how it would be
To see that empty chair.
You filled my world, we were as one,
The loss is hard to bear.

You're now in God's care, my love,
I know it's for the best.
Your suffering is now over,
In peace, my love, you rest.

Life goes on, friends all tell me,
Time heals a broken heart.
The years slip by so quickly,
Why did we have to part?

Take my heart, my all, my love,
The thoughts we used to share,
I need all your strength now, dearest,
When I see that empty chair.

But we shall be one again, my love,
To laugh, to talk, to play.
Never again to be apart,
That tomorrow will be our today.

E. V. Dance

Professional Disappointment

Thirty odd years of frustrated desire,
Waiting for senior staff to retire;
Assistant, adviser, consultant and guide -
Always a bridesmaid, never the bride!

So many incumbents of manager's chair,
They come and they go, it seems grossly unfair;
You keep your nose clean, oft times laugh at his jokes,
To stay in the race with those vile other blokes.

By the subtlest of means you both kowtow and fawn,
In the high expectation your bright day will dawn;
Have patience, you muse, he retires next July -
The time seems to drag when you'd like it to fly.

"Could we have him to dinner?" you enquire of the wife,
She responds unequivocally "Not on your life!",
Perhaps just as well, you so sadly conclude,
She's no Delia Smith in the enhancement of food.

Then the great day arrives and you're biting your lip,
To hear of their choice for the managership;
Alas, when you get home she sees from your frown -
The unspeakable twerps have promoted old Brown!

Roy Perry

Borstal Boy

A Borstal boy came home one night
To find his house without a light.

As he sat there on his bed,
A sudden thought came to his head.

He rushed into his girlfriend's room,
To find her hanging in the gloom.

He reached into his pocket for a rusty knife,
And cut her down to find she had no life.

As he stood there in shock and fear,
He cried "My Love" with a tear.

He looked in anger all around,
And on her chest these words he found.

My darling dear I died in shame,
As I could not bear your child without a name.

My love was strong, my love was dear,
My only wish is that you were near.

As I died I heard songs of prayer
wherever I am, please understand you are always there.

Lester McKie

Passing By

This morning, I searched the garden,
To find out what was wrong,
For some days now, my blackbird friend,
Hadn't answered my imitation of his song.

Tears were near when I found him,
Half eaten, half hidden 'neath a bush,
There alas beside him, the remains
Of a lovely, spotted thrush,

With stray dogs or cats I've no quarrel,
Nor that squirrel, who cheeky as can be,
Will take cob nuts from my hand
When there's none left on the tree.

It's with those big, nasty magpies
Where my patience ends,
They seem to delight in persecuting,
My defenceless little friends.

Now they really have upset me,
Deprived me of so much fun,
Made me so mad, made me mutter to myself,
"Wish I had a gun".

W. E. Nicholls

Paradise Found

A dream, a scheme, a plan of mine,
To whisk me through the sands of time.
To a faraway beach with a faraway name.
A golden sun, and sand the same.

Chocolate brown bodies with glistening glow,
Drinking cooling cocktail, "Siberian Snow."
Shimmering sea with frothy, white surf,
Bubbling up like the suds of the earth.

Powder blue sky with cotton wool clouds,
Creating a backdrop on all that it shrouds.
Piney palm trees with juicy fruits,
Promising flavour right down to the roots!

Hear the steel band in the distance play.
"Come and join in!", it seems to say.
The world was built 'round this beautiful place,
But only a few see its heavenly face.

The music is fading, it sounds far away...
The sun's going down on another hot day.
I open my eyes and wonder just when,
I'll visit my island of dreams once again?

Linda A. Moore

'Maxie's Light'

Candlelight beside my bed
Unlike the leaves that fall down dead
Unlike the days that change to dark
Unlike chained gates that front a park
But flowing water endlessly
Forever full, forever free.
Oceans blue and pastures green
Of all the beauty we have seen
Of stars that make the dark turn light
Of all the moons that shine for night
Of rain and wind and sleet and snow
A place always where roses grow
Not a day of thoughts, nor hour nor minute
Can pass me by without you in it.
And while you sleep within your dreams
When your fears turn into screams
Turn to me your candle bright
To guide you through and give you sight.
Your fears will gently ease away
To dream until the light of day.

Rosemaris Jesson

National Identity

Layer upon layer digging deeper
Until you find, a visible darkness.
A history of time forgotten
A time of broken loyalties,
Broken dreams, broken pacts.

A time of evasion, rape, torture,
Annihilation of a race forever lost
From who they are; who they could be.

Fighting, blaming, killing
Each others blood. Preventing
Union between the essence of who we are.

War with ourselves; war with who will contend,
Opposites, difference, grievance,
Or just for the sake of a fight.

Drawing blood, scoring a point,
Winning, beating the underdog.
Teamwork united as one.

Tania Donnelly

Little Bird Child Fly

Fly little bird you're not a child
Up into the sky
Let your tiny wings flutter wild
As the clouds go by.

Up in the sky there is a heaven
Where there is abundances of love
You will find your little heart will then open
So make haste tiny dove.

So goodbye my little boy
You're now a bird
Fly very high with joy
And let your wisdom be heard

And you know we will remember your name
It still will remain the same.

Ronald MacDonald

Nethershore

Oh! To wander evermore
Upon the straits of Nethershore
Knowing naught of this nor that;
To see the truth in mortal lie,
To measure naught by tongue, ear or eye
Beyond each new wave that breaks
Lies an endless, signless; virgin shore;
Where I'll wander, wander evermore,
Upon the straits of Nethershore

Neil Bannister

The Desperate Concealment

I decided to open my heart to the grief
To let out the pain.
Stored in the darkness of my hidden memories
Sad, suffering remorse
Buried in the contours of my brain.

Death has a sting,
But first feelings fringe on numbness
As if tranquillity bathes itself in care.
A bewildered heart, born of despair
I'm at peace now, but the pain is there
It will be buried there until the time is right
To open up the door and see its flight.

Proud heart, mourn,
Between the laughter of love, the desperate concealment,
The refusal and the scorn.
I decided to open my heart to the grief,
Let out the pain.

I decided to live again.

Marion Elizabeth Sherwood

Lachrymal

She stumbles restlessly from room to room
Tunelessly humming her never-ending song.
Her dim watery eyes brighten briefly
At something half remembered from time long past.
The words emerging from her smiling mouth,
Are often tangled, like a kitten's ball of wool.
My children all have grown, reached independence,
Giving me independence of my own -
Short-lived, snatched from me,
Full circle now complete
As I become the mother
Of an eighty-two year babe;
A stranger who resembles one I once knew well,
Someone much-loved. But, all feeling numb
The dreaded burden is assumed
And shouldered down the weary nights and days.

Pam Lowe

Sunset on a Norfolk River

Peace and stillness on the river,
Trees like black lace
'Gainst the golden wonder of the setting sun.
Little fleecy clouds, pink and flaming,
Drifting from their mother-fire,
Drifting gently, dispersing,
And becoming lost in eternity.
The river runs red,
Red with blood of the dying sun,
And the world pauses,
Before plunging into the abyss of night
To be born anew to the waiting dawn.

Dede Banks

From Here, I Can See It All

From here I can see everything
To my left, the endless forest
Untouched by human hands
Unspoilt by human nature.

From here I can see everything
The sun setting on the horizon
Streaking the sky with a myriad of colours
And announcing the coming night.

From here I can see everything
The birds flying freely
The horses in the distance
Grazing happily, safely away from man.

Then I look to my right
The concrete road runs through the countryside
Shattering the peace, spoiling the tranquillity
Reminding me of the damage we do.
From here, I can see it all.

J. P. Simpson

Untitled

Heart over matter is the
way I feel about you.
You gave me a love and
promised to be true.
There I was all alone, at home,
No evidence, no clues.
all I wanted was the truth.
You have to hurt to understand the
mind of your man.
No matter where I turn, I always fail to learn.
Is it a spell or is it a curse
or have you just stolen my
heart from my purse.

Nunisa Lee

The Garden of Life

All alone in a garden with the wind - the rain,
We all have to manage somehow to keep sane,
The days are so short, we have to race everywhere,
So much beauty around us, it doesn't seem fair,
That we haven't the time to stop and stare.
Sometimes the hailstones of winter we feel
The earthquakes and tremors and floods from the sea.
We stop, shed a tear and then move on to our next toil and strife.
The storms they do pass and people feel free to build and restore.
Even those who are devastated by war.
Yes, they find in themselves a power so strong,
They cry for a while and then they move on.
Yes they move on, but not for a while.
Have time to decide what to shelve and to store
Time to comfort yourself and recover from the war.
Then you move on to a future that's bright,
Because of our hope we can see the light.

Valerie M. Robb

Untitled

The lives of great men all remind us
we can make our lives sublime
and departing leaving behind us
foot print on the sand of time.

I've stood on the bridge at midnight as the
clock was sticking the hour and the moon rose
dare the city behind the dark church tower,
I've seen her bright reflection in the water's
under me like a golden goblet falling and
sinking into the sea, and like those waters come
rushing among the wooden peers a flood of thought
came done me that fill my eyes with tears.
And forever and forever as long as heart
hath passion as long as life hath woe the moon
and its broken reflection shall appear like
the symbol of love in heaven.

G. Stewart

The Garden

I spend many hours, in your garden I tend
To know you'll not see it, sends me 'round the bend
It gives me no pleasure, just sheer bloody pain
To know you'll not sit, in this garden again
I spend many hours, to make the garden look fine
Yet in the end, I find I'm wasting my time
It was not the garden, that had beautiful life
It was you darling, you, my very own wife
You were the beauty, the pleasure, the joy.
'Cause when you were in it I felt like a boy.
With your little fingers, the garden did grow
You made it lovely, of that I now know.
My efforts are fruitless, my work is no good
'Cause the plants that I grow, never grow as they should
You were the garden, the summer, the spring
And now you're in heaven, the angels will sing
'Cause you tend their garden, in summer and spring
And they see the pleasure, and joy that it brings.

R. Walker

Freedom In Sane!

I walked across the desert shore.
To find the unknown, to explore.
To ride the foreboding ocean wave,
and taste the aroma that I crave.

I walked the waters to the land of Sane,
and close behind my spirit came.
To mind my home, my new salvation,
to be united with an untouched Nation.

Running through my freedom land,
welcomed by riches from the people's hand.
from ancient gold to tunics in bright arrays,
A haven found to spend my days.

Old to grow in peace, without poverty or disease,
away from corrupt people who deceive.
A place to rest my weary head,
A million days from the place I fled.

J. Prentice

A Wise Barn Owl and a Guinea Fowl

A wise barn owl and a guinea fowl
Were discussing the intemperate weather
"Don't you think my dear
It's this north hemisphere
That infernally dampens one's feather?
'Tis foul, for a fowl, in a fog I feel,
I feel terribly foul," said the owl,
"And with ice on one's beak
One can hardly speak
And my tail's at the end of its tether."
"I agree," said the guinea who's name was Minnie,
"To sojourn is folly indeed.
Let us board for abroad
On that big bird Concorde."
So they hastened away with all speed.

Lucienne Francis

'Spring Song's Memory'

At 6 a.m. I awoke with a start,
were my ears hearing right?
A bird was singing with full heart,
welcoming the dawn in the early morn.
My heart gave a lift, spring was here.
Hearing that sound my memories were clear,
like a note from a song, of births and joy,
on the path, from oh, so long,
that reached back in life, of all I hold dear.
And the depth of the memory, seems so near.
As the years unfold and birthday's are told,
none of us really want to grow old.
But wisdom of life is a wonderful thing,
treasure and share it is, something I do,
to those, who will listen,
which are only,
the few.

D. L. Daubeney

Past Times

What happened to the years gone by when we
were young and free?
When every day was clear and warm and we lived happily.
When children wore school uniforms they all
looked smart and neat.
And boys would stand on buses so that ladies had a seat.
When we could go out after dark without being afraid,
When offspring thought that parents' rules
were there to be obeyed,
When money was in short supply and treats were very few,
Why were we all so happy when we had something new?
The best things in this life are impossible to buy.
I wish that people could perceive this fact before they die
If love and care and thoughtfulness consumed the human race,
The world would be as God desired, a placid, happy place.

J. H. Ridgeon

425

K. Z.

She trudges slowly, head down, eyes fixed
Upon the narrow gauge of a railway track.
The line once used to carry them . . .
Like lambs to the slaughter.

The gates draw nearer and the prominent watch towers,
Like triffids in the skyline, form an evil horrorizon.
The fields once mined now mind themselves
Though a scent of charred flesh still hangs in the wind.

Eventually she comes to the gate and enters the yard, where
Half a century ago, she last laid eyes upon her mother.
She took the left queue. Her mother, the right queue. The wrong queue.
Decided as being too old to live but never too young to die.

A tear forms and trickles down her cheek. Flowing like
Her aggression, her hatred but also like blood.
Remembers that last look and wave from her mother
Before she disappeared into the kiln of death.

The billowing smoke, absorbed by the rain, so that
Death rained in and on the camp.
So ironic they were killed in a shower.
And although she still lives, her life is inert.

Mark Keeble

Hill Lambs

It really is an awesome sight
To see the lambs in full flight,
They gallop back and forth with glee
It really is a sight to see.

Into little gangs they get
Feed times, to Mother go don't fret,
They really are so full of fun
Especially when they feel the sun.

I wonder what are the games they play
The jump and frolic all the day,
The hills now really are alive
With bleating, as they jump and jive.

So our thanks we give to thee
For such wonders now we see,
Many thanks for these gifts
They really give our hearts such lifts.

Every year this scene we see
The country is the place to be,
Thank you God for things so rare
And letting us your wonders share.

E. R. Shepherd

The Arrival

Imperceptible as Life's first breath, she came.
Uncertain, as the first faint shafts of dawn
That pierce the night, and bid the stars to fade,
She came, and like a thought, was born.

So deftly did she move to touch the Earth
That mortal souls were scarcely made aware.
But tiny creatures in their sleeping, stirred.
And dreamed of dappled sunlight, balmy air.

Too early yet to waken from thy sleep -
Leave not the womb for this forsaken place.
The ice is not yet melted on the brook,
And hoarfrost hangs like softly glistening lace.

Deep snows still linger o'er the distant hills
Borne by winds that left the landscape bare.
Yet what could this sweet creature be but Spring
That brushed the senses, made the soul aware?

The pulse of Life beats quiv'ring through the land,
Though all yet held in Winter's mighty spell.
Now soon the Spring will cast her mantle green.
Thy God is in His Heaven - all is well!

J. P. Goulden

Mothers

I did not know what mothers were supposed to be.
Till I was old.
My loved children had left home.
I had loved them.
I was proud and happy to do so.
It was easy.
But I had not quantified what a mother was supposed to be.

A phrase I had heard many times struck me one day.
"Well, of course, you'd praise me; you're my mother."
It struck me like a bucket of cold water.

My mother had seen the worst in me
Because she was my mother.
She had been hard to me because she was my mother.
She criticised me always because she was my mother.
I had to do all I did for her because she was my mother.
All this I knew,
All this I had lived,
I suddenly saw she had failed me and made me guilty for her failure.

P. Joy Anthony

There's Only One World

Big grey elephants playing in water,
Then the humans come to slaughter,
Beautiful tigers playing around,
Then they're shot to the ground,
Why do people do this for a sport
Why not play tennis in a tennis court?
Can our planet really live on.
When all the plants and animals are gone?
What will it be like with nothing here?
Lots of people will shed a tear
from the great big whale to the tiny snail
Each and everyone can tell a tale.
Can our planet really live on
When all the plants and animals are gone?

Yvonne Wyllie

Dawn

The early morning dew lays like a blanket on the grass,
waiting for the break of dawn that soon will come to pass.
The heavy mists roll lazily across each vale and field,
expectant of the warmth to come that each new day will yield.
Darkness fades, relenting, as the sky melts into grey,
in deference to the might and power of this brand new day,
and shadows of the night depart before the rising sun,
while all around the world awakes, the spell of night undone.
The sun, ablaze, pushes herself above the distant trees
and shares the warmth that she creates with everything she sees.
The mists depart, thus giving way unto a clear, bright day,
as gentle clouds way up above, drift slowly on their way.

Paul Thompson

Beware

Warm water lapping, wrapping our feet in liquid love,
Waves, not distressing or possessing, sending
Messages through us of secrets
Not yet unfolded, not yet told.
The water warm and gentle, pure. No anger here,
No sorrow; only tomorrow it may change
When the skies darken and the waves
Will rearrange the sifting sand
Beneath the feet, to make us feel unsure.

And such is love, catching us looking
In the wrong direction. Blinding us with affection.
Beware the gentle waves, the kind caressing ripples,
Beware the alluring sun, the soft sea breezes
The sparklers and the stars upon the water
The last and lulling wave now lapping over.
The taste of salt. Denial of fault.
Take care, for after that the tide may
Well desert us - or return and hurt us.

Nancy Bateman

426

Chockie

Chockie whose name ought to be love.
Was Gods gift to you, sent from above.
Her intelligence, devotion, her winning ways,
Bring comfort to you, on lonely days.
To care for Chockie, is no easy thing.
But think of the happiness, that she brings.
Ever loyal, faithful and true.
Love is what Chockie means to you.
Yes Chockie was sent from heaven above.
And this little dog represents love.

I. J. Woolston

Spring Song

O spring, you lift the mists of winter gloom,
Time warms the earth, brings flowers to bloom,
Late frosts keep a crispness in the air,
Bright sunlight beams across meadows bare,
Song birds' early chorus greets the silent dawn,
They lift the heart from yesterday forlorn,
The hedgerows shoot young saplings too,
Wild creatures join play in the early dew.
Blossoms enrich the bowers along the leas,
Make varied colours to draw the bees.
O spring, you wake up everything again, renew,
Bring special things, with harsh winter bid adieu.
Full buds burst forth in colourful display,
Leafless trees become showers of green array,
Every year nature's beauty is unfurled,
Rest awhile, observe, enjoy, this wondrous world.
The mind refreshed, is activated to proclaim,
Each month ahead needs plan, restrain.
When lovers meet, soft hands entwine,
Fond hopes lead on to happiness and summertime.

P. J. Benham

Big Sister

When I was young, you were always there
To wash my face and to comb my hair,
When I did wrong, you were quick to chide,
And I couldn't find a place to hide.
When I was sad, you comforted me
As you held me close upon your knee.
When I was hurt, you would dry my tears,
Kiss me better and soothe all my fears.
When I was in need, I'd turn to you
And know you'd always see me through.
When all my troubles I shared with you
You always told me just what to do.
But now you are gone, there's no-one there,
No-one to turn to - no-one to care
Yet though there's a gap no-one can fill
I know in my heart you're with me still
And if there's another life to share
I know that you'll be waiting there.

M. B. Holden

Silent

What is anger, inside my head
twisting and turning, a definite red
now I can see you, grey vertical line
but did I want to find you, are you
really mine

Uncontrollable, ferocious, dare I let you escape
is it me you are after, or am I the bait
snake swirling inner tubes attached to your core,
I'm scared to give in, for surely there's more

I can see pink then you turn to red
like a raging bull you scream in my head
trying to turn the red into blue
passing through purple making myself new

Who is the anger for, is it for me
could I have shouted when I was three
now I will shout but not so silently
from red to blue, set myself free

Nicky Helm

The Stranger

The sadness in her tired eyes
To all around was no surprise
For she was poor and so forlorn
Her clothing rags and badly torn.

She struggled through the darkness
Up the narrow winding stair
Of an old condemned back building
Where she lived no one to care.

The world was cruel the shelter none
Food was sparse no where to run
Nights were cold and days were long
The only thrill was the busker's song.

He seemed to come from nowhere
When summertime appeared
The crowd's all gathered 'round him
His wit and songs to hear.

One sunny day he spoke with her
His voice was kind and low
This man she would remember
When winter's cold winds blow.

Morag Sutherland

My Braveheart

This wounded heart of mine doth try,
To hide its ache from mine own eye.
This wounded heart of mine cries out,
On mine deaf ears it would shout.

I carry on without a show,
As big as life, so no one would know.
Torn apart my heart sings out,
Cleaved in two without a doubt.

To mask my sorrow I would say,
Heart of mine live for today.
Do not falter, do not fail,
Let your beat carry us down this trail.

Will it end my heart replies,
Will it end my hearts desires.
Will it cause me to reject,
To sit and ponder and reflect.

Let us heal this pain and sorrow,
It will lessen by tomorrow.
Life goes on for you and I,
On and on until we die: My braveheart.

D. B. Allan

My Life

I would have loved,
to have gone away today
a trip down to the sea,
but here I sit alone, am I
just little old me.

I am on holiday this week
the first of the week, to start
but I had to go to Hospital
at the very first part.

Another visit again this week,
to rid me of my pain, I would
rather have gone to the sea this
week, before the rains come again.

Two visits have now gone, another
two next week, I think that will
be the last, but oh Dear me, my
Holiday will have passed.

I would have liked to have gone
away this week, the weather has been fine,
I would like to travel for miles, and miles when I get the time.

Peter R. Beard

The Rainforest

Stand in awe and look awhile
Upon this your majesty
Your life borne in the branches
Your breath held by the leaves

Stand in awe and listen awhile
To the silence of life hidden within
Broken only by unseen rustles
as life springs from tree to tree
and whispers of wings under leaves

Stand in awe and breathe awhile
Smell the life that lives therein
The sweet, sweet smells keeping you alive
with scent of essence to light your fire

Stand in awe and feel awhile
Kiss the air, touch the leaf

Stand in awe and look awhile
If you blink you will miss it all
Stand and look before it goes
For man can destroy as well as grow

Stand in awe and think awhile - before it's too late

Teresa Scully

Far Away Lands

I long to venture far away,
To lands that I have seen,
In book and magazine;
Where mountains reach into the sky;
And rivers rage, and condors fly;
And torrents plunge from places high,
To forests deep and green.

Volcanoes with strange sounding names;
Chimborazo, El Misti, Sangay, Cotopaxi,
Where infernal gods from fiery depths,
Spew forth rocks, on sulphurous breath,
Invading life and bringing death,
With pyrotechnic brilliancy.

I'd love to wander lonely tracks,
Untrodden by human feet,
My solitude complete.
I'd view the world from lofty heights,
Where pumas lurk, and cold winds bite;
And the mountain air is clear and bright.
A grandiose retreat.

Sandra L. Hopwood

"Human Frailty"

I walked across the sand dunes today,
toward the cliff top at Hartley Bay.
Sat within a lonely creek
delicate wild flowers growing at my feet.

Old stone steps carved in the rock
creating a pathway to the beach.
The sea was calm, the sky bright blue
A crimson horizon, a coppery hue.

Seagulls stalking in the sand
for fossils and seashells,
Close at hand leaned an old wooden cross
marked "DANGER - NO ENTRANCE" I was banned

From treading the path down memory lane.
I could hear voices singing again,
As they swam abreast in the cold North sea,
Then, walking home in the moonlight
So young and carefree.

The onslaught of War has taken its toll.
Merely names alphabetically listed on the "HONOURS ROLL"
of a War Memorial.

Mary Bridges

Quiet

Wind blowing in the background.
Two people quietly whispering.
The sun reflecting off the ground.
The sound of the wind whistling.
This peaceful thought is in my head,
In fact I am alone.
The rest of the world could be dead.
The gentle wind has blown
Them away. It never really liked me.
I never really did appreciate
The beauty of what you cannot see
Until it was too late.
And all is silent and all is sound
And all is peaceful when I look around.

O. C. C. McSweeney

"No Problems"

We read it in the paper - we see it on TV
Tragedy and torment - pain and misery.
Everywhere, and anywhere - around us all the while,
But suddenly superseded by my tiny Grandson's smile.

Innocently chuckling - reaching out for Mummy -
Eyes wide - mouth a rosebud - toothless, gummy!
Outdoors it is raining - the dratted car has stalled -
All superseded by his joy (although completely bald!)

Washing dripping everywhere - machine declines to go!
Engineer is busy. "See you next week!"! - When LO!
A gurgle grabs attention - bootees leave his feet -
Family and strangers - all-comers he will greet.

We may not get our pensions, NHS is on decline -
Prices may be soaring - the weather isn't fine.
But Springtime brings me flowers - Summer brings the sun
And for my tiny Grandson, life's path has just begun.

Margaret Smith

Lost Sheep

Despairing haul on twitching rope,
Transforming into plead
The call by single man of hope,
To those long lost to greed.

But new-found shrines do not receive
Discordant peals of pain,
For loss of time the flock will grieve
If spent away from gain.

Each chime craves reason for the cause
Of vacant, unshared pews,
No more the Squire's bidding draws.
The sheep decide to choose.

In saddened mind old thoughts are filed,
The Ringer kneels to pray
For flock abandoned to the wild.
The Shepherd let them stray.

M. J. Notley

Four Seasons

We have four seasons in a year,
We start off in the spring,
That's when the flowers start to grow,
Then summer time begins,
It is the time that I like best,
The season I like most,
You just look up and see the sun,
And feel as warm as toast,
Autumn is the one that's next,
It's getting rather cold,
The trees are losing all their leaves,
And looking rather bald,
And last, not least, it's winter time,
The worst one of the lot.
I'll just have to wait for summer time,
To feel all warm and hot!

J. A. Downes

The Gift of Love

I made a wish and you came true,
Truer than a Spring day's freshness and hue.
I prayed to God and He blessed me
With his gentle, loving creation, thee.

Your love for me is wondrous to behold.
Pure, warm, glowing as Autumn's gold,
Deep, deep as your eyes - clear blue,
Eyes that reflect my love for you.

As the water lily glides serene on the pool, dark and deep,
As the breeze gently ruffles a field, yellow with wheat,
As the Spring flowers burst from the earth, alive and new,
True as all these miracles is my love for you.

Love, warmth, compassion and humanity.
These are the wonders you bring to me.
The gift of love is mine, because of you.
I made a wish and you came true.

Margaret Eileen Taylor

Capriati Is Not the Same

Shall I go to Capriati when the summer comes again shall I
visit all our loved ones, will it ever seem the same
Now I think of all we could have talked about had I learnt
the language well yet still we joked and laughed a lot now
only I can tell,

And yet we knew each other fine where it most tells
'mind to mind' for words don't count too much when heart
and mind reach out and touch,

He'd smile whenever I came near, there was laughter in
his eyes I'll never forget those happy carefree days
the summer sunshine the bright blue skies,

We saw that he was growing old and age had bough him pain
yet I could never see him that way, to me he was always the same

And now he's gone from us and his passing brings us pain
and I can only miss him so
And Capriati can never be the same.

W. Venna

The Glorious Dead

I hear noises in my head
Voices of men who are long since dead
Times wrong-way telescope may look askance
At men now dead, through pure mischance.
But through that lens I can see them still
And hear their voices, loud and shrill
"Remember me" they said as they went
But from this world, there is no lament.
Of the world deserving, mention better
All that comes is a black-edged letter
"We are sorry to inform you" and so it goes on
To someone who might have lost a favourite son.
All in all, what a way to be told
That a loved one has come
To the end of their world.

Raymond Stuart Thomson

A Dream of Peace

The dove of peace, its wings unfurled,
Visits the peoples of the world,
As it travels, to far off places,
It spreads its joy amongst the races.
With worldwide peace and happiness gleaned
I awoke to find it was just a dream.
Oh' if only the dream were true,
As the dove of peace successfully flew,
Spreading love to all mankind,
Leaving hate and fear behind.
A thankless journey it would seem,
How I wish, it was not a dream.
Pressing on with relentless vigour,
The size of the task ever bigger and bigger,
Peace and love will see it through,
How I wish the dream were true.

B. Lanigan

My Thoughts, Watching Seagulls in Eastbourne

We shouldn't laugh at the birds the way they
walk then fly for they are only a good example of how
we live and survive, when the world began and they were
food for man, the fear had not subsided yet, so the
only way on a worrying day was to take off and fly away.

I'm looking for examples for how we are today, and what
we do when life gets hard to take the pain away, we
do take off and fly away and we usually go to Spain,
we take a package holiday to smooth away our pains.

For others who can't afford to fly it's usually on a
train, they buy a ticket to London and never come back
again, so we shouldn't laugh at the birds.
They're smarter than you think, for they can fly and hover
high, the troubles down below, so rise above your
heartaches and wait until they go.

Kenneth Harris

Untitled

Mum, you're the best of the rest.
Understand that when I say I hate you know it isn't true.
Many years I have been with you
    But when I say goodbye to
    You and go my own way I think
    it will be sad for me and you
I will always be happy as long as you are there
Love is me and you and always will be
Only you can cheer me up when I am sad
Vacant - my heart is vacant without you.
Eleven years with you now - I've enjoyed every one
Yesterday was and so were the yesterdays before that
Over the years you have always been there for me
Upon the stars where ever you are I will
    always see your face.

Master Luke West

Waiting

First born, first smile, first tooth
urging to walk, run and skip
start school, find a friend
then a date
try college (high hopes)
get a job (high hopes)
get married still with high hopes
(church and bridesmaids most essential).

First born, first smile, first tooth
walk run and skip
start school, find a friend
take a year off (pre college)
have an affair (no one marries now!)
Get a job (Ha! Ha! Ha!)
First born lives up a tree with 3 kids at Newbury
His brother despises him and his unwashed brood
he works in a bank, 9-5, lives in a semi
and has 2.5 children (of course)
occasionally he allows his brother the use of his bathroom

Mary Midson

The Choice

Sitting in a drunken stupor,
Wallowing in self-indulgent pity
Living for unreciprocated love,
Praying for obliteration of the past,
Living within a cocoon of pain,
Living, learning, dying fast
If this is living, give me death,
All forgotten, gone, no more.
But hope remains, undulled, alive,
So existence rise, again to sore.
What height before the bubble bursts,
The image of hope, destruction complete?
Until then continue, keep battling within,
Keep fighting for life with death still to meet.

Vicky Burgess

Mr. Magic Man

We need the magic touch of your hand
We desperately need your magic power
Hey Mr. Magic man, help us all take a stand
Hey Mr. Magic man, where are you now?

We need and want to have peace in our hearts
For this we so desperately yearn
An eighty year old war has and is tearing us apart
Please tell us what it is we have yet to learn.

Tell us, is there a secret formula to peace?
Some special potion perhaps?
Don't let our last chance cease
Please Mr. Magic man, we've come too far for this cease-fire to lapse.

Then I suddenly hear in my head the Magic man cry
You do not need me or my magic for this horrific war to permanently die
For beneath your very noses the answer lies
It is one simple task, both parties must compromise.

You see my friends it is up to all of us
We must talk this thing through
An end to this war and tragedy is a must
So beautiful Ireland can start anew.

Rachael Birdling

Let's Help

What have we done in a previous life?
To warrant the grief that surrounds us
There's death and disease and starvation
There's trouble that hits every nation
It's time that we looked at the world as our home
And spared a thought for its children
There are food mountains and wine lakes
And all manner of things just going to waste
If man is so clever I ask myself, "Why?"
If children were starving next door
We would think this a terrible sin
Yet we let half the world go unnoticed
People just say "What can I do?"
"I'm just one" It's time the ones got together
The ones would be thousands, an army
An army for good and not harm
Let's think of all children as ours
All children should be happy and fed
Just think how we'd feel when it's not easy
Feeding the world and its children

Margaret Roe

A Day I Remember

I wandered through the meadow, with the sun on my face
Watching larks in a cornfield, and rabbits running around, as
   if in a race
Birds in the tree-tops feeding all their young
With young horses jumping about, having lots, and lots of fun

I love the country, with its fresh air, and prickly hedges
   surrounding each field
Lots of cows chewing the grass, from which milk, they will yield
Sometimes I find mushrooms, which I eat with my afternoon meal
And a kind word from Ted and farmer, as he scraped mud from
   his heel

Once I was passing a barn, when Ted shouted, "give me a
   hand please"
Some lambs had just been born, and needed cleaning, so I got
   on my knees
About two hours later, they were all clean, warm and being fed
I got cup of hot tea from the farmers wife, and there was coffee
   for Ted

Helping new life come into the world, gives one a great feeling
I was overjoyed, but for the pain in my knees from kneeling
Since that day I have watched those little lambs grow
Suckling on their mothers, and them running to and fro

William A. Laws

Summer Morning

Have you ever risen very early on a Summer morn - when all the
World was lying hushed and still,
and seen the rosy fingers of the dawn, curling o'er the distant hill
flooding the fields with golden light, setting rooftops afire
bathing in pinky pearly light, the towering Church spire.

Through the stained glass windows, steals the morning glory of
the day's first hours, enhancing every dim recess with strange and
mystic powers, suddenly the world's aflame - and birds burst into song
radiant - glorious - beautiful - another day is born

The gardens, hushed and quiet, await the sun's caress, for at its
warmth the flowers awake, and don their summer dress, the
country lanes o'erhung with trees are dappled in lacy light, the
shadowed squares in town are lit, and etched in colour gay and bright

Every heart can hope again, and every soul is blessed, when
nature sends a lovely day, and summer's at its best, life cannot be
always fair - or always sunny days, GOD shows his great love for
us in many different ways

So, when the days seem dark and dreary, and winter's gloom
depresses - Think back on Spring and Summer, search the minds
recesses, glean comfort from the knowledge that despite the fog
and rain, summer days and sunshine will surely come again

Margaret Rose

Daddy

Daddy, I only ever wanted your love
To have you look at me with pride
And to know that you were mine
I never wanted us to become strangers
Now so many years are between us
And it's too late
You walk past me in the street - can't you see me
You ignore me when we meet - don't you need me
I didn't hurt you, you left my life
When you remarried and had a new wife
I felt I was a visitor I felt I was a prisoner
In an adult world I didn't understand

In my heart I love you and always will
In reality you died when I was nine
Because that's the time I stopped being the daughter
You used to look after
I won't apologize for things I didn't do
The word "sorry" belongs to you
It's such a shame those wasted years
You didn't share my happiness or try to stop my tears

Patricia McLellan

A Nightmare

Little children in their beds,
Try to sleep, but in their heads,
Monsters lurk, waiting for their turn to live
As small eyes, heavy with sleep, finally close,
Out they do creep.

To do battle, and chase all the demons around,
Run for your life, or hide on the ground
Here comes a dragon! with thundering roar,
Eyes all flashing, with razor sharp teeth.
Oh! Why did we go to sleep?

This is a nightmare, how can we escape,
Something is shaking and pulling our legs,
Fighting for breath they struggle and shout
With one mighty tug! at last they are free.

They wake with a jump, the monster is dead,
Batted and crumpled, it lays still on the floor
Slowly they prod it back into shape,
Once more it waits at the top of the bed,
It's only a pillow, for their young sleepy heads.

Mavis Henderson

My Tennessee Joe

Bib-fronted overalls going to school
Transport in those days was never the rule.
The farm in the hillside of America's South
Organic grown produce to melt any mouth
Joe get the mule, there's fields to be tended
Rows of white cotton it just never ended.
A family of seven, each with their chores
No time for playing no time to make wars.
Joe joined the Air Force, a new role he took
Twenty good years yes becoming a cook
He travelled the world, saw many things
Settled in England life through a few stings
A change of career, new path to follow
Then cancer it struck him so hard this to swallow
Joe fought it all his way expecting to win
Admired by so many with his drawl and his grin
I held his hand right to the end
Forty years of marriage my heart will not mend
I imagine the welcome, from one and from all
As you entered in heaven and said, Hi you all

M. Lomax

Tara

Tara, Tara, you are my best friend
We walked the lanes together
Thinking this would never end

You were only a baby when we first met
I held you and loved you and gave you my heart
Our life was good and wonderful, and then we had to part.

The years flew by so quickly
The seasons come and go
Oh Tara, Tara how I feel, you'll never never know

I never had a friend like you, I never will again
Even though others will take your place
It will never be the same

The time had come for you to go, I held you close to me
I looked into your tired face
Your eyes as always true
You passed into another world, another time and place
But one thing always stays with me
My friend your loving face

We loved each other, always true
My friend, My dog, I still love you.

Mary F. Barratt

A Careless Nation

As part of the twentieth century population
We will be remembered as a nation
With little regard for the poor and needy
But ruled and managed by the greedy

The wealthy insufficiently taxed
While old age pensions were finally axed
Free medical and dental care withdrawn
And so private health care was born

We chopped down forest, slaughtered trees
Created nuclear fall-out and CCP's
Too many cars and aerosol sprays
Damaged the Ozone and let the sun's rays
Dry up the rivers, burn hot on our land
'Til only a barren waste could be scanned

We were to blame for AIDS and disease
For poison, pollutants and oil in the seas
For the destruction of good clean air
Consequences the next generation must bare

Anyone with a conscience must agree
We are leaving an horrific legacy.

S. Budd

Six Foot and Under

We are born,
We age,
We go to school,
We work hard until we are to told to do so,
We have problems,
We have friends
We have colours, shapes and sizes,
We have twisty bends,
We have love
We have children of our own,
We celebrate, Birthdays, Christmas and so on,
We been where no man has boldly gone,
We laugh, sing, and cry
What is the bloody use of all these when
we only DIE???

Just remember one thing, when you're six foot under,
You've had a life full of these memories like
NO OTHER!

Happy Ways, Come with Summer Days

Paula Thomson

Old Times

When we we're young there
was a tradition
you obeyed your parents under any conditions
there were police to keep the law
Which they could do without a flaw
To catch you scrimping was a crime
To escape there was no time
The police could box you 'round the ears
Of assault charges there were no fears
They'd take you home to Mum and Dad
Who'd give you another for being bad
It did no harm to have a clout
It's what right from wrong was all about
Today the police are just puppets
They may as well be in the Muppets

N. C. Tilley

Experience

Experience is dearly bought,
Violating hearts serene
It swiftly, ruthlessly dispels
The sweet illusions borne of dreams.

With bitterness its wake is rife
And broken faith in things once dear;
Too fragile are the shattered lives
To find a solace soon in tears.

And somehow life must still go on
Unchecked by individual pain,
Then, suddenly, when all seems lost,
The world begins to smile again.

Joan Rea

The Cliff

Rocky giant - dark, foreboding
Watching o'er the cold, grey ocean
Concealing memories, deep within you
Of life, of death, no promise broken.

Sailing ships - and coal barges
(beauty and the beast compared)
All have passed your stony bastion
Smugglers, lovers, their secrets shared.

Gulls and terns - your natural partners
Though nesting, fouling, every crevice
Love sharing in your lonely vigil
Wheeling, diving, from your surface.

Centuries old - scarred and ravaged
Still standing tall, aloof and proud
Your granite life, assured forever
A gift from God, that He allowed.

W. Elliott

Waiting

We wait for this and wait for that,
We wait for a letter to fall on the mat.
We wait for taxis, planes and trains
And bath water to run down the drain.
We wait for the bus to go to the zoo,
And wait yet again for an ice cream or two.
We wait for birthdays and Christmas cheer,
And when they are here
We wait for New Year -
Then Easter -
Then Whitsun -
We even wait for the sun,
Which never seems to come.
The trouble is -
When all this waiting ends -
Off we go again.

Shirley Nel

Curiosity

Through the woods, down to the stream
Wandering along as in a dream.
I wonder where this stream will go,
I'll follow it, I have to know.

It runs into a leafy glen, a lovely sight to see
The trees are shading mossy banks, Nature's wonders there for me.
I wander on as in a trance as sights to me unfold,
Hues of wondrous colour, in greens and browns and golds.

It crosses right across a field where cows contented graze,
In the lazy summer heat, a glorious golden haze.
And I look back to boyhood in those long lost summer days
The breeze caresses rushes, in their long and rustling waves.

The stream is up in speed, as if it has an urgent need,
As if it knows around the bend its long journey soon will end.
Then in the river each long day
Down to the sea it will make its way.

May Monaghan

If I Want You Enough

If I want you enough, will you come?
Wanting is intangible;
How can we measure it?
How could you know what it is I know
About you?
The whole presence of you lifts me to such heights,
My esteem soars at the thought of you,
My existence has its only meaning
Because I see in you everything that is life.
I am - only because you are.
I am able to see myself
Because I have seen you.
You lift my soul and warm my very being
So that just a thought of you excites my mind
In ways that are ineffable.

Sandra Shields

The Night Shift on the Children's Ward

Sitting here, watching the clock tick by,
Waiting anxiously for the babes to cry,
Wondering when the next feed will be,
Will it be at one, two or three.

Waiting to change the dirty nappies,
Just to keep the "wee" ones happy.
But it's all part of the fun,
Wash, dry and cream the bum.

At two 'o clock the ob's are done,
Pulse taken with the finger not the thumb.
The other children are sleeping tight,
Let's hope it's quiet the rest of the night.

At six 'o clock the lights go on,
The night shift is all nearly done.
At seven thirty it's off to bed,
To try and rest our weary heads.

Mandy MacKenzie

Near

Sweeping fields of fresh green sounds,
Waves of lotioned scream,
Blue, walking with myself,
Head in the clouds of a clear,
Bright sky.

I know! let's sit for a while,
Discuss peace.
Lying back, spread-eagle . . .
Can only see half a world
Anyhow.
Hey! I didn't even know it was
Night . . .
Until I closed my eyes

P. J. Smitham

The Kestrel

Across a patchwork silken sky,
Weaves the kestrel with hungry, wandering eye,
Focused on the meadow below,
Where each movement, minute, nature's trained to know,
Vole of mouse, rat or shrew,
From an ariel vantage his prey pursue,
Then the immaculate stunning dive,
Talons prepared their kill to rive.

And then an oak with branch stout and stable,
Provides for him a dining table,
At its head and prey before,
See him! Great relish, pare, tear and claw,
And if no pesticides his meal contains,
He will thrive, and others, on his meal's remains,
Of us all in judgement he circles on high,
Much nearer to God than you or I.

Robert Betteridge

Homeless

Here I sit in the pouring rain,
    watching the water run into the drain.

I hear your feet as they scurry away,
    a usual sound as I sit here each day.

You think being homeless is my choice?
    I try to explain but you dismiss my voice.

You walk towards me, you look into my eyes
    but you walk straight past, and my soul just dies.

All I ask is for you to understand,
    it is not money that I demand.

Just a little love would be a start,
    only that would restore my heart.

Next time you see me in this doorway,
    a little smile wouldn't go astray.

You don't have to have a thing to say,
    but think, 'could this be you someday?'

Paula Lawrence

Our First Night Together

So we lay there in youth, our time of fruition,
We curve upwards, an answer to summer's call.
And sure we stay in timely fission,
Too sure to sway or untimely fall.

So the contagion of love went vastly spreading
And filled my head and soul with noise,
And made me plunder all my wanting,
Through whole compulsion, not lack of choice.

So there I lay and watch you slumber,
Never more lovely than ever, when
I'd wish for all life's exquisite wonders,
Were not they by my side right then.

D. Stapleton

How My Wonder Grows

One day I met a traveller
Weary from his trails
Who endeared me with descriptions
And the enchantment of his tales
Of lands been long forgotten
And paths been long untrod
His love for all adventure
And an unwavering faith in God

This lasts to me unknown
No understanding of this I sell
For I don't believe in deities
Or a holy heaven and hell
But with the traveller I share a wonder
And a joy in things unknown
And with all experience and
Knowledge acquired as yet
How my wonder's grown

Serjane Davis

Idyll

Take me to a golden time
When fluting nymphs and piping boys
Twirled and sang of earthly joys
With dance and sport and mime.
Lead me on through seaward dreams,
Let me taste the salt-blue wind,
Fly with hawks beyond the clouds
And vanish into mist and haze.
Take me down an autumn path,
Smell the wetness of the leaves
And kiss the dew and soar again
Above the earth-bound, bold and brave,
But turning home on wings of fire
To scatter roses on your grave.

Simon Harrison

Danielle

You entered this world in a tragic way,
We thought you'd never last the day,
You proved us wrong as time went by,
Although you suffered you really tried.

We are proud of what you tried to do,
Your fight was very strong and true,
You amazed us with your fight for life,
Until that very fateful night.

Your life was so Precious and dear,
It was not ours to keep, that came quite clear,
God stretched out a helpful hand,
To keep you safe in His promised land.

The tears we find quite hard to hide,
The pain it hurts so deep inside,
It was so sad to see you go,
Danielle because we love you so.

L. J. Smith

Untitled

6:00 a.m., 6:00 a.m.
Clear empty roads
Birds take flight
Frost in the fields
Silent but still, resounding mystery
Encircled by sky formations
Feeling of solitude,
Unaccompanied thoughts
Music, expressions, desires, opinions, cries
Echoes of our hidden creatures
A yearning to commune, understanding
Our equality of concern for our home
6.00 am, too early, too late

Ann Edgars

Throw-Away Society

We're a throw-away society, but we don't throw very far.
We drop it in the street or we throw it from the car.
We dump it in the rivers, we dump it in the sea,
Just because it's out of sight should it bother you and me.

We're a throw-away society when no longer any use,
We throw rubbish in the hedgerow and the countryside abuse.
A lot we cannot even see but I am told that it is there,
That we're breathing in pollution that is floating in the air.

We're a throw-away society as our morning mail box shows,
The advertising litter in the waste dispenser goes.
We tear it up and throw away without a single care
Of the stately tree once swaying in the misty morning air.

We're a throw-away society, even love flies out the door,
When we say we can't be happy together any more.
But a child's heart is broken, dreams lie shattered on the floor.
O this throw-away society is becoming such a bore.

Rosemary Garfoot

'Walk Away'

When you're faced with the chance to tread Nick's dance,
Walk away my friend, walk away;
Should he use his charms to silver your palms,
Walk away my friend walk away.
　If want becomes need and you can't feel your greed,
　Then you're better to turn and run,
　For the light that you sought, the shadows have bought
　And Nick's grin has darkened your sun.

When passions arise but truths become lies
And you feel the chill of Nick's smile,
Show your back once again and laugh at his pain,
Lest your soul shall give to his guile.
　Nick's song of life is your song of strife
　And the words he sings are for hate;
　If you choose not to hear, what can you fear,
　You are yours and a gift to your fate.

When you're faced with the chance to tread Nick's dance,
Walk away my friend, walk away;
He may never give in but you know he can't win,
If you walk away my friend ....walk away.

Richard Goodall

Little Girl of Appalachia

Not yet five, a tear in her eye,
Children scramble for presents as a
train sped by,
She turned and looked at me,
I felt guilty about her poverty,
I paused for thought, and went on my way
This was America on Thanksgiving day.

Christine Wrightson

'Limbs of Time'

As we walk down the lane,
we glance at the view,
of tall slender trees,
of various hue.
Those trunks gnarled with age,
misshapen and bowed
the same time majestic,
towering proud.
What changes have they seen
as the seasons have passed,
from spring flowers, to autumn blasts.
Birds nesting in branches,
children climbing trees,
blackberry picking,
dogs scratching at fleas.
The limbs of time can weave a spell,
of days gone by, a sad farewell,
so treasure our trees, their beauty behold
from green in spring, to autumn gold.

Mavis Fisher

Memories

The sound of running feet across the floor
Two small voices whispering at the door
Two pairs of laughing eyes look into mine
Four little hands in mine entwine
These are the memories I treasure through the years
Knowing they will not return.

The sound of children's laughter fills my ears
Bringing back memories of those yesteryears
When around the farm the three of us would play
Have our adventures and make our plans each day
And in the evening tell stories by the fire
My heart is sad to think those days are gone

The years roll by and I older grow
More vividly the memories seem to flow
Once more I travel down the path of time
And feel again those little hands in mine
Maybe when I am gone they too
Will look back across the years remembering me.

Sarah E. Roberts

The Sea

The sea is cold and lonely
But he roars and shouts with pride
Treat me with respect, for my waves I cannot hide

Come visit me, and feel free
Enjoy my hospitality
Tread carefully my gardens
My plants and trees that sway
Explore my world, with love and care
For I will guide you on your way

I rest not yet, I must go on
My world where you had so much fun
Come back again and visit me
But bring respect
I am the sea.

Eileen Francis

Lost

I'm lost in the darkness. There's nothing to see. I reach out,
But I can't find the way. Then I wonder which way.
Which way do I want to go?

I'm lost in a maze, a maze of great height. The maze is cold
And I'm not getting any warmer.

I find myself in the centre of an ocean.
The ocean has no other life, But me and its deep blue colour.
I look to the sky, But there are no clouds.
I find myself sinking and unable to swim.

I find myself yet again in the maze. It is even colder and darker.
Every route I take is wrong. Will I ever escape?

I find myself on a mountain top.
Everything is below me,
And everything is on top of me.
I look at the sky, It is beautiful.
I look below, But it is black.
I try to fly to the beauty,
But I find myself losing balance
And falling to the never-ending darkness yet again.
Why can't I reach the light?

Houra Qadir

My First Flight

I was twenty one then, ninety now
But I remember as the 'plane soared above
My hat flew off as the wind hit my brow
I looked down, saw Hull and the Wash,
Never visited but known through King John
Then I was back on Croydon Ground
With my ruffled hair, safe and sound.

Helen D. C. Pitts

Mum

You may think I don't realize how very much you care.
But in my darkest hours of need, you always have been there.
And it hasn't gone unnoticed that however big or small
My cry for help has been, you've always come to meet my call.

In all the years you've given - never thinking of receiving,
You've shared my hopes, my dreams and gave me something to
believe in.
Each time I make a big mistake - some notions quite absurd,
You love me still, just as I am, with no reproachful word.

I know at times you wanted to . . . but never voiced your fears,
Afraid that you might hurt me, afraid to "interfere".
I've now come to appreciate each sacrifice you've made,
And thank you for the times when thanks might not have been
conveyed.

For your unselfish caring for all of those years,
For the times that you saved me from drowning in tears,
For being part of my life no-one else could ever fill,
I love you . . . from the bottom of my heart, and always will.

Juliet Ealden

To Linda My Valentine

To my old faithful Valentine
For such a long time you
Have been so true
Through all storms and weathers
Come hail sunshine and snow
And cold weathers
Who's been so brave through it all
And even through the wind and thunder
Storms twisted 'round and 'round
Through all the pain which you yourself
Have borne even through little jealousies
Along the way you bore
So you weathered the storm through all
Of your pains to be well again so unto you
My Valentine for time to be recorded
About time past for in the future for
All time my Valentine for only you really
Know that I brought it to you and not sent it
To you my Valentine

George Lightfoot

Love Is Everywhere

Thank You God, for blessing me,
For sunshine, sky and flowers, so lovely
Thank You for bird songs and "doggy love"
And all the good times I have had
Which make me forget the sad and bad

So, like a flower, my soul, can grow,
Like a tiny seed in Spring, we sow,
It blossoms in Summer's sun, then fades and dies

But, next year, it will arise,
To give new life for us to share,
If we pause, to stand and stare
And admire nature's beauty, everywhere.

Age, brings its own reward, each day
Happiness, peace and contentment stay,
Like moonlight when night covers our land,
So, shall I put my trust in God's almighty hand
And all my fears shall blow away, like wind upon the sand.

Betty Owen

The Bomb

The disaster is over, the trauma begun
for the one who is lost is a very dear one.
Who shall forget the bang of destruction?
Who will again begin the construction?
Not I, for it begins in the mind.
Yet the IRA's meaning is blind
with these murderers getting away with this deed,
as though taking lives is what they all need,
We sleep tonight with sadness and grief
and try to know why they carry out this belief.

Now war is here in England
Lives are destroyed - all for land.

IS IT WORTH IT?

The buildings rebuilt, the windows rearranged,
but many are dead, that cannot be changed.

Dorian Ralph

Untitled

Have love for each other while you can
For the river of life flows fast,
Care for each other while you can
For the seasons are soon past.

Real love, like a tree will branch and grow
And its seeds will fill and spread,
But a shallow love like a flower will bloom
Then soon, too soon, be dead.

Doreen Thompson

Your Baby

Neither of you are sculptors or artists
But between you with love, patience and God's blessing
You have created a masterpiece.
For within you lies a miracle
Almost fully developed and yet unborn.
A miracle inspired by love
A miracle instituted by God
A miracle even to the most unbelieving
Yet we believing still claim it to be a miracle.

Chris Gregory

Nethershore

Oh! To wander evermore
Upon the straits of Nethershore
Knowing naught of this nor that;
To see the truth in mortal lie,
To measure naught by tongue, ear or eye
Beyond each new wave that breaks
Lies an endless, signless; virgin shore;
Where I'll wander, wander evermore,
Upon the straits of Nethershore

Neil Bannister

"Children at Play"

Children laughing at play,
dancing skipping, all happy and gay.
Not a worry, without a care
refusing to let every day,
mundane thing, disturb their play.

Oh how I envy those childhood days,
the sound of laughter, makes me stop to think.
How quickly life, passes us by, without even a blink,
to watch young children at play, is so refreshing,
in every way, I want to stay, carry on watching them play.
But alas, it is time to go, to journey homeward through the snow.

But feeling happy and aglow, after watching those dear children
at play.
So carefree, and happy, each in their own sweet way.
I tell myself, as I journey home, how I did enjoy
watching the children, happy at play.

Joyce Treacey

Spirit

Cleanse your spirit, from negative ways,
Breathe in the light, of sunset rays,
roam the earth, live from your soul,
and from within, allow peace to flow -

Swim through the oceans with eyes open wide.
Feel your freedom, as you drift with the tide.
Gaze at the stars, a million miles away,
Live your life for each and every day.

Follow your instinct, it's there as your guide
and never give up on your spiritual side.
Feed on life's presence, let yourself grow
Have faith in your spirit wherever you go.

Drink the spring water's from fresh flowing streams
with spirit and soul nurture your dreams.
Don't give up on what's true and right,
and throughout your life just follow the light.

Ally R. Parker

Ambiguity

The black horse and his rider
   Traverse across the manege
      Like a creature of the air -
You led me a merry dance my dark beauty
Resisting my advances for so long
   I implored you
   Cajoled you
Bullied you, to no avail -
But now things have changed
I invited you
      and you accepted
With lightness and with grace -
You moved beneath me
   Your ebony skin glistening
      Until I became a centaur -
My legs wrapped 'round your ribs
You almost made me swoon
   And just for a moment there
   We caused the earth to tilt
And turn a little slower on its axis.

Muriel E. Calder

Tea Break in Winter

Groups of students assemble in clusters outside the
college foyer
Diverse laughter permutes and crystallizes the air.
Some divulge and share another fun
And circumsolar towards a low watery opaque sun.

Plastic cups and multi-coloured paper wrappers chase
the cold north wind
All waiting for that unsolicited sound to ring
Eleven bells! The clusters drop in time
And leave the territorial robin to search the
margins of its mind.

John Crabtree

The Underpass

With vacant stare and outstretched hand, dignity since passed,
Coins are cast about his feet, a meal again at last.
As winter's chill strips the trees and cuts through clothing to
   the bone,
The beggar's sunken eyes catch sight of fur-lined boots that
   hurry home.
A subway station, an underpass, cover the forgotten class,
Like a veil upon an open sore that masks the face of the modern
poor.
In cardboard boxes vagrants sleep as the world goes rushing by,
No time to stop, no time to weep or ask the reason why.
Who are these people life missed out, by many so reviled,
Someone's daughter, someone's son, once an infant, someone's
child.
The hand that gives a silver coin sets a conscience free,
As avarice walks hand in hand with social tragedy.

Alan G. Johnson

Spring

The daffodils push through the earth,
Breaking out in a golden mirth
There is a warm tinge in the air,
Telling us, that spring is there,

Birds start singing, happy are they,
The cold winter winds have at last gone away
The countryside has a new adorn.
Over at the farm, lambs are born.

We plan for the future, our hopes and dreams.
Spring - cleaning, gardening, all kinds of schemes
Holiday, outings, and picnics in the sun,
A new beginning has now begun.

Audrey Taylor

Untitled

Skipping off merrily to start a new day
Bright shiny faces ready for play
Not knowing what terror was to be in store
Laughter one minute then laughter no more.

Pray for the wee bairn's of Dunblane
The poor wee bairns so brutally slain
This place can never be the same
An air of sadness will remain

We'll all point a finger, to find someone to blame
Yet these efforts are all in vain
The relatives' grief will still be the same
Their lost little loved ones will rest in Dunblane

That fateful day will haunt us for years
How can we wipe away all the tears
This shocking deed is too much to bear
Broken hearts that are beyond repair

The whole world cries for the tragic young ones
Blown away by a sick man with guns
Please Lord help us understand why
These dear little children had to suffer and die.

Gaynor Atkins

The Empty Chair

In my mind I see you sitting there
But it is now an empty chair
I think of the memories of long ago
And all the things and people we used to know
Now you sit in another chair
At the nursing home where you needed constant care
It broke my heart to leave you there
I see the sadness in your eyes
All the tears that we both cried
Fifty-five years we spent together
Through fine and stormy weather
But now you sit in an higher chair
Safely held in the Lord's tender care
Gone the sorrow gone the pain
Goodbye my love till we meet again

Hannah Hobbs

Candle

Why do you weep little candle?
Burn, burn just for me.
Guide my life and let me see.
Shine bright and warm.
Brighten the world surrounding.
Share your warmth, kindly
like a father to a child.
Never be defeated,
always shine, be true.
Don't let the great darkness
take a hold on you.
If tragedy should come,
take comfort, don't be sad
Don't let your wax drip like tears.

Eleri Hedd James

The Umbrella Blues

Inside out and upside down
Brollies lie all over town,
In gale force winds and driving rain
Never to be used again.

Handles broken spokes askance
No one gives a second glance,
A humble brolly in high winds
Will almost always end in bins.

High in treetops there they flutter
Down below the people mutter
Soaking wet and unprotected
All are looking most dejected.

A brolly that was once regarded
To keep you dry is now discarded,
Do not mock beneath your cover
It could be you someday or other.

Janice Richer

Why Me

It only took a second to swallow this pill called E,
But now I regret it and ask God why me?
I'm leaving my family and friends behind,
Whom I loved so much I must have been blind
To take notice of those who said it was fun,
A fool I was should have said no and run.
Please help to stamp out this terrible pill,
Before more youngsters take it and die or get ill.
If only I had not taken this pill called E,
Then I would not be asking God again, why me?

Elizabeth Russell

A Cockney Shoe Shop

"Alloe Ducys" the customer says
As she comes into the shop
"I need some shoes, but not too dear
Gawd, I'm fit to drop!"

Gimme a five or five 'an 'arf,
Don't mind if I takes a seat,
Got to rest this back 'o mine
Take the weight off me plates of meat.

Blimey love, they fits a treat
'An ever so soft as well,
Just what I need for shopping,
You've done me proud there gel.

Corns and bunions, misshaped feet
Ingrown toenails too,
We get the lot from "our old dears"
Their audience is you.

It comes to us all at the end of the day
Old age is a state of mind
They may be very annoying
But try — just try to be kind.

Marion M. Hancock

Promised Land

You have the right to turn God away,
  But before you do,
Look ahead and see
  What is in store for you.
A beautiful land, as promised,
  To those who follow Him.
A land of health and laughter,
  Where illness and sadness cannot enter in.
A place where love and peace have grown
  And hate and war are quite unknown.
A land where all nations join as one
  And dwell beneath God's heavenly sun.

Oh! Lord above we pray to thee,
That we may live eternally.
To join you in your promised Land,
Where all nations live, hand in hand.

Beverley James

Inner Strength

Where it comes from we do not know
but all of a sudden we feel the adrenalin flow,

It rushes through our body with an incredible force
an inner strength for an outward course.

Your mind becomes alert, so powerful and strong
it's bursting with determination, the will to carry on,
Your confidence soars as you now become aware
of an inner strength, you didn't know was there.

Your very being, your body and soul
stretches out to reach life's own goal,
you know now that you can win the fight
because an inner strength has given you your power and might.

The ecstasy you feel as your spirits soar high
because you've succeeded in what you attempted to try,
so let your happiness out and set yourself free
as an inner strength is your path to destiny.

Jacqueline Chilton

Beaten and Broken

A cab driver whistles at a girl walking by,
But he doesn't see the tear in her eye.
He doesn't see the sadness in her face,
Or the never-ending bruises that slow her pace.

Something went wrong back down the line,
She can't quite remember or even define.
But the taste of blood in her mouth is still clear,
And that evil taunting - will it ever disappear?

Drooping like a withered flower,
She's lost her pride to fulfil his power.
Violent thoughts flood her head.
She sometimes wishes she was dead.

When will it stop? - this eroding pain
When will the sun shine and stop the rain?
Will she ever know how it feels to smile
Instead of retching blood and bile.

Fiona Palmer

A Passage In Time

This is a poem about passage in time,
But let me begin by telling you mine.
A little girl feeling lost and forlorn,
And at an early age learnt how to mourn.
Being moved from one place to another,
And me and my sister, told to love one another.
I passed through puberty without to much ado,
But adolescence brought a problem or two.
By the time my mother had stopped pulling out her hair,
I had a child of my own for me to care.
So you can see from this poem of mine,
I wasn't an angel all of the time.

Bernadette Warburton

Untitled

Here is a child that is God's gift,
But yet, I stand here watching him
in such a cradle of filth and disease that I am sickened.

The despair in this baby's eyes, the plea for life, for freedom
is so over-powering I have to turn and weep,
for this child has been dumped in such a place that
hunger and starvation is normal.

But yet I say these things when there is nothing I can do
for the illness is immobilising and cannot be stopped,

but knowing that this being will be with God in a matter of days
is reassuring, for he shall suffer no longer.

He is on a filthy cot where babies have died,
and that is what shall follow
for this poor creature has an illness that no one can stop.

I hear you say: What about his mother - why has she gone and
left him in this?

Gabby Fletcher

Always Remembering, Longing to Forget

Oh yes, I've been hurt, I've been abused,
but it's no big deal to feel so used.
My whole life really, has been a disaster,
and everyday is going faster and faster.
I tried to run, I tried to hide,
I trusted no-one, in no-one did I confide.
I rarely have bad dreams or shed a tear,
how can something so deep, still be so very near.
I don't like sex, so I'm no use to any man -
they don't really care if you can't or you can.
If you refuse them - they're heart is sunk,
they think they'll be lucky if they get you drunk.
The word "no", they cannot comprehend -
and "do not touch", simply drives them around the bend.
They don't really care, they haven't got a clue,
Only one thing matters, and it's not me or you.
But don't worry girls, we'll always soldier on -
the good will still remain, when the evil has gone.
It's a long hard road to get to the light,
but nothing is worth it, unless it's worth a fight.

Anna Marie Morse

Beauty

Mother Nature is slowly changing, the heat of a summer day has
gone, but not bird's song, only beauty remaining marking time to
rest. Majestic trees so straight and tall bow their heads, saying
farewell to summer's green and colourful coat as breezes play
hide and seek between strong arms. Pretty green leaves show off
a new look, tinges of gold, brown and red they wear, before
autumn puts them finally to bed. Little birds in formation do
gather on rooftops high, chattering with excitement, migration
time is nigh.
Autumn stretches out her arms to embrace, in all beauty and
grace her children, to slumber and rest upon her breast, her cloak
blazoned and resplendent, gives thought to friend winter now on
its way, and hastens to depart. Boisterous winds do follow on,
chilling hands and feet in strength and whining song.
Winter's sun now weak, glimmers down
upon us, a respite from days so bleak. Snow's fluttering flakes
descending on trees branches bare, a carpet of glistening white
for feet, with children's laughter and joys complete. Around the
corner the beauty of spring, new life, joys, hopes, new everything!
Little plants too curious to stay, push eager noses through Mother
Earth's soft brown blanket, to feel gentle breezes 'round pretty
heads, buds and shoots cover branches bare, God's creation and
beauty everywhere.
Greatest thanks to Him who knows best, when to play and when
to rest.

Barbara Mary Sheffield

Untitled

Again I try, though hope seems lost,
But now my spirit's broken,
In place of grief and hate and loss,
A new love has awoken.

As pain subsides, from slaughtered dreams,
And the wounds begin to heal,
Emotions charred, now gently stir;
I begin again to feel.

Through twilight lands I walk alone,
Though with me walks your shadow,
Our friendship's path was straight and clear,
But now the path grows narrow.

Before me stands a beauteous realm,
And as I long for shelter;
Yet still I trudge through winter's spring,
For I can never enter.

This way I cannot walk again,
I do not have the strength to.
Farewell, my darkness calls once more,
Forgive me, friend, I love you.

Dean Higgins

Life's Pathway

As we go down life's pathway we learn many things
But one thing we should learn is about ourselves
We should learn that we are spirit and all that is good
We come here with love from spirit above.

We should learn not to forget this and tell our
Friends this as well,
We should go forwards and tell the world this also,
For this is all worth knowing, it will build a path of
Light and love. To shine all around,

For this is life's pathway we must all go down
We may stray from the pathway many times in our
Life. But we will not be alone our forgotten for
God is the light the path and the way so let us
Remember this every day

Edwin Peace

My Treehouse (The Home of My Imagination)

I have the fondest memories of the home I called my own,
It was my very special place where I could be alone,
The roof was made of leaves, the floor of bits of wood,
The furniture I made myself it wasn't very good,
My mother used to say to me are you in there again,
The only use that she could see was sheltering from the rain.
You had to spend some time in there to really understand,
to be so near the pale blue sky with clouds so close at hand,
The peacefulness the solitude just sometimes what you need,
To think my little treehouse was started with a seed.
You know now that my treehouse meant all the world to me,
Although no longer there, I still have the memory.

Julie Haig

Baby Angel

So sweet this dear loved baby, so sweet
but she was dying,
still smiling all the while though, always
laughing never crying,
she kicked her legs all 'round her cot,
and gurgled at her dad,
she didn't know her death was soon in
the world she saw no bad,
her straw blonde hair and deep blue
eyes so precious to behold,
her sweet soft skin and baby legs
would soon be hard and cold,
her bed would soon a coffin be in
God's earth she would be buried,
why give her to her mum and dad then
make her life so hurried?
Memories soon are all that's left
and cherished they will be kept,
they began the night she feel asleep
and to the angels' world she crept.

Caroline Brankin

The Gossip

Now listen dear, you know me, a gossip I will never be
But there is something I've just heard,
Now promise not to breathe a word
Elsie Brown from number ten, has had the postie in again
Two hours on Monday, he was there
You wouldn't think that they would dare
Her poor husband's not too fit, still they say he drinks a bit
What's that you say, you already knew, who on earth's been
telling you
Shirley Jones, I might have known, she can't leave anyone alone
You say you saw her the other day, what else did she have to say,
Come on now, you know me dear, I never repeat anything I hear
Goodness me, now is that true, that was quite a thing to do
Now excuse me dear, I'll have to go, I promised I'd call in on Floe
Now listen Floe, you know me, a gossip I will never be
But there is something I've just heard
Now promise not to say a word.

Diane Marsh

Spring Is Nigh

Now March is come and spring is nigh
But winter lingers on.
The hedgerows hug the snow close by,
While feeble warms the sun.

The hoarfrost hangs its dainty fronds
From hedgerows and the trees.
Though frozen now the streams and ponds
Are thawing by degrees.

Chilled by the frost the hardened ground
Shows little sign of life
And hapless birds make little sound.
East wind cuts like a knife.

But soon the surge of life will flow
Into the sap from earth
New leaves, new flowers soon will grow,
The spring of life new birth.

Derrick J. Wooding

A Soldier's Reality

You can speak of grasses green,
But you'll never know what I have seen.
For where he goes is where he stays,
This is where he'll spend his days.
Lying there encased in mud,
Soaked in his own fresh blood.
Sadly he has finally found,
No soldier dies on English ground.

Delwin Smith

A Soldier's Return

He left his wife and children small
To go to war and answer the call
Across the sea to a foreign land
To serve his country to make a stand
The bullets they flew, the shells fell near
His thoughts went to home and his family so dear
Then suddenly everything went very black
His body went rigid, the legs had gone slack
No feelings at all as he lay on the ground
Hands gently raised him, thank God he'd been found
His legs had been shattered hush there now don't talk?
We'll do all we can to make sure you can walk
A message was sent to his wife far away
We're sending him home a month from Tuesday
How can this have happened? he'd just gone to war
She'd kissed him goodbye as he went out the door
So now she is waiting for sight of the plane
And praying that he'll never leave them again
Her mouth has gone dry and her heart's beating fast
For her soldier husband has come home at last.

Marion Richards

This Room

I love this room
To gaze out of the window and see the world rushing by,
People bustling, people hard and cruel,
Red-grey walls, grey roofs, grey roads
But here I am content. Beauty in this room
An island of warm colours and quietness
Safe from cruel people and a grey world.
Here there is peace and warmth where no-one can hurt us.

So much has happened to us in this room
I have found you, you have shown me sweetness
I have tasted the honey-taste of joy
We have held each other close
I have heard the ripple of your laughter
And known pride that I could please you.

You are not here now
Nor am I certain that I will ever be here with you again
But my heart is full
I have memories and I dream of joys to come
I love this room.

Veg Truman

Look After Your Cat

My wife: the morals of an alley cat of Seine,
But with the features of a foreign royal
Very small and lean but perfectly pristine,
And I'd thought till now quite loyal,
But if she'd met Macavity they'd have made the perfect team!

She'd always like to get out a lot
and most especially at night,
With her beautiful long hair I'd think, "look what I have got".
I'd watch her put her war paint on almost ready for a fight.
Everywhere we'd go, men would try to touch her and tie my
      feelings in a knot.

And our babies, well she guarded them like gold.
But as little children she said their independence was a must.
They've all grown up brilliant, brave and bold,
They never ask for money and none of them went bust.
I know realize when my wife was made, they surely broke the
      mould.

So if your wife's the perfect Persian, my advice to you;
Get home in time! Make sure for meals together you are sat!
Massage her everyday that's what to do.
Because I never did any of all that,
And my wife now lives with Cyril at number forty-two!

D. Bruton

"Sunset Pal"

All friends are acceptable and lovely
But you come singingly
When the ears aren't in the mood
You keep calling all sun set.

Tell a pal, your presence discomforts
He reasons and controls his movers
Despite all shakings and unreceptiveness
You perch like a colonial Lord, stinging vampire-like.

A little shake of the Legs, makes you quiver
Sending your heart abyss;
The old trespassers respected you
Now you're friend only to those who have no choice.

Even the strangers now know your sauciness
And fight you triumphantly;
You regard not the father, mother nor the child
Your belly reds on 'em all.

You leave saying not when next you call
You now even a killer above the law - what a creature!
Come next, your doom awaits you
If not he that's sustained you to living amongst nobles . . . ?

Barnny E. O. Nomorere

Transition

Your quilt's a 'Snowman' landscape; purple-and-white:
But you will not sleep beneath it, tonight;
For a blue silk-lined coffin, in shades of fresh pine,
Now holds your young body; oh, daughter of mine!

Drifting through the air, your spirit will go,
Leaving broken hearts to mourn below.
Through midnight skies your spirit will glide,
Secretly racing to the 'other side'.

Something cried deep inside, through your dark fearful night,
Compelling you onwards to seek for the light;
That light which burns brighter than any other,
Holding love's powerful secret, which binds us forever.

As your earth-body broke; life's silver thread snapped in two;
Leaving nothing, now nothing, that the doctors could do.
But your spirit lives on, not trembling, but steady,
And I know precious daughter your 'home' will be ready.

For soon you'll awaken from a deep, healing sleep:
Meanwhile, sealed in our hearts, your memory we'll keep.
As your spirit drifts forward, now steady and fast;
Gail Louise, you will find, your own peace, at last!

Jean Mary Brady

When Unemployment Is Acceptable

No need to ask who squeezed the trigger first or whether
causes are perceived as just, so long as guns spit out their
deadly burst and shells reduce the landscape back to dust.
It matters little these were once proud homes for which the
corpses now have little need, or that the churches with their
shattered domes watch helpless as their broken faithful bleed.

The smiling suits of smug, smooth salesmen shine, their
grinning teeth from wall to wall extend as each recounts
success, shareholders dine and drink their toasts to profits
that won't end.

Theirs are the firms who make these deadly wares and which
are sold to anyone who'll buy; drought stricken poor and
terrorists boost shares since profit's based on numbers who will
die.

Is it not time this ugly trade was banned so that the guns
use up their stocks and cease? With factories closed the
work force future's planned 'round drawing dole, a small price
paid for peace.

Some will protest that others will supply or that a ban
would bring financial pain. Let them console the grieving
folk who cry in Sarjevo, Belfast and Dunblane.

John Arbee

Shadows of Our Souls

There are no places for our dark shadows, nor for the light
      that deeply entwines all mankind.

No place to hide for our souls that are lost or our innermost
      thoughts that penetrate the far corner of this forsaken barren
      waste.

Where is the hope that is buried deep in the bowels of the earth
      or the smouldering heat that runs rampant, that disperses the evil
      that penetrates skin and effects our race?

Bodies immersed in light they hold the hope that from our souls we
      are transported and somehow through the very existence
      evolve into another solar energy.

Understanding, do not caste your mind or dwell too deeply for
      when you have understood the whole energy of life that is,
      when evolved you have the right to guide.

Through the blacken oasis see the bodies drift through the
      oozing matter, arms outstretched, barren waste, dead no life.

Energy comes, wind that blows silently like the dead of night,
      sparse, barren, perhaps there is hope.
For with hope comes the eternal oasis of knowledge that will
      set us free.

Joan H. Newell

The Book

The tender eyes of any child
Can suddenly turn green,
It is my book, I told you so
I thought you would have seen.
My name is there for you to see
The cover's ripped and torn,
I've had this book for ages now
It says when I was born.
You have yours upon the desk
I'll read to you one day,
I'm sure you'll clearly understand
The things it has to say.
You may be only two years old
With sticky hands and face,
But my book's mine, and yours is yours
Please, leave it in its place.
I know I shouldn't shout at you
About this thing you took
But Mummy says, you will understand
When someone takes your book.

June Meachem

"To My Husband"

With all my love to my valentine,
can you, will please be mine?
I know we don't always see eye to eye,
And we don't always know the reason why,
But whatever our faults and however we feel,
Deep down our love for each other is real.
So let's forget the past, and rekindle the fire
That's smouldering, let those flames burn higher!
I want the whole world to know how it feels
To be loved - roly poly, head over heels!
You're always in my thoughts and on my mind,
A love like ours is hard to find.
Others are fooled that we do not care,
But our love for each other is always there.
So let's begin again, and the best place to start
Is to say that I love you with all of my heart.

Angela Gilbert

What Could Have Been

All my life I have waited for you
But you came along too late
I know that we can never be
So I accept the hand of fate

It will never stop me loving you
And thinking of you all the time
Now I dream of what could have been
And wish that you were mine

I bear my thoughts, I dream my dreams
And I get by most every day
For I am strong and will carry on
I have too, come what may

I have lived my life, and it's been good
But there's only one regret
And that is that I missed you
When we two should have met

John Linsley

Memories

Chalk and things, class bells ring,
Childhood laughter, girls to run after,
Pen and Ink, science room stink;
Homework 'Scams', terrible exams,
Physical jerks, teachers' quirks,
Girls in the gym, some fat, some thin,
Boys in the gym, God, look at him,
Running in the sports, it took all sorts,
Teacher's pet, I remember him yet,
Six of the belt, I knew how that felt,
Third year girls, new found thrills,
Suddenly you're leaving, only you grieving,
So long in the past, these memories last,
of chalk and things.

Allan Bunting

The Manuscript

An ink-inebriated spider
capers incoherently across the page
its broken tipsy topsy-turvy trail
makes eye-stinging mystery of what in thought
made sense.

We who toil here
snap and speculate to trap the insect meaning -
we watch the wasted moments
tick and trickle,
far behind the swaying spider-line.

From dream to drafts
a short and simple step,
yet carried by so flawed a messenger.

We yearn for Nelson's Handwriting
and tea.
(though Jill says gin!)

Ann Crompton

Sleeping

Sleeping, sleeping in my bed
Cannot rest my dreaming head
Clocks ticking, watch pricking, spine's tingling in my bed
Times running out for me
As I cannot feel or see
I am all and all is me

Sleeping, sleeping drifting apart
From my dreams and my heart

Dreaming, dreaming in my head
A restless night is still ahead
I worry as the night goes on
About the things yet to come

The night is long the night is dark
It is too long for my heart
It beats so fast and so long
But the night still goes on

Then suddenly the sun comes out
I feel alive I jump about
But then again a night still comes
When funny things are going on

Ben Mounsey

The Good Old Days

The brightly lit streets of years gone by, children played
    without a cry,
rin, tin, tin, hide and seek, these are games that made them sleep.
With hoop and stick and top and whip, they were never of
    school sick.
Bat and ball upon the wall, skipping ropes they'd jump so tall,
they would play these games to win and you could never get
    them in.

Glass alley marbles shining bright, winking out at their delight,
conkers hanging from their strings, just waiting there to see
    who wins.
Oh what fun the children had and they were never ever bad.
Alas these good old days have gone and no one seems to
    have much fun.
These games they did not cost much money and Mum could
    always feed our tummies

Television now is their game and doing homework is a pain.
"What's on next" one would cry rubbing his tired and weary eye.
Computer games is another thrill, pressing their buttons with
    such skill.
Watching close upon the screen, they can't move, their in
    such a dream.
Designer labels, trainers bright, these are things that make
    their night.
The smiles that come upon their faces, when Mum walks in
' with her wages.
The words you hear Mum shout out: "Bring back the days
    when they played out."

Ann Dowling

Upon Life's Threatening Treacherous Vine

Rising flames go higher in thy fire,
caressing the inner walls of our desire.
Filling your fiery eyes with all that's by,
seducing the tremorous heart with dire ecstasy.
With greedy lust the hunger sighs,
with hollow breath the moon does cry.
Entwined are the alluring beings, enticing they may be,
but neither is a figment of how the soul perceives.
Why does it fade the everlasting shine,
upon life's threatening treacherous vine?
Do you not take heed of those sinful deeds,
that life throws upon the ground, our seeds.
How shall I live with every lasting lie,
since you have left and I have nigh;
but burns eternal does the glowing flame,
high up does our love still reign?

Jayson Khundkar

I Can't

I can't see you in the mornings,
Can't watch you wake, can't help you slowly rise.
I can't watch those early yawnings,
Can't see you stretch or kiss those sleepy eyes.
I can't see you in the shower,
Can't watch you shave, can't help you dry.
I can't know that breakfast hour,
Can't share your paper, can't wave goodbye.

I can't call you when I need you, can't be sure you'll hear my cry.
I can't tell how much I please you, can't ask you, can't hear
   you sigh.
I can't cope with being lovers, can't be just another one.
I can't ask about the others, can't believe that I'm the only one.

I can't tell you that I want you, can't be sure enough of you.
I can't say that I don't love you, can't do that, can't lie that
   much to you.
I can't love the way you want to, can't be with you, can't be free.
I can't play the way you want to, can't just wait, can't let it be.

I can't be with you tomorrow,
Can't explain, can't even tell you why.
I can be with you no longer,
Can't stay, can't even say goodbye.

Barbara Wade

Memories of You

Leaves of russet golden brown
cascading slowly to the ground.
Through trees, the pale old wintry sun
threw ghostly shadows all around.

How dear to me, those golden days
when once our footsteps softly trod.
Recalling all the plans we made,
dreams we dreamed like lovers do.
Now all I have are memories
and thoughts that are so dear of you.

Now you have gone, you are no more,
buried on some foreign shore
I still see your smile and hear your call,
for you are here with me once more.

Pearly drops of morning dew
and winds that blow, caress my face
as soft rain falls mixed with my tears.
I'm not alone, I have no fears.
No you're not gone, you're still here.
I feel your presence everywhere.

Gladys Bree

Untitled

Charm that's seeping out between the cracks to add a third
dimension charm that's plastered butter on the holy oak to
spiritsoak and soothe the mighty
charm that's plainly used as scaffoldry to buttress ailing rises
charm that's worked as beeswax well into the gleaming timber
charm that's autumn cuckoldry
my hand an eagle my hand an eagle my heart a golden cock
that screams my heart a golden cock that screams
my hurt I curl my fist around my hurt I curl my fist around
cromm cruaich stoops his liver burning hot
crouches sh*ts on warpath hailstones break his skull and vapour
rises
fatsie watsie waller strums races blood to beat the drums
beating one two beats the blood yearn for union hands go thud
pulses spread in veins black mans hotspot reigns
dead man's fists go busy build pressuresspaces dizzy
gutman's voice aglow tensionscrews go high and low
dead man's mettle boils the kettle
cut the finger off to write your life
one more is needed cut!
Last little left one goes "but" the argument runs out

Jon Killi

Information Technology

I need a degree to work on a checkout, bar codes, cash cards,
   credit checks.

I.T. I hear them shout, I.T. I say shrugging.
The kids love I.T. no more bat on ball, marbles, climbing trees,
instead they play in a mystical land where we cannot see.
Who controls IT or does IT control me.
They spend their lives with variables, circuitry, plastic and
electricity, surf a Net that's as daft as their virtual reality,
contact Mr. Wong in Hong Kong, don't even know their
neighbours.
Trees and Meadows a Red Admiral on a leaf, LIFE . . . Mother
Nature's gift to you and me in return we give her pollution,
devastation global catastrophe.
Like a child bored with a toy we turn our back, did we create IT
to blind ourselves to our real legacy, turn IT off look around and
you will see. No need for a flood or a rainbow this time we're
right oncourse to end IT for all time.
History will be the judge did we follow the path or lose our way.

They say you can dance with IT or you can dance for IT. USE
YOUR LOAF, DON'T DANCE, GET A LIFE . . .

Henry Charles Breiden

Napoleon Blues

Barren land, horizons blue
Columns of soldiers, no food!
Snow like a blanket, covers the scene
Wolves and hounds, howl and scream.

Day and night, troops plod on
Following leaders, whose minds have long gone!
In howling winds and biting cold
They shuffle along, souls lost and forlorn!

So cold and hungry, they march along
One by one, singing their last song!
Into the night, they shuffle along
In hope of glory, in hope of home!

Thousands and thousands, yet each man stands alone
A rifle, a treasure, life no longer his own.
Glazed, hollow eyes, pangs of hunger linger on
Tortured minds and bleeding limbs, numbness with time sets in.

Doom, approaches, and gloom like a velvet glove
Strangles morale, they just can't last!
Fate watches over, her daggers sharp
One by one, they fall, she claims her prizes fast!

Emanuela Imam

A Baby's Life

You're in the only place you've ever known,
Close to mother yet all alone.
Your world is safe and warm and dark,
But soon you'll have to make your mark.

You'll suddenly find that everything's new.
Nothing familiar remains for you.
Now it's strange and bright and cold.
So much change. Why weren't you told?

Now you're born you do so much,
You have to breath and cry and suck
And things around you tight are put,
They make you hot, enclose your foot.

Nappies are objects you must wear.
They're fixed and uncomfortable it's not fair.
Although your life will never be the same,
Everyone's glad you finally came.

You've entered the world,
There's no turning back,
'Cause here you are now - with a name - Sue or Jack!

Iona Beange

Grace and Favour

I take a breath of God's sweet air,
close to the foxes' country lair.
Far away from the smoke and grime,
where no one stops to think of time.

This is where I feel at peace,
where all hostilities seem to cease.
No such things as traffic lights,
no drugs, no thugs, no "Bloody" fight.

The buttercups of burning gold,
sheep all snugly in the fold.
The setting sun in golden splendour,
all seem to sing "love me tender"

I look up to the friendly trees,
gently swaying in the breeze.
They cuddle me in sheer delight,
like a loving mother in the night.

They try to brush my cares away,
bowing sweetly as they sway.
Whenever I feel the need to rest,
I know the place that loves me best.

Doris Gamble

Snow

Frozen images of frosty feathers float down from bird-like
clouds above,
Preening themselves free of their icy quills,
Whilst gliding across the dark, cold sky.
Lights on, curtains closed,
The world is shutting out problems and suffering.
"Next time" cries the plucked bird "when I return
My feathers will not full on ragged children, lifeless trees
and hurtful hands"
But will melt in warm hearts".

Jenny Rivett

Shadow of a Vampire

I find myself staring at the cold
Cobbles of a deserted street,
The street is dark
but as my eyes adjust, I can make out the
figure of a young man upon a bench,
His clothes are torn but yet his presence
makes me shudder,
There is such guilt and despair in his eyes
that I feel he has known sorrow beyond belief.
As I look more closely
I notice a young girl approaching the man,
I phase out my bedroom and concentrate deeper,
deeper still,
I become the girl in the velvet cape!
Now finally I can discover this stranger's torment,
Alas, I shall never know,
for he is only a shadow in a picture,
Upon my bedroom wall.

Chantal Rosalyn Harris

Valentine

Moonlight reflects the Moss Rose bud's melancholy,
Communicating the desolation felt,
Darkness conveys her solitude wholly,
Private thoughts yearning for the morning's melt.
Sunrise breaks the gloom of night,
Promising life, to dissolve anxious emotions,
Radiation of love and light,
Transforms the plight and wheels the motion.
Intensity of passionate affection,
Penetrates the bud, above,
Giving rise to the blooming Moss Rose, adoration,
Displaying voluptuous love.
If you the Sun and I the Rose,
Recognize me, dear one, and erase the woes.

Alison Stevens

"Witches Brew"

Jars and bottles and curious things
Cobwebs, candles and Butterfly wings
Stacked on shelves so dusty and dark
There's Elm and Ash and Sycamore bark

The dazzling eyes of a Peacock's tail
Staring out in the moonlight pale.
Dried up leaves from an Autumn fall
And, bright as a diamond, a crystal ball.

While there in the inglenook, firelights glow
Pokes and pries and twinkles so
On the brasses hung from the mantle shelf
Dancing about like a mischievous Elf.

And there is a broom and a pointed hat
And sitting beside them, a huge black cat.
Leather bound books of magic rhymes,
Bottles and casks full of herbal wines.

Remedies, spells and boxes of pills
Everything needed to cure most ills.
The black cat purrs, and looks at the door
Here comes her mistress, the Witch, once more!

John Unsworth

Life's Journey

Being born into life's dawn,
Colours a brand new day,
We try our best to stand the test,
of strifes along the way.
When we're young we just bounce back,
And carry on along our track,
Age progresses and with it stresses,
Which way to turn? Which path to take?
Will our choice be a lucky break?
Children will follow, we'll try to teach,
our values in life and goals to reach,
The autumn of your life begins,
The kids have left we're alone again,
Talking to each other again is fun,
Not having to shout above music's drone.
The twilight of our life is shared.
In memories of love for the lives we have cared,
When the sun decides to set all fulfilment will be met.
Our lives will not have been in vain,
For love and laughter outweigh the pain.

Catherine Spivey

The Clopping Machine

The wild-eyed professor leaned back for a rest, his latest invention complete, 'Young fellow', said he, 'you are surely impressed by this rare, technological feat.' 'Er...yes,' I replied, 'I like it a lot, but what is its purpose?...I mean...'
'You mean you can't guess?
Why, any dumb clot would know it's a Clopping Machine!'

'A Clopping Machine! Why didn't I guess? What else could it be, would you tell? A product of inspired genius, no less; I imagine it clops very well.' 'It certainly does!' the professor enthused, 'Success is rewarding and sweet, two years of my time - every minute well used - and now my research is complete.'

'Young man, since you're here, it's your privilege now to witness my brainchild's first cry.' 'This control,' he explained, 'determines just how the volume is set - low or high.' 'So now,' he continued, adjusting the dial, 'I shall press this red button, on top...' The machine sprang to life, flashed its lights for a while, then then suddenly gave a loud 'CLOP!'.

'Amazing!' I said, 'But tell me just where is the market for such a device?' He answered me quickly, 'The market is there; I believe it will fetch a good price, every modern contraption, expensive or cheap, in factory, office or shop, is designed to give out a ridiculous 'bleep'. What relief to hear something go 'CLOP!"

Frank Sutton

Dying

Darkness, deep, dark deadly
cloaks the essence of my soul;
only pain to fill the void,
emptiness, only emptiness.

Heart keeps beating
world keeps turning,
don't look 'round, life and death
two sides of the coin.

Fear, fear of dying
crying, screaming in your head,
voices, only voices.

Looking from eyes weary with the world,
scurrying like ants;
got to play the game
nothing stays the same.
Nothing changes, everything changes.

Flowers bloom and wilt,
another season, another year
growing dim, growing old.

Amanda McGivern

The Becoming of Age

The becoming of age was derelict as the day fell to an end
Come see the stars, the moon the everlasting sunset
I can dream as good as anyone
But the nightmare still remains and the memories still remain
Hanging over my head until the weight of it all crushes me
And I can dream as good as anyone
Can you hear the scream of a child call out for forgiveness
Can your ears believe your own wisdom
As the divine figure of wonders stands without answers
Ignoring the issue, and the issue will always remain
As long as I can dream as good as anyone

I awoke suddenly to find only reality again
And I wait for the time I can go to sleep to find my tranquillity
Rest my head on the concrete pollution and listen to the noise
The thousand of thoughts are there but cannot be identified
For the chance I have is a long wait
The passion is slowly slipping away and I don't want to question
Anymore . . . lead me to the missing point
The point being no longer being
To scream, to live, to dream as good as anyone

Ian Stuart Ambrose

'A Typical Day'

Well, here I sit, my morning work done
Considering I'm only a flamin' scale one
Yes sir! no sir! three bags full sir! I hear myself say
Maybe I'll reach scale two someday.

The girl across the desk is filing her nails
Maybe she's the sort to work in sales
Ever idle, never stops talking
her nail breaks, "oh my god!" she starts squawking.

Then you get the executive type
Never stops moaning about people on strike
As long as he's up top, raking in the money
People kiss his feet and call him 'honey'.

It's 11:45 and time for lunch
No-one's here to cover, well, thanks a bunch
"Oh, sod it"! I'm off for a bite to eat
let someone else take the seat.

Well, on I plod through the rest of the day
At last 5 o'clock is here
I pack up my things and leave the office
and go home and have a nice cool beer.

Carole Edwards

Dance My Name

Stood by the sun, and the dawn came
called my name
And rose to the sky, and the rain came
danced my name
And fell to the earth,
Wet the soil and washed my soul
I sang to the sea, and the waves came,
Roared my name,
I turn to the sun, as she burns -
The moon is coming soon
Touch the earth, know your worth,
Feel the rhythm beat as one -
Touch the sky, know your mind,
And the healing has begun.
Stood by the night, and the moon came cried my name
And soared to the sky, and the stars came, shone my name
I bow, to the south, and the wind breathes over me
I dance to the moon, as she chants - the sun is coming soon
Touch the sea, know your peace, feel the healing of the old
Touch the stone, know your home, feel the healing of your soul

Amanda River

The Ocean

Ocean wide, ocean deep
Grey whispers lashed, frozen by the shore's stares.
Waves wash over me as sleep
Rolled sidling with the molten green, faint-flecked clouds
Of life, of love, of death -
Arc of wood held fast by salt,
Deeps of green, skies inverted;
The rocks reflect, sea-urchin-studded
On a universe tied to the shores of common sense and frailty.

Janet Dalmar

Let This Be Home

Some times between this quiet serene
    Content may be, no soul can tell,
Chaste moon shines like an Archangel saint,
    Oh why do you melt and bid farewell,
My heart forever wished the melancholy adieu
    The sky is frowning but no showers fell,
If flowers have no scent, the birds no song,
    Nature's miraculous attire forever seems wrong,
How thankful your bliss to grant my cause,
    The grandeur, the stillness, the moonlight applause.

Oh solitude hide me in your soundless dell
    Thou and I are here and alone,
I hear the voice of water, the crystal swell,
    This is love, let this be home,
Ease my heart you silver moon
    Let me ravish the melody, with mocking tune,
Buds I'll kiss the flowers know it well
    Like the wild bee to the foxglove bell,
This amorous cool silence, with scented air,
    Natures creation with pious care.

John Leighton

Guilt

I crouched there
Crumpled up like an old sack
Writhing in my own personal Hell.

Mumbled uttering
Of the tabooed words Devil and Death,
A form seemingly synonymous.

A numb vessel
And the clammy stench of guilt
Washing over, a bloody suffocation.

Steel fingers inside
Catch and scratch for an umbilical excuse
Choking me with invisible tears.

Cristina Cooper

The Robin

Alone he sits, quietly watching;
Content to wait, my little Robin.
One laurel leaf sufficient to hide
His vermilion chest, puffed with pride -
Until, artfully and with cunning flight
He ventures swiftly, into the light
To feast, once the other birds are gone
Upon the titbits on the lawn.
Then, having taken of his fill
His departure even is swifter still -
Back to the laurels my Robin takes flight
Seeking their safety from the morning's sunlight.

Joan Povey

Nostalgia

No nightingale for me, but the sweet collared dove,
Cooing contentment from some hidden bough,
'Minds me of may-times many years ago,
The blossom-scented days when we were half in love.

For when I hear its call, that low, insistent note
Telling the pleasures of connubial bliss,
Under the lilacs, tasting our first kiss
I seem to stand again, and languor fills my soul.

Not you alone, my dear, are present to my mind:
Oxford's enchantment casts its golden dust,
Punts drift down Cherwell through the buttercups
And in its haunted dusk our youth is left behind.

Yet will I not regret that we have grown apart,
Sighing that autumn soon will strip the tree;
Those tender may-times are still part of me,
Hid, like the collared dove, contented in my heart.

Ann Ferguson

A Mother's Thoughts

Was it I, was it I, did I hear a sigh
    Did I hear the sound of a baby cry
Do my eyes, do my eyes with their sight now dim
    See a child, no two, come running in
Do my arms, do my arms, reach out to hold
    What once was mine and in them fold
Does my heart, does my heart, still beating slow
    Cry out, aching, I love you so
Do the years, do the years with the laughter and tears
    Slowly pass, as a dream and all one hears
Not a sound, not a sound as I sit alone
    In this house, so quiet, which once was home.

Ivy Eunice Brookes

Hero or Villain?

Reality's too much
Complications overwhelm the grey crisis
What next to befall in real life
Strife and tears
Hopes and fears

Fantasy takes over
Riding the roller coaster, losing the mind
The film features you
Spinning and turning, yearning
Passions burning.

Escape to transient dreams
Flowing, surging, drifting and crashing
Over and over.
The Heroes and villains, scripted, directed
Reactions selected.

Beware of the power
Wild imagination brings.
Truth becomes fantasy becomes truth.
If the dream breaks through merging true,
The victim is you.

Chris Hillier

Little Angel

Precious little angel, lying sleeping in your chair.
Dark brown eyes, skin soft and pale, and lovely jet black hair.

Lying there so helpless, and we all want to peep.
At this perfect little baby, so content and fast asleep.

May your dreams be forever happy, full of love and happiness.
As you're such a perfect little baby,
I wish you luck, and may God bless.

May He guide your tiny footsteps, keep you safe and full of health.
May He also give you wisdom, lots of love, and also wealth.

Irene Campbell

Spring

Snowdrops hold up their little heads
Daffodils line the flower beds
Lambs skipping everywhere
It is truly a wonderful sight
To live in the country is such a delight
Watching a wonderful season called Spring.

To sit in my garden is such a treat
Watching the birds they are ever so sweet
Rushing backwards and forwards with little leaves
They are so busy building among the trees.

Blue-tits, Blackbirds, Robin Red-breast
She will make a beautiful nest
In the old kettle I left out last year
Flying past me she has no fear.

I watch creatures great and small
Knowing that God loves them all
So I am thankful every day
To watch them at their work and play.

Brenda Sutton

Lauren

Lauren you lie there so peacefully, with a mint coloured blanket covering your small body. You're so beautiful, with that face of an angel and eyes that will melt ice. You are the youngest of four, and the cheekiest, but what would we do without you, your three sisters smother you like three little mothers. I am so proud, so happy, my heart is filled with love that could burst into spring time. You were not planned but I 'Thank God' you are here. I hear you say, "I spy with my little eye something beginning with, my friends". Out the mouth of our baby, our little girl so sweet so comforting, so pure!
You changed our whole life darling, you made us become a family. I enjoy life now, more than I could have ever. You made me sit down and think, you made me make the right choice. I look at you and wonder what your mind thinks about, a mind of innocence. Your hair looks like threads of silk and Lauren your cheeks become rose red, we should
have called you Snow White. And who could have thought that a two year old little girl could have brought all this.

Julie Bolam

First Love

Slowly it comes after friendship.
Creeping inside the innocent flesh,
Worming its way to the heart.
Never intended,
But falling into life as a seed to the ground,
Implanting and sprouting,
Feeding on feelings.
Until one glorious summer day
Its petals unfold and face the stark new world,
Furnishing the atmosphere with a new fragrance as pure as the wind,
And softening the air like a baby's laugh.
Slowly it blossoms.
Holding precious moments
Of fantasies and dreams.
Only to die, or so it seems,
In the frost of dawn.

Clare R. Thurgood

"The Three Sisters"

Across Rannoch Moor I chanced to gaze,
'Cross wind dipped reed, and peaty bog with orchid rare,
The purple heather caught my wandering eye
As it carpeted to the very distance, and on the horizon
The Three Sisters stood, towering with darkening crag.

Perchance I saw an antlered head,
And gentle hooves stepping lightly, across their shadowed walls?
High above, the shrieking gulls cascaded down to the fallen lamb.
The swirling mist clung deep and crowned each towering head
And from morning rain, the streams, like silver threads,
Fell into the valley, gained momentum
And pounded the rocks of the pass, finally
To slide resplendent into Loch Leven's wide, calm waters.

Brenda M. Luck

My Equilibrium

Poetry flows down my stream
Crystal clear, so pure and clean.
Never should it fall,
Or be the writing on the wall.
Days shall come and days shall go
And still the muse should flow.
The cogs will turn -
The mind shall churn,
But no, a halt in time
Is the end of a poet's line.
A tear without the eye,
The truth inside a lie -
Without the rhythm of verse
Is as barren as a washed-up mermaid's purse.
For poetry is my being -
My centralized point of living -
The path I choose to lead,
The food from which I feed.
And on your words I depend
A loyal, truthful and honest friend.

Angeline Joffe

A Child

Chubby fingers, toothless grin,
Curly hair, dimpled chin,
bottles, dummies, nappies hoo,
they say 'ga, ga' and smile at you!

They try to crawl, they try to run,
but then they sit and suck their thumb.
Their big bright eyes go really wide,
When you jump up and try to hide!

They are so innocent, when they're asleep,
You really wish you'd like to keep,
that little bundle you love so much
an innocent bundle the world can't touch!

Joanne Iley

Awakening?

I walk alone along the shore,
calm peaceful place before day ends,
then sit and watch the sky in awe,
as crimson sun though azure sea descends

The sea and sky are one,
in wondrous hues of blue and gold,
I blink, and all is gone,
the sky is dark, the stars unfold

The waves caress the shore and sigh,
lap gently 'round my soul
hypnotic like a lullaby
no then, no now, no new, no old

Beyond my comprehension lies
a paradox of time and space
so many things to understand
so little time - I must make haste.

Denise Jorgensen

To Live

To live is something precious, to remember is a secret, to love is a
desire, and to hold a moment in time in the palm of your hand, is a
miracle that will never happen again.

A sunset is a glimpse of heaven, and heaven is a reflection of earth,
Sky, so full, yet free of life and beauty, a dream escapes into the
atmosphere and surrounds us.

I watch and ponder awhile, as I am held in the elegance of life, a
time flower is picked and I drift through time itself,
The wisps land in heaven as the wind cradles them in her arms
and carries them away.

If something so precious as this is found in a lifetime, a meaning
has been found,
true love, a soul mate, a child, a friend, a dream, a fantasy, then
life has been lived.

For a piano plays the chords of my life, and who-so-ever touches
the keys, touchesmy life
and leaves a pattern of music behind.

Emma Swift

Untitled

Quickly does the night speed its
Darkened hours towards the dawn,
My sleepy head upon the pillow lay.
I am alive, I am awake, I am reborn.
Now must I rise from the misty
World of dreams.
Come forth dear day, breath life
into this still form.
Shadows of the night are fading fast.
Fantasies I weave in sleep are lost.
Am I dreaming, perhaps I am
The visions that I thought were real
Were in fact unreality and
Thinking I am waking sleeping still

Ellen Binding

The Ladder of Life

Daily I climb the ladder of life
Daughter - mother - sister - wife.
Balancing things that need to be done
Climbing slowly - rung by rung.

Ever onwards up I go,
Some days quickly - sometimes slow.
Heading to where I want to be
Holding tight to the inner me.

Sometimes I think I've climbed so high
That I can reach and touch the sky.
But then I pause, and looking down
Can see my feet still on the ground.

I often think I'm near the top,
That I've reached my goal and my legs can stop.
But just when I think my climb is done
Destiny adds another rung!

Janet Fox

The Play

Is this enough for you and me
Do we have what we need
Two characters engaged in dialogue
Acting out another scene
High drama from me, you the every essence of charm
But it's just a matter of flattery and
Flattery's a juggler only there to impress me.

I sat on the steps of the sacred heart
And thought of the play in which we both have a part
I touched the blade so sharp and cold
I touched on the ending not yet told
You murmur, I scream, I must be heard above everything
The blue sky fades to winter grey
I'm truly sorry in a dozen different ways.

Jane Moysen

Temporary Death

I can feel myself floating,
Drifting high up to the clouds,
As the blackbird flies
Towards the mighty sun.

As I turn myself I see,
But it is not me, just a body.
For I am here up above,
How can this be?

I know I am here,
Yet down below people fuss,
Around someone who resembles me.
Is it an intruder?

What is this scene?
Is this my death?
Have I travelled up,
To another world?

The sunlight blinds me.
The blackbird sings outside on the tree.
My chamber is silent,
As I wake from my dream.

Joanne Shuttleworth

The Spirit Is Dead

White, yellow, bright light,
Gives heat and comfort, there is no night.
City etched in wax below,
The people see yet do not know.

Oh foolish tranquillity!

The soul deceived, the red sky burns above,
Square box believed, but who gets our love?
As the light descends the sky rolls down,
It eats the heart from my Christmas town.

Too many wise men now, it seems.

Now the light flickers, soon it will die,
Reaching out to survive; yes, it will try.
No city left now, just pools of hot sad remains,
still the light burns, still hope in the flames?

Gone; My christmas candle dies.

No longer comfort, no heat, no light.
Gone forever. Eternal night.
We took all it had, without question, nothing put back.
From our apathy, anxiety will fester, the Saviour wears black.

Weep now friends, for soon we will join the Christmas Candle.

James Gilmartin

Nigel

Mother, could I but say, the things I hear myself a-saying,
day by day.
Your love and gentleness throughout the years,
Of laughter gaily given when I know you hide the tears.
Never do you look at me as others want to do
And ask the age old question,
"Oh God - How could you?"

Mother, your brightness glows as with me you play,
and help my fumbling fingers as I dress at start of day.
How tired you sometimes feel when your working day is through,
But you never fail to come to me and kiss me sweet adieu.

Would that I could, my mother dear, just once walk from this bed,
And do the many little things that you do in my stead,
To make the tea - or cut the bread.
But here in ghastly form my earthly prison lies,
Not even mirrored outwardly; no soul shines through my eyes.

My thoughts lie deeply buried, my limbs I do not own,
But through it all your love has gone unwasted - Have you known?
Without you, what for me? Who to care, to smile at this pitiful
mound of human decay?
Mother, could I but say: "I love you."

Corrie Francis

The Visitor

She was frightened.
Death, more terrifying than any savage beast, raised "its" hideous head.
She shivered.
Death, cold, as cold as ice, entered the room.
She protested.
Death was heavy, heavy like lead, a weight she could not move.
She was blinded.
Death so black, blacker than a hangman's hood, ensconced her form.
She was dumb.
Death silently, silent as the grave, hovered by her side.
She surrendered.
Death. The Grand Master, death, had come to claim a soul.
She kissed.
Death, inevitable death, her loved one had gone.
She cried.
Death, unfathomable death, like an ocean, accepted her tears.

Jenny Elsen

The Flame

I could be hot dangerous too
Don't play with me or I will burn you
When it is winter I could warm you
I could cook your dinner and other things too
I could be yellow, blue, or red
You blow me out when you go to bed
My flame reaches high into the sky
When the rain comes then I shall die.

Charlotte Blyth

What's in the Cardboard Box?

We had a cardboard box today,
Delivered at our door,
Mum and Dad had to pay.
What's in it, I'm not sure.

They hid it but I don't know where,
I think it's in their room,
I don't think it's very fair,
Perhaps they'll show me soon,

I'm curious to know what's in it,
I really am, I am!!
I want to know if it's my Guide kit,
Or my little sister's pram.

Tonight Mum's showing what's in it,
I really cannot wait,
Aaaaaa! I can't believe it,
IT'S DAD'S FISHING BAIT!!!

Helenelaine Hiscox

One Man, One Woman

One man, one woman, alone in life
Destined to meet? Only destiny knows
The pain of seclusion cuts like a knife
And deep down inside the willingness grows

Across a crowded room the heavens conspire
As their phoenix-like souls ascend from the fire
With a bashful exchange the touch paper glows
The river of love can explicitly flow

They gently embrace as a nocturne plays on
Contentment will rise as they sing their own song
Sealed with a kiss as he looks in her eyes
They exit together both ready to fly

Emotions run high as passion explodes
The years of frustration can finally unload
This need for acceptance is long overdue
And when he says "I love you" the words ring true

These words are never wasted
She's all he'll need to quell his strife
Because they'll always be together
One man, one woman, one life

Dean Cartwright

446

Captured by Shadows of Time

As I walk all alone.
The thoughts which hurt me, are still there.
Wondering when the sky will show the colours of dawn.
Captured by childhood memories that cannot bare.

Time carried on days go by.
Secrets are kept like a precious stone.
For yet I live, not born to cry.
In peace a while, I sit alone.

As I sit and look
Thinking how, and the wind is still
My private life is an open book
Dreams and wishes, hoping to fulfil.

There are words that reach my ear.
those who whisper tell of other things.
Behind they talk, I tend not to hear.
Wanting freedom like a bird has wings.

There is nothing more, me that pained.
True friends are understanding but far apart.
My dreams of success when having gained.
The feeling of each moment will be close to heart.

Sajida Parveen

A Place to Belong

I don't want to leave here, why am I shifted around, what
did I do, is it my fault please someone tell me now.
Another life another house another place to call home,
This is your new family, but I had a family back home.
Their memory I had but I blocked it away, it is easier
to forget than to deal with the pain.
What did I do, is it my fault please will someone explain
    They said my mother is sick, that's why I can't come home
doesn't she know where I am, can't she even phone? All she is,
is a picture on my bedroom wall, and a visit maybe
once a year with the present of a new doll.
She'll say how much she misses me, and ask me the same,
A kiss goodbye and then she's gone, until I don't know when.
What did I do, is it my fault? Will she be back again.
    Another life another house another place to call home
this is your new family, but I have a family back home.

Joanne Daly

Troubled Ulster

Please God end this wicked evil war I pray
Don't let my children go through what I have
Been through each and every day.

Just for living in Ulster you are a target they say
Fear of the unknown
Is a terrible price to pay.

May there be no more pain and sorrow
Life is too short anyway
Dear God my this troubled Ulster
Just be a memory and fade away.

April Uprichard

Poor Little Spider

Mummy Mummy there's a spider in my room,
come and get it out with your big, big broom.
I will not kill the spider,
I will not kill it dead,
the poor little spider has hardly got a head!
It's running across my floor Mummy,
it's running up my door,
watch out when you come in, look before . . .
It's running across the landing now,
it's running down the stairs.
There it goes dropping its big black hairs.
Oh no! Here comes Daddy,
watch out Dad,
Look before . . . too late
there's the spider squashed on the floor,
living no more.

Emma Morris

A Question of Emotion

When she flows through your thoughts,
Do you cry?
    When she stands at your side,
Do you smile?
    When she rejects you,
Do you try?
Or wait a while?

Andrew McCabe

He Gave Us Ears that We Might Hear

Have you heard the sighing of the breeze,
Did you feel the gentle touch upon your face?
The whispering leaves, on swaying, dancing trees.
Then darkening day, and gathering cloud,
Brings stronger winds that blow a gale.
Out of my path, it howls and wails
Leaving behind a path of horror in its place
Such changes from a gentle breeze.

Have you heard the lapping of the waves
As they gently roll towards the shore?
Seagulls sitting, riding on the sea so brave.
Then darkening sky, and gathering wind,
Stirs up the waves to make them soar,
Each wave topped with frothing white,
Fighting each other as of one mind
To rise and fall, to crash and roar,
Reaching crescents on rock and shore.
Such changes from a gentle wave.

Irene Green

Untitled

There was an old man who
didn't know what to do. He found
an old shoe that was the colour
blue, blue that went with the sea
also the blue sky. That goes away
up high down on the field where the long
grass grows bunnies and hares go on
their fares. Fairs go 'round and
'round the toad and hare play very very
fair of all lovely creatures of
the air God does right every single
night of all the good gay bad.
Jesus is up in heaven sometimes
most sad He is missed by all
and all reach out to meet
and greet - with love feast all for
life and remote I promise
them a beautiful red rose.

Christian Davidson

Regrets

When someone very close to you,
    Dies and goes away,
You feel betrayed and guilty,
    For all the things you didn't say.
You think that you're the only one,
    Who's going through all this pain.
That no-one really understands.
    Why you'll never smile again.
You don't want to go on living,
    You can't face another day.
What's the point? There's no-one there.
    You're on your own again.
And when the nights are cold and dark,
    And your pillow's wet with tears.
You wish you could turn your mind off,
    And stop thinking back over the years.
But a long way off, the time will come
    When you'll learn to live with the pain
You'll hold your memories close to your heart.
    And then slowly you'll smile again.

Barbara Andrews

Traveller of the Road

Ragged clothes, shoes downtrodden,
Dishevelled hair, face unshaven,
Wrinkled skin, well weather-beaten,
Worldly goods packed on his back.
He's the traveller of the road.
He may look sad, times can be bad, then again they can be good.
If he has a care, there's no-one to share,
Who cares, who would, who should?
He's the traveller of the road.
He's chosen this life of solitude, though lonely it may seem,
Life has its compensations, a butterfly, a bird, a dream;
Green pastures, blue skies, fresh air fills his lungs,
He has no wealth, but he has health,
He's the traveller of the road.
Life holds no luxury for him, just bare necessity.
A place to rest his weary head, food, drink, tranquillity,
Money has no meaning Mother Nature is his supply,
He reaps on her resources as he passes by.
He's the traveller of the road.
Address: "No fixed abode".

Ann E. Hackett

Untitled

Walking around grazing
Doing good not badness
But, not for long —
Their lives as soon to end in sadness
Crammed inside a lorry trailer
No food or water for the long journey
It's just not fair!
That they do not know
That soon their lives will end in sadness
Why do we do this sad thing?
For food and clothing?
But is it all worth the pain
That we put these pour animals through!
Will this cruelty ever end?
I only hope it does and soon!

Dawn McWhirter

Remember Me . . .

Remember me when I'm gone
. . . Don't cry for me,
. . . Sigh for me,
. . . or wish that I was still there . . .
For in that cry, there is sadness . . .
. . . in that sigh, there is regret . . .
. . . and in that wish, there is longing.
As I was not born . . . just to die,
. . . see my difference,
. . . see my individuality,
. . . see the part of me I have left behind . . .
. . . Just remember me when I'm gone.

Chetna Nena

This Is My England

Spring
Daffodils, snowdrops, crocuses pushing through the icy earth;
green buds appearing as signs of new birth; birds returning,
mating, laying their eggs; young lambs, baby rabbits, finding
their legs - This is my England.

Summer
Thatched cottages nestling in villages small; old country
churches with spires so tall; children playing along the sand;
older folk enjoying the village brass band - This is my England.

Autumn
Land of hope and glory from a myriad of voices; students starting at
colleges of their choices; pavements buried under carpets of
leaves; harvest thanksgivings for the corn bound in sheaves -
This is my England.

Winter
Chill winds blowing and scarves wrapped 'round tight; short dull day
and long dark night; Christmas time with its presents and fun;
celebrating the birth of God's only Son - This is my England.

Ann Lockwood

Untitled

Don't come to me in gladness
Don't come to me in strife
but come to me with heartbeat
and take me for your wife

For I am here to be smothered
to be wrapped in warmth and love
so set me there beside you
let me fit you like a glove.

That glove will travel with you
be beside you when you go
it will rest inside your pocket
and provide a warming glow.

But, don't use me as a gauntlet
don't use me as a jest
don't throw me down in anger
trust my love and do your best.

For knowing that you're travelling
and trying hard to win
that glove that will firm your handshake
and make the rest give in.

Amanda Jane Janes

Winter

The leafless trees stand silent and white,
Covered with a silky sheet of snow,
Icicles hang like transparent fingers,
Pointing to a thick white blanket, covering the floor,
All is tranquil and still,
The ground is covered with a coating of cotton wool,
Marked with a little cat's paw prints,
A layer of soft white snow is spread across the roof tops,
Glistening and twinkling like stars,
A puff of smoke drifts away through the misty air,

Snowflakes softly fall from the sky,
light as a feather,
like sparkling flowers frozen in mid-air,
Drifting silently to the ground,
Snowmen appear as if by magic,
Standing silent and frozen with crooked smiles,
Watching the world pass by,
What was water now is ice,
People slip and slither along the glass-like path,
A pale sun peeps out from behind a cloud.

Emma Cripps

Yesterday's Tomorrows

By this iron unfeeling monster life is passing, dreams are too,
from its mouth it spits relentless, plastic mouldings hot and true,
clamping, folding ever making just to try and make ends meet,
I sit daily head unbending, I sit daily, so we eat.
Where's the boy with hopes unending where's the child that
    once I knew.
When at school he dreamt a future dreams of fame and fortune too,
school days happy, joy and laughter, going hopeful down
    life's road,
never caring or regretting shoulders coping with life's load.
Where's the lad who grew to manhood, strong and handsome
    long ago.
Who liked to flirt and loved the ladies, oh tell me where did
    that man go,
dreamed that he would make a fortune be a someone in his life.
Met a beauty, lovely lady took that lady for his wife.
They had children, happy children lovely daughters, one and two,
he kept working, dreams still burning, praying someday they'd
    come true.
Did I ask too much by dreaming? Tell me please, I want to know,
where's the fame, and where's the fortune, where oh where
    did my life go?
Life keeps rolling, we get older, children marry, families swell,
they have children, many questions, what are the answers? What to tell?
Don't sit dreaming of your future, don't sit drifting mind afar,
grasp the future, climb that mountain, shake the world,
    become a star.

Brian Manning

448

The Winds of Time

The winds of time fall upon my face
Hark! "Is that me"
As I peer at the looking glass,
I see reflections of what once used to be.
Skin so sweet, eyes so blue,
No more looking glass, 'tis not
Is this the face of winds, scarred, rugged
The winds of time blow hard
Cold as ice, purple, grey, blue . . .
not you!!
Biting deep line aghast young, pure
It's not so!!
The winds of time fall upon my face,
It's the looking glass!
Turn, away!!
Stay young, Stay pure,
It's not so!
The winds of time
Fall upon my face
Hark! "Is that me?"

Anthony Flowers

Confusion

Who is that girl standing in the door?
Has she come to see me, why and what for?
She knows me!
I've never seen her before,
There is a strange man in my home,
He says he's my husband.
How can he be?
They mean nothing to me,

Memories swim in my head,
All of them in profusion,
People, places and things that have been said,
My days are filled with confusion,
Sometimes I cry,
Who am I?

Jessie Sams

The Gift

Dreams and wishes of fulfilment,
Hastening the heart and expanding the consciousness.
The dreaming moments escaping reality.
The need to go within, to renew and strengthen
We hang our fears on the hooks of emotion,
The growing cloud blocking our growth,
Surrounding and smothering the inner voice,
Blocking out the light which illuminates all.
Recognize the emotion that causes fear,
And it flees - filling the vacuum with Love and Light.
Understanding self, acceptance of self,
Loving of self - the greatest gift of all.

Jennifer Denning

Happy 60th Birthday Jenny

Hello Jenny it's us your friends to say,
Have a wonderful 60th Birthday.
Enjoy your special day and really celebrate,
Because we all think that you're just great.

The Nifty Fifty years have been and gone,
Through life you have learnt right from wrong.
The worries you have had you try to shrug away,
As you face another hectic and tiring day.

Your Pension Book and Bus Pass you now can claim,
In their neat little wallets they safely remain.
What ever you do Jenny, don't become a "Twirley",
That's when the Bus Driver says "You're too early".

Anyway Jenny enjoy your day whatever you do,
Our thoughts are with you the whole day through.
Good luck and happiness we all wish for you,
Because if anyone deserves it, you certainly do.

Iris Smith

Dad

Jimmy Parker was his name
Football was his favourite game
He loved to sit and paint the world
Good food and drink were his key words
He lived his life to the full
He took the rough with the smooth
Your friends will miss you
Your loved ones too
You left us Jimmy far too soon
You gave us all the very best
And now it's time for you to rest
You might be gone from us today
But in our hearts you will always stay

Brenda Neale

Passengers

The train left, I was aboard, unaware that I had been chosen
For a journey that began at the end of this pilgrimage,
Made by passengers transcending through an immaculate image
Taking a leap away from the frozen.

There was no seeing, no touching, but we could feel -
Feel the nothing as we rode through nowhere,
Through an emptiness the lonely silence we shared,
Floating on invisible tracks to the boundaries of the real . . .

. . . Why can I remember, only, the impression of a voice,
Whispering, breathing, asking us to remain,
A voice with no eyes, no features, no face.

In the beginning it seemed we had not a choice
Yet still, along the rails, some jumped when we experienced pain,
Some, from the sides, tried to reach up and unite though fell
    back for the pace

Was so awkward and so strange. There was no noise
Till we reached the end, then it all became too insane
For we divided when destiny, or chance, decided our gender
    and race.

We abandoned the fear and embraced rejoice
Stepping out for the platform, cautious, seeking to gain
One's paradise? Then surveyed the land . . . and saw it was
    all waste.

Edna Sackey

To My Lost Love

I love the sound of gently falling rain
For deep within its whispering refrain
I hear your voice, and you are near again

Such tender love we shared, and then such pain.
You had to go, but in the sound of rain
You come to me, and we are one again.

Joyce Riddell

Logic of Life

We must always keep a positive mind,
For it is so easy to be so blind!
Don't set your goals in life too high,
Or your enthusiasm will just simply die.
Try every day to achieve something small,
This builds your confidence, as a rule.

Stability enables us to think straight,
So don't take on too much, that's just fate!
Only your decisions find contentment,
Taking other advice leads to resentment!
Remember things don't happen just over night,
Find some patience, then you'll get it right!

Don't feel a failure if things go wrong,
Put it down to experience where it should belong!
Structure your life within your limitations,
Then you'll see a difference, great expectations!
Once you have found positive, constructive thoughts,
The logic of life is yours, it couldn't be bought!

Ann Penelope Beard

Barn Owl

Barn owl so noble and wise,
Floats across the darkened skies,
with taloned feet and scanning eyes,
He searches for his prey.

Barn owl the woodland wing through.
Plaintively crying twit twoo,
may spy a mouse or unwary shrew,
Lurking 'neath the under growth.

Hark I hear the vixen screech,
into still night air doth reach
even you owl perched in the beech,
'tis a good night for hunting.

songbirds awaken the dawn.
sunrise opens first morn,
The night's time has been well worn,
The barn owl returns to his roost.

David Tovey-Bailey

War

The guns are firing shooting dead
Flying shrapnel lumps of lead

The trees are brown the skies are grey
And the war proceeds day by day

A sniper fires from behind a wall
And in a crowd some people fall

A bomb explodes and leaves a haze
And also sets the hills ablaze

At last the dust begins to clear
And we see the victims lying near

A child sprawled out upon the ground
her pulse and breathing can't be found

The people crowding walk away
And remember the horror from the day

Running hiding from the war
The civilians rush from what they saw

War is pointless war is cruel
Who or what would plan this duel

Emily Anderson

The Answer in My Dreams

Bridged is the gap over the river of souls,
Flying through a bright and welcoming hole.

Then I reached a valley, green grass and
Luminous sky,
I stood upon the pastures, letting out an
Anxious sigh.

In my prayer to the Lord, I was lost and pleading,
Asking if this bridge before me should be so deceiving.

He was just about to answer me, the Lord who cannot lie . . .
But then I saw her standing there,
I looked up to the sky.

Thank you Lord! For taking care,
Her smile says she's just fine.
She waved, then walked away from me . . .
I could not cross that line!

Christopher Jewitt

Ducks on the River Irwell

Little ducks so wild and free
follow their leader instinctively,
instinctively in unison travelling silently;
swimming, swimming impressively
the little ducks so jauntily
wend their way so peacefully,
I wonder where, their destiny.

Joseph Hinson

A Wonderful Day

Colours in the garden grow
  Golden rays of sunshine glow.
The first song of the bird is sung,
  A new day has just begun.

The water ripples in the breeze
  And reflects the blossom on the trees.
Swans spread their slender wings
  While bluebells seem to really ring.

Then raindrops fall from way up high.
  They fall like diamonds from the sky.
A flash of lightning, a thunder clap.
  In a raging storm the world is trapped.

Then once again the sun will shine
  A rainbow in the sky I'll find.
Slowly the dark clouds roll away
  But colours, everywhere, they will stay.

Soon the sun disappears behind a hill
  It seems as though time has just stood still
It's time for the moon to shine up in the sky.
  To a wonderful day we say goodbye.

Joanne Frampton

Memories Are Forever

White is the snow freshly laid.
Gone are the footsteps where we played.
I shut out the cold and latch the door.
The cat is curled up asleep on the floor.
I close my eyes and begin to dream.
I remember the summers down by the stream.
Thinking back over the years.
Across my cheeks run salty tears.
Remembering my dear best friend,
And how her life came to an end.
But the winters come and summers go.
The sun goes down and the moon's aglow,
And only memories will live forever more.

Claire-Marie Farrell

Dunblane

A cold March morning at school in Dunblane.
"Good-bye", said innocents. Still young and shy,
they let go of safe hands in the playground.

Evil lurked, waiting to discharge its pain.
Shocked, horrified, too numbed to even cry
we saw their faces that made no more sound.

They can no longer feel the sun or rain.
We ask the question again, again, why?

Joy Aldridge

Vegetables

A carrot, a potato, a cabbage, a swede,
Got themselves into trouble, indeed!
Some hungry people said
"We need you to put in the pot, to enhance our stew"
Well, what could these poor vegetables do?
They didn't want to end in a stew!
But those hungry people pulled them right out of the ground.
Placed them in a bag that swung 'round and 'round.
To these people, it didn't matter,
If those poor vegetables were diced or splattered.
As long as their stomachs were full to the top,
By that lovely stew, to come from that pot.
Well the veg was diced and some were mashed,
And into the pot they were dashed.
The stew was cooked, the hungry people ate,
Every last drop, they even licked the plate.
But those vegetables were rotten indeed,
For after eating, those hungry people did need,
To use the toilet. They said to each other
"Next time around we'll leave alone vegetables growing in the
ground"

Duane Finch

Little Girl You've Changed Our Lives

We went to the park today
Granddad, you, and I
They forecast rain, how wrong they were!
The sun shone from the sky.

We pushed you proudly in your pram
For all the world to see.
Your soft brown eyes, and golden hair
Like Autumn on the trees.

We threw some bread by the water's edge
little ducklings came to greet you,
Their lives, like yours, have just begun
Tiny, precious, and brand new.

We sat you carefully in the swing,
and pushed you to and fro,
you laughed, you smiled, enriched our lives,
How much! You'll never know.

We've been to the park today
and no matter how hard we try,
We'll never forget the fun we had,
granddad, you, and I.
Gillian Mason

TO-DAY

TO-DAY is ours for living
Grasp it - if you can -
For Life and time are fleeting,
Gliding softly, swiftly on.

Time is quickly passing,
Slipping through our hands,
Running through our fingers
Like the hot Sahara sands.

So fill each waking moment,
Every second, minute, hour,
Fill them full, to overflowing,
Let action be your power.

Eagerness will help you
To make TO-DAY worthwhile,
For then you'll find, each inch of time,
Will soon become a mile.

However far you journey,
Whatever length Life's span,
It's each TO-DAY that makes the whole
Of Life's rich golden plan.
Eunice M. Caines

Sunset in Paradise

The forest edge where all is green
Grass grows thick and soft and clean
A place to sit at eve of day
To watch and think and nothing say.

The air feels warm with the gentlest breeze
Dying sunlight in shimmering seas
Rose petals falling like soft pink rain
Brushing my face, soothing the pain.

The sun deep red like embers dying
Strange distant sounds like mermaids crying
The splash of waves on the beach below
Sand roams the beach with the ebb and flow

Strange emotions I feel that I haven't felt before
As my heart like a bird in the clouds wants to soar
Swathed with these feelings of wonder and love
Strange garments indeed yet they fit like a glove

The sun's final bow as it dips out of sight
And all with the world is suddenly right
Open my heart, let this feeling fill the air
Let this marvel spread out for all beings to share.
Arthur Capenhurst

The Birth of Spring

The sun starts to shine on the cold frosty morns,
Forcing its rays down to touch the earth.
Spring awakens and stretches her sleepy arms.
There must be a maker to this wonderful new birth.

The snowdrops and crocuses unfold in the sun,
Their soft velvet petals forced through the crusty earth.
The animals awake, rub their eyes, spring is here.
Thank you God for this wonderful new birth.
Gillian Edwards

A Struggle

Walking slowly with her frame
Fingers light holding grip,
with all her energy, moves another pace
not getting anywhere fast.

A little struggle, another move
as patient gets closer to her room
A deep breath, a stretch of her back
A smile for me and we're off again

A "Well done. You're doing good"
From me, gives extra strength
As another move is made
Mable gets closer to her chair
The eagerness for the chair, on her face

A pleading to God, to get her there quickly
and then she's there once again.
Ready for the next struggle to move again.
Donna Inge

Scenes of Norway

Islands like jewels set in an emerald sea,
Fiords thrusting inland, - lakes, large as can be.
Fruit, lush and ripe at the water's edges,
Blueberries, cranberries, wild flowers in crevices.

Majestic mountains with ice-capped shoulders,
Spilling forth waterfalls, smoothing the boulders
To ice-cold, milky-blue rivers below,
Gurgling and rushing the waters flow.

Shrouded in mist the high mountains make
Strange shapes that drift over fiord and lake.
White glaciers tinged with blue so cold
Against the lush sparkling valleys of old.

Tall trees draped in velvet of darkest green,
Pine cones displaying their rich dark sheen.
Logs from the new-felled trees smelling sweetly
Pretty timbered dwellings with roofs turfed neatly.

Goats on the mountainside, bells lazily jangling
Whilst far below ribbons of streams are meandering.
Carved wooden churches to praise this bounty.
Majestic, idyllic Norway, a beautiful country.
Barbara J. Tipping

Hunger

Jesus held out His hand with fish and bread from the sea and land.
Five thousand did He feed that day, a miracle is what they say.
I know we cannot do the same in these days of boats and planes.
How is it that people die and little children have to cry.

They cry for help that does not come, while our children play in the sun.
Black or white we are all the same and if all people on this earth had been given the same chance at birth,
Then pain and hunger would be no more and they would not be so poor.
The little that you have to give will help someone else to live.
So hold out your hand like Jesus did to help save the people over there,
To show them that we really care.
Doreen Peck

451

City Beyond 2000

Jungles made of concrete, buildings to the sky,
Glinting glass and steel grow ever ever high.
Stalagmitic columns in gross monotony,
All vying for the honour of top monstrosity.
Hateful hateful concrete, hateful high-rise homes,
Where are the cathedrals, where all the domes?
Lost among the tall stuff dwarfing church and chapel,
All the English cities emulate BIG APPLE!
Soaring blocks of offices, penthouse in the sky,
Piercing through the stratus and cirrus cumuli

We may never know, but wonder
When the world's a little older
Will a different kind of beauty
Please the eye of the beholder?
Will tomorrow's children in a manner circumspect
Gaze upon these cities and applaud their architect?

Caroline Shore

The Colours of My Life

I look at the snow, the colours of white
Glistening and decking gardens and hedges alike
I look at the fall, with various shades of brown
Of leaves tumbling down and twirling around,
I look in spring, the fields so fresh and green
For the lambs to skip on and spring flowers to be seen.
I look at the sky with shades of blue
Then at night silver stars come into view
I look at the sun all shining and gold
A wonderment of brightness and warmth to behold
I look at the sunset the colour of red
To see it setting, leaves much to be said
These are the colours the rainbow of my life
They each in turn changing moods, sometimes happiness,
sometimes strife
But without them, what would my life be.
Nothing, nothing at all but a catastrophe

Joan I. Granahan

Arms or Alms?

Once begged a slice of life's tastiest bread
gnawed with hunger on charity's cold words,
scavenged for a while beside vulture birds,
food for thought? Ideas which lie like lead.

A stabbing pain knifes deep inside my head
a bleeding trail searching ever inwards
probing, gutting deep my very innards
contemplating whether I should be dead.

A third world citizen sits gassing fumes
belly laughs and gurgles - one funny choke;
final curtain played out in this mad war,
I hear civilized weapons speak volumes
in distant landscape advertising Coke -
Your conscience friend need trouble me no more.

Des O'Donnell

Are We Awake?

I don't want to sleep, dreams are scaring me
Constant every night
But soon darkness overcomes me.

I try to run, but cannot move
Pray for the sun, the light it does soothe
The beast beckons me, what do I do?

Other creatures flee, destroys all he sees
Chased until they tire
But still he does not chase me.

Can't resist those eyes, they don't seem to lie
Doesn't want to hurt me
I join him and hear a sigh.

Run through the night, take turns to chase
We are alive, but are we awake?

Gordon Miller

The Bench

From here there is a view for miles
Down the hill and into the world of man.

Here I can sit, exempt from my life
But be absorbed in the human hustle and bustle of the one
complete body buying the 18th birthday present
Or shoes for the little one.

Their unimportant quirks, subjectless drivel of polite conversation
"A man sat on the floor" he says,
"In WHSmith, how dare he?!!" she cries, she, a pillar of respectability
Benches are for sitting on, not floor. "No time to stop, good morrow."

Benches are ornamental, not to be sat upon.
Cannot defile the graffiti ridden, beaten down bench to watch the
world go by.
I stand on MY bench in protestation
"Must conform to the social norm, must conform" I shout angrily
(within my mind)

Why must I do what they tell me to.
A woman, soaked with the wisdom of her years
Sits down to contemplate her weary feet and worldly treasure
I am trapped, I move on.

Elaine Cotton

The Love Bite

I walked along the streets last night
dragging my feet, head bent and a heart full of sorrow
and although the rained poured down, soaking my flesh,
chilling my bones
I did not care, because for me there was to be no tomorrow.

Why did you betray me? I'm sure I gave you all I had,
think of the good times, those loving words you spoke
Why him darling do you think he's better than me?
You said you'd love me forever,
. . . well that obviously was a joke.

You will never know how much I loved you,
or that last night was to be my last
but that would have achieved nothing, nothing but more hurt,
the way you hurt me darling, when you treated me like dirt.

And then this morning looking in the mirror,
I saw the love bite on my neck your teeth had made,
it's all I have to remind me of you,
and just like my memories, it too is destined to fade.

Adrian Millichip

Impi Dawn

Now, in dawn's African mist, flows a ripple toward the reeds
Droplets from the lips of man, hint of perspiration yet to come
Then, foretold in the shimmering wet, images of war sown seeds
Go now! This warrior, to where men harken to the drum
The oncoming tread of the Boer's boot, heightens his heart's rhythm
Forward now, to where the suns above a chasm

Shadows leap and plunge before the urge of stamping feet
Limbs bedecked with oxtail hair, announce the Impi's lust
The Boer has crushed the grass, with waggon wheel and
    booted spite
Now, hear the Zulu chant, forged from Shaka's soul replete
The ground, like a drumhead taut, now resounds through
    whirling dust
Ebony limbs, through glistening sweat, wield shields of black
    and white

Surging now, the Impi's flanks, like the horns of a raging bull
Following through, the centre's thrust, to impact on the Boer
The singing sounds of rifle butts on the shafts of assegais
A sibilant hiss as a bullet strikes and arms flail to the full
The falling warrior to the spirit god, implores him at this hour.
From a position prone, through the trampled grass, he sees his
    last sunrise
Grant that where the leopard drinks, and lowers his feline head
That beside the reeds my soul shall stand, sentinel to our dead.

Brian G. Tuckey

An Inside Look

Trapped,
by staring eyes.
They're all around
burning at your soul.

Not an eyelid drops
as the hours tick by.
Morning rises once again
and you're still held
steadfast, by the gaze of
your own conscience.

Beating at your heart
guilt emerges from within.
Strong as steel no more
energy seeps from your skin.

Your world lays shattered on the floor.
Picking up the pieces
you see a new picture appearing.
Your humiliation evaporates
as you build on the new foundations
of self-discovery.

Helen Thompson

'Fame'

Ambition burned with a brief consuming fire
Drawing me close to the vagrant flame
As if to seal my fate.
Applause defied this mind naive, ego soaring
Desirous of the poisoned bait - unheeding!

But, hands that grasped this naked flame
Now waver - unpractised to its heat
As pressure serves to falsify
This talent born of me.

What future this, of wealth, acclaim, false goals and self deceit?
The questions light and burn within
Will downfall be complete?
As my chameleon clings to drama's crutch
Will conscience seek my swift retreat?

Now safe away from footlights' glare
Discordant will take heed! The error of misguided zeal
Must surely cool this fire in me.
Fantasies reined, disguises shed - but still she spark remains
Now phantoms haunt my smouldering dreams
Stirring the ashes of that stardom scene.

Elizabeth Beale

"Water Fantasy"

Fountains flashing in the sunlight
Drawn from subterranean spas,
Bright cascading showers dancing,
Weaving cloaks of shining stars.

Vaporous mists of water rising,
Lifted high on Summer air,
Drift across a garden canvas
Pure enchantment painted there.

Velvet lawns, green willows arching
Over tranquil lily pools,
Where dragonflies fan rainbow wings
And larvae spin on silken spools.

From golden Cypresses and Maples
White doves coo soft lovers' calls;
Sweet birdsong swells and mingles with
The music of the waterfalls.

Water gushing, surging, rushing,
Bubbling forth from natural springs,
Tumbling sprays of swirling splendour
Rhapsodies on nature's strings.

Jean E. Collins

Loving Eyes

Your heart, once warm, global warm,
drenched in Day-Glo red.
Now so cold; like an eclipse of the sun, you
block out all the precious things I
have said.
Whenever we meet, you can't get away
from me quickly enough, time cannot
come too soon. Such a shame, as
there was a time our love's harmony
was that of the finest symphonic tune.
Is this all that's left? Reach out your
hands, take back these memories, I
should not have kept them for so long.
They say love is a fool's blindfold, it
isn't true, I am but a man whose
loving eyes for you then, could see no wrong.

Charles Murphy

Stratheden

Here I stand at Eden's door,
Drinking in the view before,
Where sea and rolling hills both meet,
This tranquil beauty my eyes to greet.

Golden flowers standing tall,
A sea bird's lonely chilling call,
So many shades of wondrous green,
Nature's treasures to many unseen.

Primroses fighting winter's bite,
Struggle to reach spring's welcome light,
Whether sunshine bright or thunder cloud,
Nothing can dull Mother Nature's shroud.

Down the lane a lonely stream,
A wooded valley take time to dream,
A country path a well trodden mile,
How good to stop and dream awhile.

A rocky cove, an ocean deep,
How good that nature never sleeps,
A newborn lamb, spring is here,
As nature starts another year.

Edwina Crowley

The Book

Tall thin and slender, a fixer a mender.
For knowledge for fun, read with tea or a bun
It can inspire, depress you or thrill you
Bring you to tears, light up that smile, open new fears.
Until the last page, when it is read
Fold the leaf over it up
The close of the chapters the end of the book
But never forget a covers a cover
The book is inside, to be judged by its ride.
And not by a bribe, or the author inside
But the reader outside, and his own obscure mind.

Gary Ritchie

Being

If being is the sum of thought alive,
essence, perception drawn by disposition,
potential from a term some do derive,
costly frittered some in subjugation;

Each meeting point a mystery course extent
a choice to make a dream or dread unfold,
how recognise, swift moment gripping bent
of option spent, the stairway to its gold;

How sift the dross bombarded by the mass,
the timeless bounteous qualities to weave
a melody of life and love, not crass,
a quintessential harmony to leave

In final words, yet be not understood,
'Here, this was mine, I make it thine if good'?

Camilla Bissell Thomas

A Wood in County Clare 1973

This wood is prehistoric in its silence
Dripping dampness,
Insects crawling from the ancient earth
    and rotting trees.

Boulders strewn -
What brought them here?
They have lain a long time in
    the accumulating layers of soft moss.

Step lightly there -
Glance over your shoulder -
    Quick -
Was that the sun come trickling through,
Or something even older,
Surviving in the sombre twilight
    of the trees.

Elizabeth Copus

Jigsaw

Building up a Jigsaw making a frame
Each piece is different no two are the same
Building up a Jigsaw it's hard to do
When there's no picture to give you a clue
You'll get nowhere by building a part
So be guided by what's in your heart

Fitting it together it can't be wrong
Becoming clearer as you go along
Fitting it together without asking why
It'll be finished the minute you die
Picking the shapes as they come into view
Adding the colours to the outline of blue
And when it's finished the picture is you

Gary Margetts

Forever My Baby

Every inch of me yearns to hold you once more
Each time I close my eyes I see your small
face and watch pure innocence shine.
I hold your tiny fingers and caress your
little toes, touch your velvet soft skin and
stroke your silky hair.

But emptiness fills my heart and arms.

Never to see you run and play like other
children. Unable to comfort you in your hour
of need or share moments of joy.
These things are Motherhood.
In law I have no children but they are wrong.
I have a child called Jessica
Where does she live?

In my mind in my heart and in my dreams
She will forever be my baby.

Juliy Marshall

Sweet Memories

As I sit on the rocks overlooking the sea
Each wave bringing back sweet memories to me
Of some who listened to my tales of woe
Then off to sea he had to go.

I sit and remember the days gone by
With prayers in my heart sent up to the sky
He is gone for a while I know that's true
I pray for his safety what else can I do

He taught me the good things and warned of the bad
And he is the best friend I ever had
One day he will return to me
To tell of the tales while he was at sea

My dad was that sailor, all dressed in blue
The sea was his caller, what else could he do
They sent him away, far out on the sea
To fight for his country, for you, and for me

Hazel Rowe

Easter When I Was a Child

I remember Easter when I was very small
Easter eggs and flowers
I really loved them all

In the garden on my own
I would look around and sigh
Everything was beautiful
The flowers, birds and the deep blue sky

I remember Easter
The seaside trips we had
Perhaps by train, or by bus
It didn't seem to matter much

I remember Easter
The catkins on the trees
Tulips and daffs
Dancing in the breeze

To me Easter is rather special
And also very sad
But I remember Easter as a child
The best I ever had

Joan Weaver

The Seasons

Springtime is the new beginning
Earth awakened, softly growing,
Spring, to life, is new born babies
Mother rocks the cradle singing.

Summer comes with all her beauty
Sky of blue, the sun is high,
Likened to, of happy children
Free to run and free to fly.

Autumn comes in warmth and splendour
Time to reap what we have sown,
Men and women, in their prime now
Eager hope in heart and home.

Winter brings the aging season
Clouds of grey and snow-capped trees,
White-haired people are reclining
Older, wiser, living, dying.

All the world is at our feet
And blessings are too many to be counted,
Life, is as the seasons come and go
And harvest is, what we have done about it.

Evelyn M. Bristow

A Poet Is King

In a world of many nations, a poet is King.
For whether male or female one mind is just the thing,
To feed the minds of others and inspire the common goal,
That engenders social work to create one global whole.

Computers cannot do this, nor can the nations' crews,
Like the Clintons or the Yeltsins we see in the news
For such people are not thinkers to plan a universe
They may lack the inspiration to write a single verse!

Here we need a proper poet who will set all minds on fire
Not by using part-world symbols but by making us entire!
That is the secret of the ages which I reveal for all,
The entire global population who this book may enthral.

The time has come for vision of a global social scene,
Not tawdry stuff of empires that jungle life has seen.
Where those fooled by Hitlers whose ideas led to wars
As we have seen in Bosnia and its many war-made scars.

Cosmic Comrades, please believe me, we can see if we try,
A better world around us before we're doomed to die,
We are the heirs of all millennia that have gone before,
And the next one can be special through electronic lore.

Edward Graham Macfarlane

"Significance of a House"

My memory is fading, I am getting old.
Each year it becomes harder for me to remember your hold.

Through the time I often sift
To arrive at that date.
But factors have changed with my old age.

But the thing I remember without any fear,
Is the love I held for one so dear.

Now you're departed,
You've left me alone.
In a big empty house
That was our home.

It costs too much to heat, and the repairs,
Well! I simply can't meet.

But to leave it dear would be my shame.
You see . . .
I can't quite give up the palace of mine.
With the windows that rattle and damp rotten base,
It keeps me alive as your memory is this place.

Emma Reeves

Innocent Eyes

As the clock strikes twelve another year's gone, now I fear for
your future my innocent one.

So how can I protect those innocent eyes from the hatred and
violence in this world I despise.

You had no choice when you were conceived, believe me my
baby, I never believed this world that's now yours would turn out
so bad, run by murderers or men money mad.

The T.V. screen above your head beams out pictures of wounded
and dead. Pictures of wars in far away places, pictures of horror
on children's faces. Ready for death deprived of life, never a
mother, never a wife.

Your climate's warmer than your Daddy's one, but you're not
allowed to go in the sun. How do you tell your innocent child,
the generation before killed all that was wild, just to make money
for the privileged few and our ignorance cost you your ozone too.

So what will become of your sweet smiling face, my beautiful darling
don't stop just in case. Like mine you will find it never comes
back. It's hard baby when it doesn't come back.

Forgive us my princess, for what we have done. It hurts so much
baby to think you're the one to inherit this earth that a few have
stripped bare, but God's chosen you, you must start to repair.

So go now my princess, put on your crown, save this world from
falling down.

Danny O'Neill

Welcome Spring

Canter in brave season of new birth;
Draw tinge of green from torpid Mother Earth;
Dismiss the sullen spirit, clinging cold;
Re-kindle hope in every troubled soul;
Bring warm assurance of much brighter days,
When evening sunset issues golden rays.

Bold witness to insipid scene, laid waste,
Inspire, enliven every morbid place;
Fend off sad Winter's last vain thrust
Of biting frost and snowy gust,
That stiffened joints may gladly give consent
To rambling yens, for too long tightly pent.

O bubbling, vibrant Spring, so gay,
To new-sown seed and flower and blade,
Grant new release from weary ways,
Fresh vision on the routine days;
Let tree-top songs cascade as rain;
Rouse dormant Earth with loud alluring strains.

John E. Wilson

Dreaming

I am relaxing in the park
Enjoying the singing of a lark
It is so peaceful sitting here
Released from any stress or fear

The pond is but a stroll away
Where swans abound throughout the day
Majestic midst the ducks and geese
Whose quacks and gaggles never cease

I take the time to get afloat
And cast off in a little boat
Squirrels run up and down the trees
And bee sounds murmur on the breeze

Across the pond I see a goat
He really has a shaggy coat
I gaze on myriad wayside flowers
I fain would linger here for hours

Rising within me sharp and keen
Compelling urge to paint this scene
To capture for posterity
These things which captivated me

Christine Russell

Parting

Losing those you love leaves you desolate and alone
Feelings of sadness mingle with despair
People who love you offer their support and show they care

Nothing helps through the early days - memories are like
knives through your heart
Birthdays, Christmases - dates of importance serve as
reminders from the start

Only time heals the pain of memories that once hurt
Making them easier to bear
Easing the burden, the desolation and loss that placed you there

Janice Tweddle

Memories Held

Huge melon moon riding high
Etched against the evening sky
Heavy smell of fires and cooking pots
Of rubbish uncollected, left to rot
The desert with its swirling dust
Muted golds and browns, greys and rust
How gladly all this I'd exchange
For the cooling touch of rain
The cold east wind upon my face
See curd topped waves as they race
To shed their spume upon the beach
Such things are now beyond my reach
Like the setting sun taking its time
To paint sea and sky, line by line
In shades of blues, greens and softest gold
Now just memories I'll ever hold
For where I am sudden night will fall
Enclosing in its sable pall
All but a camel train passing by
Cut out figures against the darkling sky.

Diana Formby

Untitled

Cuckoo, Cuckoo - your lonesome song
Echoes through the twilight zone.
Your long lost sound floods my mind,
of childhood days and freedom.
They say you lodge in another's dwell,
Survival! - chants your haunting tune.

Ah! Cuckoo, cuckoo now hear my song,
I also live in a twilight zone.
Where memories dear can pain the mind.
Hark! Childhood days and freedom.
But unlike you, in a prison dwell,
Survival too my haunting tune.

Barry Murray

A Chance Encounter

A chance encounter dictated our paths should cross
Fate - an unexplained phenomenon
A mutual attraction was immediately evident
Fate or a chemical reaction

Each dawning day you were my life's sole purpose
My love for you blossomed from within
Instinct or intuition - you were the strong silent type
Little did I suspect your love grew deeper
For one other than I.

The betrayal cut deep leaving an invisible wound
Will this wound ever heal, heal with no scar?
I play the game - the pretending game
I wear my mask to hide the pain
Revenge is not sweet, fate dictated the way
Explain to me why, oh explain to me why
A chance encounter dictated our paths should cross.

Bernadette McGoldrick

My Dream

I saw two people, happy friends, and as the time passed by,
Fate decreed reluctantly that one of them should die . . .
The other one lived many years, remembering the friend,
But, one day fate decided that another life should end . . .
The two, who had in life and love by death been separated,
Now rested in their peacefulness, souls re-incarnated.
For, from their ashes on the ground, there sprouted two small trees.
The soul of each departed friend created one of these.
And as they grew so tall and green, everybody saw . . .
That they forever were entwined, and so would part no more.
This was my dream, so vivid, I shall forget it never . . .
Divided in this life by Death -
United by Death . . . forever.

Carol Priest

Father of Mine

You gave me life with my mother too
Father of mine, wish I could give life to you
Taken suddenly, I don't know what to do
I never knew I'd have to live without you
It haunts me that I didn't get to say goodbye
And tell you that I loved you, I keep asking why
I didn't realize you were so ill and you needed me
Never again will we be a whole family
I can't take it in, that you're gone forever
I can't hold you again, never means never
When your heart stopped beating, more than one heart broke
We're all feeling numb, wondering how to cope
All my memories are good but they're not enough
How could you be so frail? When you looked so tough
You helped so many, I wish you could help me now
To live again, without any pain, because I don't know how.

James Parker

The Sisters

Nursed within the womb with her,
Fed by the same mother's milk,
Through all the years of early youth
I planned with her and dreamt with her,
Only to find on growing up
We spoke a different tongue.

Like sparkling froth on waves that break
And dance in joy across the seas,
She is scarce conscious of the deep
Strong currents that sway our being,
Ever she skims across the shining surfaces of life
In happy thoughtlessness!

How can I know her then who live
Within the dark uneasy depths
Where numberless sensations press
Like the heavy waters of the ocean bed
Upon my pliant consciousness
Until I cry in pain!

Anne Coghill

Unbound Regrets and Memory

In its many shades the canvas of life stretches far,
Even beyond the grave though in mystery veiled.
It is brushed in the lights of the sun and fading star,
And looms gigantic as a cross where Man is nailed.
Its wars depart with times of peace through choice.

In tones for all, subtle hates do merge with loving hues,
And ships of hope are set on ebb and flow obscure,
But they all contain God's greatest prize in scattered clues,
And climb in tune to meet the whole of love so pure.
I must respond and play my part content.

To these cloistered hills I came to learn the mystery,
And found within the rapture of their quiet peace
The awesome thrill of an unpinioned memory,
Yet I weep not with the joy of its sweet release,
But from the sorrow of my forgetting.

Bert Garradley

It Has to Be Said

Black and white that's me and you
Every colour tint and hue
Catholic Moslem Seik and Jew
Buddhist Baptist and Hindu
Human beings you and me
All we want is to be free
To be together is the key
And live in perfect harmony
Let's be honest we all care
We won't admit it we don't dare
All too proud we may lose face
If we agree to just one race
Just one God just one law
Who if not us are these rules for
Persecution there's no excuse
Victimization or racial abuse
Stop it now it has to be said
Put it right or we'll be dead
Like the dodo become extinct
With no more chains in the genetic link

Gary Margetts

Eyes of Innocence

The eyes of the child are innocent eyes,
Every new day is full of surprise,
For every little girl and boy,
Always finding new things to enjoy.

Now when they become a little older,
Activities are quite a lot bolder.
But what they really wish to know,
Is just how far that they can go.

They test your patience, try you out,
Find what discipline's all about.
Then as they go through their school years,
Those innocent eyes are often in tears.

So much to do and so much to learn,
Every gold star they work hard to earn.
And when they think their learning is done,
They discover it's only just begun.

Eileen A. Morris

Life Is So Precious

Life is so precious, it's there for the taking,
Every smile, every tear, every moment on waking.

Treading each path, each moment, each day,
Sometimes the straight path is too much, and we stray.

These things aren't done to cause hurt, or to cause pain,
Most are mistakes, and are not done again.

The walk becomes easier, with someone in sight,
Life can be hard, so stand up and fight.

Take it in both hands, don't wish life away,
Tomorrow is better, make it a new day.

Jane Bradley

The Last Day

My mind had stopped;
everything became small,
I fell on the floor and climbed the wall . . .
outside the window faces laughed
and there I cowered and crawled
on the mat.

Wings grew to replace my arms
strange music weaved a magical charm
the day grew fearfully black and
there I lay, shivering in the dark . . .

Flashes of flame cut through the sky,
I heard screams - as many died . . .
whispers, I heard - saying fly! fly!!!
Out through the window I soared
to the sky.

The earth below was a cauldron of fire
the great ball became a funeral pyre;
up onwards I climbed - into a red hue,
up and into a land of bright blue . . .

    James E. Stephens

Our Precinct

Gone, the groan of bus and stink of lorry;
Exhaust of cars and no more need to worry.
We now can sit and stare and even think;
God's in His heaven and we're in our precinct.

They've covered up the tarmac of the road;
Re-laid the surface in a herringbone mode
And even built raised flower beds around,
Where scents of petunia and pelargonium abound.

When it rains, there is no need to frown,
We are covered in and all around,
The people sit at tables by 'The Bird in Hand'
And others buy their snacks from the 'Hot Dog' man.

Seats have been placed in grottos by the flowers,
Where lovers meet and chat in fragrant bowers,
They watch the shoppers hurry on their way,
Or smile at them and pass the time of day.

Grateful folk drop coins in the busker's cap;
A tramp comes by to rest or even nap;
The 'Hot Dog' man kindly offers him a drink;
God's all around us now in our precinct.

    Joseph Kynoch

Harvest

Swelling seas of golden grain, ripened, warmed by sun and rain
Flaxen fields all white and ready, patient horses, silent, steady,
Wide blue sky and larks high-singing, bells for Sunday worship
ringing; heaving horses in the traces - sun browned arms and
sweat-grimed faces; aching backs and blistered hands, fields like
rolling golden sands, hot sun
beating - thirsts to slake, black-brown earth like rich plum cake.
Brass bright morn till dew drenched night, groaning leather,
wheel shafts bright - Straining horses, sweating men, 'round the
field and back again: Snatch a hasty sandwich lunch, harness up
the Suffolk bunch Golden cartloads come and go - barns are filled
to overflow.
Wheels a whirring, voices calling, work from morn till dusk is
falling - Morning stretches into noon, evening brings a golden
moon. Stars shine out above the hill: Only one more cart to fill,
Darkness falls and home to bed - aching limbs and throbbing
head, Stumble up the narrow stair, kneel in brief and drowsy
prayer, coarse clean sheets and scent of musk, feather pillows,
kindly dusk Barn owl's cry and farm dogs bark - small farm
sounds steal through the dark. Sleep contented, dream less deep,
watch all God's good angels keep. Mind that's free from fear or
sorrow, may it be a fair tomorrow - Golden day and peaceful
night - this the harvester's delight.

    Dorothy R. Harvie

Nostalgia

Nostalgia is the name we choose to think
Explains a need to bow the knee in fake
Obeisance to a place once known; to drink
From well long dry or view some emptied lake
Glimpsed sparkling once beneath the sort of moon
Sat on a velvet cloth magicians wave,
A coaxed and floating yellow fat balloon
To dance like jokey-jerky torch of grave
Yet playful, preposterous usherette
And light the narrow aisle that leads to where
We fled from, never caring that Regret
Should gnaw and tug us to her littered lair
Of dreams and fancies. Raking smooth the track
To 'once was,' 'might have been,' we stumble back.

    Brian Harris

To Have and to Hold

I saw her in a crowded room, my girl
Eyes of blue and hair a-curl
I found myself beside her chair
I knew not how I got just there
I had neither gold nor pearl
Just my heart to give this girl
Neither mountains or rivers wide
could never keep me from her side
One day she wore my band of gold
Her love was mine to have and hold
If one day I have to go, I'll leave with her my heart to keep
Love never dies, it only sleeps.
I'll be with her in her old age dreams
For she has known what real love means
And somewhere in the mists of time
I'll find her and she I once again be mine
Nothing good is ever free, what will be, will be

    Alice Nicholls

Two Men Dead in a Pit

Two men dead in a pit
Faces decaying
Bodies rotting
Face down in the mud
As if running from the knowledge
That death is behind them.

Two men dead in a pit
Last thoughts of wife and child
Sitting on his mother's knee
Wondering if Daddy is coming home
But Daddy is coming home
In a letter of deepest regrets.

Two men dead in a pit
Amongst wire, leaves and death
The crimson blood seeps into the earth
The maggots feast on the tasty flesh
Why have war when there have been
Twenty-five million men dead in a pit.

    Amanda Conway

Why

How about the singing birds, are they happy?
For we too can sing.
But is this singing like the waves that sing forever,
No more than a creaking door,
Or a noise to mask the world's great silent loneliness?
Dawn and dusk is when the world is lonely,
And birds sing out their song so sweet so very sweet yet
somehow sad;
Like a train roaring sadly through the night,
Laden with silent people why and where,
And the one vast question never answered
Why the singing, why the sadness, why the emptiness - Why?

    Elspeth Percival

Feathers

There's a pheasant in the garden . . . what a handsome bird!
    Far from the maddening pop-guns we've just heard.
Crows and magpies keep clear as he struts around,
    Starlings scatter, wagtails and doves give ground.

Hunger and caution struggle as he nears the house;
    Head cocked to scan the grass for seeds to browse;
Then, frightened by some imagined noise . . . or real,
    Runs before his feather-tail away from his meal!

Last year all his family . . . wife and six young ones . . .
    Took shelter in our haven from the noisy guns.
Raised in peace, happy and plump and feathery-sleek
    'Til the "Glorious Twelfth" let loose the death reek.

I wonder how many survived the shots?
    How many tragic pairs ended in pots?
Now it's the "sporting" family-raising truce
    To build up numbers before the guns let loose.

You're welcome to stay . . . have your young ones in peace
    Live safely until the avid guns' release;
Display your feathers' hues . . . strut proudly your beat;
    Live long . . . wisely evade being hunter's meat!

George Prince

The Sea in Winter

The vagaries and moods of the sea,
Fascinate and give pleasure to me,
Mountainous and raging waves,
Swirling in hidden and dangerous caves.

Pounding and breaking on the shore,
They encroach with a thunderous roar,
Forwards and backwards the reluctant shingle,
Sounds that make my spine tingle.

The pale, golden and wintry sun,
A cauldron of fire has begun,
The full moon scudding across the sky,
Shines mysteriously, I can hear the sea sigh.

Comes the morning and all is calm,
Surely a gentle sea cannot do harm,
I'm not misled by the siren of the sea,
Who imposes her will by mighty decree.

It's hard to imagine the seductive sounds,
Her wiliness knows no bounds,
Lapping gently on a deserted beach,
Trying hard my feet to reach.

Irene Greenall

Take It Like It Is

Love and hate capture erotic pleasures
Enhancing belief, terror and mystery
The necessities crumble around life
With visions of dark cruel dreams

The tide and tombs of long gone masters
Relinquishments to wild sleeps of the past
Tossing and turning, tossing and turning
The illusions of time protruding

Prisoners of fools, shadows of evolution
Revelations to the seeking souls
The incantation of inamorata incalculable
A materialist momentarily alive

The rye smile from fantasy returns
Words now working poetically
Like the experts of art tricked you all
Secrets of realism with ease and ecology

The final lines of simplicity iconoclasm
Perhaps the answer to riddles within
Teachings of hypocrisy, satire?
Make me rich or understand me

Ian Lyon

The Stormy Sea

The stormy sea, like a raging battle
Fighting with the cliffs
Coming with force, like a herd of cattle,
Giving off a salty whiff.

Crashing together, the two waves meet,
Spitting a salty spray
Chalk cliffs crumble, the battle is complete,
The sea has won again

The ships are lost, on a stormy sea
As the fog is getting lower
I am the king, the sea belongs to me,
None shall have my power

Angela Bourne

Saint Valentine's Day

Pale pink cottage perched on the brim of the hill,
Fine powdery flakes alighting in the February chill,
Tawny toast stamped with "Good Morning!"
Trembling heart beats in warning!
Tea and scones in the Devonshire harbour,
Arm in arm in resplendent ardour.
Deserted Abbey in snowy splendour,
To joy and magic we surrender.

Tide of hope and brimming affection,
Gush and flow in our direction.
There is no beginning.
There is no end.
Forever linked.
Always the first,
Still the first,
The craved for friend.
Separately special; totally entwined,
Wish us joy and may fate be kind!

Diana M. Platt

2:30 AM

More snow
Flakes tumble from the city sky
driven from its dull orange glow to earth
I pray they cover the deep tracks gouged
by events of the day

Above and around me - faint voices murmur
But nothing can distract me from
the silent swirling outside my window
and your fitful sleep

I ache to wake you but fear
what you might say
- yet what is left half said
Keeps my eyes from closing
watching the night sky's burden
mend the soiled ground.

When you wake, a grey light will have come
and tracks will be covered in a virgin day.
But now I will wait, and watch
this quiet snow's fall.

Ailsa Templeton

The World Today

It is so beautiful how in life we form,
From a tiny egg and sperm a child is born,
Each day we see, hear and learn,
But as we grow older it starts to turn,
Of course it's the Era we live in today,
Lack of work causing crime, oh let us pray,
The wide spread of drugs across the U. K,
And law and order will never win their day,
People of today wish they could go back to before,
When they could leave their house without locking their door,
But we all know that, that will never be
God only knows what it'll be like in the next century.

Jackie Berry

Early Morning from a Hospital Window

London's landmarks; silhouettes of a silvery skyline.
Frustrated tower blocks reach for beckoning clouds.
A blanket of billowing mist descends on the silent stillness.
Shining, white roofs creep cautiously above each other,
Forming printed patterns of a jagged jigsaw.
Icicles hang from windows; beautiful, threatening, magical,
piercing,
Sudden flaps of a pigeon's wings break the snowy silence;
And another day has begun without me . . .

Joanna Chapman

'Dust'

On darkest deep a light was shone
For mortal man to dream upon,
And still today he cannot picture,
What came before holy scripture.

A cosmic egg, in distant space.
A waiting void, a starting place,
And then it hatched and flung its yolk,
A searing nebulae across time itself to soak.

That stellar dust so filled the ether,
The force of light, our galactic keeper.
So many globes, elliptic spinning,
Locked together, gravity winning.

This speed of light that makes us sift
Across the colours of Doppler's shift,
To attempt to measure suns afar,
To only touch the closest star!

No word invented can describe
The magnitude that does imbibe,
of this giant, that surrounds our trust,
A massive space composed of dust.

George Colley

Loving Memories

Some memories fade of those most loved and lost,
For nature in its wisdom knows that grief and pain
Should not endure forever,
Sufficient though it seemed in death's sad, early claim.

The tears we cry were cried to no avail
Except to calm our fear and ease our aching hearts
For things we knew could never be again
But memories fade and nature leads to happiness, not pain.

'Tis good that nature made it so
And those we loved, who loved us in their turn
Do surely not begrudge a fresh-found love
Taking what once was theirs alone
And adding to the lingering joys in memories tome.

Edgar Wall

Parents

Go to bed now, time to get up,
Don't spill your dinner and watch that cup,
Now stop being silly and get in the bath,
Look a car's coming, get on the path,
If you don't put the phone down I'll make you
share the bill,
And don't say I won't 'cause you know I will,
Your Gran's coming down so get out of the house,
And if all your mates are out today
Sit quiet as a mouse,
The baby's in the playpen so don't let her out.
You've got piles of homework so don't mess about,
You'll often here these phrases when you're just small,
But who needs parents they're stupid after all,
They're bossy boots and show-offs, they'll tell
you what to do.
And if you understand them I'd love to hear from you,
But they're good for all the soppy stuff
When you need someone to hold.
But nobody really needs parents just you be told.

Arianne Graven

Untitled

And the Angel feels sad,
for she now knows,
her cobweb wings are beat'n,
ready to blow,
to dust, to dust.

And the Reaper carves lines on
the face of the elderly
for; to keep time.
from ashes to ashes,
when death next awakes.

And the Angel feels sad, And the Reaper carves lines on,
for she now knows the face of the elderly,
her cobweb wings are beat'n for; to keep time.
ready to blow from ashes to ashes,
to dust to dust, when death next awakes.

Hayden Hyams

Precious Moments

Many years of waiting,
For this moment I had yearned.
My heart skipped a beat,
Why were they so concerned.
I only had a glimpse of you,
I picked Carl to be your name.
A few days later you had passed away.
In God's keeping you had gone.
It broke my heart when I heard those words,
I could not weep, or speak, I felt numb.
The pain and anguish I still feel.
When a newborn baby I do see.
Life goes on, you hide your pain.
You laugh and smile,
Then go home and cry alone.
Those precious moments when I saw you.
Will remain with me, my whole life through.

Doreen Fraser

Old Jock

Don't stop, don't look, it's best you see.
For truly only the blind can be,
oblivious to the plight of Jock.
The poor old lad's had quite a knock.

His Missus past away last year.
The one and only he held dear.
And little Jock's still wondering how?
He's nothing left to live for now.

Soon Jock had sadly taken to drink.
This way he said, you cannot think,
of golden years and tender love.
Now gone forever, like a fleeting dove.

Don't look at Jock, or the urine spilt,
on his trousers now, that seem to wilt.
Or the light gone from his bright blue eye.
For there, but for the grace of God, go I.

Frank Bennett

Santa Claus

Santa Claus is coming,
he leaves his engine running,
he goes to the bank,
then the petrol tank,
It began to snow,
blow! Blow! Blow!
Out pops Santa dressed in red,
now he wishes he was back in bed,
he puts petrol in his sleigh,
gives Rudolph some hay,
hoping everyone has a happy Christmas Day!

Jennifer Barr

Colour Blind

Have you ever had a lesson
From a little boy so small?
I had one the other day
As I watched the kids play ball.

The park was full of children
But all was not quite right
One child different from the rest
His skin was black not white.

I asked my son about this boy
He said "I know who you mean,
He was different from the rest of us
His shirt was red not green".

Len Jones

Rose

My mother rose, ninety-six years old,
forgets the stories she once told,
stories of old times, hardships and trials,
now locked away in her memory's files.

Stories of her childhood days, no food on the table,
no fire to blaze.
Sent into service at fourteen years old,
her brothers down the pit, so it was told,

A young girl still, Rose went to be married,
walked to the church, no funds for a carriage.
Heartbreak at losing son Billy, only two years old,
he died from pneumonia,
she thought was a cold.

At forty-five with her youngest just ten,
Rose could not believe she was pregnant again,
but early one bright September morn,
her last child a baby girl was born.

A child who learned stories from her mother's knee,
now tells them to you, for that child was me.

Josephine Turner

Untitled

My love for you will always be
From the beginning of time to its end
I long to be your everything
Your lover, your best friend
When there was no-one else who cared
If you should live or if you died
'Twas me who heard your broken sobs
Who held you while you cried

Gradually you turned away
From the memory of me
You didn't need me any more
I had to set you free
You made a vow to someone else
"She's everything" you say
Why, then, can't you set me free
And let me go my way

Anne Carr

Friendship

Friendship is true,
Friendship is kind,
No conditions
Rules or regulations,
No secrets.
Should have an understanding.
A gentle sense of ease
of sharing passions, pain,
Or just a cup of tea.
Should brighten many a dreary day,
Warm the sometime aching heart.
Asks for nothing, but expecting nothing
Reaps a golden harvest.

Joy Westcott

Your Life, Your World

People on the streets running scared
Frightened of what they've seen or heard
Everyone running, to where I don't know
Perhaps they're following the rest of the show.

Everyone watching where someone else goes
Watching from behind windows at what's bothering their nose
Muggings in the street, but when asked, "did you see?"
The answers the same, "Oh No Not Me!"

Babies being born one a minute
They don't ask to be here, they're just put in it
It's up to you to make it right
Stand up for yourself, it's your fight

Don't turn you back on your fellow man
Help him out, do the best you can
Stand up in the world and don't be scared
Get yourself seen, get yourself heard.

This is your world so open your eyes
Stand up for your rights, don't look to the skies
Live your life, do what you want to do
Be yourself, Just be you.

Arthur Crilly

The Last Supper

We walk along that so familiar way; the towpath by the river,
Full of loves and lives, now forever gone.
I wonder at our change, at our decay.
Reflected in those waters, deep and cold, I see the faces of
    two strangers,
Feasting in each other's bliss so fully that none can touch
    their lives.

But as in old Verona lovers lived and died, so died our love.
We walk a towpath now not strewn with flowers or blessed
    with golden sun,
But cast with shadows, deepest black,
And littered with the dross that floated up within our lover's
    minds.

When a moment spent far from your side,
Seemed as a hundred years - and many moments pass,
Then all consuming passion, once in love, burned out in
    gnawing doubts,
And hate, not love, ate out our hearts and souls.

The Spring and Summer of our love gives way to Autumn's
    doubt, .
And as the leaves give up their lives, to save their mother tree,
So we must damn our love and die a death in life,
Which scars our souls and then corrupts our sight.

Out faces in the water some winters more must see,
And human flesh consume before they die or find some place
    of peace.

From each new death our hearts must take some succour,
And feast on some new soul 'til The Last Supper.

Diane L. Brown

I Kissed the Rose

I kissed the rose - so warm and tender,
from the heart, to the heart,
to reach that never-ending part
of my loved one's life;

I kissed the kiss - that tells one that apart from
them, there can but no one be,
for ever yours, truly, for all to see;

I loved the love - so intimate, so close
that boundaries are endless,
I've found the secret of an almost hidden source,
discovered love's embrace;

The fragrance is so sweet and delicate,
as the bloom is rich and full of promise too,
I know the word, the kiss, the love;
for I - have kissed the rose.

Derick Kane

Poem

I had a job at Karner
hanger factory it be
it's located at Alpine way.
E6. You see. I've been there
15 years or more.
Cleaning toilet and floors
been of sick for 4 weeks now
redundant letter come to me
saying that's the end for thee
I am very upset you see
as no one cares for me.
So what am I going to do these days?
I take care of my husband in many ways.

Eileen Donnelly

Laura

I love you Laura, what more can I say?
From the moment I saw you my heart went astray.
From your ivory skin to your beautiful smile,
Your uplifted nose and your eyes that beguile.
Your body in motion, your scented dark hair,
Your mouth like a Rosebud breathing the air.

I've waited so long for you to be here,
Now that you are I have to be near
To look, and to listen for you I would die,
The sweetest sound - the sound of your cry.
Your hands clasp mine in firm embrace
A beautiful member of the human race.

Alas, I can't stay with you all the time.
My life runs on a different line.
The moments we meet along the way,
I'll keep in my memory fresh each day.
You're the purest creature I'll ever behold.
So small and vulnerable just two months old.

Ann L. Blampied

Boating

It is summer in England and we are boating the Thames,
From the Trout Inn at Tadpole to where boating ends,
At a small town called Lechlade, with its riverside park,
Where children play merrily, and picnic till dark.

In a narrow boat called Tarka, our pace is quite slow,
But who wants to hurry, there's no need you know,
To have us a meal, we moor up at midday,
Ducks come a-calling, they won't stay away.

We pass through the locks with their gardens of flowers,
How neat are the lock sides, it must take some hours,
By lock keepers in uniforms, with their welcoming smiles,
It's pleasant to see them, when you've travelled for miles.

Church spire in the distance, could that be journeys end,
Or just turn around point, and we go back again,
To the peace and the quiet, of the country we like,
That's why boating in England is such a delight.

Alan Winston Curtis

Silent Love

That warm, strong hand encasing mine,
Gently caressing every inch, every sinew,
Those twinkling eyes with just a hint of mischief,
Those special eyes, glinting like the morning dew,
Gaze on me knowingly, saying everything,
Just one glance is all I need to see,
To know I'm safe in your arms
As they firmly but gently encircle me
No words pass between us two
No not one word, not one utterance
For no words could say more
Than we two can say with just a glance
Those warm, sensuous, pliant lips,
Covering mine so knowingly,
Safely encircled in your loving caress
Safely ensconced for eternity.

Anne Williams

Pre-Packed Danger

Why is it that everything we buy
From socks and shirt to coloured tie,
From screws and hooks to white elastic,
Must be packed in rock hard plastic?

Plastic now plays a large part in our lives.
When seeking presents for friends and wives,
The items we purchase their glories reveal
In a transparent pack with unbreakable seal.

Look all around and what do you see?
If it isn't the one then it's P.V.C.
From door handles, hooks and rainwater chutes
To luminous 'macs' and ankle length boots.

This material supplies our everyday needs,
But beware of complacency, listen! take heed!
It has hidden powers which man does not know
And is gathering strength for one fatal blow.

When it makes its attack on our civilization
We shall one day awake to the realization
That we are in packets, plastic festooned.
Captured forever, cocooned and marooned.

James Meadows

Tomorrow's Dreams

Smiles galore, happiness in abundance,
God's earth, pure and free,
could this be real,
or just Tomorrow's Dream?

Children's angelic faces,
smiling and beaming bright,
no more fears for them,
if Tomorrow's Dream is right!

The sky, sun, moon and stars,
A gift to us all from God,
these are precious gifts to hold on to,
if Tomorrow's Dreams come true.

The birds, the trees, the flowers
the rivers and the streams,
these will all stay with us,
if we help along Tomorrow's Dreams.

If we could put right
every wrong along life's way,
there would be no need for Tomorrow's Dreams
because we would have them Today!

Doreen Haynes

Tower of Love

The lovers built a tower of love
From years of bliss and honeyed words,
A gossamer tale of lovers fair
Each one the mortar for the bricks
Of lovers' castles in the air.

Both lovers spun a web of gold
Of glances feelings and sweet joy,
The spidered threads a picture wove
Of dreams and vistas of a future life
That shone a spring-like morning mauve.

And up the heavens rose their prayers
As golden arrows killing shadows there,
Nor tainted ever by a deathlike sound!
But flying breathless in a cloudless bliss
Above the hills and meadows ageless bound.
Our lovers painted on the silken skies
A myriad stars that soon were light
In star-filled memory of a golden life,
The longing for another silvered one
Before death's shadow parted them in strife.

Desmond F. Hussey

The Heartbreaker

He's like a whirlwind,
He picks you up, stirs your feelings,
Makes your life like a heaven
Then sends you flying, shattered and hurt.

Once, you were part of his whirlwind,
Now, you are just another broken heart
Left lying where you were thrown
Trying to pick up the pieces to mend your broken heart.

Jenny Harvey

Air Raid Poem

The sirens are ringing around the town,
German planes are flying around,
In darkest hours the bombs fall down,
Devastation is all around.
People running with fear and fright,
All because of this terrible night.
Buildings and vehicles are all a-blaze,
The town has turned into a giant maze.
Fire shoots up into the air,
Causing people to stand and stare,
Inside the shelter people are sad,
But under it all they're really mad.
The German planes have flown away,
For this is the start of another day.
Bodies laying beneath the rubble,
Which causes havoc and lots of trouble.
People searching for family and friends,
Hope the war will come to an end.

James Lukic

Remember

From a picture on the wall
Gipsy brown, the wide eyes shine
Look down at me through the years
Blonde her hair and face so soft, features so rounded
Petal soft skin and peaches smooth
Gentle smile shows up the dimples by slimline lips
Where has she gone this little girl?
In my mind's eye I see her still, playing
In the garden where the willow grew
Shadow of a memory past
I see a living image that looks so real
She runs to greet me with arms outstretched
But, before the touch, she stops and turns
Backward steps to toys awaiting, red car standing by
In the garden where the willow grew
Memory fades, panic, fear instead, a treasure lost
A love has gone, lost forever
In the garden where the willow grew

John E. Paul

The Milkman

The milkmen of the dairy are very special men
From very early morning they collect all the milk they can,
For the old, the young, and the in-between.
And sometimes are very rarely seen.
So please help your friendly milkman, to stay out on his round
For everyone he loses another one is found
The price increase is a scandal
For all our milkmen to have to handle
They are all out together to fight this
And with the milkman's wish
They will get there in the end
Because they are the people's best friend
Out in the dark they go
In wind, rain and snow
You never hear them complain
No matter if in pain
They just plod on and on
Until the job is done
So please take the plunge and spend
A few extra pence with your friend the Milkman.

Barbara Gillian Berry

"S'no Dream"

Purple trees and flowers that scream,
Grow in wild profusion.
Along a road
I call a dream
In a country called confusion.

But I believe
And try to conceive,
Of a land where all this happens.
For isn't it true,
That snow is blue
When you're all reduced to atoms.

Colin Simpson

Let the Children Be Heard

We should listen and learn from our children.
Give them a chance to say what's on their minds,
They see the world so very differently.
Not hiding what they're feeling deep inside.
They never question about what they're thinking.
They always tell the truth not knowing how to lie.
Each and every individual all have their different thoughts.
When they're young and so very shy.

Some are so very pleasant and can also be very kind.
Some are so very naughty with evil racing through their minds.
No child is exactly the same.
Which you will come to realize.
When you really get to know them.
Then it will come as a big surprise.

Children are so different just like the stars shinning in the sky.
They all have their own personality.
Which makes them all one of a kind.
Try and understand them and one day you will find
That there's good in each and every one of them.
It just takes someone to look into their minds.

Jennifer Jones

Aspect of Life

A thought, a word and a good deed
Given with love to those in need
Time to gaze and appreciate
Nature's wonders before too late
Life is short, so much ahead
Messages to be given, things to be said
People think love of God doesn't matter
When tragedy strikes, their lives to shatter
They pray so hard and say, why me?
If only they had eyes to see
'Tis then that true love proves its worth
Most valuable trait to possess on earth
So make God a part of everyday life
A presence to ease all trouble and strife
And finally such peace of mind
That benefits all of mankind

Joan Brooks

My Star

Watching, waiting, standing, sitting.
Glasses poised to see my star.
The wind strikes up a chord,
Clouds unfurl to reveal a chorus of starlets,
Not yet my star.
The wind calms. The clouds close in.
When will my star appear?

Watching, waiting, standing, sitting,
Again the wind strikes up a chord.
The clouds unfurl. There is a storm!
At last my star appears in a shimmering aura
Giving a performance radiant and bright,
I was so thrilled that night.

All too soon the storm subsides,
The wind calms. The clouds close in.
When will I see my star again?

Amanda J. Dawber

God's Tailored Pie

With the ashes, and breath, the liquid, and heat in the sky
God baketh us all, into this great almighty pie
As the tools of his great mind, are but ruled by the weather
He says unto us all, "Please Come Hither"

He rotates this pie, with His great big hands
And tells us "We Must Share, This Crust Called Our Land"
He lets the heat bake us, until we are brown
Then His breath blows, to cool us all down

The Master of time, then smiles and frowns
Shall I eat this pie up? Or shall I put it back down?
Because He is so very kind in mind
We are placed back onto His wheel in time

The speed is so fast, we are sent into flight
Our flight is but a circle, or any shape of his might
And our never ending, is always in God's sight

Once more, the Great Tailor of our land
Puts us back on His potters stand
He says "I will rebake you, with my great big hands
As you are all worthy, of tasting our crusty land"

Catherine Evans James-Thompson

Who Am I

Who am I if I am: -

A bright blue sky on a cool crisp dawn, the sun high above glows
like golden corn. Teams of tadpoles in a babbling brook, a
weeping willow bent down to look. Baa lambs leaping and
bounding with glee, like a child with a new toy playing happily.

Who am I if I am: -

Daffodils dancing in the mid-day breeze, whilst blossoming
branches cover every tree. Scarecrow standing to attention in the
field, like a Palace guard on morning drill. Birds pairing off and
busily building their nest, sparrows, swallows and the robin-red-
breast.

Who am I if I am?

Bargain hunters shopping at the new season's sale, fighting and
foraging through rail after rail. The time to re-decorate and clean
out every room, "look at all that dust! quick where is that
broom?" Cleaning cars, washing windows, oh so much to do;
out with the old and in with the new!

Who am I if I am all the above?
I know I am something that most people love.

Julie Bradley

Angels Fly Because . . .

Hey you! To whom this message rings
Grab a hold of my wing
Rest yourself in the crease of its fold

Feeling the desperation of deepest blue
And that your heart wide open happiness belongs to you
Angels fly because they take themselves lightly

We understand nothing but contemplate all
Of what it would be like to return back to peace
And try to stretch farther on our wide-eyed lease.

In emotional mist she breathes in fog
And breathes it out as garden flowers
Do bleeding angels sing when close to tears?
She needs the answer.

An angel rests between the lashes of a quarter moon
And among other things we see
That compassion is the silent sound.

Thrusting forward new light shadows
If on the ascendant her soul arises
And doesn't contradict what her essence extemporizes.

Elizabeth Holmes

Safely Gathered In

He sat in the chimney corner and dreamt of the days gone by;
He thought of the things that might have been,
And his eyes were scarcely dry.
He puffed on his old churchwarden,
And his heart grew strangely fond,
For he was alone and his family passed to the "Great Beyond".
In the silent, scented evening, with the roses 'round the door,
He turned to his youth, to firm friendship's goodly store.
He'd ploughed many a furrow, seen many an acre yield
Its harvest in mellow season. His hand, and the contract sealed.
The ridges he'd cut in his lifetime, ran straight to the horizon's goal,
Just one or two that wandered around the oak tree's bole.
'Twixt shaded copse and hedgerow, a furrow, just out of sight.
He'd struggled against hate and vile malice,
Defending the weak against might.
They found him there in the morning
As the sun filled the gloom with new light
In the little grey church; the lectern,
Shining great eagle (in flight)
Safe carried the precious burden - "My servant - in whom I delight!"

Geoffrey N. Nuttall

My Spiritual Awakening

This was I, Joyce, who took a fall from
grace, into a pit of turmoil and pain;
this pain I could hardly endure or sustain;
every which way I turned was to no avail
SAD! WEARY! PALE!
I would pray by day and by night, please dear
Lord, lift this dark veil and let me see Thy Light.
Days, weeks and years passed, but I would not
give up my fight - please dear Lord, answer this plight.
My own dear father said, 'Look to spirit';
yes, I did, my prayers were answered; they have
now surrounded me with a 'blue - healing - light.'
Now I clearly see this divine light, I know now
dear Lord, I'm ready to serve Thee; a spiritual
path I hope You will lay before me and teach
me Thy wondrous ways of spirit
so I may help others, who suffer like 'I,'
that spirit does come around and never let's you down;
they are not just in Heaven and Earth but all around.
Thank you, Lord, I was lost but now I am found.

Joyce Brown

April, Come What May

Dedicated to April Ashley, the parents of Steven Donovan,
the parents of the massacred children, and the family of the
massacred teacher of Dunblane, Scotland. (1996) I thank you.

"Hush, little one, do not fret, do not cry,
Mother will sing you a sweet lullaby.
These parched leaves will turn green some day;
Then it will be April, come what may,

The angry storm is here to alarm us,
The nation is in turmoil; it has caused such a fuss!
The circle of events will turn along the way;
Then it will be April, come what may.

We have only a few grains to sustain us,
Father is off to work in his only pair of shoes to catch the bus
A the end of the month it will be a well paid day
Then it will be April, come what may.

On awakening, little one, we shall see all the lovely things
    which we may buy;
Mother will throw you to the ceiling, your beautiful sky;
From these worn, protective arms you will be released to play;
Then it will be April, come what may.

This lovely picture palace, is it really ours to keep?
Father toiled for hours when we were both fast asleep.
The lovely April Showers did fall on us on that Harvest Day,
How grateful are we to April in this Sunny Month of May."

Margaret Andrews

Dreams of America

Ghosts born of Dodge City, and tumbleweed blown.
Great men of Mount Rushmore, long-carved into stone.
Deep forests of Walden, and Jefferson's plan;
Laws crafted, free-woven for dignified Man.
From Bull Run to Shiloh, the firm rebel's tread,
And tired Grant and Sherman account for the dead.
Backwoodsmen and trappers hew solitary lives,
Adept with the long blades, Jim Bowie's feared knives
The welded Sioux Nation defies Custer's stand,
And Wells Fargo crosses the broad Rio Grande!
Young freshmen of Princeton, The Raven's renown;
And Paul Revere's gallop through Lexington town.
Grass leaves of mown Summer, the wild Prairie Rose,
Long beach high-back breakers, Nevada capped snows.
Plantations, proud Boat-Queens, warm Florida's coast;
The Iron Horse, McKinley, and Washington Post.
Bright lights of Manhattan, and Emerson's voice;
Ganglands and Depression, yet land of free choice!
And Lindbergh's free 'Spirit' flies vast seas alone;
So dreams of a Nation are fired into stone!

Christopher Rothery

"The Other Side"

Dark shadows descend on thy body, thy soul;
Guilt from within;
I am what I am,
Neither human or immortal.
I'm crossing a path untold.
Voices piercing, calling, devouring at my soul.
Where am I?
What am I?
Am I alone?
Crimson insanity floods from my body.
I am gone . . .
But not alone.

Joanna • E • Moore
(London)

Untitled

In a world of opportunism
had I the spirit of optimism
to replace thoughts of pessimism

early man practised paganism
replaced by the worship of God in the form of judaism
christians introduced the rite of baptism
then the west developed catholicism and protestantism
the east believed in buddhism
the state developed doctrines of imperialism
capitalism communism and now federalism
art gave us impressionism cubism surrealism
expressionism and minimalism
but today the following is for computerism
could this be the beginning of technological suprematism
or will this finally reduce mankind to zombieism
perhaps this is a fantasy far removed from realism

Colleen & John McDermott

Cultured Land Inspired by Africa

Skies are alight with fire
grounds dried with pain
trees blowing with breeze
animals crawl with exhaustion
searching for green lands, blue rivers
and perfect peace.

Man fires guns from hell
day and night stealing our great creatures
blood money allows man to wear gold
with no guilt they plead ignorance for
selfish greed

Damage is uncontrollable
caught up in loyalties
publicity is essential to all
sit back watch destruction
for this world lives on the edge.

Allyson Barrass

Seasons in the Wood

Awakening from winter's dark and cold
Green buds bravely push their way to light
Springtime's glorious flowers will soon unfold
To welcome those who gaze upon the sight

In summer's heat the trees give leafy shade
To strollers in the wood on lazy days
With time to pause and rest within the glade
Before they go upon their separate ways

Soon comes the autumn leaves brown, red and gold
Crisp and glowing with their colours bright
The trees stand in their glory proud and bold
And passers-by gaze wondrous at the sight

Branches bare of leaves sway in the breeze
Dramatic, dark and reaching to the sky
Autumn has made way for winter's freeze
And those who used to stroll now hurry by

Gwen Bagley

Man's Best Friend

Key in the lock, open the door
Greeted by a friendly paw
Excited whimpers, wagging tall
Feet stampeding the chewed up mail
Mischief in his eyes wanting to play
He's soon forgotten that you've been away
Now for a mad dash under the chair
To retrieve the bone he left there
Tail still wagging his bone at your feet
You cuddle and kiss him and give him a treat
Ears stand to attention at the familiar sound
Of his collar and lead, for walkies he's bound
A world full of adventure, what's to be found
Exploring in detail with nose to the ground
Walkies over, back home for a sleep
Laying in his bed, a black furry heap
Dreaming doggy dreams, contented, at ease
Man's best friend always willing to please.

Alison Wells

A Bluetit Killed by a Passing Car

She stood beside him.
Grief, bewilderment -
who knows what emotion filled her.

She stayed beside him.
Unmoved by the noise,
the wind, the hideous wheel.

Not a Bosnia or a Burundi here
but as I passed them,
raising dust over their perfect yellow breasts,
a tear formed.

Joseph J. Field

The Cheetah

The gazelles scatter
From the water-hole
Like mercury tossed around,
They must flee
As never before
Or he'll grind them to the ground.

His huge hind legs
Propel him forward
Trampolinin' o'er the plain,
Faster and faster
On and on
Is he carrying Olympia's flame?

All fear the smell
Of the cheetah's fire
All dread the tolling bell
To survive
They must outrun
This smoke-ringed sprinter from — Hell.

Catherine Thorburn

Albert

To my Husband he was a Father
He was a Grandad to my Sons
To me, the Dad, I never had
And a friend to everyone.

He was a happy cheerful man
Hardly thinking to complain
But he did have strife, within his life
That gave him sorrow and gave him pain.

He was well known for his thoughtfulness
Never missing a time or a date
He would write things down, so when time came around
He knew that he wouldn't be late.

He loved the life that was given to him
It was full - he remembered it well
The stories he told were exciting and bold
While others were too sad to tell.

He could always ease your sorrow,
He would charm away the hurt
He will be remembered for a long, long time
Our Dad, your Grandad, ALBERT.

Diane Howard

Dedicated to Nicky

(Born Spring 1966 - Died Spring 1996)

I remember the day we first met long ago
He was ever so handsome, he nickered "Hello"
A beautiful liver chestnut, part Arab bred
With a diamond shaped white blaze upon his forehead
He taught me to ride and he never complained
When I lost my balance and grabbed at his mane
The back in his young days with my husband he hunted
Competitions they entered and won at Cross Country
Border Rideouts, so many, Nicky rode at them all
Selkirk, Melrose, Jedburgh and out to Mosspaul
Our children both rode him, he was incredibly kind
So loyal and honest with an intelligent mind
But the day we all dreaded, his life we had to end
Unable to stand, our final gift to our friend
We fed him some mints, sat close by his side
And said our goodbyes as with dignity he died
Our faithful companion, his spirit had gone
But behind him a lifetime of memories live on
Such beautiful memories are all ours to recall
Of Nicky, so special - the best horse of all.

Bobbie Boustead

Trusting Eyes

He had such trusting eyes. A TOO TRUSTING heart.
He was far too naive for his years.
Such a trusting little soul. Till his whole SAFE world fell apart.

DEEP ANGER set his world on fire. That YEARS could NOT
put out the flames.
NOW - instead of the one responsible - ONLY - HE HIMSELF
does HE BLAME.
With such deep and embittered feelings - ALL aimed straight
BACK HIS WAY.
Although all the fury binds him tight as he makes it through
another day.

The story's never ending - only magnified with time.
His anger is COLOSSAL. His FURY - knows NO BOUNDS.
But he keeps it deep inside him - but the ANGER never goes
underground
It's ALWAYS waiting to trap him though he tries so to break free.
Heaven only knows - what the FINAL outcome will be.

He's went STRAIGHT THROUGH - SUICIDAL - coming OUT
the other end.
He has a hurt child deep inside him now - except for his wife -
that child's his only TRUE friend.

Eric Mitchell Phillips

Magical Woods

Soft green,
Grey green,
Blue green,
Brown green,
Sea green?
Softly dappled,
The world is in the triple-trunked
   beech tree in the woods,

With the blue grey,
Green grey, map markings.
Speckled,
Striped,
Dappled,
Spattered,
Smooth and horizontally marked
Or rugged as an oak.

Softest, softest,
Green grey lichens,
Seaweed?
Spangled like stars? Silvery, silvery grey.

Anne Chadwick

That Boy I Despise

He walks up behind me - his tip-a-tap feet.
He calls me rude names, right up the street.
He tells me I'm stupid.
He tells me I'm dumb,
He tells me I'm uglier than everyone.
I still keep walking, with tears in my eyes.
That boy I despise!
I round the corner,
My last few steps.
I've never been happier to see Mrs. Keps.
But as I think about what he has said
That I am so ugly:
I wish I were dead!

Danielle Bikhaze

The Dark Mirror

The soldier has returned from the East.
He comes home like a stranger to another country
and little known places. To the village
that was his God-given birthright.

He walks through the quiet woods. When
boughs snap off somewhere close, the explosions
seize the contours of his fear. The past, the dark mirror,
splinters shards of jungle whispers deep in the flesh
of memory and love.

He, the soldier, has brought back sounds and names,
the fragrance of frangipani
in her yellow-ribboned hair, the cry of dark-plumed birds
to these English lanes.

The confused silence around him
and the hiddenness of truth in it
will guide him along forever. And always there if need be,
the white stick that knows where to go.

Bernard Durrant

Winter

Winter came and froze the autumn solid.
He looked at the world he had conquered,
The trees were bare, but for a few
These he blessed and made part of Christmas
The others he pitied and gave a brilliant white fur coat.

The animals were weary, he told them to rest
Some were too busy
So he commanded the moon to stay longer.
Making the day short.
But the sun was annoyed and left the world cold,
Winter thought to himself, I have ruined the earth
And hid himself in the clouds, wallowing in self pity
Till spring, struck him down with a beam of sunlight

Graham Parkings

The Start or the Finish

Adam was the first man to dwell upon this earth
He must have been a lonely man till Eve made it well worth
How many men on Earth today, would sacrifice a rib
To gain a living partner, that would talk and talk Ad-Lib

Now Eve was made from hard stuff, or shall we call it bone
Her favourite foods were off the trees, that grew around her home
They could eat fruit off all the trees, except the juicy one.
From the tree of knowledge of good and evil, but to Eve this
   was just fun.

Now Eve was quite a charmer, and always had her way

She soon enticed poor Adam, to eat apples every day
The tree of good and evil, was a fruitful apple tree
With delicious golden apples for both of them to see.

It's a sin to yield to temptation but it's easier said than done
We all know it is difficult, for each and everyone
Eve told Adam, you must eat this fruit, or I shall say goodbye
So Adam ate these golden ones, for he knew she'd never lie.

So let this be a warning, for everyone to heed
Temptation is always with us whatever is our creed
It could be just an apple, or something very cheap
But stealing is still stealing, so look before you leap.

Islwyn Davies

My Plea

Surely it just can't simply be me?
Having lived on this earth for three score and three
who doesn't have any reason to see
why things are so wrong with society

Daily one gets the reports from 'ere
of guns and bombs and blades that sear
places at home and countries afar
persons who cannot just be what they are

They won't let others calmly live in peace
nor be allowed their borders to keep
there's greed and terror, power gone mad
it only serves to make the world sad

Help us find pleasure to enjoy the day
not pollute our land 'til everything's grey
let bird and fish and creature, us too
live in harmony without more ado

This race has achieved so many great things
why destroy all the goodness it brings
Life should be having more quality now
Remember! 'Tis short for us to endow

Ivy McKechne

Warsawa

The bombers roar across the morning sky,
waves of destruction with no reason.
Black uniforms, young men, mouths full of lies,
bleak, windowless buildings, melancholy seasons.

Broken glass, grateful silence, dark suffering,
the people with disjointed memories, daisies in hell.
Grey photographs of days past differing.
Calls to God, stars of David, souls to sell.

Brown-shirted morons, stride the streets,
in seas of destruction, urban decay.
Killing and maiming, in jack-booted feet,
after the holocaust, all past, hid away.

With a blankness in their eyes, they wait,
for the trains that will take them to their doom.
Death camps, no more for a future fate,
human refuse, dust and ash, all too soon.

Nothing fails like the failure to hear,
to speak of the horrors, we'll always regret.
We have to live our lives with no fear,
we must try to remember lest we forget.

Mik Hussey

Mister Doctor

Woke up this morning
Had nothing to say
Red lights warning
As I spent my hard-earned pay

Mister Doctor stood standing there
With bright blue hair
Laughing and joking
At the old man choking

I sat over there
Breathing the stench of fumes
From the night before
I stood up and ran to the door

No escape from Mister Doctor
Sitting there with his bright blue hair
With his pen he wrote another endless page
His face bright red with rage
As he wrote another page

Gordon Nairne

Fragments

Treasures scarce recalled across Time's distance;
half-remembered pleasures of lost youth;
friendly rooms vacated by both party guests and hosts;
empty rooms where shadows flicker sadly on their ghosts.

Symbols of acquisitive insistence;
apostatic jetsam of past faith;
debris of the urgent search for novelty and change;
people, places, things once familiar, now strange.

Disconnected fragments of existence;
atomising particles of life;
sad, neglected gardens, half-projected dreams.
Nothing is forever, nothing as it seems.

  Kaleidoscopic images, half-seen as they are tossed,
  perhaps in time will capture all the fragments that were lost.

Brian Chaplin

Untitled

I sit all day, penning poems,
I should be doing work,
My mind to wander, when on my own,
A pen, a pad, alert.

I cannot rest in my mind,
My body growing fat,
Writing endless rhyming lines,
Resembling a cheshire cat.

I think too much, I do not do,
I write till I'm run dry,
Emotionally drained, I go to bed,
Another idle sigh.

S. Roberts

Happiness

Happiness, is smelling the earth,
Fresh after rain.
Knowing the plants will rise again.
Seeing the birds flying free in the sky,
Hearing them sing, not knowing why.
Seeing the fox, and the badger run free,
Knowing this is how it should be.
Seeing babies asleep in their prams,
And the sheep with their lambs,
Who gambol in the fields of green.
Knowing this is how it should be.
Seeing the flowers look to the sun,
And the trees reaching high.
Seeing the seasons changes,
As they have since time begun.
Knowing it all as in your arms I lie,
Seeing your face every day my dear,
Hearing your footsteps, as you draw near.
That is my happiness.

Grace Maycock

The Colours of the Wind.

Have you ever painted the colours of the wind,
Have you ever heard the wolves cry to the moon,
Have you ever had snow in June,
Have you ever jumped down a waterfall into a river,
Have you ever seen a ghost that made you shiver,
Have you ever sailed the ocean wide,
Have you ever been on a river ride,
Have you ever heard a bird sing in the dark,
Have you ever sailed Noah's ark,
Have you ever swum to the bottom of the sea,
Have you ever touched a bumble bee,
Have you ever jumped off a plane,
Have you ever lion-tamed,
Have you ever balanced on a rope high up,
Have you ever won the F.A. cup,
Have you ever jumped through a flamed ring,
Have you ever met the king,
Have you ever been struck by lightning,
Have you ever seen a monster that's frightening,
Have you ever painted the colours of the wind.

Amy Thompson.

Capri Journey North

Let's load the car with bag and case
We'll travel far, a long night's chase.
Now with our load; the engine whines.
We hit the road and follow lines.

Tonight's the night that I must keep
Awake, deprive myself of sleep
Driving onward through the night
Insomnia till we arrive.

The unlit motorway's surreal
We race under each bridge
I gently guide my steering wheel
Through dip and bend and ridge.

It's time at three to take a rest
Some food and coffee would be best,
A cigarette - I feel the need,
A routine check, get back to speed.

When Scottish sunshine hit our screen
The darkness hours were gone
And at Loch Rannoch's silver shore
Our long night's work was done.

Roderick MacLean

Destiny

He was drawn to her side like a magnet, the orchestra played destiny
waltz oblivious to people they danced until dawn, his angel in blue
blue met her prince.
Sun shone fit to burst throughout summer, as especially laid on
from above, they laughed and they sang, not a cloud in the sky.
Fiery sunsets as never before.

Sunday walks up the Wrekin', glow worms peeping through grass.
Escaping from friends to their woods.
Stars sparkled above - one, brightest of all.
"That one's ours", he said "Star of the North".

Hand touching hand - like crossing of cables,
First kiss - Chemistry gone mad,
"Our love", he said "is too prefect to spoil"
Jealous gods. Did they hear - were they glad?

So proud of his wings off to Aden - the war.
Then a love-drenched letter he wrote,
"Your face ever lovely. Is always before me,
Yet more so - much closer tonight",

Cruel moon why so bright on that night of all nights why mar
perfection so rare?
Dreams of the future together - forever. Turning to fear and despair.
Sweet precious memories remain crystal clear, happy laughter
with loving and living. Their hopes - swept away - vanished with
words, one of our aircraft is missing.

Gwendoline Tallon Dunkley

Is This Hell?

Bombs were exploding, fires burning,
Guns were shooting as well.
The tear-stained boy was just learning
What it's like in hell.
His mother and father have been shot,
Their bodies lay right there.
He couldn't understand just what,
Or who, all he could do was stare.
He wanted to run,
He wanted to shout,
He wanted to fire a gun.
What was it all about?
A gentle arm went 'round his shoulder,
It was a lady crying there.
Standing nearby was a soldier
Looking at this stricken pair,
"I've just lost my son" she said
"Come we will start again".
They walked hand in hand, looking straight ahead,
The tears had washed away the pain.

Doreen Benham

Untitled

To offend, to comprehend,
To summer breeze, lent freeze of time
Can stop to see her beauty.
I cast a glance and hold for an eternity
The blue-eyed flare,
For that moment still drives me
From all reality. Never to know.
To haunt, to taunt me for all my being.

Andrew Burton

Love a Broken Heart

A traveller came with tales to tell, and landed at my door
He bid me that, I do his work, my soul he wants and more
He'd watched me work, and watched me play, he'd seen me
laugh, and cry. He said I'm the answer to your dreams, I never
questioned why. At first we always had such fun, and life was
never grim. Until the day he was controlling me, and not me
controlling him. A prisoner he had me as, he has the rest, a
prisoner of despair. No dream is he, no answer, only a never-
ending nightmare. He is not made of flesh and blood, but it
doesn't really matter he comes in many shapes and forms, his
aim your life to shatter. I don't need him now he's gone away, I
got my soul away but he's always there and you never know, I
may feel that weak again one day. He takes the weak he sucks
them in; he'll promise you the earth but it's all false hope, and
then you see him, for what he's really worth. So if he knocks
upon your door, don't let him in, you see, I did! And if you do,
you may, just end up exactly the same as
me. Just look away say no, get out, and his power you'll reverse.
It's better to be down and sad sometimes, because false happi-
ness is worse.

Andrew Winterbottom

The Rhymester's Tale

Writing poetry is my scene.
Having something published is my dream
Mind you this would be hard for me to do,
As I've never sent even on thing "in" to make
My dream come true!!
That's up to now I'll confess to you!!
I've had a poem accepted "Oh Joy! Oh happy day"
And it came out of the blue!!
Just hurry and print and publish it!!
If I don't see it soon I'll have a fit!!
There's only one thought that makes my heart sink!!
What if the publishing firm is on the brink
And goes bankrupt without a trace?
And like the Chinese I "lose face"?
Oh! Well, I probably wouldn't make it in the
"Rat Race"!!

Flora Divers

Hear the Cottage

Hear the stone begin to crumble
Hear the woodwork now decay
The greedy mould is taking over
The shattered glass down to lay

The final grave of happy moments
lays silently, no mourners come
Gentle screams of forgotten faces
The years roll by, one by one

Alone it sits in empty greenness
The old cottage that is no more
The roof has long since died and fallen
And grass and weeds become the floor

Hear the stone begin to crumble
Hear the woodwork now decay
The greedy mould is taking over
The shattered memories down to lay

Dana Stevens

The Poor Little Badger

There once was a badger who was black and white,
He danced through the meadow all through the night,
One night he was startled by a noise he heard,
He thought it was a mouse, he thought it was a bird.
He was certain he saw the figures in the dark,
And then he heard a voice and a very nasty bark.
Shocked at the movement he began to run,
Then he turned and saw the barrel of a gun,
Back to his set he made his way,
Unaware of the price he would have to pay.
His home was suddenly filled with light,
Huge claws and a spade what a terrible sight.
He turned his back and felt fangs in his hind.
And a cold sharp metal hit him from behind.
The badger couldn't breath let alone run,
And the last sound he heard was a shot from a gun,
The man was happy and his pleasure increased,
As the badger was ripped from piece to piece.

Emma Barlow

Reflection

Withering roses, dormant in the snow.
Vibrant colours merely thoughts of long ago.
Emerald blades from under the snow peek,
While summer blooms underground sleep.

Winter skies as white as lace,
Ferocious winds that bite your face.
Bare branches incline awkwardly in the wintry breeze,
Footsteps fall heavily upon the rustling leaves.

Beautiful roses, where have you gone?
Come back springtime and don't be long.

Gemma Dawkins

Accused and Naked

I am weak as I stand accused and naked
Weary having had questioned my beliefs so sacred
Holding back tears of anger from flowing
As gloved suspicious hands probe my clothing

Like a clap of thunder the iron door slams shut
This is the final blow, the salt on my cut
The almighty slam, it echoes all 'round
As my body shudders and gives way to the sound

Helpless with despair, onto my knees I fall
As the convicting noise rebounds off the wall
The ringing in my ears like a tolling bell
Now I'm alone in this cold, empty cell

Shattered, I lie on the icy stone floor
All sealed in except the slot in the door
The guilty walk away along with my pride
While I've stood accused and naked inside

Lynda Hamilton

The Beauty Before the End

The deepest blue of the boundless sea
was spreading until far
to the dark horizon of the sky.
A seagull,
white as the midnight nymph,
was flying, looking for
its olympian companion.
The white houses of the small island
looked like proud lilies in the sun
made from purest marble.
A sweet, muffled voice
was heard near a sceptic massive rock.
Someone was singing
the endless happiness of life.
All this beautiful
like fairy tale place
was the epigram of the dream,
before the catastrophe.

Rena Platirrahou

Dream Weaver

I lay in bed staring up at the ceiling,
Watching the Dream Weaver doing her weaving,
Praying that soon, I shall be with her,
Uttering words and making potions galore.

Suddenly she turned and stared straight in my eyes,
My lids flickered shut and, to my surprise,
There I was in a field full of flowers,
Springing and jumping and dancing for hours.

I arrived at a river and suddenly turned,
The sun was being covered by big fluffy clouds.
I looked for the flowers but they were all gone.
With a tear in my eye, I knew my dream had gone wrong.

I woke with a jerk, bolt upright in bed,
And realised it was a dream that had a sad end.
I lay in my bed and stared up at the ceiling,
And again watched the Dream Weaver, weaving.

Keely Simone Weatherall

Remembrance

Standing there in the rain.
Thinking back to the very day.
Friends, families people die.
A tear drops from your eye.
Standing there in the rain
Thinking back to the very day.
Brave, scared, frightened all the time
Just think of those people.
Who laid down their lives.

Holly Kernot

A Glimpse

I will never understand;
We come from two separate worlds.
Where does he live?
Where is he going?
What is he doing here?
I packed a lunch this morning.
What will he eat?
It's so hot.
Where will he find water?
I am lost without a map
And friends.
He is here alone.
Proud and free,
the Maasai tribesman stares
Across the dividing gulf
At me; I'm the odd one here.
He turns and walks
Purposefully into the barren emptiness
of Africa.
I return to my guidebook.

Susie Jones

Beauty

Beauty is in the eye of the beholder,
well, tonight I beheld,
whilst longing for the beauteous thief, who hath surreptitiously
obtained my heart, the one who evokes all the emotions contained
within, my eyes beheld such a beautiful scene,
almost religious, calm,
serene, and angelic, like her sleeping face.

So many colours, Mother Nature's resplendent,
so little sound, so many thoughts,
so little anger, for once, one felt no hatred, only joy.

Words cannot describe, one could do it no justice,
only a twinge of sadness,
that the two beauties of which I have beheld,
could not be shared together,
but gladness to have known them both.

Laurence Taylor

Think On My Friend?

Think on, when someone is crying.
Think on when one is smiling.
Deception is a clever tool, in which can make or break.
The mechanics of life.
The analytic masters theories on reversals.
. . . thus to smile, feign happiness is to
turn the wheel full circle . . . ongoing bleakness.
. . . A cycle of black.
. . . To cry, to shed those clear tears . . . shed them.
Wildly, shed them openly. The wheel is slowing
Allowing for time, no squeaks. It is oiled, tears and soiled.
The machinery is working effectively.
How can a preacher know so little about his clergy?
Think on
Am I not worthy?

Bissy Thomas

Grains of Hope

Grains of hope with each passing day
To help us on our way
The tiredness that we feel inside makes us feel so low of life
We try so hard to reach for that golden star
That is always just out of reach for us
But when the time is right
This golden star will shine around us
To lift us out of the tired ways in which we live.
The helpless ways we may feel will vanish with a touch of hope
Loneliness will be replaced with showers of love forevermore
Kindness will be replaced in your heart for everyone to see
And you will be given the will to carry on
And make this world full of your dreams.

Denise Lean

The Bridge of Life

He sat there with his eyes closed,
He wasn't really there,
He opens up the gates of love
For those who really care
He feels their anguish and their love
Their joy, the hurt and pain
He lives through each emotion.
It runs through every vein.
This medium sits before us
He gives us faith and hope
When our hearts are heavy
He gives us strength to cope.
We know he is a mortal
But to us a link so strong
Our loved ones now surround him,
To guide when we are wrong.
Our sitting is soon over,
It's time to say goodbye,
They say "we'll meet you at the bridge of life,
And there is no need to cry."

Helen Padmore

Sky Brooch Jewels

The porcelain aquatic moth, sparks for eyes
Under the pavilion restaurant lights
The river's silver calligraphy spelling beauty
Sways against the banks boulder cobbled pebbles
Kaleidoscope cascades under notched brown hanging branches
As the Chinese weeping willow covers with gold
Making shadows on the water
As catkins dive glowing like fireflies
And float towards the white seraphic swan
Salisbury's high lit cathedral spire
Surrounded by shining marbled sparkling dimple dots
Of stars and sacred satellites in silver shoals of sparklers
Sprinkled all over in galaxy and sky
Splash zone glittering glowstars, a passing lightning comet
Look down on a city's million lower house glitters
Battling to compete with the marvel on high
The giant brooch of jewel stars
Then they drift towards the moon
Of magnet and mystique and manoeuvres away
To planets galactic wild and afar.

Stuart Munro

Old Love

When we first met I fell in love
We fitted like a hand in a glove
I thought you were the one for me
But six months later I began to see.

You changed so much you didn't want me around
You used me right down to the ground.
When your friends came along you didn't care,
But when they went out "I love you" you'd swear.

I got used to you not being there
So I didn't stop to care.
But by the time you realized
It was all too late!

I know you still love me,
but my feelings have changed
I don't want you back
You've only yourself to blame.

You're too late for sorry's
You're now in the past
I'm getting on with my life
Without you at last.

Lindsey Sinclair

A Prayer

Once there was a Priest who dared
To ask for favours in his prayers
Oh Lord says he, I must relate
There is no money in the plate

From what I find, it makes me think
The congregation must be skint,
For foreign coins, and buttons too
All fill the plate along the pew

As read in Scriptures most divine
The water that was turned to wine
Lord from your Heaven of Milk and Honey
Please turn the buttons into money

Audrey G. Taylor

If Only . . .

If only you were here again with your quiet, gentle ways,
To help us through life's trials and brighten our darkest days,
If only you had lived to see another year or two,
To view the little faces of the children you never knew.
If only you could hear us when we talk of 'what might have been'
And reminisce till the 'wee sma' 'ours' the days of yester'e'en,
If only we could have you back, just for a little while
Just to say the things we meant to, and to see your kindly smile.
But alas this cannot be for God has called you home,
Where we will meet again someday by the Grace of Him alone.

Helen B. Lyon

The Seagull

Sleek white bird with strutting legs,
With beady eye and fishing beak,
Poised upon the Prom you stand
To view the various passers-by.
Behind you, wild and overcast,
The grey storm clouds amass to burst;
The ocean rollers pound and crash
Upon the bruised and battered shore.
Your calmness, peace, tranquillity
Bring solace to this troubled world,
Till - taking flight, you raise your voice
And foul expletives screech abroad.
You swoop and dive, you fish and plunge,
Until you glide to rest once more
And stand - and stare - upon the shore,
Your beady eye surveying all.

Effie Devenish

The Tapestry

Life is like a tapestry GOD weaves with gentle hands.
With blues like the sea and golds like the sand.
Pink like a blossoming rose and white like a peaceful dove.
Greens or reds or yellows GOD weaves them all with love.
But the tapestry He weaves isn't all a mass of light
There must be blacks and browns to highlight the bright.
He leaves the tapestry for forthcoming years to mend
And we must help to weave until our life comes to an end.

He made His son's tapestry according to plan
And I don't think Jesus could quite understand
Why His Father wanted Him to die
And make His mother Mary cry.
But on the cross He hadn't breathed His last breath
He rose again victorious and triumphant over death.
We try to model ourselves like our LORD
Until we are in Heaven reunited with our GOD.

Jennifer Louise Sneddon

The Vista

Upon a hill I stand and gaze, upon a sky ablaze
with colour of such wondrous hue.
A rainbow glows with promise of new life and sun.
It sets my heart aglow, to see this glorious, heavenly show.
Beside the clouds the sun appears,
The clouds have ceased to shed their tears,
And from the woods and meadows sweet,
All life awakes the sun to Sreet.
Gone the dusk the sun will sink, trailing its glory.
But as the glory fades away.
It foretells another day when the rising sun will bring.
Fresh life and hope to everything.

Eva Taylor

Heaven

With every step she took she grew weaker,
With every breath she breathed she grew more tired.
And her heart beat like a soldier's drum,
And she could not find a place to rest her weary feet,
No she must go on, no time to sing a song.
She must keep going, she must reach the summit.
No-one must question her,
No-one must help her.
Where is she going?
What is she doing?
Is it her choice or someone else's?
Who will answer our questions?
Only the girl.
Answer our questions girl
Why?
We need to know.
I am finishing my journey.
To where are you going?
To a better place
What is it called? Heaven.

Joy Quillinan

The Field

How does it work, that field over there
With frost on the ground, and a chill in the air
How does it work, when the frost's gone away
and this field seems to change from day to day

How does it work, now this field is just brown
with furrows all over, going up and down
How does it work, when spring comes along
when the seedlings appear and the birds sing along

How does it work, as the sun starts to shine
and the seedlings are plants, growing all the time
How does it work, now the days are warm
now the plants are tall and rise at dawn.

How does it work, now the harvest is here
Now the crop has been taken for another year
How does it work, now the field's bare, and then
the year starts anew, and the cycle again

How does it work, mother nature I mean
when things seem to grow without being seen
How does it work, this wonderful world
If only we knew, how wise we would be

Julie Heath

For the Children

This world we are creating, is it a Hell on Earth?
With guns and bombs, pollution, what will it all be worth?
What will we leave behind us? What sad inheritance?
Will our children thank us? Will they have a chance?

We've felled the great Rainforests, laid bare the fertile soil,
Polluted all the Oceans with Nuclear waste and oil.
Look at the children's faces, see inside their minds,
Are they all in terror of what we'll leave behind?

Their eyes are full of sadness, deep pools of fear and woe,
Come the day of judgement where will they have to go?
What can we do about this? Pray God it's not too late,
Can we reverse this horror and start to re-create?

Put smiles upon their faces, wipe away the tears,
Show them life is beautiful, they need not live in fear.
The power is within us, we must put all things right,
Let us work together and make their future bright.

Give them a world of wonder, of peace and harmony,
With fish in every Ocean and birds in every tree.
Don't leave it up to others, stand up and tell them all,
Do it for the children before the curtains fall.

Jim Sargant

Mulberry Rose

What a beautiful sight, the girl on the bench
With her cream faded dress all laced,
Her cream satin shoes, and her ivory skin,
Her blonde hair hangs straight to her waist.

She twists in her fingers, a blood red rose,
And she hums as she swings her feet,
Then as I get near, she becomes very still,
Then moves to the end of the seat

She clutches the flower tight to her breast,
Smiling she says 'it's a mulberry rose',
And as she moved the flower about
Its fragrance reached my nose.

At the sound of footsteps I turned my head,
But as I looked back she had gone
I searched all the park, for some sight of the girl
Just a clue, but there was none.

Each day I visit that same park bench,
hoping that that's where she goes
but she never does, yet the strangest thing is,
I can smell that mulberry Rose.

Debra Weston

Smiles

From: From far away I see your smiles,
which seems to take away the miles,
smiles can be seen far and wide,
even as far as the countryside
smiles can say that you want to stay,
smiles can show warmth from within the heart
smiles can say you want to make a new start.
smiles can go from ear to ear.
Smiles can even protect you from fear.
A smile is like a budding rose
it brings happiness as it grows.
Remember to always keep in mind
even when you're in a bind.
A smile can show you're really kind.

Giulietta Pecchia

Forever

It was a Hidden Shadow in the night,
Which showed no signs of becoming light.
I thought there was to be no ending,
But I knew I had to keep pretending.

The Night passed by me, haunting my heart,
It took all my security, every part,
Now I feel the loneliness brought about,
I wonder if there's a right way out.

When the Sun burns out the blackened night,
An end will be put to the struggled fight.
My heart will be filled with no more pain,
The Shadow and I will not meet again.

Joanne Robinson

Remembering a Friend

You were always my friend: With me to the end.
While others abandoned me, you were always there.
When others were angry at me, you were always there.
When it was dark and I couldn't make my way through,
you were the light, you were the angel, who guided me through.
No one knew but me and you, that we were kindred spirits:
whatever I said, you listened — not in dread;
but sat there silently, your ears twitching to every word I spoke.
There are folk that will say you were just "a dog".
But they're wrong, for so long as I live you were so much more
—
to me you were human.

Alison Clarke

The Third Battle of Newbury

Now all is peace and quiet in woodlands green and pastures brown
While traffic fumes, pollution choke the centre of the town.
The residents are desp'rate for relief to the congestion;
'Where does the Newbury by-pass go?' is local burning question.

With route decided, plans drawn up, dates jotted in the diary,
It's now the chance to put one's views at the public enquiry.
To those protestors who don't live near here - now please take note;
The democratic way is how the locals want to vote.

But all along the route, tree houses, camp sites are erected
By people, with this region absolutely not connected.
They try to stop the clearance men from felling all the trees,
And some resort to sabotage, the clash with the police.

Security is tightened with an extra band of men;
Despite this the objectors outmanoeuvre them again.
Meanwhile two guards who've recently their innocence assured
Admit now that they have a previous criminal record.

When all is said and done, the problem has to be resolved
With sensible discussions 'tween the parties all involved.
But shame the by-pass penetrates this quiet Berkshire corner,
With loss of habitat and all its glorious flora, fauna.

Alan E. Wiseman

Sunrise in My Pocket

Sunrise in my pocket, and night stars in my eyes,
When the mist hangs in the valleys
And the sun decides to rise.
Then the hills cry gentle tears, crying from the skies.
Down the streams to the valleys, that have been lost
For a thousand years.
Like pure, dream - clean waterfalls that settle gently
in an absent wind.
In straight, unchanging gullies, the steep, green slopes tolerate
the sunrise in my pocket.
A dreaming, sleepy village that opens yawning - like a lonely
lover's locket.
The only sound is that of these, running water trickling
and meandering though there is no wind to rustle
through the stark, unbending trees.
I only want to be with you sharing all of these
and be the sunrise in your pocket.
And the night star in your eyes.
Like the wind you are free.

Doreen Morris

Celebration

The long sandy beaches are there now as they were in forty-four
When the roaring tangle of machines and men disembarked
   along that shore.
Fighting for peace they were then, for some, death an inevitable
   fate.
So that we, all these years later, have a cause to celebrate.

And above the shrub strewn sand dunes are white crosses all in line.
Simple names inscribed on them, names just like yours and mine.
When the bloody task was finished, under those crosses by design
They laid the now sung heroes with names like yours and mine.

They too had celebrations, for them it was part of life's living.
A birthday, promotion or some success, brought joys without
   misgivings
Then they danced and sang and jollied the days or nights away
In company with good friends they met along life's way.

But they fell and crawled and spluttered, as dying fighting men do.
And the others, they went onwards, bringing peace for me and you.
The long sandy beaches are still there now but filled with
   tourists galore
And the memorabilia is abounding in the towns along the shore.

There are flags and trinkets for sale there, and museums of
   military fame
But still on those little white crosses, there is but a single name
They are there by the monotonous thousands, orderly and all in line
Names, that are our cause for thanksgiving, names, just like
   yours and mine.

Gwynfor Davies

Forgotten

Silently it came,
When the room was shrouded in darkness
And all was still, but for the clock
Ticking tirelessly into the night.
A chill crept over the grate
Where embers had long since groaned and died.
Outside, soft snowflakes fell
Quietly changing the face of the narrow street.

Suddenly, and without warning
The church clock struck midnight.
Revellers shouted and pelted each with snowballs
"Happy New Year"!
Tramping, sliding, noisily through the glistening drifts.

It was several days before anyone noticed milk bottles
Collecting at the front door
And when police broke in
And Annie's tiny frozen body was carried away
Silence fell once more
As neighbours bowed their heads in shame.

Jackie Brough

Untitled

Last night I had a dream!
Where there was not a democracy and slaves
had not been freed.
There were still Victorian days, when people's minds
were kept enslaved.
It was still a policy when blacks and whites resorted
to celibacy and could not even have babies

Last night I had a dream!
Where people stared at you and me.
I was bent before your knees and
Whipped until the people who stared were pleased.

Last night I had a cruel dream!
I screamed and screamed, until I felt your
Kiss and warm caress, I woke up.
Then later hand in hand, we walked outside
And in the dark pools of some people's eyes
I realize they were living my dream, but had no one
To wake them up.

Janice Lawlor

To an Old Caledonian Pine in Glen Falloch

Defiantly, though shattered by the storm
Which flung your proud head to the ground below,
Your trunk remains, in almost human form,
a sculpture carved by lightning, frost and snow.

Your roots still clasp the soil where from a cone
You first appeared three centuries ago,
and even though life from your limbs has flown
You still stand up to all the winds that blow.

You saw patrols of Redcoats in the glen
Hunting, perhaps, for Rob Roy and his men.
The road was built, the railway line arrived,
A thousand trees were felled but you survived.
Men left these hills to start their lives again,
But in this land their roots, like yours, remain.

Ian Purvis

Time

Time
which has always been there
since the beginning of time
the beginning of my time
time with people
I've spent my time like money
except I don't get any change
and these poems and memories are my receipts
but I can't take them back
to exchange my time with people for better times

Time
on a clock
always clocks and such
My brain will stop thinking
in time with seconds of my life
and I will have my last memories
of time I've spent with people
and the valuable time I've spent with you
while I finally decide it's time
to shut my eyes and die

Andre Dais

Forever

My body merely entertains that
which is eternal,
Death is no barrier for our love,
only an obstacle.
My spirit, desires, hopes and love
are all alive in your presence.
Your feelings and warmth course through
my weary soul,
My eternity is in your remembrance.

Amanda Jayne Rowse

Merry England

They called it Merry England in those medieval times
When God Queen Bess was on the throne and Shakespeare
    wrote his lines.
On the village green, a happy scene, as jesters played and pranced,
And children in their carefree ways, around the Maypole danced,
While the minstrels sang their songs of praise and played
    enchanting sound,
The Englishman stood proud and tall, to his country he was bound.

When the Spanish Great Armada on our foreshores showed
    its might,
Those heroic men of England chose to sail and fight.
Sir Francis Drake, made no mistake, and made those galleons run,
As they trembled at the power of the mighty English gun.

With adventure for the New World and thoughts of treasures
    on their mind,
The buccaneers with Drake set sail in his sip, the Golden Hind.
For three years they sailed the seven seas in circumnavigation
    of the globe,
And they brought back with them the treasures of spices,
    silks and gold.

Walter Raleigh, for the Queen, he lay his cloak upon the ground
Showing chivalry, with victory and romance was all around.
Ah yes! Those days of English glory, in that Golden Tudor reign
Could we hope to see once more the likes of it again.

David Colloby

KADAM

I'll never forget the day he knocked,
when I opened the door I nearly dropped.

"Kadam," I said, "my little soul,
have you been down that muddy hole?"

The hole was three feet deep and full of water.
I said, "Get in the bath or there'll be slaughter!"

He said, "But Mama I was a mole
I really liked it down that hole!"

I looked into his little face,
he was so dirty and such a disgrace.

He laughed and giggled when I scrubbed his feet,
his face was all shiny and he looked so sweet.

If you find a hole in your heaven up there,
you will get dirty, but little one don't despair.

Stand under the moonbeams, they'll wash you clean,
you'll be happy and laughing - you'll be serene.

Beth Rogers

Moods

When I'm annoyed, I count to ten
When I'm pleased, I write now and then
When I'm happy, I sing a song
But today I'm tearful, something's wrong.

When I'm excited, my heart skips a beat
When I'm hungry, I eat cold meat
When I'm sick, I retire to bed
And place a pillow over my head.

When I'm serious, I knit my brows
When I'm cheating, I think I'm a louse
When I'm meditating, I'm usually calm
Because meditation acts like a balm.

When I'm really angry, I always shout
I must be having some serious doubt
When I'm depressed, I really can't help it
I feel I'm now in a bottomless pit.

But when I'm in a good mood, I laugh quite a lot
Like a baby smiling in its newly bought cot
I like feeling chirpy if it takes me all day
It's nice to be joyful and dance all the way.

Brenda LaRose

The Lampingtoole

Way down deep in the woods each night,
   unbeknown to the jolly sprite,
underneath the wazookey stool,
   floating happily in a coolie pool,
Lurks the snaky Lampingtoole.

Ears all nobly pink and green,
   Such a happy shade of sheen,
Glistening under woogie beams,
   whistling tunefully scary themes.

Unexpectedly he creeps, upon whoever dares to sleep,
   taking it upon himself, Go foodleize the kindly elf,
Jumping wake the elf does see, a mystifying yum-yum tree,
   Leaves all webbed with tooley threads,
Ecstatic through moonbeams he treads.

In the blink of his hip not eye, the Lampingtoole gave a funny cry,
   Laughing at the pranerks snoozing,
Choking shamelessly and oozing,
   tiptoeing upon each foot, covering all about with glut,
When at last he's true kerput, back into his coolie:splut!!

Julia Robertson

Untitled

You sit there with your unseeing eyes,
Unhearing ears
Sometimes you laugh
What are you thinking?
I wish I could share your thoughts once more
The raindrops fall steadily down
I see a tear trickle from your eye,
Life can be so cruel
Your withered hands clutch at your skirt,
With fingers twisted and bent
How they once held me tight to your breast,
Long ago, before time played its cruel trick
Your eyes still sparkle
Sometimes it's hard to remember how you were
You look at me
See to see me
Then look away
"Who are you?" you cry
Oh Mother
What I'd give for you to know me.

Angela Graham

Zero Permanence

We flit like moths up to the candle's flame,
Unresisting, we are drawn into the light
Though fatal to be pulled too close, too hot,
Existence stands and blinks in Phoebus' sight.
Each life, though most essential as it seems,
Through time's vast span, lasts only for a day
And as a spark that, held up to the sun,
Is lost in dazzling, radiant array.
We shine as brightly as we are allowed,
In myriad attempts to leave our mark
Bur glorious as life's flare seems to burn,
We fade and pass forever into dark.
To overcome the trivial transience of our run,
We darlings of the gods burn brightly
And die young.

Duncan James Steward

Unseen, yet Felt, Unaware

In the streets they walk with heavy loads,
Unseen, yet felt, unaware,
Bore deep the nails into their skins
Meshed deep the thorns the iron pins,
The blood runs deep, deep in their veins
Seeps from the wounds, the Lord's remains,
The mindless rushing and what's it for,
Life is a cross, a crucifix, a crucifixion.

Claudine Shapcott

J. R. R. Tolkein

Horn commences battle,
Trolls mount their steeds
and cloaks flowing gallop
from their majestic castle.
To the bleak battlefield,
Where a troll crouches,
wielding his broken sword.
Arrows piercing him,
Face screwed in agony.

Tolkein contemplates,
sucking his pipe,
rubbing his twisted fingers,
over sheets of yarn.
The story descending, like a glistening waterfall.
Each drop reflecting the jealousy, love, hate and anger of
the tale.

Gazing over the coffee-stained desk,
and bookshelf coated in dust.
He sighs and with weary eyes,
sits and returns to his livelihood.

Catherine Burt

Alone

I live alone in my own little world,
With the people I love life can be so cold,
Weeks pass by, year's go on
In my heart I feel my life is gone.
I often wonder, what's the point of it all,
When people around me make me feel so small.
I lie in bed thinking it would be so nice,
If someone would love me without a price.
A little love goes along long way,
And when I've found love I know I'll stay.

Claire McDonnell

The Spider and the Fly

Distressed, she wriggles to secure her life,
Trying to break free from this web of fear.
Buzzing so loudly to express her strife,
The footsteps of the spider she can hear.
So slowly with his thread he binds her up,
First starting at her head then to her feet.
Fly stew is on the menu for his sup,
Which he can't wait to make and cook, then eat.
He mends his web of fear with glistening threads,
To catch another victim flying by.
Then carefully back to his home he treads,
To watch an unsuspecting fly fly by.
If you don't want to end up in his stew,
Then stay clear of his web I'm telling you!!!

Julie Puttock

Peaks

Glistening peaks, sparkling air
Tumbling streams and waterfalls
On some high tor an eagle's lair
Hear the eagle's shrill and lonely call.
To be high above the valley and clouds
The cold crisp wind upon my cheek
To feel the silent peaceful sounds
This is a place for lonely souls to seek.

Soft new virgin snow slopes now call
So with speedy skis gliding on downwards
Soon to be among the pines so tall
Swiftly gliding in and out of the pinewoods.
Down, down to the valley from the peaks
Back to all worldly things
Only to return to those distant peaks
For the solace only they can truly bring.

Glenys Simner

473

Calvary

How could He send His only Son,
To die at Calvary?
I know that in the same place,
I couldn't have, if it were me.
But it's all because of His love for us
And His will to set us free,
Yet still I'll never understand how He could care so much for me.
He's made his love apparent through His sacrificial Son
And through this ultimate gift of love
Our salvation has been won.

So now it's up to us to show
Our Father that we care,
By telling others of our faith so that it can be shared.
This gift from Him is oh so rare.
It is our second chance.
But at least now we can express our love,
In song in verse, in dance.

Jennette Munday

Old Age

Now I am old I have to walk with a cane
to ease my body of ache and pain.
My bones are now so fragile and old
I need heaps of clothes to keep out the cold.
Everyone thinks I am very fat
and now, I've taken to wearing a hat.
They say that your body heat goes out through your head
and now, I will wear a hat in bed.
Nobody looks and nobody cares
for when you are old and you walk with a cane,
there is no time to think of being vain.
Those days have long gone and your youth has flown
It's hard and it's sad to be left all alone.

Helen Brown

The Tormented Spirit

Flame of life in youth burns fiercely
To find his love is his endeavour
As a bee seeking nectar
From a flower in rainbow colour
In Spring sunshine promenading
With his love upon his arm
The admiring world approving
At this youth's display of charm
Summer and Autumn pass with a sigh
But in Winter bleak the youth did die
For his love had deserted him
And for another left his side
His heart lay in broken pieces
Scattered by each passer-by
Buried 'neath the snow so deep
E'en the willow o'er head did weep
And in the night his spirit wails
From the depths of river deep
"Oh, my love, where art thou hiding
Come and join me in my sleep."

Ian Platt

I

I've come out of the depths of despair
To find that there is life out there
I want to laugh I want to sing
I want to do most anything.

I want to be what I want to be
Happy, loving, joyful and carefree
To fill my life with hope and gladness
Forgetting all my thoughts of sadness

I know it's possible to have these things
Like a bird that's just discovered its wings
To soar so high up in the sky
That's where I want to be that is I.

Janet Williams

Flower Power

In sunshine or showers
They delight us for hours
Those wonderful, colourful, beautiful flowers

We need flowers for each celebration
In life as we journey ahead.
They shine forth on every occasion
Where natural beauty is spread.

The old church receives a new lease of life
As the Bride holds her blossoms so gay.
When 'mid the flowers the Groom meets his wife
To find joy on their own wedding day.

Then mother love when a child is born
With flowers the joy is complete.
Peace and love are spread this happy morn
In magical beauty the infant to greet.

No matter how many years have gone
We remember the friends we have had so long,
And so for lingering Birthday delight
A bouquet of flowers is always just right

Jessie Smith

Time

Days go by, we can't catch up
They fly so fast from dawn to dusk
There are many things we want to do
But before we know it the day is through

So helping out for charity
A good cause so they say.
So, giving up a bit of time
It helps you on your way.

So when the day comes to retire
And working days are through.
But don't give up there's many things.
That you can find to do.

Just take a look around you.
And give a helping hand
Then you'll think it's all worthwhile,
I'm sure you'll understand.

Ada Louisa Foley

Lottery Letdown

In my mind I can see rings of rubies and pearls,
Tiaras of diamonds fit for daughters of earls,
Bracelets of sapphire entwined with pure gold,
Emerald necklaces of value untold.
Earrings and brooches of flawless design
Glitter and sparkle, more heady than wine.
These jewels I craved when our numbers dropped through,
But this week's Lottery you forgot, didn't you?

Helena Kerr

The Passing of a Storm

Soft, silky silence, a saturated scene.
They stood, stayed, nothing the silence could break,
even silent the stream.
Secure they were, standing, feeling, the Earth, the Sun were still.
Together in that solstice, no wind, no sound, locked in the arms
of Paradise.
One dare not move, breath-rationed, held back, its very
expulsion dreaded, was it Peace on Earth?

Suddenly a stirring, are links so tenuous, should they despair
in this beautiful set, a revolution to occur?
The secure, special link, threatened by offshore breeze,
sound-spoiled silence, intrusive, shattering, still no more.
Sadly Nimbus climbing the White Mountains of the Sky,
Sharpened, twisting, turning, tenacious, terrible and tearing wind.

Then lo, abruptly, the air swirling, yet sensitive as it stills,
sweet the smell, fresh, roses, scent, succour for the sad.
Clear perception, all peace, no more malevolence,
Sun-kissed, soothing, satisfying - life once more begins.

Harry McDonnell

Mum's New Mug

O Mum I love you dearly you mean the world to me I brought
you all these lovely mugs from which you drank your tea, but
there seems to be a problem for which I can't explain for all these
lovely mugs you've broke, it is a crying shame, I don't know
what you do to them perhaps you could explain I've seen you
drop them on the floor or wash them down the drain. Claire says
"it's all to do with age" to this Dad does agree for now that you
are 48 and nearly on your knees perhaps you think it's a better
way for you to drink your tea.

But never fear dear mother this problem I have solved, for in this
little package there's a new mug for you to hold. I know it's
plain and simple I'm sure that you won't mind, in fact when I did
buy it the man was very kind and took the trouble to tell me it
was the latest kind. A demonstration he did give I did not think
it funny I wouldn't have minded half as much but I had parted
with me money. He took that there mug and threw it on the floor
it did bounce twice then flew out the shop front door. It landed
on the pavement and on its side did rest
and upon examination it looked its very best.

I know it's plain and simple, but I'm sure you must agree that,
that's the type of mug from which to drink YOUR TEA.

Gary Ingham

Gifts of Life

My world revolves around them
They are my 'treasure trove',
They fill my life with happiness
They fill my heart with love,
They came into my life
True blessings from above,
I have so many blessings
And I'm thankful for each one
But the greatest gifts that God bestowed,
Are my darling grandchildren.

I'm such a lucky person
Though, sometimes, I forget
My life is so much richer
Than others I have met.
I have no silver, I have no gold
But the love of my family
Is a wealth untold.

Christine Heptinstall

Brotherly Love

His face is soft and gentle
Two ear lobes so special we know
Two little eyes as blue as the sea
One set of lips as cute as can be.

He lies so silently
Sleeping throughout the day
And when night falls the baby awakes
He opens his eyes and stirs and shakes
So unaware of the world outside
So cold and frightening it seems from deep, deep inside.

Joanne Seekings

'Twixt the Sea and Shore

As the waves roll back to the sea
they leave jewels of colours for us all to see
these flecks of foam on the ribbed
wet sand left by the waves of an
out-going sea with all the colour
of fairyland magic and mystery
thousands of tides have come and gone
fierce gales of autumn and spring
millions of summoning moons have
shone to bring to birth
this lovely thing a fleck
of foam on the shining sand
left by the waves of an out-going sea
leaving to us the mystery of this
fleck of coloured foam magic
and mystery

Elizabeth Lippe

Mr. and Mrs. Blackbird's Dilemma

Mrs. Blackbird in her nest did lay
Two eggs and then she flew away
On her return she said "Goodness me"
"I laid two eggs, but now there are three"

As the time passed, the chicks hatched out
Two were normal, but the third did shout
Forever hungry, he was never full
Life certainly was far from dull

He grew to such an enormous size
Mrs. Blackbird couldn't believe her eyes
Mr. Blackbird said "I'm know I'm not wise
But we couldn't have produced a chick that size"

Time passed by and they did their best
To raise the three chicks in their nest
Then one day the large one spoke
And Mr. Blackbird began to choke

"Oh no! You know what we have done
We've raised a cuckoo as our son!"

June M. Shaw

Siren Call

A village maid, I was born and bred
until one day when I was led
To the city, with its lights aglow
which beckoned me away from a life so slow.
I fell in love with the city's allure.
And left behind the windswept moor.

Oh! not for me the meadows and rills
The sheep and the corn, the rolling hills,
Oh no! for me the city's roar,
The noise and the bustle at the city's core.
The pavement hard upon the feet -
Oh, give me the sound of the city's beat.

The peace and the quiet, and the village stream
cannot make up for the distance gleam
of Old Father Thames at the city's heart,
And Eros with his magic dart -
My heart is in rhythm with the city's pace,
And I am in tune with the madcap race!

Ivy Woodhead

Death

Everyone has to die
Up and up to heaven we fly
Past the clouds and birds we go
Weather this is true we will never know
When we die we will find out
What it's really all about
Do we see our lives at either side of a tunnel
Or is it like getting poured down a giant funnel
Do we walk to the light in front of us
Or do we catch the double-decker bus
It will be an experience we won't forget
But hopefully it won't happen yet

Claire Kula

Cruit Island, Donegal

Cruit Island Bay and Arland Strand,
Vast acreage of no-man's land.
Stretching as far as the eye can see,
A haven of tranquillity.
Old granite stone, just the slightest of traces,
of sheep tracks, wild, rugged, remotest of places.
And cold the wind that here doth roam.
With wild and melancholy moan.
And seas, a whirlwind of spray and proud waves crashing
Beating like a heart that never stops dashing!
This paradise, I see thee nigh,
Belongs to God, a deity high!

Gillian Anne Faulkner

Untitled

In flanders field where poppies
they crossed the seas to fight the foe
they dug their trenches made their stand
as they defended this foreign land

They fought long and hard in wind and rain
they said it was not fought in vain
a poppy field, a terrible grave
for those boys so young, so brave.

Now the day has come of remembrance
and we pray for those who made their stance
people recall the horror of those years
and for their loved ones shed some tears

But despite these memories of yesterday
the fear of war still comes our way
let's hope the past has left a scar so deep
that countries for ever the peace will keep

John McNally

Time's Up

This isn't the time,
They haven't grown or known the way.
When the saunter, when to run,
Or for me to lay the line.

Life's not just fun,
Darkness, light, ups and downs.
Inside out, all around,
In the mid but lonesome.

Pain torments my heart,
Tears and laughter, their sunny days.
Life's fulfilments left undone,
To linger or depart.

There is no change,
Follow closely watch, observe.
The line is straight it has no curve,
That simple, that strange.

Daphne Cole

Feelings

Another place, another time
They may have passed so quickly by
But fate had struck and for awhile
Although among many, they were alone
To enjoy their thoughts, the secret smiles
A gentle touch, and much - much more
The knowledge that the joy they'd found
Would forever last no matter what
The paths they took, together - or apart
Their memories were installed for evermore
Part of their lives lived to the full
Expressive - thoughtful - giving - wonderful
Must it all end or would they find
Within their lives the peace of mind
That inner strength to carry them
Along life's path till journey's end

John Sutton

Your Life and Mine

My love for you will break
This rock,
Send memories crashing through
The ocean's sky.
You'll walk on alone and I will
Find you screaming
In the wind
Seagulls will swoop
Around our fiery head, calling
For our souls,
And I will touch you warm and silently
At dawn and cry
For what has gone before.
It's been so long since I've seen you.

Joanne Pugh

Sonnet - What of the Future?

When I reflect on words you spoke to me,
Those tender words I was so charmed to hear,
My thoughts are birds that fly away to see
Into the future, bright and crystal clear.
Together we will true contentment find,
And if we stumble love will help us through
And guide us forward though the pathways wind,
And mists obscure the final perfect view.
Together, there is music in the sound,
A promise of the days that lie ahead,
Days where both joys and sorrows will abound
And we'll remember all the words we said.
Come let us forward go with hearts so light
That we will falter not and win the fight.

Freda Lee

My Cathedral

My cathedral boasts no stone,
Though it's high and cloud-filled, cathedral dome,
No brass plates or organ sound,
Just green leafed branches, sky to ground,
No music echoes 'round a wall,
Just trill of burn, or plash of fall.

No books to read, no collection plate,
Just wild rose and buttercup, daisy collate,
My cathedral still gives peace,
For tired minds from care release,
Come then enter, an oak for your chair,
All nature your healer, release from care.

My cathedral boasts no choir,
Except call of curlew, lark flying higher,
My cathedral was not built by man,
Just like Topsy "growed" as it can,
But here it is open wide, please call,
A warm welcome waiting for one and all.

For each who have the gift to see,
It's there in abundance, - nature's sanctity.

Grace Wade

My Garden

I have such a pretty garden
    Though rather small.
I'll tell you just the little things
    I can recall.
A little Lad's Love - a little one, and that comes first of all
And then some Buddleias, more than one, because they're
    nice and tall.
Enough, not overmuch, Gold Rod;
And Rosemary, that fragrant herb
    Which is a favoured one of God.
A little Lilac bush and a Laburnum tree where birds do sing

And I have in my garden small another thing -
    The atmosphere of Perfect Peace
Where one may work and rest
    For nature only can release
One's spirit at its best.

Dorothy E. Coombe

Me

I have had many a great time in my name,
though suffering comes with me.
I am the shot that killed,
your mother, wife or son,
your only close family.
I am a thing people run from,
I am the force of millions.
I am the whole world's problems.
Many a death I hold in my mind,
many a life I've surrendered.
I am the blood splattered over the earth,
peace is my enemy.

Christine Dickens

A Poem of Peace

What have they done to You, oh my Lord?
They scourged and spurned You, the angry horde
A crown of thorns they placed on Your head
They did not care how much You bled.

No pity or compassion did they show
But Your boundless love for them did grow
From the shores of Galilee
Right up to the hill on Calvary.

Though You died, it was not the end
Only the beginning for those who would lend
An ear to the words, that You did impart
Giving comfort and hope, to those heavy at heart

Oh joyous day! When you rose again
Glorious and triumphant, was that day of Your reign
Your message was simple, and clear to all
That we live in peace and harmony, 'til the day we are called.

Elsie Gallagher

The Dog

The dog is said to be man's best friend,
They will stick by you until the end,
Always there when we come home,
Sit by the door and expect a bone,
Dogs are used for many things,
For the blind, police, even to protect kings!
Their owners they really do adore,
If they don't go out, they think we are
A big bore,
They love to sit on your lap,
And have a quiet, peaceful nap,
A dog's life isn't much,
They understand different languages
Including Dutch,
So as you can see why the dog is said to be
Man's best friend,
They will stick by you until the end!

Anna Lebbern

My Way

My poems are not epic with thoughts profound and deep
They're not designed with you in mind to make you laugh or weep,
They don't rely on pathos, or politics and such
And in the great big scheme of things, don't matter very much.
They're just my observation of things as time goes by
The everyday occasions that occur to you and I.
If they give you pleasure then that's an added treat
That gives me satisfaction and makes the verse complete.
The words come crowding in my head and flooding out my pen
I have to drop my daily chores until they're writ, and then
I've got another poem for everyone to see
Not centred upon any one, but written just for me!

Barbara Avery

World at War

The German Bombers out at night,
They won't give up without a fight.
They have their orders, crystal clear,
To spread the anger, pain, and fear.

The blacked-out windows of the streets,
Around the world, the many defeats.
The shouts of soldiers, far and near,
As homeless people shed a tear.

As bombs drop down on the old city square,
People stand, and watch, and stare.
The culprits of this awful deed,
Drop more in a quest of perilous greed.

I've just explained some wonders of life
You've heard of killings, husband and wife.
So maybe you knew this, maybe you saw,
What it's like in a world at war.

Chris Stubbs

Life Goes On

All happiness must pay! Can this be really true?
We start the road of life as happy, chuckling babes
And life goes on . . .

As kids we work and play, and lark about.
We cultivate our skills - we choose our path.
And life goes on . . .

The teenage years - we fall in love
Oh joy of joys! We make our choice,
And life goes on . . .

A happy couple now create a family,
A home that's filled with laughter, joy and tears.
And life goes on . . .

Too soon they're grown, they've flown the nest.
A white haired couple sit and dream their sweet contented
dreams
And life goes on . . .

But now the cruel blow! Such grief, such searing pain!
All happiness must pay? Ah yes, how well we know that now.
But - somehow - life goes on.

Brenda Eyles

"Tribute"

My beautiful friend, your life was not long
We were together, now you are gone
I miss you more, a little each day
I gaze at your photo, and here's what I say
My beautiful friend, so big and black, I know
That I can't have you back,
But in my heart, I know that we,
Always together, will truly be.

Only a whisper away.

Hazel Smith

To Linda

May the gods look down on you and say
We will help my dear this day
We look into your heart and see the pain
The fear you feel to be alone again
Time itself such a magical thing
Will take away care and let your heart sing
There are those who love you so
And feel sad to see you low
Who pray to God most every night
That He will cast his shining light
Upon you and let you know
True love and happiness you will know
Lovely cool waters run through your life
Taking away all struggle and strife
Your world become a clear blue sea
And within it grow the happiness tree

Daisy Annetts

The Missing Half

We were born together and lived as one,
We wore the same clothes and shared in our fun.
We stayed side by side, through thick and thin,
This was our downfall and greatest sin.

The day of departure lurked deep in our mind,
It destroyed our ensemble; harsh and unkind,
Nobody prepared us for life far apart;
The greatest nightmare locked away in our heart.

The hangman's rape violently swung,
trying to capture not two, but one.
Her hands were tied; he hauled her away.
He left me behind, the sun less a ray.

Torn asunder in gloom and despair,
Loneliness is empty, tragically unfair.
In this strange world, we cannot win.
Feels hard as death, life without your twin.

Deirdre Crowley

Strength of My Land

Born out of chaos, then cut from the whole
This land that is reaching deep into my soul
Its beauty is boundless, its spirit is free
It nurtures my feelings, allows me to see
That anger and fury have created such might
And bred in the mountains a passion to fight
Their scars through the ages tell of their battles
Against seasons and elements and even man's shackles
They gaze upon glens and cradle their lochs
Whilst daring the winds to perish their rocks
Dressed up in heather from hilltops to seas
This land is still willing and able to please
Protecting her children with tolerance so great
She shelters and feeds us not knowing her fate
Embracingly wild, yet perfectly planned
So honest and loyal, my purest Scotland

Chris Cunningham

Is This Me?

Is this me on the ground?
This poor lost soul simply sitting around?
His only possessions his life and his clothes,
You know the man all society loathes?

He won't make an effort or so they proclaim,
But who will employ him? It's always the same,
Their petty excuses but it's clear what they think,
"He's scruffy and useless; I'm sure he must stink"

For a man like this one thing is true,
His life is all over, because of you,
You won't give him work, you're prejudiced you see,
He's trying the handle but you've got the key.

Jason Marshall

"The Haircut"

Today is the day for my haircut,
This trip to the barber's I hate,
My mum says I'm needing it badly,
When I get there I know I will wait.

The shop is always so smoky,
Old men queuing up for a trim,
I don't know why they all bother,
They were bald before they came in.

My best friend at school says, "He's a butcher."
If you complain he will cut off your ears,
A few of his mates went there for a cut,
He said he's not seen them for years.

I told my mum this morning, just one hour away from my fate,
My stomach was hurting, I felt really sick,
My haircut will just have to wait.

Anthony Wray

Nostalgia

Can we remember those bygone years
Those halcyon days of yore;
Will we ever forget those times in our lives
When our spirits did soar and soar.

Will you, dear friend, ever be as you were
Like I was, so carefree and bright;
Can we turn back the clock and be hopeful again,
Can we alter our darkness to light.

Have those happy years gone forever, my friend
To be lost in the depths of time;
Will they ever return to us just as before
And bring joy to your heart and to mine.

If we remember those far-off years
And think how we were in those days;
Then we'll find, my dear friend, that those years are still here,
It is us who have changed in our ways!

John Carr

You are a rainbow

If words were reflected in colours, I would call you a rainbow
Violet for your tenderness and caring - often shown and always there
Indigo for the depths within you I've yet to plumb
Blue - the colour of your eyes penetrating mine
Green for your calmness and quiet between life's storms
Yellow for your brightness and humour - effervescent and
shining through
Orange for your fervour in all that you do
Red for your passion kindling the essence of you
- Like a rainbow you are all of these colours
- But unlike a rainbow you will never fade

Beverley Dipper

Within Reach

It was within reaching distance,
They wouldn't let me go. I couldn't do it.
I wanted to.
They held me back
I pushed forward
They screamed at me
I sat and listened, silent
I went to talk
They wouldn't let me
Once again they held me back
I tried to tell you
Tried to show you
Nothing happened
Desperation, filling me with guilt
Frustrated, furious with myself
Those repeating voices in my head holding me back from
being myself
I couldn't do it.

Joanna Stacey

The Little Blue Smurfs

The little smurfies, they live in their land
They've even formed their own little band
If you want to know how they get along
You come and listen while they play a song

There's violin smurf playing away
And grandpa smurf is having a grand day
Little flute smurf, he's there on the side
And xylophone smurf, in his playing he takes pride

They're all on herb tea, or so I am told
It keeps them young looking, they'll never grow old
So all you fine people, you listen to me
You put on your laugh and join in their glee

Old Father Abraham, he keeps them in hand
So if you're all good people, he'll let you into their land
Anyone naughty outside he must stay
Twiddling his thumbs, while you go and play

Fae Clark

This Human Child

Into this world we've created through our love together
This baby born to us, the outcome of such love;
Oh! So tiny little one with tenderness we care
This human child, what joy, for us to share as one.

Excitement filled our hearts that day, the day we realized
Success we had in creating so, this image now so real;
Perfect form, so small, untouched by any stain
Flawless human form, born to us a couple true.

The pain of birth just disappeared, of the product sown and reaped
Forcefully pushing with such haste into this planet we call earth;
Leaving with determination a nest so moist and warm, secure
To be a part, to play a role, within this Universe.

Love and joy in abundance, this treasure sure our own
This vision of a mortal one of skin so soft and pale;
Innocent, this angel one, its presence in a crib
Smiling sweetly, peacefully, this one designed with love.

Catherine O'Kane

It Could Happen to You

No one can be really sure.
They'll ever fall in love,
But hopefully when you mature,
The earth will really move.

In youth, attraction's just skin deep,
We all wear "Rosy Glasses",
Sometimes we laugh, sometimes we weep,
It happens to the masses

In middle age it means much more,
Because you're so much wiser,
You'll meet someone you can adore,
There's simply no one nicer

And if you're really fortunate,
You'll get that special glow,
You'll be his "Wrinkly" Juliette,
He'll be your Romeo,

Suddenly love songs all seem true,
You're happy all day long,
Every day the sky is blue,
You're living your own love song.

Doreen M. Carne

Shades in All Colours

What is the matter with mankind, I wish we were all colour blind,
This black and white issue, why is it a problem between me and you?
You didn't make me, I didn't make you,
God has the right to do what He wants to do,
He made us brothers and sisters,
He gave us shades in all colours.

Look at the flowers and the rainbow, look at the plants around
    and below,
See their harmony, see their colour, they have no hate for one
    another, they are beautiful shades in all colours.

Prejudice is wrong and doesn't belong, God gave us love to
    all get along, humans can be as beautiful as the flowers,
We have shades in all colours,

We happen to be made by the Almighty. Out of one man,
    came you and me,
United colours are great to see, all races should live in unity,
We have the will, we have the powers, we have beautiful
    shades in all colours.
We know what is wrong and what is right, to love one another
    and to unite, we are beautiful people, black and white,
We should be lovers, not haters, we have shades in all colours.

Barrington Delevante

Summer Hol's
(or 'An Old Dog's Advice to the Puppies')

"Off you go boys - be good." - What a cheek!
What else can we be in the kennels this week?
Whilst they disappear, away to the sun,
Off on their hol's, to the sea and the fun.

Don't be sad lads, for in spite of their glee,
It will take them a long time to get to the sea.
There'll be long traffic jams, then they'll miss the boat,
The rain will pour down - now boys, don't you gloat.

When they return don't feel sorry for them,
'Cos even though Lindy, our maid's such a gem,
We were left, abandoned, as off they did race,
So pity for them would be quite out of place.

Ignore them when they come running to us,
Gnaw your bone, have a stretch - just don't make a fuss.
Remember, we must make it most frightfully clear.
That to us summer hol's are so terribly drear.

Now steady young lads - that's their voices we hear,
And here come our leads - Damn, we've one choice - that's clear.
To bounce, bark, wag our tails - show how happy we are,
'Cos our walks can resume now they've brought back our car!

Brian Booth

The Moon through My Window at Night

Oh Magic Mystical Moon that shines
through my window at night,
What beauty you display in the heavens high.
I felt the spirit of God was in the Moon,
such greatness and majesty.
I love you dear Moon, just as I feel you love me.
Brighter by the minute,
now appearing full view in my room
suddenly you're gone.
I say goodnight my lovely Moon - until next we meet
Magic Mystical beauty of the night.

Jacqueline Beyba

My Jesus

Stand up Jesus and let them see You,
Those proud cocky people, who don't know the truth.
To them You are a nursery rhyme character
With brown curly hair.
They don't realize the pain that You had to bear.
They think You're a model fresh from the parlour,
They don't realize You were sent by Your Father.
They don't realize You were human like me,
Coming in love, to set us all free.
They don't realize how terribly You died,
That nail hitting wood brought tears to Your eyes.
You had the power to squash me like a bug.
But instead You poured out Your love.
My sins are forgiven because of Your bravery,
Now I'm no longer tied to the devil in slavery.
Thank You Jesus for loving me so,
Your promise to me is You'll never let me go.
I could never repay You for what You've done for me,
By dying on the cross and setting me free.

Amanda-Jayne Hill

The Piano Keys

A hundred setting suns align on the horizon
"Grand" says Gran, as the mantle piece burns
The corps are out, one by one
Down on Cherry Tree Road silence is old
Past broken cars and Yamaha's we found our forgiveness
The joy we borrowed was safe to doubt
We dreamt the future
Up to heaven in roaring black laughter
I wanted to fly, melancholy, in tandem with the autumn shade
Always shadow what harrows England
I looked at kindness with her goldsmith locks
There was a constellation of senses that will not bring dawn
Yet smile a proposal and give language an arrow
So to sleep in cold sinew like a marble horse
Slowly entire zest befell a J.C.B. widow
Crawling for a jinx of spirit she opened the bottle
I prayed for a father to reap society
With church tails high I kissed the remedy as a bride
And sang and sang and sang
Looking back I remember the piano keys

Adam Stancer

Life

Thumpety Thump Thumpety Thud
Thus beats the heart pumping the blood
Thump Thumpety Thump, now beats there are two
Sounds of new life that grows within you.

A kiss, a caress, a joining as one
A love full of passion, a new life begun
Steadily slowly the new life grows stronger
Your patience runs out, you can wait no longer.

Pant Pant and Push, then suddenly Whoosh,
A miracle happens it's hard to explain
An explosion of joy through all the pain
The child in your arms unaware of the fuss
A child born of love, an extension of us.

Brenda Roberts

479

A Highwayman on Shooter's Hill

The eyes that glitter behind the mask are black as the clothes he wears. And the heart that beats within his breast is black as the cross he bears. The stallion too on which he sits is black as the night around, as they stand in the shadows and patiently wait for the coach which is London bound.

Not a sound in the dark but the sigh of the wind and the far-off cry of a hound. And something creaking as it gently sways in the wind above the ground. Was that once a man? That thing hanging there upon the Gallows tree. Hanging in chains with sightless eyes, a warning for all to see.

The Gent of the Road looks up and sighs and talks to the thing above. Alas, poor Tom, I knew you well, so fair and full of love. No more will you dandle a wench on your knee down in the Rising Sun. And the High Street of Eltham will miss your sweet laugh, but remember the things that you've done.

No more will you gallop across Blackheath with the thought of a promise so dear. The brush of her lips as she sets down your ale, a smile and a word in your ear. "Dear Tom, let it finish before it's too late", so often she said with a sigh. "A Gent of the highway I know you are, but without you I'll surely die."

They came with the dawn and took you away to hang on Tyburn's tree. Then brought you back here to Shooter's Hill in chains for all to see. The one who betrayed you will surely come tonight on the Dover run. And shall be here to hold up the stage and avenge my only son.

Gordon Hoare

The Homecoming

The universal call back to home,
To seat you on your secret throne.
Throw back your robes of gold delight,
To take upon the perfect flight.

Of heavenly angels, from God's breast,
To free you now, at His behest.
The silken threads that we do weave,
To form the way and to receive
The answer, that will take us back.

The search is over, we do not lack,
The love that God endowed us with.
The heavenly Father there to give
His heart to us at any time,
His love for us is so sublime.

The quantum leap, is our last test,
Upon this earth we cannot rest.
Until we hear His voice, at last,
The purest voice come from our past.
From ages long, so long ago,
Piercing the heavens, so now we know.

Elaine Lathbury

Brummie Rush Hour

Birmingham exudes its working hordes.
Thick as treacle, factory gates and office doors
pour out the cans of people
and destination fever spurs a fleeting dash;
gears crash as ratty hooters blare
harsh arguments of heated irritation.

Veins of brummie streets bulge varicose.
Fuming clots, pulsating tail to nose
clutter up each way the choking roads
and silting freeways block the tubes of infiltration;
vents arteriole seep metallic blood
that swell the necks with thick coagulation.

Fever burns the hour that peaks its virulence.
Radiating beams of plaguing metal streams
cast wide its agitation
like some erupting crucible of metalliferous blood;
spewing out its molten heart of raw metallic guts
in surging waves of hot regurgitation.

Edwin Cobb

Schizophrenia

I'm a complex personality
Three people in one
There's a fourth in my wardrobe
And he's not alone
Got a friend at the local
Likes lager and black
But his mates, one a shandy
'Cos he's driving back
Democracy rules in this chaotic mess
One person, one vote
Though under duress
My mood swings are frantic
One second unhappy, the next I am glad
Part of us sane, most of me mad
I'm not paranoid, but I know for a fact
The others talk about me behind my back
It's getting quite puzzling
My new family tree
The problem is knowing
Which one's really me?

Dave Downes

Spring Time

Now the ice, and snow, have gone,
We can now look forward to Spring, which is yet to come.
Bring in with it, lots of showers,
Which will bring froth, May flowers,
Birds will be whistling, up on high.
Dipping and diving, through the sky.
Bring in lighter evenings, and warmer weather,
Which everyone, will enjoy, together

Dennis Calvert

Just Someone

Several times he took me home to share his marital bed,
To listen to his music and the lovely things he said,
But he didn't think of afterwards and all the envious pain
That I would feel deep inside to haunt me over again.
I can close my eyes and easily see her picture on the wall,
While making love I'd wonder if she could see it all.
We wrongly said it gave us satisfaction to be there,
But how could he have respect for her, how could he even care?
And how could I be like this, this really isn't me,
I don't like cheats or cheating, was my love so blind to see,
That I suppose, if he knows, when he's lying there with her,
That I've been there with the love we share, he can make his mind a blur,
And pretend he's got me there to give him mental variation,
When in fact, to his marriage, I'm just giving it salvation.

Gillie Pactat

Lifetime

Today it is time,
Time to be born.
Time to thrust a way,
upon this gentle morn.
Time to make that journey,
From the darkness of the womb,
Upon an unknown way.

Today it is lifetime! A lifetime released.
Without a sign of how it will unfold,
Or what the future of that life will hold,
Or what path that life will take,
Or what changes that life will make,
To its generation.
it may lead a nation.
Perhaps for right, perhaps for wrong.
It may be short, it may be long.

But today a mother's arms will cradle,
That new life, as in the stable.
A husband's arms, will hold his wife.
Today it is time! Time for life!

Jean Fenton

Spring

Here she comes pushing up her green spikes
Through earth sodden wet
Here she comes waving her wand on tree and shrub
She dabs her paint so delicate on first crocus and daffodil
And favours pink malus most with blossoms that strain her
 slender branches
Here she comes with rainbow and cool wind
Her bright sunlight stabs the earth and bulbs bathe
Thrush and blackbird sing and ready themselves
Here she comes with wind swept cloud casting quick shadows
Dropping her icy jewels that bounce and dance on earth's stage
Here she comes scenting her air decorating her body with
 bright colours and pins them with shafts of sunlight
Now she is ready
She blooms with health
Summer waits and blows a warm kiss
Lying together as one, begin their annual courtship.

Edward Roome

Dunblane

Take a walk in the Scottish countryside
To the people of Dunblane.
Feel the grief they will be feeling
Since that gunman went insane.
Imagine a mother and father.
Who has no child to kiss goodnight.
His toys still in his bedroom.
Unplayed with, yet in sight.
And the other children cry.
For the mates they will never see.
Their peace, their lives in ribbons.
Oh God why should it be.

Jenny Bosworth

Walk of Death

So gentle is the one that stalks,
Through grass in lands afar
He walks.

Like a coiled-up spring and then he goes,
Unleashed, the bloody river flows.

Through greed and gore he carries on,
And on and on till there's no more,
The stuff he fills his walls within.
So strong he is, so lean, so thin.

Empty carcass, blood and bone,
A shallow grave not marked with stone.
Through pain and fear, but not a tear,
Did die a life so full, so dear,

And shall we mourn, what can we do,
As guilty as the lion too.
Our life does stretch the normal chain,
And keeps us safe and free from pain.

Alan Garvey

Armistice

We strive to remember their valour
We care to remember why - they gave their lives so freely,
Over land, and sea, and sky.

It was for this land we call Britain -
Whose boundaries are so wide -
They fought with all their weapons - made stronger
By their pride!

Still now - years on
Our soldiers fight in battles - and come back
with their scars -
Their lives are always tainted, because they fought for ours!

So - let's keep the Great in Britain -
Let's stand up - one and all,
At the eleventh hour, on the eleventh day of the eleventh month
We will remember - all of them
For they will never grow old.

Brenda Cook

Waters of Love

Waters of "Love"
Through streams, keep it flowing
Down into rivers, keep it going
Into the sea, it is flowing
Tides are turning, twisting, turning,
Moon reversing,
Earth is tilting.
Waves of waters, splashing,
Washing rocks, as it may go.
To and thro', to and thro',
With a spiritual flow
Trying to tell us, all is well,
As we all, shall know,
Waters are now, calmer down below,
Fill our hearts "Lord"
With Your spiritual flow
Which is your "Love"
We shall always know,
And let it,
"Flow," "flow," and "flow".

John Robinson

Three Wishes

If I had three wishes
What could they be?
I think I'd have lots of
Sweets to share them all 1,2,3.

For my second wish I'd
Wish to be a millionaire,
and then I could say I don't care.

For my very last wish what could it be?
I think I'll wish for everyone to be happy.

Clare Jones

Reflections

Look in the mirror deep.
What do I see?
The face of a man fast asleep.
Wake up your heart!
Wake up your soul!
Tormented by life's harrowing woes.

No more the face of a man asleep,
Look into the mirror deep
What do I see?
The face of a child staring back at me.
Wide innocent eyes veil tales of woe,
The hurt, the anguish and oh, the pain,
And then the mask appears again.

Once more look into the mirror deep.
What do I see?
A reflection of an inner me.
Step inside the imagery.
What do I see?
The person I would like to be.

Gaynor Lounds

The Children of Tomorrow

Look through the eyes of the children of tomorrow,
what do you see?
A cold harsh world of anger and sorrow, fashioned by you and me.
Do the coloureds honestly have their freedom, do they honestly
have their rights?
Should there be on every other corner riots, killing and fights?
Do the children of the third world have enough to eat?
Should our children be unsafe to play in their own street?
Should there be homeless in the cold?
Why shouldn't there be homes for everyone?
So for the children of tomorrow something must be done.
So united we will stand and together we will fall.
The whole world hand in hand will rise above it all.
The world will be at peace again, there will be no war.
The children of tomorrow will see it as it was before.

Danielle Jeffery

'When Love Dies'

When your love for me dies, as die it surely must,
Will it be a slow and lingering end, or will it be a killing
By sharp cruel words, like rapier thrust
Into my heart?b Oh let it not be so - I could not bear the pain
But rather let me hope awhile that love will live again.
Let it lie patient on its gentle bed, and give me time
For my farewell, when each tender glance of yours,
Each kindly, word however lightly meant;
Will give me hope that love again will burn
And bring your swift return to me.
If you must go away, and in my heart I know that you will go
You say you cannot stay because I ask
Too much of you - more than you have to give,
And I must learn to live
Without your love, for it has died.
It was too frail to mend.
There is no more to do, but to weep upon its grave
and mourn its passing until the end.

Beti Howe

House Viewers

Tension rises: Will they like it?
Will they want to buy?
Twice today they've driven past,
They must be wondering why,
Why we seek to leave this house,
Why it's up for sale,
They won't find out by cruising 'round
Ignorant of our tale.
We like the house and would not move
If I still had a job.
The mortgage now we can't afford -
It's not just a few bob.
They're coming in with list in hand
So know the price we ask.
They're looking 'round; he seems quite stunned
But she's up to the task.
Standard questions asked and answered,
There is no need to pack.
The body language says it all;
We know they won't be back.

David Turner

Daydream Wonder

As you gaze into the tunnels of wrongs and rights,
Will you do as it says or will you might?
It's hard to trust from within your views,
Does it depend who is who?
It all shatters as you're still looking through,
You're thinking now who am I, am I you?
You look out the window into the world beyond,
The sunset's glow is bright and strong,
From the deep depths in to the world we go,
What will any of us gain or know?.

Joanne Mary Sharlott

Grieve Not for Me

Will you weep for me when I am gone?
Will your tears flow when my life is done?
Will you mourn for me at my grave side?
Will your grief show once I have died?

Why weep for me when I cannot hear?
Why shed for me your sorrowful tear?
Why mourn for me while I turn to clay?
Why grieve for me as I mould away?

Weep for those who suffer a living Hell,
Shed tears for those whose souls scream and yell,
Mourn for those cut down in their prime,
Grieve for those dead before their time.

Weep for those tortured and maimed,
Shed tears for those shattered and shamed.
Mourn for those who silently plea,
Grieve for all those, but grieve not for me.

David Mantle

Happiness Is . . .

Happiness is a family, safe and secure.
Times shared are precious, memories are fond
From beginning to end.

Happiness is a friendship, warm and fun -
A loyalty, honesty, caring, sharing;
Forever.

Happiness is a lover, tender and sweet.
Touch, emotion, passion and open arms,
Hope.

Happiness is nature, beautiful and free -
Sky, sea, earth and all things bright,
For as long as nature intends.

Happiness is a soul, a personal dream.
A spirit of love, hope, faith with
No beginning and without an end.

Happiness is . . .

Emma J. Wright

Away Reality

When the outside world has hurt you
With all its cruel and viscous ways,
When of its torment you've grown weary
And its callousness you've felt the pain,
Then float, retreat into the world inside
With all its endless peace, that only you can find
With its unbridled beauty that it holds as it hides,
Keep it clean from trespass, solely yours,
Keep it locked up in your mind.

Edward John Borrill

The Lonely Woman

My life is like an empty room
With all the people gone
The parties are all over
And I am quite alone.

Or is it more an empty house
As still as any grave
Save phantom calls of fair-haired children
I shall never have?

Reflections in the pool of life
Are like a random stone
Thrown rippling through the shadows
Now all the birds have flown.

The memories of my golden days
With azure flecks and green
Flash across my vision
And vanish like a dream.

My brain has rainbow coloured cells
And in this cosmos my past dwells.

Gill Morgan

A Trucker's Lament

Sitting alone, staring out into space,
Through the frost-coated windscreen
that looks like lace,
Thinking to myself in a forlorn tone,
Why the hell aren't I sitting at home,
In a comfortable chair watching T.V.
With my wife beside me and a G and T.
Having come home at a respectable time,
A day's work done and the night is all mine,
To do what I want, anything at all,
Go down to the pub and drink till I fall.
Or just stay at home and laze about,
Relax on the sofa and occasionally shout,
At the kids to be quiet, as my favourite programme is on,
Do your homework, or go out and play on the lawn.
But as I sit here alone, far from content,
I know others are thinking, a trucker's lament.

Gordon Johnston

The Messenger

Tuesday morning, bleak and grey.
Through the streets I make my way.
Nine o'clock, no birds sing,
Only the noise of the sirens ring.
In my pocket I hold the note,
That brings such misery to other folk.

I see the house down the lane,
Already, I can feel their pain.
Next door's garden, shattered by a bomb,
What's left of the house? Only some!
I tread the path up to the door, wishing I was not there at all,

Tears fall as she reads the note,
Her eldest son has gone down with the boat.
Her family cries as I walk away,
I know it off by heart, it happens every day.
On the tram, I'm riding home,
Feeling impossibly alone. All at once the people shout,
The lights come on, the bells ring out.
The war is over; There's endless joy. But it's all too late,
For the sunken boy!

Helen Norton

Simulation (Fantasy No. 2)

Although you do not know it,
 We have walked together hand in hand
 On many an ocean shore,
 Crinkling our toes in the hot dry sand
 Cooling our feet in the on-rushing waves.

Although you cannot know it,
 We have wandered through many a woodland glade,
 And o'er many a lakeland fell,
 Scenting the clear fresh mountain air,
 Trampling the springy turf beneath our feet.

Although you will not know it,
 I have often kissed your luscious lips,
 Finding them soft, and warm, and sweet,
 Softer, warmer, sweeter, than I had ever dreamed.

Although you should not know it,
 I have often held your pliant body
 Close against my own,
 Until its gentle stirring
 Bespoke our urgent mutual need.

 This is how it seems to be in my own "virtual reality."

Gillian L. Sumner

I Wonder

I wonder what it feels like
To sit there every day
And just hope to see a friendly face
Give a smile or wave your way.

I wonder what it feels like
To always be alone
With no one to ever speak to
Apart from salesmen on the 'phone

I wonder what it feels like
With just your memories of the past
To fill your lonely days
And give some joy at last.

I wonder what it feels like
When your loved ones are all dead
And there is no one there to hold you
As you lie motionless in bed

I only wonder what it feels like
Because I am young you see
But I dread to think that one day
It could even happen to me

Josephine Wood

The T.V. Soaps

We sit down with a cup of tea, to catch up on the soap.
With all the problems on the box, peace of mind, "no hope".

Brookside, Coronation street, East Enders, Neighbours too,
Emmerdale, Home and Away, I just don't know who's who.
Dirty Dave, or is it Des, I don't know who is what,
I try to follow what goes on, but mix up all the lot.

If Annalise goes out with Grant, Peggy will have a fit,
will Liz our trusty barmaid start serving at the Vic.

Gail lives with Philip Martin, Nigel acts the clown,
while Marlene goes off to church, Frank is feeling down.

Mike Baldwin had a short affair, with Cody the other night,
Phil Mitchell came in the room, and gave them both a fright.
Does Brett go out with Tiffany, Bianca out with Shane,
I'm trying to get the story right - it's driving me insane.

Can someone please explain to me, all you EAR-HOLE benders,
If Brookside and Coronation Street are Neighbours of East Enders.

Derek Harding

Reflections

My mind was wandering far and wide
to bygone times and evening tide
to summer days in endless measure
of winter winds and nights to treasure.

I thought of all the happy days
of hours spent in lots of ways
of children laughing in the sun
I counted blessings one by one.

I saw while dreaming in my sleep
the countless mysteries of the deep
of clean fresh air, the bluest skies
of good roast beef and apple pies.

And then I walked through, in my mind
the fields and by-ways I could find
I climbed the style, just by the brook
and walked the lanes to school we took.

As here I viewed a spectre vast
We can reflect our pleasures past.

Christine Wheeler

Thorns

I have sown the seeds of thorns,
Walking on thorns, I have become thorns.

My life is a bed of thorns,
When I sleep, my body is pierced by thorns.

Whenever I speak,
They ignore me, like thorns.

My life is sullen within me,
Even flowers, look like thorns.

What else is there to have in life,
When Darshan (Master) has written Lachhman's fate, with thorns.

Das Lachhman Das

No More War!

War in Bosnia, here and there -
War is almost everywhere,
and I'm asking myself why
nations are reaching for this kind of crime?
Children, mothers, broken arms, shot in the eye,
paralysed, disable, dead . . . Why?
Nagasaki, Hiroshima, World War One and Two -
Who's to blame, tell me Who?
Hitler, Hussain? Evil leaders yes that's true,
but you are guilty too,
because you are follow them, and it's very sad
to be scared of someone who is absolutely mad.
So please be brave and say no, more
to the madness, to the War!

Ewa Demus

Love Lost

Into the midst beyond
We shall walk hand-in-hand
With blue sky yonder
And waves upon the sand
The ships upon the horizon
A flock of seagulls scream
The very smell of life
Wanders into our dream
Some children playing on the beach
Their smiles and faces appear
Then why do I feel this uncertainty
And an overwhelming fear
I turn to see an expressionless face
As our hands begin to part
I knew this moment would arrive sometime
When you finally break my heart

Andrew Darren Goor

This Earth

"Oh" what a world is this.
We should all be living in bliss.
Instead of hurting each other,
We should be at peace with our brother,
trying to do the best we can,
to heal the wounds of this earth's man,
Together we have to live on this earth,
And it would be far easier,
Without the hurt.

Ann Marie Kidd

And It's All Over Now

Once upon a time, we had a love,
We would sit under the blue moon above.
Going around together, nothing to break us apart,
We were both tucked inside each other's heart.

You would tell me that you loved me,
I thought that it would always be.
That fatal night we broke up,
deep down, my heart, got deeply cut.

So now we go around, so alone,
the love we have had, has now all gone.
All the sharing we used to do,
now all I have left are my dreams about you.

Not forgetting how it used to be,
how it feels so uncomfortable to be free.
Hoping some day we'll make up and be a couple again,
but all I feel in my heart, is the pain.

It's been so long now, I realize you're never coming back,
I haven't seen or heard from you, I've lost all track.
Trying to remember all the lovely things you would do,
hoping I will see you again because I still love you.

Carole Thompson

To Be Beyond

To be beyond, and dutiful,
To be, to see the beautiful,
To smell, to feel, to know, to gain,
Why can't it stay the same?

To hold so close and hear,
To touch this "oh so dear",
To laugh aloud, the sheer delight,
Why can't it just be right?

To be deprived of all, and sigh,
Time to think our thoughts, and cry.
Rise above ourselves to be,
Ourselves, as others would like to see.

Extinct, no function left at all,
To go across the boundary wall,
Quiet, still, and safe to go,
Deservedly, utterly, rightly so.

Alison O'Dwyer

Dougal

We lost our Dougal, he didn't survive
To be with us for Christmas 95.
A sad Christmas in truth, without our pet
But in thoughts he remains, we'll never forget.
We got him by chance (but for no small fee!)
For we'd set out to purchase a Cherry tree,
A Cherry tree of the Japanese kind -
With never a thought of a dog in our mind.
On the way, however, some kennels we passed
Saying 'Douglas for Sale, one left, he's the last'
The last of a litter of Lhasa apso
(From Tibetan monasteries of long long ago)
So we had to enquire, did he look the same
As his namesake of Magic Round about fame?
And surely he did in every way
So our visions of Cherry blossom faded away,
As with whimpers of joy and excited leaps
He showed us he meant to be ours for keeps.
Happy years we kept him - now in memory
We have planted that Cherry tree.

Doreen Yewdall

No Other Rose

No other rose I wanted in my garden
To bud and blossom and to scent the air.
No other rose I planted in my garden,
My only rose, the one I chose, is there.

Each year I prune the rose that's in my garden
And gently use the sharply-cutting knife,
To take away the dead and useless branches
And so make way for new and better life.

In summer's eve I walk into the garden,
The sweetest fragrance all around me blows.
I take delight in knowing that it came from
My tended one, my loved and chosen rose.

Diana Myatt

The Christmas Gift Token

Through the streets and shops I tramped
to buy a gift and postage stamp
with a man in mind who's so complex
may be a 17th century text
books perhaps for the intellectual
or a mobile with swing perpetual
something creative or slightly comical
the Beano or some scribe's chronicle
sad at heart feet overheated
looks to me I've been defeated
unimaginative may be this card
even though I did try hard
no need to grovel or to flatter
for to you it will not matter
whilst smiling at this awful rhyme
you'll appreciation it all took time
enjoy it for that's all what counts
and savour spending this huge amount

Elizabeth Skidmore

V.E. Day

How they would love this special day.
With adults and children alike happy and gay.
To celebrate the ending of life how it really was.
No more bombs no more rubble
No more ladies in American trouble.
Oh yes they would love - this day.
And how they do it the great - British way.
Flags would be flying.
Drink would be flowing,
To celebrate that long ago homecoming.

But they're not here, with a glass to cheer.
So we will celebrate this fiftieth year.
Remembering that they did their bit.
And us being British, very proud of it.

Dawn Benoit

Never to Be Forgot

He stood in the dusky air,
Where red poppies bob their heads in the breeze,
As red as the blood spilt there many years ago,
The huge craters that once scarred the bloodied mud
Now has tall grasses and daisies stained by
the setting sun.
The smell of gas and rotting flesh is now no more
Only the scent of wild flowers fill the air,
He smiles, all the pain and suffering now has gone
The groans of the dying are replaced by innocent
children at play.
A child comes gathering daisies and stops and stares.
He gives a mock salute she returns it back.
He watches her go as he fades with the evening sun,
A man who is not really there but died on that spot years ago,
On the tenth day of the eleventh month
During a time that should never be forgot.

Helen Whapshott

Untitled

All along the watch tower,
Where the eagles lay.
Above the flight of ravens,
The night scratches morning to start
Another day.
Underneath a rainbow where Somme poppies
Lay
A tear fell on a marble stone
That spoke the weathered words of wars
In a foreign land
The sounds of bugles calling out
The sight of victory.
They fought and fell they went
Through hell
The men of yesterday.

Charles Gordon Love

The Lonely Flower

I was lost like a flower that grew alone
Where the tall dark trees were fully grown.
At the mercy of the elements, it was hard to survive;
If I was trod on by anything I could not hide.
An innocent flower trusting, loving and kind
to forgive what was happening but sad about life
Never knew in this world, what mystery could be
Until all these different spells happened to me.
O the golden sunshine, the gentle rain,
this brings joy to my heart once again
I look up to the trees to the heavens above,
could I reach to the stars to those I love?
But those tall dark trees prevent the views from the skies.
Make sure I never see too much with my eyes,
I really like my colour of the palest blue
and to others and myself will always be true,
If I am to live in these woods all alone,
I'll have strength from God, then those dark trees will moan.

Ivy Land

I Looked Out of My Window to See

I looked out of my window.
To see what I could see.
There was a robin redbreast.
Staring at me.
A bumble bee came by.
And oh robin redbreast did fly.
The bumble bee chased robin.
Way up high into the sky.

Pussy cat, pussy cat.
Wither can ye be.
Way up high in the old apple tree.
Pussy cat, pussy cat.
Why are you up there.
Says the cat "Because I wanted to eat.
That big blackbird up there."

Angela Jane Titley

"Can You Imagine"

Can you imagine
What life would be like
Without food, water and clothes
And for a child without a bike

Think of the poverty
In the countries that are poor
Think of the dying children
Crying, heartbreak and despair

Think of the fighting
Between countries and towns
Between Catholics and Protestants
Punishment beatings and being shot down

Claire Hamilton

Ambition

What is it that spurs me on
to greater heights than otherwise
attained;
But leaves me flat, alone
and uninspired just on the brink of possible
success . . .

Why do these feelings, until this moment unbeknown
spring suddenly from depths
unfeigned;
But without warning, slink away
and leave me floundering in a
wilderness

Of perplexity. Will I achieve my
ambitions, or be forever
chained
to unimportant phenomena of life
which cloud the mind and dim the eye with
hopelessness.

Jennifer Young

Visionary

John Willie published a 1940's magazine,
Titled 'Bizarre' a new face on the scene.
Catering for a public just after a war,
Their tastes existed of that he was sure.
Artwork, articles, photographs and letters,
He encouraged abandonment of sexual fetters.
Artwork by himself both sensual and sublime,
Producing provocative illustrations time after time.
Delving into the mystery of the sexual fetish,
Printing his material with enthusiastic relish.
Influencing a generation following close behind,
Irving Claw and Eric Stanton and all their kind.
Photographers and artists and shapely beauties,
Comic strips and posing with rope bound cuties.
Silk stockings and waspies and six inch heels,
Teasing the imagination and how it all feels.
Fifty years forward his dream lives on,
John Willie's vision far from long gone.
Rubber wear and corsets now all the rage,
Fetishism booms and takes centre stage.

John Carter

Untitled

Flowers - the joy and perfume of the soul,
We look and wonder with delight,
A thousand shapes and countless colours
carpets of purple, pink, blue and white
Spotted and frilled, some very shy
Others so bold in colour and scent
They seem to hold an argument.

Perhaps they represent the people here on earth
Sent to teach us how to live -
We all have a different shape and hue,
We bloom, we die - yet perhaps like flowers
We return to life, lovelier and much more wise,
For we have lived in Paradise.

Anna Hepburn

485

Granddad

It's not easy telling of your love
to someone like yourself
like a grand hotel, untouched by time
standing so very tall and proud
keeping us sheltered from the weather
like the bitter winds and rains

In its own special way telling of old,
of the good times and the bad
making history as the years go by
being strong, yet never a word is said
making the young abide by rules
yet not letting them know it's him

Like that grand hotel standing tall
you get younger each time we talk
you have all those hidden stories
that make you proud of your life to date
from one generation to another
I love you just because you're you.

Jenna G. Sparkes

Others Call

It always happens, it never fails
to wait until I'm busy.
For you to shout your urgent tone,
you, the annoying telephone.

I get settled to watch T.V,
but you, have other plans for me.
You are persistent in your ringing,
your bur bur you keep singing.

But why, I ask myself,
when in the house there are others,
do they go deaf to your bring bringing,
leaving me, to answer your insistent ringing.

I sigh a sigh and lift your receiver.
I say hello and listen a while,
then I give a patient smile, you see
It's never for me.

Barbara Stainton

Dunblane

Go home, we do not want you here.
To watch our weeping, hear our prayers.
You are intruding on our sorrow.
We face today but not tomorrow.
We do not want your prying eyes
To see our tear-stained faces, hear our sighs.
We just need to be alone,
Not beamed into everybody's home
By newsreel and by satellite
Day by day, night by night.
Once you've filed your last report, said all there is to say,
Please pack your bags and go away.
We need some peace and quiet and space
To come to terms with what's happened in this place.
We need to grieve, we need to mourn
And then we need to try and carry on.

Dorothy T. Harries

The Garden of Love

Peace just sits there waiting for us
Waiting in the Garden of Love,
It nestles behind the tree of grace
There in our Heaven Above.

The end of pain, the end of sorrow
The end of all that is blind
But the beginning of, the new tomorrow
With all ugliness left behind.

We need fear not, our new world above
Or dread our time to move on,
As the sun shines bright in our Garden of Love
And the peace, lives on - and - on.

Glenys Benjafield

Minds

Stargazing with thought of the mind.
To heights beyond the great divine.
What are the thoughts of mankind.

Stargazing still curious to know.
To look at Earth, its beauty unfold.
With Colours of Nature, no man could have told.

Stargazing may minds still, continue to wonder,
admire, and praise at the glory of this.
That such splendour belongs to us all.

Stargazing with thoughts flooding in.
Its free beauty of wealth, minds, taking it in,
to explore, discovering and research.

Stargazing, give thanks, for autumn and winter,
Its memories kept safe. New birth of spring and
Summer about to begin. All bright, fresh and new

Stargazing bringing thoughts down to earth,
Let's stride now into the future, with, warmth
And love so divine. Give thanks.

Irene Marshall

"Peppe"

Ears alert
To hear a call soft red coat
Like a fluffy ball

Green eyes bright
To see at night

Four white paws to walk him around
Telling his foe
"This is my ground"

Long straight tail
High in the air
Moving around without a care

Pretty pink nose
To sniff his scent guiding him home
From a night well spent

Homeward bound without a fuss
A loving "Miaow"
From a lovely red puss

A purr and a cuddle
And now to be fed
Washes whiska's and face and so to bed.

Ellen Hill

Melting Moments

Long winds the road of life that leads us on
To pastures new; the rocky path that climbs
Forever on until the battle's won.
Now for a resting place to ease our minds.

Much needed is a moment of pure pleasure;
A blossom bursting on a wind-swept bough.
Time to be still and contemplate the leisure
Of a peaceful mind, unfurrowed brow.

Fond thoughts of past delights bring solace sweet
And dreams of future joys will raise the soul
To further effort; strength anew to meet
What lies ahead; clear vision for the goal.

So steal away to find a quiet nook,
Secluded from the beaten track, and say
A prayer of thanks, and take a closer look
At present blessings, lest they slip away.

Hold on to precious moments lest they melt
And face away, lost through those careless hands.
Sustained with tender care and love heart felt
A store of joy they bring to life's demands.

Helen Ratcliffe

A Minute for Dunblane

I walked on the hill at Gretton
To the sound of church bells across the valley
From Winchcombe;
The noises of the countryside -
Machinery, animals, bird noises sweet and sour -
Passed through the air.

Then at 9:30 a.m.
An eerie silence, broken only by the wind
Whistling through trees;
Suddenly a songbird
Began his sweet solos, not realising the mourning
On that morning;

And when the minute passed
The bells burst into peals once more to ring
A song of hope;
The songbird joined by crows
And pheasant, as if all the country 'round
Had come to terms.

We are All victims of Dunblane;
Perhaps we can All learn for the future?

Bill Pullen

Food for Thought

The sweetness has disappeared from my life,
what was luscious has now become humbled.
Once feathery, golden, delicious white bread,
to contemptible brown has now crumbled.

Formerly surfaced with succulent cream,
daily bounty reduced, separated.
Potato once sliced, fried and served crisply,
consumed whole, undecorticated.

Where once no concern of magnitude share,
appears contemptible, measured amount.
Energy creating abundance,
moderated and made to account.

What used to remain must now proceed through,
therefore fibrous consuming ensured.
Change of old manner, practice and habit,
must now be forever endured.

But I suppose if I look on the bright side,
now is wholesome what used to run riot,
and I'm sure I'll soon be accustomed,
to this desolate, bland low fat diet.

Douglas J. Clarke

Hard Times

The country lane is long and winding
with high bushes on each side,
tiny green buds hard on finding,
from the frost - away do hide.

Now the winter's really biting
the earth is crunching at my feet,
to keep my balance I am fighting,
visions ahead - I have to keep.

I must try to keep on walking,
though the distance seems so far,
when I hear voices talking
who has left the door ajar? Of my mind in disarray -
wondering can I put it in perspective? Make it work for me today!!

People talking 'round in circles,
nothing easy but resigned,
trying to solve my personal problems
just to give me peace of mind.

Though it's getting even harder,
like the ground beneath my feet,
to keep pace and keep on walking
to make my life seem complete.

Barbara Johnson

Inspiration

The sun inspires me most
With its bright beams enveloped with cloud,
And infra colours being sent out,
It stands "mighty" strong and proud.

Cool clear water is also a masterpiece
Built from God's handiwork.
The bloom of a new plant,
Like another birth to nature.

No human being can compare
His handiwork with that of gods,
Man or God can destroy it all
Who will be the first?

Is it God's handiwork that inspires us,
Or is it our feeble knowledge about beauty?
The atomic bomb or God,
"Who is the stronger?"

The moon takes the place of the sun,
But what takes the place of the earth?
Is it faith in God?
That makes me believe in life after death?

Franklin Chetwood

Bye Gone Days

"Going to the shop", you happily call,
To the next door neighbour you knew,
Door left unlocked, you trusted all,
Your friendships remained all so true.

Children out playing in the park,
As they merrily run free.
Walking along the lane in the dark,
having picnics by the sea.

Windows left open, to let in the air,
Out in the back garden to weed.
No fear in our minds to cause despair,
Or to make our hearts want to bleed.

What happened to people, what happened to trust?
Be careful who you speak to.
Is bad behaviour really a must?!
So morals become such a few.

Do what you want! Who seems to care,
Turn back the clock to the past.
Where is the joy? We used to share,
I wish it had continued to last.

Angela Carvell

"Memories"

I often think of my childhood days, so happy and full of fun
When in summertime we would go to the seaside with our dad
and mum.
We'd take our buckets and spades, and sandwiches galore
Then board the busy train to reach the lovely shore.

At last we'd reach the seaside, a magnificent sight to see,
We would run ahead and try to be the first to paddle in the sea
We could not afford bathers, but no one seemed to mind
It never really bothered us, we weren't the worrying kind.

When we finished paddling we'd run back up the sand,
Start to build a sand castle, hoping Dad would give a hand.
Our castle was always the biggest, or so we always thought,
Then it was time for sandwiches that our mum had brought.

The sandwiches were always tasty, bread and jam so sweet,
We'd devour every mouthful, it was such a lovely treat.'
To swill them down we'd have water, sometimes tea from a flask,
To have prepared it all, must surely have been a task.

All too soon the day would be over, and off we'd go again
We'd have to wait at the station and finally board the train,
We'd all be happy and exhausted and usually fall asleep
These are happy memories to treasure and to keep.

Jean O. Gray

My Love for You

I love you from the ground below
To the highest point in heaven above
I never ever, want you to be apart from me
Or ever say to me that, "You must go"
For if you do my love, you lose me and my love
You don't realise, I am a part of you
You also are a part of "Loving me"
Onward through our old years we go
Praying hard that "we don't let go"
The years are rolling by one by one
We often say, "we are almost done
But our true love will never fade
Or slip from our grasp", nor stray
For it is steadfast as it will always stay
To give us strength to carry it on
With all our ups and all our downs
On with life we both abound

Bertha Shuttleworth

Clockwork

Who am I?
Who are You?
I'm not me, I'm just you.

Can you see inside my brain,
And spy the cogs twisting 'round?
Ticking. Tick-tock. Clockwork.

Wind me up, shut me down.
Press the nob, turn me 'round.

I am here, trapped in a sea of deep blue orange.
Holding on.
Swimming. Surviving.
Clockwork.

Ticking.
Tick-tock.
Clockwork.
Swimming.
Surviving.
Clockwork.

Julie Sheldon

The British Red Cross

A Team of Dedicated Workers,
    Who care for the disabled, and sick
They help you, in every possible way
    To brighten your life, if just for a day
It means so much, when you can't move about,
    So thank God, for such people as these
For the outings and parties they give to you
    To help you through another day

Dorothy Shaw

Care in the Community

It's the early morning carer, who gets you up each day
Who makes you that first cuppa
As you sit and chat away
You talk of hair and fashion
You talk of sun and rain
You talk of things that used to be
But will never be again
You go right back, to years gone by
Oh my, those were the days
When hair was bobbed
And clothes were smart
And the Charleston, was the craze
But today is something different
There are guns and bombs about
And people, being terrorized
And frightened to go out
There are drugs and bars up windows
Doors locked, throughout the day
Bring us back, the good old days
And take, today away

Janet Lees

Fait Accompli

Admired, envied or coveted by most of her kith and kin,
With pleasure and pride she accepted, her fair and flawless skin.

Natural births for her babies - so no caesarian mark,
No aftermath of ailments left rashes or roughness like bark.

Advancing years made no difference, her skin stayed good and fair,
Then suddenly - quite suddenly - her heart required repair.

Required a vein the length of her leg, leaving a ghastly scar -
To be used when her sternum - carved open - revealed arteries
    quite bizarre.

No matter, the fair and flawless skin, her thanks to the surgeon
    cum knife
With pleasure and pride she's accepted the scars, and hopes
    of a better life

Eleanor Stephenson

Untitled

To a bedridden friend.

Today on your ninety-eighth birthday
What can I wish for you my friend?
There are many things I could wish for you
But alas, they could never come true.
You have family love and true friendships
May they continue to blossom and grow.
So I wish you continued enjoyment
Of conversations with friends who call,
Fond memories to give you pleasure
In the long quiet moments alone.
May your faith and your courage be steadfast
And your fine sense of humour blend
With feelings of peace and contentment -
These are wishes, my friend.

Ethel M. Clark

I Wonder

When my spirit goes into the blue yonder
Towards Heaven - I wonder
Will God reveal, or still conceal
The mystery of the Universe for real
Those who claim their souls have taken flight
Tell of tunnels, peace and light
Of meeting their loved ones for a fleeting spell
Funny - nobody ever glimpses Hell
Strange, no mention of dogs, cats, pets
Even in these fleeting moments nobody gets
To see past monsters of human breeds
Maybe none repented of their evil deeds
And do you think those billions gone
Can see on Earth what's going on
What frustrations are they feeling
Watching us killing, maiming, stealing
Do they see God shed a tear
For us poor mortals living here
I wonder . . .

Brian Cross

Life

For what is life but life itself
Who are we to judge its wealth
As each day passes, a month goes too
Before you know it so do you
Who says we cannot discover or judge life
For are we not life itself
What is life?
What good does it do for me or you?
What purpose does it serve?
Questions impossible to answer or to try to explain
Could this all be in vain?
No, for what we do know, is life is here and is to
stay
It is only us who go away

Amanda Hunt

Untitled

Hello, a wave, each time we meet.
Too afraid, to stop and talk.
Then in the very bright light of day.
This familiar face, wobbled at my gate.
Her frame, it seems would not hold her still.
"Guide me home? Please would you?
My eyes, my legs, are all askew."
Shoes and coat, I stood erect.
Look left, look right, my arm outstretched,
it seems a yes.
Each staggering; step, she took,
My arm, was held, in her tight embrace
Two steps, she took; then stopped, to talk.
"The last friend I had has gone and died.
Will I be the next to lie?
Cold and stiff and all alone."
"No, no," I said, "that's all nonsense.
I will guide you home."
Next when we meet, I will stop to
say, "hello!"

Beverley Hutchinson

All That Glistens

The headaches of this world we're in, the pressures,
torment, pain and strife.
Can tempt you to eternal sin,
a folly of this earthly life.
To keep your spirits soaring high, avoid the 'pleasures'
you are sold.
Then it will come as no surprise,
when all that glistens is not gold.

Those mindless deeds of mindless thoughts, will lead you
nowhere,
so I've found.
A house of cards, without support,
collapses, built on shaky ground.
To feel the glow, let goodness reign, when fire dies,
the ash lies cold.
To understand a wider frame,
see, all that glistens is not gold.

Dawn Johnson

Intensity

The poem has no ruled standard, yielding (as it does) to social trends.
What holds true in one age lies dead soon after. Let us make amends.
Let us at last call 'dead' the lie that poetry can be complete,
And meditate instead upon the duties of the aesthete.

To justify a piece while teasing into sight its voice and brain,
To twine both plot and substance, then to bring the reader 'round
again,
To make available to all the boundless planes of thought and mind;
These, in all their aesthetic charm, are serious: for we are blind.

The smallest fancy of a mind long frozen in a textual world
Has more impact than fattened thought, more passion and more
to unfold.
When concentration's central to the exploration of a theme
The author's focus designates the reader viewer of a dream.

Iain Matheson

To All

We all have an angel to guide us,
We all have a star shining bright.
We all have the chance to help others,
Through even the darkest night.

We all have to carry out God's purpose,
We all have a duty to fulfil.
Even though the way may be lonely
And often rough and uphill.

We all reach the end of our journey
When the aches and the pain shall be eased.
I pray we shall hear God saying,
"This is my child, in whom I'm well pleased"

Janet Watson

Between Two Worlds

Oh God, I get so confused, please help me to be strong.
Torn between two worlds, not sure where I belong.
Home is where the heart is, or so they say,
but where, dear God, is my heart today?
Is it with my dog, who is lying by my side?
Of course, she'll always have my love and my pride.
What about my parents, asleep in their bed?
Dear God, to be without them I'd rather be dead!
Now my brother, we've had some fun,
but our life isn't over, it's only just begun.
Every little bird has to leave its nest,
to survive on their own, that's life's big test.
And now the place where I work and live,
a beautiful new country with so much to give.
For myself I plan to make a better life,
to plough through fate's obstacles and conquer all my strife.
My dreams and ambitions, it is here they lie,
so I have to catch them before they die.
Dear God, please help me to be strong,
for it's in two worlds, at the moment, I belong!

Clarissa Oxenham

A Message from Bonnie Jean

You were my first-born joy, you brought
Wee daughter in a carry-cot,
We watched you grow, our family life
Was happy, healthy, free from strife.
And then with cries of "all the best"
We waved you off - you flew the nest,
Perhaps to visit other lands . . . ?
We just held tight with open hands.

And then a man became your life,
You were his love but not his wife,
You did not bring him home with you
Until, one day, out of the blue
You asked your family for a meal,
You both were charming - made us feel
Your life was happy - I relaxed
And you flew off to foreign parts.

My dear, you phoned, your holiday o'er,
I couldn't speak, my tears did pour,
How could I know that in your case
Had been a wedding-gown of lace?

Dorena Blincow

A Tree

She stands there in her glory
with arms stretched towards the sky.
Never did she look so beautiful -
a wonder to the eye.

As the sun shines down upon her
she shimmers in the breeze;
her favourite dress adorns her
along with other trees.

Who can compare the colours
she drapes around her arms;
the yellows, golds and reds, she knows
all add towards her charms.

As days pass by, she shares with us
her dress - which can be found
just like a deep-piled carpet
beneath her body, on the ground.

Then naked she stands in the wind and rain
and wonders what winter will bring.
In her white winter coat, she will feel like a bride,
awaiting to blossom in spring.

Joan Zambelli

Memories of 'My Dear Cyril'

The ten years of our time together,
Towards the end, you were a bit under the weather.
When the time had finally come,
Your body became 'cold and oh so numb'.

The times we shared,
To show each other how we cared.
The talks we had,
Some 'Good' and some 'Sad'.

Now 'My Dearest One', my heart is broken,
And all I have to show, is my tears as a token.
We had a great companionship,
And an 'Understanding' relationship.

I will never hear your voice again,
It will never be the same.
I miss your 'Good mornings' and 'Good Nights',
But I can now see your glowing light.

Crezet Freeman

"Happy Days"

Boat, moving from side to side showing its bottom to all.
Water, racing along the deck foam flecked and angry.
Wind, pulling at anything not lashed down, poking its nose
around every corner.
Spindrift, skipping across the sea, playing leap-frog with the waves.
A sky, so sullen it talks of foul weather with a smile.
Ropes, twanging like violin stings against their will, covers
trying to stay in one piece.
Sea horses, jumping across the bow desperately washing
everything clean.
Below deck stomachs walk the plank, 'head down' becomes the
order of the day.
Smells from the galley waft into every corner smiling on the inert
bodies, each one trying to breathe untainted air.
The boat's inner soul resting quietly waiting for signals from above.
Engine, pulsating with life, chattering to the sea, throwing a tail
high in the air. The old man of the sea, talking to anyone that
will listen, sometimes whistling a merry tune. Grey clouds slowly
roll aside making room to shake hands with the changing sea.
Oh Happy days.

Edwin Alexander Turner

The Swirling Clouds of Misery

Amid the fog before my eyes,
What waits inside to injure me?
I cannot see what the future holds
For me, inside that cloud. The pain,
The agony is building up
Inside my soul; I enter.
There, before myself, I see a
Deep, dark hole; I cannot stop,
I keep on walking, nearer, nearer,
Till I fall. I see the swirling
Clouds of misery, the pattern
Of my life, before I drown in
All my sorrows, 'til I breathe the
Air no more. The swirling clouds of
Misery are gone; likewise am I.

Alison R. Beal

Behind Your Eyes

I love you and yet I shall never know
What you carry behind your eyes
I cock my head like a listening bird
But I never can sort out the truth from the lies.

I think we are one momentarily
But I always find out my mistake
And see we are two pressed together
Whom a word may separate.

Pity us, we're learning the hard way
What living together may mean . . .
Unlimited misunderstanding
Till we turn aside to dream.

Judith Williams

Leonie

You were born into our world
When we needed you the most
A little child for us to love
A babe for us to hold

You came into our life
A small, free spirit
You've only been here a short time
But it's as though you've always been in it

Time, it waits for no one
And now life's an open book . . .
The angels sing and play their harps
And the fairies stop to take a look

With deep blue eyes
And raven hair
You'll be in our hearts forever
We shall always care

When you smile
You are everything we hoped you'd be
We love you
Leonie . . .

Deborah Tomlinson

My Love

I met my love and loved my love
When we were by the sea,
I knew at once this was true love
And knew that he loved me.

In course of time, I wed my love,
Together we would be
To fill our lives with joy, my love,
But fate chose differently.

A few short weeks we had, my love,
When war came ruthlessly.
For six long, frightful years, my love,
Parted then we'd be.

At last the bells rang out, my love,
The lights shone, brilliantly,
And you came home to me my love,
We met so joyously.

When you were old and ill, my love,
I nursed you tenderly,
But you left me, alone, my love,
With just a memory.

Elizabeth Gardfall

Absent Friends

We think of those whom we once knew,
When we were young and tender.
When reminiscing in the past,
We are happy to remember.

We lived together side by side,
Our friendship strong did grow.
And when they moved to distance far,
We missed each other so

We helped each other such a lot,
In good times and in bad.
The knowledge that we had a friend,
Made all of us feel glad.

At Christmas time we send a card,
Just to keep in touch.
And prove that friendship through the years,
Still means to us as much.

And at this special time of year,
For absent friends we pray.
And hope that in the future time,
We'll meet again one day

Iris E. Covell

490

Losing Your Horizon

Rushing around
Velocity of sound
No jet required, life's enough.

"I cannot halt - life will pass"
Objective near?
Horizon unclear.

Follow their lead
Always right, yes indeed
Originality alarms.

Always must be 'him' to choose
The time the place
A wool-bearing race.

Dream on! Why not?
Escape slide from 'your lot'
Think it, guide it. Follow your sights.

Facing forward, thinking back
No beaten track
All dimensions yours.

The time's around
Horizon found.

Julie Park

Wanderer

There is a place inside a dream, beyond infinity,
'tis there for all the unawake if they would only see.
I strayed there once when slumber deep took me so far away,
and nameless hues through spectrums strange in colours lit my way.
The great bear Ursa looked at me, and lumbered on toward
safety from the mighty sweep of Orion's starry sword.
A fireball lit the heavens vast, a chariot meteor,
colossal, straining, hands on reins the valiant Auriga.
Misty galleons emerging from iridescent cloud, drives Cetus,
whale with mournful low and songful voice, yet proud.
Awesome giant Jupiter, in orbit's net ever caught
disregards the wondergaze of craftless astronaut.
Then Mercury, ever swift across the heavens in a dash
With winged heels and lightning speed creates a silver flash.
No dark of night no sunrays here, no Earthly sight nor sound.
Just all the things once mused about when eyes were heaven bound.
And then a voice a gentle voice was softly drawing me
along the blueish silver cord which spans all eternity.
I looked towards this marbled place this misty cloudy home
my wanderings interrupted 'til the next time I might roam.

Elaine Petersen

Wonderland

The white-capped mountains stand so tall
Waiting for the next snow to fall
It won't be today, the sky is too blue
The sun shines brightly, the clouds too few.

It is a winter wonderland
This scene before my eyes
I really am in Switzerland
The beauty I see is no surprise

It's just as I had hoped for
When I poured over magazines and books
The chalets, the views, I couldn't ask for more
This place certainly has me hooked

As I walk through the forest
My boots crunching on the snow
The air is so clean and fresh
The white covered branches hang low

The peacefulness and joy I found there
Will for the rest of my days stay in my heart
Feelings of contentment were around me everywhere
And my love for this place will not depart.

Hazel Matthews

How Cool It Is

How tiresome it can be when you don't want to play with me.
We could be the best of pals and later on
in life go out with all the gals
If only you could see how cool it is to play with me.
But you're busy having a sulk.
How on earth can we be tops if you won't pull out all the stops!
Casper's the latest craze but you're still sitting in a daze
If your Mum says you can, we'll go down the street and join a gang
Buck up, shift it, move those wimpy legs I say. How can I?
When I don't even want to play.
You could be the roll-over jackpot to my Rocky 6 or 7
and we could be in Hamburger Heaven
If you could only see what a true friend I am to thee
As I stand here like a Wally while you try and fix that flaming lorry
You told me it was an XR7.
Still the insurance's cheaper by heaven!
But somehow we're out of luck with this clapped out pick-up truck
Maybe tomorrow you'll see, how
Cool it is to play with me!

Mandy New

"When They're Gone"

When they finally lay to rest
Was their life really just a test!
Where do they go when they slip away
As we sit beside them and pray.
Do they find the peace at last
That they dreamt about in the past.
What kind of journey do they endure
perhaps they live on for ever more.
A second chance in another way
just a different world and another day.
I guess it's only they who know
and we'll find out, when we do go.
It's such a mystery to us down here
But I don't believe it's something to fear,
A chance to meet up with the past
to be with our loved one's at last.

Joanna T. McAndrew

World in Crisis

If our world could talk, I bet she would say,
"What have I done to be treated this way?
My rivers polluted, my forests no more,
My air is dirty and my lungs are sore."

People are trying, but is it enough?
There are still those who think our world is tough,
That she will survive no matter what we do.
Well, I'd just like to say, I've got news for you.

Our world is dying, she's going to blow,
I think she's decided that we're her foe,
We've got to convince her, once and for all,
We're going to love her and answer her call.

Clare Fencott

A Poet's Dream

I see it now a poet's dream
To capture this, a winter scene
Covered now by driven snow
A landscape full of magic glow

Lying there a blanket white
Reflecting diamonds shining bright
I listen now there is no sound
To this magic scene all around

How I love the snow so deep
To feel the softness on my feet
To this scene I could keep
On that blanket I could sleep

Then I see a change take place
The snow is melting without trace
Such changing moods of a winter scene
Gone at last, a poet's dream.

Ann Parker

Seasons of Life

Spring is the moment of birth,
    when all new things are born,
Green shoots appear from the earth,
    to herald a brand new morn.

Summer is our youth,
    of sunshine and blue skies,
When the sheer joy and loving and living
    shines from our bright eyes.

Autumn is the time of life,
    when leaves of red and gold,
Fall like pages in our memory book,
    which gently we unfold.

Winter comes upon us, grey,
    with no birds to sing,
The time has come for growing old,
    we must make way for Spring.

        Hilda May Houghton

Untitled

Trees stand tall, and very bare
When autumn comes, and takes its fare
Trees look, stately, white with snow
But even winter has to go
Trees with growing buds again
For spring it comes, with dashing fame
Trees in summer look their best
They dance and shimmer, in green dress
And life, like trees, have changing months
In one season, you hold the triumphs
Then suddenly, you loose a game
But don't give in, just try again
For what is life, if there is no pain
Just like a summer, with no rain
And like the coming of each season
Except life, and don't look for reason.

        Ann Castleman

Mother's Lament

Hell! On that bloody battlefield it's hell,
    where men are torn asunder
By steel and flame, by cannon shell from iron guns that thunder
See that mother's son, who bravely went to war.
Lying in a death trench, not knowing what it's for?
There must have been a reason?
"For Honour" they may shout
But where is the Honour? when your guts are hanging out
Where is the honour to see a brave man cry.
When he can't help his comrades, as they shed their blood and die.
When he's honour bound, to hold his ground - although he
    knows he's beat
Or be branded as a coward, if he beats a quick retreat.
Oh! Why do mothers suffer just to raise their sons?
To finish up as fodder, for those blasting greedy guns!!

        Hilda Richardson

'Childhood Days'

Long years ago I lived in Mandalay
Where my parents danced the 'Lancers,'
At monthly balls such grand affairs,
Each function giving pleasure.

Our house was large with rambling rooms
With nursery floor and gardens too,
All trim and neat, cool and shady
Beneath the bower of blooms.

Where servants padded softly by,
Serving with loyal pleasure,
For me and mine in old Mandalay
During those long gone days of leisure;

Though wars may come and years roll by,
Those memories I will keep by me,
Of happy days and childhood years,
In grand and ancient Mandalay.

        Gretta Johnson

What Is Love?

Is love when you want him?
When you long to hold him?
Long to kiss and long to own him?
Is love protection
When you want to be sheltered?
Is love caring and sharing
And feeling your heart melting?
Is love a feeling?
Is love a motion?
Is love a cream or a powerful potion?
What is love, does anyone know?
Once you've found love,
Can love go?
Is there love?
Or is love just a dream?
That people have,
And wish to feel?

        Cassy Evans

Eyes of a Stranger

Does it make you want to cry,
when you see pain in the eyes of a stranger,
does it make you want to cry,
when you see small kids in danger.

Does it make you want to cry,
when you see this world at war,
does it make you want to cry,
when you see bodies torn and raw.

Does it make you want to cry,
for this world that's dying out,
does it make you want to cry,
and yell and scream and shout.

Does it make you want to cry,
when you see small kids in danger,
does it make you want to cry,
when you see pain in the eyes of a stranger.

        Dave Stainer

Such Mortals Tread

The world in space is looming up
Volcanic craters in turn erupt
All nature's plans they disappear
A silent plain with thinning air.

The magic touch of dusty soil
A throbbing heart the sweat and toil
Eyes wide to wonder so obsessed
A starry trail that brings success.

To stand and look upon the world
To see the wondrous earth unfurled
Defiant courage plays its part
Space travellers born with mighty heart.

To see this world it casts some doubts
Among all mortals with faith devout
To marvel in this universe
The earth and moon in turn reversed.

        Alexander Taylor

A Sonnet of At-One-Ment

As I walk along this chosen track
with life's testing ways,
I put my head up to the sky, in silence I do gaze.
In my hour of weakness temptations rears its head.
It wheedles and cajoles, me Lord
I must learn to pray instead.
Teach me to arise from sin, and help me not to falter,
As you arose, from lawlessness, pressures and the pain
How did it feel Lord, to be tortured, so I might live again?
Reflecting often makes the lesson as a boon,
I realize the time is near, and I will see you soon.
forgive me Lord, so I am free, to take this lovely chance,
to live my life with love and grace in mind,
and change my circumstance.

        Jane Margaret Clark

This War

There was a war in all our hearts
Well hidden, and submerged
We smile, and clasp hands
Well hidden
The acid that drips from your tongue burns me
I will be burnt in this war
The truth is submerged
I fear for my safety
This war, well hidden
Something touched me, and I saw too much
I heard what they really said
I laughed at this facade
I thought that I could never stop
They named me mad
Well hidden in my soul
You burn me softly

Josie Sutherland

Sea Shore Impressions

I love to go down by the sea
where the waves wash backwards
and forwards silently.

The soft sea breeze
blows through my hair
but I don't really care.

Shells and sea creatures
wash up on the shore
scattered all over the sandy floor.

Glistening sun rays fill the sky
the seagulls drift up so high.

I see a dolphin in the distance
he dances in between the waves
and heads towards the sheltered caves.

Emma Trevis

Time and Emotion

I gaze into the distant hills
Where patchy snow still hugs the ground.
My arms stretch out, and my heart fills
With longing just to touch each curve, each mound:
The sun breaks through the heavy-laden sky
Casting its beams with teasing provocation
Stirring the memories that deep within me lie
of yesteryear - a haunting fascination.
Deep shadows form like weaving apparitions
Darting from ridge to crag in frantic silhouette
Changing the landscape now from calm to friction
Making the outline gloomy, cheerless . . . yet
In a flash I can see the strong allurement
That held me spellbound through my childhood years -
'Twas the majesty of those great mountains
That brought such comfort and allayed my fears.

Hannah Kinsey-Jones

Lost Love Never Lost

And when he comes to you, in the hush of night,
warm to his nearness, reach for his embrace,
fear not his name to call, nor his hand to seek,
stroke his ruffled hair, trace the fondness in his face.

Yes deep in the stillness, your lonely darkest hours,
his silken touch tender, and soft whisper soothes your ear,
your dreams can but conjure, as you hold him very close,
through the dark he'll stay, and dry your every tear.

Then in the twilight dim, as dawn awakens day,
sense his presence fleeting, as he takes his leave,
the door now stands ajar, his dancing shadow looms,
silent footfall on the stair, your love you can perceive.

Blow your abiding kiss, and smooth his pillow crease,
the crisp linen furrow, where he'd been there lain,
be sure to mark the page, in his book of verse,
for with next night, he'll come to you again.

Frank Payne

Dunblane Remembered

Oh it's so tragic
What more can you say
why did a madman
kill the children that day

The fatal wounding of sixteen tots
all killed in a shower of gunshots
the school is closed now
you could hear the people say
most of the parents cried that fatal day

The press men gathered in a mass
questioning parents as they tried to pass
letters appear in papers two days late
seems a madman is filled with hate

Yes another madman strikes yet again
now Dunblane will never be the same
It makes you wounder who will be next
so many madmen out there to vex

Annette Smith

My Dear Father

You were never meant to be a dad
What one would describe as a bit of a lad
With your film star looks and smart sense of dress
And attitude of couldn't care less.
Your knowledge of the world was on a wide scale
But on the domesticated front
You surely did fail
Your conversation was second to none
Your laugh, your jokes, your great sense of fun
You were never there when I needed you most
But at all the parties you were the perfect host
How I longed for you just to be with me.
Though that was never to be
Now the years have gone
You're no longer here
Still I'll never forget you father dear.

Hilda Vass

Soulful Ramblings

What is left within my soul
When love has gone and life decayed?
Where is the spark of human fire
to motivate my future days?

Where's the music to revive my soul
When life becomes a discordant dirge?
Where's the score of harmonic joy
for mind and body to emerge?

What of the future for my disquiet Soul
When cruelty and conflict are no more?
When man's acceptance is the norm -
not judgement of the bigot's law.

What light shines from my anguished Soul
when life is past and Earth reviewed?
Where is my spark - or has it died
or does it roam in life renewed?

Annabelle Page

Memories

I returned to the hills on Saturday
Where as a child I used to play
Where later walked with friends now dead
Alas, how quick the years have sped.

It's not the same as it used to be
Fences are built where it once was free
Seats are broken, the grass grown tall
I'm sad I came to see it all.

I close my eyes and think of days
When children once could roam and play
When all around was safe and free
So sadly now just a memory.

Alfreda Gladys Westmacott

Something to Smile About

Pick up a paper - look at TV
What is it you hope to see?
Someone who's happy, someone who's glad
Perhaps something funny not the world going mad
We all of us have our highs and lows
And life's not all roses as we all know
But surely it's not all gloom and doom
And shouldn't we all try to make some room
For a little laughter and fun times too
There's plenty around for me and you

I'm fed up with seeing faces downcast
And being told that nothing will last
Let's look to the future and be uplifted
The sands of time have already shifted.
Jot down your blessings then tuck them away
And when you are having a really down day
Take out the list - read what you've got
You'll see your good fortune - you've got such a lot
So come on good people let's raise a shout
And hope that it's heard Nations throughout
Please give us something to smile about

Joan Garden

Sturgie

He came as a kitten, a wee ball of fluff
With a tail one could scarcely see.
Two beautiful eyes, his necklet a muff
And straight to my heart went he

When I put him out of doors for a little run
The tiny cries were pitiful for me to join the fun
And then he would keep me romping until I thought
he would never tire
My precious little kitten was indeed a lively wire

Up and down the chimneys, up and down the trees
Went my little kitten with the greatest ease
Climbing up the curtains, sitting on the rails
Calling to be rescued with tiny frantic wails

But now my precious treasure is 18 years and more
They say that cats have nine lives - he has easily lived a score
Chased by two Alsatians with a mere cat's whisker from doom
Then buried beneath some floorboards which nearly proved his
tomb

But praise the Lord who created all pets Sturgie is with me still
And though in form, a huge big puss, he still has a kitten's will
It is he who decides if the food is right, it is he who chooses his bed
I have an idea he thinks he is the boss and I am just Big Puss
instead! Miaow!!

Dorothy Boyd

My Brother Jim

Where are you, my brother Jim
What really happened to you,
Your only crime, I can see,
As a schizophrenic, you were put out
To fend for yourself in the community.

The Certificate said, self-neglect.
You froze, to death, on a London Street,
On a cold January night.
Was this really, meant to be your plight.

As your only next of kin
I don't know what they did with you,
Whatever was their whim.
Nobody let me know you see,
The above was you, my brother Jim.

The pain of searching, has taken its toll.
I don't have any more tears.
Where are you, my brother Jim
What really, happened to you,
As my search begins anew.

Audrey Fidge

"How Things Are"

Life seems full of danger now
We even have to beware of the cow
Our dairy products were recommended
But now it seems all that is ended.

There is something wrong with eggs and butter.
The rest of the list I dare not utter.
We should not smoke or enjoy a drink
For fear of what the others think.

Let's get back to former days.
When animals could be left to graze.
Hens and poultry could peck around,
To take their pleasure from the ground.

Fruit and vegetables grown for taste.
Not for quick profit in man's haste.
Do not destroy our country scenes.
If it is not beyond our means.

Things that once made England great
Should not be allowed to deteriorate
Life is precious although short
It is one commodity that cannot be bought.

Audrey Margaret Brushett

A Dying Planet

The world is in a terrible mess
which lessens people's happiness.
The sky is grey with dust and smog
and the planet is turning into a bog.

The hole in the ozone is getting bigger
and cancer it can often trigger.
CFC's make the greenhouse effect
and the world turns into a total wreck.

The tropical rain forests humans fell
and earth turns into a living hell.
Wildlife lose their habitat
but developers don't care about that.

Wars start out between each race
and fighting now is commonplace.
There's no religious toleration
and blood is shed in every nation.

So if you understand what I say,
then there's no time to delay.
Don't read this, then sit around and wait,
do something to help before it's too late.

Alison Elwood

Crazy War

Bringing sadness to us,
Wars are made by criminals.

If politicians had listened to
children a little,
They still wouldn't understand,
What is a peace that we desire,
Nobody wants their homes set on fire.

All the people waiting in fear,
What is next to happen,
Will they perish and disappear, in gale of war.

Various sites, homes burning.
The flames of fire extending, more and more,
Criminals pretending, that
they are not to be blamed
for their evil work.

At every blast, people jerk,
hastened beats of their hearts choked with horror.
They never dreamed of the war to happen,
but now from their faces
one can only read what is a rigid, painful sorrow.

Elma Mustafic

False Dawn

Nobody cared for the entrails of rust,
twisted by hate and pitted with dust,
metallic shards of shine dulled by time,
so graceful in the desert,
amongst the grime.

Like fallen gods they came down to earth,
ceasing the merriment and silencing the mirth,
the once mighty roar crushed and choked,
left by the wind,
as the landscape smoked.

Through fiery skies the warlords had raced,
the sounds of life their bellies replaced,
with the golden blood-light of a new false dawn,
leaving nothing behind,
to whisper or scorn.

The story unfolded of men too bold,
of feelings so noble and pain untold,
until the cries ceased and teeth were bared,
there was no-one left,
and nobody cared.

Andy Ridge

"Life in the Park"

Sitting on a park bench
With nothing to do all day
A couple of cans of Carlsberg
Safely tucked away

No money in my pockets
No sole left in my shoes
I've got nowhere to sleep tonight
But I suppose my bench will do

Some people throw me money
Thinking society's to blame
But money isn't everything
It only helps to ease the pain

A pain I caused all myself
I've got no one to blame
Just by putting myself on the shelf
To display my awful shame

I used to be a normal man
With a life and lots of friends
But now I choose the booze
To hide from my emotions till the end.

Alan Carrick

The Ploughman

Beyond the hedgerows stretch the furrowed lines
whilst seagulls swoop and screech with mocking cry.
The fresh brown earth the ploughman leaves behind
for food and worms the gulls each other vie.

The morning sun then glinting as it shines
reflecting from the moist and polished soil.
As drab and fallow, fields are freshly turned
and teams of horses plough and sweat and toil.

Now rests the team awhile for mid-day break
the welcome bag of mixed oats as their feed.
The birds now flock around their chance they seize
as if they understand the horses need.

Then all too soon the work must start again
they plough until the western sun is low.
O'er tree lined hills now turning into gold
now dusk, and horse and ploughman they must go.

Their stabled rest is waiting down the lane
clean straw and fresh cool water he has earned.
The ploughman finished with his task today
knows all too soon the daybreaks swift return.

Alan J. Vincent

The Eagle

He is magnificent bird, the Eagle
with a wing span of fire feet, with his
eyes darling to and fro
he misses nothing with his telescopic eyes

He is on one of his many hunting
expeditions, he is an astute hunter,
as he covers the hunting field,
off the Scottish glens

This is where his cunning comes
to the fore, with his keen eye sight
he can see the slightest movement
far below.

Swaying this way and that his
quarry comes into his view, then
he swoops with talons extended,
the unsuspecting he plucks with
ease from the ground.

His power has to be seen, to be
admired, for he commands the
clear skies of the Scottish Alps.

Ester Rehill

Her First Day at School

It's nigh on five years since she was born
When you woke her gently one wintry morn.
The wind is cold, the sky is grey
And our baby is starting school today.

Smartly dressed in uniform new
Skirt of grey and jumper blue.
In a school bag neatly packed
A lunch box filled with tasty snack.

At last it's time, with lump in throat
To help her on with her little coat.
In the classroom does she cling?
No, she's off to play with everything.

You're redundant for a while it seems
As she waves goodbye, her eyes a-gleam.
Emotions in turmoil you leave the place,
And dab with hankie at tears on face.

Tears were expected, that was true
But tears from her, not tears from you.
For it's not easy when your heart is full
And it's your child's first day at school.

Freda Pilton

Man's Best Friend

Comes a time when you know you are near the end,
When your master pats you on the head and calls you old friend.
When he takes you silently down to the local vet,
And brings you home again, whispering no no, not yet.

Oh, I can remember all the good times still,
When the children were small, and I always had my fill.
They would take me for walks across fields so green,
I was drained from watering the biggest trees I've ever seen.

The children have grown up and have fled the nest,
I dream of those days that were truly the best.
Now I'm constantly left to play on my own,
I dig up the garden looking for the elusive bone.

I'm very old and find it hard even to walk,
I waggle my tail at my master, but he is too sad even to talk.
He'll take me back to the vet sometime this week,
Lay his hand upon my head, and put me to sleep.

It is said that I'm man's best friend?
And that I will be, right to the very end?
I love my master, and I guess I always will,
Even on the day my beating heart is made still.

Brian Kelly

Another Day

Another day when the wind blows hard,
When driving rain blows hard and fast.
How long will it last?

Another day when the sky is dark,
And birds are few and far between.
I feel so sad and dark inside,
If only they could feel my pain;
But enough of all this sorrow,
Let's look forward to a brighter tomorrow.

Another day when the sun shines bright,
And all those dark clouds are out of sight,
And the pain is softened by a longing for a brighter tomorrow,
When we can walk and lose this sorrow.
Another day, another tomorrow,
And I'm so grateful for all my tomorrows.

Jean Steer

The Dreaming Pool

I once came across a dreaming pool,
Visited by wise men and many a fool.
By day the pool is blue like the sky
and admired by all that pass by.
By night it is so still and grey,
and all that make a wish, will have to pay.
It's like a mirror, so clean and clear,
But it's only our own reflection that will appear.
We sit there dreaming of what we'd like to be,
But do we really want to know. for what will be,
will be.

We look again and see the hidden pain,
And all our yesterdays of hidden strain.
Are there enough dreams left here in the pool?
Or is it now only visited by a fool.
For all we know, we can wish in a well.
But no one even if they knew would tell.
So we must take each day as it comes,
Face all troubles each day, and we have won.

Caroline Gill

Winter Love

When the rain falls, it reminds me of you
When the wind blows, I remember you too.
You were my love in winter
But when summer's golden dawn
Arose above the fields of green
I found my love had gone.

Gone like the winter storms
With the first sign of spring
Gone are my lover's arms - leaving me wondering.

When the sun shines, it reminds me of you
When the lark climbs, I remember you too
All summer I tried to forget you
Wishing I'd never met you
Hoping that I could start to live my life anew.

Jane McLean

My First Holy Communion

On the eighteenth of June 1995
Was the day for me when Jesus came alive
He entered my body in the form of bread
But only I knew it was my heart He fed
For I feel so much bigger
I feel Oh so strong
For I'm a Soldier of Christ now
And nothing can go wrong

I'll say my prayers night and morning
And offer each day
To God our Father in Heaven
He'll show me the Way,
To be kind to others, be Honest and True
And, I'll do all things the way Jesus would do
I'll pray to Mary my Mother and my Guardian Angel too
For I know they'll help me as all Mothers do

Brian A. T. Godfrey

A Tribute to the Children of Dunblane

The children of Dunblane
Will be like the Springtime rain.
They will never be forgotten
like the Springtime blossom.
Their lives were very short,
but in our hearts they are caught
Our memories are so sweet
of all those tiny feet
You can never take away
for in our hearts they will stay.
Our love for them will never die,
even though in our hearts they lie
Oh so heavy.
We love you children of Dunblane.
We'll think of you like Springtime rain.
Not with us for so very long
such sweet memories do live on.

Denise Walters

Spectacular World

The balance of nature was perfect designed by a dynamic force
Winter, Spring, Summer and Autumn each had their own
    useful course
Colourful flowers and plant life displayed a style of their own
Showering fields and hillside scenting the air where they had grown
Birds and butterflies took to the air exotic shades painted their
    wings
Flew over hedgerows and treetops where gifted, the song bird sings
Numerous animals grazed on the plains feeding on luscious
    green shoots
Protecting their young as they grew, hiding them in bracken
    and roots
Tranquil blue seas rolled and glistened golden sun sparkled
    on waves
Dolphins raced and played in the depths fish swam through
    endless caves
This world where we live is spectacular with magnificent
    sights for free
We have everything to support us will our siblings enjoy all
    we see.

Christine Allison

The Move

We moved from South Wales to West Wales
We haven't been here long.
Family and friends said we'd be lonely and bored
They couldn't have been so wrong.
We bought a two bedroomed cottage
Doing it up was fun
We even fitted a new kitchen
with the help and aid of our son
The garden's a riot of colour.
With flowers and fruit trees galore
With wonderful views all around us
Who could ask for anything more.
And the villagers are so friendly
Yes, we've got it made
Would we move back to Cardiff
No, not even if we were paid.

Connie Morgan

Wish

You are the tears in my eyes
Who once filled the skies
With smiles
And paved my path with stars.

And when you were near
You became
My friend I always longed for;
A dream forever dreamed;
The demise of loneliness, the love and hate
Of passion spent and discovered too late,
The soul-mate
I searched for yet never found -
But I wish you were here.

Alexandra Wilson

496

A Lady Died the Other Day

This legal system puzzles me.
When inmates strike for higher pay.
Where villains walk the streets quite free.
    A Lady Died The Other Day.

It wasn't murder, wasn't rape
She took some tins, she didn't pay
Concealed from view, beneath her cape
    A Lady Died The Other Day.

They found her guilty of the charge.
But could she really have her say?
The total cost was far too large.
    A Lady Died The Other Day.

Left alone to face the shame.
Scourged by the media in every way.
With no one else to take the blame.
    She Took Her Life The Other Day.

How many others break the law?
Causing misery, and sorrow.
Who go undetected by the score.
    They won't all die tomorrow.
        Colin C. Thomas

At Peace

On Exmoor, in a spot you and I loved the best,
We scattered your ashes there to rest.
Under a gorse bush as bright as the sun,
Near where we watched the deer graze and run.

For evermore, you may wander free,
Over heather moorland, rolling down to the sea.
No more in pain from your troublesome heart,
Of this Exmoor landscape, you are now a part.

Lonely Combes with clear trickling streams,
Fast flowing rivers, their waters gleam.
Glimpse a buzzard floating, on a thermal high,
An artist's palette is the sunset sky.

Thickly wooded slopes sheltering valleys so deep,
Under moonlight and stars, you can slumber and sleep.
Waking to sparkling dews, and soft grey mists,
The wild beauty of Exmoor you can embrace and kiss.

You were a most caring family man,
We miss you, but on the other hand you are there.
And so now your presence is felt all around,
To embrace us with the peace, that you have found.
        Barbara D. Rogers

The Plague of Age

I'm growing older
What does it matter,
My dentures fall out
with a big clatter

My eyes are all 'misty'
Oh! Where are my glasses?
Upstairs? Downstairs?
maybe in "ashes"!!

The family comes home
whatever's the noise
"television" the boys "say",
Granny can't hear them
whate'er the "ploys."

Then when they are weary
back home they go
Granny and Granddad are "free" and so off to a "show"
Maybe tomorrow we'll have a large platter
as when "age" begins to "glimmer"
"inches" don't matter!!
        Elizabeth Redge

The Waiting Room

I sit here in this room today.
With people all around,
I can see some are tall,
Some are small and some are very round
There are the old, and the young,
Them that smile, and them that frown.
Them that talk,
And them that moan and groan,
The clothes are an array of colours,
There are reds, greens, and blues,
There are yellow, pinks and browns.
And lots of other hues.
Some of them are depressed,
And some with aches and pains.
There are some that cough
And some that wheeze and sneeze.
Well my waiting time is over
It is my turn at last,
And I can hear others saying
It must be my turn next.
        Carole Johnson

Memories of the Thirties

Memories? - They're what you've left
When, of your youth and strength bereft
Your mind casts back to former days
With unashamed nostalgic gaze.

Old age tears holes in memory's net
But some things one cannot forget
No rockets went to Moon or Mars
When only 'toffs' had motor-cars.

Woodbines in little paper packs
Five for twopence, including tax
Fry's chocolate came in penny bars
And Virol in Ali Baba jars.

No plastic bags the hedgerows filled
But all the little songbirds trilled
No litter in the streets was seen
And no graffiti marred the scene.

No yobbos then came into sight
The streets were safe to walk at night
But I am glad I'm seventy-one
For now those better days have gone.
        Arthur J. Greene

A Christmas Story

Remember a spider of long ago,
Who weaved his web to and fro,
Across the entrance of a cave
To deceive King Herod's knave.

For in that cave lay a Child,
Mary and Joseph by His side,
Praying that He would not cry
They didn't want their Son to die.

The night was cold and very bleak,
Neither one a word did speak.
Frost on the web brightly glistened
As the couple intently listened.

They heard the knave as he spoke:
"No-one's in there, the web's not broke."
The soldiers horses galloped passed,
The Family slept, safe at last.

Now look at the tinsel on your tree,
'Tis meant to be a memory,
Of that web weaved long ago,
Though this story, few do know.
        Felicity Neil

First Performance

The four-sided space in the grip of the people is bright
With the hall's fluorescent, unsteady belligerent light.
I sit in a corner seeking to smother a yawn
That heaves like a tide in my throat till the story is born.
How I envy the gatherer's ease, his skill and delight!
But the magic he musters I lose in my shadow of fright.
For I grope through the centre in sickness that threatens to stifle:
Each tongue is a sword and each eye is the point of a rifle
And the fall of a foot on the floor is the drumming of war
As stripped and untrained, I stumble and flounder before.
I pass from my part with a throat in the swelling of tears
And the grin on my lips is a death wish that nobody hears.

Jenny Gage

Back to Sea

Craggy stones from the banks do jut
Waters grey, green-hurtling glut,
Tumbling gravels over in glee,
Make their bubbling dash to mother - sea.

Anchored aquatics rock sad farewells
No splash plop or swirl unique as gathered all
the strange haunting murmur swells.

Sweep and rush the gleaming grains along
Granite, marble, quartz and flints,
Sol's rays flash frantic frenzied glints.
All in vortex hurry helter-skelter back to sea.

Ripped from the shores, clay soils the limpid mass
Brown mud and muck cast their cloudy slicks
Whirlpools spin hapless twigs as torrents pass.

Raging waters bear the roots of shading trees
Crazed headlong churning concourse in serried
swathes of molten might plunge into the welcoming
arms of mother - sea.

Gerard McCormack

My Star

Have you ever lay late at night
Watching the stars it's a glorious sight
They shine and twinkle, dull then fade
As if you're watching a massed parade
The clouds shuffle past, spoiling your vision
Which one is brighter, what a decision
Then I see one that draws my eyes closer
The more I look the more I am sure
Not very close and not very bright
But strong and dependable always in sight

I smile with my eyes closer and fall fast asleep
Wake up in the morning, the clocks peep, peep, peep
I look at that long satin gown, sparkling white
And smile as I remember that star from last night
You see that star was talking to me
The doubts in my mind were being set free
At two when I walk down the isle at the church
I'll understand now why I love you so much!

Carla Ann Brown

Untitled

You were my life, my heartbeat, my each breath,
Without you I am missing half my whole -
My body goes on still - but oh! my soul -
How hollow is existence since your death.
How could you leave me to face life alone?
To reach out for your hand, and touch just air;
To dream I hold you close - with what despair
I clutch my pillow, when that dream is flown.
We had such plans, such schemes, all gone to dust.
Now they mean nothing. I must plan anew,
To try to build a future lacking you
And half myself: I plan because I must.
My only aim will be to see me through
The lonely days till I can be with you.

June Moss

Just One Week

I saw you on Thursday, you smiled - you were as happy as a child.
With your new car, just like a toy, given to an excited little boy.

I saw you on Friday, when you left, I couldn't help feeling bereft.
My heart was so heavy as if filled with pain, I knew I'd not see
    you again.

On Saturday came the phone call, when I took it, I punched the wall.
I waited there with baited breath, while they told me the news
    of your death.

On Sunday, I don't know, I wasn't here, my body filled with an
intense fear - wondering, worrying, just what to do, now that I
was without you.

On Monday the black car came, with flowers that spelled out
    your name.
I tried so very hard to be brave, as they lowered you into your grave.

On Tuesday I was all alone, just waiting by the telephone,
    when I realized you weren't going to ring, I was numb, I felt nothing.

On Wednesday I spoke to you, the doctor said it would help me to,
to say all the things that I should have said
and now I can't because you're dead.

Today, it's Thursday, just one week, since you could laugh
    and love and speak.
Now I'm alone, you've left, you're gone and I wonder how on
    earth I can carry on.

Barbara Dawn Woods

Untitled

The shadow cast about my face
Was hiding me from mock disgrace
As happy-go-lucky as I may be
My only comfort is the sea.
For as I sit alone, at last
I see the sailing of a mast
Bobbing along the red horizon.
By then my step is quick to liven.
This is my saviour, my chance at last
To stop the memories of my past.
As I jump and wave and shout,
I see the ship just turn about!
As the bow stops where I stand,
The captain gently takes my hand
And here my foot touched wooden planks
My memory very quickly blanks.

A few years passed, in my old age
I reflect upon my worst of days
And as I smile, I close my eyes
And sail up into clear blue skies.

Jade Fletcher

Staying Mum

The hardest thing I've ever done
Was the day I gave away my son
Not as a baby, but as a man
And other mothers will understand.

When I heard the words "Mum this is June"
And turned to see love in full bloom
Number one all the time he grew
But from now on only number two.

No use to rant, no good to rave
You'd only be lonely to your grave
I smiled and greeted with all my charm
Though the feeling inside was one of alarm

No more would he be my whole life
Sometime soon he'd take a wife
And I will find a path anew
There must be a million things to do

So when I've found myself again
The one I was before he came
He'll visit me, and I hope he'll know
That the love of this mother, just never will go.

Helen E. Pym

Your Scattergun

We all clutch at love sometimes
We may steal a feel of some divine
It's the little stabs of joy that see us through
I've seen this play a hundred times
The universal pantomime
from the cheaper seats you get a better view
One day you'll wake to find your dreams have all been scattered
Like sand reeling in the midst of a desert wind
And it all becomes clear in a blinding flash of insight
And insecurity starts kicking in
We all feel alone sometimes
The silence once the curfew chimes
You're not the only one to feel this way
Consider this as interlude
Then shift your mood and attitude
Turn around the face a brighter day
Maybe you'll wake to find your destiny has been twisted
Your guiding star not for the first time crashes down
In your state of mind you feel inclined to take a shot at everyone for
all our sake please don't take your scattergun to town.

David Webb

Water Life

Water shines up to heaven.
Water glows in the dark.
Water keeps its little secret.
Water is special.
Water is mine.
Water is soft.
Water is morning and all day.
Water is so delicate.
Water sings songs in its own way.
Water whales,
Water fish.
Water gives us good dreams.
Water is good thoughts.
Water is the secret of love.
Water is stuck in a shell.
Water is our life.
Water has a reflection
Which is ME!

Jeanne Tara Morell

Without You

Without you the grass would be grey not green,
Without you the flowers would die in the spring,
Without you the sky would be black and never blue and there
would be no more laughter and nothing to do.

Without you all the lights would fade and there would be no
bright colours just gloom and shade,
Without you the hours would never pass and the winner of the
race would keep coming last,
But . . . most of all my life would not be worth living if I have to
keep on being Without you.

Carrie-Lee Luckings

The Error of Human Principle

To err is human or so they say
Yet make a mistake and soon you'll hear, "hey,
Why haven't you done this, and why not that",
Words spoken by people who know not squat.
As if the phrase belongs to a privileged few
Who would have problems thinking of any thing new.
But the world is unfair and few things are equal
Completing a circle of day to day ritual.
You'll protest till you're blue
Or threaten to sue,
But you'll be ignored with disdain
And called a great pain
In the ass no doubt, that causes ladies to pout
But this is the world as made by man
Who says to himself, if we can't who can?

A. Casim Andrews

An American Journey

We were once in Phoenix in Arizona State,
When we had an invitation to view the Golden Gate.
The Golden Gate we all had seen, we said with gay abandon,
But we'd love an invitation to view the great Grand Canyon.
No sooner said, than it was done, and into trucks we poured,
Allowing only thoughts for the treat we had in store.

The aircraft that we boarded was small in the extreme,
In all six people seated, Oh what good fun it seemed.
The pilot offered paper bags, though there was nought inside.
What we great travellers airsick? We'd crossed Atlantic wide.

The scenery was grand indeed, and we were captivated,
Until we reached the Canyon wide, and ground all undulated.
The little plane was buffeted up, down, in quick succession,
With thermals throwing us around, Oh yes, we learned our lesson.
Our gills turned green, and we were sick, we learned our lesson
late,
Next time we get an invite we'll view the GOLDEN GATE.

Hilda Hazlewood

A Sonnet to Thomas Jefferson

One of Virginia's greatest sons was he,
Whose legendary genius would be crowned
With wit imbued with wisdom, rarely found.
He loved both art and science equally.

To be a skilful statesman was his aim,
Able to bargain and negotiate
The epic purchase of the Gallic state.
He was the master of the power game.

He penned the famous words which roused the nation,
And would become his country's battle cry.
Thus "Liberty for all" was the quotation
Which spurred his fellow-men to fight and die.
His glorious gift would lay the firm foundation
On which democracy would truly lie.

Celia G. Thomas

'It'

Without 'it' he cannot cope.
Without 'it' he knows no hope.
Without 'it' he cannot wake.
Or conversation attempt to make.
He needs 'it' to feel secure.
As his dependency develops more.
Something in life upon which he can depend.
'It' won't leave without warning like a lover or a friend.
He lacks the willpower he needs to stop.
Keep reaching higher to touch the top.
Each day in the shadow of the habit.
The confrontation of the addict.

Claire Preece

Destiny

How did I know you were the one
When you stood at my door
What did you do to make me think
I'm yours forevermore
What was it made me dream the dream
I knew would just be mine
Why was I sure that I'd be yours
Until the end of time
When did our lives merge into one
How did it all begin
When others told us we were wrong
Why did we not give in
There is no answer, reason or rhyme
It must be some rich plan
Of fate that brings two lives together
The love of woman and man
So we will wander down life's path
And when we have to part
We'll always know the ties that bind
Start deep within the heart.

Anona Dugmore

Last Saturday I Fell in Love

I was alone at the party,
you came into the room,
you looked stunning in your red dress,
your lovely smile, your jet black hair,
your beautiful saucer eyes, they knocked me out.
I plucked up courage to ask you for a dance,
I held you close, but not too tight,
I didn't want to damage my beautiful China doll,
I found out your name,
it was Natalie
every girl's name in every love song became Natalie
I sang them all for you,
when it was time to go, you cried,
I turned away,
I didn't want you to see the tears in my eyes
we promised to see each other again
you made me so very happy
Natalie is seven years old
Natalie has Cerebral Palsy
last Saturday I fell in love

Ian Sangster

Paranoia

A terminal illness is not a vocation,
you can live without that - no hesitation,
there's a hate in your heart which tears you apart,
your head's in a hole, you're losing control.

The birth of a fever, the lapse of a mind,
a cruel taunt telling you life is unkind.
To rekindle a dream of something that you've not seen,
yet your mind is a desert that is barren and mean.

A tumour that burrows from your head to your toe,
violates your body, it tells you "soon you must go".
Trapped in a body, you didn't choose it by choice,
when it evicts from this world your mind will surely rejoice.

A sigh of relief, forget that unwanted grief,
you just want to die and fly up in the sky.
Just drifting in space, gone without trace,
just to reach paradise, all memories gone would suffice.

Billy Adair

Loneliness

Sharing and caring make life worthwhile.
You can share a kiss - you can share a smile.
When you were two and now are one
Your purpose in life seems to have gone
Loneliness is a tangible thing,
It can tear at your heart and make it ring
With sadness when you close your door
And family and friends are with you no more.
When all your friends belong in pairs,
You sometimes feel that no-one cares.

Freda Richardson

"You"

You never said goodbye, when you decided to go
You chose a place so quiet, so no one else would know
You slipped away and left our lives, you left us all alone
Feeling sad and lonely, now that you have gone.
You must have been hurting deep inside, but couldn't
tell us why.

I wish I could understand the reason why you're gone.
A simple note, a line or two just to say goodbye.
It saddens me to think of you that day;
Sitting there alone.
Deciding to do what you did;
No one could have known.
A silence feels our lives; the pain is deep inside
You were so very special
Your memory never dies.
You were a father, brother and a son;
Please tell us all just why you're gone.

Anita Johnson

Our Final Call

Our holidays in Devon.
Were our idea of heaven,
The rolling hills, the sea, blue skies,
All are heaven in our eyes.
The flowing of "the Dart",
Is a sight to hold apart.
No rush, just a leisurely pace
And to see a friendly face.
Their welcome and their greeting,
Will always take some beating
The memories we hold so dear,
To last us through the year.
Thank God for this view of heaven
And our holidays in Devon.
But now at last we've come to live
Our help to others we will give,
Friends and neighbours good and true,
We are so happy, never "blue",
Our roots put down once and for all,
Glorious Devon our final call

Jean Chappell

Moon

Moon, pale cadaver of the sun
Your fitful silvered glances come
From the dappled aspen now,
Murmuring breezes stir and sough,
And waking from their fitful sleep,
Glimmering forms of conies creep,
Spangled into life once more,
Play on the forest's flickering floor.

In the distance, foxes bark
Silent shadows of the dark.
Up above, the clouds float by,
Drifting continents of that vast sky.
Stars flash intermittent blue and green,
Icons of celestial screen.
Moon - wanton mistress of the night,
Ambivalent - both pale and bright.

Betty Cobb

'Lambs to the Slaughter'

Oh Thomas Hamilton, what have you done?!!!
You really should have put down your gun.
A minute's silence is just not enough.
For your license should have been rebuffed.
An entire nation was united in grief,
Through this awful tragedy; seconds brief
Is there a heaven or is there is a hell?
Hark the sound of the old school bell.
Like lambs to the slaughter in they go.
Damn you Thomas Hamilton.
Each one a son, a daughter you know.

Jan Rennie Gray

Friends

Friends are those who when we're down are there to lift us up,
Who when life's waves o'ertake us, will share the bitter cup.
Who cry with us in sorrow's hour, and cheer us when we're sad,
Who laugh with us and share our joy when life has made us glad.
They seek no compensation, ask nothing in return,
Are happy just to be there, showing love and deep concern.
Friends are those who know our faults and love us just the same,
Forgive us when we wrong them, though they know that we're to
blame.
Friends are never spiteful or possessive or untrue,
But quick to give encouragement in all we try to do.
Friends are like rare precious stones, more precious far than gold;
And if you're blessed with only one, you're blessed with wealth
untold.
If no such blessing comes your way, don't sink into despair,
But think of all the folk you know and find somebody there.
Just ask the Lord for guidance, from whom all blessings stem,
Then find someone who needs a friend and be a friend to them.

Iris Wilcocks

Violent Man

Cowering in the corner as the night draws near,
Your life is restricted, ruled by fear.
A figure looms over you, hand raised in fury,
You have no defence, he is the judge and the jury.
A sorrowful tear runs down a once beautiful face,
He only smiles after 'putting you in your place'
The unmistakable odour of alcohol hits you when he breathes,
A painful sigh escapes your lips as he finally leaves.
You feel so intimidated, you have no power with which to fight,
Your hopes and aspirations faded long ago, along with your rights.
Hopes and dreams, just like your heart are totally shattered,
Your mind as well as your body, left blood-stained and battered.
A lonely red-tinted tear falls to the floor,
Another day ends just like the one before.
Month after month you have suffered in silence,
Your life in ruins due to one man's violence.
And so yet another day ends, the same as it began,
Physical abuse at the hands of a violent man.

Dawn Rumsey

Path of Hope

I'll never abandon the path of hope
what lies at the top of the slope?
the answer is beyond my eyes' scope
pains and aches devour my back
I never for once think of going back
my tongue dry and thirsty
my feet weary and dusty
from whence a drop of water?
is no little laughing matter
thorns thrust deep into my soles
unscathed remains my soul of souls
these troubles of mine so heavy
make my mind wavy and hazy
I sometimes stumble to the wayside
but God's hand is always on my side
onlookers and mockers laugh and despise
do they know the beauty of sunrise?
oh, what manner of life?
yet the Creator gave all abundant life
I'll never think hopeless.

Jato Nyanganji

The Good Time

Do you remember when you could leave your doors unlocked,
You didn't read in the papers, and what you see, leaves you shocked.
People were not mugged or attacked in the street,
You could walk out at night, your friends you could meet.
You didn't need alarms on your house or your car.
Crime's much worse now, people forget the law.
There wasn't graffiti on the walls,
Nor damaged swings, in children's parks.
You were proud of your town, you could hold your head up high,
The nineties why do they do it, why?

Janet Elizabeth Isherwood

Mary

Dear little fragile doll, sitting propped up in the bed,
With sparse white hair and cheeks of fiery red,
Whose worn, stiff legs and tiny feet lie useless now
And gnarled wee fingers try to grasp the crockery.
Endearing smile and eyes light up your delicate face,
What were you like before Time played the Game of Life with you?
And left the trace of sheer hard work and drudgery
Down through the years, until eventually
Your frail, worn body is sitting here in front of me.
You crave affection and bask in the warmth of a loving cuddle,
As you sit with medicine in one hand and your
Crumpled Kleenex tissues in a muddle.
Ah! Mary, close your faded blue eyes and rest awhile,
Sleep brings blissful release from pain and life's trial.
Snuggle deep into your soft, white pillow,
Sweet dreams, wee Mary, life may be a little kinder tomorrow.

Enid Olphert

Sweet Lady of Mine

A big-bottomed lady with such vibrant motion,
You send my heart racing into rapid commotion,
My fantasy and more, not just a drop in the ocean,
And in my mind your image weaves a magic potion.
I've caressed your skin of pearly white sheen,
Acting like a lady in waiting on the silver screen.
Projecting a film of light for us all to see,
Though deep down inside you are pure mystery.
Turning many a head as you pass on by,
Such a heavenly body which fell from the sky.
A body that teases with each twist and turn,
My longing for you, I could in no way spurn.
My odyssey has met with humbled pleasure,
And no man can steal my priceless treasure.
And to my final resting place my body must go,
To free my soul in your veins which forever flow.
You must be the daughter of old father time,
Oh never run dry, sweet lady of mine.
For fondest memories and auld lang syne,
Sweet darling, sweet angel, sweet river of mine.

Gary Mooney

The Star

Star so bright in the sky
You shine in the nights
You dazzle my eyes twinkle bright
little star you shoot from here to there
You are visible in my sights
But gone in the morning, star star
You shine bright but you are so far away
I don't know how I see you, night night
You shine so bright you
ARE BEAUTIFUL

Jermaine Edwards

Ann

In the tranquil hours of darkness, you rambled through my mind,
You swam the sea of madness, but left the book unsigned,
I looked out through my window into your emptiness,
I prayed for my survival, and donned my battle dress,
One thousand screaming banshees, they did not stand a chance,
Sent to meet their maker with my psychiatric lance,
You heard my last confession, tales of silk and lace,
A hyperbolic function, an absolute disgrace,
And although your tears were salty they didn't sting at all,
I held you in my arms my little china doll,
Now the day is breaking, sunlight fills the sky,
So until you next come calling,
Adios, Au revoir, Goodbye.

Ian Rodger

Pepsi Cola

Beige and white striped,
you were a cute little mite,
with your tiddly small paws,
you crept on all fours.

Pouches filled with food, that you stored,
the pieces of wood, that you gnawed,
the wheel that you could run around,
holes in the carpet, that I found.

I loved it when you twitched your nose,
the friendship you gave, the love that rose,
all the hours that we spent together,
how I wished, they'd go on forever.

I'm so sorry for your last night,
to leave you alone, just was not right,
in my bed, while I was asleep,
I didn't hear you call, and now I weep.

Your cage is now empty, and so bare,
to you I pledge, this I swear,
I'll remember you always, and when we met,
Pepsi Cola, my hamster, I'll never forget.

Ann Coulstock

Time

What would happen if we had no time?
Would we get lost, would we know what to do?
Would we abandon the time pattern made,
Or has the time rule already been laid?
Is time embedded so deep in our soul,
That escape is such an impossible goal?
And when it is reached you know you have tried,
And now you know that it's time that you died.

Clare Ellerby

A Fantasy of Death

While I dream beneath this dark and toxic earth,
What rabid fantasies can harm me now.
There is no fear or pain,
Desires have passed.

I am knowledge
What joyous truths could I reveal,
For am I here?
Or am I around the next corner,
Just out of sight,
Always.

Can you hear my voice in spring's sweet breath,
Feel my radiance in the summer sun,
Do my footsteps echo through autumn shadows,
Or my warmth melt filigreed flakes of snow.

There is no fear, there is no pain,
No boundary that can contain me
And so
I ask
Is death the fantasy,
Or life itself.

Chris Powell

The Godman Is Coming

In some time-distant ocean he stirs the breeze,
he is conceived.
The Godman is coming.
Pitiful his wailing, stranded infant flaying the seas,
He moves the storm, He is born.
The Godman is coming.
Curiosity of a child, he is the gale grown wild,
He shakes the orb, wrecks the sky,
He perceives he's born to die.
The Godman is coming.
In majestic splendour he is raised,
Multi-coloured his rage,
Inland he wades, wreaks revenge against immortal shades,
He is forlorn.
The Godman is coming.
The threads of time weave his shroud,
He his the hurricane spent,
Ruin his legacy, is he you is he me,
He is left forgotten.
The Godman is coming.

David Shaun Wright

Silent Tears

The mists of time pass like tangled dreams
Within the mind.
That quiet lonely thought, doth now unwind.
Can we but clear the flotsam,
And the clouds? Which now divide.

So much we thought we knew, 'twas but nothing,
Just a waste of time; of such it was.
And things of matter we discarded and destroyed.
Now we have between us, just an aching void.

Gently the raindrops on my face
Like tears unbidden fall,
Memories so bittersweet those passing years recall,
So much we had of nought account.
When we thought we had it all.

Glady Jane Spill

'Night'

Night, even you betray me,
You are never never long enough to be still in,
To be in to be in,
To love in,
To See in,
To hear in,
To Cry in - To Like in.

Night!
Wrap Your Blanket Around
All those Who are Forlorn,
Forever Unfinished NIGHT!

Jackie M. Maginn

To Whom It May Concern

To whom it may concern,
You are the flower which shines in my heart,
With your dazzling silky petals delicately blowing in the soft
gentle breeze,
Your nectar is sweeter than honey,
Your sweet smelling fragrance fills my lungs with delight and
pleasure,
Your unblemished skin is purer than snow,
Your hair is like strands of gold precious and priceless,
Your eyes are like priceless gems glittering and twinkling,
You are my untouched rose,
My roaring passionate and flourishing wave which turns and stirs
as it comes towards me,
But always turns away.

Cem Baglarbasi

Day and Night

Sweet desire of everyone
You are the morning sun,
With eyes of crystal blue,
And skin the whitest dove.

Cool breeches kiss your tender cheeks,
The pure beauty of one so sweet,
Blessed by the gods for all to see,
A smile to calm the troubled sea.

When sister comes,
Her hair so raven black,
Birds their songs have done,
And the wind is slack.

She smiles a silvery smile
And dons her hair,
With diamonds for a crown,
For each and everyone, to sleep in peace.

John Harper

Special Care Baby

You're mine - yet you're not mine.
You belong to the tubes, the wires,
The monitors, the oxygen, the doctors -
All these are keeping your tiny body alive,
Helping you, while I stand helpless.
I'm your mother - mothers should help their children,
They should be there to hold them, comfort them, protect them.
But I stand here looking at you struggling to stay alive,
Watching you breathing, wondering whether this breath
   will be your last.
I want to put out my hand to touch you.
I want to hold you close to my breast.
I want to know you and love you - but I am so afraid.
If you die, then loving you will make the loss more painful.
Can I bear that pain?
Will part of me die with you?
So I stand and watch.
I stand and wait.
I stand and pray.
I am helpless. — As helpless as you are my newborn son.

Joan Evans

Untitled

I love to wander the hillside
With the wind blowing in my hair
To feel the dew and the sunshine
It's quite beyond compare.

The stillness, the shadows and the dew
are all there waiting for you
Come, come the hail, rain and snow
And give us a magnificent show.
The daffodils, snowdrops and Narcissi to.
Walk amongst them in barefoot, sock or shoe.
Touch them gently, the flower and the leaf.
Some will still remain low and deep.
I wait each year for spring to come 'round.
To see all the wonder that grows from the ground.
The warmth of the sunshine after the cold winter's day.
Each day I pray that spring has come to stay
I want to wonder the hillside
With the wind blowing in my hair.

June Hodgson

Winter Feast

From my window I can see
Wondrous sights to feast on,
A blanket of snow on a carpet of green
Casting a sparkling glittering sheen,
A stage for the antics of squirrels and birds
Their detail and beauty too precious for words.
The robins arrive and queue up for a bite
Then blackbirds and thrushes - what a delight!
Blue tits and great tits there on site
Surely they were there all night.
Hordes of starlings - gobbling madly
Then come the magpies, behaving badly,
Welcome all you feathered friends
For when winter's gone, the feeding ends
No longer are my actors there
All have taken to the air.

Ann Boyd

Heavenward

Cutting through the water like a knife
Yacht and I tip sharply in the wind,
Sails swell, bloated, strong as if with life
Full and white with winds of strength within.

We sail fast and straining on the air
Boat and sailor stretch out to be free,
Smile, I think I am in heaven here
Happy, as a curlew calls by me.

If there is a heaven it could be
Very like this place where I feel good,
Somewhere where the curlew nears the sea
Calling always calling heavenward.

Barbara Pearton

Silver Rose

Single silver rose and golden stem,
With stardust leaves, soft as dew,
On velvet emerald green,
So sublime so supreme!

You stand alone in field of corn
And bring the eve, as we perceive, you call the dawn.
On lightly dusted cloud you sing,
And rain of crystal pure you bring.

With summer's heat, yellow gold
You'll see the winter come in white snow,
Virgin cold.
Where lovers walk then stop and lay
You'll hear the secrets that they say,
And turn your head when bird does sing
You watch it glide on translucent wing.
Oh! Silver rose of life
What a precious, precious thing you are.

Alan Clarke

Solace

Your face the first I saw when I was Born,
Your eyes, alight with love and tenderness,
Yours the first smile, bright as a summer's morn,
Your lips, which gave my first soft sweet caress,
Yours were the arms which cradled me to sleep,
Your gentle hands, which tended all my needs,
You were there at my first faltering steps and showed the path
Where faith and honour leads.
You watched me play, learn, work and grow,
To be a man, to love all nature's things,
To climb the hills and watch the rivers flow,
To find the sweet content their songs can bring.
Your face the last, when death last closed my eyes,
My face the first you'll see in paradise.
When tears fall, dwell on these things awhile - and then you will
remember me and smile.

Irene Davies

Video

Cold eyes, cold heart, cold steel are all you'll ever be.
You reproduce the images we see.
The workings of your design get dated by the minute
In nineties technology.
Remote control is all you know - obeying every code
You signal when it's over and rewind my soul.
Remote control.
There's no emotion, no voluntary response,
Everything you do is controllable, predictable and cold.
Your images played can touch my heart,
But I'm in control.
Play, pause, fast-forward, rewind, stop, eject,
You record this memory; emit - that sound,
You turn life all around.
Captured moments flickering inside, rewind my soul
Remote control.

Anna Bradford

Requiem for a Friend

Can you be dead? You who have lived so free
You who with joy and laughter lived to love
and loved to live

Can you be silent? You who would shout with pleasure
At the sight of the early spring as she danced
over daffodils.

Can you be still? You who danced with the winds
You who ran on the open road and rejoiced
at the wind in your face.

Can you not sing? You who led my heart carolling
Over the hills of your fancies and would not suppress
the music that poured from your heart.

Can you be buried? You who hated the dark.
You who were free as a bird.
It must not be.
Oh but it is . . . it is.

Eileen Holmes

Don't Go Too Far?

Get a grip on reality,
You know you can't always,
live in a fantasy.
It's nice to float into your dreams.
But remember, never take it
to the extreme.
You can't always live in a fantasy.
So get a hold of reality.

If you take it too far
You'll never get home.
Never stray, where you shouldn't roam.
You might be mistaken for being mad.
If you ever stray.
Make sure you get back to reality.

Helen Mayle

503

Spring Is Different Now

Spring came in with an icy wind,
With scurries, and flurries of snow,
And if you didn't look at the date,
The season, you never would know.

Once - not so very long ago,
In spring, girls went into their frocks,
Away went the boots and stockings,
For Easter meant sandals and socks.

The boys all wore short trousers then,
No jeans or apparel like that.
Grey ones for school, khaki for play,
And white when they went into bat.

We'd go out in groups for a walk,
To find the first pussy willow,
Coming back to find the washing
In the gardens all a-billow.

Spring to us meant a lot of time
To explore the fresh countryside,
We had great times, but always knew
Our home time must not be defied.

Isobel Crumley

Yesterday, Today, Tomorrow

Yesterday, today, tomorrow
Yesterday, the eldest, today the youngest
Tomorrow, still to come

Yesterday, known to all
Today, the black sheep of the family,
Tomorrow still to come, of mystery
and speculation.

Tomorrow comes forth, becomes older
and adopts the mannerism of Today,
no longer the mystery of before
and Today becomes like Yesterday

As Today becomes more like
Yesterday, we remember and wonder
where Yesterday has gone

To the place where memories are kept,
while Today remains with us
to constantly remind us of how we are
and before joining Yesterday,
urge some of us to shape the manner of
Tomorrow.

Jason Umusu

The Willow Tree

A baby is born into a world of which he knows nothing.
Yet his is a world of love and happiness.
Now - all his memories are beautiful.
His tender years, nurtured by the ones he trusts.
Sunny days, green grasses and warm waters are all his.
One day his mother turns to him
She tells him that she is planting a tree - a willow tree
But the tree is weak and defenceless, so she helps it.
Both boy and tree grow, helped by love
The tree is still there - strong and proud
Its strength lies in its roots, and the care taken in its
    early years.
This tree will stand the test of time
Many will find shade beneath its branches
Many will admire it, children will climb it
It will be many things to many people
But there is one, there will always be one who is different,
The patient, kind one, who made the tree what it is today.
She is the one who will find most pleasure in it,
She can close her eyes and think of that tree
'That's my tree, I did that, it was all worthwhile'.

Jonathan Owen

Reflections on Life

Just two rooms, but it's wonderful, our very first home.
With second-hand furniture, and a few things on loan.
After long years of waiting, we've got a flat, what a thrill
At last to build a dream home we set to with a will
We've got our new carpet, what pleasure it gave
There's so much we need, how we work, and we slave
That new suite's lovely, but just look at that wall
Ah well, that rooms looking grand, but we'll have to do the hall
Now those folks over the road have a new car, we must have one too
Down the road, they've had it tiled and carpet in the loo
Now I'm looking around, and wondering where the pleasure went
For now, there's always something new but no one is content
He's got an insatiable appetite, that big fellow greed
For it seems the more you get, the more you seem to need
You have to stand well back, to see, you'll need a will of steel
If you're ever to break the chain, and, get off that wanting wheel.
You can work yourself to a stand still, then learn that wisdom,
old but true
It just doesn't matter however much
You've got, you just can't take it with you.

Eva Sutherland

Night Moves

Late at night when you are sleeping,
you hear no sound nor see no creeping,
but in some dark and dismal corner,
a devilish creature is lurking.

In the eerie shadows toiling,
contriving to gain from her deceiving,
manipulating, moulding, threads entwining,
strand by strand the mesh is forming.

The trap is set, work concluding,
poised, concealed, she lies in waiting.
An insect, hovers, cautiously lingering,
too late, the mesh ensnaring.

She feels the violent tremouring,
frantic attempts to free but failing.
Her injured victim, she is closing,
they struggle but her strength prevailing.

Calmly, precisely she is wrapping,
coating her prey to save, preserving.
She repairs her damaged webbing,
preparing for her next trapping.

Claire Awberry-Beck

An Angler's Wish

When I go fishing it's quite late at night
With the stars up there twinkling and the moon
nice and bright.
I opened me tuck box and took out me flask
And then came the maggots, what more could one ask
You've guessed I'm an angler and it's my only wish
To sit here in silence and catch a few fish.
It's really quite tranquil just sat here at night
Waiting for hours just for one fish to bite
And then when it does start turning the reel
It could be a roach or a chub or an eel.
And then when you've played it right into your net
You're still not quite sure just what you've caught yet.
I love sitting here, there's no one but me
Just eating me sarnies and drinking me tea
Now when I get home after fishing all night
The wife will say now then did the fish start to bite
I said to her yes love the night was just fine
Do you want me to lend you a rod and a line.
You'll love it I'm sure, just give it a try
Just you and me fishing 'neath the lovely night sky.

Anthony Akrill

Winter Rhapsody

The earth is bare - or so to casual glance at first it seems.
Yet, here and there, bravely,
Upward through the ground,
Delicate spear of snowdrop,
Crocus, purple, yellow, gleams.
Wintry frost spreads lacework delicately around.

Scarlet and black, two dancers glide
In wondering exhilaration, o'er frozen lake
Heedless of encircling trees, jasmine entwined
On branches, silver rime encased,
Which resting place provide,
For bluetit, robin or daring magpie
In separate scavenge combined.

Of hyacinth pink, mauve, and blue
The heady perfumes delight
The onlooker who chances by
This private winter's reverie.
Chill blue all-encompassing sky,
With dazzling sun so bright,
Backdrop is, so apt for this wondrous dramatic tapestry.

Irene Pacitti

Lost Love

I looked into your eyes, they were brown,
You always said I wore a pretty gown,
You made me laugh, just like a clown,
When I was with you, I was never down,

When I was with you we had lots of fun,
Even when it was raining there was always sun,
When I looked at you I thought my heart was won,
From you, my love, I will never run,

But one day a pretty girl come along,
To her, you said, you do belong,
The bluebird suddenly stopped its song,
Then you suddenly said to me so long,

One day it eventually came to an end.
Millions of love letters I had to send,
My friend gave me a shoulder to lend,
Yet my broken heart will never mend.

So just like a flower, you withered by my side,
Just like the sea, you disappeared with tide,
Just like the snail, you go and hide,
Just like a fairy tale, I still want to be your bride.

Jillian A. Millar

Forbidden Love

For one day in my life I was a princess
You did that for me
You touched me and kissed me gently
Your embraces set me free
Gentle words like poetry
Of which I had never heard
You touched my body you kissed my hand
Not having to say a word
I never wanted those moments to end
Nor did I want to let you go
I was captured in a world where time stood still
Everything moved so slow
I knew our time was ending
And back to reality once more
Just one last kiss then I must leave
Have I said those words before?
We held each other tightly
With each embrace it was harder to part
Those magical hours of happiness and love
Will forever live on in my heart

Dorothy Nash

A Boy's Best Friend

I think of you Mother, each night and each day,
You enriched my life and guided my way,
Throughout the days of many years,
You brought me laughter and stemmed my tears.
You calmed my fears with a soft spoken word,
In a tone of voice, most soothing when heard.

You were known as an angel, sent down from above,
You toiled hard for others and gave of your love,
Unstinting and generous, to the end of your life,
You adored good music and quelled any strife,
You tended the sick and helped the poor,
Never a beggar was turned from your door.

You enrolled for service to Country and King,
In the helping those folk who had lost everything,
Brought out to the country to live in peace,
Away from the cities, the bombs and the guns,
You comforted mothers, mourning lost soldier sons,
You helped with provision of food and of song,
Giving strength to the weak and assisting the strong.

Douglas White

Each New Flame

As each new flame reaches for the sky
Young flames are growing while new flames die
Flames moving in slow motion as the fire flickers
Bright
Embers glowing forming shadows
in their fading light
Dancing leaping flames crackling all around
glowing shades of orangy-yellow surround

Waters on the fire now fire has died down
ashes burning lightly
The fire has been drowned

There are only memories a few ashes just swept away
beautiful hearth of brass
glistening in the day

The night before such a tremendous display of beauty
ebony new coal replace the old that's thrown away
another night of wonder just a fantasy
the first glow from the hearth will come burn flicker
lift to the sky then fade into the fresh burnt ashes
then slowly die

Dismay
Julie Deason

Life's Lonely without Bill

She sits there staring into space.
You ought to see her lonely face.
Lots of people stand and stare,
And walk straight passed without a care.
Her clothes are ragged, her hair is jagged
Her shoes are tatty and torn
She sits in her coat with a scarf 'round her head
Just trying to keep herself warm.

She has little food, and has lost all her pride.
her only companion's the stick by her side.
Nobody bothers, no body cares.
She thinks of her days gone by.
She used to be married her husband passed on
But she's never been able to cry
She carries his photo close to her heart, since the day
She said goodbye, she can't wait till tomorrow
I asked her why?, I wasn't amazed at her reply.

My life has now ended, so I ask God above,
If He will take me tomorrow, and one day he will.
Then I can return to my husband Bill.

Joanne Ousey

505

Lorraine

You gave your life so easy - it was worthless.
You gave your life so others - they might see.
You gave your life so easily - left others off the hook.
You gave your life to write a history book.

You gave your life so others - they might see.
You gave your life for him, and her, and me.
You gave your life in tumult but your spirit never died.
Your life began to write the book that sighed.

And when you spread your hand across the land,
And when you see the tribes at your command,
You know your spirit's rising with the eagle far above;
You'll know the book was written out of love.

And when the time will come for us to weep
And when the time will come for us to sleep,
I'll sing your name, I'll shout your name,
I'll walk across the strand.
You give your life to free this native land.

Catherine O'Shea O'Brien

Dedicated to Goldie

Why did you have to leave me, the only canine friend I had,
You helped me through the good times, and also the bad,
You were always there to guide me, and show me the way,
But Goldie how I feel for you, in words I just cannot say.
The bond we had was sure, or so I'd like to think,
When I was sad you'd look at me, and always give the wink,
The walks we took together, were always fun for you,
The scents and smells were different, everything anew,
Well Goldie the time has come, for me to shed more tears,
That happens when you lose a loved one, a friend that has been
for years,
I know you'll be safe, in heaven up above,
And I know our prayers are coming to you, brandishing our love,
Heaven is a wonderful place, where all you doggies go,
But don't turn that clock back, as bad things will happen, that
you know,
Well my little poodle, this poem has to end,
It's dedicated to Goldie, a true and trusty friend.

Clare Anderson

Elvis Superstar

Gone from this world, but not from our hearts,
You were the king right from the start.

So young and good looking, a rebel at heart.
You sang 'Love Me Tender' and then 'Surrender'
Swayed to 'Don't Be Cruel',
jiggled to 'All Shook Up'
and rocked to 'Blue Suede Shoes'.
'The Wonder of You' took the waved by storm.
'I Just Can't Help Believin' 'How Great Thou Art'.

Helen Barrie

Daddy

Daddy, my everything, my nothing.
You've gone without saying good-bye;
Leaving us unforgettable feelings,
Unfinished dreams and forgotten truth.
How it would be nice if you were here -
Everything would have a meaning again.
But you have gone and didn't even say good-bye.
Between the life and the death
There was an inconstant conflict,
And on this tireless fight,
Your wish was strong and inaccessible -
Life was your desire.
With the suffering you fought,
But you were already tired and fragile.
Your end arrived without us knowing
With an extinguished smile upon your face.
The breath of your life gone, leaving us only tears,
Tears which never will dry,
Never.

Ana Maria de Souza Carter

Eggshells

Life is like a tree
You said.
Climb its branches
To success.
So I held out my timid hand
And you crushed it into
The sticky sap.

Welcome to the new world
Where we live for you.
We'll improve your self-confidence
By using your eggshell body.
We'll suck you dry
And spread your juices over the stars
Coating each and every
Spark of youth.

We'll card your golden locks to wool
And we'll whitewash
Those rose-coloured glasses.
We'll pierce your nose with a rusty ring
And lead you to the slaughter.

Alison Gregory

A Scene from Remembrance Day

I weep for you, pale youth
you lie so quiet and still
one could not think that death
could ever treat you ill.
He left you as in sleep
with fingers softly curled
while others lie with shattered limbs
and faces locked in their last pain
who were you? Friend or foe?
It does not matter now
These dead are all the same
For none will ever tread this
road again.

Decima Anderson Browne

Spring

As you drive along country lanes, in the Spring,
You will notice the beauty, this season can bring,
Mother Nature awakens from her winter sleep,
As leaves and flowers begin to peep
Under the hedgerows, that you may notice too
Trimmed neatly each year, with machine, as they do,
But do you notice the hedge, that has been cut and laid
By a man who knows, about this old country trade,
An untidy hedge is not good, for farmer or bird,
So during the winter, the chopping axe can be heard,
Cutting each 'pleach' near the bottom, but not quite through,
Then laid at an angle, while stakes hold it true,
Different styles display a finish so fine,
You can't help but praise the cutter's line,
Then in the Spring, the hedge starts to grow
New life from each cut, soon will show,
A good hedge again, where small birds can nest
As the season moves on and hedge-cutters rest.

Chris Key

Grandchildren

How lucky I am to be blessed
With seven grandchildren of the best
they bring their laughter, joy and tears
I've seen it all throughout the years
I love each child so very dear
their visits and voices I love to hear
each child is different in many ways
they fight and argue and think they know
they're growing up it's all a show
they'll have to learn the same as us
give them time, try not to fuss
they'll learn about life everyday
and make mistakes along the way
at least I've tried and had my say

Barbara Harpin

Treasures

What do you treasure most in life,
Whispered a voice one day,
The path one treads is fraught with strife
What helps you on your way?

First, I treasure the rising sun
That greets me every morn,
Without its steadfast daily run
This world would be forlorn.

And then the precious gift of sight
Enabling me to see
The beauty of day and of night
'Tis more than wealth to me.

Ah, there is the song of a bird
That helps me on my way,
In the song of a bird I've heard
Hope on a gloomy day.

Above all I treasure the peace
I find in my wee cot,
It is here that my worries cease
Contentment is my lot.

Clarissa Jones

"That Perfect World"

I am dreaming of a place,
Where people only laugh and dance,
Where no one ever cries,
- A place where hate and tears are distant memories.

Forward thinking for that new generation,
Plant the seed, watch it grow - into that perfect world.

I am dreaming of a place,
One of sheer delight,
Somewhere people talk all day,
And dream all night,
- Where cheating and sin are forbidden thoughts.

I need this feeling to grow,
Just like a tree,
- Using only inner strength.

I can remember the past pain,
I can think of the present time,
I can dream for the future years,
- but I can only pray for that perfect world.

Alexine Wilson

A Look in the Mirror

Breathless as I look at you
your smouldering eyes are so alive.
Your voice is filled with wisdom
and your moves are full of grace.
Oh I long to touch you but you don't belong to me.
You are in love with someone else, you see . . .
and me, you never seem to see . . . even in your company.

I start to talk to you, and you end it there
so I go and sit back in my chair.
If only you knew how much I have to share
maybe you would care.

You are wrapped up materialistically
you don't have the time to notice the reality.
Oh but those smouldering eyes
that hide the lies of vulnerability.
Your pecking dress . . . you think you're the best
but you're not, you're just like the rest. We are all equal when
undressed.
Stripped of our fortunes, then we can see
how deep the beauty lies within thee!

Carol Wyche

Absent Lover

Waves lapped gently upon the shore.
You were by the water's side, and I, by yours.
Meticulous though my memory may be,
Time steals the moment away from me.

The distant, twinkling, neon lights.
Eyes peering from the August night.
Watch as witness to my lonesome walk.
Our eternal path soon reached a fork.

The time we spent seems oh so brief,
Compared to the crawling days of stabbing grief.
Beginning with the first sunburst of dawn
And is with me still, this night, as I walk alone.

For I, there cannot be another
Than you, my one companion, my absent lover.
The very recollection initiates the tears,
Spilling painfully across the years.

Forming a vast pool, a reservoir so deep
From which my bitterness still seeps.
I have learnt that life, far from being fair,
Is like a malignant god that wreaks despair.

Andrew Murray

Israel

Love lingers on the fringe of desire,
Your body wars with the need to be free,
Oblivion becomes the silent movement of your Mind
Loud voices explode like wild shrapnel blazing
Deep into the star-kissed night

You reach out like a wild tiger soaring through
The derelict heart of your lonely lover
Eyes meet under the purple moon.
We two souls drifting through uncertainties
Stand alone, then connect.
In this your country forceful fusion melts the
barriers of barbed wire
Loud voices exult the sunsets of desire.
Passion moves like a gale over our tremulous
inexperienced lips, which quiver slowly and seductively against
the deceiving wall. Time does not fool us!
Youth forgets the fragility of life.
Now love bursts a New Horizon
As Israel SHINES ABOVE the betrayal of a Million Nations!

Camille Alicia Malone

Everlasting Peace

Twenty-five years of heartaches, destruction, tears and pain,
Wondering what it was all about, and what any of it would gain,
Families have lost their loved ones, which no other can replace,
Although left with lots of memories, in their hearts lies an empty space.

Finally the talking startled, to get the violence to cease, So we
could finally be on our way, to everlasting peace. Everyone danced and
sang in the streets, when the news did finally come through.
There was now an end to the bombing, and the guns were silent too.

Our city came to life once more, new businesses came to town,
The soldiers were being sent back home, tower and checkpoints
were taken down.

The on Friday the 9th February, after seventeen months had passed,
Came the news that no one wanted to hear, that peace wasn't
going to last. Just one hour later in a quiet London town, a
massive bomb exploded, pulling a business premises down.

One hundred people were injured, two more were found to be dead,
All our hopes of going forward, were now back in reverse instead
I was only nine when the troubles started, things were fine until
then, I've been told, my one wish for myself and my family now,
is that peace returns before we grow old.

Frances Meenan

My Musical Jigsaw

It's a beautiful day, sunshine, light of the world,
Landscape, greenfield leisure, waterfall - cascades,
Sky, a flock of seagulls, exploding seagulls,
Trees, black crowes, stone the crows, cranes,
Zoo, lions of judah - untamed, cheetahs, cougars,
Tygers of pantang, teddy bears, jaguars, def leppard,
Herd - crazy elephant, camel, hammersmith gorillas,
Warriors, flux of pink indians, redskins, scrotum poles,
Talking heads, spooky tooth, tonto's expanding head band,
Poni-tails, bangles, charms, pearls before swine,
Blodwyn pig, sam apple pie, ugly custard, help yourself,
Taste, april wine, matthews southern comfort,
Drunks with guns, egg, beans-human beans, cannibals,
Suburban studs, freaks of nature, heavy pettin',
Juicy lucy, aphrodite's child, raped, holy mackerel,
Dire straits, bad company, first offence, judge dread,
Ten years after, writing on the wall, humble pie,
Crazy world of Arthur Brown, cardiac arrest, grateful dead.

Hedley Lawson

Sleeping Weakness

Sleepy foetus gripping tight in despair.
Last breaths heaving from the chest.
Flushed with heat, gasping for air.
Tangled and strangled in a wed of hair.

Continuous sheets of falling perspiration.
Endless tears from the madness of wake.
The will, the want and the frustration.
Feeling disarray and no co-ordination.

The monotonous clock ticks on,
But the time takes forever.
All known sounds have now long gone.
Eternity, to face alone.

Yearning to rid insomnia.
Does it end? Never.
Will this night end? No.
It will continue forever.

Angharad Lock

Summer Love

We run amidst grass knee high,
Laughter echoing around us,
Into bowing heads of trees their arms outstretched,
Welcoming us into their shade,
The sun, glimmering its way amid never-ending leaves,
Dancing in graceful shadows,
Come with me my love and dream,
The breathless hush our lips meet with whispering touch.
No word or sound lest we break the spell,
Warm embracing arms of tenderness,
Sweet kisses and laughter so real,
We exist where time stands still,
In peaceful tranquillity.

Greta Dickinson

Sweet Revenge

My advice is "never"
Let your daughter cut your "hair"
I did once and rued it - and
That sweet "Mona Lisa" smile on her face
I completely misconstrued it

She was thinking of all of her teen-age years - when
I forbade her this - that - and the "other" - and
Her childhood years - what an old grump I was
Not a bit like "Fennella White's mother"
Fennella could go to bed when she chose - and
Watch "grown-up" things on TV
Her mother was sweet and gentle and kind
Not an old fashioned mum like me
So - never - no - not ever - let your daughter cut your hair
You could find that when she's finished
There's little of it left there.

Gladys Barton

When Christ Went Forth to Pray

The night was dark; the hour was late
When Christ went forth to pray
To ask the cup be passed from him,
To tread another way.
His followers, though they were there,
Knew nothing of his plight.
They fell asleep, not knowing
That this would be the night
When Jesus Christ gave up his all
To die upon the tree.
To save poor sinners from their trials
And save, yes, even me!
For all of us are sinners,
And all have done their wrong.
But Jesus died to save them,
We sing the glorious song.
Hallelujah, Praise the Lamb
Who died upon the tree.
Who died to save poor sinners
And save, yes, even me!

Angela Holt

You Are My Life

My heart's an empty landscape, your love the missing trees.
My tears like the raindrops falling in the deep blue sees.
My emptiness like the dark, your life the vacant light.
My loneliness like the sand as the sea goes out of sight.

You are my every season, my winters to my springs.
You are my precious elements, my belongings and my things.
You are my every year, my every week and day.
You are my life's direction, my sign to guide the way.

You are my life!

Claire Forrest

Life's Journey

Safe arrival, not too soon.
Whipped into the air from the womb,
Crying out, heart steady beating
Wrapped up warm, a joyful greeting.

As time goes by with family and friends
The journey never seems to end,
Playful days, learning ways,
Right and wrong in good stead
Trying not to be easily lead.
Keeping to the straight and true
Always the best thing to do.

The years have flown
Happiness and sorrow known,
As we journey on life's way
Rejoicing living day by day.
We hope to enjoy what's in store
Thanking God for the years before.

Ivy Baker

Christmas

At this peaceful time of year
When my thoughts of You are clear,
My mind turns to a baby lying in the hay;
For You came into this land
And with Your loving, caring hand
Taught us how to live Your gentle way.
You showed us peace, gave us salvation
The healing of our nation
Yet how many hearts just simply turn away?
They leave You and they hate You
Despise You and forsake You
Yet You love them more with every passing day.
This Christmas, Father, touch the lives
Of brothers, sisters, husbands, wives
Let "peace to all" this coming year
Be the message sounding clear;
So Father, then the world may know
Why the babe was born so long ago.

Elizabeth Sutherland

I Understand Why Old Men

I understand why old men once I knew
When still a child
Loved digging cloddy earth in frost or dew
Or the wind wild.
From earth and air their souls a oneness drew
And they were one with what their garden grew.

I understand why men loved carving wood
Or blocks of stone.
Tough fingers feel a bond of soul and blood
With what was grown
Or wrought or mined in earth. They could,
Sculpting, moulding, sense a brotherhood.

I do not understand why these days we
In central-heating,
In plastic double-glazed sterility,
Insulating
Ourselves from Brother Wind and Sister Clay
Severed from our Spirit Mother, spend our day.

David Hanson

Ode to a Cornish Cairn

I wander o'er the moor, so wild, so free,
Where grow wild orchids, shy anemone,
Towards a rugged cairn upon the hill.
Haunt of sly woodcock, snipe in winter's chill
There, mighty rocks are reaching to the sky,
While others on the sward, recumbent lie.
Sculpted by wind and rain, strange shapes I see,
Like birds and beasts in fable, legendry
One upright holds sweet water in a bas'n,
St. Francis caring for the birds of heav'n.
"Oh rocks! Tell me, frail human here alone,
What secret's hidden in your hearts of stone!"
Soft, like falling dew, they communed with me.
"In aeons past, a mountain range were we;
By clash of mighty forces in the Earth;
Flung up in throes of a chaotic birth.
A noble cairn are we, immovable.
Obey the laws of God immutable.
Keep faith, O man, in all humility,
Bow the knee and worship the Divinity."

Dorothy Richards

What to Look for in Love

The universe shows no bounds to love.
Open arms, await, as arms unfold.
Love shows its friendly face, in many ways.

Awaiting, around corners, hidden by shadows.
Of insincere feelings, which address
all corners, of the world.

The intriguing world, material by
nature, of its inhabitants.
Pronounces, to all, this timeless
bond, Love.

Janice E. Gilbert

One Day at a Time

When sunbeams waken at the dawn
Or frosty patterns trace the panes,
And cat curls tight near embers low
The new day starts - Halloo! Halloo!
And you with me, and me with you,
Yet, so it goes, and on and on
With things undone to dwell upon,
Or smiles recurring, melon wide,
The warmth within, or cold outside.
Time only changing, never we,
And happiness tenfold or more
With added blessings by the score,

To bring about a tapestry
Entwined by threads from me, and thee.

Alan J. Chester

Disused Railway

We walk, my dog and I, along the track
where once puffed trains,
on which my children went to School
with satchels on their back.

Where much was noise, now all is peace.
Wild strawberries grow.
A Badger Sett shows signs of recent occupation,
Willow sweeps low.

Once I deplored the axing of the trains
Now, new joys I find.
Though overgrown, fox-gloves and king-cups bloom,
Old man's beard does bind.

Would that I could preserve always nor lack,
music of birdsong,
While walking with my dearly loved companion
Along the disused track.

Ivy Mengell

New Love

Spring is here the dark
Nights start to fade
The smell of new life starts to unwind
Baby I have got love on my mind

Spring it's the time for new life and love to begin
Will it still be the same
When winter's dark cloak comes again

I see her in the early morning mist
Her eyes and golden hair by soft
Spring breezes kissed
She stands motionless in time
But come summer will she be mine

John W. Cookson

Dusk till Dawn

To the moon at night I feel strangely drawn
No child of light - a lunar pawn
When dusk has come and day is over
Out sneaks the moon like a secret lover.

Night holds a magic all of its own
A mystical wonder in me is born
The shadows dance and tease the light
That magical, wonderful beautiful night

Everything changing, nothing stays still
Soon the cold light of day the shadows fill
Another hour and day shines bright
Another day until the night.

Jane Anne McKloud

Silent Scream

Where are you? I've searched high and low,
when did you leave? Where did you go?
Where are you? You're my only friend,
without you here this pain won't end.
I try to think, I've searched my soul,
you've hidden in the blackest hole.
Are you out there somewhere on the breeze
as it whistles gently through the trees?
Or somewhere in the maddening crowd,
trying not to scream out loud?
In every mirror there's your face
fighting with the human race.
Where are you? Please don't stay away,
you get more distant every day.
You need to jump across the track
and start the long hard journey back.
Come home to us I hear them plea.
Are you trapped? Alone? In company?
They don't know if you can break free,
but I should know, for you are me.

Garelan F. Peters

"The Butcher of Baghdad"

Armed forces in the gulf, sent to fight Iraq.
Sent to liberate Kuwait, with orders to attack.
Overthrow Saddam Hussein, a tyrant who is mad,
Wipe out this dictator, the Butcher of Baghdad.

The allies start the bombing, with sorties by the score,
Saddam hears his air force, is a threat no more.
The butchers in his bunker, makes a quick retreat,
Contemplates his next move, before he tastes defeat.

Saddam fires at Israel, a neutral country too,
Wants to show that Arabs, are enemies of the Jew.
Disregard for human life, women and children die,
Genocide and torture, that we must rectify.

All the allied air force, superior in the skies,
Better planes and pilots, it comes as no surprise.
But what about the air force, belonging to Saddam,
The pilots have defected, and now live in Iran.

Now the war is over, and now Kuwait is free,
But Saddam's still in power, so cautious we must be.
Monitor his movements, let's hope the battles cease,
And then the allied forces, can leave the Middle East.

David O'Rourke

Once Seen, Forever Smitten

Stallion strength seriously strong in serving
Serenity; striking sublimity of strength of
Being with emotions evoke in ecstasy in witnessing
Widely wonderful; awe! Witnessed once one
Component of creator a notion not known
Before but to be beheld peripheral to rivals
Ranting raving anxious over all material meaning
Only to miss masterly marvels.
Every component recognized more creator disclosed
in a mirror being shattered. Every piece broken
Is a clue lost from the mystery
Every peace broken is a part to be seen gone
A simple tree surviving idyllically, a river
Running random, a cloud careless, reflect Him.

Gerry Wickham

Wasted Time

Voices of confusion
Shallow mumbles of boredom
Sticking into my brain like pins,
Killing eager thoughts but creating new ones,
How to kill time.
Confusion of the latter,
Licking at my fingers like a cat,
Pushing me to continue.
I try to hit it, kill it
But the throbbing carries on.
Endless pain, timeless hatred,
Life is anxious to end but my soul still lives on fire,
Ice burns in my heart and mind,
But time makes it easy to stay.
Time kills no man
Yet sends him to sleep.
Tick tock tick tock.

Fiona Darley

The Artist

When she comes with the attitude envied by all.
She changes the focus of others and leaves grinning faces.
She knows there's no time for cross words, and makes the
most of two worlds which she has control of.
Filled with grubby hands and sketched-out places in the time
of her travels.
She wants to see it all but she knows where her place is.
Using nature's goods builds her expression.
In time when the hands are tired and the imagination slow,
it will be shown to others.
So that they may understand what goes through the mind of
a genius.

Helen Phillips

The Planet We All Call Home

This planet is so beautiful, it is a living breathing
Pulsating, devastating recycling work of art
It provides us with everything we need
It feeds our body and the beauty feeds our soul
I just ask that you remember not everyone is so fortunate.

One cannot carry the burden - but together if we don't
Brush it under the carpet we can start with ourselves
Just by being nicer to each other

Elizabeth Serena Taylor

Untitled

For years I've been targeted with abuse
Put down and told I was no use.
I wish people would leave me alone
And not cut me to the bone.
People say fight back and stand tall
Sometimes I just wanted to end it all
At school, work, or in the street
It's always the same people I meet
They think I'm only here for their fun,
Leaving me feeling empty when they're done.
Don't they know it's a person they see.
Well I do not react when they hurt me,
Grown men aren't supposed to cry.
Well I know that's just another lie.
I don't want to be a victim anymore
Ridiculed and beaten till I'm sore.
Do I have to endure it till I drop
Oh please God make them all stop
Can I make it go away in my head
Or will it only stop when I'm dead.

Donald Davies

Morning

I woke up this morning at half past nine
Put on my slippers and my dressing gown
Went downstairs to let the dog out
Opened the curtains and had a look out

It was dull and dreary as it always is
So I thought to myself, "oh sod this"

The dog had started to bark
I thought he's just a little nark
I opened the door and let him in
And went up the stairs and cuddled in

The next thing I know I had woken up
I went to stroke my faithful mutt
He wasn't there next to me
He'd gone downstairs and was lying on the settee

Fiona Lattimer

Begging

How would you feel with no water and no food,

Who stand out begging,
Why do people stare and be crude.
They don't give a damn about what you wear,
All they seem to do is say we don't care,
How dare they beg on our street with nothing even on their feet,
But why are people so cruel and unfair,

How would you feel with no water and no food,
Don't stare, why not start to care,
Put yourself in their position you're right it's not like a cushion,
So don't stare, go on help somewhere,
But why are people so cruel and unfair,

How would you feel with no water and no food,
Children as young as five beg upon the street,
Would you stop on your beat,
And look how they sleep,
Or would you walk on by for a treat,
But why are people so cruel and unfair.

Anna-Marie Scott

The Legend of Mad Dog Riley

Make way for Mad Dog Riley, the maddest dog in town, he's
trained to kill and yes he will, Mad Dog will shoot you down.

He mounts his wily stallion, and rides across the glen, and as he
rides, he screams the words "Mad Dog rides again."

Now standing in the moonlight his strong hands on his hips, his
eyes are cold, his muscles taut, the word death, plays on his lips.

His face is still and stony as he reaches for his gun, Mad Dog will
not rest in peace until his deed is done.

With a steady hand that aims to fire his victim now is near, he
pulls the trigger, points his gun, Mad Dog knows no fear.

As shots ring out throughout the air, Mad Dog removes his hat, and
waving it high above his head screams "take that! and that!
And that!"

Mad Dog turns to go now his mission is complete, swallowed
into darkness he makes a fast retreat.

Mad Dog's legend lives on, but anyone who's sane, will pray that
Mad Dog Riley, will never ride again!!!

Cathryn Robinson

Hope and Despair.
An Old Forward's Lament.

Continual rugby over three decades,
Knackered my legs, toes, knees and hips.
Countless twists from the memory fade,
And numerous muscular rips.

For three score years it held in check,
Then descended Hell let loose,
Griping arthritis my sleep to wreck,
My mobility to reduce.

Ten endless months on a waiting list,
A hip replacement performed at last,
The light of hope shone through the mist,
The racking pain was in the past.

But infection struck with hateful spite!
The replaced hip refused to mend,
Three more ops - a hundred dreadful nights,
A second hip at the end.

Now home I go to try once more.
God grant that this time I succeed.
It will be nice to walk - as before
A normal life to lead.

Gordon Davies

The Truly Greatest Show on Earth

When old winter's had its throe, leaving mortals down and low
See that spring has sprung along, to put us back on song
So come on all you sleepy heads, cock-a-doodle-doo,
    out of your beds
The sun is peeping o'er the hills, and looking at your window sills
Rise and shine to greet a new day dawning, thank the Lord
    this beautiful spring morning
Cherry pink and orange white, blossom for the eyes delight
Bill and cooing overhead, two little doves just newly wed
The countryside is lovely in the springtime, lots of pretty
    flowers have their fling time
Jinking by on flutter byes, those happy flappy butterflies
Busy bees thro' petals roam, then buzz off home to honeycomb
Evening church bells ding-a-ding-dong-ding, in this green and
    pleasant land the congregation sing
Daytime dons an evening suit, blackbird toots a twilight flute
All is peaceful and serene, a nicer day was never seen
Sunset spreading gold across the lea, bright moon shining
    thro' the branches of a tree
Silver starlight over all, time to let the curtain fall
Gentle breeze a-whispering "Take a bow . . . you joys of spring"
By courtesy of the Creator of this open air theatre
Step outside, just look around and see . . . THE TRULY
    GREATEST SHOW ON EARTH . . . for free

Eric Mellors

Dissipated Thoughts of a Faded Bloom

It seemed to me, just strolling down the Ealing High,
Past gardens fronting semis with colourful display
    . . . And then the common on the right,
Where youths, indulging cricket, think of love
For girls who wander giggling by
Hand in hand, that I had missed an early
Chapter in my life through discipline
So hard. And now, in middle age I have
Become obsessed with nature's oft compelling laws . . .
Ah! That I were young again!
And then "The Baker's Arms", inviting any passer-by
Into its cool interior, glassware twinkling
In a gentle light, with beer on tap to cherish any thirst!
And waiting there, all warmth and rounded softness
The buxom barmaid stands . . . ah me!
Such carnal thoughts, but nice and very natural.
And, on going in, her smile of greeting
Quite upsets any notion of drinking two cool soothing pints.
Oh no! A half will do, I could not stand the pace!
Silly greying man, go home and study stamp collecting.

Edward Colson

What Is Peace?

Killings and shootings an endless stream,
Peace is just a long lost dream.
Tears of anger and despair,
Yet the merciless killer does not care.

Sixteen children faces of fear,
How could it possible happen here?
Everyone asks the question,
But no-one receives the answer.

Everyone wants to run,
But there is no escape.
Torment, pain and misery,
The perils of our society.

What can be done to stop it?
When will it come to and end?
Government looks to the people,
But the people look away.

The situation gets steadily worse,
An everlasting curse.
Killings and shootings an endless stream,
Peace is just a long lost dream.

Jemma Simmons

Our Kids

Five little children we have had
People think we're stupid, we must be mad,
But all the joy they do give
Makes us all just want to live
We have our ups and we have our downs,
We have our smiles and we have our frowns.
Sleepless nights, well that is a fact,
We often have tears and smacks.
But all and all we get by,
They are the apples of our eyes.

Donna Taylor

As a 30 Year Old Looks Back

Children of seven, up to eleven,
Played by the waters,
Learned at the schools,
Played in the park, but not after dark,

Girls and boys all happy together,
Teachers were the monsters,
Home time was heaven,
But little did they know,
They'd just lived the best days of their lives.

Jacqueline Goodchild

Prisoner

Transported through of Elysian Bliss
Kilted demons had died in defence of this
Resplendent in amethyst, sapphire and greens
Nature proudly displayed a jewel-box of schemes.
Music drifts from a ferryboat, plying alone,
And nostalgia returns for your Austrian home.
From the bright little craft on a mirror of blue
An old concertina played a tune they all knew.
Guard and guarded alike hum the lilting refrain
Everyone is in love with Vienna again!
Now its craggy magnificence, with day almost done,
Tinted fiery hues in the setting sun.
Night descends over Parkland where forests are deep;
Behind turreted walls a castle sleeps.
And lulled for a while in this blessed release
Drawn into the deep soothing chasm of peace,
You wander alone in the realm of dreams,
Lost in Labyrinth of fantasy where you seem
To be seeking the clue of what yet is to be;
Only the coming dawn possesses the key.

Isabelle Gorra

Prayer for a Friend . . .

Death, I have watched you stalk the one I love -
Layers of black, upheld on breaths of ages past,
A shiftless, shapeless guardian of all men dead
But I'll not let you lay a claim on her . . .

Be gone, dark herald of the Underworld!
Return to count the souls already thieved
When men's bodies lay broken and defenceless
And through their fatal wounds they let you in . . .

But you know I am strong enough
To banish your decrepit form into oblivion -
Death - you will not steal her soul this night
For life is for the living - and I live on . . .!

Julie Parkinson

April

April, when fields turn green.
Lambs on the hillside call.
Blackbirds sing, weeping willows swing
Snows of Spring silently fall.

April, when new leaves appear
Golden daffodils wave.
Golden trumpets in hands of green
Like soldiers on parade.

April when new life appears
Bulbs return from earth's dark grave,
Where they slept undisturbed through the winter,
April sends her rays of heat
Penetrating through to bulbs' growing feet.
Soon they make a brilliant show
Tossing their heads to and fro
Tossing their heads, as if to say,
No need to worry, no need to fear
Spring has called us - another year.

Frances Gibson

Niall

Teasing, bleeding, eerie
Pulling, sulking, deepening
Pain. Game. Insane, insane, insane.
Smile through eyes betraying
A lack of trust in the world.
Fake an air, a mood, an attitude,
And on the inside crumble, tumble
Wonder. If only, if when, if now, if then.

His smile in world of confusion.
In the labyrinth of mind and soul
The flood lights are lit and warmth
Drowns every corner that is grey and cool.

Then he has to go.
Oh God no. Please no.

Catherine O'Byrne

The Portable Loo

Imagine royalty squatting astride the portable loo
Kings, queens, princesses and all such noble breeds;
Imagine whilst on tour in deepest Africa
Her majesty announces, "where's the loo"
Immediately, and without further ado her secret army erects the
portable loo
There are chamber maids, ladies in waiting . . . waiting
Soldiers standing, stiffly guarding and as she
enters the portable loo it expands like the Tardis in Dr. Who.
When motion is completed the stench that lingers on is quickly
doused with perfumed spray
All other evidence is hastily collected, wrapped neatly in
Union Jack napkins and flown back to England
where it is flushed down the British loo
On its way to mingle with fifty million common turds
gushing through miles and miles of murky drain pipes
leading to the sea
where all excreta is inane
smelling just the same as common s***.

Jai B. Lloyd

The Knockdown

If you fall down with no friends around
knee deep in the vipers of despair
when your only consolation is your art of conversation
but it's void when no one is there,
so dig into a book with your sunken night
look and skim across the page that is yellow with age,
but the neon God you made stays implanted
in your brain and reverberates in pain, a protest in vain.

The on offbeat of the music machine spews memory's from
the past, like a forgotten tape that you lost in hate but
the feeling didn't last,
so get out of the slipstream, ignore what you
heard, close the door on adolescence, discontent from
the world find your destination look for the path,
keep right on course and never look back.
So build a wall a thousand feet height
with golden turrets to impale the sky.

David Foster

Poetry is . . .

Liquid thought
  painting with words,
my playground,
  mental urination,
a ventage of the soul,
  mind carpentry,
cerebral orgasm,
  amanuensis for those whose hands no longer write,
the only constant when people fade like shadows,
  my sanctuary, my fortress, my tomb.

Beverley Whitehall

Special Needs

He needs my care, both night and day,
leave him, I would not dare!
I love him more than words can say,
even though I'm worse for wear.

This child is very special to me,
he's found things harder than most,
great progress he's made, I can see,
he deserves a champagne toast!

In the beginning he didn't understand,
he was as difficult as can be,
he'd shout and scream, let go of my hand,
his frustration was plain to see.

He understands the world more now,
the local school he's attending,
Read, English, Maths, he knows how,
I'm glad it's a happy ending.

Caroline Hiles

Tunnel Vision

Artist - with light brush of his imagination
Pallets dove-grey skyline.
Watery, white-speckled clouds
Like anchor-free drifters.
Autumn scenery.
Melancholy offering of falling leaves.
Crumpled, dirty brown
Artist carefully selects, dilutes.
Sky, orange-clad sunset
Smudges bright make-up
'Gainst distant chalk hills.
Artist tracing bleak skeletal -
Branches, gnawed and hard-boned,
Fruitless.

Sultry winter geese
Make splashes of movement
Scoff at slow earthworms.

A shallow, undetailed stream,
A man, walking his dog
Comes in from the cold.

Anthony Gapper

Consequences of War

A waif at my feet so pale and thin
Palms spread sad eyes open wide
Looking up at me he begged for food
A starving victim - a mere child

Far too young to have their say
Or to alter such grim circumstance
But why will not the powers that be
End it all - let kids have a chance?

Chance to lead a normal and happy childhood
One full of laughter and hope and love
Not hunger or fear and dread
Of the incessant bombing from above

If this carnage and self-destruction
And outrageous horrors were to cease
Then maybe all these little people
Could claim their right to live in peace

Annie Riley

Romeo and Juliet

Romeo and Juliet to be together their
parents would not let.
To be there and to love each other
no one could understand this, not even Juliet's mother.

Alas, Romeo got sent out of the city
The nurse told Juliet this was a pity
Juliet came up with a plan
So they could be together as fast as they can

But Romeo heard that she was dead
he came back 'cause he was lead
When he saw her laying down
he drank some poison and gave a frown
Juliet awoke and saw him there
She picked up a knife and killed herself with no care.

Emma Rock

Freedom's Last Stand

Out of the grass the greyness came
merging into dusk
with trumpet roar and thundering foot
A bulk with smell of musk
The leathery hide with crinkles made
with clink of tusk and ears to shade
The baby playful at her feet
Runs to aunt and cousin for a treat
Guarded nurtured beloved of family group.

Muddied water is sprayed in air
As playful trunks the water share
the eyes so wise, the memory old
of elephant graveyard,
so we are told.
Have right to range on crowded earth
Uniqueness and splendour
such creatures of dearth.

Jane Darnell

Circles of Dawn

Wrapped up in my idle thoughts
Midnight and I'm still wide awake.
Seeing you pack your clothes and leave,
Was more than I could take.
The things you did, the words you said
Left me crying on the floor.
But the pain was so great and I was so weak;
I needed you so much more.
Still I fight my way through each day
And pray for you by night;
Yet I'm left alone and lost
With each day's first ray of light.
So now every week's a pattern
Every month a pure routine
The salt burns, my heart bleeds
When I think what might have been.
So here you leave me, still lost in thought
To find what I'm searching for
Till the next dawn comes around
And I wake alone once more.

Deborah Tapp

Massacre

Blood spilt on a superstitious Wednesday
Mingles with the flowing grief of Dunblane.
One psychopath; eighteen deaths. A world in mourning.

Scenes of bloody corpses
Linger in the minds of thousands;
Innocence destroyed and purity shattered.
Families weep at the obnoxious disappointment.
Immense depression crushes both
Strong and weak.
Messages of meticulous sincerity
Arrive amid confusion
And misunderstanding.

United sympathy emanates from
Our hearts
Condolences.

David Peters

The Wise Old Cat

Two bright eyes peep over the chair,
Mischief written all over him there.
What shall I do to make her see me?
I'll run and jump all over the settee.
Oh, I've overdone it I can clearly see.
She's coming right over to chastise me.
I'll fall on my back with my legs in the air.
It's sure to work, I'll get 'round her,
She will rub my tummy, and scratch here and there,
I told you, oh yes, that I would get 'round her.

Blanche Divit

'For Him'

The loneliness reaches my tearless eyes,
Like that wave of deceit, feeding despise
'For Him'. The 'truths' unfold into such lies,
Each shedding its unnatural disguise
Like snake's skin. And yet I am just afraid
Of the power, on me, 'he' had. That made
Seeing 'him', 'his' face near, like coming home
On a cold winter's night. Now it's the tone
Of 'his' voice, once music haunting my head,
In my sleep, in my dreams, now it's my dread.

Will it go away, this pain that I bear?
A headdress for all to witness, I wear
it. What did I do, to tear us apart?
Except for love 'him', with all of my heart.

Caroline Harding

A Love So Strong

A cold, chilling sensation ran down my neck,
Like the summer breeze skimming the sea so blue
I could feel gentle loving lips caress mine but no one was there,
Sweet nothings were being whispered into my ear,
Shivers rippled down my spine,
I could here my name being echoed over and over again,
Even though we are so distant from one another,
I knew his love was strong,
Why won't he start afresh,
Why won't he let me go,
As I glanced down from heaven,
A fresh warm tear ran down my pale face,
I know it's difficult to understand,
But I'm never coming home.

Amanda Tweedale

Losing Someone Close

The walls around you come closing in,
Like the waves that crash upon the shore,
Helplessness and sadness wash over you,
And seep down to your inner core.

Your mind it wanders to distant places
Of happy times you'd shared in the past,
The pain it brings is vivid now,
You wish it to go; but on it lasts.

Your life seems oh so empty now
Like the hollowness of an echo,
But keep your memories close to your heart,
They are a treasure you can never let go.

Little one can offer now
To comfort you in your sorrow,
But may God guide you, and hold your hand,
Today and in every tomorrow.

Jill Sullivan

Lambs at Play

They frolicked in the gym that day
Like wee lambs in a field at play
Jumping for joy and skipping away
Watched by their shepherdess in a caring way
as their wondrous skills they did display

Then suddenly a dark and evil cloud rolled by
With a clap of thunder rained bullets from the sky,
Devastation, death and destruction lay before our very eye
Like slaughtered lambs our little babies lie

Cut down so suddenly in the midst of play
And now all we can do is pray
And ask the question WHY? God, WHY?
That our poor innocents should die

With eyes raised to heaven on high
We hope that one day, by and by,
We too will play in that big gymnasium in the sky
Under The Great Shepherd's watchful eye.

Audrey Marilyn Davies

Love?

Every star that's in the skies,
Let us see with the same eyes.

Every tree, with its rustic charms,
Let us hug with the same arms.

Every day of every week,
Let us see break, cheek to cheek.

Every animal that in nature survives,
Let us join in being free and alive.

For every person in need we see,
Let us together feel sympathy.

Every day I see your face,
Let my finger a gentle line trace.

Every day you find life too much,
Let my words your misery touch.

Whether I'm here and whether you're there,
Let us, together, breathe the same air.

For every moment we are alive,
Let us, together, prosper and thrive,

If there comes a day you want me too,
Let it be as much as I want you.

Jo-Anne Farley

Through the Eyes of Wounded Men

Life must have a meaning, fear alone is not enough.
Life you must believe in, through the scary, through the rough.
Who is there to turn to when the darkness overwhelms,
    when the hurt becomes so great that the lonely see themselves.

Mirrors see the faces, show the eyes without the tears.
Sometimes I am screaming and yet still nobody hears.
Once you've seen the shadows that just no one dares describe,
    then you understand what it must mean to be alive.

People without faces and no mouths can have no say.
Watch them as they wallow in the hopes of yesterday.
Freedom is a luxury we seldom can afford,
    yet on a boat to nowhere watch the pitiful aboard.

Watch them as they scramble in a bid to see the light.
Cold, afraid and hungry see them struggle see them fight.
Nowhere in the love songs can the careful show the way,
    and still we run to buy those words that might just save the day.

A harbour is a haven as a kiss is love itself.
A gentle breath of tenderness is richer than all wealth.
Reach out and grasp the beauty that can turn your life around,
    for once you lose the feeling it can never be re-found.

Joy Duxbury

Untitled

I walk in sleep Through waters deeper by far
Than ocean's darkest reaches, And in this profoundness where I am,
Abiding in endless spaces out of Time,
Wherein my shadow may encounter its premise,
Veiled in attire no earthly eye may see,
To this blessed place of retire I flee.

Constant in motion, Ever changing in circumstances and renewal
Pervading in this immensity, Which in 'Time' may not conceive of in
flesh, nor bear witness to the wonders of this creation,
Melting all in the fulfilment of His design.

We sing in union with the stars His praise,
Where no night or day may end this place.

O great spirit, that hat cast away my bones,
And rendered my flesh to dust, you who brought me hither,
    out of the mouths of dragons'
And thence from the cold womb of earth I wore in sleep,
To these cosmic reaches blessed before I am,
And from whence I am come,
Reborn like unto Thine own substance,
To reside forever in Thy keep.

Anthony John Doyle

My Life

Life is happy life is sad
Life is good life is bad
Life is living life is sharing
Life is loving life is caring
Life is funny life is serious
Life is not knowing life is mysterious

Life is empty life is full
Life is wonderful life is cruel
Life is friendship life is hate
Life is loyalty life is fate
Life is the best thing I have ever known
I love my life because it's my own.

Julie Ryan

'The Lamp Street'

Darkness. Silvered, stone-flagged crests
Leading over nowhere's brow,
As I, starry eyed, walk Luca's yellow alleys
While the memories softly mingle,
By the light from careless panes
Where the player hides no detail from the viewer.

I remember the beginnings,
In browning attic rooms
Overlooking mildewed squares of bland indifference.
Chimney pitted buildings
Bore their overhanging cares,
In the shadows of their crackle-bare branched cousins.

Care must wander in this wonder;
Future. Present. Memories past.
Seeking solace in the appetite of hunger.
Can the wage of death be sin?
When an innocent looks back -
To realize that life is getting younger.

Justin Walker

A Dangerous World

Should murderers have the right to live,
When someone's life they take, not give?
Should criminals be allowed to run free,
When they are a danger to you and to me?
Should serial killers be stopped, before they kill more?
Should burglars so easily get through your door?
Should motorists cut down on their speed?
Should joyriders and drink drivers really be freed?
Should drug pushers make teenagers hooked on drugs?
Should prisons and detention centres, be more strict on the thugs?
Should stabbers and gunmen carry guns and sharp knives?
Will wars carry on endangering our lives?
Should racists beat others because of their skin?
Do these people realize they have committed a sin?
Should all notorious people be put on Death row,
Left to suffer and sweat, like only their victims know?
The world that we live in should be a safe place,
The extinct population should be the criminal race,
I look to the future, and what do I see?
That one of these victims could even be me.

Donna Howe

Be Brave

Stand fast, stand fast, and hold your fire,
Let not your trembling finger fail
Your heart though thudding at the test,
Courageous calls within your breast.

Courageous calls within your breast,
As shot and shell about you fly,
"Be brave," it says, and fear not Death,
'Tis more important how you die.

But more important still, my friend,
A thousand times more so, it says,
Is that you DIE - if living be
A future life-long debt to me.

George S. C. Davis

Ballet of Trees (A Picture of Your Mind's Eye)

Reaching out towards, a vacant sky,
leaves and branches, stretch on high,

A maze of roots run aground,
trunks, twisting, turning, 'round, and 'round,

Natures vibrant tune they're a-dancing
In winds, that blow from afar,
North and South, some from Africa
creating silhouettes of shadow, figurine

A ballet of trees with gilded autumn
leaves, free-fall into, nature's
verdant green
spring, summer, winter's scene

On this stage,
an opera, a chorus,
nature's play,
unearthed for us.

Joe Lasley

Alone

I step outside,
Leaving the feeling of warmth and safety inside,
It is 6 p.m., the cold air hits me,
It makes my body freeze over and ache.

Even the trees have stopped swaying,
As though they've been glued into place by the frost,
The street seems so empty and silent,
I am alone, just me and the fading lights of the lampposts.

I slowly walk through a small bunch of trees,
The shadows seem to disguise me,
I hear a noise, my heart thumps fast, I start to run,
The cold air and sparkling frost following close behind,

I finally reach the back of a factory and walk inside,
I lie down on a dry patch in the corner and look up at the ceiling,
It is damp and looks as though it is going to fall on top of me,
Everything on top of me, me crushed beneath the whole world,

I open my eyes and see a light coming in through a small window,
I get up, the smell of dampness seems stronger than the night before,
I pick up my coat and walk out into the fresh cool air,
I walk on, alone, into the world that has been waiting, waiting for me.

Julie Srih

A Valentine Wish for Love

A picture of beauty, a work of art
One look was all, you stole my heart
What can I do? What will you say?
If I was to ask you, marry me someday
Wanting your love, so happy we would be
Pleading to you on my bended knee
Return my love, be honest if you dare
Accept this proposal, show me you care
Birds would sing I'd rejoice and dance
This Valentine's Day just give me a chance

Ann Dulon

'Perchance to Dream'

The melody plays as the waltz fills the air,
one must lift one's dress as one comes down the stairs.
The girls and I giggle at the passing young men,
the orchestra plays, so we sing once again.
With our heads held high, we glide and we float,
our femininity oozing with every note.
    I feel like a princess, I feel such a glow,
then comes the applause and the end of the show.
The make up comes off and the dresses are hung.
Again I'm a housewife, once more I'm a mum.
Last night felt so wonderful, I recall now,
"What would Ivor Novello think of me now"?
In my jeans I'm here now, as I dust and I clean,
I'm thankful for a little taste of how it might have been.

Gwen Curling

A Sad Farewell

Gently, softly, silently
Like a autumn mist descending on a cold, still river
His lips brushed her hair.
No words were spoken
Just stillness and silence filled the air.

Rain drizzled on the bedroom pane
In empathy with the teardrops falling from her eyes
Pane reflecting pain,
The one inanimate, the other animate.

She knew the time had come
No more pleading
No more tenacious grasping of hands.
Just a sad farewell,
A silent kiss
And a lost long awaited fragile caress.
And still the rain fell.

Amanda Elizabeth Bellamy

Air Raid

The raucous wailing summons,
Light invades the room,
Distant bombs cause chaos,
Suffocation from the fumes.

A demented bolt to refuge,
Aluminium heedless and cold,
Our only protection from shrapnel,
And unforeseen dangers foretold.

My sister was left in the kitchen,
Perturbed and condemned by the fear,
Mother turned sharply to retrieve her
Not knowing that death was so near.

The metal case shook so violently,
Outside, my family - deceased,
Disguised, lying, blood covered silently,
I drop to my knees and pray - peace.

Angela Triffitt

Lighten Up!

Be as a feather,
Lighten up,
Float on life's paths,
Bolders do not float,
They weigh heavy in life's water,
Be as a feather through life,
Float on life's wind,
Be carried to your spiritual path of enlightenment.

Janet Burton

Time Stand Still

Oh silent, silent time, how quickly you pass me by
Leaving behind fleeting shadows, that I perchance to spy
Can I, by reaching out my hand, hold you standing still
No - as onward you rush, like water over a water mill

You just keep rushing on, through all the sounds of life
From the bubbling laughter, to the crying, screaming strife
I wish that I could hold you, to still the pain within
To stop the aching loneliness, of my life without him.

Lost love of my illusion, floating high with Father Time
Drifting far away as if a dream, flowing silent and sublime
I see through my reflections, striving hard to hold time still
That love is cruel and blind, inflicted by ourselves at will.

What a wondrous web of deception, we will ourselves to see
Believing that true love when found, is always going to be
Oh, time, stop your endless motion, if only for a while
I want to re-capture the memory, of his tender loving smile.

To hold the beauty, of all that we shared, in our passionate love
A blissful paradise, where our desire, soared on the wings of a dove
To re-live but an hour again, of the most precious time we shared
Knowing in my heart, he loved me and yes - he truly cared.

Janet Snook

A Traveller's Explanations!

On the day of the year, of the year I was born,
Life was a game and I became a pawn.
A pawn to be used.
A pawn to be subdued.
But then life came to me.
Not quick not suddenly.
It came in dribbles.
It came in strings.
In very big puzzles.
In all kinds of things.
I understood what it was all about.
It was to live in awe, puzzle and doubt.
For if life was easy.
Oh what a big bore.
To read a book and know the score.
No I like my life the way it is.
Puzzle and doubt and lots of fizz.
For me I must say whole and hearty.
I live my life as one great party!!

David Counsell

Listen

Listen Listen to the silent whisper
Listen Listen to the heart that trembles
Be not fooled by bold words -
Look behind them, there's a message
Listen Listen to the voice
Listen Listen to the tears -
To the sighs and to the screams
The message is there waiting to be heard
Listen Listen to the voice within -
To the birds, waves and trees
There's a message there -
A message waiting to be heard -
Listen!

Bernadette McGovern

Ladybird Eternity

The day crept up upon me,
Like a stalking cat.
Waking up was something, I didn't want
to do without you.

It's not what you think, as
you read these lines.

Before you went, into the chasm of eternity
We played with our toys
Innocent childhood soon to be snatched away,
Tell me do you remember the ladybirds we caught
in the summer sun
Encased in your cupped palm
you whispered
"Your house is on fire"

Well you flew away too
and now the ladybirds have lost their vibrant colour.
To me they just remind me of you

Eleri Sian Lewis

Survival

And all of a sudden the insect stops
Like in suspended animation
It flutters and flaps around for a bit
And then stops suddenly
As if it were dead
On a huge spider's web
The complex silk arena
The arena of death
As the insect prepares for its hideous fate
The hostile spider crawls down from its lair
On a pathway as thin as a hair
The insect is stuck
It cannot move
Just another meal for the spider

Jamie Jackson

You

Emerald eyes that sparkle and shine.
  Like fairy-dust's magic,
  They'll fade given time.
Precious pink lips that promise delight
  Like angels in heaven,
  Where hearts burn so bright.
You are my heaven, my night and my day.
  Like stars in the dark sky,
  That come out to play.
Forever and always, you'll stay in my heart.
  Like Juliet's Romeo, they
  Never did part.

Helen Moore

Mountains

There, the mountains stand, so old and wise,
Like a tombstone to giants of old.
With Eagles flying and praising their glory
At ancient battles when bold.

The rain pours down thrice every week,
To mourn the death of those heroes gone
In battles of old, when they fought with leeks
In their caps to show who they were.

Old myths and legends hollow around
Those mountains so wise in history,
But no one knows the true tales that abound
Of the history of all of the Nations.

Tho' the air is so cold in those mountains so old
The people are merry and happy
So maybe I'll go to those mountains so old
And stay 'til I go to the giants.

Gwilym James Edwards

Remember the Flowers of Dunblane

Blown away in a puff of air
Like petals on a windy day.
Taken from life, from youth so fair,
Why, we all ask? Who can say?
Young voices stilled, no laughter now,
Only weeping and silent tears,
As those who remain ponder how
They can face the oncoming years.
Remembrance tokens quickly fade,
Words and gestures are comforts brief,
The Nation, as one, homage made,
A corporate expression of grief.
Perceive the future, think of the past,
Never let the memories wane.
Names of martyrs will always last -
Those bright young flowers of Dunblane.

Bethan M. Dyson

Moon and Sea

The sea is a melancholy place,
When on the shore alone
I feel its sadness.

Obsessed, it slithers to and fro
Clawing back the granules,
Meticulously sifting through its collection,
Should knowledge of its past incriminate

Its sweet salt smell odourated
By the fodder of countless harvests,
In the light it shimmers, glistening,
Returning light to light,
As jewels in a treasure trove.

When moonbeams in the night
Caress and kiss the waves,
It takes them to itself
And moon and sea blend
In their cold harmony,
Like sterile lovers.

Alex Laird

The Refugee

The stench of blood, the smell of fear, the innocent are dying.
Men dragged away and slaughtered, women and children crying.
Screams of fear, shouts of pain,
blood flows on the ground like a river of rain,
To the sound of gunfire the lucky ones flee,
Here starts the journey of the refugee.

Thousands of people on their way
to who knows where, they have nowhere to stay.
Starving and tired but they march on
to the sound of the guns, the tanks and the bomb.
Mother hangs on to her frightened child,
petrified faces with eyes dancing wild
terrified by the suffering they see.
Oh, Heartless war, why should it be? From your womb you give
birth to the refugee.

A man gives his commands from an ivory tower
surrounded by wealth, basking in power.
These are the ones who should not be free,
they should do the walk of the poor refugee.
Oh heartless war, why should it be? through you is born the
refugee.

Jean Atherton

The Harbour

Fishermen, trapping more tourists than fish
Mending their nets for pleasure!
  The Post Office will not open this day!

Seagulls far inland, making friends with a plough
Their juveniles facing the wrong way on St. Michael's roof
  Bread greedily accepted from a stranger

Low tide and early sun, bringing scent from the sea
The school bus on its way with more homework
  "You're early today Miss Rigby" (John Potter's milk round)

Tired shops begin to yawn at "nine"
The paperboy was whistling hours ago
  Second thoughts shade the harbour wall with a heart
Mrs Hugget's mongrel selects today's flagstone
Mr Hobbit, the street cleaner, reverses to avoid abuse

  Travel case, a waiting room for middle-aged children

Hands held for love on a bus ride to heaven
"Two singles please to the station"

  Miss Rigby's moment: not to look back!
"It's a disgrace!" snaps the school entrance to the playground
"Good luck to them!" scream the Juveniles without knowing

Graham Morris

A Woman's Dreams

A woman dreams of many things
like finding a man to love or a romance
Playing and singing silly love songs
Thinking she feels her heart dance.

Then when a woman has a child
A daughter the image of her mother
Her thoughts, her dreams all change
To spend time with each other

The woman's dreams then change
with plans just for her child,
Watching her daughter grow up
acting youthful and so wild.

Then before you know it
Fate then takes a nasty twist
One minute she's there playing
The next you see her through a mist

That's when my dreams became a nightmare
six months later I still hear her cry
I hope she knew I loved her
So to my Catherine-Anne finally "Goodbye!"

Colette Stewart

'Spring'

Awaking to the dawn chorus basking in the morning sun
Listening to life being created, oh how wonderful that it's begun
The pealing of church bells, sweet music to my ears
Smelling the fresh mimosa as it so magically appears

Bright yellow cornfields contrast an azure clear sky
Larks gloriously singing while others soar so high
Above clear tranquil waters and trickling blue streams
A kaleidoscope of colours creating breathtaking scenes

Newborn bleating lambs, stir quaint old sleepy towns
With gaiety in their hearts they dance with leaps and bounds
Embracing all the wondrous things that only this season can bring
A season for all seasons, that miraculous gift called 'spring'

Angela Donovan

Time's Consequences

Seconds ago, everything seemed fine,
Little did I know of the consequence of time.
The chemistry was there and each time we met
The love that I felt is hard to forget
I can't see him now a week since the day
of our walk through the park
what a price I must pay
for feelings of magic
for the shortest of time
for someone I know now
can never be mine.

Angelina Corlett

She Wonders

She stands at her window watching the people go by
and wonders why
Lives go on but the ache is still inside and she wonders why.
How could anyone harm something so young and defenceless,
She wonders why her little girl will never have the chance to play
and laugh again. A child passes by with one hand holding on to
her doll and the other held by the mother, she wonders why she
will never be able to hold onto her little girl's hand and cuddle
her. The ache inside is like
no other it cannot be filled by words of comfort and sorrow. She
wonders if the ache will go away but knows that part of her is
lost and can never be replaced. She wanders into the kitchen and
her little girl's doll is on the table; she wonders why her little girl
will never have the chance to play with it again. As tears run
down her cheeks,she wonders if they will ever stop and if the
ache inside will go away. Others grieve but do they have this
ache and loss? Inside she wonders, as she buries her face in the
doll's hair, she remembers the time at Christmas when her little
girl was full of life — opening presents She wonders when the
suffering will be over and asks the same question why her little
girl, and as the ache begins to get worse she wonders if there is a
God, she wonders.

Alison Caulton

The Silent Stalker

Is that he, who passes by,
With measured step, and twisted lip?
Dark glasses shade his murky eyes.
My thudding heartbeats dip, and flip,
As from my sight he slides away,
To hide, until some other day.

What does he carry in that bag,
That dangles from his bony hand?
Is it my death-knell hidden there?
Pistol, knife, or just a strand
Of rope, to tighten 'round my throat,
As into black oblivion I float?

Or could it be that woman.
Who loiters on the corner there?
From her black raincoat hood,
Protrudes a pointed nose, and wispy hair.
That shabby handbag on her arm,
What does it hold, to do me harm?

Freda E. Allen

A Lobster's Tale of Woe

I was a lobster a short while ago
Living quietly at the bottom of the sea.
In spite of my claws I didn't do any harm
And I assumed that no-one would hurt me.

Naive you all cry and maybe that's true,
Looking back I'd agree you are right.
But no-one told me, when I was at school
That lobsters were supposed to be bright.

I was mooching around, looking out for some lunch
Dodging the occasional curious seal.
How could I know that the morsel I ate
Was merely the bait in a creel.

I was pulled up to a boat, then to market I went
A chef bought me and threw me into a pot.
I don't usually complain, but seriously folks
The water in there was bloody hot.

I wasn't always like this, bright pink on a plate
I walked tall(ish) with never a slouch.
It doesn't seem fair for a creature once proud
That my last word on earth was just OUCH!!!!

Gillian H. Britton

Individuality

Individuality is the power within your being.
Locked deep into the darkness of your soul,
Or out into the brightness of your mind.
It revolves around the entity of your life
like a glowing orb of what is you.
As you reach for what you want your
individuality takes you to the success.
Of your efforts of reaching beyond normality.
The strengths of individuality are
stronger than ourselves and those
of us that use its powers shall
take themselves higher than the others
and awaken the cloud of their dreams,
and eliminate the mask of uncertainty.

Claire O'Connell

The Road Ahead

Trudging along, the world a daze,
Look around a morbid haze,
Look above, into the sky,
Will today be the day I die?

Shuffling along, slow and weak,
The thought of loved ones keeping them peak.
What about Harry? What about Fred?
Should it be me who ought to be dead?

Love and peace, hate and deception,
Those in power want all the attention.
Who's more important them or us?
Who needs fighting? Who needs fuss?

At the end, what will there be?
What will it take for the leaders to see?
No more torture, no more pain.
Can't they all be friends again?

Amanda Nield

Summer Ride

Wind, dodging through branches,
like a villain trying escape capture.

Sun, beating down on weathered brows,
creating rivers of sweat down red
and puffing cheeks.

The even beat of the horses hooves
on the sun-baked ground, keeping
time with the rider's heart beat.

And all around the once green fields,
stretched out, now baked into a golden
carpet, shimmering in the afternoon heat.

Annie Cartwright-D'Arcy

What's in a Smile?

A smile can hide so many things
loneliness, anxiety or grief,
but to you, no peace it brings
when you're not smiling underneath.

How many times do you smile each day,
without it feeling true?
None of your troubles fade away
but it's the easy thing to do.

A genuine smile is truly meant
and requires that 'special glow.'
That feeling which is Heaven-sent
and only you can know.

Without this warmth, your spirit's lost,
a smile looks out of place.
It's colder than a morning's frost
and unsettled on your face.

Suddenly and without doubt
someone special returns that glow.
You're smiling from the inside-out,
now, true emotions show.

Geoff Durham

Jessica

Skin so pure and fair,
Long, thick, wavy red hair,
So innocent as the day is long,
That's our little Jessica.

So innocent she does remain,
Kept away from life within.
Some freckles dotted upon her skin,
So beautiful and so thin.

Beautiful baby protected from the world,
Within my womb so warm.
So innocent and away from harm.
Our little Jessica so pure.

Bernice Pirie

Imaginary Train

She feels like she's waiting on Platform B,
Longing and yearning for something to see,
Hoping and praying the train is near,
Listening and wishing for something to hear.

Sitting there deserted she feels so alone,
Wondering if she'll ever get back home,
Realizing now her shadow is her only friend,
And praying to God for a future around the bend.

Finally she decides to get up and move,
The train isn't ready to arrive and there's nothing she can do.
So silently she waits for no more pain,
Secretly she waits for an Imaginary Train.

Jennifer Carlton Woodworth

Growing Up

Lost, lonely miles from happiness,
Lost, lonely a child's madness,
Life has no meaning,
You search but cannot find it.
You sip thoughts deep enough to drown in,
Like a sorrowful well with no bucket.
You utter words harsh enough to choke on,
Like a car without brakes.
Childhood is behind you,
Your life is now your own,
People still care, but no-one comprehends
that kindness is what you can't cope with,
Their hearts are near but they're not penetrating yours.
Despair cannot be rushed and shouted away,
You need time for the fog to rise,
You need time for the knots to straighten,
You need time to begin your life.

Chloe Lewis

Look over There

Wow!! Look over there,
look at that boy, do I dare!
With big brown eyes and brown curtain hair.
Wow!! Look over there.

I don't believe it,
He has spoken, his voice
Wow!! Look over there.

We spoke for hours
I felt like the world stopped spinning,
Wow!! Look over there

I knew I had to go, I didn't want to leave,
The boy of my dreams is sitting there,
Wow!! Look over there.

Will I ever see this beauty of mine
Just one kiss before I go
Wow!! Look over there.

When his lips touched mine,
It felt like the joy of a million children
Rolled into one, wow!! Look over there.

Is this love! Or am I dreaming
Wow look over there.

Heidi Baker

Life's Too Short

Wash away life's stresses and strains,
look in the mirror and what remains?
One human being like any other . . .
Son, Daughter, Father or Mother.
Why do we take on a mantle of woes
when each of us into the workplace she goes,
for life is too short to be looking back
and too stressful when always on the attack.
Life is for living for doing our best,
for loving and giving, to hell with the rest.
What's competition when stripped to the core?
Somebody's greed to always want more!
What more do they want when looking around . . .
than health, peace and happiness where friendships abound.

M. C. Warner

Untitled

He is the man who 'just walks along',
Looking at this and comparing that
Down past the park and on up the hill,
Walking the streets he sees from his flat.

Stopping and thinking, remembering still
Here fell the bombs,
That killed many people
The church that was saved, apart from its steeple.

The planners who came, saw what was left
Preserved the church, and tore down the rest.
Down with the modest, up with the tall
Towering blocks and the church coffee stall.
Seeing a world where he cannot belong,
for he is 'the man who just walks along'.

Alan E. Tanner

Beauty

Beauty mystifies the eyes.
Petals curl and pencil slim stalks
Reach upwards to the sky
Streams that trickle out of view
Gardens august with their summer hue.
Dappled sunlight filters through the trees
And ripples on a pond move free.
It all adds sweetness to the mind.
This beauty that mystifies the eyes.
Leaving my heart full of wonder, love and hope.
For always, for all mankind.

Hazel Faulkner

Burning Flame

First encounters not a word spoken, everything understood.
Magic hovering beneath apprehension, a mutual desire unfulfilled.
Mood recreating the past, embarrassed silence no part of an
expression in their language, both vanishing into a fast running
stream, its intenseness of rich ruby wine bathing their souls.

Rays of bright light, moist drops of rain cascading through the
sun cloud of hope . . . hope in the events of the future. Moments
held in memory like petals of rosebuds in their hands.
Of what I speak only a few live to taste; it is the taste of
illogical overpowering emotion, the substance of life that can
last a thousand nights, and light up a thousand grey days.

Passing through the corridor of time you can look, you may
search but many don't ever find the other half of themselves,
people come and people go like the turning pages of a book . . . but .
. . If by some chance you stumble across your burning bush . . .
Will you stop to take the heat from the flame . . . Will you hold
your hand to the fire and risk the burn of flesh whose pain will
never sleep . . . or will you walk on . . . to travel the unknown
wasteland of distant future . . .

Elizabeth Ann Harse

Taut

Eyes bore into blank t.v. screen,
Malevolent, at the foot of the room,
Silence taunting me with sheer volume
And humidity like a hand around my throat.
My frustration matches the incessant span of night.

Each nerve is taut, each thought is bitter,
Cold, dry panic gnaws my inside face.
Every thought heralds the direst threat.
Imagination claims command, and
Red-rimmed eyes are too dry to weep.

We are lost, and fearful; yet ever vigilant,
But knowledge is worthless, and ignorance bliss.
Too scared to move, muscles rigid as stone,
The beauty of sleep is one I will not know.
A day is too short, it passes only in dread of night.

Angela Cavenor-Shaw

Penitence

Many a word written in anger.
Many a phrase sewn together from rags.
Many's the time I thought before saying
The many and terrible things that I have.
Many the tempers that flared in my eyes.
Many the plots that were wove in my mind.
Many and varied the dooms I prepared,
For the many and various Fools I despised . . .
Many the hours I withdrew and repent,
Many the wandering walks that I went,
Many the hours all alone I have spent,
Reading the letters my misery sent.

David B. H. Barton

A Heavy Heart

This world is fabricated, my heart feels like stone
Many a thought I will perceive, that never will be known.
The soul is willing, the flesh is weak, tell me what to do
The heart is often dangerous, can mine see me through.
The good, the bad, the ugly times when life just gets you down
Can my heart take it all, will I bear a frown.
Will I want it over, or will I see it through
My destiny is in your hands, please tell me what to do.
My heart is very heavy, I feel I'm all alone
I think about what's happened that I cannot condone.
It's in my dreams at night, my thoughts in daytime too
The days when I don't give a damn are numbered very few.
I need someone to help me, to get me through my pain
My heart can't see the sunshine but constantly the rain.
The pain I feel ain't physical, but it hurts me till I cry
And I'll carry all the memories until the day I die.

Arleen O'Hara

The Jaffa Orange Box Kids

As the Jaffa Orange box goes down.
My tearful father he wears a frown
Where the hell is Father Brown
Promised he'd come and say a prayer
Only me and my poor old Dad were there
The child a victim of convulsions
Will go into the ground without extreme unction.
I cover the porcelain like little face
With an old rag, just a bit of waste
No chance for you my little boy
You were born I'm afraid just to die
I hold the carbide lamp real still
As my dad begins to fill
The soil it thuds in the midnight air
Covering my little brother lying there
If only my dad had had the half crown
My little brother wouldn't be in the ground.

Denis Murphy

Unexpected Visitor

Hello.
My underwire rides squewiff to my breast,
Headdress of lemon conditioner wrapped in
Carrier bag and toothpaste stained towel turban.
Indiscretion breeds infidelity,
I think.
Only it happened to be an evening of soap opera
and cigarettes.
So I turn to tune into music that
Makes me feel brave.
Was he ever to decipher the will of each whim,
My perfect womanhood,
Her hair curling at my neck,
Tentatively, each moment, I am shameful.
So I threw off the damp towel,
And plastic bag and,
Flicked the switch on the kettle.

Hayley Sykes

Destiny

The air is stuffy: It stifles,
My walk is slow and stiff,
This limp it hinders my thinking,
My thinking is slow like my pace.
The leaves are swept by the wind,
They decay as the warm rain falls,
It soaks through my trousers and skin,
My throat becomes dry like before
They say my hair is too long,
It's true it gets in the way,
Like spiders it crosses my face,
Like spaghetti collects at my mouth.
I'm here if you wish to find me,
My leaves are a path in the dark.

Anita Clarke

Enlightenment

Twilight . . . Neither day or night.
Mystery . . . Shapes after strangely.
The eye thinks itself deceived.
What is in the noonday sun is clear and definite
Changes imperceptibly as night approaches.
Any conclusion drawn regarding an issue
Of itself presents another face
And one is forced to reconsider
By the following noon it has changed yet again confusing the
   uncertain mind.
I watch the fading light
Deliberately seeking an answer from something I cannot see
Yet know is there hiding itself in shadow
Lest I come upon it and recognise the face of truth.
The face of truth . . .
I need seek no more.

I. M. Goodley

The Illusive Spirit of Life

I was so far away in my mind
Looking for the answers, but there were none to find
The spirit I grasped and almost took
Has disappeared without a second look.

There are so many things I want to do
Not just for myself, but for you
Wishing on a dream kept in my soul
My head has leapt the fence and gone A.W.O.L.

Wishes will soon turn to dust
They last as long as lust
Walking down the road, head held high
Wanting to succeed, but when will I begin to try?

Voices argue inside a confused head
Asking me why I am so easily lead
I want to hear the angels sing their praises
For this isn't one of those teenage phases.

Alexandra Johnston

'If Only'

She lay against the flattened grass
looking up at me with loving eyes
with loving eyes I knew could last.
He hair tied behind her head,
her cheeks flush her voice hush
sighing but not speaking.
Her soft breasts swaying with the momentum
Of her lips, with my lips,
her slender long legs tightly squeezing me
and lovingly teasing me.
Beneath me this dream of all dreams
this angel stolen from heaven
pure as pure is and ever will be.
Our joy splitting my seams or so it seems.
I do love her too
I do need her
but she is not you.

Julian F. Wall-Hayes

Untitled

We walk through the flooded forest.
Like fearful creatures in the dark.
Trees shake with mirthful laughter.
If we are alone,
where are our
mothers?
(who will shatter the tiger's eyes?)

The war reigns —
to die or lie?
Who are angels in the midst of all this?
Prognosis of death.
Prepare.
Who calls upon these morbid angels to stalk our people?
Was it the devil?
Or was it God himself?
Ghost children
walk in the red hot flames of death.
An end to all worthless life,
led by souls consigned to death,
sowing seeds of immortality.

Emma Campen

Whisper

Fast asleep in a mother's womb
Perfect and beautiful, ready to be born.
The essence of life is within you now,
God's whisper, as you take your breath,
will gently touch your brow.
Listen carefully little one
to the secrets spoken at your dawn,
Always remember the wisdom that you heard
before you were born.

Elizabeth Anne Jones

Life Goes On

Life goes on, so easy to say,
When it's not your loved one who's passed away,
When it's not your tears that are falling fast.
And not your time just racing past,
When things have come to a sudden stop,
And no way can you turn back the clock.
Smile, they say, throughout your sadness,
Let fond memories bring back the gladness.
But it's so much easier said than done
When in your lonely world there is no more sun
When only clouds hang overhead
And there's no one to kiss as you go to bed,
No one to say "Thanks for a lovely day,"
So you lay in silence, and pray and pray
That you'll live again despite all the fray.
For 'TIME' doesn't heal, that's the oldest myth,
And I miss all the love that you could give.
But "Life goes on", or so I'm told,
Maybe one day, I'll return to the fold.

Doreen McDonald Banks

Morning on Ham Hill

Sky, vast and commanding
mist softens the scene
Hilltops forced like bosoms to the sky

Valley of mist soft as down
Sunshine filters spills and settles
like gold filings
Hovering on the surface
fearful it may sink
out of sight
out of beauty
Crunchy wheels on yellow stones speed along
All's not lost
I will come back
I will not forget

Bernadette Huggett

The Winds of March

Chill winds of March, bare through my bones and sigh
Moaning through trees, fast bending them at will
Swirls paper, twigs and dust away on high.
Will earth's vibrations anymore be still.
The sun breaks through and everything's arrayed
In golden haze, that warms both heart and mind
A heartening glimpse of summer now portrayed
Tranquillity, a place that's hard to find
Too soon, the sun, her shutters close again
Rain whips like needles 'gainst my tender skin
The icy blasts condemn my heart to pain.
Take heart, 'cause even yet the sun may win.
May warm the earth to bring forth all her prize.

Dora Watkins

Oh Boy

When I turn back the pages, hey I was real cool.
Monkeying around, just wasting my time at school.
Could not think straight, did not know my left from right.
Head never in a book, always looked for a fight.

Life is no rehearsal, don't get a second chance.
No shy guy, life is one long party filled with romance.
Stoke up the fires of desire and let it flow.
Oh Boy! If you need some instruction just let me know.

Headache gone tomorrow. Boy I spread my net wide.
Sampled the field prayed my rivals didn't collide.
Laid my head to rest on any young girl's pillow.
Talk of any commitment then off I would go.

Opened my heart, then shut it in the nick of time.
In case a pretty young chick thought she would be mine.
Damned if I cared, as long as I got my pleasure.
String them along, I could pick them at my leisure.

John Neal

Pollution

Chimneys smoking from factory towers
rubbish thrown on the road it piles
car exhaust fumes put lead in the air
Rivers flowing with oil everywhere

Man is too lazy to walk to the bin
The smoke in the air that we breath in
Desolated lands that man has ruined
From pesticides sprayed to poison the ground

Slime is dripping from the sewerage pipes
Making a home for dirty little rats
Food gone off and thrown into bins
The cats tip it over and rummaging within

Life is disgusting filled with filth and abuse
And swearing that comes from the mouths of youths
It wouldn't hurt us to do our best
To clean up the rubbish and not make a mess

Trying to be a bit less of a lout
Clean the language that comes from the mouth
Caring not for the world we live in
Going on daily doing nothing but sin

Gillian P. Stannard

Through My Eyes

I see motorways jammed with cars
sad, lonely men drunk in bars
children playing in the street
who knows who they might meet
on the news every day I see
people dying far from me
of starvation people are dying
while all alone children are crying
this is what I see
maybe you should look through the eyes of me

Jennifer McCluskey

Poem for Louise

We traced dust patterns on lazy summer days,
Sat in our place.
Counted freckles on each other's face
Told the time by the position of the shadows.

Draped in daisy chains - wilted at the edges.
Not blood brothers
Acquainted mothers.
Daisies braided for growing friendship.

Grubby hands - nail polish chipped at the edges.
Flicked through the covers of magazines,
The glamour queens.
Compared hand-me-downs.

The sun winked at us through abandoned clouds,
Like the countless men
Who invaded our den,
As we closed our eyes and dreamt of being tall.

Anna Jones

Visit 'Round the Planets

When people ask, how you know all life is one,
say it is easy to know, and tell how it is done,
you sail through the heavens, and swing from
the stars,
fly past Jupiter, wave to angry old Mars;
you drift by the Moon, and wave to the Sun,
visit beautiful Venus, where love began;
say hello to the Great Bear, and the brilliant
North Star;
and you can slide down, the long Milky Way,
sit yourself down on a bright golden tray;
you can make this journey from when the Sun sets,
and be back in your home, before it comes up in
the West.

Josephine Brown

Unspoken Thoughts

If I should have to live without your gentle smile
    Or spend each day without a hope of seeing you,
My heart would cease to beat in just a little while,
    For you're the one I'm living for - what would I do?

No matter where I am it's always you alone I see,
    It's always you my every silent thought contains.
I dream your eyes of velvet brown smile just for me
    And even when I wake the dream of you remains.

How could I ever tell you just how much I care,
    Or just how much it means to me to be your friend?
Oh, how I wish that I could take your hand and share
    Each moment of your life until all life shall end.

But you will never know the love I feel inside
    Or how my sad heart longs for you when you're away,
And so these tender thoughts for you I have to hide
    As I can never one of them to you betray.

So just for now I'll smile and let you think I'm fine,
    But secretly my heart will beat for only you.
Each day I'll hope in case you give to me a sign
    To say that deep inside you feel the same way too.

Doreen Stanbury

Deepness

Loneliness is sadness, a deep mysterious emotion
lost in the mist of love, an agitation that creates a
deep depression, a deep pain.
Forty-eight hours seems so long when love and
loneliness are combined. Combined so strong that it
motivates a striking pain in the depth of one's heart.

Words are screaming out in one's mind
ready to be exploded, words that are so hard to speak,
speech that may end in misery. Words that could create
a battle, a battle of hate and a battle of love.
To be able to express one's feelings is a gift in itself,
a gift of self freedom, a gift of happiness.

Too many blocks forced by pressure will soon crash
and explode with the creation of a beauty.

The human eye speaks for the speechless.
All wrapped up in emotions and scared to express,
emotions causing lust, love and misery.

The power of one's mind is so strong and explosive,
so intense and yet so dignified. Too many people are trapped in a
frame that is unbreakable. Unbreakable until the last breath fades.

Eavan Dowling

Where Wild Garlic Grows

Bowed down and grown weary of bleak city toils,
Of noise and pollution and consumer spoils,
I searched for a haven and verily chose
One favoured by Nature, where wild garlic grows.

The mountains stand sentinel, guarding my days,
And lift my eyes heavenwards to sing and to praise
The glory of Nature, her will to impose
A timelessness here where the wild garlic grows.

The deer come to nibble my plants in the night,
The owl and the bats celebrate the moonlight,
The stars stud my window and ere my eyes close
I thankfully rest where the wild garlic grows.

When winter's upon us and thunder clouds roar,
And savage winds race icy waves high on shore,
I sit burning driftwood in seemly repose
And dream of the season when wild garlic grows.

The thyme and the heather and sweet briar rose,
The fruit of the forest, and God only knows,
From dawn's early calling until even's close
My soul is at peace where the wild garlic grows.

Janette Valentine

Now to a Future

Just look around and what do you see
Lots of people so healthy and free, growing up just like me

Sports and healthy living was my life
Then came the being of a mother and wife
It's so good to remember those times
Canoeing, climbing, skiing and sports
Then came a day when it came to naught.

We all learn to walk and talk as a child
But now your bodies have been defiled
We become so lost and have so many fears
It's all so different as we have lost first gear
The deadly letters of M.S. appear
Confidence goes and life disappears

But 'round the corner when help is around
Build your life in a new body found
Try to laugh and not look back
I'm so tired I must hit the sack
While I'm asleep I hope there's a chance
Researchers have found a technical advance

Anne Ward

"River Days"

I sit about the river bank with
ludicrous contraption in hand.
The fine float of gossamer line; it's grand to be alive.
The sun beams it captivating light
which warms and glows your face.
The baited hook descends with vigour to its eager base.
Tranquil awareness is soon disrupted within this flowing friend.
Tugging with such virility and power.
What is it to be?
Another eel submerges just right for my tea.
Rabbits play on crowded bank, mink
slink down with no obvious fear and fish in waters nearby.
Night imprisons day owl and bat, they fly,
Time for angler to gamble home as badger grunts on by.

Daniel Joseph Groom

A Bouquet of Love

Long-stemmed red roses - just a few
Remind me of my love for you
Chrysanthemums with their bright cheerful faces
Bring memories of good times and places
Roses so fresh - such a delicate hue
Lilies stand tall with petals of blue
Little white daisies looking so sweet
I think of the day you swept me off my feet
Freesias, carnations - what a beautiful scent
Oh - those happy days in the garden we spent
Our lives intertwined just like this bouquet
Makes me thank God for each and every day.

Colleen Peaty

"Homeward Bound"

Through wisp of mist all milky grey
Loom high and dark above my head the stark and cruel cliffs of stone
That show me I am nearing home.
Away I've been for three long years
Often my cheeks were wet with tears as memories filled my
wakeful nights
Some filled with joy and some with fright,
The raging gales and lashing rain
Of seagulls crying out in vain against the harshness of the night.
The joy of days all filled with sun,
Of deer all in a playful mood, they frolic as they hunt for food.
Puffins droop sleepily in the haze that rises above the dazzling waves.
Ledges along the lee of the rocks are nature's gift to the nesting flocks.
Pools that glimmer sparkle and shine, reflecting colours in every hue
Green of the weeds and the water so blue,
The shimmering backs of a fish or two.
A walk on the shore gives sheer delight.
Lapping waves on the shingle bright, the feel of the gravel
between my toes. I'm home, back in my Lundy roads.

Jean Lesslie

Stolen Child

She battled for months:
She felt the pain as a sharp knife
It was a traumatic start for her
would it be happy by the end of the hunt?

The mother breaking down and shouting
my baby is being stolen!

Could the people hear her words?
And what if she could have run as fast as a cheetah
to stop the black car, to open the door
and take her baby back home?

Will ever be a tomorrow for the mother?
Will the baby be in a healthy environment?
Will his small organs be taken away?
She doesn't care to know.

Elizabeth Faitarone

The Heartstrings of a Child

Her face is all dirty; her dress is torn.
She has one shoe, the other has gone.
She is tired and hungry, as she tries to keep in line.
She is one of thousands on the bread line.

Christmas means nothing to her.
The cold and the rain are too much to bear.
She goes on her knees and says a prayer,
Wondering, is GOD really there?
With her eyes averted she looks to the sky,
And feels the tears fall from her eyes.
She gets to her feet, and scrambles into line,
Whispers to GOD, "Now I'll be fine."
She finds a potato, one that's raw.
She didn't care, it had been on the floor.
She was hungry; she had no bed.
They didn't tell her, her mother was dead.
As she lay there on the ground,
That was where her body was found.
Did GOD answer her prayer,
And tell her why she was There?

Bessie Thackeray

Memories

Sunset kisses, moonlight walks
Feeling closeness, midnight talks
All they had is in the past
They both knew it could not last
Slowly time has passed them by
There's no longer time to cry
But even though their love is gone
The memories in their minds live on

Astrid Galtung Lihaug

Spring She Came A-Calling

Spring dropped in one April day,
She said, "Has winter gone away,
And taken all the driven snow,
So now the woodland flowers can grow.

And has the frost all disappeared,
So that the Partridge can be reared,
And has he taken all the rime,
So that the Skylark sings on time,

And did he take the hoar about,
Can sleepy Squirrels venture out,
And has the ice gone from the pool,
That made the Mallards play the fool?"

To this, then April answered, "Yes",
So Spring changed Mother Nature's dress,
Then all the flowers came out to see,
The Squirrel ventured from the tree,
And all around the birds did sing,
To welcome back once more sweet Spring.

John E. Sharpe

Determination

Be the master of your subconscious mind,
Search for your powers hidden inside,
Say 'yes' to the challenges and you will find,
Great courage and achievement and a sense of pride.

Very sensitive people, don't shut your eyes.
Forget the traumas of the past,
Don't sit under your problems and hide,
Positive thinking, brings happiness at last.

Channel your energies, they are more precious than wealth,
Take the initiative, stop moaning, and Go,
Find magical moments and riches and health,
Congratulate yourself and never feel low.

Unlock your energy and bring in success,
Real living achievement is what you'll get,
Discover, true-self, and have a well-earned rest,
Enjoy it forever and no need to fret.

Take note of this message, it's important to you,
Don't let your subconscious weaken your will,
Conquer 'fear' and you'll never be blue,
Look outwards, not inwards, and your stress will be nil.

Joan Y. Matthews

Peace in My Heart

The stars in the sky,
Seem to cover a lie,
Of the life we lead down below.
Of caring and loving,
Of green fields and trees
And watching the rivers flow.
How long must it take,
Before we awake,
From a life of destruction and woe?
I know in my heart
It's still at the start,
But the arrow has left its bow.

Anna Christina Jackson

The Sounds in My House

That music from my sisters' room it's
Seeping under the door,
The TV's on downstairs, I think its starting a war
Dad's in the kitchen Mum is too,
I think they're starting another fight
It'll probably go on all night.
There goes the water running for the bath,
Here come's the football man strolling up the path,
Tick tock there goes the clock striking nine.
Time for my bed I think
Now there's a bed-time rhyme.

Gabrielle Louise Potter

Love

Love is a word. Used in so many ways.
Love has been written in verse.
In songs that we love.
Love is sent in our letters, to our love ones away.
Love gives them strength, in the love that we send.
Love can be so angry, when that person still cares.
Love is a healer of one's inner fears.
Love that is given, can dry up your tears.
Love can describe so much, and care is but one.
Love has to learn to let go, and can still love from afar.
Love will always be given by this Parent,
If her child reaches out.
Love comes from within you, cannot be bought in a shop.
For each living thing in this world, where
We live, should be touched every day with
this gift we can give.
You can send your love to those that are gone.
But the love of a family, is a love so divine.
And it's been given to me, by the family, that
I can call mine.

Christine Ivy Hosier

Untitled

I lost my mum the other day,
She closed her eyes and passed away.
I wasn't with her when she died,
But when I heard, oh, how I cried!
That honour went to my youngest brother,
He held her hand, said 'Goodbye Mother!'
I can't believe she's gone away,
I feel her with me every day.
She loved her garden, stayed for hours,
I see her smile in all the flowers.
Worked with patchwork, dressed small dolls,
And sold them on the charity stalls.
She loved to paint the countryside
And flowers and birds both far and wide.
I'll always miss her everyday,
I wish she hadn't gone away.

Iris Patricia Goodhand

Suffer the Little Children to Come unto Me

Sixteen kiddies go to school
All are smiling, all have charm
Soon their blood lies in a pool
Who'd think learning they'd come to harm?

Fifteen kiddies wrapped in wool
Go out for firewood, have no school
Pick up coloured plastic 'toys'
Their legs blown off - boys will be boys?

All kiddies have a right to live
Warmth, fun, charm they give
Sadly the risks are grave to play
In doing that, here's their mayday

Who are the madmen who plot to kill
The loved, good, innocent at will?
And Women of the World, what of us
Who give them life, love warmth and fuss?

We bring them to a world of strife and guns
Smother them with love in tons and tons
Men toss their lives, more mines on the way
To cripple the kiddies on their way to play.

Joy Pattinson

Discontentment

If you are fed up with your lot,
Look around see what others have got.
It may surprise you when you find,
That you have left them all behind.
In this life we are never glad.
To count the good, only the bad.
Have you good health and some money,
Well you are really lucky honey.
See the homeless out of their house,
They can't afford a meal for a mouse.
Doesn't this make you very sad.
Think of the things that they once had.
So count your blessings though they be small
You could end up with nothing at all.

Catherine Lindsay

Present Paradise - Future Lost (To Development)

Devon is full of hills and dales, character and colour,
no two fields look quite alike 'tho next to one another.
Each season, in the woods are colours never seen before,
and a carpet thick with gorse and heather runs right across the moor.
This truly glorious patchwork of purples, golds and greens
is nature made quite perfectly - all 'round God's love is seen.

If you gaze down on the valleys, then another joy you'll find,
with tiny streams and winding lanes and crops of every kind.
Cows and sheep and horses - some grazing, some asleep,
and little country cottages make the scene almost complete -
but - deep down in the valley where the red soil's at its best,
the sea is shimmering silver as the sun sets in the West.

Jean Meecham

The Anchor of Our Lives

Mother, we are boats on the sea of life,
Praise the day our father said 'be my wife'
When the waves of life came crashing down on us,
Together you created shelter in a harbour of love.

As we have grown, you have broadened our horizons,
If fear and doubt have surfaced, entering waters unknown
You have shone a beam of light, for
us to avoid rocky outlets,
Then with wind in our sails, you have
watched us sail off into many sunsets.

Lucy Morgan

Gallipoli 1915 - 1994

Silent stones, honouring fallen heroes
preside with martial precision
over this beautiful, blood-fed place.
The anonymity of hasty, universal death
unites brother enemies, mutely condemning
those brutalities which usurp history.
Now, idle yawping sun-burned trippers
desecrate this sacred plot
with empty indifference,
while scorched black earth
and skeletal trees
witness to continuing conflict,
where the silence of remorse
and the sibilant sighing voice
of the quiet singing sea
should protest the vanity of man
which wrought that first, hideous,
angry moment.

James Wheatley

Sunset of Life

The old man sits and stares into space, no longer part of life's
 Rat Race,
Greying hair and faded eyes, no longer a picture of youth.
The frail hands folded neatly on his lap; content to let time pass by,
He does not seem to care, that he is dismissed as being long
 in the tooth,
He has the greatest gift of all; time to think and time to stare.

Thoughts, memories, hopes and dreams drift by,
In the Autumn of his life, he has a lifetime of sadness and joy
 to share,
But he is old and lonely, no one to care.
His bride of many years is gone, and his children scattered far
 and wide,
No one to sit at his side.

The sun of his life is sinking fast, and he will be together at last,
With all his loved ones already departed,
No longer will he be dismissed, as having outstayed his
 welcome in this life,
Soon he will be reunited with his soul mate, his wife,
Till we meet again he sighs.

Anne Anderson

Somalia

We were a nation once
Like any other
We lived in peace, harmony and tranquillity
With each other
We once experienced the joy and pride of being with one another

Why weren't we strong though, to withstand the forces of destruction
Where is the vision of peace that we were once shown as a nation
What has happened to the Somalia we all once knew

Why do my brothers have to die
Why do the mothers have to suffer
Why do the children and women have to be the target of unwanted hate
When we are all the creation of Allah

We might not be one nation any longer
But we will not give up the struggle,
for the existence of a unified Somalia

Isabella Odowa

Heaven and Earth

Could life be an illusion
Love, hate, confusion
If the world were to end
Would it be soon
Would there be any stars
Would there be a moon
Would we still breathe the air
Lives of frustration
Lives of despair
Your needs are hunger
They never disappear
Like the sky up above
Is never completely clear
Like the rock which you stand on
Is slippery when wet
When you fall get back up
One day your needs will be met
Does this world exist with a heaven above
Filled with care, feeling
A strong power of love

Helen Rees

Lovers in Love

The leaves are on the ground
Lovers walking holding hands
taking each day, come what may
the birds singing in the trees
Lovers feeling so at ease
the wind blows, comes and goes
like their love how long who knows
for the future they cannot see

Lovers cherish the time spent together
they pray their love will last forever
many lovers have a past
where other relationships didn't last
Lovers should express and confess the way they feel
many carry scars that won't heal

So they seek the perfect partner
and say within themselves
that the right person has come along
regardless if they're right or wrong
they hope their love remains
ever till the end.

Darren Paul

Country Scene

The wild and beautiful neglect that runs through
my summer dream,

Once left silently to Mother Nature will envelope around
with delight

Wild life, Wild flowers run free and flourish,

Crazy bracken vigorous growth along winding
roads and pathways,

A light blue sky topped with a gentle breeze,

Matched with a lazy sunshine to complete and
compliment my scene, my dream.

E. J. Ward

The Anchor of Our Lives

Mother, we are boats on the sea of life,
Praise the day our father said 'be my wife'
When the waves of life came crashing down on us,
Together you created shelter in a harbour of love.

As we have grown, you have broadened our horizons,
If fear and doubt have surfaced, entering waters unknown
You have shone a beam of light, for
us to avoid rocky outlets,
Then with wind in our sails, you have
watched us sail off into many sunsets.

Deborah Haigh

Life's Tapestry

In life's tapestry are woven
Many strands, some dull, some bright.
Each decade unfolds a story
Pools of darkness, rays of light.
Carefree childhood, eager school days
Slow but sure the patterns grow,
Happy teenage, loving friendships
Marriage, children, laughter, woe.
Through it all the strong weft glimmers
Shining silver, gleaming gold,
Then suddenly the picture changes
We realize we're growing old.
Precious memories of those dear ones
We have loved and lost awhile
Are now scattered 'mid the weaving
'Oft remembered with a smile.
All the changes we've experienced
All the grief, the joy, the strife,
Indelibly recorded
In the tapestry of life.

Annie Leaver

Afterwords

In the confiding dark, her dreams bereaved
me softly of her, where I lay awake
and in the blessing of her arms believed
that at its time, only the dawn would break.
But now the cruel ordinary day
drowns all our whispers in its busy sky,
farewells perplexed with shadows, blown away
unspent (goodbye, my Love. Goodbye,   Goodbye . . .)

You were the voice I cannot swear I heard
before I woke into a silent place.
You were the lover gone before I stirred,
you were the sweet-limbed innocence of sleep,
you are the eyes that cannot let me weep,

I am the dying echo of your face.

John Dolben

Granddad

The sun, the moon, the stars and sky
Meadows, rivers, mountains high,
Spring flowers, summer trees and autumn leaves
All these, you Granddad are to me.

If I could wish for anything,
The whole world at my feet,
This is the wish that I would bring,
A wish of which the poets sing,
That the love that shared 'tween you and I,
Should live on and on and never die,
Lasting through all eternity.

Annette Sexton

Have You Ever Wondered

Have you ever wondered 'what will the future be'?
Maybe it is better that we cannot see.
Could we foretell the coming of another bloody war?
Could we foretell the sorry time when love will be no more?
Maybe there is suffering, bitter tears and pain,
When goodness has surrendered to the tyrant's evil reign.

Perhaps there is a paradise where peace and beauty dwell,
A re-created Eden where everything is well.
Could there be a future when God and man unite?
Our weapons all be laid aside without the need to fight.
Could there be a golden age when honour reigns supreme?
With brotherhood of every race no longer just a dream.

Life is a fleeting moment in the vast expanse of time,
In vain we search for purpose, for reason and for rhyme.
Sufficient is our knowledge for this, the present day,
Take heed of past experience to guide us on our way.
And when we often wonder 'what will the future be',
Just trust in God who made us, for He alone can see.

Jenny Porteous

Maybe Someday

Maybe someday, our troubles in this world will all be over
Maybe someday, when reason makes its stand.
Maybe someday, the laughter will return and bubble over
Filling hearts with gladness - maybe someday.

Maybe someday, we'll find the way to trust in one another
Maybe someday, we'll come to understand.
Maybe someday, we'll be prepared to call each other 'brother'
Joining hands in friendship - maybe someday.

Someday, maybe, we'll live in perfect harmony
A world so full of joy will be our prize
Someday, maybe, the wars will just be memories
And gleams of hope will shine in children's eyes

Maybe someday, we'll have the chance to show what we believe in
That Dove of Peace will soar above this land.
Maybe someday, there'll be no hate, no strife, no fears, no grieving
Love will find the answer - maybe someday . . . maybe someday . . .
   maybe someday.

Donald Robert Lennard

Confusion

Why is there so much confusion
More than life, or what there is left,
Everything has to be definite,
Yet the only certainty is death.

There are too many side-salads of distraction,
That challenge us on our way,
And no-one informs us of the real facts,
Because they're too frightening to say.

And I can't help thinking there's more to do,
Why would it end like this?
To end our time here a stranger,
Lost souls, that no-one will miss.

Anna Philpott

A 'Penwood' Reverie

   The garden's winding rivulet
Meandering 'tween its green and whitened banks.
From tinkling sparkling fountain borne
Crystal clear on barmy summer morn
Tho' brief its course it doth freely run
To quickened carp who with sinuous grace
In richest garb doled food to taste.

   A minuscule landscape
Lily-shaded pond and trees.
Rippling water from gentle breeze.
Tree-patterned carpet of emerald green
with miniature bridge, linking bank between
A realized dream of innate skill,
One man's heart, mind and steadfast will.

Albert J. Bradshaw

Coming to Terms

My years fly past as I see my face in the glass
My body gets weaker and my memory fails fast.
Suddenly it's yesterday where has it all gone
The past youth becomes dimmer but my dreams live on.
It's no joy to get up and no joy to go to bed
And there's no joy to go out or even rest my head.
There's no-one who cares or comes to see me
The kids have all grown and where can they be.
They are off in a world of their own making
And I am left sadly alone and forsaken.
The nights are the hardest where I spent them alone
And after divorce I fine I'm left on my own.
The house is emptied and cold and chill
And there's no-one but me to tend to its will.
So why for do I ask myself do I care
Why so has life changed it doesn't seem fair.
One puts one life in this little old rhyme
And if I went tomorrow one's had a good time.

Josephine Millington

Waiting for Freedom

Curtains closed, windows shut, lights off.
Me sitting huddled in the corner, just waiting now. Looking now.
Looking in the direction of the phone. Hoping for it to ring.
Ringing to tell me the waiting is over, finished, freedom.
Ten minutes later, still here in.
silence, silence, silence, apart from the old clock.
  Tick. Tick. Tick.
The alarm sounds. I jump. I feel the walls collapsing around me.
I wish they would.
It's a habit now, after days, months, years, sitting here in the
  damp dark dungeon.
Like something out of hell. I close my eyes,
picturing the image of the man, or woman coming through the door.
My eyes jolt open as the phone rings, once, twice, three times.
I freeze and force myself further into the corner where not
  even rats would venture.
The phone still ringing. A man walks in. picks it up.
Could I be free?
Would it be the end? He slams the phone down. I say my prayers.
He walks out of the door in some farcical rush.
I still sit, waiting for freedom.

   Gary Marlow

The Mystic's Choice

Where the crashing blue of the ocean,
Meets the sun-kissed golden sand,
A billion spindrift swirlings,
Dance wildly onto the land.

Here on that razor's edge in time,
That curls under tumbling waves,
Lies a corridor between the worlds,
And doors to mythic caves.

In this mighty rushing, roaring frantic foam,
Accept no limitations - claim your rightful throne.
For you're in the realm of magic now, life's future lie's unfurled,
Stand like a man upon the sand - a foot in both the worlds.

Ethereal, you're wreathed in shimmering powers,
——— your moment of choice is here,
You stand invisible, awash with surf,
Grasp now! and have no fear.

The sword of Mystic Mastership,
Will give you living power,
So, take it now, in pride and truth,
In this enchanted hour.

   John C. Sutton

'Poem to a Wounded Heart'

Jeannie, Jeannie - ma cherie,
None can hold a light to thee,
For upon thy matchless brow,
Lie treasures of eternity.

Not ermine, silver, diamonds, gold,
But one greater treasure as of old,
Nor greater preciousness behold,
One heart of sweet love - yet untold.

None can compare, to this treasure here,
Nor word express e'en with a tear,
What sweetness there does lie - deep locked,
Where divinity has dropped - this precious gift.

But one can see and can espy,
What golden lustre there doth lie,
And what the gift which is - will be,
A heart of true sincerity.

A heart that's bled - nay bleedeth still,
Which angels would copy - could they will,
A rose - blood red - of Nature's skill,
Cannot compare until - the Daybreak!

Neither Nature's rose, nor angel's wing,
Can ever cause a soul to sing,
A sweeter song, fit to describe
Nor match the feeling - or imbibe - a deeper thought.

   John Burgan

The Main in the Moon

Kiss me slow -
Moon angel, enchanted child.
Weave me now to sleep.
Let me descend -
To the black darkness below.
Glints of silver hope above.
Your army has come,
And will come again.

Your father stays locked
Inside his crystal ball.
Condemned to light, the eternal night.
"Oh, Moon angel, does he cry
The silver stardust from the sky?"
Which streaks his black wasteland
With rich white diamonds.
  - I am overcome with dreams . . .

   Alison Shaw

Musings on Mozart (1756-91)

Can you imagine Mozart in this age and day?
With pony tail and denim gear - an earring on display!
Because he was an artiste, could be that's how he'd dress
For he'd be unconventional - flamboyant to excess.
He'd appear before the queen, as with George The Third
On television chat shows, would be seen and heard.
Interpreters may be required on a British show
Though music is a language many love and know.
Even on "This is Your Life" some evening could appear
Perchance star too on "Top of the Pops," how teenagers would cheer!
He would fly around the world, with orchestras to play,
Or conduct an opera rehearsed a previous day.
Harmonies from heaven through his gifted pen,
Symphonies - concertos - music not of men.
I'm sure he would fraternize with stars of present fame
Whatever form artistry takes, the breed is just the same.
So! Immortal Wolfgang, happy in rebirth
Thank God we hear your music whilst living on this earth.

   Frances Veale

Like Remnants of a Burning Star

Like remnants of a burning star
My heart for you would travel far
Beyond the clouds of destiny
On moonbeams that is where I'd be.

To rest my head, the Planet Queen
Would let me sleep and study dreams
Of when my journey 'cross the skies
Finds you waiting and finally dies.

My heart would cry and never rest
Until I concluded my final quest
To search the skies so clear and blue
So I can say that I love you.

   Janet Woolway

Nature's Grace

Why is nature at her best as she's about to sleep
When leaves are falling from the trees in hues of copper deep
The air turns cold but even frost improves her beauty too
As, clad in white, she shines her best with sunlight glistening through.

How sly the fog when she consumes all undiscerning folk
And those in fields stand unaware they are within her cloak
But when pale warmth of morning sun intrudes on her advance
She sneaks away like thief in night to wait another chance

Those little ones who cannot fend when winter's grip is tight
Bury deep in warm dark hole and sleep extended night
But even though their sleep is such that all in death they seem
As warmth invades their comfy nest they waken from their dream

Upon reflection, I'm not sure that nature's at her best
when wind is chill and like us all she feels it's time to rest
Her beauty, true, does show itself when nights are drawing in
But then she wakes and charm shines through when life begins again.

   Jean Webb

Lonely

The leaves are wet with dew,
My eyes are wet with tears,
The desert is dry, the sand is dry,
I feel dry - my lips are all dry,
The thunder roars in the night,
My heart pounds like the thunder that roars,
This season has slipped away,
Just like when you slipped away,
Now it's winter - it's cold -
Just like my world,
When that season slipped away
and gave way to winter,
I knew it was the best for you,
But I didn't know,
I'd be lonely without you.

Akira A. Ourisa-Ansah

Candlelight

My thoughts of you are soft and gentle,
My feelings - a delicate light,
Offering warmth in the coldness of winter,
Dawn in the dark of the night.
Sometimes they flare up like a flame in the wind,
Then glimmer not quite out of sight,
But always they're warm and forgiving;
Like candlelight.

Your thoughts of me are insubstantial,
Your feelings - a shadowy sprite,
That flicker in the coldness of winter
And only flare in the dark of the night.
A slight change in the wind and they're gone
Like birds on the wing taking flight.
A ghostly, spectral, intangible thing;
Like candlelight.

Christine Taylor

Homeward Bound

The road home was long and winding, the sky was growing dark,
My feelings were uncertain, my loneliness was stark,
I stumbled homeward heavily, my heart felt like a stone,
I was so very troubled, I had to get back home.

But what would be my welcome there? I really did not know.
For years I had not written them. Would they say "stay" or "go"?
A light flickered in a window, my childhood home's still there.
The old oak tree standing proud, I had to stop and stare.
Those fields were my playground, that cottage was my cell,
Some years ago, I ran away, from boredom into hell.
I got things wrong, I made mistakes, I had to find my way
And I worked hard and I grew strong until that fateful day,
The doctor did not mince his words, there is no help to give;
The cancer is inoperable, I have only months to live.
I know I don't deserve their love but I have to say goodbye;
If my family will have me, I've just come home to die.

Anne-Marie Smith

Goodbye My Friend

I did all I could to save you.
My best and dearest friend
There was nothing that would ease your pain
so your life it had to end
It broke my heart when I gave consent
and the pain it goes so deep.
I lost my best and dearest friend
when I had you put to sleep.

I could not bear to see you suffer
there was no more I could do
I did not want to let you go.
but I had to think of you
So many happy memories
I will treasure to the end
Of you and I together
my best and dearest friend.

Ellen Roberts

Short Love

Caressing with eyes, the shyness all gone,
moonlight on their faces intensely it shone
she pictured them naked, she took off her dress,
Together they lay, tenderly touched till they rest.

One night he spoke highly of his sort of life,
and how he had once murdered for the sake of a wife
She looked at him strangely, not sure what to say
for it was too late her heart was in play.

She loved him so deeply he was her special knight,
She thought that their happiness could make it alright,
She held him so closely they heard not a sound,
the gun cocked behind, them she fell to the ground.

The stranger had stood there enraged with despair,
Waving a lock of some curly blond hair,
you murdered my daughter, now you must feel pain,
He turned 'round to face him the gun charged again.

The lovers lay dying their hands, squeezing tight,
fighting for life with all of their might.
He moved close beside her, he was in great pain,
He told her he loved her and took all the blame.

Alexandra Thornton

Let Me Sleep during This War

Let me sleep
Must close my eyes
I'm tired, so tired
To sleep would be wise

Let me sleep, the light is still on
Turn it off
Please be gone

Let me sleep
Please, my aching heart
You're hurting my people
We need a new start

Let me sleep
I'm cold, bitter, frozen
I want to survive
I want to be chosen

Let me sleep, what is that noise?
The shooting of guns silly boys, evil toys.

Let me sleep, let me die
Then my pain will disappear just show me a place,
Far away from here

Carly Rich

A Happy Worker

In 1981 a new domestic star was born
My badge of office proudly worn
Mopping, dusting, polishing, cleaning
Life took on another meaning.

For the health service I did my bit
Dirty ward! I'd have a fit
Attended meeting went on courses
Had my say, used my resources

See the patient, keep them happy
Clean the ward remove the nappy
Bring their food, watch them eat it
Keeping dirt at bay. I'll try to beat it.

Times are changing in 1996
An old dog learning new tricks
Health and safety, patients charter
I'm feeling like a new starter

In a two years I must retire
To carry on working is my desire
My job has given me so much pleasure
I'll worry how to spend my leisure

Elsie Hume

Forever Entwine

The time has come to say - good bye
Never to find the reasons why

Where he's gone is far away
I feel so lost - so alone today

Everyone's tried to help me through
When all I want - is to be with you

We shared so much as time went by
I think of us - then more - I cry

I can't believe that you're not here
When yesterday - I held you dear

So close to me away from harm
So tenderly - you - in my arms

I lived for you each and every day
To hear "love you" as you'd often say

My love for you will carry on
Even though - today you're gone

The time has come to say - good bye
But my love for you will never die

I'll just be waiting until again you're mine
For our souls to join - and forever entwine
Heather Knapp

Men, Who Needs Then?

If it weren't for men,
My life would by easy.
If it were legal,
I'd marry my dog - for
It wouldn't answer back
When told what to do!

I pay for his dinner,
He runs out of petrol,
He calls me gorgeous
Because he can't remember my name!

There's nothing he wouldn't do for me,
At least he's once nothing so far.
His idea of being economical
Is to shower once a week.
He says he'll make me happy,
I tell him I'll miss him.

Why do we love them?
Who says we do?
Men don't grow on trees
They swing from them!
Fiona S. MacLean

Wisdom of the Leaves

As we leave footprints in the sands of time
 No matter how discouraged we may be,
Hope is born anew when we hold
 Leaves budding on a sapling tree.

Or when we see a fragile plant
 Whose life has just begun,
Blossom forth in sheer delight
 Cheered by the warming sun.

Someone designed such splendour
 To keep faith within our soul,
To uplift our sinking spirits
 When sadness takes its toll.

We regain hope from the buds and blossom,
 And wisdom from the leaves,
They offer solace top a broken heart
 A peace to one that grieves.

And though there may be showers and storms
 The sunshine will forever glisten
Upon the leaves of flowers and trees
 Where man can pray and God will listen.
Charles F. Chandler

Time

Was it not yesterday
On homeward way from school
We criss-cross jumped that meandering
Stream
And tunnel crawled its watery way;
On four wheeler boxes
Hurtled down that castle hill,
Dare devil drivers every one;

With bent pin hook
Mullet fished a sun-kissed harbour tide,
Perpetually optimistic,
Yet contented with a bite?
You dare tell me
It was three score year and more?
Charlie Delaney

The Day

There were rainbows 'round my shoulders
On that one whole and perfect day
When Earth stood at peace.
Not a single shot was fired
Not a single soul lay dead
One could not know the reasons
One could only wait and hope.

Alas, the axis turned again
And 'twas as it was before
With pain and grief and heartache.
One could not know the reasons
For the shattering of hope
But there had been rainbows 'round my shoulders
On that day of perfect peace.
Joan Roberts

Untitled

I never knew your name lost in the waste land,
On the plateaux of Siberia,
Recalling a summer day in fields of scented Jasmine,
Can you remember his music,
He was working for you a labour of love,
Seeking the north star, the heroic moon,
On winter nights hearing your voice,
As he played the piano,
Trapped in a private Auschwitz,
Could he touch the hand that bled just beneath the thumb,
He was everything to you,
The frozen ground binding your souls,
With the promise of reunion,
Silently you waited,
For that familiar knock on the door,
Without the legacy of flesh and blood,
To cover your despair,
Of course he never came,
Can I bear this gift for you now,
Sculpted with LOVE.
John Liam Sullivan

After the Frost on New Year's Day

 The birds awaken a new dawn,
on this 1996 new morn.

 Stillness awakes at the church gates,
the sound of the church bells ring,
and the congregation start to sing,
with words of welcome to this New Year's day.

 As the people leave the church, goodwill wishes they say
to the priest, as they leave to go on their way.

 Doves and wood pigeons flapping their wings,
as to the ground these bird he brings,
that evil sparrow hawk then pounces on his prey.
Does this bird not know, that of all days today,
if he is wicked, he will remain so, the whole year through.
Heather Sephton Taylor

"Account 88888"

Restricted action in the chest
Polluted rust, Sunday best
City sky, orange glow
Poisoned animals are burned to flow

Let's run out of maybe days
Avoidance again, don't change your ways
Really wish to be left in peace
Use your strength and then we'll see

Wonderful time to yet be had
Once it's over you'll be glad
That what we've gambled and what we've won
Has certainly been a lot of fun

Egotist confidence will never wane
Perilous reactions occur just the same
People are forced to fight for their lives
Some may leave husbands, children and wives

Tolerance of pain, so hard to withhold
Integrity for a Pound, so cheaply sold
Sardonic vitality, falsified accountancy
Ignorant stupidity is making me weary

Andrew Waite

Little Green Men

Weirdos and ghoulies and little green men
Race through the town on the stroke of ten.
Where are they going? What will they do?
Perhaps they're coming for me or you.

With their grotesque heads and bulging eyes
They'd never win a beauty prize.
Floating 'round them a haze of blue,
Perhaps they're coming for me or you.

Vaulting over walls and hedges,
Dancing the charleston on the edges,
There's the spacecraft still quite new.
Perhaps they're coming for me or you.

I hide in a doorway and cover my face,
Longing to be in a safer place.
They may be here till the morning dew,
Unless they capture me or you.

They creep quite close. I shudder with fear.
They touch my face and laugh and sneer.
I open my mouth to scream and shout.
A voice says "O.K. now, your tooth is out".

Gwenda Bleasdale

At Dawn

At dawn, retire to the cool
redolent remnant of night, listen to
the beach echoing from the unrest of tides,
  of waves, in continuous repeated lament of welcome and farewell,
  of tighten and loosen.
We harvest the scent of seaweed
and the sharp taste of salt from
water's liquid kiss.
The sea-moan swallows your laughter
and another surge, washed ashore,
steals your footprints from the radiant beach.
Eastern horizon, the purple twilight
competing with the dark - ordinary armageddon
shrinking our shadows.
Now awake, leave the gentle web of
your dim dream and enter my eyes,
exit: The outside reerected by perception.
And seashells we take home,
their whisper, to sing from wilderness
while we are being tamed.

Edgar Leidel

Time Taken Away

Bereavement is strange, I am going through it now
my partner who had cancer, has thrown in the towel.
My recent memories, are of his suffering and pain,
but work, family & friends have fortunately kept me sane,
the weekends are lonely and seem extra long
and a tear you will spill, when on the radio, is your song.
Filled with grief, the last thing you need at this time,
is long lost relations, suddenly appear, looking for a dime.
But, death seems to bring out the worst
why does greed flourish with a burst.
You force a smile on your face and try to find your feet,
but in your mind you can still see him sitting in his favourite seat.
I try to keep thinking of all the good times we shared and had
and as I think back we really did not have many that bad.
So the moral of this tale is enjoy things while you can,
because it is not easy to find a replacement for that special man,
you might moan about doing their washing and ironing their shirt,
cooking their dinner and cleaning up their dirt,
but suddenly, when they are not there,
you realize how much you did really care.

Jill Weightman

The Whale

Crashing over the ocean blue.
My mind is swirling, what to do.
Waves around me, hitting my face.
I used to swim with style and grace.

Close behind me, gaining fast.
A sudden urge, I hear a blast.
If my life is taken, my son is free.
Free and alone; please can't you see.

A shot of pain; is now the end?
Listen, a message, to you I send.
Your make-up is a hidden mask.
And if you want your looks to last.
Your painted face will age in time.
For every lipstick, a life, like mine.

Alone in this enormous sea.
My dad has gone, now there's just me.
My wits about me all the time.
I'll never leave a son of mine.
These very words my father had spoken.
Inside I cry, my heart is broken.

Charlotte Louise Hall

Moments

Looking out - from this darkness
Onto a world of peace and light . . .
My heart cries out for friendship
Between the people out of sight . . .

For all of those - whose dreams and wishes
Never ever - fade away . . .
Sharing moments with a loved one
Feelings stronger day-by-day . . .

Demolish words and ways of anger
Even though justice is sought . . .
Remember those there - far above us
A place where friendship - is always thought . . .

What of this world with all its problems
And of the people here within . . .
What we should do - is love one another
Then we will know - that we will win . . .

Teach our children ways of wisdom
Help them combat sorrow and pain . . .
Our compassion need ne'er be forsaken
New life will continue - forever and again . . .

Colin Adrian Paternoster

Quattro Stagioni

Happiness, oh, happiness
Why hast thou forsaken
The heart that once leapt with joy
When Spring sunshine did pour
upon the strands of time,
Weaving with such myriads of silken twine
To gain with love the Summer solstice night.
Oh blissful happy days, why did the tide of time erode,
When leaves of russet and of gold
drifted upon the autumnal fall.
An ice chill wind besieged us all.
Bitterness, sorrow, discontent
Did eat amidst the web of woe
So Winter in its prime laid
the snow that fell upon our languished souls.
Amidst the silence of a broken heart
Forgiveness had forsaken all.
As blossoms on the bough will surely spring again
We must arise, forgive and let live
To find again the promise of our goal.

Anne Christabel Davey-Young

Guardian Angel

Perhaps 'twas day though maybe night
More darkness in my room than light
Only stillness filled the air when I awoke
And was aware
Of a figure standing there
Someone I didn't know

Even then I felt no fear, although
I'd never seen before
This girl/woman/child
Who was watching over me
Many years ago

Time has passed by as it can
I've two lovely girls and a boy called Dan
Twenty years, it can't be less
Sad to say I've developed M.S.

I really can't walk very well
But I'm damned if I know who I can tell
It doesn't really matter through
Now I know who came to see me
Many years ago

Frances Joan Torbett

The Girl

Been found in a cardboard box one night,
No home, no parents had been her life,
Tears jerk down from aching cheeks,
Stimulated, drugged tears are the kind she weeps.

She dresses in a way to ward others off,
Inwardly afraid of love, which she scoffs,
Nobody has ever shown her real care,
So she feels prostitution is no cross to bear.

She is punishing herself for a deed never done,
Being hated is her crime, a permanent one,
Alone she feels mocked and scorned by the world,
Pressure for the next drug is bearing down on this girl.

Penniless and alone are the key words for her,
Kept alive by strange men, in cars which stealthily purr,
Stealing any respect or divinity from within,
Her mind and her body are ridden with sin.

She hangs around with crowds of noisy boys,
They use each others company as a kind of sick joy,
And other kids hang at different places of wreck,
Each individual is a separate case of neglect.

Carol Potter

Rainforest Lament

There is no song in the forest
No flash of colour flits from bough to bough,
The birds have all but vanished
From their homes they've all been banished,
The forest sounds are harsh and angry now.

There is no peace in the forest,
No Tamarin sentry sitting on a bough,
Though their struggles are unending
Doom is certain and impending,
The forest's full of trucks and loggers now.

There is no home in the forest,
No hiding from the saws that rake the bough,
Both Kaiapo and Yanomami
Flee like a beaten army,
The forest is ablaze and dying now.

There is no rain in the forest,
No water drops on green and leafy bough,
For timber men were greedy
So destruction then was speedy,
The forest's just a barren desert now.

B. C. Smith

Vanished Bushman

No more upon the great sand face his mark.
Night's curtain has fallen on his last sunset.
Little big man, born to run, to lead his band
on the trackless, desert paths of life.

Who once gathered, hunted, danced
and thrived where mortal man succumbs,
now writhes enmeshed in progress snare,
his last life tide long ebbed.

Now silent the playful apricot children,
whose mirth meandered on the evening wind.
A future overtaken, swept aside,
like dancing dust devil, come and gone.

Suppressed sixth sense, now dagger dulled,
diseased and drowned in seas of lager beer.
Standpipes supplant his secret sip wells.
Survival skills are lost to modern peer.

We notice not his passing
in one blink of history's eye.
Now he runs with nomad spirits,
in that desert in the sky.

Harry Mulford

Rejection

The sun is shining, the sky is blue,
My heart is aching because of you,
I know I will never see you again!
And even though you caused me so much pain,
I loved you!
In my heart I knew it couldn't last
But I still cling to the past,
The future seems very grim and the road ahead seems very lonely!
Friends say you were no good for me,
As you could not accept me the way I am,
I laughed too loud,
I coughed and sniffed,
My legs are less than perfect,
My hair was long, I cut it short,
But still I was not suitable,
There must be someone, who likes me the way I am,
Why should I change and be someone else!
I feel better already!
My friends say, think positive,
The future's bright, you will find Mr. Right!

Cherrill Seward

Grand Slam

Grand-slam, wham! Wham!
Muscle-built testosterone man.
Kick, flick, hook, punch;
Now it's down to the final crunch.

Grand-slam, wham! Wham!
St. Andrews crossed faced fan.
Fast, last, tears, cheers;
The excitement builds up over the years.

Grand-slam, wham! Wham!
Scottish against the Englishman.
Throttle, bottle, tap, slap;
Euphoria happens, and the crowds clap.

Grand-slam, wham! Wham!
Muscle-built testosterone man.
Kick, flick, hook, punch;
Now it's down to the final crunch:
Grand-slam, wham! Wham!

David Maxwell

Daydreaming

As I sit here numb in the tired classroom
My mind often slips away to a Knoydart Corrie
Which sang to me the sweetest song
And made my soul leap in my aching body.
The Corrie,
Encircled by a ridge that cut into the sky
Making it bleed cloud
That spilt down in a silent torrent
For the landscape possessed a harsh and dangerous beauty
But a beauty that moved me . . .
Like a vast picture it lay before me
One of nature's masterpieces framed in a gallery of mountains
But, here I sit with only mountains of work
And a hope that one day I will return.

Colin A. Clouston

My Chair

Here I sit, upon my chair
My legs are numb, just hanging there
I've been like this, for many a year
At first the pain, caused many a tear
But now I'm used to it, you see
Don't need no one, to push for me
People always, stand and stare
They'd cross the street, when I was there
They look at you, in a funny way
With nothing really, much to say
I'm no different, from them you see
They to, could have a chair like me
I wheel around, on my merry way
And live my life, from day to day
But I'm not cruel, like them you see
I'd not wish this, on my enemy.

Anthony Fidler

50 Years of My Life

The future was as bleak as a long dark motorway,
Never ceasing to exist,
Gloomy was my past,
But never knowing how to return to my normal status,
I knew things would never return to normal,
But having to go on like that same dark motorway,
My room, was as large as an enclosed corner
My life, like a one way street, the operative root being death,
Life had been a grave disappointment to me,
If only,
If only I had a proper job then my life would go on till old age,
Where dying would be the fault of natural causes,
Not my immature behaviour and unworthy desires,
If only cleanliness was my main priority not, a quick monkey in
the back of my pocket,
5 minutes of fun,
Took 50 years off my life.

Elizabeth Harknett

Untitled

Oh Ludlow town I know it well
My heart is always there
If only I had the time of tales to tell
Of its beauty and soul so bare
How I love to wake in the morning
And know I am in Ludlow Town
The night has gone, day is dawning
And I am with you, without a frown
Oh the peace, and the hush and the beauty
I would that my life forever would last
Because my heart is always with you
And has always been many years past.
I get up and go out
Where the gentle breeze blows
On the southern side
Where the River Teme flows.
Then I walk into the fields.
Or through them if I choose
And I tread on the green grass
Under my shoes.

Frank Tipton

The Journey

We wander through the woods at night,
My Spirit and I in the soft moonlight.
The trees are dim, the shadows strong;
The path is straight and very long.

My Spirit says when we get there
We'll find a life we both can share.
Between the trees we stroll along.
My Spirit sings a spiritual song.
It has no words, nor even a tune.
It's made from pieces of the moon.

The rabbits see us going by.
They look right through us to the sky.
My Spirit and I go hand in hand.
Forwards to the promising land.
I wonder if it will be as good
As this happy wandering through the wood.

Denys Kendall

Exeter Youth

A sorry sight?
Nay, pity dare not
Trespass near that
Youthful pride found dwelling there.

See, huddled there,
On draughty stair,
(As yet unswept of trash)
A boy, unkempt,
Unruly hair hangs long, in matted clumps.

Boy? Nay, young man,
Who from childhood ran,
Like the wolf cub, keen for lust,
And in his eyes a silent cry,
And an ancient, wild mistrust.

Elizabeth Manning

The Budding Artist

He stands by his easel engrossed in a dream
Of what his mind's eye has already seen,
The bare canvas beckons, the ideas flow,
His paintbrush is poised over palette aglow
With colours and hues of every shade
From palest blue to the richest of jade.
He makes his first stroke, it stands out bright
On the empty background in the full north light,
His confidence grows as he pours out his heart
In glorious colour, for the love of his art.

Elizabeth N. S. Gray

Tainted Innocence

Gone is the flesh,
Of another innocent child,
Now just a rotting mess,
A virgin pure defiled.

In undergrowth she lays,
She pains no more,
Now she plays,
Behind heaven's door.

And so the plague continues,
The virus it seems has no cure,
Because restrictions on its growth are too loose,
Our children just aren't safe anymore.

Gwynneth R. Jones

Ragnarok

Place in your mind a dream
of deathly players, kings and queens.
They know where you want to go
They've seen what you want to be shown

And if we leave right now
we can enter Doomsday Town

Trained, we can find a way
to build a city from mind - clay.
Becoming ostracized but free
Clear our minds of social debris

And if we leave right now
we can construct Doomsday Town

In our city strangers roam
Now we know we're far from home
Pale new friends are smiling down
old inhibitions begin to drown

And we feel free right now
We've constructed Doomsday Town.

Charlotte McCrea

Dinosaurs

T. Rex, T. Rex, T. Rex, T. Rex,
Of dinosaurs he was the best.
Other dinosaurs were his slaves,
Angrily he dragged them to his cave.

Triceratops was a horny dinosaur,
He could be knocking at your door.
He had bones in his back and bones in his neck,
If a human had seen him they'd have said "FLIPPIN' `ECK!!!"

Stegasaurus had a small head,
One swipe of its tail and you would be dead.
On its back were bony diamond shaped plates,
I don't think Steggy had many mates!!!

Beverley Edwards

A Dream by the Stream

A clear blue sky with sun so bright
No clouds around to spoil our sight
Birds are flying high in the sky
Singing songs for us all to enjoy

The gentle stream just flowing by
Lapping stones upon its way
It's all so peaceful sitting here
Your troubles and cares just disappear

Why can't our life always be this way
With peace and quiet every day
All we can do is sit here and dream
For this short time sitting by the stream

The sky it changes from blue to black
Raindrops start falling upon your back
You feel someone is trying to say
You know your life will never change!

Barry Vincent

The Gifts of Love

The gifts of love are all about us
on earth divine, the sea and sky.
Fresh green meadows, flowers in bloom
Birds that sing their heavenly tunes.

All loving creatures great and small
The summer sun which sheds its warmth
the rustle of the falling leaves
And trees that give their fruitful treats.
The cries and laughter of children playing,
Newborn babies born each day.
Kind friends and neighbours, old and new
to have and to hold, to love and be loved.

And in these times of troubles around us.
Of war-torn strife, the grief and the famine,
Let us give thanks to our Lord and
Master. For in His loving creations,
comes out gifts of true love.

Jim Carlin

Precious Time

Time is precious, time is life,
On where do you go so swiftly
To some there is too little,
To others there is too much.
I listen to the singing of the birds,
And watch the squirrels and young puppies at play.
Holding those precious moments of time.
In my mind I drift to the beach and the sea,
I listen to the sound of the gulls,
A sound I simply adore, and watch the ships sailing to foreign lands.
This brings back memories of my happy childhood days,
Of wonderful parents, sunshine and laughter
Sadly my parents are no more,
Just a loving memory in the lanes of time.

Inga L. Samuel

Perfection

Multitudes of colours are everywhere.
One blink of an eye, a cloudless sky.
Trees and flowers in their prime.
Such beauty and grace, lights up my face.
Birds chirping their special tunes,
as if knowing, the month of June.
Sense the warmth all around.
Bees buzzing amongst the flowers,
I could gaze for hours and hours.
Treasured moments of pure delight.
Every morning, noon and night.

Ellen Jean Jones

Life!

Before us humans, it was good
No one died, cause on one could,
Now there are weapons, so killings too,
What's the point, I'm asking you.

People have lives, good or bad,
We see people, happy and sad.
You've got a life, so make it good
Enjoy yourself, like you know you should.

Whatever age, your end will come,
So don't sit around, looking dumb.
Get outside, please don't cry
'Cause the very next day, you just might die.

So people live, and people die,
All I want, is the reason why.
What really happens, when we go,
Is it the end - we'll never know.

After dark, do we rise
In spirit form, begin new lives,
A second chance to get it right,
Giving love and spreading light.

Darren Lapping

My Love

Never was life so lonely
Never was life so sad;
Thinking of our years together
And all the joy, we had,
Thinking how I love you
And how much, that you loved me;
Wishing we were together
Until eternity.
But God, perhaps with wisdom
Took you from my side,
All I am left, is memories
And tears I try to hide;
In dreams, you're still beside me
Then, comes the Cruel Dawn,
Reality takes over
And I realize you're gone.
I know that fate decreed this
I must soldier on in vain
Until, "Please God" just hear my prayer,
Let me meet my love again

Constance E. Mellish

The Death of Love

May blossoms bend the sapling bough:
New fledglings take flight on the breeze;
Sweet flowers grow in leafy glades;
Fair summer soon will hold its lease.
But I shall care for none of these.

For in my haunted heart, there dwells
The sad, still ghost of dreams long past.
Dreams, gently nurtured in love's spring,
That died in winter's icy blast;
Freezing my soul while time shall last.

My eyes cannot see summer's blaze;
The tripping, bubbling stream is still
Since you left me in this dark world,
Where winter reigns with dreaded chill -
For love is dead, and all is ill.

Beryl M. Laithwaite

It's Only When

It's only when we've lived a while and found
that answers are not easy,
It's only when we've found that the little things
are not little any more.
It's only when we recognise the truth that we come to a moment
in our lives when reason outgrows self-interest and strangers
become important,
It's only when we have trod the path that the world has trod
before that we must realise that we grow from our own mistakes,
(triumph overcoming disaster)
It's only when we accept that we cannot guarantee tomorrow for
those we love, we open their eyes, their minds and their hearts
and allow them to make their own mistakes.
It's only then that we can say "now it's up to you", and having
said it we can truly know that our job is almost done.

Ian Comrie

Tomorrow's Stream

Tomorrow's stream won't be so dank.
No lifeless mist to fill its bank.
No falling leaf swallowed by that mist.
Tomorrow's stream will be sun-kissed.
Today's stream skulks past under shrouds.
Tomorrow there will be no clouds.
When the clock has turned its face
The stream will glide its natural grace
Darting silver, pebbles bright
What a change overnight.
Gurgles will reveal their source.
A kingfisher will flash along its course
Tomorrow's stream won't hide in mist.
Tomorrow's stream, will be sun-kissed.

George Smith

Mangrove Swamps

Nestling in the sheltered retreats,
Of river mouths and quiet bays,
Enjoying the warmth of subtropical water;
Few tidal forests are left today.
The Mangrove Swamps on Natal's warm coast
Have shrunk to struggling remnants.
Sensitive to the slightest disturbance,
As are their many inter-dependants.
Leaping in the soft brown earth,
The Mud-Skippers search for food;
These strange amphibious little fish are
Harmonious to the Mangroves' quiet mood.
Also the Fiddler Crabs who are guarding
Their snug muddy borrows below
The tangled roots speckled with molluscs,
And the distinctive trees that grow.

This system works with divine order,
As it traps and protects the earthy border:
Nature in her wisdom knows how best,
To protect and clothe the earth in sensible dress.

Gillian Clapham

Last Frontier

O' splendid desolation, O' land of virgin snow
Of sculptured hills and valleys, where most men fear to go
Keep your wind-blown beauty, where man has seldom trod
You savage freezing wilderness, belongs to nought but god
Blow your blizzards bitter, with paralysing cold
Keep politician, and business men, from all that they would hold
They've already raped your sky above, in your land of
'The Mid-Night sun'
And they'll defile your sacred earth, before their
Greedy deals are done
Do not grow a blade of grass, nor nurture bush or tree
For that will let the dealers in to put an end to thee
Stow all your oil and minerals, far beneath your permafrost
Guard them at sixty degrees below, lest the last frontier be lost
Keep faith with Arctic wolf, and bear, and the life of long ago
Of 'seal', and 'whale', and fox, and tern, and harmless Eskimo

James J. McAleer

The Morning Sound

On being of sad and lonely face,
Of the past, do not onward pace.
Leave past mistakes, go where they die,
And be where love at last will lie.
To chance of love when hearts are broken,
Now do marry thoughts unspoken.
Can the ever rewarding song be found,
The future hears the morning sound.
Greet the dawn's sun of life anew,
Your father's wishes will all come true.

Dorothy Iris Pearson

Our City Streets

People crying in the cold air,
No one to help them through the night,
turning to crime to survive
Turning their back on the sin of guilt.

No one cares anymore.
Finding little comfort on dark corners of buildings
Begging city gents for spare change
Holding their cold hands to the people of work
Ignored most of the time.
People, tourists, shaking heads ignoring the dark
ugliness of our city streets.

Charities trying desperately to help in anyway they can.
But, people are still suffering in our streets.
People shaking under blankets in our streets
No hope, no future
Someone please help us they cry.
The forgotten people of our City Streets.

Chris Antoniou

Very Much Alone

The only sounds that I hear, are just in my head,
No movements beside me in my bed.

My feelings for you are still just the same.
Now and again the wind echoes your name.

Why, oh why did you have to go?
The reason for this, I still do not know.

My heart remains open, it still will not close.
My love for you will not die like an unwatered rose.

Oh why did you exit out of my life?
One day I'd have wanted to make you my wife.

Without your love, I know I won't make it,
Being this lonely, I just cannot take it.

The way you were was too good to be true.
All I dream of lately, is being with you.

There's still lots of love, for us to live in,
So come back to me as all is forgiven.

Billy Bray

No One Else but You

No one else could be so thoughtful as a friend,
No one else would try so hard not to offend,
No one else could make my failures seem success,
No one else would take my slights without redress.
No one else could wish to please me half so much,
No one else has got the measure of your touch.

No one else would like my friends because I do,
No one else would be so keen to see my view.
No one else could be so happy when I'm pleased,
No one else knows when to stop when I am teased.
No one else would stand by me when I am wrong,
No one else would give support to make me strong.

No one else would see my faults and yet not say,
No one else but you — my friend in every way.

Dale Galbraith

The Silent Place

There is a place where earth and heaven meet
On Dartmoor, where the white clouds softly fall
To lay their misty magic at your feet
And carry you away beyond recall.
There is a place where you can lift a hand
And touch the sky; where happiness abounds
And love with gentle enshrouds the land
In her tranquillity of peace. No sounds
Break thro' the stillness. Where it almost seems
Our dead, lost world is but a fantasy
And here is truth - the answer to our dreams.
Where we could stay for all eternity
Our souls uplifted, standing face to face
With God, in silence, wondering, complete,
If we can only seek and find that place
On Dartmoor, where our earth and heaven meet.

Freda L. Norton

The Army of Life

The spring, summer flowers coming alive,
Now starts a battle only the strongest survive,
The daffadowndillies turn into soldiers with swords,
And tulips into noblemen, knights on horseback and Lords,
The snapdragons breath fire, sneeze smoke and roar flames,
A lone rose becomes a circus master, with the animals he tames,
A crocus in the corner, a trumpet that makes a loud sound,
To rally the people and animals around,
A daisy, a milkmaid in a field all day,
But when she hears the cries of the soldiers she runs far away,
A baby cactus stands by with a thousand defenses,
A castle, a moat, with dangerous fences,
After in the corner stands a shovel and spade,
The last treasured memories of a victorious crusade.

Gemma Wallis

Life's Observer

Sitting back and observing
People watching
Detached from the world
Seeing friends and strangers pass by
Quietly observing
There are pictures but no sound
To and fro they go about their business,
as I sit quiet and cosy in my room
New and familiar faces
Shall I continue to watch or take part,
join them running around with a purpose or job to do,
or observe quietly in my room

Claire Turner

Bert

My dear Bert was a quiet man,
No ostentatious fuss.
Just a gentle, genuine little man
Who just liked to be 'one of us.'

I met him when I was just a lass
And he married me after a while.
We've had fifty happy years
Since we both walked down the aisle.
I was happy then to be his bride,
And I want you now to know,
I was privileged to be his wife,
And now, sadly, he's had to go.

I feel as if half of myself has died,
But for his sake I must carry on.
I hope that now he's in heaven
For I'm sure that's where he's gone,
That God has freed him from his pain
And the suffering he has been through.
And don't worry Darling, "I'm here",
And one day I'll again be with you.

Beryl Barrett

Alone

The house is so silent I walk alone.
No wagging tails to greet me, when I come home.
My dogs were so special, it makes my heart ache.
Through good times and bad, they were my special mates.
Their love was unyielding, my heart cries out.

My two faithful friends, I miss so much.
But age took its toll, without a doubt,
my two special boys have now left home.

It only seems like yesterday, when they were so small,
causing chaos around the home.
The silence is deafening without a doubt,
They were so special one black and one white.
For thirteen years they shared my life.
They gave me their love, all day and at night.
I miss them so much my two faithful friends,
who sat on my lap and never once complained.

Jean Taylor-Watson

'Dunblane'

No more the time no more to play
Of earthly daily pleasure
Where lay ye down we contemplate
The consequence in measure
No more to see the hour of day
Nor yet the setting sun
The anguish of the passing hours
For the heart and mind of anyone
No more, no more in anguish cry
In echo to this day
But rest in peace where ye lay down
For ye can't come out to play
What then for us but cry no more
When we've quietly walked away
But remember well these saddest hours
When we watch our children play.

Edward J. Costello

Smugglers

Six hundred casks of brandy,
  Of gin three hundred more,
Across the English Channel,
  The laughter makes for shore.

Two hundred casks of rum,
  Best French silk and tea,
The smugglers bring their contraband,
  They do not pay a fee.

Two excise cutters 'round the bay,
  They drive the lugger to the beach,
Quickly closing in,
  The ship now in their reach.

The lugger tips upon its side,
  The smugglers run along the bay,
The cutters reach the stricken ship,
  The smugglers with their lives will pay.

Six hundred casks of brandy,
  Of gin three hundred more,
The Revenue it wins the night,
  The lugger broken on the shore.

        Anthony Webb

Smugglers

Six hundred casks of brandy,
  Of gin three hundred more,
Across the English Channel,
  The laughter makes for shore.

Two hundred casks of rum,
  Best French silk and tea,
The smugglers bring their contraband,
  They do not pay a fee.

Two excise cutters 'round the bay,
  They drive the lugger to the beach,
Quickly closing in,
  The ship now in their reach.

The lugger tips upon its side,
  The smugglers run along the bay,
The cutters reach the stricken ship,
  The smugglers with their lives will pay.

Six hundred casks of brandy,
  Of gin three hundred more,
The Revenue it wins the night,
  The lugger broken on the shore.

        Anthony Webb

"Mistress"

I dreamt last night, the sweetest dream,
of my mistress, princess, queen.
Sedately painting, with wonderful taste,
a picture of the lake in the rolling mist.
The beauty that was captured there,
I could not tell if it was picture, or her.
A closer look at canvas told,
she had arrested my very soul.
The detail captured flickered and danced, as life itself,
glorious scenery, fisherman, little elf.
The sun emblazoned in heavenly skies,
spilled warmth, gently over my eyes.
The birds perfect, yet! different every one,
as flight carried them gliding, beyond the sun,
The clouds a whisper of white, leafy forest a sea of green,
what mixture, oaks, firs, chestnuts, the best I've seen.
This idyllic splendour transformed into art,
I know now mistress, we will never part.
For when I, from this passionate slumber awake,
forever our hearts will entwine, never to break.

        Gerald MacEwan

Inheritance

It's their world now. "Illiterate and selfish."
"Obsessed with sport, noise, sex and speeding cars."
Yet can we claim the world we now bequeath to them
Is better than the one which once was ours?

We had our chances. On the whole, we lost them,
Too busy chasing rainbows, money, fame.
New hope is needed now, ideals, young strength, forgiveness too.
Their world is in a mess, and we're to blame.

It's their world now. The better ones still study,
Play instruments, help wildlife, read and write,
Though manners may be minimal and language shocks our ears.
Unscrupulous we were, but *so* polite.

We oldies are redundant now, and hated.
We clog the system and refuse to die.
Yet some young people care for us, and for the planet too.
They shame us there. We didn't even try.

It's their world now. The legacy we leave them:
Pollution, over-population, crime;
An ecosystem threatened by destruction, profit, war,
Is now their problem. Wish them well, this time!

        Audrey Forbes-Handley

Today's Date

He'll call tonight, I'm sure he will,
Not that I'm sitting in for Bill.
I wasn't doing anything anyway,
Well, that's what I'm supposed to say.

It's all a game in the end you know,
All I have's one date to show,
Table for two - on expenses I think,
Well, he must like me to risk such a stink.

A chat about him and a thing or two,
He wasn't sure which knife to use.
He's down to earth, I like that in a bloke,
It's his wife and three kids that makes it a joke.

Well, what can I expect at thirty-three?
Who's single and desperately looking for me?
. . . why my children of course, my little men
They don't have to leave me by half past ten.

     Julie Dunningham

Secret Love

I didn't want last night to end
nor the morning light to come
I didn't want the world to turn
nor see the rising sun
I wanted it to be just us
together and alone
I wanted the impossible
forever on our own

Did you have to be so nice
it's harder to let go
Did you have to be so sweet
my heart is breaking so
Why do you seem to care so much
I'm starting to believe
Why did you make me fall in love
when you know you have to leave

You don't know how it lifts my heart when you phone each day
You don't know how I hang on to every word you say
I wish each night that you might come, if I could cast a spell
I'd wish that we could have all time eternity as well

        Doreen Fisher

536

Yearn

Yearn for the days of yesteryear
When life was much more calm
When people were safe to walk the streets
Without attracting harm

Yearn for the time law and order
Was for all, not just the select
When the village bobby walking his beat
Was treated with respect

Yearn for that time not too long ago
When a door was never locked
With the rent man, milkman and the rest
Walking in when they had knocked

Yearn for the time when employment
Was there for young and old
When summers were hot and hazy
And winters bitingly cold

Yearn for the time before drugs
When our children had little temptation
And pray that someone will come along
To halt this present stagnation.

Doreen Young

"Joys of Life"

Taken for granted are the joys of life
One can too easily be caught up and lost in strife
Just look around us, look what we've got
There are so many things to cheer us up

So pretty the flowers that bloom in the spring
So beautiful the sound of birds as they sing
They sing so gaily as they fly 'round the sky
Cheeping chirping cheerily as they fly by

The bees suck the nectar from the flowers they find
Butterflies clap their wings - they are one of a kind
Listen to the laughter and giggles of bairns
They sound so joyfully happy as they play their games
Animals moo they baa and they bleat
To name but a few the cows and the sheep

The next time you feel so sad and so down
Take my advice get up look around
Don't let yourself be caught up in strife
Go out - enjoy - the "Joys Of Life"

Collette-Anne Smith

Nobody Understands Me

It hurts inside, an unwelcome aching,
refusing to exit, refusing to subside.
Not one mortal halts to listen,
pauses to understand,
lingers to find out more.

This aching, pulling, dragging me down,
burrowing its way deeper inside,
taking me, a mere mortal under its wing.
Against my will, kidnapping my soul,
my inner strength ceases to exist.

Sinking, drowning within myself.
My only request, say a prayer for me.
Hope and faith are no longer.
Answer my prayer.
Please, understand me.

Save my soul, not my life.
I no longer desire the freedom to live,
my body should be laid to rest,
accompanying my hope, faith and ambition.
Will you not pause to understand, to save me.

Christine Jackson

Separation

Attached by a cord that bonds us together
Right from birth remain close forever
Then the cord breaks, the closeness falls apart
Like something reaching in and taking your heart.

For one person's happiness -
Causes a lot of people pain
Doesn't matter about your feelings
To them it's some game.

Trying to keep in contact
That's a hard thing to do
Remembering the love they now give to others
Once belonged to you.

There's always going to be a part of you
That remains empty and gone
But others have gone through it
So you're not all alone.

Time's a great healer
That's what they always say
But that's no reassurance
The hurt won't go away.

Amanda J. Fudge

The Four Seasons

Spring comes along with leaps and bounds
Refreshing rain and daffodils spring from the ground
Young love comes alive, hope lives anew
Young lovers go leaping hand in hand
Over the fields wet with morning dew.

Now summer is here with flowers in full bloom
The garden all colour with windows open wide
Sweet scent of roses drift into the room
Love too has grown from a blossom sweet and fresh
Love fully grown not at is best.

Autumn creeps in still beautiful with calor
The sweetness of summer gone with the fading sun
So young love too passes into its autumn
Still holding hands they cling to each other
Sadly now their work is done.

Now comes the winter cold and chill
Snow and cold rain sweep over the hill
The flowers have gone, time marches on
The winter of life has completed its work
The lovers have loved and gone.

Dee Shields

My Songbird

I woke up one morning sad and forlorn,
not knowing what the lonely day would bring;
when I heard your sweet voice: I smiled and rejoiced,
"Oh Songbird, you sang your song for me."

Each morning thereafter I listened for you
you always were steadfast and true,
your melody echoed in my heart,
I could not imagine life without you!
You gave me joy divine, in that song of thine.

Then one morn' in Autumn I listened, and heard
no sweet song from my favourite songbird.
My heart grew sad and I smiled no more;
till the following Spring, when the early dawn
brought your loving song to me once more.
My heart filled with laughter, my soul full of glee,
"Oh Songbird, you sang your song for me."

Doris Bright

Solace

I have to leave you for a little while,
Not very far, just out of sight.
Shed your tears, for they are the antidote to sorrow,
which will surely pass and fade away,
and you will know comfort.
Think only of the love, the joy and the secrets
that we shared, and nothing is lost.
Let light enter your heart,
and no shadows will fall.
Remember me gently, as I remember you,
and of the sweet contentment that was,
forever ours, of which so many never find.
Accept with dignity and grace,
that which is irreversible,
For this is but an interlude,
a passing phase.
Smile for me,
I am not far away.

Jack W. Jenkinson

Ode to the One I Love

Our love is like the ocean,
Oh so deep, so clear
On which we drift slowly, calmly further from others
And closer to a land of our own.
Oh so peaceful, so tranquil
This feeling that's surrounding us
When we're alone together.
The water shallows to the shore but our love is ever deep.
The sun will fade behind the sea but our love keeps on shining.
Oh so warm, so natural.
What is this place that keeps us bound
Where time stands still, where we can go and be as one?
Is it heaven? Or maybe paradise?
Oh so wonderful, so beautiful.
Only we know the answer:
When your warm hands caress me, with your tender lips touching mine
Oh so softly, so gently,
This is where I want to be . . . forever

Celine Fabian

The Tiger Car

The car is a roaring tiger
Roaring the whole day through
Passing objects at tremendous speed
And then it stops to gather some feed
It gulps it all down and runs into town
Terrorizing people as it runs 'round the bend
The Tiger car has not got a friend
And then it dozes off to sleep softly silently.

Adam Christopher Owen

Gloves

Of all the clothes we often wear
One particular item, comes in a pair
And guess what; this is the glove
Which we all like to wear and love

Take for a start, there are children's mittens
All lovely and warm like cuddly kittens
Then there are oven gloves, you use to bake
So you don't burn you fingers, taking out your cake

We also wear gloves, for all sorts
From driving a car, to all kinds of sports
Next are the leather, that are rather posh
But that's ok, if you have lots of dosh
In the garden, you would be lost
Without your gloves in the cold & frost
Even doctors wear plastic gloves, take heed
In case a slip up and one starts to bleed

So you see gloves play a big part in your attire
Whether for work, play, warmth or mire
But to wear silk and lace is very grand
To go out in the evening, and to shake someone's hand

Jean Linney

Winter's Embrace

Together we walked through a temple of trees,
On a wintry morning in a windswept breeze.
The snow had laid even on the feast of Stephen,
For it smothered the land like ivory sand.
Only the church bells tolled in this eternal cold,
For all else was still by winter's will.

Together we strolled through a carpet of snow,
Our laughter echoing in a vale of silence.
Tears that flowed, frozen as they left our eyes,
Falling like snowdrops as from the sky.
The snowflakes in our hair like diamonds sparkled,
While we danced away to winter's play.

Together we skated across the frozen lake,
Never afraid that the ice may break.
We ran up the hill by sheer power of will,
Then exhausted we lay in an old-fashioned way,
Alone and as one, embracing the sun.

Jason Cooke

Mists

Fog, haze, mist and smog, you appear in many guises
One day a friend and then a foe
No man nor beast surmises

The cliff-top horn bemoans its woe of wrecks and sailors dead
While brooding rocks more souls await who onto them are lead

But then again another guise of rose and early morn
Your hazy breathe soft in its wake proclaims each glorious dawn

The low ground mist the tombstones coil
Another morbid stage
Grey fingers tracing names and verse long since obscured with age

And then it takes upon itself an apparition foul, an evil, vile
and loathsome thing stooped in a smoky cowl
The buildings stand with shoulders drooped, their faces streaked
with grime
As fragile man with blood and sweat attempts life's upward climb

Anita Barnes

In Mourning

I alone weep in the long lonely night
Remembrance, sorrow; memories are sought
Of laughter together, cries of delight
Painful recollections made in deep thought
No chance to say to each other goodbye
My love and feelings time will not decay
But grow stronger so I tearfully cry
Oh, Why aren't you here? Why didn't you stay?
This vile world now cold and uncaring
I loved more deeply than I cared to show
Took you for granted now I despising
Wish I had told you how I loved you so
Through your death love has made me truly see,
Just how the love in life should always be.

Emma Treasure

Manaton Woods

In winter woods at Manaton,
of mist enshrouded trees like ghosts,
bracken bent, brown and dead,
and peaty earth as soft as bed.

Down below the River Dart would tumble,
Froth and spill,
and everywhere was still.

Fallen trees across the path
victims of more bitter times,
now moss covered, emerald green,
adorned with silver lichen,
for woodland creatures, food and haven.

We walk in silence here,
for just a word seems like a shout,
and who are we to trespass on tranquillity?

Joanna Caton

"Paula"

Long fair hair that curls with the touch of a finger
Rosebud lips remind me of a fresh spring day
Your grey-blue eyes reveal the purity of heaven
your smile reveals your gentle caring way

A little upturned nose, kissed by the sun in summer
Spreading freckles on skin so smooth and fair
The most exquisite flower plucked from heaven's garden
With you only I can compare

Tiny kittens, babes, and puppies too
Love to nestle within your arms
They can feel the love that radiates there
And know they will come to no harm

So young, so lovely, and full of fun
So gentle, caring and mild
You're a bright shining light in this dark, dark world
Dear Paula, you're a beautiful child.

Elizabeth Collins

Changing Seasons

Seasons come and seasons go,
'Round and 'round and 'round they flow,
Spring prepares for bulbs and flowers,
With a little help from April showers.

Summer brings and abundance of blooms,
Brightly coloured and sweet perfumes,
Autumn breezes in ordering trees to shed,
A carpet of leaves in orange, brown and red.

Winter arrives and so does snow and frost,
Birds fly away or pay the cost,
But seasons come and seasons go,
Always and forever they will flow.

Celia Law

Recompense?

He's a hero? We'll give him a mention!
(Say nothing of heat, flies and fear.
When people are fighting for freedom
That's not what they're ready to hear.)

Served in Burma? We'll give him some medals
For fighting for King, Home and Peace!
When fathers are dying for freedom
They're nice for the children to keep.

You're a widow? We'll give you a pension.
Not enough for your own way of life?
But you've cuttings and medals and babies
Of the pilot who made you his wife...

Geraldine Palin

The Future of the World

A man alone on a silvery steed
Rides through the night,
Black, lightened only by the faint moon,
The moon that once shone bright.

This moon that used to light his path,
Silver against the gold of the sun,
No longer rides proud through the midnight sky
For the things man has not done.

Man, the highest of animals,
Yet the most destructive of all,
No respect for fellow beings,
Ignoring them when they call.

They cry out for help, desperate,
Sinking into the choking mire,
Yet man still survives, floating somehow
And all around him is fire.

A man and his horse,
The last of their kind,
Searching for a solution
They are doomed never to find.

Julia Mariner

Dunblane

Dunblane, Dunblane,
our hearts go out to you.
The evil one
who took our angels knew,
exactly of the pain he'd cause,
when bullets flew
and took the lives of those young treasured ones.

Dunblane, Dunblane,
we hang our heads,
for fives and sixes that are dead,
for those that have been injured too
Thank God, their lives were not pursued!

Dunblane, Dunblane,
We'll ne'er forget,
the bairns or teacher who have met,
the evil one
but then gone on,
to Heaven's World of sweet protect.

Dalys de Relya

Trustee, Trust Who?

They made us. Whatever we are, however we think. Our manner, yes our manner, bad or even good, is still a lengthy process of creation, yet this still has been made by them. Some have the chance of changing all this but even that asks of their permission. Do we trust them. The question is NO, so what hope is there for the answer.

They did not make us but fraternize with us, relieve us, accompany us, and also help to keep us sane through times of illness, and perhaps cure what we have already been made as before. But they forget us and leave us or leave us and forget us, whichever comes first, and it will come. Now there is no question, so mentioning the word answer is an effort, as there is no such word.

Not relieve us but confuse us, that is what WE do. There is no need for these other two for we spiritually destroy ourselves, whether this has been learnt or not, it is feasible to blame our creator, and we are right to do so. Blame others is the answer, but the question still is to be found. NO I cannot trust myself!

Glenn Richard Alder

Silent Perceptions

As I lie in quite solitude
Reflecting all life's busy ways
There gradually steals over me
A calm and tranquil state
To contemplate what has been done
To others much less fortunate
For those in such improvised lands
And those in war-torn states
Who have not heard of that great love
Much less what it could do
That we as "Christians", may hear the call
And answer to its clarion sound
Thus fulfil, that, that our Master taught
  Love One Another

Denis N. Holt

Lost Cries

The house was aglow with raging fire,
Screams of the children in the heights of the loft,
The mother cried, "Dear God, help us."
Her plea went unnoticed,
Her children were lost.
Smoke blackened rooms,
Ashes which smoulder,
Echoes of the children,
Never to grow older.
The father cried, "Dear God, why?"
"It should be me, I should of died".
His pain and anger went unnoticed,
His children were lost . . .

Gillian Harvey

The Best

"We are looking for a labrador" we told the sanctuary boss,
she showed us you, sitting in your cage, a labrador/collie cross.
We fell in love with you there and then, and you seemed to like
us too, we didn't know how much joy you'd bring, with all the
things you'd do.
You loved to be with people, always wanting them to play,
our ever growing family of cats didn't get in your way.
When you went out 'walkies' the cats would go along too,
wanting to run around and play, wanting to be with you.
The teenagers who were our 'family,' never tired of your games,
you loved every one of them, always recognized their names.
Time went past too quickly, and we realized you were getting old
your coat turned grey, you slowed down and started to feel the cold.
Then came that dreaded day last year, when we know it was the end,
we said a last, tearful, goodbye to our wonderful faithful friend.
The five years that we had you Rigs, were full of love and joy
we always told you that you were the best, we still believe it boy.

Celia Pearson

The Loss

She stands by the graveside with a heart of stone
She stands by the graveside feeling so alone
In life he was her dearest friend
She loved him dearly right to the end
Suddenly she's filled with so much love
And knows that he's watching from above
She hears him whisper in her ear
'Don't cry my love wipe away your tear
I'll always walk beside you
I'll guide you every day
Until God unites us both once more
I'll love you come what may!'

Betty Crawford

Love-in-the-Mist

We met in the early morning mist,
Out with our nannies for a healthy walk.
Our world was contained by the tree-lined park —
And I only had eyes for your curls so dark.

In the early mist of our early lives.

I held your hand in the noonday mist,
And the sun so high with the rising heat.
Our world was contained by children and home —
And I only had eyes for your curls so brown.

In the mid-day mist of our middle lives.

I hold your hand in the evening mist,
With the setting sun beginning to wane.
Our world is contained by our fading sight —
Though I still have eyes for your curls so white.

In the evening mist of our evening lives.

Beryl Saltmarsh

Legacy

Wakeful, I await my final hour
No escape, no place to hide
Alone yet not alone at all
Soft whispers in my ear as though I'm but a sleeping child
Yet I am here inside, as I always was
Phantoms whirl around my bed in ghostly ritual
A door bangs, then remembering, closes gently
Faceless shapes reach out and stroke my hand
Their fear at my unknown terminus cruelly manifest
My weary mind dances along tangled threads of reason
Stripping away the web of illusion binding me like a shroud
To glimpse a time when tendrils of my life reached out and
    touched the moon
I now exist within the orbit of my dying world
Strangely calm, my life has run its course
Soon vultures will descend, dissecting every action,
thought and word
They need not linger long for I will leave the only thing that counts
A legacy of Love

Gillie Threadgold

Black Dog

Black Dog,
Roaming in your empty fog,
Upon the razor's edge you eternally tread,
With a sable glance, you raise the grateful dead.
Travelling across desert denied of their own dust,
Your bowels ACHE with a fledging lust,
Visiting unknown soldiers in their ignorant soil,
You know of the futility of human toil.
You are the black dog; poet, prophet, sham and martyr,
For the palace of wisdom you constantly barter.
As mankind shops for a life in society's malls -
While a mad God bangs his head against heavenly rubber walls.
When shrinks, politicians and priests play 'poker' with tarot cards.
And another promised land is broken into tiny shards.
And day by day, and hour by hour,
The milk of human kindness turns sour . . .
You are the black dog: The king without a throne . . .
In a world of rain and failure you search desperately for a bone.

Earl-David Dick

Winter Is Here

The winter's here and it's so cold
Not good for those who have grown old
The knees both creak, the muscles moan
The cold gets into every bone
The days grow short, the nights grow long
The birds no longer sing their song
Henry my hedgehog has gone to sleep
He's probably under my compost heap
A hungry fox comes creeping in
He would love to raid my rubbish bin
The ground is too hard to dig or hoe
And so the garden has to go
I've varnished my fence, I've varnished my gate
And now I think I'll hibernate!

Edna Weston

The Mist Must Not Obscure the Heights

The road we followed was an ever upward wind,
Into mists, so damp, bleak, frightening unkind.
Yet, kind enough to keep heather and bracken in view,
But then unkind, that mountain heights appeared untrue.
At times we were fooled into thinking we had reached the top,
Desperately we searched for the summit, but we found it not.
Yet still we followed that mountain road, as it continued along its wind,
When suddenly the gradient ended, there was no more road to climb.
When from the summit, the mist pleasingly cleared away,
We viewed the valley as the delightfully passed that way,
But yet, with the sun, with the dump mist too,
life was awakening, making all things seem new.
When the journey of life appears an upward wind.
The mist of life's way tries to obscure the mind.
It would be well to remember in some kind of way,
Heather and bracken becomes oasis in the day.
Whilst the road may wind and seemingly wind up,
You can reach the summit, if you reach up and touch.

Charlotte J. Dougherty

'I Love You'

I love you as I've always said so many time before
but for all the times it's been said,
no one had meant it more

When I say I love you, I mean it in every way
I love you for the way you look and
what you do and say

I love you because you're so special and
you make my life worthwhile,
I love you because you're so honest
and I love your warming smile.

Now you know I love you and you're the
one I adore
Mum I hope you'll never forget, I'll love
you forever more.

Stuart O'Neill

Blind Accidents of Life

Gliding through the forest, flying like a bird,
Over logs and bushes, yet I never heard the rumbles of the motor
I was deaf against the wind, living in my private world
where Death could never find me;
in my private heaven brighter than the stars,
living life for all it was - though now I'm in the wars.

I never heard the motor car; I was racing through the trees.
But now, oh God, I'm dying
and I'm down here on my knees.

The sound of bones on metal still crashes in the air.
Why, oh why did I never ride with greater care?

Not only me, the horse is dead; still lying in the road.
I thought that I'd heard thunder;
racing home before lightening showed.

The only lightening I then saw
was reflecting on the car.
My body with my stallion's
uniting as a star.

Brigitte May

Morrison's Grave

An honoured idol
resting in your Parisian death bed
You've been gone so long
but still they flock
they come to stare in awe
and say a silent prayer.
Even now you can't escape
we won't allow you
never will you wake in a good mood again.
The others point your way
Their magnificent splendour
show us to your humble rest.
Flowers lay at your feet
a feast of friends, alive they cry
I've seen you
I've touched your hollow grave
the world misses its poet,
The cavalier, the shaman.
I never got to say hello
But a least I got to say goodbye.

Jonathan Chown

'Hawk on High'

The hawk soars high over fir and birch
over river, fields, streams and hills
in the search for food she eyes her terrain
ready to swoop, to dive for the kill
salmon leap and rabbit scour
mammals jump and take to heal
but one lone morsel is all she seeks
to fatten her young and provide a good meal
then all of a sudden she spots a sole rat
scuttling around on a river bank
so with careful precision and gentle ease
she lowers to execute her rank
talons outstretched, wings a-poise
she grasps at the vermin, a master supreme
and heads for a branch on trees upon high
to finish her task, to tear the food clean
now bloody and covered with remnants of cull
she heads for her nest where chicks lie await
the raw meat mother has butchered for them
to share between them: her chicks and her mate.

Alan Domhnull Lang

Be Yourself to Be Free

Fascist, homophobic jokes
Painful thoughts of past revoke
Racist people stop and stare
Others just don't seem to care
They see us lying in the gutter
Tears we're crying make them mutter
Short change falling in a tin
They've already thrown us in the bin
The cars they drive are fast and new
But they just leave us there to queue

We are no-ones

The foreigners, the different, the strange
If only we could make them change
They could look inside and see
I'm not a colour, I'm just me
Across the oceans and the seas
It's up to us, to you and me
And someday we will show them how
To be themselves and set us free

Emmalouise Potter

Castle Eventide

Aware of penetrating memory of music
Sea mesmerises lasting echoes
From warm multiplicity of notes,
While concert from estuarine castle reigns
Like breath of forgotten perfume.
Theorbo casts its sounds of harmony
Through quiet, lazy expectancy
In low ceiling dungeon, listeners in space
Sitting absorbed on clusters of hard chairs
As though sea waves were slanting potent messages,
Bass booms across outer ears, inner eyes.

Music from medieval past catches iron
Of sixteen century cannons to remember
Days of old feuds like rambling
Scatter clouds dispensing raindrops of power.

Light clothes bathe in cool air as Cornish mist
Brings immobile balm - someone maybe
Hears their own heart beat.
Bass viol and merry violin stand and evoke
The key to ancient music's imagery.

Juliet Fowler

Forbidden - Love

Roll back the curtains of your mind.
Remember all the love you gave
Those precious hours you gave to me.
When I was helpless to be free.

Our love blossomed every day
We were so happy long ago
You went away without a word
You could not forget, it's too absurd.

You didn't ring or write a word
If you were ill, I would have heard
Don't bother now to get in touch
I've other friends who mean so much

I still remember long ago
When we were young, you so - and - so.
I still look back
In case you're there

To see your smiling face once more
You needn't call, I know the score
'Cos, I don't love you any more.

Joan M. O'Reilly

Summer Seasons

Summer is here once again
brighter I thought it would be
As I sit in the garden each day
I look around what do I see
You're not there anymore
A hectune in my mind I adore

Oh my darling the flowers are bright
The grass is greener and in sight
Yet in my heart the garden is lane
For you're not sitting in your chair
My thoughts for you will never die
As I sit in the garden I look at the sky.

Oh my darling I wish you were here.
To sit in the garden beside me dear
We use to sit in the bask of the sun of the sun
The two of us had laughs and fun
No longer are we together
You've gone at peace forever.

Mary Gilfillan

Untitled

I'll see my darling and do what I can
I think very soon I'll be using the pan
Just a little frying and what will emerge
Such a delicious omelette in every sense of the word
She eats it with relish I am pleased about that
One cannot go wrong with such a
Nice snack now is the time for a
Piping hot drink there is nothing
Better than tea I'm daring to think
I've made her happy that is a fact
I'll do a bit of cleaning and try
And relax what now brown cow
Just be wary of the bull don't be
Presumptions you must keep your cool
I go back to my pal and see how she's
doing not at all bad she knows I am wooing

Leslie Frederick Eshem

He Really Did Love Me

He really did Love me he paid for me everywhere we went he
wanted me to move in with him without paying rent. He used to
kiss me put his arms around me and say that he loves me. Now
he has deserted me and now I'm feeling lonely. One night when
he walked me home he took me to my door
and kissed me till my knees fell to the flour.
He got on his bike and rode away down the motorway.
He said he was coming back but I waited a year and he never did.
All I got was letters no photographs or postcard and now I'm
trying to cope but it's hard.

R. C. Mitchell

Mammy Kathleen

In early days and even later life
She talked she sang and moved around with joyful ease
Until one day the hand of fate caused strife
Within herself and lo! one leg and arm would please
To move in its own way and no direction take.
And later too, the smile that lit those brown brown eyes
Did substitute for speech.
Our Mother was Samaritan good to every class and creed
And in her present silent life they ask for her indeed.
The smile that grows, the joy that bursts envelop her so fast
'Tis heaven on earth to be around to share her happy past.
She listens, listens, says "AH SUN"
Then grasps your hand with her left hand to show a job's well done.
Though strokes clear four and others too did ransack her light heart
She never mourned nor burden saw in HIS swift touch, her part.
Her favourite songs at dances many she sang at home for us
And in her songs did SALLY join, our joyous days, no fuss.
What she did say or tell to us belongs all to the past
No more to speak or to impart her dear heart's wish at last.

Iris McEvoy

High Tech

I switched on the computer
And then surfed the net
A world of data to unveil
I launched myself into cyberspace
And picked up my e-mail
I downloaded through my modem and
Telephone line
A little something for,
 the electronic grapevine
I'm a digital fly in the worldwide web
But I am not in danger
For every spider is a friend
Not one of them is a stranger

Len Galvin

Moonlight

The valley hushed, so still the night,
Softly bathed in the moons golden light.
A lake shines like mirrored glass
Shadows cast on the mountain pass.
All is still, the valley sleeps
The night so cold the sleep so deep.
The stars glitter like a sequined gown
The glorious moon shining down.
Soft the light, soft as a mothers kiss,
A magical time of legends and myths.
Nothing stirs so deep the night,
All will sleep till the dawn brings light.

June Pearce

Where Is My God?

I stare at the stars with a frown on my face
I need someone here who'll plead my case
My body is aching
My bones show right through
I can't lift my head
But that's nothing new.

Where is my God?
The one that I love
Where is my God?
My help from above.

The camp is so crowded
There's a smell of death
I gasp all of a sudden
My final breath.

Kerri-Anne Clark

An Evolving Past!

How often,
How many times each day.
Does the smell of death,
Or the sight of piled bodies.
Or close pitiful, wanting screams.
Flesh across your consciousness?

You gave me the orders,
You made me pull the trigger,
Your history trading my life for theirs,
Your ghost causing destruction,
Victims of hate,
The children of an evolving past.

Do you not hear those screams,
Smell the stench of death,
See the bloody rivers.

Have you not burnt a lesson,
Witnessed this scene before,
Seen the futility.

Do you not feel for
The children of Bosnia!

John Finlayson

Free

The long shape quivered as from a troubled dream
From which she wakened to a distant sound
Deep within the forest, the call of the wild,
Instantly alert, tail swishing slowly
Body low on the ground.

She knew he was calling her, he of the awesome mane
King of the forest, she his queen.
She had slept long, tardy crossing the plain
Now padding swiftly to their chosen lair
Yet never seeming to lessen the miles between.

She crashed through the forest not heeding those who trembled
   in her wake
Nor stayed to slake her thirst.
She heard again the roar that called her,
Louder and louder, but the way was long;
Perhaps he would reach her first.

She felt him nuzzle her head, sensed the softness of his tawny mane
As she slept.
The keeper gently stroked her, she who now lay still,
Then quietly left the cage,
"You're free now, old girl," he said, and wept.

Kathleen Hilton-Foord

Confusion

A million things in my head so I walk
A million solutions in their mouths so I stop
Head on my knee's I sit
Thoughts in my head I contemplate
The answer eludes my mouth so I watch
I see him run around a track I time
I sit and wonder the point I rise
No solutions in my head so I walk

I walk all the way home
and all the way back.
Still it sits and festers
rots, smells and pesters.

Till I lose my temper
and throw it all out.
The million things in my head
What was it all about?

Claire Page

Candy

I often look at the photo, hanging on the wall,
Of my dog, That wasn't very tall,
A little Yorkie, Black and tan,
A friend to every one, child woman or man,
The memories of you are very clear,
You were wonderful, beautiful and very dear,
Why did all those years, go by so fast,
I know my love for you, will always last,
One day I will see you again,
Till then goodnight, God bless, my special friend.

Jeanette Mary Freemantle

Progress

We said we'd fight
make a stand
form a protest hand in hand
the trees still fall
the buildings rise,
I still wipe brick dust from
my eyes.
Here a road where an oak once stood
still our cries do no good.
We said we'd fight
make a stand
form a protest hand in hand
so let us stand
hear our word
let the futures voice be heard.

Julie Anne Burr

Fear

Only fear.
Only fear ever held my hand.
Only fear ever gently brushed my neck,
made hair stand on end.
Only fear held me tight.
Slid cold lips across my chest.
Only fear ever wrapped me in chill limbs,
drew me down on her.
Only fear crept behind me,
stroked fingernails down my spine,
bit gently into my shoulders.
Only fear ever pushed herself onto me,
teased peaked flesh across my skin.
Only fear moved against me, around me,
held me close while I shudder to a halt.
Only fear.
Never you.
Never anyone.
So why should I stop being afraid.

Thomas Henry Frost

Plight of the Third World Mother

The coldest part of the North Pole burns tonight.
The dullest of the stars in shining bright,
And she is in her haven her jewel hidden away,
Waiting for the heavens to open, with the break of day.

The crystal drops should fall on earth this morn.
But the cockerel does not wake to bring the dawn,
For although the heavens are heavy, whilst her treasure lays by her side,

Her jewel is crumbling rapidly and her whole world has died
Her jewel is not bright as it should be,
Though she cradles it and rocks it constantly.
She is not enough, for what it really needs,
Is for the sky to open with a string of crystal beads.

Tonight she's very cold and full of fear,
For she will be left alone without him near.
She's never had to face deprivation of this kind,
For God's should has fallen over her and robbed her of her child.

Tracy Richards

I Will Destroy You

Why does trust turn in to lies,
I let you in only to be locked out of my own world.
I will relent and one day attack the hearts that have deceived me.
The sound of thunder crashes around my heart,
as lightening pierces my eyes.
I have been blind.
I will rise one day, but for now my soul will lie in wait.
In wait for the day that I am reborn.

Christina Barclay

Respect

Respect is a hard thing to be earned,
Respect is one thing I have learned,
Respect the man and not his clothes,
He may look noble in his fancy Robes,
He'll put you down, stab you in the back,
Won't bat an eyelid he never looks back,
I'm a common man that's plain to see,
No fancy clothes or regalia just me,
I respect my family and close friends.
on whom I can depend,
To a discourteous man this may seem funny,
Treading on a man because of his
lack of money
Give respect where respect is due,
you'll find it coming back to you
I'm a common man as plain as you
respect me please that's all I ask,
is this such a daunting task,
come from behind that noble mask,
Have respect

David Weatherill

Untitled

You've gone. Abandoned us,
Left us to struggle with our own imagination,
Like twilight hanging on to a day already dead.
Not knowing how to come to terms with the sudden parting,
Life just finished.
As though it never existed,
Like some huge void snatched you away for its own purpose.
But you were there,
For many more years than I could ever conceive,
Quietly, calmly there, being you.

B. A. Blake

In a Winter Dusk

The field silent as a graveyard
Seemed in the evening light.
Kind-faced cattle were made grotesque
As they stood dark against the mist
Which gathered in the grave-markers.
Flapping crows fell to distant trees
Lost in the rising dark,
The winter air caught at my face.

Then nothing at all moved.
It seemed the light itself drew deep,
Held breath and then was gone
Only the first new stars
Stopped my hopes from falling
Into the winter night.

Amanda Attfield

"Memories"

Soft silent snowflakes falling in the night,
Making every place so smooth, so bright
Bringing back memories of Christmas long ago
When Santa came on his Reindeer and a loud Ho-Ho.

We never saw him, or even heard his voice,
But for weeks before we were as quiet as nice
Waiting for the Happy day, with all its fun and cheer,
We had at home together, at Christmas and the New Year.

One Christmas morning I was awakened by my big brother Jack,
Who swore to all us younger folk that he had caught Santa and his sack,
Up we jumped even though it was break of day,
To hear the hall-door bang- He told us Santa got away.

As the years went on I had my children too,
Three were born in December, in Summer the other two
I often felt so weak, I cold hardly dress the tree,
But on Christmas night as I fed my babe, my heart was full of glee.

Many years have gone, three score and ten
The memories live on, of the happy times then,
And I still love Christmas, when I'm greeted with the words I
    love to hear
Happy Christmas Patt and a bright New Year.

Elizabeth M. P. Beecher-Cantillon

Windows of the Soul

They lie in their beds immobile
Each twist and turn costing energy
Dependant on the nursing staff, daily.

The world is just outside the window
Every tree, building, road an escape.
Birds large and small fly free
Soaring, swooping, effortless it seems
Graceful, on the wind.
Large planes sail smoothly through the air
No noise is heard, they are shapes of silver in the sun
Soon they will land, but where have they been?
Now carrying people from a far
Soon to take others far away.

Behind the windows minds travel
Bodies remain immobile.

Bargie Bidmead

A Mother's Lament

She will never see or feel another lovely
    summers day
She will never run all through the grass or smell
    the new mowed hay
Make a lovely daisy - chain to wear upon her head
Dear Lord can you please tell me why my
    little girl is dead

I sent her off this morning with her bag
    upon her back
Never thinking for a moment that she would
    not come back
If only for a second we could see ahead
    and take a precious moment forever to suspend
To be used and cherished in our hour of pain
Bringing with it comfort when our darkest moment came
But then Lord I remembered the gift you gave to me
That all our precious moments are stored in our memories

Norma Boyle

"The Meaning of Words"

Words are just words
Until written or said
They can sometimes, bring happiness
But could also, cause us dread

Thee are funny words, and naughty words,
And words, that sound so nice
There are even, words of wisdom
And words given, in advice.

There are harsh, words said in Anger
And softer, words of love
There are written, words in prayer
To our creator, up above.
There are words, in many languages
That are spoke, every day
And said to us, in foreign tongues
Have nothing, to convey.

But the words, that when translated.
For this world, to see and hear
Should be, peace and joy to fellow men
And all wars, to disappear.

Jean Brigden

Secret Lives

Tonight is the night, when lovers meet.
In the moonlight sun, and grass so deep.
They dance and sway in rhythm with the wind.
And walk hand in hand by the whistling trees.
Then when the time has come for the lovers to part,
A kiss full of life and energy sends then spinning a far.

Fay Barnes

Wild Winter

Still summer some prefer
Of idle trees, lethargic lakes,
Beautiful blossoms, silent seas,
Whispering woods, those lazy days
Forever evenings, still summer.
Summer fades, a crescendo of colour
Rustling russet rivers and sky's dour
Whispering winds warn woeful weather
Wild winter loosed from her tether.
Wild winter returns roiling and raging
With wind whipped white wreathed waves
Flailing trees and racing clouds
Raw and wrathful seas surge
Wild winter returns in awesome anger.
Places placid is still summer,
Lethargic and lazy a rainbow of colour.
Untamed and raw is wild winter
Dark and grey, irresistible but dour.

Kevin A. Bratherton

View from Below

When I'm in my wheelchair lots of people stare,
Some are very critical yet many others care,
With wheels as legs we feel so lucky, caring people say we are plucky,
Then we meet the other kind who through their ignorance are
quite blind,
When I venture into a crowd I often feel like screaming loud,
"Here I am I can talk" despite the fact I cannot walk,
I've just had the door slammed in my face, somehow I've got
inside this place,
Going through shops can be quite a pain, wow there's that door
slammer again,
If I catch them with my wheel I have no doubt they will squeal,
Let them hurt I won't care until they decide to treat us fair,

Then I meet someone who show they care talk to me and not my chair,
May I help you they sincerely ask they make me feel I'm not a task,
With a smile I can say thank you kindly you've saved my day,
So to all those people who ignore our plight,
Please be thoughtful and treat us right,
We are quite human, we also bleed it's just understanding we
desperately need.

Dorothy Barker

Time . . .

Time will never stop and watch
Though years go sailing by
Time will never keep those lives, who surely are to die,
And yet we find a tiny space,
To keep those years inside,
To surely prove to everyone
We've lived a happy life.
And because our life is precious
We only have one chance,
One Sunrise in the morning,
One endlessness to dusk.
And when we reach our final dreams
Time still cames on,
Never stoping just to glance
Incase the time is wrong
And yet in life we pass our pleasure,

Debbie Pattison

Goodbye Cruel World

The feeling returns, the heartache begins,
The tears start to fall as my problems set in.
I reach out for the answer, but the answers not there,
My tears full of loneliness as if nobody cares.
People say there's a tunnel and that you soon reach the light,
But the lights always drifting away out of sight.
Sometimes I get so low, sometimes feel so down,
Feel people wouldn't miss me if I was no longer around.
I sometimes get the feeling I could just walk away,
Leave it all behind me, never face the next day.
I grasp out for the happiness, I grasp out for the love,
But the answers not with me, it's with God up above.
If I left you all behind, I'd never feel the pain,
If I shut my eyes forever, I'd never cry again.

Katie Luckes

Untitled

Forgive me.
Yesterday my path was my own.
Though it was harsh and desolate
It was not lonely.
The sight of a bright sunset can be blinding.

Today I stumbled and fell,
And I saw your image.
But your expressions were distant and faded.
I had tripped over my own feet.

Please,
Let those colours return to my eyes once more.
Forgive me.

Jonathan Olsen

Single Mother versus the World

Feel my pain as I kiss the path, of which devious
politicians have let loose their wrath.
Taste my anguish as I play their game, of welfare
and benefits and other such shame.
But do not offend me by feeling pity, if anything
I don't deserve that,
I am the sacrificial pawn in this game of chess,
and to you I take off my hat.
I ride the cloud that soars my mind, and not an ounce
of pride can I at all find.
Instead just an emptiness that shall be passed onto my kin,
what right have I to commit this
unwarranted sin.
And as I reflect on a future of deprivation
of which life definitely reaps,
I look at my reflection with contempt and disgrace,
as my internal warrior weeps.

Anthony Blackman

Meeting

A child touched my sleeve today,
So gently
And with such concentrated care.
As if her finger tips were feeling there
Not just the texture of my clothing.
But some crystal beaded abacus
Slowly telling the sum of my being.

Sue Coulson

Open Plan

Open plan, the scourge of man,
no fences, no domain in which to reign and take some pride,
instead it is open wide, open plan.

Where that safe haven for your child?
secure to play, from which to watch the world outside,
Instead he just runs wild, a constant worry or worse,
a victim of a car or man, each one a threat or curse.

Free, I do agree but free for what?
No one to care, no one to see,
Oh yes, he's running free, no one to teach or guide,
all are busy with jobs inside.

He wanders far and wide until so tired and spent,
turns, pauses,
and wonders where that safe haven went.

A big cold world, no warm familiar sight,
as he whimpers with sudden fright.
his mother, always there in sight, is all he needs,
to solve his plight.

Barbara Terry-Short

"Good" . . . "Bye"

Girlfriend . . . Congratulations, the show was great, well, done!
    It was great to see you, you made it fun.
Director . . . Tell Mr Burton to stay behind.
    Where's that invoice I couldn't find.
Girlfriend . . . Your diction was great, we could here every word,
    You've got one of the nicest voices I've heard.
Director . . . You left the door open, didn't put magazines away,
    I'm going to have to ask you to finish today.
Girlfriend . . . I'm really enjoyed watching you,
    I could see all your moves, I had a good view,
Director . . . No, I'm not finding fault or nit-picking you,
    It is not the sort of things that I do,
Girlfriend . . . You've got a great personality and smile
    Can I stay and talk with you for a while.
Director . . . You've not been working my way,
    So I think that we had better call it a day.
Girlfriend . . . I'm looking forward to tomorrow night,
    Got a great personality, nice and polite.
Director . . . Just leave your jumper and your tie,
    Goodbye Mr. Burton, Bye, Bye.

Andrew G. Burton

The Vase

The vase was a turquoise blue, sent by a
boyfriend she once knew,
Wild flowers the colours of the rainbow,
mostly muted blues.
His words of passion could easily turn her mind,
Like the sails on the windmill,
and the flour it grinds.

His love is lost amid the passions of time,
Her feelings for him so long buried and sublime;
But every time the vase has flowers of muted blue
She should be thinking of me - but alas, I know it's you.

With buttercups and cowslips, poppies and bluebells,
The glaze on the vase used every day is cracked and gone brown.
A shattering sound could be heard as the vase fell to the ground;
But the sound of the teardrop falling on the one thing
to remind of such beauty.
Went unnoticed to those standing, all around.

Peter Gurney

Shattered Dreams

Shattered Glass
Broken into a million pieces
Checking for cuts
On passing pilgrims
A terror bomb
Fire engine on the scene
Condemnation from all angles
Press reporting in
Mindless murder without borders
Lost lives, shattered dreams
Politicians playing political games

Bryan Heavey

'My Gun Words' under the Willow Tree

Under the willow tree
  down by the river -
We sat and made our vows.
We didn't know what the future held
we were alone —
  'Cept for the sheep and cows.
It was a lovely springtime day
All the flowers were in bloom
We were so in love with each other
Together we would overcome troubles
Under us - or above
We felt we'd survive them all
Because of our deep love
Now fifty years together
He died - and there's only me.
But I still go
  down by the river.
To sit under our
  favourite willow tree.

Hazel Bowen

Woman Is Life

Shirts ironed with love, by the hands of a woman,
Wrap and hug with intangible arms.
Warm silk, a white dove, the piety of this woman,
Seeps through the fabric to tranquillise and calm.

Prepared with the love and care of a woman,
The meal of Ambrosia, is her inside you, and her,
Viands of the Gods themselves from this woman,
Her touch can be tasted, her love and her care.

Fluffy pillow, crisp sheets and warm with a woman,
Wholesome and unfeigned, her love craves the man.
Her body accepts and absorbs to completion,
What toll can be placed on the gold on her hand?

A friend and a lover, a mate and all woman,
She gives and she loves and fulfils man life
Children born, life given, loves largesse of a woman,
All treasure is nothing, to the love of a wife.

Dino Wilson

Memories

I treasure all the memories in which you've played a part
And every time I think of them, warm feelings fill my heart,
Because it's meant so much to me to have someone like you,
A nan who's wonderful and such a good friend too.
I treasure all the memories of you and I together,
I miss you now with so much love,
Until were together forever,
I loved you right from the start and
at the moment were apart it may seem it's forever and ever,
but someday we'll be back together;
when I think of you, I know that it's true,
that when I'm free, you will be there waiting for me;
I love you my nana, more than these few words can ever say
I can't wait for the day, that I'll never be away,
As ill be home forever with you to stay.

Stuart O'Neill

Untitled

The sky at night
Is a wonderful sight
And is the sun through the day
The snow that falls on a
frosty night and quickly blows away.

The rain that falls
The trees that grow
A rainbow in the sky
So deep is the sea
And the still of the sand
And the stars in the sky.

We are born and we, grow old
But alas we must die
But these great things
And their beauty
Will last till the end of time.

Doreen Hunt

Brave Mave

Courage borne silently with no heroines flair
An invisible barrier that even the closest could not penetrate
A pain suffered in silence for half a decade
Half a decade more than she expected to suffer
An ache tossed aside with a flick of the wrist and a flickering smile
An agony that few of us can imagine, not only physical pain,
but the mental torture that only those few who can foresee their
own future suffer
Yet still she battled like an invincible warrior, shielding those
around her from the countless unnamed faceless enemies that
were her cancer
Protecting her children until the very end, not only protecting
them but revelling in their company and most unselfishly of all,
sharing her last strength with them till her final breath
Even now at her journeys end, if we were to ask her how she
was, she would look, pause and say,
"NOT TOO BAD"

Neil Bellamy

Take Time

Take time to look behind the smile,
  that tells you all is well
The loneliness that it may hide,
  is very hard to tell
Take time to listen to the words,
when they tell what might have been.
Take time to look into the eyes,
  and read the tale between

For a smile can hide the deepest heart ache
  with a longing to be heard.
  For a kind soul just to listen,
  and be concerned of every word.
  For smiling is a way of saying
  Please will you be a friend
  Then I'll be glad to listen to,
  your story without end.

Jill Wiseman

546

Lunar Limelight

The Spring moon, giant tangerine,
rising in the black of night
takes the stage, probes the darkness,
spotlights the slumbering world.
The world, lulled into soft serenity:
The world as it might be.

Behind the peaceful facade,
away from the lunar limelight,
the world still wars,
death hovers in the wings,
humanity hell-bent on destruction:
The world as it is.

When humanity reads the Author's Script,
follows directions, the play will change.
He set the stage, supplies all needs;
when each player finally accedes
there will be a shifting of the scenes:
The world as it should be.

Joan Butler

Freedom

Let the wind blow,
Let it ride high
Scudding the clouds,
Hurrying them by.
Let the birds sing
Their sweet, mellow song
Let us do right,
Try not to do wrong.
Let us love each other
Whatever we be.
Let us stand up straight
Tall as a tree.
Let the sky be blue,
And green the grass.
Let the Lord love you
You have only to ask.

K. M. Fletcher

A Dying Wish

I wish that I could be like you
And go out in the weather
I would not mind the wind or rain
I would not mind the weather
To feel the cold rain on my face
The wind blow through my hair
Just to be outside again
And breath in good fresh air
To walk the old familiar Road
The road that takes me home
I would not mind the weather
I'd be going home

Emily Doyle

Bullets, Debris and Glass

I walked in darkness, the night was cold,
I thought on you and in my arms I'd hold . . . You,
but how could that be . . . for you
were gone, gone so far that no-one could reach,
You were gone, so many more lessons to teach.

I ran on the beach, the sand was wet,
I thought on the first time that we both met . . .
Remember the bullets, debris and glass,
You were quiet but somehow brave, 'cause it was
You they wanted and I was saved.

I stopped by the grave that read your name,
It made me realise that this fighting wasn't a game.
'Cause they took your life and let me live . . . but
what good is life when part of me is with you,
Under the clay so cold and so blue,
They may take my life and let me be
Rid of this fighting and at last free.

Lorna Goudie

City

Faces, faces and the dust of feet,
Quick sidelong glances as you cross the street,
A tired toneless voice, a wave of scent
That swiftly faded yet in passing went
Bound each to each in one brief memory -
No time to wonder that this fact should be.
Red ties, red buses and red shiny lips,
Long bony arms and large unlovely hips
And letters on a board that twist and blur
And leave no hint of what their meanings were
And rushing here to 'phone and there to tea
And vainly chasing punctuality.
Wet drooping hats and paths of wavy light
Like moonbeams on the sea one summer night,
Hot gusts of food and shabby clothes and rings
And longings for the grass that traffic brings
And thoughts that come and finish incomplete
In faces, faces and the dust of feet.

Lucy Antrobus

The Unknown

Sometimes when you are just
Not sure where life is going,
You wish to see past the here and now,
But know there's no way of knowing.

One day you think you've found your aim,
The next day you're not so sure.
Decisions and pressure seem constant,
What lies ahead, outside your door?

Suggestions of this, hints to do that,
Don't seem to help your delusion.
The future is yours, not his or hers,
You just need to push past the confusion.

So although you know that you'll never know,
Just where your seeds will be sown,
You wish that there was a way to prevent,
Heading, towards the unknown.

Clare Barton

In Memory of My Father

Consider his position - old and grey,
His usefulness outspent his life near done,
He sits alone and whiles away the day
And welcomes with a sigh the setting sun.
There's not a single sign which might suggest
That once the bloom of youth his brow did grace,
Long years of toil have put him to the test
And etched the lines of age upon his face.
He won respect from all who came his way
And scarce a harsh word spoke of any man,
Embedded in the twilight of his day
With quiet content, he's ready for God's plan.
    And when the chosen few are called on high,
    If he's not there, what chance have you or I?

Donal J. Healy

My School

My school's the best,
it beats all the rest.
If only more people know,
then they would come to.

My school's totally are,
cause it's such friendly place.
We never feel lonely,
cause this school's the one and only.
My school's really cool,
cause everyone rule's.
When it come's to dinner time,
we always find somewhere to spend our time.
It's a really nice place
it's made for the entire human-race.
If you're black or white.
This place has got to be right.

Cassandra Anne Crabtree

My Dream

I always see him day and night,
He's always here right next to me.
In his arms he holds me tight,
In his eyes love is all I see.

I start to shed my tears of joy,
For being with him is a dream come true.
I start to gaze at his dark brown eyes,
And then he whispers "I Love You"

He's my one and only love,
He's the one I'll never forget.
His name engraved deep in my heart,
He's the best man I've ever met.

He takes my hand and off we go,
To the loveliest place my eyes have seen.
We sing a song, we walk along,
The greenest gardens I've been in.

I don't want to leave, I don't want to go.
With my love I'd like to be.
Unfortunately, when I open my eyes,
All I'm left with is . . . reality.

Nesreen E. Zarrouk

Twilight Years

You lie there at rest
Your misty grey eyes deep in sleep
I hear your shallow breathing
And I watch the rise and fall
Of your chest

You stir momentarily
And through the flutter of lashes
I can see your eyes dance
It must be a dream of a life
Long past

Your brow is unfurrowed
There are no wrinkles to be seen
It reminds me that you were
Once young and keen

You wake slowly, gently
Stretching each limb
The lines on your face return
And I realize then that I am
Seeing myself in the twilight years to come

Anne E. Whitaker

Springtime of My Heart

It seems only like a season
Blooming in full flower
Since I found you in life's spring field
You were mine from that hour

Yet life has not been kind to us
And soon our time is spent
Wondering on the joys and pain
Where all the days have went

The mind a vision does create
Of days both far and near
The fact that winter has now come
Of all the things so dear

Each petal falls down one by one
I can hear the world's outcry
He loves me no he loves me not
When through time the beauty dies

But though the veil of flesh decays
A fickle work of art
The spirit of my love is framed
In the springtime of my heart

John Bernard Elford

Loneliness

The wooden house stood above the shore
Four-square like a child's drawing
Right in the path of the strong sea-winds
Which scoured with salt and sand
To make its bare wood the colour of bone.
Nothing there to soften this stark outline
Except, at an upstairs window, lace curtains.

Perhaps a girl lived there once
Who hung the curtains as a challenge to the grey sea.
She would open the window and let the lace billow out,
Luxuriant, catching the light
In its rich pattern of scrolls and flowers,
Like Rapunzel letting down her hair
Saying "Here I am - this is me -"

But now the house is empty
And only the waves answer
The waves, and the seagull's sad cry.

Clemency Emmet

"The Yank Came Back"

Marie Jones was his only next of kin,
A Welsh American daughter conceived in sin,
Yankee Joe was to have married her mum, next leave,
But all he could do now was sit and grieve,
For his lovely Megan had died giving birth,
Now there would be no one else for him on earth,
So he went back to the U S A without a wife
From that day forth he led a lonely life,
The years dragged OH! so slowly away,
He'd always hoped to see Marie again one day
He took an off chance visit back to Wales,
And called at the Tavern he and Megan once sipped ales
"Marie Jones Yankee 'sir did you say?"
"Ah! yes "the landlord said. "She jetted out to the U S A yesterday".

Mona Jenkins

Paranoia

Shades of green, flashes of red
Envy, suspicion, jealousy, dread
Watching, looking, peering, prying
Frowning, scowling, pouting, sighing
Monsters lurking in dark recess
Full intent with no regrets,
Why, what, when, questions asked
A relentless river, sanity's past
Who, where and how, the flow spills forth,
Anger bubbles over, malice and wrath
The world gets smaller, the mind shuts tight
The battle rages, the negative fight:
Dark shadows of the mind, looking for prey
Savage poison of the soul, a tune to play.
Paranoia, paranoia, my food, my light
Paranoia, paranoia, bonfire burning bright.

David Joste

Shed No Tears At All

This creaking frame, this mortal guise,
Shall hinder me no more,
For I'm restored, reborn, made whole,
As I was once before,
Though we shall never walk again,
Together stride for stride,
I will be your unseen guardian
Forever at your side.
You never asked, you only gave,
Never wavered as a friend,
Providing love, support, companionship;
Unto the bitter end.
So as I leave this weary frame
To meet my makers call,
Remember me with happiness;
And shed no tears at all.

W. Heelan

The Change

The sun goes, down, the hot evening changes to twilight,
The flowers drop their heads, the sky darkens now it's night.
The moon emerges, brightening the earth below,
The stars twinkle overhead, giving the land a faint glow.

Everything's quiet and away of the creatures creep,
The days been long and hard and how it's time to sleep.
Except of course for the owl, out pops its little face,
And the black and white old bagger rummaging in every place.

Some noises fill the earth, both loud and shrill,
But other than that the air is quiet dark and still.
Suddenly the cock crows on the distant farm, the darkness fades away,
The sun rises, sets in the sky, the rays light the earth now it's day.

The creatures pop their heads out of their nests now,
The black crow caws, the young dog barks, the old cat says meow.
The whole world awakens in a hurry.
Out of bed the school children scurry.

The owl goes to sleep and the badger goes into the ground,
The milkman and the baker wake to do their round.
And nobody notices, It's all so strange,
The world, the happenings and the earth's change.

Mary Howlett

Baby Grandson

A baby sleeping softly,
Like an unfurled petalled rose,
Smooth warm skin and crescent eyebrows
She'll ears and button nose.
So innocent and sweet he seems,
I wonder what he really dreams.
A life of warmth of trust of love
Is surely what. Should be.
For all these little one's on earth,
    As unaware as he.
You can only take him forward
    Helping through the years
    Doing your best as he grows
Through laughter, pain, or tears.
God has given you a miracle
To treasure and to love.
Be not neglectful of that trust
He watches from above.

Olive J. Hirst

Untitled

In two's and three's they bent their knees and fell to the dust to die.
They killed a race and laid to waste a land of God's own souls.
Nero eat his oath of hate and forgot his place in Rome.
For now he had a vast expanse of people who loved God's home.
And it was not St. Peter but just his lonely crew who were
murdered to the bone.

Esther Dempsey

My Life

Days of darkness autumn gloom
Pacing 'round a tiny room
Thinking thinking no resolve
Moving on going nowhere
Is this my life?

Memories of days gone by
Just a few that make me cry
All mixed up these thoughts of mine
Aware of so much wasted time,
Is this my life?

Dreams when young seem possible so simple
Unselfish love prepared to share
Receiving love from one who cares,
Now faded dreams alone somewhere
Is this my life?

Children grown they move on
Your dreams for them still, bright and strong
Do I now move on or is this my life?

Jane Barbara Bell

"Somewhere" (Out There You Live)

Somewhere out there you live
And somewhere inside, within me
You my friend still live
I've often began to wonder
Just what you are thinking now!

The sun from your life
Will eternally glow in my heart
I see the sun shining against my bedroom window
But not as golden
As I keep you here in my heart

Somewhere out there you live
Somewhere's become, so far out of my reach
I've ached, moaned, sadness
I'm so aware I stand alone

Like a change of seasons
You left to live somewhere
Somewhere out there
Without exchanging me your reasons
To want to live, without me
Somewhere out there

Catherine Doherty

Reunited

I dreamt a dream with you last night
    I called out from the dark,
I dreamt and called aloud again,
    I dreamt you called me back.

I tried to climb the high high hill
    That kept us both apart,
I crept, I crept, I could not stand,
    I struggled with the dark.

At last I heaved a final heave,
    I gained the topmost rung,
I saw you there, you looked and said
    "I've waited here so long."

They heard me crying in my sleep
    They heard my scream, they heard my tears
They tried to wake me from my dream
    But I had fled, across the years.

Philip Brady

Out There

Go out there and seek,
For out there, there is
The one who is out there.

We all know who is out there
And off course why he is out there
If you have forgotten why he is out there
It is because we need him out there
To love and fancy.

Nicola Boyle

Ship of Dreams

There is a ship that sails
with her masts on high
her sails are made of dreams
pale blue as a summer sky

Along the seas of yesterday
blown by the winds of time
she glides along so easily
this old ship of mine

My ship of many memories
brings a light into my eyes
a day dream full of happy thoughts
with gladness and surprise

And when my ship goes sailing
on soft cloudless skies
it takes me back through the years
I just sit back and sigh.

Grace Jack

A World Filled with War

We spend our lives fighting for peace
So what is the point on being put upon this place
When one war is over another beings
Are people ever grateful for what they receive
There is too much resentment and not enough love
Circling this planet that we stand above
People take life as though it's food upon a plate
Make it and take it then put the rest to waste.
This world is used as a battle ground under the blazing sun
Killing and fighting, until victory is won
Just take a step back and look at what your doing
Can't you see it's future lives that you are going to ruin

Nicola Jayne Burnside

Lover to Dust

Lover turned to stranger,
Stranger turned to dust.
A must to keep away from you,
A must to sweep the dust
From the shelves of my memory,
Where books of ancient history lie,
Waiting to be read and read again,
Or waiting to be destroyed
Once and for all.
Destroying them means losing you,
And lose you I must.
Reading them means loving you,
Loving you is lust.
Lust is insatiable,
When its object is of dust,
Dust is irrecoverable,
And so must you be,
My lover turned to dust.

Raghda Butros

Window Pain

When I look out the window,
Having my cup of tea,
I like to watch the people,
And wonder, "Will that be me?"

Will that be me in 10 years,
Hurrying to get to work under the wire.
Will that be me in 20 years,
Just waiting to retire.

Will that be me in 30 years,
No rushing left to do.
Just time to do some shopping,
And spend some time with you.

Time to finally relax,
And enjoy my cup of tea,
Sitting by the window,
Glad that I am who you see.

Joanne Bargioni

Torment in Somalia

With the dreaded wake of morning,
  And the spirit soul unfed,
The body lies here groaning
  For a particle of bread.

The children no longer wailing,
  They cannot lift their head,
Nor hear a mother's calling -
  All now painless and dead.

And the 'vaults' of christian - galling,
  All seem forget the key,
When the weather here is failing -
  Their coffers not run free.

But, remember once 'it' was sea,
  Now the cursed barren land,
And this cruel fate may befall thee -
  To eat the fruits of sand.

Brian Coffey

Freedom

Ready for dinner, what day is today?
Ready for dinner, what more could I say.
I need to start thinking
Endeavour to write
It's where I find happiness
Where everything is bright.
My spirit grows stronger
With each written word
The ink just keeps flowing
I know it sounds absurd.
But my heart fills with happiness
My mind feels Oh so free,
Who cares whose ready for dinner
Today, I care only for me.

Rachael Crowley

Living Pictures

One eye is triangular, the other has fallen or dripped
A mouth, or just a set of teeth, this sad face is unlipped

It resembles a jig saw puzzle, a human face, no it can't be
I'll enquire, "excuse me, can you explain?" "Why yes, the
  portrait, it's abstract you see"

The horse to the left, on the wall by the door, is a perfect
  representation
You don't have to guess, you can see it's a horse, an equestrians
  greatest temptation

Did it move? Yes I think, is it real? Or just a mere image
The horsehair seems to breath, the eyes have a living visage

Now the gallery's closed, I'm all alone, I'm at home with the
  silence prevailing
I ponder on the woman, the woman in bits, with the pain in her
  face remaining

My solitary thought, is the way I'd feel, to be portrayed in that
  way, do you see?
Then terror strikes as I feel the breath, of the horse there right
  beside me.

Jane Carr

The Rose

Romance is in the air when a sweet smelling rose is in the room,
The long stem, the red bud waiting to bloom.
How delicate the red rose is, with long fine green leaves,
So romantic, like the wind blowing through an old willow tree.

The red rose means love, a love so deep and strong,
A kind of relationship that lasts so very long.
When two hearts beat as one, and the love is always there,
The kind of relationship that is so very rare.

If the rose is dried it keeps all the colour, the smell and the love inside,
It doesn't die and the love stays in the soul, the heart and the mind.
If you get hurt with a thorn it is a test of love,
But the wound will heal in time and the relationship will be a
stronger scent of love.

Karen Browne

Snot

My friend Jonathon's got a snotty nose.
He's never got a hanky so he wipes it on his clothes,
You can see the silver 'snail's-trails' running all along his sleeves,
And just see me run for cover every time he goes to sneeze!
The teachers all say, "Jonathon, why don't you use a tissue!
But he just smiles and sprays them with a dirty great "ATISHOOO!"
Other kids miss swimming 'cos of measles or verrucas,
But John can't go in case he fills the pool with strings of mucus.
And on the football field he just can't seem to learn to shoot,
He's always slipping over when his nose drips on his boot.
With Jonathon around you know I'm not the boy to step on,
'Cos he'll spring to my defence with his deadly secret weapon,
His big proboscis, fully armed will always save the day,
When at point blank range he hits you with his sticky, lethal spray.
So Jonathon's my hero though his habits are quite grotty,
I'm proud to say my best friend is a first class champion snotty.

Jenny Purnell

Michael

He says his life is on the stage
His soul is in the glove
He says he wouldn't harm a child
His heart is like a dove

His mind is the earth's own heart
Their trusting bond shall never part
As long as he has the strength, the power
His dance and song will be a growing flower

Budding in the sun's own rays
His dance will flower in different ways
As long as he's the dance, the song
His mystery will be forever long

Kelly Porr

The Countryman

The Countryman begins to sing,
his thoughts are of the coming spring.
He sees the signs, those shoots of green,
with Winter past, the worst he's seen.

The cuckoo comes and swallow soon,
and countryside gets into tune.
Dawn chorus welcoming the morn,
he's feeling good, glad he was born.

Moorhen builds her nest upon the stream,
everywhere is like a dream.
Mowing grass to make the hay,
as sun shines on another day.

The Countryman enjoys the life,
he shares it with his darling wife.
The seed is sown, away the plough,
he's thinking of the summer now.

Raymond J. Hobbs

Lonesome Melody

Hear him strumming to the busy beat of life,
Homeless figure in a doorway.
Plays a melody recalled from bygone days,
Years of loneliness his story.
Who is he standing there? fighting cold and despair!
Doesn't anybody care?

Cold wind whistles to his 'Lonesome Melody',
Takes the rhythm from his fingers.
Through the years he's lost his friends and family,
But his hope in life still lingers.
Who is he standing there? fighting cold and despair!
Doesn't anybody care?

O won't you bring a smile to those sad and lonely eyes,
Playing in his disguise - won't you show him that you care?

Drop a coin down on the other side of life conveniently forgotten,
Take a look - it could be you that's standing there, lost and lonely
and forsaken!
Who is he standing there? fighting cold and despair!
Why doesn't anybody care?

People walking on the other side of life, can you hear my melody?
Lonesome Melody!

Yvonne Lyons

Heavenly Heights

Dawn chariots of cloud
Hoofing it down the scudding wind
Race on forever across the world of blueness
To shadow furtively the lower green of earth
Wakening in throbbing blinks between the grey.
Cease not the turning of thy carriage wheels
Scarce kissing the hilltops of thy journey
Floating ecstatically into space-oblivion.
We shall do likewise - our time is brief
And there is no returning

J. J. MacGregor

Punishment

You've been vulnerable, violated, viciously abused,
Humiliated, beaten, battered and bruised.
Understandably shaken, shattered; subdued,
And frightened, forced and furious -
How could you become so used?

C. Beardmore

Pilgrimage

Father died in '43, the middle of the war,
He had a sudden headache and collapsed upon the floor.
I was only thirteen and didn't know the score,
But twenty-four hours later Father was no more.

Father died at 43, a soldier in his prime.
He just overdid things and went before his time.
He left me lofty mountains I must singly climb
Without a Father's guidance or yet his extra dime.

After nearly fifty years I saw his lonely tomb
In the annex graveyard, because there wasn't room
To bury a mere stranger, many miles from home,
In the nearness of the Church from which he hadn't come.

I never saw his body. The funeral I missed.
I never said my Farewell to the man I never kissed.
They sent me off to Granny by a steam engine that hissed
With a once-white hanky clutched within my fist.

Just what would have happened, if he'd lived a normal span?
Would his life have made me a different sort of man?
Would at least his ashes lie beside our Gran,
So I could put a flower there, anytime I can?

Patrick Davies

Racist

Once there was a black boy walking down the street,
He had ragged clothes on and no shoes upon his feet,
Once there was a white boy walking down the street,
He was dressed as royalty with new shoes upon his feet,
There were definitely differences at each side of the road,
The black boy's grass was long and the white boy's had been mowed,
On one side the houses glistened and looked pretty in the spring,
On the other they were dirty and looked horrible and grim,
How many spiteful angry snowballs have been thrown?
How many dirty looks and fights had happened on this street?
Something bad always happened when both sides agreed to meet,
But despite all the anger there was one friendship going on,
Between the two most different boys Simon and Tom,
They smiled and laughed together despite the colour of their skin,
And I just hope that one day their two peopled side is going to win,
People are really trying hard to get the message through,
It does not matter what colour your skin is, what matters is you.

Karen Waite

Valhalla

Their names are carved in stone all over the World.
Heaven is where they will be. Eighteen to what ever age, it made
no difference.

Ready always to serve their country.
Obstacles were no hindrance in their quest for victory.
Youth; too many died in theirs.
Adored by everyone, family, friends, and comrades.
Loyal in their allegiance to their sovereign and country.

Barracks were their home, except in battle.
Religion - each to their own belief.
Identification; only by their tags.
They were all active, nimble and strong. Ideologist, everyone.
Sacrifice; they gave their lives for the free world.
Hammock: used by the Navy for a bed.

Lament by those of us who survived. Every one a hero
Gallant to all who knew them.
Immaculate always; but difficult in battle.
Offered their services willingly, without thought for their own safety
Names we must never forget. "WE WILL REMEMBER THEM".

Stanley Naylor

551

The Dunblane Disaster

The moment you are born, A candle sets alight
And stands up tall and proud, In view of every sight
For everyone to see and love, And cherish in its prime.
Occasionally the candle flickers, And will blow out in time.
But unfortunately every now and then, A whirlwind will arise
And knock the candle off its stand, To leave behind the cries.
But the children of Dunblane, Were not knocked off their stands.
They were thrown across the room, By murderous and killing hands.
The only question left right now, Is why-oh-why-oh-why?
Why a class of six year-olds, So innocent should die?
Their flames once stood so tall, And burnt so strong and bright.
But now are drowned among the tears, At such a ghastly sight.
Why such a man had ever lived, Is far beyond my say.
But my love, thoughts and prayers, Go out to Dunblane today.

Caroline M. Lamerton

Wingless Flight

When I was a child,
I dreamt of a beautiful life
for they told me I could fly -
when I was a child and I could *dream*.

When I grew up,
I realised I couldn't fly
for I had no wings -
when I grew up and I could *think*.

Now that I am old,
I discovered I can fly
even without wings
now that I am old - and I can only *dream* . . .

Gabriel Zembylas

Through a Glass Darkly

Look not, fair lady, in thy glass to see
Thy beauty there, as frail as winter's frost,
Lest there the lady looking back at thee,
With brooding eyes, should love thee, and be lost.
Then, in those eyes, where heaven once was sought,
Reflections of thyself shall constant shine;
And, in those lips, for benedictions wrought,
Self-adoration shall importune thine.
Yet earthly vanity hath holy grace:
That Love we crave, and blindly seek in vain,
Reflected was in that lost, lovely face;
Time-tarnished now the glass showeth not again.
Forsaken heart, seek thou the vision still,
Till love, at last perfected, yield Love's will.

Bernard Brown

Autumn Jewels

As through the woods I gaze and see
Autumn unfolding magic all around me,
Leaves in silence descend upon my head,
Carpeting the ground to soften my tread.

A squirrel gathering its winter store,
Scurries off, then back for more.
Raindrops, that fall upon the trees, now seep
Their branches, in jewelled perfection, weep.

Soon they will be standing bare
Exposed to the winter's chilling air.
Rays of the sun, when the rain gives way
Brilliant orange take the last glimpse of day.

A harvest mouse slips silently by
A wary fox, so sleek, so sly.
A badger sniffs the evening air
Wood pigeons cooing haven't a care.

Soon the moonlight, casting its light so pale,
Will cover everything with its silver veil.
And through the silence of the night,
Around me, autumn's magic, sheer delight!

J. R. Saundercock

Muttering Retreats

Torn in half between the memories and the temptation.
Like little seeds of passion killed by the storm.
Like a clown's smile that drowns the desperation.
Like a snowman melting in the April sun.

A thought or two - a desperate denial
The falling star won't make the wish come true.
A lonely child deprived of its salvation
A single tear, the asylum of the heart.

Pray my friend - life, it is so cruel
As the sunset melts across the evening sky
For the spark of madness hidden in the sadness
For the mermaid songs to cherish once again.

Galina Davis

An Epitaph to a Fool

Charlie made no secrets of his hopes and fears
Hoping for much happiness, and a lot of long years
Attention to detail, was his guiding light,
Reality and the essentials, he was apt to lose sight
Looking to something, perhaps castles in the sky
Invariably disillusioned, and wondering why
Expecting too much, in trying to fulfil his dreams
    and refusing to accept all that life seems
Wanting perfection in every thought and deed
Always a struggle, to satisfy that need
Looking and questioning in every possible way
Keeping on striving day after weary day
Eventually he learned, after giving his all
Removed from this life, he lost his soul

The found God didn't need his worldly goods
    and he only took his soul
    and so it closed his little pose
    and asked why live at all!

Charlie Walker

Morning Glory

Early morning sunshine in rays of golden light
Sparkle on the waters of the loch
The hills rise up in rugged lines
And by the curving bay
The ebbing tides leave sandy tracks
Glinting in each sunbeam's ray
Fields brightly massed with wild flowers
The silence broken only by the curlew's cry
The trees forming their green bowers
A picture of beauty set by nature to delight
A mix of gentle colours to please the eye
Topped by a brilliant blue
Of skies stretching to horizons new.

Hazel Smith

Smoke (A Rondeau)

The smoke from
            your havana curls an 'S'.
        Blase, amidst the blitz of
    my distress, where shellfire of
recriminations burst,
        You smile, exhaling
            easy lies rehearsed -
                A smog of falsehood,
        failing to impress. Once,
    captive to the charms of
your finesse, I loved you, let
your blandishments caress
        My heart, and kissed the lying lips that pursed
            To blow the smoke. Now, constrained
                by fidelity's duress, I own that,
                though I love, I like you less, And
    coward-like would leave you if I durst,
        Abandoning illusions fondly nursed
To evaporate to nothingness -
            Just like the smoke.

Kathleen Collier

Hesitation

An important person passed my way
and I didn't know quite what to say.
I wanted to say how much I cared,
but I felt really shy, so I didn't dare.
I wanted to say you're not alone,
but I find it easier to talk on the phone.
I wanted to say I think you're great,
but feared that friendship might turn to hate.
I wanted to say how much you're admired,
but decided instead to gaze into the fire
and dream of what I would like to say,
when that important person passes my way.

Katrina M. Anderson

Remembrance

The garden of remembrance was full of flowers in splendid bloom,
Their perfect shapes, their fragrance seemed to pass away all too soon.
Yet implanted in our memory are seeds of what they used to be,
And in our eyes they are still there for everyone to see.

Their length of stay — not long, still could not have been more sweet,
Each morning, noon and night they stood to wave and greet.
Their petals now have faded and the flowers are all gone,
But their time of blooming in our heart lives on, and on, and on.

The ground now is dormant, a space of barren soil is seen,
But soon the earth will break, to let through new shoots of green.
Thus is nature's true wonder, that although nothing can really last,
There is no such thing as 'ended', for new life comes from what
has passed.

Pym Ruperti

The Stain on the Floor

Behind the glass panel,
The body lies motionless on the floor.
Doctors run from room to room.
From room to body.
From body to ambulance.
Next door, the old lady's breathing is stifled.
Yet, the child continues to play.
When we enter the room -
The window is open, and his life is let out.
Will he be remembered by anyone else except the people that day?
The people whose last memory of him,
Was the stain on the floor.

Catherine Sargeant

The Killing Smile

Glow
with the sun on your cheeks
Pale is so sickly and weak
Strengthen
your colour and worship the circle that
smiles

Slow
with its rays it breaks through
warmly caressing your skin
Perspiring
with pleasure you throw back your head
feeling good

Kill
off your menial troubles
relaxing you sleep in the heat
Parched
you wake up hot and bothered gasping
to drink

Life's
bottle will soon be empty
breathing will shortly cease
Glowing
you throw back your head
Will others learn when you're dead?

Lucy Sealy

Love

Each day goes by and the next one comes
While I continue mourning, for her presence sorely missed,
Those disturbingly vivid memories
Continue to hog my confused mind.

Her touch so nourishing, her looks unique,
Her soothing voice used make me weak.
Her confidence, her devoted love for me,
I saw no simple reason for it not to be.

It seemed so natural,
The sex, the gelling, the sense of a combined unit
The truths of real love.
Until one selfish bastard took it all away.

She lay across my legs with her head resting on my breast,
She had been stabbed repeatedly on her stomach,
her eyes hovered in her head,
And gradually she dwindled away and my heart with her.

Mark Phillips

Let Her Know Love Again

She was a child before we were born
Now she is helpless old and forlorn
She was a bride long years ago
Walking in beauty cheeks aglow
She was a mother babes at her breast
Caring for others giving her best

She is a woman salute her for this
Now she is withered harder to kiss
Speak to her gently nurse her with pride
Now as she waits to sail with the tide
Ours are the last hands she will ever hold
Let her know love again now she is old

Mary Sadie Law (nee Hay)

Bewitched

With the softest look in your eye
With your warmest smile
Our lives touched one another
But for the briefest moment
Even that was long enough to know
I will always love you
As you bewitched me

But my life's not worth living now that you've gone
I can never replace the love that I've lost
I've looked and I've tried
But there's no one out there
That comes close to your beauty, your kindness, your warmth
So I'm destined to live all alone

The emptiness bit, it hurt and it scared
The pain now is easing with the time that has passed
But the love that I gave you will always be there
With the passing of time the weeks and the years
I will always love you
'Cause you bewitched me.

P. Booth

Aimer C'Est Mourir Un Peu

When hurt, love is a night-closed flower
Closing petals tight around its heart,
Knowing with the first cold stinging shower
Come storms of pain and desolation dark.
When wrecking winds do force the calyx open
They scatter pollen far where nothing grows,
Then stinging rains reclaim the desolation,
and sunshine's warmth a stronger, wilder rose.

Kathleen McCormack

Easter.

I lie
Cold,
Wrapped,
Still
On a cold stone slab.
I feel nothing
But, I am awake
In the dankness of this cave
++++++++++++++++++++++++++

I am wounded.
Pierced with holes
But no blood runs,
No pain feels.
It is still . . .
Silent . . .
Almost peaceful . . .
Strange . . . almost restful

In shock . . . I . . .
I am . . . realising
I . . . who am I . . . ?
I AM I. I AM
Before the world began.
I AM
The world's creator . . .GOD'S SON
+++++++++++++++++++++++++++

I . . . Have work to do.
Energy I have . . .
I must need.
It is I.
I AM ENERGY.
I confound and explode my body
Into a new thing.

I move, I walk,
I am still, I talk.
I AM I before the world began

CREATOR,
GOD'S SON,
REDEEMER OF MAN.

G. M. Haviland

The Witch

For her beloved grandchildren

I saw her picking cowslips, and marked her where she stood,
She never knew I watched her, whilst hiding in the wood.
Her skirt was brightest crimson, and black her pointed hat,
her broomstick lay beside her, I'm positive of that.
Her chin was sharp and pointed, her eyes I don't know,
for when she turned towards me, I thought it best to go!

Glenis K. Glover (Haxey)

Heresy

Extinction was forever, yet geneticists today
Try to clone God's animals, from clumps of DNA.
And if Science should succeed, making ev'ry living thing
Now God-Mankind could be well pleased - and then file everything
When a kind became extinct, scientists would not fret -
They'd simply build another one and make it better yet.
And then they'd ask, 'But, are our lives the best?' -
Then file and check their DNA - just like all the rest.
Our DNA would be improved - New Man would be complete
But soon our new creations, would make us obsolete.
New Man, he would hunt us down and start killing Humankind
Just like the book by Shelley 'bout a certain Frankenstein.

Andrew Healy

Reflection

Time to reflect upon the past, at my life, and what I have done.
A tear for the loved ones I have lost, to the friends and relatives gone.
When one is young, time seems to drag, speed is of the essence,
it's not till it's gone we realize, we should live our lives in the present.
Make the most of what you have, our elders used to say,
I never thought I would echo those sentiments one day.
I love this house, and the gardens and I love the view,
so many plans, and ideas, and so much I want to do.
I'm not one who gives way to panic, but must admit that now,
I feel a sense of urgency, to get jobs done somehow.
If I plant a tree, or buy some bulbs, or get some seeds to sow,
will I get the chance, will I have the time to watch the magic grow?
To sit beneath the apple tree, the branches heavy with their flowers,
with birds singing harmoniously, between the sunshine and showers.
A shaft of light pierces through the clouds, a rainbow begins to form,
a wondrous sight for all to see, after a summer storm.
Time to reflect has now past, the mood has gone away,
with so much beauty all around, on such a glorious day.
Let's not waste our time, but enjoy what's now,
make the most of everything.
Life is precious, so take care, remember the joy that laughter can bring.

Yvonne O'Gara

The Citadel of Gozo

The knights of good Saint John
Built here a citadel,
High upon this rocky hill -
Fortress walls and steep stone steps,
Such unexpected beauty -
As gazing out across the patchwork fields
Bright flowers are everywhere in bloom
In this Mediterranean spring.

People walk along the road
Like bobbing birds below.
And in the distance one white sail
Glides slowly on the sea,
Catching the brightness of the sun.

Did some great giant long ago
Flatten these Gozo hills?
For they are as table tops
To spread a feast upon.
And hills and sea are met in a haze of blue,
As through the air the Angelus bells ring,
Calling the faithful people to their prayer.

Barbara Higgins

Grandmother's Bedroom Suite

My own dear Grandmother's bedroom suite
Is very dear to me,
It holds such special memories
Of happiness and glee.

She left it to me when she died,
And I treasure it with love
Knowing what each drawer contained
Her beads, her purse, her gloves.

The washstand with its jug and bowl
In the corner stood
And when the sun shone through the glass,
It brought the red out in the wood.

This beautiful redwood bedroom suite
Will come to you one day
Never sell it for its value
A more princely sum could not repay.

She would like for you to have it,
And I know just what she's say
I love you like I loved your Nannie,
That's right - your "Nannie JJ."

Joan Jelley

"Mummy's Not Dead! She's in Heaven"

My mum went to live in heaven last year.
She went ever so quickly, without a tear.
They took her in an ambulance, Daddy went as well.
When he came back he was very upset, I could tell.

A week after Mummy had gone to heaven,
I spotted men in black coats, in the church yard,
Today was Sports Day - doing my best was hard,
Because Daddy never came, and I wasn't taken home till seven.

There are trees in heaven aren't there!
Of course — came the reply.
Good - she'll be able to breathe then,
And I'll try not to cry.

I can see heaven Daddy through my binoculars.
And guess what! Mummy's driving a car.
She doesn't have to pay for it, and petrol is free.
Be careful Mum! You nearly hit a tree!

We've got photos of our mum,
And to us she'll stay forever young.
Of course - she will live for ever.
When I get there, she'll waiting to meet me, whatever the weather.

Geoff Payne

September

September morns and winter mists
It's been four months since your lips
I kissed.
With open arms and beating heart
Four months to long to be apart.
It can't go on it must stop now, I
feel the sweat upon my brow.
I call her name it was in vain, I
call again, again, again.
God help me now your strength I need, and
give me guidance this I plead
For I was young never to be old, let this
my story now be told.
I came to help and try and solve, a problem
That was centuries old.
But nothing I could do would change, the ways
of people old and strange. And so to them my
life I give and pray it was so they could live.

Brian Hobbs

New Year's Resolutions

I vowed to clear all clutter up - it has to go I said
I turned out drawers and cupboards too and laid my treasures on the bed.
There were loads of photos, slides and books
Recipes for modern cooks.
Knitting patterns for all sizes, scents and soaps
Might do for prizes.
China cats, dogs and mice - now what is this?
Looks rather nice.
I put it back, can't part with that - my daughter made that pretty mat.
These animals look too appealing - my character is so revealing.
How can I throw these things away?
I put them back for another day.
The photos too - there's far too many - I really cannot part with any.
My doll stares back - you wouldn't dare
The memories are all laid bare.
I've just unearthed a long lost token
My New Year's vows alas are broken.

Phyl Jennings

Thick Black Muck

Another oil spill has hit the news
Which way will greedy man choose
Thick Black Oil Floats on water
What will we leave for son or daughter?
As fish gasp, choke and oil drink
One wonders what they think
Birds' feathers coated with oil
Unable to fly lest they fall
Fishermen losing job after job
Now a cockle shortage makes me sob
God created a beautiful world
But man is bent to destroy it all
Nature is balanced - perfectly on land
The oil spills and coats the sand
What, I wonder will we leave for our children.

Meg Gaspar

Lullaby

Sleep Sleep
It will be alright
Wrap up your fears in the veil of the night
Bind them up tightly and throw them away
To the care of tomorrow to the light of the day

I've watched you in waking sensing your pain
Your loving and living your trying in vain
Stop all this struggle give up the fight
Surrender your soul to the arms of the night

Healing the potion soothing the balm
Envelope your spirit in its magical charm
Strengthen your will as soon as you may
For night's nearly over it soon will be day

Sleep Sleep

Tony Nolan

The Luring Pipes of Pan

Pandora created by the Gods of yore,
To settle a matter of battle score,
To punish mankind for his theft of fire,
You came to earth with a mission dire.
Endowed with beauty, art and charm,
You came to do us mortals harm.
Curiosity opened wide the lid,
Releasing ills your box had hid.
Recall those scabs, the weeping sore,
The wasted limbs, and many more.
The mental anguish, shame and blame,
For man has learned he has no claim.
To pyrite your eternal flame,
There are no winners in your hellish game.
Pyrite, Fools Gold, Angel Dust, Witches Milk or Devils Grip,
Takes us on a lethal trip.
Recall the luring pipes of Pan,
Restore the gift of life to man.

Maureen Corrigan

War Zone

You go down the war - torn streets,
Strewn with death.
Loneliness, sickness, and poverty follow you,
Day in, day out,
Don't look back,
There is only death and danger there.

A door opens, another dying friend
Is taken into the light,
Leaving you alone in the dark street,
With your fear and great grief.

But, Please, look forward,
With hope, to happiness and love,
Life and all its treasures
Are waiting for you at the end of the street,
Grasp them firmly with both hands.

Wars, must be ended!
Not by weapons, but by caring hearts,
With thoughts for others, in words and deeds,
So that you, your family, and friends,
Can walk, once more in the bright streets of peace.

Jean Cooper

My Brother

I have a brother
Who is like no other.
He kicks me here,
He kicks me there.
The way Mum treats him it isn't fair.
If he went out on the street,
and murdered someone at Mum's feet.
She would tell him to run along and play,
and to never to do it again.
If I murdered someone at her feet.
She would take me to court,
Hoping for defeat!
THAT'S WHY I HATE MY BROTHER!

Sheryl Ellis

The Space Age

The Moon has been invaded,
No longer is he alone.
Men who ride the universe
Have taken him for their own.
He who has shone his light upon us
And taken us all from the dark,
Has become another object to explore
And leave their mark.
Perhaps when men have conquered him
And all the world knows his worth,
They will leave him alone,
And be content
With the wonderful things on earth.

Gilderson

Thoughtfulness

If I should die before I'd lived,
    I'd wonder why I'd been born.
Just to see sorrow, hurt and fear,
    No fun, no laughter, just scorn.

If I should die before I'd lived,
    I'd wonder why the sun shone above.
When all my life had been darkness, no light,
    And in my life, no love.

Linda M. MacKenzie

Glory Summer's Evening

The red sun sets
At another days ending
And the dew wets
The lands of all God's sendings

The cold air turns our breath into
Heavens dust before our eyes
The country side surrounding
Now silver tells no lies
Steep slopes echo laughs and cry's
All sounding of glory days hear and past by

The evening star rises
And shy is the moon as it creeps from behind clouds
Each little star surprises
As they form together in crowds
All in unique shapes and sizes

Glory days hear and past by now fading
Like the shy moon into the dusky evening of our lives

Tonya Kehoe

"To My Mother"

You are to me, so very special,
Like no-one else could be,
You're part of my world
And part of my heart
But mostly part of me.
You brought me into this very world
And then you showed the way,
You've always cared and listened
Whenever-night or day.
You're the one who gave birth to me,
Which no-one else could do
And that is why I want to say
So many thanks to you.
I want to say so many things
Which I don't know how to do
But I think there's a line which seems
Them up,
And that is
"I Love You."

Ciara Kelly

A Love Song

I will build for you a dwelling house
On a sunny wave lapped shore.
Fashioned in love and built in hope, what can I offer more.

I will walk beside you all my days,
keeping in step, and in hand in hand,
Sorrows and joys leaving marks on our lives like footprints in the sand.

I will love you through the sunlight the sunlit years,
Our children playing by our side,
Youth retreating from our grasp, like the ebbing tide.

I will set my love to music in lyrical rhapsody
and sing it soft and sing it low like the whispering sea.

I will sit with you in the twilight
when our hair is streaked with grey,
watching the fingers of moonlight touching the silvery spray.

I will love you 'til the end of time not buried with the grave,
on and on for evermore, like the endless wave.

Patricia Rose

Secret Love

All us lasses want to know.
What would you say if I let my love show.

My love's a secret to all but a few.
What would you say if ever you knew.

I think these thoughts for the entire day.
As I turn around to look your way.

When I think of you I'm lost in dreams.
Each time I see you the more my love seems.

If I tell you will you want me too.
If you reject me what will I do.

You stare at me in such a way.
That you make my feeling go astray.

My love for you has grown so true.
A bond I've made to share with you.

So sweetheart you know you're mine.
One day our love shall be entwined.

Now take my hand and walk my side.
To show our love could never die.

Cecile L. Hermine

They Ask Me

They ask me brusquely
If I wrote, am writing, or write anything.
My answer is three brusque no's.
"Wasted talent", they sneer, and leave.

"Wasted talent!"
What talent have I,
Lost between two languages?
I winked at Telugu,
And English winks at me
A bilingual tragedy -
I have no key.

"What are you writing?"
"Words."
But words are words are words,
Not great writing,
Though they pass for it at present.

In the beginning was the word in the West,
The OUM of the East is not even a word,
But a strange creative sound
The little of Hindu wisdom.

N. A. Yajulu

Dunblane Angels

Comfort these Dunblane angels in your arms Lord and welcome them to their new home,
Friends for the rest of eternity, together in heaven their new place to explore and roam.
They were wiped out before their little lives began, without a chance or a second thought,
For their grieving families it's a nightmare never to end, and a lifetime they'll never forget.

These heartbroken families are numbed with grief, with the realization their wee little loved ones are gone,
Their minds tell them they could be dreaming but their hearts tell them they're wrong.
We the world can only imagine their sorrows and try to share their pain,
As we picture the faces of these little children who'll never return home again.

Their stricken families brought together by their grief, wishing it was all a mistake,
Alone in their thoughts and wondering why their sleeping children will never again wake.
And never again to hear their voices or watch them playing again their school yard,
Emptiness fills their souls with tremendous grief unable to come to terms with their loss or their broken hearts.

Paul O'Brien

Untitled

As surely as houses will fall when built on sand,
I know dear God you have taken my hand!
Since I made my abode in this pleasant land
My gratitude's constantly abound.
For your earth is endowed with
wondrous creations
The magnificent seas —
The hard working bees so zealous
for the task you gave them —
This momentous task, one year
or seasons, I ask, Oh! that I
Could be like them
Their product just a thimble of
such goodness, the quality high
no matter where they labour.
This tiny creatures energy
seemingly lost but so blessed
Could be a lesson not to our cost
but to our eternal good and Your praise

William Turner

Mum's Hot

Gran is sleeping
Dad's still eating
The baby's crying
Mum is sighing -
For the days past
When she married Dad at last!
And was full of love and dreams.
Not laden down, by mortgages and schemes.
For bedrooms, nurseries and a vegetable garden
Wall paper, paint and waiting for peltry to harden,
Poor Mum thinks of what might have been.
The days she like to be seen -
In her white bikini in the beach.
Those days have gone are out of reach!

Shirley Spearing

Shreds of a Misadventure

Looking down your nose at me
Tell me what you want to see
Watching me fail and squirm
Waiting for me to finally learn
That I am not I

All my life I struggle through
And I see you laughing too
Hate like raindrops falling down
Holding my breath while I drown
Why I don't know why

Feel the stillness of your stare
Trapping me in its lonesome lair
Break my soul what I have left
The stain shows clear of your theft
A lie more than a lie

Vicky Lee Strachan

Give Me Love

Give me love as I am smashing your car
Give me love as I'm braking, your rear view mirror window
Give me love as I'm unhanging your car doors
Give me love as I'm levering out your brake pasts
Give me love as I'm smashing out your bumper
Give me love as I'm gratifying and vandalizing your doors
Give me love as I'm recycling your boots
Give me love as I'm beating up your gromy
Give me love as I'm killing anyone and everyone you ever cereal about
Give me love as I'm crow baring your already defined dissolute space
Give me love as I knock you unconscious and send you to outer space
Give me love as I take everything you ever had
Give me love as I make a fool of you
Give me love as I am jealous of you
Give me love as you or I have never had
Give me love even though I'm in the natural front
Give me love even though I don't deserve it

Karen Jeevaratnam

A Child's Cry

Watching on TV
What's happening outside,
Killing, wars, starvation
But people lied,
They told me that everything was alright
But it's not,
People fight.
Petty wars over who's land is who's,
Why don't they give it up and move?
The answer is simple
It's as easy as 1, 2, 3.
Stop being greedy,
Stop accusing.
Yes there is a key
To open the door,
I will treat you
As you treat me,
See the answer's easy!

Laura Rowley

The Rose Garden

Can there not be a secret place such as a rose garden
wherein a soul may walk at ease
where peace prevails
tranquillity fills one's being
until the soul reharmonises
a hidden place where love meets love to merge as one

Can there not be a rose garden as seen within the mind
where a soul may walk at peace
where the rosy pinks of myriad vibrant petals
heal the soul
sustain its needs
and gradually release its withering shoots

Can there not be a rose garden
with sunny bench 'pon which to sit and dream
a place where honeybees still hum as birds do sing
and cooing doves murmur in the noonday heat
where shadows soothe beneath the sheltering boughs of trees
is there not a rose garden for every maid and man

Rose Helen Symes

"Chills Me"

I'll come over
sober
just to see you
portrayed as a babe

White moister
on a warm sommersday
my own icecream in the shade
and your sister will come over
complaining somebody stole her Rover
but she is happy
and disparately untrue and not to so unlike you
she tells you stories you've heard before
but her eyes is bloody sore
and I imagine her tongue is bored
'cause last night I scored

But I seem to remember
me and you
faithful through the whole of December

Erik Vibe Simonsen

The Rainbow

Every time after the rain,
A rainbow comes to play,
Different colours in the sky
Red, yellow, blue, and green up so high.

Every time after the rain,
When you look out you may see a rainbow.
Dazzling rays of colours
smiling down upon you.
Then in the evening the rainbow fades away.

Sarah Lane

Ode to a Drunk

A sober man knows where his wife might be
A drunk man is too drunk to care
A fool doesn't know to worry
But the wise man knows where
Who are you?
Since you're not the fool . . .
You're the intelligent man
Who is ignorant of himself
Who buys an illusion in a bottle
An illusion of mirth
But it is only an illusion
For what you really feel is guilt
You're sad and pathetic
Causing nothing but pain
Who doesn't know where he is
Nor if he has a wife at all
And underneath all your bravado
You're the "tin god"

Susan McAuley

Marmaduke Fat Cat

Marmaduke fat cat from kitchen window sill,
Sat smacking his whiskers from mid morning fill,
He green eyed the garden with feline disdain,
His working day ruined by troublesome rain.
With professional traverse avoiding footprints of water,
Carelessly imprinted by someone's young daughter,
Marmaduke fat cat headed for favourite repose,
To his linen cupboard office, to luxury he knows,
Satsuma striped fat cat, rained off, hence no play,
But a desk-bound relegation for a drizzly Friday.
For a last calculation before sleep he did pause.
Counting never past twenty, for he owns no more claws,
Proposal resolved, what's for six o'clock dish,
Marmaduke the happy, it's Friday, it's fish.
Cinnamon striped dreamer, nil intention of toiling,
Curled into blankets, above water tank boiling.

Marion McCall

Western Trail

There's some oak trees in the distance, walk till you come to them
Turn right and take the little path into the hidden glen
Wander through the beauty of nature undisturbed
The butterflies fly freely and the birds are unperturbed
There's thousands of varieties of grass and flowers wild
And the breeze that blows across this glen is gentle, warm and mild.
The peace is so becoming you will breathe the air and smile
Sit amidst the long cool grass and ponder for a while
List while you're drifting, the birds will sing to you
The bees will hum a tune and the trees will whisper too.
Stroll a little further you'll come by a babbling stream
Hear it as it gurgles through the rocks into your dream.
Hidden by the shadows of the ferns and shady plants
Watch the antics of the spiders, the beetles and the ants
The fish make shivering circles as they surface for the fly.
Kingfishers swoop to catch them, silhouettes against the sky.
Then homeward bound you'll follow the path from peace and rest.
The clouds are burning embers, as the sun sets in the West.

Sandra Guthrie

Soul of Life and Spirit

Shotguns are nasty, Fires burn their peat
A knife in the chest, a heart cease to beat.
Open wounds leak their blood, Life soon runs dry
The limits are reached, Your body will die.

If your soul is caring, loving and free
Enter the destination, smiling with glee
But if you are evil, murderous and bad
You will fall beneath us, with no safety pad

Our lives may be worthless, we may mourn our dead
The key to our hearts, the voice in our head
Violence and disaster, fill life with anger
Retreat from our battles, life can last longer.

Ricky Gall

Grainan Alech

Stone on stone
Winnowed by ancient tools.
Moulding history
Stone circling stone
Distant voices interrupting the wind
Lost and faded in past mists
A stronghold a lookout
Imprinted on the moss landscape
Walking here
Remembering the smell of damp earth
Under bare feet
Looking into bearded faces of ancestors
Feeling the vibration of past existence
Emergence of life began here.
In stone and earth and moss
Beginning the circle.

Ivy M. Jamison

Roll of Thunder

In the distance cries, a roll of thunder
   Can hardly hear myself, above the waves
In the distant skies, a cloud of anger
   How many of mankind can we give save.

The birds are flying south, the birds are leaving
   Is more danger coming? Are we doomed?
Did we make this happen? Us, the humans
   Is this the life for us, which we ourselves have groomed?

Maybe, if we cleanse our souls, in the water
   Maybe then we can all, start anew
We can all join hands, sons and daughters
   Like new flowers soaking in morning dew

Come little children, see what we've done to you
   we couldn't even get the art of killing right
Instead there's suffering, it becomes your friend
   As the days fade into night

In the distance cries, a roll of thunder
   can hardly hear me screaming, above the waves
In the distant skies, a cloud of anger
   How many of mankind should be saved?

Amber S. Kelly

Jewels of the Earth

If you have seen the sun on high
Sparkling in the day-time sky
Looked up to see the moonlight glow
Then jewels of the earth you'll know.
No greater scene upon this earth
Is Mother Nature giving birth
The budding trees in early spring
Butterflies and birds on wing
Snowballs billowing as they fly
As winds blow swiftly across the sky
The pitter patter of gentle rain
Snowflakes and a fine glowing through a window pane.
All these things are treasures aglow
Jewels of the earth, for us on show.

Pat Howard

Action Man

The great man walks in with expanded chest
Action man, demolition man, builder - the rest
What needs doing today he nods
furniture moving, gardening, sweeping jobs?

The jobs I need doing, all cause disruption
so he thinks with a smiling interruption
He's swift and agile, quick as lightning
done with a flurry, and to him quite exciting

He enjoys the challenge of these, my chores
He'll do anything to help, so as not to be bored
Good job he doesn't claim any pay
Alexander the great, is just one today

Doreen Hough

What Is a Mother

A mother is sweet, loving and kind
Also a friend I think you'll find.
A mother is someone you can trust,
And joke with if you feel you must.
She'll tend to you when you are sad,
And in the end she'll make you glad.
A mother is someone you can't beat,
And a better one you'll never meet.
A mother may criticise,
But really she's an angel in disguise.
She'll tend to you, when you're young or old,
Whether it is fine or cold.
She'll always be on your side,
And in her you can confide.
She'll comfort you when nightmares make you scream,
But she'll join in the fun when you dream.
Let's not forget grandma's too,
As they deserve something for all they do.
So as we go along our merry way,
Let's show our love every single day.

Jackie Ollett

Sonnet to John Clare

There was a post long ago called Clare
of late become a legend and I dare
To say these poets you can not compare
All great in their respective right or wrong
Suffered mortally although in their rhymes
A touch of madness heighten up the song
Which can be so repeated time on time
And very simple, thus defying sense
Southey - Coleridge Shakespeare lies Betjeman
To name a few who raised the heart of men
To me this clare out shadows and for where
He said with pointing I do not agree
Stops commas colours were not meat for me
Read once again his verse and you will see.

D. M. Pearson

Untitled

Fly! Fly! I can fly, I can fly!
I'm in the air, I'm in the trees,
darting and dipping between the leaves.
I hear the buzz of buzzing bees
beneath me, and the breeze
lifts to the sky, so high,
no one can hear my cry.

Wings! Wings! I have wings, I have wings!
I soar above, I dive below,
drift and float where the clean winds blow,
where hills of cloud as soft as snow
support me, come and go,
swirl in circles and rings.
With me the skylark sings.

Bruce Ogilvie

"I Love You"

For many years it has been asked,
"What is love?"
Many have tried to answer,
but to no real avail.
That is until I met you.
One is in love,
When their love is their life
And their life evolves around their loved one.
And in the case of me and you,
this is definitely true.

My love for you is eternal.
Like life itself, it continues on forever ever after death

And on this day I give you these lines,
instead of beautiful gifts,
and hope that they will show you
I love you more than life itself.

Jason Neary

The Fire

A spark it was which awakened the beast,
Stirred from its slumber to devour a feast.
It stormed through the house and crept up the walls,
From the roof it uttered crackling calls.

The flaming tongue wicked the house clear,
Leaving behind its black sooty sheen.
As I look through the cage where the Beast once stayed,
It looks empty, dark, cold and decayed.

Through the charcoaled window was a blackened box.
The debris left by the Beast astounds and shocks.
The silence radiated from the ashes,
On its way to another the beast dashes.

C. L. Morris

Reawakening

Winter depression has taken its toll,
taped into the very source of my soul.
New life is dawning like a fresh spring morning.
Watery sunshine wearily greets the day,
Trying to say: "I'm here to stay!"

With a whirling icy wind, winter challenges
Spring to a duel,
Reawakening begins new shoots appear,
Strong and inspired by the warming earth.
Beautiful blossoming buds, burst into life.
Winter breathes a frosty torrent of air across the country.
Springs sunshine shimmers behind dreary clouds,
Melting the menacing frost.

Spring has won the duel and winter lost,
Smiles an grey faces - light up the cocoons
We spin ourselves every winter.
Like caterpillars we transform ourselves into happy,
Shining people.
Reawakened from winter slumber.

Katharine H. D. Louw

Untitled

Majestic fragile, surviving waters of life
A clog to her surface, shock, hinder the species
Ocean of time, so pure scarred, survival is hers
Natured creatures in her bosom, dead, scattered
plumage bright colours in shreds
Grief to the heart-strings, a lesson in wisdom
Craving for the Oily black monster
It's turning our wheels, it's the love of our life
Blind to the fumes, children in distressed
Challenge extinction, now is the hour.
Life, beauty mysteries. will be music and song.
Heaven on earth, a shinning so peaceful.
Mother earth, centuries of life, greedy for food
tragedy of chemicals, space is the aim
feeling her roots shrinking of wild-life
Silence so dismal, hollow - sad thoughts
Major step forward will alter the course
the loud is now, no backward thoughts
tranquillity, peace will be our joyful reward.

Dympna McManus

Him

He was standing on the docks,
Watching the sun go down,
The moon rose behind him,
His black shadowy figure emerged, in the sea.

A light wind blew,
His shirt waved in the wind.
His hair moved out of place,

Then he dived into the moon lit sea,
Then after a moment he emerged on
The surface of the water,
Then swam to the sandy shore.

L. Back

Still

Sweet death
although the taste I had of you was all encompassing and wild
I know something sweeter still
I know something that burns my soul more
that takes me on higher voyages
and deeper plunges

I have tasted a love that made your slaked wings
seem flushed and fat like a rosebud
I have seen a love that still did not bear your mark
on its forehead
I saw
I live
still

sweet death
do not tell me your lies
I do not need them
I have lived them
I do
still

Line Neesgaard

Today's Reality

The strings of our sanity grow over thin.
They become worn, are frayed,
With other peoples lack of care, and
The strings need care so they may be played.

And the stage of our hearts find little comfort,
In the fact that so few graze the floor.
So few that are worthy to perform,
So many the audience never saw.

And the novels that our faces show,
Become less interesting as the days go by.
But still they tell our stories,
The ceaseless sagas till the day we die.

And the world becomes a painting,
An item to be bought and sold.
Observes smile, a pretty picture,
But the painted men stay cold.

Anna Morgan

Evolution

Evolution is a tide causing waves through time:-
Deprivation becomes a way of life, some find.
Every bad driver downs a few more scotches.
Violence has evicted the newly formed neighbourhood watches.
Even hopes for peace become those abandoned packages in the city
somewhere black-clad assassins dish out "justice" then expect our pity.
The bogeyman (just a dream) comes out from under our beds
And becomes our family, a friend, or neighbour instead.
The poor blackbird flounders in the oily wake of man's "evolution"
It's progress that's now the problem, no longer the solution.
Once upon a time there was a future for our children to see
Now civilization is the white flag around the last dead tree.
Evolution may not be "the way forward" it seems
What lies in those waves that might yet be unseen?

Sharron M. Harries

The Rose

It arrived in one of those gift boxes
encased in ribbon fine
of hearts strewn in chorus line,
and lid featured with bow sublime.

When seen after the unmasking
amidst rolled colour loud,
perfumed petals were poised as veiled leaves crowd
all - displayed in a tissue shroud.

Exposed from the shielded casing,
caught in the thorns of time essence and pallor waned,
and with willowed stoop brittle decay did disdain
that endearing message claimed.

Loves sentiment professed - a statement now wept!

Hazel M. Hall

John Wilmot

The Earl of Rochester, Restoration poet,
(And what some would call a sexist git)
Thought that he had women sussed
As unworthy of men's time or trust.

Which is not to say he couldn't be fussed
To chase the occasional piece of t*t,
But preferred "drinking to engender wit"
(Part of me always liked that bit)
And mocked his own excessive lust
With the ardent hypocrisy of the upper crust.

One arm 'round a bottle, one arm 'round a bust,
He'd sing the praises of the former but omit
To mention that the latter, if you let it,
Can easily lead from pleasure to disgust
If you don't know when to quit.

Sean Moran

Crosshaven

The little cares that fretted me.
I lost them yesterday
Among the fields above the sea,
Among the winds at play,
Among the lowing of the herds,
The swaying of the trees,
Among the singing of the birds,
The humming of the bees
The foolish fears of what might pass
I cast them all away,
Among the clover in the grass,
Among the fresh mown hay,
Among the whispering of the corn,
Where sleeping poppies nod,
Where sick thoughts die,
And good are born,
Out in the fields of Corn.

Anthony Walsh

No Illusion

In the air so fresh, in a gentle breeze
In the warmth of the sun, in the midst of the trees
Looking down in wonder and filled with glee
Looking down we ponder at the beauty we see
There is only silence on if life stands still
There is only our gasps for this wondrous thrill
The children's eyes were at last awake
The children's memories that no one can take
A loch, trees and fields was all that we had seen
A birds, eye - view just like in a dream
We were high above where the birds do soar
We were, I'm sure, at Heaven's door.

James Binnie

To Mum

When I was small, you held my hand
and helped me on the way.
and listened to my chatter
at the end of every day . . .

You patched my knee,
and dried my tears -
You even helped me through the fears
of spiders, ghosts and other frights,
assuring me - "it will be alright" . . .
And now I'm being a Mother too,
How hard it seems, so much to do,
The best of teaching, I received
You showed me all I'd ever need . . .

I want to say so much to you,
but no amount of words will do.
I cannot thank you for all you've done,
There are no words, except,
"Thank you Mum."

Diane Jenkins

Rendezvous

Upon my birth you set the time for this rendezvous,
my first tear was for you . . .
for when I started to live,
I also started to die . . .
You were always real
turning my arteries cold,
jealous of my laugh, youth and joy . . .
I wanted to dodge you
in artful acrobatics
that served only to push me closer to you . . .

I am at your mercy,
powerful stranger and eternal sovereign.
I cannot portray you . . .
You are painted with a scythe
in your fleshless hand . . .
Rather .., and above all ..,
you may be the light,
And . . . in this rendezvous,
relentless and cold,
I want to shake hands with you as a friend . . .

Yolande Anzelius

Epitaph

Lie me in six foot solitude, let my playmates file by.

Never, for one instant think, it was not my time to die.
Leave a litre of vodka, quite close to my right side.
So may I journey happy, on this last, and special ride.
Save your money on flowers, they also made me sneeze.
Instead, spare a pound for the homeless,
and some meat for their scruffy dogs please.
Sell my few things of value, let some hungry mouth be fed,
Let nothing left be wasted, possessions are no use to the dead.
Burn all my books of poems, we all knew they could never sell,
Or turn them into nursery rhymes, for my words
always rhymed too well.
Wear no dark colours to mourn me, black never pleased my eye,
Life will be quiet without me, say farewell, but not goodbye.

Anne Davis

A New Born

In the sun she lay,
The beauty of day.

You must be careful, as silent as night,
The slightest sound and she will give fright.

Her coat is white, her eyes are blue,
She is the symbol for all that is true.

She would be a horse but for one single trait,
A great spiralling horn that dismisses all hate.

Yes it is true the beauty is born,
And this beauty is a sacred unicorn.

Christopher Atkinson

My Memory Friends

They are my memory friends
and the thoughts I'll never forget
are held in a special place
from the day we first met

They are my respective friends
so unique in every way
such wonderful distant memories
but unforgotten to this day

As fresh and clean as spring air
so photographic in my mind
as if inscribed by Egyptians
from way bade in time

They were my holiday friends
and every time I close my eyes I find
I see everyone of their smiling faces
still kept alive in my mind.

Keri Hemming

Facets of Winter

A golden, luminescence of winter's sun, misty apparition
merged behind scudding clouds and spiky fingered trees,
herald of winter's cool presence felt and dying essence
of autumn's fiery flora seen.

At dusk the blizzards teeth bit the earth violently,
embracing all nature in its cloak.
Drifting in meringue shaped peaks,
unyielding in glistening sheen.

A cacophony of sound high-pitched, discordant, screaming,
endlessly attacking the ear, making the heart fearful.

Respite came short-lived with the dawn,
birds, anxiously swooping, fleeing,
using the pulsing, gliding eddies, to seek shelter from the blast.

Leaves lately held by fingers of sleeping giants,
now whorl in corners, a leaping dry applause, lacking direction.

Soft, at last, rain, gently dripping, melting, soothing the hurt.
Fitful sunlight, warming, challenging winter's cold,
a herald bringing forth spring with energy born of its light and
hope renewed.

Dorothy Emerson Hawley

Combined Operations (Ascension 1995)

I'm drawn by aerial tumult to the scene;
By wheeling, hungry fighters, folding back
Wings and plummeting head-first, with certain
Graceless artistry, into the attack

Upon a sub-marine prey, vulnerable
Through shallow water and a total lack
Of defence, save that provided shoaling
In numbers turning blue seas into black.

The water's surface pock-marked at each point
Of entry, as flight on flight of charger
Splashes down in ceaseless daylight bombard
Of the fleet forced shoreward by much larger,

Radar-guided, wolf-pack hunter-killers,
Launching torpedo-like into the fray,
While other overhead marauders prowl
To snuff the lives of beached and fallen prey,

Red-throated frigate birds contest each catch.
Sleek tuna using natural cunning
Shepherd the victims boobies dive upon,
Steenbass fry along their annual running.

W. A. Wilkie

To Love in Life, to Love in Heaven

The love that we have, the happiness we share
The laughter, the tears, just show that we care.
A hand in the day, held tight in your own
A kiss in the night, the sweetest I've known.

You are the candle, love is the flame,
My light in the darkness, I whisper your name.
True to the colour, faithful as the sea,
Like the endless rising sun, you're always there for me.

You've given me love, like I've never known,
Wonderful memories, that we'll always own.
Gentle, kind and patient, caring to the end,
You're my life, my love, you're my best friend.

As years pass on by, no time is left here,
The light at the end of the tunnel is near,
High above the clouds, our souls are to go,
And this love that we have, will continue to grow.

Remember the happiness, the laughter, the tears,
The days and the nights, the number of years.
This love that we have, we'll always believe in,
There's not just the memories, but a whole new beginning.

Louise Bourdon

Solitude

My life has changed so very much
Since you have passed away
That moment in time I will never forget
It was a terrible terrible day
You gave me life and all your love
Security, strength and more
But death my love is a shattering thing
Like the slamming of a door
My world ended too that awful day
Of heartbreak, desolation and sorrow
Only memories of yesterday's
And the loneliness of tomorrow's
Some months have passed and still I'm trying
To give my life some meaning
But without you love my hopes and dreams
Are fast disappearing
All I see now are the endless years
Like a dark and desolate lane
And a hope that at the end of it
Is light and you again.

Kay Davidson

Looking Back

Looking back you will wonder why you stood back helplessly,
To watch loves smouldering embers burn with muted misery.
Looking back you will wonder why the ending had to be.
Leaving you to drift the ashes of bitter memories
Looking back you will see too clearly where you both went wrong.
Why in the little things of life you failed to get along.
When from the beginning you were meant to meet you two.
Tools to let a dream so lovely slip away from you.

Hilda Cowan

Sat Dreaming by a Waterfall

The sound of water crystal clear.
Splashing on stones smooth with wear.
Colours changing in the evening sunset.
Dreaming of endless days to come yet.
Dreaming of yesteryear when all was calm,
No stress, no pain, no one to harm,
Playing as a child; so innocent and young,
No fear, any thinking that everyone
Was so perfect in them way,
But then things change day by day;
And as we live it all seems the same.
But it isn't and no ones to blame
It happens and we wonder when,
But this is life over any over again
Just like the water relentless in its way.
It surges in any sees no change to any day.
Except by way of rains that swell,
The cold clear liquid on which we dwell.
And watch it went away to pastures new.
Perhaps it's time I moved on to.

Brian Damms

Raceless Days

The heat of the sun beating down on his back,
is eased by the breeze hitting his flank.
cool water enters his mouth, relieving the thirst,
the green grass will be next.
The flies are dislodged by the shake of his mane,
a flick of his tail whips off the rest.

The fall of an apple is caught in his eye,
he wanders over and tastes its sweet demise.
He watches a dog running free,
feeling the harmony in the shade of a tree.
Old in his age, he'll do as he please.

The drop of the sun, takes with it his strength,
the need for sleep overpowers his rest,
He walks to the gate and waits to be led,
to the warm dark stable, where his friends are bed.

Lesley Clarkson

Futile

Beds in a row - neat and trim,
bodies just lying there
all life trapped within
no-one stirred - no-one moved,
except the nurse on call
they try to hide their heartache
but the look in their eyes say it all.

Beds in a row, tidy and clean
lives that were wrecked, their plans now a dream
things that should have been, things that could have been
all shattered by a fall
they chat awhile, they even smile
but the look in their eyes - say it all.

Their fate is a sentence inflicted by chance
no more will they run no more will they dance.
Windows long and narrow look out on mountains green,
but the beauty that is there
remains to them unseen!

Beds in a row - sterile and white
no sign of the tunnel - not even a light!

Oonagh Lee McNamara

Reality Bites!

When I walked out of my home,
I didn't realise I would be alone
My past gone, my future unclear
and my present to fear.

The streets are so cold,
and my life is untold,
but I can never go back
to the place I used to call home.

Now the world is a cold and lonely place
and I am so ashamed I can't
look myself in the face.

What I had is gone,
Whilst my life is undone,
My feelings so confused
and my life blown
up just like a fuse.

Sophie Gregory

Requiem

There is no music that can mourn your death
No voice, no sound, tho' the whole earth should cry!
Great grief is dumb; silence alone can match
The endless silence in whose depths you lie.
O that Alcestis and Euridice
Could plead with Fate their precedent, and sue
For your return! That the still blood might flow,
The dumb voice speak, and prove this loss untrue!
The earth we both so loved, forever now
Is your vast tomb; and in my heart the tide
That gave it Life is turned back to its source
And lies forever buried, at your side.

Phyllis Anderson

To Have a Mum?

What would it be like to have a mum,
Being normal having fun,
I hold no memories of her,
When I think of her I often shed a tear.

A happy family altogether,
Knowing each alter having thoughts forever,
When bed times you have to face,
You have someone there you don't have
to stare into space.

She would lead me down the right path,
Speak to each other joke and laugh,
Why does this world have to be a mystery
The pain the hurt and mist of all misery.

Shareen Gould

Love Is Dead

Love is dead. Long live, what?
What do you put in that space.
An empty, dark, lonely place of
no light, no warmth, no colours.
No laughter. Nothing shared any more.
No touching, no caring.
no sharing.
No comfortable knowing that you are cared for, and care about.
No place to go; nowhere to belong.
Nobody belongs to you.
No right to expect to be happy.
What right have you got anyway?
Impaled upon the hurt, afraid to move anyway at all.
It will only hurt more.
Be still. Endure.

Pamela Baker

My Boys

The children are in bed fast asleep.
Seeing them so peaceful is a memory I will keep

I feel so proud of my two lovely Boys
Especially when I watch them play with their toys

I enjoy looking after them from day to day
Please give them health and happiness I pray

I cannot believe my babies are growing up
Instead of crawling around the floor like little pups

Gone are the days of dummies and rattles
Now I have to sort out their daily battles

I'm trying to teach them their toys they must share
Because deep down inside I really care.

When I'm down and feeling low
Seeing their smiles I start to glow

My darling boys mummy loves you both so dearly
I hope through your eyes you will see that so clearly

Susan Brittle

Essence Feeds

Play the heart and make it dance
  beat on beat to cause a trance
Take a chance and move it more
  eat into the very core
Different moods do sounds impel
  when lost in space yet need to tell
Rainbow music many hues
  of reds and yellows, greens and blues
The mind is full but never fail
  bombard the soul and make it sail
  beyond the reach of body needs
Play the heart and essence feeds

P. G. M. Curtis

"You Are All Those Things"

You are all those things, that mates my heart
Sing, you are my hearts, rhythm, that beats
With sheer joy unexpectedly; the inward glow,
Unseen; the inward space "Just for you"
Where no other can invade the utter sweetness
Of that invisible, "You only fill my soul,"
And, you alone stills all its longings;
Separate, yet, as together bound,
As one, that is perfect love, when it is
Found; that colours of pure crystal are
Found too, in the many little ways I
Discover daily about you, the way you talk,
The way you laugh and smile, the gentle ways
And, the words said, cowvey, yet conceal so
Much, yet still to come; the never ending
Golden thread, that binds together, forever,
Those who have found that perfect love,
"The well of happiness,"
A blessing from above.

K. Baber

Fill a Blank

To fill a blank I first need words,
Not too obtuse , not too absurd,
Bridge the gap, in one big span
Fill in the blank spaces if I can.

I've started now, so lets get on,
The flow has begun to enlarge upon,
The very thing I have to do,
Is keep on going, will I pull through.

Another line is on me here,
Will it continue for long, I fear
That time is not on me side,
As I try and try not to let it slide.

Maybe one more verse and that will be all,
At least I'm still going, but I'm set for a fall.
One more line and it's going to be tally,
That's it gone now I've gone do'wally.

Raymond J. S. Hay

Falling

As I share into the black hole, I realize that I'm feeling,
And there is no one at the edge, who I can hear calling,
I just feel deeper and deeper, until I can't see the top,
It seams never ending, will I ever stop?
Will I ever be saved, I am so hopeful,
I don't want to fall because this falling's so painful,
And the more I fall, the darker it seams to get,
And passing by I see love, hate and regret.
Can't tell if my eyes are opened or closed.
When will this end, never I suppose
And in a desperate moment, I feel for a grip
But as before like my hope, I just start to slip,
So I'll just keep on falling 'til I hit the floor.
I'll just keep on falling, until I can't fall anymore.

Philip Robert Lees

The Scar of Time

In times of trouble,
Children huddle, and other people unite,
And when terror raises its ugly head.
Basic instinct makes them stand and fight,
But sometimes, only sometimes,
Events are so appalling.
It shocks people right through to their soul,
The mind stutters, and the heart flutters,
And it rocks the nation as a whole.
No-one knows why it happened,
They cannot believe that it did.
But time carries on regardless,
Leaving behind bad memories,
And a scar on the face of time.

Royston Bristow

Untitled

The Sun shone brightly on that fine day
That I first saw your face
My troubles and sorrows melted away
And joy did them replace.
I thought that we were right together
I felt we'd get along
Being strong in stormy weather
I guess that I was wrong.
I made mistakes, that I know
They are my biggest regret
But though I'm left now feeling low
I'm oh so glad we met.
The pain will fade in time I'm told
Though right now it's fairly bad
Not having you here to touch, to hold
Leaves me feeling sad.
And when I think of you, Audrey
Your smile it cuts my heart
And leaves me wondering endlessly
Just why we had to part.

Stephen Power

I Watch

I watch her standing in the rain her face
says it all, it reveals the pain
She can speak no words, she can cry no tears
She is full of anger, she is full of fears
Alone she stands, and alone she will wait
for a life full of love, not one full of hate
she stands alone as the rain still falls
Where there once stood open doors, now stood walls
She knows she has to keep going she has to be strong
To pick herself up to make sense of all
that's gone wrong
I want to help her, but can only stare
God knows what I'd do if I was standing there
As she starts to walk I wait to see
and much to my horror the girl I was
watching was me.

Natasha Bentley

The Dolphins

You glide through the waves
With a skilful grace
Like gleams of quicksilver
But steady of pace
Pilots of the sea
Through its fathomless depths
Your powers so boundless
That we can but guess.

To your own kind you're social, caring and true,
Fending off danger so constant with you.
Stricken seafarers, you save when you can,
Lifting them between you so the story ran.

May you always be here,
In your element so free,
And your click-click call
Sounding over the Lee.

A. Hunt

Why

Why do we strive for this and that
And kill ourselves to get them,
Yet haven't time to call on friends,
And birthdays - we forget them.

We only are aware of this
When our youth has passed us by,
For youth is full of promise
And ambitions reach the sky.

Achievements are like mountains,
Hard climbed, to reach the top
The prize of our endeavours,
Yet some, know not when to stop.

But death is always waiting
To stop the sands of time,
And we must go with Him - to where?
And leave it all behind.

Phyllis Joan Jenkin

For Faith

Green trees grow old, go brown and wither down,
When flowers melt they turn towards the sun,
But never did he show disgruntled frown,
Never was her life more filled with fun.
Like his daughter I was near him every day,
Like sisters we were never far apart,
I loved, respected, praised in every way,
And never did I think one day he'd part.
The sun went down, the clouds just disappeared,
Nothing I could say would make her smile,
Never was a child so filled with tears,
She said they'd have to leave just for a while.
The dad she'd loved had left her with his smile
And taken hers with him just for a while.

Sophie Louise Baldock

Nostalgia

I remember, yes! I remember,
The house where I was born,
It stands beneath the Malvern Hills,
Amidst the fields of corn,
The corpse that runs long side it,
Where we used to play,
Picking primroses and bluebells,
As we went out merry way,
Summer night we'd hear the nightingales,
On the air so warm and still,
I'd love to hear them once again,
But I guess I never will,
Many years have passed since then,
Now I am old and grey,
But I often think about these things,
The joys of yesterday,
My parents both long gone now,
So loving and so tender,
Now in the twilight of my life
I remember, yes! I remember.

Josephine Hill

Closed Curtains

Summer, winter! It's hard to tell, the air is so still, like that the breath of a deadman. Not a whisper, even the old house is quite. Tonight there is no pain, its bones do not crack, nor does it groan in anguish. Tonight I alone sit and wander. If I were to rise up from my bed now and walk along the silver ribbon, winding its way across hill and dale. If I could gaze upon the horizon and see the land disappear into the darkness which surrounds me. If I could whistle aloud and wait for the night creatures to jump, and dart, starring back at whence the sound came, with frightened eyes, still fixed with the glaze of sleepiness from a days rest. If I could, so many things, what would it be like? But here I sit and wonder, here I am safe, I have light so that my eyes may see all and heat to keep my body warm. I have no fear, in the room I know so well, Oh! but to be below the skies, a million light's faded behind a black sheet, the cool grass brushing against my feet, distant sounds and near noises, many creatures spying at me from beyond, then would I, could I, be so sure?

Nicky Aston

Nana

Nana's are special in lots of different ways,
Even when you're going through that difficult phase.
No matter how many grandchildren there is to come.
They manage to share out love to each and every one.

Nana is a very special and meaningful name,
It means love and beloved equally the same.
They cheer you up when you are down,
And keep you smiling without a frown.

Nana, I love you for just been there,
Whenever I need someone to care.
I love you for everything you say and do,
But most of all for just being you.

Lynette D. Cope

"Winter"

In the midst of winter
Among the fallen leaves,
The cold wind was tugging
Hard at the sleeves,
I looked at the sky
Where the sun had been,
But only grey clouds, could be seen.
Oh my sun, why did you have to go,
And leave behind a blanket of snow.
The animals of the forest,
Are hiding away.
They know for a while,
They cannot play.
Over the hills they would like to roam
But it was getting colder -
I turned for home.

Diana Thomas

Ten Rounds

When the going gets tough the ground very rough,
Boxed in from all sides no where to hide.
Feels like ten rounds with Bruno knocked down in the first
Oh God help! it can't get any worse.
Take a deep breath, steady your nerve
You go the distance, ahead in the third.
New prospects, new horizons, one step at a time
You will find new direction with new focus and perception,
Reaching round ten way ahead of the herd
A little shaken and bruised
But with great honesty and worth.
You will, believe me, achieve everything
You so rightly deserve.
I know I have backed a winner I know I am right
Points will go to your corner
This will be your Title Fight

Heather Claxton

Solemn Sunday

Red-frocked, with glowing flames
they search the stave for notes to weave
wrapping themselves in holy chords
hot candle wax stuck to the sleeve

While the faithless pomp lovers survey the time
it takes to worship idols of stone
praying, 'give me more bread or it's Satan instead,
am I Christian or am I clone?

The leader pours water from jug to jug
straining his eye under tarnished felt
there are no glowing objects in the pulpit of course
he must be afraid he might melt

Fantasy drives the hypocrite and fool
into thinking he's one step ahead
but, when the dawn breaks and he finally awakes
he will find himself still in his bed

Barry Bryn Childs

My Best Friend

For many years
We have travelled along
The same path together
In work and in pleasure
In all kind's of weather
With a friendship is depth and sincere
Now you have gone a head
And opened the door
To the green pastures beyond
Where the sun always shines
And darkness never fall's
One day I will reach that door
I will knock
It will open
Then once more our hand's will clasp
In the friendship we enjoyed

A. P. Cherry

March

Through blue air,
Vaporous puffs and swirls of cloud
Move swiftly;
Lace edge and chiffon frill
Constantly changing, never still.

Across their face
Joyful and high,
Relishing the airy space
The rooks wing by.

Long twigs, spiky,
Wider than wing span,
Ungainly seem,
Yet unhampering their flight,
Are carried from tree of source
To chosen tree top height,

Audrey Caton

Reuptake Inhibitor

I feel so tired, I feel confused,
My love is true but I've been used.
I feel so calm, I feel so tired,
My job is great but I've been fired.

My friends are always here for me -
That's what they're always telling me.
But when I'm here alone with me
I find I have to disagree.

I trust the one who lies to me,
Who sleeps with me, keeps telling me
That I am hers and she is mine -
Why do I trust her every time?

My life's gone, I want it over -
All these fools say "talk it over".
But what's to say when in my head
I think of me and wish me dead.

James Lander

My Toy

Remembering back to when I was a boy,
Daddy once bought me a very special toy.
I've kept this toy for all of my life,
Even though, now married with a wife
It to me was a friend with no name.
But, I loved it dearly, just the same.
Something to cuddle each night in bed,
It used to listen to everything I said.
Mum knitted clothes for it to wear,
But, now when I look, he's got a bit thread-bear.
Every child has one, but, mine was the best,
Even now, much more useful than all the rest
Some poor Teddy Bears end up in the bin,
Which I always think of as being such a sin.
Others in the cupboard, put away,
And that's where the poor things stay.
But, no not mine, he sits on the floor,
And with great pride, props open the door.

John Banks

Reflections

Deep into the pool I look and see
Who is that reflection? - Could it be me?
Peaceful and happy I do look
Like in a dream or story book.
Deep into my reflecting eyes
I gaze and see myself, knowledged and wise.
Deep into my soul I know I am
Gentle and soft like a new spring lamb.
Drawing the energy from the pool within
I know that I can now begin
On my path of truth and love
Confident and assured of the help from above.
And all through life I know I can.
Stop and reflect from where it began
With healing light from heaven above
Peace to all, with all my love.

Tina Buckberry

Time

Time is a bound from the moment of life.
Recorded on paper by attending midwife,
Clocks and timepieces then rule our days
From waking to sleeping in so many ways.
Time can be fleeting, time can be slow,
Time can say stop. Time can say go.
Unseen and unfelt untouchable and unsmelt.
It touches us with its tender hands,
Our hair turns white and wrinkles appear.
Our eyesight dims and our bones get brittle.
Time has the ball and we are the skittle.
Time can be our enemy and also our friend.
Time is with us from beginning until life's end.

June Ann Wood

Song Bird

When you're all alone and I'm not there,
can you sense my spirit touching your hair.
Pretend that I am with you that you can see my face,
Pretend we are hiding in our secret place,
I am the song bird I can fly,
My spirit is with you shining in the sky,
I will watch you from above
Looking down with adoration and love,
Can you feel me I'm with you now
I can feel your skin smell your scent touch your brow
I press my kisses on your skin
let the moisture sink its way in,
Inside your body I'll move around
finding the places wanting to be found
In deep movements that are sacred to us all
Hold me now or I might fall.
Can you feel my breath behind your ear
I'm letting you know that I am near
A love so strong it's you my spirit will find
It will go and leave my body behind.

Kirsty Johnson

Caledonian Antisyzygy

On the shore of a storm-lashed loch
I cling to a tree-
It still has its roots.
My one sure anchor
In a night of black chaos.
I know how Lear felt on his mad moor-
White waves pound on dark stones,
Trees are devils dancing.
The earth is storm-tossed, lost,
Ripped from its cradle.

In a golden blaze of vine leaves
I lean from my window
Scented by dying red roses,
And see with a shock of happiness
Two goldfinches eating sorrel seed.
In a flash of scarlet and gold
Zipping across the garden in a mad burst of gaiety,
Flying in perfect unison
To circle the earth
As the sun strikes the meridian.

Lorna Ferguson Kirk

My Dad Loves Me

My dad told me he loved me today,
On a card from O.K.
It's the first time he's told me,
in this adult way.

He must have found it hard to, say
as he wrote it in an affectionate way
It said he missed me, and cared for me, my wife too,
it also said he loved us two.

It must have come from deep inside
much pain, so much he no longer hides,
this feeling of fatherly pride
So many empty days have long gone past
his feelings out now, now at last.

There are many stories, I've yet to tell
a victim of a victim, my father as well.
Yes this story is much like mine,
when he told it, it made me cry.

Because he is my father yes he is my dad
Because of this I'm so very glad
Oh yes I am and, I love you to Dad.

E. Thomas

Our Future

Take care of the little children
For they are here on loan
Take care of the little children
and they'll always come back home.

Take care of the little children
For soon they will grow, and then
you'll sit and wonder,
where all the years have gone.

Take care of the little children
For they are honest and full of love.
No matter what we say or do, it will never
come again
that childish laughter and loyalty,
Your child is your best friend.

Take care of the little children,
Teach them sensibility, fairness and
compassion, and they will have learned well.
To make their world a better place
instead of a mighty Hell.

Patricia Henfryn Duffy

Hospitality

What are we doing to each other,
Why can't we act like sister and brother
Why use guns to settle a row,
A nice long chat would be better some how.

Innocent people killed and maimed for life,
Why oh why is there so much strife.
Why can't we all turn over a new leaf,
We don't have to kill to prove our belief.

Hostages imprisoned for many years
Causing their families unnecessary tears.
What satisfaction do they get from this
Suffering and killing can't be bliss.

Blood thirsty leaders wanting to be on top,
Surely your God would want you to stop.
He must be appalled at what he is seeing,
As he created the human being.

His hospitality we have abused on earth,
Is this the way to show him what it's worth.
We should thank the Lord in every way,
For the privilege of allowing us to stay.

Dora E. Cooper

Woman

The violence at home was too much to bear,
The kicking, the beating, the throwing of chairs.
Her got drunk, he lashed out, he beat her about,
The husband just didn't care.
She stayed with him-she had nowhere to go,
He beat her, she screamed and kept saying 'No'.
He tried to throw her out of the door-
That was it, that was all-she could take no more.
The knife in her hand went into his chest-
She could do no more, she had tried her best.
In a cold prison cell the woman waited,
A man she had loved had now become hated.
Her life was gone for a man who had beat,
Who had almost killed her-it felt such a cheat.
"For a man I once loved, for a man who once cared,"
As she said these words the wardens stared,
"For the years of hurt, the bruises, the pain,
The beatings from hands, from sticks, from canes.
A man who once called me a bitch and a cow,
If he had cared I would not be here now."

Caroline Larner

A Dream Come True

When I was a little girl,
I longed to be married to give it a whirl,
My husband would be handsome and strong
A lovely home where I belonged
Then came along our lovely baby
Who I'm sure will become a lady
She's so sweet and kind
Little bossy boots, blows your mind,
But beware her temper is bad
For this she takes after her dad
When I try to get her in her own bed at night,
She cries and says I just want you to hold me tight.
So what can I do. I love her so
Maybe one day she'll get married and go
She too will have these dreams
And no doubt make up lots of schemes
Just like the song says
I've got sunshine on a cloudy day
What can make me feel this way
My girl Chelsey Summerscales.

Pam Summerscales

A Walk in Springtime

Just take a stroll down a well worn track
Let your cares drift away, no need to look back
So much beauty to see, sounds abound to hear
Spring is a wonderful time of year.

You can hear the leaves whisper and play in the breeze
Right at the top of those gnarled old trees
See that carpet of bluebells, they were laid just for you
Sit and soak up the sunshine under skies oh so blue.

Stop and look at the stream with the fish darting by
Sun splashed crystal clear water gives a chuckle and sigh
As it laps over stones and swirls under the bridge
Make its way far beyond and over the ridge.

If you search in the hedgerows you may find a nest
Full of featherless babies taking a rest
After filling themselves from mums busy beak
She'll be backwards and forwards for many a week.

Pick a primrose with petals just kissed by the sun
Nestling in clusters where shy rabbits run
As you go through the gate into meadows so green
Take with you the memories of springtime you've seen.

J. Sanders

Early Retirement from Offshore

Long gone the days,
Of choppers, rigs and big pays,
The dirt and grime,
So now you can shine.

You will miss the banter and the myths,
Along with the 12 hour shifts,
The food offshore,
Was really a bore,
But the ice cream machine will miss you,
So you better send it a tissue.

You hated lifeboat drills,
But now you're home it's brill,
You will miss the cinema, snooker and the darts,
But now we will never be apart,

Your list of jobs now will keep you going,
While your wife is gardening and sewing,
You will have time to play with your son,
You're lucky there is only one,
So relax and enjoy your RETIREMENT.

Carole Anne Gillespie

Five or Six or Maybe Ten

Laughter echoes across the sands,
Children running holding hands,
faces tanned, hair bleached white,
barefoot, naked - what a sight!
Skipping and jumping o'er the waves
dashing off to explore the caves,
endless hours playing in the sun
idyllic days, with worries none,
I close my eyes, I am back then
was I five or six of maybe ten.

Blue, blue skies and warm golden sands,
Ice cream, lollipops and sticky hands,
rock pools, shells and donkeys to ride,
castles washed away by the incoming tide,
and oh what sadness as the sun went down,
it was home to bed, with tears and a frown,
As my memory fades and I grow older,
days aren't so warm - the beach seems colder;
oh how it all seemed so much better then,
when I was five or six or maybe ten.

Joyce Miller

When the Miracle of Life Can Again Be Found

In each glorious colour and joyful sound
Which sets, the countryside alight once more
Such is the splendour of the adventure which awaits
  for us to explore

The springtime, its every shade
Designed by God, as only he could have made
To blossom upon hedge 'row and tree
Then to attract, the butterfly and bee.

While upon the meadow green, the lambs now play
Yet another miracle of life, which arrives with the
  coming of each springtime day
A blaze and alive, each country lane
Beneath the warmth of the sunshine and each
  refreshing shower of rain.

The springtime, welcomed by
A variety of creatures and birds of the sky
The springtime, to set our hearts alight
Such is the gift of the miracle of life.

David Stradling Floyd

Old Mother Nature

I listen to those sounds of storm,
that chill. I feel no longer warm,
like moods of man that are so strange,
are Mother Natures sounds of change,
when howling winds, as if on wings,
it seems to try and tell me things,
Those winds are signs of her in anger,
perhaps she feels the world's in danger,
when man destroys those beauty spots,
for all those buildings, roads and shops.
When the rain falls down, it seems to say,
That Mother Nature's sad that day,
The hazy mists, say she's confused,
Maybe she thinks the worlds misused,.
Her tears of laughter in the April showers
Remind me then of her great powers,
She could send gales, and snow and ice,
When man doesn't treat the world very nice,
The hail and winds can come crashing around,
Revenge on those buildings, by knocking them down,

Alexa Lawrence

The Bowl

It stood resplendent on a deep dark shelf
Its beauty rather out of place
Deep maroon, and Roman figures, bands of gold
Down in its depths moved figures of black.

My mother lay on her sick bed
Could gaze, admire and dream perhaps?.
At Christmas it was filled with treats
Apples, bananas nuts and pears.

Then came the day my mother died.
Sometime later off went the bowl
To join my father and new wife.
I felt so sad.

Visiting, watching and seeing
It stood dusty and neglected
Time has passed and both have died
All was shared and sorted.

What feelings of relief I felt
When back into our house it came
Maroon, white and gold
Standing on a white shelf.

Judy Parfitt

The River

The river blue in its intensity reflects a haunting mood of
love-eternity leaves tingle, taunt each limitless pool. The hawk in
varying mood enjoys his reflection, hovers as a decoy duck and
swoops on his merciless prey. Twists of fate prevail like an
anthem in the night. Hollows call out, the river swiftly moves on.
Yet underneath this perpetuating light this inviting harmony of
life, a murky coil lies beneath, submerged life forms, a tail frog
reclines in his 'oblivion of slime', the darkness pulls you in doors
close, coating a velvety silence. A waterfall heralds us, sporting a
spirit so free, clad in sparkle, inviting high ideals, Torrents run in
abandon. Two lovers, embalmed in their silence aroused by soft
urges, seduced by a throb a power intertwines the mind, in gay
assault, twisting it over the edge falling, falling, the evocative,
provocative call to come with me, in a twist of pain and pleasure,
releases as in silent arcadian, to be plunged, thrown in discourse
free spirits exuberantly unfold, deafening urges in feeble ascent,
we are taken through this chastening laughing mural, lost inside
torrents, the gender and power afloat captive we continue, no
choice left but to surrender. The losing of the mind like a vessel
in the sea beauty calls, lively in nature's
harness, a new mood as if to coo a waning day, gnats flirt the
rivers surface nothing to beckon me now but a few bird calls, as
night extinguishes the murmur of the day.

—*Jill C. Smith*

On the Beach

Looking out from soft white sand
gazing out at the calm blueness
broken only by the peaks of cold rocks.
The bitter freshness of the salt
bites the cheeks and stings the eyes,
bring soft blue tears to the lashes

But everything was different last night.
The deep white foam, raced fiercely,
crashing wildly
breaking over cold, sharp rocks,
and rushing to the dark sand.

White horses rode over high, black crescents,
rushing freely, towards the horizon,
silhouette against the orange sky.
while seagulls swooped towards them
shrieking shrilly as they rise.

But now it's like a different scene
fresh and still with rocks of green.
waves lapping softly on the shore
until the wind picks up once more.

Annie Robertson

My Valentine

It's hard the rocky path we tread
Since that first day that we were wed
But sunshine hides behind the clouds then in
Full force it shouts aloud.
I'm here I'm bright I smile again, just let the
cloud roll by and wain.
And so in human terms it says your smile your wit
your joy of life if never lost in all of strife.
It's there to brings back to therefore the
confidence you had before
In love in life in self esteem it's just our
thinking we must redeem.
To start a new with clear new thought, banish
The old that cause distraught.
Each day a new page of a book a script to
Follow, a brand new look

A prayer of thankfulness for anything, the
house, the garden, the joy children bring.
It's there for each of us to hold
And value our love till we grow old.

M. A. Trickett

"Love and Deceit"

It's hard to accept you could be so cruel,
Only yesterday it was love and kissing,
Now all I feel is a compleat fool,
Sure my caress you are not missing.

Thrown away like a used old rag,
Onto new exciting pastures,
Feeling frustrated mourn full and map,
You couldn't have moved on any faster.

Was I not special in your life?
It was so easy for you to cheat,
You said it was I who's become your wife,
Me alone - no others to meet.

But I tell you now you misjudged me badly,
I have at last regarded my pride,
Although I once loved you madly,
I know I never want to be your bride.

I never again want you in my home,
You are not and never will be a friend of mine,
I would simply prefer to live alone,
Than ever again experience your kind.

Laura Jane Milne

The Learning of Life

For the promises that life makes to us,
And the goals as to what we achieve,
Are down to us all both woman and man,
In the completely of life vast weave.

Decisions made can be those gone wrong,
And the reverse is often the way,
The choice is ours both yours and mine,
For in life's theatre we all have a play.

Is it human nature to blame not us,
With the finger pointed elsewhere,
But the resolve of problems is all mankind's,
And the awareness and need to repair.

So the better we deal with life's troubles
And the unity applied to succeed,
The better our living the better we are,
And the greater the things we achieve.

So awaken we must with lessons learned,
And strive for the one major night,
To know ourselves and care what we do,
And for peace and our love to unite.

Richard Northcote

Minding My Own Business

Could it really have been innocence I saw
Shining on the face of that child

From all the commotion I hear
She's obviously driving them wild.

Last night her eyes sparkled like emeralds
And from her bath with her hair not yet dry

She looked up and smiled in my face
And I had to force myself not to sigh.

Bumps and bruises are really quite obvious
When worn by a child such as that

And just how many times can a toddler
Trip over the family cat?

I kept meaning to do something about it
When I couldn't bear to listen to her cry.

Now I have to live with the fact
That I sat and listened to her die.

Sue Trenerry

The Master's Hand

The Greatest master his canvas prepared
He sprinkled the earth with dew
And then because he loved and cared
He painted the world for you

Gently with the soft winds brush
He worked in colours pale
And slowly appeared the first dawns flush
The misty hues of hill and dale

He used for the sky all shades of blue
Hung with jewels of silver and gold
These were the moon and stars he drew
And the sun so warm and bold.

Of water colours he made the sea
Reflecting the blue of the sky
He painted this canvas for you and me
And I marvel and wonder why.

A picture by a master's hand
He left it in our care
This masterpiece that is our land
A gift beyond compare.

Dorothy Mouton

The Storm

Humid, hazy heart turns to deepest gloom,
the storm builds around an electric sky,
huge ice cream clouds plume,
where eagles float on thermals high.
almost lost to naked eye.

Impulsive lightning flashes down,
amid bellicose rumbles and torrid rain,
turning sodden earth to sombre brown,
squalls lift debris with no height to gain,
dashing it hard back to a ground in pain.

Fast rising waters becomes a real peril,
dribbling river beds turn to angry flood,
fiercely scouring rocks laced with beryl,
pheasants wings cover a sopping brood,
chirping warnings at washed away food.

After a spell the stormy deluge abates,
the Lord never again will engulf the earth,
a rainbow appears hiding heavens gates,
where angels rejoice at a souls rebirth,
bright sun bursts through with radiant mirth.

Richard McCoull

Kieran-Vice Cpt

Seventeen years and one day,
I awoke to hear you had gone;
Your clowning image - a memory -
"A Happy Birthday" shattered.
A tear trickled from my eye,
One of a lake which was to follow.

You saved others, under a bridge you were a guard.
One of a team, you mastered a regal sport,
In time you moved.
   Now time has stopped.
You lie asleep, so quiet no jokes.

My hand tight.
I passed around; an emotional sponge.

You were lowered your height.
The birds that cried your fate
Flew like the wind -
Your dream was cancelled.
Silence echoed home.
Your finale, was through upright oars -
In honour. Carried on grieving, loving shoulders.

Gabrielle McManus

They Deserve More

Sometimes I just break down and cry, honestly I really try
I just fall down onto my knees
And shout - who chopped down the trees?
Who took all the food - and left them lying nude,
Who took all the drink - and let families unlink?
While the children cry for shelter and her little brother felt her
What he felt were bones and heard were massive tummy moans.
Just think of being in the war and risking all your life
There should be some law not to split a husband and wife.
Just think of all the animals - just lying there - dead
There should be rules that both animals and human beings
   should be fed.
Let them walk through the valley of fantasy
   not through the valley of hell
Don't let them suffer from illness, let them be fit and well.
Just sit there and think what they all go through
And think of a way to make their dreams come true.
Sometimes I just wonder why - it is so unfair
I hate to see the people die and think that people don't care.
Lots of people die each day - all kinds of races
I'd really like to see the world have happy smiling faces.

Amie Proffitt

The Little Donkey

There there little donkey, as you plod along,
Your poor little legs, they have to be strong,
   As you plod along the weary road,
With Mary and Joseph, and a heavy load,
   Your head hangs low, and your eyes are sad,
But Mary and Joseph, they tell you be glad,
   For baby Jesus this night will be born,
And you little donkey with us will adorn,
   For without you little donkey,
We could not survive, the stable at the inn, we would not arrive,
And without you to help us, and guide us along,
   Without your strength, and your body so strong,
Without your power, as you pull along,
   We would not have made the stable at all,
And poor baby Jesus, as He made His first cry,
   Alone in manger, and under a star,
And you little donkey, as you stand so tall,
   Proud and happy, the wonder of it all,
And only for you, a little donkey small,
   Might never have been, no christmas at all.

Iris McFarland

'Seeds'

In the garden of my mind, seed were planted
The seeds of "Love" grew, never to be daunted!
Seeds of "Happiness", scattered all around.
"Loyalty" too, grew strong, in this fertile ground.

Seeds, all nourished, by the river of my heart.
Every pulse, encouraging new growth to start.
Buds of "Faith", surely did blossom.
"Courage" and "Hope: The last seeds to open.

Seeds of "Hate And Malice", most, of the thorny kind
Unwanted weeds, in this hallowed ground.
The seeds of "Evil" - surely must go.
To let the "Seeds Of Live", eternally grow.

Maisie Roberts

Peace in Our World

Dear Lord may we ask that you always will stay,
Close by us at night, and throughout all the day.
Your love will enfold and forever we'll know,
That you'll be our comfort wherever we go.

The world as we know it is changing so fast,
The only sure knowledge is your love will last.
Take care of our dear ones across land and sea,
Unite us in service dear Father with thee.

Our home and our children need you ever near,
Without you the darkness will ne'er disappear.
Oh Jesus, our Guide and our Saviour and Friend,
Stay with us we pray you through life to the end.

Your still voice we hear at the close of the day.
As quietly we thank you for work and play.
We know in the morning the skies will be blue,
If we trust and confess all our sins Lord to You.

Winifred F. Shaw

A Sad Story

There's an old woman living in my house,
She's elusive, but I know she's there,
Because she uses my brush,
It's often full of white hair.
As I hurry past the mirror in the morning,
I see her. When I creep back in stealth,
She has gone. Does anyone else see her?
Or do I delude myself.

When I go out for the night,
She is well hidden from sight,
But I know she's at home . . . waiting.
I see her more than I will admit,
By my mirror she'll patiently sit,
I know she waits for a sign,
When she can make my hairbrush her own
And know it's hers. It won't then be mine.

And maybe, she'll catch a glimpse of me
Now and then, that only she can see.

Heather Rayne

Yesterday's Child

When you're a child
you wish for time to go,
But always waiting
seems so slow.
Now I'm older looking to my past never waiting
Time seem' to go so fast
When's my birthday
wonder what I'll get now I'm older
Birthdays I want to forget
People always telling you what to do
Now if it's wrong it's down to you
When I was younger.
I wished for time to go
Now I wish only for time to slow

Christina Worby

Untitled

Endlessly I search for you.
But I never seem to move.
How often I have seen you.
Only to open my eyes and lose you.
I reach out my hand and touch you.
All that I touch is a ghostly memory.
If but dreams were substance.
Then you would be more than air.

Every tear that's shed for wanting you.
One day shall from into you.
A body of glistening sorrow.
No more to hold onto than a dream.
For a dream is as much as you shall ever be.
And my only gifts to you.
A body of tears.
And a life of fears.

Michael J. Wood

Dunblane

An evil presence entered their midst
To deliver an evil kiss;
The children bustled to the school
And entered the dark abyss.

A gun is fire upon a child,
His hopes and dreams are gone;
The derelict buildings soar above,
To a sky without a sun.

A cruel and loathsome person
Has touched the weak and mild;
But who can tell the old and needy?
Who can tell a child?

And so we read another chapter
In this book of vicious lies;
But there's a question to be answered -
Please do answer . . . WHY!

Sion Rogers

The Bride

Seeking consolation, not emotional constipation,
lacking confirmation: Devotional contemplation,
Seeking consistency, not a novitiate sisterhood;
Looking, consoling; that true initiating brotherhood.
Seeking truthfulness, not the apposition of living,
Looking good, in the path of discipleship of giving;
Seeking womanhood, to really compliment man.
Looking evangelical, decimating her plan.
Seeking sweet sisterhood to complement her loving brother,
Looking pater, denominationally mother;
Seeking perfection, the virgin, the perfect union,
Looking wifely-wise, the only and Christ communion.
Where is that Shangri-La? Not the end - Armageddon!
Golf-club raised;
sacramentally searching for that bright Heaven.

Michael Ruxton

Cindy

Sometimes life hurts and pains
Others joys and gains.
I knew her once, so young, beautiful
but not the same.
To have lived and died within twelve years.
To have smiled, hoped and prayed
and then to cascade away.
I full of joy, she only of sorrow and pain.
I wish I had known when Ashley-
James was born you were loosing the war
You had won all the battles, been so brave
Then why God? Send this matter,
the matter of death at her door.
My memories of the era so bittersweet
Goodbye sweet angel Cindy. I wish you
hadn't died and gone away forever.

K. Tucker

The Face of God

"Day beckoned to the soulless night,
Whilst in the ash a robin sang
Each burst expressing hope and life;
As through my humbled being each note rang.
In distant pastures ewes and lambs
Their mournful sounds were making
And with each cry that echoed forth
A part of me was waking.
Of all the blessings that I own;
Contained inside the wisdom of my heart
Best I love the tenfold gifts of nature
Which the creator gives to mortals such a part.
Rapt in this state of ecstasy and feeling,
Upon this wet and windswept place;
I felt again the voice of beauty calling,
And for a second met God face to face."

Michelle Parrish

Home Coming

I tiptoed up those rickety stairs
Crossed bare boards with bated breath
For in that room so cold and stark
Lay a trail old woman close to death

Not tears cascade down my cheeks
Dripped upon that threadbare counterpane
With anguished heart I cried aloud
"Your prodigal son is home again"

Her eyelids flickered open wide
Her lips moved slowly as in prayer
I sank on my knees to catch what she said
As she fixed me with that last glazed stare

Those final words she softly spoke
Will haunt me all my lifetime through
For was it non-recognition or reproach
Those last three word of "Who are you"?

T. Wheeler

You May Not Know This But?

You may not know this but, I was born rich!
I don't mean the fancy yacht and Chateau in France type of rich,
Although I don't remember ever wanting for anything.

What I mean is the kind of rich that comes from being loved,
From being brought up with a code to live by and standards,
With a sense of what's right and valuing opinions.

I guess when you are a parent, you question what you've done
And as a Son or Daughter you take things for granted
Too busy with things and spending what you've got.

Sometimes when you are born my kind of rich,
It takes a lot of years to see or comprehend it,
But now I understand the endowment you gave me.
Thank you for making the investment.

Ken De Carlo

Cindy

Sometimes life hurts and pains
Others joys and gains.
I knew her once, so young, beautiful
but not the same.
To have lived and died within twelve years.
To have smiled, hoped and prayed
and then to cascade away.
I full of joy, she only of sorrow and pain.
I wish I had known when Ashley-
James was born you were loosing the war
You had won all the battles, been so brave
Then why God? Send this matter,
the matter of death at her door.
My memories of the era so bittersweet
Goodbye sweet angel Cindy. I wish you
hadn't died and gone away forever.

K. Tucker

Daddy

Me and my dad get on really great
Remembering the wave I gave at the gate
His little girl had grown.
If only he had known
How much his daughter loved him so
He always said, one day I'd go
Far away to start a new life
Like always my dad was right.

The tears streamed down my face that day
I never really wanted to go away
I needed a place where I could go
Without my dad, time went slow
Moving around place to place
I never forgot my fathers face
I guess I neglected him as I grew up
I sort of found a different kind of love

I didn't see my dad for a while
It was now I was missing his friendly smile
He taught me everything this made me survive
I never want you, my daddy, to die

Carole Eileen Hickman

Granny's Wee Treasure

She's the bonniest baby I ever did see.
As she sits there and smiles and wees on my knee.
Opens her mouth as if to say,
"Am I here with you for the rest of the day."

"I want my milk and I want it now."
Dear Lord we may go and buy her a cow.
It's in one end and out the other.
But to her Granny it's no bother.

Will you be dark or will you be fair,
cries Granny as she lugs out a lump of her hair
In a while it's down to rest.
Granny and Granda have done their best.

We Really did enjoy our day
We're glad wee Kerby came to stay
I'll get her bag for you to pack
Granny wearily hands the baby back

Night night our wee treasure says
my Granny and Granda need their rest.

Vivenne Ellen Patria McMullan

She Knew

She sits there sometimes, alone in the field,
surrounded by the grasses of life,
her hair blows like a soft golden shield.

Her eyes closed,
a tear trickles down the milky flesh,
if but only for a short time,
she knew he loved her.
If she knew a way to find him,
to get to him, she would,
but now she sits full of shame,
should she try? Maybe she should . . .

Open now, her eyes were red,
the grass firing her emotion . . . she left,
this place was to remain her that her love is dead.

Why, why did he have to go,
she knew he loved her so,
hurt now, she couldn't stop crying,
by now he'd be flying,
flying away to a new life . . .

Without her.

David J. Amos

I Need Someone to Love Me

As I sat dreaming into space
I thought my life was such a waste
And just as I had started to cry
A flock of little birds flew by

Then I thought of happiness, freedom and peace
And with that my heart, it started to ease
For life is for the living, get that into you head
Enjoy yourself, have fun, you are a long time dead

With so much love to spare
I need someone loving to share
Is there someone out there
someone who would really care
I have warmth and love in abundance for you
And I just pray you have the same for me to
And then the world can all see
Someone can really love me.

Edith McCullough

Jamie

Now when the catkins blow
We will remember Jamie,
Small martyr of our evil days.
And when the snowdrops grow
In innocence, then will we grieve
For Jamie - little victim of our time
Smiling through the news
In all its ghastly truth -
That little boys can be so cruel
And silence his small voice forever.

Then as we stood - heads bowed
In biting winds, and heard the
Unfamiliar prayers,
Would we - when sunny crocus
Starred the grass - another cold and windy day
Remember Jamie?
And resolve that no more innocents
Shall ever fall sad prey
To wicked cruelty
And our neglectful ways?

Polly Wates

The Old Water Mill

By the old water mill, I saw her standing still.
Waiting for her love to come by.
With tears in her eyes, and to my surprise.
Flung her arms 'round my neck and began to cry.
As my heart began to race, I wiped her sad face
And asked why she was so sad.
Twenty years had gone by, and with a big sigh.
Said she had not seen him since he was a lad.
She poured her heart out, and without a doubt.
The description she gave was true.
Blue eyes and fair hair, a scar on his ear,
And at once I really knew.
I was that lad, and how I am glad.
By chance I climbed the steep hill,
For the girl I love most, and thought I had lost
Found her standing by the old water mill.
In a loving embrace, I kissed her warm face
And held hands, as we walked down the hill.
Now together for life, as future husband and wife.
All thanks to the old water mill.

Patricia Robinson

Untitled

Can't find anywhere -can't find you,
can't see, can't talk, can't dance,
 can you?
You see: There was an invisible man, who knew himself well,
but no one knew he wasn't invisible,
they thought him through, they said to him:
"Hey! how are you doing?"
"Fine chum, how are you?"
That's how it goes.
I know that some people hide theirs
and so well: Wide world hide inside,
it's small, forgotten,
'til uncurled at a time of retching,
then it's there, and all hell!
because he doesn't realize it's out, or it's there at all!
Not many people see themselves,
maybe you're invisible too?
there was invisible man, who knew himself well,
but no one knew he wasn't invisible,
 do you?

Andrew P. Walters

Sorrow and Joy

I feel my way, I am not bold
I find faults that are not there
I ought to know without being told.

I'm lost, empty, left out in the cold
I cry for help that isn't there
I feel my way, I am not bold.

My friends desert me, leave the fold
What do they want, what must I do
I ought to know without being told.

I am so hapless, I've lost my hold
On all that life can offer me
I feel my way, I am not bold.

Please someone help me break the mould
Dampen the pain, lift the spirit
I ought to know without being told.

This cry has made me happy I behold
Bared my feelings, bared my soul
Now I know my way, now I'm bold
Now I know without being told.

Margaret Trimby

Autumn

Oh close the door now summer lady
make way for autumn queen so grand the entry.
She must be of golden falling leaves
A carpet of red she will lay on a damp breeze she will play.

Through every tree and forest green turning colours can
be seen she plays the noble part with
such a light heart till every leaf is shed
bare to turn and face the winter fayre.
Then over night and day she seems to stray
like a gypsy turned all tattered and brown
no more the regal lady grand all tattered
and torn fallen to the ground a gently
breeze of ice cold sneeze of winter abound.
She lays to die on a diamond land gone
till seasons fill and spill their wonders nigh.
She will be back next year without any fear
so noble and grand that lady of autumn so dear.

Lynn Wayth

The Tempest of Life

Swirling clouds of cotton wool surround the earth;
Opening on us to pour out their tears;
Tears of sadness, tears of despair,
Full of regret with a warning, beware!

Beware, the clouds are gathering,
All the earth's anger is going to erupt;
With flashes of light and crashes of thunder;
The rain beats down like lava pouring from a live volcano.

The clouds are parting,
The earth is in peace and tranquillity;
The earth's light is shining bright;
I'm wondering why things change so fast.

Time goes by without a glance,
As one lets slip by the passing chance;
The chance to be happy, the chance to be great,
Hurry and take it before it's too late.

Why do things change so much?
And in such a short time.

Julie Yvonne McCafferty

Individual

An individual is a person,
whose different to another.
I know one, she is my Mother.

She's elegant, charming and kind,
my love for her forever does bind.

With an air of sophistication the earth's
gravity gave a pull,
and sent the world a spinning to make
everyone pay attention,
to learn to their full.

Your mother you must cherish,
just as if she were a delicate rose,
which imparts a fragrance that gladdens,
the heart and nose.

Its time glides along, the petals descend,
and the rose has to perish.
Wasn't it a while ago so beautiful in bloom,
and yet quite frail?
Yet the heady scent cloth prevail.

A. Povey

Sea of Love

Her sweet love has gone like the sea from the shore
Leaving rock pools of memory behind
Her face is reflected in crystals of light
Sending ripples of hope 'cross my mind

Words are like footprints that trail in the sand
Castles of dreams built so high
Feeling so helpless just watching them fade
And crumble away with the tide

Time is a mist rolling in from the sea
Distorting the things that were said
Clouding emotions that pull at the heart
And reel like the gulls over head

But love is rock and slow to erode
Or maybe I'll just never learn
I'll stay on the beach for the rest of my life
And wait for the sea to return.

Kevin Holmes

Don't Give Up

When things go wrong as they sometime will when
The road you're trudging seems all uphill when the
funds are low and the debts are high. And you want
To smile but you have to sigh — when care is pressing
You down a bit — rest if you must but don't you quit
Life is queer with its twists and turns —-
As everyone of us learns —-
Any many failure turns about —-
When he might have won. Had he stuck it out
Don't give up though the pace seems slow
You may succeed with another blow —-
Success is failure turn inside out —-
The silver tint of the cloud of doubt and you
Never can tell how close you are —-
It may be near when it seems so far —-
So stick to the fight when you're hardest hit —-
It's when things seems worst
You must not quit

R. E. Myhill

A Sad Story

There's an old woman living in my house,
She's elusive, but I know she's there,
Because she uses my brush,
It's often full of white hair.
As I hurry past the mirror in the morning,
I see her. When I creep back in stealth,
She has gone. Does anyone else see her?
Or do I delude myself.

When I go out for the night,
She is well hidden from sight,
But I know she's at home . . . waiting.
I see her more than I will admit,
By my mirror she'll patiently sit,
I know she waits for a sign,
When she can make my hairbrush her own
And know it's hers. It won't then be mine.

And maybe, she'll catch a glimpse of me
Now and then, that only she can see.

Heather Rayne

Ode to a tree

Put your trust in the strength of a tree take refuge under its shade,
Embrace it with love and your soul will feel free, rejoice and
    don't be afraid.
Hear God's voice in the song of the bird's as they sour thro' the air.
See his mercy in the waves of the sea.
All to kens of love and his mercy and care
These thinks are constant and for ever will be
So when your heart is heavy and fainting with fear,
And you know not what the morrow may bring.
When they say it's all over and the ending draws near
Because of mans madness and greed.
Just remember the tree and its message of hope
Tho' perished lives on thro' its seed
And the promise of Jesus comes down from above.
To all things that live, yes even you.
Remember his words - be still know that I am god.
And behold "I Make All Things New"

Gladys M. Locke

Biographies
of
Poets

ABBOU, LEILA
[b.] 27 March 1977, Leamington Spa; [p.] Houmada Abbou and Edwina Abbou; [ed.] Bishops Itchington Combined School, Southam School, Mid-Warwickshire College; [occ.] Awaiting entrance into university to study art; [hon.] J Spencer White Award for Academic Achievement, Modular Science Award for Academic Achievement; [pers.] This poem was written in response to the tragedy that took place in Dunblane. The sadness I felt inspired these words of comfort.; [a.] Leamington Spa, Warwickshire, UK

ADAMS, KATHLEEN GLADYS
[pen.] Catherine Rouse/Kate Conway; [b.] 5 August 1916, Harrow, Middx; [p.] Gladys May, Edmund Clarke; [m.] Christopher Frederick Adams, 17 September 1964; [ch.] One son ('Sim'); [ed.] Harrow County School; [occ.] Pensioner/Widow/Mother/Scribe; [oth. writ.] Various poems, published odd wimes, here and there. Also, short stories, not condemned, but not accepted.; [pers.] For my work I aim for a basic rhythmic pulsation, plus perfect symmertry... I sense 'something' coming from a man in a dark cap and gown. Very valuable! For morale, not for material help.; [a.] Peterborough, Cambs, UK

ADAMS, NIKKI
[pen.] Nikki Adams; [b.] 2 January 1980, Southampton; [p.] Gary Adams, Maureen Adams; [ed.] Redbridge Community School, Southampton City College; [occ.] Student; [hon.] School Commendations; [pers.] My poem was written to make people try and understand that no matter how wrong something maybe there is usually a reason why it happens.; [a.] Southampton, Hampshire, UK

ADAMS, SARAH
[pen.] Sarah Anne; [b.] 28 December 1972, Stoke-on-Trent; [p.] Harold Lowndes and Winnie Lowndes; [m.] John Craig Adams, 5 August 1995; [ed.] Birches Head high School, Stoke-on-Trent, Staffs, Stoke-on-Trent City College, Shelton, Staffordshire; [occ.] Nursery Nurse at Townsend primary School Bucknall; [hon.] Gold Leadership Award, Diploma in Nursery Nursing; [pers.] I have always desired to have a poem published and hope that one day I will achieve success with my other poems. I would like to dedicate this poem to my mum and dad and my husband John as a special thanks for all the encouragement.; [a.] Stoke-on-Trent, Staffordshire, UK

ADAMSON, MRS. ELSA
[pen.] Florence; [b.] 12 November 1912, Hull, Yorks; [m.] Deceased; [ch.] Two; [ed.] Just ordinary school in Hull; [occ.] Retired; [memb.] Ladies Guild, and Tapestry class. Also Dancing Class.; [pers.] Being my first ever poem, I was thinking out loud, works just flowed from my pen, about the days, when I was ten.; [a.] Hessle, East Yorks, UK

AITKEN, MANDY
[b.] 1 April 1959, Guildford, Surrey; [p.] Sheila and Arthur Richardson; [m.] Neill Aitken, 1 April 1989; [ch.] Tony Aitken (Now deceased); [ed.] Broadwater County Secondary School, Registered General Nurse Training, St. Lukes Nurse Education Centre, Guildford, Surrey; [occ.] Clinical Ward Manager - Unstead Park Rehabilitation Hospital; [memb.] U.K.C.C., R.C.N.; [hon.] ENB 998 Dip.; [oth. writ.] Numerous poems, - 'A Fireman's Widow' was published in "In Touch", Surrey Fire

Brigade Magazine, I am currently writing my son's biography; [pers.] I write a lot of poetry, usually influenced by my observation of people and events in my life. My greatest inspiration was my thirteen year old son, who died very suddenly, last year. I hope, one day, to see his book published. He was an extraordinary child and a very special son.; [a.] Godalming, Surrey, UK

AKHTAR, SHAMSHAD
[pen.] "Light of the World"; [b.] 14 April 1957, West Pakistan; [p.] Mazir Ahmed, Ramzan Biri; [m.] 8 November 1977; [ch.] Muhummed Akhtar; [ed.] C.S.E. and G.C.E. Level in variety of subjects, Qualified Paralegal in Criminology Level 1: The Sociology of Crime and Deviance; [occ.] Law Student; [memb.] Have served as school governor and on Love Mental Health Committee of my Union, member of Socialist Workers Party, Workers Revolution Party; [hon.] Community Sports Leadership Award; [oth. writ.] I am a known established community and union resource: my unpublished work is to be found Internationally within our Community and the world.; [pers.] I support and uphold the weak and vulnerable, encourage goodwill and protect the essence of life, beauty and nature.; [a.] London, Peckham, UK

AKUA, OWUSU-ANSAH
[pen.] Akua; [b.] 9 May 1979, Ghana; [p.] Millicent Asamoa - Krodua K. Asamoah; [ed.] Christ The King School, Ghana. Aburi Girls Sec. Sch. Ghana; [occ.] Student; [memb.] Intercultural Exchange Programme; [pers.] I strive to express my thoughts, emotions, and imagination through my writings. Also to let people understand the meaning of my writings

ALDER, GLENN RICHARD
[b.] 20 August 1978 in Barnet.; [p.] Richard Alder, Brenda Alder.; [ed.] Edge Grave School, Merchant Taylors' School.; [occ.] Student Cassio College Waterford BTEC ND in Caring Services (2 year); [oth. writ.] First poem to be published at 18 years old. Hopefully the first of many.; [per.] I strive to convey my deep personal thoughts, which have been greatly influenced by my own experiences and insights. We live to make memories.; [a.] Watford, Hertfordshire.

ALDRIDGE, RACHAEL
[pen.] J. S. Collett; [b.] 11 December 1979, Buckinghamshire; [p.] Sandy Aldridge and A. G. Aldridge; [ed.] Highworth Warneford Comprehensive, Cirencester College; [occ.] Student; [memb.] National Trust, The Wharf Theatre Devices; [oth. writ.] None published; [pers.] "Carry on regardless!!!" no matter what life brings.; [a.] Highworth, Wiltshire, UK

ALLAN, JANET
[b.] 25 September 1950, Dundee, Scotland; [p.] Ellen and Aubrey Evans; [m.] Divorced; [ch.] Jennifer; [ed.] Left school 1964/65 with a school leavers certificate. Gained standard grade english as a mature student 1986/87; [occ.] Matron of Fettes College Edinburgh; [hon.] Handwriting compt for the Magazine Look and Learn - 1963/64 A silver medal for Scottish song compt.; [oth. writ.] Christine (Forever Friends Arrival Pres), The Driving Test (Arrival Press); [pers.] This is dedicated to: Mr. J. L. Ness my headmaster from Linlathen Sec School Proff. Donald G. McLarty and my daughter Jennifer, their influence has encouraged me to never doubt one's ability; [a.] Edinburgh, Scotland, EH4 1QX

ALLIS, NICOLA JANE
[pen.] Nicky Allis; [b.] 17 September 1953; [m.] Michael Allis, 3 September 1984; [ch.] Melanie, Maddy, Jimmy; [pers.] My inspiration is gleaned from the changing seasons and the beauty surrounding my somerset home, and my writing is both visionary and reflective aspects of life, love and nature.; [a.] Castle Cary, Somerset, UK

ALLSOP-SEWARD, CHERRILL
[pen.] Cherrill A. Seward; [b.] 15 March 1950, Johannesburg; [p.] Alice and Cyril Allsop, Stepfather Jack Seward; [ed.] Secondary Modern School, Art School (for 3 years); [occ.] Purchasing Assistant in a college; [memb.] Whitby Yacht Club, Leo Walmsley Society; [pers.] My poem reflects the modern trend in society for some men to expect perfection in women, trying to mould them into what they would like them to be, and not seeing them for what they are.; [a.] Whitby, N. Yorkshire, UK

AMBROSE, JENNY
[b.] 5 September 1937, Uxbridge in a Police House; [p.] Arthur and Gladys Hudkin; [m.] Colin T. Ambrose, 25 March 1961; [ch.] Five Children; [ed.] Greenway Sec. Modern, Left School at 15 no qualifications. My education Started 30 years ago with adult education.; [occ.] Housewife, Caring for two grandchildren (looking after animals) Domestic and wild.; [memb.] Classed in A.E. included Chinese Cookery, Typings, Needlework, Water colour Miniatures, Sculpture China Paintings, (Public Speaking and Psychology by incredible teacher Dr. Sussanne Band); [oth. writ.] Four small true stories in Anthology "Moments of contemplation" Poem "The Still Pool" 3 Stories Booklet" Out of Uxbridge Frays Writers Circle. True story about a kestral in P.A.W.S. wildlife magazine.; [pers.] Let peace fill your heart and mind and life.; [a.] Uxbridge, Middx, UK

ANDERSON, CYRIL VINCENT
[b.] 4 May 1944, Anston, Lindrick; [p.] Cyril Vincent and Bertha; [ed.] Hamilton Road Country Primary, Grave County Secondary Modern, Stoke-on-Trent College of Technology; [occ.] artist-photographer; [memb.] Endon Cricket Club, Vice President; [hon.] Books at school for English Literature and Language, Cricket trophies and honours with Longton Cricket Club and Endon Cricket Club; [oth. writ.] A Young Psychologist (book), Industrial Science (book), Six Towns Magazine (feature stories), National Geographic Society, University of Sheffield (psychology texts); [pers.] An artist and photographer of high reputation and an excellent poet, with an interest in psychology, sociology and philosophy. [a.] Stoke-on-Trent, Staffordshire

ANDERSON, ELIZABETH
[b.] 14 January 1942, Morham Mains; [p.] Isabella and Thomas Mason; [m.] James William Anderson, 18 September 1965; [ch.] Dawna Michele, Mark Adam and Julie Louise; [ed.] Haddington Infant School, Knox Academy Secondary, Ross High, For further education; [occ.] Housewife now on incapacity benefit - was secretary; [memb.] None now, was in Haddington Amateur Operatic Society which has now been abandoned.; [hon.] English I and II Burns Certificate for Scottish Literature, Scottish Leaving Certificate, Pitmans Shorthand Cert., Typing and Book-Keeping; [oth. writ.] None, except letters to local press; [pers.] I have always enjoyed writing poetry but have never submitted any as I never knew how to do so till I saw your advert. I also enjoy logic puzzles and am a keen reader.; [a.] Haddington, East Lothian, UK

ANDERSON, IRENE
[b.] 1 January 1951, Lampeter; [occ.] Medical Secretary; [oth. writ.] Poem published in "1993 Poets" poem published in "Connecting New Poetry" 1995; [pers.] "If more people wished for peace, the wish might come true."; [a.] Glasgow, Strathclyde, UK

ANDERSON, KATRINA M.
[b.] 7 December 1947, Springfield, Fife; [p.] Margaret and Zymunt Tomaszewski; [m.] William Anderson, 13 July 1984 (Second Marriage); [ch.] Edward 31, Loma 26, Tanya 19; [ed.] Bell-Baxter High School Cupar. H.N.C. Glenrothes College Dundee University; [occ.] Student, 2nd year at Dundee University, M.A. Honors Social Work; [oth. writ.] Printed in College; [pers.] In poetry I am free to be myself; [a.] Glenrothes, Fife, UK

ANDERSON, PHYLLIS R.
[b.] 5 May 1907, London, Dartmoor; [p.] Ada and Herbert Mann; [m.] Dr. C. S. Anderson, 15 June 1946; [ed.] Wycombe House School, I had very little, I was always ill; [occ.] Housewife and Artist and Musician (Piano and Cello); [hon.] Kenneth Clarke (P.R.A.) Award for Painting; [oth. writ.] The Dartmoor book 3 chinese fairy tales in the V and A children's section. A novel on Dr. Anderson, a children's story, several stories, 3 plays on the life of St. Peter.; [pers.] I have a had a very sad life - but I wouldn't have missed it. I have been greatly influenced by St. Francis of Assissi, Tho' Not at all religious.; [a.] Taunton, Somerset, UK

ANDERSON, ROBERT
[pen.] Bob Anderson; [b.] March 10, 1949, Forfar; [p.] Robert and Margaret Anderson; [ch.] Tracy Elizabeth; [ed.] Forfar Academy; [occ.] Forklift Driver; [memb.] Canmore Bowling Club, Forfar Bridge Club; [oth. writ.] The Expert, Night Time Caller, Business Mans Vacation; [pers.] When your best in not good enough, there is no shame in defeat.; [a.] Forfar, Angus

ANDERSON, SUZANNE MARY
[b.] 6 November 1955, Exeter, Devon; [p.] Raymond Jeffrey and Elsie Jeffrey; [m.] Partner: Michael Melvern; [ch.] Joanne, Ian, Brennan, Desnie; [ed.] Hitchin, High School; [occ.] PCB Assembler; [pers.] When you experience pain it, helps to put into words how you feel. When you're happy, you want to share it with the world.; [a.] Letchworth, Herts, UK

ANDREW, GILLIAN LESLEY
[b.] 4 August 1942, Derby; [p.] Doris Cormish, Leslie Cornish; [m.] Vivian Ward Andrew, 8 September 1965; [ch.] Melanie Jane (daughter), Ashley Ward (son); [ed.] St Philomena's Convent High School, Derby; [occ.] Medical Receptionist; [oth. writ.] Poems and short stories.

ANDREWS, LEONARD
[b.] 12 February 1927, Rotherham; [p.] William Andrews, Sarah Andrews; [m.] Marion, 26 December 1953; [ch.] Robert, Susan; [ed.] Spurley Hey School, Rotherham, English Revision in 1993 and 1994 at Rotherham College of Arts and Technology; [occ.] Retired; [hon.] First class certificate in Orthopedic Nursing Exam. when 23 years old; [oth. writ.] Songs, lyrics, poems, short stories; [pers.] It is never too late to learn and christianity helps; [a.] Rotherham, South Yorkshire, UK

ANGUS, JEAN
[b.] 27 September 1934, Birmingham; [p.] Kathleen Angus and James Angus; [ed.] Cotteridge Secondary Modern; [occ.] Retired; [oth. writ.] Other poem published in Anthology 'World Poets 1972'; [pers.] Life's a rich tapestry of emotions. If my poetry touches someone's heart or stirs a memory, then that is enough. I shall always continue.; [a.] Birmingham, Warwickshire, UK

ANNETTS, MRS. DAISY
[b.] 20 September 1922, Barnsley; [p.] Robert Benjamin Emmerson, Ada Emmerson; [m.] Colin Annetts, 16 September 1943; [ch.] Demise, Robert Edward; [ed.] Royston Comprehensive; [occ.] Retired; [memb.] Royston Salvation Army Corps Council, Home League Birthday Sergeant; [hon.] Band of Hope with honours as a child, won two books for writing essays; [oth. writ.] Poems have not sent for publication; [pers.] I try to show love and concern for my family and all mankind. Try hard to live a good christian life and always aim at the highest that being God of course.; [a.] Barnsley, Yorkshire, UK

ANSLOW, ROSEMARY
[b.] 19 August 1937, West Midlands; [p.] John Patrick Payton, Doris Payton; [m.] Alfred Terence Edward Anslow, 6 September; [ch.] Adrian Anslow Johanna Anslow; [ed.] "St. Chads" Roman Catholic School Sedgley, West Mislands; [occ.] Housewife, retired Sales Manager; [memb.] Tettenhall and Perton Drama Group "Pattco"; [hon.] Senior Acting Gold Medal "Lamda" the London Academy of Music and Dramatic Art; [oth. writ.] "How still was the night," "Elsie and the Whale (humorous), "A Day that I Recall."; [pers.] My poem is dedicated to my son Adrian Anslow he was lost at sea during the Falklands war may 25th 1982. He was royal navy fleet air arm. Just 20 yrs. old. I try to communicate with him, in poetry.; [a.] Wolverhampton, Tettenhall, West Mid, UK

ANSTIS, DICK
[b.] 17 January 1928, Bermuda; [p.] Jim and Nell Anstis; [m.] Divorced in 1966; [ch.] Richard, Katharine, Eleanor; [ed.] City of Bath Boys School Jesus College, Oxford; [occ.] Retired London Local Government Officer; [memb.] Labour Party, National Trust, Rambler's Association, Chelsea Football Club, Institute of Public Relations; [oth. writ.] Children's Stories; [pers.] I would hope my writing might open windows on life's miseries and magic to help me and readers (not least grandchildren) to cope, to improve and to enjoy.; [a.] Cobham, Surrey, UK

ANTONIOU, MR. CHRIS
[b.] 6 March 1964, London; [p.] Anthony and Emily; [m.] Chrisoulla, 25 September 1994; [ed.] Secondary Education, Further Education, correspondence courses; [occ.] Civil Servant; [memb.] Royal Naval Association Chelsea Football Club Member, Player Recommendation Adviser (unpaid), Birmingham City FC Shareholder; [hon.] Special Honour Recently for Achievements in the Civil Service; [oth. writ.] Taken from my book called "A Book Of Poems" some years ago.; [pers.] I speak out through my words, and if you can understand them, then you may understand me. We need peace, and to be loved.; [a.] London, Norbury, UK

ANTROBUS, EDNA LUCY
[pen.] Lucy Antrobus; [b.] 19 August 1908, Sydenham; [p.] William Ernest Chard, Lucy Elizabeth Chard (Maiden name Godfrey); [m.] Harvey Antrobus, 29 August 1934; [ch.] Celia Rosemary, Yvonne Daphne; [ed.] St. Anns Oxford (Modern History Degree), now music teacher, R.A.D.A. trained actress - worked in T.V. film and stage (Yvonne antrobus); [occ.] With BBC for 15 years prior to retirement; [oth. writ.] Articles published in 'Bygone Kent' also 'Family Tree' including poem. Poems published in poetry review and 'Poetry Today' also local poetry societies; [a.] Beckenham, Kent, UK

APPLEBY, STEPHEN
[b.] 25 October 1960, Gateshead; [p.] Joyce and Ralph; [m.] Margaret, 25 March 1995; [ed.] Sunderland University degree in Law; [occ.] Writer; [hon.] Degree in Law at Sunderland University; [oth. writ.] Novels - Too Much Spring - The Touch Stone; [pers.] I am a writer of novels I have two published, I am a writer full time and spend. 5-6 hours per day writing.; [a.] Gateshead, Durham, UK

ARMSTRONG, JOAN
[pen.] Pandora; [b.] 24 August 1947, City Westminster; [p.] David Robert, Dorothy Elizabeth; [ch.] Stephen Anthony Smith, Lee Richard; [occ.] Unemployed; [hon.] Commencing Degree English Literature this year, Kingston University; [oth. writ.] Discovered by the International Library of Poetry; [pers.] A quiet moments reflection, recorded for all to share, to feel, to see is life's contentment.

ARNOLD, MAUREEN B.
[pen.] Maureen B. Arnold; [b.] July 19, 1939, Edmonton; [p.] Mr. and Mrs. Goodrich; [m.] Brian S. Arnold, March 5, 1960; [ch.] Tracy and Ryan; [ed.] Secondary Modern; [occ.] Housewife; [memb.] Eastern Enfield Royal British Legion; [hon.] None as I have never entered anything before.; [oth. writ.] Poems and articles for Eastern Enfield Royal British Legion Bl. Monthly Magazine.; [pers.] I write as a hobby for myself, my family and friends about everyday life and current affairs.; [a.] Enfield, Middlesex

ARORA, RENU
[b.] 14 December 1978, Gwent; [p.] H. Arora (BA. ACA.) CP. Arora (Teacher); [ed.] Rougemont School Newport. I am currently studying A levels in English, Drama and Art.; [occ.] Student at school; [memb.] Local Youth Theatre. Gwent Badminton Squad; [hon.] I was invited to take part in a radio programme where I sang my own songs and recited my own poetry. I was interviewed live.; [oth. writ.] Several poems published in school magazine. One poem published in a book by the 'Forward Press' called 'Head Over Heels'.; [pers.] I think that we should all be at ease with our mind - the key to serenity; [a.] Cwmbran, Gwent, UK

ARORA, SOPHIE DE COURCY NORMAN
[pen.] Sophie De Courcy Norman Arora; [b.] 15 April 1967, Gerard's Cross; [p.] David and Helen De Courcy Norman; [m.] Birinder Arora, 6 August 1994; [ed.] More House Grammar, North London Polytechnic; [occ.] Housewife/Voluntary Worker; [hon.] B.A. in English and Classical Civilisation; [pers.] I enjoy using poetry as a means of projecting a variety of different emotions. Special thanks to my husband for inspiring me, to write this poem.; [a.] Isleworth, Middlesex, UK

ASH, SHARON
[pen.] Sharon Ash; [b.] 28 November 1969, Lewisham; [p.] Colin Ash, Joan Ash; [ch.] Kelly-Marie, Jamie Alexander; [ed.] Bideford College; [occ.] Full - time Mother; [memb.] Bideford and District Angling Club; [oth. writ.] None published

at present.; [pers.] Live life to the full don't worry about what others think, its what you think that matters; [a.] Bideford, Devon, UK

ATKINSON, BETTY MARGARET
[pen.] Elizabeth Atkinson; [b.] 26 July 1923, London; [p.] Wm. J. Gamlin, Leah Emily (Nee Hunt); [m.] Gordon Atkinson (Deceased), 10 March 1956; [ed.] L.C.C. Junior and Secondary Schools, further Education - various, Qualified Teacher Ballroom dancing 1951, Qualified Account 970, B.A. degree (Open) University 1979, B.A. degree Hons. (Open) 1994; [occ.] Singer/Manager, Elizabeth Atkinson Enterprises; [hon.] B.A. Hons (Open), F.F.A., A.I.D.M.A. (BB), A.N.A.T.D. (BB Comm.); [oth. writ.] Three poems published.; [pers.] I dedicate 'A Fragrant Memory' to my dear sister Grace.

ATKINSON, MRS. OLIVE
[b.] 13 May 1927, Blyth, Notts.; [m.] Arthur Atkinson, 24 November 1951; [ch.] Alan; [ed.] Village C of E School, Everton, Doncaster; [occ.] Housewife; [hon.] A badge for work done re, Poppy Collections - etc.; [pers.] I have suffered with Parkinson's disease for the past ten years.; [a.] Doncaster, S. Yorks, UK

ATTON, JOAN MONICA
[b.] 7 September 1939, Ghana; [p.] Albert Atton and Mary Briandt; [ch.] Sheila Bannerman-Williams, Andrew Frimpong; [ed.] St. Mary's Secondary School, Accra, Ghana; [occ.] Occupational Health Nurse Adviser, Registered Nurse, Midwife, Theatre Trained; [memb.] Royal College of Nursing; [hon.] Diploma in Occupational Health Nursing at the Royal College of Nursing Caverdish Square, London,; [oth. writ.] I am a new song writer. I am now trying to have them published.; [pers.] In my poem I strive to reflect the power of God working in everything and working in our daily lives. The Holy Spirit is the power of God and was given to mankind as a gift on the Perto Costal day. I have been influenced by the wonders of creation and great ability of mankind.; [a.] London, UK

AUSTIN, ANDREA
[b.] 15 April 1960, Dumfries; [p.] Maitland Austin, Stella Austin; [ed.] Marchmount High School, Dumfries College, Paisley University; [occ.] Retail Manager; [memb.] NCDL; [hon.] BA Business Administration; [pers.] Writing for myself is the positive side of my negativity.; [a.] Dumfries, Dumfries and Galloway, UK

AUSTIN, JAIME
[b.] 7 July 1978, Harrow; [p.] Barbara Austin; [m.] (Engaged) Russell Cox; [ed.] Barnhill Secondary School, Walford High School, Ealing Tertiary College; [occ.] Student; [oth. writ.] Various short stories, a story called "A Joint Betrayal" earning me a WH Smiths certificate of commendation; [pers.] I use both my poetry and stories to express myself, and my views on issues over which I have no control. My own life has influenced most of my work.; [a.] Ashford, Middlesex, UK

AVERY, BERNARD E.
[pen.] Bernard E. Avery; [b.] 25 February 1932, Oxford; [p.] Rev. and Ann Avery; [m.] Olive Avery, 30 March 1957; [ch.] One Boy and Two Girls (Adopted); [ed.] Cheltenham Grammar; [occ.] Sales Rep (Part Time); [hon.] Oxford School Cert. (1948); [oth. writ.] "From Storm to Sunshine" (story) 1948, "Bible Messages in Verse" 1994,

"More Bible Messages in Verse" 1996, (Plus several poems in anthologies) (and articles in Christian Magazines); [pers.] Our youngest daughter was murdered (in 1986) for insurance money. My poetry is something positive which I feel has resulted from the tragedy and I trust will help readers. For God's Glory; [a.] Malvern, Worcs, UK

AYLWARD, SOPHIE CLARE
[b.] 13 December 1984, Chichester; [ed.] A pupil at East Court School for Dyslexic children; [occ.] 11 years old, School girl at East Court School for Dyslexic children; [pers.] I like to paint pictures with my words.; [a.] Sandwich, Kent, UK

BABER, KATHLEEN
[pen.] C.C. Pearce Baber; [b.] 5 December 1915, Avonmouth; [p.] Alfred Albert Pearce and May Pearce; [m.] Deceased: We divorced 1953 (Mine), June 1941 (Wartime Disaster); [ch.] One daughter Mary and one son Philip; [ed.] I was Educated at the only school in Avonmouth. The Church of England School, we had very good and dedicated Headmaster McWilliam Powell and Teachers.; [occ.] Housewife of many lively interests, but now housebound owing to A Fall in 1983, thro' which, I lost my balance, so I need a Mobile Walking Aid, like one used in Super - Markets. Very good. I have had a very busy life and try to use my time and life to and for, the love of God, and those who have need of love like his, he never excludes anyone", is the life here allotted to the seven ages of man, the father hood of God is perfect and absolute religous mainly, through daily prayer, my faith has been truly rewarded in more than one personal encounter, I am honoured, and humbly grateful to my dear Father Creator, always "Re-Newing."; [pers.] My catholic faith, and all, through my trials, follies, and tribulations, I am ever aware, as the days slip away, I am in the Holy presence of our Blessed Savior Christ Jesus, I awe "This Gift and Inspirations for Writings."; [a.] Bristol, Gloucestershire, UK

BACON, LORRAINE
[b.] 29 September 1965, Hackney; [p.] Kenneth Moore, Anita Moore; [m.] William Bacon, 25 August 1990; [ch.] James, Michael, Katie, Louise; [ed.] Sandy Upper School, Sandy Place Middle School; [occ.] Housewife; [oth. writ.] I have written a number of childrens poems and am currently working on an adventure story, this has yet just been a hobby for me.; [pers.] I am greatly influenced by a childs imagination and try to see through their eyes to create my poems and stories; [a.] Biggleswade, Bedfordshire, UK

BAGLARBASI, CEM
[b.] 21 July 1977, Enfield; [p.] Meyrem Baglarbasi, Ahmet Baglarbasi; [ed.] Winchmore School, Waltham Forest College; [occ.] Manufacturing Student; [memb.] Churchills Snooker Club, Pool and Track Fitness Room User; [pers.] I strive to reflect and blend the rhythm and goodness of the music which I listen to, which inspires and influences my poetry.; [a.] Walthamston, London, UK

BAILEY, BETTY
[b.] 12 October 1927, Eccles, Lancashire; [p.] John and Florence Eckersley; [m.] Thomas Bailey, 25 March 1950; [ch.] Joyce Susanne, David Keith; [ed.] Stretford Technical College; [occ.] Retired; [memb.] President - Astley women's Institute, Hon. Life Vice President (Hon Sec 1971-1990), North of England Airedale Terrier Club, Airedale Broad Council Sec. 1984-990; [oth. writ.] Various articles for dog papers on Airedale Terriers. Piece

of prose - entry for competition 1993, WI Denman Cup. (finalist from Lancashire).; [pers.] I am greatly influenced by the beauty of Nature and to me a poem must paint a picture in words.; [a.] Tyldesley, Lancashire, UK

BAILEY, JENNIFER
[b.] 25 February 1947, Gorleston; [m.] David Bailey, 19 April 1974; [ch.] Two adult sons; [ed.] Great Yarmouth High School for Girls, Nottingham University; [occ.] Supply Teacher; [memb.] South Somerset Choral Society, Somerset Wildlife Trust; [oth. writ.] 1993 Assembly of poems above Primary School Life "Every Monday Morning". Own Imprint ISBN 09522557-07, 1995 Choral Work "Ego Aethelredus" based on Ilminster's History, with composer Nigel Variety of Poems Articles, Folk Harris. Songs published, Performed.; [pers.] As an incurable `people watcher', I write about the behaviour and characteristics of both children and adults, both past and present. Everyday life, local history and legends provide a rich source of inspiration.; [a.] Ilminster, Somerset, UK

BAKER, DERYK ALAN LEE
[pen.] Lee Baker; [b.] 28 September 1952, Aalyesbury, Bucks; [p.] Mr. Frederick Seymour Alan Baker and Ms. Margret E. Baker; [ch.] Steven David, Simon, and Derek; [ed.] The Grange Secondary Modern School, Aylesbury, Bucks; [occ.] Research Criminologist and Ethnic Minority Counsellor; [memb.] Amnesty International (U.K.), Liberty (U.K.); [hon.] too many: B.A. Humanities: Middlesex University 1975, Diploma in Socio-Legal Studies: Ealing College, Certificate in Counselling: The Lincoln Memorial Clinic for Psychotherapy, Postgraduate certificate in criminology: Middlesex University 1994; [oth. writ.] "Cracks in the Fabric!", "An Examination and Review of the United States Drug Control Strategy": The Library of Congress & Middlesex University, "Sales" [pers.] I live the life I love and I love the life I live. I do not love and live global decay, only unity within the "world melting-pot". [a.] Hackney, London

BAKER, HEIDI THERESA
[b.] 4 January 1981, Rochford, Essex; [p.] Keith Baker, Joy Watts; [ed.] Shoeburyness County High School; [occ.] Pupil; [oth. writ.] Several poems, none submitted for publishing; [pers.] I never plan to write a poem, the thoughts just come to me and I have to write them down. My poems are often about my feelings at that time.; [a.] Shoeburyness, Essex, UK

BALDOCK, SOPHIE
[b.] 8 February 1979, Kingston; [p.] David Baldock, Jorita Baldock; [ed.] Surbiton High School, United World College of South East Asia (Singapore), Hurtwood House College; [occ.] Student; [oth. writ.] Other poems and sonnets but not published due to the personal nature of them.; [pers.] My poems are always influenced by my love for people and nature, I try to concentrate a life time of thoughts into one short sonnet.; [a.] Esher, Surrey, UK

BALL, MRS. J. M.
[b.] 20 January 1917, Hinckley; [p.] David - Emily Savage; [m.] Mr. Ernest Ball (Deceased), 10 June 1939; [ch.] David - Janet; [ed.] Just a Council (Mine) School. Children went to Grammar Schools; [occ.] Retired; [oth. writ.] I have several poems but this is the first time I have sent any in. I have several too in Cyril Fletcher Stye.; [pers.] I have always been interested in poetry and also in oil painting.; [a.] Leicester, Leics, UK

BALLARD, IRIS ROSEMARY MICHAEL
[b.] 17 May 1929, Bottle, Sussex; [p.] Kathleen Foord, Benjman Chesson; [m.] Alan Frank Ballard (Deceased 1985), 30 September 1950; [ch.] David, Glen, Piers, Peter, and Heidi; [ed.] Hastings Sacred Heart College, then one Girls School, recently, St. Vincent College, for Adult Education, Courses; [occ.] Retired, from Nursing and Motherhood; [memb.] I belong to the Brotherhood of the White Eagle Lodge. German Shepard Rescue Centre British Association for German Shepards, German Shepards Dog Welfare Charity, Lee on Solent Sailing Club, no longer active member.; [hon.] Poems published by budding editors Chris Woltons (Lights from within) Phil Rampton, small article in Stella Poluris and Poem in Science Thought Review. In the 60's, and 70's awards for writing directing and making Cine Films, second one with Children of Saint Johns School Crowbough; [oth. writ.] The films, were show to Local people in the 60's for School Building Fund. I've written a few short stories.; [pers.] I was influenced by, the old poets but I write from my heart, hoping I can sway a few people, that need comfort, and to prompt, others to, be aware of the needs of poverty stricken, victims of war, also the beauty of our Mother Earth.; [a.] Lee on Solent, Hants, UK

BANKS, DOREEN
[pen.] Doreen McDonald Banks; [b.] Hull, East Yorks; [p.] Harry and Grace Bates; [m.] John McDonald Banks; [ch.] Nigel, Anthony, John Banks; [ed.] St. Mary's Secondary school Hull; [occ.] Dance Teacher, Run my own School; [memb.] R.S.P.B., Am also a fund raiser for the P.D.S.A. and R.S.P.C.A and Hospice charity shops; [hon.] Fellow - Idta member - B.A.T.D and B Bo. and elementary Rad. All are dance qualifications.; [oth. writ.] Article in the "Smart Dogs magazine (July/95). This was a true story about our dog and family. 8 poems published by forward press - anchor books and triumph house. And other local press writings.; [pers.] My greatest love was my dear late husband, a wonderful kind honorable man, all animals, the countryside and all God's wonderful creations. I try through my poetry, to assure people that this world is a beautiful place if you just open your eyes to everything around you.; [a.] Woodmansey, Beverley, East Yorks, UK

BANKS, SUSAN GEORGINA
[pen.] Georgina George; [b.] 20 December 1941, Pentilly Castle, Cornwall; [p.] Edward and Muriel Sharpe; [m.] Divorced; [ch.] Deborah, Matthew and Harvey; [ed.] Joseph Wright School of Art, Derby and Derbyshire College of Art; [occ.] Resident warden of a sheltered housing scheme for elderly people; [memb.] Association of American Tap Dancing; [hon.] Silver Medalist, all England dance championships, B.T.E.C. National Wardens Certificate, Art Scholarship 1956; [oth. writ.] Several poems published in local magazine; [pers.] A photograph captures the moment, a story will capture the mind, but the lilt and the rhyme of a poem can capture the soul of mankind. It has been a very pleasant surprise for me to have my writing chosen and published.; [a.] Allestree, Derby, Derbyshire, UK

BARBER, SERENA ELLEN
[b.] 27 June 1972, Ashford, Midx; [p.] Norah Ann Barber; [ch.] Stephanie Norah and Sophie Ellen; [ed.] St. Teresas RC School, St. Ignatius Infant; [occ.] Mother; [pers.] To my mother and grandmother thank you, I love you both forever.; [a.] Chertsey, Surrey, UK

BARKER, HARRY MILNER
[b.] 10 March 1928, Leeds; [p.] Harry and Emma; [m.] Evelyn, 23 December 1950; [ch.] Christine; [ed.] Middleton Council School Leeds; [occ.] Retired; [oth. writ.] Poems not published, The Demise of Toffee Row, The Passing of a Friend, Friendship, Left Home, Benny the Breadman; [pers.] I like writing poems, but my main ambition is to write a full length novel.; [a.] Leeds, West Yorks, UK

BARNES, JAMES
[pen.] Jim; [b.] 25 February 1935, Halifax, Yorks; [p.] John William, Kathleen; [m.] Marjorie, 11 August 1956; [ch.] Patricia, David, Sharron, Kirth, Mark Michelle; [occ.] Self employed sales; [memb.] Institute of Sales Management; [oth. writ.] The Advent of Summer, The Meaning Of Life; [pers.] A statement from the heart is more than you could dream a statement from the heart can make your life supreme.; [a.] Southend on Sea, Essex, UK

BARRON, GRAHAM ROBERT
[b.] 4 May 1971, Dunstable; [p.] George Barron, Iris Barron; [m.] Philip McLaughlin; [ed.] Northfiels Upper School; [occ.] Unemployed; [oth. writ.] One other poem published in a National Anthology; [pers.] This is only the second poem I have submitted to be, and successfully had, published. Through this, I hope to gain the patience to write and the courage to submit more of my works.; [a.] Brighton, East Sussex, UK

BARTON, DAVID B. H.
[pen.] Holman; [b.] 28 August 1972, Nottingham, England; [p.] Nicholas J. and Margaret A. J. Barton; [ed.] Nottingham High School, Demontfort University; [occ.] Writer; [oth. writ.] Various songs performed in Leicester. The telekine - a graphic novel. Xenobios - speculations on the nature of life elsewhere. All so far unpublished.; [pers.] Poetry is redundant if it speaks of things which have been put in better words elsewhere. It should not.; [a.] Leicester, Leicestershire, UK

BASELEY, PEGGIE
[b.] Rugby, UK; [p.] Perc and Alice Baseley; [ed.] Rugby High (Grammar); [occ.] Impoverished Idle; [oth. writ.] Technical articles, short stories; [pers.] All my creative writing - poems and prose - is based on my observations of people in real life situations. But my humorous verse - which I enjoy because it is happy - seems to be most popular; [a.] Rugby, Warwicks, UK

BASKEYFIELD, KATHLEEN
[pen.] D. J. Lauren; [b.] 29 December 1927, Nantwich; [p.] Fredrick and Alice Browness; [m.] Richard Leonard Baskeyfield, 26 March 1949; [ch.] John Leonard Thomas Baskeyfield; [ed.] Ludford St. Elementary - Crewe. Ches; [occ.] Housewife; [memb.] Wistaston Gardeners Society; [oth. writ.] Several poems, two short stories, not published; [pers.] Enjoy life, and bless each new day.; [a.] Wistanton Crewe, Cheshire, UK

BATCHELOR, MRS. JACQUIE
[b.] 23 November 1956, Hillingdon; [p.] Mrs. A. H. Clover (Deceased), Mr. J. F. Clover; [m.] Mr. David Graham Batchelor, 7 September 1991; [ed.] Edgebarrow Comprehensive School (Berkshire); [occ.] Housewife (formerly mortgage underwriter); [oth. writ.] School magazine, no other competitions entered. Many other poem which I have not as yet submitted for publishing.; [pers.] I started writing again after running out of other poets verses to express my love for David, my husband, which I like to include in cards I send him. Inspiration came one day while walking our dogs. The beauty of the day, made the words flow; [a.] Desborough, Northants, UK

BATCHELOR, RUTH
[b.] 5 September 1953, London; [p.] Alan and Joyce Batchelor; [ed.] John Howard Grammar School, Clapton, Birmingham Polytechnic; [occ.] Photographer; [memb.] North Norfolk Camera Club, United Photographic Portfolios, Bureau Freelance Photographers; [hon.] C.R.C.C.Y.P. (Birm. Poly 1975) (Cert. in Residential Care of Children and Young People); [oth. writ.] Several poems published in local church magazines. Also produce own 'Poems and Pictures' series of postcards.; [pers.] I trained as a residential social worker, now working as Freelance Photographer. I enjoy writing poetry, and am usually inspired by major events or situations in my life.; [a.] Sheringham, Norfolk, UK

BATHURST, DOROTHEA
[pen.] Thea Bathurst; [b.] 28 April 1911, London; [p.] Joseph Eyre, Rebecca Eyre; [m.] Harry Wolf Hanagan and Edgar Bathurst, 25 January 1933 and 15 May 1971; [ch.] Susan; [ed.] Sacred Heart Convent Rochampton London new Woldington Surrey and Trinita dei Mondi Rome; [occ.] Housewife (Widow); [memb.] La Moye Golf Club La Moye St Brelade Jersey Ch Islands; [oth. writ.] Other poems not sent in for publication; [pers.] It has always been an ambition of mine to get either a novel or poem published - I am a great advocate of bringing back Religion in Schools; [a.] St. Brelade, Jersey, Channel Islands, UK

BATICKCHARI, SHAFIULLAH
[b.] 30 March 1940, Chittagong; [m.] Rakeba Chowdhury, 7 December 1975; [ch.] Three Daughters - Saafia, Faiza and Rahaymin Chy; [ed.] B.SC. Engineering, Dip - in C. Elec; [occ.] Engineering; [oth. writ.] Shangramee - Banglee (struggle for Blengalee Nationalism) published 1971.; [pers.] Writing is my hobby. I enjoy writing about my personal experience.; [a.] Denton, Manchester, UK

BAXTER, SHIRLEY
[pen.] Shirley Baxter; [b.] 1 December 1933, Oldham, Lancashire; [p.] Both Deceased; [m.] Divorced; [ch.] Philip - 41, Karen - 38; [ed.] Wirral Grammar School, Bebbington, Cheshire; [occ.] Retired, Ex-Nurse; [memb.] British Legion, Crown Green Bowling Association, 5 Bowling Clubs including League Bowling; [hon.] Rose Bowl 1995 (Crown Green Bowls), Pairs Winner (Indoor Bowls) 1995; [oth. writ.] Many poems, some published by poetry now Peterborough, 2 short stories, 1 published by 'New Fiction'. One novel entitled 'Cockroach Cottage' looking for a publisher.; [pers.] Although I enjoyed English and poetry at school, I never attempted to write anything until later in life, then only for my own amusement, to be destroyed once it was written. Only in the last five years have I written seriously.; [a.] Formby, Merseyside, UK

BAYLISS, JESSICA HELEN
[b.] 30 January 1985, Stoke-on-Trent; [p.] Ken and Helen Bayliss; [ed.] Thursfield C.P. now at Pikemere C.P.; [occ.] School girl; [memb.] Local swimming club (Biddulph); [oth. writ.] None published; [a.] Kidsgrove, Staffs, UK

BEALE, ELIZABETH ANNE
[b.] 22 January 1942, Bedfordshire; [ed.] Grammar School Bedford, Mander College Bedford, Diploma in Psychology; [occ.] Writing poems; [oth. writ.] Several poems published over 30 yrs. Parnasus publications and competitions. (N.B. I have never won a prize.); [pers.] My poems strive to form simplicity out of complexity of human emotions. I have been influenced by Brian Patten.; [a.] Flitwick, Beds, UK

BEAN, JOAN E.
[b.] 21 February 1914, Scarborough; [p.] Ernest and Elizabeth Lawrence; [m.] William Bean (Deceased), 3 August 1940; [ch.] Lawrence and Jane; [ed.] Convent of the Ladies of Mary Queen Street Scarborough Yorks; [occ.] Housewife (Retired); [pers.] I am interested in Drawing, Painting, Collecting Antiques also Floral Art, having won a few cups at the Local Horticultural shows, for Floral displays over the years, (My Philosophy is. "Keep Believing"); [a.] Scarborough, Yorks, UK

BEARD, ANN PENELOPE
[pen.] Penelope Ann; [b.] 12 November 1951, Bognor, Regis; [m.] Divorced; [memb.] The Welsh Academy; [oth. writ.] Many poems published in books by poetry now, anchor books triumph house. Plus poems and short story for East Anglian archives magazine.; [pers.] Writing is like an artist who portrays color and feelings on canvas. As we have the opportunity to do it through words.; [a.] Clanfield, Hampshire, UK

BEASLEY, KEITH
[b.] 9 August 1958, Banbury; [p.] Kath and Cecil Beasley; [ed.] MCS Brackley: UCNW; [occ.] Therapist and Trainer of Reiki Natural Healing; [memb.] SMN, Mensa. Heyford Players and Morris Men; [oth. writ.] 3 Business Improvement books, articles for Mensa Magazine, etc.; [pers.] I believe that my role in life is to awaken the spirit in the community, in business and in each of us.; [a.] Northampton, UK

BEATTS, WILLIAM
[b.] 20 June 1983, Paisley Maternity; [p.] William and Carol Ann; [ed.] 2nd Year Eastwood High School, Eastwood; [memb.] Neilston Swimming Club, Scouts, Pace (Amateur Dramatics); [pers.] I had fun composing my poem as part of a school project in primary 7.; [a.] Barrhead, Renfrewshire, UK

BECKER, DOUG
[pen.] Doug Becker; [b.] 23 October 1973, England; [p.] Micheal and Cheryl Becker; [ed.] Latimer School, Tresham College; [occ.] Security Guard; [hon.] BTEC Diploma in Fine Art Foundation studies; [oth. writ.] Small self publication "unsung songs from the streets"; [pers.] In being only one human being, be a happy human being.; [a.] London, UK

BEECH, LYNN
[b.] 24 May 1949, Crewe; [p.] George and Bessie Kidson; [m.] Divorced; [ch.] Lisa - 24, Matthew - 21; [oth. writ.] My first poem was submitted to anchor books and was published in the over the wall issue. This is my second poem submitted and I am very pleased to say also published.; [pers.] I write my poems about life, feelings and thoughts. They are simple to understand and easy to read a poem for everyone.

BEER, DELIA
[b.] 23 April 1947, Worcester Pk, SY; [p.] Dick and Doll Scrivener; [m.] Stanley Beer (30 years together); [ch.] Stuart (26), Duncan (22), Angus (16); [occ.] Housewife; [oth. writ.] Several novels - Humour, SCI-FI, Romance, Thrillers, (none published yet) many poems.; [pers.] I write because I must and hope that it pleases others. Humour helps to retain sanity in this crazy world.; [a.] Surbiton, Surrey, UK

BELL, KATHLEEN ANN
[b.] 17 May 1936, Canterbury, England; [p.] Charles and Kathleen Baker; [m.] Anthony George Bell, 8 April 1954; [ch.] Anthony, Kathrine, Georgina, Derek; [ed.] St John's County Girls School, Northgate Kent, left school at 15 years I was encouraged to write by my teacher Mrs Hugill; [occ.] Housewife looking after my husband, writer; [hon.] Amateur writers encouragement programme. Several poems published in newspaper two A.W.E.P. anthologies. With many certificates of merit and encouragement; [oth. writ.] Short child's story in local newspaper. I write for myself but strive to please my family and friends. I enjoy writing about anything and everything.; [pers.] I've written for 50 yrs for Birthday poems for family. The past ten years I branched out into children's stories and a series of stories on verse about a house named "Edgar". Favorite author is Wilbur Smith. I'm a compulsive writer; [a.] Townsville, Queensland, Australia

BELLERBY, ANNA-MARIE
[b.] 15 July 1979; [p.] Chris and Hellen Bellerby; [ed.] Fishguard High School; [occ.] Studying for A-level English lit, History and Sociology,; [memb.] Fishguard Young conservatives and South Wales cult TV Society (Shangri-LA).; [hon.] Duke of Edinburgh Bronze Award; [pers.] I just write what I see. Good or bad.; [a.] Scleddan, Pembrookshire, UK

BELLIS, THOMAS
[pen.] Tom Bellis; [b.] 22 October 1907, Shildon; [p.] Thomas William and Clara Bellis; [m.] Edith Bellis Nee Stephenson (Deceased), 8 September 1934; [ch.] Geoffry, Maureen; [ed.] All Saints School, Shildon; [occ.] Retired; [memb.] Former Member of Church Choir, Boy To Man, Lesson Reader Old Testament For Three Consecutive Years, Ex-member Local Operatic Society; [hon.] 5 years Royal Air Force, Defence Medal, 1939-1945 War Medal; [oth. writ.] Three books published, two short stories and several poems included in anthologies, one read on Tyne-Tees Television by Maxwell Dees.; [pers. Elementary School Education. 45 yrs service British Rail, Office Boy to Supplies Manager, Prolific Writer of Stories and poetry. All clean well plotted material for family reading.; [a.] Shildon, Durham, UK

BENJAFIELD, GLENYS
[pen.] Faith Strong; [b.] 29 May 1947, East London; [p.] George and Florence Day; [m.] Recently Divorced, 30 March 1968; [ch.] Grant and Kerrie (twin), Granddaughters 3 years; [ed.] Deanery High School Stratford E.15. Correspondence Course, several courses, relating to people with learning disabilities. Self taught cake decorating and sugar craft.; [occ.] Aux. Nurse, as "associate carer" spencer close Epping Essex; [memb.] St. Johns Ambulance. Thornwood Line Dancing. Member of the Epping Spiritualist Movement. Awards. F.A.W. St. Johns Mencap. P.P.1. support workers, aromatherapy, and food and hygiene course certificates.; [oth. writ.] Publications in local spiritual newsletter the N.H.S. Focus

Magazine. I have had one publication in a paperback anthology, of which I do hold the sole copyright. I have been writing poems and converting true stories into verse (which I enjoy most) since 1968. I call my work "My Diary". My ultimate aim is to eventually produce "My Diary" as my own autobiographical anthology. I feel my inspiration comes from pure, situation and circumstance, life, though I feel some emerges from a spiritual source. I have no particular favorite author or poet, I simply enjoy writing and reading what appeals to me, which covers a wide variety.; [a.] Epping, Essex, UK

BENN, LINDA
[b.] 4 November 1959, Ellsmere Port; [p.] Raymond and Betty Francis; [ed.] Stanney Comprehensive John Moores University Liverpool; [occ.] Management Consultant own business; [memb.] British Association of Woman Entrepreneurs. (Bawe), Institute of Personal Development (IPD); [oth. writ.] Several poems written but unpublished first poem submitted for evaluation.; [pers.] My poems reflect my life and experiences. Poetry has helped me to understand people, a form of therapy.; [a.] Chester, Cheshire, UK

BENNETT, DAVID A.
[b.] 18 February 1953, Leeds, West Yorks; [p.] Frank Bennett and Monica M. Bennett; [ed.] St. Peters, Leeds, Agnes Stewart, Leeds Park Lane College, Leeds, Aberdeen College of Commerce; [occ.] Media Specialist/Broadcaster; [memb.] British Equity, F.O.E., RSPB, N.C.A., A.A.C.A., Friends of Aberdeen International Youth Festival Friends of Aberdeen Art Gallery and Museums Scottish Eco-Linc; [oth. writ.] Poems, short stories monologues, children's stories and play, letters T.V. and radio scripts newspaper copy; [pers.] The written word gives vent to ideas.; [a.] Aberdeen, Aberdeenshire, UK

BENNETT, FRANK
[pen.] Frank Bennett; [b.] 27 April 1930, Acton, London; [p.] Christoper John, Ethel Mary; [m.] Sylvia Rose, 8 October 1956; [ch.] Jacqueline, Jillian, Denise; [ed.] Finchley Grammar St. Albans College. Hertfordshire University. London University, Goldsmiths; [occ.] Freelance Journalist, Professional Artist; [memb.] Freelance Press Services Bureau, Brent Artists Register, Dollis Hill Vice Chairman, Art Group, Transatlantic Photography; [hon.] Oxford and Cambridge Joint School Certificate. Certificate Art and Design. Art and Design (Access), Certificate Art and Communication; [oth. writ.] Short story, entitled 'Nearly Mine', Full Length Novel, entitled, "The Old Man's Nurse', various other poems, short stories, articles for Press, (etc.); [pers.] In my writing and poetry, I try to paint pictures with words. Sometimes I find it easier to express my feelings and emotions in written form, than on canvas.; [a.] London, Middlesex, UK

BENNETT, HELEN
[b.] 6 November 1976, Slough; [p.] John Bennett, Pauline Hounsome; [ed.] Westgate School, Slough Middlesex Training Center Hayes; [occ.] Child Carer; [hon.] Guides- Baden Powell- Highest award in guiding; [oth. writ.] None- this is my first publication; [pers.] My writing has been greatly influenced by my friends and family, who I'm entirely grateful too. My greatest thanks goes to my Godmother Pam Hounsome and my grandfather George Hounsome for all this encouragement and support without them this poem would never be.; [a.] Slough, Berkshire, UK

BENNETT, PETER
[b.] 1 July 1960, Co. Offaly; [p.] John Bennett, Elizabeth Bennett; [ed.] Standard Education; [occ.] Painter/Decorator; [memb.] The Local Gym; [oth. writ.] More poems.; [pers.] I like to write poems that are easily readable, but have a great emotional and perceptive quality about them. I would like my poems to represent a moment in time, in the sense that they relate to, other peoples moments.; [a.] Kilcormac, Ireland

BENNETT, ROGER
[pen.] Roger Thornton; [b.] 19 July 1947, Burton-on-Trent; [p.] Deceased; [ed.] Salisbury Memorial Private School, Burton-on Trent and other Educational Establishments; [occ.] Work with Disabled People; [memb.] Worked with the Yorkshire Poetry Society, Success Writers Peterborough Staple, Publications (Derbyshire); [hon.] Won the Burton Festival of Music and Drama, Poetry Section for Poem (Nagasaki); [oth. writ.] Intak' Yorkshire Poets Association, West Midlands Arts, People to People are poetry now; [pers.] My thoughts revolve round classical poetry to contemporary verse and prose.; [a.] Burton-on-Trent, Staffordshire, UK

BENNETT, THERESA MAY YUILL
[b.] 1 April 1958, Mancot Hospital; [p.] Archibald and Sheilah Yuill; [m.] Divorced, 31 May 1980; [ch.] One daughter and one son; [ed.] Average; [occ.] Unemployed; [pers.] When I think of a poem about something I try to bring out the beauty of something, in an underlying moral tone!; [a.] Buckley, Flintshire, UK

BENSON, LISA REBECCA
[pen.] Lisa Rebecca Benson; [b.] 26 January 1972, Leigh; [p.] John and Ruth Benson; [ed.] Penwortham Priory High School; [occ.] Community Support, Worker - Social Services; [oth. writ.] Several poems, short stories and statements.; [pers.] In our world, the way it is today - we need words and so I knock on the door of knowledge to strengthen my wall of wisdom.; [a.] Leyland, Lancashire, UK

BERRY, BARBARA GILLIAN
[b.] 7 December 1943, Leamington Spa, Warwickshire; [p.] Evelyn and Reginald Berry; [m.] Divorced 1994, 10 March 1962; [ch.] 2 daughters, 1 son; [ed.] Secondary Education all the way through; [occ.] Secretary; [hon.] 1 Charity Swin Award Excellent References from places of work and excellent report from school. Now I have achieved my poem being published.; [oth. writ.] I am always making things and writing poetry mostly for Charity work and helping anyone who needs my help. I have two wonderful grandchildren and love being with them as much as I can.; [pers.] I am a workaholic and will push myself to the limit in whatever I do. I love writing, mostly poetry but have writen a short children's story. I love making things for charity raffles etc and love helping others. Others always come before myself.; [a.] Nottingham, Stapleford, UK

BERRY, KATHY
[b.] 5 April 1958, Barne, Herts; [p.] Albert Edward, Patricia Joyce Blake; [m.] John Edward, 28 April 1979; [ch.] Cassandra Elizabeth, Leannarose; [ed.] Campions Sec Mod, Nicholas Hawlesmoor Comp; [occ.] Interior Designer, House Technician; [memb.] RSPCA Farley Volunteer Group; [oth. writ.] Poem published in 'A Passage in Time' Numerous others I've not had the courage to show

anyone!; [pers.] We are here for but the bat of an eyelid so we must make the most of it whilst considering others at all times. I only hope my poems give us much pleasure to read as to write.; [a.] Luton, Beds, UK

BEVAN, MARJORIE
[b.] 5 May 1934, Swansea; [p.] Jack Johnson, Gladys Johnson; [m.] Kenneth Bevan, 2 March 1957; [ch.] Julie, Tina, Lynne; [ed.] Glanmor Secondary School for girls Swansea; [occ.] Housewife; [pers.] This is the first time I have written a poem. I just wanted to show how proud I am of my seven beautiful grandchildren and how much I love them.; [a.] Swansea, Glamorgan, UK

BEVERIDGE, JANET TRACEY YOUNG
[b.] 8 February 1940, Dunfermline; [p.] Barbara and William Buchanan; [m.] Andrew Westwater Beveridge, 10 May 1958; [ch.] Yvonne and Elaine, grandchildren - Lisa and Nicki; [ed.] Helsby County Grammar School Queen Anne, Dunfermline; [occ.] Retired; [memb.] Dunfermline Abbey; [oth. writ.] Other poems recently published and participation in local events various private writings; [pers.] A late starter I enjoy this new-found aptitude of expression. Each one is spontaneous heartfelt emotion of this life I cherish with the hope that goodness shall always prevail.; [a.] Dunfermline, Fife, UK

BEYBA, JACQUELINE
[b.] 30 November 1939, Wales; [pers.] The beauty of Jehovah's Creation has inspired me to write about the moon.; [a.] Newbridge, Gwent, UK

BEZZINA, MARIO F.
[b.] 29 April 1950, Malta; [p.] Anthony and Maria Stella; [m.] Mary Rose, 26 March 1977; [ch.] Annabelle and Maria Clara; [ed.] Secondary Education of the Technical School of St. Joseph, Paula and University of Malta and University of Perugia (Italy); [occ.] Assistant Principal with the Government of Malta; [memb.] President: "Movement for Literary Revival," Chairman "Literary Group," One of the Founders of the "Maltese Poets Association," Editor of "Hegga Letterarja."; [hon.] Several Prizes in Poetry Competitions - in Malta, Italy, U.S.A., Scotland, and `Il Premio Citta' Di Valletta given by the President of the Rep of Malta; [oth. writ.] Author of 17 poetry collected booklets in maltese (1970-1996) selections in various anthologies (6) in all - published in Scotland, France, Italy, Zabreg, South Korea, the figures in the Directory of International Writers (University of Colorado - USA).; [pers.] Mario feels in him the urge to communicate with others his innermost emotions, his views on actual life, the love he nurtures for humility and his disappointment when he sees that he is discarded by friends and foes alike, for the simple reason that his poems are the product of love for all concerned, for those who do not appreciate truth and are guilty against their breather in more ways then one.; [a.] Birkirkara, Malta

BHASKARAN, SALIM BASHIR
[pen.] Sajoo; [b.] 7 May 1971, Port Dickson; [p.] Bashir Abdullah, Aisha Hassan; [ed.] Port Dickson High, International Islamic University, University of East London; [occ.] Bar Final Student; [memb.] Malaysian Debating Society, University Squash Club; [hon.] United Nations mediation Council representative. University English Literary and Poetry Prize. Law Degrees.; [oth. writ.] A few poems and sonnets were published in the University

magazines; [pers.] This achievement is a dedication to the person whom had inspired my passion towards crafting this poem; [a.] Barking, Essex, UK

BIRCH, KATRINA
[b.] 10 November 1959, Kidderminster; [p.] Cecilia and Geoffrey Morgan; [m.] Eric Birch, 30 March 1996; [ch.] Daniel and Kara (From previous marriage); [oth. writ.] Have collection of poems, as of yet unpublished; [pers.] I started writing poetry, for my children, I'd like to thank them both for prompting me to do so.; [a.] Stourport on Severn, Worcs, UK

BJERKESET, OLE ANDREAS
[pen.] Savio Sampaio Sorrates de Souza; [b.] 25 December 1977, Oslo, Norway; [occ.] Student; [memb.] Sodalicium Eruditionis; [oth. writ.] The Balcony (poems), Jammin' (poems), Albert (play); [pers.] Poetry is not the noblest manifestation of the force of art, but I write all the same.; [a.] Trondhjem

BLACK, VERONICA
[b.] 28 May 1947, St. Helens, Lancashire; [p.] John Kenny, Veronica Kenny; [m.] Ronald Francis Black, 31 July 1968 to 22 July 1974; [ch.] Stephen John Black; [ed.] Lowe House, Girls School St. Helens, Lancashire; [occ.] Formers, - Service Co-Ordinator ACE concern St. Helen/welfare Visitor, Pilkinton trust fund/deputy to Manager, Downhurst, Residential home, Ealing London 1992-1994 semi Retired from Dec '95, registered sick.; [oth. writ.] Several poems published in various Anthologies for: Anchor Books, poetry now, Triumph house; [pers.] For the most part my poetry is an expression of gratitude for people, places, times in my life, written as a tribute, to present as a gift of thanks.; [a.] Saint Helens, Lancashire, UK

BLACKBURN, JANET JODIE GEMMA BETHANY
[b.] 6 January 1954, Mansfield; [p.] Donald Hardy, Agnes Hardy; [m.] Divorced; [ed.] Basic Education enrolled at 'Future Business College' as a mature student; [occ.] Secretary, teach evening class 'Computer skills'; [oth. writ.] Short stories as well a poetry; [pers.] An admirer of Pam Ayres, who I feel I have been inspired by.; [a.] Mansfield, Notts, UK

BLACKBURN, MARGARET
[pen.] Peggy; [b.] 5 January 1934, Liverpool; [p.] Margaret and George Bayliss; [m.] Norman Blackburn, 25 September 1955; [ed.] Very little, until I started at my local College in November, 1994. Since then I have discovered myself.; [occ.] Dressmaker; [memb.] Going on a Pre-Access course at Rupert Road College, Huyton, Knowsley, Merseyside; [hon.] Achievement tests in Literacy, Level one 90%, Level two, 75%, Level three 90%, Numeracy level one 90%; [oth. writ.] For College only, C.V. Thesis on Dr. Barnardo who devoted himself to the protection and education of children everywhere.; [pers.] Since my quest for education as a mature student my life now is completely whole and my message to older people who may think it's too late for them to learn, 'take it from me', 'it's never too late'. So keep learning and enjoy; [a.] Liverpool, Knowsley, UK

BLACKHAM, MR. DAVID ANDREW
[b.] 15 January 1974, Rotherham; [p.] Harold and Nancy Blackham; [ed.] Thomas Rotherham College, Sheffield Halamshire University; [hon.]

Diploma in Business Management; [oth. writ.] Poem published in "Sunlight and Shadows."; [pers.] Don't walk through life, dance. Happy travels down life's track.; [a.] Rotherham, S. Yorks, UK

BLACKWELL, NANCY SHIPWAY
[b.] Cleeve Hill, Cheltenham; [p.] Bob and Vera Watkins; [m.] John Blackwell; [ch.] Robert (One Son); [ed.] Our Lady's Convent Chesterton House Cirencester previous establishment of the White Raja Robert Brook of Sarawak; [occ.] Author; [memb.] West Country Writers Association, Cheltenham Steeplechase Club, Friend of Leckhampton Court Sue Ryder; [hon.] Cutswold Hunt Supporters Club; [oth. writ.] The sporting formed from rags to riches (books) impressions of prestbery many articles for bokwolel life magazine. Take a break the pony magazine family circle.; [pers.] I write for pleasure I just pick up a pen and ideas flow. I write complimentary articles for church magazine and charity magazines and clubs I. like to write fact or fiction.; [a.] Cheltenham, Glos, UK

BLAIR, GRAHAM
[b.] 25 March 1975, Glasgow; [pers.] The queen of my heart, I did it my way, you changed me so much, this one's for you. My little Miss Moodswings.

BLAKESTON, MRS. VIOLET
[pen.] Vi Blakeston; [b.] 27 July 1924, Clumber Park, Notts; [p.] James and Clara Howard; [m.] George Frederick Blakeston (Deceased), 27 April 1947; [ed.] Hardwick C of E - School, One year Cookery course at Workshop Grammar School - Notts - I had to cycle for 5 miles, every friday; [occ.] Housewife; [memb.] Founder chairman of G.M. Ladies Club 1972, C.P.R.E. 18 year of the Executive Com. E.U.W. 1976 onwards, The W.I. Womens Institute for 48 years and still a member R.S.P.B., A contributor to the W.N. magazine, I wrote Nature Articles and was congratulated by Sandy Lodge - committee on my 5 years work; [hon.] Diploma awarded for "Best in Show" Bracknell, Berkshire. "Roses", Paintings hung in Ashmolan Museum, Oxford and Daily Telegraph Foyer, Fleet St, London, plus other Exhibitions, Kings Lynn Art Group.; [oth. writ.] Many poems published in various poetry books since 1972, "Stockwells of Devon", "London" Peterborough. Poems printed in The Lynn News and Advertizer, E.D.P. and the local papers, Citizen and Murcury. Poems in various Church Magazines.; [pers.] In deep and tragic situations all my emotions are released through the written word, the poet in me comes to the love.; [a.] Snetthisham, Kings Lynn, Norfolk, UK

BLAMPIED, ANN LYDIA
[pen.] Ann Lydia Blampied; [b.] 13 December 1932, Walton-on-Thames, Surrey; [p.] Alexandra Forbes, Maud Lydia Forbes; [m.] Michael Philip Blampied, 26 June 1973; [ch.] David Thomas, Lydia Ruth and Gina; [ed.] Mayfield Girls School Watton-on-Thames Left School A. Fourteen; [occ.] Retired from Nursing now working as Security Agen.; [memb.] Houses under Probaie cci: on holiday. Folkestone Cancer Counseling Assn. Etching Hill Bridge Club; [hon.] Rewards - Watching my children grow up, all three have exceeded my expectations.; [oth. writ.] I have written dozens of poems over the past decade. This is the first, I have submitted for publication, due to my daughters persuasion. People and incidents are intriguing subjects, I never tire of.;

[pers.] I have had an extremely varied and demanding life. My mother died when I was 13 years. From then on I was on my own. I lived in hostels, joined the W.R.N.S. at 18 years. Married twice. Survived cancer 10 years ago. Travelled extensively.; [a.] Etching Hill, Kent, UK

BLOXHAM, LUCY-MAY
[pen.] Lucy-May Bloxham; [b.] 12 October 1938, Midlands; [p.] Lucy and James Stokes; [m.] Richard, 23 March 1968; [ch.] David - Accountant; [ed.] Grammar School and Secretarial College; [occ.] Retired Real Estate Agent and Solicitor's Secretary; [oth. writ.] Several poems in International Society of Poetry's various anthologies newspapers and magazines. My own poetry book to be published in the Autumn.; [pers.] I love nature and my poems often include religious connotations - William Blake and Tennyson are my favorite poets; [a.] Saint Austell, Cornwall, UK

BLUMSCHEIN, JASON KARL
[pen.] Joseph Jarral; [b.] 14 May 1971, Newton Abbot; [p.] Peter and Carol Blumschein; [ed.] Teignmouth High School; [occ.] Clerical; [hon.] English, NVQ Business and Administration; [pers.] All of my work comes from within. It is the only way I can show true feelings in the writings that I produce.; [a.] Teignmouth, Devon, UK

BLYTH, GARY KRISTIAN
[b.] 2 November 1968, Hampshire; [p.] Dennis and Moreen Blyth; [m.] Kathryn Ann Blyth, 14 April 1991; [ch.] Jordan Elizabeth Blyth; [ed.] Penyrheol Comprehensive; [occ.] Steelworker; [pers.] To Kathryn the inspiration behind my words. If love is like sunlight then surely, without it one must wither away and die.; [a.] Swansea, West Glam, UK

BOAST, LEANNE
[b.] 5 April 1980, Peterborough; [p.] Tanya Boast, Malcolm Boast; [ed.] Sir John Leman High School Beccles; [occ.] Student, Sir John Leman High School Sixth Form, Beccles; [memb.] The Louise Elizabeth School of Dance (Lowestoft); [pers.] I do not consider myself to be a poet. My writing comes from within, it's my personal message to the world.; [a.] Beccles, Suffolk, UK

BOGARD, JOHN
[b.] 12 December 1950, Mirecourt, France; [p.] Roger Bogard and Noelle Bogard; [m.] Phulbassia Bogard, 8 July 1978; [ch.] Natacha, Daniel, Paul; [ed.] Lycee in Mirecourt - France University of Nancy France IPC in Epinal France; [occ.] Hospitality Management; [oth. writ.] Two books, 'Tomorrow the Cosmos' (in French) by La Pensee Universelle-Paris, 'The Message From The Cosmos' by Castle of Dreams - Darlington and several unpublished poems; [pers.] Let us live simply, so that others can simply live on our blue planet.; [a.] Birmingham, UK

BOLDEN, JOHN
[pen.] John Bolden; [b.] 25 August 1957, Oxfordshire; [m.] 19 September 1992; [ch.] One Son (born 8 August 1995); [ed.] Held Top Open Music Scholarships, Winchester College, and Magdalene College, Cambridge, Hold Cambridge Degree M.A., Mus. B.; [occ.] Composer, Pianist, Music Lecturer, Oxford University, Member of Winchester Cathedral Choir; [memb.] 1. Composer's Guild of G.B., 2. Performing Right Society; [hon.] 4 National Awards for Musical Composition Since 1981. Compositions heard in

fifteen countries world wide, and published and recorded on CD. many broadcasts.; [oth. writ.] Musical Compositions, Organ, Religious Choral, Piano, Chamber Orchestral. Currently Composing Piano Concerto, other poems, Working Towards A Small Volume for Possible Publication.; [pers.] Debussy said, "Music begins where words are powerless to express, and stravinsky said, "Music is powerless to express anything". My training is in music and I find an expressive outlet in poetry often when stuck with composition. This allows me to explore the contradiction (or is it?) of the above and the meeting point to literal and abstract, meaning.; [a.] Winchester, Hampshire, UK

BONNEYWELL, CLAIRE
[b.] 26 September 1960, Rochester; [p.] Jim Gifford, Iris Gifford; [m.] Ian Bonneywell, 30 March 1986; [ch.] Miles, Lance; [ed.] Maidstone Technical High School for girls, Mid-Kent College of Higher and further Education, Maidstone; [pers.] I very much appreciate this opportunity of being able to share my love of writing with you.; [a.] Cuxton, Kent, UK

BOOTH, PHILIP
[b.] 7 January 1957, Nottingham; [p.] William Harry and Mary Elizabeth; [ch.] Philip James; [occ.] Chef, Writer of Children's Stories; [oth. writ.] Adventures of "Garageman Stan" A scenes of Children's books yet to be published.

BORAKOVA, VERONIKA FEJESOVA
[b.] 8 December 1969, Hnusta, Slovakia; [p.] Julius Fejes, Veronika Fejesova; [m.] Peter Borak, 21 October 1995; [ed.] 1988-1993 Faculty of Philosophy, P. J. Safarik University in Kosice, Slovakia; [occ.] Translator; [hon.] Master Degree in English and Slovak Language and Literature - 1993, Laureate of the Slovak National Amateur Poetry Competition - 1996; [oth. writ.] Poems on Slovak radio Bratislava '87-93, Literary Magazine 'Nove Slovo - Deilna Mladych (New Word - young Workshop) '94-95,' Dotyky (Touches)," magazine for literature and art '94-96, debut collection "step" to be published by Odkaz Publishers, Slovakia later this year.; [pers.] My world has no time for long novels...but it is still waiting for that single poem.; [a.] Birmingham, UK

BOROS, ALEXSANDER
[b.] 27 February 1926, Warsaw, Poland; [p.] Jan, Teofila Boros; [m.] Margaret Evelyn, 16 July 1949; [ch.] Stephen, Peter, Janet; [ed.] Primary Education; [occ.] Retired; [pers.] Started writing poetry in 1994 after being unable to do much manuel work due to arthritis.; [a.] Oswaldtwiste, Lancs, UK

BOTLEY, CLARE ANN
[b.] 11 June 1973, Taplow; [p.] Roger Botley, Jackqueline Botley; [ed.] Burnham Upper School, Thames Valley University; [pers.] My poems are influenced by life and come from my soul.; [a.] Slough, Bucks, UK

BOURNE, RUTH
[b.] 13 November 1973, Dublin; [p.] Marjorie and William Bourne; [ed.] Scoil Carmel Secondary School, University of Limerick; [occ.] Materials and Design Engineer; [memb.] Amateur Artists Society, Alumni - University of Limerick; [hon.] Bachelor of Engineering; [oth. writ.] Once Published in school magazine; [pers.] To my parents: I know I should say it more often, but thank you, love always.; [a.] Limerick City, Ireland

BOWEN, VICTOR
[b.] 1 May 1948, Langley, Norfolk; [p.] Victor and Peggy Bowen; [m.] Happily divorced; [ch.] Kirsty (19); [ed.] Bungay Grammar School Suffolk; [occ.] Taxi Driver; [oth. writ.] Entering this competition is the first time I have admitted to writing poetry, now, as 'Arfur' would say, "The World is my Lobster."; [pers.] If only we could all view the world through the eyes of a poet. Peace, perfect, peace!; [a.] Lincoln, Lincs, UK

BOWERY, MAUREEN EVA
[pen.] Moby; [b.] 4 August 1934, Finsbury; [p.] Harriet and Gilbert Edwards; [m.] (Ex) Michael Edwin Bowery, 20 July 1957; [ch.] Nil; [ed.] LaussAnne Secondary, Modern - Kent; [occ.] Retired Ex-Met: Police Officer and Malawi Police Africa; [memb.] J.P., British Legion - Crawley Branch, League of Friends - Crawley Hosp., Soroptimists International; [hon.] "Silver Mike" Award 1956 Baghdad Broadcasting Corp., Top Sales Award Natal/Transvaal and Orange Free State, South Africa 1975, (2000.00) Wraf Service in Action Medals for Baghdad and Cyprus 1952-55; [oth. writ.] Enid Blyton (first ever published) called "Bowl Of Fruit" as a Child Arrival press 3 poems Rhyme arrival magazine (few) recent books "Circle of Life", "Childhood Memories", "Growing Up" published one poem each; [pers.] I've travelled since I was 17 years Middle East/America/all the Africa's and Australia and my writing reflects emotions experienced in each country. Africa is special influence in/on many poems and articles.; [a.] Crawley, West Sussex, UK

BOYLE, PETER LAWRENCE
[pen.] The Pete's Pen and Peter The Pot-Headed Professor; [b.] 24 January 1951, Greemock; [p.] James and Margaret Boyle; [ed.] Notre Dame College of Education, Bearsdem, Glasgow (Diploma in Education); [oth. writ.] 1990 Glasgow year of cultural, collaborated with 9 others writers to write "Govan Stories" for 7:84 Theatre Company - performed during May fest 1990, in Starathclyde and won an award; [a.] Glasgow, Lanarkshire, UK

BOYLE, WILLIAM MULHOLLAND
[b.] 14 March 1920, Hamilton, Scotland; [p.] Deceased; [m.] May Alexandra Boyle, 29 October 1988; [ch.] Four; [ed.] Normal day school; [occ.] Retired; [oth. writ.] Previous efforts local press, books; [pers.] Ex. Railway Man (G'vard.) 1936 'S'2, Pro. Boxer. (Bantam.) Scotland. From 1936, '46. Ex. MIHLR. - Coal - England. From 1952, '80.; [a.] Cannock, Staffs, UK

BRADLEY, D. H. E.
[b.] 24 October 1927, Swindon, Wilts; [occ.] Retired actor/singer; [oth. writ.] "Taking The Epistle" 1985, Merlin Books Ltd., "More Moronic Rubbish" 1986 Merlin Books Ltd., "Nutty Notions" 1986 Merlin Books Ltd., "Random Ruminations" 1987 Vantage Press, Inc., New York 10001, USA; [pers.] Words, a blessing, publication, a bonus!; [a.] Cheltenham, Glos., UK

BRADLEY, JANE FRANCES
[b.] 18 December 1965, Nottingham; [p.] Rex Coker, Gillian Coker; [m.] Mark Russell Bradley, 16 June 1995; [ch.] Matthew, Melissa, Warren; [ed.] Gladehill Infant and Junior School, Padstow Comprehensive School, Arnold and Carlton College of Further Education; [occ.] Mum and Housewife; [hon.] Air gun shooting, numerous Certificates from St. John Ambulance Brigade. Numerous CSE's O levels and CFE's, based on a Nursing background; [oth. writ.] A number of unpublished poems, an adult short story.; [pers.] From the deepest emotions from my heart and soul, the magic slips through the ink in my pen. I adore all varieties of poetry.; [a.] Top Valley, Nottingham, UK

BRADSHAW, ALBERT J.
[b.] 6 August 1908, Birmingham; [p.] Albert Bradshaw, Rose Bradshaw; [m.] Winifred Francis, 29 March 1937; [ch.] Michael John, Robert Gordon; [ed.] Elementary Board School I left School 1922 worked on the factory floor. Until 1973; [occ.] Retired; [pers.] Greatly influenced by gentlemen teachers throughout four last years at school. Especially by English lit teacher, recited poetry. Deplore bad language read and enjoy tennyson wordsworth; [a.] Birmingham, Staffs, UK

BRADY, JEAN MARY
[pen.] Jean Mary Brady; [b.] 19 October 1950, Barkisland, West Yorkshire; [p.] Pauline and James Wheelwright; [m.] Divorced; [ch.] Gail Louise, Diane Carol, Kathryn Rose, Christopher Michael; [ed.] Elland Grammar, Manchester Metropolitan University; [occ.] English Teacher; [hon.] BA (hons) Humanities/Social Science PGCE (FAHE) (Post-graduate certificate in education further adult and higher education).; [oth. writ.] Several picture-script stories, short stories, and poems published in a children's comic - "Twinkle" presently working on research for Local History book - (as final year MA); [pers.] My best creative writing comes from personal experience and deeply felt emotions. Even my "Writing for children" is inspired by my own little one's play and personalities; [a.] Manchester, Lancashire, UK

BRAITHWAITE, LYNNE JANINE
[b.] 1 July 1934, Nr Sawrey, Hawkshead, Lancashire; [p.] George and Elizabeth Braithwaite (Deceased); [ed.] Hawkshead County Primary School, Royal Airforce; [occ.] Retired/Unemployed ex Royal Airforce (39 1/2 yrs.); [memb.] "All now ceased", Society of Licensed Aircraft Engineers and Technologists. Jim Russell Racing Drivers School (Snetterton) Institute of Advanced Motorists. Registered Silver Smith-Sheffield Assay Office. Royal Airforces Association; [hon.] Long service a good conduct medal with clasp. British Empire Medal; [oth. writ.] Non published! 1. An Ode to Life or Two Into One Will Go 2. The Cards 3. An Ode to Survival 4. To Aunty Doris 5. What Patients Charter? L.J.B. Life Vol. 1 Vol. 2 Vol. 3 In progress of being written; [pers.] Being born 1 July 1934 and scrowled in the Hawkshead area of the Lake District gives one a real sense of beauty that lives with you forever. This followed by 34 1/2 yrs. in the R.A.F. suitably enhanced my education in the "University of Life". Undergoing a change of gender at the age of 59 1/2 compels one to look in great depth at ones life, past, present, and future.; [a.] Morecambe, Lancashire, UK

BRANLEY, JANICE
[b.] 25 November 1955, London; [p.] Marjorie Settle, Ralph Settle; [m.] Steve Branley; [ch.] Thomas, Megan, Duncan; [ed.] Thomas Bennett Comp., City of Leicester Poly.; [occ.] Artist; [hon.] B.A. (Hons) Art and Design, M.A. Textile Design; [oth. writ.] Poems published in 'Siud and Eilean' (Acair Press) 1994, 'Emergency' (Forward Press) 1996, 'Closet Poets' (Forward Press) 1996; [pers.] I have lived for most of my adult life on remote Scottish Islands, including Eigg, Muck and for the last nine years the Isle of Lewis in the outer hebrides.; [a.] Isle of Lewis, UK

BREATHNACH, EILIS
[b.] 6 August 1961, Burton-on-Trent; [p.] Thomas and Marie Brennan; [m.] Shane Walsh, August 6, 1988; [ch.] Thomas and Oran; [ed.] Knock N.S. Conent-of-Mercy, Borris-in-Ossory (Qualified Nursery Nurse and Montessori Teacher); [occ.] Mother and Housewife; [memb.] Aras Chronain (Irish Cultural Center) Clondalkin and Aras Chronain Patchwork Group; [pers.] Inspiration for my poetry comes from my family and everyday events.; [a.] Clondalkin,, Dublin 22, Ireland

BREEZE, RACHAEL L.
[b.] 26 May 1985, Billinge; [p.] Darren Breeze and Lynne Breeze; [ed.] St. Peters Junior School, West Leigh High School; [memb.] Leigh Life Saving Association, Horse Riding Club; [oth. writ.] Several poems wrote but not published; [pers.] This is my first poem to be published and I hope it will not be my last. I love reading Roald Dahl's books and have been influenced by his work.; [a.] Leigh, Lancs, UK

BRETHERICK, SHEILA
[b.] Bradford; [p.] Lewis Hey, Cecilia Hey; [m.] Widow; [ch.] Three; [occ.] Was designer sample Mailler in Carson Industry; [hon.] Awarded employee of the year 1993 out of the whole of the english and Irish snurfit group; [pers.] Words can be so meaningful, have such depth, be such a comfort, in our hour of need; [a.] Leeds, Yorks, UK

BRIDGEMAN
[pen.] John Henry; [b.] 16 July 1915, Twenty Lincs; [p.] William and Rose Bridgeman; [m.] Phyllis, 25 September 1939; [ch.] Noel and Shirley; [ed.] Bourne Fen Elementary left school at the age of 13 1/2 yrs started to work on a farm with Livestock; [occ.] Retired previous - farm foreman; [memb.] Gardening Club Age Concern, Bourne Lincs, Bourne Abbey Church; [hon.] Mayor of Bourne 1952 Gardening Cups, Herdsmen Cup from Agriculty Shows; [oth. writ.] Several poems published in local papers.; [pers.] I started writing poetry in 1993 at the age of 78 yrs I lost my wife in 1992 we were married 53 yrs. I was a gift given to me in my loneliness.; [a.] Bourne, Lincoln, UK

BRIDGES, MARY MAUREEN
[pen.] Burton; [b.] 30 March 1921, Northumbria; [p.] Arthur and Elizabeth Wensley Burton; [m.] Charles Bridges (Deceased - 1985), 9 June 1945; [ch.] Pamela, Romans, Kenneth; [ed.] Astley Central - Seaton Delavala North Oxfordshire Technical College and School of Art, Banbury, R.S.A. - 1 yr. Course, 1 yr. Postal Course L.S.J.; [occ.] Sen. Aux. Nurse Iweluding (War Service); [memb.] Arvon Foundation, Poetry Society; [hon.] 3 Poems Published in Anthology. "Poems Immortal" 1974 - Certificate of Merit on Programme. "Talk About Complete Re Novel. "Geordie Pride" 1980 (Remains Unpublished); [oth. writ.] Five chapters of second novel completed to date "Fridays Child" - no publisher - Editor's choice award from the international society of pets 1996 for entry "The Mediterranean Sea"; [pers.] Writing Poetry brings me peace and tranquility - An understanding of people and places - where in I can express my innermost thoughts, as I travel around this wonderful. World of "Life".; [a.] Bicester, Oxfordshire, UK

BRIEN, ANDREW
[b.] 17 December 1970, Plaistow, E London; [p.] Mrs. A. J. Tilley; [m.] Mrs. Yuki Brien, 14 September 1996; [ed.] Langdon Comp. School, Southend College of Technology, Plymouth University; [occ.] Police Officer; [oth. writ.] Knights in shining armour published in "A Passage In Time"; [pers.] To Yuki, whom I love so dearly forever and always

BRIGGS, SHARRON
[b.] 14 August 1963, Southeast London; [p.] Edward and Sheila Briggs; [ed.] Stratford Comprehensive; [occ.] Secretary; [pers.] This poem is dedicated to my mum and her poor feet. And everyone else who suffered from them!; [a.] Forest Gate, London, UK

BRIGHTWELL, YVONNE
[pen.] Eve Laurie; [b.] 18 September 1960, Dumfries, Scotland; [p.] David Patterson, Janet Patterson; [m.] Stephen Petty; [ch.] Mark, Debbie, Lee, Michelle and Ricky; [a.] Trowbridge, Wilts, UK

BRISTOW, EVELYN M.
[b.] Born in Canada of English parents.; [pers.] I am a dreamer, which inspires me to turn some of my thoughts into poetry.; [a.] Tetney, Grimsby, South Humberside UK

BRITAIN, MARY GWENDOLINE ANNIE
[pen.] Mary G. A. Britain; [b.] 31 March 1910, Pickhill; [p.] John and Gertrude Britain; [ed.] Church of England School Pickhill Nr Thirsk. Before her marriage my mother a teacher - teaching 5 to six years olds, and father a farmer; [occ.] Never been employed; [hon.] The only certificate I ever won, was when I was still at school, aged 13 years old, was for writing, about nature after reading a book on nature. Never tried any kind of Writing since, until now writing poetry for your Library.; [a.] Thirsk, North Yorkshire, UK,

BROCKING, JEREMY STEPHEN
[pen.] J. S. Brocking; [b.] 14 September 1960, London; [p.] Yvonne Ellen, William Percy; [m.] Pat Yorke (engaged), 3 May 1997; [ed.] Norwood Primary School, Henry Thornton Secondary School, Brixton College; [oth. writ.] Although I have been writing poetry since my school days, 'Quiet Moments' is my first attempt at publication.; [pers.] My poems reflect all walks of life. I have been greatly influenced by John Lennon whom I greatly admire.; [a.] Streatham, London, UK

BROOKES
[pers.] To my darling Ben, with all the love in my heart, mummy.

BROWN, ANITA FLYNN
[b.] 11 May 1961, Lancashire; [p.] Alice and Larry Flynn; [m.] Andy Brown, 5 September 1987; [ed.] Comprehensive; [occ.] Residential Care Officer; [oth. writ.] Poem "Hell Be There", to be published in September 1996 in the Anthology - messengers from the North West.; [pers.] Through my writing I try to project my innermost feelings. I plan to write a novel.; [a.] Newton-le-Willows, Merseyside, UK

BROWN, BERNARD
[b.] 1933, Deal; [m.] Joycie; [occ.] Retired; [oth. writ.] The Holy Boy; [a.] Emsworth, Hants, UK

BROWN, DIANE
[b.] 12 November 1955, Chatham, Kent; [p.] Trevor and Margaret St. John-Murphy; [m.] Philip, 2 August 1989; [ed.] Windsor High School for girls; [occ.] Partner in Land Consultancy Firm; [memb.] RSPB, RNLI; [hon.] Headmaster's Prize and Art Prize at school; [oth. writ.] Poems, short stories and book "Tales Of Bramble Mill" (unpublished); [pers.] I draw inspiration from all the sadness and despair in the world yet strive to offer hope. I am indebted to Miss Meech, English mistress at high school, who so encouraged and inspired my writing and love of english literature.; [a.] Windsor, Berkshire, UK

BROWN, LEANN DENISE
[b.] 14 September 1982, South Shields; [p.] Dianne Brown (Mother); [ed.] Harton Comprehensive School, year 8, class- 8RT; [occ.] Scholar; [memb.] Speedwell (Netball Association), School Athletics Team.; [hon.] Subject Commendations, effort recomendations.; [pers.] I am honored to have a poem published, and have it appear in Quiet Moments. It was unexpected and I am thrilled.; [a.] South Shields, Tyne and Wear, UK

BROWN, PAMELA
[pen.] Libra; [b.] 26 September 1928, Gillingham, Kent, UK; [p.] Charles Henry and Florence Mary Weston; [m.] Frederick Thomas Brown, 22 December 1951; [ch.] Kevin John, Gary Richard, Jillian Carol; [ed.] Elementary; [occ.] Retired Clerical Worker; [memb.] A.A.W. (Association of Anglican Women) Ladies Guild, Senior Kiwi Grey Power; [oth. writ.] One or two poems in free weekly paper, also senior Kiwi Magazine.; [pers.] I prefer rhythmic poetry. I write of family, experiences, pets, observations of nature etc.; [a.] Blenheim, Marlborough New Zealand

BROWNE, DECIMA PROSSER ANDERSON
[pen.] Anderson Browne; [b.] 16 July 1901, Jersey; [p.] Teachers; [ed.] High School, Leamington Spa Warwickshire; [occ.] Retired; [oth. writ.] Short stories; [a.] Torquay, Devon, UK

BROWNE, KAREN
[pen.] Karen Browne; [b.] 10 April 1977, Gosford; [p.] Judy and Noel Browne; [ed.] Corpus Christi College College of Tafe - various Courses; [occ.] Full-time student; [oth. writ.] "Feelings of Love," "Peace, Love and Understanding," "The Fall of Emotions," "The Moon and the Sea," "Waterfall of Love," "Ocean Blue Eyes," "Alive with your Love," "Lightning Reaches Out," and "My Heart."; [pers.] I focus solely on `romantic' poetry. Writing about my personal experiences, with the special people who have influenced the way I perceive love and the feelings and many emotions that surround these experiences, both positively and negatively.; [a.] Killarney, Vale, Australia

BRUCE, KATHLEEN RUTH
[pen.] Kathleen Ruth Bruce; [b.] 10 August 1962, Winchester; [p.] Anne and William Burner; [m.] David Gordon Bruce, 23 March 1985; [ch.] Danielle, Annaliece, Kieran Bruce; [ed.] Winchester, Comp., Eastleigh College of Further, Ed. Eastbourne, In House Management College; [occ.] Housewife; [oth. writ.] Varied selection of unpublished work; [pers.] Through the value of words, I strive to make a point and make people aware of life and the living world.; [a.] Winchester, Hants, UK

BRUFORD, PETER
[b.] 1 April 1960, Islington; [p.] John Masters, Irene Masters (Nee Bruford); [ed.] Islington Green School (Comprehensive); [occ.] Care Assistant; [memb.] The Writing School Former Member Titanic Historical Society British Titanic Society; [pers.] Oh what would I do is the first piece of poetry that I've ever had published and I feel very proud of both my achievement, and the fact that the publishers have considered it worthy enough for inclusion in this volume.; [a.] London, UK

BRUSHETT, AUDREY MARGARET
[pen.] Audrey M. Brushett; [b.] 20 July 1931, London; [p.] Rose Emma and Charles Brushett; [ed.] Church of England Elementary Schools; [occ.] Retired; [oth. writ.] Some, but only for my own pleasure. One inscribed on a memorial to my mother, and sisters Rose Ivy Brushett and Betty Louise.; [pers.] I have always felt the need to put my feelings on current affairs and personal happenings on paper.; [a.] London, London, UK

BRYAN, PAMELA
[pen.] Mary Short; [b.] Bristol; [a.] Hereford, UK

BRYAN, WENDY LYNNE
[pen.] Noddy; [b.] 20 January 1954, Barry, S. Glam; [p.] Mr. J. H. and Mrs. G. V. Bryan; [ed.] Gladstone Rd Infants and Junior School, Holton Rd Senior for Girls; [occ.] Sales Assistant; [memb.] Barry East Girl, Guide Association, Barry and Cardiff SNU Spiritualist Church; [hon.] Took 1st Prize in the Poetry Competition at the South Wales District S.N.U. Summer School Pageant Rooms Penarth August 1985 and 86; [a.] Barry, South Glam, UK

BRYANT, WENDY MARIAN
[pen.] Lee; [b.] 23 November 1953, Folkestone; [p.] Edward Rouse Epps, Irene Winifred Epps; [m.] Roger John Bryant, 15 October 1988; [ch.] Deborah, Stephen, Natasha; [ed.] Holywell Sec. Mod Folkestone, Kent; [occ.] Administrator/ Partner Training Company; [oth. writ.] I write poems, short stories and articles for a local magazine that I produce each month called the black down view.; [pers.] Writing poetry is elating, for other to enjoy reading it gives me the ultimate satisfaction.; [a.] Wellington, Somerset, UK

BRYCE, ALEXANDER
[pen.] Pike; [b.] 11 June 1966, Alexander Hospital, Coatbridge; [p.] Francis and Elizabeth; [ch.] Lewis Alexander Bryce; [ed.] Rose Hall High and Coatridge College. Scotvec First Aid, Photography, Karate Coach Level 2.; [occ.] Factory Worker Manufacture of Marine Products; [memb.] Lenbukan Karate Club (coach) Pool Team - (Galleria) Snooker Crucible, 1st C/B Scouts. When Younger, Photographic Club, Fishing Club.; [hon.] 1st Dan Black Belt - Karate, First Aid, Flower Growing Winner, Photographic Courses Completed, Chess Trophy Winner; [oth. writ.] Short story winner (Sunday Post) newspaper, worked on local newspaper-voluntary.; [pers.] All men who have great ideas are sometimes called mad or crazy just because no-one wants to know what they have to say. So remember my name forever and I will pray for the well-being of all mankind even in heaven.; [a.] Coatbridge, UK

BUCKLEY, RAYMOND
[b.] 27 March 1938, Ireland; [p.] Christopher and Mary Ann Buckley; [m.] Philomena, 28 June 1960; [ch.] Seven Stanley, Raymond, Derek and Robert, Jacqueline, Colette and Jane; [ed.] C.B.S. Primary and Secondary School; [occ.] Reflexologist, Writer and Musician; [memb.] London and Counties Society of Physiologist, Int. Inst. of Reflexology, Irish Reflexologists Institute, Irish Massage Therapy Assoc. N.I.M. Cooper by trade also Professional Musician; [hon.] Northern Institute Massage Dip. or Honor, Higher Grade. Former Irish Youth Athletic Champion. Saxophone Tapes successfully released, composed and played by self and orch.; [oth. writ.] Articles for Reflexology Mags. Articles on Aviculture Large No's Musical Compositions. Two Novels to date. Approx 600 poems to date.; [pers.] Living is a life long experience! Some times it is possible to determine the pre-determined circumstance of one's death, based on God knowing all things.; [a.] Drogheda, Ireland

BULLMAN, SUSAN
[pen.] Susan Carole Stephen; [b.] 8 November 1951, Castleford; [p.] Sydney and Margaret Hinchcliffe; [m.] Paul Arthur Bullman, 8 May 1978; [ch.] Matthew and Dominic; [ed.] Secondary Modern; [occ.] Housewife; [oth. writ.] 'Kindness in all Things,' 'Byron,' 'Cool Tide Ebb Away,' 'All Children Treasure,' 'The Spring Lamb.'; [pers.] I began writing poetry at the age of ten. Reading poems by T. S. Eliot, and poems such as 'Tiger Tiger Burning Bright,' and 'The Snare,' gave me a deep and lasting insight into the joy and pain of animals.; [a.] Castleford, West Yorks, UK

BUNDY, LOUISA-MARY
[pen.] Louise Bundy; [b.] 1 January 1916, Kirby Stephen; [p.] Thomas Allen and Nellie Smith; [m.] Alfred Herbert Bundy, 9 May 1953; [ch.] Elizabeth Narissa Bundy; [ed.] Finished my education at the Capelles Comprehensive School in Guernsey, at the age of 14 years.; [occ.] Retired; [oth. writ.] Several poems published in magazines. A poem published by Anchor Books "Joyful Harvest" Edited by Michelle Abbott.; [pers.] I'd always led a very active life until osteospondylosis struck, coupled with the hardening of the arteries - in 1990. I was told by the specialist it was to far gone for therapy, nothing could be done (only pain killers) they suggested I go in a nursing home. Six years later I am (with help) still lining in my own bungalow. I am not able to do much, despite all the things I'd enjoyed doing being taken from me. Some how I always "have a go" at something else. Oh, yes, I get very frustrated at times, but very happy. I still have my faith, life is still good and I have a lot to thank God for. I started scribbling poetry in 1994 to keep my mind active. (I think I would go crazy if I did not have a try at something.) My advice would be to all those who are house bound is to try what you may think impossible and you'll find life much easier to cope with. God is good and he does care. I saw my daughter, Elizabeth through 4 years at the Royal College of music and I am very proud of her. She is now married to Graham healing and living in Potter's bar, in Hertfordshire - they are both very much involved in music and drama; [a.] Bournemouth, Dorset, UK

BUNTING, ALLAN
[b.] 28 May 1928, Glasgow; [p.] John and Janet (Deceased); [m.] May Bunting (Deceased), 18 June 1956; [ch.] Alison and Stuart; [ed.] White Hill Senior Secondary School Eng. Apprentice and Night - Class" Eng. Tech. Drawing, National Service RAF Flight Mechanic. Finally Tech. Manager Print and Photo Copiers; [occ.] Retired (Semi-Pro Jazz-Drummer) Modern Jazz Group; [memb.] Musicians Union. R.S.P. - "Hamilton Collection" for North American Indian Artefacts. Glasgow Libraries Plus "Mitchell Reference Library".; [hon.] Technical Awards and 25 years Service Gold Watch with my Company - Winning Contestant on Televisions "Sale of the Century"; [oth. writ.] Publication of Letters to "Jazz Magazines" Letters to T.V. programmes - and BBC Radio - To Home Office Regard "Time" Change in Scotland - Prime Minister, and Michael Hezectine and Sunday Times; [pers.] I am a very Sentimental Person with regard to music, nature, and my fellow man. Much influenced in the poetry of Robert Burns, I have a New Lady in my Life, I have written many poems to her-about Love!; [a.] Glasgow, Lanarkshire, UK

BURCHMORE, HEIDE MARIE
[b.] 25 March 1974, Munster, W Germany; [p.] Susan Ann Burchmore, Roger Beker Burchmore; [ed.] GCSE - Maths/English (Lang)/English Lit/ Biology/French/Rural Science/ RSA Typing/ Geography/History/Eng Oral; [occ.] RAF (ASOP) Aerospace Systems Operator; [oth. writ.] Just write for personal interest. Doing a poetry course with the London school of Journalism.; [a.] Clacton-on-Sea, Essex, UK

BURGAN, REV. JOHN
[b.] 7 August 1942, Derby; [p.] Robert Burgan, Grace Burgan; [m.] Jeanette, 3 September 1966; [ch.] Richard, Stephen, Phillip, Ruth; [ed.] Derby Secondary Education, then Theological training followed by grad - and post - grad at London Univ. - King's College; [occ.] Minister of Religion; [hon.] Dif. TL. RD (Hons) Mphil/PMD (cand); [oth. writ.] 'Paul's Letter to Pastor', 'Secret Knowledge Through The Eyes' (awaiting pub.) 'Pentecostal Distinctives (one chapter of - also awaiting publication). Many articles on Sunday religion matter.; [pers.] I have only just started writing poetry and it gives me a fresher of varied outlet from purely academic writing.; [a.] Crawley, W. Sussex, UK

BURN, SARAH
[pen.] Sarah-Lou; [b.] 14 May 1980, Gravesend, Kent; [p.] Andria Burn and James Burn; [ed.] St. John's RC Comp., Rochester Road, Gravesend, Kent; [occ.] Student (Part time job at McDonald's); [memb.] St. John's Percussion Ensemble; [hon.] North West Kent Young Musician of 1996, Typing - Elementary 1st class pass, Intermediate pass; [oth. writ.] Two novels, a book of poems (none published), numerous pieces of music; [pers.] I write poetry when I am provoked by my inner feelings and by what goes on around me. I like to see my poetry as a communicator between my soul and the outside world.; [a.] Rochester, Kent, UK

BURROUGH, PAUL
[b.] 5 May 1916, Surrey; [p.] Canon and Mrs. E. G. Burrough; [m.] Bess (Deceased), 23 May 1962; [ch.] Step-daughter only; [ed.] St. Edward's, Oxford, St. Edmund Hall, Oxford, Ely Theological College; [occ.] C of E Bishop retired from Mashonaland, Zimbabwe; [memb.] Vincent's Club, Oxford Leander Club, Henley, O.U.B.C. (Boat Races of 1937 and '38); [hon.] M.B.E. (Mil) MA; [oth. writ.] 'Lodeleigh' - Chatto and Windus 1947, 'God and Human Chance' 1984, 'Angels Unawares' 1988; [a.] Bampton, Oxon, UK

BURROWS, KENNETH HAYDN JAMES
[pen.] Ken Burrows; [b.] 16 May 1923, Derby; [p.] Hilda and James Burrows; [m.] Gwen, 15 March 1952, Deceased, 24 December 1995; [ch.] David, Eary, Michael; [ed.] Kedleston RD Elementary Boys School; [occ.] Retired Painter and Decorator; [memb.] Evington Club, Alvaston and Crewton Social Club; [oth. writ.] Several poems published, both in books and magazines; [pers.] I first won a competition at School and my headmaster told me I must always write. I didn't write any more until I went abroad in the army in 1942. Then I couldn't stop!; [a.] Derby, UK

BURTON, ANDREW
[pen.] Andy Burton; [b.] 30 April 1962, Farnworth; [p.] Mabel and Edward Burton; [ed.] St. Georges High School, Herwich, Bolton, Worsley College; [occ.] Engineer (Maintenance) Pesca Engineering, Ltd.; [memb.] Bolton Amateur Theatre Societies - Secretary of Central Point for 24 Amateur Groups; [oth. writ.] Few poems publishes in Bolton Burning news one poem published in three books; [pers.] If something is wrong. Look to the beginning because if it is wrong at his beginning it will be wrong all the way through.; [a.] Walkden, Worsley, Manchester, UK

BUSH, ANNE
[b.] 2 February 1952, Johnstone, Scotland; [p.] John and Maria Canney; [m.] James Bush; [ch.] Paul, Gayle; [ed.] Holy Family Primary, St. Stephen Secondary School, Port Glasgow, Scotland; [pers.] I have been writing poetry since childhood, and quite a lot of my poems reflect my emotions at the time.; [a.] Luton, Beds, UK

BUTCHER, SUSAN
[b.] 13 January 1972, Brisbane, Australia; [p.] Jean and Reg Butcher; [ed.] Cecil Jones High School; [occ.] VDU/Telephone Operator; [memb.] London Beatles Fan Club, Liverpool Beatle Scene; [oth. writ.] Over 200 original poems and songs, many for family and friends.; [pers.] I like to write poetry that is easily understood but has meaning.; [a.] Southend-on-Sea, Essex, UK

BUTLER, AMIE K. Z.
[b.] 29 July 1980, London; [p.] Angela Butler; [ed.] Secondary G.C.S.E level; [occ.] Not long left school; [oth. writ.] I have written many other poems for my own enjoyment, which have never been published. Which I hope to have published one day.; [pers.] "I write of only what I feel so others can share one experience with me."; [a.] UK

BUTLER, EMMA
[b.] 3 September 1977, Cork City; [p.] James and Catherine Butler; [ed.] St. Patrick's School, College of Commerce, Cork.; [occ.] Student; [pers.] In a world full of noise, the quiet moments and memories we manage to save are gilt-edged, golden centred and precious without a price.; [a.] Cork City, Ireland

BUTLER, YVONNE
[b.] 16 July 1938, Upper Barian, India; [p.] John Armstrong and Phyllis Pullinger Armstrong; [m.] Michael Butler, 5 September 1959; [ch.] Graham Butler born 1965; [ed.] British Military Schools Overseas, Amery Hill School; [occ.] Accounts Supervisor; [memb.] Hampshire Federation of Woman's Institutes; [hon.] Amateur Drama Society; [oth. writ.] Have written poetry all my life, for my own enjoyment and to celebrate special occasions

in the life of family and friends.; [pers.] I draw great inspiration from the natural world, especially from the life of Gilbert White, the 18th century naturalist and author of "The Natural History of Selborne."; [a.] Selborne, Nr Alton, Hants, UK

BUTROS, RAGHDA
[b.] 12 October 1972, Amman, Jordan; [p.] Dr. Albert Butros, Mrs. Idam M.; [ed.] Ahityyah School for Girls, Amman, Jordan Centennial School, Ottawa, Canada, Lycee Francais, London, England University of Jordan, Amman B.A. Engl. Lit. (Major) Poli. Sci. (Minor); [occ.] Assistant Manager, YAFI Design, (Graphic Design Company) Amman Jordan; [oth. writ.] Several articles on politics and culture published in Jordanian english language newspapers.; [a.] Amman, Jordan

BUTTON, GREGORY
[b.] 2 April 1972, Gooderstone; [p.] Sam Button and Joy Button; [ed.] Methwold High School, Downham Market Sixth Form Centre; [oth. writ.] Many poems published in local, parish magazine.; [pers.] The object of this work of poetry, is to express the connection between our most diverse emotions, in its truly irrational and confused state.; [a.] Gooderstone, Kings Lynn, Norfolk, UK

BUXTON, DERRICK
[b.] 1 July 1928, Renishaw; [p.] Percy Buxton, Dorothy Helen Buxton; [m.] Margaret Doreen Buston-Nee Gee, 29 March 1948; [ch.] Malcolm, Peter, Maureen Mary, Margaret Helen; [ed.] Chesterfield College of Technology most of my Career spent in mine Management and Technical Services finally forming my own Engineering Co.; [occ.] Retired MD of Quarryfields Engineering Co.; [memb.] Fellowship of Services. Fellow of Sales and Marketing Management Institute. Associate Member of Work Study Institute; [oth. writ.] I have done quotations for fellowship. Magazines and local organizations, but nothing of significance.; [pers.] I am in my 69th year and have endured same wide ranging experiencing in my career, I am gradually putting these into verse, which I shall endeavour to publish on completion.; [a.] Worksop, Notts, UK

BYRNE, SUSAN LEE NEILSON
[pen.] Skybird; [b.] 9 December 1960, Edinburgh; [p.] Agnes Huth (Russel); [m.] James Byrne (Patrick), 5 July 1980; [ch.] Jemma Sky Huth Byrne; [oth. writ.] I have more of my own, but this is my first one, I dared send (or share with anyone) to competition.; [pers.] To my daughter Jemma Sky Byrne unknown to you the seed of our life is the innocence of watching you grow cherishing you, freely eternal love mum.; [a.] Edinburgh, Scotland

BYRNE, SUSAN
[b.] 5 February 1949, Somerset, England; [p.] Harry - Ruth Regan; [m.] Thomas Patrick Byrne, October 1971; [ch.] Mark - David Byrne; [occ.] Housewife Writer for Pleasure; [memb.] Fingal Writers Club Coolock, Dublin 5, Ireland.; [oth. writ.] Have been published in group book called Woven Threads, also, had poem published in magazine called Mischief, I have also written several books, but as yet waiting to be discovered.; [pers.] I would like to dedicate this poem to my dad who died January 1989. His name Harry Regan, born in Kent, England.; [a.] Swords, Dublin, Ireland

CAINES, EUNICE MARY
[b.] 27 September 1926, Hebden Bridge; [p.] Thomas Thornber, Annie Jane Thornber; [m.] Ronald Edwin Caines; [ed.] Colden Council School, W.R.C.C. also Central Street School, Hebden Bridge; [occ.] Retired Civil Servant; [oth. writ.] Several poems published, one broadcast on air by BBC Radio Leeds; [a.] Brighouse, West Yorkshire, UK

CALDER, PAUL EDWARD
[b.] 18 April 1964, Edinburgh, Scotland; [p.] James Edward Calder, Janet Turnbell Patterson; [m.] Janet Margaret Tait, 18 April 1986; [ch.] Amy (9), Alexander (5); [ed.] Selkirk High School; [occ.] Laborer; [pers.] I consider life itself to be a reflection of all poetry for without life - there would be no poems or poets. In this I find myself shaped and influenced by personal experience.; [a.] Aberdeen, Aberdeen, UK

CALLAN, MOIRA
[b.] 27 June 1943, Fleetwood; [m.] Douglas, 12 March 1966; [ch.] Two; [occ.] Home Help; [oth. writ.] I am in the middle of writing my biography as a home help. I also wrote but unpublished six books for children called "The Flower People".; [pers.] Thank you to my wonderful daughter Jayne for the love, advice and encouragement.; [a.] Hull, East Yorks, UK

CAMERON, MICHELLE
[pen.] Shelley Scott; [b.] 8 December 1968, Northampton; [p.] Elizabeth Bishop-Bailey, Malcolm Cameron; [ch.] Rickie Scott, Jessica, Laura, Liam Alexander; [ed.] Duston Upper School; [occ.] Full-time mother; [memb.] St. Neots Operatic Society; [oth. writ.] Children's stories in verse (unpublished as yet); [pers.] Whilst I tend to draw from my own experiences for my poetry, poets such as Shelley, Barratt-Browning have been an inspiration.; [a.] Saint Neots, Cambs, UK

CAMPBELL, MRS. ANNIE E.
[b.] 31 July 1919, Dunganoon; [p.] Mr. and Mrs. Michael Kane; [m.] John J. Campbell, 26 April 1934; [ch.] Malachy, Sheila, Kitty Annie, Josie, Sean Gertie, Brian, Teresa, Michael, Kevin, Patricia, Una, Eithna, Plynkett; [ed.] To G. Level Standard; [occ.] Retired

CAMPBELL, KEVIN
[b.] 30 April 1965, Co Kildare; [m.] Annabelle, 27 September 1996; [occ.] Aux Nurse; [hon.] This will be my first publication; [oth. writ.] Poems, short stories; [a.] Clane, Kildare, UK

CAMPBELL, LES
[b.] 11 February 1945, Newcastle; [p.] Kath and Andrew Campbell (both Deceased); [m.] Lilian Campbell, 15 February 1974; [ch.] Glen Campbell (26); [ed.] Wallsend Weston Secondary Modern; [occ.] Blacksmith; [memb.] Fellowship of Christ (Baptist Church), Evangelist Team; [oth. writ.] Poems and plays for my church; [pers.] I'm a recovering alcoholic and ex-con who has been saved by the grace of God. I try to reflect in my poems that their is life, and someone who really does love us.; [a.] Rosyth, Fife, UK

CAMPION, DORIS
[b.] 30 March 1933, Stockport; [m.] Henry Campion, 27 July 1963; [ch.] 3 girls; [ed.] Elementary School left at 14 years old; [occ.] Retired; [oth. writ.] Published Little Girls Are Wonderful lots of others not published; [pers.] Poetry to me is the natural way to put feeling into being.; [a.] Stockport, Cheshire, UK

CANTILLON, ELIZABETH BEECHER
[b.] 3 March 1926, Tallow; [p.] John and Mary Beecher; [m.] Dermot Finbar Mary Cantillon, 9 April 1956; [ch.] Geraldine, Anne, Dermot, William, Eric; [ed.] Primary School, Convent of Mercy Secondary School Carrick on - Suir; [occ.] Housewife; [hon.] Hons Inter Cert, Hons Leaving Cert.; [oth. writ.] Outline history of Tallow short stories; [pers.] They also serve, who only stand and wait. (Milton); [a.] Tallow, Eire, UK

CANTRELL, PAULINE
[b.] 17 June 1943, Staffs; [p.] Edwin and Elsie Locker Cantrell; [m.] Divorced 20 years; [ch.] Four, two boys and two girls; [ed.] Primary School; [occ.] Machine Operator/Carpet Factory; [memb.] None, School of Writing, Student; [hon.] None as yet, would like to reach such a level; [oth. writ.] Short stories, writings with the school of writing, for four months, there are several other poems in folders, which I have wrote with life experiences, poems can tell of ones being, so much, whether happy or sad, or even both.; [pers.] I have always wanted to write but never really knew how, my poem was a first attempt, hearing from you, has given me a vast amount of encouragement, thank you.; [a.] Telford, Salop, UK

CAPENHURST, ARTHUR
[b.] 11 April 1949, Leicester; [p.] Trudi (83) and Arthur (Deceased); [m.] Jo Anne, 29 June 1984; [ed.] 'O' Level Maths and 'A' Level Ery taken at age 40; [occ.] Firefighter; [memb.] 'Writers Bureau' 'Writers Kramp' (Club); [oth. writ.] 2 Short stories in Nautical Magazine short story BBC Radio Various Articles in Local Magazine 2 poems in published anthologies; [pers.] Writing is an expression of my life and my life is buddhism.; [a.] Manchester, Lancs, UK

CARLIN, PETER
[pen.] Peter Carlin; [b.] 16 December 1972, Leeds; [m.] Beverley Anne Carlin, 9 March 1996; [ch.] Emily Jane Carlin; [occ.] Photographer; [pers.] If the pen doesn't work by itself, then it must not work anymore.; [a.] Leeds, Yorkshire, UK

CARR, JOHN
[pen.] John Harrison; [b.] May 14, 1941, Nottingham; [p.] Lancelot Harrison and Vera Harrison; [m.] Frances Carr (Nee Russell), September 18, 1980; [ch.] Gary, Robert, Amanda, Jacqueline; [ed.] Abingdon (John Roysse's) School, Berkshire; [occ.] Document Courier; [oth. writ.] Various, including short pantomimes, dialogue, prose and poems of which one entitled "The Tree" sent to the Green Party and to The Woodland Trust in Grantham, Lincolnshire.; [pers.] I believe "Life is now". If we worry too much about the future we can't enjoy the present therefore we have no past. The present shapes the future and creates the past.; [a.] Chorley, Lancs

CARRINGTON, JEAN
[b.] 10 January 1948, Blackpool; [p.] George and Betty Carrington; [ed.] Queen Mary Grammar School Lytham St Anne's, St Anne's College of Further Education; [occ.] Retired; [memb.] Lytham St Anne's Art Society National Trust; [oth. writ.] Short story in English teaching magazine in far east; [pers.] I try to employ my christian beliefs in all I do and write.; [a.] Lytham, St. Anne's, Lancs, UK

CARROLL, MARTIN
[b.] 14 November 1917, Portsmouth; [m.] Beryl Carroll, 3 February 1943; [ch.] Two boys one girl; [ed.] Portsmouth Grammar School Distinction in Maths; [occ.] Accountant/Taxation Specialist own Company; [memb.] Member Institute of Management Fellow Taxation Consultants Association; [hon.] Doctor of Commerce Mensa Gold Award; [oth. writ.] Various articles on Accountancy and Taxation published in professional journals. One poem "Nymph" previously published by son after his father's death; [pers.] Became interested in poetry after semi-retirement, to Spain. Poems bequeathed to wife in memory.; [a.] Ferndown, Dorset, UK

CARTER, KAREN
[b.] 29 March 1965, Havant; [p.] Alan and Sylvia Carter; [m.] Divorced, 8 August 1987; [ch.] Two Jade and Kirsty Carter; [ed.] High Bury College Casham, Portsmouth, Drama Course I also took my Lamda Exam; [occ.] Single parent; [oth. writ.] I did write a true story about myself to take a break and it was published in February this year; [pers.] I have been writing poetry and stories since the age of 11, but have never sent anything of for publication before.; [a.] Portsmouth, Hants, UK

CARTER, LORNA MAY
[pen.] Lorna Mayne; [b.] 9 October 1920, Long Eaton; [p.] Thirza and Robert Marshall Cooling (Deceased); [m.] John Carter (Deceased), 4 May 1945; [ch.] Allan, Robert and Janice; [ed.] Educated at the Wellington Street School for Girls at Long Eaton Notts; [occ.] Housewife; [oth. writ.] One poem title "Dedicated To Sean Wilson" published in "No Submission" a book of poetry published in poetry from the Midlands; [pers.] I do cross stitch, embroidery, love gardening orchids and carnations my favorite flowers, love animals, have met my favorite singer Sean Wilson, for whom I wrote the poem which won a competition in 1995; [a.] Long Eaton, Notts, UK

CARTER, MARGARET
[b.] 25 May 1938, Dublin; [p.] Richard and Elizabeth Wilson; [m.] Ivan Carter, 18 June 1963; [ch.] Alexandra and Ivan; [ed.] Wesley College, Dublin; [occ.] Housewife; [memb.] Art Class; [hon.] State Registered Nurse, Baggot Street Hospital, Dublin; [oth. writ.] Several poems in anthologies 'Poems to Enjoy' published book with illustrations of 50 of my poems.; [pers.] As I observe everyday situations I find poetry an ideal median to express any thoughts and humours and thoughtfulness, the two sides of life; [a.] Cherleywood, Herts, UK

CARTER, MARIAN
[pen.] Marian Carter; [b.] 31 January 1924, Lancashire, Blackburn; [p.] Arthur and Mary Jane Hargreaves; [m.] Terence Carter, 30 yrs. (second) husband; [ch.] Diane, Terry Jnr, Vanessa Jayne, David James; [ed.] Feniscowles School, Technical Darwen College, Blackburn Technical College; [occ.] Poetess/Artist/Pianist have had exhibitions of my own paintings. Sometimes played piano where needed, my number 011293; [memb.] Society of Amateur Artists; [hon.] Fellow of the International, Who's Who in Poetry, England Cambridge, Dictionary of Biography, The World's Who's Who of Women, Who's Who in Western Europe, Certificate of Merit - "For Distinguished Contributions to Poetry", Diploma - "Companion of Honour to Western Europe; [oth. writ.] Wrote various 'pieces' for newspapers, including poetry. A few years ago, created my own poetry book -

sold up! Still have 1/2 a book on "Sioux Indians!"; [pers.] I found out years ago, if you have a leaning towards thinking about what you wish to do - go ahead - do it! Don't fail! Follow your 'dream' - it does come true!; [a.] Darwen, Lancashire, UK

CARTER, MRS. JANET
[pen.] 'Jan'; [b.] 6 January 1941, London; [p.] Mr. and Mrs. N. A. Bain; [m.] Mr. Roy Alfred Carter, 26 December 1959; [ch.] Burton Lee, Sylvia Carter, Daryl Carter; [ed.] Greenwich Park, Secondary School London; [occ.] TEF/L Teacher; [memb.] Angling Clubs Book Clubs; [hon.] R.S.A. English French Mathematics TEF/L Certificate; [oth. writ.] Children's newspaper women's magazines voices on the wind the other side of the mirror quiet moments sound of poetry. (Int: Soc: Of Poets.; [pers.] I furthered my career, when I was a grandma, I love having six clever, Grandchildren.; [a.] St. Leonards-on-Sea, East Sussex, UK

CARTWRIGHT, DEAN
[pen.] Dean Cartwright; [b.] 9 July 1969, Hartlepool; [ed.] Self-taught Genius; [occ.] Personnel Officer with a Disreputable Local Government Office; [memb.] Hartlepool Library, World Books, Jean Alexander Appreciation Society; [hon.] Too many to mention; [oth. writ.] Mainly poetry and lyrics also, several articles published in magazines and fanzines; [pers.] Hold on to your dignity. Hold on to your individuality. Most of all hold onto your dreams.; [a.] Hartlepool, Cleveland, UK

CARVER, EILEEN
[pen.] Eileen Carson; [b.] 20 March 1949, London; [p.] Mary and John Carson; [m.] Robert J. Carver; [ch.] Dawn Mary, Mark James; [ed.] St. Angelas Ursuline Convent Forest Gate, London E7; [occ.] PA/Secretary; [oth. writ.] Complied poems to encourage colleagues to attend Blood Drawing sessions. Poem published in company magazine.; [pers.] I write 'Personalized poems' under my maiden name, to cover every conceivable occasion/celebration, and am about to launch my own company.; [a.] Barking, Essex, UK

CARVILL, PATRICK JOSEPH
[pen.] Veritas; [b.] 22 May 1932, Lucan, Co Dublin; [p.] Annie and Joseph Carvill; [m.] Frances Margaret Carvill, 23 October 1954; [ch.] Martin, Jeremy, Cindy and Brendon; [ed.] Lucan Convent, Redditch Coll.; [occ.] Retired (Engineer); [memb.] Animal Welfare, Rambling, Photographic Club, Archery; [oth. writ.] Articles in local newspapers. Unpublished poems. Poem in school magazine.; [pers.] Pollution, in all its form, is the inevitable result of man's activity and his nemesis. Our mindless disregard for the signs of imbalance in the environment sn indicative of our still primitive state.; [a.] Redditch, Worcs, UK

CASSIDY, BONNIE ZOE
[b.] 12 March, Torquay; [p.] Lionel and Elaine Cassidy; [ed.] I passed my 11 plus; [memb.] Leage Against Cruel Sports; [pers.] I have two cats and one kitten his name is Pantha, I love cats, I read about them all of the time. I have two German Sheperds, Samson and Breeze, I love writing poetry and swimming.; [a.] Torquay, Devon, UK

CASSIDY, TIM
[b.] 26 October 1957, Wimbledon; [p.] Mary Cassidy and Francis Cassidy; [ed.] St. Wilfrids West Sussex; [occ.] British Airways Mt OPS Gatwick; [memb.] Civil Air Flying Club Biggin

Hill; [pers.] A special thanks to Miss Karen Cunningham (British Airways) who inspired me to write this poem.; [a.] Crawley, Sussex, UK

CATALINOTTO, LUCIANO
[b.] 29 June 1970, Leicester; [p.] Martino and Rositta Catalinotto; [ed.] Bishop Ellis Primary School, Delisle Comprehensive School, Scuola Media Diano Marina, Scuola Alberghier; [occ.] Sous Chef; [oth. writ.] Angelina Thorn, Slack, nothing but poems and stuff; [pers.] Poetry is like jazz, hits you straight between the eyes.; [a.] Leicester, Leicestershire, UK

CATLING, TONI
[b.] 26 October 1968, Oxford; [p.] Mrs. Andreen Banister; [m.] Mr. Anthony John Catling, 2 October 1993; [ed.] Royal Alexandra and Albert School Redhill, Hevy Box School Witrey; [occ.] Sales Assistant Clerk; [oth. writ.] Only personal poems; [pers.] To understand a word is more to me that reading, it's thought or feelings that overwhelm me, my mind is what pushes me. and my heart is what carries me through.; [a.] Witney, Oxon, UK

CAVALIERE, LUCY
[b.] 21 July 1983, Eastbourne; [p.] Luigi Cavaliere and Shelagh Cavaliere; [ed.] Bishop Bell Cofe, School Eastbourne; [occ.] Attending school; [oth. writ.] This is my first attempt at having a piece of poetry published, although I have written lots of poems about cats and wish to try in the future to have them published.; [pers.] Because of my love of cats, I find when writing about them a deeper understanding. Cats are like poems, they can be small, but expressive and magical and I love to combine the two.; [a.] Eastbourne, East Sussex, UK

CHADWICK, JOYCE
[b.] 5 November 1937, Tunstall; [p.] Robert, Elizabeth Chadwick; [occ.] Enamel Kiln Cranker; [pers.] My poems are about what I see around me.; [a.] Tunstall, Staffs, UK

CHALMERS, JOANNA STAN ROSE
[b.] 24 June 1974, Plymouth; [p.] Joseph and Patricia Chalmers; [ed.] Redgeway Comprehensive, Plymouth College of Further Education; [occ.] Clerk/Typist for Wessmann Refrigeration; [oth. writ.] Many writings, poetry and short stories, never shown my work before this competition.; [pers.] My poetry is a reflection of my feelings and opinions on life today as I see it.; [a.] Plymouth, Devon, UK

CHALONER, MISS EVELYN GRETA
[b.] 15 February 1952, Liverpool; [ed.] Princess Park Secondary Modern, Lodge Lane, Liverpool, 1963-1966. Arundle Comprehensive. Lodge Lane, Liverpool. 1996-1967; [occ.] Full-time student administration NVQ Level 2; [memb.] Southcourt Baptist Church Penn Road, Aylesbury, Bucks; [oth. writ.] A story in a small book call swan song. Story was named fantasy, this was in 1981; [pers.] To be a born again christian, and to be a person in my own right. Also to be concerned about our plant and the human race.; [a.] Aylesbury, Bucks, UK

CHANDLER, CHARLES FREDERIC
[pen.] C. F. Chandler; [b.] 16 February 1915, Brighton; [p.] Frederic Chandler, Alice Chandler; [m.] Kathleen Joyce Chandler (Deceased), 6 May 1935; [ch.] Eileen, Janet, Antonette, Ian; [ed.] Dane Hill Village Church School, Hayward Heath, "Belvedere" Private School; [occ.] Monotype Operative (Retired); [memb.] Inaugurated

Haywards Heath Branch Of R.A.F.A. (Made Secretary), Royal British Legion Berkmansted Club; [oth. writ.] Poems published in local paper, "The Mid-Sussex Times" and Sussex Magazines; [pers.] I strive to write of the warming gifts of God and our earthly heritage.; [a.] Berkhamsted, Herts, UK

CHARLESWORTH, RICHARD JAMES
[pen.] Charles James; [b.] 15 March 1952, Cheltenham; [p.] Malcom and Gwendolyn Charlesworth; [m.] Sally Christine, 21 September 1974; [ch.] Bethany Jane, Oliver James; [ed.] Arle Secondary Modern Gloucester College of Art and Technology (Gloscat), O.U. Technology Undergraduate; [occ.] Project Engineer; [memb.] British Association for Shooting and Conservation (BASC) Cheltenham and District Clay Club (C.D.C.C.), University of Life; [oth. writ.] Several poems published in other anthologies; [pers.] Influential poets include: W.H. Davis, Lord Tennyson, John Masefield, C. Patmore, C. Kingsley. Some Shakespearian Sonnets "Treat the earth well, it was not given to us by our parents, it was lent to us by our children.; [a.] Tewkesbury, Glos, UK

CHESTER, ALAN
[b.] 3 April 1923; [p.] William and Emily Chester; [m.] Iris Lilian Chester, 1951; [ch.] 4 Boys, 1 Girl, 5 Granddaughters; [ed.] School of Life; [occ.] Retired, Farm Worker, Shepherd, Verderer; [oth. writ.] Many poems and short stories over the years, and not finished, yes poetry stimulated by a wonderful wife, and a great marriage.; [pers.] Schooled on Milton (Lycidas) Shakespeare. Try to emulate A.E. Copparo (Uncle on Mother's side)! But praise the Lord for what I've been given.

CHESTER, TEENA-KAY
[b.] 3 February 1976, Gillingham; [p.] Albert John Chester and Kathleen Chester; [memb.] English Heritage; [oth. writ.] I've written several other poems and short horror stories but have not been published before.; [pers.] I have been greatly influenced by the poet P. B. Shelley. And I'm a great fan of the horror writer Stephen King. I write for fun.; [a.] Gravesend, Kent, UK

CHEYNE, ANICIA MANDUK
[b.] 1 December 1981, Walthamsford; [p.] Bruce Cheyne and Barbara Manduk Cheyne; [ed.] Edward Red Head Primary School, Wilowfield Secondary School.; [occ.] Student; [hon.] An honour being in this book.; [oth. writ.] Other private poetry. eg, Danced, a hopeful love, it story of true love.; [pers.] Kiss the one you love, for they may not be there forever.

CHIRCOP, MARY DORIS
[pen.] Maria D. Kirkop; [b.] 27 November 1946, Malta; [p.] Joseph and Connie Chetcuti; [m.] Dominic Chircop A.I.A., C.P.A., 15 May 1971; [ch.] Connie, Fabio; [ed.] Maria Regina Grammar School; [occ.] Housewife, Ex Civil Servant; [memb.] Ghaqda Poeti Maltin (Maltese Poets Society) and Hon. Treasurer of same; [oth. writ.] Several poems published in local poetry publications; [pers.] The world is full of inequalities.; [a.] Gzira, Malta

CHRISTIAN, TRACY
[b.] March 7, 1969, Paignton, Devon; [p.] Ann Denny and Allan Moores; [m.] James Fernley (Partner); [ch.] Benjamin William Christian; [ed.] Priory Grammar School, Shrewsbury, Shropshire, Wolverhampton University; [occ.] Registered Psychiatric Nurse; [oth.

writ.] This is my first!; [pers.] I write poetry for fun and as a way of telling my family how much I love them.; [a.] Shrewsbury, Shropshire

CHURCH, JACQUELINE
[b.] 11 December 1980, Glasgow; [p.] June Church, James Church; [ed.] King's Park Secondary; [occ.] Student at King's Park Secondary; [pers.] Poems come from the heart. I always write what comes into my head straight away and I don't spend hours on poem. Poems should come naturally.; [a.] Glasgow, UK

CIANCI, I. H.
[b.] 11 August 1957, Rijeka, Croatia; [p.] Tullio Cianci, Natasha Bush; [ed.] Private Schools, England; [occ.] Film Writer, Director, Producer; [oth. writ.] Book of Poems "The Message", collection of short stories, "Take 24" currently writing my science fiction epic film, structured for 20 TV episodes; [pers.] One night I woke up from the loud voice inside of me which kept on telling me you have a message to give so write it, and change will come. You will see!; [a.] London, Chelsea, UK

CICCHIRILLO, PIERINA
[pen.] Kudos; [b.] 12 July 1976, Tameside; [p.] Francesco Cicchirillo, Concetta Cicchirillo; [ed.] Tameside College of Technology, University of Derby; [occ.] Student; [hon.] BTEC National in Business and Finance, Currently and Business Management; [oth. writ.] Nothing published, but my own personal writings for friends and family; [pers.] My writing comes from what has happened in my life and the lives of those around me who I love. My advice is if you love someone never give up hope on them.; [a.] Ashton-under-Lyne, Tameside, UK

CLARK, DELLA
[b.] 12 January 1962, Reading; [p.] Jan and Betty Kopanski; [ch.] Charlene Clark; [hon.] An award of Excellence for my Poetry; [oth. writ.] Various poems published; [pers.] Thank-you my friends who gave me the courage to walk away. Words from the heart, I hope will give women in my situation faith in love.; [a.] Wokingham, Berks, UK

CLARK, ETHEL M.
[pen.] Ethel M. Clark; [b.] 17 March 1909, Woodlaston, Glos; [p.] Wm. and Lizzie Williams; [m.] John Henry Clark (died 10 July 1970), 30 December 1930; [ch.] Jean (64), John (62), and Peter (58); [ed.] Gloucester Pupil Teachers Centre 1922-1927 Certificate of Education Stafford College 1949-50, Taught Juniors various Glos. Schools; [occ.] Retired Teacher Taught 29 years; [memb.] In 1950's was a Parish Counselor and on a school board of Managers. In 70's Chairman of Electrical Women's Association for Midlands area electricity; [oth. writ.] Children's poems "Happy All The Day" reflections of eventide 1973 their small learners - Biology of my childhood in village of Woolaston - extracts published in "Shadows From the Past, compiled Long Last House Editor Nenetia Murray personally signed by Ford Weymouth.

CLARK, JANE MARGARET
[b.] 20 November 1962, Chadwell, St. Mary, Essex; [p.] Stanley Clark and Joyce Clark; [m.] Divorced; [ch.] Sophie Marie Richman, Daniel, Mark, Richard; [ed.] Torells comprehensive school; [oth. writ.] My writings, I have never believed to be good enough to send off. So I keep them for private use. I only sent this off by chance, to be

shared with all Gods children.; [pers.] Justice of the highest level occurs when everyone is treated as an equal and where everyone is loved and forgiven unconditionally.; [a.] Grays, Essex, UK

CLARK, JENNI
[b.] 28 August 1982, Reading; [p.] Lynne and Graham Clark; [occ.] Pupil of South Bromsgrove School; [oth. writ.] None published; [pers.] My school is built on the site of an old flax mill whose pond still exists. A poetry workshop led by Eleanor Cooke looked at this feature and 'The Eyes of my Shoes' was the result of my efforts; [a.] Alvechurch, Worcestershire, UK

CLARK, WAYNE
[b.] 13 April 1970, Kent; [p.] Michael Clark, Ann Clark; [ed.] Ongar Comprehensive Moreton Cofe and Primary School; [occ.] Farm Worker; [oth. writ.] Several poems (never submitted for publications); [a.] Ongar, Essex, UK

CLARKE, ALISON
[b.] 7 February 1970, Derby; [p.] Haskell and Jean Clarke; [ed.] Millshaven Elementary, Killarny Junior High, Queen Elizabeth High School, University of Alberta, Grant MacEwan College; [occ.] apparell clerk, writer; [memb.] Stroll of Poets, Writers' Guild, Wordworks Society of Alberta; [hon.] was on the honour roo throughout junior high and also in high school. I obtained a Rutherford Scholarship for $500 for having an 80% average or better; [oth. writ.] was published in various high school and university publications including The Gateway, unpublished fiction, The Canadian Writers' Journal and Ariel - a journal produced by the University of Calgary. I've also had a poem recorded and performed as a song.; [pers.] I write because it gives me great pleasure. Sometimes my work is very political - striving to get acrss a serious message. Other times, my writing consists of observaitons that I have made about humankind, animals, or society in general. [a.] Edmonton, Alberta, Canada

CLARKE, ANITA
[b.] 29 January 1968, Dudley, West Mids; [p.] Geoffrey and Janet Clarke; [ed.] Kingswinford Comprehensive School, University of Essex, University of Leeds, University of Durham, Stourbridge College of Technology and Art; [occ.] Full time post-graduate student (MA in Applied Social Studies and Social Work); [memb.] World Society for the Protection of Animals, Liberty Campaign for Bears, World Wide Fund for Nature, National Assoc of Probation Officers; [hon.] B.A. Hons in English and European Literature, Post Graduate Certificate of Education, Teaching English as a Foreign Language Qualification; [oth. writ.] Have been writing for pleasure for fourteen years. This is my first published work.; [pers.] I attempt to capture a gothic, macabre, mysterious, fantasy atmosphere in my poetry. I am inspired by J.R.R Tolkien, Edgar Allan Poe and film noir. "There is more to life than reality".; [a.] Kingswinford, West Mids, UK

CLARKE, ANN
[pen.] Mac; [b.] 16 May 1940, Radgoon, Burma; [p.] Alex Newman, Doris Neman; [m.] Donald, 18 January 1987; [ch.] Jacqueline, Paul, Mark Gwids; [ed.] High School/Malaya; [occ.] Medical retired civil servant; [memb.] B.S.S.A. and pain concern; [oth. writ.] Poem published in poets of the S.E. other sent.; [pers.] My wish is to write a book. I love start! My form might be crippled but my mind steel open.; [a.] Blean, Kent, UK

CLARKE, JOHN FREEMAN
[pen.] Nobby The Mobile; [b.] 15 September 1921, Portsmouth, Hants; [p.] Edgar Charles and Nellie (Nee Daish) Clarke; [m.] Rita Ivy (Nee Manning) Clarke, 9 December 1944; [ch.] Paul Edgar and Linda Anne (Now Malsoh); [ed.] Portsmouth, Junior Technical; [occ.] Retired (Royal Naval Dockyard Shipwright, 1937-82); [hon.] I.S.M.; [oth. writ.] Too numerous to list, on any and most subjects, as they happened; [pers.] As a Royal Naval Dockyard Shipwright (1937-82), I was the unofficial Dockyard Poet, for most of that time.; [a.] Portsmouth, Hants, UK

CLARKE, NORMA EILEEN
[pen.] "Val"; [b.] 5 May 1938, Sutton Colefield; [p.] Lillian and Charles Hughes; [m.] Richard Christopher Clarke, 10 January 1959; [ch.] Angela, Mark, Natalie, Amanda; [ed.] Secondary Modern School, Lea Village Sheldon Birbingham 33; [occ.] Housewife; [memb.] "The Guild of International songwriters and Composers"; [hon.] "Mother of the Year" for having the most interests in one's life. Still hold title by the people paper and Oxo Company; [oth. writ.] Written 200 songs, consisting of, rock 'n roll, rap. reggae, ballads, country carols, heavy metal, dance disco, M.O.R. jazz, blues, soul, my poems and songs are of true life; [pers.] Eldest child of 11 children, mother died, when I was 15. Leaving 7 school children and 3 babies. The youngest was 1 year old, she died giving birth to him at Marston Green Maturnity Hospital.; [a.] Coleshill, Solihull, UK

CLARKE, SARAH
[pen.] S. E. M. Clark; [b.] 18 February 1972, Hong Kong; [p.] Robin L. Clarke and Puspa R. Serangan; [ed.] Bahrain School, Bahrain, Smith College (1 yr.) Massachusetts, U.S.A.; [pers.] This timely publication coincided with the death of one who figured strongly inily inspiration for 'Old Photographs' - a perfect, and lasting, tribute.; [a.] Oxshott, Surrey, UK

CLEMENTS, WILLIAM EDWARD
[b.] January 23, 1927, Battersea; [p.] Lillian and Alfred Clements; [m.] Freda Rosina Clements; [ch.] Six; [ed.] No. 1 Grammar School, Morden, Surrey; [occ.] Retired; [pers.] I have written several poems but this is my first attempt at publication.; [a.] Grays, Essex

CLEMMETT, DONALD RICHARD STEPHEN
[b.] 3 February 1963, Shropshire; [p.] Patricia Mary Clemmett and Colin Clemmett; [m.] Jane Klaasje Clemmett, 31 July 1982; [ch.] Anthony Stephen (13), Natalie Klaasje (11); [ed.] St. Mary's Primary and Sir Blessed William Howards Secondary School (Staffs); [occ.] Engineer/ Goodyear Type and Rubber Company - Bushbury Wolverhampton; [oth. writ.] Several poems to help the 'Drugs Awareness' campaign at my son secondary school (none published).; [pers.] I try to write about things that affect everyday people in their everyday lives i.e. - love, pain, fear, worry, etc (mainly love) and try to make it 'True to Life.'; [a.] Wolverhampton, Staffordshire, UK

CLIFFE, SHARON ANN
[pen.] S.A. Cliffe; [b.] 15 October 1970, Helsby, Cheshire; [p.] Mr A. H. and Mrs M. M. Cliffe; [ed.] The Chester Catholic High School, S. Martins College-Lancaster University; [occ.] Student of Curative Education for special needs Children/ Adults.; [memb.] Alzheimers Disease Society, Cheshire Scouting, Camphill Movement for special needs Children/Adults.; [hon.] History/Social Ethics; [oth. writ.] Various Articles for Regional National Alzheimers Society; [pers.] The words come from a bigger place than this, they will live on into Nirvana!; [a.] Chester, Cheshire, UK

COBBAN, PATRICIA
[b.] 27 March 1946, Royston, Barnsley; [p.] Robert Harrison, Eva Harrison; [m.] Douglas William Cobban, 22 August 1977; [ch.] Dawn and Steven; [ed.] Normanton Girls High School, Wakefield School of Commerce, 1986 - Adult Evening Classes - (G.C.S.E. - maths 'C' Grade, English a Grade; [occ.] Housewife; [memb.] St. Lukes, Haverigg Church, guider - Rainbow Unit (of guides) Mothers Union. Sick Visitor for Mothers Union; [oth. writ.] One poem published in local church magazine; [pers.] I write from the heart - inspired by the world as I see it today - and hope for a better one in my time - God willing.; [a.] Millom, Cumbria, UK

CODLING, LINDA J.
[pen.] Linda Codling; [b.] 19 August 1970, Tumut, Australia; [p.] Sandra and Lawrence Codling; [ed.] Galston High School and Hornsby College of Tafe; [occ.] Secretary/Acting Student; [hon.] Twice winner of short story competition, interview on Radio (Sydney) regarding my poetry. Attended "Camp for talented writers Sydney; [oth. writ.] Written for radio (volunteer) wrote 2 novels "Jued Valley" and "Ashton" as yet unpublished. Written many songs, written cast and directed several short plays (volunteer); [pers.] I am proud to be an original, and imaginative Australian writer, who will do anything to pursue my career in writing; [a.] Wahroonga, Sydney, Australia

CODY, LYNN-MARIE
[pen.] Lynn-Marie Cody; [b.] 14 July 1967, Harrogate; [p.] Susan Cody, Barry Cody; [ed.] St. John Fisher R.C. School, Harrogate, Cambridge University; [occ.] Private Language Tutor, (French, German, Spanish); [memb.] Elmet Conservative Association, The National Poetry Foundation; [hon.] Modern Languages (B.A.); [oth. writ.] Three poems published by 'Poetry Now' for three forthcoming anthologies, several poems published in local magazine.; [pers.] For me, poetry stems for the heart of emotion, be those emotions personal or directed at the concrete, objective world around us. As well as English poetry, I enjoy reading the foreign poets: Bertolt Brecht, Octavio PA2 and Cesar Vallejo.; [a.] Wetherby, West Yorkshire, UK

COLE, ASHLEE
[pen.] James Yates Cole; [b.] 22 February 1968; [pers.] For a special woman, whom I will always hold close to my heart.; [a.] Bristol, UK

COLES, GILBERT RONALD EDWIN
[b.] October 19, 1937, Saint Austell, Cornwall; [p.] Cyril Albert Norman and Edna Honor; [m.] Mary, November 19, 1960; [ch.] Susan Anne, Mary Angela, Andrew Gilbert John; [ed.] Comprehensive, Short-hand Typist in the Royal Army Service Corps.; [occ.] Senior Meat Hygiene Inspector with Ministry of Agriculture, Fisheries and Food; [memb.] Saint Mary's Church Choir, Royal Society of Health, St. Johns Ambulance, Royal Institute of Public Health and Gygiene, the Association of Meat Inspectors Several Local Choral Societies; [hon.] Medal for Blood Donations; [oth. writ.] None printed - only within my family circle for special occasions, i.e. Birthdays, Weddings, and occasionally at social functions for friends and neighbours.; [pers.] I like to think that my poems bring joy and comfort to others, particularly if they are undergoing ill health or stressful times, and that they Aid recovery.; [a.] Bideford, North Devon

COLES, HAYLEY-MARGARET
[b.] 10 October 1981, Reading; [p.] Keith and Kym Coles; [ed.] Willink School Burghfield Common; [pers.] Adopted and brought up by grand-parents Alec and Margaret Coles from the age of 6 weeks. I wrote this poem to my real Mum, in a mothers day card. The title is my special Mum because that's what she is.; [a.] Reading, Berks, UK

COLLEY, MR. GEORGE
[b.] 16 July 1949, Cardiff; [p.] Ernest and Catherine Colley; [m.] Christine Colley, 4 April 1992; [ed.] Duffryn High School Newport; [occ.] Engineer; [oth. writ.] Short stories/Discourses - Scientific/ Cosmic Rationalization of our purpose.; [pers.] To relate science to scripture wrapping love to enhance the imagery.; [a.] Cumbran, Gwent, UK

COLLIER, VIV
[b.] 8 October 1944, Wokingham; [p.] Fred and Joan Hearn; [ch.] Stephanie and Jacqueline; [ed.] Secondary Education in Wokingham followed by a year at secretarial college; [occ.] Carer for my mother; [memb.] Writers Bureau, Princess Theatre, Hunstanton; [oth. writ.] Several humorous poems in local magazine; [pers.] Brought up in a strictly "Stiff upper lip" environment I have found the written word the only outlet for my true emotions and thank God daily for the diversity of the English language.; [a.] Thornham, Norfolk, UK

COLLINS, PETER
[b.] 8 April 1944, London; [p.] Joseph and Rene Collins (Father died in 1987); [m.] Joseph (Died age 46 in 1992), 21 June 1972; [ch.] Gary (17), Melissa (14); [ed.] Brookland Primary School, Finchley, London, 1951-55, Clarks College School, Finchley, London, 1955-60; [occ.] Enquiry Officer for Royal Mail Customer Services, London for 20 years; [oth. writ.] Several poems published in local Synagogue Magazine; [pers.] I write poetry as a hobby, when there is someone who means something to me, I am inspired to write about that person, in verse. I am not influenced by any poet, I just write what I feel, e.g. when I first met my wife, and then, when she tragically died in '92.; [a.] Stanmore, Middlesex, UK

COLLINSON, J. M.
[pen.] Jean M. Collinson; [b.] 27 March 1925, Birmingham; [p.] Norman Blackham and Vera May Blackham; [m.] Norman Alan Collinson, 29 May 1954; [ch.] Paul, Ann, Michael, Karen, (all adopted); [ed.] War Disrupted Education Junior school and Queens College, Birmingham Trained in shorthand and Typing Started Employment at the age of 14 years. Worked up to the age of 65. Had time off when children were babies; [occ.] Retired housewife; [memb.] Husband and my self members of Christian Music Ministries Choir 325. Bromford Road, Hodge Hill, Birmingham B36 8ET. Roger Jones Christian Musicals Assisted by Ann Routley. Musicals are taken all over England and also Israel and Canada; [oth. writ.] Have written 66 poems up to the moment, had many published in books ie: 1996 British Poetry Review, A Trouble Shared, Poems Of The 90's, The Magic Of Love, Poems For Mum, Follow The Star, Poetry Now Christian Verse, Resurrection, The Human Kind, A Sprinkle of Seasoning. To Mention

But A Few.; [pers.] The poems I write except for a few are distinctive in the power of the holy spirit, I feel the words come into my mind and I have to write them down. Sometimes when I read them myself I say to myself "Did I really write this" I am so amazed by some of the words some of my poems come so fast I can write them in a matter of 10 mins. they also come when I least expect them.; [a.] Birmingham, Warwicks, UK

COLTMAN, IRENE MAUD
[pen.] Coltman Irene; [b.] 28 September 1930, Middlesbrough; [p.] Robert Henry Corner, Ada Robson; [m.] Henry Coltman, 29 September 1951; [ch.] Carol, Lynne, Joyce and Tracy; [ed.] Secondary Modern Archibald Girls School Middlesbrough Cleveland; [occ.] Housewife and Mother; [memb.] National Association of Women's Clubs, Centre Ladies Club Billingham Dads Music Club Stockton; [hon.] Late Commanding Officer, Girls Training Corps, (Now Venture Corps); [oth. writ.] Various poems unpublished; [pers.] I wrote the poem "Welcome Stranger" when I had to give a vote of thanks to a blind person who visited my ladies club with his guide dog. Irene Coltman; [a.] Billingham, Cleveland, UK

COMBEER, MARTIN
[b.] 14 August 1964, Redhill, Surrey; [p.] Brian and Sheila; [ed.] Woodhatch Comprehensive, Reigate College; [occ.] Clearance/Product Researcher At (M.C.P.S) Mechanical Copyright Protection Society - for Music Composers and Publishers; [oth. writ.] Sleeve Notes/Biographical Information for Music Product, releases various short stories and poems (as yet unpublished!); [pers.] I like exploring most genres in creative writing. I am currently working on a novel contemporary (thriller), a number of nonsense/children's poems and lyrics for children's songs.; [a.] Reigate, Surrey, UK

COMERFORD, ANITA
[b.] 24 February 1955, Swansea; [m.] Laurence William Comerford, 1 August 1980; [ed.] Llwyn-y-Bryn Comprehensive School, Swansea, and Manselton Secondary Girl's School, Swansea, where I was head girl; [occ.] Housewife; [oth. writ.] Some amusing letters published in a women's magazine, a number of poems and short stories published in various anthologies.; [pers.] I like to write about the good things in life.; [a.] Somerse, UK

COMLEY, MARY
[b.] Cuckfield, Sussex, England; [p.] Wonel and Eleanor Peake; [m.] Robert Comley, September 8, 1990; [ch.] Stephen Anne and Clare; [ed.] Convent Educated Lourdes Mount, Ealing St. Josephs, Reading Berkshire. I am not a Catholic but a Pentecostal Christian; [occ.] Homemaker and Enthusiastic pet owner and people encourager?; [memb.] Immigrated to Australia - flying through the Darwin cyclone and didn't surprise my U.K. friends!; [hon.] Distinction and credits H.Sc Standard. Elocution medal, honour in sports, running cup several times - I've awarded myself and overcoming medal of life's traumas to hopefully result in a character to bless"; [oth. writ.] Reading evening post published hundreds of my letters and a few human interest articles. I have this year sent my poems to friends here and overseas churches overseas a good respond; [pers.] I survived a very traumatic childhood hence life for many years a series of awesome knocks the learning from learning

to respond right created growth and later in a building relationship with my creator blessing flowed!; [a.] Glenthompson, Victoria, Australia

COMPLIN, DIANE E.
[b.] 1 July 1942, Herts; [m.] David Complin, 7 August 1960; [ch.] Tracey, Ninna, Marc; [ed.] Copland County Middx; [occ.] House wife; [memb.] Royal Academy of Art Berkhamsted Golf Club; [hon.] Classical Ballet and Art; [oth. writ.] None published.; [pers.] One of my dreams to write and publish a poem. Poems like art and ballet all woven into one. Listing to poetry of the masters being read can be very influencing.; [a.] Berkhamsted, Herts, UK

COMRIE, IAN
[b.] 24 October 1939, Broxburn; [p.] John Comrie, Jean Comrie; [m.] Elizabeth Comrie, 15 August 1962; [ch.] Jane, Fiona, John and Anne; [ed.] Lindsay High School Bathgate; [occ.] Riding School Proprietor Instructor; [memb.] British Horse Society, British Side Saddle Assoc., Association British Riding School, British Show Pony Society; [oth. writ.] Several poems published poem in poetry now. Many poems still to be published.; [pers.] My mind searches for what? I do not know. I give to you word pictures of ideas. Ideas that came not with crystal clarity, but as a portrait in a great hall viewed by flickering candle-light.; [a.] Broxburn, West Lothian, UK

COOK, PAULA
[b.] 31 March 1969, Isleworth; [p.] Maria and Burnard; [occ.] Temp (Clerical); [pers.] Thanks to my parents, for the eight wonderful years we spent in New Zealand. All my days were magical I couldn't have wished for a better childhood.; [a.] Peterborough, Cambs, UK

COOKE, ANITA
[b.] 8 February 1956, Dublin; [p.] Tom and Nita Hendy; [m.] Patrick, 4 September 1979; [ch.] Two Girls, Two Boys; [ed.] Primary and Secondary Leaving Cert.; [occ.] State Reg Nurse; [hon.] Grade 8 First Honours piano force; [oth. writ.] 2 poems 1 prose 1 song, book in the works; [pers.] There must be more to life than the daily drudgery and speed that is all around us. Our spirits are to be found in the nature which we are destroying I have lived it therefore I know; [a.] Kildare, UK

COOKE, LISA MARIE
[b.] 6 December 1986, Mansfield; [p.] Paul David Cooke, Julie Askew; [ed.] Holly Hill, School Selston Notts; [occ.] School Pupil; [memb.] School Gymnastics Club; [hon.] Top of Class in School Work; [oth. writ.] Poems written in class.; [a.] Selston, Notts, UK

COOMBES, DEBBIE
[b.] 17 December 1965, Horsham; [p.] Jill Thorn, Stan Coombes; [ch.] Carl Tuesley; [ed.] Millais, School for girls. Horsham, Sussex; [pers.] I hope that many generations of people will enjoy reading poems, like I have and a special thank you to Karl Bates, Steve Smith; [a.] Horsham, Sussex, UK

COONEY, MICHAEL JAMES
[pen.] Michael James-Cooney; [b.] 27 May 1970, Edgware; [p.] Pierce Cooney, Jean Godmon; [m.] Sarah Dimmock; [ed.] Hyde Junior, Hendon High Senior; [occ.] Graphic Designer; [memb.] Hillingdon Yacht Club, Spur Road Brat Pack; [pers.] I hope through poetry, to become a better, wiser person.; [a.] Edgware, Middx, UK

COOPER, HELEN
[pen.] Helen Ratcliffe; [b.] 29 December 1939, Birmingham; [p.] Joseph Anthony Ratcliffe, Dorothy Ratcliffe; [m.] Alan Peter Cooper, 5 July 1986; [ch.] Teresa Lake, Lorna Antunes, Helen Lake; [ed.] Kings Norton Grammar School, Birmingham, London University; [hon.] B.A. (Hons) French and German; [oth. writ.] Sermons for Church Services; [pers.] In my writing I try to reveal the presence of God in man and in nature. I have been inspired by the work of Walther Von Der Vogelweide.; [a.] Birmingham, West Midlands, UK

COOPER, MARK ANTHONY
[b.] 16 March 1971, Doncaster; [p.] John and Sandra Cooper; [ed.] Stainforth Westgate First School, Stainforth Middle School, Hatfield High School; [oth. writ.] Poem published in 'inspirations from Southern England,' articles for Hatfield School's newsletter.; [pers.] My friends have been my greatest inspirational source.; [a.] Doncaster, South Yorkshire, UK

COOPER, MARY
[b.] 25 January 1944, Boston, Lincs; [p.] Eric and Eillen Pearson; [m.] Brian Cooper, 30 July 1965; [ch.] Rachel and Sara-Jane; [ed.] Boston High School, Lincolnshire, Doncaster Training College, Nottingham University and various Courses; [occ.] Retired teacher (30 years), 13 yrs. teaching R.E. 15 years - Art Dance Drama; [memb.] Pepper Pot Players - Upton on Severn Norton Theatre Group - Littleworth Worcs; [hon.] Teaching, Certificates, Counselling and Pastoral Care Diploma; [oth. writ.] Various Magazines and Newspapers - Articles and Letter and Poems. Items of Poetry in, a) 4 Anthologist (Arrival Press), b) Writer Bureau " Lift The Veil". 3 pantomimes and some short plays.; [pers.] I want to share my feelings and thoughts with others hopefully to give both pleasure and comfort.; [a.] Worcester, UK

COOPER, PAMELA
[b.] 2 April 1953, St. Albans; [p.] Jean Joyner; [m.] Billy Cooper, 5 June 1971; [ch.] Morag, Angus, Claire; [ed.] Beech Hill High School Luton; [pers.] I find expressing my feelings on paper easier than trying to express them in words, and its an escape value to my mind.; [a.] Leighton Buzzard, Beds, UK

COREA, IVAN
[b.] 5 April 1957, Columbo, Sri Lanka; [p.] Vernon and Monica Corea; [m.] Charika Corea, 10 August 1991; [ch.] Charin Corea; [ed.] S. Thomas' College, Mount Lavinia, Sri Lanka; Chalfonts County Secondary School, Bucks; Archbishop Tenison's Grammar School, Croydon; West London Institue, Isleworth, Middlesex; Avery Hill College, Etham, London; [occ.] Head of P.R. and Marketing - FE Mulberry Tower Hamlets; Manager-Director Newsbrief (London); Editor, Sri Lanka Today; Editor, Maldives Today; Editor, Asia Pacific - Travel Days (Europe); [memb.] Institue of Travel and Tourism, Association of Teachers and Lecturers, Friends of Sri Lanka, UK - Sri Lanka Business Council; [hon.] nominated in 1981 for the 'United Nations Media Peace Prize' in London, 'Editor's Choice Award' for Enchanting Maldives Poem; [oth. writ.] Edits two of the most successful travel and tourism magazines in South Asia -Sri Lanka Today and Maldives Today, "selected poems by Ivan Corea" published in Sri Lanka, three poems on the Maldives "Enchanting Maldives", "A Maldivian Dream" and "A Man

from Utheemu" widely acclaimed in South Asia, articles written in newspapers and magazines in Europe and South Asia; [pers.] The published poem "An Ode to Charika Corea" is a tribute to Charika Corea and commemorates the birth of our first child 'a gift from God' - Charin Yasindu Corea - who was born in February 91 at the Royal London Hospital. I have been greatly influenced by British and Sri Lankan poets and other South Asian writers.; [a.] Docklands, London

CORLETT, MELISSA
[b.] 24 September 1980, Chiang Mai, Thailand; [p.] Drs. R. and S. Corlett; [ed.] Currently taking A - levels at West Island School in Hong Kong; [occ.] Student; [pers.] Through I love the work of Philip Larkin, my greatest influence is from the lyrics of songs, their rhythmic patterns and the meaning conveyed by a few spoken words.; [a.] Hong Kong

CORNWALL, PETER ALAN
[pen.] Thomas Creedence; [b.] 7 July 1954, Bury St. Edmunds; [p.] Alfred John and Vera Pamela; [m.] Wendy Carol Cornwall, 18 March 1986; [ch.] Sean, Anneka, Ivan, Lewis and Gareth; [ed.] Colonel Frank Seely Comprehensive School, Basford Hall College; [occ.] Driver; [memb.] Labour Party, British Legion, Working Men's Club; [hon.] English Literature Social Studies, Elements of Retailing First Aid; [oth. writ.] Several poems published in local magazines and one readout on Radio Nott'm.; [pers.] I hope my poems are enjoyed by people from all walks of life. I have been greatly influenced by the writings of John Lennon and John Fogerty.; [a.] Arnold, Notts, UK

CORRIGAN, MAUREEN
[b.] 10 May 1929, Dublin, Ireland; [p.] Mary Lee Noonan, Herbert J. Corrigan; [ed.] Dominicans Muckross Park Dublin Ursuline Thurles Ireland Montessori Training Center Sion Hill Blackrock Dublin Ireland; [occ.] Retired Researching Cancer as M.S.; [oth. writ.] Poetry short stories and research articles on the cause and hopefully a cure for cancer. Book on same subject A New Hope For Lupus Victims; [pers.] My dream to see the cause of war understood and a universal effort to cure illness.; [a.] Dublin, Ireland

CORRY, MRS. PATRICIA
[b.] 17 September 1944, Belfast; [p.] Ella; [m.] Ronnie, 14 October 1965; [ch.] Natalie, Wendy, Ashley; [ed.] Nowi-Dawn, Foster Child John; [occ.] Field Supervisor, Market Research Coopers and Lybhard; [oth. writ.] Bits And Pieces, Here And There Making Special, Very Special, Times; [pers.] As mother of a large family. Four daughters who have brought me 2 good sons, my beautiful granddaughter Ellie Rose and foster child John. When I can't say the words to express my joy or pain I just write my way through it in a poem.; [a.] Bangor, Down, UK

COSGROVE, LYNDA
[pen.] Shauna Westwood; [b.] 2 May 1980, Kildare; [p.] Peadar and Emily Cosgrove; [ed.] Timahoe National School, Timahoe and St Farnans Post Primary School, Prosperous; [occ.] Student; [memb.] Timahoe Historical Society; [oth. writ.] Short stories, dialogues and other poems, all unpublished; [a.] Naas, Kildare, UK

COSTELLO, EDWARD
[b.] 19 September 1926, Waterford, Ireland; [p.] Sara and Edward; [m.] Catherine; [ch.] Catherine and Jacqueline; [ed.] Convent and Monastery;

[occ.] Retired, Racing Carriage Builder; [pers.] Started writing poetry in 1945 for comrades in the forces to send home to wives and sweethearts.; [a.] Bushey-Watford, Herts, UK

COTTON, ELAINE
[b.] 7 October 1977, Cambridge; [p.] Karen Cotton, Roger Cotton; [ed.] Dyson Perrins C.E. High School (still attending); [occ.] Student; [memb.] Malvern Youth Theatre Colwall Players; [hon.] GCSE English Literature and Lang Grade 5 Piano and Theory 7 others GCSE's; [pers.] My writing is influenced very much by my observation of society and people this, being my first piece of writing published, I hope to proceed in a writing career.; [a.] Malvern, Worcs, UK

COULSON, VESTA J. A.
[b.] 8 January 1972, Congleton; [p.] George J. Ball, Rosemary A. Ball; [m.] Andrew N. Coulson, 20 August 1994; [ed.] Heathfield High School, South Cheshire College, University of Salford; [occ.] Bi-Lingual Secretary; [memb.] C.I.M.; [hon.] BSC (Hons) Dipm; [oth. writ.] Short stories greeting verses.; [pers.] Believe in yourself and anything's possible.; [a.] Bury, Lancs, UK

COURAGE, ROBERT
[pen.] "Romeo"; [b.] 4 March 1947; [ch.] Four grown up brought up on own; [hon.] Various; [oth. writ.] Articles in magazines/papers. Picture poems supplied for 5 pounds P.O. and S.A.E. work received from ant genuine recording companies, e.c.t. in future. Ex entertainment/bodyguard.; [pers.] Wanting future career in poetry/writing etc. most important to bring love and comfort in places of hate and doom and gloom and to reach people's heart with hope.

COURT, MR. ROY P.
[pen.] "Roy Perry"; [b.] Teignmouth, Devon; [ed.] Teignmouth and Ilfracombe Grammar Schools; [occ.] Retired bank official, poet and short story writer; [memb.] Having severed in the Royal Navy, I am a member of both the exeter and Teignmouth Branches of the R.N. Waste Ensign Clubs; [oth. writ.] I have had a slim volume of verses entitled "A Merry Meander Down Memory Lane" published (1995); [pers.] "The magic of devon casts a spell on us all, those God - given charms have the power to Enthral"; [a.] Teignmouth, Devon, UK

COURTNEY, JULIAN
[b.] 1 April 1974, Cardiff; [p.] Antony and Sandra Courtney; [ed.] New College, Cardiff, Surrey University; [occ.] Just completed degree and entering employment as Insurance Salesman; [hon.] BSC Sociology; [oth. writ.] Personal collection of poems (unpublished); [pers.] I would like to dedicate this poem to all those who have supported me over the years.; [a.] Treharris, Mid-Glamorgan, U

COUSINS, CHRISTOPHER JUNIOR
[pen.] Tyler Stone; [b.] 4 November 1970, Manchester; [p.] Delores Delrio Cousins and Leeford Cousins; [ch.] Daniel Christopher Cousins; [ed.] Birley High School, Manchester; [occ.] student (social work); [oth. writ.] regular contributor of poetry and short stories for local magazines newspapers; [pers.] Through my poetry I find expressing my feelings and experiences therapeutic. I enjoy the challenge of writing about real issues that can reflect on the lives of mankind.; [a.] Manchester, Lancashire

COWAN, HILDA
[b.] 27 February 1941, Liverpool; [p.] John and Hilda Birmingham; [m.] James Lumley-Cowan, 28 July 1962; [ch.] 3 - 1 daughter and 2 sons; [ed.] Anfield Grammer School for Girls, Anfield Commercial College; [occ.] Health resource Co-ordinator for age concern L.P.; [hon.] Mary McArthur Scholarship - to International Labor Organization Geneva 1981/82; [oth. writ.] Approaches to health awareness. For older people. paper presented at International Conference 'Marginalisation of Older People' Liverpool University 1990; [pers.] My emotions and thoughts are part of me. I am happy to share them; [a.] Old Skelmersdale, West Lancs, UK

COX, CHRISTOPHER STEPHEN
[pen.] Christopher Cox; [b.] 21 October 1982, Hammersmith; [p.] Stan Cox and Anna Cox; [ed.] Roxeth Manor 1st and Middle Schools, currently Rooksheath High School; [occ.] Full time student; [memb.] Press Pack, Drama Club at School; [hon.] Poem displayed in Royal Festival Hall, work commended by Witsmith Young Writers Competition 1994; [oth. writ.] Poem book called All Sorts, book of poems, several short stories about disasters; [pers.] I feel that I can express my feelings about life in my poems. I try to write a whole different range of poems.; [a.] Harrow, Middx, UK

COX, MS. RITA
[b.] 4 July 1951, Sutton Coldfield; [p.] Peter Gricmanis, Peggy Essex; [ch.] Tristan; [ed.] Fairfax High School, The University of Birmingham; [occ.] PhD Student in American Literature; [memb.] The University of Birmingham Alumni Association; [hon.] BA (Hons) English Language and Literature, MA - American Studies; [pers.] I tend to write from personal experience thus ensuring deeply significant moments are never lost. I am influenced very much by Dante Cabriel and Christina Rossetti, Gerard Manly Hopkins and John Clark authors who all write from great personal depth.; [a.] Sutton Coldfield, West Midland, UK

COX, SALLY JANE
[b.] 25 February 1952, Norwich, Norfolk; [p.] Elizabeth and Leonard Wade; [m.] Malcolm John Cox, 19 September 1970; [ch.] Alex John; [ed.] Comprehensive; [occ.] Housewife, Chief Gardener, Cook, etc HA!; [oth. writ.] This is my first published piece of poetry, I have a few other poems which I write for pleasure.; [pers.] Most of my works revolves around the love of life itself and the treasures I have been given in my family, animals and friends.; [a.] Norwich, Norfolk, UK

COX, TONI
[pen.] Toni Cox; [b.] 26 December 1925, Bristol; [m.] Divorced; [ch.] Son and Daughter; [ed.] Private Public School; [occ.] O.A.P. (Retired Nurse); [memb.] Local Organ Club Spiritualists National Union; [hon.] D.S.N.Y. (healing).; [oth. writ.] Inspirational poetry done as a hobby. A few published in various anthologies.; [pers.] I enjoy writing, be they letters to the press, or poetry! My latest being a pamphlet called "Don't Die". I love nature and music; [a.] Bristol, Bristol, UK

CRAMPTON, ANN
[b.] 3 May 1953, Northampton; [p.] Ernest Hale and Betty Hale; [m.] John C. D. Crampton, 19 July 1975; [ch.] Calvin, Lee and Nathaniel; [ed.] Breezehill Secondary Modern Wellingborough; [occ.] PA/Medical Secretary; [oth. writ.] First

Submission; [pers.] Life and people can be so cruel but if we trust our hearts and look around us, life can also be beautiful.; [a.] Wellingborough, Northants, UK

CRAWFORD, JAMES
[b.] 14 May 1984; [p.] Gratnne and Ian; [ed.] Currently 2nd year in Largs Academy; [hon.] Top 5 Academically in 1st year School; [oth. writ.] Poems printed in school magazine; [pers.] I thoroughly enjoy writing poetry and I am privileged to have my poem chosen for printing.; [a.] Largs, Ayrshire, UK

CREGG, LAURA-JAYNE
[b.] 20 January 1986, Accrington; [p.] John and Linda Cregg; [ed.] Attends Peel Park County Primary School Accrington; [memb.] Accrington Dance Centre, Arcadian Ballroom. Far Fisa School of Music Darwen, Speech and Drama. Team Excel Cycling club; [hon.] R.A.D. Ballet, N.A.T.D. Dancing, Imperial Society Dancing, School of Music, and London College of Music Speech and Drama; [pers.] Ambitions, to be a vet.; [a.] Accrington, Lancs, UK

CRITCHLEY, MATTHEW THOMAS
[b.] 18 September 1978, Blackpool; [p.] Thomas Johnson Critchley and Carole Ann Critchley; [ed.] King Edward VII School, Lytham-St-Annes, Lancs; [occ.] Student; [pers.] I have always enjoyed creative writing and enjoy writing about things true to life and fictional that will appeal to most people.; [a.] Preston, Lancs, UK

CROSKIN, RODERICK
[pen.] Roderick Croskin; [b.] 18 September 1930, Grimsby; [p.] Ernest Gilroy, Florence Louisa; [m.] Aline Croskin, 3 October 1959; [ch.] James Andrew, Sarah Louise; [ed.] Beverly Grammar, Wolverhampton Technical Teachers College; [occ.] Retired Director Scarborough International School of English; [memb.] School-Governor; [hon.] Empire-Essay Prize; [oth. writ.] Teaching-texts for English (Lang and Lit), French, German, Social Studies, and Business Studies (a life-time's attempts to make these subjects exciting and amusing). None are published but all, offering tried and tested lively teaching-techniques, support well- researched subject-matter and thus could be edited, to serve both staff and students. Other writings include extended synopses of some of the classics - also available for publication.; [pers.] Write out of emotion. Enthusiasm is the mother of genius.; [a.] Scarborough, North Yorks, UK

CROUCH, MARGARET
[b.] 20 August 1933, Henley-on-Thames; [p.] Emily Chapman, Fred Chapman; [m.] Philip Crouch, 25 November 1976; [ch.] Geoffrey; [ed.] Comprehensive School; [occ.] Retired; [oth. writ.] Several poems published in poetry books, one in a magazine; [pers.] I get my inspiration from the school of life.; [a.] Marlow, Bucks, UK

CROWE, FRANCES DIANA SPARGO WILLIAMS
[pen.] Frances Williams Crowe; [b.] 16 March 1935, Rickmansworth, Herts; [p.] Walter Reginald Williams Crowe and Dorothy Crowe; [m.] Divorced; [ch.] Sean Denis O'Sullivan and Dianne Siobhan O'Sullivan; [ed.] Northwood College, Maxwell Road, Northwood, Middx; [occ.] Clinical Chartered Psychologist; [memb.] Associate Fellow of the British Psychological Society, British Society for Protective Psychology; [hon.] Winner of the Hilda Martindale Exhibition for 2 years running prior to doing M.Sc. in clinical psychology at Univ. of Surrey 1975-77. Because Chartered Clinical Psychologist in 1988.; [oth. writ.] Professional articles; [pers.] I endeavour in my professional life as well as personally to release the healing springs of man's inner resources and nobility of spirit in adversity through art as well as science.; [a.] Tonbridge, Kent, UK

CROWLEY, DEIRDRE
[b.] 12 August 1977, Tralee, Co Kerry, Ireland; [p.] Siobhan and Denis Crowley; [ed.] St. Joesephs Secondary School, Castle Island, Co Kerry, Ireland; [occ.] Student Nurse; [hon.] I received first class honors in speech and drama. I have several trophies and medals for basketball and gaelic football.; [oth. writ.] Last year I came 3rd in Ireland for writing an essay on Family Solidarity. I was one of 5 to represent my country in Belgium as a result of further writings. I also attended a creative writing course.; [pers.] My writings are influenced by the closest comfort to my heart and the deepest love in my soul - my family and friends.; [a.] Watford, Hertfordshire, UK

CROWLEY, RACHAEL MARIE
[b.] 18 February 1969, Waterford, Eire; [p.] Richard and Elizabeth Crowley; [ed.] Presentation Convent St. Pauls College, Leinster School of Drama L.A.M.D.A.; [occ.] General Manager of Security Firm; [memb.] R.S.A. Stratford-upon-Avon, Belltable Arts Centre, Waterford Chamber of Commerce, Network; [hon.] Bronze, Silver and Gold Medals with L.A.M.D.A. Speech and Drama, Associate and L. Teachers Diploma with Leinster school of Music and Drama; [oth. writ.] A lot of poems written for personal happenings, which were read at various gatherings. Poems entered into the Bridport Competition and local magazines.; [pers.] Respect is something you earn, not something you inherit so believe in what you do and you will succeed.; [a.] Waterford, Waterford, Rep of Ireland

CUMBERBATCH, MARGARET JULIA
[pen.] Margo Martell; [b.] 4 December 1935, Barbados; [p.] Cyril and Inez Welch (Deceased); [m.] Lindsay Adolphus Cumberbatch, 7 April 1956; [ch.] Linda, Marilyn, Lindsay and David; [ed.] St. Patricks, R.C. School Barbados, St. Gabriels Convent, England, Cert. Nursing and Nursing Studies, Cert. in Counselling University West of England et Diploma in Counselling; [occ.] Pediatric Nurse; [memb.] Barbados Caribbean Association; [hon.] Cert. in Counselling Diploma Counselling; [oth. writ.] Several unpublished poems. Short stories and novels.; [pers.] To care and entertain, through my writing and present work other fellow beings.; [a.] Bristol, Avon, UK

CUMBERBIRCH, KELLY MARIE
[b.] 21 April 1986, Wigan; [p.] Correana and Brian Cumberbirch; [ed.] St. Patricks R.C. Wigan; [occ.] Student; [memb.] Wigan open Karate Club, Local Pony Club; [hon.] Karate Certificates School Certs for Hockey, C Science; [pers.] When I'm into my poetry I am anyone I want to be and anywhere I wish to go taking everybody with me.; [a.] Wigan, Lancashire, UK

CUNNINGHAM, CHRISTOPHER KERR
[b.] 11 March 1965, Haddington; [p.] Stewart Cunningham and Rena Cunningham; [m.] Corinne Cunningham; [ch.] Rory and Kieran; [ed.] Knox Academy, Haddington, East Lothian, Inverness College, Nappier University; [hon.] Winner of the bank of Scotland Quest for most outstanding student; [oth. writ.] Poems personal to me; [pers.] My heart belongs to the highlands, my mind, belongs to Scotland, but my life, belongs to my Family.; [a.] Balintore, Ross-shire, UK

CUNNINGHAM, PAULINE
[b.] 17 June 1948, Durham; [m.] 21 January 1967; [memb.] I.A.M. also, A Member of IA The Writing School; [oth. writ.] Had poem published in Josephine Austin's, "First Time Magazine", name of poem. "You Frightened To Tell" autumn 1989, 17 Edition.; [pers.] A lot of my inspiration comes from news coverages and real life events that interest the Media.; [a.] Newton Aycliffe, Durham, UK

CUNNINGHAM, SANDRA ELAINE
[pen.] Sindread; [b.] 9 February 1956, Enfield; [p.] Edith Mary Smith, Patricfrancis Smith; [m.] Terry Cunningham, 1 June 1984; [ch.] Jadeen Barbara/Terry Patrick; [ed.] Tottenham County School Wathamstow College for further education (Social work); [occ.] Domestic Engineer; [hon.] Residential social worker for care assistance including home nursing and first aid, adoption of elephant certificate, registered child minder; [pers.] I hope my writing brings hope and inspiration to all who read it, with the knowledge that the best things in life are free; [a.] London, UK

CURTIS, ALAN WINSTON
[b.] 10 October 1940, Calne, Wiltshire; [p.] Reginald and Joyce Curtis; [m.] Christine, 1 June 1963; [ch.] Ian, Paul, Nicholas; [ed.] Secondary School; [occ.] Dairy Maintenance Electrician; [oth. writ.] Other poems based on my past life and the countryside around the river thames; [pers.] I am a lover of my country Great Britain especially the English Country side; [a.] Wootton Bassett, Wiltshire, UK

CURTIS, LESLEY
[b.] 19 May 1966, Corby; [p.] Roger Curtis and Alison Curtis; [ch.] Harry; [ed.] Westminster College Oxford; [occ.] Primary School Teacher; [hon.] B. Ed. (Hons); [oth. writ.] Several poems published locally and nationally; [pers.] I write down my feelings when the spoken word is inadequate. The simplicity of a few lines can speak volumes.

CUTTS, NOELINE IRIS
[pen.] Iris Thorley; [b.] 10 July, Otatunu; [p.] Beryl and George Thorley; [m.] 30 December 1961; [ch.] Five children - 1 Adopted; [ed.] School Certificate in 5 Subjects Latin, French, Chemistry, Math and English I have 4 papers in Accounting and Certificate for Floristry, counseling and Spanish; [occ.] Accounts payable clerk with a Computer Company; [memb.] I believe in "Victim Support" to comfort people who have been victimized. Mairangi Arts Count and exhibit my Portrait Paintings; [hon.] Maston guide for thinking your people in my church. Certificate for floral arranging, counting Spanish by corresponding. A certificate for victim support training; [oth. writ.] I have written my autobiography in verse. At present I am writing a book of songs, turning the Bible into verse.; [pers.] I want to leave the world a better place than what I found it. I want my readers to enjoy the beauty in the simple things around them and see God's guiding hand in everything; [a.] Auckland, New Zealand

D'ARCY, ANN
[pen.] Annie Cartwright - D'Arcy; [b.] 13 August 1950, Lancashire; [ch.] Four Children; [occ.] House wife/mother; [oth. writ.] Several articles for local newspaper; [a.] Ashford, Wicklow, Ireland

D'CRUZE, RICHARD
[b.] 19 July 1936, Jamshedpur, India; [p.] Richard William and Doris Mary D'Cruze; [m.] Arlene D'Cruze, 15 May 1957; [ch.] Lydia Ann, Lyndon John; [ed.] Complete Course of Secondary Education in High School Section of Salesian College Sonada Darjeeling; [occ.] Employee of Royal Mail; [memb.] Founder of 'St. Paul's Home Cambridge School' Zunheboto Nagaland - India. Founder of 'Eden's English (High) School'. Birsanagar-Jamshedpur India; [oth. writ.] Just completing 'Children's Delight' (a book of poems for children); [pers.] I have been greatly influenced by the early poets and strive to describe in my writings the natural beauty that surrounds mankind and the good that exists in all humans everywhere.; [a.] Southall, Middlesex, UK

D'ROZA, PAULINE
[b.] 2 December 1916, India; [p.] Paul Hamilton Douglas Garside, Freda Garside; [m.] Swithin D'Roza (2nd marriage), 25 May 1963; [ch.] Marcus, Donella, Marcia; [ed.] Senior Cambridge Trained and Qualified Teacher; [oth. writ.] A collection of my poems I've titled "From Pictures in my Mind" a few short stories and to celebrate my 80th birthday I am writing my autobiography entitled "I am Amazed."; [pers.] I believe each one should create, plan, move forward by writing, music, embroidery, recipes for cooking, painting, but always creating, planning, moving forward to have a healthy body and healthy mind.; [a.] Fosses, Paris, France

DACCUS, ERIKA
[pen.] Erika Daccus; [b.] 8 November 1974, Wroughton; [p.] Cynthia Barraclough; [ed.] Burford School and Community College. West Oxfordshire College, Westminster College from September 1996; [occ.] Sales Assistant; [oth. writ.] No other poems published.; [pers.] Through my poetry I reflect upon feelings and emotions that can be expressed in no other way.; [a.] Carterton, Oxford, UK

DAIS, ANDRE
[b.] 22 December 1977, City of London; [p.] Katina Dais and Yiannes Dais; [ed.] St Andrews Primary Cofe, Ashmole Secondary School, Islington 6th form and Southgate College; [occ.] A-level Student; [memb.] Jubilee Campaign, Anti Nazi League (A.N.L.) World Wildlife Fund; [hon.] Grades for GCSE English Lit: A/B, Art: C, Science: C/C; [oth. writ.] Un-published short stories and poems, adult fairy tales, children's fairy tales, romantic lit; [pers.] I have improved many aspects of my life through imagination, and have used this to create my own unique storys and fairytales which inspire thoughts, feelings and everything that were about; [a.] Southgate, Enfield, UK

DALLAS, EILEEN
[b.] 12 Octber 1948, Aberdeen; [p.] John and Mary Reekie; [m.] Alexander Gordon Dallas, 25 February 1967; [ch.] Karen, Fiona and Scott; [ed.] Frederick St. Secondary School, Aberdeen College; [occ.] Day Centre Officer, Rosehill Day Centre; [hon.] Diploma in Social Work, Diploma of Higher Education; [a.] Aberdeen, UK

DALLIN, LINDA HARRINGTON
[b.] 23 May 1994, Lancs; [p.] Emily and Bernard; [m.] George Edwin, 5 October 1963; [ch.] Mark Edward; [ed.] Comprensive; [occ.] Sales Assistant; [oth. writ.] One article accepted by Sunday Telegraph, also 1 poem printed in (poetry works) by arrival press 1992 (Peterborough); [pers.] Enjoy converting the worlds problems mainly topical, into verse or lyrics.; [a.] Weston super Mare, Somerset, UK

DALTON, PHILIP
[pen.] Philip M. Dalton; [b.] 9 November 1975, Beverly; [ed.] I educated myself through the books I've read, I dreamt my way through school; [occ.] Poet and Musician; [memb.] Numerous music societies and star drops of Ryliss; [oth. writ.] Since I started writing poetry 2 years ago I have wrote about 330 poems covering my dreams and fears and the grove of my visions. Every poem I have sent off for publication has been highly praised. I hope to have my own poetry and Art book out next year. Look out for it; [pers.] I am also going to bring my poetry to life with music when I get my own band together. I am influenced by Charles Baudelaire, William Blake, James Douglas Morrison and March Bolan. I couldn't be who I am today without their eyes.; [a.] Driffield, East Yorkshire, UK

DALY, MRS. FAITH
[pen.] Veronica Robertson; [b.] 7 December 1945, Southbourne, Hants; [m.] Mr. Michael Daly, 7 January 1967; [ch.] Clare and Michaela; [ed.] Summerbee Secondary School Strouden Park Bournemouth CFE Kings Road, Devonport, Plymouth; [occ.] Classroom Assistant; [hon.] Duke of Edinburgh's Devon Award (Scheme for 26-55 yr old run by the Duke of Edinburgh's award Scheme) I was the first person in Devon to receive this award. I received it on 1st April 1996; [pers.] I enjoy challenges, and have done a lot of different things in the past 10 years. Flown a single engine plane, learned to swan/dive. And an actively involved with the sea Cadet Corps! And lots of other things!; [a.] Plymouth, South Devon, UK

DALY, JOANNE
[b.] 3 October 1975, Dublin; [p.] Margaret and David Daly; [ed.] Loreto College Swords, Co Dublin, Bel Canto School of Singing, Co Dublin; [occ.] Piano Teacher; [memb.] Bel Canto School of Singing, Co Dublin; [hon.] Musicianship; [pers.] This poem reflects the deep hurt and confusion of someone who was once part of my life.; [a.] Rush, Dublin, UK

DAMMS, BRIAN
[b.] 18 April 1936, Louth, Lincs; [m.] Edith, 31 October 1959; [ch.] Kenneth, Carchine, Graham, Auistance, Clive; [ed.] King Edweary VI Grammar School Edward St Louth, Lincolnshire; [occ.] Heating and Plumbing Consultant; [oth. writ.] Several poems published in local papers; [pers.] Years gone by seem to surface in my poems, and I enjoy most of the past, this making writing all the more enjoyable. [a.] Louth, Lincs, UK

DAVEY, ANNE CHRISTABEL
[pen.] Anne Christabel Davey-Young; [b.] 16 March 1940, Barnstaple; [p.] Leonard Young, Elsie Young; [m.] Ronald Charles Davey, 20 August 1960; [ch.] Anne-Marie (Deceased), Robert Charles Alexander; [occ.] Clerk/Part Time Music Teacher; [oth. writ.] Poems published by 'The Lady' Magazine. Also by Noeal Newspaper.

Poetry Book "Woven Threads" written in Aid of Children's Hospice.; [pers.] Writing poetry for me is the encapsulation for all seasons of God's creation.; [a.] Barnstaple, Devon, UK

DAVIDSON, D. R.
[pen.] Don Davidson; [b.] 12 May 1935, Bermondsey, London; [p.] Mary and Thomas Davidson; [m.] Edith Eileen; [ch.] Donna; [ed.] Normal Secondary Ed., due to war year, bombed out - evacuated, etc.; [occ.] Retired disabled due to injury 1993; [memb.] RAF Regular 1953-58 (Started training on Artframe Mech but went colour blind and didn't carry on with service life; [oth. writ.] One poem in "A Taste of Central England", published Dec. 93, title: (Untitled - if I were asked); [pers.] I write when I feel like writing usually when I'm down!; [a.] Clacton on Sea, Essex, UK

DAVIDSON, JOHN
[b.] 8 October 1938, Leeds, England; [p.] Stuart Davidson and Frances McDonald-Davidson; [m.] Anne Busquet-Davidson, 6 July 1968; [ch.] Jane and Paul; [ed.] Mylnhurst Convent School, Sheffield Barlborough Hall, Chesterfield Ratcliffe College, Leicesterfield Sheffield University; [occ.] Marketing Director, Quantor Limited; [memb.] Catholic Church, GK Chesterton Society; [hon.] BSc, DiP. ED.; [oth. writ.] "Verses For Christ" - Approximately 1,000 verses per year since 1982 (none published); [pers.] I try to express, in verse form, the truths and teachings of Christ and his Church, as I believe that these are the light of the world and its only real hope. I have been most influenced by Christ, the church the saints, Pope John II and the writings of G.K. Chesterton.; [a.] London, Wimbledon, UK

DAVIDSON, ROGER CHARLES THOMAS
[b.] 22 September 1949, London; [p.] Timothy and Joyce Davidson; [m.] Marion; [ch.] Lee, Ian, Claire, Gavin, Donna; [ed.] Sec, Med, in Tower Hamlets; [occ.] Banking; [memb.] Local Theatre Group plus numerous sports clubs. Which include Surrey C.C.C. Tottenham Hotspur F.C.; [oth. writ.] Some poems published in local mags. some years ago.; [pers.] For all the people who try to make the world a better place, there are those that try twice as hard to make it worse.; [a.] Hornschurch, Essex, UK

DAVIES, ANTHONY
[b.] 5 March 1946, London; [p.] Frederick and Elizabeth; [m.] Pamela Frances, 14 June 1969; [ch.] Leigh Frances and Samantha; [ed.] Forest Hill Comprehensive; [occ.] Property Consultant; [oth. writ.] None published; [pers.] Emotions can be expressed in poetry which to me are not possible in prose.; [a.] Swanley, Kent, UK

DAVIES, MR. DENNIS N.
[pen.] Dennis N. Davies; [b.] 20 February 1937, West Bromwich; [p.] Edith Davies, William Davies; [m.] Marie T. Davies, 16 June 1962; [ch.] Jason D. Davies; [ed.] All Saints. West Bromwich; [occ.] Production Worker; [oth. writ.] Goodbye Friend, Anchor Books, Publisher - Andrew Head Peterborough Inner Peace. International Society of Poets.; [pers.] Left school at fifteen, when in army at eighteen, Served as a driver in the R.A.S.C. move too Telford, Shropshire, work at G.N.N. Sankeys. For the last 30 yrs. Have one grandchild named Emma.; [a.] Telford, Shropshire, UK

DAVIES, DAWN MARIE
[b.] 18 November 1960, Brynaman, S. Wales; [p.] Peter and Sylvia Balbini; [m.] Hugh Davies, 23 September 1988; [ed.] Amman Valley Comprehensive Ammanford Technical College; [occ.] Assembly Line Operator; [hon.] Had one poem published by anchor Books Title "Leisure Time"; [oth. writ.] Always being asked by friends at work, to write poems for birthdays, weddings etc.; [pers.] I tend to put my thoughts in writing, and to keep it simple and to the point.; [a.] Brynaman, Ammanford, Carms, UK

DAVIES, GARETH
[b.] 5 July 1977, Frimley; [p.] Katherine Davies, Richard Davies; [ed.] Ashcombe School, Dorking, Guildford College; [occ.] Fast Food Worker, Burger King, Guildford; [oth. writ.] Poem published in Surrey Anthology (Arrival Press), have written several poems for Sign Post Magazine.; [pers.] My writings are a way of relieving anger and sadness for me. I feel there is always some sort of message in my poems. I like to think that in my poetry I've won peoples emotions.; [a.] Dorking, Surrey, UK

DAVIES, GLYNIS
[b.] 19 October 1953, South Wales; [p.] Amy Maud Davies and Ivor Harries; [m.] Allan Daniels; [ch.] Louise, Claire, and Phillip; [ed.] (1) Queen Elizabeths Grammar School for Girls, Johnstown, South Wales (2) Basingstoke School of Nursing, (3) University of London, (4) University of Greenwhich, (5) O.U; [occ.] Self-employed Care Assistant; [hon.] 'O' Level English Language, Biology, C.S.E. Maths, Arts foundation (AIOI), Yr 1 degree Philosophy, yr 1 degree Environmental Science, Professional Psychiatric Nurse (RMN), Teaching and Assessing in Clinical Practice (ENB 998), Mensa IQ 143, Various Volunteer Work; [oth. writ.] Various personal compositions but this is the first submission for competition, publication.; [pers.] Writing is a compulsive expression form somewhere within. The enjoyment and inspiration I draw from life itself.; [a.] Orpington, Kent, UK

DAVIES, IRENE
[b.] 13 August 1917, Barry, S. Wales; [ed.] Barry County Grammar School; [a.] Mungret, Limerick, Eire, Ireland

DAVIES, JODIE
[b.] 22 May 1981; [p.] John Davies, Jennifer Davies; [ed.] Tasker Milward V.C. School, Pembrokeshire; [occ.] Student; [pers.] I write about things that affect people in everyday life, and I strive to make my poems as realistic as possible; [a.] Haverford West, Pembrokeshire, UK

DAVIES, MISS KAY
[pen.] Kady; [b.] 7 February 1968, Hopkinstown, Pontypridd; [p.] Gordon Davies, Sheila Davies; [m.] Mark Willding (partner); [ed.] Trehopcyn Primary School, Coed-y-Lan Comprehensive School; [occ.] Artist; [hon.] London College of Art (Diploma); [oth. writ.] Numerous poems (unpublished); [pers.] With the love and support of your family and friends, there's nothing you can't achieve or overcome.; [a.] Trehafod, Mid-Glam, UK

DAVIES, PATRICK
[b.] 19 October 1929, Blackheath; [p.] Ken and Celia Davies; [m.] Lorna (Nee Blades), 23 December 1953; [ch.] Jane, Paul, John and Mark; [ed.] Bedford School and Trinity College, Cambridge; [occ.] Retired; [memb.] All Professional and Lapsed in FBIM, M/M&M,

MIMC; [hon.] BA (Hons C.M.A. (CANTAB); [oth. writ.] A variety of poems on various topics - particularly a monthly series for women in Bangladesh (1979-82).; [pers.] Poetry should rhyme and scan and contain wit or wisdom.; [a.] Chichester, W. Sussex, UK

DAVIES, RITA
[b.] Glasgow; [p.] Eliz Tennant, Thomas Berry; [ed.] Whitehill Junior Secondary, Glasgow; [occ.] Daycare Manager, Social Worker; [pers.] I am inspired by God, His wonderful creation, and the gifts of my loyal, amusing and very thoughtful friends.; [a.] Glasgow, Scotland

DAVIES, THOMAS NOEL
[pen.] T. Noel Davies; [b.] 21 September 1959, Bromborough; [p.] William Peter Davies and Hilda Davies; [m.] Samantha D. T. Davies, 4 August 1984; [ch.] Glenn Roen Davies; [ed.] Anthony Gell School, Wirksworth, Ecclesbourne School, Duffield Yale College, Wrexham Dundee University; [occ.] Dental Surgeon (BDS); [memb.] Thornhill Baptist Church; [oth. writ.] Several poems published in local magazine. Several poetry renditions in public.; [pers.] I wish to write poems in various styles, invariably my deep Christian faith is expressed and hope to publish my own anthology entitled 'Insite at Midnight'. I enjoy the poetry within Bob Dylans' work.; [a.] Southampton, Hants, UK

DAVIS, MADELINE AMY
[b.] 27 March 1949, Ryeford, Herefordshire; [p.] John Henry Purshall and Evelyn Georgina May (Mary) Purshall; [m.] Ronald Davis, 26 August 1967; [ch.] Sally-Anne; [ed.] East Dean Grammar School Cinderford Glos, and Abenhall School Mitcheldean Glos; [occ.] (Retired) Disabled with Rheumatoid Arthritis; [memb.] Arthritis Care; [a.] Newent, Glos, UK

DAVIS, SYLVONIE ELAINE
[b.] 29 December 1967, Watford, Herts; [p.] Gloria M. Davis and Franklin E. Davis; [oth. writ.] In addition to the type of poetry printed herein. I also write poems of a religious nature and poems and verses for special occasions. I am in the process of compiling any personal anthology (sponsors welcomed!); [pers.] My mother was the one who solved and nurtured the "Poetry Seed" in me and has been an inspiration. Also appreciated is the encouragement of my father and brothers, Kingsley, Aubrey and Michael.; [a.] Watford, Herts, UK

DAVISON, LINDA
[pen.] Linda Hilton; [b.] 29 October 1952, Clapmam; [p.] Violet and George Hilton; [m.] Raymond Sibley (Partner), Summer 1996; [ch.] Rober, Mark and Tracy Davison; [ed.] Sutton Common County Secondary Girls School, Sutton Arts College; [occ.] Nursery Nurse; [hon.] Diploma in Child Care; [oth. writ.] A Mother's Bond in, The Other Side Of The Mirror. Also many other poems for pleasure.; [pers.] Having been very ill myself and losing my mum of cancer. Then finding true love, I feel I need to put my feelings into words my life is very special.; [a.] Tadworth, Surrey, UK

DE BREANSKI, MR N.
[b.] 20 March 1920, Guernsey, CI; [p.] English; [m.] English; [ed.] Secondary School Education; [occ.] Retired; [pers.] I have lived near the sea most of my life and I am very much influenced by all of its moods.; [a.] Maidstone, Kent, UK

DE RELYA, DALYS
[pen.] Darrylice; [b.] 13 March, Liverpool; [p.] Paul and Alice; [ed.] Ursuline High School, Liverpool City College of further Education, Millbank College of Commerce; [occ.] Managing Director; [oth. writ.] Several poems published in book/magazine and exhibited, some unsigned. Also poems written in cards etc. on behalf of others. Previously also having written lyrics and composed.; [pers.] Various subjects written but mainly romantic poetry, which truly express my emotions. I greatly admire the poetic writings of Les Greenwood (S.A.) which are closet to my heart, and today's romantic poets/song writers of the U.S.A. and Britain.; [a.] Weaverham, Cheshire, UK

DEASON, JULIE ANNE
[b.] 10 September 1968, Brighton; [p.] Margerate Patricia and Anthony Richard Deason; [ch.] Shadi; [ed.] Portslade Community College, Davigdor Infants School; [occ.] single mother; [hon.] French certificate, Mensa certificate; [oth. writ.] Many other poems not published but are for my own personal pleasure. Pleasure, I never dreamt I would get one published. I'm elated and very proud I can share my talent with others. Thank you. [pers.] I get a great sense of achievement writing poems, also occassional art. It helps me through the obstacles life throws at me. I deal with my life in this way from past to present. It brings me much pleasure wich is rewarding; [a.] Brighton, Essex

DEEMING, CONRAD
[b.] 24 July 1965; [p.] Ann Deeming, John Deeming; [ed.] Warley High School, West Bromwich College; [occ.] Chef. Thornescroft Restaurant, Wolverhampton; [oth. writ.] I write poems for myself and friends.; [pers.] I sometimes feel todays society value the wrong things in life. I try to write about the real meaning of life.; [a.] Dudley, W. Mids, UK

DEIGHAN, REV. PATRICK
[b.] 7 April 1931, Castletown, Navan, Co. Meath; [p.] John Deighan, Ann Deighan; [ed.] St. Finian's College, Maynooth College; [occ.] Retired Priest; [hon.] B.A. (Hon's Classics), B.D. 1st Prize twice for poems at Listowel Writers' Week.; [oth. writ.] Poems published in National and local newspaper, magazines and anthologies, poems read on national and local radio, also letters and poems on TV, articles and letters in newspapers and magazines.; [pers.] Perhaps my awareness of the fact that I was born on the same date William Wordsworth has benefited my affinity with language and sense of word-magic!; [a.] Laytown, Meath, UK

DELANEY, CHARLIE
[b.] 1936, Carlingford; [m.] Jean Delaney; [ed.] St. Patrick's Grammar School Armagh; [occ.] Surgical Chiropodist, retired Civil Servant; [memb.] Civil Service Retirement Fellowship British Chiropody and Podiatry Association Age Concern; [pers.] I have loved most poetry and English Literature from my earliest schooldays.; [a.] Littlehampton, West Sussex, UK

DELANEY, YVONNE
[pen.] Yvonne Delaney; [b.] 20 January 1936, Belfast, Northern Ireland; [p.] John Rea, Ellen Rea; [m.] Denis Delaney, 9 October 1954; [ch.] Barry Delaney, Anthony Delaney, Sharon Hulme; [ed.] St. Bonifaces R.C. School, Attended further courses of Education, Widely read; [occ.] Retired Secretary; [memb.] St. Peter and Pauls Writing

Club, Ex. Member Salford Players Theatre Club (Drama); [hon.] Several articles published in local papers, poems in school and church magazines; [oth. writ.] Short stories, poems, play, novel; [pers.] Life is a gift from God, his children are on loan to us, they should be loved, cherished, cared for and treated with dignity. In my writing I endeavor to express the tremendous love I have for children.; [a.] Salford, Lancashire, UK

DEMPSEY, WILLIAM E.
[b.] 7 June 1964, Birmingham; [p.] William and Olive Dempsey; [m.] Alice Parkes, 24 June 1950; [ch.] Ann-Alicia and Edward William; [occ.] Retired - Part time Groom to my daughter's Arabian Horses; [memb.] Burmastar Ass., Royal Warwickshire Regimental Assoc.; [hon.] The Burma Star; [oth. writ.] Short stories and poems in various magazines. Articles for union magazine. Poems and editorial for military newsletters.; [pers.] I hope my poetry and stories help to guide others to the joy of creative writing.; [a.] Solihull, Warwickshire, UK

DENNING, JENNIFER
[pen.] Amber Moon; [b.] 12 September 1937, London; [m.] Trevor Denning, 23 December 1983; [ch.] Richard, Jonathan; [ed.] Convent School Trinidad (West Indies), Christchurch Secondary, Hants.; [occ.] Fund-raising, Shops Development officer for age concern, second occupation as a professional portrait artist, also run a computer astrology business; [memb.] Welsh Arts Council; [pers.] I hope that what I write reaches out and touches people and maybe adds light to their lives, and brings a global conciousness a closer reality. [a.] Hantwit Fardre, South Wales

DENTON, COLIN
[pen.] Old Grumpy; [b.] York; [p.] Frederick Arthur and Edith Denton; [m.] Jane Tait D. Denton; [ed.] Bootham School Leeds College of Building; [occ.] Retired; [memb.] Fellow Faculty of Building Fellow Guild of Incorporated Surveyors Member British Institute of Architectural Technologists; [oth. writ.] Technical papers on aspects of construction: Scripts for Technical Training videos: Awarded Bronze, Silver and two Gold Medals for papers on Road Safety and Advanced Driving.; [pers.] Watercolor painter, several paintings published, works selected by the Royal Academy, the Royal Watercolor Society and the Royal Miniature Society. Poetry takes a sometimes cynical view of human nature.; [a.] Lastingham, North Yorkshire, UK

DESMOND, LAURY
[b.] 28 May 1977, Eastbourne, Sussex; [p.] Jacquelyn Desmond, Keith Bloomfield; [ed.] St. Richard R.C. Comprehensive School, University of Wales, College of Cardiff; [occ.] Full time student, studying English Literature at Cardiff; [hon.] Twice Won the Thomas Prize at St. Richard School for Most Imaginative Use of English Language; [oth. writ.] At moment, working on completion of an anthology of poems and short stories, as yet unpublished.; [pers.] Writing, to me is as necessary for everyday survival as water to drink, and air to breath.; [a.] Hastings, East Sussex, UK

DEVENEAUX, HAROLD GUSTAVE BOLOGJE
[b.] 29 March 1923, Bombali Makeni, Seirra Leone; [p.] Francis and Agnes Deveneaux; [m.] Makuta Conteh, 29 March 1951; [ch.] Felix,

Angnes, Frances, Harry, Eldon; [ed.] Seirra Leone Grammar, London School of Journalism (correspondance course); [occ.] minister of religion; [memb.] International Academy, Society of Metaphysicans, Penman Club; [hon.] Doctor of Philosophy (by the International Academy), Academician of Honour and Merit (by Academia Universalis Amoris); [pers.] Poems of Rudyard Kipling, poems and writings of Oscar Wilde have animated my thinking and writing. My hobbies: reading, penfriendship, metaphysical research; [a.] Freetown, Sierra Leone

DHATARIYA, DR. KETAN
[b.] 14 January 1967, Alwar, India; [p.] Dr. Ramesh and Mrs. Sarala; [m.] Mrs. Vasundhara, 7 March 1994; [ed.] Woolwish College, London SE18 University College and Middlesex Hospital Medical School, London; [occ.] Doctor; [memb.] Member of the Royal College of Physicians; [oth. writ.] Personal poems - 'Born Into A World Of Harsh Reality - A Life In Verse'; [pers.] I like to write as an external manifestation of how I feel internally.; [a.] Bexleyheath, Kent, UK

DIACHUK, NAOMI
[pen.] Naomi Lange; [b.] 4 March 1948, Lancaster, Eng.; [m.] Now separated; [ch.] Roy (25), Byron (22), Emily (20); [ed.] Newark Secondary Modern and Tech 1960's; [occ.] Women's Refufe Volunteer; [oth. writ.] Book - 'Itineraries' published 1990 in New Zealand - poems under former name of Lange, which I have now reverted back to.; [pers.] Part-time writer, mostly of poetry. Writing is heaven sent work!; [a.] Auckland, New Zealand

DIACOPOULOS, PEARL JUNE
[pen.] Pearl Laker; [b.] 2 November 1935, Battersea; [p.] Robert Laker, Florince Laker; [m.] Peter Diacopoulos, 4 April 1953; [ch.] Cathy, Chris, Marina, Mark, Andrew; [ed.] Secondary School, Left at 15 years old; [occ.] Housewife: Poetry?; [pers.] I have been married for 43 years. I have 5 children, 6 grandchildren, 1 great grandchild. Started to write when I was 14 years old.; [a.] Enfield, Middx, UK

DICKENS, CHRISTINE
[b.] 24 March 1982, Cambridge; [p.] Nick Dickens, Elizabeth Dickens; [ed.] Hermitage County Primary School. Tarporley High School; [occ.] Student; [pers.] My work is mostly about aspects of life that I have personified. I am greatly influenced by what is going on in the world.; [a.] Duddon Nr Tarporley, Cheshire, UK

DICKINSON, GRETA
[b.] 9 November 1931, Bolton; [p.] Elsie M. Bell, John Bell; [m.] Leslie V. Dickinson (Ex-husband), 10 May 1952; [ch.] Leslie Vincent, John, Marie; [occ.] Retired; [memb.] Farnworth Christian Spiritualist Church, Committee Member and Trustee, Platform Medium and Spiritual Healer; [hon.] Music; [oth. writ.] Two poems accepted last year, to be published in a book.; [pers.] There is love laughter and beauty all around us in our lives, to be able to express my innermost thoughts into writing is a great gift and a wonderful bonus. Nature is beautiful in its simplicity.; [a.] Farnworth, Lancs, UK

DILLET, MOIRA
[ed.] Wishaw High School; [memb.] The Royal Zoological Society of Scotland; [oth. writ.] Several works published in National Editions of Poetry; [pers.] My pleasure is poetry.; [a.] Shotts, Lanarks, UK

DINKOVSKI, MARCIA
[b.] 24 June 1977, Crawley; [p.] Carole Dinkovski, Panche Dinkovski; [ed.] Three A Levels English Literature, Sociology Drama Thomas Bennett Community College; [occ.] Student to be (Sussex University), Degree English/Drama; [memb.] Creative Audio Techniques (Piano Lessons); [pers.] I sincerely believe in an Egalitarian Society regardless of sex, race of creed. I strive to be compassionate and honest in my poems. I have written many poems and songs and my ambition is to be a Singer/Songwriter and Poet; [a.] Crawley, Sussex, UK

DITCHBURN, BARBARA
[b.] 28 March 1934, Eastham, London; [p.] William and Elsie Ditchburn; [m.] Derek Ditchburn, 30 July 1953; [ch.] Five - four boys and one girl (youngest); [ed.] Vicarage Modern Secondary School, East - Ham; [occ.] Resting between jobs after operation byrn in caring for old people in a rest home; [memb.] Was a Member of the Sulton Coldfield Poetry Society over 10 yrs ago. Jonathan Clifford ran it then and home poetry was put in "Pause" at that time. Also did some for the "blind" tapes which were rewarded for BBC for an afternoon Programme; [hon.] N.N.E.B. (Nursery Nurses Examination Board.) also kitchen hygiene certificate. And at present attending a course for hairdressing acquire M.V.Q. at Birmingham School of Hair-dressing; [oth. writ.] Several books (not published) of fiction. Numerous poems.; [pers.] I write to give my self pleasure, that is why I've never troubled to have many published. If other people enjoy what I write it's an added bonus. I am a compulsive writer.; [a.] Erdington, Birmingham, UK

DIXON, SIMON GEORGE
[pen.] Dixie/Cave II; [b.] 13 November 1968, Stainsacre; [p.] T. A. Dixon and A. Dixon; [ed.] Hawsker School, Eskdale School, Whitby School; [oth. writ.] One poem published in a prison magazine, the poem was called, I Love You.; [pers.] I wrote Do You Feel The Same Way As I Do, after hearing a slade song, called, How Do You Feel, and I think life's an egg to crack; [a.] Whitby, UK

DOBSON, CLAIRE
[pen.] Marina Knife/Cicily Muir; [b.] United Kingdom; [ed.] Lots! Including a BA Hons Literature and Philosophy; [occ.] Avoiding the Machine and Writing and Editing Illustrator and Design work; [memb.] Stone Soup Poetry Society, Boston, MA, USA, New Writer's Collective: Boston Naked City Coffee Haus: Boston USA; [oth. writ.] "If Locomotives" a book for Anoraks with colours P:X; [pers.] In the 20th words are an illusion of meaning - language has lost it's weight - too many people have mouthed to many words and created a mass emptiness; [a.] Boston, London, UK

DOBSON, GEORGE WALTER
[pen.] George Montgomery; [b.] 20 September 1927, Darlington, Co Durham; [p.] George Walter and Lavinia; [m.] (Previous wife) Nora - Deceased, (2nd Marriage) Jean Mary Dobson, 29 September 1994; [ed.] University of Life; [occ.] Retired; [hon.] Letter of Praise from HRM Prince of Wales and very favourable comment by Lady (Polly) Feversham also a number have appeared in English Heritage Literature and local newspapers; [oth. writ.] Over 150 serious with verse including poetry for children; [pers.] A poem's an artistic expression

of mind relaxing to read. So help you unwind it may be inspired by a beautiful scene an unusual happening or events that have been it's a collection of symbols written in rhyme. For all to enjoy - whatever the time tis hoped its message will strike up a chord and awaken memories your mind has long stored. It's aim to enlighten bring joy from it's verse reflecting on 'Things' - real or diverse. Saying what is felt - when truly inspired can only be helpful, if not always admired.; [a.] Stockton-on-the-Forest, York, UK

DOCHERTY, MRS. ELIZABETH
[b.] September 21, 1935, Port Glasgow; [m.] Widow (George), November 28, 1958; [ch.] Six; [occ.] Housewife; [hon.] 12 poems. Published by triumph house. One by anchor books.

DONALDSON, JACKIE
[b.] 21 September 1945, Anna Cramp; [p.] John Donaldson and Rita Donaldson; [m.] Vivienne Donaldson, 1 August 1968; [ch.] David, Andrew, Michelle, Caroline; [ed.] The Royal School, Armagh Queen's University Belfast; [occ.] Mathematics Teacher Clounagh Junior High School Portadown; [hon.] S. Sc (applied Mathematics); [oth. writ.] Miscellaneous Jottings awaiting an orderly reconstruction; [pers.] Like Thomas Hardy 'I have no Philosophy, merely ...A confused heap of impressions like those of a bewildered child at a conjuring show'; [a.] Richhill, Armagh, UK

DONALDSON, MARY
[pen.] Margaret Reeves; [b.] 11 July 1943, Dunstable; [p.] Arthur and Phyliss Edwards; [m.] John Donaldson, 22 June 1963; [ch.] Alan and Jane; [ed.] Secondary Modeen Northfields Dunstable; [occ.] Supervisor Boots The Chemist - Dunstable; [oth. writ.] Nothing published yet have tried short stories for magazines no luck so far.; [pers.] I have been pushed into publication by friends and colleagues. I hope I don't dissapoint them.; [a.] Dunstable, Beds, UK

DONOVAN, ANGELA
[b.] 22 November 1964, Scotland; [m.] David Hallsworth; [ed.] Currently studying Computer Technology; [occ.] Mature Student; [memb.] Theatre and Jazz Club; [oth. writ.] I have had other poems published by local competitions and your good selfs; [pers.] I often find poetry impulsive like stripping off and streaking across a crowded football pitch sometimes you just have to let yourself go; [a.] Northampton, Northamptonshire, UK

DOWDALL, TINA C.
[b.] 4 March 1959, Firbeck; [m.] Christopher A. Dowdall (Jnr), 5 October 1991; [ed.] Maltby Comprehensive School; [occ.] Former Legal Secretary Currently - Temporary Clerical Worker; [pers.] Love, like currency, invested wisely, brings great dividends. My grandfather Harold Entwistle has been my influence.; [a.] Rotherham, South Yorkshire, UK

DOWNES, DAVE
[b.] 8 July 1967, Oldham; [p.] Robert and Barbara; [ed.] Comprehensive School, Oldham College of Technology, Nottingham Trent University; [occ.] Architectural Technician; [oth. writ.] I have had produced a slim bound volume of my work for close friends titled "Shadows Have No Mass", and have a bound notebook of all my work over the past three of so years.; [pers.] I'm a very positive person, very much a take it as it comes and enjoy

it type. I surprised myself at just how dark some of my work can be, and I often write from the subconscious, it's a good form of therapy!; [a.] Nottingham, Notts, UK

DUFFIELD, MARGARET
[pen.] Margaret Duffield; [b.] 9 September 1916, Halifax; [p.] Sarah, Charles Gething; [m.] Michael Joyce Adams Duffield, 21 June 1940, (Deceased); [ch.] Michael, Carol, Claire; [ed.] Sunnyside Elements, Night School, Drama, Education Lesson; [occ.] Grandma! Boy have Headquarters so called; [memb.] Authors and poets in Hilda Gledill was around the world journalist many newspapers, still feature local Barkisland; [oth. writ.] Hand - Soft backed anthologies. Songs articles local newspaper, plus poems local. Only person to perform in Jersey 200 grounds, with a song then liked, about the great Jambo, when I lived in Jersen.; [pers.] Please tell me above the song writings, Educational or numerous, love song. On tapes in arranged by musical.; [a.] Halifax, West York, UK

DUNCAN, MARGOT HELENE
[pen.] Helene Westerdale; [b.] 9 July 1937, Swinton, Yorkshire; [p.] Ernest Charity, Mary Ellen Charity; [m.] Ian C. Duncan (Deceased), 25 July 1959; [ch.] Alistair Grant, Christopher Iain; [ed.] Dexborough Grammar College of Sarum St. Michael Salisbury; [occ.] Retired; [memb.] OCA, USA, Marlborough College Choir, Marlborough Town Choral Society, Philip Larkin Society, Marlborough Music and Theatre Clubs; [hon.] Teacher's Certificate advance Scouting Grade VIII Singing Grade VIII Music Theory; [oth. writ.] Poems published in 'other poetry,' my beehive press and OCA took prize in USA National Competition Article in "Yoga and Health"; [pers.] The loss of my husband at age 46 has only served to make me enjoy every moment of every day. Life is incredibly short and heaven is here. Influences Hendy, Hopkins, Dylan Thomas, Larkin.; [a.] Marlborough, Wilts, UK

DUNN, SARAH
[b.] 6 May 1938, Belfast; [p.] Mary, William McGeough; [m.] John E. Dunn, 25 June 1994; [ch.] Six children, 30 grandchildren; [ed.] Public Elementary; [occ.] Housewife; [pers.] I wish to see peace prevail among all nations. Especially between the two different cultures in N Ireland.; [a.] Antrim, Antrim, UK

DUNNE, DANIEL G.
[b.] 28 September 1956, Mullingar; [p.] Kathleen and Christopher Dunne; [m.] Betty Mimnagh, 27 July 1988; [ch.] Gerard (6), Gregory (4), Rita (21 months); [ed.] 1963-1970 Dalystown NS, 1970-75 - St. Josephs Rochfortbridge, 1975-1978 - St. Patricks College Drumcondra Dublin; [occ.] Principal - Clonard NS Co. Meath; [memb.] Elgse - Poetry Ireland; [hon.] B.Ed. Degree 1975, Currently Studying for my M.A. in Local History Maynooth University, Co. Kildare; [oth. writ.] 'The Little Silver Bell 1995 (Book Guild) - a Childrens Novel. 'Along the Gravel Road', poems reflecting children and childhood.; [pers.] Writing should not be locked away, it is for people to enjoy, not just a literary few, but everyone. Poetry should reach out to capture the imaginations of people.; [a.] Mullingar, West Meath, Ireland

DURHAM, GEOFF
[b.] 18 September 1967, Staffordshire; [p.] Mrs. Barbara Hollins, Mr. Terry Durham; [ed.] Trinity C.E. High School, Newcastle Staffordshire

Polytechnic, Stoke; [occ.] Local Government Officer Newcastle- Under-Lyme Borough Council; [hon.] BTEC National Certificate in Business Studies Higher National Certificate in Public Administration; [oth. writ.] None actually published but I write poems for Colleagues' birthdays for fun and enjoyment.; [pers.] "True poetry comes straight from the heart and reflects the mood of the writer". Personal favorite: "The Soldier"; [a.] Newcastle-u-Lyme, Staffordshire, UK

DURRANT, BERNARD
[b.] 8 June 1924, Wimbledon; [p.] Dorothy and Archibald-Churchill Durrant; [ed.] Highfield College, Eton House College; [occ.] Retired College Lecturer Poet and Writer; [memb.] National Geographic Society; [hon.] First/Second/Third-class Military Certificates of Education, TELS (Japan) Poetry Contest 1982, Matsumoto Poetry Prize (Japan) 1983 and 1986; [oth. writ.] The heart In Exile 1964-90 (Memoirs And Paintings 1995, To A Wilder Shore (Novella) 1993, From The Butterfly's Wing (poems) 1986.; [pers.] Poetry, and the doing of it, I feel, is an essentially intimate experience, shared with the Gods - to which the reader should come quietly and alone under a roof of leaves, preferably.; [a.] Rochester upon Medway, Kent, UK

DUTHIE, VALERIE
[b.] 28 January 1936, Glossop, Derbyshire; [ch.] Two grown up daughter Tara and Kristine; [occ.] Retired Nursery Nurse; [memb.] Enjoy the facilities that the University of the Third Age have to offer to Stirling University; [hon.] Related to Nursery Nursing; [oth. writ.] Poems and articles published in various magazines; [pers.] I write from the heart.; [a.] Stirling, Stirlingshire, Scotland

DYKE, LILY MAY
[pen.] Lucinda Langley; [b.] 16 January 1911, Glamorgan, S. Wales; [p.] Artur and Edith Hellier; [m.] Jack L. Dyke (Deceased), 19 April 1934; [ch.] Gerald, Nigel, Colin; [ed.] Scotch Country School and Ogmore Vale Grammar School Glamorgan, South Wales; [occ.] Retired; [memb.] In Past Norton Sub Hamdon W.I. and Choir, over 60's club and Theatrical group. Norton Village Choir, Stoke Sub-Hamdon W.I, Working Peoples Club, Oak Tree House disabled Club, Wednesday Dinner Club; [oth. writ.] Short stories and poems published in magazine pensioner's clubs entitled "Something Different" a small book of my own poems of mine among others in a book published by a firm in Peterborough; [pers.] I have always had a love of poetry, music, and drawing and painting. Like writing poems that express my feelings or some uplifting message in them, or about the environment.; [a.] Stoke-sub-Hamdon, Somerset, UK

EAGER, MARIE ELIZABETH
[pen.] Gaby; [b.] 31 August 1982, Birmingham; [p.] Marguerita Eager, Bernard Eager; [ed.] Bordesley Green Girls, Secondary Modern and Birmingham Conservatoire, Junior School of Music; [occ.] Senior School Pupil; [memb.] Membership to Local Library; [hon.] Award for singing exam from the Royal Associate Board of Music.; [pers.] This poem was written at a very emotional time earlier this year after my father's death. I love poetry and hope to attain the best in whatever I do.; [a.] Birmingham, Warwickshire, UK

EBERT, KATHLEEN
[pen.] Tassi Bone; [b.] 3 January 1910, London; [p.] Ada and Sydney Bone; [m.] Peter Ebert (Divorced), June 1946; [ch.] 3 girls, born by 1st marriage to late John Mainden - photographer, 2nd Judith, 3rd Tabitha, 6 grandchildren, and one great grandson; [ed.] Convent (French), Highgate Grammar School, London, Painting Scholarship, Dartington Hall, Pottery - Elmgrant - Central School, London; [occ.] Pottery, Painting, Poetry, previous occupation: Art Therapist, Crafts Instructor, Social Worker, Writer; [memb.] Friends of Tate, A Royal Academy, Poetry Soc: RSPB and W.W.F.; [hon.] Occasional Prizes: Painting, Pottery, Exhibiting; [pers.] "Losses on the Roundabouts means Profits on the Swings."; [a.] Highgate, London, UK

EDINBORO, MS. DONNA LESLEY
[b.] 27 May 1959, Fulham; [p.] Horace Alverton, Eunice Beryl; [ch.] Simone, Nicole, David Leon; [occ.] Project Worker Housing Association; [oth. writ.] I have written other poems. A compilation entitled 'Betrayal of Thoughts'.; [pers.] My poems are expressions of how I view issues in the world and of my experiences.; [a.] London, UK

EDWARDS, JERMAINE S. A.
[b.] 22 June 1982, Bath Hosp., England; [p.] Margurita Edwards, Norman Edwards; [ed.] Leytonstone Secondary School; [occ.] Student; [memb.] Library and Youth Club and Maths Club; [hon.] Poem of the month, search and rescue and student of the week award; [pers.] I write poetry to reflect my feelings towards certain objects or opinions that I'm intrigued with.; [a.] London, UK

EDWARDS, MARGARET
[pen.] Margaret Edwards; [b.] 20 May 1936, Norwich; [p.] Bessie Winifred and Cecil Henry Cooper; [m.] Ken Edwards, 29 September 1956; [ch.] Ray, Roy, Maria; [ed.] Secondary Modern "Angel Road" School; [occ.] Housewife; [pers.] I find it much easier to express feelings in verse, I love nature and beautiful scenic surrounding I enjoy art. My husband and I are blessed with six lovely grandchildren.; [a.] Norwich, Norfolk, UK

EDWARDS, MARY
[b.] 23 August 1936, Plymouth; [p.] William Baker and Grace Baker; [m.] Gordon Edwards, 24 May 1980; [ch.] Susan Toni, Vincent Mark; [ed.] Notre Dame High School; [occ.] Retired Civil Servant; [memb.] Rainbow's Penfriend's Group. Jaguar Car Club (spouse); [hon.] GCE's in English Law and Human Biology; [pers.] I strive to treat others, as I myself would like to be treated.; [a.] Plymouth, Devon, UK

EDWARDS, RACHEL
[b.] 1 December 1979, Gillingham, Kent; [p.] John and Betty Edwards; [ed.] Robert Napier G.M. School, Gillingham, Kent; [occ.] Student; [hon.] Award Certificate in Business French; [oth. writ.] Am currently creating a book of poetry.; [pers.] I have been influenced by my own feelings when writing my poetry. The words come from within me as they flow together.; [a.] Gillingham, Kent, UK

ELDEN, MYRTLE
[pen.] Myrtle Elden; [b.] 27 December 1932, Ipswich; [p.] James and Alice Parkins; [m.] Paul Elden, 10 October 1953; [ch.] Two Girls, Two Boys, Six Grandchildren; [ed.] Nacton road Secondary School for Girls. I left school at the age of 14; [occ.] Retired; [oth. writ.] (Memories. The Cream of Eastern England. Vanishing Waistline. Addictive Poetry) (Aspiring Watchdog. In from the Cold) (Sounds of Years Gone By. The Marching Of Time.) These books are all Anthology's; [pers.] I started to write as therapy after the death of my beloved husband in 1995.; [a.] Ipswich, Suffolk, UK

ELDER, PAUL
[pen.] Paul Carlisle; [b.] 29 August 1970, Doncaster; [p.] Valerie Elder, Alexander Elder; [ed.] Hatfield High School; [occ.] Meadowhall Security; [oth. writ.] This is my first published work, but my first fiction novel is well into development amongst other projects that are screaming to be allowed to see the light of day; [pers.] My dreams are to become a published writer, whose work is taken seriously and whose message is clear, to accomplish your dreams you need to take the first step.; [a.] Doncaster, South Yorkshire, UK

ELFORD, JOHN BERNARD
[pen.] Gilgalad; [b.] 18 May 1967, Mackay, Australia; [p.] Trevor and Shirley Elford; [m.] Wendy Elford, 15 May 1993; [ch.] Jessica Anne; [ed.] Year 12 Aldridge State High School Maryborough Qld. Australia; [occ.] Carpenter; [oth. writ.] A poem published in an Australian anthology and also many unpublished poems.; [pers.] When I read the works of the great poets these essence touches me from beyond the grave. Regardless of the era there were people with the strengths and weaknesses of all mankind. I write not for any pretence of fame or fortune but just because I live. Life is so short and I am just one crying down the corridors of time...I have hoped and dreamed, tried and failed and loved and hurt, yes I have lived.; [a.] Kingaboy, Queensland, Australia

ELLIS, SANDRA ELIZABETH
[pen.] Sandra Ellis; [b.] 28 October 1943, Wickford, Essex; [p.] Ruth (Nee Carter) and Leslie Flexman; [m.] Kenneth Peter Ellis, 28 September 1963; [ch.] Tracy Jane, Kerry Ann and Kristy Ruth; [ed.] Brentwood County High School for girls, Mid-Essex Technical College and School of Art, MALA School of Dancing; [occ.] Secretary - S. Essex Health Authority (Following 12 years in Banking); [memb.] Member of the Royal Academy of Dancing, Fellow of the Imperial Society of Teachers of Dancing (Operatic Ballet and Stage Branch), Hon. Secretary - Wickford Lawn Tennis Club, Member of the Institute of Advanced Motorists; [hon.] Cadburys Junior Writers Award; [oth. writ.] Various poems - school/church magazines etc. Biography - (with pinch of salt!) "Little Potatoes Are Small", (The Carter Family in Wickford from 1907) - unpublished; [pers.] I have always loved writing - even letter-writing is a literary challenge and one that I hope delights the recipient.; [a.] Wickford, Essex, UK

ELLOTT, GUY HEWITT
[pen.] Hewitt Ellott; [b.] 2 September 1959, Redhill; [p.] James Ellott, Jeannie Hewitt Ellott; [m.] Caroline June; [ch.] Jo, Sas, Megs and Jake; [ed.] The College Of Life; [occ.] Motor Vehicle Examinations and Medication; [memb.] Royal British Legion Green Peace; [oth. writ.] Eglathius ring super tankers; [pers.] Cave men ruled O.K; [a.] Horley, Surrey, UK

ELSON, KAREN ELIZABETH
[pen.] Gypsy, Beth Martin; [b.] 17 July 1976, Grays, Essex; [p.] Robert and Margaret Elson; [ed.] William De Ferrers Secondary School; [memb.] Member of the RSPCA; [pers.] If someone tells you you're not good enough, prove them wrong! Quitting is not worth the regret; [a.] Essex, UK

EMERY, SID
[b.] 19 April 1945, Dudley; [p.] George Emery and Harriet Emery; [m.] Margaret Patricia Emery, 27 June 1970; [ch.] Jason, Paul Emery; [ed.] Mount Pleasant Secondary Modern; [occ.] Furnaceman; [oth. writ.] Several poems published locally and winner of National Competition. Conservation poetry for charities.; [pers.] My inspiration comes from a deep love and concern for the protection and preservation of the natural world and all life in whatever form.; [a.] Dudley, West Midlands, UK

EMERY, MR. WALTER LEONARD
[pen.] Mr. Walter Leonard Emery; [b.] 6 May 1916, Cradley; [p.] Now Deceased; [m.] Gwendolen Emery (Second Marriage), 1 June 1983; [ch.] One daughter (Christine); [ed.] Colley Lane Council School Halesowen; [occ.] (Retired) Disabled War Veteran; [memb.] Corn bow Dance Club Pensnett Snooker Club. Cradley Heath Liberal Club Honery Member; [oth. writ.] Over 200 poems of various subjects. Seven books containing poems and pictures to match, made up myself.; [pers.] I have been interviewed by a local newspaper who published one of my poems entitled (Black Country Days) other poems I have written include (The limping boatman) a very dear friend. A canal barge.; [a.] Rowley Regis, Worcester, UK

ENGLISH, JASON
[pen.] Leonard Young; [b.] 4 September 1977, Cork City, Rep of Irl; [p.] Sean English, Helen English; [ed.] St Josephs College, Cahir, Co Tipperary, Republic of Irl completed my leaving Certificate 1995; [occ.] Night Porter in a Hotel; [oth. writ.] This is the first serious poem I have ever written and this is the first competition I have entered. I am a virgin poet starting off.; [pers.] Everyone has a duty to look deep within themselves, recognize and acknowledge their ability's and use them positively so that they can find happiness and self-fulfillment in their lives.; [a.] Cahir, Tipperary, UK

EVANS, LEANNE
[b.] 3 April 1976, Newport, Gwent; [p.] Lesley and Adrian Evans; [oth. writ.] I have a number of unpublished writing, this includes short stories, I also keep a diary for thoughts and feelings, this has helped no end.; [pers.] This poem is dedicated to Keith, who I love very much. Also if wasn't for my Mom and Dad telling me I had talent I wouldn't be writing this now.; [a.] Blaenavon, Gwent, UK

EVANS, SARAH
[b.] Preston; [oth. writ.] One previous published poem poetry now North West 1996 Anthology; [pers.] "Faith In the Beautiful".; [a.] Manchester, UK

EVENDEN, MARIE AMELIA
[b.] 4 July 1939, Dagenham, Essex; [p.] Edith and Basil Sandford; [m.] Divorced/partner now Colin Francis Byrne; [ch.] 2 girls 1 boy - Julie Sue, Steven Evenden (all married); [ed.] Secondary

Girls School Parsloe Avenue Dagenha Essex; [occ.] T.S.S.U. Assistant Princess Alexandra Hospital, Laying out instruments for operation; [oth. writ.] More poems a song and a story I am still writing. None published; [pers.] I sometimes write poems on how I feel or how I think others maybe feeling I do also like to read poetry; [a.] Harlow, Essex, UK

EVERINGHAM, DIANE
[b.] 1 June 1958, London; [p.] Ivy and Gerry Butcher; [ch.] One - 17 years old - Michael; [ed.] Barstable Comprehensive, Basildon College, Anglia Poly' B.Ed Honours Degree; [occ.] Teacher of English, the Cornelius Vermuydon Comp', Canvey Island; [pers.] I have always loved poetry and have written my own since an early age. For me it represents emotions on a page.; [a.] Basildon, Essex, UK

EWINS, RODNEY
[b.] 23 November 1967, Belfast, Northern Ireland; [m.] Keshwari Ewins, 26 February 1991; [ch.] Aron and Declan; [ed.] Drumgor Primary, Lismore Comprehensive - Northern Ireland; [occ.] Intensive Home Care Worker, Social Services; [oth. writ.] Articles on Elvis Presley published in monthly magazine in England and U.S.A.; [pers.] As a wise man once said, "Don't judge a man until you've walked in that man's shoes." --Elvis Presley 1935-1977; [a.] Craigavon, Armagh

EYLES, BRENDA M.
[pen.] Brenda Eyles; [b.] 29 May 1926, Devon; [p.] Elizabeth and William Hallett; [m.] Stanley Arthur Eyles, 10 September 1947; [ch.] Rodney and Antony David; [occ.] Garage Proprietor; [memb.] West Buckland W.I., Taunton Conservations, Conservatives Abroad; [hon.] Several prizes won in various Poetry Competitions; [oth. writ.] Several poems published; [pers.] I like to write simple verse which can be enjoyed and, more importantly, understood by ordinary people.; [a.] Wellington, Somerset, UK

EYRE, BRIDGET E.
[b.] 19 December 1934, Bilby, Nottinghamshire; [p.] Emily and Jack Barker; [m.] Harry; [ch.] Five children; [pers.] Poetry has been a great comfort to me and I nave to thank my mother who said they should be written down and encouraged me. My other hobbies include gardening, painting and breeding Shih Tzu dogs we also enjoy the beautiful scenery since retiring to North Wales

FAITARONE, MISS ELIZABETH
[b.] 10 January 1974, Buenos Aires, Argentina; [p.] Alej Andro Faitarone (Argentinian) and Rosa Benitez (Spanish); [ed.] High School and Teachers Training College; [hon.] Previously published in a poetry anthology called "Symphonies of the Soul" by the Poetry Guild in America; [oth. writ.] Poetry and short stories in English and Spanish; [pers.] Poetry is the brightness of passion where in mystery words, soul and spirit, describe my world.; [a.] Horsham, West Sussex, UK

FARISH, ADAM
[pen.] Fez; [b.] 13 October 1977, Germany (B.M.H.); [p.] Rose and Frank Farish; [ed.] Elizabeth College, Guernsey, Grammar School Guernsey; [occ.] Student; [memb.] NHC Basketball Club, Guernsey R.U.F.C. St Saviors CC; [hon.] National Finalist in team "Youth Speaks" competition; [oth. writ.] Personal poems and short prose, none previously published; [pers.] As a

young man I try to give a voice to the struggles and challenges of young people in the 90's. My influences are not other poets but the world around me, in particular my close friends - Chris, Laura, Natalie, and Kerry.; [a.] Guernsey, Britain

FARMER, JOYCE
[pen.] Lively Pensioner; [b.] Witham, Essex; [p.] Muriel Messent, Ernest Messent; [m.] Alexander Farmer, 18 November 1995; [ch.] Susan, Grandchildren, Daniel, Samantha; [ed.] Tabor School, Braintree; [occ.] Retired; [memb.] Dancing, Bowling Clubs, Meditating; [oth. writ.] Several poems published in books of anthology; [pers.] I have inspirations often unexpected, sometimes at night, or early mornings there is a story in all my poems.; [a.] Rayleigh, Essex, UK

FAULKNER, MISS GILLIAN ANNE
[b.] 12 September 1963, Belfast, Northern Ireland; [ed.] 'Richmond Lodge' Grammar School for Girls, 'Stranmillis' - Teacher Training College - Belfast; [occ.] Primary School Teacher - Seaview Primary School, North Belfast; [memb.] Member of "Belfast Chorale - School of Music, Grade 8 - singing and theory of music B.ed. D.A.S.E (teaching degree); [pers.] I feel closest to God when I am appreciating the beauty of nature all around me. I have been greatly influenced in literature by the poetry of Wordsworth and Coleridge.; [a.] Belfast, Antrim, UK

FAULKNER, NORAH
[b.] 28 May 1928, Long Buckby, Northamptonshire; [p.] Minnie Elizabeth Hunt and Frank George Hunt; [m.] Sidney Charles Faulkner, 15 January 1947; [ch.] Peter, Michael, Mary, Sheila, Kevin, Julie; [ed.] Long Buckby C. of E.(Church of England) mixed school; [occ.] Housewife, retired leather workers; [memb.] Brownsover "Golden Age" Club; [hon.] I have been awarded several trophies for bowling competitions and matches; [oth. writ.] I have several poems - I have written years ago - and submitted to various companies. One who been put to music and this I have a recording of.; [pers.] I try to see the good in people as well as the not so good that we often find. I accomplish as much pleasure from music-books-and flowers as one may get from the most expensive forms of pleasure; [a.] Rugby, Warwickshire, UK

FEGAN, VIVINNE LYNDA MCGINN
[ed.] High School Sandymount University, Opera Singing Music; [occ.] Romantic Writer; [oth. writ.] Poetry, songs, and romantic stories school stories for girls 10 years up to sixteen.; [pers.] I can express my feelings in my poetry, tomorrow the world. My interests, are romantic poets and chamber music.; [a.] Castle Town Fine, West Meath, Mullingar, Ireland

FENNELL, MRS. ANNE
[b.] 1 March 1947, Mirfield, West Yorks; [p.] Mr. and Mrs. J. Woodward; [m.] Graham Fennell, 25 February 1967; [ch.] Lisa, Russell and Melissa Fennell; [occ.] Nursery Manager (Child Care); [a.] Swinton, South Yorks, UK

FENWICK, CYNTHIA
[b.] 29 September 1929, Scunthorpe; [p.] George and Maud Camplin (Deceased); [m.] Dennis Fenwick (Deceased), 19 December 1951; [ch.] Peter John and Joy Elaine, Grand Daughter Chloe Joy; [occ.] Retired Legal Cashier/Acctnt.; [oth. writ.] Published Poems: - The Gardener, Ward 22, Freedom, Why?, Childhood Memories,

Grammy's Face, My Bundle of Joy, Villains, Frosted Lace; [pers.] I see a face, I see a flower, I see a bird shake off a shower, the words begin to flow again? Its then I reach out for my pen.; [a.] Scunthorpe, North Lincs, UK

FERGUSON, ANN
[b.] 23 November 1936, Leeds; [p.] Arthur and Betty Ferguson; [ed.] Leeds Girls High School, Lady Margaret Hall, Oxford; [occ.] Retired Head of Modern Languages; [memb.] Southport Bach Society, Association for Language Learning, National Trust, R.S.P.B. etc; [hon.] M.A. (Oxon) Cert. Ed. (Cantab); [oth. writ.] Poems published in school and church magazines; [pers.] Finds writing poetry, like gardening both therapeutic and enjoyable.; [a.] Southport, Merseyside, UK

FIELD, MRS. PAULINA DIGNOS ARONG
[pen.] P. D. Field; [b.] 6 June 1940, Cebu City, Philippines; [p.] Juan R. Arong and Gala D. Arong; [m.] Malcolm Roderick Field, 11 February 1982; [ch.] (3 Step-children); [ed.] High School (2nd year) Undergraduate, Primary and Secondary School at Colegio Del Santo Nino, Cebu City, Phils.; [occ.] Retired Nurse, Trained as Enrolled Nurse at St. Thomas Hosp. London, 1975; [memb.] U.K.C.C.; [pers.] "It is never too late to make your dreams come true" I have always admire the poems of William Wadsworth and stories written by Catherine Cookson.; [a.] Spalding, Lincs, UK

FINNEY, VERA
[pen.] Ann Berry; [b.] 11 October 1941, Farnworth, Bolton; [p.] William Berry, Nelly Berry; [m.] Ian Donald Finney, 11 February 1989; [ch.] Andrew Geoffrey (from first marriage); [ed.] Farnworth Grammar School, St. Katharine's College, Liverpool, The Open University; [occ.] School Librarian/Supply Teacher; [memb.] Past Member of Farnworth Amateur Operatic and Dramatic Society, Present Member of Bolton Academy of Dance and Stage; [hon.] B.A. Degree, Certificate of Education, C.E. Certificate of Religious Teaching, I.S.T.D. Adult Tap Dancing: Levels 1-5, Bronze and Silver Medals; [oth. writ.] I am at present studying with 'The Writing School.' I have had 'A Diary' published in a woman's magazine and am submitting articles and short stories in the hope of publication and/or recognition.; [pers.] The pleasure in writing is in the sharing of experience.; [a.] Bolton, Gt. Manchester, UK

FIRTH, LYNDA MARGARET
[b.] 29 February 1948, Huddersfield; [p.] Joseph Moss and May Moss; [m.] Geoffrey Firth, 18 March 1967; [ch.] Mark, Andrew, Darren, James; [ed.] New some County, Secondary School Huddersfield Technical College, The University of Huddersfield; [occ.] House Wife; [memb.] Rawlins School of Dancing; [hon.] Silver, Bronze, Gold Medals for Ballroom Dancing and Latin American Dancing, Husband, Partner several poems published in local magazines. Combined Artwork Huddersfield Gallery; [oth. writ.] A study of grammar, Vocabulary, Lexis, Syntax, title, to May from Miss Lorna a project by 'Photic Communion' by Lees of Union are created by a mere exchange of words.; [pers.] I strive to reflect the goodness of mankind in my own ties of language, which have been greatly influenced by important writers times past and present.; [a.] Huddersfield, Yorkshire, UK

FISHER, JOHN SAMUEL
[b.] 7 August 1933, Dunedin, NZ; [p.] Robert and Gertrode Fisher; [ch.] Samuel, Carmela, Jonathan; [ed.] Christchurch Boys' High School, College House (Christchurch), University of New Zealand, St. John's Theological College (Auck); [occ.] Retired (Anglican Priest); [pers.] I am passionate about social justice treaty or waiting issues and aspects or struggles for equality. I try to capture internalized fragments of human experience in my writing. I am eclectic in tastes admiring Thomas Hood and T. S. Eliot.; [a.] Christchurch, New Zealand

FISHER, KENNETH
[pen.] K. Jay; [b.] 16 October 1944, Portsmouth; [p.] Mr. and Mrs. J. Fisher; [m.] Pamela Jones, 6 July 1987; [ed.] St Brinus Secondary Modern, Didcot - Oxon; [occ.] Medically Retired was HGU Driver, Ex Navy; [hon.] Duke of Edinburough Gold; [oth. writ.] Article on Aviary Birds Published in Cage and Aviary Magazine, several poems written unpublished; [pers.] I try to reflect things that happen in life into words, enjoy the classics such as Keats and Shelly.; [a.] Alrewa, Staffs, UK

FISHER, PAUL ANTHONY
[b.] 22 July 1963, Wrexham; [p.] Colin Fisher, Hazel Fisher; [m.] Patricia Jayne Fisher, 28 September 1985; [ch.] Sarah Jayne, Danielle Jaid; [ed.] Darland Comprehensive Rossett; [occ.] Section Leader at F. Bender Ltd; [memb.] Wrexham Library Local Fishing Club; [oth. writ.] Have written other poems for friends and family, also for myself.; [pers.] I do enjoy to write poetry. Some funny but others quite serious.; [a.] Wrexham, Wales, UK

FITZGERALD, VANNESA
[pen.] Vannesa Sinclair; [b.] 17 July 1957, Hartlepool; [p.] Jeane Alton and John Metcalf; [ed.] High School for Girls Hartlepool; [oth. writ.] Numerous poems none published; [pers.] I have been greatly influenced by my travels in North Africa in the past seven years. My personal philosophy in life is 'Never Give Up'; [a.] Hartlepool, UK

FLEMING, JUNE MARY
[b.] June 28, 1938, Consett Co., Durham; [p.] Hannah and Barron Griffith Williams; [m.] Rev. William Hillis Fleming, August 25, 1965; [ch.] James Alexander, Martha Elizabeth; [ed.] Annfield Plain Sec. Mod. Consett Grammar, Shotley Bridge Gen. Hosp. Dudley Rd, Maternity Hosp. B'Ham, Forest Gate Maternity Hosp. Londoney; [occ.] Housewife and Duties Associated with being a Minister's wife; [oth. writ.] None published; [pers.] Some deeply felt feelings and thoughts are difficult to express. Eg appreciation of beauties of nature and complexities of human nature coping with living. My poems seem to be an attempt to put these thoughts into words, to help and inspire others. I think the greatest poet is the Psalmist David.; [a.] Liverpool, Merseyside

FLETCHER, SANDRA DENISE
[b.] 24 April 1945, Paddington; [p.] Dorothy May Milner, Father Deceased; [m.] Divorced; [ch.] Jacqueline and Anthony John and Nicola; [ed.] St. Pauls Primary School, Tottenham N17, St. Katherine's Secondary Modern School: Tottenham; [occ.] Care Assistant at Yew Tree Cottage: Ipswich Rd: Swainsthorpe, Norwich; [oth. writ.] No other writings published; [pers.] "It wasn't until I started writing a book that I realize how much English I did not know.; [a.] Norwich, Norfolk, UK

FLINT, JOHN J.
[b.] 3 March 1925, Sotherton; [p.] William and Kathleen Flint; [m.] Elizabeth; [ch.] 5 Boys, 4 girls; [occ.] Retired; [pers.] Ex Hertford Regiment/ 1st Oxf and Bucks Lt. INF.; [a.] Halesworth, Suffolk, UK

FLYNN, CORRINNE
[b.] 15 August 1974, Pembury; [p.] Tim and Heather Flynn; [ed.] Beechwood in Tunbridge Wells, and King Alfreds College in Winchester; [occ.] Client Services; [memb.] Jeanine Greville and Dance School; [hon.] BA Honours in History and Drama Ballet, Tap and Modern Awards, Cross Country Cup; [oth. writ.] Publishing in School Magazine 1st prize and poem published Youth Hostel Assoc. Magazine; [pers.] Makes me think maybe God is a woman too!! Influenced by Historical events.; [a.] Basingtoke, Hants, UK

FOGG, JACQUELINE LYDIA
[b.] 10 November 1969, Bexley, Kent; [p.] May Somerton, Kennedy Fogg; [ed.] Highcliffe Comprehensive, Brockenhurst College; [occ.] Administrator; [memb.] Animal Aid, Amnesty International Greenpeace; [oth. writ.] Many campaign letters published in Bournemouth echo and National charity newsletters.; [pers.] Humour is essential. A campaigner for animal rights, human rights and the environment, I write about what I see and what I hear. The enclosed poem is for my cat, Teddy.; [a.] Bournemouth, Dorset, UK

FORD, MARY BEATRICE
[pen.] Clare Leigh; [b.] 28 July 1914, Wood Green, London; [p.] Hugh Osbornie Browne, Ethel Beatrice Brownie; [m.] John William George Ford, 3 April 1937; [ch.] David Hugh, Edwin Michael, Helen Rose Mary, Timothy Julian; [ed.] St. Matthias Church School Dalston Secondary (item), Germiston Intermediate (item), S.A. Germiston High South Africa; [occ.] Housewife; [a.] Westerham, Kent, UK

FORGAN, MISS SARAH
[b.] 13 May 1906, Johannesburg, South Africa; [p.] Irvine Forgan and Sue Forgan; [ed.] Matric and University Exemption at Ran Park High school in Randburg, South Africa; [occ.] Second year fine arts student at the University of the wit waters rand (Wits); [memb.] Transvaal horse society fine arts student union at the University of Wits. South Africans for the abolition of Vivisection (SAAV); [hon.] Honours for oral communication from S.A. guild of speech and drama. Three matric graduation distinctions in English, Fine Arts and Biology, full academic colours in matric, editor of Wits S.A.A.V. newsletter, student representative at Wits Fine Arts; [oth. writ.] Bronze award for poetry from Eisteddfod Foundation and publication. And Editorial material for Wits S.A.A.V.; [pers.] I have developed simultaneously a great love and a great wariness for humanity. To find yourself different in society is an alienating yet encouraging phenomenon and I hope to reflect this is my writing; [a.] Johannesburg, Midran, South Africa

FORM, MALCOLM G.
[pen.] Gordon M. G.; [b.] 10 May 1946, Edgware; [p.] Glady and Albert Form; [m.] Christine M. Form, 23 May 1972; [ch.] Brean and Helen; [ed.] Secondary Modern Rosceth Manor, now Rooks Heath. Eastcote Lane Harrow Middx; [occ.] Medically Retired was Ex Coldstream GDS Now Clearer Part time; [memb.] Guards Association Royal Engeans Club, Royal Observe Assoc., Royal Airforce Assoc., Piccadilly Poets London; [hon.] Except G.S.M. South American T.A. Long Service; [oth. writ.] 3 poems published War poem title Men of Action Poetry now and Twa in Mag and one in Anthologies living in 20th century.; [pers.] I try to depict celtic History and English History. Another and Richard himself and War poems of conflict I have been involved in.; [a.] Luton, Bedfordshire, UK

FORREST, MRS. B. B. BEATRICE
[pen.] Betty; [b.] 8 January 1926, Calverton; [p.] Emma Harrison, Harold Harrison; [m.] Jim Forrest (Deceased), December 1951; [ch.] Angela, Bryonny, James; [ed.] C/E School studied at A level, Ceramics, Art and Sociology; [occ.] Retired Nurse and Midwife; [memb.] Thoroton Society, W.E.A. Nott., City Hospital Retirement Club, also several ladies meetings; [hon.] SRN, SCM; [oth. writ.] Play, called "Stockingers in the Home". Poems inc - the closure of special shops in Nottingham. Historical poems of village life. The Nottingham Slaves - about children down the mines - also poems of the country side.; [pers.] I write when I feel very strongly about something, either in the past or present. I could feel happy or very sad at the time.; [a.] Arnold, Nottingham, UK

FORREST, HAZEL
[b.] 7 September 1950, Wallsend on Tyne; [p.] Richard William Brooks, Audrey Magaret Helena Brooks; [m.] David Forrest, 12 December 1970; [ch.] Paul David Forrest; [occ.] Sales Distributor; [oth. writ.] Poems published in local newspaper; [pers.] The spiritual preparation for writing a poem is influenced by life itself, as long as there is life, I shall endeavour to write poetry.; [a.] Whitley Bay, Tyne and Wear, UK

FOTHERGILL, KARIN HILDA
[b.] 15 June 1923, Ardrossan, Ayrshire; [p.] Mr. and Mrs. Nils Olof Lundholm; [m.] The Odore Fothergill (Deceased), 31 March 1958; [ch.] One daughter, Gerda, Anita; [ed.] Ardrossan Academy and St. Leonards School, St. Andrews, as a boarder; [occ.] Housewife; [memb.] The Royal Overseas League and Bridge Section Edinburgh; [hon.] M.C.S.P. Trained as a Physiotherapist at the Royal Infirmary in Edinburgh; [oth. writ.] Several other poems. But have not tried to get them published.; [pers.] I obtained prizes for elocution and reciting, poems at Ardrossan Academy. My mother was very keen on acting and was a member of the Ardrossan and Saltcoats Players Club, taking principal parts. She came from a very musical family and I inherited sense of rhythm, which come into poetry.; [a.] Edinburgh, UK

FOUNTAIN, NIGEL STEPHEN
[b.] 4 January 1956, Luton; [p.] Dorothy Ellen, Alec; [m.] Christine Anne Fountain, 20 January 1996; [ch.] 1 Boy, 1 Girl grown-up; [ed.] Challney High for boys Luton Bedfordshire; [occ.] Security Dog Handler; [memb.] IWA, RAC; [hon.] Won many school prizes in poetry and writing competitions; [oth. writ.] 1,000's but never inclined to get any published; [pers.] 2 quotes! Always do your best and never do a man a bad turn. You don't have to do him a good turn just don't do him a bad one. Poetry is to be written, not necessarily to be read.; [a.] Sawtry, Cambs, UK

FOWLER, JAYNE
[b.] 25 August 1960, Aldershot; [p.] Anthony Dixon and Jean Courtney; [m.] Harold Fowler, 21 May 1988; [ch.] Kelly Anne and Amy Martha; [ed.] Holt Grammar School; [occ.] School

Secretary; [pers.] I dedicate my poem to my two beautiful daughters whom I love with all my heart and who bring me endless happiness.; [a.] Basingstoke, Hants, UK

FOX, JANET
[b.] 5 March 1956, Castleford, W. Yorks; [p.] Doreen and Desmond Wood; [m.] Garry Fox, 2 March 1977; [ch.] Alison Louise Fox; [occ.] Secretary for Pontefract Firm of Law Costs Draftsmen; [pers.] I write for fun, to get my thoughts, and feelings down on paper and often to convey what I find difficult to say in person. My work is very personal-filled with memories and future hopes.; [a.] Pontefract, West Yorks, UK

FOX, SANDRA ELIZABETH
[b.] 1 August 1942, Longton, Staffordshire; [p.] Leonard Ruffell; [m.] John Fox, 5 May 1965; [ch.] One daughter age 26, one son age 24; [ed.] Broadway Secondary Cheadle, Cheshire; [occ.] Lady of Leisure, Ex-School Registrar; [memb.] Writers News; [hon.] 'A' level in EA/English Lit/ Language at Adult Education Class; [oth. writ.] Always trying, submitting and hoping for success.; [pers.] Inherited a love of words from my father. Would like to write something profound.; [a.] Beaconsfield, Bucks, UK

FRANCIS, MARILYN ROSEMARY
[pen.] Mal Francis; [b.] 19 September 1952, Wrexham, Clwyd; [m.] Frank H. Francis; [ch.] One son - aged 21 yrs.; [ed.] Secondary Modern Previous Occupation Manageress, Supervisor, Exports/Despatch, Shop Assistant P.T.; [occ.] Housewife; [memb.] R.S.P.B W.R.V.S.; [oth. writ.] Not entered for publishing 35-40 poems on natural world entitled there is a little creature there is a little bird, children's stories.; [pers.] I am greatly influenced by "Nature" itself, it never ceases to amaze me be way of my writing I try to capture a vision or a moment for I fear it may be lost forever and to Mother Nature I most humbly bow.; [a.] Mourn Villa, Chirk Bank, Clwyd, UK

FRANKLING, KAY
[b.] 4 February 1971, Farnborough, Kent; [p.] Marion Grant and Graham Grant; [m.] Peter Frankling, 1 September 1990; [ch.] Ronni-Kaye, Maxine-Fern and George-Ellen; [ed.] Beaverwood Walsingham; [occ.] Housewife; [pers.] A fairwell message, I wrote for my Auntie Eileen (mum's sister) to say fairwell to her husband Lewis Green away from herself her son Paul and daughter Christine.; [a.] Bexhill-on-Sea, East Sussex, UK

FREER, DENISE MARIE
[pen.] Denise Marie O'Shea; [b.] 14 June 1953, Coalville; [p.] Patrick and Barbara O'Shea; [m.] David Michael Freer, 21 September 1991; [ch.] Warwick, Clare, Joanne; [ed.] St. Peter's and Paul, Earl Shilton, St. Martins Convent, Stoke Golding; [occ.] Housewife; [oth. writ.] My Personal Book of Poetry. Some of which I have put to music.; [pers.] I feel my poetry brings out my thoughts and inner feelings to share with other people.; [a.] Coalville, Leicester, UK

FROST, THOMAS
[b.] 31 December 1976, Colchester; [pers.] All my poems were actual letters to a girl I loved, I still love her, more than ever, so I still write poems.; [a.] Tolleshunt Major, Essex, UK

FRY, ELIZABETH LOUISA
[pen.] Eliza Lippa; [b.] 26 May 1948, Henley, Berkshire; [p.] Harry Fry and Elizabeth Fry; [m.] John Lippe, 8 August 1976; [ch.] Six daughters; [occ.] Caring for children; [hon.] Best Letter Writer in the school Honours List 1939 name in Gold Letters on School Plaque of best school pupils list; [oth. writ.] A letter I wrote to the principal cologne college in Germany whilst 9 was looking after his son he put the letter in the college for students to study.; [pers.] Some of us are big ships some of us are small were gracefully achts and rusty tramps but there's one thing overall we have the same wide seas to sail the same part to make so here's a happy wish to you and to me while wave and wave let's break.

FUDGE, AMANDA JAYNE
[pen.] Amanda J. Fudge; [b.] 7 August 1975, Church Village; [p.] Kevin and Lynda Fudge; [ed.] Ysgol Heol-y-Celyn, Ysgol Gyfun Rhydfelen, Bridgend College of Further and Higher Education; [occ.] Nursery Nurse; [hon.] Nursery Nurse Education Board (N.N.E.B/C.A.C.H.E) (Merit), English Speaking Board (Merit), World Champion Bell-Lyre Player; [oth. writ.] I write for personal release and self enjoyment. Also for family and friends. (This is the first time that I have ever entered a poetry competition or had any work published.); [pers.] I strive to reflect life experiences in my work either through personal experience or through empathy. The subjects I write about are universal and therefore can be identified by anyone.; [a.] Pontypridd, Mid-Glamorgan, UK

FULLMAN, ANTHONY DENNIS GRAHAME
[pen.] Tony Fullman; [b.] 22 February 1962, Romford, England; [p.] Stan Fullman, Elsie Fullman; [ed.] Marshalls Park Comprehensive; [occ.] Ceramic tiler; [hon.] 4 Certificates for Piano Playing and Music; [oth. writ.] I have written numerous poems but this is the first poem I have offered for publishing; [pers.] In all of my poems there is a state of mind. Sometimes happy, sometimes sad, sometimes light, sometimes deep, but always accurate.; [a.] Romford, Essex, UK

GALE, SHANE
[b.] 2 November 1969, Witham, Essex; [p.] David George Gale and Linda Baily; [m.] Tracy Bernadette Mary Fitzgerald, 14 February 1990; [ed.] Bramston Comprehensive; [occ.] Retail Hygiene Manager; [oth. writ.] First submission of work for publication; [pers.] "Divinity abides within poetic prose and seeks to expound it's law. Yet who amongst you has dared to rend the veil?"; [a.] Witham, Essex, UK

GALL, RICKY
[pen.] Knight; [b.] 3 June 1979, Peterhead; [p.] Freda Gall, Gunther Gall; [ed.] Ellon Academy; [occ.] Trainee Private Detective, Shadow Investigations; [memb.] Scottish Aeromodellers Association/Computer Clubs/Warplanes Collector's Club; [hon.] Multiple Computing Certificates, Diploma in Private Investigation; [oth. writ.] A number of poems against war and the dark side of mankind.; [pers.] Only peace and freedom for the people of planet Earth can lift us from limbo. The world need not be bad.; [a.] Hatton, Aberdeenshire, UK

GALLOWAY, JOHN HENRY
[pen.] Johnson; [b.] 22 July 1916, Poplar Elk, London; [p.] William, Ellen Elizabeth; [m.] Ada Winifred (Deceased); [ch.] Patricia and Margaret; [ed.] Hay Currie Secondary School from Infants to

Senior Level, at Ten and a half years, seconded to Dempsey St. Myopic School, London E.I. now a Training College (Further Education); [occ.] Retired; [memb.] R.A.O.B., Fully paid and Member T.G.W.U. have represented various committees i.e. Manpower Services, Youth Employment D.H.S.S., Tribunals Walthamstow, Barking - Romford and Dagenham, Seventeen and Half Years - Disablement Advisory at Poplar and Stratford East, Trade Union Secretary Ten years and Community Health Councilor 2 1/2 years; [oth. writ.] I looked out of my window and what.; [pers.] I enjoy life, through many good friendships I was promised a literary careers from a composition about a school journey to Hastings 1926/7 at Dempsey St. Myopic School.; [a.] London, UK

GAMBRIEL, MELANIE
[b.] 20 March 1962, Windsor; [p.] Raymond and Angela Gambriel; [ed.] Bulmershe Comp. Woodley, Nr Reading; [occ.] Shop Manageress Recently made Redundant; [memb.] Writers successful School for beginners; [oth. writ.] Mothers Day poem published in daily newspaper many many poems and short stories written and listed not submitted for publication.; [pers.] The pen is a very powerful tool and in the hands of the correct user of it's worth, can ultimately rewrite and change this world we live in to one of peace and harmony. I strive to be the one; [a.] Southampton, Hampshire, UK

GAROFALL, ELIZABETH WISE
[b.] September 24, 1907, Plumpstead; [p.] John and Elizabeth Doswell; [m.] John Garofall, July 1, 1939; [ch.] Two sons (both with honours degrees); [ed.] Grammar School, Teacher's Training College, Diploma English at King's College London; [occ.] Retired (widow) Deputy Headmistress; [hon.] Distinction/English, 1st prize (all London) for Essay on League of Nations. 3 years exhibition roan grammar school for best scholar of the year; [oth. writ.] VF or Fun Humorous verses on birthday cards; [a.] Eaton Bray, Beds

GARRADLEY, BERT
[b.] 30 March 1919, Birmingham; [p.] Walter Garradley, May Ellen Garradley; [m.] Irene May Garradley, 21 December 1946; [ed.] Icknield Street Elementary School, Birmingham; [occ.] Retired/Building site manager; [oth. writ.] Nothing hither to published, or submitted.; [pers.] With my self as part, I endeavour still to learn the love and the mystery of God that sublimes the universe.; [a.] Birmingham, Warwickshire, UK

GARRETT, PATRICK JOSEPH
[pen.] Pat Garrett; [b.] March 12, 1946, Perth, Scotland; [p.] Peter Garrett, Maria Garrett; [m.] Patricia Garrett, August 22, 1970; [ch.] Mark (Deceased), John, Joseph; [ed.] Bishop Wulstan High School; [occ.] Warehousing; [memb.] Leicestershire Microlight Aircraft Club; [hon.] 96824 B.G.A. Pilot; [oth. writ.] Works magazine, M.C.N. Cruse Chronicle; [pers.] Life is what happens to our dreams. I try to "fix" time by writing. Poem in memory of Mark Anthony.; [a.] Rugby, Warwickshire

GARRETT, PETER JOHN
[b.] 29 June 1931, St Pancras, London; [p.] Irish Origin; [m.] Maureen Garrett (Nee Neill), 20 February 1954; [ed.] Secondary (Blitz Child) Poor Education. A Bomb went off out in the street a head came through the classroom window - as the eye flickered as the brown was dying in the skull I head my teacher say - Peter its the 'I' before 'E'

except after; [occ.] Book-Keeper/'C' Accountant; [memb.] Late - Guildford Choral Society (First Tenor), I am a full Range Tenor - Operatic - Dramatic Type; [hon.] NIL - but I got good marks at the Godalming Music Festival, also recited 2 Canto's by Byron; [oth. writ.] NIL - but would like to write book - (could be a best seller.); [pers.] Over population is Dan's Downfall.; [a.] Gomshall, Surrey, UK

GASPAR, MARGARET ELIZABETH
[pen.] Tosca - Lulu - Meg - "Alien" - "Hot-Hot-Lady"; [b.] 24 August 1947, Southern Rhodesia now Zimbabwe; [p.] Jack Donald Baker, Sophia Elizabeth Earle; [m.] Manuel Domingues Gaspar, 6 April 1968; [ch.] Mandy Elizabeth (15) adopted!, Anthony Manuel (28) natural son; [ed.] Very little - due to parents divorce - I have not had a single poetry lesson!; [occ.] Live-in-home-care with two-counties-community care; [memb.] Joined the writing school of London - but no time to pursue studies; [oth. writ.] I adore pushing a pen!; [pers.] I am a totally philosophical person - who puts my faith in God - I love all fellow human - and do my best for them all.; [a.] Halstead, Essex, UK

GEDDES, YONA ELISE
[b.] November 24, 1918, Alton, Hants; [p.] Ralph, Rhoda Hinkins; [m.] Deceased, 1st 1938, 2nd 1960; [ch.] Rhoda, Diana, Vincent, Frances; [ed.] Tutored at home until the age of eight by grandfather then church schools till the age of fourteen; [occ.] Retired, teacher taught art-craft, pottery, to mentally handicapped; [oth. writ.] Short stories as hobby as a child none published; [pers.] I feel my background is my spur. Mother, Romany, and Father, Pioneer Photographer, Artist, Illustrator and many other talents, a very liberal upbringing for the time.; [a.] Prevensey Bay, E. Sussex

GEE, MARGARET
[b.] 15 July 1936, Stockport; [p.] Florence Maud Humphries, Peter Sharples Humphries; [m.] Alfred Keith Gee, 25 September 1965; [ed.] Secondary Modern School; [occ.] Retired; [pers.] I have always written poetry and have always enjoyed reading poetry.; [a.] Stockport, Cheshire, UK

GENTLES, RUTH
[pen.] Heather Lynn; [b.] 28 October 1940, Perth, Scotland; [p.] Flora Stewart Chalmers McLean, Campbell Lawson; [m.] Robert Gentles, 27 October 1960; [ch.] Five daughters; [ed.] Shawlands Academy, Coatbridge Technical College, Cumbernauld College; [occ.] Home Carer, (Social Work Department); [memb.] Church of Scotland, Colville Park Recreational Club, Swimming Club, Girl Guide Association Helper; [hon.] The Royal Society of Arts Examination Shorthand. Scot Bec Junior Secretarial Certificate Shorthand and typing stage 1. Mensa Certificate First and Certificates Scotvec National Certificate modules preparing to work with people with special needs. Domiciliary care staff training certificate extended caring skills in home care.; [oth. writ.] Some school magazine poems enjoyed many books my first being 'little women' Jane Austen love of Wordsworth in poetry thorn birds Coleen McCullough.; [pers.] A greater hand guides the pen and thoughts of the mind persuading us to use any hidden talents.; [a.] Coatbridge, Lanarkshire, UK

GEORGE, MRS. LINDA
[b.] 17 February 1951, Gower, Swansea; [p.] Anna and Robert William Phillips; [ch.] Gaynor George, Anna George, Helen George.; [ed.] Mynyddbach Comprehensive School for Girls in Swansea, South Wales.; [occ.] Secretary; [memb.] Runrig Fan Club Member; [oth. writ.] I have written 40 poems to date. A poem called "That Special Moment" is to be published in a book called "The Other Side Of The Mirror" (October 1996). All the poem I write reflect true experiences that have actually happened to me; [pers.] The most precious thing in life, is to love and be loved. This happened to me. The very special person that I wish to thank for my inspiration to write, I still love deeply, thank you Stuart Williams for coming into my life, and making the living good for me,; [a.] Swansea, West Glam, UK

GEORGIADES, MISS LEA
[b.] 1 November 1945, Cyprus; [occ.] English and History Teacher in a Secondary School; [hon.] Won essay competitions as a child; [oth. writ.] Because writing poetry in 1995, had poems published in three anthologies, 1. Poetry Now - London 1996, 2. Out Of The Closet 3. Poets in London And The Home Counties; [pers.] A poet's soul must be capable of feeling genuine anguish, pity, indignation and love. Poets must be witnesses to their epoch, and in the face of negativism, imagine the potential moral trans for motions poetry, supported by conscience, can help us to learn to live like human beings; [a.] London, UK

GIBBONS, STEPHEN
[b.] 27 October 1970, Greenock; [p.] James Gibbons, Elizabeth Gibbons; [ed.] St. Columbas High School; [occ.] Undecided; [oth. writ.] Thank God for window's - Glasgow and Strathclyde poetry anthology, an honest love - a message of faith - anthology.; [pers.] In my life time I will try to experience every kind of experience and hopefully reflect this in my writing for the benefit of others.; [a.] Greenock, Strathclyde, UK

GILBERT, MARLENE M.
[b.] 17 June 1937, Nottingham; [p.] Edgar Cox, Ida Cox; [m.] Michael L. Gilbert (Recently deceased), 20 April 1957; [ch.] Wendy Ann, John William, 10 grandchildren; [ed.] Very little - parents moved house many times attended 15 schools in 10 yrs.; [occ.] Retired - disabled extensive arthritis - (but mobile); [memb.] Society of Amateur Artists, Writers Viewpoint - Rhyme Arrival Mag. - Anchors Aweigh Mag. - Poetry now mag. - Saga - Choice - Arthritis Care - Good Times (ARP 050) magazines - Springfields Horticultural Society Ltd.; [hon.] NIL - but - 'writers viewpoint' for children's story - Good Ideas, commended for effort - encouragement award - free critique; [oth. writ.] Over 150 poems many with drawings - 21 published in anthologies - one in church magazine - story with drawings for children - music (March) plus other pieces - letter in magazine.; [pers.] Although I read and write I have a learning difficulty - I enjoy writing poetry, I write how I feel and see life, nature, etc. I have also taught myself to play the organ - piano - also paint - some with poems.; [a.] Spalding, Lincolnshire, UK

GILES, VICKY
[b.] 3 January 1981, Boston, Lincs; [memb.] Endurance Horse and Pony Society; [pers.] As a pianist I have been greatly influenced my music, and I find that poetry and music complement each other. May my poetry be a light for many dark minds.

GILL, MARY
[pen.] Mary; [b.] 12 April 1946, Ealing; [p.] Mr. and Mrs. Harrison (Deceased); [m.] Divorced, 11 June 1966; [ed.] Sec-modern school left school at 15. Did 3 years training for hairdressing completed 10 years.; [occ.] Early retirement due to dystomia.; [hon.] Certificates for Hairdressing and also for 10 years as a warden for the elderly. No special Awards. I just gave support and care to people; [oth. writ.] I have never sent my poems before for competitions. I am proud now to have been selected for publication.; [pers.] I love situation poetry and I am a romantic person and enjoy all sentiments that life gives us.; [a.] Ponders End, Emfield, UK

GILL, RUSSELL
[b.] 8 March 1958, Neath; [p.] Denzil Gill, Adeline Gill; [m.] Annette Gill, 17 January 1978; [ch.] Stephanie Louise, Helen Elaine; [ed.] Glan-Afan-Comprehensive Port Talbot; [occ.] Truck Driver (Chemicals); [memb.] Ex Scout Leader Port Talbot; [oth. writ.] A short story for the Good Morning Programme Competition (unpublished).; [a.] Port Talbot, West Glam, UK

GILLIBRAND, CATHERINE S.
[b.] 13 February 1932, Peasdown, St. John, Nr Bath; [p.] Arthur I. Flynn, Lucy E. Flynn; [m.] John Gillibrand, 29 December 1956; [ch.] Antony, Carol, John, Valerie, Diane, Julia and Barbara; [ed.] Talbot Girl's School Ashworth's Secretarial College Moor Lane Computer Research and Technology; [occ.] Secretary/Housewife; [memb.] St. Vincent de Paul Society St. Oswald's Ladies St. Oswald's Choir Amnesty International; [oth. writ.] I have written a variety of poems over the years. The 'Shoe Shine Girl' is the only one I have submitted for publication; [pers.] Poetry illustrates in words the deepest thoughts and emotions in the recesses of our hearts and minds; [a.] Preston, Lancs, UK

GODDARD, WILLIAM
[b.] 17 June 1934, Spexhall, Suffolk; [p.] William Valentine and Lily Goddard; [m.] Rosalind Helen Goddard, Lram Dram, 18 May 1968; [ch.] Angela Marie and Allan David; [ed.] Broome Junior School, Bungay County Modern and Royal Navy; [occ.] Managing Director of Consultancy and Travel Company; [hon.] Astronautical Engineering 22 years in Fleet Air Arms; [oth. writ.] Poems and stories, interview, airline profiles, for various magazines and travel magazines; [a.] Epsom, Surrey, UK

GOIS, MARIA E. M.
[pen.] Elisabete Gois; [b.] 2 August 1975, Portugal; [p.] Maria Gois and Jose Gois; [ed.] Secondary School; [pers.] I have always had this natural poetry talent since I was a little girl and it has always been willing to come out of my soul to be free and known.; [a.] London, UK

GOLDSMITH, CHRISTOPHER
[pen.] Chris Gilchrist; [b.] December 1942, Bournemouth; [p.] Leslie and Pamel Goldsmith; [ed.] Haileybury College; [occ.] Sales Executive London; [memb.] Itchenor Sailing Club; [oth. writ.] Several Articles for magazines; [pers.] I have been greatly influenced by the sea and the Sussex Country Side where I grew up.; [a.] West Wittering, West Sussex, UK

GONSALVES, PATRICIA VERBENA
[pen.] Pattie; [b.] 28 September 1944, Antigua, W Indies; [p.] Deceased; [m.] Divorced, 23 May 1964; [ch.] Rosie, Marjorie, Michael, John, Jr. Vernon, Verbena; [ed.] High School, Grammar School, Night School; [oth. writ.] I have a lot of

unpublished poems.; [pers.] I write poems as these help to express my inermost feelings, my deep concern for the love of God and others, with a desire, that others might be encouraged regardless of what circumstance of life maybe.; [a.] Nottingham, UK

GONZALEZ, ALZAGA SATURNINO
[b.] 19 March 1974, Argentina; [p.] Augusto G. A., Mara Maciel; [ed.] St Georges College (Quilmes) Club De Teatro (CAP); [occ.] Student of Theatre at Buenos Aires; [memb.] Old Georgian Club; [hon.] IB Diploma IGCSE. Progress in English, Plastic Arts. Theatre Festival (Went to "Cuba" as an observer from the Club De Teatro with a scholarship); [oth. writ.] Several poems published in local magazine from Club De Teatro name: Talento short tales and reflections; [pers.] I strive to reflect men decadence. Showing solutions to some cases but not every time. "Pedes In Terra Ad Sidera Visus"; [a.] Buenos Aires, Argentina

GOODCHILD, MISS JACQUELINE
[b.] 5 December 1965, Highbarnet, Hertfordshire; [p.] Dorren Goodchild; [ed.] Livingstone Primary School, and Queen Elizabeth's Girls School; [occ.] Post Woman and Avon Rep.; [hon.] None as yet, but hoping with this one my first.; [pers.] This is a first for me, but in my teens I wrote many songs in my bedroom, only to lock them away from most people. I now hope to rekindle my love for writing, as I'm sure I will have more poems to share with people very soon.; [a.] New Barnet, Hertfordshire, UK

GOODCHILD, STEPHEN WILLIAM
[b.] 11 November 1955, Chatham, Kent; [p.] Richard and Mary; [ch.] Brett, Kelly, Elaine; [ed.] Comprehensive school, private studies; [occ.] Manager, Taxi Concern; [oth. writ.] small stories with meanings and of course poems; [pers.] My writings give messages and something to think about along the lines of life, love, hope, charity, etc.; [a.] Sittingbourne

GOODER, PAUL
[pen.] Spank; [b.] 24 March 1976, Sheffield; [ed.] Kirk Balk, Comprehensive; [oth. writ.] I have two poems published in the book Heart and Soul, one in the book Timely Poets, one in the regional book of anthologies.; [pers.] Through writing songs and poetry I aim to discover, understand and portray my thoughts, feelings and dreams.; [a.] Barnsley, S. Yorks, UK

GOODLEY, IVY MARGARET
[b.] 11 April 1918, London, Eng.; [p.] May and William Hills; [m.] Ronald Ernest Goodley, 24 January 1943; [ch.] Christopher and Jeffrey Goodley; [ed.] Elementary; [occ.] Retired; [oth. writ.] Poetry. Spiritual Meditations; [pers.] I try to reflect all areas of life in what I write, my spiritual life is the most important element and I am guided entirely from what I receive from this; [a.] Holbeach Spalding, Lincs, UK

GOODMAN, GEORGINA
[b.] 26 January 1981, Essex; [p.] Peter Goodman and Pamela Goodman; [ed.] Currently studying at Felsted School; [occ.] Student (currently studying for GCSE's.); [memb.] Thespian Society, Choir, Raf Squad, Shooting Team, various sports clubs (Tennis, Hockey, Netball); [hon.] School prizes for English, History, Religious Studies. Several poems and pieces of art work published in local magazines. I also have an art scholarship at

school.; [oth. writ.] Several poems and pieces of art published in local magazines; [pers.] I hope to portray my concepcions and inner feelings concerning delicate subjects, in my writing.; [a.] Thaxted, Essex, UK

GOODWIN, PAUL
[b.] 18 September 1941, Bermondsey; [p.] George and Grace Goodwin; [m.] Jean Anne, 6 March 1965; [ch.] Karen Denise, Debrah Louise; [ed.] Credon RD sec Mod Bermondford/Ockendon - Lennards Sec' Mod Essex; [occ.] Checker; [oth. writ.] Several, but as yet nothing published; [pers.] I have not been influenced by any poets, I tend to write from personal instances, news media, especially the triviality of wars (IE) Bosnia, Viet Nam, etc.; [a.] Gillingham, Kent, UK

GOOLD, YVONNE C.
[b.] 10 August 1974, Cardiff; [p.] Jeff Goold, Lynda Goold; [ed.] Howardian High School Cardiff, Portsmouth University; [occ.] Student; [hon.] B.A. Honours Geography; [a.] Cardiff, UK

GORDON, MR. AIDEN JOSEPH
[b.] 20 July 1940, Ireland; [p.] Hugh and Bridget Gordon; [m.] Mary Ann, 27 February 1961; [ch.] Aiden, Gerard, Paul, Thomas, Anna Teresa, Joan, Frances; [ed.] Technical College until 16 yrs old Balliwasloe, Co, Galway Eire; [occ.] General Foreman, Building; [oth. writ.] Lyrics for musicals songs etc. Never tried to get them published.; [a.] Birmingham, Warwickshire, UK

GORDON, MARY
[b.] 23 May 1947, Co Cork, Ireland; [m.] 1969; [ch.] Two Daughters; [ed.] B.A. Durham University; [occ.] Housewife; [oth. writ.] Some poetry published in a National Women's Magazine.

GORDON, TANYA
[pen.] Peyton-Lee Paris; [b.] 21 February 1977, Brampton; [p.] Malcalm Gordon and Gail Van-Limbeek; [ed.] Brampton Infants, Brampton Junior William Howard School, Carlisle College; [occ.] Student; [pers.] I hope I reflect in my poetry the feelings and thoughts I've had touching the hearts of others would be a great achievement and an honour.; [a.] Brampton, Cumbria, UK

GOTTING, LYNNE
[pen.] Justienne Tymme; [b.] 1 September 1937, India; [p.] Mr. and Mrs. F. A. Packwood (Deceased); [m.] Divorced (1980), 15 July 1961; [ch.] Gary Andre Philip and Tracey-Anne Mary; [ed.] St. Mary's Convent (Cambridge Cert) and Secretarial; [occ.] Legal Secretary; [memb.] "Reader's Digest"and "Which"; [oth. writ.] A very special poem for my daughter and son-in-law for their wedding day; [pers.] I always only write verse when I need to express my feelings - through floods of tears or peels of laughter in my heart.; [a.] Worthing, West Sussex, UK

GRANT, NICOLA JANE
[b.] 12 August 1970, Banbury, Oxon; [ed.] St Mary's University College (A College of the University of Surrey) and The University of Durham; [occ.] Civil Servant and Student (Medieval History); [hon.] B.A. (Hons) Upper Second Class Theology, RS and History; [oth. writ.] My poem 'The Strange' was published in inspirations from Eastern England in the spring of 96; [pers.] I enjoy reading gothic horror. My favorite poet is Wilfrid Owen.; [a.] Peterborough, Cambs, UK

GRAY, JUDITH A.
[b.] June 7, 1958, Lincoln; [p.] Aileen and Malcolm Elvidge; [ch.] Gemma L. Gray; [ed.] Robert Pattinson School, North Hykeham, Lincs North Lincs College, Inter Business and Admin. College; [occ.] Managing Part Charity Clothing Agency Voluntary Work with Oxfam; [oth. writ.] Selection poems written for my own personal reasons.; [pers.] Poetry for me is a way of bringing the inside out. You could say I'm a "Secret Scribbler" let out of the closet.

GREATOREX, TESSA MARIE
[b.] 5 July 1978, Workington; [p.] Marion and Frank Greatorex; [ed.] Collegiate High; [occ.] Receptionist; [hon.] An award in English Literature and a cert in 'Junior Story Writer; [oth. writ.] I have written other poems but only for my own enjoyment.; [pers.] My main aim in my work is that I carry on writing things I enjoy - I believe if you enjoy doing something, you'll do it with more heart!; [a.] Blackpool, Lancs, UK

GREEN, DAVINA
[b.] 7 December 1976, Hamilton; [p.] Ethel and David Green; [ed.] Hamilton Grammar School, (previously) Beckford Primary. College: Glasgow College of Building and Printing; [occ.] Student of Graphic Design; [memb.] Unicorn Car Club; [oth. writ.] Only my collection of poetry which date back from my first real poem at age 13.; [pers.] In my poetry I strive to see the best in everything, and to enlighten the ignorant. Life is full of magic, we just need to open our eyes.; [a.] Hamilton, South Lanarkshire, UK

GREEN, PHILIP
[b.] 25 May 1950, Lingdale, N. Yorks; [p.] Harold and Violet; [m.] Avril, 15 July 1995; [ch.] Two (Martin and Tracey); [ed.] Brotton County Modern, Sunderland Polytechnic; [occ.] Self-employed Illustrator/Teacher working also for C.C. Education Authority; [hon.] H.N.D. Tech Illustration; [oth. writ.] "Todays The Day", "You Ask Me If I Love You", "As A Kid" and many others unpublished; [pers.] A feeling of being guided spiritually revealing the true sensitive person inside releasing thoughts of love and caring for others!!! Through writings of verse, poems etc.; [a.] Billingham, Cleveland, UK

GREENWOOD, CARON LUCY
[b.] 23 April 1975, Exeter, Devon; [p.] Robert Greenwood, Judith Greenwood; [ed.] Knowles Hill Comprehensive, South Devon Technical College; [hon.] The youngest person in the country (at the time) to pass NVQ level three (Business Administration and Secretarial) doing the first two years of the course in just over a year.; [pers.] After 2 1/2 years Caron became disatisfied with office work and began searching for a new direction. It was a very unsettled period for her. So in order to try and sort herself out she began to write poetry "Soul Searching", being the first. She left her job and entered college to acquire enough qualifications to go to university with the ultimate goal of going into psychiatric nursing. Sadly she never reached her objective as Caron passed away on 25 February 1996 - 2 months before her 21st birthday.; [a.] Newton Abbot, Devon, UK

GREGORY, MRS. PENNY
[pen.] Penny Gregory; [b.] 27 September 1939, Tunbridge Wells, Kent; [p.] Walter and Maud Page; [m.] William George Gregory, 15 November 1958; [ch.] Paul, Mark, Marie and Sean; [ed.] Blessed Sacrament Convent T/Wells Tunbridge

Technical School Tunbridge Wells County Grammar School; [occ.] Financial Consultant; [memb.] School Governor St. Catherine's Littleham from St. Catherine's R.C Church Choir; [pers.] Inspiration comes from many varied occasions whether funny sad or even therapeutic I.E. the loss of a loved one; [a.] Rustington, West Sussex, UK

GREGORY, SOPHIE LOUISE
[pen.] Sophie Gregory; [b.] 27 May 1982, London; [p.] Jocelyn and Martin Gregory; [ed.] Manorhouse School Bookham; [occ.] School Girl; [memb.] Pony Club; [a.] Boxhill, Surrey, UK

GRIFFIN, BRIAN WILLIAM
[b.] 19 June 1933, Caerphilly, SW; [p.] Winifred and William Griffin; [m.] Jean, 2 April 1956; [ch.] Steven, Wendy, Kevin; [occ.] M/C Operator Packaging Industry; [memb.] Amateur Artists Assc.; [oth. writ.] Short stories, various poems (Odd Owens) reflecting events; [pers.] My inspiration stems from a lifetime of memories ranging from child to modern way events; [a.] Machen Newport, Gwent, UK

GRIFFIN, RUBY E.
[pen.] Ruby; [b.] 21 April 1926, Southwork, London; [m.] Gliff James Griffin, 11 December 1976; [ch.] Two; [ed.] Ordinary studied English at St Matthews Church School for Girls at Combervell green S.E.S (was Editor of School magazine); [occ.] Retired; [memb.] So I got was in women's Print Union S.E.1. London, I like fairness in all things look for loyalty in people. Like things of natural beauty. Believe in space. Freedom of speech. Believe in green peace. Friends of earth and believe in space items and believe in God; [hon.] Won Essay, when young temperance. Also lifeboat.; [oth. writ.] "Pondering in Voices on the Wind" of August issues 1996; [a.] Gwent, South Wales, UK

GRIFFITHS, ANDREA
[pen.] 'Angie'; [b.] 31 August 1968, Blackpool; [p.] Alan Clarke (Deceased), Doreen Clarke; [m.] Gareth Griffiths, 21 March 1987; [ed.] Numerous Schooling in the UK And abroad including St. Johns Episkopi Cyprus; [hon.] Several Poems Read out at Memorial Services also had a few Published in Local Magazines and one in a Book; [oth. writ.] I have been writing poetry since I was 15 years old when I first met my future husband to be...Gareth.; [pers.] I get great satisfaction in sharing my poetry with those close to me. My poetry reflects my personality, my thoughts and dreams - Gareth was and is my inspiration...; [a.] Thetford, Norfolk, UK

GRIME, P.
[pen.] Peter Grime; [b.] 6 November 1926, Elloughton Brough, East Yorkshire; [p.] Mr. Charls Grime, Mrs. Lillian Grime; [ed.] Village Schools, left when fourteen; [occ.] Retired; [oth. writ.] Poetry; [pers.] I have never had any poetry published but have sent poems to over thirty publishers and almost always had a good reply; [a.] Elloughton Brough, East Yorkshire, UK

GRIST, HILARY ANN
[b.] 28 January 1942, Frome; [p.] Harold Feltham, Glenys Feltham; [ed.] Oakfield Road Secondary Modern; [occ.] Unemployed; [hon.] Ballet, Tap Dancing, Piano Forte; [pers.] I enjoy writing about every day things in my life, also, in other peoples lives namely - the humorous side. I find my friends say, "A great tonic".; [a.] Frome, Somerset

GROVES, AUDREY
[b.] 8 July 1930, Ilminster; [p.] Maggie Case and Ivor Case; [m.] Malcolm Groves, 11 October 1951; [ch.] Tina Gene, Gregory Malcolm, Kevin Henley; [ed.] Church of England Girls School, Ilminster; [occ.] Retired; [memb.] Ilminster Bowling Club; [oth. writ.] Only for my own pleasure - this time, I was pushed!; [pers.] Learn to enjoy all the beautiful things around you.; [a.] Ilminster, Somerset, UK

GROVES, MRS. B.
[pen.] Bessie Groves; [b.] 17 December 1919, Wootton Courteny; [p.] Edwin and Lucy Quick; [m.] Ernest Groves, 16 December 1941; [ch.] One daughter, three sons; [ed.] Minehead Grammar School Minehead Somerset; [occ.] Retired housewife; [oth. writ.] 3 Poems in arrival press one other poem in arrival press next month.; [pers.] Being a country person I hope my poems give pleasure to someone; [a.] Minehead, Somerset, UK

GURNEY, PETER
[pen.] Basbe; [b.] 11 November 1946, Godstong, Surrey; [p.] Wilfrid and Jean Gurney; [m.] Nee: Betty Mansfield; [ch.] 3 Farm Cats: Smiley, Lily and Nelson; [ed.] St. Catherines Sec Mod., Bletchingley Surrey and Agricultural Courses and Plumpton College; [occ.] Organic Dairy Farmer; [memb.] Founder Member of "Ardingly" C.P.R.E.; [oth. writ.] Several poems written and sent to Magazine but not as yet published - articles written for Agricultural Magazines and 1st chapter on paper for a future novel - when I retire in 15 yrs.; [pers.] My poetry is like looking into a still millpond, reflecting a reversed mirror image of the past, the sadness, tho! Mostly the joy. Thanks to a happy childhood to my parents.; [a.] Aylesbury, Bucks, UK

HAGGERTY, MICHELLE
[b.] 8 May 1978, Edmonton, London; [p.] Michael and Margaret Haggerty; [m.] Single; [ed.] Northumberland Park Community School; [occ.] Office Clerk, Enfield; [pers.] My one wish would be for peace and tranquility, and for others to respect life.; [a.] Tottenham, London, UK

HAIGH, DEBORAH
[pen.] Lucy Morgan; [b.] 4 April 1959, Leeds; [p.] Lucy and Harry Turnball; [m.] Michael Haigh, 4 September 1976; [ch.] Machaela, Melanie, Claire and Lee; [hon.] English Literature; [pers.] I dedicate this poem to my parents, they have been the greatest influence on my life and I love them very much.

HAINSWORTH, KENNETH
[b.] 17 February 1935, Batley; [p.] Harry and Gladys; [m.] Jessie, 31 December 1955; [ch.] Julie and Karen; [ed.] Park Rd Secondary Modern Batley; [occ.] Wine Seller; [memb.] City and Guilds - Leeds Showstopper Entertainment Group and British Actors Equity; [pers.] Make a friend, keep a friend find an enemy make a friend.; [a.] Batley, West Yorks, UK

HAISLEY, MOORE W.
[b.] 9 July 1935, Donaghadee; [p.] Jack and Annie Moore; [m.] Jill, 30 December 1963; [ch.] Michael, Jenni, Sally; [ed.] Bangor Grammar School, Trinity College-Dublin Uni. Presbyterian College Belfast; [occ.] (Semi) retired every man; [memb.] R.A.C.L.D., R.H.F. Association, Hon. Officer 1st Glasgow, Boys Brigade Coll.; [hon.] MA Dublin Univ.; [oth. writ.] Hundreds of Sermons - unpublished, Hobbies Gardening - Golf; [pers.] Was drawn to the writings of John Donne while at

University and to the work of Robert Burns after University; [a.] Livingston, West Lothian, UK

HALL, PHILIP MARTIN
[pen.] Tam Daniel; [b.] 31 January 1950, Leeds, Yorks; [p.] James and Lorna; [ed.] Rock Ferry High School, Birkenhead, University of Life.; [occ.] Self-employed in Fire Protection Industry; [memb.] "Any club that will have me as a member...!"; [hon.] Do not seek them.; [oth. writ.] Many poems published. Currently working on 1st novel.; [pers.] Having letters after your name is no recommendation of competence. It merely means you've passed the exam and paid the fee!; [a.] Birkenhead, M'side, UK

HALL, TERESA
[b.] 15 March 1962, London; [p.] Patrick Cawley and Shirley Cawley; [m.] Terence Hall, 10 November 1990; [ch.] Peter, Richard and Aaron; [ed.] St. Augustines Comprehensive NW London; [occ.] Housewife, Mother; [pers.] Given that my son is unable to speak I hope his feeling can be heard through my writing I shall always be his voice.; [a.] Blackthorn, Northampton, UK

HALLIDAY, CHRISTINE JOY
[pen.] Joy Holden; [b.] 5 January 1953, Sheffield; [p.] Florence and Leonard Townsend; [m.] Brian Halliday, 17 May 1988; [ch.] Stuart Leonard Halliday; [oth. writ.] An entry in the anthology "Between A Laugh And A Tear"; [pers.] I often wonder at nature's creativity and find this a fascinating topic. Writing comedy verse is particularly enjoyable.; [a.] Dundee, Tayside, UK

HALSE, MISS GILLY
[b.] 24 June 1967, Farnborough, Kent; [p.] Michael Halse, Monica Halse; [m.] Martyn Tanner (Fiance), getting married 25 October 1997; [ed.] John Rigby R. C. School Westwickham, Kent; [occ.] In the Shipping/Freight Forwarding Business; [memb.] The Whimsical World of Pocket Dragons. Country Artists Club, Local Gardening Club; [pers.] I find writing poetry very relaxing and rewarding, it puts me in a peaceful state of mind - good for body and soul.; [a.] Swanscombe, Kent, UK

HAMILTON, CLARE
[b.] 21 April 1980, Belfast; [p.] Carol and Derek Hamilton; [ed.] Knockbreda High School; [memb.] Member of Young Farmers Club of Ulster since September 1993; [hon.] Bronze Duke of Edinburgh Award, RSA Clait Stage One; [pers.] I enjoy writing poems based on peace and death. I have been greatly influenced by my family and friends.; [a.] Newtownards, Down, UK

HAMILTON, LYNDA
[b.] 19 April 1978, Lanark, Scotland; [p.] Violet Elizabeth, Allan James; [oth. writ.] Other poems include City life, Chessboard, Emotions, You Do To Me And Fast Moving Beast.; [pers.] "Accused And Naked" was inspired by and written for John Dalrymple.

HAMILTON, MARLYN
[b.] 3 April 1969, Scotland; [p.] James Hamilton, Euphemia Hamilton; [ed.] St. Ambrose Comprehensive School, Lanarkshire; [occ.] Show Jumper/Riding Instructor due to an unfortunate riding accident in May of 1995, I had to give up my life with my horses when in bed recovering I started to write and also to study for a diploma in reading. My writing helps to make up for the loss of working with my horses, I love to write. It has become a passion; [hon.] Studied through London

College of Music at the Thames Valley University, for diploma in reading in December 1995 passed with 83 marks. Currently Studying for an L.L. CM. Dip. in Reading in December 1996. At Glasgow University. Also hold grade five honours in Speech and Drama; [oth. writ.] I have put together a Portfolio with several different variety's of writing including illustration in hope of publication. I have also written a children's book. Called "Stories of Holme Farm" and again will try to have it published soon.; [pers.] Beauty, lies in the simple things in life, if only we would stop and look.; [a.] Glenmavis, Nr Airdrie, Lanarkshire, UK

HAMILTON, VALERIE
[b.] 10 November 1940, Ashburton, NZ; [p.] Gordon and Susie Scott; [ch.] Debra Hamilton - Ede., Kerry Hamilton (two), 34 years old daughter and 31 years old son; [ed.] Educated at Ashburton High School, Trained and Graduated as a School Dental Nurse, Qualified Marriage Guidance and Relationship Counselor; [occ.] Housewife; [memb.] My Local Church; [pers.] I have been writing ever since someone put a pencil in my hand! I aspire to communicate my passion for life to others, through my writing.; [a.] Twizel, New Zealand

HAMMOND, STROMA
[pen.] Mary Nilmot; [b.] 9 February 1938, Salisbury; [p.] Henry Tomlin, Edith Tomlin; [m.] David Hammond, 30 June 1962; [ch.] Trudy Clare, Craig Scott; [ed.] Highbury Avenue School, Salisbury and Salisbury and South Wilts College of Further Education; [occ.] Computer Secretary; [oth. writ.] Published in "Poetry Now - Regional Anthologies - The South East" 1993; [pers.] Life is an experience.; [a.] Ashford, Middlesex, UK

HANNING, MARGARET
[b.] 23 August 1937, Cornwall; [p.] Winifred and William Carthew; [ch.] Susan and Steven; [memb.] Dancing Group (Choreographer), Cats Protection League Writing School; [oth. writ.] Many poems and stories; [pers.] I find writing relaxing. I feel I am a "young" 59 years, I keep myself very busy and active. I help others a great deal and am involved with charity work.; [a.] St. Austrell, Cornwall, UK

HARBARD, NIKKI
[pen.] Nikki Harbard; [b.] 16 October 1969, Beckenham; [p.] Joan and John Harbard; [m.] Separated; [ch.] Reece and Demi; [ed.] Warrenwood Girls Secondary, Rochester, Gravesend College of Technology; [occ.] Unemployed housewife returning to College to become a teacher; [memb.] Martial Arts/Sports Athletic Club; [hon.] None I'm starting access course in Humanities and Social Science September 96 and September 97 Hope to get a place at Greenwich University to study six subject bed in primary education; [oth. writ.] No writings 1st ever application; [pers.] I once become sad and found it hard to talk about my sadness I release my inner thoughts in writing poems. And found I had a talent I was unaware of; [a.] Rochester, Strood, Kent, UK

HARDING, CAROLINE LOUISE
[b.] 6 February 1978, Bristol; [p.] Brian and Eileen Harding; [ed.] Down End Comprehensive School 1989-1996; [occ.] Student, Part-time sales driver in Principles Retail Ltd.; [memb.] Member of Hebron Ranger Unit - Undertaking Duke of Edinburgh's Award - Level Bronze; [hon.] 9 GCSES - and awaiting results of my three A levels in English, German and History; [oth. writ.] A

collection of poetry written since the age of six, all of which is unpublished.; [pers.] I find writing poetry, both enjoyable and exciting. I think the way words and images can express emotions helps us to understand our feelings.; [a.] Bristol, Avon, UK

HARDING, DEREK
[b.] 11 November 1935, Stepney, London; [p.] Patrick Harding, Edith Harding; [m.] Diane Harding, 18 March 1989; [ch.] Andrew, Michael, Christalla; [ed.] Secondary Modern Hamlet of Ratcliffe School Stepney; [occ.] Retired Caretaker; [memb.] Instructor in the 50th Epping Forest South Scout Group and Team Manager of the 50th Scout Football League; [oth. writ.] Poem published in a regional anthology, writes children's stories and children's plays.; [pers.] Think of the time you waste, worrying what might be, instead of getting on with life.; [a.] Meldreth, Herts, UK

HARDS, ETHEL JENNIFER
[pen.] Ewen Rose; [b.] 29 August 1949, Malta; [p.] Horace and Maria Farrow; [m.] John Ronald Hards, 17 January 1996; [ch.] Annalise and Micheal Chandler; [ed.] Notre Dame Convent, Malta, Walderslade School for Girls England; [occ.] Housewife; [memb.] Catholic Women's Guild; [hon.] My 1st Publication in "Quiet Moments." I expected a critical report, please believe me, today you have changed my life forever.; [oth. writ.] Personal stories poetry for friends and family only until now. (Your news to publish my poem came this morning as I was at a how ebb, I now feel inspired again).; [pers.] To Annalise and Michael, "my heart has always ruled my head, it has been both a life saver and a hurdle, I'll never change."; [a.] Hernebay, Kent, UK

HARKNETT, SARAH
[pen.] Sarah Harknett; [b.] 5 September 1978, Milton Keynes; [p.] Norman and Lynda Harknett; [ed.] Walford High School Tertiary College; [occ.] Student at Walford High School; [a.] Northolt, Middlesex, UK

HARMER, DOLLY
[b.] 18 June 1919, Christchurch; [p.] Rev. G. Maurice Elliott and Irene; [m.] Peter (Deceased), 4 February 1940; [ch.] Four Boys; [ed.] Andover Grammar, Sought Hampstead High, Burthwick Teacher Training Open University; [occ.] Retired School Teacher; [memb.] C of E (all Saint LB) Girl Guide (now Trefoil Guild) for 66 years, U and A, Dark Horse Venturer, Table Tennis Coach and Veteran Player; [hon.] Oh BA (Hons) Certificate of Merit (ESTA Award); [oth. writ.] Stories for Children (many), A Few Features, Some Poems. All since retiring.; [pers.] Need constant activities and challenge economical and Anti-Racial enjoy family which, includes 12 grandchildren, swimming and tap dancing, and table tennis.; [a.] Leighton Buzzard, Beds, UK

HARRIS, CLAIRE
[pen.] Claire Harris; [b.] 2 September 1960, Nuneaton; [p.] Albert J. Harris, Irene M. Wilson; [ed.] Stockingford County Junior, Alderman Smith High School; [occ.] A Poor Artist; [hon.] A merit in oil painting, A certificate for good attendance at school; [pers.] I like to encourage others to develop their own artistic talents.; [a.] Bedworth, Warwks, UK

HARRIS, IRIS
[pen.] Elise; [b.] 14 March 1947, Plymouth; [p.] John, Doreen Cowl; [m.] Thomas Harris, 12 September 1970; [ch.] Christopher, Darren, Mathew; [ed.] John Kitto, Comprehensive School;

[occ.] Night Care Assistant; [oth. writ.] First time entrant; [pers.] My knowledge of poetry is limited. But the pleasure I gain from writing my own and reading others is Nirvana; [a.] Plymouth, Devon, UK

HARRIS, LYNNE
[pen.] Kathleen Day; [b.] 29 August 1946, Chesterfield; [p.] Marion and Thomas Wilks; [m.] Keith Harris, 29 September 1990; [ch.] Lorraine, Joanne, Rachel, Andrew; [ed.] Heath County Girls School, Chesterfield Technical College; [occ.] Housewife; [memb.] B.U.A.V., Dr. Hawen Trust Redwings National Trust; [oth. writ.] Several short stories and topical articles. Hope to complete a novel in the near future.; [pers.] I am proud of my families coal mining background and feel that through my writing I can keep alive my heritage.; [a.] Chesterfield, Derbyshire, UK

HARRISON, GEORGE
[b.] 25 April 1969; [occ.] Sales and Marketing; [oth. writ.] 'A New Dawn' published in "Homecounties Poets" (Arrival Press ISBN 1857863011) Volumes of personal writings over the years; [pers.] "To those who walk the lovely mile". "One Day I suddenly realized that though I am many things to many people I am also many things to myself"; [a.] Kings Walden, Herts, UK

HARRISON, JENNIFER BAILEY
[b.] 25 February 1947, Gorleston, Norfolk; [m.] David, 19 April 1974; [ch.] Two adult sons; [ed.] Great Yarmouth High School for Girls, Nottingham University, BA (Hons) 1968, PGCE, 1970; [occ.] Supply Teacher (primary, housewife/writer); [memb.] South Somerset Choral Society, Somerset Wildlife trust; [oth. writ.] 'Every Monday Morning' poems about primary school like, (own imprint) 'Ego Aethelredus' choral work based on local history with composer Nigel Harris. Various poems, articles; [pers.] As a people watcher I enjoy writing about the fables and activities of all age groups. I am particularly interested in local history, legend and love on which to base my work; [a.] Ilminster, Somerset, UK

HARRISON, PATRICIA
[b.] 13 January 1905, Worthing, GB; [p.] Stephens; [m.] Godfrey Harrison; [ch.] Five; [ed.] St Andrews and London University and Dalcroze Institute Geneva, Switzerland; [oth. writ.] Two books of Little Missenden Poems; [pers.] Childhood spent mostly in little Missenden, then continuously from 1933.; [a.] Little Missenden, Amersham, Bucks, UK

HARRISON, PETER
[b.] 7 November 1954, Cirencester; [p.] Charles, Doris Harrison; [m.] Elizabeth Bateman, Living as partners; [ch.] Step daughter Sheryl (16); [ed.] Deer Park School, Cirencester Glos 1966-71; [occ.] (Craftwork) Makes Resin Giftware, Historical Replicas and Sports Memorabilia; [memb.] Have been Member of Assorted Animal Charities ie. (WWF) (RSPB) etc. Rescue Catros (animal); [hon.] Presented to queen as winner of export and design. Award 1991, at Buckingham Palace; [oth. writ.] I have a large collection of poems, some short, some almost short stories. Few poems published in magazines.; [pers.] I like to write oil paint, photograph. Interests nature, animals, varied music especially progressive rock. I like to bring out peoples emotions by my work, perhaps touch a feeling. Would like to hear some of my words to music.; [a.] Cirencester, Glos, UK

HARRISON, PHILIP DILWORTH
[b.] 20 February 1956, Shirley, West Yorkshire; [m.] Teresa Harrison, 17 May 1980; [ed.] Bingley Grammar School; [occ.] Building Society Branch Manager; [memb.] Tavistock Rotary Club, Tavistock and District Chamber of Commerce; [hon.] Fellow of the Chartered Institute of Banker; [a.] Tavistock, Devon, UK

HARRISON, SIMON
[b.] 25 May 1950, Hayes, Middlesex; [p.] Geoffrey and Angela Harrison; [ed.] Vyners Grammar School, Middlesex Bristol University, Southampton University College of Wales, Aberystwyth; [occ.] Archivist; [memb.] Society of Archivists, Chester Archaeological Society; [hon.] Degree in History Post Graduate qualifications in Education and Archive Administration; [oth. writ.] Short stories and poems. One story published in writers own magazine. Special interest in writing Haiku; [pers.] I have been influence by the simplicity and beauty of Chinese and Japanese poetry. In my writings, I am to make every worry count, to express thoughts simply and illuminate Profound truths.; [a.] Chester, Cheshire, UK

HARSE, ELIZABETH ANN
[pen.] "Lisa"; [b.] 2 October 1944, Bristol; [p.] Charles and Betty Oppery; [m.] Rodney H. Harse, 15 January 1972; [ch.] Harse Alexander, Harse Annemarie, Harse Kimberley; [ed.] Left School age 15 years, could with read well - nor spell well my dictionary is my constant companion even today; [occ.] Own/run a small Office/home cleaning service. Successfully 6 years now; [oth. writ.] A life of living `Poetry' some writer down from early years for family's benefit truth they should all at least know the real me.; [pers.] Only you can "Caress your soul with a tender memory"...A smile on the face of every day will be yours from within my writings are my memories and my memories are my life; [a.] Cheltenham, Glos, UK

HARVEY, AMANDA
[pen.] Amanda River; [b.] 27 February 1974; [occ.] Artist, Painter; [pers.] This poem is dedicated to Lynn V. Andrews, with many thanks. It is a tribute to American Indian Healing, and is a celebration of the beauty and the wisdom of our world, and within us all.; [a.] London, UK

HASKINS, HENRY
[b.] 19 July 1947, Emsworth; [p.] Harry and Eve Haskins; [ch.] Ben and Kate; [ed.] Shoreham Grammar; [occ.] Milkman; [pers.] My basic concept of life is to care about friends and family and I try to reflect this in my writing.; [a.] Bognor Regis, Sussex, UK

HATTON, MRS. LEE GOOCH
[pen.] Lee Gooch Hatton; [b.] 12 January 1954, Tonbridge, Kent; [p.] Lawrence and Margaret Gooch; [m.] Barry Hatton, 3 October 1987; [ch.] Sharni, Sherin, Alisha (3 girls); [ed.] Hillview School for girls Tonbridge, Kent; [occ.] Technical Librarian, her Majesty's Forces, Germany; [oth. writ.] A few poems plus a short story published in British Forces magazines in Germany; [pers.] Traumatic experiences throughout my life (ie visiting a mentally handicapped children's orphanage in war torn former Yugoslavia) have always inspired to express my deepest feelings in the form of poetry; [a.] Wallenhorst, Osnabruck, Germany

HAVIARAS, LOUISA BORG
[b.] 13 December 1959, Larnaca, Cyprus; [p.] Paul Borg, Anastasia Borg; [m.] George Haviaras, 27 December 1981; [ch.] Loucas, Anastasia; [ed.] B.A. Greek and English Language and Literature Athens University; [occ.] English Language Teacher; [memb.] Cyprus Board on Books for Young People/International Association of Teachers of English as a Foreign Language; [hon.] Honorary Certificate for an unpublished Collection of poems Sponsored by the Cultural Department of the Bank of Cyprus. Honorary Certificate in the 7th Greek National Poem Competition; [oth. writ.] A collection of poems called "Pale Clouded Yellow" which is coming out in 1996-1997 in the United States.; [pers.] Life is a journey and our experiences along the way provide us with an insight to higher understanding and appreciation of the gift of existence.; [a.] Strovolos, Nicosia

HAY, SHARON
[b.] February 22, 1970, Glasgow; [ed.] Lamlash Primary, Cranhill Secondary, Glasgow College of Commerce; [memb.] International Guild of Songwriters; [oth. writ.] Lots of other songs and poems, but never have tried to get them published.; [pers.] Whatever is for you, will never go by you.; [a.] Glengormley Newtown Abbey, Co. Antrim

HAYES, MARK
[pen.] "Mazy"; [b.] 4 April 1966, Bexhill-on-Sea; [p.] David Hayes; [m.] Sharpa Devi Sharma; [ch.] Benjamin; [ed.] Bexhill High School; [occ.] Quality Assurance; [hon.] London Marathon, Manchester Marathon (sub 3 hours) Seven Sisters Marathon; [oth. writ.] Poems for radio writing poetry for fun. Love to write professionally.; [pers.] Life's too short to worry all day, strive to be happy - life can be okay.; [a.] Gosport, Hants, UK

HAYNES, MARY
[b.] 14 November 1924, Sheffield; [p.] Betsey and Walter Jones; [m.] 4 August 1945, (Divorced) 19 December 1978; [ch.] Alan Haynes and Philip Robert Haynes; [ed.] Local Council School; [occ.] Retired; [oth. writ.] None published; [pers.] I find that writing poems during stress and heartbreak is a great comfort to me, and in times of happiness, inspiration to smile at the world; [a.] Sheffield, S Yorkshire, UK

HAYSLER, MYRTLE
[pen.] Hazel; [b.] 13 June 1920, Cambridge; [p.] Florence and Walter Wright; [m.] Alfred Haysler, 24 June 1944; [ch.] Roger David and Trevor John; [ed.] Haberdasher's Aske's, Hatcham Boys School, London, Liverpool University Malory Comprehensive, London; [occ.] Retired School Secretary; [memb.] The Judy Habbitts Sch. of Dance; [hon.] Pianoforte, National College of Music, Imperial Society of Dance; [oth. writ.] Several poems, published in local daily papers; [pers.] I feel the pleasure of beauteous images that are released in writing is a passion that should be pursued.; [a.] Norwich, Norfolk, UK

HAYWOOD, MR. KENNETH
[b.] 23 June 1927, Coventry; [p.] Emley and Fredrick; [m.] Dorothy Evans, 21 December 1946; [ch.] Christine, Barry, Hazel; [ed.] Coventry Comprehensive School; [occ.] Retired Decorator; [oth. writ.] Two novels of yet unpublished.; [pers.] I have been greatly influenced by early writings of satires, my Philosophy, there's a funny side to everything,; [a.] Shrewsbury, Salop, UK

HEALY, DONAL
[b.] 2 June 1946, Cork; [p.] John Healy, Hannah Healy; [ch.] Ken, Sandra, Fergus, Deirdre, Daniel; [ed.] Fellow - Chartered Institute of Management Accountants; [occ.] Managing Director; [memb.] Lee Valley Golf and Country Club; [oth. writ.] Short stories. One published in local newspaper.; [pers.] To read is to borrow the thoughts of others, to write is to create your own.; [a.] Lowerfarran, Cork, Rep of Ireland

HEAVENS, KATHLEEN
[b.] 1 March 1920, Swindon; [p.] William and Agnes Garrett; [m.] Douglas Heavens, 29 June 1940; [ch.] Janet, Anne, Katrina; [ed.] Infants - Gorse Hill Swindon, Junior - Gorse Hill, Secondary - Euclid Street; [occ.] Retired; [memb.] Methodist Church, Red Cross Age Concern, Ecumenical Parish Choir, Ladies Co-operating Choir; [hon.] Poems published in church magazines, booklet published in Aid of Prospect Hospice, poems published in arrival press books; [pers.] I write what I call every day poetry - my own experiences of life - nothing airy fairy.; [a.] Swindon, Wiltshire, UK

HEAVER, POLLY LOUISE
[b.] 20 May 1979, Chichester; [p.] George Heaver and Shelagh Philip; [ed.] Oakwood Primary and Secondary, Lavant House School, Westonbirt School Glos, South Downs College; [occ.] Art Student; [memb.] Redwings Horse Sanctuary; [oth. writ.] A poem read out on the 'Big Breakfast' channel four. In December 1995. Appeared in 'Wilts a Glos' Newspaper about my poetry; [pers.] Poems art all very meaningful and come from within. I find I can release a great surge of energy whilst writing my poetry. Poetry and Art combined gives my great enthusiasm to control to write and explore.; [a.] Chichester, West Sussex, UK

HEDGES, CAROLE ANN
[b.] 23 November 1958, Lewisham; [p.] Joyce Townson, John Lewis; [ch.] Martin Thomas John Hedges; [ed.] Weald of Kent, High School for Girls Tonbridge; [occ.] Housewife; [oth. writ.] Nothing published until now; [pers.] My poems reflect my feelings during certain events in my life. When my son had leukaemia I found it comforting to put my thoughts down on paper.; [a.] Strood, Kent, UK

HEFFERNAN, JOHN
[b.] 29 March 1925; [ed.] Leaving School Certificate, Self Education, Interests - History - Avid Reading, My Faith - Biographies - Spiritual Poetry; [occ.] Retired - old age pensioner 71 years now - not so active now.; [memb.] Over They Ears, Poetry Classes Interaction and Exchange, History Group (Discussion), Bible Study Circle; [hon.] Yes, I have 4 prize awards. In papers and magazines.; [oth. writ.] Letters and articles for newspapers/comments of interest poetry competitions. Entry for poetry comments and appreciation; [pers.] "A pilgrim through this life" - make all life better for mankind - good friends. Inspiration reading for new poets dear readers - the psalms in the Holy Bible - the divine office - also the words of your hymn book.; [a.] Paignton, Devon, UK

HELLEWELL, JACKIE
[b.] 11 September 1964, Bromley, Kent; [ch.] David Mark Hellewell; [ed.] Presently studying at Hastings College - (3 A'levels 2 GCSE's) hoping to go on to University to get a degree; [occ.] Student; [pers.] Without the constant

encouragement and enthusiasm, combined with the love and support, shown by my brother, Mark Elliott, throughout some of the darkest times of my life, I would not be the person I am today and I thank him; [a.] Hastings, East Sussex, UK

HEMSELL, DELIA
[b.] 12 December 1948, Stanington, Northumberland; [p.] Humphrey E. Shimwell and Barbara D. Shimwell; [m.] Terence Hemsell, 27 July 1968; [ed.] Village School, Pegswood Northumberland, Jeffries Girls School, Kirby-in-Ashfield; [occ.] Disabled, retired through Illness 1981, showing and judging dogs; [memb.] The British Manchester Terrier Club, Melton Mowbray Canine Society; [hon.] S.C.E. English Lit., English Lan., History, Art and R.I. Diploma of Interflora Personel; [oth. writ.] Poems to be published by private author, poems and drawings published in "highlights" B.M.T.C. magazine; [pers.] I am mainly an artist, using my ability to paint canine plus other creatures for the benefit of M.T. rescue. Words just form whilst I am painting. I have numerous paintings in Europe, Australia, Mexico and the U.S.A., and of course the U.K. poems I hope show the unconditional love we have for our pets and vice versa.; [a.] Kirby-in-Ashfield, Notts, UK

HENDERSON, MARIE F.
[b.] 29 October 1916, Peterhead; [p.] Joseph and Jemima Allen; [m.] John George Henderson, 9 May 1944; [ch.] Roy Henderson; [ed .] Peterhead Primary Secondary Education Niagara Falls High School USA and Canada; [occ.] Retired Senior Citizen; [memb.] Ravens Craig Speakers Club, Eastern Star British Legion; [hon.] Apart from Club Presidency and Secretarial offices NIL; [oth. writ.] Stories and articles, poems for various club magazines nothing professional; [pers.] I dedicate my poem to my granddaughter Rebecca with all my love and best wishes when she reaches her eighteenth Birthday; [a.] Peterhead, Aberdenshire, UK

HENDRICKSE, JOHN
[pen.] Johanan; [b.] 15 December 1942, Cape Town; [p.] Archie Hendrickse, Eva Glendenning; [m.] Divorced/Separated; [ch.] John Guy; [ed.] Mann's College, Cape Town South London College of Commerce; [occ.] Development and Marketing Executive; [oth. writ.] Several unpublished poems and writing a biography for a musician; [pers.] Those who betray their dreams answer to the ghosts in sleepless nights. Those who have silver and look for gold will never be satisfied. Those who see their beauty above others, might as well as be blind.; [a.] Sutton, Surrey, UK

HENGEN, TOM
[b.] 15 December 1973, Luxembourg; [p.] Gust Hengen and Marceline Hengen; [ed.] Lycee Hubert Clement Esch/Alzette, Centre Universitaire De Luxembourg, University Of Wales-Aberystwyth; [occ.] Student; [memb.] Aberystwyth University Sub-Aqua Club; [oth. writ.] Unpublished poetry and working on a short story which may be published in a forthcoming anthology of new writers.; [pers.] My major interest lie in the conflicting relationship between the individual and society and the shortcomings of that society though the eyes of the marginal. I'm working on post-colonialism in am influenced by Hemingway, Graham Swift, and Music (Rage Against the Machine, Bob Marley, Nirvana); [a.] Aberystwyth, Ceredigion, UK

HERBERT, MARY
[pen.] Mary Purcell Herbert; [b.] 19 January 1928, Saul., Gloucestershire; [p.] Grace and Ivor Purcell; [m.] George Herbert, 15 May 1949; [ch.] Lorna and Nigel R. A. F.; [ed.] Central School for girls Downfield Stroud, Gloucestershire; [occ.] Retired nurse; [oth. writ.] Poems published in local newspapers and in village magazines.; [pers.] I have a great love of the countryside which was my childhood home. It's characters and customs were mine to enjoy and now, in later years, my privilege to remember.; [a.] Dawlish, Devon, UK

HERLIHY, SHEILA MARIE
[b.] 8 June 1976, Cork, Ireland; [p.] Nora and Finbarr Herlihy; [ed.] Ballingeary Secondary School, Ballingeary, Co Cork, University College, Cork, Ireland; [occ.] I hope to continue further education in September of this year; [hon.] B.A. Honors Degree in English Literature and Irish from University College, Cork; [oth. writ.] Some small amount of poems have been published in their monthly magazine by the Aquarian press in Dublin.; [pers.] Most of my poems address personal issues whilst also drawing inspiration from exterior activities around me. I am primarily interested in the romantic and the congressional poets.; [a.] Inchigeela, Macroom, Cork, Ireland

HERRMANN, GUNILLA L.
[pen.] Anne Robson; [b.] Sweden; [hon.] Grant from the Board of Culture Gotland, Sweden; [oth. writ.] Published in Sweden 1987 Maola Migettlitet Landskap 1990, Den Elaka Flickan Pataket. Poems have been published in the local newspapers.; [a.] San Pedro, Marbella, Spain

HEWIE, ALISON
[pen.] Alison Hewie; [b.] 11 June 1958, Woolwich, London; [p.] John Davidson, Rachel Olive Hewie; [m.] Divorced; [ch.] 13 yr. Daughter, Samantha Rachel McDowell; [ed.] Completed my apprenticeship as proof reader/editor with various newspapers in South Africa. Freelancing is my aim now in fiction writing; [occ.] Proof Reader/Editor; [memb.] South African Writer's Club Lodge Players Amateur Dramatics Society. Involved in children's theatre, running theatre workshops.; [hon.] Gold and Silver Awards in English literature, creative writing.; [oth. writ.] A couple of short children's stories involving insects. Two of my plays were dramatized in South African schools; [pers.] One classic author has "followed" me around - and still does. Charles Dickens. But "My" poet will always be the gentleman who penned "I wandered lonely as a cloud..."; [a.] Spalding, Lincolnshire, UK

HEWLETT, MISS CARRIE
[b.] 11 October 1962, Bristol; [occ.] Medical Secretary; [oth. writ.] Include letters, articles and mystery stories which have been published; [pers.] Always been interested in both reading and writing but this is my first published poem, although I have been composing for many years.; [a.] Bristol, UK

HICKMAN, CAROLE
[b.] 24 December 1974, Co. Durham; [p.] Sheila Hickman and James Hickman; [ed.] Willington Parkside Comprehensive, Co. Durham; [occ.] Waitress; [oth. writ.] I began writing poetry since I was a child I grew up in a small town called Crook in Co. Durham as a teenager I was a rebel moving place to place.; [pers.] I lived with my parents who I dearly love. I moved to Chesterfield alone when I was nineteen I now live in a bedsit. This town is bigger with more chance of life in it.

HICKS, JEAN
[p.] Beatrice and Thomas G. Butler; [pers.] My mother spoke poetry to me as a child, my father played the accordian and sang, it lives deep within me to this day, I can sing, play the keyboard, and read my poems to my grandchildren.; [a.] Deal, Kent, UK

HIGNETT, STEPHANIE CHRISTINE
[b.] January 3, 1975, Liverpool; [p.] Josie and Steve Hignett; [ed.] Saint John Bosco (8 G.C.SE's) 4 A-Levels Gov and Pol. English, Sociology and Psychology.; [occ.] Student, B.A. combined degree, Soc. and Psy.; [memb.] British Psychological Society, Liverpool Football Club; [oth. writ.] Many other unpublished works.; [pers.] Strive to be yourself, and all shall become clear. Thomas Hardy talks of fate, but you have the ability as a human being, to change, reinvention is the key to the disaster of what you do not want to become.; [a.] Liverpool, Merseyside

HILL, AMANDA-JAYNE
[b.] 19 April 1976, Oldham, Lancashire; [p.] Russell Hill and Carole Hill; [ed.] Crompton House C of E School, City College (Manchester); [oth. writ.] Several poems published in church magazine. Poem due to be published September, book messengers from the North.; [pers.] I hope that this gift that God has given me can be used to help and encourage other people. Battling against my rare disease has taught me to trust in God who is the real author of my poems; [a.] Middleton, Manchester, UK

HILLARY, MICHAEL ROBERT
[b.] 24 November 1951, Norwich; [p.] Robert Hillary, Alice Earley; [m.] Heather Margaret Ireland, 24 August 1974; [ch.] Kathrine, Rachel, Matthew; [ed.] Norman Secondary Modern; [occ.] Project Manager Eastern Electricity; [a.] Norwich, Norfolk, UK

HIN, HINDER
[b.] 5 February 1957, Wolverhampton; [p.] Doreen Biggs, John Biggs; [m.] Peter Reynolds; [ch.] Natalie, Sheena, Alex; [ed.] Wightwick Hall school, Wightwick W-DW; [occ.] Housewife, Freelance Interior Des.; [oth. writ.] Poem written for the local hospice; [pers.] Because of personal tragedies the suicide of my father and recently my husband. My mother's death from cancer aged 53. I write from my heart.

HINDES, MISS DEBBIE
[b.] 15 December 1967, Shrewsbury; [p.] Mr. Douglas Hindes, Mrs. Barbara Hindes; [ed.] Meole Brace School, Shrewsbury, Shropshire; [occ.] Dental Surgery Assistant; [pers.] My writing is about feelings, emotions and life, words that everybody can relate to and understand.; [a.] Shrewsbury, Shropshire, UK

HIRD, KAREN ANN
[b.] 22 January 1965, Merthyr, Tydfil; [oth. writ.] I have written many poems which have been received and enjoyed by many on a personal level. As yet I have not thought to put them all together and share them with the general public. 'Facing The unknown' will be my first publication; [pers.] Writing poetry, for me is a very spiritual experience. I am greatly influenced by my own inner feelings and thoughts. My writing tries to reflect and explain how we all try to sort out our feelings at different times in our life. It ranges from happiness and laughter to sadness and sorrow. Thus trying to put our lives into some kind of perspective; [a.] Abergavenny, Gwent, UK

HIRST, LEE
[b.] 21 October 1976, York; [p.] Janet Franks and Bob Hirst; [ed.] Archbishop Holgate Comprehensive; [occ.] Currently unemployed; [hon.] 2 Certificates of Merit from Mensa; [oth. writ.] I also write short stories as a hobby.; [pers.] My first interest in poetry came when I read a poem by Walter D. Wintle.; [a.] York, North Yorkshire, UK

HISCOCKS, MRS. OLIVE
[b.] 30 December 1912, London; [p.] William A. Sparke, Ada A. Sparke; [m.] Harold Burt Hiscocks, 15 October 1938; [ch.] Roger John, Mary Elizabeth; [ed.] Beckenham County School of Girls; [occ.] Retired Florist; [oth. writ.] Two articles in local book of war memories "War Takes Over" and "Battle Of Britain Baby" sold several paintings.; [a.] Orpington, Kent, UK

HOARE, GORDON
[b.] 3 April 1919, Edinburgh; [p.] George and Agnes; [m.] Margaret Kincaid Hoare, 10 November 1951; [ch.] David, Fred, Douglas; [ed.] West Calder High School West Lothian; [occ.] Retired; [memb.] The Royal Naval Assoc.; [hon.] Campaign Medals From 1939-45 Holder of the Malta George Cross Anniversary Medal; [oth. writ.] Many poems-unpublished; [pers.] The best laid plans of mice and men gang Aft Agley.; [a.] Coventry, West Mids, UK

HOBBS, HANNAH
[b.] 31 August 1919, Oldham, Lancs; [p.] Charlotte and Robert Swift; [m.] Harrold Hobbs (Deceased), 5 April 1941; [ch.] Rita and Kenneth Hobbs; [ed.] Elementary; [occ.] Retired; [oth. writ.] Unpublished poems; [pers.] I have been painting in oil's for 25 years and have exhibited several times sometimes I write poems to go with my paintings I like to express my feelings through poetry and painting.; [a.] Banbury, Oxon, UK

HODGSON, JUNE
[b.] 24 June 1935, South Shields; [p.] Joseph Dixon Bamford and Ivy Bamford; [m.] Raymond Hodgson, 31 January 1959; [ch.] Graham Alan, Dr. Jeffrey Mark, Michael David, Hodgson, Grandsons, Andrew and Rowan; [ed.] The Gregg High School Newcastle upon Tyne; [occ.] Retired; [memb.] W.I. Eastern Star. D.C.C., P.C.C., Brownie Leader, (Music Teacher at Home) Sunday School Teacher, produced "Oliver" 1995 with Children's Choir; [oth. writ.] Church of Venerable, Bede. 1937-1987, ISBN 0.9513644.1.3; [pers.] My christian belief has always made me feel and see the beauty in words.; [a.] Newcastle upon Tyne, Tyne and Wear, UK

HOLLIS, MRS. ELSIE
[pen.] Elsie Hollis; [b.] 25 July 1931, Tideswell; [p.] Benjamin Walter, Ella Wrag; [m.] John Hollis (my lovely John), 9 February 1957; [ch.] Elizabeth Oulsnam, my daughter; [ed.] Bishop Pursglove Cofe School, Tideswell, several diplomas in the school of life. I left school at the age of 15; [occ.] Resident Manager of a Sheltered Housing Complex; [hon.] Seven Caring Awards Dealing with Disabilities in the Elderly; [oth. writ.] Lots of poems, plus children's stories up to now, none published.; [pers.] I write about the aspects of life as I experience them. This poem is dedicated to my husband John (my lovely John) who died November 27, 1995. My favourite poets are Christina Rosetti and Malcolm Wilson Bucknell.; [a.] Tideswell, Derbyshire, UK

HOLMES, EDITH
[b.] 25 November 1941, Rothes; [p.] George Paterson, Etta Paterson; [m.] James Holmes, 1 April 1964; [ch.] Debby, Ryan; [ed.] Rothes School; [occ.] Housewife; [pers.] First poem.; [a.] Rothes, Morayshire, UK

HOLMES, LISA
[b.] 17 January 1979, Leeds; [p.] Paul and Brenda Holmes; [ed.] Island School, Hong Kong; [occ.] Student; [hon.] Several prestigious speech and drama awards and winner of the Island school short story competition (senior section) 1995; [a.] Hong Kong

HOLT, ELIZABETH IVOVIC
[b.] 27 January 1961, Kotor, Yugoslavia; [m.] Simon Holt; [ch.] Kent Pilas Holt; [ed.] B.A. Belgrade University, M.A. University of Kent at Canterbury; [occ.] English Teacher; [hon.] T.S. Eliot Poetry Award (UKC); [oth. writ.] Short stories and essays; [pers.] Writing as an instrument of survival; [a.] Reading, Berks, UK

HOLTON, KATIE
[b.] 1 August 1981, London; [p.] Pauline Holton, Patrick Holton; [ed.] St. Clares Primary and St. Benedict's College (Secondary School); [occ.] Student; [memb.] Tiffany Stage Academy of Performing Arts, Youth Theatre; [hon.] LAMDA Drama Examination - Honours, I.S.T.D. Dance Examinations - Honours, London College of Music, Drama Examinations - Honours; [oth. writ.] Poems published in school magazines, poem published in "Poetry Now"; [pers.] I have only just started writing seriously but I know its something I want to do. Reading has been the most influential thing to encourage me.; [a.] Clacton, Essex, UK

HONEYFIELD, MARY
[b.] 28 July 1957, Bristol; [p.] James and Christine Grealley; [m.] Kean Honeyfield, 14 August 1982; [ch.] Debbie and James; [ed.] St. Thomas More R.C. Comp. Bristol; [occ.] Housewife; [oth. writ.] A couple of poems have been published in anthologies; [a.] Bristol, UK

HOOKE, HELEN
[b.] 14 September 1916, Ellerslie, Auckland, New Zealand; [p.] James and Mary Newbold Brown; [m.] Richard Waldron Hooke, 8 August 1959; [ch.] One Adopted Son; [ed.] Hamilton High School (NZ) introduced to lit. By English Teacher wanted to pursue to Uni (passed Matric) 50 years later read English lit graduated Macquarie Uni, Sydney Graduated BA May 1990; [occ.] Retired worked as Private Sec. and later become Reg. Nurse and after marriage worked at home aunties and bring up son.; [hon.] Received a prize for short story - Sydney Eisteddfod 1983, while in N2 Air Force (WAAF) 1942-45 attended Auckland Uni part time under war grant unable to continue moved to Australia mind 50's; [oth. writ.] Have been a spinner since 1972 have written numerous articles for guild magazines.; [pers.] We love family if 4 started on working lives while great depression was still on. Neither of my parents had Secondary Educ., my mother didn't even finish primary, but she was proud of achievements wanted me to do well. My fathers didn't think Educ. necessary my mother died while I was a WAAF.; [a.] Chatswood, Sydney, Australia

HOPE, LYNNE M.
[pen.] Lynne Hope; [b.] 28 November 1947, Hull; [m.] Eric C. Hope, 5 October 1968; [ch.] Lisa

Michelle, Daniel James; [ed.] Wyke Hall High, Hull College; [occ.] Telephone/Telemarketing Training Consultant; [memb.] Institute of Personnel Development; [hon.] National Training Award 1994, Humberside Business Award 1993, Humberside Business Award 1992, Federation of Small Business Award 1995; [oth. writ.] Several articles published in local newspaper and magazines. Short story winner on local radio.; [pers.] My poetry reflects my feelings, cheerful or sorrowful are compiled into verse.; [a.] Swanland, East Riding of Yorkshire, UK

HOPPER, DERRICK
[b.] 4 November 1961, Bishop Auckland; [p.] Derrick Hopper (Deceased), Jean Hopper; [m.] Claire, 6 June 1987; [ch.] Callum (5); [ed.] Various 0 Levels including Maths and English Literature qualified heating engineer; [occ.] Crane Driver (Foreman); [memb.] University of Life; [pers.] My inspiration is my family, live for today for tomorrow may not be yours.; [a.] Bishop Auckland, Durham, UK

HOPWOOD, SANDRA
[b.] 22 July 1951, Bristol; [p.] Rosetta Smart and Kelvin Smart; [m.] Peter Hopwood, 5 September 1970; [ch.] Sarah Hopwood; [ed.] Lawrence Weston, Comprehensive School; [occ.] School meals, Supervisory Assistant; [memb.] R.S.P.B., Runrig Fan Club; [oth. writ.] I poem, 'To a Dying Dolphin' Published in an Anthology 'poetry now, West County Anthology. Many other unpublished poems.; [pers.] My aim is to write poems which will be enjoyed and understood by all. I refute critics that poetry can only be of merit if it is abstruse.; [a.] Yate, South Glos, UK

HORNE, MRS. JANET E.
[b.] 27 April 1958, Huddersfield; [m.] Mr. A. J. Horne, 13 September 1996; [ed.] Melbourne Australia; [occ.] Care Assistant; [memb.] Baptist Church also Supporter of Varied Charities; [hon.] Biology Award, Psychology Award, and First Aid; [oth. writ.] Awards in Australia for numerous poems.; [pers.] I enjoy creating poems concerning nature and animal welfare to which I feel strongly for.; [a.] Huddersfield, WY, UK

HORSFIELD, GORDON
[pen.] Gordon Barrie; [b.] 27 May 1926, Sheffield; [p.] George William and May Horsfield; [m.] Divorced; [ed.] Elementary Plus Private Study; [occ.] Retired/one year Suez Contractors Fire Service, 32 years Fire Service Senior Officer, 11 years Fire Advisor - Boots the Chemists; [memb.] Member of the Institution of Fire Engineers; [hon.] Medal - General Service Medal (Palestine) Jubilee Medal, Fire Service Long Service and Good Conduct Medal; [oth. writ.] Numerous poems and short stories. A number of which have been, published 'shake hands with a bayonet' an account of the experiences of 450 contractors interned by the Egyptian Government for about 8 weeks during the Suez war 1956 as yet unpublished.; [pers.] Although influenced by earlier poets I constantly strive to write poems which are different.; [a.] Newhaven, E. Sussex, UK

HORSHAM, JEAN MARGARET
[pen.] Jean Auchinleck; [b.] 16 August 1937, Plymouth; [m.] William, 1957; [ch.] Six plus fostered 100 plus; [ed.] Plymouth, Malta, Cyprus, Egypt, Hongkong, Malaysia; [occ.] Nurse, Teacher, Revenue Officer, Welfare Manager I.T. Trainor etc.; [oth. writ.] Always been a writer;

[pers.] I write what I feel I don't care if you read it but if you share my experience its nice not to be alone on this planet.; [a.] Whitley Bay, Tyne and Wear, UK

HORTON, ZENA ANNETTE
[pen.] Zena A. Horton; [b.] 24 January 1933, Wolverhampton; [p.] Olive G. Haynes and Reginald F. Haynes; [m.] Les Horton, 4 July 1954; [ch.] Janet Louise, Robert William and Caroline Anne; [ed.] The Royal Wolverhampton School, Penn Road Wolverhampton; [occ.] Chief Baby Sitter; [memb.] Family Member of the Hornby Railway Collectors Association; [hon.] R.W. School prize for Magazine Article 1950 second prize School Centeneny Essay 1950; [oth. writ.] Poems for school magazine 1950 Hornby Railway Collectors Association Magazine, and Arrival Press, School Centeneny Essay 1950; [pers.] Writing in all forms has been my interest since the age of eleven. I have kept a daily diary, every day, since January 1958 to date. Regular letter writing to my school friend June Beales, is important to me.; [a.] Ferndown, Dorset, UK

HOULDEN, PATRICK
[b.] 5 June 1969, Alton, Hants; [oth. writ.] 1) Heat of the Moment, 2) The Unspoken; [pers.] The only gift I possess is life.; [a.] Portsmouth, Hampshire, UK

HOWARD, DIANE
[b.] November 15, 1942, Portsmouth; [p.] Joy Ansell and Tom Ansell; [m.] Cliff Howard, March 31, 1962; [ch.] Andrew Francis and Julian Robert; [ed.] Cranbourne Secondary Modern, Windsor Grammar School S.E. Berks. Coll. of Further Ed.; [occ.] Administrator; [hon.] Area Finalist - Daily Mirror Mrs. Britain Award 1971; [oth. writ.] Poems published in other anthologies short plays have been staged in the past for local church youth group; [pers.] I would like to think that my poems cover any occasion and suit every emotion. My inspiration comes from everyday life and the people I meet I listen to conversations, and many of my titles and poetic content comes from them.; [a.] Bracknell, Berkshire

HOWLETT, MARY
[b.] 9 February 1982, Dublin; [ed.] Goldenbridge Secondary School, Second Year Student; [memb.] St. James Band Dublin; [hon.] Two Certificates of Merit in the Gerard Manley Hopkins Poetry Competitions 1994/1995. Runners up prize in the National Poetry Competition, category under 20 years 1993 for the European Year of Older People.; [oth. writ.] Various other poetry.; [a.] Inchicore, Dublin 8, Ireland

HRIPAC, VLADIMIR
[b.] 28 July 1968, Belgrade; [ed.] Engineer of Architecture; [occ.] Architect - Designer; [oth. writ.] A collection of poems, several essays on art, and essays on ancient, renaissance and Japanese architecture.; [pers.] I am deeply interested in Buddhist, especially zen-buddhism, trying to achieve the real human nature. I have been greatly influenced by T. S. Eliot, Jacques Prevent, Haiku and Zen-poetry, and writings of Aldous Huxley, Hermann Hesse, D. T. Suzuki and Erich Fromm.; [a.] Belgrade, Yugoslavia

HUGHES, EDITH MAY
[b.] 26 June 1918, Hengoed; [p.] William Richard and Margaret Hannah Brown; [m.] Emrys Jenkin, 20 July 1939; [ch.] Alwyn and Judith; [ed.] I was educated at the local Hengoed School; [occ.] Retired (House wife); [hon.] Bronze Medal Cooking

Award; [oth. writ.] Two poems recently published dedicated to mum "Mother" and carnival celebration Island Moods and Reflections.; [pers.] My grandchildren David Matthew Rhys and HUW keep me youthful in both spirit and out look. In my Poetry I try to reflect my views and experiences of Life. Since retiring writing poems gives me great satisfaction an sense of achievement.; [a.] Hengoed, Mid-Glam, UK

HUGHES, PAUL ROBERT
[b.] 1 March 1996, London; [p.] Eric and Sheila Hughes; [m.] Lisa Christina Hughes, 23 May 1992; [ch.] Kurtis Paul Hughes; [ed.] Bromfords Comprehensive School; [occ.] Welder (Aviation); [oth. writ.] Other poem's not as yet published; [pers.] I write how I feel on every day subjects; [a.] Chelmsford, Essex, UK

HULME, MARY
[pen.] Ditto; [b.] 13 August 1923, Stockport; [p.] Bertha and James Irwin; [m.] Allan F. Hulme, 4 February 1950; [ch.] Three; [ed.] Church of England School (St. John The Baptist-Heaton Mersey: Stockport); [occ.] Retired (Civil-Servant); [memb.] Heaton Mersey Community Centre, Revue Society Member, Civil Service Society, P.D.S.A. St. John's Church, A Founder Member of our Local Tenant's Association; [hon.] Stockport, Seroptomist runner-up of above for 1996. When young I won gold, silver, and bronze medals and certificates for ballet, tap and comedy dancing; [oth. writ.] Stories (children's) hymns, songs, and poetry. I came 12th in a hymn writing comp. run by B.B.C. (Title "I Just Want To Say Hello Lord"); [pers.] I believe in loving `all men', keeping our country beautiful, looking after our wild-life, and countryside, I can't abide cruelty to any animal, we are their voice, believe in our royal family.; [a.] Manchester, Lancs, UK

HUME, ELSIE
[b.] 31 March 1935, Sunderland; [p.] Anthony and Ethel Coyne; [m.] Norman Hume, 19 May 1955; [ch.] Norman, David, Jacqueline and Julie; [ed.] West Park Grammar School; [occ.] Domestic Charge Hand, Tywyn Cottage Hospital; [oth. writ.] I have written poems for my pleasure and I am writing my life story.; [pers.] I write for pleasure and relaxation also the written word is something for my children and grandchildren to remember me.; [a.] Tywyn, Gwynedd, UK

HUMPHREY, VIRGINIAN JEANETTE
[b.] 4 January 1952, St Albans; [p.] Fred Humphrey (Deceased), Eileen Humphrey; [ed.] Townsend Cofe Girls School Cassio College; [occ.] Production Section Manager; [hon.] G.S. Medal; [pers.] If in some way a poem lights your heart, the flame will linger for ever; [a.] Grantham, Lincs, UK

HUMPHRIES, TAMSIN
[b.] 31 October 1970, Swansea; [p.] Maisie and Peter Humphries; [m.] John Knight Clement (Deceased); [ch.] Laura Jane Humphries; [ed.] Bishop Gore Comp.; [occ.] Single Mum; [pers.] Dedicated to: John Knight Clement who died 8 August 1995, age 25. Until we meet again!; [a.] Swansea, W. Glam, UK

HUNT, MRS. ELLEN JOAN
[pen.] Nellie Atkins; [b.] 30 September 1924, London; [p.] Herbert Atkins and Mabel Atkins; [m.] Calfred William Saunders, 31 March 1945, (2nd) George John Hunt, 29 December 1984; [ch.] Thomas, Rita, Jennifer, Shelley, Beverly; [ed.] Blackfen Central, Sidcup, Kent, Bluecoat School

for Girls, Point Hill Greenwich, London. (Secondary); [occ.] Retired. (Printer) for 20 yrs. commuting to London offices.; [memb.] R.A.FA Basildon Club Labour Party, Pitsea Basildon, Essex. During working life joined Variety and Drama Associations of British Road Services for Container way. Did several shows at Cripplegate Theatre.; [hon.] Stations at Swingate, Dover, joined as Volunteer Women's Royal Air Force for 3 1/2 years. Trained as M.T. Driver in Morocambe, Lancs, during World War II was removed after marriage to have child.; [oth. writ.] None other than diaries and letters to press; [pers.] I was one of the pioneers for establishing a new St. Mary's Church in Peckham, London. I also, since moving to Basildon with half a dozen volunteers, started the (1958) Basildon Royal Air Force Association Club and was "Wings Officer for 2 years.; [a.] Basildon, Essex, UK

HUNTER, ROSS
[b.] 13 September 1977, Irvine, Scotland; [p.] Alex and Julie; [ed.] Brannock High (Newarthill); [occ.] Unemployed Fencer; [oth. writ.] Poems - Growing, Forever You, A Promise, A New Hope and Bitter Taste, although as yet unpublished; [pers.] I'm inspired by the seemingly everyday normal things in life. That others let pass them by.; [a.] Newarthill, Lanarkshire, UK

HURST, STUART D.
[b.] 1 September 1976, Wigan; [p.] Jean Hurst, David Hurst; [ed.] Abraham Guest High School; [occ.] Factory Worker; [pers.] We have no real control over events or our own lives. Something is controlling us. The closest we ever get to freedom is poetry.; [a.] Wigan, Lancs, UK

HUSSEY, MIK
[b.] 23 April 1957, Bradford on Avon, Wiltshire; [p.] Pam Blythin; [m.] Sue Hussey, 21 February 1992; [ch.] Marc, James and Nichola; [ed.] Toll Bar. Waltham, N.E. Linces, Own Promotion Company Alley Cat Promotions; [occ.] S Manager of a Reservation Home; [memb.] West End Bowling Club, British Region Social Club; [hon.] Bachelor Society, Bachelor at Heart 1994, Bachelor Society, Cultural Attache. 1995....; [oth. writ.] Gubbinz (Magazine) Lyrics for rock bands Tiggy and The Tom Cats. Crooner With A.K., Null and Void, Kissing The Peach, Baby Won (short stories); [pers.] Smash the chains that hold us all. There is no truth, only belief.; [a.] Grimsby, NE Lincs, UK

HUTCHINSON, BEVERLEY
[pen.] Beverley Hutchinson; [b.] 16 June 1952, Jamaica; [m.] March 1985; [ch.] One daughter; [ed.] Mayfield School, Putney; [occ.] Housewife; [hon.] Voice Training and speech and drama; [oth. writ.] Poems for family and friends in birthday cards; [pers.] To be able to communicate to all.; [a.] Tolworth, Surrey, UK

HYDE, ELLEN MAY
[b.] 5 May 1981, Birmingham; [p.] Angela and Anthony Hyde; [ed.] Devonshire Rd, School and Holly Lodge High School, Smethwick, Warley, W. Midlands; [occ.] Schoolgirl; [hon.] This is the first time I have entered a poetry competition, and the first publication - it's wonderful!; [oth. writ.] A few short stories and poems reflecting my view of life; [pers.] Being a teenager I know the stresses and feelings of young people - but there is world out there, life is exciting. Life is learning all the time, to 'Feel', to be 'Aware' is important.; [a.] Birmingham, West Midlands, UK

IAN
[b.] 5 March 1976, Dunstable; [p.] Ray and Jan; [ed.] Normal Schooling, Life Guard and Gym Qualifications; [occ.] Life Guard; [pers.] Enjoy life.

IMAM, EMANUELA
[pen.] Cassandra; [b.] 17 June 1963, Prague, Czechoslovakia; [p.] Italian; [m.] Pakistan, 18 March 1989; [ch.] Zac, Isabella, Anastasia; [occ.] Homemaker and Inventor; [memb.] Theosophical Society Bufora; [pers.] When we walk in the light of the Golden Orb, we walk in the shadow of our soul.; [a.] London, UK

INKER, L. DAVID
[b.] 15 November 1946, Bristol; [ed.] Ordinary, Currently Studying an Information Technology Course; [occ.] Security Engineer; [oth. writ.] The Theory of Electromagnaesis. (Writing still in progress.) The Theory of (Electromagnaesis).; [pers.] I think that everyone, should follow their dreams at least once. In their life time and who knows what might happen.; [a.] Bristol, Bristol, UK

IRWIN, SAMUEL T.
[pen.] Samara; [b.] 25 November 1957, Limavady, NI; [p.] Samuel A. and Martha Irwin; [m.] Carol M. Clean, 27 June 1981; [ch.] Christina R., Laura A., Heather S.; [ed.] Dungiven County Secondary, Limavady Technical N.W. College of Technology, Londonderry University of Ulster; [occ.] Assistant Station Chemist (Nigen) and Northern Ireland Mc Tours Guide; [memb.] EMA (EPEA), Christian Motor Cyclists Assn' (C.M.A.); [oth. writ.] 'Thought for the Way' and 'Irish Light' in motorcycling magazines. Articles in community news and secular articles in National Motorcycle magazines and papers.; [pers.] Have Jesus first in your life and you cannot be last! Write what you feel as it comes even when 'on the move' - 'polish' the material later.; [a.] Whitehead, Antrim, UK

ISWERWOOD, JANET ELIZABETH
[b.] November 21, 1952, Widnes, Cheshire; [p.] James and Violet Brookes (Father Deceased); [m.] John (Deceased) Now engaged to George McNorton; [ch.] Four; [ed.] Fairfield High School; [occ.] Part time work, full time mother; [oth. writ.] Local newspaper, church magazine, many to various poetry anthologies; [pers.] I have only been writing for a short time and have been successful. I hope to have my own book one day. I write all types of poetry which I hope will be an inspiration to others. I suddenly found my gift in poetry.

ISLAM, NINA
[b.] 21 October 1977, London; [p.] Tajul Islam, Nurun Nahar Islam; [ed.] Newham Sixth Form College (New Vic) Prince Regents Lane, Plainstow E-13 London; [occ.] Student of a levels in English Literature and Sociology (Finished a levels in June 1996); [hon.] Hoping to go on to further education to get a teaching degree; [pers.] Personally I do not know if I have been influenced or inspired by anyone to write poems, but only know that I first started to write in order to reflect my emotions, whether it be happy or sad.; [a.] London, UK

IVANS, NORAH
[b.] Birmingham; [m.] Walter Ivans; [ch.] Five; [occ.] Housewife; [hon.] Holder of Birmingham's gold medallion for poem "The Birmingham Centenary", poem in the Archives at and for Oscott College 150 years celebration; [oth. writ.] In local newspapers the Focas, The Northern Star

and The Castle Bromwich Gazette; [pers.] I read my poems at womens clubs and the proceeds go to children in creed; [a.] Birmingham, West Mid, UK

IZIKY, AMIRA DAVID
[b.] 3 July 1978, Juba, Sudan; [p.] David Iziky, Kassech Sewell; [ed.] Western Middle School, Burnside High School, North Tyneside College; [pers.] The one certain thing about life is that sooner or later everybody dies, and that the only true immortals are words.; [a.] Wallsend, Tyne and Wear, UK

JACKSON, ENID
[b.] 29 December 1931, Jamaica; [p.] Una Pennant, Joseph Pennant; [m.] Lenord Jackson; [ch.] Dalbert, Owen, Cheryl, Floyd Dennis, Byron Mark; [ed.] Thompson Town School, Mico Training College - Jamaica; [occ.] Retired Midwife, Voluntary Bereavement Visitor; [hon.] S.R.N., R.M.; [oth. writ.] Book of poems published this year 1996; [pers.] I have always loved poetry. Now I am retired and working with bereaved people many of my poems reflects life in different ways.; [a.] Neasden, London, UK

JACKSON, STEPHEN JOHN
[pen.] John Joseph; [b.] 5 April 1951, Liverpool; [p.] James Jackson, Teresa Jackson; [m.] Brenda Jackson, 17 November 1979; [ch.] Darran Nathan, Joshua Mathew; [ed.] St Andrews Sec Mod, Liverpool, Halton Technical College; [occ.] Approved Electrician, construction; [memb.] Institute of Advanced Motorists; [pers.] Life's experiences has greatly influenced my thoughts as expressed in my words; [a.] Rhuddlan, Denbighshire, UK

JACKSON, T. P.
[b.] 24 April 1953, Co. Armagh, N Ireland; [p.] Malachy and Brigid Jackson; [ed.] Currently Studying for degree in Eng. Literature and French Literature - Part-time at Kingston University; [occ.] Customs Officer; [oth. writ.] Poetry and a few short stories - nothing as yet published as I have never sent anything for publication.; [pers.] I write for pleasure and to record moments in time, memories and events that I have experienced. Nothing serious (not in the league of many others).; [a.] Cressington, Surrey, UK

JACQUES, GOANITA ERNESTA ISABELLA MARIE
[b.] 10 September 1959, Holland; [m.] Susan Goodwin, 10 September 1994; [ch.] Richard White, Yarrow Wild, Louis Wild; [ed.] Very Little; [occ.] Writer and Philosopher; [oth. writ.] Poem ("The Photo") and article included in "Bad Reputation," ed. Tina Kendal, poem ("Boots") in poetry now anthology 1996. Poem ("The Sisters Three") received commendation by judges, in '94 Margot Jane Memorial poetry price, published in booklet.; [pers.] In my poetry I explore different aspects of my inner and outer identity, and express a range of emotions, from pain to joy - hoping that the written word be a pathway to better communication and understanding.; [a.] Hebden Bridge, West Yorks, UK

JAFFRAY, FRANCES S.
[b.] 6 October 1943, Aberdeenshire; [p.] James and Margaret McKnight; [m.] George R. Jaffray, 11 May 1943, Aberdeenshire; [ch.] 2 daughters and (2 stepchildren daughter and son); [ed.] Ellon Academy then B.A. Degree - Open University; [occ.] Care Team Leader in a Church of Scotland Home for Elderly; [memb.] Country and Western

Music Clubs Interest in Handcrafts; [oth. writ.] 3 poems published in anthologies by Triumph Press Peterborough. Runner up in a local magazine poetry competition.; [pers.] I am very proud to be related (on my mother side) to the Celebrated Buchan Poetess Flora Garry. Her work has influenced me a lot, and I find it easier to write in the Doric (Buchan Dialect).; [a.] Ellon, Aberdeenshire, UK

JAMES, PAMELA
[b.] Cornwall, UK; [p.] Doris and Jack Pitts; [m.] Jimmy James; [ch.] Sara Jane; [ed.] Private School, Birmingham, UK; [oth. writ.] Poetry and short stories unpublished; [pers.] I like to remember John fleming who was chairman of our voluntary group who encouraged me to write my poetry and entertain the senior citizens and the less fortunate people in South Africa; [a.] Walkerville, Gauteng, UK

JAMIESON, ALISON
[b.] 6 August 1957, Elgin; [p.] Donald and Isabella Cuthbert; [m.] Michael, 25 July 1975; [ch.] Simon, Peter, Michelle; [ed.] Seafield Primary and Elgin Academy; [occ.] Housewife and Crofter; [oth. writ.] Short article in the farmers weekly magazine.; [pers.] I think that everyone is good at something so I am trying to discover just what it is that I might be good at. I have always had an active imagination or so many mother used to say anyway.; [a.] Helmsdale, Sutherland, UK

JEEVARATNAN, KAREN
[b.] 19 August 1967, London; [p.] Charles and Mary Jeevaratnan; [ed.] Copeland High School Wembley, south London College Knights; [occ.] Manager; [pers.] I think poetry should overcome barriers of race religion greed and love.; [a.] London, Levishman, UK

JENKINS, JOHN
[b.] 7 January 1942, London; [p.] Rose Jenkins, Jack Jenkins; [m.] Margaret Ann, 10 July 1965; [ch.] Paul John Sharon Ann; [ed.] Secondary School; [occ.] Maltings Operator in the Brewing Industry; [memb.] Riven Hall Oak Golf Club, Witham Bowls Club, Wickham Bishops Snooker Club; [oth. writ.] Two poems published in company magazine, one poem published in anthology Paths to a Poet.; [pers.] I write poetry on most any subject, some serious, but I do like to write humour into poetry. I also write short stories in rhyme.; [a.] Witham, Essex, UK

JENKINS, LINDSEY
[b.] 28 March 1952, Enfield, Middx; [p.] Ivy Rann, Joshua Rann; [m.] Anthony Gordon Michael Jenkins, 1 November 1986; [ch.] Amanda Jane and Donna Louise; [ed.] Carterhatch Jr School Enfield Middx Suffolks Sec Mod, Enfield, Middx; [oth. writ.] Several poems published in various anthologies; [pers.] I like to think that my poems communicate, and that people can relate to them, I do not think poetry should be obscure leaving and reader to search for the meaning.; [a.] Kirby Cross, Essex, UK

JENNER, WILFRED
[pen.] B. Jenna; [b.] 12 November 1929, Kent; [p.] Fathers origin Norway, English Mother; [m.] Italin, May 1958; [ch.] Four Boys; [ed.] Life; [occ.] Retired; [oth. writ.] Various poems and short stories; [pers.] I simply regard myself as an ordinary person who happens to love poetry and art; [a.] Bletchley, Bucks, UK

JENNINGS, VALERIE
[b.] 27 September 1947; [m.] Donald Jennings, December 1978; [ch.] Helene Jane, Victoria, JoAnne and Robert James; [ed.] Slough High School for Girls. Roehampton Institute of Education, London University.; [occ.] Teacher becoming mature student - restoration and conservation; [hon.] BA (open) P.G.C.E. Adv. Dip. E.D. (Technology); [oth. writ.] Previously published poetry; [pers.] I feel that poetry should be a reflection of life and it's emotions and is a much underestimated art form.; [a.] Spalding, Lincs, UK

JENSEN, MARGARET M. FOSTER
[pen.] M. M. Foster-Jensen; [b.] 20 February 1938, Liverpool; [p.] Mary and James Foster; [m.] Hans Jorn Jensen; [ch.] Dean, Russell, Jorn, Annita; [pers.] The challenge of using words provides a platform to express life.; [a.] Liverpool, Lancs, UK

JESSON, ROSEMARIS
[b.] 16 June 1959, Vermont, USA; [p.] Rosemarie A. Maryea and Gary Charles Maryea; [m.] Maxwell P. Jesson, 10 August 1991; [ch.] Krystle Anne, Sabrina Luisa, Joshua Jake; [ed.] Corona Academy Stage School - Kent College, Pembury Kent; [occ.] Housewife/Mother/Student; [hon.] Various Certificates for Verse Speaking, Qualified Ball Room/Latin American Dance Teacher to Bronze Standard. Arthur Murrays, Diploma in Child Psychology; [oth. writ.] Nothing published before but have compilation for my own Anthology of poetry. Hoping to be published one day.; [pers.] My writing comes straight from my heart giving me freedom to express my feelings, thoughts and emotions. Whenever my writing touches another persons life only then are my poems given meaning.; [a.] Coulsdon, Surrey, UK

JOHNSON, CLARE
[b.] 12 May 1971, Stoke Mandeville, Buckinghamshire; [p.] Dr. Hilary Johnson and John Johnson; [ed.] John Colet School, Wendover and Aylesbury College, Aylesbury; [occ.] Secretary; [memb.] AMSPA - Assoc. of Medical Secretaries and Practice Administrators; [pers.] I enjoy expressing my thoughts in words and dedicate this poem to Ben who is my inspiration; [a.] Wendover, Bucks, UK

JOHNSON, JOAN
[pen.] Val J. Johnson; [b.] Bristol; [m.] Doug Johnson, 9 September 1961; [ch.] Paul, Sarah, Amanda, Rachel; [occ.] Business woman, owner of two restaurants; [hon.] Hon. B.A. U.S.A.; [oth. writ.] Newspaper articles published in several newspapers; [pers.] Being a pastor's wife for thirty years, I believe nothing happensto us by accident but by the providential hand of God. Most of my inspiration is derived by the ordinary, everyday things around me.; [a.] Tooting Bec, London

JOLLY, JUNE LILLIAN
[pen.] June Carron; [b.] 14 June 1941, Margate; [p.] Elizabeth and Joseth Brewer; [m.] John Dere Jolly, 17 June 1989; [ch.] Maxine Segrue, Michele Segrue; [ed.] St. Anne's Convent; [occ.] House wife; [memb.] Drama Group Brockley SEG London; [oth. writ.] Auto Biography from the age of 4 years till 16 years called The Violation Of Innocents not published yet; [pers.] Love of writing poems, stories, drama, music; [a.] Catford, London, UK

JONES, CHARLES ALUN
[b.] 9 December 1940, Nantymoel; [p.] Alfred Thomas Jones, Sarah Margaret Boobyer; [m.]
(Partner) Valerie Mary Way; [ch.] Simon, Gregory; [ed.] Ogmore Grammar, Bridgend Tech. College; [occ.] Security Officer; [hon.] A medal for running Cardiff Marathon in 4 hrs.; [oth. writ.] Several poems published with anchor books.; [pers.] I have been influenced by poems in my mother's magazine written by "Patience Strong". I find when a poem comes to mind. You must write it down or it can be lost forever.; [a.] Bridgend, Mid-Glamorgan, UK

JONES, CLARISSA
[b.] 10 July 1911, Maerdy; [p.] Sussanah and Thomas Evans; [m.] Allin Jones, 11 August 1945; [ed.] Infants and girls schools, Maerdy Secondary School, Ferndale, Bangor Normal College - 2 yrs.; [occ.] Retired teacher was deputy head of warstones infts. school Wolverhampton; [oth. writ.] Stories; [pers.] I still believe that the romantic poets - Wordsworth, Shelley keats etc are the best in English Literature. Wordsworth's "Intimations of Immortality" voices my own beliefs.; [a.] Llandudno, Gwynedd, UK

JONES, MRS. ELIZABETH ANNE
[pen.] Elizabeth Jones; [b.] 24 April 1967, Liverpool, England; [p.] Michael James Lawson and Catherine Anne Lawson; [m.] Richard William Jones, 7 August 1993; [occ.] Student of life; [oth. writ.] 'Holly' - a children's story about the origin of Christian history. 'All God's Children' a book of verse expressing ones individual perspective on a journey through life.; [pers.] As I stretched out my hand and cried out from my heart He lifted me up. The giver of life had awakened me from my spiritual sleep. A peace, pain ceased, love and joy swept over me in great waves. My eyes were opened. I had been touched by a Gentle, Almighty, Personal God. I knew that my life had been irrevocably changed. The journey into all truth and begun. This is the source of all my expression the identity of this source is Christ.

JONES, MRS. ELSIE
[b.] 11 July 1914, Orrell, Bootle; [p.] Catherine and James Lyons; [m.] William John Jones (Deceased), 12 May 1934; [ch.] Three Daughters and Six Grandchildren; [ed.] Elementary; [occ.] Retired; [memb.] Singing Group at Church; [hon.] 19 letters from the Royal Family for poems submitted. First prize 15 pounds, Ormskirk Senior Citizens, First Ponting, 4 Publications in Anthologies (another following), publications in Newspapers, photos and write-ups, Letters from Consultants and Celebrities, (for poems), reading of my poems at various places, poems read out over radio 4 (a few years ago), (also radio Merseyside); [oth. writ.] Lyric of song - "Wilderness of Dreams"; [pers.] I have been greatly inspired by famous poets and found poetry-writing a wonderful outlet.; [a.] Liverpool, Lancs, UK

JONES, MR. ERNEST ERIC
[pen.] Mr. Richard A. Roberts; [b.] 9 October 1913, Nottingham; [p.] William Henry Jones; [m.] Georgina Elizabeth Jones, 29 December 1980; [ch.] Nine sons, six daughters; [ed.] My Education St Pauls School Secondary; [occ.] Retired; [memb.] Publishers; [hon.] Certificate Grant of Patent, Tractor Trailor, Safety Cables; [oth. writ.] Collection of Modern Poems, Book Title, To Each His Own Collection of Modern Poems For The Young; [pers.] Started writing in 1980 modern style verse served. Petty officer first class Era SRR. Seven Brothers served in the war, five came back.; [a.] Colindale, London, UK

JONES, GWYNETH
[b.] 5 March 1952, Bangor, N. Wales; [p.] Jeffrey Talbot and Buddug Mary Talbot; [m.] remarried to David Jones, 26 July 1995; [ch.] Robert John Lees, Marsha Lees; [ed.] Deiniol School, Bangor, Coleg Menia, Bangor; [occ.] housewife; [oth. writ.] Several other poems published, magazines, written book on different religions; [pers.] I am greatly inspired by the harm that the world is facing, which prompts me to write down my despair. I hope one day mankind will be aware.; [a.] Holyhead, Gwywedd

JONES, GWYNNETH
[b.] 12 April 1962, Bradford; [p.] Vera Jones and Ernest Jones; [m.] (Fiance) Geoff, Divorced; [ch.] Kayleigh, Marie; [ed.] Eccleshill Grammer School and Night School for shorthand; [occ.] Mother; [oth. writ.] Have written a book of poetry/which I'm hoping to get published. It specializes on child abuse.; [pers.] I hope through my poetry to help other victims of child abuse, to help them strive to understand and learn and also to educate society.; [a.] Bolton, Lancs, UK

JONES, MR. JOHN L. H.
[pen.] Bigfellow; [b.] 3 May 1913, Brighton; [p.] Both Deceased; [m.] Lilian Jones (Nee Plunkett), 30 March 1938; [ch.] Twelve; [ed.] Balham Grammar School Peterhouse Univ. Cambridge Reading Law; [occ.] Retired; [oth. writ.] Life story and book of short stories limited editions bound for family only. Started doing poetry last year while in hospital. Never submitted any for publication.; [pers.] I wrote many poems and short stories for the family. Others have read them and quite impressed, but I have never submitted any before this to the Library of Poetry.; [a.] Bosham, West Sussex, UK

JONES, OWEN D.
[pen.] Owen Dan Jones; [b.] 17 April 1926, Towyn, Merioneth; [p.] Lawrence Jones and Elizabeth Jones; [m.] Eileen Annette Chapman, 29 June 1948; [ch.] Martin Jones, Lawrence Jones; [ed.] Towyn High School, Gordonstoun; [occ.] Retired Jeweler; [memb.] Burton Golf Club; [hon.] F.G.A. (Fellow of the Gemmological Assoc.), D.G.A. (Gem Diamond Diploma), H.R.D. (Diamond Diploma Antwerp); [oth. writ.] Poem (The Gulf Statue) published poetry now 1996; [pers.] Influenced by nature and my view of humanity, and the works of Betjenian and Walcott.; [a.] Ashbourne, Derbyshire, UK

JONES, OWEN J.
[b.] 23 September 1920, Bettws, Bridgend; [p.] John and Gwenllian Jones; [m.] Merill (Nee Thurman) (Deceased - 1976), 12 January 1946; [ch.] Glynda and Elaine; [ed.] Bettws Council School and Garw Grammar; [occ.] Retired, (War Pensioner) RAOC 5 1/2 years; [hon.] 2nd Prize Gas Council, Paper of the year 1958, WW II Campaign Medals. France, Germany Star 1939, As Star, Defence Medal, Service Medal; [oth. writ.] Anthologies and so it goes (Arrival Press) The Marching of the (Anchor Books), Poets' Retreat (Anchor Books), Chosen Grace (Anchor Books), Voice From Wales (Anchor Books), Christian Verse From Wales (Anchor Books), Sheltered From The Cold (Anchor Book), Poets Debut (Anchor Books), Voice In the Wind (Int. Society Poets); [pers.] Admirer of early Romantic Poets. In addition to later writers such as, Robert Brooke, Masefield, De La Mare. I still think poetry should Rhyme; [a.] Bettws Bridgend, Mid-Glam, UK

JONES, PETER E.
[b.] 9 August 1921, London; [p.] Sidney and Gertrude; [m.] Jill Eira, September 1951; [ch.] Two boys and one daughter; [ed.] St Benedicts Ealing; [occ.] Retired; [oth. writ.] Some childrens books for parents to enjoy (none published); [pers.] Too old to seek fans, but would like to share some things I have written with a wider audience. Main influence has been taken, with Lewis Carroll and Kenneth Grahame and A. A. Milne; [a.] Wickham Market, Suffolk, UK

JORDAN, WILLIAM
[pen.] William D. Jordan; [b.] 17 November 1976, Co. Down; [pers.] My poems are songs and scenes in the rooms and corridors of the castle of my imagination. If I can isolate these incidents I will find inner freedom.; [a.] Down, UK

JOSEPH, MRS. MARY
[pen.] Mary Joseph; [b.] 18 January 1937, West Indies; [p.] Maria and Edgar Davis; [m.] A. S. Joseph, 21 June 1959; [ch.] Ms. Lorraine and Ms. Sharon, (grandson) Phillip (4); [ed.] All Saints School, Antigua West Indies; [occ.] Retired Lady; [memb.] The Poetry Society; [oth. writ.] Several poems published in Anchor Books, Arrival Press and Triumph House Books.; [pers.] I am striving to reflect some goodness to mankind in all my writing. I had this great influence for the love of poetry from my head master Mr. O'Maude. He gave me also that urge and appetite for books.; [a.] London, UK

JOSLYN, GWENDOLYN HAZEL
[b.] 8 January 1922, Southend on Sea; [p.] Elsie Charity (Jones Nee), Thomas Jones; [m.] Raymond Anthony Joslyn, 1942 Divorced 1971; [ch.] Three Boys, Two Girls; [ed.] Leyton School of Art; [occ.] Carer Housekeeper; [memb.] RSPB Community of Poets (Canterbury); [oth. writ.] Poems for children and odd short stories, for pleasure as yet unpublished "The Grandchild" published in community of poets publication.; [pers.] Write just for my family and my love of words. At school disliked sport or physical exercise and was punished by being made to learn poems - to my delight; [a.] Hythe, Kent, UK

KADANDARA, JOYCE
[pen.] Joyce Kadandara; [b.] 21 July 1938, Zimbabwe; [p.] Phillip and Gertrude Mbofana; [m.] Jeconiah A. T. Kadandara, (Deceased) 10 February 1968; [ch.] Two boys; [ed.] BA (hon) Sociology and Public Administration. Post graduate Dip Social Admin. Qualified Nurse/Midwife.; [occ.] Deputy Secretary Health Support Services, Minghealth, Zimbabwe; [memb.] Global Commission on Women's Health. Focal person on women's health issues: Zimbabwe member of Zimbabwe Nurses Association; [hon.] Prize winner in Nursing Schools, Whittington hospital U.K. Member ICN professional Services Committee Geneva (1989-1992); [oth. writ.] Articles to Professional Nurses Association, American Nurses Association, ICN Geneva, expression of caring in Nursing book published by the college of Nursing Florida Atlantic University USA; [pers.] I believe women are an endangered human species, whose inherent inner strength has made them survive against all odds, and are now posed for a "take off" into the 21st century.; [a.] Harare, Zimbabwe

KANE, DERICK
[pen.] D. F. Hazell; [b.] December 1955, Hamilton, Scotland; [ed.] King's College, London; [occ.] Music Teacher; [hon.] B. Mus, L.T.C.L.; [oth. writ.] Music articles written and songs published in various periodicals; [pers.] I reflect in my poetry the deep love shown to me by H. M.; [a.] London, UK

KAUR, JASBIR
[pen.] Jesse Kaur; [b.] 12 December 1979, Dudley; [ed.] King Edwards VI College, Stourbridge; [occ.] R. E., History and English A-Levels; [oth. writ.] Several other poems written and also a few short stories; [pers.] Religion is a major part of my life and greatly influences my writing.; [a.] Dudley, UK

KAYE, ZOWIE JADE
[b.] 24 April 1981, Wiltshire; [ed.] St. John's Comprehensive Marlborough, Wilts, John O'Gaunt Comprehensive Hungerford, Berks; [occ.] School student; [hon.] BBC Wildlife Magazine award for Nature Writing - Highly Commended (1991), gained 3rd position in Photography Competition run by Hungerford Camera Club (1995); [pers.] I think it is good to observe your thoughts through writing.; [a.] Hungerford, Berks, UK

KEARNEY, KIM Y.
[b.] 11 June 1956, Leicester; [p.] Yvonne and Richard Kearney; [ch.] Jade and Nathan; [ed.] English Martyrs, followed by South Fields College, qualified in Hairdressing City and Guilds; [occ.] Mother, Child Care; [hon.] City Guilds Hairdressing; [oth. writ.] A few verses several years ago but nothing ever shown to anyone, or published.; [pers.] I chose to call my poem rebirth, as I felt it, was giving birth to a part of myself, to share with others maybe to see their self, in what I had written, and that it may help them. With love Kim.; [a.] Leicester, Leicestershire, UK

KEAVEY, BRYAN
[ed.] Braken Hill (Pre-School), Burrow Natinal (Junior), Suiton Park School (Senior) all in Howtte; [occ.] Barman in Baldwyle, Dubun 13 Pub; [memb.] Life Member of Amateur Football Club can Howth Cettc; [hon.] Two Medals, Gold and Silver during a School Sports Day; [oth. writ.] Song lyrics, poems, one novel. I'm working on a series of short stories set in a new york police prescient at the moment and hope to put the last act to a play.; [pers.] I wrote this shortly after the canary wharf trembling in the hope the Northern Ireland peace process would not end.; [a.] Howtte, Dublin 13, UK

KEECH, MARIAN
[pen.] Martinella Brooks/Agnes Mae; [b.] 31 August 1938, Southampton; [p.] Berlie C. Young and Doris Young Nee Morris; [m.] Divorced; [ch.] Richard Gordon; [ed.] St. Joseph's R.C. Southampton; [occ.] Unemployed; [memb.] C. Companion; [hon.] Diploma Acc. Children's Writers, Runner Up, H. Commended several times for both Adult/Children's short stories. and runner up in 1995 Amn. (American Newsletter) competition short story. 2 Poems local paper. Engl. Lang./Lit.; [oth. writ.] Five poems in four separate anthologies re-arrow books Peterboro.; [pers.] I always do my best, and if I fail at least I tried. I have been influenced by Dickens, Shelley, and Kahlil, Gibran.; [a.] Weston-super-Mare, North Somerset, UK

KEEL, MISS JULIE ANNE D'ARRY
[b.] 13 June 1964, Ormskirk; [p.] Mrs. Sheila Keel and Duncan Keel; [ed.] Maghull Deyes High School; [occ.] Branch Manager Hospital Division; [pers.] Dedicated to a brave lady who is my sole mate she, (Sheila) a mother who I will love for ever. Thank you for everything the white Tornado!; [a.] Walton, Liverpool, UK

KEHOE, TONYA
[b.] 16 February 1981, Wexford; [p.] Theresa Kehoe, The late Michael Kehoe; [ed.] Colaiste bride Secondary Education to date; [occ.] Student; [oth. writ.] Other poems and short stories but nothing published.; [pers.] Poetry is the only way I can do justice to the beautiful things that inspire me.; [a.] Boolavouge, Wexford, UK

KELLY, BRIAN
[b.] 11 December 1946, Dublin; [p.] Patrick Kelly, Nancy Kelly; [ch.] Tara Kelly, Stuart Kelly; [occ.] Airport Police, Dublin Airport; [oth. writ.] Three poems published in (in-house Runway Magazine) several poems specially written for friends for special occasions: (Births, Deaths, Anniversaries among others). I am currently writing a book on the life 'n' times of Martin Kilgallon: A one-time legend of Dublin Airport. To be published by Aer Rianta (The Airport Authority) in 1997; [pers.] My poems and stories reflect 'Life' and the way we are affected by it.; [a.] Inglewood, Clonsiwa, Dublin 15, Ireland

KELLY, CIARA
[pen.] Ciara Kelly; [b.] 17 August 1979, Dublin; [p.] Brendan and Teresa Kelly; [ed.] Loreto Secondary School, Balbriggan, Co Dublin; [occ.] 6th year student in Loreto Secondary School; [memb.] Digges Lane - The College of Dance, Dublin; [hon.] Various awards for performing arts and dance. Various school achievements also; [oth. writ.] Various poems unpublished; [pers.] To my family, relatives and friends, thank you for being there for me. You all mean so much to me. My poems are influenced by family, friends, surroundings, experiences and feelings.; [a.] Naul, Dublin, UK

KELLY, EVA
[b.] 10 January 1930, Gateshead; [p.] Grace and Edward Iredale; [m.] Sidney (Deceased 24 July 1995), 8 July 1950; [ch.] Four - Brian, Alan, Peter, Susan; [ed.] Gateshead Central School; [occ.] Mother, Grandmother, Church Voluntary Work, Guide Association; [memb.] Guide Association, Church of England; [oth. writ.] Story, which I read on local radio. Four children's stories published in "Brownie" magazine. Several poems for guide movement and church. Songs - words and music for children's concerts.; [pers.] My husband was my inspiration and mentor. I write from the heart, and my future writings will be in Sid's memory and honor. Have written many poems for my grandchildren.; [a.] Newcastle upon Tyne, North Tyneside, UK

KELLY, MERYL ANNE LINDEN
[b.] 9 November 1941, Radcliffe; [p.] Charles A. L. Kelly, Edith Kelly; [ed.] Stand Grammar School for girls, Bury Technical College, University of Salford; [occ.] Analytical Chemist Consultant to Gilbert International; [memb.] Royal Society of Chemistry; [hon.] C. Chem., MRSC; [oth. writ.] Internal Company Scientific Reports Only.; [pers.] This poem was written during my school days. Due to its commendation by my, then, English mistress, I thought it worthy of further assessment.; [a.] Radcliffe, Manchester, UK

KELSEY, IRENE
[b.] 6 June 1919, Birmingham; [p.] Howard and Millicent Lane; [m.] Edward Kelsey, 25 April 1980 (2nd Marriage); [ch.] Roger, Lynne, Alan, Paul and Steven; [ed.] Woodstock Private School, Handsworth, Birmingham and also Elementary Schools; [occ.] Retired Sec/P.A.; [hon.] Pass with

London Writing School, Mensa Certificate for Unsupervised Work, Pass for Pitman's Script with Pitman's College; [oth. writ.] Novel (unpublished). Several short stories. Other poems accepted and published in anthologies. First and second prizes in Local Essay Competitions; [pers.] Life itself, and personal experiences, are my inspiration.; [a.] Sutton Coldfield, West Midlands, UK

KEMP, CHRISTINE LESLEY
[b.] 17 December 1960, Edmonton; [p.] Stanley Kemp, Doris Kemp; [ed.] Community School, Tottenham, Barnet College, North London Consortium, Open University; [occ.] Senior Nursery Officer. Under fives Centre; [memb.] North London Spiritualist, Church, Silver Cord Association; [hon.] N.N.E.B., D.P.Q.S.; [pers.] All poems that I have written have been inspired by the earth, heaven and my life itself; [a.] Edmonton, London, UK

KENNEDY, PAUL
[b.] 17 October 1973, Weston-super-Mare; [p.] Margaret Kennedy, Rod Kennedy; [ed.] Priory Secondary School, Weston-Super-Mare College of further Education; [occ.] Diary Operative; [oth. writ.] Published in two books, poets in the West Country, and The World At My Feet.; [pers.] Do not just read poetry, see it and feel it. There is a wealth of imagery and emotion sat behind each word that will enhance and open up your imagination.; [a.] Weston-super-Mare, Somerset, UK

KENT, KATRINA FAY
[pen.] Katrina Kent; [b.] 17 September 1976, Cornwall; [p.] Una Kent, Martin Kent, Adrian Thomas; [ed.] Richard Lander School and Truro College; [occ.] Student/Pit Sales Representative; [pers.] Within my personal poetry I portray both my vivid imagination and personal experiences through life. My words reflect issues important to myself.; [a.] Truro, Cornwall, UK

KERR, MARIAN
[b.] 12 June 1932, Vimy Ridge; [p.] James and Mary Hunter; [m.] Dead, 5 November 1951; [ch.] Two Sons; [ed.] Model School till 14 years of age Technical College Night Classes; [occ.] Housewife, Retired; [a.] Ballymoney, Antrim, UK

KERSHAW, DEREK C.
[b.] 24 February 1934, Timperley, Cheshire; [p.] Charles E. Kershaw and Winifred Kershaw; [m.] Christine Anne Kershaw, 15 August 1989 (Second Marriage); [ch.] Charles Martin, Ralph Adrian, Deborah Lynne; [ed.] Stretford Technical College; [occ.] Retail Music Shop Professor; [memb.] Too busy trying to earn a living now-a-days! Used to be a member of several Tennis Club, Golf Clubs and Art Groups; [oth. writ.] Poems in local papers; [pers.] I do not take a leaf out of any other poets notebook-nor am I influenced by any other writings - but am more influenced by my own experiences and reflections of life.; [a.] Rhos-on-Sea, Clwyd, UK

KETTERIDGE, DAVID
[b.] 12 August 1947, Birmingham; [p.] William and Mary Ketteridge; [m.] Pauline Ann, 29 September 1976; [ch.] Deana, Carrie Anne, Dale, Neal; [pers.] All through life we experience inspirational moments. We either cast them away to memory or capture them. Like the artists the poet creates a picture, rather words, for all to appreciate; [a.] Birmingham, UK

KILPATRICK, KIM
[b.] 27 April 1963, Down Patrick; [p.] Robert and Lydia Morrison; [m.] James Kilpatrick (Deceased),

20 March 1984; [ch.] James Darah and Melissa Kimberly; [ed.] Killyleagh High School; [occ.] Full time poetry writer and full time mum; [oth. writ.] Several poems published in "poetry now anthologies."; [pers.] "My wild heart", was written for my husband who passed away suddenly this year, 7 weeks after I had composed the poem. I dedicate it to his memory and to his great love for Strangford Lough over whose islands he roamed freely.; [a.] Killyleagh, Down, UK

KING, MR. A. S. G.
[pen.] Albert Samuel George; [b.] 18 September 1906, London; [ed.] Elementary; [occ.] Retired Since 1966; [oth. writ.] Unpublished, perhaps you will allow me to send the enclosed for you perusal. "The War and After" which I wrote in 1942 but never proceeds with publication.; [pers.] I have never made any application for publication of any of my poems. I leave it with you to elucidate; [a.] Worthing, Sussex, UK

KING, JOAN
[b.] 26 September 1939, Harrogate; [p.] John Pollard and Jane Pollard; [m.] Leonard King, 4 July 1959; [ch.] Linda, Michael, Shelley, Andrew; [ed.] Harrogate grammar school; [occ.] Office Manager; [oth. writ.] Short story writing and humorous verse, mainly for friends and colleagues.; [pers.] I write from the heart about life as I see it, but I particularly favour a by gone, more genteel era.; [a.] Sutton, Surrey, UK

KING, MARGARET M.
[b.] 14 June 1936, Howden, Yorks; [p.] Sydney Thompson, Ethel Thompson; [m.] George King, 18 August 1956; [ch.] Susan Heather, Stephen John; [ed.] Queen Anne Grammar School, York; [occ.] Financial/Payroll Administrator-Hotel Complex; [memb.] Emperors Fitness Club, Interval International; [oth. writ.] Previous poems have only been written for friends and local competitions quite successfully.; [pers.] I find that writing poetry is the way of expressing my personal feelings and true personality. This has been my first attempt into serious competition entry.; [a.] York, Yorks, UK

KINGSTON, JOANNA E.
[b.] 20 February 1942, Derby; [m.] David R. Kingston, 17, October 1983; [ch.] David, Paul, Dean; [ed.] P.N.E.U. Ashbourne Derbys Grammar School Ilkeston Derbys; [occ.] Clinical Specialist in Infection Control (James Paget Hospital NHS Trust); [hon.] S.R.M.: Diploma In Management Studies, Diploma in Nursing Studies, Higher Certification in Infection Disease Studies; [oth. writ.] Publication professional journals: Nursing Professional Nurse local publications; [pers.] I believe that: Effective communication leads to enhanced and mutual understanding of each others' experiences in life. I remain totally fascinated by all forms of poetry! From the earliest to the most recent.; [a.] Ormesby St. Margaret, Norfolk, UK

KIRK, ALAANA
[b.] 5 February 1966, Welling; [p.] Barbara and Williams Michael Stewart (Divorced); [m.] Graham Kirk, 5 February 1983; [ch.] Katie - 13, Dean - 12, Graham - 10 and Scott - 9; [ed.] Bexley Grammar School Welling, Kent; [occ.] Housewife; [oth. writ.] I have not had any of my work published before, (An honour at my first attempt!) Although I have my own folder, of which I have titled 'Lou's Mood)' (a nickname since childhood) full of poems that simply reflect my own emotions and moods. Be they happy or sad.; [a.] Erith, Kent, UK

KIRKUP, NIGEL BARRON
[pen.] Nigel B. Kirkup; [b.] 12 February 1963, Ebchester; [p.] James Albert Kirkup and Muriel Kirkup; [m.] Helen Kirkup, 15 August 1990; [ch.] Polly Emma Kirkup; [ed.] Blackeyne Comp School Co. Durham; [occ.] Entertainer, Singer Cartoonist; [hon.] Diploma in Cartoons and Illustration; [a.] Ebchester, Consett, Durham, UK

KNIGHT, PATRICK
[b.] 29 March 1945, Liverpool; [p.] John and Eliza Knight; [m.] Evelyn Alicia, 23 May 1992; [ch.] Bernadett, Stephen, Tina, William, Heather, Elizabeth; [ed.] Our Lady of Mount Carmel S/R School Liverpool 8; [occ.] Cleaner; [oth. writ.] Only poems for family and friends; [pers.] Poetry I find is one of the best form of self expression.; [a.] Runcorn, Cheshire, UK

KNOWLES, CHARLES PATRICK
[pen.] Pat Knowles; [b.] 17 March 1955, Derby; [p.] John and Margaret Knowles; [m.] Julia Rosa Knowles, 23 December 1992; [ch.] Lewis Charles, Rebecca Jane; [occ.] Formula One Engine Tester; [a.] Northampton, N. Hants, UK

KYNOCH, JOSEPH
[b.] 13 March 1929, Edinburgh; [p.] Deceased; [m.] Olive Marion, 23 December 1968; [ch.] One stepson; [ed.] Elementary; [occ.] Retired, Civil servant; [memb.] Society of Authors; [oth. writ.] The Naked Soldiers published by Excalibur Press of London and 'Nakne Soldater' published by Aschoug of Oslo 1995.; [pers.] Don't look at the mountain - climb it!; [a.] Stubbington, Hants, UK

LAING, ALISTAIR
[b.] 24 August 1950, East Calder; [p.] Alistair and Susan Laing Nee Cross; [m.] Marie Laing Nee Russell, 21 February 1981; [ch.] (Step) Angela, Carla, Steven; [ed.] East Calder Jun. Sec., Bathgate Tech College; [occ.] Maint' Fitter; [oth. writ.] Mostly comic verse in the work place, and personal poems.; [pers.] I was influenced by Robert Burns at an early age and tend to think there is something in his works for everybody and every occasion.; [a.] Livingston, West Lothian, UK

LAITHWAITE, BERLY
[pen.] Jessie Cook; [b.] 5 September 1934, Southampton; [p.] Claude Smith, Jessie Smith; [m.] David Laithwaite, 26 March 1960; [ch.] Perry, Darren, Kim, Scott; [ed.] Itchen Grammar School Adult Education, French, Astrology, Creative Writing; [occ.] Housewife; [oth. writ.] Poems published in nine anthologies. Interested in short story writing, but none published yet. Pen name only used in story writing.; [pers.] Writing poetry allows me to express my feelings. I admire the artistry of Elizabeth Barrett Browning and Christina Rossetti.; [a.] Southampton, Hants, UK

LAMB, CHRISTINE
[b.] Darlington; [p.] Deceased; [m.] Hoyd, 1 April 1961; [ch.] Three children; [occ.] I work in the community as Auxiliary Care Nurse; [hon] Sociology, English Language; [oth. writ.] Poet of the month is Darlington Crown Library. "My poems read out on Radio Cleveland."; [pers.] I began writing poetry in 1983. Mainly for my mother, who had a terminal illness, it gave her great, pleasure to listen to my poetry read out aloud. My poem "Leaving to Cope" was read aloud at my mother's funeral.; [a.] Darlington, Durham, UK

LAMB, LILIAN MAY
[b.] 12 February 1909, Liverpool; [p.] Alice Argyle and William Argyle; [m.] George Edward Lamb, 8 April 1933; [ch.] Veronica Jane; [ed.] Several Junior and Secondary School Leaving at Age 14; [oth. writ.] Poems published in local church magazines; [pers.] I started writing poetry in my seventies as I became increasingly housebound. I firmly believe it was a gift from God to help fill the hours. For my philosophy in life, I quote from a poem "I am aware of God's sun who gave his life to save me and claimed my love, life and service for all eternity."; [a.] Wolverhampton, West Midlands, UK

LAND, BRIAN
[b.] 8 April 1948, Plymouth; [p.] Philip Leslie, Elsie May Land; [m.] Sylvia Lillian, 8 April 1978; [ed.] Laira Green Secondary, Modern Plymouth Devon; [occ.] Retired; [memb.] Volunteer Worker, Alzheirens Disease Society, Volunteer Worker For National Schizophenia Society; [oth. writ.] Poems published, The Holocaust (2040 A.D.), Brief Affair, Last Words to Sylvia, Connie, The Disaffected, Too Late; [pers.] Poetry is the finest weapon man has ever possessed. It can convey anger, love, ideas, and humour. And is the true communicator. There are no barriers in verse.; [a.] Plymouth, Devon, UK

LANDES, ALISON
[b.] 18 June 1977, Aberdeen, Scotland; [ed.] Studying creative writing, acting, and art in first year at Regent's College; [oth. writ.] Writing short stories and poetry for my own enjoyment but hope to publish my stories one day.

LANE, MR. JACK
[b.] 21 July 1920, Clapham, South West London; [m.] Eileen, 29 September 1945; [ch.] Jennifer and Nina; [ed.] St. John's Bowyer and Lanfranc Schools; [occ.] Retired; [memb.] All lapsed....; [hon.] Awards for Music Festival achievements. Many years ago.; [oth. writ.] Through the years various essays, verse, stories... including one translated for publication in Russia. Circulated accounts of wartime experiences and travel. Happiest when writing and most comfortable resorting to the written word.; [pers.] For sheer phonetic relish and his exquisite gift of suspension my favorite poet is - Robert Burns. If a sick and tired society becomes uglier with every passing day - at least there is the consolation that things of indelible beauty become rare jewels of increasing value.; [a.] Weston-super-Mare, Somerset UK

LANE, LORRAINE ELIZABETH
[pen.] Lorraine Lane; [b.] 22 January 1959, Alton; [p.] Michael and Giana Harying; [m.] Simon Michael Lane, 23 June 1990; [ch.] Sonia-Marie, Carla-May, Lauren Giana; [ed.] All-Saints School 1964-66, Saint Laurence School 1966-70, Amery Hill Secondary School 1970-75; [occ.] Registered Childminder; [oth. writ.] Contributions, to inspirations from Southern England, A Mixed Bag, On Mother Natures Doorstep (3 separate books) by Anchor Books. I've also had poems in local papers and I write poems for family and friend; [pers.] I believe that if the words that come from my heart, can touch another, its poetry.; [a.] Alton, Hampshire, UK

LANG, ALAN DOMHNULL
[b.] 21 October 1968, Coatbridge, Scotland; [p.] Anne and Peter Lang; [ed.] Rosehall Secondary School, Coatbridge; [occ.] Warehouse Operative for Salvesen Logistics in Livingston; [memb.] Scottish Society for Prevention of Cruelty to animals (SSPCA), Scottish Wildlife Trust (SWT); [oth. writ.] Over twenty other writings so far unreleased.; [pers.] I love to write about the beauty of nature and of the wonders of the inner mind. Most of my writings deal with the subjects of fictitious creatures or historic battles. There's much more below the surface; [a.] Livingston, W. Lothian, UK

LANGFORD-JOHNSON, WILLIAM
[pen.] Langford (Sketching and Painting etc); [b.] 15 April 1913, Burton-on-Trent; [p.] Deceased; [m.] Frances Langford-Johnson, 1 October 1945; [ch.] Richard and Michael, daughter - Josephine; [ed.] Doncaster Grammar School, Leeds University School of Architecture and Leeds College of Art; [occ.] Retired Chartered Architect, Practicing professional artist; [memb.] Fellow of the Royal Society of Arts, Retired Associated of the Royal Institute of British Architects, Member of the Royal Glasgow Institute of the Fine Arts, Past membership of the Corps of Royal Engineers, serving in India and Burma, 1939-1946; [hon.] D. arch. Dist'n. (Leeds) F.R.S.A. td. A.R.I.B.A., Award for Architectural design. Award from R.N.L.I. for artistic services; [oth. writ.] Inclusion in the book of "Scottish Poets", Several poems in local press.; [pers.] One only gets out of this world that which one puts into it but there is no harm in hoping for a bonus.; [a.] Tigh-na-Bruaich, Argyll, UK

LANGLEY, MRS. NORMA
[b.] 18 May 1937, Caterham; [p.] Jack and Doris Rice; [m.] Len, 21 March 1959; [ch.] Derek, Bruce, Cathy, Tracy; [ed.] St. James Primary Brightlingsea, Colchester County High School for Girls; [occ.] Wife, mum and gran; [memb.] Scientology, Brightlingsea Video Camera Club, Brightlingsea Against Live Exports; [hon.] Scientology Clear; [oth. writ.] Around 300 poems in last eighteen months, started seriously writing poems with the start of live exports through Brightlingsea have a history of the protests in verse and many other subjects.; [pers.] I believe in spiritual freedom for mankind and that animals are sentinent beings which should be granted five freedoms - from distress, from pain and injury, from hunger and thirst, from fear and distress and to express normal behavior.; [a.] Brightlingsea, Essex, UK

LARNER, CAROLINE
[b.] 12 March 1976, London; [p.] Allan Larner, Rosalino Larner; [ed.] Roding Valley High School, Epping Forest College and Angua Polytechnic University.; [occ.] Student (at Angua Polytechnic University); [memb.] Environmental Investigation a (E.I.A.), League against cruel sports (L.A.C.S), respect for animals, world society for the protection of animals, Liberty, Redwings horse Sanitary.; [hon.] 10 Ecses, 3 A levels in English Literature, History and Psychology - presently studying a BA (Hons) Degree in English literature and Women's studies.; [oth. writ.] Many short stories and poems - as yet unpublished.; [pers.] I strive to reflect both personal and public issues in my writing. I feel it is important to draw attention to issues often avoided by other poets.; [a.] Loughton, Essex, UK

LASLEY, JOE
[b.] 16 December 1946, Liverpool; [p.] Maggie and Joe Lasley; [m.] Susan Lasley, 6 January 1973; [ch.] Stephen, Joseph, Keith; [ed.] St. Bernards R.C., St. Margarets C.E. Liverpool; [occ.] International Distribution Manager; [memb.] Institution of Freight Forwarders (A.I.F.E.), Erskine Community Council; [hon.] IATA/FIATA Diploma (Distinction); [oth. writ.] Arrival poets 1995 - poem published "Abstract Heart."; [pers.] All my utterances in the name of art are an absurd reflection upon life.; [a.] Paisley, Renfrew, UK

LATCHFORD, MARGARET JUNE
[b.] 1935, Isle of Wight; [p.] Mr. and Mrs. Morrell; [m.] Douglas Latchford, 27 October 1973; [ch.] Three; [ed.] Basic; [occ.] Housewife; [pers.] Thank you a pleasant surprise. My favorite poem by Rupert Brooks. The Voice, My Treasured possession. A leather bound poem book by, Ella Wheeler Wilcox my favorite book Sophie by Michael Dean-White!; [a.] Colwyn Bay, N. Wales, UK

LAURICELLA, JOANNE
[pen.] Lauricella; [b.] 26 May, Hay on Wye; [p.] M. A. Price and I. J. Price; [m.] A. M. Lauricella, 2 September 1965; [ch.] Two; [ed.] High School and college Worcester; [occ.] Typist and Computing for myself; [memb.]; [hon.] Art, Printing; [oth. writ.] Short story for children and adults; [pers.] Make every day and special will be with you in every way; [a.] Malvern, Worcestershire, UK

LAURIE, STEVEN
[pen.] S.W.L.; [b.] 7 January 1977, Glasgow; [p.] John, Micheline Laurie; [ed.] St. Ninians High School; [oth. writ.] Nothing published; [pers.] Politeness helps but patience is necessary.; [a.] Glasgow, UK

LAWLOR, JANICE
[pen.] Janice Lawlor, Janice Nicholls; [b.] 19 September 1968, Barbados; [p.] Mr. and Mrs. J. Nicholls; [m.] Gary Lawlor, 17 February 1996; [occ.] Data Entry Approver; [hon.] Merit in Radio and Broadcasting; [oth. writ.] Articles published in the Daily Nation Barbados, several short stories (unpublished); [pers.] I write because its the most effective and relaxed way of expressing your feelings or that of others. Its like taking an aspirin for a really bad migraine.; [a.] Whittey Bay, Tyne and Wear, UK

LAWRENCE, KERRY
[b.] 27 July 1975, Warrington; [a.] Warrington, Cheshire, UK

LAWRENCE, PAULA AINA ANTONIA
[b.] 12 March 1981, Lagos, Nigeria; [p.] Fumilayo Antonia Lawrence, Tayo Michael Lawrence; [ed.] St. Gregory's R.C. High School.; [occ.] Student; [oth. writ.] Two poems in school year book.; [pers.] I strive to share my feelings and emotions with the rest of the world through my writing.; [a.] Harrow, Middlesex, UK

LAYLAND, MRS. MABEL
[pen.] Mabel Drury Layland; [b.] 7 October 1926, Thurnscoe, Nr. Rotherham, Yorks; [p.] Jane Drury, Walter Drury; [m.] Alexander Layland (Deceased 26 January 1970), 4 September 1948; [ch.] Sandra Jean Layland now Dawson; [ed.] Thornscot Secondary Hill Modern Girls School, Sandra gained 8 O'levels with extra also 8 A levels with extra 9 years of age when Alex died; [occ.] Retired; [hon.] General Certificate of Secondary Education, North Oxfordshire College of Art English Grade A (B) (one), Summer 1993 was asked to go on to A Level Literature but didn't; [oth. writ.] "Thoughts from my Heart," Mabel Drury Layland 1975, also "Share my Thoughts," Mabel Drury Layland 1976, published by Arthur H. Stockwell Ltd. Elms Court, Ilfracombe, Devon.; [pers.] I sent you work of the Bluebell Woods of England, and "The Magnolia Tree" published by Stockwells all I wanted was an

assessment of my work I threw "The Wrestle with Experience" in for if you wanted to use something, I have much unpublished work written with depth and feeling.; [a.] Banbury, Oxfordshire, UK

LEACH, IAN
[b.] 18 August 1970, Castleford; [p.] Joan Leach, Raymond Leach (Deceased); [m.] Sarah Jayne Leach, 14 October 1996; [ed.] Airedale High School, Wakefield District College; [occ.] Administration Assistant, British Library, Boston Spa; [oth. writ.] Several scrips for British and American comic books, stories for British scifi/fantasy fanzines. Currently working on a novel: Eternity's Kiss.; [a.] Castleford, West Yorks, UK

LEE, FREDA
[b.] 9 January 1927, Chesterfield; [p.] James and Dora Alton; [m.] Gerald Lee, 2 August 1952; [ch.] Catherine Ann, Helen Mary, Jonathan Mark and Matthew Robert; [ed.] Chesterfield Girls' High School, Homerton College, Cambridge; [occ.] Retired; [memb.] The Rolling Stock Company (singing and drama); [oth. writ.] Short articles in local magazines; [pers.] Poetry reading and writing is in the the family as far back as my grandmother's uncle who published a book of poems and was named "The Belper Poet"; [a.] Chesterfield, Derbyshire, UK

LEE, PATRICIA
[pen.] Scaney; [b.] 29 June 1936, Abingdon; [p.] Deceased; [m.] Douglas Lee, 27 May 1989; [occ.] Housewife; [oth. writ.] Several poems also I book of poems published all profits given to cancer, research.; [pers.] I am in a different world when I write my poems.; [a.] Abingdon, Oxon, UK

LENNARD, DONALD ROBERT
[b.] 13 October 1932, St. Pancras; [p.] Thomas Albert Lennard, Florence Alexandra Lennard; [m.] Olive Kate Wakely, 31 March 1956; [ch.] Graham, Kathryn, Andrew; [ed.] Southall Grammar School, London School of Printing and Graphic Arts; [occ.] Printing Office Manager; [memb.] Ceydon Study Circle (Philatelists), Hounslow and District Philatelic Society, West Middlesex Family History Society, Society of Genealogists; [hon.] Diploma in Printing - London School of Printing and Graphic Arts; [a.] Wisbech, Cambs, UK

LESLIE, MARGARET
[b.] 19 November 1917, Prudhoe-on-Tyne; [p.] Frederick, Anne Mary Armstrong; [m.] Matthew Gilbert Leslie, 27 July 1940; [ch.] One son; [ed.] Prudhoe Council School; [occ.] Retired; [memb.] Past member Newcastle and Tynemouth Writer's Clubs; [hon.] Poem published Arrival Press 1994, 4 cups dialect prose morpeth gathering.; [oth. writ.] Broadcast own scripts local radio, BBC morning story numerous letters to newspapers and periodicals, 2 novels (unpublished) poems - various subjects, articles - short stories; [pers.] I am not aware of being influenced by anyone. When inspiration comes it comes quickly. I like to think my writing will give pleasure; [a.] Newcastle upon Tyne, Northumberland, UK

LEWANDOWSKI, SUSAN
[pen.] Sue Levandovska; [b.] 3 February 1951, Rotherham; [p.] Margery and Philip Horner; [m.] Mr. Zenon Lewandowski, 15 July 1972; [ch.] Rachel and Rebecca Lewandowski; [ed.] Old Hall, Kimberworth Rotherham College for Further Education; [occ.] Civil Servant; [memb.] The Poetry Society; [hon.] RSA Stages I II III, English Language, Typing; [oth. writ.] I have written my

own book of 64 poems called "From Within" which I am trying to get published plus other poems and passages.; [pers.] I have tried to highlight throughout my poems that goodness always conquers bad and I feel that if this is learned from them, I will have achieved a great deal.; [a.] Rotherham, South Yorkshire, UK

LEWIN, MRS. P. A.
[pen.] Trish Lewin; [b.] 7 February 1955, Morpeth; [p.] Edna and Tom; [m.] Peter, 5 June 1976; [ch.] Two, Emma Louse and Lisa Victoria; [hon.] Intermediate (at 13 yrs old) Brook Bond Prize Poetry in 1968 and other School Awards; [pers.] I like to reflect on life as it is like a mirror ready to walk into.; [a.] Morpeth, UK

LEWIS, DAVID JOHN
[pen.] Dave; [b.] 15 September 1951, Hornsey, North London; [p.] Sylvia and Brinley Lewis; [ed.] Priory Vale Sec. Mod Crouch End London N. 8; [occ.] Unemployed; [oth. writ.] I have written a few poems based on my personal life and people in it.; [pers.] Life is not a rehearsal take every opportunity as I do now to thank family and friends for their inspiration and encouragement. Remember words from the heart are words of truth.; [a.] Iver Heath, South Bucks, UK

LEWIS, SHIRLEY
[b.] 1 January 1925, Barry, South Wales; [p.] Isa Miles, William Miles; [m.] John Lewis, 11 August 1950; [ch.] Julian, William, Sian (Adults); [ed.] Howell's School, Llandaff Cardiff, King's College, (Then, part of) Durham University; [occ.] Retired teacher: At present, part-time English Tutor; [hon.] B.A. Hons. English, (1950) Diploma in Education; [oth. writ.] Fair amount of poetry written, some at Croxdale. None, so far, entered for publication.; [pers.] Croxdale is an estate in County Durham, where I stayed at times, in a farm cottage. Other poems have always arisen from actual occasions, localities and people. Styles and forms vary. Some are much heroic, wry or humorous.; [a.] Petersfield, Hants, UK

LEWIS, VICTOR THOMAS
[b.] 25 April 1928, Barry, S. Glam; [p.] Trever Lewis, Gwendoline Lewis; [m.] Maria Michealides, 20 March 1954; [ch.] Michael John, Matthew Simon; [ed.] Holton School Barry S Glamorgan; [occ.] Retired Business Lecturer; [memb.] Metropolitan Health and Fitness Club; [hon.] International Sportsman Business Attain-ment awards; [oth. writ.] Personal Development Courses and Business Skills Seminars to Executives of more than 1000 companies; [pers.] I abandon completely the search for security and reach out to the risk of living with both arms and will persist until I succeed.; [a.] Dinas Powys, S. Glam, UK

LIGHTFOOT, ANNA
[b.] 22 June 1963, Hampton Court; [p.] Phyllis Lightfoot, Alfred Lightfoot; [ed.] Bishop Wand C of E Secondary School, Sunbury-on-Thames, Kingston College of Further Education; [occ.] Senior Market Research Interviewer; [pers.] Poetry is forever... the greatest communicator of the creative mind... it never dies.; [a.] Sunbury-on-Thames, Middlesex, UK

LINDLEY, MATTHEW
[b.] 15 December 1971, West Drayton; [p.] Irene and Buck; [ed.] Townmead Sec School and Berkshire College of Agriculture.; [occ.] Temp Gardener; [memb.] ESCLA, Ceverton Supporters club, London Area.; [hon.] Esso 1 Certificate in

Athletics.; [oth. writ.] No other recognized poems to date maybe in the future.; [pers.] I like to put down how I feel through my perceptions of the outside world. My favorite poets include W.B. Yeats, Shelly and Keals.; [a.] West Drayton, Middx, UK

LINNEY, SYLVIA
[b.] 28 July 1921, Steyning, Sussex; [p.] Maud and Harry Camps; [ch.] Anthony and Vanessa; [ed.] Early years, Boarding School in Deal Kent, until six years of age then Aldrington and Hove High School, Hove, Sussex; [occ.] Retired, though happy to help my 'older' friends; [memb.] Brighton and Hove Albion Football Supporters Club, a respected team established nearly one hundred years one season left only at the ground, sold-no home to go to!; [hon.] Medals for sports events at School; [oth. writ.] Many of private interest only; [pers.] There is nothing so bad that couldn't be worse save the iron will and destruction force of a cold heart.; [a.] Hove, Sussex, UK

LITTLE, ANTONY
[b.] 19 October 1968, Roehampton; [p.] William and Barbara; [ed.] Yateley Comprehensive, Farnborough College of Technology; [occ.] Postman; [oth. writ.] I have poems in three other collections - Cats, Images in Ink and Sunlight and Shadows; [pers.] Never ever give up.; [a.] Yateley, Camberley, Surrey, UK

LITTLE, MARIE
[b.] 9 March 1940, Bath; [p.] Mr. and Mrs. C. Barnett (Deceased); [m.] Terry Little, 21 July 1960; [ch.] Three sons, twelve grandchildren; [ed.] Kingsdown Secondary Modern Kingsdown, Bristol; [occ.] Housewife; [memb.] Kingswood Writers Ink-Corporated; [oth. writ.] Poems published in both local and national anthologies and has had short stories published in local writer's group anthologies; [a.] Bristol, South Glos, UK

LITTLER, KATHERINE
[b.] 16 May 1979, Gloucester; [p.] Mr. and Mrs. Beale; [ed.] Gloucester, Cleve Prior and Heversham Primary School. Dallam (Cumbria) and much Wenlock Secondary School 9 GCSE's. Sixth Form College-Telford; [occ.] 3 A' Levels, 1 A/S Levels and 1 GCSE in New College (6th form) Telford; [hon.] Passing 9 GCSE's. Merit in grade 1,2 and 3 piano; [oth. writ.] Reports done on specific outings, E.G. theatre trip to Malvern to see Romeo and Juliet, for school newspaper. Also stories for display at school and college.; [pers.] Finding that poetry is my talent, which I can enjoy, I hope that reading it will bring as much enjoyment to other people, as it did for me writing it.; [a.] Broseley, Shropshire, UK

LIVESEY, ESTELLE
[pen.] Constance Lee; [b.] 6 January 1939, Manchester; [p.] Leslie and May Caplan; [m.] Darren Paul Livesey, 6 January 1984; [ed.] Grammar School for Girls; [occ.] Brickwork contractor a female "Sibbie"; [memb.] I was a chair lady and requested to be vice chair as I was too busy at the time on a residents association. I'm also director on a management company concerned with three blocks of flats; [oth. writ.] Recently a poem. The first one I ever wrote so I've decided to retire from the building trade and write which I've always wanted to do. (My poem first one sold to book company with royalties).; [pers.] I love looking for the positive in the negative and whenever possible writing about it. Eg. rushing about whilst not looking, I fell over my dog called meg, it hurts and I wasn't looking, but thank God I have a leg!; [a.] Polegate, East Sussex, UK

LLEWELLYN, MRS. ANNE
[b.] 8 August 1939, Tottenham; [p.] Kathleen Seymour, George Pipe; [m.] 27 February 1960, Divorced; [ch.] Tracy Kathleen, Stephen John; [ed.] Secondary Modern (Tottenham) Hornsey Art School; [occ.] Care Work with Quantum Care (Auxiliary); [memb.] None, but enjoy Walking, Arts, Crafts, Reading, Painting, Drawing; [hon.] General Certificates for Care of the Elderly open University (Working with Older People); [oth. writ.] Recording of nine years working at Belmont home for the Elderly (not printed) poem "The Old Walnut Tree" (not printed).; [pers.] I have gained immense insight over the last nine years, also inspiration and enlightenment. Have had time to read a great deal also seen the passing of many people that opens my eyes to the supernatural.; [a.] Wormley, Hertfordshire, UK

LLOYD, MISS DILYS ANN
[pen.] D. A. Lloyd; [b.] 1 August 1942, London; [p.] Matthew Lloyd and Jane Anne; [ed.] Queensmill Road, Fulham, London Garndolbenmaen Primary, Portmadog Secondary Modern (last two in Gwynedd); [occ.] Now disabled, formerly nurse of 30 yrs; [hon.] Nursing Certificate State Enrolled Nurse 1962; [oth. writ.] Have been published in a Welsh monthly magazine and 1 English poem in the one-to-one Christian and magazine; [pers.] I think that my first entry into writing poetry was when I was leaving school and I wrote some verses to the tune of "Thanks for the Memory". Now lost.; [a.] Garndolbenmaen, Gwynedd, W. Wales, UK

LOCKWOOD, MRS. ANN
[pen.] Annivan; [b.] 10 May 1948, Sheffield; [m.] Peter Lockwood, 23 June 1990; [ed.] City Grammar School, Sheffield Open University; [occ.] Retired on Ill Health - Ex Secretary; [memb.] Hatfield House Lane Methodist Church, Sheffield, The girls Brigade, Sheffield Band of Hope/Hope UK, Lay Preacher. Methodist Church; [hon.] BA Degree 1989, Open University, in Arts and Humanities; [oth. writ.] Poems published in two books by Triumph House, Peterborough; [pers.] As an active Christian, 90% of my poetry is based on this aspect. I prefer "Rhyming" verse to "Blank" verse. I enjoy reading as well as writing poetry.; [a.] Sheffield, South Yorkshire, UK

LOI, MAURA
[b.] 22 July 1969, Cagliari, Sardinia; [p.] Gianfranco Loi, Eventino Yolanda; [ed.] Istituto Professionale di Stato (School of Languages) Translation School (English - German); [hon.] I won for competition with my poems in Italy; [oth. writ.] To date I have penned over 450 poems and and continue to write poems virtually everyday - I completed my first novel "Life at the edge of 17, and Tom in the process of completing my second one.; [pers.] I started writing poems at the age of 6. My influences rely heavily on real life experiences that I (end those close to me) encounter - My greatest dream is to, one day, see my work published.; [a.] London, UK

LONGFORD, CARL
[b.] 17 September 1955, Bramcote; [p.] Stanley Longford and Mary Longford; [m.] Linda Susan Longford, 30 October 1993; [ch.] Jeannette Mary, Michelle Loise, Wayne Carl; [ed.] Bramcote Hills Secondary Modern Boys. Brackenhurst Agricultural College, Southwell; [occ.] Landscape Gardener; [memb.] British Institute of Innkeeping;

[hon.] Award in design. Awards in the Lincensed Trade, Awards in Horticulture; [oth. writ.] Various poems; [pers.] I like to reflect on things of reality in writing. I am especially influenced by nature; [a.] Beeston, Nottingham, UK

LONGLEY, EILEEN
[b.] 2 January 1931, Seven Kings; [p.] (Deceased) Ada Norris and Bob Norris; [m.] George Longley (Deceased), 25 May 1953; [ch.] Diane Rains and Trevor Longley; [ed.] Uphall Secondary School Ilford Essex; [occ.] Retired (Ex Civil Servant); [pers.] My poem reveals my feelings on love and sacrifice.; [a.] Southend, Essex, UK

LORING, DAVID
[b.] 21 April 1948, Gt. Yarmouth; [p.] John and Winifred (Both Deceased); [m.] Divorced; [ch.] Alexander and Anna; [ed.] Lancing College, Sussex; [occ.] Programmer; [memb.] Institute of Management; [a.] Wantage, Oxon, UK

LOUW, KATHARINE HEATHER DAWN
[b.] 26 January 1977, Zimbabwe; [p.] Schalk Louw, Laraine Louw; [ed.] English High School Swakopmind, Namibia-Africa; [pers.] My writing is special to me and at times very personal. It's a special gift passed down from my mother.

LOVE, CHARLES G.
[b.] 26 May 1948, Stirling, Scotland; [m.] Carole, 22 July 1969; [ch.] Garry, Lisa, Mitcheline, Danya; [ed.] Peters Hill School, Springburn Glasgow Scotland; [oth. writ.] Several poems I've not shown yet; [pers.] A thought. A day spent, discerning in the garden of Enlightenment is likened to a thousand years spent else where.; [a.] Birmingham, UK

LOVE, LILY ROSINA
[pen.] Rosina Turner; [b.] 5 April 1929, Leicester; [m.] Divorced; [ch.] One son; [ed.] Secondary School I consider it a good Education; [occ.] Retired; [hon.] Grade 4 examination with Merit in Singing. Never continued with it.; [oth. writ.] Some personal none published given to writing letters of complaint about bad taste in the media, T.V. etc.; [pers.] I tell it straight, as it is, keeping it simple and clear, so it is easy to understand. I am overwhelming our society. First attempt at Poetry.; [a.] Leicester, Shire

LOVELOCK, CORRINNE ANNE
[b.] 6 December 1973, Rochford; [p.] Peter Lovelock and Jean Lovelock; [ed.] King John School, South East Essex sixth from college Canterbury Christ Church College of higher education; [occ.] A student in Canterbury training to be an early years teacher; [oth. writ.] Several poems that remain unpublished.; [pers.] I owe my talent, my "gift of the gab", to my mother, Jean Marlyn Lovelock, who sadly died 15th July 1995. I know she would have been as thrilled as I am to see a poem of mine published so I dedicate this poem to her, with loving thanks.; [a.] Hadleigh, Essex, UK

LOVERIDGE, MRS. DOROTHY
[pen.] Dorothy Dyke; [b.] 22 December 1923, Basingstoke; [p.] Henry William Dyke, Daisy Elsley; [m.] Ronald Colin Loveridge, 8 August 1981 (Second Marriage, 1st husband died); [ch.] Janice Elizabeth; [ed.] All local schools then evening schools in Art, Bookkeeping, French etc.; [occ.] Housewife [memb.] I.P.A. (International

Police Assn.), Local Conservative Club, Parish Councilor Old Basing; [oth. writ.] Many, many published in local gazette (No payment) and in conservative local magazines; [pers.] I was a special sergeant for 20 yrs. Leading fireman before that, private detective many years taught safety in home to brownies and guides, my poems are from my heart and always true of real life.; [a.] Basingstoke, Hants, UK

LOWDER, MARGUERITE L.
[pen.] Marguerite Longstaff Lowder; [b.] 11 January 1941, Sunderland; [p.] Harry and Ivy Longstaff; [m.] Walter, 15 August 1959; [ch.] Paul, Nigel and Mark; [ed.] Chester Road Secondary Modern School Sunderland Co Durham; [occ.] Mother and Housewife, given 12 hrs. to live in 1961; [oth. writ.] Just to know. Turn To God. God Cares, In Love With Life, Precious Moments, In Love, Life's Path, The Dream; [pers.] My poetry is about life and experiences also nature. Poems printed locally.; [a.] Marpelt, Northumberland, UK

LOWTHORPE, DIANA M.
[b.] 22 May 1942, Lincolnshire; [ed.] Coll. Grad. NY City Univ. (USA), High School Grad. (Gt. Britain); [occ.] Self Employed As - Medical Informations Analyst, Research in Epidemiology; [hon.] Trained Nurse (USA), Accountant (USA); [oth. writ.] Anthology of poems, USA, dedicated to the men of the U.S. Boston going off to the war in Vietnam; [pers.] Lived in the USA 1966-1991 inspired by life itself, all of its wonders and horrors plus all creatures great and small their love and joy shown to me constantly!; [a.] Woodmansey, Beverley, UK

LUCEK, MARK
[oth. writ.] Writes a wide range of poetry and short stories and has a plans for a novel.

LUCKETT, MRS. DORIS
[pen.] Dorilu; [b.] 8 August 1914, London; [p.] Thomas and Ellen Luce; [m.] Leonard Charles Luckett, 2 April 1938; [ch.] Two son and daughter; [ed.] Wakefield Higher East Ham.; [occ.] Retired; [hon.] Only School Leaving Awards with Honours in History; [oth. writ.] Poems, short stories, Christian Music Compositions.; [pers.] I was always lyrically inclined, loving the rhythm in poetry, music and dancing. Once my voice was an asset also but a major stroke affected the focussing of my eyes and mini strokes the quality of my voice but I still has the ability to express myself with my pen sharing the outward flow with others and giving the glory to God.; [a.] Southsea, Hants, UK

LUCKINGS, CARRIE-LEE
[pen.] Pigeon; [b.] 11 June 1977, London; [p.] Ronnie and Elaine Luckings; [ed.] Roding Valley High School 1989-1993, Epping Forest College 1993-1995; [occ.] Secretary to the AMRC; [memb.] Epping Forest Country Club; [hon.] Black Belt Karate - Wadaro Miss Hotel Guadalupe 1995; [pers.] This poem is dedicated to my loving family and friends. Also in loving memory of Alf Fisher - still missing you.; [a.] Laughton, Essex, UK

LUKIC, JAMES
[b.] 17 April 1982, Chesterfield; [p.] Milos Lukic and Janet Lukic; [ed.] Newbold Community School Chesterfield; [occ.] School Boy; [pers.] I write for fun and this is my first published work.; [a.] Chesterfield, Derbyshire, UK

LYALL, ANANKA
[b.] 23 April 1980, Paisley; [ed.] Coltness High School; [occ.] 6th Year High School Student; [memb.] Motherwell Cricket Club, Ladies Soccer Team; [oth. writ.] Contributor to Scottish Poets 1995 (Arrival Press) published March 1995; [pers.] The universe is there to be explored, not to be hidden.; [a.] Wishaw, Lanarkshire, UK

LYNCH, NOEL
[b.] 20 December 1932, Limerick, Eire; [p.] Deceased; [m.] Margaret, 10 November 1962; [ch.] Two; [occ.] Milk Man; [pers.] I was born in Co Limerick Farmers son. Left school early to go to a racing stalk tame to Scotland worked as a miner. Salesman 2 lovely grandchildren Nicola, Gary.; [a.] Kennoway, Fife, UK

M'BAYO, TAMBA EADRIC
[b.] 29 July 1956, Bo, Sierra Leone; [p.] Joseph M'Bayo, Jane M'Bayo; [m.] Finda M'Bayo, Nee' Dabundeh; [ed.] Prince of Wales School, St. Edward's Secondary School, Fourah Bay College, University of Sierra Leone; [occ.] Social Studies Teacher, International School of Lome, Togo, Assistant Librarian, British School of Lome; [hon.] Modern History; [oth. writ.] A collection of about one hundred unpublished poems, unfinished novel.; [pers.] There is nothing mysterious about poetry. It should be read and written by all - young or old, black or white. Poetry is 'shadow-chasing'.; [a.] Lome, Togo

MACDONALD, ANNA
[pen.] Anna MacDonald; [b.] Dundee; [oth. writ.] Writes poetry, essays and short stories. Has published many collections of poetry (including poetry books for schools) most recently "Rockwell and Write" (1996) which is strong in humor with a hint of irony. Two books "Clifton and Friends" and "more about Clifton and Friends" (both stories in verse) have been transcribed to braille. Appears in numerous anthologies and magazines (medical, educational and literary) and frequently in local press and has broadcast several times on radio. Currently involved with Dundee Industrial Heritage Trust's "The Story of Jute."; [a.] Dundee, UK

MACEWAN, GERALD
[b.] 23 November 1945, Scotland; [p.] Hannah and James MacEwan; [m.] Arlene Helena MacEwan; [ch.] Maureen Jacqueline, Karma, Ged, Christopher, Jennifer; [ed.] Glasgow; [occ.] Senior Buyer; [memb.] Chartered Institute of Purchasing and supply (MCIPS); [oth. writ.] Various works reflecting life and dreams. (Although none submitted for publication).; [pers.] "Poetry is a vehicle we can use to transport our emotions."; [a.] Whitley Bay, Tyne and Wear, UK

MACKAY, CATHERINE ELIZ
[b.] 27 June 1929, Glasgow; [p.] Jane Roddy, Robert Porter; [m.] Douglas Mackay, 12 July 1952; [ch.] Jane, Catherine; [ed.] Possil Secondary School, Glas. School of Art, Jordan Hill Teacher Training College, Northern College, Dundee; [occ.] Retired (Previously, Learning Support Teacher); [memb.] Glasgow Junior, Orpheus Choir, Church Choir, Angus Dainting Group; [hon.] Dp. ED, D. Sp. ED, Article 51, Glasgow School of Art; [oth. writ.] Short stories, Discussion documents on Dyslexia, Hymns, Small Articles (Education); [pers.] I try to opens as many doors as I can for those who struggle thro life. Hopefully, in my writing, I speak for others less fortunate than I.; [a.] Carnoustie, Angus, UK

MACKERETH, JEAN
[b.] 23 April 1940, Cockermouth; [p.] J. and M. Stephenson; [m.] W. MacKereth, 6 February 1960; [ch.] S. M. Jean; [ed.] Fairfield Primary Sch. all saints, Derwents Sch's. C'Mouth; [occ.] Housewife ceramic painter from home; [memb.] Anchor's Aweigh Bronte Society C'Mouth Civic Trust, Brooke's Hospital for Animals Cairo. I. F. A. W., P.A.L.; [oth. writ.] Poem published in a mixed bag.; [pers.] Always a compulsing writer single 7 year old. (Poetry) greatly influenced by Wordsworth Coleridge, Emily Bronte and Byron; [a.] Cockermouth, Cumbria, UK

MACKIGGAN, COLLINE
[b.] 29 April 1947, Oban; [m.] 20 June 1974; [ch.] 2 Daughters; [occ.] Housewife; [oth. writ.] One hundred fifty poems. 10 Christian songs as yet unpublished 'God's Perfect Plan' published this year by Christian Publishers Triumph House; [pers.] I trust those who read this poem will be as blessed as I was in writing it.; [a.] Argyll, UK

MACNEILL, ELIZABETH ANN
[pen.] Lisa; [b.] 9 April 1955, Cuckfield; [p.] Emma and Ron(ald) MacNeill; [a.] Eastbourne, East Sussex, UK

MADDOCKS, KIM
[b.] 8 April 1982, Manchester; [p.] David Maddocks and Barbara Maddocks; [ed.] Helmshore County Primary School. Haslingden High School; [memb.] R.A.Y.S. - Rossendale Amateur Youth Society Drama and Operatic.; [oth. writ.] Poems and essay printed and published in High School Magazine.; [pers.] Imagination is no special talent, everyone has it, you just have to find it.; [a.] Rossendale, Lancashire, UK

MAGGS, MRS. CHRISTINA ROSE
[b.] 22 October 1941, Amesbury; [p.] George and Nancy Reasey; [m.] Peter Maggs, 28 April 1962; [ch.] Christopher, Richard and Michael; [ed.] South Wilts Grammar School, Salisbury; [occ.] Secretary, Midland Bank; [oth. writ.] 6 poems published in previous anthologies, 4 more to be published 1996/97.; [pers.] I love putting my thoughts into verse and it gives me pleasure when people say they have enjoyed my work. If I can evoke an emotion from the reader then I know I have succeeded in my aim. It is very exciting to see my work in print.; [a.] Amesbury, Wiltshire, UK

MALONE, CAMILLE
[b.] 7 January 1972, London; [p.] Sonja Malone, Joseph John Malone; [ed.] New Hall School (Chelmsford), Landsdowne Independent Sixth form College (London); [occ.] Student I am currently studying Classical studies with English at King's College London (Strand Campus); [memb.] King's College Poetry Society, King's College English Society, King's College Drama Society, Member of BECTU (The British Entertainment Cinematography Trade Union); [oth. writ.] I have written several pieces of work mainly for esoteric pleasure and for the people I have loved this is the first time that I have endeavored to get my work published (to share it among many people so to speak.); [pers.] This poem was written in Israel in 1994. It is written from direct experience. The beauty of the country and the strength of the people despite many problems is truly inspirational.; [a.] London, UK

MANFREDI, NICOLINA
[pen.] Nicolina Manfredi; [b.] 10 March 1970, Hitchin; [p.] Alfonsina Manfredi, Sabino Manfredi; [ed.] St. Albans - Stevenage College; [occ.] Care Assistant; [memb.] (Stevenage) New Age and Spiritualist Group, The Astrological Association (London); [hon.] Certificate - City and Guilds English/Communications; [oth. writ.] Several poems - various themes published in books and a range of anthologies; [pers.] Find love from within to express for it is love breeds the rewards of success - at soul level free from the shackles of time.; [a.] Stevenage, Herts, UK

MANLEY, RONA
[b.] 31 August 1956, Yeovil; [p.] Ronald Joseph and Mary May; [m.] Stephen Manley, 29 December 1973; [ch.] Ashley John; [ed.] Beaminster Comprehensive School Dorset; [occ.] Store Manager; [memb.] National Grocers Benevolent Fund (Charity Group Caring for the Elderly from a Retail or Food Industry); [pers.] I would like to dedicate this poem to my mum, whom we lost last year. A talented lady, who enjoyed writing herself in her later years. She had the pleasure of reading my poem before she died, and would be very proud to see it printed. 'A Tribute To My Mum'.; [a.] Crewkerne, Somerset, UK

MANNING, ELIZABETH
[b.] 19 April 1961, Taunton; [occ.] Ward Sister in Rehabilitation of Young Disabled Adults; [oth. writ.] Various unpublished poetry and prose.; [pers.] I like to be able to look beyond the material world, and see and experience the spiritual presence in all life. This can be intensely joyous or painful, and for me, can only be expressed in poetic form.; [a.] Taunton, Soms, UK

MANTLE, DAVID
[b.] 18 April 1975, Hitchin; [p.] Ian Mantle and Valerie Mantle; [ed.] Fearnhill School, Letchworth Bournemouth University; [memb.] English Heritage R.S.P.B.; [hon.] BSC (Hons) Heritage Conservation; [pers.] Main poetical influences are World War I poets, Dante, Mediaeval Romances and Folk Music. External influences are my family, my friends and Michelle! Six Foot of Earth Makes Us All of One Size".; [a.] Letchworth, Herts, UK

MARIA
[pen.] Sasha; [b.] 11 June 1972, Svetozarevo; [hon.] Dozens of poetry awards at poetry contests and festivals in the former Yoguslavia. Published in lots of magazines as a teenager; [oth. writ.] I've been writing diary for ten years parts of which ar in verse. At the moment, I am working on publishing my children's book "The Adventures of the Blue-eyed Popcorn" - A cycle of fable-poems about a naughty popcorn. I write love poems and poems on the frustration, depression and indoctrination whose shadows are cast over the young people in my unfortunate country.; [pers.] Let the other party speak as well.; [a.] London, UK

MARIE, JUNE
[b.] 14 June 1962, Jersey, C.I.; [p.] L. and J. Baratte; [m.] Steve Marie; [ch.] Harrison and Emily; [ed.] Convent F.C.J., Jersey and Jersey College for Girls; [occ.] Mother and wife; [oth. writ.] Wisdomless was published in "Voices On The Wind"; [pers.] I enjoy writing poetry on the people, the nature and the history of Jersey.; [a.] Saint Saviour, Jersey, UK

MAROSEK, KATHERINE ANNE
[pen.] Kate O'Connor; [b.] 28 March 1974, Johannesburg, South Africa; [p.] Mrs. Jeanne Bonney, Mr. Eamonn O'Connor - Deceased, Stepfather: Mr. Ken Bonney; [m.] Captain Scott Marosek, 1 June 1996; [ed.] The Towers Convent, Sussex studying GCSES, Chichester College of Technology College of Technology studying Secretarial skills, languages and A-Level Communications Studies; [occ.] Legal Secretary for a Lawfirm in Virginia, USA; [memb.] I was once a member of the Chichester Youth Theatre Group which was entered and won the Lloyds Bank Theatre Challenge - we performed at The National Theatre, London; [hon.] Sporting awards for Long Jump and Gymnastics; [oth. writ.] Since I compose a lot of music for the piano, I use my poetry in constructing lyrics/I also enjoy writing short stories of events in my life.; [pers.] Life is short and death is inevitable - so make an effort to express your love to your friends and family before it's too late. It's just not worth being nasty, so why not just be nice. I learned this form my mother and found it to be invaluable advice. Now, I make sure I tell Scott, my husband, every day, that he is very precious to me and that I love him more than life itself.; [a.] Chichester, West Sussex, UK

MARSH, A. C.
[b.] 20 February 1910, Woodbridge; [p.] Lilian and Edward Marsh; [m.] Hilda, 28 May 1938; [ch.] Five; [ed.] Church of England; [occ.] Retired; [memb.] British Legion, Working Mans Clubs Life Member; [oth. writ.] One published in local press, others private, family pleasure.; [a.] Camberley, Surrey, UK

MARSH, JANET ROSE
[b.] 5 February 1959, Poplar, London; [p.] Jessie Marsh, Herbert Marsh; [ed.] St. Pauls Way School Bow E.3; [occ.] Clerical Administrator; [pers.] Poem written for Dennis many years ago.

MARSHALL, IRENE
[ch.] Foke granddaughter and one grandson, fostered children after my own children married; [ed.] Attended a course at NCC City College, for care of the elderly, various course for children needing care; [occ.] Working as a care assistant in a residential home; [a.] Nr Dereham, Therford, Norfolk, UK

MARTIN, BRENDAN
[pen.] Voisier, Spiv, Breno.; [b.] 21 July 1959, Mullingar, Ireland; [p.] Kevin and Maisie Martin; [m.] Monica Nee Foley, 14 November 1986; [ch.] Paul Aidan and Kim-Lisa; [ed.] Primary and C.B.S. Secondary Mullingar County Westmeatt, Ireland; [occ.] Telecommunications Technician.; [memb.] Catholic Boy Scout of Ireland, Extel Golf Society; [hon.] 10 year Service Award for Scouting.; [oth. writ.] Two volumes of my poems and songs called 'Smaointe' and 'Withered Words', neither of which have been published; [pers.] Dreams are not real, life is, and much stricter. Death is the conqueror, but love, is the Victor. Breno.; [a.] Clondalkin, Dublin 22, Ireland

MARTIN, DAVID
[pen.] M. Decker, R. Tollon; [b.] 7 September 1962, Ipswich; [p.] Pauline D. Martin and Ben St. Romaine; [ed.] Tower Ramparts - Secondary Modern, Westbourne High 6th Form, Suffolk College; [occ.] Disabled; [oth. writ.] Several poems in local magazines, one poem in a regional anthology "Eastern Poets" and a large collection of poems and short stories awaiting publication.; [pers.] "If

you're in a rut you've gotta get out of it" (M. Owen - the Ruts) and special thanks to Diane for the inspiration.; [a.] Ipswich, Suffolk, UK

MARTIN, KEITH GERHARD JAMES
[b.] 9 February 1959, Billericay; [p.] James Martin, Ursula Martin; [ed.] Beauchamps Comprehensive Essex University; [oth. writ.] Poetry and Prose, Song Lyrics, Music Theory Textbook, Guitarist, Composer. Founder member original rock band. Appeared in Kerrang!, making music and evening echo publication. Air-play on BBC radio Essex.; [pers.] In my poem tried to combine Music, Religion, Philosophy, Physics and Mathematics within the challenge of a disciplined set framework. Word is vibration is music is creation.; [a.] Wickford, Essex, UK

MASON, DAVID B.
[pen.] David B. Mason; [b.] 26 October 1919, Hadleigh, Suffolk; [p.] Ben Mason and Gertrude Mason; [m.] Phyllis Mason, 16 August 1946; [ch.] Jennifer, Patricia and Philip; [ed.] Church School (Hadleigh) (No schooling after 10 years of age due to accident); [occ.] Retired from farming and soldiering; [memb.] Many National Farmers Union, Ioiu Farming and Wildlife Group, many Literary Society, Centre For Many Studies, Society for Protection of many Countryside, Parish Commissioner; [hon.] Still Waiting!; [oth. writ.] Short stories, poetry, articles editor of farming and wildlife newsletter (quarterly) (Short stories and poetry intended for publication in book farm); [pers.] All my writing is inspired by nature and wonderful women. I am not merely a countryman but part of the ecology! Now celebrating 50 years of happy marriage.; [a.] Braddan, Isle of Man, UK

MASON, JOAN
[b.] 24 June 1935, Chippenham, Wilts; [p.] Canon and Mrs. W. H. Barkwell; [m.] Robert Guthrie Mason (Deceased), 3 January 1967; [ch.] Two lovely daughters Susan and Sally Mason; [ed.] Very varied due to the war and fregment evacuation from Bristol's bombs. Convent 45/46 Chippenham Grammar 46/51 Lackham Agricultural College; [occ.] Voluntary Driver for Red Cross, C.V.S., Social Services, Double Decker Play Bus; [pers.] I enjoy putting pen to paper-but my recent playing Accordian and Melodian in a small Irish Group has caused a different inspiration and I do compose little tunes with words sometimes.; [a.] Williton, Taunton, Somerset, UK

MASSINGHAM-APPLEBY, KATIE MAY
[pen.] Katie May; [b.] 4 August 1978, London; [p.] Jackie Appleby, Barry Appleby; [ed.] Cleeve Park Secondary School; [occ.] Unemployed; [oth. writ.] I have only one other published poem. 'Precious Jewel', published in the spring of 1996 in 'First Time' Literature Magazine.; [pers.] I have nothing but love to give this world and that's all I want to receive.; [a.] Sidcup, Kent, UK

MATHERS, MRS. SHEILA
[pen.] Shela Nee Desio; [b.] 20 September 1930, Cathays Terrace, Cardiff; [p.] The Late Mr. Giusseppe Desio and Mrs. Louise Desio; [m.] Mr. Anthony Arthur Mathers, 25 August 1958 (38 years); [ch.] Two boys age 31 yrs. and 36 yrs.; [occ.] Housewife; [hon.] So near yet so far. Never had the converdence to enter any of my work. Knelting sewing embroidery tap. every one that has seen my work all say that I am very gifted and have a great talent in many things; [oth. writ.] Just that I am very senative person, not a very good mixer, must be with the right people, love children,

I hope to write more poetry in the near future!; [pers.] Sober, level, headed, malistic, prodigal down to earth, cool, patient, cool headed, even tempered like reason for seeking truth and knowledge of reality the cause of nature of the causes of the nature of things beliefs and human behaviour like to get things stride.; [a.] Cardiff, Glam, S. Wales, UK

MATHESON, MARGARET
[pen.] Margaret Matheson; [b.] 1 May 1948, Edinburgh; [p.] William Woodhouse, Margaret Woodhouse; [m.] William Matheson (Deceased), 2 June 1972; [ed.] Tower Bank Primary, Portobello Secondary, Telford College Edinburgh, Royal 'Dick' school of Veterinary Studies, Edinburgh; [occ.] Technical Officer; [hon.] Book awards on subjects studies at school and college IE Scottish Literature and Animal Health; [oth. writ.] Poems from 1971-1972 + The Dream, The Fox, The Cat and Us, The Fox The Hedgehog and The Cat, The Boys, Where Are You?; [pers.] Poetry writing has become my friend and saviour through a turbulent life when no one else could listen. I can express myself by composing verse. I respect all poetry.; [a.] Portobello, Midlothian, UK

MATTHEWS, JOAN YVONNE
[b.] 3 November 1940, Birmingham; [p.] Edward and Violet Crook; [m.] Derek George Matthews, 29 March 1958; [ch.] Jacqueline, Annette and Philip, 6 Grandchildren - Katie, Lauren, Jay, Liam, Joseph and Jessica; [ed.] Secondary Modern School; [occ.] Retired Sales Consultant; [memb.] Local Women's Institute also, Patron of Local Operatic Society; [hon.] School Diplomas in, Art and Design, Hand Writing and Elocution also, Painting Displayed in Glyn Vivian Ant Gallery at the age of twelve 1952; [oth. writ.] Other poems being published in Anthologies; [pers.] Most of my poems are about the Trials of Life, and they have a message within them I hope they bring wisdom and understanding and hope to the reader.; [a.] Swansea, Glam, UK

MATTHEWS, RAY
[b.] 28 August 1921, Woolston, Southampton; [p.] Dorothy and Frank Matthews; [m.] Phyll Froud, 26 December 1944; [ed.] Taunton's Grammar School, Southampton Emergency Teacher - Training College, Eastbourne, 1947-8 (Special Subjects Religious Education, English); [occ.] Teacher - now retired - teaching at Bitterne C.E. school Southampton 1948 - 1982. Special responsibility post religious knowledge, English, Games Hon. Sec. Parent - Teacher Association; [memb.] National Federation of Community Organizations, National Fed-n Chairman 1971-1976, (Now honorary life-member), Sholing Community Centre - Chairman Hampshire, Fed'n Community Assns' - Chairman Southampton Liaison Committee C.A's - Chairman Woolston C.A. Member, Lyndhurst C.A. Member, School Drama Group, 2 Community Centre Drama Groups, Bitterne Court Tennis Club, Weston Sports Cricket Club and Table Tennis, Bitterne Court Men's Singles 1958 - 1963 Tennis Champion, Association Football Qualified Referee Class I; [oth. writ.] Special Pictorial Television Presentation of Commemorative poem - 'Ode to Southampton City (Granted City Status - 11 February 1964 small collection of children's poems prepared for publication - hopefully? A fair member of personal and general poems and various local poetry contributions.; [pers.] Inspired and guided by a proven knowledge of continuous existence in the 'unseen' world around us, which offers an

awareness and capacity to benefit all creation.; [a.] Lymington, Hants, UK

MATTHEWS, MR. ROBERT A.

[pen.] Sisco; [b.] 6 May 1951, Dagenham; [p.] William Arthur and Elisabeth Margaret; [m.] Ann Patricia, 23 January 1971; [ch.] Lisa and Tammy; [ed.] Comprehensive; [occ.] Semi Retired; [oth. writ.] Why Do We Love Them So, My Mother's Gone, Love Is A Happy Thing; [pers.] I believe everybody loves someone or something but very few people know how to show it, in these cold and hard times. Reading or writing poetry could help bring more love into our otherwise great society telling of their dreams hopes fears loves and desires.; [a.] Tilbury, Essex, UK

MAYERS, JOAN

[pen.] Joan Mayers; [b.] 1 September 1920, Ashton-u-Lyne, Lancs; [p.] Fred and Jeannie Roberts; [m.] Fred E. Mayers, 7 February 1941; [ch.] Patricia A. Mayers (now 'Eyres); [ed.] Ashton-u-Lyne Grammar School. Margaret McMillan Teacher Training College.; [occ.] Retired School Teacher; [memb.] Women's Institute, `The Glen Singers' (large choir which sings for charity); [hon.] `Women of the Year' for the Business and Professional Women's Association for 1975 for the West Lancashire area. (For work with young `difficult' teenagers); [oth. writ.] Some short plays and some `Cameos' about personalities. Also `Letters' for people who find it difficult to express themselves.; [pers.] `Words' and humorous writings, with `Punch Lines', nearly always. Am at the moment doing a revision course in Latin which I found fascinating at school. I have formed a Drama Group in the W.I. and am writing plays suitable for performance.; [a.] Ben Rhydding, Ilkley, West Yorks, UK

MAYLE, HELEN

[b.] 10 November 1978, Nottingham; [p.] Mr. and Mrs. P. J. Mayle; [m.] Fiance Dave Hibbitt (Musician); [ed.] The Grove School, Balderton, Newark, Notts.; [occ.] College Student; [pers.] I write poetry from how I feel about the situations I find myself in, every day life, as a teenager, life has so many up's and down. "Life is like a nightmare" with good times along it's highway.; [a.] Newark, Notts, UK

MAYNE, BRYAN STUART

[b.] 22 August 1969, Burton-on-Trent; [p.] Linda Mayne and Terry Mayne; [m.] Anna Turner (Engaged); [ch.] Rhea, Samara, Michael, Eleanor; [ed.] Paulet High School, Burton-on-Trent Staffs, Burton-on-Trent Technical College, Staffs; [occ.] Presently Unemployed Awaiting Fire Service; [memb.] Royal British Legion; [hon.] Gulf War Medal, United Nations Medal, Liberation of Kuwait Medal; [oth. writ.] 'Fantasy' (first time poets), 'Mixed Emotions' (off the wall) presently in process off compiling my own book.; [pers.] "To me, poetry is the hidden voice of the mind, and the world is a foundation from which it reflects. By freeing those emotions I am able to understand the world and its people from a different perspective."; [a.] Ferndown, Dorset, UK

MCAULEY, SUSAN

[b.] 30 March 1947, Donegal, Ireland; [ch.] Three daughters ages: 20,18,12; [ed.] BA Sociology Classical Studies M Phil in Womens B.A. from University College Galway M.Phil Trinity College Dublin; [occ.] Residential Care/Educator with the Mental Handicapped; [pers.] My inner thoughts bring me some small reward and the feelings is good.

MCBEAN, LAURENCE KITCHENER

[b.] 11 September 1914, Hartlepool; [p.] Alfred McBean, Margaret McBean; [m.] Vera Wildbore, 20 November 1937; [ch.] Brian and Keith McBean; [ed.] Jesmond Road Elementary, Elwick Road Central; [occ.] Retired; [oth. writ.] Number of poems published in local evening paper and read out on local radio station.; [pers.] Like to study people and events which inspire my poems.; [a.] Hartlepool, UK

MCBRIDE, SARAH ELIZABETH

[pen.] Sally McBride; [b.] 30 April 1946, Belfast; [m.] John McBride, 20 March 1965; [ch.] Three sons and one daughter; [ed.] Secondary Education; [occ.] Housewife; [pers.] I write poetry as a form of relaxation.; [a.] Belfast, Down, UK

MCCANDLESS, PAULINE

[pen.] Pauly Centinelli; [b.] 9 June 1976, Glasgow; [p.] Robert McCandless and Janet McCandless; [ed.] Saint Stephen's High School, Port Glasgow, Glasgow University; [occ.] 3rd year student at Glasgow University, studying English Lit. MA (Hons); [memb.] SPUC Paisley Youth to Lourdes Group; [oth. writ.] Sonnets, poems and children's stories; [pers.] Writing is my dream-having "Sandblaster" published is the first step of my dream coming true. I have been greatly inspired by the works of William Shakespeare, John Donne and Charles Dickens.; [a.] Port Glasgow, Renfrewshire, UK

MCCARTHY, VAL

[pen.] Vaf; [b.] 19 January 1978; [p.] Hannah McCarthy, Joe McCarthy; [ed.] Convent Primary School, Mitchelstown St. Fanahans College, Mitchelstown; [occ.] Student; [memb.] An Forsa Cosanta Aituilt - an F.C.A. as the 2nd line reserve for the Irish Army; [pers.] I was always messing around with my poetry, but I was never that serious about it. Maybe now since my poem is being published I might get a little more serious I'm only 18 years old. I've plenty of time to get serious.; [a.] Mitchelstown, Co. Cork, UK

MCCONNACHIE, THOMAS

[pen.] Tammy Troot; [b.] 4 August 1936, Dundee; [m.] Frances, 26 August 1958; [ch.] Five (One Deceased); [ed.] Logie Secondary - Dundee; [occ.] 'Caretaker' Dundee, City Council Housing Division; [memb.] Kiethick Angling Club, Coupar Angus; [hon.] School Dux for Art, Former Teacher of Fishing and Fly Tying Dundee Education at Kirkton Evening Institute and Lawside Academy; [oth. writ.] Published 'Our Heilan Coo' by Anchor press (Anchor Books, poets Choice 134 Yarwell Court Kettering), I have large amount, untapped work at hand over 40 of numerous. Type many to do with fishing; [pers.] A game lad Thon Tammy Troot. Aye by Water Like Coot. Creepin' crawling Fa'in catching caulds a muckle sin airms outstretched shows fishs size forever mocked firtellin' lies.; [a.] Dundee, Tayside, UK

MCCONNELL, MARK D.

[pen.] Roman McCknell; [b.] 7 January 1967, Paris, France; [p.] H. Desmond McConnell, Myra J. McConnell; [ed.] Island School, Hongkong University of Arizona, Tucson U.S.A.; [occ.] Writer; [memb.] Royal Shakespeare Company; [oth. writ.] Poems published in Community and College magazine. Published in Contemporary Anthology of poetry.; [pers.] My verse is influenced by the Contemporary American poet William Carlos Williams, and from reading the classics.; [a.] Fleet, Hampshire, UK

MCCORMICK, RUSSELL

[b.] 28 May 1926, Dublin; [m.] Jean, 18 June 1955; [ch.] Four; [ed.] Mount Joy School Dublin, Dublin University Trinity College; [occ.] Retired; [memb.] Naval Club London, Royal Southern Yacht Club, Hamble; [hon.] M.A., M.S.C., C.E.N.G., M.I.E.E.; [oth. writ.] Scientific papers; [pers.] Use your imagination!; [a.] Hamble, Hants, UK

MCCORMICK, SUZANNE

[b.] 4 November 1964, Stanley; [p.] Ron (Deceased) and Pauline McCormick; [ed.] Pewsey Secondary Grammar School, Darwin Boarding School, Falklands; [occ.] Horelier; [memb.] Local Society for Poets, Local Clairvoyance, Healing and Mediumship Society; [hon.] English Literature, English Language; [oth. writ.] Many poems published in local papers.; [pers.] Always strive to capture feelings and meanings in my writing. When I sit out in and reflect on the beauty of this earth and mother nature, feel this inspires me in my writing.; [a.] Birchington, Kent, UK

MCCORQUODALE, MS. LINDA

[pen.] Kris Tophar; [b.] 3 February 1964, Forfar, Scotland; [p.] Mrs. Sheila Thomson and Mr. Ronald Thomson; [m.] Geoffrey McCorquodale, 17 July 1987; [ch.] Two - one son of 5 1/2 Kristopher, daughter 12 1/2 Kelly; [ed.] Arbroathe Montrose Academy; [occ.] Self Employed Poet, Catering and Housekeeping; [oth. writ.] Private short stories and poems.; [pers.] Personal experience is the food of life to learn and grow from mistakes so that each mistake gets better.; [a.] Perth, UK

MCDERMOTT, PAUL

[b.] 24 November 1977, Liverpool; [p.] Linda and Marry; [ed.] Maghull High School, Hugh Baird College, Bootle; [occ.] I have just left college and currently work in a wholesalers in Liverpool called Parfetts; [oth. writ.] I have been writing stories and poetry all my life, but until now I have never had it published, when you wrote to me and offered to publish my poem, it was like a dream come true.; [pers.] The constant encouragement by my family and friends help make it possible to write poetry. My poems always reflect something that concerns me. Peace was written about a contrast between war and peace.; [a.] Liverpool, Merseyside, UK

MCDONALD, ARLENE

[b.] 21 May 1955, Manchester; [p.] Ethel and Herbert Reid; [m.] John Joseph, 16 August 1975; [ch.] Gary Martin; [ed.] Broughton High School for Girls; [occ.] Home Care Assistant; [oth. writ.] Several poems published by known publisher in 1995.; [pers.] I am in awe of God's creation of our world, and of my life poetry is my humble attempt to portray the soul and emotion of this creation.; [a.] Manchester, Lancashire, UK

MCDONALD, KATH

[b.] 5 August 1953, Manchester; [p.] Maurice and Jean Brown; [m.] Michael Richard, 5 August 1980; [ch.] Samantha and Debbie; [ed.] Two Trees Secondary Modern Haughton Green, Denton.; [occ.] Housewife/Cashier; [hon.] English Speaking Board (Hon) Trained at 32 years and Passed Nursery Nurse (NNEB); [oth. writ.] "Have You Ever Wondered" published in "Poets Of The North West" and "The Inevitable Vow" published in "First Time Poets"; [pers.] "My Writing has been influenced by personal findings and events within my life".; [a.] Stockport, Cheshire, UK

MCDONNELL, MAURA
[pen.] Maura McDonnell - Fairthlough; [b.] 16 May 1922, Eire; [p.] Michael and Fran Fairthlough; [m.] Martin McDonnell; [ch.] 2 Sons and 2 daughters; [ed.] Primary school and won scholarship to secondary school; [occ.] Old age pensioner and great - grandmother; [memb.] Write Away Writers Association of Ireland and oldest member of Drogheda creative writing class; [oth. writ.] Short stories and rhymes. Poems read on local radio and on Irish television.; [pers.] I started writing four years ago, at the age of seventy. I find it a great hobby and especially at my age, I find it keeps my brain active.; [a.] Drogheda, Louth, UK

MCDONNELL, PATRICIA
[pen.] Patricia McDonnell; [b.] 20 October 1955, Birmingham; [m.] Patrick, 11 March 1976; [memb.] Am involved in Gatehouse publishing. I'm secretary of a magazine Gatehouse voices and various local committees; [hon.] English language GCSE Grade B English literature GCSE Grade A distinction in RSA Core Text Word Processing. Currently working on my CLAIT; [oth. writ.] Have had a poem published in beauty and the beast magazine. Poems published in Gatehouse voices. Am working on a book currently; [pers.] I enjoy writing, poems, stories. I like reading historical novels, romances. I would like one day to write a book, which will be my dream.; [a.] Manchester, UK

MCEVOY, KATHLEEN
[pen.] Kathleen McEvoy; [b.] 28 November 1962, Stone House, Stroud Gloucester; [m.] Joseph McEvoy, 30 November 1983; [ch.] Two boys one girl; [ed.] 2nd Level 4th year; [occ.] Housewife; [oth. writ.] Several other poems written.; [pers.] My poetry is a written expression of my emotional self. Early influenced by W.B. Yeats and Patrick Kavanagh; [a.] Portlaoise, Co Laois, UK

MCEWAN, HASTIE CATHERINE
[pen.] Kay Hastie; [b.] 10 May 1960, London; [p.] Catherine Sword Huntly, Andrew Hastie Huntly; [m.] Gordon McEwan, 29 December 1980; [ch.] Lana Louise, Lee Gordon; [ed.] Copland High School, Wembley; [occ.] Home Carer; [memb.] 'Just For Youth' Youth Magazine; [hon.] Diploma in Short Story Writing/English from International Correspondence School (ICS) Glasgow/Certificate of Competence as a published writer from: Writer Bureau, Manchester; [oth. writ.] Articles and letters in Magazines, articles for Youth Magazine, 'Just For Youth' - (Local Magazine) Editor for Church Magazine: Belhaven News (Cane 3rd in Library live short story comp.); [pers.] "If you feel it in your heart - do it!"; [a.] Dunbar, East Lothian, UK

MCEWAN, MIKE
[b.] October 11, 1939, Glasgow; [ed.] Professional RMN, REN, RNT, DNA, M Phil, FRSH, Graduate of Dundee College of Technology Mediploma in Nurse Administration (DNA), Graduate of University of Glasgow (M Phil EDST); [occ.] University of Lecturer in Health Studies University of York; [memb.] Fellow of the Royal Society of Health Member of General Council University of Glasgow; [hon.] Territorial Decoration (TD) and Clasp, Gulf Medal, Saudi Arabian Medal, Kuwait Liberation Medal; [oth. writ.] A number of papers on military subjects presented at conversions/courses etc., thesis on stress as a curriculum development 1995 dissertation of nursing schemes 1988.; [pers.] Poetry used as a method of personal expression sometimes to express feeling or reaction to events or experiences and sometimes just for a bit of amusement.; [a.] Scarborough, N. Yorks

MCFARLAND, IRIS
[b.] 18 September 1954, Omagh; [p.] John and Frances Deery; [m.] Kenny McFarland, 13 March 1983; [ch.] Ryan, Colin, Clive, Dale, Amy; [ed.] Omagh High School; [occ.] Mother/Housewife; [memb.] Swimming Club, Pre-school Committee; [oth. writ.] Genealogy-Family History, Personal Journal.; [pers.] I enjoy writing short poems and personal/family poems. I also do a lot of folk art painting.; [a.] Omagh, Tyrone, UK

MCGANN, RAY
[b.] 7 September 1951, Longford; [m.] Liz; [ch.] Ross, Stacey, Kayleigh; [pers.] I dedicate this poem to nature.

MCGEE-OSBORNE, DOREEN
[b.] 2 January 1930, Staffordshire; [m.] John Edward McGee-Osborne, 8 April 1950; [ch.] Robert, Patricia, Christopher, Catherine; [occ.] Retired; [oth. writ.] Several poems published in magazines and anthologies, small booklet of my poems, "Indelible Impressions" published in June '96; [pers.] Married to an aviator, my poems reflect the nomadic lifestyle I have lived, the things I have seen having moved me to write; [a.] Canewdon, Rochford, Essex, UK

MCGOVERN, BERNADETTE
[b.] 16 September 1964, London; [p.] Mary and Peter McGovern; [pers.] Chance the tide draw forth the uniqueness in all our children; [a.] Aberdeen, UK

MCGOWAN, MARGARET ELIZABETH
[pen.] Elizabet Skidmore; [b.] 19 March 1948, Sheffield; [p.] Kenneth William, Hilda Murial Skidmore; [m.] Patrick McGowan, 22 June 1968; [ch.] Marianne, Joanne, Claire Louise, Tammy Jane; [pers.] This poem was intend for an intelligent charming and unpretentious man who inspired but never received it, to ashley, Wir Thanks.; [a.] Chesham, Bucks, UK

MCGREGOR, MRS. CLAIRE ELIZABETH
[b.] 31 May 1940, Haverton Hill, Billingham; [p.] Mary and Vincent Maddren; [m.] Alexander McGregor, 28 September 1963; [ch.] Karen, Allison, Joanne, Alexandra; [ed.] Haverton Hill, County Girls; [occ.] Housewife; [hon.] Giving birth to my four beautiful daughters; [pers.] After bringing up my four daughters, I have finally found time in my life to put my thoughts into rhyme and finding it so relaxing. This competition is the first I have entered and feel very privileged to be mentioned.; [a.] Billingham, Cleveland, UK

MCGUCKIN, ARNOLD
[b.] Ireland; [m.] Wendy Mathen McGuckin, 22 March 1975; [ch.] Angela, Helen; [ed.] Technical College (N. Ireland) to A-Level standard distinctions (95%) English, German credits (75%) Art, Physics, Social Studies etc.; [occ.] Marketing Manager; [hon.] Basic academic qualifications ref, above. Career- Wise Sales and Service Awards, A Beautiful Wife, Children and Good Health.; [oth. writ.] Numerous poems and prose on family, politics, occult emotion, spirituality etc. ect have received offers, in past - to have work included (published) in novel of author and magazines of organizations (but declined); [pers.] Since age 7 I have been quite prolific in expressing thoughts, feelings and reactions - 'on paper'. Began a novel - still incomplete on record but intact 'within' I live - I writer.; [a.] South Normanton, Derbyshire, UK

MCGUFFOG, KYLIE
[b.] 19 March 1980, Falkirk; [p.] David McGuffog, Jane Smith; [ed.] Larbert High School for 5 years attending Falkirk College; [occ.] Student; [hon.] Swimming certificates; [oth. writ.] Poems published in school magazine; [pers.] I have been influenced by past experiences in my life.; [a.] Stenhousemuir, Central, UK

MCHALE, IRENE
[pen.] Kirsty Lee-Brooke, Irene McHale; [b.] 2 April 1937, Manchester; [p.] Ethel McHale and Albert McHale; [m.] Divorced; [ch.] Jaqueline Susan Claridge, Mandy Veronica Claridge and Cheryl Jane Claridge; [hon.] English/Writing; [oth. writ.] Poems and short stories (unpublished); [pers.] I try to reflect natural beauty and the freedom it exudes. I have been inspired greatly in my writings by the beautiful yorkshire Moors and Surrounding area's, especially Haworth, home of the Bronte's.; [a.] Worthing, West Sussex, UK

MCKEAG, PAUL
[pen.] Kristian Phoenix; [b.] 15 November 1973, Newtownards; [p.] Margaret and Billy; [m.] Gay/ single; [ed.] Primary Model School Newtownards, Secondary Scrabe School Newtownards; [occ.] Unemployed writer, volunteering to help disabled and AIDS/HIV; [oth. writ.] Two short stories. The Piper and Out of the Attic. Also book of poetry. The letters of a Deviant, none of which are published.; [pers.] I live for the day when equality will no more be a theory but a practice. All men and women are equal.; [a.] Newtownards, Down, UK

MCKEARNEY, JAMES A.
[b.] October 24, 1957, Dungannon; [p.] Marylouise and James Joseph McKearney; [m.] Gail Lorraine McKearney, June 2, 1990; [ch.] Nicole, Louise and James; [ed.] Bishop Challoner Rlc; [occ.] Sales Engineer; [hon.] Diploma in travel and tourism; [oth. writ.] None other than 2 books that I have wrote for my own pleasure; [pers.] I have been writing ever since I can remember. I have not been influenced by any one writer. I tend to express my emotions on life, the good, the bad and the anguish we experience.; [a.] Kings Heath, Birmingham

MCKEEVER, JOHN JR.
[pen.] John J. Moore-McKeever/Jack J. Moore; [b.] 15 January 1973, Co. Louth; [p.] Catherine Moore and John McKeever; [ed.] Dublin Institute of Technology Mountjoy Square; [occ.] Filmmaker; [memb.] Ely Artist Awareness Group; [hon.] D.I.T.'s Certificate in Design (Usual Media); [oth. writ.] Screenplay shorts, currently working on 2nd Feature script.; [pers.] I'd like to thank God for all my wonderful gifts.; [a.] Ardee, Louth, UK

MCKEOWN, FRANCIS
[pen.] Frank McKeown; [b.] 30 March 1925, Belfast; [p.] Joseph McKeown, Mary McKeown; [m.] Lilian Margaret, 2 March 1956; [ch.] Beverley Ann, Susan Jane; [ed.] Newport Boys Council School (Barton Isle of Wight); [occ.] Retired; [memb.] Institute of Company Accountants; [oth. writ.] Everyday humorous rhymes, poems on history, philosophy etc., anti-war poems and songs, limericks.; [a.] Christchurch, Dorset, UK

MCKIE, LESTER RONALD
[b.] 27 May 1954, West Indies; [p.] Corneilous and Nanett McKie; [m.] Cynthia McKie, 16 August 1980 (Now divorced); [ch.] Three; [ed.] Mill End Secondary School, further Education at Goldsmiths

College London; [occ.] Fenth and Community Worker; [memb.] Member of St. Mark, Methodist Church High Wyncombe; [oth. writ.] Taken a 12 months correspondence course in writing. I have written two short stories none publish yet.; [pers.] I tend to write personal along the lines of one life experience, I like love stories and romantic novels. I put a lot of passion, emotion and feeling in my writing.; [a.] High Wycombe, Bucks, UK

MCKLOUD, JANE ANNE
[pen.] Jane McCairn; [b.] 24 June 1969, Greenock; [p.] James McCairn and Jane McCairn; [m.] Heath Richard McKloud, 4 August 1990; [ch.] Andrew James and Emily Jane; [ed.] Notre Dame High School, Dumbarton Glasgow Western College of Nursing and Midwifery; [occ.] Casualty Staff Nurse; [memb.] British Organ Donation Society; [pers.] At the end of the day comes the night.; [a.] Greenock, Renfrewshire, UK

MCLEAN, MRS. JANE
[b.] 7 July 1943, Londonderry City; [p.] Catherine Hunter McDeomiett; [m.] Alexander Michael McLean (Deceased), 6 July 1990; [ch.] One daughter (Miller) and twin sons by previous marriage; [ed.] Primary School, Londonderry High School, Open University; [occ.] Staff Nurse, Rush Hall Private Nursing Home; [memb.] Royal College of Nursing; [hon.] RMN, RGN; [oth. writ.] No other publications some poems published in church magazine; [pers.] I write for enjoyment and hope that my work may bring enjoyment and light with other lives.; [a.] Castlerock Coleranie, Londonderry, UK

MCLELLAN, JAN
[pen.] Kaye Morgan; [b.] 30 January 1960, London; [ch.] Philip James, Sarah Louise; [ed.] Spencefield Secondary Modern Wigston College F.E.; [occ.] Community Care Worker; [oth. writ.] Poems included in other anthologies. Currently researching for a work in human nature.; [pers.] So many ways to have or to be... so few have we experienced... so many others to explore...; [a.] Leicester, UK

MCMANUS, D.
[pen.] Dympna Elizabeth; [b.] 5 July 1928, Fermanagh; [p.] William Margaret Keown; [m.] Hugh McManus, 26 August 1959; [ch.] Two girls; [ed.] Secondary; [occ.] Housewife; [hon.] 1982, 1983, 1984, sat for general certificate of education at Fermanagh College of further education and achieved subjects in English Literature, English language, History, Sociology, 1953 Certificate of Proficiency Mannequin Beauty Culture, Modelling, Makeup; [pers.] I am grateful my poem been published, it will let the world see the pollution of our beautiful planet. Fields of cattle we can't survive on meat. But the hour is upon us slaughtering the innocent dreadful man needs to change fast, we used to be self-sufficient, etc., potatoes, vegetables wildflowers, birds, insects, fish, frogs, scarce crickets, grasshopper extinct.; [a.] Lisnaskea, Fermanagh, UK

MCMILLAN, MISS DIANE
[pen.] Diane McMillan; [b.] 26 May 1976, Dunoon; [p.] Marion and Norrie McMillan; [ed.] Dunoon Grammar School 19-; [occ.] Childminder/Nanny; [pers.] I have written poetry since I can remember, for my own pleasure, I am now very happy and hopefully that maybe somebody will receive pleasure from my writing.; [a.] Dunoon, Argyll, UK

MCNAMARA, WINIFRED
[pen.] Oonagh McNamara; [b.] 21 December 1941, Dublin; [p.] John Lee and Catherine Lee; [m.] Joseph McNamara, 14 August 1966; [ch.] John, Robert, Fiona, Paula one Grandchild Jessica; [occ.] Along with my Husband. We Manage our own Farm; [memb.] Member of the Royal Canal Restoration Committee; [hon.] Certificate from the Royal life saving Society, Certificate of Merit from Mensa; [oth. writ.] Numerous poems at the moment, I am compiling some Anecdotes of things remembered.; [pers.] When I write a poem it relieves the trauma of the inspiration that inspired it.; [a.] Abbeyshrule, Longford, Ireland

MCRAE, DANIEL
[b.] 24 August 1930, Glasgow; [p.] Daniel McRae, Angelina McRae; [m.] Margaret McRae, 9 February 1951; [ch.] Daniel, Carol, Marie, Lyn, Mark, Ann, Charles; [ed.] Bernard Street Junior Secondary; [occ.] Retired, painter signwriter; [memb.] Telegraph Amateur Radio Society; [hon.] City and Guilds on Amateur Radio and Electronics; [oth. writ.] Ghosts Ghouls and Witches, Follow The Star, several poems published in Amateur Radio Magazines and local press; [pers.] To get through life with as little hassle as possible.; [a.] Slamannan, Stirling, UK

MCTAVISH, SANDY
[pen.] Sandy McTavish; [b.] 22 January 1947, Paisley; [p.] Edward and Roseann; [m.] Myra, 9 November 1968; [ch.] Dawn and Scott (Grandson Ross); [ed.] St. Mirins Academy, Senior Secondary, Reid Kerr College; [occ.] Security Guard; [memb.] Anchor Bowling Club, Dykebar Social Club; [hon.] Work printed honour enough for me; [oth. writ.] Work printed in book 'Inspiration from Scotland' Poem title: A Much Needed Language, re: Gaelic language should be taught in all schools and homes.; [pers.] Help and consider people who 'really' need it!; [a.] Paisley, Renfrewshire, UK

MCWHIRTER, DAWN
[b.] 3 February 1981, Stranraer; [p.] Thomas McWhirter; [ed.] Kirkcolm Primary School and presently at Stranraer Academy; [occ.] In full time education; [pers.] I enjoyed writing my poem very much as it is on a topic that I feel strongly about. I enjoy writing very much and hope that the success of this poem is the first of many others.; [a.] Stranraer, Dumfries and Galloway, UK

MEEKINS, SHAUN ANTHONY
[b.] 30 May 1977, Maidstone; [p.] (F) - Anthony Meekins, (M) - Karen Meekins; [ed.] The Maplesden Noakes School, Winchester University; [occ.] Literary, Drama Student at Winchester University; [hon.] Head Boy (1994-1995) The Maplesden Noaks School. First Prize Pianist, Folkestone Performing Arts Festival, Commendations in Amateur Dramatics; [oth. writ.] Articles published in county newspaper. 'The Kent Messenger!'; [pers.] "What better way to glorify our world than to Personify The Beauty Within It." My Inspiration derives from 'Metaphysical Poetry.'; [a.] Maidstone, Kent, UK

MELLOR, MISS TRACY
[b.] 20 June 1981, British Forces, Iserlohn, Germany; [p.] Moya Cudworth and Ian Mellor; [ed.] Edinburgh School Munster, Germany, Heritage School Clowne Chesterfield, Kings School Gutersloh Germany; [occ.] School Pupil; [pers.] This is my first piece of work, and I am very proud to be having it published.; [a.] Padderborn, Germany

MENDOZA, CELESTE
[b.] 2 November 1979, Trinidad; [p.] George, Chundra Mendoza; [ed.] Cheadle Hulme High School; [occ.] A Student; [pers.] I hope to keep up the good work in my writing.; [a.] Cheadle Hulme, Cheshire, UK

MEREDITH, TERRY
[pen.] Terry Meredith; [b.] 3 April 1954, South Wales; [p.] William and Lucy; [m.] Fiona, 26 December 1994; [ed.] Cymmer Alan Comprehensive, Port Talbot, Swansea College of Technology; [occ.] Sales and Marketing Director; [oth. writ.] A number of poems in local magazines, various public renditions given including BBC Radio Wales, plus one poem included in the Wales 1996 anthology published by poetry now.; [pers.] I use the gift of words to share my thoughts and hopes and dreams with others with a view to giving a little sunshine into rainy lives.; [a.] Chepstow, Gwent, UK

MERRIGAN, NIKOLA
[b.] 19 February 1946, Dublin; [p.] Dr. Michael O'Donnell and Joey; [m.] Patrick Merrigan, 14 November 1968; [ch.] Michael Patrick, Nicholas and Richard; [ed.] Our Lady's School, Templelougue St. Louis, Ruthmines, St. Marys, Arklow; [occ.] Freelance Water Colour Artist; [oth. writ.] Never published any of my poetry before; [pers.] The nuns in school said I was always day dreaming, I still do, and escape from real life with my painting and poetry. I like to reflect on life from the outside.; [a.] Cork, Cork, UK

MERRIMAN, SHEILA JOAN
[b.] 11 December 1936, Redditch, Worcs; [p.] Harold Crump, Ada Crump; [m.] Roy Merriman, 4 October 1958; [ch.] Wendy Ann, Trudi Alison, Neil Andrew; [occ.] Retired; [pers.] I write poems for my own pleasure and relaxation; [a.] Redditch, Worcs, UK

METIN, BONNY
[pen.] Bonny Metin; [b.] 18 February 1967, Gravesend, Kent; [p.] Mr. Stanly and Mrs. Jean Greenfield; [m.] Mr. Sahin Metin, 1 October 1987; [ch.] Yasemin, Sam; [ed.] Southfields Comprehensive school a couple of GCSES gained as a mature student; [occ.] Housewife; [oth. writ.] A few poems published in books such at "Poetry Now '96", "Auld Lang Syne '96".; [pers.] The only way to truly express my emotions is through poetry and the thought that someone gets joy through my writing is totally exhilarating.; [a.] Leyton, London, UK

MIDDLETON, JEAN
[pen.] J. Middleton; [b.] 19 September 1914, Bedford; [p.] Mrs. E. and Mr. A. W. Coleman; [m.] Maurice B. Middleton, B. Com., B.A., 26 December 1938; [ch.] One son, Michael, one daughter, Ann; [ed.] Bedford High, Bedford Coll. husband head of Local High School when he died at 53; [occ.] Retired; [memb.] Local Tennis Club National Trust Local Choir; [oth. writ.] School Magazine Local Magazine; [pers.] Have been to H. Kong 16 times son worked there hence have travelled widely in Far East. Philippines, Thailand, China, Macau, Malaysia, and Europe. My father worked on the great airships.; [a.] Bexhill-on-Sea, East Sussex, UK

MIDDLETON, JOAN
[pen.] Joan Flint; [b.] 29 July, Market Harborough; [p.] Phylis Flint and Harry Flint; [ch.] Tina Whitbread, Steven Whitbread; [ed.] Market Harborough High School; [occ.] Fashions; [memb.] Swimming Club, Gardening Club; [oth. writ.] Children's stories creative writing unpublished; [pers.] To give peace of mind in reading my poems how to feel life and realize the importance of living.; [a.] West Bridgeford, Notts, UK

MIDDLETON, SAMANTHA JANE
[pen.] Sam Middleton; [b.] 16 January 1970, Aylesbury, Bucks; [p.] Sidney Middleton, Pauline Middleton; [ed.] Temple Cowley - Oxford, Cowley St. John - Oxford, University of London; [occ.] Law Clerk - Rixons Solicitors; [pers.] My work is relevant to the people around me and my environment, I reflect my personal thoughts and observations.; [a.] Folkestone, Kent, UK

MILES, PATRICK
[pen.] Patrick Miles; [b.] 5 September 1928, Croxley; [p.] Thomas and Sarah; [m.] Catherine, 5 September 1967; [ed.] The city of London School, St Peters, York and Trinity College, Dublin University; [occ.] Career Development Consultant and International Marketing Consultant; [memb.] Royal Society of Arts Institute of Marketing, Blisworth Art Society (Exhibitor); [hon.] FRSA 1951-1995, MA Dublin 1960 English and Economics; [oth. writ.] Poems 1991 entitled "Wisdom Smiling". Published by Arthur Stockweil Humorous Group of Tracts - "How to Succeed in Life" - "Networking"; [pers.] As a poet, musician, and painter I just cannot escape the conclusion that God is everywhere. All the time, and this is reflected in my writing.; [a.] Blisworth, North Hants, UK

MILLAR, JILLIAN A.
[b.] 8 November 1976, Paisley; [p.] Eileen McCready, Ronald Millar; [ed.] St. Lukes High School, Barrhead; [occ.] Electronic Assembler; [memb.] British Mensa; [a.] Barrhead, Glasgow, UK

MILLER, CAROL-ANN
[b.] 28 June 1977, Dundee; [p.] Maureen Miller; [ed.] St. Saviours High School Dundee and in the future I will study social work at university; [occ.] Care Assistant; [pers.] The poems I have written reflect emotions and experiences I have found hard to express in any other way. I hope that when others read my work they are able to extract a part of it which they can identify with. I also try to poetry how special life is in my work.; [a.] Bampton, Oxfordshire, UK

MILLER, GORDON
[b.] 7 April 1976, Glasgow; [p.] Thomas Miller, Teresa Miller; [ed.] Kings Park Secondary School; [occ.] Customer Service Assistant; [memb.] Several Computer Programmer Clubs; [oth. writ.] Several poems published by computer programming club; [pers.] I prefer to write about the emotions and fears people keep private.; [a.] Glasgow, Strathclyde, UK

MILLICHIP, ADRIAN
[b.] 5 October 1963, Stourport; [p.] Rosina Trotman, Roger Millichip; [ed.] Stourport and Wolverhampton Schools, Wolverhampton University.; [occ.] Driver; [hon.] Diploma of higher Education, BA (Hons) Humanities; [pers.] The idea for the poem was firs penned about 16 years ago when I was still a teenager and adjusted about 4 years later. It is the result of not one but

various experiences and attempts to reflect the feelings of being a youth. It was entered on the Philosophy of "Nothing Ventured, Nothing Gained".; [a.] Stourport, Worcs, UK

MILLS, GHLADYS
[b.] 16 January 1921, Dorset; [p.] Ellen and William Thomas; [m.] Widowed, 4 August 1941; [ch.] Three sons; [ed.] Educated in Finchley London, then known as Central School equivalent to the now comprehensive school; [occ.] Retired from Local Government at age 64; [oth. writ.] I write for friends my son has my poems and stories put into book form for me, this is the first time I've submitted to a competition. I write for pleasure to myself and others.; [pers.] Most of my poems reflect situations we all experience at times during our cries and I am fortunate to be able to put this into poetry. Therefore people can relate themselves to my words.; [a.] Canvey Island, Essex, UK

MILLS, THURZAH
[pen.] Thurzah Berry; [b.] 11 January 1961, London; [p.] Archibald Neville and Jean Rita Berry; [m.] Paul Mills, 7 May 1996; [ch.] Danny Christopher; [ed.] Rock Hills School for Girls; [occ.] Part Time Cashier; [memb.] Company Theatre Group; [pers.] I have always found writing to be very therapeutic. It gives me a greater understanding of the hurdles in our pathway of life. Several poems written, as gifts, for family and friends - none submitted before for publishing!; [a.] London, UK

MILNE, LAURA J.
[pen.] "LJ"; [b.] 3 October 1972, Yorkshire; [p.] Margaret and Raymond Milne; [ed.] Elgin Academy '84-'89, Cults Academy '89-'90, Robert Gordons Uni '91-'95, Aberdeen University '96-'99; [occ.] Law Student; [memb.] Keen Sportsman, enjoy Mini Triatrilons, 1/2 Marathons former Scottish Swimmer, Member of Local Gym; [hon.] BA (Hons) in Law and Management, currently studying an accelerated LLB; [oth. writ.] None (this is all very new to me!) I do like to write personal poems and ditty's for my friends and family.; [pers.] Always try to do the best for yourself achieving your own goals do what you feel is right for yourself not simply to please others.; [a.] Aberdeen, UK

MILNE, PAULA ELIZABETH
[pen.] Paula Milne; [b.] 10 February 1964, Belfast; [p.] Mr. and Mrs. J. L. Milne; [ed.] Killard House School and Gilnahirk Primary School; [occ.] N.V.Q. Level 2 Award in Catering; [hon.] I love to write poems and I have entered some poems in our Local Magazine; [oth. writ.] For the last year I have been at night school doing english learning the basic's doing poetry reading poems, this has greatly help me with every day life.; [pers.] I have been greatly influenced by poems and poetry and I enjoy writing poems and I am delighted that my poem was chosen to be published.; [a.] Dundonald, Belfast, UK

MITCHELL, GRAHAM
[b.] 14 May 1960, Derby; [p.] Alan and Emma; [ed.] A sound and enjoyable State Education; [occ.] Production Worker; [memb.] The Internation Society of Poets, The Poetry Society, Poetry Digest; [oth.writ.] Day After Day. War of the Veg! Julie, I love you truly! for my love of Julie! Figure of eight it's a joy when we kiss!; [pers.] Live your life as if in clover, because when you're dead you're dead all over!; [a.] Derby, Derbyshire, UK

MITCHELL, PATRICIA K.
[b.] 23 May 1922, Ealing; [p.] Florence Marchbank, William Marchbank; [m.] The late Ernest George Mitchell, 12 June 1948; [ch.] Alan John and Andrew Peter George; [ed.] Ranelagh School, Bracknell, Hampton Emergency Training College; [occ.] Widow, Retired teacher; [memb.] A.R.I.P.H.H. for life I belong to Thursday Centre, run by help the aged. A member of the Methodist Church. A member of the Mengo Hospital in Kampala, Friendship Association; [hon.] 2 Certificates and 1 Diploma from R.I.P.H.H. qualified teachers certificate 1947; [oth. writ.] I have written several stories for children, 5-9 yrs. not yet published.; [pers.] Try to be content and grateful for what you have in life. When over to, go on learning. Be friends with all people. Pray more each day.; [a.] Craven Arms, Shropshire, UK

MITCHELL, RACHEL CLAIRE
[b.] 16 August 1979, Poole, Dorset; [p.] Michael John and Sandra; [m.] Teresa Mitchell; [ed.] Redhill Comprehensive; [occ.] Student, Nursing Nurse; [pers.] I have written many poems. And hope they too may be published one day. I hope my poems will inspire others. My poems are expressions of my feelings.; [a.] Arnold, Nottingham, UK

MONIE, EILEEN ROSE
[b.] 7 June 1954, Barking, Essex; [p.] Roseina and Joseph; [m.] 28 August 1976; [ed.] Sacred Heart Convent School for Girls Dagenham Essex; [occ.] Credit Controller; [memb.] Social Clubs as I enjoy Dancing Immensely; [hon.] Several Prizes at School for Poetry and Creative Writing; [oth. writ.] A selection of poems on numerous subjects however I am usually called upon my friends to compose personalized birthday wishes and also I have written verse for headstones as although a selection are offered to the bereaved from a book it is so nice to create one of your own especially if you have known the deceased.; [pers.] My interest in poetry came about when I was 7 years of age as I used to enjoy composing religious prayers in poem form and have been enthralled ever since. I have a great love of life and believe that there are no dress rehearsals do not harm anybody and life will take care of you along with it is nice to be important but it is more important to be nice.; [a.] Barking, Essex, UK

MOON, PATRICIA
[pen.] Pat; [b.] 22 October 1940, Sunderland; [p.] Violet Alexandra Strain and Ernie Strain; [m.] Alfred Patrick Moon, 26 March 1960; [ch.] Clifford and Julia; [ed.] Barnes School for Girls Sunderland; [occ.] Receptionist; [hon.] Awards in oral communications; [oth. writ.] Brief Autobiography written in verse; [pers.] Portraying one's thoughts in poetry, helps to express deep feelings.; [a.] Bedworth, Warwickshire, UK

MOONEY, GARY
[b.] 17 February 1963, Broxburn; [p.] Thomas Mooney, Selina Reid; [m.] Diane Mooney; [ch.] Kirsten Louise; [ed.] Broxburn Academy Public School; [occ.] Electrical Transformer Test Engineer; [memb.] Uphall Golf Club; [oth. writ.] None others enclosed or submitted for publishing by myself, though I have written many poems as a personal hobby since primary school age; [pers.] To be dedicated and contented in everything I do.; [a.] Uphall, West Lothian, UK

MOONEY, RACHAEL
[b.] 3 July 1979, Letter Kenny; [p.] Linda Gallagher and Kevin Mooney; [ed.] Lore to Convent, Milford Leaving Cert. Student; [occ.] Student; [memb.] Ceoltas Ceolteoiri Cirinn; [hon.] 'The New Girl' awarded 10th place in Windows Publications, Cavan, Ireland.; [oth. writ.] Several poems published in local newspapers. Booklet of poems produced and pointed locally for Guises award. (President's Award).; [pers.] I don't set time aside to write poetry the mood just takes me over and I have to write. It's a great way to express yourself; [a.] Carrigart, Ireland

MOORE, MR. A. S.
[pen.] A. Moore; [b.] 18 May 1917, East London; [p.] Deceased; [m.] (Deceased) Doris Moore, 1980; [ed.] Elementary; [occ.] Disabled O.A.P.; [memb.] Ex Master Builder. Ex-Chief Technician, Hospital Ex. Special constable (London) 25 yrs Younger Days (Swimming, Life Saving Arts St. John's Ambulance Member. Passed driving test, age 69 But do not drive now; [hon.] Home Service Medal, Battle Britain Medal, 1st ever (presented) diploma Morbid Anatomy, Long Service Medal, 25 yrs Metropolitan Police.; [oth. writ.] I have compiled various poems in a book, or my stop family at my Demise.; [pers.] Sorry about my writing, but I get cramps in my fingers at time.; [a.] Ashford, Kent, UK

MOORE, MRS. GLADYS
[b.] 18 August 1906, Barnsley; [m.] Mr. T. Moore; [occ.] Housewife; [a.] Barnsley, South Yorkshire, UK

MOORE, MRS. VIOLET M.
[b.] 17 July 1915, Co. Durham; [p.] Mr. and Mrs. F. Harrison; [m.] Widow of Ex. Sgt. S. F. Moore Fepow, 8 October 1939 (war time); [ch.] Two sons also one daughter; [ed.] Church of England Schools; [occ.] Retired Pensioner; [oth. writ.] I wrote my war time memories 2nd world war bride also my husband badly wounded as a far east prisoner of war in Changi Jail Singapore from 1942 to 1945 also my life earlier ref the 1st world war. My book called "Bouquet of Memories", published by myself 1915 to 1990 then I was 75 years old.; [a.] Bury Saint Edwards, Suffolk, UK

MORCIANO, VESNA KOLACKO
[pen.] V. K. Morciano; [b.] 3 May 1969, Australia; [p.] Joseph and Carol Kolacko; [m.] David Morciano, 13 April 1994; [ed.] Diploma in Business Operations, Cert. in Public Administration and Clerical, Cert. in Office and Business Studies; [occ.] Sales and Service, Co-Ordinator; [memb.] Health and Fitness Club; [oth. writ.] Working on a novel; [pers.] Man's mind is a wonderful playground of ideas that I love to get hold of and put them on paper to keep immortal. All stories are worth being told!; [a.] Geneva, Switzerland

MORCOMBE, ANDREW
[pen.] Drew Morcombe; [b.] 2 March 1965, Glasgow; [p.] James and Mary Morcombe; [m.] Angela Gallagher Morcombe, 24 April 1992; [ch.] Megan Fiona, Ciaran Brian; [ed.] Saint Anne's R.C. Primary, Saint Mungo's Academy, Saint Andrew's College of Education; [occ.] School teacher, Saint Bride's Primary, Cambuslang; [memb.] General Teaching Council for Scotland, Educational Institute of Scotland; [hon.] Bachelor of Education; [oth. writ.] 'Ode to Angela' a poem for my wife.; [pers.] Many writers are inspired by the depressingly morose or moribund but I have been inspired only twice by the joys of family.; [a.] Hamilton, South Lanarkshire, UK

MORRIS, EILEEN
[pen.] Eileen Morris; [b.] 3 April 1935, London; [p.] William Smith, Alive Smith; [m.] Divorced 1969; [ch.] Leslie Albert, Lorraine Alison; [ed.] Rainham Secondary, St. Albans College; [occ.] Retired Higher Clerical Officer, Community Health Clinic; [memb.] Retirement Fellowship, Rainham Horticultural Society; [hon.] Book Keeping to Trial Balance together with Pitmans Shorthand and Typing Certificates 1950; [oth. writ.] Several poems published in Rainham poets annual anthology (1994 to 1996), a poem published in moving picture, (forward press, 1996); [pers.] For many years I have entertained family and friends by writing personalized poems on special occasions. Since retiring I have been encouraged by my family to expand on my literary interests.; [a.] Upminster, Essex, UK

MORRIS, HELGA
[b.] 21 July 1931, Liverpool; [p.] Alf and Edith Kristensen; [m.] Gordon Morris (Deceased 1981), 9 September 1954; [ch.] Dan, Kathy, Nicola, Louise, Karla; [ed.] Elementary School Technical College; [occ.] Pensioner; [hon.] N.N.E.B.; [oth. writ.] 2 Poems (age 11) 4 poems 1996, Newspaper article; [pers.] I am housebound I have time on my hands so writing helps to pass that time at the same time giving pleasure, humour, sometimes sadness recalling memories from the past.; [a.] Scunthorpe, North Lincs, UK

MORRIS, MARY
[b.] 28 September 1929, Aspull; [p.] Wilfred and Dora Prescott; [pers.] For myself and others; [a.] Hindley, Lancashire, UK

MORRIS, PATRICIA MAE
[b.] 17 May 1924, Calcutta, India; [p.] Maurice and Daisy Morris; [ed.] Convent of Jesus and Mary Junior Overseas University Examination of Cambridge; [occ.] Free Lance Writer; [memb.] Association Member Song Writer Guild Of Great Britain; [hon.] Graduate in Bible Studies Old and New Testament. First Class Honours in English Literature; [oth. writ.] H. M. The Queen's Coronation, the wedding of Princess Margaret and Mr. Armstrong Jones Charles and Diana's Wedding and Andrew and Sarah's Wedding. Just for a while, smile love thy neighbour thank you Lord.; [pers.] I have one passion in life to show kindness to all those who come my way the years are slipping by so fast who knows I may not be around tomorrow.; [a.] London, UK

MORRIS, PETER JOSEPH
[pen.] Peter J. Morris; [b.] 26 October 1965, Kelsall; [p.] Robert James Morris, Patricia Ann Morris; [ed.] Ponteland First School, (About 9 years old) Percy Hedly (special school) Man Power Service Centre, Killing Worth Yr. S Winncomblee Walker/New Job Hordons Woodcrafts West Denton, (Two times); [occ.] Bedpacker (Remploy); [memb.] British Philaeic Bureau Stamp Active, Royal Mail Collectors Club, Voyager Stamp CC (Eire) B. This stamp travellers Club Canada; [hon.] C.S.E. English oral grade 3, english written G-4 English lictoer G-3; [pers.] I write poems because I like to, and I collect stamps.; [a.] Newcastle-upon-Tyne, Tyne and Wear, UK

MORSE, MRS. ELUNED
[b.] 25 November 1931, Denbigh, N. Wales; [p.] Morris and Ellen Owen; [m.] Douglas Morse/Widow of Deceased Harry William 1966, 7 August 1971; [ch.] Four Sons and Nine Grandchildren; [ed.] Denbigh Grammar School; [occ.] Housewife,

Former Nurse and D'Receptionist; [oth. writ.] Write for own Amusement. Never entered a competition before.; [pers.] I write about subjects I feel deeply about, am able to express inner feelings, better in poetry. I love the sounds of words. Being a welsh speaker, I also write in welsh; [a.] Dinas Powys, South Glamorgan, UK

MORSE, JEAN
[pen.] Janet Esrom; [b.] 4 May 1936, Johannesburg; [p.] William and Alleten Parry; [m.] Thomas, 5 June 1957; [ch.] Gregory, Bryn, Russell, Kathryn; [ed.] Wynberg Girls High Ex commercial school teacher; [occ.] Home maker; [memb.] Stellenbosch Food and Wine Guild, Flower Club, Cape Writers Circle, SA Kennel Club; [hon.] Eisteddfod Awards for music and singing; [oth. writ.] Articles for local newspaper - poems and short stories; [pers.] I believe in dreams am a born optimist love people and travel. Breed laboratories and study French; [a.] Stellenbosch, South Africa

MORTIMER, SUSAN
[b.] 7 May 1951, Sydney, Australia; [m.] Divorced; [ch.] Three children; [ed.] Burwood Girls High School in Sydney; [hon.] I participated as a soprano in performances by the Tamworth Opera Society and the Tamworth Musical Society and sang a Amateur and professional venues; [pers.] These works are channelled from Metatron, to encourage mankind to greater heights. In November last year, that which truly believe, began to flow through me in words that inspired and taught me greater spiritual understanding, these works continue to flow. I read about your competition in a magazine, whilst at my hairdresser in London, and entered your competition because I felt that it would give me some technical guidelines for future works. Your words of praise have greatly encouraged me, and I am delighted that others will read and perhaps experience through this work, the love that is there and constant for them.; [a.] Tamworth, New South Wales, Australia

MOYSEN, JAYNE
[b.] North Wales; [p.] Dorothy and Cyril; [ch.] Emma (One Daughter); [ed.] Ruabon School and Wrexham College; [memb.] Wrexham Tennis Club; [hon.] English, Music and Business Studies; [oth. writ.] I write songs and have had some success with recording but I really enjoy performing them live.; [pers.] I write from my heart.; [a.] Wrexham, UK

MULLEN, KAMIRIA
[b.] 25 January 1942, Wellington; [p.] Ngamate Tamati and Henry Mullen; [m.] Divorced; [ch.] Roera Wendy Thomas, Helen Moana Mataki, Terence Stevens (adopted out) plus 9 grand children; [ed.] Left High School with no qualifications at 15, worked as Newspaper Librarian, Aerial Photograph Librarian, Shop Assistant, Film Projectionist, Film Production Ass. Prison Officer (10 yrs). Graduated as a Trained Bilingual Primary School Teacher in 1992 (at 50 yrs old) have about five papers to finish on a degree in Maori Law and Philosophy, plus 5 papers to complete a Bachelor of Education; [occ.] Maori Language Teacher (Children and Adults), Writer, Part-time Actress; [memb.] Te Atoarangi Incorporated Society. (Organization set up to promote the realization of the indigenous language of New Zealand, Maori) Hongoeka Marae Incorporated Society. Committee that runs my tribal meeting place (Marae) in my home town Plimmerton.) I am a member of the Ngati Toarangatira and Te Atiawa tribes on my Mothers side. On my Father's my great grandparents came from Derry and Antrim respectively in Ireland;

[hon.] If I win a prize in this competition this will be my first Award; [oth. writ.] Short story about children published in Te Ao Marama Contemporary Maori writing for children 1994. Currently writing a book on sexual abuse and domestic violence based on my own experiences and romance for mills and boons for money! I am perpetually broke.; [pers.] A survivor of sexual and physical abuse I am dedicated to working on ways to eradicate violent behavior. I have been involved in a campaign to promote tougher legislation against offenders which has taken affect on the 1-7-96 in N2. I do not really know the rules for good poetry - I write what I feel.; [a.] Hongoeka, Plimmerton, New Zealand

MULLER, CHARLES HUMPHREY
[pen.] Harry Denton; [b.] 11 August 1942, Ladybrand, South Africa; [p.] Aubrey J. Muller, Winifred L. Muller; [m.] Carolyn Joanne (Nee Moore), 6 January 1979; [ch.] Winifred Blair, Valerie Kotkin-Smith, Carol Bathgate, Angus and Bruce Muller; [ed.] Grey College, S.A., BA (Natal) Bahons (OFS), MA (Wales), Ph.D. (London), D. Litt. (OFS), D.Ed. (SA); [occ.] Owner, Proprietor of the Kenmore Bank Hotel, Jedburgh, Scotland; [memb.] British Interplanetary Society, London, AUETSA (Assoc. of University English Teachers of Southern Africa), SBTB (Scottish Borders Tourist Board), STB (Scottish Tourist Board, Edinburgh); [hon.] Best Student Pilot: PMB Aero Club 30 May 1964, British Council Senior Scholarship 1993, M.Ed. (Univ. S.A.) awarded with distinction (1980). Editor of UNISA English Studies Editor of Communique Chair of English, University of the North, 1979-1988; [oth. writ.] You can have anything you really want (diadem books), several books on English lit teaching, literary stylistic, victorian and modern novel, and teletuition (Distance Learning) and Didactics. (McGraw-Hill, OUP, MacMillan). Various poems.; [pers.] I grapple with the personal's consciousness in a sometimes bewildering world. Over arching the bleakness is hope. Influenced by the novels of Graham Greene and the positive thinking of Norman Vincent Peale and Christian faith.; [a.] Jedburgh, Roxburghshire, UK

MULLINS, FIONA LOUISE
[b.] 23 October 1976, Bradford; [p.] Moira Mullins, Kenneth Mullins; [ed.] Bingley Grammar School, Hull University; [occ.] American Studies, Undergraduate Student, Hull University; [memb.] Hull University Ski Club, Hull University Fencing Club; [oth. writ.] One poem in the "Poetry Now, Young Writers" Regional Anthology (W. Yorks) and one in the "Poetry Now" anthology "The Forbidden Fruit"; [pers.] I write about how I feel. So don't laugh!; [a.] Bingley, W. Yorks, UK

MULLINS, SARAH JANE
[b.] 28 November 1981, Nuneaton; [p.] (Step Father) Paul and Vivien Shortland and (Birth Father) Tony Mullins; [ed.] Hartshill Grant Maintained School, Nuneaton; [occ.] School girl; [oth. writ.] Personal anthology; [pers.] I always wanted something published.; [a.] Nuneaton, Warwickshire, UK

MUNN, ALLAN F.
[b.] 17 August 1941, Zimbabwe; [m.] Gillian; [ch.] Five; [ed.] Boarding School at Churchill in Harare. Member of the Chartered Institute of Marketing; [occ.] Chairman of Companies and Consumer Magazine Publisher; [hon.] Jaycees Andrew Dunlop Award in Leadership; [oth. writ.] Children's and Adult Poetry - The Book "Extinction

if Forever" - Prize Winner in the Canadian Poetry Competition, poem 'First Love.'; [pers.] All life has an ending and becomes extinct nature has its time and its ways. But the humans are racing and trying to outwit their creator, by shortening the days.; [a.] Harare, Zimbabwe

MURPHY, AIDAN
[pen.] Audie; [b.] 20 February 1967, Dublin, Ireland; [p.] Patrick and Veronica; [ed.] Primary and Secondary; [occ.] Soldier Irish Defence Forces; [memb.] Cobh Youth Services, Collins Bk. Squash Club; [hon.] 2 Military Service medals, for service over seas.; [oth. writ.] A poem titled "All For The Children" printed in Unifil magazine "Litani."; [pers.] We are more than any one person can see.; [a.] Cobh, Cork, UK

MURPHY, ELIZABETH MARY
[b.] 14 May 1965, Enniscourthy; [p.] Mathew and Ann Murphy; [ed.] Ballyraeburk N.S, and F.C.J. Convent Bundody; [occ.] Completed 2.2 year course with Vtos; [memb.]; [hon.]; [oth. writ.]; [pers.] Never give up when the chips are down, in other words don't give up, when things don't go according to plan; [a.] Ferns, Wetford, UK

MURPHY, FRANCIS HAZEL
[b.] 14 September 1957, Surrey; [p.] Peter and Jean Murphy; [m.] To be Clive Bryant, getting married 19 October 1996; [ch.] Wayne Valentine George Semark, I will have 4 step children when I nmarry; [ed.] Yeoman's Bridge County School, Ash, Aldershot Hants; [occ.] Partner in a Printing Firm "Butterfly Press"; [pers.] I like to write poems that relate to circumstances and express feelings.

MURRAY, NORAH
[b.] 13 April 1944, Linton, Morpeth; [m.] James Murray, 1 November 1963; [ch.] Graham James, Brian Gregg; [ed.] Uddingston Grammar; [occ.] Housewife; [memb.] Lares Amateur Operatic Society Lares Flowers Club; [a.] Lares, Ayrshire, UK

NAAKTGEBORELL, BIDMEAD V. A. L.
[pen.] "Bargie"; [b.] 5 November, Ruscombe; [p.] Lottie Whittaker, Percival Bidmead; [m.] Peter Naaktgeborell, 24 April; [ch.] Son, daughter; [oth. writ.] Poems, one printed in Local Paper. (Short stories never offered for print).; [pers.] "I often wonder," have we ever considered how much our lives weigh in the balance of "if."; [a.] The Hague, Holland

NEESGAARD, LINE
[b.] 20 January 1968, Dublin; [p.] Bitten Neesgaard Kaspersen and Johnny Kaspersen; [ch.] Pablito; [ed.] Newbold College, Blacknell Napier University, Edinburgh; [occ.] Freelance Photographer; [hon.] B.A. with Distinction in Photography, Film and T.V.; [oth. writ.] Extensive Personal Work, nothing published; [a.] Holte, Denmark, UK

NEIL, PATRICIA A.
[b.] 23 March 1932, Sheffield; [p.] Marjorie and Harry Richardson; [m.] Stanley Neil, 9 December 1978; [ch.] David Nigel/Judith Helen/Anne Marie; [ed.] Abbeydale Girls, Grammar School (Sheffield); [occ.] Retired - was fultime postwoman for 14 yrs.; [pers.] I strive to reflect the beauty of nature in my writing, as the countryside has always held an irresistible source of joy and pleasure for me.; [a.] Skegness, Lincolnshire, UK

NELSON, PATRICIA
[pen.] Claudia; [b.] 25 March 1956, Sefton Park; [p.] Mary; [ed.] Plumstead Manor School London; [occ.] Model; [hon.] French, Geography Math's SCE; [oth. writ.] Poems published in anchor books - established in 1992. (5 so far.) on Love - Twilight - Rape.; [pers.] I melt with a shimmer of mystery when I write. 'Life is a creation - to feel and touch your emotions.' (A) Oscar Wilde - intrigued me. 'Dramatic And wild.'; [a.] Bournemouth, Dorset, UK

NELSON, ROBERT
[b.] 1916, Northampton; [m.] Edith Page, 1946; [occ.] Retired; [oth. writ.] "Financial Management" (F.T. Publication Ltd - 1973). Many articles and study manuals on finance and accountancy.; [a.] Thaxted, Essex, UK

NEWALL, AUDREY
[m.] Arnold D. Newall; [ch.] Derek, Jayne, Lynne; [oth. wri.] Various other poems on a wide range of subjects; [pers.] I live with my husband in beautiful Shropshire, have three lovely children all of whom have now left home. Poetry is my first love and I admire the work of both early and modern writers. I enjoy painting too, in watercolour and pastels.

NEWELL, JOAN H.
[pen.] Tara; [b.] 5 March 1944, Highgate; [p.] Alfred Newell and Minnie Newell; [ed.] Lyndhurst Secondary Modern School, Boreham Wood; [occ.] Senior Administrator one 2 one, Mercury; [oth. writ.] Modern poets '85 poetry now 1991 - Vol 2; [pers.] Poetry is an expression of life and a fragment of eternity; [a.] Boreham Wood, Herts, UK

NEWMAN, JOAN DOROTHY
[b.] 17 September 1930, Warley, Worcs; [p.] Nellie-Rose and Cyril Bruton; [m.] John Clyde, Richard Newman, 18 July 1953; [ch.] Richard Paul Anthony Clyde Newman; [ed.] Ware (Herts) Grammar for Girls School; [occ.] Retired Medical Secretary; [hon.] Matriculation 1946, 6th form Modern Languages Prize 1947, 1st Price Children's story Coma 1945 (Hertfordshire "Advertiser"); [oth. writ.] Saga "Letters" Magazine 1st Prize 1995, "Breakfast Special" Radio Colour Names Competition Winner 1970; [pers.] My poems are "Snapshots" of phases in my life from age 21. "Sweet Marigold" is addressed to a doll whose wardrobe was my Hobby for a while. Other poems are more personal, in varying moods.; [a.] Cheltenham, Glos, UK

NEWMAN, PATRICIA ANN
[b.] 28 January 1940, Staffordshire; [p.] William Ernest Kings, Lilian May Kings; [m.] Richard Leslie Newman, 28 March 1959; [ch.] Lorna Ann, Jared Kingsley Richard; [ed.] Smethwick Hall Girls Schools; [occ.] Special Support Ass. in a school for Emotional and Behaviour Difficulties (children 5 yrs. to 12 yrs.); [memb.] Stourport Cruiser Club and Marina; [hon.] Trinity College of Music London Oxford Modular Scheme for Behaviour Management; [pers.] Being an artist I am sensitive to all that is around me and I feel that sensitivity is my philosophy on life.; [a.] Kidderminster, Worcs, UK

NICHOLAS, RONALD
[b.] 30 August 1972, Sussex; [p.] Angela Alban and Tony Ronald; [ed.] Licensed Victuallers School, American College, Liverpool University, BA Honours Sociology and English Literature; [occ.] Was student, now currently travelling the

world; [memb.] Amnesty UK Mensa; [oth. writ.] Many unpublished poems, some pieces for school magazines, and local paper; [pers.] I see poetry as a window to the imagination, where one can rekindle past glories, hopes and unfulfilled dreams. I have been influenced by the works of Aldous Huxley and William Blake; [a.] Beaconsfield, Bucks, UK

NICHOLS, BRYAN

[pen.] Nicholas Bryans; [b.] 1 May 1929, London; [ed.] City of London College; [occ.] Writer; [memb.] Ex. Member of New National Operatic Society and West Wickham Operatic Society; [hon.] I.S.T.D. Gold Medalist; [oth. writ.] Numerous poems, currently writing autobiography; [pers.] Boy Sailor in Second World War. Assisted to sing German U-Boat March 1945 at age of fifteen. Acted as a reporter in the Film "Niagara".; [a.] Llandrindod Wells, Powys, UK

NICHOLS, JOYCE

[b.] 24 December 1935, Wakefield; [p.] Oswald Nassau, Amelia Nassau; [m.] Arthur Nichols (Divorced), 12 November 1969, 14 November 1959; [ch.] Debra Elizabeth, Daryl Edward; [ed.] Batley Art College; [occ.] Care Assistant (Res Home) Knowle Manor, Morley; [memb.] Founder Member of the 'Siegen Circle' - Morleys Twin Town of Germany, Former member of Nap-Colour Netball Team; [hon.] Pianoforte, Art Scholarship, several competitions; [pers.] I strive to do my best wholeheartedly and to keep on keeping on with optimism.; [a.] Morley, Yorkshire, UK

NIGHTINGALE, DOREEN

[pen.] Gale, Night; [b.] 26 March 1931, Lewisham; [p.] Maurice Stanley, Booth Shorrock; [m.] Dorothy Shorrock, 11 August 1956; [ch.] Philip Andrew Nightingale; [ed.] Hither Green Secondary; [occ.] Retired; [memb.] Institute of Advance Motorists nine years; [oth. writ.] "Silent Prayer" Church Magazine Holy Trinity Larkfield; [pers.] The English language being one of the most beautiful what better way to express the wonders of the world and its progress.; [a.] Maidstone, Kent, UK

NOBBS, IRENE

[b.] 29 June 1932, Hillsborough; [ed.] Maze Public Elementary School; [occ.] Housewife; [hon.] National Literary Award in Feb. 1992 for Short Story Writing. Made by TV Presenter Esther Rantzen; [oth. writ.] Several poems published in magazine, also story read out on several radio stations.; [pers.] I try to convey peace and hope to all who read my writing.; [a.] Hillsborough, Down, UK

NOBLE, MRS. ANGELA

[b.] 10 February 1935, Liverpool; [p.] Anthony and Anne Palmeria; [m.] Divorced; [ch.] Yvonne Anne, Bernard Anthony, Linda Marie; [ed.] St. Sylvesters, Modern Secondary School; [occ.] VDU Operator (part-time); [hon.] None for writing, medals for dancing; [pers.] The poems is my sole literary work my main hobbies are dancing, Calligraphy swimming and playing at guitar and keyboard.; [a.] Chiswick, London, UK

NOBLE, JEAN

[pen.] Jane Farraday; [b.] 31 July 1938, Walton; [p.] Minnie and Albert Crosshan; [m.] Robert Noble, 13 February 1960; [ch.] Julie, Mark, Paul and Tim; [ed.] Elmhurst, Grammar School, left at sixteen after Taiting O levels; [occ.] Chefs Assistant; [hon.] O level passer in english language literature and biology; [oth. writ.] 2 poems in anthologies

one story cabbage and kettles, currently writing short stories based on my parent lives.; [pers.] Deeply interested in spiritual subjects, inclined to write, against violence, greed and corruption, in my efforts.; [a.] Street, Somerset, UK

NOMORERE, EGBE OKUOIMOSE

[pen.] Izzy Barnny; [b.] 7 September 1970, Benin, Nigeria; [p.] Victoria and Okuoimose Nomorere (Deceased); [m.] Roslyn Smart Gbenoba, Engaged; [ch.] Miss Ivy Melina Egbe Okuoimose; [ed.] Baptist High School, Benin City, Nigeria; [occ.] Free-Lance writer; [memb.] Pan-African Association-Athens, Greece Consciousness for better Nigeria-C.B.N., Athens, Greece; [hon.] "Sunset Pal" my very first break-through; [oth. writ.] An African play and a novel in the making, several articles published in local magazine; [pers.] The 21st century: "Your coming undoubtedly, unstoppable, though you've been so mystified, your era is the delivery of an expectant mother, your joy, those that wish that the survival of the sons and daughters of men wouldn't be able to overcome".; [a.] Athens, Attikis, Greece

NORCUP, KATIE LAUREN

[b.] 23 July 1982, North Staffordshire; [p.] Ann Rita Norcup, Gary Norcup; [ed.] Woodlane Primary School, Newscastle-under-Lyme Independent School; [memb.] Whale and Dolphin Conservation society (WDCS), British Union for the Abolishment of Vivisection (BUAV), World Society for the Protection of Animals (WSPA); [hon.] Credit mark for the English Board (International); [pers.] I wrote the poem to show my appreciation towards my friend, who has always been there for me, and to show how much I value our friendship. Friends are often taken for granted, so, this is my way of saying thank you. To others, our friendships may seem petty, but to me, they mean a lot.; [a.] Stoke-on-Trent, Staffordshire, UK

O'BRIEN, DEBORAH ANN

[b.] 6 February 1968, London; [p.] Mr. Andrew O'Brien, Mother died; [occ.] Secretary; [pers.] I would like to dedicate my poem, if at all possible "To my grandmother, who recently died, Mrs. Evelyn Caston, an inspiration to her family"

O'BRIEN, MICHAEL L.

[b.] 25 March 1953, Limerick; [p.] Sean O'Brien and Kathleen O'Brien; [m.] Eileen, 27 November 1971; [ch.] Tony, Debbie, Sean, Jamie, Jennifer; [ed.] Municipal Technical Institute, Limerick; [occ.] Fitter/Welder; [memb.] Fair-view Rangers F.C School Boy, Manager and Coach; [hon.] First poem, "Jamie", published this year by Rivacre, in Poetry Review" 1996 "Book 3"; [oth. writ.] Several poems written but unseen; [pers.] I like my poems to reflect what I see and feel in my heart. I have only started writing, seriously this year. At the moment "Yeats" is my hero.; [a.] Limerick, UK

O'BYRNE, CATHERINE

[b.] 10 November 1969, Kilkenny, Ireland; [p.] Michael O'Byrne and Sheila O'Byrne; [ed.] Presentation Secondary School, Ballingary, Co. Tipperary, St. Patricks College, Maynooth, Co. Kildare; [occ.] German Teacher and History; [hon.] B.A. German and Sociology; [pers.] I don't consider myself to be a poet, but once upon a time, in a moment of deep despair and after much agonizing about a relationship, I picked up a pencil and this is the result. The poem is named after the person who caused the teasing, bleeding, errie, pulling...etc!!!; [a.] Jerpoint West, Thomastown, Co. Kilkenny, Ireland

O'CONNOR, KELLY ELIZABETH

[pen.] Kelly Elizabeth Paterson; [b.] 6 March 1961, Kirkcaldy; [p.] Alexander Lawson Anderson, Ann Bridget Anderson; [m.] Peter Patrick O'Connor, 19 July 1995 (2nd Marriage); [ch.] Dawn Kelly-Ann Paterson (one daughter) and I am pregnant with child due to be born December 1996; [ed.] Kent School, Hostart, Germany, Glenwood High School, Glenrothes, Scotland; [occ.] Bakery Shop Assistant; [hon.] 7 'o' grades, R.S.A. awards, Scotbec Awards; [oth. writ.] Article for Womans' Own/Poetry publication in Island Moods and Reflection/Poem published on behalf of those who died in the Dunblane tragedy.; [pers.] I dedicate this poem to my beloved father Alexander Lawson Anderson, who died September 22, 1995. He was a wonderful father, to Kelly, Karen and Cameron and grandfather to Dawn and husband to Ann. We all love and miss him dearly.; [a.] Glenrothes, Fife, UK

O'CONNOR, W.

[b.] 14 August 1920, Abercarn, Wales; [p.] Anne Eveley, John O'Connor; [m.] Vera Florence O'Connor Nee Webber, 26 November 1940; [ch.] Son Brian Lee; [ed.] Village School and Self Education; [occ.] Retired Railwayman and Reflexologist; [oth. writ.] Quite a number of poems but only one published in church magazine. Some short stories for my grand children. Nothing much seen in the light of day.; [pers.] Edit please! Although I like writing for my own pleasure, I did nothing serious until after retirement. It is said that retirement is the start of deteriation mentally and physically. This is a great falacy I can assure you. It is the start of a wonderful future and to seeking a means of extending life well beyond three score and ten. There is not enough hours in the day for myself or my wife but we love every moment of it.; [a.] Rogiet, Gwent, UK

O'DAOIRIN, PADGRAIG

[pen.] Patrick O'Dea; [b.] 14 May 1940, Co. Wicklow, Ireland; [p.] Mark and Rosaleen Deering; [m.] Bernadette, 28 August 1972; [ch.] two boys: Adam and David; [ed.] 3 GCSE's. 'A' level and 4 'O's; [occ.] Hospital Administration (Medical Records' Officer or Archivist); [memb.] 'Fine Gael' political party, Lapsed Tenis Club; [oth. writ.] Poems, lampoons, limericks, but none of note or at least not sent for publication.; [pers.] 'Do unto others as they should do unto you.'

O'DONNELL, DES

[b.] 14 March 1941, Newark-on-Trent; [p.] Terence and Hannah O'Donnell; [m.] Therese Clark, 7 April 1969; [ch.] Donna Jane and Anne Marie; [ed.] St. Thomas A Becket, Grammar Nottingham and St. Hugh's College Tollerton Notts; [occ.] Avionies Fitter (Ex Fleet Air Arm); [oth. writ.] Some poems published by Anchor Press; [pers.] Poetry reflects man's inherent need to nourish his soul I hope mine gives some crumb of comfort.; [a.] Port Patrick, Wigtown, UK

O'DONNELL, HANNAH

[b.] 1 November 1942, Cork; [p.] Deceased; [m.] Divorced; [ch.] Four children; [ed.] Primary Education Graijue W.S. Kildornery, Co. Cork; [occ.] Housewife; [hon.] Had a short story published in May '95 in a book entitled No Shoes In Summer title of story "The Fair Day"; [oth. writ.] Have a host of short stories yet to be published I'm currently writing stories and poems etc.; [pers.] To be able to express one self on paper in an anthology in its self.; [a.] Knockanevin, Limerick, Kilmallock Eire, UK

O'DONOVAN, THERESA
[b.] 5 October 1979, Cork; [p.] Mary and Michael O'Donovan; [ed.] Ballyheada National School, Colaiste Na Toirhbhirte; [occ.] Student; [memb.] Ballinhassig Badminton Club; [pers.] My poem is dedicated to the families who suffered a tragic loss in Dunblane, and who will have to live with the pain and the sorrow 'for eternity'.; [a.] Ballinhassig, Cork, UK

O'KEEFFE, BERNARD
[pen.] Barney O'Keeffe; [b.] November 17, 1963, The Curragh; [p.] Barney and Ber Okeeffe; [m.] Wendy McBride, September 21, 1991; [ch.] Sally and Anna; [ed.] Brownstown Primary and Kildare Post Primary Schools; [occ.] Electrician; [oth. writ.] Several poems of historical interest (local); [pers.] I would like my poems to increase people's awareness in local history and folklore; [a.] Brownstown, The Curragh, Kildare

O'LEARY, GABRIELLE
[b.] 16 April 1981, Port Talbot; [p.] Aileen O'Leary; [ed.] Student at Saint Joseph's Roman Catholic Comprehensive School in Port Talbot; [occ.] Student Awaiting GCSE Exams; [oth. writ.] I have written quite a few poems which have impressed my teachers and fellow students but this is the first poem I have entered for publication.; [pers.] I write my poems with a lot of thought and imagination. I use my poems as symbols for my emotions, this is because they are made up from my feelings, thoughts and frustrations of the going's on around us.; [a.] Port Talbot, W. Glamorgan, UK

O'LEARY, JOHN
[b.] 8 August 1983, Cork, Ireland; [p.] Patrick and Maura O'Leary; [ed.] Finished Primary School 20 June 1996. Starting Secondary School 2 September 1996. At Glen National School, Ballinskellings, Co Kerry, Southern Ireland; [occ.] Student/Summer Vacation; [memb.] Local Gaelic Football team, Local Youth Club; [hon.] 2nd in Gaelic skills Competitions February '96, Runner-up Captain in Soccer '93; [oth. writ.] "Winter", "Autumn", "Fantasy", "The Carpenter", "My Family", "Waves"; [pers.] My poetry writing is most "locality" based. I write only when I get inspiration. I support, Aston Villa F.C. and one day I'd like to play for them.; [a.] Saint Finan's Boy, Kerry, Southern Ireland

O'LEARY, MAUREEN
[b.] 23 January 1938, Glyncorring; [p.] Rhys Gray, Emma Gray; [m.] Michael O'Leary, 16 July 1977; [ch.] Two sons, Keith and Michael; [ed.] Cymmer Comprehensive School; [occ.] Stewardess, Constitutional Club Port Talbot; [pers.] The poem, "The Soldiers" was written while living in Saudi Arabia, at the start of the gulf war. Over the years I've written many poems, but this is my first entry every into any contest.; [a.] Port Talbot, W. Glamorgan, UK

O'NEILL, CAMPBELL
[b.] 14 June 1942, Northern Ireland; [p.] John O'Neill, Sarah O'Neill; [m.] Elizabeth O'Neill, 2 October 1993; [ed.] Coleraine Primary School, Coleraine Intermediate School, Coleraine Technical College; [oth. writ.] Poems and short stories; [pers.] After becoming disabled in 1993 through contacting listeria meningitis. With the help of the staff at the day centre where I attend I was encouraged to start writing poetry and short stories.; [a.] Bootle, Merseyside, UK

O'NEILL, DANNY
[b.] 9 May 1973, Birmingham; [p.] Terence David O'Neill and Jean O'Neill; [m.] Miranda; [ch.] Abi Jade O'Neill; [ed.] I left school at 15 years old with no qualifications, opting instead to work with my gather.; [oth. writ.] I have numerous songs and poems that I have already written and I am now writing quite regularly.; [pers.] Before my fathers death in 95' I had never written any poetry what so ever. Now writing is more of a necessity than a pleasure as a way of releasing the turmoil and emotions that I'm now experiencing for the first time. As for all my work past, present and future this is dedicated to him.; [a.] Birmingham, West Mids, UK

O'NEILL, ELAINE SUZZANNE
[b.] 4 August 1955, Staffordshire; [p.] Audrey and George Bayliss; [m.] Walter Edward O'Neill, 24 August 1974; [ch.] Tony, Edward O'Neill; [ed.] Bedlinog Sec Mod Mid Glam. Ystrad Mynach College Mid Glam; [occ.] Housewife; [pers.] With a special thanks to my husband and son's for all their support. And to my english tutor June lane for the advice and encouragement she gave me; [a.] Nelson, Mid-Glam, UK

O'ROURKE, CATHERINE
[b.] November 1955, Neilston, Glasgow; [p.] Michael Higgins, Janet Higgins; [m.] Dr. Jeremiah O'Rourke, July 1982; [ch.] Jane, Tony, Michael; [ed.] Aberdeen University Moray House College-Edinburgh; [occ.] I currently teach and perform the flute; [hon.] MA (Hons) (English Lit. and Lang.) Teaching Certificate (English and History), LTCL (Flute); [oth. writ.] Several poems published elsewhere 'Understanding', 'Darius Poetry Anthology' 1995; [pers.] Poetry grants me the unconditional freedom to celebrate and challenge those issues and themes which touch me most, a rare opportunity to be perfectly candid.; [a.] Inverness, UK

O'SHAUGHNESSY, MR. SHANE
[pen.] Shane O'Shaughnessy; [b.] 21 May 1970, Derby; [p.] Gerald and Catherine O'Shaughnessy; [ed.] Bemrose Comprehensive School, Derby; [occ.] Sound Engineer; [memb.] The International Songwriters Association; [oth. writ.] Several songs performed and recorded by various artists; [pers.] Writing is writing what you do not yet know. Writing what you already know is not writing, that's typing.; [a.] Derby, Derbyshire, UK

OCKELFORD, MRS. G. J.
[pen.] Gwendoline Ockelford; [b.] 10 August 1939, Southampton; [p.] Leslie Bishop, Irene Bishop; [m.] Brian Ockelford, 9 April 1960; [ch.] Micheal, Leslie, Malcome Brian; [ed.] Bitterne Park Sec. School; [occ.] House-wife, not working at moment; [memb.] National Trust; [oth. writ.] I write a lot of poems. But I had one put into my local, echo. have sent one to Triumph House.; [pers.] I have learn in my life that you never get any thing our of life if you don't put any thing in to life.; [a.] Southampton, Hampshire, UK

OGDEN, DENISE SONIA
[pen.] Ogden - Young; [b.] 20 December 1947, Swinton, Manchester; [p.] Mr. David Young and Mrs. Kathleen Young; [m.] Mr. Harold Ogden, 1 September 1972; [ch.] Sonia Elaine Ogden, Verity Leanne Elizabeth Ogden; [ed.] Cromwell Rd. Sec. Mod. Girls School, Salford University College; [occ.] School Secretary; [hon.] Diploma Principles - Practices of Teaching, Secretarial Certificates; [oth. writ.] Awaiting a published for "Environmental" poems written; [pers.] I am to structure my poems towards the younger generation, bringing to them important issues of todays society and era-simplicity.; [a.] Kearsley, Lancashire, UK

OLPHERT, MRS. ENID A.
[b.] 10 September 1943, Devon; [p.] Mr. and Mrs. J. Goldrich; [m.] Mr. S. Olphert, December 1970; [ch.] Two Catherine (25 yrs.) Jonathan (20 yrs.); [ed.] English Private School Istanbul, Turkey. Stoke Damerel Grammar School, Devonport, Plymouth, Devon, England.; [occ.] Staff Nurse; [memb.] RCN; [oth. writ.] "Leaving" accepted for "Voices on the Wind".; [pers.] "Humanity" look at the stars and inky black sky, wonder what life is all about and why. What is there beyond what we see? Is there something for you and me? Is there happiness, tranquility somewhere, where the spirit runs free. The prejudice and injustice that is here, until then we just tolerate the nastiness, unhappiness and hate. Look for the good and not the bad, try to bring, joy to those who are sad. Find strength in weakness and frailty, be a friend to those who need me.; [a.] Antrim, Co Antrim, UK

OMOLADE, OLUMIDE HENRY
[pen.] Knightmare; [b.] Ondo, Ondo, Nigeria; [p.] Mr. and Mrs. Omolade; [ed.] C.A.C. Grammar School Akure Federal University of Tech. Akure (B.Tech Biochemistry); [occ.] Chemist (Quality Control); [hon.] Best Performer (Male) Best All Rounder (Male); [oth. writ.] Extremities poem Collection Primal Fear - novel.; [pers.] The colativity and actuality of poetry lies in the deep canals rife and too por and torrent of the heart.; [a.] Ihagamu, Ogunstale, West Africa

OSBORN, DORIS
[b.] 7 July 1942; [p.] Albert Flower, Florene Flower; [m.] Frank Osborn, 23 March 1963; [ch.] Simon, Mandy, Maria; [occ.] Housewife/Care Assistant; [memb.] Local Residents Council Group/ Friendship Club for the Elderly; [oth. writ.] I enjoy writing short stories although none of which have been published as yet. Now I am finally having some of my work published and I am overjoyed about it.; [pers.] When I am sitting at home in my cottage. I like to reflect the way I feel by writing poetry. When I am feeling happy I write about happy things. And when I am sad I write about sad things.; [a.] Milton Keynes, Buckinghamshire, UK

OSBORNE, PATRICIA
[pen.] Trisha Osborne; [b.] 2 March 1938, London; [p.] Joe Lloyd, Daisy Lloyd; [m.] Laurie Osborne, 2 March 1988 (Photographer); [ch.] Roderick, Stuart; [ed.] Tottenham High School for Girls; [occ.] Secretary, FCO, London; [oth. writ.] Many poems written for members of my family unpublished.; [pers.] My love for my family is the driving force in my life, and is expressed in my poems.; [a.] Croydon, Surrey, UK

OSBORNE, STEVEN
[b.] 19 June 1973, Belfast; [p.] Samuel and Lorna Osborne; [m.] Miss Liza Megarry (Girlfriend); [ed.] 'Model School for Boys', Belfast Institute of Futh and Higher Education; [occ.] An employee of Isaac Mercedes Benz, Agnews, Job - Service Advisor; [memb.] Church, Bethshan Assemblies of God; [hon.] GCSE'S in Eng. language and Literature Maths, Physics, Economics, Geography

and History 2 HNC's in Engineering and Management and Psychology A-Level; [oth. writ.] Various poems for youth meetings and church member.; [pers.] "Life without words is like a broken pencil. Pointless." All influences come from the bible.; [a.] Belfast, Antrim, UK

OSMUNDSEN, GRACE WYNNE
[pen.] Rorke; [b.] 17 November 1930, Rangoon, Burma; [p.] Michael and Enid; [m.] Qistein Osmundsen, 1977; [ch.] Five; [ed.] Private School Abroad Burma Then India; [occ.] Freelance Actress and Director; [memb.] Equity - Life Member Arts Centre Group Questors Theatre - Ealing; [hon.] In sport, won many cups etc in International Sport in India. As a child in children's hour - did Recitations after winning in competitions; [oth. writ.] Musical - based on the ordinary man's experience in Jesus day 3 part story. other shorts write sketches and plays for outreach for churches etc. Other works also about 50 poems.; [pers.] I think poetry - for me anyway comes from the inner man. reflecting the truth that he knows is within himself. And seeing the world with that inner eye and putting in the written word - what is otherwise hard to express.; [a.] Kilkhampton, Cornwall, UK

OXLEY, LOUISE
[b.] 30 October 1979, Wallasey; [p.] Diane Clare Oxley and Kevin Paul Oxley; [ed.] Greenleas Primary School at present Wallasey School; [occ.] At school waiting for GCSE results then will take A-levels in Maths, English, Literature and History; [memb.] Soprano in Wallasey Girl Choir; [hon.] Bronze and Silver Duke of Edinburgh. Gained grand Prior in St. John Ambulance; [oth. writ.] Poems published in Carousel Merseyside, and in School newspaper, also wrote and edited school pupils magazine.; [pers.] I enjoy reading and writing poetry. I wrote my first poem at the age of eight but became really enthusiastic about my writing when I started my GCSE literature course. My poems remain personal, but I'm working on broadening my horizons.; [a.] Wallasey, Merseyside, UK

PACTAT, GILLIE
[b.] Esher, Surrey; [p.] Joseph Borton, Nella Borton; [m.] Divorced; [ch.] Lucienne, James; [ed.] St. Maur's Convent, Weybridge, SY., Weybridge College of Technology and Science; [occ.] Proprietor of Ladies Dress Hire Business; [oth. writ.] Poems and Editorials published in local newspapers and magazines; [pers.] My writings reflect the high's and lo's of everyday life and love that we can all relate to at some time in our lives.; [a.] West Byfleet, Surrey, UK

PAGE, AMANDA MARGARET
[b.] 17 August 1956, Norfolk, England; [p.] Ronald and Margaret Hewitt; [m.] Christopher Brian Page, 4 October 1975; [ch.] Joanne Amanda and Emma Louise; [ed.] Claydon Secondary Modern and Ipswich Civic College Suffolk England; [occ.] Post Shop Officer Australia Post; [pers.] I moved to Australia in November 95 with my Husband and Daughters after a holiday there 2 years previous for the wedding of my eldest brother (Another Chris) the inspiration behind the poem; [a.] Dolan's Bay, New South Wales, Australia

PALMA, ALFRED
[b.] 8 September 1939, Malta; [p.] Late Carmelo and Maria Fava; [ed.] Elementary and Higher; [occ.] Author; [memb.] Society of Maltese Poets, Society Chopin a' Paris; [hon.] Citta' Di Valletta, Winner of many Local Poetry, competition, 2nd Prize 'Carlo Goldeni' Prize (Rome) 1996; [oth. writ.] Radio plays, short stories, poetry anthology, 2 novels, translations, dante'n divina commedia in Mattere, 9 plays by shakespeare in Mattere, several publications in the U.K. currently writing on all Shakespeare's works.; [a.] Zabbar, Malta

PALMER, COLIN
[pen.] Colin Palmer; [b.] 22 June 1982, Kings Lynn, Norfolk; [p.] Jack Palmer, Pauline Palmer; [ed.] The Priory School, Orpington, Kent; [oth. writ.] Several poems published, one in the British poetry review 1996 and the other in family pets anthology published by Rivacre Ltd.; [pers.] I enjoy creative writing and sharing my work with others. I have been greatly encouraged by my English teacher and my parents.; [a.] Orpington, Kent, UK

PALMER, SUSAN THERESA
[b.] 8 July 1949, London; [p.] Lillian and Louis Cooper; [m.] Geoffrey Keith Palmer, 22 June 1968; [ch.] Adam, Mark, Luke, Paul; [ed.] Sir Humphery Gilbert, Secondary School, London; [occ.] Teacher, Scott Wilkie, Primary, London; [memb.] P.A.D.I.; [hon.] N.N.E.B. Combined Studies diploma in higher education; [oth. writ.] Other poem been published in paper back anthology; [pers.] I try to reflect my inner feelings in my poems, to express the way that society looks on "lower" classes, how these people strive to succeed.; [a.] Loughton, Essex, UK

PAPIER, KIETA SUZANNE
[b.] 24 December 1983, Kalulushi, Zambia; [ed.] Lechwe Education Trust, Kitwe, Zambia; [occ.] student; [hon.] Scholarship Book Award for creative writing 1994 and 1996, Award of Merit for English Literature 1996; [a.] Kitwe

PARK, JULIE
[b.] 17 June 1971, Jersey, CI; [p.] Reg and Joyce Brooker; [m.] Ken Park; [ed.] Beaulieu Convent School, Jersey; [occ.] Writer; [oth. writ.] Poems published in seven volumes to date; [pers.] If music be the food of love and prose the food for thought let poetry be the food of wonder through a happy life, liberally sprinkle all three.; [a.] Jersey, Channel Isles, UK

PARKER, ALLY
[b.] 30 August 1972, London; [p.] Frank Parker, Wendy Parker; [ch.] Adam, Lee, Francis Praker; [ed.] Plashet Girls School, London; [occ.] Mother; [oth. writ.] I have written numerous poems and stories but this is the first time I have submitted any of my work for competitions or publication.; [pers.] This poem is dedicated to my son Adam (Oidee). I hope one day he will understand it and live his life for peace in everlasting love.; [a.] Bideford, Devon, UK

PARKER, ANDREW BENNETT
[pen.] Androo B. Parker; [b.] 26 November 1960, Huddersfield; [p.] Jim Parker and Elaine Bennett; [ch.] Brad Parker, Danielle E. J. Parker; [occ.] 'Lost' Poet; [memb.] Y.H.A. (Life Membership), Ramblers Association Dewsbury, Local Writers Group; [oth. writ.] Some poems printed in Associated Publication; [pers.] There is something in me that calls from beyond the horizon. I can only follow, bear good hope and do my best to write it down... and be grateful.; [a.] Heckmondwyke, W. Yorkshire, UK

PARKER, DIANE
[b.] 29 January 1950, Stockport, Berry; [p.] Richard and Doreen; [m.] Mike Parker, 13 June 1970; [ch.] Daniel; [ed.] Reddish Vale Comprehensive School; [occ.] Housewife (trying to find time to write my own book); [oth. writ.] One poem published in a book. A compilation of poems, titled "And All That" published by arrival press. Also one poem in a local magazine; [pers.] Never write to make money. Write only for your own personal pleasure. (But if money is offered, treat it as a bonus, not to be refused.); [a.] Stockport, Cheshire, UK

PARKER, MICHAEL L. GAUDOIN
[b.] 1 November 1939, Madura, India; [p.] Joseph Parker and Elaine Gaudoin; [ed.] St Patrick's College, Wellington (N.Z.) Gregorian University, Rome Divinity School, Cambridge (U.K.); [occ.] Roman Catholic Priest Hermit - Writer; [oth. writ.] Heart in Pilgrimage (Alba House Publ. New York) The Real Presence (Alba House New York) Window on the Land of St Francis (in Prep. Alba House—); [pers.] My writings are focused on responding to Christ's presence in bread and Wine, signs of the yruth of communication, unity and justice.; [a.] Valfabrrica, Italy

PARKES, LAUNA
[b.] 12 April 1982; [p.] Jane and Douglas Parkes; [ed.] Currently a Pupil at Gordonstown Sch., Scotland; [occ.] Pupil at Gordonstown School; [pers.] I've written poetry since I was 11 almost as a diary to express my current feelings, thoughts about life.; [a.] Orpington, Kent, UK

PARKHURST, ANNA
[b.] 28 February 1923, London; [p.] Late H. H. Marks, B.C. as Military Cross; [m.] Ida Hughes-Stanton; [ed.] Private - 6 Schools, MA Pathology: Oxford; [occ.] Retired Writer; [memb.] British Legion Assoc. of W.R.N.S.; [hon.] ORA levels (at 40), OU Degree (at 60), War Medals WRNS (WRNS 1941-1946); [oth. writ.] Ten books which my poems (anthologies), book for equation (I contributed).; [pers.] Worked: Typist 47-77, Interests: History, Art collecting, Driving, Music Class) part DSD now (broken hip); [a.] Richmond, Surrey, UK

PARKINSON, DEBORAH E.
[pen.] 'The Fortune Teller'; [b.] 10 February 1064, Exeter, Devon; [p.] Kenneth Parkinson, Josephine Parkinson; [ed.] Ayminster Schools Colyton Grammar School, Devon; [pers.] Love is the greatest inspiration, its gain or its loss. One gain is another man's loss. A loss, another gain. Love all, and all will come around. Live for love.; [a.] Chayofa, Tenerife, Canary Island

PARSLEY, MISS JAYNE YVETTE
[pen.] Jayne Parsley; [b.] 18 March 1973, Hertford; [p.] Jennifer Parsley and James Parsley; [ed.] St. Joseph's School Hertford, The Sele Secondary School Herts Regional College; [occ.] Sterile Operator; [memb.] Arab Horse Society Grundy Park Gym, Herts country Club; [hon.] Poems published in Regional Arab Horse Magazine, beauty, therapy diplomas; [oth. writ.] Several articles in equestrian magazines "The Arabian Horse"; [pers.] No matter who we are, or what our crime is, we are all a person that someone else, is trying to be...; [a.] Hertford, Hertfordshire, UK

PARVIN, MR. MAURICE
[pen.] David Marks; [b.] 3 September 1935, Middlesbrough; [p.] Fred and Lily Parvin; [m.] Widower; [ch.] David, Julie, Mark; [ed.] Secondary Modern; [occ.] Painter and Decorator; [pers.] I try to write about things and people I see on my every day activities and I have been influenced by the wonderful victorian poets; [a.] Stockton, Cleveland, UK

PATEL, DAKSHA
[b.] 18 October 1975, England; [memb.] Karate Union of Great Britain; [oth. writ.] Published: 'Survival' in the anthology, 'Aspect of Life' August 1995, ISBN (Softback) 1 857,31 695 9. 'Under the Stars' in the Anthology 'Point of No Return' August 1996, ISBN (Softback) 186188 401 X ISBN (Hardback) 186188 406 0; [pers.] I do not turn a blind eye to the sufferings and the discontents of humans. Life is cruel and unjust for many it is merely a Universal fact. There is always a place for the truth in poetry.; [a.] London, Gt. London, UK

PATERNOSTER, COLIN A.
[pen.] Adrian Price; [b.] 1 March 1960, Derby; [p.] Cyril Henry Paternoster, Joyce Paternoster (Both Deceased); [ed.] Ashe Hall - Derbyshire Derby college - Derby University; [occ.] Technician Writer-Director; [hon.] R.S.A. Technology (Dist), N.V.Q. Business Administration; [oth. writ.] Short stories - Stage And Screen Works, Poetry And Prose, Letters Of Enlightenment; [pers.] I endeavour to entertain and please through my works to write for one and all be they the very young to the more mature; [a.] Derby, Derbyshire, UK

PATIENCE, DONALD
[b.] 28 June 1928, Blair Atholl, Perthshire; [p.] Charles J. M. and Ann Patience; [m.] Flora Bell Patience, 31 August 1961; [ch.] Charles M. and Jan Patience; [ed.] Duthil School Kingussie School, Dux of Both Schools University of St. Andrews M.A. 1950; [occ.] Church of Scotland Minister Retired; [oth. writ.] Booklet, Kirk of Kilmaurs, Editor Kingussie School Magazine 1946; [pers.] The words of Thomas Ken 1637-1711, "Praise God from whom all blessings flow! Praise Him above ye heavenly host! Praise father son and Holy Ghost!; [a.] Kilmaurs, Ayr, UK

PATTERSON, RAY
[b.] 15 February 1946, Glasgow; [p.] Harry and Betty; [m.] Patricia Patterson, 10 September 1966; [ch.] Gillian and Raymond; [ed.] Holyrood Senior Secondary Glasgow; [occ.] H.G.V. Driver; [pers.] Poetry, is my way of expressing my views on life. I simply write about events whether they be happy. Funny or sad. Poetry is my window on the world.; [a.] East Kilbridge, Glasgow, UK

PATTINSON, JOY
[pen.] Harris Smith; [b.] June 1935, Lowestoft, Suffolk; [p.] Elsa-Kate Harris and Douglas Smith; [ed.] St. Mary's Convent High School, Lowestoft, awarded Master of Business Admin., L'Universite De La Romande in 1989; [occ.] Retired from United Nations, mainly with United Nations, elected editor of the official UN staff journal (Geneva), after contributing over 40 articles and poems for that in house publication. Have taken part in several live BBC World Service phone-ins (posed questions to former NATO Secretary-General Manfred Werner, John Le Carre and President Iliuesco of Romania. Worked in Ethiopia as personal secretary go HRH Eskinda Desta

(executed) in his capacity as Commodore of Royal Ethiopian Navy Day, organizing visit of HRH The Princess Anne.; [memb.] Women in Management, former member of IQPS (Institute of Qualified Private Secretaries), BRA (British Resident Abroad), AFICS (Association of Former International Civil Servants), now: British Residents Abroad, AFICS: Association of Former International Civil Servants, followed courses: London School of Journalism in freelance writing; [hon.] Awarded Masters Degree in Business Administration in June 1989 at age of 54 years by Correspondence Course at Open University (Isle of Man); [oth. writ.] Whilst with UN, was elected Editor of Official Staff Journal and contributed 67 articles and poems. All were published by the journal but not considered "published" in true sense of the word!; [pers.] I maintain that education does not end when school days finish. It commences. I proved this by being awarded a Degree of Master of Business Administration at the age of 54. Writing must interest the reader in the first line, bringing forth smiles, laughter, tears. Making the reader ponder, above all, wonder.; [a.] Saint George, Switzerland

PAUL, DARREN
[b.] 31 May 1965, Waltham Forest; [p.] Iceleen Paul, Hopsow Paul; [ch.] Racheal Paul; [ed.] Sidney Chaplin Junior High School, Folly Lane Walthamstow McKeniee Senior High; [occ.] Student in poetry; [a.] London, UK

PAUL, JOHN
[b.] 30 May 1940, Epping, Essex; [p.] Henry Alfred and Lucy Paul; [ch.] Tara, Michael, Divina, Samantha; [ed.] Belfairs High School, Basingstock College; [occ.] Restoration - Property; [pers.] Communication - The worlds view is of the outside. Feelings are from the inside. We should all try to get the inside on the outside. Then the world will be more aware.; [a.] Basingstoke, Hampshire, UK

PAYNE, SYLVIA
[pen.] Sylvia Rose (Payne); [b.] 16 March 1950, Hinckley, Leics; [p.] Ralph Jackson and Ethel Jackson; [m.] Michael A. Payne; [ch.] David Payne, Joy Dawson; [ed.] Local Grammer School; [occ.] Dressmaker and Freelance Designer; [memb.] Hinckley Concordia Theatre Group, P.S. Hinckley is nicknamed "Tin-Hat" after a blacksmith made a hung and giant tin-hat outside a public House beginning of 1900's.; [oth. writ.] A few poems and scribblings, not published; [pers.] From my nowhere "Tin-hat" town, I voice my yesterday dreams!. Although, the romantic poets have given inspiration, I am greatly influenced by Dylan Thomas; [a.] Hinckley, Leicestershire, UK

PEACE, MRS. MOLLIE
[b.] 25 May 1920, Highclere, Berks; [p.] William and Amy Messenger; [m.] Ronald Peace, 19 July 1941; [ch.] Elaine - Nigel; [ed.] Primary schools and "College of Life"; [occ.] Housewife (Widowed); [memb.] W. Wildlife R.N.L.I., SASA; [oth. writ.] Short stories in local mags also poetry, poetry read at poetry workshop in West Mindlands.; [pers.] My lasting hobby has been people. Fascinating, also I have always felt a great affinity with nature. Trees to me are "People"; [a.] Banbury, Oxon, UK

PEARMAN, SUSAN C.
[b.] 2 December 1980, Middlesbrough; [p.] Alan and Carol Pearman; [ed.] Studying for GCSE's; [memb.] Stage one Theatre Company, The Caxton

Players; [oth. writ.] Another poem, "The Doll," published in the anthology, "The Next Step."; [pers.] I write from the heart with encouragement from Elle, Kell Bell, Cawowine and Waffy.; [a.] Grimsby, NE Lincs, UK

PEARSON, CELIA
[b.] 18 April 1954, Maidstone; [p.] Dennis and Margaret Sidwell; [m.] Michael, 14 February 1991; [ch.] Jay and Tracey; [ed.] Senacre Secondary School; [occ.] Relief Guest House Manager; [oth. writ.] One or two articles in Women's Magazines and Local Paper; [pers.] My husband and family provide love and support while my cats give me inspiration. Thank you.; [a.] Maidstone, Kent, UK

PECEHIA, GULIETTA
[b.] 25 June 1961, Watford; [p.] Mr Orazio, Mrs Lucia Pecehia; [ed.] Comprehensive School "Leggatts"; [pers.] It is in everyone of us to have the gift to heal; [a.] Watford, Herts, UK

PEGG, MRS. PAM
[b.] 4 September 1953, Leicester; [p.] Leslie and Marjorie Wilkins; [m.] James Pegg, 10 May 1992; [ch.] Zoe Louise, Kelly Yasmin; [ed.] New Parks Girls School; [occ.] Spiritual Tarot Reader; [oth. writ.] Unpublished poems; [pers.] My writing expresses life experiences that have affected me profoundly. To witness deep emotions in another gives me an insight to all human suffering.; [a.] Leicester, Leicestershire, UK

PELIDIS, MARY
[pen.] Mary Pelidis; [b.] 4 February 1948, Gwelo, Rhodesia; [p.] Michael and Zaharoula; [ed.] Bulawayo Teachers College (Rhodesia); [occ.] T.O.E.F.L in Language Schools; [memb.] Sacristan's Guild of St. Paul's Anglcan Church Athens; [oth. writ.] Poetry of a lighter/humorous nature.; [pers.] Give pleasure to both the reader and the listener by reciting not only my own poetry but that of the great "spirits" of this Art; [a.] Kaisariani, Athens, Greece

PEMBERTON, MAVIS
[b.] 17 August 1929, Coventry; [p.] Harold Cook, Dorothy Cook; [m.] William Pemberton, 26 February 1949; [ch.] David, George, Susan, Jennifer; [ed.] Broad Street, Secondary Girls; [occ.] Retired R.G.N. O.N.D.; [hon.] Attended Queens Garden Party 1991; [oth. writ.] The Cricket At Tudor Lake, District Nurses, Working Mother; [pers.] Each poem reflects a part of a life experience.; [a.] Coventry, Warwickshire, UK

PENDLEBURY, MR. KENNETH
[pen.] Ken Pendlebury, Bluey Pendlebury; [b.] 3 November 1937, Atherton; [p.] William, Lily Pendlebury; [m.] Patricia Pendlebury, 7 October 1963; [ch.] Karen Pendlebury (Daughter); [ed.] Hesketh/Fletcher, C.E. School, Mining College Leigh; [occ.] Retired Miner; [memb.] Tyldesley RU and Wigan RL Rugby Clubs "Atherton" Soldiers Sailor's Club Libelal Club; [hon.] Town Leigh Team Rugby League, Leigh School Boy and open age Lancashire under 19's "Amateur"; [oth. writ.] I write every month for Atherton Parish Church Magazine. I have had seven poems published, all in different books, I have wrote a full book that I hope will get published.; [pers.] It is a wonderful feeling to know people enjoy reading my poems in the church magazines. I try to help younger poets to go forward, in this new and rewarding hobby.; [a.] Atherton, Gt. Manchester, UK

PEREIRA, PEDRO BARRY YEON
[pen.] Sweet "P."; [b.] 30 January 1970, High Wycombe; [p.] Rita Pereira; [ed.] Guinions primary School, Wellesbourne Secondary School, Amersham College, University of Luton; [occ.] Student; [hon.] BSC (Hons) Computer Science and Management Science, "Best School Poet of 1985, "Best Dancer" in various competitions; [oth. writ.] A published poem "Who Am I?"; [pers.] My poems are deep reminiscent and emotional rhythms from the heart, pieced together by carefully chosen words - from a yesterday survivor much wiser and stronger than tomorrows.; [a.] High Wycombe, Bucks, UK

PERKINS, CLAIRE E.
[pen.] E. Claire; [b.] 14 December 1969, Cheshire, England; [p.] Barbara Alcock and Don Perkins; [m.] Partner: David Mayer; [ed.] Only 3 CSE'S City Guilds Florist, "Miss Spent Childhood"; [occ.] Unemployed, studying writing course; [memb.] Book Clubs Various; [hon.] This is my 1st!; [oth. writ.] Unpublished, `We're Talkin' "Un-Sure Heath" "That It I moan..." and "Black Sheep"; [pers.] "When once the itch of Literature comes over, nothing can cure but the scratch of a pen", Samuel Lover.; [a.] Knutsford, Cheshire, UK

PEVERI, SIMONE
[b.] 23 March 1967, Hackney, London; [p.] Rudolph Peveri and Marie Peveri; [ed.] Onslow Secondary School, Hatfield Herts, Youth Training Scheme, Hatfield Herts, St. Albans Oaklands College - NVQ Levels II and III Decorating; [occ.] Unemployed; [oth. writ.] Short stories, screenplays, songs and in the process of writing a novel. Poem fist published work.; [pers.] Writing is my therapy. It keeps me sane.; [a.] Hatfield, Herts, UK

PHILLIPS, GEORGE K.
[b.] 21 June 1913, Edmonton Middx; [p.] Henry Phillips, Frances Phillips; [m.] Alice Dorothy Phillips (Late), 3 September 1939; [ch.] Brian Anthony and Pamela Anne; [ed.] Elementary. No Exams Passed; [occ.] Retired; [hon.] Mentioned in Destpaches, Occupation Army in Germany, British Army of the Rhine (1947); [oth. writ.] Book - Not 'The Satanic Verses' published by Pentland Press Durham. Poems published in other Anthologies; [pers.] Of romantic nature. I believe in poetry that rhymes. Do not hold with modern poetry - prose cut down into short lines looking like poetry. I like nature - Countryside - Seaside flowers beauty of nature.; [a.] Margate, Kent, UK

PHILLIPS, MRS. JENNIFER ELIZABETH
[b.] 8 July 1950, Llanbradach; [p.] Danny Seaborne and Ann Seaborne; [m.] Wayne Phillips, 9 September 1992; [ch.] Nadina; [ed.] Caerphilly Sec. Mod., Rhydfelin College; [occ.] Pharmacy Assistant; [hon.] City and Guild - Hairdressings; [oth.writ] (Pub Writ) "Life", Poetry Now 1994 (Wales). (Pub Writ) "The Return", Christian Poets from Wales, 1995. (Pub Writ) "Food", Island Moods and Reflections, Poetry Institute of the British Isles.; [pers.] I find great satisfaction in the fact that my poems are being recognized and put into print.; [a.] Blackwood, Gwent, UK

PHILLIPS, MARK
[b.] 20 August 1979, Dublin, Ireland; [p.] Ken and Nuala Phillips; [ed.] Terenure College (1988 to date); [occ.] Student; [memb.] Templeague Tennis Club; [hon.] U/11 Gold all Ireland medal for rugby, 1994/95 silver junior cup medal, highly covered in Texaco Art 1991; [pers.] I like my poetry to reflect the realities of life as I see them; [a.] Dublin 16, Ireland

PHILLIPS, SOPHIA
[b.] 13 March 1976, Huntingdon; [p.] Robert Phillips, Elizabeth Phillips; [ed.] Farnborough VI Form College, Leeds University; [occ.] Student; [memb.] Farnborough Dra Amateur Operator Society; [oth. writ.] Articles for Leeds student paper; [pers.] 'Love is like the tide - it comes and goes with waves of destruction' it is with this parallel that one can interpret my poetry.; [a.] Ewshot, Surrey, UK

PHILPOTT, MISS LISA
[b.] 23 June 1972, Minster Sheppy; [p.] Martyn and Iris Philpott; [ed.] Rowena School for Girls Swanstree Ave, Sittingbourne Kent; [occ.] Statistical Analysis Clerk Kent Police; [memb.] Friend of the Marlowe Theatre Canterbury; [hon.] Drama Award Rowena Girls School; [oth. writ.] Poem published in 'Voices In The Wind', my first competition entry in 1995 his early years on a great Monday morning; [pers.] I would like to dedicate this poem to a special friend who unknowingly has kept me going through sad times, and whom without him my poem would not have been thought of - Paul Shepherd; [a.] Sittingbourne, Kent, UK

PICKEN, JUNE E. M.
[pen.] Nadine; [b.] 21 June 1934, Worcester; [p.] Reginald and Edith Caseley; [m.] Alan John Picken, 10 September 1995; [ch.] Mark and Anna; [occ.] Run canal family business (Museum-Tea shop crafts and horse drawn passenger boat); [memb.] Womens Institute and Monmouth and Brecon Canal Society; [hon.] Have won several W.I. competitions local and county - two poems published by Anchor; [oth. writ.] The Navvies, Peace, St Maugan's Gift Brecon Beau Hauler; [pers.] Lived on boats and travelled the waterway for eighteen years. Inspired to write poetry after moving to Wales 10 years ago; [a.] Brecon, Powys, UK

PICKERS, AMANDA JANE-STEWART
[b.] 1 April 1968, Watford, England; [p.] Mrs. Margaret and Mr. Idris Pickers; [occ.] Art and Photography Student; [oth. writ.] I have written a few other poems, among them one called "The Sin" and I hope that one day I shall perhaps get another one of them published one can life in hope.; [pers.] I dedicate this poem to all those who are in constant search for their peace of mind, but to no avail.

PIKE, CECIL VINCENT
[pen.] "Pikey"; [b.] 3 June 1909, London, NW; [p.] Maud and Charles Pike; [m.] Florence, 9 August 1930; [ed.] Elementary; [occ.] Retired, Engineer; [hon.] Tunstall Tellecon National Caring Award 1990; [pers.] I was 5 years old when the great war broke out, so my education suffered. When I was 12 I was still in standard 2. My parents kept moving house.

PILTON, FREDA
[b.] 31 October 1936, Tiverton; [p.] Elizabeth and Sidney Heard; [m.] Frank Loder, 27 March 1958; [ch.] Wendy Ann, Andrew John, Judi May; [ed.] Tiverton Girls Grammar School; [occ.] Retired; [oth. writ.] Three poems published in poetry anthologies. One poem publishing in a newspaper in Texas USA; [pers.] I get my inspiration from nature and the people around me, and I hope my poems give pleasure to the reader.; [a.] Tiverton, Devon, UK

PITTS, DOROTHY CECIL
[pen.] Helen Pitts; [b.] 20 September 1906, London; [p.] John and Constance Pitts; [ed.] Kings College, London; [occ.] Pensioner; [memb.] The Progressive League, Trie Labour Party; [hon.] Matriculation, B.A. Hon's 1st class, two other poems published; [oth. writ.] The patient replies to the psychiatrist 'to Doris on her 70th birthday amateur plays.; [pers.] Be lies in reincarnation and matreya's coming. Much influenced by Keats - Wordsworth and adder and spender and McNeice.; [a.] London, London, UK

PLACE, C. ROSE
[b.] 10 February 1933, Romford; [p.] Alan Waters and Hilda Waters; [m.] Frederick Place, 30 September 1967; [ch.] Colin, Hilda, Douglas; [ed.] Endsleigh Private Girls School, Colchester, Cambridge School Certificate; [occ.] Housewife; [memb.] General Church of the New Jerusalem, British New Church Academy; [hon.] Cam. School Certificate, special mention English Literature and Art N.N.E.B.; [oth. writ.] Poems in church magazine. One poem published in anthology; [pers.] I have been greatly inspired by the works of Emmanuel Swendenborg especially by his teachings of the life after death and Gods creation.; [a.] Harston, Cambs, UK

PLATIRRAHOU, RENA
[b.] 14 May 1967, Kouroutes, Crete; [p.] Charidimos and Maria Platirrahou; [m.] Junior Poon, 14 May 1990 in Bristol; [ch.] Two Adorable Germ. Shepard Dogs; [ed.] Completed High School (in Greece), English Language Courses (in England), Business Studies Course (in England); [occ.] Overworked self employed, Part-time writer; [hon.] Was awarded first prize in 1982 International Greek Poetry Competition of all Greek Schools in the World. Also, won two other Local Competitions in Crete 1984, 1985; [oth. writ.] Some of my Greek poems were published in Local Newspapers and Magazine in Greece.; [pers.] I am fascinated and inspired by Society problems, by people's inner world, feelings, desires, dreams, Phobias and confusions. Poetry is the only expressing icon and freedom for me.; [a.] Bristol, Avon, UK

PLATT, JOHN LAW LITTLEWOOD
[pen.] John Lawrence; [b.] 26 June 1928, Hadfield, Derbyshire; [p.] John Cooper Platt, Hilda Platt; [m.] Divorced; [ch.] Janice, Howard, Karen; [ed.] Glossop Grammar School, Glossop Derbyshire, Grimes College Manchester, Manchester College of Art; [occ.] Retired (Voluntary work with learning disabled); [memb.] Fishbourne Bowling Club, Fishbourne West Sussex; [oth. writ.] Poems and lyrics, mainly for my own pleasure. Although many were in a book of poems, all proceeds to Cancer Research (soft back 1970's); [pers.] Being a cancerian and an extrovert, the majority of my poems deal with thoughts and feelings of love.; [a.] Bognor Regis, W. Sussex, UK

PLICIO, KEVIN JAMES
[b.] 10 August 1970, London; [p.] Santiago Plicio, Maria Jesus Pages; [ed.] St Thomas Apostle Secondary, St Francis Xavier College; [occ.] General Store Manager; [memb.] King Georges Tennis Club, Peckham Liberal Club of Snooker; [pers.] I try to put into words, the emotions that everyone feel, but fail to put into practice. I am influenced only by time and the way it affects life.; [a.] Wandsworth, London, UK

PORTER, KERENSA
[b.] 12 August 1973, Edgeware; [p.] William Porter, Carole Porter; [ed.] Chailey Comprehensive, Haywards Heath College, University of the West of England, Bristol; [hon.] BA Honors Degree in Politics and Sociology (2:1), Piano - Grade 7, Flute - Grade 8; [oth. writ.] Poem published by anchor books; [a.] Lewes, East Sussex, UK

POTTER, CYRIL GEORGE
[b.] 19 October 1962, Rustington, West Sussex; [p.] Cyril G. Potter (Snr.), Lena Jean Potter; [m.] Karin Potter, 12 August 1995; [ch.] Katie Jane Potter; [ed.] Littlehampton Comprehensive Secondary School; [occ.] General Laborer; [oth. writ.] Many poems published in books of anthology - locally known for poetry writing, but sadly not related to Beatrix Potter.; [pers.] A poem is a heartfelt list of sentences - carefully selected and put into rhyme.; [a.] Angmering Village, West Sussex, UK

POWER, STEPHEN
[b.] 26 December 1966, Nottingham, England; [p.] Edward Power, Deirdre Power; [ed.] St. Patricks Comprehensive School, Shannon, University of Limerick; [occ.] Electronic Engineer; [a.] Shannon, Clare, Ireland

POZNANCZYK, IRENE
[b.] 26 September 1976, France; [p.] Boleslaw and Liliane Poznanczyk; [ed.] A-Levels in Economics and French literature at the Sorbonne University in Paris; [occ.] Student; [oth. writ.] Some articles in the secondary school newspaper; [pers.] I have been deeply influenced by international legends and mythologies, I try to give a great place to dreams in my reality.; [a.] Argenteuil, France

PRICE, GILLIAN ALICE
[b.] 17 July 1948, Hereford; [p.] Horace Taylor, Lita Taylor; [m.] Geoffrey Ronald Price, 31 August 1974; [ch.] Caroline, Mandy Heather, Annabelle; [ed.] Saint Martins Primary, Blue Coat Secondary Modern; [occ.] Housewife; [pers.] I dedicate my poems to my Husband Geoffrey who I love and adore and to my Daughter and to my 10 grandchildren. Shelley, Marie, Natasha, Terri-Ann, Teisha, Jamie, Charlene, Jessica, Michelle and Jastin also my brothers Robert and Paul Taylor.; [a.] Hereford, UK

PRICE, HANNAH MARY
[b.] 20 September 1922, Tumble; [p.] John T. Griffiths, Mary Hannah Griffiths; [m.] David A. Price, 30 December 1958; [ed.] Gwendraeth Grammar, Cartrefle College, Wrexham; [occ.] Retired Teacher; [memb.] Hermon Baptist, Llanon, Llannon W.I., Gwendraeth Historical Soc, Dyfed and Glamorgan Family History Soc, Hon. President of local newspaper: Leader of Mother Toddler Group; [oth. writ.] At present in Hospital; [a.] Llanelli, Carmarthen, UK

PRIME, JAYNE
[b.] 13 September 1976, Hull; [p.] Barbara and Geoff Prime; [ed.] David Lister School Hull College of further Education; [memb.] Hull Vixens Women's Rugby League Club; [pers.] I like to write my poetry on things I take part in, but I also write poetry for Birthday cards etc and every day life, what ever comes into my head I write down on paper; [a.] Hull, East Yorkshire, UK

PRINCE, RAYMOND PAUL
[pen.] Paul Price

PRINGLE, JAMES DOUGLAS
[pen.] James Douglas; [b.] 2 June 1925, West Hartlepool; [p.] Edward Douglas and Phyllis Pringle; [m.] Winifred Collins, 13 June 1953; [ch.] Colin Douglas; [ed.] Elementary, Technical College, Marine School (Eng.); [occ.] Retired; [hon.] H.H.C., Marine Eng. Cert. - (Heat Winner of "Epson Worldwide Bridge Contest") Diploma; [oth. writ.] Numerous short stories never published - also poems currently my autography.; [pers.] Spent ten years in the Merchant Navy as a Marine Engineer, thus many stories based on experiences.; [a.] Berkhamsted, Herts, UK

PRITCHARD, LORRAINE
[pen.] Teresa Green; [b.] 1 November 1952, Hereford; [m.] James Barry Pritchard, 6 October 1973; [ch.] Caroline, Mary, David; [ed.] Kingstone Secondary Modern, Hereford; [occ.] Housewife; [memb.] Radnorshire Association for the Disabled; [oth. writ.] Unsuccessful story for the Brecon and Radnor Express.; [pers.] I am just an ordinary housewife, and I come from Knighton Mid Wales - and the countryside inspired me.; [a.] Knighton, Powys, UK

PROCTOR, ALICIA C. M.
[pen.] "Lisa"; [b.] 13 February 1928, Gosport; [p.] Fredrick and Irene Redman; [m.] Dennis Claud Proctor, 27 September 1947; [ch.] Anne Gilbert (BA, B.Ed.) Gill Hughes (H. N.C.); [occ.] Retired Youth Leader and Founder of Youth Clubs; [oth. writ.] This is my first attempt; [a.] Broughton Astley, Leics, UK

PRYOR, SAMANTHA M.
[b.] 27 August 1976, Hyson Green; [p.] Gillian Ford, Ronald Hartley; [m.] Mr. David Lilliman; [ed.] Kirkby Centre School, West Notts College, Clarendon College; [occ.] Student, West Notts College Mansfield; [memb.] British Epilepsy Association, Leeds; [oth. writ.] One Night, would you like me to tell you a story; [pers.] I strive to reflect my feelings and what goes on in the world around me.; [a.] Mansfield, Notts, UK

PUDNEY, CHRISTOPHER
[pen.] Chris Pudney; [b.] 6 February 1983; [p.] Pauline and Roland Pudney; [ed.] Chislehurst and Sidcup grammar school; [occ.] Students; [pers.] In finding happiness we find ourselves, and our loved ones shall follow.; [a.] New Eltham, Kent, UK

PULLEN, BILL
[b.] 28 December 1947, Cheltenham; [p.] M. S. F. and M. L. Pullen; [ed.] Cheltenham Grammar School To 'O' Levels; [occ.] Office Administration (Bourton-on-the-Water); [memb.] Glos-Warwicks Railway, Severn Valley Railway, Gothorington Cricket Club, (Poss.) Gloucester Rugby Club, Various Folk Clubs and Blugs/Jazz Clubs (Officially and unofficially!); [hon.] Finalist in "Folkwrite" song contest (writers) and Worcester Blugs Harmonica Players Competition; [oth. writ.] Various poems and songs - The Latter In Many Cases written in a Blues Idiom Around my Harmonica Playing (I also play percussion) - I work solo (Folk) and in various duos, trios, bands etc. As a singer/player (Amateur and semi-pro); [pers.] Events, people and places inspires me - I like to think that, like Nostradamus, I occasionally "Foretell" something in a song or poem to the extent of saying "I Told You So!" Something in the future.; [a.] Winchcombe, Cheltenham, Glos, UK

QADIR, HOURA
[b.] 20 January 1981, Kabul, Afghanistan; [p.] Mr. Nabi Qadir and Mrs. Parwin Qadir; [ed.] Ellen Wilkinson High School for Girls; [occ.] Student; [pers.] We are all lost in the maze of the Creator. Some of us find our way out, but most of us remain lost forever.; [a.] Northolt, Middlesex, UK

RABBETT, SARAH MARIE
[b.] 14 May 1980, Harrow; [p.] Angela Rabbett and Colin Rabbett; [ed.] Currently awaiting my G.C.S.E. results.; [hon.] I have not entered one of my poems into my other competitions, but have had merits for piano exams I have sat.; [oth. writ.] I have written many poems and songs.; [pers.] My philosophical statement, life is to short to hold grudges and hate. Two things I could not live without my family and friends.; [a.] Ammanford, Dyfed, UK

RADLEY, TAMMY LOUISE
[pen.] Tammy Radley; [b.] 8 January 1979, Orsett; [p.] Peter and Denise Radley; [ed.] Cornelius Vermuyden School; [pers.] My poems reflect my emotions at the time of writing, and I like to think that other people can relate to my poems as well as enjoy them.; [a.] Canvey Island, Essex, UK

RAFIQ, HUMERA
[pen.] Humera; [b.] 27 March 1980, Rochdale; [p.] Mohammad Rafiq, Shahnaz Rafiq; [ed.] Falinge Park High School, Hopwood Hall College, Middleton; [occ.] "A" Level Student; [memb.] Wardleworth Women's Welfare Association, Wardleworth Community Centre St, John's Ambulance (3 Cross Award); [hon.] Nominations in English Language and Literature (GCSE Level) "Distinction" from Oxford University in "Young Enterprise"; [oth. writ.] Many poems and creative piece of writings for High School use, in art promotions; [pers.] I have a close personal tie to all types of poetry especially pre twentieth century ones like William Shakespeare. I enjoy writing romantic poetry and I also love to perceive all aspects of nature in my work.; [a.] Rochdale, Lancashire, UK

RALLY-HYDREOU, MARIA
[pen.] "Thracian Woman"; [b.] Xanthi, Greece; [p.] Demetrius and Christian Rally; [m.] Gregory Hydreou, 26 October 1975; [ch.] Antony, Demetrius, Christina-Paschalina; [ed.] English, French, Italian Language and Literature in the University of Thessaloniki, History-Archaeology (Univ. of Athens), Balkan Languages (Russian, Turkish, Romanian, Bulgarian) in the Balkan Studies Institutes of Thessaloniki, Art; [occ.] English Teacher in Arsakeio, Lykeio (Teaching CPE, CAE, PCE). Giving Lectures in public about Literature, History, etc.; [memb.] Company of Greek Literary Persons, ENAM: Club Operatori Arte e Cultura, Accademia Universale "Federico II di Svevia" Italy, Center of Thracian Studies, "Aesop" Club of Kutahya Greek people (my origin is from Minor Asia), The House of Europe, etc.; [hon.] "Ipektsi" Turkish-Greek prize, Italian Poetry prize (Roma, Bari, Pisa, Genova), Greek poetry prize, essay and short novel, as well; [oth. writ.] Several pieces of Translation from English, French and Italian (essay, articles, poems) participation in anthologies (Greek, Italian, Indian) Literary Critic in magazines, critical analysis and presentation of literary works, science-fiction.; [pers.] I believe in man and I hope that he can live in peace, love and freedom. Nature is the best we have, so we must

protect it. I have been greatly influenced by Shakespeare's wise thoughts and witty motto's. I have also been moved by Shelley's poems. My poetry has mostly philosophy and lyricism. It is often epigrammatic.; [a.] Athens, Attiki, Greece

RAVENSCROFT, FRANK
[b.] 17 June 1922, Preston; [p.] William and Alice Ravenscroft; [m.] Olga Claire Ravenscroft (Deceased), 11 May 1946; [ch.] Barbara, Bryan, Robert, Frances, Jacqueline; [occ.] Retired Computer Service Engineering Manager; [oth. writ.] Numerous poems and works of prose, novels and manuscripts for TV and stage, illustrated children's books. None published to date.; [pers.] My writings reflect my environment and life in general - sentiment and reality.; [a.] Leyland, Preston, Lancashire, UK

RAWLINSON, FRANCIS
[pen.] Frank Arthur; [b.] 6 February 1937, Stockport; [p.] Jeanne Hodkinson, Jimmy Rawlinson; [m.] Deceased; [ed.] Stockport and Military; [occ.] Retired; [oth. writ.] Poem (Tree of Youth) Anchor Books Peterborough, (Inspirations of Yorkshire), Sleep Matters PO Box 3087 London W4 4ZP (Insomniacs) Poem Peridicle, Articles (Whippet Notes), Dog World, (Yuletide Tide), Voice on the Wind? In Poets.; [pers.] Amuse oneself with your scribble is may be published or pay dividends eventually.; [a.] York, UK

RAWSON, AMANDA
[b.] 18 November 1980, Doncaster; [p.] Linda Rawson, Trevor Rawson; [ed.] The Hayfield School; [occ.] Student; [memb.] R.S.P.B.; [hon.] 1, 2, 3, 4, Progressive riding test. (B.H.S.) level 1, 2, 3, swimming awards,; [oth. writ.] Five poems published in school newsletters; [pers.] I want to thank my mum for encouraging me and helping me to reveal my talent.; [a.] Doncaster, South Yorks, UK

READ, MRS. KATHLEEN G.
[b.] 24 September 1912, Thornton Heath, Surrey; [p.] Alfred G. Wolfe and Mercy E. Wolfe; [m.] Arthur J. Read, 18 June 1977; [ch.] One step-daughter; [ed.] Council Schools, until Scholarship to South-Eastern Home Training School, Lewisham, Pitmans College, Lewisham and Evening Pitmans College Croydon; [occ.] Retired Civil Servant, with Air Ministry at R.A.F. Kenley, and later with The Land Commission, Croydon; [memb.] Over 60's Club, Boscombe, and two Women's meetings, past member of Old Coulsdon Camera Club; [hon.] Three Cups and 1 Shield, Awarded Old Coulsdon Camera Club 13th First Exhibition 1959, Pictorial Class, First prize for which I was given a Silver Tankard, Top prize winner for my year at the S.E Home Training School, Lewisham.; [oth. writ.] I have written my Father's Life Story and am waiting news of it's publication. I have written children's plays. In the past I wrote 12 poems for children, with the idea of producing a Children's Birthday Book. I am told by my family and many friends that they look forward to receiving my letters.; [pers.] I think I take after my Father who was a poet and writer of Devotional Songs. He was a Salvation Army Officer. My hobbies are Tapestry work, sewing and thinking and writing poetry. I have been a widow for six years - my husband died in Teneriffe Whilst on our holiday, it set me back a little.; [a.] Bournemouth, Dorset, UK

READING, TRACY ANITA
[b.] 11 August 1970, Exmouth, Devon; [p.] David and Isobel Reading; [ed.] Polesworth Comprehensive School, Then at: North Warwickshire College of Technology and Art; [occ.] Resident Cook at Farleigh School, Andover; [memb.] A Member of Farleigh Singers Choir, Polesworth Congregational Church; [hon.] City and Guilds in General Craft Catering Cake Decorating Certificates, Awarded in Competition; [oth. writ.] A collection of poetry as yet, unpublished. Numerous pen-friends world wide.; [pers.] I write about things that I enjoy, take pleasure in, and feel strongly about. Especially, the environment.; [a.] Polesworth, Staffordshire, UK

REID, ALLAN
[b.] 15 October 1958, Buckie; [p.] Alexander and Norma Reid; [m.] Irene, 3 April 1981; [ch.] Kerry and Allan; [ed.] Buckie High School; [occ.] Nightshift worker in local factory. (Was in the Gordon Highlanders for 13 years); [oth. writ.] Have written over 200 poems, wrote to Yonkly magazine for a year and have entered only one other competition.; [pers.] I don't read other peoples poetry and write for the pleasure and nothing else. My wife and kids read my poems before I put them away into an old briefcase. I write in different styles and class myself as an abstract poet. I will be buying the book in the near future.; [a.] Portknockie, Buckie, Banffshire, UK

REID, DANNY
[pen.] Daniel T. Reid, D. T. Reid; [b.] 14 April 1968, Plaistow, London; [p.] Gordon Terence and Barbara Reid; [m.] Michelle Norris (Reid), 20 July 1996; [ed.] Langdon, Hall Mead Comp; [occ.] Audio Visual Technician, Projectionist; [memb.] The Painthouse (Musical Collective), East Ham Syndicate (Football) X1; [hon.] English Lan, Lit. various sporting; [oth. writ.] Forthcoming poem collection "The Magpie Returns", songwriter for promising musical project (Bullfrog) - various compositions Inc. "House The Sea"; [pers.] In my poems and songs I translate personal experience, interweaving elements of romance, love, ambition, inner turmoil and a quest for knowledge and understanding. Influenced by Wilfred Owen, Shelley Byron, William Blake and Spike Milligan.; [a.] Elmstead Woods, Kent, UK

REYNOLDS, MATTHEW
[pen.] Matthew Reynolds; [b.] 19 May 1985, Walsall, W. Mids; [p.] Keith Reynolds, Sandra Reynolds; [ed.] Mayfield Preparatory School, Walsall W. Midlands; [occ.] Still at school; [memb.] Harlequin Drama Club West Bromwich Youth Operatic Society; [hon.] L.A.M.D.A. speech exams grade 1 - distinction grade 2 - distinction grade 3 - Pass.; [oth. writ.] Several poems; [pers.] I want people to take care of their world and to understand nature and treasure all living things.; [a.] Walsall, West Midlands, UK

RHODES, VICTORIA
[b.] 6 May 1980, Bradford; [p.] Stanley and Catharine Rhodes; [ed.] Ripon City School; [occ.] Pupil at Ripon City School; [memb.] Y.M.C.A. Red Triangle Drama School; [oth. writ.] Poems published in inspirations from Yorkshire; [pers.] My outlook on life seems very pessimistic through my poetry. But I am very optimistic young women. I am not influenced by other poets. But I am encouraged by the people I know. Especially Mrs. Anne Towse.; [a.] Ripon, North Yorks, UK

RICH, CARLY ELISA
[pen.] Carly E. Rich; [b.] 18 September 1982, Harrow; [p.] Shelley and David Rich; [ed.] Hatch End High; [occ.] School Student; [oth. writ.] Various greeting card verses, journalist for school magazine, short story.; [pers.] I endeavour to portray in my writings my understand of other peoples' struggles and emotions and also being able to express my own feelings.; [a.] Stanmore, Middx, UK

RICHARD, ANN
[b.] 29 December 1953, Forfar, Angus; [p.] James Todd, Annie Todd; [m.] Donald Richard, 7 August 1976; [ch.] Laura, Alison, John; [ed.] Grove Academy, Broughty Ferry; [oth. writ.] Several works in local publications and excerpts on radio; [pers.] For my writing I draw on my own experiences and sometimes I write in my native tongue of Doric so that it does not become a dying language.; [a.] Carron, Moray, UK

RICHARDS, DOROTHY
[b.] 3 June 1902, Penzance; [p.] Charles Richards, Emma Richards; [ed.] West Cornwall College for Girls, Bedford College, Regent's Park, University of Bordeaux, University of Grenoble; [occ.] Retired French-Mistress; [memb.] Cornish Bard, Cornish Wane - Lelder, Member of Cornish Gorseth; [oth. writ.] Two publications in the Cornish Language - 1. Whethlow Tushuvel (stories of simple folk), 2. Ystoy Plu Senar, History of Zennor Parish; [a.] Pendeen Penzance, Cornwall, UK

RICHARDSON, PHYLLIS V.
[b.] 21 February 1913, Ipswich; [p.] Deceased; [m.] Deceased, 28 December 1932; [ch.] Margaret and Michael; [ed.] Copleston Secondary Modern School

RICKWOOD, MRS. JEAN
[pen.] Jean Rickwood; [b.] 10 January 1940, Bradford; [p.] Mr. and Mrs. Wood who brought me up; [m.] Mr. Brian Rickwood, 24 May 1958; [ch.] Steven and Sandra 37 and 34 age; [ed.] Backward School Meltham Nr Hudersfield; [occ.] Cleaning all my life; [memb.] Now magazine and Harrogate College; [hon.] Won Elegant Grandmother At Pontains 1988 At Southport, had awards for Collecting for Children in need and Swimming; [oth. writ.] Had six poems published up to now. I have sent two more to publishers. Have had a story in a magazine called do it now. I am going to be in Sega magazine I have been on my local radio stray Fm and in my local paper.; [pers.] I am dyslexic I only found our 5 years ago. I have been going to my local college it helps me with my autobiography. In September I am going to learn painting. I have shaken hands and had a Chat with Pam Ayres. Meet Hank Marvin he siged his name on my work for my book meet Rodey Bouwers of the Lakley Lads. He wished me all the best in my writing.; [a.] Harrogate, North Yorkshire, UK

RIDGES, ROY DAVID
[b.] 18 December 1946, Queensborough; [p.] Betty and Charlie Ridges; [m.] Separated; [ch.] Ian and Philip; [ed.] Secondary Modern School; [occ.] Stevedore; [memb.] The Guild of International Songwriters and Composers; [oth. writ.] Have written several other poems. But the great whale never sleeps is the first one I have attempted to have published.; [pers.] I have written poems over the last five years and my main inspiration has been Ian Anderson the singer songwriter of Jethro Tull and I hope from this poem to have others of mine published.; [a.] Sheerness, Kent, UK

RIDGWAY, KEVIN
[pen.] Krazy Kev; [b.] 19 December 1974, Spelthorne; [p.] Roberta Ridgway, Arthur Ridgway; [ed.] Dartford Grammar School For Boys; [occ.] Administrative Officer, Metropolitan Police Service; [memb.] National Federation of 18plus groups, Kent Area; [hon.] Winner of the Norbury Trophy (Best Magazine) for "Grapevine" (Kent Area 18plus Magazine) in 1995 as editor; [oth. writ.] Numerous articles for grapevine; [pers.] My poems tend to reflect the darker nature of the human soul. My greatest influences have been Homer and Dante.; [a.] Crayford, Kent, UK

RIDLEY, SYLVIA YVONNE
[pen.] Gerina Lomoder; [b.] 20 August 1955, Scotland; [p.] Mrs. Jane Moore - Reginald Moore; [m.] Edward Ridley, 3 April 1987; [ch.] Neville, Jacqueline, Amanda Jason; [ed.] Longfield Comprehensive School, Darlington; [occ.] Cook; [memb.] Willington Ladies Darts and Dominoes; [hon.] Honours, Food and Safety; [oth. writ.] Many poems but this is the first I have submitted to anyone. My poems are on life and reality.

RIGNALL, SHEILA ANN
[b.] June 30, 1934, Manchester; [p.] Ellen and Charles Royle; [m.] Divorced; [ch.] Karen and Gregory; [ed.] Secondary Modern; [occ.] Retired hairdresser; [oth. writ.] Poems and short stories. None published as yet, only started writing poetry in September 1995.; [pers.] A near death experience in 1991 altered my conception of life as a whole, and I had the urge to set down my thoughts and analyse them. Creative writing was the result. I feel I have been given a new lease of life in more ways than one.; [a.] Walkden, Worsley, Lancs

RILEY, PAULETTE URSULA
[pen.] P. Ursula; [b.] 9 June 1966, Dudley; [p.] Enid Johnson, E. Riley; [ed.] Hillcrest School and Community College, Dudley College of Technology; [occ.] VDU Operator/Clerk; [oth. writ.] Next of kin-short story (not published) several poems (not published) several song lyrics.; [pers.] Children are the future mankind should cherish them, show them love and understanding so the world can be a happier peaceful place than the evil within it today.; [a.] Dudley, West Mids, UK

RIST, CAROLE
[b.] 20 August 1949, Dunkirk, Kent; [p.] Mr. and Mrs. Myde; [m.] Peter, 3 August 1968; [ch.] Shane, Mandy, Robin; [ed.] Lady Capel School, Favasham, Kent; [occ.] Housewife, but I now in a wheelchair, due to (Myotonic Dystraphy); [oth. writ.] I have written many poems but none as yet have been published; [pers.] When my children were small I often told them about the youth fairy and I've always enjoyed reading poems.

RITCHIE, GARY
[pen.] Gary Ritchie; [b.] January 26, 1971, Kirkcaldy; [p.] Maureen and Peter Ritchie; [m.] Heather Brynes, not married; [ed.] West Wemyss Primary and Buckhaven High School; [occ.] General Labourer; [oth. writ.] Have had several poems published in high school magazines.; [pers.] To cheer people up even a little, when reading my poems.; [a.] Thornton, Fife

ROBB, VALERIE
[b.] 29 October 1946, Hornsea; [p.] Florence Walton and Vittorio Porru; [m.] Alexander Robb, 20 October 1979; [ch.] Julie Marie, Christine, Elizabeth Ann, Laura Eva; [ed.] Penistone Grammar School and Barnsley College as a mature

student learning the Italian Language; [occ.] Housewife; [oth. writ.] Poems and essays that I have kept for my own personal library; [pers.] For me poetry is a way to express feelings and thoughts that everyday speech does not allow.; [a.] Penistone, S. Yorkshire, UK

ROBERTS, JOYCE
[b.] 24 September 1935, Homa Point, Kenya; [p.] Marguerite and Francois Verlaque; [m.] John Roberts (Deceased), 21 July 1956; [ch.] Mandy Jane - Daughter; [ed.] Kenya preliminary exam. Cambridge Overseas School Certificate; [occ.] Retired (Secretary); [oth. writ.] One other poem selected for "Between A Laugh And A Tear"; [pers.] Certain events and experiences have inspired me to capture them in verse; [a.] Dinas Powys, S. Glamorgan, UK

ROBERTS, JO
[b.] 14 August 1935, Putney, SW; [p.] Harry and Dorothy Roberts; [ed.] Putney High School Exeter University; [pers.] Interests, Travel, Language, Christianity, Birds and Animals, People; [a.] Woodbridge, Suffolk, UK

ROBERTS, SHEILA
[b.] 19 June 1956, Edmonton; [p.] Reginald Miles (Deceased), Brenda Miles; [m.] Divorced; [ch.] Kevin Richard, Kerrie Lee-Anne, Emma Jodie; [ed.] William Foster Comprehensive School, Self taught Accountancy Diploma; [occ.] Book-keeper, self empl., but unemployed at present; [oth. writ.] None published to date, as never regarded myself as proficient enough to achieve this standard.; [pers.] I love to write, albeit poetry or novels, I like to pen humorous verse, and fictional novels, influenced and admire Edward Lear, George Arwell and M.G. Wells.; [a.] Northampton, Northamptonshire, UK

ROBERTSON, A. SCOTT
[b.] 21 February 1967, Mansfield; [p.] Elizabeth and Charlie Robertson; [occ.] Freelance Writer; [pers.] It's over before it begins bust still we try.; [a.] Worksop, Notts, UK

ROBERTSON, GEORGE
[pen.] Robbie; [b.] 10 March 1955, Leith; [p.] John and Janet Robertson; [m.] Gillian McCabe Robertson, 26 August 1994; [ch.] Grant Robertson; [ed.] Parson's Green Primary Sch., Portobello High Sec. Sch., Stevenson Coll. For. Edu.; [occ.] Boiler/Plant attendant, Scottish Courage Brewers; [memb.] Liberton Golf Club, Hibernian Football Supp. Clubs, Tartan Social Club; [hon.] City and Guild Cert. in Motor Vehicle Engineering; [oth. writ.] Letters and poems to local newspaper retirement poems for employees.; [pers.] Coming from a large family I write about the changes over the years in family circles. Influences include burns and recently late Norman McCaig.; [a.] Edinburgh, Midlothian, UK

ROBERTSON, JULIA MARY
[b.] 29 December 1954, Farnworth; [p.] John Benson, Joan Hannah Benson; [m.] Graeme John Robertson, 29 December 1977; [ch.] Robin, Amanda, Jayne, Wesley Graeme Richard; [ed.] Derby Street School for Girls Bolton Lancashire; [oth. writ.] Poem published in International Magazine 'Donovans Friends'.; [a.] Farnworth, Lancashire, UK

ROBERTSON, KATHLEEN
[b.] 23 December 1939, Dundee; [p.] Margaret McLaren; [m.] Sandy Robertson, 17 October 1993;

[ch.] Two; [ed.] GCE; [occ.] Housewife; [memb.] Muirhead - Birkhill Bowling Club; [oth. writ.] I've written about 500 poems and I've have sent you two. The rest of them have never been entered into my competition.; [pers.] I love quiet times when words bubble up from inside me, the ink flow's and makes sense to me.; [a.] Dundee, Angus, UK

ROBILLIARD, MRS. JANINE
[b.] 9 January 1958, Guernsey; [p.] Donald and Daphne Leech; [m.] Roy Robilliard, 16 June 1983; [ch.] Four children; [occ.] Care assistant for the elderly and housewife; [oth. writ.] Too many to mention; [pers.] I find profound joy when I'm writing poetry, it's a tranquil way to express my thoughts and feelings on paper.; [a.] Saint Martins, Guernsey, UK

ROBINSON, BARRY
[b.] 21 June 1934, Bristol; [p.] Reginald Robinson, Ethel Robinson; [m.] Pamela (nee Lewis) Robinson, 21 November 1959; [ch.] Luvene Annette, Andrew Paul; [ed.] Redcliffe Secondary Modern School (Bristol); [occ.] Principal Electrical Engineer - Local Government; [memb.] Fellow of the Institute of Electrical and Electronic Incorporated Engineer, Member of Chartered Institution of Building Services Engineers; [hon.] (As above), F.I.E.T.E. and C.I.B.S.E.; [pers.] The poem written is basically what I truly believe and hold to be true. Have been influenced and admire works of 'Rudyard Kipling' especially 'If'.; [a.] Bristol, Avon, UK

ROBSON, KEITH
[pen.] Melancholy; [b.] 18 March 1979, London; [p.] Irene Robson, Colin Robson; [ed.] St Georges RC Primary School, St. Michaels Secondary School, Learning Support Centre; [memb.] Music Direct, Terrorvision Fan Club, Smashing Pumpkins Fan Club; [hon.] Duke of Edingbough, 10 Star decaflon, First aid course 1 and 2, National record of Achievement 94-95, Literacy Level 2; [oth. writ.] Apart from personal writings; [pers.] Life is a vicious circle that goes around and around I'm a peaceful person who feels he's in the wrong environment, all of these and my psychology of life influence me to write what I write.; [a.] London, UK

ROBY, MRS. PAULINE ELIZABETH
[pen.] P.E.R.; [b.] 28 September 1962, Billinge; [p.] Harold and Eva Bold; [m.] David Roby, 4 October 1986; [ch.] Elizabeth Helen Roby; [ed.] Up Holland High School, Wigan College Of Technology.; [occ.] (Had to finish work due to an Injury to leg) I was a clerk for greater manchester police.; [hon.] The Hilda Derbyshire Prize for Commercial Subjects.; [oth. writ.] Wrote quite alot of poetry for personal keepsake; [pers.] My work comes from the heart there is no planning I just put pen to paper. I hope to put my own book together and Illuminate it.; [a.] Wigan, Lancs, UK

RODOY, LORRAINE
[b.] 12 January 1952, Newcastle upon Tyne; [p.] Joseph and June Moore; [m.] Divorced; [ch.] Victoria Louise and Katie Louise; [ed.] Western Comprehensive; [occ.] None Teaching Assistant Whitgift School, Grimsby; [memb.] Royal Life saving society, Amateur Swimming Society; [hon.] RLSS Bronze Cross, RLSS Silver Cross, RLSS Award of Merit; [pers.] Life is so unpredictable. We should meet the challenges facing us with hope and determination; [a.] Grimsby, North East Lincolnshire, UK

RODRIGUES, CHRISTINE
[b.] 11 September 1981, Jersey, C.I.; [p.] Jose Rodrigues and Maria Rodrigues; [ed.] Rouge Bouillon School (primary) D'Hautree School; [occ.] Student; [oth. writ.] Poems which are unpublished and unknown.; [pers.] Poems for me, are both descriptive and successful ways of expressing all kinds of expressing all kinds of good or bad feelings.; [a.] Saint Melier, Jersey, Channel Islands, UK

ROE, MARGARET
[b.] 4 November 1939, Slough, Berks; [p.] Emmin and Margaret Hall; [m.] Robert Henry, 4 August 1957; [ch.] Jeffrey, Debra, Matthew. All married with children.; [ed.] The Orchards Slough; [occ.] Housewife; [oth. writ.] Since starting to write on the 20-1-96. I have done only (smile) about. 96 Too long a list for these few lines. Roots. The Mirror, Death, Love, Hate, The Bottle, The Sky, Dragons, Birth, The Three Depression, escape, The Tower, A Gift, Life.; [pers.] What does one say about oneself. I have know love, joy happiness pleasure, I have know the other side of the coin, pain worry and grief. I am blessed with an Optimistic disposition, a good sense of humour, they will see me through the maze that we call our life.; [a.] Bedworth, Warks, UK

ROGERS, BETTE
[pen.] Beth Rogers; [b.] U.K.; [ed.] U.K. general education with further college studies, Aust. communication skills, Social Science = Credit Pass; [occ.] writer; [oth. writ.] Children's - "WiniBella the Winsome Witch" - first book published by Dorrance Publishing Co. U.S.A. to be released the end of October 1996, theme: helping each other; [pers.] To be able to draw attention to this world we live in and to understand the best and beautiful things in life are certainly free.; [a.] Limassol, Cyprus

ROGERS, FRAN
[b.] 27 July 1952, London; [p.] Noel J. Godwin, Violet Godwin; [m.] Colin Rogers, 26 February 1972; [ch.] Samantha-Jane, Michael Geoffrey; [ed.] Tolworth Girls Comprehensive; [occ.] Working with disabled and handicapped people.; [memb.] Thames Valley Arts Society; [oth. writ.] Written poems since the age of eleven and many stories and poetry for children; [pers.] I try to keep an element of humour in my poetry. I think a smile and good humour is essential to everyone.; [a.] New Malden, Surrey, UK

ROGERSON, GERARD
[b.] 12 May 1969, Kendal, Cumbria; [p.] Geoffrey Rogerson, Eleanor Rogerson; [ed.] Keswick School, Manchester Polytechnic, The College of Law, York; [occ.] Solicitor, Whitehaven in Cumbria; [memb.] Play drums in local rock group; [hon.] English Literature, Advanced Level Creative Writing; [oth. writ.] Several poems published in anthology of modern poets. Searching for publisher to publish my collection of poems covering a ten year period.; [pers.] I have no significant influences I draw my inspiration from the paths of life around me and the sardonic humour of a limited existence.; [a.] Workington, Cumbria, UK

ROOKE, DEIRDRE ANN
[b.] 19 December 1931, Kent; [p.] Mr. and Mrs. J. W. Bell (Deceased); [m.] John Desmond Rooke, 6 August 1951; [ch.] One son; [ed.] Private High School Low-Fell, Co. Durham; [occ.] Retired;

[oth. writ.] Lyrics (Songs) not published; [pers.] My writings are mainly inspirations of happenings in my life.; [a.] Wokingham, Berkshire, UK

ROSS, JULIA
[b.] 27 June 1969, Gravesend; [p.] Carol and Alexander Ross; [ed.] Gordon Secondary; [occ.] Residential Social Worker; [memb.] Global Taekwondo International; [oth. writ.] First poem published, many more available for publication.; [pers.] I reflect upon very private and personal thoughts, feelings and experiences, and a knowledge my surroundings!; [a.] Gravesend, Kent, UK

ROSSI, DANIEL
[b.] 13 March 1977, London; [p.] Rosanna and Amelio Rossi; [ed.] St. Charles College - London 9 G.C.S.E.'s; [occ.] Part-time musician. Pastry Chef. (full-time); [oth. writ.] Various songs and various poetry but none submitted until now for publication.; [pers.] I have been greatly influenced by Pete Townsend on my musical likes and by Jim Douglas Morrison for my thoughts in poetry.; [a.] London, UK

ROWE, HAZEL
[pen.] Hazel Rowe; [b.] 12 January 1926, Lerryn; [p.] John and Ivy Collins; [oth. Writ.] On The Other Side Of The Mirror; [pers.] I am an O.A.P. and cannot offord another 20 pounds. Its a lot for the little bit of information.; [a.] Lostwithiel, Cornwall, UK

ROWSE, AMANDA JAYNE
[pen.] Amanda Jayne Rowse; [b.] 15 July 1975, Sheffield; [p.] Donald Rowse, Daphne Rowse; [ed.] Sheffield High School for Girls, Thomas Roherham Sixth Form College, Roherham College of Art and Technology, Helsinki Business Polytechnic University of Sunderland; [occ.] Student; [memb.] The Poetry Club, Glamorgen Rag Society, University; [oth. writ.] Poem published in previous "Times" book, articles for finnish magazine; [pers.] I write to reflect my thoughts and feelings, a release of emotions.; [a.] Rotherham, S. Yorks, UK

ROXBURGH, KATIE LOUISE
[b.] 1 November 1983, Chatham; [p.] Sandra and Malcolm Roxburgh; [ed.] Still at School; [occ.] At School, Chapter Girls School, Strodd, Kent; [memb.] Love Horses and Riding, belongs to West Kent Meopham Pony Club; [oth. writ.] Many poems and story's for school, english lessons.; [a.] Cuxton, Rochester, Kent, UK

RUSSELL, ROWEENA
[b.] 1 July 1975, Ireland; [p.] Rosaire, Michael Russell; [ed.] Secondary St. Mary's College Arklow. Studied Child Care currently studying social care; [occ.] Student Working part time in a nursing home Rath gar; [memb.] Arklow Rowing Club Arklow Arts Group; [hon.] Highly commended in poetry competition in Arklow musical festival. Published with Arklow Arts Group; [oth. writ.] I have written over 700 poems and hope to publish a number of my works in the future; [pers.] Alter not what you have for what which you shall never have!; [a.] Arklow, Wicklow, UK

RUTTER, LESLEY
[pen.] Lesley Mattimoe; [b.] 10 April 1964, Co Durham; [p.] Frank Mattimoe and Margaret Mattimoe; [m.] Neville Rutter, 1 March 1996;

[ch.] Michael Anthony Mattimoe; [ed.] Bishop St. Johns Comp.; [occ.] Catering Assistant; [pers.] I write poetry to express myself and it has proved great therapy for me. Also to inspire people there is light at the end of every tunnel.; [a.] Newton Aycliffe, Durham, UK

RUXTON, MICHAEL
[b.] 26 March 1956, Blantire, Malawi; [p.] Mr. T. D. Ruxton, Mrs. M. Ruxton; [ed.] Fircroft College, Birmingham Polytechnic; [occ.] Unemployed; [memb.] Pentagraph Poets; [hon.] Degree in English Literature; [oth. writ.] Self published books Running With The Bewildered Beat, I've Got Pockets, I've Got Pockets 2, Moods and Meditations of the Masque (other magazines first time); [pers.] Writing has been very useful in overcoming mental health problems and I write to had people to identity. I also write on man's other topics and enjoy it.; [a.] Portslade, Sussex, UK

RYAN, ANN
[b.] 7 September 1978, London; [p.] Nancy Ryan; [ed.] St. Agnes Primary School, John Kelly Girls School, John Kelly 6th from College; [occ.] Student; [hon.] I took part in a Mensa Challenge. I passed and received a certificate on merit. I also received a prize for my Outstanding English work at school - 1995; [oth. writ.] I've never had anything published. But I have my own poetry book which is full of my own personal poems.; [pers.] Sometimes life isn't easy. You need to put up your umbrella and protect yourself from everything that life hurls at you.; [a.] Neasden, London, UK

RYDQVIST, MILINDA ELIZABETH
[pen.] Milinda Elizabeth, Milinda Weaving; [b.] 14 February 1945, Romford, Essex; [ch.] Gary Weaving, Gavin Weaving; [hon.] President's Award, Ballroom and Latin Dancing; [oth. writ.] Several poems published in various anthologies, first works published in 1972.; [pers.] Writing allows me to express my unspoken thoughts.; [a.] Laindon, Essex, UK

SACKEY, EDNA DINA
[b.] 6 July 1979, Ghana, Africa; [p.] Monica Akroa and David Sackey; [ed.] Salisbury Secondary School, Edmonton, Hertford Regional College, Turnford, Herts; [occ.] Student; [memb.] Edmonton Green, SLMS GYM; [hon.] Diploma in Vocational Ed. 9 pass grades over 'C' at GCSE Level (1=Ak, 5=A's, 1=B, 2=C); [oth. writ.] Several, none published; [pers.] Poetry is a reflection of the soul. The voice of the soul, given the chance respect, expresses a beauty and an understanding beyond the physical, the visual and the audible, enticing the mind to wonder in realms unavailable to the physical world.; [a.] Edmonton, Enfield, UK

SACRE, SONIA
[pen.] Sonia Sacre; [b.] 24 June 1939, Rothwell; [p.] Ethel and Dennis Coleman; [m.] Gordon Sacre, 18 January 1969; [ch.] Cheryl, Denise, Karen, Mandy, Darren; [ed.] Secondary Modern; [occ.] License Public House; [oth. writ.] Many published poems; [pers.] I consider my poetry to be poems of life - emotions that are felt that are kept within and never spoken of. I am prompted to write when something. I have seen or heard effects are emotionally or have experienced in my life. They are in fact real life stories.; [a.] Caldecoh, Leicestershire, UK

SAINSBURY, IRIS
[b.] 4 June 1925, Swindon; [p.] Ruby and Len Bamford; [m.] Roy Sainsbury, 4 June 1949; [ch.] Two girls, Glenis and Carol; [ed.] Wroughton Primary School, English Reading Top Marks; [occ.] Housewife Retired was Shop Assistant; [memb.] Club, Marks and Spencers, RSA retired Marks and Spencers; [hon.] School Prizes for English, and Reading; [pers.] Four grandchildren: two boys and two girls ages 22, 19. Two boys, 16, youngest granddaughter. I am now 71. Hobbies: Poetry. Dancing and travelling. Widow for 22 years, age 71 but still have hobbies of poetry dancing and travelling.; [a.] Swindon, Wilts, UK

SALT, MICHAEL JOSEPH
[pen.] Joseph Michaels; [b.] 27 January 1943, Oldham; [p.] Silas and Elizabeth; [m.] Sheila, 19 December 1964; [ch.] Sharon Tracy, Stephen Michael; [ed.] Waterloo Secondary Modern School, Oldham; [occ.] Craftsman Gardener (Ret.); [memb.] Institute of Supervisory Management. Associate Member; [hon.] City-Guilds Horticulture, National Examination Board of Supervisory Management; [oth. writ.] Short poem "Footsteps" in school magazine and a pome entitled "Within The Bower" published by the Poetry Institute of the British Isles, in their anthology "Sunlight and Shadows".; [pers.] My aim is to give pleasure with my writings. If I can do that then I have achieved my ambition and will strive to maintain that pleasure.; [a.] Oldham, Lancs, UK

SALTER, PAULA JANE
[b.] 12 March 1983, Kingston; [p.] Anne and Michael; [ed.] Hawkedale First School, Springfield Middle School, St. Pauls Catholic; [occ.] Student; [pers.] I have been writing poetry from a very young age, and I hope that I will continue to do so many years to come.; [a.] Sunbury, Middlesex, UK

SAMUEL, INGA LOUISE
[b.] 22 March 1938, Redcae, Cleveland; [p.] Robert (Deceased) and Daphne Robinson; [m.] Ivan David Samuel, 14 July 1966; [ch.] One son 23 years old, 1 daughter 25; [ed.] Private Suite High School, Private Rosebank High School Hartlepool Cleveland, Coverdales Secretarial College Hartlepool Cleveland; [occ.] Promotions on Conservatories; [hon.] First attempt poetry in my life; [oth. writ.] Inga's diet health glamour for young and old (8 yrs age), small booklet (for a bright new you) and short true animal stories only in Rough Stage (hoping to write more soon).; [pers.] My new book should be ready end October its only to do with diet and health etc "Oh No Not Another Diet" running very late due to divorce ill health etc.; [a.] Poole, Dorset, UK

SAMUELS, KELLIE-ROSE
[pen.] Henri (Harriet Webster); [b.] 27 November 1978, Nottingham; [p.] Joseph and Rose Samuels; [ed.] Joseph Whitaker Comprehensive; [occ.] Student; [memb.] Whymsical World of Pocket Dragons. Rock Band in Local Village/I sing in a Church Choir/Penfriend Trio Club; [hon.] 10 G.C.S.E.'s/Student Training Enterprise Project/St. John Ambulance Three Cross Award/Work Experience Certificate/Dance/Drama Certificate/Junior Chorister of the Month/2nd Prize Book Quiz at School/'Walk to Beat Epilepsy' Award; [oth. writ.] I have never dreamt of such happiness as I feel now. I'm a personal writer myself and it is a great love in my life. I never thought that a poem of mine would have been published.; [pers.]

I tend to reflect on my own life and personal feelings. My writings are about past lovers, love lost and friendship and disabilities of body, mind and soul. I owe a lot to Mr. P. Allan of Joseph Whitaker school, for helping me through my troublesome school years and Mr. D. Greasley also.; [a.] Mansfield, Notts, UK

SANDER, DENISE
[b.] 16 May 1938, Corsham; [p.] John and Frances Lucas; [m.] Anthony, 12 March 1960; [ch.] Michael, Helen, Jayne; [ed.] St. Michaels Church; [occ.] Domestic at Local Old Peoples Home; [memb.] G.E.C. Sports; [oth. writ.] Have 35 anthologies accepted in British Institute of Poetry. Printed in 'A Passage Of Time' last year; [pers.] To be accepted last year was an honour. So I feel very pleased about being in again this year.; [a.] Melksham, Wiltshire, UK

SANDERS, MISS ANGELA
[pen.] Ann Sandwill; [b.] 13 January 1935, Barking, Essex; [p.] John and Ethel Sanders; [m.] Deenis Wilson (Divorced - 1975), 2 April 1956; [ch.] Robert John; [ed.] Convent, Westcliff, Essex Convent, Deal, Kent; [occ.] Baby and Young Child Carer; [oth. writ.] Composed children and adult short stories and poems since an adult - not published success to date. Village correspondent on two vocal newspapers; [pers.] I draw from my children for their stories. I look forward to showing them my first book.; [a.] Streatham, London, UK

SANDERSON, SYDNEY
[pen.] Mistral; [b.] 23 August 1941, Blackpool; [p.] Harry and Daisy Sanderson (Deceased); [m.] Divorced; [ch.] Sarah Jane Sanderson; [ed.] Attended Blackpool Technical College and School of Art., Dist. Science, Calc, Drawing; [occ.] Freelance Artist Exhibitions in Northwest; [memb.] Blackpool and Fylde Art Society; [hon.] Olevel English Distinction in Science Calculations and Drawing; [oth. writ.] Mostly poems and ghost story which appeared in the local paper; [pers.] Inspired by the great poets: Tennyson, Coleridge and Kipling, I have a devout love of history, and feeling for the way our forebears strived. For freedom and peace; [a.] Blackpool, Lancs, UK

SATU, LINDGREN
[b.] 28 February 1966, Helsinki, Finland; [ed.] BA, Univ. of Helsinki; [occ.] Student, Univ. of Helsinki; [oth. writ.] One poem published in a local Catholic Magazine, one short story included into a National Competition Anthology (vision). I write in English, Italian and finish.; [a.] Helsinki, Finland

SAUNDERS, EVELYN F.
[pen.] Ruth Evelyn; [b.] 21 October 1921, Woking; [ed.] Secondary, Clark's College; [occ.] Tour Operator; [memb.] Various Flying Clubs. British Women Pilots Association. 99's.; [hon.] Jean Lennox Bird Trophy for noteworthy performance in aviation.; [oth. writ.] Quite a few poems published in books and magazines. Writes articles on tourism and flying.; [pers.] Obtained pilot's licence at age of 68 and still actively flying. Am known as a person who gives inspiration to others. Hope to spend more time at creative writing in the future.; [a.] Guildford, Surrey, UK

SAYER, SIMONE LEE
[b.] 26 January 1982, Durban, South Africa; [p.] Mr. G. and Mrs. D. Bolton; [ed.] Grantham Park-

South Africa, Chantry Middle School-Morpeth, presently student in year 9 at King Edward VI School-Morpeth; [hon.] Various awards eg. Accomendation Awards for Good School Work; [oth. writ.] Write short stories, poems and songs; [pers.] I have an inner love for putting words together, on thoughts I feel to reflect inner emotions. My greatest ambition is to use my skill to my best ability for a successful future.; [a.] Cambo, Morpeth, Northumberland, UK

SCARLETT, SIMONE ANGELA ELLIS
[b.] 5 October 1982, Aylesbury; [p.] Pearline Ellis and Henry Scarlett; [ed.] Currently attending the Mandeville Upper School, Aylesbury, Bucks; [occ.] Secondary School Pupil; [oth. writ.] Poem: Walking Alone At Night - published in a local anthology, various other poems so far unpublished.; [pers.] "My imagination is my inspiration."; [a.] Aylesbury, Bucks, UK

SCARRATT, PETER JAMES
[b.] 19 September 1964, Ormskirk; [p.] Philip Scarratt, June Scarratt; [m.] Lesley Almond; [ed.] Bebington Secondary School for Boys; [occ.] Train Guard; [memb.] Met Railway Athletics Association; [hon.] Winner Birkenhead Old Society Cup; [oth. writ.] Small article on running published in house magazine; [pers.] I have to thank the infinity of sky and space for my inspiration, and the fact that one life time can never be enough; [a.] Kingsbury, Middlesex, UK

SCOTT, SKYE
[b.] 13 September 1980, Dunbar, Thurso; [p.] Mrs. S. MacKay, Mr. D. Scott; [ed.] Dollar Academy - 1991-1993, Golspie High School - 1993-1996 (Moray College 1996?); [occ.] Waitress/Chamber Maid; [pers.] I have been writing poems for many years although have never had any published; [a.] Tongue, Sutherland, UK

SCULLY, TERESA
[b.] 27 August 1955, Dagenham; [p.] Cornelius and Catherine Scully; [ed.] Sacret Heart of Mary Cowvent School Upminster; [occ.] Admin. Manager; [memb.] Royal Geographical Society Essex Wildlife, Life watch; [pers.] This poem came from my heart the sadness caused by seeing the rainforest destroyed. Let us rid man's inhumanity to man.; [a.] Chadwell Heath, Essex, UK

SEACOMBE, AUDREY JOYCE
[b.] 1 January 1931, Withington, Manchester; [p.] William Spencer, Ivy Spencer; [m.] John Seacombe, 30 March 1959; [ch.] Three sons, three daughters-in-law, two step grandchildren, four grandchildren; [ed.] Urmston Grammar School, Manchester College of Technology, St. Matthias College, Bristol; [occ.] Retired formery Librarian, then Teacher, now Pastoral Assistant, Christ Church, Swindon; [memb.] Fellowship of Christian Writers, Creation Science Movement; [hon.] 1958 fellow of the Library Association 1975 Postgraduate Certificate in Education (Bristol University); [oth. writ.] Magazine Articles; [pers.] I endeavour to honour God the father, God the son and God the Holy Spirit in my life and in my writing.; [a.] Swindon, Wiltshire, UK

SEEDHOUSE, DARREN
[pen.] Darren Seedhouse; [b.] 22 May 1973, Weston-s-Mare; [p.] Lyn Seedhouse, Alec G. Seedhouse; [ed.] Worle Comprehensive School, Brunel College of Technology (Bristol); [occ.]

Unemployed; [oth. writ.] Until now I only wrote for personal satisfaction; [pers.] I take my inspiration from experiences of harsh environments. I think I may appeal to the younger generation who may reflect on parts of their lives through my writing.; [a.] Weston-super-Mare, North Somerset, UK

SEMERARO, LARA

[pen.] Lara The Cat; [b.] 5 July 1974, England; [p.] Lynn and John Semeraro; [occ.] Hair Stylist part time and Poet part time; [memb.] Rauqes Sharki - Eygptian Dance School. Ponana, North African Theme Dancing Bar; [hon.] None until now, I am shy with my writing; [oth. writ.] Books full of poetry and short stories for children but nothing published.; [pers.] The whole world inspires me everything in and around it, especially the things that you can't see.

SEYMOUR, EDWARD G.

[pen.] Edward G. Seymour; [b.] 30 May 1924, Christchurch; [p.] George and Ida Seymour; [m.] Dorothy Eileen Seymour, 13 March 1961; [ed.] National School, Poole; [occ.] Retired; [memb.] Royal British Legion (Christchurch) Ex-Servicemen Club (Leytonstone); [oth. writ.] Poems published in 1992 poets. World of Poetry 1995. One held in Department of Documents Imperial War Museum. Many as yet unpublished.; [pers.] Have you ever stopped to think that life, at least the way we know it, is an infinitesimal fraction of time, so whatever you do, don't blow it.; [a.] Leytonstone, London, UK

SHANDLEY, ALMA

[b.] 4 June 1906, Liverpool; [p.] Sidney and Gertrude Shandley; [ed.] St. Edmunds College, Liverpool Truro Diocesan Training College Cornwall; [occ.] Retired (teacher); [memb.] L'pool Music Group Merseyside Museums and Galleries L'pool Historical Society RNLI (Shoreline member), can no longer attend these meetings; [hon.] Margaret Sackulle Prize (Exeter Univ.) Arch Bishops Teachings Certificate (Holy Scripture); [oth. writ.] Poems printed in Educational Magazines broadcast on radio Merseyside plat broadcast (N. Regional); [pers.] I have always written poetry simply because I like doing so.; [a.] Liverpool, Lancs, UK

SHARLOTT, JOANNE MARY

[b.] 30 December 1981, Oxford; [p.] Ralph Christopher and Jacqueline Mary Sharlott; [ed.] William Fletcher School, Yarnton Oxford, Marlborough School Woodstock Oxford; [occ.] Full time Education, Part-time at a Local Garden Centre Coffee Shop; [hon.] Swimming certificates many Scout Badge; [pers.] Imagination is the key to all learning.; [a.] Yarnton, Oxford, UK

SHARP, MISS CLAUDIA

[b.] 12 April 1969, Cheshire; [p.] Dr. D. M. Sharp, Beryl Sharp; [m.] Mr. Jonathan D. Bradford; [ch.] Laura and Steffanie (4 1/2), Daryl (3); [ed.] Hallow Park School, Hallow Worcestershire; [occ.] Domestic/Mother; [hon.] Canoe and Kayak Ability Award, St. John's 1st Aid Certificate, English Long, Art; [pers.] I write how I feel as children of the world are so precious.; [a.] Saint Albans, Hertfordshire, UK

SHARPE, JOHN EDWARD

[b.] 22 August 1938, Birmingham; [p.] Albert Sharpe, Vera Sharpe; [m.] Jean Sharpe, 29 September 1962; [ch.] Jayne Irene, Ian Andrew; [ed.] Folden Millock Road, Secondary Modern School, Carretts Green Tech. College; [occ.] General Operator, Rover Cars, Long Bridge; [memb.] Vile Chairman, Earlswood Town Football Club; [hon.] City and Guilds of London Inst. Sheet Metal Work; [oth. writ.] Several poems published in books and magazines.; [pers.] I find writing poetry very relaxing and like to specialize in writing poems about the countryside especially the Cotswold area where I spend holidays and long weekends.; [a.] Birmingham, West Mids, UK

SHAW, ANGELA CAVENOR

[pen.] E. Cavenor; [b.] 26 May 1971, Stoke-on-Trent; [p.] Joan Cavenor Evans and Edward Cavenor (Deceased); [m.] Andrew Cavenor Shaw, 4 September 1993; [ed.] Trentham High School, Stoke-on-Trent Sixth form College, University of Warwick (Bahons and MA); [occ.] Student - preparing Ph.D. proposal; [memb.] Mensa, National Canine Defence League (NCDL); [hon.] BA (hons) Sociology and Education, MA Social and Political thought. Various music grade Awards (piano and flute); [oth. writ.] Poem published in an anthology, other poems published in magazines.; [pers.] Time is one thing we can't fight, so I write poetry both to capture and remember feelings or events that are important to me. If just one person is moved by, or thinks about, what I write then I feel it's worthwhile.; [a.] Tamworth, Staffordshire, UK

SHAW, DOROTHY

[b.] 1 August 1906, Lytham; [p.] John Bonney, Elizabeth Brown; [m.] James Shaw, 1 September 1934 (Deceased June 1995); [ed.] Secondary School, Oxford Grove School, Bolton, Sunninghill School, Morris Green Bolton, Art School; [occ.] Retired; [hon.] Award of Merit Poetry for age concern; [oth. writ.] Have 3 poems in a Hard Back Book called Tomorrow's Poets; [a.] Bolton, Lancs, UK

SHAW, GEORGE

[b.] 9 June 1937, Newcastle-under-Lyme; [p.] George A. Shaw and Gladys Shaw; [m.] Irene Pamela Shaw, 12 March 1960; [ch.] Jeff, Rob and Jon; [ed.] St. Mary's C. of E. Tunstall and later at HMS Collingwood R.N. Electrical School, Fareham; [occ.] Technical writer; [mem.] North Staffs, Road Runners Association (NSRRA); [oth. writ.] Several poems (unpublished) and a - part finished novel (some day to become a cinema smash hit). Recorder for local walking group "The Dippers."; [pers.] My poems are like the `last bus' (proverbial) on Christmas Eve. Full of spiritual expectation mixed with sense of humour.; [a.] Madeley, Crewe, Cheshire, UK

SHAW, IAN

[b.] March 6, 1967, Heywood; [p.] Tony and Brenda Shaw; [ed.] Sutherland Road High School; [occ.] Set Builder; [oth. writ.] Some poems published in various anthologies.; [pers.] I strive to explore the emotional ties that we all share. If just one reader can associate and draw something from it. Everything I've written has been worthwhile.; [a.] Bury, Lancs

SHAW, JUNE M.

[b.] June 28, 1947, Halifax; [p.] Herbert Whitworth-Irene Whitworth; [m.] John, November 26, 1966; [ch.] David Andrew and Michael John; [oth. writ.] "Easter" (Anthology of the Cross), currently working on a book of poems for children; [pers.] I would like children to grow up appreciating the arts. By writing simple poetry I hope to introduce them to an enjoyable pastime.

SHAWCROFT, ANGELA

[b.] 15 June 1978, Chesterfield; [p.] Patricia Shawcroft, Robert Shawcroft; [ed.] Violet Markham Secondary School, Chesterfield College; [occ.] Freelance Artist and Art Student; [pers.] A poet is born, not made.; [a.] Chesterfield, Derbyshire, UK

SHEARON, MICHAEL

[b.] 25 June 1954, Morley; [p.] William Shearon, Sarah Shearon; [m.] Susan Jacqualine Shearon, 19 July 1979; [ch.] Michael, Lisa, Rebecca, Claire, Craig; [ed.] Various High Schools; [occ.] Carer of Disabled Wife; [oth. writ.] One poem published by 'Anchor Books' Dream Ride in C'est La Vie!; [pers.] Twelve years ago my daughter 'Lisa' and her teacher, Mr. Hall of Whitebridge Primary encouraged me to start writing.; [a.] Leeds, Yorks, UK

SHEFFIELD, MS. BARBARA MARY

[b.] 26 June 1928, Watford, Herts; [p.] Mr. and Mrs. Ernest James Sheffield of Harrow Middx Freeman of the City of London; [ch.] Family of Four; [ed.] Elementary, Technical College; [occ.] Retired, Handicrafts and creative work are important hobbies.; [memb.] 'Garston Brotherhood of Spiritualists' Watford Hearts 'Home Counties Association of Spiritual Healers.; [hon.] Painting, and sport in my youth, plus handwork and crafts from te age of fight.; [oth. writ.] The Rose, Twilight, A Special Love Spring, Heaven, A Thought, Strength, A Travellers Delight, My Love. etc.; [pers.] The love of natural beauty surrounding me brings fresh joy into my life each day. My purpose in life is to help others to the best of my ability, showing love and compassion, to transform, sadness into joy, and keep my simplicity of life with a sense of humour always.; [a.] Watford, Herts, UK

SHEPHERD, NICHOLA

[b.] 4 August 1972, Doncaster; [p.] Philip and Ann Bussey; [m.] Tobias Shepherd, 14 August 1993; [ed.] Danum School, University of Hertfordshire; [occ.] Disability Employment Consultant, Help People with Disabilities to find Work - Herts County Council; [hon.] Business Administration, British Sign Language; [oth. writ.] I have written poems, but I have not attempted to get them published before.; [pers.] My work is very much based on my personal experiences. I try to make art out of words of expression.; [a.] Milton Keynes, Buckinghamshire, UK

SHIELDS, HAIDEE

[pen.] Dee Shields; [b.] August 12, 1917, Wiltshire; [p.] Albert Stacey, Mabel Stacey; [m.] Jack Shields (Deceased), September 11, 1976; [ch.] Sidney Bruce, Haidee Penelope; [ed.] Aldbourne C of E School Educated until the age of fourteen at this Village School; [occ.] Retired; [memb.] Berkshire Blind Society; [oth. writ.] Several poems published in local magazines. Interview and reading of a poem on tape for berkshire blind society.; [pers.] I began writing poetry as an expression of my inner thoughts when losing my sight restricted many activities.; [a.] Thatcham, Berks

SHORT, SUZANNE LOUISE

[b.] 25 July 1978, Birmingham; [p.] Lynette Short and Kenneth Short; [ed.] Coleg Powys, Newtown; [occ.] Student at Coleg Powys; [hon.] RSA Diploma in Business Administration; [oth. writ.] Articles published in local newspaper; [pers.] The feelings of each and every person, can be expressed in one word, that word is poetry; [a.] Newtown, Powys, UK

SHREEVE, GRAVE EVELYN
[b.] 28 April 1911; [p.] Mr. and Mrs. Ben Lyon; [m.] Widow, 14 August 1932; [ch.] Three, 2 girls 1 boy; [ed.] Elementary School; [occ.] House wife; [memb.] Mothers Union Member of the British Cgoin; [oth. writ.] Like Singing, Dancing, Classical Music, Amateur/Dramatics, 11 grandchildren 15 great grandchildren; [pers.] I am with my husband a very successful business retired at 59. Went on to provide breakfast for 20 malajunted boys, been a caretaker for the local village school. Been an SRN for 10 years. Retired at 80 years.

SIDMAN, RUTH
[b.] 26 February 1975, Merthyr, Tydfil; [p.] Joel and Sylvia Sidman; [ed.] 6 CLSE's, 2 A-Levels French and English; [occ.] French/Drama Student; [oth. writ.] Not as yet as it's the first time I have ever entered a poetry competition but I have written many poems based on death i.e., "The Calling" the time of the holocaust "Why God, Why?"; [pers.] Poetry is the highest form of communication. It's a means of evoking emotion and response in the reader so we search our souls and consider various facets of this fantastic journey called Life; [a.] Swansea, Wales, UK

SIMMONS, BERNARD
[pen.] Ben Simon; [b.] 10 May 1925, London; [p.] Ben Simmons and Hattie Simmons; [m.] Agustina Maria, 9 August 1956; [ch.] Robert Salvador, Jeannie Rebecca, Tanya Alexandra; [ed.] Stepney Grammar, Raines Foundation; [occ.] Retired; [memb.] Radlett Poetry Soc., R.M. Old Boys Assoc.; [hon.] Poems Published in School and College Publications; [oth. writ.] Short story writing - short plays; [pers.] I try to encompass the experience of life into poetic terms.; [a.] Radlett, Herts, UK

SIMMONS, RONALD H.
[b.] 20 November 1920, Shropshire; [p.] Walter Simmons, Dorothy Simmons; [m.] Katherine Mary, 5 March 1946; [ch.] Rosemary Anne - Andrew Douglas Henry; [ed.] Berhamsted School, Herts; [occ.] Retired; [oth. writ.] Children's short stories, children's poems - romantic poems as a "Pastime" and family "Entertainment". Never sought publication!; [pers.] Strong desire to portray a true appreciation of life and our general environment. Partly influenced by my experienced of service in World War II as a pilot in the Royal Air Force.; [a.] Louth, Lincolnshire, UK

SIMNER, GLENYS
[b.] 22 August 1945, Walsall; [p.] Ivy Turner, Bill Turner; [m.] Widow; [ch.] Nigel Simner; [ed.] Great Barr High School and Commercial College, Walsall College of Art and Technology; [occ.] Tutor (Business Administration); [oth. writ.] Plays written for local amateur drama groups; [pers.] My special thanks to Peter Paul Camilleri, Nadur, for all his encouragement and support; [a.] Walsall, West Midlands, UK

SIMONSEN, ERIK VIBE
[pen.] E. V. Simonsen/Tim Kernett; [b.] 23 October 1970, Bergen; [p.] Lill and John Simonsen; [ed.] University degree in Media and Literature, (University of Bergen - Norway); [memb.] The Poetry Library, Royal Festival Hall (London); [oth. writ.] Poems accepted for publication in "Nineties Poetry," "First Time," and "Never Bury Poetry."; [pers.] I have spent the last six months in London, trying to get established as a poet. Now I'm leaving, and London can fuck off.

My poems I write with one overall thing in mind: Not to be boring.; [a.] Bergen, Norway

SIMPSON, COLIN MORRISON
[b.] 9 August 1945, Kirriemuir; [p.] George and Mary Simpson; [m.] divorced; [ed.] Webster's Seminary, Kirriemuir. Montrose Academy, Montrose; [occ.] Incapacity benefit due to long-term illness; [pers.] Deeply committed to world socialism and implacable enemy of capitalism and fascism.; [a.] Kirriemuir, Tayside DD8 5AL

SIMPSON, TRISTAN
[pen.] Tristan Simpson; [b.] 3 June 1977, Aberdeen; [p.] Raymond and Katherine; [ed.] Newtonhill Primary School Portlethen Academy; [occ.] N.D.T. Technician (non-destructive testing engineer); [pers.] Poetry is a way of seeing life in a different perspective my perspective is a way of seeing poetry in life; [a.] Newtonhill, Stonehaven, UK

SINOTT, DARRAGH
[b.] 3 April 1978, Dublin; [p.] Charles and Bridget; [ed.] Glenstal Abbey School, Co. Limerick; [occ.] student, first year; [memb.] Inland Waterways Association of Ireland, Connemara Coast Leisure Centre, Glenstal Society; [oth. writ.] published selection of own work and friends' work in annual school booklet; [pers.] Children suck their mothers when they are young and their fathers when they are older.; [a.] Oughterard, Galway

SIRETT, CLIVE HUGH WESTON
[pen.] Clive Weston Sirett; [b.] 18 October 1945, West Drayton, Mddx; [p.] H. H. Sirett (Journalism) and Phyllis Model Manning (1930's Model Fashion); [m.] Doreen M. Sirett (Abstract Painter), 9 July 1983; [ch.] 1 Daughter aged 25 (from previous marriage) 1 stepson aged 36 (both Artists); [ed.] 1957-61 Alfred Sutton Central 1976-77 Art Foundation at Basingstoke College of Art and Design. 1977-80 West Surrey College Art and Design Farnham 1980-1981 Reading University; [occ.] Retired Lecturer in Art and Design Working Towards joint exhibition sculpture poetry, painting with wife 1997; [memb.] Hoping to publish complete book of poetry 1956-61 Reading Natural History Society; [hon.] 1959 and 1961 Laffan Prize for Natural Science. 1977. Foundation prize Bek Academic Student for 6 years. 1980 BA Honrs. Fine Art 1981 Post graduate certificate in Education 1982 Certificate Health Safety in Ceramics (London Poly); [oth. writ.] 1972/3 Several poems pub. by Southern Arts and Berkshire Countryside Mags. June 1996 poem pub. in anthology "Mightier than the sword" by forward press (New Poets) Peterborough. Thesis 21,000 words on post-wan fashion 1980 currently working on collection of 30 poems for book; [pers.] I write only about the ideas and images I have experienced at first hand. My ambition now is hopefully, through my writing, to encourage others towards a greater awareness of, and respect for, the earth and all it's life forms.; [a.] Purley-on-Thames, Berkshire, UK

SLAUGHTER, VIVIENNE MARGARET
[b.] 8 October 1941, London; [p.] Gladys and Frank Chambers; [m.] John; [ch.] Steven and Reggie

SMALL, ANNE
[b.] 2 October 1955, Hertfordshire; [ch.] Caroline, Robert and Clementine; [ed.] North London Comprehensive School. I left school at 15 years. I did not have the opportunity to continue with my education; [occ.] Mother and housewife; [oth.

writ.] First poem in "The Other Side Of The Mirror". Second two in "Between A Laugh And A Tear". These are the only poems I have ever entered in any competitions; [pers.] Words in verse, I enjoy. It is my way of expressing myself and feelings; [a.] Wickford, Essex, UK

SMALL, NOLA BETTY
[pen.] Nola B. Small; [b.] 12 November 1936, Sydney, Australia; [p.] Kathleen Burrows, Stanley Burrows; [m.] John Oliver Small, March 1967; [ch.] Nicholas, Jodi, Jonathan, Christopher; [ed.] Bankstown, Sydney "Meriden" Grammar School, Sydney, Australia. Adelaide University - Psychology, English, History, Statistics, Education. Dip. O. Therapy (Aust.) O.T. Reg. (Canada) O.T.R. (U.S.A.) A. Mus.; [occ.] Teacher and Editor - Freelance in Art, Drama, Writing, Music; [memb.] Reader at Hastings National Poetry Festival. Leader of Creative Writing Group "Small Times"; [hon.] Northam Poetry Festival, Australia - Finalist. "Runner-up" - Forward Poetry Competition, (1994); [oth. writ.] Over 20 anthologies published, some fiction, some plays, short stories and essays. Poetry published in many anthologies. Biography "International Encyclopedia of Poetry" - 1993 and 1996.; [pers.] My writing began as a result of an accident. I have been greatly influenced by Yannis Ritsos, modern Greek, poet. Seeing beauty revitalizes the soul - "A Thing of Beauty is a Joy, Forever!" (Keats).; [a.] Bromley, Kent, UK

SMITH, ALEXANDER
[b.] 26 September 1946, Helmsdale; [p.] Alexander and Ida Smith; [m.] Kathleen, 9 December 1965; [ch.] Suzanne, Steven, Tonya and Tracey; [ed.] Bonar Bridge School; [occ.] Salmon Fisherman; [a.] Ardgay, Sutherland, UK

SMITH, ANGELA
[pen.] Angela Smith; [b.] 16 January 1960, Bolton, Lancashire; [p.] Marilyn Burniston and Albert Burniston (Deceased - 14 June 1996); [m.] Robert Smith, 2 August 1982; [ed.] Fleetwood Grammar School, Lanchashire; [oth. writ.] Several poems and short stories as yet unpublished.; [pers.] My writing comes from my heart and from a truth within myself. In turn I try to reach the truth in others. I would like to dedicate this poem (The Arts) to my father, Albert Burniston, who dies recently on 14 June 1996. He taught me everything I know.; [a.] Thornton, Cleveleys, Lancashire, UK

SMITH, AUDREY LOUVENE
[b.] 9 October 1935, Birmingham; [p.] Harry and Elizabeth Hassam; [m.] Sidney Smith, 22 May 1952 (Deceased); [ch.] Gwenneth, Deborah, Dawn Ann; [ed.] Secondary Modern Education Leaving School at 15 yrs. of Age.; [occ.] Housewife; [pers.] My poetry mostly reflects my thoughts and the day to day happenings in life I wrote this one to help my granddaughter Carly.; [a.] Birmingham, West Mids, UK

SMITH, MRS. CAROLYN
[b.] 21 August 1959, Liverpool; [p.] Robert Lowe, Maureen Lowe; [m.] Rod Smith, 19 August 1994; [ch.] Jamie, Samantha; [ed.] Coombe County Comprehensive School; [occ.] Accounting Technician; [memb.] British Mensa, Association Accounting Technicians; [pers.] My writings reflect my inner moods, and my attempts, to understand other people's predicaments.; [a.] Sutton, Surrey, UK

SMITH, CHRISTOPHER J.
[b.] 1 May 1971, London; [p.] Victor Smith and Ingerborg Smith; [ed.] Blairgowrie High School and Edinburgh University; [occ.] Writer and Poet; [oth. writ.] A book called "Strangeworld" which is an adult fairytale mixed; with curiuos sci-fi and about seven hundred poems and some short stories [all unpublished]; [pers.] I try and extend the boundaries of concepts to view life from a peculiar angle on the fringes of light and darkness. I'm influenced by Jimi Hendrix, Luc-Besson and T.H. White; [a.] Blairgowrie, Perthshire, UK

SMITH, DUNCAN EARL
[pen.] James Earl; [b.] 26 May 1930, Thurgoland, Sheffield; [p.] James Smith, Alice Smith; [m.] Audrey Smith, 10 March 1973; [ch.] Dawn, Stephen, Andrew; [ed.] Barnsley Technical College Newbury Technical College; [occ.] Retired Filtration Eng; [hon.] Dale Carnegie Diplomas in Sales and Management, HNC Mech Eng; [oth. writ.] Several as yet unpublished; [pers.] I have been inspired and a long admirer of Sir John Betjeman, my poems tend to reflect emotional feelings as applied to life experiences.; [a.] Wakefield, West Yorks, UK

SMITH, GILLIAN
[b.] 10 November 1930, Middlesex; [oth. writ.] Includes comic poems, under the title Insect - Asides.; [pers.] I have written ever since I can remember first holding a pencil. The songs of 'weeping men' was written in 1964 when I was thirteen and has remained a favorite.; [a.] Banham, Norfolk, UK

SMITH, JILL
[b.] 7 October 1950, Birmingham; [p.] Francis Thomas Cooper, Doris May Cooper; [m.] William Smith, 30 December 1995; [ch.] Stuart Bailey, David Bailey and Christine Turnel; [ed.] Secondary Modern; [occ.] Hospital Receptionist; [oth. writ.] A short novel (Ghost story) and various poetry written as a hoby.; [pers.] A tribute to my father 1-6-1904, 24-9-90 a hard working man who lost his dignity and self respect.; [a.] Minehead, Somerset, UK

SMITH, MRS. JOAN
[pen.] Joan Kent; [b.] 19 September 1920, Norwich; [p.] Sidney and Christianna Ingate; [m.] Mr. Norman Smith, 22 August 1950; [ch.] One Son; [ed.] Church of England School; [occ.] Housewife; [hon.] Volunteer Work Doing War Time Service with the Civil Defense and WRVS. Part Time Youth Leader for 17 years. Speaker on Atomic Warfare for WRVS. Charity work and caring for the elderly.; [oth. writ.] Article "Caring To The End" Published in Church Times, "Flowing Gently", At The End Of The Day", "A New Life", "A Player For Every Day", "Try", "Hands", "The Picture", and several other poems; [pers.] Things I love countryside, oil painting, mountains, music, the sea breaking on a lonely shore, sitting quietly in a church, waking in my garden at eventide, and waiting poetry.; [a.] Norwich, Norfolk, UK

SMITH, LAWRENCE
[b.] 30 December 1918, Hartlepool; [p.] Deceased; [oth. writ.] Garcia Lorca, Bull Ring, Mayakousky, Recognition, Captured By A Butterfly, After The Bomb; [pers.] Epitaph beneath this stone dwells poor fool Smith who in the world but sought three things: the truth of luck and a cup of tea, pray for him; he found all three; pray for him; he prayed for thee; [a.] Seaford, E. Sussex, UK

SMITH, MARJORIE JOAN
[pen.] Marjorie Joan; [b.] 19 October 1925, Leeds; [m.] William Smith, 25 March 1972; [ed.] Gipton County Council School, Surrey Farm Institute of Agriculture and Horticulture, Staff at Askham Bryan College; [occ.] Retired Florist; [memb.] East Yorkshire Womens Institute; [hon.] Part one and part two City and Guilds in Floristry; [a.] Bugthorpe, E. Yorkshire, UK

SMITH, MARLENE
[b.] 21 January 1938, New Zealand; [p.] Aubry and Doris Shaw; [m.] divorced; [ch.] four; [ed.] left school at fifteen; [occ.] housewife; [memb.] Theosophical Society; [oth. writ.] None as yet I have never sent anything to be published.; [pers.] I have learned many things in my time on earth and feel a need to share my thoughts before I die.; [a.] Dunedin, New Zealand

SMITH, R. PETER
[b.] 30 October 1939, York; [p.] Reginald and Mary; [m.] Joan Valerie, 25 March 1961; [ch.] Maria Jane; [ed.] The Manor School York, University College Scarborough; [occ.] School Teacher; [memb.] Chairman 1st Scalby Scouts and Guides Scarbrough, Swimming Instructor Scarborough Swimming Club; [hon.] B.A. (Open University) 1982; [oth. writ.] Various poems published "Yorkshire Voices", "Christian Verse", "Butterfly Box", "Poetry Magic"; [pers.] I enjoy writing poetry as it is means of using rhyme and rhythm to concisely express and idea, mood, or memory.; [a.] Scarborough, North Yorkshire, UK

SMITH, TREVOR J.
[b.] 6 January 1951, Gillingham, Kent; [m.] Jean Helen; [ed.] Secondary Modern at Leatherhead; [occ.] Self employed gardener/man-friday; [oth. writ.] "Autumn by the Mole" inspired to write this poem one sparkling late October morning, while walkint the Mole Valley River Basin. "Arrival Press Publication" "Home counties Poets."; [pers.] "Beached" was written while back packing around Scotland Western Isles, as is a lot of my poetry, in seeking out wild lonely places in these islands around the U.K. which is spiritually uplifting, as are the seashore caves I lie in!; [a.] Leatherhead, Surrey, UK

SMITH, VIDA
[b.] 8 September 1926, Derbyshire; [p.] John Baxter, Edith Baxter; [m.] Ernest Smith, 21 January 1950; [ch.] One; [ed.] Elementary School; [occ.] Retired; [oth. writ.] Poems of love and romance, every day living that's comical, good deeds and prayers. Nature.; [pers.] I have never had any printed I never thought they were good enough, when I've read to great poets they seem to put my effort in the shade.; [a.] Barnsley, South Yorks, UK

SMITHAM, PAUL
[pen.] P. J. Smith; [b.] 27 March 1966, Penzance; [p.] Alan, Jean Smitham; [m.] Rachel, 5 November 1994; [ch.] Ashleigh Jade and Jeska Ebony; [ed.] Penzance Grammar School; [occ.] Government Service; [oth. writ.] Only ever written for personal pleasure; [pers.] I feel poetry to be a very personal, inner secret perhaps, its time to share.; [a.] Penzance, Cornwall, UK

SMYTH, ANN MARIE
[b.] 30 May 1964, Dublin, Ireland; [p.] John F. Smyth, Louise Smyth; [ed.] Loretto College, The National College of Art and Design, Dublin; [occ.] Jewellery Designer and Astrologer; [memb.] Raja

Yoga Meditation; [hon.] Art, Poetry; [oth. writ.] Written and illustrated a monthly newsletter for Raja Yoga, also written several poems and novels not yet published; [a.] Dublin, Ireland

SMYTH, GEORGE M.
[b.] 28 April 1922, Belfast; [p.] William and Matilda Smyth; [m.] Elizabeth Jean Smyth, 29 September 1945; [ch.] Three boys and One girl; [ed.] I left school at the age of 14 years - then my education began; [occ.] Retired; [memb.] Royal British Legion; [hon.] 2nd World War and - Campaign Medals I served in the fleet Air Arm (South East Asia Command) also a Badge" For Loyal Service"; [oth. writ.] My antrim home the choir planting a seed everywhere I look and others (none of which I offered for publication); [pers.] I wrote the poem "The passing years" for our 50th, wedding anniversary as a tribute to my wife for the love and devotion she has given me throughout all those years.; [a.] Belfast, Northern Ireland

SMYTH, LOUISE CLARE
[b.] 28 May 1976; [p.] Michael Smyth, Sally Smyth; [ed.] Epsom and Ewell High, N.E.S.C.O.T.; [occ.] Short Story and Poet; [hon.] C.P.V.E. Certificate; [oth. writ.] Just starting on a novel; [pers.] With every dedication to my heroes in the poem and with love and honour to my family and friends, especially to my man for inspiring me.; [a.] Worcester Park, Surrey, UK

SNEDDON, JENNIFER LOUISE
[b.] September 16, 1985, Glasgow; [p.] Eunice Sneddon, John Sneddon; [ed.] St. Leonard's Primary School East Kilbride; [occ.] School Girl; [memb.] East Kilbride Youth Choir 6th A East Kilbride Guide Company, choir member of the Royal Scottish National Orchestra; [oth. writ.] Articles published in annual school magazine; [pers.] I thank God for the talents I have been blessed with. May He continue to inspire me throughout my life.; [a.] East Kilbride

SOMERSET, MARIE
[b.] 8 March, Buckingham, Bucks; [p.] Charles Somerset Esther Somerset; [m.] Married/Divorced; [ch.] Nigel Milton, Joanne Bryony; [memb.] Royal Photographic Society; [hon.] L.R.P.S. (Royal Photographic Society Distinction), IQ 152 (Mensa); [oth. writ.] Several poems published in magazines and newspapers; [pers.] To force a dream into reality is to lose it forever; [a.] Bracknell, Berks, UK

SOMJEE, MISS SHEHNAZ
[pen.] Miss Shehnaz Somjee; [b.] Karachi, Pakistan; [p.] Rahim Somjee (Judge); [ed.] Ear, nose, throat, head and neck surgeon, currently studying law part-time; [occ.] ENT/head and neck surgeon; [memb.] Active in medical organisations and bodies; [hon.] Gold medalist as College student numerous medals and prizes for debates, singing, quiz competitions, flower-arranging. Academic distinctions throughout school College and Medical College; [oth. writ.] "Some time somewhere" (Collection of poems in Pakistan. Freelance newspaper articles, Medical Research Papers, was editor of College Magazine, some poems published in souvenirs of Karachi American Centre (with presentation), Invented a surgical instrument "Somjee-crab tree temporal above support.; [pers.] My poems reflect my medical profession, insight into life, Piscean dreams, and mixed interests and travels. They are my living dreams. They shall live for me and after me; [a.] Liverpool, Merseyside, UK

SONDHI, RINA
[b.] 27 June 1968, London; [p.] Mr. Ram P. Sondhi, Mrs. Janak Sondhi; [ed.] B. Ed. (Hons) English and Drama, MA English and Language Studies in Education (Sheffield and Rothampton); [occ.] Language Co-Ordinator in a Primary School in Paddington; [hon.] Mollie Page Award for contribution and endeavour to the community.; [oth. writ.] CD Rom Teachers Pack for Thomas Nelson publications Teachers Resources Packs.; [pers.] Life is a journey of the soul, venturing through obstacles, completing the circle of love, satisfaction and "Peace and Mind".; [a.] Walkern, Herts, UK

SORENSEN, MARK E. W.
[b.] 29 August 1977, Oxford; [p.] Margaret Sorensen, Erik Sorensen; [ed.] Barley Hill Primary School, Thame, Oxfordshire (82-89), Lord Williams School, Thame, Oxfordshire (89-96); [occ.] Student; [memb.] Thame Youth Theatre; [hon.] International Toastmasters Certificate, Head Boy (1995-1996) Lord Williams's Sixth form, Lord Williams's School, Thame, Oxfordshire; [oth. writ.] Persistent letter writer to media and personalities, articles for school publications and year book, poems and short stories for personal enjoyment, comedy sketches - a view to maturing to writing plays.; [pers.] I wrote and re-wrote "Empty House" in the back cover of Hardy's "The Mayor of Casterbridge" during a level english. This my first poem, was a gift to a very special friend - Katherine. I try disparately to write truthfully, reflecting my ideas and emotions with precision and not pretension.; [a.] Thame, Oxfordshire, UK

SPACKMAN, PAMELA
[b.] 2 April 1930, Redhill, Surrey; [p.] Bessie and Frank Harding; [m.] Bernard, 28 April 1951; [ch.] Kenneth, Stephen, Nigel and Adrian; [occ.] Retired; [oth. writ.] This is my first to be printed.; [pers.] I've written several poems for fun and friends. Its something I enjoy, and would like to write a book with a few poems on different subjects.; [a.] Camborne, Cornwall, UK

SPARKLES, JENNIFER GAIL
[pen.] Jenna; [b.] 29 October 1963, Hampton Court; [p.] Tiny and Shirlie Winter; [m.] Chris, 23 September 1989; [ch.] 1st child due December 13th 1996; [pers.] In memory of my own granddad Cox and my father would have made a wonderful granddad.; [a.] Egham, Surrey, UK

SPENCER, MRS. SHARRON
[b.] 31 October 1954, Bladon, Oxford; [p.] Raymond and Cynthia Palmer; [m.] Mr. John Derek Spencer, 8 March 1975; [ch.] Twin boys - Andrew and Stephen; [ed.] Marlborough Secondary School Woodstock, Oxon; [occ.] Bank Clerk - Barclams Bank Plc.; [memb.] Member/Treasurer Plough Ladies Darts Team in Bicester; [oth. writ.] Collection of poems written over last few years, on various subjects. None published to date.; [pers.] My ability to write poetry came to light a few years ago when I was requested to write a verse for a member of staff leaving work. This idea has stuck and it is expected of the time to create a poem about them. I also write poems on any subject that comes to mind.; [a.] Bicester, Oxfordshire, UK

SPINK, DEBBIE
[pen.] Debbie Chase; [b.] 17 April 1959, Portsmouth, Hampshire; [p.] Michael Chase, Ann Chase; [m.] Howard Spink, 28 July 1984; [ch.] Lara Leigh; [ed.] Warblington County, Secondary

School, Southdowns College of Further Education; [cc.] Word Processor Operator, Bradford Social Services; [oth. writ.] Short stories published in children's magazines; [pers.] The death of my sister and my happy childhood has greatly influence my writings of both poetry and stories.; [a.] Bradford, West Yorks, UK

SPIVEY, CATHERINE
[b.] 12 October 1948, Leigh; [p.] Harry Smith, Catherine Smith; [m.] Charles Spivey, 4 May 1972; [ch.] Angela, Lynne, Joanne, Jason; [ed.] St. Mary's R.C. Secondary Modern; [occ.] Shop Assistant; [oth. writ.] One poem published.; [pers.] I like to make friends smile by writing funny poems about them.; [a.] Leigh, Lancs, UK

STAGGS, ARTHUR ALBERT GEORGE
[b.] 17 November 1912, Bow, London; [p.] English; [m.] Elizabeth Gladys, 6 July 1942; [ch.] One daughter; [ed.] Left School 1925 Linguist; [occ.] Retired "Sales Executive"; [memb.] Special Forces Club" London, (S.D.E.), (FFI) Forces "Francaise De L'Interieur" No. 3442; [hon.] British 1939-1945 War Medals ie (4) French "Commemorative Medal" with "Liberation Bar" 1942-1945, "French Resistance"; [pers.] "Philosophical Reason" The Year's Come And Go With Reason", The Season's Advance The Year's With Reason! But Why Grow Old Without Reason.; [a.] Thame, Oxon, UK

STAINER, MISS MARJORIE
[b.] 9 December 1933, Farnborough; [p.] Lillian and Victor Stainer; [ed.] Cove Secondary Modern School; [occ.] Retired Print Room Operator Practising Christian; [memb.] Friends of St. Columbia's House for Retreats Woking registered RNIB but I am partially sighted; [hon.] 20 years Service Broach Schlumberger "Instruments" print room; [oth. writ.] Love Beats with Jesus, Stimulating Awareness, Five Caligraphy Retreater's, Women Priests, A Ripple, several more; [pers.] My heart is in religious verse have had some printed in cove parish church magazine. I have written other types never published anything have written my life story.; [a.] Farnborough, Hants, UK

STAINTON, BARBARA
[pen.] Irene Stone; [b.] 23 July 1946, Dormanstown; [p.] Cissie Stonehouse, Ben Stonehouse; [m.] Joseph Stainton, 22 January 1969; [ch.] Lorraine and Lyndsey; [ed.] Lady Claria Dorman, Secondary Modern (Dormanstown); [occ.] House wife; [oth. writ.] Short stories, with a twist in the tail. Crime stories and novel's as yet unpublished.; [pers.] I enjoy being a prolific writer as I am confined. To the house with a disabled husband.; [a.] Hemlington, Cleveland, UK

STARKS, MANDY
[b.] 28 September 1963, Plymouth; [p.] Michael Starks, Pamela Starks (Mother Deceased); [m.] Michael Conibeer (partner); [ch.] One son James Starks; [ed.] St. Joseph's Primary School King-Alfred School comprehensive. I only took mock exams. Would have passed English lit and sociology 0 level; [occ.] Laundry assistant; [hon.] Stagei Youth Work course; [oth. writ.] "A Secret Land" published in "Poems of the Southwest" 1993; [pers.] I first started writing poetry at 18, influenced by the "Diary of an edwardian lady" and "Keat's Ireland". I usually write from experience and current affairs. Favorite book "Weathering Heights".; [a.] Burnham-on-Sea, Somerset, UK

STEELE, GEMMA ANNE
[b.] 11 November 1985, North Wales; [p.] Kate Steele; [ed.] Age 2 1/2 - 10 at Penrhos Prep School. Sat Scholarship 12 months early at the age of 10 won Academic Scholarship to Royal Penrhos Girls Division; [memb.] Pig Taiis (Love collecting pigs of all kinds), B.K.K.S British Koi Keepers Society; [hon.] Poetry Society Silver Medal, Honours. (Spoken verse), Lamda grade 6 Distinction. (Verse and Prose). Academic Scholarship. Poetry Society Spoken Verse, Primary Credit, Primary Advanced Credit, Junior Credit, Junior Advanced Honours, Junior Silver Honours, Lamda Verse and Prose, Grade 1 Pass, Grade 2 Distinction, Grade 3 Distinction, Grade 4 Distinction, Grade 5 Honours, Grade 6 Distinction, Royal Academy of Dancing Pre-Primary Pass, Primary Bronze H-Commended, Swimming, 1000 Meters Award, S.T.A. award, Music Academy Technics, Introductory Keyboard Honours, Grade 1 Merit, Chester Competitive Music Festival Society, Verse Speaking 1993 Merit, Verse Speaking 1994 Merit, Solo Drama 1994 Merit, Sight Reading 1995 Merit, Solo Drama 1995 Merit, Prepared Reading 1995 Merit, Bible Reading 1995 Distinction, Verse Speaking 1995 Distinction, Cheshire Festival Music and Drama, Verse Speaking 1992 Distinction, Sight Reading 1993 Merit, Solo Drama 1994 Merit, Sight Reading 1996 Honours, Bible Reading 1996 Merit; [pers.] I strongly believe that what I have achieved is by studying hard and always being supported by my mum who convinced me that whatever I put my mind to I can do. Please may I dedicate this to Kate Steele for her convincing me.; [a.] Colwyn Bay, Clwyd, UK

STEVENS, DANA
[b.] 16 April 1980, Northern Ireland; [p.] Martina and Ken Stevens; [ed.] I have recently completed 9 GCSE's at St. Teresa's School, Darking and I am going to study 3 A-levels in English; [occ.] Student; [hon.] Lamda-Drama exams to Level 8; [oth. writ.] None, apart from material towards school exams; [pers.] The inspiration for my poem came from the beautiful and tranquil contryside of Kellybegs, Donegal in Ireland. I also believe life is for living!; [a.] Reigate, Surrey, UK

STEVENS, MRS. VERA
[pen.] Vee; [b.] 15 January 1918, Barking; [p.] Lily and Harry Sheldrake; [m.] Divorced; [ch.] Marian; [ed.] Public School; [occ.] Retired Civil Servant; [oth. writ.] Have written several poems. But as yet, haven't had them published.; [pers.] I pray for mankind for strive for peace, harmony and freedom. To be happy, to help others, whatever their colour and creed, and be kind to animals.; [a.] Barking, Essex, UK

STEVENSON, JOHN DAVID
[pen.] Leicester Fox; [b.] October 3, 1959, Leicester; [p.] Desmere Lacht; [ed.] Average; [occ.] Cower; [pers.] In the memory of the spirit of Des

STEVENSON, LEE DAVID
[b.] 15 October 1972, Saltburn; [p.] Alan and Susan Stevenson; [m.] Andrea Sweeney, 25 June 1996; [ed.] Park View Comprehensive, Sunderland University; [occ.] Police Officer; [hon.] Degree in Education BA ED (Hons), Community Sports Leaders Award; [oth. writ.] Several unpublished poems and short stories; [pers.] Everybody needs hope and inspiration thanks to life and Andrea for being mine.; [a.] Chester-le-Street, Durham, UK

STEWART, CLINTON
[b.] 10 February 1929, Montego Bay, Jamaica; [p.] Henethia and Nehemiah Stewart; [m.] March 1957; [ch.] Ingrid, Norson, Lorna, Lola, Lorna, Geraldene; [ed.] Elementary Standard Six with Distinction; [occ.] Retired factory fitters process operator

STINCHCOMBE, ABIGAIL HELEN
[pen.] Abigail Helen Stinchcombe; [b.] 20 July 1981, Rotherham; [p.] Mr. Paul Stinchcombe and Mrs. RoseAnne Stinchcombe; [ed.] Ferham Junior and Infant School, Wingfield Comprehensive School; [occ.] GCSE Student, Wingfield Comprehensive; [memb.] Member of council for the protection of Rural England (CPRE), Royal Society for the protection of birds (RSPB) and MENSA the high IQ society; [hon.] Accomplished pianist with grades 1, 2, 3, 4, and 5. Swimming achievement, grades 1 and 2, open water test. Mensa high IQ award; [oth. writ.] Several poems published in various magazines; [pers.] I find that poetry is brought to life when you express your inner most emotions and emphasis the beauty of mother nature rather than materialism.; [a.] Rotherham, South Yorkshire, UK

STIRLING, MS. CHRISTINE
[b.] 21 December 1957, Bally Money; [p.] John Lyle Stirling (Deceased), Annie Mary Stirling; [ed.] Coleraine Girl's Secondary School; [occ.] Career for Elderly Mother; [oth. writ.] This poem has just been accepted for publication in "Inspirations from the West Country" by Anchor Books, if a wish to have it published.; [pers.] This being the first poem I've written, it has given me great pride and a feeling of accomplishment to have become a semi-finalist in the 1996 International Amateur open poetry contest, and to have it published in "Quiet Moments."; [a.] Coleraine, Londonderry, UK

STIRLING, THERESA
[pen.] Theresa Shields Stirling; [b.] 8 September 1958, Glasgow; [p.] Edward Shields, Mary Shields; [m.] Michael Stirling, 19 May 1978; [ch.] Jacqueline, Michele; [ed.] St. Philomena's Primary, All Saints Secondary, Provanmill, Glasgow; [pers.] Dedicated to the memory of my Brother John.; [a.] Glasgow, UK

STOCKDALE, DAVID
[b.] 15 March 1955, Rochdale; [occ.] Author, Freelance Journalist, Landscape Photographer; [hon.] My writing has been complimented, but I don't usually enter competitions, several photographic awards.; [oth. writ.] Several books and poems published, many articles, collection of own poetry being prepared.; [pers.] Poetry is essential to me and I have always felt compelled to write it. Much of my own work describes profound spiritual experiences, human nature, suffering, and the lake district where I live.; [a.] High Lorton, Cumbria, UK

STOCKS, PAULINE
[b.] 23 September 1942, Sheffield; [p.] Ernest Judge, Beatrice Judge; [m.] Divorced; [ch.] Kay (1961), Tina (1964); [ed.] Secondary School; [occ.] Housewife; [oth. writ.] Several poems published; [pers.] Writing poetry reflects personal experiences and is my way of expressing thoughts and feelings.; [a.] Sheffield, South Yorkshire, UK

STONER, ERIKA
[b.] 3 May 1982, Raf Weaberg, Germany; [p.] Eileen and Chris; [ed.] Currently attending Princes Risborough Upper School, Princes Risborough Bucks; [oth. writ.] I have written other poems but this is the first but hopefully not the last to be published; [pers.] I wrote this poem when I was 10 years of age and my family/friends and myself are very proud of it. I was inspired by my registered blind.; [a.] High Wycombe, Bucks, UK

STONER, LESLIE JAMES
[pen.] James Leslie; [b.] 19 June 1932, London; [p.] Mr. Joseph Stoner, Mrs. Lily Stoner; [m.] Mrs. Violet Stoner, 23, July 1957; [ch.] Son, daughter; [ed.] Watford Grammar; [occ.] Retired Aircraft Engineer; [memb.] Hounslow Symphony Orchestra (Violin) Big Band Jazz (Trumpet) String Orchestra, Quartette, London Ragtime Orchestra, Traditional Jazz Band; [hon.] English Grammar, Cups - certificate (music festivals) Aero Engine Maintenance; [oth. writ.] Poems published in local papers. Essays (not published) in philosophy and spiritual subjects; [pers.] I am not impressed with humanity as a whole including myself, but there are exceptions; [a.] Southall, Middlesex, UK

STRATTON, VERA AILEEN
[pen.] "Molly" Kirkham; [b.] 5 April 1918, Drayton, Norwich; [p.] Anthony Kirkham, Eileen Fayers; [m.] George Stratton, 23 December 1939; [ch.] Anthony, Rosalie, Mike; [ed.] Notre Dame High "For Young Ladies" Norwich - I won the 11-plus scholarship from the Model Girl's School 4 credits Oxford exam at 16 school leaving; [occ.] Shorthand-typist 5 years, 1941 Civil Defence, Accounts Etc. until 1943; [oth. writ.] When my disabled husband started with the land settlement near Chichester with 100 savings. (Farmers' Suicides" read (partly) on BBC "On Your Farm" programme Rodacres) We were chosen for this tenancy-difficult soils 10 spring gardens LNDN. The British Council Feb. 1986. Several poems sent to China for use in their magazine promoting cultural, educational and technical co-operation between Britain and other countries-(My poem on the difficulties of farming (Tenant), etc. Poems on Smoking-Need For Cycle Tracks, etc. Poems sent to Ted Heath and Gillian Shephard-she replied with copies of her speeches from parliament. Supporting pig farming in the early 90's when over-importing pork ruined the pig industry and led to suicides.; [pers.] I've cycled across Britain after a strict upbringing as an only child, the struggle of the 1920's and 1930's father with "superior ability" in Royal Flying Corps" yet unable to find his previous rep. job for our country. Love of the soil and gardening, food. I find relief in writing verse-concise, powerful!; [a.] Kings Lynn, Norfolk, UK

STREET, REBECCA
[b.] 4 December 1976, Bournemouth; [p.] Ivor James and Elizabeth Rita Street; [ed.] Grange Comprehensive School, Bournemouth and Poole College of Further Education; [occ.] Administrator for a Nursing Agency; [hon.] Nine GCSE's including 2 A's 2 B's and 4 C's. First Class Pass in Word Processing; [oth. writ.] Several poems published in a local magazine.; [pers.] I write my poetry for personal pleasure and it helps me over-ride and understand my feelings. I find it rewarding if other people can appreciate my writing also.; [a.] Christchurch, Dorset, UK

STRITCH, THOMAS
[b.] 19 December 1971, Salford; [p.] Thomas Stritch, Mary Stritch; [ed.] Our Lady of Mount Carmel, R.C. High School, Salford; [occ.] Artist; [pers.] The love of my girlfriend and friends is the strength with which I write and paint, I thank them for their belief in he.; [a.] Salford, Gt. Manchester, UK

STUART, EDWARDS
[b.] 7 February 1977, Barking; [p.] Thomas and Beryl Edwards; [ed.] The Forest School, Reading College, York University Southampton University; [occ.] Student; [oth. writ.] Many other poems (not yet published) and song lyrics.; [pers.] Humidity was my first poem, but since I have enjoyed writing many more. I have realized the importance of expressing thoughts and feelings in same form, in my case through my poems.; [a.] Wokingham, Berkshire, UK

STUBBERFIELD, MARTIN
[b.] 17 April 1953, Trowbridge; [p.] Frederick and Joan Stubberfield; [ed.] Bath School of Art The University of Wales College of Cardiff; [occ.] Yoga Teacher; [memb.] The British Wheel of Yoga; [hon.] Honours English Literature; [oth. writ.] Poems and short stories.; [pers.] Happiness is to be found only in what moves and develops.; [a.] Bath, Banes, UK

SUDDELL, PAULINE-MARIAM
[b.] February 1, 1948, England; [p.] Lawrence and Levy; [m.] Peter John Suddell, February 6, 1981; [ch.] Debbie (6-8-69), Patsy (16-10-89); [ed.] Secondary Modern School, London E14; [occ.] Housewife; [a.] London, Middlesex

SULTANA, FIORELLA
[b.] 15 October 1979, Italy; [p.] Karmel and Dorothea Sultana; [ed.] Currently attending the Sixth Form of St. Mary's School, Shaftesbury, Dorset; [memb.] Dorset Philharmonic Orchestra, Amnesty International Catholic History Society; [hon.] National Modern Languages Competition 1st prize Italian poetry; [oth. writ.] Several articles published in "The Catholic Herald", another poem published in poetry now, young writers anthology several articles and poems in local magazines and in school magazines.; [pers.] I want to use my talents as a witness to my deep christian belief and commitment; [a.] Warminster, Wiltshire, UK

SUMNER, ALLAN
[b.] 23 February 1930, Salford Redhill, Surrey; [p.] Deceased; [m.] Margaret Mary Sumner, 12 August 1950; [ch.] Five, 14 grandchildren; [ed.] Spent school days in Air Raid Shelters, left school age 13 yrs. to work in Armament Factory; [occ.] Served 8 yrs. RAF, NCO, now retired; [hon.] Long Service Badge in Civilian Occupation; [oth. writ.] Song lyrics poems without success; [pers.] Self taught organist, playing memory interested in nature, travel, and people not so fortunate as myself.; [a.] Totnes, Devon, UK

SURNAN, PHILIP RAYNOND
[b.] 26 June 1964, Cheltenham; [p.] Mrs. M. Newsome; [m.] Wendy Frances Surman, 19 May 1984; [ch.] Kelly Marie, Sean Gary; [ed.] Rowan Field Infants, Junior Nonkscroft Secondary; [occ.] Disabled; [oth. writ.] Their Crying Prayers, As Time Goes By, What Peace, My Weird Dream, Until Next Time, The Meaning of Life, Living Again, Biding My Time, The Handicap, The Cost of Living; [pers.] My work is based on true feelings and experiences encountered since becoming disabled in 1991.; [a.] Cheltenham, Gloss, UK

SUTTON, B.
[pen.] Brenda May; [b.] 11 May 1946, Birmingham; [p.] Thomas Donaldson and May Donaldson; [m.] Gordon Samuel Charles Sutton, 21 October 1963; [ch.] Sharon, Angela, Tania, Helen; [ed.] Bessbrook Primary School, Ashgrove Comprehensive School; [occ.] Housewife; [hon.] Getting my Poems Published; [oth. writ.] Two poems published. I also write poems for friends, special occasions.; [pers.] I always had a love of poetry. I would like to dedicate this poem to my mother, husband, and my four girls, Sharon, Angela, Tania and Helen, also my grandchildren for whom I have no greater love.; [a.] Newry, Down, UK

SUTTON, FRANK
[b.] 27 May 1932, Dronfield, Derbys; [p.] Sidney Sutton, Jessie Sutton; [m.] Brenda Sutton, 2 June 1956; [ch.] John Francis, Benita Jane; [ed.] Dronfield Grammar School; [occ.] Singer/ songwriter with own recording studio; [memb.] Associate Member of the Performing Right Society; [oth. writ.] Poems in several anthologies, songs written and performed for radio, television and films.; [pers.] My broadcast work has taught me to aim for clarity and simplicity in writing, for immediate impact. Where appropriate, I like to incorporate a little humour.; [a.] Coal Aston, Dronfield, Derbyshire, UK

SWANN, JOAN SYLVIA
[pen.] Sylvia Clayton; [b.] 2 March 1934, London; [m.] Roger G. Swann; [ed.] Secondary Modern; [occ.] Occupational Health; [memb.] Life-boat (shore-line), Nurses League, Royal College of Nursing, Saga Magazine Club, Natural Treat; [hon.] Ophthalmie Nursing Diploma; [oth. writ.] One poem published 1992 in "Eastern Voices" editor.; [pers.] I have always been interested in poetry since only childhood. But have taken many years to compile my arm private thoughts onto paper.; [a.] Bury St Edmunds, Suffolk, UK

SYMES-EARLE, ROSE HELEN
[b.] 18 September 1938, Hutton, Essex, England; [p.] M. V. and B. R. Symes; [ch.] Anton and Quentin; [ed.] St. Felix, Southwold, Suffolk, Mon Fertile, Switzerland Chelmsford, Essex, Polytec Trinity College, London; [occ.] Writer/Poet/ Composer/Artist/Creativity Therapist/Regression Mediator/Healer/International Lecturer; [memb.] N.F.S.H. England, A.S.H.A. Australia, N.F.S.H.N.Z. Inc - New Zealand Greypower, New Zealand; [hon.] Cert. Eff. Spkg. Hons. Trinity College London; [oth. writ.] "Timelessness of Words", "A Voice Within", "In Harmony", "4 Cassettes of Healing Music, Two With Poems"; [pers.] A world travellers, and specialize in Dyslexia and special needs and learning difficulties, using my own creativity as examples. I was assessed dyslexic when I was aged 50 years and try to help others to understand this difficulty.; [a.] Nelson, New Zealand

TALLON, GWENDOLINE
[pen.] Gwendoline Tallon; [b.] 21 June 1916, Wrexham; [p.] William Tallon and Elizabeth Tallon; [m.] George Edward Jones, 3 August 1940; [ch.] Cynthia Gwendoline, Rosalind Carole, and John Edward Tallon; [ed.] Victoria School, Wrexham Clwyd North Wales; [occ.] Retired, reside - over looking North Sea Sheringham. Widowed, Married, John William Dunkley, 16 December 1989; [memb.] Wrexham Writers Circle, St. John Ambulance Brigade, Divisional Superintendent of Nursing Cadets Brymbo Clwyd, North Wales;

[oth. writ.] Articles published in periodical maldon. Essex. Several poems published in local community newspaper.; [pers.] I acquire pleasure, plus invigoration, whilst dancing in Spain - Wintertime inspired by the realistic depth of W. Shakespeare's sonnet "True Love" I find a sense of humor is a God send when meditating on life's human frailties.; [a.] Sheringham, Norfolk, UK

TAPP, DEBORAH
[b.] 31 October 1977, Dartford; [p.] Ron Tapp and Kathleen Rayner; [ed.] Dartford Grammar School for girls; [occ.] Store Supervisor; [hon.] 9 GCSE Certificates: English Language, English Literature, Art, German, Maths, Science, History, Home Economics; [pers.] There are some people who have a knack of making life special. My friends and family, you have made my life special, I love you all. Thank you for always being there for me.

TAYLOR, ANGELA
[b.] 29 June 1983, Port Elizabeth, South Africa; [p.] Patricia Taylor and Peter Taylor; [ed.] Alderman Smith High School Nuneaton, Warks; [occ.] Scholar; [hon.] Academic Achievement 4 years running, 2 Commendetions Certificates Honours, Bronze and Silver Awards for Dancing; [oth. writ.] Poem about Earth published in 'Voices On The Wind'; [pers.] My aim is to open the eyes and hearts of people to cruelty to both animals and earth.; [a.] Nuneaton, Warwicks, UK

TAYLOR, BETTY GUNSOM
[b.] 3 October 1919, Millom, Cumbria; [p.] Hugh and Man Fulton; [m.] E. W. Alan Hughes, George Ch. Taylor, M.B.E., 9 September 1986; [ch.] Jane Miles, Helen Allen; [ed.] Barrow-in-Furness County Grammar School for girls. Spennithorne College Barrow-in-Furness. Regent Street Polytechnic, London; [occ.] Retired Admin. Officer Teacher; [memb.] Oxfam - Group Secretary Constituency Contact. Liberal Democrat - Executive Committee (Secretary 3 years); [hon.] Matriculation with distinctions. First class business studies R.S.A. distinction in wartime crash degree course radio and electrical engineering held cup for several consecutive years for "Original Poem" in Borton festival of music and drama; [oth. writ.] Have written prose and poetry during my life for business publications and local. Broadcast my own work nationally (once) and locally; [pers.] This poem was written in 1962, while I walked down a Salford Street towards a factory I had to visit as a government inspector. All my poetry has risen spontaneously from a moment and mostly reflects my Lakeland roots - and the love I know.; [a.] Burton-upon-Trent, Staffordshire, UK

TAYLOR, CAROLE MARIAN
[b.] May 6, 1944, Winchester; [p.] Joan and Percy Flux; [m.] Michael Richard Taylor, March 28, 1964; [ch.] Samantha and Justin; [ed.] Danemark Secondary School Winchester; [occ.] Catering Supervisor; [memb.] Body Sound Health Club; [oth. writ.] Poems; [pers.] My poems reflect mainly on things that have personally affected my life; [a.] Chandlersford, Hants

TAYLOR, DAVID S.
[b.] 17 June 1927, Stonehaven; [p.] Andrew and Ella Taylor (Both Deceased); [ed.] Mackie Academy, Stonehaven, King's College, Aberdeen Univ. MA (Hons), Modern Languages; [occ.] Retired (Ex-Teacher); [oth. writ.] Two published novels!; [pers.] I think of myself as a rationalist, but am sometimes more a pagan at heart, suspending disbelief in favour of Zeus and Apollo.; [a.] Stonehaven, Kincards, UK

TAYLOR, DONNA MARIE
[b.] 1 September 1958, Virginia, USA; [p.] Paul and Wendy Grimwood; [m.] Roger William Taylor, 20 December 1975; [ch.] Paul, Mark, Sarah, Darren, Thomas; [ed.] St. Ivo Comprehensive School; [occ.] Housewife and mother; [oth. writ.] I have written several other poems and just recently I have started writing short stories for children.; [pers.] You will find some of my poetry is family based, but its all to do with everyday life.; [a.] Hemingford Grey, Cambs, UK

TAYLOR, ELIZABETH SERENA
[pen.] Panadora; [b.] 5 July 1943, Peebles, Scotland; [p.] Mr. Harold Vasey and Alice Worsley Nee; [m.] Peter Joseph Taylor-Toal, 28 October 1961; [ch.] Serena, Sonya, Sharon (three girls); [ed.] Secondary School in Flixton Lancashire; [occ.] Housewife/Mother/Gran; [oth. writ.] Childrens stories for my children and maybe in the future published; [pers.] I am a dreamer and inventor. "Imagination is my second name". A Humanitarian who loves life, who hates injustice of all kinds. We are all children of God, therefore, I told no allegiance to any religion (you are either good, bad or inbetween) no matter what label you go by. I am politically minded simply because I care but of late, have become a touch cynical. Above all else, I am a mother first, last and always.; [a.] Bournemouth, Dorset, UK

TAYLOR, G.
[pen.] "Spud Murphy"; [b.] 1 April, Tomworth; [ed.] Secondary Modern; [occ.] Retired; [a.] Slough, Berks, UK

TAYLOR, MR. GUY DENNIS
[b.] 24 October 1939, Oxford; [p.] George Taylor, Edith Taylor; [m.] Edna Doreen; [ed.] Secondary (Comprehensive) Education to G.C.E. Standard; [occ.] P.C.V. Driver; [oth. writ.] Selection of Verse (as yet unpublished); [pers.] A great deal of my writing tends to be humorous attempting to bring laughter into peoples lives - also concerned with conservation.; [a.] Oxford, Oxon, UK

TAYLOR, LAURENCE
[b.] 21 August 1974, Lisburn, N. Ireland; [p.] Robert and Jennifer Taylor; [ed.] Down High School University of Wolverhampton; [occ.] Student; [memb.] British Camde Union Rock Face Climbing Wall (Birmingham); [oth. writ.] Northern Ireland 1995 (Poetry now), life images 1995 (poetry now), sunlight and shadows (poetry inst. of British Isles).; [pers.] I am a product of my society, I only say what I see. To analyze is to rape and savage the soul from where it came.; [a.] Walsall, West Midlands, UK

TENNENT, IRIS
[b .Forever and a Day (Transfer of poem and any applicable orders) Elizabeth Lowe; [m.] James Young Tennent, 16 April 1949; [ch.] Stephen James, David Young, Paul Martin, Martin Scott; [ed.] Chapel Street School Levenshulme Manchester; [occ.] Retired Screen PrintixDesigner Textiles; [oth. writ.] Stories and poems not published; [July 3, 1996 see the things going on around them. If we appreciated our world more, it would be a better place to live in. This is where I get my inspiration from.; [a.] Earby, Lancs, UK

TERRY-SHORT, BARBARA
[b.] 30 April 1933, Uttoxeter; [p.] Doris and Frederick Hudson; [m.] James Terry-Short, 29 March 1952; [ch.] Greg, Lyn, Ang, Kim; [occ.]

Reflexology Student Crochet Tutor and Miniturist; [memb.] Knitting and Crochet Guild the British RForever and a Day (Transfer of poem and any applicable orders) [oth. writ.] Collection of Poems, two short stories none submitted; [pers.] I write from the heart on whatever influences my frame of mind at that moment in time, (be it, life's pleasures , hardships or nature itself.); [a.] Leominster, Herefordshi UK

THEAKSTON, BRYAN J.

[b.] 1935; [m.] Eileen Elizabeth; [ch.] Four sons; [occ.] Sales Adviser; [oth. writ.] Several short stories (unpublished); [pers.] Encouraged to write poetry by youngest son Clay; [a.] Shropshire, UK

THOMAS, BISSY DENISE

[pen.] B.T., Bis.I; [b.] 9 April 1967, Hampstead, London; [p.] Bertha and John Mal amah-Thomas; [ed.] Parliament Hill. Lansdowne I.S.F.G. - 'A' LevEnglish Sociology. Bucking Hamshire College, Bsc - Sociology andJuly 3, 1996 [oth. writ.] Many, a considerable number that remained filed in my index linder poetry; [pers.] I write when I need to express me, takes place anywhere, it is spontaneous and therapeutic. Writing is a part of me, that releases itself continually. My first inspirations were Hardy and Bob Marley. They wrote how they felt. That is how I write; [a.] Hendon, London, UK

THOMAS, COLIN C.

[b.] 31 December 1937, Tenby, Dyfed; [p.] David M. Thomas, Doris H. Thomas; [m.] Valerie Ann, 8 February 1987; [ch.] Tracy, Donna, Steven; [ed.] Greenhill Comprehensive School Tenby, Studied Art - St. Loyes College, Exeter; [occ.] Retired; [memb.] Kingstanding Chess Club, Birmingham Chess League; [oth. writ.] Poem published in local paper, other works submitted to national poetry magazine, several other works, at present, continuing to write.; [pers.] I hated poetry at school, and never really acquired a liking for it until I started to write myself, my inspiration comes from topical themes which stir my emotions.; [a.] Birmingham, Warks, UK

THOMAS, MAXINE CORDELIA

[b.] 13 November 1978, Haverfordwest; [p.] Ken Thomas, Gill Thomas; [ed.] The Church in Wales Primary School, St. Davids, Ysgol Gyfun Deawi Sart Secondary School, St. Davids; [occ.] Student - studying English Literature, German and Welsh A' Levels; [memb.] International Penfriend Society, Linking British Modern Foreign Language Learners with Students Abroad; [hon.] Welsh Panasonic Student Innovation Award '95, S.C.S.E.'s - 10, J.J. and Elenor Welsh Memorial Prize - Best Welsh G.C.S.E. Result. Merit Award - for Academic Excellence; [pers.] "A woman who writes feels two much." "The world is what you make it, it's outcome your input."; [a.] St. Davids, Pembrokeshire, UK

THOMPSON, DOROTHY

[b.] 8 December 1920, Salford, Lancs; [p.] Charles Vernion and Louie Critchley; [m.] Stanley James (Jimmy) Thompson, 15 December 1941; [ch.] Valerie Carol and Michael James; [ed.] St. Joseph's Convent, Lincoln Manchester Repertory Theatre School of Acting; [occ.] Tour guide; [memb.] British Actors Equity Association, Stratford-upon-Avon Shakespeare Club, Member Association of Stress Counsellors, The Poetry Society Bronze Medal for Verse Speaking; [hon.] A.L.C.M. (Speech), A.L.A.M. (Speech) Hons, A.L.A.M.

(Acting) Hons, L.G.S.M. Speech and Drama (Teaching), M.A.S.C. (Relax); [oth. writ.] Poems published in three anthologies for three difference publishing houses. More accepted for publication.; [pers.] 'Do not push the river let it flow! This is so: I no longer act' which once was my creative outlet - suddenly, I am writing poetry. Creative energy will find an outlet!; [a.] Stratford-upon-Avon, Warwicks, UK

THOMPSON, SHERYL

[pen.] Sheryl Roach. [b.] 8 December 1971, Norwich [p.] Christopher Roach, Monica Roach. [m.] Steven Robert Thompson, 15 June 1996. [ed.] Norwich Comprehensive, The Norfolk College of Arts and Technology, Norwich School of Art and Design. [occ.] Artist. [hon.] Editor's Choice Award for outstanding achievement in poetry presented by the International Society Of Poets, 1996. [oth, writ.] Poems published in anthologies by arrival press; Fur Coats and Feathers, and Animals Forever. Also a collections of further poems waiting for a captive audience. [per.] The inspiration for my poems come from my fears, my dreams, my deepest feelings and ambitions but most of all from life experience. [a.] Norwich, Norfolk.

THOMPSON, STUART CHARLES

[pen.] SC Thompson; [b.] 16 February 1974, Aberdare; [ed.] Porth County Comprehensive University of Hertfordshire; [occ.] Nature Reserve Warden; [memb.] Royal Society for the Protection of Birds Wildfowl and Wetlands Trust; [hon.] Cadbury's Literature Award 1983, Agriculture and Environmental Biology; [oth. writ.] Many poems spanning over twelve years.; [pers.] The underlying theme of my writing is the role of fate in our lives.; [a.] Pontypridd, Mid-Glamorgan, UK

THOMSON, JACQUELINE

[b.] 31 March 25, Normanton; [p.] John Poole Bolton and Elizabeth Harriet Bolton; [m.] John Hugh Thomson, 10 April 1943; [ch.] John Stuart, Andrea, Hugh Alexander; [ed.] Art School, Tech College Wakefield, Yorkshire; [occ.] Retired; [oth. writ.] "Reams" unpublished; [pers.] Words are vital to the communications we used in our daily lives. Emotions of love, understanding and comfort, help us colour the rich tapestry of our individual lives, and maybe enrich the lives of others, as solomon wrote in Proverbs 25:11.; [a.] Skegness, Lincolnshire, UK

THURNBER, PAUL J.

[b.] 2 April 1945, Birmingham; [p.] William Thurnber, Frances Thurnber; [m.] Erning Thurnber, 23 September 1967; [ch.] Louise Erma, Matthew Paul; [ed.] St. Philips Grammar School; [occ.] Safety Professional; [memb.] Institution of Occupational Society and McAlin; [hon.] Honorary Membership of the University of Life; [oth. writ.] Several poems published in Anthologies, and Newpapers.; [pers.] I am offended by waste of any sort. Either haste of emotion, feeling or life itself, and by writings on a romantic, or war commentary level reflect this stance; [a.] Birmingham, West Midlands, UK

TIERNEY, NEIL

[p.] Aline and James William Tierney; [m.] Joan Free Pugh, 12 August 1950; [ch.] Kathleen Jane; [occ.] Author and Music Critic; [memb.] President, Crosby Recorded Music Society; [hon.] British Empire Medal, Commander-in-chiefs Certificate

(Arnhem Campaign) Awarded by Field Marshal Montgomery; [oth. writ.] Biographies of Sir William Walton and Igor Stravinsky, published by Robert Hale. Many published articles and literary features.; [pers.] I believe that an innate simplicity, an aura of humility, exists at the heart of all really great art, whether it be Michaelangelo's Pieta in sculpture or Handel's Zadok the Priest in music. True inspiration is inseparable from these qualities.; [a.] Liverpool, Merseyside, UK

TILZEY, MISS PENELOPE C.

[b.] 12 September 1962, Bromley; [p.] Gilbert and Eileen; [ed.] Reigate Country School, Sixth Form College - A'Levels, Hotel Career Centre, Bournemouth - Travel and Tourism Diploma; [occ.] Unemployed as recovering from M.E.; [oth. writ.] Poems published by the Poetry Institute of the British Isles, Poetry Now and the Poetry Guild; [pers.] I discovered how poetry can convey deep feelings through the first world war poets. I write in order to explore my reactions and emotions as well as in the hope of reaching others.; [a.] Woolpit, Suffolk, UK

TIMMS, BERTHEI RAYMOUND

[b.] 22 November 1909, Home; [p.] Arnold, Harriet Timms; [m.] Kathleen Timms, 1951; [ch.] Council School; [a.] Criccieth, Gwynedd, UK

TINDALL, ANTHONY

[b.] 23 March 1974, Co Durham; [p.] George and Dorothy Tindall; [ed.] University of Newcastle Upon Tyne, Newcastle College, Lord Lawson of Beamish Comprehensive; [occ.] Pipeline Analyst; [hon.] B Sc. (Hons) Mapping information Science; [pers.] My poetry explores love, sex, lust, emotions and experiences and I try not to be held back by societies narrow mind. Influences Jim Morrison.; [a.] Chopwell, Newcastle upon Tyne, UK

TIPTON, KIM MARIE

[pen.] Kim Marie Tipton; [b.] 22 August 1959, Bloxwich, Walsall; [p.] Eileen Mary Perry, Samuel Perry; [m.] Stuart Tipton, 7 April 1979; [ch.] Craig Stuart, Zoe Marie Tipton; [ed.] Forest Comprehensive School, Lichfield College 'O' Level Maths, English, Sociology; [occ.] Housewife; [memb.] Multiple Sclerosis Society; [oth. writ.] Personal story published in well known weekly magazine poems retained by the London Poetry Society hopefully for publication in the future.; [pers.] My poetry strongly reflects the many obstacles which disabled people face, the biggest being the attitude of society towards them, their 'Disability' and their refusal to accept things we cannot change, but have to learn to accept.; [a.] Burntwood, Staffs, UK

TOMASSO, ANNE

[b.] 11 June 1951, Glasgow; [m.] Divorced; [ch.] Stacey, Stephen and Sonja; [ed.] North Kelvinside School Anniesland College Glasgow Caledonian University; [occ.] Social Worker/Day Care Centre Manager; [hon.] Diploma in Social Work; [oth. writ.] Lesson on from a snowdrop published in the People's Friend God's surprise - published in The Science Of Thought Review A Raindrop and The Magic Cauldpon Puppet Presentation - performed at "The Arts Is Magic" Glasgow; [pers.] I have been greatly influenced by radical feminist writers and also by the work of Emily Dickinson. As a result I strive to highlight the strong feminine influence which is at work in the whole of creation.; [a.] Glasgow, UK

TOMSETT, ANN E. G. F.
[pen.] 'Pixie' also known as 'Frederica-Ann'; [b.] 12 November 1953, Essex; [p.] Fred and Maria Tomsett; [ed.] St. Bernards High Westcliff, Southend Techicole, R.A.D.A. London, London College Art, S.E.V.I.C. Thundersly, London Academy of Modeling; [occ.] "Being Eccentric and Flamboyant"; [memb.] Art/Littery Guild/ Honory, Ordinator of the Freddie Mercury Phoenix Trust (Queen) for Aids a wearness/Honory Member Act for Equity Variety Club, Whale and Dolphin Conservation/'Soloman Whitebread' Art Club/ Society Giuseppe De' Art/Pocket Dragons; [hon.] Grade 7 Guild Hall Music - Drama/Graduated London Accad Modeling, Diploma 'Art-Graphic Design; [oth. writ.] Poems published in Oxford Press Anthology '76 and London Poets; [pers.] "Age is immaterial - all time is precious - the written word - immortal" 'Pixie' Frederica Ann Tomsett.; [a.] Hadleigh, Essex, UK

TOWNSEND, JOAN
[b.] 15 August 1940, Ilford, Essex; [p.] Doris, Douglas Burgoyne; [m.] Keith John Townsend, 30 June 1978; [ch.] Sharon Muriel and Neil Robert; [ed.] Beal Grammar School, Ilford, Essex; [occ.] Retired Financial Accountant; [pers.] I have derived such great pleasure and comfort from poetry all through my life, it is a bonus to have written a poem myself.; [a.] Chippenham, Wiltshire, UK

TRAVERS, EDWARD
[b.] 7 November 1947, Dublin; [p.] Thomas and Mary Travers; [m.] Antoinette, 19 March 1973; [ch.] Julia-Ann, Louise and Gillian; [ed.] DE, La Salle, Ballyfermont, Dublin 20; [occ.] P.S.V. Driver (Taxi); [memb.] Astronomy Ireland; [a.] Dublin, UK

TREWEEKS, GORDON
[b.] 29 November 1935, Eaton; [p.] Freda Treweeks, Percy Treweeks; [ch.] Karen, Paul Maria, Nicola, Ruth; [ed.] Elementary School; [occ.] Managing Director; [memb.] Glamorganshire Golf Club, Penarth Music and Variety Company; [oth. writ.] "Memories" published in an Anthology by Arrival Press. September 1996. Numerous unpublished poems; [pers.] A tranquil life besets peace of mind.; [a.] Penarth, South Glam, UK

TRUEMAN, DENNIS JOHN
[b.] 3 May 1944, New Ollerton; [p.] Edward Dennis and Mary Louise; [m.] Ann Melody Strange, 1 March 1964; [ed.] Secondary Modern, Whinney Lane, New Ollerton, Newark, Notts; [occ.] Fork Truck Driver for Hanson Brick, Kirton, Notts; [memb.] Ollerton Collery, Cricket Club; [hon.] Local Sporting Awards, Football, Cricket, Table-Tennis, Darts Dominoes; [oth. writ.] Only private none previously published my taste in poetry is A.E. Houseman; [pers.] I write mostly about love and laughter nothing else matters. Being a cricketer, on my head stone I would like - "Out!" "Bowled Neck and Crop!"; [a.] Edwinstowe, Mansfield, Notts, UK

TRUMAN, VERONICA
[pen.] Veg; [b.] January 2, 1948, Leicester; [p.] Arnold Granger and Florence Granger; [m.] John Truman, May 29, 1982; [ed.] Ravenhurst Road Junior, Market Bosworth Dixie Grammar School.; [occ.] Housewife; [memb.] Midland Golden Retriever Club: Vice Chairman Coalville Canine Society: Pat Dogs: Mensa.; [a.] Groby, Leicestershire

TUCKER, KASHMIR
[pen.] Kash Tucker; [b.] 15 April 1969, Wolverhampton; [p.] Mohinder Singh and Shindo Kaur; [ch.] One, Ashley-James (son); [ed.] Colton Hills Secondary, Walsall Technology College, Birbingham Polytec; [occ.] Housing Management Officer; [oth. writ.] Private Collection, on personal encounters emotions through one's life; [pers.] I write to gain perception and thoughts into words. A clarity of meanings and emotions of life and times of oneself for the interpretation open to all others.; [a.] Wolverhampton, West Mids, UK

TURNER, EDWIN ALEXANDER
[b.] 27 April 1938, Stoke-on-Trent; [p.] John, Christina Turner (Deceased); [m.] Patricia May, 20 May 1967; [ch.] Scott, Anglia; [ed.] Secondary Modern, Technical College, Night School, Inhouse Tutorial, Business Management, Seamanship M.N. - R.N.R.; [occ.] Jobbing Contractor; [memb.] Theatre (Stage Musicals) (Memb) of "Spotlight" Beccles; [oth. writ.] Children's stories (published), Newspaper articles (business), Poetry (abstract papers) i.e. Naval News; [pers.] To make words sound like music to the ear. Coming alive with the vibrations of every day life. My "Mentor" is the writings of "Dylan Thomas."; [a.] Lowestoft, Suffolk, UK

TURNER, WILLIAM P. T.
[b.] 20 November 1915, Gt. Crosby, Lancs; [p.] Frank Turner, Florence A. Turner; [m.] 2nd wife Jessie I. Turner, 10 October 1988; [ch.] Steven Turner; [ed.] Liverpool Collegiate Public School, Skerrios, Lancs, Inner City; [occ.] Retired at 80; [oth. writ.] Articles for 'prevention' magazine.; [pers.] Always loved mechanical things from my early days. Fascinated by growing things, especially trees and the country. Abhored the war. Left England in 1949, emigrating, then overflowing itself with poetry. Propelled away from England by nervous breakdown into my love of horticulture instead of medicine. My love has increased over the years of knowledge gained of the wonderful Creator of this universe and lovely earth, becoming especially dear to me but not in any way from a religious sense. I feel sad at the worlds lack of Bible knowledge and ignorance of his purpose.; [a.] Killarney, Kerry, Eire, UK

TYLER, EDWARD GRAHAM
[b.] 1 October 1933, Leicester; [p.] Edward Tyler and Edith Archel; [m.] Sybil June Clark, 24 June 1954; [ch.] Jillian Carol, Paul Graham Edward, Ruth Helena Wendy; [ed.] Queen Elizabeth's Grammar - Blackburn, Keele University; [occ.] Retired University - Chemistry - Lecturer; [memb.] Royal Society of Chemistry, Geological Society of London; [hon.] Head Boy at School, State Scholar, Church - Warden at Local Parish Church; [oth. writ.] Several poems published in local magazines; [pers.] As a Franciscan Tertiary I have been much influenced by the astonishing beauty of the English Countryside, of richness and poverty in the human spirit and of man's interaction with his environment. Greatly admire the poetry of Gerard Manley Hopkins.; [a.] Stoke-on-Trent, Staffordshire, UK

TYLER, THERESA
[pen.] Mick Terri; [b.] August 16, 1945, Coventry; [p.] Bill and Kathleen Hirons; [m.] Divorced; [ch.] Three 2 boys 1 girl; [ed.] None very sick child until 16 then I taugh myself. I became Care Asst. Aromatherapist/Reflexologist; [occ.] Now disabled.; [oth. writ.] Poems published in inspirations S.F. writing now on 2nd book.; [pers.] I would like to thank Pam who cares for me. And is also my friend. Also Dr. Alan

Done. Who without I would have given up. For both of you thank you.; [a.] Wootton, Beds

TYRRELL, THERESA
[b.] 27 August 1966, Birmingham; [p.] Theresa and Edward; [m.] James Tyrrell, 3 August 1985; [ch.] John, Stephen, Shauna; [ed.] St. Elizabeth's primary as St. Francis of Assisi Secondary; [occ.] Playschool teacher and housewife and mother; [oth. writ.] More poems; [pers.] Write for yourself and to help others.; [a.] Enniscorthy, Wexford, UK

UDOGARANYA, FRANCIS BENSON
[b.] 35 August 1933, Oguta, Nigeria; [p.] Nwafor Udogaranya; [m.] Mary (Maria) Udogaranya, 6 February 1960; [ch.] Seven; [ed.] Administrative Accountant at Present - Studying Law; [memb.] In Associate Member - Institute of Administrative Accountants London. A Member of the Saint Patrick's College, Old Boys Association - Nigeria; [pers.] Ease in writing comes from art, not change: As those move easiest, who have learnt to dance. A good writer may not be a good speaker at the same time. Strong memory and a good sense of imagination rarely exist together.

UNDERWOOD, TOM
[b.] 22 November 1922, Wombleton; [pers.] I have a deep sincere feeling to all mankind.; [a.] Harrogate, Nr Yorkshire, UK

UPRICHARD, APRIL
[b.] 14 April 1966, Belfast; [p.] Robert Barry (Deceased), Joyce Barry (Deceased); [m.] George Uprichard, 14 April 1993; [ch.] Andrew McMaster, Daniel Uprichard; [ed.] DunDonald Girls High School; [pers.] The troubles in Ulster have affected everyone living in the province and further a field. Physiologically and physically. But most importantly the victims themselves who have died in the troubles. My poem is dedicated to them.; [a.] Portadown, Armagh, UK

UYGUR, YELIZ
[b.] 24 August 1981, London; [p.] Selim Uygur (Father), Sonay Uygur (Mother); [ed.] Kingsmead Secondary School; [occ.] Secondary Education; [memb.] The Challis School of Dancing; [oth. writ.] I have written many poems from the age of ten, however have never actually considered them for publication.; [pers.] All of my poems are written based on thought, past, present and future, therefore are invaluable to me and hopefully the person reading them.; [a.] Enfield, Middlesex, UK

UZELE, JENNIFER W.K.
[pen.] June Junipher. [b.] 12 July 1957, Nairobi. [p.] James and Josephine Kabiru. [m.] Lamech Wayio Uzele, 1 February 1986. [ch.] Uvonti Uzele age 10. [ed.] High School, Bible College. [occ.] Singer, song writer, Bible teacher. [mem.] Swimming clubs, weights and aerobics, Quiet Moments with God. [hon.] Long distance runner, musical awards, performers awards. [oth. writ.] I compose music and write songs. I write jingles. [per.] Genesis 1:1(a) In the beginning God...... with God being in the lead - nothing fails check and when everything fails there is one left... In the beginning God..... [a.] Machakos, Kenya.

VANCE, SUZANNE
[pen.] Suzanne Vance; [occ.] Singer/Songwriter; [memb.] PRS, G.I.S.C.; [oth. writ.] Large catalogue of songs on perceptions of life and own philosophy. Recordings on C.D. and tape. Influences contemporary folk artists of the female

kind.; [pers.] I always endeavour to surrender my talents to the life or good I feel within me. In this way God's creativity flows through, playing me like an instrument and the song is thus His creation, not mine.; [a.] Glasgow, UK

VAUGHAN, HERBERT SKEFFINGTON
[b.] 2 April 1917, Gateshead; [p.] Frederick and Elinor Vaughan; [m.] Elizabeth Joy (Aslat), 3 August 1940; [ch.] Four Sons and a Daughter, 8 Grandchildren; [ed.] Kingsbridge Grammar School 1929-1936, Downing College, Cambridge (Under F. R. Leavis) 1936-1939; [occ.] Retired (Immediate Previous: 1971-1982 Tutor - Organizer, Northumberland W.E.A.); [a.] Kingsbridge, Devon, UK

VAUGHAN, KATHRYN LAWTON
[b.] 23 July 1966, Macclesfield; [p.] The late Geoffrey Moss and Pauline Mills; [m.] Robert M. F. Vaughan, 31 July 1993; [ed.] St. John's C.E. Primary School, Macclesfield County High School, The University of Exeter, The University of Bristol; [occ.] Secondary Mathematics Teacher, Worle Comprehensive School; [memb.] Association of Teachers of Mathematics (Local chairperson), Eating Disorders Association, (Media Contact), Local Church; [hon.] 2 (ii) Hons. B.Sc. in Mathematics, Post graduates Certificate of Education; [oth. writ.] Mathematical articles and reviews published in the Association of teachers of Mathematics journals: Mathematics teaching and micro Math, Working on Mathematics book with Thomas Nelson writing team; [pers.] Browning first opened my mind to enjoying literature. I now reflect on images to convey pure emotion in my writings.; [a.] Bristol, Bristol, UK

VEALE, KYMBERLEY
[pen.] Kymberley Veale; [b.] 12 May 1966, Horsham, W Sussex; [p.] Mrs. L. M. Green and Mr. R. Smith; [m.] Mr. Nick Veale, 20 July 1996; [ed.] Millias School for Girls, Depot Road Horsham, West Sussex (O'Level passes, English, Maths, Art, History, Geography, Human Biology); [occ.] (Fruit Picker); [oth. writ.] A poem for Shropshire, Published in the Shropshire Star, and now waiting for an appointment with the Shropshire Tourism Board. A child's story book called 'Jungle Tots'.; [pers.] I have taken a verse from a recent poem, to explain the style of my writing, wanting the outside to feel so much the inner passion, beauty of such to awaken man's depth of being: Writings from the heart...feels...can touch!; [a.] Crawley Down, West Sussex, UK

VINALL, RODNEY HORACE
[b.] 2 October 1915, London; [p.] James H. Vinall, Maud Ellen Vinall; [m.] Margaret Anne Davis, 30 July 1960; [ch.] Beverley Anne and Neil Roy; [ed.] Clarks College, Pitmans College, Ecole Hoteliere, Lausanne Switzerland; [occ.] Retired Merchant Navy Officer, including 36 years service in the Royal Naval Reserve, retiring with rank of Commander; [memb.] Institute of Advanced Motorists, Royal Society of St. George, British Trials and Rally Drivers Association, British Automobile Racing Club, British Motor Racing Narshals Club, British Racing and Sports Car Club; [hon.] Reserve Decoration, Coronation Medal, Cross of St. Isabella, (for service in the Spanish Civil War), United Nations Korea Medal, British Korean Medal, French Resistance Medal, Croix de Geurre, 2nd class, 4 WW 2 Campaign Medal, Defence Medal, War Medal, 2nd WW; [oth. writ.] "The Motor Ship," subject - The Greater Use of Frozen Foods by Ferry Operators,

November 1966, New Zealand, Official Bulletin of the New Zealand Automobile Association, "Co-Driver in Monte Carlo Rally visits Auckland." Eskimo News, and several others.; [pers.] I have always in my travels around the world, to represent my country in the best possible manner, and to support the principals of free speech, and freedom at all times. I have been much influenced by the late Admiral Lord Nelson, in my approach to this end.; [a.] Leigh-on-Sea, Essex, UK

VINCENT, BARRY
[b.] 15 March 1950, Chesham Bucks; [p.] Joan and Ashley Vincent; [m.] Patricia, 23 May 1970; [ch.] Emma and Wayne; [ed.] Raans County Secondary School Amersham Bucks; [occ.] Motor Engineer; [hon.] City and Guilds part 1 and 2 for Motor Engineer; [oth. writ.] Several poems published in various books.; [pers.] I have to be in the mood to write, but then it flows, I loving writing love song/ballard's but as of yet I have done nothing to release them.; [a.] Rickmansworth, Herts, UK

VINTERS, PAULINE
[b.] 29 July 1932, Grimsby; [p.] Sidney Martin, Frances Martin; [m.] William Vinters, 26 September 1953; [ch.] Paul William; [occ.] Retired; [oth. writ.] Several poems published and I also write and frame poems for friends and relations wedding anniversaries and special occasions; [pers.] I like to express my work in simple language but with feeling from my heart for others to enjoy; [a.] Tattershall, Lincolnshire, UK

WADE, HELEN ELIZABETH
[pen.] Helen Wade; [b.] 14 September 1981, Leeds; [p.] Lesley Wade and Andrew Wade, divorced; [ed.] currently in year 9 at Benton Park Secondary School - Rawdon Leeds; [occ.] student; [memb.] Guisley Music Centre - Studying Drama; [pers.] I try to give people my views of the way I see today's society and I try to write about issues that matter, not just to me but other people too. [a.] Rawdon, Leeds, West Yorkshire

WADLEY, MRS. HELEN SIAN
[b.] 2 May 1962, Hengoed, S. Wales; [p.] Allen Thomas (Deceased), Barbara Thomas; [m.] John Beresford Wadley, 27 June 1992; [ed.] Hengoed Primary/Junior School Ystrad Lewis Girls Comprehensive School Mynach Ystrad Mynach College of further Education; [occ.] Civil Servant; [oth. writ.] Unpublished poetry of love written to spouse.; [pers.] Thanks to my loved ones here and gone without whom I would not have life or inspiration to write from this heart. Words cannot express where your heart is full of happiness. Life's been good to me so far....; [a.] Penpedairheol, Mid-Glamorgan, UK

WADSWORTH, PATRICIA
[b.] 18 July 1922, Pontefract; [p.] Robert Steerment, Maud Steerment; [m.] E. Wadsworth; [ch.] John and Jenny; [ed.] Convent, Gravesend, Kent; [occ.] Retired; [hon.] Defence Medal, 1939-45 medal; [oth. writ.] Private book of poems to my dead son, killed through lightning.; [pers.] The only thing we bring into this world when we are born is love, and the only thing we can take out of it is love, or hate when we die, I hope I take love.; [a.] Wolverhampton, West Midlands, UK

WAITES, ANNE
[b.] 27 February 1964, Runcorn; [p.] Alfred and Jean Perry; [m.] Andrew Robert Waites, 19 August 1995; [ch.] Harriet Katie Waites; [ed.] Helsby

Grammar; [pers.] Influenced by grandma Perry.; [a.] Cheshire, UK

WALDOCK, PAUL
[b.] 16 July 1963, Tidworth; [p.] June Waldock, Philip Waldock; [oth. writ.] A few poems published in books.; [pers.] I write and have my poems published for the moments of pleasure the readers receive from reading them.

WALKER, JEAN
[pen.] Jean Walker; [b.] 25 May 1948, Walsall at Home; [m.] James Charles Walker, 5 April 1980; [ch.] Natalie and James; [occ.] Housewife; [memb.] "Walsall Society of Artists", "Royal Birmingham Society of Artists"; [hon.] Award of Distinction from "London Art College", From which I did a correspondence course in June '95"; [oth. writ.] This is my first poem, but I hope to write some more.; [pers.] The poem was how I felt when Jim (my husband) and myself were apart in our early courting days.; [a.] Walsall, West Midlands, UK

WALKER, JOSEPH
[b.] 28 May 1947, Stepney; [p.] Nellie and Henry; [m.] 1968; [ch.] Three; [ed.] Secondary Modern, plus living in the East End of London; [occ.] London Licensed Taxi Driver; [hon.] Semi Finalist in Passage in Time; [oth. writ.] Show Me The Way I'm Looking For, which was featured in "A Passage in Time" page 151, plus 30 unpublished poems.; [pers.] Everyday events inspire me to put pen to paper.

WALKER, JUSTIN IVAN
[b.] December 10, 1956, England; [ed.] Middlesex University, Salisbury College (Wiltshire); [occ.] Further Education Tutor; [memb.] Middlesex University Alumni; [oth. writ.] Full length novel 'The Mirrabelle Letters' (Mystery Thriller as yet unpublished) more poems and short stories.; [pers.] 'The Mirrabelle Letters' is a cross between Wilkie Collins and Kafka! - I love Georgian Poetry (The Edwardian Kind).

WALKER, MICHELLE
[pen.] Shelly; [b.] 8 April 1963, Wolverhampton; [p.] Graham Walker, Doreen Walker; [ch.] Raechel Lue, Kaisha Lue; [ed.] Deansfield High, Bilston College; [pers.] I write to express what I see and feel.; [a.] Bilston, West Midlands, UK

WALKER, MR. RAY
[pen.] R. Walker; [b.] 24 September 1941, Beccles; [p.] Bertie Walker, Emma Walker; [m.] Marge Walker (Deceased); [ch.] Lorraine, Joanne, Mark; [ed.] St Helena Secondary Modern; [occ.] Manager (Private Nursing Home.), (Registered-Mental-Nurse); [pers.] In memory of Marg. My dear departed wife; [a.] Colchester, Essex, UK

WALKER, STEVEN
[pen.] Steve Walker; [b.] 17 October 1982, Chesterfield; [p.] David and Elizabeth Walker; [ed.] Studying all different subjects at Highfields School - Matlock. Special interests in English, Geography, P.E. and Foreign Languages; [occ.] Attends School; [memb.] Plays Football for Matlock Town Under 13 Team. Represents Highfields at Cross Country Running and Athletics; [hon.] 1995-96 Season Awarded Players of the Year, and Managers Player of the year, and Parents Player of the year. Also won a Cup final playing for Matlock Town Under 12's; [pers.] I like to write poems about different subjects. I support Everton Football Club.; [a.] Matlock, Derbyshire, UK

WALL-HAYES, JULIAN F.
[b.] October 10, 1969, Aldershot; [p.] Frederick Wall-Hayes and Beryl Greenhalgh; [ed.] Courtmoor Secondary School Fleet; [occ.] Forte PLC M3 Service Area; [memb.] Fleet Broadway Club, Joe Bananas, Camberley; [oth. writ.] "Looking By Myself" in poetry now - Regional Anthologies London 1993.; [pers.] Love yourself before you can love others. Always try to be happy, enjoy the good things in life and just experience the bad things, without bad times there cannot be good times.; [a.] Fleet, Hampshire

WALLACE, SHARON
[b.] 15 July 1979, Perth; [p.] Christie, Sandra Wallace; [ed.] Kinross Primary/Secondary; [occ.] Live in Nanny; [hon.] 2nd prize for school poetry competition; [a.] Kinross, UK

WALLACE-DUNLOP, ELIZABETH
[b.] 5 November 1937, London, United Kingdom; [p.] Richard and Elizabeth Bertram; [m.] Keith Wallace-Dunlop, 14 December 1967; [ch.] James (Stuart), Philippa (Elizabeth), Alexandra (Clare); [ed.] Wincery House School, Bexhill-on-Sea, London College of Secretaries, St. Luke's College, Exeter (Teacher Training); [occ.] Homemaker/living in the country growing food and reclaiming our old orchards, Writer, Healer; [oth. writ.] Articles for organizations/to which I've belonged (in the past). Currently assembling my first volume of poetry.; [pers.] My work comes from a desire to help mankind on its spiritual journey. I am to show the balance between the physical and spiritual and to evoke a consciousness of wholeness.; [a.] Hatherleigh, Devon, UK

WALSH, ANTHONY
[b.] 22 October 1938, Ireland; [p.] Richard and Mary Walsh; [m.] Elizabeth Walsh, 25 June 1963; [ch.] Richard, Jacinta, Eilis, Don. Teresa; [ed.] Christ The King Schools, Turners Cross Cork City; [occ.] Communications; [oth. writ.] 2,000. 'Urbanites', 'Dawn', 'Reality'; [pers.] My Poetry Reflects, Mankinds Journey, Through Life.; [a.] Cork, Cork, UK

WALTERS, AGNES LILIAN
[pen.] Rita Savio; [b.] 18 June 1920, Burslem, Stoke-on-Trent, Staffs; [p.] William and Gertrude Pickering; [m.] Eddie Walters, 15 July 1973; [ch.] Four by previous marriage; [ed.] Private School; [occ.] Retired; [memb.] I attended college and worked with professional artist and amused myself "Portraying Drama"; [hon.] I was presented with flowers, they also made me a wine evening, and they put it in the Press and all the people who had any connections with me came from Keele University.; [oth. writ.] `Private School Commercial'. Poem, written for Princess Ann, another one for Queen Elizabeth of England, and also Princess Diana and Prince Charles about their wedding and I had an edited programme on the Radio. The late Hen Lord Wilson also sent me a birthday Card and letter I wrote a full book of poems, which Keele University published.; [pers.] Poetry and other things; [a.] Eastbourne, East Sussex, UK

WALTERS, DENISE
[b.] 24 June 1956, Carcroft; [p.] Josephine and Raymond Lount; [m.] Raymond Walters, 24 June 1974; [ch.] Martin and Julia; [ed.] Adwick High School, Doncaster College; [occ.] House wife; [oth. writ.] Several poems yet to be published.; [pers.] My children are my greatest achievements, everything else is a bonus.; [a.] Doncaster, S. Yorks, UK

WALTERS, LEIGHTON WILFRED
[pen.] Poet Nelvius; [b.] 8 April 1956, Pontneathvaughan; [p.] Marilyn Walters, John Walters; [ed.] Vaynor and Penderyn Secondary School, Garnett Teachers Training College, Coventry Polytechnic, The Fashochshule Konstanz; [memb.] Shooters Rights Association, Institute of the Motor Industry, Institute of the Road Transport Engineers; [hon.] Motor Vehicle and Raft Studies Motor Vehicle Technicians Cert, Full Technology Cert, Nelding Craft Practice, Certificate of Education Bachelor of Science Hon, Deg; [oth. writ.] Other poems but not published; [pers.] I discovered this poem among my son's belongings shortly after he died. It is my most treasured possession, and if he was alive today, I am sure he would be delighted. With the recognition that it was had.; [a.] Glynneath, West Glam, UK

WALTON, ELEANOR
[b.] 12 March 1968, Suffolk; [p.] Marlene and Bernard Walton; [occ.] H. M. Forces Royal Army Veterinary Corps Dog Handler; [oth. writ.] Unpublished; [pers.] Our memories are our strength, through harder times, in life.; [a.] Saxmundham, Suffolk, UK

WARD, ELIZABETH
[pen.] Elizabeth Pemberton-Ward; [b.] Manchester; [p.] Martha Alice Pemberton; [m.] Harold Edwin Ward; [ch.] Noel Edwin, Lynn Elizabeth, Julie Ann, and Jayne Margaret; [ed.] Saint Phillips, Bradford Rd, Manchester And Loreburn College, Spring Gardens, Manchester; [occ.] Retired person. B.B.C. Oxford Rd, Manchester; [memb.] Philharmonic Choir of Manchester (Registered Charity), Performance of Dream of Gerontius Elgar, Royal Albert Hall, London, 14 July '96; [a.] Manchester, UK

WARD, HANNAH
[b.] 27 January 1980, Poole, Dorset; [p.] Cheryl Ward, John Ward; [ed.] The Blandford School (upper) presently in 6th Form; [oth. writ.] One poem published in a local paper and one published in a school magazine.; [pers.] My poems create themselves they are spontaneous, and I never set out with a specific subject in mind; [a.] Blandford Forum, Dorset, UK

WARD, MRS. JOYCE LUCY
[b.] 10 April 1920, Witney, Oxon; [p.] Arnold and Clara Dix; [m.] Donald George Ward, 10 April 1939; [ch.] Son and Daughter; [ed.] Witney Grammar School; [occ.] Housewife; [memb.] Wychwood Handicrafts Soc. Mothers Union Wychwood Singers; [pers.] I have always been a reader of prose and poetry. My interests include welfare work, painting, with oils acrylics and water colour, also the garden gives me great pleasure.; [a.] Chipping Norton, Oxon, UK

WARD, RUTH M.
[b.] 16 August 1971, Solihull; [p.] Peter Ward and Janet Ward; [ed.] Moseley Secondary School, Birmingham College of Food; [occ.] Cake Decorator; [memb.] British Sugarcraft Guild; [hon.] Aston Cup for Excellence in Cake Design, various diplomas and awards in Bakery and Cake Decoration; [oth. writ.] Extensive unpublished private collection; [pers.] Poems are from the inside, they can capture a feeling or a memory forever.; [a.] Birmingham, West Midlands, UK

WARDLE, MICHAEL ROBERT
[b.] 8th August, 1962, Portsmith Hampshire; [m.] Jenny Ruth Wardle on 25 June 1988, No children

yet. [ed.] Prince's Grammar School Fareham, gaining 9 O levels and 3 A Levels. B.A. (honours) Philosophy from Reading University 1983. Currently 3rd year under-graduate at Portsmouth University studying for B.S.C. (honours) Diagnostic Radiography. [occ.] University Student. [mem.] Student Member of the Society of Radiographers. [hon.] Qualified 1st aider, self defense, P.A.D.I. open water scuba diver, advanced driver, RAC/AUC motorcycle graduate. [oth. writ.] Poems published in previous anthology. Currently writing a book about travelling the U.S.A. [pers.] I have found love with my wife Jenny and together we embark on this great adventure called life. We have recently returned from a two year tour of the United States and hope to go back someday. [a.] Fareham Hampshire, UK

WARING, MARCUS
[pen.] Marcus Waring; [b.] June 1, 1974, Chichester, W. Sussex; [p.] Susan and Patrick Waring; [ed.] Westbourne House Prep School, Seaford College, South Devon College, Worchester College of H.E.; [occ.] Temporarily Working at boatyard in Sussex; [memb.] Bosham Sailing Club; [hon.] Diploma of H.E. in "Life and Literature in Shakespeare's England" B.A. (Hons) English studies; [oth. writ.] A collection of other poems (unpublished); [pers.] After studying Conrad's "Heart of Darkness" and forster's "A Passage to India." And "Howard's end, I am fascinated by the modernist's search for self, and plan to commence a career in writing by starting on a short story concerning a young man's psychological quest.; [a.] W. Sussex

WARNER, MARY CAROLINE
[b.] 22 January 1959, Macclesfield; [p.] Norman Baum and May Baum; [m.] David Warner, 2 March 1985; [ed.] Wilmslow County High for Girls, Fielden Park College Manchester; [occ.] Medically Retired Day Nursery Manager: Junior Church Teacher; [memb.] Knutsford and District Motor Club, Church of England Childrens Society, Committee Member (Northwich) Team Manager W.Gt Motorsport Really Division; [oth. writ.] Poem/song for church occasions/magazines; [pers.] I use my own experiences in my poetry to offer hope, love and friendship to those around me. My greatest influence has been "the moody blue" and their inspirational songs/writing.; [a.] Northwich, Cheshire, UK

WARRIER, DEBBIE
[b.] 6 March 1970, Kuching, Malaysia; [p.] Quin Warrier, Matthew Warrier; [ed.] Servite College 1983 to 1987 - High School Certificate, Curtin University (Western Australia) 1988 - 91 Bachelor of Social Work; [occ.] Hospital Social Worker; [memb.] The Poetry Society, 22 Betterton Street, Convent Garden, London; [oth. writ.] Presently attempting to publish book "Reflections" collection of poems written between 1985 to 1996 which I have dedicated to my family.; [pers.] Grew up on Australia and an presently on working holiday with my sister Daphne in London. Have been travelling around the world since 1995. I believe strongly in following your dreams.; [a.] Waterloo, London, UK

WATKINS, DORA
[b.] 21 April 1927, Shapwick, Som; [p.] William and Ada Haggett; [m.] James Watkins, 11 July 1948; [ch.] Trevor, Rosemarie, Ronald; [ed.] Elmhust Grammar Street (Som); [occ.] Canteen assistant; [memb.] W.I, USA, Dram club Village Hall Committee-Member of Church Council.; [oth. writ.] Several poems-one small one act ray "Life

Was Different Then" book about village life in the 30's Book of country savings.; [pers.] I love writing, if it gains recognition that's a bonus, if it doesn't it has pleased me.; [a.] Shapwick, Nr Bridgwater, Somerset, UK

WATKINS, GAVIN MARK
[b.] 1 January 1974, Morriston; [p.] Barbara Watkins, Roy Watkins; [m.] June 1997 (Hopefully); [ed.] Ysgol Gyfun Y Strade, University of Glamorgan; [occ.] Unemployed; [oth. writ.] Poem to be published in collection of poems by Welsh Poets by Anchor Books called 'Inspirations from Wales'. I also have many more poems unpublished and also some short stories.; [pers.] I found myself in my first year on a HND course in computing when I suddenly realize that I did not want to do it. Instead I put pen to paper and started writing poems. I find expression through poetry stimulating and enjoy others reading them.; [a.] Llanelli, Dyfed, UK

WATKINS, KEITH ALAN
[pen.] Keith Watkins; [b.] 17 September 1945, Bristol; [p.] Lorna and Alan Watkins; [m.] Verona Marion Watkins, 18 March 1972; [ed.] Downend County Primary, Chipping Sodbury Grammar; [occ.] Technically Unemployed, but writing poems, life story etc.; [memb.] None - Prefer to be a free soul/spirit. Don't want to be influenced by others, or alter style. (Might soon be a member of A.A.!!); [hon.] None in writing as yet. I was in the motor trade as a mechanic, served a five year apprenticeship passed city and guilds and the National Craftsman Certificate (nothing glamorous there, sorry!) Oh, I've read loads of poems on B.B.C. Radio Bristol.; [oth. writ.] I've one book (Cheap and Cheerful) Printed. It's sponsored by 'Action Print' of Bristol. I've already 50 poems for book two. Book 3 will be the best of one and two. Also writing humorous and serious autiobiography.; [pers.] I write because I think it's a terrible shame to let your thoughts etc. Just disappear. Why shouldn't other people share them and hopefully enjoy them?! I'll still be here when I'm gone.; [a.] Bristol, Bristol, UK

WATKINS, MAVIS
[b.] 16 September 1925, Cardiff; [p.] Robert and Edina Callow; [m.] Elwyn James Watkins (Died 18 January 1993), 28 February 1944; [ch.] Edna, Robert, Brian (all grown up); [ed.] Windsor Business College Neath; [occ.] I am retired, but my interests are gardening, and looking after my pets two cats and a dog named Susie.; [oth. writ.] Story 'Old Man' published in New Writes of Wales, Persistent Phone Eisteddfod Cardiff 50 and 2nd 1987, Story Ely 50 and Eisteddfod 1992, Aberystwyth 50 and Eisteddfod (one 2nd two 3rd); [pers.] I've been very lucky, God has looked after me always. My wish is that all people would love one another.; [a.] Cardiff, South Glamorgan, UK

WATSON, GUY H. R.
[b.] 24 May 1958, Sutton; [p.] Mr. and Mrs. G. R. Watson; [ch.] Two daughters - Aimee and Rachael; [ed.] Reed's School, Cobham Surrey, London University; [occ.] Assistant Manager, Mental Health Project (Leonard Cheshire foundation); [hon.] B.Sc (Hons) London University, Psychology and Behavioral Sciences; [oth. writ.] Several, "I Observe" published in your anthology, "Voices on the Wind" 1996; [pers.] All my work in written from "The Heart". Usually in difficult times and/ or situations.; [a.] Denmead, Waterlooville, Hants, UK

WATSON, JANET
[b.] Warwickshire; [p.] Elizabeth Watson, Thomas Watson; [ed.] Tamworth Girls High School, City of Leeds Training College; [occ.] Retired Headmistress, Huntington County Primary; [memb.] Member of Education York, Advisory Committee, Member of British Drama League; [oth. writ.] Children's stories baby Jetty.; [pers.] I am a Christian with a strong faith after recovering from cancer, I believed I'd been saved with some special work to do. I prayed about this, and awoke with a complete poem at 3 am, this has happened ever since, I believed the poems were to help other hence my book. "In Praise of God" I now have enough for my next book and still they come, as simple direct messages.; [a.] Retford, Nottinghamshire, UK

WATSON, LINDA
[pen.] Kerry J.; [b.] 13 January 1960, Scotland; [ed.] Tower Hamlets Comprehensive Girls School Studied Music/Singing Privately at Trinity College/ Royal Academy - Schools of Music; [occ.] Cabaret Singer; [pers.] Make every day count.; [a.] London

WATSON, PENELOPE J. R.
[b.] 30 June 1945, Waltham Forest; [ed.] Sydney Burnell, Secondary Modern Higharis Park; [pers.] This poem was written in 1960, read in assembly, and my head master never found out who wrote it.; [a.] Harlow, Essex, UK

WATSON, VANESSA HELEN
[pen.] Vanessa W.; [b.] 4 July 1958, Wolverhampton; [m.] (Sep) Dr. Joachim Reidiess, 14 December 1985; [ch.] Alexander, Georgia; [ed.] Queen Mary's, London School of Economics; [occ.] Poet; [memb.] My multiplicity of poetic voices, orchestrated in counter points, of form, mood, rhythm, language and tempo, represent an cappella woman's search for meaning, truth and love in the life games challenge to exist in a chaotic world of random; [hon.] Coincidence tempered by free will. Ignorabimus; [oth. writ.] Uninvited Guests, A Skyrian Anthology, published in the united states.

WATTS, MISS SARAH
[pen.] Sarah Watts; [b.] 29 October 1966, Northampton; [p.] Mr. James Watts; [ch.] Kallom and Katie; [oth. writ.] None to speak of, and hundreds never shown; [pers.] I have written poetry for years, purely for my own pleasure never imagining it being of any interest to others.; [a.] Coventry, UK

WAY, PAM
[b.] 18 May 1932, Wallasey, Cheshire; [p.] Herbert and Florence Winstanley; [m.] Kenneth Way, 2 November 1980; [ch.] Derek, Keith, Mandy and Debby; [ed.] Wallasey High School; [occ.] Computer Operator; [oth. writ.] 6 'Manxie' childrens books and BBC TV Series of first one in 'Playdays'; [a.] Peel, Isle of Man, UK

WEAVER, DARREN
[b.] 14 February 1979, Merthyr Tydfil; [occ.] Student; [pers.] Poetry is a unique form of art as they are short and can be remembered easily, while novels are long and cannot be completely remembered.; [a.] Merthyr Tydfil, Mid-Glamorgan, UK

WEBB, DAVID
[b.] 9 December 1968, Watford; [ed.] Southbourne Comprehensive Ruislip Manor, Middx; [occ.]

Frustrated singer/songwriter (full time Clerical Farnborough Hants Todder); [memb.] Bob Dylan Appreciation Society I support West Ham F.C.(!?); [oth. writ.] Although I have written many songs 'your scattergun' is my first real attempt at writing words without music; [pers.] I'd like to think my writing expresses both strengths and weaknesses of the human condition and the eternal paradox that is life's rich pageant; [a.] Farnborough, Hants, UK

WEBB, KIRSTY LOUISA
[b.] 13 March 1978; [p.] Linda and Keith Webb; [ed.] Queen Elizabeth Mercian School Tamworth; [occ.] 'A' Level Student; [hon.] Duke of Edinburgh Awards Bronze and Silver; [pers.] My poetry is an outlet for my emotions and innermost feelings.; [a.] Tamworth, Staffordshire, UK

WEIR, MRS. LYNDA JUNE
[b.] 23 July 1953, London; [p.] Beryl and "Mike" Harrison; [m.] Stephen Weir, 23 July 1988; [memb.] R.S.P.C.A.; [oth. writ.] I have written verses since I was very young. I have never had anything published before.; [pers.] I would like my poem to be dedicated to my parents. Beryl and Mike Harrison who now, sadly, are both deceased. God bless them. My love went with you.; [a.] Welwyn Garden City, Herts, UK

WELLS, ALBERT WILLIAM
[pen.] William Wells; [b.] 19 August 1929, London; [p.] James Wells, Amelia Wells; [m.] Mary Wells, 9 January 1960; [occ.] Retired; [memb.] Gratton Bowling Club, Art Classes; [oth. writ.] I write verses for birthday cards that I design.; [pers.] I enjoy reflecting on the years of my childhood, and my poetry is a record of journeys back.; [a.] Copthorne, West Sussex, UK

WELLS, CHRISTINE DENISE
[pen.] Kes; [b.] 26 February 1950, Erdington; [p.] Iris and Dennis Kesterton; [m.] Gerald Alan Wells, 7 August 1971; [ch.] Rachel, Melanie, Emelia; [ed.] Fentham Girls Secondary Modern Night School Classes; [occ.] Housewife and Chief Bottle - Washer; [memb.] Birmingham Stage School: United Reform Church, L.A.M.D.A. (Drama group); [hon.] Keep fit: Bronze, Silver, Gold, Gold bar, Gold Award, Musical Comedy, Bronze, Silver in mime - Honours L.A.M.D.A in Speech: Distinction L.A.M.D.A. Improvisation - Distinction; [oth. writ.] Other poems published in various books; [pers.] There is insufficient communication, love, and understanding in this world without these is hard for mankind to survive. I use poetry as a form of communication one which people hopefully will enjoy.; [a.] Erdington, Birmingham, West Midlands, UK

WELLS, COLIN
[pen.] C..; [b.] 19 October 1967, Leicester; [p.] Victor and Joan Wells; [ch.] Stefan; [ed.] Mary Lindwood School (Leics); [occ.] Crown Court Security Officer; [hon.] Gulf Medal and Rosette - 1991; [oth. writ.] Various for family and friends none published; [pers.] I started to write poetry whilst serving in the Gulf Conflict in 1991 and now try and reflect the world as I see it.; [a.] Leicester, Leicestershire, UK

WENDON, MR. U.
[b.] 4 April 1939, Erith, Kent; [m.] Fran; [ed.] Sean, Ryan, Ross; [pers.] Enjoy the natural world with all its beauty. Don't live in a world of make-believe.; [a.] Farnborough, Hants, UK

WENSLEY, JOHN
[b.] 10 September 1929, Taunton, Somerset; [ed.] Taunton School, Kings College, London; [occ.] Retired; [memb.] R.N.L.L., West Country Association for Counselling, Society of Mary and Martha, Friends of the Earth; [pers.] I am interested in the inter play between opposites and working towards reconciliation and personal healing. As a priest, I am interested in the relation between religion and therapy, especially gestalt.; [a.] Wellington, Somerset, UK

WEST, LUKE JAMES
[pen.] West Luke James; [b.] 6 March 1985, Essex; [p.] Mrs. Josephine Snelling and Mr. Perry West; [ed.] De Vere C/P School Castle Hedingham Essex; [occ.] Student - About to Embark on Secondary Education; [oth. writ.] No other writings have been published; [pers.] I have always enjoyed writing both poems and stories. I find it's a good way to express my feelings. School is O.K. I enjoy gymnastics and going to car boot sales. I wrote "Mum, you're the Best of the Rest" in school, just before Mother's Day this year Poetry is my way to show feelings, I may not always have time to tell.; [a.] Castle Hedingham, Essex, UK

WEST, PENNY
[pen.] Penny West; [b.] 15 January 1946, Dorset; [m.] Philip West, 1972; [ch.] One girl and one boy; [ed.] Brandford Grammer, Nurse/Midwife; [occ.] Educational Support Ass.; [memb.] Charter 88, Republic, Learning Through Handscapes; [oth. writ.] None published. This was He first time, I've submitted any of my poetry for competition or publication.; [pers.] I'm always surprised at the restrictions society puts on mankind and the disdain when someone breaks them.; [a.] Blumsdon, Swindon, Wilts, UK

WESTON, JEAN MAUREEN
[b.] Birmingham; [m.] Divorced; [ch.] Neil, Annette, Ian, Nathan; [ed.] Secondary Modern, Worcester College; [occ.] Retired Civil Servant; [hon.] English Literature; [oth. writ.] Articles for the Civil Service magazines, lyrics for songs (not recorded) Poetry and book (unpublished) Leisure writing; [pers.] Literature is a source of knowledge and inspiration to all who seek them.; [a.] Kidderminster, Worcs, UK

WESTON, MAUREEN
[pen.] Ashley O'Neill, Maureen Weston; [b.] 1 July 1944, Chorley, Lancs; [p.] Edward Hullock and Olga Isaballe Dugdale; [m.] James Richard Weston, 23 September 1994; [ch.] Robert Ian Edward Eccles, Simon Andrew Eccles; [ed.] St. Johns School, Whittle-Le-Woods Chorley Lancashire, no further education; [occ.] Admin. Assistant, Decantae Mineral Water Limited; [oth. writ.] None published as yet; [pers.] I try to put kindness, love and understanding into my writing. Feeling, love and understanding into what I write and hope that the reader will have the same emotional understanding of my work.; [a.] Llanrwst, Gwynedd, UK

WESTWOOD, LEANNE
[b.] 19 June 1981, Birmingham; [p.] John and Diane Westwood; [ed.] Torc High Secondary School; [occ.] School girl; [pers.] I have always been interested in writing poetry, and hope to continue throughout my life.; [a.] Tamworth, Staffs, UK

WHARTON, ELEANOR EMMA
[pen.] Ellie Wharton; [b.] 19 March 1981, Margate; [p.] Raymond Wharton and Valerie Wharton; [occ.] Student; [hon.] Grade 5 Piano, Swimming Awards; [oth. writ.] Numerous poems, published in a school magazine. One story read out on the local radio.; [pers.] I enjoy writing poems as it can allow you to escape reality and lose yourself in your own created world. I am greatly influenced by different cultures and changing seasons.; [a.] Canterbury, Kent, UK

WHEATLEY, JAMES
[b.] 6 December 1940, Newcastle-on-Tyne; [p.] James and Alice Wheatley; [m.] Mary Wheatley, 13 February 1993; [ch.] Alison, Step Children Anne, Susan David; [ed.] Heaton Technical School Newcastle, Brasted Place College, Lincoln Theological College, Open University (B.A. Hens); [occ.] Parish priest: Parscen Cross, Sheffield; [memb.] Julian Society, Thomas Merton Society, Former member Mid-Northumberland Chorus, Morpeth Operatic Society, Sheffield Philharmoic Chorus; [hon.] % BA Hons E General Ordination Exam Distinction in New Testament set books, Julia Garford Price: Thesis the church in England to 664; [oth. writ.] Several poems published by Wainam Press, Triumph House. Specialist Piece on Thomas Merton, at Present working on a series of Short Stories on New Testament Personalities; [pers.] My poems in the main reflect the Christians approach to God, at times the unknowable "wholly other". Greatly influenced by the English medieval mystics, especially Julian of Norwich and the cloud of unknowing. I believe in "The Grace of Doubt". R.S. Thomas has bean a seminal influence.; [a.] Sheffield, South Yorks, UK

WHEATLEY, DR. PETER
[b.] 28 July 1922, Wimbledon, London; [p.] Ruby and Kenneth Wheatley; [m.] Sylvia Mary, 6 June 1953; [ch.] Barnaby James; [ed.] Tiffin School, London Univ., (Med. Fac); [occ.] Medicine Retired; [memb.] Carlisle and Border Art Society; [oth. writ.] Short story, The Sniper 1986 poems (pub.) Naughty Billy 1984, Poems (Unpub.): Blood Red Poppy 1986, My Pretty Jenny '94, Travellers Joy '93, Cowslips '94; [pers.] Greatly moved by the pathos and futility of war, and the simple innocent beauty of love and nature. Inspiration, the war poets, especially Owen, Blunder and Aldington.; [a.] Wethearal Carlisle, Cumbria, UK

WHEELER, JEFFREY C.
[pen.] Jeffrey Charles; [b.] 18 May 1936, Coventry, Eng; [m.] Susan Mary Wheeler, 4 April 1964; [ch.] Stephen Howard, Jane Louise, Anne Elaine; [ed.] John Gulson Grammar, Coventry, Coventry Univ.; [occ.] Photographer; [hon.] Photography exhibited by Royal Photographic Soc., Bath, England and other U.K. Venues; [oth. writ.] Novels, 'Throwing Stones at the Sun,' 'The Broken Voice,' (being assessed for publ.) several poems (unpubl.) short stories, 'The Visitor,' 'The Tales of Tommy,' 'Uneasy Rider' (collection for pub.); [pers.] Like Albert Camus, I enjoy the absurdity of the world. Most influenced by William Golding.; [a.] Nuneaton, Warwicks, UK

WHISTON, KERRY SUSANNE
[b.] 7 July 1976, Northwich, Cheshire; [p.] Susan Whiston, Terence Whiston; [ed.] Regis Secondary School, Wulfrun College of Further Education; [occ.] Sales Administrator; [memb.] West Midlands Special Constabulary; [pers.] I endeavor to write thought provoking material in an attempt to weaken

humanities preconceived ideas and beliefs. Difference is not wrong only unfamiliar.; [a.] Wolverhampton, West Midlands, UK

WHITE, CHRISTOPHER
[b.] 27 May 1984, Watford; [p.] Martin White, Margaret White; [ed.] St. Martin's School, Northwood; [memb.] Eastcote Cricket Club, Broadwater Sailing Club; [oth. writ.] Several poems published in school magazine; [pers.] I particularly enjoy writing about wildlife and the elements. Poetry gives a source of continual enjoyment, and can put across those feelings which are not easy to say directly to another person. Eventually I hope my poetry collection may be published in a book.; [a.] Ruislip, Middx, UK

WHITTINGHAM, MRS. YVONNE
[b.] 24 October 1950, Walsall; [p.] Mr. and Mrs. Simms; [m.] Stephen Whittingham, 7 December 1974; [ch.] Daughter Nicola aged 19; [occ.] Due to ill health, I'm no longer in employment.; [pers.] My poem was written from the heart. Most of my poems are written from personal experiences. I have written quite a few, this is the first one I've tried to get published.; [a.] Tipton, West Mids, UK

WIELAND, SUSAN MARY
[b.] 28 August 1960, Ramsgate, England; [p.] William Plumbridge, Maureen Plumbridge; [m.] Christian Wieland, 26 October 1984; [ch.] Steven Daniel, Sara Susan; [ed.] Charters Towers, England, Academie De Langues Et Commerce, Geneva; [occ.] Housewife; [oth. writ.] Several poems published in 1979, 1980 in an easter anthology, contemporary poets of 1979, treasury of modern poets 1980 and spring poets 1980. All books by Regency Press London and New York.; [pers.] Poetry touches the soul and heart of humankind, spreading joy and hope for all. I have always written and adored poetry since an early age.; [a.] Geneva, Switzerland

WILBY, MARY
[m.] Peter, 29 July 1955; [ch.] Nicholas; [occ.] Retired; [memb.] Norwich R.A.F.A., Poringland Women's Institute, Fram. Earl Art Class; [oth. writ.] Poems in W.I. Magazine, Poem in Local Paper; [a.] Poringland, Norwich, Norfolk, UK

WILD, CAROL
[b.] 25 February 1962, Glasgow; [p.] Angus and Sarah; [m.] (Partner) Philip; [ed.] Reid Kerr College, Scotland; [occ.] Accountant; [pers.] I believe poetry comes from the heart, not from what we remember.; [a.] Derby, Derbyshire, UK

WILFRED, FISHER
[b.] 28 September 1927, St. Annes-on-Sea; [m.] Dora May Poole, September 1954; [ch.] Grown up son and daughter; [ed.] Blackpool Grammar School, RAF Halton Apprenticeship; [occ.] Retired Royal Air Force Officer; [pers.] Nearly forty years in the RAF, mostly as a pilot, travelling to many parts of the world taught me the beauty of everything to be found in this world. I like to this my poetry reflects this beauty.; [a.] Harrogate, N. Yorks, UK

WILKES, TRACEY
[b.] 24 September 1962, Hove, East Sussex; [m.] Tanya Levene, Divorced; [ch.] Jasmine, Zoe, Millie; [occ.] Counsellor; [memb.] British Association Counselling; [hon.] Sen., Dip. Couns.; [pers.] Look within and gain strength and courage from yourself.; [a.] Hove, East Sussex, UK

WILKINSON, B. R.
[pen.] Beth Charles; [b.] 21 March 1926, Forest of Dean, Gloucs; [p.] Frank and Janet Charles; [m.] L. Wilkinson, 21 March 1968; [ch.] Paula and Sandra; [occ.] Retired; [oth. writ.] Poem published in local book of poetry - Mansfield - Notts.; [pers.] Always an enquiring mind, feel at one with nature, and a belief in a supreme being, or power.; [a.] Mansfield, Notts, UK

WILKINSON, ELIZABETH ANN
[pen.] Elizabeth A. Wilkinson; [b.] 22 February 1935, Runcorn; [p.] Harry and Catherine Chimes; [m.] John Wilkinson (now died 1989), 9 March 1956; [ch.] Three Sons, Two Daughters; [ed.] All Saints Parish girls school Runcorn, Dutton Training school in Nursing for State enrolled Nurse. Retired from Halton General Hospital Runcorn; [occ.] Now retired after 42 years Nursing in N.H.S.; [hon.] Red Cross certification Nursing subject swimming at school. Qualified in 1955 enrolled Nurse presented to the mayor of Runcorn and other certificates in Nursing. Recent Award 96 was the Editors Choice Award from International Poets Society; [oth. writ.] Had poems published by poetry now, Press Arrival, some to be published in the Passage of Time the other side of the mirror and now this one is Quiet Moments.; [pers.] I enjoy helping others and writing my poetry delighted I'm lucky ot be having some published. I enjoy crosswords music my friend types up my work for me. I enjoy my grandchildren and family, I am one of eight children 4 brothers and 3 sisters.; [a.] Runcorn, Cheshire, UK

WILLIAMS, ALAN JAMES
[pen.] Alan Williams; [b.] 6 February 1943, Manchester; [p.] Ethel and James (Both Deceased); [m.] 23 September 1972, (Now divorced 3 years); [ch.] Helen; [ed.] Worsley Technical College; [occ.] Poet; [memb.] Manchester Chamber of Commerce and Industry; [hon.] O.N.C. Mechanical Engineering G.C.E. 'O' levels - Maths, English Language, Geography and Engineering Drawing, Ecicles and Dist. League - Bowler of the year 1980. Several Brewers buy my printed and framed poems, to hang on pub walls.; [oth. writ.] Specialized personal poems - printed and framed. Specific theme poems for pubs etc., standard poems for pubs-both printed and framed. Poems applicable to high St. Businesses. Poems written for company advertising purposes, orthodox poems on all subjects.; [pers.] At the end of the day, there'll come a time, when life will depart, from this body of mine. As I leave, I'd like to think, I've helped you all, enjoy a drink. I have been greatly influenced by the writing of Roy Orbison.; [a.] Eccles, Gt. Manchester, UK

WILLIAMS, ANNE
[b.] 6 October 1951, Birmingham; [p.] Annie and Alfred O'Neill; [m.] 30 August 1969 but now separated; [ch.] Sharron, Sandra and Christopher; [ed.] Holte Grammar Commercial School; [occ.] Community Hall Caretaker; [oth. writ.] One poem previously published in 'poems for the open mind' 2nd edition and three poems published in 'poems for the open mind' 4th edition.; [a.] Birmingham, W. Midlands, UK

WILLIAMS, HARVEY STEPHEN
[pen.] Harvey Williams; [b.] 25 February 1948, Mill Rd, Cambridge; [p.] Doris Williams and Harry Williams; [m.] (Ex) Alice, 5 December 1970; [ch.] Amanda Louise, Jason Harvey; [ed.] Netherhall Secondary School Cambridge; [occ.] Unemployed, Poet; [memb.] Argyle Street Housing Co-op 3 Fletchers Terrace Cambridge; [oth. writ.] Recital of selected poems on Cambridge Community Radio. Half hour poetry recital at Cambridge boat race. (Music venue).; [pers.] Having will power is the key to survival.; [a.] Cambridge, Cambs, UK

WILLIAMS, JOHN HENRY
[pen.] Henry Clifton; [b.] 8 December 1928, Worcester; [p.] Robert and Ruby Williams; [m.] Marjorie Violet (Nee Shellam), 6 December 1952; [ch.] Four Sons (Lost one); [ed.] Not enough!; [occ.] Difficult to Describe! Not age - also ex Bankcruft (Fraud); [memb.] None now - other than the "Ex" Club!; [hon.] None - other than the above!; [oth. writ.] Regency press 1971; [pers.] Phone me very upset country business, tradesman - see letter. True personal addresses are blue shot. and the upper house lower sapey, Clifton-on-Teme Worcestershire.; [a.] Worcestershire, Worcs, UK

WILLIAMS, MELANIE DALE
[pen.] Melanie Dale Williams; [b.] 20 November 1977, Munster, Germany; [p.] Donald and Jaynemarie Williams; [ed.] Edinburgh School, Munster, Kings School Gutersloh; [occ.] Student; [memb.] None, have been member of many chairs, art and drama clubs whilst at school. I am soon to become a member of "Nottingham's Hospital Radio"; [pers.] I enjoy all aspects of creative writing and poetry etc. My ambition is to be either a broadcast or print journalist. I am strongly approved to ignorance and prejudism.; [a.] Nottingham, Notts, UK

WILLIAMS, OWAIN
[pen.] Francis Wells; [b.] 22 December 1948, Kidwelly, Dyfed; [p.] Winifred Eileen and Caradog Williams; [m.] Janet Margaret Williams, 22 December 1977; [ch.] (Twins) Eleri and Rhiannon Williams; [ed.] 5 "O" Levels: English Literature and Language, Physics, Mathematics, Engineering and Technical Drawing. City and Guilds of London: Mechanical Craft Studies.; [occ.] Serving Member of Armed Forces (RAF) nearing completion of 22 years Service; [memb.] British Orienteering Association; [hon.] Long Service and Good Conduct Medal (RAF); [pers.] As an amateur poet, I try to reflect people's nature and my love of the simple pleasures in our natural world. My writing is deeply effected by my love for the genius of Dylan Thomas and the power he had by writing in a manner that will always reflect the passion that truly is the Welsh People.; [a.] Ely, Cardiff, S. Glam, UK

WILLIAMS, PAUL
[b.] 21 March 1964, Worcester; [p.] Albert and Beryl Williams; [ed.] Perdiswell Secondary; [occ.] VDU Operator; [memb.] Worcester Dog Training Club, Evesham Greyhound Rescue; [hon.] DEBSM Cert. in Business Management City and Guilds 9231 Photography Distinctions in Portraiture and Landscape. Clait 1 Distinction and Clait II Pass.; [oth. writ.] Poem published by Anchor Books help published in complete magazines.; [pers.] The Greyhound so graceful, yet treated so badly by society. As sadly so are many animals.; [a.] Worcester, Worc'shire, UK

WILLIAMS, RACHEL-LOUISA
[b.] 4 June 1980, Wakefield; [p.] Stevens Williams, Kathleen Williams; [ed.] Outwood Grange School; [occ.] Student; [pers.] I'm only 16 years old. It's hardly like I've had chance to do anything with my life yet, so my poetry is generally influenced by my experiences of the life I have led so far. Forgotten? Is my first published work, I hope it will not be my last.; [a.] Wakefield, West Yorkshire, UK

WILLIAMS, REBECCA
[b.] 19 February 1981, Cardiff; [p.] Ivor Williams, Lynda Williams; [ed.] St. Cyres Comprehensive School, Penarth, S. Glamorgan; [occ.] Student; [pers.] In my writing I endeavour to reflect my feelings about the experiences and events which have affected my teenage years.; [a.] Dinas Powys, South Glam, UK

WILLIAMSON, HELEN
[pen.] Nelly; [b.] 4 March 1957, Dundee; [p.] Catherine Reid, George Williamson; [m.] Duncan; [ch.] Seven; [ed.] Jamestown Alexandria, Central District Perth, St Ninians, Perth High SC; [occ.] Very busy housewife and career; [memb.] P.W.A.M.M., S.P.F., T.C.F.; [hon.] Three burns Awards for Rabbie Burns; [oth. writ.] Several poems and one printed in local school magazines; [pers.] I give to you my friends a few lines roped together to form a rope. Will you take hold of its end.; [a.] Perth, UK

WILLIAMSON, MARK ANTHONY
[pen.] Mark Williamson; [b.] 6 June 1966, Sunderland; [p.] Ann Watson; [ch.] One son, Luke; [ed.] At Thornhill Comprehensive School, Sunderland; [oth. writ.] Several short stories and poems; [pers.] Inside the life's blood of every pen, are the greatest, sweetest words that may ever be written, some people strive to free them, some people thirst for them, all it takes is imagination, imagination and a pen. I'll keep striving.; [a.] Sunderland, Tyne and Wear, UK

WILLIS, ORLA
[pen.] Orla; [b.] 6 September 1978, Cork City; [p.] John Willis, Lynda Willis; [ed.] Presentation Sec. School, Ballyphehane, Cork City in Leaving Certificate Year; [occ.] Student; [memb.] School Choir; [oth. writ.] Have written many poems but came 3rd with a poem in school.; [pers.] Poetry to me comes from the heart and I have been greatly influenced by family and friends.; [a.] Cork City, Ireland

WILLSHER, LYNN
[pen.] Catherine Evans, James Thompson; [b.] 1995, Leeds; [p.] Margeret Thompson Nee Jones; [m.] Ronald Willsher; [ch.] Seven - Life span of 24 years; [ed.] Hillside Sec Modern, Beeston, Leeds, Outwood Sec Modern, Nr Wakefield, "Sight and Sound College", Leeds public servant and Transport; [occ.] Now Retired, Compiling Biography; [memb.] Coach Drivers Club; [oth. writ.] Logos for private companies and poems; [pers.] "With this picture from the mind. The powers within, will only be kind."; [a.] Leeds, Yorkshire, UK

WILSON, CAVIN DOUGLAS JOHN
[pen.] Douglas Gunn; [b.] 11 July 1962, Irvine, Ayrshire; [p.] James J. H. Wilson, Lesley P. S. Wilson; [m.] Partner: Nikki Gill; [ed.] Inverness Royal Academy; [occ.] Medically Retired H.M. Forces (Army); [oth. writ.] The Ghost Dancer Chronicles 1995, Co-written with Nikki Gill (awaiting publication) and an array of individual poems as yet unpublished.; [pers.] I find the poem is an ideal medium for capturing snapshots of thoughts and feelings. I prefer using a tight close-up to the slow panning shot of longer forms of writing. Poetry provides the best framework for my endeavors.; [a.] Whitley Bay, Tyne and Wear, UK

WILSON, DAWN
[b.] 28 July 1978, Durham; [p.] Jacqueline Wilson and Margaret Rennie; [occ.] Attending College and Part-time Bar work in Public House; [pers.] All we can do, is give our best in life, even if we don't succeed. As long as I know, that I give my best, I will always be satisfied.; [a.] Brandon, Durham, UK

WILSON, KAREN
[b.] 24 June 1954, Guildford; [p.] Kenneth James Wilson, Lieselotte Wilson; [ed.] Thornbury Castle School (Secondary) Boksburgh Commercial High School, South Africa IHK, Business School, Frankfurt, Germany; [occ.] Treasury Assistant; [memb.] National Geographic, Survival International; [pers.] I draw my inspiration from life around me, and my poems reflect how I feel or what I seen, in the hope that others learn to appreciate the gifts of life; [a.] Guildford, Surrey, UK

WINDSOR, SHEILA MARY
[b.] 2 April 1949, Twickenham; [p.] Geoffrey James Jones and Sarah Jane Jones; [m.] Alexander Richard Windsor, 11 July 1981; [ch.] Thomas and Mark; [ed.] Shrewsbury Technical College, The University of Keele; [occ.] Special Support Assistant, Stoneport on severn High School; [hon.] A level English prize, Keele University Foundation year prize; [oth. writ.] 'Dragonfly' published in 'Between A Laugh and A Tear'; [pers.] 'Finale' describes my last visit to 'Mayfield' my childhood home. It is about the eternal nature of love and is dedicated to my mother, Sarah Janes.; [a.] Stourport on Severn, Worcs, UK

WOOD, A. LOUISE
[b.] 12 November 1924, Ilford, Essex; [p.] Arthur Howes and Florence Howes; [m.] Stanley Wood, 24 December 1950; [occ.] Retired; [pers.] Poems are the means of expressing ones inner thoughts - bringing contentment.; [a.] Herne Bay, Kent, UK

WOOD, JUNE ANN
[b.] 4 April 1938, London; [p.] William Charlesworth, Catherine Charlesworth; [m.] Ernest Sidney Wood, 29 November 1958; [ch.] Ann Carol, Tina (two daughters); [ed.] Secondary Modern; [occ.] Housewife; [pers.] Absorb nature and live your life to the full.; [a.] London, UK

WOOD, RUZENA
[pen.] Ariela Valda; [b.] 17 March, Macclesfield, UK; [ed.] MA Honours English Literature, Edinburgh University, 1959, musical composition with Ronald Stevenson; [occ.] Music Archivist, National Library of Scotland Music Department, Edinburgh EH1 1EW, 1959-1997; [memb.] Jewish Literary Society; [hon.] Founder Member of Board of Institute for Scottish Music, Glasgow University, 1995; [oth. writ.] The Palace of the Moon (Czech Folk Tales) published by Audri Dentsch, London, 1981, Contributed to: Recording of and edition of: 6 Concertos by John Hebden, (critical edition in progress), reviews for The Edinburgh Star, musical compositions and humour.; [pers.] Ruzena Wood is a Scottish Jewis, resident in Edinburgh. Her time has been divided between music and literature, with a particular interest in Czech literature, musical composition and Jewish studies. From April 1997 she will be working commercially freelance, with an interest in reviewing Jewish educational materials and broadcasting.; [a.] Edinburgh, Scotland

WOOD, SHEILA FRANCES
[pen.] "Penny Wilson"; [b.] 16 August 1943, Liverpool; [p.] Deceased; [m.] John Haslam (Common Law); [ed.] Convent of Notre Dame Birkdale Southport Lancs, Loretta School of Dancing Southport Lancs.; [occ.] Pro. Tennis Teacher, Actress, Sportswear Designer, Art Agent; [memb.] Lancashire Lawn, Tennis Association, Equity. R.A.D. (Royal Academy) (Of Dancing); [hon.] Passed all the R.A.D. Ballet exams. Won many Ballets Cups. Won many Tennis Tournaments. Design Exclusively for "Harrods" sportswear.; [oth. writ.] "Best of Modern Verse 1968", "New Times Poetry" 1970 Working on a play. For 1997 based on artists and poets.; [pers.] People expect life to always have an end product. Unfortunately, life is not like that, enjoy the moment and appreciate what you have.; [a.] Crosby, Liverpool, Merseyside, UK

WOOD, VIVIENNE
[b.] 16 March 1947, Edinburgh; [p.] John Thomson, Molly Thomson Nee Cockburn; [m.] Divorced; [ch.] Angela and Richard; [ed.] Mary Erskine School for Girls, Napier University; [occ.] Administrative Officer, Napier University; [memb.] Institute of Management; [oth. writ.] Institutional Research Papers published (various); [pers.] To my children - follow your dreams; [a.] Edinburgh, Midlothian, UK

WOODHOUSE, ANDREW
[b.] 30 January 1940, Leiston, Suffolk; [p.] Hector Davis and Elsie; [m.] Elizabeth Jennifer, 24 October 1964; [ch.] Annabel and Hayley; [ed.] Silcoates: Belper Grammar Leeds College of Art: Goldsmith's, London University Notts. University, Northern Ordination Course - Manchester; [occ.] Artist: Now Stipendiary Ministry C.E.; [memb.] Chaplain Royal British Legion Bedale; [hon.] National Dip. Design (Leeds), Art Teachers Certificate (Distinction) London, Dip. Ed. Nottingham, Dip. N.O.C. Manchester; [oth. writ.] Personal unpublished poems.; [pers.] Creativity is a gift from heaven blown from the hand of God. Or to put it simply creativity is a gift to cherish: A miracle to share.; [a.] Bedale, North Yorks, UK

WOODMAN, DEREK
[b.] 8 April 1944, Ebbw Vale; [p.] Raymond John Woodman, Doris Woodman; [ed.] Willow Town Secondary Modern School; [occ.] Materials Controller British Steel (Tinplate) EBBW Vale Galvinising Section; [memb.] EBBW Vale Conservative Club; [hon.] Monmouthshire Certificate of Education. Distinctions in English lit, Religious Knowledge E; [oth. writ.] Some poems published in Poetry Magazines; [pers.] My poems reflect sometimes the hope and sometimes the sadness of life.; [a.] Ebbw Vale, Blaenau Gwent, UK

WOOLLACOTT, TREVOR
[b.] 16 September 1965, Winchester; [p.] Harry Woollacott, Noreen Woollacott; [ed.] Priory Comprehensive (Worle, Weston-Super-Mare); [occ.] Clerical Assistant; [memb.] Manchester United Supporters' Club Bridgwater and South West Branch, Registered Blood Donor. Recently Registered as Television and Film Extra.; [oth. writ.] Several joke poems in the style of John-Cooper-Clark "The Punk Poet"; [pers.] I would simply like to dedicate my poem to the memory of Matthews Lloyd Jennings, who passed away sadly on 19 March 1996, aged 25 years.; [a.] Weston-super-Mare, North Somerset, UK

WOOLWAY, JANET
[b.] 17 January 1956, Gosport, Hants; [p.] Sheila Hawkes and Roy Hawkes; [m.] Philip Woolway, 28 May 1977; [ch.] Matthew John, Adam Philip, Samuel Joseph James; [ed.] Privett Secondary Modern; [occ.] Playgroup Leader; [oth. writ.] Poems published in local magazine; [pers.] I would like my future generations to feel they know me through my writing.; [a.] Gosport, Hampshire, UK

WOOTTON, CLIVE THOMAS
[b.] 26 May 1950, Pretoria; [p.] Liese Wootton; [oth. writ.] Wide-Range of Poetry; [pers.] "Not to no Avail". Deep in mud, triumphant archfiend slaked his thirst on human blood. Noble the naked savage buried, humble poetry in baleful wake. Weep not on his woeful tale, slow and harsh the celestial march, thwarting, but not to no avail.; [a.] Hammersmith, London, UK

WRIGHT, DAVID SHAWN
[b.] 27 September 1963, Rotherham; [p.] Les and Pauline Wright; [m.] Kryan Wright, 24 August 1990; [ch.] Cheryl Ann, Charlotte Cassandra, Jacob Daryl; [ed.] Old Hall Camp Rotherham; [occ.] Night Store Manager; [oth. writ.] Many short poems written as forms of exorcisms; [pers.] To ask is but a moment of ignorance, not to ask is a lifetime of stupidity my greatest influence is John Milton; [a.] Preston, Lancs, UK

WRIGHT, IRENE ROSE
[pen.] Rose Wright; [b.] 11 October 1940, Rotherham; [p.] Stanley Clare, Irene Clare; [m.] William Wright, 14 October 1961; [ch.] Jacqueline, Mandy, Claire; [ed.] South Grove Secondary Modern School for girls, Wellgate Rotherham; [occ.] Retired Nurse; [oth. writ.] For family and friends for weddings occasions etc; [pers.] I just write what I feel at any given time. Request etc.; [a.] Leeds, Yorkshire, UK

WRIGHTSON, CHRISTINE
[b.] 18 August 1946, York; [p.] Henry and Kathleen Leng; [m.] John Wrightson, 19 March 1987; [ed.] Joseph Rowntree Secondary School, New Earswick, York; [occ.] Disabled/Housewife; [pers.] I have always been aware of social problems.; [a.] York, North Yorks, UK

WYLES, STEPHEN JOHN
[pen.] S. J. Wyles; [b.] 19 July 1955, Forestgate; [p.] Walter and Doreen; [m.] Sandra, 19 August 1978; [ch.] Jessica and Daniel; [oth. writ.] Poems published in Triumph House Books "The Christian Poetry collection 1996 and Christian verse from East Anglia"; [pers.] The pen is mightier than the sword, therefore there can be no greater force than Gods word. As a Christian I am but a pen in the master's hand and unselfish love is but one of the wondrous facets of the crystal clarity of God's word.; [a.] Basildon, Essex, UK

YADAV, YESHA
[b.] 11 August 1981, Lucknow, India; [p.] Pradeep Kumar Yadav, Mamta Yadav; [ed.] High School of Glasgow, Hutchesons' Grammar School, Garnetbank Primary; [occ.] Student at High School of Glasgow in Secondary III; [memb.] School Literary and Debating Society, Asian Artistes Association; [hon.] Glasgow Educational and Marshall Trust 1994 prize for Literature, School French prize for 1996; [oth. writ.] The Hutchesonian School Magazine; [pers.] I enjoy entertaining disadvantaged social groups through Indian classical dancing. I have given more than

100 dance performances in Scottish Residential Homes and Day Centers for the elderly and the disabled because I feel that my little effort means a lot to them.; [a.] Glasgow, Lanarkshire, UK

YATMAN, MICHELLE
[pen.] Michelle Wilson; [b.] 17 July 1974, London; [ch.] 2 Girls age 2 - age 3; [ed.] 7 GCSE's additional education = Art and Textiles Computering; [pers.] Things in my life have not been very easy but I have always tried to keep up with my education and for the first time in my life things have never been better.; [a.] London, UK

YOUNG, VALERIE
[b.] 15 February 1939, Birkenhead; [p.] Joseph and Rose Phillips; [m.] William (Bill) Young, 18 March 1961; [ch.] Alan; [ed.] St Annes, Rock Ferry, Birkenhead; [occ.] Retired; [hon.] First prize in an essay competition in senior school; [oth. writ.] I love to write poetry for my friends and relatives, mostly humorous.; [a.] Bromborough, Wirral, UK

ZARSADIAS, PRIZZI
[b.] October 2, 1985, London; [p.] Rafael and Phoebe; [ed.] A junior at St. Mary's Roman Catholic School, London; [occ.] Student; [memb.] Wants to be a Brownie or a girl scout.; [hon.] 1. Ballet Primary - Honours Royal Academy of Dancing 2. Tap Primary - Highly Commended Imperial Society of Teachers of Dancing 3. Grade 2 Piano - Associated Board; [oth. writ.] Several poems and short stories with excellent remarks and high grades; [pers.] Great minds think alike. Kudos to my parents and teachers.; [a.] East Acton, London

ZERMAN, TAMARA
[pen.] Tobic Byron; [b.] 16 February 1911, Rostov-on-Don, South Russia; [p.] Francise John Zerman, Elizabeth Zerman; [ed.] Privately educated by Governesses, Boarding School, private tutor for music and art attended elite art school, Royal Drawing Society, Studios at Queensgate, London; [occ.] Now retired, in the past Tutor of Art and Music and eventually Dress Designer and Stage Decor; [memb.] R.D.S. membership; [hon.] I had a great honour bestowed upon me and was made an Honourable member 'Of The Kings Regiment', The Queen Mother is the Colonel in Chief, and Sir Geoffry Errington was Colonel at the time in 1983; [oth. writ.] I composed my first Concerto and several other pieces a few years ago and still play.; [pers.] One morning when I was six years of age my Governess was dressing me up ready to go up with the whole family for a picnic in the Caucasus in South Russia where there were boiling lava wells which had good effect on health. I asked her to tie a wide pink sash around my waist. She refused to do so, I started to cry and made much noise, my Father came to see what was happening, the Governess told him, he said, 'do as the child ask.' She said 'But Sir Madam would not like it.' 'Do as the child asks' Father repeated. With great anger she tied the pink sash with a double knot round my waist very tight. On arriving a picnic was laid on a rug and everybody was busy doing something. Little by little I departed from the rest without being noticed and to my horror when I reached one of the boiling lava wells I lost my balance as the ground was sloping towards the well I shouted 'Papa, Papa.' My Father on hearing my voice took his walking stick and ran after me, and just in time with a hook of his stick caught me by my pink and pulled me towards him, he stood there a long time recovering. Afterwards I heard him saying to my Mama 'Do you know that pink sash has saved that child's life.'

Index
of
Poets

Sheffield, Barbara Mary 437
Sheldon, Julie 488
Shell, Scott D. 279
Shelley, Mark 351
Shelton, Holly 51
Shelvock, F. 378
Shenton, Townley 83
Shephard, H. J. 414
Shephard, Lotus 371
Shepherd, David J. 329
Shepherd, E. R. 426
Sherin, Georgina 130
Sherlock, Laura 352
Sherriff, E. A. 107
Sherwood, Diane 307
Sherwood, Marion Elizabeth 424
Sherwood, Stephen 98
Shewring, K. 397
Shields, Dee 537
Shields, Sandra 432
Shier, Rhiannon 187
Shiner, Finlay 312
Shipway-Blackwell, Nancy 118
Shone, Hayley 38
Shore, Caroline 452
Shore, Dave 310
Short, Beth 306
Short, Odette 364
Short, Suzanne Louise 399
Shreeve, G. 227
Shreeve, Jan 315
Shrubsole, Joy 327
Shurety, Ferrelyn 147
Shuttlewood, J. 268
Shuttleworth, Bertha 488
Shuttleworth, Joanne 446
Sidman, Ruth 363
Siglioccolo, M. 197
Sillifant, Tessa 232
Sillince, Carole 166
Silvester, Sarah 292
Sime, I. F. 161
Simmonds, Jill 41
Simmonds, Pauline B. M. 240
Simmonite, Michael 281
Simmons, A. K. 242
Simmons, Bernard 311
Simmons, Clare 319
Simmons, Jemma 511
Simmons, Ronald H. 209
Simms, D. 403
Simner, Glenys 473
Simonsen, Erik Vibe 557
Simpkins, Nicola M. 176
Simpson, Colin 462
Simpson, J. 248
Simpson, J. P. 424
Simpson, S. 383, 384
Simpson, Tristan 167
Simpson, W. 272
Sinclair, Ian 60
Sinclair, Janet 28
Sinclair, Lindsey 469
Sinclair, Susan 340
Singleton, Ruby 183
Sinnott, Darragh 333
Sirett, Clive Weston 325
Sisco 356
Sisk, Emma 42
Skeet, Sue 104
Skidmore, Elizabeth 484
Skidmore, Rebecca 291
Skilton, Peter J. 223
Skinn, Gordon 306
Skinner, Colin D. 338
Skinner, J. M. 284

Skipper, B. 170
Skitch, Karen 122
Slade, J. L. 221
Slate, Pauline 208
Slatter 335
Slattery, J. 225
Slaughter, V. M. 258
Slavin, M. H. 388
Slimjim, Ol' 22
Slinn, M. 106
Slinn, Richard 355
Sloan, Charles James 171
Sloanes, Gill 65
Small, Anne 31
Small, Nola B. 174
Smart, Barbara 50
Smith, A. L. 335
Smith, Alan 8
Smith, Alan 147
Smith, Anne-Marie 528
Smith, Annette 493
Smith, B. C. 531
Smith, Carolyn 61
Smith, Christopher J. 33
Smith, Collette-Anne 537
Smith, D. F. 383
Smith, D. M. 359
Smith, Delwin 438
Smith, Dorothy 8
Smith, E. 196, 390
Smith, Elizabeth 34
Smith, Eric W. 7
Smith, F. B. 190
Smith, Frances 331
Smith, George 534
Smith, Gillian Patricia 141
Smith, Hazel 51, 477, 552
Smith, Irene 308
Smith, Iris 37, 449
Smith, J. M. 391
Smith, Jaclynn-Sarah 45
Smith, Janet E. 304
Smith, Janet R. 62
Smith, Jean 22
Smith, Jessie 474
Smith, Jill C. 568
Smith, Joan M. 10
Smith, John W. 166
Smith, Karen 351
Smith, L. J. 433
Smith, Lawrence 91
Smith, Lesley-Anne 366
Smith, Margaret 428
Smith, Marion 126
Smith, Marjorie Joan 407
Smith, Mark 96
Smith, Marlene 388
Smith, Melanie 87
Smith, Michael 296
Smith, Michelle 235
Smith, Pamela 177
Smith, Patricia 339
Smith, R. 198
Smith, R. Peter 380
Smith, Roy 398
Smith, Ruth 285
Smith, Sharon 206
Smith, Suzanne T. 349
Smith, Trevor J. 393
Smith, V. 207
Smith, Winklet 73
Smith, Zoe 252
Smitham, P. J. 432
Smyth, B. A. 78
Smyth, G. M. 90
Smyth, Louise 285

Snape, Doris 154
Sneddon, Jennifer Louise 470
Snelling, Eileen 338
Snelling, Hazel Lea 323
Snook, Janet 516
Snow, L. 205
Snowsill, J. 110
Solazzo, Linda E. 69
Sollie, Kai H. 301
Soma, Anita 157
Somerset, Marie 264
Somjee, Shehnaz 117
Sondhi, Rina 373
Sorensen, Roy 333
South, Marilyn J. 248
Southall, D. J. 410
Southall, Rowena M. 170
Spackman, Pamela 365
Spalding, Delia 319
Sparkes, I. 406
Sparkes, Jenna G. 486
Sparrock, Jean Hopper 312
Spearing, Shirley 557
Speck, Vera E. 209
Spencer, I. 230
Spencer, Lesley 284
Spencer, M. 390
Spencer, Sharron 111
Spencer-MacKay, Moira 296
Spill, Glady Jane 502
Spivey, Catherine 442
Spokes, Marjorie 239
Spooner, Phyllis M. 87
Spraggs, Gwynedd 49
Spreadbury, K. S. 97
Sprigings, Dorothy May 190
Spurr, Jill 39
Srih, Julie 515
Stacey, Donna 330
Stacey, Joanna 478
Staggs, A. A. G. 379
Staien, Sue 334
Stainer, Dave 492
Stainer, Marjorie M. 231
Stainsby, Judith A. 329
Stainton, Barbara 486
Stakely, George E. 147
Stanbury, Doreen 522
Stancer, Adam 479
Standage, Sandra 299
Stanger, Arabella 327
Stanley, Roberta 359
Stannard, Gillian P. 522
Stanworth, George 58
Stapleton, D. 432
Starkie, Michelle 181
Starks, M. 105
Staughton, Donna 317
Staveley, B. J. 280
Steele, Gemma Anne 56
Steele, Ruth 269
Steer, Jean 496
Steggles, Richard 260
Stephens, C. 386
Stephens, Elizabeth 20
Stephens, James E. 457
Stephenson, Eleanor 488
Stephenson, Lily 366
Stevens, Alison 442
Stevens, Dana 468
Stevens, Gary 58
Stevens, Jacqueline 32
Stevens, Vera 275
Stevenson, Gordon G. 334
Stevenson, J. D. 200
Stevenson, Lee 175

Stevenson, Millicent D. 216
Stevenson, Robert Earl 132
Stevenson, S. M. 411
Steward, Duncan James 473
Steward, K. M. 184
Stewart, Betty 23
Stewart, Christine 138
Stewart, Colette 517
Stewart, G. 425
Stewart, George 303
Stewart, Jamie 51
Stewart, Kelly A. 252
Stewart, Kerry 295
Stewart-Condron, Maureen 134
St. John, Kate 275
Stichler, Maureen 133
Stilwell, Laura 275
Stinchcombe, Abigail Helen 155
Stirling, Christine 147
Stock, A. C. 296
Stockdale, David 320
Stoker, Sara 287
Stone, Nicholas 186
Stone, Tyler 344
Stoner, Erika 326
Stopford, Rebecca 375
Stormonth, James 6
Stott, G. J. 209
Strachan, Vicky Lee 557
Strain, Mandy 118
Strange, Nicole Le 256
Stratton, Harry 70
Street, Rebecca 111
Street, Ros 362
Stretton, Keri 293
Stritch, Thomas 254
Stubberfield, Martin 300
Stubbs, Chris 477
Stubbs, Lorraine D'or 280
Styles, Susan 343
Suddell, Pauline 292
Sullivan, Jill 514
Sullivan, John Liam 529
Sullivan, Patrick 417
Sultana, Fiorella 306
Summerfield, Judith 322
Summerscales, Pam 567
Sumner, Allan 149
Sumner, Gillian L. 483
Sumsion, Annalisa Maria 34
Surman, P. R. 97
Surman, Patricia 166
Sutherland, Carole A. S. 321
Sutherland, Elizabeth 508
Sutherland, Eva 504
Sutherland, Jane 300
Sutherland, Josie 493
Sutherland, Karen 285
Sutherland, Morag 427
Sutton, Anita 30
Sutton, Brenda 444
Sutton, Frank 442
Sutton, John 476
Sutton, John C. 527
Sutton, Mark A. 240
Sutton, Patrick 274
Sutton, Vic 289
Swann, Susan 387
Swanwick, Maureen 412
Sweeney, Deirdre 334
Sweeney, Edith 66
Sweeney, Niamh 340
Sweetman, Lois 298
Sweetman, S. T. 403
Swift, Emma 445
Swindells, Janet 307

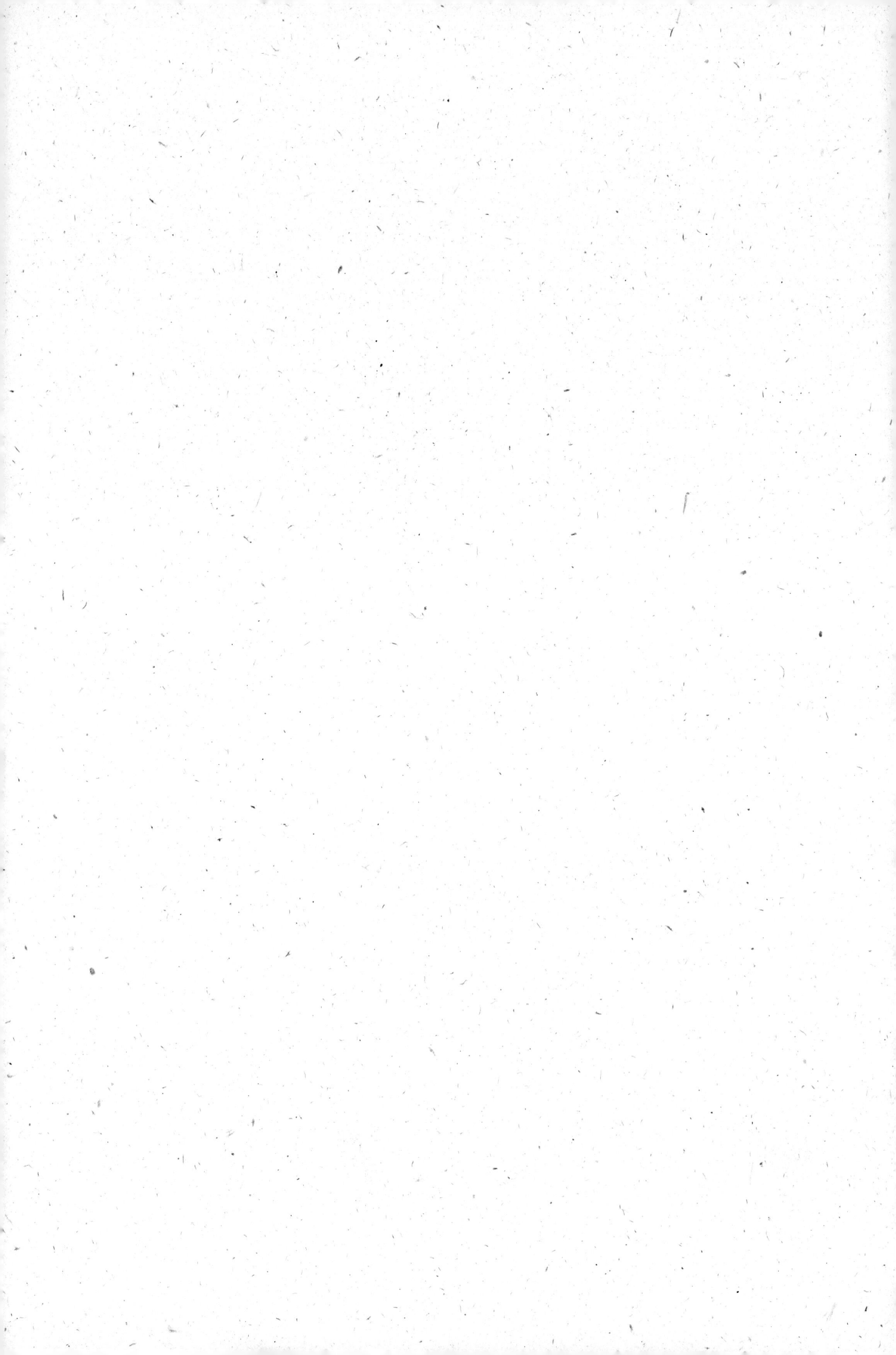